south america
on a shoestring

Regis St. Louis

Sandra Bao, Gregor Clark, Aimée Dowl, Beth Kohn, Carolyn McCarthy,
Anja Mutić, Mike Power, Kevin Raub, Paul Smith, Andy Symington, Lucas Vidgen

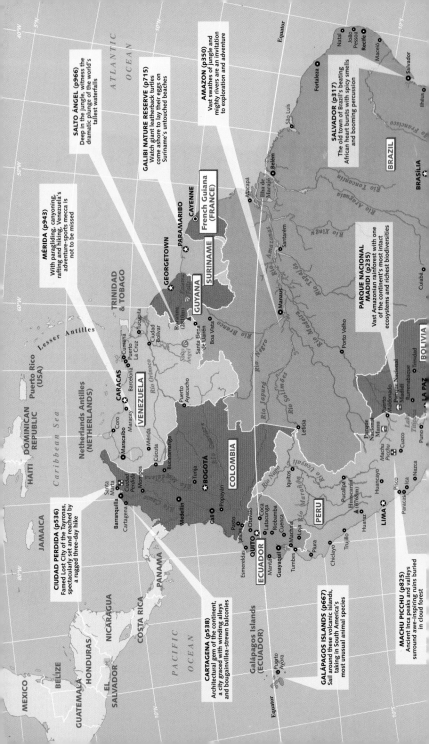

SALTO ANGEL (p966)
Deep in the jungle, witness the dramatic plunge of the world's tallest waterfalls

GALIBI NATURE RESERVE (p715)
Watch giant leatherback turtles come ashore to lay their eggs on Suriname's untouched beaches

AMAZON (p350)
Vast swathes of jungle and mighty rivers are an invitation to exploration and adventure

MÉRIDA (p943)
With paragliding, canyoning, rafting and hiking, Venezuela's adventure-sports mecca is not to be missed

SALVADOR (p317)
The old town of Brazil's beating African heart bursts with spicy smells and booming percussion

PARQUE NACIONAL MADIDI (p235)
Vast Amazonian rainforest with one of the continent's most intact ecosystems and richest biodiversities

CIUDAD PERDIDA (p536)
Famed Lost City of the Tayronas, spectacularly sited and reached by a rugged three-day hike

CARTAGENA (p538)
Architectural gem of the continent, a city graced with winding alleys and bougainvillea-strewn balconies

GALÁPAGOS ISLANDS (p667)
Sail around these volcanic islands, taking in South America's most unusual animal species

MACHU PICCHU (p825)
Ancient Inca peaks and valleys surround awe-inspiring ruins buried in cloud forest

ATLANTIC OCEAN

PACIFIC OCEAN

Caribbean Sea

Lesser Antilles

Netherlands Antilles (NETHERLANDS)

Puerto Rico (USA)

TRINIDAD & TOBAGO

DOMINICAN REPUBLIC

HAITI

JAMAICA

MEXICO

BELIZE

GUATEMALA

HONDURAS

EL SALVADOR

NICARAGUA

COSTA RICA

PANAMA

VENEZUELA

COLOMBIA

ECUADOR

PERU

BOLIVIA

BRAZIL

GUYANA

SURINAME

French Guiana (FRANCE)

CARACAS

BOGOTÁ

QUITO

LIMA

LA PAZ

BRASÍLIA

GEORGETOWN

PARAMARIBO

CAYENNE

Galápagos Islands (ECUADOR)

Puerto Ayora

Equator

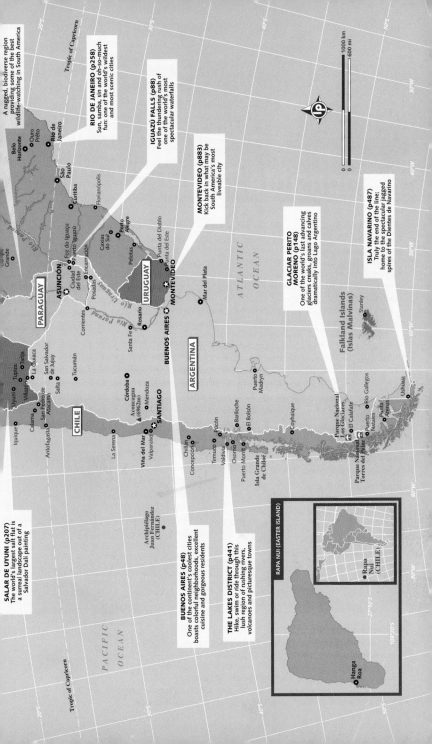

A rugged, biodiverse region providing some of the best wildlife-watching in South America

SALAR DE UYUNI (p207)
The world's largest salt flat is a surreal landscape out of a Salvador Dalí painting

RIO DE JANEIRO (p258)
Sun, samba, sin and oh-so-much fun: one of the world's wildest and most scenic cities

IGUAZÚ FALLS (p88)
Feel the thundering rush of one of the world's most spectacular waterfalls

MONTEVIDEO (p883)
Kick back in what may be South America's most liveable city

GLACIAR PERITO MORENO (p148)
One of the world's last advancing glaciers creaks, groans and calves dramatically into Lago Argentino

ISLA NAVARINO (p487)
Truly the end of the line; home to the spectacular jagged spires of the Dientes de Navarino

BUENOS AIRES (p48)
One of the continent's coolest cities boasts colorful neighborhoods, excellent cuisine and gorgeous residents

THE LAKES DISTRICT (p441)
Hike, swim or ride through this lush region of rushing rivers, volcanoes and picturesque towns

PARAGUAY

ASUNCIÓN

URUGUAY

MONTEVIDEO

BUENOS AIRES

ARGENTINA

CHILE

SANTIAGO

Falkland Islands (Islas Malvinas)

ATLANTIC OCEAN

PACIFIC OCEAN

Tropic of Capricorn

Tropic of Capricorn

RAPA NUI (EASTER ISLAND)

Rapa Nui (CHILE)

Hanga Roa

1000 km
600 mi

Responsible Travel

Travel offers some of the most liberating and rewarding experiences in life, but it can also be a force for positive change in the world, if you travel responsibly. In contrast, traveling without a thought to where you put your time or money can often do more harm than good.

Throughout this book we recommend ecotourism operations and community-sponsored tours whenever available. Community-managed tourism is especially important when visiting indigenous communities, which are often exploited by businesses that channel little money back into the community.

Some backpackers are infamous for excessive bartering and taking only the cheapest tours. Keep in mind that low prices may mean a less safe, less environmentally sensitive tour (especially true in the Amazon Basin and the Salar de Uyuni, among other places); in the marketplace unrealistically low prices can negatively impact the livelihood of struggling vendors.

See also p24 for general info on social etiquette while traveling, Responsible Travel sections in individual chapter directories for country-specific information, and the GreenDex (p1062) for a list of sustainable-tourism options across the region.

TIPS TO KEEP IN MIND

- **Bring a water filter or water purifier** Don't contribute to the enormous waste left by discarded plastic water bottles.

- **Don't litter** Sure, many locals do it, but many also frown upon it.

- **Hire responsible guides** Make sure they have a good reputation and respect the environment and communities you'll visit.

- **Learn the lingo** Take a Spanish or Portuguese class (and stay with a local family if possible). Locals appreciate the effort.

- **Pay your porter, tip your guide** Porters, guides and cooks are often ridiculously underpaid. Tip as much as you can.

- **Respect local traditions** Dress appropriately when visiting churches, shrines and more conservative communities.

- **Buyer beware** Don't buy souvenirs or products made from coral or any other animal material.

- **Spend at the source** Buy crafts directly from artisans themselves.

- **Support the community** Seek out community-based services that keep dollars local. Ask where your operator is based and where the money ends up.

- **Don't haggle over every penny** Excessive bargaining can leave locals with a bad impression of foreign travelers.

INTERNET RESOURCES

www.ecotourism.org Links to businesses devoted to ecotourism.
www.mongabay.com Wildlife- and conservation-focused website.
www.nature.org Worthwhile articles on ecotourism and sustainable development.
www.planeta.com Ron Mader's outstanding ecotourism website.
www.tourismconcern.org.uk UK-based organization dedicated to promoting ethical tourism.
www.transitionsabroad.com Focuses on immersion and responsible travel.

South America Highlights

You haven't really traveled until you've taken on South America. Thirteen countries strong, the continent is home to astounding natural and cultural wonders, including the snowcapped peaks of the Andes, thousands of kilometers of magnificent white-sand beaches, captivating colonial towns and indigenous villages, and the Amazon rainforest – home to more plant and animal species than anywhere else on earth.

The challenge is deciding where to begin. Here, a selection of Lonely Planet authors, staff and travelers like you share their most memorable South America experiences. You can add your highlights at www.lonelyplanet.com/south-america.

WES WALKER

1 MACHU PICCHU, PERU

We had been hiking for days on the Inca Trail. The journey itself had been so incredible that I had almost forgotten where the trail led. On the final day, we began at the break of dawn to catch a glimpse as the sun rose. Finally, there it was: Machu Picchu (p825). I had seen hundreds of photographs but none could do it justice. It was pure magic to see it in person.

Karlee Palms, traveler, USA

BUENOS AIRES NIGHTLIFE, ARGENTINA

Dinner at 10pm, cocktails at midnight, clubbing by 2am…you will never be at a loss for somewhere to eat, drink or dance until the wee hours of the morning. From hot Palermo clubs to unexpected swanky lounges in the *microcentro* (city center) to bona fide steakhouses in San Telmo, I felt constantly invigorated by Buenos Aires' (p48) palpable energy.

**Mary Polizzotti,
Lonely Planet staff, USA**

JEFF GREENBERG

2
OTAVALO MARKET, ECUADOR

Although a visit to Otavalo's Saturday market (p618) is ostensibly about buying Andean handicrafts, the real treasures are the people. I love chatting with the folks, who have their portion of uplifting and sorrowful tales, and seem keen to share a bit of their lives with those curious enough to ask.

**Regis St. Louis,
Lonely Planet author**

3

MICHAEL Ta

4
COLONIA DEL SACRAMENTO, URUGUAY

Explore the Unesco-listed Barrio Histórico (p889), with its basilica, lighthouse and drawbridged Puerta de Campo. The cobblestoned streets lined with historic homes are fabulously photogenic when the ceiba trees bloom.

Debra Herrmann, Lonely Planet staff, Australia

SALAR DE UYUNI, BOLIVIA

Not many places on this third rock from the sun are more otherworldly than the blindingly white Salar de Uyuni (p207), the world's largest salt flat high up in the almost surreal Bolivian *altiplano* (Andean high plain), best visited on a multiday trip around the country's stunning southwest. You won't believe your eyes – guaranteed!

Annelies Mertens, Lonely Planet staff, Australia

6

WOODS-WHEATCROFT

BEACHES, BRAZIL

I wasn't much of a 'beach person' until I experienced the splendors of coastal Brazil (see p276). With thousands of kilometers of perfect white-sand options ranging from bikini-laden scenes to empty, idyllic escapes, you're bound to find the paradise you've been seeking.

Lou LaGrange, Lonely Planet staff, USA

7

MANFRED GOTTSCHALK

JOHN ELK

5

THE 'W' TREK, TORRES DEL PAINE, CHILE

Everything they say about the weather in Patagonia is true! We fought horizontal snow, howling winds and sleet. In between we saw breathtaking mountains, glacial lakes and spectacular skies. The 'W' route (p485) was a truly spectacular hike and well worth the effort. Fortunately, my warm-blooded companion was able to put up our tent and cook dinner in crazy conditions while I worked on getting the feeling back in my fingers and toes. It was an absolutely fantastic adventure!

Emma Cashen, traveler, Australia

CENTRAL SURINAME NATURE RESERVE, SURINAME

After a rickety bus journey and a couple more hours in a dugout canoe, I arrived on rugged, lush Foengoe Island (p714). Days were spent hiking, bird-watching, monkey-spotting and admiring the views from atop the steep and sleek Voltzberg. At night, the mosquito net provided little muffling of the howler monkeys that sang me to sleep.

**Emily K Wolman,
Lonely Planet staff, USA**

EMILY WOLMAN

8

PIES SPECIFICS

SALTO ÁNGEL (ANGEL FALLS), VENEZUELA

After an 11-hour flight, a 10-hour bus journey, six hours on a motorized rowing boat and a four-hour hike, the clouds parted as we sat at the bottom of the falls (p966) and it literally took our breath away – the group collectively gasped, in total awe of the amazing sight in front of us. All that effort was worthwhile for just the briefest glimpse.

James Andrews, traveler, UK

KRZYSZTOF DYDYNSKI

10

9

CIUDAD PERDIDA TREK, COLOMBIA

It wasn't just the 2000 steps up to the jungle-covered lost city (p536), it was also swimming and wading through crystal clear water to get there, and passing indigenous tribal villagers going about their daily lives.

**Jennifer Mullins,
Lonely Planet staff, Australia**

PAUL

11 **TRINIDAD, PARAGUAY**

While in Paraguay, make it your mission to check out the Jesuit *reducciones* (settlements) at Trinidad and Jesús (p752). Resurrected from the rubble, these beautifully preserved religious ruins don't see many visitors and you'll likely have them to yourself.

Paul Smith, Lonely Planet author

Contents

The Authors

REGIS ST. LOUIS
Coordinating Author, Ecuador

After his first journey to the Andes in 1999, Regis returned home, sold all his belongings and set off on a classic journey across South America. Since then, he's returned numerous times to travel the continent, logging thousands of miles on dodgy jungle and mountain roads, and he's learned to speak Spanish and Portuguese. Regis is the coordinating author of Lonely Planet's *Ecuador, Brazil* and *Rio de Janeiro* guides, and he has contributed to more than two dozen Lonely Planet titles. His work has appeared in the *Chicago Tribune* and the *Los Angeles Times,* among other publications. He lives in New York City.

SANDRA BAO
Argentina

Being born in Buenos Aires has made Sandra a *porteña* (BA citizen) for life. She left Argentina for the United States at age nine, with thoughts that 'Midnight Special' and 'Yellow Submarine' were creations of Argentine musicians. Now she knows the harsh truth, but remains proud of her original country's famous steaks, *fútbol* and tango. Sandra has traveled extensively throughout the world, but especially loves Patagonia's Andean spine. She's the author of Lonely Planet's *Buenos Aires* guide and has contributed to *Argentina, Mexico, Venezuela* and several other titles.

GREGOR CLARK
Brazil

Gregor has been hooked on South American travel ever since making his first trip across the equator in 1990. Over the past two decades, he's visited everywhere from Caracas to Tierra del Fuego, from the Galápagos to Machu Picchu to Easter Island. But Brazil remains his favorite country of all, thanks to the warmth, exuberance and graciousness of its people, the lyrical beauty of the Portuguese language, the music and the food, and the country's remarkable array of wild and beautiful places. Gregor has contributed to Lonely Planet's *Brazil* and *Argentina* guides.

LONELY PLANET AUTHORS

Why is our travel information the best in the world? It's simple: our authors are passionate, dedicated travelers. They don't take freebies in exchange for positive coverage so you can be sure the advice you're given is impartial. They travel widely to all the popular spots, and off the beaten track. They don't research using just the internet or phone. They discover new places not included in any other guidebook. They personally visit thousands of hotels, restaurants, palaces, trails, galleries, temples and more. They speak with dozens of locals every day to make sure you get the kind of insider knowledge only a local could tell you. They take pride in getting all the details right, and in telling it how it is. Think you can do it? Find out how at **lonelyplanet.com**.

AIMÉE DOWL
The Guianas

Aimée didn't think much about the Guianas until rumors of strange wildlife compelled her to visit Suriname (and generally prompted friends to ask 'is that in Africa?'). Her Guianese adventure for Lonely Planet delivered even more cultural surprises and jungle critters – enough, she hopes, to lure a few Shoestringers that way. When Aimée is not in such out-of-the-way places, she lives at a cool 2850m in Quito, Ecuador, where she is a freelance writer. Her work has appeared in the *New York Times, Viajes, Ms. Magazine, BBC History* and four Lonely Planet guides.

BETH KOHN
Venezuela

An *aficionada* of Latin American rhythms and culture since her Miami childhood, Beth has claimed the window seat on buses throughout the Spanish-speaking world. A longtime resident of San Francisco, she navigates the hills of her adopted hometown by beater bicycle and spends way too much time scheming up summer backpacking trips. She is also a photographer, and an author of Lonely Planet's *Venezuela, Mexico* and *California* guides. You can see more of her work at www.bethkohn.com.

CAROLYN McCARTHY
Chile

Carolyn first met Chile as a tourist, returned seasonally as a trekking guide and moved there in 2003 on a Fulbright grant to document pioneer Patagonia. On this trip she found out what happens with uninsured rental cars, befriended more street dogs and endured a heady case of *soroche* (altitude sickness). Her work has appeared in the *National Geographic, Boston Globe, Salt Lake Tribune,* on lonelyplanet.com and in other publications. For Lonely Planet she recently authored *Trekking in the Patagonian Andes* and *Central America, Chile, South America* and *Yellowstone & Grand Teton National Parks* guides. Visit her blog at www.carolynswildblueyonder.blogspot.com.

ANJA MUTIĆ   Bolivia

While growing up in Croatia, New York–based Anja had a deep fascination with the ancient civilizations and mysterious rainforests of South America. In 2002 she spent six weeks traveling around Bolivia, immediately enchanted with its remote landscapes and indigenous cultures. She descended into the mines of Potosí, swam in Inca hot springs, found herself in the midst of a coca peasants' roadblock and got lost in the Amazon. For this book, she was repeatedly hit by water balloons leading up to Carnaval. Still, she'd go back in a snap.

MIKE POWER   Colombia

Mike is an English freelance journalist specializing in Latin American current affairs. He became fascinated by Colombia during an extended freelance assignment there in 2007–08. During research for this book he was dazzled by the beauty of Salento, dazed by the toughness of La Guajira and awed by the infinite dimensions of the Amazon. He has reported extensively from Panama for Reuters, from Haiti for CBC, and from Colombia for Glasgow's *Sunday Herald*, www.thefirstpost.co.uk and London's *Guardian* newspaper. Next time he goes on assignment, he'll be packing more tea bags.

KEVIN RAUB   Brazil, Peru

Kevin grew up in Atlanta and started his career as a music journalist in New York, working for *Men's Journal* and *Rolling Stone* magazines. The rock 'n' roll lifestyle took its toll, so he needed an extended vacation and took up travel writing. His first trip to Peru involved eating palm grubs and jungle rat while cruising the Amazon, and a little shimmy and shake from the aftershocks of the devastating quake of 2007. He lives in São Paulo, which he is determined to turn the world onto.

PAUL SMITH   Paraguay

From an early age, and with a vague and naive ambition to be the next David Attenborough, Paul dreamed of exploring the remotest areas of South America in search of wildlife. After spending two months in Bolivia as a student, that dream started to come true, but with David Attenborough still going strong he changed his career plans, became a travel writer and moved to Paraguay permanently in 2003. While researching this edition Paul came face to face with a puma in Enciso, fell in a reedbed near Asunción and lamented the lack of space to include more places.

ANDY SYMINGTON   Brazil

Andy first visited Brazil in the last millennium, and saw in the new one in style on Copacabana Beach in Rio. Though based in northern Spain, he gets back to Brazil often, for those untranslatable Amazonian juices, for the nightlife, for *moquecas* (seafood stew), and for the people, but especially for the crisp, cold crack of the machete-opened green coconut, the world's best breakfast.

LUCAS VIDGEN   Argentina, Uruguay

Lucas has been dropping in and out of South America for the last 20-odd years – traveling, staying put, working, slacking off. He's contributed to several *Central America*, *South America* and *Argentina* Lonely Planet titles. Lucas loves the wide open spaces (best experienced from the back of a pickup truck) of Argentina and Uruguay, a perfect contrast to their cosmopolitan cities. When not on the road, he lives in Quetzaltenango, Guatemala, where he publishes the nightlife and culture magazine *XelaWho*.

Itineraries

THE BIG LOOP

This is it – the time-is-not-an-issue journey of a lifetime. Ease into Latin American culture in **Buenos Aires** (p48). Go east to **Bariloche** (p130) and follow the Deep South route (p17) back to Buenos Aires. Continue north to **Córdoba** (p91) and **Salta** (p103) and cross over to Chile's desert oasis of **San Pedro de Atacama** (p421). Head into Bolivia to experience the surreal **Salar de Uyuni** (p207). Continue to **La Paz** (p174) and on to Peru via **Lake Titicaca** (p806). Linger at **Cuzco** (p811) and **Machu Picchu** (p825) before going to **Lima** (p775), **Huaraz** (p846) and on to Ecuador. Visit colonial **Cuenca** (p634) and enchanting **Quito** (p600). Pass into Colombia to see bustling **Medellín** (p550) and the spectacular **Zona Cafetera** (p557), then go to **Cartagena** (p538) to chill out on the Caribbean. See **Parque Nacional Tayrona** (p534) and **Ciudad Perdida** (p536) before bussing from **Santa Marta** (p530) to **Maracaibo** (p941) in Venezuela. Hang out in **Mérida** (p943) before moving to **Salto Ángel** (p966) and **Roraima** (p969). Cross into Brazil at **Santa Elena de Uairén** (p970), travel to **Manaus** (p360) and boat down the Amazon to **Belém** (p351). Then hit **Parque Nacional dos Lençóis Maranhenses** (p350), **Jericoacoara** (p345), **Olinda** (p336) and **Salvador** (p317). Take in the beaches and nightlife of **Rio de Janeiro** (p258) and go to **Campo Grande** (p314) for a wildlife tour of the **Pantanal** (p311). Cross into Paraguay for a look at the biodiversity of the **Chaco** (p758) and urban exploring in **Asunción** (p742). Visit the engineering marvel of **Itaipú Dam** (p755) and the thundering **Iguazú Falls** (p88). Route back through Brazil on to charming **Montevideo** (p883) before boating to Buenos Aires for a grand ending of the South American tour.

How long?
5-8 months

When to go?
Year-round; consider Carnaval in Feb/Mar; in Patagonia, Dec-Mar is best

Budget?
Daily average if you scrimp: US$35-45

From the Argentine pampas to the chilly Andean *páramo* (grassland), from the Caribbean to the Amazon and onto the cerulean beaches of Brazil, the 26,000km Big Loop winds through 10 South American countries, giving the unbound wanderer heaps to write home about.

ANDEAN HIGH

For rugged adventure, unparalleled alpine vistas, rich indigenous cultures, fabulous crafts and some of the best, most colorful markets on the continent, journey down the Andes from Colombia to Argentina.

How long?
2 months

When to go?
Year-round

Budget?
Per day US$20-35

Fly into **Bogotá** (p510), taking in the old historic center and lively nightlife. Take day trips to the striking underground salt cathedral at **Zipaquirá** (p519) and to the outdoor adventure spot of **Suesca** (p520). Continue on to the colonial town of **Popayán** (p566), near the **Parque Nacional Puracé** (p570), where you can take some fantastic treks into the Andes. Then go to **Pasto** (see boxed text, p575) and on to the beautifully set **Laguna de la Cocha** (see boxed text, p575). Cross the Ecuadorian border at Ipiales and visit **Quito** (p600), wandering the streets of colonial Old Town before heading south through the volcano-studded Andes. Do the **Quilotoa Loop** (p625), hit the hot baths in **Baños** (p627) and visit colonial **Cuenca** (p634). Cross into Peru and pause at **Huaraz** (p846) for Peru's best trekking and climbing. Leave plenty of time to linger in traveler-favorite **Cuzco** (p811), gateway to Peru's big must-see, **Machu Picchu** (p825). Skip the overrun Inca Trail, however, and try an alternative **trek** (see boxed text, p832). From there head south across shimmering **Lake Titicaca** (p806) into Bolivia for more hiking, trekking and mountaineering in the **Cordillera Real and the Yungas** (p189). Continue south to the hallucinogenic landscapes around **Salar de Uyuni** (p207), before crossing to Argentina by way of **La Quiaca** (see boxed text, p109) and the spectacular **Quebrada de Humahuaca** (p108). Travel through the majestic Argentine Andes until you hit **Mendoza** (p118), near massive **Cerro Aconcagua** (p122), the western hemisphere's highest peak.

The Andean High route winds through more than 5000km of rugged Andean highlands, passing snow-capped volcanoes, windswept *páramo*, indigenous villages, incredible vistas and some of the western hemisphere's highest peaks. Primary transport: the bus, a (white-knuckle) South American adventure in its own right.

THE DEEP SOUTH

Mysterious, windswept, glacier-riddled Patagonia is one of South America's most magical destinations. For tent-toters, outdoors nuts, climbers and hikers, it's a dream. Patagonia – and the archipelago of Tierra del Fuego – is best visited November through March, and you can see more for cheaper if you camp. Remember, the going can be *slo-o-o-w.*

Start in busy **Bariloche** (p130), in the Argentine Lake District. The Andes here are magnificently forested and studded with azure lakes. Don't miss **Parque Nacional Nahuel Huapi** (p133) or **Parque Nacional Lanín** (p128). From Bariloche head south to **Esquel** (p135). Travel west into Chile to the Andean hamlet of **Futaleufú** (p470) for some of the continent's best rafting. Take the scenic Carretera Austral to **Coyhaique** (p473) and on to the striking scenery of the green-blue **Lago General Carrera** (p476). Head to the windswept **Chile Chico** (p476), then cross into Argentina to **Los Antiguos** (p144). Bounce down the desolate RN 40 to **El Chaltén** (p144) in spectacular **Parque Nacional Los Glaciares** (p148). Hike and climb your brains out before having them warped by the **Glaciar Perito Moreno** (p148) near **El Calafate** (p146). Cross back into Chile to hike beneath the granite spires of **Torres del Paine** (p484); rest up in **Puerto Natales** (p481). Head to **Punta Arenas** (p477), before traveling south into Argentina's **Tierra del Fuego** (p149) and bottoming out at **Ushuaia** (p150). After severe southern exposure, work back north along the Atlantic, stopping for penguins in **Reserva Provincial Punta Tombo** (p143) and whales in **Reserva Faunística Península Valdés** (p141). After days in the wilderness, treat yourself to well-deserved recovery in civilization, so beeline to **Buenos Aires** (p48).

An alternate (pricey) route south is aboard Chile's world-famous **Navimag ferry** (p385), sailing through majestic fjords from Puerto Montt to Puerto Natales.

How long?
1-2 months

When to go?
Mid-Nov–mid-Apr

Budget?
Per day US$40-50
(cheaper if you camp)

By the end of this epic adventure, you'll have traveled over 5000km and seen the very best of Patagonia. Bus and hitchhiking are the cheapest modes of travel, but lake crossings are possible and flights make things faster. Argentina's RN 40 is covered by private minivan.

SAILING THE MIGHTY AMAZON

Few rivers fire the imagination like the Amazon. Ever dreamt of going down it? You can. But there's a reason everything west of **Manaus** (p360) in Brazil is off the beaten track: boat travel on the Amazon can be bleak, boring, sightless, uncomfortable, hot and dirty. Truthfully, it's *hard-core.*

Just to make the journey as long as possible, set off from **Yurimaguas** (see boxed text, p867) in Peru. Start with a 10-hour warm-up float to **Lagunas** (p867) and check out the **Reserva Nacional Pacaya-Samiria** (see boxed text, p867), before heading on to **Iquitos** (p864) on the Río Marañón (which becomes the Amazon). From Iquitos (inaccessible by road), get a three-day boat (or a fast eight-hour speedboat) to the tri-border region of Peru, Colombia and Brazil, and take a break – and a jungle excursion – in Colombia's **Leticia** (p576). From Leticia, it's three more arduous days to Manaus, but breaking the trip at a jungle lodge in the amazing **Reserva de Desenvolvimento Sustentável Mamirauá** (see boxed text, p365), makes it all worthwhile. Once you do hit Manaus, you're getting into well-traveled territory. But, having come this far, the journey is only over when you hit majestic **Belém** (p351), 3½ days away on the Atlantic. Break the journey in **Santarém** (p357) to visit beautiful **Alter do Chão** (p359).

For those who really want a challenge, an interesting alternative would be starting this journey in the Ecuadorian oil town of **Coca** (p644) on the Río Napo. From here it's a 12- to 15-hour journey to **Nuevo Rocafuerte** (p646) on the Peruvian border. You can spend the night (or a few weeks, if you don't time the cargo-boat departure right) before undertaking the six-day boat ride to Iquitos in Peru. In Iquitos, pick up the first part of the itinerary.

How long?
3-4 weeks

When to go?
Year-round

Budget?
Per day US$30-45

By the time you finish this maniacal journey, you'll have motored over 4000km, slapped hundreds of mosquitoes, eaten loads of lousy food, met some true characters and seen a *lot* of water. Most importantly, you'll have floated the Amazon from its Peruvian headwaters to the Atlantic.

EXPLORING THE GUIANAS

They're expensive, they're hard to reach, they're largely unpopulated, and they can be very, very captivating. And they're *definitely* off the beaten path. Where you start depends on where you're coming from: Guyana via New York, Cayenne via Paris or Paramaribo via Amsterdam. For the sake of argument, let's say you're traveling overland from Brazil.

From **Oiapoque** (see boxed text, p357) in Brazil hire a dugout canoe (unless the bridge is complete) across the Rio Oiapoque into French Guiana. You're now officially off the beaten track. Make your way by bus across the verdant, forgotten landscape (complete with burned-out cars along the roadside) to **Cacao** (p694). From here, embark upon the two-day hike along **Sentier Molokoï de Cacao** (p695) for some wildlife-spotting fun. Then make your way up to **Kourou** (p696), where you can witness rockets blast off from South America's only satellite launcher. Take a ferry (or a more comfy catamaran) across shark-infested waters to the **Îles du Salut** (p697), a former island prison where you can sling up a hammock in the old prison dormitories! Back on the mainland, head up the coast and watch the turtles nesting (April to July only) at **Awala-Yalimapo** (p701) before crossing into Suriname. Hang out for a few days in weirdly wonderful **Paramaribo** (p708), and set up a tour into the majestic **Central Suriname Nature Reserve** (p714). From Paramaribo, continue west to **Nieuw Nickerie** (p715), where you cross into Guyana. Head up to **Georgetown** (p723), and make a detour by boat up to isolated **Shell Beach** (p728) or to see the spectacular **Kaieteur Falls** (see boxed text, p729). Back in Georgetown, get a bus south across the majestic Rupununi Savannas, stopping in **Annai** (p730) and **Lethem** (p731) to savor the vast isolation.

How long?
3-5 weeks

When to go?
Year-round; ideally Jul-Dec

Budget?
French Guiana per day US$60; Suriname and Guyana per day US$30-40

Exploring the Guianas means leaving the beaten path behind and journeying some 2500km. You'll see fascinating capital cities, tropical jungle, unadulterated cowboy country and a couple of the continent's most pristine beaches.

LET THE PARTY BEGIN

South America offers some pretty incredible options when it comes to rocking a few sleepless nights. Some towns have infamous nightlife scenes, while in other places the action peaks only at big festivals or in summer. For an overview of the big fêtes, see Festivals & Events in each country chapter's Directory.

Start things off with a bang in **Rio de Janeiro** (p258), not missing the frenetic samba scene in Lapa. Continue the Brazilian *festa* by hitting the non-stop party scene of **Porto Seguro** (p328), **Salvador** (p317) and fun but laid-back **Jericoacoara** (p345). From there travel north to the Guianas. The Guyanese will tell you that **Georgetown's** (p727) Sheriff St is the hottest party in the Caribbean. Next, it's on to **Caracas** (p919) for steamy salsa-filled nightclubs, tropical **Porlamar** (p959) for island allure, and **Mérida** (p943) for a university vibe and all-night music scene. Colombia keeps the party going in comely **Cartagena** (p538) and even livelier **Cali** (p563). In Ecuador, the small-town beach scene of **Montañita** (p660) is a nice contrast to the bar-and-club-land of **Quito's** (p613) Mariscal district. In Peru, spend a night crawling **Lima's** (p787) Barranco neighborhood, before moving the party to festive **Arequipa** (p798). The good-time scene of Bolivia's **La Paz** (p174) is next, followed by the journey to Chile's bohemian seaside city of **Valparaíso** (p400) – New Year's Eve here is particularly spectacular. Afterwards hit the student party scene of **Córdoba** (p91) in Argentina, then move on to the great nightlife of **Buenos Aires** (p48), with mandatory bar-hopping in Palermo Viejo. Hop the ferry to reach the bars and discos in **Montevideo's** (p887) Old Town. Time things right to catch the summer-long party at swanky **Punta del Este** (p898) in Uruguay. Next it's on to Brazil, to hit the island revelry on **Ilha de Santa Catarina** (p298). End the journey with a few nights in São Paulo (p282) for a final send-off of drinking and dancing in the city's unrivaled club scene.

How long?
6-12 weeks

When to go?
Year-round

Budget?
Per day US$35-50

This big nightlife journey around the continent takes in 10 countries and some 17,000km. The tour offers plenty of big-city intrigue, as well as some welcome respites at festive beach spots and colonial towns.

Getting Started

Planning for the big trip is half the fun. This section is intended to help you decide when to go and predict what kind of cash you'll drop, plus offer some tips on good films and books to check out before heading to South America. Also browse the South America Directory (p984), which covers subjects ranging from activities to volunteering. The Transportation chapter (p1000) will give you a good overview of bussing, boating and jetting around the continent.

WHEN TO GO

South America stretches from the tropics – where sweltering lowlands can lie only hours from chilly Andean highlands – nearly to Antarctica, so when to go depends on where you go.

Climbing and trekking in the Andes of Ecuador, Peru and Bolivia is best in the drier months from May to September but possible year-round. Travel in the Amazon is also possible year-round, though regional rainy seasons throughout the Amazon make river travel easier (it's generally driest from July to November). Ski season in Argentina and Chile is June to September. Patagonia is best visited during the region's summer months of December to April, but hotels and campgrounds book solid and prices are highest during the peak months of January and February.

See Climate Charts, p987, and Climate in the Directory section of each country chapter for country-specific information.

The continent's wild array of colorful festivals (see p991) is also a consideration; Carnaval, the most famous celebration of all, is in late February and early March. It's well worth seeing, but prices are high (expect to pay about triple normal rates during Carnaval).

You should also take into account high- and low-season rates for the places you plan to visit. In Brazil, for instance, prices are high from December through Carnaval, and immediately drop the week after Carnaval. South Americans love to travel during the two- to three-week period around Semana Santa (Holy Week or Easter) and during the Christmas–New Year holidays. Both foreign and national tourists are out in droves in July and

---

DON'T LEAVE HOME WITHOUT

Remember this: you can buy just about anything you'll need in South America. Certain items, however, can be hard to find. For more on what to bring, flip through the South America Directory (p984). And don't forget the following:

- alarm clock – for those early-morning bus rides
- insect repellent (containing 30% DEET) – useful no matter where you're going
- photocopies of important documents – plus scanned copies in your email as a backup
- duct tape – make your own miniroll around a pencil stub or lighter
- pocket USB-type flash drive for digital storage
- earplugs – accessory of choice for snoring bunkmates, relentless traffic and psychopathic roosters
- Swiss Army knife or multitool (with corkscrew)
- first-aid kit – be prepared
- universal sink plug – for washing clothes on the road
- flashlight or head lamp – essential for unreliable power sources

August. During these tourist high seasons prices peak, hotels fill up and public transportation gets slammed. The flip side is a celebratory, holiday atmosphere that can be quite contagious.

COSTS & MONEY

Brazil is by far the most expensive country in South America, though prices vary depending where you go – Rio, the South and the Southeast being more expensive than the Northeast. Chile is also expensive relative to the rest of South America, as is Argentina, which has been hit by runaway inflation in recent years. Travel costs in Uruguay run slightly lower than Argentina, while the Guianas are a mixed bag, but generally tend toward the pricey end of the scale (French Guiana still uses the euro after all). The cheapest countries on the continent are Bolivia, Paraguay, Ecuador and Colombia. Traveling in Venezuela can be pricey (the wildly fluctuating black-market exchange rate is much better value than the official rate, but of course it's illegal and there is a greater risk of being ripped off). See p980 for more details.

At the beginning of each country chapter, we give a thumbnail sketch of costs. Generally, it will cost less per person if you travel in twos or threes, spend little time in big cities, travel slowly and cook your own meals or eat at markets. Costs rack up as you tag on comforts like air-conditioning and a private bathroom, expensive tours to places such as the Galápagos Islands, or activities like skiing or clubbing.

ATM cards provide the most convenient way of getting cash on the road. ATMs are available in most cities and large towns – though in remote destinations, you'll want to get ample funds before heading out. Many ATMs accept personal identification numbers (PINs) of only four digits; find out whether this applies to your destinations before heading off. Traveler's checks (best if in US dollars) are less convenient. They usually entail waiting in lines during standard bank hours, and many banks even refuse to accept them.

WHAT YOU'LL PAY

To give a very rough idea of relative costs, let's assume you're traveling with another person, mostly by bus, staying in cheap but clean hotels, eating in local restaurants and food stalls, with the occasional splurge on sightseeing or a night out dancing. Not including juicy side trips or tours into interior regions, you could expect the following as a minimum per person/per day budget:

- Argentina – US$35 to US$45
- Bolivia – US$15 to US$25
- Brazil – US$45 to US$50
- Chile – US$40 to US$50
- Colombia – US$20 to US$30
- Ecuador – US$20 to US$25
- French Guiana – US$50 to US$60
- Guyana – US$40 to US$50
- Paraguay – US$25 to US$35
- Peru – US$20 to US$30
- Suriname – US$30 to US$40
- Uruguay – US$35 to US$45
- Venezuela – US$60 to US$120 (at official exchange rates)

TIPS TO STAY ON A BUDGET

There's no need to bargain locals out of every last coin when other tried-and-true techniques will save you more. Try the following:

- Consider traveling out of season (weather permitting) to get low-season rates for lodging and airfare.
- Plan your days around free activities, like exploring city neighborhoods and parks, catching free concerts and shows, and hanging out on the beach.
- When asking about accommodation rates, always ask about low-season discounts or for staying multiple nights.
- Always ask about the *almuerzo, menú* or *prato do dia* (set meal).
- Form a group for tours; your bargaining power increases the more people you have.
- Instead of eating at restaurants, buy food at open-air markets or cook your own food at your hostel/guesthouse.
- Take overnight buses in countries such as Argentina, Brazil and Chile to save a night's hotel costs.
- Camp whenever you can (only when it's safe), especially in Patagonia and in hostel backyards.
- Wash your clothes in hotel sinks (where permissible).
- Travel slowly.

Note that we use local currencies for costs in this book. Owing to often volatile exchange rates, it's wise to research the latest financial situation, both before and during your trip. This is particularly important in inflationary countries like Venezuela and Argentina, less so in more economically stable Chile.

For more detailed info, see the country chapter directories at the end of each country directory, and the South America Directory (p993).

LIFE ON THE ROAD

Whether you're thumbing a ride in Chilean Patagonia, waiting curbside for a milk truck in the Ecuadorian Andes or listening to the air brakes hiss on a hair-raising ride through the Bolivian *altiplano* (Andean high plain), South America kicks out unforgettable experiences on the road. In fact, some argue the road *is* the experience.

And then there's *life* on the road. In South America, it's never short on challenge. But that's what makes it South America. Travel here is about struggling awake for a dawn departure after being kept up all night by a blaring soccer game. It's about sucking dust on a long bus ride while manically trying to guess which of the towns you keep passing through is the one you intended to visit. It means peaceful relief when you finally arrive and find your pack still on the roof. It's the sight of begging children, the arduous haul to the hotel, a screaming bladder and the excitement of a new town all catapulting your mind from one emotional extreme to another.

The hotel manager says the showers are hot, but the water hitting the skin is as cold as a Patagonian glacier. There's no seat on the toilet. (At least the bowels are behaving.) You call that a fan? It sounds like a helicopter! OK – food. Leave the pack in the corner, get out the map, locate the market, grab the passport (or leave it behind?) and go. The sun feels great. Then you get lost, your mood turns sour as your blood sugar crashes, you find the market, you smell the mangoes, and you try to haggle but have no clue what the fruit seller is saying. You finally hand over the cash – did you just get ripped off? – and walk out to find a good place to eat. And when you do, it's sheer and incomparable bliss.

CONDUCT
Introductions

In general, South Americans are gregarious, not easily offended, and will want to exchange pleasantries before starting a conversation; skipping this part of any social interaction is considered unrefined and tactless. Public behavior can be very formal, especially among government officials, who expect respect and deference. Casual introductions, on the other hand, are relaxed and friendly. In countries like Argentina, Chile and French Guiana men and women kiss other women on the cheek, rather than shaking hands – in Brazil it's two kisses, one on each cheek (go to the left first). Men usually shake hands with other men, unless they're real pals, in which case they give a hug. If in doubt, wait to see what the other person does and then respond.

Indigenous People

The word *indígenas* refers to indigenous people, who are especially present in the Andes and in the Amazon Basin. You may hear the term *indio/a* batted around among *mestizos* (people of mixed indigenous and European descent) but it is considered very derogatory.

Access to many remote Amazon Basin areas where people retain the most traditional ways of living is heavily restricted, and it is essential to respect these restrictions. Such regulations help to deflect unwanted interference and protect the communities from diseases to which they have little immunity.

Other indigenous groups or subgroups have opened their doors to travelers who want to learn about their culture. Community tourism is one of the highlights of South America, but remember to take ceremonies and rituals seriously, despite the fact that they may be organized for your sake. *Ayahuasca* and other psychoactive drugs play an important part of religious life for some rainforest communities; it is illegal for foreigners to take these drugs, although you may be offered a trip down shaman lane by certain opportunists. Do your research.

Dress

Casual dress is widely accepted, but most South Americans still take considerable pride in their personal appearance, especially in the evening. Foreign visitors should, at the very least, be clean and neatly dressed if they wish to conform to local standards and be treated with respect by officials, businesspeople and professionals. When going out at night, you'll stand out in typical travelers' attire in all but the most gringo-haunted hangouts. Try to keep one 'going-out outfit' on hand for nights out. It's also advisable to look respectable when crossing borders, as police and military officials are less likely to detain you.

DOS & DON'TS

- Do tip 10% if *servicio* (service) isn't included in the bill.
- Do be respectful when haggling for anything.
- Do approach eating with an adventurous attitude.
- Don't take pictures of people without permission.
- Don't feel uncomfortable in the Andean countries (Bolivia, Ecuador and Peru) when people stare.
- Don't hesitate to refuse food or drink from strangers.

TOP 10

RECOMMENDED FILMS

1 *Central do Brasil* (Central Station, 1998); set in Brazil; directed by Walter Salles

2 *Cidade de Deus* (City of God, 2002); set in Brazil; directed by Fernando Meirelles

3 *Diarios de Motocicleta* (The Motorcycle Diaries, 2004); set in various parts of South America; directed by Walter Salles

4 *La Historia Oficial* (The Official Story, 1985); set in Argentina; directed by Luis Puenzo

5 *Maria Full of Grace* (2003); set in Colombia; directed by Joshua Marston

6 *The Mission* (1986); set in Paraguay; directed by Roland Joffé

7 *Nueve Reinas* (Nine Queens, 2000); set in Argentina; directed by Fabián Bielinsky

8 *Orfeu Negro* (1959); set in Brazil; directed by Marcel Camus

9 *The Revolution Will Not Be Televised* (2002); set in Venezuela; directed by Kim Bartley and Donnacha O'Briain

10 *Stranded* (2007); set in Uruguay and Chile; directed by Gonzalo Arijón

MUST-READ BOOKS

1 *Dona Flor and Her Two Husbands* by Jorge Amado (Brazil, 1978)

2 *Ficciones* by Jorge Luis Borges (Argentina, 1944)

3 *Hopscotch* by Julio Cortázar (Argentina, 1963)

4 *House of Spirits* by Isabel Allende (Chile, 1982)

5 *In Patagonia* by Bruce Chatwin (England, 1977)

6 *The Lost City of Z: A Tale of Deadly Obsession in the Amazon* by David Grann (USA, 2009)

7 *One Hundred Years of Solitude* by Gabriel García Márquez (Colombia, 1967)

8 *Open Veins of Latin America* by Eduardo Galeano (Uruguay, 1971)

9 *The Story Teller* by Mario Vargas Llosa (Peru, 1987)

10 *The Villagers* by Jorge Icaza (Ecuador, 1964)

To people of modest means, even shoestring travelers possess considerable wealth. Flaunting items such as iPods, expensive-looking watches and jewelry is likely to attract thieves. In addition to leaving the name-brand goods at home, one way of blending in is to buy clothes at the local market after you arrive.

Sex

Sexual contact between locals and visitors, male and female, straight and gay, is quite common, and some areas could be described as sex-tourism destinations. Prostitution exists everywhere, but is more visible in some places than in others (as in certain parts of Copacabana in Rio, Brazil). Child prostitution is not common but, sadly, exists. There are harsh penalties for those convicted of soliciting children as well as real risks of entrapment. AIDS is widespread among gay and straight people alike, so always protect yourself. Around 1.3 million South Americans are currently living with HIV or AIDS. Brazil, with over 700,000 sufferers, has the highest incidence rate.

Taking Photographs

Don't photograph individuals without obtaining their permission first, especially indigenous people. If someone is giving a public performance, such as a street musician or a dancer at Carnaval, or is incidental to a photograph, in a broad cityscape for example, it's usually not necessary to request permission – but if in doubt, ask or refrain. Also, if you do take photos of street performers or musicians, it's common courtesy to give a little change. See p995 for more information.

Snapshots

CURRENT EVENTS

Great changes are sweeping through the continent, bringing peace and prosperity to some regions, tension and uncertainty to others. South America's biggest success story is Colombia, a country that has made significant strides toward ending its 40-year internal war. Although the conflict isn't over, Colombians are enjoying a previously unimagined period of stability, along with newfound financial confidence. Not surprisingly, President Álvaro Uribe remains popular – a recent poll rated him as one of Colombia's most popular presidents in history.

Brazil also has cause for optimism. After paying off its debts to the IMF ahead of schedule, a vast offshore oil field was discovered in 2007, promising even greater riches to an already energy-independent nation. For most Brazilians, however, the biggest successes are landing both the 2014 World Cup and the 2016 Olympics, which Rio de Janeiro will host. Both are major milestones, not only for Brazil, but for South America, as the Olympics will be the first ever held on the continent. Despite a few scandals, Brazilian President Lula enjoys record-high approval ratings for his economic and social successes – notably raising the standard of living for Brazil's poorest citizens. There's even talk of revising the constitution to allow him to run for a third term.

Speaking of rewriting constitutions, a lot of ink has spilled in South America in the past few years. Citizens of both Ecuador (in 2008) and Bolivia (in 2009) voted to draft new constitutions. Both set ambitious goals toward addressing social injustices (providing free health care, education and basic services to all citizens) and even protecting the environment. To the benefit of those in charge, term limits were also abolished, allowing elected presidents to serve indefinitely. Not everyone had warm feelings. Violent protests erupted in Bolivia led by those who saw the document as yet another step toward the anticapitalist Bolivarism of Venezuelan President Hugo Chávez.

Chávez, South America's most controversial leader, has also benefited from constitutional tinkering. Although he failed in initial efforts to be made 'president for life,' in 2009 citizens approved an amendment ending presidential term limits, ensuring his days in power are far from over. Since US President Obama took office, Chávez' fiery anti-American rhetoric has cooled, with internal problems (the nationwide rise in crime and economic woes brought on by falling oil prices) eclipsing other concerns.

Political shake-ups have occurred all across the continent. In Paraguay, after over 60 years of Colorado party rule, former bishop Fernando Lugo was elected president in 2008, bringing a new era of hope (marred slightly by allegations that he sired three illegitimate children by different women). Argentina, meanwhile, faced a leadership crisis as President Cristina Fernández de Kirchner lost power in congress during midterm elections. Her popularity took a nosedive as the economy faltered while she focused on raising farm export taxes. Even more serious troubles plagued Peru. President Alan García, who launched a campaign to open traditional indigenous lands to gas and mineral exploration, encountered fierce resistance from Amazon-based peoples. The conflict reached a boiling point in 2009, during a bloody encounter between protestors and police that left dozens dead. García's administration has presided over sustained economic growth in its push for development and free trade, but it has also been rocked by corruption scandals.

According to the treaty of the newly created Union of South American Nations (Unasur), the headquarters of the Union will be in Quito, Ecuador. The South American Parliament will convene in Cochabamba, Bolivia; its bank, the Bank of the South, will be in Caracas, Venezuela.

Exploiting the land in the name of economic development is a familiar topic in South America. The fate of Chilean Patagonia remains uncertain. Plans are underway for nearly a dozen hydroelectric projects that could transform one of the world's most pristine wildernesses into another industrial engine. The Guaianas, on the other hand, are moving in the opposite direction. Ecotourism is the hot topic, with Suriname and Guyana promoting their rainforests as the setting for an African-style safari at a fraction of the price.

Despite a legacy of border disputes and skirmishes among some South American nations, the continent may be on its way to forging an ambitious new union. In 2008 the leaders of 12 South American nations (all but French Guiana) met in Brazil to sign the treaty of the Union of South American Nations (Unasur). Modeled on the EU, this regional body aims to boost economic and political integration in the region, improve trade and possibly even establish a single currency. The treaty envisions a revolving presidency and biannual meetings of national representatives. In 2009 representatives were still hammering out the details for the creation of the new regional development bank, the Bank of the South. By 2014, Unasur aims to remove tariffs for most products, which will be a significant step toward the creation of a single market.

HISTORY
The First South Americans

At its peak, the Inca empire governed at least 12 million people from 100 separate cultures and 20 language groups. Its highways traversed more than 8000km of the Andes.

Back in the salad days (sometime between 12,500 and 70,000 years ago), humans migrated from Asia to Alaska over a land bridge across the Bering Strait and slowly hunted and gathered their way south. Settled agriculture developed in South America between 5000 BC and 2500 BC in and around present-day Peru, and the emerging societies ultimately developed into major civilizations, of which the Inca empire was the most sophisticated.

Enter the Spanish

At the time of the Spanish invasion in the early 16th century, the Inca empire had reached the zenith of its power, ruling over millions of people from northern Ecuador to central Chile and northern Argentina, where native peoples of the Araucanian language groups fiercely resisted incursions from the north.

The Spanish first arrived in Latin America in 1492, when Christopher Columbus, who was bankrolled by Queen Isabella of Spain to find a new route to Asia's spice islands, accidentally bumped into the Caribbean islands. Meanwhile, the Portuguese navigator Vasco da Gama founded the new sea route to Asia. These spectacular discoveries raised the stakes in the brewing rivalry between Spain and Portugal and, to sort out claims of their newly discovered lands, they came to the negotiating table.

Published in 1552, Bartolomé de las Casas' impassioned *Short Account of the Destruction of the Indies* is one of the only accounts written during the Spanish Conquest that is sympathetic to indigenous Americans.

Dividing & Conquering

Spanish and Portuguese representatives met in 1494 to draw a line about 48° west of Greenwich, giving Africa and Asia to Portugal and all of the New World to Spain. Significantly, however, the treaty placed the coast of Brazil (not discovered until six years later) on the Portuguese side of the line, giving Portugal access to the new continent.

Between 1496 and 1526, Spanish exploration from Panama intensified. Rumors surfaced of a golden kingdom south of Panama, prompting Francisco Pizarro to convince Spanish authorities to finance an expedition of some 200 men.

When Pizarro encountered the Inca, the empire was embroiled in a civil war and proved vulnerable to this invasion by a very small force of Spaniards. Pizarro's well-armed, mounted soldiers wreaked havoc on the population, but his deadliest weapon was infectious disease, to which indigenous people lacked immunity. The Inca ruler Huayna Capác died, probably of smallpox, in about 1525.

Lima, founded in 1535 as the capital of the new viceroyalty of Peru, was the base for most of the ensuing exploration and conquest, and became the seat of all power in Spanish South America. By 1572 the Spanish had defeated and killed two successive Inca rulers – Manco Inca and Túpac Amaru – and solidified Spain's dominance over much of the continent.

> During the long bleak epoch of slavery, over six million Africans were captured and brought to South America. The majority (around 3.6 million) ended up in Brazil. Others were brought to present-day Venezuela, Colombia, coastal Peru and Ecuador and northwestern Argentina.

Silver, Slavery & Separation

Following the conquest, the Spaniards, who above all else sought gold and silver, worked the indigenous populations mercilessly in the mines and the fields. Native American populations declined rapidly, however, due to introduced diseases. In several parts of the continent, African slaves were introduced in huge numbers to replace the dwindling indigenous labor, notably in the plantations of Brazil and the mines of Bolivia.

The movement for independence by the Spanish colonies began around the end of the 18th century, when domestic problems at home siphoned Spain's interest from its colonies. The Peninsular War which erupted in 1807 was an even greater drain on resources as Spain and Portugal fought off the invading French army under Napoleon. By the end of the war in 1814, Venezuela and Argentina had effectively declared independence from Spain and, over the next seven years, the other Spanish colonies followed suit. Brazil became autonomous in 1807 and declared independence in 1822.

Independence & Dependence

After independence, conservative rural landowners, known as *caudillos,* filled the power vacuum left by the departed colonial regime. Strong dictatorships, periods of instability and the gross inequality between powerful elites and the disenfranchised masses have since characterized most South American countries.

> One of the great heroes of South America is Simón Bolívar ('the Liberator'), who helped secure independence for present-day Venezuela, Colombia, Ecuador, Peru and Bolivia. Gabriel García Márquez wrote a fictionalized account of his last days *(The General in His Labyrinth)* and Hugo Chávez even had Venezuela renamed in his honor (the Bolivarian Republic of Venezuela).

After WWII, which marked the beginning of industrialization throughout South America, most countries turned to foreign loans and investment to make up for their lack of capital. This set the stage for the massive debt crises of the 1970s and 1980s, as South American governments accelerated their borrowing, and profits from industry and agriculture made their way into Western banks and the pockets of a tiny South American elite. Dictatorships provided a semblance of stability, but oppression, poverty and corruption bred violent guerrilla movements in many countries, most notably (and most recently) in Peru and Colombia. Many of the problems facing South America today are a direct result of foreign debt and the systems of corruption and inequality that date back to colonial and postindependence years. The upsurge of populist and nationalist leaders in the early 2000s, with left-leaning presidents elected in several South American countries, was largely a democratic response to years of corruption and incompetence under fiscally conservative and often military-linked ruling parties.

THE CULTURE
Indigenous Culture

When foreigners think of indigenous South Americans, odds are they imagine either the colorfully dressed *indígenas* (indigenous people) of the Andean highlands or the people of the Amazon rainforests. The Quechua and other linguistic groups of the Bolivian, Ecuadorian and Peruvian highlands have coexisted with the *mestizo* (people of mixed indigenous and European descent) majority – although not without conflict – for centuries. Their cultures are strong, autonomous and reticent to change and have influenced their country's culture (through music, food, language and so on) to its core. For travelers, experiencing these highland cultures firsthand can be as simple as getting on a bus, shopping in a market or hanging around a village. Many indigenous people are friendly with foreigners, but many are wary of them, as outsiders have brutally oppressed their people for centuries.

The lives of rainforest peoples are usually vastly different from what the tourist brochures floating the world suggest. Except under unique circumstances, travelers generally will not encounter indigenous people of the rainforest traditionally dressed, unless they're doing so specifically for the sake of tourism – not an inherently negative situation, but one to approach with awareness. Most rainforest communities have only recently been hit with the Western world. Many are facing the complete upheaval – if not annihilation – of their cultures and lives, and the culture one encounters as a visitor is one in the throes of dramatic change.

Bolivia, Peru and Ecuador have the highest percentages of indigenous people, most of whom live in the highlands. Other important groups include the Tikuna, Yanomami and Guaraní of Brazil, the Mapuche of northern Patagonia, the Aymara of the *altiplano* (Andean high plain of Peru, Bolivia, Chile and Argentina) and the Atacameños of Chile.

> For the best collection of online music links, visit the Humanities section of the Latin American Network Information Center (Lanic; www.lanic. utexas.edu). The Music page has dozens of links on nearly every country in South America (except for the Guianas).

Music

Music in South America is a big part of life. Turn it off, and the continent would simply grind to a halt. South America's musical landscape is incredibly varied, which is not surprising given how disparate its roots are. Influences that helped shape the continent's music scene stretch across the globe, taking in African rhythms, North American jazz, indigenous sounds, Spanish flamenco, Cuban and Italian singing styles and even Eastern European polkas and mazurkas – all play a part in forging the great soundtrack of South America. For a complete rundown on the music scene, country by country, see p32. For a list of recommended albums, see opposite.

Population

Over three-quarters of all South Americans live in cities, while large areas such as the Amazon Basin and Atacama Desert are relatively uninhabited. Population growth and internal migration have led to the emergence of supercities, such as São Paulo, Buenos Aires, Rio de Janeiro, Lima and Bogotá.

Infant mortality rates are shockingly high in some countries, most notably Bolivia, Peru and Paraguay. South America has a high proportion of people younger than 15 years old (hovering around 27%), but some of the countries (in particular Bolivia, Colombia, Ecuador, Peru and Venezuela) have even more youthful populations.

> Brazil's diversity is astounding: it has a larger black population than any other country except for Nigeria; São Paulo has the largest Japanese community outside of Japan.

Although the majority of South Americans are *mestizos,* self-identified indigenous peoples make up a large percentage of the population in Bolivia (55%), Peru (45%) and Ecuador (25%). Owing to a legacy of immigration, Brazil has one of Latin America's most ethnically diverse populations, with a sizable portion of the population (around 39%) claiming African heritage. The Guianas are a mosaic of East Indians, Indonesians, Africans, Creoles, Chinese and their descendants. Even the most racially homogeneous countries (eg Argentina, Chile and Paraguay) have Syrians, Chinese, Japanese and other immigrants and their descendants represented in the population.

THE SOUTH AMERICAN SOUNDTRACK

Painful as it was, we winnowed this list down to a lean 25 selections. Here's our highly subjective pick of top albums, country by country.

Argentina

- *Sur o no sur* – Kevin Johansen
- *Tres cosas* – Juana Molina
- *Chaco* – Illya Kuryaki and the Valderramas
- *Gracias a la vida* – Mercedes Sosa

Bolivia

- *Charangos famosos* – Celestino Campos et al

Brazil

- *África Brasil* – Jorge Benjor
- *Tropicália ou Panis et Circensis* – Caetano Veloso, Gilberto Gil et al
- *Chega de Saudade* – João Gilberto
- *Elis & Tom* – Antonio Carlos Jobim and Elis Regina
- *Cartola* – Cartola

Colombia

- *La vida es un ratico* – Juanes
- *La candela viva* – Totó La Momposina
- *¿Dónde están los ladrones?* – Shakira

Chile

- *Miedo escénico* – Beto Cuevas
- *Leyenda* – Inti Illimani
- *Gran Santiago* – Teleradio Donoso

Ecuador

- *Ecuafornia* – Esto es Eso
- *Mis mejores pasillos* – Julio Jaramillo

The Guianas

- *Is We Ting* – Roy Geddes et al

Paraguay

- *Kchiporros* – Kchiporros

Peru

- *Eco de sombras* – Susana Baca

Uruguay

- *Eco* – Jorge Drexler
- *Aunque cueste ver el sol* – No Te Va Gustar

Venezuela

- *The Venezuelan Zinga Son* – Los Amigos Invisibles
- *El rey de los soneros* – Oscar D'León

LA VIDA MUSICAL

Welcome to one of the world's great music destinations. This vast continent, with snowcapped peaks, lush jungles and sparkling coastline, boasts a soundtrack as diverse as its geography. South America's best-known music styles – Brazilian samba and bossa nova, Colombian salsa, Argentine tango and Andean *música folklórica* (traditional music) – receive airtime across the globe. But there are countless other forms of music, some little known outside a particular region, that are well worth seeking out.

Argentina

The famous sound of tango emerged from the rough-edged immigrant neighborhoods of Buenos Aires in the late 19th century. Born from a clash of musical styles, tango peaked under international legends such as Carlos Gardel and Astor Piazzolla. Today's greats include Susana Rinaldi and Adriana Varela, along with cutting-edge groups fusing acoustic and electronic sounds (dubbed electrotango) such as the Gotan Project and BajoFondo.

Argentina, together with Chile and Uruguay, nurtured *nueva canción*, folk music with political undertones that emerged in the 1950s and '60s. Still-going-strong Mercedes Sosa is one of *nueva canción's* great figureheads, along with Atahualpa Yupanqui and León Gieco.

Charly García is Argentina's best-known rocker. Other contemporary Argentine bands making waves are Bersuit Vergarabat, Catupecu Machu, Gazpacho and the multitalented Argentine-American Kevin Johansen.

Brazil

This great musical powerhouse is home to a dizzying array of talent. Samba, born in early 20th-century Rio, has strong African influences and is intimately linked to Carnaval. Great sambistas include Dorival Caymmi, Ary Barroso and Noel Rosa, followed by Cartola, Nelson Cavaquinho and Clementina de Jesus in later years. Contemporary singers carrying the samba torch include Teresa Cristina, Diogo Nogueira and Maria Rita.

Bossa nova arose in 1950s Rio and gained the world's attention in classics like 'Garota de Ipanema' by Jobim and Vinícius de Moraes. Bossa nova's founding father, guitarist João Gilberto, still performs, as does his daughter Bebel Gilberto, who combines smooth bossa sounds with electronic grooves.

Tropicalismo (aka Tropicália) appeared in the late 1960s, fusing Brazilian samba and bossa with North American rock and British psychedelic sounds. Major Tropicália figures include Gilberto Gil, Gal Costa, Os Mutantes and Caetano Veloso.

Música Popular Brasileira (MPB) covers everything from bossa nova–influenced works to more mainstream pop. MPB first emerged in the 1970s under talented musicians such as Milton Nascimento, Elis Regina, Djavan and others. Two great MPB stars still around are Jorge Benjor (who melds funk, samba and African beats) and master songwriter Chico Buarque.

Brazilian hip-hop continues to evolve, under stylists such as Marcelo D2 and actor-musician Seu Jorge. Regional musical styles include *forró*, a lively, syncopated northeastern sound, and *axé*, the samba-pop-rock-reggae-funk-Caribbean fusion music that comes from Salvador. Daniela Mercury and Ivete Sangalo are the big *axé* names.

Chile

The contemporary Chilean scene spans '60s revolutionary folk to modern and alternative rock. La Nueva Canción Chilena revitalized Chilean folk with social and political issues. Important figures include Violeta Parra, Victor Jara (murdered by the military) and the still-touring Inti-Illimani.

Groups in exile found success abroad, such as Los Jaivas, Los Prisioneros and La Ley. Joe Vasconcellos created energetic Latin fusion. Contemporary bands hogging the spotlight are Lucybell, Tiro de Gracia, Los Bunkers, Javiera y Los Imposibles, Mamma Soul and former La Ley front man Beto Cuevas. Look for the Strokes-like Teleradio Donoso and Chico Trujillo, whose *cumbia chilombiana* has Manu Chao–like elements.

Colombia

Along the Caribbean coast you'll find African-inspired rhythms such as cumbia, *mapalé* and *porro*. The coast is also the birthplace of the accordion-based *vallenato*, Colombia's most popular musical genre. Colombia's most famous mainstream musicians are Shakira, Carlos Vives (Latin-pop vocalist), Totó La Momposina (singer of traditional Afro-Caribbean music), and Juanes (Latin-rock vocalist).

Notable contemporary groups include the eclectic cumbia-powered sound of Pernett and the Caribbean Ravers, the space-rock-meets-cumbia of Bomba Estéreo and Choc Quib Town, a Pacific Coast hip-hop and funk band. For salsa, Bogotá's LA 33 are tops.

Ecuador, Peru & Bolivia

Música folklórica (traditional Andean music) has a distinctive, haunting sound that is inescapable in the highlands. Essential highland instruments are the ukulele-like 10-string *charango*, the *quena* (reed flute) and the *zampoña* (pan flute). Catch live performances at a *peña* (folk-music club). When it comes to youth culture, Caribbean-born reggaeton is the anthem on the streets.

Ecuador has a rich *folklórica* tradition, but the country's true national music is the soulful *pasillo*, made famous by Julio Jaramillo. Northwest Ecuador is home to Afro-Ecuadorian marimba music. Cumbia, originally from Colombia, also appears in Ecuador. Rock, metal and alternative groups are also emerging from Ecuador. Esto es Eso, a US-Ecuadorian duo, blend hip-hop, pop, rock, *pasillo* and traditional sounds. Sudakaya is known for reggae, while RoCola Bacalao plays a mix of ska, punk and merengue.

In addition to emotive pre-Columbian *música folklórica*, Peru is known for its coastal *música criolla*, which has African and Spanish roots. Also sharing African-Spanish roots, the bluesy *landó* often tackles complex social issues. Caribbean salsa is omnipresent, as are cumbia and *chicha*, both originally from Colombia. *Chicha* is a cheerful Andean fusion of traditional panpipes with electronic percussion and guitars. Top artists include Euforia and Rosy War, along with newer bands such as Agua Marina and Armonía 10, who play a kind of Peruvian techno-cumbia.

Bolivia is home to both the haunting Andean sound and more up-tempo music from lowland areas such as Tarija. Major artists include *charango* masters Celestino Campos, Ernesto Cavour and Mauro Núñez. Also keep a look out for Altiplano, Savia Andina and Yanapakuna.

The Guianas

Reggae plays in heavy rotation in the Guianas, though in Guyana you might catch the rapid-fire rhythms of steel-pan drumming, which has Caribbean roots. For a primer on the steel-pan sound, see the Roy Geddes Steel Pan Museum (p725) in Georgetown.

Paraguay & Uruguay

Paraguay is known for its harp music, including a song called 'Pajaro Campana' (also played on guitar), which uses the bizarre call of the bellbird (Paraguay's national bird) as the main rhythm. Traditional dances include the lively polkas *galopadas* and the *danza de la botella*, with dancers balancing bottles on their heads.

Tango is big in Uruguay, with much spillover from neighboring Argentina. *Candombe*, an African-derived rhythm is occasionally heard, particularly during Montevideo's lively Carnaval. Top Uruguayan musicians are singer-songwriter Jorge Drexler, hard-rocking La Trampa and No Te Va Gustar.

Venezuela

Salsa is big in Venezuela, with greats like Oscar D'León achieving nationwide recognition. Other music competing for airtime includes merengue, reggaeton and *vallenato* from Colombia. The country's most popular folk rhythm is *joropó* (also called *música llanera*), which is usually sung and accompanied by the harp, *cuatro* (small, four-stringed guitar) and maracas.

Caracas is a major center for Latin pop and *rock en español*, which fuses Latin rhythms with a rock sound. The scene's most famous band is the Grammy-winning Los Amigos Invisibles.

Religion

About 300 million South Americans (81% of the population) are at least nominally Roman Catholic, though the number of those who actively practice hangs much lower (only 20% in the case of Argentina). The presence of Catholicism is still quite visible – virtually every town and village on the continent has a central church or cathedral – and Catholic-related festivals are an important part of the calendar.

Among indigenous peoples, allegiance to Catholicism was often a clever way to disguise traditional beliefs that were ostensibly forbidden by the church. Similarly, black slaves in Brazil gave Christian names and forms to their African gods, whose worship was discouraged or forbidden. Syncretic beliefs and practices such as Candomblé in Brazil have proliferated to this day, but they do not exclude Christianity. There is no conflict between attending mass one day and seeking guidance from a *mãe de santo* (Candomblé priestess) the next.

In recent decades, various Protestant sects have made inroads among the traditionally Catholic population. There is also a small number of Jews and Muslims sprinkled throughout the continent.

Sports

Volleyball, baseball, motor racing, cock-fighting, even the rodeo all have a place (albeit an often tiny one) in the pantheon of South American sports. However, nothing unites (or more often *divides*) South Americans like a bang-up game of *fútbol* (soccer). It's the national passion in nearly every country on the continent and can be a source of great pride or utter disgust come tournament time. Speaking of tournaments, Brazil won its fifth World Cup final in 2002, snatching the world record for most titles taken (it's also the only country to have played in every World Cup). Having last hosted the World Cup in 1950, Brazil proudly plays host nation again in 2014. National hysteria is already sweeping through the country. Other important tournaments include the annual South American club-team championship, the Copa Libertadores. Teams from Brazil and Argentina, the continent's powerhouses, often battle for first place, though upsets occasionally occur, as happened in 2008 when Ecuador's LDU Quito team beat Brazil's team Fluminense in the final. The Copa América is a continent-wide championship played in odd-numbered years, with two non–South American teams invited.

Volleyball is popular throughout South America, especially in Brazil. There, people also play a variation called *futevôlei,* in which players use their feet instead of their hands. *Béisbol* (baseball), while not widely followed on the continent, is hugely popular in Venezuela.

Rallies (dirt- and off-road auto races) are big in Chile, Argentina, Bolivia and Brazil. Argentina is famous for polo, Buenos Aires being the best place to see a match.

Stay up to date on all South American soccer games and tournaments played throughout the continent and the world at www.latinamerican football.com.

ENVIRONMENT
The Land

The Cordillera de los Andes, the longest continuous mountain system on earth, forms the western margin of the continent, snaking nearly 8000km from Venezuela to southern Patagonia. Riddled with volcanoes, the Andes are part of the volcanic 'Ring of Fire' running from Asia and Alaska to Tierra del Fuego. East of the Andes, the Amazon Basin – the largest river basin in the world – covers parts of Bolivia, Venezuela, Colombia, Peru, Ecuador, the Guianas and Brazil. In the center of the continent (parts of Brazil, Bolivia and Paraguay), the vast Pantanal is the largest inland wetland on earth.

On the geographical side-stage, other physical features include the Orinoco River Basin, which drains the *llanos* (plains) of Venezuela; the barren Chaco of southern Bolivia, northwestern Paraguay and the northern tip of Argentina; the extensive Paraná–Paraguay river system; the fertile pampas of Argentina and Uruguay; and arid, mystical Patagonia, in the far south.

Wildlife
Plant and animal life are generally unique to their habitats. There are numerous habitats throughout South America, but the following are the most important.

AMAZON BASIN RAINFORESTS
Biodiversity seems an insufficient word to describe the seven million sq km of the Amazon. The world's greatest rainforest is home to more plant and animal species than any other place on earth. It contains one in 10 of the world's known species, including over 40,000 plant species, 1300 bird species, over 400 mammal species, 4000 fish species and 2.5 million insect species (bring repellent). In some of its two-hectare plots, it's possible to find more than 500 tree species; a comparable plot in a mid-latitude forest might have three or four. One study found 3000 species of beetle in five small plots and estimated that each tree species supported more than 400 unique animal species. The rainforest canopy is so dense, however, that little to no sunlight penetrates to the forest floor, and nearly all life is found in the trees.

The Amazon River, from its inconspicuous source in the Peruvian highlands to its mouth near Belém, Brazil, measures some 6275km. Its flow is greater than the next eight largest rivers combined, and it carries one-fifth of the world's freshwater.

More than 75 monkey species reside in the Amazon, and they're wonderful to spot. Other Amazonian animals include sloths, anteaters, armadillos, tapirs, caiman, pink and grey dolphins, the Amazon manatee and the western hemisphere's greatest feline, the jaguar.

TROPICAL CLOUD FORESTS
In remote valleys at higher elevations, tropical cloud forests retain clouds that engulf the forest in a fine mist, allowing wonderfully delicate forms of plant life to survive. Cloud-forest trees have low, gnarled growth; a dense, small-leafed canopy; and moss-covered branches supporting orchids, ferns and a host of other epiphytes (plants that gather moisture and nutrients without ground roots). Such forests are the homes of rare species such as the woolly tapir, the Andean spectacled bear and the puma. Some cloud-forest areas host over 400 species of birds.

HIGH-ALTITUDE GRASSLANDS
Even higher than the cloud forest, the *páramo* (humid, high-altitude grassland of the northern Andean countries) is the natural sponge of the Andes and is characterized by a harsh climate, high levels of ultraviolet light and wet, peaty soils. It's an enormously specialized habitat unique to tropical America and is found only from the highlands of Costa Rica to the highlands of northern Peru. Flora of the *páramo* is dominated by hard grasses, cushion plants and small herbaceous plants, and features dense thickets of the *queñoa* tree, which, along with Himalayan pines, share the world-altitude record for trees. Animals of the *páramo* include Andean foxes, deer and *vicuña*, a wild, golden-colored relative of the llama.

CENTRAL ANDEAN REGION
Another unique ecosystem exists between the coast and the *cordillera*, from northern Chile to northern Peru. The coastal Atacama Desert, the world's driest, is almost utterly barren in the rain shadow of the Andes. The cold

Peru current (also called the Humboldt Current) moderates the temperature at this tropical latitude and produces convective fogs (*garúa* or *camanchaca*) that support *lomas* (hillside vegetation) in the coastal ranges.

SAVANNAS

Savannas are vast, low-altitude, primarily treeless tropical and semitropical grasslands. Because of their openness, they can be the best places to observe wildlife in South America. The most famous example is Brazil's Pantanal, which spills over into Bolivia. Other savannas include the Venezuelan *llanos* and, to a lesser extent, the pampas of southern Brazil and Argentina.

TROPICAL DRY FORESTS

Hot areas with well-defined wet and dry seasons support the growth of dry forests. In South America these climatic conditions are mostly found near the coast in the northern part of the continent. Because many of these coastal regions have a dense and growing population, tropical dry forest is a fast-disappearing habitat – only about 1% remains undisturbed. The majestic bottle-trunk ceiba (kapok) tree is the forest's most definitive species. It has a massively bulging trunk and seasonal white flowers that dangle like lightbulbs from otherwise bare tree branches. Parrots, parrotlets, monkeys and a variety of reptiles inhabit these forests.

MANGROVES

Found in coastal areas of Brazil, Colombia, Ecuador, the Guianas and Venezuela, mangroves are trees with a remarkable ability to grow in salt water. They have a broadly spreading system of intertwining stilt roots to support the tree in unstable sandy or silty soils. Mangrove forests trap sediments and build up a rich organic soil, which in turn supports other plants. Mangrove roots provide a protected habitat for many types of fish, mollusks and crustaceans, while the branches provide nesting areas for sea birds.

National Parks

There are over 200 national parks in South America and a staggering number of provincial parks and private reserves. They are undeniably one of the continent's highlights, covering every terrain imaginable, from tropical rainforest and cloud forest to Andean *páramo* to tropical and temperate coastal regions. The most popular parks have well-developed tourist infrastructures, attract high-season crowds and are fairly easy to reach. Some parks have only faint trails, basic camping facilities or refuges and, if you're lucky, a park ranger to answer questions. Others are impossible to reach without 4WD transport or a private boat. Maps are generally tough to come by, so if you plan to do any trekking, research the park first and check larger cities for topographical map sources. See Maps in the South America Directory (p993) and in individual country directories for information on where to obtain maps.

Environmental Issues

One of the gravest environmental threats to South America is well known. Every day wide swaths of forest are felled at an alarming rate across the continent. Deforestation is happening in the Amazon rainforest; the temperate forests of Chile and Argentina; the Atlantic rainforest of Brazil, Argentina and Paraguay; the coastal mangroves and cloud forests of Ecuador; and the Chocó bioregion of pacific Panama, Colombia and Ecuador.

The forest is being destroyed for many reasons, including farming (particularly soy, one of the fastest-growing farming industries in South America), oil drilling, mining and cattle ranching. Oil exploration has opened pristine

Believe it or not, there are still uncontacted tribes in the Amazon. Survival International estimates that there are 15 uncontacted tribes in Peru alone, living in the deepest regions of the Amazon. Most have refused all attempts at contact by the outside world, sometimes with violence.

tracts of Amazon rainforest to colonization and has led to large-scale toxic spills and the poisoning of rivers and streams. Urban sprawl has also wreaked havoc on local ecosystems, as cities and shantytowns spread into national parks and environmentally sensitive areas. Pulp mills, which pollute rivers, and uranium mining are other destructive practices.

Overdevelopment of certain areas (notably the northeastern coast of Brazil) also plays a role in environmental degradation, as do unsustainable fishing and farming practices. Patagonia faces profound changes to its natural environment, with proposals under consideration to build a series of hydroelectric dams in Chile. Desertification is another issue facing Patagonia, where global warming has melted glaciers at rates even faster than experts predicted.

You can read more about conservation and environmental threats in South America on the following websites:

Amazon Watch (www.amazonwatch.org)
Ancient Forests International (www.ancientforests.org)
Birdlife International (www.birdlife.org)
Conservation International (CI; www.conservation.org)
International Rivers (www.internationalrivers.org)
Rainforest Action Network (RAN; www.ran.org)
World Land Trust (www.worldlandtrust.org)
World Wildlife Fund (WWF; www.wwf.org)

For news on the indigenous struggles in South America and beyond, check out the website of Survival International (www.survival-international.org).

Argentina

HIGHLIGHTS

- **Buenos Aires** (p48) This is one sophisticated capital that's full of life and beauty – eat, shop, tango and party all night long.
- **The Lake District** (p125) From fishing to skiing to hiking to white-water rafting, an outdoor lover's paradise graced with gorgeous mountains and lakes.
- **Córdoba** (p91) Argentina's second-largest city and an attractive mix of historical buildings and alternative, youthful culture – all surrounded by quaint mountain villages.
- **Iguazú Falls** (p88) A must to see before you die – the world's most amazing waterfalls, stretching almost 3km long and 70m high.
- **Off the Beaten Track** (p102) Explore the lonely road from Cachi to Cafayate, a combination of rugged landscapes, scenic adobe villages, and vineyards producing *torrontés* (white-wine grape).
- **Best Journey** (p102) North of Jujuy is the lovely Quebrada de Humahuaca, a Unesco World Heritage Site of harsh yet vivid mountainsides dotted with *cardón* cacti.

FAST FACTS

- **Area:** 2.8 million sq km (roughly the size of India)
- **Budget:** US$35 a day
- **Capital:** Buenos Aires
- **Costs:** hostel US$10, steak dinner US$10, five-hour bus ride US$16
- **Country code:** ☎ 54
- **Languages:** Spanish; Quechua in the Andean northwest
- **Money:** US$1 = AR$3.84 (Argentine pesos)
- **Population:** 40 million
- **Seasons:** Patagonia (November to February), skiing (June to September), Buenos Aires (March to May and September to November)
- **Time:** GMT minus three hours

TRAVEL HINTS

Pack light, but bring foul-weather gear for Patagonia. Family photos bring locals closer, and MP3 players are great for long bus rides.

OVERLAND ROUTES

Argentina has three border crossings each with Bolivia, Paraguay, Brazil and Uruguay, and many, many border crossings with Chile.

The secret is out: with its gorgeous landscapes, cosmopolitan cities and lively culture, Argentina is a traveler's paradise. It stretches almost 3500km from Bolivia to the tip of South America, encompasses a wide array of geography and climates, and is almost the size of India. Nature-lovers can traverse the Patagonian steppe, climb South America's highest peak, walk among thousands of penguins and witness the world's most amazing waterfalls. Hikers can sample the stunning scenery of the lush Lake District – with its glorious lakes and white-tipped mountains – and revel in Patagonia's glacier-carved landscapes and painted Andean deserts. City slickers will adore fabulous Buenos Aires, full of opportunities to learn Spanish, watch *fútbol* (soccer), dance the sexy tango and interact with dynamic and beautiful *porteños* (people from Buenos Aires). You'll be out shopping for designer clothes at affordable prices and eating the world's best steaks every day while partying at nightclubs all night long.

Argentina is safe, friendly and – compared to Europe or the US – very affordable. Now is a great time to visit, so get your spirit in gear and prepare for an unforgettable adventure!

CURRENT EVENTS

After years of boom, Argentina's inflation remains high and the economy continues to sputter. The country teeters on the edge of recession, but there is also good news for travelers – a weakening peso means that hard currency goes a long way.

Cristina Kirchner, Argentina's first elected woman president, lost much of her power during the June 2009 legislative elections. Her husband, ex-president Néstor Kirchner, later resigned as the leader of the Peronist party, soundly ending their hopes for an extended political dynasty.

In other news, Argentina will be celebrating its bicentennial in 2010, rejoicing in 200 years of independence from Spain. Expect to visit several newly renovated museums and buildings, such as the famous Teatro Colón which shut down popular tours for over two years during its facelift.

HISTORY
The Good Old Days

Before the Spanish hit the scene, nomadic hunter-gatherers roamed the wilds of ancient Argentina. The Yámana (or Yahgan) gathered shellfish in Patagonia, while on the pampas the Querandí used *boleadoras* (weights on cords) to snag rhea (ostrich-like birds) and guanaco (the llama's cousin). Up in the subtropical northeast, the Guaraní settled down long enough to cultivate maize, while in the arid northwest the Diaguita developed an irrigation system for crops.

In 1536 the Querandí were unfortunate enough to meet pushy Spaniards in search of silver. They eventually drove the explorers away to more welcoming Paraguay. (Left behind were cattle and horses, which multiplied and gave rise to the legendary *gaucho* – cowboy).

The Spanish were persistent, however, and in 1580 they returned and managed to establish Buenos Aires, though trade restrictions from Spain limited the new settlement's growth. The northern colonies of Tucumán, Córdoba and Salta, however, thrived by providing mules, cloth and foodstuffs for the booming silver mines of Bolivia. Meanwhile, Spaniards from Chile moved into the Andean Cuyo region, which produced wine and grain.

Cutting the Purse Strings

In 1776 Spain designated the bootlegger township of Buenos Aires as 'capital of the new viceroyalty of the Río de la Plata,' a nod to its strategic port location. A rogue British force, hoping to snag a piece of the trade pie, invaded in 1806 but was given the boot soon after by the rallied settlers. With newfound power, the confident colonists revolted against Spain, which they held a grudge against for the trade restrictions. Complete independence was their reward six years later in 1816.

Despite this unity, the provinces resisted Buenos Aires' authority. Argentina split allegiances between the inhabitants of Buenos Aires (Unitarists) and the country folk (Federalists). A civil war ensued, and the two parties' bloody, vindictive conflicts nearly exhausted the country.

In 1829 Juan Manuel de Rosas came into power as a Federalist, but applied his own brand of Unitarist principles to centralize control in Buenos Aires. He built a large army, created the *mazorca* (a ruthless secret police), institutionalized torture and forced overseas trade through the port city. Finally, in 1852, Justo José de Urquiza (once Rosas' supporter) led a Unitarist army that forced the dictator from power. Urquiza drew up a constitution and became Argentina's first president.

ARGENTINA

The Fleeting Golden Age

Argentina's new laws opened up the country to foreign investment, trade and immigration. In the following decades, sheep, cattle and cereal products were freely exported, while Spanish, Italian, French and other European immigrants came in search of a better life. Prosperity arrived at last, and Argentina became one of the richest countries in the world at that time.

The prosperity was tenuous, however, as global economic fluctuations brought about new foreign trade restrictions that mostly benefited rich producers of wheat, wine and sugar. After the 1880s poor immigrants continued flooding into the city, nearly doubling Buenos Aires' population to one million residents. The city's face changed: old colonial buildings were torn down, major streets were widened and urban services improved. The industrial sector couldn't absorb all the immigrants and their needs, however, and the gap between rich and poor widened. In 1929 the military took power from an ineffectual civilian government, but an obscure colonel – Juan Domingo Perón – was the first leader to really confront the looming social crisis.

The Peróns – Love 'em or Hate 'em

Today the Peróns have become Argentina's most revered – as well as most despised – political figures. Many people believe that Argentina has never recovered, either economically or spiritually, since Perón's first presidency.

From a minor post in the labor ministry, and with the help of his charismatic soon-to-be wife, Eva Duarte (Evita), Juan Perón won the presidency in 1946. His social welfare and new economic order programs helped the working class, which benefited from improved wages, job security and working conditions. His heavy control over the country, however, was tinged with fascism: he abused his presidential powers by using excessive intimidation and squelching free press. Dynamic Evita, meanwhile, had her own sometimes vindictive political ends, though she was mostly championed for her charitable work and women's rights campaigns.

Rising inflation and economic difficulties (due especially to a shortage of capital from war-torn Europe) undermined Perón's second presidency in 1952; Evita's death the same year was another blow. After a coup against

him in 1955, Perón retreated to Spain to plot his return. The opportunity came almost two decades later when Héctor Cámpora resigned the presidency in 1973. Perón won the elections easily, but his death in mid-1974 sucked the country back into the governmental coups and chaos that had plagued it since his exile. In 1976 military rule prevailed once again, and Argentina entered its darkest hour.

Dirty War (1976–83)

In the late 1960s, when antigovernment sentiment was rife, a left-wing, highly organized Peronist guerrilla group called the Montoneros was formed. The mostly educated, middle-class youths bombed foreign businesses, kidnapped executives for ransom and robbed banks to finance their armed struggle and spread their social messages. On March 24, 1976, a military bloodless coup led by General Jorge Videla took control of the Argentine government and ushered in a period of terror and brutality. Euphemistically called the Process of National Reorganization (aka El Proceso), this movement became an orgy of state-sponsored violence and anarchy, and their primary target was the Montoneros.

Some estimate that up to 30,000 people died in the infamous Guerra Sucia (Dirty War). Zero tolerance was the theme: the dictatorship did not distinguish between the revolutionary guerrillas or those who simply expressed reservations about the dictatorship's indiscriminate brutality. To 'disappear' meant to be detained, tortured and probably killed, without legal process. Ironically, the Dirty War ended only when the Argentine military attempted a real military operation, the repossession of the Islas Malvinas (Falkland Islands).

Falklands War

Argentina's economy continued to decline during military rule and eventually collapsed into chaos. El Proceso was coming undone.

In late 1981 General Leopoldo Galtieri took the presidential hot seat. To stay in power amid a faltering economy, a desperate Galtieri played the nationalist card and launched an invasion in April 1982 to dislodge the British from the Islas Malvinas (Falkland Islands).

The brief occupation of the Malvinas, claimed by Argentina for 150 years, unleashed a wave of nationalist euphoria that lasted about a week. Then the Argentines realized

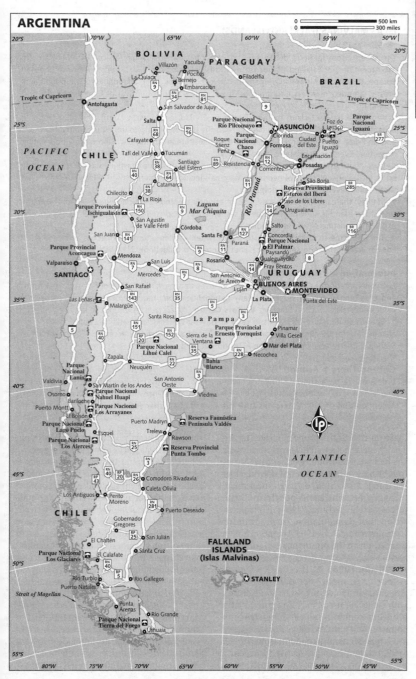

ARGENTINA

| 0 | 500 km |
| 0 | 300 miles |

ISLAS MALVINAS (FALKLAND ISLANDS)

☎ 500 / pop 3100

The sheep boom in Tierra del Fuego and Patagonia owes its origins to the Islas Malvinas (to the Argentines) or Falkland Islands (to the British). During the mid-19th-century wool boom in Europe, the Falkland Islands Company became the islands' largest landholder. The population, mostly stranded mariners and *gauchos*, grew rapidly with the arrival of English and Scottish immigrants.

Argentina has laid claim to the islands since 1833, but it wasn't until 1982 that troubled Argentine president Leopoldo Galtieri invaded the islands, hoping to unite his country. However, English Prime Minister Margaret Thatcher didn't hesitate in striking back, thoroughly humiliating Argentina. Even today relations remain chilly.

Bays, inlets, estuaries and beaches create a tortuous, attractive coastline that is home to many birds, including a plethora of penguins. Mammals include elephant seals, sea lions, fur seals, killer whales and several species of dolphins.

Stanley, the capital, is an assemblage of brightly painted metal-clad houses. 'Camp' – as the rest of the island is known – is home to settlements that provide lodging as well as a chance to experience pristine nature and wildlife.

The best time to visit is October to March, when wildlife returns to beaches and headlands. For general information see Lonely Planet's *Antarctica* guidebook.

Information

Everyone entering the Falkland Islands by air needs an onward ticket, proof of sufficient funds and prearranged accommodations. Many nationalities don't require visas, but double check at www.visitorfalklands.com. Stanley's **Visitors Centre** (☎ 22215) is at the public jetty.

Pounds sterling and US dollars in cash or traveler's checks are readily accepted, but the exchange rate for US currency is low. Visa and MasterCard are widely accepted. The only bank is Standard Chartered Bank in Stanley; ATMs do not exist.

Getting There & Around

Unless you're on a cruise ship, you'll likely arrive by air. LANChile heads to Mt Pleasant (near Stanley) once weekly from Santiago, Chile, via Punta Arenas. Once monthly it flies via Río Gallegos, Argentina. Chilean airline **Aerovías DAP** (www.dap.cl) offers charter flights.

---

that iron-clad British prime minister Margaret Thatcher was not a wallflower, especially when she had political troubles of her own. Britain fought back, sending a naval contingent to set things straight, and Argentina's mostly teenage, ill-trained and poorly motivated forces surrendered after 74 days. The military, stripped of its reputation, finally withdrew from government. In 1983 Argentina handed Raúl Alfonsín the presidency.

Argentina Today

Alfonsín brought democracy back to Argentina and solved some territorial disputes with Chile. He also managed to curb inflation a bit but couldn't pull the long-struggling country back onto its feet again.

Carlos Menem, president from 1989 to 1999, brought brief prosperity to Argentina by selling off many private industries and borrowing heavily. He also practically stopped inflation in its tracks by pegging the peso with the US dollar, but this was only a quick fix. After a few years the peso became so overvalued that Argentine goods weren't competitive on the global market. Toward the end of Menem's rule unemployment spiraled steadily upwards.

In 1999 Fernando de la Rúa was sworn into office. He inherited an almost bankrupt government which witnessed yet another economic downturn, even higher unemployment and a widespread lack of public confidence. By 2001 the economy teetered on the brink of collapse, and in December Fernando de la Rúa resigned. The country went through three more presidents within two weeks before finally putting Eduardo Duhalde in charge. Duhalde devalued the peso in January 2002, defaulting on AR$140 billion in debt.

After some instability, the peso settled to around three to the US dollar, which, due to Argentina's suddenly cheap exports, created a booming economy. In 2003 the left-leaning Néstor Kirchner was handed the presidential reins and became an immensely popular leader. He kept the economy growing strong, paid some of Argentina's debts to the IMF and curbed corruption to a degree. Argentina was living high and there was optimism in the air.

In 2007 Kirchner's term was up, but he wasn't through with politics. His wife, Cristina Fernández de Kirchner, easily won the nation's highest office – becoming Argentina's first elected woman president. Her tenure has been much rockier than his, however, and has seen the occasional corruption scandal, a major tax-hike conflict, high inflation rates and a worsening economy. With time still left in her term, the country can only hope these problems are merely bumps in the road towards recovery – yet again.

THE CULTURE
The National Psyche
Argentines have a worldwide reputation for being spoiled, stuck-up and egotistical. They tend to think they're better than anyone else and that they belong in Europe rather than at the tail end of a third-world continent like South America. And they undergo more cosmetic surgery and psychoanalysis than anyone else in the world. It's no wonder people make fun of them.

But frankly, most Argentines just don't fit this profile. And this stereotype usually refers to *porteños*. While a huge number of people do live in the capital and its suburbs, a full two-thirds live in the rest of Argentina, where attitudes and egos are more modest. In fact, many folks outside the capital don't even like *porteños*. And, not all *porteños* are sniffy aristocratic wannabes – quite a few, as you'll find out, are friendly, helpful and curious about where you come from.

It's easy to see how Argentines got their reputation. They live in a fabulous country with vast natural resources, a gorgeous capital and rich culture. Yet they've seen their country (once one of the richest in the world) collapse into almost third-world status that has had to ask for financial handouts. With years of unstable economies, rapidly rising inflation and inept governments, if Argentines can maintain their proud spirit, then more power to them.

Lifestyle
Over a third of Argentines are considered to be living in poverty. To save resources and maintain family ties, several generations often live under one roof.

Families are pretty close, and Sundays are often reserved for the family *asado* (barbecue). Friends are also highly valued and Argentines love to go out in large groups. They'll give each other kisses on the cheek every time they meet – even introduced strangers, men and women alike, will get a kiss.

Argentines like to stay out *late*; dinner is often at 10pm, and finishing dessert around midnight on a weekend is the norm. Bars and discos often stay open until 6am or so, even in smaller cities.

The important culture of maté is very visible in Argentina; you'll see folks sipping this bitter herb drink at home, work and play. They carry their gourds and hot-water thermoses while traveling and on picnics. Consider yourself honored if you're invited to partake in a maté-drinking ritual.

Population
About 90% of the country's population lives in urban areas. Argentina's literacy rate is over 97%.

Nineteenth-century immigration created a large population of Italians and Spanish, though many other European nationalities are represented. Newer mixes include Japanese, Koreans and Chinese (rarer outside the capital), and other South American nationalities such as Peruvians, Bolivians, Paraguayans and Uruguayans.

Indigenous peoples make up less than 1% of Argentina's population, with the Mapuche of Patagonia being the largest group. Smaller groups of Guaraní, Tobas, Wichi and Tehuelche, among others, inhabit other northern pockets. Around 15% of the country's population is *mestizo* (of mixed indigenous and European ancestry); most *mestizo* reside up north.

SPORTS
Rugby, tennis, basketball, polo, golf, motor racing, skiing and cycling are popular sports, but soccer is an obsession. The national team has twice won the World Cup, once in 1978 and again in 1986, when Diego Armando Maradona (Argentina's bad-boy, rags-to-riches soccer star) surreptitiously punched in a goal

to beat England in the quarterfinals. Today, Lionel Messi is Argentina's biggest *fútbol* star.

The game between River Plate and Boca Juniors is a classic match not to be missed, as the rivalry between the two teams is intense (see p67).

RELIGION

Most of Argentina's population is Roman Catholic (the official state religion), with Protestants making up the second most popular group. Buenos Aires is home to one of the largest Jewish populations outside Israel, and also claims what is likely South America's largest mosque.

Spiritualism and veneration of the dead are widespread: visitors to Recoleta and Chacarita cemeteries will see pilgrims communing with icons like Juan and Evita Perón, Carlos Gardel and psychic Madre María. Cult beliefs like the Difunta Correa of San Juan province also attract hundreds of thousands of fans.

ARTS
Literature

Argentina's biggest literary name is Jorge Luis Borges, famous for his short stories and poetry. Borges created alternative-reality worlds and elaborate time circles with vivid and imaginative style; check out his surreal compendiums *Labyrinths* or *Ficciones*. Internationally acclaimed Julio Cortázar wrote about seemingly normal people while using strange metaphors and whimsical descriptions of people's unseen realities. His big novel is *Hopscotch*, which requires more than one reading.

Ernesto Sábato is known for his intellectual novels and essays, many of which explore the chasm between good and evil. Sábato's notable works include *Sobre héroes y tumbas* (On Heroes and Tombs), popular with Argentine youth in the '60s, and the startling essay *Nunca más*, which describes Dirty War atrocities. Other famous Argentine writers include Manuel Puig *(Kiss of the Spider Woman)*, Adolfo Bioy Casares *(The Invention of Morel)*, Osvaldo Soriano *(Shadows)*, Roberto Arlt *(The Seven Madmen)* and Silvina Ocampo (poetry and children's stories).

Contemporary writers include Juan José Saer, who penned short stories and complex crime novels, and novelist and journalist Rodrigo Fresán, who wrote the best-selling *The History of Argentina* and the psychedelic *Kensington Gardens*.

Cinema

In the past, Argentine cinema has achieved international stature through such directors as Luis Puenzo (*The Official Story*, 1984) and Héctor Babenco (*Kiss of the Spider Woman*, 1985).

More recent notable works by Argentine directors include Fabián Bielinsky's witty and entertaining *Nueve reinas* (Nine Queens; 2000), Lucrecia Martel's dysfunctional-families saga *La ciénaga* (The Swamp; 2001) and Pablo Trapero's gritty *El bonaerense* (2002). Carlos Sorín's *Historias mínimas* (Minimal Stories; 2002) is a rich yet minimalist character study.

Juan José Campanella's *El hijo de la novia* (The Son of the Bride) was Oscar nominated for best foreign-language film in 2002, while Martel's *La niña santa* (The Holy Girl; 2004) won acclaim for its take on sexual awakening. Sorín's *El perro* (Bombón, the Dog; 2004) is a captivating tale of man's best friend and changing fortunes. Tristán Bauer's award-winning *Illuminados por el fuego* (2005) follows a soldier of the Falklands War. And in 2005 Juan Diego Solanas won top prize at the Stockholm Film Festival for his well-executed and mature *Nordeste* (Northeast), which tackles difficult social issues like child trafficking.

Other recent Argentine films include Damián Szifron's hilarious *Tiempo de valientes* (2005), Israel Adrián's *Crónica de una fuga* (2006) – which chronicles an escape from a torture camp during Argentina's Dirty War – and Lucía Puenzo's *XXY* (2007), the story of an intersexual teenager.

Music

Legendary figures like Carlos Gardel and Astor Piazzolla popularized tango music, and contemporaries such as Susana Rinaldi, Adriana Varela and Osvaldo Pugliese carry on the tradition. Recent tango 'fusion' groups include Gotan Project and BajoFondo Tango Club.

Folk musicians Mercedes Sosa, Leon Gieco, Atahualpa Yupanqui and Los Chalchaleros are popular performers.

Rock star Charly García is Argentina's best-known musician, but past popular groups have included Fito Páez, Sumo, Los Pericos, Babasónicos, Divididos and Los Fabulosos Cadillacs (who in 1998 won a Grammy for best alternative Latin rock group).

Contemporary Argentine musical artists include wacky Bersuit Vergarabat, alternative Catupecu Machu, versatile Gazpacho and the multitalented Kevin Johansen.

Córdoba's edgy *cuarteto* is Argentina's original pop music, played in working-class bars throughout the country. Coarse *cumbia villera* was born in shantytowns, fusing cumbia with gangsta rap, reggae and punk. Finally, *murga* is a form of athletic musical theater composed of actors and percussionists; they often perform at Carnaval.

Visual Arts

Well-known painters include Xul Solar, who did busy, Klee-inspired dreamscapes; Guillermo Kuitca, who experimented with cartographic illustrations; and Víctor Hugo Quiroga, who concentrated on provincial topics. Benito Quinquela Martín depicted the hard-working laborers on the docks of Buenos Aires' La Boca neighborhood. Painter, poet, songwriter and '60s icon, the multifaceted Jorge de la Vega dabbled in mixed media and geometric abstracts.

Famous sculptors include Graciela Sacco, who worked in audio, video and with life's common objects; Rogelio Yrurtia, whose art chronicles the struggles of the working people; and Alberto Heredia, who enjoyed ridiculing solemn official public art.

Buenos Aires' Galerías Pacífico, on Av Florida, has restored ceiling murals by Antonio Berni and Lino Spilimbergo, two Italian-Argentine artists who studied in Europe and dealt with political themes. For street art keep an eye out for creative stencils (www.bsasstencil.com.ar) and graffiti (www.bagraff.com).

Theater & Dance

Buenos Aires' monumental Teatro Colón is one of the world's finest acoustic facilities, offering classical music and ballet, among other things. The capital also has a vibrant theater community, and there's live theater in the provinces as well.

Tango is Argentina's sultry dance, thought to have started in Buenos Aires' bordellos in the 1880s (though Montevideo in Uruguay also stakes a claim to the dance's origin). It wasn't mainstream until it was filtered through Europe, finally hitting high popularity in Argentina around 1913. Carlos Gardel is tango's most famous songbird.

ENVIRONMENT

Argentina doesn't have a huge rainforest to destroy, but does have some environmental problems. Rapid growth in some cities (El Calafate comes to mind), related to the country's tourist boom, is seldom thought out well enough. Air and noise pollution is always a problem in Buenos Aires and other large cities. Some rural areas suffer soil erosion from improper land use or flood control, as well as river pollution from pesticide or fertilizer runoff.

Argentina has lost about two-thirds of its forests in the last century. Practically all of the pampas is now cattle grazing land, and the Patagonian steppe region suffers from overgrazing and desertification. Some celebrities, such as Kristine Tompkins (ex-CEO of clothing company Patagonia) and Ted Turner, have bought huge tracts in Patagonia with the idea of protecting much of the land. For more information check www.conservacion patagonica.org or www.vidasilvestre.org.ar.

One recent environmental issue is the Pascua Lama gold and silver mine, soon to be constructed along the Chilean border; though most of the mining would be in Chile, there would be a major waste dump in Argentina.

The Land

Argentina is huge – it's the world's eighth-largest country. It stretches some 3500km north to south and encompasses a wide range of environments and terrain.

The glorious Andes line the edge of north-west Argentina, where only hardy cactus and scrubby vegetation survive. Here, soaring peaks and salt lakes give way to the subtropical lowland provinces of Salta and Santiago del Estero. To the south, the hot and scenic Tucumán, Catamarca and La Rioja provinces harbor agriculture and viticulture.

Drier thornlands of the western Andean foothills give way to the forked river valleys and hot lowlands of Formosa and Chaco provinces. Rainfall is heaviest to the northeast, where swampy forests and subtropical savannas thrive. Densely forested Misiones province contains the awe-inspiring Iguazú Falls. Rivers streaming off these immense cataracts lead to the alluvial grasslands of Corrientes and Entre Ríos provinces. Summers here are very hot and humid.

The west-central Cuyo region (Mendoza, San Juan and San Luis provinces) pumps out

ARGENTINA

most of Argentina's world-class wine vintages. Central Argentina has the mountainous Córdoba and richly agricultural Santa Fe provinces. The Pampas is a flat, rich plain full of agriculture and livestock. Along the Atlantic Coast are many popular and attractive beaches.

Patagonia spans the lower third of Argentina. Most of this region is flat and arid, but toward the Andes rainfall is abundant and supports the lush Lake District. The southern Andes boasts huge glaciers, while down on the flats cool steppes pasture large flocks of sheep.

The Tierra del Fuego archipelago mostly belongs to Chile. Its northern half resembles the Patagonian steppe, while dense forests and glaciers cover the mountainous southern half. The climate can be relatively mild, even in winter (though temperatures can also drop below freezing). The weather in this region is very changeable year-round.

Like several other countries, Argentina lays claim to a section of Antarctica.

Wildlife

The famous Pampas is mostly sprawling grasslands and home to many birds of prey and introduced plant species; most of the region's remaining native vegetation survives up north along the Río Paraná. Also in the northern swamplands live the odd-looking capybara (the world's largest rodent), swamp deer, the alligator-like caiman and many large migratory birds.

The main forested areas of Argentina are in subtropical Misiones province and on the eastward-sloping Andes from Neuquén province south, where southern beech species and coniferous woodlands predominate; look for the strange monkey-puzzle tree (*Araucaria araucana* or *pehuén*) around the Lake District. In the higher altitudes of the Andes and in much of Patagonia, pasture grasses are sparse. Northern Andean saline lakes harbor pink flamingos, and on the Patagonian steppe you're likely to see guanacos, rheas, Patagonian hares, armadillos, crested caracaras and gray foxes. Pumas and condors live in the southern Andean foothills, but sightings are rare.

Coastal Patagonia, especially around Península Valdés, has dense and viewable concentrations of marine fauna, including southern right whales, sea lions, southern elephant seals, Magellanic penguins and orcas.

National Parks

Argentina has a good range of national parks. A wide variety of climates is represented, such as swamps, deserts and rainforest – and highlights include giant trees, waterfalls and glaciers.

Some cities have their own national park information office; in Buenos Aires you can visit **Administración de Parques Nacionales** (National Park Office; Map pp52-3; ☎ 011-4311-6633; www.parques nacionales.gov.ar; Av Santa Fe 690).

Some of Argentina's best national parks:

Parque Nacional Iguazú (p88) World-renowned for its waterfalls.

Parque Nacional Los Alerces (p137) Site of ancient *alerce* (false larch) forests.

Parque Nacional Los Glaciares (p148) Awesome for its glaciers and alpine towers.

Parque Nacional Nahuel Huapi (p133) Offers vivid alpine scenery.

Parque Nacional Tierra del Fuego (p154) Exceptional beech forests and fauna.

Parque Provincial Aconcagua (p122) Boasts the continent's highest peak.

Reserva Faunística Península Valdés (p141) Famous for coastal fauna.

Reserva Provincial Esteros del Iberá (p80) Home to swamp-dwelling wildlife.

TRANSPORTATION

GETTING THERE & AWAY
Air

Cosmopolitan Buenos Aires is linked to most of the capitals in South America. Argentina's main international airport is Buenos Aires' Aeropuerto Internacional Ministro Pistarini (known as Ezeiza). Aeroparque Jorge Newbery (known simply as Aeroparque) is the capital's domestic airport. For information on getting into town from the airports, see p49. A few other Argentine cities have 'international' airports, but they mostly serve domestic destinations. The national airline is Aerolíneas Argentinas.

DEPARTURE TAX

International passengers leaving from Ezeiza are required to pay a US$18 departure tax in pesos, euros, US dollars or by credit card. Other airports such as El Calafate and Ushuaia also charge departure taxes.

GETTING TO CHILE

For most travelers, crossing the border from Argentina into Chile is a relatively quick, easy procedure. Usually the same bus takes you right through and there are no fees. Border outposts are open daylight hours; Dorotea (near Puerto Natales) is open 24 hours in summer. Just have your papers in order, don't take anything illegal (including fresh food) and you should be golden. And try to get your ticket as soon as possible, as Chile-bound buses often fill up quickly. For crossing from Chile, see p385.

Boat

Ferries link Buenos Aires to several points in Uruguay. For more information, see p68.

Bus

It's possible to cross into Argentina from Bolivia, Paraguay, Brazil, Uruguay and Chile.

GETTING AROUND
Air

The airline situation in Argentina is in constant flux; minor airlines go in and out of business regularly. Ticket prices are unpredictable, though they are always highest during holiday times (July and late December to February). Certain flights in extensive Patagonia are comparable to bus fares when you consider time saved.

The major airlines in Argentina are **Aerolíneas Argentinas** (AR; www.aerolineasargentinas .com), **Austral** (www.austral.com.ar) – AR's domestic partner – and **LAN** (www.lan.com). For a list of principal airline offices, both international and domestic, see p68). Addresses of regional offices appear in each city entry.

There may be special air-pass deals available; check with a travel agency specializing in Latin America, since deals come and go regularly. These passes may need to be purchased outside Argentina (sometimes in conjunction with an international ticket), you need to be a foreign resident to use them, and they're often limited to travel within a certain time period.

For more information, see p1005.

Bicycle

Cycling around the country has become popular among travelers. Beautiful routes in the north include the highway from Tucumán to Tafí del Valle and the Quebrada de Cafayate. Around Mendoza, there's touring that includes stops at wineries. The Lake District also has scenic roads, like the Siete Lagos route. Drawbacks include the wind (which can slow progress to a crawl in Patagonia) and reckless motorists. Less-traveled secondary roads with little traffic are good alternatives. Rental bikes are common in tourist areas and a great way to get around.

For information on biking around South America see p1006.

Bus

Long-distance buses are modern, fast, comfortable and usually the best budget way to get around Argentina (remember that overnight trips save accommodation costs). Journeys of more than six hours or so will either have pit stops for refreshments or serve drinks, sweet snacks and sometimes simple meals. All have bathrooms, though they're often grungy, lack water (bring toilet paper) and are usually for 'liquids only.' The most luxurious companies offer more expensive *coche-cama* (literally 'bed-bus,' deluxe sleeper bus), *ejecutivo* or *suite* recliners, most of which lay back horizontally. But even regular buses are usually comfortable enough, even on long trips.

Bus terminals usually have kiosks, restrooms, cheap eats and luggage storage. In small towns you'll want to be aware of the timetable for your next bus out (and possibly buy a ticket), since some routes run infrequently. In summer there are many more departures. During holiday periods like January, February or July, buy advance tickets. If you know your exact traveling dates, you can often buy a ticket from any departure point to any destination, but this depends on the bus company.

Car

Renting a car in Argentina is not cheap, but can get you away from the beaten path and start you on some adventures. Figure AR$250 per day average for a cheap model with some free mileage. The minimum driving age in Argentina is 18, but car rental offices require drivers to be at least 21.

Forget driving in Buenos Aires; traffic is unforgivable and parking is a headache, while public transport is great. See Legal Matters (p159) for dealing with police.

The **Automobile Club Argentina** (ACA; Map pp58-9; ☎ 011-4802-6061; www.aca.org.ar; Av del Libertador 1850, Palermo) has offices, service stations and garages in major cities. If you're a member of an overseas affiliate (like AAA in the United States) you may be able to obtain vehicular services and discounts on maps – bring your card. ACA's main headquarters is in Buenos Aires.

Hitchhiking

Good places for a pickup are gas stations on the outskirts of large cities, where truckers refuel their vehicles. In Patagonia, distances are great and vehicles few, so expect long waits and carry snack foods and warm, windproof clothing. Carry extra water as well, especially in the desert north. Realize that many cars are full with families.

Haciendo dedo (hitchhiking) is fairly safe for women in Argentina; however, don't do it alone, don't get in a car with two men and don't do it at night. There is nothing especially unsafe about hitchhiking in rural Argentina, but don't hitchhike in Buenos Aires.

Having a sign will improve your chances for a pickup, especially if it says something like *visitando Argentina de Canadá* (visiting Argentina from Canada), rather than just a destination. Argentines are fascinated by foreigners.

For more information, visit www.autostopargentina.com.ar.

Local Transportation

Even small towns have good bus systems. A few cities use magnetic fare cards, which can usually be bought at kiosks; Buenos Aires has a plan to add this system, but we'll believe it when we see it. Pay attention to placards indicating an ultimate destination, since identically numbered buses may cover slightly different routes.

Taxis have digital-readout meters. Tipping isn't expected, but you can leave extra change. *Remises* are taxis that you book over the phone, or regular cars without meters; any hotel or restaurant should be able to call one for you. They're considered more secure than taxis since an established company sends them out. Ask the fare in advance.

Buenos Aires is the only city with a subway system, known as Subte.

Train

The British-built train system in Argentina is not as widespread as it once was, and currently bus travel is faster, more flexible and more reliable. There are long-distance services from Buenos Aires to Rosario, Córdoba, Tucumán, Posadas, Santiago del Estero, Bahía Blanca and some Atlantic beach towns. There's also service from Viedma to Bariloche.

The very scenic, famous and expensive Tren a las Nubes (www.ecotren.com) chugs from Salta, in the north, toward Chile. It's notoriously undependable, however, so check and double-check the situation before getting your hopes up.

In Patagonia there are a couple of short touristy train rides (both narrow-gauge) such as La Trochita, which originates in Esquel or El Maitén, and El Tren del Fin del Mundo, in Ushuaia.

BUENOS AIRES

☎ 011 / pop 13 million (greater BA)

Believe everything you've heard – Buenos Aires is one of South America's most electrifying cities, graced with European architecture, atmospheric neighborhoods and bustling nightlife. It has the charm of an unshaved Casanova, the mind of a frenzied lunatic and the attitude of a celebrity supermodel. And BA's passionate residents are prideful and even haughty, but once you get to know them they'll bend over backwards to help.

After Argentina's economic collapse in 2002, BA bounced back and created a renaissance that's still keeping the city aglow today. Argentines found the 'outside' world

---

DON'T MISS...

- Shopping and eating in Palermo Viejo (p57)
- Looking for finds at San Telmo's bustling Sunday antiques fair (p56)
- Wandering through Recoleta's amazing cemetery (p56)
- Experiencing a *fútbol* game's passion (p67)
- Taking in the high kicks at a tango show (p65)
- Soaking up Buenos Aires' second-to-none nightlife (p65)

GETTING INTO TOWN

If you fly into Buenos Aires from outside Argentina, you'll probably land at **Ezeiza Airport** (off Map p51; ☎ 5480-6111; www.aa2000.com.ar), about 35km south of the city center. Ezeiza is clean and modern and has food services, shops, (expensive) internet access and luggage storage. There's also a 24-hour information counter (☎ 5480-6111).

The best way into town is the frequent, comfortable shuttle service by **Manuel Tienda León** (MTL; AR$45, 40 minutes); its booth is just outside customs. Another option is **Hostel Shuttle** (☎ 4331-4041; shuttle@hostelsuites.com), which goes five times daily from Ezeiza to certain downtown hostels (AR$35), but you'll need to reserve 48 hours in advance.

For taxis, avoid the shuttle companies' hiked-up prices and head behind the shuttle booths to the city taxi booth, which charges around AR$98 (including tolls). *Do not* go with a taxi tout; make sure you find the booth and pay up front. Hard-core penny-pinchers can take bus 8 (AR$2, 1½ to two hours) from outside the Aerolíneas Argentinas (domestic) terminal, which is a short walk away. Get small change in bills and coins at the bank before getting on the bus.

If you need to change money, avoid the *cambios* (exchange houses) as their rates are bad. Instead, head to the nearby Banco de la Nación, which has fair rates and should be open 24 hours. There are several ATMS in Ezeiza (withdraw uneven denominations – ie AR$290 instead of AR$300 – to get change).

Most domestic flights land at **Aeroparque Jorge Newbery** (Map p51; ☎ 5480-3000; www.aa2000 .com.ar), only a few kilometers north of the city center. Manuel Tienda León shuttles to the city center take 15 minutes and cost AR$15. Bus 45 (AR$1.10) also goes to the center; take it going south (to the right as you leave the airport). Taxis cost about AR$20.

Shuttle transfers from Ezeiza to Aeroparque cost AR$45.

Retiro bus station (Map pp52–3) is about 1km north of the city center; it has shops, cafes, telephone and internet services and luggage storage (don't leave luggage unattended). Dozens of BA's local bus lines converge here; outside, it's a seething mass and not to be figured out after a 14-hour bus ride. You can take the Subte if your destination is near a stop, and taxis are cheap; try to get one marked 'radio taxi' on the doors. The tourist information office (look for it under bus counter 105) is only open 7:30am to 1pm Monday to Friday, and Sunday.

---

prohibitively expensive, and turned their energy inwards – with impressive results. New restaurants, boutiques and businesses keep popping up not only to serve the locals and their pesos, but also to cater to the influx of foreign tourists bringing hard currency and taking advantage of good deals.

Yet every great metropolis has a poor side. Cracked sidewalks, ubiquitous graffiti and rough edges – even in the wealthiest neighborhoods – speak volumes about this city. Poverty and beggars exist, and at night the *cartoneros* (garbage recyclers) appear. There's a deep melancholy here – an acknowledgement of Argentina's riches coupled with the despair of not realizing its full potential. The undeniable reality is that BA comes with a darker side.

So throw yourself into this heady mix and hold on tight, 'cause you're going for a wild ride. And don't be surprised if you fall in love with this amazing and sexy city – you won't be the first, or the last.

ORIENTATION

Buenos Aires is a very large city, but most sights are within the compact downtown area. Interesting surrounding *barrios* (neighborhoods) are easily accessed via public transport. The major thoroughfare is broad Av 9 de Julio; all north–south streets (except for Av 9 de Julio) change names at Av Rivadavia.

The *microcentro* (city center; roughly bordered by Av Córdoba, Av 9 de Julio and Av de Mayo) is the heart of BA's downtown bustle. To the north are chic Retiro, Barrio Norte, Recoleta and Palermo, while to the south lie the working-class neighborhoods of San Telmo and La Boca. The waterside *barrio* Puerto Madero, with its modernized brick warehouses and promenades, lies east of the center.

INFORMATION
Bookstores

El Ateneo (Map pp52–3; Av Florida 340) Has some books in English, including Lonely Planet guides. There's another branch at Av Santa Fe 1860 in a gorgeous building.

Walrus Books (Map pp52-3; ☎ 4300-7135; Estados Unidos 617; ☑ noon-8pm Tue-Sun) Used books in English; run by an American. Buys books in excellent condition.

Cultural Centers

Biblioteca Lincoln (Map pp52-3; ☎ 5382-1528; www.bcl.edu.ar; Maipú 672) English-language books and newspapers; to check out materials you must join up (AR$80 per year).

British Arts Centre (Map pp52-3; ☎ 4393-6941; www.britishartscentre.org.ar; Suipacha 1333) Workshops, a cinema and library.

Centro Cultural Borges (Map pp52-3; ☎ 5555-5358; www.ccborges.org.ar; Viamonte 525) Tango shows, art exhibitions and plenty more.

Centro Cultural Recoleta (Map pp52-3; ☎ 4807-6340; www.centroculturalrecoleta.org; Junín 1930) Inexpensive exhibitions, theater, classes etc.

Centro Cultural Ricardo Rojas (Map pp52-3; ☎ 4954-5521; www.rojas.uba.ar; Av Corrientes 2038) Zillions of inexpensive, art-oriented classes.

Emergency

Ambulance ☎ 107
Police ☎ 911
Tourist Police (Map pp52-3; ☎ 4346-5748, 0800-999-5000; Av Corrientes 436; ☑ 24hr) Has interpreters for crime reporting.

Immigration Offices

Immigration (Map pp52-3; ☎ 4317-0200; www.migraciones.gov.ar; Av Antártida Argentina 1355; ☑ 7:30am-1:30pm Mon-Fri)

Internet Access

Internet access is everywhere and connections are generally fast. Charges are about AR$3 per hour.

Medical Services

Most of BA's hospitals have English-speaking staff; call for appointments.
British Hospital (www.hospitalbritanico.org.ar) Perdriel (Map p51; ☎ 4304-1081; Perdriel 74); Marcello T de Alvear (Map pp52-3 ☎ 4812-0040; Marcello T de Alvear 1573)
Dental Argentina (Map pp58-9; ☎ 4828-0821; www.dental-argentina.com; Laprida 1621, 2B) Dental professionals who speak English.
Hospital Municipal Juan Fernández (Map pp58-9; ☎ 4808-2600; Av Cerviño 3356)

Money

There is a gray market for US dollars, and you may hear people on pedestrian Av Florida call out 'cambio, cambio.' However, it's wiser to change money at a bank or *cambio* (exchange house) – scams and counterfeit bills do exist.

Some banks won't change less than AR$100 and may require ID; lines can be long. *Cambios* have slightly poorer exchange rates, but are quicker and have fewer limitations. US dollars are accepted at many retail establishments at a pretty fair rate.

Traveler's checks are very hard to cash (try exchange houses rather than banks) and incur bad exchange rates; one exception is **American Express** (Map pp52-3; Arenales 707). ATMs are commonplace, though there are withdrawal limits (from AR$300 and up) that depend on your banking system. Visa and MasterCard holders can get cash advances, but ask your bank before traveling.

Post

National post branches are all over the city.
Correo Postal Internacional (Map pp52-3; ☎ 4891-9191; www.correoargentino.com.ar; Av Antártida Argentina) For international parcels 2kg to 20kg; see website for rates. Contents must be checked. Boxes sold here.
FedEx (Map pp52-3; ☎ 0810-333-3339; www.fedex.com; Maipú 753) Has several branches across the city.

Telephone

The easiest way to make a call is from a *locutorio* (small telephone office), where you enter a booth and make calls in a safe, quiet environment. Costs are comparable to street telephones and you don't need change. Most *locutorios* offer reasonably priced fax and internet services as well.

Public phones are numerous; use coins, or buy a magnetic phone card from any kiosk.

Tourist Information

Buenos Aires' many small tourist offices (www.bue.gov.ar) are spread out in key tourist locations throughout the city. Hours vary throughout the year.
Tourist Office Florida (tourist kiosk; Map pp52-3; cnr Avs Florida & Diagonal Roque Sáenz Peña); Puerto Madero (tourist kiosk; Map pp52-3; Av Alicia Moreau de Justo, Dique 4); Recoleta (tourist kiosk; Map pp52-3; cnr Av Quintana & Ortiz); Retiro bus station (Map pp52-3; ste L83, under bus counter 105; ☑ 7:30am-1pm Mon-Fri & Sun)
Secretaría de Turismo de la Nación (Map pp52-3; ☎ 4312-2232, 0800-555-0016; www.turismo.gov.ar; Av Santa Fe 883; ☑ 9am-5pm Mon-Fri) Mostly info on Argentina but helps with BA.

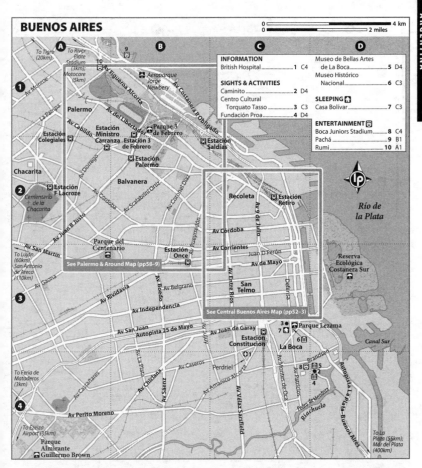

BUENOS AIRES

INFORMATION
British Hospital...................... 1 C4

SIGHTS & ACTIVITIES
Caminito................................. 2 D4
Centro Cultural
    Torquato Tasso.................. 3 C3
Fundación Proa..................... 4 D4

Museo de Bellas Artes
    de La Boca........................ 5 D4
Museo Histórico
    Nacional............................ 6 C3

SLEEPING
Casa Bolívar.......................... 7 C3

ENTERTAINMENT
Boca Juniors Stadium............ 8 C4
Pachá.................................... 9 B1
Rumi..................................... 10 A1

South American Explorers (Map pp52-3; ☎ 5275-0137; www.saexplorers.org; Roque Sáenz Peña 1142, 7th fl, ste A; ☼ 10am-5pm Mon-Fri, to 1pm Sat) Membership-based organization that offers excellent South American travel information. Also stores luggage, receives mail, offers internet and wi-fi, has library with book exchange, puts on events and maintains a bulletin board.

Travel Agencies

Say Hueque (www.sayhueque.com) Downtown (Map pp52-3; ☎ 5199-2517; Viamonte 749, 6th fl); Palermo Viejo (☎ 4775-7862; Guatemala 4845, ste 4, 1st fl) Mostly books adventure trips for travelers around Argentina, but also offers BA activities like tango shows.

Tangol (Map pp52-3; ☎ 4312-7276; www.tangol .com; Av Florida 971, Suite 31) Books adventurous activities

such as skydiving, *estancia* (ranch) visits, helicopter flights and night tours of BA. Also has typical travel agency services.

DANGERS & ANNOYANCES

Petty crime exists in Buenos Aires like in any big city. In general, BA is pretty safe. You can walk around at all hours of the night in many places, even as a lone woman (people stay out late, and there are often other pedestrians on the streets). Most tourists leave unscathed – they tend to be travel-smart and don't wear fancy jewelry or go around with their wallets hanging out or purses left carelessly on a chair. They're cautious of pickpockets in crowded places, aware of their surroundings and at least *pretend* to know where they're going.

CENTRAL BUENOS AIRES

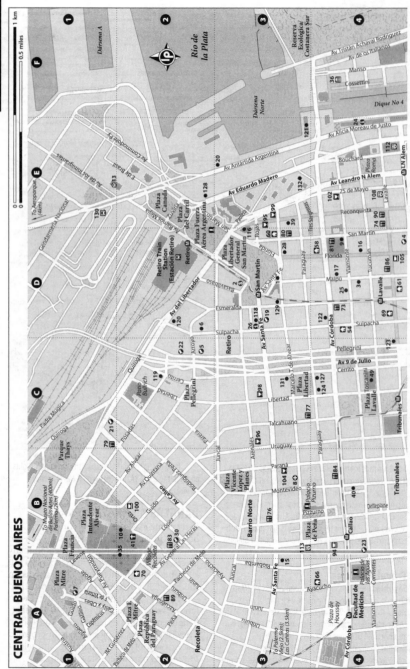

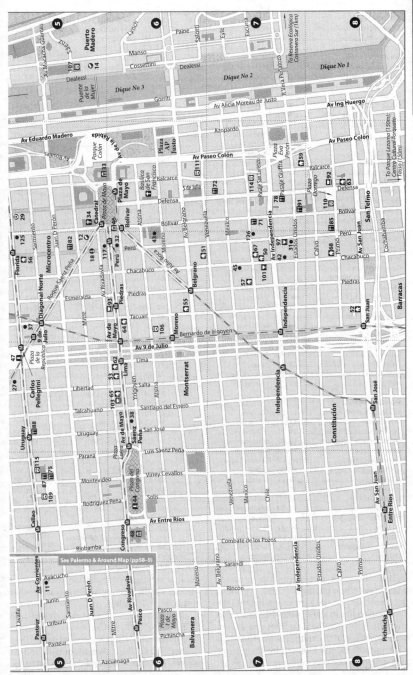

See Palermo & Around Map (pp58–9)

ARGENTINA

If anything, BA is besieged more by minor nuisances. When buying anything, try not to get shortchanged and keep an eye out for fake bills, especially in dark places like taxis and nightclubs (search for clear lines and a good watermark). Watch carefully for traffic when crossing streets, and look out for the piles of dog droppings underfoot. Note that fresh air is often lacking – air pollution and smoking are big issues. Dealing with taxis is another thing; see p70 for tips.

Every city has its edgy neighborhoods, and in BA these include Constitución Estación (train station), the eastern border of San Telmo and La Boca (where, outside tourist streets, you should be careful even during the day). Av Florida can be edgy only very, very late at night. See p50 under Emergency for the tourist police.

SIGHTS

At Buenos Aires' heart is its *microcentro*, which holds many of the city's historical buildings and museums. To the north lies upper-crust Recoleta, with its famous cemetery, and park-filled Palermo, home to many great restaurants and bars. Down south is where the blue-collar class hangs: this includes tango mecca San Telmo and colorful, roughhousing La Boca. There's enough bustle in this city to keep you trotting around all day and all night.

City Center

Buenos Aires' *microcentro* holds many 19th-century European buildings, which surprises many travelers expecting a more Latin American feel. The liveliest street here is pedestrian **Av Florida**, packed with masses of harried businesspeople, curious tourists, angling leather salespeople and shady money changers. Make sure to stop at **Galerías Pacífico** (Map pp52–3), one of BA's most gorgeous shopping malls; peek at the ceiling paintings inside. South of Av Florida is busy Av Corrientes, and if you head west on this thoroughfare you'll cross superbroad Av 9 de Julio (run!). It's decisively punctuated by the famously phallic **Obelisco** (Map pp52–3), a major symbol of Buenos Aires. Just beyond is the city's traditional theater district, also full of many cheap bookstores.

The 18th-century **Museo del Cabildo** (Map pp52-3; admission AR$1; ⏰ 10:30am-5pm Tue-Fri, 11:30am-6pm Sun) is all that's left of the colonial arches that once surrounded Plaza de Mayo. Nearby, the neoclassical **Catedral Metropolitana** (Map pp52–3), finished in 1827, contains the tomb of liberator José de San Martín, Argentina's most venerated historical figure. A block east you'll see the pink presidential palace, **Casa Rosada** (Map pp52–3) and the famous balcony where vibrant Evita energized adoring crowds during her heyday in the 1940s. Around the southern side of the building is **Museo de la Casa Rosada** (Map pp52-3; ☎ 4344-3804; www.museo .gov.ar), the most interesting feature of which is the catacombs of the Fuerte Viejo, an 18th-century colonial ruin. The museum was being renovated at research time, so call or check the website for details and to see if their tours of the Casa Rosada have been reinstated.

A block south of Plaza de Mayo is **Manzana de las Luces** (Block of Enlightenment; Map pp52–3), a solid square of 18th-century buildings that includes **Iglesia San Ignacio**, Buenos Aires' oldest church, and **Colegio Nacional**, an elite secondary school. Underground are old defensive military tunnels.

Over to the west, at the other end of Av de Mayo, you'll find the green-domed **Palacio del Congreso** (Map pp52–3). Modeled on Washington, DC's Capitol Building, it was completed in 1906 and faces pigeon-filled Plaza del Congreso and its **Monumento a los Dos Congresos**, the granite steps of which symbolize the Andes.

Since its opening in 1908, visitors have marveled at magnificent **Teatro Colón** (Map pp52-3; ☎ 4378-7100; www.teatrocolon.org.ar; Cerrito 618), a luxurious seven-story building that seats 2500 spectators on plush red-velvet chairs and surrounds them with tiers of gilded balconies. This world-class facility for opera, ballet and classical music was being renovated at research time – check to see if their daily tours have been reinstated.

East of the city center is BA's newest *barrio*, **Puerto Madero** (Map pp52–3). This renovated docklands area is lined with pleasant pedestrian walkways, expensive lofts, trendy restaurants and bars and some of the city's priciest hotels. Art lovers should check out the **Colección de Arte Fortabat** (Map p51; ☎ 4310-6600; www.coleccionfortabat.org.ar; Cossettini 141; admission AR$15; ⏰ noon-9pm Tue-Fri, 10am-9pm Sat & Sun), a fancy art museum showing off the collection of multimillionaire Amalia Lacroze de Fortabat.

Further east is the completely different world of **Reserva Ecológica Costanera Sur** (Map p51; ⏰ 8am-7pm Nov-March, to 6pm Apr-Oct), a large marshy ecological reserve with dirt paths and natural landscapes. The entrance is east of San Telmo, via the street R Vera Peñaloza.

San Telmo

Six blocks south of Plaza de Mayo, San Telmo – home of BA's main tango culture – is full of cobbled streets and aging mansions. Historically its low rents have attracted artists, but these days you'll see more boutiques than studios. The neighborhood was a fashionable place until 1870, when a series of epidemics over 20 years drove the rich elite northwards; many houses were then subdivided and turned into cramped immigrant shelters.

On Sundays, **Plaza Dorrego** (Map pp52–3) packs in the crowds with its famous **antiques fair**. Hordes of tourists clash elbows for rusty pocket watches, vintage dresses, ancient crystalware, delicate china and old coins. Good tango street shows add excitement and photo ops, but don't forget to drop some change into the hat. Surrounding the plaza are pleasant cafes where you can sip anything from cognacs to *cortados* (coffee with milk) while lazily people-watching. Afterwards, stroll the atmospheric streets to window-shop for that perfect Victrola – you just may find it. At night check out the clubs that put on those famous tango shows.

Four blocks south at Defensa and Brasil is leafy **Parque Lezama** (Map p51), the location where Buenos Aires was founded; you can mix with the locals playing chess, or visit the well-presented **Museo Histórico Nacional** (Map p51; ☎ 4307-1182; ⏱ 11am-6pm Wed & Fri-Sun, to 9pm Thu).

La Boca

Vivid, working-class La Boca, situated along the old port and at the *boca* (mouth) of the Río Riachuelo, was built by Italian immigrants from Genoa. Its main attraction is colorful **Caminito**, a short pedestrian walk lined with corrugated-metal buildings. Local artists display their brightly colored paintings, adding to the vibrant ambience. The neighborhood is also home to the Boca Juniors soccer team (p67).

Boca's standing as an artists' enclave is the legacy of painter Benito Quinquela Martín; his old home and studio is the **Museo de Bellas Artes de La Boca** (Map p51; Pedro de Mendoza 1835; admission AR$5; ⏱ 10am-6pm Tue-Fri, 11am-7pm Sat & Sun). Also, don't miss the excellent **Fundación Proa** (Map p51; ☎ 4104-1000; www.proa.org; Pedro de Mendoza 1929; admission AR$10; ⏱ 11am-7pm Tue-Sun), which exhibits cutting-edge contemporary art; there's a wonderful view from its rooftop.

Be aware that this is one of the poorer *barrios* of Buenos Aires and, whether day or night, you shouldn't wander from the beaten path of tourist hangouts. Buses 29, 130 and 152 run to La Boca.

Recoleta

One of Buenos Aires' prime tourist attractions, **Cementerio de la Recoleta** (Map pp52-3; ⏱ 7am-6pm) sits in the plushest of neighborhoods, ritzy Recoleta. High walls surround this necropolis where, in death just as in life,

generations of Argentina's elite rest in ornate splendor. It's fascinating to wander around and explore this extensive mini-city of lofty statues, detailed marble facades and earthy-smelling sarcophagi. Follow the crowds and you'll find Evita's grave.

Next to the cemetery is the 1732 **Iglesia de Nuestra Señora de Pilar** (Map pp52–3), while out front a hippie fair – complete with lively performers and crowds of tourists – takes place on most days (especially weekends). Sit at a cafe and take in the nearby attractive greenery of **Plaza Intendente Alvear**; note the giant *ombú* trees. If you're lucky you'll spot a *paseaperros* (professional dog-walker) strolling with 15 or so leashed canines of all shapes and tails.

The **Museo Nacional de Bellas Artes** (off Map pp52-3; ☎ 5288-9900; Av del Libertador 1473; ⏱ 12:30-7:30pm Tue-Fri, 9:30am-7:30pm Sat & Sun) houses works by famous French impressionists and Argentine artists. It's well worth a visit.

Palermo

Full of green parks, imposing statues and elegant embassies, Palermo on a sunny weekend afternoon is a *porteño* yuppie dream. **Jardín Botánico Carlos Thays** (Botanical Gardens; Map pp58-9; ⏱ dawn-dusk) is good for a stroll, while the **Jardín Zoológico** (zoo; Map pp58-9; ☎ 4011-9900; cnr Avs Las Heras & Sarmiento; admission AR$9-16; ⏱ 10-6pm Tue-Sun) has mostly humane animal enclosures and some attractive classic structures to boot. There's also the pleasant **Jardín Japonés** (Japanese Gardens; Map pp58-9; ☎ 4804-4922; cnr Avs Casares & Berro; admission AR$5; ⏱ 10am-6pm) and lovely **Rosedal** (Rose Garden; Map pp58–9). On weekends, rent bikes and cruise the lakes of **Parque 3 de Febrero** (Map pp58–9).

Not too far from these green spots is the cutting-edge **Museo de Arte Latinoamericano de Buenos Aires** (Malba; Map pp58-9; ☎ 4808-6511; www.malba.org.ar; Av Presidente Figuero Alcorta 3415; admission AR$15, Wed AR$5; ⏱ noon-8pm Thu-Mon, to 9pm Wed), which has exhibitions by Latin American artists. Another interesting place is **Museo Evita** (Map pp58-9; ☎ 4807-9433; www.museoevita.org; Lafinur 2988; admission AR$12; ⏱ 11am-7pm Tue-Sun), chronicling this legendary and effervescent woman's life and work. Palermo also contains the **Campo de Polo** (Polo Grounds; Map pp58–9), where polo matches are played, **Hipódromo** (Racetrack; Map pp58–9) and **Planetario** (Observatory; ☎ 4771-9393; www.planetario.gov.ar; cnr Avs Sarmiento & Belisario Roldán; astronomy shows AR$4).

Make sure to stroll through the subneighborhood of **Palermo Viejo** (Map pp58–9), just south of the parks. It's further divided into Palermo Soho and Palermo Hollywood. Here you'll find BA's hippest restaurants, trendiest boutiques and some lively nightlife. Its beautiful old buildings make for some great wanderings.

ACTIVITIES

Porteños' main activities are walking, shopping and dancing tango. Those searching for greener pastures, however, head to Palermo's parks, where joggers run past strolling families and *fútbol* scrimmages (join in only if you're very, very confident of your skills).

Safe cycling is possible in this city, but only in specific places. Good places to pedal are Palermo's parks (see opposite) and Puerto Madero and its nearby Reserva Ecológica Costanera Sur (see p55). You can rent bikes from bike tour companies, who also do guided tours (see below under Tours).

Other than at certain major hotels and gyms, tennis courts and swimming pools can be found in Palermo's **Club de Amigos** (Map pp58-9; ☎ 4801-1213; www.clubdeamigos.org.ar; Av Figueroa Alcorta 3885).

Some companies like **Tangol** (Map pp52-3; ☎ 4312-7276; www.tangol.com; Av Florida 971, ste 31) offer activities such as skydiving, helicopter tours and *estancia* visits, which often include horse riding.

COURSES
Language

BA is a popular destination for Spanish students. There are plenty of schools and even more private teachers, so ask around for recommendations. All offer social excursions and can help with accommodation; some have volunteer opportunities.

Weekly group rates range from AR$525 to AR$775 for 20 hours (some charge for materials too); private classes run AR$53 to AR$70 per hour. Check websites for specifics; also try www.123teachme.com, where students rate language schools.

For something fun and different, check out www.spanglishba.com – sort of a speed-dating concept, but with language.

Academia Buenos Aires (Map pp52-3; ☎ 4345-5954; www.academiabuenosaires.com; Yrigoyen 571, 4th fl)
ELEBaires (Map pp52-3; ☎ 4383-7706; www.elebaires.com.ar; Av de Mayo 1370, 3rd fl ste 10)
Estudio Buenos Aires (Map pp52-3; ☎ 4312-8936; www.ebatrust.com.ar; Reconquista 962, 3rd fl)

Hispanaires (Map pp52-3; ☎ 4815-6953; www.hispanaires.com; Montevideo 744)
Instituto de Español Rayuela (Map pp52-3; ☎ 4300-2010; www.spanish-argentina.com.ar; Chacabuco 852, 1st fl, ste 11)
Mundo Español (Map pp52-3; ☎ 4362-4647; www.mundo-espanol.com; Chacabuco 649)

Tango

Tango classes are available everywhere – your own hostel may offer them. All *milongas* (dance halls, or the dances themselves) offer inexpensive classes. They can also put you in touch with private teachers, some of whom speak English. Cultural centers (see p50) often have affordable classes as well. For citywide tango events, see www.tangobuenosaires.gob.ar. For a list of tango show venues, see p65.

Centro Cultural Torquato Tasso (Map p51; ☎ 4307-6506; www.torquatotasso.com.ar; Defensa 1575) Afternoon tango classes.
Confitería Ideal (Map pp52-3; ☎ 5265-8069; www.confiteriaideal.com; Suipacha 380) One of BA's tango meccas, with continuous classes (some in English), frequent *milongas* and nightly shows.

TOURS

If you have little time and want to take a tour, that's OK. Just avoid those big buses full of languid sightseers – much more creative tours exist.

Cultur (☎ 15-6575-4593; www.cultour.com.ar) Good walking tours for AR$55. Private tours also available.
Cicerones (☎ 4431-9892; www.cicerones.org.ar) Nonprofit organization that relies on volunteers to show visitors key parts of Buenos Aires. Free tours given.
Eternautas (☎ 5031-9916; www.eternautas.com) Economical weekend walking tours in Spanish (AR$10) and English (AR$55). Also does tours with a political, artistic, social or historical bent (AR$515 and up). Guides speak various languages and are certified historians.
Gobierno de la Cuidad de Buenos Aires (☎ 0800-999-2727; www.bue.gov.ar/recorridos) Free guided tours of the city, including self-guided tours. Ask if English-speaking guides are available.
Urban Biking (☎ 4568-4321; www.urbanbiking.com) Bike tours of BA and Tigre.

FESTIVALS & EVENTS

A few of Buenos Aires' biggest celebrations:
Tango festival (www.festivaldetango.gob.ar) Late February to early March.
Fashion BA (www.buenosairesmoda.com) March and September.

PALERMO & AROUND

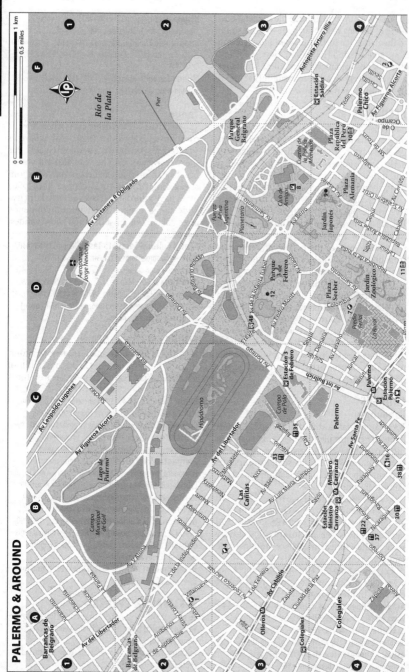

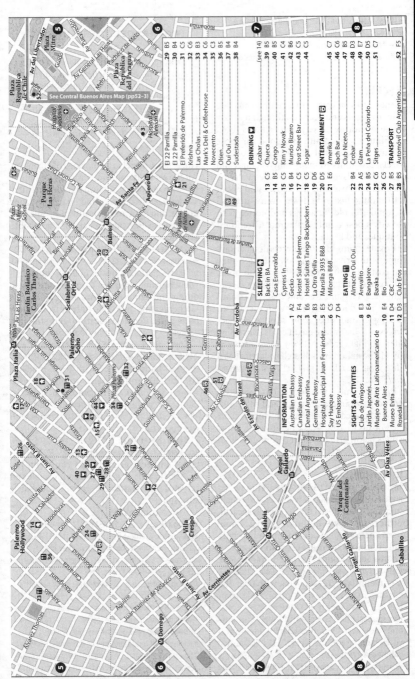

See Central Buenos Aires Map (pp52–3)

El 22 Parrilla	29 B5
El 22 Parrilla	30 B4
El Preferido de Palermo	31 C5
Krishna	32 B3
Las Cholas	33 B3
Mark's Deli & Coffeehouse	34 C6
Novecento	35 C3
Olsen	36 B5
Oui Oui	37 B4
Sudestada	38 B4

DRINKING 🍷
Acabar	(see 14)
Chueca	39 B5
Congo	40 B5
Kim y Novak	41 C4
Mundo Bizarro	42 B6
Post Street Bar	43 C5
Sugar	44 C5

ENTERTAINMENT 🎭
Amerika	45 C7
Bach Bar	46 C6
Club Niceto	47 B5
Crobar	48 D3
Glam	49 E7
La Peña del Colorado	50 D5
Sitges	51 C7

TRANSPORT
Automóvil Club Argentino	52 F5

SLEEPING 🛏
Back in BA	1 A2
Casa Esmeralda	2 F4
Cypress In	3 E6
Gecko	4 B3
Hostel Suites Palermo	5 E5
Hostel Suites Tango Backpackers	6 C5
La Otra Orilla	7 D4
Mansilla 3935 B&B	8
Milonga B&B	

EATING 🍴
Almacén Oui Oui	22 B4
Arevalito	23 A5
Bangalore	24 B5
Baraka	25 C6
Bio	26 C5
CBC	27 B5
Club Eros	28 B5

INFORMATION
Australian Embassy	8 E3
Canadian Embassy	9 E4
Dental Argentina	10 E4
German Embassy	11 D4
Hospital Municipal Juan Fernández	12 D3
Say Hueque	
US Embassy	

SIGHTS & ACTIVITIES
Club de Amigos	13 C5
Jardín Japonés	14 B5
Museo de Arte Latinoamericano de	
Buenos Aires	16 B4
Museo Evita	17 C5
Rosedal	18 C5
	19 D6
	20 D5
	21 E6

ARGENTINA

Festival Internacional de Cine Independiente
(www.bafici.gov.ar) Mid to late April.
Arte BA (www.arteba.com) Mid-May.
La Rural (www.ruralarg.org.ar) Agricultural/livestock fair;
July to August.

SLEEPING

Buenos Aires' *microcentro* is central and close to many sights and services, though it's busy and noisy during the day. San Telmo is about 15 minutes' walk south and good for those seeking old colonial atmosphere, cobbled streets, proximity to many tango venues and a blue-collar flavor around the edges. Palermo Viejo is northwest of the center and about a 10-minute taxi ride. It's a pretty area full of wonderful old buildings and dotted with the city's best ethnic restaurants, trendiest boutiques and liveliest bars.

Private rooms in some hostels don't always come with private bathroom, though they can cost more than rooms in a cheap hotel. All hostels listed here include kitchen access, light breakfast and free internet; most have free wi-fi and lockers (bring your own lock). The bigger ones offer more services and activities, and many take credit cards. Hostelling International cards (AR$55) are available at any HI hostel or BA's **Hostelling International office** (Map pp52-3; ☎ 4511-8723; www.hostels.org.ar; Av Florida 835).

BA has some good budget hotel choices. Most offer a simple breakfast and cable TV; some take credit cards, which might incur a fee of up to 10% – ask beforehand. Most listings below also have internet and/or wi-fi available for guests.

City Center

Lime House (Map pp52-3; ☎ 4383-4561; www.lime house.com.ar; Lima 11; dm AR$28-40, d AR$120-160) Small, funky and rustic hostel that's centrally located, but next to busy 9 de Julio – expect some noise. There's a great pool room, and upstairs is an enormous rooftop area with views.

Hostel Suites Florida (Map pp52-3; ☎ 4325-0969; www.hostelsuites.com; Av Florida 328; dm/d AR$36/160; 🕸) Argentina's largest hostel, with over 300 beds and an awesome location on pedestrian Florida. Offers plenty of services, large common spaces, good dorms and lovely contemporary doubles. A basement bar/nightclub and two Jacuzzis are in the works. HI Discount.

Milhouse Avenue (Map pp52-3; ☎ 4343-9383; www.milhousehostel.com; Av de Mayo 1245; dm/d AR$38/175; 🕸)

> **TWO-TIER COSTS IN ARGENTINA**
>
> A few hotels, some museums, most national parks and one major airline have adopted a two-tier price system. Rates for foreigners are double (or more) locals' prices. While it's somewhat useless to complain to service personnel at government-run entities about this discrepancy, you can choose to stay at hotels that don't discriminate – just ask.

Huge, fancy hostel in a renovated old mansion. All the services you could ask for, and more: bar with draft beer, rooftop terrace, basement TV lounge/kitchen area and DJ parties. Good dorms, and doubles are beautiful – some have original clawfoot tubs. Wheelchair accessible; HI discount.

Trip Recoleta Hostel (Map pp52-3; ☎ 4807-8726; www.triprecoletahostel.com.ar; López 2180; dm AR$45-63, s/d AR$140/210) Small hostel in a tall building – you'll be climbing stairs. Large sex-segregated dorms and tight bathrooms, along with a tiny kitchen/eating area. The only reason to stay is its great Recoleta location and stunning cemetery views from the small terrace.

Goya Hotel (Map pp52-3; ☎ 4322-9269; www.goyahotel.com.ar; Suipacha 748; s/d from AR$105/150; 🕸) A good budget choice with forty modern, comfortable and carpeted rooms. 'Classic' rooms are older and have open showers; 'Superior' rooms are newer with bathtubs. The presidential suite (AR$210) comes with jets in the tub.

Regis Hotel (Map pp52-3; ☎ 4327-2605; www.orlo-hoteles.com.ar; Lavalle 813; s/d AR$322/385; 🕸) Quiet and central midrange choice on pedestrian Lavalle. It has good, comfortable and carpeted rooms, attentive service and old-style atmosphere.

Also recommended:
Milonga (Map pp52-3; ☎ 4815-1827; www.milonga hostel.com.ar; Ayacucho 921; dm AR$35, d AR$118-155) Old house with simple rooms facing outdoor hallways. Pool room covered in graffiti 'art.' Nicer is their annex, Milonga B&B (Map pp58–9), at Agüero 1389.
BA Stop (Map pp52-3; ☎ 4382-7406; www.bastop .com; Av Rivadavia 1194; dm AR$35-40, s/d AR$100/140) Good small hostel in old building. Art murals on walls and tranquil back room with table tennis.
Milhouse (Map pp52-3; ☎ 4345-9604; www .milhousehostel.com; Yrigoyen 959; dm/d AR$38/175; 🕸) Large and central; BA's original 'party hostel.' Great facilities and tons of activities and services. HI discount.

Hotel Central Córdoba (Map pp52-3; ☎ 4311-1175; www.hotelcentralcordoba.com.ar; San Martín 1021; s/d from AR$140/160; ⛬) Good-value rooms; within swilling distance of two popular downtown bars.

Hotel El Cabildo (Map pp52-3; ☎ 4322-6745; Lavalle 748; s/d from AR$170/195; ⛬) Surprisingly nice rooms and unbeatable location right on pedestrian Lavalle. Superior doubles are best; no breakfast.

San Telmo

Puerto Limón (Map pp52-3; ☎ 4361-9649; www.puerto limonhostel.com; Chacabuco 1080; dm AR$36, d AR$160-190; ⛬) This very laid-back hostel has funky touches, a bright common area and a pleasant open patio in back. Rooms vary widely: the best double is room 2, and the best dorm, room 9.

Hostel-Inn Tango City (Map pp52-3; ☎ 4300-5776; www.hostel-inn.com; Piedras 680; dm/d AR$38/139; ⛬) Large hostel in a tall, almost claustrophobic building. Rooms are cramped but decent. Good basement barlike area, complete with pool table and small kitchen. Another branch nearby at Humberto Primo 820. HI discount.

Ostinatto (Map pp52-3; ☎ 4362-9639; www.osti natto.com.ar; Chile 680; dm AR$38-52, d AR$170-185; ⛬) This snazzy hostel has a ground-floor bar-lounge, catwalks in its airy central well (not for those with vertigo), a small rooftop terrace and a slick penthouse. Room rates include one free tango and Spanish class.

Hostel Rayuela (Map pp52-3; ☎ 4342-5951; www .rayuelahostel.com; Av Belgrano 887, 1st fl; dm/d AR$39/160; ⛬) Intimate hostel on a busy street (it's quiet inside) and near good public transport. The atmosphere is pleasant enough. Good rooms line a long brick hallway, but there aren't many bathrooms for the number of dorm beds. Run by three couples.

America del Sur (Map pp52-3; ☎ 4300-5525; www .americahostel.com.ar; Chacabuco 718; dm/d AR$50/180; ⛬) Gorgeous boutique-like hostel with bar-bistro area near reception and large, elegant wood patio in back. Clean dorms with four beds all have well-designed bathrooms. Private rooms tastefully done. Cheap *asado* dinners available.

Ayres de San Telmo (Map pp52-3; ☎ 4362-0131; www.ayresdesantelmo.com.ar; Av San Juan 907; dm AR$63, d AR$145-160; ⛬) Good, clean hostel with artsy touches, in an elegant old building on a busy street. The top-floor lounge area has a kitchen, and there's a tiled rooftop terrace nearby.

Hotel Babel (Map pp52-3; ☎ 4300-8300; www.hotel babel.com.ar; Balcarce 946; d AR$350-420; ⛬) Just nine beautiful rooms are available at this colorful boutique hotel. Standard rooms have queen beds; superior rooms have two twins or a king. All are arranged around a bright covered patio. Reception is a small affair with bar counter and lounges.

Palermo Viejo

Back in BA (Map pp58-9; ☎ 4774-2859; www.backinba .com; El Salvador 5115; dm AR$35, d AR$110-145) Intimate, friendly and casual hostel with *buena onda* (good vibes). Newly remodeled, offering comfortable beds and common areas painted in bright colors. Reception is a bar counter and there's a small central patio for Thursday-night *asados*.

Gecko (Map pp58-9; ☎ 4771-0910; www.gecko hostel.com.ar; Bonpland 2233; dm AR$35, d AR$112-162; ⛬) Sporting a colorful Boca-themed paint job is this casual, funky and artsy hostel. There's a bar/pool table room in front and covered patio hallways in back. Popular for long-term stays.

Casa Esmeralda (Map pp58-9; ☎ 4772-2446; www .casaesmeralda.com.ar; Honduras 5765; dm/d AR$42/130) Homey, small and rustic hostel with a casual vibe and a pleasant garden area. There's also a sunny rooftop patio and a friendly dog on the premises.

Hostel Suites Tango Backpackers (Map pp58-9; ☎ 4776-6871; www.tangobp.com; Paraguay 4601; dm/d AR$43/150; ⛬) HI hostel in an old converted house with sunny rooftop patio. Nice bar-lounge reception area as well. Three blocks to Plaza Italia (metro and bus lines). HI discount.

Hostel Suites Palermo (Map pp58-9; ☎ 4773-0806; www.hostelsuites.com; Charcas 4752; dm/d AR$46/190; ⛬) This somewhat upscale hostel is in a beautiful renovated old building with high ceilings, a nice interior patio and a great rooftop terrace. The best rooms are the two doubles with balcony. Nightly events; HI discount.

Mansilla 3935 B&B (Map pp58-9; ☎ 4833-3821; www.mansilla3935.com.ar; Mansilla 3935; s/d AR$158/210; ⛬) Family-run B&B offering a great deal. Each of the six simple but lovely rooms comes with its own bathroom. Ceilings are high, and a few tiny patios add charm. Sauna available.

La Otra Orilla (Map pp58-9; ☎ 4867-4070; www .otraorilla.com.ar; Álvarez 1779; r AR$170-590; ⛬) Just seven luxurious and romantic rooms

ARGENTINA

are available in this beautiful guesthouse, located off the beaten path in Palermo Viejo. All rooms have private bathroom except for two. There is a cute garden patio, and the service is friendly.

Cypress In (Map pp58-9; ☎ 4833-5834; www .cypressin.com; Costa Rica 4828; d AR$230-315; ⌘) This contemporary guesthouse boasts a slick lounge/lobby area, and though the 13 small rooms are comparatively plain, they're still good. A rooftop patio makes for a great hangout area, and the best room is located up here.

EATING

Buenos Aires is overflowing with excellent food, and you'll dine very well at all budget levels. Typical restaurants serve a standard fare of *parrilla* (grilled meat), pastas and/or *minutas* (short orders), but for something different head to Palermo Viejo and Cañitas, where a large number of international and ethnic eateries can be found. Another food-oriented neighborhood is Puerto Madero, but most of the restaurants here are very fancy, relatively expensive and lean more toward steaks than stir-fries.

Vegetarians rejoice: unlike in the rest of Argentina, there is a good range of meat-free restaurants in BA – you just have to know where to look. Most nonvegetarian restaurants offer a few pastas, salads and pizzas – but not much else is meat-free.

City Center

Pizzería Güerrín (Map pp52-3; Av Corrientes 1368; slices AR$4) Great for good, fast and cheap pizza slices; you can eat standing up, like the thrifty locals, or sit down for a rest.

El Cuartito (Map pp52-3; Talcahuano 937; slices AR$4-5) Another excellent, inexpensive stand-up or sit-down pizzeria, and a BA institution. The line goes out the door on weekend nights.

Pura Vida (Map pp52-3; Reconquista 516; juices AR$10-14) US-style juice bar with lots of choice (think carrot-ginger-orange or banana-pineapple-coconut. Also makes a few sandwiches, salads and wraps. Another branch in Recoleta at Uriburu 1489.

Lotos (Map pp52-3; Av Córdoba 1577; mains AR$10-15; ⌚ 11:30am-6pm Mon-Fri) Fast and efficient vegetarian cafeteria serving fresh and healthy meals. Choose what looks good and pay at the end of the counter. Its store downstairs sells tofu, whole wheat bread and organic tea.

Parrilla al Carbón (Map pp52-3; Lavalle 663; mains AR$16-30) For fast, cheap and tasty grilled meats in the city center you won't do much better than this hole-in-the-wall. Order a set meal (steak, fries and cola) for AR$4.25 or grab a *choripan* (sausage sandwich) for a ridiculous AR$5.

Cumaná (Map pp52-3; Rodríguez Peña 1149; mains AR$17-24) The low-priced pizzas, empanadas and *cazuelas* (hearty stews) pack in the crowds. Great rustic atmosphere. Just get here early to avoid a wait.

CBC (California Burrito Company; Map pp52-3; Lavalle 441; burritos AR$19; ⌚ 8am-11pm Mon-Fri) Megapopular for its California-style burritos; choose your fillings while you're waiting in line. Even sells house margaritas. Another branch at Godoy Cruz 1781 in Palermo Viejo.

Filo (Map pp52-3; San Martín 975; mains AR$25-40) Hip and artsy restaurant offering a mind-boggling selection of salads, pizzas, pastas and desserts – all of it good.

Chiquilín (Map pp52-3; Sarmiento 1599; mains AR$25-45) Popular and long-running *parrilla* restaurant with an upscale atmosphere, suited waiters offering good service and hanging hams for decoration.

Also recommended:

Pippo (Map pp52-3; Montevideo 341; mains AR$15-26) Something of a BA institution. Cheap, casual and open late.

El Sanjuanino (Map pp52-3; Posadas 1515; mains AR$20-35) Cheap Recoleta eats – *locro* (traditional hearty stew), tamales and empanadas.

Grant's (Map pp52-3; Av General Las Heras 1925; set menus AR$22-33) One of the city's better all-you-can-down places.

Galerías Pacífico (Map pp52-3; cnr Avs Florida & Córdoba; meals under AR$25) Downstairs food court in a fancy mall.

Broccolino (Map pp52-3; Esmeralda 776; mains AR$25-40) Excellent pasta, with too many choices.

Granix (Map pp52-3; Av Florida 165; meals AR$33; ⌚ lunch Mon-Fri) Large, popular vegetarian cafeteria; on 1st floor in Galería Güemes.

San Telmo

Origen (Map pp52-3; Primo 599; mains AR$10-30; ⌚ 8:30am-10pm Sun-Tue, till 12:30am Wed-Sat) Smart corner cafe with a small menu highlighted by fancy sandwiches, salads and pizzas. *Licuados* (fruit shakes) available, plus lots of desserts. Grab a sidewalk table for people-watching.

El Desnivel (Map pp52-3; Defensa 855; mains AR$15-22; ⌚ closed Mon lunch) Hugely popular with both locals and tourists. Get a table in the original room in front: this way you can keep an eye on the grill, where *bife de lomos* (tenderloins) and *vacío* (flank steaks) lie sizzling.

Territorio (Map pp52-3; Estados Unidos 500; mains AR$15-27) Casual eatery focusing on *tablas* (meat and cheese platters) and *picadas* (meat/cheese plates and appetizers). Also serves sandwiches with exotic meats such as venison and wild boar. Craft beer and wines smooth it all down.

Abuela Pan (Map pp52-3; Bolívar 707; daily menus AR$18; ☺ Mon-Fri 8am-7pm) Tiny but atmospheric spot with just a handful of tables. The vegetarian special changes daily – expect things like eggplant *milanesas* (thin breaded steaks), stuffed cannelloni or vegetable stews.

Brasserie Petanque (Map pp52-3; Defensa 596; mains AR$35-50; ☺ closed Mon dinner & Sat lunch) Fabulous bistro serving all the French classics: escargot, steak tartare and terrine de foie gras, as well as more exotic dishes like *estofado de conejo* (rabbit stew). For a good deal, get the *menú del día* (daily special; AR$25 to AR$33).

Palermo Viejo

El 22 Parrilla (Map pp58-9; Carranza 1950; mains AR$12-42) Wonderfully local and unpretentious steak house with family atmosphere, serving large portions of all the typical cuts of meat. There are pastas for vegetarians and cheap wine for everybody. Also at the corner of Gorriti and Godoy Cruz.

El Preferido de Palermo (Map pp58-9; cnr Borges & Guatemala; mains AR$15-22) This local joint has an old general-store atmosphere, with jars of olives in the window and tall tables *not* made for comfort. Great varied menu, however: homemade pastas, Cuban rice, Spanish veal, seafood stew and tripe.

Krishna (Map pp58-9; Malabia 1833; mains AR$16-25; ☺ closed Mon all day & Tue dinner) Tiny, hippie-style place full of Indian drapes and low, colorful mosaic tables. Wash down your *thalis* (set meals), tofu and seitan (wheat gluten) with a *lassi* (yogurt drink) and *chai* (tea).

Baraka (Map pp58-9; Gurruchaga 1450; mains AR$16-28; ☺ 9am-9pm Mon-Sat, 10am-8pm Sun) Trendy and casual cafe with a creative menu highlighted by exotic choices: *ceviche* (marinated raw seafood), vegetable stir-fry and Thai chicken curry. Great homemade pastries, along with *licuados* and many exotic teas.

Arevalito (Map pp58-9; Arévalo 1478; mains AR$20; ☺ 9am-midnight Mon-Sat) The menu is hardly extensive at this tiny eatery, but everything is

good and very healthy. There's homemade yogurt, and the coffee is exceptional.

Mark's Deli & Coffeehouse (Map pp58-9; El Salvador 4701; mains AR$20-30) Very popular cafe-deli serving excellent soups, salads and sandwiches, with iced coffee for hot days. Modern decor, pleasant outside seating and a guaranteed wait on sunny weekends.

Oui Oui (Map pp58-9; Nicaragua 6068; mains AR$25; ☺ 8am-8pm Tue-Fri, 10am-8pm Sat & Sun) Cute as a bug is this tiny French bistro serving mostly gourmet salads and outstanding sandwiches. Weekend brunch is awesome – arrive early to get a table. There's an annex, Almacén Oui Oui (Map pp58-9), on the corner at Nicaragua 6099.

Bio (Map pp58-9; Humboldt 2199; mains AR$25-35; ☺ closed Sun & Mon dinner) Small corner bistro serving tasty and creative vegetarian fare, like seitan curry, quinoa risotto, and great salads. Organic ingredients are used. The ginger lemonade is a must on a hot day.

Sudestada (Map pp58-9; ☎ 4776-3777; Guatemala 5602; mains AR$25-65; ☺ closed Sun) Upscale corner restaurant serving magnificent dishes from Thailand, Vietnam, Malaysia and Singapore. A refreshing change: the spicy food here is really spicy! The weekday lunch menu is a good deal (AR$27). Reserve for dinner.

Bangalore (Map pp58-9; ☎ 4779-2621; Humboldt 1416; mains AR$30-45) It's a popular British-style pub on the ground floor, but upstairs there's a small space with just a few tables. Indian food is the focus here; the menu changes monthly, but it's always good. Reserve ahead.

Also recommended:

Club Eros (Map pp58-9; Uriarte 1609; mains AR$10-15) Dirt-cheap eatery stuffed with local diners.

Las Cholas (Map pp58-9; Arce 306; mains AR$16-28) Good-value northern Argentine food in hip Las Cañitas. Upscale rustic and very popular, though dishes tend to be salty.

Novecento (Map pp58-9; ☎ 4778-1900; Av Báez 199; mains AR$30-45) Fancy Italian bistro in Las Cañitas serving gourmet pastas, meats, fish and salads. Great weekend brunch.

Olsen (Map pp58-9; ☎ 4776-7677; Gorriti 5870; mains AR$35-55; ☺ closed Mon) Gorgeous space, luscious food, high prices. Popular Sunday brunch.

DRINKING

BA is all about the night, and there are plenty of cafes, bars and live-music venues in which to drink the night away. Cafes have very long hours: they're usually open early morning until late into the night. Bars and live-music venues open late and stay open even later; on weekends they'll often be hopping until 6am the next day.

For a night of rowdy drinking, join the expat-run **Pub Crawl** (☎ 15-5115-9053; www.pub crawlba.com). For AR$60 you get food, drinks and transport to several bars and one nightclub.

Cafes

Buenos Aires has a heavy cafe culture, which is obvious once you see the number of cafes in the city. Some are famous institutions, full of elegant old atmosphere and rich history; most are modern and trendy. *Porteños* will spend hours solving the world's problems over *media-lunas* (croissants) and a *cortado* (coffee with a little milk). Many offer full menus too.

Bar Plaza Dorrego (Map pp52-3; Defensa 1098) One of San Telmo's most atmospheric cafes, on the edge of Plaza Dorrego. The dark wood surroundings (check out the graffiti) and old-world ambience can't be beat; grab a window seat for the best people-watching. Large food menu.

Café Tortoni (Map pp52-3; Av de Mayo 829) The Cadillac of BA's cafes and too popular for its own good – it's expensive, the waiters are known for their surliness and there's even a souvenir counter inside. Still, it has a charming old atmosphere and nightly tango shows (AR$60 to AR$70; see p66).

Richmond (Map pp52-3; Av Florida 468; ☺ closed Sun) Take a java break from Av Florida's hustle and bustle at this elegant cafe, which also offers plenty of snacks, meals and cocktails. The Richmond was a popular meeting point for BA's famous writers (including Borges), and the atmosphere could well take you back in time.

La Biela (Map pp52-3; Av Quintana 600) The upper-crust elite dawdle for hours at this classy joint in Recoleta. Prices are relatively high, and the outside-seating menu costs even more, but it's simply irresistible on a warm sunny day, especially weekends.

Clásica y Moderna (Map pp52-3; Av Callao 892) Classic, cozy cafe with a heavy bohemian vibe. These brick walls have seen famous poets, philosophers and singers; these days it's a venue for intimate music shows. Small bookstore inside, otherwise there's usually a Spanish-language newspaper or two.

Los 36 Billares (Map pp52-3; Av de Mayo 1265) A long-running spot, with wood details and classic surroundings. It's popular as a billiards hall, with plenty of tables and occasional competitions. Tango shows take place in the evenings (see p66).

Bars

Palermo Viejo has BA's highest concentration of trendy and upscale bars, though there are a few good ones downtown and in San Telmo as well. *Porteños* aren't big drinkers, and getting smashed is generally frowned upon. For a very happening scene, hang out with the masses in Plaza Serrano (in Palermo Viejo) on a weekend night – there are plenty of bars with sidewalk tables.

Gibraltar (Map pp52-3; Perú 895) One of BA's most popular expat pubs that also attracts a heady mix of backpackers and locals. It has a good, unpretentious atmosphere and serves tasty international foods like roast beef with gravy and green Thai curry, plus plenty of whiskeys. There's a pool table in the back.

Milión (Map pp52-3; Paraná 1048) Bar-restaurant located in a richly renovated old mansion. The drinking happens on the 2nd and 3rd floors, and happy hour is 6pm to 9pm. Very popular, with a nice terrace overlooking the leafy garden.

Gran Bar Danzón (Map pp52-3; Libertad 1161) Upscale restaurant–wine bar with a good selection of wines by the glass. There are also fresh fruit cocktails, exotic martinis and Asian-inspired dinner selections. It's very popular, so come early for happy hour and snag a good seat on a sofa.

Acabar (Map pp58-9; Honduras 5733) Among BA's most eclectic bar-restaurants, Acabar is bohemian, flowery and has a colorful 'anything goes' decor. Board games for everyone and good music keep this large place packed with fun-seekers. Serves food earlier on.

Mundo Bizarro (Map pp58-9; Serrano 1222) Mundo Bizarro is a cool and very red Palermo Viejo watering hole with a retro loungy feel, a jukebox, a video screen for cartoons or movies and even a pole to dance around. Serves international food including sushi, plus tasty cocktails.

La Puerta Roja (Map pp52-3; Chacabuco 733) Hit the buzzer to get into this San Telmo joint; there's no sign. Upstairs is a good bar area, a pool table in back and a smoking room overlooking the street. Come early for good, cheap food and mellower vibe – it gets busy later on. Expat-run.

Sugar (Map pp58-9; Costa Rica 4619; closed Mon) From 8pm to midnight at this megapopular Palermo Viejo bar, it's happy hour: drinks are AR$5. It's partially US-run, and all servers speak some English. There's a singles scene on Wednesdays, and lines on weekends (AR$20 drink minimum). Very loud and red.

Congo (Map pp58-9; Honduras 5329; closed Sun & Mon) A great Palermo Viejo drinking den, best on warm nights when you can relax out back in one of BA's best patio gardens. Cool, superhip and upscale; be prepared to wait in line on weekends, when there are DJs and a drink minimum to enter.

Kilkenny (Map pp52-3; Marcelo T de Alvear 399) BA's most famous Irish pub is fashionable with businesspeople on weekdays after work, and crammed full of everyone else on weekend nights. Good, dark atmosphere, but on weekends it's uncomfortably packed inside – try for a sidewalk table.

Druid In (Map pp52-3; Reconquista 1040) Half a block from Kilkenny, with a much cozier pub atmosphere, the Druid offers classic Irish pub fare like steak-and-kidney pie, Irish stew and curries. There's also live jazz, rock and Celtic music on Fridays and Saturdays (and the occasional Thursday).

Le Cigale (Map pp52-3; 25 de Mayo 722) A hip and moody downtown lounge with a retro-Euro atmosphere and excellent cocktails, it's especially popular for its Tuesday DJ 'French night.' Good party crowds on weeknights, when tables are supremely hard to find.

El Alamo (Map pp52-3; Uruguay 1175) American-run bar unsurprisingly popular with expats. Lots of US sports on TV. Huge pitchers of AR$40 beer during happy hour (weekdays until 10pm). Has a good way to draw women in: they drink free beer all day from Monday to Friday.

Post Street Bar (Map pp58-9; Thames 1885) Very casual and funky bar with colorful stencils covering the wall from top to bottom. This makes you feel like you're hanging out drinking in an artsy ghetto. The music runs to rock, reggae and blues and there's a small art gallery upstairs in the back.

ENTERTAINMENT

Buenos Aires never sleeps, so you'll find something to do every night of the week. There are continuous theater and musical performances, and tango shows are everywhere. On weekends (and even some weeknights) the nightclubs shift into high gear.

Every modern shopping center has its multi-screen cinema complex; most movies are shown in their original language, with subtitles. Check the English-language newspapers *Buenos Aires Herald* or *Argentimes* (www.theargentimes.com) for screening times. For general information about BA happenings, see www.whatsupbuenosaires.com.

Discount ticket vendors (selling tickets for select theater, tango and movie performances) include **Cartelera Vea Más** (Map pp52-3; 6320-5319; www.veamasdigital.com.ar; Av Corrientes 1660, ste 2), **Cartelera Baires** (Map pp52-3; 4372-5058; www.carterabaires.com; Av Corrientes 1382) and **Cartelera de Espectáculos** (Map pp52-3; 4322-1559; www.123info.com.ar; Lavalle 742).

Ticketek (5237-7200; www.ticketek.com.ar) has outlets throughout the city and sells tickets for large venues.

Tango Shows

Most travelers will want to take in a tango show in BA, as they should. It's a bit futile to look for 'nontouristy' shows, however, since tango is a participatory dance and so its shows are geared toward voyeurs. If you want less sensationalism, then look for cheaper shows; they'll tend to be more traditional. *Milongas* are where dancers strut their stuff, but spectators don't really belong there.

There are many dinner-tango shows oriented at wealthier tourists. Some have a Las Vegas-like feel and often involve costume changes, dry ice and plenty of high kicks. The physical dancing feats can be spectacular, though this is not considered authentic tango (which is much more subtle). Reservations are usually necessary.

There are 'free' (donation) street tango shows on Sunday at San Telmo's antiques fair (p56) and in front of Galerías Pacífico (p55) in the Microcentro. You might also see it on weekends on El Caminito in La Boca. Schedules can be hit-or-miss, so catching them can be a matter of luck. Some restaurants in BA (especially in San Telmo and La Boca) offer free tango shows while you eat. Cultural centers are also good places to search, especially Centro Cultural Borges (p50).

Centro Cultural Torquato Tasso (Map p51; 4307-6506; www.tangotasso.com; Defensa 1575) Excellent San Telmo venue, but has only tango *music* shows (not dancing), along with many other offerings (including courses, see p57). Show prices vary.

Los 36 Billares (Map pp52-3; ☎ 4381-5696; www .los36billares.co.ar; Av de Mayo 1265; admission AR$40) Old-time restaurant-bar with many billiard tables in back and downstairs. Tango shows Tuesday to Sunday at 9pm; a historic local place. Dinner available.

El Balcón (Map pp52-3; ☎ 4362-2354; Primo 461) Small San Telmo restaurant offering tango-dinner shows on Sundays from 1pm to 7pm. Shows are free, but you must eat or drink there.

Café Tortoni (Map pp52-3; ☎ 4342-4328; www .cafétortoni.com.ar; Av de Mayo 829; admission AR$60-70) Tango in the back of a historic, elegant cafe (p64). Shows run twice nightly; the less expensive one has more singing, and the more expensive one more dancing. Call ahead to reserve.

Taconeando (Map pp52-3; ☎ 4307-6696; www.taco neando.com; Balcarce 725; dinner & show AR$180, show only AR$140) One of the smaller and more reasonably priced upscale shows.

Confitería Ideal (Map pp52-3; ☎ 5265-8069; www .confiteriaideal.com; Suipacha 384; dinner & show AR$190) The mother of all tango venues offers shows Wednesday to Sunday, along with lots of classes (see p57) and *milongas* daily.

Classical Music & Performing Arts

Av Corrientes, which is between 9 de Julio and Av Callao, is Buenos Aires' answer to Broadway.

Teatro Colón (Map pp52-3; ☎ 4378-7133; www .teatrocolon.org.ar; cnr Tucumán & Cerrito) The capital's most prestigious performing-arts venue is richly opulent and an excellent place to see opera, ballet, theatre and classical music.

Teatro General San Martín (Map pp52-3; ☎ 0800-333-5254; www.teatrosanmartin.com.ar; Av Corrientes 1530) Inexpensive shows and events (half-price on Wednesdays) are on offer at several auditoriums and galleries here, but practically all are in Spanish.

Luna Park (Map pp52-3; ☎ 5279-5279; www.luna park.com.ar; cnr Av Corrientes & Bouchard) Takes up a whole city block and serves as a venue for operas, dances, rock concerts, sporting gigs or any other large event. Check its website for schedules.

Nightclubs

Buenos Aires is all about the night, and clubbing is no exception. The action doesn't even start until 2am, and the later the better. Those in the know take a nap before dinner, then stay up till the early-morning light – or even until noon the next day!

Porteños are fickle and hot spots change, so it's always best to ask where the hottest night spots are during your stay and double check the hours/days.

Asia de Cuba (Map pp52-3; ☎ 4894-1328; Dealessi 750) By day it's an upscale restaurant, but at night Asia de Cuba becomes one of BA's slickest clubs. The location is pretty darn romantic, and the exotic dockside lounges don't hurt. Dress well and look important.

Bahrein (Map pp52-3; ☎ 4315-2403; Lavalle 345) On Tuesdays this popular downtown spot offers up the best drum and bass in town. Chill-out spaces and eclectic decor add to the cool-vibe mix, and each floor has a different beat. Check out the old vault in the basement; the building used to be a bank.

Club Niceto (Map pp58-9; ☎ 4779-9396; Vega 5510) One of BA's biggest crowd-pullers. Best on Thursday nights, when theater company Club 69 takes over and puts on a raucous transvestite show that's popular with both gays and hets. Also a good venue for creative international music groups visiting BA.

Crobar (Map pp58-9; ☎ 4778-1500; cnr Av de la Infanta Isabel & Freyre) Located in Palermo's parks is this fashionable, multilevel nightclub with several different spaces playing house, rock, salsa and '80s remixes. Less elite than many more upscale clubs, but still a fun and very popular hot spot.

Rumi (Map p51; ☎ 4782-1307; Av Figueroa Alcorta 6442) A wonderland of electronica, hip-hop and house music, with famous DJs spinning on Friday 'Glamour Nights.' To avoid the hefty admission and snag a booth, come early for dinner. It's popular with rich youth, celebrities and models, so dress well.

Pachá (Map p51; ☎ 4788-4280; Av Costanera R Obligado) Famous international guest DJs spin tunes for spruced-up and sniffy clientele at this huge, riverside mecca. An excellent sound system pumps out the electronica, while the laser light shows dazzle the crowds. Best on Saturdays, but don't arrive until 4am. Lines outside are long – try to get a VIP invite.

Live Music

Some bars have live music too.

Notorious (Map pp52-3; ☎ 4813-6888; www.no torious.com.ar; Av Callao 966) Small place with great intimate feel, and one of BA's premier venues

GAY & LESBIAN BUENOS AIRES

Buenos Aires is one of South America's top gay destinations, and offers a vibrant range of gay bars, cafes and clubs. You'll have to know where to look, however; despite general tolerance for homosexuality, this ain't SF or Sydney yet. BA's lesbian scene also definitely exists, though it's not nearly as overt as the boys' (but is it ever?).

Look up current sweetheart spots in free booklets such as **La Otra Guía** (www.laotraguiaweb .com.ar), **The Ronda** (www.theronda.com.ar) and **Gay Map** (www.gaymapbuenosaires.com), all available at tourist or gay destinations. A good website with general information is www.thegayguide .com.ar.

San Telmo is a popular neighborhood for gay-run hotels and B&Bs, including **Axel Hotel** (www .axelhotels.com/buenosaires), **Casa Bolivar** (www.casabolivar.com) and **Lugar Gay** (www.lugargay.org).

In November there's a **gay and lesbian film festival** (www.diversafilms.com.ar) as well as a **gay pride parade** (www.marchadelorgullo.org.ar). There's even a **gay tango festival** (www.festivaltangoqueer .com.ar) in December. Gay pride has arrived in Buenos Aires, and it's here to stay.

Popular gay nightspots:

Alsina (Map pp52-3; ☎ 4334-0097; Alsina 940) Palatial like a fairy tale, with hot dancers and packed floor.

Amerika (Map pp58-9; ☎ 4865-4416; Gascón 1040) All-you-can-drink madness; large crowds, dark corners and thumping music.

Bach Bar (Map pp58-9; Cabrera 4390) Rowdy fun, especially for lesbians. Intimate and packed, with occasional stripper shows.

Chueca (Map pp52-3; ☎ 4834-6373; Honduras 5255) Upscale restaurant-bar in Palermo Viejo with near-nightly drag shows.

Glam (Map pp58-9; Cabrera 3046) A fun and crowded gay club in a big old mansion. Plenty of lounges, bars and young pretty boys.

Kim y Novak (Map pp58-9; ☎ 4773-7521; Guemes 4900) Small, trendy corner bar with nice casual vibe. Stripper pole and basement dance floor.

Sitges (Map pp58-9; ☎ 4861-3763; Av Córdoba 4119) Loud bar/club and a big check-out scene for both girls and boys. Has wall phones for calling strangers.

---

for live jazz music. Other offerings include Brazilian, piano and tango. Dinner available; up front is a CD shop where you can listen before buying.

La Trastienda (Map pp52-3; ☎ 4345-0411; www .latrastienda.com; Balcarce 460) International acts specializing in salsa, merengue, blues, Latin pop and tango play at this large venue (600 seats, plus 150 standing room), but rock rules the roost. Check website for schedules. There's a restaurant in front.

La Peña del Colorado (Map pp58-9; ☎ 4822-1038; www.lapeniadelcolorado.com.ar; Güemes 3657; admission AR$20-25) Wonderfully local music venue with nightly folk shows; after midnight, the clientele themselves start strumming guitars. It also serves northern Argentine food specialties like spicy empanadas, *locro* and *humitas de Chala* (similar to tamales), and maté to drink.

Sports

If you're lucky enough to witness a *fútbol* match, you'll encounter a passion unrivaled in any other sport. The most popular teams are **Boca Juniors** (Map p51; ☎ 4362-2260; www.bocajuniors .com.ar; Brandsen 805) in La Boca and **River Plate** (off Map p51; ☎ 4789-1200; www.carp.org.ar; Alcorta 7597) in Belgrano, northwest of Aeroparque Jorge Newberry.

Ticket prices ultimately depend on the teams playing and the demand. In general, however, *entradas populares* (bleachers) are the cheapest seats and attract the more emotional fans of the game; don't show any signs of wealth in this section, including watches, necklaces or fancy cameras. *Plateas* (fixed seats) are a safer bet. There are also tour companies that take you to games, like **Tangol** (Map pp52-3; ☎ 4312-7276; www.tangol.com; Av Florida 971, ste 31).

Polo in Buenos Aires is most popular from October to December, and games take place at Campo de Polo in Palermo. Rugby, horse racing and *pato* (a traditional Argentine game played on horseback) are some other spectator possibilities.

SHOPPING

If you earn hard currency, Buenos Aires is a good place to spend money. The city is full of modern shopping malls, along with long, flashy store-lined streets like Avs Florida and Santa Fe. You'll find decent-quality clothes, leather, accessories, electronics, music and homewares, but anything imported (like electronics) will be very expensive.

Palermo Viejo is the best neighborhood for boutiques and creative fashions. Av Alvear, toward the Recoleta cemetery, means Gucci and Armani. Defensa in San Telmo is full of pricey antique shops. There are several weekend crafts markets, such as the hippy *feria artesanal* in front of Recoleta's cemetery (p56). The famous San Telmo antiques fair (p56) takes place on Sunday. For cheap third-world imports head to Av Pueyrredón near Estación Once (Once train station; Map p51); you can find just about anything there.

Feria de Mataderos (Map p51; ☎ 4342-9629, 4687-5602; www.feriademataderos.com.ar; cnr Av de los Corrales & Lisandro de la Torre; ☯ 6pm-midnight Sat Jan-Mar, 11am-8pm Sun Apr-Dec) Way out west in the Mataderos *barrio* is this exceptional street market. People flock here for the cheap *asado,* a good crafts market, traditional folk dances and *gauchos* on horseback. Call for exact dates. Buses 180 and 155 get you there in about an hour.

GETTING THERE & AWAY

Air

Most international flights leave from **Ezeiza Airport** (Map p51; ☎ 5480-6111; www.aa2000.com.ar). **Manuel Tienda León** (MTL; Map pp52-3; ☎ 4314-3636; www.tiendaleon.com; cnr Av Eduardo Madero & San Martín) runs frequent shuttles to/from Ezeiza (AR$45, 40 minutes). There's also a **Hostel Shuttle** (☎ 4331-4041; shuttle@hostelsuites.com) that goes five times daily from Ezeiza to certain downtown hostels (AR$35) and back again, but you need to reserve 48 hours in advance.

Penny-pinchers can take bus 8 (AR$2, 1½ to two hours). Taxis cost around AR$98, including tolls.

MTL charges AR$15 for the 15-minute ride to **Aeroparque Jorge Newbery** (Map p51; ☎ 5480-3000; www.aa2000.com.ar). Or take city bus 45 from Plaza San Martín (AR$1.10). Taxis cost around AR$20.

Argentina's international departure tax is US$18 (around AR$60), payable in pesos, euros, US dollars or by credit card. The domestic tax is US$8.

Airline offices in Buenos Aires:

Aerolíneas Argentinas/Austral (Map pp52-3; ☎ 0810-222-86527; Av Leandro N Alem 1134) Another branch at Perú 2.

American Airlines (Map pp52-3; ☎ 4318-1111; Av Santa Fe 881)

British Airways (Map pp52-3; ☎ 0800-222-0075; Pellegrini 1141, 12th fl)

Continental (Map pp52-3; ☎ 0800-333-0425; Pellegrini 529)

Delta (Map pp52-3; ☎ 0800-666-0133; Av Santa Fe 895)

KLM (Map pp52-3; ☎ 4317-4711; San Martín 344, 23rd fl)

LADE (Map pp52-3; ☎ 0810-810-5233; Perú 714)

LAN (Map pp52-3; ☎ 0810-999-9526; Cerrito 866)

Transportes Aéreos de Mercosur (TAM; Map pp52-3; ☎ 0810-333-3333; Cerrito 1026)

United Airlines (Map pp52-3; ☎ 0810-777-8648; Av Eduardo Madero 9000)

Boat

Buquebus (Map pp52-3; ☎ 4316-6500; www.buquebus.com; cnr Avs Antártida Argentina & Córdoba) offers several daily ferries to Colonia via a fast boat (AR$130, one hour) or a slow boat (AR$93, three hours). One boat daily also goes directly to Montevideo (AR$240, three hours), though boat/bus combinations via Colonia are cheaper. There are also seasonally available boat-bus services to Punta del Este, Uruguay's top beach resort. Buquebus has other offices at Av Córdoba 867 (Map pp52–3) and in Recoleta's Patio Bullrich mall. There are more services and higher prices in the summer season, when it's a good idea to buy your ticket an hour or two in advance. Some nationalities need visas to enter Uruguay (see p907).

Bus

Retiro (Map pp52-3; ☎ 4310-0700; cnr Avs Antártida Argentina & Ramos Mejía) is a huge three-story bus terminal with slots for 75 buses. Inside are cafeterias, shops, bathrooms, luggage storage, telephone offices with internet, ATMs, and a 24-hour information kiosk to help you navigate the terminal. There's also a **tourist information office** (ste L83; ☯ 7:30am-1pm Mon-Fri & Sun); look for it under bus counter 103.

The following lists are a small sample of very extensive services. Prices will vary widely depending on the season, the company and the economy. During holidays, prices rise; buy your ticket in advance.

Domestic destinations:

BUS FARES		
Destination	**Cost (AR$)**	**Duration (hr)**
Bariloche	250	21
Comodoro Rivadavia	320	24
Córdoba	125	10
Mar del Plata	79	6
Mendoza	150	15
Puerto Iguazú	180	19
Puerto Madryn	250	20
Rosario	50	5
Salta	250	21
Tucumán	250	16

International destinations:

BUS FARES		
Destination	**Cost (AR$)**	**Duration (hr)**
Asunción, Paraguay	140	18
Foz do Iguazú, Brazil	145	19
Montevideo, Uruguay	140	10
Rio de Janeiro, Brazil	460	42
Santiago, Chile	250	20
São Paulo, Brazil	415	34

Train

With very few exceptions, rail travel in Argentina is limited to Buenos Aires' suburbs and provincial cities. It's cheaper but not nearly as fast, frequent or comfortable than hopping on a bus.

Each of BA's train stations has its own Subte stop. Useful stations and their services:

Estación Constitución (Map p51) Services by Metropolitano (☎ 0800-122-358736) and Ferrobaires (☎ 4306-7919; www.ferrobaires.gba.gov.ar) to Bahía Blanca and Atlantic beach towns.

Estación Once (Map p51) Service by Trenes de Buenos Aires (☎ 0800-333-3822; www.tbanet.com.ar) to Luján, Bahía Blanca, Atlantic beach towns.

Estación Retiro (Map pp52-3; ☎ 4317-4400) Service by Trenes de Buenos Aires, Metropolitano and Ferrovías (☎ 0800-777-3377; www.ferrovias.com.ar) to Tigre and Rosario.

GETTING AROUND
Bicycle

Buenos Aires has several companies that offer guided bike tours to select destinations, including Urban Biking (see p57). They also rent out bikes, but be aware that downtown motor vehicles in this city consider bikes a pest – and very low on the traffic totem pole. If you must, ride bikes in safer neighborhoods like San Telmo and Palermo (both with some cobbled streets) or Puerto Madero and the nearby Reserva Ecológica Costanera Sur. And if you want to live another day to eat another steak, ride defensively!

Bus

Sold at many kiosks, the Guía T (pocket version costs AR$6) details some 200 bus routes. Fares depend on the distance, but most rides cost AR$1.25; say *'uno veinte cinco'* to the driver, then place coins in the machine behind him (change is given). You should offer front seats to elderly passengers or those with kids.

If you read Spanish and have a good BA map, see www.xcolectivo.com.ar for bus routes.

For information on BA's coin shortage, see boxed text, p159.

Car & Motorcycle

We don't recommend you rent a car to drive around Buenos Aires. *Porteño* drivers turn crazy behind the wheel and you shouldn't compete with them. Also, public transport is excellent. Cars are good to explore the countryside, however. Try **Avis** (Map pp52-3; ☎ 4326-5542; www.avis.com; Cerrito 1527), **New Way** (Map pp52-3; ☎ 4515-0331; www.new-wayrentacar.com.ar; Marcello T de Alvear 773) or **Hertz** (Map pp52-3; ☎ 4816-8001; www.hertz.com.ar; Paraguay 1138). Rentals cost around AR$260 with 200 free kilometers.

For more information on renting cars, see p156.

For motorcycle rentals (about US$100 per day) contact **Motocare** (off Map p51; ☎ 4761-2696; www.motocare.com.ar/rental; Echeverría 738) in the *barrio* of Vicente Lopez.

Subway

Buenos Aires' Subte (www.subte.com.ar) is fast, efficient and costs only AR$1.10 per ride. The most useful lines for travelers are Líneas A, B, D and E (which run from the *microcentro* to the capital's western and northern outskirts) and Línea C (which links Estación Retiro and Constitución).

Trains operate from approximately 5am to 10:30pm except Sunday and holidays (when hours are 8am to 10pm); they run frequently on weekdays, less so on weekends.

Taxi & Remise

Black-and-yellow cabs are very common and reasonably priced. In early 2009, meters started at AR$3.80; tips are unnecessary, but leaving extra change is appreciated. If you're taking a taxi into town from Ezeiza airport, head to the city taxi counter (with posted prices), just behind the first row of transport booths. This is important – don't just go with any driver.

Many people might warn you it's not safe to take street taxis in Buenos Aires because of robbery. It's all a matter of luck, and usually it's OK to take a taxi off the street – even as a lone woman. In fact, taxi drivers are much better at ripping you off. Make sure the driver uses the meter: it's good to have an idea of where you're going, and make sure the meter doesn't run fast (it should change only every three blocks or so). Know your money: fake bills feel fake and either don't have watermarks or have a bad one. Finally, try to pay with exact change or at least with low-denomination bills: some drivers deftly replace high bills with low ones, or switch your real bill for a fake one. And try to remember that most *taxistas* are honest people making a hard living.

If you want to play it safest, however, call a *remise*. They're considered safer than street taxis, since an established company sends them out. Any business should be able to phone a *remise* for you.

AROUND BUENOS AIRES

TIGRE

About an hour north of Buenos Aires is this favorite *porteño* weekend destination. You can check out the popular riverfront, take a relaxing boat ride in the Delta del Paraná and shop at **Mercado de Frutos** (a daily crafts market that's best on weekends).

Tigre's **tourist office** (☎ 011-4512-4497; Mitre 305) is next door to McDonald's. Nearby are ticket counters for commuter boats that cruise the waterways; the tourist office is good and can recommend a destination.

The quickest, cheapest way to get to Tigre is by taking the Mitre line from Retiro train station (AR$1.35, 50 minutes, frequent). The most scenic way is to take buses 59, 60 or 152 to the Tren de la Costa, a pleasant electric train whose final station is in Tigre.

SAN ANTONIO DE ARECO

☎ 02326 / pop 22,000

Dating from the early 18th century, this serene village northwest of Buenos Aires is the symbolic center of Argentina's diminishing *gaucho* culture. It's also host to the country's biggest *gaucho* celebration, **Día de la Tradición**, on November 10th. There's a cute plaza surrounded by historic buildings, while local artisans are known for producing maté paraphernalia, *rastras* (silver-studded belts) and *facones* (long-bladed knives). Buses run regularly from BA's Retiro bus terminal (AR$15, two hours).

URUGUAY

Day trips to small, charming, cobbled **Colonia** are popular, and it's also possible to travel to nearby **Montevideo** (Uruguay's capital) for a couple of days. A good summer destination is the beach resort of **Punta del Este**, only a few hours away from Buenos Aires. For more information on these destinations, see the Uruguay chapter.

NORTHEAST ARGENTINA

From the spectacular natural wilderness of Iguazú Falls in the north to the chic sophistication of Rosario in the south, the northeast is one of Argentina's most diverse regions. Wedged between the Ríos Paraná and Uruguay (thus earning it the nickname 'Mesopotamia'), the region relies heavily on those rivers for fun and its livelihood, while next door, the Chaco is sparsely populated, and often called Argentina's 'empty quarter.'

HISTORY

This was Guaraní country first. They were semi-sedentary agriculturalists, raising sweet potatoes, maize, manioc and beans and eating river fish until the Spanish arrived in 1570, pushing their way south from Paraguay. Santa Fe was founded in 1573, Corrientes a few years later. The Jesuits came soon after, herding the Guaraní into 30 *reducciones* (settlements) in the upper Paraná in the hope of converting them by way of prayer and labor. The *reducciones* were doing a roaring trade in yerba maté

NORTHEAST ARGENTINA

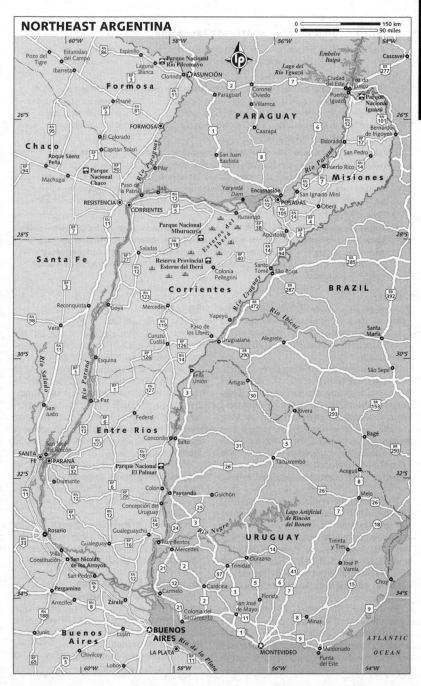

REMOTE NATIONAL PARKS IN NORTHEAST ARGENTINA

Northeast Argentina is home to some incredible parks that take some getting to, but are well worthwhile. Listed below are a few. For more information, log on to www.parquesnacionales .gov.ar.

- **Parque Nacional El Palmar** (☎ 03447-493053; elpalmar@apn.gov.ar; RN 14, Km 199; admission AR$20) Home to capybara, *ñandú* (rhea) and poisonous pit vipers, this 8500-hectare park protects the endangered yatay palm. There's cheap camping, good walking trails, and swimming holes. The park lies in between Colón and Concordia, on the Uruguayan border; both are easily accessible from Gualeguaychú (p78).

- **Parque Nacional Chaco** (☎ 03725-499161; chaco@apn.gov.ar) Protecting 15,000 hectares of marshes, palm savannas and strands of the disappearing *quebracho colorado*. Birds far outnumber mammals – there are plenty of rhea, jabiru, roseate spoonbill, cormorants and common caracaras – but mosquitoes outnumber them all. Bring repellent. Camping is free, but facilities are basic. Capitán Solari (5km from the park entrance) is the nearest town, and is easily accessed from Resistencia (p82).

- **Parque Nacional Río Pilcomayo** (☎ 03718-47-0045; riopilcomayo@apn.gov.ar) This 600-sq-km park is home to caiman, tapirs, anteaters, maned wolves and an abundance of birdlife, particularly around the centerpiece, Laguna Blanca (where piranha make swimming a bad idea). Access is via the small town of Laguna Blanca (9km east of the actual lagoon) which can be reached from Formosa (p84).

production until Carlos III, busy with nation-building back in Spain, decided that the Jesuits' growing power base was too much of a distraction, and booted them all off the Americas in 1767.

Some Guaraní were still out there, though, in the steamy thorn forests of Chaco and Formosa, resisting the newcomers. They lasted until 1850, when the woodcutters from Corrientes came through, looking for the *quebracho* (axe-breaker) tree and its tannin-heavy wood. After the land had been cleared (in more ways than one), the Guaraní who were left were kept busy picking the newly planted cotton and raising cattle.

The War of the Triple Alliance (1865–70) put an end to Brazil and Paraguay's claims on the territory, and for a few years Entre Ríos was an independent republic before joining the Buenos Aires–based Unitarist coalition under Rosas. Local *caudillo* (chief) Justo José Urquiza brought about Rosas' defeat and the eventual adoption of Argentina's modern constitution.

By the late 19th century, Rosario had become the regional superstar (it even vied for capital status for a while there) as its port did a roaring trade, and thousands of rural dwellers poured in from the countryside in search of a better life.

ROSARIO
☎ 0341 / pop 1,235,500

So, you dig the vibe of the capital, but the sheer size of it is sending you a little loco in the coco? Rosario may be the place for you.

Located just a few hours north, this is in many ways Argentina's second city – not in terms of population, but culturally, financially and aesthetically. The city's backpacker scene has been growing slowly, and the huge university and corresponding population of students, artists and musicians give it a solid foundation.

Nighttime, the streets come alive and the bars and clubs pack out. In the day, once everybody wakes up, they shuffle down to the river beaches for more music, drinks and a bit of a lie-down.

It's not all fun and games, though. Culture vultures won't be disappointed by the wealth of museums and galleries, and Che Guevara fans will want to check out his birthplace.

Orientation & Information

The long-distance **bus terminal** (☎ 437-2384; Cafferata 702) is 4km west of center. Many local buses go to the center; buy AR$1.75 magnetic cards at kiosks beforehand. Bus 138 leaves from the train station.

The informative **tourist office** (☎ 480-2230; Av del Huerto) is on the waterfront.

Cambios along San Martín and Córdoba change traveler's checks; there are many banks and ATMs on Santa Fe between Mitre and Entre Ríos.

Sights

Prices, dates and hours change throughout the year. Check with the tourist office to be sure.

The colossal **Monumento Nacional a la Bandera** (Monument to the Flag; ☺ 2-7pm Mon, 9am-7pm Tue-Sun), located behind Plaza 25 de Mayo, contains the crypt of flag designer General Manuel Belgrano. You can take the elevator (AR$1) to the top for a dizzying view of the river and surrounds.

Parque Independencia's **Museo Histórico Provincial Dr Julio Marc** (☺ 9am-7pm Tue-Fri, 2-6pm Sat & Sun, closed Jan) has excellent displays on indigenous cultures from all over Latin America, colonial and religious artifacts and the most ornate collection of maté paraphernalia you ever did see. The **Museo Municipal de Bellas Artes Juan B Castagnino** (cnr Av Carlos Pellegrini & Blvd Oroño; admission AR$1; ☺ 9am-6pm Tue-Fri, 2-8pm Sat & Sun) focuses on European and Argentine fine art.

Renowned architect Alejandro Bustillo designed the apartment building at **Entre Ríos 480** where, in 1928, Ernesto Guevara Lynch and Celia de la Serna resided after the birth of their son Ernesto Guevara de la Serna, popularly known as El Che.

Wanna go to the beach? For a more relaxed, family-oriented scene, take the red 153 bus from the corner of Corrientes and Córdoba 6km north to Av Puccio (here the bus turns inland). Stroll up the boardwalk along **Catalunya beach** and look for a spot to lay the towel. There are plenty of restaurants around. Keep walking and in 20 minutes you'll hit the private beach **Av Florida**, which charges AR$3 for access to a wider stretch of sand. Beyond it is **Estación Costa Alta** (the boat dock), where you can take a 15-minute ride across the Paraná (round-trip AR$3) to **Isla Invernada**, land of woodsier, more natural beaches (camping possible). To get to the boat dock without the stroll, take bus 103 from the local bus terminal on San Luis; it stops close by.

For a younger, noisier experience, catch a ferry (AR$7 one-way) from the Estación Fluvial (Ferry Station) to **Isla Espinillo**, where

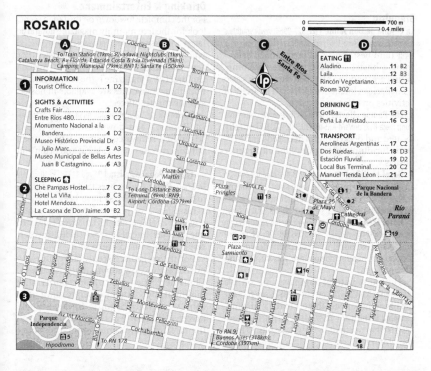

ROSARIO

0 —— 700 m
0 —— 0.4 miles

INFORMATION	
Tourist Office..............1 D2	
SIGHTS & ACTIVITIES	
Crafts Fair........................2 D2	
Entre Rios 480................3 C2	
Monumento Nacional a la	
Bandera......................4 D2	
Museo Histórico Provincial Dr	
Julio Marc...................5 A3	
Museo Municipal de Bellas Artes	
Juan B Castagnino........6 A3	
SLEEPING	
Che Pampas Hostel........7 C2	
Hotel La Viña 8 C3	
Hotel Mendoza...............9 C3	
La Casona de Don Jaime.10 B2	

EATING	
Aladino.............................11 B2	
Laila.................................12 B3	
Rincón Vegetariano.........13 C2	
Room 302.........................14 C3	
DRINKING	
Gotika...............................15 C3	
Peña La Amistad..............16 C3	
TRANSPORT	
Aerolineas Argentinas 17 C2	
Dos Ruedas.......................18 D3	
Estación Fluvial................19 D2	
Local Bus Terminal..........20 C2	
Manuel Tienda Léon 21 C2	

To Train Station (1km); Rivadavia Nightclubs (1km); Catalunya Beach, Av Florida, Estación Costa & Isla Invernada (5km); Camping Municipal (7km); RN11; Santa Fe (150km)

To Long-Distance Bus Terminal (4km); RN9; Airport; Córdoba (397km)

Parque Nacional de la Bandera

Río Paraná

Parque Independencia

To RN 178

To RN 9; Buenos Aires (318km); Córdoba (397km)

you'll find a selection of restaurants and bars, music, hammock space and water sports on offer, such as water skiing (AR$40 per hour), jet skiing (AR$80 per hour) and windsurfing (AR$30 per hour).

Out at the airfield, **Paracaidismo Rosario** (☎ 15-641-7799; www.paracaidismorosario.com.ar) offers one-off tandem skydives as well as longer certification courses.

Back in town, there's a weekend **crafts fair** on Av Belgrano, south of the tourist office.

Festivals & Events

Every June Rosario celebrates **Semana de la Bandera** (Flag Week), climaxing in ceremonies on June 20, the anniversary of the death of Manuel Belgrano, the flag's designer. In early October the **Semana del Arte** includes a poetry festival and theatre, comedy and dance performances. From mid-October to early November, the **Festival de Jazz** takes place in various venues around town. Also in November, the national **Encuentro de las Colectividades**, a tribute to the country's immigrants, is celebrated with fancy dress, music and food stalls.

Sleeping

La Casona de Don Jaime (☎ 527-9964; www.youthhos telrosario.com.ar; Roca 1051; dm/d AR$32/110) Rosario's first (and best) hostel is pretty much everything a hostel should be. There are comfy sitting areas and an attached bar. There's also a small, clean kitchen, lockers and a variety of activities on offer.

Che Pampas Hostel (☎ 424-5202; www.chepampas .com; Rioja 812; dm/s/d AR$40/130/140; 🖳) Centrally located and decked out in deep reds and low-slung furniture, this is one of the city's better hostels.

Hotel La Viña (☎ 421-4549; 3 de Febrero 1244; s/d AR$70/100) Sporting dark but spotless rooms with TV, this is a reliable budget hotel. Rooms vary substantially in size, so check out a few.

Hotel Mendoza (☎ 424-6544; mendoza@arnet.com .ar; Mendoza 1246; s AR$120-200, d AR$150-220; 🌂) Cool and spacious rooms in an excellent downtown location. Cheaper rooms are fan-cooled and unrenovated.

The most natural campsites are on **Isla Invernada** (☎ 455-0285; per person AR$4); see p73 for details on how to get there. On the mainland, **Camping Municipal** (☎ 471-4381; campsites per person AR$4) is 9km north of the city; take bus 35 from the center to Barra 9.

Eating

If you feel like exploring, take a wander along Av Carlos Pelligrini between Maipú and Moreno. This is Rosario's restaurant strip – 10 blocks dedicated to the pillars of Argentina cuisine: pizza, *parrilla*, pasta, *tenedores libres* (all-you-can-eat buffets) and ice cream, sometimes all gloriously available in the one location. Otherwise, there's a *confitería* (cafe/snack bar) on just about every street corner.

Rincón Vegetariano (Mitre 720; buffets AR$13) With over 50 dishes to choose from and a tad more atmosphere than your average all-you-can-eat joint, this is Rosario's best bet for staying meat-free.

Aladino (Italia 969; set lunches AR$25) Good, authentic Middle Eastern food. Weekend nights they have dinner and a show (belly dancers) for AR$65. For a cheaper, simpler variation, check out Laila (Italia 1075; mains AR$5) one block south.

Room 302 (3 de Febrero 893; mains AR$30-50; 🌣 dinner Tue-Sat) Surprisingly good Thai food and an excellent cocktail list. Dress up, but not too much.

Drinking & Entertainment

For the complete lowdown on the tango scene, look for the free monthly magazine **Rosario de Tango** (www.rosariodetango.com), which lists classes, *milongas* and other tango-related news. For general cultural events, the monthly Agenda Cultural (AC) magazine is the one to look for. Both these magazines are available in hostels and the tourist office.

Gotika (Mitre 1539; admission AR$8-20; 🌣 24hr Thu-Sat) Rosario's best downtown dance club is set up in a renovated church. Music varies, but concentrates on breakbeat and drum and bass.

ourpick **Peña La Amistad** (Maipú 1111; 🌣 10pm-late Fri & Sat) *Peñas* (clubs/bars that host informal folk-music gatherings) have been enjoying a resurgence of popularity among young Argentines of late, and if you haven't checked one out, this, one of Rosario's oldest and best respected, is a fine place to start.

For the megadisco scene, make your way northwest of downtown along Rivadavia. Clubs here open their doors shortly after midnight, but remain deserted until after 2am, when lines begin to form. Any taxi driver will know where you're going, and the fare from the center should be about AR$20.

Getting There & Around

Aerolíneas Argentinas (☎ 420-8138; Córdoba 852) flies four times weekly to Buenos Aires (AR$220).

Sol (☎ 0810-444-4765; www.sol.com.ar) flies daily to Buenos Aires (AR$230) and Córdoba (AR$280). A *remise* to the airport (8km from town) should cost around AR$30.

Bus services from Rosario's **terminal** (☎ 437-3030; www.terminalrosario.com.ar; cnr Cafferata & Santa Fe), 4km west of town, include Buenos Aires (AR$58, four hours), Córdoba (AR$66, six hours), Santa Fe (AR$28, 2½ hours), Mendoza (AR$100, 12 hours) and Montevideo, Uruguay (AR$184, 10 hours).

Manuel Tienda León (☎ 409-8000; www.miguel canton.com.ar; San Lorenzo 935) offers door-to-door shuttle service to Buenos Aires hotels and airports (AR$135, four hours).

The **train station** (☎ 436-1661; Av del Valle 2700), 3km northwest of the center, has services to Buenos Aires (AR$19 to AR$39, 6½ hours), on Mondays, Thursdays and Sundays, Tucumán (AR$31 to AR$243, 18 hours) on Mondays and Fridays and Córdoba (AR$19 to AR$51, eight hours) on Mondays and Saturdays. Due to the poor condition of tracks and carriages and frequent delays, you'd have to be a true train buff to appreciate these services.

Dos Ruedas (☎ 15-571-3812; www.bikesrosario.com .ar; Zeballos 327) offers bike hire (AR$30/45 per hour/day) and guided bike and kayak tours.

SANTA FE

☎ 0342 / pop 506,300

Santa Fe would be a fairly dull town if not for the university population. Thanks to this, there's a healthy bar and club scene, and plenty of fun to be had during the day.

Relocated during the mid-17th century because of hostile indigenous groups, floods and isolation, the city duplicates the original plan of Santa Fe La Vieja (Old Santa Fe). But a 19th-century neo-Parisian building boom and more recent construction have left only isolated colonial buildings, mostly near Plaza 25 de Mayo.

Orientation

Av San Martín, north of the plaza, is the main commercial artery. The airport is 15km south of town. The bus marked 'A (aeropuerto)' goes past San Luis and Yrigoyen (AR$1.50, 45 minutes). From the bus terminal, ask at Tata Rápido or Río Coronda for their express airport bus service (AR$1.50). A taxi costs about AR$20.

Information

There are several ATMs along the San Martín *peatonal* (pedestrian mall).

Municipal tourist office (☎ 457-4123; www.santafe -turistica.com.ar; Belgrano 2910) In the bus terminal.

Post office (Av 27 de Febrero 2331)

Tourfe (Av San Martín 2500) Collects 3% commission on traveler's checks.

Sights & Activities

Some colonial buildings are museums, but churches still serve their ecclesiastical functions, like the mid-17th-century **Templo de Santo Domingo** (cnr 3 de Febrero & 9 de Julio). The exterior simplicity of the 1696 Jesuit **Iglesia de la Compañía** (Plaza 25 de Mayo) masks an ornate interior. The restored, two-story **Casa de los Aldao** (Buenos Aires 2861) dates from the early 18th century.

Built in 1680, the **Convento y Museo de San Francisco** (Amenábar 2257; ⏱ 8am-noon & 3:30-7pm Mon-Fri, 3:30-5pm Sat & Sun), south of Plaza 25 de Mayo, is Santa Fe's most important landmark. Its meter-thick walls support a roof of Paraguayan cedar and hardwood beams fitted with wooden spikes rather than nails. The doors are hand-worked originals, while the baroque pulpit is laminated in gold. Its museum covers secular and religious topics from colonial and republican eras.

The **Museo Etnográfico y Colonial Juan de Garay** (25 de Mayo 1470; ⏱ 8:30am-noon & 4-7pm Mon-Fri, 4:30-7pm Sat & Sun) has a scale model of Santa Fe La Vieja, but the real show-stopper is the *gaucho* 'camp chair' – made entirely of cow bones and leather. Gruesome – but comfortable! There are also colonial artifacts, indigenous basketry, Spanish ceramics and a stuffed horse.

The big buzz in town surrounds the newly renovated port area, which features a casino, fancy restaurants, multiplex cinema, food court, shopping mall etc. The real reason to come here, though, is the **Centro Cultural Ribera** (⏱ 9am-9pm), a converted silo complex showcasing local contemporary artists.

Santa Fe has its own brewery, **Cervecería Schneider** (☎ 450-2237; www.cervezaschneider.com; Calchines 1401), and brand of beer (called, uh, Santa Fe). Free guided tours of the ultramodern facility culminate in a tasting session, which consists of one glass per person, regardless of wheedling. Reservations are necessary and you must wear long pants and closed shoes.

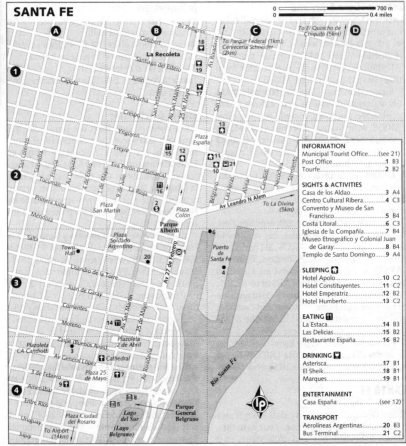

SANTA FE

0 — 700 m
0 — 0.4 miles

INFORMATION
Municipal Tourist Office	(see 21)
Post Office	**1** B3
Tourfe	**2** B2

SIGHTS & ACTIVITIES
Casa de los Aldao	**3** A4
Centro Cultural Ribera	**4** C3
Convento y Museo de San Francisco	**5** B4
Costa Litoral	**6** C3
Iglesia de la Compañía	**7** B4
Museo Etnográfico y Colonial Juan de Garay	**8** B4
Templo de Santo Domingo	**9** A4

SLEEPING
Hotel Apolo	**10** C2
Hotel Constituyentes	**11** C2
Hotel Emperatriz	**12** B2
Hotel Humberto	**13** C2

EATING
La Estaca	**14** B3
Las Delicias	**15** B2
Restaurante España	**16** B2

DRINKING
Asterisca	**17** B1
El Sheik	**18** B1
Marques	**19** B1

ENTERTAINMENT
Casa España	(see 12)

TRANSPORT
Aerolineas Argentinas	**20** B3
Bus Terminal	**21** C2

Costa Litoral (☎ 456-4381; www.costalitoral.net; Puerto Santa Fe) offers two-hour riverboat cruises (AR$27 per person).

Festivals & Events
Santa Fe's **beer festival** takes place on the last weekend in January and first weekend in February in the Parque Federal, just north of town. Festivities include plenty of live music and a certain carbonated alcoholic beverage.

Sleeping
The surprisingly seedy area around the bus terminal is the budget hotel zone. It's not dangerous – just the town center for various unsavory transactions.

Hotel Humberto (☎ 455-0409; Crespo 2222; r AR$50) Slightly cramped, aging rooms. But considering you get a TV and bathroom for less than the price of a dorm elsewhere, it's not a bad deal.

Hotel Apolo (☎ 452-7984; Belgrano 2821; s/d AR$70/90, without bathroom AR$50/70) Solid budget rooms with TV a few steps from the bus terminal.

Hotel Constituyentes (☎ 452-1586; San Luis 2862; s/d AR$80/110) A block from the bus terminal, this hotel has large carpeted rooms with TV. Get one at the back to avoid street noise.

Hotel Emperatriz (☎ 453-0061; emperatrizhotelsf @hotmail.com; Freyre 2440; s/d AR$100/120, with air-con AR$130/150; ❄) The lobby, with its fabulous Moorish tiling may raise hopes unfairly, but the rooms are still OK.

Eating

On Belgrano, across from the bus terminal, several places serve Argentine staples like empanadas, pizza and *parrillada* (a selection of grilled meats). The bus terminal sports a 24-hour snack bar serving huge portions of decent grub.

Las Delicias (San Martín 2882; cakes & pastries from AR$1.50, mains AR$10-24) Not the cheapest cafe in town, but the marble tabletops and brass trims make it one of the most atmospheric. Good bakery items.

Restaurante España (San Martín 2644; mains AR$14-25) A huge menu covers the range of seafood, steaks, pasta, chicken and crepes, with a few Spanish dishes thrown in to justify the name. The wine list is a winner, too.

La Estaca (Corrientes 2633; mains AR$24) A traditional *parrilla* offering surprisingly good value for its swank downtown location.

`our pick` **El Quincho de Chiquito** (cnr Brown & Vieytes; set meals AR$39) Think you like fish? Put that to the test at this local-favorite restaurant, where a few fish-based entrees are followed by seven different fish dishes. Still hungry? Unlikely, but you can reorder any of the dishes, as many times as you like. Take bus 16 on Blvd Pelligrini and tell the driver where you're going.

Drinking

Santa Fe's rock-steady nightlife centers on the intersection of Av San Martín and Santiago del Estero, an area known as La Recoleta. Bars come and go in this area; it's worth going for a wander and seeing where the crowds are. Here are a few to get you started:

Marques (cnr 25 de Mayo & Gelabert; 6pm-late Wed-Sat) One of many 'predance' options in the area, with good music, beautiful people and sidewalk seating.

El Sheik (25 de Mayo 3452; 7pm-1am Tue-Sat) Attracts a young crowd with its cheap drinks and good music.

Asterisca (Rivadavia 3237; 6pm-late Thu-Sat) Minimal stylings, laid-back music. Good for a few quiet drinks without the crowds and the hassle.

Entertainment

La Divina (Costanera Este s/n; 1pm-late Tue-Sat; admission free-AR$30) This is the city's definitive summertime disco, playing everything from cumbia and *marcha español* (aggressive drum beats, bleepy noises and chanted lyrics) through to mainstream house and techno.

The best Cultural Center in town is the **Casa España** (456-6538; www.ate.org.ar; Rivadavia 2871) which hosts live theater, exhibitions and concerts.

Getting There & Around

Aerolíneas Argentinas (452-5959; 25 de Mayo 2287) flies regularly to Buenos Aires (AR$250). **Sol** (0810-444-4765; www.sol.com.ar) flies to Rosario daily (AR$260).

The **bus information office** (457-2490; www.terminalsantafe.com) at the bus terminal posts fares for all services.

Buses leave hourly for Paraná (AR$4, one hour). Other services include Rosario (AR$28, 2½ hours), Buenos Aires (AR$74, six hours), Corrientes (AR$100, 9 hours) and Posadas (AR$149, 10 hours).

International services go to Rio de Janeiro, Brazil (AR$465, 39 hours); Asunción, Paraguay (AR$150, 13 hours); and Montevideo, Uruguay (AR$160, 11 hours).

PARANÁ

 0343 / pop 279,900

Although less famous than its sister city across the river, Paraná is, in many ways, a more attractive place.

Built on the hilly banks of its namesake river, the historical center is largely intact, and the city boasts a couple of majestic plazas. As is the rule in this part of the world, fun-seekers hit the riverbanks at night to choose from an array of restaurants, clubs and bars.

Orientation

The city's irregular plan has several diagonals, curving boulevards and complex intersections. From Plaza Primero de Mayo, the town center, San Martín is a *peatonal* for six blocks. Bus 1 goes from the bus terminal past the center to the riverside.

Information

There are several ATMs along the San Martín *peatonal*.

Municipal tourist office (423-0183; Buenos Aires 132) Paraná's municipal tourist office has branches at the bus terminal and at the Oficina Parque on the riverfront. The free-call number (0800-555-9575) is handy if you find yourself in need of on-the-spot tourist information.

Post office (cnr 25 de Mayo & Monte Caseros)

Provincial tourist office (422-3384; Laprida 5)

Sights & Activities

Plaza Primero de Mayo has had an **Iglesia Catedral** since 1730, but the current building dates from 1885. When Paraná was capital of the confederation, the Senate deliberated at the **Colegio del Huerto**, at the corner of 9 de Julio and 25 de Mayo.

At the west end of the San Martín *peatonal*, on Plaza Alvear, the **Museo Histórico de Entre Ríos Martín Leguizamón** (⏰ 9am-12pm & 4-8pm Mon-Fri, 9am-12pm Sat) flaunts provincial pride, as knowledgeable guides go to rhetorical extremes extolling the role of local *caudillos* in Argentine history. The adjacent subterranean **Museo de Bellas Artes Pedro E Martínez** (⏰ 9am-noon & 4-9pm Mon-Fri, 10:30am-12:30pm & 5:30-8pm Sat, 10:30am-12:30pm Sun) displays works by provincial artists. Both museums welcome the AR$1 voluntary contribution.

The modern **Museo de la Ciudad** (Parque Urquiza; ⏰ 8am-noon & 4-8pm Mon-Fri) focuses on Paraná's urban past and surroundings. Winter opening hours are slightly shorter.

Baqueanos del Río (☎ 423-4893; tours per hr from AR$25) organizes fascinating tours of the river and islands, with special attention paid to wildlife and the traditional lifestyle of the islands' inhabitants. Departs from riverfront tourist office regularly from 1pm to 8:30pm Thursday to Saturday, and by appointment on other days.

Costanera 241 (☎ 423-4385; www.costanera241.com.ar; Buenos Aires 212) offers river tours, fishing trips and kayak safaris.

Medano's Bikes (☎ 15-4290-016; medanosbikes@hotmail.com) rents bikes and offers bike tours of the city.

Sleeping

Camping Balneario Thompson (☎ 420-1583; Bravard s/n; campsites per person AR$12) The most convenient campground. Buses 1 and 6 ('Thompson') link it to downtown.

Paraná Hostel (☎ 422-8233; www.paranahostel.com.ar; Pazos 159; dm AR$36, d without bathroom AR$80; 🖥) In a new and improved location, Paraná's only hostel is all class – central, clean, spacious and well equipped.

Hotel Itatí (☎ 423-1500; hoteles_itati@hotmail.com; Belgrano 135; s/d AR$55/80; 🆒) The best of the budget hotels in the downtown area.

Paraná Hotel (☎ 423-1700; www.hotelesparana.com.ar; 9 de Julio 60; s/d AR$115/146; 🆒) A wonderfully atmospheric lobby leads to some decent rooms. Note that AR$60 buys you an upgrade to a 'Superior,' which are larger and more modern.

Eating

A good place to stock up on food is the **Mercado Central** (cnr Pellegrini & Bavio).

Bauci's Beach (Costanera s/n; mains AR$15-35) Down on the waterfront, this laid-back place has a deck overlooking the river and a good stretch of sandy beach. The menu's your average *parrilla* fare, and the sunset drinks are superb.

Bugatti (☎ 15-504-0770; Portside; mains AR$25-40) No surprises on the menu here – meat, chicken, pasta and fish – but the elegance of the dining room in this renovated post office makes the trip worthwhile. Even if you're not hungry, the balcony bar is a great place to take a breather.

El Viejo Marino II (Av Laurencina 341; mains AR$30) Spend five minutes in this town and people will be telling you that you have to try the fish. Stay another couple of minutes and they'll be telling you to check this place out. They're right, too – the atmosphere is loud and fun, the servings huge, and the specials, like *surubí milanesa* (river fish fried in breadcrumbs, AR$32), keep the locals coming back.

Drinking & Entertainment

Weekends are the real party nights in Paraná, and most of the action centers on the eastern end of the riverfront, by the port. Here, **Kravitz** (Figueroa s/n; ⏰ 10pm-late Fri & Sat) plays the usual mix of mainstream *marcha*, house and salsa. **Anderson** (Lineal 334; ⏰ Thu-Sat) is a spot for a drink or a dance, but only if you're 25 or over. There are many other bars and discos in the area.

Getting There & Around

The **bus terminal** (☎ 422-1282) is on Ramírez between Posadas and Moreno. Buses leave hourly for Santa Fe (AR$4, one hour). Other services and fares closely resemble those to and from Santa Fe.

GUALEGUAYCHÚ
☎ 03446 / pop 83,500

Gualeguaychú is a summertime river resort for families. As such, you're likely to see several men who have taken their tops off who really shouldn't have. It's also the site for some of the country's most outrageous Carnaval celebrations in February, featuring young people who have taken their tops off and should do so more often.

GETTING TO BRAZIL

The small, largely uninteresting town of **Paso de los Libres** (area code ☎ 03722) is the gateway to the Brazilian town of Uruguaiana. The border crossing is marked by a bridge about 10 blocks southwest of central Plaza Independencia. Taxis charge about AR$4 to get you to immigration from downtown, but they cannot cross. The border is open 24 hours. The nearest town covered in the Brazil chapter is Porto Alegre (p302).

Between Paso's bus terminal and the center are some very dodgy neighborhoods – it's well worth investing in the AR$1.25/8 bus/taxi fare to get you through.

Across from the bus terminal, **Hotel Capri** (☎ 42-1260; Llanes s/n; s/d AR$50/80) is the place to be if you need a lie-down between buses. More central and much more comfortable is **Hotel Las Vegas** (☎ 42-3490; Sarmiento 554; s/d AR$80/120; 🐱). There are resto-bars all along Colón between Mitre and Sitja Nia. The best restaurant in town is **Casaredo** (Madariaga 950; mains AR$20-45).

Moving on from Paso de los Libres, there are regular buses to Mercedes (AR$12, two hours), Buenos Aires (AR$110, nine hours), Corrientes (AR$40, five hours), Santa Fe (AR$54, eight hours) and many other destinations.

Orientation & Information

Plaza San Martín marks the city center. The **tourist office** (☎ 42-2900) is on the Plazoleta de los Artesanos. Several banks have ATMs.

Sights & Activities

At the former Estación Ferrocarril Urquiza, at the south end of Maipú, the **Museo Ferroviario** has a free open-air exhibit of locomotives, dining cars and a steam engine. Alongside the station, the **Corsódromo** (Blvd Irazusta) is the main site for Gualeguaychú's lively Carnaval.

Cross the river bridge and follow signs 2km for the **Termas de Gualeguaychú** (☎ 49-9167; www .gualeguaychutermal.com.ar; RP 42, Km 2.5; admission AR$20; ☺ 8am-midnight), a popular complex of shallow thermal pools at various temperatures.

Sleeping & Eating

Confiterías and snack bars line Av 25 de Mayo, while the *costanera* (riverside promenade) has shoulder-to-shoulder *parrillas* between Bolívar and Concordia.

Camping Costa Azul (☎ 42-3984; campsites per person AR$15) Good facilities overlooking the Río Gualeguaychú, 200m north of Puente Méndez Casariego.

Hostel Gualeguaychú (☎ 42-4371; www.hostelguale guaychu.com.ar; Méndez 290; dm incl breakfast AR$25) The best of the three hostels in town by a long, long margin.

Hotel Alemán (☎ 42-6153; Bolívar 535; s/d AR$100/115; 🐱) A solid budget choice a few blocks from the river. There are other, similar hotels on the same block.

Aguay Hotel (☎ 42-2099; www.hotelaguay.com.ar; Av Costanera 130; s/d AR$230/290; 🐱 🖥 🐶) The town's best-looking (and best-located) hotel drops its rates considerably in the off-season.

Punta Obeliscos (cnr Costanera & Bolivar; mains AR$15-30) Right down on the riverfront with an excellent raised outdoor deck. Tends to open only in summer.

Campo Alto (cnr Costanera Nte & Concordia; mains AR$20-40) With its tree-shaded terrace and occasional live music, this casual restaurant has a better atmosphere than most.

Getting There & Around

The **bus terminal** (☎ 44-0688; cnr Blvd Jurado & Artigas) is 1km southwest of downtown. Departures include Buenos Aires (AR$35, three hours), Paraná (AR$39, four hours), Corrientes (AR$100, 10 hours). Note that the border crossing to Fray Bentos, Uruguay, was closed indefinitely at the time of research.

Bicitour (Caballería 871) hires bikes for AR$5/40 per hour/day.

YAPEYÚ

☎ 03772 / pop 2200

Mellow little Yapeyú lies 72km north of Paso de los Libres and has exactly two attractions: the birthplace of national hero General José de San Martín and some remnants from its Jesuit mission past. It once had a population of 8000 Guaraní, who tended up to 80,000 cattle. After the Jesuits' expulsion, the Guaraní dispersed and the mission fell into ruins. Tiny Yapeyú is trying its hardest. What few sights exist are well signposted in Spanish, English, Portuguese and Guaraní.

The **Museo de Cultura Jesuítica**, consisting of several modern kiosks on the foundations of mission buildings, has a sundial, a few other mission relics and interesting photographs.

It's a measure of the esteem that Argentines hold for the Liberator that they have built a building to protect the **Casa de San Martín**, the house where he was born, even though it's mostly been eroded to its foundations.

Near the river, **Camping Paraíso** (☎ 49-3056; www.termasdeyapeyu.com.ar; cnr Paso de los Patos & San Martín; campsites per person AR$12, bungalows s/d AR$70/100) has good hot showers for campers and some excellent bungalows. Insects can be abundant, and low-lying sites can flood in heavy rain. **Hotel San Martín** (☎ 49-3120; Cabral 712; s/d AR$60/90) has cheerful rooms that face an inner courtyard.

Comedor El Paraíso (Matorras s/n; mains AR$20-35) serves passable meals and has good river views. It's next to the Casa de San Martín.

Buses stop three times daily at the small **bus terminal** (cnr Av del Libertador & Chacabuco), en route between Paso de los Libres and Posadas.

RESERVA PROVINCIAL ESTEROS DEL IBERÁ

Esteros del Iberá is a wildlife cornucopia comparable to Brazil's Pantanal do Mato Grosso. Aquatic plants and grasses, including 'floating islands,' dominate this wetlands wilderness covering 13,000 sq km. The most notable wildlife species are reptiles like the caiman and anaconda, mammals like the maned wolf, howler monkey, neotropical otter, pampas and swamp deer, and capybara, and more than 350 bird species.

Bird-watchers and nature nuts from all over the world converge on the village of Colonia Pellegrini, 120km northeast of Mercedes, to take advantage of the ease of access to the park (Colonia Pellegrini lies within the park's boundaries). It's a charming enough place in its own right: dirt roads, little traffic and plenty of trees. There is a **visitors center** across the causeway from Colonia Pellegrini with information on the reserve and a couple of short self-guided walking trails. The **tourist office** (☉ 8am-1pm & 2pm-7pm) at the entrance to the village is helpful and also rents bikes for AR$25/90 per hour/day. Two-hour **launch tours** (AR$70), available everywhere, are good value. Horse tours (AR$20 per hour) are pleasant, but you'll see more wildlife from the boat.

Many hotel operators in Mercedes (the gateway town) will try to railroad you into buying a package tour with tales of overbooking,

closed hotels etc. If you want to book ahead and go all-inclusive, fine, but there's really no need to panic – there are way more beds available than there will ever be tourists and it's easy (and much cheaper) to organize your room, food and tours on the spot. The tourist office in Colonia Pellegrini has a complete list of accommodations and eateries in town, and www.camaraturismoibera.com is an excellent source of information.

Camping is possible at the **municipal campground** (AR$20 per person) in Colonia Pellegrini, which has excellent, grassy waterfront sites.

A number of *hospedajes* (basic hotels) offer rooms with private bathroom for around AR$50 per person, the best of which is probably **Posada de la Luna** (☎ 03773-15628-823; cnr Capivára & Ysypá), down by the waterfront.

At the end of the village, **Rancho Ibera** (☎ 03773-1541-2040; www.posadaranchoibera.com.ar; room incl full board per person AR$480) is set in a beautiful house with simple, pleasant rooms. The price includes three excellent meals and one excursion per day.

Buses run from Corrientes and Paso de los Libres to Mercedes, where *combis* (small buses) to Colonia Pellegrini (AR$25, four hours) leave at noon Monday to Saturday, and return to Mercedes at 5am Monday to Friday, and 11am on Saturday. Heading north, there is a bus on Saturdays at 5pm to Ituzaingó (AR$50, three hours), where you can catch onward buses passing between Posadas and Corrientes. Another option is to get a group together to pay for a private transfer to Virasoro (AR$450, three hours) for onward buses to Posadas.

CORRIENTES
☎ 03783 / pop 360,300

It's hard to love Corrientes, but you're welcome to try. It's a big, serious city with a couple of decent museums and a reputation for being very budget-unfriendly. Once the sun starts setting, a walk along the riverfront might make you feel a bit happier about being here. The once-moribund **Carnaval Correntino** (www.carnavalescorrentinos.com) has experienced a revival and now attracts crowds of up to 80,000.

Orientation
Plaza 25 de Mayo is the center of Corrientes' extremely regular grid plan. The commercial center is the Junín *peatonal,* between Salta

and Catamarca, but the most attractive area is the shady riverside along Av Costanera General San Martín. Bus No 106 runs between San Lorenzo downtown and the bus terminal.

Information

There are several banks with ATMs around 9 de Julio.

Cambio El Dorado (9 de Julio 1341) Changes cash and traveler's checks.

Municipal tourist office (☎ 42-8845; Plaza JB Cabral) More central than the provincial tourist office, but hopelessly disorganized.

Post office (cnr San Juan & San Martín)

Provincial tourist office (☎ 42-7200; 25 de Mayo) The best in town.

Sights

The east side of San Juan, between Plácido Martínez and Quintana, is a shady, attractive area. The **Monumento a la Gloria** there honors the Italian community; a series of striking **murals** chronicles local history since colonial times.

The **Museo de Bellas Artes Dr Juan Ramón Vidal** (San Juan 634; www.culturacorrientes.gov.ar; 9am-noon & 6-9pm Tue-Sat) emphasizes sculpture and oil paintings from local artists and hosts the occasional international exhibition.

The **Museo Histórico de Corrientes** (9 de Julio 1044; 8am-noon & 4-8pm Mon-Fri) features exhibits of weapons, coins and antique furniture, and displays on religious and civil history.

Visit the **Santuario de la Cruz del Milagro**, on Belgrano between Buenos Aires and Salta.

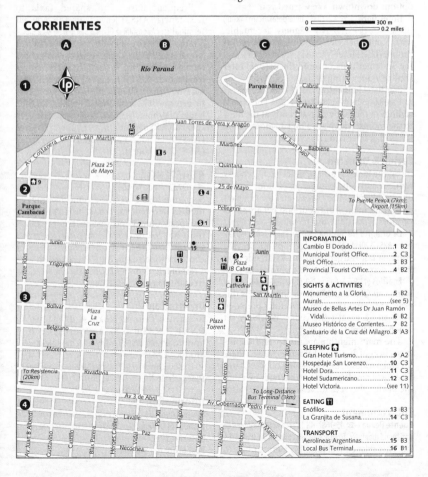

CORRIENTES

0 — 300 m
0 — 0.2 miles

ARGENTINA

According to local legend, the 16th-century cross here defied indigenous efforts to burn it.

Sleeping

Corrientes offers no joy for those in search of budget accommodation: what there is isn't cheap, and what's relatively cheap isn't very good. If you're watching the pesos and really want to check out the city, nearby Resistencia (right) is just down the road and much more wallet-friendly. During Carnaval, the tourist office maintains a list of *casas de familia* offering rooms for AR$35 to AR$100 per person.

Hospedaje San Lorenzo (☎ 42-1740; San Lorenzo 1136; r AR$90) Small, badly ventilated, some say overrun by cockroaches, and offering rooms by the hour, this is one of the only budget options downtown. We warned you.

Hotel Dora (☎ 42-1053; hoteldora@hotmail.com; España 1050; r AR$120; 🖳) Vaguely acceptable, with somewhat clean rooms in a good location. The Hotel Victoria (next door) and the Sudamericana (around the corner) offer similarly unexciting deals.

Gran Hotel Turismo (☎ 43-3174; www.ghturismo.com .ar; Entre Ríos 650; s/d AR$180/210; 🖳 🖳) The classic stylings of the lobby stop abruptly at the door to the rooms, which are a bit run-down. Still, it has character and river views.

Eating & Drinking

Be on the lookout for *chipas* (crunchy, cheesy scones) and *sopa paraguaya* (a flour-based, quiche-like pie). They occasionally turn up on restaurant menus, but your best bet are street vendors around the bus terminal.

La Granjita de Susana (cnr San Lorenzo & Yrigoyen; mains AR$12-20) A good budget option, serving empanadas, burgers and steaks at sidewalk tables across from Plaza JB Cabral.

Enófilos (43-9271; Junín 1260; dishes AR$18-44) What some call Corrientes' one saving grace is this excellent restaurant, with carefully prepared food and a great wine cellar. Weekday set lunches (AR$40) are a bargain.

The main nightlife area is around the intersection of Junín and Buenos Aires, where several bars and clubs get going on weekends. The *costanera* (riverside promenade) west of the bridge also sees some action.

Entertainment

Puente Pexoa (☎ 45-1687; RN 12 at La Rotonda Virgen de Itatí roundabout; 🕒 from 8:30pm, 1st band at 11:30pm Fri & Sat) This relaxed restaurant is a great place to check out *chamamé*, a sort of Guaraní version of polka dancing. Sound deadly? It actually gets very rowdy and is sometimes hilarious. People show up in full *gaucho* regalia, and up to four bands play each night. From downtown, take bus 102 marked '17 de Agosto' 7km out of town to the Virgen de Itatí roundabout. It's just off the roundabout; the driver will point it out. A taxi back costs AR$15 or AR$20.

Getting There & Around

Aerolíneas Argentinas (☎ 42-3918; www.aerolineas .com; Junín 1301) flies daily to Buenos Aires (from AR$430). Local bus 105 (AR$1.25) goes to the **airport** (☎ 45-8358), about 15km east of town on RN 12. A *remise* should cost around AR$15.

Frequent buses and shared taxis to Resistencia (AR$3) leave from the **local bus terminal** (cnr Av Costanera General San Martín & La Rioja). Shared taxis also leave from the corner of Santa Fe and 3 de Abril. The **long-distance bus terminal** (☎ 47-7600; Av Maipú) has departures for Paso de los Libres (AR$40, five hours) via Mercedes (AR$31, 3½ hours) for access to Esteros del Iberá, Posadas (AR$40, four hours), Formosa (AR$20, three hours), Puerto Iguazú (AR$65, nine hours), Buenos Aires (AR$90, 11 hours) and Asunción, Paraguay (AR$40, six hours).

RESISTENCIA

☎ 03722 / pop 403,000

Sculpture-lovers wallow around like pigs in mud in Resistencia. A joint project between the local council and various arts organizations has led to the placement of over 500 sculptures in the city streets and parks, free for everyone to see. Delightful Plaza 25 de Mayo, a riot of tall palms and comical *palo borracho* trees, marks the city center.

Orientation

Resistencia's airport is 6km south of town on RN 11; bus 3 (marked 'Aeropuerto/Centro') goes to Plaza 25 de Mayo. A taxi will cost around AR$15.

Buses 3 and 10 go from the bus terminal to Plaza 25 de Mayo (AR$1.50).

Information

There are ATMs near Plaza 25 de Mayo.

Cambio El Dorado (Paz 36) Changes traveler's checks at reasonable rates.

Post office (cnr Sarmiento & Yrigoyen) Faces the plaza.

Tourist kiosk (☎ 45-8289; Plaza 25 de Mayo) About 450m away from the tourist office. Handy.

Tourist office (☎ 42-3547; Santa Fe 178) Well stocked.

Sights

There's insufficient space here to detail the number of **sculptures** in city parks and on the sidewalks, but the tourist office distributes a map with their locations that makes a good introduction to the city. The best starting point is the **Museo de Escultura** (🕑 8am-noon & 3-8pm Mon-Sat) an open-air workshop on the north side of Parque 2 de Febrero. Several of the most impressive pieces are on display here, and this is where, during the **Bienal de Escultura** (www.bienaldelchaco.com), held on the third week of July in even years, you can catch sculptors at work.

El Fogón de los Arrieros (Brown 350; admission AR$5; 🕑 8am-noon Mon-Sat) is the driving force behind the city's progressive displays of public art and is famous for its eclectic assemblage of art objects from around the Chaco province, Argentina and the world.

The **Museo del Hombre Chaqueño** (Museum of Chaco Man; Justo 150; 🕑 8am-noon & 4-8pm Mon-Fri, 10am-1pm Sat) focuses on the colonization of the Chaco and has exhibits and information on the Guaraní, Mocoví, Komlek and Mataco provincial indigenous cultures.

Sleeping

Camping Parque 2 de Febrero (Avalos 1100; campsites AR$10) Has excellent facilities.

Hotel Alfil (☎ 42-0882; Santa María de Oro 495; s/d AR$50/80) Surprisingly good value for the price. No frills, but a few charming touches.

Residencial Bariloche (☎ 42-1412; Obligado 239; s/d AR$70/90; 🏊) A good deal: spacious, clean and quiet rooms with cable TV. Pay an extra AR$10 for air-con or just get blown away by their industrial-size room fans.

Hotel Colón (☎ 42-2861; hotelcolon@gigared.com.ar; Santa María de Oro 143; s/d AR$100/150; 🏊 🖳) A slick lobby leads on to large, unrenovated rooms a half block from the main plaza.

Eating

Fenix Bar (Don Bosco 133; meals AR$12-25) The menu runs the usual gamut of pizza, meats and pastas, but the food is well presented, the decor atmospheric and the wine selection excellent.

Pizza Party (cnr Obligado & San Martín; pizzas from AR$20) Despite the name, this is the most popular pizzeria in town, with excellent thin-crust pies and shady courtyard seating.

Charly (Güemes 213; meals around AR$25) Carefully prepared meat and fish dishes are the winners here, but there's also an excellent selection of salads and wines. Budget fiends can eat the same dishes at lower prices in the restaurant's *rotisería* around the corner at Brown 71.

Several attractive *confiterías* and ice-cream parlors have rejuvenated the area north and northwest of Plaza 25 de Mayo; try, for instance, the bohemian **Café de la Ciudad** (Pellegrini 109; mains AR$15-30), formerly a sleazy bar, for slightly pricey sandwiches, burgers and beer.

Drinking & Entertainment

Weather permitting, there are often free folk concerts in the Plaza 25 de Mayo on Sunday nights. The **Centro Cultural Guido Mirada** (Colón 146) shows art-house films and hosts live theater and dance performances.

Clover (cnr French & Ayucucho) Because every town must have an 'Irish' pub, even out here in the Chaco.

Zingara (Güemes; 🕑 6pm-late Wed-Sat). This hip, minimally decorated bar wouldn't be out of place somewhere like Milan or Paris. Cocktails feature heavily on the drinks menu.

Getting There & Away

Aerolíneas Argentinas (☎ 44-5550; www.aerolineas.com; Justo 184) has daily flights to Buenos Aires (from AR$430). The recently launched **Aero Chaco** (☎ 0810-345-2422; www.aerochaco.net; Sarmiento 1685) flies to Buenos Aires, Puerto Iguazú and Cordoba but had not fixed its prices at the time of writing.

The **bus terminal** (☎ 46-1098; cnr MacLean & Islas Malvinas) has an urban service (marked 'Chaco–Corrientes') between Resistencia and Corrientes for AR$1. You can catch it in front of the post office on Plaza 25 de Mayo.

You can save yourself a trip out to the bus terminal by buying tickets in advance at the **telecentro** (cnr Brown & López y Planes).

La Estrella goes to Capitán Solari, near Parque Nacional Chaco, four times daily (AR$14.50, 2½ hours). Other destinations include Buenos Aires (AR$160, 13 hours), Santa Fe (AR$80, seven hours), Rosario (AR$115, nine hours), Córdoba (AR$125, 12 hours), Salta (AR$87, 10 hours), Formosa (AR$14, 2½ hours), Posadas (AR$40, five hours), Puerto Iguazú (AR$65, 10 hours) and Asunción, Paraguay (AR$40, five hours).

ARGENTINA

FORMOSA
☎ 03717 / pop 239,800

Way out here on the Río Paraguay, this town has a much more Paraguayan feel than others in the region. The riverfront has been tastefully restored and makes for an excellent place to go for a wander once the sun starts going down. In November, the weeklong **Fiesta del Río** features an impressive nocturnal religious procession in which 150 boats from Corrientes sail up the Río Paraguay.

Hotel San Martín (☎ 42-6769; 25 de Mayo 380; s/d AR$90/120; ✼) Good for the price but otherwise uninteresting, the San Martín is surprisingly quiet for its central location. Some rooms are definitely better than others, so have a look around if you can.

Mercotur (☎ 43-1469; Lelong 899) has regular buses to Clorinda, Laguna Naick-Neck and Laguna Blanca (Parque Nacional Río Pilcomayo), departing at 5am and midday daily. **Minibus Fede** (☎ 42-4430; Lelong 875) makes the same trip at 5am, 10am and 4pm (AR$20, 2½ hours).

POSADAS
☎ 03752 / pop 339,000

If you're heading north, now's about the time that things start to feel very tropical, and the jungle begins to creep into the edges of the picture. Posadas is mainly interesting as an access point, both to Paraguay and the Jesuit mission sites north of here, but it's a cool little city in its own right, with some sweet plazas and a well-developed eating, drinking and partying scene down on the waterfront.

Orientation
Plaza 9 de Julio is the center of Posadas' standard grid. Streets were renumbered several years ago, but local preference for the old system occasionally creates confusion.

All addresses in this section use the new system. The bus terminal is almost 6km from the downtown area. Buses 8, 15 and 24 travel between the two (AR$1.40). A taxi costs about AR$10.

Information
There are several downtown ATMs.
Cambios Mazza (Bolívar 1932) Changes traveler's checks.
Post office (cnr Bolívar & Ayacucho)
Provincial tourist office (☎ 555-0297; turismo @misiones.gov.ar; Colón 1985) Has a wealth of printed material.

Sights & Activities
The natural history section of the **Museo de Ciencias Naturales e Historia** (San Luis 384) was closed at the time of research, but focuses on fauna and the geology and mineralogy of the province. The museum also has an excellent serpentarium, an aviary, aquarium and a historical section that stresses prehistory, the Jesuit missions and modern colonization.

In the cool of the afternoon, the **costanera** comes alive. It's a favorite spot for joggers, cyclists, dog walkers, maté sippers, hot-dog vendors and young couples staring wistfully at the lights of Paraguay across the water.

Sleeping
Residencial Misiones (☎ 43-0133; Av Azara 1960; s/d AR$40/60) Crumbling and basic, this is the best budget deal in town.

Hotel Colón (☎ 42-5085; Colón 2169; s/d AR$70/80) Reasonable-size rooms in a decent location just off the plaza. Get one upstairs for ventilation.

Posadas Hotel (☎ 44-0888; www.hotelposadas.com .ar; Bolívar 1949; s/d AR$150/170; ✼) With by far the best-looking interiors of any hotel in town, the Posadas' rooms are spacious, comfortable and well decorated.

GETTING TO PARAGUAY

Launches across the Paraná to Encarnación (AR$3) continue to operate despite the bridge. They leave from the dock at the east end of Av Guacurarí. At the time of writing, immigration procedures were carried out at the dock, but this changes often – call ☎ 42-5044 for the latest.

Buses to Encarnación (AR$3) leave every 20 minutes from the corner of Mitre and Junín, passing through downtown before crossing the bridge (get off for immigration procedures and hang on to your ticket; you'll be able to catch another bus continuing in the same direction).

Buses also go from Puerto Iguazú to Ciudad del Este (AR$3).

Both borders are open 24 hours. Most non-EU citizens require a visa to enter Paraguay. For info on entering Argentina from Paraguay, see p752.

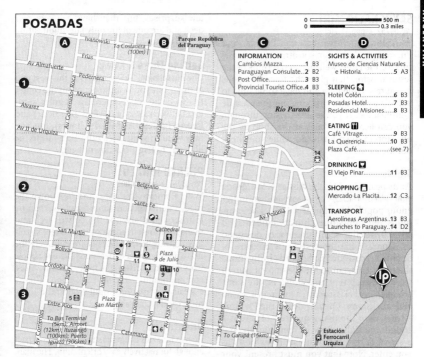

POSADAS

INFORMATION			SIGHTS & ACTIVITIES		
Cambios Mazza	1	B3	Museo de Ciencias Naturales		
Paraguayan Consulate	2	B2	e Historia	5	A3
Post Office	3	B3			
Provincial Tourist Office	4	B3	SLEEPING		
			Hotel Colón	6	B3
			Posadas Hotel	7	B3
			Residencial Misiones	8	B3
			EATING		
			Café Vitrage	9	B3
			La Querencia	10	B3
			Plaza Café	(see 7)	
			DRINKING		
			El Viejo Pinar	11	B3
			SHOPPING		
			Mercado La Placita	12	C3
			TRANSPORT		
			Aerolíneas Argentinas	13	B3
			Launches to Paraguay	14	D2

Eating & Drinking

For cheap eats with few surprises, head for the semipedestrian intersection of Bolívar and San Lorenzo, where there's a range of pizza and pasta joints with sidewalk seating.

Café Vitrage (cnr Bolívar & Colón; mains AR$12-35) With its brass fittings and dark wood features, the Vitrage oozes style. Mostly a bar/cafe, it can also whip up a juicy steak any time of the day or night.

Plaza Café (Bolívar 1979; mains AR$20-40) The most innovative menu in town features tempura, risotto and some good seafood dishes.

La Querencia (Bolívar 322; mains AR$25-40) Posadas' spiffiest *parrilla*, with a wide-ranging menu and a good wine list.

The balcony bar at **El Viejo Pinar** (San Lorenzo 1782) is a good spot for midweek drinks. Weekends, the action moves down to the waterfront.

Shopping

There's something for everyone at the indoor **Mercado La Placita** (cnr Sarmiento & Av Roque Sánez Peña), from counterfeit sneakers to Paraguayan handicrafts and homemade cigars.

Getting There & Around

Aerolíneas Argentinas (☎ 42-2036; www.aerolineas .com; cnr Ayacucho & San Martín) flies daily to Buenos Aires (AR$460).

Bus 8 from San Lorenzo between La Rioja and Entre Ríos goes to the airport, 12km southwest of town, and Aerolíneas Argentinas runs its own shuttle service. A *remise* costs about AR$20.

International departures from the **bus terminal** (☎ 45-26106; cnr Ruta 12 & Santa Catalina) include São Paulo in Brazil (AR$285, 20 hours).

Domestic fares include Corrientes (AR$40, four hours), Resistencia (AR$43, five hours), Puerto Iguazú (AR$45, 5½ hours), Buenos Aires (AR$125, 13 hours; AR$150 in *coche-cama;* deluxe sleeper bus) and Salta (AR$160, 17 hours). Buses to San Ignacio Miní (AR$8, one hour) leave frequently.

Trains run on Wednesdays and Saturdays from nearby Garupá to Buenos Aires (AR$65 to AR$223, 24 hours). Shuttle services leave from Posadas' **railway station** (☎ 43-6076; cnr Madariaga & Estación) about 15 minutes before departures.

SAN IGNACIO MINÍ
☎ 03752 / pop 11,200

A mellow little town between Posadas and Puerto Iguazú, San Ignacio attracts most visitors for the large, well-preserved ruins of the Jesuit mission that gives the town its name. If you're staying here and have some time to kill, it's well worth checking out the Casa de Quiroga, too. If you're just passing through, you can leave your bags at the shop by the bus stop in town for AR$4 while you check out the ruins.

Sights
At its peak, in 1733, the **mission of San Ignacio Miní** (admission AR$25; ☺ 7am-8pm) had an indigenous population of nearly 4500. The enormous red-sandstone church, embellished with 'bas-relief sculptures, was designed in 'Guaraní baroque' style (a mixture of Spanish baroque style and indigenous themes). Adjacent to the tile-roofed church were the cemetery and cloisters; the same complex held classrooms, a kitchen, a prison and workshops. On all sides of the Plaza de Armas were the living quarters. There is a sound and light show at 7pm nightly and a set of fairly bizarre museum exhibits as you enter. Note that you must present your passport to enter here.

Casa de Quiroga (Quiroga s/n; admission AR$3) is at the southern end of town, offering grand views of the Río Paraná. A small museum contains photos and some of the famous Uruguayan writer's possessions and first editions.

Sleeping & Eating
our pick Adventure Hostel (☎ 47-0955; www.si hostel.com; Independencia 469; dm/s/d AR$34/100/140; 🅿 🖃 🖳) A beautifully set-up hostel with air-con dorms, a great pool area, huge kitchen and plenty of hammock action. More like this, please.

Hotel San Ignacio (☎ 47-0422; cnr Sarmiento & San Martín; s/d/cabañas AR$60/90/160; 🅿 🖃) For a combination hotel/bar/restaurant/internet cafe/pool hall/teen hangout, the San Ignacio's actually a pretty mellow place. Rooms in the main building are spotless, and the A-frame *cabañas* (cabins) out back sleep four and are great value.

Rivadavia between the bus stop and the ruins is lined with small restaurants serving *milanesas*, pizzas etc. The menu at **La Aldea** (Los Jesuitas s/n; mains AR$15-25, set meals AR$15) holds few surprises, but they have a lovely rear deck and are one of the only late-night eating options in town.

Getting There & Away
The **bus terminal** (Av Sarmiento) is at the west end of town, but you want to get off in the center to avoid the walk. There are regular services between Posadas (AR$8, one hour) and Puerto Iguazú (AR$40, 4½ hours), but you may want to walk or cab the 1km out to the highway to flag a bus down there.

PUERTO IGUAZÚ
☎ 03757 / pop 34,000

With a world-class attraction just down the road, Puerto Iguazú should feel overrun by tourists, but it absorbs the crowds well and manages to retain some of its relaxed, small-town atmosphere. The falls are definitely the drawcard here: you'll meet your share of people who have come straight from Buenos Aires, and are heading straight back again. There's a steady backpacker population and a lively hostel and restaurant scene.

Orientation
Puerto Iguazú's irregular street plan is compact enough for relatively easy orientation. The main drag is the diagonal Av Victoria Aguirre.

Information
The Brazilian Consulate here arranges visas in half a day, much better than the week that it takes their Buenos Aires counterparts to do the same job.

Banco de Misiones ATM (Av Victoria Aguirre 330)

Post office (Av San Martín 780)

Tourist office (☎ 42-0800; Av Victoria Aguirre 311) This is the main office. There's also a tourist kiosk downstairs at the bus terminal.

Sleeping
Camping El Pindo (☎ 42-1795; per tent AR$12, plus per person AR$12) At Km 3.5 of RN 12 on the edge of town, this campground has good facilities and is easily reached by local buses.

Hostel Guembe (☎ 42-1035; www.elguembehostel house.com.ar; Av Guaraní s/n; dm/r AR$35/110; 🅿) Mellower than most hostels in town, with OK dorms and a pretty garden area.

Hostel Sweet Hostel (☎ 42-4336; www.hostelsweet hostel.com.ar; El Mensú 38; dm/r AR$35/120; 🅿 🖳) Spacious dorms, an excellent pool/bar area, friendly staff and stylish doubles.

Residencial Lola (☎ 42-3954; Av Córdoba 255, s/d AR$50/80) No-frills budget rooms that may well be the cheapest in town.

Los Troncos (☎ 42-4337; www.hotellostroncosiguazu.com; San Lorenzo 154; r AR$200; 🅿 🅿) Excellent rooms for two to five people a short walk from the bus terminal. The leafy setting and excellent pool/deck area make up for the removed location.

Some other good options:

Marco Polo (☎ 42-5559; www.marcopoloinniguazu .com; Av Córdoba 559; dm/d AR$40/140; 🅿 🅿) Huge complex with a good pool and bar. Book ahead.

Residencial Los Ríos (☎ 42-5465; Av Misiones 70; s/d AR$80/120; 🅿) Big modern rooms by the bus terminal. A good budget deal.

Colonial Iguazú (☎ 42-2898; Av Guaraní 57; s/d AR$80/120; 🅿 🅿) Lovely, simple rooms facing a large patio and good-size swimming pool.

Eating & Drinking

El Andariego (Moreno 229; mains AR$15-24) This no-frills neighborhood *parrilla* does good, cheap meat and pasta dishes.

Plaza Pueblo (Av Victoria Aguirre s/n; mains AR$15-30) A pleasant outdoor eatery offering a wide-ranging menu and football-size calzones.

Terra (Av Misiones 145; mains AR$20-35) Decent pastas, excellent stir-fries and assorted Asian dishes at this cool little cafe/restaurant.

Going out in Puerto Iguazú is so much fun that even Brazilians come here to dance. Imagine that. Most of the action revolves around the six-way intersection of Avs Brazil and San Martín. Keep an eye out for **Cuba Libre** (cnr Av Brasil & Paraguay), which has long happy hours and occasional live music, and **La Barranca** (Moreno s/n), for all your megadisco requirements.

Getting There & Around

AIR

Aerolíneas Argentinas (☎ 42-0168; www.aerolineas .com; Av Victoria Aguirre 295) flies daily to Buenos Aires (AR$530).

Andes Líneas Aéreas (☎ 42-2681; www.andeson line.com; Av Tres Fronteras 499, Loc 3) flies to Buenos Aires (AR$505), Córdoba (AR$533) and Salta (AR$533).

The recently launched **Aero Chaco** (☎ 0810-345-2422; www.aerochaco.net) flies to Resistencia, but had not fixed its prices at the time of writing.

PUERTO IGUAZÚ

0 — 500 m
0 — 0.4 miles

To Camping El Pindó (1km);
Parque Nacional Iguazú
(15km); Airport (18km)

GETTING TO BRAZIL & PARAGUAY

Buses to Foz do Iguaçu (AR$3) leave regularly from Puerto Iguazú's bus terminal. The bus will wait as you complete immigration procedures. The border is open 24 hours, but buses only run in daylight hours. For info on entering Argentina from Brazil, see p307.

Frequent buses go from Puerto Iguazú's bus terminal to Ciudad del Este, Paraguay (AR$3, one hour) and wait at the border as you complete customs formalities. For information on coming here from Paraguay, see p755.

Remises to the airport cost about AR$70. Various companies offer shuttle service for AR$15. Ask at your hotel.

Ride Cataratas (☎ 42-2815; Av Argentina 184) rents 105cc motorbikes for AR$12.50/120 per hour/day. **Internet Iguazú** (Aguirre 552) rents mountain bikes for AR$7/40 per hour/day.

BUS

The **bus terminal** (☎ 42-3006; cnr Avs Córdoba & Misiones) has departures for Posadas (AR$45, 5½ hours), Salta (AR$221, 23 hours), Buenos Aires (AR$175, 20 hours) and intermediate points. Frequent buses also leave for Parque Nacional Iguazú (AR$10, 30 minutes), and there are international buses to Foz do Iguaçu, Brazil (AR$3, 35 minutes) and Ciudad del Este, Paraguay (AR$3, one hour).

TAXI

For groups of three or more hoping to see both sides of the falls as well as Ciudad del Este and the Itaipú hydroelectric project, a shared cab or *remise* can be a good idea; figure about AR$200 for a full day's sightseeing, but make sure you account for visa costs. Contact the **Asociación de Trabajadores de Taxis** (☎ 42-0282), or simply approach a driver.

PARQUE NACIONAL IGUAZÚ

People who doubt the theory that negative ions generated by waterfalls make people happier might have to reconsider after visiting the **Iguazú Falls**. Moods just seem to improve the closer you get to the falls, until eventually people degenerate into giggling, shrieking messes. And this is grown men we're talking about.

But getting happy isn't the only reason to come here. The power, size and sheer noise of the falls have to be experienced to be believed. You could try coming early, or later in the day (tour groups tend to leave by 3pm), but you're unlikely ever to have the place to yourself. The **park** (☎ 03757-49-1445; admission AR$60; ☾ 8am-7pm) quickly fills with Argentines, backpackers, families and tour groups – but who cares? Get up close to the Garganta del Diablo (Devil's Throat) and the whole world seems to drop away.

Guaraní legend says that Iguazú Falls originated when a jealous forest god, enraged by a warrior escaping downriver by canoe with a young girl, caused the riverbed to collapse in front of the lovers, producing precipitous falls over which the girl fell and, at their base, turned into a rock. The warrior survived as a tree overlooking his fallen lover.

The geological origins of the falls are more prosaic. In southern Brazil, the Río Iguazú passes over a basalt plateau that ends just above its confluence with the Paraná. Before reaching the edge, the river divides into many channels to form several distinctive *cataratas* (cataracts).

The most awesome is the semicircular Garganta del Diablo, a deafening and dampening part of the experience, approached by launch and via a system of *pasarelas* (catwalks). There's no doubt that it's spectacular – there's only one question: where's the bungee jump?

Despite development pressures, the 55,000-hectare park is a natural wonderland of subtropical rainforest, with over 2000 identified plant species, countless insects, 400 bird species and many mammals and reptiles.

If you've got the time (and the money for a visa – see p375), it's worth checking out the Brazilian side of the falls, too, for a few different angles, plus the grand overview. For more information, see p304.

Information

Buses from Puerto Iguazú drop passengers at the Centro de Informes, where there's a small natural-history museum. There's also a photo-developing lab, gift shop, bar and many other services, including restaurants and snack bars.

Dangers & Annoyances

The Río Iguazú's currents are strong and swift; more than one tourist has been swept downriver and drowned near Isla San Martín.

The wildlife is potentially dangerous: in 1997, a jaguar killed a park ranger's infant son. Visitors should respect the big cats and, in case you should encounter one, it's important not to panic. Speak calmly but loudly, do not run or turn your back, and try to appear bigger than you are by waving your arms or clothing.

Sights

Before seeing Iguazú Falls themselves, grab a map, look around the museum, and climb the nearby tower for a good overall view. Plan hikes before the mid-morning tourbus invasion. Descending from the visitor center, you can cross by free launch to **Isla Grande San Martín**, which offers unique views and a refuge from the masses on the mainland.

Several *pasarelas* give good views of smaller falls, and, in the distance, the **Garganta del Diablo**. A train from the visitors center operates regularly to shuttle visitors from site to site. At the last stop, follow the trail to the lookout perched right on the edge of the mighty falls.

Activities

Best in the early morning, the Sendero Macuco nature trail leads through dense forest, where a steep sidetrack goes to the base of a hidden waterfall. Another trail goes to the *bañado*, a marsh abounding in birdlife. Allow about 2½ hours round trip (6km) for the entire Sendero Macuco trail.

To get elsewhere in the forest, you can hitch or hire a car to take you out along RN 101 toward the village of Bernardo de Irigoyen. Few visitors explore this part of the park, and it is still nearly pristine forest. **Iguazú Jungle Explorer** (☎ 03757-42-1696; www.iguazu junglexpolrer.com), based at the visitors center, can arrange thrilling 12-minute speedboat trips below the falls (AR$75), as well as 4WD excursions on the Yacaratía trail to Puerto Macuco.

Moonlight walks (☎ 03757-49-1469; www.iguazu argentina.com; guided walks with/without dinner AR$130/80) offers walks to the falls at 8pm, 8:45pm and 9:30pm on the five nights around the full moon. Call to reserve a place.

Getting There & Away

Regular buses run to Puerto Iguazú (AR$10, 30 minutes).

NORTHWEST ARGENTINA

With a very tangible sense of history, the northwest is Argentina's most 'indigenous' region, and the sights and people here show much closer links with the country's Andean neighbors than the European character of its urban centers.

HISTORY

The Central Andean population spread never got much further than what is now northwest Argentina. Before the Spanish arrived, this region hosted an array of indigenous tribes: the Lule south and west of modern Salta, the Tonocote of Santiago del Estero, and the Diaguita, doing the roaming nomad thing. Even today, Quechuan communities reach as far south as Santiago del Estero.

Diego de Almagro's expedition came through Jujuy and Salta on the way from Cuzco to Chile in 1535, but it wasn't until 1553 that the first city of the region, Santiago del Estero, was established. Local resistance meant slow going for the conquistadors in these parts, but eventually San Miguel de Tucumán (1565), Córdoba (1573), Salta (1582), La Rioja (1591) and San Salvador de Jujuy (1593) were founded. It took Catamarca another 100 years to find its feet.

As the double horns of disease and exploitation decimated indigenous populations and the *encomiendas* (grant of land and indigenous inhabitants given to settlers) lost their economic value, the region's focus shifted. Tucumán provided mules, cotton and textiles for the mines of Potosí, and Córdoba became a center for education and arts. The opening of the Atlantic to shipping in late colonial times diminished Jujuy's and Salta's importance as trade posts, but Tucumán grew in stature as the local sugar industry boomed.

The region's continued reliance on sugar and tobacco farming meant that it was hard hit during recession times, and even today Jujuy province is one of the poorest in the country. There's an air of optimism, though, as the booming tourist industry brings much-needed income to the area.

ARGENTINA

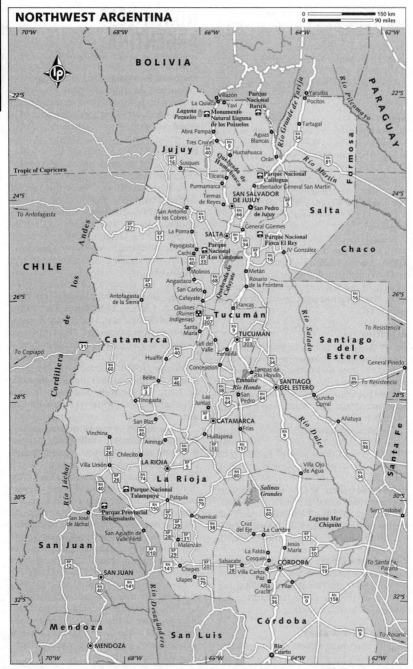

NORTHWEST ARGENTINA

0 — 150 km
0 — 90 miles

CÓRDOBA

☎0351 / pop 1,531,500

Argentina's second city is everything it should be – vibrant, fun, manageable in size and (in places) gorgeous to look at. Culture vultures beware: you may get stuck here. Music, theater, film, dance: whatever you want, you can be pretty sure it's going on somewhere in town. The city also rocks out with seven universities, and has a buzz that some say is unmatched in the whole country.

Orientation

Córdoba is growing rapidly – what started as a humble settlement on the south bank of the Río Primero (or Sequoia) now sprawls to the north and south and out into the countryside. Its attractive downtown comprises a labyrinth of plazas and colonial architecture.

Plaza San Martín is the city's nucleus, but the commercial center is northwest of the plaza, where the 25 de Mayo and Rivera Indarte pedestrian malls intersect. Local buses don't serve the bus terminal, but it's an easy eight-block walk to the center; just keep moving toward the big steeple. A taxi should cost AR$8.

Information

There are ATMs near Plaza San Martín.

Cambio Barujel (cnr Buenos Aires & 25 de Mayo) For changing traveler's checks.

Municipal tourist office (☎ 428-5600; www.visitecordobaciudad.com.ar; Rosario de Santa Fe 39) There's a satellite office (☎ 433-1980) at the bus terminal.

Post office (Av General Paz 201)

Provincial tourist office (☎ 428-5856) In the historic *cabildo* (colonial town council) on Plaza San Martín.

Sights

To see Córdoba's colonial buildings and monuments, start at the **cabildo**, on Plaza San Martín. At the plaza's southwest corner, crowned by a Romanesque dome, the **Iglesia Catedral** (begun in 1577) mixes a variety of styles.

While guided tours of the **Universidad Nacional de Córdoba** (☎ 433-2075; guided visits per person AR$10; ⏲ 10am, 11am, 5pm & 6pm Tue-Sun) may sound a little dry, they get rave reviews. The tour (in perfect English) takes you on a whirlwind ride through the ages, encompassing the history of Córdoba, Argentina, the Jesuits and the university's museum and library.

There's not a whole lot of joy at the **Museo de la Memoria** (San Jerónimo s/n; ⏲ 9am-noon & 2-8pm Tue-Sat), but that's kind of the whole point. Set in a former detention/torture facility, it's a somber documentation of Dirty War atrocities, which are told through photographs of the (often startlingly young) 'disappeared' of the era.

South of the center is Córdoba's **Milla Cultural** (Cultural Mile) – 1.6km of theaters, art galleries and art schools. The highlights here are the **Paseo del Buen Pastor** (Av Hipólito Yrigoyen 325; ⏲ 10am-10pm) which showcases work by Córdoba's young and emerging artists, the **Palacio Ferrerya** (Av Hipólito Yrigoyen 551; ⏲ 8am-7pm Tue-Sun), housing 400 works of fine art, and the **Museo Provincial de Bellas Artes Emilio Caraffa** (Av Hipólito Yrigoyen 651; ⏲ 11am-7pm Tue-Sun), which features a rotating collection of top-shelf contemporary art.

Activities

There's plenty to do in and around Córdoba: paragliding, skydiving, trekking, rafting, rock climbing, horse riding and mountain biking, to name a few options. **Latitud Sur Travel Agency** (based in Tango Hostel; see p93) offers all this and more, and has been recommended for its willingness to give advice on how to do things independently.

Courses

SET Idiomas (☎ 421-1719; www.learningspanish.com; Corrientes 21) Offers 20 hours of Spanish classes for AR$560/1120 in group/individual classes. Homestays available.

Tsunami Tango (☎ 15-313-8746; www.tsunamitango.com; Lapidra 453) Tango classes and *milongas* Tuesdays to Saturdays. Check the website for times.

Sleeping

Municipal campground (☎ 433-8012; per person AR$6) Spacious but basic, in the Parque General San Martín, 13km west of downtown. Bus 1 from Plaza San Martín goes to the Complejo Ferial, about 1km from the park.

Le Grand Hostel (☎ 422-7115; www.legrandshostel.com; Buenos Aires 547; dm AR$39-50, d AR$100; ✕ 💻) The best-looking hostel in town would be a madhouse if it ever hit its 108-bed capacity, but until then it's an excellent option. Need a good night's sleep? Look elsewhere.

Hostel Alvear (☎ 421-6502; www.alvearhostel.com.ar; Alvear 158; dm AR$40; 💻) The best of the downtown hostels, Hostel Alvear is set in a rambling building with good common areas, pool table, foosball etc.

ARGENTINA

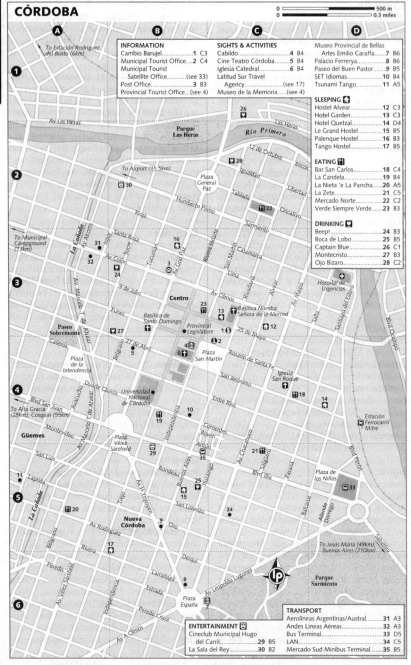

CÓRDOBA

0 — 500 m
0 — 0.3 miles

INFORMATION
Cambio Barujel...................**1** C3
Municipal Tourist Office....**2** C4
Municipal Tourist
  Satellite Office..........(see 33)
Post Office.......................**3** B3
Provincial Tourist Office...(see 4)

SIGHTS & ACTIVITIES
Cabildo............................**4** B4
Cine Teatro Córdoba........**5** B4
Iglesia Catedral................**6** B4
Latitud Sur Travel
  Agency.....................(see 17)
Museo de la Memoria.....(see 4)

Museo Provincial de Bellas
  Artes Emilio Caraffa......**7** B6
Palacio Ferrerya...............**8** B6
Paseo del Buen Pastor......**9** B5
SET Idiomas....................**10** B4
Tsunami Tango................**11** A5

SLEEPING
Hostel Alvear..................**12** C3
Hotel Garden..................**13** C3
Hotel Quetzal.................**14** D4
Le Grand Hostel..............**15** B5
Palenque Hostel..............**16** B3
Tango Hostel..................**17** B5

EATING
Bar San Carlos................**18** C4
La Candela.....................**19** B4
La Nieta 'e La Pancha......**20** A5
La Zete..........................**21** C5
Mercado Norte...............**22** C2
Verde Siempre Verde......**23** B3

DRINKING
Beep!............................**24** B3
Boca de Lobo.................**25** B5
Captain Blue..................**26** C1
Montecristo...................**27** B3
Ojo Bizaro.....................**28** C2

TRANSPORT
Aerolíneas Argentinas/Austral.........**31** A3
Andes Líneas Aéreas......................**32** A3
Bus Terminal.................................**33** D5
LAN...**34** C5
Mercado Sud Minibus Terminal.......**35** B5

ENTERTAINMENT
Cineclub Municipal Hugo
  del Carril....................**29** B5
La Sala del Rey..............**30** B2

Hotel Garden (☎ 421-4729; 25 de Mayo 35; s/d AR$80/110, deluxe AR$130/160; 🖳) About as central as it gets. Standard rooms are OK value, but the deluxe are several steps up in quality and a very good deal.

Hotel Quetzal (☎ 422-9106; San Jerónimo 579; s/d AR$100/150; 🍴 🖳) The neighborhood's a bit run-down, but the prices on these clean and spacious modern rooms are excellent.

Córdoba's hostel scene is exploding. Some more good ones:

Tango Hostel (☎ 425-6023; www.latitudsurtrek.com .ar; Rivera 70; dm/d AR$36/100; 🖳) Friendly if slightly cramped and noise-prone.

Palenque Hostel (☎ 423-7588; www.palenquehostel .com.ar; Av General Paz 371; dm AR$40, d with shared bathroom AR$100; 🖳) In a classy and atmospheric old building.

Eating

Cheap set lunches can be found in and around the **Mercado Norte** (cnr Tablada & San Martín). On weekends *choripan* vendors sell juicy Spanish chorizo in a bun for AR$6.

La Candela (Duarte Quirós 69; mains AR$12-15) A rustic student hangout featuring tasty and cheap empanadas and *locro*.

Bar San Carlos (Plazoleta San Roque, cnr Salgüero & San Jerónimo; mains AR$12-20) A neighborhood *parrilla* right in the center. The set lunches (AR$12) are a bargain, and plaza-side seating is a bonus.

La Zete (Corrientes 455; mains AR$15-25) The smells that hit you as you walk into this authentic Middle Eastern eatery are guaranteed to get your mouth watering, and the kebabs, empanadas and salads won't disappoint.

Verde Siempre Verde (9 de Julio 36; mains AR$15-25) Delicious, fresh, mostly vegetarian food, homemade bread and wholemeal pastas.

La Nieta 'e La Pancha (☎ 468-1920; Belgrano 783; mains AR$25-35; 🍴 dinner) An excellent menu of delectable regional specialties, creative pastas and house recipes. Grab a table on the lovely upstairs terrace.

Drinking

Córdoba's drink of choice is Fernet (a strong, medicinal tasting, herbed liquor from Italy), almost always mixed with Coke.

For bar-hopping, head straight to Calle Rondeau, between Independencia and Ituzaingo – two blocks packed with bars. If you can get a spot at **Boca de Lobo** (Rondeau 157), that'll make a fine start.

For a little more edge, check out **Ojo Bizaro** (Igualdad 176; 🕙 11pm-late Wed-Sat), featuring funky stylings in four rooms with DJs playing everything from '80s electrotrash to underground grooves.

Discos are mostly north of the center, along Av Las Heras. Music styles vary – listen for something you like and look for people handing out free passes. **Captain Blue** (Las Heras 124) gets seriously crowded, especially when bands play; there are plenty of others in this area.

The best disco in the downtown area is **Montecristo** (27 de Abril 350; admission AR$10-25). Come late and dress well. Nearby **Beep!** (Sucre 171; entry incl drink AR$10) is a recommended gay club.

Entertainment

Friday nights, the city hosts the Patio del Tango (admission AR$3, with dance lessons AR$6) in the historic *cabildo* (weather permitting), kicking off with two-hour tango lessons.

Cuarteto music (Argentina's original pop, a Córdoba invention) is predictably big here and played live in many venues. But it's also the gangsta rap of Argentine folk music and tends to attract undesirable crowds. **La Sala del Rey** (Primero 439) is a respectable venue and the best place to catch a *cuarteto* show. The hugely popular band La Barra plays on Sundays.

For art-house flicks at rock-bottom prices, check out the **Cineclub Municipal Hugo del Carril** (www.ccmunicipal.org.ar; Blvd San Juan 49; admission AR$10; 🕙 box office 9am-late).

Getting There & Away

AIR

Aerolíneas Argentinas/Austral (☎ 482-1025; www .aerolineas.com; Av Colón 520) flies regularly to Buenos Aires (from AR$415). **LAN** (☎ 0810-999-9526; www .lan.com.ar; San Lorenzo 309) flies the same route for AR$360.

Sol (☎ 0810-444-4765; www.sol.com.ar) flies to Rosario (AR$280) and Mendoza (AR$268).

Andes Líneas Aéreas (☎ 426-5809; www.andes online.com; Av Colón 532) flies to Salta (AR$355), Buenos Aires (AR$398) and Puerto Iguazú (AR$533).

The recently launched **Aero Chaco** (☎ 0810-345-2422; www.aerochaco.net) flies to Resistencia, but hadn't fixed its prices at the time of writing.

The **airport** (☎ 465-0392) is about 15km north of town. Bus A5 (marked 'Aeropuerto') leaves from Plaza San Martín. Buy an AR$1.25 *cospel* (token) from a kiosk before traveling. Taxis to the airport cost about AR$20.

ARGENTINA

DETOUR: COSQUÍN

Up in the hills, 55km outside Córdoba, this sleepy little town springs to life once a year for the world-famous nine-day **Festival Nacional del Folklore** (www.aquicosquin.org), held every January since 1961. Aside from that, there's not a whole lot going on, but the **aerosilla** (chairlift; AR$18) up Cerro Pan de Azúcar (1260m), 15km out of town, gives some great views over the valley. A taxi there costs AR$65, including waiting time.

Hotels in town include the basic **Hospedaje Remanso** (☎ 03541-45-2681; Paz 38; s/d AR$60/100) and the more comfortable **Hospedaje Siempreverde** (☎ 03541-45-0093; www.cosquinturismo.com .ar; Santa Fe 525; s/d AR$100/120). Accommodation can get tricky during festival time – book early or consider commuting from Córdoba.

San Martín between the plaza and the stadium is lined with cafes, restaurants and *parrillas*. **La Casona** (cnr Corrientes & San Martín; mains AR$12-25) has good homemade pastas plus the standard *parrilla* offerings. **Mama Rosa** (cnr Perón & Catamarca; mains AR$25-35) is probably the best restaurant in town. Frequent buses run to Córdoba (AR$8, 1½ hours).

BUS

Córdoba's **bus terminal** (☎ 433-1988; Blvd Perón 380) has departures for Tucumán (AR$96, 11 hours), Buenos Aires (AR$95, 10 hours), Mendoza (AR$100, 10 hours), Posadas (AR$180, 15 hours) and Salta (AR$165, 13 hours). International services include Florianópolis, Brazil (AR$421, 32 hours), Montevideo, Uruguay (AR$210, 16 hours) and Santiago, Chile (AR$185, 16 hours).

TRAIN

Córdoba's **Estación Ferrocarril Mitre** (☎ 426-3565; Blvd Perón s/n) has departures for Buenos Aires (AR$41 to AR$240, 15 hours) via Rosario. Book tickets well in advance.

Trains to Cosquín (AR$6, two hours) leave from **Estación Rodriguez del Busto** (☎ 568-8979) on the northwest outskirts of town daily at 10:25am and 4:25pm. Buses A4 and A7 from the central plaza go to the station or it's an AR$15 taxi ride.

AROUND CÓRDOBA

Frequent minibuses leave from the **Mercado Sud Minibus Terminal** (Blvd Illia), near Buenos Aires, to Cosquín, Jesús María and Alta Gracia.

Jesús María
☎ 03525 / pop 27,500

After losing their operating funds to pirates off the coast of Brazil, the Jesuits produced and sold wine from Jesús María to support their university in colonial Córdoba. The town is located 51km north of Córdoba via RN 9.

If you're only planning on seeing one Jesuit mission, **Museo Jesuítico Nacional de Jesús María** (admission AR$5) should probably be it. Easily accessed, but in a peaceful rural setting, it's been wonderfully preserved and restored and is crammed full of artifacts. For some reason there's a contemporary art exhibition on the top floor. Go around the back to check out the antique wine-making gear.

Buses run between Córdoba and Jesús María (AR$7, one hour).

Alta Gracia
☎ 03547 / pop 43,000

Only 35km southwest of Córdoba, the colonial mountain town of Alta Gracia is steeped in history. Its illustrious residents have ranged from Jesuit pioneers to Viceroy Santiago Liniers, Spanish composer Manuel de Falla and revolutionary Ernesto 'Che' Guevara. The tourist office, located in the clocktower opposite the museum Virrey Liniers, has a good town map.

From 1643 to 1762, Jesuit fathers built the **Iglesia Parroquial Nuestra Señora de la Merced** on the west side of the central Plaza Manuel Solares; the nearby Jesuit workshops of **El Obraje** (1643) are now a public school. Liniers, one of the last officials to occupy the post of Viceroy of the Río de la Plata, resided in what is now the **Museo Histórico Nacional del Virrey Liniers** (www.museoliniers.org; admission AR$5; ☼ 9am-1pm & 4-8pm Tue-Fri, 9:30am-12:30pm & 5-8pm Sat, Sun & holidays), alongside the church.

Though the Guevaras lived in several houses in the 1930s, their primary residence was **Villa Beatriz**, which has now been converted into the **Museo Casa Ernest 'Che' Guevara** (Avellaneda 501; admission AR$5, free Wed; ☼ 9am-7pm daily, 2-7pm Mon in winter). The museum focuses heavily on the legend's early life, and, judging by the photographs, Che was a pretty intense guy by the time he was 16, and definitely had his cool look down by his early 20s. Particularly touching are some of Che's letters that he wrote to his parents and children towards the end of his life.

For horse treks in the surrounding countryside, contact **Turismo Ecuestro** (☎ 43-2067; Liniers 158). **Rent-a-bike** (☎ 43-2116; www.altagraciabike.com .ar; Sarmiento 406) does what you would expect, for AR$5/40 per hour/day.

The **Altagracia Hostel** (☎ 42-8810; Paraguay 218; dm AR$35) offers spacious, clean dorms a few blocks downhill from the clocktower.

The long, narrow rooms at **Hostal Hispania** (☎ 42-6555; Vélez Sársfield 57; s/d AR$70/100; ⬚) are supermodern and set around a lovely garden area featuring a beautifully tiled swimming pool. Many of the rooms have balconies.

Parrillas and sidewalk cafes line Av Belgrano in the few blocks downhill from the Estancia. Out by Che's house, **Sol de Polen** (☎ 42-7332; www .hectorcelano.com.ar; Avellanada 529; mains AR$20-30) has good Cuban-inspired set lunches and a couple of basic rooms (doubles AR$100) out back.

From the **bus terminal** (cnr Perón & Butori), buses run every 15 minutes to and from Córdoba (AR$6, one hour). You can flag them down as they pass through town.

LA RIOJA

☎ 03822 / pop 181,400

This is siesta country, folks. Between noon and 5pm *everything* shuts down (except, for some reason, bookstores). Once the sun starts dipping behind the surrounding mountains, people emerge from their houses, and the city and its three gorgeous central plazas take on a lively, refreshed feel.

In 1591 Juan Ramírez de Velasco founded Todos los Santos de la Nueva Rioja, at the base of the Sierra del Velasco, 154km south of Catamarca. The 1894 earthquake destroyed many buildings, but the restored commercial center, near Plaza 25 de Mayo, replicates colonial style.

Information

La Rioja's **tourist office** (☎ 42-6345; www.larioja.gov .ar/turismo; Luna 345; ◷ 8am-9pm) Has a decent city map, good accommodation information and many kilos worth of brochures covering other provincial destinations.

La Rioja has no *cambios,* but several banks have ATMs. The **post office** is at Perón 764.

Sights

The **Museo Folklórico** (Luna 811; ◷ 8am-1pm & 5:30-9pm Mon-Sat) is set in a wonderful 19th-century house and displays ceramic reproductions of mythological figures from local folklore as well as *gaucho* paraphernalia and colorful weavings. The **Museo Inca Huasi** (Alberdi 650; ◷ 8am-1pm & 5:30-9pm Mon-Sat) exhibits over 12,000 pieces, from tools and artifacts to Diaguita ceramics and weavings. Both museums welcome the AR$5 voluntary contribution.

The **Convento de San Francisco** (cnr 25 de Mayo & Bazán y Bustos) houses the Niño Alcalde, a Christ-child icon symbolically recognized as the city's mayor. The **Iglesia Catedral** (cnr San Nicolás & 25 de Mayo) contains the image of patron saint Nicolás de Bari, another devotional object.

Festivals & Events

The December 31 ceremony **El Tinkunako** re-enacts San Francisco Solano's mediation between the Diaguitas and the Spaniards in 1593. When accepting peace, the Diaguitas imposed two conditions: resignation of the Spanish mayor and his replacement by the Niño Alcalde.

Sleeping

Accommodation in La Rioja suffers from two problems: it's overpriced and often booked out. The tourist office keeps a list of homestays where you can get a decent room with private bathroom for AR$50/70 (singles/doubles).

Country Las Vegas (campsites per person AR$10) The campground is at Km 8 on RN 75 west of town; to get there, catch city bus 1 southbound on Perón.

Hotel Mirasol (☎ 42-0760; Rivadavia 941; s/d AR$50/90) Nothing fancy, but a good budget choice in an excellent downtown location.

Gran Hotel Embajador (☎ 43-8580; www.granhotel embajador.com.ar; San Martín 250; s/d AR$65/85; ⬚) The best-value midrange option in town. Some upstairs rooms have balconies.

Pensión 9 de Julio (☎ 42-6955; cnr Copiapó & Vélez Sársfield; s/d AR$70/100) Large rooms with private bath and a lovely shaded courtyard overlooking Plaza 9 de Julio.

Eating

Rivadavia east of Plaza 9 de Julio is lined with cafes, restaurants and *parrillas.*

Café del Paseo (cnr Luna & 25 de Mayo; snacks AR$6-10) The coziest cafe in town offers great people-watching opportunities.

La Aldea de la Virgen de Lujan (Rivadavia 756; mains AR$15-25) Serves excellent homemade pasta and, very occasionally, regional specialties.

Stanzza (Dorrego 160; mains AR$25-40) Arguably La Rioja's finest dining. The steaks and pastas are good – creatively and carefully prepared – but the seafood dishes are the standouts.

Entertainment

New Milenium (San Martín 62; Thu-Sat) If you're in the mood for a megadisco (and aren't we all, always?), this is a central option for shaking that thing.

Getting There & Away

Aerolíneas Argentinas (42-6307; www.aerolineas.com; Belgrano 63) flies Monday to Saturday to Buenos Aires (AR$510).

La Rioja's new **bus terminal** (42-5453; Perón s/n) is 5km from the center. Bus 8 (AR$1.50) runs between the two. A taxi costs around AR$10. There are departures for Chilecito (AR$22, three hours), Catamarca (AR$23, two hours), Tucumán (AR$60, six hours), Córdoba (AR$66, 6½ hours), San Luis (AR$45, eight hours), San Juan (AR$66, six hours), Mendoza (AR$90, eight hours), Salta (AR$135, 10 hours) and Buenos Aires (AR$160, 16 hours).

CATAMARCA

03833 / pop 208,200

Surrounded by mountains and centered on shady Plaza 25 de Mayo, Catamarca is an attractive place. The only problem is that it lacks anything of any real substance to do. Once a year, the town gets mobbed by hard-core religious types, groupies of the Virgen del Valle. After that things quieten down quickly.

Orientation

The bus terminal is five blocks south of the center: walk out of the terminal, turn right, follow Güemes to the other side of Plaza 25 de Agosto, then hang a right up the pedestrianized Rivadavia until you bump into Plaza 25 de Mayo.

Information

Several downtown banks have ATMs.

Banco Catamarca (Plaza 25 de Mayo) Can change traveler's checks in 24 hours.

Municipal tourist office (43-7743; turismocatamarca@cedeconet.com.ar; República 446) Has a wealth of material on the town and surrounds.

Post office (San Martín 753)

Sights

The neocolonial **Iglesia y Convento de San Francisco** (cnr Esquiú & Rivadavia) contains the cell of Fray Mamerto Esquiú, famous for his vocal defense of the 1853 constitution. After being stolen and left on the roof years ago, a crystal box containing his heart is now on display in the church.

The **Museo Arqueológico Adán Quiroga** (Sarmiento; admission AR$3; 7am-1pm & 2:30-8:30pm Mon-Fri, 10am-7pm Sat & Sun), located between Esquiú and Prado, is a classic – crammed full of precolonial pottery, mummies, skulls, metalwork, and colonial and religious artifacts. It's not pretty, but it is interesting.

Festivals & Events

On the Sunday after Easter thousands of pilgrims from across Argentina honor the Virgen del Valle in the **Fiesta de Nuestra Señora del Valle**. On December 8, a colorful procession carries the Virgin through the town.

The **Fiesta del Poncho** is a more provincial event, held during two weeks in July.

Sleeping

Autocamping Municipal (campsites per tent/person AR$10/5) Gets heavy use on weekends and holidays, and has some ferocious mosquitoes. It's about 4km from downtown. To get there take bus 10 (marked 'camping') from Convento de San Francisco, on Esquiú.

San Pedro Hostel (45-4708; www.hostelsanpedro.com; Sarmiento 341; dm AR$30, d with shared bathroom AR$80;) A surprisingly hip little hostel just off the plaza. An annex around the corner is quieter and houses the double rooms. Free bike hire.

Residencial Tucumán (42-2209; Tucumán 1040; s/d AR$60/90;) The best of many options around the bus terminal.

Hotel Colonial (42-3502; República 802; s/d AR$100/130) The lobby's wrought-iron banisters and classy tilework mark this as the only hotel with any real style in town. Rooms are much blander, but comfortable.

Eating & Drinking

There's a bunch of restaurant/cafe/bars along the northern edge of the plaza. Some serve good-value set lunches.

Los Troncos (Mota Botello 37; mains AR$15-27) A neighborhood *parrilla* that gets two thumbs up (often while they're driving) from Catamarca's taxi drivers. And you know they know their stuff.

Sociedad Española (Virgen del Valle 725; mains AR$20-35) The Spanish Society is always worth hunting down for traditional Spanish dishes, including seafood.

Bars and discos can be found on Av Galindez (the western extension of Prado), reasonably close to the center; a taxi out here should cost about AR$5.

Getting There & Away

Aerolíneas Argentinas (☎ 42-4460; www.aerolineas .com; Sarmiento 589, 8th fl) flies to Buenos Aires (AR$510) from Monday to Saturday.

Catamarca's **bus terminal** (☎ 42-3415; Güemes 850) has departures to La Rioja (AR$23, two hours), Tucumán (AR$32, 3½ hours), Santiago del Estero (AR$28, four hours), Córdoba (AR$66, 5½ hours), Salta (AR$106, eight hours), San Juan (AR$89, eight hours), Mendoza (AR$114, 10 hours) and Buenos Aires (AR$150, 16 hours).

SANTIAGO DEL ESTERO
☎ 0385 / pop 370,100

Due to its central location, Santiago is a major transport hub, but unfortunately for 'modern' Argentina's oldest city, its list of charms pretty much ends there. If you're here on a Sunday, the Patio del Indio is a don't-miss, but after that even the tourist office is kinda stumped about what to do.

The provincial **tourist office** (☎ 421-3253; Libertad 417) is on the plaza. Several banks have ATMs. The post office is at the corner of Buenos Aires and Urquiza.

The **Museo Wagner de Ciencias Antropológicas y Naturales** (Avellaneda 355; ⏱ 8am-8pm Mon-Fri, 10am-9pm Sat & Sun) offers free guided tours of its fossils, funerary urns, Chaco ethnography and dinosaur findings.

On Sundays, the best place to be is the **Patio del Indio** (☎ 431-1227; www.indiofroilan.desantiago.net.ar; Av del Libertador s/n, Barrio del Tigre), an open-air venue hosting folk concerts starting around midday. The space is the brainchild of José Froilan Gonzalez, an internationally renowned drum maker who has made drums for Cirque du Soleil and Shakira's percussionist, amongst others. Midweek you can stop by to see him at work. Catch a taxi (AR$6): the area between here and downtown is definitely sketchy.

Sleeping & Eating

Campamento Las Casuarinas (Parque Aguirre; campsites per person AR$5) Offers shady campsites less than 1km from Plaza Libertad.

Residencial El Sauce (☎ 421-5893; Misiones 75; s/d AR$50/70) The best budget deal in town. The spacious, spotless rooms are out back, with shared balconies.

Hotel Savoy (☎ 421-1234; www.savoysantiago.com.ar; Tucumán 39; s/d from AR$125/180; 🛇) The eye-popping grandeur of the facade and lobby here make up for the fairly ordinary rooms. Pay an extra AR$30 for a balcony and wi-fi.

Mia Mamma (24 de Septiembre 15; mains AR$15-25) Santiago's all-purpose restaurant does good pastas, cheap *parrilla* (*bife de chorizo* AR$21) and some tasty homemade desserts.

Getting There & Away

Aerolíneas Argentinas (☎ 422-4335; www.aerolineas .com; 24 de Septiembre 547) flies daily to Buenos Aires (AR$702).

The **bus terminal** (☎ 422-7091; cnr Chacabuco & Perú) has frequent departures to Tucumán (AR$20, two hours), Catamarca (AR$28, four hours) and Buenos Aires (AR$90, 12 hours).

Trains leave from **Estación La Banda** (☎ 427-3918), 7km out of town, for Tucumán (AR$12 to AR$29, 3½ hours) at 7am on Tuesday and Saturday and Buenos Aires (AR$41 to AR$366, 21 hours) at 9:30pm Wednesdays and 12:15am Sundays.

TUCUMÁN
☎ 0381 / pop 830,300

A big city with a small-town feel, Tucumán is definitely improving in terms of the backpacking scene. There are some good hostels, a pumping nightlife and some excellent adventures to be had in the surrounding hills. Independence Day (July 9) celebrations are especially vigorous in Tucumán, which hosted the congress that declared Argentine independence in 1816.

Orientation

The bus terminal is a few blocks from the center, a decent walk if you don't want to fork out the AR$6 cab fare. Tucumán's **airport** (☎ 426-4906) is 8km east of downtown. To get there, catch bus 121, which passes the center and the bus terminal (AR$2), or take a taxi (AR$15).

Information

ATMs are numerous.

Maguitur (San Martín 765) Cashes traveler's checks (2% commission).

Post office (cnr 25 de Mayo & Córdoba)

TUCUMÁN

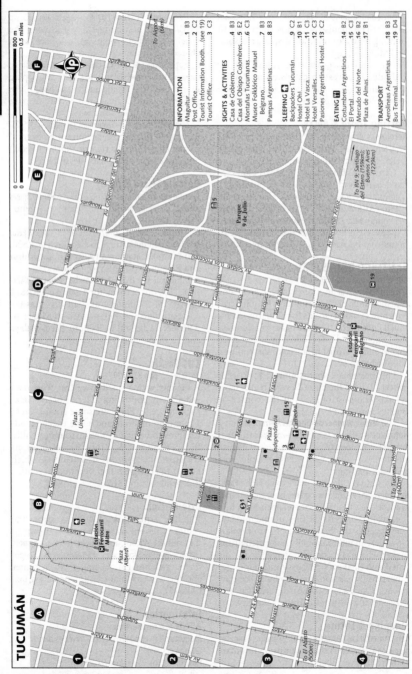

INFORMATION
Maguitur	1	B3
Post Office	2	C2
Tourist Information Booth	(see 19)
Tourist Office	3	C3

SIGHTS & ACTIVITIES
Casa de Gobierno	4	B3
Casa del Obispo Colombres	5	E2
Montañas Tucumanas	6	C3
Museo Folklórico Manuel Belgrano	7	B3
Pampas Argentinas	8	B3

SLEEPING 🛌
Backpackers Tucumán	9	C2
Hostel Oh!	10	B1
Hotel La Vasca	11	C3
Hotel Versalles	12	C3
Pasiones Argentinas Hostel	13	C2

EATING 🍴
Costumbres Argentinas	14	B2
El Portal	15	C3
Mercado del Norte	16	B2
Plaza de Almas	17	B1

TRANSPORT
Aerolíneas Argentinas	18	B3
Bus Terminal	19	D4

Tourist office (☎ 430-3644; Av 24 de Septiembre 484) On Plaza Independencia. There's also a booth at the bus terminal.

Sights & Activities

Spectacularly lit up at night, Tucumán's most imposing landmark is the **Casa de Gobierno**, which replaced the colonial *cabildo* on Plaza Independencia in 1912.

Museo Folklórico Manuel Belgrano (Av 24 de Septiembre 565; ☺ 9am-1pm Tue-Fri) displays horse gear, indigenous musical instruments, weavings, woodcarvings and Quilmes pottery.

Casa del Obispo Colombres (Parque 9 de Julio; ☺ 8am-1pm & 2-8pm) is an 18th-century house that preserves the first ox-powered *trapiche* (sugar mill) of Tucumán's post-independence industry. Guided tours in Spanish explain the mill's operations.

Montañas Tucumanas (☎ 467-1860; www.montanas tucumanas.com; Laprida 196, 1st fl) offers regular day and multiday trips involving rappelling, trekking, mountain biking, horse riding, rafting and more.

Courses

Pampas Argentinas (☎ 497-6125; www.ltargentina .com.ar; San Martín 980, 6th fl) offers individual Spanish classes for AR$52. Can arrange accommodation and homestays with advance notice.

Sleeping

Hostel Oh! (430-8849; www.hosteloh.com; Santa Fe 930; dm AR$30, d with shared bathroom AR$80; ☐ ☎) In nearly every way a wonderful hostel - spacious, friendly and atmospheric. The one downfall? The bed-to-bathroom ratio is heavily skewed in favor of long waits.

Pasiones Argentinas hostel (☎ 421-8131; www .pasionesargentinas.com.ar; Paz 336; dm/d AR$30/80; ☐) This is a basic hostel that wins points for being run by a group of young, enthusiastic travelers.

Backpackers Tucumán (☎ 420-2716; www.backpack erstucuman.com; Laprida 456; dm/d AR$33/85; ☐) An excellent downtown location, good atmosphere and spacious dorms. Tourist info and cheap meals offered.

Tucumán Hostel (☎ 420-1584; www.tucumanhostel .com; Buenos Aires 669; dm/d AR$33/90; ☐ ☎) Despite the rash of newcomers, it's still one of the best, with spacious dorms, good doubles, great common areas and a leafy garden in a beautiful old building.

Hotel La Vasca (☎ 421-1288; Mendoza 289; s/d AR$69/90, with shared bathroom AR$55/72) A good budget choice, the La Vasca's rooms have classy hardwood furniture and face a pretty courtyard. Bathrooms are aging, but well maintained.

Hotel Versailles (☎ 422-9760; www.hotelversaillestuc .com.ar; Alvarez 481; s/d AR$120/150; ☒) Tucumán's hotels tend to lack style, but this one has a few classy touches. Not many, but a few. Good location, too.

Eating & Drinking

Stalls at the **Mercado del Norte**, with an entrance at the corner of Mendoza and Maipú, serve good cheap food and great pizza.

Costumbres Argentinos (San Juan 666; mains AR$10-24) The food here is decent enough, but the real reason to come is the atmosphere: there's a sweet beer garden out back and live music Thursday to Sunday nights.

El Portal (Av 24 de Septiembre; mains AR$15-25) A rustic indoor/outdoor eatery with a simple menu. It's an excellent place to try regional specialties like *humitas* (corn dumplings).

Plaza de Almas (Maipú 791; mains AR$15-25) Although it can seat well over a hundred people, the well-designed spaces here, spread out over three levels indoors and out, maintain an intimate atmosphere. The menu is simple but creative, with a range of kebabs, meat dishes and salads on offer.

The stretch of Calle Lillo to the west of the market between La Madrid and San Lorenzo - known as **El Abasto** - is the place to go out; it's five blocks of pubs, discos and bars. This area really only kicks off from Wednesday to Saturday, but when it does, it really does.

Getting There & Around

Aerolíneas Argentinas (☎ 431-1030; www.aerolineas .com; 9 de Julio 110) flies daily to Buenos Aires (AR$586).

Tucumán's **bus terminal** (☎ 430-4895; Terán 350) has a post office, *locutorios* (small telephone offices), a supermarket, bars and restaurants, all blissfully air-conditioned.

Aconquija goes to Tafí del Valle (AR$18, 2½ hours) and Cafayate (AR$45, six hours).

Long-distance destinations include Santiago del Estero (AR$20, two hours), Córdoba (AR$96, 11 hours), Salta (AR$45, four hours), Corrientes (AR$94, 12 hours), La Rioja (AR$60, six hours) and Buenos Aires (AR$140, 15 hours).

Trains run from **Estación Ferrocarril Mitre** (☎ 430-9220; Corrientes 1000) to Buenos Aires Wednesdays at 5:40pm and Saturdays at 8:30pm (AR$39 to AR$300, 25 hours).

Bike hire is available from **Pasiones Argentinas hostel** (see p99).

TAFÍ DEL VALLE
☎ 03867 / pop 4200

Set in a pretty valley overlooking a lake, Tafí is where folks from Tucumán come to escape the heat in summer months. Off-season it's much mellower (which isn't to imply that there's any sort of frenzy here in summertime), but still gorgeous and makes a good base for exploring the surrounding countryside and nearby ruins at Quilmes (p102).

Information
The helpful **Casa del Turista** (☎ 421-084) is in Tafí's central plaza. **Banco Tucumán** (Miguel Critto) has an ATM.

Sights & Activities
At 2000m, Tafí, a temperate island in a sub-tropical sea, produces some exceedingly good handmade cheese. The **cheese festival**, held during the second week in February, is well worth a look (and, possibly, a nibble). At **Parque Los Menhires**, (admission AR$3; ☿ dawn-dusk) at the south end of La Angostura reservoir, stand more than 80 indigenous granite monuments collected from nearby archaeological sites. Take any bus passing El Mollar or a taxi (AR$15) or walk the 12km downhill towards the lake.

Sleeping & Eating
Autocamping del Sauce (☎ 42-1084; campsites/cabañas per person AR$10/35) The tiny *cabañas* with bunks would be very cramped at their maximum capacity of four people.

Hostel Nomade (☎ 15-440-0299; Las Palenques s/n; www.naomadehostel.unlugar.com; dm/d AR$30/80) The best hostel setup in town, with funky doubles and slightly cramped dorms around a grassy garden. A short walk uphill from the plaza.

our pick Estancia Los Cuartos (☎ 0381-1558-74230; www.estancialoscuartos.com; Critto s/n; s/d AR$150/190, with shared bathroom AR$100/120) Sitting right by the bus terminal, it's hard to stress what a bargain the beautiful rooms in this historic homestead are. Breakfast includes a platter of cheese made on the premises.

Parrillas line Av Perón, specializing in *lechón* (suckling pig) and *chivito* (goat). **Don Pepino** (Av Perón s/n; mains AR$20-40) is the coziest of the bunch and usually has live entertainment at mealtimes, but there are many others.

Getting There & Around
Tafí's **bus terminal** (☎ 42-1031; Critto s/n) is an easy walk from the center. Departures include Cafayate (AR$37, four hours) and Tucumán (AR$18, 2½ hours). Mountain bikes can be rented from **Hostel Nomade** (see above) for AR$5/40 per hour/day.

CAFAYATE
☎ 03868 / pop 12,600

Set at the entrance to the Quebrada de Cafayate, 1600m above sea level and surrounded by some of the country's best vineyards, Cafayate provides the opportunity to indulge in two of life's great pleasures: drinking wine and exploring nature. If you're pressed for time, you can combine the two and take a bottle out into the Quebrada with you, in which case we would recommend a local *torrontés*, provided you can keep it chilled.

February's **La Serenata** music festival draws big crowds.

DIY: IT'S ALL DOWNHILL FROM HERE

One of the best day trips you can do from Tafí needs no guide at all. Hire a bike, and start off downhill past the lake and out on to the road to Tucumán. It's a 40km (mostly) downhill cruise, following the course of the Río Los Sosa, with literally hundreds of gorgeous swimming holes and picnic spots right by the roadside.

Once you lose sight of the river and houses start appearing, you know the best part of the ride is over. You can hail any Tafí-bound bus (make sure you choose a safe place for them to pull over), stash your bike underneath and ride home in style.

There's no food or water anywhere along this route, so come prepared. And check your brakes before leaving, too – you'll definitely be using them.

Information

The **tourist information kiosk** (☎ 42-2442) is at the northeast corner of Plaza San Martín.

Sights

The **Museo de Vitivinicultura** (Güemes; admission ARS2; ⓨ 9am-2pm & 4-7pm Mon-Fri), near Colón, details the history of local wines. There are 14 wineries in and around Cafayate that offer visits and tastings – the tourist office has a list of opening hours and prices. Make sure you try the fruity white *torrontés*.

From 25 de Mayo, a 5km walk southwest leads you to the Río Colorado. Follow the river upstream for about two hours to get to a 10m **waterfall**, where you can swim. Look out for hidden rock paintings on the way (for a couple of pesos, local children will guide you).

Several operators around the plaza offer tours of the Quebrada for ARS50 per person. Try to go in the late afternoon, when it's cooler and the colors and photo ops are better.

Puna Turismo (☎ 42-2038; www.punaturismo.com; San Martín 80) offers quad bike tours for ARS80 to ARS450 for one to four hours and rents mountain bikes (ARS30/40 per half/full day).

Sleeping & Eating

Camping Lorahuasi (☎ 42-1051; RN 40 s/n; per car, person & tent ARS7; ⚊) Located 1km south of town. It has hot showers, a swimming pool and a grocery store.

Hostel Rusty-k (☎ 42-2031; rustykhostal@gmail .com; Rivadavia 281; dm ARS25, d with/without bathroom ARS70/60; ⚏) A wonderfully atmospheric hostel with some good common areas and a big backyard.

El Portal de las Viñas (☎ 42-1098; www.portalvinias .com.ar; Nuestra Señora del Rosario 153; s/d ARS50/100) An excellent-value budget spot just off the plaza. Rooms have terracotta-tile floors and spacious bathrooms and are set around a vine-shaded courtyard.

Hostal del Valle (☎ 42-1039; hostaldelvalle@norte virtual.com; San Martín 243; s/d ARS100/120; ⚏) Super comfortable rooms set around a leafy patio and garden. Go for the ones out back for privacy and ventilation.

Heladería Miranda (Güemes btwn Córdoba & Almagro; scoops from ARS3.50) This place sells imaginative wine-flavored ice cream with a considerable alcoholic kick.

Baco (cnr Güemes & Rivadavia; meals ARS15-28) Crammed full of rustic decorations, this is the most frequently recommended restaurant in town. It serves up interesting variations on Argentine standards and a good selection of local wines.

El Patio (cnr Mitre & Rivadavia; mains ARS15-30) Offers nightly folk music shows and a succulent *chivito a la parrilla* (barbecued goat; ARS25).

Cheap eats can be found at the various *comedores* (eateries) inside the **Mercado Central** (cnr San Martín & 11 de Noviembre). Restaurants around the plaza do good regional dishes at reasonable prices.

Getting There & Around

El Indio (Belgrano btwn Güemes & Salta) has buses to Salta (ARS35, four hours), San Carlos (ARS5, 40 minutes), up the Valle Calchaquíes, and Angastaco (ARS14, two hours).

El Aconquija (cnr Güemes & Alvarado) has departures to Tucumán (ARS45, six hours), passing through Tafí del Valle (ARS25, five hours). Take one of the daily buses to Santa María to visit the ruins at Quilmes (p102), in Tucumán province (ARS8, one hour).

For information on the tough but rewarding backroad trip between Cafayate and Cachi, up the Valles Calchaquíes, see boxed text on p102.

AROUND CAFAYATE
Quebrada de Cafayate

From Cafayate, RN 68 slices through the Martian-like landscape of the Quebrada de Cafayate on its way to Salta. About 50km north of Cafayate, the eastern Sierra de Carahuasi is the backdrop for distinctive sandstone landforms like the Garganta del Diablo (Devil's Throat), El Anfiteatro (Amphitheater), El Sapo (Toad), El Fraile (Friar), El Obelisco (Obelisk) and Los Castillos (Castles).

Other than car rental or organized tours, the best way to see the Quebrada is by bike or on foot. Bring plenty of water and go in the morning, as unpleasant, strong winds kick up in the afternoon. At Cafayate, cyclists can load their bikes onto any El Indio bus heading to Salta and disembark at the impressive box canyon of Garganta del Diablo. From here, the 50-odd kilometers back to Cafayate can be biked in about four hours, but it's too far on foot. When they've had enough, walkers should simply hail down another El Indio bus on its way back to Cafayate.

THE BACK ROAD: CACHI TO CAFAYATE

If you're in Cachi and heading towards Cafayate, buses reach Molinos and start again in Angastaco, leaving a 42km stretch of gorgeous, lonely road unserviced. Hitching is common in these parts, but traffic is rare and even the towns that have bus service have infrequent departures.

It's hard, but not impossible. The last thing you want to do is stand on the roadside with your thumb out. The best thing to do is, when you hit town, start asking around literally everywhere – the police station, hospital, *kioskos* – to see if anybody knows anyone who is going your way. Somebody will and you won't get stuck for long. If you do, there are decent, cheap places to stay and eat in Molinos, Angastaco and San Carlos.

You may end up in the back of a pickup truck with the wind in your hair and the mountains in your face. But really – this is the sort of adventure you probably had in mind when you booked your airfare.

Sound like too much? You can always ask at the *remisería* (remise office) in front of Cachi's bus terminal if there's a group going that you can join. Remises seat four passengers and cost AR$480 from Cachi to Cafayate. The stretch from Molinos to Angastaco should cost about AR$100.

Valles Calchaquíes

In this valley north and south of Cafayate, once a principal route across the Andes, the Calchaquí people resisted Spanish attempts to impose forced labor obligations. Tired of having to protect their pack trains, the Spaniards relocated many Calchaquí to Buenos Aires, and the land fell to Spaniards, who formed large rural estates.

CACHI
☎ 03868 / pop 5600
Cachi is a spectacularly beautiful town and by far the most visually impressive of those along the Valles Calchaquíes. There's not a whole lot to do here, but that's all part of the charm. The **tourist office** (☎ 0800-444-0317; Güemes s/n) is in the municipal building on the plaza. They have an atrocious city map and good info on hotels and attractions.

While you're here, definitely stop in at the **Museo Arqueológico** (☒ 8:30am-6pm Mon-Sat, 10am-12:30pm Sun), a slickly presented collection of area finds, including an impressive array of petroglyphs.

Todo Aventura (☎ 0387-020-4466; www.todoaventura.com.ar), operating out of the Nevada de Cachi restaurant by the bus stop, is the local adventure tourism operator, offering treks, horse rides and tours on bike and quad bike. They also rent bikes (AR$10/50 per hour/day) and quad bikes (AR$60 per hour).

For accommodations, check out the **municipal campground & hostel** (campsites/dm AR$5/20) or **Hostel Inkeñan** (☎ 49-1135; luisreicolque@hotmail.com;

Güemes s/n; dm AR$25, d with/without bathroom AR$80/60), a charming little hostel with good-value doubles. The best hotel in town is the **Hostería Cachi** (☎ 49-1105; www.soldelvalle.com.ar; s/d AR$156/184; ☐ ☒), with an excellent hilltop location and stylish, modern rooms. Some cheap restaurants surround the plaza. The most interesting restaurant in town is **Ashpamanta** (mains AR$20-35; ☒ dinner), just off the plaza, where all ingredients are locally grown.

It's difficult but not impossible to get directly from Cachi to Cafayate (see boxed text, above for details). It's easier to take a bus back to Salta (AR$38, 4½ hours), via the scenic Cuesta del Obispo route past Parque Nacional Los Cardones.

QUILMES
This pre-Hispanic **pucará** (indigenous Andean fortress; admission AR$5), in Tucumán province, 50km south of Cafayate, is Argentina's most extensive preserved ruin. Dating from about AD 1000, this complex urban settlement covered about 30 hectares and housed perhaps 5000 people. The Quilmes people abided contact with the Incas but could not outlast the Spaniards, who, in 1667, deported the last 2000 to Buenos Aires.

Quilmes' thick walls underscore its defensive functions, but evidence of dense occupation sprawls north and south of the nucleus.

Parador Ruinas de Quilmes (☎ 03892-42-1075; s/d AR$130/160) also has a restaurant.

Buses from Cafayate to Santa María pass the Quilmes junction, but from there, it's 5km to the ruins by foot or thumb.

SALTA

☎ 0387 / pop 551,300

Salta has experienced a huge surge in popularity as a backpacking destination over the last few years, and rightly so – the setting's gorgeous, the hostels are attractive, the nightlife pumps and there's plenty to do in and around town.

Orientation

Salta's commercial center is southwest of the central Plaza 9 de Julio. Alberdi and Florida are pedestrian malls between Caseros and Av San Martín. Bus 5 connects the train station, downtown and the bus terminal.

Information

There are ATMs downtown.

Administración de Parques Nacionales (APN; ☎ 431-2686; España 366, 3rd fl) Has information on the province's national parks.

Cambio Dinar (Mitre 101) Changes cash and traveler's checks.

Municipal tourist office (☎ 0800-777-0300; Caseros 711) Runs an information kiosk in the bus terminal in high season.

Post office (Deán Funes 140)

Provincial tourist office (☎ 431-0950; Buenos Aires 93) Very central.

Sights

CERRO SAN BERNARDO

For spectacular views of Salta and the Lerma valley, take the **teleférico** (gondola; round-trip AR$20; ☉ 10am-6:30pm) from Parque San Martín, or climb the winding staircase trail that starts behind the Güemes monument.

DOWNTOWN MUSEUMS

The **Museo de Arqueología de Alta Montaña** (Mitre 77; admission AR$30; ☉ 11am-8pm Tue-Sun) documents the amazing discovery of three mummies found at an altitude of 6700m on the Llullaillaco volcano. The climate kept the bodies and a collection of textiles and sacred objects found alongside them almost perfectly preserved.

The **Museo de Artes Contemporáneo** (Zuviría 90; admission AR$2; ☉ 9am-8pm Tue-Sat, 4-8pm Sun) exhibits the work of contemporary artists from the city, as well as pieces by Argentine and international artists. The space itself is world-class, well lit and expertly curated. Exhibits change rapidly, so it's always worthwhile popping in to see what's on there.

CHURCHES

The 19th-century **Iglesia Catedral** (España 596) guards the ashes of General Martín Miguel de Güemes, a hero of the wars of independence. So ornate it's almost gaudy, the **Iglesia San Francisco** (cnr Caseros & Córdoba) is a Salta landmark. Only Carmelite nuns can enter the 16th-century adobe **Convento de San Bernardo** (cnr Caseros & Santa Fe) but anyone can admire its carved *algarrobo* (carob-wood) door or peek inside the chapel during Mass, held at 8am daily.

EL TREN A LAS NUBES

From Salta, the Tren a las Nubes (Train to the Clouds) makes countless switchbacks and spirals to ascend the Quebrada del Toro and reach the high *puna* (Andean plateau). The La Polvorilla viaduct, crossing a broad desert canyon, is a magnificent engineering achievement at 4220m above sea level. The tracks have been plagued by maintenance issues in recent years and departures are not at all guaranteed. When it is running, most trips take place on Saturday only from April to November but can be more frequent during July holidays. The AR$600 fare includes meals. Contact **Tren a las Nubes** (☎ 422-3033; www.ecotren.com; cnr Ameghino & Balcarce) to get the latest news.

Activities

Whitewater rafting outside of town is available with various companies along Buenos Aires, near the plaza. **Extreme Games** (☎ 421-6780; www.extremegamesalta.com.ar; Buenos Aires 68, Loc 1) can take care of all your bungee-jumping (AR$78), Jet Ski (AR$85), horse riding (from AR$170) and whitewater rafting (AR$140) requirements. Transportation costs another AR$48. If that all sounds a bit much for you, **pedal boats** (per 20 minutes AR$8) are available on the lake in Parque San Martín.

Sleeping

Camping Municipal Carlos Xamena (☎ 423-1341; Libano; campsites per person/tent AR$5/5; ☒) Features a gigantic swimming pool. Take bus 3B from the corner of Mendoza and Lerma near the Parque San Martín.

Sol Huasi (☎ 422-2508; www.abaco.ya.com/solhuasi-web; Av Belgrano 671; dm/d AR$25/70; ☐) This is a basic hostel located in a cool old house. The traveler-run vibe and supercentral location are pluses.

ARGENTINA

SALTA

El Andaluz (☎ 422-9414; www.hostelandaluz.com
.ar; Córdoba 191; dm AR$28, d without bathroom AR$70;
🖳) Centrally located in an atmospheric old
house. Frayed but friendly.

Hostel los Cordones (☎ 431-4026; www.loscordones
.todowebsalta.com.ar; Av Entre Ríos; dm AR$30, d with/without
bathroom AR$80/100; 🖳) A sweet little hostel of-
fering a good range of rooms. The location
near the Balcarce nightlife zone is a bonus
for party people.

Residencial Balcarce (☎ 431-8135; www.residencial
balcarce.com.ar; Balcarce 460; s/d AR$60/80, without bath-
room AR$35/50) An honest little budget hotel in
a good spot. The beds aren't that great, but
everything else is.

Posada del Marqués (☎ 431-7741; www.posadadel
marques.com.ar; Córdoba 195; s/d AR$159/169; 🍴 🖳)

There are some lovely touches in this sedate
little inn a few blocks from the plaza. Rooms
are nothing special but the common areas
are charming.

Eating & Drinking

The west side of Plaza 9 de Julio is lined with
cafes and bars with tables out on the plaza;
there are some great spots for coffee, snacks
or a few drinks.

Mercado Central (Florida & Av San Martín) At this
large, lively market you can supplement inexpensive pizza, empanadas and *humitas* with
fresh fruit and vegetables.

Dubai (Leguizamón 474; mains AR$10-15) A small
but excellent selection of authentic Middle
Eastern dishes. Save room for dessert.

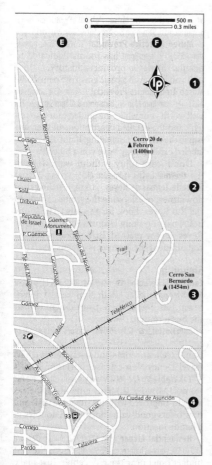

La Monumental (cnr Av Entre Ríos & López; mains AR$20-30) A straight-up local *parrilla* featuring excellent meat at good prices. House wines are average.

Cordova (Balcarce 653; set meals AR$25) In the stately dining room of the Spanish Society, this restaurant serves up some regional goodies plus excellent seafood and paella.

The **Mercado los Cerros** (cnr Ameghino & Zuviría) has been renovated and converted into a food court offering regional foods and upscale *parrillas*. Live music weekend nights.

Balcarce south of the train station is Salta's very happening *zona viva* – four blocks stacked with restaurants, bars and clubs.

Smaller bars include **Uno** (Balcarce 996), or check out **Bowling Pub** (cnr Necochea & 20 de Febrero)

for a full bar and eight lanes of 10-pin bowling. **Macondo** (Balcarce 980) is the place for a few quiet drinks (midweek, anyway).

Entertainment

For the megadisco experience, check out **XXJ** (Balcarce 915) and **Inside Club** (Balcarce 836). **La Vieja Estación** (www.viejaestacion-salta.com.ar; Balcarce 885; mains AR$15-40; ☺ dinner) is one of the best-known of Salta's many *peñas* (live folk-music venues).

Getting There & Away

AIR

Aerolíneas Argentinas (☎ 431-1331; www.aerolineas .com; Caseros 475) flies daily to Buenos Aires (AR$626).

Andes Líneas Aéreas (☎ 437-3514; www.andesonline .com; España 478) flies to Buenos Aires (AR$611), Córdoba (AR$355), and Puerto Iguazú (AR$533). **LAN** (☎ 0810-999-9526; www.lan.com.ar; Buenos Aires 92, Loc 1) flies to Buenos Aires regularly (AR$565).

Transport to Salta's **airport** (☎ 423-1648), 9km southwest of town on RP 51, leaves from airline offices about 1½ hours before the flight (AR$8).

BUS

Salta's **bus terminal** (☎ 401-1143; Yrigoyen) is southeast of downtown, an easy walk from most of the hotels listed here.

Géminis services the Chilean destinations of San Pedro de Atacama (AR$190, eight hours) and Calama, Chile (AR$200, 12 hours) on Tuesday and Friday mornings, connecting to Antofagasta, Iquique and Arica.

There are daily departures to Jujuy (AR$21, two hours), Cafayate (AR$35, four hours) and Cachi (AR$38, four hours), and departures to Molinos on Fridays only (AR$52, seven hours).

Long-distance services include Tucumán (AR$45, 4½ hours), La Quiaca (AR$57, seven hours), Resistencia (AR$114, 12 hours), Rosario (AR$185, 16 hours), Mendoza (AR$250, 18 hours) and Buenos Aires (AR$200, 21 hours).

Getting Around

Bus 5 runs between the bus terminal, downtown area and train station. **Pura Vida** (☎ 431-7022; Mendoza 443) rents bikes for AR$10/50 per hour/day.

SAN SALVADOR DE JUJUY

☎ 0388 / pop 333,000

If you're heading north, Jujuy is where you start to feel the proximity to Bolivia; you see it in people's faces, the chaotic street scenes, the markets that spill out onto sidewalks, the restaurant menus that offer *locro, humitas* and *sopa de mani* (spicy peanut soup) as a matter of course, rather than as 'regional specialties.'

Originally a key stopover for colonial mule-traders en route to Potosí, Jujuy played an important part in the wars of independence when General Manuel Belgrano directed the evacuation of the entire city to avoid royalist capture; every August Jujuy's biggest event, the weeklong Semana de Jujuy, celebrates the **éxodo jujeño** (Jujuy exodus).

Orientation

The colonial center of the city is Plaza Belgrano. Belgrano (the main commercial street) is partly a pedestrian mall. To get to the center from the bus terminal, walk north along Av Dorrego and across the river, keeping the hill at your back.

Information

ATMs are common on Belgrano, and banks should be able to change traveler's checks. The **post office** is at the corner of Lamadrid and Independencia.

Staff at the **municipal tourist office** (☎ 422-1326; Av Urquiza 354; ☾ 8am-10pm) in the old railway station are helpful and have abundant maps and brochures on hand. There's another kiosk just outside the bus terminal and a **provincial tourist office** (☎ 402-0254; www.turismo.jujuy.gov.ar; Gorriti 295; ☾ 7am-8pm) right on the plaza.

Noroeste (☎ 423-7565; www.noroestevirtual.com.ar; San Martín 134) is a recommended tour operator offering trips to provincial highlights plus more offbeat options like paragliding, snowboarding and community tourism.

Sights & Activities

Opposite Plaza Belgrano, Jujuy's **Iglesia Catedral** (1763) features a gold-laminated Spanish baroque pulpit, built by local artisans under a European master. In a small square next to the church is the **Paseo de los Artesanos** (9am-12:30pm & 3-6pm), a colorful arts market. On the south side of Plaza Belgrano, the imposing **Casa de Gobierno** is built in the style of a French palace and houses Argentina's first national flag. On the north side of the plaza, the colonial **cabildo** deserves more

attention than the **Museo Policial** (☾ 8:30am-1pm & 3-9pm Mon-Fri, 9am-noon & 6-8pm Sat & Sun) within.

Museo Histórico Provincial (Lavalle 256; admission AR$3; ☾ 8am-8pm) has rooms dedicated to distinct themes in provincial history.

If you have even a basic grasp of Spanish, the **Museo Arqueológico Provincial** (Lavalle 434; admission AR$3; ☾ 8am-8pm Mon-Fri, 8am-noon & 4-8pm Sat & Sun) is well worth your while: the guided tour is excellent, and the detailed descriptions of shamanism in the area are fascinating. If not, the poorly labeled exhibits may leave you a bit cold.

Don't leave Jujuy without wallowing in the **thermal baths** (admission AR$5; ☾ 9am-7pm) at **Hostería Termas de Reyes**, 20km northwest of downtown, overlooking the scenic canyon of the Río Reyes. Look for the bus (AR$2, one hour) passing along Urquiza with 'Termas de Reyes' on the placard. Bring food, since the restaurant at the *hostería* is expensive.

Sleeping

Camping El Refugio (☎ 490-9344; RN 9, Km 14; per tent AR$4 & per person AR$4) About 3km west of downtown. Bus 9 goes there from downtown or the bus terminal.

Club Hostel (☎ 423-7565; www.noroestevirtual.com.ar; San Martín 134; dm/d AR$35/120; ▢ ▣) Decent location, excellent rooms and friendly staff. The travel agency Noroeste (see left) is on site.

Yok Wahi (☎ 422-9608; www.yokwahi.com; Lamadrid 168; dm/d AR$30/90; ▢) This cute little hostel's actually improved with age (imagine that) and now offers good-value dorms and doubles in a handy location.

Residencial Alvear (☎ 422-2982; Alvear 627; s/d AR$70/90, without bathroom AR$50/70) This is the best budget hotel near the city center. Just make sure you're at the back, away from the noisy restaurant downstairs.

SPLURGE!

Posada El Arribo (☎ 422-2539; www.posada elarribo.com.ar; Belgrano 1263; s/d AR$210/230; ▣ ▣) An oasis in the heart of Jujuy, this highly impressive family-run place is a real visual feast. The renovated 19th-century mansion is wonderful, with high ceilings and wooden floors, and there's patio space galore and a huge garden. The modern annex behind doesn't lose much by comparison, but go for an older room if you can.

SAN SALVADOR DE JUJUY

INFORMATION	
Bolivian Consulate	1 B2
Municipal Tourist Office	2 D1
Post Office	3 C2
Provincial Tourist Office	4 D2
Tourist Information Kiosk	(see 23)

SIGHTS & ACTIVITIES	
Cabildo	5 D2
Casa de Gobierno	6 D2
Iglesia Catedral	7 D2
Museo Arqueológico Provincial	8 C1
Museo Histórico Provincial	9 C2
Museo Policial	(see 5)
Paseo de los Artesanos	10 D2

SLEEPING	
Posada El Arribo	11 B2
Residencial Alvear	12 C1
Yok Wahi	13 B2

EATING	
La Quebrada	14 C2
Madre Tierra	15 C2

Mercado Municipal	16 C1
Viracocha	17 C2
Zorba	18 C2

DRINKING	
Carena	19 C2
La Peluquería	20 D1

TRANSPORT	
Aerolíneas Argentinas	21 B2
Andes Líneas Aéreas	22 B2
Bus Terminal	23 C3

Eating & Drinking

Mercado Municipal (cnr Alvear & Balcarce) Upstairs, several eateries serve inexpensive regional specialties that are generally spicier than elsewhere in Argentina; try *chicharrón con mote* (stir-fried pork with boiled maize).

La Quebrada (Lavalle 289; mains ARS12-20) This great-value local eatery serves up a spicy *sopa de maní* and an even spicier *picante de pollo* (chili chicken with rice and vegetables).

Viracocha (cnr Independencia & Lamadrid; mains ARS18-28) Some places say they offer regional food, but this one delivers, with plenty of quinoa, llama and spicy favorites to choose from alongside a good range of steak and fish dishes.

Zorba (cnr Necochea & Belgrano; mains ARS25-35; ☯ breakfast, lunch & dinner) While they deleted all the Greek food from the menu (bummer!), the gut-busting Americano breakfast remains (sweet!) and it still offers the most interesting menu in town.

Madre Tierra (Belgrano 619; set lunches ARS30; ☯ breakfast, lunch & dinner) The vegetarian food here is excellent, and the salads, crepes and soups can be washed down with either carrot or apple juice.

As far as drinking in Jujuy goes, you have two options: the hip, minimalist **Carena** (cnr Balcarce & Belgrano; ☯ lunch & dinner Tue-Sat) or down-home and rowdy **La Peluquería** (Alvear 546; ☯ Wed-Sat), with live folk music on Wednesdays and Thursdays and your regular pub/disco scene on weekends.

Getting There & Around
AIR

Aerolíneas Argentinas (☎ 422-2575; www.aerolineas .com; Av Pérez 341), flies to Buenos Aires (ARS645) Tuesday to Friday.

Andes Líneas Aéreas (☎ 431-0279; www.andeson line.com; San Martín 1283) flies to Buenos Aires via Salta.

Jujuy's **airport** (☎ 491-1103) is 32km southeast of town. The airlines provide transport to the airport.

BUS

Jujuy's scruffy **bus terminal** (☎ 422-1375; cnr Av Dorrego & Iguazú) blends in with the Mercado del Sur. It has long-distance and provincial bus services, though Salta has more alternatives.

Chile-bound buses from Salta to Calama (AR$190, 13 hours) stop in Jujuy Tuesdays, Thursdays and Sundays. Make reservations in advance at the Andesmar office at the terminal.

El Quiaqueño goes to La Quiaca (AR$35, five hours), Humahuaca (AR$16, 2½ hours) and Tilcara (AR$16, 1½ hours). Cota Norte goes daily to Libertador General San Martín (AR$13, two hours), for access to Parque Nacional Calilegua.

Long-distance services include Salta (AR$21, two hours), Tucumán (AR$57, 5½ hours), Córdoba (AR$151, 12 hours), Mendoza (AR$201, 16 hours), Resistencia (AR$114, 14 hours) and Buenos Aires (AR$266, 24 hours).

QUEBRADA DE HUMAHUACA

North of Jujuy, RN 9 snakes its way through the Quebrada de Humahuaca, a painter's palette of color on barren hillsides, dwarfing hamlets where Quechua peasants scratch a living growing maize and raising scrawny livestock. On this colonial post route to Potosí, the architecture and other cultural features mirror Peru and Bolivia.

Earthquakes leveled many of the adobe churches, but they were often rebuilt in the 17th and 18th centuries with solid walls, simple bell towers, and striking doors and wood paneling from the *cardón* cactus.

Tilcara
☎ 0388 / pop 6800

The most comfortable of the Quebrada towns, Tilcara is also one of the prettiest, and it hosts a number of fine eating and sleeping options.

Tilcara's hilltop *pucará*, a pre-Hispanic fortress with unobstructed views, is its most conspicuous attraction, but the village's museums and its reputation as an artists colony help make it an appealing stopover. The tourist office, in the municipal offices, distributes a useful map. Banco Macro, on the plaza, has an ATM.

Tilcara is full of trekking and tour operators. Check with the tourist office for flyers. **Caravana de Llamas** (☎ 15-408-8000; www.caravanade llamas.com) offers llama trekking (the llamas carry luggage, not people) of varying lengths and difficulties from AR$160.

SIGHTS

The well-organized **Museo Arqueológico Dr Eduardo Casanova** (Belgrano 445; admission AR$10, free Mon; ☼ 9am-6pm), run by the Universidad de Buenos Aires,

features some artifacts from the site of the *pucará*. The room dedicated to ceremonial masks and their manufacture is particularly impressive. The museum is in a striking colonial house on the south side of Plaza Prado. Admission is also good for El Pucará.

The **Museo José Antonio Terry** (Rivadavia 459; admission AR$2; ☼ Tue-Sun) features the work of the Buenos Aires–born painter whose themes were largely rural and indigenous; his oils depict native weavers, market and street scenes, and portraits. Also featured is work from local and regional artists.

Rising above the sediments of the Río Grande valley, an isolated hill is the site of **El Pucará** (admission AR$10; ☼ dusk-dawn), 1km south of central Tilcara. There are fantastic views of the valley from the top of the fort, which has been brilliantly reconstructed in parts. The admission fee includes entry to the Museo Arqueológico Dr Eduardo Casanova.

Only a few kilometers south of Tilcara, the hillside cemetery of **Maimará** is a can't-miss photo opportunity.

SLEEPING & EATING

Autocamping El Jardín (☎ 495-5128; campsites per person AR$10) It's at the west end of Belgrano near the river and has hot showers and attractive vegetable and flower gardens.

Casa los Molles (☎ 495-5410; www.casalosmolles .com.ar; Belgrano 155; dm/cabin AR$30/90) Set in a beautiful old building just up from the plaza, the dorms here are spacious and simple. The cabins, set at the back of a pretty garden, are a real bargain.

Uwa Wasi (☎ 495-5368; www.uwawasi.com.ar; Lavalle 564; s/d AR$120/170, without bathroom AR$60/120) Beautiful, medium-size rooms around a vine-shaded courtyard. The mountain views from out back are alone worth the price.

La Chacana (Belgrano 472; mains AR$18-30) This place is set in a sweet little courtyard and offers nouveau Andean dishes featuring quinoa, wild mushrooms and local herbs.

Cheap places to eat line Belgrano between the bus terminal and the plaza. **El Cafecito** (cnr Belgrano & Rivadavia) is the place for coffee and croissants. The homemade cakes (AR$5) are worth keeping an eye out for.

ENTERTAINMENT

Nightlife is limited in Tilcara, but there are plenty of *peñas* around, hosting live folk music every night. **La Peña de Carlitos** (cnr Rivadavia & Lavalle) is probably the most consistent.

GETTING THERE & AROUND

Both northbound and southbound buses leave from the bus terminal on Exodo, three blocks west of Plaza Prado. Sample destinations include Jujuy (AR$11, 1½ hours), Humahuaca (AR$6, 40 minutes) and La Quiaca (AR$20, four hours).

Tilcara Mountain Bike (Belgrano s/n), opposite the bus terminal, rents bikes for AR$8/40 per hour/day. It also provides good area maps for day-trip options.

Humahuaca

☎ 03887 / pop 12,200

A popular stopover on the Salta–Bolivia route, Humahuaca is a mostly Quechuan village of narrow cobbled streets lined with adobe houses. There's plenty to do in the surrounding countryside, and the town provides some great photo opportunities. The **tourist office** (cnr Tucumán & Buenos Aires) underneath the clock tower keeps irregular hours but has excellent information on accommodation and local attractions.

Hasta las Manos Expeditions (☎ 42-1075; www .hlmexpeditions.com.ar; Barrio Milagrosa s/n) are the resident adventure-tourism specialists, offering sand-boarding at Abra Pampa (AR$120 full day) and trekking to remote locations.

SIGHTS

From the clock tower in the **cabildo**, a life-size figure of San Francisco Solano emerges daily at noon. Make sure you arrive early, because the clock is erratic and the figure appears only very briefly.

Humahuaca's patron saint resides in the colonial **Iglesia de la Candelaria**, which contains 18th-century oil paintings by Cuzco painter Marcos Sapaca. Overlooking the town is Tilcara sculptor Ernesto Soto Avendaño's **Monumento a la Independencia**.

Museo Arqueológico Torres Aparicio (Córdoba 249; admission AR$2; ☯ Thu-Sat 11am-2pm) has a small but interesting collection of local archaeological finds.

Ten kilometers north of Humahuaca by a dirt road, on the east side of the bridge over the Río Grande, northwestern Argentina's most extensive pre-Columbian **ruins** cover 40 hectares at **Coctaca**. Many appear to be broad agricultural terraces on an alluvial fan, but there are also obvious outlines of clusters of buildings.

FESTIVALS & EVENTS

Carnaval celebrations are particularly boisterous here, and on February 2, the village holds a **festival** in honor of the town's patron saint, the Virgen de la Candelaria.

SLEEPING & EATING

Hostal La Antigua (☎ 0388-15587-8969; www.hos talantigua.com.ar; La Pampa 81; dm AR$25, d without bathroom AR$80) The best dorms in the downtown area, set in a spacious house with friendly owners.

Posada del Sol (☎ 42-1466; www.posadadelsol.com .ar; Barrio Milagrosa s/n; dm AR$30, d without bathroom AR$90) One of the most atmospheric options around, just 1km over the bridge. Upstairs doubles have great views, and dorms are plain but comfortable. Call for free pickup from the bus terminal.

Casa Vieja (cnr Buenos Aires & Salta; mains AR$15-25) One of the more appealing restaurants in town, featuring regional dishes alongside Argentine standards.

GETTING TO BOLIVIA

Cold, windy **La Quiaca** is a major crossing point to Bolivia. It has decent places to stay and eat, but little to detain the traveler. However, If you arrive late at night, it's best to stay here as services are much better than across the border in Villazón. La Quiaca has no tourist office, but the ACA station on RN 9 has maps. The best place to stay in town is **Hotel de Turismo** (☎ 42-2243; cnr Av San Martín & República de Árabe Siria; s/d AR$70/120), but **Hotel Frontera** (☎ 42-2269; cnr Belgrano & República de Árabe Siria; s/d without bathroom AR$30/40) will do for a night if you're on a budget. Both places serve meals. From the **bus terminal** (cnr Belgrano & Av España), there are frequent connections to Jujuy (AR$35, five hours), Salta (AR$57, seven hours) and intermediate points, plus long-distance services.

The border is a 1km walk from the bus terminal. There is no public transport, but if there's a taxi around, they should be able to take you for AR$5. The border is open 6am to 8pm daily. For information on entering Argentina from Bolivia, see p209.

Quinoa (Buenos Aires 457; mains AR$24-28) specializes in 'Andean Gourmet' – think goat-cheese provoleta, coca-leaf mousse etc.

Many restaurants around town feature live folk music most nights.

GETTING THERE & AWAY

From the **bus terminal** (cnr Belgrano & Entre Ríos) there are several departures to Salta (AR$45, five hours) and Jujuy (AR$16, two hours), and northbound buses to La Quiaca (AR$16, two hours).

ATLANTIC COAST

The beaches along the Atlantic coast form Buenos Aires' backyard, and summer sees millions of *porteños* pouring into towns like Mar del Plata and Pinamar for sun and fun. The rest of the year, and in smaller towns, the pace of life rarely approaches anything resembling hectic.

MAR DEL PLATA

☎ 0223 / pop 589,300

On summer weekends, the beach in Mardel (as it's commonly known) gets really, seriously, comically crowded. We're talking people standing shoulder to shoulder, knee-deep in water. During the week, and in the nonsummer months, the crowds disperse, hotel prices drop and the place takes on a much more relaxed feel.

Founded in 1874, this most popular of Argentine beach destinations was first a commercial and industrial center, then a resort for upper-class *porteño* families, Mardel now caters mostly to middle-class vacationers.

In November, the **Mar del Plata Film Festival** (www.mardelplatafilmfest.com) attracts serious international attention, both for films that debut here and celebrities that attend.

Orientation

The airport is 9km northwest of town (take bus 542); taxis there cost AR$22, more in summer. To get from the bus terminal to the center, take bus 511, a taxi (AR$6) or walk 20 minutes.

Information

The **tourist office** (☎ 495-1777; Blvd Marítimo 2240) is near Plaza Colón. Most *cambios*, banks

and ATMs are near the intersections of San Martín and Córdoba and Avs Independencia and Luro. Free **walking tours** of the city (conducted in Spanish) leave from in front of the cathedral on Wednesdays and Saturdays at 5pm. Call ☎ 15-686-4333 to arrange one in English.

Sights

Now the Italian consulate, 1919 **Villa Normandy** (Viamonte 2216) is one of few surviving examples of the French style that was *en vogue* in the 1950s. A block away near the top of the hill, **Iglesia Stella Maris** has an impressive marble altar; its virgin is the patron saint of local fishers. On the summit, **Torre Tanque** offers outstanding views.

Museo del Mar (Av Colón 1114; admission AR$18; ☾ 10am-9pm) is probably the most extensive seashell museum you'll ever see. Based around central cafes on two floors are a small tide pool and an aquarium. It's a good place to rest and have tea.

Mardel's excellent new **aquarium** (Illia 5600; admission AR$55; ☾ 10am-7pm), 6km south of town, has all your regular fishy attractions, plus dolphin shows, swim with the sharks (AR$130) and water-ski and wakeboard classes (from AR$100). Bus 221 from the center gets you here.

Activities

AMBA (☎ 474-2320; Justo 3680) organizes scuba-diving trips from AR$150 per dive, including equipment.

Arcangél (☎ 463-1167) offers tandem parachute jumps for AR$120 and videotapes the experience for AR$70.

Escuela Argentina de Surfistas (☎ 15-400-2072; Yacht Club, Playa Grande) gives surf lessons on Playa Grande for AR$50 per hour, including equipment.

Club Mitre (www.josecordobatango.com.ar; Bolívar 3367) hosts group tango classes (AR$15), followed by a *milonga* on Mondays, Wednesdays and Fridays at 9pm.

Sleeping

Prices are about 30% higher in January and February, when it's worth making reservations.

Hostel Urbano (☎ 491-9083; www.hostelurbano.com .ar; San Martín 2445; dm/s/d AR$50/130/150; ☐) A spotless new hostel that's surprisingly tranquil for its central location. Kitchen access.

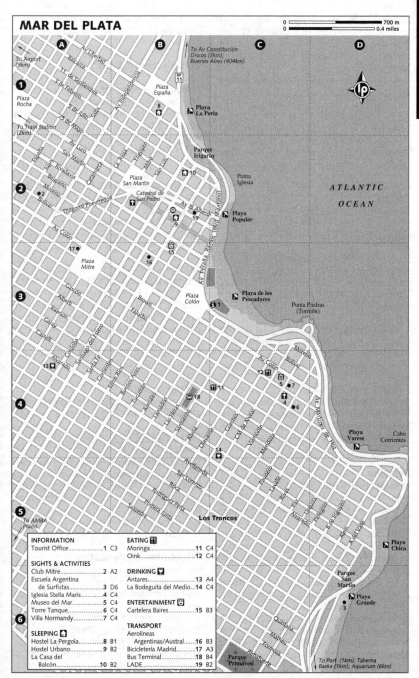

MAR DEL PLATA

Hostel La Pergola (☎ 493-3695; www.lapergola hostel.com.ar; Yrigoyen 1093; dm/d AR$50/150; ☐) Set in a beautiful 1929 stone house a block from the beach, this is one of the better-looking hostels in town.

La Casa del Balcón (☎ 491-5609; www.lacasadel balcon.com.ar; 3 de Febrero 2538; dm AR$50, d without bathroom AR$150; ☐) Antique-packed, with walls covered in contemporary art, this one feels more like a boutique hotel than a hostel.

Rates at Mardel's crowded campgrounds, mostly south of town, are around AR$10 per person; the tourist office has information about their facilities.

Eating

There are many *tenedores libres* in the center of town for AR$20 to AR$30, not including drinks. They're a great deal if you're a big eater.

Moringa (Alsina 2561; mains AR$25-40) This upscale Middle Eastern restaurant serves an excellent assortment of authentic dishes, including falafel, *kebbe* (a mixture of ground lamb and cracked wheat) and shish kebabs.

Taberna Baska (12 de Octubre 3301; mains AR$30-50) Forget the overpriced tourist joints down by the port – the best seafood in town is at this authentic Basque restaurant a few blocks away.

Oink (☎ 486-5251; Güemes 2364; mains AR$50-70; ☿ Tue-Sat) A slightly misleading name for one of the country's best nouvelle Argentine restaurants. Plenty of *juses* (juices) and reductions, and the seven-hour baked Patagonian lamb (AR$58) is a treat.

Drinking

La Bodeguita del Medio (Castelli 1252) This bar takes a fair stab at the whole Cuban thing, offering two-for-one-mojitos happy hours and a range of Cuban dishes.

Antares (Córdoba 3025) This microbrewery serves up seven of its own brews and a range of German-influenced dishes and meat-and-beer stews.

Weekends, the place to be is Calle Alem, down near Playa Grande – a strip of bars, discos and restaurants.

The discos on Av Constitución heat up late on the weekends. Check out **Chocolate** or **Sobremonte**, both of which charge AR$20 to AR$40 admission. Bus 551 runs from the center all night.

Check the monthly *Guía de Actividades* (available from the tourist office) for cultural happenings.

Getting There & Away

AIR

Aerolíneas Argentinas (☎ 496-0101; www.aerolineas .com; Moreno 2442) and **Austral** (☎ 496-0101; Moreno 2442) scoot to Buenos Aires (AR$293). **LADE** (☎ 491-1484; www.lade.com.ar; Corrientes 1537), is cheapest to Buenos Aires (AR$239) and also serves Patagonia.

BUS

Mardel's busy **bus terminal** (☎ 451-4506; Alberti 1602) has departures to Buenos Aires (AR$80, 5½ hours), Pinamar (AR$23, 2½ hours), Villa Gesell (AR$19, two hours), La Plata (AR$75, five hours) and Bahía Blanca (AR$95, seven hours).

TRAIN

The **train station** (☎ 475-6076; cnr Av Luro & Italia) is about 20 blocks from the beach, but there's an **office** (☎ 451-2501) at the bus terminal. In summer there are trains seven times daily to Buenos Aires for AR$52 in *turista* and AR$69 in *primera* (those under 25 get a discount in the off-season). The trip takes about seven hours.

Getting Around

You can rent bikes at **Bicicletería Madrid** (Yrigoyen 2249; per hr/day AR$8/40) on Plaza Mitre.

VILLA GESELL

☎ 02255 / pop 25,800

This laid-back dune community sleeps off-season, but in summer it's a favorite for young *porteños*, who stream in to party the warm nights away. It's one of the prettiest coastal towns: small, with windy, sandy roads sporting charming summer cottages (and grander retreats).

Orientation & Information

The lively main street, Av 3, sees most of the action; a section of it becomes a pedestrian mall in summer. Banks and their ATMs are also on Av 3.

There's a central **tourist office** (www.gesell .gov.ar; Av 3; ☿ Nov-Feb) near Paseo 108; another **tourist office** (☎ 45-8596; Buenos Aires), about a 20-minute walk northwest of town, is open all year.

The main **bus terminal** (cnr Av 3 & Paseo 140) is south of town; bus 504 or an AR$15 taxi ride will get you to the center.

Sights & Activities

Gesell's long **beach** and boardwalk draw swimmers, sunbathers and horse riders. There's year-round **fishing** from the pier. Surf classes are available from **Windy** (Paseo 104; per 3hr class AR$300) on the beachfront. Ask about kitesurfing classes – they rent gear to experienced kitesurfers only. Bikes are rented at **Rodados Luis** (Paseo 107; per hr/day AR$7/50) between Avs 4 and 5.

El Ultimo Querandi (☎ 46-8989; cnr Av 3 & Paseo 132) offers four-hour 4WD tours to the nearby lighthouse (AR$50 per person) that are a combination of hair-raising dune-bashing and excellent photo opportunities.

Feria Artesanal (Regional y Artística; Av 3), between Paseos 112 and 113, is an excellent arts and crafts fair that takes place every evening from mid-December through mid-March. The rest of the year it's a weekend-only event.

Sleeping

The most affordable *hospedajes* are north of Av 3. It's important to book ahead in summer, especially in the second half of January, when prices rise even more.

La Deseada (☎ 47-3276; www.ladeseadahostel.com.ar; cnr Paseo 119 & Av 6; dm AR$50; 🖳) One of the best-looking hostels on the coast, tucked away six blocks from the beach and a 15-minute walk from the center.

Surf Hostel (☎ 47-3277; www.danubiohostel.com.ar; Paseo 105 btwn Avs 2 & 3; dm AR$50; 🖳) Nothing special to look at, but an excellent location a couple of blocks off the beach.

Hotel Walkirias (☎ 46-8862; Paseo 102 btwn Av 2 & Buenos Aires; s/d AR$100/150) Rampantly ugly from the outside, the Walkirias has a good cozy feel to it on the inside, with exposed beams and spacious modern bathrooms.

Gesell's campgrounds charge AR$10 to AR$20 per person. Most close off-season, but **Casablanca** (☎ 47-0771) and **Monte Bubi** (☎ 47-0732), clustered at the south end of town on Av 3, are open all year.

Eating & Drinking

Av 3 is the place to go for pizzas, sandwiches, ice cream and *parrilla*.

Sutton 212 (cnr Av 2 & Paseo 105; mains AR$25-40; 🕙 breakfast, lunch & dinner) With its fabric-covered ceilings and Rajasthani lamp shades, this is one of the hippest places along the coast. Surprisingly, the food, imported beers and cocktails are all reasonably priced.

Rias Baixes (Paseo 105 No 335; meals AR$30-40) With its strip lighting and plastic chairs, this local *marisquería* (seafood restaurant) isn't about to win any interior-design prizes, but it definitely serves some of the freshest, best-value seafood in town.

The biggest concentration of bars is on Paseo 105, between Avs 2 and 3. The beachside restaurants are great places to have a few drinks and a snack at sunset, or have a meal if your wallet is up to the challenge.

Entertainment

Anfiteatro del Pinar (☎ 46-7123; cnr Av 10 & Paseo 102) Performances in January, February and Semana Santa. Gesell's Encuentros Corales (a choir music festival) take place annually in this lovely amphitheater.

Cine Teatro Atlas (☎ 46-2969; Paseo 108 btwn Avs 3 & 4) Such rock-and-roll greats as Charly García and Los Pericos have played this small theater, which doubles as a cinema during off-season months.

Pueblo Límite (☎ 45-2845; www.pueblolimite.com; Buenos Aires 2600; admission incl drink AR$20) A small-town megadisco, this complex has three dance clubs, two bars and a restaurant in summer. In the low season, it's just two discos – one for Latin pop, the other electronica.

Getting There & Away

Bus destinations include Buenos Aires (AR$78, five hours), Mar del Plata (AR$20, two hours) and Pinamar (AR$5, one hour).

PINAMAR

☎ 02254 / pop 23,200

Rivaling Uruguay's Punta del Este in the fashion stakes, Pinamar and the surrounding towns are where wealthy Argentine families come to play in summertime.

Orientation & Information

Libertador, roughly paralleling the beach, and perpendicular Av Bunge are the main drags; streets on each side of Bunge form large fans. The **tourist office** (☎ 491-680; Av Shaw 18) has a good map. The **bus terminal** (cnr Shaw & Calle del Pejerrey) is 12 blocks from the beach and seven from the center. The train station is a couple of kilometers north of town, near Bunge.

ARGENTINA

Sights & Activities

Many places are only open on weekends and in summer, but at other times you can stroll peacefully in bordering pine forests and along the wide, attractive **beach** without being trampled by holidaymakers.

Skydiving, glider and balloon flights can be arranged at the **Aerodromo Pinamar** (☎ 49-3953) and windsurfing with **Kuyen** (☎ 011-3561-8358 www.windsurf-kuyen.com). Bike hire is available from **Bike Store** (☎ 48-8855; Bunge 1111; per hr AR$5), quad bikes from **ATV house** (☎ 40-1279; www.atv house.com.ar; Cangrejo 1575) and dune buggies from **Buguilar** (☎ 49-2809; Av del Cazón 1354).

The **Pinamar film festival** (www.pantallapinamar .com) draws crowds in early March.

Sleeping

Several campgrounds, charging AR$15 for two, line the coast between Ostende and Pinamar.

Albergue Bruno Valente (☎ 48-2908; cnr Mitre & Nuestras Malvinas, Ostende; dm AR$50) The painstakingly slow renovations at this former hotel continue, but it still remains a good, cheap option in summer and a cold and dreary one in winter. It's close to the beach and far from the center, and some of the front rooms have balconies with sea views.

Hotel La Gaviota (☎ 48-2079; Calle del Cangrejo 1332; s/d AR$100/200) Spotless, smallish rooms and a comfortable patio area out back. There are others similarly priced on this block.

Eating & Drinking

Av Bunge is lined with restaurants, snack bars and ice cream parlors.

Con Estilo Criollo (cnr Av Bunge & Marco Polo; mains AR$20-30) Straight-down-the-line old-school *parrillada* – but it's well done, and the AR$30 set meal is a bargain.

Cantina Tulumei (Av Bunge 64; mains AR$30-40) Pinamar's best seafood restaurant is still going strong. Check out the seafood *parrilla* for two (AR$68).

Tavóla (Av Bunge 64; pizzas AR$30-40) Stone-fired pizzas in a traditional Italian setting. A good wine list seals the deal.

During summer the restaurants along the beachfront turn into bars and discos (don't worry – you'll hear 'em) and generally go until the break of dawn. In the low season, check the area bounded by Avs Bunge, Libertador and de las Artes. Solid bets are **Antiek Bar** (Av Libertador 27) and **Paco** (cnr Avs de las Gaviotas & de las Artes). Not

cool enough for you? Try **Black Cream** (cnr Jones & Av Libertador), possibly the Atlantic coast's only dedicated funk club, or **La Luna** (Av Bunge 1429), an almost impossibly hip bar playing electronica and reggaeton.

Getting There & Away

Bus schedules resemble those of Villa Gesell. Trains run in summer to Buenos Aires on Sundays (AR$70, six hours). Purchase tickets at the bus terminal.

BAHÍA BLANCA
☎ 0291 / pop 292,600

Mostly a stopover point for people headed elsewhere, Bahía Blanca is surprisingly cosmopolitan for its size, and boasts Argentina's worst-signposted museum.

Information

For the lowdown on music, art and theater happenings around town, pick up a copy of the *Agenda Cultural*, available in the tourist office, restaurants and bars.

Post office (Moreno 34)

Pullman Cambio (San Martín 171) Changes traveler's checks.

Tourist office (☎ 459-4007; Alsina 45) Almost overwhelmingly helpful.

Sights

The most worthwhile sight is **Museo del Puerto** (Torres 4180, Puerto Ingeniero White; ☺ 8am-11am Mon-Fri), a whimsical tribute to the immigrant population of Bahía Blanca. From downtown, buses 500 and 501 drop passengers a few blocks away – ask for plenty of directions.

On weekends there's a **feria artesanal** (crafts fair) on Plaza Rivadavia.

Sleeping

Balneario Maldonado (☎ 452-9511; campsites per person AR$8) The campground is 4km southwest of downtown. Bus 514 gets you there.

Bahía Blanca Hostel (☎ 452-6802; www.bahiablanca hostel.com; Soler 701; dm/s/d AR$35/55/80; 🖳) A new hostel set up in an old-school way, this one's short on charm but long on value.

Hotel Victoria (☎ 452-0522; www.hotelvictoriabb.com .ar; Paz 84; s/d AR$90/130, with shared bathroom AR$40/80) Has a good range of rooms in a classy old building. This well-kept old building has a range of basic, comfortable rooms set around a leafy central courtyard.

Eating & Drinking

Piazza (cnr O'Higgins & Chiclana; mains AR$12-25) A popular lunch spot right on the plaza, with an imaginative menu and a fully stocked bar. Chocoholics should not miss the chocolate mousse (AR$8).

Your best bet for midweek drinks is the strip of bars on Alsina between Mitre and Alvarado. Weekends, the place to go is **Fuerte Argentina**, a cluster of bars and discos at the north end of Salta. You can walk to there, but a taxi from the center should cost about AR$6.

Getting There & Around

The airport is 15km east of town. **Aerolíneas Argentinas/Austral** (☎ 456-0561; www.aerolineas .com; San Martín 298) has flights to Buenos Aires (AR$120).

The **bus terminal** (☎ 481-9615) is about 2km east of Plaza Rivadavia; there are many local buses heading into town (AR$1; buy magnetic cards from kiosks). To avoid the trek out to the terminal you can buy bus tickets at the handy downtown **office** (cnr Chiclana & Alsina) right on the plaza. Destinations include Sierra de la Ventana (AR$20, two hours), Buenos Aires (AR$94, nine hours), Santa Rosa (AR$55, six hours), Mar del Plata (AR$95, seven hours) and Neuquén (AR$70, seven hours).

The **train station** (☎ 452-9196; Cerri 750) has services to Buenos Aires Tuesday to Friday and Sundays. Fares are AR$39/63 in *turista/ Pullman* class.

SIERRA DE LA VENTANA
☎ 0291 / pop 3400

Sierra de la Ventana is where *porteños* come to escape the summer heat, hike around a bit and cool off in nearby swimming holes. The nearby mountain range of the same name in Parque Provincial Ernesto Tornquist attracts hikers and climbers to its jagged peaks, which rise over 1300m.

Near the train station you'll find the **tourist office** (☎ 491-5303; www.sierradelaventana.org.ar; Av del Golf s/n).

For a nice walk, go to the end of Calle Tornquist and cross the small dam (which makes a local **swimming hole**). On the other side you'll see **Cerro del Amor**; hike to the top for good views of town and pampas.

El Tornillo (Roca 142) rents bikes for AR$5/30 per hour/day.

Sleeping & Eating

There are several free campsites along the river, with bathroom facilities nearby at the pleasant and grassy municipal swimming pool (AR$4).

Camping El Paraíso (☎ 491-5299; Diego Meyer; per person AR$7) This full-facility campground opposite the municipal swimming pool is one of the best setups in town.

Hostería Maiten (☎ 491-5073; Iguazú 73; s/d AR$60/100) Spotless, older-style rooms around a lush courtyard. A good budget deal.

Hotel Atero (☎ 491-5002; cnr San Martín & Güemes; s/d AR$80/150; ⬚) One of the most comfortable options in town, with large, homey rooms right on the main street.

Sol y Luna (cnr San Martín & Tornquist; mains AR$20-40) An excellent menu of carefully prepared dishes. The trout with almond sauce (AR$36) is a standout.

Sher (Güemes s/n; mains AR$25-40) Of the various *parrilla* joints around town, this one has the best atmosphere and service.

Getting There & Away

Expresso Cabildo (San Martín 141) and **El Condor** (cnr San Martín & Namuncura) both leave twice daily for Bahía Blanca (AR$20, 2½ hours), La Plata (AR$107, 13 hours) and Buenos Aires (AR$99, nine hours). If times don't suit, there are various *combi* companies, including **Ventana Bus** (☎ 15-468-5101) and **Combi Dido** (☎ 456-4400), which run slightly quicker minibuses to Bahía Blanca for a similar price.

The train station is near the tourist office. Tuesdays to Saturdays, there's train service from here or nearby Tornquist to Bahía Blanca (AR$10, three hours) and Plaza Constitución in Buenos Aires (AR$41, 11 hours).

AROUND SIERRA DE LA VENTANA

Popular for ranger-guided walks and independent hiking, the 6700-hectare **Parque Provincial Ernesto Tornquist** (admission AR$10) is the starting point for the 1136m summit of **Cerro de la Ventana**. It's about two hours' routine hiking for anyone except the wheezing *porteño* tobacco addicts who struggle to the crest of what is probably the country's most climbed peak. Leave early: you can't climb after 11am in winter, noon in summer.

Friendly **Campamento Base** (☎ 0291-494-0999; RP 76, Km 224; campsites per person AR$10, dm AR$30) provides shady campsites, clean bathrooms and excellent hot showers.

Buses traveling between Bahía Blanca and Sierra de la Ventana can drop you at the park entrance, and there are also buses directly to the park from the village (AR$5, one hour).

CENTRAL ARGENTINA

Containing the wine-producing centers of Mendoza, San Luis and San Juan (which themselves comprise an area known as Cuyo), there's no doubt what Central Argentina's main attraction is. But once you've polished off a few bottles, you won't be left twiddling your thumbs – this is also Argentina's adventure playground, and the opportunities for rafting, trekking, skiing and climbing are almost endless.

HISTORY

Back in the 16th century, Spaniards crossed from the Pacific over Uspallata Pass toward Mendoza to manage *encomiendas* among the indigenous Huarpe. Though politically and economically tied to the northern viceregal capital in Lima, Cuyo's isolation fostered a strong independence and political initiative which later provided the basis for present-day Cuyo's defined regional identity.

Irrigated vineyards became important during later colonial periods, but Cuyo's continued isolation limited the region's prosperity. It wasn't until the arrival of the railway in 1884 that prosperity arrived; improved irrigation systems also allowed for expansion of grape and olive cultivation, plus alfalfa for livestock. Vineyard cultivation grew from 6400 hectares in 1890 to 240,000 in the 1970s, and many vineyards remain relatively small, owner-operated enterprises to this day.

SAN LUIS

☎ 02652 / pop 212,400

San Luis is coming up as a backpacking destination, but it still has a long way to go. Most people come here to visit the nearby Parque Nacional Sierra de las Quijadas. The commercial center is along the parallel streets of San Martín and Rivadavia, between Plaza Pringles in the north and Plaza Independencia to the south.

The **San Luis International Film Festival** (www .festivalsanluiscine.com) is held in the first week of November.

Several banks, mostly around Plaza Pringles, have ATMs. The **tourist office** (☎ 42-3957; www.turismo.sanluis.gov.ar; cnr Av Illia & Junín) has an almost overwhelming amount of information on San Luis' surrounding areas.

The large, multibed dorms at **San Luis Hostel** (☎ 42-4188; www.sanluishostel.com.ar; Falucho 646; dm AR$35) are a bit of a turnoff, but the rest of the hostel is beautiful. Staff can arrange trips to Sierra de las Quijadas and tours of local gold mines.

Av Illia, which runs northwest from the delightful Plaza Pringles, is the center of San Luis' moderately hopping bar scene. There are plenty of fast-food options along this street. **Las Pircas** (Pringles 1417; mains AR$15-30) is a more serious restaurant/*parrilla*. The menu is pretty wide-ranging, and touches like balsamic vinegar for your salad really make the place.

Austral (☎ 45-2671; Illia 472) flies daily to Buenos Aires, and the **bus terminal** (España btwn San Martín & Rivadavia) has departures to Mendoza (AR$42, 3½ hours), San Juan (AR$50, five hours), Rosario (AR$86, 11 hours) and Buenos Aires (AR$125, 12 hours).

REMOTE NATIONAL PARKS IN CENTRAL ARGENTINA

Central Argentina has an amazing range of landscapes, which is reflected in its national parks. For more information, log on to www.parquesnacionales.gov.ar. A couple of hard-to-reach, but extremely worthwhile examples:

Parque Nacional Lihué Calel (☎ 029-5243-6595; lihuecalel@apn.gov.ar) In a desert-like landscape in the middle of the pampa, this 32,000-hectare park is surprisingly biodiverse, playing host to puma, jaguarondi, armadillos and many birds of prey, such as the *carancho* (crested caracara), alongside flowering cacti and petroglyphs. Santa Rosa (p125) is the nearest town (226km away), but access is still complicated – hiring a car is the best way to see the park.

Parque Nacional Sierra de las Quijadas (☎ 02652-44-5141; usopublicoquijadas@apn.gov.ar; admission AR$8) Covering 150,000 hectares, this park features spectacular, surreal rock formations and dinosaur tracks and fossils. Hiking is excellent and camping is free, but be careful of flash flooding. The nearest town is San Juan (p123); its park office can help with transportation and logistics.

CENTRAL ARGENTINA

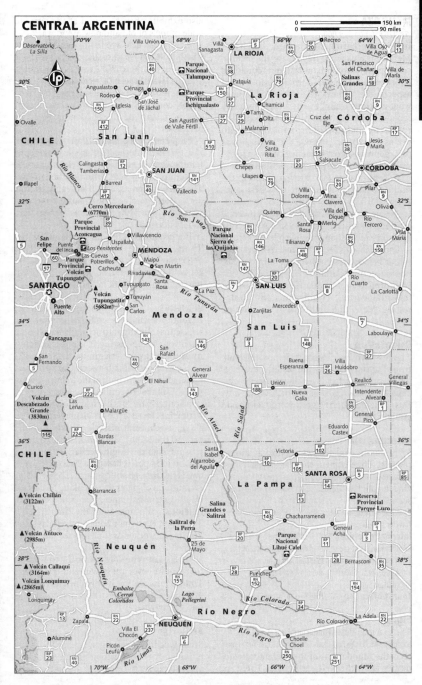

MENDOZA

☎ 0261 / pop 929,000

In 1861 an earthquake leveled the city of Mendoza. This was a tragedy for the *mendocinos* (people from Mendoza), but rebuilding efforts created some of the cities most-loved aspects: the authorities anticipated (somewhat pessimistically) the *next* earthquake by rebuilding the city with wide avenues (for the rubble to fall into) and spacious plazas (to use as evacuation points). The result is one of Argentina's most seductive cities – a joy to walk around and stunningly picturesque.

Add to this the fact that it's smack in the middle of many of the country's best vineyards (the region produces 70% of the country's wine) and the base for any number of outdoor activities, and you know you'll be spending more than a couple of days here.

Early March's **Fiesta Nacional de la Vendimia** (wine harvest festival) attracts big crowds; book accommodation well ahead. The surrounding countryside offers wine tasting, mountaineering, cycling and whitewater rafting. Many different tours of the area are available.

Orientation

The bus terminal is about 15 minutes' walk from the center; catch the Villa Nueva trolley if you don't feel like walking. Mendoza's **airport** (☎ 448-7128) is 6km north of the city. Bus 60 (Aeropuerto) goes from Calle Salta straight there.

Information

Wine snobs and the wine-curious should pick up a free copy of the **Wine Republic** (www .wine-republic.com), an English-language magazine devoted to Mendoza's wining and dining scene.

Cambio Santiago (Av San Martín 1199) Charges 2% for traveler's checks.

Information office (☎ 431-5000) In the bus terminal. Another kiosk is at the corner of Avs Las Heras and Mitre.

Tourist kiosk (☎ 420-1333; Garibaldi) This helpful kiosk near Av San Martín is the most convenient information source.

Tourist office (☎ 420-2800; Av San Martín 1143)

Sights

The spacious **Museo Fundacional** (cnr Alberdi & Castillo; admission AR$5; ☻ 8am-8pm Mon-Sat, 3-10pm Sun) protects the foundations of the original *cabildo*, destroyed by the 1861 earthquake. There are also exhibits of items found at the site and scale models of old and new Mendoza.

The Virgen de Cuyo in the **Iglesia, Convento y Basílica de San Francisco** (Necochea 201) was the patron of San Martín's Army of the Andes. Unique **Museo Popular Callejero**, along the sidewalk at the corner of Av Las Heras and 25 de Mayo, consists of encased dioramas depicting the history of one of Mendoza's major avenues.

Parque General San Martín, 2km west of town, is a forested 420-hectare green space containing **Cerro de la Gloria** (nice views), several museums and a lake, among other things. There have been reports of muggings in this park. Don't go alone, near dark or carrying valuables. Bus 110 gets you here from Plaza Independencia.

Plaza Independencia has a **crafts fair** Thursday through Sunday night, while Plaza Pellegrini holds its own weekend **antiques market** with music and dancing. Also check out the beautiful tile work in Plaza España.

WINERIES

Argentina's wines are constantly improving and, consequently, attracting international attention. Wine-tasting is a popular activity at the many wineries in the area. Bus 173 leaves from La Rioja between Garibaldi and Catamarca to get to both of the following vineyards. Call first to confirm opening hours.

About 17km southeast of downtown in Maipú is **Di Tomasso** (☎ 499-0673; Urquiza 8136; tours AR$10), a beautiful, historic vineyard dating back to the 1830s. The tour includes a quick pass through the original cellar section.

Also in Maipú is **Bodega La Rural** (☎ 497-2013; www.bodegalarural.com.ar; Montecaseros 2625; tours AR$10). Its museum displays wine-making tools used by 19th-century pioneers, as well as colonial religious sculptures from the Cuyo region. Tours run every half hour on weekdays and hourly on weekends, but less frequently in English.

Cyclists can consider biking a 40km circuit that would cover these wineries and more. Tourist information in Mendoza has an area map. See also boxed text, opposite, for details on visiting vineyards.

Activities

Scaling nearby Aconcagua (see p122) is one of the most popular activities here, but there are also plenty of operators offering rafting,

---

THE GRAPE ESCAPE

It would be a crime to come to Mendoza and not visit at least one vineyard. A crime, people. Depending on your budget and time frame, there are a few options:

■ Bussing around Maipú and Luján (see opposite)

■ Bussing to Maipú, then renting a bike/moped (AR$40/60) for a self-guided tour. Established operators in Maipú include **Bikes & Wines** (☎ 410-6686; www.bikesandwines.com; Urquiza 1606) and **Coco Bikes** (☎ 481-0862; Urquiza 1781). They provide basic maps and reasonable rides, but check your wheels (brakes, seat etc) before heading out.

■ A low-cost (around AR$70) tour, available through any hostel or tour operator. These are fine for your average Joe, but they can get crowded and rushed and tastings certainly won't include any of the good stuff.

■ A high-end wine tour with outfits like **Trout & Wine** (☎ 425-5613; www.troutandwine.com; Espejo 266, Loc 12) or **Ampora Wine Tours** (☎ 429-2931; www.mendozawinetours.com; Av Sarmiento 647). These start at around AR$400, but you'll be visiting some exclusive wineries in small groups and be getting samples of some of the finest wines that the region has to offer.

---

climbing, mountain biking and trekking, among other things. All the hostels listed in the following Sleeping section can organize these.

Inka Expediciones (☎ 425-0871; www.inka.com.ar; Justo 345) offers fully serviced guided treks to the summit of Aconcagua as well as logistical support for independent climbers.

Internacional Mendoza (☎ 423-2103; www.internacionalmendoza.com; Av San Martín 1020, Loc 3) offers rafting (AR$85), parasailing (AR$200), rock climbing (AR$150), and horse riding (AR$100). They rent bikes for AR$40 per six hours with an MP3 audio tour of the city included.

Ski equipment rental places operate along Av Las Heras during winter.

Courses

Fundación Brasilia (☎ 423-6917; www.fundacionbrasilia.com.ar; Villanueva 251) offers individual Spanish classes for AR$432/816 per 10/20 hours.

Sleeping

Note that hotel prices rise from January to March, most notably during the wine festival in early March. Some hostels in Mendoza will only rent you a bed if you buy one of their tours. Needless to say, none are listed below.

Parque Suizo (☎ 444-1991; campsites per 2 people AR$15) About 6km northwest of town, in El Challao, this woody campground has hot showers, laundry facilities and a grocery. Get here on Bus 110, which leaves from Av Alem just east of Av San Martín and from Av Sarmiento.

Quinta Hostel (☎ 420-4478; Olascoaga 1323; dm AR$35, d without bathroom AR$90; 🖵) A sweet little back-to-basics hostel. None of the frills of the larger hostels, but if all you want is a bed, this is a good deal.

Break Point (☎ 423-9514; www.breakpointhostel.com.ar; Villanueva 241; dm/d AR$50/150; 🖵 🐾) Large dorms (sleeping eight) in a big old house. The pool and lounge areas are excellent, but it loses points for undersupply of bathrooms and the noisy bar downstairs.

Damajuana Hostel (☎ 425-5858; www.damajuanahostel.com.ar; Villanueva 282; dm/d AR$60/150; 🖵 🐾) Mendoza's best-looking hostel is all class – great lounge areas, fast, free internet and a good grassy backyard with a decent-size pool.

Hospedaje Sao Paolo (☎ 423-1763; Gutiérrez 490; r AR$80) A serious budget hotel. There's no frills here, but for the location the price is right.

Hotel Casino (☎ 425-6666; Gutiérrez 668; s/d AR$100/120; 🗗) Some good, spacious rooms and some smallish, ordinary ones. They're all clean and comfortable, but have a look at a few before deciding.

Eating

Sidewalk restaurants on pedestrian Av Sarmiento are fine places to people-watch. The restaurants along Avs Las Heras and San Martín offer good-value set meals; see signboards for details. The renovated **Mercado Central** (cnr Av Las Heras & Mendocinas) is a good hunting ground for cheap pizza, empanadas and sandwiches.

MENDOZA

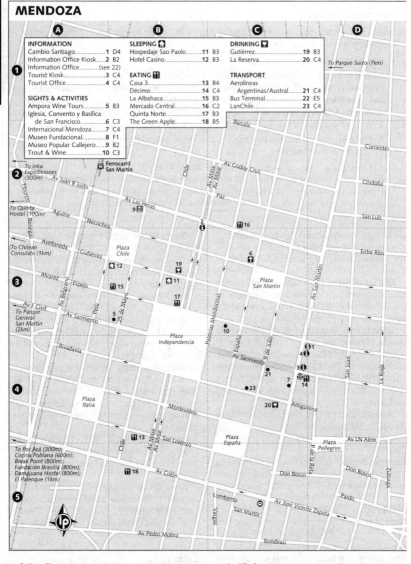

INFORMATION
Cambio Santiago................1 D4
Information Office Kiosk....2 B2
Information Office............(see 22)
Tourist Kiosk......................3 C4
Tourist Office....................4 C4

SIGHTS & ACTIVITIES
Ampora Wine Tours............5 B3
Iglesia, Convento y Basílica
   de San Francisco............6 C3
Internacional Mendoza.......7 C4
Museo Fundacional............8 F1
Museo Popular Callejero.....9 B2
Trout & Wine...................10 C3

SLEEPING
Hospedaje Sao Paolo........11 B3
Hotel Casino....................12 B3

EATING
Casa 3.............................13 B4
Décimo...........................14 C4
La Albahaca....................15 B3
Mercado Central..............16 C2
Quinta Norte...................17 B3
The Green Apple..............18 B5

DRINKING
Gutiérrez.........................19 B3
La Reserva.......................20 C4

TRANSPORT
Aerolíneas
   Argentinas/Austral........21 C4
Bus Terminal...................22 E5
LanChile..........................23 C4

Quinta Norte (cnr Espejo & Av Mitre; mains AR$20-30) A good range of daily specials and shady sidewalk seating make this one a winner.

El Palenque (☎ 15-454-8023; Villanueva 287; mains AR$20-40) Popular for years and still going strong, this casual restaurant/bar serves up some good standards with a few surprises thrown in. Come early or book ahead.

La Albahaca (Espejo 659; mains AR$22-35) In a country where 'Italian' food is abundant but can often disappoint, this is the real deal. The *fettucine puttanesca* (AR$26) is everything it should be.

Décimo (cnr Av San Martín & Garibaldi, 10th fl; mains AR$25-40) This place is worth it for the views alone, but it has a small, creative menu, too.

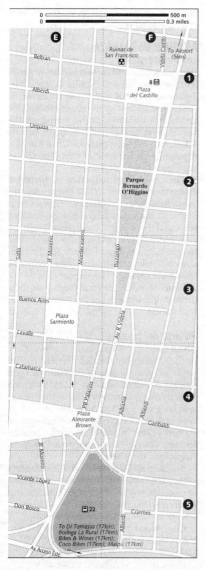

There's no sign at street level – get the elevator from the entrance on Garibaldi.

The Green Apple (Av Colón 460; buffets AR$30; ⏰ Mon-Sat) Vegetarian restaurants are a bit light on the ground around here, but this one's been doing it for years. Good salads, pies and desserts.

There are literally dozens of excellent restaurants in Mendoza. A couple more:

Casa 3 (San Lorenzo 490; mains AR$15-20) A hip little bar/restaurant. Good music, tasty food and lots of cocktails.

Cocina Poblana (Villanueva 217; mains AR$15-25) Tasty, inexpensive Middle Eastern food comes as a welcome break from all that steak.

Drinking

Av Villanueva, west of the center, is ground zero in terms of Mendoza's happening bar scene. Going for a wander is your best bet, but here are a few to get you started.

Por Acá (Villanueva 557) Purple and yellow outside and polka-dotted upstairs, this bar-cum-lounge gets packed after 2am, and by the end of the night, dancing on the tables is not uncommon. Good retro dance music.

La Reserva (Rivadavia 34; admission free-AR$15) This small, nominally gay bar packs in a mixed crowd and has outrageous drag shows at midnight every night, with hard-core techno later.

Gutiérrez (Gutiérrez 435; admission AR$10-30) The best downtown dance club, with various theme nights, including Tuesday's 'hostel night.'

Getting There & Away

AIR

Aerolíneas Argentinas/Austral (☎ 420-4185; www.aerolineas.com; Av Sarmiento 82) has daily flights to Buenos Aires from AR$514.

Sol (☎ 0810-4444-765; www.sol.com.ar) flies to Córdoba (AR$268) and Rosario (AR$410).

LANChile (☎ 425-7900; Rivadavia 135) flies twice daily to Santiago de Chile (AR$1152).

BUS

The **bus terminal** (☎ 431-1299) is about 10 blocks east of the town center. See the table on the next page for sample destinations and fares.

Getting Around

Mendoza buses take magnetic fare cards, sold at kiosks in multiple values of the AR$1.10 fare. Trolleys cost AR$1.10 in coins.

Internacional Mendoza rents bikes; see p119 for more information.

USPALLATA

☎ 02624 / pop 3800

In an exceptionally beautiful valley surrounded by polychrome mountains, 105km west of Mendoza at an altitude of 1751m, this crossroads village along RN 7 is a good base for exploring the surrounding area, which served as a location for the Brad Pitt epic *Seven Years in Tibet*.

BUS FARES

Destination	Cost (AR$)	Duration (hr)
Aconcagua	30	3½
Buenos Aires	170	14
Córdoba	100	9
Las Leñas	80	7
Los Penitentes	48	4
Malargüe	50	6
Neuquén	120	12
San Juan	20	2
San Luis	42	3½
Tucumán	165	14
Uspallata	20	2
Valparaíso	85	8

Sights

One kilometer north of the highway junction toward Villavicencio, a signed side road leads to ruins and a museum at the **Bóvedas Históricas Uspallata**, a metallurgical site since pre-Columbian times. About 4km north of Uspallata, in a volcanic outcrop near a small monument to San Ceferino Namuncurá, is a faded but still visible set of **petroglyphs**. The **tourist information office** (☎ 42-0009; RN 7 s/n; ☺ 9am-8pm) is opposite the YPF station.

Sleeping & Eating

Camping Municipal (campsites AR$8; ☒) Uspallata's poplar-shaded campground is 500m north of the Villavicencio junction.

Hostel International Uspallata (☎ 15-466-7240; www.hosteluspallata.com.ar; RN 7 s/n; dm/d AR$40/140) A beautiful, spacious hostel set in breathtaking countryside 5km out of Uspallata (aka the middle of nowhere). From Mendoza or Uspallata, tell the driver you're getting off here. Otherwise it's a AR$12 *remise* ride from town.

El Portico del Valle (☎ 42-0103; porticodelvalle@hotmail .com; cnr Las Heras & RN 7; s/d AR$110/150; ☒) Comfy and airy rooms by the junction. Further up Las Heras are a couple of good, cheaper hotels.

El Rancho (cnr RN 7 & Cerro Chacay; mains AR$20-30) The coziest *parrilla* in town, serving all the usual, plus a good roasted *chivo*.

Getting There & Away

The bus terminal is tucked behind the new, rampantly ugly casino on the main drag. There are departures for Mendoza (AR$15, 2½ hours) and Puente del Inca (AR$10, one hour) and points in between. Santiago-bound buses will carry passengers to and across the border but are often full; in winter, the pass can close to all traffic for weeks at a time.

AROUND USPALLATA
Los Penitentes

Both the terrain and snow cover can be excellent for downhill and Nordic skiing at Los Penitentes (☎ 02624-42-0229), two hours southwest of Uspallata at an altitude of 2580m. Lifts and accommodations are very modern; the maximum vertical drop on its 21 runs exceeds 700m. A day ski pass costs AR$75 to AR$115, depending on the time of year. The season runs from June to September.

The cozy converted cabin of **Hostel Los Penitentes** (in Mendoza ☎ 0261-438-1166; www.penitentes .com.ar; dm AR$70) accommodates 38 in very close quarters, and has a kitchen, wood-burning stove and three shared bathrooms. Meals are available for AR$15, and dorm rates are halved in summer. The hostel offers Nordic- and downhill-skiing trips in winter and Aconcagua treks and expeditions in summer.

From Mendoza, several buses pass daily through Uspallata to Los Penitentes (AR$48, four hours).

Puente del Inca

About 8km west of Los Penitentes, on the way to the Chilean border and near the turnoff to Aconcagua, is one of Argentina's most striking wonders. Situated 2720m above sea level, Puente del Inca is a natural stone bridge spanning the Río Mendoza. Underneath it, rock walls and the ruins of an old spa are stained yellow by warm, sulfurous thermal springs. You can hike into Parque Provincial Aconcagua from here.

The little, no-frills hostel of **La Vieja Estación** (in Mendoza ☎ 0261-452-1103; www.incahostel.com.ar; campsites per person AR$8, dm AR$35) offers mountain climbing, glacier trekking and snowshoeing. A cheap restaurant and bar are also on the premises.

Cozy, wood-paneled rooms and a big dining hall give **Hostería Puente del Inca** (☎ 02624-42-0222; s/d AR$120/140) a real ski-lodge feel.

Daily buses to Mendoza take about four hours (AR$52).

PARQUE PROVINCIAL ACONCAGUA

On the Chilean border, Parque Provincial Aconcagua protects 71,000 hectares of high country surrounding the western hemisphere's highest summit – 6962m Cerro Aconcagua. There are trekking possibilities to base camps and refuges beneath the permanent snow line.

Reaching Aconcagua's summit requires at least 13 to 15 days, including some time for acclimatization. Potential climbers should get RJ Secor's climbing guide, *Aconcagua*, and check www.aconcagua.com.ar and www.aconcagua.mendoza.gov.ar for more information.

Mid-November to mid-March, permits are mandatory for trekking and climbing; these permits vary from AR$60 to AR$600 for trekkers and AR$1500 to AR$2000 for climbers, depending on the date. Mid-December to late January is high season. Purchase permits in Mendoza in the main **tourist office** (☎ 0261-420-2800; Av San Martín 1143).

Many adventure-travel agencies in and around Mendoza arrange excursions into the high mountains. See the Mendoza Activities section (p118) for details.

SAN JUAN

☎ 0264 / pop 486,600

Smelling kerosene? Don't panic – that's just the proud folks of San Juan *polishing their sidewalks*. Uh-huh. An attractive enough place, San Juan's big claim to fame are the nearby wineries and access to Parque Provincial Ischigualasto.

Rather than changing names as they intersect the central plaza (which is what happens in most Argentine towns), streets in San Juan keep their name but are designated by compass points, with street numbers starting at zero at the plaza and rising from there. Thus there will be two Laprida 150s - one Laprida 150 Este and one Laprida 150 Oeste.

The **tourist office** (☎ 422-2431; www.turismo.sanjuan.gov.ar; Sarmiento 24 Sur) also has a smaller branch at the bus terminal. **Cambio Santiago** is at Gral Acha 52 Sur, and there are several ATMs. The **post office** is on Roza near Tucumán.

Sights

The **Museo de Ciencias Naturales** (cnr España & Maipú; ☾ 9am-1pm), now in the old train station, has exhibits of Triassic dinosaur skeletons found in the area, and you can see the preparation labs.

Museo de Vino Santiago Graffigna (Colón 1342 Nte; ☾ 9am-5:30pm Mon-Sat, 10am-4pm Sun) is a wine museum that's well worth a visit if you're not planning on visiting any of the area wineries. Take bus 12A from in front of the tourist office on Sarmiento (AR$1.50, 15 minutes).

Sleeping & Eating

Camping El Pinar (RP 113, Km 14; campsites per person AR$2, per tent AR$5) Buses go to this woodsy municipal site on Benavídez Oeste, located about 6km west of downtown.

San Juan Hostel (☎ 420-1835; www.sanjuanhostel.com; Córdoba 317 Este; dm/s/d AR$35/80/100; ◻) Simple, spacious and friendly, this hostel is in a good spot between the terminal and center. Good info on tours and local attractions.

Zonda Hostel (☎ 420-1009; www.zondahostel.com.ar; Caseros 486 Este; dm/d AR$40/100; ◻) The coziest hostel in town, set in a great house a couple of blocks from the bus terminal. Good facilities, mediocre staff.

Hotel Alhambra (☎ 421-4780; www.alhambrahotel.com.ar; Acha 180 Sur; s/d AR$120/150; ⌨) Comfy, slightly cramped rooms in an excellent location just off the plaza.

Remolacha (cnr de la Roza & Sarmiento; mains AR$15-30) The best *parrilla* in town features a lovely garden area out front.

Soychú (Roza 223 Oeste; buffets AR$12) At the other end of the carnivore scale, this friendly vegetarian eatery has a seriously good selection of food and fresh juices.

The pedestrian section of Rivadavia is crammed with sidewalk cafes and fast-food joints.

Getting There & Away

Aerolíneas Argentinas/Austral (☎ 421-4158; San Martín 215 Oeste) fly daily to Buenos Aires for AR$528.

The **bus terminal** (☎ 422-1604; Estados Unidos 492 Sur) has buses to Mendoza (AR$23, three hours), Córdoba (AR$72, nine hours), San Agustín de Valle Fértil (AR$32, four hours), La Rioja (AR$66, six hours) and Buenos Aires (AR$150, 15 hours).

For car rental, try **Classic** (☎ 422-4622; Av San Martín 163 Oeste). If you're heading to Ischigualasto, one of the cheapest ways to do it is to get a group together in your hostel and hire a car for the day.

AROUND SAN JUAN

San Agustín de Valle Fértil

This relaxed, green little village is 250km northeast of San Juan and set amid colorful hills and rivers. It relies on farming, animal husbandry, mining and tourism. Visitors to Parques Ischigualasto and Talampaya use San Agustín as a base, and there are also nearby **petroglyphs** and the Río Seco to explore.

The tourist office, on the plaza, can help set you up with tours of the area. There's camping and cheap accommodation, and a couple of good *parrillas*. Change money before you get here.

Buses roll daily to and from San Juan (AR$32, four hours).

Parque Provincial Ischigualasto

At every meander in the canyon of Parque Provincial Ischigualasto, a desert valley between sedimentary mountain ranges, the intermittent waters of the Río Ischigualasto have exposed a wealth of Triassic fossils and dinosaur bones – up to 180 million years old – and carved distinctive shapes in the monochrome clays, red sandstone and volcanic ash. The desert flora of *algarrobo* trees, shrubs and cacti complement the eerie moonscape, and common fauna include guanacos, condors, Patagonian hares and foxes.

Camping is (unofficially) permitted at the visitors center near the entrance, which also has a *confitería* with simple meals and cold drinks. There are toilets and showers, but water shortages are frequent and there's no shade.

Ischigualasto is about 80km north of San Agustín. Given its size and isolation, the only practical way to visit the park is by vehicle. After you pay the AR$40 entrance fee, a ranger will accompany your vehicle on a two- or three-hour circuit over the park's unpaved roads, which may be impassable after rain.

If you have no transport, ask the San Agustín tourist office about tours or hiring a car and driver, or contact the **park** (☎ 0264-49-1100). Tour operators in San Juan do tours here, but it's way cheaper to make your own way to San Agustín and line something up there. Some tours can be combined with **Parque Nacional Talampaya**, almost 100km northeast of Ischigualasto.

MALARGÜE

☎ 02627 / pop 25,200

From precolonial times, the Pehuenche people hunted and gathered in the valley of Malargüe, but the advance of European agricultural colonists dispossessed the original inhabitants of their land. Today petroleum is a principal industry, but Malargüe, 400km south of Mendoza, is also a year-round outdoor activity center: Las Leñas (right) offers Argentina's best **skiing**, and there are archeological sites and fauna reserves nearby, plus organized **caving** possibilities. Hotel prices go up in ski season. The hotels listed here offer guests a 50% discount on ski tickets at Las Leñas. Ask at the desk before checking in.

The **tourist office** (☎ 47-1659; www.malargue.gov.ar; RN 40, Parque del Ayer) is at the north end of town, directly on the highway.

Open all year, **Camping Municipal Malargüe** (☎ 47-0691; Alfonso Capdevila; campsites AR$8) is at the north end of town.

Facing the park, **Hostel Nord Patagonia** (☎ 47-2276; www.vallesuraventura.com.ar; Inalican 52 Oeste; dm/s/d AR$55/130/160; 🖳) is the coziest hostel in town. Also on site is a travel agency – summer activities include volcano treks, rafting and horse riding. In winter it offers transfers to Las Leñas for AR$25 per person.

Half a block from the plaza, the homey little **Kathmandú Hostel** (☎ 15-41-4899; www.hostel-kathmandu.com.ar; Torres 121; dm AR$35) offers comforts like hammocks, a Ping-Pong table and an open fireplace.

Don't let the shabby exterior of **Hotel Theis** (☎ 47-0136; San Martín 938; s/d AR$130/150) fool you – these are some of the sweetest rooms in town.

Restaurants line the five blocks of San Martín south of the plaza. **El Quincho de María** (San Martín 440; mains AR$20-30) has arguably the finest food in town. **Don Gauderio** (cnr San Martín & Torres; mains AR$15-25) is about as hip as Malargüe gets – it works better as a bar, with occasional live music, but has a couple of interesting pizzas and sandwiches on offer.

The **bus terminal** (cnr Roca & Aldao) has regular services to Mendoza (AR$50, six hours) and Las Leñas (AR$25, 1½ hours). There's a weekly summer service across the 2500m Paso Pehuenche and down the awesome canyon of the Río Maule to Talca, Chile.

If you're heading south, there is a daily bus to Buta Ranquil (AR$60, five hours) in Neuquén province, with connections further south from there. Book at least a day in advance at **Transportes Leader** (☎ 47-0519; cnr San Martín & Roca).

LAS LEÑAS

Wealthy Argentines and foreigners alike come to Las Leñas, the country's most prestigious ski resort, to look dazzling zooming down the slopes and then spend nights partying until the sun peeks over the snowy mountains. Summer activities include hiking, horse riding and mountain biking. Despite the fancy glitter, it's not completely out of reach for budget travelers.

Open from approximately July to October, Las Leñas is only 70km from Malargüe. Its 33 runs reach a peak of 3430m, with a maximum drop of 1230m. Lift tickets run about AR$136 to AR$209 (depending on the season) for a full day of skiing. The **ticket office** (☎ 011-4819-6000; www.laslenas.com; ☒ mid-Jun–late Sep) can provide more information.

Budget travelers will find regular transport from Malargüe, where accommodations are cheaper. Buses from Mendoza (AR$70) take seven hours.

SANTA ROSA
☎ 02954 / pop 124,100
One of the only towns of any size out on the Pampas, Santa Rosa doesn't offer a lot to the average traveler, except for being a staging point for nearby Parque Nacional Lihué Calel, an isolated but pretty park that's home to a surprising assortment of vegetation and wildlife.

Information
You'll find several ATMs near Plaza San Martín.
Post office (Lagos 258)
Tourist information center (☒ 24hr) At the bus terminal.
Tourist office (☎ 43-6555; www.santarosa.gov.ar; cnr Luro & San Martín) Opposite the bus terminal.

Sights
The **Museo de Bellas Artes** (cnr 9 de Julio & Villegas; ☒ 7am-1:30pm & 2-8pm Tue-Fri, 6:30-9:30pm Sat & Sun) is an unexpectedly modern gallery containing work by local and national artists.

Laguna Don Tomás is the place where locals boat, swim, play sports or just stroll. In March and April, the tourist office organizes deer-watching trips in **Reserva Provincial Parque Luro** (☎ 02954-49-9000; www.parqueluro.gov.ar), 35km south of town.

Sleeping & Eating
There are restaurant/cafes scattered around the main plaza.
Centro Recreativo Municipal Don Tomás (☎ 45-5358; campsites per person AR$5) Provides decent campsites at the west end of Av Uruguay. From the bus terminal, take the El Indio bus.
Hostería Santa Rosa (☎ 42-3868; Yrigoyen 696; s/d AR$75/85, without bathroom AR$65/75) A back-to-basics budget hotel one block from the bus terminal.

Hotel San Martín (☎ 42-2549; www.hsanmatin.com.ar; cnr Alsina & Pelligrini; s/d AR$100/160; ☒) Reasonable value for comfortable if unexciting rooms near the old train station.
Abarca (Urquiza 336; mains AR$25-35) A huge salad bar and friendly service make this otherwise ordinary neighborhood *parrilla* a good choice.

Getting There & Around
Aerolíneas Argentinas (☎ 43-3076; cnr Lagos & Moreno) flies to Buenos Aires from AR$360. Taxis to the airport, which is 3km from town, cost about AR$8.

The **bus terminal** (☎ 42-2952; Luro 365) has services to Bahía Blanca (AR$100, six hours), Puerto Madryn (AR$150, 10 hours), Buenos Aires (AR$100, 7½ hours), Mendoza (AR$150, eight hours), Neuquén (AR$87, 7 hours) and Bariloche (AR$175, 12 hours).

Rent Auto (☎ 43-5770; cnr Luro & Harris) is one of the recommended car rental agencies in town.

THE LAKE DISTRICT

Extending from Neuquén down through Esquel, Argentina's Lake District is a gorgeous destination with lots of opportunities for adventure. There are lofty mountains to climb and ski down, rushing rivers to raft, clear lakes to boat or fish and beautiful national parks to explore. From big-city Bariloche to hippie El Bolsón, the Lake District's towns and cities each have their own distinct geography, architecture and cultural offerings. There's something fun to do every month of the year, so don't miss visiting this multifaceted region.

The Lake District's original inhabitants were the Puelches and Pehuenches, so named for their dependence on pine nuts from the *pehuén,* or monkey-puzzle tree. Though Spaniards explored the area in the late 16th century, it was the Mapuche who dominated the region until the 19th century, when European settlers arrived. Today you can still see Mapuche living around here, especially on national park lands.

NEUQUÉN
☎ 0299 / pop 250,000
Palindromic Neuquén is a provincial capital nestled in the crook of where two rivers, the Limay and the Neuquén, meet. It's the

ARGENTINA

gateway to Patagonia and the Andean Lake District as well as an important commercial and agricultural center. Neuquén isn't a major tourist magnet, but it isn't unpleasant either – and if you're interested in old bones, those belonging to the largest dinosaurs ever have been found in the surrounding countryside.

Information

There are several banks with ATMs.

Cambio Pullman (Alcorta 144) Changes traveler's checks.

Chilean consulate (☎ 442-2727; La Rioja 241).

Post office (cnr Rivadavia & Santa Fe)

Provincial tourist office (☎ 442-4089; www.neuquentur.gov.ar; San Martín 182) Sells fishing licenses.

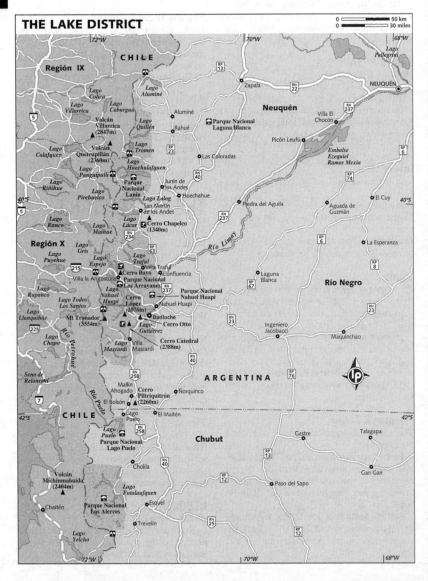

THE LAKE DISTRICT

Sights

Museo Nacional de Bellas Artes (cnr Mitre & Santa Cruz; ⏰ 10am-9pm Tue-Fri, 10am-2pm & 6-10pm Sat, 6-10pm Sun) has exhibitions of work by Argentine and international artists. The small **Museo de la Cuidad** (cnr Independencia & Córdoba; ⏰ 8am-9pm Mon-Fri, 6-10pm Sat & Sun) tells Neuquén's history.

Sleeping

Punto Patagónico Hostel (☎ 447-9940; Roca 1694; dm AR$45, s AR$65-100, d AR$100-130) Neuquen's only hostel is decent but not central (taxis to downtown cost AR$12). There are five rooms total; those with private bath are spacious. There's a Ping-Pong table and a nice patio.

Hospedaje Alberdi (☎ 448-1943; Alberdi 176; s/d/tr AR$70/120/140) Seven good, simple rooms. Stay here and you can get 10% off your meal in the restaurant (see Restaurant Alberdi, below).

Hotel Alcorta (☎ 442-2652; alcortahotel@infovia.com.ar; Alcorta 84; s/d AR$85/125) A homey maze of decent, mostly carpeted rooms. Triple and quad rooms also available; reserve ahead.

Hostería Belgrano (☎ 442-4311; Rivadavia 283; s/d AR$100/130) Central and attractive, with dark, nonsmoking rooms.

Hotel Ideal (☎ 442-2431; www.interpatagonia.com/hotelideal; Olascoaga 243; s/d AR$150/200; ⏣) Well-located, larger hotel with comfortable mid-range rooms and cable TV. Get a room in back for more peace.

Eating & Drinking

Restaurant Alberdi (Alberdi 176; mains AR$10-25) Cheap and popular local eatery that's been running for 30 years. Good meats and homemade pastas.

Cabildo (Rivadavia 68; mains AR$10-30) Family-friendly place with sandwiches, waffles, omelettes and 27 kinds of pizzas.

Club 32 (cnr Roca & Av Argentina; mains AR$26-38) Upscale restaurant with a loungy feel. Its large menu includes salads, stir-fries and sushi – if you dare. Lots of alcoholic drinks too.

For food supplies go to **El Norte supermarket** (cnr Olascoaga & Moreno).

Getting There & Around

The airport is 6km away (bus from center AR$1.60, taxi AR$20). **Aerolíneas Argentinas** (☎ 442-2409; Santa Fe 52), **LADE** (☎ 443-1153; Brown 163) and **LAN** (☎ 444-1210; airport) have services.

Neuquén's modern bus terminal is 4km west of the center; there's a tourist office inside. To get downtown take a 'Pehueche' bus (AR$1.50; ticket local 41) or a taxi (AR$15).

DO IT YOURSELF!

Neuquén province has one of the world's richest concentrations of dinosaur bones. A few hints: Plaza Huincul, Villa El Chocón, Centro Paleontológico Lago Barreales – all within a few hours' drive. The greater region also boasts lakes, hot springs, a few *bodegas* (wineries), a notable bird sanctuary, and some world-class fishing. Renting your own vehicle is the way to go. For information and maps, visit the tourist office.

Destinations include Bariloche (AR$68, six hours), Bahía Blanca (AR$90, eight hours), Buenos Aires (AR$180, 16 hours), Junín de los Andes (AR$55, six hours), Mendoza (AR$135, 12 hours), Viedma (AR$55, 10 hours) and Temuco, Chile (AR$90, 10 hours). Most local buses take magnetic cards, bought at kiosks.

JUNÍN DE LOS ANDES

☎ 02972 / pop 12,000

Cute and pleasant, Junín proclaims itself Argentina's 'trout capital' – and there are indeed some beautiful, trout-filled rivers in the area. It's a tranquil and slow-paced hamlet on the beautiful Río Chimehuín, 42km north of San Martín de los Andes. There's nothing much to do except wander around, explore the river or mountains and visit gorgeous Parque Nacional Lanín (p128).

Information

There's a bank (ATM) on the plaza.
National Park Office (☎ 492-748) On the plaza, next to tourist office.
Tourist office (☎ 491-160; junindelosandes.gov.ar; Milanesio 596; ⏰ 8am-9pm) Issues fishing permits.

Sights & Activities

Hike 15 minutes from the western edge of town to hillside, pine-dotted **Parque Vía Christi** (admission AR$5), where you can wander the 19 stations of the cross (open daylight hours). It's a very creative, well-done effort fusing Christian themes with Mapuche struggles. For indigenous artifacts, visit **Museo Mapuche** (Ponte 540; ⏰ 9am-2:30pm & 4:30-7pm Mon-Fri).

Sleeping & Eating

Laura Vicuña (☎ 491-149; mallinlaura@gmail.com; Ponte 867; campsites per person AR$20, cabañas AR$120-140) Pleasant and open all year, with sunny riverside sites. Just beyond is another camping place, but not quite as nice.

La Casa de Marita y Aldo (☎ 491-042; casademaritay aldo@hotmail.com; cnr 25 de Mayo & Olavarría; dm AR$34, with sleeping bag AR$30) Homey small house with two 5-bed dorms and rickety wood floors.

Hostería Rüpú Calel (☎ 491-569; www.rupucalel.com .ar; Suárez 560; s/d/tr AR$100/150/190) Ten comfortable rooms in a large family home.

Centro de Turismo (Milanesio 590; mains AR$10-30) Modern, comfortable restaurant with an unfortunate name, serving good-value food. It's next to the tourist office.

Ruca Hueney (cnr Milanesio & Suárez; mains AR$20-45) Junín's classiest restaurant, serving meats, pastas and trout. You can pick up something at the cheaper takeout counter next door and picnic at the park across the street.

Getting There & Away

The airport is 19km south, toward San Martín de los Andes.

The bus station is three blocks west of the plaza. Destinations include San Martín de los Andes (AR$6, 45 minutes), Bariloche (AR$30, three hours) and Neuquén (AR$55, six hours). Chilean destinations include Pucón (AR$70, four hours) and Temuco (AR$70, seven hours).

PARQUE NACIONAL LANÍN

At 3776m, snowcapped Volcán Lanín is the dominating centerpiece of this tranquil **national park** (admission AR$30), where extensive stands of *lenga* (southern beech) and the curious monkey-puzzle tree flourish. Pleistocene glaciers left behind blue finger-shaped lakes, excellent for fishing and camping. For more information and maps, contact the National Park Office in Junín (p127) or San Martín (right).

In summer **Lago Huechulafquen** is easily accessible from Junín; there are outstanding views of Volcán Lanín and several worthwhile hikes. Mapuche-run campgrounds include Raquithue, Piedra Mala and Bahía Cañicul; charges per person are AR$8 to AR$15. Free campsites are also available. Bring supplies from town. The forested **Lago Tromen** area also offers good hiking and camping.

From San Martín you can boat west on **Lago Lácar** to Paso Hua Hum and cross by road to Puerto Pirehueico (Chile); there's also bus service. Hua Hum has camping and hiking trails. Fifteen kilometers north of San Martín, serene **Lago Lolog** has good camping and fishing.

Summer vans from Junín's bus station go all along Lago Huechulafquen to Puerto Canoas (AR$15, three times daily in summer). Buses to Chile over the Hua Hum and Tromen passes can also stop at intermediate points, but are often crowded.

SAN MARTÍN DE LOS ANDES
☎ 02972 / pop 28,000

Attractive San Martín is a small, fashionable destination crowded with rowdy Argentines in summer. Nestled between two verdant mountains on the shores of Lago Lácar, the town boasts many wood and stone chalet-style buildings, many of them chocolate shops, ice cream stores and souvenir boutiques. But behind the touristy streets lie pleasant residential neighborhoods with pretty rose-filled gardens, and the surrounding area has wonderful forested trails perfect for hiking and biking.

Information

There are several ATMs around town.

Andina Internacional (Capitán Drury 876) Changes traveler's checks.

National Park Office (☎ 427-233; Frey 479) Sells fishing licenses.

Post office (cnr Pérez & Roca)

Tourist office (☎ 427-347; www.sanmartindelosandes .gov.ar; cnr San Martín & Rosas) Near the plaza.

Sights

The 2.5km steep, dusty hike to **Mirador Bandurrias** (admission AR$2) ends with awesome views of Lago Lácar; be sure to take a snack or lunch. Tough cyclists can rent bikes at **Rodados** (San Martín 1061), and reach the *mirador* (lookout) in about an hour via dirt roads.

Walk, bike or hitch to **Playa Catrite**, 4km away down RN 234 (there's a bus three times daily in summer). This protected rocky beach has a laid-back restaurant with nice deck; there's camping nearby. Cerro Chapelco is a ski center 20km away.

From the pier you can take daily boat tours to Paso Hua Hum (round-trip AR$140) to access walks and a waterfall, and to Quila Quina (round-trip AR$40) for beaches and water sports.

Sleeping & Eating

Reserve accommodation ahead in high seasons (January to March and July to August).

Camping ACA (☎ 429-430; servicioaca@smandes .com.ar; Koessler 2176; campsites per person AR$30, cabañas

AR$200-460) Spacious campground a 15-minute walk east of center, with shady dirt sites (avoid ones near the road). Get a *cabaña* for some luxury. There's also good camping at Playa Catrite (campsites per person AR$35), 4km south of town.

Secuoya Hostel (☎ 424-485; www.hostelsecuoya .com.ar; Rivadavia 411; dm AR$55, d/tr AR$140/180) Small hostel in a plain house, with a dark kitchen and rustic dining area.

Bike Hostel (☎ 424-117; www.bikehostel.com.ar; Koessler 1531; dm AR$60) Interesting hostel in an attractive, spacious house with huge beamed ceilings. Good, large dorms (some with balcony) and antique furniture in the dining room.

Puma Youth Hostel (☎ 422-443; www.pumahostel .com.ar; Fosbery 535; dm/d AR$60/175) This good, clean HI hostel has a great kitchen and spacious dorms. Nearly all rooms have their own bathrooms. HI discount.

Hostería Cumelen (☎ 427-304; www.interpatagonia .com/cumelen; Elordi 931; d/tr AR$160/220) Central, with 18 pleasant older rooms, some brighter than others. Management can be gruff.

Las Lucarnas Hostería (☎ 427-085; hosterialaslu carnas@hotmail.com; Pérez 632; r AR$200) Ten beautiful, comfortable rooms, some with bathtubs. Upstairs rooms have sloped ceilings, and there's an apartment with limited kitchen use (AR$370).

Dublin Pub (San Martín 599; mains AR$15-25) Popular contemporary pub with great front patio and upper balcony. Cooks up mostly sandwiches, along with a few pastas and salads. Cocktails and local beers also.

Pulgarcito (San Martín 461; mains AR$20-40) Great for pastas – it offers a wide variety, with 30 different sauces. Also lots of meats, seafood, soups, salads and omelettes.

Ku (San Martín 1053; mains AR$25-60) Elegant restaurant serving meats, homemade pastas and regional cuisine.

Getting There & Away

The **airport** is 23km north of town. Airlines include **Aerolíneas Argentinas** (☎ 410-588; Belgrano 949, Loc 2) and **LADE** (☎ 427-672), with an office at the bus station.

The bus station is five blocks west of Plaza San Martín. Destinations include Junín de los Andes (AR$6, 45 minutes), Villa La Angostura (AR$23, 2½ hours) and Bariloche (AR$35, four hours). Chilean destinations include Pucon (AR$75, five hours) and Temuco (AR$75, seven hours).

VILLA LA ANGOSTURA
☎ 02944 / pop 11,000

Tiny Villa La Angostura is a darling chocolate-box town that takes its name from the *angosta* (narrow) 91m neck of land connecting it to the striking Península Quetrihué. There's no doubt that Villa is touristy, but it's also charming; wood-and-stone alpine buildings line the three-block-long main street. There's skiing at nearby Cerro Bayo in winter.

El Cruce is the main part of town and contains the bus terminal and most hotels and businesses; the main street is Arrayanes. Woodsy La Villa, with a few restaurants, hotels and a nice beach, is 3km southwest and on the shores of Lago Nahuel Huapi.

Information

ATMs are available around town.

Andina (Arrayanes 256) Changes traveler's checks.
National Park Office (☎ 494-152; La Villa)
Post office (Las Fuschias 121) In a shopping gallery behind the bus terminal
Tourist office (☎ 494-124; cnr Arrayanes & Av Siete Lagos)

Sights & Activities

The cinnamon-barked *arrayán*, a myrtle relative, is protected in the small but beautiful **Parque Nacional Los Arrayanes** (admission AR$30) on the Península Quetrihué. The main *bosque* (forest) of *arrayanes* is situated at the southern tip of the peninsula; it's reachable by a 40-minute boat ride (one-way/round-trip AR$70/120) or a walk on a relatively easy 12km trail from La Villa.

Experienced bike riders should rent a bike to reach the *arrayán* forest. It's possible to boat either there or back, hiking or biking the other way (buy your return boat ticket in advance). Take food and water; there's an ideal picnic spot next to a lake near the end of the trail.

At the start of the Arrayanes trail, near the beach, a steep 30-minute hike leads to panoramic viewpoints over Lago Nahuel Huapi.

From the El Cruce part of town, a 3km walk north takes you to the **Mirador Belvedere** trailhead; hike another 30 minutes for good views. Walk three minutes beyond the mirador, then take an unmarked side trail to the right; after 20 minutes you'll reach a trail leading to views of **Cascada Inayacal**, a 50m waterfall. Get a map at the tourist office as the trails around here can be confusing.

Sleeping & Eating

The following are all in or near El Cruce. Reserve ahead in January and February.

Camping Unquehué (☎ 494-103; www.campingun quehue.com.ar; Av Siete Lagos 727; campsites per person AR$26, tent AR$10) Attractive and well-run campgrounds 500m west of the terminal. Great grassy sites, excellent facilities and a nearby supermarket. Tent and mattress rental available.

Hostel El Hongo (☎ 495-043; www.hostelelhongo .com.ar; Pehuenches 872; dm AR$50) This homey and very intimate hostel is in an old house about 10 blocks northwest of the center. Dorms are spacious and carpeted, but there are only two bathrooms for 19 beds.

Italian Hostel (☎ 494-376; www.italianhostel.com .ar; Los Marquis 215; dm/d AR$50/140; ☽ mid–Oct–mid-Apr) Great-vibe hostel with pleasant garden and friendly owners who bike-tour during their vacations. Dorms are very large (six to 10 beds) but good. There are three cozy private rooms with shared bath upstairs.

Hostel La Angostura (☎ 494-834; www.hostel laangostura.com.ar; Barbagelata 157; dm/d AR$55/170) Wonderful central hostel with comfy lodge-like spaces and clean, modern rooms. There's a nice deck in front for smokers; bike rentals available. HI discount.

Hostal Bajo Cero (☎ 495-454; www.bajocerohostel .com; Av Siete Lagos 1200; dm/d AR$65/230) About 1200m west of the bus terminal is this gorgeous hostel with large, well-designed dorms and lovely doubles. It has a nice garden and kitchen, plus airy common spaces.

Las Cumbres (☎ 494-945; www.hosterialascumbres .com; Confluencia 944; d/tr AR$230/270) Lovely, intimate guesthouse with eight beautiful and cozy rooms. The bright, relaxing common room has great wood-trunk details and a deck. It's 1km east of center and just off the highway.

Gran Nevada (Arrayanes 106; mains AR$15-25) Family-friendly place mega popular for its cheap and plentiful meats, pizzas and pastas. Come early or be prepared to wait.

La Buena Vida (Arrayanes 167; mains AR$35-50) Modern restaurant good for traditional dishes, along with some more exotic choices: try the Hungarian goulash, crepes, risotto or borscht.

Tinto Bistro (☎ 494-924; Huapi 34; mains AR$50-65) Upscale restaurant serving up dishes like Thai shrimp cakes and lamb in wine sauce. Owned by the Dutch princess's Argentine brother.

Getting There & Around

From the **bus terminal**, buses depart for Bariloche (AR$14, 1¼ hours) and San Martín de los Andes (AR$23, 2½ hours). If heading into Chile, reserve ahead for buses passing through. Buses to La Villa (where the boat docks and park entrance are located) leave every two hours.

There are at least a half-dozen bike-rental places in town.

BARILOCHE

☎ 02944 / pop 100,000

The Argentine Lake District's largest city, San Carlos de Bariloche attracts scores of travelers in both summer and winter. It's finely located on the shores of beautiful Lago Nahuel Huapi, and lofty mountain peaks are visible from all around. While Bariloche's center bustles with tourists shopping at the myriad chocolate shops, souvenir stores and trendy boutiques, the city's real attractions lie outside the city: Parque Nacional Nahuel Huapi offers spectacular hiking, and there's also great camping, trekking, rafting, fishing and skiing in the area. Despite the heavy touristy feel, Bariloche is a good place to stop, hang out, get errands done and, of course, have some fun.

Information

Internet cafes and ATMs are common. For good travel information in English, look around for a free copy of **The Traveller's Guru** (www.travellersguru.com).

Cambio Sudamérica (Av Bartolomé Mitre 63) Changes traveler's checks.

Club Andino (☎ 527-966; 20 de Febrero 30) Topo maps and *refugio* (a usually rustic shelter in a national park or remote area) information.

Hospital Privado Regional (☎ 525-000; cnr 24 de Septiembre & 20 de Febrero)

Immigration office (☎ 423-043; Libertad 191)

Information kiosk (cnr Moreno & Villegas)

Librería Cultura (Elflein 78) For Lonely Planet guides.

Municipal tourist office (☎ 429-850; www.bariloche patagonia.info; Centro Cívico).

National park office (☎ 423-111; San Martín 24)

Post office (Moreno 175)

Sights & Activities

The heart of town is the Centro Cívico, a group of well-kept public buildings built of log and stone (architect Ezequiel Bustillo originally adapted Middle European styles into this form of architecture, now associated with the Lake District area). The **Museo de la**

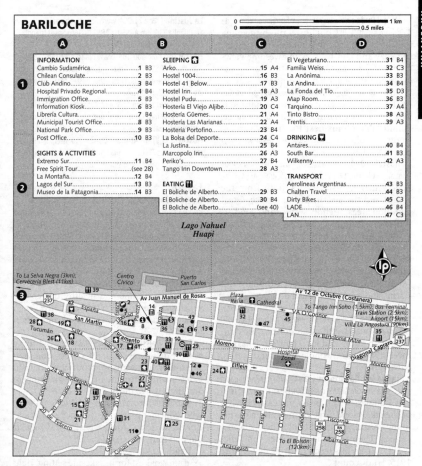

BARILOCHE

0 ____ 1 km
0 ____ 0.5 miles

Lago Nahuel Huapi

To La Selva Negra (3km);
Cervecería Blest (11km)

Centro Cívico

Puerto San Carlos

Av Juan Manuel de Rosas

Plaza Italia

Cathedral

Av 12 de Octubre (Costanera)

To Tango Inn Soho (1.5km); Bus Terminal;
Train Station (2.5km);
Airport (15km);
Villa La Angostura (90km)

RN 237

España

San Martín

Tucumán

Salta

Belgrano

24 de Septiembre

20 de Junio

9 de Julio

Elflein

Morales

Moreno

Hospital Zonal

Onelli

Elordi

Diagonal Capraro

Moreno

Av Bartolomé Mitre

RN 237

Quaglia

Villegas

Beschtedt

Frey

O'Connor

Gallardo

Tiscornia

Ruiz Moreno

Sarmiento

Rivadavia

RN 258

RN 258

To El Bolsón (120km);

Anasagasti

Albarracín

Patagonia (admission AR$5; 🕑 10am-12:30pm & 2-7pm Tue-Fri, 10am-5pm Sat), located here, offers a history of the area, along with good displays of stuffed critters and archaeological artifacts.

Rafting and kayaking trips on the Río Limay (easy class II) or Río Manso (class III to IV) are very popular; **Extremo Sur** (☎ 427-301; www.extremosur.com; Morales 765) has good tours and guides. Other activities include hiking, trekking, rock-climbing, biking, paragliding, horse-riding, fishing and skiing.

Many agencies and hostels offer tours. One backpacker-oriented agency is **Lagos del Sur** (☎ 458-410; www.lagosdelsurvt.com.ar; Rolando 287, 1st fl, Oficina 2), with several interesting area offerings. For something different, the **Free Spirit Tour** (☎ 15-584-927; www.freespirittour.com), run out of

Tango Inn (see p132), takes you to a hostel at a nearby lake, with various outdoor activities on the roster.

Courses

La Montaña (☎ 524-212; www.lamontana.com; Elflein 251) is a good Spanish school. It also offers accommodations, volunteer work programs and social excursions.

Sleeping

Make reservations in January, February and during holidays.

La Selva Negra (☎ 441-013; campingselvanegra@ speedy.com.ar; Av Bustillo Km 2950; campsites per person AR$33) Pleasant shady camping sites. It's 3km west of town; take buses 10, 20 or 21.

Hostel Pudu (☎ 429-738; www.hostelpudu.com; Salta 459; dm/d AR$40/130) Cool hostel run by a young Argentine and an Irish couple. A bit mazelike, but cozy and laid-back, with awesome views from every room. Great vibe, tiny bar downstairs and small garden for *asados*.

Arko (☎ 423-109; www.eco-family.com/hostel; Güemes 685; dm/d AR$45/150) Draped down a hillside is this renovated guesthouse with a few large, comfortable rooms next to a pretty garden. Rooms in older buildings cost less; kitchen access available.

Hostel 1004 (☎ 432-228; www.penthouse1004 .com.ar; San Martín 127, 10th fl, ste 1004; dm/d AR$45/120) Spectacular five-star views, both from the rooms and the awe-inspiring terrace. Great common areas, friendly service and good atmosphere. Inquire about their mountainside hostel, La Morada, perfect for a getaway.

Periko's (☎ 522-326; www.perikos.com; Morales 555; dm/d AR$45/140) Beautiful, well-run hostel with pleasant atmosphere, grassy yard and wonderful kitchen/dining areas. Well-thought-out dorms and four exceptional doubles.

Hostel 41 Below (☎ 436-433; www.hostel41below .com; Juramento 94; dm AR$50, d without bathroom AR$150) Intimate hostel with clean dorms, fine doubles (with view) and a mellow vibe. Easy to meet others in the wonderful common room. Kiwi-run.

Tango Inn Downtown (☎ 430-707; www.tangoinn .com; Salta 514; dm AR$55, d AR$200) Best for its superior doubles, which boast unbeatable views of the lake. Good large dorms, plus a purple lounge room with pool table. There's even a Jacuzzi! Their other hostel, Tango Inn Soho, is 500m from bus terminal at 12 de Octubre 1915. HI discount.

Hostería Güemes (☎ 424-785; fax 435-616; Güemes 715; s/d AR$100/150) Quiet family guesthouse sporting plain but comfortable rooms. Nice airy living room with central fireplace and city views. Spanish-speaking owner Cholo is an expert on the area's fishing.

Hostería Las Marianas (☎ 439-876; www.hosteria lasmarianas.com.ar; 24 de Septiembre 218; r AR$260) Friendly and homey family guesthouse with 16 fine rooms, some with partial lake views. Vaulted breakfast room. Great midrange option.

Also recommended:

La Bolsa del Deporte (☎ 423-529; www.labolsa deldeporte.com.ar; Palacios 405; dm/d AR$40/130) This is an artsy, hobbit hole–like compound with a fun hangout garden.

La Justina (☎ 524-064; www.lajustinahostel.com. ar; Quaglia 726; dm AR$50, r AR$130-160) Small friendly hostel; good kitchen and dining areas.

Hostel Inn (☎ 400-105; www.hibariloche.com; Salta 308; dm/d AR$55/200) Great modern hostel with awesome views and free dinners. Their other hostel, Marcopolo Inn, is at Salta 422. HI discount.

Hostería Portofino (☎ 422-795; Morales 435; s/d/t AR$100/150/180) Clean, quiet and well-run guesthouse with eight small rooms.

Hostería El Viejo Aljibe (☎ 423-316; nsegat@infovia .com.ar; Frey 571; d/tr/q AR$200/250/320) Homey place with a pretty garden and simple rooms.

Eating

Regional specialties include *jabalí* (wild boar), *ciervo* (venison), and *trucha* (trout). **La Anónima** supermarket is on Quaglia near Moreno.

La Fonda del Tío (Av Bartolomé Mitre 1130; mains AR$20-35) Where locals go for large portions of good, inexpensive food. Arrive early to avoid a wait.

El Vegetariano (20 de Febrero 730; set menus AR$25; ⊙ closed Sun) Simple and healthy five-course vegetarian menu, which changes daily. Vegan substitutions available, and the takeout option is AR$17.

Familia Weiss (Palacios 167; mains AR$25-45) Family restaurant always full of diners enjoying specialties like venison, trout and goulash. Convenient picture menu, good atmosphere and nightly live music.

Map Room (Urquiza 248; mains AR$25-40) Smoky bar with gourmet pizzas, large fancy salads and fine sandwiches. Meats, pastas and regular old pub grub too. Good coffee.

Trentis (Av Juan Manuel de Rosas 435; mains AR$25-40 ⊙ closed Mon) Best for its lakeside setting, right above the water. Serves pizzas, pastas and sandwiches and has a good casual atmosphere.

La Andina (Quaglia 95; pizzas AR$30) Long-running, friendly and no-nonsense corner eatery with good but inexpensive pizzas and empanadas.

El Boliche de Alberto (Villegas 347; mains AR$30-45) Bariloche's most famous *parrilla*, boasting excellent meats. There's another branch around the corner at Elflein 158, plus an equally good pasta restaurant at Elflein 49.

Tarquino (cnr 24 de Septiembre & Saavedra; mains AR$38-45) Fine meats, homemade pastas and good wine selection; worth visiting for the gorgeous, hobbit hole–like architecture alone. Exceptional service; French spoken.

Tinto Bistro (San Martín 570; mains AR$47-60; ⊙ closed dinner Sun) Upscale place with well-prepared, exotic dishes like trout teriyaki with wasabi dressing. Spicy selections are actually spicy! Owned by the Dutch princess's Argentine brother.

Drinking

Trentis (opposite) and The Map Room (also opposite) are great drinking spots also.

Wilkenny (San Martín 435) Bariloche's biggest and loudest drinking attraction, this popular pub comes with a wraparound bar.

South Bar (Juramento 30) Intimate, laid-back bar with dim lighting and dartboard. Great music and a talkative bartender.

Cervecería Blest (☎ 461-026; Bustillo km 11) Touristy brewery/restaurant, but with a nice atmosphere. Try pilsner, lager, bock and even raspberry beers. It's 11km west of the city; take bus 20.

Antares (Elflein 47) Very popular contemporary bar; score a loft table for people-watching. Copper-hued beer dispensers hold craft beers, and there are live cover bands Thursday to Saturday nights.

Getting There & Around

AIR

The **airport** (☎ 405-016) is 15km east of town; take bus 72 (AR$2.50) from the town center or a taxi (AR$50).

Aerolíneas Argentinas (☎ 422-144; Av Bartolomé Mitre 185), **LAN** (☎ 431-077; Av Bartolomé Mitre 500) and **LADE** (☎ 424-812; Villegas 480) provide services.

BICYCLE

Dirty Bikes (☎ 425-616; O'Connor 681) rents bicycles and organizes bike tours. For information on biking the Circuito Chico, see right.

BUS

The bus terminal is 2.5km east of the center; it's AR$1.60 by bus or AR$15 by taxi.

BUS FARES

Destination	Cost (AR$)	Duration (hr)
Buenos Aires	265	20
Comodoro Rivadavia	145	15
El Bolsón	18	2½
Osorno, Chile	80	5
Puerto Madryn	175	13
Puerto Montt, Chile	80	7
San Martín de los Andes	35	4
Villa La Angostura	12	1¼

Chalten Travel (☎ 423-809; www.chaltentravel.com; Moreno 126) has a two-night transport package to El Calafate for AR$480.

CAR

There are plenty of car rental agencies in town. Car rental rates are around AR$200 (with 200km) per day.

TRAIN

The **train station** (☎ 423-172) is next to the bus terminal. There's train service to Viedma (AR$44/102 in *turista*/Pullman class, 17 hours) twice weekly.

PARQUE NACIONAL NAHUEL HUAPI

Lago Nahuel Huapi, a glacial relic over 100km long, is the centerpiece of this gorgeous national park (admission AR$30 to the Tronador area and on Puerto Pañuelo boat tours). To the west, 3554m Monte Tronador marks the Andean crest and Chilean border. Humid Valdivian forest covers its lower slopes, while summer wildflowers blanket alpine meadows.

The 60km **Circuito Chico** loop is a popular excursion. Every 20 minutes, bus 20 (from San Martín and Morales in Bariloche) heads along Lago Nahuel Huapi to end at Puerto Pañuelos, where boat trips leave a few times daily for beautiful **Puerto Blest**, touristy **Isla Victoria** and pretty **Península Quetrihué** (see p129). Bus 10 goes the other way, inland via **Colonia Suiza** (a small, woodsy Swiss community), and ends at Bahía López, where you can hike a short way to the tip of the peninsula Brazo de la Tristeza. In summer, bus 11 does the whole Circuito, connecting Puerto Pañuelos with Bahía López, but in winter you can walk the 6km stretch along the nonbusy highway, with much of that being on a woodsy nature trail. There's a beautiful two-hour side hike to Villa Tacul, on the shores of Lago Nahuel Huapi. It's best to walk from Bahía López to Puerto Pañuelos rather than the other way around, since many more buses head back to Bariloche from Pañuelos. Confirm bus schedules in Bariloche's tourist office.

Cyclists can hop a bus to Km 18.600 and rent a bike at **Bike Cordillera** (☎ 02944-524-828; www.cordillerabike.com). This way you'll bike less, avoid busy Av Bustillo and take advantage of the loop's more scenic sections. Call ahead to reserve a bicycle.

ARGENTINA

Skiing is a popular winter activity from mid-June to October. **Cerro Catedral** (☎ 409-000; www.catedralaltapatagonia.com), some 20km west of town, is one of the biggest ski centers in South America. It boasts dozens of runs, a cable car, gondola and plenty of services (including rentals). The best part, however, is the views: peaks surrounding the lakes are gloriously visible.

Area hikes include climbing up Cerros Otto, Catedral and Campanario; all have chairlifts as well. The six-hour hike up Monte Tronador flanks to Refugio Meiling usually involves an overnight stay as it's a three-hour drive to the trailhead (Pampa Linda) from Bariloche. Summiting Trondador requires technical expertise.

If trekking, check with Club Andino (p130) or National Park Office (p130), both in Bariloche, for trail conditions; snow can block trails, even in summer. Club Andino has *refugio* information, while the National Park Office knows about the area's camping scene.

EL BOLSÓN
☎ 02944 / pop 27,000

Hippies rejoice: there's a must-see destination for you in Argentina, and it's called El Bolsón. Within its liberal and artsy borders live alternate-lifestyle folks who've made their town a 'nonnuclear zone' and 'ecological municipality.' Located about 120km south of Bariloche, nondescript El Bolsón is surrounded by dramatically jagged mountain peaks. Its economic prosperity comes from a warm microclimate and fertile soil, both of which support a cadre of organic farms devoted to hops, cheese, soft fruits such as raspberries, and orchards. This, and El Bolsón's true personality, can be seen at its famous **feria artesanal** (craft market), where creative crafts and healthy food are sold; catch it on Plaza Pagano on Tuesdays, Thursdays and weekends (best on Saturdays).

The **tourist office** (☎ 492-604; www.elbolson.gov .ar) is next to Plaza Pagano. Get maps and *refugio* information at **Club Andino** (☎ 492-600; Av Sarmiento), near Roca. There are two ATMs, and lines can get long. The post office is opposite the tourist office.

For area activities like rafting on Río Azul, paragliding and horse riding, contact **Grado 42** (☎ 493-124; www.grado42.com; Av Belgrano 406) or **Huara** (☎ 455-000; www.huaraviajesyturismo.com.ar; Dorrego 410).

Sleeping

Surrounding mountains offer plenty of camping opportunities, including at *refugios* (sites AR$10, bunks AR$35).

Camping Refugio Patagónico (☎ 483-888; Islas Malvinas s/n; campsites per person AR$20) Premier camping with both sunny and shady sites, mountain views and expansive fields.

La Casa del Viajero (☎ 493-092; aporro@elbolson .com; near Libertad & Las Flores, Barrio Usina; dm/d AR$35/80) Totally laid-back, rustic and artsy backwater. It's hardly luxurious – that's the appeal. Across the main bridge and 200m north; look for a sign and bushy entrance. Call for pickup.

Hospedaje Salinas (☎ 492-396; Roca 641; s/d without bathroom AR$40/80; cnr Roca & Feliciano) Five no-frills older rooms (all with twin beds), tiny cooking facilities and nice garden patio in which to hang.

Albergue El Pueblito (☎ 493-560; www.elpueblito hostel.com.ar; dm/d AR$43/150) Tranquil and rustic countryside hostel with creaky-floor dorms and three *cabañas*. Cozy hangout area; bike rentals available. Incongruous but cool bar area in separate building. HI discount. Take a bus (it's 4km north of town, down an unmarked dirt road) or *remise* (AR$8).

Posada Pehuenia (☎ 483-010; www.hospedajepehue nia.com; Azcuenaga 140; dm/d AR$45/120, cabañas AR$150) Friendly hostel with good intimate vibe and small dorms. Backyard *cabañas* and bike rentals available, and there are *asados* twice a week.

Refugio Patagónico (☎ 483-628; www.refugio patagonico.com; Islas Malvinas s/n; dm/d AR$45/120) Wonderful hostel in a country-like setting. Each dorm rooms has its own bath. Beautiful, large and airy common area.

Altos del Sur (☎ 498-730; www.altosdelsur.bolsonweb .com; Tres Cipreses 1237; dm/d AR$50/150) New, modern and lovely hostel with pleasant common areas and good dorms. Occasional pizza nights, and basic groceries sold. A bit isolated, it's four kilometers uphill from town, and there are no buses (remise AR$12). HI discount.

Residencial Los Helechos (☎ 492-262; San Martín 3248; s/d/apt AR$100/150/200) Family-run guesthouse with six modern rooms and two apartments, a flowery garden, and kitchen access. A great deal for what you get; look for the 'Kioscón' sign.

La Posada de Hamelin (☎ 492-030; www.posada dehamelin.com.ar; Granollers 2179; s/d/tr AR$120/170/200) Just a handful of wonderfully cozy rooms in this sweet, friendly and vine-covered family home. Excellent breakfast (AR$15).

La Casona de Odile (☎ 492-753; www.welcomear
gentina.com/odile; s/d AR$140/280) Five kilometers
north of the center is Frenchwoman Odile's
parklike haven on two hectares. There are four
homey rooms, with fabulous dinners available
(AR$85). Reserve ahead.

Eating & Drinking

Food at the *feria artesanal* is tasty, healthy
and good value.

Jauja (San Martín 2867; ice cream AR$6-9) Best for
its famous ice-cream counter; the restaurant
food is just so-so.

Apunto (Sarmiento 2434; mains AR$20-35) Well-
regarded *parrilla* with some options available
for noncarnivores.

Patio Venzano (cnr Sarmiento & Hube; mains AR$25-40)
Great cozy atmosphere and nice patio add to
the tasty *parrillada* and pasta offerings here.

Otto Tipp (cnr Islas Malvinas & Roca; mains AR$27-36;
☾ dinner only) Large brewery restaurant with
plenty of pizzas, along with some homemade
pastas.

Pasiones (cnr Belgrano & Beruti; mains AR$30-40) Well-
prepared food that includes gourmet pizzas,
fish and pastas. Not too fancy, with outdoor
seating and live entertainment.

Cervecería El Bolsón (☎ 492-595; Ruta 258)
Relaxing place that brews about a dozen beers
and also serves food. It's 2km north of town.

Boulevard (cnr San Martín & Hube) Irish Pub atmosphere with organic wood details, a dozen
cocktails and craft beer. Snag a sidewalk table
for fresh air.

Getting There & Around

LADE (☎ 492-206; Sarmiento 3238) occasionally flies
to El Bolsón.

There's no central bus terminal; several
bus companies are spread around town, with
Via Bariloche having the most departures
to and from Bariloche. Destinations include
Bariloche (AR$18, 2½ hours), Esquel (AR$27,
2½ hours), Puerto Madryn (AR$150, 12 hours)
and Buenos Aires (from AR$305, 22 hours).

Rent bikes at Peuman, at the **Club Andino**
(☎ 492-600; cnr Roca & Sarmiento), for AR$40/50 a
half-/full day (summer only).

AROUND EL BOLSÓN

The spectacular granite ridge of 2260m **Cerro
Piltriquitrón** looms to the east like the back
of some prehistoric beast. From the 1100m
level, reached by *remise* (AR$120 round-trip;
negotiate waiting fee), a further 30- to 40-

minute hike leads to **Bosque Tallado** (admission
AR$8), a shady grove of about 40 figures carved
from logs. Another 20-minute walk uphill is
Refugio Piltriquitrón, where you can have a
drink or even sack down (bunk AR$25, bring
sleeping bag; camping free). From here it's
2½ hours to the summit. The weather is very
changeable, so bring layers.

On a ridge 6km west of town is **Cabeza del
Indio** (admission AR$2), a rock outcrop resembling
a man's profile; the trail has great views of
the Río Azul and Lago Puelo. There are also
a couple of **waterfalls** (admission each AR$2) about
10km north of town.

A good three-hour hike reaches the narrow
canyon of **Cajón del Azul**, which has some glorious swimming holes. At the end is a friendly
refugio where you can eat or stay for the night.
From where the town buses (AR$6) drop you
off, it's a 15-minute steep, dusty walk to the
Cajón del Azul trailhead.

About 18km south of El Bolsón is windy
Parque Nacional Lago Puelo. You can camp, swim,
fish, hike or take a boat tour to the Chilean
border (AR$90). In summer, regular buses run
from El Bolsón (AR$4.25, 15 minutes). For
information on taking tours to El Maitén's
railroad workshops, see below.

ESQUEL

☎ 02945 / pop 30,000

Homely Esquel doesn't look like much at first
glance, but it boasts a dramatic setting at the
foothills of western Chubut province and is
the transition point from Andean forest to the
Patagonian steppe. It's also the starting gate
for the Old Patagonian Express and gateway
to Parque Nacional Los Alerces. There's good
hiking, rafting, kayaking, horse riding and skiing in the area, and the pleasant Welsh stronghold, Trevelin, is a good day trip away.

Information

Banks with ATMs are located on Alvear and
on 25 de Mayo near Alvear.

Club Andino (☎ 453-248; Pellegrini 787)

Post office (Alvear 1192) Next to the tourist office.

Tourist office (☎ 451-927; www.esquel.gov.ar; cnr
Alvear & Sarmiento)

Sights & Activities

La Trochita (Old Patagonian Express; ☎ 451-403; www
.latrochita.org.ar) is Argentina's famous narrow-
gauge steam train. It does short tourist runs
from the station near the corner of Brown and

Roggero to Nahuel Pan, 20km east (AR$50, 1¼ hours). At the other end of the tracks, 140km away, is El Maitén; the railroad's workshops and a museum are here. El Maitén is accessible from El Bolsón; there is no regular train connection from Esquel. Check the website or tourist office for current schedules.

For adventure tours and activities try **EPA** (☎ 454-366; www.grupoepa.com; Rivadavia 484) or **Patagonia Verde** (☎ 454-396; www.patagonia-verde .com.ar; 9 de Julio 926). Good hikes in the area go to Laguna La Zeta (two hours), Cerro La Cruz (four hours) and Cerro Nahuel Pan (six hours). For mountain guides contact **Cholila Mountain Explorers** (☎ 456-296; www.cholilaexplorers.com).

Sleeping

El Hogar del Mochilero (☎ 452-166; cveron@ar.inter.net; Roca 1028; campsites per person AR$15, dm AR$20) A shady little camping paradise; kitchen available. Also has a huge 31-bed dorm; bring sleeping bag and earplugs. Doubles are planned. If Carlos isn't around, check the house across the street.

Planeta Hostel (☎ 456-846; www.planetahostel.com; Alvear 2833; dm AR$35) Small and intimate hostel with few amenities and one small double (AR$90). Mini-bouldering wall in the back; motorcycle parking available. About 10 blocks west of the bus terminal.

Casa de Familia Rowlands (☎ 452-578; Rivadavia 330; s/d AR$40/80) Friendly and family-run, with three homey, basic rooms (two share bathrooms). About seven blocks from the center.

Anochecer Andino (☎ 450-321; www.anocheerandino .com.ar; Ameghino 482; dm/d AR$45/120) Clean, plain new hostel with friendly owner up on the region's outdoor attractions. Cheap dinners are available, and there's an apartment (AR$180).

Casa del Pueblo (☎ 450-581; www.esquelcasadelpue blo.com.ar; San Martín 661; dm/d AR$46/130) Mazelike but good hostel with cozy common areas. Good kitchen and grassy garden with hammock. The bar in front building has a Ping-Pong table. Bike rentals available; HI discount.

Parador Lago Verde (☎ 452-251; Volta 1081; s/d/ tr AR$70/90/120) Six tiny and dark rooms, but there's a small grassy lawn and some rose bushes. About six blocks from the center.

Eating & Drinking

La Anónima supermarket (cnr Roca & 9 de Julio) Has a cheap takeout counter.

Mirasoles (Pellegrini 643; mains AR$20-30; ⏲ dinner Tue-Sat) Intimate, upscale restaurant with just a few good dishes that include homemade pastas, salads and fish.

María Castaña (cnr 25 de Mayo & Rivadavia; mains AR$25-35) Popular cafe with sidewalk tables and plenty of menu choices like sandwiches, pastas and cheese boards.

La Luna (Fontana 656; mains AR$25-40) Great for its outdoor deck and pizzas; also serves craft beers.

Hotel Argentino (25 de Mayo 862) Old-time Wild West saloon bar and pool tables. Funky atmosphere worth checking out.

Killarney's Irish Pub (Sarmiento 793) Irish pub wannabe with typical food offerings and good beer. DJ nights are Thursday, and there's tango dancing twice weekly.

Getting There & Around

The airport is 20km east of town (taxi AR$50). **Aerolíneas Argentinas** (☎ 453-614; Fontana 408) and **LADE** (☎ 452-124; Alvear 1085) provide services.

Esquel's modern bus terminal is six blocks north of the center, at the corner of Alvear and Brun. Destinations include El Bolsón (AR$26, two hours), Bariloche (AR$50, 4¼ hours), Puerto Madryn (AR$150, 10 hours) and Comodoro Rivadavia (AR$80, nine hours). Buses go to Trevelin (AR$5, 25 minutes) from the terminal, stopping along Av Alvear on their way south.

TREVELIN
☎ 02945 / pop 9500

Historic Trevelin is a calm, sunny and laidback community only 24km south of Esquel. The **tourist office** (☎ 480-120) is on Plaza Fontana.

Landmarks include the historical **Museo Regional** (admission AR$4; ⏲ 9am-9pm), in a restored brick mill, and **Capilla Bethel**, a Welsh chapel from 1910. **Tumba de Malacara** (admission AR$10; ⏲ 10am-12pm & 3-8pm), two blocks northeast of the plaza, is a monument to the horse that saved John Evans, Trevelin's founder.

The best budget accommodation in town is the friendly and serene **Hostel Casaverde** (☎ 480-091; www.casaverdehostel.com.ar; Los Alerces s/n; dm/d AR$40/145, cabañas AR$220-340), at the top of a small hill. The rooms, kitchen, atmosphere and views are so welcoming you'll be tempted to extend your stay. HI discount.

You can have afternoon tea (3:30pm to 7pm) and conquer a platter of pastries at **Nain Maggie** (☎ 480-232; Perito Moreno 179) and **Las Mutisias**

(☎ 480-165; San Martín 170), while keeping your ears pricked for locals speaking Welsh.

Half-hourly buses run from Esquel to Trevelin (AR$5).

PARQUE NACIONAL LOS ALERCES

Just 33km west of Esquel, the spacious Andean **Parque Nacional Los Alerces** (admission AR$30) protects extensive stands of *alerce (Fitzroya cupressoides)*, a large and long-lived conifer of humid Valdivian forests. Other common trees include cypress, incense cedar, southern beeches and *arrayán*. The *colihue* (a bamboo-like plant) undergrowth is almost impenetrable.

The receding glaciers of Los Alerces' peaks, which barely reach 2300m, have left nearly pristine lakes and streams with charming vistas and excellent fishing. Westerly storms drop nearly 3000mm of rain annually, but summers are mild and the park's eastern zone is much drier. An **information center** (☎ 471-015) can help you plan excursions.

A popular boat tour sails from Puerto Chucao (on Lago Menéndez) and heads to **El Alerzal**, an accessible stand of rare *alerces* (AR$110). A two-hour stopover permits a walk around a loop trail that passes Lago Cisne and an attractive waterfall to end up at **El Abuelo** (Grandfather), a 57m-tall, 2600-year-old *alerce*.

In the park there are organized **campgrounds** (campsites per person AR$10-30), along with some free sites. Lago Krüger, reached by foot (12 hours) or taxi boat from Villa Futalaufquen, has a campground, restaurant and expensive *hostería*. See Esquel's tourist office for a complete list of accommodation options.

There are frequent buses from Esquel (AR$15, 25 minutes).

PATAGONIA

Few places in the world inspire the imagination like mystical Patagonia. You can cruise bleak RN 40 (South America's Route 66), watch an active glacier calve house-size icebergs and hike among some of the most fantastic mountain scenery in the world. There are Welsh teahouses, petrified forests, quirky outpost towns, penguin colonies, huge sheep *estancias* and some of the world's largest trout. The sky is wide, the clouds airbrushed and the late sunsets nearly spiritual.

Patagonia was thought to be named after the Tehuelche people's moccasins, which made their feet appear huge – in Spanish, *pata* means foot. Geographically, the region is mostly a windy, barren expanse of flat nothingness that offers rich wildlife only on its eastern coast, and rises into the spectacular Andes way into its western edge. It's attracted an interesting range of famous personalities, however, from Charles Darwin to Ted Turner to Bruce Chatwin to Butch Cassidy and the Sundance Kid. Despite the big names, however, Patagonia maintains one of the lowest population densities in the world.

VIEDMA
☎ 02920 / pop 52,000

Patagonia's eastern gateway is this unremarkable provincial capital. Viedma is the finish line for January's **La Regata del Río Negro**, one of the world's longest kayak races, which starts 600km away in Neuquén. Other attractions include a couple of museums and a scenic riverside walk. Nearby Carmen de Patagones (p139) takes most of the family charm.

The **tourist office** (☎ 427-171; www.viedma.gov.ar; cnr Costanera & Colón) is by the river. There's a **post office** (Rivadavia btwn Mitre & Tucumán), ATMs and plenty of internet access.

Sights & Activities

The history of local indigenous cultures can be seen at **Museo Antropológico Histórico** (San Martín 263; ◷ 9am-6pm Mon-Fri, 10:30am-12:30pm & 4:30-6:30pm Sat). **Museo Salesiano** (Rivadavia 34; ◷ 8am-noon Mon-Fri, 8am-12:30pm & 7-9pm Tue-Thu) has some amazing ceiling paintings and a neat fish-vertebrae cane.

Summer activities include **kayaking** and weekend **catamaran rides** (ask at riverside venues). The riverside makes for pleasant walking.

The Atlantic shoreline, Patagonia's oldest lighthouse and the town of **Balneario El Cóndor** lie 30km southeast of Viedma; daily buses go from Plaza Alsina (AR$4). A further 30km south is **Punta Bermeja**, a sea-lion colony. In summer only, buses from Viedma drop you 3km from the colony (AR$15).

Sleeping & Eating

Camping Municipal (☎ 15-524-786; campsites per person AR$4) About 1km northwest of the center; riverside with bleak gravel sites. A taxi will cost AR$10.

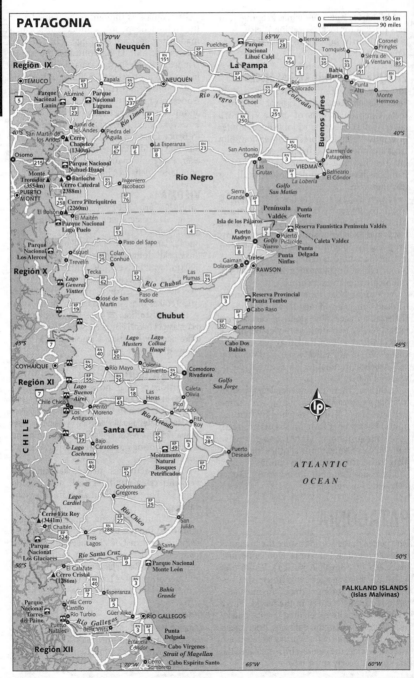

Hotel El Vasco (☎ 430-459; hotelelvasco@yahoo.com
.ar; 25 de Mayo 174; s/d AR$100/120) A good deal for its
small, attractive rooms and nice patio. Reserve
ahead – it's popular.

Residencial Tosca (☎ 428-508; residencialtosca@
hotmail.com; Alsina 349; s/d AR$110/150; 🔀) Mazelike
place with simple and hardly luxurious but
adequate rooms that have cable TV.

Camila's Café (cnr Saavedra & Buenos Aires; snacks
AR$10-20) Good for sandwiches, *cazuelas* (stews)
and lots of drinks.

Sal y Fuego (Villarino 55; mains AR$30-40) Upscale
riverside restaurant with outside seating;
there's a cafe side that's less expensive but
with the same views.

Getting There & Around

The airport is 4km southwest of town (taxi
AR$15). **LADE** (☎ 424-420; Saavedra 576) and **Aerolíneas
Argentinas** (☎ 422-018; Colón 246) have services.

Viedma's bus terminal is 13 blocks south of
the center, at the corner of Guido and Perón.
Buses (AR$1.50) and taxis (AR$10) head
downtown. Destinations include Bahía Blanca
(AR$40, 3½ hours), Puerto Madryn (AR$75,
seven hours), Comodoro Rivadavia (AR$150,
13 hours), Bariloche (AR$116, 15 hours) and
Buenos Aires (AR$170, 13 hours).

The **train station** (☎ 422-130) is on the southeast outskirts of town; there's a Friday service
to Bariloche (from AR$40, 15 hours).

CARMEN DE PATAGONES
☎ 02920 / pop 24,500

Just across the Río Negro is picturesque
'Patagones,' with historic cobbled streets and
lovely colonial buildings. There's not much
to do other than stroll around and take in the
relaxing atmosphere, and it's just a short boat
ride from busy Viedma. For walking maps visit
the **tourist office** (☎ 461-777, ext 253; Bynon 186).

Across from the boat dock is the good
Museo Histórico (☎ 10am-12:30pm & 8-10pm Mon-
Fri, 7-9pm Sat); check out the cane with hidden
stabber. Salesians built the **Iglesia Parroquial
Nuestra Señora del Carmen** (1883); its image of
the Virgin, dating from 1780, is southern
Argentina's oldest. Note the flags captured
in the 1827 victory over the Brazilians.

Residencial Reggiani (☎ 461-065; Bynon 422;
s/d AR$70/110) has small, decent rooms (those
upstairs are brighter). Better is **Hotel Percaz**
(☎ 464-104; reservas@hotelpercaz.com.ar; Rivadavia 384; s/d
AR$100/150), offering good budget rooms with
worn carpets.

The **bus terminal** (cnr Barbieri & Méjico) has services to Buenos Aires and Puerto Madryn
(among other places), but long-distance buses
are more frequent from Viedma.

Patagones is connected to Viedma by frequent buses, but the *balsa* (passenger boat)
is more scenic. It crosses the river every few
minutes (AR$1.75, two minutes).

PUERTO MADRYN
☎ 02965 / pop 66,000

Founded by Welsh settlers in 1886, this sheltered port city owes much of its popularity
to the nearby wildlife sanctuary Península
Valdés. It holds its own as a modest beach
destination, however, and boasts a lively tourist street scene and popular boardwalk. From
June to mid-December visiting right whales
take center stage.

Information

There's a **tourist office** (☎ 453-504; www.madryn.gov
.ar/turismo; Av Roca 223) both in the center and at
the bus station. There are many internet cafes
and banks with ATMs, and **Cambio Thaler** (Av Roca
493) changes traveler's checks.

Sights & Activities

The **Museo Provincial del Hombre y el Mar** (cnr García
& Menéndez; admission AR$6; ⏲ hrs vary) has some fine
natural history exhibits, especially on orcas.
Well-done **EcoCentro** (☎ 457-470; Julio Verne 3784;
admission AR$25) offers excellent exhibits of local
sea life, complete with a touch pool and lofty
glass tower. Take the Linea 2 bus to the last
stop, then walk 1km. Hours are erratic, so
call beforehand.

Other area activities include kayaking,
windsurfing, scuba diving and horse riding.
You can pedal (or just taxi) 17km southeast
to **Punta Loma** (admission AR$25; ⏲ dawn-dusk), a sea-
lion rookery, or 19km northwest to **Playa El
Doradillo**, which offers close-up whale-watching
in season. See p141 for info on bike rentals.

Tours

Countless agencies sell tours to Península
Valdés (p141) and Punta Tombo (p143). Rates
are between AR$150 and AR$180; most hotels
and hostels will also sell tours.

When choosing, it's always best to get recommendations from fellow travelers. What
was the group size, and was there an English-
speaking guide? And take water, as it's a very
long drive to both reserves.

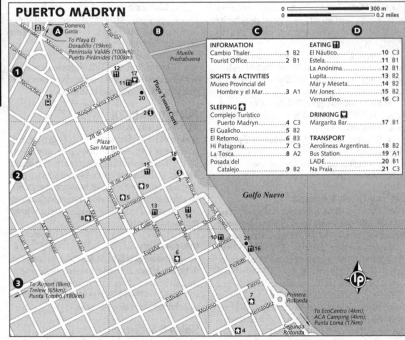

PUERTO MADRYN

INFORMATION
Cambio Thaler.................1 B2
Tourist Office..................2 B1

SIGHTS & ACTIVITIES
Museo Provincial del
Hombre y el Mar.........3 A1

SLEEPING
Complejo Turístico
Puerto Madryn.............4 C3
El Gualicho....................5 B2
El Retorno.....................6 B3
Hi Patagonia..................7 C3
La Tosca........................8 A2
Posada del
Catalejo.......................9 B2

EATING
El Náutico.....................10 C3
Estela..........................11 B1
La Anónima...................12 B1
Lupita.........................13 B2
Mar y Meseta................14 B2
Mr Jones.....................15 B2
Vernardino..................16 B2

DRINKING
Margarita Bar...............17 B1

TRANSPORT
Aerolíneas Argentinas.......18 B2
Bus Station..................19 A1
LADE...........................20 B1
Na Praia......................21 C3

Sleeping

Prices listed are for the high season, approximately October to March. In January it's a good idea to reserve ahead.

ACA Camping (☎ 452-952; campsites per 2 people AR$43, d AR$75) Shady sandy sites; simple bunk doubles. Some food is available (but it's best to take your own). It's 4km south of the center; take Linea 2 bus to the last stop, then walk 800m (taxi AR$15).

La Tosca (☎ 456-133; www.latoscahostel.com; Sarmiento 437; dm AR$40-45, d AR$120-130) Friendly hostel with great common area. Small, darkish rooms line a pleasant grassy yard excellent for hanging out. Dinners are available (AR$25 to AR$35).

Posada del Catalejo (☎ 475-224; www.posadadel catalejo.com.ar; Mitre 446; dm/d/tr AR$40/170/200) Small and peaceful place with a tiny patio and rustic kitchen in back. The one dorm has eight beds.

El Gualicho (☎ 454-163; www.elgualicho.com.ar; Zar 480; dm AR$45, d AR$150-170) Great hostel with clean dorms, a good-vibe living room, spacious kitchen and grassy garden. Hotel-quality doubles. Bike rentals; HI discount.

El Retorno (☎ 456-044; www.elretornohostel.com .ar; Mitre 798; dm/d AR$45/150) Nonfancy, mazelike hostel with owners attending guests. It lacks a large common area but has several smaller ones spread out here and there.

Hi Patagonia (☎ 450-155; www.hipatagonia.com; Av Roca 1040; dm/d AR$45/150) Simple hostel best for its backyard bar-patio, which is great for socializing. Bike rentals and bouldering wall too.

Complejo Turístico Puerto Madryn (☎ 474-426; www.advance.com.ar/usuarious/hi-pm; 25 de Mayo 1136; d/tr AR$180/220, apt AR$300) Large complex with good, clean modern rooms, including 11 large apartments with kitchens. Doubles and triples also have kitchen access. Grassy backyard.

Eating & Drinking

La Anónima (cnr Yrigoyen & 25 de Mayo) has takeout.

Lupita (Av Gales 191; mains AR$10-38) For something different try this Mexican joint, which serves up tacos, burritos, fajitas, nachos and quesadillas.

Mr Jones (9 de Julio 116; mains AR$15-34; ⏰ from 7pm) Popular spot with relatively exotic cuisine (goulash, pot pies, satay with venison) along with 30 kinds of pizza and imported beers like Negro Modela, Guinness and Budweiser.

El Náutico (Av Roca 790; mains AR$22-45) Long-running seafood restaurant with good service and great local atmosphere. The huge menu has something for everyone – try the AR$35, three-course meal.

Estela (Roque Sáenz Peña 27; mains AR$25-45; ☽ dinner only, closed Mon) Popular, intimate and excellent *parrillada;* also serves seafood and homemade pastas.

Vernardino (Blvd Brown 860; mains AR$25-50) Best for its breezy wood deck, which overlooks the beach – or sit at a table on the sand. Typical menu of meats, pastas, pizzas and sandwiches.

Mar y Meseta (Av Gales 32; mains AR$25-50) Fine restaurant serving tasty, creative dishes like blue-cheese *ñoqui* (gnocchi) and salmon with champagne cream.

Margarita Bar (Roque Sáenz Peña 15) Hip pub with brick walls, food menu, international cocktails and great atmosphere.

Getting There & Around

Madryn has an airport, but most flights arrive 65km south at Trelew (door-to-door shuttle per person AR$25, taxi AR$150). **Aerolíneas Argentinas** (☎ 451-998; Av Roca 427) and **LADE** (☎ 451-256; Av Roca 119) have services.

The bus station is on the corner of Yrigoyen and San Martín. Destinations include Puerto Pirámide (AR$16.50, 1½ hours), Trelew (AR$11, one hour), Comodoro Rivadavia (AR$90, six hours), Viedma (AR$75, seven hours), Esquel (AR$150, 10 hours), Bariloche (AR$240, 14 hours) and Buenos Aires (AR$260, 18 hours).

Rental cars are easily available; rates run about AR$300 (no km limit) per day. For bike rentals check out **Na Praia** ☎ 455-633; Blvd Brown 860); they also rent kayaks and organize windsurfing classes.

RESERVA FAUNÍSTICA PENÍNSULA VALDÉS

☎ 02965

Gouged by two large bays, this oddly shaped peninsula is mostly a flat, bleak and dry landscape of unrelenting low shrubs, with the occasional guanacos or rheas to add interest. Once you get to the coastlines, however, the real celebrity wildlife awaits: sea lions, elephant seals, southern right whales, Commerson's dolphins, Magellanic penguins and – if you're very, very lucky – orcas (who have been filmed here beaching themselves to snatch

pinnipeds). June to mid-December is whale-watching season, penguins waddle around from October to March, and elephant seals and sea lions lounge around all year. Commerson's dolphins are best seen from September to November, while dusky dolphins are spotted year-round. The orca phenomenon happens during high tide (February to April).

As you enter the **Reserva Faunística Península Valdés** (admission AR$45; ☽ 8am-8pm daily) you'll pass the thin 5km neck of the peninsula. If you're on a tour bus, it will stop at a good interpretation center and lookout. Squint northwards for a glimpse of **Isla de los Pájaros**. This small island inspired Antoine de Saint-Exupéry's description of a hat, or 'boa swallowing an elephant,' in his book *The Little Prince* (from 1929 to 1931 Saint-Exupéry flew as a postal manager in the area). Also, keep an eye out for salt flats **Salina Grande** and **Salina Chico** (42m below sea level) – South America's lowest spots.

Caleta Valdés is a bay sheltered by a long gravel spit and favored by elephant seals. Just north of here lives a substantial colony of burrowing Magellanic penguins. At **Punta Norte** a mixed group of sea lions and elephant seals snoozes, with the occasional orca pod keeping an eye out offshore.

Puerto Pirámide – a sunny, sandy, shrubby, one-street kinda town – is home to 500 souls. You can stay here, the peninsula's only sizable settlement, to enjoy a calm spot and be closer to wildlife attractions. Services, however, are much more limited than Puerto Madryn's: for example, there's only one ATM in town (that may not work), and there are no car rentals. Scuba diving and some limited tours are available, however. Boat rides (AR$100) outside whale-watching season aren't really worth it unless you adore shorebirds and sea lions, though there's a chance of seeing dolphins. For information there's the **tourist office** (☎ 495-048; www.puertopiramides.gov.ar).

Sleeping & Eating

There are several accommodation options in Puerto Pirámide; in summer it's a good idea to reserve ahead.

Camping Puerto Pirámides (☎ 15-200-521; campsites per person AR$15) Gravel sites sheltered by shrubs and dunes; beach access available.

Hostel Bahía Ballenas (☎ 15-567-104; www.bahiaballenas.com.ar; dm AR$50) Fairly modern hostel with two large 12-bed, sex-segregated dorms. Good kitchen and common area.

ARGENTINA

Posada Pirámides (☎ 495-040; www.posadapira mides.com; dm/d AR$60/180) Plain hostel with 11 basic rooms and dorms. Good restaurant available.

Among food options, **La Estación**, across from the YPF gas station, has a nice deck and atmosphere. There are many restaurants by the water, down the first street to the right as you enter town; **La Posta**, with a wood deck out front, is a good inexpensive choice.

Getting There & Away

Buses from Puerto Madryn leave for Puerto Pirámide twice daily in summer (AR$16.50, 1½ hours). Schedules are less frequent in the off-season.

TRELEW
☎ 02965 / pop 96,000

Trelew is not an exciting city, but does have a pleasant bustling center with leafy plaza and some historical buildings. There's an excellent dinosaur-oriented museum, and it's a convenient base for exploring the nearby Welsh villages of Gaiman and Dolavon, along with the noisy Punta Tombo penguin reserve.

Trelew's major cultural event is late October's **Eisteddfod de Chubut**, celebrating Welsh traditions.

Information

There's a **tourist office** (☎ 420-139; cnr San Martín & Mitre) on the plaza, where many banks with ATMs can be found, along with the **post office** (cnr Av 25 de Mayo & Mitre).

Sights

In the former railway station, the nicely pre-sented **Museo Pueblo de Luis** (cnr Fontana & 9 de Julio; admission AR$2; ☼ 8am-8pm Mon-Fri, 2-8pm Sat & Sun) has good Welsh artifacts; check out the de-formed skull. Nearby is the excellent **Museo Paleontológico Egidio Feruglio** (admission AR$25; ☼ 9am-8pm), with realistic dinosaur exhibits including crystallized dinosaur eggs.

Tours

Several travel agencies organize tours to Península Valdés (p141) and Punta Tombo (opposite). Tours are similarly priced to those from Puerto Madryn – around AR$150 to AR$180. There are also tours to see black-and-white Commerson's dolphins (AR$100, best viewed September to November).

Sleeping & Eating

Hostel El Ágora (☎ 426-899; hostelagora@hotmail.com; Roberts 33; dm/d AR$40/80) Five blocks northwest of the bus terminal is this nothing-special hostel. There are only two bathrooms for 16 beds and a small patio for *asados*.

Hostel Soñadores (☎ 436-505; hosteltrelew@speedy .com.ar; Lamadrid 1312; dm AR$40) Fifteen blocks south of the bus terminal is this hostel with a strange vibe. There's one 14-bed dorm upstairs, a four-bed 'private' room (AR$200; actually part of a larger room) and a tiny kitchen. All share 2½ bathrooms.

Residencial Rivadavia (☎ 434-472; www.cpatagonia .com/rivadavia; Rivadavia 55; s/d with shared bathroom from AR$90/105) Go for the upstairs rooms, which are newer and brighter, at this plain guest-house. Every two rooms downstairs share a bathroom.

Hotel Touring Club (☎ 433-997; www.touringpat agonia.com.ar; Fontana 240; s/d AR$120/190) An institu-tion, with a downstairs cafe that exudes classic old atmosphere. Rooms upstairs are plain, dark and small, with those on the inside a bit depressing.

La Bodeguita (Belgrano 374; mains AR$15-30) This modern, popular place is big on pizzas, but it also does meats, pasta and seafood. Attentive service, family atmosphere and huge menu.

Confitería Touring Club (Fontana 240; mains AR$10-30) Excellent for its old-time atmosphere and serious, suited waiters. Breakfast, sandwiches and lots of alcoholic drinks available; check out the dusty bottles behind the bar.

El Viejo Molino (Gales 250; mains AR$25-50) Beautifully renovated old mill, with lofty and artsy interior. Look for the BBQ window grill; also fish, pastas and fancy salads. Tango les-sons upstairs.

Getting There & Around

The airport is 6km north of town (take Puerto Madryn bus and walk 300m; taxi AR$18). **Aerolíneas Argentinas** (☎ 421-257; 25 de Mayo 33) and **LADE** (☎ 435-740), with offices at the bus station, fly here.

Trelew's bus station is six blocks northeast of downtown. Destinations include Puerto Madryn (AR$10, one hour), Gaiman (AR$3.80, 30 minutes), Comodoro Rivadavia (AR$75, five hours), Bariloche (AR$200, 14 hours) and Buenos Aires (AR$270, 18 hours).

Car-rental stands are at the airport and in town; cheapest rentals run about AR$170 with 200km.

AROUND TRELEW
Gaiman
☎ 02965 / pop 5700

For a taste of Wales in Patagonia, head 17km west of Trelew to Gaiman. The streets are calm and wide and the buildings are nondescript and low; on hot days the local boys swim in the nearby river. The real reason travelers visit Gaiman, however, is to down pastries at one of several good **Welsh teahouses**. Most open around 3pm and offer unlimited tea and homemade sweets for AR$35 to AR$40 (make sure you eat a very light lunch). To get oriented visit the **tourist office** (☎ 491-570; www.gaiman.gov.ar; cnr Rivadavia & Belgrano).

The small **Museo Histórico Regional Gales** (cnr Sarmiento & 28 de Julio; admission AR$2; ☉ 3-7pm) details Welsh colonization with old pioneer photographs and household items. Support Joaquín Alonso's eccentricity at **Parque El Desafío** (admission AR$10; ☉ dawn-dusk), a garden-forest area methodically strewn with bottles, cans, and even old TV sets.

Gaiman is an easy day trip from Trelew, but if you want to stay, try homey **Dyffryn Gwirdd** (☎ 491-777; www.dwhosteria.com.ar; Tello 103; s/d AR$90/140), with seven simple but good rooms and a pleasant atmosphere. And just outside town there's **Hostería Gwesty Tywi** (☎ 491-292; www.hosteria-gwestytywi.com.ar; Chacra 202; s/d AR$150/180), on parklike country grounds complete with farm animals; the six rooms here are fine and comfortable.

Frequent buses go to/from Trelew (AR$3.80, 30 minutes).

Reserva Provincial Punta Tombo
From September to April, over a half-million Magellanic penguins breed at **Punta Tombo** (admission AR$35; ☉ dawn-dusk Aug-Apr), 120km south of Trelew and 1½ hours by road. It's the largest penguin colony outside Antarctica. Other area birds include rheas, cormorants, giant petrels, kelp gulls and oyster-catchers. You may also spy some land critters such as armadillos, foxes and guanacos on the way there.

You can get very close to the birds for photos, but don't try to touch them – they'll nip. To get there, arrange a tour in Trelew or Puerto Madryn (from AR$120 to AR$180) or hire a taxi (AR$400 round-trip; negotiate waiting fee). Car rentals are possible from Puerto Madryn or Trelew.

COMODORO RIVADAVIA
☎ 0297 / pop 144,000

Petroleum-rich Comodoro Rivadavia is popular only as a convenient pit stop along Argentina's long eastern coastline. It's a nondescript city with busy streets and the ugliest cathedral you'll likely ever see. If you're stuck here and are desperate, check out the **Museo del Petróleo** (Petroleum Museum; cnr San Lorenzo & Calvo; admission AR$10; ☉ 9am-5pm Tue-Sat), 3km north.

Information
There are ATMs and internet cafes along San Martín.
Cambio Thaler (Mitre 943)
Post office (cnr San Martín & Moreno)
Tourist office (☎ 446-2376; www.comodoro.gov.ar; Rivadavia 430)

Sleeping & Eating
Comodoro is a transport hub, and hotels can get full. Many offer a shared bathroom option for less.

25 de Mayo (☎ 447-2350; 25 de Mayo 989; r from AR$85) Very basic, with most rooms facing a small outdoor hallway. Kitchen access available.

Hostería Rua Marina (☎ 446-8777; Belgrano 738; s/d from AR$100/140) Worn dark rooms, stuffy in hot weather and most facing an indoor hall. The best ones are rooms 18, 19 and 20 – they're in the back and upstairs, and boast outside windows.

Cari-Hue (☎ 447-2946; Belgrano 563; s/d from AR$120/150) Boring and dark, yet decent enough budget rooms with cable TV.

Hotel El Español (☎ 446-0116; hotelespanol_patagonico @hotmail.com; 9 de Julio 940; r from AR$130) Decent simple rooms with cable TV; some have bathtubs. The upstairs rooms are brighter.

Patio de Comidas (cnr Güemes & San Martín; meals under AR$5) Good and cheap. Next to La Anónima supermarket.

Molly Malone (San Martín 292; mains AR$15-35) Small and funky bar/restaurant serving breakfast, sandwiches, burgers and pastas. Wi-fi available.

La Barra (San Martín 686; mains AR$25-50) Very popular cafe which serves pastas, salads and sandwiches, along with plenty of cocktails.

Getting There & Around
The **airport** is 8km east of the center (bus AR$1.10, taxi AR$25). **Aerolíneas Argentinas** (☎ 454-8126; Rivadavia 156) and **LADE** (☎ 447-0585; Rivadavia 360) operate flights here.

The bus terminal is in the center of town. Destinations include Trelew (AR$60, 5½ hours), Los Antiguos (AR$82, 7½ hours), Esquel (AR$80, nine hours), Bariloche (AR$170, 14 hours), Río Gallegos (AR$150, 11 hours) and Buenos Aires (AR$310, 24 hours). Buses to El Calafate all go through Río Gallegos.

LOS ANTIGUOS
☎ 02963 / pop 2500

Situated on the shores of Lago Buenos Aires, Los Antiguos is a calm little town with rows of poplar trees sheltering *chacras* (small, independent farms) of cherries, strawberries, apples, apricots and peaches. Travelers come to cross the border into Chile, but getting here via RN 40 can be an adventure in itself.

Los Antiguos' **Fiesta de la Cereza** (cherry festival) occurs the first or second weekend in January, and the nearby countryside has good **hiking** and **fishing**. The **tourist office** (☎ 491-261; www.losantiguos.gov.ar; 11 de Julio 446) has information. There's one bank with an ATM.

A 20-minute walk east of the center is the cypress-sheltered **Camping Municipal** (☎ 491-265; campsites per person AR$5, tents AR$15, cabins AR$80-120). **Albergue Padilla** (☎ 491-140; San Martín 44 Sur; dm AR$35-40, d/tr AR$120/150) is a family-run place right where Chaltén Travel buses stops. For more comfort, try **Hotel Los Antiguos Cerezos** (☎ 491-132; hotel_losantigoscerezos@hotmail.com; s/d AR$120/160). A good place to eat is the chalet-like **Viva El Viento** (mains AR$23-40), on the main drag. These places are all around the main drag.

Buses cross the border to Chile Chico a few times daily. From November through March, **Chaltén Travel** (www.chaltentravel.com) goes to El Chaltén on even-numbered days (AR$190, 12 to 16 hours). Other destinations include Perito Moreno (AR$19, one hour), Río Gallegos (AR$155, 16 hours) and Comodoro Rivadavia (AR$82, six hours). There are thrice weekly Tacsa buses to both Esquel (AR$154, 12 hours) and El Chaltén (AR$150, 14 hours). The gradual paving of RN 40 and changing demand will keep transport options in flux, so get current information from the tourist office.

EL CHALTÉN
☎ 02962 / pop winter 600, summer 1800

Argentina's trekking capital and one of Patagonia's top traveler magnets, this small but growing village is set in a pretty river valley. Travelers come for the extraordinary snowcapped towers of the **Fitz Roy range**, offering world-class hiking and camping – along with astounding mountain scenery. Climbers from around the world make their bid to summit the premier peak **Cerro Fitz Roy** (3441m), among others. Pack for wind, rain and cold temperatures even in summer, when views of the peaks can be obscured. If the sun is out, however, El Chaltén is paradise on earth – but come and see it soon, as the road to El Calafate is being paved and changes are sure to come.

Note that El Chaltén is within national park boundaries, and rules regarding fires and cleaning distances from rivers must be followed. El Chaltén mostly shuts down from April to October.

Information

On the left just before the bridge into town, **park headquarters** (☎ 493-004) has maps and hiking information; day buses automatically stop here. You need to register for anything longer than a day hike. The **tourist office** (☎ 493-270) is to the left after crossing the bridge into town.

Bring enough Argentine pesos for your stay in El Chaltén. There are no banks or exchange houses, and only one undependable ATM. Few places take traveler's checks, credit cards or US dollars – and if they do, exchange rates are poor. Many travelers have left sooner than they wanted to because they ran out of money.

Locutorios and limited internet access (slow and expensive) are available. A decent selection of camping food and supplies is readily available at the small supermarkets in town. Gear like stoves, fuel, sleeping bags, tents and warm clothes can be bought or rented from Camping Center, Eolia and Viento Oeste, all on San Martín (the main drag).

If you need a mountain, climbing or ice-trekking guide, visit **Casa de Guías** (www.casa deguias.com.ar) on San Martín.

Hiking

One popular hike goes to **Laguna Torre** and the base camp for skilled technical climbers attempting the spire of **Cerro Torre** (3128m); it's three hours one way.

Another hike climbs from the end of town to a signed junction, where a side trail leads to backcountry campsites at Laguna Capri. The main trail continues gently to Río Blanco, base camp for the Cerro Fitz Roy climb, and then very steeply to **Laguna de los Tres** (4.5 hours one way).

The hike to **Lago Toro** is seven hours one way, so most folks camp overnight.

Sleeping

Prices listed are for January and February, when you should arrive with reservations. Not all accommodations include breakfast.

Confluencia is a free campsite (seven night limit) right at the entrance to town; there's an outhouse and potable river water nearby. Campfires are not allowed; do all washing at least 100 steps from the river. Ask nearby hostels about showers.

Rancho Grande Hostel (☎ 493-005; www.rancho grandehostel.com; San Martín 724; dm/d/tr/q AR$50/200/230/260) Large hostel with spacious, modern dorms and common areas. Good services and busy atmosphere. Great doubles, all with bathroom. Takes credit cards and traveler's checks; HI discount.

Albergue Patagonia (☎ 493-019; patagoniahostel @yahoo.com; San Martín 392; dm AR$50, d AR$140-230) A cozy hostel with an intimate feel, small dorms and cramped bathrooms. The newer double wing has larger, more comfortable doubles. Bike rentals available.

Condor de los Andes (☎ 493-101; www.condor delosandes.com; cnr Río de las Vueltas & Halvorsen; dm AR$50-60, d AR$220) This small hostel has good common spaces and a backpacker feel. Each dorm has its own bathroom. HI discount.

Posada La Base (☎ 493-031; Hensen 16; d AR$200-300) Friendly place offering spacious rooms facing outside; kitchen access available. Two rooms share a kitchen/dining area; great for large groups. Video loft in reception area.

Also recommended:

El Relincho (☎ 493-007; www.elchalten.com/elrelincho; San Martín s/n; campsites per person AR$20) Large grassy complex with pleasant campsites near river. Rustic hangout area. Three large and comfortable *cabañas* available.

Albergue del Lago (☎ 493-245; hosteldellago_el-chalten@yahoo.com; Lago del Desierto 135; campsites per person AR$20, dm AR$40) Very basic, with rather bare dining area and small dorms. Rooms out back are better. Big with camping climbers.

Nothofagus B&B (☎ 493-087; www.nothofagusbb .com.ar; cnr Hensen & Riquelme; s/d AR$200/210, with shared bathroom AR$140/150) Wonderfully homey, friendly and cozy guesthouse with spotless carpeted rooms.

Inlandsis (☎ 493-276; www.inlandsis.com.ar; Lago del Desierto 480; d AR$160-210) Eight great carpeted rooms, all with views. Friendly and intimate.

Hostería Lago Viedma (☎ 493-089; www.elchalten .com/lagoviedma; Arbilla 71; d AR$260) Just four tidy and simply decorated rooms at this small guesthouse.

Eating & Drinking

Pack lunches are available at most hostels/hotels and at some restaurants.

Patagonicus (cnr Güemes & Madsen; pizzas AR$20-50) Popular pizzeria baking 20 kinds of pies, as well as pastas, salads and sandwiches.

El Bodegón Cervecería (San Martín s/n; mains AR$30-42) Wonderfully cozy pub with creative driftwood decor, good homemade brews and feisty beer master. Pizza, pastas and *locro* available.

El Muro (San Martín 948; mains AR$30-50) Good meats and homemade pasta dishes like lamb lasagna and pizzas topped with venison or boar. Nice atmosphere; located towards the end of town.

Fuegia Bistro (San Martín 493; mains AR$30-50; ☾ breakfast & dinner only) Upscale restaurant with great service and fine cuisine that's heavy on the meats.

Estepa (cnr Cerro Solo & Rojo; mains AR$40-60; ☾ closed Mon) Well-prepared and tasty dishes like lamb with Calafate sauce and salmon ravioli. Plenty of pizzas; also makes lunch boxes.

CROSSING FROM EL CHALTÉN (ARGENTINA) TO VILLA O'HIGGINS (CHILE)

This two-day trip can be completed between November and March. Bring provisions and Chilean pesos (if possible); check boat schedules beforehand.

From El Chaltén, take the morning shuttle to Lago del Desierto (AR$80, 1½ hours), where you can either take the **Patagonia Aventura boat** (☎ 02962-493110; www.patagonia-aventura.com.ar; AR$90) or hike along the eastern shore (15km, 4½ hours). At the northern end of the lake is Argentine immigration. From here it's a five-hour walk to Candelario Mansilla (where basic accommodations, camping and meals are available) and Chilean immigration. Chilean boat Hielo Sur (www.hielosur .com) goes from Candelario Mansilla to Villa O'Higgins (CH$33,000) thrice weekly.

Getting There & Away

The following schedules are for December through February; during other months services are less frequent or nonexistent. When paving work is done, the travel time to El Calafate will be much shorter.

Chaltén's first bus terminal should be finished by the time you arrive. There are several daily buses to El Calafate (AR$70, four hours). **Chalten Travel** (☎ 493-005; cnr Guemes & Lago del Desierto; www.chaltentravel.com) provides transport to Lago del Desierto (AR$80, 1½ hours), where it's possible to do boat/hiking combinations into Chile. Its buses also go to Los Antiguos (AR$150, 13 hours) and further points north from mid-November to mid-April, but only on odd-numbered days.

EL CALAFATE

☎ 02902 / pop 20,000

Fast-growing El Calafate has become a gung-ho destination, but despite its touristy facade, it makes a pleasant-enough pit stop for a few days. Its prime location between El Chaltén and Torres del Paine (Chile) also means that most Patagonian travelers pass through here at some point or another, and fortunately, there is one incredible, unmissable attraction: the dynamic Glaciar Perito Moreno, located 80km away in Parque Nacional Los Glaciares (p148).

Information

There are several banks with ATMs in town (If you're planning on visiting El Chaltén, withdraw enough money in El Calafate).

Cambio Thaler (Libertador 963, Local 2) Changes traveler's checks.

La Cueva (☎ 492-417; Moyano 839; jorgelemos322 @hotmail.com; ☼ Sep-May) Basic mountaineers' *refugio* that organizes area treks.

National Park Office (☎ 491-545; Libertador 1302) Issues trekking permits and fishing licenses and provides hiking information.

Post office (Libertador 1133)

Tourist office (☎ 491-090; www.elcalafate.gov.ar; cnr Libertador & Rosales) Also at the bus terminal.

Sights & Activities

Within town there's not much to do besides souvenir shopping and people-watching, but a few distractions exist. **Centro de Interpretación Histórica** (☎ 492-799; cnr Brown & Bonarelli; admission AR$19; ☼ 10am-8pm) explains the history of Patagonia via photos, diagrams and a video.

It's just north of the center. **Laguna Nimez** is a wetlands sanctuary 15 minutes' walk from town. Walk north on Alem, go over the small white bridge, and at the restaurant, jog right, then left. There may be a small admission charge. There's also good horse riding in the area.

Sleeping

In January and February reservations are recommended.

Camping El Ovejero (☎ 493-422; www.campinglove jero.com.ar; Pantín 64; campsites per person AR$15-20, dm AR$35-45) Relatively pleasant but busy camping spot with shady creekside sites, picnic tables and fire pits. Kitchen access available with hostel bunks.

Hospedaje Jorgito (☎ 491-323; Moyano 943; campsites per person AR$15; d with/without bathroom AR$120/80) Offers twelve bright, warm and old-fashioned rooms, all in a large family house with kitchen access. Pleasant orchard camping sites in back.

Hostel del Glaciar Pioneros (☎ 491-243; www.gla ciar.com; Los Pioneros 255; dm AR$42, d AR$156-203) Good, long-running hostel with spacious common areas and cool hangout restaurant-pub. Dorms are small but clean; superior doubles are excellent. HI discount.

Che Lagarto (☎ 496-670; www.chelagarto.com; 25 de Mayo 311; dm/d AR$45/238) Slick hostel with pool table, contemporary sofas and flat-screen TV in reception/bar area, plus wooden front deck. Small but tidy dorms, social atrium with fireplace, cheap *asados* and nightly movies.

America del Sur (☎ 493-525; www.americahostel .com.ar; Puerto Deseado 153; dm/d AR$60/240) One of Calafate's best hostels, with great views, loft hangout space, spacious modern dorms (each with its own bath) and good service. Clean and tidy, with floor heating. Cheap *asados*.

Hospedaje Alejandra (☎ 491-328; Espora 60; d AR$90, cabañas AR$300) Seven plain rooms, with shared bathroom, along a hallway in a small family house. Much better are the three *cabañas* in back, which sleep up to five people and have kitchens.

Las Cabañitas (☎ 491-118; lascabanitas@cotecal .com.ar; Feilberg 218; r & cabañas AR$180-315) This friendly place has just five small and dark but cute *cabañas* with tiny bathrooms. A few larger, more modern rooms are also available.

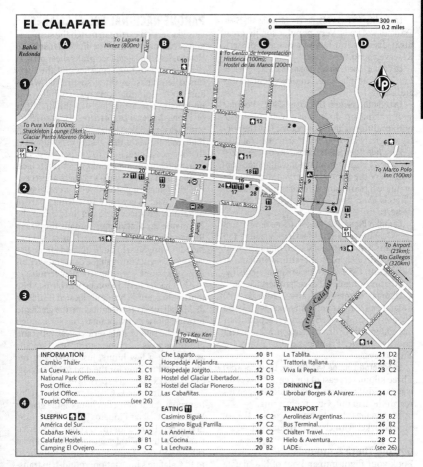

EL CALAFATE

Also recommended:

Hostel de las Manos (☎ 492-996; www.hostelde
lasmanos.com.ar; Feruglio 59; dm AR$40-45, d AR$180)
Lovely small hostel with bright common area. Dorms in
new wing are much larger. It's 300m north of the center.

Calafate Hostel (☎ 492-450; www.calafatehostels
.com; Moyano 1226; dm AR$43-50, d AR$180) Huge log
cabin hostel surrounded by balconies inside and out. A bit
impersonal, but good for large groups. Small restaurant;
HI discount.

Marco Polo Inn (☎ 493-899; www.marcopoloinn
calafate.com; Calle 405 No 82; dm/d AR$45/200) Large
hostel with good dorms and common area. Nightly events
and pool table. Located a 15-minute walk west of the
center. HI discount.

i Keu Ken (☎ 495-175; www.patagoniaikeuken.com.ar;
Pontoriero 171; dm/d AR$45/210) Pleasant intimate hostel

about 10 minutes' walk uphill from bus terminal. Chill
atmosphere, great views and good dorms.

Hostel del Glaciar Libertador (☎ 492-492; www
.glaciar.com; Libertador 587; dm/d AR$49/253) Big modern
hostel with spacious kitchen and dining areas. Clean, well-
thought-out dorms and lovely doubles. HI discount.

Cabañas Nevis (☎ 493-180; www.cabanasnevis
.com.ar; Libertador 1696; cabañas AR$380-590) Four-
teen comfortable, two-story A-frame *cabañas* with
four to eight beds and kitchen. Great for large groups;
English spoken.

Eating & Drinking

Viva la Pepa (Amado 833; mains AR$25-40) Delicious,
creative and well-prepared dishes like savory
and sweet crepes, beautifully constructed
salads and huge tasty sandwiches.

La Tablita (☎ 491-065; Rosales 28; mains AR$25-60; ◌ closed Wed lunch) Very popular for its great meat dishes, with lots of sides and dessert. Reserve ahead.

La Cocina (Libertador 1245; mains AR$30-50; ◌ closed Tue) Intimate place serving excellent pastas and salads.

La Lechuza (Libertador 1301; pizzas AR$30-65) Popular spot baking up dozens of excellent pizzas, both traditional and more exotic (try the stir-fry veggies with whiskey-marinated crab).

Pura Vida (Libertador 1876; mains AR$40-60; ◌ closed Wed dinner) Creative healthy food and huge portions. Try the meat stew served in a squash, or the eggplant tart with mashed potatoes. There's even apple pie with ice cream for dessert.

Casimiro Biguá (☎ 492-590; Libertador 963; mains AR$50-70) Fine restaurant serving Calafate's top food and wine. Also has a *parrilla* nearby at Libertador 993, plus a Trattoria Italiana at Libertador 1359. All have exquisite cuisine, good atmosphere and excellent service.

Librobar Borges & Alvarez (Libertador 1015) Calafate's best hangout cafe-bar, with good people-watching views from its second-floor loft. Offers a large drink selection, a few snacks and live music. Front patio downstairs for sunny days.

Shackleton Lounge (☎ 493-516; Libertador 3287) Three kilometres east of the center, this place was closed at research time, but if it's open it's worth the trip out. Give them a ring.

La Anónima (cnr Libertador & Perito Moreno) Supermarket with cheap takeout food.

Getting There & Around

Book your flight into and out of El Calafate well ahead of time. The **airport** is 23km east of town; the departure tax is AR$20.

Ves Patagonia (☎ 494-355) has door-to-door shuttle services for AR$26; taxis cost AR$80 (though sometimes negotiable for less).

Aerolíneas Argentinas (☎ 0870-222-86527; 9 de Julio 57) and **LADE** (☎ 491-262; at bus terminal) operate flights here.

Bus destinations include Río Gallegos (AR$45, 4½ hours), El Chaltén (AR$70, 3½ hours) and Puerto Natales, Chile (AR$50, five hours).

In summer, **Chalten Travel** (www.chaltentravel.com; Libertador 1174) does the multiday trip from El Calafate to Bariloche via adventurous Ruta 40 (AR$480). Car rentals in El Calafate will cost you from AR$250 per day with 200km.

PARQUE NACIONAL LOS GLACIARES

Few glaciers on earth can match the suspense and excitement of the blue-hued **Glaciar Perito Moreno**. Its 60m jagged ice peaks sheer off and crash land with huge splashes and thunder-ous rifle-cracks, birthing small tidal waves and large bobbing icebergs – while your neck hairs rise a-tingling. It's the highlight of **Parque Nacional Los Glaciares** (admission AR$60) and measures 35km long, 5km wide and 60m high. What makes this glacier exceptional is that it's advancing – up to 2m per day – and constantly dropping chunks of ice off its face. While most of the world's glaciers are reced-ing, the Glaciar Perito Moreno is considered 'stable.' And every once in a while, part of its facade advances far enough to reach the Península de Magallanes to dam the Brazo Rico arm of Lago Argentino. This causes tre-mendous pressure to build up, and after a few years a river cuts through the dam and eventu-ally collapses it – with spectacular results.

The Glaciar Perito Moreno was born to be a tourist attraction. The ideally located Península de Magallanes is close enough to the glacier to provide glorious panoramas, but far enough away to be safe. A long series of catwalks and platforms gives everyone a great view. Hanging around for a few hours, just looking at the glacier and waiting for the next great calving, can be an existential experience.

Most tours from El Calafate cost AR$110 for transport, guide and a few hours at the glacier; Hostel del Glaciar Pioneros (p146) and Hostel del Glaciar Libertador (p147) offer an 'alterna-tive' tour that includes a short hike and boat ride (AR$175). If you don't want a tour, head to El Calafate's bus station; round-trip trans-port costs AR$80 and gives you several hours at the glacier. Groups of up to four can hire a *remise* for about AR$300 (negotiate!). Also, consider seeing the glacier later in the after-noon, when many of the crowds have gone and more ice falls after the heat of the day.

There's a cafeteria at the site, but for best selection and price bring a lunch from El Calafate.

Boat tours to other glaciers are also avail-able, but a more adventurous option is to hike directly on the Moreno glacier in crampons (AR$400 to AR$530, including transportation but not park admission). There are two op-tions available, and they're well run by **Hielo & Aventura** (☎ 492-205; www.hieloyaventura.com; Libertador 935) in El Calafate.

RÍO GALLEGOS
☎ 02966 / pop 90,000

Río Gallegos is not a very interesting destination, but it's not terribly boring either. The main drag downtown is lively, the low tides amazingly low (they dip down 14m) and some of the continent's best fly-fishing is nearby. You can even see penguins – if you don't mind the trip 140km southeast, to Cabo Vírgenes. Still, most travelers stop here just long enough to catch the next bus to El Calafate, Puerto Natales or Ushuaia.

Information
Most banks with ATMs are on or near Av Roca.

Municipal tourist office (☎ 436-920; www.turismo
.mrg.gov.ar; cnr Av Roca & Córdoba)
Post office (cnr Avs Roca & San Martín)
Provincial tourist office (☎ 438-725; Av Roca 863)
Thaler Cambio (cnr Av San Martín & Alcorta)
Tourist office (☎ 442-159) At the bus terminal.

Sleeping & Eating
Polideportivo Atsa (☎ 442-310; cnr Asturias & Yugoslavia; campsites per person AR$10, tents AR$10) Remodeling at the time of research; about 500m southwest of bus terminal.

Casa de Familia Elcira Contreras (☎ 429-856; Zuccarrino 431; dm/d AR$40/120) Simple home run by an elderly woman, with clean rooms and kitchen access. One eight-bed apartment available. It's about 10 blocks from the center and a 15-minute walk from the bus terminal (taxi AR$9).

Hotel Covadonga (☎ 420-190; hotelcovadongargl @hotmail.com; Av Roca 1244; r with/without bathroom AR$160/130) Old hotel with some retro charm – and they're not even trying for style. Inside rooms share bathrooms.

Hotel Sehuen (☎ 425-683; www.hotelsehuen.com; Rawson 160; r from AR$134) Attractive modern hotel with bright lobby and spacious, comfortable rooms.

El Viejo Miramar (☎ 430-401; hotelviejomiramar@ yahoo.com.ar; Av Roca 1630; s/d AR$150/180) Friendly place with just 10 tidy, carpeted rooms. Don't let its location, next to a gas station, put you off.

Restaurante Chino (9 de Julio 27; buffets AR$38) The bad news: the food isn't that great. The good news: it's all-you-can-eat.

Restaurant RoCo (Av Roca 1157; mains AR$20-60) Slick and contemporary, at least for Río Gallegos. Typical menu with plenty of choices.

Lagunacazul (cnr Lista & Sarmiento; mains AR$30-70; ☽ closed Mon) Río Gallegos' best restaurant, close to the shore and with attentive service.

Getting There & Away
The airport (☎ 442-340) is 7km from the center (taxi AR$27). **Aerolíneas Argentinas** (☎ 0810-222-86527; Av San Martín 545), **LAN** (☎ 457-189; at airport) and **LADE** (☎ 423-775; Fagnano 53) operate services.

The bus terminal is about 2km from the center, on RN 3 (bus 'B' AR$1.75, taxi AR$13). Destinations include El Calafate (AR$45, four hours), Ushuaia (AR$180, 12 hours), Comodoro Rivadavia (AR$90, 11 hours), Río Grande (AR$120, eight hours) and Buenos Aires (AR$330, 36 hours). Buses to Punta Arenas (AR$40, five hours) run only twice weekly; try buying your ticket in advance. Buses to Puerto Natales (AR$45, six hours) often include a transfer and wait in Río Turbio.

TIERRA DEL FUEGO

Reluctantly shared by Argentina and Chile, the 'land of fire' really is the end of the world. The archipelago, surrounded by the stormy South Atlantic and the Strait of Magellan, offers plenty of natural beauty: scenic glaciers, lush forests, astounding mountains, clear waterways and a dramatic coast. The largest city, Ushuaia, boasts the title 'southernmost city in the world' – and is the main gateway to Antarctica. Tierra del Fuego is isolated and hard to reach, but for true adventure-seekers it's a must.

Passing ships gave Tierra del Fuego its name: they spotted distant shoreline campfires that the Yámana (or Yahgan) people tended. In 1520 Magellan paid a visit, but he was seeking passage to the Asian spice islands. As ships sailed by, the indigenous Ona (or Selknam) and Haush continued hunting land animals, while the Yámana and Alacalufe lived on seafood and marine mammals. The early 1800s, however, brought on European settlement – and the demise of these indigenous peoples.

RÍO GRANDE
☎ 02964 / pop 68,000

Windy Río Grande is just a bleak pit stop for most travelers, though fishers come from all over the world for their chance to hook gigantic trout in the surrounding countryside. For information, contact the friendly **tourist office** (☎ 431-324; www.riogrande.gov.ar) in the main plaza.

TIERRA DEL FUEGO

The closest thing to a hostel, homey **Albergue Hotel Argentino** (☎ 422-546; San Martín 64; campsites per person AR$20, dm/d AR$40/80) has simple facilities in an old house.

Río Grande's airport is 4km west of town. **Aerolíneas Argentinas** (☎ 424-467; San Martín 607) and **LADE** (☎ 422-968; Lasserre 445) provide air services. The bus terminal is at Finocchio 1149; destinations include Ushuaia (AR$60, 3½ hours), Rio Gallegos (AR$120, eight hours) and Punta Arenas (AR$120, eight hours).

USHUAIA

☎ 02901 / pop 60,000

Nestled on the shores of the Beagle Channel, as far south as roads go on earth, lies charismatic Ushuaia. Boasting 1500m Fuegan Andes

peaks as a spectacular backdrop, this touristy yet pleasant city attracts all sorts of travelers: the independent backpackers, the cruisers, the Antarctica-bound and those who finally end their South American biking, motorcycling or driving journeys here – at the southernmost city in the world. But there's more than just this quirky novelty at hand, as adventurous souls also come to explore nearby pristine mountains, lakes and glaciers, as well as partake in the area's many other outdoor possibilities.

Originally established as a penal colony, Ushuaia became a key naval base in 1950. Gold, lumber, wool and fishing brought in revenue over the years, but today tourism drives this fast-growing city's economy. In the summer high season (December through March), cruise

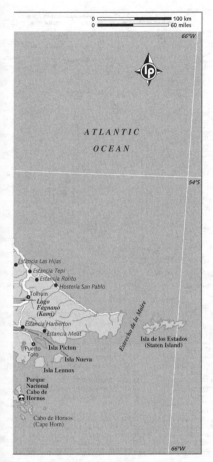

ships visit almost daily – and the main drag, Av San Martín, fills with Gore-Tex-wearing tourists. Antarctica has become a major destination for bold travelers, and Ushuaia is the closest city from which to jump off to the White Continent. Like a star at her peak, Ushuaia's popularity won't be waning anytime soon.

Information

Internet cafes are common. Most banks in town have ATMs.

Boutique del Libro (25 de Mayo 62 & Av San Martín 1120) Carries Lonely Planet guides.

Cambio Thaler (Av San Martín 209) Changes traveler's checks.

Club Andino (☎ 422-335; www.clubandinoushuaia .com.ar; Juana Fadul 50) Trekking maps and guidebooks.

Immigration office (☎ 437-718; Fuegia Basket 187)

Municipal tourist office (☎ 424-550; www.turis moushuaia.com; Av San Martín 674) There's also a tourist information office at the pier.

National Parks Administration (☎ 421-315; Av San Martín 1395).

Sights & Activities

The small but good **Museo del Fin del Mundo** (Av Maipú 175; admission AR$20; ☒ 9am-8pm summer) explains Ushuaia's indigenous and natural histories; check out the bone implements and bird taxidermy room. It has a nearby annex in a historical building at Maipú 465. The excellent **Museo Marítimo** (cnr Yaganes & Paz; admission AR$45; ☒ 9am-8pm) is located in an old prison that held up to 700 inmates in 380 small jail cells. There are interesting exhibits on expeditions to Antarctica, plus an art gallery. Tiny **Museo Yámana** (Rivadavia 56; admission AR$15; ☒ 10am-8pm summer) has some history on the area's indigenous people.

After seeing the Glaciar Perito Moreno in El Calafate, the **Glaciar Martial** here will seem like a piddly ice cube – but at least it's located in a beautiful valley with great views of Ushuaia and the Beagle Channel. Walk or taxi (AR$20) to a short chairlift (AR$35 round-trip) 7km northwest of town; from here it's about two hours' walk up to the glacier (slightly shorter if you take the chairlift).

Hop on a **boat tour** to *estancias*, a lighthouse, Puerto Williams, bird island and sea-lion or penguin colonies. Ask about the size of the boat (smaller boats get closer to wildlife), whether there are bilingual guides and if there are any landings (only Pira Tour actually lands at the penguin colony, which is active October through March). Tours range from AR$50 to AR$240; tickets are available at the pier, travel agencies and hotels.

Founded by missionary Thomas Bridges and located 85km east of Ushuaia, **Estancia Harberton** (☎ 422-742; admission AR$25; ☒ mid-Oct–mid-Apr) was Tierra del Fuego's first *estancia*. This 200-sq-km ranch boasts splendid scenery and alluring history. There's a good museum, and you can take an optional boat trip to the area's penguin colony. Buses to Harberton cost AR$140 per person round-trip and take 1½ hours; they leave from near Av Maipú and 25 de Mayo.

Hiking and trekking opportunities aren't limited to the national park: the entire mountain range behind Ushuaia, with its lakes and rivers, is an outdoor person's wonderland. Many trails are poorly marked, however, so

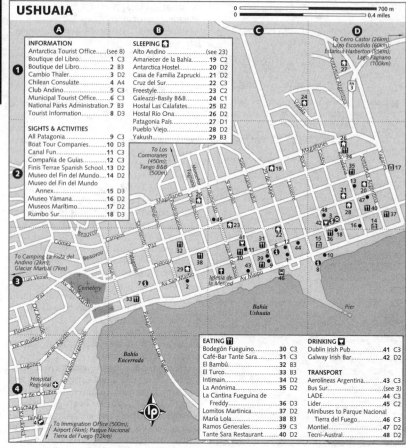

USHUAIA

INFORMATION
Antarctica Tourist Office......(see 8)
Boutique del Libro..............1 C3
Boutique del Libro..............2 B3
Cambio Thaler......................3 D2
Chilean Consulate................4 A4
Club Andino........................5 C3
Municipal Tourist Office........6 C3
National Parks Administration.7 B3
Tourist Information................8 D3

SIGHTS & ACTIVITIES
All Patagonia........................9 C3
Boat Tour Companies..........10 D3
Canal Fun...........................11 C3
Compañía de Guías.............12 C3
Finis Terrae Spanish School..13 D2
Museo del Fin del Mundo....14 D2
Museo del Fin del Mundo
 Annex..............................15 D3
Museo Yámana....................16 D2
Museos Marítimo.................17 D2
Rumbo Sur..........................18 D3

SLEEPING
Alto Andino........................(see 23)
Amanecer de la Bahía.........19 C2
Antarctica Hostel................20 D2
Casa de Familia Zaprucki.....21 D2
Cruz del Sur.......................22 C3
Freestyle............................23 C2
Galeazzi-Basily B&B.............24 C1
Hostal Las Calafates............25 B2
Hostal Río Ona....................26 D2
Patagonia País....................27 D1
Pueblo Viejo.......................28 D2
Yakush................................29 B3

EATING
Bodegón Fueguino.............30 C3
Café-Bar Tante Sara............31 C3
El Bambú............................32 B3
El Turco..............................33 B3
Intimain..............................34 D2
La Anónima........................35 D2
La Cantina Fueguina de
 Freddy..............................36 D3
Lomitos Martinica................37 D2
María Lola..........................38 B3
Ramos Generales................39 C3
Tante Sara Restaurant.........40 D2

DRINKING
Dublin Irish Pub..................41 C3
Galway Irish Bar.................42 D2

TRANSPORT
Aerolíneas Argentina..........43 C3
Bus Sur.............................(see 3)
LADE.................................44 C3
Lider.................................45 C2
Minibuses to Parque Nacional
 Tierra del Fuego................46 C3
Montiel..............................47 D2
Tecni-Austral.....................48 D2

hire a guide from **Compañía de Guías** (☎ 437-753; www.companiadeguias.com.ar; Av San Martín 628), which has guides for trekking, mountaineering, ice/rock climbing, kayaking, sailing and fishing.

Plenty of ski resorts dot the nearby mountains, with both downhill and cross-country options. The largest resort is **Cerro Castor** (☎ 499-302; www.cerrocastor.com), about 27km from Ushuaia, with almost 20 slopes. Ski season runs from June to October.

Tours

Many travel agencies sell tours around the region. You can go horse riding, canoeing or mountain biking, visit nearby lakes, spy on birds and beavers, and even get pulled by husky dogsleds during winter. **Canal Fun**

(☎ 437-395; www.canalfun.com; 9 de Julio 118) is one of the better adventure tour organizers, with prices to match.

Courses

Learn Spanish at **Finis Terrae Spanish School** (☎ 433-871; www.spanishpatagonia.com; Rivadavia 263). They offer various after-school activities, and can also help with accommodations.

Sleeping

Reservations are a good idea in December and January.

Camping La Pista del Andino (☎ 435-890; www.lapistadelandino.com.ar; Alem 2873; campsites & RV sites per person AR$18; ☼ Oct-Apr) About 2km uphill from the center (taxi AR$10), this camping spot has pleasant sites with views. Cooking facilities, good common areas and snack services are available. Free pickup.

Amanecer de la Bahía (☎ 424-405; www.ushuaia hostel.com; Magallanes 594; dm AR$46, d without bathroom AR$140) A short walk uphill lies this friendly, cozy hostel with creaky floors and small dorms. Some rooms have views. There are two dogs on premises.

Antarctica Hostel (☎ 435-774; www.antarcticahostel .com; Antártida Argentina 270; dm AR$50, d without bathroom AR$170) Popular, good-vibe hostel with relaxing reception lounge area, kitchen/eating loft and grassy backyard.

Freestyle (☎ 432-874; www.ushuaiafreestyle.com; Paz 866; dm AR$50-60) Modern five-star hostel with fine spacious dorms and all the services. Top-floor lounge has awesome mountain and water views, faux-leather sofas and a pool table.

Galeazzi-Basily B&B (☎ 423-213; www.avesdelsur .com.ar; Valdéz 323; s/d with shared bathroom AR$115/150, cabañas AR$210-280) Wonderful B&B with friendly, polyglot hosts. Newer *cabañas* out back have private bathrooms and kitchens. Two dogs on premises.

Hostal Los Calafates (☎ 435-515; www.loscalafates hostal.com.ar; Fagnano 456; s/d/tr/q AR$170/190/210/240) Just seven homey and warm rooms at this clean, friendly, family-run guesthouse. Kitchen access is also available.

Casa de Familia Zaprucki (☎ 421-316; zaprucki @hotmail.com; Deloquí 271; apt AR$190-400; ☽ Oct-Apr) A little garden of Eden run by an elderly woman. Four clean, homey and private apartments (all with kitchen) that hold up to six. One has three bedrooms.

Tango B&B (☎ 422-895; www.tangobyb.com.ar; Valdéz 950; r AR$270) Just four rooms, all with private bathroom, are on tap at this cozy home with views over the city. Your host Raúl puts on a tango music show twice a week.

Alto Andino (☎ 430-920; www.altoandinohotel.com; Paz 868; d AR$420) Eighteen luxurious rooms and suites (with kitchenettes) with slick, minimalist design. Spectacular views from the top-floor breakfast/lounge area. Worth the splash-out.

Also recommended:

Cruz del Sur (☎ 434-099; www.xdelsur.com.ar; Deloquí 636; dm AR$50) Intimate, casual hostel with funky decor and small four- to eight-bed dorms. Pleasant library room; family-run.

Los Cormoranes (☎ 423-459; www.loscormoranes .com; Kamshen 788; dm/d AR$50/200) Hillside hostel with small six- and eight-bed dorms facing outdoor plank hallways. The best double is room 10. HI discount.

Patagonia Pais (☎ 431886; www.hostelpatagoniapais .com.ar; Alem 152; dm AR$50-55) Small, intimate and very casual hostel just north of the center.

Yakush (☎ 435-807; www.hostelyakush.com.ar; Piedrabuena 118; dm AR$50-55, d AR$160-200) Colorful, clean hostel with good dorms, awesome upstairs lounging room and attractive kitchen/dining area.

Pueblo Viejo (☎ 432-098; www.puebloviejo.info; Deloquí 242; s/d AR$140/160) Guesthouse with just eight small, clean and tidy rooms, all of which share bathrooms.

Hostal Río Ona (☎ 421-327; www.rioona.com.ar; Magallanes 196; s/d AR$155/175) Ten comfortable rooms, only four with kitchenette but all with fridge and coffee-maker.

Eating & Drinking

Café-Bar Tante Sara (Av San Martín 701; mains AR$3-5.50) Popular corner bistro with big menu: breakfast, pasta, sandwiches, salads, snacks and cocktails. Also has a restaurant at Av San Martín 175.

Ramos Generales (Av Maipú 749; mains AR$17-31) A wonderful old-time atmosphere here is reminiscent of an old general store. There's great bread, pastries and panini, plus a selection of exotic coffees and teas.

Intimain (Rivadavia 451; mains AR$18-28; ☽ closed Sun) Artsy, veggie-oriented eatery that occasionally holds intimate events. Simple menu of salads and sandwiches available.

Bodegón Fueguino (Av San Martín 859; mains AR$20-45; ☽ closed Sun & Mon) Located in a cute yellow house, this place serves great homemade pizzas and pastas, along with 12 kinds of *cordero* (lamb).

María Lola (Deloquí 1048; mains AR$40-76; ☽ closed Sun) Upscale restaurant cooking up dishes like seafood risotto and *cordero fueguino* (Patagonian lamb). Good service and great views.

Galway Irish Bar (cnr Av San Martín & Roca) Popular drinking hole with semiauthentic decor and Beagle beer (Ushuaia's own) on tap.

Dublin Irish Pub (9 de Julio 168) Intimate pub with good atmosphere and dim lighting. Popular with foreigners.

Also recommended:

El Turco (Av San Martín 1040; mains AR$13-33; ☽ closed Sun) Popular for its good-value meats, pizza and pasta.

Lomitos Martinica (Av San Martín 68; mains AR$14-22) Cheap *parrilla* with huge sandwiches.

El Bambú (Piedra Buena 276; per kg AR$22; ☽ closed Sat & Sun) Good vegetarian takeout.

La Anónima (cnr Paz & Rivadavia) Supermarket.

Getting There & Around

In January and February, book your passage in and out of Ushuaia in advance.

Ushuaia's airport is 4km south of the center (taxi AR$18); the departure tax is AR$13. **Aerolíneas Argentinas** (☎ 0810-222-86527; cnr Av Maipú & 9 de Julio), **LADE** (☎ 421-123; Av San Martín 542) and **Aerovías DAP** (www.dap.cl; at the airport) provide services.

Ushuaia does not have a bus terminal, but the tourist office can help with transport options. **Tecni-Austral** (☎ 431-412; Roca 157), in the Tolkar travel agency, has almost daily services to Río Grande (AR$60, three hours) and Río Gallegos (AR$180, 12 hours). **Lider** (☎ 442-264; Paz 921) and **Montiel** (☎ 421-366; Deloquí 110) head to Río Grande (AR$60, three hours) up to eight times daily. **Bus Sur** (☎ 430-727, Av San Martín 245) goes to Punta Arenas three times weekly (AR$190, 12 hours) and to Puerto Natales on Saturdays (AR$210, 15 hours). You can also go to Puerto Natales from Río Gallegos.

Taxis around town are fairly cheap. Rental cars cost around AR$260 per day with 200km free. For transport to Parque Nacional Tierra del Fuego, see below.

For information on getting to Puerto Williams (Chile), see p151.

PARQUE NACIONAL TIERRA DEL FUEGO

West of Ushuaia by 12km lies the beautiful **Parque Nacional Tierra del Fuego** (admission AR$50; ☽ dawn-dusk), which extends from the Beagle Channel in the south to beyond Lago Fagnano in the north. Only a small part of the park is accessible to the public, and despite a tiny system of short trails, the views along the bays, rivers and forests are wonderfully scenic. For information on the park's walks, get a map from the tourist office or National Parks Administration in Ushuaia.

Keep your eyes peeled for *cauquén* (upland geese), cormorants and grebes. The most

---

BEYOND THE EDGE OF THE WORLD – ANTARCTICA

A trip to awe-inspiring Antarctica is a once-in-a-lifetime adventure. It's expensive but worth every penny, and is so much more than just a continent to tick off your list. The land and ice shelves pile hundreds of meters thick with kilometers of undulating, untouched snow, while countless glaciers drape down mountainsides. Icebergs loom like tall buildings and come in shapes you didn't think were possible, from triangles to dragon-silhouettes to graceful sculptures with circular arches. The wildlife is magnificent; you'll see thousands of curious penguins and a wide variety of flying birds, seals and whales. Antarctica is an astounding place, and its tourism industry is growing fast as more and more people visit. We can only hope that careful management will assure that this glorious continent remains beautiful.

For the average person, cruising is the easiest and best way to visit the White Continent. The season runs from November to mid-March; peak-season voyages often get sold out. Last-minute tickets might be available later in the season, but sailings on reasonably small ships will still cost around US$3500. Regular tickets run from around US$5000. Ask how many days you will actually spend in Antarctica – as crossing the Southern Ocean takes up to two days each way – and how many landings will be there. The smaller the ship, the more landings per passenger (always depending on the weather).

Because of its relatively close location to the Antarctic peninsula (1000km), most cruises leave from Ushuaia. Travel agencies such as **Rumbo Sur** (☎ 422-275; www.rumbosur.com.ar; Av San Martín 350), **All Patagonia** (☎ 433-622; www.allpatagonia.com; Fadul 40) and **Canal Fun** (☎ 437-395; www.canalfun. com; 9 de Julio 118) offer 'last-minute' packages, though there are many more. **Alicia Petiet** (www. antarcticatravels.com) is a tour consultant who helps travelers with Antarctic cruises.

If booking from home, check that your company is a member of **IAATO** (www.iaato.org), whose members must abide by strict guidelines for responsible travel to Antarctica. For basic info in Ushuaia, visit the **Antarctica tourist office** (☎ 421-423) at Ushuaia's pier.

Lonely Planet's *Antarctica* guidebook is an indispensable guide to the region's history and wildlife, and has a section on various ways to reach the Big Ice. Also, Lonely Planet's *The Falklands & South Georgia Island* guidebook is useful for those whose Antarctic cruise also visits these islands.

One last thing: bring more film and/or extra memory cards than you think you'll need. You'll thank us later.

common land critters you'll see are the European rabbit and North American beaver – introduced species that have wreaked havoc on the ecosystem. Foxes and the occasional guanaco occasionally visit, and marine mammals are most common on offshore islands.

The only organized campground is **Lago Roca** (☎ 02901-433-313; ◷ Oct-Apr). Pitch a tent for AR$12 per person; a restaurant and tiny grocery (expensive and not always open) are nearby. Free campsites are also available.

Minibuses to the park charge AR$50 per person. They leave about every half-hour from 9am to 8pm daily, from near the corner of Av Maipú and 25 de Mayo. Taxis to the park charge AR$120.

ARGENTINA DIRECTORY

ACCOMMODATIONS

There's an excellent range of affordable hostels throughout Argentina. Most hostels are friendly and offer tours and services. All include kitchen access and sheets; most have towel rental, internet access, free wi-fi, luggage storage, light breakfast and double rooms (book these ahead). Typical prices for dorm rooms are AR$45 to AR$50, while doubles are AR$150 to AR$200. Hostel organizations include **Hostelling International** (www.hostels.org.ar), **Minihostels** (www.minihostels.com) and **HoLa** (www.holahostels.com); membership is not required to stay at any of the participating hostels, but discounts are given to members.

Residenciales are small hotels, while *hospedajes* or *casas de familia* are usually family homes with extra bedrooms and shared bathrooms. Hotels can range from one to five stars, and rooms usually come with private bathroom and a light breakfast (coffee, tea and bread or croissants with jam). Some hotels in Buenos Aires and other tourist destinations operate on a two-tier system, charging foreigners more than locals. As far as we know, the accommodations we've listed here don't use this system.

Camping is cheap and popular in Argentina, though sites aren't always near the center of town. National parks usually have organized sites, and some offer distant *refugios* (basic shelters for trekkers).

Peak tourist months in Buenos Aires are July, August and November to January, when accommodation prices are at their highest. Patagonia is busiest during the summer (November to February), though ski resort towns fill up fast in July and August. Northern destinations and the Atlantic beach towns attract the most travelers in December and January (the latter are practically ghost towns the rest of the year). In peak season it's wise to make reservations ahead of time.

We've listed general high-season rates here, but not ultrapeak rates (Easter week or Christmas). In low season, or if you're staying for more than a few days, you should ask for a discount.

ACTIVITIES

Argentina has plenty for the adventure-seeking traveler. A multitude of beautiful national parks offer awesome summer hiking and trekking, especially around Bariloche (p133) and Patagonia's Fitz Roy range (p144). For the highest peak outside Asia there's lofty Aconcagua, at 6962m (p122).

Skiing is world-class, with major resorts at Cerro Catedral (p134), near Bariloche; Las Leñas (p124), near Malargüe; Los Penitentes (p122); and Chapelco (p128), near San Martín de los Andes. The ski season runs from about mid-June to mid-October. In summer, these mountains turn into activity centers for mountain biking.

Cycling is a popular activity in Mendoza (p118), the Andean northwest, the Lake District and Patagonia (where winds are fierce!). Mountain bikes are best for pedaling the sometimes remote and bad roads, many of which are gravel. Many tourist cities have bike rentals, though the quality is not up to Western standards.

The Lake District and Patagonia have some of the world's best fly-fishing, with introduced trout and landlocked Atlantic salmon reaching epic proportions. The season runs from November to mid-April. It's almost always catch-and-release.

White-water rafting can be enjoyed near Mendoza (as well as in the Lake District) and horse riding and paragliding are popular in many tourist areas.

BOOKS

Lonely Planet's *Argentina* guidebook and *Buenos Aires Encounter* are *número uno* for exploring Argentina in greater depth.

Travelogues on the country include *The Voyage of the Beagle* (Darwin on *gaucho* life), *The Uttermost Part of the Earth* (Lucas Bridges

ARGENTINA

on Tierra del Fuego's indigenous people), *In Patagonia* (Bruce Chatwin's classic) and *The Motorcycle Diaries* (Che Guevara on adventurous travel with a dilapidated motorcycle).

WH Hudson's *Idle Days in Patagonia* tells of the naturalist's adventures in search of the region's fauna; see also his *Tales of the Pampas,* a compendium of short stories. Mountaineers should check out Gregory Crouch's *Enduring Patagonia,* a detailed account of his Cerro Torre climb. Richard W Slatta's *Gauchos and the Vanishing Frontier* depicts the engaging frontier life of Argentina's favorite icon.

For something fun pick up a copy of Miranda Frances' timeless *Bad Times in Buenos Aires,* or Marina Palmer's sexy *Kiss and Tango.*

BUSINESS HOURS

Traditionally, businesses open by 9am, break at 1pm for lunch and then reopen at 4pm until 8pm or 9pm. This pattern is still common in the provinces, but government offices and many businesses in Buenos Aires have adopted the 9am to 6pm schedule.

Restaurants generally open noon to 3pm for lunch and 8pm to midnight for dinner. On weekends hours can be longer. Cafes are open all day long; most bars tend to open their doors late, around 9 or 10pm.

Opening hours aren't listed in reviews unless they vary widely from these standards.

CLIMATE

January and February are oppressively hot and humid in the subtropical north (including Iguazú Falls) and Buenos Aires. These are the best months, however, to visit the high Andes and southern Patagonia – where you'll need warm clothes. Buenos Aires is best in spring or fall. Skiers enjoy the Andes during the winter months, June to September. For more information and climate charts see above.

DANGERS & ANNOYANCES

Don't let anyone tell you otherwise: despite the public's constant dissatisfaction with its government and a lumbering economy that gives rise to occasional crime waves, Argentina remains one of the safest countries in Latin America. Most tourists who visit Buenos Aires leave happy and unscathed. Outside the big cities, serious crime is not common. Lock your valuables up in hostels, where, sadly enough, your own fellow travellers are occasionally to blame for thefts.

In general, the biggest dangers in Argentina are speeding cars and buses: be careful crossing streets, and *never* assume you have the right of way as a pedestrian. If you're sensitive to cigarette smoke, be aware that Argentines are truly addicted to nicotine: they'll light up in banks, post offices, restaurants, cafes and everywhere else. Other small concerns include air pollution (in big cities), cracked sidewalks, ubiquitous dog piles and the occasional hole in the ground. Stray dogs are common but usually don't bite. For information on the coin shortage problem, see boxed text, p159.

For big-city advice, see Buenos Aires (p51). For general advice on traveling safely, see the South America Directory (p989).

DRIVER'S LICENSE

To rent a car in Argentina you must be 21 years old and have a credit card and valid driver's license from your country. An International Driving Permit is useful but not always necessary.

ELECTRICITY

Argentina's electric current operates on 220V, 50Hz. Most plugs are either two rounded prongs (as in Europe) or three angled flat prongs (as in Australia).

EMBASSIES & CONSULATES

The following is not a complete list. For locations of these and other consulates see individual city maps.

Australia (Map pp58-9; ☎ 011-4777-6580; Villanueva 1400, Buenos Aires)

Bolivia Buenos Aires (Map pp52-3; ☎ 011-4394-1463; Corrientes 545, 2nd fl); La Quiaca (☎ 03885-422-283; cnr San Juan & Árabe Siria); Salta (Map pp104-5; ☎ 0387-421-1040; Boedo 34); San Salvador de Jujuy (Map p107; ☎ 0388-424-0501; Independencia 1098)

Brazil Buenos Aires (Map pp52-3; ☎ 011-4515-6500; Pellegrini 1363, 5th fl); Paso de Los Libres (☎ 03772-425-444; Mitre 842); Puerto Iguazú (Map p87; ☎ 03757-421-348; cnr Córdoba & El Mensu)

Canada (Map pp58-9; ☎ 011-4808-1000; Tagle 2828, Buenos Aires)

Chile Bariloche (Map p131; ☎ 02944-523-050; Av Juan Manuel de Rosas 180); Buenos Aires (Map pp52-3; ☎ 011-4331-6228; Diagonal Roque Sáenz Peña 547, 2nd fl); Esquel (☎ 451-189; Molinari 754); Mendoza (Map pp120-1; ☎ 0261-425-4844; Paso de los Andes 1147); Neuquén (☎ 0299-442-2727; La Rioja 241); Río Gallegos (☎ 02966-422-364; Moreno 148); Salta (Map pp104-5;

☎ 0387-431-1857; Santiago del Estero 965); Ushuaia (Map p152; ☎ 02901-430-909; Jainén 50)

France (Map pp52-3; ☎ 011-4312-2409; Av Santa Fe 846, 4th fl, Buenos Aires)

Germany (Map pp58-9; ☎ 011-4778-2500; Villanueva 1055, Buenos Aires)

Ireland (Map pp52-3; ☎ 011-5787-0801; Av Libertador 1068, 6th fl, Buenos Aires)

Netherlands (Map pp52-3; ☎ 011-4338-0050; Cossetini 831, 3rd fl, Buenos Aires)

New Zealand (Map pp52-3; ☎ 011-4328-0747; Pellegrini 1427, 5th fl, Buenos Aires)

Paraguay Buenos Aires (Map pp52-3; ☎ 011-4814-4803; Viamonte 1851); Posadas (Map p85; ☎ 03752-423-858; San Lorenzo 179); Puerto Iguazú (Map p87; ☎ 03757-424-230; Córdoba 370)

UK (Map pp52-3; ☎ 011-4808-2200; Agote 2412, Buenos Aires)

Uruguay Buenos Aires (Map pp52-3; ☎ 011-4807-3040; Av General Las Heras 1915); Gualeguaychú (☎ 03446-426-168; Rivadavia 510)

USA (Map pp58-9; ☎ 011-5777-4533; Colombia 4300, Buenos Aires)

FESTIVALS & EVENTS

This is just a brief list; see city listings for more. For Argentine public holidays see p158.

Festival Nacional del Folklore (www.aquicosquin.org) Cosquín's nine-day folklore festival (p94).

Carnaval Late February/early March. Especially rowdy in Gualeguaychú (p78) and Corrientes (p80).

Fiesta Nacional de La Vendimia (www.vendimia .mendoza.gov.ar) Late February/early March. Mendoza's (p118) famous wine harvest festival.

Día de la Tradición November 10. Gaucho celebrations, especially in San Antonio de Areco (p70).

FOOD & DRINK

Eating reviews throughout this chapter are given in order of budget, with the least expensive options first.

Argentine Cuisine

As a whole, Argentina does not have a widely varied cuisine – most folks here seem to survive on meat, pasta and pizza – but the country's famous beef is often sublime. At a *parrilla* (grillhouse) or *asado* (private barbecue) you should try *bife de chorizo* (thick sirloin), *bife de lomo* (tenderloin) or a *parrillada*. Ask for *chimichurri*, a spicy sauce of garlic, parsley and olive oil. Steaks tend to come medium *(a punto)*, so if you want it rare, say *jugoso*. You're on your own with well-done.

The Italian influence is apparent in dishes like pizza, spaghetti, ravioli and chewy *ñoquis* (gnocchi). Vegetarian fare is available in Buenos Aires and other large cities. *Tenedores libres* (all-you-can-eat buffets) are popular everywhere and often good value. Middle Eastern food is common in the north, while the northwest has spicy dishes like those of Bolivia or Peru. In Patagonia lamb is king, while specialties such as trout, boar and venison are served around the Lake District.

Confiterías usually grill sandwiches like *lomito* (steak), *milanesa* (a thin breaded steak) and hamburgers. *Restaurantes* have larger menus and professional waiters. Cafes are important social places for everything from marriage proposals to revolutions, and many also serve alcohol and simple meals.

Large supermarkets often have a counter with good, cheap takeout. Western fast-food chains exist in larger cities.

Breakfast is usually a simple affair of coffee, tea or maté with *tostadas* (toast), *manteca* (butter) and *mermelada* (jam). *Medialunas* (croissants) come either sweet or plain. Lunch is around 1pm, teatime around 5pm and dinner usually after 8pm (few restaurants open before this hour).

Empanadas are baked or fried turnovers with vegetables, beef, cheese or other fillings. *Sandwichitos de miga* (thin, crust-free sandwiches layered with ham and cheese) are great at teatime. Commonly sold at kiosks, *alfajores* are cookie sandwiches filled with *dulce de leche* (a thick milky caramel sauce) or *mermelada* and covered in chocolate.

Postres (desserts) include *ensalada de fruta* (fruit salad), pies and cakes, *facturas* (pastries) and flan, which can be topped with *crema* (whipped cream) or *dulce de leche*. Argentina's Italian-derived *helados* (ice cream) are South America's best.

The usual *propina* (tip) at restaurants is 10%. At fancier restaurants, a *cubierto* (a service charge separate from the tip) of a few pesos is often included in the bill to cover bread and 'use of utensils.'

Drinks
ALCOHOLIC DRINKS

Argentines like to drink (but not to excess), and you'll find lists of beer, wine, whiskey and gin at many cafes, restaurants and bars. Both Quilmes and Isenbeck are popular beers; ask for *chopp* (draft or lager). Microbrews are widely available in the Lake District.

Some Argentine wines are world-class; both reds *(tintos)* and whites *(blancos)* are excellent, but Malbecs are especially well known. The major wine-producing areas are near Mendoza, San Juan, La Rioja and Salta.

Argentina's legal drinking age is 18.

NONALCOHOLIC DRINKS
Soft drinks are everywhere. For water, there's *con gas* (carbonated) or *sin gas* (noncarbonated) mineral water. Or ask for Argentina's usually drinkable *agua de canilla* (tap water). For fresh-squeezed orange juice, ask for *jugo de naranja exprimido*. *Licuados* are water- or milk-blended fruit drinks.

Even in the smallest town, coffee will be espresso. *Café chico* is thick, dark coffee in a very small cup (try a *ristretto,* with even less water). *Café cortado* is a small coffee with a touch of milk; *cortado doble* is a larger portion. *Café con leche* (a latte) is served for breakfast only; after lunch or dinner, request a *cortado*.

Tea is commonplace. You shouldn't decline an invitation for grasslike maté, although it's definitely an acquired taste.

GAY & LESBIAN TRAVELERS
Argentina is a strongly Catholic country, but enclaves of tolerance toward gays and lesbians do exist. This is especially true in Buenos Aires, which is a top gay tourist destination. In fact, BA was the first city in Latin America to accept civil unions between same-sex couples (in 2002).

Argentine men are more physically demonstrative than you may be used to, so behaviors such as cheek kisses or a vigorous embrace are commonplace. Lesbians walking hand in hand should attract little attention, as heterosexual Argentine women sometimes do this, but this would be suspicious behavior for males. In general, do your thing – but be discreet.

For more information about gay- and lesbian-friendly travel in Buenos Aires see boxed text, p67.

HEALTH
Argentina requires no vaccinations. In 2009 there was a dengue outbreak in some parts of northern Argentina, and malaria is always a minor concern in the more rural, lowland border sections of Salta, Jujuy, Corrientes and Misiones provinces. In the high Andes, watch

for signs of altitude sickness and use more sunscreen. For more information see wwwn.cdc.gov/travel/destinations/argentina.aspx.

Urban water supplies are usually potable, making salads and ice safe to consume. Many prescription drugs are available over the counter. Seek out an embassy recommendation if you need serious Western-type medical services. For more information, see the Health chapter (p1011).

HOLIDAYS
Government offices and businesses close on most national holidays, which are often moved to the nearest Monday or Friday to extend weekends. Provincial holidays are not listed here.

Año Nuevo (New Year's Day) January 1
Semana Santa (Easter) March/April
Día de la Memoria (Anniversary of 1976's military coup) March 24
Día de las Malvinas (Malvinas Day) April 2
Día del Trabajador (Labor Day) May 1
Revolución de Mayo (May Revolution of 1810) May 25
Día de la Bandera (Flag Day) June 20
Día de la Independencia (Independence Day) July 9
Día de San Martín (Anniversary of San Martín's death) August 17
Día de la Raza (Columbus Day) October 12
Día de la Concepción Inmaculada (Immaculate Conception Day) December 8
Navidad (Christmas Day) December 25

INTERNET ACCESS
Argentina is online: every city and town in the country, no matter how small, has internet cafes. In downtown Buenos Aires they're on practically every corner. Most *locutorios* (telephone offices) also offer internet access. Costs are very affordable, from AR$3 to AR$5 per hour depending on the city.

To type the @ *(arroba)* symbol, hold down the Alt-key while typing 64 on the keypad. Or ask the attendant *'¿Cómo se hace la arroba?'*.

INTERNET RESOURCES
Argentina Turística (www.argentinaturistica.com) All about Argentina.
Budget Buenos Aires (www.budgetba.blogspot.com) Tips on cheap BA.
Buenos Aires Expatriates Group (www.baexpats.org) Also good for travelers.
Bloggers in Argentina (http://bloggersinargentina.blogspot.com) People's personal experiences with this great country.

Expose: Buenos Aires (www.exposebenosaires.com)
Great info about BA.

Lanic (http://lanic.utexas.edu/la/argentina) A massive list
of Argentine websites.

Lonely Planet (www.lonelyplanet.com) The internet's
best, with awesome forum.

Sectur (www.turismo.gov.ar) Argentina's official tourism
site.

The Argentine Post (www.argentinepost.com) Current
news about Argentina.

LANGUAGE

Besides flamboyance, the unique pronunciation of *castellano* – Argentina's Italian-accented
version of the Spanish language – readily identifies an Argentine elsewhere in Latin America
or abroad. If you're in Buenos Aires you'll also
hear *lunfardo*, the capital's colorful slang.

Some immigrants retain their language as a
badge of identity. Quechua speakers, numerous in the northwest, tend to be bilingual in
Spanish. Many Mapuche speakers live in the
southern Andes, while most Guaraní speakers live in northeastern Argentina. English is
understood by many Argentines in the tourist
industry.

See the Language chapter (p1020) for more
information, and pick up a copy of Lonely
Planet's *Latin American Spanish* phrasebook
to avoid cluelessness.

LEGAL MATTERS

Argentina's police have a reputation for
corruption and abuse of power, so do your
best to obey the law. Marijuana and many
other substances that are illegal in the US
and most European countries are also illegal
here. Though constitutionally a person is innocent until proven guilty, people are regularly held for years without a trial. If arrested,
you have the constitutional right to a lawyer,
a telephone call and to remain silent.

If you behave, it's unlikely you'll run into
trouble with the police. Politely mention contacting your consulate if you do have a run-in.
Drivers sometimes take care of matters on
the spot by saying '*¿Cómo podemos arreglar
esto más rapido?*' (How can we sort this out
faster?). In all events, it's a good idea to carry
identification (or copies in a pinch) and always be courteous and cooperative when dealing with police or government officials.

MAPS

All tourist offices will have decent maps for
general sightseeing. In many cities, newspaper
kiosks and bookstores stock good maps. For
detailed hiking maps check with the local Club
Andino or any National Parks office, which
have outlets in outdoors-oriented cities.

The **Automóvil Club Argentino** (ACA; www.aca.org
.ar), the main branch of which is in Buenos
Aires (Map pp58-9; ☎ 011-4802-6061; Av del Libertador
1850), publishes some excellent city and provincial maps; members of ACA's overseas
affiliates get discounts with their card.

MEDIA

The English-language daily *Buenos Aires
Herald* (www.buenosairesherald.com) covers
the world from an international perspective.
The expat-run newspaper *Traveller's Guru*
(www.travellersguru.com) has both a BA and
a Patagonia version, while the *Argentimes*
(www.theargentimes.com) is another good
expat-run, English-language newspaper.

The most important Spanish dailies are
the upper-class *La Nación* and the fun tabloid *Clarín*. *Página 12* gives a refreshing leftist
perspective and often breaks important

SPARE SOME CHANGE...PRETTY PLEASE?

You will very quickly notice that change in small bills – but especially coins – is very hard to come
by in Argentina, and especially Buenos Aires. Some vendors won't sell a small item if it involves
giving up precious *monedas*. Theories abound as to why this problem exists, but the situation is
certainly exacerbated by bus companies. Buses take in only coins which aren't deposited at banks.
Instead, they're sold on the black market for a 5-10% markup. In BA a magnetic card system is
theoretically in the works to ease this ridiculous situation.

In the meantime, break large bills when making big transactions, like at restaurants. Save up a
stash of small bills and coins for small purchases, and never give up coins unless you're begged to –
and you will be. Some people line up in special queues at Retiro and Constitución train stations,
where you can get up to AR$20 in coins without a 'fee.' (Surprisingly, banks only give out a few
pesos' worth). One silver lining – you'll never be weighed down with too much change.

stories. *Ámbito Financiero* is the voice of the business sector, but it also provides good cultural coverage.

Argentina has dozens of channels on cable TV, with plenty of radio stations across the country as well.

MONEY

Carrying a combination of US dollars, Argentine pesos and ATM/credit cards is best.

ATMs

Cajeros automáticos (ATMs) are the best way to go in Argentina, whether you're in a big city or small town. Practically every bank has one, transactions are straightforward and exchange rates are reasonable. Most ATMs have English instructions. Savvy travelers bring more than one card, just in case.

One big problem with ATMs is that there's a limit on how many pesos you can withdraw per transaction. This limit can be anywhere from AR$100 to AR$1000 (usually AR$300), with the amount depending on your network system. You can usually make more than one transaction per day, but your bank may charge you a per-transaction fee. It's good to check with them before traveling.

When getting cash out, consider withdrawing an odd number like 290 pesos, instead of 300. This will guarantee you some small bills; just *try* breaking a 100 peso note for a 10 peso sale – you'll get groans for sure.

Bargaining

Bargaining might be possible in the northwest and in craft fairs countrywide, especially if you buy several items. But it's not the sport that it is in some other countries in Latin America.

If you stay several days at a hotel, you can often negotiate a better rate. Many higher-range hotels will give discounts for cash payments.

Cash

Bills come in denominations of two, five, 10, 20, 50 and 100 pesos. One peso equals 100 centavos. Coins come in five, 10, 25 and 50 centavos and one peso. Always carry small denomination bills and coins.

US dollars are the easiest currency to exchange, though euros are also widely accepted at *cambios* (exchange houses). Although many businesses in Argentina will accept US dollars, not all places will. This is especially true for small purchases, patriotic merchants and government offices. In Buenos Aires especially, be aware of fake bills, which tend to look and feel a little fake and either have a bad watermark or be missing one altogether. They're often given out in dark places like nightclubs or taxis.

Credit Cards

The larger a hotel is, the greater the chance it will accept credit cards. Ditto for stores and other services like bus tickets. Some businesses add a *recargo* (surcharge) of up to 10% to credit card purchases; always ask before charging. Note that restaurant tips can't be added to the bill and must be paid in cash.

MasterCard and Visa are the main honchos, but American Express is also commonly accepted. Let your company know you'll be using your card(s) abroad. Limited cash advances are possible (try Banco de la Nación) but are difficult, involving paperwork and fees.

Exchanging Money

US dollars and certain other currencies can be converted to Argentine pesos at most banks or *cambios* (exchange houses). Some banks will only exchange a minimum amount (say, AR$100) so check before lining up. *Cambios* offer slightly poorer rates but have fewer restrictions.

Since the major currency devaluation in January 2002, Buenos Aires' Av Florida has seen a proliferation of shady figures offering 'cambio, cambio, cambio' to passing pedestrians. Using these unofficial street changers is not recommended; there are quite a few fake bills floating about.

Traveler's checks are very difficult to cash (even at banks) and suffer poor exchange rates. They're not recommended as your main source of traveling money.

Exchange rates at press time included the following:

EXCHANGE RATES		
Country	**Unit**	**AR$**
Australia	A$1	3.33
Canada	C$1	3.55
euro zone	€1	5.60
Japan	¥100	4.28
New Zealand	NZ$1	2.74
UK	UK£1	6.12
USA	US$1	3.84

You should double-check the exchange rate when you travel, as Argentina's peso is volatile.

POST

Letters and postcards (up to 20g) to the US, Europe and Australia cost around AR$5. You can send packages under 2kg from any post office, but anything heavier needs to go through the *aduana* (customs office).

Correo Argentino (www.correoargentino.com.ar) – the privatized postal service – has become more dependable over the years, but send essential mail *certificado* (registered). Private couriers, such as OCA and FedEx, are available in some larger cities – but are much more expensive.

RESPONSIBLE TRAVEL

Unlike Bolivia or Peru, modern Argentina doesn't have huge numbers of indigenous peoples with delicate cultures. Most responsible travel here includes how you behave in the country's more pristine areas, such as the village of El Chaltén (which is inside a national park). Common sense rules: keep water sources potable by washing 100 steps away from rivers and lakes, don't litter (this includes cigarette butts) and avoid walking off-trail.

STUDYING

Since the devaluation of the peso, Argentina has become a hot destination for learning Spanish. For a partial list of Spanish schools in Buenos Aires, see p57. Other large cities, such as Bariloche, Mendoza and Córdoba, also have Spanish schools.

TELEPHONE

Telecom and Telefónica are the major Argentine phone companies. *Locutorios* are very common in any city; you enter private booths, make calls, then pay at the front counter. These may cost more than street phones but are better for privacy and quiet, and you won't run out of precious coins.

Calling the US, Europe and Australia from *locutorios* is best on evenings and weekends, when rates are lower. Least expensive is buying credit phone cards at kiosks or calling over the internet via Skype or another system.

Cell phone numbers start with ☎ 15. Toll-free numbers in Argentina start with ☎ 0800.

To call someone in Argentina from outside Argentina, you'll need to dial your country's international access code, then Argentina's country code (☎ 54), then the city's area code (leaving out the first 0), then the number itself. (When dialing an Argentine cell phone from outside Argentina, dial your country's international access code, then ☎ 54, then ☎ 9, then the area code without the 0, then the number – leaving out the ☎ 15).

Argentina operates mainly on the GSM 850/1900 network. If you have an unlocked, tri-band GSM cell phone, a cheap option is to buy a prepaid SIM chip in Argentina and insert it into your phone. You can also buy or rent cell phones in Argentina. This is a fast-changing field, so check websites like www.kropla.com for current information.

TOILETS

Argentina's public toilets are better than most other South American countries, but not quite as good as those in the West. Head to restaurants, fast-food outlets, shopping malls and even large hotels to scout out a seat. Carry toilet paper and don't expect hot water, soap or paper towels to be available. In smaller towns, some public toilets charge a small fee for entry.

TOURIST INFORMATION

All tourist-oriented cities in Argentina have a conveniently located tourist office, and many of them have English-speaking staff.

In Buenos Aires, each Argentine province has a tourist office. Also in BA is the excellent **Secretaría de Turismo de la Nación** (Map pp52-3; ☎ 011-4312-2232; 0800-555-0016; www.turismo.gov.ar; Av Santa Fe 883; ⊙ 9am-5pm Mon-Fri), which dispenses information on all of Argentina.

TRAVELERS WITH DISABILITIES

Mobility-impaired folks will have a tough time in Argentina, where sidewalks are often busy, narrow and cracked. Ramps don't exist at every corner, and in smaller towns the side streets are gravel. Higher-end hotels tend to have the best wheelchair access; with restaurants and tourist sights it's best to call ahead.

There are some kneeling buses in Buenos Aires (forget the Subte), but taxis are so common and cheap that it's definitely best to use them. Call radio taxis or *remises* beforehand to ask for a proper-sized vehicle that can take a wheelchair.

These websites have no Argentina info but are good for general travel tips: www.access-able.com and www.sath.org.

ARGENTINA

VISAS

Residents of Canada, the US, Australia, and many western European countries do not need visas to enter Argentina; they receive an automatic 90-day stamp on arrival. It's smart to double-check this information with your embassy before you leave, as changes often occur.

For visa extensions (90 days, AR$300), visit *migraciones* (immigration offices) in the provincial capitals. There's also an immigration office in Buenos Aires (see p50). For information on obtaining Argentine residency, see www.argentinaresidency.com.

For more Argentina visa information, see www.lonelyplanetcom/argentina/practical-information/visas.

VOLUNTEERING

Volunteer opportunities in Argentina include the following:

Buenos Aires Volunteer (www.bavolunteer.org.ar)
Foundation for Sustainable Development (www.fsinternational.org) Hooks up volunteers with worldwide NGOs.
Fundación Banco de Alimentos (www.bancodealimentos.org.ar)
Help Argentina (www.helpargentina.org)
La Montaña (www.lamontana.com/volunteer-work)
Parque Nacional Los Glaciares (☎ 02962-430-004) Summer work with park rangers in El Chaltén. Spanish language skills preferred.
Patagonia Volunteer (www.patagoniavolunteer.org)
South American Explorers (www.saexplorers.org) Contact its Buenos Aires clubhouse (p50) for more information.
WWOOF Argentina (www.wwoofargentina.com) Organic farming in Argentina.

WOMEN TRAVELERS

Being a woman traveler in Argentina is not difficult, even if you're alone. In some ways Argentina is a safer place for a woman than Europe, the USA and most other Latin American countries. Argentina is a *machismo* culture, however, and some men will feel the need to comment on a woman's attractiveness. They'll try to get your attention by hissing, whistling, or making *piropos* (flirtatious comments). Much as you may want to kick them where it counts, the best thing to do is completely ignore them – like Argentine women do. After all, most men don't mean to be rude, and many local women even consider *piropos* to be compliments.

On the plus side of *machismo*, expect men to hold a door open for you and let you enter first, including getting on buses; this gives you a better chance at grabbing an empty seat, so get in there quick.

WORKING

Argentina's economy is currently in the slumps, and many Argentines are unemployed or underemployed. Jobs are hard to come by, especially for foreigners.

Teaching English is the best bet for casual labor. There are some English-teaching jobs in Buenos Aires and other major cities, but most teachers make just enough to get by – about AR$25 per hour (this does not count prep or travel time). A TESOL or TESL certificate will be an advantage in acquiring work.

Many teachers work illegally on tourist visas, which they must renew every three months (in BA this usually means hopping to Uruguay a few times per year). Work schedules drop off during the holiday months of January and February.

For job postings, check out www.craigslist.com or www.olx.com.ar, and the classifieds in the English-language newspapers **Buenos Aires Herald** (www.buenosairesherald.com) or **The Argentimes** (www.theargentimes.com). You could also try posting on expat website forums like www.baexpats.org.

Bolivia

HIGHLIGHTS

- **Salar de Uyuni** (p207) Venture into the surreal salt deserts and take in spurting geysers, towering volcanoes and colored lagoons.
- **Carnaval** (p201) Join the revelrous crowds in Oruro and devour La Diablada and other boisterous dancing delights.
- **Lake Titicaca** (p197) Hike the length of Isla del Sol on the sapphire-blue waters of what's considered the world's largest high-altitude lake.
- **Amazon Basin Trips** (p231) Penetrate deep into the lush pampas and rainforest of the Amazon lowlands on a riverboat.
- **Tupiza** (p207) Trot, cycle and hike your way through the red rock country around the pretty town of Tupiza.
- **Off the Beaten Track** (p235) Stay in a remote community-run ecolodge in Parque Nacional Madidi and marvel at the wildlife.

FAST FACTS

- **Area:** 1,098,580 sq km (France and Spain combined)
- **Budget:** US$15 to US$25 a day
- **Capitals:** Sucre (constitutional), La Paz (de facto)
- **Costs:** La Paz bed US$3 to US$5, 1L bottle of domestic beer US$1, four-hour bus ride US$2.50
- **Country Code:** ☎ 591
- **Languages:** Spanish, Quechua, Aymara, Guaraní
- **Money:** US$1 = B$6.97 (bolivianos)
- **Population:** 9.8 million
- **Seasons:** high (June to September), low (October to May), rainy (November to April)
- **Time:** GMT minus four hours

TRAVEL HINTS

Take it easy at altitude. Visit a toilet before boarding buses. Choose your tour operator carefully.

OVERLAND ROUTES

Bolivia's border crossings include Guajará-Mirim and Corumbá (Brazil), La Quiaca and Pocitos (Argentina), Tambo Quemado and Hito Cajón near San Pedro de Atacama (Chile), Yunguyo and Desaguadero (Peru) and Fortín Infante Rivarola (Paraguay).

BOLIVIA

BOLIVIA

A place of mind-boggling superlatives, landlocked Bolivia really packs a punch. The hemisphere's highest, most isolated and most rugged nation, it's also among the earth's coldest, warmest and windiest spots with some of the driest, saltiest and swampiest natural landscapes in the world. It's a land of paradoxes: South America's poorest country, Bolivia is the richest on the continent in natural resources. But the superlatives don't end here. Over 60% of the population claim indigenous heritage, including Aymara, Quechua and Guaraní, making it South America's most indigenous country.

Bolivia's natural treasures are many and marvelous, from soaring mountain peaks and surreal salt flats to steamy jungles and wildlife-rich grasslands. The cultural aspect – exploring the country's vibrant ancient traditions and preserved colonial cities – offers unparalleled delight. Most visitors stick to the well-worn paths of the *altiplano* but there's plenty to see and do elsewhere, including dense rainforests and snowcapped cordilleras.

While Bolivia is now well and truly on the travelers' radar, it's still largely raw and undeveloped. This may be a boon for intrepid travelers but it's a perennial source of problems for Bolivians. As of the last few years, notable changes have been sweeping Bolivia's formidable landscapes.

CURRENT EVENTS

Since 2005 Bolivia has been undergoing a revolution of sorts virtually synonymous with former *cocalero* (coca grower) Evo Morales, Bolivia's first indigenous president. In January 2009 he pushed through a groundbreaking new constitution approved in a nationwide referendum by 67% of the population, granting previously unheard-of rights to the country's indigenous majority and allowing the president to seek a second five-year term.

This was stellar news for the working classes and the indigenous of the western highlands but not for everyone in Bolivia. In fact, many middle- and upper-class Bolivians, especially in the energy-rich eastern provinces, are openly critical of Morales' anticapitalist stands and socialist ideologies. This opposition led to violent protests in autonomy-hungry Santa Cruz in September 2008 (with 11 people dead) and the alleged attempt at presidential assassination in April 2009.

Another hot topic is the trial of former president 'Goni' Sánchez de Lozada who stands accused, together with 16 members of his cabinet, for 67 deaths during the 2003 protests in La Paz. The trial opened in May 2009 in absentia; Goni still lives in Maryland and the unheeded request to the US for extradition is one of the several sore points (including the controversial coca; see p167) between Bolivia and US. Since the diplomatic talks in spring 2009, the worn ties have been mending slowly.

In addition to Bolivia's internal strife, Morales has other things on his plate, such as the management of Bolivia's so far untapped lithium reserves (the world's largest) and the upcoming election in December 2009. With his approval ratings still high, he's slated to run a second term. How he will manage to keep his polarized country in check remains to be seen. As the Bolivians themselves say, *vamos a ver…*

HISTORY
Pre-Gringo Times
Sometime around 1500 BC, Aymara people, possibly originating from the mountainous region of modern central Peru, swept across the Bolivian Andes to occupy the *altiplano* (high plain of Peru, Bolivia, Chile and Argentina). The years between AD 500 and AD 900 were distinguished by imperial expansion and increasing power and influence of the Tiwanaku (Tiahuanaco) culture. The society's ceremonial center near Lake Titicaca rapidly became the highland's religious and political heart. In the 9th century AD, however, Tiwanaku's power waned. Ongoing submarine excavations in Lake Titicaca are attempting to identify the cause of Tiwanaku's downfall.

Before the Spanish Conquest, the Bolivian *altiplano* had been incorporated into the Inca empire as the southern province of Kollasuyo. Modern Quechua speakers around Lake Titicaca are descended from immigrants who arrived under an Inca policy of populating newly conquered colonies with Quechua-speaking tribes.

There's considerable speculation that ruins on the scale of Machu Picchu, possibly the lost Inca city of Paititi, may be buried in the Bolivian rainforest.

Conquistadors

By the late 1520s, internecine rivalries began cleaving the Inca empire. However, it took the arrival of the Spaniards – initially thought to be emissaries of the Inca sun god – to seal the deal. The Inca emperor Atahualpa was captured in 1532, and by 1537 the Spanish had consolidated their forces in Peru and securely held Cuzco.

After the demise of the Inca empire, Alto Perú, as the Spaniards called Bolivia, fell briefly into the hands of the conquistador Diego de Almagro. Before long, Francisco Pizarro dispatched his brother Gonzalo to subdue the rogue, silver-rich southern province. In 1538 Pedro de Anzures founded the township of La Plata (later renamed Chuquisaca and then Sucre), which became the political center of Spain's eastern territories.

In 1545 huge deposits of high-quality silver were discovered in Potosí. The settlement grew into one of the world's richest (and highest) cities on the backs of forced labor: appalling conditions in the mines led to the deaths of perhaps eight million African and indigenous slaves. In 1548 Alonso de Mendoza founded La Paz as a staging post on the main silver route to the Pacific coast.

In 1574 the Spaniards founded the granaries of Cochabamba and Tarija, which served to contain the uncooperative Chiriguano people. Then colonialism and Jesuit missionary efforts established settlement patterns that defined the course of Bolivian society.

Coups de Grâce

In 1781, a futile attempt was made to oust the Spaniards and reestablish the Inca empire. Three decades later a local government was established in the independence movement stronghold of Chuquisaca (Sucre). Chuquisaca's liberal political doctrines soon radiated throughout Spanish America.

In 1824, after 15 years of bloodshed, Peru was finally liberated from Spanish domination. However, in Alto Perú, the royalist general Pedro Antonio de Olañeta held out against the liberating forces. In 1825, when offers of negotiation failed, Simón Bolívar dispatched an expeditionary force to Alto Perú under General Antonio José de Sucre. On August 6, 1825, independence was proclaimed, Alto Perú became the Republic of Bolivia, and Bolívar and Sucre became the new republic's first and second presidents.

In 1828 *mestizo* (a person of mixed indigenous and Spanish descent) Andrés de Santa Cruz took power and formed a confederacy with Peru. This triggered protests by Chile, whose army defeated Santa Cruz in 1839, breaking the confederation and throwing Bolivia into political chaos. The confusion peaked in 1841, when three governments claimed power simultaneously.

Such spontaneous and unsanctioned changes of government continued throughout the 1980s in a series of coups and military interventions. At the time of writing, Bolivia had endured nearly 200 changes of government in its 181 years as a republic.

Chronic Territorial Losses

By the mid-19th century, the discovery of rich guano and nitrate deposits in the Atacama Desert transformed the desolate region into an economically strategic area. Since Bolivia lacked the resources to exploit the Atacama, it contracted Chilean companies. In 1879, when the Bolivian government proposed taxing the minerals, Chile occupied Bolivia's Litoral department, prompting Bolivia and Peru to declare war on Chile.

During the War of the Pacific (1879–83), Chile annexed 350km of coastline, leaving Bolivia landlocked. Though Chile offered to compensate Bolivia with a railway from Antofagasta to Oruro and duty-free export facilities, Bolivians refused to accept their *enclaustramiento* (landlocked status). The Bolivian government still lodges coastal claims but diplomatic relations with Santiago appear to be improving since the rise to power of the country's first indigenous leader, President Evo Morales and Chile's leader Michelle Bachelet.

Bolivia's losses continued. In 1903 Brazil annexed a huge chunk of the rubber-rich Acre region, which stretched from Bolivia's present Amazonian border to halfway up Peru's eastern border.

After losing the War of the Pacific, Bolivia was desperate to have the Chaco, an inhospitable region beneath which rich oilfields were mooted to lie, as an outlet to the Atlantic via the Río Paraguay. Between 1932 and 1935, a particularly brutal war was waged between Bolivia and Paraguay over the disputed territory (more than 80,000 lives were lost). Though no decisive victory was reached, both nations had grown weary of fighting

BOLIVIA

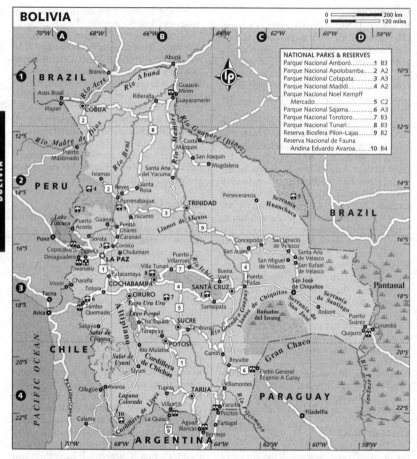

BOLIVIA

NATIONAL PARKS & RESERVES	
Parque Nacional Amboró	1 B3
Parque Nacional Apolobamba	2 A2
Parque Nacional Cotapata	3 A3
Parque Nacional Madidi	4 A2
Parque Nacional Noel Kempff Mercado	5 C2
Parque Nacional Sajama	6 A3
Parque Nacional Torotoro	7 B3
Parque Nacional Tunari	8 B3
Reserva Biosfera Pilon-Lajas	9 B2
Reserva Nacional de Fauna Andina Eduardo Avaroa	10 B4

and peace negotiations in 1938 awarded most of the territory to Paraguay. To this day no oil has ever been found in the disputed region, though prospectors are still searching.

Revolution & Counterrevolution

Following the Chaco War, friction between disenfranchised miners and their absentee bosses escalated. Radicals, especially in Oruro, gathered beneath the banner of the Movimiento Nacional Revolucionario (MNR). The turbulent 1951 presidential elections brought victory to the MNR's Victor Paz Estenssoro, but a military coup prevented him from taking power. The bloody revolution of 1952 forced the military to capitulate and Paz Estenssoro finally took the helm.

The new government spearheaded reforms aimed at ensuring the participation of all social sectors. Mining properties were nationalized and the sole right to export mineral products was vested in the state. The government introduced universal suffrage and an unprecedented policy of agrarian and educational reform, including a redistribution of estates among *campesinos* (peasant farmers) and universal elementary education. For the first time since the Spanish Conquest, indigenous people felt that they had a voice in the government.

The MNR government lasted an unprecedented 12 years but had trouble raising the standard of living. Paz Estenssoro became increasingly autocratic as dissension in his own ranks percolated. Shortly after his second re-election in 1964, he was overthrown by his vice president, General René Barrientos, reviving Bolivia's political instability.

A series of repressive military governments ensued, starting with that of the right-wing general Hugo Banzer Suárez (1971–78). In 1982 a civilian government returned under Hernán Siles Zuazo and his left-wing Movimiento de la Izquierda Revolucionaria (MIR), but the country suffered from labor disputes, monetary devaluation and staggering inflation.

Under the Bolivian constitution, a candidate must earn 50% of the popular vote to become president in a direct election. When no candidate emerges with a clear majority, congress makes the decision, usually via a backroom deal between the major candidates. In 1989 the right-wing Acción Democrática Nacionalista (ADN) made a deal with the MIR, and the MIR's leader Jaime Paz Zamora was appointed president. In 1993 MNR leader Gonzalo Sánchez de Lozada ('Goni'; the Gringo) garnered the most votes, but had to ally with a *campesino* party to secure the presidency. He embarked on an ambitious privatization program, notable because much of the proceeds were invested in a public pension program. The new economic policies were met with protests and strikes, while antidrug programs sparked more unrest.

In the 1997 elections, comeback king Hugo Banzer Suárez and his rightist ADN party won just 23% of the vote. Due to pressure from the International Monetary Fund (IMF), neoliberal economic reforms were instituted, the currency was stabilized and many major industries were privatized. In August 2001 Banzer resigned due to cancer and handed over the reins to his vice president Jorge Quiroga Ramirez. With strong US backing, Sánchez de Lozada returned to power in the 2002 elections, only to face a popular uprising in February 2003 over the privatization of the gas industry, which forced him from office and into exile in the US. His deputy and successor Carlos Mesa held a referendum to permit Bolivia to export gas through Chile, but the questions were deemed complicated and the results uncertain. With this crisis and unrest on his hands, Mesa tried unsuccessfully to resign but Congress did not accept his offer. However, street demonstrations and unrest escalated, and as thousands marched into La Paz in June 2005, his resignation was accepted.

Former leader Eduardo Rodríguez was appointed as interim president until the elections in December 2005. In these elections, Evo Morales won in a landslide, having promised to change the traditional political class and empower the country's poor majority. Indeed, he was quick to act, nationalizing the country's gas reserves in 2006. Morales also ceased the US coca-crop eradication, integral to the US War on Drugs program, by kicking out the DEA (Drug Enforcement Administration) in 2008. But the most radical change for Bolivia came in January 2009, when 67% of the voters backed the new constitution that granted greater rights to the indigenous majority population, in the face of powerful opposition from the affluent elites in the natural resource-rich eastern provinces.

Although the GDP grew steadily in the 1990s, Bolivia remains the continent's poorest nation. Foreign debt (US$4.6 billion), infrastructure shortcomings and high unemployment rates continue to plague the country.

Coca Quandary

Coca has always been part of Bolivian culture: the Inca love goddess was represented holding coca leaves. Chewing the bitter leaf increases alertness and reduces hunger, cold and pain (see boxed text, p168). It's believed that the Spanish conquistadores reaped the rewards of coca's lucrative regional trade. The world's (in)famous cola company incorporated derivatives into its 'secret' recipe, and some 19th-century patent medicines were based on coca. The raw leaf is neither harmful nor addictive and is said to be high in calcium, iron and vitamins.

But when its derivative – cocaine – became the recreational drug of choice (particularly in the USA), demand for Bolivian coca leaves rocketed. Since 1988 Bolivian law has permitted 12,000 hectares (30,000 acres) of coca to be cultivated for local (legitimate) use, but in reality, experts say that actual cultivation exceeds this limit.

In the '80s, in a desperate bid to curb Bolivia's status as primary producer of coca, the US sent its DEA squadrons into the primary coca-growing regions of Chapare and Beni to assist in coca eradication. It also injected

BOLIVIA

THE COCA CRAFT

Chewing coca leaves into an *akullico* – a soggy wad of golf-ball proportions – is an important ritual in Andean culture and is said to reduce fatigue, hunger and cold, as well as the effects of altitude. Most travelers try it, at least once. The following is a novice's guide to a good chew.

- Buy a good-quality leaf (*elegida* or *seleccionada*). 'Prime' leaves are moist, green and healthy.

- De-vein the leaves one by one and insert them into the side of your mouth, between your cheek and choppers. Start macerating – not chewing! – the leaves. (The Bolivians say *pijchar*.) Sufficient maceration can take up to 45 minutes or more.

- Resist the urge (or not) to spit out the bitter-tasting mass!

- When the leaves are sufficiently soggy and the mass resembles a 'ball,' add a pinch of the alkaline substance *llipta* (also called *lejía;* these are plant ashes, normally from *quinua*) or sodium bicarbonate (baking soda). The easiest way is to crush the *llipta* into a powder and add it to a leaf before putting it in your mouth. This alkaline substance helps release the leaves' alkaloids.

- Sense (or not) a strong tingling and numbing sensation in your cheek. (Resist the temptation to slap your face and declare 'I can't feel anything!' – like any anesthetic it wears off.)

- Enjoy a mild sensation of alertness, reduction of appetite and resistance to temperature fluctuations. (Coca leaves do not produce a rush or a 'high.')

- Spit out when sated or before your mouth is the color of the Incredible Hulk. If imbibing is more to your taste, opt for a coca leaves tea.

millions of development aid into the regions to develop alternative agricultural industries. This program largely failed: the alternative crops grew slowly, profits were negligible and, as poverty increased among *cocaleros,* they shifted their cultivation to other areas. There were reports of brutality and human-rights abuses initiated by the DEA against the *cocaleros.*

In Chapare, it was Evo Morales – a former coca grower and by then a union organizer – who lead the resistance against the eradication policies. Soon after his election as president, Morales was quick to reinforce the slogan *'coca sí, cocaína no'* ('coca yes, cocaine no'), an emphasis on solving the cocaine problem – at the consumer, not the *campesino,* end. He also suspended eradication programs by expelling the DEA in 2008 and wishes to increase cultivation while seeking export opportunities for alternative coca-based products. At a UN meeting in March 2009, he announced that Bolivia would start the process to remove the coca leaf from the 1961 Single Convention that prohibits the traditional chewing of coca leaf. Some see Morales' recent acts as opting out of the war on drugs while others view it as a move toward establishing a new market for legal coca-based by-products.

THE CULTURE
The National Psyche

Bolivian attitude varies widely depending on climate and altitude. *Kollas* (highlanders) and *cambas* (lowlanders) enjoy expounding on what makes themselves 'better' than the other. Lowlanders are said to be warmer, more casual and more generous to strangers; highlanders are supposedly harder working but less open-minded. The reality is that seemingly every *camba* has a kind *kolla* relative living in La Paz and the jesting is good-natured.

Bolivians are all very keen on greetings and pleasantries. Every exchange is kicked off with the usual *buen(os) día(s)* (hello/good day), but also with a *¿Cómo está?* or *¿Qué tal?* (How are you?). Bolivian Spanish is also liberally sprinkled with endearing diminutives such as *sopita* (a little soup) and *pesitos* (little pesos, as in 'it only costs 10 little pesos').

Lifestyle

Day-to-day life varies from Bolivian to Bolivian, depending on whether they live in the country or city, their class and cultural background. Many *campesinos* live a largely traditional lifestyle in small villages, often without running water, heat or electricity, while those in the cities enjoy the comforts and modern conveniences and follow more

Western practices. Clothing customs vary dramatically, from the women (Cholitas) of the *altiplano* in their pleated skirts and hats, to those who opt for the latest in designer wear.

Nevertheless, from ritual offerings to Pachamama (Mother Earth) to the habitual chewing of coca, Bolivia is long and strong in traditional culture. An entire canon of gods and spirits are responsible for bountiful harvests, safe travels and matchmaking. One especially unique tradition is the *tinku,* a ritual fistfight that establishes a pecking order, practiced during festivals (in May) in the northern Potosí department. The bloody, drunken battles (some fatal) go on for days, may feature rocks or other weapons and don't exempt women.

Population

Thanks to its geographic diversity, Bolivia is anything but homogenous. Around 60% of the population claims indigenous identity. Many *campesinos* speak Quechua or Aymara as a first language and some still live by a traditional lunar calendar. Miraculously, the frigid *altiplano* region supports nearly 70% of the populace.

Most Bolivians' standard of living is alarmingly low, marked by substandard housing, nutrition, education, sanitation and hygiene. The country has a high infant mortality rate (45 deaths per 1000 births); a birth rate of 3.17 per woman and a literacy rate of 86.7%.

Bolivia's economic landscape is bleak, but not completely dire, thanks to the oil exports to Brazil and Argentina, a thriving informal economy of street vendors and contraband and coca exports.

SPORTS

Like in most of Latin America, the national sport is *fútbol* (soccer) and the national side typically fares quite well in *futsal* or *fútbol de salón* (five-versus-five minisoccer) world championships. Professional matches happen every weekend in big cities and it's easy to pick up impromptu street games. On the *altiplano,* liberated women have been playing more and more in recent years – in full skirts. *Lucha libre* (wrestling) is becoming popular among a small but growing group of hardy *altiplano* females. Racquetball, billiards, chess and *cacho* (dice) are also huge. The unofficial national sport, however, has to be festing and feting – competition between dancers and drinkers knows no bounds.

RELIGION

Roughly 95% of Bolivia's population is Roman Catholic, with varying degrees of commitment. Particularly in rural regions, locals mix the Inca and traditional beliefs with Christianity, resulting in syncretism, an amalgamation of doctrines and superstitions.

Natural gods and spirits form the beliefs of these indigenous religions, with Pachamama, the earth mother, central to sacrificial offerings. The Aymara believe in mountain gods: *achachilas* and *apus* are spirits of high mountains.

Talismans are also popular to guard against evil or bring good luck, as is Ekeko, a little elf-like figure and the Aymara household god of abundance, and the *cha'lla* (ritual blessing) of vehicles at the cathedral in Copacabana.

ARTS
Music

Despite motley, myriad influences, each of Bolivia's regions has developed its own musical styles and instruments. Andean music, from the cold, bleak *altiplano,* is suitably haunting and mournful, while music from the warmer lowland areas like Tarija has more vibrant, colorful tones.

Under the military regimes, *peñas* (folk-music shows) were a venue for protest; today, cities host *peñas*. Major artists to look for include *charango* masters Celestino Campos, Ernesto Cavour and Mauro Núñez (the recording is *Charangos Famosos*). Also sound out Altiplano, Savia Andina, Chullpa Ñan, K'Ala Marka, Rumillajta, Los Quipus, Wara, Los Masis and Yanapakuna.

The ukulele-like *charango* originally featured five pairs of llama-gut strings and a *quirquincho* (armadillo carapace) sound box that produced the pentatonic scale. Modern *charangos* are now usually made of wood as armadillos are a protected species.

Before the *charango,* melody lines were 'aired' exclusively by woodwind instruments. Traditional musical ensembles use the *quena* (reed flute) and the *zampoña* (pan flute). The *bajón,* an enormous pan flute with separate mouthpieces in each reed, accompanies festivities in the Moxos communities of the Beni lowlands.

Bolivia has its share of pop groups. Those in the mix include longtime Azul Azul, Octavia and Los Kjarkas. The last are best known for their recording of 'Llorando se fue,' which was lifted and reshaped (without permission) into the blockbuster hit 'Lambada.' Inevitably, rap music has hit the scene, with some of the youngsters in El Alto catching on to its beat.

Dance

Traditional *altiplano* dances celebrate war, fertility, hunting prowess, marriage and work. The Spaniards' European dances blended with those of the African slaves to evolve into the hybrid dances of Bolivian contemporary celebrations.

Bolivia's de facto national dance is the *cueca*, derived from the Chilean original and danced by handkerchief-waving couples, primarily during fiestas. The most colorful dances are performed at *altiplano* festivals, particularly during Carnaval: Oruro's La Diablada (Dance of the Devils) fiesta draws huge international crowds.

Architecture

Tiwanaku's ruined structures and a handful of Inca remains are about all that's left of pre-Columbian architecture in Bolivia. The classic Inca polygonal-cut stones that distinguish many Peruvian sites are rare in Bolivia, found only on Isla del Sol and Isla de la Luna (Lake Titicaca).

Renaissance (1550–1650) churches were constructed primarily of adobe, with courtyards and massive buttresses, such as that in Tiwanaku.

Baroque (1630–1770) churches were constructed in the form of a cross, with an elaborate dome, such as the Compañía in Oruro, San Agustín in Potosí and Santa Bárbara in Sucre.

Mestizo style (1690–1790) is defined by whimsical decorative carvings including tropical flora and fauna, Inca deities and gargoyles. See the wild results at San Francisco (La Paz), San Lorenzo, Santa Teresa and the Compañía (Potosí).

In the mid-18th century, the Jesuits in the Beni and Santa Cruz lowlands went off on neoclassical tangents, designing churches with Bavarian rococo and Gothic elements. Their most unusual effort was the mission church at San José de Chiquitos.

Since the 1950s many modern city highrises have been constructed. There are some gems: look for triangular pediments on the rooflines, new versions of the Spanish balcony and hardwoods of differing hues.

Weaving

Weaving methods have changed little in Bolivia for centuries. In rural areas, young girls learn to weave and women spend their spare time with a drop spindle or weaving on heddle looms. Before colonization, weavers used llama and alpaca wool, but today, sheep's wool and synthetic fibers are the cheaper options.

Bolivian textiles have wonderfully diverse patterns. The most common pieces include the *manta* or *aguayo,* a square shawl made of two handwoven strips, the *chuspa* (coca pouch), the *falda* (skirt) which has patterned weaving on one edge and woven belts.

Each region boasts a different weaving style, motif and use. Zoomorphic patterns feature in weavings from Charazani country (near Lake Titicaca) and in several *altiplano* areas outside La Paz (Lique and Calamarka). Potolo, near Sucre, is renowned for its distinctive red-and-black designs. Finer weavings originate in Sica Sica, a dusty and nondescript village between La Paz and Oruro, while the expert spinning in Calcha, southeast of Potosí, produces an extremely tight weave and some of Bolivia's finest textiles.

ENVIRONMENT

The 1990s saw an enormous surge in international and domestic interest in Amazonian ecological issues. Though environmental organizations have crafted innovative ways to preserve selected spots (including external funding), in other areas intensive development continues, often – in the past at least – with governmental encouragement. The jury is still out on how the Morales government will help the environmental cause. Contact the following nonprofit groups for information on countrywide environmental conservation efforts.

Asociación Armonía (www.armonia-bo.org; www.birdbolivia.com) Everything you need to know about Bolivian birding and bird conservation.

Conservación Internacional (CI; www.conservation.org.bo) Promotes community-based ecotourism and biodiversity conservation.

Fundación Amigos de la Naturaleza (FAN; www.fan-bo.org) Works in Parques Nacionales Amboró and Noel Kempff Mercado.

Servicio Nacional de Áreas Protegidas (SERNAP; www.sernap.gov.bo; Bedregal 2904, Sopocachi) Bolivia's national park service manages all reserves and protected areas.

Wildlife Conservation Society (WCS; www.wcs.org) Works with local institutions and communities through conservation programs in the Madidi and Kaa-Iya regions.

The Land

Despite the loss of huge chunks of territory in wars and concessions, landlocked Bolivia is South America's fifth-largest country. Two Andean mountain chains define the west, with many peaks above 6000m. The western Cordillera Occidental stands between Bolivia and the Pacific coast. The eastern Cordillera Real runs southeast past Lake Titicaca, then turns south across central Bolivia, joining with the other chain to form the southern Cordillera Central.

The haunting *altiplano*, which ranges from 3500m to 4000m, is boxed in by these two great *cordilleras*. It is an immense, nearly treeless plain punctuated by mountains and solitary volcanic peaks. At the north end of the *altiplano*, straddling the Peruvian border, Lake Titicaca is often described as the world's highest navigable lake. In the bottom left corner, the land is drier and less populated. Here are the remnants of two ancient lakes, the Salar de Uyuni and the Salar de Coipasa, which form an ethereal expanse of blindingly white desert plains when dry, and hallucinogenic mirror images when under water.

East of the Cordillera Central are the Central Highlands, a region of scrubby hills, valleys and fertile basins. Cultivated in this Mediterranean-like climate are olives, nuts, wheat, maize and grapes.

North of the Cordillera Real, where the Andes abut the Amazon Basin, the Yungas form a transition zone between arid highlands and humid lowlands. More than half of Bolivia's total area is in the Amazon Basin. The northern and eastern lowlands are sparsely populated and flat, with swamps, savannas, scrub and rainforest.

In the country's southeastern corner lies the flat, nearly impenetrable scrubland of the Gran Chaco, which extends into northern Paraguay.

Wildlife

National parks and reserves comprise 18% of Bolivia's territory and harbor myriad animal and bird species. Several national parks and protected areas (Parque Nacional Amboró, for example) boast one of the world's greatest densities of species concentration. The *altiplano* is home to camelids, flamingos and condors. The harsh Chaco hides jaguar, tapir and *javeli* (peccary). The Amazon Basin boasts an amazing variety of lizards, parrots, snakes, insects, fish and monkeys. Bolivia has several rare and endangered species including giant anteaters and spectacled bears.

River travelers might spot *capybaras* (large rodents), turtles, caimans and pink dolphins. Anacondas exist in the Beni, as do armadillos, sloths, rheas and *jochis* (agoutis).

National Parks

Bolivia has 22 officially declared parks, reserves and nature areas under the National Park Service, Sernap. Areas that are accessible to visitors, albeit often with some difficulty, include the following:

Amboró (p230) Near Santa Cruz, home to rare spectacled bears, jaguars and an astonishing variety of birdlife.

Apolobamba Excellent hiking in this remote mountain range abutting the Peruvian border, with Bolivia's densest condor population.

Cotapata Most of the Choro trek passes through here, midway between La Paz and Coroico in the Yungas (p191).

Madidi (p235) Protects a wide range of wildlife habitats; home to more than 1100 bird species.

Noel Kempff Mercado (p230) Remote park on the Brazilian border; contains a variety of wildlife and some of Bolivia's most inspiring scenery.

Reserva Nacional de Fauna Andina Eduardo Avaroa (p207) A highlight of the Southwest Circuit tour, including wildlife-rich lagoons.

Sajama Adjoining Chile's magnificent Parque Nacional Lauca; contains Volcán Sajama (6542m), Bolivia's highest peak.

Torotoro Enormous rock formations with dinosaur tracks from the Cretaceous period, plus caves and ancient ruins.

Tunari Within hiking distance of Cochabamba; features lovely nature trails through mountain scenery.

TRANSPORTATION

GETTING THERE & AWAY

Air

There are only a few airlines offering direct flights to La Paz' Aeropuerto El Alto (LPB), so airfares are as high as the altitude. There are direct services to most major South American cities; the flights to/from Chile and Peru are the cheapest. Santa Cruz is an increasingly popular entry point from Western European hubs.

BOLIVIA

> **DEPARTURE TAX**
>
> The international departure tax, payable in cash only at the airport, is US$25 (US$31 if you stayed in Bolivia for more than three months). There's also a 15% tax on international airfares purchased in Bolivia.

Flights from La Paz or Santa Cruz or both serve Iquique, Arica and Santiago (Chile); Asunción (Paraguay); Bogotá (Colombia) via Lima; Buenos Aires, Cordoba and Salta (Argentina); Caracas (Venezuela) via Lima; Cuzco and Lima (Peru); and Manaus, Río de Janeiro and São Paulo (Brazil).

Boat

The Brazilian and Peruvian Amazon frontiers are accessible via irregular riverboats. A more popular crossing is across the Río Mamoré by frequent ferry from Guajará-Mirim (Brazil) to Guayaramerín (see boxed text, p236). From there, you can travel overland to Riberalta and on to Cobija or Rurrenabaque and La Paz.

Bus

Daily *flotas* (long-distance buses) link La Paz with Buenos Aires (Argentina) via Bermejo or Yacuiba; Salta (Argentina) via Tupiza/Villazón; Corumbá (Brazil) via Quijarro; and Arica and Iquique (Chile) via Tambo Quemado. Increasingly popular is the crossing to San Pedro de Atacama (Chile) as a detour from Salar de Uyuni tours (see p206). The most popular overland route to and from Puno and Cuzco (Peru) is via Copacabana (see boxed text, p197), but traveling via Desaguadero is quicker. Several bus services from Santa Cruz via Villamontes run the route to Asunción in Paraguay on a daily basis. Note that Bolivian customs formalities take place at Ibibobo, about an hour before the Paraguayan checkpoint of Infante Rivarola; the customs are down the road at Mariscal Estigarribia. This is a notorious smuggling route so expect to be lined up with your bags as customs officials and sniffer dogs rifle through your private possessions.

Car & Motorcycle

Motoring in Bolivia is certain to try your patience (and mechanical skills!), but will be a trip of a lifetime. Most rental agencies accept national driver's licenses, but if you plan on doing a lot of motoring bring an International Driving Permit. For motorcycle and moped rentals, a passport is all that is normally required. See also p1008.

Train

Bolivia's only remaining international train route detours west from the Villazón–Oruro line at Uyuni. It passes through the Andes to the Chilean frontier at Avaroa/Ollagüe then descends precipitously to Calama, Chile (see p206). Other adventurous routes dead end at the Argentine frontier at Villazón/La Quiaca (see boxed text, p209) and Yacuiba/Pocitos and in the Brazilian Pantanal at Quijarro/Corumbá (see boxed text, p229).

GETTING AROUND

You can get anywhere cheaply via bus, hitchhiking or *camión* (truck). The most common (and locally popular) option is buses, which come in all shapes and sizes (as do their wheels) – and in all states of luxury or disrepair. Think twice about booking the cheapest ticket – a 24-hour-plus torture trip into the jungle at the end of rainy season (many stop operating during the rainy season). Boats, planes and trains are a much better choice when river crossings are high and unpaved roads have turned to mud. Trains are always the best option in the far south and in the north while mototaxis will zip you around cheaply in every Beni town. Whatever your mode of transport, always take a stash of snacks, warm clothes, water and toilet paper.

Air

Bolivia's national carrier, **Lloyd Aéreo Boliviano** went defunct in February 2008. **AeroSur** (☎ 3-336-7400; www.aerosur.com) is now the main domestic airline, which offers regular flights to seven destinations in Bolivia as well as international flights to Miami, Madrid, Cuzco, Buenos Aires and more.

Transporte Aéreo Boliviano (☎ 2-268-1111), the rough-and-ready military airline known as TAM often offers discounted flights to and from smaller towns within Bolivia, although it is infamous for its cancellations and delays (and enforcing its 15kg baggage limit). **Amazonas** (☎ 2-222-0848; www.amaszonas.com) flies small planes from La Paz to Rurrenabaque (frequently delayed or cancelled due to adverse weather conditions – allow two days to arrive or return), Trinidad, Santa Cruz and other lowland destinations. The small airline **Aerocon** (☎ 3-351-1200; www.aerocon.bo) connects the country's major cities as well as some more remote corners. A new airline, **BOA** (☎ 2-211-7993; www.boa.bo) was just starting to fly between major cities at the time of research, with rates even cheaper than TAM; however, it wasn't particularly reliable yet.

Note that Aasana, the government agency responsible for airports and air traffic, charges a domestic departure tax (B$11 to $B16), payable at its desk after check-in.

Boat

Half of Bolivia's territory lies in the Amazon Basin, where rivers are the main (and during the rainy season often the only) transport arteries. The region's main waterways are the Beni, Guaporé (Iténez), Madre de Dios and Mamoré Rivers, all Amazon tributaries. Most cargo boats offer simple accommodations (cheap hammocks and mosquito nets are available in all ports) and carry everything from livestock to vehicles. Patience and plenty of spare time are key to enjoying these off-the-beaten-path journeys.

Bus, Camión & Hitchhiking

Thankfully, the Bolivian road network is improving as more kilometers are paved. Unpaved roads range from good-grade dirt to mud, sand, gravel and 'only at own risk.' Modern coaches use the best roads, while older vehicles ply minor secondary routes.

Long-distance bus lines are called *flotas*. Large buses are called *buses* and small ones are called *micros*. A bus terminal is a *terminal terrestre*. Each terminal charges a small fee, which you pay to an agent upon boarding or when purchasing the ticket at the counter.

To be safe, reserve bus tickets at least several hours in advance; for the lowest fare, purchase immediately after the driver starts up the engine. Many buses depart in the afternoon or evening, to arrive at their destination in the wee hours of the morning. On most major routes there are also daytime departures. It's a lot safer to travel and the views are better during the day. Drunken driving is illegal, but bus drivers have been known to sip the hard stuff on long nighttime hauls.

There have been numerous reports of items disappearing from buses' internal overhead compartments. Hold on tight to your day packs and bags if they are with you in the

bus. Backpacks and bags are generally safe when stored in the baggage compartment but watch them as they load your luggage. You will be given a baggage tag which you must show when reclaiming your bag.

An alternative on many routes is a *camión* (truck), which normally costs around 50% of the bus fare. This is how *campesinos* travel, and it can be excruciatingly slow and rough (you're better off only attempting these on shorter routes). *Camiones* offer the best views of the countryside. Each town has places where *camiones* gather to wait for passengers; some even have scheduled departures. Otherwise, the best places to hitch a lift will be the *tranca*, the police checkpoint at every town exit. Don't assume the rides are free – make sure to ask the price when boarding.

On any bus or *camión* trip in the highlands, day or night, layer well for the freezing nights and take food and water. Expect much longer travel times (or canceled services) in the rainy season when roads are challenging or impassable.

Taxi & Mototaxi

Taxis are cheap but few are metered. Confirm the fare before departure or you're likely to be overcharged. Cross-town rides in large cities rarely exceed B$15 (except to and from the airport) and short hops in smaller towns are less than B$8. Fares are sometimes higher late at night, with excessive luggage and are always more for uphill runs. Full-day taxi hire is often cheaper than renting a car. Hourly mototaxi rentals are common in balmy Beni towns, as are quick mototaxi jaunts.

Train

Since privatization, passenger rail services have been cut way back. The western network runs from Oruro to Uyuni and Villazón (on the Argentine border); a branch line runs southwest from Uyuni to Avaroa, on the Chilean border. Between Oruro, Tupiza and Uyuni, the comfortable *Expreso del Sur* trains run twice weekly. The cheaper *Wara Wara del Sur* also runs twice weekly between Oruro and Villazón. See www.fca.com.bo for schedules.

In the east, there's a line from Santa Cruz to the frontier at Quijarro, where you cross to the Pantanal in Corumbá, Brazil. An infrequently used service goes south from Santa Cruz to Yacuiba on the Argentine border twice a week.

BOLIVIA

Rail travel in Bolivia requires patience and determination. Most stations now have printed timetables, but they still can't be entirely trusted. In older stations, departure times may be scrawled on a blackboard. When buying tickets, take your passport. For most trains, tickets are available only on the day of departure, but you can usually reserve seats on better trains through a local travel agent for a small commission – a wise idea in high season.

LA PAZ

☎ 02 / 1.5 million (including El Alto)

La Paz is dizzying in every respect, not only for its well-publicized altitude (3660m), but also for its quirky beauty. All travelers enter the city via the flat sparse plains of the sprawling El Alto, an approach which hides sensational surprises of the valley below; the first glimpse of La Paz will, literally, take your breath away. The city's buildings cling to the sides of the canyon and spill spectacularly downwards. On a clear day, the imposing, showy, snowy Mt Illamani (6402m) looms in the background.

The posher suburbs, with skyscrapers, colonial houses and modern glass constructions, occupy the city's more tranquil lower regions, but most of the daily action takes place further up the incline where a mass of irregular-shaped steep streets and alleys wind their way skywards. Here, locals embrace their frenetic daily life. Women, sporting long black plaits, bowler hats and vivid *mantas,* attend to steaming pots or sell everything from dried llama fetuses to designer shoes while men, negotiating the heavy traffic and its fumes, push overladen trolleys.

La Paz must be savored over time, not only to acclimatize to the altitude, but also to experience the city's many faces. Wander at leisure through the alleys and markets, marvel at the many interesting museums, chat to the locals in a *comedor* (basic cafeteria), or relax over a coffee and newspaper at many trendy cafes. There is a happening night scene and some interesting day trips outside of the city.

La Paz was founded by Alonso de Mendoza in 1548, following the discovery of gold in the Río Choqueyapu. Although gold fever fizzled, the town's location on the main silver route from Potosí to the Pacific assured stable progress. By the mid-20th century, La Paz had grown rapidly as thousands of *campesinos* migrated from the countryside. Today it is the country's governmental capital (Sucre remains the judicial capital.)

The sky-high altitude means that warm clothing, sunscreen and sunglasses are essential. In the summer (November to April), the harsh climate assures afternoon rainfalls and the steep streets are awash with water torrents. In winter (May to October), days are invigoratingly crisp. While the sun shines, temperatures may reach the high teens, but at night they often dip below freezing; see p1016 for advice on dealing with altitude sickness.

ORIENTATION

You are more likely to get winded than lost in La Paz. There's only one major thoroughfare, which follows the canyon of the Río Choqueyapu. Often referred to as the Prado, it changes names several times from top to bottom: Autopista El Alto, Av Ismael Montes, Av Mariscal Santa Cruz, Av 16 de Julio (the Prado) and Av Villazón. At the lower end, it splits into Av 6 de Agosto and Av Aniceto Arce. If you become disoriented and want to return to this main street, just head downhill. Away from this thoroughfare, streets climb steeply uphill, and many are cobbled or unpaved.

The city has a number of districts, including the Zona Central (the blocks around and down from Plaza Pedro D Murillo), Sopocachi (the upmarket commercial and residential zone around Av 6 de Agosto), Miraflores (climbing the slope east of Zona Central) and Zona Sur (the most expensive residential area, further down the valley). A handful of Zona Sur suburbs, including Obrajes, Calacoto and Cotacota, have clinics, government offices and other services of interest to travelers.

A free map of La Paz is available from any one of the information kiosks (Map pp176–7).

Instituto Geográfico Militar (IGM; Map pp180-1; ☎ 237-0118; Juan XXIII 100, Oficina 5) offers original 1:50,000 topographic maps (B$40) or photocopies (B$35) if a sheet is unavailable. Another outlet is located at Saavedra, Estadio Mayor, Miraflores.

INFORMATION
Bookstores

Andean Base Camp ('Ex-Etnic'; Map pp180-1; ☎ 246-3782; www.andeanbasecamp.com; Illampu 863) This helpful place stocks a large range of Lonely Planet guides and excellent maps.

GETTING INTO TOWN

The main bus terminal is 1km uphill from the center. *Micros* and minibuses (B$1) marked 'Prado' and 'Av Arce' pass the main tourist areas but are usually too crowded to accommodate swollen backpacks. If walking, snake your way down to the main drag, Av Ismael Montes, and keep descending for 15 minutes until you see San Francisco Church on your right, from where Sagárnaga, the main tourist street, goes uphill.

Heading into town from El Alto airport (10km outside the center) between 7am and 8pm, catch *micro* 212 directly outside the terminal, which will drop you anywhere along the Prado. A proper taxi from the rank to the center should cost no more than B$50 for up to four passengers. If arriving by bus in Villa Fátima or the cemetery district, take particular care. At night, it's best to take a cab (around B$8), but approach an official driver or call for a radio taxi and *never* share with strangers. By day, frequent *micros* run to the center from both locations.

SpeakEasy Institute (Map pp180-1; ☎ 244-1779; www.speakeasyinstitute.com; Arce 2047) Stocks hundreds of fantastic reads. Fifty percent of earnings go to a local knitters association to provide their children with homework support.
The Spitting Llama Bookstore & Outfitter (Map pp180-1; ☎ 7039-8720; www.thespittingllama.com; Linares 947) Located inside Posada de la Abuela, stocks new and used guidebooks.

To trade books, the best library is Oliver's Travels bar (p186). Or try Gravity Assisted Mountain Biking (p182) or Café Sol y Luna (p186).

Cultural Centers

Centro Boliviano-Americano (Map pp176-7; ☎ 234-2582; www.cba.com.bo; Parque Zenón Iturralde 121) Language classes and current US periodical library.
Goethe Institut (Map pp176-7; ☎ 243-1916; www.goethe.de; Av Aniceto Arce 2708) Films, language classes and good German-language library.

Emergency

Tourist Police (Policía Turística; Map pp180-1; ☎ 222-5016; Plaza del Estadio, Puerta 22, Miraflores) To report a crime or file a *denuncia* (police report), contact the English-speaking tourist police.

Immigration Offices

For information on embassies and consulates in La Paz, see p239.
Immigration (Migración; Map pp180-1; ☎ 211-0960; Av Camacho 1468; ⏰ 8:30am-4pm Mon-Fri) Extensions to length of stay granted here.

Internet Access

La Paz has nearly as many internet cafes as shoeshine boys. Hourly rates range from B$1 to B$3 per hour. Many hostels offer internet access; smarter cafes have wi-fi access.

Internet Alley (Map pp180-1; Pasaje Iturralde) Just off Av Villazón near Plaza del Estudiante. Fastest, cheapest connections in town.

Internet Resources

Bolivia Travel Guide (www.gbtbolivia.com) A privately run site with excellent coverage of La Paz.
La Paz (www.lapaz.bo) La Paz's municipal website has good cultural and tourism sections.

Laundry

Lavanderías are the cheapest and most efficient way of ensuring clean (and dry) clothes in La Paz.

Illampu, at the top of Sagárnaga, is lined with laundries. Most *residenciales* (budget accommodations) offer cheap hand-washing services. For quick, reliable same-day machine wash-and-dry service (B$5 to B$10 per kg), try **Limpieza Express** (Map pp180-1; Aroma 720).

Left Luggage

Most of the recommended places to stay offer inexpensive or free left-luggage storage, especially if you make a return reservation. However, think twice about leaving anything valuable in deposit on a short- or long-term basis as there have been numerous reports of items, including cash, going missing. Always put a lock on your luggage items if possible.

Media

La Razón (www.la-razon.com), **El Diario** (www.eldiario.net) and **La Prensa** (www.laprensa.com.bo) are La Paz's major daily newspapers. National media chains **ATB** (www.bolivia.com) and **Grupo Fides** (www.radiofides.com) host the most up-to-date online news sites.

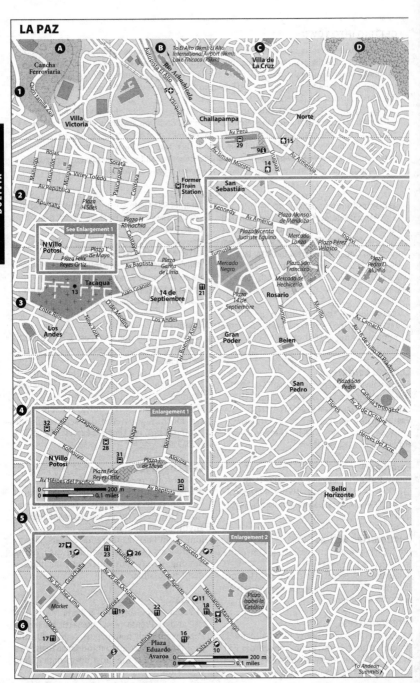

LA PAZ

BOLIVIA

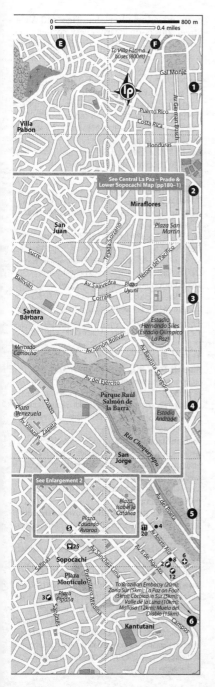

BOLIVIA

Medical Services

After-hours *farmacias de turno* (pharmacies) are listed in daily newspapers.

24-hour pharmacy (Map pp180–1; cnr Av 16 de Julio & Bueno) A good pharmacy on the Prado.

Centro Epidemiológico Departamental La Paz (Centro Pilote; Map pp176–7; ☎ 245-0166; cnr Vásquez 122 & Peru; ⏱ 8:30-11:30am Mon-Fri) Off upper Av Ismael Montes near the brewery. Cheap antimalarials as well as rabies and yellow-fever vaccinations – bring a sterile needle from a pharmacy.

Dr Elbert Orellana Jordan (☎ 242-2342, 7065-9743; asistmedbolivia@hotmail.com) Gregarious and caring English-speaking doctor makes 24/7/365 emergency house calls.

Dr Fernando Patiño (☎ 7722-5625; curare27@gmail.com) US-educated, English-speaking general practitioner.

Dr Jorge Jaime Aguirre (Map pp176-7; ☎ 243-2682; Edificio Illimani, Arce 2707, 1st fl) Frequently recommended dentist for everything from routine cleaning to root canals.
High Altitude Pathology Institute (☎ 224-5394; www.altitudeclinic.com; Saavedra 2302, Miraflores) Offers computerized high-altitude medical checkups and can help with high altitude problems. English spoken.

Money

Watch out for counterfeit US dollars, especially with *cambistas* (street money changers), who loiter around the intersections of Colón, Av Camacho and Av Mariscal Santa Cruz. Outside La Paz you'll get 3% to 10% less for checks than for cash.

Casas de cambio (authorized currency exchange houses) in the city center are quicker and more convenient than banks. Most places open from 8:30am to noon and from 2pm to 6pm weekdays and on Saturday morning. Outside these times, try Hotel Gloria (p184).

The following places change traveler's checks for around 2% to 3% commission:
Cambios América (Map pp180-1; Camacho 1223)
Casa de Cambio Sudamer (Map pp180-1; cnr Colón 206 & Camacho; ☺ 8:30am-6:30pm Mon-Fri, 9:30am-12:30pm Sat) Also has Moneygram service for money transferal.

Cash withdrawals of US dollars and bolivianos are also possible at ATMs at major intersections around the city. For Visa and MasterCard cash advances (bolivianos only) with no commission and little hassle, try:
Banco Mercantil (Map pp180-1; cnr Mercado & Ayacucho)
Banco Nacional de Bolivia (Map pp180-1; cnr Colón & Camacho)
DHL/Western Union (Map pp180-1; ☎ 233-5567; Perez 268) For urgent international money transfers. Outlets are scattered all around town.

Post

Ángelo Colonial (Map pp180-1; Linares 922; ☺ 8:30am-7:30pm Mon-Fri, 8:30am-6pm Sat, 9am-noon Sun) Convenient, gringo-friendly branch with an outgoing-only service.
Central Post Office (Ecobol; Map pp180-1; cnr Santa Cruz & Oruro; ☺ 8am-8pm Mon-Fri, 8:30am-6pm Sat, 9am-noon Sun) Holds *lista de correos* (poste restante) mail for two months – bring your passport.

Telephone

You'll find convenient Punto Entels scattered around the city. Competitive communications companies include Cotel, Tigo and Viva. Street kiosks on nearly every corner offer brief local calls for B$1 per minute. Hawkers with mobiles on a leash offer cellular calls for B$1 per minute. You can buy cell phone SIM cards *(chips)* for around B$10 from Entel (see below) or any carrier outlet.

International calls can be made at low prices from the **international call center** (Map pp180-1; Galería Chuquiago, cnr Sagárnaga & Murillo; ☺ 8:30am-8pm).
Entel office (Map pp180-1; Ayacucho 267; ☺ 8:30am-9pm Mon-Fri, 8:30am-8:30pm Sat, 9am-4pm Sun) is the best place to receive calls and faxes.

Tourist Information

Information kiosks main bus terminal (Map pp176-7); Casa de la Cultura (Map pp180-1; cnr Mariscal Santa Cruz & Potosí)
InfoTur (Map pp180-1; ☎ 265-1778; cnr Mariscal Santa Cruz & Colombia; ☺ 8:30am-12:30pm & 3-7pm Mon-Fri, Sat 9am-1pm) A handy spot on the Prado, with friendly staff and limited information on La Paz and Bolivia.
Tourist information center (Map pp180-1; ☎ 237-1044; Plaza del Estudiante; ☺ 8:30am-12:30pm & 3-7pm Mon-Fri) The original tourist office, with English-speaking staff and some printed matter, including city maps. Ask to see a copy of *Jiwaki*, a listing of the month's activities.

Travel Agencies

America Tours (Map pp180-1; ☎ 237-4204; www.america-ecotours.com; 16 de Julio 1490 No 9) Highly recommended English-speaking agency specializing in community-based ecotourism in Madidi, Sajama, Rurrenabaque and the Salar de Uyuni. Environmentalist owners are especially good on new routes.
Andean Summits (off Map pp176-7; ☎ 242-2106; www.andeansummits.com; cnr Muñoz Cornejo 1009 & Sotomayor, Sopocachi) Mountaineering and trekking all over Bolivia, plus adventure tours, kayaking, 4WD and archaeology trips. The owners are professional UIAGM/IFMGA mountain guides.
Bolivia Milenaria (☎ 2-291-1275; www.millenariantours.com; Av Sanchez Lima 2193, Sopocachi) This agency manages the lauded Tomarapi community-run lodge in Sajama and offers a variety of culture-focused tours around Bolivia.
Bolivian Journeys (Map pp180-1; ☎ 2-235-7848; www.bolivianjourneys.org; Sagárnaga 363) Specialists in climbing, mountaineering and trekking, they organize daily guided climbs to Huayna Potosí at affordable prices.
Fremen Tours (☎ 2-244-0242; www.andes-amazonia.com; Oficina 6-C, Edificio V Centenario, cnr Av 6 de Agosto & Perez) Upmarket agency specializing in soft adventure in the Amazon and Chapare; there is also an office in Cochabamba (see p213).

La Paz on Foot (off Map pp176-7; ☎ 211-8442, 7154-3918; www.lapazonfoot.com; Moreno, E22, Calacoto, Zona Sur) Run by the passionate English-speaking ecologist, Stephen Taranto, they offers a range of activities, including walks in and around La Paz, the Yungas, Chulumani and Titicaca.

Travel Tracks (Map pp180-1; ☎ 2-231-6934; www .travel-tracks.com; Sagárnaga 213 & Sagárnaga 366) This English-speaking agency is an excellent choice for guided hikes as well as customized trips around the country.

DANGERS & ANNOYANCES

While living the high life in La Paz is fun, it's important to take it easy, no matter how well you think you're feeling at nearly 4km above sea level. To avoid *soroche* (altitude sickness), take local advice '*camina lentito, come poquito…y duerme solito*' ('walk slowly, eat only a little… and sleep by your poor little self'), especially the first day or two. More annoying than dangerous, ski mask–clad *lustrabotes* (shoeshine boys) hound everyone with footwear, but for B$3 you can support their cause.

SIGHTS

The steep city is a breathtaking attraction in itself, especially when the sun shines. The city's colorful and rowdy markets swirl to the beat of indigenous cultures. For a break from the hectic rhythm of everyday street life, head to the museums or wander through the cobblestone alleys and among the colonial buildings. Keep your eyes peeled for fantastic glimpses of Illimani towering between the world's highest high-rises.

Plaza Murillo Area

This plaza marks the formal city center, with various monuments, the imposing **Palacio Legislativo** (Map pp180–1), the bullet-riddled **Palacio Presidencial** (Map pp180–1) and the 1835 **cathedral** (Map pp180–1).

Just off the west side of the plaza, the **Museo Nacional del Arte** (National Art Museum; Map pp180-1; ☎ 240-8600; www.mna.org.bo; cnr Comercio & Socabaya; admission B$10; ⏱ 9:30am-12:30pm & 3:30-7pm Tue-Sat, 9:30am-12:30pm Sun) is in the superbly restored pink granite Palacio de los Condes de Arana (1775). The collection of indigenous, colonial and contemporary arts is small but rewarding.

Calle Jaén Museums

Five blocks northwest of Plaza Murillo, colonial Calle Jaén has four small **museums** (Map pp180-1; ☎ 228-0758; combo admission B$4; ⏱ 9:30am-12:30pm & 3-7pm Tue-Fri, 9am-1pm Sat & Sun) that can easily be appreciated in a few hours. The **Museo de Metales Preciosos Precolombinos** (Jaén 777) has dazzling gold and silver artifacts; **Casa de Murillo** (Jaén 790) displays items from the colonial period; **Museo del Litoral** (Jaén 798) laments the 1864 war in which Bolivia lost its Pacific coast; and **Museo Costumbrista Juan de Vargas** (cnr Jaén & Sucre) has good displays on the colonial period.

BOLIVIA

SCAMS

Sadly, La Paz seems to have caught on to South America's common ruses. Fake police officers and bogus tourist officials are on the rise. Note: authentic police officers will always be uniformed (undercover police are under strict orders not to hassle foreigners) and will never insist that you show them your passport, get in a taxi with them or allow them to search your person in public. If confronted by an imposter, refuse to show them your valuables (wallet, passport, money etc), or insist on going to the nearest police station on foot. Of course, if physically threatened, hand over valuables immediately!

Another popular Bolivian bother is the bogus South American tourist who, on engaging you in conversation in English, is confronted by the aforementioned fake tourist police. The 'tourist' abides by an 'order' to show the policeman his bag/papers/passport, and 'translates' for you to do the same. During the search, the cohorts strip you of your cash or belongings, or both.

Fake 'taxi drivers' are working in conjunction with gangs who steal from or – as has tragically been the case – assault or kidnap unsuspecting travelers (to extort ATM pin numbers). Beware of hopping into shared cabs with strangers or of accepting a lift from a driver who approaches you (especially around dodgy bus areas).

And finally, psst my friend! This popular scam involves someone spilling or spitting a phlegm ball. While you or they are wiping it off, another lifts your wallet or slashes your pack; the perpetrator may be an innocent granny or young girl. Similarly, don't bend over to pick up a valuable item which has been 'dropped.' You risk being accused of theft, or of being pickpocketed.

BOLIVIA

CENTRAL LA PAZ – PRADO & LOWER SOPOCACHI

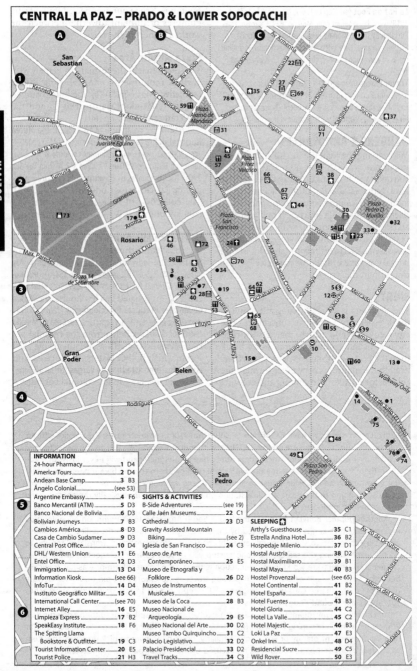

INFORMATION

24-hour Pharmacy	1 D4
America Tours	2 D4
Andean Base Camp	3 B3
Ángelo Colonial	(see 53)
Argentine Embassy	4 F6
Banco Mercantil (ATM)	5 D3
Banco Nacional de Bolivia	6 D3
Bolivian Journeys	7 B3
Cambios América	8 D3
Casa de Cambio Sudamer	9 D3
Central Post Office	10 D4
DHL/ Western Union	11 E6
Entel Office	12 D3
Immigration	13 D4
InfoTur	14 D4
Instituto Geográfico Militar	15 C4
International Call Center	(see 70)
Internet Alley	16 E5
Limpieza Express	17 B2
SpeakEasy Institute	18 F6
The Spitting Llama	
Bookstore & Outfitter	19 C3
Tourist Information Center	20 E5
Tourist Police	21 H3

SIGHTS & ACTIVITIES

B-Side Adventures	(see 19)
Calle Jaén Museums	22 C1
Cathedral	23 D3
Gravity Assisted Mountain	
Biking	(see 2)
Iglesia de San Francisco	24 C3
Museo de Arte	
Contemporáneo	25 E5
Museo de Etnografía y	
Folklore	26 D2
Museo de Instrumentos	
Musicales	27 C1
Museo de la Coca	28 B3
Museo Nacional de	
Arqueología	29 E5
Museo Nacional del Arte	30 D2
Museo Tambo Quirquincho	31 C2
Palacio Legislativo	32 D2
Palacio Presidencial	33 D2
Travel Tracks	34 C3

SLEEPING

Arthy's Guesthouse	35 C1
Estrella Andina Hotel	36 B2
Hospedaje Milenio	37 D1
Hostal Austria	38 D2
Hostal Maximiliano	39 B1
Hostal Maya	40 B3
Hostel Provenzal	(see 65)
Hotel Continental	41 B2
Hotel España	42 F6
Hotel Fuentes	43 B3
Hotel Gloria	44 C2
Hotel La Valle	45 C2
Hotel Majestic	46 B3
Loki La Paz	47 E3
Onkel Inn	48 D4
Residencial Sucre	49 C5
Wild Rover	50 E3

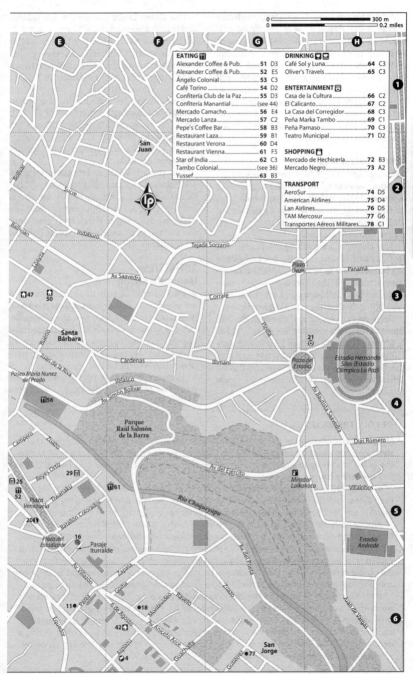

BOLIVIA

EATING 🍴
Alexander Coffee & Pub	**51**	D3
Alexander Coffee & Pub	**52**	E5
Ángelo Colonial	**53**	C3
Café Torino	**54**	D2
Confitería Club de la Paz	**55**	D3
Confitería Manantial	(see 44)	
Mercado Camacho	**56**	E4
Mercado Lanza	**57**	C2
Pepe's Coffee Bar	**58**	B3
Restaurant Laza	**59**	B1
Restaurant Verona	**60**	D4
Restaurant Vienna	**61**	F5
Star of India	**62**	C3
Tambo Colonial	(see 36)	
Yussef	**63**	B3

DRINKING 🍷 📺
Café Sol y Luna	**64**	C3
Oliver's Travels	**65**	C3

ENTERTAINMENT 🎭
Casa de la Cultura	**66**	C2
El Calicanto	**67**	C2
La Casa del Corregidor	**68**	C2
Peña Marka Tambo	**69**	C1
Peña Parnaso	**70**	C3
Teatro Municipal	**71**	D2

SHOPPING 🛍️
Mercado de Hechicería	**72**	B3
Mercado Negro	**73**	A2

TRANSPORT
AeroSur	**74**	D5
American Airlines	**75**	D4
Lan Airlines	**76**	D5
TAM Mercosur	**77**	G6
Transportes Aéreos Militares	**78**	C1

A must for musicians is the impressive **Museo de Instrumentos Musicales** (Map pp180-1; ☎ 240-8177; Jaén 711; admission B$5; ☯ 9:30am-1pm & 2-6:30pm), with an exhaustive hands-on collection of unique instruments from Bolivia and beyond. If you don't happen on an impromptu jam session, check out museum founder and *charango* master Ernesto Cavour's Peña Marka Tambo (p186) across the street. Check out the *charango* and wind-instrument lessons here for around B$50 per hour.

Other Central Museums

Travelers love the slightly worn but very interesting **Museo de la Coca** (Map pp180-1; ☎ 231-1998; Linares 906; admission B$10; ☯ 10am-7pm), which gives an educational, provocative and evenhanded look at the sacred leaf and its uses. Written translations are available.

The cloisters, cells, the garden and roof (for views!) of the recently opened **Museo San Francisco** (Map pp180-1; ☎ 231-8472; Plaza de San Francisco; admission B$20; ☯ 9am-6pm Mon-Sat) beautifully revives the history and art of the 460-year-old cathedral, the city's landmark.

Between the plaza and Calle Jaén, the free **Museo de Etnografía y Folklore** (Map pp180-1; ☎ 240-8640; www.musef.org.bo; cnr Ingavi & Sanjinés; ☯ 9am-12:30pm, 3-7pm Mon-Sat, 9am-12:30pm Sun) explores the fascinating Chipaya culture and has an astounding exhibit of the country's finest textiles.

The **Museo Tambo Quirquincho** (Map pp180-1; ☎ 239-0969; admission B$3; ☯ 9:30am-12:30pm & 3-7pm Tue-Fri; 9am-1pm Sat & Sun) is a former tambo (wayside market and inn) displaying old-fashioned dresses, silverware, photos, artwork and Carnaval masks. It's off Evaristo Valle at Plaza Alonzo de Mendoza.

Near Plaza del Estudiante, the **Museo Nacional de Arqueología** (Map pp180-1; ☎ 231-1621; Tiahuanacu 93; admission B$10; ☯ 9am-12:30pm, 3-7pm Mon-Fri, 9am-noon Sat) holds an interesting collection of Tiwanaku pottery, sculptures, textiles and other artifacts.

The private **Museo de Arte Contemporáneo** (MAC; Contemporary Art Museum; Map pp180-1; ☎ 233-5905; Av 16 de Julio 1698; admission B$15; ☯ 9am-9pm) is more notable for its 19th-century mansion designed by Gustave Eiffel, with glass roof and stained-glass panels, than for its Bolivian art collection.

ACTIVITIES
Mountain Biking

For an adrenaline rush at altitude, head off on wheels with **Gravity Assisted Mountain Biking** (Map pp180-1; ☎ 231-3849; www.gravitybolivia.com; Edificio Av, Av 16 de Julio 1490 No 10). Two of the most popular full-day options are to zoom down from Chacaltaya to La Paz or from La Cumbre down the 'World's Most Dangerous Road' to Coroico (B$600 per person). Many other outfits on Sagárnaga offer the La Cumbre to

---

DEADLY TREADLIES

Many agencies offering the La Cumbre to Coroico mountain-bike plunge give travelers the T-shirts boasting about surviving 'The World's Most Dangerous Road' (WMDR). Keep in mind that the gravel road is narrow (just over 3.2m wide), with precipitous cliffs with up to 600m drops and few safety barriers.

In March 2007 a new replacement road opened. This means the old road – the WMDR – is now used almost exclusively for cyclists, support vehicles and the odd tourist bus. Prior to this, the road's moniker was well deserved: an average of 26 vehicles per year disappeared over the edge.

Around 15 cyclists have died doing the 64km trip (with a 3600m vertical descent) and readers have reported close encounters and nasty accidents. Ironically, the road – now traffic-free – can be more dangerous to cyclists, especially for kamikaze freewheeling guides and overconfident cyclists who think they don't have to worry about oncoming vehicles. (One fatal accident occurred during our research period.) Other accidents are due to little or no instruction and preparation and poor-quality mountain bikes; beware bogus rebranded bikes and recovered brake pads.

Unfortunately, there are no minimum safety standards in place for operators of this trip, and no controls over false advertising, or consequences for unsafe operating practices. In short, many agencies are less than ideal. This is one activity where you don't want to be attracted by cheaper deals. Cost cutting can mean dodgy brakes and poor-quality parts; in other words, a deadly treadly. This, plus inexperienced guides and little or no rescue and first aid equipment, is a truly scary combination on the WMDR.

Coroico trip for a few bucks less but consider what corners are being cut before you go plunging downhill. Also, think twice before going with any of the agencies who offer these trips during the rainy season (January/ February). Also see boxed text, opposite. Also recommended for the Coroico trip is **B-Side Adventures** (Map pp180-1; ☎ 211-4225; www.bside -adventures.com; Linares 943).

Trekking & Climbing

Except for the altitude, La Paz and its environs are made for hiking. Many La Paz tour agencies offer daily 'hiking' tours to Chacaltaya, a rough 35km drive north of La Paz, and an easy way to bag a high peak. This formerly offered the world's highest downhill skiing run (5320m down to 4900m). Some companies offer hiking trips with a cultural, environmental or nature-based focus (see p178). For trekking and climbing in the Cordilleras around La Paz, see p191.

TOURS

There are many tour operators in La Paz (see p178), especially around Sagárnaga; others are based at the larger hotels and cater to individuals or tour groups. Note that many are not formally registered; check carefully if choosing between those on Sagárnaga. Many specialize in particular interests or areas. Most agencies run day tours (US$10 to US$60 per person) in and around La Paz, to Lake Titicaca, Tiwanaku, Chacaltaya and other sites. Speak to travelers for recommendations.

FESTIVALS & EVENTS

Of the major festivals and holidays during the year, Alasitas (January 24), the festival of abundance, and El Gran Poder (late May to early June) are the most interesting to visitors. The Fiestas Universitarias take place during the first week in December, accompanied by riotous merrymaking and enough water-balloon bombs to sink the Chilean navy.

SLEEPING

Most backpackers beeline for central La Paz to find a bed. The downtown triangle between Plazas Mendoza, Murillo and 14 de Septiembre is full of popular budget hostels and *residenciales* and midrange hotels, the vast majority of which are around Sagárnaga and to the east of upper Montes.

The area around the Witches' Market (between Illampu, Santa Cruz and Sagárnaga) is about as close as Bolivia gets to a travelers ghetto. If you want to live closer to movie theaters, a wider array of restaurants and a bar or two, consider staying closer to Sopocachi around Plaza San Pedro.

In the cheapest accommodations, expect communal bathrooms, cold showers, no heat and lots of partying, although some impose a curfew. Spend a bit more if you need your sleep.

West of the Prado & Mariscal Santa Cruz

Hotel Continental (Map pp180-1; ☎ 245-1176; hotel continental626@hotmail.com; Illampu 626; r per person with/without bathroom B$60/50) This older, two-star HI-affiliate is clean, well located and popular among thrifty tour groups.

Hostal Maya (Map pp180-1; ☎ 231-1970; maya host_in@hotmail.com; Sagárnaga 339; s/d/tr B$80/140/180, without bathroom B$55/110/150; ☐) This is a friendly, if basic place. The most appealing rooms have windows (note: a few don't), although rooms at the front can be noisy.

Hostel Provenzal (Map pp180-1; ☎ 231-0479; Murillo 1014; s B$90, d B$160-165) This place offers pleasant light and breezy rooms in neat surroundings and with good storage. Being so close to Oliver's Travels (see p186) can raise the decibels.

Hotel Majestic (Map pp180-1; ☎ 245-1628; Santa Cruz 359; s/tr B$100/220, d B$145-160) Its pink bathrooms, smart parquetry floors and cable TV provide distraction from its nondescript retro yet clean surrounds in the heart of things.

Hotel Fuentes (Map pp180-1; ☎ 231-3966; www .hotelfuentesbolivia.com; Linares 888; s/d/tr B$140/195/250; ☐) Cozy place in the heart of tourist mecca with friendly, helpful management and basic but neat rooms (some on higher levels with superlative views).

Estrella Andina Hotel (Map pp180-1; ☎ 245-6421; www.estrellaandina.com; Illampu 716; s/d incl breakfast US$24/34/45) Clean, well-run and central place where rooms come with Andean murals, Inca themed paraphernalia and cable TV.

East of the Prado & Mariscal Santa Cruz

Hospedaje Milenio (Map pp180-1; ☎ 228-1263; hospedaje milenio@hotmail.com; Yanacocha 860; r per person B$27) A simple, laid-back joint, run by friendly staff. The best rooms are upstairs and outward facing (note: most singles have internal windows).

BOLIVIA

Hostal Austria (Map pp180-1; ☎ 240-8540; Yanacocha 531; dm/s/d/tr B$35/45/70/105; 🖳) This shabby, rambling and friendly number offers short beds (some in windowless cells), dicey shared baths, hot showers and cooking facilities.

Hotel La Valle (Map pp180-1; ☎ 245-6085, 245-6053 (annex); www.lavallehotel.com; Valle 139 & 153; s/d/tr annex B$50/80/110, s/d/tr B$75/120/150) Particularly popular with locals for its clean rooms, all with bathrooms, at fair prices. The older annex has no-frills but adequate rooms; next door, the newer fancier section offers rooms with cable TV and breakfast.

Hotel Gloria (Map pp180-1; ☎ 240-7070; www.hotel gloria.com.bo; Potosí 909; s/d/tr B$320/420/490) Above the snarling traffic of the Prado, this midrange place has a red-shag pile look but helpful and friendly staff.

Only mentioned because they'd be obvious by their absence:

Wild Rover (Map pp180-1; ☎ 211-6903; www.wild roverhostel.com; Comercio 1476; dm B$40-56, d with/ without bathroom B$75/70)

Loki La Paz (Map pp180-1; ☎ 211-9034; www .lokihostel.com; Loayza 420; dm B$45-55) Self-promoting, party pumper and one of the chain of insomnia-crowd-attracting hostels. Upfront warning: if you don't already know about it you probably shouldn't stay here.

San Pedro & Sopocachi

Residencial Sucre (Map pp180-1; ☎ 249-2038; Colombia 340; r per person B$40, s/d B$80/120) Management is helpful and the spotless rooms are set around a secure and pleasant colonial courtyard (good for cycle storage).

Onkel Inn (Map pp180-1; ☎ 249-0456; www.onkel -inn-highlanders.com; Colombia 257; r per person B$60-200, d B$160-250; 🖳) This HI-affiliated place is in a fabulous location – between San Pedro and El Prado. It's generally quiet although the inside bar is close to a couple of the rooms. Of two dorms (on top of singles and doubles), the upstairs one is more airy.

Hotel España (Map pp180-1; ☎ 244-2643; 6 de Agosto 2074; s/d/tr B$190/270/360; 🖳) This colonial place is a bit like a great aunt – friendly with a colorful personality but ever-so-slightly worse for wear. There's a lovely, sunny courtyard and an inexpensive restaurant.

Near the Main Bus Terminal

Some of the city's best choices are handy to the main bus terminal.

Hostal Maximiliano (Map pp180-1; ☎ 246-2318; hostalmaximiliano@yahoo.com; Inca Mayta Kapac 531; s without bathroom B$35, d B$90) An extremely basic, but secure place where you come for little, or no, action. It's in a handy location to Plaza San Francisco.

Hostal Tambo del Oro (Map pp176-7; ☎ 228-1565; Armentia 367; s/d B$70/100, without bathroom B$40/70) A pleasantly quiet, cozy and colonial-style place, with good-value, slightly run-down carpeted rooms and gas showers.

Adventure Brew Hostel (Map pp176-7; ☎ 246-1614; www.theadventurebrewhostel.com; Montes 533 & 641; dm B$46-60, d/tr B$160/210) This popular abode offers designer-style rooms, funky communal spaces, pancake breakfasts (included in price), BBQs, a microbrewery on site as well as activities and fun on tap. The owners opened another one just down the road, appropriately named Adventure Brew Hostel Too. Book ahead.

Arthy's Guesthouse (Map pp180-1; ☎ 228-1439; www.arthyshouse.tripod.com; Montes 693; r per person B$70) This clean and cozy place hidden behind a bright orange door deservedly receives rave reviews as a 'tranquil oasis.' The friendly, English-speaking owners will do all they can do to help you. It has single, twin and quadruple rooms, with kitchen facilities and a midnight curfew.

EATING

La Paz enjoys an abundance of inexpensive eateries offering everything from local treats to more Western-style dishes. For local fare, your cheapest bets are the *almuerzos* (set lunches) in the countless hole-in-the-wall restaurants; look for the chalkboard menus out front. Common dishes include *lomo* (tenderloin), *churrasco* (steak), *milanesa* (breaded and fried beef or chicken cutlets) and *silpancho* (beef schnitzel). Street stalls offer tasty morsels and there are vegetarian restaurants around. Calle Sagárnaga is lined with hordes of cafes of reasonable price and quality.

Restaurants

Restaurant Laza (Map pp180-1; Bozo 244; almuerzo B$8) This lunchtime hole-in-the-wall is a winner.

Coroico in Sur (off Map pp176-7; Patino 1526; almuerzo B$15; 🕑 lunch & dinner Mon-Sat, lunch only Sun) A great place to join the locals for typical Bolivian lunch dishes of *plato paceño* in a tranquil garden setting.

Paceña La Salteña (Map pp176-7; 20 de Octubre 2379, Sopocachi; 🕑 8:30am-2pm) The peach walls, chintz curtains and gold trimmings give the fare a gilded edge at this award-winning *salteñería*. Vegetarian *salteñas* (filled pastry shells) only on weekends.

Restaurant Verona (Map pp180-1; Colón near Santa Cruz; mains B$15-20) Open daily for sandwiches, pizzas and *almuerzos*.

Yussef (Map pp180-1; Sagárnaga 380; mains B$20-45; lunch & dinner) Cheap, cheerful and Middle Eastern. Hummus, kebabs and the like are purchased by portion.

Restaurant Paladar (Map pp176-7; Guachalla 359; almuerzo Tue-Fri B$20, mains B$40-60; lunch Tue-Sun) This cavernous place serves recommended Brazilian fare, including *feijoada*. Heavy drapes, bow-tied waiters and smartly-dressed locals would have you think it's a pricey joint.

Ángelo Colonial (Map pp180-1; 236-0199; Linares 922; mains US$2.50-5) A ramshackle collection of antiquities – pistols, swords and portraits – is featured inside this quirky colonial-style restaurant, as are excellent soups, salads and veggie lasagna. Service is slow.

Armonía (Map pp176-7; Ecuador 2284; buffet B$25; lunch Mon-Sat) A recommended all-you-can-eat vegetarian lunch is found above Librería Armonia in Sopocachi, using organic products where possible.

Star of India (Map pp180-1; mains B$30-40; 9am-11pm Mon-Fri, Sat & Sun 4-11pm) Worthy of a London curry-house (the owner is British), this place is hot. It receives rave reviews by foreign residents and travelers for its broad menu of tasty Indian foods and lassi breakfasts.

Restaurant Vienna (Map pp180-1; 244-1660; www .restaurantvienna.com; Zuazo 1905; mains B$30-65; lunch & dinner Mon-Fri, closed Sat, lunch only Sun) Worth the splurge: this place is classy and arguably La Paz' best continental restaurant.

Cafes & Quick Eats

Tambo Colonial (Map pp180-1; Hotel Rosario, Illampu 704; mains US$3-6; breakfast & dinner) Offers an excellent fruity breakfast buffet and great salads and soups in the evening, plus fantastic chocolate mousse.

Café Torino (Map pp180-1; Hotel Torino, Socabaya 457; snacks B$5-30, almuerzo B$20-30; 7am-11pm Mon-Fri, to 3pm Sun;) A somewhat quirky, old-world cafe with '80s music and a good selection of snacks.

Kuchen Stube (Map pp176-7; Gutiérrez 461; cakes B$8-20) Espresso coffee, German pastries and other decadent homemade goodies.

Pepe's Coffee Bar (Map pp180-1; Jimenez 894; snacks B$10-25) Take a spell from the Witches Market and linger at this arty spot over a coffee or fruit salad.

Confitería Club de La Paz (Map pp180-1; cnr Camacho & Mariscal Santa Cruz; mains B$10-30) For a quick coffee or empanada, hit this spot formerly renowned as literary cafe and haunt of politicians and today better known for its strong espresso and cakes.

Alexander Coffee & Pub (mains B$10-40; until 1am) Prado (Map pp180-1; 16 de Julio 1832); Prado (Map pp180-1; cnr Potosí & Socabaya); Sopocachi (Map pp176-7; 20 de Octubre 2463) Popular cafe chain serving all manner of java drinks, sandwiches and pastries. Don't miss the quinoa tart.

Fridolin (Map pp176-7; Av 6 de Agosto 2415; snacks B$18-60) Austrian-flavored place with several branches around town popular for its large variety of *tortas* (cakes), *pastelitos* and everything in between, from breakfasts to salads.

Confitería Manantial (Map pp180-1; Potosí 909; buffet B$25; lunch Mon-Sat) This place in Hotel Gloria has a good-value and popular veggie buffet. Arrive before 12:30pm.

Markets & Street Food

For cheap, filling eats hit the markets. Cheap DIY meals can easily be cobbled together from the abundance of fruit, produce and bread sold there.

Mercado Camacho (Map pp180-1; cnr Av Simon Bolivar & Bueno) Stands sell empanadas and chicken sandwiches, while *comedores* serve up daily fare.

At **Mercado Lanza** (Map pp180–1), in the streets surrounding Evaristo Valle and Figueroa, is a mass of stalls selling anything and everything. While hygiene in the *comedor* is questionable, don't miss the rank of fruit drink stalls at the Figueroa entrance.

The *comedor* at **Mercado Uruguay** (Map pp176–7), off Max Paredes selling set meals (of varying standards and in basic surrounds), including tripe and *ispi* (similar to sardines) for less than B$8.

Groceries

If you're headed off for a picnic, load up on everything from olives to cheese, crackers and beer at **Ketal Hipermercado** (Map pp176-7; Arce near Pinilla, Sopocachi). There's also the decent but more basic **Ketal Express** (Plaza España). Just up the road from Kuchen Stube is **Hipermaxi**, a well-stocked supermarket.

BOLIVIA

BOLIVIA

DRINKING

There are scores of inexpensive, local drinking dens where men go to drink *singani* (distilled grape spirit), play *cacho* (dice) and eventually pass out. Unaccompanied women should steer clear of these dens (even accompanied women may have problems).

There are a few great bars with a mixed traveler/Bolivian scene.

Café Sol y Luna (Map pp180-1; cnr Murillo & Cochabamba) A relaxed Dutch-owned joint where cocktails, coffee, occasional live music and salsa nights are on the menu.

Mongo's (Map pp176-7; Hermanos Manchego 2444; ⏰ 6pm-3am) Long-standing hip, hot (it gets crowded) and happening spot. There's after-dinner music, and live salsa on Tuesday.

Oliver's Travels (Map pp180-1; Murillo 1014) The worst (or best?) cultural experience in La Paz is to be had at this pub thanks to its crowd of mainly foreign revelers, beer, football, typical English food (including curries) and popular music.

RamJam (Map pp176-7; Medina 2421; ⏰ 6pm-3am) A trendy spot with the lot: great food and drinks, mood lighting and live music. There are vegetarian options, English breakfast and microbrewed beer. They're proud of their reputation: 'come for a meal and stay until far too late…'

Reineke Fuchs (Map pp176-7; Jáuregui 2241; ⏰ from 6pm Mon-Sat) Sopocachi brewhaus featuring imported German beers, schnapsladen and hearty sausage-based fare.

Thelonious Jazz Bar (Map pp176-7; 20 de Octubre 2172; admission around B$25; ⏰ 7pm-3am Mon-Sat) Bebop fans love this charmingly low-key bar for its live and often impromptu performances and great atmosphere.

The local gilded youth mingle with up-market expats at trendy bars and clubs along 20 de Octubre in Sopocachi and lower down in Zona Sur, where US-style bars and discos spread along Av Ballivián and Calle 21. You'll need more than a backpacker's clothes (and budget) to fit in here.

ENTERTAINMENT

Pick up a copy of the free monthly booklet *Kaos* (available in bars and cafes) for a day-by-day rundown of what's on in La Paz. The tourist information center (p178) and **Casa de la Cultura** (Map pp180-1; Mariscal Santa Cruz & Potosí) has a free monthly cultural and fine arts schedule. **Teatro Municipal** (Map pp180-1; cnr Sanjinés & Indaburo) has an ambitious theater and folk-music program.

Peñas

Typical of La Paz are folk-music venues called *peñas*. Most present traditional Andean music, but they often include lavish guitar and song recitals. Admission ranges from B$30 to B$80 and usually includes the first drink; meals cost extra. Check newspapers for advertisements about smaller unscheduled *peñas* and other musical events.

El Calicanto (Map pp180-1; ☎ 240-8008; Sanjinés 467; mains B$25-50, dinner buffet B$30)

Peña Parnaso (Map pp180-1; ☎ 231-6827; Sagárnaga 189; mains B$35-40, admission B$80; ⏰ show 8:30pm)

Peña Marka Tambo (Map pp180-1; ☎ 228-0041; Jaén 710; mains B$40, admission B$30; ⏰ from 8pm Thu-Sat)

La Casa del Corregidor (Map pp180-1; ☎ 236-3633; Murillo 1040; food & show B$80, admission B$25; ⏰ 7pm-late Mon-Sat)

SHOPPING

Street stalls are the cheapest place to buy pretty much everything from batteries and film to bootleg CDs.

Tight travelers can grab a bargain at the **Mercado Negro** (Map pp180–1), a clogged maze of makeshift stalls that sprawls over several blocks. It is, however, notorious for pickpockets and recently, a few 'spitters' have been reported here (see p179).

Calle Sagárnaga is the street for tasteful and kitsch souvenirs as well as CD shops and the nearby **Mercado de Hechicería** (Witches' Market; Map pp180–1) is the place for oddities such as shriveled llama fetuses, which locals bury under the porches of their new homes for luck and good fortune. If you're lucky, you might convince a *yatiri* (Aymara healer) to toss the coca leaves and tell your fortune, but they usually refuse gringo customers. Make sure you ask politely before taking photos here. For less expensive llama or alpaca sweaters, bowler hats and other non-tourist clothing items, stroll along Graneros and Max Paredes.

Many La Paz artisans specialize in *quenas, zampoñas, tarkas* and *pinquillos*, among other traditional woodwinds. There's a lot of low-quality or merely decorative tourist rubbish around. Visit a reputable workshop where you'll pay a fraction of gift-shop prices, and contribute directly to the artisan rather than to an intermediary. Several shops sell instruments along Sagárnaga, Linares and Illampu.

GETTING THERE & AWAY
Air
Call **El Alto International Airport** (LPB; ☎ 281-0240) for flight information. Airline offices in La Paz include these ones:

AeroSur (Map pp180-1; ☎ 244-4930; www.aerosur .com; Edificio Petrolero, Av 16 de Julio 1616)

Amazonas (☎ 222-0848; Saavedra 1649, Miraflores)

American Airlines (Map pp180-1; ☎ 237-2009; www.aa.com; Edificio Hernann, Plaza Venezuela 1440)

LAN Airlines (Map pp180-1; ☎ 235-8377; www.lan .com; Edificio Ayacucho, Av 16 de Julio 1566, ste 104)

Taca (Map pp180-1; ☎ 215-8202; www.taca.com; Edificio Petrolero, Av 16 de Julio 1616)

TAM Mercosur (☎ 244-3442; Gutiérrez 2323)

Transportes Aéreos Militares (TAM; Map pp180-1; ☎ 268-111, 277-5222; Montes 738)

Domestic flight prices vary little between airlines, except for TAM, which is sometimes cheaper. Most travel agents sell tickets for internal flights for the same price as the airlines. The following schedule and price information is subject to change. Prices quoted are one way. Many domestic flights are not direct and often involve a stopover or more to pick up passengers, with legs usually lasting less than an hour. Be aware that some flights cannot go during wet season, especially to the Beni region.

Cobija B$956, twice daily with Aerocon (via Trinidad), three times weekly with AeroSur, four times weekly with TAM.

Cochabamba B$340-386, three daily with AeroSur and three weekly with TAM.

Guayaramerín B$1174, twice daily with AeroSur, twice daily with Aerocon (via Trinidad) and one direct daily with Aerocon.

Puerto Suarez B$814-1373, daily flights with Aerocon (via Santa Cruz), twice weekly with AeroSur (via Trinidad) and three weekly with TAM (via Cochabamba and Santa Cruz).

Riberalta B$949-1174, three daily with AeroSur (via Trinidad), six weekly with Amazonas (via Trinidad), five weekly with TAM (via Cochabamba and Trinidad) and twice daily with Aerocon (via Cochabamba and Trinidad).

Rurrenabaque B$420-525, four daily with Amazonas and five weekly with TAM.

San Borja B$645-856, two daily via Rurrenabaque and two daily via Trinidad with Amazonas and six weekly via Rurre with Aerocon.

Santa Cruz B$699-856, two to four daily with AeroSur, five weekly with TAM (via Cochabamba) and two daily with Aerocon (via Trinidad).

Sucre B$420-553, daily direct flight with AeroSur and five weekly with TAM.

Tarija B$783-863, daily with AeroSur (some with layover) and two direct flights weekly with TAM.

Trinidad B$469-535, four daily with Amazonas/Aerocon and five weekly with TAM.

Yacuiba B$868, twice weekly with TAM (via Cochabamba and Tarija).

Bus
There are three *flota* departure points in La Paz: the main terminal, the cemetery district and Villa Fátima. Fares are relatively uniform between companies, but competition keeps prices low. Allow for longer travel times (often double or canceled) in the rainy season.

MAIN TERMINAL
Buses to all places south and east of La Paz as well as international destinations leave from the main **terminal** (Map pp176-7; ☎ 228-0551; Plaza Antofagasta; terminal fee B$2) a 15-minute uphill walk north of the city center. Prices are relatively uniform between companies.

Approximate one-way fares and journey times from the main terminal are shown in the table below. Buses provide connections between major cities several times daily, and more expensive *bus-cama* (sleeper) services are available on long overnight runs.

BUS FARES

Destination	Cost (B$)	Duration (hr)
Arica, Chile	100-150	8
Cochabamba	45-90	7-8
Cuzco, Peru	100-150	12-17
Iquique, Chile	150-200	11-13
Oruro	15-45	3-4
Potosí	52-80	11
Puno, Peru	50-80	8
Santa Cruz	170	16
Sucre	70-135	14
Tarija	90-180	24
Tupiza	115	20
Uyuni	90	13
Villazón	115-140	23

CEMETERY AREA
Micros and minibuses run to the *cemeterio* (cemetery) constantly from the center: catch them on Av Mariscal Santa Cruz or grab *micro* 2 along Av Yanacocha. Heading into the city from the cemetery by day you

BOLIVIA

can catch *micros* along Av Baptista. At night always take a taxi.

Several bus companies, including **Trans Manco Capac** (Map pp176-7; ☎ 245-9045) and **TransTurs 2 de Febrero** (Map pp176-7; ☎ 245-3035), run frequent services to Copacabana (B$15 to B$20, three to 3½ hours) between 5am and 8pm from José María Aliaga near Plaza Felix Reyes Ortíz (Plaza Tupac Katari). For B$25 to B$30 try the more comfy tourist buses that do hotel pickups. From Copacabana, lots of *micros* and minibuses sprint to Puno (B$30, three to four hours).

Between 5am and 6pm, **Autolíneas Ingavi** (Map pp176-7; José María Asín) has departures every 30 minutes to Desaguadero (B$10, two hours) via Tiwanaku (B$10, 30 minutes). Nearby is **Trans-Unificado Sorata** (Map pp176-7; ☎ 238-1693; cnr Kollasuyo & Bustillos), which operates two daily buses to Sorata (B$20, 4½ hours). You need to reserve buses on weekends, so book your ticket early. Sit on the left for views.

VILLA FÁTIMA

You can reach Villa Fátima by *micro* or minibus from the Prado or Av Camacho. **Flota Yungueña** (☎ 221-3513) minibuses to Coroico (B$15 to B$25, three hours) leave from the *ex-surtidor*, a former gas station. Flota Yungueña also has departures to Rurrenabaque (B$50 to B$80, 18 to 20 hours) from their second office at Las Américas 341, just north of the former gas station. Nearby **Trans Totaí** (San Borja) and **Trans San Bartolomé** (☎ 221-1674) serve Chulumani (B$15 to B$20, four hours) – a heinous trip in the rainy season. There are also buses to Guayaramerín (B$160 to B$180, 35 to 60 hours), Riberalta (B$140, 35 to 60 hours) and Cobija (B$180, 50 to 80 hours).

GETTING AROUND

La Paz is well serviced by public transportation. There are full-size buses and *micros*, which charge around B$1 for trips around the city center. Buses, *micros* and minibuses announce their route with signs on the windshield; barkers shout out destinations on minibuses ad nauseam. *Trufis* are shared taxis that follow a fixed route and charge B$3 per person around the center and B$4 to Zona Sur. Any of these vehicles can be waved down anywhere, except in areas cordoned off by the police.

Radio taxis, which you can phone or flag down, charge about B$4 around the center, B$8 to B$10 (more in peak hour) from

Sagárnaga to Sopocachi, or Sopocachi to the cemetery district and B$15 to B$20 to Zona Sur. Charges are for up to four passengers and include pickup, if necessary. Charges are a little higher after 11pm.

AROUND LA PAZ

TIWANAKU

Tiwanaku is Bolivia's most significant archaeological site, 72km west of La Paz on the road toward the Peruvian frontier at Desaguadero.

Little is known of the people who constructed this great ceremonial center on Lake Titicaca's southern shore. Archaeologists generally agree that the civilization that spawned Tiwanaku rose in about 600 BC but after AD 1200 the group faded into obscurity. However, evidence of its influence has been found throughout the area of the later Inca empire.

There are a number of megaliths (more than 130 tons in weight) strewn around the site, including a ruined pyramid and the remains of a ritual platform. Much has been restored, not always with total authenticity, and travelers fresh from Peru may be disappointed. The highlights include the new onsite **Museo Lítico Monumental** (admission B$10; ☾ 9am-5pm) with finds from the earliest Tiwanaku periods and the ongoing excavation of **Puma Punku** (Gateway of the Puma). For a greater appreciation of Tiwanaku's history, hire a guide. A major research and excavation project is ongoing, which means that some of the main features may be cordoned off during your visit.

You can stop at Tiwanaku en route between La Paz and Puno, Peru (via Desaguadero), but most travelers prefer to travel from La Paz to Puno via Lake Titicaca (p197) and visit Tiwanaku as a day trip from La Paz. **Autolíneas Ingavi** (Map pp176-7; José María Asín, La Paz) leaves for Tiwanaku (B$10, 1½ hours) about eight times daily, as does **Trans Tiwanaku** on José Aliago (B$10, two hours). To return to La Paz, flag down a bus (expect to stand), or catch a minibus from the village's main plaza. Sometimes minibuses will pass the museum entrance if they're not full, looking for passengers. Several La Paz agencies (p178) offer guided tours to Tiwanaku for US$10 to US$20, including transportation and a bilingual guide.

THE CORDILLERAS & THE YUNGAS

Two of South America's icons – the Amazonian jungle and the peaks of the Andes – meet in this fabulously diverse zone. The Yungas, beautiful subtropical valleys where steep forested mountainsides fall away into humid, cloud-filled gorges, contain several Afro-Bolivian settlements and form a natural barrier between the *altiplano* and the Amazon. Tropical fruits, coffee and coca all grow here. The climate is moderate with misty rain possible at any time of year. Above these steamy forested depths rise the near-vertical slopes of the Cordillera Real northeast of La Paz and the Cordillera Quimsa Cruz to the south.

COROICO

☎ 02 / pop 4500

Perched on the shoulder of Cerro Uchumachi (2548m) at an elevation of 1500m to 1750m, Coroico is a Bolivian Eden. It serves as a lowland retreat for middle-class *paceños* (citizens of La Paz), an enclave for a few European immigrants and a popular base for short treks into the countryside. As many expats can attest, it's so laid-back that it's hard to break away.

Orientation & Information

Coroico is 7km uphill from the transport junction of Yolosa. There's a **tourist office** (☎ 7401-5825; ☾ 8am-8pm daily) on the plaza and a small information kiosk at the bus terminal. The former can also provide guides for local hikes. Online try www.coroi.co.cc for information.

Únete (Plaza García Lanza; ☾ 10am-10pm daily) offers the most reliable access in town, for B$3 per hour.

There are no foreign-card accepting ATMs in Coroico. **Prodem** (Plaza García Lanza; ☾ 8:30am-noon & 2:30-6pm Tue-Fri, 8:30am-4pm Sat & Sun) changes dollars at a fair rate and does cash advances for 5% commission.

Sights & Activities

For pretty views, trek an easy 20 minutes up to **El Calvario**, where the stations of the cross lead to a grassy knoll and **chapel**. To get there, head uphill toward Hotel Esmeralda. There are two good trailheads from El Calvario. The one to the left leads to the **cascadas**, a trio of waterfalls

5km (two hours) beyond the chapel. The trail to the right leads up to **Cerro Uchumachi** (a five-hour round trip), which affords terrific views of the valley.

You can also rent horses from **El Relincho** (☎ 7192-3814), located between the hotels Esmeralda and Sol y Luna, 10 minutes' walk above town, for B$50 per hour or B$700 for a two-day camping trip around Uchumachi, all including guide.

Friendly **Cross Country Coroico** (☎ 7127-3015; www.mtbcoroico.co.cc; Pacheco 2058) offers mountain biking day-trips for all levels of rider from B$280 per person, including a guide and packed lunch. Readers have reported the trips as being good-natured if a little disorganized. La Paz-based biking company **Gravity Assisted Mountain Biking** (p182) were, at the time of writing, about to launch a new zip-line in the Coroico area at Yolosa. Check their website, www.ziplinebolivia.com, for details.

Siria León (☎ 7195-5431; siria_leon@yahoo.com; Manning s/n) is recommended for Spanish lessons (B$35 an hour).

Sleeping

Rates rise as much as 100% on holiday weekends and hotels are often booked on weekends from June to August. Bargain midweek and for longer stays. There are many more places to sleep than those listed here and most have restaurants as well.

Hostal Sol y Luna (☎ 7156-1626, in La Paz 244-0588; www.solyluna-bolivia.com; camping B$20, s/d B$110/160, without bathroom B$70/120, apt/cabaña s/d B$110/160; ☟) Set on a jungly hill, this splendid gringo-friendly retreat is well worth the 20-minute walk east of town (B$12 in a taxi). It has scenic campsites, self-contained *cabañas* (cabins), apartments and comfortable rooms with shared bathroom. Bonuses include restaurant with veggie options, book exchange, shiatsu massage, two pools and a slate hot tub.

Hostal de la Torre (☎ 289-5542; Cuenca s/n; r per person B$25) Sunny and clean, this is Coroico's cheapest acceptable accommodation. A modern block of mini-apartments (per apartment for up to five people B$250) was to open shortly at the time of research.

Hostal El Cafetal (☎ 7193-3979; danycafetal@hotmail .com; Miranda s/n; r per person B$35; ☟) A superlative option with stunning views, reputedly the best eats in Bolivia and a pool in a lush garden setting. Follow your nose (and the signs) from the plaza.

BOLIVIA

Hostal 1866 (☎ 7159-5607; Cuenca s/n; r per person with/without bathroom B$60/35) Inside this curious building, a hybrid of medieval and Moorish style, the interior rooms are windowless and dingy but the en-suite rooms are spacious, light and breezy.

Hotel Esmeralda (☎ 213-6017; www.hotel-esmeralda .com; Suazo s/n; r per person B$100, with balcony B$90, without bathroom B$50, ste B$150; 🖳 🖵) There's a variety of rooms; the cheapest are tiny and dark, with shared bathrooms, but the suites are nicer, with hammock-equipped balconies. Facilities include pool table, laundry and a buffet restaurant. Some readers report that service has been erratic of late.

Hostal Kory (☎ 7156-4050; Kennedy s/n; s/d B$60/100; 🖵) Southwest of the plaza, the most 'solid' and plain of the budget options, with fabulous views, a large pool and a restaurant that serves decent food in smallish portions.

Hotel Don Quijote (☎ 213-6007; Iturralde s/n; s/d B$80/150; 🖵) A flat 10-minute walk east of the plaza, this friendly pad is popular with Bolivian families for its inviting pool. Pick-up from the plaza is free.

Eating & Drinking

Coroico has a decent choice of eateries; you'll sometimes wonder which country you're in. The plaza is ringed by a number of inexpensive local places and pizzerias. Local volunteers swear that the average **Pizzeria Italia** on Ortíz is the best of the mediocre bunch.

La Senda Verde (Ortíz; snacks B$5) This courtyard cafe dishes out home-produced coffee from the refuge in nearby Yolosa and good breakfasts.

Villa Bonita (Héroes del Chaco s/n; mains B$12-30; 🕙 10am-6pm) Delicious homemade ice creams and sorbets and an eclectic range of vegetarian dishes served outside at this delightful garden-cafe 600m from town.

Luna Llena (mains B$15-35) The small outdoor restaurant at Hostal Sol y Luna is run with a motherly hand by doña María. Order the Indonesian buffet (B$35 per person for eight to 20 people) a day in advance.

El Cafetal (Miranda s/n; mains B$15-40) Bolivia's culinary gold medal goes to this French-run restaurant. It's worth every step of the 15-minute walk uphill from the plaza for its phenomenal salads, crêpes, curries and breezy atmosphere.

Back-Stube Konditorei (Kennedy s/n; mains B$22-40) Excellent breakfasts, tempting cakes and pastries and memorable *sauerbraten* (marinated pot-roast beef) with *spätzle* (Swabian dough noodles).

For a candlelit drink or two, try **Bamboo's Café** (Iturralde 1047; mains B$20-40) with good-value spicy Mexican food.

For a game of pool and the two-for-one happy hour, head to **Bar Mosquito** (Sagárnaga s/n; 🕙 daily after 6pm).

Getting There & Away

The new La Paz–Coroico road has replaced the 'World's Most Dangerous Road' (see p182) as the town access route. Asphalted along its whole length, it has already suffered from several landslides that have cut up some sections. Buses and minibuses (B$20, 3½ hours) leave hourly (between 7:30am and 8:30pm) from La Paz' Villa Fátima neighborhood. En route they stop in Yolosita where you can connect with buses and *camiones* north to Rurrenabaque (B$100, 15 to 18 hours) and further into Bolivian Amazonia.

In Coroico, buses leave from the bus terminal at Av Manning. It's a steep walk uphill to the plaza, or you can hop a taxi (B$5). **Turbus Totaí** run comfortable taxi services to La Paz from the terminal, leaving when full (B$20, two hours).

For Chulumani, the quickest route is to backtrack to La Paz. Although the junction for the Chulumani road is at Unduavi, few passing minibuses have spare seats at this point.

CHULUMANI
☎ 02 / pop 3000

This placid town is the terminus of the Yunga Cruz trek (see opposite) and a great detour off the gringo circuit. Located in a coca-growing region, it's also the capital of Sud Yungas province.

Chulumani's tourist office is in a kiosk on the square but the hours are whimsical. There's no ATM; Banco Unión changes traveler's checks for 5% commission; Prodem changes US dollars and gives cash advances on credit cards (5% commission). The Cotel office on Plaza Libertad is one of several phone offices. Internet connections are sporadic; on a good day head to **Enternet** (Sucre s/n).

For great views, head to the **mirador** two blocks south of the plaza. The English-speaking owner of the Country House (see opposite) is full of ideas for hiking, biking, river tubing and camping outside the town.

An interesting day trip is to the **Apa-Apa Reserva Ecológica** (☎ 213-6106; apapayungas@hotmail.com; r per person B$50, camping one-off fee B$70 plus per person per night B$15; ⚑), a cloud forest rich in birds and flora 8km from town. You can stay in the beautiful historic hacienda or camp at the well-equipped site above it. The reserve runs four-hour guided forest walks (B$50 per person with a B$200 minimum) and has a cafe. A taxi from Chulumani costs B$15.

Sleeping & Eating

Hostal Dion (☎ 213-6070; Bolívar s/n; r per person B$70, without bathroom B$50) At this friendly, clean and well-maintained choice just off the plaza, rates include a simple breakfast.

our pick **Country House** (Tolopata 13; r per person B$70; ⚑) The nicest place to stay is Javier Sarabia's rustic guesthouse, 10 minutes' walk from the plaza. There's a mineral pool, great breakfasts, homey bar and delicious meals on request. The owner can organize all sorts of local excursions.

El Castillo (☎ 235-9881; www.hotelcastilloloro.com; r per person B$150; ⚑) Along the Chulumani road at 1934m, this unique riverfront castle functions as a hotel and restaurant. The swimming pool, waterfalls and subtropical climate make it an appealing weekend getaway.

For cheap chow, try the fried chicken at **Snack San Bartolomé** on the plaza or the basic *comedores* near the *tranca*. The best *almuerzos* for just B$10 can be had at **El Mesón** (Plaza Libertad s/n) and **Conny** (Sucre s/n), which has a pleasant dining room with views and is also open in the evenings. Also on the plaza, **Restaurant Chulumani** has an upstairs dining terrace.

Getting There & Away

From Villa Fátima in La Paz, around the corner of San Borja and 15 de Abril, different companies depart when full for Chulumani (B$25, four hours) from 8am to 4pm. From Chulumani, La Paz-bound buses wait around the *tranca*. Theoretically, there are several departures before 10am and after 4pm but services are frequently cancelled. Buy your ticket in advance; even if your company doesn't depart, it will be valid for one of those that does.

It's possible to go to Coroico via Coripata: take a La Paz-bound bus and get off at the crossroads just after Puente Villa at Km 93. Here, wait for a bus or *camión* to Coripata and then change again for a lift to Coroico (for a lo-o-o-ng, dusty trip).

TREKKING IN THE CORDILLERAS

Several worthwhile treks run between the *altiplano* and the Yungas. Most popular are the **Choro** (La Cumbre to Coroico, 70km), **Takesi** (Taquesi; 45km) and **Yunga Cruz** (114km). These two- to four-day treks all begin with a brief ascent, then head down from spectacular high-mountain landscapes into the riotous vegetation of the Yungas. This area is also home to **Huayna Potosí** (6088m), the most popular major peak to climb; many agencies in La Paz can organize the ascent (see p178).

The best time for these treks is during the May to September dry season. Security is a concern as nasty incidents have been reported so it's best to check the situation ahead of time and avoid solo hiking. Many tour agencies in La Paz offer these as a two- to three-day trip for around US$60 to US$190 – note that negotiating the price down will affect the quality of the services and often won't include park entrance fees, porters or transport. Hikers should carry the *Alpenvereinskarte Cordillera Real Nord* (Illampu) 1:50,000 map; this can be bought at Buho's Internet Café in Sorata (on the south side of the plaza).

SORATA

☎ 02 / pop 2500

Sorata is the kind of place in which the hardiest soccer thug would consider taking up yoga. Surrounded by green mountains, and at the confluence of the Ríos San Cristobal and Challa Suya, its calm beauty attracts tourists needing relaxation, as well as mountaineers and trekkers seeking adventure in the surrounding snowcapped peaks of Illampu (6362m) and Ancohuma (6427m). On Sunday, jeeps and buses ferry flocks of locals to the market. On Tuesday, many places are closed.

Activities

WALKING

More for the walk than the site is the 12km trek to the **Gruta de San Pedro** (admission B$5; ⏰ 8am-5pm), a four-hour round trip from Sorata (or B$30 by taxi). Bring water and snacks. Otherwise call the San Pedro community (☎ 238-1695) who manage cave visits and might be able to arrange transport. The community has also set up two simple *albergues* to overnight in.

BOLIVIA

HIKING

Peak hiking season is May to September. Ambitious adventurers can do the seven-day **El Camino del Oro trek**, an ancient trading route between the *altiplano* and the Río Tipuani gold fields. Alternatively, there's the steep climb up to **Laguna Chillata**, a long day trek with multiple trails (it's best to take a guide; you can't see the lake until you get there); **Laguna Glacial** (5100m), a two- to three-day high-altitude trek; the challenging five-day **Mapiri Trail**; or the seven-day **Illampu circuit**. Although this is one of the best trails, there have been ongoing incidents and this should not be attempted without well-informed guides.

The **Sorata Guides & Porters Association** (☎ /fax 213-6672; guiasorata@hotmail.com; Sucre 302) can help organize many different treks and rents equipment. Budget on around B$200 per day for a guide plus food for you and the guide. It costs B$40 extra to hire a mule.

MOUNTAIN BIKING

Andean Epics Ride Company (☎ 7127-6685; www .andeanepics.com; inside Lagunas) runs a series of awesome rides around Sorata for all levels from April to December. Where else in the world can you cycle on pre-Inca paths, jump at 6000m and plunge thousands of meters downwards? A minimum of four people is required for the longer rides; prices range between B$350 and B$500 per ride. The main gig is a bike-boat extravaganza: a five-day trip from Sorata to Rurrenabaque with two days riding followed by a three-day boat journey with hikes as side trips (B$1400, all inclusive, departures every Monday). Mountain-bike guru and owner Travis is always building downhill trails and plotting out new routes.

Sleeping

Altai Oasis (☎ 7151-9856; www.altaioasis.lobopages.com; camping B$12, s/d B$70/100, without bathroom B$40/70, cabins for 2-5 people B$300-420; 🖳) Beautiful riverside retreat with a lush garden, hammocks, caged macaws, a balcony cafe-restaurant and a range of lodging options. To get there, follow the downhill track past the soccer field to the river, climb back up to the road and turn left before reaching Café Illampu.

Residencial Sorata (☎ 279-3459; r per person B$30-70) Friendly ghosts loom in this rambling colonial mansion on the northeast corner of the plaza. New rooms come with private bathrooms and

there's a wild garden. Manager Louis is great on local trekking information.

Hotel Santa Lucia (☎ 213-6686; r per person with/ without bathroom B$70/40) This cheerful, bright yellow place with carpeted rooms and laundry sinks has a friendly owner, Serafin, who'll do his utmost to make your stay comfortable.

Hostal Panchita (☎ 213-4242; s/d B$50/70) Built around a clean courtyard on the south side of the plaza, this pleasant spot has spacious rooms with private or shared bathrooms. The attached cafe-restaurant does arguably the best of the town's pizzas.

Hostal Mirador (☎ 289-5008; hostellingbolivia@yahoo .com; Muñecas 400; s/d B$50/80) Perks include a sunny terrace, a cafe, decent rooms and lovely views down the valley. There's a 10% discount for HI members.

Hostal Las Piedras (☎ 7191-6341; Ascarrunz s/n; r per person B$50, s/d B$100/140) The nicest of Sorata's *hostales*, with pretty rooms named after precious stones, some featuring valley views. Head to the soccer field, a 10-minute walk from the plaza, down Ascarrunz (a rough track).

Hotel Paraíso (☎ 213-6671; Villavicencio s/n; r per person B$60) Central location, a bright flowery patio, a series of roof terraces with nice views and solid rooms with bathrooms.

Eating & Drinking

Small, inexpensive restaurants around the market and the plaza sell cheap and filling *almuerzos*.

The main square should be renamed Plaza Italia, such are the number of (identical) pizzerias (oh! plus a Mexican).

Café Illampu (snacks B$10-20; ☽ closed Tue) On the road to San Pedro, this tranquil cafe, run by a Swiss master baker, is where you'll find good coffee, sandwiches on homemade bread and great cakes.

El Ceibo (Muñecas 339; mains B$15-25) One of a row of simple Bolivian eateries serving hearty portions of typical Bolivian dishes.

Pete's Place (Esquivel s/n; almuerzo B$15, mains B$15-40) For the latest trekking news and great food, this is the place, with a yummy selection of veggie and international dishes. Look for the signs on the plaza.

Altai Oasis (mains B$20-50) The balcony restaurant of Altai Oasis Hotel serves coffee, drinks and its trademark steaks, veggie treats and Eastern European dishes like borscht and goulash, all paired with nice valley views.

For beer, cocktails and homemade liquor, head to **Lagunas** with a worldly vibe and vegetarian dishes.

Getting There & Away

Sorata is far removed from the other Yungas towns and there are no direct connections to Coroico.

From La Paz **Trans Unificado Sorata** (☎ 238-1693) and **Perla del Illampu** each leave hourly from Manuel Bustillos with Angel Babaia between 4am and 5:30pm (B$15, three hours). From the plaza in Sorata, La Paz-bound *micros* depart when full and *flotas* leave on the hour between 4am and 5pm.

For Copacabana you must get off at the junction town of Huarina and wait there for another bus.

LAKE TITICACA

Lake Titicaca is deservedly awash with gushing clichés. Considered the largest high-altitude lake in the world, this incongruous splash of sapphire amid the stark plains of the *altiplano* is rightly described as one of the most beautiful sights in the region.

At an elevation of 3808m, the lake is a remnant of Lago Ballivían, an ancient inland sea. Covering 8400 sq km, it straddles both Peru and Bolivia. The lake's traditional Aymara villages, ancient legends and snow-topped peaks of the Cordillera Real in the background together provide a magical landscape and experience.

COPACABANA
☎ 02 / pop 54,300

Nestled between two hills and perched on the southern shore of Lake Titicaca, Copacabana (Copa) is a small, bright and enchanting town. It was for centuries the site of religious pilgrimages, and today the pilgrims flock to its fiestas.

Although it can appear a little tourist-ready, the town is a pleasant place to wander around, with excellent cafes, and lovely walks along the lake and beyond. It's the launching pad for visiting Isla del Sol, and makes an agreeable stopover between La Paz and Puno or Cuzco (Peru). At 3800m, the days are pleasant and sunny (with rain in December and January) but nights are chilly the rest of the year.

BOLIVIA

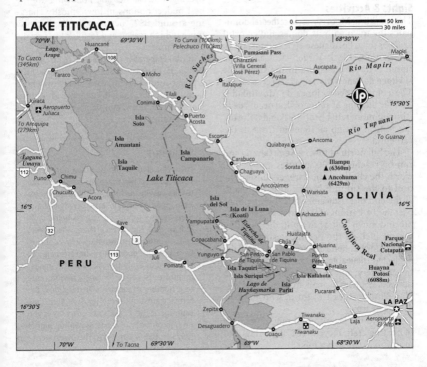

LAKE TITICACA

BOLIVIA

Information

The best book exchange is at **Hotel La Cúpula** (Pérez 1-3; www.hotelcupula.com). Travelers beware: there's no ATM in town! Calle 6 de Agosto is the Wall St of Copacabana with many change booths.

Lavanderías are noticeably scarce, although many hotels will do your washing (B$10 to B$20 per kg). Cheaper laundry services are offered along 6 de Agosto.

Centro de Información de Comunitario (Plaza Sucre; ☒ 9am-1pm & 3-7pm) This NGO-sponsored project encourages tourism to three of the area's communities (Isla de la Luna, Cha'llapampa and Las Islas Flotantes) with a photographic exhibit and shop.

Centro de Información Turística (☎ 7191-5544; cnr Av 16 de Julio & Plaza Sucre; ☒ 9:30am-5pm Tue-Sat) Helpful English-speaking attendant gives out rudimentary information here.

Entel Internet alf@net (6 de Agosto; ☒ 9am-11pm; per hr B$10) The town's best connections.

Prodem (cnr 6 de Agosto & Pando; ☒ 2:30-6pm Tue, 8:30am-12:30pm & 2:30-6pm Wed-Fri, 8:30am-3pm Sat & Sun) Cash advances on a Visa and MasterCard (5% commission).

Sights & Activities

The sparkling Moorish-style **cathedral** dominates the town with its domes and colorful *azulejos* (blue Portuguese-style ceramic tiles). The famous black Virgen de Candelaria statue is housed upstairs in the **Camarín de la Virgen de Candelaria** (☒ all day but unreliable). The colorful Bendiciones de Movilidades (*cha'lla;* blessing of automobiles) occurs daily (though more reliably on weekends) during the festival season at 10am in front of the cathedral.

The hill north of town is **Cerro Calvario** and can be reached in 30 minutes and is well worth the climb, particularly at sunset. The trail to the summit begins near the **church** at the end of Destacamento 211 and climbs past the 14 stations of the cross. Other sights around town (all with sporadic opening hours) include the pre-Inca astronomical observatory at **Horca del Inca** (admission B$5); the neglected **Tribunal del Inca** (admission B$5) north of the cemetery; and the community of **Kusijata** (admission B$5) with a small archaeological display 3km northeast of town, with the **Baño del Inca** nearby.

Head to the lakeshore to rent all manner of boating craft, bicycles (B$70 per day) and motorbikes (B$50 per hour).

Festivals & Events

A Bolivian tradition is the blessing of miniature objects, like cars or houses, at the **Alasitas festival** (January 24), as a prayer that the real thing will be obtained in the coming year. These miniatures are sold in stalls around the plaza and at the top of Cerro Calvario.

Following Alasitas, the **Fiesta de la Virgen de Candelaria** is celebrated from February 2 to February 5. Pilgrims from Peru and Bolivia perform traditional Aymara dances amid much music, drinking and feasting. On **Good Friday**, the town fills with pilgrims, who join a solemn candlelit procession at dusk. The biggest fiesta lasts for a week around **Independence Day** (during the first week in August), featuring parades, brass bands, fireworks and lots of alcohol.

Sleeping

There is an incredible variety of cheap places to snooze. During fiestas, however, everything fills up and prices can jump threefold. Most places will store backpacks for free while you overnight at Isla del Sol. Following are the best budget options in town, mostly charging around B$25 per person (significantly more in high season and festivals), especially along Jáuregui.

Hostal Emperador (☎ 862-2083, La Paz 242-4264; Murillo 235; r per person B$25, without bathroom B$20) Upbeat and colorful with hot showers, a laundry service, shared kitchen and luggage storage. The new section has en-suite rooms and a sunny terrace.

WARNING

Particular care should be taken during festivals, particularly those for Semana Santa (Easter Week) and Independence Day week. Petty theft is common, and there have been more serious reports of tourists being tackled around the neck – these maneuvers cause you to faint, whereupon you are relieved of your goods. Also, travelers are encouraged to avoid the taxis and the smaller minibuses to La Paz for safety reasons, due to a number of incidents. Instead take the formal tourist buses or the larger *flotas;* any tour agency in Copacabana can book you on one of these. The cost is slightly higher (B$25 to B$30) but worth the investment.

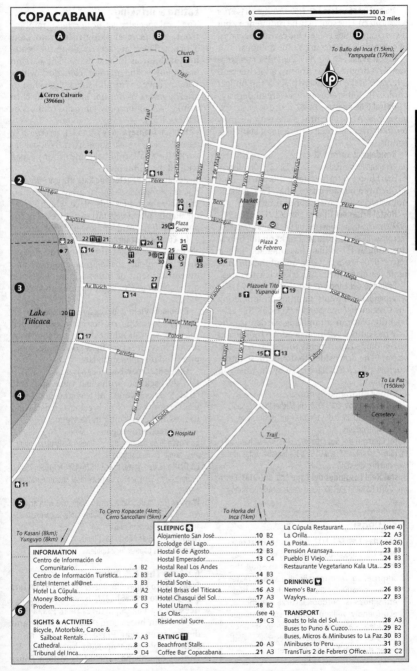

COPACABANA

Alojamiento San José (☎ 7150-3760; Jáuregui 146; r per person B$20-25) This spot may be rudimentary but it's as clean as they come. One caveat: the claims of constant hot water are a little dubious.

Hostal Sonia (☎ 862-2019; Murillo 256; r per person from B$25) Bright cheery rooms, a kitchen and a terrace make this lively place a top budget choice. In 2009 renovations were underway.

Hostal 6 de Agosto (☎ 862-2292; 6 de Agosto; r per person B$25) A rosy central place with a sunny outlook over a garden and clean, if standard, rooms.

Residencial Sucre (☎ 862-2080; Murillo 228; r per person with/without bathroom B$35/25; f B$140) Clearly a smart hotel in former days, this place – now a little tired but adequate – has TVs, reliable hot water, courtyard and restaurant.

Hostal Brisas del Titicaca (☎ 862-2178, La Paz 245-3022; www.hostellingbolivia.org; cnr 6 de Agosto & Costañera; r per person B$50; 🖳) Situated right on the beach, this popular HI-affiliate has amenable (albeit retro 1970s) rooms. Grab one of the en-suite units featuring their own lake-view terraces.

Ecolodge del Lago (☎ 862-2500, La Paz 245-1138; r per person B$100) Twenty minutes on foot along the Costanera (or a quick taxi ride), this eco-friendly place in a rambling garden on the lake has quirky self-heated adobe rooms and self-equipped apartments with solar-powered water. (The downside: no doubt these introductory prices will have risen by the time you read this.)

Other midrange options:

Hotel Utama (☎ 862-2013; cnr Michel Peréz & San Antonio; s US$10-15; d US$10-20) Clean, reliable and popular with groups.

Hotel Chasqui del Sol (☎ 862-2343; www.chasquidelsol.com; Costañera 55; s/d US$20/35) Massive vistas of the lake and friendly staff.

Hostal Real Los Andes del Lago (☎ 862-2103; Busch s/n; s/d/tr B$100/120/180) Good value, clean and breezy.

Eating & Drinking

The local specialty is *trucha criolla* (rainbow trout) and *pejerrey* (king fish) from Lake Titicaca. These are served along the **beachfront stalls** for as little as B$20. The bargain basement is the market *comedor*, where you can have an 'insulin shock' breakfast or afternoon tea of hot *api morado* (hot corn drink; B$2) and syrupy *buñuelos* (donuts or fritters; B$1).

Pensión Aransaya (6 de Agosto 121; almuerzo B$15, mains B$25-40; 🕑 lunch) Superfriendly local favorite for a tall, cold beer and trout heaped with all the trimmings.

Restaurante Vegetariano Kala Uta (cnr 6 de Agosto & 16 de Julio; mains B$20-30) An artsy Andean atmosphere pervades this place which serves up slightly bland vegetarian choices. Try the *poder Andino* (Andean power) breakfast.

La Cúpula Restaurant (Peréz 1-3; mains B$20-50; 🕑 closed Tue lunch) At this hotel restaurant, local ingredients make up an extensive and inventive menu of international and local dishes, with great veggie options and scenic views.

Pueblo El Viejo (6 de Agosto 684; mains B$20-50) Readers love this rustic, cozy and chilled cafe-bar, with its ethnic decor and laid-back atmosphere. It serves up a good burger and pizza and it's open until late.

Coffee Bar Copacabana (6 de Agosto s/n; mains B$25-45) Laid-back spot with great value *almuerzo* (B$15), extensive list of teas and good coffees (proper espresso!), breakfasts, pastas and nachos and everything in between.

Also recommended:

La Posta (6 de Agosto s/n; 🕑 dinner) Tasty pizzas in a cozy, tango-themed setting.

La Orilla (6 de Agosto; mains B$25-45; 🕑 10am-10pm, closed Sun) Serves up tasty local and international dishes.

Waykys (cnr 16 de Julio & Busch) Warm den with graffiti-covered walls and ceilings, a billiards table, book exchange and a varying range of music.

Nemo's Bar (6 de Agosto 684) Dimly lit late-night hangout that's popular for a tipple.

Getting There & Away

Trans Manco Capac (☎ 862-2234) and **TransTurs 2 de Febrero** (☎ 862-2233) have booking offices for La Paz departures near Plaza 2 de Febrero but buses sometimes arrive at and depart from near Plaza Sucre. The more comfortable nonstop tour buses from La Paz to Copacabana – including Milton Tours

GETTING TO PERU

There are two options to enter Peru: the first one is via Copacabana and the Kasani–Yunguyo border crossing, while the faster but less interesting route is via Desaguadero (8:30am to 8:30pm) on the southern side of Lake Titicaca. If you're leaving direct from La Paz, the easiest way is to catch an agency bus to Puno (Peru); the bus breaks in Copacabana (the Copa–Puno trip departing from Av 6 de Agosto costs B$30 and takes three to four hours) and again for immigration formalities in Yunguyo. Similar buses go direct to Cuzco (B$85 to B$150, 15 hours) with a change in Puno. A cheaper way from Copacabana is by minibus from Plaza Sucre to the Kasani–Yunguyo border (B$3, 15 minutes). On the Peruvian side, micros and taxis will ferry you to Yunguyo (15 minutes; around six Peruvian soles). From here, you can catch a bus to Puno.

For information on travel from Peru to Bolivia, see p809. Keep in mind that Peruvian time is one hour behind Bolivian time.

and Combi Tours – cost around B$25 to B$30 – and are well worth the investment (see boxed text, p194). They depart from La Paz at around 8am and leave Copacabana at 1:30pm (3½ hours). Note, at the time of research, these were departing from the top of 16 de Julio, several blocks south of Plaza Sucre. Tickets can be purchased from tour agencies.

ISLA DEL SOL

Isla del Sol (Island of the Sun) is the legendary Inca creation site and the birthplace of the sun in Inca mythology. It was here that the bearded white god Viracocha and the first Incas, Manco Capac and his sister-wife Mama Ocllo, made their mystical appearances.

With a permanent population of around 2500, Isla del Sol is dotted with several villages, of which **Yumani**, **Cha'lla** and **Cha'llapampa** are the largest. The island's Inca ruins include **Pilko Kaina** and **Escalera del Inca** (admission B$5, valid for both & Yumani) at the southern end and the **Chincana** complex in the north (admission B$10), which is the site of the sacred rock where the Inca creation legend began. At Cha'llapampa, there's a **museum** (admission B$10) with artifacts from Marka Pampa, referred to by locals as La Ciudad Submergida (The Sunken City). The museum entry ticket is also valid for the Chincana complex and vice versa; a guide will accompany you to both.

A network of **walking tracks** make exploration easy but the sunshine and the 4000m altitude can take their toll. You can see the island's main archaeological sites in one long day, but it's best to stay overnight – plus you're contributing to local economy. Bring food, water and sunscreen.

Sleeping

Isla del Sol's infrastructure has exploded in recent years, with more restaurants and accommodation options than sun rays. Note though that shops for self-catering are still rather scarce. If camping, it's best to ask permission from the local authority and then set up away from villages, avoiding cultivated land.

Water is a precious commodity – the island does not yet have access to water mains – as supplies are carried by person or donkey. Please bear this in mind; think twice before taking frequent showers. Also note that in high season (June to August and festivals), prices listed here may double.

The most scenic place to stay is Yumani – high on the ridge – where guesthouses are growing faster than coca leaves. Ch'allapampa and Ch'alla have basic accommodations options.

Hostal Qhumphuri (☎ 7152-1188, La Paz 284-3534; hostalqhumphuri@hotmail.com; s/d B$20/40) This simple, family-run spot has clean rooms in a mustard-colored construction on the hill behind the beach at Cha'lla.

Hostal Cultural (☎ 7190-0272; r per person B$35, without bathroom B$20) Behind the beach, this is the only option in Ch'allapampa with private bathrooms.

Hostal San Francisco (r B$25) The neatest of a choice of very basic options in Ch'allapampa, a flowery place to the left of the landing site.

Inti Wasi Lodge (☎ 7196-0223; museo_templodelsol @yahoo.es; dm per person B$25, cabins with bathroom & breakfast per person B$70) Four basic but cozy cabins in Yumani with smashing views and a recommended restaurant, Palacio de la Trucha, attached.

ISLA DEL SOL

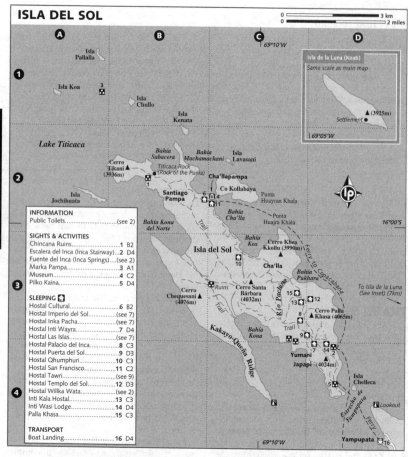

0 —————— 3 km
0 —————— 2 miles

Isla de la Luna (Koati)
Same scale as main map

▲ (3925m)
Settlement ●

Lake Titicaca

INFORMATION
Public Toilets.............................(see 2)

SIGHTS & ACTIVITIES
Chincana Ruins.............................1 B2
Escalera del Inca (Inca Stairway)....2 D4
Fuente del Inca (Inca Springs)....(see 2)
Marka Pampa.............................3 A1
Museum.....................................4 C2
Pilko Kaina................................5 D4

SLEEPING
Hostal Cultural............................6 B2
Hostal Imperio del Sol.............(see 7)
Hostal Inka Pacha.....................(see 7)
Hostal Inti Wayra........................7 D4
Hostal Las Islas........................(see 7)
Hostal Palacio del Inca.................8 C3
Hostal Puerta del Sol....................9 D3
Hostal Qhumphuri......................10 C3
Hostal San Francisco..................11 C2
Hostal Tawri............................(see 9)
Hostal Templo del Sol.................12 D3
Hostal Willka Wata...................(see 2)
Inti Kala Hostal.........................13 C3
Inti Wasi Lodge.........................14 D4
Palla Khasa.............................15 C3

TRANSPORT
Boat Landing............................16 D4

Hostal Imperio del Sol (☎ 7196-1863; r per person with/without bathroom B$100/35) This peachy, modern and central place in Yumani has spotless rooms. The shower room is rarely open due to limited water supplies.

Hostal Inti Wayra (☎ 7194-2015, La Paz 246-1765; r per person from B$45) The amicable and rambling Inti Wayra affords great views from most rooms; these vary a great deal – some are larger and more open.

Other basic, budget options – all charging around B$25 to B$30 (more in high season) – include the following, in geographical order from south to north.

Hostal Inka Pacha (☎ 289-9160)
Hostal Willka Wata (☎ 7325-0242)
Hostal Las Islas (☎ 7193-9047)
Hostal Tawri (☎ 7352-7194)
Hostal Puerta del Sol (☎ 7195-5181)
Hostal Templo del Sol (☎ 7122-7616)
Hostal Palacio del Inca (☎ 7151-1046)

This list is by no means exhaustive. Within this category (B$20 to B$30), hostel standards (read basic) and prices (read fair price to quality ratio) are almost identical. This is a fun place to DIY exploring.

Two midrange places worth mentioning, both with private bathrooms and breakfast included:

Palla Khasa (☎ 7622-9180; palla-khasa@hotmail.com; r per person B$80) Around 400m uphill out of Yumani, with stellar views, a pleasant ambience, comfortable rooms and a wonderful restaurant.

Inti Kala Hostal (☎ 7194-4013; javierintikala@hotmail
.com; r per person B$80) A massive deck and small neat
rooms. At the time of research it was expanding.

Eating

There are more cafes in Yumani than Titicaca
has *trucha*. We suggest you follow your nose
and taste buds, plus fellow travelers' recommendations (and see how far your feet can take you)
and choose what appeals to you. Most mid-
and top-range accommodation options have
good eateries. Most restaurants are blessed with
lovely views, and those on the ridge are special
for the sunset. Nearly all menus are identical;
set lunches and dinners cost between B$25 to
B$30. Pizzas are the go; Isla del Sol rivals Rome
for its per capita number of pizzerias.

Getting There & Away

Boats depart from Copacabana Beach around
8:30am and 1:30pm daily. Buy tickets at the
kiosks on the beach or at agencies in town.
Depending on the season and the company,
they may drop you off at a choice of the island's
north or south (check with the agency). Most
full-day trips (about B$25 return) go directly
north to Cha'llapampa (two to 2½ hours).
Boats anchor for 1½ hours only – you'll have
just enough time to hike up to the Chincana
ruins, and return again to catch the boat at
1pm to the island's south. Here, you'll spend
around two hours before departing for Copa
and arriving back between 5pm and 6pm.
Those who wish to hike the length of the island
can get off at Cha'llapampa in the morning
and walk south to Yumani for the return boat
in the afternoon – it's a moderately strenuous
three- to four-hour walk along the ridgeline.

Half-day tours to the island's south are available (B$15 to B$20) but are hardly worthwhile.
Alternatively, you can opt to stay overnight or
longer on the island (highly recommended to
fully experience it and give something to the
community), then buy a one-way ticket to
Copacabana (B$15 to B$20) with any of the
boat companies in Yumani or Cha'llapampa.

THE SOUTHWEST

Nowhere tantalizes the senses as much as
Bolivia's southwest. Picture windswept basins, white-capped volcanic peaks and blinding white salt deserts. Feel indeterminable
distances. Taste red dust. Further east, enjoy

silence as the *altiplano* drops into ethereal
and spectacular rainbow-rock surrounds.
And as you head lower again, breathe in the
alluring scent of the region's orchards and
vineyards.

ORURO

☎ 02 / pop 260,000

Set at 3706m around a range of mineral-rich
hills, on the dusty and dry plains of the *altiplano*, the distinct city of Oruro has a flavor
all of its own.

Accommodations and transportation are
in high demand during festivals and events,
especially the Carnaval, so advance booking is essential and inflated prices are the
norm.

The city is about three hours south of La
Paz on a decent paved road, and is the northern limit of Bolivia's limited rail network. It's
fiercely cold and windy year-round, so come
prepared.

Information

There are a couple of ATMs on the plaza.
Watch your cash stash – local pickpockets and
bag-slashers are quite competent, especially
during drunken festivals.

Banco Bisa (Plaza 10 de Febrero) Cashes Amex traveler's
checks into B$ without commission (for US dollars, there's
a $6 fee).

Immigration (☎ 527-0239; Soria Galvarro btwn
Ayacucho & Cochabamba; ☺ 8:30am-12:30pm &
2:30-6:30pm Mon-Fri) Extend your stay here (last door
on the left).

Lavandería (cnr Sucre 240 & Pagador) Charges B$10 per
kg for 24-hour service.

Mundo Internet (Bolívar 573; per hr B$3) The best of
several places in town.

Municipal tourist bureau (☎ 525-0144; Plaza 10 de
Febrero; ☺ 8am-noon & 2:30pm-6:30pm Mon-Fri) On
the top floor of Cine Palais Concert, the tourist office isn't
really designed for walk-ins but can be helpful and gives
out maps.

Tourist police (☎ 528-7774) Round-the-clock operation at the bus terminal, which shares the kiosk with the
tourist info point and gives out maps.

Sights & Activities

Museo Patiño (☎ 525-4015; Soria Galvarro 5755; admission
B$8; ☺ 8:30-11:30am & 2:30-6pm Mon-Fri, 9am-2:30am
Sat) is a former residence of tin baron Simon
Patiño. Exhibits (by guided tour only) include
period furnishings, paintings, photographs
and fine toys.

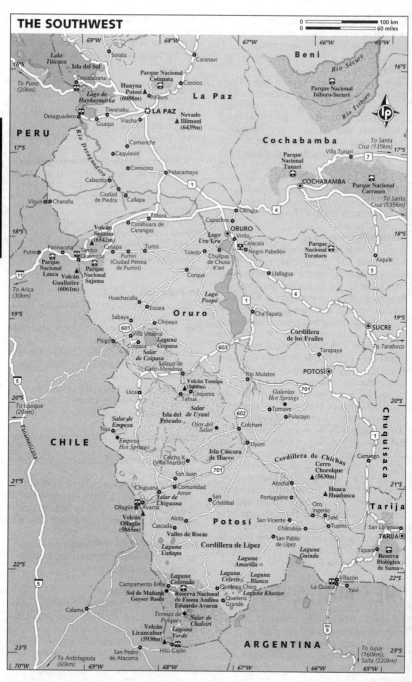

THE SOUTHWEST

Adjacent to the **Santuario de la Virgen del Socavón** is the **Museo Sacro, Folklórico, Arqueológico y Minero** (☎ 525-0616; Plaza del Folklore s/n; admission both museums B$10, camera use B$3, video use B$20; ⊙ 9am-11:15am & 3:15-5:30pm), part of which is in a defunct mine, with displays on mines, miners and the devilish miners' god, El Tío.

At the south end of town, the **Museo Antropológico Eduardo López Rivas** (☎ 527-4020; España s/n; admission B$3; ⊙ 8am-noon & 2-6pm Mon-Fri, 10am-6pm Sat & Sun) has artifacts from the early Chipaya and Uru tribes. Take a *micro* marked 'Sud' from the plaza's northwest corner or opposite the train station and get off just beyond the tin foundry.

Don't miss the whimsical home and studio of a seven-member artist family, **Museo Casa Arte Taller Cardozo Velasquez** (☎ 527-5245; juegue oruro@hotmail.com; Junín 738; admission B$8), worth a trek to the edge of town. There are no specific opening hours – best to call ahead.

The **Obrajes hot springs** (admission B$10), 25km northeast of town, are the best of several nearby soaking options. From the corner of Caro and Av 6 de Agosto, catch an 'Obrajes' *micro* (B$5, 30 minutes), which departs from 7:30am to 5pm daily. On weekends, local rock climbers flock to the area called **Rumi Campana**, 2km northwest of town; contact the **Club de Montañismo Halcones** (www.geocities.com/msivila).

Festivals & Events

During the spectacular **Carnaval**, from the Saturday before Ash Wednesday, the city turns into a parade of party animals. Revelers – including proud locals, 90% of whom call themselves *quirquinchos* (armadillos) – pitch water at each other (which, frankly, can be downright tiresome). Several parades (including the **Entrada** and **La Diablada**) feature dancers in intricately garish masks and costumes.

Sleeping

Near the train station on Velasco Galvarro there are quite a few handy, if not classy, *alojamientos* (accommodations).

Residencial San Miguel (☎ 527-2132; Sucre 331; s/d B$40/60, without bathroom B$30/50) Handy for both the train station and the center but pretty rock-bottom in terms of comfort.

Pub the Alpaca (☎ 527-5715, 523-2707; wcamargo_gallegos@yahoo.com; La Paz 690; r per person B$40) Three simple, sunny and spacious rooms share a kitchen, plus you've got the city's best pub in your front room. Email ahead.

Hotel Bernal (☎ 527-9468; Brasil 701; s/d B$70/100, without bathroom B$40/70) Good-value and friendly place with appealing rooms featuring back-friendly beds, decent hot showers and even cable TV.

Residencial 21 de Abril (☎ 527-9205; simon21deabril @bolivia.com; Montecinos 198; s B$50, d with/without bathroom B$120/80) Family-run *residencial* a short walk from the center with tidy bright rooms, all with TV and hot water.

Alojamiento Copacabana (☎ 525-4184; Velasco Galvarro 6352; aloj.copacabana@hotmail.com; d B$70) The best of the budget spots opposite the train station – bright, clean, cheerful and secure.

Other solid options:

Hostal Hidalgo (☎ 525-7516; 6 de Octubre 1616; s/d/tr B$50/100/150) A modernish central option with clean windowless rooms and pricier newer ones (s/d/t B$100/180/250).

Residencial Boston (☎ 527-4708; Pagador btwn Caro & Cochabamba; d with/without bathroom B$100/80) A class above most Oruro *residenciales*.

Hotel Repostero (☎ /fax 525-8001; Sucre 370; s/d/t B$100/135/155) Worth paying extra to stay in the renovated wing (s/d/t B$145/150/195) with carpeted rooms.

Hotel Samay Wasi (☎ 527-6737; samaywasioruro @hotmail.com; Brasil 232; s/d/t B$150/210/270; 🖳) Attractive European-style hotel by the bus terminal.

Eating

Life doesn't really get going here until 11am, so Mercado Campero and Mercado Fermín López are your best bet for an early breakfast. Stalls serve mostly *api* and pastries in the morning, but look out for *thimpu de cordero* (a mutton and vegetable concoction smothered with *llajhua*, a hot tomato-based sauce) and *charquekan* (sun-dried llama meat with corn, potatoes, eggs and cheese). For bargain lunch specials, check out the small eateries around the train station.

Govinda (Junín btwn 6 de Octubre & Soria Galvarro; almuerzo B$9-16, mains B$11-13; ⊙ closed Sun) For Hare Krishna veggie fare, try this serene place.

El Huerto (Bolívar near Pagador; almuerzo B$10; ⊙ closed Sat) Friendly hole-in-the-wall eatery with veggie lunches, tasty cakes and snacks.

Paprika (Junín 821; mains B$18-40) Join the locals for some lively banter. Where else can you be served a B$15 lunch by bow-tied waiters?

Bravo's Pizza (cnr Bolívar & Soria Galvarro; pizzas B$19-30, pastas B$28-45) More than 20 pizza varieties, including a spicy one with dried llama meat.

BOLIVIA

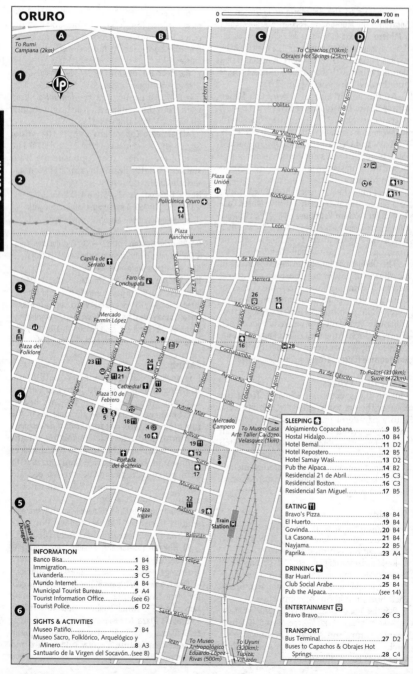

ORURO

0 — 700 m
0 — 0.4 miles

BOLIVIA

To Rumi Campana (2km)

To Capachos (10km); Obrajes Hot Springs (25km)

Plaza La Unión

Policlínica Oruro

Plaza Ranchería

Capilla de Serrato

Faro de Conchupata

Mercado Fermín-López

Plaza del Folklore

Cathedral

Plaza 10 de Febrero

Portada del Beaterio

Mercado Campero

To Museo Casa Arte Taller Cardozo Velasquez (1km)

Plaza Ingavi

Train Station

Canal de Desague

To Museo Antropológico Eduardo López Rivas (500m)

To Uyuni (320km); Tupiza; Villazón

To Potosí (310km); Sucre (472km)

La Casona (Montes 5969; pizzas from B$20) Out-of-the-oven *salteñas* by day, quick sandwiches for lunch, and pizza and pasta at night.

Nayjama (cnr Aldana & Pagador; mains B$30-55; ☽ closed Sun for dinner) High-quality traditional Oruro food with an innovative touch and lamb as the specialty. The English menu is slightly more expensive so try to ask for the Spanish one.

Drinking & Entertainment

Pub the Alpaca (La Paz 690; ☽ Thu-Sat 8pm-1am) At this intimate Swedish- and Bolivian-run pub, the good-mood feel is helped with good mixed drinks.

Bar Huari (cnr Junín 608 & Soria Galvarro) Not much seems to have changed in this series of high-ceilinged rooms since the 1930s. Great for a beer with locals.

Club Social Árabe (Junín 729; ☽ closed Sun) A slice of old-fashioned Oruro, this 2nd-floor spot has occasional live music on weekends.

Bravo Bravo (cnr Montecinos & Pagador) The best karaoke in town.

Getting There & Away

BUS
All buses arrive and depart from the **bus terminal** (☎ 527-9535; terminal fee B$1.50), a 15-minute walk or short cab ride northeast of the center. Buses to La Paz (B$20, three hours) run every half-hour or so. There are daily services to Cochabamba (B$25, four hours), Potosí (B$20, five hours), Sucre (B$40, eight hours), Tupiza (B$86, 14 hours) and Villazón (B$86, 16 hours). Several night buses depart daily for Uyuni (B$40, eight hours) but the train is the ticket on this rough route. For Santa Cruz, you must make a connection in Cochabamba; buses depart on Saturday.

Several daily services ply the route to Arica, Chile (B$100, 10 hours), via Tambo Quemado and Chungará (Parque Nacional Lauca). There are a lot more buses going to Iquique (B$80, eight hours) via the Pisiga border crossing. Most travelers, however, prefer to enter Chile further south at San Pedro de Atacama via Uyuni and a *salares* (salt plains) tour (see p206).

TRAIN
Oruro became a railroading center thanks to its mines, but the only surviving passenger connection is with Uyuni and points south.

You must take your passport to the **ticket window** (☎ 527-4605; ☽ 8:15-11:30am & 2:30-6pm Mon & Thu, 8:15am-6pm Tue & Fri, 8:15am-noon & 2:30-7pm Wed, 8:15-11am & 3-7pm Sun); arrive early and purchase your ticket at least a day ahead to avoid long lines.

The train service is run by the **Empresa Ferroviaria Andina** (FCA; www.fca.com.bo) and offers two services. The top-notch *Expreso del Sur* has two classes: the quite serviceable salon and top-of-the-line executive premier, which includes meals, videos, heaters and a dining car. It departs Oruro at 3:30pm Tuesday and Friday to Uyuni (*salón/ejecutivo* B$52/101, seven hours), Tupiza (B$92/202, 13 hours) and Villazón (B$109/236, 16 hours). It's a thoroughly enjoyable trip with beautiful scenery as far as Uyuni, but unfortunately the stretch to Tupiza is after dark.

The *Wara Wara del Sur* is the 2nd-class train, departing Oruro on Wednesday and Sunday at 7pm to Uyuni (*popular/salón/ejecutivo* B$31/40/86, 7½ hours), Tupiza (B$54/69/153, 13½ hours) and Villazón (B$65/86/185, 17 hours). For the *popular* class, prime your wrestling persona before joining the fray. There's no dining car but snacks are peddled at every stop.

UYUNI
☎ 02 / pop 20,000
This 'climatically challenged,' otherworldly and isolated community (elevation 3669m) today seems to exist only for the tourist hoards who venture out to the extraordinary *salares*. The town itself has two notable sights: the archaeology museum and the rubbish-strewn Cementerio de Trenes (a graveyard of rusting locomotives 2km southwest of town).

Information
Banco de Crédito (Potosí btwn Arce & Bolívar) The lone ATM in town here is often out of service, especially on weekends. The bank breaks big boliviano notes and changes cash. Otherwise, try the street changers near the bank, bigger tour companies or popular restaurants; several places on Potosí buy Chilean and Argentine pesos.

Immigration (Ferroviaria btwn Arce & Sucre; ☽ 8:30am-noon & 2:30-6pm Mon-Fri, 8:30am-noon Sat & Sun) If traveling to Chile, it's best to pick up your exit stamps here (B$21).

Lavarap (cnr Ferroviaria & Sucre; ☽ 7am-10pm) Charges B$10 per kg. Some hostels and hotels offer the same service.

Reserva Nacional de Fauna Andina Eduardo Avaroa (REA; ☎ /fax 693-2400; www.bolivia-rea.com; cnr Colón & Avaroa; ☻ 8:30am-12:30pm & 2:30-6:30pm Mon-Fri) You can buy your park entry (B$30) at the administrative office if going under your own steam.

Rowl@and (Potosí btwn Bolívar & Arce) One of the more reliable and cheaper spots, opposite the ATM (B$4 per hour). Minuteman Pizza inside Hotel Toñito has wi-fi.

Tourist office (cnr Potosí & Arce; ☻ 8:30am-noon & 2pm-6:30pm Mon-Fri) Inside the clock tower, this tourism office has unreliable hours and scarce printed materials.

Sights

The **Museo Arqueología y Antropológico de los Andes Meridionales** (cnr Arce & Colón; admission B$5; ☻ 8:30am-noon & 2-6:30pm Mon-Fri) features mummies, loads of skulls and Spanish-language descriptions of mummification and deformation.

Tours

A drive across the *salar* and surrounds is a surreal and must-do experience: salt plains, hot springs, geysers, lagoons, volcanoes and flamingos are the tour trademarks. In the wet season some areas can't be reached.

STANDARD TRIPS

The most popular tour is a jeep trip: a three-day circuit visiting the Salar de Uyuni, Laguna Colorada, Sol de Mañana and Laguna Verde. If you want to head into Chile, you can do three days of the tour, hop off at Laguna Verde and connect there with transport to San Pedro de Atacama (often the price is the same; check whether transfer is included in fee; see p206). There is a border outpost at Laguna Verde but it's best to get the Bolivian exit stamps in Uyuni; better tour agencies often arrange stamps outside office hours.

CUSTOM TRIPS

Shorter trips traverse the northern crescent of the Salar de Uyuni for one to two days but these have angered some locals as they don't give much to the local communities. Depending on the season and usually at higher cost (but worth every *peso*), you can arrange longer custom trips visiting the less-visited attractions of the remote and beautiful Los Lípez region, the Salar de Coipasa and on

---

CHOOSING AN OPERATOR

Operators are piled high in Uyuni: there are currently over 80 agencies offering trips to the *salar* (salt plain). Most offer Spanish-speaking drivers who take you on the identical three-day trip. While the competition may mean more choice, it also means lowered quality as many dodgy and fly-by-night operators try to make a fast buck. It's your right to negotiate but remember that cost-cutting leads to operators cutting corners – at the expense of your safety and the environment! Common exploits include trying to cram an extra body into the jeep (six people should be the maximum), or they join forces with other agencies to make up the numbers.

The results of this have included deadly accidents. At least 16 people, including 13 tourists, have been killed in jeep accidents on the Salar de Uyuni salt plains since May 2008. There have been alarming reports of ill-equipped vehicles, speeding tour operators, a lack of emergency equipment, breakdowns, drunk drivers, poor food and service, and disregard for the *salar's* once pristine environment. Environmental no-nos include the following:

▪ Using the facilities of the Playa Blanca salt hotel (see p207).

▪ Chasing flamingos to get a good in-flight photo.

▪ Leaving garbage – including toilet paper – behind.

The best operators have written itineraries outlining meals (vegetarians can be catered for if specified), accommodations and trip details. The average costs for a standard three-day trip are between B$600 and B$850. Four-day circuits cost between B$800 and B$1000, with many ending up in Tupiza. Day trips start at B$150 (not recommended) while two-day stays cost between B$200 and B$400. In most cases, price reflects quality. Trips are often slightly cheaper if you form a group of four to six.

When choosing the operator in Uyuni, your best bet is to talk to travelers to get the latest scoop. The market is so volatile that it's impossible to recommend operators with confidence. We strongly suggest that you speak to several companies after doing some research of your own in town.

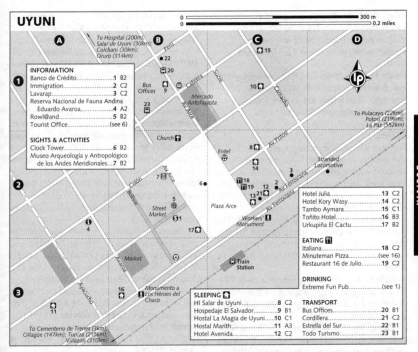

UYUNI

0 ___ 300 m
0 ___ 0.2 miles

BOLIVIA

to Tupiza. You can even tack on a day to climb one of the region's volcanoes.

Sleeping

Uyuni's tourism boom means that new hotels are opening all the time and older properties are being refurbished to keep up with the competition. The best of the bunch fill up fast in the high season so reservations are recommended.

Cheap places near the station come in handy as most trains arrive and depart at ungodly night hours. Only better hotels offer heating and there are water rations in Uyuni year-round.

Hostal Marith (☎ 693-2096; Potosí 61; r per person with/without bathroom B$50/30) This no-nonsense backpackers' favorite is often full. Hot water is sporadic. Extras include laundry sinks and a patio that's good for socializing.

Hotel Avenida (☎ 693-2078; Ferroviaria 11; s/d B$60/120, s/d/tr without bathroom B$30/60/90) Near the train station, a popular and clean option for pre-departure and return trips. Laundry sinks and hot showers between 7am to 9pm (in theory).

Hospedaje El Salvador (☎ 693-2407; Arce 346; s/d B$50/90, s/d/tr without bathroom B$40/70/100) Convenient if you're arriving by bus late at night, with friendly service, clean simple rooms with TV and a cafeteria.

HI Salar de Uyuni (☎ 693-2228; cnr Potosí & Sucre; dm B$45-50, d B$120-150) A real labyrinth of varying rooms, a bit on the dark side but clean.

Hotel Julia (☎ /fax 693-2134; juliahotel5@hotmail.com; cnr Ferroviaria & Arce; s/d B$80/150, without bathroom B$60/100; ☐) Central choice with no-frills but adequate rooms and internet room off the lobby (B$5/hour).

Hotel Kory Wasy (☎ /fax 693-2670; Potosí 350; r per person B$80) Rooms are poky and dark but all have private bathrooms (some are external) and the management is friendly.

Hostal La Magia de Uyuni (☎ /fax 693-2541; www.hostalmagiauyuni.com; Colón 432; s/d/tr B$190/280/415) The pricier upstairs rooms are well-kept and the darkish backpacker rooms downstairs (double B$130) arranged around an indoor courtyard.

Other options:
Urkupiña El Cactu (☎ 693-2032; Arce 46; r per person B$55) Handy shelter near the train station with hot water and plenty of blankets.

Toñito Hotel (☎ 693-2094; www.bolivianexpeditions .com; Ferroviaria 60; s/d/tr B$200/280/420; 🖳) Top choice for pleasant rooms in the old wing (new wing is pricier), laundry service, free wi-fi and Uyuni's best breakfasts.

Tambo Aymara (☎ /fax 693-2227; www.tamboaymara .com; Camacho s/n; s/d/tr/ste B$220/350/500/380) The most stylish option in town, with an ethnic theme and earth-toned rooms around a flower-filled patio.

Eating

For quick eats, cheap meals are on offer at the market *comedor* and nearby street food stalls, if you've got a strong stomach. A fast-food **kiosk** next to the clock tower has a few tables outside and cheap bites (B$8 to B35) like sandwiches and hamburgers.

Restaurant 16 de Julio (Arce 35; almuerzo B$18, mains B$18-45) A good place to escape the fellow gringos, this no-frills resto has a full spectrum of international and Bolivian dishes.

Italiana (Arce btwn Potosí & Ferroviaria; mains B$24-33) Buzzing travelers' hangout with bamboo decor and a menu heavy on Mexican and Italian dishes.

ourpick Minuteman Pizza (Ferroviaria 60; personal pizzas B$30-40; 🕑 breakfast & dinner) When Chris from Boston built a purpose-built pizza kitchen, he meant business – and he got it. Uyuni's best all-round eating choice offers gourmet pizzas, Budweiser, Tarija wines and a huge range of breakfasts.

Extreme Fun Pub (Potosí 9; mains B$35-45) Cool atmosphere, cocktails, decent grub, book exchange, occasional concerts, dice games and drinking competitions.

Getting There & Away

Arrive from Tupiza via the badlands to avoid the crowds. In high season, it can be tricky to get out of isolated Uyuni. Buy your bus ticket the day before or ask a tour agency how much they charge to purchase train tickets (or buy yours days ahead); lines are long and *quién es más macho* (literally 'who is the most macho') shoving matches can break out for the limited seats.

BUS & JEEP

All buses leave from the west end of Av Arce, a couple of minutes' walk from the plaza. There's a choice of companies to most destinations, so ask around to get the best price or service.

Several companies offer daily evening buses to Oruro (B$40, seven hours), where you can change for La Paz. It's a chilly, bone-shaking trip, so you might prefer **Todo Turismo** (☎ 693-3337; www.touringbolivia.com; Cabrera 158 btwn Bolívar & Arce), which runs a heated bus service with friendly staff and an onboard meal (B$230, 10 hours) via Oruro (8pm daily, except Wednesday and Sunday). The cheaper option with reliable buses and good drivers is **Omar**, right next to the post office, with daily 8pm departures to La Paz (B$100 to B$130; 11 hours). There are daily departures for Potosí (B$40, five to six hours) with connections to Sucre (B$60, nine hours). Direct buses depart daily for Tupiza (B$60, seven to eight hours) and Villazón (B$80, 10 hours), where you can connect to Salta.

There are buses at 3:30am on Monday and Thursday and at 5am on Sunday and Wednesday to Calama (B$100, nine hours) in Chile. You will have to change buses in Avaroa at the Chilean border. An alternative route to Chile is with an organized tour, which will leave you in San Pedro de Atacama. The best companies are **Estrella del Sur** (☎ 693-3132; toursestrelladelsur@hotmail.com; Arce at bus terminal) and **Cordillera** (☎ 693-3304; cordilleratravel_927@hotmail .com; Ferroviaria 314).

TRAIN

Uyuni has a modern, well-organized **train station** (☎ 693-2320). Tickets often sell out so buy your ticket several days in advance or get an agency to do it for you. Confirm hours on the noticeboard inside as the train can be delayed, especially during the rainy season.

Comfortable *Expreso del Sur* trains ramble to Oruro (*salón/ejecutivo* B$52/101, seven hours) on Wednesday and Saturday at 12:05am (arriving the next morning, on Thursday or Sunday) and southeast to Tupiza (B$41/101, 5½ hours) and Villazón (B$63/152, 8½ hours) on Tuesday and Friday at 10:40pm.

Wara Wara del Sur trains chug out of the station at 1:45am on Monday and Thursday night for Oruro (*popular/salón/ ejecutivo* B$31/40/86, 7½ hours) and on Sunday and Wednesday night at 2:50am for Tupiza (B$24/33/64, six hours) and Villazón (B$36/48/99, 10 hours).

Depending on size, you may have to check your backpack/case into the luggage compartment. Look out for snatch thieves on the train just before it pulls out.

> **WARNING**
>
> In the past couple of years, predeparture robberies have been increasing, where farewelling 'friends' enter the train and relieve others of their goods. Don't store your belongings in the overhead compartments.

On Monday at 3:30am a train trundles west for Avaroa (B$32, five hours) on the Chilean border, where you cross to Ollagüe and may have to wait a few hours to clear Chilean customs. From here, another train continues to Calama (B$91 from Uyuni, six hours from Ollagüe). The whole trip can take up to 24 hours but it's a spectacular, if uncomfortable journey. Taking a bus to Calama is more reliable.

SOUTHWEST CIRCUIT

Different times of year offer different experiences: from April to September, the *salares* are dry and blindingly white. In the rainy season, they're under water, projecting a perfect mirror image of clouds, sky and land to the horizon. At this time, roads may be quagmires, making passage difficult and potentially dangerous, and hail and snow are always a possibility.

Salar de Uyuni

The world's largest salt flat sits at a lofty 3653m and blankets an amazing 12,106 sq km. It was part of a prehistoric salt lake, Lago Minchín, which covered most of southwest Bolivia. When it dried up, it left a few seasonal puddles and several salt pans, including the **Salar de Uyuni** and **Salar de Coipasa**.

The salt-extracting town of **Colchani** on the eastern shore is the easiest point to access that great salt flat, and the place to go if you just want a glimpse of it without going on a tour. A maze of tracks crisscrosses the *salar* and connects nearby settlements and several islands that pepper this white desert. **Isla del Pescado** (also known as Isla Incahuasi) at the heart of the *salar* is a hilly outpost covered in Trichoreus cactus and surrounded by a flat white sea of hexagonal salt tiles.

It is illegal to actually construct buildings on the *salar* itself – Playa Blanca salt hotel, a morning stop on many tours, falls into this category due to its sewage system polluting the salt pan. Local environmentalists strongly recommend that you don't give them any business. There are several salt hotels on the edge of the *salar;* try the cozy **Maya Hostal** (room B$35 per person) run by a local Aymara family in the village of **Coqueza**, under the Tunupa volcano.

Far Southwest

Several startlingly beautiful sights are hidden away in this remote corner. The surreal landscape is nearly treeless, punctuated by gentle hills and volcanoes near the Chilean border. Wildlife in the area includes three types of flamingos (most notably the rare James species), plus plenty of llamas, vicuñas, emus and owls.

The following sites comprise the major stops on most tours. **Laguna Colorada** is a bright adobe-red lake fringed with cake-white minerals, 25km east of the Chilean border. The 4950m-high **Sol de Mañana geyser basin** has boiling mud pots and sulfurous fumaroles. Tread carefully when approaching the site; any damp or cracked earth is potentially dangerous. The nearby **Termas de Polques** hot springs spout comfortable 30°C (86°F) sulfurous water and provide a relaxing morning dip at 4200m.

Laguna Verde, a splendid aquamarine lake, is tucked into Bolivia's southwestern corner at 5000m. Behind the lake rises the dramatic 5930m cone of **Volcán Licancabur** which can be climbed; take a local guide.

GETTING THERE & AROUND

The easiest way to visit the far southwest is with a group from Uyuni (see p204); the above attractions are all visited on the standard three-day trip. Alternatively, you can set out from Tupiza (see p208) and end up in Uyuni, a very worthwhile option.

TUPIZA

☎ 02 / pop 22,300

If ever there's a place where you want to throw your leg over a horse, brandish spurs and say, 'ride 'em cowboy,' this is it. Reminiscent of the American Wild West but more spectacular, this tranquil settlement is set at 2950m and ringed by an amazing landscape of rainbow-colored rocks, hills, mountains and canyons of the Cordillera de Chichas. It was the apt setting for the demise of Butch Cassidy and the Sundance Kid: after robbing an Aramayo payroll at Huaca Huañusca, some 40km north of Tupiza, the pair reputedly met their makers in the mining village of San Vicente in 1908.

BOLIVIA

Hiking, biking and horse-riding opportunities abound. The variety of bizarre geologic formations, deep gorges and cactus forests form a dramatic backdrop. Unsurprisingly, it's finally been discovered by travelers and is well and deservedly on the gringo trail. Many people who visit for a day end up staying for a week to enjoy a tranquil and friendly experience.

Information

Several internet places on the plaza have slow connections for B$3 an hour.

Most accommodations can do a load of washing for you. There's a **laundry place** (per kg B$10; Mon-Sat) on Florida.

Most agencies distribute small maps of the town and the surroundings.

Tupiza Tours (694-3003; www.tupizatours.com; Hotel Mitru, Chichas 187) is a wealth of information, has a book exchange and gives cash advances. You can change cash or get cash advances at **Banco de Crédito** or **Prodem** on the plaza.

Sights & Activities

Tupiza's main attraction is the spectacular surrounding countryside, best seen on foot or horseback. Recommended destinations in the vicinity, all less than 32km away, include the following canyons and rock formations: **Quebrada de Palala**, **Quebrada de Palmira**, **El Cañon del Duende**, **Quebrada Seca** and **El Sillar**.

A short trek up **Cerro Corazón de Jesús** reveals lovely views over the town, especially at sunset. Lively **street markets** convene on Thursday and Saturday morning near the train station. Hotel Mitru enthusiastically promotes its solar-heated **pool** (B$20 for half-day).

Tours

Tour companies are being trotted out at a pace in Tupiza. Ask other travelers for recommendations. All the agencies offer the triathlon, an active full-day tour of the surrounding area by jeep, horse and mountain bike (B$200 to B$300 with lunch, based on four people). The best operators have safety equipment for the triathlon (helmets and jackets for bike trips, and hard hats for horse riding).

Horse riding is available in short jaunts (B$25 and B$30 per hour) and longer rides (up to four days).

All companies offer four-day trips to the *salar*. Expect to pay between B$1200 and B$1350 per person for the standard trip, based on four people in a jeep during the high season. The below agencies offer all of the above.

Alexandro Adventure Travel (694-4752; ale adventure4x4@hotmail.com; Arraya s/n) This friendly agency shows travelers off-the-beaten path spots around Tupiza and specializes in volcano climbs (Tunupa, Uturuncu or Licancabur) further afield.

El Grano de Oro Tours (694-4763; elgranodeoro tours@hotmail.com; Arraya 492) The owner's father has a working farm 12km from Tupiza, where it's possible to arrange a stay for B$40 per night as part of a two-day horse-riding route.

La Torre Tours (694-2633; www.latorretours-tupiza .com; Hotel La Torre, Chichas 220) Run by a friendly couple, this agency rents bikes for B$70 per day during the dry season. They also offer all the standard Tupiza tours.

Tupiza Tours (694-3003, La Paz 2-224-4282; www .tupizatours.com; Hotel Mitru, Chichas 187) This outfit, the largest in Tupiza, pioneered many of the Tupiza area routes now also offered by competitors. It offers daily departures to the *salar*. There have been mixed reports about the quality of their tours.

Sleeping

The cheapest options are basic *residenciales* opposite the train station.

El Refugio del Turista (694-4811; Santa Cruz 244; r per person B$40) At the time of research, Hotel Mitru was about to open this new budget option. It's five blocks from the train station featuring six rooms with shared bathrooms, a kitchen and a garden for BBQs.

Hostal Tupiza (694-5240; Florida 10; r per person B$25) Family-run affair with small but decent rooms on the 2nd floor, around a courtyard with a giant fig tree.

Alexandro Hostal (694-4752; aleadventure4x4 @hotmail.com; Arraya s/n; r per person with/without bathroom B$40/35) Friendly spot with three clean rooms around a terrace upstairs from the agency, as well as a shared kitchen, a laundry sink and TV room.

Hostal El Grano de Oro (694-4763; elgranode orotours@hotmail.com; Arraya 492; r per person B$40) Four simple and sunny rooms with large comfortable mattresses, cactus furniture, a shared bathroom and family vibe.

La Torre Hotel (694-2633; latorrehotel@yahoo.es; Chichas 220; r per person B$40, s/d B$60/120) This rambling house with clean rooms is a good place to meet travelers. Guests have use of a kitchen, a safe, a roof terrace and a TV lounge.

Hostal Valle Hermoso (694-2370; www.bolivia .freehosting.net; Arraya 478 & Arraya 505; r per person B$40, s/d

B$60/120) An HI hostel with a book exchange, optional breakfast and laundry service. Boards advertise group tours with the hotel agency. The same family has the bright, newer annex up the road, near the bus station.

Hotel Mitru (☎ 694-3003; www.tupizatours.com; Chichas 187; r per person B$40, s B$80-160, d B$140-200, ste B$320; 🔊) The best and most reliable hotel in town, the bright and airy Mitru with a pool is just the ticket after a dusty day out on horseback. Its annex (☎ 694-3002; Avaroa at Serrano; room per person B$40, single/double B$70/120) near the train station is excellent value.

Eating

Affordable street meals are served outside the train station and at the *comedores* around the market.

Alamos (cnr Avaroa & Santa Cruz; mains B$9-15) A green light outside marks this saloon-style spot where locals and tourists mingle in the funky two-floor space with a Mexican vibe. The portions are huge and meat-heavy.

Il Bambino (cnr Florida & Santa Cruz; almuerzo B$12) Excellent *salteñas* (B$3) in the morning and filling *almuerzos* at noon are the highlight of this friendly corner eatery.

Rinconcito Quilmes (Suipacha 14; almuerzo B$10, mains B$16-30) You'll see few other gringos in this little spot known for filling meat-heavy lunches served in a spacious dining room.

Sede Social Ferroviaria (cnr Avaroa & Chichas; mains B$15-30; ☙ closed Sun) Locals flock to this no-trimmings railway workers' club for the *parrilladas* (B$60 for two people).

Tú Pizza (Plaza Independencia s/n; mains B$18-30) This stylish little eatery on the main plaza has the whole gamut of pizzas, pastas and lasagna as well as mains with local goat's cheese and quinoa.

Italiana (Florida near Plaza Independencia; mains B$18-35) Perhaps the best of several tourist places in town – all offer almost identical decor and menus offering wide and varied choices.

Getting There & Away
BUS

Note that the upper prices of the range reflect high-season bus costs. Several *flotas* leave the **bus station** (terminal tax B$4) in the morning and evening for Potosí (B$50 to B$100, seven to eight hours); the road to Potosí is being paved and, when finished, should reduce travel time by a couple of hours. There are multiple departures daily for Villazón (B$15 to B$25, three hours); once you cross the Argentine border at La Quiaca you can catch a bus to Salta, with five daily departures (US$18). There are evening departures for Tarija (B$60, eight hours), with connections for Villamontes and Santa Cruz. Several buses head daily to La Paz (B$90 to B$180, 15 hours) in the evening via Oruro (B$70, 11 hours). Evening buses also leave for Sucre (B$80, 10½ hours) and Cochabamba (B$100, 18 hours). There are regular morning departures for Uyuni (B$50 to B$80, six hours).

BOLIVIA

GETTING TO ARGENTINA

The Bolivian side of the main border crossing to Argentina is a sprawling, dusty, chaotic sort of place. Watch out for the usual scammers who tend to congregate at borders; dodgy banknotes and petty theft are not unknown.

All northbound buses depart from the **Villazón bus terminal** (fee B$2). Regular bus services head to Tupiza (B$15, 2½ hours), La Paz (B$140 to B$170, 21 hours) via Potosí (B$80 to B$120, 11 hours), Oruro (B$140 to B$160, 17 hours) and Tarija (B$40, seven to eight hours).

The Villazón train station is 1.5km north of the border crossing – a taxi costs B$5. The *Expreso del Sur* departs Wednesday and Saturday at 3:30pm for Tupiza (*salón/ejecutivo* B$22/51, 2¾ hours), Uyuni (B$63/152, 8½ hours) and Oruro (B$109/236, 16½ hours). more basic *Wara Wara del Sur* departs Monday and Thursday at 3:30pm for Tupiza (*popular/salón/ejecutivo* B$13/17/38, three hours), Uyuni (B$24/48/99, 11 hours) and Oruro (B$30/86/185, 18 hours).

On the north side of the international bridge, **Bolivian customs & immigration** (☙ 24hr) issues exit and entry stamps (the latter normally only for 30 days) – there is no official charge for these services. Argentine immigration and Argentine customs are open from 7am to 11pm. Formalities are minimal but the wait and exhaustive custom searches can be very long. In addition, those entering Argentina may be held up at several control points further south of the border by more customs searches. For information on travel from Argentina to Bolivia, see p109.

TRAIN

You miss most of the brilliant scenery on the train route to Uyuni, so you might consider the less comfortable bus service. The **ticket window** (☎ 694-2527) at the train station opens irregularly on days when there's a train, so it's easier to have an agency buy your tickets for a small surcharge.

The *Expreso del Sur* trundles north to Uyuni (*salón/ejecutivo* B$60/101, five hours) and Oruro (B$101/202, 12 hours) at 6:40pm on Wednesday and Saturday. At 3:30am on Tuesday and Friday the *Expreso* speeds south to Villazón (B$22/51, three hours), arriving on Wednesday and Saturday morning.

The *Wara Wara del Sur,* which is often delayed, leaves at 6:50pm on Monday and Thursday evenings for Uyuni (*popular/salón/ ejecutivo* B$24/33/64, six hours) and Oruro (B$54/73/150, 13½ hours), and at 8:40am on Monday and Thursday for Villazón (B$13/17/38, 3½ hours).

TARIJA

☎ 04 / pop 132,000

Befitting of a viticultural city, Tarija is like an aging red wine: it's modest, displays positive attributes and consistently improves over time. The city is almost Mediterranean in nature and design: stately date palms line the beautiful plaza, colonial houses abound and a central market pulsates with life and flavors. The city's numerous cafes, plazas and museums provide a pleasant place to relax. A significant student population adds action to the ambience.

The surrounding area has many sights and activities, bottled for the traveler. Vineyards, Inca trails and fossilized regions occupy a range of habitats, from lush fertile valleys to desert-type plains (the start of the Chaco region). With planning, these areas are accessible by hiking or on a tour with the growing number of operators. The valley's springlike climate is idyllic. *Chapacos* (as *tarijeños* refer to themselves) are in many ways more Spanish or Argentine than Bolivian. They're proud of their fiestas, unique musical instruments and local food and drink, including the fortified wine *singani*.

Orientation

Street numbers are preceded by an O *(oeste)* for those addresses west of Colón and an E *(este)* for those east of Colón; addresses north of Av Las Américas (Av Victor Paz Estenssoro) take an N.

Information

Internet places are ten a penny and usually have phone cabins incorporated as well. Try along Bolívar for decent connections (per hour B$3 to B$4). ATMs are numerous around the plazas.

Casas de cambio (Bolívar) Changes US dollars and Argentine pesos. Banco Bisa and Banco Nacional, both on Sucre, will change traveler's checks.

Departmental tourist office (☎ 663-1100; cnr 15 de Abril & Trigo; ☺ 8:30am-noon & 3-6pm Mon-Fri) Has basic town maps and will answer queries regarding sites within and around town.

Immigration (☎ 664-3594; Ingavi 789) Friendly and worth visiting about border crossings or to extend your visa.

Lavandería La Esmeralda (☎ 664-2043; La Madrid 0-157) Does a quick machine wash and dry service for B$12 per kg.

Municipal tourist office (☎ 663-3581; cnr Bolívar & Sucre; ☺ 8:30am-noon & 3-6pm Mon-Fri) Not much material or information, but friendly staff.

Sights & Activities

It's worth a stroll around the center to see what remains of the colonial atmosphere. For fossil frolickers, the free university-run **Archaeology & Paleontology Museum** (cnr Lema & Trigo; ☺ 8am-noon & 3-6pm Mon-Sat) houses a good overview of the region's geology and prehistoric creatures.

Wealthy Tarija landowner Moisés Navajas left behind the partially restored **Casa Dorada** (☎ 664-4606; Ingavi 0-370; ☺ 8am-noon & 2:30-6:30pm Mon-Fri) – now the **Casa de la Cultura** – which houses a quirky extravaganza of European furniture, imported by a Spanish couple in 1903.

A popular weekend retreat is **San Lorenzo**, 15km northwest; you can pop into the former home of the *chapaco* hero Moto Méndez. *Micros* and *trufis* (B$3, 30 minutes) leave from the corner of Domingo Paz and Saracho every 20 minutes. Another getaway is **Tomatitas**, 5km northwest. Have a dip in the natural swimming hole or trek to the 60m-high **Coimata Falls**. Tomatitas *micros* leave frequently from the corner of Av Domingo Paz and Saracho in Tarija (B$1.50). For Coimata Falls, walk or hitch 5km to Coimata; the falls are a 40-minute walk upstream.

As the region's viticulture center producing both wine and *singani*, Tarija caters to those who love a good drop. *Bodegas* (wineries) include Bodega La Concepción, Bodega Casa Vieja, Campos de Solana/Casa and Kohlberg.

Note: many of these wineries have offices in town where you can buy the wine at lower prices than the shops. **Viva Tours** (☎ /fax 663-8325; cnr 15 de Abril & Delgadillo) can quench your thirst with excellent and reasonably priced winery tours (between B$80 and B$150 per person for half or full-day tours). Full-day trips incorporate surrounding areas, including the stunning **La Reserva Biológica de Sama**, Inca trail, colonial villages of the countryside and the varied Gran Chaco hinterlands.

Recommended companies, offering similar routes, include:

Sur Bike (☎ 7619-4200; Ballivian 601) For biking and hiking in the area.

VTB Tours (☎ 664-3372; Ingavi 0-784)

Sleeping

Residencial El Rosario (☎ 664-2942; Ingavi 777; s with/without bathroom B$70/35, d B$70) This budget place is well-tended, with rooms looking onto a quiet patio. There are gas-heated showers, laundry sinks and a TV room.

Hostería España (☎ 664-1790; Corrado 0-546; s/d B$60/120, without bathroom B$40/80) Hot showers, a flowery patio and tonnes of tourist info at reception. Slightly overpriced rooms are pretty cold in winter.

Residencial Zeballos (☎ 664-2068; Sucre N-966; s/d B$80/140, without bathroom B$40/80) Dozens of potted plants and climbers give this place a fresh, spring feel. The basement rooms are grim and dark so go for something upstairs.

Hostal Libertador (☎ 664-4580; Bolívar 0-649; s/d B$100/180) This central and welcoming place has dated en-suite rooms with phones and TV. No fan or air-conditioning.

Victoria Plaza Hotel (☎ 664-2600; hot_vi@entelnet.bo; cnr La Madrid & Sucre; s/d B$170/250; 🖳) The 1950s rooms at this charming spot are decked with gleaming wooden floors, comfy beds and retro furnishing.

Hotel Luz Palace (☎ 664-2741; Sucre N-921; s/d B$180/250) Modern, spacious rooms at this recently refurbished colonial hotel offer great value. The on-site tourist agency will help you plan your trip.

Also recommended:

Grand Hotel Tarija (☎ 664-2684; Sucre N-770; s/d B$160/300) One of the town oldies, comfortable and central.

Hostal Costanera (☎ 664-2851; cnr Estenssoro & Saracho; s/d B$180/280; 🐾 🖳) Splurge on one of the elegant rooms here, with spacious bathrooms, great showers and other perks.

Eating

At the northeast corner of the market, street vendors sell snacks and pastries unavailable in other parts of Bolivia, including delicious crepe-like *panqueques*. Breakfast is served out the back, other cheap meals are upstairs and fresh juices are in the produce section. Don't miss the huge bakery and sweets section off Bolívar.

Café Campero (Campero near Bolívar; mains B$10-30; 🕑 dinner only Tue-Sun) Dive into the fabulous range of breads, cakes and pastries, including *cuñapes* (cassava and cheese rolls).

Club Social Tarija (15 de Abril E-271; almuerzo B$15; 🕑 lunch only Mon-Fri) Old-fashioned *almuerzos* are the favorite of the loyal crowd of monthly meal-plan subscribers.

Serenata (Trigo; almuerzo B$15) *Palapa*-roofed restaurant and an atmospheric place to enjoy the great value *almuerzo*.

Café Mokka (☎ 665-0505; Plaza Sucre; mains B$16-38) For coffee, decent cocktails and light grub, head to this stylish place with a pavement terrace overlooking the square.

Chingo's (Plaza Sucre; meals B$20-45) Juicy steaks are the name of the game here, specializing in hefty Argentine beef *parrillada* (barbecued or grilled).

Bufalo (Plaza Luis Fuentes; mains B$26-55) Bufalo's ranch house setting is a clue to the meat-based menu, with some usual offerings such as *medallones de lomito con salsa de mariscos* (beef medallions in seafood sauce).

Taberna Gattopardo (Plaza Luis Fuentes; mains B$26-58) European-run tavern with good espressos and cappuccinos, well-prepared salads and *ceviche*, and delicious chicken fillets.

Heladería Napoli (Campero N-630; per kg B$36) Serves simply divine scoops of ice cream until 8pm.

Chifa Hong Kong (Sucre N-235; mains B$40) Cheap cocktails, huge lunches and an extensive Chinese menu.

Drinking & Entertainment

La Candela (Plaza Sucre; 🕑 9am-midnight Mon-Fri, 9am-2am Sat & Sun) French-owned, this thriving little bar-cafe has a boho ambience and live music at weekends.

Thai Kaffe (Plaza Sucre; 🕑 9am-midnight Mon-Fri, 10am-2am Sat & Sun) Popular with trendy twenty-somethings who gossip over a milkshake in the afternoon and gulp *singanis* in the evenings.

BOLIVIA

Keep an eye out for flyers advertising *peñas,* usually held at restaurants on weekends. After 6pm, chess heads can pick up a game at the **Asociación Tarijeña de Ajedrez** (Campero), where you can play for free if you respect club rules: no smoking and quiet.

Getting There & Around

AIR

The airport (off Av Victor Paz Estenssoro) is 3km east of town. **TAM** (☎ 664-2734; La Madrid 0-470) has Monday and Friday flights to Santa Cruz (B$558); flights to La Paz (B$783) via Sucre (B$477) depart on Tuesday, Wednesday, Friday and Sunday. The short hop to Yacuiba (B$308) leaves on Wednesday and Saturday. **AeroSur** (☎ 901-1015555; 15 de Abril) flies three times weekly to La Paz (B$850) and daily to Santa Cruz (B$661).

Taxis into town (B$20) cost almost twice as much from the terminal as from the road 100m outside. Otherwise, cross the main road and take a passing *micro* A or *trufi,* which pass by the bus terminal and the Mercado Central.

BUS

The **bus terminal** (☎ 663-6508) is at the east end of town, a 20-minute walk from the center along Av Victor Paz Estenssoro. Cross the street from the bus stop to catch *micro* A (B$2.50) to the center.

Several buses travel daily to Potosí (B$70, 12 to 15 hours), Oruro (B$90, 20 hours), Cochabamba (B$100, 26 hours) and Sucre (B$90, 18 hours). Expreso Tarija runs a morning service to La Paz; buy your ticket in advance. Services to Santa Cruz (B$100, 24 hours) pass through Villamontes (B$50, seven hours) from where there are connections to Asunción (they involve long waits). Buses to Yacuiba (B$40, nine hours) leave between 6:30pm and 7:30pm.

COCHABAMBA

☎ 04 / pop 608,200

With a massive statue of Christ looming over the metropolis, busy buzzy Cochabamba is one of Bolivia's boom cities, with a distinct, almost Mediterranean vitality and a prosperous feel in sections. The old center features beautiful colonial houses, balconies, overhanging eaves and large courtyards, while the more modern area to the north is home to a standard strip of high-rises and glitzy cafes.

A definite plus is the weather – warm, dry and sunny (with the odd downpour) – a welcome relief after the chilly *altiplano.* There's a pleasant tree-lined plaza, vibrant markets and some interesting museums. The town's congenial nightlife is thanks to the university population. Don't leave without sampling some *chicha cochabambina,* a traditional fermented corn brew quaffed throughout the region.

The city was founded in 1574 and soon blossomed into the country's primary granary, thanks to its fertile soil and mild climate.

Orientation

Addresses north of Av de las Heroínas take an N, those below take an S. Addresses east of Av Ayacucho take an E and those west an O. The number immediately following the letter tells you how many blocks away from these division streets the address falls. Good maps are available from the tourist office or at the well-stocked Los Amigos del Libro, which also carries guidebooks.

Information

Internet places, most charging B$3 to B$4 per hour, are as common as empanadas. Banks and *casas de cambio* will change traveler's checks and there are ATMs located all around town. You'll find street money changers on Av Heroínas; they only accept US cash.

Brillante (Ayacucho 923) For laundry.

Immigration (☎ 453-3331; cnr Galindo & Torrez; ⏰ 8:30am-4pm Mon-Fri) For visa and length-of-stay extensions. Ignore the queues; they are for a separate department.

Los Amigos del Libro (several branches incl España near Bolívar) Stocks the best range of paperbacks plus Bolivian literature and guidebooks.

Tourist office (☎ 425-8030; Plaza 14 de Septiembre; ⏰ 8am-noon & 2:30-6:30pm Mon-Fri) Hands out good city material. There are several info kiosks, which also open Saturday morning, including at the bus station and airport.

Tourist police (☎ 120 or 451-0023; Achá 0-142)

Dangers & Annoyances

The streets south of Av Aroma near the bus station are best avoided and are positively dangerous at night – don't be tempted by the cheaper accommodation in this area. Pickpocketing and petty thefts are common in the markets. Do not climb the San Sebastián hill as assaults have been reported.

Sights & Activities

Museo Arqueológico (☎ 425-0010; cnr Jordán E-199 & Aguirre; admission B$10; ☺ 8:30am-5:30pm Mon-Fri, 8:30am-2:30pm Sat) has a fine collection of Bolivian mummies and artifacts in three sections: paleontology, fossils and archaeology.

Tin baron Simón Patiño never actually lived in the **Palacio Portales** (☎ 424-3137; Potosí 1450; admission with guide B$10; ☺ gardens 3-6:30pm Tue-Fri, 9am-noon Sat & Sun; ☺ tours Spanish/English every half hr 3:30-6pm Tue-Fri, 9:30-11:30am Sat, 11-11:30am Sun), a French-style mansion in the *barrio* of Queru Queru, north of the center. It was built between 1915 and 1927 and everything, except perhaps the bricks, was imported from Europe. Now used as an arts and cultural complex and a teaching center, entrance is by guided tour only. Take *micro* E north from east of Av San Martín.

The **Cristo de la Concordia** statue, which towers over the city's east side, can be reached by taxi (B$30 for the round trip with wait time) or a **teleférico** (cable car; return B$6; ☺ closed Mon) that climbs all the way to the top.

Courses

Cochabamba is a good spot for studying Spanish or Quechua. The following cultural centers offer courses (B$35 per hour) as well as advice on private language teachers.

Centro Boliviano-Americano (☎ 422-1288; info @cbacoch.org; 25 de Mayo N-365)

Instituto Cultural Boliviano-Alemán (☎ 412-2323; www.icbacbba.com; Lanza 727)

Volunteer Bolivia (☎ 452-6028; www.volunteer bolivia.org; Ecuador 342) Also arranges short- and long-term volunteer work, study and homestay programs throughout Bolivia.

Tours

To visit nearby national parks and reserves, contact **Bolivia Cultura** (☎ 452-7272; www.bolivia cultura.com; España 301) or **Fremen Tours** (☎ 425-9392; www.andes-amazonia.com; Tumusla N-245).

Sleeping

Don't be tempted by the rock-bottom prices for accommodations in the market areas and around the bus station. It's cheap for a reason, as the area is positively dangerous after dark.

Hostal México (☎ 452-5069; México near Ayacucho; r per person with/without bathroom B$25/20) Very basic but clean and central.

Residencial Familiar (☎ 422-7988; Sucre E-554; r B$30, s/d B$50/80) Set in a lovely old building around a secluded patio, this recently renovated place has plenty of character and en suite rooms.

Residencial Familiar Anexo (☎ 422-7986; 25 de Mayo N-234; r per person with/without bathroom B$60/35) Similar to Residencial Familiar (above) but with slightly more faded charms and a slightly more central location.

Hostal Jardín (☎ 424-7844; Hamiraya N-248; s/d B$50/80) In a quiet part of town, this long-time favorite is centered around a likeably chaotic garden with an enormous starfruit tree. Rooms come with bathrooms and hot water.

ourpick Hotel Gina´s (☎ 422-2295; www.ginashotel .web.bo; México 346 near España; r per person with/without bathroom B$90/80, ste B$250-280) Modern, bright and freshly furnished hotel. The suites, equipped with kitchen and living room, are superb value.

Hostal La Fontaine (☎ 425-2838; hostalfontaine @hotmail.com; Hamiraya 181; s/d B$95/160; ☐) Odd religious paintings adorn the stairwells of this great value little hotel. Rooms are spacious with cable TV, minibar and breakfast included.

City Hotel (☎ 422-2993; www.cityhotelbolivia.com; Jordán E-341; s/d/f B$100/140/180; ☐) This spotless and friendly hotel has bright and well-equipped rooms with firm beds. There's a laundry service, cable TV and breakfast included.

Hotel Boston (☎ 422-4421; hboston@supernet.com .bo; 25 de Mayo N-167; s/d B$145/220) The reliable old Boston is past its heyday but offers a central location, cable TV, breakfast and a warm welcome.

Monserrat Hotel (☎ 452-1011; www.hotelmonserrat .com; España N-342; s/d B$160/200; ☐) Renovated historic building at the heart of the dining scene with elegant and comfy rooms. Great views of the *Cristo* from the second floor.

Eating

Markets are cheap for simple but varied and tasty meals; keep an eye on hygiene levels and don't leave your bags unattended. Great *salteñas* and empanadas are ubiquitous; for the latter, try **Los Castores** (Ballivián 790; B$2.50). The *papas rellenas* (potatoes filled with meat or cheese) at the corner of Achá and Villazón are particularly delicious.

Uno's (cnr Heroínas & San Martín; almuerzo B$7; ☺ 8am-1pm Mon-Sat) Tasty and cheap vegetarian buffet served on plastic, prison-style trays.

BOLIVIA

BOLIVIA

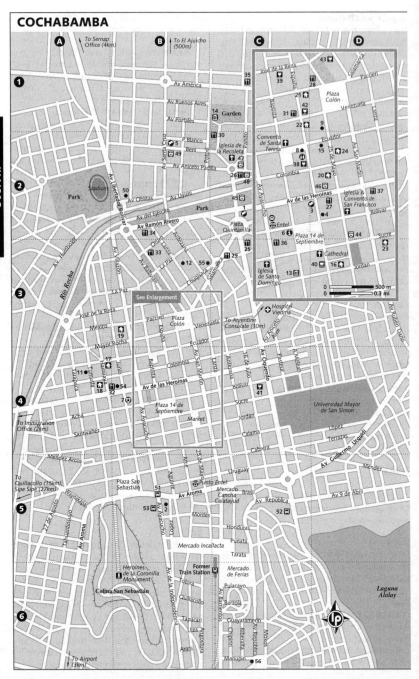

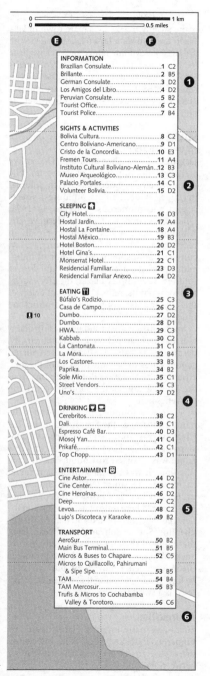

Dumbo (Heroínas E-345; B$10-40) This jumbo-size place (also at Ballivián 55) serves a range of eats throughout the day, from pancakes to decent burgers. Popular for a late-afternoon *helado* (ice cream) and coffee.

Kabbab (Potosí N-1392; mains B$15-25; ☺ dinner only) A thousand and one variations on Persian kebabs and Turkish coffee are served in an intimate space.

Páprika (cnr Rivero & Lanza; mains B$20-35) One of the 'in' spots, this quiet leafy place is popular for its food – both Bolivian and international.

La Mora (cnr Hamiraya & Heroínas; mains B$20-40) Handwritten menus, bizarrely painted furniture, Italian food and *singani* fruit cocktails.

HWA (Salamanca 868; mains B$20-40) If you like Asian food, you are in for a treat – tasty Korean and Japanese dishes are on offer.

Sole Mio (América E-826; pizzas B$25-50; ☺ dinner only Mon-Fri, lunch & dinner Sat & Sun) The best pizzas in town, wood-fired, robust and fittingly conjured up by owners from Napoli.

Casa de Campo (Pasaje Boulevar 618; mains B$25-50) A Cochabamba classic, this loud traditional spot is the place to meet, eat grilled meats and play *cacho* (dice).

La Cantonata (cnr España & Rocha; mains B$35-60; ☺ closed Mon) One of the city's best restaurants, one of the country's best Italian splurges.

Búfalo's Rodizio (Torres Sofer, Oquendo N-654; buffet B$40; ☺ lunch only Sun, dinner only Mon) A great all-you-can-eat Brazilian-style grill made for carnivores.

Drinking
CAFES

Mosoj Yan (cnr Bolívar & Plaza Busch; buffet B$40; ☺ lunch only Mon-Fri) A light and airy cafe, Mosoj Yan is part of a support center for street kids so your coffee bolivianos go to a good cause.

Espresso Café Bar (Arce 340) This one wins the 'best coffee in town' award.

BARS

There's plenty of drinking action along El Prado (Av Ballivián), where **Top Chopp** is a typical Bolivian beerhall. Calle España is also fertile territory, with an everchanging parade of bohemian cafe-bars. Try the grungy **Cerebritos** (España N-251; ☺ 8pm-late), the artsy **Dali** (Plazuela Barba de Padilla, Reza E-242) or the cozy candlelit **Prikafé** (cnr España & Rocha).

BOLIVIA

BOLIVIA

Entertainment

Deep (Pando) and **Levoa** (Paseo de la Recoleta) are trendy clubs charging at least B$30 to get in. For cheaper dancing, try **Lujo's Discoteca y Karaoke** (Beni E-330; ☺ 8pm-late Wed-Sun).

Cinemas include the **Cine Center** multiplex (Ramón Rivero s/n), the bright **Cine Heroínas** (Heroínas s/n) and the smaller **Cine Astor** (cnr Sucre & 25 de Mayo).

Getting There & Around

AIR

To reach the **Jorge Wilsterman Airport** (CBB; domestic/international departure tax B$14/170) take *micro* B from the main plaza (B$2) or a taxi (around B$20). The airport is served regularly by **AeroSur** (☎ 440-0912; Villarroel 105), **TAM** (☎ 441-1545; Hamiraya N-122) and **Aerocon** (☎ 448-7665; office at airport). There are daily flights to La Paz, Santa Cruz, Sucre and Trinidad. **TAM Mercosur** (☎ 452-0118; Plazuela Constitución) flies to Asunción, Buenos Aires and São Paulo via Santa Cruz daily except Sunday.

BUS

Cochabamba's **main bus terminal** (☎ 422-0550; Ayacucho near Aroma; B$4 terminal fee) has an info point, luggage storage and ATMs. Comfortable *bus-cama* service is available on the main routes for roughly double the regular price. There's frequent service to La Paz (B$45, seven hours) and Oruro (B$25, four hours). Most Santa Cruz buses (B$54 to B$66, 10 to 13 hours) depart before 9am or after 6pm. A few afternoon buses daily depart for Sucre (B$40, 10 hours); some continue on to Potosí (B$52, 15 hours).

Micros and buses to Villa Tunari (B$20, three hours) in the coca-growing Chapare region leave almost hourly from 8am to 7pm from the corner of Oquendo and República.

AROUND COCHABAMBA

A 2½ hour cross-country (but well-signed) walk from the village of **Sipe Sipe**, 27km southwest of Cochabamba, are the ruins of **Inca-Rakay**. It makes a good side trip for the scenery rather than any archaeological grandeur, but there have been several serious reports of campers being assaulted here. Sunday is market day in Sipe Sipe. Direct *micros* run on Wednesday and Saturday; otherwise go via **Quillacollo**, which is reached by *micro* from Cochabamba.

About 160km northeast of Cochabamba is the steamy, relaxed Chapare town of **Villa Tunari** and **Inti Wara Yassi** (Parque Machía; www.inti warayassi.org), a wildlife refuge and mellow place to warm up after the *altiplano*. Volunteers are welcome (15-day minimum) and you can camp for B$10. In town, there are numerous places to stay and eat, though there is no ATM.

SUCRE

☎ 04 / pop 215,800

Dazzling whitewashed buildings. Decorative archways. Rooftop views of terracotta. The stunning city of Sucre has a rich colonial heritage, evident in its buildings, streetscapes and numerous churches. In 1991, Unesco declared it a Cultural Heritage site. Although the city has expanded rapidly in recent years, the center maintains a cozy, convivial atmosphere, with colorful indigenous markets, upmarket shops and diverse eateries. The flowery plazas, the city's social and focal points, reflect the vibrant colors of the city and its people, many of whom are indigenous.

Sucre citizens are proud people and maintain that the heart of Bolivia beats in their city, despite the fact that La Paz usurped Sucre's capital status to become the seat of the government and treasury. But Sucre remains as the judicial capital; the supreme court still convenes here.

Sucre was founded in 1538 (under the name La Plata) as the Spanish capital of the Charcas. In 1776, when new territorial divisions were created by the Spaniards, the city's name was changed to Chuquisaca. During this time, it was the most important center in the eastern Spanish territories and heavily influenced Bolivia's history. Independence was declared here on August 6, 1825, and the new republic was created and named after its liberator, Simón Bolívar. Several years later, the name of the city was changed again to Sucre in honor of the general who promoted the independence movement, but you could be forgiven for thinking that it means 'sugar,' for it is a sweet treat.

Information

Sucre has many internet places, including numerous Entel and Punto Viva call centers where you can also get online; hourly rates are between B$3 and B$4.

There are numerous ATMs around the city center but not at the bus station or at the airport. Street money changers, who operate outside the market along Av Hernando Siles, are handy on weekends but check rates beforehand.

Immigration (☎ 645-3647; Bustillos 284; ⊙ 8:30am-4:30pm Mon-Fri) Extends visas and lengths of stay.

Limpecable (☎ Pérez 331; ⊙ daily) Does laundry for B$12 per kg. Inside Supermercado SAS.

Municipal tourist office (☎ 643-5240; Argentina 65) On the first floor on the Casa de la Cultura, staff can provide information on the city and good maps. Also runs the kiosks at the airport and bus terminal.

Oficina Universitaria de Turismo (☎ 644-7644; Estudiantes 49; ⊙ 8-11am & 3-5pm Mon-Fri) Information office run by university students, sometimes offering guides for city tours.

Post office (cnr Estudiantes & Junín) The main post office has an *aduana* (customs) office downstairs for *encomiendas* (parcels). Open all day.

Tourist police (☎ 648-0467; Plazuela Zudáñez)

Sights

Ride the Dino Bus to a cement quarry 5km north of the center where you'll find **Cretaceous Park** (www.parquecretacicosucre.com; admission B$30; ⊙ 7am-7pm Mon-Fri, 10am-3pm Sat & Sun), a slick theme park with around 5000 dinosaur tracks of at least eight species of dinosaur. It departs from the plaza daily at 9:30am, noon and 2:30pm.

For a dose of Bolivian history, visit the **Casa de la Libertad** (☎ 645-4200; www.casadelalibertad .bo; Plaza 25 de Mayo 11; admission incl optional guided tour B$15; ⊙ 9am-noon & 2:30-7pm Tue-Sat, 9am-noon Sun), an ornate museum where the Bolivian declaration of independence was signed in 1825; it displays the era's artifacts.

The excellent **Museo Textil Indígena** (ASUR; ☎ 645-3841; www.bolivianet.com/asur; San Alberto 413; admission B$16; ⊙ 9:30am-noon & 2:30-6pm Mon-Fri) features fine Jalq'a and Candelaria (Tarabuco) weavings; ask for English translations of the labels. It's part of a successful project to revitalize handwoven crafts. You can see weavers in action and browse the superb works for sale.

The new **Museo de Etnografía y Folklore** (☎ 645-5293; www.musef.org.bo; España 74; ⊙ 9:30am-12:30pm & 2:30-6:30pm Mon-Fri, 9:30am-12:30pm Sat), known locally as MUSEF, showcases a series of fascinating displays that vividly illustrate the great diversity of Bolivia's ethnic cultures, including masks and artifacts from the Uru-Chipaya culture.

Sucre boasts several lovely colonial churches but opening hours are unpredictable. The **cathedral** (Plaza 25 de Mayo) dates from the 16th century, though major additions were made in the early 17th century. Just down the block is the **Museo de la Catedral** (Ortíz 31; admission B$20; ⊙ 10am-noon & 3-5pm Mon-Fri, 10am-noon Sat), which holds one of Bolivia's best collections of religious relics.

The beautiful **Convento de San Felipe Neri** (Ortíz 165; admission B$10; ⊙ 4-6pm Mon-Sat, entry via the school) has good rooftop views. If you're interested in sacred art or antique musical instruments, the **Museo y Convento de Santa Clara** (Calvo 212; admission B$10; ⊙ 9am-noon & 3-6pm Mon-Fri, 9am-noon Sat) inside a 17th-century convent has a renowned collection.

For spectacular city views, trek up to **Museo de la Recoleta** (Plaza Pedro Anzures; admission B$10; ⊙ 9-11:30am & 2:30-4:30pm Mon-Fri, 3-5pm Sat) inside a 1601 Franciscan convent, which now houses religious paintings and sculptures and colorful courtyard gardens.

Activities

Sucre's surrounding valleys offer the perfect venues for action-packed adventure – hiking, mountain biking, tubing, horse riding, you name it. Paragliding is the latest thrill on the adventure menu. Popular destinations include the pre-Hispanic Chataquila (Inca) trail, the seven waterfalls (by bike or hike), rock paintings, and villages of Yotala, Ñucchu and Q'atalla, and the 4WD and hike tour combo to the Maragua Crater.

There are as many prices as there are trips. Based on a group of four people, half-day hiking trips start at about B$180, mountain-bike trips B$155 per person and horse riding B$190 upwards.

Recommended operators:

Bolivia Specialist (☎ 643-7389; www.boliviaspecialist .com; Ortiz 30)

Candelaria Tours (☎ 646-1661; www.candelariatours .com; Audiencia 1)

Joy Ride Bolivia (☎ 642-5544; www.joyridebol.com; Ortiz 14)

Locot's Aventura (☎ 691-5958; www.locotsadventure .com; Bolívar 465)

Courses

The number of language courses available here has exploded over recent years. There are several reliable options.

Academia Latinoamericana de Español (☎ 646-0537; www.latinoschools.com; Dalence 109) Comprehensive program featuring cultural classes and homestay options.

BOLIVIA

SUCRE

0 _____ 400 m
0 _____ 0.2 miles

BOLIVIA

INFORMATION
Brazilian Consulate.............................1 B4
German Consulate...............................2 A3
Immigration..3 A5
Limpecable...4 A6
Municipal Tourist Office....................5 B4
Officina Universitario de Turismo....6 B4
Peruvian Consulate.............................7 C5
Post Office..8 B4
Tourist Police......................................9 B5

SIGHTS & ACTIVITIES
Academia Latinoamericana de
    Español..10 B5
Bolivia Specialist...............................11 B5
Candelaria Tours................................12 B5
Capilla de la Virgen de Guadalupe..(see 20)
Casa de la Libertad...........................13 B4
Cathedral...14 B4
Convento de San Felipe Neri...........15 B4
Fox Language Academy.....................16 C4

Iglesia de la Recoleta & Museo
    de la Recoleta..............................17 D6
Instituto Cultural Boliviano-Alemán..18 C5
Joy Ride Bolivia...............................(see 47)
Locot's Aventura.............................(see 43)
Museo de Etnografía y Folklore......19 C4
Museo de la Catedral........................20 B5
Museo Textil Indígena (ASUR).........21 D5
Museo y Convento de
    Santa Clara..................................22 C5

SLEEPING
Alojamiento San Marcos..................23 C3
Grand Hotel.......................................24 C4
Hostal Charcas..................................25 B4
Hostal Colonial..................................26 B4
Hostal de Su Merced........................27 B5
Hostal Las Torres..............................28 C4
Hostal Sucre......................................29 B5
Hostal Veracruz.................................30 B3
Hostel Amigo.....................................31 B5
La Posada..32 B5
San Francisco.....................................33 C4

EATING
Café Tertulias.....................................34 C4
Chifa New Hong Kong......................35 C4
El Germén...36 C4
El Paso de los Abuelos......................37 B5
El Patio...38 C4
Florín..39 C5
Freya...40 A4
Kultur Café Berlin...........................(see 18)
La Taverna..41 B4
Las Bajos..42 A4
Locot's..43 C4
Market..44 C3
Pastelería Amanecer..........................45 B5

DRINKING
Bibliocafé...46 B5
Joy Ride Café.....................................47 B5
Salfari...48 A5

ENTERTAINMENT
Centro Cultural los Masis.................49 C5

TRANSPORT
AeroSur...50 B5

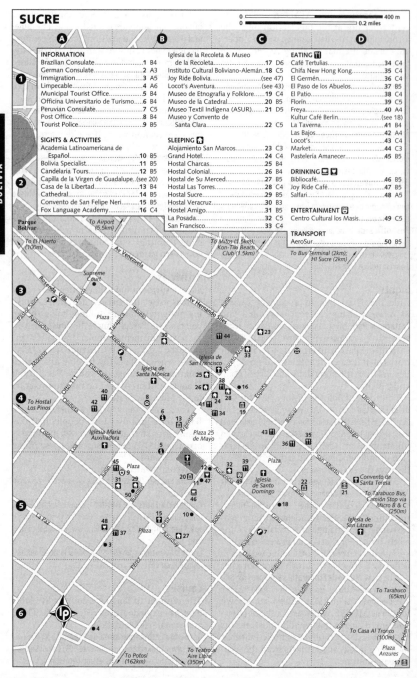

Fox Language Academy (☎ 644-0688; www.fox academysucre.com; San Alberto 30) Runs volunteer schemes. Learning Spanish or Quechua here subsidizes English classes for underprivileged local kids.

Instituto Cultural Boliviano-Alemán (☎ 645-2091; www.icba-sucre.edu.bo; Avaroa 326) Offers recommended Spanish and Quechua lessons with homestay options.

Festivals & Events

Sucre loves an excuse for a celebration. It's worth checking out the list of many religious festivals at the tourist office. On the weekend closest to September 8, people from all over the country flock to join local *campesinos* in a celebration of the **Fiesta de la Virgen de Guadalupe** with traditional songs and dance.

Sleeping

While accommodations in Sucre are among Bolivia's most expensive, there are also plenty of budget options around the market and along Ravelo and San Alberto. It's also a good place to splurge on something more stylish. Homestay options are available through Candelaria Tours (p217) from B$85 per night (minimum five nights).

Alojamiento San Marcos (☎ 646-2087; Arce 233; r per person B$30) Friendly owners, clean quiet rooms with shared bathrooms (new en-suite rooms were being added at the time of research), kitchen and laundry access.

Hostel Amigo (☎ 646-1706; www.hostelsucre .com; Colón 125; dm B$30, s/d B$70/80, without bathroom B$35/40; ☐) This backpacker haven is well-equipped with kitchen and BBQ terrace. A basic breakfast is included and Spanish lessons are offered.

Hostal Charcas (☎ 645-3972; Ravelo 62; s/d B$60/100, without bathroom B$40/60) A travelers' favorite with central location, laundry service, 24-hour hot water and simple but clean, attractive rooms.

HI Sucre (☎ 644-0471; www.hostellingbolivia.org; Loayza 119; dm B$40, s/d B$90/150, without bathroom B$50/80; ☐) In an attractive building, Sucre's HI hostel is clean and friendly, with a shared kitchen and some private rooms with spa baths and cable TV. Handy for the bus station.

Hostal Veracruz (☎ 645-1560; Ravelo 158; s/d B$45/70; ☐) At this consistently popular place, a fair variety of rooms is available, some nice and sunny, some a little echoey from the central vestibule. Breakfast and laundry available.

San Francisco (☎ 645-2117; Arce 191; s/d B$60/120) A stunning entry hall and eye-catchingly ornamental staircase greet you. The rooms are more modest but adequate.

Grand Hotel (☎ 645-2461; Arce 61; s/d B$100/140) Central location, excellent staff, tastefully decorated rooms, a popular restaurant and a plant-filled courtyard make this a favorite for all budgets.

Hostal Las Torres (☎ 644-2888; www.lastorres hostal.com; San Alberto 19; s/d B$110/170) This light and pleasant hotel is entered down an alleyway. Rooms have comfy beds, TV and good baths. Breakfast is included.

Hostal Sucre (☎ 646-1928; Bustillos 113; s/d B$135/180; ☐) Another HI affiliate, this typically white hotel has a beautiful double courtyard, complete with well and fountain. Rooms are a little dingy but acceptable.

our pick **Casa Al Tronco** (☎ 642-3195; Topater 57; r B$140) Charming new guesthouse in the Recoleta district with three rooms, glorious city views from two terraces, kitchen and discounts for stays over five nights. Book ahead.

La Posada (☎ 646-0101; www.laposadahostal.com; Audiencia 92; s/d B$250/350; ☐) Worth the splurge, this classy place has spacious rooms with colonial ambience. There are views over town, an intimate feel and a recommendable courtyard restaurant.

Other worthy upscale options:

Hostal Colonial (☎ 644-0309; www.hostalcolonial -bo.com; Plaza 25 de Mayo 3; s/d/tr/ste B$210/280/ 350/490) Handsome colonial hotel.

Hostal de Su Merced (☎ 645-1355; www.boliviaweb .com/companies/sumerced; Azurduy 16; s/d B$240/360) Charming and beautiful, with great views from the rooftop terrace.

Eating

With a variety of quality restaurants, Sucre is a great place to spend time lolling around cafes while observing Bolivian university life.

The central **market** (⏰ 7am-7:30pm Mon-Sat, Sun breakfast only) has good snacks and fantastic fresh juices and fruit salads.

Good *salteñerías* include **El Patio** (San Alberto 18; ⏰ 10am-12:30pm) and **El Paso de los Abuelos** (Bustillos 224); get there early as they sell out fast.

Pastelería Amanecer (off Junín btwn Colón & Olañeta) This petite non-profit bakery has delightful homemade goodies. Proceeds benefit local children's projects.

BOLIVIA

Kultur Café Berlin (Avaroa 334; mains B$12-30; ☺ closed Sun; ▣) This dark German-themed spot offers filling dishes such as *papas rellenas* (spicy filled potatoes). It's a fine spot for an evening beer.

Café Tertulias (Plaza 25 de Mayo; mains B$15-25) An intimate bohemian hangout for chats over coffee, beer or light fare such as pizza, salads and pasta.

Freya (Loa 751; almuerzo B$15; ☺ noon-2pm Mon-Sat) This likeable place does tasty vegetarian *almuerzos*.

Las Bajos (Loa 759; mains B$15-35) One of the oldest and most typical *choricerías* in Sucre, though it's not just sausage on the menu.

Florín (Bolívar 567; mains B$15-35) The place to be seen in Sucre, this bar-restaurant serves a mixture of *comida típica* and international dishes, including a 'full English' breakfast. Good spot for happy hour too.

Locot's (Bolívar 465; mains B$15-40; ☺ 7am-late; ▣) Relaxed and attractive, Locot's has candle-lit tables, original art, a gringo-friendly vibe and a small menu of Bolivian, Mexican and international food.

Chifa New Hong Kong (San Alberto 242; mains B$20-35) Great value Chinese food with huge portions. Watch your head on the ceiling upstairs!

La Taverne (Arce 35; mains B$20-40) Sophisticated atmosphere, a French-flavored menu, excellent daily specials, live music every Friday night and weekly film screenings.

El Germen (San Alberto 237; mains B$25-40) This service-with-a-smile spot is a favorite for its tasty vegetarian dishes; meat is also good as are the curries and cakes.

El Huerto (Cabrera 86; mains B$25-40) Sucre's people in the know favor this spot in a secluded garden for its classy feel and stylishly presented traditional plates.

Drinking

Some of the bars and restaurants on and near the plaza have live music and *peña* nights.

Salfari (Bustillos 237; ☺ 8pm-3am) This little gem of a pub has friendly service, potent home-made fruit liqueurs and a loyal local crowd playing lively games of poker and *cacho*.

Joy Ride Café (Ortiz 14; mains B$20-40; ☺ 7:30am-2am Mon-Fri, 9am-2am Sat & Sun) Wildly popular gringo-tastic cafe, restaurant and bar with a bit of everything, including midnight vodkas, nightly movies and weekend dancing.

Bibliocafé (Ortiz 80; mains B$15-25; ☺ closed Mon) This unpretentious spot with two adjacent

locations is dark and cozy on one side and a little smarter on the other. Drinks served until late plus there's regular live music.

Entertainment

For *discotecas* (weekends only), check out the basement **Mitos** (Cerro s/n; admission women/men B$5/10) or the student-frequented **Kon-Tiki Beach Club** (Junín 71; admission women/men B$5/10). The **Centro Cultural los Masis** (☎ 645-3403; Bolívar 561; ☺ 10am-noon & 3:30-9pm Mon-Fri) hosts concerts and other cultural events. Southeast of the town center, the **Teatro al Aire Libre** is an outdoor venue for musical and other performances.

Getting There & Away

AIR

The airport is 9km northwest of the city center. **AeroSur** (☎ 646-2141; Arenales 31) and **TAM** (☎ 645-1310; airport) have flights to most major cities.

BUS & SHARED TAXI

The bus terminal, a 15-minute walk uphill from the center, is accessed by *micro* A or 3 from along España but the *micros* are too tiny to accommodate lots of luggage. There are numerous daily buses to Cochabamba (B$80, 12 hours), departing between 6pm and 8pm. Direct buses to Santa Cruz (B$70 to B$120, 15 to 20 hours) run daily in the afternoons. Numerous companies leave daily for Potosí (B$20, three hours) where you can connect to Tarija, Villazón and Uyuni. Alternatively, most hotels can arrange shared taxis to Potosí (B$30 for up to four people). Lots of *flotas* have departures for La Paz (B$70 to B$120, 14 to 16 hours) via Oruro (B$50 to B$70, 10 hours).

Getting Around

Local *micros* (B$2) take circuitous routes around Sucre's one-way streets. Most seem to congregate at or near the market; they can be waved down virtually anywhere. You can reach the bus terminal on *micro* A or the airport on *micros* F or 1 (allow an hour) or by taxi (B$25).

AROUND SUCRE

The small, predominantly indigenous village of **Tarabuco**, 65km southeast of Sucre, is known for its beautiful weavings, the colorful, sprawling **Sunday market** and the festival of Pujllay on the third Sunday in March when hundreds of indigenous people from the surrounding countryside descend on the town in local costumes.

The Sunday market is plenty touristy but also the most photogenic of places. Do request a shot beforehand and take care of your things. The spitting scam is, unfortunately, becoming more common (see p179). There are amazing woven ponchos, bags and belts as well as *charangos* (buy only wooden ones – have mercy on endangered armadillos). However, much of the work for sale is not local but acquired by traders, so don't expect many bargains.

You can visit Tarabuco with a charter bus (B$35 round trip, two hours each way) from Sucre, which leave from outside Hostal Charcas on Ravelo around 8:30am and return between 1pm and 3pm. Buy advance tickets from bigger hotels or any travel agent. Alternatively, *micros* (B$10, two hours) leave when full from Av de las Américas on Sunday between 6:30am and 9:30am and return around 3:30pm.

For scenic trekking opportunities, head to **Cordillera de los Frailes**, a spectacular mountain range that runs through much of western Chuquisaca and northern Potosí departments. Home to the Quechua-speaking Jalq'a people, it has a string of sites worth visiting, including the rock paintings of **Pumamachay** and **Incamachay**, the weaving village of **Potolo**, the dramatic **Maragua Crater** and the **Talula hot springs**. There are plenty of hiking routes but they traverse little-visited areas; to minimize cultural impact and avoid getting hopelessly lost, hire a registered guide (around B$150 per day plus costs) either in Sucre or call ahead at **Maragua Entel** (☎ 693-8088) a couple of days in advance. Several Sucre travel agencies arrange excursions (see p217) although day trips aren't advised – spend at least one night in the area in order to contribute to the local communities.

POTOSÍ

☎ 02 / pop 149,200

Potosí shocks. A visit to the world's highest city (4070m), a Unesco World Heritage Site, reveals a former and current splendor and past and present horror, tied to its one precious metal – silver. Potosí is set against the backdrop of a rainbow-colored mountain, the Cerro Rico. The city was founded in 1545 following the discovery of ore deposits

in the mountain, and Potosí veins proved the world's most lucrative. By the end of the 18th century the streets were 'paved' with silver; it grew into the largest and wealthiest city in Latin America, underwriting the Spanish economy for over two centuries.

Millions of indigenous people and imported African slaves laborers were conscripted to work in the mines in appalling conditions, and millions of deaths occurred. Today thousands continue to work in the mines: although the silver has been depleted, miners work in spine-chilling conditions to extract minerals. To protect them in the hell below, they worship their devil, known as Tío. Above ground, echoes of the once-grand colonial city reverberate through the narrow streets, bouncing from the formal balconied mansions and ornate churches. This city is not to be missed, but go slowly, be prepared for the harsh climate and brace yourself for a jolt.

Information

There are numerous places to get online, mostly charging B$2 to B$4 per hour, including **Café Internet Candelaria** (Ayacucho 5) – where 15 minutes is free with breakfast.

ATMs are common in the town center. Lots of businesses along Bolívar, Sucre and in the market change US dollars at reasonable rates; stalls along Héroes del Chaco also change euros and Chilean and Argentine pesos.

There is a helpful **tourist information center** (☎ 622-7477; Ayacucho near Bustillos; 🕑 8:30am-noon, 2-6pm) in the ornate Torre de la Compañía de Jesús.

Sights

Potosí's central area contains a wealth of colonial architecture. At the time of research, the **cathedral** was closed for long-term restoration but you can climb its **bell tower** (🕑 11am-12:30pm & 2:30-6pm Mon-Fri; admission B$7) for nice views of the city.

The **Casa Nacional de la Moneda** (National Mint; ☎ 622-2777; cnr Ayacucho & Bustillos; admission for mandatory 2-3hr guided tour B$20; 🕑 9am-noon & 2:30-6:30pm Tue-Sat, 9am-noon Sun; English tours depart at 9am, 10:30am, 14:30pm & 16:30pm) is worth its weight in silver; it's one of South America's finest museums. Constructed between 1753 and 1773 to control the minting of colonial coins, the restored building now houses religious art, ancient coins and wooden minting machines.

BOLIVIA

The highlight of the **Museo & Convento de San Francisco** (cnr Tarija & Nogales; admission B$15, photo permit B$10, video camera permit B$20; ⏱ 9am-noon & 2:30-6:30pm Mon-Fri), Bolivia's oldest monastery, is the view from the roof. The **Museo & Convento de Santa Teresa** (cnr Santa Teresa & Ayacucho; admission by guided tour B$21, photo permit B$10; ⏱ 9am-12:30pm & 2:30-6:30pm, last tour 11am & 5pm Mon-Sat, 9-11am & 3-5pm Sun) explains how young girls from wealthy families entered the convent, still home to Carmelite nuns.

Activities

A visit to the **cooperative mines** is demanding, shocking and memorable but potentially dangerous (see boxed text, below). Tours typically involve scrambling and crawling in low, narrow, dirty shafts and climbing rickety ladders – wear your gnarliest clothes. Working practices are medieval, safety provisions nearly nonexistent and most shafts are unventilated; chewing coca helps (see p168). Work is done mostly by hand with basic tools, and underground temperatures vary from below freezing to a stifling 45°C (113°F). Miners, exposed to myriad noxious chemicals, often die of silicosis pneumonia within 10 years of entering the mines. They work the mine as a cooperative venture, with each miner milking his own claim and selling his ore to a smelter through the cooperative. (Look out for the multiaward-winning US-made film *The Devil's Miner*; 2005.)

Most tours start at the **miners' street market** where you buy gifts for the miners: coca leaves, alcohol and cigarettes to start. You may also visit a **mineral refinery**. Then you're driven up to **Cerro Rico** where guides often give a **demonstration blast** – this can not only be dangerous but is also detrimental to the environment so we urge you to request a tour without dynamite explosion when signing up or to politely turn it down.

After donning a jacket and helmet, the scramble begins. You can converse with the miners, take photos (with flash) and share gifts as a tip.

All guides work through tour agencies, and must be licensed. Ask around the agencies if you need an English-speaking guide; some are former miners themselves. Expect to pay around B$80 to B$100 per person for a four-to five-hour group tour (10 people or fewer is best); slightly lower rates may be available during the low season. This price includes a guide, transportation from town and equipment: jackets, helmets, boots and lamps. There are many agencies (all also offer trekking excursions and day trips to the nearby Tarapaya hot springs); some of those recommended by travelers include the following:

Andes Salt Expeditions (☎ 622-5175; www.bolivia-travel.com.bo; cnr Bolívar & Junín) Run by ex-miner Raul Braulio Mamani who worked as the guide for *The Devil's Miner*.

Greengo Tours (☎ 623-1362; www.greengotours.com.bo; Quijarro 42) The environmentally conscious owner is fighting to stop dynamite explosions.

Koala Tours (☎ 622-4708; ktourspotosi@hotmail.com; Ayacucho 3) Runs some of the best mine tours; Efrain Mamani is a highly recommended guide.

Potosí Specialist (☎ 622-5320; jhonnybolivia@hotmail.com; Padilla 10) Friendly agency run by knowledgeable Jhonny Montes.

Sleeping

Only top-end hotels have heating, and there may be blanket shortages in the cheapies, so you'll want a sleeping bag. Hard-core budget places may charge extra for hot showers.

Residencial Sumaj (☎ 622-3336; hoteljer@entelnet.bo; Gumiel 12; s/d/tr B$30/60/90) Stay on the skylit top floor of this budget standby. There's shared kitchen for B$15 per day and 10% discount for HI members.

WARNING!

The cooperatives are not museums, but working mines and fairly nightmarish places. Anyone undertaking a tour needs to realize that there are risks involved. Anyone with doubts or medical problems – especially claustrophobes, asthmatics and others with respiratory conditions – should avoid these tours. Medical experts including the NHS note that limited exposure from a few hours' on a tour is extremely unlikely to cause any lasting health impacts. If you have any concerns whatsoever about exposure to asbestos or silica dust, you should not enter the mines. Accidents also happen – explosions, falling rocks, runaway trolleys etc. For these reasons, all tour companies make visitors sign a disclaimer absolving them completely from any responsibility for injury, illness or death – if your tour operator does not, choose another. Visiting the mines is a serious decision. If you're undeterred, you'll have an eye-opening and unforgettable experience.

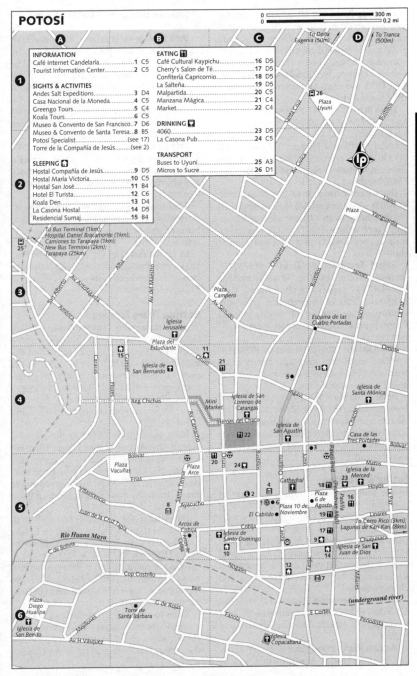

POTOSÍ

BOLIVIA

BOLIVIA

La Casona Hostal (☎ 623-0523; www.hotelpotosi
.com; Chuquisaca 460; dm B$30, s/d/tr B$81/122/183, without
bathroom B$45/70/105) Rave reviews are already
given to this restored colonial house recently
opened as a hostel. There's a money exchange,
a shared kitchen, free breakfast, a small cinema (B$3 per film) and internet terminals
(B$2 per hour).

Koala Den (☎ 622-6467; ktourspotosi@hotmail.com;
Junín 56; dm B$35-50, d B$130-150) A favorite for its
backpacker-social vibe and amenities, this
colorful spot has a kitchen, TV room with
DVDs, book exchange, free internet, hot
showers, heating at night and a lounge area.
Small breakfast included.

Hostal María Victoria (☎ 622-2132; Chuquisaca 148;
s/d B$70/90, without bathroom B$40/70) A whitewashed
colonial home with a tree-shaded courtyard
and a roof terrace. Small breakfast included,
tour agency on site and an eight-minute
shower limit.

Hostel Compañía de Jesús (☎ 622-3173;
Chuquisaca 445; s/d/tr B$70/110/140, without bathroom
B$50/80/110) For sparkling clean rooms, firm
mattresses, lots of blankets and a friendly
atmosphere in this old but freshly painted
Carmelite monastery with a leafy courtyard
and two patios.

Hostal San José (☎ 622-4394; Oruro 171; s/d B$60/120,
d with bathroom B$160) Cheap and cheery place
with a decent location; a second floor was
going up at research time.

Hotel El Turista (☎ 622-2492; hotelturistapotosi
@hotmail.com; Lanza 19; s/tr/ste B$140/280/300, d B$200-220;
🖳) Recently revamped, this midrange spot
with a vibrantly colored patio offers spacious
and comfortable rooms with heating, electric
showers and TVs.

Eating & Drinking

In the morning, food stalls in the market
comedor serve inexpensive breakfasts of
bread, pastries and coffee. For juicy *salteñas* (B$3.50), you don't need to go further
than **La Salteña** (Padilla 6) or **Malpartida** (Bolívar
644). Meat and cheese empanadas are sold
around the market until early afternoon; in
the evening street vendors sell cornmeal and
cheese *humitas*.

Confitería Capricornio (Pasaje Blvd 11; mains B$6-
17; 🕙 9am-10pm) Quick-bite eatery notable for
its old-school vibe and affordable meals and
snacks.

Manzana Mágica (Oruro 239; mains B$8-20; 🕙 8:30am-
3pm, 5:30-10pm Mon-Sat) A worthwhile, strictly

vegetarian spot known for its ultrahealthy
meals.

Doña Eugenia (cnr Santa Cruz & Ortega; dishes B$10-
40; 🕙 9:30am-12:30pm, closed Wed) Head to this
convivial local fave at the northern end of
town around 10am to ensure a taste of the
legendary *kala purca* (thick maize soup with
a hot rock in it).

Cherry's Salon de Té (☎ 622-5320; Padilla 8; mains
B$12-25; 🕙 8am-10pm) The spot for apple strudel,
chocolate cake and lemon meringue pie.

Café Cultural Kaypichu (Millares 14; mains B$17-
30; 🕙 7:30am-2pm & 5-11pm Tue-Sun) A peaceful
and relaxed retreat with healthy breakfasts,
mainly vegetarian food and folk music on
weekends.

4060 (Hoyos 1; mains B$18-60; 🕙 4pm-midnight)
Contemporary cafe-bar known for its pizzas,
burgers and Mexican food. Also a sociable
spot for a drink.

La Casona Pub (Frías 41; 🕙 6pm-midnight Mon-
Sat) Memorable friendly watering hole with
pub grub, good cocktails and live music on
Friday.

Getting There & Around

The bus terminal is 1km northwest of town
(15 minutes' walk downhill from the center),
reached by frequent *micros* (B$1) from the
west side of the cathedral or by taxi (B$4 per
person). Several companies offer a daily overnight service to La Paz (B$40 to B$60, eight
hours) via Oruro (B$25, five hours) departing
around 8pm; you can also opt for a *bus-cama*
(B$60 B$80).

Most buses to Sucre (B$20, three hours)
leave daily between 7am and 5pm. There are
shared taxis to Sucre (B$30 for up to four
people, 2½ hours) if you're rushed, and *micros* all day (B$15 to B$20, five hours) if you're
broke, from the *tranca* 500m north of Plaza
Uyuni.

Buses leave for Tupiza (B$60 to B$100,
seven hours) and Villazón (B$60 to B$100,
nine hours) daily in the evening. Buses to
Tarija (B$50 to B$70, 12 hours) run twice,
early in the morning and in the evening; *bus-
cama* is available (B$70 to B$100). There are
nighttime services to Cochabamba (B$40 to
B$60, eight hours).

Buses to Uyuni (B$30 to B$40, six hours) –
a scenic route – depart three times daily
(11am, noon and 6:30pm) from just below
the railway line, higher up on Av Antofagasta
with Av Tinkuy.

THE SOUTHEAST

The vast lowlands of the Bolivian Oriente are rich and varied, and home to much of the country's natural resources. Numerous cultural highlights include stunning Jesuit missions and natural wonders like Parque Nacional Amboró and the more remote Parque Nacional Noel Kempff Mercado. Che Guevara fans can follow his footsteps, while stalwart travelers can venture into Paraguay through the wild Chaco. Brazil is a hop, skip and a train ride away.

SANTA CRUZ

☎ 03 / pop 1.54 million

Santa Cruz de la Sierra (elevation 417) prides itself on being more Brazilian than Bolivian. Indeed, thanks to the warm and tropical ambience, the *cambas,* as the locals call themselves, seem more laid-back than their *kolla* (Andean) countrymen.

The city was founded in 1561 by Spaniard Ñuflo de Chaves, 220km east of its current location. It proved vulnerable to indigenous attack and was moved to its present position, near the Cordillera Oriental foothills. Santa Cruz mushroomed from a backwater town to Bolivia's largest city. Renowned as one of the main centers of the cocaine trade, today it is more in the news as the center of the controversial energy sector and its overwhelming desire for the region's autonomy from the rest of Bolivia.

The modern area to the north, with its stylish shops and smart cafes, hasn't monopolized the city's colonial center; the terracotta-tiled and balconied buildings maintain a delightful ambience, particularly around the tree-lined plaza. (If you're lucky you might see a sloth. Despite their relocation, the odd one makes an appearance.)

Santa Cruz is an excellent base for exploring still-pristine rainforests, the Che Guevara trail and 18th-century Jesuit missions.

Orientation

The city center is laid out in a straightforward grid. Ten numbered *anillos* (ring roads) form concentric circles around the compact city center, indicating separate suburbs or regions. *Radiales* (spokes) connect the rings. The city's cheaper options are in the center, within the first *anillo;* the smarter restaurants and hotels are on Av San Martin, known as Equipetrol, to the north.

Information

BOOKSTORES

Los Amigos del Libro (Ingavi 114) and **Lewy Libros** (Junín 229) near the plaza have limited selections of foreign-language books for sale or trade.

EMERGENCY

Tourist police (☎ 322-5016; north side of Plaza 24 de Septiembre)

IMMIGRATION OFFICES

Immigration (☎ 333-2136; ⏲ 8:30am-4:30pm Mon-Fri) is north of the center, opposite the zoo entrance. Visa extensions are available. There's an office at the **train station** (⏲ supposedly 10am-noon & 1:30-7pm), which is more convenient but which is reportedly plagued by phony officials. The most reliable office is at the airport.

For information on consulates in Santa Cruz, see p239.

INTERNET ACCESS

There are numerous internet places on Junín including **Punto Entel** (Junín 140; per hr B$3; ⏲ 8am-11pm).

LAUNDRY

Central, efficient wash-and-dry places offering same-day service (drop-off before noon) for around B$12 per kg:
España Lavandería (España 160)
Lavandería La Paz (La Paz 42)

MONEY

Cash advances are available at most major banks, and ATMs line Junín and most major intersections.
Casa de Cambio Alemán (east side of Plaza 24 de Septiembre) The easiest place to change cash or traveler's checks (2% to 3% commission).
Magri Turismo (☎ 334-4559; cnr Warnes & Potosí) The American Express agent but doesn't cash traveler's checks.

TELEPHONE

There are telecom stores along Bolívar for making cheap international internet calls.
Punto Entel (Junín 284) Office near the plaza has landlines.

TOURIST INFORMATION

Departamental de Turismo (☎ 333-3248; Plaza 24 de Septiembre) Inside the Palacio Prefectural, on the north side of the plaza.

BOLIVIA

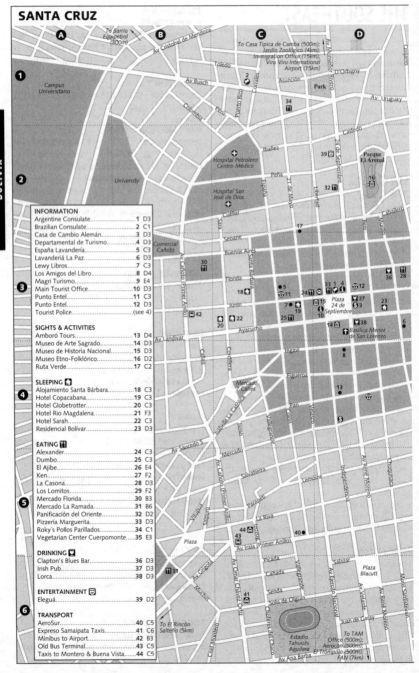

SANTA CRUZ

BOLIVIA

Fundación Amigos de la Naturaleza (FAN; ☎ 355-6800; www.fan-bo.org; road to Samaipata Km 7.5) Has information on Amboró and Noel Kempff Mercado national parks. West of town (*micro* 44).

Main tourist office (☎ 334-5500; Plaza 24 de Septiembre) On the ground floor of the Casa de la Cultura, west side of the plaza.

Sights

There are few attractions in Santa Cruz proper, but the shady **Plaza 24 de Septiembre** with its **cathedral** is an attractive place to relax by day or night. There are good city views from the **bell tower** (admission B$3; ☽ 10am-noon & 4-6pm Tue, Thu, Sat & Sun). A block away is the little **Museo de Historia Nacional** (☽ 8am-noon & 3:30-6pm Mon-Fri), which houses a permanent display of Chiquitania art and photo exhibits that explain the customs of this little-known indigenous group.

Locals relax around the lagoon at **Parque El Arenal**, north of the center, where there's a handicrafts market and paddle boats for rent. Overlooking the lagoon is the **Museo Etno-Folklórico** (☽ 8am-noon & 2:30-6:30pm Mon-Fri), with a small collection of regional anthropological finds. Don't dawdle here at night.

The **Jardín Zoológico** (☎ 342-9939; adult/child B$10/5; ☽ 9am-6:30pm) is worth a visit for its collection of South American birds, mammals and reptiles; don't miss the sloths. Take any 'Zoológico' *micro* from the center.

Discover the wonder of sequins, big hats and gold rope trim at the cathedral's air-conditioned **Museo de Arte Sagrado** (Plaza 24 de Septiembre; admission B$10; ☽ 8:30am-noon & 2:30-6pm Tue, Thu & Sun), with a dazzling collection of gowns, jewels and gold and silver relics.

Sleeping

In a bind, there are several cheap, indistinguishable places to crash across from the terminal bimodal. Otherwise, there are few reasonable cheapies.

Backpackers Santa Cruz Hostel (☎ 334-0025; Irala 696; dm B$20-30) A basic backpacker crash pad close to the old bus station.

Alojamiento Santa Bárbara (☎ 332-1817; Santa Bárbara 151; s/d B$35/50) This is a low-key place that's cheap and central, with a courtyard and bare rooms with hospital-like beds.

Hotel Rio Magdalena (☎ 339-3011; Arenales 653; dm/s/d B$50/110/120; 🖧 🛝) Former Peace Corps hangout, this is a top-notch option with comfy rooms, an inviting pool and a roof terrace with glorious city views.

BOLIVIA

ourpick Hotel Sarah (☎ 332-2425; Sara 85; s/d B$70/120; 🖭) New hotel with a great location, jungle-themed walls and spotless rooms with cable TV.

Residencial Bolívar (☎ 334-2500; Sucre 131; s/d B$75/130) Leafy tropical patios with hammocks, a toucan snoozing on a branch and clean smallish rooms. Breakfast is included and Spanish lessons available.

Also recommended for midrange stays:

Hotel Copacabana (☎ 336-2770; Junín 217; s B$139-213, d B$196-251)

Hotel Globetrotter (☎ 337-2754; Sara 49; s/d B$160/200; 🖭)

Eating

For simple, cheap eats, try **Mercado La Ramada** but consider hygiene levels carefully before indulging. **Mercado Florida** is wall-to-wall blender stalls serving exquisite juices and fruit salads for B$5.

Panificación del Oriente (24 de Septiembre 501; pastries from B$3) Mouthwatering variety of cakes, buns, pastries and tarts.

Dumbo (Ayacucho 247; ice creams B$5-15, mains B$20-50) Copious food portions and gourmet frozen yogurt.

Alexander (Junín s/n; mains B$10-30) This is a true haven for delicious breakfasts and good coffee, including the local Madidi kind.

Vegetarian Center Cuerpomonte (Aroma 54; buffet per kg B$15; 🕑 9am-7pm Mon-Sat) A stellar buffet selection of wholesome goodies such as quinoa cake, mashed sweet potato and veggie soups.

Los Lomitos (Uruguay 758; mains B$15-70) If you are a beef fanatic look no further than this Argentine-style *churrasquería*.

Roky's Pollos Parrillados (Cañoto 50; chicken B$20-30) Great charcoal-grilled roosters.

Ken (Uruguay 730; mains B$20-35; 🕑 closed Wed) Everybody's favorite Japanese eatery.

El Aljibe (Ñuflo de Chavez; mains B$25-40) An atmospheric little resto specializing in *comida típica*, increasingly difficult to find in cosmopolitan Santa Cruz.

Pizzería Marguerita (Plaza 24 de Septiembre; mains B$25-50) Long known for its high-quality pizza, pasta and salads.

Casa Típica de Camba (www.casadelcamba.com; Mendoza 539; mains B$25-55) A typical *cruceña/camba* experience: juicy meat comes sizzling off the grill while live crooners holler traditional tunes and straw-hatted waiters roam. Take *micro* 35 or 75 from the center.

La Casona (www.bistrolacasona.com; Arenales 222; mains B$35-80; 🕑 closed Sun) One of Santa Cruz's best places to eat, this German-run splash of California gourmet has diverse food offering and a shady courtyard.

Drinking

Irish Pub (Plaza 24 de Septiembre) A travelers' second home in Santa Cruz, it's on the pricey side but great for watching the goings-on in the plaza below.

Lorca (Moreno 20; admission for live music B$20; 🕑 8am-late) The meeting place of the city's artsy crowd.

Clapton's Blues Bar (cnr Murillo & Arenales; admission B$20; 🕑 Sat & Sun) Local bands play at this tiny dark bar till very late.

Entertainment

Many *boliches* (nightclubs) are spread out along Av San Martin in Barrio Equipetrol, northwest of the city, between the second and third *anillos*. You'll need to take a taxi (around B$10). Cover charges run from B$20 to B$20 and drinks are expensive.

Cinecenter (☎ free phone 900-770077; 2nd anillo; admission B$30-50) This 12-screen US-style cinema shows all the latest Hollywood releases.

Eleguá (24 de Septiembre) Groovy Latino disco where you can swing your thing to the latest samba sounds on weekends.

El Rincón Salteño (cnr 26 de Enero & Charagua; 🕑 from 10pm Fri, Sat & Sun) Best traditional *peña* in town.

Getting There & Around
AIR

The modern **Viru Viru International Airport** (VVI; ☎ 338-5000), 15km north of the center, handles domestic and international flights.

AeroSur (☎ 336-4446; cnr Irala & Colón) has daily flights to Cochabamba, La Paz and Sucre, with connections to other Bolivian cities. **TAM** (☎ 353-2639) flies direct to La Paz daily in the morning and twice weekly to Puerto Suárez. **Aerocon** (☎ 351-1200; Aeropuerto El Trompillo) flies several times daily to Trinidad from El Trompillo airport just south of the center.

Taxis to the airport charge a standard B$50. Minibuses leave Viru Viru for the center (B$3, 30 minutes) when flights arrive.

BUS

The full-service **bimodal terminal** (☎ 334-0772; terminal fee B$3), the combo long-distance bus

---

GETTING TO BRAZIL

From Quijarro, taxis (B$5) shuttle passengers to the Brazilian border town of Corumbá, 2km away. You can change dollars or bolivianos into *reais* on the Bolivian side, but the boliviano rate is poor. Note that there's no Brazilian consulate in Quijarro, so if you need a visa, get it in Santa Cruz. **Customs offices** (8am–noon & 2-5:30pm) are on opposing sides of the bridge. Bolivian officials have been known to unofficially charge for the exit stamp, but stand your ground politely. From Corumbá there are good bus connections into southern Brazil but no passenger trains.

You won't be allowed to enter Brazil without a yellow-fever vaccination certificate: there's a medical van at the border. Brazilian entry stamps are given at the border or at the Polícia Federal at the *rodoviária* (bus terminal); it's open until 5pm. Get your stamp as soon as possible to avoid later problems.

For information on travel from Brazil to Bolivia, see p316.

BOLIVIA

and train station, is 1.5km east of the center, just before the third *anillo* at the end of Av Brasil.

There are regular services to Cochabamba (B$30, eight to 10 hours), from where there are connections to La Paz, Oruro, Sucre, Potosí and Tarija. Direct overnight buses to Sucre (B$80, 15 to 25 hours) have onward connections for Potosí. There are a couple of daily services to La Paz (B$130, 15 to 23 hours) around 5pm.

There are also late afternoon buses south to Yacuiba, with connections to Salta. International routes have offices at the left-hand end of the main terminal as you enter. Daily services connect Santa Cruz with Buenos Aires (B$500, 36 hours), whilst Yacyreta run the most comfortable service to Asunción, Paraguay (B$320, 24 hours). Buses to Vallegrande (B$35, six to seven hours) leave in the morning and afternoon.

The Jesuit missions and Chiquitanía *flotas* leave in the morning and early evening (7pm to 9pm) to San Xavier (B$40, five hours) and Concepción (B$40, six hours). Departures at 8pm continue on to San Ignacio de Velasco (B$50, 10 hours). *Micros* run throughout the day every two hours or so but only go as far as Concepción (B$35, five hours).

To Trinidad (B$50 to B$120, at least nine hours) and beyond, a number of buses leave every evening (rough trip in the rainy season).

TRAIN

There are three opportunities to travel to the Brazilian border: the efficient and upmarket *Ferrobus*, the *Expreso Oriental* and the *Regional* (or *mixto*), predominantly a cargo train with a few passenger seats. For access

to the platform you need to buy a platform ticket and show your passport to the platform guard.

The most comfortable and efficient option is the *Ferrobus*, which departs on Tuesday, Thursday and Saturday at 7pm (*semi-cama/cama* B$222/257) to Quijarro on the Brazilian border and returns Monday, Wednesday and Friday at 7pm. (Note: these schedules change.)

Next in line in terms of quality is the *Expreso Oriental*, which operates a single comfortable Super Pullman class. It departs Santa Cruz on Monday, Wednesday and Friday at 4:30pm, arriving at Quijarro (8:45am; B$127) the following day. The train departs Quijarro on Tuesday, Thursday and Sunday at 4:30pm, arriving at Santa Cruz at 8:40am.

The slowest and most frequent is the *Tren Regional*. It departs Santa Cruz Monday to Saturday at noon, arriving at Quijarro (7:10am; *semi-cama/cama* B$52/115) the following day. The return departs Quijarro at 12:45pm and arrives at Santa Cruz at 9:25am.

The rail service to Yacuiba on the Argentine border, via Villamontes (for bus connections to Paraguay), is a reasonably quick and comfortable *Ferrobus* (*semi-cama/cama* B$120/135, 11 hours), which departs at 6pm on Thursday and Sunday, returning on Friday and Monday at 6pm.

AROUND SANTA CRUZ
Samaipata
The beautiful village of Samaipata (1650m) is set amid the stunning wilderness in the foothills of the Cordillera Oriental. One of the top gringo-trail spots in Bolivia and a popular weekend getaway for *cruceños*, it's brimming with foreign-run stylish hotels and

restaurants. It's the perfect base to chill, hike or explore the numerous sights. Those include the mystical pre-Inca site of El Fuerte just uphill from the village, the Che Guevara trail (the iconic leader was assassinated in the nearby village of La Higuera) and Parque Nacional Amboró further afield.

Samaipata is small enough to discover independently with just a few pointers. You can read up on it at www.samaipata.info or www .samaipataturistica.com. Once in town, get all the info you need at the following spots: **Michael Blendinger Nature Tours** (☎ 944-6227; www.discovering bolivia.com; Bolívar s/n) – great for orchid, birdwatching and full-moon tours; **Jucumari Tours** (☎ 7262-7202; Bolívar) with packages to the Ruta del Ché and mission circuits; and **Roadrunners** (☎ 944-6294; www.the-roadrunners.info; Bolívar) for self-guided hikes with GPS and guided treks to Amboró's waterfalls and cloud forests.

Four-passenger **Sindicato El Fuerte** (☎ in Santa Cruz 359-8958, in Samaipata 944-6336) vehicles leave Santa Cruz for Samaipata (weekdays/weekends B$25/30, three hours) when full from Calle Aruma near Grigota. Returns for Santa Cruz depart from the main plaza in Samaipata. *Micros* leave from near the plaza daily around 4:30am and between noon and 5pm on Sunday.

Parque Nacional Amboró

This extraordinary park crosses two 'divides': the warmer northern Amazonian-type section, and the southern Yungas-type section, with cooler temperatures (and fewer mosquitoes!). The village of Buena Vista, two hours (100km) northwest of Santa Cruz, is a staging point for trips into the spectacular forested lowland section of Parque Nacional Amboró.

For a park entry permit and cabin reservations visit Buena Vista's **SERNAP office** (☎ 932-2055; ⏰ 7am-7pm), a block south of the plaza. English-speaking **Amboró Tours** (☎ 314-5858; www .amborotours.com; Pari 81, Santa Cruz) runs adventurous trips to the park.

Jesuit Mission Circuit

From the late 17th century, Jesuits established settlements called *reducciones* in Bolivia's eastern lowlands, building churches, establishing farms and instructing the indigenous in religion, agriculture, music and crafts in return for conversion and manual labor. A circuit north and east of Santa Cruz takes in some mission sites, with buildings in various

stages of reconstruction or decay. (Get in now before mass tourism takes over!) Santa Cruz and Samaipata agencies organize tours, or you can do it on your own (allow time). Basic food and lodging are available in most of the towns. Going clockwise from Santa Cruz:

San Xavier The oldest mission (1691) and popular getaway for wealthy *cruceños*.

Concepción An attractive town with a gaudy 1709 church and restoration studios.

San Ignacio de Velasco The commercial heart of the Jesuit mission district.

San Miguel de Velasco A sleepy town with a beautiful painstakingly restored church (1721).

Santa Ana de Velasco A tiny village with a rustic 1755 church.

San Rafael de Velasco The 1740s church is noted for its fine interior.

San José de Chiquitos Frontier town with the area's only stone church (restoration nearing completion at time of research).

You can take the Santa Cruz–Quijarro train to San José first and then proceed counterclockwise. The bus schedules for seeing the missions also synchronize better if you're going counterclockwise from Santa Cruz, starting the circuit at San José. Renting a car in Santa Cruz is another option, affordable between a few people.

Parque Nacional Noel Kempff Mercado

The remote Parque Nacional Noel Kempff Mercado lies in the northernmost reaches of Santa Cruz department. Not only is it one of South America's most spectacular parks, but it also takes in a range of dwindling habitats of world-class ecological significance. Its 1.5 million hectares encompass rivers, waterfalls, rainforests, plateaus and rugged 500m escarpments. On top of this, there's an awe-inspiring variety of Amazonian flora and fauna. **Ruta Verde** (☎ 339-6470; www .rutaverdebolivia.com; 21 de Mayo 332) in Santa Cruz has information on how to get there.

THE AMAZON BASIN

Bolivia's slice of the magical Amazon Basin encompasses over half of the country's entire territory and is a prime place to experience pristine rainforest and savanna lands. The Amazon includes some of the best-known national parks and reserves, including the incredible Parque Nacional Madidi (p235). But the Amazonian paradise is not without its problems: much of the area is heavily populated and degraded through logging and mining. There's been an influx of highland settlers and an upsurge in slash-and-burn agriculture. There is also large-scale cattle ranching in the lowland areas, around Trinidad.

Boat trips provide a wonderful chance to view life from the water. Be aware that cargo vessels that ply the northern rivers lack scheduled services or passenger comforts – monotonous menus, river water and no cabins are de rigueur. Throw in a hammock or a sleeping bag. Other necessities are snacks, a water container, water-purification tablets, antimalarials and mosquito protection. The most popular river routes are Puerto Villarroel to Trinidad on the Río Ichilo and Trinidad to Guayaramerín on the Río Mamoré. Tour agencies offer comfortable river trips focused on wildlife-watching.

Towns that have air services include Cobija, Guayaramerín, Reyes, Riberalta, Rurrenabaque, San Borja and Trinidad, but flights are often delayed or canceled, especially during the rainy season.

RURRENABAQUE
☎ 03 / pop 15,000

The bustling and friendly frontier town of 'Rurre' (elevation 105m) is Bolivia's most beautiful lowland settlement. The town thrives on tourism: travelers head up the Río Beni to visit the surrounding lush jungle and the savanna-like grasslands, or to the stunningly precious Parque Nacional Madidi and its ecolodges. Hammocks are a way of life and relaxing in one is part of an otherwise hot, humid (and occasionally mosquito-infested) visit.

Information

There's no ATM in town, so beware. You can get cash advances at **Prodem Bank** on Visa and MasterCard. Tours can usually be paid for with credit cards, and *simpático* bars, agencies and hotels may be willing to facilitate cash advances.

At about B$8 per hour, internet access is pricier than in rest of Bolivia; try **Internet** (Comercio).

Immigration (Arce btwn Busch & Bolívar; ⏱ 8:30am-4:30pm Mon-Fri) Extend your stay here.

Laundry Service Number One (Avaroa) Same-day laundry service for B$12 per kg.

Municipal tourist office (cnr Vaca Diez & Avaroa; ⏱ 8am-noon & 2:30-6pm Mon-Sat) Happy to answer questions but short on material.

Parque Nacional Madidi/SERNAP Office (☎ 892-2540) Across the river at San Buenaventura. Provides information on the park; independent visitors must pay a B$95 entrance fee.

Sights & Activities

You can relax by the swimming pool at Hotel El Ambaibo on Santa Cruz for B$20 (for non-guests). Just south of town, a short uphill trek away, there's a **mirador** (lookout).

Tours
JUNGLE & PAMPAS

Jungle and pampas tours are Rurre's bread and butter. Operators are as common as mosquitoes. To choose an operator, the best bet is to speak to other travelers who've returned from a trip. Cheaper does not mean better; see boxed text on below.

Jungle tours typically include a motorized canoe trip up the Beni and Tuichi Rivers, with camping and rainforest treks along the way. Basic huts or shelters (with mosquito nets) are the main form of accommodation.

DON'T PAT THE PIRAÑAS!

'Ecofriendly' operators of pampas and jungle tours are increasing faster than mosquito larvae. Unfortunately, many of these undercut the official prices and, despite claiming to be ecofriendly, don't seem to practice what they preach, especially regarding the removal of inorganic waste from campsites and the handling of animals. As much as it's great to see the Amazonian animals, bear in mind that spotting caiman, anaconda, piranhas and the like is a privilege and not a 'right.' Operators and guides should not promise animal sightings (this encourages their unethical capture), are not supposed go looking for wildlife and should under no circumstances feed or handle any animals. Unfortunately, this is not always the case.

Your demands can put the 'friendly' back into the 'eco.' In short, your choice is vital to the ongoing protection of this wilderness area.

THE AMAZON BASIN

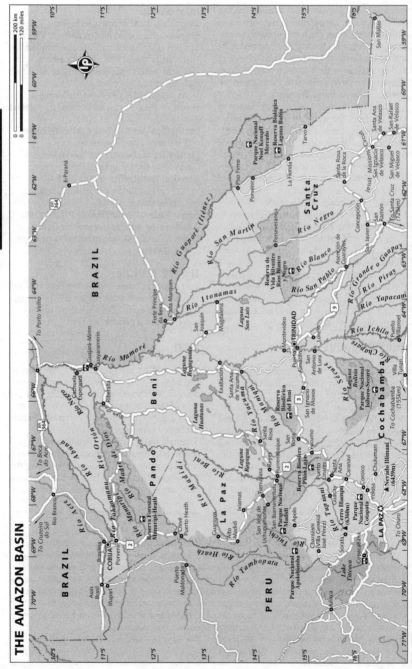

(Note that rain, mud and insects can make the wet season, especially January to March, unpleasant for some jungle tours.)

If you're more interested in watching wildlife, opt for a pampas tour, which visits the wetland savannas northeast of town. They include rewarding guided walks and daytime and evening animal-viewing boat trips.

Jungle and pampas tours are great trips but the guides' (often poor) treatment of the wildlife depends upon travelers' demands. In short, animals should not be fed, disturbed or handled. Stock up on bottled water and insect repellant. Ask to see the guide's *autorización* (license). The best guides can provide insight on the fauna, flora, indigenous people and forest lore without pushing the boundaries. Most agencies have offices on Avaroa. Recommended agencies:

Bala Tours (☎ 892-2527; www.balatours.com; cnr Santa Cruz & Comercio) Has its own jungle camp and a pampas lodge.

Fluvial Tours/Amazonia Adventures (☎ 892-2372; Avaroa s/n) Rurrenabaque's longest-running agency.

COMMUNITY-BASED ECOTOURISM

Other outstanding alternatives are the community-run and community-based ethno-ecotourism projects. Most are based several hours upriver and offer all-inclusive (with comfortable individual *cabañas*, food and *simpático* guides) overnight visits to the local communities, as well as activities such as bow-and-arrow fishing and rainforest trekking.

A Day for the Communities Tours (☎ 7128-9884; turismoecologicosocial@hotmail.com; cnr Santa Cruz & Avaroa) provides a fascinating day visit (B$200 per person, 21% goes to communities) to unique *altiplano* immigrant communities and alternative sustainable development projects, including agroforestry, organic foods and *artesanía* (handicrafts) projects.

An outstanding example of responsible community-run tourism, **Mapajo Lodge** (☎ 892-2317; www.mapajo.com; Santa Cruz btwn Comercio & Avaroa) offers all-inclusive overnight visits (B$500 per day) to the Mosetén-Chimane community three hours upriver from Rurre.

A project of the Macana community, **San Miguel del Bala** (☎ 892-2394; www.sanmigueldelbala.com; Comercio btwn Vaca Diez & Santa Cruz) ecolodge is 40 minutes upstream by boat from Rurre. The price is B$450 per day.

Sleeping

La Perla Andina (☎ 7283-5792; 18 de Noviembre s/n; r per person B$15) A block from the bus station, this bottom-end option is useful if you are looking to catch an early bus.

our pick **El Curichal Hostal** (☎ 892-2647; elcurichal @hotmail.com; Comercio 1490; s/d B$30/50, r B$70) Clean jungle-themed rooms, a BBQ terrace, shared kitchen and several hammocks.

Hotel Pahuichi (☎ 892-2558; Comercio; r per person with/without bathroom B$70/30) A Jekyll and Hyde hotel: older rooms with shared bathrooms are uninspiring, the newer en-suite rooms are worth every boliviano.

Hostal Santa Ana (☎ 892-2614; Avaroa near Vaca Diez; s/d B$70/80, without bathroom B$35/60) Decent value place with a hammock garden.

Centro de Recreación del Ejército (☎ 892-2375; Plaza 2 de Febrero; s/d B$40/60) A good, modern budget hotel converted from army barracks, featuring a river terrace and a Chinese restaurant.

Hotel los Tucanes de Rurre (☎ 892-2039; www.hotel-tucanes.com; cnr Bolivar & Aniceto Arce; s/d B$60/90, without bathroom B$50/70) This thatched-roof house offers neat rooms, a sprawling garden with hammocks, a roof terrace and sweeping river views.

Hotel Asaí (☎ 892-2439; Diez near Busch; s/d B$50/80) Bright-white rooms with bathrooms center on a shaded courtyard with hammocks under a *palapa* (palm-thatched umbrella).

Hotel Oriental (☎ 892-2401; Plaza 2 de Febrero; s/d B$70/90) Excellent place right on the plaza with comfy rooms, great showers, garden hammocks and big breakfasts included in the price.

More upscale choices include **La Isla de los Tucanes** (☎ 892-2127; Bolívar; www.islatucanes.com; cabins B$550-900; ▓ ▣), an ecological cabin complex in the north of town, and **Hotel Safari** (☎ /fax 892-2210; Comercio Final; s/d B$220/300; ▣), Rurre's poshest option right on the river.

Eating & Drinking

The Mercado Municipal is full of good *comedores* and juice bars.

Several fish restaurants line the riverfront: **La Cabaña** and **Playa Azul** grill or fry up the catch of the day (B$20 to B$30).

Camila's (cnr Campero & Avaroa; breakfast B$10-15, mains B$25-45) The best value breakfasts in town, jungle murals and a nightly happy hour on bottled beer.

Restaurant Tacuara (cnr Santa Cruz & Avaroa; mains B$18-35) This open-air eatery with shaded sidewalk seating is popular for its lasagna and huge sandwiches.

BOLIVIA

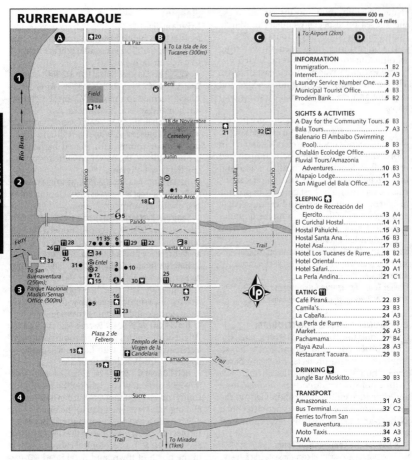

RURRENABAQUE

Pachamama (☎ 892-2620; Avaroa; mains B$20-30; ✌ lunch & dinner only, closed Sun) Restaurant-cum-cultural center with good food, lounging area, movie rooms, a billiard table upstairs, book and music exchange, arts classes and shows.

Café Piraña (Santa Cruz near Avaroa; mains B$25-40) Delicious vegetarian and meat dishes, yummy breakfasts, fresh juices, a library and nightly film screenings in the garden.

La Perla de Rurre (cnr Bolívar & Diez; mains B$30-45) Everyone's favorite in Rurre serves some mean fresh fish dishes in an unassuming environment.

Jungle Bar Moskkito (www.moskkito.com; Vaca Diez s/n) An undisputed travelers' favorite, with happy hour from 7pm to 9pm, pool tables, darts and good music. Great spot to form tour groups.

Getting There & Around
AIR

The number of flights to Rurre is increasing all the time but they are often sold out or canceled in the rainy season. Have your tour agency purchase your return ticket in advance. The humble airport is a grassy landing strip a few kilometers north of town. Airport transport costs B$5 by *micros* into town. If you're traveling light, catch a mototaxi for B$3.

Amazonas (☎ 892-2472; Comercio near Santa Cruz) has four daily flights to La Paz (B$525). Reconfirm your ticket the day before your flight. **TAM** (☎ 892-2398; Santa Cruz) flies between La Paz and Rurre (B$480) at least once a day. Flights are occasionally diverted to the nearest airport in Reyes in the rainy season.

BOAT

Taxi ferries across to San Buenaventura (B$1) sail frequently all day.

BUS

When the roads are dry, buses run daily between Rurrenabaque and La Paz (B$90, 18 to 24 hours), but it's best to break the journey at Coroico, which is 'only' 14 hours from Rurre; actually, you get off at Yolosita (B$75), the hop-off for Coroico.

Daily buses to Trinidad (normal/sleeper, B$120/150, 17 to 30 hours) go via Yucumo, San Borja and San Ignacio de Moxos in the dry season – this route is one of the worst in the country. There are also daily buses to Guayaramerín (B$120, 18 hours to three days).

AROUND RURRENABAQUE
Parque Nacional Madidi

The remarkable Río Madidi watershed features the greatest biodiversity of the earth's protected regions. The most ecologically sound section is protected by Parque Nacional Madidi (B$95 entry), which encompasses a huge range of wildlife habitats, from torrid rainforests to Andean glaciers at 6000m. Researchers have observed over 1000 kinds of birds and more protected species than any other park in the world.

The populated portions of the park along the Río Tuichi have been accorded a special Unesco designation permitting indigenous inhabitants to utilize traditional forest resources but the park has also been considered for oil exploration and as a site for a major hydroelectric scheme in the past. In addition, illicit logging has affected several areas around the park perimeter and there's been talk of a new road between Apolo and Ixiamas that would effectively bisect the park. Although the hydroelectric scheme has been abandoned, the debate continues over whether road building and oil exploration will take place and many suspect that illegal loggers will use the opportunity to benefit from these projects.

GETTING THERE & AWAY

The most accessible and popular access point is Rurre. The easiest way to visit the park is a trip to Chalalán Ecolodge (see left) or one of the ecotourism projects (see p233). Those erring on the side of adventure can visit the park's fringes independently but must register with the SERNAP office in San Buenaventura (see p231) and must be accompanied by an authorized guide. For a taste of just how wrong things can go, read *Return from Tuichi* (also published as *Heart of the Amazon*) by Yossi Ghinsberg.

TRINIDAD

☎ 03 / pop 86,500

There's more than meets the eye to 'Trini' (elevation 235m), Beni's capital. Trinidad is the place you'll come to if you're after a trip down the long and deep Río Mamoré or on your way between Santa Cruz and Rurrenabaque. An enjoyably lazy modern town centers on the tropical main square and offers plenty to do, with a little effort: from the mission route to the pre-Hispanic route, featuring the unique system of water channels attributed to the *Moxeñas*.

The Spanish-funded **ethno-archaeological museum** (admission B$5; ☯ 8am-noon & 3-6pm) at the university, 1.5km out of town, exhibits artifacts such as traditional instruments and tribal costumes. Motorbikes are not just transport, but a pastime: for B$12 per hour or B$80 for a full day, you can rent a bike and join the general public in whizzing around the square.

Information

The helpful **tourist office** (☎ 462-4831) tucked away inside the Prefectura building has good brochures on surrounding sights and a town map. ATMs are near the main plaza.

SPLURGE!

The Bolivian Amazonia's most notable community-based ecotourism project is **Chalalán Ecolodge**, fronting a wildlife-rich lake six hours up the Río Tuichi from Rurre. Since 1995 it has provided employment for the Tacana villagers of San José de Uchupiamonas and is often cited as a model for sustainable tourism, with the profits going directly back into the community. It's an awesome place, with an extensive trail system, excellent meals and night hikes. An all-inclusive four-day, three-night stay costs around US$320 per person. For details, visit the **Rurrenabaque office** (☎ 892-2419; Comercio near Campero; www.chalalan.com) or contact the **La Paz office** (☎ 2-231-1451; Sagárnaga 189).

BOLIVIA

For information on tours and activities in the surrounding area, including horse-riding trips, river outings, trekking, visits to local communities and bird-watching, try **Turismo Moxos** (☎ 462-1141; turmoxos@entelnet.bo; 6 de Agosto 114).

Sleeping

Residencial Patujú (☎ 462-1963; Villaviciencio 473; s/d B$50/100) A homey budget option with a bright but cool courtyard.

Residencial Santa Cruz (☎ 462-0711; Santa Cruz 537; s/d B$80/140, s without bathroom B$60) Rooms on the 1st floor of this cheery place are airier (worth the slight price difference).

Hotel Copacabana (☎ 462-2811; Villaviciencio 627; s/d with fan B$80/140, with air-con B$140/210; 🔀) Friendly place with tiled clean rooms.

Hostal El Tajibo (☎ 462-2324; cnr Santa Cruz 423 & 6 de Agosto; s/d with fan B$100/150, with air-con B$200/250; 🔀) Trini's best-value budget option has stylish rooms, some featuring balconies. Air-con rooms include breakfast.

Eating & Drinking

Trinidad is cattle country, so beef is bountiful. If budget is the priority, hit the Mercado Municipal, where for a pittance you can try the local specialty, *arroz con queso* (rice with cheese), plus shish kebabs, *yuca* (cassava), plantain and salad. There are several decent places around the plaza.

Club Social (Suárez; almuerzo & dinner B$20) The lovely social club in a shady courtyard off the main plaza is a local family favorite, with generous portions.

El Tabano (Villaviciencio near Mamoré; mains B$25-40) Cool beers and cocktails, excellent food and Trinidad's young crowd are all on offer at this courtyard bar-pub.

La Fonda Mojeña (18 de Noviembre; mains B$25-40) Typical food is the order of the day at this little restaurant famous for its local specialties.

Getting There & Around

AIR

The airport (B$7 terminal tax) is northwest of town, a feasible half-hour walk from the center or a quick ride by taxi (B$15) or moto-taxi (B$10). **Amazonas** (☎ 462-2426; 18 de Noviembre 267) shuttles daily between La Paz and San Borja. **Aerocon** (☎ 462-4442; Vaca Diez near 18 de Noviembre) handles several daily flights to Santa Cruz, Riberalta and Cobija. **TAM** (☎ 462-2363; cnr Bolívar & Santa Cruz) has a couple of weekly flights to Cochabamba and La Paz.

BOAT

If you're looking for river transportation north along the Mamoré to Guayaramerín, or south along the Mamoré and Ichilo to Puerto Villarroel, inquire at the *Capitanía*, in Puerto Almacén 8km southwest of town. The Guayaramerín run takes up to a week (larger boats do it in three to four days) and costs around B$250 including food, B$200 without. To Puerto Villarroel, smaller boats take five days and cost about B$100 including meals.

GETTING TO BRAZIL

The cheerful little town of **Guayaramerín** (elevation 130m) on the banks of the Río Mamoré is Bolivia's back door to Brazil. This frontier settlement thrives on legal and illegal trade with the Brazilian town of Guajará-Mirim, just across the river.

There are daily buses to Trinidad (B$140, 22 hours) from the bus terminal at the south end of town. Flying is the way to go though – there are daily flights to Trinidad with **Aerocon** (☎ 855-5025) and **TAM** (☎ 855-3924), which also has daily flights to La Paz and several weekly to Cochabamba and Santa Cruz.

The relatively efficient **Brazilian consulate** (☎ 855-3766; cnr Beni & 24 de Septiembre; ⏰ 9am-5pm Mon-Fri), a block east of the plaza, issues visas in three days. Money changers hanging around the port area deal in US dollars, Brazilian *reais* and bolivianos.

Popping into Guajará-Mirim is really easy. Day visits are encouraged, and you don't even need a visa. Motorboats (B$10) across the river leave from the port every half an hour from 6am to 6pm, and less frequently later. To travel further into Brazil or to enter Bolivia, you must pick up an entry/exit stamp. For departure stamps from Bolivia, head to **Bolivian immigration** (⏰ 9am-5pm Mon-Fri) in the Prefectural building on the main plaza or the other branch at the airport. A yellow-fever vaccination certificate is officially required to enter Brazil; have it handy in case of a 'spot (the tourist) check.'

For information on travel from Brazil to Bolivia, see p316.

BUS

The rambling bus terminal is a 10-minute walk east of the center. *Flotas* depart nightly for Santa Cruz (normal/*bus-cama* B$50/80, eight to 10 hours) and road conditions permitting. Several companies head daily to Rurrenabaque (B$70, 12 hours) via San Borja. *Camionetas* run to San Ignacio de Moxos (three to four hours) when full from *paradas* (stops) at Santa Cruz with Mamoré and 1 de Mayo near Velarde; buses occasionally run from the terminal around 9am. There are also daily dry-season departures to Guayaramerín.

BOLIVIA DIRECTORY

ACCOMMODATIONS

Bolivian accommodations are among South America's cheapest, though price and value are hardly uniform. Prices in this chapter reflect high-season rates (late May to early September); prices can double during fiestas. Negotiate during slow times; a three-night stay may net you a deal. Room availability is only a problem during fiestas (especially Carnaval in Oruro) and at popular weekend getaways (eg Coroico).

The Bolivian hotel-rating system divides accommodations into *posadas, alojamientos, residenciales, casas de huéspedes, hostales* and *hoteles*. This rating system reflects the price scale and, to some extent, the quality.

Posadas are the cheapest roof and bed available. They're frequented mainly by *campesinos* visiting the city, cost between B$8 and B$15 per person and provide minimal cleanliness and comfort. Shared bathrooms are stinky, some have no showers and hot water is unknown.

Most *alojamientos* (B$15 to B$35 per person) – some clean and tidy and others disgustingly seedy – have communal bathrooms with electric showers (to avoid electric shock, don't touch the shower while the water is running and wear rubber sandals). Most travelers end up at *residenciales,* which charge B$60 to B$140 for a double with private bathroom, about 30% less without. *Casas de huéspedes* (family-run guesthouses) sometimes offer a more midrange, B&B-like atmosphere.

In this chapter, we assume that *residenciales* and *casas de huéspedes* (and some *hostales,* depending on the city) have shared bathroom facilities (unless specified otherwise), while hotel rooms come with separate bathroom and include breakfast.

Warning: several readers have alerted us to instances of improper use of propane heaters in Bolivia. These are not meant to be used in enclosed spaces and can be dangerous so refrain from using them, if supplied.

Hostelling International (HI; www.hostellingbolivia .org) is affiliated with a network of 16 accommodations in different parts of Bolivia. Atypical of other 'hostelling' networks, members range from two-star hotels to camping grounds, but few offer traditional amenities like dorm beds or shared kitchens. HI membership cards may be for sale at the flagship hostel in Sucre (p219), although rumor has it that some are yet to learn about offering the 10% discount to members.

Bolivia offers excellent camping, especially along trekking routes and in remote mountain areas. Gear (of varying quality) is easily rented in La Paz and popular trekking towns like Sorata. There are few organized campsites, but you can pitch a tent almost anywhere outside populated centers. Remember that highland nights are often freezing. Theft and assaults have been reported in some areas; inquire locally about security.

ACTIVITIES

Hiking, trekking and mountaineering in and around the Andes top the to-do list; opt for camping or fishing if you're feeling lazy. The most popular treks (see p191) begin near La Paz, traverse the Cordilleras along ancient Inca routes and end in the Yungas. Jungle treks (see p231) are all the rage around Rurrenabaque.

An increasing number of La Paz agencies organize technical climbs and expeditions into the Cordillera Real and to Volcán Sajama (6542m), Bolivia's highest peak; see p178.

Mountain biking options around La Paz (p182 and p192) are endless. Kayaking, wilderness canoeing and white-water rafting are gaining popularity near Coroico, in the Chapare (in the lowlands around Cochabamba) and in Parque Nacional Noel Kempff Mercado. Horse riding is hugely popular throughout the red-rock country around Tupiza (p207).

BOLIVIA

BOLIVIA

BOOKS

For in-depth coverage, pick up a copy of Lonely Planet's *Bolivia*.

If walking is on your itinerary, add *Trekking in Bolivia* by Yossi Brain to your kit. *The Andes of Bolivia,* by Alain Mesili, is a must for madcap mountaineers.

For a good synopsis of Bolivian history, politics and culture, check out *Bolivia in Focus,* by Robert Werner. If you are going to be in the country for the long haul, pick up *Culture Shock! Bolivia,* by Mark Cramer. *The Fat Man from La Paz: Contemporary Fiction from Bolivia,* a collection of short stories edited by Rosario Santos, makes great roadside reading.

English-, German- and French-language publications are available at Los Amigos del Libro in La Paz, Cochabamba and Santa Cruz. There's an ample selection of popular novels, Latin American literature, dictionaries and coffee-table books.

Bibliophiles rejoice: used-book outlets and dog-eared book exchanges are now commonplace along the Bolivian part of the Gringo Trail.

BUSINESS HOURS

Few businesses open before 9am, though markets stir awake as early as 6am. Cities virtually shut down between noon and 2pm, except markets and restaurants serving lunch-hour crowds. Most businesses remain open until 8pm. If you have urgent business to attend to, don't wait until the weekend as most offices will be closed. Restaurants are generally open between 8am till 10am for breakfast, noon till 2:30pm or 3pm for lunch and 6pm till 11pm for dinner, unless specified otherwise in the listings.

CLIMATE

Bolivia has a wide range of altitude-affected climatic patterns. Within its frontiers, every climatic zone can be found, ranging from stifling rainforest heat to arctic cold.

Adventurers will likely encounter just about every climatic zone, no matter when they visit. Summer (November to April) is the rainy season. The most popular, and arguably most comfortable, time to visit is during the dry winter season (May to September).

August is the most popular month of the high tourist season, which runs from late May to early September.

The rainy season lasts from November to March or April. Of the major cities, only Potosí receives regular snowfall (between February and April), though flakes are possible in Oruro and La Paz toward the end of the rainy season. On the *altiplano* and in the highlands, subzero nighttime temperatures are frequent.

Winter in Cochabamba, Sucre and Tarija is characterized by clear skies and optimum temperatures. The Amazon Basin is always hot and wet, with the drier period falling between May and October. The Yungas region is cooler but fairly damp throughout the year.

For more information and climate charts, see p987.

DANGERS & ANNOYANCES

Crime against tourists is on the increase in Bolivia, especially in La Paz and, to a lesser extent, Cochabamba, Copacabana and Oruro (especially during festival times). Scams are commonplace and fake police, false tourist police and 'helpful' tourists are on the rise. Be aware, too, of circulating counterfeit banknotes. See p179 for a detailed rundown of *en vogue* cons.

There is a strong tradition of social protest in the country: demonstrations are a regular occurrence and this can affect travelers. These are usually peaceful happenings, but police occasionally use force and tear gas to disperse crowds. *Bloqueos* (roadblocks) and strikes by transportation workers often lead to long delays.

The rainy season means flooding, landslides and road washouts, which means more delays. Getting stuck overnight behind a slide can happen: you'll be a happier camper with ample food, drink and warm clothes on hand.

Note that the mine tours in Potosí (see boxed text, p222) and the 4x4 excursions to the salt flats of Uyuni (see p204) have become so hugely popular that many agencies would rather make money than conform to any semblance of safety regulations. Make sure you do your research before signing up for the tour.

DRIVER'S LICENSE

Most car-rental agencies will accept a home driver's license, but it's wise to back it up with an International Driving Permit.

ELECTRICITY

Most electricity currents are 220V AC, at 50Hz. Most plugs and sockets are the two-pin, round-prong variety, but a few anomalous American-style two-pin, parallel flat-pronged sockets exist.

EMBASSIES & CONSULATES

Argentina La Paz (Map p180-1; ☎ 2-241-7737; fax 2-242-2727; Aspiazu 497); Cochabamba (☎ 4-425-5859; fax 4-422-9347; Blanco 929); Villazón (☎ 2-596-5253; Saavedra 311); Santa Cruz (Map pp226-7; ☎ 3-334-7133; fax 3-334-8200; Junín 22)

Australia La Paz (Map pp176-7; ☎ 2-211-5655, 242-2957; Av 20 de Octubre 2396, 3rd fl)

Brazil La Paz (☎ 2-216-6400; fax 2-244-0043; www .brasil.org.bo; Av Aniceto Arce, Edificio Multicentro); Cochabamba (Map pp214-15; ☎ 4-425-5860; fax 4-411-7084; Av Oquendo N-1080); Guayaramerín (☎ 3-855-3766; fax 3-855-4695; 24 de Septiembre 28); Santa Cruz (Map pp226-7; ☎ 3-334-4400; fax 3-335-0488; Busch 330); Sucre (Map p218; ☎ 4-645-2661; Arenales 212)

Canada La Paz (Map pp176-7; ☎ 2-241-5141; fax 2-241-4453; Sanjinéz 2678, 2nd fl)

Chile La Paz (☎ 2-279-7331; fax 2-212-6491; www .cgchilelapaz.com.bo; Calle 14 N 8024, Calacoto); Santa Cruz (☎ 3-343-4272; www.consulado-chile.scz.com; Edificio Torre Equipetrol, 9th fl)

France La Paz (☎ 2-214-9900; www.ambafrance-bo.org; cnr Siles 5390 & Calle 8, Obrajes)

Germany La Paz (Map pp176-7; ☎ 2-244-0066; fax 2-244-1441; Av Aniceto Arce 2395); Cochabamba (Map pp214-15; ☎ 4-425-4024; fax 4-425-4023; Edificio La Promontora, cnr España & Heroínas, 6th fl); Sucre (Map p218; ☎ 4-645-2091; Avaroa 326)

Paraguay La Paz (Map pp176-7; ☎ 2-243-3176; Edificio Illimani, Salazar 351)

Peru La Paz (Map pp176-7; ☎ 2-244-0631; fax 2-244-4199; www.conperlapaz.org; Edificio Hilda, Av 6 de Agosto 2455); Cochabamba (Map pp214-15; ☎ 4-448-6556; Edificio Continental, Blanco N-1344); Santa Cruz (☎ 3-341-9091; Viador Pinto 84); Sucre (Map p218; ☎ 4-645-5592; Avaroa 472)

UK La Paz (Map pp176-7; ☎ 2-243-3424; fax 2-243-1073; www.ukinbolivia.fco.gov.uk/en; Av Aniceto Arce 2732); Santa Cruz (☎ 3-353-5035; Santa Cruz International School; Km 7.5)

USA La Paz (Map pp176-7; ☎ 2-216-8000; http://lapaz .usembassy.gov; Av Aniceto Arce 2780); Santa Cruz (☎ 3-351-3477; Av Roque Aguilera 146)

EMERGENCIES

Emergency service numbers in major cities:
Ambulance (☎ 118)
Fire department (☎ 119)

Police (RadioPatrol; ☎ 110)
Tourist Police (☎ 02-222-5016)

FESTIVALS & EVENTS

Bolivian fiestas are invariably of religious or political origin and typically include lots of music, drinking, eating, dancing, processions, rituals and general unrestrained behavior. Water balloons (gringos are sought-after targets!) and fireworks (all too often at eye level) figure prominently.

Alasitas (Festival of Abundance) January 24. Best in La Paz and Copacabana.

Fiesta de la Virgen de Candelaria (Feast of the Virgin of Candelaria) First week in February. Best in Copacabana.

Carnaval Held in February/March; dates vary. All hell breaks loose in Oruro during La Diablada.

Semana Santa (Easter Week) March/April; dates vary.

Fiesta de la Cruz (Festival of the Cross) May 3. May or may not have anything to do with the cross Jesus hung on.

Independence Day Fiesta Held August 6, this highly charged event sees excessive raging nationwide.

FOOD & DRINK

Eating reviews in this chapter are given in order of budget, with the least expensive options first.

Bolivian Cuisine

Generally, Bolivian food is palatable, filling and ho-hum. Figuring prominently, potatoes come in dozens of varieties, most of them small and colorful. *Chuño* or *tunta* (freeze-dried potatoes) often accompany meals and are gnarled-looking, but some people love them. In the lowlands, the potato is replaced by *yuca* (cassava).

Beef, chicken and fish are the most common proteins. Campesinos eat *cordero* (mutton), *cabrito* (goat), llama, alpaca and, on special occasions, *carne de chancho* (pork). The most common altiplano fish is *trucha* (trout), which is farmed in Lake Titicaca. The lowlands have a great variety of freshwater fish, including the delicious *surubí* (catfish). Pizza, fried chicken, hamburgers and *chifas* (Chinese restaurants) provide some variety.

The tastiest Bolivian snack is the *salteña*. These delicious meat and vegetable pasties originated in Salta, Argentina, but achieved perfection in Bolivia. They come stuffed with beef or chicken, olives, egg, potato, onion, peas, carrots and other surprises – watch the squirting juice. Empanadas (dough lined with cheese and deep-fried) are toothsome early morning market treats.

BOLIVIA

Standard meals are *desayuno* (breakfast), *almuerzo* (lunch; the word normally refers to a set meal served at midday) and *cena* (dinner). For *almuerzo*, restaurants – from backstreet cubbyholes to classy venues – offer bargain set meals consisting of soup, a main course, and coffee or tea. In some places, a salad and simple dessert are included. *Almuerzos* cost roughly half the price of à la carte dishes: less than B$8 to B$35, depending on the class of restaurant. Reliable market *comedores* (basic eateries) and street stalls are always the least expensive option.

Some popular Bolivian set-meal standbys include the following:

chairo (*chai*·ro) Beef or mutton soup with potatoes, *chuño* and other vegetables.

milanesa (mee·la·*ne*·sa) Breaded and fried beef or chicken cutlets.

pacumutu (pa·koo·*moo*·too) Chunks of beef grilled on a skewers with veggies.

pique a lo macho (*pee*·ke a lo *ma*·cho) Heap of chopped beef, hot dogs and French fries topped with onions, lettuce, tomatoes and *locoto* chilli peppers.

silpancho (seel·*pan*·cho) Thinly pounded beef schnitzel.

Drinks

ALCOHOLIC DRINKS

Bolivia's wine region is centered around Tarija. The best label is La Concepción's Cepas de Altura (from the world's highest vineyards). The same winery also produces *singani,* a powerful spirit obtained by distilling grape skins and other by-products. The most popular cocktail is *chuflay,* a refreshing blend of *singani,* 7-Up (or ginger ale), ice and lemon.

Bolivian beers aren't bad either; popular brands include Huari, Paceña, Sureña and Potosina. Beer is ridiculously fizzy at the higher altitudes, where it can be difficult to get the brew from under the foam.

The favorite alcoholic drink of the masses is *chicha cochabambina,* a fermented corn brew. It is made all over Bolivia, especially in the Cochabamba region. Other versions of *chicha,* often nonalcoholic, are made from sweet potato, peanuts, cassava and other fruits and vegetables.

NONALCOHOLIC DRINKS

Beyond the usual coffee, tea and hot chocolate, *maté de coca* (coca-leaf tea) is the most common boiled drink. *Api,* a super-sweet, hot drink made from maize, lemon and cinnamon, is served in markets. Major cola brands are available and popular. Don't miss *licuados,* addictive fruit shakes blended with milk or water. *Mocachinchi* is a ubiquitous market drink made from dried peaches and more sugar than water.

GAY & LESBIAN TRAVELERS

Homosexuality is legal in Bolivia but still not widely accepted. In 2004 parliament attempted (unsuccessfully) to introduce Law 810, allowing homosexual couples to marry and foster children.

Gay bars and venues are limited to the larger cities, especially Santa Cruz and La Paz, but these are still somewhat clandestine affairs. As for hotels, sharing a room is no problem – but discretion is still in order.

Gay rights lobby groups are active in La Paz (MGLP Libertad), Cochabamba (Dignidad) and most visibly in progressive Santa Cruz, which held Bolivia's first Gay Pride in 2001. La Paz is known for La Familia Galan, the capital's most fabulous group of cross-dressing queens who aim to educate Bolivians around issues of sexuality and gender through theater performances. The feminist activist group Mujeres Creando is based in La Paz and promotes the rights of oppressed groups.

HEALTH

Sanitation and hygiene are not Bolivia's strong suits, so pay attention to what you eat. Most tap water isn't safe to drink; stick to bottled water if your budget allows (your bowels will thank you). Carry iodine if you'll be trekking.

The *altiplano* lies between 3000m and 4000m, and many visitors to La Paz, Copacabana and Potosí will have problems with altitude sickness. Complications like cerebral edema have been the cause of death in otherwise fit, healthy travelers. Diabetics should note that only the Touch II blood glucose meter gives accurate readings at altitudes over 2000m.

Bolivia is officially in a yellow-fever zone, so a vaccination is recommended; it is in fact obligatory for US citizens requesting visas and for onward travel (such as Brazil, which requires the certificate). Anyone coming from a yellow-fever infected area needs a vaccination certificate to enter Bolivia. Take precautions against malaria in the lowlands.

While medical facilities might not be exactly what you're used to back home, there are decent hospitals in the biggest cities and passable clinics in most towns (but *not* in remote parts of the country). For more information on altitude sickness and other critical matters, see the Health chapter (p1011).

HOLIDAYS

On major holidays, banks, offices and other services are closed and public transport is often bursting at the seams; book ahead if possible.

Nuevo Año (New Year's Day) January 1
Semana Santa (Easter Week) March/April
Día del Trabajo (Labor Day) May 1
Día de la Independencia (Independence Day) August 6
Día de Colón (Columbus Day) October 12
Día de los Muertos (All Souls' Day) November 2
Navidad (Christmas) December 25

Not about to be outdone by their neighbors, each department has its own holiday: February 10 in Oruro, November 10 in Potosí, April 15 in Tarija, May 25 in Chuquisaca, July 16 in La Paz, September 14 in Cochabamba, September 24 in Santa Cruz and Pando and November 18 in Beni.

INTERNET ACCESS

Nearly every corner of Bolivia has an internet cafe. Rates run from B$1 to B$12 per hour. Note that smaller towns often have a very slow dial-up connection.

INTERNET RESOURCES

Bolivia.com (www.bolivia.com) Current news and cultural information.
Bolivia web (www.boliviaweb.com) Good portal with a variety of links, including cultural and artistic links.
Boliviacontact.com (www.boliviacontact.com) Quite thorough, searchable index of Bolivian sites.

LEGAL MATTERS

Regardless of its reputation as the major coca provider, drugs – including cocaine – are highly illegal in Bolivia, and possession and use brings a jail sentence. Foreign embassies are normally powerless to help (or won't want to know!). In short, don't even think about it.

MAPS

Government topographical and specialty maps are available from the Instituto Geográfico Militar (IGM; see p174). For Cordillera Real and Sajama trekking maps, the contour maps produced by Walter Guzmán Córdova are good. Freddy Ortiz' widely available, inexpensive *Journey Routes* map series covers the major tourist destinations. The excellent *New Map of the Cordillera Real*, published by O'Brien Cartographics, is available at various travelers' hangouts. O'Brien also publishes the *Travel Map of Bolivia*, which is about the best country map. The **South American Explorers Club** (www.saexplorers .org) has maps of major cities.

MEDIA
Newspapers & Magazines

Major international English-language news magazines are sold at Amigos del Libro outlets. Bolivian towns with daily newspapers include Cochabamba, La Paz, Potosí and Sucre.

Radio

Bolivia has countless radio stations broadcasting in Spanish, Quechua and Aymara. In La Paz, tune into noncommercial 96.5FM (Radio Top) for folk tunes or 100.5FM for a catchy English-Spanish language pop mix. For a 24/7 stream of Andean artists, browse **Bolivia Web Radio** (www.boliviaweb.com/radio). **Radio Panamericana** (www.panamericana-bolivia.com) is popular all around Bolivia.

TV

The government-run Canal 7 has its main opposition on UNITEL out of Santa Cruz. There are several private TV stations. Cable (with CNN, ESPN and BBC) is available in most upmarket hotels.

MONEY

Bolivia's unit of currency is the boliviano (B$), which is divided into 100 centavos. Bolivianos come in 10, 20, 50, 100 and 200 denomination notes, with coins worth five, two and one bolivianos as well as 10, 20 and 50 centavos. Often called pesos (the currency was changed from pesos to bolivianos in 1987), bolivianos are extremely difficult to unload outside the country. See also p22.

ATMs

Just about every sizable town has a *cajero automático* (ATM); we've noted those that don't. ATMs dispense bolivianos in 50 and 100 notes (sometimes US dollars as well) on

Visa, MasterCard, Plus and Cirrus cards. Be aware that some British and European travelers have reported access problems with this system outside of larger cities.

Cash

Finding change for bills larger than B$10 is a national pastime as change for larger notes is scarce outside big cities. When you're exchanging money or making big purchases, make sure you request small denominations. If you can stand waiting in the lines, most banks will break large bills.

Credit Cards

Brand-name plastic, such as Visa, MasterCard and (less often) American Express, may be used in larger cities at better hotels, restaurants and tour agencies. Cash advances (according to your limit at home) are available on Visa (and less often MasterCard), with no commission, from most major bank branches. Travel agencies in towns without ATMs will often provide cash advances for clients for 3% to 6% commission.

Exchanging Money

Visitors generally fare best with US dollars. Currency may be exchanged at casas de cambio and at some banks in larger cities. You can often change money in travel agencies. Cambistas (street money changers) operate in most cities but only change cash dollars, paying roughly the same as casas de cambio. They're convenient after hours, but guard against counterfeits. The rate for cash doesn't vary much from place to place and there is no black-market rate. Currencies of neighboring countries may be exchanged in border areas and at casas de cambio in La Paz. Beware of mangled notes; unless both halves of a repaired banknote bear identical serial numbers, the note is worthless.

Exchange rates at press time included:

EXCHANGE RATES

Country	Unit	B$
Australia	A$1	6.02
Canada	C$1	6.47
euro zone	€1	10.17
Japan	¥100	7.68
New Zealand	NZ$1	4.90
UK	UK£1	11.63
USA	US$1	6.97

International Transfers

The fastest way to have money transferred from abroad is with **Western Union** (www.westernunion .com). An alternative option is through **Money Gram** (www.moneygram.com), with offices in all major cities – watch the hefty fees. Your bank can also wire money to a cooperating Bolivian bank; it may take a couple of business days.

Traveler's Checks

Changing traveler's checks in smaller towns is often impossible. You'll usually be charged a commission of up to 5% (the rates are lowest in La Paz) or a flat fee of US$6. American Express is the most widely accepted. Bring your passport.

POST

Even small towns have post offices; some are signposted Ecobol (Empresa Correos de Bolivia). The post is generally reliable in major towns, but when posting anything important, pay the small fee to have it certified.

Reliable free lista de correos (poste restante) is available in larger cities. Mail should be addressed to you c/o Lista de Correos (Poste Restante), Correo Central, La Paz (or whatever city), Bolivia. Using only a first initial and capitalizing your entire LAST NAME will help avoid confusion. Mail is often sorted into foreign and Bolivian stacks, so those with Latin surnames should check the local stack.

Airmail postales (postcards) cost from B$7.50 to B$10.50 depending on where you are sending it. A 1kg parcel to the USA will cost around B$150 by air. Posting by sea is s-l-o-w but considerably cheaper.

RESPONSIBLE TRAVEL

Traveling responsibly in Bolivia is a constant struggle. Trash cans (and recycling bins) are few and far between and ecological sensitivity is a relatively new if growing concept. Nearly every tour operator in the country claims to practice 'ecotourism,' but don't take their word for it. It's best to grill agencies about their practices and talk to returning travelers to see if their experiences match the propaganda.

On the personal behavior level, there are several things you can do to leave minimal impact or maximize the positive impact on the country. If you're taking a jungle or pampas tour around Rurrenabaque, request that your guide doesn't catch or feed wildlife for the benefit of photo opportunities. Before visiting indigenous communities, ask if the guide is from the community or make sure the agency has permission to visit. On the Salar de Uyuni, encourage drivers to carry garbage and to follow existing tire tracks to minimize damage to the fragile salt flats. In the Beni, don't eat fish out of season and resist the urge to buy handicrafts made from endangered rainforest species.

When it comes to dealing with begging, think twice about indiscriminately handing out sweets, cigarettes or money. Instead, teach a game, share a photo of family or friends, or make a donation (basic medical supplies, pens or notebooks) to an organization working to improve health, sanitation or education. If invited to someone's home for a meal, take something that won't undermine the local culture, such as a handful of coca leaves or fruit.

SHOPPING

Compact discs and cassettes of *peñas,* folk and pop music make good souvenirs. Cassettes, however, may be low-quality bootlegs; higher-quality CDs cost around B$75. Selection is best in La Paz.

Traditional instruments (eg *charangos, zampoñas*) are sold widely throughout the country but avoid buying ones made from endangered armadillos.

Bolivian woven ware is also a good buy. Touristy places such as Calle Sagárnaga (La Paz) and Tarabuco (near Sucre) have the greatest selection, but may be more expensive than buying direct from a craftsperson. Prices vary widely with the age, quality, color and extent of the weaving: a new and simple *manta* might cost B$150, while the finest antique examples will cost several hundred. Another good buy is alpaca goods, either finished or raw wool.

STUDYING

Sucre, Cochabamba and La Paz are all loaded with Spanish schools. Private lessons are starting to catch on in smaller retreats like Sorata and Samaipata. In bigger cities, it's also possible to find one-on-one music, weaving and other arts lessons. Instruction ranges from between B$40 and B$60 per hour.

TELEPHONE

Entel, the Empresa Nacional de Telecomunicaciones, has telephone offices in nearly every town (as increasingly does Cotel, Viva, Tigo and other competing companies), usually open from 9am to noon and from 2pm to 5:30pm Monday to Friday (plus on Saturday morning). Local calls cost just a few bolivianos from these offices. *Puntos* are small, privately run outposts offering similar services. Street kiosks are often equipped with telephones that charge B$1 for brief local calls.

One-digit area codes change by province: ☎ 2 for La Paz, Oruro and Potosí; ☎ 3 for Santa Cruz, Beni and Pando; and ☎ 4 for Cochabamba, Sucre and Tarija. When making a long-distance call from a public telephone, you must dial a '0' before the single-digit area code. In this chapter, a 0 has already been added to the codes and these are presented – as two digits – at the start of each town section. Drop the initial code if you're calling within a province. If you're calling from abroad, drop the 0 from the code. If you're ringing a local mobile phone, dial the eight-digit number; if the mobile is from another city, you must first dial a 0 plus the two-digit carrier number. These range from 10 to 21.

Bolivia's country code is ☎ 591. The international direct-dialing access code is 00. Some Entel offices accept reverse-charge (collect) calls; others will give you the office's number and let you be called back. For reverse-charge calls from a private line, ring an international operator: for the **USA** (AT&T toll-free ☎ 800-10-1110; MCI ☎ 800-10-2222), **Canada** (Teleglobe ☎ 800-10-0101) or **UK** (BT ☎ 800-10-0044) – beware that these calls can be bank-breakers.

Calls from telephone offices are getting cheaper all the time; these vary between B$1.50 and B$8 per minute. Much cheaper Net2Phone internet call centers, charging as little as B$0.20 a minute to a fixed line abroad, exist in major cities; the connections can be shaky. Most internet shops have Skype installed, which you can use at no extra cost, just paying for the time online.

TOILETS

Take your 'toilet humor' – stinky *baños públicos* (public toilets) abound. Learn to live with the fact that toilet facilities don't exist in many buses. Carry toilet paper with you wherever you go at all times! That, and learn to hold your breath. In remote areas, you may have to pay B$5 to use the facilities.

TOURIST INFORMATION

The national tourist authority, the Viceministerio de Turismo, has its head office in La Paz. It assists municipal and departmental tourist offices. These are merely functional and, when open, distribute varying amounts of printed information.

TOURS

Tours are a convenient way to visit a site when you're short on time or motivation, and are frequently the easiest way to visit remote areas. They're also relatively cheap but the cost will depend on the number of people in your group. Popular organized tours include Tiwanaku, Uyuni, and excursions to remote attractions such as the Cordillera Apolobamba. Arrange organized tours in La Paz or the town closest to the attraction you wish to visit.

There are scores of outfits offering trekking, mountain-climbing and rainforest adventure packages. For climbing in the Cordilleras, operators offer customized expeditions including guides, transport, porters, cooks and equipment. Some also rent trekking equipment. See p178 for recommended agencies.

TRAVELERS WITH DISABILITIES

The sad fact is that Bolivia's infrastructure is ill-equipped for disabled travelers. You will, however, see locals overcoming all manner of challenges and obstacles while making their daily rounds. If you encounter difficulties yourself, you're likely to find locals willing to go out of their way to lend a hand.

VISAS

Passports must be valid for one year beyond the date of entry. Entry or exit stamps are free. Attempts at charging should be met with polite refusal; ask for a receipt if the issue is pressed. Always carry a photocopy of your passport (and visa), and if possible, store your valuables safely elsewhere when not in transit.

Bolivian visa requirements can be arbitrarily interpreted. Each Bolivian consulate and border crossing may have its own entry requirements, procedures and idiosyncrasies.

Citizens of most South American and western European countries can get a tourist card on entry for stays up to 90 days. US citizens now need a tourist visa to enter Bolivia. At the time of writing, it was possible to obtain the visa (US$135, valid for five years) upon arrival to Bolivia; check with the **Bolivian embassy** (☎ 202-483-4410; www.bolivia-usa.org; 3014 Massachusetts Ave NW, Washington, DC) before traveling. Citizens of Canada, Australia, New Zealand, Japan and many other countries are usually granted 30

days. This is subject to change; always check with your consulate prior to entry. If you want to stay longer, you have to extend your tourist card (easily accomplished at the immigration office in any major city; it's free for some nationalities and costs B$198 per extension for others). The maximum time travelers are permitted to stay in the country is 180 days in one year.

Overstayers can be fined B$14 per day (or more, depending on the nationality) – which is payable at the migration office or airport – and may face ribbons of red tape at the border or airport when leaving the country.

More about up-to-date visa information can be found online at lonelyplanet.com.

VOLUNTEERING

Volunteer organizations in Bolivia include:
Parque Machía (☎ 4-413-6572; www.intiwarayassi .org; Parque Machía, Villa Tunari, Chapare) Volunteer-run wild animal refuge; minimum commitment is 15 days and no previous experience working with animals is required.
Sustainable Bolivia (☎ 4-423-3786; www.sustaina blebolivia.org; Julio Arauco Prado 230, Cochabamba) Non-profit with a variety of short- and long-term volunteering programs in Bolivia through 22 local organizations.
Volunteer Bolivia (Map pp214-15; ☎ 4-452-6028; www.volunteerbolivia.org; Ecuador 0342, Cochabamba) Arranges short- and long-term volunteer work, study and homestay programs throughout Bolivia.

WOMEN TRAVELERS

Women's rights in Bolivia are nearing modern standards. That said, avoid testing the system alone in a bar in a miniskirt. Conservative dress and confidence without arrogance are a must for foreign women. Men are generally more forward and flirtatious in the lowlands than in the *altiplano*.

WORKING

There are many voluntary and nongovernmental organizations working in Bolivia, but travelers looking for paid work shouldn't hold their breath. Qualified English teachers can try **Centro Boliviano-Americano** (CBA; ☎ 243-0107; www .cba.edu.bo; Parque Zenón Iturralde 121) in La Paz; there are also offices in other cities. New, unqualified teachers must forfeit two months' salary in return for their training. Better paying are private school positions teaching math, science or social studies. Accredited teachers can expect to earn up to US$500 per month for a full-time position.

Brazil

HIGHLIGHTS

- **Rio de Janeiro** (p258) Succumb to the fever of the *cidade maravilhosa* (marvelous city): wild samba clubs, sizzling sands, soaring peaks and sexy sundowns.
- **Salvador** (p317) Revel in the distinctive smells, addictive percussion and thriving Afro-Brazilian culture of the beachside capital of Bahia.
- **Ouro Prêto** (p290) Meander along history-oozing cobblestones and over hillsides topped with stunning baroque churches in one of South America's dramatic colonial towns.
- **Pantanal** (p311) Commune with caimans in the Americas' largest wetland, where toucans and macaws fill the skies and jaguars prowl behind the scenes.
- **Off the Beaten Track** (p367) Head deep inland to Acre's riverfront capital Rio Branco, a launchpad for visiting the house of martyred environmentalist Chico Mendes.
- **Best Journey** (see boxed text, p350) Hug the coast through buttock-bruising potholes and spectacular dunes on a 4WD truck between Tutóia and Parque Nacional dos Lençóis Maranhenses.

FAST FACTS

- **Area:** 8,456,510 sq km (about the size of the continental United States)
- **Budget:** US$45 to US$50 a day
- **Capital:** Brasília
- **Costs:** double room in a comfy *pousada* (hotel) US$40 to US$60, per-kilo lunch US$6 to US$8, bus ride from Rio to Ouro Prêto US$48
- **Country Code:** ☎ 55
- **Languages:** Portuguese and 180 indigenous languages
- **Money:** US$1 = R$1.76 (*reais* or reales)
- **Population:** 199 million
- **Seasons:** high (December to Carnaval, July to August), low (April to May)
- **Time:** GMT minus three to five hours, depending on the region

TRAVEL HINT

There's no heartier cheap meal than those offered at Brazil's ubiquitous per-kilo restaurants.

OVERLAND ROUTES

Brazil's many border crossings include Oiapoque (French Guiana); Bonfim (Guyana); Boa Vista (Venezuela); Tabatinga (Colombia and Peru); Brasiléia, Guajará-Mirim, Cáceres and Corumbá (Bolivia); Ponta Porã (Paraguay); Foz do Iguaçu (Paraguay and Argentina) and Chuí (Uruguay).

Brazil is a tale of contrasts – a fairy tale for some, the tail end of a hard-knock life for others; but its cerulean shores and pristine beaches, its enchanting colonial towns and rugged natural landscapes, its pristine rainforests and dense jungles have all enthralled visitors for centuries, despite often being lost on many of its own socially ill-fated inhabitants. Brazil offers much to the visitor: count 7500km of powdery white-sand beaches giving way to deep blue Atlantic waters; visit stuck-in-time colonial towns, music-filled metropolises and idyllic tropical islands; see majestic waterfalls, crystal-clear rivers, rugged mountains, red-rock canyons and unspoiled jungle. It's all here in dramatic abundance.

Opportunities for adventures are endless (kayaking, rafting, trekking, snorkeling and surfing are just a few ways to spend a sun-drenched afternoon in nearly any region in Brazil), as are prospects for doing little beyond digging your toes into warm sands and sucking down a parade of *caipirinhas*, Brazil's national cocktail.

Though Brazil's most famous celebration, Carnaval, storms though the country's cities and towns like a best-of Blitzkrieg of hip-shaking samba, dazzling costume and carefree lust for life, the Brazilians hardly regulate their passion for revelry to a few weeks of the year – this is, after all, a country where, 'Have a good beach!' is not only something uttered regularly but also practically part of the national anthem! Spend a little time here and the Brazilian Way – *O Jeito Brasileiro* – will seize you in its sensational clutches.

CURRENT EVENTS

After Brazil paid off its debts to the UN and the IMF *ahead* of schedule in 2006, fat pockets abound for a blossoming middle class. But the prosperous news didn't end there for the World Bank's eighth-largest economy – a massive underwater oil field was discovered by Brazil's state-owned Petrobras off the coast in 2007, potentially catapulting the country overnight into one of the world's largest oil exporters. Just two years after becoming both energy independent and the largest consumer of plant-based biofuels in the world – a long-harnessed dream dating back to the 1970s – suddenly Brazil had won an audience among the world's oil mafia.

Despite weathering the recent economic recession better than other developing nations, Brazil's two biggest nemeses remain: the economic disparity between rich and poor still lingers nationwide; and violent crime still dominates the headlines (though actual statistics put Brazil's crime rate on par with that of the US and Japan). Elsewhere, an aviation crisis broke out in 2007 after two high profile crashes just 10 months apart put Brazil's airline infrastructure issues front and center. The country's defense minister, in charge of civil aviation, was fired.

Though Brazil's national soccer team has stumbled short of expectations in the last few years, their Confederations Cup triumph in 2009 could prove a prelude to redemption: Brazil was announced as the host nation for the 2014 FIFA World Cup. If they don't win, heads will roll. But the world spotlight won't stop there: Rio de Janeiro will host the 2016 Olympic Games just two years later.

HISTORY

The Tribal Peoples

Little is known of Brazil's first inhabitants, but from the few fragments left behind (mostly pottery, trash mounds and skeletons), archeologists estimate that the first humans may have arrived 50,000 years ago, predating any other estimates in the whole American continent.

The population at the time of the Portuguese landing in 1500 is also a mystery, and estimates range from two to six million. There were likely over 1000 tribes living as nomadic hunter-gatherers or in more settled, agricultural societies. Life was punctuated by frequent tribal warfare and at times, captured enemies were ceremonially killed and eaten after battle.

When the Portuguese first arrived, they had little interest in the natives, who were viewed as a Stone Age people; and the heavily forested land offered nothing for the European market. All that changed when Portuguese merchants expressed interest in the red dye from brazilwood (which later gave the colony its name), and slowly colonists arrived to harvest the land.

The natural choice for the work, of course, was the indigenous people. Initially the natives welcomed the strange, smelly foreigners and offered them their labor, their food and their women in exchange for the awe-inspiring metal tools and the fascinating Portuguese liquor. But soon the newcomers abused their customs, took their best land and ultimately enslaved them.

The indigenous people fought back and won many battles, but the tides were against them. When colonists discovered that sugar-cane grew well in the colony, the natives' labor was more valuable than ever and soon the sale of local slaves became Brazil's second-largest commercial enterprise. It was an industry dominated by *bandeirantes*, brutal men who hunted the indigenous people in the interior and captured or killed them. Their exploits, more than any treaty, secured the huge interior of South America for Portuguese Brazil.

Jesuit priests went to great lengths to protect the indigenous community. But they were too weak to stymie the attacks (and the Jesuits were later expelled from Brazil in 1759). Natives who didn't die at the hands of the colonists often died from introduced European diseases.

The Africans

During the 17th century African slaves replaced indigenous prisoners on the plantations. From 1550 until 1888 about 3.5 million slaves were shipped to Brazil – almost 40% of the total that came to the New World. The Africans were considered better workers and were less vulnerable to European diseases, but they resisted slavery strongly. *Quilombos,* communities of runaway slaves, formed throughout the colonial period. They ranged from *mocambos,* small groups hidden in the forests, to the great republic of Palmares, which survived much of the 17th century. Led by the African king Zumbí, Palmares had 20,000 residents at its height.

More than 700 villages that formed as *quilombos* remain in Brazil today, their growth only stopped by abolition itself (1888).

Survivors on the plantation sought solace in their African religion and culture through song and dance. The slaves were given perfunctory instruction in Catholicism and a syncretic religion rapidly emerged (see p251). Spiritual elements from many African tribes, such as the Yorubá, were preserved and made palatable to slave masters by adopting a facade of Catholic saints. Such were the roots of modern Candomblé and Macumba, prohibited by law until recently.

Life on the plantations was miserable, but an even worse fate awaited many slaves. In the 1690s gold was discovered in present day Minas Gerais, and soon the rush was on. Wild boomtowns like Vila Rica de Ouro Prêto (Rich Town of Black Gold) sprang up in the mountain valleys. Immigrants flooded the territory, and countless slaves were brought from Africa to dig and die in Minas.

The Portuguese

For years, the ruling powers of Portugal viewed the colony of Brazil as little more than a moneymaking enterprise. That attitude changed, however, when Napoleon marched on Lisbon in 1807. The prince regent (later known as Dom João VI) immediately transferred his court to Brazil. He stayed on even after Napoleon's Waterloo in 1815, and when he became king in 1816 he declared Rio de Janeiro the capital of a united kingdom of Brazil and Portugal, making Brazil the only New World colony to serve as the seat of a European monarch. In 1821, Dom João finally returned to Portugal, leaving his son Pedro in Brazil as regent.

The following year the Portuguese parliament attempted to return Brazil to colonial status. According to legend Pedro responded by pulling out his sword and shouting out *'Independência ou morte!'* (Independence or death!), crowning himself Emperor Dom Pedro I. Portugal was too weak to fight its favorite colony, so Brazil won independence without bloodshed.

Dom Pedro I ruled for nine years. He scandalized the country by siring a string of illegitimate children, and was finally forced to abdicate in favor of his five-year-old son, Dom Pedro II. Until the future emperor reached adolescence, Brazil suffered a period of civil war. In 1840 Dom Pedro II ascended the throne with overwhelming public support. During his 50-year reign he nurtured an increasingly powerful parliamentary system, went to war with Paraguay, meddled in Argentine and Uruguayan affairs, encouraged mass immigration, abolished slavery and ultimately forged a state that would do away with the monarchy forever.

The Brazilians

During the 19th century coffee replaced sugar as Brazil's primary export, at one time supplying three-quarters of world demand. With mechanization and the building of Brazil's first railroads, profits soared and the coffee barons gained enormous influence.

In 1889 a coffee-backed military coup toppled the antiquated empire, sending the emperor into exile. The new Brazilian Republic adopted a constitution modeled on the USA's, and for nearly 40 years Brazil was governed by a series of military and civilian presidents through which the armed forces effectively ruled the country.

One of the first challenges to the new republic came from a small religious community in the Northeast. An itinerant holy man named Antônio Conselheiro had wandered for years through poverty-stricken backlands, prophesying the appearance of the Antichrist and the end of the world. He railed against the new government and in 1893 gathered his followers in the settlement of Canudos. Suspecting a plot to return Brazil to the Portuguese monarchy, the government attempted to subdue the rebels. It succeeded only on the fourth try, in the end killing every man, woman and child and burning the town to the ground.

Coffee remained king until the market collapsed during the global economic crisis of 1929. The weakened planters of São Paulo, who controlled the government, formed an opposition alliance with the support of nationalist military officers. When their presidential candidate, Getúlio Vargas, lost the 1930 elections, the military seized power and handed him the reins.

Vargas proved a gifted maneuverer, and dominated the political scene for 20 years. At times his regime was inspired by the Italian and Portuguese fascist states of Mussolini and Salazar: he banned political parties, imprisoned opponents and censored the press. He remained in and out of the political scene until 1954, when the military called for him to step down. Vargas responded by writing a letter to the people of Brazil, then shooting himself in the heart.

Juscelino Kubitschek, the first of Brazil's big spenders, was elected president in 1956. His motto was '50 years' progress in five.' His critics responded with '40 years of inflation in four.' The critics were closer to the mark, owing to the huge debt Kubitschek incurred during the construction of Brasília. By the early 1960s, inflation gripped the Brazilian economy, and Castro's victory in Cuba had spread fears of communism. Brazil's fragile democracy was crushed in 1964 when the military overthrew the government.

Brazil stayed under the repressive military regime for almost 20 years. Throughout much of this time the economy grew substantially, at times borrowing heavily from international banks. But it exacted a heavy toll on the country. Ignored social problems grew dire. Millions came to the cities, and *favelas* (shantytowns) spread at exponential rates.

Recent Events

The last 20 years have been very good to Brazil. After its first democratically elected president in 30 years was removed from office on charges of corruption in 1992 – Fernando Collor de Mello was accused of heading a group that siphoned more than R$1 billion from the economy – a period of widespread economic growth has stabilized and blessed the South American workhorse.

Collor's replacement, Itamar Franco, introduced Brazil's present currency, the real, which sparked an economic boom that continues to this day, though it was his successor, former finance minister Fernando Henrique Cardoso, that presided through the mid-1990s over a growing economy and record foreign investment. He is often credited with laying the groundwork that put Brazil's hyperinflation to bed, though often at the neglect of social problems.

So it wasn't surprising that sooner or later a presidential candidate would campaign solely on a platform of social reform. In 2002 socialist Luíz da Silva ('Lula'), running for the fourth time, won the presidency. From a humble working-class background, Lula rose to become a trade unionist and a strike leader in the early 1980s. He later founded the Workers Party (PT), a magnet for his many followers seeking social reform.

His accession initially alarmed investors, who had envisioned a left-leaning renegade running the economy amok. In fact, he surprised friends and foes alike with one of the most financially prudent administrations in years, while still addressing Brazil's egregious social problems. Lula's antipoverty program of Fome Zero (Zero Hunger) collapsed under poor management, though its successor Bolsa Familia (Family Purse) did bring hardship relief to more than eight million people. Lula has made employment a top priority, and an estimated three million jobs were added under his watch. Lula also raised the minimum wage by 25%, which had an immediate impact on many working families.

Unfortunately, Lula's administration had some setbacks, including a wide-reaching corruption scandal in 2005 that saw a number of his PT party members resigning in disgrace, although the scandal never quite touched the president – his approval rating reached 90% at one point.

Lula's second term brought more economic prosperity as Brazil became a net foreign creditor (as opposed to debtor) for the first time in 2008 and the country weathered the economic recession at the end of the decade better than any other developing country. By 2020, São Paulo is expected to be the 13th richest city in the world. Despite all the good economic news, many among the middle class and intellectuals believe Lula is merely sailing on the glory of policies and successes originally initiated by his predecessor, Cardoso. As the next presidential election looms in 2010, Brazil's future looks brighter still, but as history has proved, administration change always keeps *brasileiros* guessing.

THE CULTURE
The National Psyche
Despite the country's social and economic woes, Brazilians take much pride in their country. The gorgeous landscape is a favorite topic, and although every Brazilian has a different notion of where to find paradise on earth, it will almost certainly be located within the country's borders. Soccer is another source of pride – less the national pastime than a countrywide narcotic to which every Brazilian seems to be addicted.

Famed for their Carnaval, Brazilians love to celebrate, and parties happen year-round. But it isn't all samba and beaches in the land of the tropics. At times, Brazilians suffer from *saudade,* a nostalgic, often deeply melancholic longing for something. The idea appears in many works by Jobim, Moraes and other great songwriters, and it manifests itself in many forms – from the dull ache of homesickness to the deep regret over past mistakes.

When Brazilians aren't dancing the samba or drowning in sorrow, they're often helping each other out. Kindness is both commonplace and expected, and even a casual introduction can lead to deeper friendships. This altruism comes in handy in a country noted for its bureaucracy and long lines.

There's the official way of doing things, then there's the *jeitinho,* or the little way around it, and a little kindness – and a few friends – can go a long way. One need only have patience, something Brazilians seem to have no shortage of.

Lifestyle
Although Brazil has the world's eighth-largest economy, with abundant resources and developed infrastructure, the living standard varies wildly. Brazil has one of the world's widest income gaps between rich and poor.

Since the mass urban migration in the mid-19th century, the poorest have lived in *favelas* that surround every city. Many dwellings consist of little more than a few boards pounded together, and access to clean water, sewage and healthcare are luxuries few *favelas* enjoy. Drug lords rule the streets and crime is rampant.

The rich often live just a stone's throw away, sometimes separated by nothing more than a highway. Many live in modern fortresses, with security walls and armed guards, enjoying a lifestyle similar to upper classes in Europe and America.

Population
In Brazil the diversity of the landscape matches that of the people inhabiting it. Officially 55% of the population is white, 6% black, 38% mixed and 1% other, but the numbers little represent the many shades and types of Brazil's rich melting pot. Indigenous people, Portuguese, Africans (brought to Brazil as slaves) and their mixed-blood offspring made up the population until the late 19th century. Since then there have been waves of immigration by Italians, Spaniards, Germans, Japanese, Russians, Lebanese and others.

SPORTS
Futebol (soccer) is a national passion. Most people acknowledge that Brazilians play the world's most creative, artistic and thrilling style of football (Brazil is the only country to have won five World Cups – 1958, 1962, 1970, 1994 and 2002), but the national team has bailed out on the early side of recent World Cups and Olympic Games. Folks in the street blame superstars like Ronaldo and Ronaldinho for being more worried about sponsorship deals and lavish lifestyles than playing as part of a team. That had better

BRAZIL

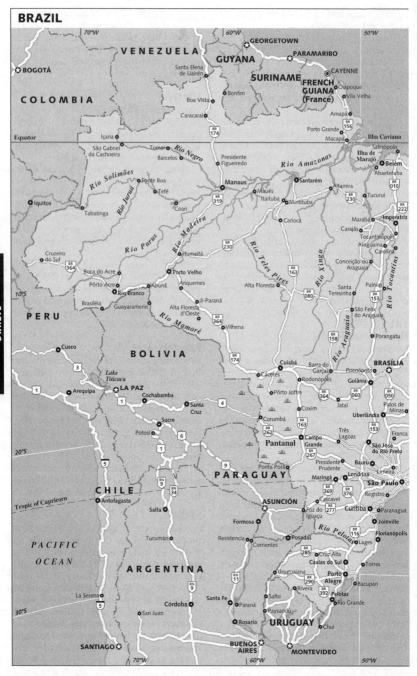

change, though, as the country is slated to host the 2014 World Cup, where pressure on the national team is sure to reach an all-time frenzy – the country couldn't possibly tolerate another World Cup championship loss on their home soil á la 1950.

Games are an intense spectacle – one of the most colorful pageants you're likely to see. Tickets typically cost between R$20 and R$30. The season goes on nearly all year, with the national championship running from late July to mid-December. Major clubs include Botafogo, Flamengo, Fluminense and Vasco da Gama (all of Rio de Janeiro); Corinthians, Palmeiras and São Paulo (all of São Paulo); Santos (of Santos), Bahia (of Salvador), Sport (of Recife) and Cruzeiro (of Belo Horizonte).

RELIGION

Brazil is the world's largest Catholic country, but it embraces diversity and syncretism. Without much difficulty you can find churchgoing Catholics who attend spiritualist gatherings or appeal for help at a *terreiro* (the house of an Afro-Brazilian religious group).

Brazil's principal religious roots comprise the animism of the indigenous people, Catholicism and African religions introduced by slaves. The latest arrival is evangelical Christianity, which is spreading all over Brazil, especially in poorer areas.

The Afro-Brazilian religions emerged when the colonists prohibited slaves from practicing their native religions. Not so easily deterred, the slaves simply gave Catholic names to their African gods and continued to worship them. The most orthodox of the religions is Candomblé. Rituals take place in the Yoruba language in a *casa de santo* or *terreiro*, directed by a *pai de santo* or *mãe de santo* (literally, 'a saint's father or mother' – the Candomblé priests).

Candomblé gods are known as *orixás* and each person is believed to be protected by one of them. In Bahia and Rio, followers of Afro-Brazilian cults turn out in huge numbers to attend festivals at the year's end – especially those held during the night of 31 December and on New Year's Day. Millions of Brazilians go to the beach at this time to pay homage to Iemanjá, the sea goddess, whose alter ego is the Virgin Mary.

ARTS

Brazilian culture has been shaped by the Portuguese, who gave the country its language and religion, and also by the indigenous population, immigrants and Africans.

The influence of the latter is particularly strong, especially in the Northeast where African religion, music and cuisine have all profoundly influenced Brazilian identity.

Literature

Joaquim Maria Machado de Assis (1839–1908), the son of a freed slave, is one of Brazil's early great writers. Assis had a great sense of humor and an insightful – though cynical – take on human affairs. His major novels were *Quincas Borba, The Posthumous Memoirs of Bras Cubas* and *Dom Casmurro.*

Jorge Amado (1912–2001), Brazil's most celebrated contemporary writer, wrote clever portraits of the people and places of Bahia, notably *Gabriela, Clove and Cinnamon* and *Dona Flor and her Two Husbands.*

Paulo Coelho is Latin America's second-most-read novelist (after Gabriel García Márquez). His new-age fables *The Alchemist* and *The Pilgrimage* launched his career in the mid-1990s.

Peter Robb's *A Death in Brazil* weaves attempted murder, politics, history and travel into a fascinating contemporary commentary on Brazil's national psyche.

Chico Buarque, better known for songwriting, has written several books. *Budapest,* his best and most recent novel, is an imaginative portrait of both his hometown of Rio de Janeiro and Budapest. Another famous Brazilian musician, Caetano Veloso, also penned an interesting memoir of music during Brazil's military dictatorship, *Tropical Truth: A Story of Music and Revolution in Brazil.*

Cinema

Brazil's large film industry has produced a number of good films over the years. One of the most recent hits is 2007's *Tropa do Elite (Elite Troop),* a gritty look at Rio's crime and corruption from the viewpoint of its most elite police force, BOPE (Special Police Operations Battalion).

The same director, José Padilha, initially garnered Brazilian cinema attention with 2002's *Ônibus 174 (Bus 174),* a shocking look at both the ineptness of the Brazilian police and the brutal reality of the country's socioeconomic disparities. It tells the story of a lone gunman who hijacked a Rio bus in 2000 and held passengers hostage for hours live on national TV. A dramatic version of the events, *Última Parada 174 (Last Stop 174),* surfaced in 2008.

One of Brazil's top directors, Fernando Meirelles, earned his credibility with *Cidade de Deus (City of God),* which showed the brutality of a Rio *favela.* Following his success with *Cidade de Deus,* Meirelles went Hollywood with *Constant Gardener* (2004), an intriguing conspiracy film shot in Africa; and the more recent thriller *Blindness* (2008), partly filmed in São Paulo.

Walter Salles, one of Brazil's best-known directors, won much acclaim (and an Oscar) for *Central do Brasil (Central Station;* 1998), the story of a lonely woman accompanying a young homeless boy in search of his father.

For a taste of the dictatorship days see Bruno Barreto's *O Que É Isso Companheiro* (released as *Four Days in September* in the US, 1998), based on the 1969 kidnapping of the US ambassador to Brazil by leftist guerrillas.

Another milestone in Brazilian cinema is the visceral film *Pixote* (1981), which shows life through the eyes of a street kid in Rio. When it was released, it became a damning indictment of Brazilian society.

Music & Dance

Samba, a Brazilian institution, has strong African influences and is intimately linked to Carnaval. The most popular form of samba today is *pagode,* a relaxed, informal genre whose leading exponents include singers Beth Carvalho, Jorge Aragão and Zeca Pagodinho.

Bossa nova, another Brazilian trademark, arose in the 1950s, and gained the world's attention in the classic *The Girl from Ipanema,* composed by Antônio Carlos Jobim and Vinícius de Moraes. Bossa nova's founding father, guitarist João Gilberto, still performs, as does his daughter Bebel Gilberto who has sparked renewed interest in the genre, combining smooth bossa sounds with electronic grooves.

Tropicalismo, which burst onto the scene in the late 1960s, mixed varied Brazilian musical styles with North American rock and pop. Leading figures such as Gilberto Gil and Caetano Veloso are still very much around. Gil, in fact, was Brazil's Minister of Culture from 2003 to 2008.

The nebulous term Música Popular Brasileira (MPB) covers a range of styles from original bossa nova–influenced works to some sickly pop. MPB first emerged in the 1970s under talented musicians like Edu Lobo, Milton Nascimento, Elis Regina, Djavan and dozens of others.

The list of emerging talents gets longer each day, but Brazilian hip-hop is reaching its stride with talented musicians like Marcelo D2 (formerly of Planet Hemp) impressing audiences with albums like *A Procura da Batida Perfeita* (2005). Actor/musician Seu Jorge, who starred in *Cidade de Deus*, has also earned accolades for the release of *Cru* (2005), an inventive hip-hop album with politically charged beats. His follow-up, *America Brasil O Disco* (2008), was also well received.

Brazilian rock (pronounced 'hock-ey') is also popular. Groups and artists such as Zeca Baleiro, Kid Abelha, Jota Quest, Ed Motta and the punk-driven Legião Urbana are worth a listen.

Wherever you go in Brazil you'll also hear regional musical styles. The most widely known is *forró* (foh-*hoh*), a lively, syncopated Northeastern music, which mixes *zabumba* (an African drum) beats with accordion sounds. *Axé* is a label for the samba-pop-rock-reggae-funk-Caribbean fusion music that emerged from Salvador in the 1990s, popularized especially by the flamboyant Daniela Mercury and now worshipped stadiums over by the sexy Ivete Sangalo. In the Amazon, you'll encounter the rhythms of *carimbo,* and the sensual dance that accompanies it.

Architecture

Brazil's most impressive colonial architecture dazzles visitors in cities like Salvador, Olinda, São Luís, Ouro Prêto, and Tiradentes. Over the centuries, the names of two architects stand out: Aleijadinho, the genius of 18th-century baroque in Minas Gerais mining towns and Oscar Niemeyer, the 20th-century modernist-functionalist who was chief architect for the new capital, Brasília, in the 1950s and designed many other striking buildings around the country.

ENVIRONMENT

Sadly, Brazil is as renowned for its forests as it is for destroying them. At last count more than one-fifth of the Brazilian Amazon rainforest had been completely destroyed. All its major ecosystems are threatened and more than 70 mammals are endangered.

Though rapid deforestation in the Amazon slowed after a swath of jungle the size of Greece was cleared between 2000 and 2006, 2008 proved a disturbing year: on top of the 12,000 sq km that were razed, an additional 25,000 sq km were lost to fires and logging, according to Brazil's National Institute of Space Research. Recent surges in commodities (driven by China) and a sharp rise in worldwide biofuels interest, along with the passing of a controversial road-paving law that gives the go ahead to the long-fought paving of the 765km BR-319 between Manaus and Porto Velho, insure the Amazon remains a threatened environment.

Brazil first began chopping down the forest on a grand scale in the 1970s when the government cleared roads through the jungle in order to give drought-stricken northeasterners a chance to better their lives on newly created cropland of Amazonia. Along with the new arrivals came loggers and cattle ranchers, both of whom further cleared the forests. The few settlers that remained (most gave up and moved to the *favelas* of Amazonia's growing cities) widely employed slash-and-burn agriculture with devastating consequences.

The government continues development projects in the Amazon, although the protests have become more vocal in recent years. In 2005 a Roman Catholic Bishop went on a hunger strike to protest the government's R$2 billion plan to divert water from the Rio São Francisco to help big agricultural businesses. Though President Lula declared a temporary halt to the project that same year, election year concessions won over and plans went ahead. The army began initial work on the project in 2007 and despite continued protests and petitions, judicial cessation of the project remains elusive.

The Land

The world's fifth-largest country after Russia, Canada, China and the USA, Brazil borders every other South American country except Chile and Ecuador. Its 8.5 million sq km area covers almost half the continent.

Brazil has four primary geographic regions: the coastal band, the Planalto Brasileiro, the Amazon Basin and the Paraná-Paraguai Basin.

The narrow, 7400km-long coastal band lies between the Atlantic Ocean and the coastal mountain ranges. From the border with Uruguay to Bahia state, steep mountains often come right down to the coast. North of Bahia, the coastal lands are flatter.

The Planalto Brasileiro (Brazilian Plateau) extends over most of Brazil's interior south of the Amazon Basin. It's sliced by several large rivers and punctuated by mountain ranges reaching no more than 3000m.

The thinly populated Amazon Basin, composing 42% of Brazil, is fed by waters from the Planalto Brasileiro to its south, the Andes to the west and the Guyana shield to the north. In the west the basin is 1300km wide; in the east, between the Guyana shield and the *planalto* (plateau), it narrows to 100km. More than half the 6275km of the Rio Amazonas lies not in Brazil but in Peru, where the river's source is also found. The Amazon and its 1100 tributaries contain an estimated 20% of the world's freshwater. Pico da Neblina (3014m) on the Venezuelan border is the highest peak in Brazil.

The Paraná-Paraguai Basin, in the south of Brazil, extends into neighboring Paraguay and Argentina and includes the large wetland area known as the Pantanal.

Wildlife

Brazil has more known species of plants (55,000), freshwater fish (3000) and mammals (520 plus) than any other country in the world. It ranks third for birds (1622) and fifth for reptiles (468). Many species live in the Amazon rainforest, which occupies 3.6 million sq km in Brazil and 2.4 million sq km in neighboring countries. It's the world's largest tropical forest and most biologically diverse ecosystem, with 20% of the world's bird and plant species and 10% of its mammals.

Other Brazilian species are widely distributed around the country. For example the biggest Brazilian cat, the jaguar, is found in Amazon and Atlantic rainforests, the *cerrado* (savanna) and the Pantanal.

Many other Brazilian mammals are found over a broad range of habitats, including five other big cats (puma, ocelot, margay, oncilla and jaguarundi); the giant anteater; 75 primate species, including several types of howler and capuchin monkey, the squirrel monkey (Amazonia's most common primate) and around 20 small species of marmosets and tamarin; the furry, long-nosed coati (a type of raccoon); the giant river otter; the maned wolf; the tapir; peccaries (like wild boar); marsh and pampas deer; the capybara (the world's largest rodent at 1m in length); the pink dolphin, often glimpsed in the Amazon and its tributaries; and the Amazon manatee, an even larger river dweller.

Birds form a major proportion of the wildlife you'll see. The biggest is the flightless, 1.4m-high rhea, found in the *cerrado* (savanna) and Pantanal. The brilliantly colored parrots, macaws, toucans and trogons come in dozens of species. In Amazonia or the Pantanal you may well see scarlet macaws and, if you're lucky, blue-and-yellow ones. Unfortunately, the macaws' beautiful plumage makes them a major target for poachers.

In Amazonia or the Pantanal you can't miss the alligators. One of Brazil's five species, the black caiman, grows up to 6m long. Other aquatic life in the Amazon includes the *pirarucú*, which grows 3m long. Its red and silvery-brown scale patterns are reminiscent of Chinese paintings. The infamous piranha comes in about 50 species, found in the river basins of Amazon, Orinoco, Paraguai or São Francisco or rivers of the Guianas. Only a handful of species pose a risk, and confirmed accounts of human fatalities caused by piranhas are *extremely* rare.

National Parks

Over 350 areas are protected as national parks, state parks or extractive reserves. Good parks for observing fauna, flora and/or dramatic landscapes:

Parque Nacional da Chapada Diamantina (p324)
Rivers, waterfalls, caves and swimming holes make for excellent trekking in this mountainous region in the Northeast.

Parque Nacional da Chapada dos Guimarães (p314)
On a rocky plateau northeast of Cuiabá, this canyon park features breathtaking views and impressive rock formations.

Parque Nacional da Chapada dos Veadeiros (p310)
200km north of Brasília, among waterfalls and natural swimming holes, this hilly national park features an array of rare flora and fauna.

Parque Nacional da Serra dos Órgãos (p277) Set in the mountainous terrain of the Southeast, this park is a mecca for rock climbers and mountaineers.

Parque Nacional de Aparados da Serra (p302) Famous for its narrow canyon with 700m escarpments, this park in the Southeast features hiking trails with excellent overlooks.

Parque Nacional dos Lençóis Maranhenses (p350) Spectacular beaches, mangroves, dunes and lagoons comprise the landscape of this park in the Northeast.

Parque Nacional Marinho de Fernando de Noronha (see boxed text, p338) Pristine beaches, cerulean waters, world-class diving and snorkeling and one of the world's best spots to view Spinner Dolphins highlight Brazil's island Eden.

TRANSPORTATION

GETTING THERE & AWAY

Brazil has several gateway airports and shares a border with every country in South America except Chile and Ecuador.

Air

The busiest international airports are Aeroporto Galeão (formally known as Aeroporto Internacional António Carlos Jobim) in Rio de Janeiro (p258) and São Paulo's Aeroporto Guarulhos (p282). Brazil's flag-carrying airline, **Varig**, was bought out by discount airline **Gol Airlines** (www.voegol.com .br) after filing for bankruptcy in 2005 and a complete phase-out of the former was slowly ongoing at the time of writing. **TAM** (www.tam .com.br) is the other major carrier.

ARGENTINA

Round-trip flights from Buenos Aires to Rio or São Paulo are available on Varig/Gol, TAM, British Airways or Aerolíneas Argentinas. Other flights from Buenos Aires go to Porto Alegre, Curitiba, Florianópolis and Puerto Iguazú in Argentina, a short cross-border hop from Foz do Iguaçu.

BOLIVIA

Varig/Gol flies from Santa Cruz to Campo Grande (and onto São Paulo). Inside Bolivia,

---

DEPARTURE TAX

The departure tax for Brazil is included in the price of the ticket.

Aerosur and Aerocon fly from other Bolivian cities to Cobija, Guayaramerin and Puerto Suárez, across the border from the Brazilian towns of Brasiléia, Guajará-Mirim and Corumbá respectively.

CHILE

Varig/Gol, TAM and LANChile fly from Santiago to Rio and São Paulo.

COLOMBIA

Aero República and Satena fly from Bogotá to Leticia, from where you can walk, taxi or take a *combi* (minibus) across the border into Tabatinga, Brazil. Avianca and Varig/Gol fly direct from Bogotá to São Paulo. Flights to Rio usually stop in São Paulo as well.

ECUADOR

There are no direct flights between Quito or Guayaquil and Brazil. Taca and LAN tend to run the best deals to Rio or São Paulo, usually via Lima.

THE GUIANAS

Meta, a Brazilian regional airline, flies from Georgetown (Guyana), Paramaribo (Suriname) and Cayenne (French Guiana) to Belém and Boa Vista. French Guiana carrier Air Caraïbes also flies between Belém and Cayenne. Puma, a Brazilian carrier, flies from Macapá to Oiapoque, just across the border from St Georges, French Guiana.

PARAGUAY

TAM flies direct between Asunción and Rio or São Paulo. Varig/Gol flies from Asunción to Curitiba. You can also fly from Asunción to Ciudad del Este, a short cross-border hop from Foz do Iguaçu, Brazil.

PERU

TAM, LAN, Taca and Varig/Gol fly from Lima to Rio or São Paulo.

URUGUAY

TAM, Varig/Gol and Pluna fly direct from Montevideo to São Paulo. Pluna also flies direct to Rio. Varig/Gol also flies direct from Montevideo to Porto Alegre.

VENEZUELA

TAM and Varig/Gol fly direct from Caracas to São Paulo and Rio as well as via Manaus.

BRAZIL

Boat

From Trinidad in Bolivia, boats take about five days to sail down the Río Mamoré to Guayaramerín (Bolivia), opposite Guajará-Mirim (Brazil).

From Peru fast passenger boats make the 400km trip along the Rio Amazonas between Iquitos (Peru) and Tabatinga (Brazil) in eight to 10 hours. From Tabatinga you can continue to Manaus and Belém.

Bus

ARGENTINA

The main border crossing used by travelers is Puerto Iguazú–Foz do Iguaçu, a 20-hour bus ride from Buenos Aires. Further south, you can cross between Uruguaiana (Brazil) and Paso de los Libres (Argentina), which is also served by buses from Buenos Aires. Other crossings are at San Javier-Porto Xavier and Santo Tomé–São Borja on the Rio Uruguai.

Direct buses run between Buenos Aires and Porto Alegre (R$195, 18 hours) and Rio de Janeiro (R$325, 42 hours). Other destinations include Florianópolis (R$216, 25 hours), Curitiba (R$230, 34 hours) and São Paulo (R$285, 36 hours).

BOLIVIA

Brazil's longest border runs through remote wetlands and forests, and is much used by smugglers.

The busiest crossing is between Quijarro (Bolivia) and Corumbá (Brazil), which is a good access point for the Pantanal. Quijarro has a daily train link with Santa Cruz, Bolivia. Corumbá has bus connections with Bonito, Campo Grande, São Paulo, Rio de Janeiro and southern Brazil.

Cáceres, in Mato Grosso (Brazil) has a daily bus link with Santa Cruz (Bolivia) via the Bolivian border town of San Matías.

Guajará-Mirim (Brazil) is a short river crossing from Guayaramerín (Bolivia). Both towns have bus links into their respective countries, but from late December to late February rains can make the northern Bolivian roads very difficult.

Brasiléia (Brazil), a 4½-hour bus ride from Rio Branco, stands opposite Cobija (Bolivia), which has bus connections into Bolivia. This route is less direct than the Guayaramerín–Guajará-Mirim option, and Bolivian buses confront the same wet-season difficulties.

CHILE

Although there is no border with Chile, direct buses run between Santiago and Brazilian cities, such as Porto Alegre (R$312, 36 hours), Curitiba (R$312, 54 hours), São Paulo (R$330, 54 hours) and Rio de Janeiro (R$362, 62 hours).

COLOMBIA

Leticia, on the Rio Amazonas in far southeast Colombia, is contiguous with Tabatinga (Brazil). You can cross the border on foot, by *combi* or taxi, but river and air are the only ways out of either town.

FRENCH GUIANA

The Brazilian town of Oiapoque, a rugged 560km bus ride (or a quick flight) from Macapá, stands across the Rio Oiapoque from St Georges (French Guiana). A road connects St Georges to the French Guiana capital, Cayenne, with minibuses shuttling between the two. (Get there early in the morning to catch one.) Another option is to fly directly from Belém to Cayenne, which if booked early enough can often be cheaper than ground transportation (see p255).

GUYANA

Lethem (southwest Guyana) is a short boat ride from Bonfim (Roraima, Brazil), a two-hour bus ride from Boa Vista.

PARAGUAY

The two major border crossings are Ciudad del Este–Foz do Iguaçu and Pedro Juan Caballero–Ponta Porã. The latter gives access to the Pantanal. Direct buses run between Asunción and Brazilian cities such as Florianópolis (R$158, 22 hours), Curitiba (R$108, 14 hours), São Paulo (R$145, 20 hours) and Rio de Janeiro (R$201, 26 hours).

PERU

The only land access to Peru is via Iñapari, a five-hour *combi* or truck ride north of Puerto Maldonado (Peru). This route is only open during the dry season. You wade across the Rio Acre between Iñapari and the small Brazilian town of Assis Brasil, a three- to four-hour bus or 4WD trip from Brasiléia.

SURINAME

Overland travel between Suriname and Brazil involves first passing through either French Guiana or Guyana.

URUGUAY

The crossing most used by travelers is at Chuy (Uruguay)–Chuí (Brazil). Other crossings are Río Branco–Jaguarão, Isidoro Noblia–Aceguá, Rivera–Santana do Livramento, Artigas–Quaraí and Bella Unión–Barra do Quaraí. Buses run between Montevideo and Brazilian cities such as Porto Alegre (R$150, 12 hours), Florianópolis (R$209, 18 hours) and São Paulo (R$285, 30 hours).

VENEZUELA

Four daily buses run to Boa Vista (R$90 to R$110, 12 hours) from Manaus. A direct daily bus to Caracas (R$250, 36 hours) stops in Santa Elena de Uairén and Puerto La Cruz.

GETTING AROUND
Air
DOMESTIC AIR SERVICES

Brazil's major national carriers are TAM and Varig/Gol. Upstart low-cost carrier **Azul** (☎ 0800-702-1053; www.voeazul.com.br), owned by JetBlue, began operating in late 2008 out of Campinas, 100km northwest of São Paulo, to Curitiba, Fortaleza, Manaus, Recife, Rio de Janeiro, Salvador, Porto Alegre and Victória. A free shuttle to Campinas' Viracopos airport runs from Barra Funda metro station in São Paulo.

Airline tickets can be purchased at any travel agent. Supposedly, both Varig/Gol and TAM now accept all major foreign credit cards through their websites (though it didn't work for us) – otherwise you'll have to pay in cash at a travel agency.

Overall, Brazilian airlines operate efficiently, but delays are common. National telephone numbers for reservations and confirmations:

OceanAir (☎ 0300-789-8160; www.oceanair.com.br)
TAM (☎ 0800-570-5700; www.tam.com.br)
Trip (☎ 0300-789-8747; www.voetrip.com.br)
Varig/Gol (☎ 0300-115-2121; www.voegol.com.br)

In order to secure a seat, book as far ahead as possible during busy seasons (Christmas to Carnaval, Holy Week and Easter, July and August). At other times, you can buy tickets for same-day flights, with no added cost.

AIR PASSES

If you're combining travels in Brazil with other countries in South America, it's worth looking into the TAM South America Airpass, which allows for travel of up to 8200 miles between Argentina, Bolivia, Brazil, Chile, Paraguay, Peru, Uruguay and Venezuela. High-season prices start at US$402 and vary depending on distance. Other South America passes include the Mercosur Airpass (see p1005) and LAN.

For flights solely within Brazil, the TAM Brazil Airpass offers travelers up to nine domestic legs and is sold in increments of four starting at US$551. This can be an excellent investment, but shop around as Brazil's low-cost carriers often offer unbelievably low fares during seasonal blowout sales.

Consult respective websites for additional rules and regulations.

Boat

The Amazon region is one of the world's last great bastions of river travel. The Rio Negro, the Rio Solomões and the Rio Madeira are the highways of Amazonia, and you can travel thousands of kilometers along these waterways (which combine to form the mighty Rio Amazonas), exploring the vast Amazon Basin traveling to or from Peru or Bolivia. Travel may be slow and dull along the river (with distances measured in days rather than kilometers), but it is cheap.

For more information see also the boxed text, p351.

Bus

Buses are the backbone of long-distance transportation in Brazil and are generally reliable, frequent and comfortable. Unfortunately, you pay for the privilege – bus ticket prices in Brazil are among the highest in South America. **Itapemirim** (www.itapemirim.com.br) and **Cometa** (www.viacaocometa.com.br) are two of the best. If you can navigate the Portuguese, you can consult the **ANTT** (www.antt.gov.br) website, Brazil's ground transportation authority, for a national database of bus schedules.

There are three main classes of long-distance buses. The cheapest, *convencional*, is fairly comfortable with reclining seats and usually a toilet and sometimes air-con. The *executivo* provides roomier seats, costs about 25% more and makes fewer stops. The more luxurious *leitos* can cost twice as much as *comum* (taxi) and have spacious, fully reclining seats with pillows, air-conditioning and sometimes an attendant serving sandwiches

BRAZIL

and drinks. Overnight buses, regardless of the class, often make fewer stops.

Most cities have one central bus terminal (*rodoviária*, pronounced 'hoe-doe-vee-*ah*-rhee-ya'). Usually you can simply show up at the station and buy a ticket for the next bus out, but on weekends and holidays (particularly from December to February) it's a good idea to book ahead.

Car

Brazilian roads can be dangerous, especially busy highways such as the Rio to São Paulo corridor. There are tens of thousands of motor-vehicle fatalities every year. Driving at night is particularly hazardous because other drivers are more likely to be drunk and road hazards are less visible.

That said, driving can be a convenient if somewhat expensive way to get around Brazil. A small four-seat rental car costs around R$100 to R$120 a day with unlimited kilometers (R$140 to R$160 with air-con) and basic insurance. Ordinary gasoline costs around R$2.20 to R$2.50 a liter, ethanol (known as *álcool* and produced from sugarcane) about 50% less (most cars take both).

You should carry an International Driving Permit if you rent a vehicle.

Hitchhiking

Hitchhiking in Brazil, with the possible exception of the Pantanal and Fernando de Noronha, is difficult and likely unsafe. The Portuguese for 'lift' is *carona*.

Local Transport

BUS

Local bus services are frequent and cheap, with extensive routes. Many buses list their destinations in bold letters on the front, making it easier to identify the one you need. Drivers don't usually stop unless someone flags them.

Typically, you enter the bus at the front and exit from the rear. The price is displayed near the money collector, who sits at a turnstile and provides change for the fare (usually between R$2 and R$2.50). You'll have difficulty getting a bulky backpack through the narrow turnstile. Avoid riding the bus after 11pm and at peak (read packed) times: noon to 2pm and 4pm to 6pm in most areas, and keep a watchful eye for pickpockets and thieves.

TAXI

City taxis aren't cheap, though they are quite useful for avoiding potentially dangerous walks and late-night bus rides, or if your baggage is too bulky for public transport. Most meters start around R$4.30 and rise by R$1.20 or so per kilometer (prices increase at night and on Sunday). Make sure the driver turns on the meter when you get in. In some small towns, prices are fixed and meters are nonexistent.

The worst place to get a cab is where the tourists are. Don't get one near one of the expensive hotels. One caveat, in Rio, where walking at night can be sketchy, don't be afraid of taxis. Unlike most Latin cities, taxis in Rio tend to be honest and trustworthy.

TRAIN

There are very few passenger trains in service. One remaining line well worth riding runs from Curitiba to Paranaguá, descending the coastal mountain range (p297).

RIO DE JANEIRO

☎ 0xx21 / pop 6.1 million

At once both a cinematic cityscape and a grimy urban front line, Rio de Janeiro, known as the *cidade maravilhosa* (marvelous city), is nothing if not exhilarating. Flanked by gorgeous mountains, white-sand beaches and verdant rainforests fronting deep blue sea, Rio occupies one of the most spectacular settings of any metropolis in the world. Tack on one of the sexiest populations on the planet and you have an intoxicating tropical cocktail that leaves visitors punch-drunk on paradise.

With the seductive sounds of samba as their rallying cry, Rio's residents, known as *cariocas,* have perfected the art of living well. From the world-famous beaches of Copacabana and Ipanema to the tops of scenic outlooks of Corcovado and Pão de Açúcar to the dance halls, bars and open-air cafes that proliferate the city, *cariocas* live for the moment without a care in the world. This idea of paradise has enchanted visitors for centuries, and there are dozens of ways to be seduced. You can surf great breaks off Prainha, hike through Tijuca's rainforests, sail across Guanabára, dance the night away in Lapa or just people-watch on Ipanema Beach.

While Rio has its share of serious problems, there are plenty of residents (expats included)

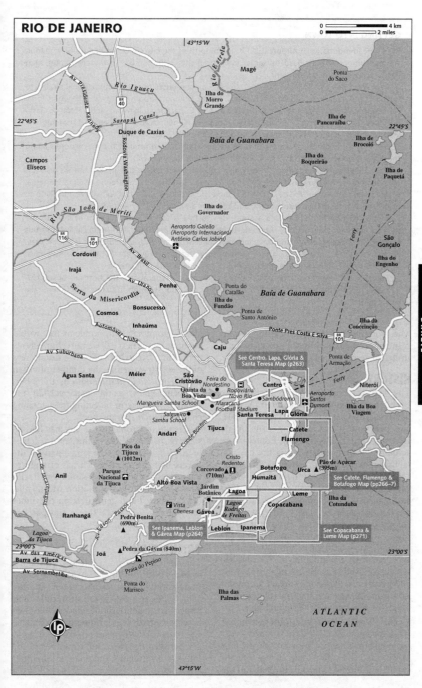

RIO DE JANEIRO

See Centro, Lapa, Glória & Santa Teresa Map (p263)

See Catete, Flamengo & Botafogo Map (pp266-7)

See Ipanema, Leblon & Gávea Map (p264)

See Copacabana & Leme Map (p271)

BRAZIL

GETTING INTO TOWN

Rio's Galeão International Airport (GIG) is 15km north of the city center on Ilha do Governador. Santos Dumont Airport, used by some domestic flights, is by the bay in the city center, 1km east of Cinelândia metro station.

Real Auto Bus (☎ 0800-240-850) operates safe air-con buses from the international airport to Novo Rio bus station, Av Rio Branco (Centro), Santos Dumont Airport, southward through Glória, Flamengo and Botafogo and along the beaches of Copacabana, Ipanema and Leblon to Barra da Tijuca (and vice versa). The buses (R$7) run every 30 minutes from 5:30am to 11pm and will stop wherever you ask. You can transfer to the metro at Carioca station.

Heading to the airports, you can catch the Real bus from in front of the major hotels along the main beaches, but you have to look alive and flag them down.

The safest course is a radio taxi for which you pay a set fare at the airport, but it's also the most expensive. A yellow-and-blue common *(comum)* taxi should cost around R$60 to Ipanema. A radio taxi costs about R$$80. From the domestic airport, a radio taxi runs R$37 and R$46 to Copacabana or Ipanema, respectively; and *comums* are around R$22 and R$28.

If you arrive in Rio by bus, it's a good idea to take a taxi to your hotel, or at least to the general area you want to stay. **Rodoviária Novo Rio** (☎ 3213-1800; Av Francisco Bicalho), the bus station, is in a seedy area – and traveling on local buses with all your belongings is a little risky. A small booth near the ATMs on the 1st floor organizes the yellow cabs out front. Sample fares are R$45 to the international airport and R$21 to Copacabana or Ipanema.

Local buses leave from stops outside the station. For Copacabana, the best are buses 127, 128 and 136; for Ipanema, buses 128 and 172. For the budget hotels in Catete and Glória, take bus 136 or 172.

---

who wouldn't dream of relocating. It's no coincidence Christo himself sits arms outstretched across the city, either.

HISTORY

The city earned its name from early Portuguese explorers, who entered the huge bay (Baía de Guanabara) in January 1502, and believing it a river, named it Rio de Janeiro (January River). The French were actually the first settlers along the bay, establishing the colony of Antarctic France in 1555. The Portuguese, fearing that the French would take over, gave them the boot in 1567 and remained from then on. Thanks to sugar plantations and the slave trade their new colony developed into an important settlement and grew substantially during the Minas Gerais gold rush of the 18th century. In 1763, with a population of 50,000, Rio replaced Salvador as the colonial capital. By 1900, after a coffee boom, heavy immigration from Europe and internal migration from ex-slaves, Rio had 800,000 inhabitants.

The 1920s to 1950s were Rio's golden age, when it became an exotic destination for international high society. Unfortunately the days of wine and roses didn't last. By the time the capital was moved to Brasília in 1960, Rio was already grappling with problems that would continue for the next half-century. Immigrants poured into *favelas* from poverty-stricken areas of the country, swelling the number of urban poor. The *cidade maravilhosa* by the 1990s was better known as the *cidade partida* (the divided city), a term reflecting the widening chasm between rich and poor.

Despite its problems the city has had its share of successes, hosting the Pan Am games in 2007. Rio was also the launchpad for the Favela-Bairro project, which has brought to the *favelas* better access to sanitation, health clinics and public transportation. Meanwhile, urban renewal and gentrification continues in Centro, Lapa, Santa Teresa and parts of the *zona sul*.

ORIENTATION

The city can be divided into two zones: the *zona norte* (north zone), consisting of industrial, working-class neighborhoods, and the *zona sul* (south zone), full of middle- and upper-class neighborhoods and well-known beaches. Centro, Rio's business district and the site of its first settlement, marks the boundary between the two, and a number of the important museums and colonial buildings are there.

The parts of Rio you are most likely to explore stretch along the shore of the Baía de Guanabara and the Atlantic Ocean. South from Centro are the neighborhoods of Lapa, Glória, Catete, Flamengo, Botafogo and Urca dominated by the peak of Pão de Açúcar (Sugar Loaf). Further south are Copacabana, Ipanema and Leblon.

Other areas of interest include the colonial hilltop neighborhood of Santa Teresa overlooking Centro, and the looming statue of Cristo Redentor (Christ the Redeemer), atop Corcovado.

Aside from the bus station, Maracanã football stadium and the international airport, most travelers have few reasons to visit the *zona norte*.

INFORMATION
Bookstores
Livraria Letras & Expressões (Map p264; Visconde de Pirajá 276, Ipanema) English-language newspapers and magazines, a good cafe and internet.
Nova Livraria Leonardo da Vinci (Map p263; Edifício Marquês de Herval; Av Rio Branco 185, Centro) Rio's largest bookstore.

Emergency
Tourist police (Map p264; ☎ 3399-7170; cnr Av Afrânio de Melo Franco & Humberto de Campos, Leblon; ☼ 24hr) Provides robbery reports for insurance companies.

Internet Access
Most youth hostels and hotels provide internet access.
Central Fone (Map p263; basement level, Av Rio Branco 156; per hr R$8.30) Also a good spot for international phone calls.
Cyber Point (Map p271; Av NS de Copacabana 445, Copacabana; per hr R$6)
Cybertur (Map p264; loja B, Vinícius de Moraes 129; per hr R$6.50)

DON'T MISS...

- sunsets on Ipanema
- samba clubs in Lapa
- the view from Pão de Açúcar
- a stroll through Santa Teresa
- the funicular ride to Cristo Redentor
- football madness at Maracanã

Euro Cyber Café (Map pp266-7; Correia Dutra 39B, Catete; per hr R$3)

Medical Services
Cardio Trauma Ipanema (Map p264; ☎ 2247-8403; Farme de Amoedo 88)
Hospital Ipanema (Map p264; ☎ 3111-2300; Antônio Parreiras 67, Ipanema)

Money
Be cautious when carrying money in the city center and take nothing of value to the beach. *Nothing*.

ATMs for most card networks are widely available but often fussy. Try Banco24Horas ATMs or Bradesco, Citibank and HSBC when using a debit or credit card. Don't even waste your time (or sanity) with Itaú, Unibanco or Caixa – they are Brazilian-only. The international airport has Banco do Brasil machines on the 3rd floor and currency-exchange booths on the **arrivals floor** (☼ 6:30am-11pm). ATMs cluster on the 1st floor near the main entrance of Rio's Novo Rio bus station.

Banco do Brasil Centro (Map p263; Senador Dantas 105); Copacabana (Map p271; Av NS de Copacabana 594); international airport (Map p259; Terminal 1, 3rd fl)
Citibank Botafogo (Map pp266-7; cnr Praia de Botafogo & Marqués Olinda); Centro (Map p263; Rua da Assembléia 100); Copacabana (Map p271; Av NS de Copacabana 828) Ipanema (Map p264; Visconde de Pirajá 459A) Leblon (Map p264; Visconde de Pirajá 1260A)
HSBC Centro (Map p263; Av Rio Branco 108) Leblon (Map p264; cnr Visconde de Pirajá & Rainha Guilhermina)

For exchanging cash, *casas de cambio* (exchange offices) cluster behind the Copacabana Palace Hotel in Copacabana and along Visconde da Pirajá near Praça General Osório in Ipanema. In Centro, exchange offices are on Av Rio Branco, just north of Av Presidente Vargas.
Bradesco Câmbio Exchange (Map p271; Av Atlântica 1702, Copacabana) Authorized AMEX exchange house.
Casa Aliança (Map p263; Miguel Couto 35B, Centro)
Casa Universal (Map p271; Av NS de Copacabana 371, Copacabana)

Post
Correios (post offices) are prevalent throughout Rio.
Central post office (Map p263; Primeiro de Março 64, Centro).
Post office Botafogo (Map pp266-7; Praia de Botafogo 324); Copacabana (Map p271; Av NS de Copacabana 540); Ipanema (Map p264; Prudente de Morais 147)

BRAZIL

Tourist Information

Alô Rio (☎ 0800-285-0555; ☯ 9am-6pm Mon-Fri) Toll-free, English-speaking assistance.

Riotur Centro (Map p263; ☎ 2271-7000; Praça Pio X 119; www.riodejaneiro-turismo.com.br; ☯ 9am-6pm Mon-Fri); bus station (off Map p263; Rodoviária Novo Rio; ☯ 7am-11pm); Copacabana (Map p271; Av Princesa Isabel 183; ☯ 9am-6pm Mon-Fri); international airport (Map p259; ☯ 6am-10pm) Very useful city tourism bureau.

DANGERS & ANNOYANCES

There's no sugarcoating it: Rio sees a devil's share of crime and violence, but much of the city's headline-grabbing ferocity rises from an ongoing urban war between police and drug traffickers, who control some *favelas* around the city. These situations, while extremely serious, don't often affect tourists. Security elsewhere in the city has seen improvements of late. There is a heavier police presence around high-traffic tourism areas, and installations of more CCTV cameras clustered around hotels in Copacabana have both contributed to less tourist crime. If you travel sensibly and follow a few precautions to minimize the risks, you will likely suffer nothing worse than a few bad hangovers.

Buses are well-known targets for thieves. Avoid taking them after dark, and keep an eye out while aboard. Take taxis at night to avoid walking along empty streets and beaches. That holds especially true for Centro, which you should avoid on weekends when it's deserted and dangerous.

The beaches are also targets for thieves. Don't take anything valuable to the beach, and always stay alert – especially during holidays (such as Carnaval) when the sands get fearfully crowded. The pickpockets are magicians here.

Take extra precautions when walking along streets that dead end or backup against *favelas*. This means the northern end of Farme de Amoedo in Ipanema and the northwest end of Djalma Ulrich in Copacabana.

Maracanã football stadium is worth a visit, but take only spending money for the day and avoid the crowded sections. Don't wander into the *favelas* unless going with a knowledgeable guide.

If you have the misfortune of being robbed, hand over the goods. Thieves are only too willing to use their weapons if given provocation. It's sensible to carry a fat wad of singles to hand over in case of a robbery.

See p370 for other tips on how to avoid becoming a victim.

SIGHTS

In addition to sand, sky and sea, Rio has dozens of other attractions: historic neighborhoods, colorful museums, colonial churches, picturesque gardens and some spectacular overlooks.

Ipanema & Leblon

Boasting a magnificent beach and pleasant tree-lined streets, Ipanema and Leblon (Map p264) are Rio's loveliest destinations and the favored residence for young, beautiful (and wealthy) *cariocas*. Microcultures dominate the beach: Posto 9, off Vinícius de Moraes, is the gathering spot for the beauty crowd; nearby, in front of Farme de Amoedo, is the gay section; Posto 11 in Leblon attracts families.

Arpoador, between Ipanema and Copacabana, is a popular surf spot. All along the beach the waves can get big, and the undertow is strong – swim only where the locals do.

Copacabana & Leme

The gorgeous curving beach of Copacabana (Map p271) stretches 4.5km from end to end, and pulses with an energy unknown elsewhere. Dozens of restaurants and bars line Av Atlântica, facing the sea, with tourists, prostitutes and *favela* kids all a part of the wild people-parade.

When you visit Copacabana, take only the essentials with you, and don't ever walk on the beach at night. Take care on weekends, when few locals are around.

Santa Teresa

Set on a hill overlooking the city, Santa Teresa (Map p263), with its cobbled streets and aging mansions, retains the charm of days past. Currently the residence of a new generation of artists and bohemians, Santa Teresa has colorful restaurants and bars and a lively weekend scene around Largo do Guimarães and Largo das Neves.

Museu Chácara do Céu (Map p263; Murtinho Nobre 93; admission R$2; ☯ noon-5pm Wed-Mon) is a delightful art and antiques museum in a former industrialist's mansion with beautiful gardens and great views.

Don't miss Rio's most famous staircase, the **Escadaria de Selarón**, a lengthy work in progress by an eccentric Chilean artist who,

CENTRO, LAPA, GLÓRIA & SANTA TERESA

0 ___ 400 m
0 ___ 0.2 miles

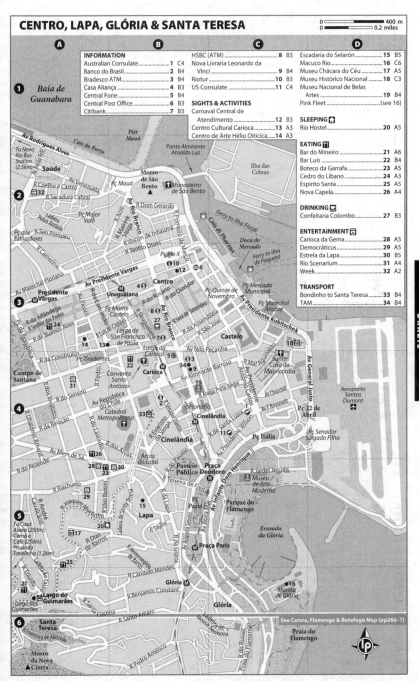

INFORMATION
Australian Consulate	**1**	C4
Banco do Brasil	**2**	B4
Bradesco ATM	**3**	B4
Casa Aliança	**4**	B3
Central Fone	**5**	B4
Central Post Office	**6**	B3
Citibank	**7**	B3
HSBC (ATM)	**8**	B3
Nova Livraria Leonardo da Vinci	**9**	B4
Riotur	**10**	B3
US Consulate	**11**	C4

SIGHTS & ACTIVITIES
Carnaval Central de Atendimento	**12**	B3
Centro Cultural Carioca	**13**	A3
Centro de Arte Hélio Oiticica	**14**	A3
Escadaria do Selarón	**15**	B5
Museu Chácara do Céu	**17**	A5
Museu Histórico Nacional	**18**	C3
Museu Nacional de Belas Artes	**19**	B4
Pink Fleet	(see 16)	

SLEEPING
Macuco Rio	**16**	C6
Rio Hostel	**20**	A5

EATING
Bar do Mineiro	**21**	A6
Bar Luís	**22**	B4
Boteco da Garrafa	**23**	A5
Cedro do Líbano	**24**	A3
Espirito Santa	**25**	A5
Nova Capela	**26**	A4

DRINKING
Confeitaria Colombo	**27**	B3

ENTERTAINMENT
Carioca da Gema	**28**	A5
Democráticus	**29**	A5
Estrela da Lapa	**30**	B5
Rio Scenarium	**31**	A4
Week	**32**	A2

TRANSPORT
Bondinho to Santa Teresa	**33**	B4
TAM	**34**	B4

BRAZIL

BRAZIL

IPANEMA, LEBLON & GÁVEA

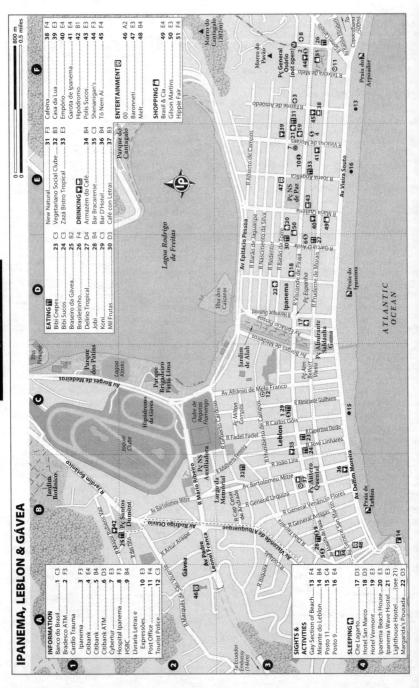

0   800 m
0   0.5 miles

since 1990, has been covering some 215 steps from Santa Teresa to Lapa with over 2000 tiles from 120 countries in mosaic-like fashion. Bring your camera.

To reach Santa Teresa, take the **bondinho** (streetcar; Map p263; tickets R60c; ☒ 6:40am-8:40pm) from the station on Professor Lélio Gama, behind Petrobras. On weekends take a taxi to the tram station, as robberies have occurred on neighboring streets.

Urca & Botafogo

The peaceful streets of Urca (Map pp266–7) offer a welcome escape from the urban bustle. Good places for strolling are along the seawall facing Corcovado, the interior streets and the nature trail **Trilha Claudio Coutinho** (Map pp266-7; ☒ 8am-6pm).

Pão de Açúcar (Sugar Loaf; Map pp266-7; ☎ 2546-8400; www.bondinho.com.br; adult/child R$44/22; ☒ 8am-7:50pm), Rio's iconic 396m mountain, offers fabulous views over the city. Sunset on a clear day is the most spectacular time to go. To reach the summit you can go by cable car, changing lines at Morro da Urca (215m), where you can stop for a short historical film or just watch the airplanes nearly scrape the side of the mountain on approach to Santos Dumont; you can also climb up (p268). To get there take an 'Urca' bus (bus 107 from Centro or Flamengo; bus 500, 511 or 512 from the *zona sul*).

Cosme Velho

Atop the 710m-high peak known as Corcovado (Hunchback), the looming statue of **Cristo Redentor** (Christ the Redeemer; Map p259), voted one of the New Seven Wonders of the World in 2007, offers similarly fantastic views over Rio. The best way to reach the summit is by **cog train** (☎ 2558-1329; www.corcovado.com.br; round trip R$45; ☒ 8:30am-6:30pm), which leaves from Cosme Velho 513. To reach the train, take a taxi or a 'Cosme Velho' bus (180, 184, 583 and 584). If you want to take a vehicle up, vans depart every 15 minutes from Paineiras (R$30) from 8am to 5:30pm. Choose a clear day to visit.

Centro

Rio's bustling commercial district has many remnants of its once-magnificent past. Looming baroque churches, wide plazas and cobblestone streets lie scattered throughout the district. It's well worth an afternoon look-see.

Occupying the former 18th-century colonial arsenal, the large **Museu Histórico Nacional** (Map p263; ☎ 2562-6042; www.museuhistoriconacional.com.br; off Av General Justo near Praça Marechal Âncora; admission R$6, Sun free; ☒ 9am-5pm Tue-Sun) contains thousands of historic relics relating to the history of Brazil, from its founding to its early days as a republic.

The avant-garde **Centro de Arte Hélio Oiticica** (Map p263; ☎ 2242-1012; Luis de Camões 68; ☒ 11am-6pm Mon-Fri, to 5pm Sat & Sun) hosts good contemporary shows in a 19th-century neoclassical building.

The small **Museu Nacional de Belas Artes** (Map p263; ☎ 2240-0068; www.mnba.gov.br; Av Rio Branco 199; admission R$5, Sun free; ☒ 10am-6pm Tue-Fri, noon-5pm Sat & Sun) houses fine art from the 17th to the 20th century, including Brazilian classics like Cândido Portinari's *Café*.

Catete & Flamengo

South of Centro, these working-class neighborhoods have several worthwhile sights.

The **Museu da República** (Map pp266-7; ☎ 3235-2650; www.museudarepublica.org.br; Rua do Catete 153; admission R$6, Wed & Sun free; ☒ noon-6pm Tue-Fri, 2-6pm Sat & Sun) occupies the beautiful 19th-century Palácio do Catete, which served as Brazil's presidential palace until 1954. It houses a collection of artifacts from the republican period and the eerily preserved room where President Getúlio Vargas killed himself.

Behind the **Parque do Catete**, the former palace grounds contain a pleasant outdoor cafe and a small pond.

The **Centro Cultural Oi Futuro** (Map pp266-7; ☎ 3131-6060; www.oifuturo.org.br; Dois de Dezembro 63, Flamengo; ☒ 11am-8pm Tue-Sun) has contemporary multimedia installations, a theater and various art galleries.

Jardim Botânico & Lagoa

This verdant **Botanical Gardens** (Map p259; Jardim Botânico 920; admission R$5; ☒ 8am-5pm), with over 5000 varieties of plants, is quiet and serene on weekdays and fills with families and music on weekends. To get there take a 'Jardim Botânico' bus, or any other bus marked 'via Jóquei.'

Just north of Ipanema stretches the **Lagoa Rodrigo de Freitas** (Map p264), a picturesque saltwater lagoon ringed with a walking-biking trail. The lakeside kiosks provide a scenic spot for an outdoor meal, with live music on weekend nights.

BRAZIL

CATETE, FLAMENGO & BOTAFOGO

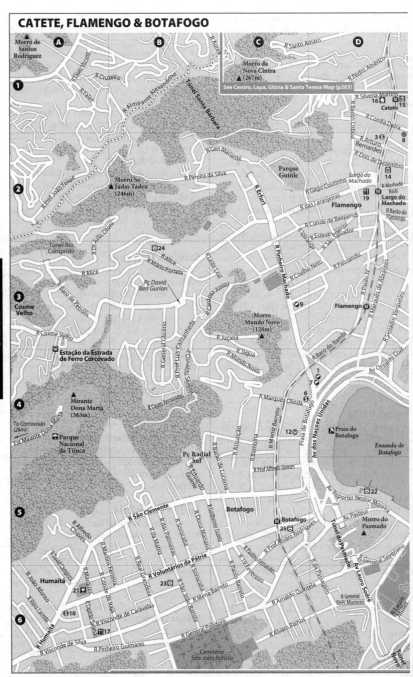

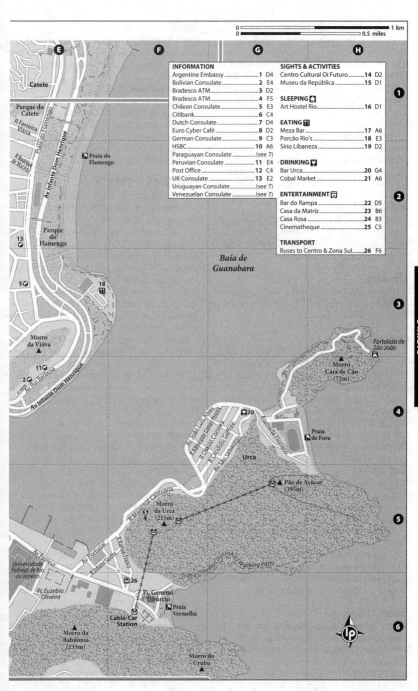

INFORMATION	
Argentine Embassy	**1** D4
Bolivian Consulate	**2** E4
Bradesco ATM	**3** D2
Bradesco ATM	**4** F5
Chilean Consulate	**5** E3
Citibank	**6** C4
Dutch Consulate	**7** D4
Euro Cyber Café	**8** D2
German Consulate	**9** C3
HSBC	**10** A6
Paraguayan Consulate	(see 7)
Peruvian Consulate	**11** E4
Post Office	**12** C4
UK Consulate	**13** E2
Uruguayan Consulate	(see 7)
Venezuelan Consulate	(see 7)

SIGHTS & ACTIVITIES	
Centro Cultural Oi Futuro	**14** D2
Museu da República	**15** D1

SLEEPING	
Art Hostel Rio	**16** D1

EATING	
Meza Bar	**17** A6
Porcão Rio's	**18** E3
Sírio Libaneza	**19** D2

DRINKING	
Bar Urca	**20** G4
Cobal Market	**21** A6

ENTERTAINMENT	
Bar do Rampa	**22** D5
Casa da Matriz	**23** B6
Casa Rosa	**24** B3
Cinematheque	**25** C5

TRANSPORT	
Buses to Centro & Zona Sul	**26** F6

BRAZIL

Parque Nacional da Tijuca

Lush trails through tropical rainforest lie just 15 minutes from concrete Copacabana. The 120 sq km refuge of the **Parque Nacional da Tijuca** (Map p259; ⊗ 7am-sunset), a remnant of the Atlantic rainforest, has excellently marked trails over small peaks and past waterfalls. Maps are available at the craft shop inside the entrance.

It's best to go by car, but if you can't, catch bus 221, 233 or 234 or take the metro to Saens Peña, then catch a bus going to Barra da Tijuca and get off at Alta da Boa Vista, the small suburb close to the park entrance.

ACTIVITIES

Rio's lush mountains and glimmering coastline just cry out for attention, and there are hundreds of ways to experience their magic on a sun-drenched afternoon.

Climbing

Rio Hiking (☎ 2552-9204; www.riohiking.com.br; rock climbs/hikes from R$165/150) offers highly rewarding climbs up Pão de Açúcar.

Hang-Gliding

The fantastic hang glide off 510m Pedra Bonita, one of the giant granite slabs towering over the city, is a highlight of any trip to Brazil. Many pilots offer tandem flights (from around R$240 including transportation), but reputable picks include **Just Fly** (☎ 2268-0565; www.justfly.com.br), **SuperFly** (☎ 3322-2286; www.riosuperfly.com.br) and **Tandem Fly** (☎ 2422-6371; www.riotandemfly.com.br).

Bay Cruises

Macuco Rio (Map p263; ☎ 2205-0390; www.macucorio.com.br; Marina da Glória; boat tours R$100) organizes two daily tours (at 10am and 2pm) in high-velocity boats.

Pink Fleet (Map p263; ☎ 2555-4063; www.pinkfleet.com.br; Marina da Glória; cruise R$80; ⊗ 9:30pm Fri, 11:45am Sat) runs two-hour weekend cruises to all of Rio's best water-accessible attractions in a German-made luxury cruise ship (skip the non-included, unmemorable meal).

Dance Classes

Centro Cultural Carioca (Map p263; ☎ 2252-5751; www.centroculturalcarioca.com.br; Sete de Setembro 237, 3rd fl, Centro; ⊗ 11am-8pm Mon-Fri) offers one-hour classes in samba and *forró*, which meet around twice a week.

TOURS

Favela Tour (☎ 3322-2727; www.favelatour.com.br; R$65) Marcelo Armstrong's insightful tour pioneered *favela* tourism – his three-hour excursion takes in Rocinha and Vila Canoas.

Santa Teresa Tour (☎ 2509-6875; www.santateresatour.com.br; tours from R$35) Offers twice daily culture and architecture tours through Rio's most historic neighborhood.

Tamandoa Adventure (Map p271; ☎ 3181-1750; www.tamandoa.com.br; Av NS de Copacabana 613 No 601; tours from R$40) Kayak, climbing and rappel excursions around Rio and Niterói.

FESTIVALS & EVENTS

One of the world's biggest and wildest parties, **Carnaval** in all its colorful, hedonistic bacchanalia is virtually synonymous with Rio. Although Carnaval is ostensibly just five days of revelry (Friday to Tuesday preceding Ash Wednesday), *cariocas* begin partying months in advance. The parade through the *sambódromo*, featuring elaborate floats flanked by thousands of pounding drummers and twirling dancers, is the culmination of the festivities, though the real action is at the parties about town.

Nightclubs and bars throw special costumed events. There are also free live concerts throughout the city (Largo do Machado, Arcos do Lapa, Praça General Osório), while those seeking a bit of decadence can head to various balls about town. *Bandas,* also called *blocos,* are one of the best ways to celebrate *carioca*-style. These consist of a procession of drummers and vocalists followed by anyone who wants to dance through the streets of Rio. Check *Veja*'s 'Rio' insert or Riotur for times and locations. *Blocos* in Santa Teresa and Ipanema are highly recommended.

The spectacular main parade takes place in the **sambódromo** (Map p259; Marques do Sapucaí) near Praça Onze metro station. Before an exuberant crowd of some 30,000, each of 14 samba schools has its hour to dazzle the audience. Top schools compete on Carnaval Sunday and Monday (March 6 and 7 in 2011, February 21 and 22 in 2012, February 12 and 13 in 2013). The safest way of reaching the *sambódromo* is by taxi or metro, which runs round the clock during Carnaval.

For information on buying *sambódromo* tickets at official prices (around R$110 to R$300), stop by Riotur or Carnaval's **Central de Atendimento** (Map p263; ☎ 2233-8151; Alfândega 25; ⊗ 10am-4pm Mon-Fri); or visit the Carnaval site (www.rio-carnival.net). By Carnaval weekend most tickets are sold out, leaving you to the mercy of the scalpers (they will find you), or to simply show up at the *sambódromo* around midnight when you can get grandstand tickets for 50% less or more, depending on the hour and location.

Keep in mind that Carnaval is costly: room rates can quadruple and some thieves keep in the spirit of things by robbing in costume.

SLEEPING

Dozens of hostels have opened in recent years, making Rio an increasingly popular backpacker destination. Ipanema and Leblon are by far the most appealing neighborhoods to base yourself, but not the cheapest. Most budget accommodation clusters around the grimier, working-class areas of Catete and Gloria.

From December to February reservations are wise and they're absolutely essential around New Year's Eve and Carnaval, even months in advance.

Ipanema & Leblon

Ipanema Wave Hostel (Map p264; ☎ 2227-6458; wavehostel.com; Barão da Torre 175 No 5, Ipanema; dm R$35-39; 🖳) Popular with a youthful, bohemian crowd; offers hardwood floors and well-maintained common areas and a brand new TV lounge on the roof housed inside a recycled water tank. It's located on Ipanema's Hostel Row. Bring your local soccer gear – they collect it.

Che Lagarto (www.chelagarto.com) Ipanema (Map p264; ☎ 2512-8076; Paul Redfern 48; dm R$38-50, d with/without bathroom R$152/133; 🍴 🖳); Copacabana (Map p271; ☎ 2256-2778; Anita Garibaldi 87; dm R$35-48, d from R$131; 🍴 🖳) This popular five-story hostel (and rowdy bar) attracts travelers who want to be close to Ipanema Beach. It's short on decor and rooms are spartan, but nightly drink specials and well-healed traveler infrastructure make it an excellent choice.

Lighthouse Hostel (Map p264; ☎ 2522-1353; www.thelighthouse.com.br; Barão da Torre 175 No 20, Ipanema; dm R$45, r without bathroom R$120; 🖳) Next door to the Ipanema Wave, this colorful, small-scale hostel has bright rooms. They only run the air-con at night, though.

our pick **Ipanema Beach House** (Map p264; ☎ 3202-2693; www.ipanemahouse.com; Barão da Torre 485, Ipanema; dm R$45, d without bathroom R$140; 🍴 🐾 🖳) This converted two-story house dating to 1918 is probably Rio's most atmospheric hostel, with six- and nine-bed dorms, private rooms, spacious indoor and outdoor lounges, a small bar and a beautiful pool – though it receives its share of complaints. A newer spot on the same street, Bonita, was in the works from the same owners at press time with more private rooms.

Margarida's Pousada (Map p264; ☎ 2239-1840; margaridacaneiro@hotmail.com; Barão da Torre 600, Ipanema; s/d/tr R$100/150/180; 🍴 🖳) This well-located guesthouse has cozy rooms in a small two-story house.

Hotel San Marco (Map p264; ☎ 2540-5032; www.sanmarcohotel.net; Visconde de Pirajá 524, Ipanema; s R$150-198, d R$167-215; 🍴 🖳) A simple midrange with clean rooms, TV, minibars and in-room safes, though the turquoise elevators are a paradise killer.

Hotel Vermont (Map p264; ☎ 2522-0057; hotelvermont.com.br; Visconde de Pirajá 254, Ipanema; s/d/tr R$286/308/385; 🍴 🖳) A long-needed renovation has turned this shabby midrange into a pricier and more stylish choice, though the rooms aren't as smart as the lobby.

Copacabana & Leme

Rio Backpackers (Map p271; ☎ 2236-3803; www.riobackpackers.com.br; Travessa Santa Leocádia 38, Copacabana; dm from R$35, d/tr from R$100/120; 🍴 🖳) Young backpackers flock to this popular hostel in Copacabana. The rooms are small but clean and nicely maintained, and some feature balconies. Leave your old clothes behind and they donate them to the homeless.

Hotel Toledo (Map p271; ☎ 2257-1990; www.hoteltoledo.com.br; Domingos Ferreira 71, Copacabana; minis/s/d R$90/115/250; 🍴 🖳) A block from the beach, the Toledo offers elevated prices for its outdated but clean rooms (though some have been renovated). The coffin-sized singles (minis) are a decent deal.

Jucati (Map p271; ☎ 2547-5422; www.edificiojucati.com.br; Tenente Marones de Gusmão 85, Copacabana; s/d/tr R$110/120/130; 🍴 🖳) Overlooking a small park on a tranquil street, this unsigned hotel gathers its share of budget travelers with some of Copacabana's most spacious and best value rooms (most have living areas and kitchenettes). It's great for groups as the price for a six-person room comes to just R$26 each.

Pousada Girassol (Map p271; ☎ 2256-6951; www.girassolpousada.com.br; Travessa Angrense 25A, Copacabana; s/d/tr R$120/150/170; 🍴) One of two small *pousadas* (guesthouses) off busy Av NS de Copacabana, Girassol has simple en-suite rooms with wood floors and adequate ventilation.

Hotel Santa Clara (Map p271; ☎ 2256-2650; www
.hotelsantaclara.com.br; Décio Vilares 316, Copacabana; s/d/
tr R$120/150/180; 🍴 🖳) One of Copacabana's
most peaceful streets hides this very friendly
three-story hotel. Upstairs rooms are best,
with wood floors, shutters and a balcony.

Santa Teresa & Lapa

Pousada Favelinha (off Map p263; ☎ 2556-5273; www
.favelinha.com; Almirante Alexandrino 2023, Santa Teresa;
s/d R$35/75; 🖳) Intrepid travelers will enjoy
this small *pousada* inside the Pereira da Silva
favela above Santa Teresa. Each room offers postcard views over Rio. Finding it is a
considerable challenge.

Rio Hostel (Map p263; ☎ 3852-0827; www.rio
hostel.com; Joaquim Murtinho 361; dm/d from R$37/110;
🖳 🖳) This beautiful, welcoming hostel is
ideally placed for exploring Rio's most bohemian neighborhood. There's ample lounge
space and lively evening gatherings on the
poolside patio.

Cama e Café (off Map p263; ☎ 2225-4366; www
.camaecafe.com; Laurinda Santos Lobo 124, Santa Teresa;
s/d from R$75/95) This excellent B&B network
links travelers with local residents (musicians, poets, architects, chefs) who rent spare
rooms in their homes. Accommodations
range from modest to lavish; check website
for listings.

Casa Áurea (off Map p263; ☎ 2242-5830; www.casa
aurea.com.br; Áurea 80, Santa Teresa; s/d from R$130/150)
Though a makeover catapulted this former
hostel into the *pousada* category, it still
oozes rustic charm from one of the neighborhood's oldest homes (1871). It's within a
short walking distance from the tram.

Catete & Flamengo

Art Hostel Rio (Map pp266-7; ☎ 2205-1083; Silveira
Martins 135, Catete; dm/s R$29/58, d R$90-115; 🍴 🖳)
An architect smashed up a classic Catete
hotel in a 125-year-old home and turned it
into an artsy, bohemian hostel featuring extra
low ceilings and bathrooms in all rooms.
The breakfast is *mineiro*-style – substantial!

EATING

Rio has a wealth of dining options, though
not always at low prices. The best places for
cheap dining are self-serve lunch buffets and
juice bars, which you'll find all over the city.
Here you can grab a sandwich or burger for
R$4 to R$10. For fancier fare, Leblon has the
best options, particularly along restaurant-

packed Dias Ferreira. Another atmospheric
choice is along Joaquim Murtinho in
Santa Teresa.

Ipanema, Leblon & Gávea

Bibi Sucos (Map p264; Visconde de Pirajá 591A; açaí R$3.40-
8.30) Bibi does one of Brazil's best *açaís* (sorbet-
like dish made from an Amazonian fruit).
They also do crepes around the corner on
Cupertino Durão.

Mil Frutas (Map p264; Garcia D'Ávila 134, Ipanema;
ice cream from R$7) Beat the heat at Rio's top
spot for ice cream. Of the ridiculous flavor
options on offer, guava and cheese is the
most popular.

Koni (Map p264; Av Altaufa de Paiva 320, Leblon;
items R$7-10.50) This bright orange *Japazillian*
hotspot has exploded in Rio – 15 outlets since
opening in late 2006. They do fresh tuna or
salmon in sushi cones *(temaki)*, the best of
which is salmon with crunchy wasabi peas
and shoestring leeks.

Delírio Tropical (Map p264; Garcia D'Ávila 48, Ipanema;
salads US$7.40-11.10) Famed for its delicious salads,
the airy Delírio Tropical serves many varieties along with soups and hot dishes (veggie
burgers, grilled salmon).

Vegetariano Social Clube (Map p264; Conde Bernadotte
26L, Leblon; mains around R$12-24) Most Brazilians
scoff at the thought, but this Zen-like spot
serves a mean tofu *feijoada* (stew with beans
and rice) on Wednesday and Sunday.

Jobi (Map p264; Cupertino Durão 81, Leblon; executive
lunch specials R$15-30; 🕑 noon-1am) This tiny, old-
school *boteco* (neighborhood bar) has been a
Rio institution for over 50 years. The *picanha*
(beef steak) is divine.

Braseiro da Gávea (Map p264; Praça Santos Dumont,
116, Gávea; mains for 2 people R$27-56) Voted best place
to flirt by *Veja Rio*, the singles scene com-
mences here over brews and grilled meats.
Service is inexcusably negligent, but the food
is solid. It's popular with actors – presumably
because nobody flirts with them!

New Natural (Map p264; Barão da Torre 167; per kg R$33)
Featuring an excellent vegetarian lunch buffet,
this travelers' favorite has fresh soups, rice,
veggies and beans.

Zazá Bistro Tropical (Map p264; Joana Angélica 40,
Ipanema; mains R$36-49; 🕑 dinner) For a splurge,
sexy Zazá sits inside a handsomely converted house in Ipanema with retro-tropical
French-colonial decor. The inventive seafood and Asian-inspired curry dishes are
spicy and fun.

Brasileirinho (Map p264; Jangadeiros 10, Ipanema; feijoada R$38.90) The same owners as the more formal Casa de Feijoada around the corner, here you get the same version of Rio's signature black bean and salted pork dish for R$11 cheaper and in a more colorful and rustic atmosphere.

Copacabana & Leme

Bakers (Map p271; Santa Clara 86B; items R$2.90-16.90) Good place for flaky croissants, strudels, decadent cakes and coffee. Deli sandwiches are also good value.

our pick **Le Blé Noir** (Map p271; Xavier da Silveira 19-A; crepes R$5-51; ☾ closed Sun) Amid artsy mosaic candlelit tables and moody French lounge music, this sexy gourmet *creperia* will change your perception of pancakes. Choose from designer savory or sweet options; or pair your favorite artisan French cheese with a combination of your choice. Worth the splurge!

Cervantes (Map p271; Av Prado Junior 335B; sandwiches R$6-14) A Copacabana institution, Cervantes is famous for its filet mignon, cheese and pineapple sandwiches. Its soggy fries, however, will not be re-writing history.

Amir (Map p271; Ronald de Carvalho 55C; mains R$9-35) Cozy Middle-Eastern restaurant with fabulous hummus, falafel and other authentic fare.

Temperarte (Map p271; Av NS de Copacabana 266, Copacabana; all-you-can-eat R$17.90; ☾ lunch Mon-Sat) This pay-by-weight restaurant also offers an all-you-can-eat option of salads, roast meats and vegetables.

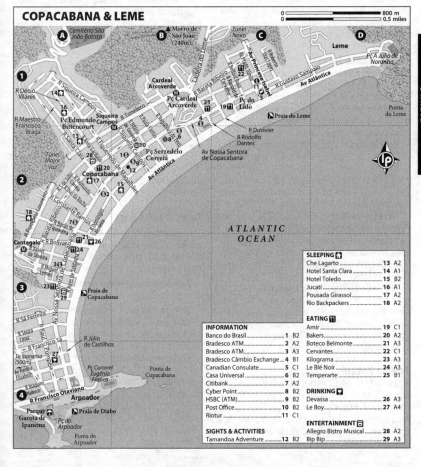

Boteco Belmonte (Map p271; Domingos Ferreira 242, Copacabana; mains for 2 people R$27.50-88) This wildly popular *boteco*, a chain started by a poor Northeasterner in the 1950s, offers good people-watching and great food. The *moqueca* (*Bahian* seafood stew) is half the price of most places, and every bit as good.

Kilograma (Map p271; Av NS de Copacabana 1144; per kg R$36.90) An excellent self-serve restaurant with salads, meats, seafood and desserts.

Centro

Cedro do Líbano (Map p263; Senhor dos Passos 231; meals R$11.50-29.50; ☺ lunch Mon-Fri) Rio's oldest Arab restaurant serves an excellent *kafta* lunch plate along a wild pedestrianized market street.

Bar Luís (Map p263; Rua da Carioca 39; mains R$15-60; ☺ closed Sun) A Rio institution since 1887, Bar Luís serves filling portions of German food chased by dark beer.

Lapa & Santa Teresa

Bar do Mineiro (Map p263; Paschoal Carlos Magno 99, Santa Teresa; mains R$18-58; ☺ closed Mon) A Santa Teresa favorite, with a menu of traditional Minas dishes like *carne seca* (dried meat with spices), *lingüiça* (pork sausage) and Saturday *feijoada*. Also packs in the drinkers.

Espirito Santa (Map p263; Almirante Alexandrino 264, Santa Teresa; mains R$27-53; ☺ closed Tue) In a beautifully restored building, Espirito Santa has excellent Amazonian dishes that can be enjoyed on a back terrace with sweeping views.

Nova Capela (Map p263; Av Mem de Sá 96; mains from R$30-68) Serving traditional Portuguese cuisine, old-fashioned Nova Capela attracts a garrulous crowd, especially after the samba clubs wind down (it's open until 5am!). The *cabrito* (goat) is tops.

Boteco da Garrafa (Map p263; Av Mem de Sá 77, Lapa; mains for 2 R$34-69) This fun *boteco* is the pre-show hangout of choice in Lapa, located on its liveliest corner. Fill up on succulent *picanha* and ice-cold bottles of Original beer before shaking the calories off later in the clubs.

Jardim Botânico & Lagoa

Pizzaria Bráz (Maria Angelica 129, Jardim Botânico; pizza R$33.50-49.50) If you don't get a chance to sample *pizza paulistana* in São Paulo (see boxed text, p287), then don't miss this unforgettable pizzeria, their only outlet outside Sampa.

Botafogo & Urca

Meza Bar (pp266-7; Capitão Salomão 69, Botafogo; tapas R$10-25) Botafogo's see-and-be-seen hotspot serves up delectable, Brazilian-slanted tapas to a sophisticated and trendy crowd. Creative cocktails and a delightful staff round out the fun here.

Glória, Catete & Flamengo

Sírio Libaneza (Map pp266-7; Largo do Machado 29, Loja 16-19, Flamengo; items R$4.50-15) Awesome and cheap Syrian-Lebanese cuisine and great juices, too. It's always a madhouse. It's inside the Galleria Condor on Largo do Machado.

Porcão Rio's (Map pp266-7; Av Infante Dom Henrique-Aterro, Parque do Flamengo, Flamengo; all-you-can-eat R$73) Don't judge a restaurant by its communist-era interrogation facility-evoking exterior, this is one of Rio's best all-you-can-eat *churrascarias* with delectable grilled meats and views of Pão de Açúcar.

DRINKING

Few cities can rival the dynamism of Rio's nightlife. Samba clubs, jazz bars, open-air cafes, lounges and nightclubs are just one part of the scene, while the *boteco* is practically a *carioca* institution. If you can read a bit of Portuguese, there are many good sources of information: the *Veja Rio* insert in *Veja* magazine, Thursday and Friday editions of *O Globo* and *Jornal do Brasil* and the Rio Festa website (www.riofesta.com.br).

Cafes & Juice Bars

Rio's numerous juice bars are a must. For coffee culture and people-watching, head to the sidewalk cafes scattered about Ipanema and Leblon.

Polis Sucos (Map p264; Maria Quitéria 70; juices R$3.50-5) A top juice bar.

Cafeína (Map p264; Farme de Amoedo 43; desserts R$4.60-6.90) This attractive cafe makes a fine spot for espresso and scrumptious desserts while the city strolls by.

Confeitaria Colombo (Map p263; Gonçalves Dias 34; snacks R$3.90-18.50) Step back in time at this gorgeous belle époque cafe that recalls Rio's colonial heyday. Opened in 1897, the massive mirrors, marble tables and gargantuan encased glass bar likely haven't changed since. A stop here is worth the trip to Centro alone.

BRAZIL

BAR-HOPPING 101

When it comes to bars, nearly every neighborhood in Rio has its drinking clusters. While Ipanema has scattered options, Leblon has many trendy choices along the western end of Av General San Martin. Near Lagoa, a youthful population fills the bars around JJ Seabra, and there's almost always a fun crowd packing the bars facing Praça Santos Dumont. The lakeside kiosks (in Parque Brigadeiro Faria Lima) are a favorite date place, with live music in the open air. Copacabana's Av Atlântica packs many sidewalk bars and restaurants, but the strip gets seedy after dark. Botafogo has authentic *carioca* bars, particularly around Visconde de Caravelas and in the Cobal market, a market during the day that turns into a lively multi-bar drinking den at night. In Centro the atmospheric Travessa do Comércio is recommended for weekday evening drinks. Lapa's liveliest street is Av Mem de Sá, which is lined with samba clubs. In Santa Teresa you'll find colorful bars around Largo do Guimarães and Largo das Neves.

For more cafe culture:

Armazém do Café (Map p264; Rita Ludolf 87B, Leblon)

Café con Letras (Map p264; Av Bartolomeu Mitre 297, Leblon)

Bars

Empório (Map p264; Maria Quitéria 37, Ipanema) An eclectic, alt rock crowd of *cariocas* and eager gringos stirs things up over nightly DJ at this battered Ipanema favorite.

Devassa (Map p271; Bolivar 8A, Copacabana) The best beer *not* brewed in the south of Brazil is served all over *zona sul* but this location has beach views. Five homebrews on tap.

Bar D'Hotel (Map p264; Marina All Suites, Av Delfim Moreira 696, 2nd fl, Leblon) One of Leblon's most stylish bars and beautiful crowds – a magnet for the young and the restless.

Shenanigan's (Map p264; Visconde de Pirajá 112A, Ipanema) Overlooking the Praça General Osorio, this Irish pub attracts a mix of sunburnt gringos and young-ish *cariocas* looking to make international connections. A good place to catch European soccer and US sports – if you can concentrate over the live rock music.

Bar Bracarense (Map p264; José Linhares 85, Leblon) *Cariocas* of all creeds descend on this simple bar for Rio's liveliest Happy Hour and good, cheap savory bar snacks (try the *bolinho de aipim* with shrimp).

Garota de Ipanema (Map p264; Vinícius de Moraes 49) Plenty of tourists pack this open-air bar, but it would be a sin not to mention the place where Jobim and Vinícius penned the famed song 'Girl from Ipanema.'

Bar Urca (Map pp266-7; Cândido Gaffrée 205, Urca) After Sugar Loaf, after the beach, after whatever…as the sun sets, *cariocas* gather along the Urca seawall to take in views of the bay over thirst-quenching *chope* (draught beer).

Waiters dash back and forth between the bar and the crowds.

Hipódromo (Map p264; Praça Santos Dumont 108, Gávea) In an area referred to as Baixo Gávea, Hipódromo attracts a late teen and twenty-something crowd. The best nights are Monday, Thursday and Sunday, when the whole square turns into a free-for-all party.

ENTERTAINMENT
Live Music

Lapa's samba clubs are still a fantastic night out, but the underground scene here has moved on under the weight of a tourist onslaught – try Botafogo to escape fellow gringos. Cover charges typically range from R$10 to R$30 (females pay less).

Allegro Bistro Musical (Map p271; www.modernsound .com.br; Barata Ribeiro 502, Copacabana; ⏲ 9am-9pm Mon-Fri, to 8pm Sat) This small cafe inside Modern Sound (Rio's best record store) is a great spot for hearing free live bands playing most nights.

our pick **Bip Bip** (Map p271; Almirante Gonçalves 50, Copacabana; ⏲ from 6pm, closed Thu) One of the hidden gems among the *cognoscenti*, Bip Bip is a simple storefront with great informal music. Famous for its quality of musicians, it has such a following, most folks, unable to get in, gather around the sidewalk and sing along.

Bar do Rampa (Map pp266-7; Av Reporter Nestor Moreira 42, Botafogo; ⏲ 8pm Wed, 7pm Sun) This local's secret inside the Guanabara yacht club offers down-home *pagode* samba in the round in a simple, open-air setting right on the water. It's beautiful – and not a tourist in sight.

Carioca da Gema (Map p263; Av Mem de Sá 79, Lapa) One of numerous samba clubs on this street, Carioca da Gema is a small, warmly lit setting for catching some of the city's best samba bands. A festive crowd fills the dance floor.

BRAZIL

GAY & LESBIAN RIO

Rio's gay community is neither out nor flamboyant most of the year, except at Carnaval. On the beaches, you'll find gay-friendly drink stands across from the Copacabana Palace Hotel in Copacabana and opposite Farme de Amoedo (Rio's gayest street) in Ipanema. On Ipanema Beach, the gay-friendly spot to dig your toes into the sand is between Posto 8 and 9.

Le Boy (Map p271; Raul Pompéia 94; ☼ closed Mon) One of Rio's best (and largest) gay clubs. DJs spin house and house tribal. Drag shows are tossed in the mix. The ladies gather next door at Le Girl.

Casa da Lua (Map p264; Barão da Torre 240A, Ipanema) This lesbian bar is in a leafy part of Ipanema and serves great drinks.

Tô Nem Aí (Map p264; cnr Farme de Amoedo & Visconde de Piraja, Ipanema) Slang for 'I couldn't care less,' this is the relaxed hangout of choice for devotees of Rio's laid-back GLS (Gay, Lesbian and Sympathetics) scene.

Week (Map p263; Sacadura Cabral 154) The 2007 importation of this massive São Paulo institution inside a historical *carioca* mansion near the port was a smash hit from go. Saturdays are the biggest, with international DJs and the lot.

Cinematheque (Map pp266-7; Voluntários da Pátria 53, Botafogo; ☼ 6pm-late) A wildly eclectic crowds spills out into the street at this Botafogo gem with a lush outdoor patio restaurant downstairs and small live stage above. The music ranges from *chorinho* (samba variation) to hip-hop to bossa nova.

Democráticus (Map p263; Rua do Riachuelo 91-93, Lapa; ☼ Wed-Sat) This ancient classic has an enormous dance floor and excellent samba, *chorinho* and *gafieira* bands. It skews younger on Thursday.

Estrela da Lapa (Map p263; Av Mem de Sá 69, Lapa; ☼ Wed-Sun) A more intimate choice (good for couples), this air-conditioned space serves up samba, rockabilly, MPB and *sambalanço* nightly. When the live music ends (around 1am), doors open for R$10 and a DJ stirs a younger crowd into a late-night frenzy.

Rio Scenarium (Map p263; www.rioscenarium.com.br in Portuguese; Rua do Lavradio 20, Lapa; ☼ closed Sun & Mon) One of Lapa's cinematic nightspots, Rio Scenarium pioneered Lapa's samba renaissance. There are three floors, each lavishly decorated with more than 10,000 antiques and movie set props. It's the most touristy, but that doesn't mean the mile-long line to get in doesn't feature its share of *cariocas*.

Nightclubs

Nothing happens before midnight. Cover charges range from R$40 to R$100, and women generally pay less than men. Often a portion of the charge covers drinks *(consumo)*.

Casa da Matriz (Map pp266-7; Henrique Novaes 107, Botafogo; ☼ from 11pm) This avant-garde space in an old two-story Botafogo mansion attracts a younger (there are video games!), alternative crowd, who pack its various little rooms.

00 (Map p264; Zero Zero; Planetário da Gávea, Av Padre Leonel Franca 240, Gávea; ☼ 8pm-late) Housed in Gávea's planetarium, 00 is a restaurant by day and swanky, design-forward lounge by night. Good DJs and excellent rotating parties attract throngs of the beautiful but beware of tiny cocktails at Los Angeles prices.

Casa Rosa (Map pp266-7; Alice 550, Laranjeiras; ☼ 11pm-late Fri & Sat, 5pm-late Sun) This former brothel straddles the fence between dance club and samba club when its cavernous rooms get packed with sweat-soaked *cariocas*. There are DJs and live samba, *sambarock* and *forró*. The Sunday samba *feijoada* for R$20 is a steal.

Baronneti (Map p264; Barão da Torre 354, Ipanema; ☼ Wed-Sat) Hip-hop, funk and house are the genres of choice for the throngs of young *cariocas* that descend on this Ipanema hotspot. Entrance is 'free' but *consumo* minimums are R$100 (men) and R$30 (women).

Melt (Map p264; Rita Ludolf 47, Leblon) This upscale Leblon destination has an upstairs dance floor and live music lounge and a slinky lounge down below. There's always a line.

Samba Schools

Starting in September, the big Carnaval schools open their rehearsals to the public. These are lively but informal affairs where you can dance, drink and join the party. The schools are in dodgy neighborhoods, so don't go alone, but by all means go. Most hostels organize outings if you want to hook up with a group. Check with Riotur for schedules and locations. The best ones for tourists:

Mangueira (☎ 2567-4637; www.mangueira.com.br; Visconde de Niterói 1072, Mangueira; admission R$20; ⊗ 10pm Sat)

Salgueiro (☎ 2238-5564; www.salgueiro.com.br; Silva Teles 104, Andaraí; admission R$10-30; ⊗ 10pm Sat)

Sports

Maracanã (Map p259; ☎ 2299-2941; www.suderj.rj.gov .br/maracana.asp; cnr Professor Eurico Rabelo & Av Maracanã; ⊗ 9am-5pm) Rio's enormous shrine to football hosts some of the world's most exciting matches – the 2014 World Cup championship match will be here – with fan behavior no less colorful. Games take place year-round and can happen any day of the week. Rio's big clubs are Flamengo, Fluminense, Vasco da Gama and Botafogo.

To get to the stadium take the metro to Maracanã station then walk along Av Osvaldo Aranha. The safest seats are on the lower-level *cadeira*, where the overhead covering protects you from descending objects like dead chickens and urine-filled bottles (no joke!). The ticket price is R$20 to $R30 for most games.

SHOPPING
Markets

Feira do Nordestino (Map p259; Pavilhão de São Cristóvão near the Quinta da Boa Vista; admission R$1; ⊗ Fri-Sun) Northeastern in character with lots of food, drink and live music, this fair is well worth a visit.

Hippie Fair (Map p264; Praça General Osório; ⊗ 9am-6pm Sun) An Ipanema favorite, this place has good souvenirs and Bahian food.

Gilson Martins (Map p264; Visconde de Pirajá 462B, Ipanema) Unique and colorful, these artisan handbags and wallets make unique gifts.

Brasil & Cia (Map p264; Maria Quitéria 27, Ipanema) Brazilian handicrafts.

GETTING THERE & AWAY
Air

Most flights depart from Aeroporto Galeão (also called Aeroporto António Carlos Jobim), 15km north of the center. Shuttle flights to/from São Paulo, and some flights for other nearby cities, use Aeroporto Santos Dumont in the city center. Also see Getting into Town (p260).

Varig/Gol tickets can be purchased at any travel agency. Many international airlines have offices on or near Av Rio Branco, Centro.

TAM (Map p263; ☎ 3212-9300; Av Rio Branco 181, 36th fl, Centro)

Varig/Gol (☎ 3398-5136; Aeroporto Galeão, Terminal 1, Setor Verde)

Bus

Buses leave from the **Rodoviária Novo Rio** (Map p259; ☎ 3213-1800; Av Francisco Bicalho) 2km northwest of Centro, which was undergoing a US$10 million facelift at research time, including the implementation of 52 security cameras. Several buses depart daily to most major destinations, but it's a good idea to buy tickets in advance. Excellent buses leave Novo Rio every 15 minutes or so for São Paulo (R$55 to R$102, six hours). Sample *executivo* fares to popular destinations:

BUS FARES		
Destination	**Cost (R$)**	**Duration (hr)**
Belém	427	52
Belo Horizonte	89	7
Buenos Aires, Argentina	325	42
Campo Grande	207	22
Florianópolis	234	18
Foz do Iguaçu	215	22
Ouro Prêto	95	7
Mangaratiba	21	2
Paraty	49	4½
Petrópolis	15	1½
Porto Alegre	223	26
Porto Velho	365	56
Recife	297	38
Salvador	249	18
Santiago, Chile	362	62

GETTING AROUND
Bus

Rio buses are frequent and cheap, and because Rio is long and narrow it's easy to get the right bus and usually no big deal if you're on the wrong one. Nine out of 10 buses going south from the center will go to Copacabana, and vice versa. The buses are, however, often crowded, stuck in traffic and often driven by raving maniacs. They're also the site of many of the city's robberies, and it's not wise to ride late at night. You saw *Ônibus 174*, right?

Metro

Rio's two-line subway system is an excellent way to get around some parts of the city. It's open daily from 5am to midnight (R$2.80).

BRAZIL

Taxi

Rio's taxis are useful late at night and when you're carrying valuables. The flat rate is R$4.30, plus around R$1.20 per kilometer – slightly more at night and on Sunday. **Transcootur** (☎ 2590-2300) is 30% more expensive than *comuns*, but safer.

THE SOUTHEAST

Rio usually digs its paradisiacal claws into most tourists, refusing to let go before sunburns are unbearable and hangovers are unshakable, but those who manage to tear themselves away from its charming clutches will find some of Brazil's most endearing attractions right in its backyard. North of town is the Costa do Sol (Sun Coast), home to the upscale beach resort of Búzios – a weekend city escape for hot to trot *cariocas* – and its more humble neighbor, Arraial do Cabo. The spectacular Costa Verde (Green Coast) stretches south from Rio to São Paulo, boasting rainforest-smothered islands (Ilha Grande), perfectly-preserved colonial villages (Paraty) and postcard-perfect beaches (the whole stretch).

Once sun and sand induce tropical overload, head inland to the breezy mountain towns of Petrópolis, once the summer home to Portugal's ruling elite, and the nearby peaks of Parque Nacional Serra dos Órgãos, with Rio state's best trekking; or, bring your appetite

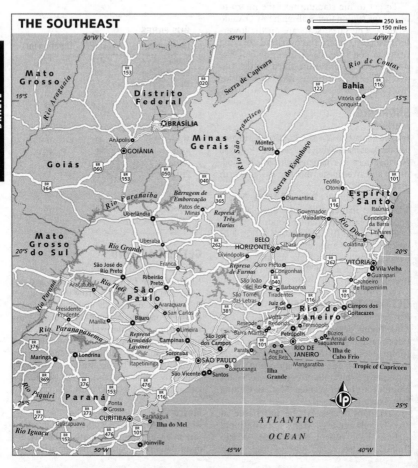

THE SOUTHEAST

and head to Minas Gerais, famous throughout Brazil for its hearty cuisine and friendly population. Here time has frozen colonial-era gold-mining towns like Ouro Prêto or sleepy villages like Tiradentes, where magical historical delights beckon around every corner. It all culminates in South America's intimidating cultural capital, São Paulo, where you'll find some of the best museums, nightclubs and restaurants in South America.

Getting There & Around

Rio de Janeiro is the major gateway to the coastal regions, though if coming from the south or west you can reach the Costa Verde via São Paulo. Belo Horizonte, Brazil's third-largest city, is the gateway to the old gold-mining towns in Minas Gerais.

Numerous flights connect the three major cities of the Southeast – Belo Horizonte, Rio and São Paulo – with plenty of bus links covering Southeastern destinations. Ilha Grande is reached by ferry from Angra dos Reis or Mangaratiba (p280).

PETRÓPOLIS

☎ 0xx24 / pop 306,000

Tucked away in the Atlantic rainforest 65km above Rio de Janeiro, the airy mountain town of Petrópolis is an important epicenter in Brazilian history. Once the summer home of the Portuguese imperial family, Petrópolis has some striking vestiges of the past, including a former palace and streets lined with gorgeous colonial mansions. It works as a great day escape from the penetrating heat of Rio, or as a place to hole up for a few days enjoying the wealth of outdoor adventures in the area. The popular 30km Petrópolis–Teresópolis trek (as the name implies) begins from here.

The city's top attraction is the **Museu Imperial** (Rua da Imperatriz 220; admission R$8; 11am-5:30pm Tue-Sun), which exhibits royal finery in the former palace of Dom Pedro II (including the astonishing 639-diamond, 77-pearl imperial crown). Nearby is the 19th-century **Catedral São Pedro de Alcântara** (Sao Pedro de Alcântara 60; 8am-noon & 2-6pm), housing the tombs of Brazil's last emperor, Dom Pedro II, his wife and daughter.

Near the municipal bus station, **Hotel Comércio** (☎ 2242-3500; Dr Porciúncula 55; s/d R$45/75, without bathroom R$22/49) has get-what-you-pay-for rooms. Nearby, the Santos Dumont-themed **Pousada 14bis** (☎ 2231-0946; www.pousada14bis.com.br;

Buenos Aires 192; s/d from R$80/140;) is a wonderful option along a quiet residential street. The owners also arrange treks and rafting in the area. **Fred´s** (☎ 2242-2301; Ipiranga 439; s/d R$99/149) offers two casual, B&B-style rooms in a spacious colonial home.

Don Sappore (Rua do Imperador 1008; crepes R$8.50-14) serves yummy crepes and ice cream. The deli-style **Tony´s** (Rua do Imperador 700; pizza R$10-44) draws a packed house for pizza but has a little bit of everything. Adjoining the Plaza Dom Pedro II, **Casa D'Angelo** (Rua do Imperador 700; mains from R$12.50) is an atmospheric cafe and restaurant with affordable *pratos executivos* (set lunches) and cold *chope*.

Buses run from Rio to Petrópolis every half hour from 5am to midnight (R$15, one hour). There are seven buses daily to Teresópolis (R$10 to R$12). The bus station is located in Bingen, 10km from town. From there, take bus 100 or 10 (R$2.20).

TERESÓPOLIS & PARQUE NACIONAL DA SERRA DOS ÓRGÃOS

☎ 0xx21 / pop 150,300

Though the town itself is dull as daisies, Teresópolis is framed by mountain scenery and well positioned for excursions into the lush-capped peaks of the Parque Nacional da Serra dos Órgãos, Rio state's best park. Some 96km north of Rio, Teresópolis itself boasts an excellent local brew but little else beyond a transit hub.

About 5km south of Teresópolis is the main entrance to the **Parque Nacional da Serra dos Órgãos** (☎ 2642-1070; Hwy BR-116; admission day/camping R$3/6; 8am-5pm). The best walking trail is the Trilha Pedra do Sino (admission R$12), which takes about eight hours round trip. Most trails are unmarked but it's easy and inexpensive to hire a guide at the national park visitors center.

One group that arranges a wide variety of treks, rafting, rock climbing and rappelling excursions is **Tamandoa Adventure** (☎ 3181-1750; www.tamandoa.com.br) in Rio (p268).

A few kilometers outside of Teresópolis, off the road to Petrópolis, there's **Camping Quinta da Barra** (☎ 2643-1050; www.campingquintadabarra.com.br; Antônio Maria, Quinta da Barra; camping per person R$15). **Hostel Recanto do Lord** (☎ 2742-5586; www.tereso polishostel.com.br; Luiza Pereira Soares 109; dm/s/d with YHI card R$20/40/55; without YHI card R$25/45/65) is a homey hostel 2km above town and offers excellent views of the park's peaks, though there's no internet. The **Várzea Palace Hotel** (☎ 2742-0878; www.varzea.palace.nafoto.net; Prefeito Sebastião Teixeira 41/55; s/d R$60/85, without bathroom R$35/45; 🖳) is a relic only saved these days by a bit of antiquated charm. The *Shining*-esque spot sits in a great location just near the church Igreja Matriz. A great value, all-you-can-eat spread with loads of homey food ison offer at **Laranja da Terra** (Av Dr Aleixo 77; buffet week/weekend R$15.20/21.20), run by a Dutch ex-backpacker.

Buses run between Rio and Teresópolis every half hour from 6am to midnight (R$20.75, 1½ hours). From Teresópolis, there are seven daily buses to Petrópolis (R$12, 1½ hours). To get to the national park's main entrance from central Teresópolis, take the hourly 'Soberbo' bus (R$3), or the more frequent 'Alto' bus to the Praçinha do Alto, then walk a short way south to the entrance.

ARRAIAL DO CABO
☎ 0xx22 / pop 25,300

If Búzios suddenly had a falling out with the *carioca* cool, what you'd have left is modest Arraial do Cabo – blessed with powdery-white sand dunes and some of Rio state's loveliest beaches, but none of the hoopla of its more famous next-door neighbor. Lying 150km east of Rio along Brazil's Costa do Sol, Arraial is somewhat of a long forgotten son, a working-class beach town left to fend for itself. Crowds descend on the beaches during summer months, so avoid holiday weekends if possible.

Arraial's beaches not to be missed: Praia do Forno, reachable by a 1km walking trail over a steep hill adjoining Anjos, is a perfect patch of sand. Other good choices within walking distance of town are Prainha to the north and Praia Grande to the west.

The unspoiled Ilha de Cabo Frio is accessible by boat from Praia dos Anjos. Praia do Farol, on the protected side of the island, is a gorgeous beach with fine white sand. The Gruta Azul (Blue Cavern) on the southwest side of the island is another beautiful spot. Be alert, though: the entrance to the cavern is submerged at high tide. Numerous agencies offer crowded package tours to these spots. **Arraial Tur** (☎ 2622-1340; www.arraialtur.com .br) runs boat trips at 11am daily for around R$30 per person. For diving, contact **Acqua World** (☎ 2622-2217; www.acquaworld.com.br; Praça da Bandeira 23).

Marino dos Anjos Albergue (☎ 2622-4060; Bernardo Lens 145; www.marinadosanjos.com.br; dm without breakfast R$28, dm/d with YHI card R$45/140, without YHI card R$55/170; 🖳 🐾) is a lovely hostel flush with Zen-like touches, retro designs and a manager you'll fall in love with. It's one block from Praia dos Anjos. Nearby, the aging **Porto dos Anjos** (☎ 9232-9058; pousadaportodosanjos@ig.com.br; Av Luis Correa 8; r with/without bathroom R$100/80; 🐾 🖳) has simple rooms with sea views.

Saint Tropez (Praça Daniel Barreto; mains for 2 R$22-80) is a French-owned spot serving a wealth of seafood and meat dishes on a breezy patio. In low season, there's a good-value set meal for R$11. On Praia Grande, **Meu Xodó** (Epitácio Pessoa 26; mains for 2 people R$25-65) is a classic seafooder famous for its fish in shrimp sauce.

Buses run about hourly throughout the day from Rio to Arraial, starting at 3:40am (R$28, three hours). The bus station is on Nilo Peçanha, a 10-minute walk to Praia dos Anjos (or a 20-minute walk to Praia Grande).

BÚZIOS
☎ 0xx22 / pop 24,600

Búzios is to Rio de Janeiro what the Hamptons are to New York City – a summer playground for the blessed and beautiful, located 167km east of the city in a setting fit for shock and awe. But the beauty of Búzios and its 26 fabled beaches – once a sun-soaked hideaway for French starlet Brigitte Bardot – is that for every 10 chic shops and minimalist design *pousadas*, there is a rustic hideaway and other low-key infrastructure catering to those on a less hedonistic budget. During the day, caramel-hued hard bodies beach-hop via water taxis from one sugary stretch of sand to another, eating just-grilled fresh fish on the beach chased by perfect *caipirinhas*. At night, the rich, famous and foreign descend on pedestrianized Rua das Pedras, Búzios rowdy strip of upscale restaurants, swanky clubs and rambunctious bars, where there is enough eye candy to shake your sweet tooth by its very foundation.

Búzios was a simple fishing village until the early 1960s, when it was 'discovered' by Bardot, sealing its fate as Brazil's St Tropez.

Orientation & Information

Búzios, aka Armação dos Búzios, is one of three settlements on the peninsula. It lies between Ossos, on the peninsula's tip, and hectic

Manguinhos, on the isthmus. Búzios' main street is Rua das Pedras, where you'll find many *pousadas*, restaurants, bars and internet cafes. As the road passes the pier, it turns into Orla Bardot, which is used interchangeably with Av José Bento Ribeiro Dantas. Praia Rosa, a fourth settlement, lies northwest along the coast.

Malízia Tour (Rua das Pedras 306) changes money. You'll find foreign-friendly ATMs bookending Rua das Pedras – on Praça Santos Dumont on the east end and inside Shopping No 1 on the west end. **Tourist information** (www.visitebuzios .com; Travessia das Pescadores 151, Armação; 8am-10pm) sits just off the southeast corner of Praça Santos Dumont.

Sights & Activities

You can dive, windsurf, sail or snorkel in Búzios, but the main activity is beach-hopping. Water taxis run R$5 to R$20 depending on distance. In general, the southern beaches are trickier to get to, but are prettier and have better surf. Geribá and Ferradurinha (Little Horseshoe), south of Manguinhos, are beautiful beaches with good waves, but the Búzios Beach Club have built condos here. Next on the coast is Ferradura, large enough for windsurfing. Praia Olho de Boi (Bull's Eye Beach), at the eastern tip of the peninsula, is a pocket-sized beach reached by a little trail from the long, clean Praia Brava. It attracts nudists. Near the northern tip of the promontory, João Fernandinho, João Fernandes (full of people and beach restaurants) and the topless Azedinha and Azeda are all good for snorkeling. Praia da Tartaruga is idyllic and home to 12 bars.

Tour Shop (2623-4733; www.tourshop.com.br; Orla Bardot 550; 3hr trips R$60) offers three daily all-you-can-drink excursions (beers are solid – *caipirinhas* are watered down) by catamaran past beaches and several islands.

Sleeping

Budget lodging is thankfully on the rise in Búzios, but still scarce during summer.

Yellow Stripe (2623-3174; www.yellowstripehostel .blogspot.com; Rua da Mandrágora 13; dm from R$35, d with/ without air-con R$99/89;) Brand new and overly-friendly, this Canadian-Brazilian hostel offers segregated and mixed dorms and a lovely pool in an old renovated house. It's 15 minutes on foot from Rua das Pedras in Portal de Ferradura and there's parking available.

Nomad Búzios (2620-8085; www.nomadbuzios .com.br; Rua das Pedras 25; dm/d from R$49/250;) This new place has expensive private rooms, but also an unbeatable dorm rate of R$49 – it's right on Rua das Pedras in a completely new, air-conditioned seaside motor court.

Pousada Mandala (2623-4013; www.pousada mandalabuzios.com.br; Manoel de Carvalho 223; s/d/tr R$110/150/200;) Passing through the lush garden courtyard, you'll find another good-value *pousada* with worn but otherwise cheery en-suite rooms, some with tiny balconies.

Zen-do (2623-1542; www.zendobuzios.com.br; João Fernandes 60, Ossos; d from R$140;) This charming (and just renovated) guesthouse in Ossos is run by a sweetheart of a lady, who puts her heart and soul into the three rooms on offer. Note that it's not the João Fernandes 60 on the hill, but rather the *other* João Fernandes 60 down the hill to the left.

Eating & Drinking

Brava, Ferradura and João Fernandes beaches have simple thatched-roof fish and beer restaurants.

Chez Michou (Rua das Pedras 141; crepes R$8-22) Legendary open-air *creperia* in the heart of the action.

Bistrô da Baiana (Manoel de Carvalho 223; snacks R$8-9, mains R$11-35) Glorified snack shack for *acarajé* (bean fritters with shrimp fried in *dendê* palm oil), *moquecas* and other Bahian delights.

Restaurante Boom (Turíbio de Farias 110; buffet per kg R$43.90) Excellent and varied buffet in airy surroundings.

Privilège (Orla Bardot 550; female/male from R$60/80; Thu-Sun) Head to this sleek seaside nightclub for house music among the A-list crowd.

Also recommended:

Koni (Rua das Pedras 151; items R$7-10.50) Hyper-cool Japanese *temaki* from Rio.

Café Maré Mansa (Oscar Lopes Campos 4) Coffee culture delivered by hip *mulatas* (persons of mixed African and European heritage).

Getting There & Away

There is no bus station. Only **1001** (2623-2050; Estrada Velha da Usina 444, Loja 13) serves Búzios – a few buses run daily from Rio (R$30.50, three hours). **Salineira** runs municipal buses between Búzios and Cabo Frio (R$3.15), a 50-minute, 20km trip. Buses depart every 20 minutes or so along stops on Estrada Velha da Usina. From there you can reach Arraial do Cabo.

BRAZIL

Getting Around

Queen Lory (☎ 2623-1179; www.queenlory.com.br; Orla Bardot 710) organizes six daily trips by schooner out to Ilha Feia, and to Tartaruga and João Fernandinho beaches (costs start from R$40 for a three-hour trip including all-you-can-drink *caipirinhas*). You can rent bicycles and buggies at **Búzios Dacar** (☎ 2623-0419; Manoel de Carvalho 248; bike/buggy per 24hr R$45/120).

ILHA GRANDE

☎ 0xx24 / pop 3600

Located 150km southwest of Rio de Janeiro, Ilha Grande was once a tranquil hideaway that saw more bait and tackle than pa-parazzi, but these days it's a full-blown party nearing Thai island proportions. Most of the international jet-setters party on private yachts and islands around Baía de Angra, while backpackers, middle-class Brazilians and international nomads collect in and around Vila do Abraão, Ilha Grande's main settlement.

The increase in popularity of Brazil's third-largest island is a no brainer: gorgeous beaches (one of which, Lopes Mendes, ranks among the country's most beautiful) flank hillsides covered in lush forests, important remnants of the rapidly disappearing Mata Atlântica ecosystem.

There are no banks or private cars on Ilha Grande, so get cash before you relax. Just off the dock, there is a small tourist booth where you can pick up an island map.

Sights & Activities

From Abraão, you can hike to other beaches around the island. It's a 2½-hour walk to stunning Lopes Mendes beach, and a three-hour hike to Dois Rios, which also has a lovely beach just beyond the ruins of the old prison. There's also Bico do Papagaio (Parrot's Beak), the highest point on the island at 982m (reached in three hours, guide recommended). As elsewhere, be smart: don't hike alone and be mindful of poisonous snakes in the forests.

You can hire kayaks and arrange excursions at **Sudoeste SW Turismo** (☎ 3361-5516; www.sudoestesw.com.br; Travessa Buganville 719-A). For diving, contact **Elite Dive Center** (☎ 3361-5509; www.elitedivecenter.com.br; Travessa Buganville). You can rent snorkel equipment for R$10 in the village.

Sleeping & Eating

Santana's Camping (☎ 3361-5287; www.santanascamping .com; Santana s/n; per person R$15) One of Abraão's better-located campgrounds, with commend-able kitchen and bathroom facilities.

Che Lagarto (☎ 3361-9669; www.chelagarto.com; dm from R$40, s/d R$120/140; ⚅ 🖳) This South American staple is the island's *en vogue* hostel, offering stylish private rooms and dorms, all with private bathrooms. There's live music nightly on the atmospheric deck. To arrive, take a left from the dock and head 1km along the beach. Book well ahead.

Jungle Lodge (☎ 3361-5569; www.ilhagrande expeditions.com; Camino de Palmas 4; r per person R$50, cha-let R$150; 🖳) Tucked away above town in the rainforest, this rustic, five-room guesthouse and open-air chalet is run by a wild-haired Pantanal guide and his German wife. It's an entirely different experience than sleeping in Abraão, a 1.5km hike away. The view from the outdoor shower is miraculous.

ourpick O Pescador (☎ 3361-5114; opescadordailha @uol.com.br; Rua da Praia; s/d with balcony R$200/220, without balcony from R$180/190; ⚅ 🖳) Cozily fur-nished rooms and friendly Italian service are the appeal of this lovely midrange beach-facing guesthouse, but the island's best res-taurant (mains for two people R$54 to R$84) round out the irresistible combination.

Manaloa Creperia (Getúlio Vargas 719; crepes R$10-15; ☉ from 4pm) One street back from the beach, this outdoor cafe serves sweet and savory crepes, juices and huge bowls of *açaí*.

Bier Garten (Getúlio Vargas 161; per kg R$31.40) A shady *por kilo* restaurant and stylish tapas bar.

Lua y Mar (Rua da Praia s/n; mains for 2 people R$42-82) Excellent seafood risottos, *moquecas* and fresh fish, right on Praia do Canto's sands.

Café do Mar (Rua da Praia s/n) Candlelit beach bar and lounge perfect for sundown cocktails.

Getting There & Away

There are now several boat options to Abraão from Mangaratiba or Angra dos Reis on the mainland. The Conerj ferry leaves Mangaratiba at 8am and returns at 5:30pm (R$6.50, 1½ hours). From Angra dos Reis, Conerj departs Cais de Lapa at 3:30pm Monday to Friday (R$6.50) and 1:30pm Saturday to Sunday (R$14, 1½ hours). From Abraão to Angra, it departs at 10am daily. Faster catamarans depart Angra's Cais de Santa Luzia Monday to Friday at

8am, 11am and 4pm for Abraão, returning at 9am, 12:30pm and 5pm (R$20, 40 minutes). On weekends, they depart Angra at 8am, retuning at 5pm on Sunday – there is no Saturday return. Various slower *escunas* depart Angra's Cais de Lapa at 2:30pm, 3:30pm and 5pm Monday to Friday (R$20, 1½ hours), returning at 7:30am and 10am. On Saturday, departures leave Angra at 11am and 3pm. On Sunday, only one *escuna* departs for Angra at 11am. Weekend *escuna* returns are at 9:30am, 1pm and 5pm. There are also private door-to-door options from Rio.

Costa Verde buses depart Rio hourly to Angra (R$28, 3½ hours) from 4am to 9pm. Four daily buses from Rio go to Mangaratiba (R$20.50). Eight daily buses connect Angra with Paraty (R$7.85, two hours).

PARATY

☎ 0xx24 / pop 32,900

You know a place is authentic when cobblestones are so uneven, it's actually painful to walk the streets. That's Paraty for you. Endlessly charming and strikingly picturesque, Paraty is not only the gem of Rio de Janeiro state, but is also one of Brazil's most cinematic destinations, a staunchly preserved colonial village that can be overly touristy at times, but a sleepy dream of cobblestones and whitewash at others, only upset by the kaleidoscopic hues that pepper its historic walls. On summer weekends Paraty's plazas, sidewalk cafes and open-air restaurants come to life with live music. Paraty is crowded from Christmas to Carnaval and most weekends, but at other times is delightfully quiet.

Information

Atrium (Rua da Lapa s/n) Changes cash and traveler's checks.

Banco24Horas ATM (Av Roberto Silveira 49; ☑ 6am-10pm)

Centro de Informações Turísticas (☎ 3371-1222; Av Roberto Silveira 1; ☑ 9am-9pm) Good town info.

Sights & Activities

The small but interesting **Casa da Cultura** (☎ 3371-2325; Dona Geralda 177; admission R$5; ☑ 10am-6:30pm Wed-Mon) offers a fascinating permanent exhibition that includes interviews with and stories from local residents (audio and video) in both English and Portuguese.

Paraty's 18th-century prosperity is reflected in its beautiful old homes and churches. Three main churches served separate races. The 1725 **Igreja NS do Rosário e São Benedito dos Homens Pretos** (cnr Samuel Costa & Rua do Comércio; admission R$2; ☑ 9am-noon & 2-5pm Tue-Sat) was built by and for slaves. The 1722 **Igreja de Santa Rita dos Pardos Libertos** (Praça Santa Rita; admission R$2; ☑ 9am-noon & 2-5pm Wed-Sun) was the church for freed *mulatos* and now houses the worth-a-peak **Museu de Arte Sacra** (☑ 9am-noon & 2-4pm Wed-Sun) – though the African-Brazilian draped in chains posing with tourists as a slave here is odd, if not offensive. The 1800 **Capela de NS das Dores** (cnr Dr Pereira & Fresca; ☑ closed) was the church of the colonial white elite.

BEACHES

Paraty's biggest draw is its astounding assortment of 55 islands and 100 beaches nearby. The first beach you reach heading a few minutes' north of town is **Praia do Pontal**, the town's beach. Its sands aren't the most enticing but the *barracas* (food stalls) backing it make a nice pit stop. Another 10 minutes' walk further and on the side of the hill is the small, hidden **Praia do Forte**. **Praia do Jabaquara**, 2km past Praia do Pontal, is a spacious beach with great views, a small restaurant and a good campground. About an hour from Paraty by boat are the **Vermelha** and **Lulas** beaches, both to the northeast, and **Saco**, to the east. These beaches are small and idyllic; most have *barracas* serving beer and fish and, at most, a handful of beachgoers. **Praia de Parati-Mirim**, 27km east of Paraty, is hard to beat for accessibility, cost and beauty, and it has *barracas* and houses to rent. You can get there by municipal bus (R$2.60, 40 minutes) from Paraty bus station, with nine daily buses.

To visit the less accessible beaches, many tourists take one of the schooners from the docks. Tickets cost R$35 to R$40 per person. The boats usually call at Praia Lula, Praia Vermelho, **Ilha Comprida** and **Lagoa Azul**. An alternative is to hire one of the many small motorboats at the port. For R$60 per hour, the skipper will take you where you want to go.

For an unforgettable three-day hiking adventure from Laranjeiras to Praia Grande, taking in remote beaches and fishing villages like Praia do Sono and Martine de Sá along the way, contact **Rio Hiking** (☎ 0xx21-2552-9204; www.riohiking.com.br).

BRAZIL

Sleeping

Book ahead if you're coming from December to February. Once you hit the cobblestones, prices rise substantially.

Casa do Rio Hostel (☎ 3371-2223; www.paratyhostel .com; Antônio Vidal 120; dm with/without YHI card R$30/35, r with/without YHI card R$80/95; ⚞ ▯ ⚞) A 10-minute walk from the old town and across the river, this popular hostel provides cozy lodgings with a garden, Jacuzzi-sized pool and riverside deck out back.

Don Quixote Hostel (☎ 3371-1782; www.donquixote hostel.com; Rua da Lapa 7; dm R$40; ▯) All colonial charms are lost on this basic hostel with three-tiered bunk beds, but its location at the entrance to the old town and attached internet cafe make it the cheapest, high-value sleep on the cobblestones.

Hotel Solar dos Gerânios (☎ 3371-1550; kirkovitz @paratyweb.com.br; Praça da Matriz 2; s/d from R$80/100; ▯) This excellent value colonial *pousada* overlooking the Praça da Matriz offers thick, stone flooring, rustic antiques and several dogs and cats. Ramshackle rooms ooze history.

Casa da Colônia (☎ 3371-2343; zeclaudioaraujo@15 @hotmail.com; Marechal Deodoro 502; s/d R$80/100) Although it's 100m outside of the old town, this guesthouse has abundant colonial charm. Kitchen access.

Flor do Mar (☎ 3371-1674; www.pousadaflordomar .com.br; Fresca 257; s/d from R$100/140; ⚞ ▯) Another charmer in the old part of town, this guesthouse is a little den of tranquility with cheery rooms and a bright, airy courtyard.

Eating & Drinking

Don't miss the sweet carts rolling around town as well as the *caipirinhas* – Paraty is second only to Minas Gerais in *cachaça* (a high-proof sugarcane spirit) fame.

Farandole (Santa Rita 190; crepes R$7-21) Cute, colorful *creperia* tucked away on a quiet side street.

O Café (Rua da Lapa 237; items R$8-35) In the old town, this laid-back place serves sandwiches, breakfast and lighter meals in a garden setting. Try the pasta-free palm heart lasagna.

Punto Divino (Marechal Deodoro 129; pizza from R$20-39, mains R$24-50) This cozy Italian restaurant has wonderful thin-crust pizzas and pastas. Live music adds to the romance.

Sabor da Terra (Roberto Silveira 80; per kg R$24.90) To beat the inflated prices in the old part of town, try this self-serve.

Entertainment

Expect cover charges around R$5 to R$7 when live music is present.

Places to enjoy cocktails and bossa nova/ MPB are **Che Bar** (Marechal Deodoro 241), **Paraty 33** (Maria Jacomé de Mello 357) and **Margarida Café** (Praça do Chafariz).

Getting There & Away

The bus station is on Jango Pádua, 500m west of the old town. Eight daily buses run to/from Rio (R$45, four hours) and four to/from São Paulo (R$41, six hours). Buses leave nearly hourly to Angra dos Reis (R$7.85, two hours). They sell tickets here as if you can take a direct bus to Belo Horizonte but the bus actually departs from Angra.

SÃO PAULO

☎ 0xx11 / pop 19 million

There's no denying it: São Paulo is a monster. The gastronomic, fashion and finance capital of Latin America is a true megalopolis in every sense of the word, home to 19 million people (metropolitan) and more skyscrapers than could ever possibly be counted.

The city lacks the natural beauty of Rio but far more cosmopolitan Sampa – as locals affectionately call it – has much going for it. This is, after all, the cultural capital of Brazil. The numbers are dizzying: first-rate museums and cultural centers (110), world-class restaurants (12,500), experimental theaters and cinemas (402) – not to mention the avant-garde art galleries and numerous concert venues. Sampa's nightclubs and bars are among the best on the continent (15,000 bars makes for one hell of a pub crawl) and the restaurants among the best in the world. Trendsetting *paulistanos* (inhabitants of the city) believe in working hard and playing harder, and despite constantly complaining about street violence, clogged highways and pollution, most wouldn't dare consider moving from the largest city in the southern hemisphere.

São Paulo's charms lie in its manageable districts, from the wealthy upscale neighborhoods of Jardim Paulista (home to Oscar Freire, Brazil's Rodeo Drive) to the artsy bohemian quarter of Vila Madalena to the Japanese neighborhood of Liberdade.

Orientation

You may find it difficult to orient yourself while here – taxi drivers and residents who have lived here for years often still can't make sense of it. But just for fun: São Paulo's layout is in more of a rectangle than a traditional circle, flanked by two river-hugging expressways: Marginal Tietê to the north and Marginal Pinheiros to the south (the two join up to the west). The key downtown squares are Praça da Sé with the Metrô Sé interchange station and Praça da República with República metro station.

Av Paulista, running southeast to northwest a kilometer or two southwest of downtown and accessible by metro, is an avenue of skyscrapers and is the financial pulse of the country. South of it is Jardim Paulista, with many upscale restaurants and boutiques; north of Paulista is Baixo Augusta, a grittier, alternative neighborhood full of bars and clubs. Traveler-friendly Vila Madalena, an artistic and nightlife area, is about 6km west of downtown.

Information

Internet is ubiquitous, including free access inside Metrô Praça da Sé. Exchange houses line the first two blocks of Av São Luis near Praça da República.

Citibank (Av Paulista 1111) One of many international ATMs on this street.

CIT OLIDA (Map pp284-5; ☎ 3331-7786; www.cidade desaopaulo.com; Av São João 473, Centro; ♥ 9am-6pm) Near Praça da República; the most helpful tourist information center for non-Portuguese speakers. Other booths are on Av Paulista, Ibirapuera Park, Terminals 1 and 2 at the airport and Tietê bus station.

Deatur (Map pp284-5; ☎ 3151-467; Rua da Consolação 247; ♥ 8am-8pm Mon-Fri, 1-6pm Sat & Sun) A special tourist police force.

Einstein Hospital (off Map pp284-5; ☎ 3747-1233; www.einstein.com.br; Av Albert Einstein 627, Morumbi) One of the best hospitals in Latin America. Catch bus 7241 to Jardim Colombo from Xavier de Toledo.

HSBC Centro (Map pp284-5; Antonio de Godói 53) Bela Vista (Av Paulista 949A)

Livraria da Vila (Map p286; Fradique Coutinho 915, Vila Madalena) Impressive English section, loads of travel guides.

Post office (Map pp284-5; Praça do Correios s/n, Centro) The main branch on Parque Anhangabaú.

Dangers & Annoyances

Crime is an issue in São Paulo, though it is safer than Rio, mainly due to the proximity of the *favelas*, which are further out in the outlying suburbs than in Rio. Be especially careful in the center at night and on weekends (when fewer people are about). Watch out for pickpockets on buses and at Praça da Sé.

Sights & Activities

The atmospheric old center of São Paulo lies between Praça da Sé, Luz metro station and Praça da República (which also has a lively Sunday market). The city's pride is the baroque/art-nouveau **Teatro Municipal** just west of Viaduto do Chá on Praça Ramos de Azevedo. Another beloved landmark is the 41-story **Edifício Itália** (Map pp284-5; ☎ 2189-2997; cnr Avs São Luís & Ipiranga, Centro; www.edificioitalia.com.br; ♥ noon-12:30am Mon-Fri, noon-1am Fri & Sat, noon-11pm Sun; admission R$15), which has a restaurant/piano bar/viewing terrace at the top (non-dining patrons can take it in for free from 3pm to 4pm during the week). São Paulo's oldest museum is also its most striking, the contemporary art-filled **Pinacoteca do Estado** (Map pp284-5; ☎ 3324-1000; www.pinacoteca.org.br; Praça da Luz 2, Centro; adult/student R$4/2, Sat free; ♥ 10am-6pm Tue-Sun). A foodie's dream, the awesome **Mercado Municipal** (Map pp284-5; ☎ 3223-3022; www.mercadomunicipal.com .br; Rua da Cantareira 306, Centro; ♥ 7am-6pm Mon-Sat, to 4pm Sun) is one of Brazil's best urban markets, inside a neoclassical building dating back to 1928. Don't skip lunch here.

Fascinating neighborhood strolls are found in Liberdade, Sampa's Japan town (and home to other Asian communities); and Vila Madalena, the artistic quarter. The former hosts a lively **street market** at Praça da Liberdade.

Museu de Arte de São Paulo (off Map pp284-5; MASP; ☎ 3251-5644; www.masp.art.br; Av Paulista 1578, Bela Vista; adult/student R$15/7, free Thu; ♥ 11am-6pm Tue-Wed & Fri, 11am-8pm Thu & Sat) has Latin America's best collection of Western art, with more than 8000 pieces. The metro stop is Trianon-Masp.

The massive **Parque do Ibirapuera**, 4km from Centro, contains several museums, monuments and attractions, notably the **Museu de Arte Moderna** (☎ 5085-1300; www.mam.org.br; adult/ student R$5.50/2.75; ♥ 10am-5:30pm Tue-Sun) offering revolving temporary exhibitions. Take bus 5154 'Term. Sto. Amaro' from Estacã da Luz. Free on Sunday.

Soccer fans should bolt for the new and spectacular **Museu do Futebol** (off Map pp284-5; ☎ 3663-3848; www.museudofutebol.org.br; Praça Charles Miller s/n; adult/student R$6/3; ♥ 10am-5pm Tue-Sun), a modern, interactive, R$32.5 million congratulatory slap-on-the-ass to Brazilian football. Housed under the bleachers of Corinthians' pseudo home stadium, Estádio do Pacaembu, it is unmissable for fans and non-fans alike. The *torcida* (cheering section) exhibit is the

BRAZIL

CENTRAL SÃO PAULO

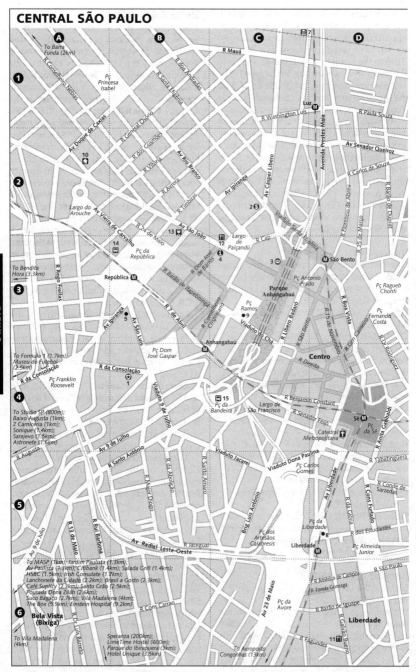

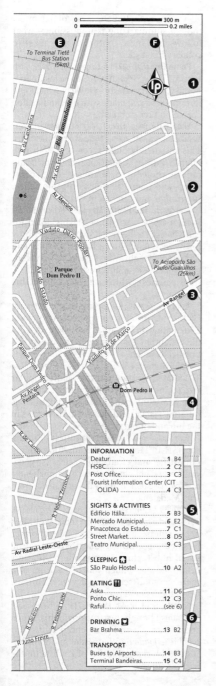

next best thing to attending a match and perhaps the best use in history of space underneath a stadium. Take bus 177C-10 'Jardim Brasil' from Teodoro Sampaio just outside Metrô Clínicas.

Sleeping

The best spot for travelers is the bohemian *bairro* of Vila Madalena, aka Soho Paulistano, 6km west of Praça da Sé, which has recently added hip hostels to its resume of artsy boutiques, cutting-edge galleries and boisterous nightlife; and the cozy, upscale district of Jardim Paulista, 5km southwest of Centro. If you opt for Centro, the areas surrounding Estação da Luz train station and central downtown are rife with cheap hotels, but also crime and prostitution – use extreme caution and don't walk around at night.

Sampa Hostel (Map p286; ☎ 3031-6779; www.hostel sampa.com.br; Girasol 519, Vila Madalena; dm with/without YHI card R$31.50/35, s with/without YHI card R$51.50/55, d R$95; 💻) The best of Vila Madalena's newly-founded hostel scene is also the veteran, dating all the way back to 2008. There's four- and eight-bed dorms, good value private rooms, a funky TV room and kitchen facilities. Female friendly.

São Paulo Hostel (Map pp284-5; ☎ 3333-0844; www. hostel.com.br; Barão de Campinas 94, Centro; dm with/without YHI card R$35/40, s/d/tr R$65/83/103; 🐾 💻) This secure, non-smoking backpackers near Praça da República offers dorms and rooms, all with private bathrooms. The 7th floor houses a kitchen, laundry and bar. Very helpful staff.

Casa Club Hostel (Map p286; ☎ 3798-0051; www .casaclub.com.br; Mourato Coelho 973, Vila Madalena; dm from R$35; 💻) Part hostel, part bar on one of Vila Madalena's best nightlife streets. There's a large kitchen and happening bar/restaurant serving by the kilo for lunch, and burgers and pasta by night. Obviously, it's the party choice.

LimeTime Hostel (off Map pp284-5; ☎ 2935-5463; www.limetimehostels.com; 13 de Maio 1552, Bela Vista; dm from R$35, s/d R$70/100; 💻) Another new, superbly located hostel, within walking distance of Av Paulista, Metrô Brigadeiro, the airport bus stop at Hotel Maksoud Plaza and, ambitiously, even Jardins. Apple TV, wi-fi and flat-screens give it a hi-tech edge, while dorms are less hip, more functional, in four- and eight-bed configurations.

BRAZIL

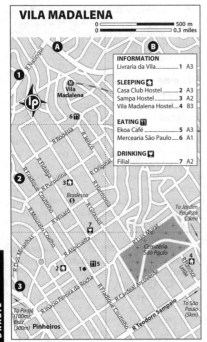

VILA MADALENA

0 _____ 500 m
0 _____ 0.3 miles

INFORMATION		
Livraria da Vila	1	A3

SLEEPING 🏠		
Casa Club Hostel	2	A3
Sampa Hostel	3	A2
Vila Madalena Hostel	4	B3

EATING 🍴		
Ekoa Café	5	A3
Mercearia São Paulo	6	A1

DRINKING 🍸		
Filial	7	A2

go wrong with Italian, Arab or Japanese, though summarizing is impossible – what follows is a mere toothpick in a massive culinary haystack.

Ponto Chic (Map pp284-5; Largo do Paíçandú 27; sandwiches R$4-17.70; ⓨ closed Sun) A Sampa institution, Ponto Chic serves tasty sandwiches, including its famous *bauru*, made with beef and melted cheese on French bread.

Ekoa Café (Map p286; Fradique Coutinho 914, Vila Madalena; menu R$16, mains R$6.50-23.80; ⓨ closed Sun) This sustainably built, green-conscious cafe offers a mostly vegetarian menu, including organic choices. There are awesome soups, salads and mains as well as organic coffee, *caipirinhas* and Eisenbahn suds.

Mercearia São Pedro (Map p286; Rodésia 34, Vila Madalena; appetizers for 2 R$7.50-28) This down-to-earth *boteco* has been at it since 1968. It's busy for its reasonable lunch buffet (R$9.80) and slammed at night, when packs of sexy *amigos* swill cold beer and fresh *pastels* (stuffed, fried pastries), which waiters deliver table to table.

Aska (Map pp284-5; Galvão Bueno 466, Liberdade; mains R$8-13; ⓨ closed Mon) Steaming-hot bowls of pork ramen draws in legions at this Liberdade noodle restaurant that's entirely too cheap. It's practically Japan.

Raful (Map pp284-5; Rua da Cantareira 306, Centro; items R$11.50-24.90; ⓨ lunch) On the wildly popular mezzanine level overlooking the fascinating Mercado Municipal, Raful serves up delicious hummus, falafel and skewered Arab treats to the hip and hungry.

Pirajá (off Map p286; Av Brigadeiro Faria Lima 64, Pinheiros; mains R$14-43) Tangerine saketinis, Rio-inspired sandwiches and a four-pepper steak (so good, you'll cry) highlight the wares at Sampa's most *carioca*-style *boteco*. It's walking distance from Vila Madalena.

ourpick Z Carniceria (off Map pp284-5; Augusta 934, Baixo Augusta; mains R$15-19.50; ⓨ closed Mon) Meat hooks still hang from the bar in this former butcher shop, now a killer Baixo Augusta social hub fueling eclectic alterna-hipsters before and after a mighty night out. Ironically, there's a good selection of veggie options. Good food. Good people.

Salada Grill (Padre Manoel 213; buffet R$15.50; ⓨ lunch) Though institutional, this lunch spot packs 'em in for its cheap buffet and reliable *feijoada* on Wednesday and Saturday. It's two blocks southwest of Paulista on the Jardin's side.

Vila Madalena Hostel (Map p286; ☎ 2305-6601; www .vilamadalenahostel.com.br; Francisco Leitão 686, Vila Madalena; dm from R$38, s/d without bathroom R$90/100; 🧺 🖥) The low-key alternative, full of artistic touches, period furniture and an eccentric owner none too keen on rowdy backpackers.

Formule 1 (off Map pp284-5; ☎ 3886-4600; www .formule1.com.br; Rua da Consolação 2303; d R$99; 🧺 🖥) For price versus location, this concept budget hotel – almost Japanese in nature with pod-like rooms and a lobby convenience kiosk – is hard to beat for its vicinity to Jardim Paulista, MASP, Av Paulista and one of the city's best art-house cinemas. Telephone, internet, baggage storage and breakfast are all extra, but you can sleep three at the above price.

Pousada Dona Ziláh (off Map pp284-5; ☎ 3062-1444; www.zilah.com; Alameda Franca 1621, Jardim Paulista; s/d/tr from R$135/180/200; 🧺 🖥) The rooms at this tranquil guesthouse are very simple, though the space itself and the international bistro are both lovely – a charming urban hideaway.

Eating

Eating is Sampa's godsend, boasting quality unrivaled in South America. You cannot

Lanchonete da Cidade (off Map pp284-5; Alameda Tietê 110, Jardim Paulista; burgers R$17.50-25) This modern diner is one of the best spots to immerse yourself in São Paulo's killer burger culture. Don't discount the memorable veggie burgers.

Brasil a Gosto (off Map pp284-5; Azevedo do Amaral 70, Jardim Paulista; mains R$36-62; ☿ closed Mon) Practically everyone's favorite Brazilian restaurant, both for its tasteful modern decor and Chef Ana Luiza Trajano's precision-perfect mix of country-wide influences in her splurge-worthy cuisine.

Drinking

Traditional bar neighborhoods are Vila Madalena (witness the corner of Aspicuelta and Mourato Coelho on weekends!) and along Mario Ferraz in Itaim Bibi, but of late the GLS scene (Portuguese slang for Gay, Lesbian and Sympathetics) is turning Baixo Augusta, once a red-light district, into a gentrified, edgy nightlife potpourri for all.

If a secret admirer sends you a note on a napkin, you're in for an interesting evening.

CAFES & JUICE BARS

Café Suplícy (off Map pp284-5; Alameda Lorena 1430, Jardim Paulista; items R$2.50-15) Probably Brazil's best coffee, with Sampa's sexiest inhabitants sipping it.

Suco Begaço (off Map pp284-5; Haddock Lobo 1483, Jardim Paulista; juice R$4-8, items R$10-15) The city's best juice spot – this trendy cafe burns through 600 glasses daily, mixed with either water, orange juice, tea or coconut water. Also offers awesome-value, build-your-own salads and sandwiches.

Santo Grão (off Map pp284-5; Oscar Freire 413, Jardim Paulista; mains R$24-43) This stylish indoor-outdoor cafe is popular for cappuccinos, wine, eclectic bistro fare and people-watching (that *includes* the staff).

BARS

Bar Brahma (Map pp284-5; Av São João 677, Centro; admission R$7-55) On the corner made famous by Caetano Veloso's love song to the city ('Sampa'), modernized Bar Brahma is the city's oldest drinking establishment. There's dueling live MPB and samba nightly and all day on the weekends in one of the three rooms, including the sleek new Esquinha da MPB. It's packed.

Filial (Map p286; Fidalgo 254, Vila Madalena) An extensive *cachaça* menu, creamy *chope* and fantastic Brazilian bar munchies (try the *bolinhos de queijo*, or fried cheese balls) served late draws swarms of the young and fun to this popular Vila Madalena *boteco*.

BRAZIL

PIZZA PAULISTANA

Forget New York, Chicago (or even Naples, for that matter): one of the world's best-kept secrets is São Paulo's excellent *pizza paulistana*. Locals say the city's pizza is so good, even the Italians are jealous! It shouldn't be a surprise, though, as swarms of Italian immigrants settled here in the late 19th century, giving the city one of the largest Italian populations in the world outside Italy. Today, nearly 6000 or so pizzerias pepper the sprawling cityscape. It *is* the best in the world. Do not depart without trying one of following:

Bráz (off Map p286; Vupabussu 271, Pinheiros; pizza R$31.50-52.50) Start to finish, the experience here will leave you forgetting pizza ever originated in Italy. Do as Brazilians do and order a Brahma draft beer *(chope)* followed by an appetizer of warm sausage bread *(pão de calabresa)* dipped in spiced olive oil, then let the feast commence. *Fosca* (smoked ham, *catipury* cheese, mozzarella and tomato sauce) is a current favorite. You can duplicate this unforgettable experience at its Rio outlet (p272) if São Paulo is not in your itinerary.

Bendita Hora (off Map pp284-5; Vanderlei 795, Perdizes; pizza R$33-62) This cavernous candlelit pizzeria was one of only three in the city to receive a star from Brazil's gourmand bible, *Guia Quattro Rodas*, in 2009. Classic vinyl records dot the walls and the liberal outdoor space draws legions of *Mauricinhos* and *Patricinhas* – as the city's hip and trendy are affectionately known – all of whom come to indulge in favorites like zucchini, mozzarella and parmesan.

Speranza (off Map pp284-5; Treze de Maio 1004, Bixiga; pizza R$35-51) One of São Paulo's oldest and most traditional pizzerias in the Italian neighborhood of Bixiga, where the Famiglia Tarallo has been serving the best margarita pizza you could ever imagine since 1958. It's housed inside a former brothel.

Skye Bar (off Map pp284-5; Av Brigadeiro Luís Antônio 4700) The top floor bar of the chic Hotel Unique, a favorite among fashionistas and rock stars, is Sampa's most astonishing cocktail with a view.

Astronete (off Map pp284-5; Matias Aires 183, Baixo Augusta; admission R$10-15; ✆ Wed-Sat) Decked out in retro-red (the Brazilian owners honed their bar skills in Williamsburg, Brooklyn), Astronete mixes cocktails with B-movies on Wednesday and '60s and '70s ditties on Friday, its hottest night.

Entertainment

Clubbing here rivals the excitement of New York and prices of Moscow. The hottest districts are Vila Olímpia (flashy, expensive, electronica) and Barra Funda/Baixo Augusta (rock, alternative, down-to-earth). Expect cover charges averaging R$10 to R$40 unless otherwise noted (sometimes recoupable in drinks, called *consumo*). Vila Olímpia's Pink Elephant was the hottest (and priciest) at press time.

Sarajevo (off Map pp284-5; Augusta 1397, Baixo Augusta; www.sarajevoclub.com.br; ✆ closed Mon) All nooks and crannies – very Eastern Bloc – and a history that includes movie production and murder, this artsy mainstay on the clubbing scene caters to a well-behaved mixed crowd for its jazz, soul/R&B, dub and hip-hop nights.

Studio SP (off Map pp284-5; Augusta 591, Baixo Augusta; www.studiosp.org; ✆ 11pm-late Tue-Sat) This large, alt-bent cultural space is Sampa's hottest spot for live local music. Early sessions are free.

Sonique (off Map pp284-5; Bela Cintra 461, Baixo Augusta; www.soniquebar.com.br; ✆ closed Mon) GLS-friendly and all dressed up in concrete and art deco lighting, this happening *pre-balada* (preparty) ultra-lounge hosts DJs nightly and staffs a clubbing concierge to direct everyone to the hotspots afterwards.

The Box (off Map pp284-5; Pequetita 189, Vila Olímpia; www.theboxlounge.com.br; admission men/women R$120/60; ✆ Fri & Sat) Full of 'playboys' (Brazilian for yuppies) and kilt-skirted waitresses, this intimate, shotgun-style NYC transplant is one of many Vila Olímpia hotspots catering to the rich, beautiful and restless.

Getting There & Away

AIR

São Paulo is the Brazilian hub for many international airlines and thus the first stop for many travelers. Before buying a domestic ticket, check which of the city's airports the flight departs from.

Aeroporto Guarulhos (✆ 6445-2945), the international airport, is 25km east of the center. Flights to Rio (Santos Dumont Airport) depart every half hour (or less) from **Aeroporto Congonhas** (✆ 5090-9000), 14km south of the center.

BUS

South America's largest bus terminal, **Terminal Tietê** (✆ 3235-0322), with buses to destinations throughout the continent, is adjacent to Tietê metro station. Avoid bus arrivals during early morning or late afternoon – traffic jams are enormous.

International buses from here go to Buenos Aires (R$285, 36 hours), Santiago (R$330, 54 hours), Asunción (R$145, 20 hours) and Montevideo (R$285, 30 hours). Frequent buses go to Rio de Janeiro (R$78, six hours). Other destinations within Brazil include Angra dos Reis (R$52, 7½ hours), Belo Horizonte (R$85, eight hours), Brasília (R$136, 15 hours), Curitiba (R$75, six hours), Florianópolis (R$120, 11 hours), Foz do Iguaçu (R$143, 15 hours), Paraty (R$41, six hours) and Salvador (R$293, 32 hours). Buses to the Pantanal – Cuiabá (R$178, 26 hours) or Campo Grande (R$161, 13½ hours) – leave from **Barra Funda bus station** (✆ 3866-1100). A direct bus to São Paulo's international airport also leaves from here (R$29).

Getting Around

São Paulo's immense public transport system is the world's most complex, boasting 15,000 buses and 1333 lines. Buses are crowded during rush hours and confusingly thorough. The main transfer points are Praça da República and the bustling Terminal Bandeiras. The tourist booths are excellent sources of bus information. The **Airport Bus Service** (www.airportbusservice.com.br; R$30) is the most efficient way to/from the international airport, making stops at Congonhas, Tietê, Praça da República and various hotels around Av Paulista and Rua Augusta. The *cheapest* way is to catch a **Pássaro Marron** bus from Metrô Tatuapé, which departs every 30 minutes (R$3.65, one hour) between 5:15am and 10:25pm. For Congonhas, catch bus 875A-10 'Perdizes-Aeroporto' from Metrô São Judas.

You can reach many places on the excellent metro, São Paulo's subway system. A combination of metro and walking is the best way to see the city. The metro is cheap, safe, fast and runs from 4:40am to midnight. A single ride costs R$2.55.

BELO HORIZONTE
☎ 0xx31 / pop 2.5 milion

Brazil's third-largest city is more or less a charmless concrete jungle but with one very important caveat: Belo Horizonte, the sprawling capital of Minas Gerais, is a very good place to eat and drink. Fueling the city's backbone as a rapidly growing industrial giant are hundreds of *botecos*, each with its own distinct personality and character. Its plethora of drinking dens has earned Beagá (the city's nickname, named for the pronunciation of its initials, BH) the title of the Bar Capital of Brazil. Though most travelers only come here en route to the colonial towns of Ouro Prêto or Tiradentes, those that stay longer will not leave on an empty stomach.

Information

Belo Horizonte has its share of crime. Pay close attention to your surroundings in the crowded area around the bus station. Don't wander late at night.

Belotur (☎ 3277-6907; www.belotur.com.br; Praça Rio Branco, Terminal Rodoviário; 8am-10pm Mon-Fri, to 4pm Sat & Sun) Extraordinarily helpful municipal tourist organization; publishes excellent monthly guide in English. Additional booths are located at Mercado Central and the international airport.

Soleá (Sergipe 1199; per hr R$4) Part dance school, part internet cafe.

Sights

The one don't-miss attraction in Beagá is the fantastic **Mercado Central** (☎ 3277-4691; Augusto de Lima 744; 8am-8pm Mon-Sat, 8am-1pm Sun), full of artisan cheese, *cachaça*, sweets and all kinds of gourmet and practical goods.

Sleeping

Pousadinha Mineira (☎ 3423-4105; www.pousadinha mineira.com.br; Espirito Santo 604; dm R$16) It's vaguely institutional and there's an extra charge for linens (R$5) and no breakfast, but this well-located choice (it's within walking distance from the bus station) is both friendly and clean. All beds are in 18-bunk dorm rooms.

Sorriso do Lagarto (☎ 3283-9325; www.osorriso dolagarto.com.br; Christina 791, São Pedro; dm R$25.50, s/d without bathroom R$45/70; ☐) The best hostel-like choice on a residential street in Sã Pedro, located next door to Savassi (about a five-block walk north). Here you'll find basic dorms and a nice outdoor patio with city views.

Formule 1 (☎ 3343-6400; www.formule1.com.br; Av Bias Fortes 783; d R$85; ☐) This budget concept hotel is great value for shoestringers – it provides you with all the mod cons in a pay-what-you-use setup: telephone, internet, baggage storage and breakfast are all extra. The small rooms can sleep three people at this price.

BRAZIL

DETOUR

A museum like no other, **Inhotim** (☎ 3227-0001; www.inhotim.org.br; admission adult/child R$10/5; 9:30am-4:30pm Thu-Fri, 9:30am-5:30pm Sat & Sun), located 60km from Belo Horizonte in Brumadinho, is a must-see in the area. Though it houses 350 works from over 80 artists, Inhotim is as much about the space itself as its inventory of contemporary art. Formed by a nonlinear sequence of pavilions in the midst of a botanical garden, Inhotim's galleries pepper a lush and mesmerizing landscape that is a museum in itself.

Around every corner of the 3.5-hectare environmental park, there are works of art built into the landscape or housed in one of nine galleries. That means a line of multihued Volkswagen Beetles along the lake or a sailing boat hanging upside down in the Burle Marx gardens. Inhotim was the private collection of *mineiro* entrepreneur Bernardo Paz until 2004, when he turned his private playground and farm into the Instituto Cultural Inhotim, a not-for-profit institution dedicated to the conservation, exhibition and production of contemporary art works and environmental preservation. Today, it's the most astonishing museum you've never heard of.

Weekends are the best time to visit, when **Saritur** (☎ 3272 8525; www.saritur.com.br) runs a direct bus from Belo's bus station at 9am, returning at 4pm (R$13.55).

Eating & Drinking

Lanchonetes (stand-up snack bars) and fast-food places cluster around Praça Sete on Av Afonso Pena, 400m southeast of the bus station. The neighborhood of Savassi has many top restaurants, including the lion's share of *botecos* that Beagá is famous for.

Boi Lourdes (Curitiba 2069, Lourdes; mains R$8-31) This sidewalk *boteco*-style version of a popular Beagá restaurant fills nightly with a fun crowd, taking in *frango ao catipury* (grilled chicken with *catipury* cheese) by the weight, tasty *picanha* and cold beer.

Pinqüim (Grão Mogol 157, Sion; sandwiches R$9.50-17.50, mains R$24-51) This always-crowded *boteco* serves legendary *chope* in a modern, impressive space with bold lighting and curvy ceilings, one block south of Savassi. It's one of the few open on Sunday.

Casa Cheira (Augusto de Lima 744, Mercado Central; mains R$12-14; ☻ lunch) Inside the northeast corner of Beagá's mesmerizing Mercado Central, this popular *boteco,* as the name implies, is always full. Daily lunch specials feature down-home *mineiro* dishes on the cheap.

Café com Letras (Antônio Albuquerque 785; sandwiches R$12-16.50) Wine and dine among the bindings at this stylish bookstore/cafe featuring snacks, larger meals and *chope.*

San Ro (Prof Moraes; per kg R$24.90) This is an Asian-vegetarian *por kilo* – if you're not a carnivore, you'll be beelining for it in Minas!

Getting There & Away

Belo's two airports have flights to just about anywhere in Brazil. Most airlines use Aeroporto Confins, 40km north of the city, but some use Aeroporto da Pampulha, 7km north of the center.

The **bus station** (Praça da Rodoviária) is in the north of the city center, near the north end of Av Afonso Pena. Buses will take you to all major points in country, including Rio (R$89, seven hours), São Paulo (R$99, 9½ hours), Brasília (R$129, 12 hours) and Salvador (R$120, 22 hours). There are 17 daily departures for Ouro Prêto (R$20, 2¾ hours), and one departure weekly on Friday at 5pm to Tiradentes (R$45, 4½ hours). To reach Tiradentes at other times, catch a bus to São João del Rei (R$37, 3½ hours) and switch there.

OURO PRÊTO
☎ 0xx31 / pop 67,000

One of South America's colonial-era greatest hits, Ouro Prêto, nestled among gorgeous mountain scenery 114km southeast of Belo Horizonte, rises from the lush landscape like a bygone living museum unyielding in its grip on the 18th century. Here numerous stunning baroque churches perched high on surrounding hillsides stand sentinel over picturesque plazas and winding cobbled streets that were once the gilded paths of the crown jewel of the Minas Gerais gold-mining towns.

As one of Brazil's best preserved colonial towns and a Unesco World Heritage Site since 1980, Ouro Prêto can be overloaded with visitors, especially on weekends and holidays; but much like Venice, its sheer beauty overcomes any resentment of being caught up in the tourist crush.

Information

Unfortunately, the town can be a bit seedy at night, particularly around the bus station. Anyone lodging near there should absolutely not walk around after dark.

Centro Cultural e Turístico da FIEMG (☎ 3559-3269; Praça Tiradentes 4; ☻ 9am-7pm) A useful and friendly source of information. You can hire official guides here starting at R$78 for four hours.

Compuway (Praça Tiradentes 52A; per hr R$4; ☻ 8am-9pm Mon-Fri, 8am-6pm Sat) Extra-pleasant internet cafe.

HSBC (São José 201) ATM.

Tourist information (☎ 3559-3287; Cláudio Manoel 61; ☻ 8am-6pm Mon-Sat) Office of the Secretary of Tourism.

Sights & Activities

Ideally, start out at about 7:30am from Praça Tiradentes and walk along Rua das Lajes for a panoramic morning view. In the east of town, the **Capela do Padre Faria** (Rua do Padre Faria s/n; admission R$3; ☻ 8:30am-4:30pm Tue-Sun) is one of Ouro Prêto's oldest chapels (1701–04) and among the richest in gold and artwork.

Descending back toward town, you'll come to the **Igreja de Santa Efigênia dos Prétos** (Santa Efigênia s/n; ☻ 8am-4:30pm), built between 1742 and 1749 by and for the black slave community. This is Ouro Prêto's poorest church in terms of gold and its richest in artwork.

The **Igreja NS da Conceição de Antônio Dias** (Rua da Conceição s/n; ☻ 8:30am-noon & 1:30-5:30pm Tue-Sat, noon-5pm Sun) was designed by Aleijadinho's father, Manuel Francisco Lisboa, and built

OURO PRÊTO

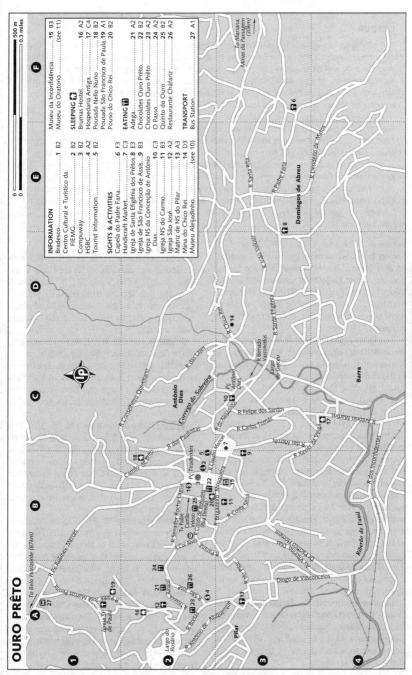

DETOUR

The otherwise unremarkable small town of **Congonhas**, 72km south of Belo Horizonte, would attract few visitors if not for the Basílica do Bom Jesus de Matosinhos and, more importantly, its magnificently carved sculptures by the Brazilian Michelangelo, Aleijadinho. Son of a Portuguese architect and an African slave, Aleijadinho lost the use of his hands and legs at the age of 30 but, with a hammer and chisel strapped to his arms, advanced art in Brazil from the excesses of baroque to a finer, more graceful rococo.

His masterworks and one of Brazil's finest Unesco offerings, the 12 Old Testament Prophets, were sculpted from soapstone at the Basílica do Bom Jesus de Matosinhos in Congonhas between 1800 and 1805. Aleijadinho was also responsible for the six chapels here and their wooden statues representing the Passion of Christ, which together are just as impressive as the prophets.

Seven daily buses run from Belo Horizonte to Congonhas (R$21.35, 1½ hours). Seven daily buses connect Congonhas with São João del Rei (R$21.35, two hours). From Ouro Prêto you must first catch a bus to Conselheiro Lafaiete (R$12.85, two hours), and then connect on to Congonhas (R$4.10, 45 minutes) on frequently departing daily buses. Local Profetta buses run between Congonhas bus station and the Basílica (R$1.85, 15 minutes), 1.5km away.

---

between 1727 and 1770. Aleijadinho (see boxed text above) is buried near the altar of Boa Morte. An extensive homage to his life, the **Museu Aleijadinho** (admission R$6) is also here, full of intricate crucifixes, elaborate oratories (niches containing saints' images to ward off evil spirits) and a vast collection of religious figurines.

The **Igreja de São Francisco de Assis** (Rua do Ouvidor aka Cláudio Manoel; admission R$6; ⏲ 8:30-11:50am & 1:30-5pm Tue-Sun), two blocks east of Praça Tiradentes, is the most important piece of Brazilian colonial art after the *Prophets* in Congonhas (see boxed text, above). Aleijadinho carved its entire exterior and his long-term partner, Manuel da Costa Ataíde, painted the inside.

On Praça Tiradentes, the excellent **Museu da Inconfidência** (admission R$6; ⏲ noon-6pm) has documents of the Inconfidência Mineira, a memorial to Tiradentes, torture instruments and important works by Ataíde and Aleijadinho.

The **Igreja NS do Carmo** (Brigadeiro Mosqueira; admission R$2; ⏲ 9-11am & 1-4:45pm Tue-Sat, 10am-3pm Sun), southwest of Praça Tiradentes, was built as a group effort by the most important artists of the area. Built between 1766 and 1772, its facade and two side altars are by Aleijadinho. The **Museu do Oratório** (admission R$2; ⏲ 9:30am-5:30pm), next door, houses a fabulous, well-displayed collection of oratories.

Further southwest, the **Matriz de NS do Pilar** (Brigador Mosqueira Castilho Barbosa s/n, in Praça Monsenhor João Castilho Barbosa; admission R$5; ⏲ 9-10:45am & noon-4:45pm) boasts 434kg of gold and silver in its ornamentation and is one of Brazil's finest showcases of artwork.

Sleeping

Pousada São Francisco de Paula (☎ 3551-3456; www .pousadasaofranciscodepaula.com.br; Padre José Marcos Penna 202; dm/s/d R$25/50/70; 🖳) A short walk from the bus station, this friendly place is tucked away in a run-down forest and offers expansive views to Igeja do Carmo from its outdoor deck.

Brumas Hostel (☎ 3551-2944; www.brumashostel .com.br; Padre José Marcos Penna 68; dm with/without YHI card R$25/32, s/d from R$50/70; 🖳) This welcoming hostel has colorful, clean rooms and kitchen access. There's a large and homey common area with lots of great old tables and places to lounge.

ourpick Pouso do Chico Rei (☎ 3551-1274; www .pousodochicorei.com.br; Brigadeiro Musqueira 90; s/d from R$110/154, without bathroom R$66/120; 🖳) The best midrange in town, oozing colonial charm. There's a lovely antique-filled breakfast room and crotchety old hardwood floors throughout. All the rooms are unique and individually priced.

Pousada Nello Nuno (☎ 3551-3375; www.pousadanello nuno.com; Camilo de Brito 59; s/d/tr from R$85/130/176) A few blocks northeast of Praça Tiradentes on a very steep incline, this lovely *pousada* has lots of colonial charm, with comfy rooms and plentiful artistic touches.

Hospedaria Antiga (☎ 3551-2203; www.antiga .com.br; Xavier da Veiga 01; s/d/tr from R$90/120/160; 🖳) Warped colonial floors, breakfast in a stunning, medieval-summoning basement room and a small garden round out the pluses at this friendly 18th-century guesthouse. Downstairs rooms are bigger and brighter.

Eating

Many restaurants and bars line Conde de Bobadela and São José. Typical Minas dishes include *tutu,* a puréed black-bean side dish; and *Feijão Tropeiro,* a mix of brown beans, kale, onions, eggs, manioc flour and sometimes bacon.

Chocolates Ouro Prêto (Getúlio Vargas 72; snacks R$2-4) This quaint cafe and dessert shop serves tortes with chicken or hearts of palm, as well as artisan chocolate treats. A newer location just opened on Praça Tiradentes.

O Passo (São José 56; pizza R$17-38) Pizza and pasta served in an old house with a priceless outdoor terrace overlooking the Burle Marx gardens.

Restaurante Cháfariz (São José 167; all-you-can-eat buffet R$31) Journey through *comida Mineira* at this atmospheric all-you-can-eat, the town's favorite. *Cachaça* included!

Two great *por kilo* options are **Adega** (Teixeira Amaral 24; all-you-can-eat R$15, per kg R$23), a buffet by day, pizzeria by night; and **Quinto do Ouro** (Conde de Bobadela 76; per kg R$25.90), full of exceptional quality *Mineira* cuisine.

Getting There & Away

The **bus station** (Rolimex-Merces) is 500m northwest of Praça Tiradentes (catch a 'Circular' bus to/from the plaza). Numerous daily buses run between Belo Horizonte and Ouro Prêto (R$19.35, 2¾ hours). During peak periods, buy your tickets a day in advance. From Ouro Prêto there are three daily buses to Rio (R$91, seven hours), and two daily buses to São Paulo (R$97.50, 11 hours).

TIRADENTES

☎ 0xx32 / pop 6600

Sleepy Tiradentes, one of the quaintest colonial villages in Brazil, is full of camera-ready charm, from its peaceful, cobbled streets to its mountain vistas, with a wandering river

trickling through town. There are two things to do here: shop and eat. Tiradentes is home to the highest concentration per capita of starred restaurants in Brazil. There are five, so a blowout meal here is a must, and no secret: the otherwise serene village swarms with Brazilians on weekends and holidays.

The town's colonial buildings run up a hillside, where they culminate in the beautiful 1710 **Igreja Matriz de Santo Antônio** (Padre Toledo s/n; admission R$3; ☉ 9am-5pm); it has a facade by Aleijadinho and an all-gold interior rich in Old Testament symbolism.

Built by slaves, the **Igreja Nossa Senhora Rosário dos Pretos** (Direita s/n; admission R$2; ☉ 9am-5pm), is Tiradentes' oldest church, dating from 1708; it contains several images of black saints. The **Museu do Padre Toledo** (Padre Toledo 190; admission R$3; ☉ 9-11:30am & 1-4:30pm Thu-Fri, 9am-4:40pm Sat & Sun) is the former mansion of another hero of the Inconfidência, and is full of antiques and 18th-century curios.

Not five minutes' walk from the cobblestones and bus station is **Hotel do Hespanhol** (☎ 3355-1560; Rua dos Inconfidentes 479; s/d R$60/90), a simple budget option with threadbare but clean rooms next door to a decent artisan shop. The wonderful **Pousada da Bia** (☎ 3355-1173; www.pousadadabia.com.br; Frederico Ozanan 330; s/d R$80/120; ☐ ☒) is a longtime favorite with rooms set around a grassy courtyard and swimming pool. Breakfast is divine. **Pousada Tiradentes** (☎ 3355-1232; www.pousadatiradentesmg .com.br; São Francisco de Paula 41; s/d R$96/110; ☒ ☐) is next to the bus station, offering just-renovated rooms decked out in modish white with large, well-maintained bathrooms.

Jardins de Santo Antonio (Ministro Gabriel Passos 308; mains R$5-22; ☉ closed Mon-Tue) serves brick-oven pizza, crepes, and cold Backer *chope* (from Minas) in a stylish spot with a fantastic front patio for people-watching. On

---

SPLURGE!

It would be a crying shame to come to Tiradentes and not shell out for one of its starred culinary offerings. Pinch *centavos* elsewhere, go big here. Three of the most affordable: **Pau de Angu** (Estrada para Bichinho Km 3, mains for 2/4 people from R$43/71) features select *Mineira* specialties (pork, chicken or beef), served with all the traditional fixings on a farm 3km out of town. **Estralgem da Sabor** (Ministro Gabriel Passos 280; mains for 2 people R$46-69) offers simple but excellently prepared *Mineira* classics. **our pick** **Tragaluz** (Direita 53; mains R$35-52) This place entices diners with a 32-page, pocket-sized contemporary menu that's laid out comic book-style and features all sorts of cute tales about the history of the town and current staff. Don't miss desert: dried guava fruit rolled in cashews nuts and fried, served over a bed of Brazilian cream cheese with guava ice cream. *Delícia!*

Largo das Forras, **Bar do Celso** (Largo das Forras 80A; meals R$14-21; ⊙ closed Tue) has a small selection of *Mineira* dishes at decent prices. **Empório das Massas** (Frederico Ozanan 327; pastas for 2/4 people from R$15/45; ⊙ closed Mon-Wed) has a wealth of pastas and sauces –you play matchmaker for a reasonable price.

Getting There & Around

The best approach to Tiradentes is the wonderful train trip from São João del Rei. The **Maria Fumaça** (São João station; one way/round trip R$18/30) is pulled by 19th-century steam locomotives and chugs along a picturesque 13km track from São João. It departs São João at 10am and 3pm and returns at 1pm and 5pm. Numerous buses connect Tiradentes with São João daily (R$2.15, 30 minutes).

THE SOUTH

Spectacular white-sand beaches, pristine subtropical islands and the thunderous roar of Iguaçu Falls are a few of the attractions of Brazil's affluent South. While often given short shrift by first-time visitors, this region offers a radically different version of what it means to be Brazilian. Here *gaúchos* still cling to the cowboy lifestyle on the wide plains bordering Argentina and Uruguay, while old-world architecture, European-style beer, blond hair and blue eyes reveal the influence of millions of German, Italian, Swiss and Eastern European immigrants.

The South comprises three states: Paraná, Santa Catarina and Rio Grande do Sul. The climate is generally subtropical, but snow is not uncommon in the interior highlands in winter.

Getting There & Away

The major air gateways are Curitiba, Florianópolis, Porto Alegre and Foz do Iguaçu, which borders both Argentina and Paraguay. All these cities have good bus connections to São Paulo.

Getting Around

Short flights and longer bus journeys connect the four major cities of the South. If you're heading to Ilha do Mel, don't miss the scenic train ride from Curitiba through the Serra do Mar to Paranaguá, where you can hop a ferry to the island.

CURITIBA

☎ 0xx41 / pop 1.8 million

Known for its eco-friendly design, Curitiba is one of Brazil's urban success stories, with pleasant parks, well-preserved historic buildings, little traffic congestion and a large university population. Paraná's capital is a good place for a pit stop, but there's not much to hold your attention beyond a few days.

Information

Cybernet XV (Rua das Flores 106; internet per hr R$2.50; ⊙ 9:30am-midnight Mon-Sat)
HSBC (15 de Novembro) One of many pedestrian zone ATMs.
Post office (15 de Novembro 700)
Tourist offices (www.turismo.curitiba.pr.gov.br) bus station (☎ 3320-3121; ⊙ 8am-6pm); Largo da Ordem (☎ 3321-3206; Praça Garibaldi 7; ⊙ 9am-6pm Mon-Sat, to 4pm Sun)

Sights & Activities

Strolling is the best way to enjoy Curitiba. The cobbled historic quarter around **Largo da Ordem** has beautifully restored buildings, art galleries, bars and restaurants, with live music after dark. Nearby, the pretty pedestrianized **Rua das Flores** (a pedestrianized section of 15 de Novembro) is lined with shops, restaurants and colorful flowers. For more greenery, visit the **Passeio Público** (Av Presidente Carlos Cavalcanti; ⊙ Tue-Sun), a park with shady walks and a lake. Curitiba's attractions outside the center – including botanical gardens and the excellent Oscar Niemeyer art museum – are accessible via the **Linha Turismo Bus** (see Getting Around, p297).

Sleeping

Curitiba Eco Hostel (☎ 3274-7979; www.curitibaeco hostel.com.br; Tramontin 1693; dm/s/d with YHI card R$20/50/60, without YHI card R$25/55/70) Hammocks, chirping insects, an outdoor deck and a pretty breakfast area are among the welcoming features at this hostel 7km from the center. Catch the 'Tramontina' bus (R$2.20) from Praça Rui Barbosa.

Roma Hostel (☎ 3224-2117; www.hostelroma.com.br; Barão do Rio Branco 805; dm/s/d with YHI card R$22/33/50, without YHI card R$28/39/60) Despite its somewhat surly atmosphere, this no-frills hostel is conveniently located between the bus station and downtown.

Palace Hotel (☎ 3222-2554; www.palacehotelpr.com .br; Barão do Rio Branco 62; s/d/tr R$38/60/82) Near Rua das Flores, the funky, faded Palace features an antique elevator and good natural lighting from big old-fashioned windows.

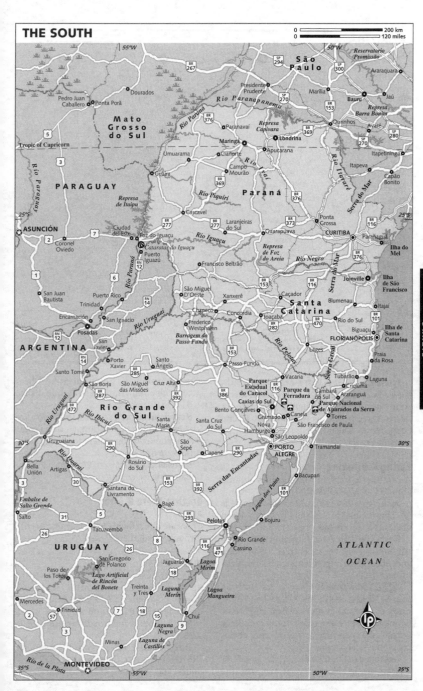

THE SOUTH

BRAZIL

0 200 km
0 120 miles

São Paulo

Reservatório Promissão

Araraquara

BR 267

SP 294

SP 300

Dourados

Presidente Prudente

Marília

Bauru

Jaú

Pedro Juan Caballero

Ponta Porã

Rio Paranapanema

SP 270

BR 153

Represa Barra Bonita

Mato Grosso do Sul

Paranavaí

Rio Paraná

BR 376

Represa Capivara

Ourinhos

BR 369

Avaré

Maringá

Londrina

Apucarana

SP 270

SP 280

Tropic of Capricorn

5

Umuarama

Cianorte

Campo Mourão

Rio Ivaí

Itapetininga

3

Guaíra

BR 369

Itapeva

Capão Bonito

PARAGUAY

Rio Paraná

Rio Piquiri

Paraná

BR 376

Serra do Mar

Represa de Itaipu

Cascavel

BR 277

Laranjeiras do Sul

BR 277

Ponta Grossa

BR 116

25°S

ASUNCIÓN

2

7

Ciudad del Este

Foz do Iguaçu

BR 373

Quarapuava

CURITIBA

Paranaguá

25°S

Coronel Oviedo

Cataratas do Iguaçu

Puerto Iguazú

BR 12

Rio Iguaçu

Ilha do Mel

1

6

RN 12

Francisco Beltrão

Represa de Foz do Areia

Rio Negro

BR 376

Joinville

Ilha de São Francisco

San Juan Bautista

Puerto Rico

BR 153

São Miguel D'Oeste

Xanxerê

Caçador

BR 116

Blumenau

Itajaí

BR 101

Trinidad

RN 14

Santa Catarina

Encarnación

San Ignacio

Chapecó

Concórdia

Joaçaba

Rio do Sul

Biguaçu

Ilha de Santa Catarina

Posadas

RN 12

San Javier

Frederico Westphalen

BR 153

BR 282

BR 470

FLORIANÓPOLIS

ARGENTINA

Rio Uruguai

Barragem do Passo Fundo

Lages

Serra Geral

Praia da Rosa

RN 14

Porto Xavier

Santo Ângelo

BR 153

Rio Pelotas

BR 285

Passo Fundo

Vacaria

Tubarão

Laguna

Santo Tomé

São Borja

São Miguel das Missões

Cruz Alta

BR 392

BR 386

Parque Estadual do Caracol

BR 116

Parque da Ferradura

Caxias do Sul

Cambará do Sul

Criciúma

Araranguá

Rio Uruguai

BR 287

BR 472

Rio Grande do Sul

Santa Maria

Santa Cruz do Sul

Bento Gonçalves

Gramado

Nova Hamburgo

Canela

Parque Nacional de Aparados da Serra

Torres

Rio Ibicuí

São Francisco de Paula

30°S

Uruguaiana

BR 290

São Sepé

Capané

BR 290

São Leopoldo

PORTO ALEGRE

Tramandaí

30°S

Rio Quaraí

Rosário do Sul

Serra das Encantadas

Bacupari

Bella Unión

Artigas

BR 153

BR 392

BR 101

Lagoa dos Patos

3

Santana do Livramento

Bagé

Embalse de Salto Grande

31

BR 293

Bojuru

Salto

5

Pelotas

ATLANTIC OCEAN

26

Tacuarembó

8

BR 116

Rio Grande

URUGUAY

26

BR 471

Cassino

San Gregorio de Polanco

Jaguarão

18

Lagoa Mirim

Paso de los Toros

Lago Artificial de Rincón del Bonete

Treinta y Tres

Laguna Merín

Lagoa Mangueira

Mercedes

2

57

Trinidad

7

18

15

Chuí

9

3

Minas

Laguna Negra

Laguna de Castillos

Rio de la Plata

MONTEVIDEO

35°S

55°W

50°W

35°S

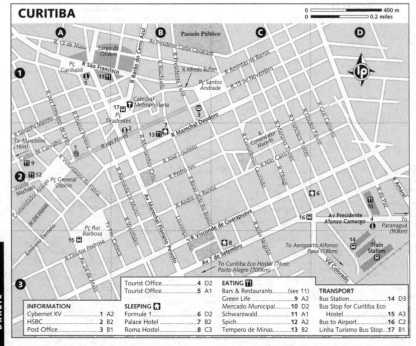

CURITIBA

INFORMATION		
Cybernet XV	**1**	A2
HSBC	**2**	B2
Post Office	**3**	B1
Tourist Office	**4**	D2
Tourist Office	**5**	A1

SLEEPING		
Formule 1	**6**	D2
Palace Hotel	**7**	B2
Roma Hostel	**8**	C3

EATING		
Bars & Restaurants	(see 11)	
Green Life	**9**	A2
Mercado Municipal	**10**	D2
Schwarzwald	**11**	A1
Spich	**12**	A2
Tempero de Minas	**13**	B2

TRANSPORT		
Bus Station	**14**	D3
Bus Stop for Curitiba Eco		
Hostel	**15**	A3
Bus to Airport	**16**	C2
Linha Turismo Bus Stop	**17**	B1

Formule 1 (☎ 3218-3838; www.accorhotels.com.br; Mariano Torres 927; r R$69; ✖ ▣) This modern, comfy chain hotel, charging a fixed rate for one to three people, is the nicest of several budget options near the bus station. Breakfast costs R$6 extra.

Eating & Drinking

Atmospheric bars and restaurants abound around Largo da Ordem.

Spich (Vicente Machado 18; buffet R$4.50; ✖ lunch Mon-Sat) This popular lunch spot offers two dozen dishes at absurdly low prices.

Green Life (Carvalho 271; buffet R$13; ✖ lunch) All-you-can-eat veggie entrees, salad, soup and juice; most ingredients come from the owners' farm.

OUR PICK Schwarzwald (Claudino dos Santos 63; mains for 2 people from R$18.90; ✖ 11am-2am) Filling plates of wurst, cold steins of beer and classic German desserts like apfelstrudel and Black Forest cake keep the crowds buzzing at this cozy, convivial beer hall.

Tempero de Minas (Deodoro 303; per kg R$23.90; ✖ lunch Mon-Sat) This airy, award-winning eatery harmonizes hearty meat-and-bean stews with abundant vegetable side dishes.

Also recommended:

Mercado Municipal (Carneiro s/n; ✖ 8am-6pm Mon-Sat) Opposite the bus station, Curitiba's municipal market is convenient for fruit, cheese, coffee or a quick bite.

Marcolini (Carvalho 1181; ✖ 7:30am-9pm) Excellent Italian-style ice cream.

Getting There & Away

AIR

There are direct flights from Curitiba to cities throughout southern Brazil.

BUS

Frequent buses run to Paranaguá (R$18, 90 minutes), Florianópolis (R$41, 4½ hours), São Paulo (R$55, 6½ hours), Foz do Iguaçu (R$102, 10 hours), Porto Alegre (R$93, 11 hours) and Rio de Janeiro (R$106, 12½ hours).

International buses run to Asunción (R$108, 14 hours), Buenos Aires (R$230, 34 hours) and Santiago (R$312, 54 hours).

BRAZIL

TRAIN

The **Serra Verde Express** (☎ 3888-3488; serraverde express.com.br) railway from Curitiba to Paranaguá is the most exciting in Brazil, with sublime panoramas.

The train leaves Curitiba at 8:15am daily, descending 900m through the lush Serra do Mar to the historic town of Morretes, arriving at 11:15am and returning at 3pm. On Sunday it continues beyond Morretes to the port of Paranaguá, arriving at 1:15pm and returning at 2pm. One-way economy/ tourist-class tickets to either Morretes or Paranaguá cost R$32/58. Sit on the left side for the best views.

Buy tickets in advance on weekends.

Getting Around

Alfonso Pena Airport is 18km from the city. An Aeroporto-Centro bus leaves every 30 minutes (R$2.20, 30 minutes) from Av 7 de Setembro. A classier 'Aeroporto Executivo' shuttle (www.aeroportoexecutivo.com.br; R$8) goes direct every 20 minutes to the center making only select stops, including the bus station and Praça Tiradentes.

The double-decker Linha Turismo bus (www.viaje.curitiba.pr.gov.br; R$20) is a great way to see the sights outside Curitiba's downtown. It leaves Praça Tiradentes half-hourly from 9am to 5:30pm Tuesday to Sunday. You can get off at any four of the 23 attractions and hop on the next bus.

PARANAGUÁ

☎ 0xx41 / pop 134,000

Paranaguá is both the terminus of the scenic train ride from Curitiba and the embarkation point for ferries to idyllic Ilha do Mel. Colorful but now faded buildings along the colonial waterfront create a feeling of languid tropical decadence, belying Paranaguá's status as Latin America's largest soybean port. The **tourist office** (☎ 3422-6882; Carneiro 258; ☸ 8am-6pm) and other places listed below are near the harbor, an easy 200m stroll from the bus terminal.

Hostel Continente (☎ 3423-3224; www.hostelconti nente.com.br; Carneiro 300; dm/s/d R$25/40/65) has clean if cramped dorms and doubles in an enviable location across from the ferry dock.

Try the local specialty *barreado* (meat stew cooked in a clay pot) or the *prato feito* (fixed-price lunch, R$8) at the inexpensive **Mercado Municipal do Café** (Carneiro s/n).

Frequent buses to Curitiba (R$17, 1½ hours) and Morretes (R$3.40, 50 minutes) leave from the terminal just inland from the waterfront. For details on the Sunday train service to/from Curitiba, see left.

ILHA DO MEL

☎ 0xx41 / pop 1200

As sweet as its name, Ilha do Mel (Honey Island) is Paraná state's most enchanting getaway. This oddly shaped island at the mouth of the Baía da Paranaguá offers excellent beaches, good surfing waves and scenic coastal walks. Cars are not allowed, so traffic consists mostly of boats and surfboard-toting Brazilians on bicycles. A young party crowd descends from January to Carnaval and over Easter. Otherwise it's a tranquil, relatively isolated place.

Sights & Activities

Ilha do Mel consists of two parts joined by the beach at Nova Brasília. The larger, northern part is mostly an ecological station, little visited except for Praia da Fortaleza, where an 18th-century fort still stands.

For fine views, visit Farol das Conchas (Conchas Lighthouse), east of Nova Brasília. The best beaches are east-facing Praia Grande, Praia do Miguel and Praia de Fora. It's a 1½-hour walk along the coast from Nova Brasília to Encantadas.

Sleeping & Eating

Rooms book up fast in peak season, but you can always pitch a tent or sling a hammock in Nova Brasília (R$10 to R$15 per person).

The biggest concentrations of *pousadas* are along the track heading east from Nova Brasília to Praia do Farol and at smaller Encantadas, near the island's southwest corner.

our pick **Hostel Zorro** (☎ 3426-9052; www.hostel zorro.com.br; dm/d R$30/90; ☐) The island's best value, this popular hostel facing Encantadas beach offers a generous breakfast, comfy common areas, a communal kitchen, a beachfront deck, and bike and surfboard rentals (per hour/day R$10/30).

Pousadinha (☎ 3426-8026; www.pousadinha.com.br; d with/without bathroom R$110/80) About 100m from the Nova Brasília dock, Pousadinha's rooms range from rustic shared bathroom affairs to newly constructed suites. The attached restaurant serves pasta and Brazilian standards (meals from R$12).

BRAZIL

EIN BIER, POR FAVOR! (BLUMENAU BEER DETOUR)

Brazil's mainstream brews – Skol, Brahma and Antarctica – are fine for staving off the tropical heat, but let's face it: taste is not their strong suit. Luckily, the German immigrants of Blumenau (Santa Catarina state) are here to help. There is a true beer culture here dating back to the mid-1800s, with *real* beer like pale ale, bock, wheat and pilsen.

The four breweries below are the region's best, and all have fantastic tasting rooms in and around Blumenau. With a car and a designated driver, you can visit them all in a day.

Cervejaria Bierland (☎ 0xx47-3337-3100; www.bierland.com.br; Zimmermann 5361, Blumenau)
Cervejaria Das Bier (☎ 0xx47-3397-8600; www.dasbier.com.br; Haendchen 5311, Gaspar)
Cervejaria Eisenbahn (☎ 0xx47-3488-7307; www.eisenbahn.com.br; Bahia 5181, Blumenau)
Cervejaria Schornstein (☎ 0xx47-3399-2058; www.schornstein.com.br; Weege 60, Pomerode)

Even better, raise a stein with the locals at Blumenau's annual **Oktoberfest** (www.oktoberfest blumenau.com.br), Brazil's second biggest party after Carnaval.

Frequent buses connect Blumenau with Curitiba (R$31, four hours) and Florianópolis (R$29, three hours).

O Recanto do Francês (☎ 3426-9105; www.recanto dofrances.com.br; d R$100) The shady garden setting, friendly French owners and afternoon crepes are the big draws at this *pousada* east of Encantadas.

Spyro Gyro (drinks & snacks R$2.50-9) Serving smoothies, fruit salad, sandwiches and *caipirinhas*, this simple juice shack on the isthmus is perfect for cooling off after a hike to the fort or the lighthouse.

Mar e Sol (meals from R$10) En route to the lighthouse, Mar e Sol serves delicious home-cooked daily specials. Junior, the local pet parrot, offers recommendations.

Praça de Alimentação (mains from R$12) This beachside restaurant complex located south of Encantadas serves seafood along with live music on weekends.

Grajagan Surf Resort Opposite Praia Grande, a classy surfers' bar whimsically decorated in carved wood and mosaics.

Getting There & Away

Abaline (☎ 3425-6325) runs boats (R$13.50) at least twice daily (more frequently in summer) from the jetty opposite Paranaguá's tourist office, stopping first in Nova Brasília (1½ hours), and afterwards in Encantadas (two hours).

Alternatively, take a bus from Curitiba to Pontal do Sul (R$23, 2½ hours), on the mainland opposite Encantadas, where you can embark for the 30-minute crossing to Nova Brasilia or Encantadas (R$10). In high season, boats leave at least hourly from 8am to 5pm.

ILHA DE SANTA CATARINA
☎ 0xx48

For years, gorgeous Ilha de Santa Catarina has been luring surfers and sun worshippers from all over Brazil, Argentina and Uruguay. Recently, visitors from other countries have begun to catch on. The island's varied landscape includes tranquil pine forests, dunes large enough to surf down and mountains covered by Mata Atlântica (Atlantic rainforest); there are also two pretty lagoons: tranquil Lagoa do Peri and the more urbanized Lagoa da Conceição. Beaches remain the island's main attraction, however, from long sweeps of unbroken sand to secluded little coves tucked into the wild, verdant shoreline.

While the north of the island is heavily developed, the south remains more tranquil, with a pleasant mix of old Azorean fishing settlements and empty, unspoiled beaches.

Activities

Surfing, **kitesurfing** and **diving** outfits line the beach at Barra da Lagoa, on the island's eastern shore. A few kilometers south, try your hand at **sand boarding** (R$10 per hour) on the dunes at Praia da Joaquina.

The island's southern tip offers excellent **hiking**, including the one-hour trek through lush forest from Pântano do Sul to pristine Lagoinha do Leste beach.

From December through March, **Scuna Sul** (☎ 3232-4019; www.scunasul.com.br) and **Lagomar** (☎ 3232-7262; centraldopasseio@gmail.com) offer six-hour **boat tours** (R$40 to R$45) from Barra

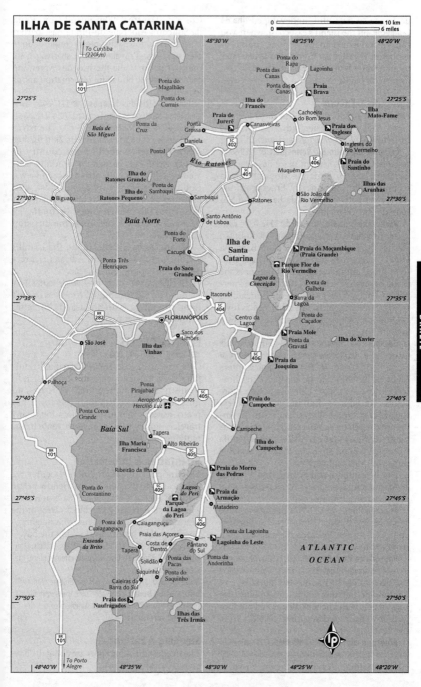

ILHA DE SANTA CATARINA

| 0 | 10 km |
| 0 | 6 miles |

To Curitiba (220km)

BR 101

48°40'W 48°35'W 48°30'W 48°25'W 48°20'W

27°25'S

Ponta do Magalhães
Ponta dos Currais
Ponta da Cruz
Ponta Grossa
Daniela
Pontal

Ponta do Rapa
Ponta das Canas
Ponta das Canas
Lagoinha
Praia Brava
Praia de Jurerê
Ilha do Francês
Canasvieiras
Cachoeira do Bom Jesus
Ilha Mato-Fame
Praia dos Ingleses
Ingleses do Rio Vermelho
Ilhas das Aranhas

SC 402
SC 403
SC 406

Praia do Santinho

Baía de São Miguel

Rio Ratones

Ilha do Ratones Grande
Ilha do Ratones Pequeno
Ponta de Sambaqui
Sambaqui

SC 401

Muquém
São João do Rio Vermelho

27°30'S

Biguaçu

Baía Norte

Santo Antônio de Lisboa
Ponta do Forte
Cacupé
Ponta Três Henriques
Praia do Saco Grande

Ratones

Ilha de Santa Catarina

Praia do Moçambique (Praia Grande)
Parque Flor do Rio Vermelho

Lagoa da Conceição
Ponta da Galheta

Itacorubi

SC 404

FLORIANÓPOLIS

BR 282

São José

Saco dos Limões
Centro da Lagoa

Barra da Lagoa
Ponta do Caçador

27°35'S

Ilha das Vinhas

SC 406

Praia Mole
Ponta da Gravatá
Ilha do Xavier

Praia da Joaquina

Palhoça

Ponta Pirajubaé
Aeroporto Hercílio Luz
Canasvieiras

SC 405

Praia do Campeche

27°40'S

Ponta Coroa Grande

Baía Sul

Tapera
Alto Ribeirão

Campeche
Ilha do Campeche

Ilha Maria Francisca

SC 405

BR 101

Ribeirão da Ilha

SC 405

Praia do Morro das Pedras

27°45'S

Ponta do Constantino

Lagoa do Peri
Parque da Lagoa do Peri

Praia da Armação
Matadeiro

SC 406

Ponta do Cuaiaguçu
Caiaganguçu
Praia das Açores
Costa de Dentro
Pântano do Sul
Ponta da Lagoinha
Lagoinha do Leste

ATLANTIC OCEAN

Enseado da Brito
Tapera
Solidão
Saquinho
Ponta das Pacas
Ponta do Saquinho
Ponta da Andorinha

Caieiras da Barra do Sul

27°50'S

Praia dos Naufragados

Ilhas das Três Irmãs

BR 101

To Porto Alegre

48°40'W 48°35'W 48°30'W 48°25'W 48°20'W

BRAZIL

da Lagoa to beautiful, undeveloped **Ilha do Campeche**, off the island's east coast, where you can check out ancient inscriptions, snorkel or sunbathe. For excursions on **Lagoa da Conceição**, catch a **water taxi** (R$8) beside the bridge in Centro da Lagoa town.

Sleeping & Eating

Heading from north to south, these are our picks. Also watch for signs advertising rooms for rent (*'se aluga quarto/apartamento'*).

Camping Escoteiro Rio Vermelho (☎ 3269-9984; per person R$9) This pleasant place lies near the northern end of Praia do Moçambique, a stunning 14km-long beach. Enter from the main road between Barra da Lagoa and São João do Rio Vermelho.

Backpackers Share House (☎ 3232-7606; www .backpackersfloripa.com; per person dm/d/tr R$40/50/45; 💻) Across the pedestrian bridge from Barra da Lagoa beach, that crazy white fortress with the souped-up motorcycle on the roof is the Backpackers Share House. It attracts an international party crowd with amenities including free use of surfboards and other beach toys, excursions, evening BBQs and an 'honesty system' bar.

Backpackers Sunset (☎ 3232-0141; www.back packersfloripa.com; Rodovia Menezes 631; per person dm/ d/tw/tr R$43/75/55/55; 💻 🐕) This place offers identical amenities to its cheaper sister hostel (Backpackers Share House) but feels more resort-like, with a swimming pool and access to parties at the adjoining dance club. Its impressive perch on a mid-island hilltop affords fabulous views and easy access to Lagoa da Conceição, Praia Mole and the huge surfable dunes of Praia da Joaquina.

On the southern end of the island, Praia da Armação (another surfer favorite) has several inexpensive guesthouses.

Pousada Pires (☎ 3237-5370; pousadapires@yahoo .com.br; Fonseca 745; d/ste R$90/100) Offering kitchen-equipped rooms, Pousada Pires is only 50m from the beach.

Pousada do Pescador (☎ 3237-7122; www.pousada dopescador.com.br; Vidal 257; 1-/2-/4-/6-person chalet R$70/120/180/200) In the old fishing village of Pântano do Sul, this family-run *pousada* has nice chalets with kitchens, patios and outdoor grills in a shady garden setting one block from the beach.

Albergue do Pirata (☎ 3389-2727; albergue @alberguedopirata.com.br; Ferreira s/n; dm/s/d R$30/40/80; 💻) Continuing 3km down the main road to Costa de Dentro (500m inland from Praia da Solidão), Albergue do Pirata has spartan hostel rooms downstairs plus a couple of doubles upstairs. Travelers trade stories on its outdoor patio, while the friendly Argentine owners provide bountiful information about local hikes.

Pousada Sítio dos Tucanos (☎ 3237-5084; www .pousadasitiodostucanos.com; Ferreira 2776; s/d high season R$130/170, low season R$80/130; 💻) The pavement ends as the road meanders 2km further south through peaceful farm country to this German-run *pousada*, splendidly situated on a hillside with distant ocean views. Rooms are rustic but elegant, most with balconies; common areas are flooded with light from tall French doors. If coming by bus, call ahead for pickup at the bus stop 600m away.

Adriana (per kg R$16.90) Among the island's countless seafood eateries, Adriana is a recommended option in Armação.

OUR PICK **Arante** (mains for 2 people R$38-85) A Pântano do Sul institution, Arante is draped floor to ceiling with thousands of notes penned by former patrons.

FLORIANÓPOLIS

☎ 0xx48 / pop 397,000

Gateway to Ilha de Santa Catarina, beautifully sited Florianópolis sits on the island's western edge, surrounded by bay and mountain vistas. Although the town has pretty features that invite exploration, many travelers simply pass through en route to the outlying beaches.

Orientation & Information

Florianópolis' pleasant colonial center revolves around the pedestrian-friendly Felipe Schmidt and leafy Praça XV de Novembro. The bus station lies a few blocks west of the praça, while the upscale Beira-Mar neighborhood lies 2km north, overlooking the bay.

@café (Schmidt 80; per hr R$3; 🕑 8:30am-8:30pm Mon-Fri, 8:30am-2:30pm Sat) One of several internet places in the pedestrian zone.

HSBC (Schmidt 376) ATM linked to multiple networks.

Information booth (☎ 3228-1095; www.visitefloripa. com.br; 🕑 8am-7pm) At the bus station, provides city and island information.

Sleeping & Eating

The liveliest drinking spots are along the bay-facing Beira-Mar Norte.

Floripa Hostel (☎ 3225-3781; www.floripahostel
.com.br; Schutel 227; dm/r with YHI card R$28/68, without
YHI card R$37/78) This welcoming HI hostel is a
10-minute walk from the bus station.

Hotel Central Sumaré (☎ 3222-5359; Schmidt 423;
s/d R$58/78, without bathroom R$39/60) Dingy, but
conveniently situated on Florianópolis' main
pedestrian thoroughfare.

Cecomtur Executive Hotel (☎ 2107-8800; www
.cecomturhotel.com.br; Paiva 107; s/d from R$78/98;
❄ 💻 ⚒) Centrally located, with abundant
perks for weary travelers, business-oriented
Cecomtur offers excellent deals on its 18
inward-facing rooms.

Café das Artes (Esteves Júnior 734; sandwiches R$5-13;
⏲ 11:30am-11pm Mon-Fri, 3-10pm Sat & Sun) This artsy,
upscale cafe in the Beira-Mar Norte area sells
sandwiches, good coffee and baked goods.

Vida Restaurante Natural (Visconde de Ouro Prêto
298; buffet R$10; ⏲ lunch Mon-Fri) This all-vegetarian
joint in a high-ceilinged colonial building
spreads an appetizing buffet.

Mirantes Grill (Praça XV de Novembro 348; per kg
R$27.90; ⏲ lunch Mon-Sat) On the main square,
Mirantes' ample lunch buffet revolves around
fresh-grilled meat.

Getting There & Away

Daily flights serve São Paulo and Porto Alegre.
Long-distance buses link Florianópolis with
Curitiba (R$40, five hours), Porto Alegre
(R$59, 6½ hours), São Paulo (R$99, 10 to 12
hours), Foz do Iguaçu (R$125, 14 hours), Rio
de Janeiro (R$150, 18 hours), Montevideo
(R$209, 18 hours), Asunción (R$158, 22
hours), Buenos Aires (R$216, 25 hours) and
Santiago (R$312, 45 hours, Tuesday only).

Getting Around

Local buses leave from the brand new TICEN
terminal one block east of Florianópolis' intercity bus terminal.

Connections to the island's beaches are
made via three outlying terminals: TIRIO (Rio
Tavares Terminal), TILAG (Lagoa Terminal)
and TICAN (Canasvieiras Terminal).

For southern beaches, including Armação,
Pântano do Sul and Costa de Dentro, catch
bus 410 'Rio Tavares' from TICEN platform
C, then transfer at TIRIO to bus 563.

For eastern beaches, catch bus 330 'Lagoa
da Conceição' from TICEN platform B, then
transfer at TILAG for a second bus to your

BRAZIL

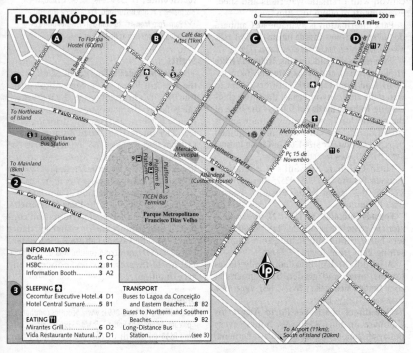

FLORIANÓPOLIS

INFORMATION		
@café................................1	C2	
HSBC..................................2	B1	
Information Booth............3	A2	
SLEEPING 🏠		**TRANSPORT**
Cecomtur Executive Hotel..4	D1	Buses to Lagoa da Conceição
Hotel Central Sumaré.......5	B1	and Eastern Beaches.....8 B2
		Buses to Northern and Southern
EATING 🍴		Beaches.........................9 B2
Mirantes Grill....................6	D2	Long-Distance Bus
Vida Restaurante Natural..7	D1	Station........................(see 3)

0   200 m
0   0.1 miles

final destination, for example bus 360 to Barra da Lagoa.

For Canasvieiras and northern beaches, catch bus 210 from TICEN platform C to TICAN.

A single fare of R$2.70 (paid at the TICEN ticket booth) covers your initial ride plus one transfer. Less frequent yellow express microbuses (R$4.50) accept surfboards and bypass the intermediate terminals.

To reach the airport, 12km south of Florianópolis, take local bus 183 'Corredor Sudoeste' (R$2.70, 30 minutes) from TICEN terminal. Taxis cost R$25 to R$35.

The island is a good place to rent a car. **Yes Rent a Car** (☎ 3236-0229) offers rates from R$75 a day.

PARQUE NACIONAL DE APARADOS DA SERRA
☎ 0xx54

This magnificent **national park** (admission R$6; ☺ 9am-5pm Wed-Sun) is 18km from the town of Cambará do Sul, approximately 200km northeast of Porto Alegre. The big attraction is the **Cânion do Itaimbezinho**, a fantastic narrow canyon with dramatic waterfalls and sheer escarpments of 600m to 720m.

Park information is available at Cambará do Sul's brand-new **Casa do Turista** (☎ 3251-1320; www.cambaraonline.com.br; Av Getúlio Vargas 1720).

Two easy self-guided trails, **Trilha do Vértice** (1.5km return) and **Trilha Cotovelo** (6km return), lead from the park's visitors center to waterfalls and canyon vistas; the more challenging **Trilha do Rio do Boi** follows the base of the canyon for 7km, requires a guide and is closed during the rainy season. For guided trips, try **Acontur** (☎ 8124-1766) or **Cânion Turismo** (☎ 3251-1027; www.canionturismo.com.br).

Near Cambará do Sul's bus station, **Pousada Paraíso** (☎ 3251-1352; Raupp 678; s/d R$35/70) has good-value upstairs rooms with balconies.

Pousada Corucacas (☎ 3251-1123; www.corucacas .com; r per person with breakfast/half-board R$60/80) offers horse riding and fishing in a country setting 2km from town.

A friendly Italian-Brazilian family serves fondue, pizza and garden-fresh greens at cozy **Cantina Menegolla** (☎ 3251-1053; Vargas 1304; pizzas from R$15; ☺ dinner).

One direct bus leaves Porto Alegre for Cambará do Sul (R$30, 3¼ hours) every Friday afternoon, returning Sunday afternoon.

On other days you have to change in São Francisco de Paula (five hours total travel time).

A taxi to the national park costs R$60 to R$80 round trip. Buses from Cambará do Sul to Praia Grande (R$7.40, 1½ hours, daily except Sunday) at the park's eastern edge can also drop you at the park entrance, but return travel to Cambará do Sul is only available on Wednesday and Friday.

PORTO ALEGRE
☎ 0xx51 / pop 1.4 million

The flourishing port town of Porto Alegre is a good introduction to progressive Rio Grande do Sul. Built on the banks of the Rio Guaíba, this lively, modern city has a well-preserved neoclassical downtown, with handsome plazas, good museums and a vibrant arts and music scene.

Information
Citibank (7 de Setembro 722) Has ATMs.
News Cyber Café (Rua dos Andradas 1001; per hr R$3.50; ☺ 9am-9pm Mon-Sat, noon-8pm Sun) Internet cafe inside Shopping Rua da Praia.
Tourist office (☎ 3358-2048, 0800-51-7686; www .portoalegre.rs.gov.br/turismo; Praça 15 de Novembro; ☺ 9am-7pm Mon-Fri, to 6pm Sat) Helpful office at Mercado Público; also at the airport.

Sights
The 1869 **Mercado Público** (Public Market) and the adjacent Praça 15 de Novembro constitute the city's heart. Shops in the market sell the *gaúchos'* characteristic *cuia* (gourd) and *bomba* (silver straw), used in drinking maté tea. The interesting **Museu Histórico Júlio de Castilhos** (Duque de Caxias 1205; ☺ 10am-6pm Tue-Sat) contains objects related to Rio Grande do Sul's history, while the **Museu de Arte do Rio Grande do Sul** (Praça da Alfândega; www.margs.rs.gov.br; ☺ 10am-7pm Tue-Sun) has a good collection of *gaúcho* art.

Near Lake Guaíba is the **Usina do Gasômetro**, an abandoned thermoelectric station converted into a showcase for visual art, dance and film. The **Casa da Cultura Mario Quintana** (☎ 3221-7147; www.ccmq.com.br; Rua dos Andradas 736) hosts theater, movies, concerts and art exhibitions.

Sleeping
Hotel Ritz (☎ 3225-0693; www.geocities.com/hotelritz _palegre; Av André da Rocha 225; s/d R$39/59, without bathroom R$30/48) South of the center, Ritz's tiny,

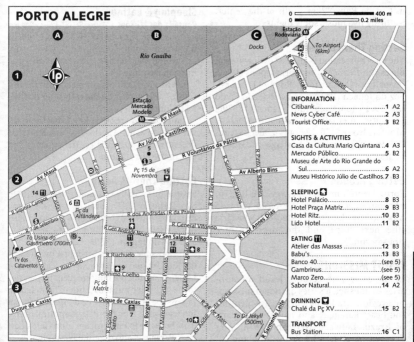

PORTO ALEGRE

INFORMATION	
Citibank	1 A2
News Cyber Café	2 A3
Tourist Office	3 B2

SIGHTS & ACTIVITIES	
Casa da Cultura Mario Quintana	4 A3
Mercado Público	5 B2
Museu de Arte do Rio Grande do Sul	6 A2
Museu Histórico Júlio de Castilhos	7 B3

SLEEPING	
Hotel Palácio	8 B3
Hotel Praça Matriz	9 B3
Hotel Ritz	10 B3
Lido Hotel	11 B2

EATING	
Atelier das Massas	12 B3
Babu's	13 B3
Banco 40	(see 5)
Gambrinus	(see 5)
Marco Zero	(see 5)
Sabor Natural	14 A2

DRINKING	
Chalé da Pç XV	15 B2

TRANSPORT	
Bus Station	16 C1

BRAZIL

clean rooms surround a sweet courtyard – a good place to meet travelers. No breakfast.

Hotel Palácio (☎ 3225-3467; Inácio 644; s/d from R$38/60) This older hotel's best rooms are flooded with sunlight (and noise) from the sizable windows.

Hotel Praça Matriz (☎ 3225-5772; Largo João Amorim de Albuquerque 72; s/d from R$45/70) Housed in a neoclassical mansion, complete with marble staircase and stained glass, this aging hotel has some rooms with French doors opening onto Praça da Matriz.

Lido Hotel (☎ 3228-9111; www.lidohotel.com.br; Neves 150; s/d R$73/126; ✷ ▢) Simple, sparkling rooms with free wi-fi provide a welcome retreat in the heart of downtown.

Eating
Porto Alegre's **Mercado Público** is packed with atmospheric eateries for all budgets. Recommended options include **Banco 40**, home of the incomparable *bomba royal* (a showy ice cream and fruit salad concoction); **Marco Zero**, featuring nightly happy hours and meals from R$13; and **Gambrinus**, an old-world Portuguese seafood restaurant (mains from R$22).

Babu's (Neves 133; fixed-price buffet R$8.50; ✷ lunch Mon-Sat) This *churrascaria*'s varied offerings include fresh-grilled meats, lasagna and salads.

Sabor Natural (Campos 890 2nd fl; all-you-can-eat buffet R$10; ✷ lunch Mon-Fri) A long-standing lunchtime favorite thanks to its excellent, vegetarian-friendly buffet.

Atelier das Massas (Riachuelo 1482; mains R$16-29; ✷ lunch & dinner Mon-Sat) Draws crowds day and night with delicious, artfully presented homemade pasta.

Casa da Cultura Mario Quintana and MARGS (see Sights, opposite) both have excellent cafes, the latter serving award-winning cakes in an elegant setting brightened with avant-garde art.

Drinking
Chalé da Praça XV (Praça 15 de Novembro; ✷ 11am-11pm) This ornate place, built in 1885, is a traditional favorite with *alegrenses* (residents of Porto Alegre) for late-afternoon beers.

Dr Jekyll (Travessa do Carmo 76; ✷ 11pm-dawn Mon-Sat) One of several late-night watering holes in Cidade Baixa, 2km south of the center, featuring live music some nights.

Getting There & Away
The busy bus station is just east of downtown. Buses run frequently to Florianópolis (R$60, seven hours), Curitiba (R$94, 11 hours), Foz do Iguaçu (R$127, 14 hours), São Paulo (R$139, 18 hours) and Rio de Janeiro (R$206, 24 hours). International destinations include Montevideo (R$150, 12 hours), Buenos Aires (R$195, 18 hours) and Santiago (R$312, 36 hours, twice weekly).

Getting Around
Porto Alegre's metro (one-way fare R$1.70) has convenient stations at Estação Mercado Modelo (by the port), Estação Rodoviária (the next stop) and the airport (three stops beyond).

JESUIT MISSIONS
In the early 17th century Jesuit missionaries established a series of Indian missions in a region straddling northeast Argentina, southeast Paraguay and neighboring parts of Brazil. Between 1631 and 1638, after devastating attacks by Paulista slaving expeditions and hostile indigenous people, activity was concentrated in 30 more easily defensible missions. These places became centers of culture as well as religion – in effect a nation within the colonies, considered by some scholars an island of utopian progress and socialism, which at its height in the 1720s had over 150,000 Guaraní indigenous inhabitants.

Seven of the now-ruined missions lie in the northwest of Brazil's Rio Grande do Sul state, eight are in Paraguay and 15 in Argentina.

Orientation & Information
The town of Santo Ângelo is the main jumping-off point for the Brazilian missions; the most interesting and intact site is **São Miguel das Missões** (admission R$5; ⊙ 9am-noon & 2-6pm; evening sound-&-light show R$5), 53km southwest of Santo Ângelo.

São Miguel's **tourist office** (☎ 0xx55-3381-1294; www.rotamissoes.com.br) is directly adjacent to the mission, 500m west of the bus station.

See p86 and p752 for information on Argentine and Paraguayan missions.

Sleeping & Eating
Pousada das Missões (☎ 0xx55-3381-1202; www.pousadatematica.com.br; dm/s/d R$39/60/96) São Miguel's most convenient lodging is this well-run, HI-affiliated *pousada*, 100m beyond the mission entrance.

On São Miguel's main street (Av Borges do Canto), **O Guarani** and **Kaipper Ely** offer dueling R$12 lunch buffets.

Turis Hotel (☎ 0xx55-3313-5245; Antônio Manoel 726; s/d R$40/80) In Santo Ângelo, the Turis Hotel has decent rooms near the central square, 1km east of the bus station.

Getting There & Away
Several buses daily run from Porto Alegre to Sânto Angelo (R$77, seven hours), where you can make onward connections to São Miguel das Missões (R$8, one hour, two to four daily) and Foz do Iguaçu (R$98, 12 hours).

It's possible to enter Argentina by crossing the Rio Uruguai via Porto Xavier, São Borja or Uruguaiana, but the most frequent bus service to the Argentine missions is from Puerto Iguazú (across the border from Foz do Iguaçu) to San Ignacio Miní. For the Paraguayan missions, daily buses go to Encarnación from Ciudad del Este, Paraguay, also opposite Foz do Iguaçu.

FOZ DO IGUAÇU
☎ 0xx45 / pop 311,000
The stupendous roar of 275 waterfalls crashing 80m into the Rio Iguaçu seems to create a low-level buzz of excitement throughout the city of Foz, even though the famed Cataratas (falls) are 20km southeast of town. Apart from the waterfalls, which should be visited on both sides, you can dip into the forests of Paraguay or check out Itaipu Dam, one of the world's largest hydroelectric power plants.

Information
Along Av Brasil there are many banks and exchange houses.
Foztur information booth (☎ 0800-45-1516; www.iguassu.tur.br) airport (⊙ 9am-9pm); downtown (Praça Getúlio Vargas; ⊙ 7am-11pm); long-distance bus station (⊙ 6:30am-6pm); local bus station (⊙ 7am-7pm) Provides maps and detailed info about the area.
HSBC (Av Brasil 1151) ATM serving all major networks.
Police (☎ 3523-1828; Av Jorge Schimmelpfeng)
Post office (opposite Praça Getúlio Vargas)
US Net (☎ 3523-7654; Av Brasil 549; per hr R$3; ⊙ 9am-8pm Mon-Sat) Internet access.

Dangers & Annoyances

Robberies are fairly common along the bridge to Ciudad del Este in Paraguay; avoid walking near the riverfront at any time.

Sights & Activities

To see the falls properly, you must visit both sides. Brazil gives the grand overview and Argentina (p88) the closer look. The single not-to-be-missed experience on the **Brazilian side** (admission R$21; ☺ 9am-5pm) is the **Trilha das Cataratas**, a scenic 1km trail leading to **Garganta do Diabo** (Devil's Throat), where the broad Rio Iguaçu makes its single most dramatic plunge, splitting into dozens of waterfalls. A regular shuttle bus loops around from park headquarters to the trailhead

(stop number three). Visiting towards sunset is especially nice, with fewer crowds and a golden glow illuminating the falls.

Costs are high for other activities on the Brazilian side. **Macuco Safari** (www.macucosafari .com.br) offers kayaking, hiking and rafting trips under the falls (R$169, sometimes cheaper from local hostels). Park-approved guides also lead four- to five-hour outings (R$135) along the **Trilha Poço Preto**, a 9km trail leading to a small lagoon where you can observe monkeys, jacaré and birdlife.

Five minutes' walk from park headquarters is the worthwhile **Parque das Aves** (Bird Park; www .parquedasaves; admission R$22; ☺ 8:30am-5:30pm), whose 5m-tall netted cages permit an up-close-and-personal look at 800 different bird species.

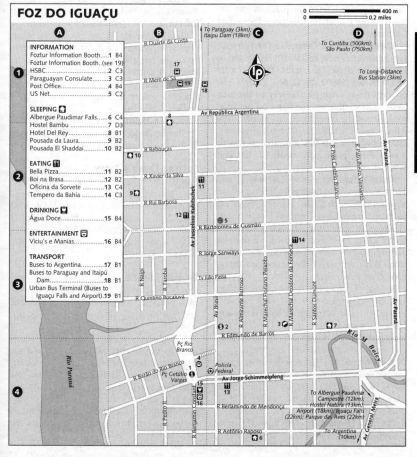

FOZ DO IGUAÇU

INFORMATION	
Foztur Information Booth.....1	B4
Foztur Information Booth..(see 19)	
HSBC..........................2	C3
Paraguayan Consulate........3	C3
Post Office...................4	B4
US Net.......................5	C2

SLEEPING	
Albergue Paudimar Falls......6	C4
Hostel Bambu.................7	D3
Hotel Del Rey................8	B1
Pousada da Laura.............9	B2
Pousada El Shaddai..........10	B2

EATING	
Bella Pizza.................11	B2
Boi na Brasa................12	B2
Oficina da Sorvete 13	C4
Tempero da Bahia 14	C3

DRINKING	
Água Doce..................15	B4

ENTERTAINMENT	
Viciu's e Manias.............16	B4

TRANSPORT	
Buses to Argentina...........17	B1
Buses to Paraguay and Itaipú Dam...18	B1
Urban Bus Terminal (Buses to Iguaçu Falls and Airport).19	B1

BRAZIL

North of town, **Itaipu Dam** (☎ 0800-645-4645; www.complexoitaipu.tur.br; hourly tours R$13; ✆ 8am-4pm) is another jaw-dropping attraction, especially when learning how much was destroyed to create it (indigenous villages, 700 sq km of forest and waterfalls to rival Iguaçu's). Buses (R$2.10, 40 minutes) marked 'PTI' (Parque Tecnológico Itaipu) leave every 15 minutes from the army base opposite Foz's local bus station. For further information see p755.

Sleeping

Most hostels offer trips to the Argentine side of the falls.

Albergue Paudimar Falls (☎ 3028-5503; www.paudimarfalls.com.br; Raposo 820; camping/dm/r with YHI card R$14/18/65, without YHI card R$15/22/70; ✵ ▣ ▣) This simple but friendly place is the in-town sister hostel to Albergue Paudimar Campestre.

Albergue Paudimar Campestre (☎ 3529-6061; www.paudimar.com.br; Av das Cataratas Km 12; camping R$15; dm with/without YHI card from R$20/25, r with/without YHI card R$80/90; ✵ ▣ ▣) Twelve kilometers from town on the way to the falls (walk 1km south from the bus stop on main road, or use the free shuttle bus marked '100 Alimentador' daily till 7:20pm), this well-established hostel is like a mini-resort, with a swimming pool, bar, meals (R$12) and internet access.

Hostel Natura (☎ 3529-6949, 9116-0979; www.hostelnatura.com; Av das Cataratas Km 12.5; camping/dm per person R$20/38; ✵ ▣ ▣) Earning raves for its food, *caipirinhas*, tranquil location and abundantly welcoming hosts, this newer hostel 13km from Foz is down a tree-lined driveway on a lovely piece of land with two small lakes, 2.5km off the main road (same turnoff as Paudimar).

Pousada da Laura (☎ 3572-3374; www.pousadalaura.com; Naipi 671; dm/d R$30/70; ▣) This pleasant hostel/*pousada* is operated by affable and ultra-experienced tour guide Luis Hernán; his nearby travel agency arranges day trips to lesser-known attractions in Paraguay.

Hostel Bambu (☎ 3523-3646; www.hostelbambu.com; Edmundo de Barros 621; dm/s/d/tr/q R$30/50/75/100/130; ✵ ▣ ▣) This laid-back hostel has ample lounge space, a bar, a guest kitchen and an outdoor patio with small pool.

Pousada El Shaddai (☎ 3025-4493; www.pousadaelshaddai.com.br; Rebouças 306; dm/s/d/tr/q R$30/48/78/120/150; ✵ ▣ ▣) Clean, wholesome and family-run, El Shaddai also has a guest kitchen, patio and pool.

Hotel Del Rey (☎ 2105-7500; www.hoteldelreyfoz.com.br; Tarobá 1020; s/d/tr R$80/110/150; ✵ ▣ ▣) A modern three-star hotel with spacious, comfy rooms and a good buffet breakfast.

Eating & Drinking

Boi na Brasa (Av Juscelino Kubitschek 439; lunch buffet/all-you-can-eat BBQ R$8/13) This all-you-can-eat *churrascaria* serves good cuts of meat at very reasonable prices.

Bella Pizza (Xavier da Silva 648; pizza R$11; ✆ dinner) Fill up on unlimited pizza at Bella's nightly *rodizio*.

Tempero da Bahia (Deodoro 1228; lunch per kg R$18.90, mains for 2 R$40-62; ✆ lunch & dinner) Serves excellent Bahian fare, with live music most nights.

Oficina do Sorvete (Av Jorge Schimmelpfeng 244; per kg sandwiches/ice cream R$28/25; ✆ 3pm-1am) Sidle on up to the bar and build your own baguette sandwich, salad or ice cream concoction.

Água Doce (Constant 63; ✆ 6pm-late Mon-Sat) *Cachaça* lovers will appreciate this bar's endless drinks list.

Viciu's e Manias (☎ 3523-9161; Constant 107; ✆ 11pm-late Thu-Sat) A popular dance club, often featuring local performers.

Getting There & Away

Frequent flights link Foz to Asunción, Rio, São Paulo and Curitiba. Buses go to Asunción (R$45, five hours), Curitiba (R$102, 10 hours), Florianópolis (R$116, 12 hours), Campo Grande (R$98, 14 hours), São Paulo (R$142, 15 hours) and Rio (R$195, 23 hours).

Getting Around

City buses marked 'TTU' (R$2.10) cover the 6km between the long-distance bus station and the local terminal downtown. A taxi costs R$10 to R$12.

Bus 120 'Aeroporto/P Nacional' (R$2.10) runs to the airport (30 minutes) and the Brazilian side of the waterfalls (40 minutes) every 20 minutes from 5:25am to 7pm, and after that every 45 minutes until midnight. Catch it at the local bus terminal or any stop along Av Juscelino Kubitschek south of Barbosa. A taxi from town to the airport costs R$35 to R$40.

GETTING TO ARGENTINA & PARAGUAY

Most nationalities can enter Argentina without a visa, but double-check before you arrive. Americans and several other nationalities need a visa to enter Paraguay. Get this in advance.

At all immigration posts, be sure to request the relevant exit and entry stamps; these may not be given automatically, and a missed stamp can create serious hassles later.

From Foz do Iguaçu, Brazil, to Puerto Iguazú, Argentina: if traveling by bus, ask to be dropped off at the border, get your passport stamped, then grab the next bus into Argentina (most bus drivers won't wait around while you finish formalities). Note that many hotels and hostels have private vans that ferry passengers to and from the falls in Argentina to save time and avoid hassle. Both borders are open 24 hours but bus service ends around 7pm.

To Ciudad del Este, Paraguay: it's inadvisable to walk across the bridge because of robberies. Take a bus or taxi to the border, get your passport stamped, then catch the next bus or a taxi to Ciudad del Este.

From Ponta Porã, Brazil to Pedro Juan Caballero, Paraguay, day visitors can simply walk across the border. If traveling further into Paraguay, you'll need to complete formalities with Brazil's Policia Federal (Av Presidente Vargas) and the Paraguayan immigration authorities (Av Dr Francia).

For information on entering Brazil from Argentina and Paraguay, see p79 and p755.

For the Argentine side of the falls, catch a Puerto Iguazú bus (R$3.50) across from the local bus terminal or at any stop along Av Juscelino Kubitschek. They pass every half hour (50 minutes on Sunday) until 7pm. At Puerto Iguazú bus station, transfer to a bus to the falls (p86).

Buses run every 15 minutes (40 minutes on Sunday) to Ciudad del Este, Paraguay (R$3.50, 30 minutes) from the army base opposite Foz's local bus terminal.

THE CENTRAL WEST

A land of breathtaking panoramas and exceptional wildlife, Brazil's Central West is a must-see for nature lovers and outdoors enthusiasts. The Pantanal, one of the most important wetland systems on the planet, is the region's star attraction. Its meandering rivers, savannas and forests harbor one of the densest concentrations of plant and animal life in the New World. Other regional attractions include dramatic *chapadas* (tablelands), which rise like brilliant red giants from the dark-green *cerrado,* punctuated by spectacular waterfalls and picturesque swimming holes. In the region's southwest corner, Bonito is another natural attraction inviting adventurous exploration. Here you can snorkel down crystal-clear rivers teeming with fish or rappel into the Abyss (one of Bonito's caverns).

The central west region also offers its share of urban pleasures, which include Brazil's surreal, master-planned capital Brasília and the historic silver-mining town of Pirenópolis.

BRASÍLIA

☎ 0xx61 / pop 2.5 million

As it celebrates its 50th anniversary, Brazil's once futuristic capital is showing its age, but it remains an impressive monument to national initiative. Built from nothing in about three years, Brasília replaced Rio de Janeiro as Brazil's center of government in 1960 under the visionary leadership of President Juscelino Kubitschek, architect Oscar Niemeyer, urban planner Lucio Costa and landscape architect Burle Marx.

For travelers on a tight budget, Brasília presents numerous challenges. Its sprawling ground plan was built for cars, so getting around by foot or public transport isn't that easy. Accommodation is expensive, and the city's best restaurants and nightlife are concentrated far from the downtown hotel districts. Even so, Brasília's retro-futuristic vibe may actually grow on you once you learn to navigate its acronym-rich jungle of planned streets.

Orientation

The central area is shaped like an airplane. Government buildings and monuments are concentrated in the fuselage (a long strip called Eixo Monumental). Hotels, banks and shopping centers are immediately adjacent, in sectors known by their abbreviations:

BRAZIL

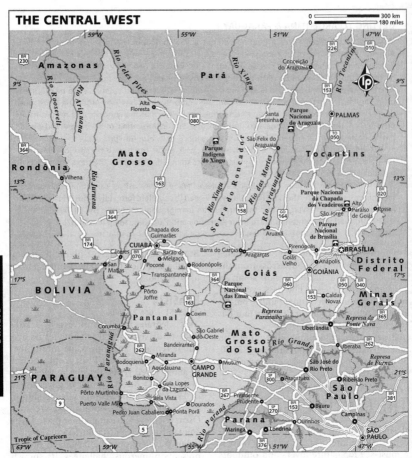

THE CENTRAL WEST

SHN/SHS (hotel sectors north and south), SBN/SBS (banking sectors) and SCN/SCS (commercial sectors). Residential neighborhoods, each with its own SC (commercial sector) lie further out along the airplane's wings: Asa Norte (North Wing) and Asa Sul (South Wing).

Information

Citibank (SCS Quadra 6, Bloco A) One of several downtown banks with international ATMs, across from the Pátio Brasil shopping center.

Tourist office (☎ 3325-1518; www.brasiliatur.com.br; ☼ 8am-6pm) A single office under the Museu Nacional was operating at the time of research; new branches are scheduled for 2010 at the airport, TV Tower and *rodoviária* (local bus station).

Sights & Activities

Brasília's major edifices are spread along a 5km stretch of the Eixo Monumental and are listed in northwest–southeast order here. To visit them you can rent a car or combine local buses 104 and 108 with some long walks. Guided city tours (R$40 to R$80) are available from many hotels and from travel agencies outside the **Hotel Nacional** (SHS Quadra 1).

Start at the **Memorial JK** (admission R$4; ☼ 9am-5pm Tue-Sun), which houses President Kubitschek's tomb plus exhibits on Brasília's construction. Next take the elevator to the observation deck of the **TV Tower** (☼ 9am-6pm Tue-Sun, 2-6pm Mon) for a bird's-eye view of Brasília.

Detour 1km southwest along Via W3 Sul to see the beautiful stained-glass windows of **Santuário Dom Bosco** (☯ 8am-6pm), then return to the Eixo Monumental, where the **Museu Nacional** (☏ 3414 6167; ☯ 8am-5pm) hosts rotating exhibits. The adjacent **Catedral Metropolitana** (☯ 8am-5pm) with its curved columns, stained glass and haunting statues of the four evangelists is one of Brasília's architectural gems. Further south, in the 'cockpit' of the airplane ground plan, are the most interesting government buildings: **Palácio do Itamaraty**, **Palácio da Justiça** and **Palácio do Congresso**.

Sleeping

Brasília suffers from a severe dearth of budget accommodations, though many downtown hotels slash prices on weekends.

Inexpensive *pousadas* were traditionally clustered in a residential area along Via W3 Sul, but in May 2008 the government closed these down, invoking zoning laws. Plans to relocate low-budget operators to a new Vila das Pousadas were under discussion at the time of research.

Brasília Hostel (☏ 3343-0531; www.hostel.org.br, Camping de Brasília; camping/dm/d with YHI card R$15/35/77, without YHI card R$18/42/87; ▣) Brasília's only dependable option under R$100, desolately situated 6km from the center (take bus 143 from the *rodoviária*), this squat hostel has 19 dorms, one double room, a tiny guest kitchen and campsites in an exposed field.

Hotel Diplomat (☏ 3204-2010; www.geocities.com/hoteldiplomatbsb; SHN Quadra 2; s/d/tr R$119/149/179; ✷ ▣) Near the TV Tower, this otherwise uninspiring place wins votes for its ample breakfast, free wi-fi and substantial weekend discounts (basement rooms are the cheapest).

Eating & Drinking

You'll find cuisine from dozens of countries in Brasília's cosmopolitan Asa Sul. Prime venues for restaurant-, bar- and club-hopping include the neighborhood commercial districts SCLS-209 and SCLS-403, both near brand-new metro stops.

Bar Beirute (SCLS-109; light meals from R$5) A lively bar with Middle East-themed dishes and outdoor seating.

Quitinete (SCLS-209; mains R$19-43; ☯ 7am-2am) This trendy restaurant/bakery serves American-style breakfasts, exquisite desserts and superb coffee.

Chiquita Bacana (SCLS-209; ☯ 5pm-late) Popular for its early evening happy hour and daily drink specials.

Gate's Pub (SCLS-403; ☯ 9pm-3am Tue-Sun) One of Brasília's most popular music and dance venues.

For cheap eats, visit the food courts in the air-conditioned downtown malls: **Shopping Brasília**, **Pátio Brasil** and **Conjunto Nacional**.

Getting There & Away

Brasília's airport, 12km south of the center, offers flights throughout Brazil.

From the *rodoferroviária* (long-distance bus station) 6km northwest of the center, buses go almost everywhere, including Belo Horizonte (R$99, 11 hours), São Paulo (R$136, 14 hours), Rio (R$152, 17 hours), Cuiabá (R$113, 18 hours), Salvador (R$194, 23 hours) and Belém (R$271, 36 hours).

CENTRAL BRASÍLIA

INFORMATION	
Citibank................................1	A2
Tourist Office.......................2	A4

SIGHTS & ACTIVITIES	
Catedral Metropolitana.........3	A4
Hotel Nacional.....................4	A2
Museu Nacional...............(see 2)	
Travel Agencies................(see 4)	
TV Tower..............................5	A1

SLEEPING	
Hotel Diplomat.....................6	B2

EATING	
Conjunto Nacional................7	B2
Pátio Brasil..........................8	A1
Shopping Brasília.................9	B1

TRANSPORT	
ITS Rent-a-Car.................(see 4)	
Local Bus Station...............10	A3

Getting Around

Brasília's *rodoviária* is right in the heart of town. From here, bus 131 runs frequently to the *rodoferroviária* (R$2, 15 minutes) and bus 102 heads to the airport (R$2, 40 minutes). Taxis to the airport cost R$30 to R$35.

Brasília's **metro** (www.metro.df.gov.br; weekends/weekdays R$2/3; ☼ 6am-11:30pm Mon-Fri, 7am-7pm Sat & Sun) runs south from the *rodoviária* to the suburbs. Recently opened stations near Asa Sul nightspots have enhanced its tourist appeal but beware the early weekend closing time.

There are plenty of car-rental agencies at the airport. Downtown, **ITS Rent-a-Car** (☎ 3224-8000; Hotel Nacional; www.itsrentacar.com.br) charges R$20 per day plus a per-kilometer surcharge.

PARQUE NACIONAL DA CHAPADA DOS VEADEIROS

This spectacular park 220km north of Brasília showcases the high-altitude *cerrado*, a sublime landscape where maned wolves, giant anteaters and 7ft-tall rheas roam amidst big skies, canyons, waterfalls and oasis-like stands of wine palms. The closest towns to the park are Alto Paraíso de Goias (40km east) and São Jorge (2km south).

Information

Alto Paraíso's **tourist office** (☎ 0xx62-3446-1159; altoparaiso.sectur@gmail.com; ☼ 8am-5pm) is 200m from the bus station; its smaller São Jorge branch keeps irregular hours.

Sights & Activities

Outside the national park, **Vale da Lua** (Moon Valley; admission R$5; ☼ 7:30am-5pm) is named for the pockmarked rocks lining its riverbed, though the surrounding hills exuberant greenery make it feel anything but lunar. The trailhead for the self-guided 600m walking loop, passing lovely natural pools, is 10km southeast of São Jorge.

Visitors to the national park must go with an accredited guide; book one at the park entrance or at most local hotels (full-day hike from R$60). Main attractions include the canyons (**Cânion I** and **Cânion II**) along the Rio Preto, the waterfalls (**Salto do Rio Preto I & II**; 80m and 120m, respectively) and **Morro da Baleia**, a humpback hill with a 2.5km trail to the top.

Sleeping & Eating

In São Jorge, sleeping options range from abundant backyard **campsites** (per person R$8-10) to the ultra-comfy **Pousada Trilha Violeta** (☎ 0xx61-9985-6544, 3455-1088; www.trilhavioleta.com.br; s/d R$65/80).

Pousada Rubi (☎ 0xx62-3446-1200; www.pousadarubi.com.br; Paulino 732; s/d from R$35/53; 🖳) This friendly *pousada* makes a great overnight base in Alto Paraíso.

Lua de São Jorge (pizzas from R$18; ☼ Thu-Sun) This is a laid-back, outdoor bar with wood-fired pizzas and live music on weekends.

Getting There & Away

From Brasília's local bus station (*rodoviária*), one daily bus goes to São Jorge (R$35, six hours) via Alto Paraíso. Buses from Brasília's long-distance *rodoferroviária* only go as far as Alto Paraíso (R$31, four hours).

Daily buses also connect Alto Paraíso to Goiânia (R$59, six hours).

GOIÂNIA

☎ 0xx62 / pop 1.2 million

The modern capital of Goiás state, 205km southwest of Brasília, Goiânia is mainly of interest as a transit hub.

Centrally located **Goiânia Palace** (☎ 3224-4874; Av Anhanguera 5195; s/d/tr from R$60/78/100) is among Goiânia's best budget hotels. For excellent per-kilo food nearby, try **Danove** (Rua 9 No 468; per kg R$14.99; ☼ lunch). Internet is available in the bus station.

TAM and Varig/Gol fly to Goiânia. Frequent buses depart the *rodoviária* 3km north of the center for Brasília (R$30, 3½ hours) and Cuiabá (R$100, 15 hours). One bus daily serves Pirenópolis (R$14, two hours), Alto Paraíso (R$60, six hours) and Palmas, Tocantins (R$80, 12 hours).

PIRENÓPOLIS

☎ 0xx62 / pop 20,500

A Brazilian National Heritage site backed by lovely mountains, Pirenópolis attracts weekend escapees from Brasília (165km east) with picturesque 18th-century architecture and abundant waterfalls.

Pirenópolis' **tourist office** (☎ 3331-2633; www.pirenopolis.tur.br; ☼ 8am-7pm), near central Praça da Matriz, arranges guides to local nature reserves (from R$60 a day). **Planeta Cyber** (internet per hr R$3; ☼ 7:30am-11pm) and a **Bradesco ATM** are nearby on Sizenando Jayme.

BRAZIL

Within 20km of town, **Parque Estadual da Serra dos Pireneus** and **Reserva Ecológica Vargem Grande** both have beautiful waterfalls and swimming holes; while **Santuário de Vida Silvestre Vagafogo** (www.vagafogo.com.br) offers a self-guided forest walk and a delicious weekend brunch (R$25).

The family-run **Rex Hotel** (☎ 3331-1121; Praça da Matriz 15; s/d R$35/60) is on the main square. West of the bus station, **Pousada Arvoredo** (☎ 3331 3479; www.arvoredo.tur.br; Abercio 15; s/d from R$50/80; ❂ ❑) offers midweek deals on comfy rooms surrounding a pool and garden. Cheap snacks abound along cobbled Direita and Nova, while restaurants and bars line Rua do Rosario.

From the bus station, 500m west of the center, four daily buses run to Brasília (R$18, three hours) and one to Goiânia (R$13, two hours).

THE PANTANAL

This vast natural paradise is Brazil's major ecological attraction and offers a density of exotic wildlife found nowhere else in South America. During the rainy season (October to March), the Rio Paraguai and lesser rivers of the Pantanal inundate much of this low-lying region, creating *cordilheiras* (patches of dry land where animals cluster). The waters rise as much as 3m above low-water levels around March in the northern Pantanal and as late as June further south. This seasonal flooding, while severely limiting human occupation of the area, provides an enormously rich feeding ground for wildlife. The waters teem with fish; birds fly in flocks of thousands and gather in enormous rookeries.

Altogether the Pantanal supports 650 bird species and 80 mammal species, including jaguars, ocelots, pumas, maned wolf, deer, anteaters, armadillos, howler and capuchin monkeys and tapirs. The most visible mammal is the capybara, the world's largest rodent, often seen in family groups. And you can't miss the *jacarés* (caimans), which, despite poaching, still number in the millions.

Orientation & Information

The Pantanal covers some 230,000 sq km (89,000 sq miles) and stretches into Paraguay and Bolivia, although the lion's share is Brazil's. Much of this territory is only accessible by boat or on foot. It's muggy at the best of times, and in the summer the heat and mos-

quitoes are truly awesome. Stock up on sunscreen and bug repellent before you arrive.

Bringing tourists into the Pantanal is a big business, and the three cities that serve as jumping-off points to the region are flooded with tour operators – some of dubious repute. Whether you arrive in Cuiabá, Corumbá or Campo Grande you're likely to be approached by a guide fairly rapidly. Some are simply opportunists looking to make a buck out of Brazil's ecotourism, but there are still several venerable old-timers and dedicated newcomers working to protect the environment while sharing its tremendous diversity with visitors. It can be hard to tell the good from the bad, but here are some suggestions to ensure you have a safe and enjoyable trip:

- Resist making a snap decision, especially if you've just come off an overnight bus.
- Talk to other travelers who have just returned from a Pantanal trip – they're often your best source of up-to-the-minute information.
- Go to the local tourism office. They generally can't give independent advice because they're government funded but many keep complaints books that you're free to peruse.
- Remember that the owner or salesperson is not always your guide and it's the guide you're going to be with in the wilderness for several days. Ask to meet your guide if possible.
- Get things in writing and don't hand over your cash to any go-betweens.
- Compare your options. Many operators work out of the local bus station or airport so it's easy to shop around.

There's no obligation to go with a tour operator. You can drive or hitchhike along the Transpantaneira, a 145km-long road originating in Poconé, south of Cuiabá (Mato Grosso state), or the Estrada Parque that loops around the south (Mato Grosso do Sul). You'll see wildlife even without a guide.

Tours

Tours generally include transportation, accommodations, meals, hikes, horse-riding excursions and boat rides.

Operators out of Campo Grande typically charge less but only include one-way transport into the Pantanal; at trip's end you'll be dropped at Buraco das Piranhas (Estrada

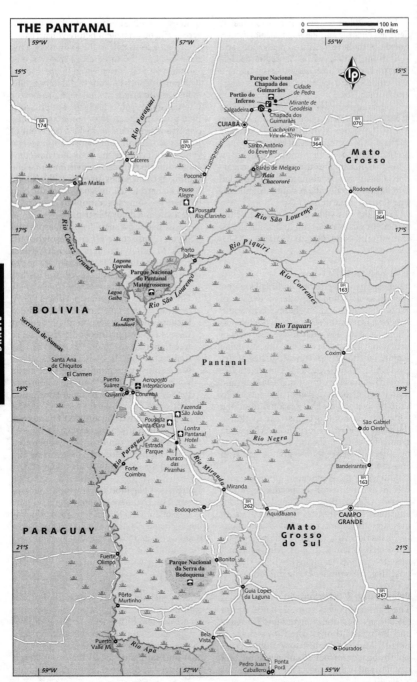

THE PANTANAL

0 ——— 100 km
0 ——— 60 miles

Parque's southern terminus), where you can catch a bus to Bonito, Corumbá or back to Campo Grande.

NORTHERN PANTANAL
Joel Souza Ecoverde Tours (☎ 0xx65-3624-1386; www .ecoverdetours.com; Av Getúlio Vargas 155, Cuiabá; per day R$150-200) Naturalist Joel Souza's agency has offered high-quality, customized Pantanal tours for nearly three decades.

Natureco (☎ 0xx65-3321-1001; www.pantanaltour.net; Leite 570, Cuiabá; per day from R$250) Another time-tested Cuiabá agency, run by Munir Nasr.

Pantanal Nature (☎ 0xx65-3322-0203, 9955-2632; www.pantanalnature.com.br; Campo Grande 487, Cuiabá; per day from R$190) Outstanding, locally raised guide Ailton Lara is highly recommended for his youthful vigor, solid professionalism and contagious passion for wildlife, birds and foreign languages.

SOUTHERN PANTANAL
EcoAdventures (☎ 0xx67-3356-4138, 9902-2076; www .ecoadventures.com.br; Lacerda 205, Campo Grande; per 3 days sleeping in hammock/dm/r R$300/400/460) A depend-able operator selling tours via the internet; owner Alisson Buzinhani designs itineraries for all budgets.

Ecological Expeditions (☎ 0xx67-3042-0508; www .ecologicalexpeditions.com.br; Nabuco 185, Campo Grande; per 3 days R$350-400) Affiliated with Campo Grande's youth hostel, this long-established budget op-erator has a checkered history (including the government's 2008 shutdown of its Pantanal camp); still, its prices remain competitive and tour quality was improving at the time of research.

Pantanal Discovery (☎ 0xx67-3383-9791; www .gilspantanaldiscovery.com.br; Campo Grande; per 3 days from R$400) A perennial Campo Grande operator with a polished sales pitch; owner Gil is as-sertive but generally well-reviewed; feel free to bargain and press for details.

Sleeping & Eating
TRANSPANTANEIRA
There are numerous accommodations on and off the road. Prices below include meals and daily excursions.

Pousada Rio Clarinho (☎ 0xx65-9998-8888; Transpantaneira Km 40; per person R$120) This rustic *fazenda* (large farm) offers non-motorized boat trips, a treetop wildlife viewing platform and authentic *pantaneira* food cooked on the woodstove.

Pouso Alegre (☎ 0xx65-9981-7911; www.pous alegre.com.br; Transpantaneira Km 33; d with fan/air-con R$260/280) A delightfully traditional *fazenda* with excellent horse riding and macaw-spot-ting opportunities, peacefully tucked 6km off the Transpantaneira.

SOUTHERN PANTANAL
Pousada Santa Clara (☎ 0xx67-9612-3500; www .pousadasantaclara.com.br; Estrada Parque Km 20; 3-day/2-night package per person in campsite/dm/r R$300/350/380; 🐾) The southern Pantanal's most versatile low-cost option, this *fazenda* has comfort-able rooms surrounding a poolside patio, plus hammock space and camping adjacent to the Rio Abobral.

Lontra Pantanal Hotel (☎ 0xx67-3231-9400; www .pesqueirodotadashi.com.br; Estrada Parque Km 7; 3-day/2-night package per person in dm/r R$290/450) Less remote than other options listed here, this *pesqueiro* (fishing lodge) overlooks the local river traffic near the Rio Miranda bridge.

CUIABÁ
☎ 0xx65 / pop 527,000
The capital of Mato Grosso state, Cuiabá is a sprawling frontier boomtown near the edge of three distinct ecosystems: the northern Pantanal, the *cerrado* of nearby Chapada dos Guimarães and the southern Amazon.

Sedtur (☎ 3613-9340; faleconosco@sedtur.mt.gov .br; Voluntários da Pátria 118; 🕐 8am-6pm Mon-Fri) pro-vides information about attractions through-out Mato Grosso. **HSBC** (Av Getúlio Vargas 346) has ATMs. For internet, try **Onix Lan House** (Celestino 8; per hr R$2; 🕐 8am-8pm Mon-Sat).

Sleeping
Hotel Ramos (☎ 3624-7472; Campo Grande 487; s/d with fan R$25/50, with air-con R$30/60; 🖳) Worn but friendly, this family-run hotel has large pri-vate rooms with free wi-fi at prices cheaper than dorms at the local hostel.

Pousada Ecoverde (☎ 3624-1386; Celestino 391; s/d R$30/50) In a charmingly funky historic home strewn with antique radios and books about the Pantanal, tour operator Joel Souza offers simple rooms adjoining a courtyard strung with hammocks. Bus station or air-port pickup can be arranged if you give advance notice.

Hotel Mato Grosso (☎ 3614-7777; www.hotelmato grosso.com.br; Costa 2522; s/d R$85/100) This more modern, centrally located hotel is part of a small local chain.

BRAZIL

Eating & Drinking

Sorveteria Nevaska (Barão de Melgaço 2169; 2-11pm) South of the center, take the edge off Cuiabá's heat with dozens of tropical ice-cream flavors.

Mistura Cuiabana (cnr Celestino & Mariano; per kg R$15; lunch Mon-Fri) A good cheap downtown lunch spot.

our pick **Choppão** (Av Getulio Vargas s/n; meals for 2 people R$35-55; 10am-late) This animated Cuiabá classic features old-school waiters serving obscenely large plates of meat or fish and the coldest *chope* in town.

Getting There & Away

Multiple airlines connect Cuiabá with cities throughout Brazil. For long-haul destinations, airfares are often competitive with bus fares.

The bus station is 3km north of the center. Buses run frequently to Cáceres (R$38, 3½ hours), Campo Grande (R$81, 10 to 11 hours), Goiânia (R$110, 15 hours), Brasília (R$122, 18 hours) and Porto Velho (R$139, 23 hours).

Car-rental agencies outside the airport tend to be cheaper than those inside. The best vehicles for the Transpantaneira are a VW Gol or Fiat Uno; beware treacherous road conditions in wet weather, especially south of the Rio Pixaím bridge at Km 65.

Getting Around

The airport is in Varzea Grande, 7km south of Cuiabá. Buses for the center leave from opposite the Las Velas Hotel on Av Filinto Muller. Buses from the center to the airport depart from Praça Ipiranga.

Frequent local buses (R$2.05, 10 minutes) run from the bus station into town, dropping you along Av Isaac Póvoas.

AROUND CUIABÁ
Parque Nacional da Chapada dos Guimarães

This high plateau 60km northeast of Cuiabá is a beautiful region reminiscent of the American Southwest. Its three exceptional sights are the 60m falls **Cachoeira Véu de Noiva**, the **Mirante de Geodésia** lookout (South America's geographical center) and the colorful rocky outcrops known as **Cidade de Pedra** (Stone City). You can reach all three by car or the first two by a combination of bus and walking. Access to Cachoeira Véu de Noiva is restricted to 100 people per day; for advance bookings, contact **park headquarters** (0xx65 3301 1133; pncg.mt@icmbio.gov.br). The park's

website (www.icmbio.gov.br/parna_guimaraes) lists approved guides who can take you to additional waterfalls, swimming holes and other attractions deeper inside the park.

Buses leave Cuiabá hourly for the charming town of Chapada dos Guimarães (R$10, 1¼ hours), just outside the park. Chapada's bus station is two blocks from the main plaza (Praça Dom Wunibaldo). For town maps, visit the **Secretária de Turismo** (0xx65-3301-2045; cnr Terres & Gomes).

Just off the plaza, **Hotel São José** (0xx65-3301-2934; Neves 50; s/d from R$18/36) has basic rooms. On the plaza itself, **Pousada Bom Jardim** (0xx65-3301-1244; Praça Dom Wunibaldo; s/d from R$40/70) is a step up in comfort and location. Nearby restaurants include the popular pizzeria **Cantinho da Maga** (Caldas s/n; pizzas from R$14; dinner).

Cáceres
0xx65 / pop 84,000

This relaxed town on the Rio Paraguai 215km west of Cuiabá is 115km from the Bolivian border town of San Matías.

There are several cheap sleeps near the bus station; if the heat's killing you, there's always the pool at **La Barca Hotel** (3345-5047; labarcahotel @terra.com.br; Osório; s/d R$50/90;).

A bus leaves Cáceres daily for the border at San Matías (R$10, 1¾ hours), where you make onward connections to Bolivia. Get the Brazilian exit stamp from Cáceres' Polícia Federal, 4km from the center on Av Getúlio Vargas.

Poconé
0xx65 / pop 31,000

Poconé, 100km southwest of Cuiabá, is the gateway to the Transpantaneira. From here, the 'highway' becomes little more than a pockmarked dirt track as it heads 145km south into the Pantanal, terminating at Porto Jofre.

The motel-like **Pousada Pantaneira** (3345-3357; pousadapantaneira@hotmail.com; s/d R$30/50) is just south of town, convenient for hitching a lift down the Transpantaneira. **Skala Hotel** (3345-1407; www.skalahotel.com.br; Praça Rondon; s/d/tr R$40/70/85) is an in-town alternative on Poconé's main square.

Six daily buses run from Cuiabá to Poconé (R$18.50, 2½ hours).

CAMPO GRANDE
0xx67 / pop 725,000

Mato Grosso do Sul's lively capital city is a major jumping-off point for the Pantanal.

The city's main thoroughfare, Av Afonso Pena, runs west–east, passing central Praça da República (alternately known as Praça do Rádio) en route to giant Parque das Nações Indígenas. The airport lies 7km west of the center; the new bus station is 5km south.

Campo Grande's **tourist office** (☎ 3314-9968; turismo.sedesc@pmcg.ms.gov.br; Av Afonso Pena; ☼ 8am-7pm Tue-Sat, 9am-noon Sun), five blocks west of Praça da República, maintains a comments book for travelers returning from the Pantanal.

Sleeping & Eating

Inexpensive hotels surround the old bus station, at the western end of Av Alfonso Pena. Nightlife is concentrated further east along the same avenue.

Turis Hotel (☎ 3382-2461; www.turishotel.com.br; Kardec 200; s/d with fan R$35/50, with air-con R$50/80; ☒) First floor rooms with fan and free wi-fi are excellent value; avoid the dark and claustrophobic basement cheapies.

Campo Grande Hostel (☎ 3382-3504; www.ecological expeditions.com.br; Nabuco 185; s/d/tr/q R$35/55/70/85; ☒ 🖳 ☎) Recent price hikes have made this rather grim hostel less appealing, but the swimming pool's still tempting.

Pousada Dom Aquino (☎ 3384-3303; pousada_dom _aquino@hotmail.com; Aquino 1806; s/d/tr R$60/90/110; ☒) A relaxed oasis in the city center, with international cable TV and free wi-fi, just northwest of Praça da República.

Feira Central (cnr 14 de Julho & Av Calógeras; mains from R$9; ☼ 7pm-late Wed & Fri, 5pm-late Sat) For a classic Campo Grande experience, join the locals for *sobá* and *yakisoba* (Japanese noodles) or *espetinho* (skewers of grilled meat) at the countless food booths in this lively indoor market.

Fogão de Minas (Aquino 2200; per kg R$24.90; ☼ lunch) Northeast of Praça da República, this popular per-kilo joint specializes in the hearty cuisine of Minas Gerais.

Getting There & Away

TAM and Varig/Gol provide daily flights to/ from São Paulo, Cuiabá, Rio and Brasília.

At the time of research, Campo Grande's bus station was moving south from the center to its new location on Av Costa e Silva, near the university and soccer stadium. Several daily buses run to Corumbá (R$77) via Buraco das Piranhas (gateway to Estrada Parque and the southern Pantanal). Other daily services include Cuiabá (R$85, 10 to 11 hours), Bonito (R$55, five hours), Ponta Porã (R$42, five hours), São Paulo (R$135, 12 to 14 hours) and Foz do Iguaçu (R$91, 14 hours).

To reach Campo Grande's airport, follow Av Afonso Pena and Av Duque de Caxias 7km west from the center.

Getting Around

Regular buses (R$2.70) run from the airport and the bus station to the center.

CORUMBÁ
☎ 0xx67 / pop 96,000

This historic port is a gateway to both the Pantanal and to Bolivia, which lies just across the Rio Paraguai. The river sunsets are beautiful, and despite Corumbá's reputation for illegal trafficking, travelers are generally left alone.

HSBC and **Bradesco** have ATMs on Delamare, and shopkeepers on 13 de Junho exchange currency. Internet is available at the **Palace Hotel** (Delamare 903; per hour R$3; ☼ 7am-midnight).

Fundtur (☎ 3231-2886; www.corumba.ms.gov .br/turismo; 15 de Novembro 659; ☼ 8am-noon & 2-6pm Mon-Fri) provides information on hotels and Pantanal guides.

The brand-new **Museu da História do Pantanal** (☎ 3232-0303; www.muhpan.org.br; Cavassa 275; ☼ 1-6pm Tue-Sun) has excellent exhibits on Pantanal history and ecology.

Corumbá Hostel (☎ 3231-1005; www.corumbahostel .com.br; Colombo 1419; dm/s/d with YHI card R$23/32/50, without YHI card R$28/38/60; ☒ ☎) was temporarily closed during research but scheduled to reopen in 2010.

Santa Mônica Palace Hotel (☎ 3234-3000; www.hsantamonica.com.br; Coelho 345; s/d R$100/120, ☒ 🖳 ☎) is a well-appointed, centrally located alternative for anyone overdosed on trans-Bolivian travel.

Churrascaria Rodeio (13 de Junho 760; per kg R$26; ☼ lunch daily, dinner Mon-Sat), Corumbá's snazziest buffet, features dozens of delicious dishes.

There are planes (one hour) and a dozen daily buses (R$75, 6½ hours) to Campo Grande, plus a 2pm bus to Bonito (R$60, 5½ hours, daily except Sunday).

See boxed text, p316, for details on crossing the Bolivian border.

BONITO
☎ 0xx67 / pop 17,000

Amid spectacular natural wonders, Bonito is the epicenter of Mato Grosso do Sul's ecotourism boom, luring visitors with

---

GETTING TO BOLIVIA

The Fronteira bus (R$1.75) goes from Corumbá's Praça Independência to the Bolivian border every 30 minutes. A taxi costs R$30.

All Brazilian border formalities must be completed with the **Polícia Federal office** (🕙 8-11am & 2-5pm Mon-Fri, 9am-1pm Sat & Sun) in Corumbá's bus station; if you arrive outside of its limited office hours, be prepared to overnight in Corumbá.

Money changers at the frontier accept US, Brazilian and Bolivian cash.

The Bolivian border town of Quijarro is little more than a collection of shacks. Taxis run the 4km between the border and Quijarro train station for around B$20. See p229 for details about onward travel from Quijarro to Santa Cruz.

---

crystal-clear rivers and opportunities for rappelling, rafting, horse riding and bird-watching. Despite its popularity, the town is still fairly relaxed outside the December to February high season.

Most local attractions require a guide, easily arranged through one of the travel agencies charging identical prices along Bonito's main street. Better-established agencies include **Muito Bonito Turismo** (🕿 3255-1645; contato @hotelmuitobonito.com.br; Rebuá 1444) and **Ygarapé Tour** (🕿 3255-1733; www.ygarape.com.br; Rebuá 1853). Trip prices generally include wetsuits and snorkel gear but not transportation; taxis to attractions below cost R$40 to R$120.

The most affordable swimming spot is the **Balneário Municipal** (admission R$15), 7km from Bonito, a natural riverside pool with lots of fish (and no guide needed), easily reached by mototaxi or bike path; **Ciclomax** (29 de Maio 625) rents bikes for R$15 a day.

Other nice snorkeling sites include **Aquário Natural Baía Bonita** (3hr trip R$125) and the crystal-clear **Rio Sucuri** (3hr trip R$107), 7km and 20km from Bonito, respectively. Even more sublime is the **Rio da Prata** (5hr trip incl lunch R$132), 50km from Bonito, which combines a 3km float downstream among 30 varieties of fish with an excellent buffet lunch featuring local meat and produce. Nearby, the **Buraco das Araras** (admission R$25) offers the opportunity to observe scarlet macaws circling out of a deep red-rock chasm.

Two other wonders 20km west of Bonito are the **Gruta do Lago Azul** (half-day excursion R$25), a large cave with luminous subterranean waters, and the **Abismo de Anhumas** (full-day excursion incl snorkeling/diving R$360/$530), where an adventurous rappel leads down a 72m abyss to another underground lake.

Sleeping

Book ahead in summer.

Bonito Hostel (🕿 3255-1462; www.ajbonito.com .br; Borralho 716; camping R$18, dm with/without YHI card R$30/38; 🖳 🖭) Drawing an international crowd, this lively hostel 1.5km from the center has six-bed dorms, a swimming pool, a covered patio, pool table, hammocks, computers (R$2 per hour), guest kitchen and book exchange. The helpful staff can arrange van excursions.

Pousada São Jorge (🕿 3255-4046; www.pousadasao jorge.com.br; Rebuá 1605; s/d from R$35/60; 🗱 🖳) This simple po•usada on Bonito's main street is a good alternative when Muito Bonito (below) is full.

ourpick Pousada Muito Bonito (🕿 3255-1645; www.hotelmuitobonito.com.br; Rebuá 1444; s/d R$45/70; 🗱 🖳) Three blocks from the bus station, this lovely family-run pousada is Bonito's best value, with comfortable en-suite rooms, an inviting courtyard and helpful multi-lingual owners with an exhaustive knowledge of the local area.

Eating

Most restaurants are along Pilad Rebuá.

Restaurante da Vovó (Muller s/n; buffet R$12.90; 🕙 lunch) Serves excellent per-kilo regional food.

O Casarão (Rebuá 1835; buffet R$14.90, rodizio de peixe R$29.90; 🕙 lunch & dinner) Popular for its all-you-can-eat rodizio de peixe, where multiple local fish specialties swim past your table on waiter's trays.

Taboa Bar (Rebuá 1837; 🕙 5pm-late) This lively bar features sandwiches, full meals, creative drinks and occasional live music. Don't miss its trademark taboa (R$3), a shot of cachaça mixed with honey, cinnamon and guaraná.

Getting There & Away

Four daily buses run from Bonito to Campo Grande (R$53, five hours). For Corumbá (R$60, six hours), there is a single 6am departure (daily except Sunday).

At the time of research, **Trip Airlines** (www
.voetrip.com.br) had just initiated flights from
Campo Grande to Bonito's new **airport**
(BYO; ☎ 0xx67 3255-4452; www.aeroportodebonito.com
.br). The airport is 13km south of town on
highway MS-178.

THE NORTHEAST

Year-round warm climate, physical beauty
and sensual culture rich in folkloric traditions all make Brazil's Northeast a true
tropical paradise. More than 2000km
of fertile coastline is studded with idyllic white-sand beaches, pockets of lush
rainforest, sand dunes and coral reefs. A
spectrum of natural environments creates
the perfect backdrop for a wide variety of
outdoor activities.

These parts of the country also breathe
colonial history. The picturesque urban
centers of Salvador, Olinda and São Luís are
packed with beautifully restored and satis-
fyingly decaying architecture. Add to this
the lively festivals, myriad music and dance
styles and exotic cuisine loaded with seafood,
and you will find Brazil's most culturally
diverse region.

SALVADOR
☎ 0xx71 / pop 2.9 million
Salvador da Bahia is among Brazil's brightest
gems. It's the African soul of the country; this
is where the descendants of slaves preserved
their African culture more than anywhere
else in the New World, successfully creating
thriving culinary, religious, musical, dance
and martial-arts traditions. Salvador's vibrant historic center, the Pelourinho, is a
treat for the senses with its dendê oil aromas,
thundering percussion and renovated colonial architecture. It has an anarchic quality
that makes its party nights memorable.

Don't be fooled into thinking the Pelô is
nothing more than a tourist ghetto. Many
of the studios here are at the cutting edge
of contemporary Brazilian movement,
dance, music and art. Underlying much of
Salvador's culture is the Afro-Brazilian religion Candomblé, in which Catholic and
animistic traditions blend to form rituals
that involve direct communication with the
spirit world. The surrounding area, however,
is desperately poor.

Orientation
Salvador sits on a peninsula on the Baía
de Todos os Santos. The center is bay-
side and divided by a steep bluff into two
parts: the Cidade Baixa (Lower City), containing the commercial center and port,
and Cidade Alta (Upper City), containing
the Pelourinho. The Pelô is the center of
Salvador's history, tourism and nightlife.
Cidade Baixa and the stretch between Praça
da Sé and Praça Campo Grande are noisy by
day and deserted by night. South, at the tip
of the peninsula, is affluent beachside Barra.
Residential neighborhoods stretch northeast
along the coast, with Rio Vermelho and
Itapuã the most interesting.

Information
ATMs exist throughout the center as well
as at the bus station, airport, and shop-
ping centers. Travel agents along Largo do
Cruzeiro change cash and travelers' checks.
Internet cafes and call centers cluster in the
Pelô and Barra.

Baiafrica Internet Café (Mattos 32, Pelourinho; per hr
R$3) Fast internet.

Banco do Brasil (Cruzeiro de São Francisco 9)

Bradesco (Mattos s/n)

Deltur (☎ 3322-1168; Cruzeiro de São Francisco 14,
Pelourinho) Main tourist police office.

Hospital Espanhol (Av Sete de Setembro, Barra)

Sebo Brandão (☎ 3243-5383; Barbosa 15) Huge
multilingual second-hand bookstore to buy or exchange
two-for-one.

Tourist offices airport (☎ 3204-1244; ☼ 7am-11pm);
bus station (☎ 3450-3871; ☼ 8am-5pm); Mercado Modelo
(☎ 3241-0242; ☼ 8am-5:30pm Mon-Sat, 8am-2pm
Sun); Pelourinho (☎ 3321-2133; cnr Laranjeiras & João
de Deus; ☼ 8am-9pm); Praça Municipal (☎ 3321-3127;
☼ 9am-8pm Mon-Fri, 9am-6pm Sat, 9am-1pm Sun) Helpful multilingual tourist offices. Also see www.bahia.com.br.

Wash & Dry (Ladeira da Praça 4; ☼ 9am-6pm Mon-Fri,
9am-2pm Sat) Quick laundry service at R$22 per load.

Dangers & Annoyances
If you're going to be pickpocketed or mugged
in Brazil, Salvador is likely to be the place.
This shouldn't prevent you from visiting but
play it safe, especially at night. Avoid empty
areas. Travelers report 'feeling like a protected
species' in the Pelô, but wandering off the
beaten path there has proven to be unsafe. The
stretch from the Largo do Pelourinho north to
Santo Antônio has a reputation for nighttime
muggings – take a taxi.

BRAZIL

Sights

PELOURINHO

The Pelô has numerous churches, galleries, workshops, and museums to browse as you wander its cobbled streets.

Museu Afro-Brasileiro (Terreiro de Jesus; admission R$5; 9am-6pm Mon-Fri, 10am-5pm Sat & Sun) has a room devoted to gorgeous carved wood panels of the *orixás* (Afro-Brazilian gods) by the multi-talented 20th-century Argentine-Brazilian Carybé. These were temporarily in the Museu de Arte Moderna at the time of research.

The church most deserving of your attention is baroque **Igreja São Francisco** (Cruzeiro de São Francisco; admission R$3; 8am-5pm Mon-Sat), with a majestic sandstone facade and marvelous

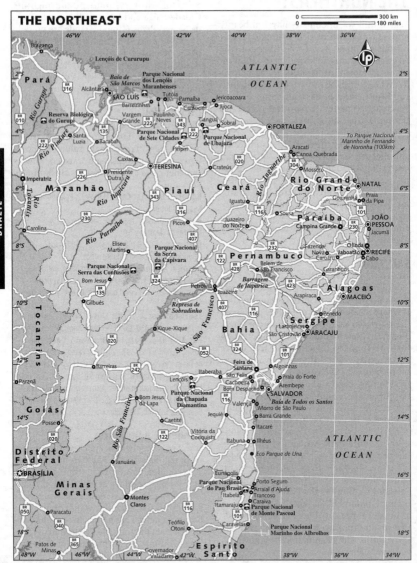

THE NORTHEAST

panels of Portuguese *azulejos* (tiles) depicting Lisbon landmarks.

The attractive **Centro Cultural Solar Ferrão** (Mattos 45; ☉ 10am-6pm Tue-Fri, 1-6pm Sat & Sun) is a newly restored building holding three permanent exhibitions – of African art, Bahian folk art and religious art – as well as temporary displays.

Steep **Largo do Pelourinho** is where slaves were auctioned and likely publicly beaten on a *pelourinho* (whipping post).

CIDADE BAIXA & BARRA

Solar do Unhão, an 18th-century sugar estate mansion on the bay, houses **Museu de Arte Moderna** (Av Contorno; ☉ 1-7pm Tue-Sun, to 9pm Sat), with a beachside sculpture garden, waterfront cafe and good temporary exhibits. It's a short walk from Mercado Modelo; cab it after dark.

On the Barra waterfront, view the sunset at Bahia's oldest fort, **Santo Antônio** (1598).

ITAPAGIPE PENINSULA

Built in 1745, **Igreja NS do Bonfim** (☉ 7-11am & 2-5pm Tue-Sun) houses a Christ who inspires extraordinary popular devotion. He's famous for effecting miraculous cures; the collection of photos, ex-voto limbs, offerings and tokens of thanks, mostly displayed in an upstairs museum (R$3) is moving. This is Candomblé's key church and fundamental in getting to grips with Bahian culture. *Fitas* (ribbons) are a popular memento that'll be pushed on you (in shops they cost R$1 for 30). Take the 'Bonfim' or 'Ribeira' bus from the base of Elevador Lacerda.

Activities

Much Bahian life revolves around the Afro-Brazilian religion Candomblé. A visit to a *terreiro* promises hours of ritual and possession, and will deepen your understanding of Bahian culture. Wear clean, light-colored clothes (no shorts) and go well-fed. **FENACAB** (Brito 39) can provide addresses and schedules.

Praia do Porto in Barra is a small, usually packed beach with calm waters. For less crowded beaches and cleaner water, head out to **Piatã** (25km), **Itapuã** (27km) or beyond.

Courses

Associação de Capoeira Mestre Bimba (☎ 3322-0639; www.capoeiramestrebimba.com.br; Laranjeiras 1, Pelourinho) runs classes in *capoeira* (martial art/dance), *maculelê* (stick fighting) and percussion. It also puts on shows.

Festivals & Events

CARNAVAL

Salvador's Carnaval is the second largest in Brazil and, for many, the best. It's characterized by parades of *axé* and *pagode* bands atop creeping *trios-electricos* (long trucks of huge speakers). A *trio* or drum corps, together with its followers grouped in a roped-off area around it, form a *bloco*. People pay hundreds of reales for the *abadá* (shirt required for entry to the *bloco*) for a top band, mostly for prestige and the safety of those ropes. Choosing to *fazer pipoca* (be popcorn) in the street is still a fine way to spend Carnaval.

There are three main areas: the beachside Barra to Rio Vermelho circuit (most touristy), the narrow Campo Grande to Praça Castro Alves circuit and the Pelourinho (no *trios* here, mostly concerts and drum corps). Check www.portaldocarnaval.ba.gov.br.

Safety Tips

Crowds clearing to escape a fight pose the greatest threat, so be aware of your surroundings. Police are a noticeable presence. Hands will be all over you, searching your pockets and groping your person. Costumes aren't common – shorts and tennis shoes are usual. A few tips:

- Form small groups and avoid deserted areas.
- Women shouldn't walk alone or wear skirts.
- Carry little money, stashed in your shoe.
- Leave *any* jewelry, watches or nice-looking sunglasses behind.
- Don't challenge pickpockets – the ensuing fight isn't worthwhile.
- Carry a photocopy of your passport.

OTHER FESTIVALS

Salvador stages many festivals. After Carnaval, the largest and most colorful:

Lavagem do Bonfim Second Thursday in January.
Festa de Iemanjá February 2.

Sleeping

Staying in the Pelô (packed with improvised hostels) means being in the action, but it can be noisy and/or draining. Mellower, beachside Barra has easy transport to the Pelô and the conveniences of a residential neighborhood. Reservations are essential for Carnaval.

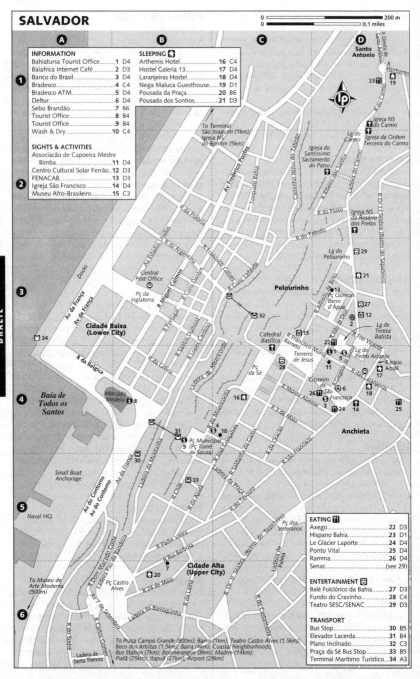

SALVADOR

0 — 200 m
0 — 0.1 miles

INFORMATION
Bahiatursa Tourist Office.........1 D4
Baiafrica Internet Café............2 D3
Banco do Brasil.....................3 D4
Bradesco.............................4 C4
Bradesco ATM.......................5 D4
Deltur................................6 D4
Sebo Brandão.......................7 B6
Tourist Office.......................8 B4
Tourist Office.......................9 B4
Wash & Dry........................10 C4

SIGHTS & ACTIVITIES
Associação de Capoeira Mestre
  Bimba..............................11 D4
Centro Cultural Solar Ferrão...12 D3
FENACAB............................13 D3
Igreja São Francisco...............14 D4
Museu Afro-Brasileiro............15 C3

SLEEPING
Arthemis Hotel.....................16 C4
Hostel Galeria 13...................17 D4
Laranjeiras Hostel..................18 D4
Nega Maluca Guesthouse.......19 D1
Pousada da Praça..................20 B6
Pousada dos Sonhos..............21 D3

EATING
Axego..................................22 D3
Hispano Bahia.......................23 D1
Le Glacier Laporte..................24 D4
Ponto Vital...........................25 D4
Ramma.................................26 D4
Senac...............................(see 29)

ENTERTAINMENT
Balé Folclórico da Bahia...........27 D4
Fundo do Cravinho.................28 C4
Teatro SESC/SENAC................29 D3

TRANSPORT
Bus Stop..............................30 B5
Elevador Lacerda....................31 B4
Plano Inclinado......................32 C3
Praça da Sé Bus Stop..............33 B5
Terminal Marítimo Turístico.....34 A3

Santo Antonio

Igreja NS do Carmo
Igreja do Santissimo Sacramento do Passo
Igreja da Ordem Terceira do Carmo
Igreja NS do Rosário dos Pretos

To Terminal São Joaquim (Tkm);
Igreja NS do Bonfim (5km)

Pelourinho

Lg do Pelourinho

Pç Quincas Berro d'Água

Lg de Tereza Batista

Lg do Pedro Arcanjo

Catedral Basílica

Terreiro de Jesus

Cruzeiro de São Francisco

Anchieta

Cidade Baixa (Lower City)

Central Post Office

Pç da Inglaterra

Docks

Av da França

Baía de Todos os Santos

Mercado Modelo

Small Boat Anchorage

Naval HQ

Pç da Sé

Pç Municipal (Pç Tomé de Souza)

Cidade Alta (Upper City)

Pç Castro Alves

Pç dos Veteranos

To Museu de Arte Moderna (500m)

To Praça Campo Grande (800m); Barris (1km); Teatro Castro Alves (1.5km);
Beco dos Artistas (1.5km); Barra (4km); Coastal Neighborhoods;
Bus Station (7km); Boomerangue (8km); Madre (14km);
Piatã (25km); Itapuã (27km); Airport (29km)

Ladeira de Santa Thereza

BRAZIL

PELOURINHO & AROUND

Pousada dos Sonhos (☎ 3322-9901; www.pousada dossonhos.com; Largo do Pelourinho 5; dm R$24, s/d without bathroom R$48/72) Expect a big welcoming smile at this well-located spot. The dorm packs 'em in but is airy; rooms with a window go for more than the clean but tight interior ones. Prices drop in low season.

Nega Maluca Guesthouse (☎ 3242-9249; www .negamaluca.com; Marchantes 15, Santo Antônio; dm R$26, d with/without bathroom R$80/70; ❷) This friendly, super laid-back hostel run by travelers has good dorm rooms just outside the Pelô's noisy zone. There's a kitchen and free internet.

Pousada da Praça (☎ 3321-0642; www.pousada dapracahotel.com.br; Barbosa 5; dm R$27, s/d with air-con R$50/80, s/d without bathroom R$40/70; ❷) A short stroll from the Pelourinho, this reliable hotel does the simple things well and wins extra points for its enthusiastic staff. Decent breakfast. Discount for cash payment.

Hostel Galeria 13 (☎ 3266-5609; www.hostel galeria13.com; Ordem Terceira/Accioli 23; dm R$30) Darkish compact dorms have sturdy wooden bunks and floorboards at this newish spot well-loved by travelers, with cushioned area and patio for chilling out. Free internet, breakfast till midday, sociable dogs and helpful English-speaking owner.

Laranjeiras Hostel (☎ 3321-1366; www.laranjeiras hostel.com.br; Ordem Terceira/Accioli 13; dm R$38, d with/without bathroom R$160/100; ❷) The highest-quality and most attractive Pelô hostel, noisy, busy Laranjeiras has high-ceilinged dorm rooms with triple bunks, and good bathrooms. The private rooms are overpriced. Price drops after Carnaval. A HI discount is offered.

Arthemis Hotel (☎ 3322-0724; www.arthemishotel .com; Praça da Sé 398, 7th fl; s/d R$40/60, with view R$60/70) Secure, traveler-friendly Arthemis has an excellent location and a breakfast veranda with a fantastic view. Cheap, spacious rooms are no-frills, with ceramic breeze-block windows, but are colorful and have hot water.

BARRA

Albergue do Porto (☎ 3264-6600; www.alberguedoporto .com.br; Barão de Sergy 197; dm R$38-46, d R$105; ❷) Barra's primo hostel has airy, high-ceilinged dorm rooms of various sizes, a living room with beanbags, and a kitchen. It's in an early 20th-century building with kindergarten-esque decor. Great staff; HI discount.

Âmbar Pousada (☎ 3264-6956; www.ambarpousada .com.br; Celso 485; dm/s/d R$40/100/116; ❷) Rooms aren't huge but the hang-out space and cheerful ambience makes this the best of a string of *pousadas* on this street two blocks back from the beach.

Che Lagarto Hostel (☎ 3235-2404; www.chelagarto .com; Av Oceânica 84; dm/d R$40/120; ❷) This popular hostel chain's Salvador offering ain't cheap, but dorms are air-conditioned, staff are friendly and the beachfront location great. Social life is guaranteed with a bar, pool table and regular parties with live samba in the front yard. It's on the corner of Leoni Ramos about 100m west of the Christ statue.

Pousada La Villa Française (☎ 3245-6008; www .lavilafrancaise.com; Recife 222, Jardim Brasil; dm R$35, r per person R$45-55; ❷) By a little nest of bars and restaurants near Barra Shopping a few blocks back from the beach, this impeccable French-run spot has cute, spotless rooms, use of a kitchen and a relaxing, cordial atmosphere.

Pousada Acácia (☎ 3264-4113; www.pousadaacacia .com.br; Oliveira 46/210; s/d R$80/100; ❷) A motherly welcome awaits at this peaceful and pretty *pousada* occupying a charming 1950s house with wooden floors, plenty of hanging-out space and a great breakfast.

Eating

Salvador is well known for its African-influenced Bahian cuisine. A street-food staple is *acarajé*.

PELOURINHO

Le Glacier Laporte (Largo do Cruzeiro 21; ice creams R$4-6; ❧ lunch) Delicious artesanal ice creams and tropical fruit sorbets to cope with the heat.

Hispano Bahia (Carmo 68; per kg R$17; ❧ lunch) Service is rude but the views out back over the bay are great at this cheap lunch spot that also does a range of Spanish omelettes.

Senac (Largo do Pelourinho 13; per kg R$19; ❧ lunch Mon-Fri) Get here early and try the creative salad fare at this top-value per-kilo lunch spot run by a restaurant school. In the same complex is a smarter all-you-can-eat buffet; open evenings, too.

Ponto Vital (Laranjeiras 23; mains for 2 people R$20-32) If there are two of you, well-made traditional plates like *arrumadinho* (sun-dried beef, beans, salad and *farofa* tossed together) are good value at this friendly spot.

Ramma (Largo do Cruzeiro 7; per kg R$29; ❧ lunch Mon-Sat) High-quality organic and vegetarian food at this upstairs restaurant. There's another branch in Barra.

Axego (João de Deus 1; most dishes for 2 people R$30-42) Warm service and fair prices are to be had at this attractive upstairs restaurant. Delicious *moquecas* are the highlight, and half-portions, a substantial feed for one, are available with no surcharge.

COASTAL NEIGHBORHOODS

Barra and Rio Vermelho are full of restaurants, particularly the two parallel streets back from the Praia do Farol beach in Barra, and Rua Feira de Santana in Rio Vermelho.

Acarajé da Dinha (Largo de Santana, Rio Vermelho; dishes R$5-25) Locals line up at this street stall for Salvador's most renowned *acarajé*.

Brasil Legal Churrascaria (Celso 110, Barra; per person R$10; ⊗ lunch) This all-you-can-eat BBQ restaurant has an excellent spread and gets packed.

Maria de São Pedro (Mercado Modelo; moquecas R$30-45; ⊗ 10am-8pm) On the top floor of the market this specializes in traditional Bahian food. The terrace has a great view over the harbor, a classic sundowner spot.

Drinking
PELOURINHO

Plazas and cobbled streets fill with revelers sharing beer at plastic tables or dancing behind roaming bands of drummers. Tuesday is the big night. There's free live music in the inner courtyards *(largos)* of the Pelô and on the Terreiro de Jesus.

COASTAL NEIGHBORHOODS

Leave the Pelô! Barra's nightlife centers in Jardim Brasil, with cool open-air bars attracting a hip, mostly affluent crowd. Largo de Santana and Largo da Mariquita in bohemian Rio Vermelho pack with people drinking beer and eating *acarajé*. Hip bars surround these squares.

Entertainment

Grab the free publication *Guia Pelourinho Cultural* from the tourist office.

FOLKLORIC SHOWS

Salvador is home to world-class choreographers and performers. Shows include displays of *afro* (Afro-Brazilian dance), *samba de roda* (flirtatious samba performed in a circle), dances of the *orixás*, and *maculelê* and *capoeira* that will blow your mind, all to live percussion and vocals.

Balé Folclórico da Bahia (Teatro Miguel Santana, Gregório de Matos 49; admission R$25; ⊗ shows 8pm Wed-Mon)

Teatro SESC/SENAC (Largo do Pelourinho 19; admission free-R$10) Regular shows of various types.

LIVE MUSIC

Singers, bands and Carnaval groups hold weekly *ensaios* (rehearsals), essentially concerts, in the months leading up to Carnaval. The brotherhood Filhos de Gandhy is an *afoxé* (group tied to Candomblé traditions) that has come to represent Salvador itself. Excellent *blocos afros* (Afro-Brazilian groups with powerful drum corps) are Ilê Aiyê, Male Debalê and Dida; more poppy but still with strong percussion sections are Olodum (an institution), Araketu and Timbalada (brainchild of Carlinhos Brown).

Teatro Castro Alves (Praça Campo Grande) Salvador's finest venue for quality performances. Its Concha Acústica (amphitheater) holds fun weekly shows.

Museu de Arte Moderna (Av Contorno) Readers rate the Saturday evening jazz here (R$4).

Fundo do Cravinho (Terreiro de Jesus) Live samba nightly (R$3) from about 8pm.

DANCE CLUBS

Salvador's dance clubs dot its waterfront, and are mostly frequented by the hip and wealthy.

Boomerangue (www.boomerangueeventos.com.br; Paciência 307, Rio Vermelho; admission R$15; ⊗ 11pm-late Fri & Sat) Three floors of different sounds in this friendly-feeling place.

Madrre (www.myspace.com/madrre; Av Mangabeira 2471, Pituba; admission men/women R$25/15) Salvador's best spot for electronic music.

GAY & LESBIAN VENUES

Beco dos Artistas (Artist's Alley; Av Cerqueira Lima, Garcia) A meeting point for a young gay crowd. To find it, walk a few blocks down Leovigildo Filgueiras from the Teatro Castro Alves.

Off (Dias D'Ávila 33, Barra) A well-established club. The bars around it on this laneway are also popular.

Shopping

Mercado Modelo (⊗ 9am-7pm Mon-Sat, to 2pm Sun) The two-story, enclosed tourist market has dozens of stalls selling local handicrafts. Arriving slave shipments were kept in the watery depths of this 19th-century building.

Shopping Iguatemí Salvador's largest mall, opposite the bus station.

Getting There & Away

AIR
Several airlines serve Salvador domestically. TAP and American Airlines fly directly to Europe and the USA respectively.

BUS
Buses from the south take the lengthy trip around the bay. Alternatively catch a ferry to Salvador's Terminal de São Joaquim from Bom Despacho (R$4, 45 minutes) on Ilha Itaparica, accessed by regular buses (R$9, 1½ hours) from main-road Valença. Getting off at Valença and coming this way saves up to R$60 on long-distance bus journeys from southern destinations.

BUS FARES

Destination	Cost (R$)	Duration (hr)
Belo Horizonte	196	24
Brasília	198	22
Ilhéus	81-128	7
Natal	161	21
Porto Seguro	127	12
Recife	106-126	11-16
Rio	225	24-28
São Paulo	220-265	33

Getting Around

For Barra and Cidade Alta, cross the footbridge from the bus station (8km from the center) to Shopping Iguatemí and catch the Praça da Sé minibus (R$4). Catch the same bus from the airport (30km from the center). For a cheaper but crowded ride (R$2.15), there are city bus terminals in front of both the bus station and the airport. Buses between Praça da Sé and Barra are regular.

Linking the lower and upper cities in the center are the fabulous art deco **Elevador Lacerda** (admission 5¢; ⊙ 24hr), and the exciting **Plano Inclinado** (admission 5¢; ⊙ 7am-7pm Mon-Fri, to 1pm Sat).

PRAIA DO FORTE
☎ 0xx71

Praia do Forte is an upmarket but laid-back holiday village with white fluffy beaches. It's pleasant enough, but the artificial feel and elevated prices make it day-trip territory for many backpackers.

Excellent **Projeto TAMAR** (www.tamar.org.br; admission R$10; ⊙ 9am-6pm), by the church, is the main draw. It's part of a highly successful national project working with local communities to preserve sea-turtle breeding and feeding grounds. As well as informative display panels, there are tanks of sea turtles and other marine life. Hatchings happen from August to April.

Pousadas cluster along streets parallel to the central pedestrian avenue. Most offer weekday discounts in the low season. **Praia do Forte Hostel** (☎ 3676-1094; www.albergue.com.br; Aurora 3; dm/d R$38/85;) has pleasant dorms with tile floors and their own bathrooms, all surrounding a grassy central courtyard. Turtle entrance fee is included, and bikes and surfboards are rented. HI discount. Near the bus stop, **Pousada Tia Helena** (☎ 3676-1198; Estrelas; s/d R$60/80) is simple, cheap-for-here and friendly. Restaurants line the main street – Casa da Nati does a good per-kilo lunch.

Buses run from Salvador's *rodoviária* to Praia do Forte (R$9.40, 1½ hours, eight daily), as do regular and slightly cheaper vans. Some buses drop off at the main road junction, where cars nip you into town for R$2 per person.

CACHOEIRA & SÃO FÉLIX
☎ 0xx75 / pop 47,500

Gently steaming in the heat, sleepy Cachoeira and São Felix face each other across the Rio Paraguaçu. This is a good day trip, giving you a glimpse of the fertile Recôncavo, whose sugar and tobacco plantations made it the economic heartland of colonial Brazil. These towns are also renowned as centers of Candomblé.

Cachoeira's **tourist office** (Nery 7; ⊙ 8am-6pm Mon-Fri, 9am-2pm Sat, 9am-noon Sun) has maps. There's a Bradesco ATM on nearby Praça Milton.

Sights & Activities
Cachoeira has an uplifting ensemble of colonial buildings in its peaceful old center. Several house art galleries, a couple of which are also cafes. The **Igreja da Ordem Terceira do Carmo** (Bonaventura) features a gallery of suffering Christs with genuine ruby blood. Atop a small hill, the picturesque chapel of **Nossa Senhora de Ajuda** is the town's oldest building.

Across in São Felix, the riverfront **Centro Cultural Dannemann** (Av Salvador Pinto 39; ⊙ 8am-5pm Tue-Sat, gallery only 1-5pm Sun), in addition to first-class contemporary art displays, is still a working cigar factory; watch the team of women at work hand-rolling them, as they've done since 1873.

Festivals & Events

Festa de São João Interior Bahia's largest popular festival, held June 22 to 24.

Festa da NS de Boa Morte Fascinating three-day event commencing on the Friday closest to August 15. Descendants of slaves pay tribute to their liberation with dance and prayer in a mix of Candomblé and Catholicism.

Sleeping & Eating

Unremarkable, clean *pousadas* charging R$30 per person cluster in Cachoeira's old-town streets near the tourist office, and more upmarket options can be found on nearby Praça da Aclamação.

Pensão Tia Rosa (☎ 3425-1792; Nery 12; s/d R$30/60) Tia Rosa is a cheap choice.

Pousada do Paraguassú (☎ 3438-3386; Pinto 1; s R$45, d from R$65-120; ☒) This *pousada* is a step up. It's on the riverfront in São Félix, with rooms in various grades facing a flowery central courtyard.

Beira Rio (Filho 19; mains R$14-26; ☒ lunch & dinner) Overlooking the river, the excellent Beira Rio does single and double portions. Starters like fried fish (R$10) are meals in themselves.

Rabbuni (Nery 1; per kg R$18.90; ☒ lunch Mon-Sat) Back in Cachoeira, Rabbuni has a popular lunch spread; profits go to charitable projects.

Getting There & Away

Daily buses depart Salvador's bus station for Cachoeira/São Félix (R$15.60, two hours, hourly). They stop in both towns, whose bus stations face each other across the bridge. There are connections to Feira de Santana for onward travel.

LENÇÓIS

☎ 0xx75 / pop 10,000

Lençóis is the prettiest of the old diamond-mining towns in the Chapada Diamantina, a mountainous wooded oasis in the dusty *sertão* (dry interior). While the town itself is very pretty, it is the surrounding area bursting with caves, waterfalls and plateaus promising panoramic views that's the real attraction. Lençóis is a hiking hotspot.

The tourist office is in the market building next to the bridge. Internet places charge R$3 to R$4 per hour. There's a Banco do Brasil with ATMs on the main square. Shops sell a useful English/Portuguese guide to the region (R$15) and trekking maps.

Sights & Activities

WALKING & SWIMMING

These walks are easily taken without a guide. Walk past the bus stop and follow the Rio Lençóis 3km upstream into Parque Municipal da Muritiba. You'll pass a series of rapids known as **Cachoeira Serrano**, the **Salão de Areias Coloridas** (Room of Colored Sands), where artisans gather material for bottled sand paintings, **Poço Halley** (Halley's Well), **Cachoeirinha** (Little Waterfall) and finally **Cachoeira da Primavera** (Spring Waterfall). Or follow São Benedito 4km out of town to **Ribeirão do Meio**, a series of swimming holes with a natural waterslide.

HIKING

To the southwest of Lençóis is **Parque Nacional da Chapada Diamantina**, comprising 1520 sq km of breathtaking scenery, waterfalls, rivers, monkeys and striking geology. The park has little infrastructure (trails are unmarked) and bus services are infrequent, making it difficult to penetrate without a guide. Make sure you only use certified guides; the **ACVL** (☎ 3334-1425; 10 de Novembro) guide association, local agencies or your *pousada* can hook you up with one.

Ultra-knowledgeable English-speaking guides are **Roy Funch** (☎ 3334-1305; funchroy@ yahoo.com) and **Olivia Taylor** (☎ 3334-1229; www .h2otraveladventures.com) at Pousada dos Duendes. Readers also rate **'Feijão'** (☎ 8131-9640; feijoada @hotmail.com) at the restaurant of the same name by the bus station.

Treks last from two to eight days, and usually involve a combination of camping, staying in local homes and *pousadas*. Prices, which usually include food and accommodation, are around R$100 to R$170 per day. Necessary gear can be rented from agencies.

CLIMBING

An adventure operator specializing in rock climbing and abseiling is **Fora da Trilha** (☎ 3334-1326; www.foradatrilha.com.br; Pedras 202).

Tours

Lençóis agencies (there's one on every corner) organize half-/full-day car trips (around R$60/105) and guided hikes from a couple of hours to a week or more. Various admission fees apply in the area; these are usually included in the tour price. Agencies pool customers to send daily groups out. There's a rotating schedule of trips.

Standout sights include **Poço Encantado**, a cave filled with stunningly beautiful blue water, **Lapa Doce**, another cave with impressive formations and **Cachoeira da Fumaça**, Brazil's highest waterfall (420m). Near Lençóis, **Morro do Pai Inácio** is a mesa-style peak affording an awesome view over a plateau-filled valley. Evening trips here cost R$30; it's a half-hour climb to the top.

Sleeping

Reserve for major holidays, particularly for São João, the town's major festival at the end of June.

Camping Lumiar (☎ 3334-1241; lumiar.camping @gmail.com; Praça do Rosário 70; campsites per person R$15, r per person R$40) Grassy campsites shaded by flowering trees in a gorgeous garden beside a church. Bar, restaurant and guest-use kitchen.

Hostel Chapada (☎ 3334-1497; www.hostelchapada .com.br; Boa Vista 121; dm/d R$30/60) Simple, uncrowded dorm rooms, a kitchen and small garden are the features of this decent little central hostel. Bike hire and HI discount are available.

Pousada dos Duendes (☎ 3334-1229; www.pousada dosduendes.com; Pires; dm R$30, s/d R$60/80, without bathroom R$45/70) This brilliantly relaxed place offers cute rooms, very friendly atmosphere, a kitchen and internet. Upstairs rooms with their own balcony and hammock cost R$20 more. The English-speaking owner runs good excursions and can also advise on local guides.

Pousada Grisante (☎ 3334-1527; www.pousada grisante.com; Florêncio; s/d R$50/80) With water views up close and personal, this laid-back choice is decorated with black-and-white photos and has crisp, modern rooms. It hangs over the rapids in the center of town, which change through the year from a trickle to a foaming torrent of cola in a kid's daydream.

ourpick **Pousada Casa de Hélia** (☎ 3334-1143; www.casadehelia.com.br; Muritiba; s/d R$50/80; �) With some of the nicest budget rooms we've seen in this part of Brazil, this tranquil, leafy retreat has numerous artistic touches and a great breakfast spread. There's good walking info, and it's close to the bus stop – keep going as the bus was, and take the first right up the hill.

Eating

Fazendinha & Tal (Pedras 125; dishes R$13-22) This handsome and original spot does tasty pasta and pizza, but specializes in *cachaça* infusions (R$1.50) ranging from cinnamon to pineapple. Don't bank on trying them all on the first visit – there are four dozen.

Neco's Bar (Praça Pacheco; per person R$14) Place orders 24 hours in advance at this Lençóis institution offering serious home cooking.

Os Artistas da Massa (Baderna 49; dishes R$15-20) This sweet spot serves really excellent fresh pasta dishes accompanied by prints of Dutch masters and quality jazz tunes you pick off the menu.

O Bode (Beco do Rio; per kg R$18; ☺ lunch) Tucked away off the main square, this sweet riverside spot does the best-value lunch in town.

Cozinha Aberta (Barbosa 42; dishes R$20-25; ☺ 1-11pm) Treat yourself at this gourmet bistro following slow food principles (everything is as fresh, organic and local as possible). In high season, their lip-smacking Thai and Indian curries are served in a different restaurant, Etnia, at Baderna 111.

A Picanha na Praça (Praça Otaviano Alves 62; meat for 2 people R$30-50; ☺ lunch & dinner) Short menu of excellent grilled meats and a salmon option. Single portions (R$20 to $40) can feed two.

Getting There & Away

Three daily buses run from Salvador (R$48.40, at 7am, 4:30pm and 11:30pm, six hours), returning from Lençóis at 7:30am, 1:15pm, and 11:30pm. All stop in Feira de Santana, where onward connections can be made.

MORRO DE SÃO PAULO
☎ 0xx75

Unique, isolated Morro, across the bay from Salvador and reached by boat, is pretty trendy these days and known for never-say-die nightlife but still has a tranquil charm along its single street that runs between three jungle-topped hills. The beaches, with their shallow, warm water, disappear with the tides, liberating you for a hike to the waterfall, a boat trip to quiet **Boipeba** or sunset-watching from the fort.

There are a few ATMs and heaps of internet places (R$3 per hour).

Orientation

Walk up the hill from the boat dock and, after paying your tax, turn right for the town, a

BRAZIL

one-street affair. Heading down the main road from the plaza, the beaches are named in numerical order, with most of the action around Segunda (Second) and Terça (Third) Praias, a 10- to 15-minute walk from the Praça.

Sleeping

Reservations are required for holiday periods, especially Carnaval and *ressaca* (five days of post-Carnaval hangover). These prices are for January; they halve off-season.

Pousada Kanzuá do Marujo (☎ 3652-1152; kanzua @hotmail.com; Terça Praia; dm/s/d R$35/105/120; ⊠) A super-bright two-story complex of modern rooms set back from the ocean. Lots of greenery.

Pousada Passarte (☎ 3652-1030; www.pousada passarte.com.br; s/d R$45/70) Small, simple rooms that are a good deal in the high season. On the square. More upmarket rooms are on offer at Rua da Biquinha 27.

Hostel Morro de São Paulo (☎ 3652-1521; www .hosteldomorro.com.br; dm/d R$45/115; ⊠) A social hostel with a green outdoor breakfast area and good dorms. Take the first left-hand passageway off Rua da Fonte Grande. HI discount available.

Pousada Albatroz (Terça Praia; pousadaalbatroz@hot mail.com; s/d R$80/120; ⊠) Tucked up an alley back from the beach, this has a charming owner and clean spacious slate-tiled rooms. You can spot monkeys and birds from the breezy upstairs patio area.

Pousada Natal (☎ 3652-1059; pousada.natal @hotmail.com; d R$100; ⊠) This laid-back main street budget spot has decent rooms with fridge and air-con and helpful folk who'll let you leave your stuff and hang around after checkout time.

Eating & Drinking

There's a wide choice. Numerous places offer all-you-can-eat pizza *(rodízio)* for R$17 to R$20. The party scene focuses around Segunda Praia. Makeshift stalls serve cracking fruit cocktails here.

Fragola (Segunda Praia; ice reams R$5-8) Great ice creams beautifully presented, and decent fruit salads available. Also on the main square.

Espaguetaria Strega (pastas R$9-20) On the main street near the square, this no-frills spot stands out for its excellent, fairly priced fresh pasta and eerie-looking bar with curious *cachaça* infusions.

Tinharé (mains R$12-25) Huge portions of the *moqueca de peixe* are excellent at this family-run restaurant hidden down some stairs off the main street.

Ponto de Encontro (mains R$14-30) Comfortably stylish, this main-street spot combines cordial service with a range of creative salads and great daily specials alongside decent Bahian dishes.

Getting There & Away

Various boats (R$70, two hours, first 8am, last 2pm) cross six times daily to Morro from Salvador's Terminal Marítimo Turístico. It can be rough, so come with a fairly empty stomach. The first return from Morro is 8am, the last is 3pm. From the south, or from Salvador saving money, go to Valença (see p323) from where regular boats (R$6, 1½ hours, hourly) head to Morro. There are also regular fast boats (R$14, 50 minutes). At low tide, buses take you part of the way. Morro agencies offer transfers to Itacaré (R$60, 3½ hours).

ITACARÉ

☎ 0xx73 / pop 25,000

Mesmeric Itacaré offers postcard-pretty surf beaches backed by wide stretches of Biosphere Reserve Atlantic rainforest. The laid-back surfer vibe makes it a great place to kick back, especially outside of peak season. A river-mouth fishing town, Itacaré hasn't been spoiled by tourism (but fingers crossed once improved road and air access is complete) and locals and visitors mingle here, discussing waves and football.

There are ATMs and several internet cafes (R$3 per hour). **Urso de Óculos** (Av Castro Alves 71) is a sweet multilingual bookstore that does two-for-one exchanges and proper cups of tea.

Activities

Surf lessons and rental are widely available. The pretty town beaches are river-mouth **Praia de Concha**, and four tiny surf beaches like manicured fingernails in a row along the ocean. A trail from the last of these leads to the thumb, idyllic **Prainha**, but don't walk it alone. Remoter paradises lie beyond; head out to **Engenhoca**, **Havaizinho** and **Itacarezinho**, 12km south of town, or cross on the ferry to explore the Península de Maraú, which includes stunning **Praia Taipús de Fora**, with excellent snorkeling and swimming. Local agencies can arrange trips here; readers recommend staying overnight to really enjoy it.

Base d'Aventura on Praia da Concha rents mountain bikes, kayaks and boats.

Sleeping

Numerous budget *pousadas* line the main drag; midrange ones back Praia da Concha. Prices reflect Christmas to Carnaval season (book ahead); they halve the rest of the year.

Albergue O Pharol (☎ 3251-2527; www.albergue opharol.com.br; Praça Santos Dummont 7; dm R$38, r R$80-120; 🖳) Great cat-and-dog-filled hostel situated handily for everything. It's clean, friendly and helpful with excellent rooms with verandas and hammocks. Kitchen, internet and comfy living rooms. Top value off-season.

Itacaré Hostel (☎ 3251-3037; www.itacarehostel .com.br; Almeida 120; dm/d R$40/110; 🖳 🖳) A warm welcome is guaranteed at this central option, with rooms opening onto a peaceful forest garden with hammocks. Free internet, kitchen and DVDs are all on hand. Book well ahead for summer. HI discount.

Pousada Estrela (☎ 3251-2006; www.pousadaestrela .com.br; Longo 34; d R$80; 🖳) At the town end of the strip, this excellent spot keeps a lid on the crazy summer prices. Rooms upstairs (R$90) and with balcony (R$100) are worth the extra investment for light and breezes. Hammock garden out back.

Eating & Drinking

Sahara (Longo 500; dishes R$5-16; 🕙 noon-10pm Wed-Mon) The Arab Plate (pita, falafel, hummus, tomato salad and fried potatoes) is mouthwatering at this handsome place at the beach end of the main drag.

Casa de Taipa (Longo 345; dishes R$9-30) Popular indoor-outdoor main-street spot for OK pasta, but best-loved for its tasty R$9.90 evening salad-and-soup buffet.

Boca do Forno (Almeida 108; pizzas R$18-35; 🕙 6-11pm) You'll find cheaper pizza than this along the main strip, but you'll not find better, nor a more beautiful setting.

Tia Deth (Av Castro Alves; dishes for 2 R$25-45) Despite the ominous name, Tia Deth offers great traditional Bahian-style seafood and fish served in a simple dining room by the gas station. Economical *pratos feitos*.

Zé Senzala (Av Castro Alves; per kg R$27; 🕙 noon-10pm) Best 'kilo food' in town, but you get better quality going at lunchtime not dinnertime.

our pick **Favela** (Longo s/n; 🕙 5pm-late) Chatty buzz, good range of music, smooth Minas Gerais *cachaça*, and the longest, tastiest *caipirinhas* in town.

Getting There & Around

Buses run between Itacaré and Ilhéus (R$9.50, 1½ hours, roughly hourly) and there's a morning bus to Porto Seguro (R$44.50, eight hours). Access from the north will be easier once the river bridge is finished. This will likely mean direct buses to Itacaré from Valença and/or Salvador.

A minibus circuits local beaches; Ilhéus-bound buses provide access to beaches further south of town.

ILHÉUS

☎ 0xx73 / pop 220,000

Bright turn-of-the-century architecture and oddly-angled streets lend Ilhéus a vibrant and playful air, and make the compact center a satisfying wander. Ilhéus's fame derives from cocoa and from being the hometown of illustrious novelist Jorge Amado.

ATMs and internet places are easily located in the center near the cathedral. A tourist-information kiosk lies between the cathedral and the water.

Sights & Activities

Igreja de São Jorge (Praça Rui Barbosa; 🕙 Tue-Sun), built in 1534, is among Brazil's oldest churches. The fans-only **Casa de Cultura Jorge Amado** (Amado 21; admission R$2; 🕙 9am-noon & 2-6pm Mon-Fri, 9am-1pm Sat) is where the author was raised; a small collection of memorabilia includes a typewriter and some of his trademark colorful shirts. The wooden floors are beautiful.

The best beaches, such as **Praia dos Milionários**, are to the south.

Sleeping & Eating

Pontal – a short bus ride from the center on the other side of the bay – has several modern midrange *pousadas*.

Pousada Mar del Plata (☎ 3231-8009; Lemos 3; s/d R$40/60) Super-central, this is a well-enough kept *pousada* whose upstairs rooms are lighter than the somewhat dingy ones on the ground floor.

Pousada Brisa do Mar (☎ 3231-2644; Av 2 de Julho 136; s/d R$40/60; 🖳) On the beachfront a couple of blocks behind the cathedral, this modern home turned *pousada* has parquet floors and sea views from front rooms.

BRAZIL

Maria de São Jorge (Lavigne de Lemos 33; per kg R$21.90; ☺ lunch Mon-Sat) The streets in front of the cathedral have several cheap lunch options, but pay the extra couple of reales to eat at this warmhearted family-run spot. Lebanese-influenced salads and tasty stewed meats get the thumbs-up.

Vesúvio (Praça Dom Eduardo; mains R$25-60) This bar featured in Amado's work; the man himself sits larger-than-life at one of the tables appreciating the great view of the cathedral. The food is pricey but you can't beat chope on the terrace.

Getting There & Away

From the rodoviária, 4km from the center (local buses connect the two), buses run to Itacaré (R$9.50, 1½ hours, roughly hourly), Salvador (R$81 to R$128, seven hours, three daily) and Porto Seguro (R$38, six hours, four daily).

PORTO SEGURO

☎ 0xx73 / pop 114,500

Bland but fun, Porto Seguro is a popular Brazilian vacation destination with active nightlife and picturesque lengths of sand just out of town. It's also a gateway to the smaller seaside hideaways of Arraial and Trancoso. Porto is famous as the official first Portuguese landfall in Brazil, and for the lambada dance, so sensual it was once forbidden.

Banks with ATM include **HSBC** (Av Getúlio Vargas), while **Gigabyte** (Periquitos 10; per hr R$2) has good internet access.

Sights & Activities

Stairs lead to the picturesque heights of the **Cidade Histórica** (among Brazil's earliest European settlements). Rewards include a sweeping view, colorful old buildings, venerable churches and capoeira demonstrations.

The beach is one long bay of calm water, north of town, lined with barracas and clubs. Take a 'Taperapuã' or 'Rio Doce' bus (R$1.90) to the beach, a 'Campinho' or 'Cabralia' to return.

Festivals & Events

Porto Seguro's Carnaval lasts an additional three or four days – until the Friday or Saturday after Ash Wednesday – and is a smaller and safer version of Salvador's.

Sleeping

There are numerous options.

Camping Mundaí Praia (☎ 3679-2287; www.camping mundai.com.br; campsite per person R$15; ☻) Opposite the beach, 4km north of town. Plenty of shade and excellent facilities.

Pousada Casa Grande (☎ 3288-2969; Av dos Navegantes 151; s/d R$20/40) The central location, good rooms, generous summer prices and a green inner courtyard have made Casa Grande the backpacker pousada in Porto. Kitchen facilities available.

Pousada Brisa do Mar (☎ 3288-1444; www.brisado marpousada.com.br; Praça Coelho 188; s/d R$30/60) Value-packed pousada handy for restaurants and the Arraial ferry, this long, narrow house has spotless rooms and a kind welcome. A budget gem.

Eating & Drinking

Barracas and beach clubs provide eating the length of the beach; Barraca do Gaucho does excellent grilled meats.

Primo (Golfo 112; skewers R$3-4) Packed with locals not tourists, this is the spot to go for Brazilian atmosphere, cheap beer and little skewers (espetinhos) of meat, fish, chicken and cheese.

Ventos do Sul (Cidade Fafe/Faffi 72; per kg R$19) Opposite the back entrance of Av Shopping, this isn't the place for a romantic dinner-date but the food (R$12.50 all-you-can-eat) is great value.

Tia Nenzinha (Passarela 180; mains for 2 R$26-60) An excellent choice for succulent picanha and quality seafood dishes. Miles better than the competition on this touristy stretch.

Portinha (Marinho 33; per kg R$28; ☺ 11am-9pm) Fire-warmed dishes, succulent salads, attractive outdoor tables and desserts to tempt the sourest heart. Some of the best per-kilo eating you'll do in Brazil. Near the ferry.

Passarela do Álcool (Alcohol Walkway; ☺ nightly). Stands sell fruit cocktails and crafts. There is usually live music and often capoeira. Vendors here sell tickets for the nightly parties.

Getting There & Around

Porto Seguro's airport is near the bus station 2km northeast of town.

Frequent buses hit Ilhéus (R$38, six hours, four daily), Valença (R$65, 8½ hours, nightly), Salvador (R$127, 12 hours, nightly) and beyond. To save nearly R$50 going to

PORTO PARTYING

Porto Seguro is famous for nightly parties. Including *lambada*, *capoeira*, live *axé*, *forró* and samba, they are impressive spectacles. Each beach club hosts one *luau* (party) a week. The closest, Tôa-Tôa, is about 5km from town; further is Barramares, usually the most extravagant. Friday night, head across on a boat to the Ilha dos Aquários, where tanks of fish add to the ambience. Saturdays are normally at **Bombordo** (Av 22 de Abril), the only club in town. Admission ranges from R$15 to R$40, and is a bit cheaper if you buy tickets from vendors around town beforehand. If the party is up the coast, there are courtesy buses from the *trevo* (roundabout). Things start at about 10pm.

Salvador, jump off at Valença, hang around in the early hours until the first bus to Bom Despacho and nip from there across on the ferry across the bay.

ARRAIAL D'AJUDA
☎ 0xx73 / pop 13,000

Perched on a bluff above long sandy beaches, Arraial has a curious blend of upmarket tourism and chilled backpackerdom. Squat buildings painted bright colors surround a traditional plaza; roads lined with *pousadas*, bars and restaurants slope down to the beaches. Arraial caters for both party animals and those looking to unwind in the tropics.

The closest beach to town is crowded Praia Mucugê, but a short walk south brings you to dreamy Praia de Pitinga and other gorgeous beaches beyond. Several ATMs and internet places cluster around the center.

Arraial Ecoparque (☎ 3575-8600; www.arraialeco parque.com.br; Praia d'Ajuda; adult/child R$55/28; ☼ Jul-Apr) has water slides, a wave pool and hosts big-name concerts; hours change seasonally. Friendly **Groupo Sul da Bahia** (Rua da Capoeira) offers Afro-Brazilian dance in addition to *capoeira*.

Sleeping & Eating

Prices halve outside of high summer. There are cheap eats on Praia Mucugê.

Pousada Alto Mar (☎ 3575-1935; www.pousada altomar.net; Bela Vista 114; dm/s/d R$20/30/60) Human warmth makes up for the simple structure at this funky, pretty cheapie with basic *apartamentos*.

Arraial d'Ajuda Hostel (☎ 3575-1192; www.arraial dajudahostel.com.br; Campo 94; dm/d R$50/130; ☼ ☐) Hostelling hits the luxury class at this super spot, with ornate plasterwork and an upbeat orange color characterizing the rooms and dorms, which surround a great pool area. Helpful staff, pool table, kitchen and internet are other facilities. Some rooms are available in a nearby annex. HI discount (30%).

Pousada Tamarindo (☎ 3575-2519; www.porto .tur.br; Praça Igreja; r R$100; ☒) Near the church, this simple and welcoming spot has dark but faultless rooms that cost just R$30 outside the peak months.

Miloca (Estrada Mucugê; crepes R$9-11; ☼ 10am-10pm) Delicious sweet and savory crepes near the center on the way to the beach. There's a takeaway outlet on the same street.

Paulo Pescador (Praça São Bras; dishes R$13; ☼ 10am-8pm) Serving only *pratos feitos*, this well-loved spot has typical Brazilian food that's fresh and yummy, with the added benefit of superfriendly service.

Portinha (Campo 1; per kg R$27; ☼ 11am-9pm) You can't go wrong at this wonderful per-kilo spot, with a picturesque shady dining area and dozens of delicious dishes kept warm by a wood fire. Great salad bar and lip-smacking desserts.

Drinking & Entertainment

Beach parties *(luaus)* at places like Magnólia are most frequent during the summer. Ask around for the latest *forró* hot spot.

Esquina do Zikita (Travesia São Bras) Turn your back on the boutiques and join the locals at this no-frills spot with cheap beer, plastic tables and self-service.

Beco das Cores (Estrada Mucugê) A small galleria with magical ambience and live music on weekends.

Girassol (Estrada Mucugê) Great for people-watching while lounging on colored pillows or playing pool.

Getting There & Away

Passenger and car ferries run frequently between Porto Seguro and Arraial (R$2.50 to Arraial, free return, five minutes) during the day, and hourly on the hour after midnight. From Arraial's dock, you can jump on a bus or *combi* to the center (R$1.90,

BRAZIL

10 minutes) or walk the lovely 4km along the beach – this is not recommended when beaches are empty.

TRANCOSO
☎ 0xx73 / pop 10,000

This small tropical paradise is, like Arraial, perched atop a tall bluff overlooking the ocean. It centers around its utterly picturesque **Quadrado**, a long grassy expanse with a white church flanked by low colorful houses, that has its roots in the town's history as a Jesuit mission. At night everyone turns out to lounge in the outdoor seating of the restaurants that line the twinkling Quadrado. The beaches immediately to the south of Trancoso are gorgeous, but don't miss **Praia do Espelho** (20km south), off the road to Caraíva.

Trancoso has ATMs and internet places.

Sleeping & Eating

Most accommodations are pricey. Reservations are necessary during holidays.

Pousada Cuba Libre (Cuba; s/d R$30/40) Dirt paths connect simple cabins perched on a hillside at this happy, tenement-like *pousada*. Kitchen available.

Café Esmeralda Albergue (☎ 3668-1527; cafe esmeralda@terra.com.br; Quadrado; r with/without bathroom R$100/80) Right on the beautiful grassy plaza, this place has a row of simple rooms, a cocoa tree and hammock chill-out space. No breakfast.

Pousada Quarto Crescente (☎ 3668-1014; www .quartocrescente.net; Itabela; s/d R$90/110; 🔀) A very sweet, tree-shaded spot with spacious gardens, a well-stocked library, comfortable rooms and a superb breakfast. A short walk from the Quadrado.

Du Blè Noir (Telégrafo 300; crepes around R$8) The chocolate and banana crepe is legendary at this crepe stand in a small galleria near the Quadrado. Savory flavors too.

Masala (Telégrafo 10; meals R$25-35; 🕒 dinner Tue-Sun) This serves gourmet Thai curries, 'boomerang' burgers and potato wedges among other traveler favorites on an eclectic Australian-influenced menu.

A Portinha (Quadrado; per kg R$28; 🕒 noon-9pm) This excellent buffet restaurant wins over diners with its wide selection of excellent fresh food and seating under a towering tree on the Quadrado.

Getting There & Away

The 13km walk along the beach from Arraial at low tide is beautiful. Hourly buses depart from Arraial's dock and center (R$6.50, one hour). Buses to Eunápolis allow you to connect with northbound and southbound services.

CARAÍVA
☎ 0xx73 / pop 6400

The march of development has reached remote, beautiful Caraíva, a sandy hamlet tucked between a mangrove-lined river and a long churning surf beach. It's still magical, however, made all the more tranquil by the absence of cars. In the low season, Caraíva all but shuts down. There are no ATMs as yet.

Boat journeys upriver, horse rides or walks to a Pataxó community are easily organized. A 14km walk north (or hop on a bus) brings you to celebrated **Praia do Espelho**.

Darkness reveals Caraíva's magic, so staying the night is recommended. The several *pousadas* include simple beachside **Casa da Praia** (☎ 6979-7691; www.pousadapraiacaraiva.com.br; s/d R$70/110) and spotless **Brilho do Mar** (☎ 3668-5053; d R$80). Mosquito nets are essential. Seek out Cantinho da Duca for excellent vegetarian *pratos feitos* (set meals, R$12).

Buses for Caraíva via Trancoso leave from Arraial's port and center (R$13.50, 2½ hours, two to three daily). The journey is completed by canoe (R$2.50). For connections north or south, head for Itabela (R$10, two hours, two daily).

PENEDO
☎ 0xx82 / pop 59,000

This riverfront colonial town is worth a stop for its rich collection of beautiful 17th- and 18th-century churches. Attractions include the opportunity to travel the waters of the Rio São Francisco and to browse the bustling markets that crowd downtown streets.

There's a Bradesco ATM off the main riverfront square. The **tourist office** (☎ 3551-2727; Praça Barão de Penedo; 🕒 9am-3pm) gives out maps.

A comfortable, friendly budget lodging is **Pousada Estilo** (☎ 3551-2465; Praça Calheiros 79; s/d with fan R$30/50, with air-con R$50/65; 🔀) on a beautiful square. They've got another decent spot above a cybercafe a block up from the river at Dâmaso do Monte 86. Across from the ferry, **Pousada Colonial** (☎ 3551-2355; Praça 12 de Abril 21; r R$80; 🔀) is a step up; a coolly elegant restored colonial house with stained-wood

BRAZIL

floors and antique furniture. Some rooms have river views.

By the river near the ferry, **Oratório** (Av Beira Rio 301; dishes R$22-60; ☉ 11am-midnight) does tasty *petiscos* (plates of bar food designed for sharing) and better seafood (*pitú*, giant river shrimp, is an expensive but memorable treat).

Three daily buses run from Maceió (R$12.50, three or five hours); the slow one gives a thorough tour of this picturesque coast. There's a daily bus from Salvador (R$59, 11 hours); the return journey leaves Penedo at 6am. If you don't do early mornings, you can get the ferry from the center of town across to Neópolis (R$1.50), from where there are connections to Aracaju, which has several daily buses to Salvador. The bus station is riverside, two blocks east of the ferry that marks the town center. Vans *(topiques)* also make the journey to Maceió.

MACEIÓ

☎ 0xx82 / pop 897,000

Maceió offers reef-sheltered swimming in vivid blue-green sea along its lengthy waterfront, and is the best stop of the northeast coast's somewhat bland small-state capitals. The swaying palms of the city beaches are seductive, but the real beach jewels are out of town, just an hour away. Maceió Fest is an out-of-season Carnaval in the second week of December.

Information

Banco do Brasil Centro (Pessoa s/n); Ponta Verde (Av Alvaro Otacílio)

Bradesco (Av Sílvio Viana) ATM, one of many along the beach avenues.

Maximu's (Lessa de Azevedo 130; per hr R$1) One of few cybercafes to open on Sunday.

Tourist office (☎ 3315-1914; www.maceiotour.com .br; Cicero s/n; ☉ 8am-7pm Mon-Fri, 4-7pm Sat & Sun) Underneath the Republic memorial. Also at airport.

Tourist police (Av Alvaro Otacílio; ☉ 24hr) Doubles as tourist information office and gives out maps.

Sights & Activities

Alagoan folk art is displayed at **Museu Théo Brandão** (Av da Paz 1490; admission R$2; ☉ 9am-5pm Tue-Fri, 2-5pm Sat & Sun), including festival headpieces weighing up to 35kg. You can browse local handcrafts at the **Mercado do Artesanato** (☉ 7am-6pm Mon-Sat, 7am-noon Sun) in the district of Levada. There's a smaller version at Praia Pajuçara.

Picturesque *jangadas* sail 2km out to bathe in natural pools formed by the reef (R$15) from Praia de Pajuçara. **Praia de Ponta Verde** and **Jatiúca** are good city beaches with calm water. **Praia do Francês** (24km) is pretty and lined with beach bars – it is Maceió's major weekend destination and has lots of *pousadas*. Incredibly idyllic **Praia do Gunga** sits across a river from Barra de São Miguel (34km) – get there before 9am for easiest/cheapest boat transport.

Sleeping

The beachside *bairros* of Pajuçara and Ponta Verde are more pleasant than the center.

Maceió Hotel (☎ 3326-1975; Pontes de Miranda 146; s/d R$10/20) Very cheap but very basic rooms in the center of town. Those on the second floor have windows.

Pousada Albergo (☎ 3231-2246; Abdon Arroxelas 327, Ponta Verde; dm/s/d R$38/75/95; ⊠) Rooms are overpriced at this moribund hostel. But it's three blocks from the beach and prices almost halve between February and May. Confusingly, there's another 'Arroxelas' street nearby. HI discount.

Pousada Glória (☎ 3337-2348; Jangadeiros 1119, Pajuçara; s/d R$40/60; ⊠) A block from the waterfront, this has surprisingly good, clean rooms with fridge and air-con. The amiability of the family that run it above their bakery make this Maceió's best budget option.

Pousada Baleia Azul (☎ 3327-4040; www.hp baleiaazul.com.br; Av Sandoval Arroxelas 822; s/d R$60/80; ⊠) Welcoming and well-located, the 'blue whale' has cute, well-equipped rooms, all with veranda/balcony with a hammock to swing in. Good value.

Eating

Barracas are dotted along the beachfronts, and stands make *tapioca recheada* (R$2 to R$5) filled with savory or sweet fillings. A few blocks back from Jatiúca beach a row of blockbuster family eateries offer excellent Italian, meat *rodízio*, fish and sushi, with particularly good deals midweek.

Sarah's Esfihas (Azevedo 59; esfihas R$2-4, other dishes R$6-15; ☉ 3-10pm) Sarah's is a popular Middle Eastern diner that makes *esfihas* (fluffy breads topped or filled), in addition to passable hummus, tabouleh, vineleaf and cabbage rolls. Try the *chopp de vinho* (sweet fizzy draft wine).

BRAZIL

MACEIÓ

Paraíso Lanches (Av Gouveia 877, Pajuçara; snacks R$3-10) This simple cafe serves innovative sandwiches, salads, savory whole-wheat pancakes, *açaí* and a huge variety of fresh fruit juices.

Don Burguer (Av Sílvio Viana 1875; burgers R$13.50; 4pm-midnight) Gourmet burgers and posh salads are the fare at this popular indoor-outdoor eatery across the road from the beach. They're pretty good but they'll overcook them unless you ask.

Divina Gula (Paulo Brandão Nogueira 85, Jatiúca; mains R$16-30; closed Mon) The spiritual heart of the Jatiúca eating area, this place specializes in Minas Gerais and Northeastern dishes and boasts over 50 different kinds of *cachaça*.

Stella Maris (Paulo Brandão Nogueira 290, Jatiúca; rodízio R$18.90 Mon-Thu, R$24.90 Fri & Sun, R$31.90 Sat) Next to Divina Gula, Stella Maris does an excellent all-you-can-eat meat feast.

Drinking & Entertainment

Rapa Nui (Av Sílvio Carlos Viana 2501; 4pm-late Mon-Fri, 11am-late Sat & Sun) This giant and fashionable beer bar packs out at weekends, with a cheerful buzz brought on by tasty *chope* and shared food platters.

Orákulo (Barão de Jaraguá 717; admission R$10; Tue-Sun 9pm-late) Popular bar has different live music daily. There are several other weekend bars in this otherwise deserted area. Get a cab at night.

Lampião (Av Álvaro Otacílio, Jatiúca) Beachfront bar playing *forró*.

Getting There & Away

Maceió's airport, 25km north of the center, has domestic connections. The bus station is 5km north of the center. Buses head to Recife (R$36, four hours, 10 daily), Penedo (R$12.50, three or five hours), and Salvador (R$80, nine hours, four daily).

RECIFE

☎ 0xx81 / pop 1.54 million

Recife, one of the Northeast's major ports and cities, has a dance and music heritage that brings it fame across the country. The center of town, with water on all sides, is bustling and vital if a touch gritty, while quieter Recife Antigo has picturesque colonial buildings. Most travelers stay in Boa Viagem, an affluent suburb

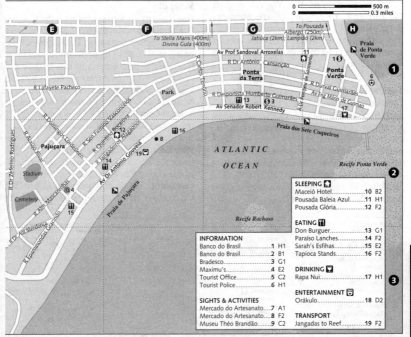

INFORMATION
Banco do Brasil.................1 H1
Banco do Brasil.................2 B1
Bradesco...........................3 G1
Maximu's............................4 E2
Tourist Office.....................5 C2
Tourist Police....................6 H1

SIGHTS & ACTIVITIES
Mercado do Artesanato....7 A1
Mercado do Artesanato....8 F2
Museu Théo Brandão.......9 C2

SLEEPING
Maceió Hotel...................10 B2
Pousada Baleia Azul........11 H1
Pousada Glória.................12 F2

EATING
Don Burguer.....................13 G1
Paraíso Lanches...............14 F2
Sarah's Esfihas................15 E2
Tapioca Stands.................16 F2

DRINKING
Rapa Nui..........................17 H1

ENTERTAINMENT
Orákulo...........................18 D2

TRANSPORT
Jangadas to Reef.............19 F2

BRAZIL

backing a long golden beach or Recife's more peaceful sister-city, Olinda.

Orientation

Recife's commercial center is busy during the day and deserted at night and on Sunday. Ilha do Recife holds the quiet, historical Recife Antigo district. Boa Viagem is an affluent neighborhood south of the center, backing a long beach.

Information

Bradesco (Av Guararapes)
Caravelas Cybercafé (Bom Jesus 183; per hr R$2.50)
Livraria Cultura (Cais da Alfândega) Bookstore with impressive range of foreign-language titles.
HSBC (cnr Av Ferreira & Filho, Boa Viagem) ATMs.
Tourist information (☎ 3232-8409; www.destino pernambuco.com.br; Praça Artur Oscar; ⏰ 8:30am-9pm) Also offices at the airport (24 hours), the bus station and at Praça Boa Viagem in Boa Viagem.
Tourist police (☎ 3322-4867; airport)

Sights & Activities

The old city has many noble buildings, better cared for these days, with explanatory panels in English outside many of them. Strolling through Recife Antigo, you can admire the colorful houses and historic synagogue on **Rua Bom Jesus** and the customs-building-turned-shopping-mall **Paço Alfândega**. Across in Centro, **Pátio de São Pedro** is a pretty cobbled square lined with characterful buildings under the gaze of a handsome baroque church.

Museu do Homem do Nordeste (Av 17 de Agosto 2187, Casa Forte; admission R$4; ⏰ 8am-5pm Tue-Fri, 1-6pm Sat & Sun) is a very worthwhile anthropological museum with historical and cultural exhibits covering everything from slavery to Carnaval.

Serpents stare, buttocks bulge and jaws gape at **Oficina Cerâmica Francisco Brennand** (Várzea; admission R$4; ⏰ 8am-5pm Mon-Fri), a seemingly exhaustive exhibition of the artist's peculiar sculptures. A trip here is a regional highlight, so bring a picnic to enjoy on the extensive grounds. Take the UR7-Várzea bus from downtown on Av Guararapes to the end of the line (35 minutes). From there, catch a taxi (R$10) as the long walk is unsafe.

Long, sandy Praia Boa Viagem is great for sun and strolling but shark warnings deter plenty of locals from more than a paddle. Other worthwhile beaches are further south at **Praia Pedra do Xaréu** (20km) and **Praia Calhetas** (23km).

Festivals & Events

Carnaval (www.carnavaldorecife.com.br) Recife holds one of Brazil's most colorful and folkloric Carnavals. Groups and spectators deck themselves out in elaborate costumes such as *maracatu* (headpieced warrior), harlequin, bull and *frevo* (crop tops with ruffled sleeves for both genders and a tiny umbrella) and shimmy for days to frenetic *frevo* and African-influenced *maracatu* beats.

Recifolia (www.recifolia.com.br) An out-of-season, Salvador-style Carnaval held in the last week in October.

Sleeping

Boa Viagem is a better area than the Centro.

Albergue Maracatus do Recife (☎ 3456-9541; www.geocities.com/alberguemaracatus; Maria Carolina 185, Boa Viagem; dm R$30; 🖳) The pool and central location are the best aspects of this slightly depressing hostel. The dorms are fairly crowded and noise travels. It has lockers and a kitchen. Near bus stop 10 on Av Domingos Ferreira.

Hotel Central (☎ 3222-2353; s/d with fan R$50/75, with air-con R$60/90, s/d without bathroom R$35/50; 🖳) Bright rooms with high ceilings and fabulous faded art deco character make this 1930s jewel the best budget option in the center.

Boa Viagem Hostel (☎ 3326-9572; www.hostelboaviagem.com.br; Lins 455, Boa Viagem; dm/d R$38/90; 🖳) On a quiet street a couple of blocks back

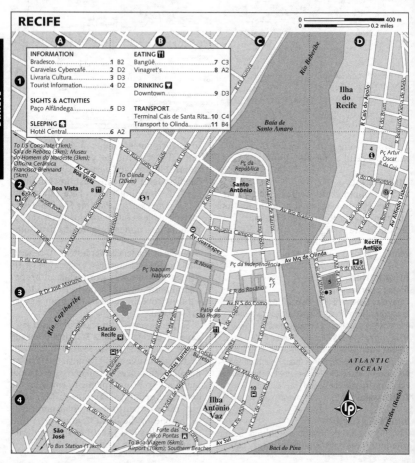

RECIFE

0 — 400 m
0 — 0.2 miles

INFORMATION
Bradesco.............................1 B2
Caravelas Cybercafé..............2 D2
Livraria Cultura....................3 D3
Tourist Information................4 D2

SIGHTS & ACTIVITIES
Paço Alfândega....................5 D3

SLEEPING
Hotél Central.......................6 A2

EATING
Banguê..............................7 C3
Vinagret's...........................8 A2

DRINKING
Downtown...........................9 D3

TRANSPORT
Terminal Cais de Santa Rita..10 C4
Transport to Olinda..............11 B4

To US Consulate (1km);
Sala de Reboco (3km); Museu
do Homem do Nordeste (3km);
Oficina Cerâmica
Francisco Brennand
(5km)

Boa Vista

To Olinda
(20km)

**Santo
Antônio**

**São
José**

To Bus Station (13km);

Forte das
Cinco Pontas
To Boa Viagem (6km);
Airport (10km); Southern Beaches

**Ilha
Antônio
Vaz**

Av Sul

Baci do Pina

Rio Beberibe

**Ilha
do
Recife**

*Baía de
Santo Amaro*

Pç Artur
Oscar

**Recife
Antigo**

*ATLANTIC
OCEAN*

Arrecifes (Reefs)

BRAZIL

from the avenue (off Farias), this darkish hostel has fairly unremarkable dorms but a nice garden with a pool to relax in. Internet, kitchen and HI discount.

Hotel Uzi Mar (☎ 3326-6746; hoteluzi@uol.com.br; Av Conselheiro Aguiar 1015, Boa Viagem; s/d R$48/63;) Bland, clean, spacious and, despite the main road location, quiet: adjectives that add up to good value. There's a sister-hotel across the road.

Hotel Julieta (☎ 3326-7860; Brandão 135, Boa Viagem; s/d R$72/79;) It's not a great deal for single travelers and space is at a premium in the tight rooms but the near-beach location, friendly staff and quiet cleanliness make this a reliable choice among more expensive Boa Viagem options.

Pousada Casuarinas (☎ 3325-4708; www.pousada casuarinas.com.br; Figueiredo 151, Boa Viagem; s/d R$80/105;) Lots of folk art spices up the modern architecture at this quiet *pousada* shaded by mango trees. Rooms which boast a veranda with hammock cost a few reales more.

Eating

Padaria (cnr Av Conselheiro Aguiar & Atlântico, Boa Viagem; dishes R$10-40) This big and breezy corner spot up the north end of Boa Viagem has tasty special-offer *pratos feitos* for R$10.90; they also do decent grilled meats at fair prices.

Bangüê (Pátio de São Pedro 20; mains R$12-35) The best of several bars on this beautiful square, unsigned Bangüê stars in the great travel book *A Death in Brazil*. It serves good-value portions and a range of tasty *petiscos* like *charque* (dried beef).

Vinagret's (Hospício 203; per kg R$22.50; lunch Mon-Fri) One of the best buffet lunch spots in the heart of the center's bustle.

Parraxaxá (Pereira 32, Boa Viagem; per kg R$29.50) Festive decor and cowboy-costumed wait staff spice up your meal at this folklore-themed restaurant. The per-kilo food is pricey but worthwhile, with lots of typical Pernambuco dishes.

Drinking & Entertainment

In the Centro, the Patio de São Pedro is a popular hangout, especially on Terça Negra (Black Tuesday), a night of Afro-Brazilian rhythms. Boa Viagem attracts affluent youth, with spread-out options the length of the main avenue. Cover charges are high. Recife Antigo has a few bars with outdoor tables along Bom Jesus that are active in the early evenings.

Downtown (Tenório 105; Wed-Sun 10pm-late) Has pool tables, a happening dance floor and plays rock. It gets particularly busy with live music on Wednesday and Sunday nights.

Jardins (Av Domingos Ferreira 2045, Boa Viagem; admission weekends R$20; 6pm-late) A sociable bar midweek and one of the most popular Boa Viagem nightspots at weekends with live music and/or DJs. It's cheaper to get in before 11pm; expect to queue.

Nox (Av Domingos Ferreira 2422, Boa Viagem; admission R$30; 10pm-late Thu-Sat) Huge club that's Recife's trendiest, with good electronic music. Long queues, but talk to the bouncer like you're desperate to spend some reales over the bar and you may get waved through.

Bar do Paulinho (cnr Av Domingos Ferreira & Capitulino, Boa Viagem; 11am-late Tue-Sat) Sociable corner spot that's a cheaper and homier place for a drink than the posher clubs nearby. Drop in after a night's dancing and tuck into delicious sausages or chicken hearts straight from the grill.

Sala de Reboco (www.saladereboco.com.br; Junior 264, Cordeiro; admission R$8; 10pm-4am Thu-Sat) It's worth the taxi trip (think R$20 from downtown Boa Viagem) out to this friendly, down-to-earth place, with a 'real Brazil' feel and cheerful live *forró*.

Getting There & Around

Several operators fly domestically from Recife's airport, 10km south of the center. TAP connects Recife with Europe, and American Airlines with the USA. Delta offers sporadic seasonal service to Recife from the USA.

From the airport, the Aeroporto bus goes to Boa Viagem and the center. Eschew fixed-rate taxis at the terminal, cross the avenue and hail one there. Recife's airport is now connected to the metro system, and it's a R$1.40 journey from the terminal to the central metro station.

Recife's **bus station** is 14km southwest of the center. Catch a metro train to the central Recife stop (R$1.40, 25 minutes) otherwise it's a fixed R$36 to R$44 cab fare.

From the central metro station, for Boa Viagem, catch the 'Setubal (Príncipe)' bus. For Olinda, catch the 'Rio Doce' bus. From the center to Boa Viagem, take any bus marked 'Aeroporto,' 'Shopping Center,' 'Candeias' or 'Piedade' from Av NS do Carmo. To return, take any bus marked 'Dantas Barreto.'

BRAZIL

Bus tickets can be purchased from **Disk Passagems** (☎ 3452-1211), a bus-ticket delivery service. Buses run to João Pessoa (R$18, two hours, hourly 5am to 7pm), Natal (R$55, 4½ hours, nine daily), Maceió (R$36, four hours, 10 daily), Salvador (R$106 to R$126, 11 to 16 hours, three daily) and other big Brazilian cities.

OLINDA

☎ 0xx81 / pop 384,000

If Recife feels like a blue-collar worker who is scrabbling hard to make ends meet, Olinda is the sibling who dropped out of the rat race to get in touch with its artistic side. This picturesque colonial town is bohemianism itself, with streets that are crammed with painters' studios, and with impromptu musical events and *cachaça*-fueled parties sprouting like mushrooms. It also has a fistful of architectural aces: gorgeous pastel-colored houses flank a stunning ensemble of baroque churches on the historic center's hillside overlooking the sea.

Information

Major banks are located northeast of Praça do Carmo, once Av Marcos Freire turns into Av Getúlio Vargas. Catch any *combi* heading in that direction from Av Marcos Freire by the Praça do Carmo.

Empório do Carnaval (cnr Prudente de Morais & Veira de Melo; per hr R$3) Fast internet among Carnaval figures.

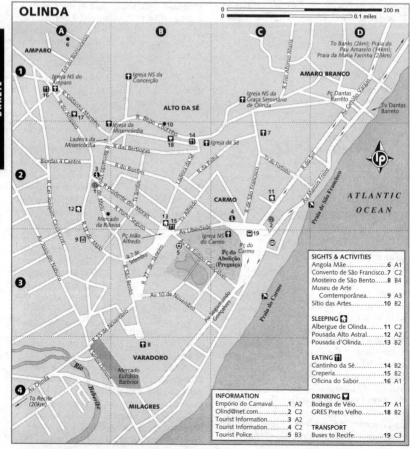

OLINDA

0 — 200 m
0 — 0.1 miles

SIGHTS & ACTIVITIES
Angola Mãe.....................6 A1
Convento de São Francisco....7 C2
Mosteiro de São Bento......8 B4
Museu de Arte
  Comtemporânea..........9 A3
Sítio das Artes...............10 B2

SLEEPING
Albergue de Olinda.........11 C2
Pousada Alto Astral........12 A2
Pousada d'Olinda...........13 B2

EATING
Cantinho da Sé..............14 B2
Creperia......................15 B2
Oficina do Sabor............16 A1

DRINKING
Bodega de Véio..............17 A1
GRES Preto Velho...........18 B2

TRANSPORT
Buses to Recife..............19 C3

INFORMATION
Empório do Carnaval........1 A2
Olind@net.com................2 C2
Tourist Information...........3 A2
Tourist Information...........4 C2
Tourist Police.................5 B3

Olind@net.com (Rua do Sol; per hr R$2.50)
Tourist information Carmo (☎ 3305-1048; Praça do Carmo 100; ☼ 8am-8pm); Casa do Turista (☎ 3305-1060; casadoturistaolinda@gmail.com; Prudente de Morais 472; ☼ 8am-8pm)
Tourist police (Av Justino Gonçalves)

Dangers & Annoyances

Crime does exist in Olinda. Avoid walking alone along deserted streets or carrying valuables at night. Guides assail you, hoping to show you the sights for a tip or sell you anything from oysters to cocaine.

Sights & Activities

The historic center is easy to navigate and delightful to wander. Every second building houses an artist's workshop, particularly along Rua do Amparo, and historic mansions and churches abound.

At the top of the town, Alto da Sé, there's a lively street-food scene, the **cathedral**, great evening views to Recife's skyscraper skyline and **Sítio das Artes** (☎ 3429-2166; www.sitiodasartes. com.br; Coutinho 780; ☼ 9am-10pm), a smartly converted historic building housing antique furniture, a wide range of embroidery and art for sale, a cafe and an upstairs restaurant.

The *capoeira* school, **Angola Mãe** (Cunha 243), welcomes visitors for classes or to watch a *roda* (circle) at 6pm on Sunday. Look for a metal gate painted in zebra stripes.

There are numerous churches; particularly worthwhile are baroque **Mosteiro de São Bento** (São Bento; ☼ 8:30am-noon, 2-5pm), with an elaborate gilt altarpiece and a 14th-century Italian painting of Saint Sebastian; and **Convento de São Francisco** (São Francisco; ☼ 7-11:30am, 2-5pm Mon-Fri, 7am-noon Sat), with a memorable tiled cloister.

The **Museu de Arte Contemporânea** (13 de Maio; admission R$5; ☼ 9am-5pm Tue-Fri, 2-5pm Sat & Sun) has a past as an 18th-century Spanish Inquisition jail. Prisoners were kept on the 2nd floor – check out the hole in a wall that extends to the basement (a toilet) and the ominously heavy wooden doors. Temporary exhibitions of contemporary art accompany a permanent collection of mostly 1930s works.

Festivals & Events

You can get a taste of Carnaval on weekends (especially Sunday night) in the months leading up to it, when *blocos* rehearse in the streets.

Carnaval Traditional, colorful and has an intimacy and security not found in big-city Carnavals. Fast and frenetic *frevo* music sets the pace, balanced by the heavy drumbeats of *maracatu*. Costumed *blocos* and spectators dance through the streets in this highly inclusive, playful and lewd festival.
Festival de Folclore Nordestino Showcases dance, music and folklore of the Northeast at the end of August. Recommended.

Sleeping

Book well ahead for Carnaval, though it can be cheaper to rent a room or house.

Pousada d'Olinda (☎ 3493-6011; www.pousada dolinda.com.br; Praça João Alfredo 178; dm/s/d R$25/40/75; s/d with air-con R$70/85; ☒ ☒) Adequate dorms, overpriced rooms with fan and excellent air-con ones out the back are available at this popular *pousada*. There's attractive old furniture, a restaurant and pool area. Good location.

Albergue de Olinda (☎ 3429-1592; www.alberguede olinda.com.br; Sol 233; dm/s/d R$32/60/75; ☒) Modern rooms in a historical building are complemented by a nice garden with hammocks, pool and an outdoor kitchen. Downsides: you're not quite in the pretty old part and there's noise from the busy road. HI discount.

Pousada Alto Astral (☎ 3439-3453; www.pousada altoastral.com.br; 13 de Maio 305; d R$60; ☒ ☒) This enchanting spot is decorated top to bottom with Carnaval figures and paraphernalia. All rooms are colorful, comfortable and cheerful; the best (R$80) are upstairs, with their own balcony looking over the leafy garden and pool below. Very friendly.

Eating & Drinking

For a no-frills snack or a sunset drink, hit Alto da Sé, where stalls serve *tapioca* with various fillings, as well as ice-cold coconuts and mixed drinks. There are parties organized nearly every night somewhere or other; just ask for the *festa*.

Creperia (Praça João Alfredo 168; dishes R$10-24) Enjoy a sweet or savory crepe or tasty salad in a palm-shaded patio or in the dining room hung with decorative plates and street signs at this charming restaurant.

Cantinho da Sé (Ladeira da Sé; mains for 2 people R$14-28) Typical Brazilian meat dishes are complemented by a view over Recife at this unassuming spot just below the cathedral. It's good value, and a fine spot for a sundowner too.

BRAZIL

DETOUR

An hour's flight from Recife or Natal is Brazil's greenest destination, **Parque Nacional Marinho de Fernando de Noronha** (www.noronha.pe.gov.br), on the idyllic island of the same name. Only 700 people per day can visit this tiny, pristine place, home to Brazil's most postcard-perfect beaches and staunchly protected marine life. Noronha's not only a sea turtle sanctuary, but also the world's best place to see Spinner Dolphins. Throw in Brazil's best surfing and diving and you're rewarded with an unforgettable paradise.

Noronha only opened for tourism in 1988 (it was formerly a military installation and prison). Since then, no new construction has been allowed on its beaches, giving floury patches of sand like Baía de Sancho and Praia do Leão a dreamlike quality. There are restrictions on vehicles, boats and people as well – Brazilians aren't even allowed to live here unless they were born here (all others get hard-to-secure temporary residence permits). No condos, no chain hotels, no beach vendors, no *people*. In short, it's an environmental success story and true treat to visit.

But paradise comes at a price. Round-trip flights from Recife/Natal (with Trip, TAM or Varig/Gol) run around R$1000, in addition to an exponential daily environmental tax from R$36.69. Contact **Your Way** (☎ 0xx11-9491-1307; www.yourway.com.br) for English assistance with accommodation and activities on the island.

ourpick Oficina do Sabor (☎ 3429-3331; Amparo 335; mains for 2 people R$30-70; ☺ lunch only Sun) Olinda's famous gourmet bistro is small, quaint and has a view over Recife. Baked pumpkin (*jerimum*) stuffed with a variety of tasty fillings is the house specialty.

Bodega de Véio (Amparo 212; ☺ closed Sun) Grocery store sells beer. People drinking beer impede customers. Owner solves by installing tables and sound system alongside. The three-sentence history of Olinda's most popular bar.

GRES Preto Velho (Coutinho 681; ☺ 9pm-late) Has regular live *afoxé*, *axé*, samba and reggae sessions.

Getting There & Around

Any 'Rio Doce,' 'Casa Caiada' or 'Jardim Atlantico' bus connects central Recife to Olinda. 'Rio Doce/Piedade' and 'Barra de Jangada/Casa Caiada' buses run between Olinda and Boa Viagem. From the airport, change in central Recife, or grab a cab for around R$25.

JACUMÃ

☎ 0xx83 / pop 3000

Accessed via the pleasant beachside city of João Pessoa, laid-back Jacumã gives you the chance to kick back on fairly deserted, boutique-free beaches. The village itself, full of weekend homes, is nothing special. The southern beaches, however, with tall, arid red cliffs, palms and green water, are stunning. There are no banks.

The best beaches are **Praia de Tabatinga**, 4km south of Jacumã, **Praia do Coqueirinho** (8km) and **Praia de Tambaba** (14km), which is a regulated (man needs woman to enter) nudist beach. Mototaxis are the only transport on this stretch.

There are plenty of *pousadas* in town and strung out along the southern beaches. In the center, signposted off the main street, **Pousada do Beija-Flor** (☎ 3290-1822; Amélia; s/d with air-con R$40/70, with fan R$30/50; ☒ ☒) has a row of spotless rooms with hammocks, and a great grassy area with a small pool. At Tabatinga, a 40-minute walk from town, **Pousada dos Mundos** (☎ 3290-1356; www.pousadadosmundos.com.br; Praia de Tabatinga; d with fan/air-con R$55/60; ☒ ☒) is a top spot to laze away a few days. Decent-sized rooms have private verandas with hammocks looking over a river (free kayaks); a pool, gym equipment, friendly people and a restaurant serving crepes are other drawcards. Call for a ride from the center. It's R$5 cheaper without breakfast.

From João Pessoa, accessible by regular buses from Natal and Recife, leave the bus station, turn right, then take the first left on Cicero Meireles. From this street, catch a Jacumã-bound bus (R$3.30 to R$4.80, around one hour). A shared-taxi service (*lotação*) is also peddled here (R$5 per person).

PRAIA DA PIPA

☎ 0xx84 / pop 3000

Pristine beaches backed by handsome cliffs, and dolphins frisking in the water near you mean Pipa is one of the Northeast's premier beach destinations. It's no secret any more and old-time travelers understandably shake their heads at the resort strip that the once-peaceful main street has become. Pipa is still a peaceful place outside high season however, and the quality of accommodation and food make it easy to lose a week here.

The long main drag has traveler-friendly installations like internet, ATMs, laundries and numerous bars and restaurants. Just off it, laid-back Bookshop rents and sells dog-eared Euro-language paperbacks. Look out for the useful free Pipa map-guide.

Sights & Activities

Guiana dolphins rest and frolic in the bay at Praia dos Golfinhos, accessible via the main beach at low tide only. Let them choose whether to approach you or not; don't chase or feed them. Quick boat jaunts also leave from the main beach to watch them but it seems more intrusive. Above the beach, accessed from the main road into town, **Santuário Ecológico** (admission R$5; ✆ 8am-5pm) is a small flora and fauna reserve and turtle station worth visiting for the spectacular views.

Several other worthwhile beaches nearby are easily accessed by walking or van. Pipa has some decent surf – boards and lessons are available.

Sleeping

Reservations are recommended for all major holidays. There are a couple of campsites.

Vilma Hostel (✆ 3246-2501; www.vilmahostel.com; Arara 19; r per person R$25) Darkish rooms have private verandas with hammocks by the grassy lawn at this spotless, colorful place.

Albergue da Rose (✆ 8844-8371; comsorriso78 @yahoo.com.br; Mata; dm/s/d R$25/35/70) Compact and delightful, this has a little hammock patio, kitchen use and a benevolent welcome a couple of minutes' walk uphill from the main street. First to the dorm gets the double bed. There's another place on the main road near the Santuário.

Pousada Vera My House (✆ 3246-2295; veramhouse @uol.com.br; Mata; r per person R$30) Rooms off a shady courtyard have marine-colored sheets and dolphin murals at this relaxed, no-frills spot. There's a kitchen (R$3 one-time charge).

Pipa Hostel (✆ 3246-2151; www.pipahostel.com.br; Arara 105; dm/d R$38/90; ✷ ✺) Book ahead for this popular hostel. Spacious dorms face

the great grassy pool area out back; private rooms look over it from above. HI discount, kitchen facilities and internet access all available.

ourpick Pousada Xamã (✆ 3246-2267; www.pousada xama.com; Cajueiros 12; s/d R$60/90; ✷ ✺) The dynamic, artistic owner has made this one of the Northeast's best budget *pousadas*. Rooms are faultless, with minibar, air-con and hot-water; the best surround the pretty pool area, with hammocks, wi-fi and hummingbirds. Great breakfast and numerous services add value. Prices drop fast for two days or more. It's at the far end of town.

Pousada Aconchego (✆ 3246-2439; www.pipa online.com.br; Céu 100; s/d R$60/100) Simply constructed bungalows with hammocks and extra touches in a pretty garden. Central location, friendly staff and regular events like BBQs.

Eating & Drinking

There's a wide eating choice in Pipa, much of it pricey. Nightlife is focused along the main drag and at a couple of beachside *barracas*, particularly Garagem.

Yaah (Galeria Beco do Adobe, Av Baía dos Golfinhos; ✆ 5-11pm) Tucked away up an alleyway, this takeaway-with-stools does decent sushi and sashimi (R$1.50 per unit) to order, as well as chunky temaki wraps (R$7 to R$9). If you fancy a tipple, try their *saqueroska*, a fruity sake concoction.

Papaya (Gameleira; light meals R$4-12; ✆ 4-11pm) Expensive but excellent juices and a range of healthy light meals are made with a smile at this sweet little spot just above the main street.

Taverna (Bem-te-Vis; dishes R$9-13; ✆ lunch) Just below the main drag opposite Restaurante Dalí, it's worth seeking out this tree-shaded terrace for its excellent lunchtime specials, which include the tasty house salad.

Papillon (Av Baía dos Golfinhos; mains R$10-30) You can't miss this spot with its hand-shaped chairs. Readers rate the pizza downstairs; the breezy, romantic open upper floor serves daily pasta specials and top-notch dishes like tuna steak with sesame-seed crust.

Peixe & Cia (Av Baía dos Golfinhos; mains R$15-27) Comparatively good-value for its tasty steaks and yummy oysters. Save cash by ordering mains with just salad rather than the rice and *farofa* you've already had enough of.

BRAZIL

Getting There & Away

Buses (R$9.50, two hours, eight to nine daily, four on Sunday) and vans (R$12, three to four daily, 1½ hours) run between Natal and Pipa. If you're coming from the south, get off at Goaininha and catch a frequent *combi* (R$3, 40 minutes) from behind the church. It's easy enough to flag down a Recife- or João Pessoa-bound bus in Goaininha (tell your van driver to drop you at the stop).

NATAL

☎ 0xx84 / pop 774,000

Sun and sand draw people to Natal, a bland but relaxed capital near the nation's northeast corner. The kilometers of beaches and dunes are kissed by very regular sunshine; the tourist board talks the town up as 'Sun City' thanks to 10 months' tanning time per year. **Carnatal** is Natal's Salvador-style, out-of-season Carnaval in the first week of December.

Orientation

Occupying a long sandy peninsula, Natal is a very spread-out place, so you'll find the local bus network useful. Fourteen kilometers south of the center, the beach suburb of Ponta Negra has numerous places to stay and eat; it's the most rewarding part of town to hang out in.

Information

Several ATMs and change offices are on Ponta Negra's beachfront.

Internet (Av Erivan França, Ponta Negra; ⊗ 9am-midnight) Cybercafe with international phone calls.

Internet Express (Av Praia de Ponta Negra 8956; per hr R$3) Near the craft market.

Setur airport (☎ 0800-841-516); Rodoviária Nova (☎ 0xx81-3205-2428) Maps and limited information. Also at Praia Shopping.

Sights & Activities

In the center, **Centro de Turismo** (Figueiredo 980; ⊗ 8am-7pm Mon-Sat, 8am-6pm Sun) has a gallery, craft shops and a restaurant with great views in a former correctional facility. At the northern end of town, views are fantastic from the 16th-century **Forte dos Reis Magos** (admission R$2; ⊗ 8am-4:30pm).

Between the center and Ponta Negra, the **Parque das Dunas** (Av Alencar, Tirol; admission R$1 plus R$1 per trail; ⊗ 8am-6pm daily) is an enormous city park with picnic areas and three marked trails through the dunes and vegetation.

Dune-buggy excursions to beautiful **Genipabu** are offered by would-be Ayrton Sennas. Trips *com emoção* (with excitement), include thrills like the Wall of Death. Accredited drivers can be more trustworthy. A half-day trip costs about R$250 (for up to four) and can be arranged through *pousadas* or agencies. Before you go, consider the damage these trips do to the dune ecosystem.

Of Natal's city beaches, **Praia Ponta Negra** (14km south of the center) is urbanized but the nicest. **Morro de Careca** – a steep, monstrous dune that drops into the sea – towers over its southern end. Bus 56 runs from here along the other city beaches, so just hop off wherever the water looks good.

Sleeping

Most backpackers stay in Ponta Negra.

Albergue da Costa (☎ 3219-0095; www.albergue dacosta.com.br; Av Praia de Ponta Negra 8932, Ponta Negra; dm/d R$33/70; ⊠) This is a great hostel with comfortable dorms, a tiny pool and super-friendly, laid-back management. Double rooms are also worthwhile here. Other attractions include kitchen, free internet, bike hire (R$20 per day) and *capoeira* or surfing lessons.

Lua Cheia Hostel (☎ 3236-3696; www.luacheia .com.br; Araújo 500, Alto de Ponta Negra; dm/d R$48/100) Complete with drawbridge, turrets, gothic doorways and replica renaissance paintings, this curious hostel is modeled after a castle. Dark dorms (bring padlock) are pretty loud and there's a nightclub on the premises, so this is one for party animals. R$10 cheaper for HI members.

Pousada Recanto das Flores (⊗ 3219-4065; www .pousadarecantodasflores.com.br; Av Engenheiro Roberto Freire 3161, Ponta Negra; s/d R$55/85; ⊠ ⊠) Spacious, spotless rooms named after flowers, excellent bathrooms, minibar, a pool and central Ponta Negra location make this peaceful (despite some traffic noise) *pousada* a great bet. Good pool.

Eating

Casa de Taipa (Araújo 130, Alto de Ponta Negra; dishes R$4-18; ⊗ 5pm-midnight) Colorful tables and a corner location make this one of the favorite launchpads for a night out in Alto. Imaginative couscous and tapioca creations with a variety of fillings do a decent job of soaking up *caipirinhas* that might fall your way later.

Tempero Mineiro (cnr Praia de Tibáu & Av Praia de Ponta Negra; daily specials R$9-12) With open-air tables in a craft market at the northern end of Ponta Negra, this family place offers good-value daily specials, solid fish and meat plates, and, at weekends, tasty *feijoada* (R$15.90 per person).

Terra Brasilis (Algas 2219, Alto de Ponta Negra; 🕙 dinner) Simple dynamics work well on this quiet suburban corner. Convivial wooden tables and a *rodízio* of either pizza (R$9.90) or *espetinhos* (R$13.90 includes soft drinks.

Erva Doce (Av Estrela do Mar 2239, Ponta Negra; half-portions R$30-40) They overdo the lighting a bit at this neighborhood restaurant but at least it's carbon-friendly. Don't be dissuaded by the prices; these half-portions of meat or seafood can feed at least two people. If you go alone, you'll be leaving with a doggie bag.

Entertainment

Ponta Negra is Natal's nightlife center. There are a few dance clubs and a compact zone of cool, charismatic bars around Araújo. The beachfront is touristy.

Chaplin/NYX (Av Presidente Café Filho 27, Praia dos Artistas; www.nyxclub.com.br; admission R$20; 🕙 Thu-Sun) Live *pagode, forró* and electronica rock feature in this popular dance club with six separate dance floors. Half-price before 11pm or by printing a voucher off its website.

Forró com Turista (Centro de Turismo, Figueiredo 980; 🕙 Thu) This local staple may sound cheesy; live *forró* in a historical courtyard is actually a blast.

Getting There & Around

Flights operate from Natal's airport, 15km south of the center. There are connections to Europe from Natal.

Long-distance buses leave the Rodoviária Nova, 6km south of the center, for Fortaleza (R$69 to R$90, eight hours, nine daily), Recife (R$55, 4½ hours, eight to nine daily), João Pessoa (R$35, three hours, eight daily) and Salvador (R$161, 21 hours, two daily).

Coming from the south and heading for Ponta Negra, get off at Shopping Cidade Jardim and catch a bus to Ponta Negra.

From the Rodoviária Nova to Ponta Negra, take bus 66. For Praia dos Artistas, take bus 38. Buses 48 and 54 run between Ponta Negra and the center, while 56 runs along all the city beaches. Bus fare is R$1.85.

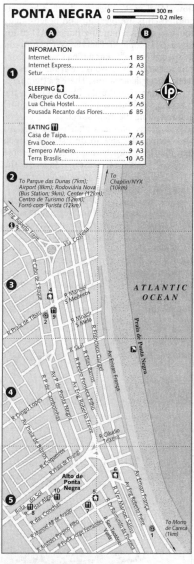

PONTA NEGRA 0 300 m / 0 0.2 miles

INFORMATION		
Internet	1	B5
Internet Express	2	A3
Setur	3	A2

SLEEPING		
Albergue da Costa	4	A3
Lua Cheia Hostel	5	A5
Pousada Recanto das Flores	6	B5

EATING		
Casa de Taipa	7	A5
Erva Doce	8	A5
Tempero Mineiro	9	A5
Terra Brasilis	10	A5

To Parque das Dunas (7km); Airport (8km); Rodoviária Nova (Bus Station; 9km); Center (12km); Centro de Turismo (12km); Forró com Turista (12km)

To Chaplin/NYX (10km)

ATLANTIC OCEAN

Praia de Ponta Negra

Alto de Ponta Negra

To Morro de Careca (1km)

CANOA QUEBRADA

☎ 0xx88 / pop 2800

This fishing village turned hippy hangout has moved upmarket these days, but still represents a relaxing seaside spot for a few days' downtime or a bout of kitesurfing. It's easily reached from Fortaleza and the new Aracatí airport will only increase the tourist flow. Hard-packed beaches backed by rust-colored cliffs are pleasant and beach-buggy tours to the surrounding dunes (R$120 for up to four people) or **Ponta Grossa** (R$200) can be spectacular. The **kitesurfing** season is from July to December; lessons are available, as are **tandem paragliding** jaunts. There's a (temperamental) Banco do Brasil ATM near where the bus stops and internet cafes (R$3 per hour) abound along the main street.

Numerous *pousadas* offer pools, gardens and plenty of space to do as little as you like. They are mostly midrange but become very affordable off-season. Maps on the main street indicate where all of them are. Charming **Pousada Europa** (☎ 3421-7004; www.portal canoaquebrada.com.br; s/d R$30/35; ☒) has a garden filled with coconut and banana palms and a swimming pool, as well as great-value rooms reached by rickety wooden staircase, each with sea views, wave noise and breezes on their individual hammock balconies.

On the beach, a long string of *barracas* offers excellent seafood and other dishes at lunchtime (R$10 to R$25). Order a couple of hours beforehand for the widest choice. Other eateries are in the center; daily specials (R$12 to R$16) range from garlic shrimp to chicken lasagna at friendly **Café Habana** (Principal; mains R$11-28; ☒ lunch & dinner); they also do decent salads and pastas. Nightlife is focused along the main street; there are also weekend beach parties in high season.

From Natal, catch a bus to Aracatí (R$50, six hours, six to seven daily) and then a bus or *combi* (R$2) the remaining 13km to Canoa. For transport from Fortaleza, see p345.

FORTALEZA

☎ 0xx85 / pop 2.4 million

This sprawling coastal center is a popular beach resort destination but offers little to the backpacker besides a couple of days on the sand and facilities to get you sorted before setting out again. Fortaleza can be glitzy, gritty, tacky or chilled, depending on which part of town you find yourself in. The city has impressive nightlife and numerous upmarket beach restaurants for a splash-out. **Fortal** (www.fortal.com.br) is a Salvador-style, out-of-season Carnaval in the last week of July.

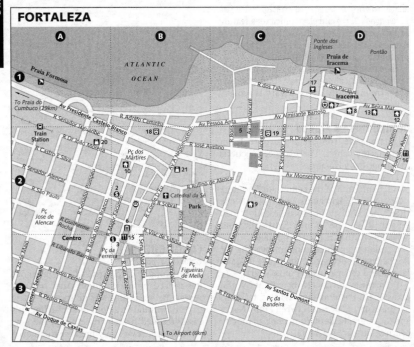

Information

Internet is widely available. ATMs and change offices cluster along the Meireles strip, particularly around the Club Náutico; there are also ATMs at the airport, bus station and Mercado Central.

Bradesco (cnr Alencar & Facundo, Centro) ATMs.

Tourist information (☎ 3257-1000; Av Beira Mar, Mucuripe; ☼ 9am-8pm) On Meireles beach. Good English map-guides. Also a kiosk on Praça da Ferreira (☼ 9am-5pm Mon-Fri), at the bus station and airport.

Tourist police (Av Barroso 805)

Dangers & Annoyances

Things have got less sleazy but there's still a lot of prostitution in Iracema and petty theft on beaches and buses.

Sights & Activities

Fortaleza's number one spot for culture is the brilliant **Centro Cultural Dragão do Mar**, a complex of walkways, restored buildings and cultural spaces spanning three blocks and including planetarium, cinema, theater, galleries, numerous restaurants and bars, and worthwhile **Museu de Arte Contemporânea** (☼ 9am-7pm Tue-Thu, 9am-9pm Fri-Sun). This is also the city's best place to hang out in the evenings.

The **Museu do Ceará** (São Paulo 51; ☼ 8:30am-5pm) has temporary exhibits downstairs and a higgledy-piggledy, scantly labeled collection upstairs with exhibits ranging from indigenous ceramics to a stuffed goat named Iôiô who was a city character in the twenties.

Praia do Meireles has an attractive waterfront promenade with homey beer *barracas* on the sand side and smart air-con restaurants alternating with hotels on the other side of the road. The fish market and evening craft fair are other draws. Further east, **Praia do Futuro** is the cleanest and most popular of the city beaches. Just northwest, tranquil **Praia do Cumbuco** has dunes and *jangada* (traditional sailboat) trips. Beach-buggy excursions to **Morro Branco** (White Hill; per person R$35) are enjoyable and sold along Meireles's promenade.

Sleeping

Iracema has most of the budget options, though a few backstreet Meireles options have worthwhile off-season prices. Both are preferable to the center.

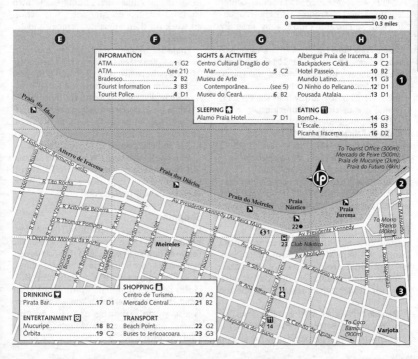

BRAZIL

Backpackers Ceará (☎ 3091-8997; www.pousada backpackers.hpg.ig.com.br; Av Dom Manuel 89; s/d without bathroom R$20/40) Fortaleza's cheapest hostel is also its best. You get your own room, and each is individually hand-decorated with charming colors. Shared bathrooms are spotless. The safe, enclosed space includes a patio, kitchen and you're just steps from the Centro Dragão. The welcoming young owners are a delight, too.

Albergue Praia de Iracema (☎ 3219-3267; www .aldeota.com/albergue; Av Barroso 998; dm R$25) This easygoing place in a restored building has dark but spacious dorms, some with their own bathroom, and a kitchen area out the back. Don't confuse with the Atalaia hostel's annex next door.

Pousada Atalaia (☎ 3219-0755; www.atalaiahostel .com.br; Av Beira Mar 814, Iracema; dm/s/d R$37/60/80; 🕃) Set in a pretty building on the beach in the nice part of Iracema (some rooms are in an annex a block away), this hostel offers segregated dorms, an internet cafe, cooking facilities, a TV room and a front patio. Small discount for HI members.

Hotel Passeio (☎ 3226-9640; João Moreira 221; s/d with fan R$40/75, with air-con R$55/95; 🕃) For city-center accommodation, the rooms at this hotel opposite a leafy square aren't too shabby. Friendly and family-run.

Álamo Praia Hotel (☎ 3219-7979; www.alamohotel .com.br; Av Barroso 885; s/d R$70/90; 🕃) Faded leopard-skin sheets, lingering odors and traffic noise are features, but this hotel is a decent-value Iracema base handily near the Pirata if partying is your aim. Skip breakfast.

Also recommended:

O Ninho do Pelicano (☎ 3219-0871; oninhodo pelicano@hotmail.com; Av Beira Mar 934, Iracema; s/d R$60/90; 🕃) This offshoot of a popular restaurant is beachside and will offer sharp off-season prices.

Mundo Latino (☎ 3242-8778; www.mundolatino .br; Bilhar 507, Meireles; d R$100; 🕃) Convenient Meireles location a short walk back from the beach. Cheap off-season.

Eating

Restaurants abound in Iracema; those around Av Beira Mar are mostly much better than those around Rua dos Tabajarás. Centro Cultural Dragão do Mar is also good for dinner. Smart restaurants line the Meireles strip.

Mercado de Peixe (fish market; Praia de Mucuripe) Buy fish, shrimp or lobster (from R$15 per kg) at one stall and have it prepared in garlic and oil

(around R$3 to R$5) at another. At the junction of the beachside road and Av Aboliçao.

Coco Bambu (Canuto de Aguiar 1317; mains R$15-40) Enjoy a buffet lunch or pizzas, *beiju de tapioca* (manioc-flour 'taco'), crepes or sushi with sand underfoot and palms overhead at this Caribbean-themed eatery.

Picanha Iracema (Alves 89; meat per kg R$20-50) There are a few meat-meat-meat restaurants on this quiet Iracema backstreet; this offers the best price-vs-quality deal. You get better value ordering by weight and there are a few cheap salads to accompany the *carne*.

BomD+ (Av Desembargador Moreira 469; per kg R$23.80; 🕃 lunch Mon-Sat) It's worth tearing yourself away from the beach and up the hill to lunch at this jolly open-air spot. The buffet is excellent and (R$2 extra per kg) includes great grilled meats and pleasant service.

L'Escale (Guilherme Rocha; per kg R$24; 🕃 lunch Mon-Sat) The excellent spread has tons of veggies at this buffet upstairs in an elegantly restored colonial building near the state museum.

Drinking & Entertainment

Iracema has legendarily lively nightlife; the bars and clubs surrounding the Centro Cultural Dragão do Mar see some action all week on their sociable terraces and fill at weekends.

Pirata Bar (www.pirata.com.br; Rua dos Tabajaras 325; admission R$30; 🕃 8pm-late Mon & Thu) The happy Mondays here are one of Brazil's biggest nights, with a great live show and fabulous atmosphere that make it worth the hefty cover.

Órbita (www.orbitabar.com.br; Dragão do Mar 207; admission R$10-20; 🕃 8pm-late Thu-Sun) One of several options in this zone, with reggae, rock, live music and electronica all regular themes.

Mucuripe (www.mucuripe.com.br; Travessa Maranguape 108; admission R$25; 🕃 10pm-late Fri & Sat) A stylish club with five dance floors popular with Fortaleza's well-heeled youth.

Shopping

Ceará has a strong craft tradition (Brazil's best hammocks!). Once a prison, the cells of the **Centro de Turismo** (Pompeu 350; 🕃 8am-5pm Mon-Sat, 8am-noon Sun) now house fabric and craft shops, as well as an upstairs folk art museum (R$1, closes between noon and 2pm). Not too far away, the **Mercado Central** (Av Nepomuceno; 🕃 daily) is also worth exploring, as is the evening market on the beach in Meireles near the Club Náutico.

Getting There & Around

Several airlines operate domestically from Fortaleza's airport, some connecting Fortaleza with Europe.

Buses run to Natal (R$69 to R$90, eight hours, nine daily), São Luís (R$118, 16 hours, three daily) and other major cities. These services are mostly run by Guanabará; prepare to queue for tickets.

Buses run to Canoa Quebrada (R$18.80, 3½ hours, five daily); you can pick up the Canoa bus in front of Albergue Atalaia in Iracema or Club Náutico in Meireles before it passes the bus station. Along the Meireles strip at places like **Beach Point** you can also book trips (R$40) on air-con buses that will pick you up at your hotel.

The 'Siqueira/Mucuripe' bus (078, R$1.60) connects the bus station to Iracema and Meireles.

JERICOACOARA

☎ 0xx88 / pop 2000

A truly special place, Jericoacoara (pronounced 'je-ri-kwah-*kwah*-ra,' or just Jeri) combines nightlife, a range of activities and a yummy variety of cuisine, enhanced by the remote setting. The sand-street village faces a broad gray beach, shouldered by a huge yellow sand dune and rolling green hills. The relaxed vibe keeps hip Brazilians and travelers staying longer than planned. It's one of South America's best destinations for wind sports and there's a longboarding wave great for learning to surf.

Avoid *bichos de pé* (burrowing foot parasites) by not walking barefoot. There are heaps of internet places (around R$4 per hour) and laundries (think R$9 per kg) but no banks: the closest ATM is at Jijoca. Upmarket *pousadas* and restaurants accept credit cards.

Orientation

Jeri consists of six parallel *ruas* running down to the beach. Starting from the big sand dune and heading east, they are: Nova Jeri, Dunas, São Francisco, Principal, Forró and Igreja.

Sights & Activities

The 3km walk to the rock arch **Pedra Furada** is beautiful and buggy trips (R$40 to R$80) to surrounding dunes and lakes, like **Lagoa do Paraíso**, are highly recommended. Surfing and wind-sport lessons are offered and gear is available to rent. **Kite Club Preá** (☎ 3669-2359;

www.kiteclubprea.com) offers great kitesurfing lessons. At sunset, catch a *capoeira* circle (classes available) on the beach.

Sleeping

We gave up counting after reaching a hundred *pousadas* so you won't be short of a bed. Most are excellent, so wander around and take your pick. During the wet season (March to June) prices drop dramatically and midrange places are a real bargain. A few to get you started:

Pousada Tirol/Jericoacoara Hostel (☎ 3669-2006; www.jericoacoarahostel.com.br; São Francisco; dm/d R$36/80) In the quiet period you can get your own room elsewhere for the price of a dorm in this central hostel but it becomes a better deal in high season. Dorms have space and face a sociable courtyard area. There are also tents for overflow. HI discount.

Pousada Isabel (☎ 3669-2069; www.jericoacoara.it; Forró 84; s/d R$50/80; [image]) A few steps from the beach, this cordial guesthouse has cool rooms with marine colors and motifs. They teach windsurfing and you can stash boards here. Confusingly, there's another *pousada*, Izabel, two doors down.

Pousada Bangalô (☎ 3669-2075; www.jericoacoara praia.com; Novo Jeri; s/d R$60/80; [image]) A tall wall creates an intimate compound at this rustic, pretty *pousada* with a lush garden.

Pousada Calanda (☎ 3669-2285; www.pousadacalanda .com; Dunas; s/d R$90/140; [image] [image]) On the dune side of town, this excellent spot has sweet, very comfy rooms opening onto a lovely garden with hammocks, loungers and a swimming pool. It's a steal in low season when the price halves.

Eating & Drinking

There are simple places offering cheap *pratos feitos*, as well as a good selection of traveler-friendly set-ups with good salads, wood-fired pizzas and fresh seafood.

Zchopp (Principal; sandwiches R$3-6) As the name implies, lip-smacking cold draft beer is available here in four unusual varieties. But it's open all day for good-value sandwiches too.

Café Brasil (btwn Principal & São Francisco; light meals R$5-15) This sweet little cafe serves quality coffee drinks, *açaí* and light meals.

Restaurante do Sapão (São Francisco; dishes R$9-24) Good-value-for-Jeri daily specials and a long menu of everything from sandwiches and pizzas to stingray stew, all served at tables in the sand under a towering tree.

Carcará (Forró; dishes for 1 person R$15-35) Set a couple of blocks back from the action, this tranquil place offers some of the best food in town at comparatively reasonable prices. Imaginatively prepared fish and meat dishes use fresh herbs and are served with a smile.

Planeta Jeri (Principal; ☺ 8pm-late) There are other party places in town but this is a reliable starting point from about 10pm. *Caipirinhas,* confusingly small pool tables, and casual sand 'n' surf vibe drive it. Outside, carts sell mixed drinks to crowds of revelers.

Getting There & Away

Getting to Jericoacoara can be tricky, but that's half the magic. Buses (www.redencao online.com.br) from Fortaleza (R$38, seven hours, two daily at 10:30am and 6:30pm) stop at Praiano Palace Hotel in Meireles and the airport before the bus station. Also included in the ticket price is a one- to two-hour transfer in an open 4WD truck from Jijoca to Jeri. From Jeri to Fortaleza, the bus leaves at 2pm and 10:30pm from Pousada do Norte, where tickets are sold. There's usually an extra bus from July to February. Various drivers offer direct transfers, costing around R$100 per person, though you may be able to get it for less, with a two-hour stop at Lagoa Paraíso thrown in. Hotel Isalana Praia, on São Francisco in Jericoacoara, is especially helpful with arranging transfers to Fortaleza.

If coming from the west or heading that way, go via Camocim, accessed by bus from Parnaíba (R$16.40, two hours, two daily at 7:15am and 5:39pm). From Camocim, transports leave for Jericoacoara (R$30, 1½ to three hours) around 9am and 10:30am Monday to Saturday from the Mercado Central. Otherwise, there's a lot of buggy traffic between Camocim and Jeri (an exciting ride); a buggy seats four and costs around R$150 to R$200. Buggy drivers may meet you at the bus station and lie about there being no other transport available. If you're on your own, head to the river ferry in town and try and negotiate prices with buggies making the crossing. From Jeri to Camocim, a truck leaves at 7am Monday to Saturday from Jeri's Rua Principal; it links more or less with a minibus (R$25, 10:30am) from Camocim to Parnaíba.

Hourly transports run between Jeri and Jijoca (R$5), which is useful for ATM runs.

PARNAÍBA

☎ 0xx86 / pop 141,000

Parnaíba is an unremarkable river-mouth port that you'll likely pass through on your way to or from Jericoacoara, the Lençóis Maranhenses or the Sete Cidades. While here, check out the Porto das Barcas, the town's quiet but prettily restored riverfront warehouse area, which has handcraft shops, tour agencies, cafes and bars. You can take a cruise out into Parnaíba's famous **delta**, a 2700 sq km expanse of islands, mangroves and abundant birdlife.

Casa Nova Hotel (☎ 3322-3344; Praça Lima Rebelo 1094; s/d R$30/50, with air-con R$50/70, without bathroom R$15/30; 🖭) is spotless and offers truly excellent value, with proper ceiling fans and good bathrooms in the mid-priced rooms. In Porto das Barcas itself, **Pousada Porto das Barcas** (☎ 3321-2275; www.pousadaportodasbarcas.com.br; s/d R$35/55) has plenty of character to its high-ceilinged rooms. Anti-mosquito weaponry is handy throughout Parnaíba.

Parnaíba is a launchpad for the Lençóis Maranhenses (see boxed text, p350), the Sete Cidades national park (see boxed text, opposite) or Jericoacoara (left).

In addition to the transport links to the places above (see the relevant sections), Parnaíba has bus connections to Fortaleza and São Luís.

SÃO LUÍS

☎ 0xx98 / pop 956,000

With its gorgeous colonial center offering just the right blend of crumbling elegance and unobtrusive renovation, São Luís is a real jewel in the Northeast's crown. The cobbled streets are lined with Unesco World Heritage–listed, colorfully painted and appealingly tiled mansions. Even some of the traffic lights boast these typically Portuguese ceramic *azulejos.* São Luís has a rich folkloric tradition embodied by its colorful festivals and has become Brazil's reggae capital.

Orientation

São Luís is divided into two peninsulas by the Rio Anil. On the southernmost, the Centro sits on a hill above the historic core of Praia Grande (aka Projecto Reviver), where many streets have multiple names. On the northern peninsula lie affluent suburbs (São Francisco) and city beaches (Calhau).

Information

Banco do Brasil (Travessa Boa Ventura) ATM.
Bradesco (Av Dom Pedro II) ATM.
Neti@ndo (Vital de Matos 48; per hr R$2.50) Internet until 11pm.
Poeme-se (Humberto de Campos; per hr R$2.50) Internet access in cool second-hand Portuguese bookstore.
Tourist information (☎ 3212-6211; www.turismo.ma.gov.br; Praça Benedito Leite; 8am-7pm) Hands out a free map and has boat and bus timetables. Also at nearby Portugal 165 (same hours), bus station and airport.
Tourist police (☎ 190; cnr Estrela & Alfândega)

Sights & Activities

Projeto Reviver has successfully restored life to the historic center, which now juxtaposes government offices, handcraft shops, galleries, cultural centers, *pousadas,* restaurants and bars. In the heart of the old-town area, the **old market** is a curious, onion-like space whose interior has stalls selling dried shrimp, beans, souvenirs and potent local liquors.

Worth visiting in the old town are the **Casa do Maranhão** (Trapiche; 9am-7pm Tue-Sun), which has what amounts to a multimedia state tourism brochure and an upper floor dedicated to the regional flavors of Bumba Meu Boi festival costumes. Items from Maranhão life, from delicate wooden fish traps to children's toys made from trash, are displayed at the **Casa do Nhozinho** (Portugal 185; 9am-7pm Tue-Sun).

Local beaches are broad and flat; some disappear at high tide. Locals pack windswept **Praia do Calhau** on weekends.

Festivals & Events

Carnaval A big event in São Luís; February/March.
São João & Bumba Meu Boi These festivals are combined from late June to the second week of August. The latter celebrates a legend of the death and resurrection of a bull with music, dance and theater. Year-round rehearsals are a great way to get a taste of these festivals – ask the tourist office for locations.
Marafolia A Salvador-style Carnaval in mid-October.

Sleeping

Hostel Solar das Pedras (☎ 3232-6694; www.ajsolardaspedras.com.br; Palma 127; dm R$20, s without bathroom R$45, d R$60) This hostel has good facilities and dorms with space and lockers. Best: the restored colonial house, with exposed rock walls; worst: the subdued atmosphere created by the undermotivated staff. HI discount.

Pousada Internacional (☎ 3231-5154; Estrela 175; s/d without bathroom R$25/40) Friendly, family-run, and in the attractive heart of the old town, this is the best of the cheap *pousadas,* with parquet floors and rooms and hallways bright with colorful murals. Rooms without a window cost slightly less, but aren't worth the saving.

Lord Hotel (☎ 3221-4655; Nazaré 258; s/d R$50/65, with air-con R$65/80, without bathroom R$35/50;) What was once probably rather smart is now

DETOUR

It's worth getting away from the coast for a day to explore the **Parque Nacional de Sete Cidades** (8am-5pm), easily reached on a day trip from Parnaíba. The small park is named the 'Seven Cities' for its bizarre, spectacular geological formations, which 19th-century explorers thought were the remains of palaces and fortresses from a lost or alien civilization.

At the park, report to the visitors center, where an obligatory guide will take you round on foot (R$40, four to five hours), by bike (R$25 plus R$2 hire per hour, three to four hours) or by car (ie the taxi you turned up in, R$20, two to three hours). You'll see all sorts of weird and wonderful sandstone shapes, all imaginatively named, as well as several walls of excellent rock paintings from 3000 to 10,000 years old. It's hot out there, though there's plenty of shade. Take water, sunscreen, walking shoes (even for the car tour) and spray for the biting flies. There are two natural pools, one at a waterfall, to cool off.

The two gateway towns, Piracuruca and Piripiri, are 20km from the park's northern and southern entrances respectively. Both are accessed on Teresina-bound buses from Parnaíba (seven daily, R$22 and 2¼ hours to Piracuruca, R$26 and 2¾ hours to Piripiri). Piripiri also has night-bus connections to Fortaleza and São Luís. Both have decent *pousadas;* there are also two hotels near the park's southern entrance. From either town, a return taxi to the park, including the trip around it but not the guide's fee, costs R$70 to R$80, about half that on a mototaxi. If you're waiting in Piracuruca for your bus, head a block down to the *praça* to check out the beautiful 18th-century baroque church.

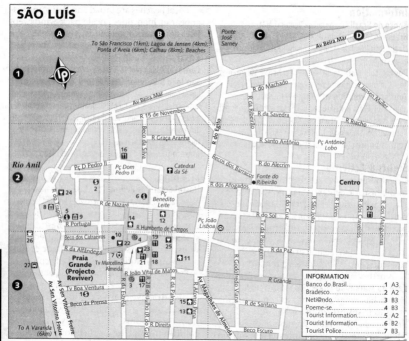

SÃO LUÍS

INFORMATION
Banco do Brasil...................1	A3
Bradesco.............................2	A2
Neti@ndo...........................3	B3
Poeme-se.............................4	B3
Tourist Information............5	A2
Tourist Information............6	B2
Tourist Police.....................7	B3

badly in need of renovation but the beds are comfortable enough, there's hot water, minibar and the location's great. Check a few rooms before you settle; some of the bathrooms are grim.

Pousada Vitória (☎ 3231-2816; Pena 98; d with fan/air-con R$70/80; ﹩) Pick your pad if you can at this friendly family spot, as some of the rooms, which face an interior patio, get a bit musty in the wet season. A good and welcoming choice.

Pousada Colonial (☎ 3232-2834; www.clickcolonial .com.br; Pena 112; s/d R$96/117; ﹩) Noble corridors and quiet elegance characterize this refurbished old-town mansion. Although the rooms don't quite live up to the ambience, they have crisp sheets and, in some cases, there are great views over the old town. In addition, there's usually a substantial discount operating.

Eating

Padaria de Valery (Giz 164; pastries R$1-3; ⌚ closed Sun) This French-owned bakery has tasty pastries, croissants, quiches and fantastic breads.

Dom Francisco (Giz 155; lunch per kg R$19, mains R$15-19; ⌚ closed Sun) Run with quiet good humor, this handsome restaurant offers excellent, fairly priced portions of, among other things, *carne de sol* (sundried beef) with yummy fried manioc and a cheapish lunch buffet. Daily dinnertime specials for R$10, too.

Base da Lenoca (Praça Dom Pedro II; mains for 2 people R$18-44) Enjoy a beer and a breeze with your seafood meal at this spot overlooking the river, popular with lunching government types.

Crioula (cnr Giz & Vital de Matos; per kg R$21; ⌚ closed Sun) This popular corner has high warehouse ceilings and a wall enlivened by a cheerful mural. Dish of the day is R$6; good traditional stews are on offer in the buffet.

A Varanda (Rego 185, Monte Castelo; mains for 2 people R$30-50; ⌚ closed Sun) The lush patio and excellent fish, shrimp and beef dishes will distract you from the slow service. Take a 'Vicente Fiaro' or 'Santa Clara' bus from inside the Terminal de Integração, get off at CEFET and take your first right. Worth the trip.

Also recommended:

La Pizzeria (Giz 129; pizza R$11-26; ⌚ dinner) Popular and attractive old-town pizza joint.

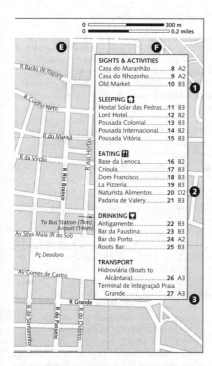

Naturista Alimentos (Sol 517; per kg R$17; ☺ lunch Mon-Fri) Worthwhile vegetarian lunch.

Drinking & Entertainment

At weekends, the reggae pumps loud at bars on Travessa Marcellino Almeida, where people down beers on the street, never really sure which bar they're being served by. **Bar da Faustina** is a classic here; nearby **Roots Bar** (Palma 86; ☺ 6pm-2am Wed-Fri) is another fine reggae choice.

Antigamente (☎ 3232-3964; Estrela 220; ☺ 11am-1am Mon-Sat) It's touristy but the evening buzz on the terrace here will prompt you to sit down and lap up the São Luís atmosphere. Beers come in ice-buckets and the *caipis* pack a kick – try one made with *tiquira*, a manioc spirit. There's a long menu of decent food as well (dishes for two people R$25 to R$40).

Bar do Porto (Trapiche 49; ☺ from 5pm Mon-Sat) It's all about the plastic terrace looking out towards the water at this casual bar near the boat dock. Casual, that is, until their pumping Friday night live reggae sessions when the cavernous interior packs out.

Getting There & Around

The São Luís airport is 15km southeast of the center. There are European connections with São Luís.

Buses run to Belém (R$89 to R$109, 12 hours, four daily), Barreirinhas (R$29, four hours, five daily) and Fortaleza (R$118, 16 hours, three daily). Long-distance buses leave from the bus station, 8km southeast of the center (taxi R$17 or bus 903 to/from the old center, R$1.80).

São Luís has that rarest of Brazilian beasts, a working train station. There's only one line, which heads to Marabá every Monday, Thursday and Saturday at 8am (returning the following day). Tickets cost R$30/68 in economy/executive class and the journey takes 14 hours. From Marabá you can head on to Santarém in the Amazon, or north to Belém.

Readers have reported armed assaults on the night buses between São Luís and Belém, so consider flying as an alternative.

ALCÂNTARA
☎ 0xx98 / pop 21,000

This picturesque colonial treasure, slipping regally into decay, lies across the Baía de São Marcos from São Luís. Built in the early 17th century, Alcântara was the hub of the region's sugar and cotton economy and home to Maranhão's rich landowners. Today the seat of Brazil's space program lies outside of town. Alcântara makes for a memorable day trip. There are two banks with ATMs, but take cash in case. It's well worth buying the excellent map-guide of the town, easily purchased in São Luís or here (R$6).

The streets around the village's highest point contain the finest architecture. On the Praça de Matriz, by a picturesque ruined church, is a grisly reminder of the days of slavery, a **pelourinho** (whipping post). On the same square is the **Museu Histórico** (admission R$2; ☺ 9am-2pm Tue-Sun), displaying personal effects from the 18th- and 19th-centuries.

There are several places to stay; especially charming is **Pousada dos Guarás** (☎ 3337-1339; pousadadosguaras@terra.com.br; Praia da Baronesa; s/d/tr with fan R$35/60/75, with air-con R$65/85/100; ☺) on the beach (or a short boat ride from it, in the wet season) and surrounded by scarlet-ibis-filled mangroves. Individual cottages are in a coconut-palm garden and are clean and pretty with mosquito nets and a hammock out front. Pack bug spray. The island's restaurants serve none-too-cheap fish dishes; if you fancy lunch,

---

ALTERNATE ROUTE

Transport between Parnaíba and Barreirinhas involves rattling on a wooden bench over a track between sand dunes, past isolated communities and gorgeous scenery. It is a recommended adventure. From Parnaíba, buses to Tutóia (R$14, 2¼ hours) leave five times daily (twice on Sunday). From Tutóia, 4WD trucks to Paulino Neves (R$8, 1½ hours) leave at 10am and 5:30pm Monday through Saturday, and 4pm on Sunday. The 4WD ride onward to Barreirinhas (R$13, two to three hours) is rougher and more scenic; in the wet season you can expect to wade through muddy puddles and/or push your vehicle out of them. Departures are at 6am and 12:30pm Monday through Saturday, and 6am on Sunday. From Barreirinhas, departures for Paulino Neves are at 9am and 4pm; these are timed to coincide with onward transport to Tutóia. There are *pousadas* in Paulino Neves (and Tutóia) and dunes within walking distance.

Agencies in Barreirinhas offer direct transfers to Jericoacoara via the scenic coastal route for about R$250 per person (with a minimum of three). The trip takes around eight to 10 hours.

Cantaria (Largo do Desterro; dishes for 2 people R$25-40; ☺ 10am-4pm) has amazing decorations, great water views and sits alongside a chapel. Stop by Rua das Mercés 401 to try *doce de especie*, the local cookie-sweet made from coconut and the juice of orange-tree leaves.

Launches to Alcântara (R$24 return, one hour, 7am and 9:30am daily, returning at 8:30am and 4pm) depart from São Luís's *hidroviária* (boat terminal), or, at low tide, from Praia Ponta d'Áreia (bus from the *hidroviária* included in ticket price). A catamaran and other sailboats also make the slow, rolling crossing. Check departure times at the dock the day before. These often vary, so this is essential. Keep an eye out for scarlet ibis.

PARQUE NACIONAL DOS LENÇÓIS MARANHENSES

Fifteen hundred square kilometers of rolling white dunes make up this spectacular national park, which is best visited from March to September, when rainwater forms crystal-clear lakes between the sandy hills. The main access point is the town of Barreirinhas, prettily set on a bend in a river. From here, numerous agencies offer the standard four- to five-hour trip by jeep (R$50, usually departures at 9:45am and 2pm daily) to the edge of the park; motorized vehicles are not permitted to enter it. From here you walk a short way into the dunes; wear beach gear, as it's basically a sand-and-swim experience. If you want to venture further into the park, you can organize memorable two- or three-day hikes, or a spectacular half-hour flyover (R$160 per person).

From Barreirinhas, too, you can take a day trip (R$60) or the daily ferry (R$5), downstream to the remote villages of Atins and Caburé, tranquil places with access to dunes, activities and peaceful *pousada* accommodation.

Barreirinhas has a **Banco do Brasil** (Av Carvalho) with Visa ATM and a few doors down is **Net Point** (Av Carvalho 693; per hr R$3). There are many *pousadas* in and around town. **Pousada do Porto** (☎ 0xx98-3349-1910; Anacleto de Carvalho 20; s/d R$30/60, with air-con R$35/70; ☒) is welcoming, clean and good value; get a room with river views. **Marina Tropical** (Praça do Trabalhador; lunch per kg R$23; ☺ lunch & dinner) does an excellent lunch, with dishes in clay pots, all labeled, plus pizzas and other dishes in the evenings, when there's live *forró* music. Nearby, good fish restaurants are along the river. In town, a small army of young fixers tries to organize every aspect of your visit. They get commissions and are actually helpful as long as you're clear about what you want.

Barreirinhas can be a jumping-off point for Parnaíba and Jericoacoara (see boxed text, above). Five daily buses run between São Luís and Barreirinhas (R$29, four hours). Vans and collective taxis (R$35 to R$40) also run the route.

THE NORTH

The Amazon conjures a romantic, near-mythical image in our minds, but also nowadays an urgently real one. The future of this immense expanse of rivers and jungle, a vital lung for the world, is of huge importance.

The numbers alone are mind-boggling: the Amazon Basin contains 6 million sq km of river and jungle, and just over half is in Brazil. It contains 17% of the world's fresh water and the main river-flow at its mouth is 12 billion liters per minute.

While you can still have amazing wildlife experiences in the vastnesses of the forest here, it's important to realize that pouncing jaguars and bulging anacondas are rare sightings. Nevertheless, a trip into the jungle ecosystem is deeply rewarding, both for the wildlife-watching and the chance to appreciate how local communities have adapted to this water world. Manaus is a popular base for such trips, but there are other good possibilities. The main city, Belém, is a launchpad to the region that deserves plenty of your time, while the tranquil white sands of Alter do Chão make a peaceful stopover on your way upriver.

GETTING THERE & AROUND

Bus travel is limited to a few routes in the North, so rivers serve as highways. Flights are usually at least twice the price of hammock-boat fare but check for specials.

BELÉM

☎ 0xx91 / pop 1.4 million

Prosperous Belém has a cultural sophistication unexpected from a city so isolated. Its wealth comes from its position at the gateway to the Amazon, meaning that any extracted (timber) or cultivated (soybeans) products pass through here before going to market. Belém has recently invested in tourism and the resulting renovations and constructions are fantastic. If you take some time to wander the mango tree–lined boulevards and investigate the bohemian arts and music scenes, this attractive city will reward like few others in Brazil.

Orientation

The Comércio, roughly between Av Presidente Vargas and Av Portugal, is a compact commercial district, noisy by day and deserted by night. The Cidade Velha (Old City) is quiet and contains Belém's historical buildings. East of the center, prosperous Nazaré has some chic shops and restaurants.

BRAZIL

RIVER TRAVEL

Riverboat travel is a unique Amazonian experience. Be warned that boats are always slow and crowded, often wet and smelly, sometimes dull and never comfortable. Do you like *forró* music? You won't after this trip! Luckily, Brazilians are friendly and river culture is interesting. Some tips:

- Downstream travel is considerably faster than upstream but boats heading upriver travel closer to the shore, which is more scenic.
- Boats often moor in port a few days before departing – check boat quality before committing.
- Fares vary little between boats. Tickets are best bought onboard or at official booths inside port buildings. Street vendors may offer cheaper prices but you run the risk of being cheated.
- *Camarotes* (cabins) are usually available and afford additional privacy and security. Ensure that yours has a fan or air-con. *Camarotes* are usually the same price as flying.
- Put up your hammock (available at any market for R$10 to R$40, don't forget rope!) several hours before departure. There are usually two decks for hammocks; try for a spot on the upper one (the engine's below), away from the smelly toilets. Others are likely to sling their hammocks above and/or below yours. Porters may offer to help you tie yours for a small tip: well worth it if knots aren't the ace in your pack.
- Bring a rain jacket or poncho, sheet or light blanket, toilet paper and diarrhea medication.
- Meals (included) are mainly rice, beans and meat, with water or juice to drink. It's advisable to bring a few liters of bottled water, fruit and snacks. There's usually a snack bar on the top deck.
- Watch your gear carefully, especially just before docking and while at port. Lock zippers and wrap your backpack in a plastic bag. Keep valuables with you. Get friendly with people around you, as they can keep an eye on your stuff.

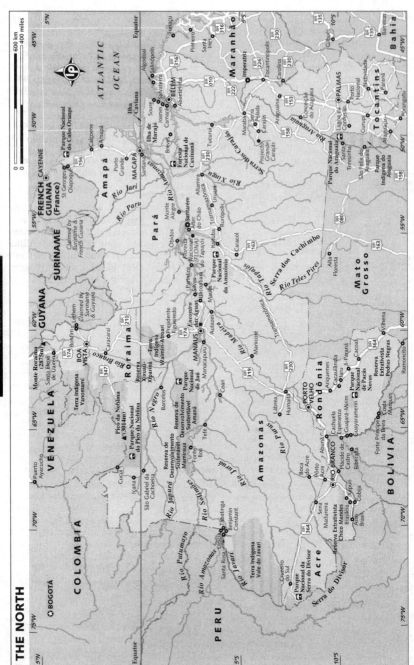

THE NORTH

Information

Estação das Docas (Av Castilho Franca) Has a cybercafe, ATMs, police, bookstore, currency exchange and tour agency.

Hospital Adventista (☎ 3084-8686; Av Almirante Barroso 1758)

HSBC (Av Presidente Vargas 670 & João Diogo 140) ATMs.

Paratur (☎ 3212-0575; www.paraturismo.pa.gov.br; Praça Waldemar Henrique; ☼ 8am-6pm Mon-Fri) More helpful office at the airport.

Porão Virtual (Barata 943; per hr R$2) Internet access.

Tourist police (Estação das Docas)

Dangers & Annoyances

Comércio has a reputation for muggings when fairly empty (at night and on Sunday). Take a taxi at night. Pickpocketing is common at Mercado Ver-o-Peso.

Sights & Activities

The Cidade Velha centers around Praça Brandão, dominated by the city's **cathedral**. With cannons covering the river, the 17th-century **Forte do Presépio** (admission R$2; ☼ 10am-6pm) was built by the Portuguese after they kicked out the Dutch and French. It has an excellent archaeological museum with great indigenous ceramics, artistically displayed. Also on the square is **Museu de Arte Sacra** (admission R$2; ☼ 10am-6pm), housed in a former Jesuit college, with a really worthwhile collection of wooden religious art. The cafe has seats in the pretty garden. Opposite, attractive **Casa das Onze Janelas** (☼ 10am-6pm) holds exhibitions of local contemporary artists.

The sedate atmosphere here is quite a contrast to the bustle of the nearby **Mercado Ver-o-Peso** (☼ 7:30am-6pm Mon-Sat, to 1pm Sun), where smells of Amazonian herbal remedies and dried shrimp mingle, and vendors trade tropical fruits and river fish. One of the two historic buildings holds a small, free exhibition on indigenous culture.

Next door, **Estação das Docas** (Av Castilho Franca; ☼ 9am-1am) is something of a gated community but nevertheless a fabulous conversion of long waterside warehouses that now offer, as well as picturesque strolling under yellow derricks, a host of facilities including cybercafe, ATMs, exchange office, tourist police and pricey but excellent eating.

Central **Theatro da Paz** (Praça da República; admission R$4, Wed free; ☼ guided visits every hr 9am-5pm inclusive Mon-Fri, 9am-1pm inclusive Sat) is one of Belém's finest rubber-boom buildings. If you can't catch a show, take the guided tour round the lavish interior.

The 1909 **Basílica de NS de Nazaré** (Praça da Basílica, Nazaré; ☼ 6am-8pm) has a vast and ornate marble interior housing the tiny image of the Virgin of Nazaré, a miraculous statue believed to have been sculpted in Nazareth.

The riverfront **Mangal das Garças** (Praça do Arsenal; sights each R$2, for all 4 R$6; ☼ 9am-6pm Tue-Sun) is a small but relaxing park featuring plenty of birds including the scarlet ibis, a butterfly house, an observation tower, a naval museum, restaurant and cute gift shop.

Bosque Municipal Rodrigues Alves (Av Barroso; R$2; ☼ 8:30am-5pm Tue-Sun) is a 15-hectare piece of thick rainforest in grand old botanical garden style. It has macaws, coatis, monkeys and the world's largest water lilies.

Museu Emílio Goeldi (Av Barata; park, aquarium & museum each R$4; ☼ 9am-5pm Tue-Sun, ticket office closed 11:30am-2pm weekdays) has snakes, big cats, manatees, crocodiles and other Amazonian species in a beautiful piece of rainforest, as well as an aquarium and good museum of indigenous culture.

Valeverde (☎ 3212-3388; Estação das Docas) runs boat trips to see wildlife, and evening cruises with live entertainment. Activities start at R$25 per person.

Festivals & Events

During the **Círio de Nazaré**, which happens on the second Sunday in October, a million people accompany the image of the Virgin of Nazaré from the cathedral to the Basílica de NS de Nazaré. Two weeks of serious partying follow.

Sleeping

Hotel Amazônia (☎ 3222-8456; www.amazoniahostel .com; Ó de Almeida 548; dm R$13, s without bathroom R$18, s/d/tr/q R$25/40/55/70) Not the hostel of the same name, this central option offers basic rooms with thin walls, and a ten-bed dorm. It's not luxury, but it's traveler-focused, friendly and mighty cheap. Breakfast and internet are available for extra.

Amazônia Hostel (☎ 4008-4800; www.amazoniahostel .com.br; Av Gov José Malcher 592; dm/s/d/tr R$32/60/80/110; ✖) A lovely renovated building holds this bright and caring hostel that makes an effort with solar power and recycling. Prices for

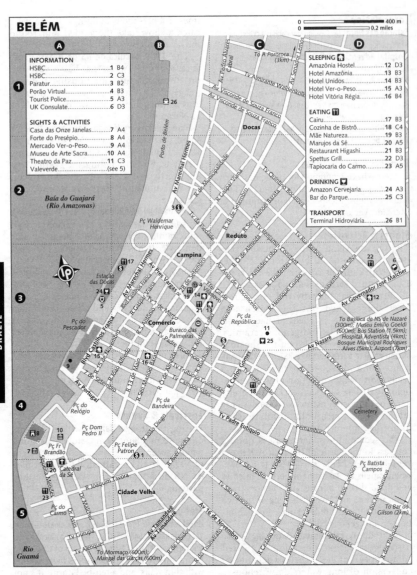

BELÉM

BRAZIL

secure, segregated dorms include sheets and air-con. It's a safe district but convenient to the center. HI discount offered.

Hotel Vitória Régia (☎ 3212-0793; Travessa Frutuoso Guimarães 260; s/d R$40/45; ✴) In the heart of Comércio, this run-down but OK spot has musty, cleanish rooms and a proper hotel structure. Air-con costs R$10 more. There

are other reasonable cheapies alongside and opposite.

Hotel Ver-o-Peso (☎ 3241-2022; www.hotelveropeso .com.br; Blvd Castilhos França 208; s/d R$65/80; ✴) A modern hotel with good-value rooms and decorated hallways. You're right opposite the bustling market (get a taxi late at night) and just a few paces from the Estação das Docas. For R$20 upgrade to a larger, better-equipped room.

Hotel Unidos (☎ 3224-0660; www.hotelunidos .br; Ó de Almeida 545; s/d/tr R$70/82/105; 🅿) Excellent service and clean, big air-con rooms on an OK street make this midrange choice worth the spend. Big breakfast spread, minibar, hot showers and free fast internet add value.

Eating

Belém is known for *pato no tucupi* (duck in a manioc juice and tongue-tingling jambu leaf sauce), *tacacá* (a gummy soup made from manioc root, dried shrimp and jambu leaves) and *maniçoba* (black beans, pork and manioc leaves).

The **Mercado Ver-o-Peso** has a big area where you can suck on cheap juices, munch on R$1 *salgados* or chow down on bargain R$4 to R$5 *pratos feitos*. Near Basílica de NS de Nazaré, a row of **tacacá stands** sells steaming bowls of this delicious stuff for R$4 a shot.

The **Estação das Docas** is wall-to-wall eating, with a row of places offering lunch buffets and pricey à la carte dinners, with riverside seating indoors or outdoors, and live music in the evenings on a moving overhead platform.

Cairu (Estação das Docas; single cone R$3) This Belém institution with several branches offers ice creams galore, with Amazon fruits served alongside sexed-up classics and decadent treats like Ferrero Rocher.

ourpick Cozinha de Bistrô (Travessa Ferreira Cantão 278; dishes R$12-25; 🕑 lunch Mon-Sat) This enchanting, discreet backstreet spot has a dark, romantic feel, a jazz theme and an excellent French-influenced bistro plates like *coq au vin*. Blackboard specials are cheaper but tasty.

Restaurante Higashi (Ó de Almeida 509; buffet R$12.99, with sushi R$25.99; 🕑 lunch) Very popular, this Japanese-Brazilian restaurant has a couple of outdoor tables and tasty salad options to go with the hot buffet and the decent sushi. Cheap lunch specials for R$7.

Marujos da Sé (Praça Brandão; most dishes R$15-40; 🕑 lunch & dinner) A nice spot with wooden outdoor tables in the heart of the old town. Waiters wear sailor suits but the food is good, particularly shared specialties like *caldeirada* or paella. Better value than the branch at Estação das Docas.

Mãe Natureza (Barata 889; per kg R$20; 🕑 lunch Mon-Sat) Fabulous vegan lunch buffet. Mãe Natureza ('Mother Nature') make their own soy milk and use unrefined sugar. It all tastes great.

Also recommended:

Tapiocaria do Carmo (Mendes 144; tapiocas R$1-6; 🕑 4-10pm Tue-Sun) Savory and sweet tapiocas (kind of like crepes) with a wide range of toppings.

Spettus Grill (cnr Balbi & Travessa Quintino Bocaiuva; skewers R$4-8; 🕑 lunch & dinner) Popular suburban beer place; specializing in *espetinhos*.

Drinking & Entertainment

Amazon Cervejaria (Estação das Docas; 🕑 from 5pm Mon-Fri, from noon Sat & Sun) Deservedly the Estacão's most popular spot with a long, convivial terrace, this microbrewery produces five tasty draft beers. Scarily, the consumption ticket goes up to 60. The food here is good but pricey.

Bar do Parque (Praça da República; 🕑 24hr) This curious beer kiosk and its mosaic-floored open terrace is a Belém classic. In the evenings everyone from students to businessfolk to sex-workers can be found at its tables, served by bow-tied waiters.

A Pororoca (www.apororoca.com.br; Av Senador Lemos 3316, Sacramenta; admission R$4-10; 🕑 10pm-late Thu-Sat, 6pm-midnight Sun) A simple but super-popular dance club playing various styles like *pagode*, reggae and *brega* (a fast and free couples dance of Pará), usually with live bands.

Bar do Gilson (Travessa Padre Eutíquio 3172, Condor; 🕑 8pm-3am Fri, noon-3am Sat, 8pm-midnight Sun) Under a tin roof and fueled by cheap beer, *chorinho* (a samba variation) rules the house at one of Belém's most celebrated live-music spots.

Getting There & Away

AIR

Abundant domestic connections as well as flights north to Miami via the Guianas fly from the airport, 8km north of the center. Bus 'Pratinha–P Vargas' runs between the traffic circle outside the airport and Av Presidente Vargas (R$1.50, 40 minutes). Taxis cost R$30.

BOAT

Boats use Belém's Terminal Hidroviária. Tickets are sold at booths inside. Boats to Santarém (hammock/cabin R$120/250, three days) and Manaus (hammock/cabin R$180/400, five days) depart on Tuesday, Wednesday and Friday. Boats to Macapá (hammock/cabin R$130/200, 23 hours) depart on Wednesday and Saturday. See boxed text, p351.

BRAZIL

BUS

Buses run to Marabá (R$46, 12 hours, six daily), São Luís (R$82 to R$103, 12 hours, daily), Fortaleza (R$195, 25 hours, one to three daily), Salvador (R$265, 36 hours, daily), Brasília (R$136, 34 hours, daily) via Palmas, and Rio de Janeiro (R$250 to R$450, 50 to 55 hours, two daily).

The bus station is on Av Almirante Barroso, 3km east of the center. For a city bus to Av Presidente Vargas, catch any 'Aero Club' or 'P Vargas' bus from across the road. Going to the bus station, take an 'Aeroclube' or 'Pratinha–P Vargas' bus from Av Presidente Vargas. Taxis to points along Av Presidente Vargas cost around R$12.

Readers have reported armed assaults on the night buses between São Luís and Belém, so consider flying as an alternative.

ALGODOAL

☎ 0xx91

Accessible only by boat, Algodoal is a simple village in an idyllic situation. Its sand streets, lack of cars, cheap accommodation and white beaches means it ticks a lot of boxes for a relaxed few days kicking back in a hammock, exploring the island or doing some low-key surfing.

The village consists of three long parallel streets. At the far end cross a small river (wade at low tide, canoe at high) to lovely Praia do Farol, which turns a corner and becomes Praia da Princesa, which is 8km long. There are other small hamlets on this island, cut by channels into three main parts. Make your way around on foot, horsecart or canoe.

Algodoal fills up during holidays and weekends, but there's always plenty of accommodation. Some hotels accept credit cards but there are no banks.

Every second home is nominally a *pousada,* most of which offer very basic rooms (make sure you get a mosquito net), hammocks and maybe a place to camp. Competition (and quality) keeps the prices low and there's not much to choose between: **Paraíso do Norte** (☎ 3854-1155; s/d R$25/45, R$5 less without breakfast) has thin mattresses and halfway walls but a pretty waterside location, while **Pousada Kakuri** (☎ 3854-1156; Principal; hammock R$10, s/d without bathroom R$25/30) on the main street has basic stick cabins and a backpacker vibe.

More upmarket choices include **Estrela Sol Hotel** (☎ 3854-1107; www.estrelasol.algodoal.com; d R$70-100; 🔁 🏊), which has the blessing of a pretty pool, and **Jardim do Éden** (☎ 9997-0467; http://algodoal.chez.com; hammock or tent R$25, r without bathroom R$75, cabin R$130-150) right on Praia do Farol (look for the driftwood sign). They offer comfortable rooms, brick cabins and good meals using local produce.

Most accommodation choices offer food, typically tasty fresh fish dishes.

Access is via mainland Marudá. Buses (R$16.50, four hours, six to seven daily) leave Belém's bus station for Marudá, and quicker minibuses (R$15) leave from just behind it. Either will drop you at Marudá's port, where boats for Algodoal (R$5.50, 40 minutes) leave six to seven times daily. Horsecarts await the boats to take you to the village, only a 10-minute stroll away anyway. To return, buses and minibuses leave the port until about 5pm. If you're coming from, or going to, the east, jump off at Castanhal, the main-road junction town where all buses stop.

ILHA DE MARAJÓ

☎ 0xx91 / pop 250,000

Lying at the mouth of the Amazon, this verdant island is larger than 70 of the world's countries but much of its interior is swampy and inaccessible. Though the main settlement, Breves, is in the island's southwest, three southeastern villages are easily reached from Belém and make for a relaxing visit. The island is notable for its hospitable people and *carimbo* – a colorful folkloric dance. Buffalos are another trademark and their meat appears on most restaurant menus.

Joanes and Salvaterra make the most appealing bases. Do as the locals do and hire a bike to get around.

Joanes

Closest to Camará, where the boat comes in, Joanes is a tiny hamlet with the fragments of an old Jesuit church and a good sandy beach. Livestock wander grassy streets lined with a few shops and sandwich stands. Attractive **Pousada Ventania do Rio-Mar** (☎ 3646-2067; www.pousadaventania.com; s/d R$55/85) sits atop a breezy headland overlooking the beach and has individually decorated rooms. The owners (who organize various projects in the local community) rent bikes and can organize activities.

BRAZIL

GETTING TO FRENCH GUIANA

Right on the Equator on the north side of the mouth of the Amazon, **Macapá** can be reached by boat or plane from Belém (see p355). The capital of Amapá state offers little in the way of sights except the 18th-century Fortaleza (fortress), but the riverfront is pleasant and you can have your equatorial moment at the monument 5km southwest of the center. The city has all services. **Hotel América Novo Mundo** (☎ 3223-2819; Av Coaracy Nunes 333; s/d R$50/70, without bathroom R$30/50;) is a cheap spot to lay your head – get a breezy front room. **Peixaria Amazonas** (cnr Beira Rio & Macacoari; 2-person mains R$20-35; lunch & dinner Mon-Sat, lunch Sun) has river views and good fish.

From Macapá's bus station, 3km north of town, you can take the improved bus trip north to **Oiapoque** (R$65, 12 to 15 hours). This rough-and-ready town is across the river from nicer but pricier St Georges (see boxed text, p696) in French Guiana. Get stamped out at the **Polícia Federal** (6am-10pm Mon-Sat) on the main street, 500m from the market where the bus stops, then take a boat (R$15, 20 minutes) across the river. An international bridge is due to open in 2010. If you want to stay in Oiapoque, crash at safe, clean **Arizona Hotel** (☎ 3521-2185; Av Coaracy Nunes 551; s/d R$50/65;).

Salvaterra

About 18km north of Joanes, slow-paced Salvaterra has more of a town feel and a decent beach, Praia Grande. A tourist information kiosk is on the plaza near the river.

Warmly welcoming **Pousada Bosque dos Aruãs** (☎ 3765-1115; Segunda Rua; s/d/tr R$60/70/80;) has good, simple wooden cabins on stilts in an attractive natural yard looking out over the water. It's a top spot to relax and serves fantastic meat and seafood dishes (for two R$15 to R$30), soups and salads. The young owners know Brazilian music well and play great tunes. Bicycle are available for rent (R$2/12 per hour/24 hours). Walking up from the jetty, take your second left.

Soure

Soure is the biggest town on this side of the island and has a spread-out grid of streets that peter out into buffalo paths. **Banco do Brasil** (Rua 3 btwn Travessas 17 & 18) has ATMs. **Bimba** (Rua 4 btwn Travessas 18 & 19) rents bicycles (per day US$3). There are a few cybercafes.

Ceramicist Carlos Amaral combines Aruã and Marajoara ceramic traditions with award-winning results. Check out his workshop **Mbara-yo** (Travessa 20 btwn Ruas 3 & 4) – small, affordable pieces are for sale. After exploring Soure's streets, bicycle out to **Praia Barra Velha** (3km); shacks sell drinks and seafood. Head on to **Praia de Araruna**, which is long, starkly beautiful and practically deserted. There's an intervening river, which requires a boat at high tide. Follow Rua 4 inland to **Praia do Pesqueiro** (11km), Soure's popular weekend beach.

There are several places to stay. **Pousada Asa Branca** (☎ 3741-1414; Rua 4 btwn Travessas 12 & 11; s/d R$25/45 with fan, R$45/70 with air-con;) has a laid-back welcome, clean rooms (some across the road) and a good-value restaurant. **Paraíso Verde** (Travessa 17 btwn Ruas 9 & 10; mains for 2 people R$20-30) has plenty of island chat and serves typical buffalo and fish dishes in the midst of a gorgeously peaceful leafy garden.

Getting There & Around

Boats travel between Belém's Terminal Hidroviário and Camará (R$14.57, three hours) twice daily (6:30am and 2:30pm) and once on Sunday (10am), returning at 6:30am and 3pm (Sunday at 3pm only). Buses and minibuses to Joanes, Salvaterra and Soure meet the boats. The centers of Salvaterra and Soure are linked by boat (R$2), which can take a while to fill up; a few kilometers outside of Salvaterra, small motorboats (R$1.50, five minutes) zip across to Soure more frequently; there's also a free, near-hourly vehicle ferry. *Mototaxis,* taxis and infrequent vans move people around the island.

Ask in Belém about the fast boat, which there's talk of reinstating. It would run directly from Belém to Soure in just two hours (R$25).

SANTARÉM

☎ 0xx93 / pop 274,000

Most travelers rush between Belém and Manaus, skipping over the very thing they are desperate to see: the Amazon. A stop in riverfront Santarém not only breaks up a long boat trip, but it also provides a chance to investigate the jungle and communities seen from your hammock. Santarém is relaxed and easygoing but it's the lovely river-beach town and beautiful rainforest preserves nearby that will entice you to prolong your stay.

Information

Amazon's Star (Av Tapajós 418; per hr R$3; 8am-10pm Mon-Sat, 10am-10pm Sun) Reliable internet access.

Bradesco (cnr Av Rui Barbosa & Travessa 15 de Agosto)

HSBC (Av Rui Barbosa) ATMs.

Tourist office (3523-2434; 8am-5pm Mon-Fri) On the water by the Praça do Pescador. Eager to help but not especially useful.

Sights & Activities

The tea-colored Rio Tapajós flows into the café-au-lait Rio Amazonas in front of Santarém. The two flow side by side for a few kilometers without mingling.

Contact **Amazon Tours** (3522-1928; www .amazonriver.com; Travessa Turiano Meira 1084) for interesting half-day English-speaking botanical tours through the **Bosque de Santa Lúcia**, including in-depth coverage of deforestation issues.

The **Museu Dica Frazão** (Peixoto 281; daily) is run by eccentric 80-something Dona Dica herself. Here she displays and sells the beautiful clothing and tapestries she makes from Amazonian root fibers.

Sleeping & Eating

Hotel Brasil (3523-5177; Travessa dos Mártires 30; s/d without bathroom R$30/50;) This budget staple is basic but it's central and just-about clean. Rooms are high-ceilinged and noisy; the friendly owner will do her best to put you in one with a window, much better than the dingy camphor-scented interior ones.

Brisa Hotel (3522-1018; Av Bittencourt 5; s/d R$60/80;) Small rooms and tiny bathrooms are modern and sterile but it's by the water and OK value for Santarém. Windows aren't useful – you'll need the air-con.

New City Hotel (3523-3149; Travessa Francisco Corrêa 200; s/d R$75/80;) Rooms vary in size and quality and have mismatching furniture, but are comfortable with minibar and air-con in all. Bargain hard as it's a bit overpriced.

Brasil Grande Hotel (Travessa 15 de Agosto 213; rodízio R$13; lunch) This old-fashioned central hotel does a cheap but decent lunch-hour *rodízio* as well as a good-value buffet spread, or *prato feito* for R$6.

Restaurante O Mascote (Praça do Pescador; mains R$15-30) Fish is the specialty of this cheery restaurant with a big outdoor terrace near the water. At lunchtime on weekdays, it's all-you-can-eat for R$17, while at weekends it's R$25 but includes *feijoada* or other special dishes.

Sabor Caseiro (Peixoto 521; per kg R$23.90; lunch) With comfy black padded booths and plenty of juices, this is a great place for lunch. The buffet is well above average, with regional and coastal specialties and hearty stews like *feijoada* at weekends.

Getting There & Around

AIR

Domestic flights operate from Santarém's airport, 15km west of the center. A taxi costs R$43. The 'Aeroporto' bus (R$2.20, 40 minutes) runs irregularly from early morning until about 6pm. Be careful not to catch the 'Aeroporto V' bus, which goes to where the airport used to be.

BOAT

Boats to Manaus (hammock/cabin R$140/300, 2½ days, Monday to Saturday) and Belém (hammock/cabin R$100/250, 48 hours, Friday to Sunday) use the Docas do Pará, 2.5km west of the center. Booths outside the entrance sell tickets. Boats to Macapá (hammock/cabin R$120/250, 36 hours, daily) depart from both here and Praça Tiradentes, 1km west of the center. See also boxed text, p351, for more information and tips.

The 'Orla Fluvial' minibus (R$1) connects the center with both ports every 20 minutes until 7pm. The 'Circular Esperanza' bus runs directly from the center to the Docas do Pará but deviates on the return. A taxi costs R$10 to R$12 to Docas do Pará.

BUS

Buses to Alter do Chão (R$2.30, 55 minutes, roughly hourly) or the airport can be caught on Av Rui Barbosa between Travessa Matos and Av Barão do Rio Branco.

Irregular buses leave Santarém's bus station (5km west of town) for Cuiabá (R$300, about three days). The journey is difficult, and can

BRAZIL

take a week in the rainy season. Similarly, you can reach Marabá (R$140, from 30 hours) if conditions are OK; from there you can continue to Belém (R$46, 12 hours) or São Luís.

AROUND SANTARÉM

Floresta Nacional (FLONA) do Tapajós

This 6500 sq km primary rainforest reserve on the Rio Tapajós is notable for giant trees, including behemoth *sumaúna* (a type of ceiba tree). Its *igarapés* (channels connecting rivers) and, in the rainy season, *igapós* (flooded forests) promise wildlife viewing; sloths, monkeys, river dolphins and birds are relatively common. Much of the charm of a visit is experiencing life in the forest's indigenous communities. Visits can be arranged through agencies in Santarém or Alter do Chão (see http://tinyurl.com/lsdb3m for a list), or go on your own by bus or by hiring a boat in Alter do Chão.

Four small communities within FLONA have ecotourism schemes and welcome visitors for homestays and tours with local guides. The two most commonly visited are Maguary and Jamaraquá. You will sleep (bring a hammock) and eat (typically rice and fish) with a family. Bring bottled water, toilet paper, a flashlight and any additional food you may want; there are no shops.

To visit, authorization (per day R$3) from **ICMBIO** (☎ 0xx93-3523 2964; flonatapajos.pa@icmbio.gov .br; Av Tapajós 2267, Santarém; ✆ 7am-noon & 2-7pm Mon-Fri) is required; in practice it can be paid at the reserve entrance. Guides are obligatory in the park. Fees for hikes and canoe trips (around R$30 per group) are accompanied by a community charge (per person R$5 to R$8).

Buses for Maguary and Jamaraquá (R$10, three to four hours) leave Santarém 11am Monday to Saturday from Av São Sebastião near the Telemar building.

ALTER DO CHÃO

☎ 0xx93 / pop 7000

Bank on spending longer at this wonderfully relaxed riverside haven than you planned to. With its white-sand river beaches and tropical ambience, Alter do Chão is one of Amazonia's most beautiful places to unwind. River beaches are largest from June to December but Alter is worth a visit at any time of year.

Right across from the center of town, the **Ilha do Amor** is an idyllic sand island in the Rio Tapajós featured on numerous postcards.

Nearby, the large **Lago Verde** lagoon is great to explore by boat or canoe. The area is surrounded by rainforest under various levels of protection, including the FLONA do Tapajós (left). Also accessible is the **Rio Arapiunes**, with blindingly white beaches and clear waters.

Bring cash from Santarém – there are no banks. There's a friendly but largely useless tourist office at the pier a few blocks from the *praça*. Watch out for a multilingual middle-aged scammer with an elaborate sob story.

Activities

Paddle across (watch for stingrays) or when the water's higher, take a boat (R$4 return) to the Ilha do Amor. Kayak or canoe (rental R$5 per hour) the Lago Verde alone or take a guided trip (R$60 to R$100). **Mãe Natureza** (☎ 3527-1264; www.maenaturezaecoturismo.com.br; Praça Sete de Setembro) offers many things, including trips in riverboats to visit the FLONA do Tapajós primary forest and/or intriguing honey-making and fish conservation community projects on the Rio Arapiuns. The tours are multilingual and use local indigenous guides; think R$250/400 per person for one-/two-day trips. Pop in anyway to see the beautiful photo exhibition, swap books or use the slow internet (R$3.50 per hour).

Festivals & Events

Alter do Chão fills during the **Festa do Cairé**, a lively folkloric festival with dancing and processions held in the second week of September.

Sleeping & Eating

There are many places to stay, most of them backpacker-friendly *pousadas,* which are great for relaxation.

Albergue da Floresta (☎ 9928-8888; www.albergue pousadadafloresta.com; Travessa Antônio Pedrosa; hammock per person R$15, d without bathroom R$30, d R$45) Set away from the center of the village, this jungle retreat offers open-air thatched-roof hammock accommodation as well as appealingly treehouse-like wooden cabin rooms. It's as laid-back as you can get. Turn right along the water from the *praça* and continue on straight up the dirt road; it's signposted left after 400m. It has kitchen facilities and prices are somewhat negotiable.

Pousada Tia Marilda (☎ 3527-1140; Travessa Antônio Lobato 559; s/d R$30/50; 🞫) This friendly, simple place is just above the *praça* and makes an attempt to decorate its decent-sized rooms. Second-floor rooms are breezier and larger.

ourpick Pousada Tupaiulândia (☎ 3527-1157; Teixeira 300; s/d R$50/80; 🞫) Excellent value is to be had at this spot halfway between the bus stop and the square. Odd-shaped rooms with bags of space and a stocked fridge occupy two circular buildings in the friendly owner's garden. A bargain.

Tribal (Travessa Antônio Lobato; dishes R$8-36) This laid-back spot on the way down to the *praça* specializes in local fish in a variety of tasty sauces and mixed-grill skewers (*churrasquinhos*) with tongue, sausage, chicken, and beef. Portions easily feed two; there are some halves available.

Shopping

Arariba (Travessa Antônio Lobato) This excellent indigenous art store unites the artwork of eight different Amazonian tribes.

Getting There & Away

Buses run between Santarém and Alter do Chão (R$2.30, 45 minutes, roughly hourly). There are also air-con minibuses (R$3). From the airport ask to be dropped off at the Alter do Chão intersection and wait for the bus. From the bus station in Alter do Chão, head right, then turn left to reach the center of things.

MANAUS

☎ 0xx92 / pop 1.65 million

The mystique of Manaus, the city in the heart of the Amazon jungle and a major port 1500km from the sea, wears off fairly fast – it's a sprawling, largely unromantic spot that doesn't make the most of its riverside position. But this is changing little by little, with restoration of noble buildings from the rubber-boom days. Manaus is a friendly place, the transport hub of the Amazon region and the most popular place to organize a jungle trip (see p364). Once you're back from a few days in the wild, things like air-conditioning will make you feel friendlier towards the place.

Orientation

The area encircled by a U-shape created by Av Epaminondas, Av Floriano Peixoto and Av Getúlio Vargas, is a noisy commercial district that is busy by day and deserted at night and on Sunday. The Praça da Matriz is seedy at night, as is the Zona Franca and waterside area. The immediate surroundings of Teatro Amazonas are slightly upscale.

Information

There are numerous cybercafes throughout the city. Many accommodations have free wi-fi.

Amazon Cyber Café (cnr Av Getúlio Vargas & 10 de Julho; per hr R$3.50; 🕑 9:30am-11pm Mon-Thu, 9:30am-10pm Fri, 10am-9pm Sat, noon-8pm Sun) Not the cheapest but reliable.

Amazônia Turismo (Av Sete de Setembro 1251; 🕑 9am-5pm Mon-Fri, to noon Sat) Changes euros, US dollars and traveler's checks.

Bradesco (Av Eduardo Ribeiro) International card ATMs.

Centro de Atendimiento ao Turista (☎ 3182-6250; www.amazonastur.com; Av Eduardo Ribeiro; 🕑 8am-5pm Mon-Fri, 8am-noon Sat) Helpful central tourist office. There are also branches at the port, airport and bus station.

HSBC (24 de Maio) ATMs.

Juliana Cyber Café (Av Nabuco; per hr R$2; 🕑 8am-11pm)

Tourist police (☎ 3231-1998; Av Eduardo Ribeiro) Same building as the tourist office.

Unimed (☎ 3633-4431; Av Japurá 241) Private hospital with emergency facilities.

Dangers & Annoyances

At the airport, avoid the vultures touting jungle trips or city accommodations. After 11pm steer clear of the port area and the Praça da Matriz. If arriving late by boat, take a taxi to a hotel – muggings are common.

Sights

Strikingly domed **Teatro Amazonas** (Praça São Sebastião; admission R$10; 🕑 9am-5pm) is the city's emblematic rubber-boom building. A short but worthwhile English-speaking guided tour takes you into the opulent interior. There are fairly regular shows; check www.culturamazonas.am.gov.br for details. The square out front, Praça São Sebastião, has colorful restored buildings with terraced cafes, craft shops and live music or cultural displays most nights from 7pm.

Newly and beautifully restored, **Palacete Provincial** (Praça Heliodóro Balbi; 🕑 9am-5pm Tue-Fri, 10am-7pm Sat, 4-9pm Sun) houses various exhibitions, which enthusiastic English-speaking guides will talk you through. Best is the art gallery; other collections of replicas of famous sculptures and coins stand alongside displays on archaeology and the military police. There's also a sound-and-film archive and a good cafe.

The **Museu do Indio** (Duque de Caxias 296; admission R$5; 8:30-11:30am, 2:30-6:30pm Mon-Fri, 8:30-11:30am Sat), set in a former convent hospital, has an excellent collection of indigenous artifacts let down by the lack of information about them. On the way there you pass Palácio Rio Negro, an ostentatious rubber baron's mansion now used for cultural events.

Tranquil **Bosque da Ciência** (Forest of Science; Otávio Cabral; admission R$6; 9am-4pm Tue-Sun, ticket office closed 11am-2pm weekdays) contains giant otters, manatees, caimans, and free-roaming turtles, monkeys, sloths and other creatures on 130 sq km of rainforest. Take bus 519 from the Praça da Matriz.

Beyond here, the **Museu de Ciências Naturais** (Estrada Belém s/n, Colônia Cachoeira Grande; admission R$12, camera R$2; 9am-noon, 2-5pm Mon-Sat) displays preserved and well-labeled regional fish, and amazing butterflies and beetles. There's also an aquarium where you can see the enormous *pirarucú* (Amazon cod). Take bus 519 from

Praça da Matriz or onward from the Bosque da Ciência. Follow the 'Museu' signs from the stop (10-minute walk).

There are **Bumba Meu Boi** (a legend of the death and resurrection of a bull celebrated with music, dance and theater) festival rehearsals at the *sambódromo* on Saturday at 9pm from September to June. It's R$10 ($5 for students) to get in; catch bus 10, 201, or 214 to get there.

Activities

The **Encontro das Águas** (Meeting of the Waters) is where the dark Rio Negro meets the café-au-lait Rio Solimões. The two flow side by side without mingling for several kilometers (differences in speed, density and temperature), before finally combining to create the Amazon. Many jungle trips include the Encontro, but if yours doesn't, take bus 713 from Praça da Matriz to Ponta do Catalão (last stop) and take a motorboat (R$8, 40 minutes) or the hourly car ferry (free) across to Careiro; you'll see the Meeting of the Waters on the way. Otherwise, a day tour from Manaus including other dubious attractions is about R$80.

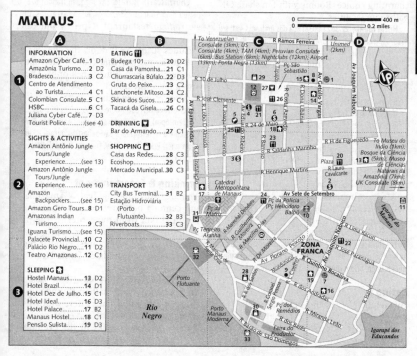

Sleeping

There are numerous budget accommodations in the Zona Franca, most of very low quality. Near the Teatro Amazonas is the ideal location. Competitors commonly post fake criticisms about popular places on travel websites.

Manaus Hostel (☎ 3231-2139; www.manaushostel .com.br; Costa Azevedo 63; dm/d R$20/65; ✖) Handily located just downhill from Praça São Sebastião, this sweet spot is quiet and warm hearted. Security is good, with a front gate and lockers in the tight-packed but decent dorms. Rooms are a little claustrophobic. Kitchen facilities and internet access available.

Hostel Manaus (☎ 3233-4545; www.hihostelmanaus .com; Cavalcante 231; dm R$22-26, r R$55-65; ✖) Popular hostel with a kitchen and a pleasant terrace area to hang out. Dorms are comfortable and not crowded; rooms aren't as great value once you factor in paying for extras like towels and internet. HI discount.

Pensão Sulista (☎ 3234-5814; Av Joaquim Nabuco 347; s/d with air-con R$40/50, s/d without bathroom R$25/40; ✖) High ceilings and colonial character are the features of this basic but rather charming choice. Rooms with fan share OK bathroom facilities.

Hotel Ideal (☎ 3622-0038; Rua dos Andradas 491; s/d R$25/35, with air-con R$35/45, with TV & minibar R$45/56; ✖) Painted in battleship gray and white high-gloss, this is one of the most reliable of the budget hotels in this zone. Rooms are clean but oppressive if you don't get a window. Air-con ones are identical.

Hotel Dez de Julho (☎ 3232-6280; www.hoteldezde julho.com; 10 de Julho 679; s/d R$65/70; ✖) Reliable traveler favorite in a great location and handy for jungle tour agencies. Rooms lack color but are modernized and comfortable; you pay R$15 extra for hot-water showers. Bring a padlock for the room safes.

Also recommended:

Hotel Brazil (☎ 2101-5000; www.hotelbrasil.tur.br; Av Getúlio Vargas 657; s/d R$69/79; ✖) Reliable spot offering good value. It's a little more if you don't pay upfront.

Hotel Palace (☎ 3622-4622; www.palacemanaus.com; Av 7 de Setembro 593; s/d R$85/105; ✖) Ornate facade shields large, bright rooms with wooden furniture.

Eating

Av Getúlio Vargas and Praça São Sebastião are good places to find food at night. Try a steaming bowl of delicious *tacacá*, an Amazon hot-and-sour soup made from manioc gum, salty dried shrimp and tongue-tingling *jambu* leaves.

Skina dos Sucos (cnr Av Eduardo Ribeiro & 24 de Maio; juices R$2-4, snacks R$3-5; ⏰ 8am-8pm Mon-Fri, to 7pm Sat) Drop into this busy blue-tiled corner spot to hog out on those weird Amazonian fruit juices. Try super-anti-oxidant *açaí* with caffeine-kick *guaraná* if you had a late one last night.

Budega 101 (Cavalcante 101; per kg R$17; ⏰ lunch Mon-Fri) Workers queue down the stairs at midday at this reliable buffet lunch spot. Things quieten a bit by one, when you have more chance of grabbing a table on the long covered patio.

Casa da Pamonha (Barroso 375; per kg R$18.50) Cool and friendly, this vegetarian place has art exhibitions, soy burgers, juices, couscous and tasty cakes served all day, and a creative, flavorful lunch buffet.

Gruta do Peixe (Marinho 609; per kg R$18.90, mains R$18-30; ⏰ lunch Mon-Sat) In a pleasant stone-faced basement with check tablecloths, this friendly family business has a lunch buffet with plenty of fish but also decent chargrilled meats.

Churrascaria Búfalo (Av Joaquim Nabuco 628; per person dinner/lunch R$34.90/44.90) Manaus's classic *rodízio* restaurant is pricey but offers tasty cuts of meat and a sizeable buffet that includes sushi. Next door, the cheaper but still delicious *por kilo* (R$25) alternative, Bufolete, is open lunchtimes only. There's also a takeaway outlet.

Also recommended:

Lanchonete Mitoso (Moreira 365; juices R$2-3; ⏰ 7am-6pm) Great combo smoothies and cheap juices.

Tacacá da Gisela (Praça São Sebastião; tacacá R$10; ⏰ dinner) Pricey but handy, friendly and delicious *tacacá* kiosk.

Drinking & Entertainment

The area surrounding Teatro Amazonas is the center's best area to hang out. Ponta Negra (13km from the center) is the main nightlife zone, with a river beach, promenade, bars and restaurants. Popular nightspots sit on the Estrada de Ponta Negra just before this area.

our pick Bar do Armando (10 de Julho 593; ⏰ 5pm-1am) A big Brazilian thumbs-up for this old-fashioned bar, where a down-to-earth local crowd and travelers converge on the streetside tables in the evening. A Manaus classic.

GETTING TO VENEZUELA & GUYANA

The capital of Roraima state, **Boa Vista** is a spot without great traveler thrills but it's a useful gateway to both Venezuela and Guyana. It's linked with Manaus by several daily buses (R$100 to R$120, 12 hours). Crash at the **Hotel Monte Líbano** (☎ 0xx95-3224-7232; Av Benjamin Constant 319W; s/d R$30/40, with air-con R$35/45, without bathroom R$20/30; ⚇), a basic cheapie. From Boa Vista, there are four daily buses to little Bonfim (R$15, 1½ hours) on the Guyanese border, and five to Pacaraima on the Venezuelan border. One daily bus heads on into Venezuela to Caracas, first stop Santa Elena (p970).

For Venezuela, determine whether you require a Venezuelan tourist card from the consulate in Manaus or Boa Vista before boarding a bus. Buses stop at a Brazilian Polícia Federal border post for exit stamps before entering Venezuela.

For Guyana, get an exit stamp from the Polícia Federal near the river where you cross to Guyana. Some of the Boa Vista–Bonfim buses stop here and then continue to the river. If you take an earlier or later departure, catch a taxi from Bonfim's bus station to the Polícia Federal (R$10); from there it's a short walk to the river. Motorized canoes cross the river (R$3). Lethem (p731) is 5km from the other side of the river and has better accommodation options than Bonfim. Get this journey done early to avoid arriving after dark.

Porão do Alemão (Estrada da Ponta Negra 1986; ⚇ 11pm-late Mon-Sat) Live rock is a regular feature at this spot popular with a university-student crowd.

Coração Blue (Estrada de Ponta Negra 3701; ⚇ 9pm-late Mon-Sat) A big popular dance club with different themes every night.

Shopping

Casa das Redes (cnr Rocha dos Santos & Miranda Leão) One of several hammock shops for your boat trip needs. They range from R$10 to R$35. Haggle and remember to buy rope.

Ecoshop (www.ecoshop.com.br; 10 de Julho 495) Handicrafts from a variety of indigenous artisans.

Mercado Municipal (☎ 6am-6pm Mon-Sat, to noon Sun) This sprawling, cast-iron, art-nouveau *mercado* has been operating since 1882. Shop here for Amazonian herbal remedies and crafts.

Getting There & Away

AIR

Several airlines operate domestic flights from Manaus. International flights go to Ecuador, Atlanta and Miami. Smaller airlines use Terminal 2, 'Eduardinho,' about 600m east of Terminal 1.

BOAT

Large passenger boats use the Estação Hidroviária (aka Porto Flutuante), a tranquil modern terminal with a cybercafe, ATMs, eateries and a good outdoor bar. Inside,

Agência Rio Amazonas sells tickets on behalf of most boats, the majority of which dock further east, near the market. Sellers on the street may sell cheaper tickets, but if something goes wrong you'll be on your own. See boxed text, p351, for information and tips.

AJATO runs a fast boat upriver to Tefé (R$190, 14 hours) on Thursday from a pier east of the port, which is also where tickets are sold. Services to Santarém and Tabatinga were suspended at the time of research.

BOAT FARES		
Destination	**Cost hammock/ cabin (R$)**	**Duration**
Belém	220/800	3½ days
Porto Velho	150/500	4 days
Santarém	115/400	30-36 hr
Tabatinga	340/1000	6½ days

BUS

Four daily buses run to Boa Vista (R$90 to R$110, 12 hours). A direct daily bus to Caracas, Venezuela (R$250, 36 hours) stops in Santa Elena de Uairén and Puerto La Cruz among other places. Road travel south to Porto Velho has been suspended indefinitely.

Getting Around

The airport is 13km north of the center. Bus 306 (R$1.50, 30 minutes) and air-conditioned

BRAZIL

bus 813 (R$2.50) run roughly every half hour until 11pm. Taxis are set at R$49 but you can bargain a cheaper rate from town. Only get official taxis from the airport.

The bus station is located 6km north of the center, and it's passed by several bus lines including 205, 209, 311 and 315. From the station cross the footbridge out front, walk with traffic to the closest bus stop and take one of the buses listed under 'Centro' on the stop's sign.

Buses (around R$1.50) to the center pass the Praça da Matriz, loop up on Av Floriano Peixoto and either head right on Av Sete de Setembro or straight on Av Getúlio Vargas.

For Ponta Negra, get bus 120 from Praça da Matriz. It's best to get a cab late at night though.

AROUND MANAUS
Jungle Trips

Many visitors to Amazonia expect to stare down a growling jaguar or trade beads with spear-toting indigenous people just outside Manaus. This isn't going to happen. On a typical trip, you are likely to glimpse pink and gray river dolphins, caymans, monkeys, tarantulas and plenty of birds. Sloths are relatively common. Manatees, anacondas, tapirs and jaguars are extremely hard to spot. The more remote, unpopulated and pristine the area, the better wildlife-viewing will be. Manaus is a big city and the numbers of tourists are high; you might feel that you'll have a more authentic jungle experience leaving from elsewhere in the Brazilian Amazon.

While anything's possible, the typical jungle trip is two to four days. Most agencies offer a similar program, which usually includes piranha fishing, nighttime caiman-spotting, a jungle walk focusing on traditional medicinal and food plants, a night forest camping, a visit to a local home and a sunrise boat trip to see macaws or dolphins. Canoeing through *igarapés* and *igapós* – which have more flora and fauna than channels and rivers – is a priority. This is one reason the high-water period (roughly March to July) is the best time to visit.

'White' rivers, like the Lago Mamorí region, tend to have a higher density of wildlife than 'black' ones, like the Rio Negro. But they also have more mosquitoes and somewhat thicker vegetation, which inhibits wildlife-viewing.

Things to consider while researching trips:

- The guide's proficiency in your common language.
- Levelt of guide's experience within trip's ecosystem.
- Is the trip focused on 'jungle experiences' or serious wildlife viewing?
- Group size.
- Ratio of travel time to time spent at the destination.
- Amount of non-motorized boat/canoe time.
- Availability of lifejackets.
- Cost breakdown for nontypical trips.
- How eco-friendly is the company really going to be? Plenty of 'ecotourism' guides pull sloths out of trees for photo opportunities.

You'll need sturdy shoes or boots, long pants, a long-sleeved shirt, a raincoat, insect repellent, a flashlight and a water bottle. High-power binoculars really improve the experience. Ask how much water is on-site and how much you'll need. Bring your passport.

DANGERS & ANNOYANCES

You name it, it's happened on a jungle trip outside Manaus. Consider that you are placing your personal safety in another's hands in an unknown, isolated natural environment. It's best to use agencies or guides registered with Amazonastur (don't believe the certificates; check online at www.amazonastur.com). Using a registered agency or guide means a better chance of being refunded should something go wrong. Women should consider being part of a group of three or more to avoid being alone in a remote location with a guide.

SCAMS

Manaus is brimful of scammers. Never pay for a tour anywhere other than the registered office of a tour agency. As the industry has become more competitive, scammers have gone so far as to create false IDs and receipts, fake confirmation phone calls to agencies, and falsely represent or impersonate guides and agencies listed in guidebooks. These scammers are most often found at the airport but also work on the street and at hotel receptions. The battle is also waged online, where reputable agencies are criticized on travel websites by 'dissatisfied tourists,' who are actually rival agencies.

AGENCIES & GUIDES

Manaus has scores of agencies. Those listed are recommended budget options offering a reasonably genuine and adventurous experience. Some agencies have a minimum-group-size requirement to set out, while others maintain a constant flow of clients in and out of a set spot. Yet other agencies pool their clients. Agencies can set up almost anything but most have expertise in a certain geographical area. Fees should be all-inclusive (lodging, meals, drinking water, transfers, activities and guides). Unless the agency is very well established, insist on paying a portion of the fee up front and the rest upon return. Most prices vary slightly according to numbers.

Take time to research the options. Many travelers have left Manaus disappointed with their once-in-a-lifetime Amazon experience because they rushed into booking the trip.

Amazonas Indian Turismo (☎ 0xx92-9198-3575; amazonasindian@hotmail.com; Rua dos Andradas 311) This welcoming and nontrendy English-speaking indigenous set-up is recommended for off-the-beaten track experiences; you'll spend much more time in the jungle than hanging around the lodge. You travel by public bus then boat to a rustic camp on the Rio Urubú. Trips from two to nine days; three-day, two-night trips are R$465, less if there's more than one person.

Amazon Gero Tours (☎ 0xx92-3232-4755; www.amazon gerotours.com; 10 de Julho 679) This friendly agency is run by English-speaking guides and piloted by helpful Gero himself. The typical trip is to the Lago Juma area, where a comfortable new lodge offers hammock, dorm or room accommodations and decent bathrooms. Prices start from R$150 per day. Honest, flexible and not pushy.

Iguana Turismo (☎ 0xx92-3633-6507; www.amazon brasil.com.br; 10 de Julho 679) Iguana's typical trip to Lago Juma costs R$140 per person per day. Comfortable hammock or cabin accommodations with flush toilets is located next to Guyanese owner Gerry Hardy's riverfront home. His wife and her family are from the area and staff the lodge. Flexible itineraries. Based in the Hotel 10 de Julho.

Amazon Backpackers (☎ 0xx92-3302-1571; www .amazonbackpackers.com.br; 10 de Julho 679) Inside the Hotel 10 de Julho, this agency has a laid-back

boss and a lodge in the Mamori lake area with good food and an adjacent riverside bar. Trips are fun and focused on the standard activities; you'll see plenty of wildlife without ever feeling miles from civilization. Two-/three-/four-day trips are R$300/460/600.

Amazon Antônio Jungle Tours/Jungle Experience (☎ 0xx92-9961-8314; www.antonio-jungletours.com; Cavalcante 231 & Andradas 491) Based at both Hostel Manaus and the Hotel Ideal, this agency doesn't want for customers and can feel a little self-satisfied as a result. Nevertheless, their lodge, in the Rio Urubú area, reached via public bus, is basic but good, with an observation tower and activities. Trips go from R$140 per day for more than one person.

Amazon Riders (☎ 0xx92-8175-9747; www.amazon riders.com) They have two lodges, one at Lake Mamori. The standard trip is four days, with two nights spent in the jungle, and costs R$480 to R$520. The trips are water-focused, with lots of fishing and canoeing; another concentrates on indigenous communities. They are moving to a new location inside the passenger port.

JUNGLE LODGES

Within reach of Manaus are many jungle lodges ranging from rustic (hammocks) to luxurious (suites). Visits are normally by (somewhat costly) packages that include activities. The experience is in many ways similar to the jungle trips above, only with better accommodations. Travel agents offer deals.

Amazon Rainforest Adventure Station (☎ 0xx92-3656-6033; www.naturesafaris.com; 4-day & 3-night packages per person US$599) A small floating lodge on Lago Juma, 60km southeast of Manaus, this lovely place caters to 28 guests. Rooms have shared facilities.

Aldeia dos Lagos (☎ 0xx92-3528-2045; www .aldeiadoslagos.com; 4-day packages per person US$405) Community-run Unesco-funded ecotourism initiative in a lakeside setting on Silves Island with good bird-watching and various mostly water-based activities. Basic accommodations.

Uakari Lodge (☎ 0xx97-3343-4160; www.uakari lodge.com.br; 3-night packages from US$550 per person) Excellent, comfortable, beautiful eco-tourist setup near Tefé, halfway between Manaus and the Triple Frontier. Part of the Mamirauá reserve, its 1.24 million hectares of protected forest combine nature conservation and scientific research leading to improved opportunities for the communities within the reserve.

BRAZIL

BRAZIL

GETTING TO PERU & COLOMBIA

Before leaving Brazil, get an exit stamp from the **Polícia Federal** (Av da Amizade 650; ☎ 8am-6pm) in Tabatinga.

For Peru, boats depart from the Porto da Feira to Santa Rosa (R$2, five minutes, ☾ 6am-6pm), from where you can travel onwards to Iquitos (see boxed text, p868).

For Colombia, it's a short walk, a R$10 taxi ride or R$4 on a mototaxi to Leticia, or you can take one of the frequent *combis*. See p580 for onward travel.

TRIPLE FRONTIER

On the Amazon's northeast bank – about 1100km west of Manaus – Tabatinga (Brazil) and Leticia (Colombia) are separated by an invisible international border. The opposite bank of the river and the islands in the middle of it, are part of Peru. Santa Rosa, Peru's border settlement, is on an island. This 'triple frontier' has travel routes linking all three countries and is a good base for jungle trips. Leticia is the largest and most pleasant of the three border towns and has the best services (see p576).

Tabatinga is linked by air with Manaus. Boats leave Tabatinga on Wednesday and Saturday for Manaus (hammock/cabin from R$150/800, 3½ to four days). Fast boats run as far as Tefé.

PORTO VELHO

☎ 0xx69 / pop 369,000

Baking on the banks of the wide Rio Madeira, Porto Velho is Rondônia's capital but doesn't have a great deal to offer the traveler. Its status as a river port, conduit for Mato Grosso's soybean output, has brought a certain prosperity. You won't linger long, however, before jumping on a riverboat to Manaus or a bus to more inviting Rio Branco.

Information

Amazon House (Av Pinheiro Machado 753; per hr R$3) Internet access, one of many.

Bradesco (Av Sete de Setembro 711) Has ATMs.

Sleeping

Hotel Tia Carmem (☎ 3221-7910; Av Campos Sales 2895; s/d R$30/45, without bathroom R$25/40; ❄) Safe and reliable family-run budget stalwart.

The cheap rooms have no fan – you'll need one, so upgrade. Free wi-fi, onsite cafe and a peaceful location.

Vitória Palace Hotel (☎ 3221-9232; Duque de Caxias 745; s/d with fan R$40/60, with air-con R$50/80; ❄) Handily placed to stagger home from the Pinheiro Machado nightlife zone, this quiet spot offers OK rooms that you'll forget fast.

Hotel Tereza Raquel (☎ 3223-9234; Aranha 2125; s/d R$50/80; ❄) They get a gleam out of the white tiles at this friendly spot just off the main shopping street. Spacious, bright rooms with decent bathrooms make this a good bet.

Eating & Drinking

Down by the river, alongside the sheds of the old train station, a string of **food kiosks** blends into one shady beer-and-meal terrace, which is particularly happy and rowdy on Saturday and Sunday. Three blocks north, Praça Aloisio Ferreira becomes a sort of fairground at weekends and has a string of cheap but decent **eateries** offering typical dishes and snacks.

Frigideira (Prudente de Morães 2570; R$15 per kg; ☾ lunch Mon-Fri) Just off Av Sete de Setembro, Frigideria is one of several places in these streets offering cool, cheap lunches with plenty of salad options.

Mirante II (Barbosa 269; dishes for 2 R$20-35; ☾ lunch & dinner Wed-Mon) The city's most atmospheric spot however, is Mirante II, featuring a terrace with awesome views over the wide river. There's a *por kilo* lunch for R$15 and live music weekend nights.

Two blocks east of Praça Ferreira, on Av Pinheiro Machado, a boisterous young middle-class nightlife zone centers around trendy **Estação do Porto** and **Antiquarius**, with **Buda's Bar** supplying down-to-earth cheap beer in the middle.

Getting There & Around

AIR

Domestic flights run from Porto Velho's airport, 6km from the center. A taxi costs R$26 or take bus 201 from Av 7 de Setembro near Praça Rondón.

BOAT

Boats to Manaus (hammock R$120, cabin R$400, 2½ to three days) leave around 6pm on Tuesday and Friday from the river port in the center. Agencies line the road down to the water; **Agência Amazonas** (☎ 3223-9743; Alfredo 265) is reliable. See boxed text, p351, for information and tips.

BUS
Buses run to Guajará-Mirim (R$36.50 to R$40.50, 4½ to six hours, six daily), Rio Branco (R$53 to R$66, eight hours, five daily) and Cuiabá (R$150, 21 to 24 hours, three daily). Collective taxis also leave the bus station for Guajará-Mirim (R$50, 3½ hours). From the bus station to the center (3km), take bus 201 or a cab (R$10).

GUAJARÁ-MIRIM
☎ 0xx69 / pop 39,000
In this pleasant town just opposite Guayaramerín (Bolivia), bushy trees shade sidewalks, stained red by the earth, from the relentless sun. It's a backwater, but a pleasant one, and a useful border crossing.

Playnet Games (Av Dom Pedro; per hr R$3) offers internet access inside a gas station until late. **Bradesco** (Leopoldo de Mateos) has ATMs. Change bolivianos and reales with the money changers at the port in Guayaramerín.

There are several places to stay. On the main street in the heart of things between the bus station and the port, the family-run **Hotel Mini-Estrela** (☎ 3541-1205; 15 de Novembro 460; s/d R$30/60; 🗗) is a sound bet with ageing but adequate rooms. Grab one near the back at weekends. Restaurants are nearby, including **Oásis** (15 de Novembro 460; per kg R$19), whose worthwhile lunch buffet includes freshly grilled meats. A couple of blocks away, **Restaurante Tropical** (15 de Novembro 640; half-portions R$8-13; 🕑 lunch & dinner) is a bright and breezy no-walls spot serving enormous, delicious portions (order a half if you're alone) of fish, chicken or tasty *carne de sol* (sundried beef).

GETTING TO BOLIVIA
Passenger launches (R$4, five minutes) to Guayaramerín (p236) depart regularly from the port at the end of the main street 15 de Novembro. You can get stamped out of Brazil at the port on weekdays; at weekends, head to Migracão at the **Policía Federal** (cnr Dutra & Bocaiúva; ☎ 8am-10pm), two blocks forward and three left, walking away from the port. There's a Bolivian consulate (p370) here too.

Buses run from the bus station, 2km east of the port, to Porto Velho (R$36.50 to R$40.50, 4½ to six hours, six daily) and Rio Branco (R$49, eight hours, daily). Collective taxis also leave from here to Porto Velho (R$50, 3½ hours). A taxi between the station and the center is R$10.

RIO BRANCO
☎ 0xx68 / pop 291,000
Remote Acre state is famous as one of the key battlegrounds fought over by the Brazilian environmental and logging lobbies. For travelers, it's a zone for off-the-beaten-track Amazon exploration and a gateway to the jungly north of Bolivia, which it once belonged to. Rio Branco, the state's very laid-back riverfront capital, makes a great stop for a day or two.

Beige-green **Palacio Rio Branco** (Praça Povos da Floresta; 🕑 8am-6pm Tue-Fri, 4-9pm Sat & Sun) is a restored art deco masterpiece holding a historical exhibition. Just below here, the **tourist office** (🕑 8am-6pm Mon-Sat, 4-9pm Sun) is willing but largely useless. Banks with ATMs are alongside. Get online at air-con **Viarena** (Barbosa 507; per hr R$3; 🕑 8am-8pm Mon-Fri).

The **Museu da Borracha** (Rubber Museum; Av Ceará 1441) in a noble mansion, was closed for restoration at the time of research.

Cheapie hotels cluster around the bus station but there's more atmosphere in the center, where you'll find **Hotel do Papai** (☎ 3223-2044; Peixoto 849; s/d R$50/80; 🗗). It suffers from daytime road noise but makes up for it with cool, spotless rooms (some in gaudy green and pink) with fridges, and a benevolent boss. Nearby, tranquil **Hotel AFA** (☎ 3224-1396; Ribeiro 99; s/d R$55/80; 🗗) has spacious, recently renovated rooms and a welcoming, helpful attitude.

The riverbank, with picturesque bridges and cutely colorful houses, is the town's nicest part. Here, the **Mercado Velho** (Praça Bandeira) has craft stalls and a food court with *pratos feitos* for R$5 to R$9. Also here, **Café do Mercado** (dishes R$7-15; 🕑 3-11pm Tue-Sun) has a great riverside terrace, perfect for evening beers, *salgados* and *petiscos*. The AFA's restaurant, **Bistrô d'Amazônia** (per kg R$30; 🕑 lunch) ain't the cheapest lunch buffet but it's brilliant, with Lebanese-inspired salads, gourmet vegetarian dishes, succulent roast meats and weekend seafood (R$45 per kg).

Rio Branco's airport is 20km west of the center. Buses (R$1.90, 40 minutes) run roughly hourly to the center of town.

Buses run to Porto Velho (R$53 to R$66, eight hours, four daily), Guajará-Mirim (R$49.50, eight hours, one daily), Xapurí (R$20.50, 3½ hours, two daily) and Brasiléia (R$24, four hours, five daily). From the bus terminal to the center (1.5km), catch a 'Norte-Sul,' 'Taquari' or 'Domoacir' bus or a mototaxi (R$3 to R$4).

XAPURI

☎ 0xx68 / pop 14,000

Xapuri, whose sweet houses, thriving trees and red-dirt roads make it a charming stop, was home to rubber-tapper and world-famous environmental martyr Chico Mendes, murdered in 1988 after years of successful campaigning against the destruction of forests by loggers and ranchers. The **Fundação Chico Mendes** (☯ 8am-6pm), a block from the bus station, displays touching Mendes photos and memorabilia, including bloodstained clothing and international awards. Staff guide you through Mendes's rustic house opposite, where he was gunned down. The activist's death sparked outrage that has led to extensive forest protection in the state.

Several fine budget *pousadas* rent comfortable rooms. A park near the plaza on Branão has laid-back spots to sit outdoors with a pizza or beer.

Buses run to Rio Branco (R$20.50, 3½ hours, two daily) and Brasiléia (R$7, 1½ hours, two daily). Collective taxis to Brasiléia (R$14, 45 minutes) leave from a kiosk on Branão.

BRAZIL DIRECTORY

ACCOMMODATIONS

Brazilian accommodations are simple yet usually clean and reasonably safe, and nearly all come with some form of *café da manhã* (breakfast).

Youth hostels are called *albergues da juventude*. The HI-affiliated **Federação Brasileira dos Albergues da Juventude** (www.hostel.org.br) has over 80 hostels in the country, most with individual links on the website. Many hostels are excellent, and they're great places to meet young Brazilians. A dormitory bed costs between R$20 and R$45 per person. Non-HI members usually pay 20% extra, but you can buy a HI guest card for R$20 at many hostels and at youth hostel association offices in Brazil.

Brazil hotels are among South America's priciest, but you can still find good deals. At the low end, R$20/50 for very basic singles/doubles is possible in nonurban guesthouses. Better rooms with private bathrooms start at about R$35/70 for singles/doubles and cost substantially more in major cities like Rio. Always ask for prices, as they're often much

---

GETTING TO BOLIVIA & PERU

West of Xapuri, the town of **Brasiléia** sits across the Rio Acre from considerably more hectic Cobija, Bolivia. You can cross the bridge between the two freely, but if you're heading further into Bolivia, get an exit stamp from the 24-hour Polícia Federal in Brasiléia's neighboring town Epitáciolândia. Buses from Rio Branco or Xapuri will drop you there.

For Bolivia, take a taxi (R$10 to R$15) or *mototaxi* (R$3) from the Polícia Federal over either Epitáciolândia's or Brasiléia's international bridge. The fare includes stopping at Bolivian immigration plus onward travel to a hotel or bus station. Cobija has places to stay, an airport and arduous bus connections.

Brasiléia has a Bolivian consulate, ATMs and money changers. **Pousada Orquidia Negra** (☎ 9981-8967; Travessa 7 de Setembro 69; s/d R$30/40) is a clean and cheerful sleeping option. Buses run to Rio Branco (R$24, four hours, five daily) and Xapuri (R$7, 1½ hours, two daily). Collective taxis do the same trips for double the money and half the time.

For Peru, get an exit stamp in Epitáciolândia, catch a bus to Assis (R$10, two hours, three daily) and cross the Rio Acre to Iñapari (Peru). Assis has better accommodations than Iñapari if you need to spend the night. Buses from Rio Branco to Assis theoretically stop at the Polícia Federal en route – check beforehand. There's a Peruvian consulate in Rio Branco. For travel from Peru to Brazil, see p861.

lower than posted prices. Also, it never hurts to ask 'Tem desconto?' (Is there a discount?), which might shave a few reales off the price. Prices typically rise by 30% during high seasons. Hotels in business-oriented cities such as Brasília, São Paulo and Curitiba readily give discounts on weekends.

A pousada typically means a small family-owned guesthouse, though some hotels call themselves pousadas to improve their charm quotient.

ACTIVITIES

The options for adrenaline-fueled adventure in Brazil are endless. Popular diversions include canyoning, paragliding, kitesurfing, wakeboarding, rafting, surfing, trekking, diving and mountain climbing.

Hiking and climbing activities are best during the cooler months, from April to October. Outstanding hiking areas include the national parks of Chapada Diamantina in Bahia (p324), Serra dos Órgãos in Rio de Janeiro state (p277), Chapada dos Veadeiros in Goiás (p310) and the Serra de São José near Tiradentes in Minas Gerais.

Brazil has some choice surf spots. The best surfing in Brazil is in Fernando de Noronha between December and March (p338). Also good are the beaches in the South and Southeast: Saquarema, Ilha de Santa Catarina (p298), São Francisco do Sul, Ilha do Mel (p297), Búzios (p278) and Rio de Janeiro (p258). In the Northeast, head to Itacaré (p326) and Praia da Pipa (p338). The waves are best in the Brazilian winter (June to August).

Búzios in Rio state has good windsurfing and kitesurfing conditions, and access to rental equipment. But Brazil's hardcore windsurfing mecca is the Ceará coast northwest of Fortaleza, from July to December. Here, Jericoacoara (p345) and Canoa Quebrada (p341) are the most popular spots.

BOOKS

Lonely Planet's Brazil and Rio de Janeiro guides have all the information needed for travelers making a more in-depth exploration of the country. Guia Quatro Rodas produces the best in-country Portuguese guides, available at newsstands.

Travelers' Tales Brazil is a fine anthology of travel adventures with good portraits of life in Brazil. One of the classics of travel writing is Peter Fleming's Brazilian Adventure, a hilarious account of an expedition into Mato Grosso in the 1930s. Claude Levi-Strauss' Tristes Tropiques (1955) was an anthropological milestone for its study of indigenous peoples in the Brazilian interior.

Several worthwhile books on history are A Concise History of Brazil by Boris Fausto and Brazil: Five Centuries of Change by Thomas Skidmore. The story behind Euclides da Cunha's masterly Rebellion in the Backlands (which describes the Canudos rebellion) is told by Mario Vargas Llosa in his entertaining novel The War of the End of the World. Jorge Amado, Brazil's best novelist, wrote many wonderful books, including Gabriela, Clove and Cinnamon.

The Brazilians, by Joseph A Page, is a fascinating portrait of the country and its people. For a well-illustrated, accessible introduction to Brazilian popular music, get The Brazilian Sound by Chris McGowan and Ricardo Pessanha. Futebol: The Brazilian Way gives insight into the culture behind Brazil's national addiction.

BUSINESS HOURS

Most shops and government services (including post offices) are open 9am to 5pm Monday to Friday and 9am to 1pm Saturday. Banks are generally open 10am to 4pm. Most restaurants open from noon to 3pm and 7pm to 11pm; those open for breakfast serve from around 8am to 10:30am. Bars typically open from 7pm to 2am, and until 4am on weekends.

CLIMATE

Most of Brazil experiences only moderate temperature changes throughout the year, though southern states like Río Grande do Sul have more extreme seasonal changes.

During the summer, which runs from December to February (school holidays coinciding), Rio and the Northeast have temperatures in the high 30s. The rest of the year temperatures are generally in the mid-20s to low 30s. The South has wider temperature variations, ranging from 15°C in the winter (June through August) to 35°C in the summer.

The Amazon region rarely gets hotter than 27°C, but it is humid there, with considerable rainfall over tropical Amazonia. In some parts of the North, December to March is considered winter, since that's the rainiest season.

BRAZIL

Owing to generally temperate weather year-round, there's no bad time to visit Brazil. But unless you have your heart set on attending Carnaval, you may want to avoid the summer crowds (and heat), and visit from April to November. Treks into the Amazon and the Pantanal are best then – especially from June to August, when it's drier.

For more information and climate charts see p987.

DANGERS & ANNOYANCES

Brazil receives a lot of bad press about its violence and high crime rate. By using common sense, there is much you can do to reduce the risks, including taking the general precautions applicable throughout South America (see p989).

First off, don't start your trip by wandering around touristy areas in a jetlagged state soon after arrival: you'll be an obvious target. Accept the fact that you might be mugged, pickpocketed or have your bag snatched while you're in the country, and don't try to resist your attackers if you do. Carry only the minimum needed for the day plus a fat-*looking* wad to hand over to would-be thieves. Other tips:

- Dress down, leave the jewelry at home and don't walk around flashing iPods, digital cameras and other expensive electronics.
- Be alert and walk purposefully. Criminals will hone in on dopey, hesitant, disoriented-looking individuals.
- Use ATMs inside buildings. Before using any ATM or changing money, be aware of those around you. Thieves may watch these places looking for targets. Cover the keypad when entering in personal codes.
- Check windows and doors of your room for security, and don't leave anything valuable lying around.
- Don't take anything to city beaches except your bathing suit, a towel and just enough money for lunch and drinks. Nothing else!
- After dark, don't ever walk along empty streets, deserted parks or urban beaches.
- Don't wander into *favelas*.

DRIVER'S LICENSE

The legal driving age in Brazil is 18. Most foreign licenses are legally valid in Brazil but we recommend obtaining an International Driving Permit, as the police you are likely to encounter as a foreign driver don't always know the law.

ELECTRICITY

Electrical current is not standardized in Brazil and can be almost anywhere between 110V and 220V. Carry a converter and use a surge protector with non-dual electrical equipment.

EMBASSIES & CONSULATES

In addition to this list, nearly all countries of note have embassies in Brasília.

Argentina (pp266-7; ☎ 0xx21-2553-1646; Praia de Botafogo 228 No 201, Botafogo, Rio de Janeiro)

Australia (Map p263; ☎ 0xx21-3824-4624; Av Presidente Wilson 231, 23rd fl, Centro, Rio de Janeiro)

Bolivia; Brasiléia (☎ 0xx68-3546-5760; Meireles 236); Guajará-Mirim (☎ 0xx69-3541-8622; Av Leopoldo de Matos 451); Rio de Janeiro (Map pp266-7; ☎ 0xx21-2552-5490; Av Rui Barbosa 664 No 101, Flamengo)

Canada (Map p271; ☎ 0xx21-2543-3004; Av Atlântica 1130, 5th fl, Copacabana, Rio de Janeiro)

Chile (Map pp266-7; ☎ 0xx21-2552-5349; Praia do Flamengo 344, 7th fl, Flamengo, Rio de Janeiro)

Colombia Manaus (☎ 0xx92-3234-6777; 24 de Maio 220); Tabatinga (☎ 0xx97-3412-2104; Sampaio 623); Rio de Janeiro (Map pp266-7)

Ecuador (☎ 0xx21-3563-0380; Pintor Oswaldo Teixeira 465, Barra da Tijuca, Rio de Janeiro)

Germany (Map pp266-7; ☎ 0xx21-2554-0004; Carlos de Campos 417, Laranjeiras, Rio de Janeiro)

Ireland (☎ 0xx11-3147 7788; Al Joaquim Eugênio de Lima, 447, Bela Vista, São Paulo)

Israel (☎ 0xx61-2105-0500; brasilia.mfa.gov.il; SES, Av das Nações, Quadra 809, Lote 38, Brasília)

Netherlands (Map pp266-7; ☎ 0xx21-2157-5400; Praia de Botafogo 242, 10th fl, Botafogo, Rio de Janeiro)

Paraguay (Map pp266-7; ☎ 0xx21-2553-2294; Praia de Botafogo 242, 2nd fl, Botafogo, Rio de Janeiro)

Peru Manaus (☎ 0xx92-3236-9607; Constelação 16-A, Aleixo); Rio de Janeiro (Map pp266-7; ☎ 0xx21-2551-9596; Av Rui Barbosa 314, 2nd fl, Flamengo)

UK Belém (☎ 0xx91-3222-5074; Av Governador J Malcher 815, Ed Palladium Center); Manaus (☎ 0xx92-613-1819; Poraquê 240, Distrito Industrial); Rio de Janeiro (Map pp266-7; ☎ 0xx21-2555-9600; Praia do Flamengo 284, 2nd fl, Flamengo)

Uruguay (Map pp266-7; ☎ 0xx21-2553-6030; Praia de Botafogo 242, 6th fl, Botafogo, Rio de Janeiro)

USA Manaus (☎ 0xx92-3611-3333; Franco de Sá 310, Adrianopolis); Recife (☎ 0xx81-3416-3050; Maia 163, Boa Vista); Rio de Janeiro (Map p263; ☎ 0xx21-3823-2000; Av Presidente Wilson 147, Centro)

Venezuela Boa Vista (☎ 0xx95-3623-9285; Av Benjamin Constant 968); Manaus (☎ 0xx92-3233-6006; Río Jataí 839); Rio de Janeiro (Map pp266-7; ☎ 0xx21-2554-6134; Praia de Botafogo 242, 5th fl, Botafogo)

FESTIVALS & EVENTS

Festa de Iemanjá (Festival of Iemanjá) Celebrated in Rio on January 1 and in Salvador on February 2.

Procissão do Senhor Bom Jesus dos Navegantes Procession of the Lord Jesus of Boatmen. In Salvador, Bahia on New Year's Day.

Lavagem do Bonfim (Washing of Bonfim church) Second Thursday in January. A Candomblé festival culminating in the ritual cleansing of Bonfim church in Salvador, Bahia.

Carnaval Friday to Tuesday preceding Ash Wednesday. Carnaval celebrations usually start well before the official holiday.

Semana Santa (Holy Week) The week before Easter. Festival in Congonhas, Ouro Prêto, Goiás Velho.

Festas Juninas (June Festivals) Throughout June. Celebrated throughout in Rio state and much of the rest of the country.

Carnatal (Carnaval in Natal) First week of December. Natal's answer to Brazil's big celebration comes in December (Natalese simply can't wait for the *other* Carnaval).

FOOD & DRINK

Eating reviews throughout this chapter are given in order of budget, with the least expensive options first.

Brazilian Cuisine

Brazilian restaurants serve huge portions, and many plates are designed for two – single travelers get hosed in these cases, as the bill runs 60% of the price for two when a portion for one is ordered. The basic Brazilian diet revolves around *arroz* (white rice), *feijão* (black beans) and *farofa/farinha* (flour from the root of manioc or corn). The typical Brazilian meal, called *prato feito* (set meal, often abbreviated 'pf') or *refeição*, consists of these ingredients plus either meat, chicken or fish and costs R$8 to R$10 in most eateries.

Another good option are *por kilo* (per kilogram) lunch buffets. Here, you pay by the weight of what you serve yourself: typically around R$30 per kilogram, with a big plateful weighing around half a kilo. Per-kilo places are good for vegetarians too. The fixed-price *rodízio* is another deal, and most *churrascarias* (meat BBQ restaurants) offer *rodízio* dining, where they bring endless skewers of different meat to your table.

Overcharging and shortchanging are almost standard procedure. Check over your bill carefully.

There are regional differences in Brazilian cuisine. The *comida baiana* of the northeastern coast has a distinct African flavor, using peppers, spices and the potent oil of the *dendê* palm tree. Both the Pantanal and the Amazon region have some tasty varieties of fish. Rio Grande do Sul's *comida gaúcha* features much meat. Minas Gerais is legendary for its hearty, vein-clogging fare, often involving chicken and pork (Brazilians also say any dish in Brazil tastes better in Minas); while São Paulo, home to large populations of Italians, Japanese and Arab immigrants, is Brazil's food mecca.

Common Brazilian dishes include the following:

açaí (a·sa·*ee*) – an Amazonian fruit with a berrylike taste and deep purple color; frozen and ground up, it makes a great, sorbet-like dish to which you can add granola, ginseng, honey etc

acarajé (a·ka·ra·*zhe*) – *baianas* (Bahian women) traditionally sell this on street corners throughout Bahia; it's made from peeled brown beans, mashed in salt and onions, and then fried in *dendê* (palm) oil; inside is *vatapá*, dried shrimp, pepper and tomato sauce

bobó de camarão (bo·*bo* de ka·ma·*rowng*) – manioc paste cooked and flavored with dried shrimp, coconut milk and cashews

caldeirada (kow·day·*ra*·da) – stew with big chunks of fish, onions and tomato

carne do sol (*kar*·ne de sol) – tasty salted beef, grilled and served with beans, rice and vegetables

casquinha de caranguejo/siri (kas·*kee*·nya de ka·rang·ge·*zho/see*·ree) – stuffed crab, prepared with manioc flour

dourado (do·*raa*·do) – scrumptious catfish found throughout Brazil

farofa (fa·*ro*·fa) – manioc or corn flour gently toasted and mixed with bits of onion, egg or bacon; it's a common condiment

feijoada (fay·zho·*a*·da) – Brazil's national dish, this pork stew is served with rice and a bowl of beans, and is traditionally eaten for Saturday lunch. It goes well with *caipirinhas*

frango a passarinho (*frang*·go a pa·sa·*ree*·nyo) – small chunks of crisp fried chicken make a delicious *tira-gosto* (appetizer or snack)

moqueca (mo·*ke*·ka) – stew flavored with *dendê* (Baiana) or olive (capixaba) oil and coconut milk, often with peppers and onions; the Portuguese word also refers to a style of covered clay-pot cooking from Bahia: fish, shrimp, oyster, crab or a combination can all be done *moqueca*-style

BRAZIL

pão de queijo (powng de *kay*·zho) – famous in Minas Gerais but available everywhere, this cheese bread is a classic snack and a great accompaniment to coffee

pato no tucupi (*pa*·to no too·koo·*pee*) – very popular in Pará, this roast duck dish is flavored with garlic and cooked in the *tucupi* sauce made from manioc juice and *jambu,* a local vegetable

peixada (pay·*sha*·da) – fish cooked in broth with vegetables and eggs

picanha (pee·*ka*·nya) – Brazil's most celebrated cut of meat, somewhat inaccurately translated as rump steak

tacacá (ta·ka·*ka*) – indigenous dish made of dried shrimp cooked with pepper, *jambu,* manioc and much more

tucunaré (too·koo·na·*ray*) – tender, tasty Amazonian fish

vatapá (va·ta·*pa*) – perhaps the most famous Brazilian dish of African origin, a seafood dish with a thick sauce made from manioc paste, coconut and *dendê* oil

Drinks

The incredible variety of Brazilian fruits makes for some divine *sucos* (juices). Every town has plenty of juice bars, offering 30 or 40 different varieties at around R$4 to R$6 for a good-sized glass.

Cafezinho puro (coffee), as typically drunk in Brazil, is strong, hot and sometimes sweet, usually served without milk *(leite)*. *Refrigerantes* (soft drinks) are found everywhere. *Guaraná,* made from the fruit of an Amazonian plant, is as popular as Coke.

The two key alcoholic drinks in Brazil are *cachaça* (also called *pinga*), a high-proof sugarcane spirit, and *cerveja* (beer). *Cachaça* ranges from excrementally raw to tolerably smooth, and is the basis of that celebrated Brazilian cocktail the *caipirinha,* a laborious and wickedly sweet concoction of the former along with crushed limes and sugar – few beach drinks go down sweeter. Of the common beer brands, Bohemia and Original are generally the best. *Chope* (*shoh*·pee) is draft beer and stands pretty much at the pinnacle of Brazilian civilization. Don't whine about the head – it's considered an indicator of quality. Key phrase: '*Mais um chope!*' (Another beer!).

GAY & LESBIAN TRAVELERS

Although gay characters have begun appearing on *novelas* (soap operas), mainstream Brazil is still homophobic. Machismo dominates and being out is difficult here. Rio and São Paulo have the best gay scenes, though you'll find good gay bars in Salvador and elsewhere. These are all-welcome affairs attended by GLS *(Gays, Lesbians e Simpatizantes)* crowds of straights and gays. An excellent gay travel and excursions agency is **Rio G** (☎ 0xx21-3813-0003; www.riog.com.br; Prudente de Morais 167 C, Ipanema). Useful websites for gay and lesbian travelers are www.riogayguide.com and www.pridelinks.com/Regional/Brazil.

HEALTH

A yellow-fever vaccination certificate is required for travelers who, within three months of arriving in Brazil (or applying for a Brazilian visa), have been in Bolivia, Colombia, Ecuador, French Guiana, Panama, Peru, Venezuela or many African countries. The list of countries can vary, so check with a Brazilian consulate. At most Brazilian borders and major airports there are vaccination posts where you can have the jab (free for foreigners) and get the certificate immediately. But it's wise to do this in advance.

Malaria is a concern in certain areas of the Amazon. Travelers should consider an appropriate malaria preventative, such as mefloquine or doxycycline (chloroquine is inadequate here), and cover up as much as possible to prevent mosquito bites. Brazil has become the epicenter of mosquito-borne Dengue Fever in Latin America, especially in and around Rio and in Bahía. If you are in an area where mosquitoes are biting during the day, you are at risk and should consider repellent.

Tap water is safe but not very tasty in most urban areas. In remote areas, filter your own or stick to bottled water.

The sun is powerful here and travelers should be mindful of heatstroke, dehydration and sunburn. Drink plenty of water, wear a strong sunscreen and allow your body time to acclimatize to high temperatures before attempting strenuous activities. A good drink when dehydrated is *agua de coco* (coconut water), which contains electrolytes.

See the Health chapter (p1011) for more information.

HOLIDAYS

Brazil's high season runs from December until Carnaval (usually February). Low season runs from March to November.

Ano Novo (New Year's Day) January 1

Carnaval (Friday to Tuesday preceding Ash Wednesday) February/March. Carnaval celebrations usually start well before the official holiday.

Paixão & Páscoa (Good Friday & Easter Sunday) March/April
Tiradentes (Tiradentes Day) April 21
Dia do Trabalho (May Day/Labor Day) May 1
Corpus Christi (60 days after Easter) Sunday May/June
Dia da Independência (Independence Day) September 7
Dia da Nossa Senhora de Aparecida (Day of Our Lady of Aparecida) October 12
Finados (All Souls' Day) November 2
Proclamação da República (Proclamation of the Republic Day) November 15
Natal (Christmas Day) December 25

INTERNET ACCESS

Internet cafes are widespread in Brazil. Charges are about R$4 to R$8 per hour.

INTERNET RESOURCES

Brazilian Embassy in London (www.brazil.org.uk) Has much practical info for tourists and links to local tourism sites in Brazil.

Brazil Max (www.brazilmax.com) This nicely designed site has features on travel, culture and society in Brazil; decent selection of articles and links.

Brazzil (www.brazzil.com) Features in-depth articles on the country's politics, economy, literature, arts and culture.

Gringoes (www.gringoes.com) Expat takes on everything from politics to travel as well as gringo meet-up info.

The Gringo Times (www.thegringotimes.com) Rio-centric and national news and culture in English.

Terra (www.terra.com.br/turismo) Portuguese-language travel site with up-to-date info on entertainment, nightlife and dining options in dozens of cities around Brazil.

LANGUAGE

Portuguese is generally considered the world's sixth most spoken language. Brazilian Portuguese has many differences from European Portuguese, but speakers can understand one another in most cases. This is not the case with Spanish – if you can speak Spanish, you'll be able to read some Portuguese but comprehending others is difficult. Some Brazilians also find it a tad offensive when foreigners arrive speaking Spanish and expect to be understood. See also the Language chapter (p1020) and pick up a copy of Lonely Planet's *Brazilian Portuguese* phrasebook to get you talking.

LEGAL MATTERS

Be wary of (but of course respectful to) Brazilian police. Some allegedly plant drugs and sting gringos for bribes, though this happens less than in other South American countries.

Stiff penalties are in force for use and possession of drugs; the police don't share most Brazilians' tolerant attitude toward marijuana. Police checkpoints along the highways stop cars at random. Don't even think about drinking and driving – Brazil introduced a zero-tolerance law in 2008. Police along the coastal drive between São Paulo and Búzios are notorious for hassling young people and foreigners. Border areas are also dangerous.

A large amount of cocaine is smuggled out of Bolivia and Peru through Brazil. If you're entering Brazil from one of the Andean countries and have been chewing coca leaves, be careful to clean out your pack first.

MAPS

The best maps in Brazil are the *Quatro Rodas* series. These good regional maps (Norte, Nordeste etc) sell for around R$9.99; they also publish the *Atlas Rodoviário* road atlas, useful if you're driving, as well as excellent street atlases for the main cities.

Good topographical maps are published by the IBGE, the government geographical service, and the DSG, the army geographical service. Availability is erratic, but IBGE offices in most state capitals sell IBGE maps. Office locations can be found on the IBGE website (www.ibge.gov.br).

MEDIA

Newspapers & Magazines

The weekly Portuguese-language *Veja* is a current-affairs magazine modeled on *Time*. In seven or eight major cities it comes with *Vejinha*, a good localized edition for info on local music, arts and nightclub scenes. The *Folha de São Paulo* and Rio's *Jornal do Brasil* newspapers have good national coverage and a socially liberal stance. *O Estado de São Paulo* and Rio's *O Globo* are a little more comprehensive in their coverage and more right wing.

TV

Brazilian TV consists mostly of game shows, football matches, *Big Brother*, tabloid crime shows, bad American films dubbed into Portuguese and the universally watched *novelas* (soap operas). Globo is the major Brazilian network.

MONEY

Brazil's currency is the real (pronounced 'hay-ow,' often written R$); the plural is *reais* (pronounced 'hay-*ice*'). One real is made up of 100 *centavos*. Banknotes come in denominations 2, 5, 10, 20, 50 and 100.

ATMs

ATMs are the easiest way of getting cash in big cities in Brazil and are widely available, but these are often finicky with foreign cards. Do yourself a favor and bring a few options, then find a bank that works with one of your cards and stick with it. Four-digit PINs are standard. In general, Citibank, HSBC, Banco de Brasil, Bradesco and Banco24Horas (a conglomeration of Brazilian banks) are the best ATMs to try, though in reality only certain branches cater to foreign cards. Look for stickers on the machines that say Cirrus, Visa or whatever system your card uses – though be warned that this hardly guarantees success.

Credit Cards

You can use credit cards to pay for many purchases in Brazil and to make cash withdrawals from ATMs. Visa is the most commonly accepted card, followed by MasterCard. American Express and Diners Club cards are also useful, though far less accepted outside major metropolitan areas. Credit-card and ATM fraud is widespread here. Keep your card in sight at all times, especially in restaurants.

Exchanging Money

Cash and traveler's checks, in US dollars, can be exchanged in *casas de cambio* (exchange offices) or some banks, which give better exchange rates but are much slower (Citibank does not charge a commission). You'll usually get a 1% or 2% better exchange rate for cash than for traveler's checks.

EXCHANGE RATES

Country	Unit	R$
Australia	A$1	1.55
Canada	C$1	1.64
euro zone	€1	2.59
Japan	¥100	1.97
New Zealand	NZ$1	1.29
UK	UK£1	2.81
USA	US$1	1.76

POST

A postcard or letter weighing up to 21g costs around R$1.21 to foreign destinations. Airmail letters to the USA and Europe arrive in one to two weeks. The *posta-restante* system functions reasonably well. Post offices hold mail for 30 days.

RESPONSIBLE TRAVEL

We all have an obligation to protect Brazil's fragile environment. You can do your bit by using environmentally friendly tourism services wherever possible and avoiding those that aren't proactively taking steps to avoid ecological damage (this includes Pantanal operators that encourage touching of animals).

Using the services of local community groups will ensure that your money goes directly to those who are helping you, as does buying crafts and other products directly from the artisans or from their trusted representatives.

SHOPPING

CDs, local crafts (indigenous and otherwise) and artwork all make good souvenirs.

Air-conditioned shopping malls *(shoppings)* feature in every self-respecting city and often contain decent music stores (and amazing food courts).

For genuine indigenous arts and crafts, have a look in the Artíndia stores of Funai (the government indigenous agency) and museum gift shops.

Artisans in the Northeast produce a rich assortment of artistic items. Salvador and nearby Cachoeira are most notable for their rough-hewn wood sculptures. Ceará specializes in fine lace. The interior of Pernambuco, in particular Caruaru, is famous for wildly imaginative ceramic figurines.

Candomblé stores are a good source of curios, ranging from magical incense guaranteed to increase sexual allure, wisdom and health, to amulets and ceramic figurines of Afro-Brazilian gods.

STUDYING

It's easy but pricey to arrange Portuguese classes through branches of the IBEU (Instituto Brasil Estados Unidos), where Brazilians go to learn English. There will be one in every large city.

TELEPHONE
Domestic Calls

You can make domestic calls from normal card-pay telephones on the street (called *orelhãos*) and in telephone offices. The cards are sold in units from 20 to 75 and start around R$4 from vendors, newsstands and anywhere else advertising *cartões telefônicos*. The more units you buy, the better value.

Local calls (within the city you're in) cost only a few units. Just dial the number without any area code. To make a local collect call, dial ☎ 9090, then the number.

For calls to other cities, dial ☎ 0, then the code of your selected long-distance carrier, then the two digits representing the city, followed by the local number. You need to choose a long-distance carrier that covers both the place you are calling from and the place you're calling to. Carriers advertise their codes in areas where they're prominent, but you can usually use Embratel (code 21) or Telemar (code 31) as they cover the whole country.

To make an intercity collect call, dial ☎ 9 before the 0xx. A recorded message in Portuguese will ask you to say your name and where you're calling from, after the tone.

International Calls

Brazil's country code is ☎ 55. When calling internationally to Brazil, omit the initial 0xx of the area code.

International calls from Brazil cost 76¢ a minute to the USA, R$1.36 to Europe and R$1.45 to Australia.

The regular card-pay telephones found on the streets are of little use for international calls unless you have an international calling card or are calling collect. Most pay telephones are restricted to domestic calls, and even if they aren't, a 30-unit Brazilian phone card may last less than a minute internationally.

Without an international calling card, your best option is an internet cafe or a local call center *(posto telefônico)*.

For international *a cobrar* (collect) calls, you can get a Brazilian international operator by dialing ☎ 0800-703-2121 (Embratel).

Cell Phones

Celular (cell) phones have eight-digit numbers starting with an 8 or 9, and calls to them run through your phone card units much faster than calls to regular numbers. Mobiles have city codes like normal phone numbers, and if you're calling from another city you have to use them.

TOILETS

Public toilets are available at every bus station and airport; there's usually a small entrance fee of R$1 or so – sometimes more depending on what you need to do! Elsewhere public toilets are not common, though Brazilians are generally nice about letting you use facilities in restaurants and bars. As in other Latin American countries, toilet paper isn't flushed but placed in the smelly basket next to the toilet. Few of the country's bathrooms are wheelchair-accessible.

TOURIST INFORMATION

Tourist offices in Brazil are nearly all run by individual states or municipalities, and may be quite helpful or utterly useless depending upon who's behind the counter.

TRAVELERS WITH DISABILITIES

Unfortunately, disabled travelers don't have an easy time in Brazil. Rio de Janeiro is probably the most accessible city for disabled travelers. The streets and sidewalks along the main beaches have curb cuts and are wheelchair-accessible, but most other areas do not have cuts and many restaurants have entrance steps.

VISAS

See p1011 for details of required yellow-fever vaccinations.

Citizens of the US, Australia and Canada need a visa; citizens from the UK, France, Germany and New Zealand do not.

Tourist visas are valid for arrival in Brazil within 90 days of issue and then for a 90-day stay. The fee depends on your nationality and where you are applying; it's usually between US$20 and US$65, though US citizens are hit with a whopping US$130 bill. Plan ahead – processing times generally take 10 business days, sometimes less depending on nationality and consulate efficiency. You'll generally need to present one passport photograph, proof of onward travel and a valid passport.

People under 18 years of age who wish to travel to Brazil without a parent or legal guardian must have a notarized letter of

BRAZIL

authorization from the nontraveling parent/guardian or from a court. Such a letter must also be presented when applying for a visa, if one is required. Check with a Brazilian consulate well in advance about this.

Request a five-year visa over a 90-day – they are the same price, but the consulates love to issue the 90-day one so, if you decide to come back, you pay again.

For up-to-date information on visas check lonelyplanet.com and its links.

Entry/Exit Card

On entering Brazil, all tourists must fill out a *cartão de entrada/saida* (entry/exit card); immigration officials keep half, you keep the other. Don't lose this card! When you leave Brazil, the second half of the entry/exit card will be taken by immigration officials. If you don't have it, Brazilian law requires a payment of a lofty fine (around R$165) at Banco do Brasil, which may be far from your intended departure point. The bank will then give you a form to give to immigration officials when you leave the country (though many travelers have reported being waived on through with little hassle – best to report the loss to the Policía Federal immediately).

Most visitors can stay for 90 days, but if for some reason you receive fewer days, this will be written in the stamp in your passport.

Visa Extensions

Brazil's Policía Federal, who have offices in the state capitals and border towns, handle visa extensions. You must apply no less than five days before your entry/exit card or visa lapses. The convoluted process is as follows: fill out and print the form 'Requerimento de Prorrogação de Prazo (DPF 270)' under the 'Formulários para Estrangeiros' subheading under 'Serviços à Comunidade' from the Policía Federal website (www.dpf.gov.br); then fill out and print the 'GRU – Guia de Recolhimento da União' under a similar subheading, 'Serviços Prestados à Comunidade,' take it to Banco do Brasil and pay the R$67 fee; then head to the nearest Policía Federal office with all in hand as well as your passport and original entry card. When you go, dress nicely! Some Fed stations don't take kindly to people in shorts. Granting an extension seems to be pretty automatic, but they may ask to see a ticket out of the country and proof of sufficient funds; and sometimes they may not give you the full 90 days. If you get the maximum 90-day extension and then leave the country before the end of that period, you can't return until the full 90 days have elapsed.

VOLUNTEERING

Rio-based **Iko Poran** (☎ 0xx21-3852-2916; www .ikoporan.org) links the diverse talents of volunteers with needy organizations. Previous volunteers in Brazil have worked as dance, music, art and language instructors among other things. Iko Poran also provides housing for volunteers. The UK-based **Task Brasil** (www .taskbrasil.org.uk) is another laudable organization that places volunteers in Rio.

WOMEN TRAVELERS

In the cities of the Southeast and South, foreign women without traveling companions will scarcely be given a sideways glance. In the more traditional rural areas of the Northeast, blonde-haired and light-skinned women, especially those without male escorts, will certainly arouse curiosity.

Machismo is less overt in Brazil than in Spanish-speaking Latin America. Flirtation is a common form of communication, but it's generally regarded as innocent banter; no sense of insult, exploitation or serious intent should be assumed.

It's advisable to adapt what you wear to local norms. The brevity of Rio beach attire generally is not suitable for the streets of interior cities, for instance.

In the event of unwanted pregnancy or the risk thereof, most pharmacies in Brazil stock the morning-after pill *(a pílula do dia seguinte)*, which costs about R$20. Tampons and other sanitary items are widely available in most pharmacies, though you'll want to stock up before heading into rural areas.

WORKING

Brazil has high unemployment and tourists are not supposed to take jobs. However, it's not unusual for foreigners to find language-teaching work in the bigger cities, either in language schools or through private tutoring. The pay is not great but if you can work for three or four days a week you can live on it.

Chile

HIGHLIGHTS

- **Torres del Paine** (p484) Break a sweat trekking to these rugged spires lording above the Patagonian steppe.
- **Central Valley** (p399) Swirl, sniff and sip your way through Chile's best vineyards on a sunny wine-country retreat.
- **Valparaíso** (p400) Wander the steep passageways decked in urban art in the hills of this bohemian port.
- **Atacama Desert** (p421) Drink in the wild starscape above the driest desert in the world.
- **Off the Beaten Track** (p464) Encounter penguins, misty seascapes and mythical lore on the archipelago of Chiloé.
- **Best Journey** (see boxed texts, p473 and p461) Discover the luxuriant pace of life while riding through Patagonia's stunning back roads and river valleys.

FAST FACTS

- **Area:** 748,800 sq km land, 8150 sq km water, 6435km of coastline
- **Budget:** US$36 to US$55 a day
- **Capital:** Santiago
- **Costs:** dorm US$15 to US$18, set lunch US$6 to US$11, national park entrance fee free to US$28
- **Country code:** ☎ 56
- **Languages:** Spanish, Mapudungun, Rapanui
- **Money:** US$1 = CH$550 (Chilean pesos)
- **Population:** 16.8 million
- **Seasons:** high (December to February), low (March to November)
- **Time:** GMT minus four hours (minus three hours in summer)

TRAVEL HINTS

Order the *menú del día* (inexpensive set meal) instead of off the menu. Budget extra travel days in rural Patagonia, where infrequent transportation can strand you in towns a day or two.

OVERLAND ROUTES

Crossings include Tacna (Peru); Ollagüe and Colchane (Bolivia); and Paso Jama, Puente del Inca, San Martín de los Andes, Junín de los Andes, Villa La Angostura, Trevelin, Los Antiguos, Río Turbio and Río Gallegos (Argentina).

Spindly Chile stretches 4300km – over half the continent – from the driest desert in the world to massive glacial fields. Filling up the in-between are volcanoes, geysers, beaches, lakes, rivers, steppe and countless islands. Slenderness gives Chile the intimacy of a backyard (albeit one fenced between the Andes and the Pacific). What's on offer? Everything. With easy infrastructure, spectacular sights and hospitable hosts, the hardest part is choosing an itinerary. Consider the sweeping desert solitude, craggy Andean summits and the lush forests of the fjords. Rapa Nui (Easter Island) and the isolated Isla Robinson Crusoe offer extracontinental exploits. But don't forget that Chile is as much about character as it is setting. Its far-flung location fires the imagination and has been known to make poets out of barmen, dreamers out of presidents and friends out of strangers. A few wrong turns and detours and you too will be part of this tightly woven family who barbecues on Sunday. Don't forget to bring an extra bottle of red to the long, lazy dinners that await.

CURRENT EVENTS

When the world economic crisis spread to Latin America, Chile proved surprisingly resilient. You could even say it's been schooling the superpowers-that-be, with a national deficit that is almost nonexistent. As if expecting this rainy day, President Michelle Bachelet's administration had tucked away over 20 billion US dollars in copper earnings. So now Chile is weathering the bad times by investing in public works projects to boost employment and morale. In the meanwhile, Chile will weather the downturn in tourism well, with fewer crowds and some deals, though Región X is paying dearly for the health crisis that nearly collapsed its massive salmon industry. Presidential elections were to come at the end of 2009. Pundits were predicting change, since the Concertación, the ruling center-left coalition hoarding power since Pinochet's fall two decades ago, had grown stale and corrupt in the eyes of the public. The center-right Alianza por Chile was well positioned to grab power – voters were already leaning toward conservative candidate Sebastián Piñera, a wealthy businessman.

HISTORY
Early History
The discovery of a single 12,500-year-old footprint in Monte Verde, near Puerto Montt, marks Chile's earliest tangible roots. In the north, Aymara and Atacameño farmers and herders predated the Inca. Other early peoples include the El Molle and the Tiwanaku, who left their mark with geoglyphs; Chango fisher folk on the northern coast; and Diaguita who inhabited inland river valleys.

Shifting cultivators from the southern forests, the Mapuche were the only indigenous group to successfully hold off Inca domination.

Meanwhile the Cunco fished and farmed Chiloé and the mainland. In the south, groups such as Selk'nam and Yaghan long avoided contact with Europeans, who would eventually bring them to the brink of extinction.

Colonial Times
Conquistador Pedro de Valdivia and his men crossed the harsh Atacama Desert to found Santiago in the fertile Mapocho valley in 1541. They set up the famous *encomiendas:* forced labor systems exploiting the north's relatively large, sedentary population. In the south there was no such assimilation – the Mapuche fought European colonization for over three centuries. When the *encomiendas* lost value, agricultural haciendas or *fundos* (farms), run by South American–born Spanish took their place. These *latifundios* (estates) became the dominant force in Chilean society with many remaining intact into the 1960s.

Revolutionary Wars & the Early Republic
Spain's trade control over the Viceroy of Peru provoked discontent among the colonies. Independence movements swept South America, with Argentine José de San Martín liberating Santiago in 1818. Under San Martín's tutelage, Chilean Bernardo O'Higgins, the illegitimate son of an Irishman, became 'supreme director' of the Chilean republic.

O'Higgins dominated politics for five years after independence, decreeing political, social, religious and educational reforms, but landowners' objections to these egalitarian measures forced his resignation. Businessman Diego Portales, spokesman for landowners, became de facto dictator until his execution in 1837. His custom-drawn constitution centralized power in Santiago and established Catholicism as the state religion.

CHILE (NORTH)

0 ——— 150 km
0 ——— 90 miles

PERU
Lauca
Arica
Putre
Oruro
Paso Chungará
Colchane
Región I
IQUIQUE
BOLIVIA
20°S
Ollague
Rapa Nui (Easter Island)
Archipiélago Juan Fernández
SANTIAGO
PACIFIC OCEAN
Chuquicamata
Calama
Los Flamencos
San Pedro de Atacama
Paso Jama
Tropic of Capricorn
ANTOFAGASTA
Región II
Atacama Desert
25°S
PACIFIC OCEAN
Nevado Tres Cruces
Caldera
Bahía Inglesa
COPIAPÓ
RN 40
Región III
Llanos de Challe
Vallenar
La Rioja
30°S
LA SERENA
Vicuña
Ovalle
RN 40
RN 38
Región IV
5
San Juan
RN 141
Región V
Paso Sistema Cristo Redentor
Viña del Mar
San Felipe
VALPARAÍSO
Portillo
Mendoza
La Campana
San Luis
To Isla Robinson Crusoe (670km)
Isla Negra
SANTIAGO
RN 7
Pichilemu
RANCAGUA
RN 143
Región VI
35°S
TALCA
Curicó
Región VII
Altos de Lircay
ARGENTINA
Chillán
CONCEPCIÓN
70°W

CHILE

Expansion & Development

Chile's expansion began with its triumph over Peru and Bolivia in the War of the Pacific (1879–83), which added the nitrate-rich Atacama Desert, and treaties with the Mapuche, which added the southern Lakes District. In 1888 Chile annexed remote Rapa Nui (Easter Island).

British, North American and German capital turned the Atacama into a bonanza; nitrate prosperity also funded the government. The nitrate ports of Antofagasta and Iquique boomed until the Panama Canal (1914) reduced traffic around Cape Horn and the development of petroleum-based fertilizers made mineral nitrates obsolete.

Mining also created a new working class and a class of nouveau riche, both of whom challenged the landowners. Elected in 1886, President José Manuel Balmaceda tackled the dilemma of unequally distributed wealth and power, igniting congressional rebellion in 1890 and a civil war that resulted in 10,000 deaths, including his own suicide.

The Struggle to Form & Reform

As late as the 1920s, up to 75% of Chile's rural population still depended on haciendas, which controlled 80% of prime agricultural land. As industry expanded and public works advanced, urban workers' welfare improved, but that of rural workers declined, forcing day laborers to the cities. The period from 1930 to 1970 saw a multifaceted struggle for agrarian reform.

During this period, the copper mines, a future cornerstone of Chile's economy, were North American–run. Elected in 1964, reformist president Eduardo Frei advocated the 'Chileanization' of the industry, giving government 50% ownership of US-controlled mines.

Too reformist for the right and too conservative for the left, Frei's Christian Democratic administration faced many challenges, including from violent groups like MIR (the Leftist Revolutionary Movement), which found support among coal miners and urban laborers. Activism also caught on with peasants who agitated for land reform. As the 1970 election grew near, the Christian Democratic Party, unable to satisfy society's expectations for reform, grew weaker.

Allende Comes to Power

Socialist candidate Salvador Allende's Unidad Popular (Popular Unity or UP) coalition offered a radical program advocating nationalization of industry and the expropriation of *latifundios*. Elected in 1970 by a small margin, Allende instituted state control of many private enterprises, creating massive income redistribution. Frustrated with slow

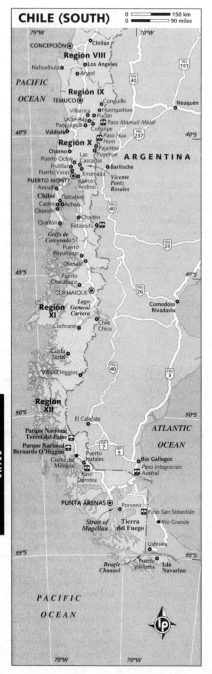

CHILE (SOUTH)

reforms, peasants seized land and the country became increasingly unstable. Declining harvests, nationalization and the courting of Cuba provoked US hostility and meddling. By 1972 Chile was paralyzed by the strikes supported by the Christian Democrats and the National Party.

After a failed military coup in June 1973, opposition gathered force and a *golpe de estado* by relative unknown General Augusto Pinochet took place on September 11, 1973. The coup resulted in the death of Allende (an apparent suicide) and thousands of his supporters. Thousands of leftists, suspected leftists and sympathizers were apprehended. In Santiago's National Stadium, many detainees suffered beatings, torture and execution. Hundreds of thousands went into exile.

The Pinochet Dictatorship

From 1973 to 1989, General Pinochet headed a durable junta that dissolved congress, prohibited nearly all political activity and ruled by decree. In 1980, voters supported a new constitution that ratified Pinochet's presidency until 1989. Progress came in the form of a stabilized and prosperous economy. Nonetheless, voters rejected Pinochet's 1988 bid to extend his presidency until 1997. In 1989, 17 parties formed the coalition Concertación para la Democracia (Consensus for Democracy), whose candidate Patricio Aylwin easily won. Aylwin's presidency suffered the constraints of the new constitution, but it did see the publication of the Rettig report, which documented thousands of deaths and disappearances during the Pinochet dictatorship.

In September 1998 General Pinochet was put under house arrest in London following investigation of the deaths and disappearances of Spanish citizens in the 1973 coup aftermath. Despite international uproar, both the Court of Appeals (in 2000) and the Supreme Court (2002) ruled him unfit to stand trial. Pinochet returned to Chile, where he died in 2006. His legacy remains extremely controversial among Chileans.

Resetting the Compass

The 21st century governments across South America became increasingly left-leaning, In Chile the trend resulted in the 2000 election of moderate leftist Ricardo Lagos, followed by his 2005 successor, Michelle Bachelet.

A watershed event, it marked Chile's first woman president, a single mother who had been detained and tortured under the Pinochet regime. Suddenly, conservative Chile looked a lot more progressive.

Unfortunately, the Bachelet presidency has been plagued by divisions within her coalition (La Concertación Democrática), which have made pushing through reforms difficult. Emerging crises like the chaotic institution of a new transportation system in Santiago, corruption scandals and massive student protests have made her tenure a difficult one. However, Chile's stability during the 2009 world financial crisis (due to the government reserves from copper exports) has been a tremendous boost.

After nearly two decades of a left-leaning government, Chileans are looking to the right for change.

THE CULTURE
The National Psyche

An 'island' between the Andes and the sea, Chile's isolation may have characterized its infancy, but recent times have brought a tsunami of outside influence. The internet, shopping malls, and Direct TV have radically recalibrated the tastes and social norms in even the most rural outposts of this once superconservative society. Chileans are known for compliance and passive political attitudes, yet this tendency is shifting. Many see new social changes as a Generation Y and Z impetus: the first generations to grow up without the censorship, curfew or restrictions of the Pinochet dictatorship. Chileans typically impress visitors with renowned hospitality, helpfulness, genuine curiosity and heartfelt eagerness to make travelers feel at home.

Lifestyle

Travelers crossing over from Peru or Bolivia may wonder where the stereotypical 'South America' went. Chilean lifestyle superficially resembles its European counterparts. There is a yawning gulf between highest and lowest incomes in Chile, and therefore a dramatic gap between living standards and an exaggerated class consciousness.

The average Chilean focuses energy on family, home and work. Chileans usually remain dependent on their parents through university years and live at home until marriage. Independence is less valued than family unity and togetherness. Regardless, single motherhood is not uncommon.

Women, while underrepresented in the workforce, are respected as professionals. For gays and lesbians, Chile is still quite a conservative culture with little public support for alternate lifestyles. Adults dress conservatively, leaning toward business formal, and their initial regard toward you will depend on your appearance.

Population

Over a third of Chile's 16.6 million inhabitants live in the capital of Santiago and its suburbs and more than 85% of the population lives in cities. In Patagonia, the person-per-square-kilometer ratio in Aisén is one to one, in the Región Metropolitana the ratio is closer to 400 to one. While most Chileans have Spanish ancestry mixed with indigenous groups, other major immigrant groups include Germans, British, Irish, French, Italians, Croatians and Palestinians. Indigenous groups include the Mapuche, 4% of the population largely based in La Araucanía, the Rapa Nui on Easter Island and Aymara and Atacameño peoples in the north.

SPORTS

Fútbol (soccer) is the most rabidly popular spectator sport, but tennis has gained ground, thanks to Nicolás Massú and Fernando Gonzáles being awarded Olympic gold medals in 2004, and Massú's silver medal in 2008. Having the perfect natural environment for it, most young Chileans who can afford it go big on individual sports like surfing, skiing and windsurfing. Chilean rodeos proliferate in the summer, when flamboyantly dressed *huasos* (cowboys) compete in half-moon stadiums.

RELIGION

About 70% of Chileans are Catholic, with Evangelical Protestantism gaining ground with 15% of the population and 8% without any religious affiliation.

ARTS
Literature

This land of poets earned its repute with Nobel Prize winners Gabriela Mistral and Pablo Neruda. Vicente Huidobro is considered one of the founders of modern Spanish-language poetry and Nicanor Parra continues the tradition.

CHILE

Chile's best known export, contemporary writer Isabel Allende bases much of her fiction in her native country, although like playwright-novelist-essayist Ariel Dorfman, she lives in the USA. Other key literary figures include José Donoso, whose novel *Curfew* narrates life under dictatorship through the eyes of a returned exile, and Antonio Skármeta, who wrote the novel *Burning Patience,* upon which the award-winning Italian film *Il Postino* (The Postman) is based. Jorge Edwards (1931–) was a collaborator and contemporary of Neruda, writing the acclaimed tribute *Goodbye, Poet.* Luis Sepúlveda (1949–) has made outstanding contributions such as *Patagonia Express* and the novella *The Old Man Who Read Love Stories.*

Marcela Serrano (1951–) is praised as the best of current Latina authors. Pedro Lemebel (1950–) writes of homosexuality, transgender issues and other controversial subjects with top-notch shock value. Worldwide, Roberto Bolaño's (1955–2005) is acclaimed as one of Latin America's best. The posthumous publication of his encyclopedic *2666* seals his cult-hero status. Alberto Fuguet (1964–) launched the McOndo movement with *Mala onda* (Bad Vibes), which discusses Latin American magic realism, presenting the disconnected reality of urban youth in a consumer culture. Fuget has since become a screenwriter and director.

Cinema

Chilean cinema has proved dynamic and diverse in recent years. Addressing class stratification, Sebastián Silva's *La nana* (The Maid) won two Sundance awards in 2009. Twenty-something director Nicolás López uses dark humor and comic-book culture to the delight of youth audiences with *Promedio rojo* (2005). *Mi mejor enemigo* (My Best Enemy, 2004) tells of not-so-distant enemies in a 1978 territorial dispute with Argentina in Tierra del Fuego. Andrés Wood's hit *Machuca* (2004) chronicles coming-of-age during class-conscious and volatile 1973. Wood's *La fiebre del loco* (Loco Fever, 2001) shows the social folly of a small Patagonian fishing village during abalone harvest. *Sub Terra* (2003) dramatizes the exploitation of Chilean miners. Iconic of their time, *Taxi para tres* (Taxi for Three, 2001), by Orlando Lubbert, and Diego Izquierdo's *Sexo con amor* (Sex with Love, 2002) are worth a look. Acclaimed documentarian Patricio Guzmán explores the social impact of the dictatorship; his credits include the fascinating *Obstinate Memory* (1997). Chile's fabulous scenery has made it a dream location for foreign movies too; contemporary films shot here include *The Motorcycle Diaries* (2004) and the James Bond movie *Quantum of Solace* (2008), a sore issue for Chileans since it is really supposed to be Bolivia.

Music & Dance

Chile's contemporary music spans '60s revolutionary folk to modern rock and alt bands. La Nueva Canción Chilena (New Chilean Song) revitalized Chilean folk with social and political issues, as in Violeta Parra's 'Gracias a la vida' (Thanks to Life). The movement included Victor Jara (later murdered in the military coup) and the still-touring Inti-Illimani.

Groups in exile found success in Europe and abroad, such as Los Jaivas, Los Prisioneros and La Ley. Joe Vasconcellos created energetic Latin fusion. Contemporary bands grabbing domestic and international attention are La Ley, Lucybell, Tiro de Gracia, Los Bunkers, Javiera y los Imposibles and Mamma Soul. Look for the Strokes-like Teleradio Donoso and Chico Trujillio, whose *cumbia chilombiana* has a bit of Manu Chao and Mano Negra.

Bars showcase new bands of all stripes while reggaeton dominates the club scene. The only 'traditional' Chilean dance is *cueca,* performed every September 18.

ENVIRONMENT

Environmental folly may be the price paid for Chile's growing prosperity. In this resource-rich country, the most notable conflicts of its pro-business policies are mining projects like Pascua Lama and hydroelectric dams planned for ten major Patagonian rivers (including Chile's biggest, Río Baker). From Region VIII south, native forest continues to lose ground to plantations of fast-growing exotics, such as eucalyptus and Monterey pine. Native araucaria and *alerce* have declined precipitously over the past decades. Salmon farming in the south threatens to pollute both the freshwater and saltwater as well as endanger marine life. A 2007 *New York Times* report revealing widespread virus outbreaks in Chilean salmon and questionable aquaculture practices has rocked the industry, and inspired tighter government controls and monitoring of this annual US$2.2-billion industry. Another issue is the intensive use of agricultural chemicals and pesticides to promote Chile's fruit exports. In the north, mining and agricultural pesticides threaten the limited water supply. The growing hole in the ozone layer over Antarctica is such a concern that medical authorities recommend that those in Patagonia use protective clothing, sunglasses and heavy sunblock to avoid cancer-causing ultraviolet radiation.

The Land

Continental Chile stretches 4300km from Peru to the Strait of Magellan. Less than 200km wide on average, the land rises from sea level to above 6000m in some areas, pocked with volcanoes, and it has a narrow depression running through the middle.

Mainland Chile, dry-topped and glacial heavy, has distinct temperate and geographic zones, with the length of the Andes running alongside. Norte Grande runs from the Peruvian border to Chañaral, dominated by the Atacama Desert and the *altiplano* (Andean high plain). Norte Chico stretches from Chañaral to Río Aconcagua, with scrubland and denser forest enjoying increased rainfall. Here, mining gives way to agriculture in the major river valleys.

Middle Chile's wide river valleys span from Río Aconcagua to Concepción and the Río Biobío. This is the main agricultural and winegrowing region. The Araucania and Lakes District go south of the Biobío to Palena, featuring extensive native forests and lakes. Chiloé is the country's largest island, with dense forests and a patchwork of pasturelands. Patagonia has indeterminate borders: for some it begins with the Carretera Austral, for others it starts in rugged Aisén, running south to the Campos de Hielo (the continental ice fields), and ending in Magallanes and Tierra del Fuego.

The country is divided into fourteen numbered administrative regions, running north to south, with the exception of Región XIV, which recently broke off from the X Region.

Wildlife

Bounded by ocean, desert and mountain, Chile is home to a unique environment that developed much on its own, creating a number of endemic species.

In the desert north, candelabra cacti grow by absorbing water from the fog (*camanchaca*). Animals include guanaco (a large camelid), *vicuña* (found at high altitudes), and their domestic relatives llama and alpaca. The gangly ostrich-like rhea (called *ñandú* in Spanish) and the plump, scraggly-tailed vizcacha (a wild relative of the chinchilla) are other unusual creatures. Birdlife is diverse, from Andean gulls and giant coots to three species of flamingo.

Southern forests are famed for the monkey-puzzle tree (*pehuén*) and *alerce*, the world's second-oldest tree. Abundant plant life in Valdivian temperate rainforest includes the *nalca*, the world's largest herbaceous plant. Puma roam the Andes, along with a dwindling population of *huemul* (Andean deer) in the south. The diminutive *pudú* deer inhabits thick forests, *bandurrias* (buff-necked ibis) frequent southern pastures and *chucao* tweet trailside. A colony of Humboldt and Magellanic penguins seasonally inhabit the northwestern coast of Chiloé.

From the Lakes District to Magallanes, you'll find verdant upland forests of the widespread genus *Nothofagus* – southern beech. Decreased rainfall on the eastern plains of Magallanes and Tierra del Fuego creates extensive grasslands. Protected guanaco have made a comeback within Torres del Paine and Punta Arenas hosts colonies of Magellanic penguins and cormorants. Chile's long coastline features diverse marine mammals, including sea lions, otters, fur seals and whales.

NORTHERN BORDER CROSSINGS

For road conditions, border-area **carabineros** (police; ☎ 133) are good resources. For Peru, Arica to Tacna is the only land crossing. Connections between Chile and Bolivia have improved, but many of these routes are long, arduous trips. The following crossings are most accessible.

Arica to La Paz Highway completely paved, goes through Parque Nacional Lauca, many buses, hitchhiking is feasible.

Calama to Ollagüe Eight-hour train ride with connections to Oruro and La Paz.

Iquique to Oruro Goes via Colchane/Pisiga; highway almost all paved, regular buses, passes by Parque Nacional Volcán Isluga; keep an eye out for wildlife.

San Pedro de Atacama to Uyuni Popular 4WD tour.

National Parks

Parklands comprise 19% of Chile, a nice number until you realize that some of these 'protected' areas allow logging and dams. Though tenuous and fragile, these wild places are some of the most stunning and diverse landscapes on the continent. In terms of visitors, Chilean parks are considerably underutilized, with the notable exception of Torres del Paine. Parks and reserves are administered by the underfunded Corporación Nacional Forestal, with an emphasis on forestry and land management, not tourism. Visit **Conaf** (Map pp392-3; ☎ 02-390-0282; www.conaf .cl; Av Bulnes 291) in Santiago for inexpensive maps and brochures.

Chile has around 133 private reserves, covering almost 4000 sq km. Highlights include Parque Pumalín in northern Patagonia and El Cañi, near Pucón (the country's first). Big projects in the works include Parque Tantauco on Chiloé and Valle Chacabuco – the future Patagonia National Park, near Cochrane.

Below are some popular and accessible national parks and reserves:

Alerce Andino (p464) Preserves stands of *alerce* trees near Puerto Montt.

Altos del Lircay (p416) A reserve with views of the Andean divide and a loop trek to Radal Siete Tazas.

Chiloé (p468) Features broad sandy beaches, lagoons and myth-bound forests.

Conguillío (p447) Mixed forests of araucaria, cypress and southern beech surrounding the active, snowcapped Volcán Llaima.

Huerquehue (p451) Near Pucón, hiking trails through araucaria forests, with outstanding views of Volcán Villarrica.

Lauca (p435) East of Arica, with active and dormant volcanoes, clear blue lakes, abundant birdlife, *altiplano* villages and extensive steppes.

Los Flamencos In and around San Pedro de Atacama, a reserve protecting salt lakes and high-altitude lagoons, flamingos, eerie desert landforms and hot springs.

Nahuelbuta (p444) In the high coastal range, preserves the area's largest remaining araucaria *(pehuén)* forests.

Nevado Tres Cruces (p416) East of Copiapó, with a 6330m-high namesake peak and 6900m-high Ojos del Salado.

Puyehue (p456) Near Osorno, with fancy hot springs and a family ski resort. Has a popular hike through volcanic desert, up the crater, to thermals and geyser fields.

Queulat (p477) Wild evergreen forest, mountains and glaciers stretch across 70km of the Carretera Austral.

Torres del Paine (p484) Chile's showpiece near Puerto Natales, with an excellent trail network around the country's most revered vistas.

Vicente Peréz Rosales (p460) Chile's second-oldest national park includes spectacular Lago Todos los Santos and Volcán Osorno.

Villarrica (p447) Volcán Villarrica's smoking symmetrical cone attracts trekkers, snowboarders and skiers.

TRANSPORTATION

GETTING THERE & AWAY

Air

Santiago's **Aeropuerto Internacional Arturo Merino Benítez** (off Map pp388-9; ☎ 02-690-1752; www.aero puertosantiago.cl) is the main port of entry. Some regional airports have international service to neighboring countries. Only LAN flies to Rapa Nui (Easter Island). Taca and LAN have nonstop flights to/from Lima, Peru. LAB and LAN fly to/from La Paz, Santa Cruz and Cochabamba (all in Bolivia). Taca and Avianca link Santiago with Bogotá, Colombia. Varig and TAM fly to Brazilian and Paraguayan destinations. LAN flies to Montevideo, Uruguay. Aerolíneas Argentinas and LAN often have internet specials from Santiago to Buenos Aires. European airlines pick up passengers in Buenos Aires before going long-haul and offer competitive fares. DAP Airlines flies between major destinations in Southern Patagonia.

Bus

Except in far southern Patagonia and Tierra del Fuego, travel to Argentina involves crossing the Andes. Some passes close in winter. Crossings in the Lakes District and Patagonia are very popular, especially in summer months, so booking early and confirming reservations is advised.

DEPARTURE TAX & ARRIVAL FEES

Chilean departure tax for international flights of under/over 500km is US$8/26 or its equivalent in local currency.

Note that *arriving* US air passengers pay a one-time fee of US$132, valid for the life of the passport. Reciprocity fees are also applied to Australians (US$56) and Canadians (US$132). This must be paid in cash and in US dollars. Officials collecting the fee most often won't have change; bring exact cash if possible. The fee is not charged to those entering overland.

CHILE

Chile Chico to Los Antiguos Frequent bus service.

Coyhaique to Comodoro Rivadavia Several weekly bus services, usually heavily booked, go through Río Mayo.

Futaleufú to Esquel Regular *colectivos* (taxis with fixed routes) service goes to the border, from where other transport is readily available.

Iquique, Calama and San Pedro de Atacama to Jujuy and Salta Paso de Jama (4200m) is most often used; Paso de Lago (4079m) is an excellent trip through little-visited *salar* (salt pans) country; book early.

Osorno to Bariloche Quickest land route in the Lakes District; frequent buses use Paso Cardenal Samoré, often called Pajaritos, year-round.

Puerto Montt and Puerto Varas to Bariloche Year-round, touristy bus-ferry combination tours.

Puerto Natales to El Calafate Many buses in summer; limited off-season.

Punta Arenas to Río Gallegos Many buses ply this six-hour route daily.

Punta Arenas to Tierra del Fuego Two-and-a-half-hour ferry ride to Porvenir, with two buses weekly to Río Grande, connecting to Ushuaia; direct buses via Primera Angostura.

Santiago to Mendoza Tons of options crossing Libertadores; *colectivos* cost more, but are faster.

Temuco to San Martín de los Andes Very popular route with regular summer buses using the Mamuil Malal pass (Paso Tromen to Argentines).

Temuco to Zapala and Neuquén Regular but thin bus service via Pino Hachado (1884m); Icaima (1298m) is an alternative.

Valdivia to San Martín de los Andes Bus-ferry combination crosses Lago Pirehueico to Paso Hua Hum, from where buses continue to San Martín de los Andes.

GETTING AROUND
Air

LAN (☎ 600-526-2000; www.lan.com) and **Sky** (☎ 600-600-2828; www.skyairline.cl) provide domestic flights. Weekly website specials released Tuesdays can shave off up to 40% on last-minute fares with LAN. Air taxis in the south link more inaccessible regions but do not insure passengers. Their weight limit for carry-on items can be as low as 10kg, with hefty charges for extra baggage.

Boat

Passenger/car ferries and catamarans connect Puerto Montt with points along the Carretera Austral, including Caleta Gonzalo (Chaitén) and Coyhaique, and also connect Quellón and Castro, Chiloé to Chaitén. Ferries from Hornopirén to Caleta Gonzalo only run in summer. Ferries to Caleta Gonzalo and

---

GETTING TO ARGENTINA

Crossing the border into Argentina is easy. Buses with international routes simply cross – no changing, no fees. Border outposts are open daylight hours, although a few long-haul buses cross at night. Dorotea (near Puerto Natales) is open 24 hours in summer. Bring your tourist card and passport. Leave that bunch of bananas back at the hostel – food's a no-no. For crossing from Argentina, see p47.

Chaitén may have interrupted service due to the activity of Volcán Chaitén.

A highlight is the trip from Puerto Montt to Puerto Natales on board Navimag's *Evangelistas*. Book with **Navimag** (off Map pp388-9; ☎ 02-442-3120; www.navimag.com; Av El Bosque Norte 0440, Santiago) far in advance. This is a cargo vessel outfitted for tourism, not a cruise ship. The cheapest beds (recliner chairs) share few bathrooms and are vulnerable to tossing waves. Meals are passable; vegetarians should give notice when booking. Pack motion-sickness remedies, snacks and drinks, which are expensive at the bar.

Known as the Cruce de Lagos (p460), a 12-hour scenic boat/bus combination travels between Petrohué, Chile and Bariloche, Argentina.

Bus

The Chilean bus system is fabulous. Tons of companies vie for customers with *ofertas* (seasonal promotions), discounts and added luxuries like movies. Long-distance buses are comfortable, fast and punctual with safe luggage holds. They usually have toilets and either serve meals or make regular food stops. Book ahead on popular long-distance routes in the summer and near major holidays. Tur Bus discounts tickets purchased online.

Car & Motorcycle

Having wheels gets you to remote national parks and most places off the beaten track. This is especially true in the Atacama Desert, Carretera Austral and Rapa Nui (Easter Island). Security problems are minor, but always lock your vehicle and remove valuables. Santiago and its surroundings frequently restrict private vehicle use to alleviate smog.

CHILE

Hitchhiking

Thumbing a ride is common practice in Chile. However, a major drawback is that vehicles are often packed with families, and a wait for a lift can be long. Traffic is sparse in Patagonia and the Atacama, so always carry warm clothes and provisions. Note that Lonely Planet doesn't recommend hitchhiking.

Local Transportation

Towns and cities have taxis, which are metered or have set fees for destinations. Confirm the price ahead. *Colectivos* are taxis with fixed routes marked on signs. Rates are about CH$400 per ride. *Micros* are city buses, clearly numbered and marked with their destination. Keep your ticket, it may be checked by an inspector. Santiago's quick and easy-to-use metro system connects the most visited neighborhoods.

Train

Train travel has fewer departures and is slower and more expensive than bus travel. **Empresa de Ferrocarriles del Estado** (EFE; ☎ 600-585-5000; www.efe.cl) runs a southbound passenger service from Santiago to Chillán, with many intermediate stops. Check the website for updates and information on shorter routes.

SANTIAGO

☎ 02 / pop 4,946,300

Santiago's postcard face is that of a modern metropolis poised under gargantuan snowtipped Andean peaks. Its courteous and orderly surface makes it the least intimidating of all South American capitals for travelers, but the city itself defies pinning down. It is a famously conservative culture which percolates into protests now and then. What is Santiago? Downtown has grit and commerce, Bellavista has trendy cafes and Barrio Brasil prides itself precisely on its lack of polish. For upscale, there's Providencia, Las Condes and the well-maintained suburbs beyond. Perhaps the most evasive face of the city is its lovely mountain backdrop, often obscured by a drapery of smog.

For visitors, Santiago is a quirky and safe city to explore and neighborhood personalities can be as distinct as grown siblings. People in the provinces are fond of saying, 'God is everywhere, but his office is in Santiago.' With over a third of the country's population, sometimes Santiago is Chile. But find out for yourself.

HISTORY

Founded by Pedro de Valdivia in 1541, Santiago's site was chosen for its moderate climate and strategic location for defense. It remained a small town until the nitrate boom in the 1880s. Gustave Eiffel designed its central station. In 1985 an earthquake shook down some of downtown's classic architecture. It's currently a major financial center for the continent and headquarters for multinationals like Yahoo!, Microsoft and JP Morgan.

ORIENTATION

'El Centro' is a compact, triangular area bounded by the Río Mapocho and Parque Forestal in the north, the Vía Norte Sur in the west, and Av General O'Higgins (the Alameda) in the south. Key public buildings cluster near the Plaza de Armas, which branches out into a busy graph of shopping arcades and pedestrian streets. North and east of the center is Barrio Bellavista, with Cerro San Cristóbal (Parque Metropolitano). To the west is Barrio Brasil, the bohemian enclave of the city. At the tip of this triangle and extending east are the wealthy *comunas* (sectors) of Providencia and Las Condes, accessed via the Alameda. Nuñoa is a residential neighborhood south of Providencia.

INFORMATION

Bookstores

Chile's 19% tax on books means high prices.
Books Secondhand (Montt, Av Providencia 1652, Providencia) The best selection of English paperbacks and some guidebooks.
Feria Chilena del Libro (Map pp392-3; Paseo Huérfanos 623) Santiago's best-stocked bookstore, some English paperbacks.

Cultural Centers

Instituto Chileno-Británico (Map pp392-3; ☎ 638-2156; www.britanico.cl; Miraflores 123)
Instituto Chileno-Norteamericano (Map pp392-3; ☎ 800-200-863; www.norteamericano.cl; Moneda 1467)

Emergency

Ambulance (☎ 131)
Fire Department (☎ 132)
Police (☎ 133)

Internet Access

All-hour internet cafes abound, charging from CH$400 to CH$800 per hour.

GETTING INTO TOWN

Aeropuerto Internacional Arturo Merino Benítez (☎ 601-9001) is in Pudahuel, 26km northwest of downtown Santiago. **TurBus Aeropuerto** (Map pp392-3; ☎ 607-9573; Moneda 1529) runs every 15 minutes between 6:30am and 9pm (CH$1500, 30 minutes). **Buses Centropuerto** (☎ 601-9883) provides a similar service (CH$1300) from Los Héroes metro station. With an airport counter, shuttles **Transvip** (☎ 677-3000; www.transvip.net) and TurBus Aeropuerto offer fixed-price taxis (from CH$11,000) and eight-seater minibuses (from CH$17,000), rates for Providencia and Las Condes are slightly higher. The main bus stations are right off the Alameda, close to metro stations.

Ciberplaza Express (Map pp388-9; Compañía 2143, Barrio Brasil; ☽ 9am-11pm Mon-Fri, to 10pm Sat)
Tecomp (☎ 333-0316; Holley 2334, Providencia; ☽ 9:30am-midnight Mon-Thu, 9:30am-1am Fri & Sat)

Laundry

Self-service isn't a concept here. Drop-off laundries charge about CH$3500 per load. Most hostels and hotels offer laundry service.
Lavandería Autoservicio (Map pp392-3; ☎ 632-1772; Monjitas 507, Centro)
Lavandería del Barrio (Map pp388-9; ☎ 673-3575; Huérfanos 1980, Barrio Brasil)

Left Luggage

All the main bus terminals have a *custodia*, ie a secure place where you can stash a bag for approximately US$2 per day. Another option is storing luggage for free at a reputable lodging.

Medical Services

Clínica Alemana de Santiago (off Map pp392-3; ☎ 210-1111; www.alemana.cl; Av Vitacura 5951, Vitacura) One of the best – and most expensive – private hospitals in town.
Hospital de Urgencia Asistencia Pública (Map pp392-3; ☎ 436-3800; Av Portugal 125, Centro; ☽ 24hr) Santiago's main emergency room.

Money

ATMs (Redbanc) are found throughout the city.
Cambios Afex (www.afex.cl; ☽ 9am-6pm Mon-Fri, 10am-2pm Sat); Centro (Map pp392-3; ☎ 688-1143; Agustinas 1050, Centro); Providencia (☎ 333-2097; Av Pedro de Valdivia 12, Providencia) Reliable exchange office.

Post

Main post office (Map pp392-3; ☎ 800-267-736; www.correos.cl; Catedral 987, Plaza de Armas;

☽ 8am-10pm Mon-Fri, to 6pm Sat) Also in the Centro at Moneda 1155 and in Providencia at Av Providencia 1466.

Tourist Information

Conaf (Map pp392-3; ☎ 390-0282; www.conaf.cl; Paseo Bulnes 291; ☽ 9:30am-5:30pm Mon-Thu, to 4:30pm Fri) Information on all of the parks and reserves, with some topographic maps to photocopy.
Municipal tourist office (Map pp392-3; ☎ 632-7783; www.municipalidaddesantiago.cl; Merced 860; ☽ 10am-6pm Mon-Thu, to 5pm Fri) Provides basic maps and information.
Sernatur (☎ 236-1416; www.sernatur.cl; Av Providencia 1550, Providencia; ☽ 8:45am-6:30pm Mon-Fri, 9am-2pm Sat) Gives out maps, brochures and advice, and can help reserve winery visits.

Travel Agencies

Sertur Student Flight Center (☎ 335-0395, 800-340-034; www.sertur.cl; Hernando de Aguirre 201, Oficina 401, Providencia) Bargains on air tickets.

DANGERS & ANNOYANCES

Santiago is relatively safe, but petty crime exists. Be on your guard around the Plaza de Armas, Mercado Central, Cerro Santa Lucía and Cerro San Cristóbal in particular. Look around you before whipping out a digital camera and avoid large, flashy jewelry. Organized groups of pickpockets sometimes target drinkers along Pío Nono in Bellavista, and Barrio Brasil's smaller streets can be dodgy after dark. As with any big city you are safer in a pair or group late at night. Also pesky is Santiago's smog, which can make your eyes burn and throat hurt.

SIGHTS
Museums

Most museums are free on Sunday and closed on Monday. Regular hours are usually from 10am to 6pm or 7pm from Tuesday to Saturday and 10am to 2pm Sunday. Unless otherwise noted, admission is CH$600.

SANTIAGO

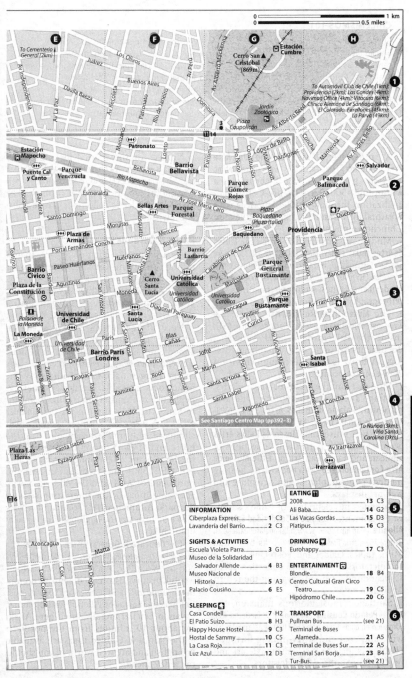

INFORMATION
Ciberplaza Express..................... **1** C3
Lavandería del Barrio.................. **2** C3

SIGHTS & ACTIVITIES
Escuela Violeta Parra................... **3** G1
Museo de la Solidaridad
  Salvador Allende..................... **4** B3
Museo Nacional de
  Historia................................... **5** A3
Palacio Cousiño......................... **6** E5

SLEEPING
Casa Condell............................... **7** H2
El Patio Suizo............................. **8** H3
Happy House Hostel.................. **9** C3
Hostal de Sammy...................... **10** C5
La Casa Roja.............................. **11** C3
Luz Azul.................................... **12** D3

EATING
2008... **13** C3
Ali Baba..................................... **14** G2
Las Vacas Gordas...................... **15** D3
Platipus..................................... **16** C3

DRINKING
Eurohappy................................. **17** C3

ENTERTAINMENT
Blondie...................................... **18** B4
Centro Cultural Gran Circo
  Teatro.................................... **19** C5
Hipódromo Chile....................... **20** C6

TRANSPORT
Pullman Bus......................... (see 21)
Terminal de Buses
  Alameda................................. **21** A5
Terminal de Buses Sur.............. **22** A5
Terminal San Borja.................... **23** B4
Tur-Bus................................. (see 21)

CHILE

CHILENISMOS 101

Chilean Spanish fell off the wagon: it is slurred, sing-song and peppered with expressions un-intelligible to the rest of the Spanish-speaking world. *¿Cachay?* (you get it?) often punctuates a sentence, as does the ubiquitous *pues*, said as '*po*.' '*Sípo*,' all clattered together actually means, 'well, yes.' Country lingo is firmly seeded in this former agrarian society who refer to guys as *cabros* (goats), complain '*es un cacho*' ('it's a horn,' meaning a sticking point) and go to the *carrete* to *carretear* ('wagon,' meaning party/to party). Lovers of lingo should check out John Brennan's *How to Survive in the Chilean Jungle,* available in Santiago's English-language bookstores (see p386). *¿Cachay?*

A must-see, **Museo Chileno de Arte Precolombino** (Map pp392-3; www.precolombino.cl; Bandera 361; admission CH$3000) chronicles a whopping 4500 years of pre-Columbian civilization throughout the Americas with breathtaking ceramics, gorgeous textiles and Chinchorro mummies.

Modern art fans shouldn't miss the **Museo de Artes Visuales** (MAVI; Map pp392-3; ☎ 638-3502; www.mavi.cl; Lastarria 307, Plaza Mulato Gil de Castro, Centro; admission CH$1000; ☽ closed Feb), with top-notch modern engravings, sculptures, paintings and photography in a stunning setting.

The **Museo Histórico Nacional** (Map pp392-3; www.museohistoriconacional.cl; Plaza de Armas 951), inside the Palacio de la Real Audencia, documents colonial and republican history. A draw is the interesting exhibit on 20th-century politics.

Modeled on the Petit Palais in Paris, Santiago's early-20th-century fine-arts museum, **Palacio de Bellas Artes** (Map pp392-3; JM de la Barra), near Av José María Caro, houses two museums: **Museo de Bellas Artes** (www.mnba.cl), with permanent collections of Chilean and European art, and the **Museo de Arte Contemporáneo** (www.mac.uchile.cl), hosting modern photography, design, sculpture and web-art displays.

Founded in celebration of Chile's socialist experiment, **Museo de la Solidaridad Salvador Allende** (Map pp388-9; www.museodelasolidaridad.cl; Herrera 360, Barrio Brasil) houses works by Matta, Miró, Tapies, Calder and Yoko Ono. During the dictatorship the entire collection spent 17 years underground, awaiting the return of civilian rule.

Santiago's most glorious mansion, the 1871 **Palacio Cousiño** (Map pp388-9; Dieciocho 438; admission on guided tour only CH$2100) was made by wine and coal and silver-mining fortunes. Highlights include the French-style art and one of the country's first elevators.

Named for the snarled locks of Pablo Neruda's widow, **La Chascona** (Museo Neruda; Map pp392-3; Márquez de La Plata 0192; admission by tour only in Spanish, CH$2500, in English CH$3500) is his shiplike house with eclectic collections. There's also a lovely cafe.

Parks & Gardens

Once a hermitage, then a convent, then a military bastion, **Cerro Santa Lucía** (Map pp392–3) has offered respite from city chaos since 1875. At the southwest corner is the Terraza Neptuno, with fountains and curving staircases that lead to the summit.

North of the Río Mapocho, 870m **Cerro San Cristóbal** ('Tapahue' to the Mapuche) towers above Santiago and is the site of **Parque Metropolitano** (www.parquemetropolitano.cl), the capital's largest open space, with two swimming pools, a botanical garden, a somewhat neglected zoo and art museum. Beam up to San Cristóbal's summit via the **funicular** (CH$1400; ☽ 1-8pm Mon, 10am-8pm Tue-Sun), which climbs 485m from Plaza Caupolicán, at the north end of Pío Nono in Bellavista. From the Terraza, the 2000m-long *teleférico* (cable car; CH$2500) runs to a station near the north end of Av Pedro de Valdivia Norte, accessing most of the interesting sites in the park. A funicular/*teleférico* combo costs US$4 or firm up those glutes with a rocky uphill hike.

The **Cementerio General** (off Map pp388-9; ☎ 737-9469; www.cementeriogeneral.cl), at the northern end of Av La Paz, is a city of tombs with a woeful history lesson. A memorial honors the disappeared, and native sons José Manuel Balmaceda, Salvador Allende and diplomat Orlando Letelier are all buried here. Walk for about 10 minutes from the northern end of Línea 2. Guided tours are available in English and are well worth it; you should call a day ahead.

ACTIVITIES

Outdoor access is Santiago's strong suit. A quick fix is to run, walk or peddle up Barrio Bellavista's Pío Nono to Cerro San Cristóbal (opposite).

Swimmers can work on their strokes at the Parque Metropolitano's gorgeous pools (see opposite).

From October to March adventure-travel companies run Class III descents of the Maipo. One popular destination is Cascada de las Animas (p400). They also organize hiking and horse-trekking trips at reasonable rates.

Excellent skiing is within sight of Santiago. The closest resort is El Colorado & Farellones (p399).

Wine enthusiasts should check out the easy day trips (see p399).

Sore backpackers can soak in hot springs **Termas Valle de Colina** (Baños Colina; ☎ 239-6797; www.termasvalledecolina.cl; entrance to springs & camping CH$5000; ☽ Oct-Feb). There's no public transportation but **Manzur Expediciones** (see p400) makes the hour trip from Plaza Italia (near metro Baquedano).

COURSES

Try one of the following language schools.
Escuela Violeta Parra (Map pp388-9; ☎ 735-8211; www.tandemsantiago.cl; Pinto Lagarrigue 362-A, Bellavista) Outstanding academic record. The school also arranges homestays and trips.
Instituto Chileno de la Lengua (Map pp392-3; ☎ 697-2728; www.ichil.cl; Riquelme 226, Barrio Brasil)
Natalis Language Center (Map pp392-3; ☎ 222-8685; www.natalislang.com; Av Vicuña Mackenna 6, 7th fl) Great for quick, intense courses.

TOURS

For basic, tick-the-boxes touring, you're better off exploring the Centro on foot than with a tour: small streets and heavy traffic mean slow progress.

Chip Travel (Map pp392-3; ☎ 737-5649; www.chiptravel.cl; Av Santa María 227, Oficina 11) Runs a human rights–oriented tour combining Parque por la Paz, a memorial for victims of the last dictatorship (see p503) with a stop at the Fundación Pinochet.
La Bicicleta Verde (Map pp392-3; ☎ 570-9338; www.labicicletaverde.cl; Santa María 227, Oficina 12, Bellavista; half-day tours CH$15,000) Two-wheel town tours with a cultural bent: one takes in the fruit and veg market, for example, while another passes political sights.

FESTIVALS & EVENTS

Santiago a Mil (www.stgoamil.cl) This major theatre festival draws experimental companies from around the world to Santiago's stages in January.
Festival del Barrio Brasil Exhibitions, theater, dance and music bring even more life to the lovely Plaza Brasil in January.
Feria Internacional del Aire y del Espacio (www.fidae.cl) Aeropuerto Los Cerrillos, southwest of town, is the site of this major international air show in late March.
Feria Internacional de Artesanía Held in the Centro's Parque General Bustamente in November, this is the city's best crafts festival.
Feria Internacional del Libro Santiago's annual book fair in Estación Mapocho attracts authors from throughout the continent in the last week of November.

SLEEPING

The bustling Centro slows way down at night so take a taxi here after dark. Hot neighborhoods for nightlife are Providencia and Bellavista while Barrio Brasil is considered up-and-coming. The swank cafe neighborhoods of Barrio Lastarria and Bellas Artes have been adopted by the gay community.

Centro

Hostal de Sammy (Map pp388-9; ☎ 689-8772; www.hostalsammy.com; Toesca 2335; dm CH$5000-7000; s/d without bathroom CH$9700/17,700; ☐) Shabby-chic Sammy is the best backpacker deal in town, with superfriendly service, games, Spanish lessons and an official hostel dog to welcome you. The owner cooks flapjacks for hungry guests and volunteers get free housing.

Ecohostel (off Map pp392-3; ☎ 222-6833; www.ecohostel.cl; Jofré 349B; dm CH$6000, d without bathroom CH$20,000) Here, the staff separate trash and recycling. This friendly hostel has single-sex dormitories with thick matching comforters (but guys get the noisy street room). It's small and orderly, with quiet time starting before midnight.

Residencial Londres (Map pp392-3; ☎ 638-2215; www.lula.cl/residencial; Londres 54; s/d without bathroom CH$9000/18,000) It's nothing fancy but Londres boasts great rates and pared-down, faded grandeur, cozied up with parquet floors and antique furniture.

Hostal Río Amazonas (Map pp392-3; ☎ 635-1631; www.hostalrioamazonas.cl; Av Vicuña Mackenna 47; s/d/q incl breakfast CH$19,000/25,000/43,000; ☐) Supercentral, this mock-Tudor mansion features plain, bright rooms and offers competitive rates.

CHILE

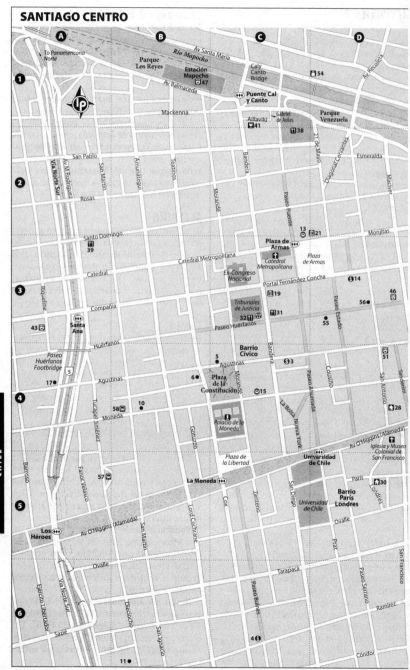

SANTIAGO CENTRO

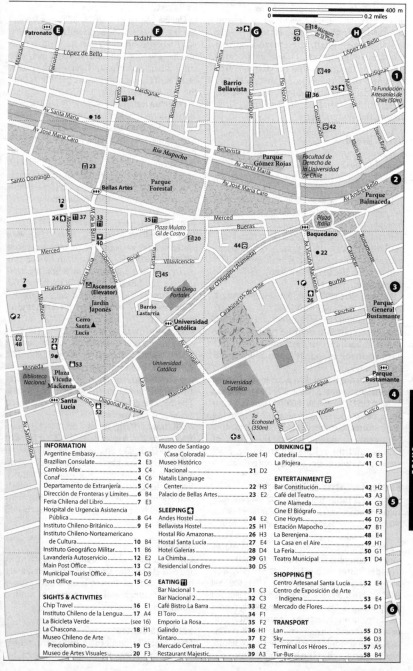

INFORMATION	
Argentine Embassy	1 G3
Brazilian Consulate	2 E3
Cambios Afex	3 C4
Conaf	4 C6
Departamento de Extranjería	5 C4
Dirección de Fronteras y Límites	6 B4
Feria Chilena del Libro	7 E3
Hospital de Urgencia Asistencia Pública	8 G4
Instituto Chileno-Británico	9 E4
Instituto Chileno-Norteamericano de Cultura	10 B4
Instituto Geográfico Militar	11 B6
Lavandería Autoservicio	12 E2
Main Post Office	13 C2
Municipal Tourist Office	14 D3
Post Office	15 C4

SIGHTS & ACTIVITIES	
Chip Travel	16 E1
Instituto Chileno de la Lengua	17 A4
La Bicicleta Verde	(see 16)
La Chascona	18 H1
Museo Chileno de Arte Precolombino	19 C3
Museo de Artes Visuales	20 F3

Museo de Santiago (Casa Colorada)	(see 14)
Museo Histórico Nacional	21 D2
Natalis Language Center	22 H3
Palacio de Bellas Artes	23 E2

SLEEPING	
Andes Hostel	24 E2
Bellavista Hostel	25 H1
Hostal Río Amazonas	26 H3
Hostal Santa Lucía	27 E4
Hotel Galerías	28 D4
La Chimba	29 G1
Residencial Londres	30 D5

EATING	
Bar Nacional 1	31 C3
Bar Nacional 2	32 C3
Café Bistro La Barra	33 E2
El Toro	34 F1
Emporio La Rosa	35 F2
Galindo	36 H1
Kintaro	37 E2
Mercado Central	38 C2
Restaurant Majestic	39 A3

DRINKING	
Catedral	40 E3
La Piojera	41 C1

ENTERTAINMENT	
Bar Constitución	42 H2
Café del Teatro	43 A3
Cine Alameda	44 G3
Cine El Biógrafo	45 F3
Cine Hoyts	46 D3
Estación Mapocho	47 B1
La Berenjena	48 E4
La Casa en el Aire	49 H1
La Feria	50 G1
Teatro Municipal	51 D4

SHOPPING	
Centro Artesanal Santa Lucía	52 E4
Centro de Exposición de Arte Indígena	53 E4
Mercado de Flores	54 D1

TRANSPORT	
Lan	55 D3
Sky	56 D3
Terminal Los Héroes	57 A5
Tur-Bus	58 B4

Hotel Galerías (Map pp392-3; ☎ 470-7400; www.hotelgalerias.cl; San Antonio 65; s/d incl breakfast CH$92,000/113,000; 😵 🖵 🐾) Mock *moai* (Easter Island statues) guard the entrance to this modern design haven. This is an obvious splurge, with impeccable service and understated, comfortable rooms that make you want to dally. Summer guests can enjoy the small outdoor pool on the 7th floor, snug among the skyscrapers.

Barrio Brasil

Sweet offerings fill this bohemian enclave, central to hip restaurants and other parts of the city. Metro stations are Los Héroes or Santa Ana.

La Casa Roja (Map pp388-9; ☎ 696-4241; www .lacasaroja.cl; Agustinas 2113; dm CH$6500, d with/without bathroom CH$20,000/16,800; 🖵) Make no mistake, you could get a better night's sleep on a long-haul bus or cattle drive than here. Yet backpackers do adore the circus atmosphere. The rent's cheap, the nightlife decent, and there's a travel agency on site.

Luz Azul (Map pp388-9; ☎ 698-4856; www.luzazul hostel.cl; Santa Mónica 1924; dm CH$7150-9500, d CH$23,800; 🖵) Congenial, slightly funky and tasteful, this small spot is a definite pleaser. While aimed at backpackers, mellow is definitely the dominant mood. It's one block from the subway.

Happy House Hostel (Map pp388-9; ☎ 688-4849; www.happyhousehostel.cl; Catedral 2207; dm/s/d/tr incl breakfast CH$11,000/25,000/33,000/45,000; 🖵) Can decor be both kooky and tasteful? Employing river stones, bamboo and bold colors, this 20th-century mansion tests the limits of whimsy and the results are stunning. Staff are informative, if not exactly outgoing.

Barrios Lastarria & Bellas Artes

Hostal Santa Lucía (Map pp392-3; ☎ 664-8478; www .hostalsantalucia.cl; Santa Lucía 168; dm CH$9000, d/t without bathroom CH$22,000/33,000; 🖵) A brand-new hostel that's intimate, stylish and central. Firm beds, white brocade covers and cozy shared spaces throughout, plus friendly management.

Andes Hostel (Map pp392-3; ☎ 633-1976; www .andeshostel.com; Monjitas 506; dm CH$11,000, s/d CH$30,000/35,000, without bathroom CH$20,000/25,000; 🖵) A hip urban hideaway for backpackers, Andes rates strong on style; think comics and zebra-print vibrancy. The downside: some rooms lack air and doubles are surprisingly bland, like the service. But the location is tops.

Bellavista

La Chimba (Map pp392-3; ☎ 735-8978; www.lachimba .com; Pinto Lagarrigue 262; dm/d incl breakfast CH$8000/20,000; 🖵) Emphasizing youth over hostel, this rambler has a modern and minimalist decor, with snug down bedding and certifiably comfy beds. Staff are friendly but the breakfasts (and the showers) are weak.

Bellavista Hostel (Map pp392-3; ☎ 732-8737; www .bellavistahostel.com; Dardignac 0184; dm incl breakfast CH$8000-8500, d incl breakfast CH$18,000; 🖵) With Santiago's best nightlife blocks away, the party crowd books this quirky hostel ('no fuckheads allowed,' says the sign) filled with knickknacks, games and a rooftop terrace. Don't come for the rooms – with metal bunks and plain doubles – they're just dull.

Providencia

Casa Condell (Map pp388-9; ☎ 717-8592; www .casacondell.com; Av Condell 114; s/d without bathroom CH$10,000/20,000) More house than hostel, this plain Jane steps away from a green corridor is a great deal. The vibe is mature. Take advantage of the shady roof deck scattered with cushioned sofas, ideal for exchanging travel tales.

El Patio Suizo (Map pp388-9; ☎ 474-0634; www.patiosuizo.com; Av Condell 847; s/d incl breakfast CH$22,000/30,000, without bathroom CH$15,000/20,000; 🖵) Fussy but in a good way, this design-conscious B&B, run by a Swiss family, offers a peaceful retreat in an often stressful city. The backyard has a barbecue, shady grape arbor and hammocks.

Vilafranca Petit Hotel (☎ 235-1413; www .vilafranca.cl; Pérez Valenzuela 1650; s/d incl breakfast CH$40,000/47,000; 🖵) Studiedly Martha Stewart, this lovely B&B has a trellised stone patio and eight rooms with big wooden trunks, firm beds in floral patterns and modern bathrooms. Breakfast includes fresh fruit like blackberries or watermelon, bread and cake.

EATING

Cheap lunches abound in the center; while Barrios Bellavista, Brasil or Providencia are better suited for dinner. Restaurants usually close after lunch and only reopen at around 8pm, forget Sundays.

Santiago Centro

Have lunch or *onces* (a snack) in the center, but don't expect to find much open for

CHILE

dinner. Along the southern arcade of the Plaza de Armas, vendors serve *completos* (hot dogs) and empanadas.

Mercado Central (Map pp392-3; 6am-4pm Sun-Thu, to 8pm Fri, to 6pm Sat) Santiago's wrought-iron fish market is a classic for long lunches (or hangover-curing fish-stew breakfasts). Skip the overpriced tourist traps in the middle, and make for one of the tiny, low-key stalls around the edge, like cheap and friendly Pailas Denisse at Local 16 (mains are CH$2500 to CH$3500).

Bar Nacional (Map pp392-3; Bandera 317; mains CH$3500-5000) An adored soda fountain bustling with bow-tie clad waiters serving scrumptious *pastel de choclo* (maize casserole). The second branch is at Paseo Huérfanos 1151.

Kintaro (Map pp392-3; Monjitas 460; mains CH$3900-4700) Ignore the chintzy digs – the sushi is reasonable value and authentic.

Restaurant Majestic (Map pp392-3; Santo Domingo 1526; mains CH$3900-6200; 7:30pm-midnight) Exquisite (and hot!) Indian dishes, including tandoori meats and vegetarian curries, are savored by diners flanked by elephant statues and batiks.

Barrios Lastarria & Bellavista

These stylish neighborhoods are top choices for dinner and drinks. JM de la Barra (between Metros Santa Lucía and Bellas Artes) is lined with cafes open until late.

Emporio La Rosa (Map pp392-3; Merced 291; ice cream CH$900-1800) Creamy, handmade ice cream with wild but oh-so-good flavors: Ulmo honey, chocolate basil, and rose petal, to name a few.

Galindo (Map pp392-3; Dardignac 098; mains CH$2900-5500) Dependable Chilean fare, with sizzling *parrilladas* (mixed grills), burgers and fries. The less-carnivorous should try *porotos granados* (bean stew), a national staple usually relegated to mom's kitchen.

Ali Baba (Map pp388-9; Santa Filomena 102; CH$2990-6990) Bedouin opulence butters you up for savory Moroccan chicken, crisp falafel and surprisingly authentic Middle Eastern classics. Upscale and vegetarian friendly.

Café Bistro de la Barra (Map pp392-3; JM de la Barra 455; sandwiches CH$4000-7000) A teacup-sized cafe with some of the best brunches and *onces* in town, serving croissants, *cortados* (coffee with a little milk) and mammoth green salad in glass bowls.

El Toro (Map pp392-3; 737-5937; Loreto 33; mains CH$5700-7200) One of those places to be seen, this cafe has both soap stars and the masses dining on filling Chilean classics or just salad. Don't leave without sampling the creative cocktails.

Barrio Brasil

Platipus (Map pp388-9; Agustinas 2099, Barrio Brasil; sushi CH$2900-4000) Candlelight and exposed brick set the scene for slow dinners, but the sushi and the *tablas* (boards of finger food) are worth the wait.

2008 (Map pp388-9; Av Brasil 84; large pizzas CH$4000-6000) Take your cheap date to this rock-and-roll pizza house with gooey thin-crust pizzas and cheap brews.

Las Vacas Gordas (Map pp388-9; 697-1066; Cienfuegos 280; mains CH$4000-6000) Always packed, this iconic, much-praised steakhouse doles out hefty portions of anything that once said 'moo.' Reserve ahead.

Providencia & Las Condes

Doner House (264-3200; Av Providencia 1457, Providencia; shawarma CH$2500; 12:30pm-10pm Mon-Sat) Shawarma is the star of this tiny eatery, but falafels and stuffed vine leaves are worth trying too.

Café Melba (232-4546; Don Carlos 2898, Las Condes; sandwiches CH$2900, mains CH$6000; 7:30am-8pm Mon-Fri, 8am-8pm Sat) Wanderlust appetites can appreciate this Kiwi-owned cafe that embraces both exotic and comfort food, with decadent all-day breakfasts, big fresh salads and a wild range from green fish curry to burgers. Service is slow.

Café del Patio (236-1251; Av Providencia 1670, Local 8-A, Providencia; mains CH$4000-5500) You'll think you've died and gone to…somewhere other than Santiago. Super-fresh salads, miso soup, and tofu stir-fries are stars in this cute restaurant with courtyard.

El Huerto (233-2690; Luco 054, Providencia; mains from CH$5000) A vegetarian mainstay, popular with both hip young things and ladies who lunch. Its adjacent cafe, La Huerta, has limited offerings but is kinder on the wallet.

Liguria (334-4346; Av Pedro de Valdivia Norte 047, Providencia; mains CH$5200-7500) A Santiago legend, this place packs 'em in, its simple recipe is cooking up a great menu at a surprisingly low price with a hefty dash of bon vivants

CHILE

and bustle. Cooking is bistro fare, seafood and Chilean comfort. There's also a branch at Av Providencia 1373.

Astrid y Gastón (☎ 650-9125; Bellet 201, Providencia; mains CH$7800-11,800; ⏰ 1-3:30pm & 8pm-midnight Mon-Fri, dinner only Sat) With expert service and cocktails, this acclaimed haute cuisine restaurant puts a modern spin on Peruvian *ceviche* (marinated raw seafood), *chupes* (fish stews) and *chochinillo* (suckling pig). Reserve ahead.

DRINKING

Bar Yellow (☎ 946-5063; Flores 47, Providencia; ⏰ 6pm-1am Mon-Wed, to 3am Thu-Sat) Small but achingly cool bar, the hands-down favorite among cocktail quaffers.

Bar Central (☎ 264-2236; Av Providencia 1391, Providencia; ⏰ 11am-2am Mon-Sat, 8pm-1am Sun) A lynchpin of Providencia nightlife, self-consciously cool Central attracts hip media types with its sleek chrome furnishings and tasty *pisco sours* (grape-brandy cocktails).

Catedral (Map pp392-3; ☎ 664-3048; cnr JM de la Barra & Merced; 12:30pm-3am Mon-Thu, to 5am Fri & Sat) Head up the stairs to a landscape of sofas, smooth tunes and soft lighting. This place is so in, and the food is much better than barworthy.

Eurohappy (Map pp388-9; ☎ 672-1016; Maturana 516, Barrio Brasil; ⏰ 7pm-midnight Sun-Thu, till late Fri & Sat) Over 400 types of beer – including local artesanal and microbrewery options – are expertly poured by Santiago's only beer sommelier.

La Piojera (Map pp392-3; ☎ 698-1682; Aillavilú 1030, Centro; ⏰ noon-midnight Mon-Sat) A bare-bones drinking den with sticky tables and faithful regulars. Try the *chicha* (hard apple cider).

ENTERTAINMENT
Live Music

Bar Constitución (Map pp392-3; ☎ 244-4569; www .barconstitucion.cl; Constitución 61, Bellavista; ⏰ 8pm-5am Mon-Sat) The hotspot of the moment has no sign: look for the gray door with a long queue of trendies. Live bands and DJs play nightly – the line up includes electroclash, garage, nu-folk, house and more.

Batuta (☎ 274-7096; www.batuta.cl; Washington 52, Ñuñoa; ⏰ 10pm-3am Wed-Sat) Enthusiastic crowds jump to ska, *patchanka* (think Manu Chao), *cumbia chilombiana*, rockabilly and surf – here anything goes.

Club de Jazz (☎ 326-5065; www.clubdejazz.cl; Av Alessandri 85, Ñuñoa; admission US$5; ⏰ 10pm-3am Thu-Sat) One of Latin America's most established jazz venues, housed in a large wooden building, within trumpeting distance of Plaza Ñuñoa (take a taxi).

La Casa en el Aire (Map pp392-3; www.lacasaenelaire .cl; López de Bello 0125, Bellavista; ⏰ 8pm-late) An alt-venue with poetry, theater and live folk music.

Nightclubs

Clubs get started at midnight. Many close their doors in February and follow the crowds to the beach.

Blondie (Map pp388-9; www.blondie.cl; Alameda 2879, Barrio Brasil; admission CH$3000-5000) With a floor of '80s hits and another of Chilean indie, Britpop or techno, this favorite of students and the gay community is usually packed.

La Berenjena (Map pp392-3; ☎ 664-2855; www .laberenjena.cl; Agustinas 676, Centro; admission CH$4000; ⏰ from midnight Fri & Sat) Indie hits from the '80s and '90s usually please the youngish crowds on one of this club's two floors.

Sofa (☎ 249-8175; www.sofa.cl; Santa Isabel 0151, Providencia; admission CH$1000-4000; ⏰ from 9pm Tue-Thu, from midnight Fri & Sat) An effortlessly cool club where drinks chill in an old bathtub and groovers move to funk, soul, hip-hop, R&B or breakbeats.

La Feria (Map pp392-3; www.clublaferia.cl; Constitución 275, Barrio Bellavista) DJs bang out euphoric house and techno.

Cinemas

Many cinemas offer Wednesday discounts. Paseo Huérfanos, in the center, has several multiplexes, including **Cine Hoyts** (Map pp392-3; ☎ 600-5000-400; www.cinehoyts.cl; Paseo Huérfanos 735).

Arthouse cinemas include the following:

Cine Alameda (Map pp392-3; Alameda 139)

Cine El Biógrafo (Map pp392-3; Lastarria 181, Barrio Santa Lucía; US$3.50)

Cine Tobalaba (www.showtime.cl; Providencia 2563, Providencia)

Performing Arts

Café del Teatro (Map pp392-3; ☎ 672-1687; Riquelme 226, Barrio Brasil; ⏰ noon-2am) Today's 'it' bar. Check out events in the old theater out back, or mingle with the welcoming regulars among the bright wall canvases.

Estación Mapocho (Map pp392-3; ☎ 361-1761; cnr Bandera & Balmaceda) Passenger trains to Viña and Valparaíso have been replaced with Santiago's main cultural center, offering live theater, concerts, exhibits and a cafe.

Performing-arts venues include the gorgeous **Teatro Municipal** (Map pp392-3; ☎ 369-0282; www.municipal.cl; Agustinas 794), home to the Ballet de Santiago, and **Centro Cultural Gran Circo Teatro** (Map pp388-9; grancircoteatro@hotmail.com; Av República 301), featuring avant-garde theater and circus performances.

Sports

Estadio Nacional (☎ 238-8102; cnr Av Grecia & Marathon, Ñuñoa) Join the throngs chanting 'Chi-Chi-Chi-Lay-Lay-Lay.' International soccer matches usually pack a crowd. Tickets can be purchased at the stadium.

Horse racing takes place every Friday and on alternate Mondays at the grand **Hipódromo Chile** (Map pp388-9; Blanco Encalada 2540), south of the Alameda near Parque O'Higgins.

SHOPPING

For artisan crafts try the following places.

Centro Artesanal de los Dominicos (Av Apoquindo 9085, Las Condes; ⏱ 11am-7:30pm, closed Mon) Next to the twin white domes of Los Dominicos church in Las Condes, this is a small market with quality crafts. From Escuela Militar metro station take orange bus 401 or 407 (they leave from stop 4) along Av Apoquindo.

Centro Artesanal Santa Lucía (Map pp392-3; cnr Carmen & Diagonal Paraguay) Located on the other side of Cerro Santa Lucía, this place sells lapis lazuli jewelry, sweaters, copperware and pottery.

Centro de Exposición de Arte Indígena (Map pp392-3; Alameda 499) Rapa Nui, Mapuche and Aymara crafts are all on offer here.

Fundación Artesanías de Chile (off Map pp392-3; ☎ 777-8643; Bellavista 0357, Bellavista; ⏱ 10:30am-7pm Mon-Sat) This is where you can get reasonably priced jewelry, carvings, ceramics and woolen goods, with fair compensation for artisans.

GETTING THERE & AWAY
Air

Aeropuerto Internacional Arturo Merino Benítez (off Map pp388-9; ☎ 601-1752, lost property 690-1707; www.aeropuertosantiago.cl) is in Pudahuel, 26km northwest of downtown Santiago. Domestic carrier offices are **LAN** (☎ 600-526-2000) Centro (Map pp392-3; Paseo Huérfanos 926); Providencia (Av Providencia 2006) and **Sky** (☎ 353-3100; Andrés de Fuenzalida 55, Providencia). The following table lists some approximate round-trip fares (cheaper than one way). Most of these flights may require a layover.

AIR FARES	
Destination	**Cost (CH$)**
Antofagasta	120,000
Arica	115,000
Balmaceda	118,000
Calama	93,000
Puerto Montt	100,000
Punta Arenas	155,000

Bus

Bus transportation is very reliable, prompt, safe and comfortable. Santiago has four main bus terminals, from which buses leave for northern, central and southern destinations. The largest and most reputable bus company is Tur Bus, which offers 10% discounts for online purchases. Pullman Bus is also reputable.

Terminal San Borja (Map pp388-9; ☎ 776-0645; Alameda 3250) is at the end of the shopping mall alongside the main railway station. The ticket booths are divided by region, with destinations prominently displayed. Destinations are from Arica down to the *cordillera* (mountain range) around Santiago.

Terminal de Buses Alameda (Map pp388-9; ☎ 776-2424; cnr Alameda & Jotabeche) is home to **Tur Bus** (☎ 778-0808; www.turbus.cl) and **Pullman Bus** (☎ 778-1185; www.pullman.cl), both going to a wide variety of destinations north, south and on the coast. They are both similarly priced and equally reliable and comfortable.

Terminal de Buses Sur (Map pp388-9; ☎ 779-1385; btwn Ruiz Tagle & Retamales, Alameda 3850) has the most services to the central coast, international and southern destinations (the Lakes District and Chiloé).

Terminal Los Héroes (Map pp392-3; Tucapel Jiménez), near the Alameda in the Centro, is much more convenient and less chaotic. Buses mainly head north along the Carretera Panamericana (Pan-American Hwy), but a few go to Argentina and south to Temuco.

Fares vary dramatically and spike during holidays, so explore options. Promotions can reduce fares by half; student reductions by 25%. Discounts are common outside the peak summer season. Book in advance to travel during holiday periods. Fares between important destinations are listed throughout the chapter, with approximate one-way fares and journey times listed in the table on the following page.

CHILE

BUS FARES

Destination	Cost (CH$)	Duration (hr)
Antofagasta	28,000	19
Arica	35,000	30
Buenos Aires, Argentina	28,000	22
Chillán	8000-13,000	5
Concepción	10,000	6½
Copiapó	21,000-35,000	12
Iquique	31,200	25
La Serena	8,000-23,000	7
Mendoza, Argentina	9000	8
Osorno	18,000	12
Pucón	10,000-24,000	11
Puerto Montt	20,000	12
San Pedro de Atacama	32,000	23
Talca	4400	3½
Temuco	14,000	9½
Valdivia	14,500	10-11
Valparaíso	3800	2
Viña del Mar	4000	2¼

Train

Chile's recently revamped train system, **Empresa de Ferrocarriles del Estado** (EFE; ☎ 600-585-5000; www.efe.cl), operates out of the **Estación Central** (Map pp388-9; Alameda 3170). You can also buy tickets inside **Universidad de Chile metro station** (Map pp392-3; ☉ 9am-8pm Mon-Fri, to 2pm Sat). Train travel is generally slightly slower and more expensive than going by bus, but wagons are well maintained and services are generally punctual.

The TerraSur rail service connects Santiago three to five times daily with Rancagua (CH$5000, one hour), San Fernando (CH$5500, 1½ hours), Curicó (CH$6000, 2¼ hours), Talca (CH$6500, three hours) and Chillán (CH$10,500, 5½ hours), from where there's a connecting bus to Concepción (from Santiago CH$12,500, 6½ hours). There's a 10% discount if you book online; first-class tickets cost about 20% more.

GETTING AROUND
Bus

Transantiago (☎ 800-730-073; www.transantiago.cl) buses are a cheap and convenient way of getting around town, especially when the metro shuts down at night. Green-and-white buses operate in central Santiago or connect two areas of town. Each suburb has color-coded local buses and an identifying letter that precedes routes numbers (for example, routes in Las Condes and Vitacura start with a C and use orange vehicles). Buses generally follow major roads and stops are spaced far apart, often coinciding with metro stations. Consult route maps at stops. You can only pay for bus rides using a Bip! (a contact-free card you wave over sensors). Transantiago operates a flat fare of CH$420 during rush hour (7am to 9am and 6pm to 8pm) and CH$380 otherwise, with discounts for Bip! cards.

Car

Renting a car to drive around Santiago is a sure-fire way to have a bad day. But if you must do it, here are some agencies. Most also have offices at the airport.

Automóvil Club de Chile (off Map pp388-9; Acchi; ☎ 431-1000; www.automovilclub.cl; Av Andrés Bello 1863)

Budget (☎ 362-3605; www.budget.cl; Bilbao 1439, Providencia)

First (☎ 225-6328; www.firstrentacar.cl; Rancagua 0514, Providencia)

Hertz (☎ 496-1000; www.hertz.com; Av Andrés Bello 1469, Providencia)

Colectivo

Quicker and more comfortable than buses, taxi *colectivos* carry up to five passengers on fixed routes. The fare is about CH$500 within the city limits. They resemble taxis but have an illuminated roof sign indicating their route.

Metro

Now part of Transantiago, the city's ever-expanding **metro** (www.metrosantiago.cl; ☉ 6am-11pm Mon-Fri, 6:30am-10:30pm Sat, 8am-10:30pm Sun) is a clean and efficient way to travel. Services on its five interlinking lines are frequent, but often crowded.

Taxi

These black-and-yellow numbers are abundant and moderately priced. Flagfall costs CH$200, then it's CH$80 per 200m (or minute of waiting time). For longer rides – out to the airport, for example – you can sometimes negotiate flat fares. It's generally safe to hail cabs, though hotels and restaurants will happily call you one, too. Most drivers are honest, courteous and helpful, but a few will take roundabout routes, so try to know where you're going.

AROUND SANTIAGO

SKI RESORTS

Chilean ski and snowboard resorts are open from June to October, with lower rates available early and late in the season. Most ski areas are above 3300m and treeless; the runs are long, the season is long, and the snow is deep and dry. Three major resorts are barely an hour from the capital, while the fourth is about two hours away on the Argentine border.

El Colorado (daily ski pass CH$30,000, students CH$25,000) and **Farellones** (daily ski pass CH$8,000), located approximately 45km east of the capital, are close enough together to be considered one destination, with 18 lifts and 22 runs from 2430m to 3330m. **Centro de Ski El Colorado** (☎ 02-398-8080; www.elcolorado .cl; Av Apoquindo 4900, Local 47, Las Condes, Santiago) has the latest information on snow and slope conditions. **Refugio Aleman** (☎ 02-264-9899; www.refugioaleman.cl; Camino Los Cóndores 1451, Farellones; dm/d incl breakfast & dinner CH$24,000/54,000) has clean dorms, two big living rooms and friendly multilingual staff. You can ski from the door to the slopes.

Only 4km from the Farellones ski resort, **La Parva** (daily ski pass CH$30,000) has 30 runs from 2662m to 3630m. For the latest information, contact **Centro de Ski La Parva** (☎ 02-339-8482; www.skilaparva.cl; Goyenechea 2939, Oficina 303, Las Condes, Santiago).

Another 14km beyond Farellones, the vast **Valle Nevado** (☎ 02-477-7700; www.vallenevado .com; Av Vitacura 5250, Oficina 304, Santiago; daily ski pass CH$32,000, students CH$26,000) can keep even cranky experts entertained, with 27 runs ranging from 2805m to 3670m, and some up to 3km in length.

In a class of its own, the ultrasteep **Portillo** (daily ski pass CH$30,000), 145km northeast of the capital on the Argentine border, has a dozen lifts and 23 runs from 2590m to 3330m, with a maximum vertical drop of 340m. The on-site **Inca Lodge** (dm per week full board from US$700) accommodates young travelers in dorms. Tickets are included in the price and low season offers some screaming deals. Contact **Centro de Ski Portillo** (☎ 02-263-0606; www.skiportillo .com) for the latest details.

Shuttles to the resorts abound. **Manzur Expediciones** (☎ 02-777-4284) goes direct to the slopes on Wednesday, Saturday and Sunday from Plaza Italia or your hotel (CH$13,000). Rentals are also available. **SkiTotal** (☎ 02-246-0156; www.skitotal.cl; Av Apoquindo 4900, Local 39-42, Las Condes, Santiago) rents equipment and can arrange transportation (CH$9500) to the resorts, with 8am departures and 5pm returns, or they can organize hotel pickup (CH$16,000).

WINERIES

Just south of the center of Santiago lies Valle de Maipo, a major wine region specializing in big-bodied reds. Santiago's most central winery, **Viña Santa Carolina** (off Map pp388-9; ☎ 450-3000; www.santacarolina.com; Rodrigo de Araya 1431, Macul; standard tour incl 2 reservas CH$7000; ☽ standard tours 10am in Spanish & 12:30pm in English Mon-Sat, icon tours 4:30pm Mon-Fri), dates from 1875, with a historical main house and cellars. At **Viña Cousiño Macul** (☎ 351-4175; www.cousinomacul .cl; Av Quilín 7100, Peñalolén; tours incl 1 varietal & 1 reserva CH$5000; ☽ tours 11am & 3pm Mon-Fri in Spanish & English, 11am Sat in Spanish) tours take in the production process as well as the underground *bodega* (winery or a storage area for wine), which was built in 1872. It is a 2¼km walk or taxi ride from the metro.

Santiago's most interesting winery, **Viña Aquitania** (☎ 791-4500; www.aquitania.cl; Av Consistorial 5090, Peñalolén; standard tours incl 2 reservas CH$5000; ☽ 9am-5pm Mon-Fri by appt only) is all about quality, not quantity. From Grecia metro station (Línea 4), take bus D07 south from bus stop 6. Get off at the intersection of Av Los Presidentes and Consistorial (you need a Bip! card). Aquitania is 150m south.

If you want to see winemaking on a vast scale, you can take a mass-market tour at **Viña Concha y Toro** (☎ 476-5269; www.conchaytoro .com; Subercaseaux 210, Pirque; tours CH$6000; ☽ 10am-5pm). To reach Pirque, go by metro from Paradero 14 at the exit of Bellavista de la Florida metro station.

At the other extreme is boutique vineyard **Viña Almaviva** (☎ 852-9300; www.almavivawinery.com; Av Santa Rosa 821, Paradero 45, Puente Alto; tours incl 1 pour CH$15,000; ☽ 9am-5pm Mon-Fri by appt only). Bus 207 from Estación Mapocho (you will need a Bip! card; see page opposite) runs past the entrance, 1km from the winery building.

Other Maipo set-ups worth visiting include **Viña Santa Rita** (☎ 362-2594; www.santarita.cl),

Viña de Martino (☎ 819-2959; www.demartino.cl) and **Viña Undurraga** (☎ 372-2900; www.undurraga.cl).

CAJÓN DEL MAIPO

Southeast of the capital, the Cajón del Maipo (Río Maipo canyon) is a major weekend destination for *santiaguinos*, who come to camp, hike, climb, bike, raft and ski. From September to April rafts descend the mostly Class III rapids of the murky Maipó in little over an hour. Half-day trips cost about CH$19,000. **Cascadas Expediciones** (☎ 02-861-1777; www.cascada-expediciones.com; Camino Al Volcán 17710, Casilla 211, San José de Maipó) and **Altué Active Travel** (☎ 02-232-1103; www.chileoutdoors .com; Encomenderos 83, Las Condes, Santiago) arrange the fun.

Near the village of San Alfonso, **Cascada de las Ánimas** (☎ 02-861-1303; www.cascada.net; d/cabañas CH$25,000/44,000) is a lovely 3500-hectare private nature reserve and working horse ranch. Hostel rooms come as doubles; the four-person *cabañas* (cabins) have kitchens and log fires. A busy restaurant serves creative offerings on a terrace with views over the valley, *and* there's a large attractive pool of natural spring water, a sauna and massage facility. You can arrange any number of hiking, riding (CH$15,000 per hour) and rafting options here, too. This is a top out-of-the-city destination. Lodging and activities are discounted from May to September.

Only 93km from Santiago, 3000-hectare **Monumento Natural El Morado** (admission CH$1500; ◷ closed May-Sep) rewards hikers with views of 4490m Cerro El Morado at Laguna El Morado, a two-hour hike from the humble hot springs of Baños Morales. There are free campsites around the lake.

Refugio Lo Valdés (☎ 099-220-8525; www.refugio lovaldes.com; r per person incl breakfast CH$17,000), a mountain chalet run by the German Alpine Club, is a popular weekend destination. Rates include breakfast, and other meals are available. Eleven kilometers from here is **Baños Colina** (☎ 02-209-9114; per person incl campsite CH$8000), where terraced hot springs overlook the valley.

Confirm the following transportation times as they are subject to change. **Buses San José de Maipó** (☎ 02-697-2520; CH$1500) leave every 30 minutes, from 6am till 9pm, from Terminal San Borja (but stopping at Parque O'Higgins metro station) for San José de Maipó. The 7:15am bus continues to Baños Morales daily in January and February and on weekends only from March to October.

Turismo Arpue (☎ 02-211-7165) goes directly to Baños Morales (CH$3500, three hours) on weekends, departures starting at 7:30am from Santiago's Plaza Italia (the Baquedano metro station). From October to mid-May, **Manzur Expediciones** (☎ 02-777-4284) also goes to the hot springs from Plaza Italia on Wednesday, Saturday and Sunday at 7:15am for similar rates. Try also **Buses Cordillera** (☎ 02-777-3881) from Terminal San Borja.

VALPARAÍSO
☎ 032 / pop 276,000

Valparaíso, or 'Valpo,' is a well-worn, frenetic port with houses stacked to gaping heights along the sea. Considered the cultural capital of Chile, this city, 120km northwest of Santiago, is a Unesco World Heritage Site with reason. While the bohemian among us love it, its rough edges won't charm all. Tangled wires and debris scatter the backdrop. The congested center is known as El Plan, with lower-level streets parallel to the shoreline which curves toward Viña del Mar. An irregular pattern of streets leads into residential hills which are also connected by steep footpaths and Valparaíso's famous *ascensores* (elevators), built in its heyday from 1883 to 1916.

The leading merchant port along the Cape Horn and Pacific Ocean routes, Valparaíso was the stopover for foreign vessels, including whalers, and the export point of Chilean wheat destined for the California gold rush. Foreign merchants and capital made it Chile's financial powerhouse. Its decline began with the 1906 earthquake and the opening of the Panama Canal in 1914. Today this V Region capital, home to the National Congress, has the highest unemployment in the nation, but its hot nightspots, restaurants and B&Bs are reviving the *cerros* (hills).

Information

Call centers are abundant in the center. Most hostels do laundry and have internet. Good Spanish-language resources are **B&B Valparaíso** (www.bbvalparaiso.cl) and **Capital Cultural** (www.capitalcultural.cl).

Cerro@legre (☎ 276-9440; Uriola 678, Cerro Alegre; per hr CH$500; ◷ 9am-9pm Mon-Sat, 10am-8pm Sun) Internet cafe.

Hospital Carlos van Buren (☎ 2204-000; Av Colón 2454)

Inter Cambio (☎ 215-6290; Plaza Sotomayor 11, El Plan; ⏲ 9am-6pm Mon-Fri, 10am-1pm Sat)

Post office (Prat 856, El Plan; ⏲ 9am-6pm Mon-Fri, 10am-1pm Sat)

Tourist information kiosks (☎ 800-322-032; www.municipalidaddevalparaiso.cl/depturismo; ⏲ 10am-2pm & 3-6pm Mon-Sat); Muelle Prat (opposite Plaza Sotomayor, El Plan); Plaza Aníbal Pinto (cnr O'Higgins & Plaza Aníbal Pinto, El Plan) With free maps.

Dangers & Annoyances

The area around the Mercado Central and La Iglesia Matriz has a reputation for petty street crime and muggings. Several readers report muggings near the market. If you go, go early, avoid alleyways and leave valuables at home. Otherwise, most people wander Valparaíso without any problem. With the usual precautions most areas are safe enough, at least during daylight. At night stick to familiar areas, avoid sketchy *escaleras* (stair passageways) and go out accompanied.

Sights & Activities

Start at **Muelle Prat**, at the foot of Plaza Sotomayor. It's lively on weekends, dare we say *touristy*. Watch your stuff. You can squeeze in a cheap harbor tour (CH$1000), but photographing naval vessels is strictly prohibited. From here, clamber through Plaza Sotomayor, where the subterranean mausoleum **Monumento a los Héroes de Iquique** pays tribute to Chile's naval martyrs of the War of the Pacific.

Take **Ascensor Cordillera** west of the plaza to the well-poised 1842 **Museo del Mar Lord Cochrane** (Merlet 195; admission free; ⏲ 10am-6pm Tue-Sun mid-Mar–mid-Sep, to 1pm & 3-8pm mid-Sep–mid-Mar), which housed Chile's first observatory. Back on the lower level take Serrano to Plaza Echaurren (stay on your guard as robberies happen here). A block north is the **Iglesia Matriz**, the site of four churches since 1559. Back by Plaza Sotomayor, near the Tribunales (law courts), **Ascensor El Peral** goes to Cerro Alegre, wander to Paseo Yugoslavo to see the Art Nouveau **Palacio Baburizza** (1916). From here, continue to Urriola to access Cerro Alegre and Cerro Concepción, the most well-known and typical of the hill areas. **Iglesia San Pablo**, on Pilcomayo and Templeman, has organ concerts Sunday at 12:30pm. Take **Ascensor Concepción (Turri)** down to reach **Reloj**

Turri (cnr Esmeralda & Gómez Carreño), a landmark clock tower.

Further east, near Plaza Victoria off Aldunate, **Ascensor Espíritu Santo** accesses Cerro Bellavista, which has become an open-air museum of abstract murals, called **Museo a Cielo Abierto**. From here, take Av Ramos and then Ricardo Ferrari to get to Neruda's least-known house, **La Sebastiana** (off Map pp402-3; ☎ 225-6606; www.fundacionneruda.org; Ferrari 692, Cerro Bellavista; admission CH$2500; ⏲ 10:30am-6:50pm Tue-Sun Jan & Feb). In this wind-whipped locale, the poet's eclectic taste, humor and his passion for ships come to life. Alternatively, take green bus O (CH$440) on Serrano near Plaza Sotomayor in El Plan.

Festivals & Events

Año Nuevo (New Year's) is a major event thanks to spectacular fireworks that bring hundreds of thousands of spectators to the city.

Sleeping

Acuarela (☎ 318-0456; www.hostalacuarela.blogspot.com; Templeman 862; dm CH$7000, d without bathroom incl breakfast CH$20,000; 🖳) Cozy ample dorms, a remodeled kitchen and spiral iron staircase make this newcomer an attractive option.

Hostal Luna Sonrisa (☎ 273-4117; www.lunasonrisa.cl; Templeman 833, Cerro Alegre; dm CH$7000, d without bathroom incl breakfast CH$22,000) Tuned to the simple appeal of a well-groomed room and thick down covers, Luna Sonrisa is clearly run by a guidebook writer (who provides local tips). Hearty breakfasts include brown bread and goat cheese.

Hostal Caracol (☎ 239-5817; www.hostalcaracol.cl; Calvo 371, Cerro Bellavista; dm/d incl breakfast CH$8000/20,000; 🖳) Say goodbye to bunk beds – the dorm consists of snug singles fitted with pirate chests. From down comforters to cereal options, this traveler-run refurbished colonial goes the extra mile.

La Nona (☎ 097-978-5808; www.bblanona.com; Galos 660, Cerro Alegre; s/d incl breakfast CH$11,000/22,000; 🖳) Ultra-attentive and comfortable, this B&B feels like Grandma's house – usurped by the next generation. Carolina and Rene prove attentive hosts and the breakfasts are big and varied. Check out their interesting city tours with a focus on social history.

Hostal Morgan (☎ 211-4931; www.hostalmorgan.cl; Capilla 784, Cerro Alegre; dm CH$15,000, d incl breakfast CH$40,000, d without bathroom CH$36,000; 🖳) Sophisticated and hush, Hostal Morgan is conspicuously aimed at travelers whose

CHILE

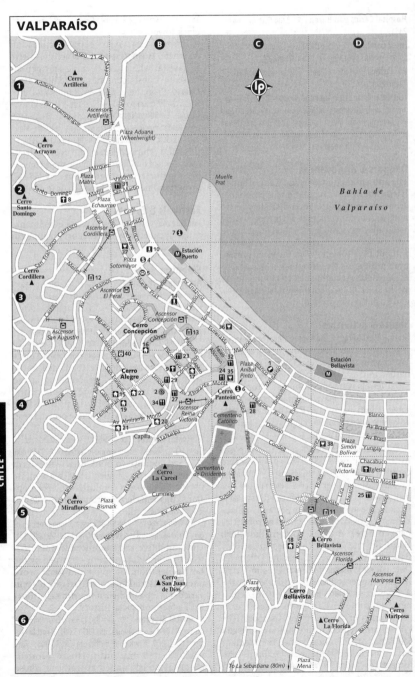

VALPARAÍSO

CHILE

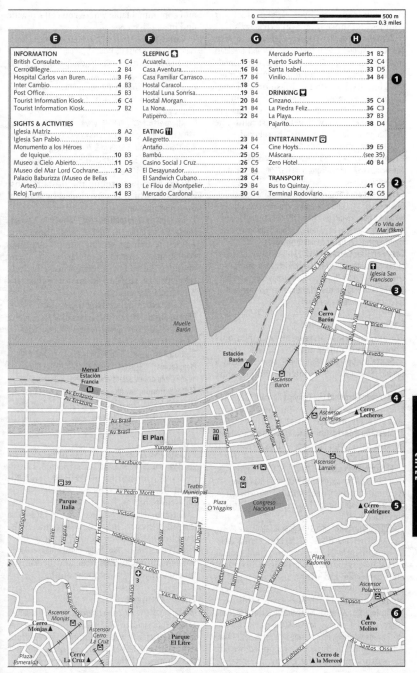

INFORMATION
British Consulate	1 C4
Cerro@llegre	2 B4
Hospital Carlos van Buren	3 F6
Inter Cambio	4 B3
Post Office	5 B3
Tourist Information Kiosk	6 C4
Tourist Information Kiosk	7 B2

SIGHTS & ACTIVITIES
Iglesia Matriz	8 A2
Iglesia San Pablo	9 B4
Monumento a los Héroes de Iquique	10 B3
Museo a Cielo Abierto	11 D5
Museo del Mar Lord Cochrane	12 A3
Palacio Baburizza (Museo de Bellas Artes)	13 B3
Reloj Turri	14 B3

SLEEPING
Acuarela	15 B4
Casa Aventura	16 B4
Casa Familiar Carrasco	17 B4
Hostal Caracol	18 C5
Hostal Luna Sonrisa	19 B4
Hostal Morgan	20 B4
La Nona	21 B4
Patiperro	22 B4

EATING
Allegretto	23 B4
Antaño	24 C4
Bambú	25 D5
Casino Social J Cruz	26 C5
El Desayunador	27 B4
El Sandwich Cubano	28 C4
Le Filou de Montpelier	29 B4
Mercado Cardonal	30 G4

Mercado Puerto	31 B2
Puerto Sushi	32 C4
Santa Isabel	33 D5
Vinilio	34 B4

DRINKING
Cinzano	35 C4
La Piedra Feliz	36 C3
La Playa	37 B3
Pajarito	38 D4

ENTERTAINMENT
Cine Hoyts	39 E5
Máscara	(see 35)
Zero Hotel	40 B4

TRANSPORT
Bus to Quintay	41 G5
Terminal Rodoviario	42 G5

rucksack days are over. It's perfect for couples and those intent on extra zzz's.

Zero Hotel (☎ 211-3113; www.zerohotel.com; Rosas 343, Cerro Alegre; d with street/sea view incl breakfast CH$90,000/140,000; ❄ 🖥 🖩) Indulge in minimalist chic – soak in an outdoor Jacuzzi or meet the Honesty Bar – an old-fashioned livingroom booze cabinet supplied with a chemist's selection of spirits and mixers. Rooms are ample and elegant, with details just right. The service is stellar but downright relaxed.

Also recommended:

Patiperro (☎ 317-3153; www.patiperrohostel.cl; Templeman 657, Cerro Alegre; dm CH$7000; 🖩) Bright, ultrasimple dorms.

Casa Aventura (☎ 275-5963; www.casaventura.cl; Pasaje Gálvez 11, Cerro Concepción; dm CH$7000; s/d without bathroom incl breakfast CH$9000/17,000) Dorms and doubles are airy, breakfast good but bathrooms need improvement. Central and English-speaking.

Casa Familiar Carrasco (☎ 221-0737; www.casacarrasco.cl; Abtao 668, Cerro Concepción; r per person CH$10,000-12,000) The colors spell preppy nightmare but this old-fashioned inn has delightful elderly owners and spectacular roof-deck vistas.

Eating

On Sunday, most restaurants are open only noon to 4pm, unless noted.

Santa Isabel (Av Pedro Montt btwn Las Heras & Carrera; ☽ 9am-9pm) Supermarket with upstairs cafeteria.

Mercado Cardonal (cnr Yungay & Rawson) Get your goat cheese and olives on this block of crisp and colorful produce.

Mercado Puerto (cnr Blanco & San Martín) Meals at the fish market are ultra fresh but nothing fancy.

El Sandwich Cubano (☎ 223-8247; O'Higgins 1224, Local 16, El Plan; sandwiches CH$1700; noon-10pm Mon-Sat) Authentic, fresh over-stuffed sandwiches. Try the *ropa vieja* (literally, 'old clothes,' shredded beef).

our pick Antaño (☎ 318-0464; Av Almirante Montt, Cerro Alegre; set lunch CH$4000-5000) Don't miss delicious, authentic Chilean comfort food such as beef slow-simmered in Carmenère, luxuriant crab casserole and fresh salads arranged as bouquets. Recipes are scrawled on the blackboard – note that each dish easily feeds two.

Vinilo (☎ 223-0665; Av Almirante Montt 448, Cerro Alegre; snacks & sandwiches CH$4000, mains CH$6900; ☽ 9am-midnight Mon-Thu, 9am-3am Fri & Sat, 10am-midnight Sun) While dinner is overpriced, we like the worn ambience, the grainy jazz records

and communal table where you can sip wine and meet travelers.

Casino Social J Cruz (☎ 221-1225; Condell 1466, El Plan; 2-person meals CH$4500; ☽ 10pm-1am Sun-Thu, to 4am Fri & Sat) A delicious hodgepodge of graffiti and laissez-faire attitude. Everybody orders *chorrillana* (a mountain of French fries under a blanket of fried pork, onions and egg).

Allegretto (☎ 296-8839; www.allegretto.cl; Pilcomayo 529, Cerro Concepción; pizzas CH$4600-5800; ☽ 1-3:30pm & 7-11pm Mon-Thu, 1-3:30pm & 7pm-midnight Fri & Sat, 1-4:30pm & 7-11pm Sun) Big, deliciously crispy pizzas come with very creative toppings here. Things get rowdy round the upstairs foosball table, which is surrounded by a mural of screaming fans.

Le Filou de Montpellier (☎ 2224-663; Av Almirante Montt 382; set menu CH$5500) A matchbox-sized French restaurant serving sumptuous fourcourse meals worthy of applause. The menu changes daily, but offerings may include fresh fish or steak in Roquefort sauce. It's not expensive either.

Also recommended are these ones:

Puerto Sushi (☎ 223-9017; Esmeralda 1138, El Plan; sushi CH$1300-2900, 2-person combos CH$4900) Good-value sushi platters.

Bambú (☎ 223-4216; Independencia 1790, 2nd fl, El Plan; set lunch CH$1900; ☽ 10:30am-5:30pm) Ultrahealthy tofu dishes, salads and wholemeal grains.

El Desayunador (Av Almirante Montt 399; breakfast CH$3000) Serves all-day breakfasts, options include juice, eggs, fruit salad or hot chocolate.

Drinking

Pajarito (☎ 225-8910; Donoso 1433, El Plan; ☽ 11am-2am Mon-Thu, to late Fri & Sat) Artsy *porteños* (residents of Valparaíso) in their 20s and 30s cram the Formica tables at this laid-back, old-school bar.

Cinzano (Plaza Anibal Pinto 1182; ☽ 10am-2am Mon-Sat) A classic, this 1896 bar is the cliché haunt of old crooners belting tangos.

La Playa (Cochrane 568; ☽ 10am-past midnight) Long bar, cheap pitchers of beer and hedonistic touches make this one great outing.

Entertainment

Máscara (☎ 221-9841; www.mascara.cl; Plaza Aníbal Pinto 1178, El Plan; admission CH$2500-3000; ☽ 11pm-late Tue-Sat) The perfect mix for music savvy clubbers, with cheap beer, a dance space and few teenyboppers – the crowd is 20s to 30s.

CHILE

La Piedra Feliz (☎ 225-6788; www.lapiedrafeliz.cl; Av Errázuriz 1054; admission from CH$3000) A massive waterfront institution featuring jazz, blues, tango, son, salsa, rock, drinking, dining and cinema.

Cine Hoyts (☎ 2594-709; Av Pedro Montt 2111; admission CH$2000) Movie theater.

Getting There & Away

The **Terminal Rodoviario** (☎ 293-9695; Av Pedro Montt 2800) is across from the Congreso Nacional. Bus service from Valparaíso is almost identical to that from Viña del Mar. Many buses go to various points north and south, with fares and times similar to Santiago. On weekends, you should get your ticket to Santiago in advance; **Tur Bus** (☎ 221-2028; www .turbus.cl) has the most departures (CH$4000, two hours). Most buses heading north leave at night, while many to the south leave in the morning.

You can reach Mendoza (CH$10,000, eight hours) in Argentina with Tur Bus or **Cata Internacional** (☎ 225-7587; www.catainternacional.com).

Sol del Pacífico (☎ 275-2030) has buses to the beach towns Horcón (CH$1100) and Maitencillo (CH$1200) every 20 minutes, and to Zapallar (CH$1500) roughly every 40 minutes. They run along Av Errázuriz and call in at Viña del Mar on their way.

Getting Around

Rent a car in nearby Viña (right). *Micros* (minibuses; CH$400 to CH$500) run to and from Viña and all over the city, as do *colectivos* (CH$400). Avoid the traffic to Viña by hopping on **Metro Regional de Valparaíso** (Merval; ☎ 252-7633; www.merval.cl), a commuter train that leaves from **Estación Puerto** (cnr Errázuriz & Urriola) and **Estación Bellavista** (cnr Errázuriz & Bellavista) to Viña del Mar (CH$900). Trains run till 10pm. Valpo's **ascensores** (from CH$250; ☾ 7am-8pm or 8:30pm) are considered both transport and entertainment. The oldest, Ascensor Cordillera, runs from 6am to 11:30pm.

ISLA NEGRA

A stirring testament to imagination, whimsy and affection, Pablo Neruda's outlandish favorite **house** (☎ 035-461-284; www.fundacion neruda.org; Poeta Neruda s/n; admission by guided tour only in English/Spanish CH$3500/3000; ☾ 10am-6pm Tue-Sun) sits atop a rocky headland 80km

south of Valparaíso (Map p379). The house includes extraordinary collections of bowsprits, ships in bottles, nautical instruments and wood carvings. His tomb is also here alongside that of his third wife, Matilde. Reservations are advised in high season. Isla Negra is not, by the way, an island, despite the Spanish name.

Pullman Bus (☎ 600-320-3200; www.pullman.cl) comes here direct from Santiago's Terminal de Buses Alameda (CH$6000, 1½ hours, every 30 minutes). **Pullman Bus Lago Peñuela** (☎ 222-4025) leaves from Valparaíso's bus terminal every 10 to 15 minutes (CH$2600, 1½ hours).

VIÑA DEL MAR

☎ 032 / pop 318,200

Trim green gardens and palm-fringed boulevards characterize this city on the sea. Known as the Garden City, because of its many parks and flowers, or just Viña for short, this city beach resort has a scrubbed, modern feel that couldn't contrast more sharply with the personality of neighboring Valpo. After the railway linked Santiago and Valparaíso, the well-heeled flocked to Viña del Mar, building grand houses and mansions away from the congested port. Viña remains a popular weekend and summer destination for *santiaguinos*.

Viña's beaches can get very crowded during holidays and are subject to cool morning fogs. The chilly Humboldt current can also put off swimmers. Summer is pickpocketing high season, so watch your belongings, especially on the beach.

Information

Afex (Av Arlegui 690) Changes traveler's checks and currency.

Hospital Gustavo Fricke (☎ 680-041; Álvarez 1532) East of downtown.

Lavarápido (☎ 290-6263; Av Arlegui 440; per load CH$3700; ☾ 10am-9pm Mon-Sat)

Municipal tourist office (www.visitevinadelmar.cl) Plaza Vergara (☎ 226-9330; Av Arlegui 715; ☾ 9am-2pm & 3-7pm Mon-Fri, 10am-2pm & 3-7pm Sat & Sun); Rodoviario (☎ 275-2000; Av Valparaíso 1055; ☾ 9am-7pm) Provides city maps and events calendars.

Post office (Plaza Latorre 32)

Tecomp (Av Valparaíso 684; ☾ 9am-midnight Mon-Sat, 11am-9pm Sun) Offers cheap international calling.

Tera Cyber (☎ 276-8091; Quinta 219; per hr CH$500; ☾ 9am-12:30am) Offers internet access.

CHILE

VIÑA DEL MAR

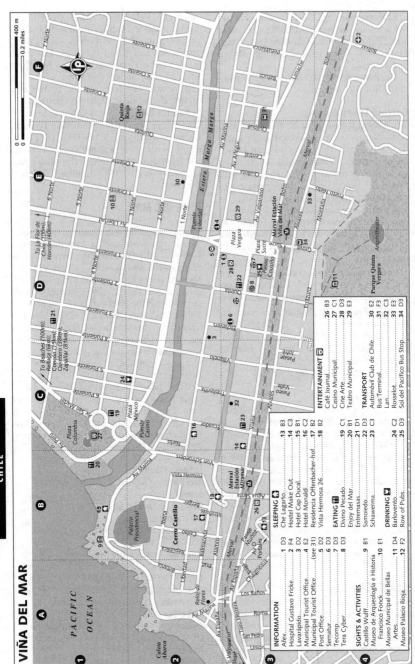

INFORMATION
Afex.....................................**1** D3
Hospital Gustavo Fricke..........**2** F4
Lavarápido............................**3** D2
Municipal Tourist Office...........**4** E2
Municipal Tourist Office........(see 31)
Post Office............................**5** D2
Sernatur...............................**6** D3
Tecomp................................**7** D3
Tera Cyber............................**8** D3

SIGHTS & ACTIVITIES
Castillo Wulff........................**9** B1
Museo de Arqueología e Historia
Francisco Fonck...................**10** E1
Museo Municipal de Bellas
Artes.................................**11** D4
Museo Palacio Rioja...............**12** F2

SLEEPING
Che Lagarto..........................**13** B3
Hostel Make Out....................**14** C3
Hotel Cap Ducal.....................**15** B1
Hotel Monaldi.......................**16** C2
Residencia Offenbacher-hof.....**17** B2
Vista Hermosa 26..................**18** B2

EATING
Divino Pecado.......................**19** C1
Enjoy del Mar.......................**20** B1
Entremasas...........................**21** D1
Samoiedo.............................**22** D3
Schaverma...........................**23** C3

DRINKING
Barlovento...........................**24** C2
Row of Pubs.........................**25** D3

ENTERTAINMENT
Café Journal.........................**26** B3
Casino Municipal....................**27** C1
Cine Arte.............................**28** D3
Teatro Municipal....................**29** E3

TRANSPORT
Automóvil Club de Chile.........**30** E2
Bus Terminal.........................**31** F3
Lan....................................**32** C3
Rosselot..............................**33** E3
Sol del Pacífico Bus Stop.........**34** D3

Sights & Activities

Specializing in Rapa Nui (Easter Island) archaeology and Chilean natural history, the small **Museo de Arqueológico e Historia Francisco Fonck** (4 Norte 784; www.museofonck.cl; admission CH$1500; ✿ 9:30am-6pm Tue-Fri, till 2pm Sat & Sun) features an original *moai* (enormous stone sculpture from Easter Island), Mapuche silverwork, Peruvian ceramics, plus insects and stuffed birds.

Viña's nickname 'the garden city' proves just at the magnificently landscaped **Parque Quinta Vergara** (✿ 7am-6pm), south of the railroad, which has plants from all over the world. Onsite is the Venetian-style **Palacio Vergara** (1908), which in turn contains the less inspiring **Museo de Bellas Artes** (admission CH$600; ✿ 10am-1:30pm & 3-6pm Tue-Sun).

On the north side of the estuary is the overly glitzy **Casino Municipal**; to the west is **Castillo Wulff**, built in 1880; and the fancy boat-shaped **Cap Ducal hotel**.

Festivals & Events

Viña del Mar's most popular event is the annual **Festival Internacional de la Canción** (International Song Festival), held every February in the amphitheater of the Quinta Vergara. Adored by Chileans, it attracts big names from the Latin American pop world and English-language has-beens.

Sleeping

Accommodations are overpriced and fill up fast in summer.

Che Lagarto Hostel (✿ 262-5759; www.chelagarto.com; Av Diego Portales 131; dm/d incl breakfast CH$10,000/36,000; 🖳) The sprawling grounds are a good start, but rooms in this sagging mansion are bare with interrogation lighting. Still, it is clean and friendly, though doubles are priced too high for the value.

Hostal Make Out (✿ 317-4150; www.makeout.cl; Viana 147; dm CH$10,000; 🖳) Despite the promise of its name, this is your regular HI hostel with a slew of acceptable bunk rooms and dated bathrooms. Supervision is minimal. Light sleepers, beware the adjoining bar.

Hotel Monaldi (✿ 288-1484; www.hotelmonaldi.cl; Av Arlegui 172; s/d incl breakfast CH$15,000/25,000, s without bathroom CH$9000; 🖳) Five old houses have been knocked together to form this labyrinthine hotel. Knick-knacks and photos clutter the walls and surfaces of the two living rooms – one has big sofas and a DVD player – and

you can use the kitchen, too. Try to bag one of the bigger, brighter upstairs rooms.

Vista Hermosa 26 (✿ 266-6820; www.vistahermosa26.cl; Vista Hermosa 26; s/d/t incl breakfast CH$17,000/24,000/33,000; 🖳) A matronly mansion on the edge of Cerro Castillo with snug doubles and squeaky clean bathrooms.

Residencia Offenbacher-hof (✿ 262-1483; www.offenbacher-hof.cl; Balmaceda 102; s/d incl breakfast CH$30,000/35,000, s/d deluxe CH$35,000/40,000; 🖳) With commanding views, this clapboard guesthouse effuses style, such as antique furnishings and bamboo bedframes. Bathrooms are sparking white, and boast thick towels. Deluxe rooms (with views) are well worth the upgrade. The glassed-in dining area serves breakfast with fruit and jams.

Eating & Drinking

The pedestrian area around Av Valparaíso has a slew of cheap eats. Paseo Cousiño is home to convivial pubs, some featuring live music.

Entremasas (✿ 297-1821; 5 Norte 377; empanadas CH$900; ✿ 10:30am-9:30pm) Prawns in cilantro, sausage and goat cheese…you won't see these empanada combinations elsewhere in Chile, so make the small investment.

Schawerma (✿ 233-6835; Ecuador 225; mains CH$1600-2500; ✿ 11:30am-9:30pm Mon-Sat) This might be the fastest food in Chile, and wow, is it tasty. The Palestinian cook expertly serves chicken or beef shawarma with slivers of roasted tomato or lemon in a lightly toasted wrap. Ask for hot sauce. There's also fresh hummus.

Samoiedo (✿ 268-1382; Valparaíso 637; set lunch menu CH$4000-6500, sandwiches CH$2200-2800; ✿ 12:30-11pm Mon-Sat) A traditional *confitería* where you can get brimming sandwiches or a classic plate of steak and fries.

Enjoy del Mar (✿ 250-0788; Av Perú s/n; sandwiches & sushi CH$3500-4500, mains CH$7500-10,500; ✿ 9am-midnight) Come for a sunset drink and bask in the panoramic views of the Pacific above the mouth of the Marga Marga. The extensive ice-cream bar will introduce you to wonders like Coca Cola ice cream. Yum? The branch on Av Perú has cheaper food but lesser views.

Divino Pecado (✿ 297-5790; Av San Martín 180; mains CH$6300-7900; ✿ 12:30-3pm & 8-11pm Mon-Sat, 12:30-4pm & 8-11pm Sun) Upscale Italian, with homemade pastas worth every calorie: think tortellini in sage butter or wasabi-salmon pansotti. Reserve ahead.

CHILE

Entertainment

Barlovento (☎ 297-7472; 2 Norte 195; ☼ 6pm-3am Mon-Sat) Hipster headquarters, this concrete-and-steel bar serves spot-on cocktails.

Café Journal (cnr Santa Agua & Alvarez; ☼ until 4am Fri & Sat) Electronic music is mixed at this boomingly popular club with three heaving dance floors, beers on tap and walls plastered in yesterday's news.

Cine Arte (Plaza Vergara 142; tickets US$6) Arthouse movies are screened here.

La Flor de Chile (off Map p406; ☎ 268-9554; 8 Norte 601; ☼ 10pm-late) Join viñamarinos young and old in the closely packed tables of this gloriously old-school bar.

Teatro Municipal (Plaza Vergara) This grand building stages plays, chamber-music concerts and arthouse movies.

Getting There & Away

LAN (☎ 600-526-2000; Av Valparaíso 276) runs a shuttle (US$10) to Santiago's Padahuel Airport from the corner of Tres Norte and Libertad. Or take a bus toward Santiago and ask to be left at 'Cruce al Aeropuerto' to shave about an hour from the trip.

All long-distance services operate from the **Rodoviario Viña del Mar** (☎ 275-2000; www.rodoviario.cl; Valparaíso 1055), four long blocks east of Plaza Vergara. Nearly all long-distance buses (some Sol del Pacífico) to and from Valparaíso stop here; see p405 for details of services.

For car hire, try **Rosselot** (☎ 382-888; Alvarez 762). The **Automóvil Club de Chile** (Acchi; ☎ 689-505; 1 Norte 901) is just north of the Marga.

Getting Around

Frequent local buses run by **Transporte Metropolitano Valparaíso** (TMV; www.tmv.cl; one way CH$460) connect Viña and Valparaíso or try the **Metro Regional de Valparaíso** (Merval; ☎ 252-7633; www.merval.cl) commuter rail (CH$900).

To reach towns north along the coast, **Sol del Pacífico** (☎ 275-2030) has buses to the stop at the corner of Grove and Álvares. Local buses also go to Reñaca (CH$1000), including green 201 (from Av España), blue 405 (from Av Marina) and orange 607, 601 or 605 (from Plaza Vergara or Av Libertad). The 601 and 605 continue to Concón.

AROUND VIÑA DEL MAR

Coastal towns immediately north of Viña have better beaches, but their quiet character has eroded with the piling on of suburbs and apartment buildings. **Concón**, 15km from Viña, is worth a trip for its unpretentious seafood restaurants. **Las Deliciosas** (☎ 903-665; Av Borgoño 25370, Concón) does exquisite empanadas, including cheese and crab (CH$850).

Another 23km beyond Concón is **Quintero**, a sleepy peninsula dotted with beaches nestled between rocks. From there it's a CH$2000 taxi ride to **Ritoque**, one of the best and least-discovered beaches around. A small group of houses (some of them built from recycled materials) is clustered around the northern end of the 10km stretch of sands. Surfing, horse riding and sea kayaking are all popular. Stay at **Dunas Hostal** (☎ 099-051-1748; www.dunashostal.com; Playa Ritoque; dm/d CH$8000/20,000), two cute beach houses with hammocks, surf rentals and good vibes. Reservations are a must. **Ritoque Expediciones** (☎ 032-281-6344; www.ritoque expediciones.cl) runs full- and half-day riding trips through the dunes, but their full-moon rides get rave reviews.

Further north, **Horcón** was Chile's first hippie haven. Now it's a clutter of bright shacks and identical seafood restaurants. Before reaching the cove, a road on the right follows a rocky, crescent-moon bay where wild camping is possible. At the far end is the nudist beach, 'Playa La Luna.'

Continue north 35km to reach **Zapallar**, the most exclusive of Chile's coastal resorts with still-unspoiled beaches flanked by densely wooded hillsides. Budget accommodations are not the norm in Zapallar but **Residencial Margarita** (☎ 033-741-284, Januario Ovalle 143; r per person CH$10,000) bucks the trend. Rooms are well kept and neat, and have reasonable bathrooms. Book ahead. Superb seafood is yours at **El Chiringuito** (Caleta de Pescadores; mains CH$8100-10,300; ☼ noon-6pm Mon-Thu, noon-midnight Fri-Sun), with crushed shells underfoot and a wall of windows that peers to the sea.

Several bus companies visit Zapallar direct from Santiago, including Tur Bus and Pullman. Sol del Pacífico comes up the coast from Viña.

NORTHERN CHILE

Traveling inland, the balmy coast of sun-bathers and surfers shifts to cactus scrub plains and dry mountains streaked in reddish tones. Mines scar these ore-rich mammoths whose primary reserve, copper, is high-octane fuel to Chile's economic engine. But there's life here as well, in the fertile valleys producing *pisco* grapes, papayas and avocados. Clear skies mean exceptional celestial observation opportunities. No wonder many international telescopic, optical and radio projects are based here. The driest desert in the world, the Atacama is a refuge of flamingos on salt lagoons, sculpted moonscapes and geysers ringed by snow-tipped volcanoes. In short, these places are an orgy for the senses and ripe for exploration.

Chile's 2000km northern stretch takes in Norte Chico, or 'region of 10,000 mines,' a semiarid transition zone from the Valle Central to the Atacama. Its main attractions are the beaches, La Serena, Valle Elqui and the observatories. The Atacama Desert occupies 'Norte Grande,' gained from Peru and Bolivia in the War of the Pacific. The stamp of ancient South American cultures is evident in enormous geoglyphs on barren hillsides. Aymara peoples still farm the *precordillera* (the foothills of the Andes) and pasture llamas and alpacas in the highlands. You can divert from the desert scenery to explore the working mine of Chuquimaquata or brave the frisky surf of arid coastal cities.

Take precautions against altitude sickness in the mountains and avoid drinking tap water in the desert reaches. Coastal *camanchaca* (dense fog) keeps the climate cool along the beach, while *altiplano* temperatures change drastically from day to night.

OVALLE
☎ 053 / pop 104,000

Chess rivals gather on the plaza of this unpretentious market town. Ovalle offers a glimpse of city life in the provinces and is the best base for Parque Nacional Fray Jorge or Valle del Encanto. The tourist kiosk sits at the corner of Benavente and Ariztia Oriente. **Tres Valles Turismo** (☎ 629-650; Libertad 496) organizes tours and exchanges money. ATMs can be found along Victoria, at the plaza.

In the grand old train station, **Museo del Limarí** (cnr Covarrubias & Antofagasta; admission CH$600, Sun free; ☎ 9am-6pm Tue-Fri, 10am-1pm Sat & Sun) displays some gorgeous ceramics that indicate trans-Andean links between the Diaguita peoples of coastal Chile and northwestern Argentina.

Sleeping & Eating
Jamies Crazy House (☎ 098-591-8686; www.jaimescrazy house.com, Tocopilla 92; dm CH$6000, breakfast CH$2000; 🖳) A welcome addition, this new hostel run by Juana Magdelena has spacious dorms and close proximity to the fruit and veg market.

Hotel Roxy (☎ 620-080; Libertad 155; s/d/tr CH$7000/9300/11,700, without bathroom CH$5600/7500/8400) This sun-drenched and serene place is adorned with lemon trees in the garden and checkered floors. On the downside, it's slightly unkempt.

Feria Modelo de Ovalle (Av Benavente; ☺ 8am-4pm Mon, Wed, Fri & Sat) A buzzing hive of market activity with scores of different fruit and vegetables.

Club Social Árabe (☎ 620-015; Arauco 255; mains CH$4000) This is a lofty atrium serving superb stuffed grape leaves, summer squash or red peppers and baklava, in addition to Chilean specialties.

Drinking
Café Real (☎ 624-526; Vicuña MacKenna 419; ☺ 9am-2:30am Mon-Sat) Cheery and cosmopolitan, with young things knocking back espressos and cold Cristal. There's a pool table and occasional live music.

El Quijote (Arauco 295; ☺ 9:30-1am) A musty bar paying homage to literary and leftist Latin America.

Getting There & Away
From the **bus terminal** (cnr Maestranza & Balmaceda) plenty of buses go to Santiago (CH$7000, five hours), La Serena (CH$1800, 1¾ hours) and more northerly points. A faster way to La Serena (CH$2300, 1¼ hours) is by **Agencia Tacso** (Ariztía Pontiente 159).

AROUND OVALLE
Petroglyphs, pictographs and ancient mortars blanket **Monumento Arqueológico Valle del Encanto** (admission CH$300; ☺ 8:15am-6pm May-Aug, 8am-8:30pm Sep-Apr), a canyon 19km west of Ovalle in a rocky tributary of the Río Limarí. These dancing stick–men and alien-like forms are remnants of the El Molle culture (AD 200 to AD 700). Visitors can camp and picnic here. From Ovalle, taxis cost CH$12,000 roundtrip, or any westbound bus will drop you at the highway marker from where it's an easy 5km walk on a clearly marked road.

An ecological island of lush Valdivian cloud forest in semi-desert surroundings, **Parque**

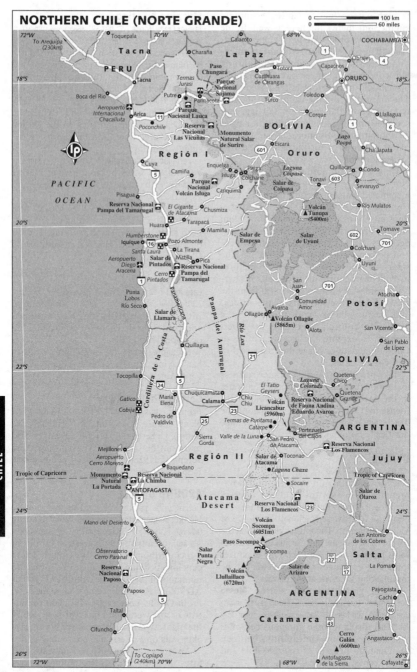

NORTHERN CHILE (NORTE GRANDE)

Nacional Fray Jorge (admission CH$1600; 🕑 9am-5pm, day-use only) is 82km west of Ovalle. This Unesco World Biosphere Reserve protects 400 hectares of truly unique vegetation nourished by moist fog. Arrive via a westward lateral off the Panamericana, 20km north of the Ovalle junction. There's no public transport, but agencies in La Serena and Ovalle offer tours.

LA SERENA

☎ 051 / pop 150,000

Blessed with neocolonial architecture, shady streets and golden shores, peaceful La Serena turns trendy beach resort come summer. Founded in 1544, Chile's second-oldest city is a short jaunt from character-laden villages, sun-soaked *pisco* vineyards and international observatories for stargazing. Nearby **Coquimbo** is quite a bit more rough-and-tumble, but lives and breathes a hearty nightlife. Mornings in La Serena often stew in chilly fog.

Information

Banks with 24-hour ATMs line the plaza.

Conaf (☎ 272-798; coquimbo@conaf.cl; Cordovez 281) Supplies brochures on Fray Jorge and Isla Choros.

Entel (Prat 571) Make calls from here.

Hospital Juan de Dios (☎ 200-500; Balmaceda 916) Has an emergency entrance at Larraín Alcalde and Anfión Muñoz.

Infernet (Balmaceda 417; per hr CH$600) Internet cafe with booths and webcams.

Lavaseco (☎ 225-195; Balmaceda 851; per kg CH$1300; 🕑 9am-1pm & 3-7pm Mon-Fri, to 2pm Sat) Laundry.

Post office (cnr Matta & Prat) Opposite the Plaza de Armas.

Sernatur (☎ 225-199; www.regionestrella.cl; Matta 405; 🕑 8:30am-10pm Mon-Fri, 9am-10pm Sat & Sun) Exceptionally attentive.

Sights & Activities

La Serena has a whopping 29 churches to its credit but relatively few takers. On the Plaza de Armas is the 1844 **Iglesia Catedral**, and a block west is the mid-18th-century **Iglesia Santo Domingo**. The stone colonial-era **Iglesia San Francisco** (Balmaceda 640) dates from the early 1600s.

Museo Histórico Casa Gabriel González Videla (☎ 215-082; Matta 495; admission CH$600; 🕑 10am-6pm Mon-Fri, to 1pm Sat) is named after La Serena's native son and Chile's president from 1946 to 1952, who took over the Communist party, then outlawed it, driving Pablo Neruda out of the senate and into exile. Pop upstairs to check out the modern art. The eclectic **Museo**

Arqueológico (☎ 224-492; cnr Cordovez & Cienfuegos; admission CH$600; 🕑 9:30am-5:50pm Tue-Fri, 10am-1pm & 4-7pm Sat, to 1pm Sun) houses Atacameño mummies, a *moai* from Rapa Nui, Diaguita artifacts and a map of the distribution of Chile's indigenous population. **Mercado La Recova** offers a jumble of dried fruits, rain sticks and artisan jewelry. Retreat into the ambience of trickling brooks, skating swans and rock gardens at **Kokoro No Niwa** (Jardín del Corazón; admission CH$600; 🕑 10am-6pm), a well-maintained Japanese garden at the south end of Parque Pedro de Valdivia.

Wide sandy **beaches** stretch from La Serena's nonfunctional lighthouse to Coquimbo. Avoid strong rip currents between the west end of Av Aguirre and Cuatro Esquinas. Choose the beaches marked 'Playa Apta' south of Cuatro Esquinas and around Coquimbo. A bike path runs about 4km by the beach. Local **bodyboarders** hit Playa El Faro, where **Maui Girl** (Av del Mar s/n), 3km south of the lighthouse, rents a board-wetsuit combo for CH$5000 per day. Playa Totoralillo, south of Coquimbo, is rated highly for its surf breaks and **windsurfing.**

Over in Coquimbo, **Cruz del Tercer Milenio** (Cross of the Third Millennium; www.cruzdeltercermilenio.cl; admission CH$1500; 🕑 8:30am-10pm) is a 96m-high concrete cross lit up at night. Ride the elevator to the top for dizzying bay views.

Excursions range from national-park visits to nighttime astronomical trips, *pisco*-tasting tours to New Age trips to UFO central in Cochiguaz. Agencies offer full-day trips through the Elqui Valley (CH$17,000), Parque Nacional Fray Jorge and Valle del Encanto (CH$26,000), and Parque Nacional Pingüino de Humboldt (CH$28,000) and stargazing at Observatorio Comunal Cerro Mamalluca (CH$15,000). The minimum number of passengers ranges from two to six.

Ingservtur (☎ 220-165; www.ingservtur.cl; Matta 611) Well-established with friendly English and German-speaking staff and discounts for students.

Inti Mahini (☎ 224-350; www.intimahinatravel.cl; Prat 214) A youth-oriented agency offering standard tours plus useful advice on independent travel.

Talinay Adventure Expeditions (☎ 218-658; www.talinaychile.com; Prat 470, Local 22) Has bilingual guides, standard and adventure options, including mountain biking, climbing, kayaking, diving, horse riding and sandboarding. They also rent bikes.

Festivals & Events

The **Festival de La Serena** attracts big-name Chilean musicians and comedians in early February. Around the same time the **Feria Internacional del Libro de La Serena** gathers prominent Chilean authors at the historical museum.

Sleeping

Hostal Nomades (☎ 315-665; www.hostalnomade.cl; Regimiento Coquimbo 5, Coquimbo; campsite per person

CH$3000, dm CH$7000; s/d without bathroom CH$12,500/ 25,000; 💻) The best budget option in the port of Coquimbo, 11km from La Serena, is this 1850 mansion which once held the French consulate. It now features dorms, on-site bar, ping-pong table and large garden area.

El Hibisco (☎ 211-407; mauricioberrios2002@yahoo.es; Juan de Dios Peni 636; s/d CH$5000/10,000; 💻) A simple

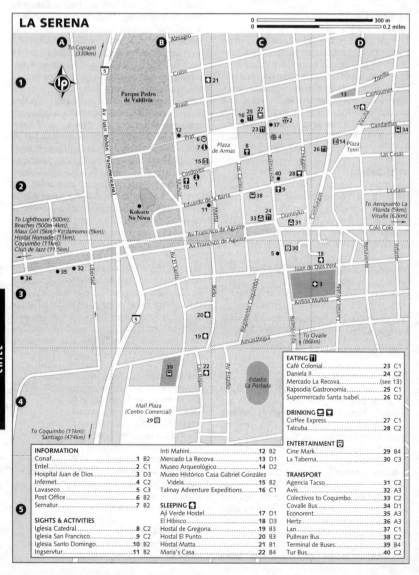

LA SERENA

0 —————— 300 m
0 —————— 0.2 miles

INFORMATION	
Conaf...**1** B2
Entel..**2** C1
Hospital Juan de Dios.................**3** D3
Infernet.....................................**4** C2
Lavaseco...................................**5** C3
Post Office................................**6** B2
Sernatur....................................**7** B2

SIGHTS & ACTIVITIES	
Iglesia Catedral.........................**8** C2
Iglesia San Francisco.................**9** C2
Iglesia Santo Domingo..............**10** B2
Ingservtur................................**11** B2

Inti Mahini................................**12** B2
Mercado La Recova....................**13** D1
Museo Arqueológico..................**14** D2
Museo Histórico Casa Gabriel González Videla..............................**15** B2
Talinay Adventure Expeditions...**16** C1

SLEEPING 🏠	
Ají Verde Hostel........................**17** D1
El Hibisco.................................**18** D3
Hostal de Gregoria....................**19** B3
Hostal El Punto.........................**20** B3
Hostal Matta.............................**21** B1
Maria's Casa.............................**22** B4

EATING 🍴	
Café Colonial.............................**23** C1
Daniela II..................................**24** C2
Mercado La Recova.................(see **13**)
Rapsodia Gastronomía...............**25** C1
Supermercado Santa Isabel........**26** D2

DRINKING 🍷	
Coffee Express...........................**27** C1
Talcuba.....................................**28** C2

ENTERTAINMENT 🎭	
Cine Mark.................................**29** B4
La Taberna................................**30** C3

TRANSPORT	
Agencia Tacso...........................**31** C2
Avis..**32** A3
Colectivos to Coquimbo.............**33** C2
Covalle Bus...............................**34** D1
Econorent.................................**35** A3
Hertz..**36** A3
Lan...**37** C1
Pullman Bus..............................**38** C2
Terminal de Buses.....................**39** B4
Tur Bus.....................................**40** C2

CHILE

family guesthouse, just not for Rastas (note the polite *'no marijuana en casa'* sign). Includes shared facilities, spongy mattresses, laundry and access to the cool glassed-in kitchen.

Maria's Casa (☎ 229-282; www.hostalmariacasa .cl; Las Rojas 18; r per person without bathroom CH$7000; 🖳) Extrafriendly backpacker stop with familial attention and simple rooms around a grassy backyard. The quietest rooms are in the far back.

Ají Verde Hostel (☎ 489-016; www.ajiverdehostal .cl; Vicuña 415; dm/s/d CH$8000/15,000/23,000, s/d without bathroom CH$12,000/16,000; 🖳) Uncomfortably close to the fish market for some, nonetheless, this is a clean and comfortable HI budget option.

Hostal de Gregoria (☎ 224-400; www.hostalde gregoria.cl; Bello 1067; d with/without bathroom incl breakfast CH$12,000/9000; 🖳) The busy decor of satin and sheen is immaculate, and the hosts are friendly. It's a shame that internet is extra.

Hostal El Punto (☎ 228-474; www.hostalelpunto.cl; Bello 979; dm CH$7000, s/d incl breakfast CH$15,000/24,000, s/d without bathroom CH$13,000/16,000; 🖳) A gorgeous German guesthouse accentuated with florid colors and sunny terraces; it also has a book exchange and laundry. It may even be a little *too* orderly. Breakfast is above average and the multilingual staff provide travel tips. To splurge, get a balcony room.

Hostal Matta (☎ 210-014; www.hostalmatta.cl; Matta 234; s/d CH$16,000/18,000; r without bathroom CH$14,000; 🖳) A deal for its snug doubles, with bright colors, friendly staff and an attractive patio.

Eating

Supermercado Santa Isabel (Cienfuegos 545; 🕙 9am-10pm Mon-Sat, to 9pm Sun) serves self-caterers.

Mercado La Recova (cnr Cienfuegos & Cantournet; 🕙 9am-6pm) Cheap eats above the market include seafood and chicken *cazuela* (stew).

Café Colonial (Balmaceda 475; breakfast from CH$2000, set lunch CH$2500, mains CH$3000-6000; 🕙 9am-late. Closed Sun) Though it's small and smoky, this homesick restaurant delivers if you're craving scones for breakfast or a lunchtime kebab or burger. Check for live music on weekends.

Daniela II (Aguirre 456; mains CH$2500-4000) This plain Jane does Chilean comfort food in generous portions to the acclaim of locals.

Rapsodia Gastronomía (☎ 543-016; Prat 470; mains CH$3000-6000; 🕙 breakfast, lunch & dinner, closed Sun) Sprawling around an interior courtyard, this old *casona* (large house) is a leisurely downtown retreat. Come for afternoon drinks or later on for occasional live music, tasty salads and sandwiches.

Kardamomo (☎ 216-060; Av del Mar 4000, 3km south of the lighthouse; mains CH$4000-7800; 🕙 lunch & dinner) A beachfront spot that rocks for cocktails with sushi or fresh tempura scallops. The service is snappy, the menu ranges from Asian to Peruvian and good live music keeps diners late on weekends. Hotel pickups are free.

More trendy and top-end eateries line the beach toward Peñuelas.

Drinking

Coffee Express (cnr Prat & Balmaceda; 🕙 9am-9pm Mon-Fri, 10am-9pm Sat) Buenos Aires–style cafe serving some of La Serena's best java.

Talcuba (Eduardo de la Barra 589; 🕙 5:30pm-late Mon-Fri, 7:30pm-late Sat & Sun) University students rub shoulders to rock and pop sounds in this dimly lit little tavern. Cheap drinks are the house specialty – try a papaya sour or Serena libre.

Entertainment

Nightclubs lining the seafront to Barrio Inglés Coquimbo go full-on in the summer season.

Cine Mark (☎ 212-144; www.cinemark.cl; Mall Plaza, Av Albert Solari 1490; admission CH$2500) Screens big-name movies.

Club de Jazz (☎ 288-784; Aldunate 739; admission CH$2500) A local icon located in nearby Coquimbo, this neoclassical house with marble stairs hosts live music on weekends from 11pm.

La Taberna (Balmaceda 824) A seedy bar in a century-old house. Come midnight on weekends, it ignites with Chilean folk music.

Getting There & Away
AIR

La Serena's **Aeropuerto La Florida** (Ruta 41) is 5km east of downtown. **LAN** (☎ 600-526-2000; Balmaceda 406) flies three times daily to Santiago (CH$60,000, 50 minutes) and twice daily to Antofagasta (CH$70,000, 1¼ hours). There's also an office with longer hours in Mall Plaza.

BUS

La Serena's **Terminal de Buses** (☎ 224-573; cnr Amunátegui & Av El Santo) has dozens of carriers

BUS FARES		
Destination	Cost (CH$)	Duration (hr)
Antofagasta	20,000–34,000	13
Arica	34,000–38,000	23
Calama	24,000–39,000	16
Copiapó	9000–18,000	5
Iquique	24,000–37,000	19
Santiago	8000–23,000	7

plying the Carretera Panamericana from Santiago north to Arica, including **Tur Bus** (☎ 215-953; www.turbus.com; Terminal or Balmaceda 437), **Pullman Bus** (☎ 218-252, 225-284; Eduardo de la Barra 435) and **Pullman Carmelita** (☎ 225-240).

Via Elqui has frequent departures to Pisco Elqui (CH$1800, two hours) and Monte Grande (CH$1800, two hours) between 7am and 10:30pm. Buses Serenamar runs several buses a day to Guanaqueros (CH$1200, 50 minutes) and Tongoy (CH$1300, one hour).

For Argentine destinations, **Covalle Bus** (☎ 213-127; Infante 538) goes to Mendoza (CH$25,000, 14 hours) and San Juan (CH$25,000, 16 hours) via the Libertadores pass on Tuesday, Thursday, and Sunday at 11pm.

COLECTIVO

Many regional destinations are more frequently and rapidly served by *taxi colectivo*. *Colectivos* to Coquimbo (CH$600, 15 minutes) leave from Av Francisco de Aguirre between Balmaceda and Los Carrera. **Agencia Tacso** (☎ 227-379; Domeyko 589) goes to Ovalle (CH$2300, 1½ hours), Vicuña (CH$1800, 1¼ hours) and Andacollo (CH$2000, 1½ hours).

Getting Around

Private taxis to Aeropuerto La Florida cost CH$5000. **She Transfer** (☎ 295-058) provides door-to-door minibus transfer for CH$1500.

For car hire, try **Avis** (☎ 227-171; laserena @avischile.cl; Av Francisco de Aguirre 063), also at the airport; **Hertz** (☎ 226-171; Av Francisco de Aguirre 0225); or **Econorent** (☎ 220-113; Av Francisco de Aguirre 0135).

VICUÑA

☎ 051 / pop 24,000

Vicuña, 62km east of La Serena, is a snoozy adobe village nestled in the Elqui Valley. It's the best jump-off point to explore the valley, visit Observatorio Mamalluca or simply indulge in its treasure groves of avocado,

papaya and other fruits. Tourist services huddle around the Plaza de Armas, including **Oficina de Información Turística** (Torre Bauer), post office, internet cafes and call centers. Banco de Estado changes US cash or traveler's checks and has an ATM (better to change money in La Serena).

Sights & Activities

Near the eastern edge of town, **Museo Gabriela Mistral** (☎ 411-223; Av Gabriela Mistral; admission CH$600) pays homage to one of Chile's most famous literary figures. The small **Museo Entomológico y de Historia Natural** (☎ 411-283; Chacabuco 334; admission CH$600) showcases insects and kaleidoscopic butterfly collections.

Sweeping panoramas of the Elqui Valley make worthwhile the hot, dusty hike up **Cerro de la Virgen**, just north of town. The summit is less than an hour's walk from the Plaza de Armas. *Pisco* fans can hoof it 20 minutes to the vigorously marketed **Planta Pisco Capel** (☎ 411-251; www.piscocapel.com; ☽ 10am-6pm Jan & Feb, to 12:30pm & 2:30-6pm Mar-Dec), where a quick tour and skimpy samples might pique your thirst. To get there head southeast of town and across the bridge, then turn left.

A highlight of the region is ogling the galaxies through the 30cm telescope at **Observatorio Cerro Mamalluca** (☎ 411-352; www .mamalluca.org; Av Gabriela Mistral 260; tour CH$3500; ☽ evenings). From September through April visits should be booked one month ahead. Bring a warm sweater. Bilingual tours run every two hours from nightfall to 12:30am. Shuttles (CH$1500), reserved ahead, leave from the administration office.

Elkinatura (☎ 412-070; Av Gabriela Mistral 549) rents bikes (CH$1500 per hour) and offers tours, horse rides, rappelling excursions and more.

Sleeping & Eating

Hostal Valle Hermoso (☎ 411-206; Av Gabriela Mistral 706; dm CH$6500; s/d incl breakfast CH$14,000/24,000) The pulse of this place is the adorable Señora Lucia, who dotes on travelers, offering yummy fruit plate breakfasts and huge smart rooms with renovated baths. The open courtyard is made for stargazing.

Hostal Rita Klamt (☎ 419-611; rita_klamt@yahoo .es; Condell 443; r per person incl breakfast CH$11,000-12,000; 🖳 🐕) A cozy three-bedroom guesthouse with gardens, swimming pool and a German-speaking hostess. One room has a private bathroom.

Hotel Halley (☎ 412-070; Av Gabriela Mistral 542; d/tr incl breakfast CH$23,500/35,000; ☒) Here, guests snooze soundly under crochet lace on rod-iron beds. There's also a lovely courtyard perfect for sharing wine. Ask for IVA-discounted. The namesake restaurant is less fancy, but certainly generous, with huge portions of roast goat, salads and Chilean classics (mains CH$2100 to CH$6000).

Getting There & Around

A block south of the plaza, **bus terminal** (cnr Prat & O'Higgins) has frequent buses to La Serena (CH$1500, one hour), Coquimbo (CH$1200, 1¼ hours), Pisco Elqui (CH$1000, 50 minutes) and Monte Grande (CH$1300, 40 minutes). Some companies have a daily service to Santiago (CH$12,000, 7½ hours), including **Pullman** (☎ 412-812).

Inside the bus terminal complex is the **Terminal de Taxis Colectivos** (cnr Prat & O'Higgins), which have fast *colectivos* to La Serena (CH$1800, 50 minutes) and Pisco Elqui (CH$2000, 50 minutes).

VALLE DEL ELQUI

Big sky observatories, muscatel vineyards, *pisco* distilleries and papaya groves all call Elqui home. Famed for its geomagnetic energy, this fertile valley offers new age–fancy alongside farms and villages whose appeal lies in their plainness. For visitors it's a funky oasis worthy of exploring.

Pisco Elqui, a bucolic village cradled in the valley, is the most accessible base for exploring the area. Sample locally made *pisco* at **Solar de Pisco Elqui** (☎ 051-451-358; ☺ 11am-7pm), which produces the Tres Erres brand, or 3km south of town at the original *pisquería* Los Nichos.

Refugio del Angel (☎ 451-292; refugiodelangel @gmail.com; campsite per person CH$3500, day use CH$1500) An idyllic riverside campground with swimming holes, bathrooms and the obligatory drum circle. The turn-off is 200m south of the plaza on Manuel Rodriguez.

Hostal San Pedro (☎ 451-061; www.mundoelqui.cl; Prat s/n; r per person without bathroom CH$5000) Small and simple, this groupie hostel's star feature is definitely the gaping valley view.

El Tesoro de Elqui (☎ 051-451-069; www.tesoro-elqui .cl; Prat s/n; dm CH$8500, d without bathroom incl breakfast CH$30,000, cabañas CH$40,000; ☒) Lemon trees and lush gardens set the scene for this romantic hideaway, featuring goodies like hammocks and skylights to stargaze. There is also an

> **EXPLORE MORE OF THE ELQUI VALLEY**
>
> Heading up the valley from Pisco Elqui, you'll find a series of small pastoral villages: Los Nichos, Horcón and Alcohuaz. With plenty of water, it would be easy enough to hike or bike to each of these from Pisco Elqui – it's only about 14km to the upper-most village of Alcohuaz. Each town has a small lodge and many have restaurants.

excellent restaurant. The dorm is small, so reserve well ahead.

La Escuela (cnr Prat & Callejón Baquedano; sandwiches CH$2000-3000; ☺ noon-late) Sandwich shop by day, hip hangout by night, La Escuela has a great open-air back patio.

Buses Via Elqui run between Pisco Elqui and Vicuña (CH$2000, 50 minutes) throughout the day; catch one at the plaza. Occasional buses continue on to Horcón and Alcohuaz.

COPIAPÓ

☎ 052 / pop 132,900

Welcoming Copiapó has little to hold travelers, but it does offer a handy base for the remote mountains bordering Argentina, especially the breathtaking Parque Nacional Nevado Tres Cruces, Laguna Verde and Ojos del Salado, the highest active volcano in the world. The discovery of silver at nearby Chañarcillo in 1832 provided Copiapó with several firsts: South America's first railroad and Chile's first telegraph and telephone lines. Copiapó is 800km north of Santiago and 565km south of Antofagasta.

Information

Añañucas (Chañarcillo; ☺ 8:30am-9pm Mon-Fri, 10am-9pm Sat) Located near Chacabuco; offers drop-off laundry service at CH$2000 per kilo.

Cambios Fides (Mall Plaza Real, Colipí 484, Office B 123) Change money here.

Conaf (☎ 213-404; Martínez 55; ☺ 8:30am-5:30pm Mon-Thu, to 4:30pm Fri) Has park info.

Sernatur (☎ 212-838; infoatacama@sernatur.cl; Los Carrera 691) Tourist info at Plaza Prat; is well-informed.

Sights

The must-see **Museo Mineralógico** (☎ 206-606; cnr Colipí & Rodríguez; adult CH$500; ☺ 10am-1pm & 3:30-7pm Mon-Fri, to 1pm Sat) is a loving tribute to the raw materials to which the city owes its existence,

YOUR NEXT ADVENTURE

Teeming with wildlife and pristine peaks with rugged ascents, **Parque Nacional Nevado Tres Cruces** is definitely an up-and-coming adventure destination. Flamingos, Andean geese, horned coots, large herds of *vicuñas* and guanacos trot around this 61,000-hectare park. Overnighters should bring sleeping bags, drinking water and cooking gas to the **refugio** (shelter; dm CH$8000). Inquire about reservations at Conaf in Copiapó (p415).

Located south from outside the park, 6893m **Ojos del Salado** is Chile's highest peak, a mere 69m short of Aconcagua, and the world's highest active volcano. *Refugios* (shelters) are at the 5100m and 5750m levels. Climbers need permission from Chile's **Dirección de Fronteras y Límites** (in Santiago ☎ 02-671-2725; Teatinos 180, 7th fl). Contact professional mountain guide **Erik Galvez** (☎ 098-911-9956; erikgalvez@hotmail.com) for mountain ascents.

English-speaking guide **Ercio Mettifogo** (☎ 099-051-3202; erciomettifogo@gmail.com) comes recommended for tailored 4WD trips. There is no public transportation; take a high-clearance vehicle, water and extra gas, and check with Conaf in Copiapó before departing.

with more than 2000 samples, some of which glow in the dark.

The remains of Copiapó's mining heyday mark its center. Shaded by pepper trees, Plaza Prat showcases the early mining era with the elegant three-towered **Iglesia Catedral**, and the musty old municipal landmark **Casa de la Cultura**. Beware the roving fortune-tellers: once they get started you'll have a hard time extricating yourself.

Sleeping & Eating

Residencial Rocio (☎ 215-360; Yerba Buenas 581; r per person without bathroom CH$5000) Simple and good value, this guesthouse has a lovely shady courtyard but the shared bathrooms see heavy use.

Hotel Montecatini (☎ 211-363; hotelmontecatini@123.cl; Infante 766; d incl breakfast CH$17,000; 🖳) An olive-facade adobe with big rambling rooms, cable TV and wi-fi. The green courtyard is pleasant and the breakfast above average, but you may have to haggle over the IVA charge.

Hotel La Casona (☎ 217-277; www.lacasonahotel.cl; O'Higgins 150; s/d incl breakfast from CH$25,000/30,000; 🖳) Heads above the competition, this immaculate country house and restaurant features a garden courtyard, snug, carpeted rooms and tile and hardwood details. Owners are bilingual.

Empanadopolis (Colipí 320; CH$1000; ☺ lunch & dinner) A quick stop for mouthwatering empanadas in the most unusual flavors.

Café Colombia (Colipí 484; snacks CH$1500) For a leisurely caffeine fix, this busy cafe turns out frothy cappuccinos and serves delectable sweets and sandwiches.

Don Elias (Los Carrera 421; set meal CH$2000; ☺ breakfast, lunch & dinner) A down-market diner serving good-value *almuerzos* (set lunches) and specialty seafood and fish.

Tololo Pampa (Atacama 291; 2-person tabla CH$8000 ☺ 8pm-late) Features *tablas*: assortments of meats and cheeses, or *ceviche* and sushi on wooden cutting boards. Locals enjoy them on the open-air patio with an outdoor fireplace. It's ideal for drinks and late-night snacks.

Getting There & Away

The recently built Aeropuerto Desierto de Atacama is 40km northwest of Copiapó. **LAN** (☎ 600-526-2000; Mall Plaza Real, Colipí 484) flies daily to Antofagasta (CH$52,000, one hour), La Serena (CH$48,000, 45 minutes) and Santiago (CH$84,000, 1½ hours). A taxi costs CH$16,000; try **Radio Taxi San Francisco** (☎ 218-788). There's also a transfer bus (CH$5000, 25 minutes).

Bus company **Pullman Bus** (☎ 212-977; Colipí 109) has a large terminal and a central **ticket office** (cnr Chacabuco & Chañarcillo). **Tur Bus** (☎ 238-612; Chañarcillo 680) also has a terminal and a **ticket office** (Colipí 510) downtown. Other companies include **Expreso Norte** (☎ 231-176), **Buses Libac** (☎ 212-237) and **Flota Barrios** (☎ 213-645), all located in a common terminal on Chañarcillo. Many buses to northern desert destinations leave at night. Sample fares include Antofagasta (CH$16,000 to CH$28,000, eight hours), Arica (CH$24,900 to CH$38,000, 18 hours), Calama (CH$20,000 to CH$33,000, 10 hours), Iquique (CH$20,500 to CH$32,000, 13 hours), La Serena (CH$9000 to CH$18,000, five hours) and Santiago (CH$21,000 to CH$35,000, 12 hours).

CALDERA & BAHÍA INGLESA

Clear waters, abundant sun and seafood make Caldera, a port, 75km west of Copiapó, bubble over with Chilean vacationers. Travelers will probably prefer to spend their beach days at nearby Bahía Inglesa, though lodging there is more expensive. In off-season prices are slashed, weather remains decent and the beach is nearly deserted. Locally harvested scallops, oysters and seaweed sweeten the culinary offerings.

Across from the plaza in Caldera, the friendly **Residencial Millaray** (☎ 052-315-528; Cousiño 331; r per person without bathroom CH$7000; ☑) is true vintage, or begging for updates, depending on your view. The ambient waterfront **Terminal Pesquero** (mains CH$3500) features seafood stalls and restaurants. Watering hole **Bartholomeo** (Wheelright 747; ☒ 7pm-4am) brings travelers and locals together with live rock and jazz on weekends.

The resort of Bahía Inglesa has white-shell beaches fronting a turquoise sea dotted with windsurfers. **Camping Bahía Inglesa** (☎ 052-315-424; Playa Las Machas; campsites for 1-6 people CH$18,000, cabañas CH$24,400-40,300) has good facilities overlooking the bay, but come in low season when rates drop. Waterfront hostal and restaurant **Domo Chango Chile** (☎ 052-316-168; www.changochile .cl; Av El Morro 610, Bahía Inglesa; dome per person CH$12,000) has three airy domes with separate baths. The food, which ranges from dripping burgers (the real deal) to fresh *ceviche,* is first-rate. They also can organize kite-surfing, surfing and 4WD excursions.

our pick **El Plateao** (Av El Morro 756; mains CH$8000; ☒ 11am-late) is a fun fusion restaurant which occupies a chic, weathered beach house in Bahía Inglesa. Meals that range from Peruvian dishes to Thai seafood curry, come hot, heaped and satisfying.

Bus stations are in Caldera and served by **Pullman** (cnr Gallo & Cousiño), **Recabarren** (Ossa Varas s/n) and **Tur Bus** (Ossa Varas & Santos Cifuentes). Buses go to Copiapó (CH$2000, one hour) and Antofagasta (CH$13,000, seven hours). Buses and fast *colectivos* run between Caldera and Bahía Inglesa (CH$800, 15 minutes). Private taxis to Aeropuerto Desierto de Atacama cost CH$12,000.

PARQUE NACIONAL PAN DE AZÚCAR

The cold Humboldt current flows up the desert coastline, bringing with it its peppy namesake penguin and abundant marine life.

The worthwhile 44,000-hectare **Pan de Azúcar** (admission CH$1600) includes white-sand beaches, sheltered coves, stony headlands and cacti-covered hills. Hired launches from the dock at Punta de Choros (up to 14 people CH$45,000) chug the east coast of the 320-hectare **Isla Choros,** viewing pods of bottle-nosed dolphins, a large sea-lion colony, otters, Humboldt penguins, and massive rookeries of cormorants, gulls and boobies.

Diving and kayak trips can be arranged through **Explora Sub** (☎ 099-402-4947; www.explo rasub.cl; 200m north of the Punta de Choros dock; 1-tank dive with rental CH$30,000), they also offer super-cute *cabañas* (double CH$30,000). From the Conaf office, trails go to El Mirador (8km) and Quebrada Castillo (12km). **Camping** (per person CH$3500) is available at Playas Piqueros and Soldado, with toilets, water, cold showers and tables. Lovely adobe cabins at **Lodge Pan de Azucar** (www.lodgepandeazucar.cl; per 2/6/8 people CH$30,000/60,000/80,000) are fully equipped; reserve with Gran Atacama in Copiapó.

Nearby, the woebegone mining port of Chañaral offers the clean but basic **Hotel Jimenez** (☎ 480-328; Merino Jarpa 561; r CH$10,000) and the business-style **Hotel Aqua Luna** (☎ 523-868; Merino Jarpa 521; s/d/tr CH$14,000/20,000/25,000), with bouncy mattresses.

Flota Barrios (☎ 480-894; Merino Jarpa 567) and **Pullman Bus** (☎ 480-213; cnr Diego de Almeyda & Los Baños) serve Santiago (CH$20,000 to CH$28,000, 15 hours) and Copiapó (CH$4000, 2½ hours). In the Pullman terminal you'll find minibuses that go to the park (one way CH$2000, 25 minutes). A taxi costs about CH$20,000 one way.

ANTOFAGASTA

☎ 055 / pop 296,900

Smelling of nicotine, brine and sweat, the port of Antofagasta is low on travelers' lists. Yet there's appeal in its antiquated plaza and the nitrate-era buildings of the Barrio Histórico. Founded in 1870, the city earned its importance by offering the easiest route to the interior, and was soon handling the highest tonnage of any South American Pacific port. It exports most of the copper and other minerals found in the Atacama, and is a major import-export node for Bolivia, which lost the region to Chile during the War of the Pacific. The forlorn surrounding area features forgotten seaside ports and eerie deserted nitrate towns easily appreciated from a bus window.

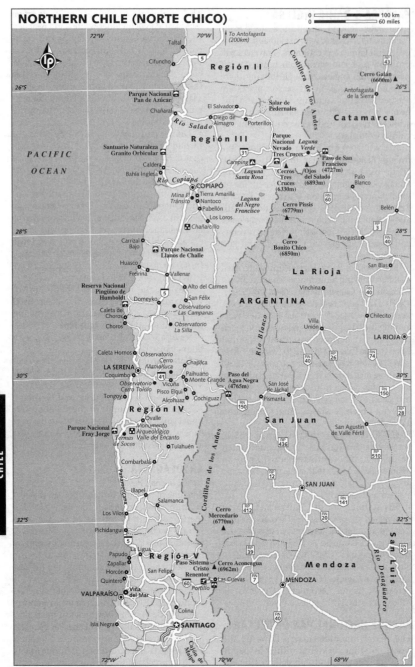

NORTHERN CHILE (NORTE CHICO)

0 — 100 km
0 — 60 miles

To Antofagasta
(200km)

Región II

Taltal

Cifuncho

Cordillera de los Andes

Cerro Galán
(6600m)

Antofagasta
de la Sierra

Catamarca

Parque Nacional
Pan de Azúcar

Chañaral

El Salvador

Salar de
Pedernales

Diego de
Almagro

Porterillos

Río Salado

Región III

Santuario Naturaleza
Granito Orbicular

Caldera

Bahía Inglesa

Río Copiapó

Parque
Nacional
Nevado
Tres Cruces

Laguna
Verde

Paso de San
Francisco
(4727m)

Palo
Blanco

Camping

COPIAPÓ

Laguna
Santa Rosa

Cerros
Tres
Cruces
(6330m)

Ojos
del Salado
(6893m)

Belén

Mina El
Tránsito

Tierra Amarilla

Nantoco

Pabellón

Los Loros

Laguna
del Negro
Francisco

Cerro Pissis
(6779m)

Tinogasta

Chañarcillo

Cerro
Bonito Chico
(6850m)

San Blas

Carrizal
Bajo

Parque Nacional
Llanos de Challe

Huasco

Freirina

Vallenar

La Rioja

Reserva Nacional
Pingüino de
Humboldt

Alto del Carmen

San Félix

Vinchina

Domeyko

ARGENTINA

Observatorio
Las Campanas

Caleta de
Choros

Choros

Observatorio
La Silla

Villa
Unión

Chilecito

Río Blanco

LA RIOJA

Caleta Hornos

Observatorio
Cerro
Mamalluca

Chapilca

LA SERENA

Coquimbo

Paihuano

Vicuña

Monte Grande

Paso del
Agua Negra
(4765m)

San José
de Jáchal

Observatorio
Cerro Tololo

Pisco Elqui

Tongoy

Alcohuaz

Cochiguaz

Pismanta

Región IV

Ovalle

Monumento
Arqueológico
Valle del Encanto

San Juan

Parque Nacional
Fray Jorge

Termas
de Socos

Tulahuén

San Agustín
de Valle Fértil

Combarbalá

Illapel

Salamanca

Cerro
Mercedario
(6770m)

SAN JUAN

Los Vilos

Pichidangui

La Ligua

Papudo

Región V

Paso Sistema
Cristo
Redentor

Cerro Aconcagua
(6962m)

Mendoza

Río Desaguadero

Zapallar

Horcón

San Felipe

Las Cuevas

MENDOZA

Quintero

Portillo

Viña
del Mar

VALPARAÍSO

Colina

San Luis

Isla Negra

SANTIAGO

Cajón de
Maipo

PACIFIC
OCEAN

CHILE

Orientation

Antofagasta drapes across a wide terrace at the foot of the coastal range. Downtown's western boundary is north-south Av Balmaceda, immediately east of the modern port. The Panamericana passes inland, about 15km east of the city.

Information

Internet businesses south of Plaza Colón charge under CH$500 per hour.

Cambio Ancla Inn (Baquedano 508) Changes money.

Hospital Regional (☎ 269-009; Av Argentina 1962)

Paris Lavaseco (☎ 222-199; Condell 2455; ☼ 9am-9pm Mon-Sat) Charges CH$7000 for up to 4kg of wash.

Post office (Washington 2623) Opposite Plaza Colón.

Sernatur (☎ 451-818; infoantofagasta@sernatur.cl; Prat 384) Has good listings and free wi-fi for visitors.

Sights & Activities

Nitrate-mining heydays left their mark with Victorian and Georgian buildings in the **Barrio Histórico** between the plaza and old port. The British-influenced **Plaza Colón** features Big Ben replica **Torre Reloj**. In the former Custom House, **Museo Regional** (cnr Balmaceda & Bolívar; admission CH$800; ☼ 9am-5pm Tue-Fri, 11am-2pm Sat & Sun) is worth a peek. Sea lions circle Antofagasta's busy fish market **Terminal Pesquero**, just north of the Port Authority.

The oft-photographed national icon **La Portada** is a gorgeous natural arch located offshore, 16km north of Antofagasta. To get there take bus 15 from Sucre to the *cruce* (junction) at La Portada, then walk 3km.

Sleeping

Options are few and reduced by the numbers of traveling miners occupying hotels.

Camping Rucamóvil (☎ 262-358; Km 11; campsite per person CH$12,000) With patchy shade and ocean views, take *micro* 2 from Mercado Central.

Casa El Mosaico (☎ 099-938-0743; Copiapó 1208; dm/d CH7000/18,000) The best of the bunch for backpackers, an ample house with BBQ pit, good tour info and options for art or scuba classes, located outside the center (reserve ahead) in Playa Huascar. Recycles and promotes low-impact tourism.

Hotel Capri (☎ 263-703; www.chilegreentours.com; Copiapó 1208; s without bathroom incl breakfast CH$7000, d incl breakfast CH$15,000) In the safe university neighborhood a bit from the center – has cleanish rooms, armchairs and kind staff.

Hotel Frontera (☎ 281-219; Bolívar 558; d US$27, s/d without bathroom CH$14,000/19,000) Dated but clean, with a bright interior passageway and florid designs that can probably camouflage any dirt.

Hotel San Marcos (☎ 251-763; Latorre 2946; s/d/tr incl breakfast CH$17,500/24,0000/34,000) Smarter than other downtown options, with soft ironed sheets and floral designs in a dated but well-kept setting. Rooms include phones and refrigerators.

Eating & Drinking

Lider (Antofagasta Shopping, Zentero 21; ☼ 8am-10pm) is a huge supermarket north of the center. Self-caterers can also hit the Mercado Central (JS Ossa) for quick *cocinería* meals and market veggies.

Battuta Café (Condell 2573, Local 1-2-3; snacks CH$1800) Come here for pies and coffee served in an ultramodern setting.

Pizzanté (www.pizzante.cl; Av JM Carrera 1857; pizzas CH$2800-6300; ☼ lunch & dinner) Your first scallop pizza just might be here, where thick crusts and inventive combinations rule an unruly menu. There are also salads.

Picadillo (☎ 247-503; Av Grecia 1000; mains CH$4500-8300; ☼ lunch & dinner) This place rates among Antofagasta's best eats. You won't mind paying a bit extra for tender steaks and fresh seafood, in a formal atmosphere with snappy service.

Wally's Pub (Toro 982; mains CH$4500-9000; ☼ from 6pm Mon-Sat) A cozy British pub serving the requisite draft with tasty curries. It also has pool tables.

Getting There & Away

AIR

Antofagasta's Aeropuerto Cerro Moreno (airport) is located 25km north of town. **LAN** (☎ 600-526-2000; Prat 445, option 8) has daily nonstop flights to Santiago (CH$85,000) and Iquique (CH$50,000, 45 minutes). **Sky** (☎ 459-090; Velásquez 890) has flights to similar destinations.

BUS

Nearly all northbound services now use coastal Ruta 1, via Tocopilla, en route to Iquique and Arica. Companies include **Flota Barrios** (Condell 2764), **Géminis** (Latorre 3055), **Pullman Bus** (Latorre 2805) and **Tur Bus** (Latorre 2751), with direct service to San Pedro de Atacama several times daily.

CHILE

BUS FARES		
Destination	Cost (CH$)	Duration (hr)
Arica	16,000	12
Calama	4000	3
Copiapó	16,000-28,000	7
Iquique	14,000	6
La Serena	20,000-34,000	12
Santiago	28,000	19

Géminis goes to Salta and Jujuy, Argentina, on Tuesday, Friday and Sunday at 9am (CH$22,000, 14 hours).

Getting Around

Aerobus (☎ 262-669; Baquedano 328) shuttles to/from Aeropuerto Cerro Moreno (CH$3000). From the Terminal Pesquero, local bus 15 goes to the airport (CH$300), but only every two hours or so. Buses arrive at their individual terminals along Latorre, in the city center.

Micro 2 from Mercado Central goes south to the campgrounds. *Micro* 14 covers downtown. Cars can be rented at **Avis** (☎ 221-073; www.avischile.cl; Baquedano 364) and **Hertz** (☎ 269-043; Balmaceda 2492).

CALAMA

☎ 055 / pop 147,600

Copper statues, copper wall etchings, copper reliefs and a copper-plated cathedral spire are pretty unsubtle reminders of the raison d'être of Calama (altitude 2700m). For travelers, though, this murky city 220km from Antofagasta makes a quick stopover before San Pedro de Atacama. Its existence is inextricably tied to the colossal Chuquicamata mine. With inflated service prices and *schops con piernas* (like *cafés con piernas*, but with beer) it clearly caters to miners.

On March 23 the city and surrounding villages celebrate the arrival of Chilean troops during the War of the Pacific with a boisterous fair featuring crafts, food, music and farm animals.

Information

Centro de Llamadas (cnr Sotomayor & Vivar; per hr CH$400; ☑ 9am-10pm) Call center with a cheap broadband connection.

Hospital Carlos Cisterna (☎ 342-347; cnr Av Granaderos & Cisterna; ☑ 24hr) Five blocks north of the Plaza 23 de Marzo.

Lavaexpress (Sotomayor 1887; ☑ 9am-9pm Mon-Sat) Offers a fast laundry service for CH$1000 per kilo.

Moon Valley Exchange (Vivar 1818) Competitive rates for money exchange.

Municipal tourist office (☎ 345-345; calamainfo tour@entelchile.net; Latorre 1689; ☑ 8am-1pm & 2-6pm Mon-Fri) Helpful and organizes tours.

Post office (Vicuña Mackenna 2167)

Sleeping

Lodging demand from the local mining industry spikes hotel costs unreasonably. Most budget places don't provide breakfast.

Camping Casas del Valle (☎ 340-056; Bilbao 1207; campsite per person CH$4000) A shady, fully equipped campground behind the stadium.

Residencial Toño (☎ 341-185; Vivar 1970; s/d CH$5000/11,000) Though spartan and visibly run down, we do like Toño's price. It's also clean and run by a welcoming family.

Hostal Nativo (☎ 347-414; www.nativo.cl; Sotomayor 2215; s with/without bathroom CH$11,000/7000, d CH$14,000) A best-buy for Calama, this sparkling budget crash pad has spotless rooms, though beds are bowed and spongy.

Hotel El Mirador (☎ 340-329; www.hotelmirador.cl; Sotomayor 2064; s/d incl breakfast CH$30,000/40,000; ☐) Vaulted ceilings, balconies and fresh, white bedding make this historic hotel stand out from competitors.

Eating & Drinking

Many options that also offer patio dining line the pedestrian mall along Ramírez.

Mercado Central (Latorre; set meals CH$1200-2000) Cheap and filling, the market *cocinerías* serve lunch to a workers' crowd between Ramírez and Vargas.

Club Croata (Abaroa s/n; set lunch CH$2600) Unexpectedly great for Chilean favorites such as *pastel de choclo*, the club is one of Calama's best traditional eateries.

Fogata Bar (Vicuña Mackenna 1973; mains CH$2800-6000; ☑ 7pm till late Tue-Sat) With the crackling outdoor firepit and live strummers, you might think you're still in San Pedro. Thankfully prices aren't. This is a hotspot for pizza or tacos washed down with a cold one.

Getting There & Away

AIR

LAN (☎ 600-526-2000; Latorre 1726) flies four times daily to Santiago (CH$35,000 to CH$64,000) from Aeropuerto El Loa. **Sky** (☎ 310-190; Latorre 1499) sometimes has cheaper rates.

BUS

In high season, purchase long-distance tickets a few days in advance. For frequent buses to Antofagasta or overnights to Iquique, Arica or Santiago, try **Tur Bus** (buy tickets at Balmaceda 1852; terminal Granaderos 3048), **Pullman Bus** (buy tickets at Sotomayor 1808; terminal Balmaceda 1802) and **Géminis** (☎ 650-700; Antofagasta 2239). Tur Bus and Pullman terminals are outside town (a $2000 taxi ride).

For San Pedro de Atacama head to **Buses Frontera** (Antofagasta 2041), **Buses Atacama 2000** (Géminis terminal) or Tur Bus.

For international destinations, make reservations as far in advance as possible. To get to Uyuni, Bolivia (CH$9000, 15 hours) ask at Frontera and Buses Atacama 2000; services go twice weekly. Service to Salta and Jujuy, Argentina, is provided by Pullman on Tuesday, Friday and Sunday mornings at 9:05am (CH$20,000, 12 hours), and more cheaply by Géminis on Tuesday, Friday and Sunday mornings at 9am (CH$30,000, 12 hours). Train service to Bolivia is discontinued.

BUS FARES

Destination	Cost (CH$)	Duration (hr)
Antofagasta	4000	3
Arica	16,000	10
Iquique	14,000	6½
La Serena	22,800-39,000	16
San Pedro de Atacama	2500	1
Santiago	30,000	20

Getting Around

From the airport, 5km away, taxis charge CH$4000. Bus companies have large terminals just outside the town center. Ask to be left at their office in *el centro* to avoid the taxi ride back.

Frequent *colectivos* to Chuquicamata (CH$1000, 15 minutes) leave from Abaroa, just north of Plaza 23 de Marzo.

Rental-car agencies include **Avis** (☎ 363-325; calama@avischile.cl; Aeropuerto El Loa) and **Hertz** (☎ 341-380; Av Granaderos 141). If heading to the geysers, you'll need a high-clearance 4WD or pickup.

CHUQUICAMATA

Just north of Calama, this mine coughs a constant plume of dust visible for miles in the desert, but then everything here dwarfs the human scale. The mine is one of the world's largest open-pit copper mines, deeper than the deepest lake in the USA. The 630,000 tons of copper extracted here annually make Chile the world's greatest copper producer.

First run by the US Anaconda Copper Mining Company, starting in 1915, the mine is now operated by state-owned **Corporación del Cobre de Chile** (Codelco; ☎ 055-327-469; visitas@codelco.cl; cnr Tocopilla & Carrera). Chuquicamata was once integrated with a well-ordered company town, but environmental problems and copper reserves beneath the town forced the entire population out by 2004.

Skip using tour agencies in Calama, as they overcharge. Instead, arrange visits through Codelco by phone or email or ask Calama's tourist office to make the reservation. Tours run from Monday to Friday, in both English and Spanish. English and Spanish tours run weekdays.

Report to the Codelco office 30 minutes before your tour; bring ID and make a voluntary donation (tip with what you are comfortable donating). The 50-minute tour begins at 2pm. Wear sturdy footwear (no sandals), long pants and long sleeves. Visitor numbers are limited, so book ahead in summer.

SAN PEDRO DE ATACAMA
☎ 055 / pop 3200
Oases attract flocks and there's no exception here. A once-humble stop on the trans-Andean cattle drive, San Pedro de Atacama (altitude 2440m) is now prime real estate. It took only a decade for a proliferation of guesthouses, eateries, internet cafes and tour agencies to wedge their way into its dusty streets, molding it into a kind of adobe-*landia*. There are all the cons of fast development (steep prices, cranky tour operators and exaggerated offers) yet…there is incredible quiet, psychedelic landscapes, courtyard bonfires under star-scattered heavens and hammock-strewn hostels. If you can sometimes set your hours contrary to the rest of the sightseers, this is a satisfying destination.

The town is near the north end of the Salar de Atacama, a vast saline lake, 120km southeast of Calama. Buses stop right near the plaza and the whole town can be explored on foot.

Water is scarce and San Pedro's water is not potable; most stores sell bottled water. Locals suggest you shower short and buy the larger containers to limit your contributions to San Pedro's growing landfill.

CHILE

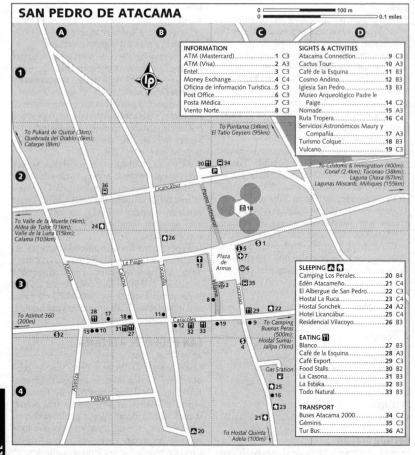

SAN PEDRO DE ATACAMA

0   100 m
0   0.1 miles

INFORMATION
ATM (Mastercard)	1 C3
ATM (Visa)	2 A3
Entel	3 C3
Money Exchange	4 C4
Oficina de Información Turística	5 C3
Post Office	6 C3
Posta Médica	7 C3
Viento Norte	8 C3

SIGHTS & ACTIVITIES
Atacama Connection	9 C3
Cactus Tour	10 A3
Café de la Esquina	11 B3
Cosmo Andino	12 B3
Iglesia San Pedro	13 B3
Museo Arqueológico Padre le Paige	14 C2
Nomade	15 A3
Ruta Tropera	16 C4
Servicios Astronómicos Maury y Compañía	17 A3
Turismo Colque	18 B3
Vulcano	19 C3

To Pukará de Quitor (3km);
Quebrada del Diablo (6km);
Catarpe (8km)

To Puritama (34km);
El Tatio Geysers (95km)

To Customs & Immigration (400m);
Conaf (2.4km); Toconao (38km);
Laguna Chaxa (67km);
Lagunas Miscanti, Miñiques (155km)

Licancábur

Paseo Artesanal

To Valle de la Muerte (4km);
Aldea de Tulor (11km);
Valle de la Luna (15km);
Calama (103km)

Le Paige

Calama

Tocopilla

Vilama

Toconao

Plaza
de
Armas

Atienza

Caracoles

To Azimut 360
(200m)

Atienza

Palpana

Caracoles

SLEEPING
Camping Los Perales	20 B4
Edén Atacameño	21 C4
El Albergue de San Pedro	22 C4
Hostal La Ruca	23 C4
Hostal Sonchek	24 A4
Hotel Licancábur	25 C4
Residencial Vilacoyo	26 B3

EATING
Blanco	27 B3
Café de la Esquina	28 A3
Café Export	29 C3
Food Stalls	30 B2
La Casona	31 B3
La Estaka	32 B3
Todo Natural	33 B3

TRANSPORT
Buses Atacama 2000	34 C2
Géminis	35 C3
Tur Bus	36 A2

To Camping
Buenas Peras
(500m);
Hostal Sumaj-
Jallpa (1km)

Gas Station

To Hostal Quinta
Adela (100m)

Information

Half a dozen internet cafes (CH$1000 per hour) dot Caracoles. For useful visitor information, see www.sanpedrodeatacama.net.

ATM (Caracoles s/n; ◷ 9am-10pm) Visa only, on the western side of the village, but it functions sporadically.

ATM (Le Paige s/n; ◷ 9am-10pm) MasterCard only, opposite the museum.

Conaf (Solcor; ◷ 10am-1pm & 2:30-4:30pm) Two kilometers past customs on the Toconao road.

Entel (Plaza de Armas) Telephone office.

Money exchange (Toconao 492) Exchanges money at poor rates.

Oficina de Información Turística (Tourist Information Office; ☎ 851-420; sanpedroatacama@gmail.com; cnr Toconao & Le Paige; ◷ 9:30am-1pm & 3-7pm Mon-Fri, 10am-2pm Sat)

Post office (Toconao s/n)

Posta Médica (☎ 851-010; Toconao s/n) Health clinic east of the plaza.

Viento Norte (☎ 851-329; Vilama 432-B; ◷ hr vary) Charges about CH$2500 per kilo of washing.

Sights & Activities

Stop in the 17th-century adobe **Iglesia San Pedro** (Le Paige) where the floorboards creak and sigh, and the massive doors are hewn from cardón cactus. North of the plaza you'll find the outdoor **Paseo Artesanal**, where you can chat up local vendors and peruse alpaca sweaters, thumb-sized dolls and trinkets galore.

Fascinating malformed skulls and mummy replicas will glue you to the glass at **Museo**

Arqueológico Padre Le Paige (Le Paige; adult/student CH$2000/1000; ☺ 9am-noon & 2-6pm Mon-Fri, 10am-noon & 2-6pm Sat & Sun). Learn about the Atacameño culture and its developments through the Inca invasion and Spanish conquest. Equally interesting is the shamanic paraphernalia (ie hallucinogenic accessories of the ancients).

You can bike or walk to nearby desert sights, just be sure to bring a map and adequate water and sunblock. Equestrian types can ride the same routes and more. **Ruta Tropera** (☎ 099-838-6833; www.rutatropera.cl; Toconao 479; per hr CH$4500) offers horse-riding tours ranging from brief to epic multiday affairs. Ambitious peak-baggers can check out **Azimut 360** (☎ 851-469; www.azimut360.com; Caracoles 66), mountain specialists with prices starting at around CH$105,000 per person (minimum two people). Or try **Nomade** (☎ 851-158; www .nomadeexpediciones.cl; Caracoles 163) – its enthusiastic trekking tours include Sairecabur (6040m; CH$83,300), Lascar (5600m; CH$83,300) and Toco (5604m; CH$54,200).

There's sandboarding on the dunes (half-day CH$15,000) as well as mountain biking (half-day CH$3000) Rent a bike from your hostel or **Vulcano** (☎ 851-373; Caracoles 317), then pedal back to the hammock for a well-deserved nap. Or cool off swimming at **Pozo 3** (☎ 08-476-7290; admission CH$3000; ☺ 7am-7pm), 3km east off the road to Paso Jama.

Stargazers won't want to miss the tour of the night sky, offered – where else? In the middle-of-desert nowhere – by an ace astronomer at **Servicios Astronómicos Maury y Compañía** (☎ 851-935; www.spaceobs.com; Caracoles 166; 2½hr tours CH$15,000).

Tours

Altiplano lakes (CH$10,000-25,000, entrance fees CH$3000-5000) Leaves San Pedro around 7am to see flamingos at Laguna Chaxa in the Salar de Atacama, the town of Socaire, Lagunas Miñiques and Miscanti, Toconao and the Quebrada de Jere, returning 5pm.

El Tatio geysers (from CH$15,000, entrance fees CH$3500) Leaves San Pedro at 4am to catch the geysers at sunrise, returning at noon. Includes thermal baths and breakfast.

Geysers and pueblos (CH$28,000, entrance fees CH$4500) Leaves at 4am for the geysers, then visits Caspana, the Pukará de Lasana and Chiu-Chiu, finishing in Calama, or returning to San Pedro by 6pm.

Uyuni, Bolivia (see below) Popular three-day 4WD tour of the remote and beautiful *salar* region.

Valle de la Luna (CH$5000, entrance fees CH$2000) Leaves San Pedro mid-afternoon to catch the sunset over the valley, returning early evening. Includes visits to the Valle de Marte, Valle de la Muerte and Tres Marías.

For further guidance, read the book of complaints at the Tourist Information Office. The following agencies attract the most positive feedback from travelers.

Atacama Connection (☎ 851-424; cnr Caracoles & Toconao s/n) www.atacamaconnection.com) Reliable agency, also does Calama airport transfers for CH$10,000 per person.

Cactus Tour (☎ 851-587; www.cactustour.cl; Caracoles 163-A) A small outfit frequently recommended for excellent service, bilingual guides, comfortable vehicles and above-average food.

Cosmo Andino (☎ 851-069; cosmoandino@entel chile.net; Caracoles s/n) Another small operation, with higher rates but with the most unblemished reputation in town.

4X4 TO BOLIVIA

High-altitude lagoons tinged crimson and turquoise, simmering geysers, flamingos in flight and Uyuni's blinding salt flats are a dreamy and extreme three-day 4WD journey from San Pedro. Given the wild uncharted terrain, it's essential to take a tour and that's where the problems start. The reasonable going rate of CH$65,000 includes transport, lodging and meals. *Quality does not come at these prices*. Service can be inconsistent and amenities are bare-bones quality. It's possible to book a four-day tour and return to San Pedro, but you might find yourself stuck in Uyuni until the tour company collects enough travelers to fill a vehicle.

The success of the trip depends largely on a plucky, positive attitude and good driver. Scout out driver recommendations from other travelers. Lodgings are at high altitudes: drink lots of water, avoid alcohol and bring an extra-warm sleeping bag and something for the thumping headaches. Try to acclimatize before going.

Turismo Colque (☎ 851-109; cnr Caracoles & Calama) has most of the departures and its reputation runs all over the board. **Cordillera Traveler** (☎ 851-966; ctravelersanpedro@123mail.cl; Tocopilla s/n) is a small, family-run business with good traveler feedback.

CHILE

Festivals & Events

Fiesta de San Pedro y San Pablo, held on June 29, is a religious festival celebrated with folk dancing groups, a rodeo and solemn processions.

Sleeping

Few budget places include breakfast but many let you boil water. Off-season prices drop. Water is scarce so make sure you limit your shower time.

Camping Los Perales (☎ 851-114; Tocopilla 481; campsite per person CH$3500) Ample grounds, hot showers and kitchen with friendly hosts.

Camping Buenas Peras (☎ 099-510-9004; Ckilapana 688; campsite per person CH$3500) Camp in a pear orchard but beware the abrupt droppings.

El Albergue de San Pedro (☎ 851-426; hostel sanpedro@hotmail.com; Caracoles 360; dm/d incl breakfast CH$6000/17,000, nonmembers CH$8000/20,000) Welcoming small HI property stuffed with skyscraping three-level bunks. Plumbing may be an issue so sniff around before check-in. The bilingual staff are friendly. Services include laundry, bike rental and sandboards.

Residencial Vilacoyo (☎ 851-006; vilacoyo@sanpedro atacama.com; Tocopilla 387; r per person CH$7000; ▣) Plain rooms (some dark) center around a hammock-strewn gravel garden. The shared bathrooms include outdoor shower stalls.

Hostal La Ruca (☎ 851-568; hostallaruca@hotmail .com; Toconao 513; dm CH$8000, d with/without bathroom CH$37,000/25,000; ▣) Ruled by a courtyard with deck chairs and thatched shelter, this friendly budget spot has cramped dorms but worthwhile doubles, spruced up with down comforters and sturdy furniture. Also very clean.

Éden Atacameña (☎ 851-154; Toconao 592; hostal eden_spa@hotmail.com; Toconao 592; s without bathroom CH$8000, d with/without bathroom CH$25,000/14,000, all incl breakfast; ▣) Remember that it's paradise on a budget, with plain brick rooms and a shady courtyard. There are also hammocks, wash basins and a communal outdoor kitchen .

Hostal Quinta Adela (☎ 851-272; Toconao 624; s/d CH$20,000/30,000) Surrounded by pear and quince orchards, this hacienda spoils you with large exposed-beam rooms with embroidered bedspreads and hardwood floors. But come to meet its captivating retired hosts. Large breakfasts cost CH$2500.

Hotel Terrantai (☎ 851-045; www.terrantai.com; Tocopilla 411; d CH$116,000-128,000; ▣ ▣) Upscale and intimate, this adobe hotel has elegant rooms and lovely shared spaces, including a sculpture garden and bonfire patio. Newer rooms are

pricier. The restaurant, run by a Peruvian chef, is quite worthwhile but exclusive to guests.

Other lodgings include the following:

Hostal Sumaj-Jallpa (☎ 851-416; sumajjallpa@san pedrodeatacama.com; El Tatio 703, Sector Licancabur; dm CH$7000, s/d without bathroom CH$12,000/15,000; ▣) Pristine Swiss-Chilean hostel located 1km outside town.

Hostal Sonchek (☎ 851-112; soncheksp@hotmail.com; Calama 370; s without bathroom CH$9000, d with/without bathroom CH$30,000/14,000) Slovenian-run; has thatched roofs and adobe walls. English and French spoken.

Hotel Licancábur (☎ 851-007; Toconao s/n; s with/ without bathroom CH$12,000/8000, d with/without bathroom CH$32,000/16,000) Friendly family atmosphere.

Eating & Drinking

Restaurant bargains are few, with gourmet concept cuisine without the gourmet standards. Since establishments only selling alcohol are outlawed, nightlife centers around restaurants' open-air bonfires. No alcohol is sold after 1am.

Food stalls (parking lot; set lunch from CH$1500) These rustic shacks behind the taxi stalls serve empanadas, *humitas* (corn dumplings) and soups.

Café de la Esquina (Caracoles s/n; meals CH$1800-3200; ☻ 8am-11pm) Pint-sized establishments with tea, fresh juices, granola, yogurt and sandwich melts.

Algarrobo (south side of plaza; set lunch CH$5000, mains CH$3500-6500; ☻ breakfast, lunch & dinner) This is a no-nonsense favorite for Chilean comfort food and sandwiches, which are big enough to share.

Todo Natural (Caracoles 271; set menu CH$5000; ☻ breakfast, lunch & dinner) Though service dawdles, customers return for wholesome vegetarian options, like goat-cheese sandwiches, fresh juice and salads.

Café Export (cnr Toconao & Caracoles; mains CH$3500-6000) Funky and candlelit, half the village squeezes in here come nightfall. Strengths include strong coffee, homemade pasta and decent pizzas.

Blanco (☎ 851-164; Caracoles 195; mains from CH$6500) Modern minimalist, it's, you guessed it, all white, down to the slick booths. The menu is fancy-pants but fresh pastas are the specialty, and there is a good selection of wines by the glass.

Popular haunts with courtyard bonfires include the friendly **La Casona** (☎ 851-004; Caracoles 195; mains CH$2800-7000) and **La Estaka** (Caracoles s/n; mains CH$3800-6500).

GETTING TO ARGENTINA

Géminis (☎ 851-538; Toconao s/n) serves Salta and Jujuy, Argentina, leaving at 11:30am on Tuesday, Friday and Sunday (CH$28,000, 12 hours). See p47 for more details about crossing from Argentina.

Getting There & Away

Buses Atacama 2000 (cnr Licancábur & Paseo Artesanal) and **Buses Frontera** (☎ 851-117; Licancábur s/n) go to Calama (CH$2500, three daily) and Toconao (CH$700, 30 minutes). **Tur Bus** (Licancábur 11) has eight daily buses to Calama, which go onward to Arica (CH$17,000, one daily), Antofagasta (CH$6000, six daily) and Santiago (CH$32,000, 23 hours, three daily).

AROUND SAN PEDRO DE ATACAMA

The crumbly 12th-century ruins of fortress **Pukará de Quitor** (adult/student CH$2000/1500; ☼ daylight hr), 3km northwest of town, afford great views of town and the oasis expanse. Another 3km on the right, **Quebrada del Diablo** (Devil's Gorge) offers a serpentine single track that mountain bikers dream of. About 2km further north are the Inca ruins of **Catarpe**. Sunset on the rolling sand peaks at **Valle de la Luna** (admission CH$2000/1500; ☼ daylight hr), 15km west of town, is a San Pedro institution. Avoid the mobs by going at sunrise. Circular dwellings **Aldea Tulor** (admission CH$2000), 9km south of town, are the ruins of a pre-Columbian Atacameño village. If biking or hiking to any of these places, take plenty of water, snacks and sunblock.

Pungent **Laguna Chaxa** (admission CH$2000), 67km south of town, within the **Salar de Atacama**, hosts three species of flamingo (James, Chilean and Andean), as well as plovers, coots and ducks. Sunsets are gorgeous. **Lagunas Miscanti & Miñiques** (admission adult/student CH$2000/1500), 155km south of town, are sparkling azure lakes at 4300m above sea level. Check with Conaf about *refugios* (shelters).

The volcanic hot springs of **Puritama** (admission CH$5000), 30km north of town, are in a box canyon en route to El Tatio, accessible by taxi or tour. A restful place with good facilities, it's a 20-minute walk from the junction along an obvious gravel track. The temperature of the springs is about 33°C, and there are several falls and pools. Bring food and water.

At an altitude of 4300m, **El Tatio Geysers** (95km north of town; admission CH$3500) is the world's highest geyser field. At sunrise tourists pilgrimage to this dragon field to gaze at puffing fumaroles. Tours depart at 4am in order to reach the geysers by 6am, when there's the most steam, but the geysers can be visited later without crowds. Camping is possible but nights are freezing; tote your sleeping bag to the no-frills *refugio* 2km before the geysers.

Tidy and tiny **Toconao**, 40km south of San Pedro, offers the authentic feel of the Atacama. Its **Iglesia de San Lucas** dates from the mid-18th century. About 4km from town, river **Quebrada de Jerez** (admission CH$1000) offers an idyllic oasis bursting with fruit trees and flowering plants. Basic lodgings, such as **Residencial y Restaurant Valle de Toconao** (☎ 852-009; Lascar 236; r per person CH$7000), are near the plaza. Buses Frontera and Buses Atacama 2000 go daily to and from San Pedro de Atacama (see p428).

IQUIQUE

☎ 057 / pop 216,400

Jutting into the sea and backed by the tawny coastal range, Iquique sits like a stage and, in fact, is no stranger to drama. It first lived off guano reserves, grew lavish with 19th-century nitrate riches, since lost momentum, and now stakes its future on commerce and tourism, manifested in the duty-free mega-zone, the sparkly glitz of the casino and ubiquitous beach resort development. The real gems of this coastal character are the remainders of lovely Georgian-style architecture, Baquedano's fanciful wooden sidewalks, thermal winds and a ripping good surf.

Orientation

Iquique, 1853km north of Santiago and 315km south of Arica, is squeezed between the ocean and a desolation-brown coastal range rising abruptly some 600m. South of the center, Peninsula de Cavancha houses the casino, luxury hotels and an attractive rocky coastline.

Information

Internet services can be found on nearly every block, including across from Playa Cavancha. Banks around Plaza Prat have

CHILE

ATMs; the Zona Franca (opposite) has more *casas de cambio* (exchange offices).

Afex (Serrano 396; 8:30-5:30 Mon-Fri, 10am-1:30pm Sat) Changes cash and traveler's checks; north of Plaza Prat.

Hospital Regional Dr Torres (422-370; cnr Tarapacá & Av Héroes de la Concepción) Ten blocks east of Plaza Condell.

Post office (Bolívar 458)

Sernatur (312-238; Pinto 436; 9am-8pm Mon-Sat, 9am-1pm Sun Jan & Feb, 8:30am-1pm & 3-5pm Mon-Fri Mar-Dec) Offers free city maps and and provides information.

Vaporito (421-652; Bolívar 505; per kg CH$1000; 9am-9:30pm) Laundry service with another branch at Juan Martínez 832, just to the east of Mercado Centenario.

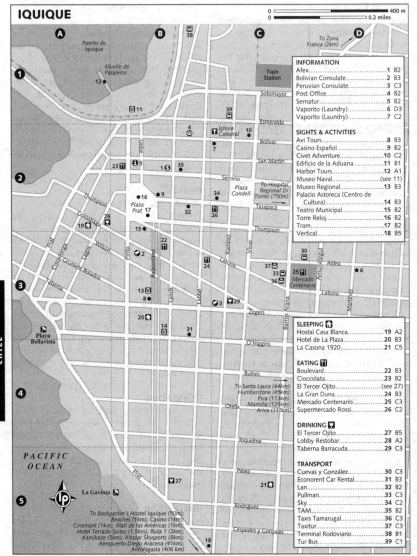

IQUIQUE

INFORMATION	
Afex	1 B2
Bolivian Consulate	2 B3
Peruvian Consulate	3 C3
Post Office	4 B2
Sernatur	5 B2
Vaporito (Laundry)	6 D3
Vaporito (Laundry)	7 C2

SIGHTS & ACTIVITIES	
Avi Tours	8 B3
Casino Español	9 B2
Civet Adventure	10 C2
Edificio de la Aduana	11 B1
Harbor Tours	12 A1
Museo Naval	(see 11)
Museo Regional	13 B3
Palacio Astoreca (Centro de Cultura)	14 B3
Teatro Municipal	15 B2
Torre Reloj	16 B2
Tram	17 B2
Vertical	18 B5

SLEEPING	
Hostal Casa Blanca	19 A2
Hotel de La Plaza	20 B3
La Casona 1920	21 C5

EATING	
Boulevard	22 B3
Cioccolata	23 B2
El Tercer Ojito	(see 27)
La Gran Duna	24 B3
Mercado Centenario	25 C3
Supermercado Rossi	26 C2

DRINKING	
El Tercer Ojito	27 B5
Lobby Restobar	28 A2
Taberna Barracuda	29 C3

TRANSPORT	
Cuevas y González	30 C3
Econorent Car Rental	31 B3
Lan	32 B2
Pullman	33 C3
Sky	34 C2
TAM	35 B2
Taxis Tamarugal	36 C3
Taxitur	37 C3
Terminal Rodoviario	38 B1
Tur Bus	39 C1

CHILE

Sights & Activities

Plaza Prat showcases the city's 19th-century architecture, with the 1877 **Torre Reloj** (Clock Tower) and the neoclassical **Teatro Municipal**, dating from 1890. At the northeastern corner, the Moorish 1904 **Casino Español** has elaborate interior tile work and *Don Quixote*–themed paintings. The 1871 **Edificio de la Aduana** (Customs House; Av Centenario) now houses **Museo Naval** (☎ 517-138; Esmeralda 250; adult CH$200; ☽ 10am-1pm & 4-7pm Tue-Sat, 10am-2pm Sun).

A handsomely restored **tram** occasionally jerks its way down Av Baquedano in the tourist high season, passing an impressive array of Georgian-style buildings. The **Museo Regional** (☎ 411-214; Av General Baquedano 951; admission free; ☽ 9am-5:30pm Mon-Fri, 10am-5pm Sat & Sun) features pre-Columbian artifacts, creepy animal fetuses, mummies and Tiwanaku skulls. Also on Baquedano is the grand **Palacio Astoreca**, housing the free **Centro de Cultura** (☎ 425-600; O'Higgins 350; ☽ 10am-5pm Mon-Fri), which exhibits paintings by local artists. **Harbor tours** (Muelle de Pasajeros; CH$3000) chug out to the sea-lion colonies.

North of downtown, the **Zona Franca** (Zofri; ☽ 11am-9pm Mon-Sat) covers an exhausting 240 hectares of duty-free shops. Take any northbound *colectivo* from downtown.

Iquique's most popular beach, **Playa Cavancha** (cnr Av Arturo Prat & Amunátegui) is worth visiting for swimming and bodysurfing. Further south, rip currents and crashing waves make the scenic **Playa Brava** better for sunbathing; take a *colectivo* from downtown or walk.

Surfing and bodyboarding are best in winter, when swells come from the north, but are possible year-round. There's less competition for early morning breaks at the north end of Playa Cavancha. **Playa Huaiquique**, on the southern outskirts of town, is also an exhilarating choice but the sea is warmer further north near Arica. For surf equipment, **Vertical** (☎ 391-031; www.verticalstore.cl; Prat 580) sells and rents it. Lessons start at CH$12,000. Sand-boarding trips to Cerro Dragón cost around CH$7000.

Iquique is a paragliding hub – its ideal conditions make you want to take a running leap. Try multilingual **Altazor Skysports** (☎ 380-110; www.altazor.cl; Flight Park, Vía 6, Manzana A, Sitio 3, Bajo Molle), an operator which offers an introductory tandem flight (CH$28,000) or more extensive courses.

Tours

Public transportation to Humberstone, Mamiña and the geoglyphs is tricky, so tours are worth considering. Tours to Pica include the Cerro Pintados.

Avitours (☎ 527-692; www.avitours.cl; Av General Baquedano 997) Offers day trips to Humberstone, La Tirana and Pica (CH$18,000) and Volcán Isluga (CH$45,000).
Civet Adventure (☎ 428-483; civetcor@vtr.net; Bolívar 684) Organizes small, fully-equipped 4WD adventure tours to *altiplano* destinations, as well as landsailing and paragliding. German and English spoken.

Sleeping

Taxi drivers earn commission from some hotels; be firm or consider hoofing it. Wild camping is free on the beaches north of Iquique near Pisagua and Cuya.

YMCA (☎ 573-596; Av General Baquedano 964; dm/d CH$6000/14,000) Lovely on the outside, cramped on the inside, where beds are firm and newish but interior courtyard rooms are dark. It's certainly secure and central but smells a bit musty.

Backpacker's Hostel Iquique (☎ 320-223; www .hosteliquique.cl; Amunategui 2075; members dm/s/d without bathroom incl breakfast CH$5500/7500/13,000, nonmembers CH$6000/7000/16,000; ☐) Steps from the beach, *the* place for backpackers in Iquique is sometimes bursting at the seams. Desk service can be a bit surly, but perks include lockers, games, laundry and storage facilities, a kitchen and a tiny roof-terrace with sea views. English-speaking staff.

La Casona 1920 (☎ 413-000; Barros Arana 1585; dm CH$8000, s/d without bathroom incl breakfast CH$10,000/17,000; ☐) Bright colors, a quiet patio and warm welcome make this old, high-ceiling guesthouse a great place to stay. It's shipshape and spotless, but a shame that the bathrooms are down a flight from 3rd-floor rooms. The owner speaks English and German.

Hotel de La Plaza (☎ 419-339; www.kilantur.cl; Av General Baquedano 1025; s/d incl breakfast CH$11,000/18,000; ☐) Quixotic but comfortable, this Georgian-style building has three stories of attractive rooms around a courtyard, but the black statues guarding the entrance are straight out of southern gothic.

Hostal Casa Blanca (☎ 420-007; Gorostiaga 127; s/d incl breakfast CH$14,000/20,500) Skip the stuffy interior rooms for better terrace options in this sedate spot. Rooms have high ceilings, wi-fi and cable TV. It's convenient to Baquedano, though the immediate vicinity is run down.

CHILE

Hotel Terrado Suites (☎ 437-878; www.terrado .cl; Los Rieles 126; s/d incl breakfast from CH$45,100/55,500; 🖾 🖵 🐾) Lording it over Playa Cavancha, this lofty hotel boasts every luxury, including both outdoor and indoor pool, wi-fi internet, sauna and gym. Smaller rooms have city views; bigger, pricier rooms look out to sea.

Eating

Baquedano has a variety of stylish eateries, though some come and go quickly.

Supermercado Rossi (Tarapacá 579; 🕘 9am-10pm Mon-Sat, 10am-2:30pm Sun) Offers variety and fresh produce.

Mercado Centenario (Barros Arana s/n; cocinería main CH$2500) Get a frills-free sandwich and fresh juice at the stalls. The upstairs *cocinerías* get packed at lunchtime.

La Gran Duna (Latorre 563; set lunch CH$2300-3000; 🕘 12pm-5pm Mon-Sat) A stylish fine-art cafe with a healthy menu featuring fresh juices and two lunch options – a cheaper home-style meal and an upscale alternative like grilled albacore and salad.

Boulevard (Av General Baquedano 790; mains CH$3000-8000; 🕘 lunch & dinner) Streetside cafe with rich fondues, goat cheese pizza and fish *papillot* (foil-wrapped), options are plenty but service is lethargic.

Cioccolata (Pinto 487; set menu CH$3100, sandwiches US$4; 🕘 8:30am-10pm Mon-Sat, 5-10pm Sun) An upscale coffee shop, its lunchtime salad bar goes big with the business crowd, but there is also a wide selection of fresh, gooey cakes and coffee.

our pick **El Tercer Ojito** (Lynch 1420; mains CH$3200-6900; 🕘 lunch & dinner) Dine on sushi, Thai curry or Peruvian fare in a candlelit courtyard filled with ferns and Buddha statues. Meals have excellent presentation and the atmosphere is utterly chilled.

Drinking

Look for the fun pubs and clubs clustered along the seafront south of town. Most happy hours are from 8pm to 10pm.

El Tercer Ojito (Lynch 1420) With tart two-for-one passion fruit sours during happy hour – suddenly you find that new age doesn't mean 'good for you.'

Lobby Restobar (Gorostiaga 142) This plush alternative lounge has groovy tunes, tinted lighting and a great terrace. Mixed drinks run pricey but the ambience is tops.

Taberna Barracuda (www.tabernabarracuda.cl; Gorostiaga 601) English pub meets US sports bar, popular with all ages.

Entertainment

Cinemark (off Map p426; ☎ 600-600-2463; Mall de las Américas, Héroes de la Concepción; tickets CH$2000) A multiplex cinema showing latest releases.

Kamikaze (off Map p426; ☎ 440-194; www.kamikaze .cl; Bajo Molle Km 7, Manzana K; admission incl drink CH$2000; 🕘 midnight-early Thu-Sat) Two floors of bamboo bars and club tunes running the gamut from salsoteca to '90s *pop en español*.

Getting There & Away

AIR

The local airport, **Aeropuerto Diego Aracena** (☎ 410-787), is 41km south of downtown via Ruta 1.

LAN (☎ 600-526-20002; Tarapacá 465) has daily flights to Arica (CH$26,900, 40 minutes), Antofagasta (CH$24,900 to CH$39,900, 45 minutes), Santiago (CH$34,950 to CH$89,450, 2½ hours), and La Paz, Bolivia (around CH$137,000, two hours). **Sky** (☎ 415-013; Tarapacá 530), with similar fares, also serves Arica, Antofagasta and Santiago as well as further south in Chile. **TAM** (☎ 390-600; www .tam.com.py; Serrano 430) flies three times weekly to Asunción, Paraguay (CH$269,000).

BUS & COLECTIVO

Most buses leave from the **Terminal Rodoviario** (☎ 416-315; Lynch); some companies have ticket offices along west and north sides of the Mercado Centenario. **Tur Bus** (☎ 472-984; www .turbus.cl; Esmeralda 594) has a cash machine.

For faster *colectivos* to Arica (CH$8000 3½ hours), try **Taxitur** (☎ 414-875; Aldea 783). **Taxis Tamarugal** (☎ 419-288; Barros Arana 897-B) runs daily *colectivos* to Mamiña (CH$6000 round trip).

SPLURGE!

A flying leap into the abyss is one way to shake off that long bus ride. Iquique's steep coastal escarpment, rising air currents and soft, extensive dunes are paradise for paragliders, ranking among the continent's top spots. Beginners can brave a tandem flight for CH$28,000. One reputable provider is Altazor Skysports at Playa Cavancha. Bring along a windbreaker, sunblock…and guts, of course.

CHILE

BUS FARES

Destination	Cost (CH$)	Duration (hr)
Antofagasta	14,000	8
Arica	7000	4½
Calama	14,000	7
Copiapó	20,500-32,000	14
La Serena	24,000-37,000	18
Santiago	31,000	26

To get to La Paz, Bolivia, **Cuevas y González** (☎ 415-874; Aldea 850) leaves daily at 1:30pm (CH$15,000, 20 hours).

Getting Around

Aerotransfer (☎ 310-800) has a door-to-door shuttle service from the airport (CH$5000), 41km south of town.

Cars cost from CH$21,000 per day. Local rental agencies often ask for an international driver's license. Try the airport rental stands or **Econorent Car Rental** (☎ 417-091; reservas@econorent.net; Labbé 1089).

AROUND IQUIQUE

Agencies in Iquique offer tours to the following sites, but they don't combine Pica and Mamiña in the same tour.

With the spark of the nitrate boom long gone cold, **Humberstone** (admission CH$1000), 45km northeast of Iquique, remains a creepy shell. Built in 1872, this ghost town's opulence reached its height in the 1940s: the theater drew Santiago-based performers; workers lounged about the massive cast-iron pool molded from a scavenged shipwreck; and amenities still foreign to most small towns abounded. The development of synthetic nitrates forced the closure of the *oficina* by 1960. Today some buildings are restored, but others are unstable; explore them carefully. A Unesco World Heritage Site, it makes their list of endangered sites for the fragility of the existing constructions. The skeletal remains of **Oficina Santa Laura** are a half-hour walk southwest. Eastbound buses can drop you off, and it's usually easy to catch a return bus (CH$1300) if you're willing to wait. Take food, water and a camera.

The whopping pre-Columbian geoglyphic **El Gigante de Atacama** (Giant of the Atacama), 14km east of Huara on the slopes of Cerro Unita is, at 86m, the world's largest archaeological representation of a human figure.

Representing a powerful shaman, its blocky head emanates rays and its thin limbs clutch an arrow and medicine bag. Experts estimate it dates to around AD 900. The best views are from several hundred meters back at the base of the hill. Don't climb the easily eroded hill. To visit hire a car or taxi, or you can go on a tour.

Amid Atacama's desolate pampas you'll find straggly groves of resilient tamarugo (*Prosopis tamarugo*) lining the Panamericana south of Pozo Almonte. The forest once covered thousands of square kilometers until clear-cutting for the mines nearly destroyed it. The trees are protected within the **Reserva Nacional Pampa del Tamarugal**, where you can also find 355 restored geoglyphs of humans, llamas and geometric shapes blanketing the hillside at **Cerro Pintados** (admission CH$1000), nearly opposite the turn-off to Pica. Pass by the derelict railroad yard, a dust-choked but easy walk from the highway, about 1½ hours each way. A Conaf-operated **campground** (campsites CH$3500, dm CH$2500) has flat, shaded sites with tables and limited space in cabins. It's 24km south of Pozo Almonte.

The oasis of **Pica** is a chartreuse patch on a dusty canvas, 113km southeast of Iquique. Its fame hails from its pica limes, the key ingredient of the tart and tasty *pisco sour*. Day-trippers can enjoy splashing around the freshwater pool, **Cocha Resbaladero** (Ibáñez; ☼ 8am-9pm; admission CH$1000), fresh fruit drink in hand. The delightful **Hostal Los Emilios** (☎ 741-126; Cochrane 213; s/d incl breakfast CH$8000/16,000; �) has some sweet rooms and an attractive orchard-side patio.

Mamiña, 125km east of Iquique (not on the same road to Pica) is a quizzical terraced town with thermal baths, a 17th-century church and a pre-Columbian fortress, **Pukará del Cerro Inca**. Plunk into a deck chair and plaster yourself with restorative mud at **Barros Chino** (☎ 057-751-298; admission CH$1500; ☼ 9am-3pm Tue-Sun), a kind of budget 'resort.' **Cerro Morado** (campsite per person CH$2000) offers fixed-price lunches and backyard camping. You'll find a few basic *residenciales* (budget accommodations) in town. All places offer full board. To splurge, check out **Hotel Los Cardenales** (☎ 057-517-000; r per person incl full board CH$30,000; �)), the coziest place in town, with springwater pool, Jacuzzis and gardens. The Lithuanian owners are multilingual. See Iquique (opposite) for transport details.

ARICA

☎ 058 / pop 200,000

Summery days of ripping big surf and warm sea currents bless this otherwise drab city, flush against Peru. Arica is an urban beach resort, with long swaths of sand reaching the knobby headland of El Morro. As far as Chile's coastal cities go, it is one of the most pleasant stops in the north. You'll find Aymara people peddling their crafts at stalls, Eiffel's iron church and a few other architectural gems. Don't miss the winding journey inland through quirky desert towns to the stunning Parque Nacional Lauca.

Orientation

Traveler services are staked out in the commercially chaotic center between the coast and Av Vicuña Mackenna. A pedestrian mall is on 21 de Mayo and the best beaches are south of the *morro* (headland) and north of Parque Brasil. The bus terminals are on Diego Portales, just after Av Santa María, accessible by bus or taxi *colectivos*, which are faster and more frequent. Take *colectivo* 8 (CH$250) along Diego Portales to get to the city center. It's about a 3km walk.

Information

Internet cafes and calling centers fill 21 de Mayo and Bolognesi. There are numerous 24-hour ATMs along the pedestrian mall (21 de Mayo). *Casas de cambio* on 21 de Mayo offer good rates on US dollars, Peruvian, Bolivian and Argentine currency, and euros.

Automóvil Club de Chile (☎ 252-678; 18 de Septiembre 1360) West of center, with maps and road information.

Ciber Tux (Bolognesi 370; per hr CH$400; ☻ 10am-midnight) Internet cafe.

Conaf (☎ 201-200; tarapaca@conaf.cl; Av Vicuña Mackenna 820; ☻ 8:30am-5:15pm Mon-Fri) Has some information on Región I (Tarapacá) national parks. From downtown, take *micro* 9 or colectivos 7, 2 or 23 (*micro* CH$300, colectivo CH$400).

Departamento de Extranjería (☎ 250-377; Angamos 990) Replaces lost tourist cards and extends visas.

Hospital Dr Juan Noé (☎ 229-200; 18 de Septiembre 1000)

Info Arica (www.infoarica.cl) For information on Arica in English and Spanish.

Lavandería La Moderna (18 de Septiembre 457; per kg CH$1800; ☻ 9:30am-9pm Mon-Fri, 9:30am-2pm Sat) Laundry.

Post office (Prat 305) On a walkway toward Pedro Montt.

Sernatur (☎ 252-054; infoarica@sernatur.cl; San Marcos 101; ☻ 8:30am-7pm Mon-Sat, 10am-2pm Sun Dec-Feb, 8:30am-5:30pm Mon-Fri Mar-Nov) Helpful locale with brochures on Tarapacá and other Chilean regions.

Dangers & Annoyances

Petty thievery is a problem at bus terminals and beaches. Take just the essentials. Strong ocean currents make some beaches more dangerous than others.

Remember to change your watches: Chile is two hours ahead of Peru from October 15 to March 15 and one hour ahead otherwise.

Sights & Activities

The imposing tawny hunk of rock looming 110m over the city, **El Morro de Arica** is reached by the footpath from the south end of Colón. Its museum commemorates the June 7, 1880 battle between Peru and Chile (a tender subject for both nationalities). Alexandre Gustave Eiffel designed the Gothic-style 1875 **Iglesia San Marcos** (☻ 9am-2pm & 6-8pm) on Plaza Colón and the **Aduana de Arica** (☻ 8:30am-8pm), the former customs house at Parque General Baquedano (before landfill, it fronted the harbor). Both buildings were prefabricated in Eiffel's Parisian studios; the church, minus the door, is entirely cast iron. **Plazoleta Estación** houses a free railroad museum.

Museo Arqueológico San Miguel de Azapa (☎ 205-555; admission CH$1000; ☻ 9am-8pm Jan & Feb, 10am-6pm Mar-Dec), 12km east of Arica, is home to some of the world's oldest mummies. There are superb local archaeological and cultural heritage displays and well-written guide booklets in English. *Colectivos* (CH$800) at the corner of Chacabuco and Patricio Lynch provide transport.

South of town, along Av Comandante San Martín, the best beaches for swimming and lounging around are **Playa El Laucho**, just past the Club de Yates, followed by the comely, sheltered **Playa La Lisera**, with changing rooms and showers. Take bus 8 from 18 de Septiembre or the northeast corner of Av General Velásquez and Chacabuco. About 7km south you'll smell a fishmeal processing plant, nearby is **Playa Corazones**, with wild camping and a kiosk. Check out the trail just past the beach steering past caves, cormorant colonies, crashing waves, tunnels and a sea lion colony. No buses serve Corazones: hire a cab or bike it.

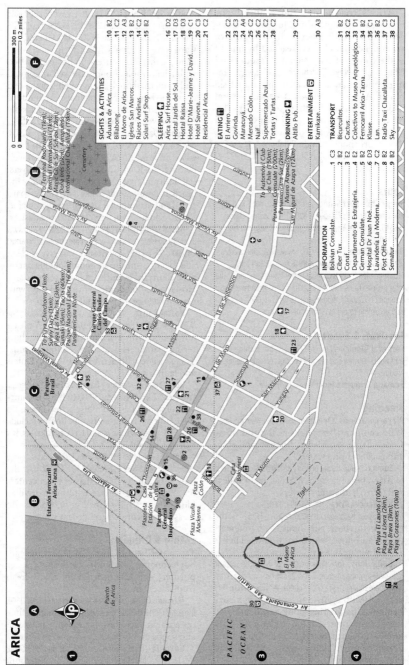

Arica's treacherous tubes host high-profile surf championships. July sees the biggest breaks. The beaches north of downtown are rougher but cleaner, reached by bus 12 at the corner of Av General Velásquez and Chacabuco. **Playa Chinchorro**, 2km away, features pricey eateries, treat shops and jet-ski rental. As well as **Playa Las Machas**, several kilometers further north, expert surfers also hit the towering waves of El Gringo and El Buey at Isla de Alacrán, south of Club de Yates. Surf shops include **Billabong** (☎ 232-599; 21 de Mayo 493) and **Solari Surf Shop** (☎ 233-773; 21 de Mayo 160).

Tours

Magic Chile Surf School (off Map p431; ☎ 311-120; www.surfschool.cl; Patagones 820) Offers surfing classes (CH$15,000) from Yoyo Sepulveda, a great resource for surf travelers.

Raices Andinas (☎ 233-305; www.raicesandinas.com; Sotomayor 195) A respectable little Aymara-run outfit, recommended for encouraging better understanding of the local people. Tours into the mountains last from two days (around CH$50,000) to four (around CH$145,000); prices vary according to the number of participants.

Festivals & Events

Carnaval Ginga Held in mid-February, this features the traditional dancing and musical skills of regional *comparsa* groups.

Semana Ariqueña (Arica Week) Early June.

Sleeping

Playa Corazones (Av Comandante San Martín; free), Wild camping 7km south at the end of Av Comandante San Martín. Sites are unkempt and packed; bring water.

Sumaki (campsite per person CH$1500), 5km north of Arica, near Playa Las Machas, has a volleyball court, baths and showers.

Residencial Arica (☎ 255-399; 18 de Septiembre 466; r with/without bathroom CH$5000/4000) Cheap is the word on this basic guesthouse with thin mattresses and huge shared bathrooms. There's TV but no breakfast or kitchen use.

Doña Inés (off Map p431; ☎ 226-372; casade huespedes@hotmail.com; Rojas 2864; dm incl breakfast CH$5500-6500, d CH$12,000-14,000) A hip little HI property with contemporary rooms, a cozy hammock patio, ping-pong and blank wall for graffiti artists. It's a 20-minute walk to downtown or take taxi *colectivo* 4 from neighboring Av Chapiquiña. Paragliding tours are available.

Arica Surf House (☎ 312-213; www.aricasurfhouse .cl; O'Higgins 661; dm/s/d CH$6000/$15,000/20,000, s/d without bathroom CH$10,000/16,000; 🖳) Geared toward wave-chasing, with surf trips and point shuttles, this nice, surfer-run hostel is staffed with friendly folk. Rooms are well appointed and modern, though the sprawling eight-bed dorm (no bunks) says orphanage. An outdoor lounge features ping-pong (legend has it Kelly Slater played here) and comfy shaded sofas.

Sunny Days (☎ 241-038; www.sunny-days-arica.cl; Aravena 161; dm CH$7000, r per person incl breakfast with/without bathroom CH$8000/7000; 🖳) Warm and welcoming, this Kiwi-Chilean run hostel delivers. It's clean and convenient to both buses and the beach. Laundry, storage, bike and boogie-board rental and a communal kitchen are all available. Rates include an 'all you can eat' breakfast.

Hostal Jardín del Sol (☎ 232-795; Sotomayor 848; www .hostaljardindelsol.cl; Sotomayor 848; r per person incl breakfast CH$8000; 🖳) This downtown property is clean and friendly, with terrace rooms looking out on a tile courtyard where breakfast is served daily. Hosts coddle newcomers (in a good way) with good travel tips and a useful local map.

Hostal Raissa (☎ 251-070; www.hotelraissa.tk; San Martín 281; s/d incl breakfast CH$10,000/16,000) A pleasant option with peaceful courtyards, chattering parakeets and high-ceiling rooms. There's a guest kitchen, cable TV, bike rentals and laundry.

Hotel D'Marie – Jeanne y David (☎ 258-231; Av General Velásquez 792; s/d incl breakfast CH$14,000/19,000) A courtyard of poinsettias and hibiscus trees livens up these large but lackluster rooms. Rooms include fans, TV, good showers and basic breakfasts. It's run by a helpful French-Chilean couple.

Hotel Savona (☎ 231-000; www.hotelsavona.cl; Yungay 380; s/d incl breakfast CH$26,000/31,000; 🖳 🐾) At the foot of El Morro, this alabaster hotel centers on an attractive terrace with bougainvillea blooms and a pill-shaped pool. Rooms are pleasantly decorated and decent value.

Eating & Drinking

Tap water here is chemical-laden; instead, buy economy-size bottles (or bring a water purifier) and benefit from the many fresh fruit-juice stands.

Mercado Colón (cnr Colón & Maipú; menu CH$800-1500, fish dishes CH$1300-2000; ⊙ breakfast & lunch) Small-time restaurants offer cheap and freshly fried fish and soups in this bustling covered market.

Govinda (Blanco Encalada 200; set meals CH$800; ⊙ 12:30-3:30pm Mon-Fri) A casual living-room ambience sets the stage for cheap and cheerful lunch menus. The imaginative three-course lunches feature fresh organic produce.

Naif (Sangra 365; breakfast CH$1000-1500; set lunch CH$1600; ☺ breakfast, lunch & dinner Mon-Sat) Hidden on a pedestrian alley, this funky cafe-cum-bar has sharp art and occasional live music. Happy hour runs from 8pm to 11pm.

Tortas y Tartas (21 de Mayo 233; mains CH$2400-5100; ☺ 9:30am-11pm) The outdoor terrace begs you to relax with a beer or sip a good cup of java at this trendy cafe. Meals are satisfying and the menu diverse, with everything from pasta to fajitas.

El Arriero (☎ 232-636; 21 de Mayo 385; mains CH$4000-5200; ☺ lunch & dinner) Steak and potatoes central, this old-fashioned *parrilla* grills meats to perfection, with alluring sides like fresh salads and fries.

Maracuyá (☎ 227-600; Av Comandante San Martín 0321; mains CH$5000-10,000; ☺ noon-3pm & 8pm-1am) An elegant (it's bow-tie service here) ocean-front restaurant with a soundtrack of waves booming below. Cuisine is international, with a fair shake of surf and turf. It's next to Playa El Laucho.

Altillo Pub (21 de Mayo 260, 2nd fl; ☺ 6pm-late Mon-Sat) Offers candlelit tables and comfy chairs overlooking the action on 21 de Mayo.

Supermercado Azul (cnr 18 de Septiembre & Baquedano) Large supermarket.

Entertainment

Kamikaze (☎ 258-136; Av Comandante San Martín 055; admission CH$1200 ☺ 7pm-3:30am Thu-Sat) At the foot of El Morro, this seafront bar and *discoteca* gets rolling after midnight.

Some of the hippest bars and discos are strung along Playa Chinchorro, including **Soho Discotheque** (www.aricaextreme.cl; Playa Chinchorro; admission CH$1500; ☺ 11pm-late Thu-Sat) and the attached pub **Drake** (admission with drink around CH$1300), both of which get a variety of DJs as well as live salsa and rock bands.

Getting There & Away

AIR

LAN (☎ 600-526-2000, option 8; Prat 391) has several daily flights to Santiago (CH$34,950, 3½ hours), sometimes with several stops. **Sky** (☎ 251-816; 21 de Mayo 356) has cheaper and less frequent domestic flights. Chacalluta Airport is 18km north. **Arica Service** (☎ 314-031) runs airport shuttles (CH$2500 per person).

BUS & COLECTIVO

The area around the terminals is notorious for petty thievery so watch your stuff. **Terminal Rodoviario** (☎ 241-390; cnr Portales & Santa María) houses major bus companies, including **Buses Géminis** (☎ 241-647), **Flota Barrios** (☎ 223 587), **Pullman Bus** (☎ 223-837) and **Tur Bus** (☎ 222-217). All southbound buses pass through a regional border inspection. For La Paz, Bolivia, **Cuevas y Gonzalez** (☎ 241-090) and comfortable **Chile Bus** (☎ 222-817) depart every morning. Sample fares:

BUS FARES		
Destination	**Cost (CH$)**	**Duration (hr)**
Antofagasta	16,000	12
Calama	16,000	10
Copiapó	24,900-38,000	18
Iquique	7000	4½
La Paz, Bolivia	8000	9
La Serena	31,600	22
Santiago	35,000	28

More services to La Paz leave from the shabbier **Terminal Internacional de Buses** (☎ 248-709; Portales 1002) just east. From here, **Trans Cali Internacional** (☎ 261-068) departs daily at 9:30am for Parinacota (CH$5000) and Parque Nacional Lauca. Tacna *colectivos* (CH$3000) are inside the terminal; their Peruvian counterparts leave from outside the terminal and have longer inspection delays. Give the driver your passport to deal with the border formalities.

For Putre, **La Paloma** (☎ 222-710; Riesco 2071) has a direct bus at 7am (CH$3000, 1½ hours).

To get to the bus terminals, hop on *colectivo* 1, 4 or 11 from Maipú or number 8 from San Marcos.

CAR

If driving to Peru, check with the consulate about the latest required forms. You'll need multiple copies of the Relaciones de Pasajeros form, found in most stationery stores, allowing 60 days in Peru; no charge. To Bolivia, take extra gas, water and antifreeze.

TRAIN

Trains to Tacna (CH$1200, 1½ hours) depart from **Ferrocarril Arica-Tacna** (☎ 231-115; Lira 889) at 10am and 7pm, Monday to Saturday.

CHILE

GETTING TO PERU & BOLIVIA

The border crossing at Challuca/Tacna is open daily from 8am to 12am and 24 hours from Friday to Sunday. Buses with international routes simply cross, although long-distance routes are best booked in Tacna, where you'll find lower prices. Have your passport and tourist card on hand and eat any stowaway fruits or vegetables before crossing. From October to February, Peruvian time is two hours behind Chilean time. The rest of the year it is one hour behind Chilean time.

For information on travel from Peru, see p798.

The most popular route to cross into Bolivia is via Parque Nacional Lauca, crossing from the Chilean town of Chungara to Tambo Quemado. Most international buses have morning departures. Immigration is open from 8am to 9pm. Have your passport and tourist card on hand. You can also reach the border of Chungara via taxi from Putre: cross the border on foot and find local transportation in Tambo Quemado. Buses with international routes simply cross.

Getting Around

Rental cars are available at **Cactus** (☎ 257-430; Av General Baquedano 635, Local 36) or **Klasse** (☎ 254-498; www.klasserentacar.cl; Av General Velásquez 762, Local 25). Prices start at just CH$21,000 per day. Mountain bikes with double shocks are available at **Bicircuitos** (Estación Ferrocarril Arica–La Paz) for CH$6000 per day.

RUTA 11 & PUTRE

The barren slopes of the Lluta Valley host hillside geoglyphs; **Poconchile** and its quake-ridden 17th-century church, candelabra cacti (consider yourself blessed if you see it in bloom, which happens one 24-hour period per year); and the chasm-side ruins of the 12th-century fortress **Pukará de Copaquilla**.

Detour in Poconchile to **Eco-Truly** (☎ 098-976-3137; www.ecotruly-arica.org; Sector Linderos Km 29; campsite per person CH$2000, r incl breakfast CH$6000), a slightly surreal Hare Krishna 'ecotown' and yoga school. We recommend their abundant vegetarian sampler lunch (CH$2500).

Aymara village **Putre** (population 2468; altitude 3530m), 150km northeast of Arica is an appealing stop for visitors to acclimatize. Take advantage of the excellent hikes among ancient stone-faced terraces of alfalfa and oregano and tranquil village ambience. Colonial architecture includes the restored adobe **Iglesia de Putre** (1670). During the frivolously fun **Carnaval** in February exploding flour balloons and live music rule the day.

There's a post office and call center in town. Baquedano is the main strip. **Tour Andino** (☎ 099-011-0702; www.tourandino.com; Av General Baquedano s/n) is a one-man show whose local guide, Justino Jirón, is warmly recommended.

our pick **Chakana** (☎ 099-745-9519; www.la-chakana .com; 750m from plaza, Putre; dm incl breakfast CH$8000, s/d/t

cabañas CH$26,000/32,000/36,000; 💻) is a cozy delight that boasts the best views and breakfast in town. The warm welcome carries over with electric heat and featherbeds. It's German-Chilean-run. Installations are new and comfortable and guests get the insider beat on nearby nature gems. It's off an unmarked dirt road but you can arrange for a free pickup with reservations.

Also in Putre, **Pachamama** (☎ 231-028; ukg @entelchile.net; r per person without bathroom CH$8000; 💻) has a communal kitchen, floral courtyard and knowledgeable staff. To get here from Baquedano, head west from the Residencial La Paloma, descending a small hill to the hostel.

Run by a supersweet couple, **Hostal Jurasi** (☎ 099-953-9858; Av Circumnavalación s/n; r per person CH$8000-12,5000) has round stone rooms. They're bubblegum-pink with space heaters and good beds. The cheaper rate is reserved for early reservations.

The following two restaurants do not offer breakfast. **Cantaverdi** (Plaza s/n; mains CH$1800-4500) is a casual place, with *humitas* and home cooking, a roaring fireplace and wi-fi. **Kuchu-Marka** (Av General Baquedano 351; mains from CH$3800) offers upscale *altiplano* cuisine (think quinoa and alpaca steaks) to live strummers.

Buses La Paloma (☎ 099-161-4709; Baquedano 301) departs for Arica (CH$3000, 1½ hours) daily at 2pm. Buses to Parinacota, in Parque Nacional Lauca, pass the turn-off to Putre, 5km from the main highway.

PARQUE NACIONAL LAUCA

At woozy heights with snow-dusted volcanoes, remote hot springs and glimmering lakes, Lauca, 160km northeast of Arica, is an absolute treasure. Herds of *vicuña*, vizca-chas and bird species including flamingos, giant coots and Andean gulls inhabit the park (138,000 hectares; altitude 3000m-6300m) alongside impressive cultural and archaeological landmarks.

At 11km from Putre, **Termas Jurasi** (admission CH$1000; dawn-dusk) has rustic thermal baths amid rocky scenery. The main road provides ample photo ops, with domestic llamas and alpacas grazing on emerald pastures among clear lagoons filled with *guallatas* (Andean geese) and ducks.

The dwindling Aymara village of **Parinacota** sits 20km away and 5km off the highway. Whitewashed adobe, stone streets and thin air make a surreal setting, capped by a lovely 18th-century church, to which one man holds the key. Don't miss the church murals, which cast Spanish conquistadors as Jesus' perse-cutors. There's also a famous tethered table. According to local fable, it used to roam town, stopping at houses where an occupant would later die. Originally the table was used to dis-play the deceased at funerals, but it must have gotten impatient when business got slow…

Call **Conaf** (☎ 058-201-225; amjimene@conaf.cl; dm CH$5000) to reserve the no-frills *refugios* at Parinacota and Lago Chungará; camp-grounds are free (and freezing). Bring enough food and a warm sleeping bag. The only lodging is **Hostal Terán** (Parinacota opposite church; per person CH$6000) Wrap yourself in cro-cheted blankets to battle the drafts in this *refugio*. Breakfast is CH$1500. Reserve with Arica-based Raices Andinas (p432).

Hiking and mountaineering opportunities are plentiful, if you can take the altitude. The twin **Payachata volcanoes** – Parinacota (6350m) and Pomerape (6240m) – are dormant. At their feet is **Lago Chungará**, at 4500m, one of the world's highest lakes. Just to the south Volcán Guallatire smokes ominously.

Adapt to the altitude gradually; do not exert yourself at first, and eat and drink moderately. Herbal-tea remedies *chachacoma,* or *maté de coca* help combat altitude sickness. Both are available from village vendors. Pack sunblock, shades and a hat. The park straddles the paved Arica–La Paz Hwy. See Arica (p433) for bus details. If you are renting a car, or have your own, carry extra fuel and antifreeze.

MIDDLE CHILE

The heartland home of Chilean rodeo and vineyards is oft skipped by travelers scram-bling further afield. But if this region existed anywhere else in the world, it would be get-ting some serious attention. The abundant harvests of the fertile central valley fill grocer's bins from Anchorage to Tokyo. Don't even mention the contribution of Chilean wine to a lively *sobremesa* (dinner conversation). Wine country is accessible by day trips from Santiago, as is great skiing. Not much further you'll find respectable surfing and the un-spoiled parks of Reserva Nacional Radal Seite Tazas and Parque Nacional Laguna de Laja.

Historically this area was a bonanza for the Spaniards, who found small gold mines, good farmland and a large potential workforce south of Concepción. The tenacious Mapuche forced the Spanish to abandon most of their settlements by the mid-17th century.

RANCAGUA
☎ 072 / pop 231,900
Industrial Rancagua is rarely a destination in it-self, unless you consider the **Campeonato Nacional de Rodeo** (www.rodeochileno.cl; admission CH$7000-12,000) held in late March. The prestigious competi-tion draws cowboys and spectators from all over. Visitors can also day trip to hot springs **Termas de Cauquenes** (www.termasdecauquenes.cl; admission CH$5000) and the underappreciated

---

TOURING PARQUE NACIONAL LAUCA

Skip the one-day blitzkriegs to Lago Chungará offered by many Arica agencies and you'll save yourself a screaming headache, known locally as *soroche* (altitude sickness). Take your time to savor the landscape. Tours lasting 1½ days (from CH$25,000) include a night in Putre, allowing more time to acclimatize; and a three-day circuit to Lauca, the Monumento Natural Salar de Surire, Parque Nacional Volcán Isluga and Iquique (around CH$90,000) returns to Arica late the third night. English-speaking guides are scarce; arrange one in advance. Outfitters include **Raices Andinas** (see p430), **Latinorizons** (Arica ☎ 058-250-007; www.latinorizons.com; Bolognesi 449) and **Parinacota Expeditions** (Arica ☎ 058-256-227; www.parinacotaexpediciones.cl; cnr Bolognesi & Thompson).

Reserva Nacional Río de los Cipreses (☎ 297-505; admission CH$2000). The reserve features waterfalls, glacial valleys and fluvial landscapes.

Traveler services include **Sernatur** (☎ 230-413; Riesco 277; ✆ 8:30am-6pm Mon-Fri), money changer **Afex** (Campos 363, Local 4; ✆ 10am-9pm Mon-Sat, 11am-9pm Sun), and **Conaf** (☎ 204-645; rancagua@conaf.cl; Cuevas 480; 9am-5pm Mon-Fri) for park guidance.

Family house **Hostal Yaiman** (☎ 641-773; Bueras 655; s/d incl breakfast CH$13,500/27,000, without bathroom CH$10,500/21,000) has carpeted rooms (with carpeted walls!) and cable TV. Local foodie favorite **Doña Emilia** (☎ 239-483; Diego de Almagro 440; mains CH$5500-7900) serves French and Spanish fare on a garden terrace.

Long-distance buses also use the **terminal** (☎ 225-425; Salinas 1165) north of the Mercado Central. From here, **Sextur** (☎ 231-342) leaves for Pichilemu (CH$3000, three hours) daily at 6:40am. To the hot springs, there are two buses daily in summer; call the terminal to confirm because the timetable changes frequently.

Tur Bus (☎ 230-341; cnr Calvo & O'Carrol) and **Pullman** (☎ 227-756; www.pullman.cl; cnr Av Brasil & Lastarria) have their own terminals. Buses to Santiago (CH$2200, one hour) leave every 10 or 15 minutes.

From the **train station** (☎ 600-585-5000; cnr Av Estación & Carrera Pinto) seven daily Terrasur trains go north to Santiago (CH$5000, one hour) and south to Talca (CH$6000, 3 hours) and Chillán (CH$10,500, 3½ hours), amongst other stops.

SANTA CRUZ
☎ 072 / pop 32,400

Thanks to the generous investments of a former arms dealer, picturesque Santa Cruz has become the nexus of area winemaking. It's best during the lively **Fiesta de la Vendimia**, the grape-harvest festival held in the plaza at the beginning of March. Worth exploring, **Museo de Colchagua** (☎ 821-050; www.museocolchagua.cl; Errázuriz 145; admission CH$3000; ✆ 10am-6pm) has fascinating collections of unusual fossils, Mapuche textiles, pre-Columbian ceramics, exquisite gold work and *huaso* (cowboy) gear. The **Tren del Vino** (☎ 02-470-7403; www.trendelvino.cl; incl transport to & from Santiago CH$62,000; ✆ 8am Sat) takes tourists on a steam-train tour. It departs from San Fernando station, with on-board wine tasting, a vineyard lunch and finishes at the museum, returning to Santiago by bus. The welcoming **Hostal D'Vid**

(☎ 821-269; www.dvid.cl; Edwards 205; d incl breakfast CH$18,000, s without bathroom CH$18,000; ▣) has crisp rooms and a lovely garden.

The **bus terminal** (Casanova 478) sits four blocks west of the town plaza. Twice every hour, **Buses Nilahué** (☎ 825-582; www.busesnilahue.com) goes to Pichilemu (CH$2500, two hours) and Santiago (CH$4000, four hours).

PICHILEMU
☎ 072 / pop 12,400

Lusty left-break waves make dusty and ramshackle 'Pichi' a hot surf spot. With bohemian *buena onda* (good vibes) and more expats every day, it isn't a bad strip of sand to kick back on.

For basic info on lodging and events, contact the **tourist office** (☎ 841-017; www.pichilemu.cl; Municipalidad, Gaete 365; ✆ 9am-6pm). On La Puntilla Beach, **Escuela de Surf Manzana 54** (☎ 099-574-5984; www.manzana54.cl; Av Costanera s/n; half-day board & gear CH$3500) offers surf rentals. Its private courses (CH$10,000 for two hours) are apt for newbies. To get there, walk to the beach end of Av Ortúzar and continue for a few minutes along the coastal road. Fronting the town center to the northeast is calm **Playa Principal** (main beach), while south is the longer and rougher **Infiernillo**, known for its fast tow. The best surfing in the area is at **Punta de Lobos**, 6km south of Pichi proper, site of the annual Campeonato Nacional de Surf (National Surfing Championship).

Campground **Pequeño Bosque** (☎ 842-071; cnr Santa Teresa & Paseo del Sol; 4-person sites US$16) is beach-accessible with full amenities. Cheap *residenciales* pop up along Aníbal Pinto in high season. Opposite Infiernillo beach, **Pichilemu Surf Hostal** (☎ 842-350; www.pichilemusurfhostal.com; Lyra 167; s/d/tr/q CH$15,000/24,000/30,000/34,000) offers sea views and expert wave advice from its windsurfing owner Marcel. Earthy, ultramodern **Posada Punta de Lobos** (☎ 09-8154-1106; www.posadapuntadelobos.cl; s/d/tr incl breakfast CH$40,000/48,000/54,000, 2-/10-person cabañas CH$48,000/90,000) sits 1km from the Punta de Lobos turn-off, surrounded by pines and eucalypti.

The low-key **Donde Pinpón** (Av Ross 9; mains CH$3000) offers seafood stews and other Chilean staples. On Infernillo beach, **El Puente Holandés** (☎ 842-350; Costanera Eugenio Díaz Lira 167; mains CH$3500-4900; ✆ 9am-11pm) ups the stakes with seafood ravioli and grilled sea bass. The terrace is spot-on for a beer.

From the **Terminal de Buses** (cnr Av Millaco & Los Alerces) on Pichilemu's outskirts, buses run frequently to Santa Cruz (CH$2500, two hours) and San Fernando (CH$3000, three hours) where there are connections north and south.

CURICÓ
☎ 075 / pop 123,800

Drawing on visitors to local vineyards and the exquisite Reserva de Radal Seite Tasas, Curicó is a laid-back city, best known for its postcard-perfect **Plaza de Armas**, complete with bandstand, palms and monkey-puzzle trees. You can find information at the **Tourist office** (☎ 543-027; www.curico.cl; Yungay 620). Mid-March's **Festival de la Vendimia**

makes merriment out of the annual grape harvest. Vineyard **Miguel Torres** (☎ 564-100; www.migueltorres.cl), located 5km south of town, conducts daily tours and serves lunch at its chic restaurant (mains CH$10,000). Take *colectivos* going to Molina and ask to be dropped off.

Cold, rambling **Hotel Prat** (☎ 311-069; hotelprat curico@yahoo.es; Peña 427; s/d incl breakfast CH$15,000/ 20,000, s without bathroom CH$7500; 💻) has cheap digs. To upgrade, try the modern **Hostal Viñedos** (☎ 222-083; www.hostalvinedos.cl; Chacabuco 645; s/d/tr incl breakfast CH$17,900/23,800/29,900, s/d without bathroom CH$15,000/20,000) with bright rooms and bouncy beds. **Mistiko** (☎ 310-868; Prat 21; mains CH$4500-6300) wows visitors with delicious Peruvian-fusion fare.

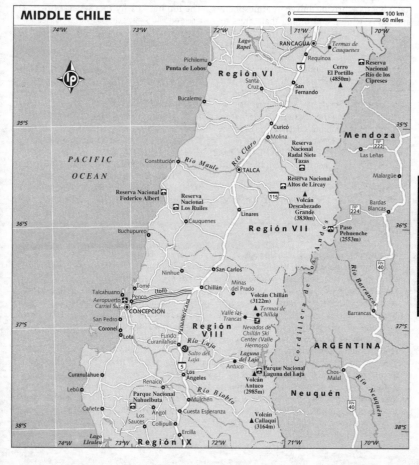

MIDDLE CHILE

The **Terminal de Buses** (cnr Maipú & Prat) and the **Estación de Ferrocarril** (☎ 600-585-5000; Maipú 657) are four blocks west of the Plaza de Armas. There are seven trains a day to Santiago (CH$6000, 2¼ hours) and Chillán (CH$7000, 2½ hours). To get to Parque Nacional Las Siete Tazas, catch a bus to Molina (CH$500, 35 minutes, every five minutes) with **Aquelarre** (☎ 314-307) from the Terminal de Buses Rurales, opposite the main bus terminal. From Molina there are frequent services to the park in January and February. Buses to Santiago (CH$3500, 2½ hours) leave about every half-hour; try **Bus Pullman Sur** (Henríquez), three blocks north of the plaza or **Tur Bus** (Manso de Velasco 0106).

TALCA
☎ 071 / pop 198,700

Talca boasts a thriving university atmosphere and savvy wining and dining that caters to gringos on the wine-country trail. Located 257km south of Santiago, it has good access to national reserves, and offers better long-distance bus connections than nearby towns. Traveler services include **Sernatur** (☎ 233-669; 1 Oriente 1150; 🕑 8:30am-5:30pm Mon-Fri) and **Conaf** (☎ 228-029; 3 Sur & 2 Poniente; 9am-5pm Mon-Fri). Occupying the house where Bernardo O'Higgins signed Chile's declaration of independence in 1818, **Museo O'Higgins y de Bellas Artes** (1 Norte 875; 🕑 10am-7pm Tue-Fri, 10am-2pm Sat & Sun) features pastoral scenes in oil and *huaso* portraits.

With big breakfasts and cozy rooms, the English-speaking **Los Castaños** (☎ 684-531; los castanostalca@gmail.com; 8 Oriente 1481; s/d without bathroom incl breakfast CH$9000/16,000) proves tuned in to traveler needs. A destination in its own right, the German-Austrian **Casa Chueca** (☎ 099-419-0625; www.trekkingchile.com/casachueca; Viña Andrea s/n, Sector Alto Lircay; dm incl breakfast CH$8500-11,000, d CH$34,000; 🕑 closed Jun-Aug; 🔲) has rustic garden *cabañas*, excellent information and adventure tour company El Caminante (below) on site. Call first from Talca terminal, then take the Taxutal 'A' *micro* toward San Valentín to the last stop in Taxutal, where you're picked up.

Canteen **Las Viejas Cochinas** (☎ 221-749; Rivera Poniente; mains CH$4000-6000; 🕑 noon-midnight), a former brothel, is a local institution. The specialty here is *pollo mariscal* (chicken in a brandy and seafood sauce), worth the wait. The hip but kitschy **Zuca Restobar** (☎ 236-124; Isidoro del Solar 5; mains CH$4900-5900; 🕑 7pm-midnight Mon-Sat) offers yummy originals like squid-ink fettuccini with razor clams.

North–south buses stop at Talca's main **bus station** (☎ 243-366; 2 Sur 1920) or there's **Tur Bus** (☎ 265-715; 3 Sur 1960). Destinations include Chillán (CH$2700, three hours), Puerto Montt (CH$12,000, 11 hours) and Santiago (CH$4000, three hours). **Buses Vilches** (☎ 235-327) has four daily services to Vilches Alto, the gateway to the Reserva Nacional Altos de Lircay.

From the **EFE train station** (☎ 226-254; 11 Oriente 1000) there are seven trains daily to Santiago (CH$6500, 2¾ hours) and south to Chillán (CH$6000, two hours). A narrow-gauge train chugs to the dune-swept coastal resort

---

YOUR NEXT ADVENTURE

Clear water ladles into seven basalt pools in the lush **Reserva Nacional Radal Siete Tazas** (admission CH$3000), with the spectacle ending at a 50m waterfall. Hiking trails abound; longer ones lead to Cerro El Fraile, Valle del Indio, and Altos del Lircay. Conaf runs two cold-water **campsites** (☎ 075-228-029; campsite per person CH$1500) at Parque Inglés. Within the park, **Camping Los Robles** (up to 6 people CH$8000) has hot showers and a BBQ area. The park is 65km from Curicó. During January and February **Buses Hernández** goes frequently from Molina to Parque Inglés (CH$1500, 2½ hours).

In the Andean foothills, 65km east of Talca, **Reserva Nacional Altos de Lircay** (admission CH$3000) offers fabulous trekking under a chattery flutter of *tricahues* and other native parrots. Those up for a strenuous 12-hour slog venture to **El Enladrillado**, a unique basaltic plateau with stunning views. At 10-hours, the hike to **Laguna del Alto** gets you off easier. Trekkers can loop to Radal Siete Tazas, but a guide is needed, as the trail is unmarked.

Conaf runs the excellent **Camping Antahuara** (campsite per person CH$2500, one-off site fee CH$8000) about 500m beyond the *administración* (headquarters), next to Río Lircay. From Talca, Buses Vilches goes several times daily to Vilches Alto (CH$1400, two hours), 5km from the *administración*.

Seasoned operator **El Caminante** (☎ 099-837-1440, 071-197-0097; www.trekkingchile.com) offers guided hikes in both parks.

of Constitución. Services (CH$1400, three hours) depart at 7:50am daily and 4:30pm on weekdays.

CHILLÁN

☎ 042 / pop 180,100

Historically battered by earthquakes and Mapuche sieges, resilient Chillán is now the gateway to some of the loveliest landscapes in middle Chile. Its new town replaced the old town in 1835. Bernardo O'Higgins' birthplace, **Chillán Viejo** has 60m-long tiled mosaic illustrating scenes from the petit liberator's life. When another quake in 1939 destroyed the new city, the Mexican government donated the **Escuela México** (Av O'Higgins 250; ☺ 10am-13:30pm & 2-6pm Mon-Fri, 10am-6pm Sat & Sun). At Pablo Neruda's request, Mexican muralists David Alfaro Siqueiros and Xavier Guerrero painted spectacular tributes to indigenous and post-Columbian figures in history; donations are accepted (and encouraged).

A tumbling sprawl of produce and crafts (leather, basketry and weaving), the **Feria de Chillán** is one of Chile's best. On Saturday it fills the entire Plaza de la Merced and spills onto adjacent streets.

Information

Banco de Chile (cnr El Roble & 5 de Abril) 24hr ATM.
Hospital Herminda Martín (☎ 208-221; Ramírez 10) Seven blocks east of the plaza.
Post office (Libertad 501)
Sernatur (☎ 223-272; 18 de Septiembre 455; ☺ 8:30-1:30pm, 3-6pm Mon-Fri) Located half a block north of the plaza.

Sleeping & Eating

Hostal Canadá (☎ 234-515; hostalcanada269chile@gmail.com; Av Libertad 269; s/d CH$6000/12,000) has character (this assessment applies both to the hostel and to its host). The rooms are impeccable.

Hostal Ñuble (☎ 321-813; 18 de Septiembre 240; conaver@gmail.com; s/d without bathroom incl breakfast CH$7500/16,000) On a leafy residential street, this quiet family-run hotel has bright, airy rooms with parquet floors and cable TV.

Mercado Central (Maipón btwn 5 de Abril & Riquelme; set lunch CH$1800) Casual eateries serve cheap *paila marina* and *longaniza* (pork sausage) by the butchers' stalls.

La Motoneta (Av Padre Alberto Hurtado 242; mains CH$2000-3100; ☺ noon-3pm & 8-11pm Mon-Sat) The best *picada* (cheap-and-cheerful restaurant)

in town: think rich pies and stews served in clay bowls.

Fuego Divino (☎ 430-988; Gamero 680; mains CH$5500-6800; ☺ 12:30-3:30pm & 8-11:30pm Mon-Sat) A stylish destination for that big night out, we found the expertly barbecued prime cuts of Temuco beef is spot-on. Reserve ahead.

Getting There & Away

Most long-distance buses use **Terminal María Teresa** (☎ 272-149; Av O'Higgins 010), just north of Av Ecuador. The other is the old **Terminal de Buses Inter-Regional** (☎ 221-014; cnr Constitución & Av Brasil), from which you can catch Tur Bus (also at María Teresa) and Línea Azul, with the fastest service to Concepción. Local and regional buses use **Terminal de Buses Rurales** (Sargento Aldea), south of Maipó.

Trains to Santiago (CH$10,500, 4½ hours, seven daily) use the **train station** (☎ 222-424; cnr Av Brasil & Libertad) at the west end of Libertad.

BUS FARES		
Destination	**Cost (CH$)**	**Duration (hr)**
Angol	2500	2¼
Concepción	2000	1½
Los Angeles	2000	1½
Puerto Montt	13,000	9
Santiago	7,200-13,000	5
Talca	2700	3
Temuco	5500	4
Termas de Chillán	2200	1½
Valdivia	8500	6

AROUND CHILLÁN

The southern slopes of the 3122m Volcán Chillán are the stunning setting of the **Nevados de Chillán ski center** (☎ 600-626-3300; www.nevadosdechillan.com; daily ski pass CH$25,000), also known for its indoor **thermal baths** (adult/child CH$8000/4500). There are 32 runs, maxing out at 1100m of vertical and 2500m long. The season attempts to run from June to mid-September, but you should check the website.

Soaks for skimpy spenders can be found at Valle Hermoso, where you'll find a **campground** (per tent CH$15,000) selling food supplies and public **thermal baths** (CH$3000; ☺ 9am-5pm). It's down a turn-off between Valle Las Trancas and the posh hotels.

The toasty but worn **Hostelling Las Trancas** (☎ 042-243-211; www.hostellinglastrancas.cl; Camino Termas de Chillán Km 73.5; dm CH$10,000, d without bathroom

CHILE

incl breakfast CH$20,000) has ski-chalet ambience, with log fires and a beer-and-burger menu. Mod-pod **Ecobox Andino** (☎ 042-423-134; www .ecoboxandino.cl; Camino a Shangri-Lá Km 0.2; 4-person cabañas CH$65,000; ⊠) pampers with cabins featuring decks overlooking the forest.

From Chillán's Terminal de Buses Rurales, **Rembus** (☎ 042-229-377) has buses to Valle Las Trancas (CH$1300, 1¼ hours) five times a day, with the 7:50am and 1:20pm services continuing to Valle Hermoso (CH$2200, 1½ hours).

Coastal villages northwest of Chillán invite exploration. Surfers and fishers head to **Buchupureo**, 13km north of Cobquecura (about 100km from Chillán), where papayas grow, oxen clog the road and houses are sheathed in local slate. **Camping Ayekán** (☎ 042-197-1756; www .turismoayekan.cl; campsites CH$15,000) is open only in high season. Once you get to Buchupureo Plaza de Armas, turn left and follow the signs. **Cabañas Mirador de Magdalena** (☎ 042-197-1890; aochoa_3000 @hotmail.com; La Boca s/n; 4-person cabañas CH$35,000) are pristine stilted cabins overlooking a river delta that twists into the sea.

CONCEPCIÓN

☎ 041 / pop 221,100

Manufacturing industries, port facilities and nearby coal deposits make Concepción Chile's second most important city. It's also left-leading, thanks to a heavy dose of local universities. A major tourist attraction it isn't. Earthquakes in 1939 and 1960 obliterated the historical buildings but downtown does offer pleasant plazas, pedestrian malls and guzzling nightlife, owing to the student population.

The city is on the northern bank of the Río Biobío, Chile's only significant navigable waterway. Plaza Independencia marks the center. Cerro Caracol blocks any easterly expansion.

Information

ATMs and cyber cafes abound downtown.

Afex (Barros Arana 565, Local 57; ☒ 9am-5:30pm Mon-Fri, 10am-1pm Sat) Changes traveler's checks.

Conaf (☎ 262-4000; Barros Arana 215, 2nd fl; ☒ 8:30am-5:30pm Mon-Fri) Info on parks and reserves.

Hospital Regional (☎ 2237-445; cnr San Martín & Av Roosevelt) Eight blocks north of Plaza Independencia.

Laverap (Caupolicán 334; per load CH$3600; ☒ 9:30am-8pm Mon-Fri, to 3pm Sat)

Post office (O'Higgins 799)

Sernatur (☎ 2741-4145; Pinto 460; ☒ 8:30am-8pm Jan & Feb, to 1pm & 3-6pm Mon-Fri Mar-Dec) Provides brochures.

Sights & Activities

On January 1, 1818, O'Higgins proclaimed Chile's independence at the city's **Plaza Independencia**. On the grounds of the Barrio Universitario, the **Casa del Arte** (cnr Chacabuco & Larenas; ☒ 10am-6pm Tue-Fri, to 5pm Sat, to 2pm Sun) houses the massive mural by Mexican Jorge González Camarena, *La Presencia de América Latina* (1965). On the edge of Parque Ecuador, the **Galería de Historia** (cnr Av Lamas & Lincoyán; ☒ 3-6:30pm Sun & Mon, 10am-1:30pm & 3-6:30pm Tue-Fri) features vivid dioramas that create a sense of life as a preconquest Mapuche or pioneer. Upstairs an art gallery features local work.

Once the epicenter of Chile's coal industry, the hilly coastal town of **Lota**, south of Concepción, offers fascinating tours (www .lotasorprendente.cl) to its mines and shantytowns. Mine **Chiflón del Diablo** (Devil's Whistle; ☎ 2871-565; tours CH$4000; ☒ 9am-6:30pm) functioned until 1976, but now former coal miners guide tourists into its chilly depths. Ask the *micro* bus driver to drop you off at Parada Calero. Go down Bajada Defensa Niño street and you'll see a long wall sporting the name. Those more aesthetically inclined can visit the magnificently landscaped 14-hectare **Parque Isidora Cousiño** (admission CH$1600; ☒ 9am-8pm), complete with peacocks and a lighthouse.

Sleeping & Eating

Catering more to businesses than backpackers, lodging can be slim pickings.

Hostal Bianca (☎ 225-2103; www.hostalbianca.cl; Salas 643-C; s/d incl breakfast CH$17,850/24,800, without bathroom CH$11,900/17,800; ☐) The best of the budgets, with bright little rooms, firm beds and cable TV. Breakfast even includes scrambled eggs.

Hotel San Sebastián (☎ 295-6719; www.hotelsan sebastian.cl; Rengo 463; s/d/tr CH$17,000/21,000/26,000, without bathroom CH$15,000/18,000/22,000) Spruced up optimistically with plastic flowers and lilac walls, the b side of this budget hotel is sagging beds and old carpets. Downstairs doubles are cleaner and brighter.

Chela's (Barros Arana 405; set lunch CH$1500; mains CH$2000; ☒ 8:30am-midnight Mon-Sat, noon-8pm Sun) Spike your cholesterol alongside other happy diners with hearty portions of *chorillana* (fries topped with onions and sausage) and steaks.

Sauré Roeckel (Barros Arana 541, Local 1; snacks CH$1800; ☒ 9am-9pm Mon-Fri, to 8pm Sat) Ups the ante of teatime with over 40 varieties of tea and dazzling cream puffs.

Crepería Jardín Secreto (O'Higgins 338; set lunch CH$2300, mains CH$2150-3450; ☯ 9am-11pm) Breakfast is a spoiler with pancakes, eggs and bacon. Teatime offers crepes topped with *manjar* (a milk caramel spread) and dinner serves them with Peking-style duck.

Sublime (☎ 279-4194; Freire 1633; mains CH$4300-6900; ☯ 7pm-midnight Mon-Sat) Done up in chrome and red leatherette, Conce's coolest eatery loves provocative combinations like hazelnut encrusted fish or steak in pear sauce.

Drinking & Entertainment

Almendra Bar (www.almendrabar.cl; Rengo 1624; ☯ 9pm-4am Wed-Sat) Bespectacled design types lounge on the low 1950s sofas at this recycled old garage, the hippest haunt in Conce. Weekdays are about cool tunes, cocktails and sushi, but the dance floor gets going on weekends.

Choripan (Prat 542; ☯ 7:30pm-late) A young, laid-back crowd gathers here for cocktails, beer and conversation over reggae and blues.

Cine Universidad de Concepción (☎ 222-7193; O'Higgins 650) Shows arthouse films on Tuesdays.

Getting There & Away

AIR

Aeropuerto Carriel Sur lies just outside Concepción. **LAN** (☎ 600-526-2000; O'Higgins 648) flies daily to Santiago (CH$40,000, one hour).

BUS

The two long-distance bus terminals are **Collao** (☎ 274-9000; Tegualda 860), in the north, and **Terminal Chillancito** (☎ 231-5036; Henríquez 2565), the northward extension of Bulnes. Most buses leave from Collao, and many companies also have downtown offices. **Tur Bus** (ticket office Tucapel 530) and other companies run frequent departures to Santiago and Viña del Mar/Valparaíso.

BUS FARES		
Destination	Cost (CH$)	Duration (hr)
Angol, Parque Nacional Nahuelbuta	1½	3500
Chillán	2000	1½
Los Ángeles	2500	2
Lota	500	½
Puerto Montt	7500-15,000	8
Santiago	8800-10,000	6½
Temuco	6000	4
Valdivia	8000	6
Valparaíso/ Viña del Mar	8000	8

Getting Around

There's no public transport to the airport, but the bright orange buses to the Universidad de las Américas (CH$500, every 20 minutes) stop 500m south on the Ruta Interportuaria. From downtown, they run east along San Martín.

Micros from the bus station run constantly to the center along San Martín (CH$300). *Micros* to Talcahuano (CH$500) run down O'Higgins and San Martín.

Concepción has several car-rental agencies to choose from. One of the best value is **Rosselot** (☎ 2732-030; www.rosselot.cl; Chacabuco 726), but deductibles may be high.

LOS ÁNGELES
☎ 043 / pop 169,900

This unprepossessing agroindustrial center is base camp for jaunts into Parque Nacional Laguna del Laja and upper Biobío. The best information can be found at **Automóvil Club de Chile** (Vicuña 684), or try **Sernatur** (☎ 317-107, Caupolicán 450, 3rd fl, Oficina 6; ☯ 9am-5:30pm Mon-Fri).

Most lodgings sit along the Panamericana, but the most reasonable options are in town. **Residencial El Angelino** (☎ 325-627; Colo Colo 335; r per person CH$8000) has clean, cheerful rooms. Resembling a 1970s chalet, **Hotel Antilén** (☎ 322-948; Av Alemania 159; r with/without bathroom incl breakfast CH$19,000/12,000) is five blocks east of the Plaza de Armas. The best digs in the region, **Hospedaje El Rincón** (☎ 099-441-5019; www.el rinconchile.cl; Panamericana Km 494; s/d CH$25,000/30,000, r without bathroom incl breakfast CH$15,000), lavishes weary backpackers with substantial breakfasts, tranquility, comfy rooms and homemade grub. German-run, they offer Spanish courses and guided hikes to Laguna del Laja. Reserve for a pickup from Los Ángeles or Cruce La Mona.

Julio's Pizza (Colón 452; pizzas CH$7000-10,000) serves good Argentine-style pizzas, pasta and other dishes. **Bife Sureño** (Lautaro 681; mains CH$6000) pleases carnivores.

Long-distance buses leave from the **Terminal Santa María** (Av Sor Vicenta 2051), on the northeast outskirts of town. **Tur Bus** (Av Sor Vicenta 2061) is nearby. Antuco-bound buses leave from **Terminal Santa Rita** (Villagrán 501).

THE LAKES DISTRICT

The further south you go, the greener it gets, until you find snow-bound volcanoes rising over verdant hills and lakes. This bucolic region makes a great escape to a slower pace.

THE LAKES DISTRICT

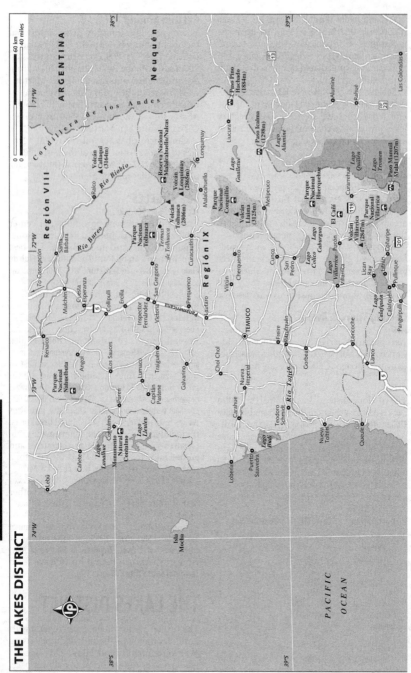

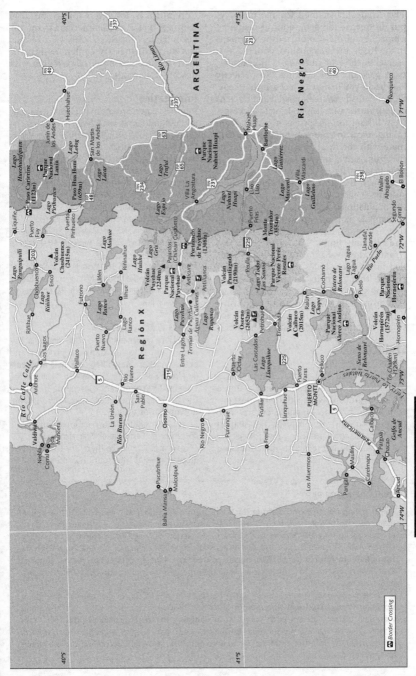

The Araucanía, named for the monkey-puzzle tree, is the geographical center of Mapuche culture. Colonized by Germans in the 1850s, the area further south is a provincial enclave of stocking-clad grannies, fruit pies and lace curtains. So perfectly laid-back, you'll start to feel a little sleepy. Don't. Outside your shingled dwelling, tens of adventures wait: from rafting to climbing, from hiking to hot-springs hopping, from taking *onces* in colonial towns to sipping maté with the local *huasos*. Hospitality is the strong suit of *sureños* (southerners), take time to enjoy it.

Though they love the malls, rural roots still mark most city dwellers (about half the population), who split wood and make homemade jams as part of their daily routine. Seek out the green spaces bursting beyond the city limits. The isolated interior (from Todos los Santos to Río Puelo), settled in the early 1900s, maintains pioneer culture thanks to its isolation, but road building signals inevitable changes. This section takes in the IX Region and part of the X, including Puerto Montt, gateway to the Chiloé archipelago and Chilean Patagonia.

TEMUCO
☎ 045 / pop 259,100

Developed and fast-paced, Temuco is a center for regional business and a transportation hub. It is also the city most intrinsically linked to Mapuche culture and, through on-and-off protests, the seat of Mapuche discontent. It has few tourist attractions, although it is also the childhood home of Pablo Neruda.

Temuco is located 675km south of Santiago via the Panamericana, on the north bank of the Río Cautín. Cerro Ñielol sits north of the city center. Residential west Temuco is a more relaxed area with upscale restaurants.

Information
Internet centers are cheap (CH$400 per hour) and ubiquitous, as are ATMs.

Conaf (☎ 298-100; Bilbao 931, 2nd fl; 9am-5pm Mon-Fri) Offers park information.

Hospital Regional (☎ 212-525; Montt 115) Six blocks west and one block north of the plaza.

Lavasec Center (☎ 234-436; Montt 250; per load CH$2500; ☺ 9am-7:30pm Mon-Sat)

Post office (cnr Portales & Prat)

Sernatur (☎ 312-857; cnr Claro Solar & Bulnes; ☺ 8:30am-8:30pm Mon-Sat, 10am-2pm Sat Dec-Feb, 9am-2pm & 3-5:30pm Mon-Thu, 9am-2pm & 3-4:30pm Fri Mar-Nov) Helpful.

Tourist kiosk (☎ 216-360; Mercado Municipal; ☺ 8am-7pm Tue-Sat, 8:30am-4pm Sun Mar-Nov, 8am-8pm Tue-Sat, 8:30am-4pm Sun Dec-Feb) Has city maps and lodgings lists.

Sights & Activities
Feria Libre (Av Barros Arana; ☺ 8am-5pm) is a dynamic and colorful Mapuche produce and crafts market. **Museo Regional de la Araucanía** (Av Alemania 084; ☺ 9am-5pm Mon-Fri, 11am-5pm Sat, 11am-1pm Sun) recounts the sweeping history of the Araucanian peoples. Take *micro* 9 from downtown or the mall.

You can salute Chile's national flower, the *copihue*, at **Cerro Ñielol** (Prat; admission CH$1000; ☺ daylight hours), where there are trails and an environmental information center.

EXPLORE MORE PARKS

The sparkling centerpiece of **Parque Nacional Laguna del Laja** (admission CH$1000) is the towering snowcone of Volcán Antuco (2979m). An amazing trek circling its skirt takes three days, or you can go for a day hike to get a taste of the action. Stay at **Centro Turístico Lagunillas** (☎ 097-4542184; campsite CH$10,000, 6-person cabañas CH$30,000) or higher up at **Casino Club de Esquí/Refugio Antuco** (dm CH$5000). Buses go from Los Ángeles' central bus station, Terminal Santa Rita, via Antuco to El Abanico, a village near the turn-off to the park (CH$1600, 1½ to two hours, up to six daily).

Pehuéns, or monkey-puzzle trees, grow up to 50m tall and 2m in diameter on the green slopes of **Parque Nacional Nahuelbuta** (admission CH$4000), a fine destination for hiking and mountain biking. You can pitch your tent at **Camping Pehuenco** (campsites CH$12,000). From Angol, 35km to the east, the **Terminal Rural** (Ilabaca 422) has buses to Vegas Blancas (CH$1600, 1½ hours), 7km from the entrance, Monday to Saturday at 6:45am, returning in the evening at 4pm and 6pm.

TEMUCO

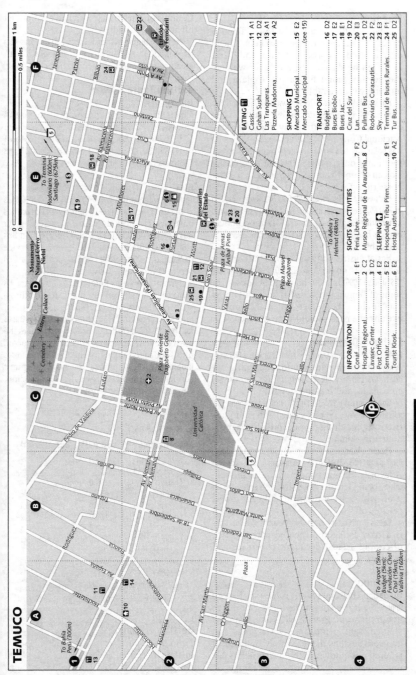

Sleeping

Fundamentally not a tourist town, Temuco proves a challenge for backpackers. Cheap digs around the train station and Feria Libre can be sketchy, especially for women; the neighborhood between the plaza and university is preferable.

Adela y Helmut (☎ 582-230; www.adelayhelmut.cl; Faja 16,000 Km 5 N; dm CH$5050, s/d from CH$16,800/21,850) Out on a small farm 48km away toward Parque Nacional Conguillío, this backpacker favorite has solar-heated water, small kitchens in every room and outstanding views of smoldering Volcán Llaima. They also rent bikes and offer horse riding.

Hospedaje Tribu Piren (☎ 985-711; www.tribupiren.cl; Prat 69; r per person CH$7000; 💻) Run by Alvaro, a friendly English-speaker, this good budget choice has clean rooms with terraces, wi-fi and cable TV.

Hostal Austria (☎ 247-169; www.hostalaustria.cl; Hochstetter 599; s/d CH$15,400/23,500, without bathroom CH$10,500/13,000) In a quaint wooden house near some of Temuco's best restaurants, this hostel is a step above the average, with homey touches like antique rugs and old-time furniture.

Eating & Drinking

Feria Libre (Av Barros Arana; 🕑 8am-5pm; mains CH$2000) A dynamic fair with vendors churning out *cazuelas* (soupy stew), *sopaipillas con queso*, empanadas and seafood stews.

Gohan Sushi (☎ 731-110; Av Vicuña MacKenna 530; rolls CH$2500-3800; 🕑 lunch & dinner) Offers innovative rolls, lunch discounts and a fun happy-hour atmosphere.

Pizzería Madonna (Av Alemania 660; pizzas CH$3800-8500, pasta CH$5200-5600; 🕑 noon-4pm & 7pm-midnight) A favorite for pizza and pasta, with the specialty being tricotta (ravioli three ways). Cap it off with velvety tiramisu. Takeout orders get 20% off.

Cassís (Mall Portal Temuco, 2nd fl; mains CH$4000) This is a cozy Patagonia-themed eatery which offers big salads, decadent chocolate and real Java.

Shopping

Fundación Chol-Chol (☎ 614-007; Camino Temuco a Imperial Km 16; 🕑 9am-6pm Mon-Fri) A Fair Trade nonprofit working with 600 rural Mapuche women, selling top-quality weavings and gorgeous textiles made entirely by hand. It is 16km out of town. From the rural bus terminal, take any bus towards Nueva Imperial, Carahue or Puerto Saavedra and ask to be let off at the Fundación.

Mercado Municipal (cnr Bulnes & Portales; 8am-7pm Mon-Sat, 8:30am-4pm Sun) One full city block with gleaming treasures hidden in the bric-a-brac.

Getting There & Away

AIR

Airport Maquehue is 6km south of town. **LAN** (☎ 600-526-2000; Bulnes 687) flies to Santiago (from CH$70,000) and occasionally to Puerto Montt (CH$45,000, 45 minutes). **Sky** (☎ 747-300; Bulnes 677) has competitive rates.

BUS

Terminal Rodoviario (☎ 255-005; Pérez Rosales 01609) is at the northern approach to town. Companies have ticket offices downtown, including **Tur Bus** (☎ 278-161; cnr Lagos & Montt) & **Pullman Bus** (☎ 212-137; Claro Solar 611), with frequent service to Santiago. **Cruz del Sur** (☎ 730-320; Claro Solar 599) serves Chiloé and Bariloche, Argentina.

Terminal de Buses Rurales (☎ 210-494; cnr Avs Balmaceda & A Pinto) serves local destinations, such as Chol Chol (CH$550, 45 minutes) and Melipeuco (CH$1300, two hours). **Buses Jac** (☎ 465-465; cnr Av Balmaceda & Aldunate) offers the most frequent service to Villarrica and Pucón, plus service to Lican Ray and Coñaripe. **Buses Biobío** (☎ 465-355; Lautaro 854) runs frequent services to Angol, Los Angeles, Concepción, Curacautín and Lonquimay.

BUS FARES

Destination	Cost (CH$)	Duration (hr)
Angol, Parque Nacional Nahuelbuta	3000	1
Chillán	5500	4
Coñaripe	2300	2½
Concepción	6000	4
Curacautín	2400	2
Osorno	4000	3
Pucón	2200	1½
Puerto Montt	8000	6
Santiago	14,000	9
Valdivia	3200	2½
Zapala & Neuquén, Argentina	14,000	10

Getting Around

From the airport, taxis cost about CH$8000 to the city center. *Colectivo* 11P goes from downtown (Claro Solar) to the bus terminal.

Colectivo 9 services west Temuco. Car rental is available at the airport with **Budget** (☎ 232-715; cnr Portales & Vicuña MacKenna).

PARQUE NACIONAL CONGUILLÍO

A Unesco Biosphere Reserve protecting the lovely araucaria (monkey-puzzle tree), **Conguillío** (admission CH$4000) also shelters 60,835 hectares of alpine lakes, deep canyons and native forest. It includes a tiny ski area, but its centerpiece is the smoldering Volcán Llaima (3125m), which last erupted on New Year's Day, 2008.

To see solid stands of monkey-puzzle trees, hike the superb **Sierra Nevada trail** (10km, three hours one way), which leaves from the parking lot at Playa Linda. At Laguna Captrén, **Los Carpinteros** (8km, approximately 2½ hours one way) accesses the Mother: the 1800-year-old, 3m-wide Araucaría Madre.

In **Laguna Conguillío**, Conaf's **Centro de Información Ambiental** (www.parquenacionalconguillio.cl) sells trail maps.

Sleeping & Eating

Campgrounds at Laguna Conguillío charge CH$15,000; other accommodations options include **El Estero** (in Temuco ☎ 045-644-388) and **Laguna Captren**, 6km from Lago Conguillío. Rates dive off-season.

Centro de Ski Las Araucarias offers dorms in **Refugio Pehuén** (dm CH$8000) and **Refugio Los Paraguas** (dm CH$8000), bring your own sleeping bag.

Ecotourism project **La Baita** (☎ 416-410; www.labaitaconguillio.cl; cabañas per person half-board CH$31,800) offers four- to eight-person cabins with slow-burning furnaces, limited electricity and hot water. In high season, meals and a small store are available. La Baita is 15km from Melipeuco and 60km from Curacautín.

Getting There & Away

To reach Sector Los Paraguas, **Vogabus** (☎ 910-134), at Temuco's Terminal de Buses Rurales, runs hourly Monday through Saturday to Cherquenco (CH$1300, one hour), from where it's a 17km walk or hitchhike to the ski lodge at Los Paraguas.

For the northern entrance at Laguna Captrén, **Buses Flota Erbuc** (☎ 272-204) reaches Curacautín (CH$1200, 1½ hours), from where a summer-only shuttle (CH$900) runs to Guardería Captrén; Mondays and Fridays *only* (6am and 5pm).

For the southern entrance at Truful-Truful, **Nar-Bus** (☎ 211-611) in Temuco has daily departures to Melipeuco (CH$1300, two hours), where the tourism office can help arrange transport to the park.

VILLARRICA

☎ 045 / pop 39,700

Villarrica has similar scenery but less fluff, zip and bustle than nearby Pucón; it bloomed and faded slightly sooner and today is a somewhat lackadaisical resort. On the southwest shore of Lago Villarrica, it was founded in 1552 and repeatedly attacked by Mapuche until treaties were signed in 1882.

Information

Banks with ATMs are plentiful.

Cyber Mundo (Bilbao 573; per hr CH$500; ☻ 9am-1pm & 3-7pm Mon-Fri, 9am-2pm Sun) Internet cafe.

Hospital Villarrica (☎ 411-169; San Martín 460)

Oficina de Turismo (☎ 206-619; Av Pedro de Valdivia 1070; ☻ 9am-1pm & 2:30-6pm Mon-Fri) Has helpful staff and lists of lodgings.

Politur (☎ 414-547; Muñoz 647; ☻ 8:30am-1:30pm, 4-9pm Mon-Sat, to 1:30pm Sun) Arranges organized tours.

Post office (Muñoz 315)

Sights

The **Museo Histórico y Arqueológico** (Pedro de Valdivia 1050; ☻ 9am-1pm & 3-7:30pm Mon-Fri), next to the tourist office, displays Mapuche artifacts. Behind the tourist office, the **Feria Artesanal** (☻ 10:30am-8pm) offers a selection of crafts.

Sleeping

Prices rise considerably in summer and during the ski season.

La Torre Suiza (☎ /fax 411-213; www.torresuiza.com; Bilbao 969; dm CH$7000, d with/without bathroom CH$25,000/16,000; ▯) Impeccably clean and wood-paneled cozy, this Swiss-run hostel has welcomed generations of backpackers. Attractions include a fully equipped kitchen, laundry, area maps and bike rental.

Hostal Don Juan (☎ 411-833; www.hostaldonjuan.cl; Körner 770; s/d CH$10,950/16,800, without bathroom CH$7600/12,600, 2-/4-person cabañas CH$23,550/29,450; ▯) With volcano views plus foosball and ping-pong games, it's a good-vibe budget choice.

Campgrounds dot the road between Villarrica and Pucón. The following have reasonably private shady sites and hot showers:

Camping Los Castaños (☎ 412-330; campsite CH$10,000) One kilometer east of town.

CHILE

Camping Dulac (☎ 412-097; campsite CH$12,000) Two kilometers east.

Eating & Drinking

Café Bar 2001 (Henríquez 379; sandwiches CH$1600-3400) The breakfast special here for CH$2000 nabs you *küchen* (cake), toast, juice and coffee, though they don't open until 9am.

El Rey del Marisco (☎ 412-093; Letelier 1030; mains CH$2200-6800; ☽ lunch & dinner Mon-Sat, lunch Sun) The place for seafood; start with shellfish empanadas and *pisco sours* and finish with delicately prepared fresh fish.

The Travellers (☎ 413-617; Letelier 753; mains CH$2950-5500; ☽ breakfast, lunch & dinner-late) Ground Zero for foreigners, this resto-bar ranges from Mexican to Thai, with a dose of eclectic pop. You can also get travel advice in German and English, in addition to half-priced happy-hour drinks (from 6:30pm to 9:30pm).

Getting There & Away

Villarrica has a main **bus terminal** (Pedro de Valdivia 621), though a few companies have separate offices nearby. Long-distance fares are similar to those from Temuco (an hour away), with fewer choices.

Buses JAC (☎ 467-777; Bilbao 610) goes to Pucón (CH$800) every 10 minutes, Temuco (CH$1700, one hour) every 20 minutes and Lican Ray (CH$700, 40 minutes) and Coñaripe (CH$1000) every 30 minutes. **Buses Regional Villarrica** (Reyes 619) also has frequent buses to Pucón.

For Argentine destinations, **Igi Llaima** (☎ 412-733), in the main terminal, leaves at 6:45am Monday, Wednesday, Friday and Saturday at 8:55am for San Martín de los Andes (CH$12,000), Zapala and Neuquén (CH$18,000, 12 hours), via Paso Mamuil Malal. **Buses San Martín** (☎ 411-584; Pedro León Gallo 599) does the same route Tuesday to Sunday at 10am (CH$12,000, six hours).

PUCÓN

☎ 045 / pop 16,900

A shimmering lake under the huffing cone of 2847m Volcán Villarrica feeds the mystique of village-turned-megaresort Pucón. Summer time draws a giddy mix of families, adventurers, package tourists and new-age gurus to this mecca. Where else in Chile can you party and play slots till dawn, leave in time to hike the volcano (alongside 300 other enthusiasts) or sleep in, go to the beach or hot springs,

drink a caramel latte, buy a gem-encrusted handbag, run into half of Santiago, get a massage, and sleep in a teepee? Something does exist for everyone here and, snootiness aside, the mix of international wanderers, the zippy social scene and backyard of natural wonders is often a blast.

Orientation

Pucón is 25km from Villarrica at the east end of Lago Villarrica, between the Río Pucón estuary to the north and Volcán Villarrica to the south. Town is walkable, with most tour operators and services on the commercial main strip of Av O'Higgins. Restaurants and shops dot Fresia, which leads to the plaza. Slightly beyond the plaza is the beach.

Information

Chile Pucón (www.chile-pucon.com) Useful internet resource.

Ciber-Unid@d (☎ 444-918; Av O'Higgins 415, Local 2; per hr CH$700; ☽ 9:30am-11pm Mon-Fri, 10am-11pm Sat, 11am-10pm Sun)

Hospital San Francisco (☎ 490-400; Uruguay 325; ☽ 24hr)

Lavandería Araucanias (Urrutia 108; per load CH$3900)

Lavandería Elena (☎ 444-370; Urrutia 520; per load CH$3000)

Oficina de Turismo (☎ 293-002; cnr Av O'Higgins & Palguín; ☽ 9am-10pm Dec-Feb, to 7pm Jun-Aug) With brochures and usually an English speaker on staff.

Post office (Fresia 183)

Supermercado Eltit (Av O'Higgins 336; ☽ 7am-9pm) Changes US cash with reasonable fees and has an ATM.

Activities

Regardless of how many people are milling about Av O'Higgins on any given day, with a little creativity you can leave the crowds behind. Don't limit your ideas to the most popular tours – ask locals and resident expats for their picks.

The masses come to **hike** the smoking, lava-spitting crater of Volcán Villarrica. The full-day excursion (CH$40,000) leaves Pucón around 7:30am. There is no technical climbing involved and people with no prior mountaineering experience frequently ascend. However, a guide is recommended unless you are an expert with your own equipment. When you book a guide service, ask how they will handle a bad-weather day. Less reputable companies head up on a

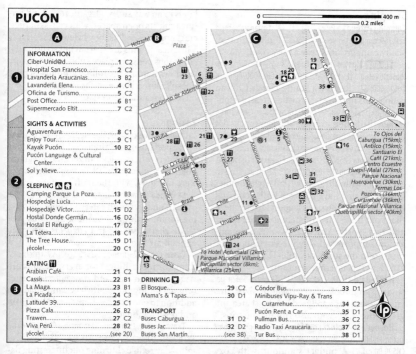

PUCÓN

INFORMATION
Ciber-Unid@d	1 C2
Hospital San Francisco	2 C2
Lavandería Araucanias	3 B2
Lavandería Elena	4 C1
Oficina de Turismo	5 C2
Post Office	6 B1
Supermercado Eltit	7 C2

SIGHTS & ACTIVITIES
Aguaventura	8 C1
Enjoy Tour	9 C1
Kayak Pucón	10 B2
Pucón Language & Cultural Center	11 C2
Sol y Nieve	12 B2

SLEEPING
Camping Parque La Poza	13 B3
Hospedaje Lucía	14 C2
Hospedaje Victor	15 D2
Hostal Donde Germán	16 D2
Hostal El Refugio	17 D2
La Tetera	18 C1
The Tree House	19 D1
¡école!	20 C1

EATING
Arabian Café	21 C2
Cassís	22 B1
La Maga	23 B1
La Picada	24 C3
Latitude 39	25 C1
Pizza Cala	26 B2
Trawen	27 C2
Viva Perú	28 B2
¡école!	(see 20)

DRINKING
El Bosque	29 C2
Mama's & Tapas	30 D1

TRANSPORT
Buses Caburgua	31 D2
Buses Jac	32 D2
Buses San Martín	(see 38)
Cóndor Bus	33 D1
Minibuses Vipu-Ray & Trans Curarrehue	34 C2
Pucón Rent a Car	35 C2
Pullman Bus	36 C2
Radio Taxi Araucaria	37 C2
Tur Bus	38 D1

CHILE

lousy day, just to turn back and not have to give a refund. Check for complaints with the tourism office and other travelers.

The rivers near Pucón and their corresponding rapids classifications are: the Lower Trancura (III), the Upper Trancura (IV), Liucura (II-III), the Puesco Run (V) and Maichín (IV-V). When booking **rafting** or **kayaking**, note that stated trip durations include transportation time. Prices range from CH$15,000 to CH$32,000 depending on the number of participants, the company and level of challenge.

Mountain bikes can be rented (CH$8000) all over town. Check shocks and brakes before renting yours. The most popular route is the Ojos de Caburgua Loop. Take the turn-off to the airfield about 4km east of town and cross Río Trancura. Bike shops should be able to provide a map.

Courses

Get fluent at **Pucón Language & Cultural Center** (☎ 444-967; Uruguay 306; week-long 10hr course CH$80,000), where you can also hook up with a homestay and free book exchange.

Tours

Disreputable outfitters in Pucón have caused accidents resulting in injury and death. Visitors may read up on traveler experiences in the tourism office complaint book. If it's new, ask to see the previous edition. Reputable outfitters include the following ones.

Aguaventura (☎ 444-246; www.aguaventura.com; Palguín 336) French-owned agency on the cutting edge of rafting, kayaking, rappelling, canyoning and snow sports.

Antilco (☎ 099-713-9758; www.antilco.com) Fifteen kilometers east of Pucón on Río Liucura; recommended horse treks in Liucura Valley.

Enjoy Tour (☎ 442-313; www.enjoytour.cl; Ansorena 123) A professional outfit with sharp new gear, and attentive staff offering myriad excursions and airport transfers.

Kayak Pucón (☎ 09-716-2347; www.kayakpucon.net; Av O'Higgins 211; ⏰ 9am-9pm Nov-Mar) Well-regarded kayak school with short and longer expeditions.

Patragon (☎ 444-606; www.patragon.net) Explore Mapuche culture with cooking classes, pottery workshops and a fascinating cultural immersion tour in Curarrehue.

Sol y Nieve (☎ 463-860; www.solynievepucon.cl; Lincoyán 361B; ⏰ 9am-midnight Jan-Feb, 11am-7pm Mar-Dec) Well regarded for anything to do with the volcano as well as rafting.

Sleeping

Camping Parque La Poza (☎ 441-435; Costanera Roberto Geis 769; campsite per person CH$3000) Fully equipped, shady campground near a busy road.

ourpick Hostal El Refugio (☎ 441-596; www.hostalelrefugio.cl; Palguín 540; dm CH$6000-8000, d CH$18,000; ⬚) Run by a young Dutch-Chilean couple, this minihostel provides great, personalized experiences. Wood-paneled rooms have lockers, beds are extrawide and hammocks dot the yard. Foreign languages spoken.

¡école! (☎ 441-615; www.ecole.cl; Urrutia 592; dm with/without bedding CH$8000/7000, d incl breakfast CH$30,000, s/d without bathroom CH$10,000/20,000; ⬚) Catering to everyone, with ultra-cozy B&B-style doubles but dorms that have received both good and bad traveler reviews. It's a good idea to check them out first. The MO here is conservation and this North American–Chilean organization supports worthwhile environmental projects in the south of Chile. Don't miss the excellent vegetarian restaurant.

Hospedaje Lucía (☎ 441-721; Lincoyán 565; r per person with shared bathroom CH$8000) Pint-sized, this family house has a trellised breakfast area and gregarious hosts who also run fishing trips.

Hospedaje Victor (☎ 443-525; www.pucon.com/victor; Palguín 705; dm with/without TV CH$9000/8000, r CH$20,000; ⬚) A budget standout, with cozy wood rooms with bright linens and new fixtures. Well insulated and very welcoming.

The Tree House (☎ 444-679; www.treehousechile.cl; Urrutia 660; dm CH$8000-10,000, d CH$24,000) Commercial and slightly masculine (or is it the curse of all tree houses?), this nevertheless spotless hostel is welcoming and well conceived, with nice shared spaces and garden hammocks. Hosts have good trip information, and breakfast costs $2500.

Donde German Hostel (☎ 442-444; www.dondegerman.cl; Brasil 645; dm CH$8500, d with/without bathroom CH$26,000/18,000; ⬚ ▨) The new and improved three-story Donde German has luxuriant dimensions, but was under renovation when we visited. Its previous incarnation got good marks from travelers.

La Tetera (☎ 441-462; www.tetera.cl; Urrutia 580; d incl breakfast with/without bathroom CH$37,000/29,000; ⬚) Ideal for couples, the 'teapot' is a German B&B with cozy rooms, toasty off season, with woven throws and a backyard garden. The breakfast is one of the best in town.

Hotel Antumalal (☎ 441-011; www.antumalal.com; Km 2; r from CH$134,500; ⬚ ▨) Luxurious and personalized, this Bauhaus hideaway effuses style but is in no way stuffy. Organic forms and textures rule its open spaces, with calf-skin rugs, crackling fires and fishbowl views of sparkling Villarrica. Rooms are spartan but stylish, with enormous beds, fireplace cubbies and picture windows framing the rolling grounds. Service doesn't skip a beat and there is an excellent on-site restaurant and spa.

Eating

Latitude 39° (Gerónimo de Alderete 324-2; mains CH$1800-4200) Specializing in gringo comfort food, this hip eatery offers juicy burgers, fat breakfast burritos, veggie tacos, BLTs, you name it. We were intrigued with the Irish nachos.

La Picada (Paraguay 215; set lunch CH$1800; ☽ lunch only) An underground eatery in someone's living room, with portions of sumptuous *pastel de choclo*, salads and *cazuelas* easily big enough for two.

Cassís (Fresia 223; mains CH$3500-5000) With something (or most things) for everyone, this hip Argentine-run cafe and *chocolatería* creates original multigrain sandwiches and salads, in addition to good coffee, homemade ice cream and fresh lemonade.

Trawen (Av O'Higgins 311; mains CH$2600-6800; ☽ breakfast, lunch & dinner) An upscale deli and rainy-day refuge churning out interesting flavor combinations: ravioli with Roquefort and roasted apples, or Antarctic krill empanadas. Service can be slow.

Pizza Cala (Lincoyán 361; pizza CH$2700-9900; ☽ lunch & dinner) Pies are brick-oven baked with fresh garden basil – this Argentine-American pizza maker does not mess around.

¡école! (Urrutia 592; mains CH$2800-5000; ☽ breakfast, lunch & dinner) The decor is Snow White meets Bob Marley and the food – Bengal curry salmon and spinach salad with sesame – is further evidence of fusion reigning, but it works deliciously. Look for occasional live entertainment.

Arabian Café (Fresia 354; mains CH$3800-5900; ☽ lunch & dinner) Get your falafel and hummus at this legit Arab restaurant.

Viva Perú (☎ 444-025; Lincoyán 372; mains CH$3900-9700; ☽ lunch & dinner Sep-Jun, lunch & dinner Thu-Sat Jul-Aug) Start with the *yuquitos* (manioc fries) and move on to the falling-off-the-bone, cilantro-heavy lamb stew. Even if you don't like spicy, you will probably love the slushy *pisco sours*.

La Maga (☎ 444-277; Fresia 125; steak 350g CH$5900; ☽ lunch & dinner, closed Mon Mar-Dec) Not the cheapest but undoubtedly the best, this

Uruguayan steakhouse serves a mean *bife de chorizo* with house-cut fries and salads.

Drinking

El Bosque (Av O'Higgins 524; 7pm-late) Offers not-so-cheap cocktails and a wine bar in a cool design ambience.

Mama's & Tapas (Av O'Higgins 587; 6pm-late) Features a good lineup on tap and an easy, relaxed atmosphere. Mexican food is discounted 30% before 9pm.

Getting There & Away

Buses go to/from Santiago (CH$10,000 to CH$24,000, 11 hours) with **Tur Bus** (443-934; Av O'Higgins 910), **Buses Jac** (443-326; cnr Uruguay & Palguín) and **Pullman Bus** (443-331; Palguín 555).

Buses JAC goes to Puerto Montt (CH$5900, six hours), Valdivia (CH$3200, three hours), and every 20 minutes to Temuco (CH$2200, 1½ hours). From the same station, **Minibuses Vipu-Ray** and **Trans Curarrehue** (Palguín 550) have continuous services to Villarrica and Curarrehue (CH$800, 45 minutes). Buses JAC and **Buses Caburga** (09-838-9047; Palguín 555) go to Caburgua (CH$1900, 45 minutes) and Parque Nacional Huerquehue (CH$1800, 45 minutes). For San Martín de los Andes, Argentina, **Buses San Martín** (443-595; Av Colo Colo 612) departs (CH$10,000, five hours) twice weekly, stopping in Junín. **Igi Llaima** (444-762; cnr Palguín & Uruguay) also goes there.

Getting Around

For car rental try **Pucón Rent a Car** (443-052; www.puconrentacar.cl; Av Colo Colo 340; per weekday CH$25,000-55,000). Alternatively, taxis such as **Radio Taxi Araucaria** (442-323; cnr Palguín & Uruguay) can prearrange trips.

AROUND PUCÓN
Río Liucura Valley

East of Pucón, the Camino Pucón–Huife cuts through a lush valley hosting a myriad of hot springs. The best value is at the end of the road: **Termas Los Pozones** (Km 36; day/night use CH$3500/4500) with the six natural stone pools open 24 hours. Light some candles and soak under the stars. Arrange a transfer with a *hospedaje* (basic hotel) or agency.

Formed by citizens to nip logging interests in this spectacular swath of native forest, the nature sanctuary **El Cañi** (Km 21; entrance with/without guide CH$6000/3000) protects some 400 hectares of ancient araucaria forest. A three-hour, 9km

hiking trail ascends a steep trail to gorgeous views. Make arrangements to visit El Cañi at ¡ecole! in Pucón (opposite), where there is also transport information.

Ruta 119

Heading toward the Argentine border at Mamuil Malal, this route provides off-piste pleasures. Immerse yourself in Mapuche culture in the quiet and colorful **Curarrehue**. The **tourist office** (197-1587; Plaza; 9:30am-8:30pm) opens in summer only. Before town, the Mapuche family farm **Kila Leufu** (099-711-8064; www.kilaleufu.cl; dm/d CH$7500/20,000) welcomes guests warmly. Must-see museum **Aldea Intercultural Trawupeyüm** (197-1574; Héroes de la Concepcíon 21; adult/child CH$500/200; 10am-8pm Dec-Mar, to 6pm Apr-Nov) explores Mapuche culture. Nearby **Cocinería La Ñaña** cooks unforgettable indigenous delicacies like *mullokin* (bean puree rolled in *quinoa*) and sautéed *piñoñes*.

Traveling 5km northeast, the rustic **Recuerdo de Ancamil** has eight natural pools on Río Maichín. Another 10km, **Termas de Panqui** (day use CH$6000; campsites/cabañas per person CH$8100/12,000) has serene hot springs and a spiritual bent.

PARQUE NACIONAL HUERQUEHUE

Rushing rivers, waterfalls, monkey-puzzle trees and alpine lakes adorn the 12,500-hectare **Parque Nacional Huerquehue** (www.parquehuerquehue.cl; admission CH$4000), only 35km from Pucón. Conaf sells trail maps at the entrance.

The **Los Lagos trail** (four hours, round-trip, 7km) switchbacks through dense *lenga* forests to monkey-puzzle trees surrounding a cluster of pristine lakes. At Laguna Huerquehue, the trail **Los Huerquenes** (two days) continues north then east to cross the park and access **Termas de San Sebastián** (045-381-272; www.termassansebastian.cl; Río Blanco; campsite per person CH$5000, 6-person cabañas CH$40,000), just east of the park boundary.

Conaf's Lago Tinquilco and Renahue campgrounds charge CH$10,000 per site. The excellent **Refugio Tinquilco** (02-777-7673 in Santiago; www.tinquilco.cl; dm with/without bedding CH$6500/5700, d CH$20,000), is a luxurious lodge with amenities like French press coffee and a forest sauna. It's at the base of the Lago Verde trailhead. Meals are available (CH$4500), or you can cook for yourself.

Buses Caburgua (09-838-9047; Palguín 555, Pucón) serves Pucón three times daily (CH$1800, 45 minutes).

CHILE

PARQUE NACIONAL VILLARRICA

Established in 1940, the park (admission CH$3000) protects 60,000 hectares of remarkable volcanic scenery surrounding the 2847m-high Villarrica. It also abuts 3746m-high Lanín (climbed from Argentina).

South of Pucón, **Rucapillán** takes in the most popular hikes (for volcano hike details, see p448) The **Challupen Chinay trail** (23km, 12 hours) rounds varied terrain on the volcano's southern side to the entrance to the **Quetrupillán** sector.

Ski Pucón (☎ 441-901; www.skipucon.cl; Pucón office at Gran Hotel Pucón, Clemente Holzapfel 190, Pucón; full-day lift ticket CH18,000; ⊗ Jul-Oct) is best for beginners but experienced skiers have good out-of-bounds options. Windy or covered conditions shut this active volcano down; check conditions before going. Agencies and hotels provide minivans (around CH$6000) to the base lodge.

LAGO CALAFQUÉN

Black-sand beaches and gardens draw tourists to this island-studded lake, to fashionable **Lican Ray** (30km south of Villarrica) and the more down-to-earth **Coñaripe** (22km east of Lican Ray). Out of season, it's dead. Lican Ray's **tourist office** (☎ 045-431-516; Urritia 310), directly on the plaza, offers maps and accommodations listings. Coñaripe's **Turismo Aventura Chumay** (☎ 045-317-287; www.lagocalafquen .com; Las Tepas 201) rents bikes and organizes treks. Coñaripe has access to rustic hot springs and parts of the park that tourists rarely tread.

Sleeping & Eating

In Coñaripe, cramped lakeside campgrounds charge a negotiable CH$10,000 per site. Try **Millaray** (☎ 099-802-7935) or **Rucahue** (☎ 045-317-210).

Hotel Elizabeth (☎ 045-317-275; Beck de Ramberga 496, Coñaripe; s/d CH$10,900/16,800) The nicest digs in town, with balconies and a well-regarded restaurant.

Hostal Hofmann (☎ 431-109; www.carmenhofmann @gmail.com; Camino Coñaripe 100; d incl breakfast CH$30,000; ⬚) Year-round digs with down comforters, strong hot showers and a filling breakfast, including excellent *küchen*.

Los Ñaños (☎ 045-431-026; Urrutia 105; mains CH$3000-6300) Excellent for empanadas, serving seafood, *cazuela* and pasta on an outdoor patio.

Getting There & Away

In Lincan Ray, **Buses Jac** (☎ 431-616; Marichanquín 240) goes often to Villarrica (CH$700, 45 minutes) and Coñaripe (CH$700, 30 minutes). Frequent buses service Panguipulli (CH$300, two hours).

LAGO PIREHUEICO

Follow the rush and tumble curves of Río Huilo Huilo on this scenic route to San Martín de los Andes, Argentina. With 60,000 acres of private land, **Huilo Huilo** (☎ 02-334-4565; www.huilo huilo.cl; admission CH$3000-25,000) is developing the area for low-impact ecotourism. The grounds include a spire-shaped hotel called **La Montaña Mágica** (d with half-board CH$95,000), equally suited to the well-heeled as to Hobbits.

The ferry **Hua-Hum** (in Panguipulli ☎ 063-197-1585) transports passengers and vehicles between Puerto Fuy and Puerto Pirehueico (1½ hours), from where land transportation departs, crossing the border at Paso Hua Hum and continuing onto San Martín. The ferry leaves year-round once daily. Cars cost CH$15,000, pedestrians pay CH$1000 and bicycles CH$2000. Basic lodging is available at both ends of the lake.

VALDIVIA

☎ 063 / pop 139,500

On a foggy riverbank, Valdivia has the hippest urban living in Chile's south. A university city, it boasts old architecture and modern attitudes, as well as a cool bar and restaurant scene. The city was the seat of German immigration in the mid-19th century (a good hint as to why chocolate and beer abounds). It has known both splendor and disaster. Ransacked by Mapuches after its founding, it fell again with the 1960 earthquake.

Orientation

Valdivia is 160km southwest of Temuco and 45km west of the Panamericana. From the Terminal de Buses, any bus marked 'Plaza' will take you to the center and Plaza de la República. Lodgings are within walking distance.

Information

Downtown ATMs are abundant, as are internet cafes. There is a tourist kiosk at the Terminal de Buses.

Hospital Regional (☎ 297-000; Simpson 850; ⊗ 24hr) South of town, near Aníbal Pinto.

THE LAKES DISTRICT •• Valdivia **453**

Lavandería Lavamatica (☎ 211-015; Schmidt 305; per load CH$4000; ☺ 9:30am-1pm & 3-7:30pm Mon-Fri, 9am-4pm Sat) Discounts for students.
Post office (O'Higgins 575)
Sernatur (☎ 239-060; Costanera Arturo Prat 555; ☺ 8:30am-5:30pm) Sits riverfront.

Sights & Activities

Head to the colorful **Feria Fluvial**, a riverside fish and vegetable market, where sea lions paddle up for handouts. The excellent **Museo Histórico y Arqueológico** (Los Laureles 47; admission CH$1300; ☺ 9am-1pm & 2:30-6pm Dec-Mar, 10am-1pm & 2-6pm Apr-Nov) occupies a nearby riverfront mansion. Displays include Mapuche indigenous artifacts and household items from early German settlements. Nearby is **Museo de Arte Contemporáneo** (☎ 221-968; Los Laureles; admission CH$1200; ☺ 10am-1pm & 3-7pm Tue-Sun), on the foundation of the former Cervecería Anwandter, a brewery felled during the 1960 earthquake. Also on Isla Teja, shady **Parque Saval** has a riverside beach and a pleasant trail to a lily-covered lagoon.

Valdivia is the seat of German culture in Chile and a tour to **Cervecería Kunstmann** (☎ 292-969; www.lacerveceria.cl; mains CH$4950-6900; ☺ noon-midnight) certainly informs: this is real beer, some of South America's best. There's ample sampling and at night you can enjoy hearty German fare (pitchers CH$4700 to CH$4900). Any bus or *colectivo* to Isla Teja can drop you off at Km 5 on the road to Niebla.

Boat cruises (CH$12,000, 6½ hours) leave **Puerto Fluvial** and float the river confluence smattered with 17th-century Spanish forts. Save some bucks by taking *colectivos* (corner of Chacabuco and Yungay; CH$1500) to Niebla. From Niebla, ferries visit Isla Teja, Corral, Isla Mancera and Isla del Rey every half-hour from 8am to 8pm; each leg is CH$1000.

For a more active approach, contact **Pueblito Expeditions** (☎ 245-055; www.pueblitoexpediciones.cl; San Carlos 188) to paddle the calm web of rivers or take a kayak course.

Festivals & Events

Noche de Valdivia, held on the third Saturday in February, is Valdivia's annual kicker, enlivened with decorated riverboats and fireworks.

Sleeping

During the school year the university crowd monopolizes cheap housing, summer has better options. The *hospedajes* near the Terminal de Buses are the cheapest but dingy.

Camping Isla Teja (☎ 225-855; Los Cipreses 1125; campsite CH$5000-8000) Good riverfront facilities in an orchard, 30-minutes' walking distance from across Puente Pedro de Valdivia, or take Bus 9 from the Mercado Municipal.

Hospedaje Karamawen (☎ 347-317; karamawen@gmail.com; Lagos 1334; r per person CH$9000; ☐) Enjoy the personal attention and artistic ambience with tasteful rooms and an engaging translator-owner. Breakfasts are excellent. English, French, German and Swedish are spoken.

Airesbuenos Hostal (☎ 206-304; www.airesbuenos.cl; Lagos 1036; dm CH$7500, s/d without bathroom CH$16,000/20,000; ☐) As agreeable as *hostal* living gets, with gorgeous wrought-iron details, spacious spaces and modern design in a 19th-century historical house. Staff are excellent and bike rentals, kitchen privileges and hot cocoa are yours for the taking. HI-affiliated.

Hostal Torreón (☎ 212-622; Pérez Rosales 783; s/d CH$12,500/25,000; ☐) Old-fashioned and elegant, it's a touch expensive but provides cozy respite on a rainy Valdivian day. Avoid the damper basement rooms.

Hostal BordeRío (☎ 214-069; www.valdiviacabanas.cl; Henríquez 746; s/d CH$22,000/27,000) Cozy with a breakfast nook, large bathrooms, colorful bedspreads and even love seats in most rooms. They also have cabins and can arrange kayaks and trips to their ecological park.

Eating

Café Hausmann (O'Higgins 394; mains CH$1350-6800) A thimble-sized shop serving *cruditos* (carpaccio), strudel and *küchen*. It's a local favorite.

Mercado Municipal (Prat s/n; mains US$4-8; ☺ lunch) Fat plates of fish and chips or *choritos al ajillo* (mussels in garlic and chilies) are served in three floors of restaurants with river views.

La Última Frontera (Pérez Rosales 787; mains CH$2500-4000) Where the university crowd gathers under portraits of Butch Cassidy and Comandante Marcos to chat and feast on superb sandwiches, lunches, fresh juices and huge beers. This funky, restored mansion makes an excellent outing. Open until late.

La Parilla de Thor (☎ 270-767; Av Costanera Arturo Prat 653; steak 400g CH$5850; ☺ lunch & dinner) A waft of cedar and *asado* (roasts) greets diners at this Argentine steakhouse on the Costanera. Reserve ahead.

La Calesa (☎ 225-467; Yungay 735; mains CH$5100-7900; ☺ lunch & dinner) Downright seductive, with sumptuous Peruvian flavors set in a sunlit room or riverfront deck. Reserve ahead.

CHILE

VALDIVIA

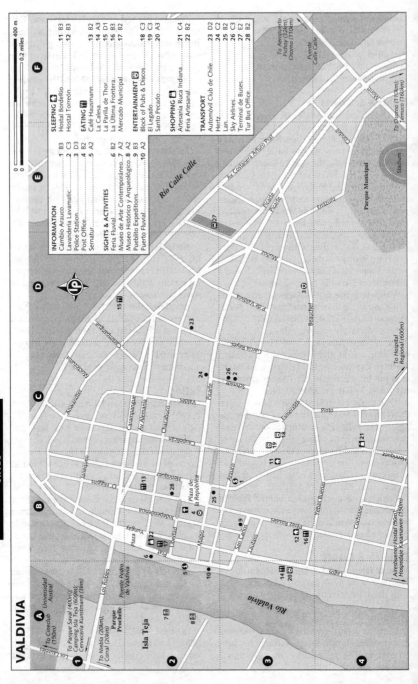

INFORMATION
Cambio Arauco.........................1	B3
Lavandería Lavamatic..............2	C3
Police Station..........................3	D3
Post Office..............................4	B2
Sematur..................................5	A2

SIGHTS & ACTIVITIES
Feria Fluvial............................6	B2
Museo de Arte Contemporáneo..7	A2
Museo Histórico y Arqueológico..8	A2
Pueblito Expeditions...............9	B3
Puerto Fluvial........................10	A2

SLEEPING
Hostal BordeRío.....................11	B3
Hostal Torreón.......................12	B3

EATING
Café Hausmann......................13	B2
La Calesa...............................14	A3
La Parilla de Thor...................15	D1
La Última Frontera.................16	B3
Mercado Municipal................17	B2

ENTERTAINMENT
Block of Pubs & Discos...........18	C3
El Legado..............................19	C3
Santo Pecado........................20	A3

SHOPPING
Artesanía Ruca Indiana...........21	C4
Feria Artesanal......................22	B2

TRANSPORT
Automóvil Club de Chile..........23	D2
Hertz.....................................24	C2
Lan..25	B2
Sky Airlines............................26	C3
Terminal de Buses.................27	E2
Tur Bus Office.......................28	B2

CHILE

Entertainment

Merrymakers should explore the block of pubs, restaurants and discos on Esmeralda (after Caupolicán); there's something for every taste and even for those without.

El Legado (Esmeralda 657) A sultry jazz bar featuring live jazz fusion, acid jazz and soul on weekends.

Santo Pecado (☎ 239-122; Yungay 745; mains CH$3200-5600; ☺ lunch & dinner Mon-Sat) An uber-trendy lounge where drinks are sipped with tasty morsels such as pesto and goat cheese.

Shopping

Feria Artesanal (Mercado Municipal) Offers a selection of wooden handicrafts and woolens. For Mapuche crafts, try **Artesanía Ruca Indiana** (Henríquez 772).

Getting There & Away

AIR

LAN (☎ 600-526-2000; Maipú 271) and **Sky Airlines** (☎ 226-280; www.skyairline.cl; Schmidt 303) fly daily to Santiago (CH$90,000, 2¼ hours).

BUS

Valdivia's **Terminal de Buses** (☎ 212-212; Muñoz 360) has frequent service to destinations between Puerto Montt and Santiago. **Tur Bus** (☎ 226-010) offers various destinations. **Buses Cordillera Sur** (☎ 229-533) accesses interior Lakes District destinations; **Buses JAC** (☎ 212-925) accesses Villarrica (US$3.50, 3½ hours), Pucón and Temuco. **Andesmar** (☎ 224-665) and **Bus Norte** (☎ 212-806) both travel to Bariloche, Argentina. **Igi Llaima** (☎ 213-542) has daily services to San Martín de los Andes.

BUS FARES		
Destination	**Cost (CH$)**	**Duration (hr)**
Bariloche, Argentina	13,000	7
Castro	8500	7
Neuquén, Argentina	20,500	12
Osorno	2200	1¾
Panguipulli	2200	2¼
Pucón	3200	3
Puerto Montt	4200	3½
San Martín de los Andes, Argentina	10,000	8
Santiago	from 14,500	11
Temuco	3200	2½

Getting Around

To and from the airport, **Transfer Aeropuerto Valdivia** (☎ 225-533) provides an on-demand minibus service (CH$3000). For car rental, try **Hertz** (☎ 218-316; Av Ramón Picarte 640).

OSORNO

☎ 064 / pop 149,400

An enormous bronze bull, balls and all, occupying prime real estate on the plaza sums up Osorno perfectly. This agricultural hub, 910km south of Santiago, has its charms, but doesn't coax most visitors into staying long. It serves as an access point to Parque Nacional Puyehue and a convenient bus-transfer point for crossing into Argentina.

The main bus station is in eastern downtown, five blocks from Plaza de Armas.

Information

Ciber Café del Patio (Patio Freire; per hr CH$400; ☺ 9:30am-11:30pm Mon-Sat, 3pm-10pm Sun) Internet access.

Conaf (☎ 234-393; Martínez de Rosas; 9am-5pm Mon-Fri) Information on Parque Nacional Puyehue.

Hospital Base (☎ 235-572; Av Bühler) On the southward extension of Arturo Prat.

Post office (O'Higgins 645)

Sernatur (☎ 237-575; O'Higgins 667; ☺ 8:30am-6:30pm daily Dec-Feb) On the west side of the Plaza de Armas.

Tourist kiosk (Plaza de Armas; ☺ 8:30am-7pm Mon-Fri, 11am-5pm Sat & Sun Jan-Feb) Info on Osorno and surrounding area.

Sights

If you're spending the day, check out the **Museo Histórico Municipal** (Matta 809; ☺ 10am-12:30pm & 2:30-5pm Mon-Fri, plus 11am-1pm & 4-7pm Sat Dec-Feb), an apt look at Mapuche culture and German colonization. The historic district is near the Plaza de Armas.

Sleeping & Eating

Run-down *residenciales* are near the bus terminal. Self caterers can stock up at **Líder** (cnr Colón & Errázuriz), next to the bus terminal, or the lunch stalls at **Mercado Municipal** (cnr Prat & Errázuriz).

Hospedaje Sánchez (☎ 232-560; crisxi@telsur .cl; Los Carrera 1595; r per person CH$5000) While the exterior could use sprucing up, this corner building has a welcoming interior. The delightful owners provide breakfast and kitchen privileges.

CHILE

Hostal Reyenco (☎ 236-285; reyenco@surnet.cl; Freire 309; s without bathroom CH$15,000, d CH$20,000; 🖳) Splurge for worthwhile creature comforts, a nice living room area and breakfast complete with eggs.

Café Central (O'Higgins 610; mains CH$1250-6100; ☯ breakfast, lunch & dinner) A plaza mainstay popular for coffee or Kunstmann draft and colossal burgers. There's a counter for solo travelers.

Club de Artesanos (Mackenna 634; mains CH$2000-5000; ☯ lunch & dinner) Ideal for a pint of local homebrew Märzen, this union house specializes in heaping plates of Chilean classics like *pastel del choclo*.

Getting There & Away

Long-distance and Argentine-bound buses use the main **bus terminal** (Av Errázuriz 1400). Most services going north on the Panamericana start in Puerto Montt, departing hourly, with mainly overnight services to Santiago. Buses service Argentina daily. Coyhaique and Punta Arenas have several departures weekly, via Ruta 215 and Paso Cardenal Antonio Samoré.

Sample travel times and fares include the following:

BUS FARES		
Destination	**Cost (CH$)**	**Duration (hr)**
Bariloche	13,000	5
Coyhaique	30,000	22
Puerto Montt	1500	1½
Punta Arenas	43,000	28
Santiago	from 15,500	12
Temuco	4000	3

Area buses use the **Terminal Mercado Municipal** (☎ 201-237; cnr Errázuriz & Prat), two blocks west of the main terminal, in the Mercado Municipal. **Expreso Lago Puyehue** (☎ 243-919) goes to Termas Puyehue/Aguas Calientes (CH$1700) and Anticura (CH$4500) from behind the northeast corner. To get to coastal towns like Maicolpué, cross the Río Rahue to the bus stops at **Feria Libre Ráhue** (☎ 269-704; cnr Chillán & Temuco).

Getting Around

Automóvil Club de Chile (☎ 255-555; Bulnes 463) rents jeeps and cars.

AROUND OSORNO

Along the coast, **Maicolpué** is a great escape off the gringo grid. It's in the area of San Juan de la Costa, a center of Mapuche Huilliche culture, with traditional communities who embrace homegrown ecotourism (inquire locally). **Campsites** (per tent CH$3500) are at the southern section of town.

Following the southern shore of Lago Puyehue, 66km east is **Termas de Puyehue** (☎ 064-232-157; www.puyehue.cl; s CH$124,200-138,000, d CH$172,800-192,000; 🖳 🐕), a top-drawer hotel with hot springs (day use from CH$30,000). Trekkers use the pools for the day or schedule a massage. From here Ruta 215 goes to the Argentine border, passing Parque Nacional Puyehue.

PARQUE NACIONAL PUYEHUE

Volcán Puyehue (2240m) blew its top the day after the 1960 earthquake, turning its dense humid evergreen forest into a stark landscape of sand dunes and lava rivers. Today, **Parque Nacional Puyehue** (www.parquepuyehue.cl) protects 107,000 hectares of this cool contrasting environment. **Aguas Calientes** (day use CH$3500-7000) is an unpretentious hot-springs resort.

Small ski resort **Antillanca** (www.skiantillanca.com; lift tickets CH$18,000, rentals CH$16,000) is 18km beyond Aguas Calientes on the flanks of 1990m-high Volcán Casablanca. Views are superb. In summer a trail leads to a crater outlook with views of the mountain range. At the base is **Hotel Antillanca** (☎ 064-235-114; s/d refugio CH$40,000/54,500, s/d CH$54,000/75,000), with rustic and more mainstream options. Trimmings include a gym, sauna and disco.

Trails abound at **Anticura**, 17km northwest of the Aguas Calientes turn-off. Pleasant, short walks lead to a lookout and waterfall. Near the park entrance, **Etnoturismo Anticura** (☎ 099-177-4672; www.etnoturismoanticura.blogspot.com; campsite per person CH$3000; dm/2-person cabaña CH$6000/25,000) is a Mapuche-run *albergue*.

Two kilometers west of Anticura, the private **Fundo El Caulle** (www.elcaulle.com; admission CH$10,000) accesses the **Baños de Caulle** trek. Visitors are refunded CH$3000 after packing out their trash. The four-day trek visits thermal fields with fumaroles, geysers and undeveloped hot springs on a barren volcanic plateau. Ask about other hikes at the *fundo* (farm).

From Osorno's Mercado Municipal, **Expreso Lago Puyehue** runs two daily buses to/from Anticura (CH$4500, 1½ hours), which drops trekkers at El Caulle. In winter there may be a ski shuttle to Antillanca; contact the **Club Andino Osorno** (☎ 064-235-114; O'Higgins 1073, Osorno).

FRUTILLAR
☎ 065 / pop 14,500

The mystique of Frutillar is its Germanness, the 19th-century immigrant heritage that the village preserved. To come here is to savor this idea of simpler times, float in the lake, eat home-baked pies and sleep in rooms shaded by lace curtains. For many it is simply too still to linger. However, the town grooves in late January and early February, when the concert series **Semana Musical de Frutillar** (www.semanas musicales.cl) brings international folk, chamber music and jazz to **Teatro del Lago** (Santiago office ☎ 02-339-2293; Av Philippi 1000; www.teatrodellago.cl), a magnificent modern amphitheatre on the lake. Midday concerts are cheapest.

The town has two sectors: Frutillar Alto is a no-frills working town, Bajo fronts the lakes and has all of the tourist attractions. The **tourist kiosk** (Av Philippi; ⏰ 10am-9pm Dec-Mar) is between San Martín and O'Higgins. **Museo Colonial Alemán** (cnr Pérez Rosales & Prat; admission CH$1800; ⏰ 10am-2pm & 3-6pm) features reconstructions of a mill, smithy and mansion set among manicured gardens.

Many visit as a day trip from Puerto Varas. **Los Ciruelillos** (☎ 420-163; 6-person campsite CH$10,000, 6-person cabaña CH$30,000), on a peninsula at the south end of the beach (1.5km from Frutillar Bajo), has fully equipped sites, a small sandy beach and fire pits. **Hostería Winkler** (☎ 421-388; Av Philippi 1155; dm CH$8000) opens an annex to independent backpackers. Some roadside stands sell snacks, but restaurant meals are pricey. Best-value grub is at **Casino de Bomberos** (Av Philippi 1065; mains CH$4000). **Hotel Klein Salzburg** (Av Philippi 663; dessert CH$3000) is a smart choice if you're after *onces*. Worth a taxi outing, restaurant and cooking school **Se Cocina** (☎ 099-757-7152; Camino a Totoral Km 2; mains CH$8500; ⏰ closed Mon)

rescues regional traditions and teaches cooking to low-income locals. The bistro atmosphere is modern cozy, serving local game and seafood, backyard produce and home brew.

Buses to Puerto Varas (CH$800, 30 minutes), Puerto Montt (CH$1000, one hour) and Osorno (CH$800, 40 minutes) leave from Frutillar Alto. Inexpensive *colectivos* shuttle along Av Carlos Richter between Frutillar Alto and Frutillar Bajo.

PUERTO VARAS
☎ 065 / pop 32,200

Every summer this staid German settlement is besieged by visitors. Take in the pleasures of its small town formality, the prim grannies alongside backpacker hordes, and the arresting lake view of Volcán Osorno when the rains pause. With a swank casino, steady growth and ready access to canyoning, climbing, fishing, hiking and skiing, Puerto Varas aspires to be the Chilean Bariloche, though in reality it still is a sleepy place where Sundays are devoted to God and barbecue.

Orientation & Information

There are numerous ATMs and internet cafes downtown.

Afex Exchange (San Pedro 410) Changes cash and traveler's checks.

Clínica Alemana (☎ 232-336; Hospital 810, Cerro Calvario) Near Del Salvador's southwest exit from town.

Municipal tourist office (☎ 232-437; San Francisco 431; ⏰ 9am-9pm Dec-Feb) Has brochures and free maps.

Parque Pumalín office (☎ 250-079; www.pumalin park.org; Klenner 299; ⏰ 8:30am-6:30pm Mon-Fri, 9am-1pm Sat)

Post office (cnr San Pedro & San José)

Sights & Activities

Visitors can stroll around town to take in the 19th-century German architecture, punctuated by the 1915 **Iglesia del Sagrado Corazón** (cnr San

---

DETOUR

Tucked in the rolling farmland, bucolic **Puerto Octay** is probably the most scenic town on Lago Llanquihue but gets few visitors. It's a great stop for cyclists circumnavigating the lake. You can get bike rentals, seriously good grub and a warm reception at **Zapato Amarillo** (☎ 310-787; www.zapatoamarillo.cl; dm CH$7000, s/d CH$26,000/30,000, without bathroom CH$15,000/20,000; 🖥), a small farm about 2km north of town. The octagonal lodge is run by a Chilean-Swiss family providing excellent dinners (CH$5000) and fondue. Excursions include treks around Lago Rupanco and Volcán Osorno. To get here, there are regular minibuses from Osorno (CH$1000) and other towns on the lake.

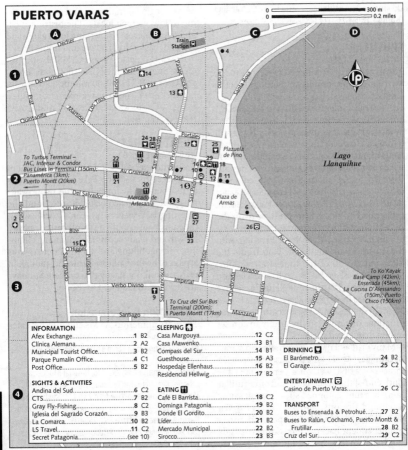

PUERTO VARAS

Francisco & Verbo Divino), based on the Marienkirche of Black Forest, Germany.

Warm summer days make braving the frigid Lago Llanquihue worthwhile. The best beaches are east of the center in Puerto Chico or along the road to Ensenada. If you're adventurous enough for that, consider rafting Río Petrohué's ice-green waters: descents down its class III and IV rapids start at US$30. Canyoning provides yet another opportunity to submerge yourself in icy waters, this time in gorgeous waterfall canyons. Secret spots to cast a line abound. If you're serious about **fly-fishing**, contact a guide.

Those who prefer solid ground can try a number of **hikes**. Volcán Calbuco (2015m) offers a moderate hike; other trails can be accessed via Petrohué. In wintertime you can **ski** the volcano (see p460). **Canopy** is another way to glimpse the forest if your own dogs are too tired to walk.

Tours

Andina del Sud (☎/fax 232-511; www.andinadelsud .com; Del Salvador 72) Offers the Cruce del Lagos (see p460) from Petrohué to Bariloche, Argentina via ferry and bus.

CTS (☎ 237-328; www.ctsturismo.cl; San Francisco 333) Tour agency for Volcán Osorno ski area, offering transportation to the mountain, canopy excursions (traveling on ziplines, tree to tree) and regional tours.

Gray Fly-Fishing (☎ 232-136; San José 192) Half-day trips on the Río Maullin starting at CH$40,000 per person.

Ko'Kayak (off Map p458; www.paddlechile.com) Reputable rafting trips on Río Petrohué (CH$30,000) and sea kayaking in Patagonia. French and English spoken. See also p460.

La Comarca (☎ 09-799-1920; www.pueloadventure .cl; San Pedro 311; ☯ 8:30am-8:30pm) Collective small outfitters with adventure trips to the Río Puelo Valley and Chiloé. Day trips include biking to Volcán Osorno (CH$30,000) and hiking Volcán Calbuco (CH$30,000). They rent bikes as well.

LS Travel (☎ 232-424; www.lstravel.com; San José 130) Friendly, with good information on Argentina, tours and car rental.

Pachamagua (☎ 09-208-3660; www.pachamagua .com) Professional canyoning outfitter with English and French spoken. Best canyoning in town.

Sleeping

Reserve ahead in January and February.

Hospedaje Ellenhaus (☎ 233-577; www.ellenhaus .cl; Martínez 239; dm/s/d CH$5000/7500/13,000) Feather duvets and knotty pine make up for the fact that most rooms are absolute shoe boxes. It's central, with kitchen use, traveler info and bike rentals.

Residencial Hellwig (☎ 232-472; San Pedro 210; s/d CH$6000/15,000) This 1915 German house is the oldest *residencial* in town and the best of the bottom end. Run by a stern matron, with large rooms and bathrooms wanting more attention.

Casa Mawenko (☎ 232-673; casamawenco@gmail .com; Pasaje Ricke 224; dm/s/d CH$7500/10,000/20,000; ☐) On a quiet pedestrian staircase, this modish house has snug, newish beds and comforters and some long-term guests. Cleaning could be more profound but breakfasts are complete.

Casa Margouya (☎ 511-648; www.margouya.com; 318 Santa Rosa; dm CH$8500, s/d without bathroom incl breakfast CH$13,000/17,000; ☐) With tidy, comfy rooms, a hippie vibe and tour planning this French-run guesthouse fosters fun. However, quarters can be cramped.

Compass del Sur (☎ 232-044; www.compassdelsur .cl; Klenner 467; dm/s/d CH$9000/17,000/21,000; ☐) Snug and Scandinavian, this hostal with chalky pastel walls, strong showers and an ample yard promises travelers some serious R & R. German, Swedish and English are spoken.

Guesthouse (☎ 231-521; www.vicki-johnson.com; O'Higgins 608; s/d incl breakfast CH$37,800/43,400) No detail is left to chance at this American-owned inn: rooms are ample and luminous, with lovely furnishings, and breakfast includes real coffee and bran muffins. Unique extras include morning yoga, hydrotherapy and a masseuse.

Eating

Líder (Av Gramado s/n) Big supermarket with a broad selection. Across the street from open-air vegetable and fruit stands.

Café El Barrista (☎ 233-130; Martínez 211; sandwiches CH$2200-3100; ☐) Everyone meets up at this popular coffeehouse serving rich Italian roast, fresh pies and sandwiches. Wi-fi available.

Sirocco (☎ 232-372; San Pedro 537; mains CH$4200-9500; ☯ lunch & dinner) Gambling a twist on Chilean cuisine, like Magellanic lamb, 'magic' mashed potatoes and seared fish. The ambience is intimate, the wine list is strong and there's a dine-out deck.

Donde El Gordito (☎ 233-425; San Bernardo 560; mains CH$4500-6000) A chaotic nook with attentive service and fresh seafood, including a delicious crab sauce. To find it, duck into the Mercado Municipal.

Dominga Patagonia (☎ 238-981; Martínez 551; mains CH$5500; ☯ dinner only, closed Sun) A hip and affordable hangout for cocktails, sushi bites and regional cuisine. Peruvian *ahí de gallina* and *ceviche* are served on lacquered black tables with low lights and fireplaces.

La Cucina d'Alessandro (Av Costanera 1290; mains CH$5000-8000; ☯ lunch & dinner Mon-Sun) This Sicilian-run pizzeria is the real deal. Choose from delectable pastas or thin-crust pizza topped with arugula, tomatoes or cured ham. Top it off with an espresso and tiramisu.

Drinking

El Barómetro (Martínez 584; ☯ 7pm-late) With leather couches and weekend DJs, this oversized bar pleases yuppies and weekend visitors.

Garage (Martínez 220; ☯ 6:30pm-late Mon-Sat) A casual space that gets started around 11pm, sometimes mixing live jazz and fusion until the wee hours, catering to Chileans' penchant for long *carretes* (parties).

Entertainment

Casino de Puerto Varas (Del Salvador 21; ☯ 24hr) A posh ambience with great views and cocktails, where out-of-towners come to spend money and console their losses with shrimp cocktail and live entertainment.

Getting There & Away

Most long-distance buses originate in Puerto Montt. Find ticket offices in town and terminals on the perimeter of town. The **Terminal Turbus** (☎ 234-163; terminal Del Salvador 1093; office San Pedro 210) houses Turbus, JAC, Intersur and Condor bus lines. **Cruz del Sur** (terminal San Francisco 1317; office Martínez 230) has the most departures, including to Chiloé (CH$5000) and Punta Arenas (CH$43,000). For Santiago, Tur Bus, and **Buses Inter** (San Pedro 210) have nightly departures.

For Bariloche, Argentina, Cruz del Sur leaves daily (CH$13,000). For information on the popular bus-boat combination to Bariloche, see boxed text, right.

Minibuses to and from Ensenada (CH$1000), Petrohué (CH$2000), Puerto Montt (CH$800), Puelo (CH$3000), Frutillar (CH$800), Ralún (CH$1300) and Cochamó (CH$1500) all leave from a small stop near the corner of Walker Martínez and San Bernardo. From the Puerto Montt airport, taxis cost approximately CH$15,000.

ENSENADA

Bendy Ruta 225 is a quaint country lane dotted with beaches and topped with the megaphone protrusion of Volcán Osorno. Horse stables **Quinta del Lago** (☎ 099-138-6382; www .quintadellago.com; Km 25; 2hr rides CH$18,725) guides horse treks up the flanks of Volcán Calbulco. Rafting outfitter **Ko'Kayak** (☎ 099-310-5272; www .kokayak.com; Ruta 225) has its base camp at Km 40. To completely get away, stay at the French-run rural **Casa Ko** (☎ 099-699-9850; r per person with/without bathroom CH$14,000/12,000), a sweet old farmhouse with homemade dinners, and walks out the back door. Call ahead to arrange transportation. **Camping Montaña** (☎ 065-235-285; campsite per person CH$3000) is in front of the police station. Next door, **Terra Sur** (☎ 065-233-140; Km 44; bike rental per hr CH$2000) rents quality mountain bikes with shocks, provides vehicle support or simply guides the way.

PARQUE NACIONAL VICENTE PERÉZ ROSALES

A long emerald lake ringed by steep Valdivian rainforest and volcanoes, Chile's second-oldest **national park** protects 251,000 hectares including Lago Todos Los Santos and snowtipped volcanoes Osorno, Puntiagudo (2190m) and Monte Tronador (3554m). Ruta 225 ends in Petrohué, 50km east of Puerto Varas, where there's park access. Minibuses from Puerto Varas are frequent in summer, but limited to twice daily the rest of the year.

Waterfalls boom over basalt rock at **Saltos del Petrohué** (admission CH$1200), 6km before the village. **Petrohué** has beaches, trailheads and

> ### THROUGH THE ANDES
>
> Once braved by Che (as told in *Motorcycle Diaries*), **Cruce de Lagos** (www.crucedelagos.cl) is a popular 12-hour bus and boat crossing (CH$127,000) between Petrohué, Chile and Bariloche, Argentina. Book this package tour ahead with **Andina del Sud** (p458) in Puerto Varas. Check for seasonal discounts and pricing for students and seniors. Another option is to trek a similar route with **Expediciones Petrohué** (below) for similar smashing views, and more bang for your buck, earned with your own sweat and blisters.

the dock for *Cruce de Lagos* (see p458) departures to Peulla (CH$22,000, 1¾ hours). The grand **Hotel Petrohué** (☎ 065-258-042; www.petrohue. com; s/d CH$99,000/130,000; 🏊) has fires crackling in inviting spaces accented with rocks and wooden beams. Lunch is available (CH$5000 to CH$10,000). If luxury isn't in the budget, try the woodsy **Conaf campground** (campsites for 1-5 people CH$7000), smoked out by family cookouts, or pay a boatman (CH$600) to cross you to **Hospedaje Kuschel** (campsite/r per person CH$4000/8000) where you'll be camping with the cow pies, if you don't score one of the few rooms. Bring provisions from Puerto Varas.

From the Conaf campground, a dirt track leads to **Playa Larga**, a long black-sand beach, from where **Sendero Los Alerces** heads west to meet up with **Sendero La Picada**. The sandy track climbs to Volcán Osorno's Paso Desolación, with scintillating panoramas of the lake, Volcán Puntiagudo and Monte Tronador. There is no road around the lake, making the interior trails only accessible by boat. Those willing to hire a boat (CH$70,000 one way – and make sure it's seaworthy) or join a hiking tour can access the **Termas de Callao** hot springs, where there's camping and a rustic family *hospedaje*. **Expediciones Petrohué** (☎ 065-212-025; www.petrohue.com), located next to the hotel, leads excursions into the area.

Access to climb or ski **Volcán Osorno** is near Ensenada. Ski area **Volcán Osorno** (☎ 065-233-445, www.volcanosorno.com; half-/full-day ski pass CH$13,500/18,000, students CH$12,000) has two lifts on 600 hectares and lovely out-of-bounds skiing for experts (watch out for crevasses). The rustic **Refugio Teski Ski Club** (☎ 099-700-0370; dm CH$11,500; 🕙 year-round) is perched mid-mountain, with sick views and little dormitory bunk slots (bring a sleeping bag for extra warmth). You'll warm up quicker with a hot-tub dip (rental CH$16,000) or two-for-one happy-hour drinks at sunset.

To get to the ski area and *refugio*, take the Ensenada–Puerto Octay road to a signpost 3km from Ensenada and continue 9km up the lateral. In Puerto Varas CTS arranges shuttle transportation.

PUERTO MONTT
☎ 065 / pop 168,200

Puerto Montt became one of the fastest growing cities on the continent, thanks to salmon farming. The current industry crisis is poised to have a great effect on this southern hub, which spent the last decade putting up malls and office buildings as fast as Lego constructions. For travelers, the city serves as a springboard to Patagonia with a port worth an afternoon visit.

Orientation

Sitting 1020km south of Santiago, Puerto Montt's downtown stretches along the sea. The waterfront Av Diego Portales turns into Av Angelmó as it heads west to the small fishing and ferry port of Angelmó. To the east it continues to the bathing resort of Pelluco, connecting with the Carretera Austral. At night the area around the bus terminal harbors petty crime; take precautions and don't walk alone here or along the waterfront.

Information

Internet places line Av Angelmó and ring the plaza. ATMs abound.

Afex (Av Diego Portales 516) For money exchange.
Hospital Regional (☎ 261-134; Seminario; ☼ 24hr) Near the intersection with Décima Región.
Latin Star (Av Angelmó 1672; per hr CH$500; ☼ 9am-10pm Mon-Sat, 10am-8pm Sun) Internet, call center and book exchange.
Lavandería San Ignacio (☎ 343-737; Chorillos 1585; per kg CH$1000; ☼ 9:30am-7pm Mon-Sat)
Municipal tourism office (☎ 261-823; Varas 415; ☼ 9am-9pm) Helpful, with plenty of national park info.
Post office (Rancagua 126)
Sernatur (☎ 256-999; ☼ 8:30am-1pm & 2:30-5pm Mon-Fri)

Sights & Activities

The town's oldest building is the 1856 **Iglesia Catedral** (Urmeneta s/n) on the Plaza de Armas. The newly renovated **Casa del Arte Diego Rivera** (☎ 261-817; Quillota 116; ☼ 9am-8pm Mon-Fri, 11am-6pm Sat & Sun) has art and photo exhibits and a theater featuring plays, dance and film.

The waterfront **Museo Juan Pablo II** (Av Diego Portales 991; admission CH$500; ☼ 9am-7pm Mon-Fri, 10am-6pm Sat & Sun) has displays ranging from history and archaeology to religious iconography, German colonization and local urbanism.

Streetside stalls line busy and exhaust-ridden Av Angelmó; their prices go up every time a cruise ship docks at port. Chew the fat with the vendors while taking in the stacks of woolens, woodcarvings and trinkets. At the end of the strip are *palafitos* (buildings terraced over the water), an excellent fish market and more crafts in the picturesque fishing port of Angelmó, 3km west. Offshore Isla Tenglo, reached by inexpensive launches from the docks at Angelmó, is a favorite local beach spot and not a bad place for a picnic.

CHILE

GET LOST: COCHAMÓ & RÍO PUELO VALLEYS

Emerald rivers and deep, pristine valleys are just some of wonders of this stunning remote region, now threatened by several dam proposals. But something this good should be shared and (we hope) preserved. Rugged and rustic, these valleys get few visitors.

Award-winning outfitter **Opentravel** (in Puerto Montt ☎ 65-260-524; www.opentravel.cl) leads treks and trail rides to remote farms and across the border into Argentina. Guests get an insider view of rural life and local guides earn fair wages – this is sustainable tourism at its best. Small-outfitter collective **Secret Patagonia** (in Puerto Varas ☎ 65-234-892; www.secretpatagonia.cl; San Pedro 311; ☼ 8:30am-8:30pm) brings adventurers to both the Cochamó and Puelo Valleys via kayak, mountain bike and hiking trails. In Río Puelo, the **Municipalidad de Cochamó** (☎ 065-350-271; www.cochamo.cl; Plaza) provides some independent guide information (in Spanish) and good area maps. Buses Fierro has five daily departures to/from Puerto Montt (CH$4000, four hours), stopping in Puerto Varas, Ensenada, Cochamó and Río Puelo.

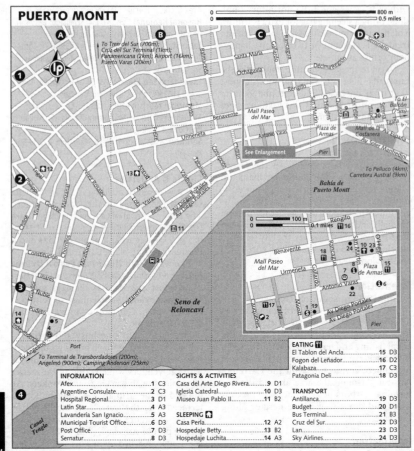

PUERTO MONTT

INFORMATION		SIGHTS & ACTIVITIES	
Afex...1 C3		Casa del Arte Diego Rivera.........9 D1	
Argentine Consulate..................2 C3		Iglesia Catedral..........................10 D3	
Hospital Regional........................3 D1		Museo Juan Pablo II...................11 B2	
Latin Star.....................................4 A3			
Lavandería San Ignacio............5 A3		**SLEEPING**	
Municipal Tourist Office............6 D3		Casa Perla..................................12 A2	
Post Office..................................7 D3		Hospedaje Betty.........................13 B2	
Sernatur......................................8 D3		Hospedaje Luchita.....................14 A3	

EATING	
El Tablon del Ancla....................15 D3
Fogon del Leñador.....................16 D2
Kalabaza.....................................17 C3
Patagonia Deli............................18 D3

TRANSPORT	
Antillanca..................................19 D3
Budget..20 D1
Bus Terminal..............................21 B3
Cruz del Sur...............................22 D3
Lan...23 D3
Sky Airlines................................24 D3

Sleeping

Travelers find wider choices in tourist-ready Puerto Varas up the road, but there are a few good options here, particularly if you want old-fashioned family lodgings.

Camping Anderson (☎ 099-517-7222; www.chipsites .com/camping/; Panitao Km 20; campsite per person CH$3000) An ecologically minded campground right on the bay where campers may work for their lodgings. Buses Bohle makes the 20km trip from Puerto Montt's bus terminal to Panitao (CH$750, nine daily).

Casa Perla (☎ 262-104; www.casaperla.com; Trigal 312; campsite per person CH$5000; dm & r per person CH$7000; 🖳) A tidy and relaxed family residence that can link you with Spanish classes and kayak trips. English and German spoken.

Hospedaje Luchita (☎ 253-762; Independencia 236; r per person CH$8000) The generous doña Luchita will likely serve you a slice of *küchen* before you've sat down in this sweet family home with waxed floors and neat, little rooms.

Hospedaje Betty (☎ 253-165; Ancud 117; r per person CH$8000) Rose-colored shingles, a sprawling old-fashioned kitchen and pastel rooms with sheer curtains cozy it up; the hostess is wonderful too.

our pick Tren del Sur (☎ 343-939; www.trendelsur.cl; Santa Teresa 643; s/d from CH$21,800/29,900; 🖳) Puerto Montt's only boutique hotel is wildly colorful and cozy, fashioned with railroad ties and featuring central heating and a skylit hallway. The hosts are warm and friendly. It's tucked in the old neighborhood of Modelo.

CHILE

Eating & Drinking

The *palafitos* (wood-shingled houses on stilts) at the far end of Angelmó have loads of ambience and good meals for about US$6 to US$8; waitresses loiter outside to coax you in. In the opposite direction, Pelluco (coastal buses CH$250) has clubs, fancy steakhouses and seafood restaurants by the beach. This is where *puerto monttinos* head for Sunday dinner or a late-night party.

Kalabaza (Varas 629; mains CH$1900-2700) A hanky-sized cafe with sandwiches, Kuntsmann beer and fixed-price lunches.

El Tablon del Ancla (cnr Varas & O'Higgins; mains CH$1900-5900) Friends pack the comfy booths on the plaza for cheap set lunches or *pichangas* (french fries with sloppy toppings).

El Balcón (☎ 714-059; Egaña 156; mains CH$2900-4200; ☺ lunch & dinner) An urban refuge streaming chill music and contemporary spins on classic dishes like *humitas del mar* (corn cooked in tusks with king crab and shrimp).

Patagonia Deli (☎ 482-898; Varas 486; mains CH$3900-6900; ☺ lunch & dinner Mon-Sat) This spot packs 'em in at lunch, when its set menu features an appetizer, main, a drink and an espresso for CH$3600. There are also sandwiches, pasta and a few veggie choices.

Fogon del Leñador (cnr Rancagua & Rengifo; mains CH$6000-9500; ☺ closed Sun) Perfect for a splurge here. Steaks singed to perfection are served with four kinds of homemade sauces and piping-hot *sopapillas* (frybread). For many, the half-portion will do.

Getting There & Away

AIR

LAN (☎ 253-315; www.lan.com; O'Higgins 167, Local 1-B) flies twice daily to Punta Arenas (from CH$105,350, 2¼ hours), Balmaceda/Coyhaique (from CH$62,100, one hour) and four times daily to Santiago (from CH$108,100, 1½ hours).

Sky Airlines (☎ 248-027; www.skyairlines.cl; cnr San Martín & Benavente) flies to Punta Arenas and Santiago with slightly cheaper fares.

BOAT

Puerto Montt is the main departure port for Patagonia. The **Terminal de Transbordadores** (off Map p462; Av Angelmó 2187) has a ticket office and waiting lounge for **Navimag** (☎ 432-360; www.navimag.com) and **Naviera Austral** (☎ 270-430; www.navieraustral.cl). Check your departure: rough seas and bad weather can cause delays.

Services to Chaitén may be suspended because of volcanic activity, call ahead. Naveira Austral leaves several times a week to Chaitén (passengers/vehicles CH$19,000/76,500). The trip takes 10 hours and usually runs overnight and is less than comfortable.

To Puerto Chacabuco you can hop on Navimag's M/N *Puerto Edén* (18 hours). Prices range from CH$143,000 for the AA single to CH$38,000 for the C berth. The company also heads to Laguna San Rafael on most Saturdays from September to April, with a stop in Chacabuco. Round-trip prices from Puerto Montt range from CH$865,000 for an AA single to CH$250,000 for C berth.

To Puerto Natales, Navimag's M/N *Evangelistas* sails the popular three-night journey through Chile's fjords; check with Navimag's Santiago offices (p1006) or on the website for departure dates and confirm your booking with the Santiago office. High season is November to May, midseason is October to April, and low season is May to September. Prices for the trip include meals. Single fares, which vary according to view and private or shared bathroom, are as follows:

BOAT FARES		
Class	**Apr-Oct (CH$)**	**Nov-Mar (CH$)**
AAA	875,000	1,325,000
AA	785,000	1,270,000
A	645,000	1,0125,000
Berths	210,000	225,000

Cars pay CH$250,000. Bikes and motorcycles can be carried along at extra cost. Those prone to motion sickness should take medication prior to crossing the Golfo de Penas, which is exposed to gut-wrenching Pacific swells.

BUS

Puerto Montt's waterfront **bus terminal** (☎ 283-000; cnr Av Diego Portales & Lota) is the main transportation hub, with a *custodia* to store belongings. Summer trips to Punta Arenas and Bariloche sell out, so book in advance.

Minibuses to Puerto Varas (CH$800, 30 minutes), Frutillar (CH$1000, one hour) and Puerto Octay (CH$1400, 1½ hours) leave from the eastern side of the terminal. Buses leave five times daily for Cochamó (CH$2000, four hours).

CHILE

BUS FARES

Destination	Cost (CH$)	Duration (hr)
Ancud	3500	2½
Bariloche, Argentina	13,000	8
Castro	5300	4
Concepción	7500-15,000	8
Coyhaique	30,000	20
Osorno	1500	1½
Pucón	5900	6
Punta Arenas	45,000	30-36
Quellón	6200	6
Santiago	12,900-27,000	12-14
Temuco	8000	6
Valdivia	4200	3½
Valparaíso/ Viña del Mar	25,800	14

For Hornopirén, where summer-only ferries connect to Caleta Gonzalo, Buses Fierro has three daily departures (CH$3500, three hours). From mid-March to mid-November, bus transportation to Hornopirén and the upper Carretera Austral is very limited.

Cruz del Sur (☎ 436-410; Pilpilco 0150) has frequent buses to Chiloé. Santiago-bound buses leave at night, stopping in various cities. 'Direct' buses stop only in Puerto Varas and Osorno; try to get one of these. **Tur Bus** (☎ 253-329) has daily buses to Valparaíso/Viña del Mar. For Coyhaique and Punta Arenas via Argentina, try Cruz del Sur or Turibús. For Bariloche, Argentina, **Andesmar** (☎ 312-123) or Cruz del Sur travel daily via Samoré pass east of Osorno.

Getting Around
ETM buses (CH$1500) run between Aeropuerto El Tepual, 16km west of town, and the bus terminal. A taxi from the airport costs about CH$9000.

Car-rental agencies **Budget** (☎ 286-277; Varas 162) and **Antillanca** (☎ 258-060; Av Diego Portales 514) facilitate a certificate (CH$58,000) to allow rental vehicles into Argentina with two days' notice. Rates start at CH$35,000 per day for unlimited mileage in an economy car.

PARQUE NACIONAL ALERCE ANDINO
Few venture to the rugged emerald forest of 40,000-hectare **Parque Nacional Alerce Andino** (admission CH$1000), despite its 40km proximity to Puerto Montt. The park protects the area's last remaining stands of *alerce*. An extremely slow-growing native conifer, the endangered *alerce* was logged to near extinction. Luxuriant montane rainforest grows – at an almost visible speed – at all but the highest elevations. Pumas, *pudús*, foxes and skunks are about, but you'll have better luck glimpsing condors, kingfishers and waterfowl.

At Correntoso, **Camping Correntoso** (per campsite CH$3000) has grassy sites. Adjacent to Guardería Sargazo, **Refugio Sargazo** (bunks CH$5000) is basic cabin accommodations with bathroom (cold water only) and kitchen.

For those without private transport, the trek begins and ends with a road walk of about 13km between the village of Correntoso, 37km east by road from Puerto Montt, and Guardería Sargazo. From the Puerto Montt bus terminal, Buses JB run up to five buses daily (fewer on Sunday) to Lago Chapo, which pass through Correntoso (CH$1000, one hour). For guided walks, consult La Comarca in Puerto Varas (p458).

CHILOÉ

In Chiloé rural ingenuity invented the *trineo,* a sled to steer through thick mud; rural necessity perfected *curanto,* meat, potatoes and shellfish vapor-smoked in giant leaves; and rural imagination created the *invunche,* a mythological gatekeeper whose price of admittance is a peck on the rear. Who are these people? With indigenous Chonos and Huilliche roots, the humble Chilote welcomed Jesuits and the Spanish, but were never an ally of mainlanders. Island insularity fostered incredibly rich traditions and myths populated by ghost ships, phantom lovers and witches, cute versions of which are whittled and sold for today's tourists. Forget the rustic souvenirs. The patient visitor needs a succession of misty rains, muddy walks and fireside chats to fathom these characters who are proud but never showy, friendly but none too talkative.

In an archipelago of more than 40 minor islands, the main island is a lush quilt of pastureland on undulating hills, 180km long but just 50km wide. Towns and farms tilt toward the eastern side, and the western shores are a nearly roadless network of thick forests lapping the wild Pacific. More than half of the 155,000 Chilotes live off subsistence agriculture, while others depend on a fishing industry that has rapidly transformed from artesanal to industrial, with the

CHILE

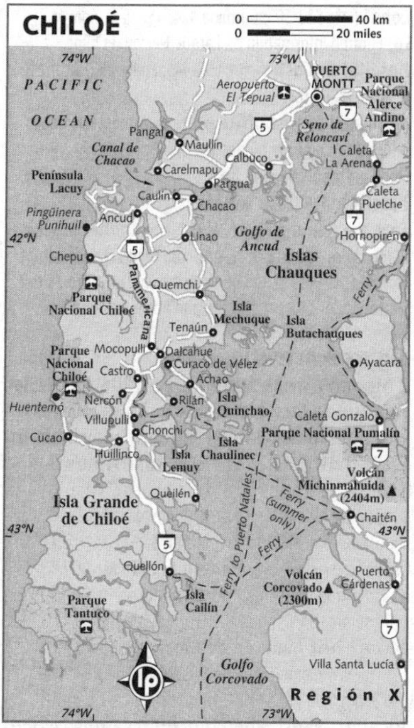

introduction of salmon farming in the mid-1990s. Visitors shouldn't miss the shingled houses and wooden churches dotting the island, some up to 200 years old, preserved as a Unesco World Heritage Site.

ANCUD

☎ 065 / pop 49,500

Bustling and weathered, urban Ancud offers an earthy base to explore the penguin colonies and walk or sea-kayak the blustery, dazzling north coast.

Information

Banco de Chile (Libertad 621) ATM.
Clean Center (Pudeto 45; per kg CH$900; 10am-4pm Mon-Sat) Laundry service.
Hospital de Ancud (☎ 622-356; Latorre 405) At the corner of Pedro Montt.
Post office (cnr Pudeto & Blanco Encalada)
La Red de Agroturismo (www.viajesrurales.cl) Organizes excursions to farming and fishing communities and rural homestays. Make arrangements via the website, or with Luisa Maldonado (☎ 643-7046).
Sernatur (☎ 622-800; Libertad 665; 8:30am-8pm Mon-Fri, 9am-8pm Sat & Sun Dec-Feb, 8:30am-5pm Mon-Fri Mar-Nov) On the Plaza de Armas, the only formal national tourist office on the island with helpful staff, brochures, town maps and accommodations lists for the archipelago.
Zona Net (Pudeto 276; per hr CH$600; 9am-midnight Mon-Sat, 2-11pm-Sun) Internet access.

Sights & Activities

The **Museo Regional Aurelio Bórquez Canobra** (☎ 622-413; Libertad 370; admission CH$600; 9:30am-7:30pm Mon-Fri, 10am-7:30pm Sat & Sun Jan-Feb) tracks island history with excellent, informative displays. Northwest of town, **Fuerte San Antonio** was Spain's last Chilean outpost. The remodeled **Mercado Municipal** (Prat) offers a colorful stroll through live crabs, fat lettuce heads and woolens.

Small, family-run **Puñihuil** (☎ 099-655-6780; www.pinguineraschiloe.cl) offers tours (CH$20,000 per person) to the penguin and sea lion colonies. On the way to the penguin colonies you'll pass **Puente Quilo** (donations only), a fabulously quirky open-air museum created by one man, Don Serafin, a regular Joe whose backyard flooded with odd treasures after the 1960 earthquake. The booty spans from whole whale skeletons to stuffed sea creatures and indigenous relics.

Festivals & Events

Ancud makes merry in the second week of January with **Semana Ancuditana** (Ancud Week). There are island-wide celebrations with music, dance and foods.

Sleeping

Camping Arena Gruesa (☎ 623-428; arenagruesa@yahoo.com; Av Costanera Norte 290; campsite per person CH$3000, s/d CH$20,000/22,000) A blufftop site with adequate rooms or grassy, fully-equipped sites with sea views, six blocks north of the plaza.

Hostal Mundo Nuevo (☎ 628-383; www.newworld.cl; dm CH$8000, s/d CH$20,000/30,000, without bathroom CH$16,000/20,000; 💻) Hunker down in this Swiss-owned seafront refuge with firm beds and sharp hardwood details. Owner Martin recommends hikes and breakfast includes homemade multigrain loaves.

Cabañas y Hospedaje Vista al Mar (☎ 622-617; www.vistaalmar.cl; Costanera 918; dm CH$8500, s/d CH$18,000/24,000, 8-person cabañas CH$55,000; 💻) With sea views, ample shared bathrooms and a spiffy dorm, minutes from the Plaza de Armas.

Hostal Lluhay (☎ 622-656; www.hostal-lluhay.cl; Cochrane 458; s/d CH$10,100/20,200; 💻) A comfortable seafront house with dear hosts, roaring fires and a tinkling piano. Don't miss breakfast.

Eating & Drinking

La Botica de Café (Pudeto 277; desserts CH$750-1500; ☺ breakfast, lunch & dinner) Rewards with real brewed coffee and a ridiculously tempting selection of international desserts.

La Hormiguita (☎ 626-999; Pudeto 44; sandwiches CH$1000-5000; ☺ lunch & dinner) Massive, sloppy sandwiches, pies, fruit juices and a few veggie choices make this cute bakery a quick hunger fix.

Retro's Pub (Maipú 615; mains CH$2500-10,000) A cozy timber tribute to rock and roll with tasty Tex-Mex and satisfying burgers. It's hopping on summer nights.

El Sacho (Mercado Municipal; mains CH$3000-5000; ☺ lunch) Fresh no-frills seafood on the market's concrete deck; the enormous plates include steamed mussels and fried fish.

Lumiére (Ramirez 278; dinner CH$5500) Awash in ocean blue and bright charm, this pub-restaurant serves *ceviche, mariscos a pil pil* (seafood with chilies and garlic) and drinks. Movies are shown in winter.

Getting There & Away

Ancud's colorful new **Terminal de Buses** (☎ 622-249; cnr Los Carreras & Cavada) is owned and operated by **Cruz del Sur** (☎ 622-249), with frequent departures to Puerto Montt (CH$3500, 2½ hours), Castro (CH$1700, 1¼ hours) and Quellón (CH$4000, 2½ hours). Taxis downtown cost CH$2000.

CASTRO

☎ 065 / pop 34,500

Castro is the attractive, idiosyncratic capital of Chiloé. With the last decade's salmon boom, this working-class town transformed its ever-casual island offerings with modern mega-supermarkets and boutique hotels. But with the current strain on the salmon industry, it's probable that Castro will backpedal to its rich everyman's roots. Don't miss its iconic wooden church and the crayon-happy *palafitos* which testify to Castro's heritage with humble beginnings in 1567.

Information

ATMs and cyber cafes are found around the plaza.

Chiloe Web (www.chiloeweb.com) Useful island website.

Clean Center (☎ 633-132; Balmaceda 220; per kg CH$1100; ☺ 9:30am-1pm & 3-7pm Mon-Sat) Laundry service.

Conaf (☎ 532-503; Gamboa 424; ☺ 9am-6pm Mon-Fri) Limited information on Parque Nacional Chiloé.

Hospital de Castro (☎ 632-445; Freire 852) At the foot of Cerro Millantuy.

Municipal tourist office (Plaza de Armas) Has good information on rural homestays.

Post office (O'Higgins 388)

Tourist kiosk (Plaza de Armas; ☺ 10am-8pm)

Turismo Pehuen (☎ 635-254; www.turismopehuen.cl; Blanco Encalada 208; ☺ 9am-6pm Mon-Fri, 10am-1pm Sat) Recommended and open year-round, with tours to nearby islands, bird-watching and horse trekking.

Sights & Activities

You can't miss neo-Gothic 1906 **Iglesia San Francisco de Castro** (Plaza de Armas) and its yellow-lavender paint job, testament to island individuality. Clever farm instruments and Huilliche relics are among the displays at **Museo Regional de Castro** (Esmeralda s/n; ☺ 9:30am-7pm Mon-Sat, 10:30am-1pm Sun Jan-Feb) Near the fairgrounds, the **Modern Art Museum** (☎ 635-454; Parque Municipal; donations accepted; ☺ 10am-8pm summer) displays innovative local works. Nonprofit **Almacén de Biodiversidad** (cnr Lillo & Blanco; www.almacendebiodiversidad.com; ☺ 9am-1pm, 3-6:30pm Mon-Fri) sells gorgeous goods made by local artisans. The colorful **palafitos** (wood-shingled houses on stilts hovering over the waters) are mostly along Costanera Pedro Montt north of town at the western exit from the city.

Festivals & Events

Festival de Huaso Chilote Cowboy festival held in late January.

Festival Costumbrista Folk music and dance and traditional foods in mid-February.

Sleeping

Seasonal lodging is advertised with hand-written signs along San Martín, O'Higgins and Barros Arana. Those interested in **rural homestays** (☎ in Santiago 02-690-8000; www.viajes rurales.cl) can also inquire at the municipal tourism office.

Camping Llicaldad (☎ 635-080; Fiordo de Castro; 4-person campsites CH$10,000) Off the Panamericana, 6km south of Castro; sites are muddy in rainy season.

our pick Palafito Hostel (☎ 531-008; Riquelme 1210; dm CH$8000-12,000, d CH$25,000; ☐) Brand new, this cool lodging perches over the Fiordo de Castro on stilts. Views are top-notch. Service is welcoming and guests stay snug under down comforters in wood-paneled rooms. It's a five-minute walk from the center.

Hostal Cordillera (☎ 532-247; hcordillera@hotmail .com; cnr Serrano & Sotomayor; r per person without bathroom CH$8000, d CH$22,000; 🖳) You'll feel part of the family at this traveler's hub, a good-value lodging with large bathrooms, comfortable beds, cable TV and wi-fi. Take in water views on the deck out back.

Hospedaje Central (☎ 637-026; Los Carrera 316; s/d CH$13,400/21,800, without bathroom CH$8400/15,500; 🖳) The nicest of the budget options, this large *hostal* has wood-varnished rooms with frilly bedcovers, cable TV and wi-fi.

Hospedaje Mirador (☎ 633-795; Barros Arana 127; s/d without bathroom CH$9000/18,000, r CH$25,000; 🖳) This red house on a steep seafront passageway has lockable rooms (small but amenable) with big beds and gasp-inducing views. Breakfasts are generous and there's wi-fi.

Eating & Drinking

Waterfront restaurants located next to the *feria artesanal* have the best bang for your peso.

Brújula del Cuerpo (O'Higgins 308; mains CH$1300-5990; ☺ breakfast, lunch & dinner) A godsend if you're sick of seafood, this noisy diner does burgers, pizza, fajitas and American-style breakfast.

Ristretto Café (Av Blanco Encalada 364; mains CH$2000-3500; ☺ 11am-late) New in town, this slick little number boasts exquisite Italian espressos, a variety of teas, fresh olive foccacia, pizzas, salads and sweets.

Don Octavio (Costanera Av Pedro Montt 261; mains CH$2500-9500) A *palafito* restaurant serving creative Chilote food that piles potatoes and sausage on fresh fish. Or you can go conservative with king crab.

Sacho (☎ 632-079; Thompson 213; mains CH$3300-5500; ☺ lunch & dinner) A top-drawer seafood restaurant with excellent crab and *pulmay*, a *curanto*-like shellfish dish featuring clams and mussels, but a little less meat and potatoes.

Kaweshkar Lounge (www.kaweshkarlounge.cl; Blanco Encalada 31; mains CH$2000-3400; ☺ 12pm-late Mon-Sat) This place is indie-cool, with an industrial vogue vibe and lounge atmosphere. The menu is vegetarian-friendly, with edgy mains such as salmon crepes.

Getting There & Away
BOAT

Occasional summer ferries to/from Chaitén (p472) were grounded at the time of writing, but these schedules tend to change frequently. It's best to check with **Naviera Austral** (☎ 65-270-430; www.navieraustral.cl; Angelmó 2187, Puerto Montt) and **Navimag** (☎ 65-432-360; www.navimag .com; Angelmó 2187, Puerto Montt).

BUS & COLECTIVO

The municipal **Terminal de Buses Municipal** (San Martín), near Sargento Aldea, has buses to Dalcalhue (CH$300, 30 minutes) and Cucao (CH$1600, one hour), with limited services off-season. The **Cruz del Sur terminal** (☎ 632-389; San Martín 486) services Quellón and Ancud as well as long-distance destinations.

For nearby destinations, *colectivos* provide a faster alternative. **Colectivos Chonchi** leave from Chacabuco near Esmeralda (CH$800), as well as from Ramírez near San Martín.

BUS FARES		
Destination	**Cost (CH$)**	**Duration (hr)**
Ancud	1700	1¼
Puerto Montt	5300	4
Quellón	1800	1½
Santiago	30,000	16
Temuco	10,000	7
Valdivia	8500	7

DALCAHUE & ISLA QUINCHAO

Dalcahue, 20km northeast of Castro, has a Doric-columned 19th-century church, well-preserved vernacular architecture, and a famous **feria artesanal** (crafts fair; ☺ 7am-5pm) selling wool imaginatively woven into fleece-lined slippers, dolls, even skirts. Artisan women weave baskets and knit at their stands, hoping the live performance will sweeten a sale. Outside of town, **Altue Sea Kayak Center** (☎ in Santiago 02-232-1103; www .seakayakchile.com) leads wonderful five- to nine-day kayak tours of the archipelago. All trips must be booked in advance.

Midway between Dalcahue and Achao, **Curaco de Vélez** dates from 1660 and has a treasure of Chilote architecture, plus an outstanding open-air oyster bar at the beach. Buses between Achao and Dalcahue stop in Curaco.

CHILE

Isla Quinchao, southeast of Dalcahue, is one of the most accessible islands, and worth a day trip. Isla Quinchao's largest town, **Achao**, features Chiloé's oldest church. Wooden pegs, instead of nails, hold together **Iglesia Santa María de Achao**.

Camping Garcia (☎ 065-661-283; Delicias; camping per person CH$2500; ☾ Dec-Mar) offers sites with a hot shower one block from the plaza. There are good lodging options at **Hostal Plaza** (☎ 065-661-283; Amunátegui 20; r per person US$10), across from the plaza, or the comfortable **Sol y Lluvia** (☎ 065-253-996; Gerónimo de Urmeneta 215; s without bathroom CH$10,000). Overlooking the pier, **Mar y Velas** (Serrano 02; CH$2900-5800) serves up mussels or clams and cold beer.

Minibuses and *colectivos* go directly to/from Castro. From Dalcahue, **Dalcahue Expreso** (Freire) has buses every half-hour to Castro (CH$300) weekdays, but fewer on weekends. Ferries for Isla Quinchao leave continuously. Pedestrians go free (but you'll need to take a bus to reach any destinations once you get on the island), and cars cost CH$5000 (round-trip).

CHONCHI
☎ 065 / pop 12,000

A somnambulant village on a tranquil bay, Chonchi defies its rebel past as the former haunt of pirates and port for cypress export. Located 23km south of Castro, it is the closest sizable town to the national park. Services center on Centenario, including a **tourist office** (cnr Candelaria & Centenario; ☾ 9am-7pm Dec-Feb). Visitors can explore **Isla Lemuy** via a free ferry departing every half-hour from Puerto Huichas (5km south). On Sunday and off-season, the service is hourly.

Camping los Manzanos (☎ 671-263; Aguirre Cerda 709; campsites for 1-4 people CH$5000) has hot showers. Beachfront haven **La Esmeralda** (☎ 671-328; www.esmeraldabythesea.cl; Irarrázaval 267; dm CH$7000, d with/without bathroom CH$30,000/20,000; 🖳) offers simple, agreeable rooms with use of the house rowboat. Owner Charles Gredy rents bikes and fishing gear and sometimes hosts seafood dinners. Seafood delights are served in a renovated *mercado:* the 2nd-floor restaurants above the crafts market have a slim deck overlooking the water.

Catch Castro-bound buses opposite the plaza on the upper level or take a *colectivo* (CH$800) opposite the church. Transportation to Parque Nacional Chiloé

(CH$1400, 1½ hours) departs a few times per day in summer.

PARQUE NACIONAL CHILOÉ

Gorgeous, evergreen forests meet taupe stretches of sand and the boundless, thrashing Pacific in this 43,000-hectare **national park** (admission CH$1000), 54km southwest of Castro. The park protects diverse birds, Chilote fox and the reclusive *pudú*. Some Huilliche communities live within the park boundaries and some manage campsites.

Access the park through Cucao, a minute village with growing amenities, and park sector Chanquín, where Conaf runs a visitors center with information. **Sendero Interpretivo El Tepual** winds 1km along fallen tree trunks through thick forest. The 2km **Sendero Dunas de Cucao** leads to a series of dunes behind a long, white-sand beach. The most popular route is the 25km **Sendero Chanquín–Cole Cole**, which follows the coast past Lago Huelde to Río Cole Cole. The hike continues 8km north to Río Anay, passing through groves of red myrtles.

Sleeping & Eating

Most accommodations and restaurants are past the bridge from Cucao.

Camping Chanquín (☎ 532-503; campsite per person CH$2000, cabañas for 1-7 people CH$25,000) In the park, 200m beyond the visitors center. Good amenities and a covered rain area. Cabins are spacious and recently renovated.

El Fogon de Cucao (☎ 099-946-5685; campsite per person CH$3000, s/d without bathroom CH$10,000/20,000) Choose between a gorgeous guesthouse with sprawling deck or waterfront camping with full facilities. The restaurant (meals CH$4500) also hosts impromptu jam sessions for those seeking nightlife. They also run horse treks (CH$40,000, three hours) and rent kayaks (CH$2500 per hour).

Parador Darwin (☎ 099-884-0702; paradordarwin @hotmail.com; r per person CH$10,000; ☾ closed May-Oct) A rainy-day score: inviting rooms with sheepskin rugs, trunk tables and electric teapots. The cafe delights with fresh juices, local razorback clams with parmesan and big salads (mains CH$3000 to CH$4900) to be enjoyed over board games and jazz.

Those making the 20km hike to **Cole Cole** stay at the **campsite** (campsite per person CH$1500), there's also a *refugio* in the works in Huentemó, to be run by the indigenous

Huilliche community. Bring your own stove and prepare for pesky sand fleas.

Getting There & Away

Buses go to/from Castro five times daily (CH$1600, one hour). Service from Chonchi (CH$1400, 1½ hours) departs a few times per day in summer. Upon arrival, stay on the bus until after the Cucao bridge. The final stop is the park.

QUELLÓN

☎ 065 / pop 23,100

Those imagining a pot of gold and rainbows at the end of the Carretera Panamericana will be surprised by a dumpy port. Even locals bemoan the pirating of Quellón's natural wealth, which has left a sad industrial air. Most travelers head this way to make ferry connections to Chaitén or Puerto Montt. It's best to change money before coming. **Banco del Estado** (cnr Ladrilleros & Freire) has an ATM.

Waterfront lodging **Hotel El Chico Leo** (☎ 681-567; Montt 325; r per person without bathroom CH$10,000, d CH$25,000; 💻) offers the best value, with fuzzy bedspreads, shell lamps and acrylic landscapes. Its decent restaurant (mains CH$2000 to CH$6500) is populated by pool sharks. Perched above the center, **Hotel Patagonia Insular** (☎ 681-610; www.hotelpatagonia insular.cl; Ladrilleros 1737; s/d CH$37,800/41,200; 💻) offers cool boutique comforts and massive views. The homespun **El Madero** (☎ 681-330; Freire 430; mains CH$2500-6000; ☽ 10am-midnight Mon-Sat) serves great grilled salmon and mashed potatoes. Take a taxi down to **Taberna Nos** (O'Higgins 150; snacks CH$2000; ☽ 8:30pm-3am Mon-Sat) for ska, cheap pints and seafood tapas, with welcoming Galician-Chilote hosts.

Cruz del Sur and Transchiloé buses leave from the **bus terminal** (cnr Aguirre Cerda & Miramar) for Castro frequently (CH$1800, 1½ hours). **Naviera Austral** (☎ 682-207; www.navieraustral.cl; Montt 457) normally sails to Chaitén (CH$19,000). Due to volcanic activity, service might be suspended so check ahead.

NORTHERN PATAGONIA

A web of rivers, peaks and sprawling glaciers long ago provided a natural boundary between northern Patagonia and the rest of the world. Pinochet's **Carretera Austral** (Hwy 7) was the first road to effectively link these remote regions in the 1980s. Isolation has kept the local character fiercely self-sufficient and tied to nature's clock. *'Quien se apura en la Patagonia pierde el tiempo,'* locals say ('Those who hurry in Patagonia lose time.'). Weather decides all in this nowhere land beyond the Lakes District. So don't rush. Missed flights, delayed ferries and floods are routine to existence; take the wait as locals would – another opportunity to heat the kettle and strike up a slow talk over maté.

Starting south of Puerto Montt, the Carretera Austral links widely separated towns and hamlets all the way to Villa O'Higgins, a total of just over 1200km. High season (from mid-December through February) offers considerably more travel options and availability. Combination bus and ferry circuits afford visitors a panoramic vision of the region. This section covers Parque Pumalín to Lago General Carrera but there's plenty more. Don't hesitate to tread off the beaten track: the little villages along the road and its furthest hamlets of Cochrane, Caleta Tortel and Villa O'Higgins are fully worth exploring (see p477).

PARQUE PUMALÍN

Verdant and pristine, this 2889-sq-km park encompasses vast extensions of temperate rainforest, clear rivers, seascapes and farmland. A remarkable forest-conservation effort, **Parque Pumalín** (www.pumalinpark.org), attracts 10,000 visitors yearly (no small number, considering that tourist season is a three-month period) to explore these tracts of forest stretching from near Hornopirén to Chaitén. Owned by American Doug Tompkins, it is Chile's largest private park and one of the largest private parks in the world. For Chile it's a model park, with well-maintained roads and trails, extensive infrastructure and minimal impact.

With the recent activity of Volcán Chaitén, Parque Pumalín has closed its infrastructure for a time and may relocate services to El Amarillo, south of Chaitén. Check the website for the latest details and transportation.

Getting There & Away

Services described in the following originate in Chaitén. Due to volcanic activity, these services may be altered or suspended. Check first.

CHILE

BOAT

The daily service from Caleta Gonzalo in Parque Pumalín to Hornopirén is suspended for the time being.

The **Naviera Austral** (☎ 731-272; www.navieraustral.cl; Corcovado 266) auto-passenger ferry *Pincoya* or new ferry *Don Baldo* sails to Puerto Montt (12 hours) three times a week. In summer ferries go to Quellón, Chiloé (six hours) twice weekly and daily to Horonpiren (CH$10,000), from where buses depart for Puerto Montt. Unless otherwise noted, all routes charge CH$19,000 for nonresidents.

BUS

The best local information resource, **Chaitur** (☎ 097-468-5608; www.chaitur.com; O'Higgins 67, Chaitén) functions as a bus terminal, makes area tours and provides up-to-date local information in English. They bus to Caleta Gonzalo (CH$6000) for the ferry; to Futaleufú (CH$7000, four hours) at 3pm daily except Sunday. **Buses Palena** (O'Higgins 67, Chaitén) goes to Palena (CH$7000, 4½ hours) on Monday, Wednesday and Friday from the terminal.

Buses Norte (O'Higgins 67, Chaitén) goes to Coyhaique (CH$17,000, 12 hours) daily except Wednesday, stopping in La Junta (CH$7000, four hours) and Puyuhuapi (CH$9000, 5½ hours).

FUTALEUFÚ

☎ 065 / pop 1800

The diamond-cut waters of the Futaleufú have made famous this modest mountain village, 155km from Chaitén. World-renowned rafting and kayaking comes at a price: the valley is starting to feel a little like Boulder, Taos, or Pucón. If the Futa or Fu (as those in the know call it) is on your destination list, make sure you slow down and say hello to locals, speak their language and share something, because these days there's more of us than them.

Information

Bring all the money you'll need; **Banco del Estado** (cnr O'Higgins & Rodríguez) is the only place to change cash.

Tours

Rafting trips on Río Espolón and segments of the more difficult Futaleufú are expensive (CH$12,000). Reliable outfitters include the following.

Austral Excursions (☎ 721-239; Hermanos Carera 500) A locally owned outfitter with river descents as well as trekking and canyoning excursions.

Bio Bio Expeditions (☎ 800-246-7238; www.bbx rafting.com) A pioneer in the region, this ecologically minded group offers river descents, horse treks and more. It is well established but may take walk-ins.

Expediciones Chile (☎ 721-386; www.exchile.com; Mistral 296) A secure rafting operator with loads of experience. Offers kayaking, mountain biking and other activities as well.

Sleeping & Eating

Camping Puerto Espolón (☎ 696-5324; puertoespolon @latinmail.com; campsite per person CH$5000; ☾ Jan & Feb) The best option close to town, it's riverside with a sandy beach.

Cara del Indio (☎ 02-196-4239; www.caradelindio.cl; campsite per person CH$3000, 8-person cabañas CH$45,000) Spacious riverside camping, 15km after Puerto Ramírez. There are kayak and raft put-in sites, hot showers, sauna and staples of homemade bread, cheese and beer are sold.

Las Natalias (shagrinmack@hotmail.com; dm CH$6000, d/tr CH$17,000/25,000, d without bathroom CH$15,000) Fully decked out and brand new, this hostel has plenty of space to socialize, and mountain views. It's a 10-minute walk from the center. Follow Cerda and the signs for the northeast sector out of town; it's on the right after the hill climb.

Adolfo's B&B (☎ 721-256; O'Higgins 302; r per person with/without bathroom CH$8000/7000; 💻) The best bargain digs in town are in this warm family home. Breakfast includes eggs, homemade bread and coffee cake.

Hotel El Barranco (☎ 721-314; www.elbarrancochile.cl; O'Higgins 172; s/d CH$70,000/80,000; 💻 🏊) Snug rooms displaying carved woodwork, colonial accents and big beds – this elegant lodge provides ambience in spades but service is slack.

SurAndes (☎ 721-405; www.surandes.com; Cerda 308; mains CH$2500; ☾ breakfast, lunch & dinner; 💻) Real coffee, fresh juices, fresh omelettes, custom burgers and veggie plates: this is gringo heaven. There's also an attractive five-person apartment (CH$14,000 per person) for rent upstairs.

Martín Pescador (☎ 721-279; Balmaceda 603; mains CH$6000; ☾ 7-11pm) Serving regional delicacies like chicken with morel mushrooms, or baked crab by a roaring fire, this is the place to put on your lipstick for.

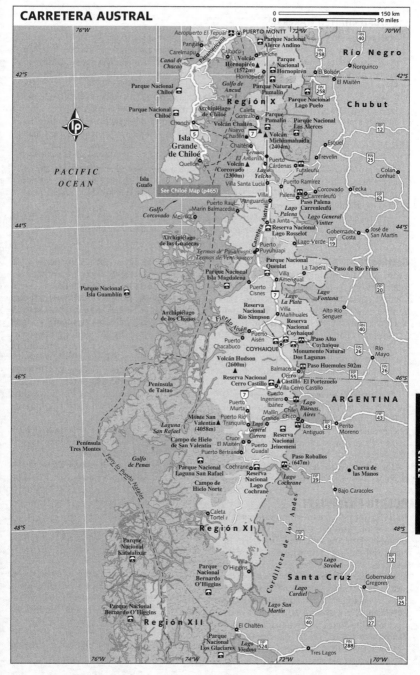

CARRETERA AUSTRAL

See Chiloé Map (p465)

CHILE

VOLCÁN CHAITÉN WAKES UP

It wasn't even ranked among Chile's 120 volcanoes, but that changed quickly. On May 2, 2008, Volcán Chaitén, 10km northeast of its namesake town, began a month-long eruption. Its ashen cone rose twenty kilometers in the air. The rampage caused flooding and severe damage to homes, roads and bridges, decimated thousands of livestock and spewed ash as far as Buenos Aires. Luckily, 8000 inhabitants successfully evacuated.

A year on, activity continued under close monitoring. As the 1112m volcano evolves, vulcanologists from Chile's Mining and Geology Service fear that a new dome complex could collapse, sending a pyroclastic flow into Chaitén in minutes. A part of one cone already collapsed on February 27, 2009. Rain also may loosen large flows of ash and debris. Explosions are a third danger, since the magma contains a high concentration of dense silicon dioxide buildup.

Plans are underway to construct Nueva Chaitén on the current site of coastal village Santa Barbara, 10km north of the former Chaitén. Regional transport and services will eventually relocate here. In the meanwhile, barring emergency status, ferries come in and out of Chaitén's port, coordinated with regional buses, but there are no official hotels or services since the town lacks electricity and running water.

Please check the current status of the region and its lodgings and services before you go. For updates, contact Parque Pumalín (www.pumalinpark.org) or local tourism offices.

Getting There & Away

From Monday through Friday, **Transportes Altamirano** (☎ 314-143; cnr Balmaceda & Prat) goes to Chaitén (CH$7000, four hours) at 7am, Villa Santa Lucía (where you can transfer south to Coyhaique), Puerto Cárdenas and Termas El Amarillo. To Coyhaique (CH$17,000, 10 to 12 hours) a bus goes at 7am on Saturday. To Puerto Montt (CH$23,000 with lunch, 10 to 12 hours) a bus goes at 8:30am Monday and Friday.

The **Futaleufú border post** (☺ 8am-8pm) is far quicker and more efficient than the crossing at Palena, opposite the Argentine border town of Carrenleufú.

There's no gas station in Futaleufú. The grocery store on Sargento Aldea sells fuel by the jug; it's cheaper in Argentina, if you make it.

PUERTO PUYUHUAPI

In 1935 four German immigrants settled this remote rainforest outpost, inspired by explorer Hans Steffen's adventures. The agricultural colony grew with Chilote textile workers, whose skills fed the success of the 1947 German **Fábrica de Alfombras** (www.puyuhuapi .com; Aysen s/n; tours per group CH$5000), still weaving carpets today. Across the inlet, **Termas de Puyuhuapi** is a high-end hot-springs resort. Located 6km south of Puyuhuapi, **Termas del Ventisquero** (☎ 067-325-228; admission CH$10,000; ☺ 9am-11pm Dec-Feb & some winter weekends), is a closer, cheaper alternative.

Camping La Sirena (☎ 325-100; Costanera 148; campsite per person CH$2500) There are tent shelters, bathrooms and hot showers at this place.

Casa Ludwig (☎ 067-320-000; www.casaludwig .cl; Uebel s/n; s/d CH$22,000/38,000, without bathroom CH$16,000/22,000) is elegant and snug – a real treat with a roaring fire and big breakfasts at the large communal table. Come out of the rain at **Cabañas & Café Aonikenk** (☎ 325-208; aonikenkturismo@yahoo.com; Hamburgo 16; d CH$30,000, cabañas for 2-6 people CH$36,000-55,000), with great cafe fare and Veronica's generous hospitality. Cabins are well appointed and it's a good stop for information about the area. The casual **Cocinería Real** (☎ 525-613; Mistral 8; mains CH$4500) serves heaped plates of fresh fish with side salads and cold cans of beer.

Between 3pm and 5pm **Buses Norte** (☎ 067-232-167; Parra 337) and Transportes Emanuel buses leave for Chaitén (CH$9000, 5½ hours) and Coyhaique (CH$8000, six hours) from the store next to the police station.

PARQUE NACIONAL QUEULAT

Queulat (admission CH$3000) is a wild realm where rivers wind through forests thick with ferns and southern beech. Its steep-sided fjords are flanked by creeping glaciers. From Conaf's **Centro de Información Ambiental** there is a 3km hike to a lookout with views of Ventisquero Colgante, a chalk-blue hanging glacier.

Just north of the southern entrance at Pudú, at Km 170, a damp trail climbs the valley of the **Río de las Cascadas** through a dense forest to a granite bowl where half a dozen waterfalls spring from hanging glaciers.

Camp at **Ventisquero** (campsites CH$5000), near Ventisquero Colgante, and **Angostura**, 15km north of Puyuhuapi.

COYHAIQUE
☎ 067 / pop 44,900

Coyhaique fills the rolling steppe at the foot of Cerro Macay's basalt massif. Ranch town and regional capital, it attracts rural workers to the timber and salmon industries and anglers to nearby fly-fishing lodges. For those fresh from the wilderness, it can be a jarring relapse into the world of semi-trucks and subdivisions.

Coyhaique's plaza occupies the heart of a disorienting pentagonal plan. Av General Baquedano skirts northeast and connects with the highway to Puerto Chacabuco. Av Ogano heads south to Balmaceda and Lago General Carrera.

Information

Banks with ATMs and internet cafes line Condell.

Cabot (☎ 230-101; Lautaro 331) A general service travel agency.

Casa del Turismo Rural (☎ 214-031; www.casa turismorural.cl; Dussen 357-B) Networks visitors to rural homestays (see below) and offers local guide services for a grassroots approach to trekking, fishing and horse riding.

Conaf (☎ 212-109; Av Ogana 1060; ☼ 9am-8pm Mon-Sat, 10am-6pm Sun) Park information.

Hospital Base (☎ 231-286; Ibar 68; ☼ 24hr) Near the western end of JM Carrera.

Lavandería QL (Bilbao 160; per load CH$3000; ☼ 9am-8pm Mon-Fri, 10am-6pm Sat & Sun)

Post office (Cochrane 202)

Sernatur (☎ 233-949; Bulnes 35; ☼ 8:30am-8pm Mon-Fri, 10am-6pm Sat & Sun summer) Excellent information on lodgings, fishing guides and the region all the way to Villa O'Higgins.

Sights & Activities

For prime river vistas, walk west on JM Carrera to **Mirador Río Simpson**. Hikers can tread trails in **Reserva Nacional Coyhaique** (admission CH$2000), 5km from town: take Baquedano north across the bridge and go right at the gravel road; from the entrance it's 3km to Laguna Verde. **Condor Explorer** (☎ 670-349; www.condorexplorer.com; Dussen 357; ☼ 10am-1pm Mon-Fri, to 2pm Sat) supplies gear and offers tailored adventures with bilingual guides. In addition to training area youth as professional guides, **Escuela de Guias** (☎ 573-096; www.escueladeguias.cl) connects local guides with clients and guides some trips, principally around Cohyaique.

Anglers can go **fishing** from November to May, with some restrictions. Brown and rainbow trout are typical catches. From June to September, skiers can make turns at the **Centro de Ski El Fraile** (☎ 231-690; daily ski pass CH$15,000), only 29km south of Coyhaique. The T-bar and pommel lift access 800m of vertical terrain. Experts can hike past the lifts to access some bowls with heavy, wet snow and lovely tree-skiing.

In town, **Museo Regional de la Patagonia** (cnr Av General Baquedano & Lillo; admission CH$500; ☼ 9am-6pm Dec-Feb, limited hr rest of year) catalogues pioneer artifacts and Jesuit regalia. The outdoor **Feria Artesanal** (Plaza de Armas) sells woolens, leather and wooden knickknacks.

DETOUR TO PIONEER PATAGONIA

When winds roar sidelong and rains persist, take refuge by the woodstove, drink a round of matés and *echar la talla* (pass the time) with the locals. Rural Patagonia offers a rare and privileged glimpse of a fading way of life. To jump-start their slack, rural economy, government and nonprofit initiatives have created local guide and homestay associations.

These family enterprises range from comfortable roadside *hospedajes* and farmstays to wild multiday treks and horse trips through wonderland terrain. Prices are reasonable – starting from CH$8000 per day for lodging.

In Coyhaique, travelers can link with rural homestays and guide services through **Casa del Turismo Rural** (www.casaturismorural.cl). Near Palena, **Aventuras Cordilleranas** (☎ 065-741-388; El Malito bridge; s incl breakfast CH$7000) provides a wonderful family lodging. The family also offers riverfront cabin accommodations and rides to rural El Tranquilo. Adventurers can ride or hike to **Rincón de la Nieve** (in Palena ☎ 065-741-269; Valle Azul; s incl breakfast CH10,000), the Casanova family farm in Valle Azul. Book a week in advance or more, as intermediaries will have to make radio contact with the most remote hosts. That's right – no phones, no electricity, no worries.

COYHAIQUE

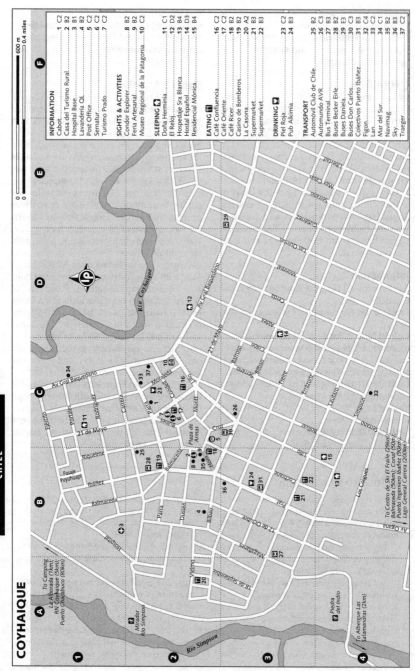

Sleeping

Rates listed here include shared bathrooms.

Camping La Alborada (☎ 238-868; campsite per person CH$2500) Clean with good amenities and sheltered sites; 1km from town.

Doña Herminia (☎ 231-579; 21 de Mayo 60; r per person without bathroom CH$6000) Herminia's affectionate service and attention to details like reading lamps and fresh towels make these impeccable rooms a steal.

Residencial Mónica (☎ 234-302; Lillo 664; r per person with/without bathroom CH$9000/6000) Well attended and warm, this prim '60s-style home is always full.

Albergue Las Salamandras (☎ 211-865; www .salamandras.cl; Km 1.5; dm/d/cabaña CH$7000/19,000/ 32,000; 🖳) On a wooded bank of Río Simpson, Coyhaique's best hostal is a rustic guesthouse with ample common spaces, two kitchens, and cozy dorm beds.

Hospedaje Sra Blanca (☎ 232-158; Simpson 459; s/d CH$12,000/16,000) Quaint and homey, Blanca's rooms are spotless, some country-style and others just kitsch, with a centerpiece rose garden.

Hostal Español (☎ 242-580; www.hostalcoyhaique .cl; Aldea 343; s/d CH$25,000/35,000; 🖳) A tasteful and modern house with fresh quilted bedding, claret carpets and a personal touch. A frigobar, central heating and wi-fi are other perks.

El Reloj (☎ 231-108; www.elrelojhotel.cl; Av General Baquedano 828; s/d incl breakfast CH$40,000/59,000; 🖳) Comfortably upscale, this renovated warehouse combines cypress walls with colonial furniture and fireplaces. Rooms are quiet, and the restaurant is excellent.

Eating & Drinking

Two large supermarkets sit side by side on Lautaro.

Café Oriente (☎ 231-622; Condell 201; sandwiches CH$3000; 🖳) A modest sandwich stop serving satisfying *ave paltas* (chicken and avocado sandwiches) on warm bread, ice cream and coffee.

Casino de Bomberos (☎ 231-437; Parra 365; fixed-price lunch CH$3500; ❂ lunch) Call it a cultural experience, this classic eatery packs with locals downing seafood plates or steak and eggs. The one thing they're short of is fresh air, with empanadas and French fries sizzling up the griddle.

our pick Café Confluencia (☎ 245-080; 25 de Mayo 548; mains CH$3000-5000; ❂ breakfast, lunch & dinner) Too chic for Coyhaique, this healthy eatery serves heaping bowls of greens and has great set lunches. At night, mint *pisco sours* are standouts. Live music on weekends ranges from rock 'n' roll to Latin acts.

La Casona (☎ 238-894; Vielmo 77; mains CH$5000) White-linen formal, this upscale eatery features grilled lamb, seafood options and steaks. Palta Victoria, an avocado stuffed with crab, makes a great start.

Café Ricer (☎ 232-920; Horn 48; mains CH$5000-7500; ❂ 9:30am-midnight) Rustic-chic, Ricer reels in tourists with its sheepskin seating, tasty pizza, salads and ice cream, but service is downright bad.

Pub Alkimia (Prat s/n) A stylish lounge for twenty- to thirtysomethings.

Piel Roja (Moraleda 495; ❂ 6pm-5am) Rumbling with late-night life, this good-time bar swarms with young locals and fishing guides.

Getting There & Away

AIR

The region's main airport is in Balmaceda, 50km southeast of Coyhaique. **LAN** (☎ 600-526-2000; Parra 402) has daily flights to Puerto Montt (CH$94,000 one hour) and Santiago (2½ hours). Another choice is **Sky** (☎ 240-825; Prat 203).

BOAT

Ferries to Puerto Montt leave from Puerto Chacabuco, two hours from Coyhaique by bus. Schedules are subject to change.

Navimag (☎ 233-306; www.navimag.com; Horn 47-D) sails from Puerto Chacabuco to Puerto Montt (CH$38,000 to CH$143,000, 18 hours) several times per week. **Mar del Sur** (☎ 231-255; Av General Baquedano 146-A) runs ferries to/from Puerto Ibáñez and Chile Chico (CH$4650, 2½ hours). Reserve at the office.

BUS

Buses operate from the **bus terminal** (☎ 232-067; cnr Lautaro & Magallanes) and separate offices. Schedules change continuously; check with Sernatur for the latest information. Unless noted, the following leave from the terminal.

For northern destinations, companies servicing Puyuhuapi, La Junta, Villa Santa Lucía and Chaitén include **Buses Becker Eirle** (☎ 232-167; Ibañez 358) and **Buses Daniela** (☎ 231-701, 099-512-3500; Av General Baquedano 1122). For Osorno and Puerto Montt, try **Queilen Bus** (☎ 240-760) or **Transaustral** (☎ 232-067).

CHILE

BUS FARES		
Destination	Cost (CH$)	Duration (hr)
Chaitén2	15,000	1
Chile Chico	13,500	12
Cochrane	11,000	7-10
La Junta	10,000	7-10
Osorno	30,000	22
Puerto Montt	30,000	24
Puyuhuapi	8000	6

For southern destinations:

Acuario 13 (☎ 240-990) Serves Cochrane.

Buses Don Carlos (☎ 231-981; Cruz 63) Serves Villa Cerro Castillo, Puerto Río Tranquilo, Puerto Bertrand and Cochrane.

Buses Interlagos (☎ 240-840; www.turismointerlagos.cl; bus terminal) Serves Cochrane and Chile Chico.

Colectivos Puerto Ibáñez (cnr Prat & Errázuríz) Door-to-door shuttle to Puerto Ingeniero Ibáñez (CH$3500, 1½ hours), where there is a ferry to Chile Chico.

Getting Around

Door-to-door shuttle service (CH$4000) to the airport leaves two hours before flight departure. Call **Transfer T&T Coyhaique** (☎ 256-000).

Car rental is expensive and availability limited in summer. Try **Traeger** (☎ 231-648; Av General Baquedano 457), **Automundo AVR** (☎ 231-621; Bilbao 510), and **Automóvil Club de Chile** (☎ 231-847; Carrera 333). **Figon** (Simpson 888) rents (per day CH$5000 to CH$14,000) and repairs bikes.

LAGO GENERAL CARRERA

Shared with Argentina (where it's called Lago Buenos Aires), this massive 224,000-hectare lake is often a wind-stirred green-blue sea in the middle of a sculpted Patagonian steppe. Its rough and twisty roads dwarf the traveler: you'll feel like you're crawling through the landscape. This section follows the Carretera Austral south from Coyhaique, around the lake's western border.

Just before reaching Balmaceda from Coyhaique, a right-hand turn-off (the sign points to Cochrane) heads toward **Reserva Nacional Cerro Castillo**. The spires of glacier-bound Cerro Castillo tower over some 180,000 hectares of southern beech forest. In Villa Cerro Castillo (Km 104) stay with the hospitable **Don Niba** (☎ public phone 067-419-200; Los Pioneros 872; r per person CH$7000) in a comfortable home with whopping breakfasts. He also offers horse treks and hikes.

Along the western shore, **Puerto Río Tranquilo** has a petrol station. Boat tours visit the gorgeous caves of **Capilla de Mármol** when the water's calm. North of town an (unfinished) glacier-lined road to Parque Nacional Laguna San Rafael bumps toward the coast. Adventure base camp **El Puesto** (☎ satellite 02-196-4555; www.elpuesto.cl; Lagos 258; s/d CH$40,000/55,000) is a lovely B&B owned by a professional guide whose ice trekking trips on Glacier Exploradores come recommended. Wild camping is possible on the windy beach, or 10km west at Lago Tranquilo.

About 13km east of Cruce El Maitén **Puerto Guadal** has petrol and provisions. Pitch a tent lakefront, or hunker down at **Terra Luna** (☎ 067-431-263; www.terra-luna.cl; 2-person huts CH$30,000, d/tr/q incl breakfast CH$80,000/90,000/110,000) with lovely cabins and a hot tub tucked into the woods. Budget travelers should check out the rustic Conejera huts with kitchen.

For transportation information, see listings (p475) under Coyhaique.

Chile Chico

☎ 067 / pop 4000

Gold and silver mines dot the roller-coaster road from Puerto Guadal, ending in Chile Chico, a sunny oasis of wind-pummeled poplars and orchards. From here, buses connect to Los Antiguos (p144) and Ruta 40 leading to southern Argentine Patagonia. **Reserva Nacional Jeinemeni** (admission CH$1000), 60km away, is a treasure of flamingos and turquoise mountain lagoons. Aside from a few expensive tours, there's little transportation. You can try to grab a ride in with **Conaf** (☎ 411-325; Blest Gana 121; 9am-5pm Mon-Fri) rangers.

There is **tourist information** (☎ 411-123; cnr O'Higgins & Lautaro; Dec-March only) and a **Banco del Estado** (González 112) for money exchange.

You can stay at **Camping Chile Chico** (☎ 411-598; Burgos 6; campsite per person CH$3000) or the ultrafriendly **Kon Aiken** (☎ 411-598; Burgos 6; per person without bathroom CH$9000, 6-person cabaña CH$35,000). They also organize excursions to nearby Reserva Nacional Jeinimeini. Farmhouse **Hostería de la Patagonia** (☎ 411-337; hdelapatagonia@gmail.com; Camino Internacional s/n; campsite per person CH$2500, d with/without bathroom CH$26,000/20,000), on the road to Argentina, has rooms among the gardens.

THE END OF THE ROAD

Ever wonder what lies beyond the guidebook pages?

The Carretera Austral doesn't end at Lago General Carrera, in fact, it rumbles nearly 300 kilometers further south to the remote village of Villa O'Higgins. Only the massive glacial barrier of the Southern Ice Field kept it from going any further, but that doesn't stop hearty adventurers from tackling the ferry-trek-ferry combination to El Chaltén, Argentina (see p47). In Villa O'Higgins, **Camping & Albergue El Mosco** (☎ 067-431-819, 098-983-9079; Carretera Austral Km 1240; campsite CH$5000, dm CH$10,000; 🖳) offers friendly lodgings and the lowdown on local hikes. Along the way, change buses in Cochrane and detour to the cool boardwalk village of Caleta Tortel, a Unesco World Heritage site.

You can find more information on transport and lodgings at Sernatur in Coyhaique (p473).

The quirky **Café Elizabeth y Loly** (☎ 411-451; González 25; mains CH$2500-5000; ☯ lunch & dinner) serves strong coffee and authentic baklava.

Getting There & Away

BOAT

Mar del Sur (☎ 231-255, 411-864; Muelle Chile Chico) ferries go to Puerto Ingeniero Ibáñez (2½ hours) almost daily. Departures change frequently so check the Entel office in Chile Chico for schedules. Rates are: for passengers CH$4650, bicycles CH$2200, motorcycles CH$5500 and vehicles CH$27,500. Reservations are highly recommended; for contact information, see p475. This is the quickest way to get to Coyhaique.

BUS

A number of shuttle buses leave from O'Higgins 420 and cross the border to Los Antiguos, Argentina (CH$2000, 20 minutes), just 9km east. Los Antiguos has connections to El Chaltén.

Transportes Ale (☎ 411-739; Rosa Amelia 800) goes to Puerto Río Tranquilo (CH$12,000, five hours), stopping in Puerto Guadal (CH$6000, 2½ hours) at 1:30pm on Tuesday and Thursday. A southbound bus goes to Cochrane (CH$12,000, six hours) at 1:30pm on Wednesday and Saturday, stopping at Puerto Guadal and Cruce Maitén (CH$7000, three hours).

SOUTHERN PATAGONIA

The wind is whipping, the mountains are jagged and waters trickle clear. This desolate area first attracted missionaries and fortune seekers from Scotland, England and Croatia. Writer Francisco Coloane described these early adventurers as 'courageous men whose hearts were no more than another closed fist.' The formation of *estancias* (extensive grazing establishment, either for cattle or sheep, with a dominant owner or manager and dependent resident labor force), and the wool boom that followed created reverberating effects: great wealth for a few gained at the cost of native populations, who were nearly exterminated by disease and warfare. Later the region struggled as wool values plummeted and the Panama Canal diverted shipping routes.

Patagonia's worth may have been hardwon and nearly lost but it is now under reconsideration. While wealth once meant minerals and livestock, now it is in the very landscape. For visitors, the very thrill lies in Patagonia's isolated, spectral beauty. Torres del Paine receives nearly 200,000 visitors a year and a growing number set sights further south to Tierra del Fuego and Antarctica.

PUNTA ARENAS

☎ 061 / pop 130,100

If these streets could talk: this wind-wracked former penitentiary has hosted tattered sailors, miners, seal hunters, starving pioneers and wealthy dandies of the wool boom. Exploitation of one of the world's largest reserves of hydrocarbon started in the 1980s and has developed into a thriving petrochemical industry. Today's Punta Arenas is a confluence of the ruddy and the grand, geared toward tourism and industry.

Orientation

Punta Arenas has a regular grid street plan with the Plaza de Armas, or Plaza Muñoz Gamero, at its center. Street names change on either side of the plaza. Most landmarks and hotels are within a few blocks of here.

CHILE

Information

Internet access is widely available and ATMs are common.

Conaf (off Map p479; ☎ 230-681; Bulnes 0309; 9am-5pm Mon-Fri) Has details on the nearby parks.

Hospital Regional (☎ 205-000; Angamos 180)

Information kiosk (☎ 200-610; www.puntaarenas.cl; Plaza Muñoz Gamero; ☑ 8am-7pm Mon-Sat, 9am-7pm Sun) South side of the plaza.

La Hermandad (Navarro 1099) Foreign currency exchange.

Lavasol (☎ 243-067; O'Higgins 969; per load CH$3000; ☑ 7am-7pm)

Post office (Bories 911) Located one block north of the plaza.

Sernatur (☎ 241-330; www.sernatur.cl; Navarro 999; ☑ 8:15am-8pm Mon-Fri Dec-Feb) Has well-informed staff as well as accommodations and transportation lists.

Sights & Activities

The heart of the city, **Plaza Muñoz Gamero**, flanks opulent mansions, including the **Museo Regional Braun-Menéndez** (☎ 244-216; Magallanes 949; admission CH$1000, Sun free; ☑ 10:30am-5pm Mon-Sat, to 2pm Sun in summer, to 2pm in winter), the luxurious seat of power of the 19th-century Braun-Menéndez family, who were sheep farmers turned land magnates. Among South America's most fascinating cemeteries is **Cementerio Municipal** (Bulnes 949), a mix of humble immigrant graves and heartfelt inscriptions and extravagant tombs of the town's first families. A monument to the Selk'nam commemorates the indigenous group that was wiped out during the wool boom.

Museo Regional Salesiano (☎ 221-001; Av Bulnes 336; admission CH$1500; ☑ 10am-12:30pm & 3-6pm Tue-Sun) touts missionary peacemaking between indigenous groups and settlers. Worthwhile material examines the mountaineer priest Alberto de Agostini and various indigenous groups. Among the historical displays at **Museo Naval y Marítimo** (☎ 205-479; Montt 981; admission CH$1500; ☑ 9:30am-12:30pm & 3-6pm Tue-Sat) is a well-told account of the Chilean mission that rescued Sir Ernest Shackleton's crew from Antarctica.

Reserva Forestal Magallanes, 8km from town, has trails through dense *lenga* and coigue. A steady slog takes you to the top of Mt Fenton where views are spectacular and winds whipping.

Tours

Worthwhile day trips include tours to the **Seno Otway pingüinera** (penguin colony; tours CH$15,000, admission CH$2500; ☑ Oct-March) and to the town's first settlements at **Fuerte Bulnes & Puerto Hambre** (admission CH$1000). Lodgings can help arrange tours, or try the following ones.

A more atmospheric alternative to Seno Otway is **Isla Magdalena** (admission/tour CH$15,000; ☑ Dec-Feb) and its thriving Magellanic penguin colonies. Five-hour tours on the *Melinka* ferry land for an hour at the island. Book tickets through **Turismo Comapa** (☎ 200-200; www.comapa .com; Magallanes 990) and bring a picnic.

Recommended agencies:

Inhóspita Patagonia (☎ 224-510; Navarro 1013) Does trekking trips to Cabo Froward, the southernmost point on mainland South America.

Turismo Aonikenk (☎ 228-332; www.aonikenk.com; Magallanes 619) English-, German- and French-speaking guides.

Turismo Viento Sur (☎ 226-930; www.vientosur.com; Fagnano 565)

Turismo Yamana (☎ 221-130, www.yamana.cl; Errazurriz 972) Kayaking trips on Magellan Strait.

Whalesound (☎ 221-076; www.whalesound.com; Navarro 1163, 2nd fl) Supports science with study-based sailing and kayak trips to the remote Coloane Marine Park. Humpback whale-watching trips are available from December to May.

Festivals & Events

At the end of July, **Carnaval de Invierno** features fireworks, parades and good cheer.

Sleeping

Hospedaje Independencia (☎ 227-572; Av Independencia 374; campsite CH$1500; dm CH$4500) Friendly but chaotic, this shoestring bet has reasonably clean rooms and guests get kitchen use and bike rentals.

Hostal La Estancia (☎ 249-130; www.backpackers chile.com/en/hostel-estancia.php; O'Higgins 765; dm CH$6500, d without bathroom CH$20,000; ☐) An old house with big rooms with vaulted ceilings and tidy shared bathrooms. Alex and Carmen are attentive hosts, generous with insider tips.

Hostal Fitz Roy (☎ 240-430; www.hostalfitzroy .com; Navarro 850; dm CH$7000, s/d/tr without bathroom CH$12,000/20,000/25,000; ☐) A country house in the city, with rambling, good-value rooms and an inviting old-fashioned living room to pour over books or sea charts. Rooms have phones, TV and wi-fi connections. Accepts credit cards.

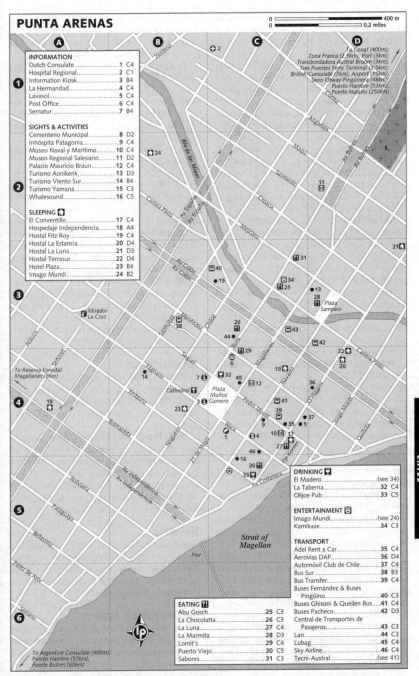

PUNTA ARENAS

0 — 400 m
0 — 0.2 miles

INFORMATION
Dutch Consulate....................1 C4
Hospital Regional..................2 C1
Information Kiosk...................3 B4
La Hermandad.......................4 C4
Lavasol.............................5 C4
Post Office.........................6 C4
Sernatur............................7 B4

SIGHTS & ACTIVITIES
Cementerio Municipal..............8 D2
Inhóspita Patagonia................9 C4
Museo Naval y Marítimo............10 C4
Museo Regional Salesiano..........11 D2
Palacio Mauricio Braun............12 C4
Turismo Aonikenk..................13 D3
Turismo Viento Sur................14 B4
Turismo Yamana....................15 C3
Whalesound.........................16 C5

SLEEPING
El Conventillo....................17 C4
Hospedaje Independencia...........18 A4
Hostal Fitz Roy...................19 C4
Hostal La Estancia................20 D4
Hostal La Luna....................21 D3
Hostal Terrasur...................22 D4
Hotel Plaza.......................23 B4
Imago Mundi.......................24 B2

To Conaf (400m);
Zona Franca (2.5km); Port (3km);
Transbordadora Austral Broom (3km);
Tres Puentes Ferry Terminal (3.5km);
British Consulate (7km); Airport (15km);
Seno Otway Pingüinera (48km);
Puerto Hambre (53km);
Puerto Natales (250km)

Mirador La Cruz

To Reserva Forestal
Magallanes (8km)

Cathedral

Plaza Muñoz Gamero

Plaza Sampaio

Strait of Magellan

Pier

To Argentine Consulate (400m);
Puerto Hambre (53km);
Fuerte Bulnes (60km)

EATING
Abu Gosch.........................25 C3
La Chocolatta.....................26 C3
La Luna...........................27 C4
La Marmita........................28 C4
Lomit's...........................29 C4
Puerto Viejo......................30 C5
Sabores...........................31 C3

DRINKING
El Madero....................(see 34)
La Taberna........................32 C4
Olijoe Pub........................33 C5

ENTERTAINMENT
Imago Mundi..................(see 24)
Kamikaze..........................34 C3

TRANSPORT
Adel Rent a Car...................35 C4
Aerovías DAP......................36 D4
Automóvil Club de Chile...........37 C4
Bus Sur...........................38 B3
Bus Transfer......................39 C4
Buses Fernández & Buses
  Pingüino........................40 C3
Buses Ghisoni & Queilen Bus......41 C4
Buses Pacheco.....................42 D3
Central de Transportes de
  Pasajeros.......................43 C3
Lan...............................44 C4
Lubag.............................45 C4
Sky Airline.......................46 C4
Tecni-Austral...............(see 41)

CHILE

Imago Mundi (☎ 613-115; www.imagomundi patagonia.cl; Mejicana 252; dm with/without bathroom CH$10,000/8000; 🖳) A young brother-sister duo channeled their wanderlust into these cool digs with just eight snug bunks, electric colors and cozy spaces. Features recycled decor and composts organic waste. On rainy days, check out the onsite climbing gym.

El Conventillo (☎ 242-311; www.hostalconventillo .com; Pasaje Korner 1034; dm CH$8000; 🖳) In the reviving waterfront district, this appealing brick hostel has remodeled, carpeted dorms and clean row showers. Bright colors mask the fact that rooms are windowless and teensy. But breakfast includes yogurt and cereal and there's 24-hour reception, laundry and a library of cool Chilean flicks.

Hostal La Luna (☎ 221-764; hostalluna@hotmail.com; O'Higgins 424; s/d without bathroom CH$8000/12,000; 🖳) Goose-down comforters and a scruffy tabby spell home at this friendly, family lodging. Six tidy rooms have shared bath and guests get kitchen and laundry privileges.

Hostal Terrasur (☎ 247-114; www.hostalterrasur.cl; O'Higgins 123; s/d CH$28,500/38,500; 🖳) Slightly upscale Terrasur nurtures a secret-garden atmosphere, from its rooms with flowing curtains and flower patterns to the miniature green courtyard. There's also friendly desk service.

Hotel Plaza (☎ 241-300; www.hotelplaza.cl; Nogueira 1116; s/d CH$50,000/62,000; 🖳) This converted mansion just off the plaza boasts vaulted ceilings, plaza views and historical photos lining the hall. Inconsistent with such grandeur, the country decor is unfortunate. But service is genteel and the location unbeatable.

Eating

Abu Gosch (Bories 647) A large, well-stocked supermarket.

La Chocolatta (Bories 852; coffee drinks CH$1200; ☯ 9:30am-8:30pm Mon-Sat, 11am-8pm Sun; 🖳) Serving bite-sized chocolates, tea and coffee, this granny-style cafe stays bustling with families and laptop addicts.

Lomit's (Menéndez 722; mains CH$3000; ☯ 10am-2:30am) Chile's answer to the sidecar diner is this atmospheric cafe where cooks flip dripping, made-to-order burgers at a center-stage griddle. Portions are generous but the service sure dallies.

Sabores (Mejicana 702, 2nd fl; mains CH$3500) Think grilled salmon, seafood stews and pasta. Low on pretense, this cozy spot serves up abundant Chilean fare at a price we like.

La Luna (O'Higgins 974; mains CH$4000-7000; ☯ lunch & dinner) Serving tasty seafood concoctions and pastas, the lively Luna caters to an international crowd with prices to match.

La Marmita (☎ 222-056; Plaza Sampaio 678; mains CH$5000-8000) Cozy and colorful, Marmita welcomes guests warmly with a crackling woodstove and personal attention. The chef prepares fresh salads and some home-cooked creations such as scallop lasagna and *causa limeña*.

Puerto Viejo (☎ 225-103; O'Higgins 1176; mains CH$5000-8000) This chic eatery sets sail with fresh options like hake in cider and warm abalone salad. New ownership means the attention may not be quite as fussy.

Drinking

La Taberna (Braun Mansion; ☯ 7pm-2am, to 3am weekends) A traveler magnet, this is a classic old-boys club with no old boys in sight. Ambience is tops, but the mixed drinks could improve.

Olijoe Pub (Errázuriz 970; ☯ 6pm-2am) Leather booths and mosaic tabletops lend pretension but this is your usual pub with good beer and bad service.

El Madero (Bories 655) A warm-up for clubbers with crowds sipping stiff drinks.

Entertainment

Kamikaze (☎ 248-744; Bories 655; admission CH$3000 with a free drink) Tiki-torches light up this most southerly dance club and, if you're lucky, the occasional live rock band. It's upstairs from El Madero.

Imago Mundi (☎ 613-115; www.imagomundipatago nia.cl; Mejicana 252; ☯ 10am-1pm Mon-Fri, 4-10pm Sat) The new heart of alt culture in PA, check the website for arthouse cinema, live jazz and cultural talks. There's also wonderful homemade treats, savory *pascualinas* (pies), sandwiches and natural juice.

Shopping

Zona Franca (off Map p479; Zofri; ☯ Mon-Sat) The duty-free zone, it offers heaps of electronics, outdoor gear, camera and film equipment. *Colectivos* shuttle back and forth from downtown throughout the day.

Getting There & Away

Check with Sernatur for bus and maritime schedules. *La Prensa Austral* newspaper lists transportation availability, contact details and schedules.

CHILE

AIR

Aeropuerto Presidente Carlos Ibáñez del Campo is 20km north of town. **LAN** (☎ 600-526-2000; www.lan.com; Bories 884) goes daily to Santiago (CH$194,000) with a stop in Puerto Montt (CH$124,000), and Saturdays to the Falkland Islands (Islas Malvinas; CH$330,000 round trip). A new service serves Ushuaia (CH$170,000 round-trip) thrice weekly. **Aerovías DAP** (☎ 223-340; www.dap.cl; O'Higgins 891) flies to Porvenir (one way CH$21,000) Monday through Saturday; to Puerto Williams (CH$55,000) Wednesday through Saturday and Monday. Luggage is limited to 10kg per person. **Sky Airline** (☎ 710-645; www.skyairline.cl; Roca 935) flies daily between Santiago and Punta Arenas, with a stop either in Puerto Montt or Concepción.

BOAT

Transbordadora Austral Broom (☎ 218-100; www.tabsa.cl; Av Bulnes 05075) sails to Porvenir, Tierra del Fuego (CH$5000, 2½ to four hours), from the Tres Puentes ferry terminal (*colectivos* leave from Museo Regional Braun-Menéndez). A faster way to get to Tierra del Fuego (CH$1500, 20 minutes) is via the Punta Delgada-Bahía Azul crossing northeast of Punta Arenas. Ferries sail every 90 minutes from 8:30am to 10pm. Call for vehicle reservations (CH$15,000).

Broom's ferry *Patagonia* sails from Tres Puentes to Puerto Williams, Isla Navarino. Passengers (reclining seat/bunk CH$95,500/CH$115,000 including meals, 38 hours) can find current schedules online.

BUS

For the airport, Bus Fernandez (CH$2500) has shuttles. Puerto Natales–bound travelers may go directly from the Punta Arenas airport with previous reservation/payment through their hotel, though this service is not 'official.'

Punta Arenas has no central bus terminal. The **Central de Pasajeros** (☎ 245-811; cnr Magallanes & Av Colón) is the closest thing to a central booking office.

Only one bus goes daily to Ushuaia, so nab reservations one week ahead. For Ushuaia, it's most efficient to bus to Río Grande where *micros* connect to Ushuaia. Companies and destinations include the following:

Bus Sur (☎ 614-224; www.bus-sur.cl; Menéndez 552) El Calafate, Puerto Natales, Río Gallegos, Río Turbio, Ushuaia and Puerto Montt.

BUS FARES		
Destination	Cost (CH$)	Duration (hr)
Puerto Montt	45,000	36
Puerto Natales	4000	3
Río Gallegos	7000	5-8
Río Grande	20,000	8
Ushuaia	30,000	10

Bus Transfer (☎ 229-613; Montt 966) Puerto Natales and airport transfers.
Buses Fernández & Buses Pingüino (☎ 221-429/812; www.busesfernandez.com; Sanhueza 745) Puerto Natales, Torres del Paine & Río Gallegos.
Buses Ghisoni & Queilen Bus (☎ 222-714; Navarro 975) Río Gallegos, Río Grande, Ushuaia & Puerto Montt.
Buses Pacheco (☎ 225-527; www.busespacheco.com; Av Colón 900) Puerto Natales, Puerto Montt, Río Grande, Río Gallegos & Ushuaia.
Tecni-Austral (☎ 222-078; Navarro 975) Río Grande.
Turíbus (☎ 227-970; www.busescruzdelsur.cl; Sanhueza 745) Puerto Montt, Osorno and Chiloé.

Getting Around

Colectivos (CH$450, more at night and Sunday) zip around town; catch northbound ones on Av Magallanes or Av España and southbound along Bories or Av España.

Adel Rent a Car (☎ 235-471; www.adelrentacar.cl; Montt 962) provides attentive service, competitive rates and travel tips. You can also try **Lubag** (☎ 242-023; Magallanes 970). All agencies can arrange papers for crossing into Argentina. The **Automóvil Club de Chile** (☎ 243-675; O'Higgins 931) offers travel assistance to drivers.

PUERTO NATALES

☎ 061 / pop 18,000

A pastel wash of corrugated-tin houses shoulder to shoulder, this once dull fishing port on Seno Última Esperanza has become the hub of Gore-Tex clad travelers headed to the continent's number-one national park. While not a destination in itself, the village is pleasant, the austral light are divine and visitor services are getting ever more savvy.

Information

Internet cafes, call centers and banks with ATMs line Bulnes.

Casa de Cambios (Bulnes 692; ☼ 10am-1pm & 3-7pm Mon-Fri, to 1pm & 3:30-7pm Sat) Best rates on cash and traveler's checks.

CHILE

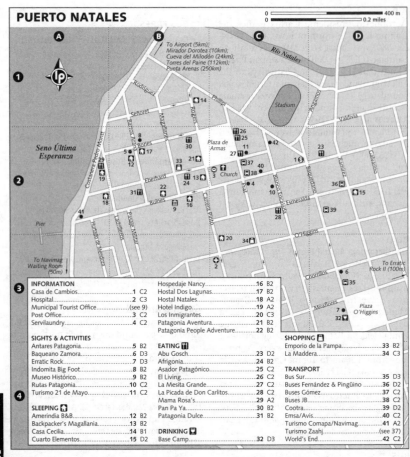

PUERTO NATALES

Conaf (☎ 411-438; O'Higgins 584; ✆ 9am-5pm Mon-Fri) Administrative office.

Hospital Puerto Natales (☎ 411-583; cnr O'Higgins & Carrera Pinto)

Municipal tourist office (☎ 411-263; Bulnes 285; ✆ 8:30am-12:30pm & 2:30-6pm Tue-Sun) In the Museo Histórico, with attentive staff and region-wide lodgings listings.

Post office (Eberhard 429)

Servilaundry (Bulnes 513; per load CH$3000) Offers laundry service, as do many hostels.

Sights & Activities

For a little context, the small **Museo Histórico** (411-263; Bulnes 285; admission free; ✆ 8:30am-12:30pm & 2:30-6pm Tue-Sun) has interesting artifacts from colonists and Yaghan and Tehuelche cultures in well-marked displays.

Warm up for the big expedition on **Mirador Dorotea**, a rocky headland less than 10km from Natales off Ruta 9. A sign at lot 14 marks the way to the lookout. The hiking trail passes through a *lenga* forest providing great views of the glacial valley and surrounding peaks.

Tours

Antares Patagonia (☎ 414-611; www.antarespat agonia.com; Barros Arana 111) Specializes in trekking in El Calafate, El Chaltén and Torres del Paine. Can facilitate climbing permits, science expeditions and made-to-order trips.

Baqueano Zamora (☎ 613-531; www.baqueano zamora.com; Av General Baquedano 534) Runs horse-riding trips and Posada Río Serrano.

Chile Nativo (☎ 411-835; www.chilenativo.cl; Eberhard 230, 2nd fl) Links visitors with local gauchos, organizes photo safaris and can competently plan your tailor-made dream adventures.

Erratic Rock (☎ 410-355; Av General Baquedano 719) Aims to keep Torres del Paine sustainable with good visitor advice (they give a free Torres del Paine introduction talk for trekkers daily at 3pm). Also promotes alternative options and rents gear. Guide service specializes in treks to Cabo Froward, Isla Navarino and lesser-known destinations.

Indomita Big Foot (☎ 414-525; www.indomita patagonia.com; Bories 206) Popular kayaking, trekking and mountaineering trips, plus ice- and rock-climbing seminars.

Rutas Patagonia (☎ 061-613-874; www.rutaspatago nia.com; Blanco Encalada 353; ☻ 9am-1pm & 3-10pm) Glaciar Grey ice trekking and ice climbing (CH$90,000), as well as kayaking on Lago Grey and Río Grey.

Sleeping

Beds abound, but the best selection fills up fast in high season, so call to reserve. Rates tumble off-season.

Hospedaje Nancy (☎ 410-022; www.nateslodge.cl; Ramírez 540; r per person without bathroom CH$5000; 🖳) Oft-praised for its adoptable hostess Nancy, this two-story home offers lived-in rooms with kitchen privileges and internet access.

Hostal Dos Lagunas (☎ 415-733; Barros Arana 104; dm CH$8000, s/d without bathroom CH$10,000/20,000) Natales natives Alejandro and Andrea are attentive hosts, spoiling guests with filling breakfasts, steady water pressure and travel tips. The rooms are ample and warm; singles occupying a double pay CH$5000 extra.

Casa Cecilia (☎ 613-560; www.casaceciliahostal.com; Rogers 60; d with/without bathroom CH$30,000/20,000) Well kept and central, Cecilia is a reliable mainstay. The only drawbacks are a small kitchen and cramped rooms. Its multilingual owners can provide good tips and there's quality camping gear for hire.

Cuatro Elementos (☎ 415-751; www.4elementos .cl; Esmeralda 813; s/d/tr CH$20,000/25,000/37,000) Eccentric-central, this eco-friendly house with a few spare rooms is coolly crafted with recycled zinc, driftwood and old woodstoves. Guests are drawn by the near-religious recycling and guided trips with an ecological bent.

Erratic Rock II (off Map p482; ☎ 412-317; www.er raticrock2.com; Zamora 732; d CH$25,000; 🖳) Ideal for couples, this snuggly home offers abundant breakfasts and spacious doubles decked in soft neutrals with throw pillows and tidy new bathrooms.

Amerindia B&B (☎ 411-945; www.hostelamerindia .com; Barros Arana 135; d CH$30,000, d/tr without bathroom CH$28,000/25,000; 🖳) With an earthy palette and retro touches, this guesthouse is a stylish retreat. Don't expect a hovering host, the atmosphere is chilled. Breakfast includes homemade bread and fruit.

Patagonic People Adventure (☎ 412-014; www .patagonicpeopleadventure.com; Bulnes 280; dm/d/tr CH$30,000/40,000/50,000; 🖳) Simple but stylish, this yuppie retreat is spotless, with hardwood floors, crisp linens and hand-woven blankets. Guests get free wi-fi and coffee and tea. Breakfast includes homemade bread, cheese, eggs, juice and yogurt.

Hotel Indigo (☎ 418-718; www.indigopatagonia.com; Ladrilleros 105; d/ste CH$97,500/132,500; 🖳) A pampered finale to your trip, with rooftop Jacuzzis and spa and plush rooms with down duvets and candles. Natural materials like eucalyptus and slate meet metal for an ultramodern feel. Service is OK, but the main star is the fjord, which captures your gaze even in the shower.

Other budget options:

Backpacker's Magallania (☎ 414-950; Rodgers 255; dm CH$6000) Bargain bunks with quirky decor.

Los Inmigrantes (☎ 413-482; Carrera Pinto 480; r per person without bathroom CH$7000) Family-run budget accommodations.

Patagonia Aventura (☎ 411-028; Rogers 179; dm CH$7500, d without bathroom CH$18,000) Full-service hostel.

Hostal Natales (☎ 410-081; www.hostelnatales.cl; Ladrilleros 209; dm/d/tr CH$9000/25,000/33,000; 🖳) Newer and stylish but impersonal.

Eating

Abu Gosch (Bulnes 472) Stock up at Natales' largest supermarket before heading out to the park.

Pan Pa Ya (Bories 349; ☻ 9am-8pm) For bread rolls or whole-wheat loaves to take on the trail, a bakery with ultrafresh products.

Patagonia Dulce (www.patagoniadulce.cl; Barros Arana 233; drinks CH$1500; ☻ 9am-8pm) Coffee and chocolate shop.

La Picada de Don Carlitos (Blanco Encalada 444; menú del día CH$2000) Abundant, hearty Chilean fare, like *cazuela de pollo* and mashed potatoes, is served at this down-home eatery. Greasy spoon it may be, but it's bursting with locals at lunchtime.

El Living (www.el-living.com; Prat 156; mains CH$3500; ☻ 11am-11pm Nov–mid-Apr) London lounge with proper vegetarian fare, real coffee and a stream of eclectic tunes. Wine or beer is advised, since

CHILE

the rest – organic salads, burritos and soups – are 100% good for you.

our pick **Afrigonia** (☎ 412-232; Eberhard 343; mains CH$4200) Personal and innovative, this is a true treat destination. Run by a friendly Zambian-Chilean couple, specialties range from ultra-fresh *ceviche* to curried chicken stuffed with spinach and mashed peanuts, served with hot bread and cool mint water.

La Mesita Grande (Prat 196; pizzas CH$5000; ☾ lunch & dinner) Happy diners share one long worn table that is not unlike a post-trek feeding trough, but it's kind of gourmet. The thin-crust pizzas are outstanding, with toppings like arugula and prosciutto or lemon-spiked salmon. Plus there are quality pastas and organic salads from a local greenhouse. Look for local Baguales beer, available on tap.

Mama Rosa's (☎ 418-718; Ladrilleros 105; mains CH$6500-9000) Located in the Indigo hotel, Rosa starts the day with big breakfasts and French pastries and finishes with king crab and local beef. It feels fully Scandinavian – from the blonde wood decor to the views of the fjord. For casual dining, try the first floor lounge.

Asador Patagónico (☎ 413-553; Prat 158; mains CH$8000) Satisfy your mastodon post-trek appetite with flame-seared lamb, steak and salads alongside quality wines.

Drinking

Base Camp (☎ 410-355; Av General Baquedano 719; ☾ 3pm-12am daily) Everyone's favorite expat information hub has added an adjoining space to sip microbrews and tell tall mountain tales.

Shopping

Emporio de la Pampa (Eberhard 302; ☾ 9am-10:30pm Sep-Apr; ☐) A wine-and-cheese shop with goodies galore for the trail.

La Maddera (☎ 413-318, 24hr emergency 099-418-4100; Prat 297; www.lamadderaoutdoor.com; ☾ 8am-11:30pm; ☐) Sells camping gear, including gas for stoves, makes repairs and does guided excursions.

Getting There & Away
BOAT
Weather and tidal conditions affect ferry arrival dates. To confirm travel with Navimag's *Magallanes* (Puerto Montt–Punta Arenas) contact **Turismo Comapa** (☎ 414-300; www.comapa.com; Bulnes 533). See p463 for fare information.

BUS
Puerto Natales has no central bus terminal. Book ahead in high season. Service is limited off-season.

To Torres del Paine, buses leave two to three times daily at around 7am, 8am and 2:30pm. If you're heading to Mountain Lodge Paine Grande in the off-season, take the morning bus to meet the catamaran (one way CH$11,000, two hours).

Companies and destinations include the following:

Bus Sur (☎ 614-221; www.bus-sur.cl; Av General Baquedano 658) Punta Arenas, Torres del Paine, Puerto Montt, El Calafate, Río Turbio & Ushuaia.

Buses Fernández & Pingüino (☎ 411-111; www .busesfernandez.com; cnr Esmeralda & Ramirez) Torres del Paine & Punta Arenas.

Buses Gómez (☎ 411-971; www.busesgomez.com; Prat 234) Torres del Paine.

Buses JB (☎ 412-824; busesjb@hotmail.com; Prat 258) Torres del Paine.

Buses Pacheco (☎ 414-513; www.busespacheco.com; Av General Baquedano 244) To Punta Arenas, Río Grande & Ushuaia.

Cootra (☎ 412-785; Av General Baquedano 456) Goes to El Calafate daily at 7:30am.

Turismo Zaahj (☎ 412-260/355; www.turismozaahj .co.cl; Prat 236/70) Torres del Paine & El Calafate.

BUS FARES		
Destination	**Cost (CH$)**	**Duration (hr)**
El Calafate	11,000	5
Punta Arenas	4000	3
Torres del Paine	8000	2
Ushuaia	28,000	12

Getting Around
Try **Emsa/Avis** (☎ 241-182; Bulnes 632) for car rentals, though rates are better in Punta Arenas.

World's End (Blanco Encalada 226-A) rents bikes.

PARQUE NACIONAL TORRES DEL PAINE
Soaring almost vertically more than 2000m above the Patagonian steppe, the granite pillars of Torres del Paine (Towers of Paine) dominate the landscape of what may be South America's finest national park. A Unesco Biosphere Reserve, the park has 181,000 hectares. Most come for the park's greatest hit but, once here, realize that other (less crowded) attractions offer equal wow power. Bring waterproof gear, a synthetic sleep-

ing bag and, if you're camping, a good tent. Weather can be wild and unpredictable, with sudden rainstorms and knock-down gusts just part of the hearty initiation. Given the high season overcrowding, it's crucial to follow all rules. In 2005 a hiker burned down 10% of the park using a portable stove in windy conditions. Be conscientious and tread lightly – you are one of almost 200,000 yearly guests. For fewer crowds, consider visiting in November or March to April.

Orientation & Information

The park is 112km north of Puerto Natales via a decent gravel road. A new road from Puerto Natales to the *administración* (park headquarters) provides a shorter, more direct southern approach to the park but no public transportation uses it. On the main route, Villa Cerro Castillo has a border crossing into Argentina at Cancha Carrera. The road continues 40km north and west to **Portería Sarmiento** (www.pntp.cl; admission high/low season CH$15,000/5000), where user fees are collected. It's another 37km to the *administración* and the **Conaf Centro de Visitantes** (9am-8pm in summer), with good information on park ecology and trail status. The park is open year-round.

Internet resources include **Torres del Paine** (www.torresdelpaine.com) and **Erratic Rock** (www.erraticrock.com), which has a good backpacker equipment list.

Activities

HIKING

Doing the circuit (the 'W' plus the backside of the peaks) requires seven to nine days, while the 'W' takes four to five. Add one to two days for transportation connections. Most trekkers start either route from Laguna Amarga and head west. You can also hike from the *administración* or take the catamaran from Pudeto to Mountain Lodge Paine Grande and start from there; hiking roughly southwest to northeast along the 'W' presents more views of Los Cuernos. Trekking alone, especially on the backside of the circuit, is inadvisable.

The 'W'

The trail to **Mirador Las Torres** is relatively easy, except for the last hour's boulder scramble. The trail to Refugio Los Cuernos is the windiest along the 'W'. **Valle Frances** is not to be missed, budget time to reach the lookout at Campamento Británico. Valle Frances to

Mountain Lodge Paine Grande can get windy but is relatively easy. The stretch to **Lago Grey** is moderate, with some steep parts. The glacier lookout is another half-hour past the *refugio*.

The Circuit

The landscape along the backside of the peaks is a lot more desolate yet beautiful. Paso John Garner (the most extreme part of the trek) sometimes offers knee-deep mud and snow. There's one *refugio* at Los Perros, the rest is rustic camping. Factor four to six hours between camps.

Other Trails

From *administración*, the three-hour hike to **Mountain Lodge Paine Grande** is an easy, level trail with fantastic views. A truly remote four-hour trail from Guadería Lago Grey follows Río Pingo to the former site of Refugio Zapata. Continue about another 1½ to two hours to a lookout over **Glaciar Zapata**.

GLACIER TREKKING & KAYAKING

Paddle through pristine corners of the park on multiday trips with **Indomita Big Foot** (061-414-525; www.indomitapatagonia.com; Bories 206, Puerto Natales). These aren't budget trips but they can be a lot of fun. Puerto Natales–based **Rutas Patagonia** (see p483) kayaks Lago Grey and Río Grey (half-day CH$40,000). They also offer Glaciar Grey ice treks (CH$70,000) from October to May. Their office by Refugio Grey has drop-in service.

HORSE RIDING

Due to property divisions, horses cannot cross between the western and privately-owned eastern sectors. **Baqueano Zamora** (061-613-531; www.baqueanozamora.com; Av General Baquedano 534, Puerto Natales) runs excursions to Lagos Pingo, Paine and Azul, and Laguna Amarga (half-day with lunch CH$27,500). **Hotel Las Torres** (061-710-050; www.lastorres.com) controls the eastern area of the park and charges CH$35,000 (snack included) for full-day trips around Lago Nordenskjöld and beyond.

Sleeping

Make reservations! Arriving without them, especially in the high season, enslaves you to bringing your own camping gear. Reserve directly through the concessions: **Vertices Patagonia** (061-412-742; www.verticepatagonia.cl) manages Mountain Lodge Paine Grande,

CHILE

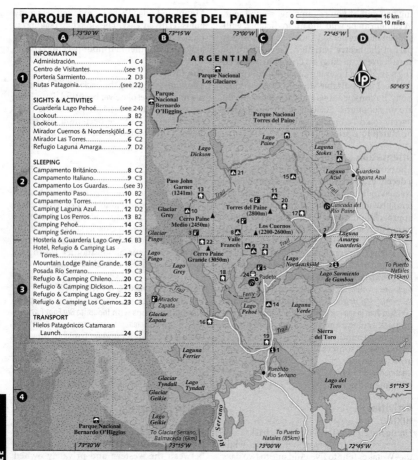

PARQUE NACIONAL TORRES DEL PAINE

0 — 16 km
0 — 10 miles

INFORMATION
Administración............................**1** C4
Centro de Visitantes....................(see **1**)
Portería Sarmiento.....................**2** D3
Rutas Patagonia.........................(see **22**)

SIGHTS & ACTIVITIES
Guardería Lago Pehoé...............(see **24**)
Lookout.....................................**3** B2
Lookout.....................................**4** C2
Mirador Cuernos & Nordenskjöld..**5** C3
Mirador Las Torres......................**6** C2
Refugio Laguna Amarga..............**7** D2

SLEEPING
Campamento Británico................**8** C2
Campamento Italiano..................**9** C3
Campamento Los Guardas........(see **3**)
Campamento Paso......................**10** B2
Campamento Torres...................**11** C2
Camping Laguna Azul.................**12** D2
Camping Los Perros...................**13** B2
Camping Pehoé..........................**14** C3
Camping Serón...........................**15** C2
Hostería & Guardería Lago Grey..**16** B3
Hotel, Refugio & Camping Las
Torres.....................................**17** C2
Mountain Lodge Paine Grande..**18** C3
Posada Río Serrano....................**19** C3
Refugio & Camping Chileno........**20** C2
Refugio & Camping Dickson.......**21** C2
Refugio & Camping Lago Grey....**22** B3
Refugio & Camping Los Cuernos..**23** C3

TRANSPORT
Hielos Patagónicos Catamaran
Launch....................................**24** C3

---

refugios Grey and Dickson and Campamento Perros. **Fantástico Sur** (☎ 061-710-050; www.fantasticosur.com) owns *refugios* Torres, Chileno and Los Cuernos, and Serón and their associated campgrounds.

Bring your passport or a copy for check-in. Staff can radio ahead to confirm your next reservation. Given the huge volume of trekkers, snags are inevitable, so practice your Zen composure.

CAMPING

Camping at the *refugios* costs CH$4000 per site, hot showers included. *Refugios* rent tents (CH$7000 per person), sleeping bags (CH$4500) and mats (CH$1500) – but potential shortages make it prudent to pack

your own gear. Small kiosks sell expensive pasta, soup packets and butane gas. Sites administered by Conaf are free but primitive. Many campers have reported mice in campsites; don't leave food around and *never* leave toilet paper.

REFUGIOS

Refugio rooms have four to eight bunk beds each, kitchen privileges (for lodgers and during specific hours only), hot showers and meals. A bed costs CH$12,500 to CH$17,500, sleeping-bag rental CH$4500 and meals CH$4000 to CH$7500. Should the *refugio* be overbooked, staff provide all necessary camping equipment. Most *refugios* close by the end of April. Mountain Lodge Paine Grande is the

---

EXPLORE PARQUE NACIONAL BERNARDO O'HIGGINS

There is no tourist trail. Encompassing the grandest of glaciers, this **park** is only accessible by boat. **Turismo 21 de Mayo** (☎ 061-411-978; www.turismo21demayo.cl; Eberhard 560, Puerto Natales) offers a full-day boat excursion (CH$60,000 with lunch) to the base of Glaciar Serrano. Or you can continue to Torres del Paine via Zodiac raft (CH$85,000), stopping for lunch at Estancia Balmaceda (included), with spectacular views of the Southern Ice Field and native forest.

---

only one that stays open year-round, but it has very limited operations.

Getting There & Away

For transportation to the park, see p484 in Puerto Natales.

Buses stop at Laguna Amarga, the catamaran launch at Pudeto and at park headquarters. Catamaran **Hielos Patagónicos** (one-way/round-trip per person CH$11,000/18,000) goes to Mountain Lodge Paine Grande at 9:30am, noon and 6pm December to mid-March, noon and 6pm in late March and November. Another launch travels Lago Grey (CH$40,000 round-trip, 1½ to two hours) between **Hostería Lago Grey** (☎ 061-712-100; www.lagogrey.cl) and Refugio Lago Grey twice daily; contact the *hostería* for schedules.

TIERRA DEL FUEGO

Foggy, windy and wet, Chile's slice of Tierra del Fuego includes half of the main island of Isla Grande, the far-flung Isla Navarino and a group of smaller islands, many of them uninhabited. Only home to 7000 Chileans, this is the least populated region in Chile. Porvenir is considered the main city, though even that status could be considered an overstatement. These parts can't help but exude a rough and rugged charm and those willing to venture this far can relish its end-of-the-world emptiness.

Isla Navarino

Forget Ushuaia – the end of the world starts where yachts roam Main St and yachts rounding Cape Horn take refuge. With more than 150km of trails, Isla Navarino is a rugged backpackers' paradise, with remote slate-colored lakes, mossy *lenga* forests and the ragged spires of the **Dientes de Navarino**. Some 40,000 beavers introduced from Canada in the 1940s now plague the island; they're even on the menu. The only town, **Puerto Williams** (population 2500), is a naval settlement, official port of entry for vessels en route to Cape Horn and Antarctica, and home to the last living Yagan speaker.

SIGHTS & ACTIVITIES

The island has fabulous trekking. Day hike to **Cerro Bandera** for expansive views of the Beagle Channel. The trail starts at the Navarino trailhead, ascending steeply through *lenga* to blustery stone-littered hilltops. Self-supported backpackers continue on for the five-day, 53.5km **Circuito Dientes de Navarino**, with raw and windswept vistas under Navarino's toothy spires.

For guided fishing and hiking, contact **Turismo Shila** (☎ 621-745; www.truismoshila.cl; Plaza de Ancla s/n; 9am-1pm, 3-7pm). The small kiosk stocks basic hiking maps and gas for camp stoves. You can also rent camping gear and bikes (CH$5000 per day) here. Multilingual guiding is available from recommended **Fuegia & Co** (☎ 621-251; fuegia@usa.net; Ortiz 049).

The gorgeous **Museo Martín Gusinde** (☎ 621-043; cnr Araguay & Gusinde; donation requested; 9am-1pm & 2:30-7pm Mon-Fri, 2:30-6:30pm Sat & Sun) explores the Yaghan legacy and has a stylish cafe and internet center.

SLEEPING & EATING

Sur Sur Hostel (☎ 621-849; sursur.turismo@gmail.com; Maragano s/n; dm CH$8000, d CH$30,000-40,000) has fair lodgings, and its gregarious Argentine owner Gustavo is eager to please. The bright hostel **Refugio El Padrino** (☎ 621-136; ceciliamancillao@yahoo .com.ar; Costanera 267; dm CH$10,000) sits right on the channel with an outdoor deck. The recommended **Residencial Pusaki** (☎ 621-116; pattypusaki @yahoo.es; Piloto Pardo 260; s/d CH$10,500/21,000) welcomes travelers with comfortable rooms, memorable meals (reserve ahead) by the dynamic Patty.

Provisions can be bought at various mini-markets in Puerto Williams, although prices are high. Bonhomie abounds at **Angelus** (☎ 621-080; Centro Comercial 151; closed Sun) a buzzing pub serving homemade pies and yummy crab pasta. The bar at the legendary **Club de Yates Micalvi**, a former German artillery vessel at the docks, comes alive after 9pm.

CHILE

DETOUR TO PORVENIR

For a slice of home-baked Fuegian life, this is it. Spending a night in this rusted village of metal-clad Victorians affords you an opportunity to explore the nearby bays and countryside and absorb the laid-back local life. **Cordillera Darwin Expediciones** (☎ 580-167, 099-888-6380; www.cordilleradarwin.com; Bahía Chilota s/n at Ferry) visits Peale's dolphins in a traditional Chilote-style fishing boat (CH$15,000 including meals). **Hotel Central** (☎ 580-077; Philippi 298; s/d incl breakfast CH$12,000/20,000) has snug rooms. For ferry information, see p481.

GETTING THERE & AWAY

Aerovías DAP (☎ 621-051; www.dap.cl; Plaza de Ancla s/n) flies to Punta Arenas (one way CH$55,000). **Aeroclub Ushuaia** (in Ushuaia ☎ 54-02901-421717; www.aeroclubushuaia.org.ar) flies to Puerto Williams from Ushuaia (one way US$120) three mornings per week.

Transbordadora Austral Broom (www.tabsa.cl) sails from Puerto Williams to Punta Arenas two or three times a month on Fridays (reclining seat/bunk CH$95,000/115,000 including meals, 38 hours).

Ushuaia Boating (☎ 061-621227, 098-269-5812; Maragano 168; one way CH$87,000) has boats to Ushuaia daily from September to March. Zodiac boats take 40 minutes but a bus (included) first transfers passengers to Puerto Navarino (1½ hours). Reserve at Angelus.

ISLA ROBINSON CRUSOE

Castaway Alexander Selkirk, the inspiration for Robinson Crusoe, spent long years on this craggy Pacific outpost. A chain of small volcanic islands, 667km east of Valparaíso, Archipiélago Juan Fernández once served as a waypoint for pirates, sealers and war ships. In modern times it has slid into anonymity. Strange, because the mysteries, jagged landscape and clear waters fall nothing short of spectacular.

A Unesco World Biosphere Reserve and national park since 1935, the island features a temperate climate and extraordinary vegetation with affinities ranging from Andean to Hawaiian. Endemic plants have suffered greatly from the introduction of mainland species, including the goats that Selkirk

supped on. Juan Fernández fur seals, nearly extinct a century ago, are repopulating. Birders look for the rare Juan Fernández hummingbird; the male is a garish red.

SAN JUAN BAUTISTA

☎ 032 / pop 600

Sheltered by steep peaks and surrounded by horse pastures, the lobster-fishing community of San Juan Bautista overlooks Bahía Cumberland. The island's sole town, it's the proverbial sleepy fishing village, down to the lobstermen in knitted caps and dusty stores that run out of cheese and beer before the provisions ship arrives. There are no ATMs or money changers, so bring cash from the mainland, preferably in small bills. **Centro Información Turista** (Vicente González) is at the top of Vicente González, 500m inland from the *costanera* (seaside road). Run by Conaf, it also has a list of registered guides and tour schedules.

Sights & Activities

Nautical lore starts at the **cementerio** near the lighthouse, where a polyglot assortment of Spanish, French and German inhabitants are buried, including the survivors of the WWI battleship *Dresden*. **Cuevas de los Patriotas** are the damp caverns where 40-plus patriots lived imprisoned for several years after a defeat at Rancagua in 1814. Directly above the caves, **Fuerte Santa Bárbara**, was built by the Spaniards in 1749 to discourage pirate raids. The fantastic island-wide **national park** (7-day admission CH$3000) offers excellent hiking. A 3km trail leads to **Mirador de Selkirk**, a spectacular panoramic viewpoint. The trail continues south, taking one hour to reach **Villagra** (4.8km) and skirts the cliffs to **Punta La Isla** (13km). Both areas have camping. On the way you'll pass **Bahía Tierras Blancas**, the island's main breeding colony of Juan Fernández fur seals. Some trails have restricted access and require guides, ask at the information center. Snorkeling with fur seals and scuba diving are other popular activities.

Sleeping & Eating

Most *hospedajes* cook for guests because restaurants are only sporadically open.

Residencial Mirador de Selkirk (☎ 275-1028; Pasaje del Castillo 251; r per person without bathroom CH$25,000) High on the hillside, this family home has three snug rooms and a sprawling deck. Don't miss Señora Julia's fantastic lobster empanadas or seafood *parol* (stew; CH$5000).

CHILE

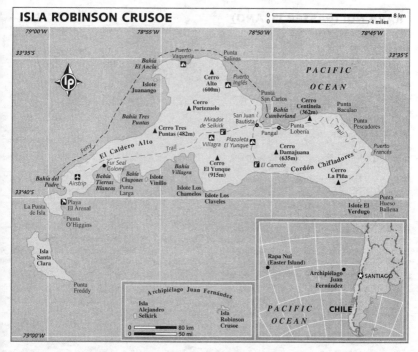

ISLA ROBINSON CRUSOE

our pick Hostal Club Pez Volador (☎ 275-1227; fabianapersia@endemica.com; Alcalde 399B; s/d CH$35,000/70,000; 🖳) Modern and chic, this B&B has happy vibes, thanks to its great hosts. Bright colors punctuate ample, spiffy rooms but best of all, its clubhouse atmosphere makes it a fun base camp, right on the water. The owners also run Endémica, a respected scuba diving and adventure outfitter.

Cumberland Restaurant (☎ 275-1030; Alcalde s/n; mains CH$4000; ⏲ lunch & dinner, closed Mon) Tasty fish sandwiches, grilled snapper and steak and salad are staples at this family spot.

Getting There & Away

Flights take roughly two hours and accept 10kg of luggage per person. Allow for an extra two or three days' stay when poor weather makes take-offs risky.

Lassa (☎ 02-273-4354; lassa@entelchile.net; Av Larraín 7941) runs flights in a 19-seat Twin Otter (round trip CH$400,000, two hours), which departs mornings. Flight payments can be made directly at Aeródromo Tobalaba upon departure.

Naval supply ships sail to the island about six times annually. A no-frills trip costs CH$8500 per day. To apply, passengers must write a letter to the Navy, **Armada de Chile: Comando de Transporte** (☎ 032-2506-354; Primera Zona Naval, Prat 620, Valparaíso), one month in advance. Call for details.

RAPA NUI (EASTER ISLAND)

Far from continents, this isolated world is a treasure trove of archaeology whose mysteries resist easy explanation. The enigmatic *moai* (huge statues) overshadow the island's subtler assets like crystalline surf, wild horses and grass-sculpted landscapes. Known as *Te Pito o Te Henua* (the Navel of the World) by its inhabitants, tiny Polynesian Rapa Nui (117 sq km) is a distant but worthwhile leap for South American travelers.

Dutch admiral Roddeveen landed here on Easter Sunday, 1722, creating the name. The island became Chilean territory in 1888,

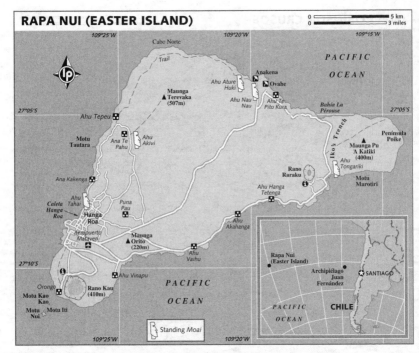

RAPA NUI (EASTER ISLAND)

though it was run as a sheep estancia, confining indigenous Rapa Nui to Hanga Roa until 1953. Finally in the 1960s they regained access. Today's islanders speak Rapa Nui, an eastern Polynesian dialect related to Cook Islands' Maori, and Spanish. Essential expressions include *iorana* (hello), *maururu* (thank you), *pehe koe* (how are you?) and *riva riva* (fine, good).

Each February island culture is celebrated in the elaborate and colorful **Tapati Rapa Nui festival**. Peak tourist season coincides with the hottest months from January to March, off-season is comparatively quiet. Allow at least three days to see the major sites. Rapa Nui is two hours behind mainland Chile, six hours behind GMT (five in summer).

HANGA ROA
☎ 032 / pop 4400

Blue skies and peaceful, meandering streets paint the unhurried appeal of Hanga Roa. While packed with tourists in high season, the pace is still leisurely. North–south Av Atamu Tekena is the main road, with a supermarket, shops, a crafts market and restaurants. Policarpo Toro sits just below along the waterfront. East–west Av Te Pito o Te Henua connects Caleta Hanga Roa, a small bay and fishing port, to the church.

Information
Lodgings provide laundry service.

Banco del Estado (☎ 210-0221; Av Pont s/n; 8am-1pm Mon-Fri) Changes US dollars and euros. MasterCard-only ATM.

Banco Santander (Policarpo Toro s/n; 8am-1pm Mon-Fri) 24-hour Visa-compatible ATM.

Hospital Hanga Roa (☎ 210-0215; Av Simon Paoa s/n)

Post office (Av Te Pito o Te Henua) Half a block from Caleta Hanga Roa.

Sernatur (☎ 210-0255; ipascua@sernatur.cl; Tu'u Maheke s/n; 8:30am-5:30pm Mon-Fri) Distributes basic maps of the island.

Taim@net (Av Atamu Tekena s/n; per hr CH$1600; 10am-10pm) Internet cafe and call center.

Dangers & Annoyances
Leave valuables locked at your lodgings. Protective clothing, sunblock, sunglasses and water are essential for the strong sun.

Sights & Activities

Rapa Nui 101 for new arrivals, **Museo Antropológico Sebastián Englert** (☎ 255-1020; www.museorapanui.cl; Sector Tahai; admission CH$1000; ☻ 9:30am-12:30pm & 2-5:30pm Tue-Fri, 9:30am-12:30pm Sat & Sun), north of town, displays *moai kavakava* (literally 'statues of ribs') and replica *rongo-rongo* tablets. Intricate wood carvings at **Iglesia Hanga Roa**, the island's Catholic church, fuse Rapa Nui tradition with Christian doctrine. It's worth attending the 9am Sunday service spoken in Rapa Nui.

Dive enthusiasts can head to **Orca** (☎ 255-0375; www.seemorca.cl; Caleta Hanga Roa s/n; ☻ Mon-Sat) for dives (CH$25,000) or snorkel trips to Motu Nui (CH$15,000 per person, minimum four). **Hare Orca** (☎ 255-0375; Caleta Hanga Roa s/n) rents body boards and surfboards (half-day CH$10,000).

Myriad operators tour the island's main sites for CH$30,000 per day, such as **Kia Koe Tour** (☎ 210-0852; www.kiakoetour.cl; Av Atamu Tekena s/n) and **Haumaka Tours** (☎ 210-0274; www.haumakatours .com; cnr Avs Atamu Tekena & Hotu Matua).

Sleeping

Book well ahead for high season. Lodgings usually provide transport from the airport.

Camping Mihinoa (☎ 255-1593; www.mihinoa.com; Av Pont s/n; campsite per person CH$4500, dm CH$7000, d CH$18,000-20,000, without bathroom CH$8000; ▯) With a fun backpacker ambience, grassy grounds, friendly attention and views of crashing surf, it's a pleasant 10-minute walk from town. Though shadeless, perks include kitchen use and bike, car and tent hire (CH$1000).

Residencial Apina Tupuna (☎ 210-0763; www.apinatupuna.com; Av Apina s/n; campsite per person CH$4500, r per person/student CH$15,000/10,000, d/tr CH$25,000/35,000) Basic but clean, this is a cast-iron bargain for budget travelers, but bungalows are worth the splurge. Campers can pitch their own tent.

Chez Cecilia (☎ 210-499; www.rapanuichezcecilia.com; Atama Tekena s/n; campsite per person CH$4500, s/d with breakfast CH$24,000/36,000, 2-person cabañas CH$30,000) Welcoming, with a variety of clean, no-frills rooms and cabins without kitchens, near Ahu Tongariki.

Te Ora (☎ 255-1038; www.rapanuiteora.com; Av Apina s/n; r CH$35,000-55,000; ▯) This snug B&B seduces with crisp tiled rooms opening onto a flourishing courtyard. Canadian host Sharon provides gracious assistance. No breakfast, but there's a communal kitchen and wi-fi.

Sunset Cottages (☎ 255-2171; www.rapanuisunset.cl; Petero Atamu; s/d/tr cabañas with breakfast CH$40,000/60,000/90,000) Four spotless, tasteful cabins with a grassy lawn, air-conditioning, TV and frigobar. Run by China, a well-regarded English-speaking tour guide.

Eating

Provisions are expensive; consider bringing some from the mainland. Av Atamu Tekena has small markets. Food carts, also on Av Policarpo Toro, serve delicious cheese and tuna empanadas (CH$2500) and cheap, filling meals.

Mikafé (☎ 255-1059; Caleta Hanga Roa s/n; cones CH$1500; ☻ 9am-8pm) Luxuriant homemade ice cream and real coffee.

Kona Yoga (☎ 255-1524; Av Pont s/n; mains CH$3000-10,000; ☻ 1-9pm) In addition to yoga, Kona offers innovative vegetarian fare, a sunny ambience and fresh fixings from the garden.

Au Bout du Monde (☎ 255-2060; Av Policarpo Toro s/n; mains CH$9000-15,000; ☻ lunch & dinner Wed-Mon) The plantain crisps, curry and ginger prawns make splurging worthwhile at this ambitious French restaurant with deck dining.

Drinking

Av Atamu Tekena is the main hotspot, with pleasant restaurants and cafes with live music in summer, including **Te Moana** (Av Atamu Tekena s/n; ☻ Mon-Sat 11am-late). Further south, **Aloha Pub-Restaurant** (Av Atamu Tekena s/n; ☻ Mon-Sat 6pm-late) has excellent *pisco sours* and tapas.

Entertainment

Groove alongside locals at disco **Topa Tangi Pub** (Av Atamu Tekena s/n; ☻ Wed-Sat 6pm-late), which is packed after midnight playing live island sounds and modern tunes.

PARQUE NACIONAL RAPA NUI

Teeming with caves, *ahu* (stone platforms), fallen *moai* and petroglyphs, this **national park** (admission CH$5000) encompasses much of Rapa Nui and all the archaeological sites. The admission fee is charged in Orongo and Rano Raraku. Respect the sites: walking on the *ahu* and removing or relocating rocks of archaeological structures are strictly taboo. Handle the land gently and the *moai* will smile upon you.

Near Hanga Roa, **Ahu Tahai** is a short hike north of town, lovely at sunset, with three restored *ahu*. Four kilometers north of Tahai, **Ahu Tepeu** has several fallen *moai* and a village site. On the nearby coast, **Ana Kakenga** has two

CHILE

windows open to the ocean. **Ahu Akivi** is the site of seven *moai*, unique because they face the sea but like all *moai* they overlook the site of a village. At the equinoxes their gaze meets the setting sun.

With white sands, clear water and leggy palms, Anakena beach is a stunning destination that abuts two major archaeological sites: **Ahu Nau Nau** and **Ahu Ature Huki**, the latter re-erected by Thor Heyerdahl and a dozen islanders.

Dazzling in scale, **Ahu Tongariki** has 15 *moai* along the largest *ahu* built against the crashing surf. A 1960 tsunami demolished several *moai* and scattered topknots, but the Japanese company Tadano re-erected *moai* in the early 1990s.

An ethereal setting of half-carved and buried *moai*, **Rano Raraku** is known as 'the nursery,' where *moai* were quarried from the slopes of this extinct volcano. It's worth a wander through the rocky jigsaw patterns of unfinished *moai*. There are 600, with the largest 21m tall. The crater holds a reedy lake under an amphitheater of handsome heads.

Visitors shouldn't miss **Rano Kau** and its crater lake, a cauldron of *tortora* reeds. Along a sea cliff 400m above, the fragile **Orongo Ceremonial Village** (admission CH$5000) is where bird-cult rituals were performed. A cluster of boulders with petroglyphs depict Tangata Manu (the birdman) and Make Make (their god). Walking (7km) or biking is possible, take water.

GETTING THERE & AWAY

LAN (☎ 210-0920; Av Atamu Tekena s/n; ✆ 9am-4:30pm Mon-Fri, to 12:30pm Sat), near Av Pont, is the only airline serving Rapa Nui, going almost daily to and from Santiago (US$500 to $900) and twice weekly to and from Papeete (Tahiti). Flights overbook, so reconfirm your ticket two days before departure. It's not uncommon for your luggage to arrive one day late.

GETTING AROUND

Taxis cost a flat CH$1500 for most trips around town.

Some hotels rent 4WDs (eight-hour day CH$25,000 to CH$45,000) or try **Rent a Car Insular** (☎ 210-0480; Av Atamu Tekena s/n), also offering scooters and motorcycles (per day from CH$25,000). **Makemake Rentabike** (☎ 210-0580; www.makemakerapanui.com; Av Atamu Tekena s/n; ✆ 9am-1pm & 4-8pm) rents sturdy mountain bikes (full day CH$10,000).

CHILE DIRECTORY

ACCOMMODATIONS

Vacation destinations book quickly during high season, so reserve ahead. Summer and holiday weekends, prices spike 10% to 20%. Sernatur and most municipal tourist offices have lists of licenced budget lodgings. The local affiliate of HI is **Asociación Chilena de Albergues Turísticos Juveniles** (☎ 02-411-2050; www.hostelling.cl; Hernando de Aguirre 201, Oficina 602, Providencia, Santiago). One-year membership cards cost CH$14,000/16,000 for under/over 30s.

Independent backpacker hostels are increasingly joining forces to advertise. Look for pamphlets for **Backpackers Chile** (www.backpackerschile.com), with many European-run listings, or **Backpacker's Best of Chile** (www.backpackersbest.cl). Especially in the Lakes District, family homes offer inexpensive rooms, most often with kitchen privileges, hot showers and breakfast. Most accommodations include breakfast, though it is usually just bread and instant coffee. Hotels often include the 18% IVA (*impuesto de valor agregado;* value-added tax) in the price, which foreign travelers are not obligated to pay. Try to settle this matter before taking a room.

The best camping resource is Turistel's *Rutero Camping* guide. Most organized campgrounds are large sites with bathrooms, fire pits and a restaurant or snack bar. Rates seem costly as they are set for groups. Try asking for per person rates. Remote areas may offer free camping without facilities. Camping gas, known as *vencina blanca*, is carried in *ferreterias* (hardware stores).

ACTIVITIES

Chile is paradise for the active. First on everyone's list is trekking, with Torres del Paine (p484) topping the list. Areas around Parinacota and Lago Chungara (p435), Parque Pumalín (p469), Nahuelbuta (p444), Puyehue (p456), Cochamó Valley (p461) and Isla Navarino (p487) are other favorites. Trails in many parks are not well marked or maintained. Some are simply old cattle roads. The government-funded **Sendero de Chile** (www.senderodechile.cl) links a network of trails north to south. For those going climbing, get permission to scale peaks on the border (Ojos de Salado) from Chile's **Dirección de Fronteras y Límites** (Difrol; ☎ 671-2725; Teatinos 180, 7th fl, Santiago).

Surfing breaks run up and down the coast of Middle and Northern Chile. Iquique also has South America's best conditions for paragliding (p428) and landsailing.

Rafting or kayaking is world-class here. Most popular is Río Futaleufú (p470), but don't overlook the Liucura and Trancura outside Pucón (p448), or the Petrohué near Puerto Varas (p457). For sea kayaking, head to Chiloé (p464) and the fjords around Parque Pumalín (p469).

Great mountain-biking destinations include around San Pedro de Atacama (p421), around Lago Llanquihue (p460) and Ojos de Caburgua (p448). On the Carretera Austral, two-wheeled travelers face rock spray from cars, summer *tábanos* (horseflies) and fierce winds in the far south. Most towns in Chile have a repair shop.

Multiday horse-riding trips access Andean terrain you can't get to otherwise. Try Pucón (p449), Río Puelo Valley (p461), Puyehue (p456) and around Torres del Paine (p485).

The skiing season runs from June to October. Santiago has some rental shops, and resorts rent full packages. Head out to Volcán Villarrica (p452), Chillán (p439) or the major resorts near Santiago (p399).

Hedonists prefer soaking in therapeutic hot springs. With volcanic activity along Chile's entire spine, hot springs run the gamut from the humble find-your-own to fancy spas with fluffy towels. Try Puritama (p421) outside San Pedro de Atacama, Los Pozones (p451), by Pucón, or Puyehue (p456). Another fun detour, wine tasting can be done in the vineyards of Middle Chile (p436) and around Santiago (p399).

BOOKS

Lonely Planet's *Chile & Easter Island* provides more detailed travel information and *Trekking in the Patagonian Andes* provides details on hikes in Southern Chile and Argentina. Chile's *Turistel* road guides are very helpful. Good travel companions include Che's *Motorcycle Diaries,* Charles Darwin's *Voyage of the Beagle,* Ariel Dorfman's *Desert Memories* and Nick Reding's *The Last Cowboys at the End of the World.* In fiction, read Francisco Coloane's *Cape Horn and Other Stories* and the anthology *Chile: A Traveler's Literary Companion* (ed Katherine Silver). Fans of verse should grab a copy of *The Essential Neruda: Selected Poems* by Pablo Neruda edited by Mark Eisner.

BUSINESS HOURS

Shop hours run roughly from 10am to 8pm, often closing for lunch between 1pm to 3:30pm. Government offices and businesses open weekdays from 9am to 6pm. Banks are open 9am to 2pm weekdays. Tourist offices keep long hours daily in summer. Most restaurants and services are closed on Sunday. Museums are often closed Monday. Restaurant hours vary widely, but most open from noon till 11pm. Few open for breakfast and most close for the lull between lunch and dinner.

CLIMATE

Northern Chile has good weather year-round but warm clothes are necessary even in summer for foggy mornings and high-altitude destinations. Rain in January and February may make some off-road travel difficult.

Santiago and Middle Chile are best from September to April, particularly during the autumn wine harvest, but avoid Santiago from December through February, when it is unbearably hot and smoggy.

Head to the Lakes District and Patagonia from October through April – but be prepared for rain. Windy conditions rule the far south, where ozone problems make sun protection absolutely essential.

Throughout Chile, mid-December to mid-March marks the high season, with higher prices, crowded lodgings, and overbooked flights and buses.

The South America Directory (p984) has more information and climate charts.

DANGERS & ANNOYANCES

Compared with other South American countries, Chile is remarkably safe. Still, watch out for petty thievery in larger cities and bus terminals (*custodias* are a secure place to leave bags). Thefts are high in beach resorts and the port area of Valparaíso. Photographing military installations is strictly prohibited. Natural dangers include earthquakes and strong offshore currents. When swimming, look for signs '*apta para bañar*' (swimming OK) and '*no apta para bañar*' (no swimming). Chile's canine gangs will follow you everywhere, but are usually harmless.

ELECTRICITY

Chile operates on 220 volts at 50 cycles. Two and three rounded prongs are used.

CHILE

EMBASSIES & CONSULATES

For information on visas, see p497.

Argentina Antofagasta (☎ 055-220-440; Blanco Encalada 1933); Puerto Montt (Map p462; ☎ 065-253-996; Cauquenes 94, 2nd fl); Punta Arenas (off Map p479; ☎ 061-261-912; 21 de Mayo 1878); Santiago (Map pp392-3; ☎ 02-582-2606; www.embargentina.cl; Vicuña Mackenna 41, Centro)

Australia (☎ 02-500-3500; consular.santiago@dfat.gov.au; Goyenechea 3621, 12th fl, Las Condes, Santiago)

Bolivia Antofagasta (☎ 055-259-008; Washington 2675); Arica (Map p431; ☎ 058-231-030; www.rree.gov.bo; Lynch 298); Calama (☎ 055-341-976; Latorre 1395); Iquique (Map p426; ☎ 057-421-777; Gorostiaga 215, Dept E); Santiago (☎ 02-232-8180; cgbolivia@manquehue.net; Av Santa María 2796, Las Condes)

Brazil Santiago (Map pp392-3; ☎ 02-698-2486; www.embajadadebrasil.cl; Ovalle 1665, Centro)

Canada (☎ 02-362-9660; enqserv@dfait-maeci.gc.ca; Tajamar 481, 12th fl, Las Condes, Santiago)

France (☎ 02-470-8000; www.france.cl; Av Condell 65, Providencia, Santiago)

Germany Arica (Map p431; ☎ 058-231-657; Prat 391, 10th fl, Oficina 101); Santiago (☎ 02-463-2500; www.embajadadealemania.cl; Las Hualtatas 5677, Vitacura)

Ireland (☎ 02-245-6616; Goyenechea 3162, Oficina 801; Las Condes, Santiago)

Israel (☎ 02-750-0500; San Sebastián 2812, 5th fl, Las Condes, Santiago)

Netherlands Punta Arenas (Map p479; ☎ 061-248-100; Sarmiento 780); Santiago (☎ 02-756-9200; www.holanda-paisesbajos.cl; Las Violetas 2368, Providencia)

New Zealand (☎ 02-290-9802; embajada@nzembassy.cl; El Golf 99, Oficina 703, Las Condes, Santiago)

Peru Arica (Map p431; ☎ 058-231-020; 18 de Septiembre 1554); Iquique (Map p426; ☎ 057-411-466; Zegers 570, 2nd fl); Santiago (☎ 02-235-4600; conpersantiago@adsl.tie.cl; Padre Mariano 10, Oficina 309, Providencia)

UK Punta Arenas (off Map p479; ☎ 061-211-535; Catarata del Niágara 01325); Santiago (☎ 02-370-4100; consular.santiago@fco.gov.uk; Av El Bosque Norte 0125, 3rd fl, Las Condes); Valparaíso (☎ 032-221-3063; Blanco 1199, 5th fl; ⏰ 10:30am-1pm)

USA (☎ 02-232-2600; santiago.usembassy.gov; Av Andrés Bello 2800, Las Condes, Santiago)

FESTIVALS & EVENTS

In January and February every Chilean locality puts on a show with live music, special feasts and fireworks; get calendars at tourist offices. Other festivities include religious holidays and Fiestas Patrias, around September 18.

Festival Costumbrista These typical fiestas take place all over. For an authentic Patagonian rodeo, go to Villa Cerro Castillo.

Festival de la Virgen del Carmen Some 40,000 pilgrims pay homage to Chile's virgin in Tirana in mid-July, with lots of street dancing and masks.

FOOD & DRINK

Eating reviews throughout this chapter are given in order of budget, with the least expensive options first.

Chilean Cuisine

Chile's best offerings are its raw materials: in the market you can get anything from goat cheese to avocados, fresh herbs and a fantastic variety of seafood. What Chilean cuisine lacks in spice and variety it makes up for in abundance. Breakfast tends toward meager with instant coffee or tea, rolls and jam. At lunch, fuel up with a hearty *menú del día* (inexpensive set meal) with soup, a main dish of fish or meat with a starch and vegetables. Central markets and *casinos de bomberos* (firefighters' restaurants) offer cheap meals. Snacks include the prolific *completo* (hot dog with mayo, avocado, tomato and ketchup) and *humitas* (corn dumplings). Empanadas are whopping and either fried, with cheese or shellfish, or *al horno* (baked) with beef they're called *pino*.

To add spice, pick up a bottle of *ají chileno*. A melted ham-and-cheese sandwich is a *barros jarpa*, with steak it's a *barros luco*, while beefsteak and green beans make a *chacarrero*. *Lomo a lo pobre* is steak topped with fried eggs and french fries. The heart-choking *chorrillana* platters include fries, onions, fried eggs and beef. Seafood is abundant and incredible. *Caldillo de…* is a hearty fish soup with lemon, cilantro and garlic. *Chupe de…* is seafood baked in a medley of butter, bread crumbs and cheese. *Paila marina* is a fish and shellfish chowder.

Southerners eat a lot of potatoes, as well as summertime lamb roasted on a spit *(asado de cordero)*. German influence means teatime includes *küchen* (fruit cakes and pies). In Chiloé look for *milcao* (potato dumplings) and *curanto*, which combines fish, shellfish, chicken, pork, lamb, beef and potato in a heaping bowl fit for two.

Drinks

Chile produces over 700 million liters of wine annually, don't miss your share. Carmenere is wonderful and unique to Chile (a phylloxera plague extinguished the variety in Europe). Cabernet sauvignon and syrah are other good bets. Decent bottles start at CH$2500.

Chile and Peru both claim authorship of the divine *pisco sour*, fresh lime mixed with grape brandy and powdered sugar. *Pisco* and Coke is a *piscola*, or *combinado* with any soft drink. In the south, tap water is safe. *Bebidas* (soft drinks, like the ultrasugary Bilz and the unfortunately named Pap, are adored). Street vendors sell *mote con huesillo*, a refreshing peach nectar made with barley and peaches.

Instant Nescafé is a national plague. Entrepreneurial would-be expats could start up more espresso bars. Maté is consumed heavily in Patagonia. *Yuyos* (herbal teas) are very common.

Kunstmann and Cólonos are Chile's best beers. A draft beer is called *schop*.

GAY & LESBIAN TRAVELERS

Chile is still a conservative, Catholic-minded country unaccepting of homosexuality; however, younger generations are more progressive. Santiago's gay scene, which had been underground for so long, is quite happening these days, with most gay bars and nightclubs in Barrio Bellavista.

Gay Chile (www.gaychile.com) has current events, Santiago nightlife, lodging recommendations, legal and medical advice and personals. Chile's first gay magazine, **Opus Gay** (www.opusgay.cl) puns with the ultra-conservative Catholic Opus Dei group. Chile's main gay-rights organization is **Movimiento Unificado de Minorías Sexuales** (MUMS; www.orgullogay.cl).

HEALTH

Public hospitals in Chile are reasonable but private *clínicas* are your best option. Outside of the Atacama Desert and Santiago, tap water is safe to drink. Altitude sickness and dehydration are the most common concerns in the north, and sunburn in the ozone-depleted south – apply sunscreen and wear sunglasses. Chile does not require vaccinations, but Rapa Nui may have restrictions or documentation requirements; check first. For more information, see the Health chapter (p984).

HOLIDAYS

Government offices and businesses close on the following national holidays:

Año Nuevo (New Year's Day) January 1
Semana Santa (Easter Week) March/April, dates vary
Día del Trabajador (Labor Day) May 1
Glorias Navales (Naval Battle of Iquique) May 21
Corpus Christi May/June; dates vary
San Pedro y San Pablo (St Peter's & St Paul's Day) June 29
Asunción de la Virgen (Assumption) August 15
Día de Unidad Nacional (Day of National Unity) first Monday of September
Día de la Independencia Nacional (Independence Day) September 18
Día del Ejército (Armed Forces Day) September 19
Día de la Raza (Columbus Day) October 12
Todos los Santos (All Saints' Day) November 1
Inmaculada Concepción (Immaculate Conception Day) December 8
Navidad (Christmas Day) December 25

INTERNET ACCESS

Most regions have excellent internet connections, wi-fi access and reasonable prices. Rates range from CH$400 to CH$2000 per hour.

INTERNET RESOURCES

Chile Information Project (www.chip.cl) Umbrella for English-language *Santiago Times;* discusses everything from human rights to souvenirs.
Chiloé (www.chiloeweb.com) Terrific information on the island of Chiloé.
Go Chile (www.gochile.cl) General tourist information.
Interpatagonia (www.interpatagonia.com) All things touristy in Patagonia.
Latin American Network Information Center (www.lanic.utexas.edu/la/chile) Links to Chilean government, politics, culture, environment and more.
Lonely Planet (www.lonelyplanet.com) Has travel news and tips, and you can interrogate fellow travelers on the Thorn Tree bulletin board.
Sernatur (www.visitchile.org or www.sernatur.cl) The national tourism organization in French, Spanish or English.

MAPS

In Santiago, the **Instituto Geográfico Militar** (Map pp392-3; ☎ 02-460-6800; www.igm.cl; Dieciocho 369, Centro; 🕑 9am-5:30pm Mon-Fri), near Toesca metro station, sells 1:50,000 regional topo maps for around CH$8600, or buy them online. These are the best maps for hikers, though some are outdated. Conaf in Santiago allows photocopying of national park maps. JLM Mapas publishes regional and trekking maps at scales ranging from 1:50,000 to 1:500,000. While helpful, they don't claim 100% accuracy.

Santiago maps are available on **Map City** (www.mapcity.cl). Some local government websites have interactive maps with search capabilities. If driving, invest in a current *Turistel* (in Spanish), an indispensable road guide with separate editions for north, central and southern regions.

MEDIA

El Mercurio (www.elmercurio.cl), Chile's oldest conservative daily is matched by the more left-leaning **La Tercera** (www.latercera.cl). English-language **Santiago Times** (www.santiagotimes.cl) translates Spanish headlines and has environmental news. Lampoon periodical **The Clinic** (www.theclinic.cl) provides cutting-edge editorials and satire about politics and Chilean society.

Chilean TV embraces vapid gossip and talent shows. Rural areas without phone service (mostly in Patagonia and the Chiloé islands) are dependent on radio broadcasting messages for communication.

MONEY

The Chilean unit of currency is the peso (CH$). Bank notes come in denominations of 500, 1000, 2000, 5000, 10,000 and 20,000 pesos. Coin values are 1, 5, 10, 50, 100 and 500 pesos. It can be difficult to change bills larger than CH$5000 in rural areas. Solicit change with an apologetic face and the words '¿Tiene suelto?' (Do you have change?).

Santiago has the best exchange rates and a ready market for European currencies. Chile's currency has been stable in recent years, with the value of the dollar lower during peak tourist season. It's best to pay all transactions in pesos. US cash may be acceptable at some tour agencies or top-end hotels (check their exchange rate carefully).

Money cables should arrive in a few days. Chilean banks can exchange for US dollars on request. Western Union offices can be found throughout Chile, usually adjacent to the post office.

ATMs

Chile's many ATM machines, known as *red-banc*, are the easiest and most convenient way to access funds. Your bank will likely charge a small fee for each transaction. Most ATMs have instructions in Spanish and English: choose 'foreign card' (*tarjeta extranjera*) when starting the transaction. You *cannot* rely on ATMs in San Pedro de Atacama (three

overused machines), Rapa Nui or in small Patagonian towns.

Bargaining

Markets are the only place to bargain. Transport and accommodation rates are generally fixed, though during off-season, you may politely ask '¿Me podría hacer precio?' (Could you make me a deal?).

Credit Cards

Most established businesses welcome credit cards although it's best not to depend on it. Consumers may be charged the 6% surcharge businesses must pay. Credit cards can also be useful to show 'sufficient funds' before entering another country.

Exchanging Money

US dollars are the preferred currency for exchange. Cash earns a better rate than traveler's checks and avoids commissions. To exchange cash and traveler's checks, *casas de cambio* are quicker than banks but offer poorer rates, as do removed destinations. Plan to exchange in larger cities. In very touristy areas, hotels, travel agencies and some shops accept or change US dollars. Street changers don't offer much difference in rates.

The American Express representative is **Blanco Viajes** (☎ 02-636-9100; Holley 148, Providencia, Santiago). Traveler's checks can be cashed at Banco del Estado and most exchange houses; ATMs are easier.

EXCHANGE RATES

Country	Unit	CH$
Australia	A$1	476
Canada	C$1	511
euro zone	€1	803
Japan	¥100	607
New Zealand	NZ$1	387
UK	UK£1	918
USA	US$1	550

POST

Correos de Chile (☎ 800-267-736; www.correos.cl), Chile's national postal service, has reasonably dependable but sometimes rather slow postal services. Within Chile, it costs around CH$120 to send a letter.

To send packages within Chile, sending via *encomienda* (the bus system) is much more reliable. Ticket offices generally have package counters. You can receive mail via *lista de correos*, or poste restante, (equivalent to general delivery) at any Chilean post office, charge per item is around CH$200. Mail is held for one month.

RESPONSIBLE TRAVEL

Hikers are obliged to carry out trash and follow a leave-no-trace ethic. Be particularly respectful to the *ahus* in Rapa Nui and with other monuments. Increasingly scarce seafood delicacies like *locos* (abalone) and *centolla* (king crab) should not be consumed during their breeding seasons. Don't buy carvings and crafts made out of protected species (cardón cactus in the north and *alerce* in the south). Put used toilet paper in the trash basket (most places). The best and easiest way to earn karma points in Chile? Be pleasant and courteous.

SHOPPING

Crafts include handknit woolens and Mapuche design jewelry and basketry from the south. Northern crafts resemble those of Peru and Bolivia. The lapis lazuli stone, used in jewelry, is almost exclusive to Chile. Irresistible edibles include *miel de ulmo* honey from the south, jams, papayas from Elqui Valley and olives from Azapa valley. **Fundación Artesanías de Chile** (Chilean Craft Foundation; www.artesaniasdechile .cl) showcases local *artesanía*.

STUDYING

Spanish-language courses are available in Santiago and several southern cities.

With Chilean headquarters at Coyhaique, the **National Outdoor Leadership School** (in USA ☎ 307-332-5300; www.nols.edu) offers a 75-day 'Semester in Patagonia,' teaching mountain-wilderness skills, sea kayaking and natural history for university credit. **Abtao** (☎ 02-211-5021; www.abtao.cl; El Director 5660, Las Condes, Santiago) organizes selective courses on Chilean ecosystems and wildlife.

Santiago's **Vinoteca** (☎ 02-335-2349; Isidora Goyenechea 2966, Las Condes) organizes wine courses. In Pucón, **Patragon** (☎ 45-444-606; www.patragon .net) offers Mapuche cooking classes and pottery workshops.

TELEPHONE

Chile's country code is ☎ 56. Entel and Movistar have call centers with private cabins; most close by 10pm. Some centers place the call for you. Long-distance calls are based on a carrier system: to place a call, precede the number with the telephone company's code: **Entel** (☎ 123), for example. For collect calls, dial ☎ 182 to get an operator.

Cell-phone numbers have seven digits, prefixed by ☎ 099 or ☎ 098. Drop the 09 when calling cell-to-cell. If calling cell-to-landline, add the landline's area code. Cell phones sell for as little as CH$10,000 and can be charged up by prepaid phone cards. The caller pays. Calls between cell and landlines are expensive and quickly eat up prepaid card amounts.

TOILETS

Put used toilet paper in the waste bin as Chile's fragile plumbing can't handle it. Public bathrooms charge (CH$150). Toilet paper is not a given – carry some with you.

TOURIST INFORMATION

The national tourist service, **Sernatur** (☎ 600-737-62887; www.sernatur.cl) has offices in Santiago and most cities. Their helpfulness varies widely but they generally provide brochures and leaflets. Many towns have municipal tourist offices, usually on the main plaza or at the bus terminal.

TOURS

The only way to get to remote calving glaciers, summit an active volcano, or raft a river is on tour. Yet opportunities for unguided activities abound, just plan carefully. Arrange ahead for English-speaking guides. Particularly in Pucón, be wary of security issues and chose the most reliable outfitter possible. Rural tourism offers local Spanish-speaking guides at a reasonable fee and access to places you otherwise would never have known about (see p473).

TRAVELERS WITH DISABILITIES

Travel within Chile is still a robust challenge for those with disabilities. **Transantiago** (www .transantiago.cl) public buses have some access ramps and wheelchair spaces. The metro is working on creating access but few hotels are wheelchair accessible. In general, Chilean hosts try to be very accommodating.

VISAS

Nationals of the US, Canada, Australia and the EU do not need a visa to visit Chile.

CHILE

Passports are obligatory and essential for routine activities.

The Chilean government collects a US$132/56/132 'reciprocity' fee from arriving US/Australian/Canadian citizens in response to these governments imposing a similar fee on Chilean citizens applying for visas. The payment applies only to tourists arriving by air in Santiago and is valid for the life of the passport. Payment must be made in cash; exact change is necessary.

On arrival, you'll be handed a 90-day tourist card. Don't lose it! If you do, go to the **Policía Internacional** (☎ 02-737-1292; Borgoño 1052, Santiago; ☽ 8:30am-5pm Mon-Fri), or the nearest police station. You will be asked for it upon leaving the country.

It costs US$100 to renew a tourist card for 90 more days at the **Departamento de Extranjería** (Map pp392-3; ☎ 02-550-2484; Agustinas 1235, 2nd fl, Santiago; ☽ 9am-2pm Mon-Fri). Many visitors prefer a quick dash across the Argentine border and back.

See p494 for information regarding embassies and consulates as well as www.lonely planet.com and follow the links to up-to-date visa information.

VOLUNTEERING

Experiment Chile (www.experiment.cl) organizes 14-week language-learning and volunteer programs. Language schools can often place students in volunteer work as well. The nonprofit organization **Un Techo Para Chile** (www .untechoparachile.cl) builds homes for low-income families throughout the country. The annual *Directorio de Organizaciones Miembros* published by **Renace** (Red Nacional de Acción Ecológica; www .renace.cl) lists environmental organizations, which may accept volunteers.

WOMEN TRAVELERS

Compared to their hot-blooded neighbors, Chilean men are often shy and downright circumspect. In north-central Chile, guys may be quick with *piropos* (come-ons), but these hormonal outbursts evaporate upon utterance – don't dwell on them. The biggest bother is being constantly asked how old you are and if you're married. Many Chilean women are intimidated by their foreign counterparts and can be difficult to befriend at first.

WORKING

Finding work as an English-language instructor in Santiago is feasible, but don't expect excellent wages. Reputable employers insist on work or residence permits (which are increasingly difficult to obtain) from the **Departamento de Extranjería** (Map pp392-3; ☎ 02-550-2400; Agustinas 1235, 2nd fl, Santiago; ☽ 9am-2pm Mon-Fri).

Colombia

HIGHLIGHTS

- **Cartagena** (p538) Get infatuated with Colombia's most romantic and perfectly preserved colonial city.
- **Bogotá** (p510) Hit the great restaurants, clubs and art galleries in this kicking capital.
- **The Amazon** (p578) Paddle through flooded rainforests to Zacambú.
- **San Agustín** (p571) Gallop around glorious countryside peppered with ancient sites and statues.
- **Off the Beaten Track** Get horizontal at Capurganá (p548) and Sapzurro (p549), the ultra-chilled-out Caribbean hideaways.
- **Best Journey** (p536) Take the awesome six-day trek through jungle to the mysterious Ciudad Perdida.

FAST FACTS

- **Area:** 1.14 million sq km (the size of France, Spain and Portugal combined)
- **Budget:** US$20 to US$30 a day
- **Capital:** Bogotá
- **Costs:** double room in a budget hotel US$10 to US$20, set meal in a budget restaurant US$2 to US$3.50, 100km inter-city bus fare US$5
- **Country code:** ☎ 57
- **Language:** Spanish
- **Money:** US$1 = COP$2000 (Colombian pesos)
- **Population:** 45 million
- **Seasons:** high season (Christmas and New Year, and the last weeks of July and August), rainy season (May to October)
- **Time:** GMT minus five hours (no daylight-saving time)

TRAVEL HINTS

Tickets for long-distance buses are not fixed so always bargain for a better deal. Night-time travel is now safe, except between Popayán and Pasto on the border of Ecuador, where armed bandits, not guerrillas, roam.

OVERLAND ROUTES

The main border crossings with Venezuela are at San Antonio del Táchira (near Cúcuta) and Paraguachón. From Ecuador, cross at Tulcán (near Ipiales).

Forget everything you've ever heard about Colombia – especially when the people telling you have never been here. For decades demonized, today Colombia is a safe, affordable, accessible and utterly thrilling destination.

Whatever you want, you'll find it here. Whether that's floating down Amazonian backwaters serenaded by scarlet macaws, wandering through perfectly preserved colonial towns saturated in tropical color and history, diving pristine Caribbean reefs patrolled by inquisitive eels, dancing till dawn in a throbbing nightclub or galloping on horseback along mountain ridges overlooking ancient indigenous burial sites, it's all in Colombia.

Not enough for you? Then go raft some of the fastest rapids on the continent, paraglide down vast canyons, hike through landscapes so perfect they seem like a Spielberg production, or wade through jungle rivers to mysterious abandoned cities.

Just to seal the deal, Colombians are friendly, welcoming and helpful people – and they receive tourists like long-lost brothers and sisters.

Security improvements have driven the continent's longest-running civil conflict into all but the most remote and inaccessible areas of the country, where travelers have no reason to visit. And best of all many Colombians, for years caged in their cities, can now enjoy their beautiful country, too.

And yet still some people think it's all just cocaine, coffee and kidnapping. They couldn't be more wrong. Spend some real time here, both on and off the gringo trail and there's a danger you might evangelize like this one day, too.

CURRENT EVENTS

For the majority of Colombians, life is better, safer and more stable today than it has been for many years. However despite a rolling back of violence, kidnapping and urban assaults, the country's 40-year civil war is not over. Nor is it likely to end, definitively, any time soon.

FARC on the Defensive

The spring and summer of 2008 was a disastrous period for Fuerzas Armadas Revolucionarias de Colombia (FARC; Revolutionary Armed Forces of Colombia). After never losing a single member of its ruling secretariat in 40 years, FARC lost three in the month of March.

First Colombia invaded Ecuadorian airspace in March 2008 and launched a deadly missile attack against a FARC encampment, and killed a key leader, Raul Reyes. A week later, another FARC leader, Ivan Rios, was murdered by his own bodyguard. He hacked off his leader's hand and delivered it to government forces as proof of his death. Two months later FARC founder, Manuel 'Sureshot' Marulanda, was reported dead of natural causes.

Then, rebels' chief bargaining pawn, French-Colombian presidential candidate, Ingrid Betancourt, kidnapped six years earlier, was snatched in an audacious and legally questionable jungle raid by Colombian soldiers. The BBC reported that one solider was wearing a Red Cross logo; a breach of the

Geneva convention since it compromises the group's international impartiality.

Hard-line right-wing President Álvaro Uribe's popularity soared to 90% soon after these events.

Non-Stick Scandals

Perhaps the biggest controversy to buffet the present government came in October 2008 when journalists discovered that the army was systematically killing civilians, dressing them in rebel uniforms and claiming them as combat kills in order to gain promotions or days off. The number of victims is believed to be in the thousands.

The story broke internationally when 19 young men from the poor Bogotá suburb of Soacha were offered high-paying work in the north of the country. They were presented as dead guerrillas, in full uniform, a few weeks later.

UN rapporteur on extrajudicial executions Philip Alston said in June 2009 the case was the 'tip of the iceberg.' He added that some of the Soacha victims were dressed in neatly pressed camouflage outfits, wearing clean jungle boots four sizes too big for them. While prosecutions were slow, the government had taken 'important steps to stop and respond to these killings,' he said.

There was a widespread purge of the army, including the dismissal of the country's top commander. However, criticism has been leveled at the government for its decision to pursue these cases through special courts, rather than employing standard criminal procedure.

Another shockwave hit the president's palace in 2008. Four million Colombians had been investing, knowingly or in ignorance, in a pyramid savings scheme, offering up to 150% returns. It collapsed, and millions were left bankrupt. Then it emerged that Uribe's sons were friends with David Murcia, a conman who investigators say ran the schemes.

Yet more embarrassment for Uribe regime came in early 2009, when it was discovered that the country's secret police, the Departamento Administrativo de Seguridad (DAS; Department of Administrative Security) had been tapping the phones of judges, opposition politicians, journalists and human rights workers.

President Uribe – A Third Term?

At the time of research the Senate had voted to allow Uribe a referendum to run for an unprecedented third term in power. The referendum needs to be approved by the country's Constitutional Court before it can be held. In a recent Gallup poll, 59% of those surveyed said they would vote in a referendum; and 84% of those said they would approve a third Uribe term.

Other possible contenders for the presidency if Uribe decides not to fight on are recently resigned Defense Minister Juan Manuel Santos and former Medellín Mayor Sergio Fajardo.

With the change of administration in the US, Uribe's aim of signing a free-trade deal with the US, allowing it tariff-free entry to valuable US markets, looked unlikely. Congressional Democrats had blocked the deal when in opposition, and during the US presidential campaign, Barack Obama repeatedly called on the Uribe administration to address a wave of assassinations of union leaders before the deal could be rubberstamped.

HISTORY
Pre-Columbian Times

Colombia's original inhabitants have left behind three main prehistoric sites: San Agustín, Tierradentro and Ciudad Perdida, along with the continent's finest gold work. They were highly skilled goldworkers and metalsmiths – their work can be seen throughout Colombia in Museos de Oro (Gold Museums). Bogotá's is the best.

Scattered throughout the Andean region and along the Pacific and Caribbean coasts, the pre-Columbian cultures of Colombia developed independently. The most notable were the Calima, Muisca, Nariño, Quimbaya, San Agustín, Sinú, Tayrona, Tierradentro, Tolima and Tumaco.

The Conquistadors Arrive

In 1499 Alonso de Ojeda was the first conquistador to set foot on Colombian soil and to see its people using gold objects. Several short-lived settlements were founded, but it was not until 1525 that Rodrigo de Bastidas laid the first stones of Santa Marta, the earliest surviving town. In 1533, Pedro de Heredia founded Cartagena, which soon became the principal center of trade.

In 1536 a general advance toward the interior began independently from both the north and south. Jiménez de Quesada set off from Santa Marta and founded Santa Fe de Bogotá two years later. On the way he conquered the Muisca, a blow that would foretell the ultimate ruin of civilizations throughout the New World.

Sebastián de Benalcázar deserted from Francisco Pizarro's army, which was conquering the Inca empire, and mounted an expedition from Ecuador. He subdued the southern part of Colombia, founding Popayán and Cali along the way, and reached Bogotá in 1539.

The two groups fought hard for supremacy, and it was not until 1550 that King Carlos V of Spain, in an effort to establish law and order, created the Real Audiencia del Nuevo Reino de Granada, a tribunal based in Bogotá. Administratively, the new colony was subject to the Viceroyalty of Peru.

With the growth of the Spanish empire in the New World a new territorial division was created in 1717, and Bogotá became the capital of its own viceroyalty, the Virreinato de la Nueva Granada. It comprised the territories of what are today Colombia, Panama, Ecuador and Venezuela.

Independence Wars

As the 18th century closed, disillusionment with Spanish domination matured into open protests and rebellions. Together with events such as the American and French revolutions and, more importantly, the invasion of Spain

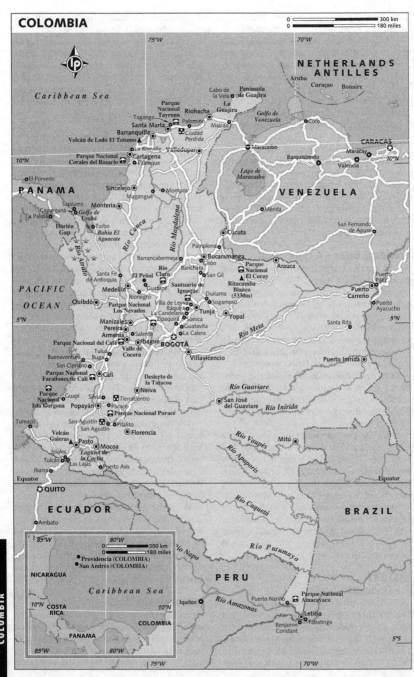

COLOMBIA

0 ———— 300 km
0 ———— 180 miles

Caribbean Sea

NETHERLANDS ANTILLES
Aruba Curaçao Bonaire

Cabo de la Vela
Península de Guajira
Parque Nacional Tayrona
Riohacha
La Guajira
Palomino
Maicao
Golfo de Venezuela
Coro
Taganga
Santa Marta
Ciudad Perdida
Barranquilla
Volcán de Lodo El Tótumo
La Boquilla
Valledupar
Maracaibo
CARACAS
Cartagena
Palenque
Parque Nacional Corales del Rosario
Barquisimeto
Maracay
Valencia

10°N

PANAMA
El Porvenir
Sincelejo
Magangué
Mompós
Lago de Maracaibo
VENEZUELA
Sapzurro
Montería
Mérida
Capurganá
Golfo de Urabá
La Palma
Darién Gap
Turbo
Bahía El Aguacate
San Fernando de Apure
Río Atrato
Río Cauca
Barrancabermeja
Pamplona
Cúcuta
Santa Fe de Antioquia
Río Claro
El Peñol
Bucaramanga
Girón
Arauca
Puerto Páez

PACIFIC OCEAN
Guatapé
Barichara
San Gil
Parque Nacional El Cocuy
Ritacunba Blanco (5330m)
Puerto Carreño
Medellín
Rionegro
Santuario de Iguaque
Duitama
Puerto Ayacucho
Quibdó
Parque Nacional Los Nevados
Villa de Leyva
Ráquira
Sogamoso
La Candelaria
Zipaquirá
Tunja
Yopal
5°N

Manizales
Pereira
Armenia
Salento
Suesca
Guatavita
La Calera
Santa Rita
Parque Nacional del Café
Ibagué
BOGOTÁ
Río Meta
Buenaventura
Tuluá
Buga
Valle de Cocora
Villavicencio
Puerto Inírida
San Cipriano
Parque Nacional Farallones de Cali
Cali
Desierto de la Tatacoa
Parque Nacional Isla Gorgona
Guapí
Silvia
Tierradentro
Neiva
Río Guaviare
Tumaco
San Agustín
Popayán
Puracé
Parque Nacional Puracé
Pitalito
San José del Guaviare
Río Inírida
San Agustín
Florencia
Volcán Galeras
Pasto
Mocoa
Mitú
Ipiales
Laguna de la Cocha
Río Vaupés
Tulcán
Las Lajas
Puerto Asís
Río Apaporis

Ibarra
Equator
QUITO
Equator

ECUADOR
Río Caquetá
BRAZIL
Ambato

Río Napo
Río Putumayo

85°W
80°W
0 ———— 300 km
0 ———— 180 miles
Providencia (COLOMBIA)
San Andrés (COLOMBIA)
NICARAGUA
Caribbean Sea
10°N
COSTA RICA
10°N
COLOMBIA
PANAMA
85°W
80°W

Iquitos
PERU
Río Amazonas
Puerto Nariño
Parque Nacional Amacayacu
Leticia
Tabatinga
Benjamín Constant
5°S

75°W
70°W

COLOMBIA

by Napoleon Bonaparte, this paved the way to independence. When Napoleon placed his own brother on the Spanish throne in 1808, the colonies refused to recognize the new monarch. One by one Colombian towns declared their independence.

In 1812 Simón Bolívar, who was to become the hero of the independence struggle, arrived in Cartagena to attack the Spanish. In a brilliant campaign to seize Venezuela he won six battles but was unable to hold Caracas, and had to withdraw to Cartagena. By then Napoleon had been defeated at Waterloo, and Spain set about reconquering its colonies. Colonial rule was reestablished in 1817.

Bolívar doggedly took up arms again. After assembling an army of horsemen from the Venezuelan Llanos, strengthened by a British legion, he marched over the Andes into Colombia. Independence was won at Boyacá on August 7, 1819.

Independence & Civil War

Two years after declaring independence, revolutionaries sat down in Villa del Rosario (near Cúcuta) to hash out a plan for their new country. It was there that the two opposing tendencies, centralist and federalist, came to the fore. Bolívar, who supported a centralized republic, succeeded in imposing his will. The Gran Colombia (which included modern-day Ecuador, Colombia, Venezuela and Panama) came into being and Bolívar was elected president.

From its inception, the state started to disintegrate. It soon became apparent that a central regime was incapable of governing such a vast and diverse territory. The Gran Colombia split into three separate countries in 1830.

The centralist and federalist political currents were both formalized in 1849 when two political parties were established: the Conservatives (with centralist tendencies) and the Liberals (with federalist leanings). Colombia became the scene of fierce rivalries between the two forces; chaos ensued. During the 19th century the country experienced no less than eight civil wars. Between 1863 and 1885 there were more than 50 antigovernment insurrections.

In 1899 a Liberal revolt turned into a full-blown civil war – the so-called War of a Thousand Days. That carnage resulted in a Conservative victory and left 100,000 dead. In 1903 the US took advantage of the country's internal strife and fomented a secessionist movement in Panama (at that time a Colombian province). By creating a new republic, the US was able to build a canal across the Central American isthmus.

La Violencia

After a period of relative peace, the struggle between Liberals and Conservatives broke out again in 1948 with La Violencia, the most destructive of Colombia's many civil wars, which left a death toll of some 300,000. Urban riots broke out on April 9, 1948 in Bogotá following the assassination of Jorge Eliécer Gaitán, a charismatic populist Liberal leader. Liberals soon took up arms throughout the country.

By 1953 some groups of Liberal guerrillas had begun to demonstrate a dangerous degree of independence. As it became evident that the partisan conflict was taking on revolutionary overtones, the leaders of both the Liberal and Conservative parties decided to support a military coup as the best means of retaining power and pacifying the countryside. The 1953 coup of General Gustavo Rojas Pinilla was the only military intervention the country experienced in the 20th century.

The dictatorship of General Rojas was not to last. In 1957 the leaders of the two parties signed a pact to share power for the next 16 years. The party leaders, however, repressed all political activity that remained outside the scope of their parties, thus sowing the seeds for the appearance of guerrilla groups.

The Birth of FARC & the Paramilitaries

During the late 1950s and early 1960s Colombia saw the birth of many guerrilla groups, each with its own ideology and its own political and military strategies. The most significant – and deadly – movements included FARC, Ejército de Liberación Nacional (ELN; National Liberation Army) and Movimiento 19 de Abril (M-19; April 19 Movement).

Until 1982 the guerrillas were treated as a problem of public order and persecuted by the army. President Belisario Betancur (1982–86) was the first to open direct negotiations with the guerrillas in a bid to reincorporate them into the nation's political life. Yet the talks ended in failure, and the M-19 guerrillas stormed the capital's Palacio de Justicia, in November 1985, leaving more than 100 dead.

COLOMBIA

The Liberal government of President Virgilio Barco (1986–90), succeeded in getting M-19 to lay down their arms and incorporated them into the political process. However, the two other major groups – FARC and ELN – are still combat-ready. FARC has lost around half its fighters in recent years, as paid desertions and endless pressure from the Colombian military have decimated ranks.

Another group emerging in the 1980s, was the Autodefensas Unidas de Colombia (AUC; United Self-Defense Forces of Colombia). The AUC, paramilitary death squads formed by rich Colombians looking to protect their lands, is responsible for dozens of massacres. This group supposedly disbanded in Uribe's second term, but many observers including Human Rights Watch say the disarmament was a sham.

All sides have committed and continue to commit atrocities, and the UN High Commissioner for Refugees says Colombia has 4.3 million internally displaced people, second only to Sudan, as the rural poor are caught in the crossfire between the guerrillas, the still-active paramilitaries and the army.

White Gold

The cocaine mafia started in a small way in the early 1970s but, within a short time, developed the drug trade into a powerful industry with its own plantations, laboratories, transportation services and protection.

The boom years began in the early 1980s. The Medellín Cartel, led by Pablo Escobar, became the principal mafia and its bosses lived in freedom and luxury. They even founded their own political party and two newspapers, and in 1982 Escobar was elected to congress.

In 1983 the government launched a campaign against the drug trade, which gradually turned into an all-out war. The cartels responded violently and managed to liquidate many of its adversaries. The war became even bloodier in August 1989 when Luis Carlos Galán, the leading Liberal contender for the 1990 presidential election, was assassinated. The government responded with the confiscation of nearly 1000 mafia-owned properties, and announced new laws on extradition – a nightmare for the drug barons. The cartel resorted to the use of terrorist tactics, principally car bombs.

The election of the Liberal President César Gaviria (1990–94) brought a brief period of hope. Following lengthy negotiations, which included a constitutional amendment to ban

extradition of Colombians, Escobar and the remaining cartel bosses surrendered and the narcoterrorism subsided. However, Escobar escaped from his palatial prison following the government's bumbling attempts to move him to a more secure site. An elite, 1500-man special unit hunted Escobar for 499 days, until it tracked him down in Medellín and killed him in December 1993.

Despite this, the drug trade continued unaffected. While the military concentrated on hunting one man and persecuting one cartel, the other cartels were quick to take advantage of the opportune circumstances. The Cali Cartel, led by the Rodríguez Orejuela brothers, swiftly moved into the shattered Medellín Cartel's markets and became Colombia's largest trafficker. Although the cartel's top bosses were captured in 1995 the drug trade continued to flourish, with other regional drug cartels, paramilitaries and, principally, the guerrillas filling the gap left by the two original mafias.

In 1999 then President Andrés Pastrana launched Plan Colombia with US backing. The plan called for the total eradication of the coca plant from Colombia by spraying fields with herbicide. Colombian coca growers – the lowest earners in the chain from field to city – and traffickers, not wanting to walk away from their COP$6 billion a year business, have in many cases moved their fields elsewhere, oftentimes into national parks which are protected against the spraying. Despite increased drug seizures and arrests of low-level traffickers, the availability of cocaine in the US and Europe remains stable and prices have dropped.

An extensive manual eradication program was trumpeted as a better way of stopping the trade in 2007. All it has done is further impoverish coca farmers, who often have no other means of surviving.

The battle to eradicate cocaine from Colombia looks Sisyphean. In 2008 the UN reported an increase of 27% of land under coca cultivation, despite a total of US$5 billion of US aid in almost 10 years. In 2009 land under cultivation decreased by 18% – meaning a net increase of 9%. As satirical US online magazine, the *Onion*, once put it in a spoof headline: 'Drugs Win War On Drugs.'

President Álvaro Uribe

Right-wing hardliner Álvaro Uribe was elected president in 2002. He inherited a country on the brink of collapse, a pariah state plagued by security problems, with many highways in the country road-blocked and controlled by the rebels. Uribe promised decisive military action against the guerrillas, and he delivered. And then some. His campaign slogan, 'Firm hand, big heart' was at least half-true. Suddenly, the country's roads were open, swamped with military, and safe.

After years of frightened lockdown, Colombians, weary of war, of kidnapping, of extortion and bloodshed relished the new freedoms they won – to travel, to work – under this tenacious, rigid man (who ironically begins each day with an intense yoga workout). Uribe's approval ratings were consistently above 70%.

Only a blind ideologue could deny that Uribe has been the most popular and successful Colombian president ever. Nevertheless this is not the full picture.

Uribe took a second term in 2006 after a constitutional amendment allowed him to run for power again. He forged on with further assaults on the guerrillas. His soldiers took the fight to the leftist rebels and pushed them back into remote jungles, where they remain today, weakened, isolated, but unbeaten.

THE CULTURE
The National Psyche

A middle-aged American couple stop on a street corner in Bogotá. Reading a large map, they are obviously lost, obviously wealthy – or wealthier than 90% of the people passing them in the street. A motorbike pulls alongside them, the driver flips his visor. What happens next?

The bike rider dismounts and the couple feel a prickle of fear. The biker smiles, asks them where they are headed, takes the map, points out the directions, shakes hands and bids them a good day and rides off. The Americans simply cannot believe it. Such a thing would never happen in a major US capital, they say.

It's a true story, and not an isolated one. Every traveler you meet who comes to Colombia with an open mind says the same thing: the people are genuinely friendly and helpful.

Kidnaps, extortion and small-scale bombings still occur, and several areas of the country are heavily mined. But the real difficulties facing Colombians today are economic.

The national psyche is remarkably robust and happiness and warmth are the default settings for most Colombians.

Everyone dreams of a *finca* (country house with land). In their hearts urban Colombians are all cowboys and they romanticize rural life. Many rural Colombians, meanwhile, struggle to survive and dream of life in the big cities.

Lifestyle

The divide between rich and poor in Colombia is enormous. The wealthiest 10% of the country controls 46% of the country's wealth (they also earn 80 times more money than the poorest 10%). Around 60% of urban Colombians live in poverty (the figure is 80% in rural areas).

Colombian families are tight-knit and supportive and, in common with most Latin Americans, children are adored. Most couples that live together are married, though this has changed in recent years. Women's rights are improving, and while abortion was legalized in 2006, it is available to women only if their life is in danger through childbirth, if the fetus is badly deformed, or if pregnancy is a result of rape. Gay rights are slowly improving, though out-and-proud behavior tends to be limited to gay nights in major cities. Poverty is widespread, as is unemployment, and all major cities have a problem with homelessness, drug abuse and begging. A firm but polite 'No' will see off all but the most persistent beggars. Drug dealers may target Western tourists, especially in cities such as Cartagena and Medellín. Shrug them off and you'll have a better, safer time.

Population

Colombia has around 45 million people, making it the third-most populous country in Latin America, after Brazil and Mexico. Population is spread fairly evenly from north to south while eastern Colombia and the Amazon is only sparsely populated. The largest cities are Bogotá (8.25 million), Medellín (2.5 million), Cali (3.5 million) and Barranquilla (1.3 million).

Colombia's diverse population, an amalgam of three main groups – indigenous, Spanish and African – reflects its history. While 58% of the country claims *mestizo* (mixed white and indigenous) heritage, other ethnicities include: 20% white, 14% mixed white and black, 4% black, 3% mixed black and indigenous, and 1% indigenous. Colombia's indigenous population speaks about 65 languages and nearly 300 dialects belonging to several linguistic families.

SPORTS

Soccer and cycling are the most popular spectator sports. Colombia regularly takes part in international events in these two fields, such as the World Cup and the Tour de France, and has recorded some successes. Baseball is limited to the Caribbean Coast. The national soccer league has matches most of the year.

RELIGION

Most Colombians are Roman Catholic. Other creeds are officially permitted but their numbers are small. However, over the past decade there has been a proliferation of various Protestant congregations, which have succeeded in converting some three million Catholics. Many indigenous groups have adopted the Catholic faith, sometimes incorporating some of their traditional beliefs. There are small numbers of Colombian Jews, and there are synagogues in most big cities.

ARTS
Literature

During the independence period and up to WWII, Colombia produced few internationally acclaimed writers other than José Asunción Silva (1865–96), perhaps the country's best poet, considered the precursor of modernism in Latin America.

A postwar literary boom thrust many great Latin American authors into the international sphere, including Colombian Gabriel García Márquez (b 1928). Gabo's novel *Cien años de soledad* (One Hundred Years of Solitude), published in 1967, immediately became a worldwide best seller. It mixed myths, dreams and reality, and amazed readers with a new form of expression that critics dubbed *realismo mágico* (magic realism). In 1982 García Márquez won the Nobel Prize for literature.

There are several contemporaries who deserve recognition including poet, novelist and painter Héctor Rojas Herazo, and Álvaro Mutis, a close friend of Gabo. Of the younger generation, seek out the works of Fernando Vallejo, a highly respected iconoclast who has been surprisingly critical of García Márquez.

Cinema

The best films of recent years in Colombia are *María, llena eres de gracia* (Maria, Full of Grace; 2004), about a pregnant drug mule seeking a new life in the US; and *Yo soy otro* (Others; 2008), a tense psychological drama about a depressed late-30s systems engineer in Cali in 2002, when the city was tight in the grip of paranarco chaos.

La Milagrosa (2008) presents a politically risky view of FARC as driven by poverty and revenge against the paramilitaries, as a rich young Colombian is kidnapped by the rebels and held in the jungle. The refusal to indulge in orthodox judgments of the FARC as one-dimensional narcoterrorists has upset many in Colombia – but the film does well to retain balance. *Paraíso Travel* (Paradise Travel; 2008) meanwhile, takes the viewer on an alternatively horrific and comic journey with illegal refugees from the slums of Medellín to their Manhattan counterparts. *Perro come perro* (Dog Eat Dog; 2008), another Cali-set thriller, is a masterly study of paranoia and betrayal among a crew of gangsters.

Music

The Caribbean Coast vibrates with African-inspired rhythms such as the cumbia, *mapalé* and *porro*. The coast is also the birthplace of the *vallenato*, based (some might say excessively) on the European accordion. This is the most popular Colombian musical genre today.

The music of the Pacific coast, such as the *currulao*, is based on a strong African drum pulse, but tinged with Spanish influences. Colombian Andean music has been strongly influenced by Spanish rhythms and instruments, and differs notably from its Peruvian and Bolivian counterparts.

Colombia's most famous mainstream musicians are Shakira, Carlos Vives (a Latin-pop vocalist), Totó La Momposina (a traditional Afro-Caribbean music singer) and Juanes (a Latin rock vocalist).

New groups pushing boundaries include Pernett and the Caribbean Ravers, who blend Berlin-esque bass lines and cumbia rhythms. Bomba Estereo mix space-rock and cumbia, and Choc Quib Town, a Pacific Coast hip-hop band, offer funky insurrection and incisive social commentary.

The more traditional *joropó* sounds of Grupo Cimarron have gained them worldwide recognition with electrifying live performances, all rapid-fire string work and blazing dance routines. Salsa is adored by everyone here, and Bogotá's LA 33 are the finest modern proponents of a tough, urban style.

Architecture

The most outstanding example of pre-Columbian urban planning is the Ciudad Perdida of the Tayronas in the Sierra Nevada de Santa Marta. Although the dwellings haven't survived, the stone structures, including a complex network of terraces, paths and stairways, remain in remarkably good shape.

After the arrival of the Spaniards, bricks and tiles became the main construction materials. The colonial towns followed rigid standards laid down by the Spanish Crown. They were constructed on a grid plan, centered on the Plaza Mayor (main square). This pattern was applied during the colonial period and long after, and is the dominant feature of most Colombian cities, towns and villages.

Spain's strong Catholic tradition left behind many churches and convents in the colony – the central areas of Bogotá, Cartagena, Popayán and Tunja are fine examples.

In the 19th century, despite independence, the architecture continued to be predominantly Spanish in style. Modern architectural trends only began to appear in Colombia after WWII. This process accelerated during the 1960s when city skyscrapers appeared.

The latest architectural phenomenon in Colombia is urban planning. The success of the TransMilenio, car-free Sunday, bike lanes and the expansion of parks in Bogotá has become a model for other cities in South America, Africa and Asia.

Visual Arts

The colonial period was dominated by Spanish religious art, and although the paintings and sculptures of this era were generally executed by local artists, they reflected the Spanish trends of the day. With the arrival of independence visual arts departed from strictly religious themes, but it was not until the turn-of-the-19th-century revolution in European painting that Colombian artists began to create original work.

Among the most distinguished modern painters and sculptors are Pedro Nel Gómez, known for his murals, oils and sculptures; Luis Alberto Acuña, a painter and sculptor who used motifs from pre-Columbian art; Alejandro Obregón, a painter tending to abstract forms; Rodrigo Arenas Betancur, Colombia's most famous monument creator; and Fernando Botero, the most internationally renowned Colombian artist. Spot a fat statue or portrait in Colombia and it's likely a Botero.

Contemporary artists worth your attention include Bernardo Salcedo (conceptual sculpture and photography), Miguel Ángel Rojas (painting and installations) and Doris Salcedo (sculpture and installations).

ENVIRONMENT

Colombia's principal environmental problem is deforestation. Every year vast areas of rainforest and other fragile habitats are indiscriminately cleared for industry, housing, farming, ranching and coca farms.

For more than 20 years guerrillas have targeted oil pipelines in order to stop multinationals depleting natural resources. Since 1986 there have been more than 950 attacks that have spilled more than two million barrels of crude oil into the environment (11 times the amounts spilled by *Exxon Valdez*), polluting rivers and land.

The US has made its military aid to Colombia conditional on the aerial fumigation of coca and poppy crops. Every year tens of thousands of hectares of coca and poppy are fumigated with a herbicide containing glyphosate, an ingredient that, besides coca plants, kills traditional crops, leading to impoverishment and displacement of thousands of peasants and indigenous people and compromising their health. Many scientists claim that the herbicide is killing microbes and fungi necessary within the rainforest ecosystem, thereby altering the whole nutrient cycling system.

The Land

Colombia covers 1.14 million square kilometers, about the same size as France, Spain and Portugal combined. It occupies the northwestern part of the continent and is the only South American country with coasts on both the Pacific (1448km long) and the Caribbean (1760km). Colombia is bordered by Panama, Venezuela, Brazil, Peru and Ecuador.

Colombia's physical geography is extremely diverse. The western part, which

---

ROMPEPIERNAS: LEG-BREAKING LAND MINES

FARC's low-tech land mines are made from hypodermic syringes, sulfuric acid, an explosive agent and a tin can. They're known to locals as *rompepiernas*, or 'leg breakers.' The syringe holds the acid, and is placed into the can, which holds the charge. The can is buried, and the plunger protrudes. Step on the plunger, the acid hits the charge and explodes. They're designed to injure rather than kill, and they're the reason you see so many amputees around Colombia. They are cheap and easy to make, and relatively risk-free to plant, and dangerous and expensive to remove. They are often planted around coca plantations to deter unwanted visitors. Colombia ranks third in the world (after Cambodia and Afghanistan) for victims of land-mine blasts. An estimated 100,000 mines are scattered around the country, but none – as far as anyone can be certain – in any of the areas we cover.

---

comprises almost half of the total territory, is mountainous, with three Andean chains – the Cordillera Occidental, Cordillera Central and Cordillera Oriental – running roughly parallel north–south across most of the country. More than half of the territory east of the Andes is a vast lowland, which is divided into two regions: the savanna-like Los Llanos in the north and the rainforest-covered Amazon in the south.

Colombia has several small islands. The major ones are the archipelago of San Andrés and Providencia (in the Caribbean Sea, 750km northwest of mainland Colombia), the Islas del Rosario (near the Caribbean Coast) and Isla Gorgona (in the Pacific Ocean).

Wildlife

Colombia has more plant and animal species per unit area than any other country in the world. This abundance reflects Colombia's numerous climatic zones and microclimates, which have created many different habitats and biological islands in which wildlife has evolved independently.

Colombia is home to the jaguar, ocelot, peccary, tapir, deer, armadillo, spectacled bear and numerous species of monkey, to mention just a few of the 350-odd species of mammals. There are more than 1920 recorded species of birds (nearly a quarter of the world's total), ranging from the huge Andean condor to the tiny hummingbird. Colombia's flora is equally impressive and includes some 3000 species of orchid alone. The national herbariums have classified more than 130,000 plants.

National Parks

Colombia has 55 national parks, sanctuaries and reserves. Only a handful of parks provide accommodations and food for visitors. The rest have no tourist amenities at all and some, especially those in remote regions, are virtually inaccessible. Some very isolated parks can be unsafe for tourists because of guerrilla presence.

National parks are operated by the Unidad Administrativa Especial del Sistema de Parques Nacionales, a department of the Ministry of the Environment. Its central office is in Bogotá, and there are regional offices in other cities. The Bogotá office handles all parks, whereas subsidiary offices only service the parks in their regions. Parks include the following:

Parque Nacional El Cocuy (p524) Spectacular alpine peaks and lakes; walking trekking.

Parque Nacional Los Nevados (p559) Snow-capped Andean volcanoes and cloud forest; hiking and mountaineering.

Parque Nacional Santuario de Iguaque (p524) Mountain lakes, historical sites; walking.

Parque Nacional Tayrona (p534) Coastal rainforest and beaches; monkeys, corals, walking, trekking and snorkeling.

TRANSPORTATION

GETTING THERE & AWAY
Air

Sitting on the northwestern edge of the continent, Colombia is a convenient and reasonably cheap gateway to South America from the US and Central America, and even from Europe. Bogotá has Colombia's major international airport, but some other cities including Cartagena, Medellín and Cali also handle international flights. The country is serviced by a number of major intercontinental airlines including British Airways, Air France, Iberia and American Airlines, and a dozen national carriers.

BRAZIL & PERU
Direct flights between these countries and Colombia are expensive. It is cheaper to fly through Leticia in the Colombian Amazon (see p580).

CENTRAL AMERICA
Colombia has regular flight connections with most Central American capitals. Sample one-way fares include: Guatemala City–Bogotá (US$400 to US$500), San José (Costa Rica)–Bogotá (US$400) and Panama City–Bogotá (US$250).

ECUADOR
You'll find one-way flights from Quito to Bogotá or Cali for around US$350, but watch out for promotions.

VENEZUELA
There are several daily flights between Caracas and Bogotá, with Avianca and Aeropostal (US$450).

Boat
BRAZIL & PERU
The only viable border crossing between these two countries and Colombia is via Leticia (p581) in the Colombian Amazon. Leticia is reached from Iquitos, Peru (p868), and Manaus, Brazil (p366).

PANAMA
There are sailboats between Colón in Panama and Cartagena in Colombia (see p543).

It's also possible nowadays to cross from Colombia to Panama via a combination of boat and land. See p548.

Bus
ECUADOR
Almost all travelers use the Carretera Panamericana border crossing through Ipiales and Tulcán. See Ipiales (p575) and Tulcán (p622).

DEPARTURE TAX

The airport tax on international flights out of Colombia is US$33. A further charge of US$23 is made if you have been in the country longer than two months. Both taxes are payable in dollars or pesos at the day's rate.

VENEZUELA
There are several border crossings between Colombia and Venezuela. By far the most popular with travelers is the route via Cúcuta and San Antonio del Táchira, on the main Bogotá–Caracas road. See p529 and p949.

Another border crossing is at Paraguachón, on the Maicao–Maracaibo road. There are buses and shared taxis between Maicao and Maracaibo, and direct buses between Cartagena and Caracas. See Maracaibo (p942) and Cartagena (p543).

There's also a popular little border crossing between Colombia's Puerto Carreño and either Puerto Ayacucho (p974) or Puerto Páez (both in Venezuela).

Car & Motorcycle
There is no overland route between Colombia and Panama, but it is possible to deliver a car between the two countries on a cargo ship. The pick-up and drop-off points are Colón and Cartagena. In Cartagena the contact is **Seaboard Marine** (☎ 5-677-2410; www.seaboardmarine .com), which charges US$850.

GETTING AROUND
Air
Colombia has a well-developed airline system and a solid network of domestic flights. The most commonly used passenger airlines include **Avianca** (www.avianca.com), **AeroRepública** (www.aerorepublica.com.co), **Aires** (www.aires.com.co) and **Satena** (www.satena.com), most of which also have international flights.

Fares and services between the companies are pretty similar; the only real reason to choose one over the other is because it better fits your schedule. Book well in advance to secure the lowest fare.

There's a COP$76,900 airport tax on domestic flights, which you normally pay while buying your ticket (this tax is included in the airfares listed in this chapter). Always reconfirm your booking at least 72 hours before departure.

Boat
With more than 3000km of Pacific and Atlantic coastline, there is a considerable amount of shipping traffic, consisting mostly of irregular cargo boats that may also take passengers. Rivers are the only transportation routes in much of Chocó and the Amazon.

COLOMBIA

GETTING INTO TOWN

El Dorado airport is relatively easy to navigate. You can change money outside customs (rates are competitive) and catch a taxi into the center (15km). There is a small taxi booth at the exit where you describe your destination and get a slip with the address and fixed price (COP$17,000 to the center), which you then pass to the taxi driver. You can save money by taking *busetas* (small buses) or *colectivos* (shared taxis) marked 'Aeropuerto'; they park about 50m from the terminal. From the center to the airport, you catch them on Calle 19 or Carrera 10.

If arriving in Bogotá by bus at the main bus terminal, you can get to the center (9km) by a *buseta* or *colectivo*, or by taxi. Prices are agreed upon beforehand at a booth – tell them your destination and you'll receive a slip with the price on it. Pay no more than that.

Bus

Buses are the main means of getting around Colombia. The bus system is well developed and extensive, reaching even the smallest villages. Buses range from ordinary bangers to modern-day luxury liners.

The best buses (*climatizado*) have plenty of leg room, reclining seats, large luggage compartments and toilets. Carry warm clothes – drivers usually set the air-con to full blast.

On the main routes buses run frequently, so there is little point in booking a seat in advance. In some places off the main routes, where there are only a few buses daily, it's better to buy a ticket some time before departure. The only time you really need to book is during the Christmas and Easter periods, when hordes of Colombians are on holiday.

Colectivos are a cross between a bus and a taxi. They are usually large cars (sometimes jeeps or minibuses) that cover fixed routes, mainly over short and medium distances. They leave when full, not according to a schedule, and are a reasonable option if there is a long wait for the next bus or if you are in a hurry.

Bus travel is reasonably cheap in Colombia. As a rule of a thumb, the *climatizado* bus costs roughly COP$4000 for every hour of travel. Always haggle – offer 25% less, politely. Discounts of 33% are not uncommon. In holiday periods, you have no chance of a discount.

Car & Motorcycle

Getting around with your own vehicle is possible, though your main danger nowadays is haphazard Colombian drivers. You'll need an International Driving Permit.

BOGOTÁ

☎ 1 / pop 8.25 million

Colombia's capital city will take your breath away – and it's not just the altitude.

Perched like a hawk at 2600m, this stylish, chic, modern and progressive city will calmly stare you down and challenge your prejudices. After years of intelligent investment and a nationwide routing by government forces of the leftist FARC guerrillas, who were at the city gates just five years ago, Bogotá is safer than ever. More than that: it's effortlessly cool with a young, educated and stylish population that welcomes outsiders with grace and passion.

It's also a city of extremes: the elegance of the colonial architecture in the historic center of La Candelaria, where most travelers hang out, is shadowed by the glittering towers of finance in the north. Both these areas look away from the ramshackle shanties of the south.

It's the geographical heart of the country, an ideal starting point for your trip. It's the seat of political and financial power, too, and *rollos*, as the residents are known, would argue that it's also Colombia's cultural heartland. And with some justification: there are more theaters, galleries, concert halls and cinemas here than anywhere else in the country.

Pack a raincoat and warm clothes – Bogotá averages 14°C, gets cold at night and it rains most of the year. Coca tea helps with altitude sickness; alcohol makes it worse. But leave your preconceptions at home. Bogotá rocks.

ORIENTATION

The city runs from north to south, and is hemmed in by mountains to the east. The city is laid out on a grid system.

The mountains, topped off by Cerro de Monserrate and Cerro de Guadalupe, have *carreras* (avenues), running parallel, and *calles* (streets), running perpendicular. Calle numbers ascend to the north, and Carrera numbers ascend to the west.

Addresses with an 'A' (eg Carrera 7A) represent a half-block. (Carrera 7A is a halfway between Carrera 7 and 8).

The north is a mix of sleek residential housing, upscale entertainment and businesses. The south is poorer and has few attractions for the visitor. The west, where planes and buses arrive, is drab, functional and industrial. The mountains' eastern slopes are rammed to bursting with houses.

The city center has some of the country's best museums, galleries, colonial buildings and historic sights.

INFORMATION
Bookstores
Authors (☎ 217-77-88; Calle 70 No 5-23) Books in English.

Emergency
Ambulance, fire and police (☎ 123)
Police station (Carrera 1A No 18A-96)
Tourist police (☎ 337-4413; Carrera 13 No 26-62; ⏱ 7am-noon & 2-7pm) Bilingual staff.

Internet Access
Candelaria NET (Calle 14 No 3-74; ⏱ 9am-9pm Mon-Sat)
OfficeNET (Carrera 4 No 19-16, Oficina 112; ⏱ 9am-9pm Mon-Sat)

Laundry
Lavandería Espumas (Calle 19 No 3A-37, Local 104) There are several budget *lavanderías* (laundries) in the center.

Libraries
Biblioteca Luis Ángel Arango (☎ 343-1212; Calle 11 No 4-14; ⏱ 8am-8pm Mon-Sat, to 4pm Sun) Library and temporary art exhibits.

Medical Services
Centro de Atención al Viajero (☎ 215-2029; Carrera 7 No 119-14) A travelers' medical center that offers various vaccinations (including yellow fever and hepatitis A and B).
Clínica de Marly (☎ 343-6600; Calle 50 No 9-67) Outpatient clinic with general doctors and specialties.
Hospital San Ignacio (☎ 594-6161; Carrera 7 No 40-62) University hospital with high standards of care, but lines are often long.

Money
Bogotá's banks have varied opening hours, normally 9am to 4pm Monday to Thursday, and 9am to 3:30pm Friday. Most banks have ATMs. Changing cash may be better and quicker in *casas de cambio* (authorized foreign currency-exchange houses). The banks listed change traveler's checks. Allow enough time – lines are often long and service slow.
Bancolombia (Carrera 8 No 13-17)
Casa de Cambio Unidas (☎ 341-0537; Carrera 6 No 14-72)
Edificio Emerald Trade Center (Av Jiménez No 5-43) There are several exchange offices here.
Expreso Viajes & Turismo (☎ 593-4949; Calle 85 No 20-32) American Express is represented here. It doesn't cash checks but gives a replacement if your checks are lost or stolen.
Titán Intercontinental (☎ 336-0549; Carrera 7 No 18-42)

Post
Adpostal Centro Internacional (☎ 341-4344; Carrera 7 No 27-54); La Candelaria (☎ 341-5503; cnr Carrera 7 & Calle 13)
Avianca Centro Internacional (☎ 342-6077; Carrera 10 No 26-53); City Center (☎ 342-7513; Carrera 7 No 16-36) The city-center branch has poste restante.
DHL (☎ 595-8100; Calle 13 No 8-11)
FedEx (☎ 291-0100; Carrera 7 No 16-50)

Telephone
Telecom (☎ 561-1111; Calle 23 No 13-49; ⏱ 7am-7pm)

Tourist Information
There are tourist information desks at the bus terminal and El Dorado airport.
Parques Nacionales Naturales de Colombia (☎ 353-2400; www.parquesnacionales.gov.co; Carrera 10 No 20-30; ⏱ 8am-5:45pm Mon-Fri) Provides information and permits, and books accommodation.
Vice Presidency of Tourism: Proexport Colombia (☎ 427-9000; www.colombia.travel/en/; Calle 28A No 13A-15, Piso 35; ⏱ 8:30am-4:30pm Mon-Fri) Nationwide tourist information.

Travel Agencies
Trotamundos (☎ 599-6413; www.trotamundos.com .co; Diagonal 35 No 5-73) Represents STA Travel. Check here for discounted student airfares.
Viajes Vela (☎ 742-3294; www.travelstc.com; Carrera 9 No 50-54, Piso 1)

DANGERS & ANNOYANCES
Like any major urban center, Bogotá requires common sense and moderate vigilance. In the

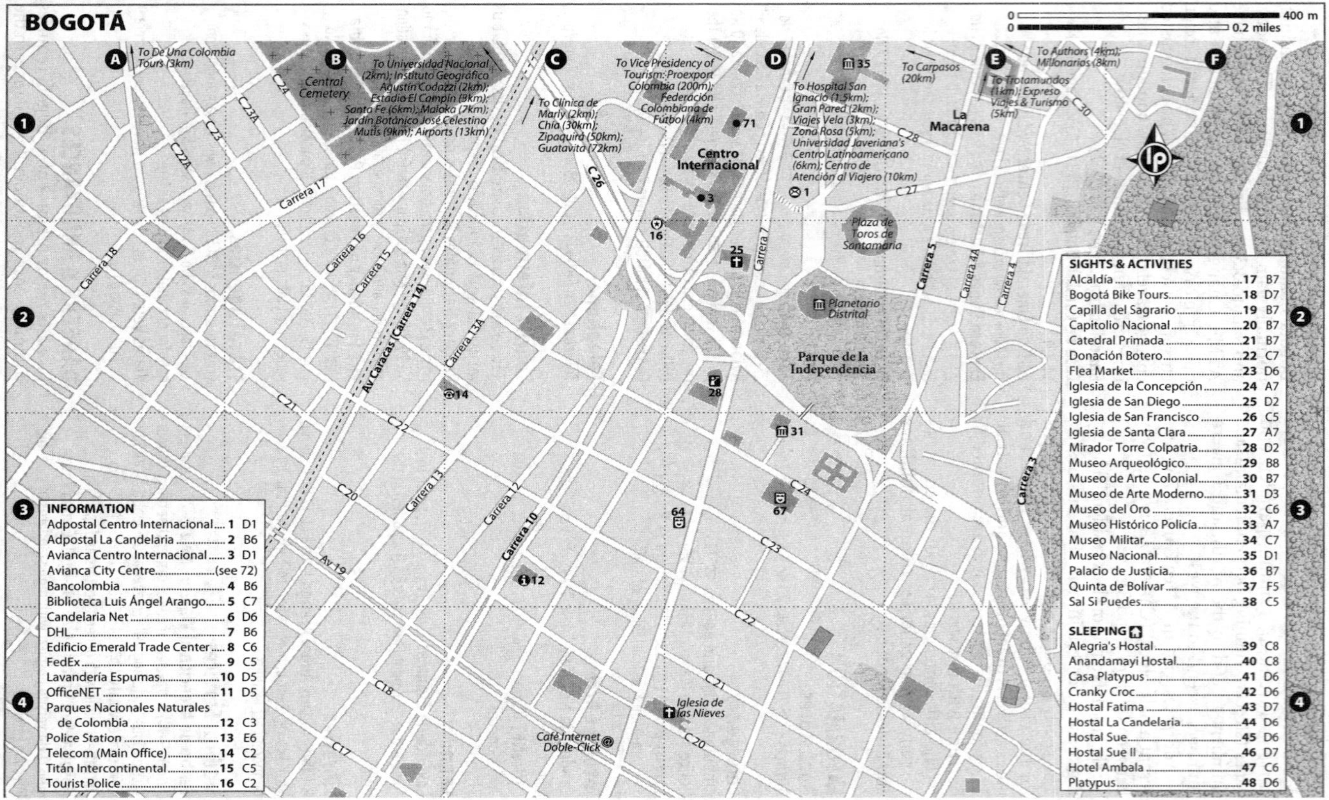

BOGOTÁ
0 400 m
0 0.2 miles
To De Una Colombia Tours (3km)
Central Cemetery
To Universidad Nacional (2km); Instituto Geográfico Agustín Codazzi (2km); Estadio El Campín (3km); Santa Fe (6km); Maloka (7km); Jardín Botánico José Celestino Mutis (9km); Airports (13km)
To Clínica de Marly (2km); Chía (30km); Zipaquirá (50km); Guatavita (72km)
To Vice Presidency of Tourism; Proexport Colombia (200m); Federación Colombiana de Fútbol (4km)
To Hospital San Ignacio (1.5km); Gran Pared (2km); Viajes Vela (3km); Zona Rosa (5km); Universidad Javeriana's Centro Latinoamericano (6km); Centro de Atención al Viajero (10km)
To Carpasos (20km)
To Trotamundos (1km); Expreso Viajes & Turismo (5km)
To Authors (4km); Millonarios (8km)
La Macarena
Centro Internacional
Plaza de Toros de Santamaría
Planetario Distrital
Parque de la Independencia
Iglesia de las Nieves
Café Internet Doble-Click
Carrera 18
Carrera 17
Carrera 16
Carrera 15
Av Caracas (Carrera 14)
Carrera 13A
Carrera 13
Carrera 12
Carrera 10
Carrera 7
Carrera 5
Carrera 4A
Carrera 4
Carrera 3
C24
C23A
C23
C22A
C26
C28
C30
C27
C21
C22
C20
Av 19
C18
C17
C24
C23
C22
C21
C20
INFORMATION
Adpostal Centro Internacional 1 D1
Adpostal La Candelaria 2 B6
Avianca Centro Internacional 3 D1
Avianca City Centre (see 72)
Bancolombia 4 B6
Biblioteca Luis Ángel Arango 5 C7
Candelaria Net 6 D6
DHL 7 B6
Edificio Emerald Trade Center 8 C6
FedEx 9 C5
Lavandería Espumas 10 D5
OfficeNET 11 D5
Parques Nacionales Naturales de Colombia 12 C3
Police Station 13 E6
Telecom (Main Office) 14 C2
Titán Intercontinental 15 C5
Tourist Police 16 C2
SIGHTS & ACTIVITIES
Alcaldía 17 B7
Bogotá Bike Tours 18 D7
Capilla del Sagrario 19 B7
Capitolio Nacional 20 B7
Catedral Primada 21 B7
Donación Botero 22 C7
Flea Market 23 D6
Iglesia de la Concepción 24 A7
Iglesia de San Diego 25 D2
Iglesia de San Francisco 26 C5
Iglesia de Santa Clara 27 A7
Mirador Torre Colpatria 28 D2
Museo Arqueológico 29 B8
Museo de Arte Colonial 30 B7
Museo de Arte Moderno 31 D3
Museo del Oro 32 C6
Museo Histórico Policía 33 A7
Museo Militar 34 C7
Museo Nacional 35 D1
Palacio de Justicia 36 B7
Quinta de Bolívar 37 F5
Sal Si Puedes 38 C5
SLEEPING
Alegria's Hostal 39 C8
Anandamayi Hostal 40 C8
Casa Platypus 41 D6
Cranky Croc 42 D6
Hostal Fatima 43 D7
Hostal La Candelaria 44 D6
Hostal Sue 45 D6
Hostal Sue II 46 D7
Hotel Ambala 47 C6
Platypus 48 D6

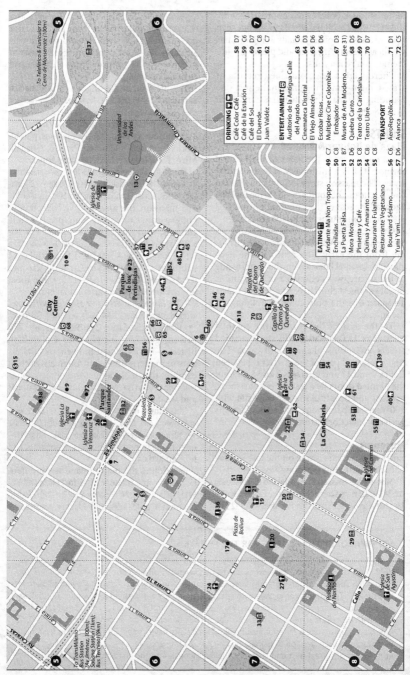

DRINKING 🍷🍸
Café Color Café..............................**58** D7
Café de la Estación.........................**59** C6
Café del Sol..................................**60** D7
El Duende....................................**61** C8
Juan Valdéz..................................**62** C7

ENTERTAINMENT 🎭
Auditorio de la Antigua Calle
  del Agrado................................**63** C6
Cinemateca Distrital.......................**64** D3
El Viejo Almacén............................**65** D6
Escobar Rosas...............................**66** D6
Multiplex Cine Colombia:
  Embajador.................................**67** D3
Museo de Arte Moderno....................**68** D5
Quiebra Canto...............................(see 31)
Teatro de la Candelaria....................**69** D7
Teatro Libre.................................**70** D7

TRANSPORT
AeroRepública...............................**71** D1
Avianca......................................**72** C5

EATING 🍴
Andante Ma Non Troppo....................**49** C7
Enchiladas...................................**50** C8
La Puerta Falsa.............................**51** B7
Mora Mora...................................**52** D6
Pimienta y Café.............................**53** C8
Quinua y Amaranto.........................**54** C8
Restaurante Fulanitos......................**55** C8
Restaurante Vegetariano
  Boulevard Sésamo........................**56** C6
Yumi Yumi..................................**57** D6

center of town, policing has improved greatly and crime has dropped significantly, but keep your wits about you, especially at night. Taxis are cheap, secure, metered and plentiful – use them if you're nervous.

There were a few confirmed reports of armed, night-time muggings in the area surrounding the main hostels in La Candelaria in 2008–09.

SIGHTS
Plaza de Bolívar & Around

Plaza de Bolívar is the heart of the historic town, but it is a mishmash of architectural styles. The massive stone building in classical Greek style on the southern side is the **Capitolio Nacional**, the seat of the Congress. Opposite is the equally monumental **Palacio de Justicia**.

On the western side of the plaza there's the French-style **Alcaldía** (mayor's office), dating from the early 20th century. The neoclassical **Catedral Primada**, on the eastern side of the square, was completed in 1823 and is Bogotá's largest church. Next door, the **Capilla del Sagrario** is the only colonial building on the square.

To the east of the plaza is the colonial quarter of **La Candelaria**, with steep cobbled streets, museums, theaters and cafes. The best-preserved part of the district is between Calles 9 and 13 and Carreras 2 and 5. Behind the painted doors lie a warren of courtyards, gardens and beautiful spaces, some still with 470-year-old bamboo roofs and adobe walls perfectly intact or restored.

Museums

Entry to museums is free on the last Sunday of each month; lines are long.

Not-to-be-missed **Museo del Oro** (Gold Museum; ☎ 343-2222; www.banrep.gov.co/museo; Carrera 6 No 15-88; adult Mon-Sat COP$2800, Sun free, child under 12 free; ☾ 9am-6pm Tue-Sat, 10am-4pm Sun) houses more than 34,000 gold pieces from all the major pre-Hispanic cultures in Colombia and is arguably the most important gold museum in the world. It's informative, accessible and curiously moving.

Bogotá's other highlight is the **Donación Botero** (☎ 343-1331; Calle 11 No 4-41; ☾ 9am-7pm Mon & Wed-Sat, 10am-5pm Sun). The 208-piece collection contains 123 of Botero's own works, including his paintings, drawings and sculptures, plus 85 works by names including Picasso, Chagall, Miró, Dali, Renoir, Matisse and Monet.

Museo Arqueológico (☎ 243-1048; www.musarq.org.co; Carrera 6 No 7-43; adult/student COP$3000; ☾ 8:30am-5pm Tue-Fri, 9:30am-5pm Sat, 10am-4pm Sun), in a colonial mansion, has an extensive collection of pottery from Colombia's main pre-Hispanic cultures, while **Museo de Arte Colonial** (☎ 341-6017; Carrera 6 No 9-77; admission COP$2000; ☾ 9am-5pm Tue-Fri, 10am-4pm Sat & Sun) has a fine display of paintings and drawings by Gregorio Vásquez de Arce y Ceballos (1638–1711), the most important painter of the colonial era.

The **Museo Nacional** (☎ 334-8366; www.museonacional.gov.co; Carrera 7 No 28-66; admission COP$3000; ☾ 10am-6pm Tue-Sat; to 5pm Sun), in an old prison, gives an insight into Colombian history – from the first indigenous inhabitants to modern times – through a wealth of exhibits that include historic objects, photos, maps, artifacts, paintings, documents and weapons.

The **Museo de Arte Moderno** (☎ 286-0466; www.mambogota.com; Calle 24 No 6-00; admission COP$4000; ☾ 10am-6pm Tue-Sat, noon-5pm Sun) has frequently changing exhibitions of national and foreign artists.

Straddling the macabre and the unintentionally comic is **Museo Histórico Policía** (☎ 233-5911; Calle 9 No 9-27; ☾ 8am-5pm Tue-Sat). Pablo Escobar's gold-adorned Harley, the jacket

---

SEPTIMAZO: BY THE PEOPLE, FOR THE PEOPLE

Every Friday from 5pm, cars are banned from Bogotá's central Carrera 7 from Calle 26 up to Plaza de Bolívar, and the whole city comes out to play, wander, nibble corn on the cob and sip hot herbal tea spiked with honey and *aguardiente* (sugarcane alcohol); it's a civil event known as 'Septimazo.' The streets come alive with spectacular and eccentric street performers: footballers juggle; transvestites mime to disco classics; stately older couples tango for cash; dwarf toreadors fight with dogs as mariachis strut by, effortlessly cool. Bogotá's B-Boys uprock as if at a New York City block party while a DJ scratches breaks. Storytellers have crowds of hundreds in hysterical laughter, who then stroll off to gamble on which box a trained guinea pig will run into. It's Bogotá at its civilized, surreal best and is an unequalled glimpse into the character of this great city.

COLOMBIA

he was wearing when police killed him in a rooftop shootout in 1993 in Medellín and a blood-stained roof tile are the standout pieces. Unconvincing dummies of the drug lord prompt stifled giggles.

The **Quinta de Bolívar** (☎ 336-6419; www.quinta debolivar.gov.co; Calle 20 No 2-91 Este; admission COP$3000; ○ 9am-5pm Tue-Fri, 11am-2pm Sat & Sun) houses Bolívar's personal effects, while **Museo Militar** (☎ 281-2548; www.ejercitonacional.mil.co; Calle 10 No 4-92; ○ 9am-4:30pm Tue-Fri, 11am-2pm Sat & Sun) has a collection including an incongruous tank, jetfighter and helicopter languishing in the courtyard of a colonial house in La Candelaria.

Churches

Iglesia de Santa Clara (Carrera 8 No 8-91; admission COP$2000; ○ 9am-5pm Tue-Fri, 10am-4pm Sat & Sun) is now open only as a museum, with more than 100 paintings and statues of saints from the 17th and 18th centuries.

Busy **Iglesia de San Francisco** (cnr Av Jiménez & Carrera 7), dates back to 1556 and has a gilded altarpiece; while **Iglesia de la Concepción** (Calle 10 No 9-50), has Bogotá's most beautiful *mudéjar* vault. **Iglesia de San Diego** (Carrera 7 No 26-37), a charming country church, is now hemmed in by high-rises.

Cerro de Monserrate

Crest the summit of the Cerro de Monserrate mountains at 3200m and test your camera's panoramic functions. There is a church on the summit, with a statue of the Señor Caído (Fallen Christ).

The most exciting trip is aboard a dubious-looking **teleférico** (cable car; COP$14,500; ○ every 15min from 9:30am-midnight Mon-Sat, 6am-5pm Sun) – or you can take the footpath. At the time of research this path was closed for repairs. A good thing, some would say – robberies have been reported and confirmed.

Other Sights

Mirador Torre Colpatria (☎ 283-6697; Carrera 7 No 24-89; admission COP$3500; ○ 11am-5pm Sat, Sun & holidays) offers 360-degree views from the 48th story of this 180m skyscraper, Bogotá's highest.

On Sunday the **flea market** in Parque de los Periodistas, has useless tat and the occasional hidden antique.

Check out the display of more than 5000 orchids at **Jardín Botánico José Celestino Mutis** (☎ 437-7060; www.jbb.gov.co; Calle 63 No 68-95;

BOGOTÁ: A SUNDAY CYCLIST'S PARADISE

Every Sunday from 7am to 2pm, 120km of Bogotá's main highways are closed to traffic and cyclists rule the roads. It's another example of how this progressive city puts its first-world counterparts to shame. To join in, either borrow a bike from your hostel (Platypus has four) or rent a 2009 model from English-speaking **Bogotá Bike Tours** (☎ 341-1027, 312-502-0554; www.bogotabike tours.com; Carrera 3 No 13-86; per 4hr COP$15,000, per day COP$25,000; ☎ 9am-6pm). Cycling at other times is more difficult, but keep to the back streets and you should be fine.

---

admission COP$2000; ○ 8am-5pm Mon-Fri, 9am-5pm Sat & Sun). It houses a variety of national flora from different climatic zones in gardens and greenhouses.

Maloka (☎ 427-2707; www.maloka.org; Carrera 68D No 40A-51; adult/student COP$10,000; ○ 10am-6pm Mon-Sun) is an interactive science and technology center. Exhibitions cover the universe, human beings, technology, life, water and biodiversity, and there's a 360-degree IMAX cinema.

ACTIVITIES

Check out the climbing wall at **Gran Pared** (☎ 285-0903; www.granpared.com; cnr Carrera 7 & Calle 50; per 1hr all-inclusive COP$17,000; ○ 2-10pm Mon, 10am-10pm Tue-Sat, 9am-5pm Sun).

For paragliding contact **Esteban Noboa** (☎ 672-8447, 310-819-4316) who charges COP$90,000 for a 25-minute tandem flight.

Horse riding in La Calera is run by **Carpasos** (☎ 368-7242, 310-261-2223; www.carpasos.com). Two hours is COP$70,000 per person.

COURSES

Universidad Javeriana's Centro Latinoamericano (☎ 320-8320; Carrera 10 No 65-48) Bogotá's best-known school of Spanish language, which offers regular one-year courses and three-week intensive courses.

Universidad Nacional (☎ 316-5335; cnr Carrera 30 & Calle 45) Best Spanish classes.

TOURS

De Una Colombia Tours (☎ 368-1915; www.deuna colombia.com; Carrera 26A No 40-18, Oficina 202) Specializes in very off-the-beaten-track destinations, including mountainous regions, Amazon tours etc. Multilingual guides.

Sal Si Puedes (☎ 283-3765; www.salsipuedes.org; Carrera 7 No 17-01, Oficina 640) An association of outdoor-minded people who organize weekend walks in the countryside. These are mostly one-day excursions to Cundinamarca, though longer trips to other regions are also arranged during holiday periods and long weekends.

Viva Bogotá (☎ 318-716-7297; leonguia@gmail.com) Tailor-made tours with bilingual guides. Local and national trips, extreme sports, emphasis on ecotourism and photography.

FESTIVALS & EVENTS

Festival Iberoamericano de Teatro Theater festival featuring groups from Latin America and beyond takes place in March/April of every even-numbered year.

Festival de Cine de Bogotá Bogotá's film festival in October usually attracts a strong selection of Latin American films.

Expoartesanías This crafts fair in December gathers together artisans along with their crafts from all around the country.

SLEEPING

Bogotá's budget hostel scene is booming. Seven of the following hostels have opened in the last two years.

Alegria's Hostal (☎ 286-8047; www.alegriashostel .com; Carrera 2 No 9-46; dm/s/d/tr incl breakfast COP$15,000/ 18,000/50,000/70,000; 🖳) Relaxed and peaceful spot away from the melee. Basic dorms are more spacious than at many of the competitors, and rooms all share bathrooms. The top room has huge windows and a glorious view.

Hostal Sue II (☎ 341-2647; www.hostalsue2.com; Carrera 3 No 14-18; dm COP$17,000, s/d without bathroom COP$27,000/45,000; 🖳) The older, (slightly) wiser sister of Sue. Table tennis and huge TV keeps the young residents busy. Many rooms are dark and a little drab.

Hostal La Candelaria (☎ 284-2348; www.hostalla candelaria.com; Calle 16 No 2-38; dm COP$17,000, s/d without bathroom COP$30,000/40,000; 🖳) On a noisy street, it's still a good option for the bars and restaurants nearby.

Hostal Sue (☎ 334-8894; www.hostalsue.com; Calle 16 No 2-55; dm/s/d COP$17,000/33,000/50,000; 🖳) Young, chaotic, raucous party hostel (pronounced 'sway'). Bring earplugs and a 'So-what?' shrug. Cramped and makeshift.

Platypus (☎ 341-2874; www.platypusbogota.com; Calle 16 No 2-43; dm COP$18,000, s/d COP$45,000/50,000, without bathroom COP$33,000/40,000; 🖳) The original and still the best, and the best value – mainly thanks to the charming and relaxed owner,

Germán Escobar, who has an encyclopedic knowledge of Colombia which he's happy to share. There's book exchange, free wi-fi, laundry and kitchen facilities, and free coffee. Clean, safe, sorted.

Cranky Croc (☎ 342-2438; www.crankycroc.com; Calle 15 No 3-46; dm/s/d incl breakfast COP$18,000/34,000/46,000; 🖳) Neat and tidy with good firm beds, a cool communal vibe and great staff.

Hostal Fatima (☎ 281-6389; www.hostalfatima .com; Calle 14 No 2-24; dm COP$18,000, s/d without bathroom COP$35,000/55,000; 🖳) Filled to the gills with a young, party-going crowd that knows what it wants and gets it here: cheap clean beds and new friends.

Anandamayi Hostal (☎ 341-7208; www.anandamayi hostel.com; Calle 9 No 2-81; dm/s/d COP$23,000/60,000/ 80,000; 🖳) Pin-drop quiet, sensitively restored colonial house with beautiful garden and heavy Buddhist vibe. Rooms come with or without bathroom, with no price difference. Chilled-out staff, beautiful rooms and dorm, thick blankets, hot water bottles, a warm kitchen and endless tea make it a great choice.

Casa Platypus (☎ 281-1801; www.casaplatypus .com; Carrera 3 No 16-28; dm/s/d/tr COP$40,000/130,000/ 150,000/170,000; 🖳) Exquisitely renovated colonial property with a glorious communal space, and modern, elegant bathrooms and kitchen. Staying here is like crashing at a rich relative's country pile. Owned by the endlessly helpful Germán from the original Platypus. Gay and lesbian couples welcome.

Hotel Ambala (☎ 342-6384; www.hotelambala .net; Carrera 5 No 13-46; s/d/tr COP$65,000/98,000/145,000; 🖳) Friendly hotel with 22 spotless but small rooms each with TV and minibar. Prices include one airport transfer and breakfast – worth at least COP$25,000. A great option if you don't like the hubbub of hostel life.

EATING

You can fill yourself to bursting with an *almuerzo corriente* (set lunch) at one of a thousand spots around Bogotá.

Mora Mora (Carrera 3A No 15-98; smoothies COP$3500, sandwiches from COP$4400; ☾ 9am-6pm Mon-Fri, 9:30am-3pm Sat) Smartly decked out, this place is popular with university students snacking on great Swiss-cheese sandwiches or a Mexican baguette.

Andante Ma Non Troppo (Carrera 3A No 10-92; dishes COP$4000-8000; ☾ 8am-8pm) Tranquil cafe and restaurant serving pastas and the best bread in La Candelaria.

La Puerta Falsa (Calle 11 No 6-50; tamale COP$5000; ⏰ 9am-11pm Mon-Fri) Bogotá institution, founded in 1816, serves sensational and filling tamales, *chocolate santafereño* (hot chocolate with cheese and bread) and lurid, dentist-worrying confections. Drop your cheese in the chocolate – it's what locals do and it's actually pretty good.

Pimienta y Café (Carrera 3 No 9-27; set menus COP$7000-14,000; ⏰ noon-4pm Mon-Fri, noon-5pm Sat & Sun) Great-value hearty Colombian food. Serves an excellent *ajiaco* (Bogotá's classic rib-sticking potato soup with corn, chicken, capers, avocado and sour cream) on weekends.

Quinua y Amaranto (Calle 11 No 2-95; set menus COP$9000; ⏰ 7am-7pm Mon-Sun) All your tofu and sprouting foodstuff needs catered for at this horrifically healthy whole-food restaurant. Great lentil burgers, seriously.

Restaurante Vegetariano Boulevard Sésamo (Av Jiménez 4-64; set menus COP$9000; ⏰ 8am-4pm Mon-Fri, to 5pm Sat) Cleanse your palate of fried chicken with a healthy set lunch including soup, fresh fruit juice and a plate of mixed vegetable dishes.

our pick **Yumi Yumi** (Carrera 3A No 16-40; salads & baguettes from COP$9000; ⏰ 9am-11pm Mon-Fri, 5pm-11pm Sat) Best baguettes and salad in town, with a Thai curry night on Monday. Killer cocktails are always two-for-one. English owners Matt and Sebastian can direct you to the cooler parties in Bogotá. The kitchen closes at 9pm.

Enchiladas (Calle 10 No 2-12; mains COP$9000-25,000; ⏰ noon-10pm Mon-Fri, 9am-10pm Sat, 5pm-10pm Sun) Authentic burritos, fajitas and tacos with clean, fresh flavors, excellent decor and a warm fireplace. Great Mexican jukebox. Highly recommended.

Restaurante Fulanitos (Carrera 3 No 8-61; mains COP$22,000-25,000) Informal but smart place that offers food typical of the Valle del Cauca in southern Colombia.

DRINKING
Cafes
Juan Valdéz (cnr Calle 11 & Carrera 4; ⏰ 7am-11pm Mon-Sat, 10am-7pm Sun) Juan Valdéz might be a chain, but the coffee is local and delicious.

Café del Sol (Calle 14 No 3-60; ⏰ 8am-8:30pm) Good coffee, snacks, sandwiches and breakfast.

Café de la Estación (Calle 14 No 5-14; ⏰ 7am-10pm Mon-Fri, 9am-8pm Sat) A great Bogotá curio, this: it's an old train carriage converted into a cool cafe.

El Duende (Calle 10 No 2-99; ⏰ noon-10pm Mon-Sat) Homely little boho hangout with decent coffee and cocktails and couples canoodling in the candlelight.

Bars
Like all Latin towns, the Zona Rosa is where the real party's at. It's the northern sector of the city, between Carreras 11 and 15, and Calles 81 and 84. Get a cab – it's 6km from La Candelaria, where most hostels are. Expect to pay around COP$6000. Dress up or you'll feel out of place. La Candelaria is cheaper, more low key, and a little more grungy.

Pub (Carrera 12A No 83-48, Zona Rosa; ⏰ noon-late) Cheerily functional Irish pub that's actually pretty good. Sells local beers brewed by the Bogotá Beer Company, an excellent microbrewery whose beers will revive a lager-jaded palate.

Café Color Café (Carrera 2 No 13-06; ⏰ noon-11pm) At the Plazoleta del Chorro de Quevedo, the seat of old Bogotá, there's a faint whiff of bohemia and marijuana on the breeze outside, where jugglers entertain or annoy. Inside, there's cheap beer.

Kea (Carrera 14A No 83-37, Zona Rosa; ⏰ 8am-3am Tue-Sat) Young, relaxed lounge bar with occasional live bands.

Ovejo (Carrera 14 No 83-70; ⏰ 6pm-3am Mon-Sat) By the sounds here you'd expect grizzled bikers to prop up the bar. Instead, it's an easy-going mixed crowd chilling to classic rock.

SPLURGE! PARTY IN A PIÑATA

Andrés Carne de Res (☎ 863-7780; www.andrescarnederes.com; Calle 3 No 11A-56, Chía; meals from COP$35,000; ⏰ noon-3am Fri-Sun) could make a vegetarian capitulate. It's a sprawling, gloriously theatrical complex that's a cross between a Cirque du Soleil show, the best steakhouse you ever visited and a liquor-drenched Colombian knees-up. More than 250,000 people eat 10 tons of meat a year here, before partying till 5am in a series of interlinked rooms and dance floors bedecked with magic-realist bric-a-brac. By midnight, it's a total madhouse with hundreds of crazed-but-friendly locals dancing on the tables to *vallenato* (Colombian accordion music), disco or cumbia and pouring rum into any passing mouth. It's in Chia – a COP$50,000 cab ride away, meaning you'll blow COP$150,000 easily, each. But you'll never forget it.

ENTERTAINMENT

See bogota.vive.in/bogota for weekly updated listings. A licensing law was passed in 2009 ruling that most clubs had to close by 3am. This may have changed by the time this book is printed. Nightlife here still thrums with an intense Latin energy. You can hear salsa, crossover (a Latin pop hybrid), merengue, rock, reggae, hip-hop and house all over town.

Nightclubs

If you're coming here to party, weekends are way livelier than weekdays.

El Viejo Almacén (Calle 15 No 4-30, La Candelaria; 6pm-2:30am Tue-Sat, 4pm-11pm Sun) Nostalgic tango bar with 4000-plus old tango LPs.

Escobar Rosas (cnr Calle 15 & Carrera 4, La Candelaria; admission COP$2500; 10pm-3am Thu-Sat) Gringolandia, with '70s and '80s rock.

Salomé Pagana (Carrera 14A No 82-16, Zona Rosa; admission COP$10,000; 7pm-3am) Fine salsa and *son cubano* (traditional Cuban music) with live bands on Friday.

Quiebra Canto (Carrera 5 No 17-76; admission COP$10,000; 8pm-3am Tue-Sat) Dependable double-level disco popular with Colombians and foreigners, playing salsa and crossover.

Cha Cha Club (Carrera 7 No 32-16, Piso 41; admission COP$15,000; 9pm-3am Thu-Sat) Thrashing house and machine-tooled techno in a converted Hilton ballroom on the 41st floor. Pristine sound system and European DJs rock a young and well-dressed crowd who dance like they mean it. Gay night on Sunday.

In Vitro (Calle 59 No 6-38; admission COP$15,000; 8:30pm-3am Tue-Sat) Tuesday nights always end up here thanks to the cheap drinks and a very flirtatious atmosphere assisted ably by cheap booze. The floor moves to hip-hop, Afrobeat, reggae, salsa and soul. Cool, student crowd.

Armando Records (Calle 85 No 14-46, Piso 4, Zona Rosa; admission COP$15,000; 8pm-3am Wed-Sat) Open terrace to beat the smoking ban, minimalist Euro decor and the city's most eclectic, open-minded music policy.

Vinacure (Av Caracas 9A No 63-32, Int 7; admission COP$15,000; 9pm-3am Fri & Sat) Bizarre burlesque, surreal stage shows with assorted drag queens and various maniacs going crazy inside a converted vintage cinema. Like the bar in Star Wars, only much, much weirder.

Penthouse (Calle 84 No 13-17, Zona Rosa; admission COP$20,000; 10pm-3am Wed-Sat) Chic, apartment-style spot full of well-dressed locals and DJs

flitting between salsa, merengue and pop. It's pricey, but worth a look.

Gotíca (Carrera 12A No 83-23, Zona Rosa; admission COP$20,000; 10pm-3am Mon-Sat) Before the licensing clampdown of 2009, this was the most reliable after-party spot in town, playing house downstairs and funk and soul in the glad-eye upstairs salon.

Cinemas

Bogotá has dozens of mainstream cinemas. Tuesday and Thursday cost COP$7000 rather than COP$16,000.

Multiplex Cine Colombia: Embajador (404-2463; Calle 24 No 6-01) Multiplex in the city center.

For something more thought-provoking, check the programs of the *cinematecas* (arthouse cinemas):

Auditorio de la Antigua Calle del Agrado (281-4671; Calle 16 No 4-75)

Cinemateca Distrital (283-5879; www.cinemateca distrital.gov.co; Carrera 7 No 22-79, Bloque 1, Oficina 905)

Museo de Arte Moderno (286-0466; www.mam bogota.com; Calle 24 No 6-00) Has regular screenings.

Theater

Teatro de la Candelaria (281-4814; www.teatro lacandelaria.org.co; Calle 12 No 2-59)

Teatro Libre (281-4834; hwww.teatrolibre.com; Carrera 11 No 61-80)

Teatro Nacional (217-4577; www.teatronacional .com.co; Calle 71 No 10-25)

Sports

Soccer is Colombia's national sport. Crowds are passionate; the atmosphere intense but friendly.

Estadio El Campín (cnr Carrera 30 & Calle 55) Home of Santa Fe and Millonarios. Matches are on Wednesday nights and Saturday evenings. Tickets can be bought at the stadium before matches (COP$8000 to COP$40,000). Plenty of touts sell tickets at face value or less just before games start at around 6pm.

For local games, tickets can also be bought at **Millonarios** (Carrera 24 No 63-68) and **Santa Fe** (Calle 64A No 38-08). For international matches (and to watch the national team), buy tickets in advance at **Federación Colombiana de Fútbol** (288-9838; www.colfutbol.org; Av 32 No 16-22).

GETTING THERE & AWAY
Air

Bogotá's airport, Aeropuerto El Dorado, has two terminals and handles all domestic and international flights. The main terminal, **El Dorado** (☎ 425-1000; Av El Dorado) is 15km northwest of the city center. Three *casas de cambio*, next to each other on the ground floor, change cash and are open 24 hours. The Banco Popular at the next window (also open 24 hours), changes both cash and traveler's checks. There are a dozen ATMs on the upper level.

The other terminal, **Puente Aéreo** (☎ 425-1000, ext 3218; Av El Dorado), is 1km from El Dorado. It handles some of Avianca's domestic flights.

There are plenty of domestic flights to destinations all over the country. Average one-way prices for the following cities are: Cali (COP$200,000), Cartagena (COP$400,000), Leticia (COP$250,000), Medellín (COP$200,000) and San Andrés (COP$350,000).

AeroRepública (☎ 320-9090; www.aerorepublica.com.co; Carrera 10 No 27-51, Local 165)

Aires (☎ 336-6039; www.aires.aero; Carrera 11 No 76-14, Local 102)

Avianca(☎ 404-7862; Carrera 7 No 16-36)

Satena (☎ 423-8530; www.satena.com; Av El Dorado 103-08, Interior 11)

Bus

The **bus terminal** (☎ 428-2424; Calle 33B No 69-13) is 10km northwest of the city center. It's large, functional and well organized, and has a tourist office, restaurants, cafeterias, showers and left-luggage rooms.

Buses travel around the clock to the following destinations: Bucaramanga (COP$60,000, eight hours), Cali (COP$50,000, nine hours) and Medellín (COP$60,000, nine hours). There are also direct buses to Cartagena (COP$140,000, 20 hours), Cúcuta (COP$90,000, 16 hours), Ipiales (COP$85,000, 23 hours), Popayán (COP$70,000 12 hours), San Agustín (COP$52,000, 12 hours) and Santa Marta (COP$120,000, 16 hours). All prices listed here are approximate for air-con buses.

GETTING AROUND
Bus & Buseta

TransMilenio apart, Bogotá's public transportation is operated by buses and *busetas* (small buses). There are few bus stops – you just wave down the bus or *buseta*. The flat fare (around COP$1100 depending on the class and generation of the vehicle) is posted by the door or on the windscreen.

Taxi

Bogotá's taxis are metered; the figure on the meter corresponds to a chart normally hanging from the back of the passenger seat.

TransMilenio

TransMilenio has revolutionized Bogotá's public transportation. Huge articulated buses charge through the main thoroughfares on their own dedicated roads. The service is cheap (COP$1500), frequent and fast, and runs from 5am to 11pm. Tickets are bought at the station. Buses get very crowded at rush hour. Watch your pockets.

The main TransMilenio route is Av Caracas, which links the center to both southern and northern suburbs. There are also lines on Carrera 30, Av 8, Av de Las Américas and a short spur on Av Jiménez up to Carrera 3. There are three termini, but the only one of real use to travelers is the **Portal del Norte** (northern terminus; Calle 170) which has bus links to Zipaquirá and Suesca.

AROUND BOGOTÁ

ZIPAQUIRÁ
☎ 1 / pop 100,000

One of Colombia's most fascinating attractions is the hauntingly beautiful underground **salt cathedral** (☎ 852-4035; www.catedraldesal.gov.co; admission COP$15,000, Wed COP$10,000; ☺ 9am-6pm) at Zipaquirá, 50km north of Bogotá.

The cathedral was born from an old salt mine, dug straight into a mountain outside the town. The mines date back to the Muisca period and have been intensively exploited, but they still contain vast reserves that will last another 500 years.

Opened to the public in 1995, the cathedral is 75m long and 18m high and can accommodate 8400 people.

Buses from Bogotá to Zipaquirá (COP$2600, 1¼ hours) run every 10 minutes from the northern terminus of TransMilenio, known as Portal del Norte, on Autopista del Norte at Calle 170. TransMilenio from Bogotá's center will take you to Portal del Norte in 40 minutes. The mines are a 15-minute walk uphill from Zipaquirá's center.

The alternative is to take the **Turistren** (www.turistren.com.co), a steam locomotive, which runs from Bogotá to Zipaquirá on weekends and holidays.

The train (return COP$32,000) departs **Sabana station** (☎ 375-0557; Calle 13 No 18-24) at 8:30am, stops briefly at **Usaquen station** (cnr Calle 100 & Carrera 9A) at 9:20am and reaches Zipaquirá at 11:30am. The return leg now leaves from Cajica, 15km south, at 3:15pm. While on the train, buy a combined ticket for the cathedral and transportation between Zipaquirá and Cajica for the return leg (COP$20,000). From Cajica, you'll reach Sabana at 5:40pm.

SUESCA
☎ 1 / pop 14,000

Suesca is an adventure-sports center near Bogotá with rock climbing, mountain biking and white-water rafting. Visit at weekends, when local outfitters are open.

To get to Suesca, take the TransMilenio to its northern terminus at Portal del Norte, and catch a frequent direct bus (COP$5300, one hour) to Suesca.

Hugo Rocha (☎ 315-826-2051; www.dealturas .com), an English-speaking guide and instructor, has 15 years' experience in the area and offers day/overnight rock-climbing trips and lessons, including all equipment. A day climb costs COP$120,000, a five-day course costs COP$500,000. Accommodation is available at COP$20,000 per night. Hugo can arrange accommodation at around COP20,000 a night.

GUATAVITA
☎ 1 / pop 5700

Also called Guatavita Nueva, this town was built from scratch in the late 1960s when the old colonial Guatavita was flooded by the waters of a reservoir. The town is an interesting architectural blend of old and new, and is a popular weekend destination for people from Bogotá.

About 15km from town is the famous **Laguna de Guatavita** (admission COP$12,000; ⓨ 9am-4pm Tue-Sun), the sacred lake and ritual center of the Muisca indigenous people, and the birthplace of the El Dorado myth. The emerald-green lake, which looks like the product of some prehistoric meteor collision, was a sacred object of worship where gold, emeralds and food were offered by the Muiscas to their gods.

Bogotá's Museo del Oro's most intricate and startling exhibit, the tiny Muisca Raft, portrays the scenes once played out here, although the piece was not found anywhere

nearby. It's an intriguing and ethereal experience to gaze at the waters and imagine shamans in jaguar masks accompanying a naked chieftain daubed in gold dust as he floated out to perform a ritual that we cannot hope to comprehend.

Dozens of greedy dreamers have tried to steal riches submerged in the lake's calm depths. Few people have ever managed it.

It's a 15-minute hike up to the lakeside hilltops from the entrance.

From Bogotá, take a bus to the town of Guatavita (departing from Portal del Norte, the northern terminus of the TransMilenio) and get off 11km before reaching the town (6km past Sesquilé), where there is a sign directing you to the lake, and walk 7km uphill along a dirt road.

NORTH OF BOGOTÁ

This is Colombia's heartland. The region of deep gorges, fast-flowing rivers and soaring peaks was the first to be settled by the conquistadors, and a number of their colonial towns stand today. It's also the revolutionary heart of the country: it was here that Simón Bolívar took on Spain in the decisive fight for Colombia's independence.

The departments of Boyacá, Santander and Norte de Santander are tourist-friendly: they're within easy reach of Bogotá on a good network of roads with bus services, and there's loads to see and do including 450-year-old colonial towns, craft markets, heart-pumping adventure sports and spectacular national parks.

TUNJA
☎ 8 / pop 160,000

Tunja, the chilly capital of Boyacá, sits at 2820m and has fine colonial architecture and elegant mansions adorned with some of South America's most unique artwork. Many travelers rush through on their way to Villa de Leyva, but fans of colonial history and ornate churches will enjoy a day or two here.

The city was founded by Gonzalo Suárez Rendón in 1539 on the site of Hunza, the pre-Hispanic Muisca settlement. Almost nothing is left of the indigenous legacy, but much colonial architecture remains. Tunja is today a bustling student center with a population of 160,000.

Information

Bancolombia (Carrera 10 No 22-43) Changes traveler's checks and US dollars.

Internet Orbitel (☎ 743-0955; Calle 20 No 10-26; per hr COP$1400; ☉ 8am-9pm) Internet and international phone calls.

Secretaría de Educación, Cultura y Turismo
(☎ 742-3272; Carrera 9 No 19-68; ☉ 8am-noon & 2-6pm) Ground floor of the Casa del Fundador Suárez Rendón, helpful staff.

Sights

The **Casa del Fundador Suárez Rendón** (☎ 742-3272; Carrera 9 No 19-68; admission COP$2000; ☉ 8am-noon & 2-6pm) and **Casa de Don Juan de Vargas** (☎ 742-6611; Calle 20 No 8-52; admission COP$2000; ☎ 9am-noon & 2-5pm Tue-Fri, 10am-4pm Sat & Sun) are worth a look for

their ceilings, which are covered with paintings featuring human figures, animals and mythological scenes.

Iglesia de Santa Clara La Real (☎ 742-5659; Carrera 7 No 19-58; admission COP$2000; ☉ 8am-noon & 2-6pm) is one of the most beautiful and richly decorated churches in Colombia. It has been converted into a museum. It was closed for renovations at the time of research. In **Iglesia de Santo Domingo** (Carrera 11 No 19-55) note the exuberant Capilla del Rosario, to the left as you enter the church.

Other churches worth a visit include **Iglesia de Santa Bárbara** (Carrera 11 No 16-62), **Iglesia de San Francisco** (Carrera 10 No 22-23) and **Catedral Santiago de Tunja** (Plaza de Bolívar). Tunja's churches are noted for their *mudéjar* art, an Islamic-

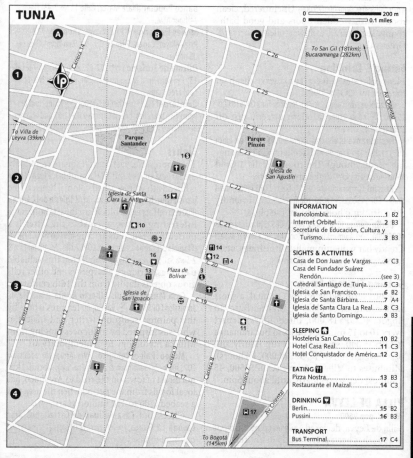

TUNJA

| 0 | 200 m |
| 0 | 0.1 miles |

To San Gil (181km);
Bucaramanga (282km)

To Villa de
Leyva (39km)

Parque
Santander

Parque
Pinzón

Iglesia de
San Agustín

Iglesia de Santa
Clara La Antigua

Plaza de
Bolívar

Iglesia de
San Ignacio

Carrera 13
Carrera 12
Carrera 11
Carrera 10
Carrera 8
Carrera 7

AV Oriental

To Bogotá
(145km)

INFORMATION
Bancolombia...................................1 B2
Internet Orbitel..............................2 B3
Secretaría de Educación, Cultura y
    Turismo....................................3 B3

SIGHTS & ACTIVITIES
Casa de Don Juan de Vargas........4 C3
Casa del Fundador Suárez
    Rendón................................(see 3)
Catedral Santiago de Tunja.........5 C3
Iglesia de San Francisco..............6 B2
Iglesia de Santa Bárbara..............7 A4
Iglesia de Santa Clara La Real.....8 C3
Iglesia de Santo Domingo...........9 B3

SLEEPING
Hostelería San Carlos...................10 B2
Hotel Casa Real...........................11 C3
Hotel Conquistador de América....12 C3

EATING
Pizza Nostra................................13 B3
Restaurante el Maizal...................14 C3

DRINKING
Berlin...15 B2
Pussini.......................................16 B3

TRANSPORT
Bus Terminal...............................17 C4

COLOMBIA

influenced style that developed in Christian Spain between the 12th and 16th centuries. It is particularly visible in the ornamented, coffered vaults.

Sleeping

Hotel Conquistador de América (☎ 742-3534; Calle 20 No 8-92; s/d/tr COP$25,000/40,000/60,000) At the corner of Plaza de Bolívar, this colonial building has 20 ample rooms with hot showers and small TVs. Some rooms are dim and boxy, but the larger doubles are noisy.

Hostería San Carlos (☎ 742-3716; Carrera 11 No 20-12; s/d/tr COP$30,000/50,000/60,000; 💻) Located in an atmospheric old home within walking distance of the sights, rooms are musty but acceptable.

Hotel Casa Real (☎ 310-852-1636; Calle 19 No 7-65; s/d/tr COP$50,000/60,000/75,000) Uncluttered, clean rooms with wooden floors and good bathrooms set around a flower-filled courtyard. Great value.

Eating & Drinking

Plenty of restaurants in Tunja serve cheap set lunches for COP$5000.

Pizza Nostra (Calle 19 No 10-36; pizza for 2 COP$10,000-15,000; 💲 noon-11pm) Modern pizzeria just off Plaza de Bolívar.

Restaurante el Maizal (Carrera 9 No 20-30; set lunch COP$11,000; 💲 7am-9pm) Excellent, daily changing menu, though the room recalls a Cold War–era airport departures lounge.

Pussini (Carrera 10 No 19-53; beers COP$2500, mixed drinks COP$4500; 💲 8:30-10pm Mon-Sun) Friendly little drinking hole right on the plaza.

Berlin (Carrera 10 No 21-49; beers COP$2500, mixed drinks COP$8000; 💲 4pm-midnight Mon-Thu, to 2am Fri & Sat) Trendy bar with minimalist furnishings, open music policy and strong drinks.

Getting There & Away

The bus terminal is on Av Oriental, a short walk southeast of Plaza de Bolívar. Buses to Bogotá (COP$18,000, three hours) depart every 10 to 15 minutes. Buses to Bucaramanga (COP$35,000, seven hours) run hourly and pass through San Gil (COP$20,000, 4½ hours). Minibuses to Villa de Leyva (COP$5500, 45 minutes) depart regularly until about 6pm.

VILLA DE LEYVA

☎ 8 / pop 9600

Villa de Leyva, declared a national monument in 1954, has been preserved in its entirety and virtually no modern architecture exists – but that's only half the story here.

Founded in 1572, Villa de Leyva enjoys a healthy, dry and mild climate, far warmer than Tunja, just 39km away (although it's 700m higher). It's close to some wonderful landscapes, with great bird-watching, ancient stone circles, impressive waterfalls, good food and excellent hiking opportunities; nature-lovers could easily spend a week here.

Villa de Leyva is a place to relax and escape the chilly heights of Bogotá, and as such, it's a popular getaway for *bogotanos*, who fill the town's many hotels, craft shops and tourist-oriented restaurants at weekends. Come early in the week for better-value hotel deals.

Information

Banco Popular (Plaza Mayor, Calle 12 No 9-43) Has a 24-hour ATM.

Money Exchange & Photocopy Shop (☎ 732-1225; Plaza Mayor, Carrera 9 No 12-36; 💲 9am-6pm) Changes US dollars.

Oficina de Turismo (☎ 732-0232; cnr Carrera 9 & Calle 13; 💲 8am-1pm & 3-6pm Mon-Sat, 9am-1pm & 3-6pm Sun) Free maps.

Quinternet I & II (per hr COP$1600; 💲 10am-1pm & 3-9pm) Two branches; one at Carrera 9 No 11-77 and another at Carrera 9 No 11-96. Decent connections in both branches.

Sights

The impressive, vast central square (reputedly the largest of its kind in Colombia), **Plaza Mayor** is lined with whitewashed colonial houses. The **parish church**, on the plaza, and **Iglesia del Carmen** (Plazuela del Carmen), a block northeast, both have interesting interiors. Next to the latter is a museum of religious art, the **Museo del Carmen** (Plazuela del Carmen; admission COP$2000; 💲 10am-1pm & 2-5pm Sat, Sun & holidays), which contains valuable paintings, carvings, altarpieces and other religious objects dating from the 16th century.

Casa Museo de Luis Alberto Acuña (Plaza Mayor; admission COP$3000; 💲 9am-6pm) features works by this painter, sculptor, writer and historian who was inspired by influences ranging from Muisca mythology to contemporary art.

Museo Paleontológico (Vía Arcabuco; admission COP$3000; 💲 9am-noon & 2-5pm Tue-Sun), about 1km northeast of town on the road to Arcabuco, has local fossils from the period when the area was a seabed (100 to 150 million years ago).

Check out **Casa de Juan de Castellanos** and **Casona La Guaca**, two meticulously restored colonial mansions on Carrera 9 just off Plaza

Mayor. They have beautiful patios and house cafes and craft shops.

There's a colorful **market** held on Saturday on the square three blocks southeast of Plaza Mayor – it's best and busiest early in the morning. Walk further southeast and climb the hill to a **viewpoint** overlooking the town.

Activities

The area around Villa de Leyva is pleasant for **hiking**, and you can visit some of the nearby attractions along the way (see p524), or go trekking in the Santuario de Iguaque (p524). The region is also good for **cycling** and **horse riding**, both run by Colombian Highlands (below). Bikes cost COP$3000 per hour; horses COP$5000 per hour.

Tours

Many locals offer excursions, but the best trips are arranged through Oscar Giledes' **Colombian Highlands** (☎ 732-1379; Carrera 9 No 11-02), which offers a variety of offbeat tours, including nocturnal hikes, rappelling and horse-riding trips. It also rents bikes and camping equipment.

Sleeping

Prices rocket and rooms become scarce during holidays and long weekends. We've listed weekday rates here.

Renacer Guesthouse (☎ 732-1201, 311-308-3739; www.colombianhighlands.com; campsite per person COP$10,000, dm/s/d COP$18,000/35,000/70,000) Very comfortable luxury hostel with fine dorms, excellent, tastefully furnished private rooms, a large kitchen for guests and a fireplace. Breakfast is also served. It's a long walk uphill from the square (1.2km northeast), but call owner Oscar Gilede when you arrive and he will pay for your first taxi.

Hospedería Colonial (☎ 732-1364; Calle 12 No 10-81; s/d COP$20,000/40,000) Basic but acceptable rooms with bathtubs, near the plaza.

Posada San Martín (☎ 732-0428; Calle 14 No 9-43; s/d/tr incl breakfast COP$30,000/60,000/90,000) This old hotel with exposed beams has bright and colorfully decorated rooms.

Hospedería La Roca (☎ 732-0331; Plaza Mayor; s/d/tr COP$40,000/80,000/120,000) Rambling hallways on two stories lead to a variety of pleasant rooms, all of which have a TV, high ceilings and a modern bathroom.

COLOMBIA

Posada de los Angeles (☎ 732-0562; Carrera 10 No 13-94; s/d/tr COP$50,000/80,000/120,000) A family-home atmosphere, with simple clean rooms and modern bathrooms.

Eating & Drinking

Not all restaurants are open on weekdays.

Pastelería Francesa (Calle 10 No 9-41; mains COP$1500-5000; ☺ breakfast & lunch Thu-Mon) Who doesn't love a French patisserie? Great apple tart and hot chocolate.

Restaurante Casa Blanca (Calle 13 No 7-16; set meals COP$6000, mains COP$15,000; ☺ 8am-8:15pm Mon-Fri, to 9:30pm Sat & Sun) Excellent-value *comida corriente* (basic set meal), mains are equally good, with trout, chicken and beef all cooked beautifully.

Los Tres Caracoles (Plaza Mayor; paella COP$23,000; lamb for 2 COP$39,000; other mains COP$12,000-15,000; ☺ noon-9pm Mon-Fri, to 10pm Sat & Sun) On Sunday the specialty is a roast leg smothered in delicious *salsa verde* (a sauce of parsley, olive oil, capers and anchovies). The owner's Spanish and knows what he's doing with a paella pan, too.

Antique (Casona La Guaca, Carrera 9 No 13-55; mains COP$12,000-26,000; ☺ lunch & dinner) Creative and inspired dishes served with style on a colonial rooftop.

Restaurante Savia (Casa Quintero; mains COP$12,000-28,000; ☺ 4-10pm Fri, 10am-10pm Sat & Sun) Good vegetarian choice, and there are good meat dishes. Elvis Presley's drummer used to play here; he died in 2006.

Zarina (Casa Quintero; mains COP$13,000-18,000; ☺ 12:30-9pm) Excellent falafel with real tahini.

La Cava de don Fernando (Carrera 10 No 12-03; beers COP$2500; ☺ 2pm-2am) Good choice for a late drink.

Getting There & Away

The bus terminal is three blocks southwest of the Plaza Mayor, on the road to Tunja. Minibuses run between Tunja and Villa de Leyva every 15 minutes from 5am to 6pm (COP$5500, 45 minutes, 39km). There are only two direct buses daily to Bogotá (COP$14,000, four hours); head to Tunja where departures are more regular.

AROUND VILLA DE LEYVA

Here you'll find archaeological relics, colonial monuments, petroglyphs, caves, lakes, waterfalls and fossils. You can walk to some

of the nearest sights, or go by bicycle or on horseback.

Estación Astronómica Muisca (El Infiernito)

The **Muisca observatory** (admission COP$3200; ☺ 9am-noon & 2-5pm Tue-Sun) dates from the early centuries AD and was used by indigenous people to determine the seasons. It was named 'Little Hell' by Catholics who wanted to put the fear of (a Christian) God into the locals, and encourage them to associate it with the devil. It was also a ritual site noted for a number of large, phallic stone monoliths. Some of these were destroyed, and in a deliciously ironic twist, some of the penis-themed rubble was incorporated into local convent walls. You can walk there in 25 minutes or take a bike (around COP$20,000 per day) or horse (COP$40,000 per half day). Taxi is COP$20,000 for a return trip with waiting time; haggle hard.

Parque Nacional Santuario de Iguaque

Iguaque is a 67.5 sq km **national park** (admission COP$31,000) northeast of Villa de Leyva. It covers the highest part of the mountain range that stretches up to Arcabuco. There are eight small mountain lakes in the northern part of the reserve, sitting at an altitude of between 3550m and 3700m. The site is named after the **Laguna de Iguaque**, a sacred lake for the Muiscas.

The **visitors center** (dm COP$28,600) is at an altitude of 2950m, 3km off the Villa de Leyva–Arcabuco road. Take warm clothing. It offers meals, dorm beds, and collects the entrance fee. If you plan on sleeping at the center, check in advance at Bogotá's national park office (p511). Dorm rates increase by COP$8000 in high season.

From Villa de Leyva take a bus to Arcabuco (four departures a day), get off after 12km at a place known as Los Naranjos and walk to the visitors center (3km). A walk from the visitors center uphill to the Laguna de Iguaque takes two to three hours. A leisurely return trip is likely to take four to six hours.

PARQUE NACIONAL EL COCUY

With snowcapped peaks, scintillating alpine lakes and glorious green valleys, Parque Nacional El Cocuy ranks as one of Colombia's most spectacular protected areas. Located in the highest part of the Cordillera Oriental, it tops out at Ritacumba Blanco, a 5330m peak.

The mountain chain is relatively compact and not difficult to reach – the gateway towns are Guicán and El Cocuy in northern Boyacá. It's an ideal place for trekking, although the routes are more suited to experienced walkers. There are no facilities in the park so you'll need to bring all your food and equipment including sleeping bags, warm clothing and a tent.

Some tour companies run trips this way. Speak to Thomas Doyer, whose company **De Una Colombia Tours** (☎ 312-450-6178) has good experience in this area and who comes recommended.

SAN GIL
☎ 7 / pop 42,900

Tiny San Gil, a busy little town on the road between Bogotá and Bucaramanga, is the beating heart of Colombia's burgeoning ecotourism and adventure sports industries. And with the mighty Río Suarez boasting some of the best Grade 4+ rapids in South America, your heart might just be stop beating.

As well as rafting, rappelling, *torrentismo* (rappelling down a waterfall), horse riding, parascending, hydrospeeding, caving and mountain biking, there are enough calmer activities to please nature-lovers who want the view without the adrenaline. There are natural swimming holes, waterfalls, beautiful rivers and easy, wonderful hikes within 30 minutes of the town.

San Gil's shady main square has huge old ceiba trees and an 18th-century cathedral and is a nice spot to relax.

If you stop in San Gil, don't miss Barichara or Guane, tranquil, immaculately preserved and renovated colonial towns nearby.

Information

The official tourism website for San Gil is www.sangil.com.co.

Bancolombia (Calle 12 No 10-44) Withdrawals up to COP$400,000. There are several other ATMs around the plaza.

Foxnet (Centro Comercial El Edén, Carrera 10 No 12-37; per hr COP$1500; ⏰ 8:30am–noon & 2-9:30pm) Internet.

Ivan's Cafe net (Calle 12 No 7-63; per hr COP$1500; ⏰ 7:30am-9pm)

Post office (Carrera 10 No 10-50; ⏰ 8-11:30am & 2-4pm Mon-Fri) Next to Cajasan Supermercado.

Tourist office (☎ 724-4617; cnr Carrera 10 & Calle 12; ⏰ 8am–noon & 2-6pm) The main tourist office; another less useful kiosk is near Parque El Gallineral.

Sights
IN TOWN

The town's best spot to escape the heat is **Parque El Gallineral** (☎ 724-4372; cnr Malecón & Calle 6; admission COP$4000; ⏰ 8am-6pm). It's a beautiful, ethereal riverside park, where the trees are covered with *barbas de viejo* – long silvery fronds of *tillandsia* (a fronded, drooping plant that grows hanging off trees). It's among some of Colombia's most beautiful public spaces. There is also a natural swimming pool.

OUT OF TOWN

Pozo Azul, is a freshwater pool just 1km north of the center of town. It's popular with Colombians at weekends; during the week it's quiet. **Quebrada Curití** is a river 12km northeast of San Gil near the village of **Curití**, with crystalline swimming pools. Best of all is the **Cascadas de San Juan Curi**, an 180m-high waterfall. Maniacs are welcome to abseil down. The falls are 22km from San Gil on the road to Charalá. There are two buses an hour to Charalá (COP$3000, 30 minutes) from the local bus station. Ask the driver to let you out at the *cascadas* (waterfalls), and walk 20 minutes up a trail to the falls. The owner of the land sometimes charges COP$5000 to enter.

Tours

More than a dozen tour agencies in San Gil run white-water rafting trips. A standard 10km run on Río Fonce (Grades 1 to 3) costs COP$25,000 per person and takes 1½ hours.

The perilous and thrilling Río Suarez is a world-class run that even seasoned experts say still scares them. It's a full day's trip, and costs COP$120,000. Most operators also offer horse riding, caving, paragliding, rappelling, rock climbing and ecological walks. Many firms act as intermediaries between the few companies that have the right to operate in each location.

Colombia Rafting Expeditions (☎ 311-283-8647; info@colombiarafting.com; Carrera 10 No 7-83) Best-equipped rafting outfit in town, with experienced, often English-speaking guides. It is pricier than the competition, but it's money well spent.

Macondo Adventures (☎ 724-4463, 311-828-2905; info@macondohostel.com; Macondo Guesthouse, Calle 12 No 7-26) Can organize dozens of activities.

Planeta Azul (☎ 724-0000; info@planetaazulcolombia .com; Parque El Gallineral) Organizes rafting trips.

Sleeping

San Gil has plenty of budget hotels in the center of town. Prices increase by up to 40% during high season.

Macondo Guesthouse (☎ 724-4463, 311-828-2905; Calle 12 No 7-26; dm COP$13,000, s COP$26,000-30,000; ☐) San Gil's backpacker nexus: with wi-fi, kitchen facilities, book exchange and laundry service. Reservations are advised. Aussie owner Shaun can advise on outdoor activities and is an expert rafter.

Centro Real (☎ 724-0387; Calle 10 No 10-41; s/d COP$15,000/25,000; ☐) A modern hotel with small rooms and no external windows, it's the best value of the budget choices nearby.

Santander Alemán (☎ 724-2535, 317-770-9188; igarnica@hotmail.com; Calle 12 No 7-63; dm COP$15,000, s/d without bathroom COP$25,000/30,000) The homely atmosphere here attracts a slightly older crowd. The rooms are large and spotless, beds are firm and the sheets are new. In the morning, try the excellent fruit smoothies and the huge breakfast (COP$7000).

Hotel Abril (☎ 724-8795; cnr Calle 8 & Carrera 10; s/d/tr COP$30,000/50,000/60,000) The best-value private rooms in town, with minibar, TV, great beds and linen and pleasant rooms set away from the road. It's cool, fresh, clean and well-managed.

Hotel Mansión del Parque (☎ 724-5662; Calle 12 No 8-71; s/d/tr COP$55,000/88,000/103,000) Set in a 300-year-old mansion at the corner of Parque Central, with some original features, some of the large rooms have balconies with views of the square. Minibars make a welcome appearance.

Eating

There are many fast-food options on Carrera 10 between Calles 11 and 12.

Plaza de Mercado (Carrera 11; set lunch COP$5000; 6am-2pm) Between Calles 13 and 14 is this covered market where locals shovel down dirt-cheap set lunches, juices and tamales.

Cafetería Donde Betty (cnr Carrera 9 & Calle 12; sandwiches COP$4000; 7am-midnight) A pleasant cafe serving breakfast, sandwiches and good fresh juice.

Restaurante Vegetariano Saludable Delicia (☎ Calle 11 No 8-40; mains COP$5000-22,000; 7am-7:30pm) Fake meat, sandwiches, salads and more at the town's only option for those who like their protein *sin sangre* (without blood).

Restaurante Rogelio (Carrera 10 No 8-09; set lunch COP$5000, a la carte COP$10,000-12,000; 7am-9pm) Popular with the ravenous postrafting crew, the huge cheap meals are tasty, if predictable: meat or chicken with rice, salad, fried bananas and yucca.

our pick **El Maná** (Calle 10 No 9-12; set meals COP$7500; 11:30am-3pm & 6-8:30pm) Very popular with locals, with great set meals including chicken in plum sauce or lasagna, with soup, fruit, coffee, salad and dessert included.

Drinking & Entertainment

Café Con Verso (Calle 12 No 7-81; drinks COP$6000-8000; 4pm-late) Artsy hangout where you can sip decent coffee and cold beer with Miles Davis playing softly as you chat.

La Habana (Carrera 9 No 11-68; CC Camino Real, Local 212; 6pm-midnight Sun-Thu, 6pm-2am Fri & Sat) Hidden away on the 2nd floor of the Camino Real shopping mall-ette is this cool nightspot with *son*, salsa, rock and reggae, with films on Wednesday and Sunday evenings.

Discoteca El Trapiche (Vía Charalá; admission COP$3000; 10pm-dawn Fri & Sat) On the outskirts of San Gil towards Charalá, head here at weekends for an authentic Colombian nightclub experience – which here means drinking and dancing to salsa and reggaeton (a blend of reggae and Latin American music), with the occasional foam party. Be sure to enter the club proper – at the entrance is a *viejoteca* where the old folks swing and sway.

Getting There & Away

The main, intercity bus terminal is 3km west of the town center on the road to Bogotá. Urban buses shuttle regularly between the terminal and the center, or take a taxi (COP$3000). Frequent buses run to Bogotá (COP$35,000, eight hours), Bucaramanga (COP$15,000 three hours), Santa Marta (COP$55,000 14 hours) and Medellín (COP$60,000 11 hours). Two buses an hour to Bucaramanga pass the Parque Nacional de Chicamocha and leave the **Cotrasangil bus office** (Carrera 11 No 8-10) until 7:30pm. Buses to Barichara (COP$3300, 40 minutes) leave every 30 minutes from 5am to 6:30pm from the **local bus terminal** (cnr Calle 15 & Carrera 10) in the center. Buses to Guane, Charalá and Curití also leave from here.

BARICHARA

☎ 7 / pop 7000

Barichara is like a film set, boasting pristinely renovated 300-year-old whitewashed buildings and stone streets.

The 18th-century sandstone **Catedral de la Inmaculada Concepción**, on the main plaza, is the largest and most elaborate building in town. The **Casa de la Cultura** (☎ 726-7002; Calle 5 No 6-29; admission COP$500; ☎ 8am-noon & 2-6pm Mon-Sat, 9am-1pm Sun) features a small fossil collection and pottery by the local Guane indigenous people.

The nearby village of **Guane**, 10km to the northwest, is the land that time forgot. It has a fine rural church and a museum with a collection of fossils and Guane artifacts.

Sleeping & Eating

La Casa de Heraclia (☎ 300-223-9349; lacasadeheraclia @hotmail.com; Calle 3 No 5-33; s/d/tr COP$25,000/45,000/ 75,000; 🖳) Beanbags on a terrace greet you as you enter, and there's a large, wide open dining area in front of the quiet, modest and lovely rooms. It's the best deal in town for backpackers.

Aposentos (☎ 726-7294; Calle 6 No 6-40; r per person COP$50,000) A small, friendly hotel right on the main plaza, offering five rooms.

Hotel Coratá (☎ 726-7110; Carrera 7 No 4-08; r per person COP$60,000) Historical hotel in a 280-year-old building decorated with antiques and wooden furnishings.

Hostal Misión Santa Bárbara (☎ 726-7163, in Bogotá 1-288-4949; www.hostalmisionsantabarbara .info; Calle 5 No 9-12; s/d/tr incl breakfast COP$120,000/ 175,000/235,000; 🖳) Housed in meticulously restored colonial mansion, this place has comfortable, old-fashioned rooms. Room 5 is very special.

There are some budget restaurants around the plaza, including **Restaurante La Braza** (Carrera 6 No 6-31; set meals COP$6500; ☺ noon-6pm), which serves cheap set meals and typical local dishes. The specialty is goat with its own innards: tasty, except for the innards. Try **Plenilunio Café** (Calle 6 No 7-74; dishes COP$7000-10,000; ☺ 6:30-11pm), a tiny Italian restaurant. **Color de Hormiga** (☎ 726-7156; Calle 8 No 8-44; mains COP$14,000-18,000; ☺ lunch & dinner Wed-Mon) specializes in ant-strewn steaks, in homage to Santanderean delicacy, the fat-bottomed ant.

Getting There & Away

Buses shuttle between Barichara and San Gil every 45 minutes (COP$3300, 40 minutes). They depart from the **Cotrasangil bus office** (☎ 726-7132; Carrera 6 No 5-74) from the plaza. Buses to Guane (COP$2000, 15 minutes) depart at 6am, 9:30am, 11:30am, 2:30pm and 5:30pm. You can hike there on the ancient, fossil-encrusted Camino Real, which starts at the north end of Calle 4. It's not strenuous, but take a hat and water.

PARQUE NACIONAL DEL CHICAMOCHA

This **national park** (☎ 7-657-4400, 313-466-4634; www.parquenacionaldelchicamocha.com; Vía Bucaramanga– San Gil Km 54; admission COP$8000; ☺ 9am-6pm Tue-Thu, to 7pm Fri-Sun & holidays) is Colombia's newest. It is located between San Gil and Bogotá; the drive between the two cities is spectacular, and brings to mind a TV car-as-hero commercial. Most of the tourist attractions in the park, however, are a waste of both time and money; the real attraction is the **canyon**. It's best seen from the new **cable car** (incl admission COP$30,000) which first swoops you down into the depths and then raises you back up on the other side of the canyon. If you want more action, there are also **zip lines** (COP$17,000) and **parascending** (COP$130,000) available. Getting here is easy: you can get on any bus heading between San Gil and Bucaramanga and ask to be dropped off at the park.

BUCARAMANGA

☎ 7 / pop 510,000

The capital of Santander is a modern, busy commercial and industrial center with a mild climate. It is noted for the famous *hormiga culona*, a fat-bottomed ant that is fried and eaten. Most travelers only stop here to break up an overland journey to the coast, though a new parascending hostel may change that.

Information

Bancolombia (☎ 630-4251; Carrera 18 No 35-02)
Click & Play (Calle 34 No 19-46, Room 115, Centro Comercial La Triada; per hr COP$1500; ☺ 8am-9pm) Internet access.
Tourist police (☎ 633-8342; Parque Santander; ☺ 24hr) Free city brochures and maps.

Sights

Museo Casa de Bolívar (☎ 630-4258; Calle 37 No 12-15; ☺ 8am-noon & 2-6pm Mon-Fri, 8am-noon Sat) contains ethnographic and historic collections. **Jardín Botánico Eloy Valenzuela** (☎ 648-0729; admission COP$500; ☺ 8am-5pm) is in the suburb of Bucarica; you can catch a bus from Carrera 15 to escape the hubbub of the city.

Sleeping

Hostel Kasa Guane (☎ 657-6960, 312-432-6266; www
.kasaguane.com; Calle 49 No 28-21; dm/s/d per person
COP$20,000/35,000/50,000; ▢) Run by a friendly,
US-trained parascending pilot, dorms and
rooms are pleasant, all backpacker facilities are present and correct. The owners
and staff can arrange parascending trips
and courses.

Eating & Drinking

The mystifyingly popular *hormiga culona* is a
snack sold by weight at around COP$50,000
per kilo. They taste just as you would expect
deep-fried insects to taste.

Restaurante Vegetariano Salud y Vigor (Calle 36
No 14-24; meals COP$6000-7000; ⊙ 7:30am-6:30pm Sun-
Fri) Inexpensive, meat-free lunches.

Restaurante El Viejo Chiflas (Carrera 33 No 34-10;
mains COP$7000-15,000; ⊙ 11am-midnight) Good
budget option, offering typical local food.

Getting There & Away

Bucaramanga's bus terminal is southwest of the center, midway to Girón; frequent city buses marked 'Terminal' go
there from Carreras 15 and 33. Taxis are
COP$6000. Buses depart from here regu-
larly for Bogotá (COP$70,000, 10 hours),
Cartagena (COP$90,000, 12 hours), Cúcuta
(COP$36,000, six hours) and Santa Marta
(COP$75,000, nine hours).

GIRÓN

☎ 7 / pop 136,000

The calm, cobbled streets of San Juan de
Girón are just 9km from Bucaramanga.
The tourist office, **Secretaría de Cultura y
Turismo** (☎ 646-1337; Calle 30 No 26-64; ⊙ 8am-
noon & 2-6pm) is in Casa de la Cultura. There
are two ATMs on the eastern side of the
Parque Principal.

The town center, founded in 1631, has
been largely restored. The **Plazuela Peralta**
and **Plazuela de las Nieves** are both pretty.
The eclectic **Catedral del Señor de los Milagros**
on the main plaza is worth poking your
head into.

Hotel Las Nieves (☎ 646-8968; Calle 30 No 25-
71; s/d/tr COP$35,000/50,000/70,00) on the main
plaza has large, comfortable rooms and a
budget restaurant.

More upmarket are the **Restaurante Villa del
Rey** (Calle 28 No 27-49; mains COP$8000-20,000; ⊙ 8am-
6pm), **Mansión del Fraile** (Calle 30 No 25-27; mains

COP$10,000-15,000; ⊙ noon-6pm) and **Restaurante
La Casona** (Calle 28 No 28-09; mains COP$10,000-15,000;
⊙ noon-6pm). Local specialties are meat-heavy
and filling.

Frequent city buses from Carreras 15 and
33 in Bucaramanga will drop you at Girón
in 30 minutes.

PAMPLONA

☎ 7 / pop 53,000

Spectacularly set in the deep Valle del
Espíritu Santo in the Cordillera Oriental, colonial-era Pamplona is a cool, fresh town of
old churches, narrow streets and a bustling
commerce. If you've just come up from the
heat of Venezuela, it makes a nice stopover
en route to central Colombia.

The best of Pamplona's museums, **Museo
de Arte Moderno Ramírez Villamizar** (☎ 568-2999;
Calle 5 No 5-75; admission COP$2000; ⊙ 9am-noon &
2-6pm Tue-Fri, 9am-6pm Sat & Sun) features about 40
works by Eduardo Ramírez Villamizar, one
of Colombia's most outstanding artists, who
was born in Pamplona in 1923.

Hotel Orsúa (☎ 568-2470; Calle 5 No 5-67; s/d/tr
COP$25,000/40,000/45,000) stands right on the
main plaza and has tidy, slightly plain
rooms with small bathrooms, and is fine
for a one-night stay.

Pamplona's new bus terminal is 600m
southwest of the main square. You can
walk to town in about 10 minutes, or pay
COP$2000 for a cab.

Pamplona sits on the Bucaramanga–
Cúcuta road, and regular buses pass to
Cúcuta (COP$10,000, 1¾ hours, 72km)
and Bucaramanga (COP$25,000, 4½ hours,
124km). The road passes through high
mountain scenery and can be very cold.

CÚCUTA

☎ 7 / pop 586,000

Cúcuta is a hot, uninspiring city; it's the
capital of Norte de Santander and is just
12km from Venezuela. Unless you're en
route to or from Venezuela, there's little
reason to visit.

Information

The bus station is very sketchy – keep your
eyes peeled and point-blank refuse the 'help'
of anyone.

**Corporación Mixta de Promoción de Norte de
Santander** (☎ 571-3395; Calle 10 No 0-30) Tourist
information.

COLOMBIA

GETTING TO VENEZUELA

If you're heading to Venezuela, take one of the frequent buses or *colectivos* (shared taxis; around COP$1000, paid in either pesos or bolívars) that run from Cúcuta's bus terminal to San Antonio del Táchira in Venezuela. You can also catch *colectivos* and buses to San Antonio from the corner of Av Diagonal Santander and Calle 8, in the center of Cúcuta. Changing transportation at the border is not necessary. Don't forget to get off just before the bridge to have your passport stamped at Departamento Administrativo de Seguridad (DAS; Department of Administrative Security). This border is open 24 hours a day, seven days a week. For information on entering Colombia from Venezuela, see p949.

There's a 30-minute time difference between Colombia and Venezuela, since Venezuelan President Hugo Chávez' 2007 time-switch decree. Move your watch forward 30 minutes when crossing from Colombia into Venezuela. Once in Venezuela, pick up a tourist card – it's issued directly by the DIEX office in San Antonio del Táchira, on Carrera 9 between Calles 6 and 7. From San Antonio there are six departures a day to Caracas, all departing late afternoon or early evening for an overnight trip.

Immigration The DAS immigration post (for an exit/entry stamp in your passport) is just before the border on the Río Táchira, on the left side of the road going toward Venezuela.

Sleeping & Eating
Avoid any hotel within six blocks of the bus station.

Hotel La Bastilla (☎ 571-2576; Av 3 No 9-42; s/d/tr COP$26,000/36,000/45,000) This is an acceptable budget option with fan-cooled rooms and private bathrooms.

Hotel Plaza Cúcuta (☎ 571-3939; Av 4 No 6-51; s/d/tr with fan COP$33,000/55,000/77,000, with air-con COP$44,000/66,000/90,000; ❄) One of the cheapest options providing air-con, it's much nicer than La Bastilla.

La Mazorca (Av 4 No 9-67; mains COP$10,000-15,000) Enjoy well-served portions of local food in this sunny courtyard restaurant.

Getting There & Away
The airport is 4km north of the city center. Minibuses that are marked 'El Trigal Molinos' (from Av 1 or Av 3 in the center) will drop you 350m from the terminal. A taxi to the center costs COP$10,000. The airport handles flights to most major Colombian cities, including Bogotá, Medellín, Cali and Cartagena.

Be wary of scams and keep your wits about you at the **bus terminal** (cnr Av 7 & Calle 1). There are frequent buses to Bucaramanga (COP$40,000, six hours). At least two dozen buses daily run to Bogotá (COP$80,000, 16 hours).

There are no direct buses to Mérida; go to San Cristóbal and change.

THE CARIBBEAN COAST

Colombia's Caribbean coast is a sun- and rum-drenched playground, stretching 1760km from the jungles of the Darién in the west to the dustbowl badlands of La Guajira in the wild, wild east.

With the lures of pristine beaches, coral reefs and virgin rainforest around Santa Marta and Parque Nacional Tayrona, or the renowned jungle trek to the ancient Ciudad Perdida (Lost City), your main problem will be packing it all in. The hippy-magnet diving resort of Taganga and the intoxicating colonial city of Cartagena – one of the continent's most beautiful and historically important destinations – suck many travelers in for months.

For more low-key times, check out Mompós, a living museum that's straight out of a Gabriel García Márquez novel, or the newly safe destinations of Sapzurro and Capurganá, where time gently vanishes into the sunset of each day. Then snap out of your hammock-swinging reverie with Colombia's most giddying party, the Carnaval of Barranquilla, a week-long Mardi Gras riot of dancing, booze and music, which rivals Rio for its size and mania.

The Caribbean coast region also happens to be Colombia's main tourist destination for the locals, which means that most people you meet will be in holiday mode and ready to rumba, or just kick back and idle the time away.

COLOMBIA

SANTA MARTA

☎ 5 / pop 415,000

Santa Marta is where Colombians go when they want sun on their backs, sand under their feet and rum in their glasses. It has a famous colonial past as one of the continent's oldest cities, and is where Simón Bolívar died after a heroic attempt to make Latin America one united republic.

Its grace as a colonial city has faded under newer concrete buildings, but its still a pleasant enough seaside town with some attractions.

Most travelers whiz through and base themselves in Taganga, or head out to Parque Nacional Tayrona. But the city's nightlife is good, the sun always shines, and the heat is drier and more pleasant than Cartagena. In the next few years Santa Marta will see restoration work that will bring back some of the old town's glorious colonial past.

Santa Marta is 10 minutes from the backpacker magnet Taganga and not far from the beautiful Parque Nacional Tayrona. It's also the place to organize a trip to Ciudad Perdida, Tayrona's great pre-Hispanic city.

Information

Some *casas de cambio* are on Calle 14 between Carreras 3 and 5.

Bancolombia (Carrera 3 No 14-10) Changes traveler's checks.

Deprisa post office (Carrera 3 No 17-26; ☺ 8am-noon & 2-6pm Mon-Fri, 8am-1pm Sat)

Macrofinanciera (Calle 13 No 3-13, San Francisco Plaza, Local 206) Private money changer.

Mundo Digital (Calle 15 No 2B-19, Local 108; per hr COP$1500; ☺ 7am-8pm Mon-Fri, 8am-8pm Sat, 9am-5pm Sun) Internet cafe.

Parques Nacionales Naturales de Colombia (☎ 423-0704; www.parquesnacionales.gov.co; Calle 17 No 4-06)

Tourist office (☎ 421-1833; Calle 17 No 3-120) The city tourist office.

Sights

The **Museo del Oro** (☎ 421-0953; Calle 14 No 2-07; ☺ 8am-11:45am & 2-5:45pm Mon-Fri) has an interesting collection of Tayrona objects, mainly pottery and gold.

The massive whitewashed **Catedral** (cnr Carrera 5 & Calle 17) claims to be Colombia's oldest church, but work was not actually completed until the e nd of the 18th century. It holds

the ashes of the town's founder, Rodrigo de Bastidas.

The **Quinta de San Pedro Alejandrino** (☎ 433-0589; admission COP$10,000; ☺ 9:30am-4:30pm) is the hacienda where the Che Guevara of the 19th century, Simón Bolívar, spent his last days and died. Take a bus towards Mamatoco from the waterfront to get there (COP$1000, 20 minutes).

Tours

Santa Marta's tour market mainly revolves around Ciudad Perdida. Tours are best organized by **Turcol** (☎ 421-2256, 433-3737; turcol24 @hotmail.com; Carrera 1C No 20-15).

Sleeping

Hotel Miramar (☎ 423-3276; Calle 10C No 1C-59; dm/s/d COP$10,000/12,000/25,000; ☐) Resembles an open prison filled with waster gringos eating greasy burgers for breakfast at 3pm. Cheap and nasty, but with a fun atmosphere – if you fit the profile.

La Brisa Loca (☎ 318-303-0666; www.labrisaloca .com; Calle 14 No 3-58; dm/s/d COP$12,000/35,000/50,000, with air-con COP$22,000/45,000/60,000; ☐ ☒) If the remaining rooms live up to the promise of the two seen during research, this vast new hostel run by two cool American brothers will wipe out every other hostel in town. It's a sprawling superhostel with a new swimming pool, a bar, a kitchen and wi-fi, and sits on top of a lovely Mexican restaurant selling fresh, delicious food.

Casa Familiar (☎ 421-1697; Calle 10C No 2-14; dm/s/d COP$15,000/20,000/30,000) A popular backpacker hangout, with private rooms and dorms. There's a nice rooftop terrace for lounging. Some of the single rooms are boxy.

Hotel Las Vegas (☎ 421-5094; Calle 11 No 2-08; s/d COP$17,000/27,000, with air-con COP$22,000/32,000; ☐) Small but functional, Las Vegas has some of the cheapest air-con rooms in town. Streetside rooms have a window and balcony but do get noisy.

Eating

There are a lot of cheap restaurants around the budget hotels, particularly on Calles 11 and 12 near the waterfront, where you can get lunch for around COP$5000.

Agave Azul (Calle 12 No 3-17; set menus COP$7000, mains COP$15,000-22,000; ☺ lunch noon-3pm Tue-Fri, dinner from 5pm Tue-Sat) Fantastic Mexican food, including great burritos and quesadillas, prepared by a

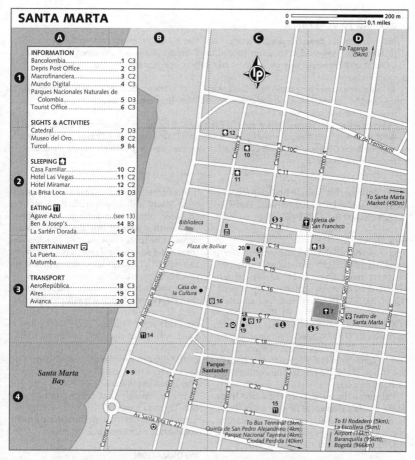

SANTA MARTA

INFORMATION
Bancolombia	1 C3
Depris Post Office	2 C3
Macrofinanciera	3 C3
Mundo Digital	4 C3
Parques Nacionales Naturales de Colombia	5 D3
Tourist Office	6 C3

SIGHTS & ACTIVITIES
Catedral	7 D3
Museo del Oro	8 C2
Turcol	9 B4

SLEEPING
Casa Familiar	10 C2
Hotel Las Vegas	11 C2
Hotel Miramar	12 C2
La Brisa Loca	13 D3

EATING
Agave Azul	(see 13)
Ben & Josep's	14 B3
La Sartén Dorada	15 C4

ENTERTAINMENT
La Puerta	16 C3
Matumba	17 C3

TRANSPORT
AeroRepública	18 C3
Aires	19 C3
Avianca	20 C3

talented New York City chef. It's owned by the same guys who have La Brisa Loca hostel upstairs and is nicely decorated, with a fresh, cool atmosphere.

La Sartén Dorada (cnr Carrera 4 & Calle 21; mains COP$10,000-14,000; ⏰ 11:15am- 3:30pm) This is one of the cheaper restaurants that serves good seafood.

Ben & Josep's (Carrera 1C No 18-67; mains COP$13,500-22,000; ⏰ dinner Mon-Sat) Great steak in pepper sauce, bad pasta and decent fish. It's the best of the waterfront eateries and worth a trip from Taganga.

Entertainment
La Puerta (Calle 17 No 2-29; ⏰ 6pm-3am Thu-Sat) A nightclub in the finest tradition: a dance floor

heaving to salsa, reggaeton, hip-hop and a side of funk, with ice-cold margaritas fueling the outrageous flirtation and dancing. It's free to get in and weekends are best.

Matumba (Calle 17 No 3-36; ⏰ 6pm-3am) Late-night club serving salsa and hard liquor – always a winning formula.

Getting There & Away
AIR
The airport is 16km south of the city on the Bogotá road. Taxis cost around COP$15,000. City buses marked 'El Rodadero Aeropuerto' will take you there in 45 minutes from Carrera 1C (COP$1500). **Avianca** (☎ 421-4018; Carrera 2A No 14-47), **AeroRepública** (☎ 421-0120; cnr Carrera 3 & Calle 17) and **Aires** (Carrera 3) service Santa Marta.

COLOMBIA

GETTING TO VENEZUELA

Half-hourly buses depart for Maicao (COP$31,000, four hours), where you change for a *colectivo* to Maracaibo (Venezuela). *Colectivos* (shared taxis) depart regularly from about 5am to 3pm (COP$20,000 2½ hours) and go as far as Maracaibo's bus terminal. Maicao is an edgy, gritty town; be alert.

There are also two buses daily from Santa Marta direct to Maracaibo (COP$95,000, seven hours), operated by Expresos Amerlujo and Unitransco/Bus Ven. They come through from Cartagena, go to Maracaibo and continue to Caracas.

Venezuelan entry formalities are done in Paraguachón, on the Venezuelan side of the border. Wind your watch 30 forward minutes (yes, 30 minutes, thanks to a 2007 Chavez decree) when crossing from Colombia to Venezuela. For information on traveling from Maracaibo, Venezuela, to Colombia, see p942.

Flight destinations include Bogotá (one way COP$300,000 to COP$400,000) and Medellín (COP$250,000 to COP$300,000).

BUS
The bus terminal is on the southeastern outskirts of the city. Frequent minibuses go there from Carrera 1C in the center. Half-a-dozen buses run daily to Bogotá (COP$100,000, 20 hours) and approximately the same number travel to Bucaramanga (COP$60,000, nine hours). Buses to Barranquilla (COP$12,000, 1¾ hours) depart every 15 to 30 minutes. Some of them go direct to Cartagena (COP$25,000, five hours), but if not, there are immediate connections in Barranquilla.

Palomino buses depart regularly from Santa Marta's **market** (cnr Carrera 11 & Calle 11) for El Zaíno (COP$5000, one hour) in Parque Nacional Tayrona, while buses for Taganga (COP$1000) leave from Carrera 1C.

AROUND SANTA MARTA
Taganga
☎ 5 / pop 5000
Taganga is a tiny fishing village that doesn't quite know what's hit it. Set around an iridescently turquoise horseshoe-shaped bay near Santa Marta with beautiful coral reefs nearby, its beauty and pace of life have attracted backpackers in their thousands. It has a reputation for cheap scuba diving and lodging, easy camaraderie and a youthful, hedonistic atmosphere. It's a great stepping stone to nearby Parque Nacional Tayrona, Ciudad Perdida, or even La Guajira.

However, popularity brings along its pitfalls, and Taganga has its share. The town's infrastructure is not built for the massive influx of visitors and litter is a serious problem. Many still-impoverished locals feel crowded out by the foreign newcomers. Add to this a small but aggravating local petty crime spree (especially on beaches and from hotel rooms) and you have to question the impact of unregulated development on small communities.

Taganga's beach is dusty and less lovely than **Playa Grande**, which is mystifyingly underused. It's a 20-minute walk or a five-minute boat ride from Taganga (COP$5000) and is lined with palm-thatched restaurants serving fresh fish. It has no electricity and is free of the distorted *vallenato* sound clash that soundtracks the seashore in Taganga by day. It also has less thieves.

It's undeniable that drugs contribute to the Taganga's popularity with foreigners. Travelers report that dealers occasionally collaborate with corrupt local police.

INFORMATION
Taganga's sole ATM is often broken, so hit the Davivienda in Santa Marta.
Centro de Salud (Calle 14 No 3-05) Pharmacy with basic essentials and not much more.
Mojito.net (Calle 14 1B-61; per hr COP$1000; ☎ 9am-2am) Internet access.
Policía Nacional (☎ 421-9561; Carrera 2 No 17-38)

ACTIVITIES
Taganga is one of the world's cheapest places to get PADI (Professional Association of Diving Instructors) certified. A four-day open-water PADI/NAUI (National Association of Underwater Instructors) course including six dives costs around COP$550,000. A two-tank dive for trained divers with lunch and all gear costs around COP$100,000.

It's a serious mistake, however, to be lured by low prices alone. See boxed text (below) for how to choose a good-quality and safe dive school.

The following schools are rock-solid: the friendly, professional, and eco-aware **Aquantis** (☎ 316-818-4285; www.aquantisdivecenter.com; Calle 18 No 1-39) is the town's best, with very high standards of training, and the newest equipment. Add to that great customer service (divers don't have to carry, clean or hang their gear and it even serves proper English tea) and it wins by a country mile. **Centro de Buceo Poseidon** (☎ 421-9224; www.poseidondivecenter.com; Calle 18 No 1-69) is well run and equipped with a training pool, but feels like a PADI-cert assembly line.

SLEEPING

La Casa de Felipe (☎ 421-9120; www.lacasadefelipe.com; Carrera 5A No 19-13; dm COP$13,000-16,000, d COP$35,000-50,000, s/tr COP$35,000/60,000, apt for 2/4 people incl breakfast COP$70,000/110,000; 🖳) Warm and welcoming, it's still the original and best backpacker hostel, offering a kitchen, travel info and advice on trips to La Ciudad Perdida and Tayrona.

Oso Perezoso (☎ 421-8041; hotelosoperezos@yahoo .com; Calle 17 No 2-36; hammock/s/d incl breakfast COP$14,000/28,000/44,000) Pokey-but-OK hotel that deserves mention only for the very cheap hammock space.

Mora Mar (☎ 421-9202; www.hostalmoramar.com; Carrera 4 No 17B-83; dm/s/d COP$15,000/25,000/40,000; 🖳) Colombian-run with a family atmosphere and a decent communal kitchen, though rooms can feel a little airless.

Hotel Pelikan (☎ 421-9057; Carrera 2 No 17-04; dm/d COP$15,000/40,000) Bright rooms, a warm welcome and great security: it's right next to the police station (a fact once missed hilariously by a joint-smoking hippy who was arrested in his hammock outside).

Bayview (☎ 421-9560; bayviewhostel@gmail.com; Carrera 4 No 17B-57; dm/s/d/tr COP$20,000/40,000/50,000/60,000; 🖳 🖳) One of Taganga's best-equipped hostels, with decent rooms, a spacious, great kitchen and barbecue area, and a bar and swimming pool that hosts raucous after-parties. However, travelers have reported the service rude and profit-driven.

Casa Holanda (☎ 421-9390; www.micasaholanda.com; Calle 14 No 1B-75; s/d COP$25,000/50,000; 🖳) Dutch owner Edwin Witjes has built a series of fresh, simple private rooms with quality mattresses, a relaxing rear terrace and attached restaurant. He also runs a neighboring Spanish school and offers reductions on courses to guests. A quarter of all school profits go to a charitable foundation for poor children in Santa Marta and Taganga. This is exactly what Taganga needs.

HOW TO CHOOSE YOUR FIRST DIVE SCHOOL

When choosing a dive school, consider the following factors:

- Is the dive center authorized by PADI or NAUI?
- Does the dive center look organized and professional?
- Is the dive equipment well-maintained?
- Is all paperwork in order?
- Will you have a certified instructor with you underwater?
- Will this same instructor sign your scuba diving forms and certification?
- Does the price include a study book and a certification for every course you take?
- When was the last hydrostatic test carried out on the tanks? (It should be every five years.)
- Ask to test the tank's air – it should be smell and taste free.
- What is the instructor-to-student ratio?
- How is the theory component of your course taught?
- Do the firm's boats have two engines?
- Is there oxygen on board?
- Are the staff certified oxygen providers?
- Do boats have adequate and sufficient lifejackets and a radio?

Divanga (☎ 421-9217; www.divanga.com; r per person COP$27,000; ⚑) Located in, ahem, glamorous, uptown Taganga, it's a fair schlep with your rucksack from the bus. But clean, cool rooms and a twinkling swimming pool await you.

EATING
Taganga has new restaurants opening every week, only to close a few months later. Most are average at best, but the following are good choices. Fishermen sell small tuna, jackfish, barracuda and snapper at decent prices at the far end of the beach.

Baguettes de Maria (Calle 18 No 3-47; mains COP$6000-11,000; ☻ lunch & dinner Sun-Fri, dinner Sat) A genius formula: massive baguettes filled to bursting with delicious, healthy ingredients fed to starving peso-pinchers in a quiet garden. But why does it always take 27 minutes to boil an egg?

Casa Holanda (Calle 14 No 1B-75; set lunch COP$7000; ☻ 8am-11pm) Newcomer that knows its market: a two-course set lunch with soup and juice for this price is a steal, and the service is friendly and fast.

Bitacora (Carrera 1 No 17-13; mains COP$7000-18,000; ☻ breakfast, lunch & dinner) Excellent steaks, lean burgers, crisp salads and fresh juices. Service can be slow; avoid the lasagna at absolutely any cost.

ENTERTAINMENT
El Garaje (Calle 8 No 2-127; ☻ 8:30pm-late Wed-Sat) The first and best nightclub in Taganga, it's open late, serves potent Cuba Libres and is set on an airy terrace with a dance floor that pulsates to a mix of the obvious hippy classics, excellent soca and tropical rump-shakers. Much better than the new and atmosphere-free Sensation club, near the beachfront, where clattering reggaeton echoes around a harsh, empty room and dull terrace.

GETTING THERE & AWAY
Taxis to Santa Marta are plentiful (COP$7000, 15 minutes), the bus is COP$1000, leaving from the junction near Poseidon dive school and arriving at Carrera 1C in Santa Marta.

Minca
☎ 5
If you need to escape the heat of the coast, head to this small village 600m high up in the Sierra Nevada above Santa Marta. It's got great coffee, a small village feel and good bird-

watching opportunities. It's very quiet and slow-paced; country walks alongside the Río Gaira, healthy food, and early nights are the order of the day.

The **Sans Souci** (☎ 313-590-9213; sanssouciminca @yahoo.com; camping with tent COP$8000-15,000, without tent COP$10,000-20,000, r per person without bathroom COP$25,000) hostel is the budget option, with great views. Guests get a discount for working on the farm.

The **Sierra's Sound** (☎ 421-9993; sierrasound .es.tl; Calle Principal; r per person COP$30,000-40,000) offers chic decor, a large terrace and a room with an incredibly comfortable bed right next to the river. You'll sleep deeply to the sound of rushing water. The hotel serves excellent food.

Minca is reached by bus from the corner of Calle 11 and Carrera 11 in Santa Marta (COP$3000). The service leaves when it's full, supposedly at 10am and noon.

Parque Nacional Tayrona
One of Colombia's most popular national parks, **Tayrona** (admission COP$35,000) is set in a supernaturally beautiful region. Its palm-fringed beaches are scattered with huge boulders that were once worshipped by the local indigenous people whom the park is named after. It has become an essential stop-off for travelers and has plenty of places to stay and eat. Beware: many of the beaches here are tormented by treacherous currents that have killed hundreds of foolhardy daredevils.

The region was once the territory of the Tayrona indigenous people and some remnants have been found in the park, the most important being the ruins of the pre-Hispanic town of Pueblito.

ORIENTATION & INFORMATION
The park's main entrance is in El Zaíno, on the Santa Marta–Riohacha coastal road, where you pay the entrance fee. From El Zaíno, a 4km paved side road goes to Cañaveral, on the seaside. Here you'll find the park's administrative center, a campground, ludicrously overpriced so-called 'ecohabs' (in reality these are just thatched cottages), a restaurant and a small museum. And the best toilets in northern Colombia.

If your budget is supertight (and you have a broad back), take food and water to self-cater at Finca Don Pedro (opposite). Food is overpriced throughout the park.

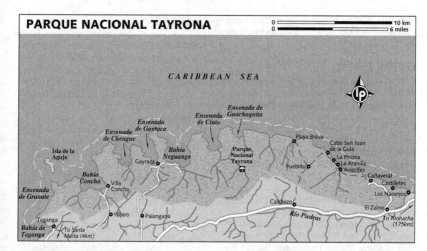

SIGHTS & ACTIVITIES

Cañaveral's small **Museo Arqueológico Chairama** displays some archaeological finds excavated in Pueblito. From Cañaveral, most visitors take a 45-minute walk west to Arrecifes, where there are budget lodging and eating facilities and the coast is spectacular, dotted with massive boulders.

From Arrecifes, a 20-minute walk northwest along the beach will bring you to La Aranilla, a sandy beach surrounded by huge boulders in a tiny bay where the water dances with light and is flecked with sparkling golden mineral flakes. Snacks are available here. Next along is La Piscina, a deep bay partly cut off from the open sea by an underground rocky chain. Another 20-minute walk will take you to Cabo San Juan de la Guía, a beautiful cape with good beaches and views. From the Cabo, a scenic path goes inland uphill to Pueblito, a 1½-hour walk away, providing some splendid tropical forest scenery. Take a flashlight, spare batteries, and watch out for snakes after dark.

SLEEPING & EATING

Most campsites around Arrecifes are not recommended – in high season they are noisy, dirty and crowded and they're a ghost town out of season.

Finca Don Pedro (☎ 315-320-8001, 301-675-7348; fincadonpedro@yahoo.es; Arrecifes; hammocks/tents per person COP$8000/15,000) The one beautiful spot in Arrecifes is the definite backpacker choice. Set among mango and avocado trees, it serves hearty food to meat-eaters and vegetarians, and has a kitchen so you can cook your own food. It also offers nature walks to spot monkeys, a bar, a pool table and a really warm welcome. True, you have to walk to a safe beach (Arrecifes has deadly undertow), but it's only about 10 minutes, and you'll pass the Panadería Vere on the way.

Panadería Vere (pastries COP$2500) Serves huge, oven-fresh chocolate loaves (calling them *pan au chocolate* doesn't do them justice) that will fill you all day.

Walk further on to Cabo San Juan de la Guía, where you can sleep in **hammocks** (with/without view COP$20,000/15,000). Choose from cheaper ones with no view (which are next to the noisy kitchen and within earshot of a rattling generator) or ones in the stunning mirador with sweeping views of the Caribbean. Best is a small **cabin** (COP$100,000) in the mirador with a double bed (we think the price is a bargain – the privacy and views are worth several million dollars). The food in the restaurant is poor and pricey; the service is slow and we found it rude, and there are no cooking facilities. The showers are open plan – but you can fall out of bed into two of Colombia's most lovely beaches. There are lockers for your gear.

GETTING THERE & AWAY

You can get to El Zaíno (COP$5000, one hour) by Palomino buses which depart regularly from Santa Marta's **market** (cnr Carrera 11 & Calle 11). From El Zaíno, catch the

COLOMBIA

jeep that shuttles between the entrance and Cañaveral (COP$2000, 10 minutes) or walk for 45 minutes.

CIUDAD PERDIDA

Ciudad Perdida (literally the 'Lost City') is one of the largest pre-Columbian towns discovered in the Americas. It was built between the 11th and 14th centuries on the northern slopes of the Sierra Nevada de Santa Marta and was most probably the Tayronas' biggest urban center. During their conquest, the Spaniards wiped out the Tayronas, and their settlements disappeared under the lush tropical vegetation. So did Ciudad Perdida for four centuries, until its accidental discovery in 1975 by *guaqueros* (robbers of pre-Columbian tombs).

Ciudad Perdida sits at an altitude of between 950m and 1300m, about 40km southeast of Santa Marta. The central part of the city is set on a ridge, from which various stone paths descend. There are about 150 stone terraces that once served as foundations for the houses. Originally the urban center was completely cleared of trees, before being reclaimed by the jungle. And this trip is all about the journey through that jungle: the scenery is memorable, the ruins not so great.

The return trip is a stiff six-day hike. The trail begins in El Mamey and goes up along the Río Buritaca. The section between Santa Marta and El Mamey is done by vehicle. Access to Ciudad Perdida is by tour only. The leaders are **Turcol** (☎ in Santa Marta 5-421-2256; www.buritaca2000.com; Carrera 1C No 20-15; per person COP$550,000) in Santa Marta (you can't hire an independent guide).

The tour includes transportation, food, hammocks, porters, guides and permits. Groups number four to 12 people, and tours depart year-round as soon as a group is assembled. You carry your own personal belongings. Take a flashlight, a water container, diarrhea medicine and masses of insect repellent. This cannot be stressed strongly enough. Some travelers have returned with hundreds of bites.

The trip takes three days uphill to Ciudad Perdida, one day at the site and two days back down. The hike may be tiring due to the heat, and if it's wet (as it is most of the year) the paths are muddy. The driest period is from late December to February or early March. There are several creeks to cross, sometimes waist-deep, on the way.

LA GUAJIRA

Say 'La Guajira' to Colombians and most people's expressions will sharpen. This remote peninsula is seen as the wild, wild east, a place beyond the back of beyond. But it rewards the intrepid with solitude and landscapes that range from immaculate beaches to arid, dustbowl beauty.

Riohacha (pop 170,000), the capital of La Guajira, is 175km northeast of Santa Marta and was traditionally the furthest east most travelers reached unless they were heading for the Venezuelan border; however, it isn't a hotbed of tourist activity and those traveling to the peninsula find more in Palomino and Cabo de la Vela.

The local indigenous people of the peninsula, the Wayuu, have a fierce reputation going back to the revolutionary days of Simón Bolívar, when they supported 'El Libertador' and were the only indigenous people in Colombia who knew how to ride horses and use firearms. They have never been ruled by the Spanish, and 20,000 of them fought the colonists with arms smuggled by the Dutch and English, contributing to Colombia's independence.

Today, the Wayuu of Cabo de la Vela offer simple lodgings to ecotourists, and all funds raised are kept by the community. But there's still a fierce pride here, a sense of otherness and resistance that pervades all interaction. The landscape is harsh, with blistering sun, dust and diesel fumes, and goats are your only friends. But as the sun dips below the horizon and you tuck into bargain lobster after a day on a deserted, pristine beach, adventurous travelers will relish the isolation of this forgotten corner of Colombia.

Palomino
☎ 5

This is La Guajira–lite, just one hour east from Parque Nacional Tayrona. Off the highway from the nondescript town of Palomino lies a stretch of archetypally beautiful Caribbean beach framed by two stunning rivers.

If the beaches of Taganga seem scruffy and rowdy, and Parque Nacional Tayrona feels like a ganja-scented social club, a trip here will reinvigorate your faith in the simple pleasures of swimming and wandering on an empty beach, buying a fish from a local, cooking it on a fire and eating it as the sun sets.

There's one budget choice by the beach – **La Sirena** (☎ 313-309-0074; martikaarellano@hotmail .com, www.ecosirena.com; hammocks/s/d without bathroom COP$15,000/50,000/60,000). Email for reservations as space is limited. The owner, Marta, is very helpful and speaks perfect English. Hammocks are right on the beach. There's one double room with shared bathroom. Attached to La Sirena is a kayak-hire firm (per day COP$60,000). To get here, take a bus to Palomino from Santa Marta or El Zaino at Parque Nacional Tayrona's entrance (COP$10,000), jump out by the *ferretería* (tool store), and turn left down to the beach. Walk about 20 minutes, then turn right at the sea and walk another 15 minutes until you see a yellow cabin with a mermaid sign outside.

Donde Tuci (☎ 315-751-8456; elmatuy@yahoo .com, www.elmatuy.blogspot.com; Playa Palomino; r per person incl full board COP$120,000), also known as Tuci's Place, is a budget millionaire's beach resort. The food is outstanding, the huge, comfortable cabins have immaculate open-door bathrooms and excellent huge beds. The beach is clean and private, and the large covered dining area is relaxed and informal. A few days here is great minisplurge. Reservations are essential and can be made by email, or by phone. Included is a free mototaxi ride to the beach, around 1km from the main highway.

There are no restaurants on the beach, so eat in town or bring your own food. There's a wonderful fish shop on the way to the beach from town that sells 10 huge langoustines at COP$15,000 or fish for a few thousand pesos. Mototaxis from Palomino village to the beach cost COP$2000 pesos and drivers will deliver beer and food for a small cost.

Palomino is about an hour further on from the entry to Parque Nacional Tayrona on the road towards Riohacha. Buses from Santa Marta cost COP$5000.

Watch out for falling coconuts. That's about your only concern here.

Mama Santa Cultural

Alongside the Río Palomino a few miles up into the Sierra Nevada stands Mama Santa Cultural, a small **lodge** (☎ 314-507-3281; caribe-colombia-mamasanta.blogspot.com; r per person COP$30,000) owned by urbane Colombian actor-poet German Latorre. Take a mosquito net and plenty of repellent. You can only stay by reservation. As you climb higher, wandering along seldom visited paths, you will see local Kogi indigenous people in traditional dress of white robes, with older males perpetually chewing on coca leaves. Marta from La Sirena (left) can help you contact the lodge and make transportation arrangements.

Cabo de la Vela

☎ 5 / pop 1500

Cabo de la Vela isn't for everybody. Really. Getting here by public transportation involves a bone-shaking ride in the back of a truck, possibly driven at lunatic speed by a man with no apparent fear of death or injury. He may spend much of the journey draining beer cans in a single slug. With luck, his assistant will be reasonably sober and will manage not to fall out of the truck at high speed. Fingers crossed.

The landscape is brutal scrub, and the local dish is *viche,* goat cooked in its own fat and served with its innards. Thankfully lobster is cheap, fresh, plentiful and exquisite. But softening the harsh landscape is the brilliantly blue Caribbean Sea that hugs a coastline of small cliffs and deserted sandy beaches, and a fantastic sunset viewed from the lighthouse.

SIGHTS & ACTIVITIES

There's absolutely nothing to do in Cabo, except swim in the sea and take a walk to El Faro (the lighthouse) to watch the sunset.

Ojo de Agua has a tiny freshwater pool hidden away next to the beach. It's less popular than Playa de Pilón, and has no facilities. It's wild, remote-feeling and craggily beautiful, with iguanas roving the clifftops.

Playa del Pilón is a nearby beach that beats anything in Cabo. It has safe and surprisingly cool waters that lap a vivid orange-sand beach framed by low, rocky cliffs.

Pilón de Azucar is a high lookout point offering views of boats laden with coal from the vast Cerrejon coal mine. Ask in town for Mikelly, a local truck driver, who on Sunday offers a round-trip tour for $5000 per stop – a real bargain. You could walk it, but beware the deadly quicksand swamp, the singeing sun and the huge dive-bombing insects that drink shots of neat DEET for breakfast.

COLOMBIA

SLEEPING & EATING

You can stay with almost any Wayuu family in Cabo, under the government's *posadas turísticas* scheme (www.posadasturisticas.com.co). You'll be sleeping in simple hammocks or in much more comfortable *chinchorros* (locally made woolen hammocks).

Tienda Mana (☎ 320-519-9990; chinchorro COP$6000) The hut next to Jorge Gomez' small shop is a bargain and he and his wife are friendly and helpful. He has a generator that runs from 6pm to 10pm, showers are via the trusty bucket method.

El Caracol (☎ 314-569-7037; hammock COP$8000, chinchorro COP$20,000, s/d COP$20,000/40,000) The first and absolutely very best restaurant in Cabo has simple cabins on the sea shore (the sea here is waist deep for about 100m). The real draw is the food: a sensational lobster in garlic mayonnaise costs around COP$15,000, and fresh octopus, shrimp and squid are seasonally priced. Great goat and fish too.

GETTING THERE & AWAY

From Riohacha, catch a *colectivo* at **Cootrauri** (☎ 728-0976; Calle 15 No 5-39) to Uribia (COP$12,000, one hour); it departs when full daily from 5am to 6pm. Leave Riohacha before 1pm in order to make the Uribia–Cabo connection. The driver will know you are going to Cabo and will bundle you from the bus onto an ongoing 4WD service to Cabo (COP$10,000 to COP$15,000, 2½ hours). Note that no service leaves Cabo on Sunday, and the return journey starts at 4am. Ask around for Mikelly, he's a safe driver.

BARRANQUILLA

☎ 5 / pop 1,112,800

Barranquilla seems like one long, intensely hot traffic jam hemmed in by heavy industry and Caribbean swamps. Colombia's fourth-biggest city is focused on trade and shipping, and other than its four-day Carnaval there's little to detain the traveler here.

The city's pre-Lenten Mardi Gras Carnaval is a one-way trip into bedlam, with revelers from all over the country descending on the town to drink the town dry, while flinging flour and water bombs at each other – you'd be mad to miss it if you're nearby. Watch for pickpockets in the crowd, buy a disposable camera and don't dress to impress.

The city center is ugly and can be unsafe after dark, but if you need a cheap bed, try the

Hotel Colonial Inn (☎ 379-0241; Calle 42 No 43-131; s/d with fan COP$30,000/40,000, with air-con COP$40,000/50,000; ▣), an atmospheric building that has fairly comfortable rooms with TV.

Hell-bent sightseers could kill an hour checking out the stained-glass windows at the **Catedral Metropolitana** (cnr Calle 53 & Carrera 46).

The bus terminal is 7km from the city center. It can take an hour to get there by local bus. Taxis are a better bet (COP$10,000, 20 minutes).

CARTAGENA

☎ 5 / pop 1.1 million

A fairy-tale city of romance, legends and sheer beauty, Cartagena de Indias is the most beautiful city in Colombia, with cobbled alleys, enormous balconies shrouded in bougainvillea and massive churches casting their shadows across leafy plazas.

Founded in 1533, Cartagena swiftly blossomed into the main Spanish port on the Caribbean Coast and the gateway to the north of the continent. Treasure plundered from the indigenous people was stored here until the galleons were able to ship it back to Spain. It attracted pirates and, in the 16th century alone suffered five sieges, the best known of which was led by Francis Drake in 1586.

In response, the Spaniards made Cartagena an impregnable port and constructed elaborate walls encircling the town, and a chain of forts. These fortifications helped save Cartagena from subsequent sieges.

Cartagena continued to flourish, and during the colonial period, the city was the key outpost of the Spanish empire and influenced much of Colombia's history.

Today Cartagena has expanded dramatically and is surrounded by vast suburbs. It is Colombia's largest port and an important industrial center of 1.1 million. Nevertheless the old walled town has changed very little.

Cartagena has also become a fashionable seaside resort. A modern tourist district has sprung up on Bocagrande and El Laguito, south of the old town. Most backpackers, however, stay in the historic part of town.

Cartagena's climate is hot but a fresh breeze blows in each evening, making this a pleasant time to stroll around the city. Theoretically the driest period is from December to April, while October and November are the wettest months.

CARTAGENA – OLD TOWN

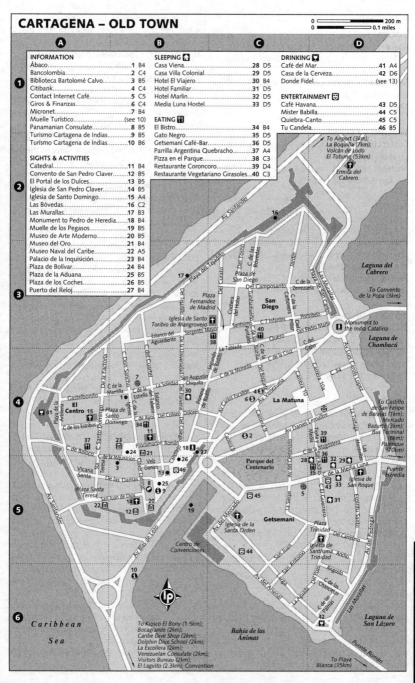

INFORMATION	
Ábaco	**1** B4
Bancolombia	**2** C4
Biblioteca Bartolomé Calvo	**3** B5
Citibank	**4** C4
Contact Internet Café	**5** C5
Giros & Finanzas	**6** C4
Micronet	**7** B4
Muelle Turístico	(see 10)
Panamanian Consulate	**8** B5
Turismo Cartagena de Indias	**9** B5
Turismo Cartagena de Indias	**10** B6

SIGHTS & ACTIVITIES	
Catedral	**11** B4
Convento de San Pedro Claver	**12** B5
El Portal de los Dulces	**13** B5
Iglesia de San Pedro Claver	**14** B5
Iglesia de Santo Domingo	**15** A4
Las Bóvedas	**16** C2
Las Murallas	**17** B3
Monument to Pedro de Heredia	**18** B4
Muelle de los Pegasos	**19** B5
Museo de Arte Moderno	**20** B5
Museo del Oro	**21** B4
Museo Naval del Caribe	**22** A5
Palacio de la Inquisición	**23** B4
Plaza de Bolívar	**24** B4
Plaza de la Aduana	**25** B5
Plaza de los Coches	**26** B5
Puerto del Reloj	**27** B4

SLEEPING	
Casa Viena	**28** D5
Casa Villa Colonial	**29** D5
Hotel El Viajero	**30** B4
Hotel Familiar	**31** D5
Hotel Marlin	**32** D5
Media Luna Hostel	**33** D5

EATING	
El Bistro	**34** B4
Gato Negro	**35** D5
Getsemaní Café-Bar	**36** D5
Parrilla Argentina Quebracho	**37** A4
Pizza en el Parque	**38** C3
Restaurante Coroncoro	**39** D4
Restaurante Vegetariano Girasoles	**40** C3

DRINKING	
Café del Mar	**41** A4
Casa de la Cerveza	**42** D6
Donde Fidel	(see 13)

ENTERTAINMENT	
Café Havana	**43** D5
Mister Babilla	**44** C5
Quiebra-Canto	**45** C5
Tu Candela	**46** B5

COLOMBIA

Information

BOOKSTORES

Ábaco (☎ 664-8338; cnr Calle de la Iglesia & Calle de la Mantilla; ☺ 9am-8:30pm Mon-Sat) English-language choices, coffee, air-con and free wi-fi.

Biblioteca Bartolomé Calvo (☎ 660-0778; Calle de la Inquisición; ☺ 8:30am-6pm Mon-Fri, 9am-1pm Sat) City library.

INTERNET ACCESS

Contact Internet Café (Calle de la Media Luna 10-20; per hr COP$1000; ☺ 8am-9pm)

Micronet (Calle de la Estrella No 4-47; per hr COP$1500; ☺ 9am-9pm Mon-Sat, to 6pm Sun)

MONEY

Cartagena has an army of money changers on the streets. Banks are a far better bet.

Bancolombia (Av Venezuela, Edificio Sur Americana)

Citibank (Av Venezuela, Edificio Citibank, 1st fl; ☺ 8am-noon & 2-4:30pm Mon-Fri)

Giros & Finanzas (Av Venezuela 8A-87) This *casa de cambio* in the old town represents Western Union.

TOURIST INFORMATION

Turismo Cartagena de Indias (☎ 6601583; www .turismocartagenadeindias.com; Plaza de la Aduana; ☎ 9am-1pm & 3-7pm Mon-Sat, 9am-5pm Sun) The main tourist office is situated in Plaza de la Aduana; there's another branch on Av Blas de Lezo.

Sights

Cartagena's old town is its principal attraction, particularly the inner walled town consisting of the historical districts of **El Centro** and **San Diego**, with many of beautiful squares, and flower-bedecked balconies. Almost every street is a postcard-worthy scene of 16th- and 17th-century architecture.

Getsemaní, the outer walled town, is not so well preserved, but money is flooding into the area as tourism booms. There are a few good drinking holes and one lovely square, Plaza Trinidad. Step briskly after dark – it's the red light district, with all that entails. Street lighting is poor.

The old town is surrounded by **Las Murallas**, the thick walls built to protect it. Construction was begun toward the end of the 16th century after the attack by Francis Drake; until that time, Cartagena was almost completely unprotected. The project took two centuries to complete, due to repeated storm damage and pirate attacks.

The main gateway to the inner town was what is now the **Puerta del Reloj** (the clock tower was added in the 19th century). Just behind it is the **Plaza de los Coches**, a square once used as a slave market. There's a **monument to Pedro de Heredia**, the founder of the city.

In the arcaded walkway nearby, **El Portal de los Dulces**, you can buy dozens of local sweets. It was featured in Gabriel García Márquez' *Love in the Time of Cholera*.

A few steps southwest is the **Plaza de la Aduana**, the oldest and largest square in the old town. It was used as a parade ground and all governmental buildings were gathered around it. At the southern outlet from the plaza is the **Museo de Arte Moderno** (☎ 664-5815; Plaza de San Pedro Claver; admission COP$3000; ☺ 8am-noon & 3-7pm Mon-Fri), with work by renowned Colombian painter, Alejandro Obregón.

Close by is the **Convento de San Pedro Claver**, built by the Jesuits, originally under the name of San Ignacio de Loyola. The name was changed in honor of the Spanish-born monk Pedro Claver, who lived and died in the convent. He spent his life ministering to the slaves brought from Africa. The convent is a monumental three-story building surrounding a tree-filled courtyard and part of it, including Claver's cell, is open to visitors as a **museum** (☎ 664-4991; Plaza de San Pedro Claver; admission COP$6000; ☺ 8am-5pm Mon-Sat, to 4:30pm Sun).

The church alongside, **Iglesia de San Pedro Claver**, has an imposing stone façade. The remains of San Pedro Claver are kept in a glass coffin in the high altar. Behind the church the **Museo Naval del Caribe** (☎ 664-2440; San Juan de Dios; admission COP$6000; ☺ 8am-noon & 3-6pm Tue-Sat) traces the naval history of Cartagena and the Caribbean.

Nearby, the **Plaza de Bolívar** is in a particularly beautiful area of the old town. Its fountains keep it cool and fresh, and local dance bands practice here in the evenings. It's a great place to spend a few hours, but bring repellent at dusk. On one side of the square is the **Palacio de la Inquisición**, dating from the 1770s with its magnificent baroque stone gateway. It is now an utterly macabre **museum** (☎ 664-4570; Plaza de Bolívar; admission COP$11,000; ☺ 9am-6pm Mon-Sat, 10am-4pm Sun) that displays Inquisitors' grisly instruments of torture, pre-Columbian pottery and works of art from the colonial and independence periods.

Across the plaza, the **Museo del Oro** (☎ 660-0778; Plaza de Bolívar; ☺ 10am-1pm & 3-7pm Tue-Fri,

10am-1pm & 2-5pm Sat, 11am-4pm Sun) has a good
collection of gold and pottery from the Sinú,
or Zenu culture. Its air-con is set to stun and
is an oasis. The **Catedral** was begun in 1575 but
was partially destroyed by Drake in 1586, and
not completed until 1612. The dome on the
tower was added early in the 20th century.

One block west of the plaza is **Calle Santo
Domingo**, a street that has hardly changed since
the 17th century. On it stands the **Iglesia de
Santo Domingo** (☎ 664-1301; Plaza de Santo Domingo;
admission COP$10,000; ☺9am-7pm Tue-Sat, noon-8pm Sun),
the city's oldest church.

At the northern tip of the old town are
Las Bóvedas, 23 dungeons built in the defensive walls at the end of the 18th century. This was the last construction done
in colonial times, and was destined for
military purposes. Today the dungeons are
tourist shops.

While you're wandering around call in at
Muelle de los Pegasos, a lovely old port full of
fishing, cargo and tourist boats, just outside
the old town's southern walls.

Several forts were built at key points outside the walls to protect the city from pirates. By far the greatest is the huge stone
fortress **Castillo de San Felipe de Barajas** (☎ 666-
4790; Av Arévalo; admission COP$14,000; ☺8am-6pm),
east of the old town, begun in 1639 but not
completed until some 150 years later. Don't
miss the impressive walk through the complex system of tunnels, built to facilitate the
supply and evacuation of the fort. Their design also cleverly amplified sound to make
the approach of enemies more apparent.

The **Convento de la Popa** (☎ 666-2331; admission COP$7000; ☺9am-5pm), perched on top of
a 150m hill beyond the San Felipe fortress,
was founded by the Augustinians in 1607. It
has a nice chapel and a lovely flower-filled
patio, and offers panoramic views of the
city. Take a taxi – there's no public transportation and there have been robberies. Pay
around COP$20,000.

Activities

Cartagena has grown into an important
scuba-diving center. However, prices are far
lower in Taganga.
Caribe Dive Shop (☎ 310-657-4507; www.caribedive
shop.com; Hotel Caribe, Bocagrande)
Dolphin Dive School (☎ 660-0814; www.dolphin
diveschool.com; Edificio Costamar, Av San Martín 6-105,
Bocagrande)

Festivals & Events
Cartagena's major annual events:
Festival Internacional de Cine International film
festival, held in March/April, usually shortly before Easter.
Feria Artesanal y Cultural Regional craft fair taking
place in June/July, accompanied by folk-music concerts and
other cultural events.
Reinado Nacional de Belleza National beauty pageant
held on November 11 to celebrate Cartagena's independence day. The event, also known as the Carnaval de
Cartagena or Fiestas del 11 de Noviembre, is the city's most
important annual bash.

Sleeping
Most backpackers stay in Getsemaní. There
are many budget hotels, some of them excellent, others are more like brothels. But things
are changing, and within a few years most
of the flophouses will be boutique hotels as
foreign money pours in.
Casa Viena (☎ 664-6242; www.casaviena.com; San
Andrés, Getsemaní; dm with air-con COP$15,000, d with/with-
out bathroom COP$40,000/32,000; ☒ ☐) The relaxed
German owner is a mine of tourist info and
can point you to trustworthy captains if you're
looking to find a yacht to Panama (p543) –
which makes up for the small rooms. Good
air-con in the (gloomy) dorm, though.
Hotel Familiar (☎ 664-2464; Calle del Guerrero 29-
66, Getsemaní; s/d without bathroom COP$17,000/32,000)
Rock-bottom prices and good firm beds, the
ground floor has the nicest rooms.
Hotel Marlin (☎ 664-3507; Calle de la Media Luna 10-
35, Getsemaní; s/d with fan COP$25,000/35,000, with air-con
COP$40,000/50,000 ☒ ☐) It's basic, but the lobby
is nice and guests can use the kitchen. Most
rooms are on the dark side – but that makes
them cooler.
Media Luna Hostel (☎ 664-2268; Calle de la
Media Luna 10-46, Getsemaní; dm COP$30,000-40,000, s/d
COP$55,0500/120,000; ☐) Cartagena has been cry-
ing out for a major hostel in Getsemaní, and
here it is. This 160-bed sensitively restored
colonial monster straddles the divide between
backpacker utilitarianism and boutique chic.
It has a bar, a cafe, a sun terrace and very high
ceilings, making every room cool and fresh.
Even the faucets are trompe l'oeil cool.
Hotel El Viajero (☎ 664-3289; Calle del Porvenir
35-68; s/d COP$40,000/60,000; ☒ ☐) Acceptable
budget bet, this 14-room hotel has a kitchen
for guests.
ourpick **Casa Villa Colonial** (☎ 664-
5421; Calle de la Media Luna 10-89, Getsemaní; s/d
COP$60,000/80,000; ☒ ☐) Personal service,

comfortable beds and air-con makes this Getsemaní's, if not Cartagena's, best option at this price. Fabulously friendly and wonderfully restored.

Eating

Cartagena is a good place to eat, especially at the top end, but cheap places are also plentiful.

Gato Negro (San Andrés 30-39, Getsemaní; mains COP$5000-6000; ☺ breakfast & lunch) A breakfast spot owned by the El Bistro crew, with great omelets and intensely welcome muesli, with free wi-fi while you wait.

Getsemaní Café-Bar (San Andrés 30-34, Getsemaní; mains COP$7000-10,000; ☺ 8am-11pm Mon-Sun) Set in an old arched building, GCB serves piping-hot a-la-carte dishes, healthy breakfasts and delicious snacks (particularly the *arepa de pollo* – grilled shredded chicken and salad on a fried cornmeal patty) and drinks.

El Bistro (Calle de Ayos 4-42; set lunches COP$9500; ☺ 8am-11pm Mon-Sat) El Bistro serves delicious set lunches with good salads and reasonably priced European-style dinners.

Pizza en el Parque (Plaza Fernando de Madrid; mains COP$15,000; ☺ 4pm-1am) Freshly cooked thin-crust pizzas served in a lovely, hidden square to the strains of ambient music, far away from the town's hagglers. Ignore the odder toppings such as pear.

Kiosco El Bony (Av 1, Bocagrande; mains COP$20,000; ☺ 10am-6pm Mon-Sun) Owned by ex-Olympic boxer Bonifacio Avila, El Bony is famous for its vast fish lunches. It's thronged with Colombians on weekends.

Parrilla Argentina Quebracho (Calle de Baloco; mains COP$40,000; ☺ noon-3pm & 7pm-midnight Mon-Thu, noon-midnight Fri & Sat) Melt-in-the-mouth Argentine steaks and a great wine list. The *solomillo* is sublime. The cabaret isn't.

Dozens of spots in the old town serve *almuerzos* for around COP$5000. One of the best is **Restaurante Coroncoro** (Tripita y Media, Getsemaní; ☺ 8am-8pm). For veggie meals, try **Restaurante Vegetariano Girasoles** (Calle Quero, San Diego; ☺ 11:30am-3pm). On Sunday, locals on Plaza Trinidad serve up excellent pizza and street food. Plaza Santo Domingo hosts six open-air cafes, serving a varied menu of dishes, snacks, sweets and drinks.

Drinking & Entertainment

A number of bars, taverns, discos and other venues stay open late. Plenty of them are on Av del Arsenal in Getsemaní, Cartagena's Zona Rosa.

Donde Fidel (El Portal de los Dulces 32- 09, El Centro; ☺ 11am-2am) The best sound system in Cartagena bar none, and definitely the best salsa collection in Colombia. Chairs in the square are a great, breezy spot to start the night. On Saturday afternoons, watch rare vintage salsa videos on the big screen. If Salsa legend Hector Lavoe were alive today, he'd own a bar like this.

Casa de la Cerveza (Baluarte San Lorenzo del Reducto, Getsemaní; ☎ 4pm-4am) Another chic spot set high atop the city's walls, similar to Café del Mar, but with stupendous views out toward Castillo de San Felipe.

Quiebra-Canto (Camellón de los Martines, Edificio Puente del Sol, Getsemaní; ☺ 7pm-4am Tue-Sat) Locals say the salsa here is even better than at Café Havana.

Café Havana (cnr Calles del Guerrero & de la Media Luna, Getsemaní; admission COP$5000; ☎ 8pm-4am Thu-Sat, 5pm-2am Sun) Live salsa and the best mojitos in Colombia, with a mixed, friendly crowd of locals and tourists. An absolutely fantastic place.

Mister Babilla (Av del Arsenal 8B-137; admission COP$10,000; ☺ 9pm-4am) A good place to dance, get drunk and flirt with Colombians.

Tu Candela (El Portal de los Dulces 32-25; admission COP$10,000; ☺ 8pm-4am) Salsa and reggaeton in this long, narrow, arched club.

Café del Mar (Baluarte de Santo Domingo, El Centro; cocktails COP$16,000-20,000; ☺ 5pm-late) One of the city's most stunning locations, out on a balustrade looking over Bocagrande, with a crowd to match. Ditch your sandals. Mediocre house music is the only drawback.

Getting There & Away

AIR

All major Colombian carriers operate flights to and from Cartagena. There are flights to Bogotá (around COP$300,000), Cali (COP$320,000), Medellín (COP$200,000 to COP$300,000) and San Andrés (from COP$300,000), among others.

The airport is in the suburb of Crespo, 3km northeast of the old city, and is serviced by frequent local buses that depart from various points, including India Catalina and Av Santander. *Colectivos* to Crespo depart from India Catalina; the trip costs COP$1000. A private cab is COP$10,000. The terminal has two ATMs, and the Casa de Cambio

América (in domestic arrivals) changes cash and traveler's checks.

BOAT

There's no ferry service between Cartagena and Colón in Panama, and there are very few cargo boats. A more pleasant way of getting to Panama is by sailboat. There are various foreign yachts that take travelers from Cartagena to Colón via the Kuna Yala (San Blas) Archipelago (Panama) and vice versa. The trip takes four to six days and normally includes a couple of days at San Blas for snorkeling and spear fishing. It costs about COP$700,000. Save hassle, time and money by asking Hans at Casa Viena – he makes no commission and has his finger on the pulse.

BUS

The bus terminal is on the eastern outskirts of the city; it can take up to an hour to get there from the old town. Large green-and-red-signed air-con Metrocar buses make the trip every 15 to 30 minutes (COP$1700, 40 minutes). In the center, you can catch them on Av Santander.

Half-a-dozen buses go daily to Bogotá (COP$100,000, 20 hours) and another half-a-dozen to Medellín (COP$85,000, 13 hours). Buses to Barranquilla run every 15 minutes or so (COP$12,000, two hours), and some continue on to Santa Marta; if not, just change in Barranquilla. Unitransco has one bus to Mompós at 7:30am (COP$40,000, eight hours).

Three bus companies – **Expreso Brasilia** (☎ 663-2119), **Expresos Amerlujo** (☎ 653-2536) and **Unitransco/Bus Ven** (☎ 663-2065) – operate daily buses to Caracas (COP$200,000, 20 hours), Venezuela via Maracaibo (COP$115,000, 12 hours).

AROUND CARTAGENA

Islas del Rosario

☎ 5

This archipelago, about 35km southwest of Cartagena, consists of 27 small coral islands, including some tiny islets only big enough for a single house. The whole area has been protected as Parque Nacional Corales del Rosario.

Cruises through the islands are well established. Tours depart year-round from the Muelle Turístico (Turismo Cartagena de Indias) in Cartagena. Boats leave between 8am and 9am daily and return about 4pm to 6pm. The cruise office at the Muelle sells tours in big boats for about COP$40,000. It's probably best (and often cheapest) to arrange the tour through one of the budget hostels in Cartagena. Tours normally include lunch, but not the entrance fee to the aquarium (COP$15,000) on one of the islands, the port tax (COP$4700) and the national-park entrance fee (COP$5300).

Playa Blanca

☎ 5

This is one of the most beautiful beaches around Cartagena. It's about 20km southwest of the city, on Isla de Barú, and it's the usual stop for the boat tours to the Islas del Rosario. The place is also good for snorkeling as a coral reef begins just off the beach (take snorkeling gear).

The beach has some rustic places to stay and eat. The most popular with travelers is **Campamento Wittenberg** (☎ 311-436-6215). It offers dorm beds (COP$18,000) or hammocks (COP$9000) and serves meals.

The easiest way of getting to the beach is with owner Gilbert, who comes to Casa Viena in Cartagena once a week (usually on

---

BENKOS BIOHO: AN AFRO-COLOMBIAN HERO

Not many Colombians even know the name Benkos Bioho. Fewer yet realize that he was the founder of the first free town for black people in the Americas. Bioho was a revolutionary slave who smashed his chains in 1603 and escaped captivity in Cartagena to establish **Palenque**, 70km southeast of Cartagena. By examining the town's complex funeral rites, dances, and language, anthropologists traced back the inhabitants' roots to the mouth of the Congo River in East Africa. Even today, Palenque feels more like an African village than a Latin one. The town lacks tourist facilities, but it is a fascinating place to spend a day.

Buses (COP$7000, 45 minutes) leave Cartagena bus terminal at 8:45am and 3pm, returning at 4.45am and noon. Local tourist officer Manuel (☎ 314-512-8858) can arrange accommodation with locals for around COP$20,000 per night.

Wednesday) and takes travelers in his boat (COP$15,000, 45 minutes).

Volcán de Lodo El Totumo

About 50km northeast of Cartagena, on the bank of the shallow Ciénaga del Totumo, is a 15m mound that looks like a miniature volcano, but instead of lava it spews mud forced out by the pressure of gases emitted by decaying organic matter underground.

El Totumo is the highest mud volcano in Colombia. You can climb to the top by specially built stairs, then go down into the crater and have a lukewarm mud bath (entry COP$5000). The mud contains minerals acclaimed for their therapeutic properties. Once you've finished your session, go down and wash the mud off in the *ciénaga* (lagoon).

To go there independently take a bus from Cartagena's city center to its bus terminal (COP$1700). There take the hourly bus to Galerazamba and get off at Loma de Arena (COP$7000). From there it is 45-minute walk or take a mototaxi (COP$2000). The whole one-way trip takes about two-and-half hours. The last bus back from Loma de Arena leaves around 3pm. Leave Cartagena before 10am – otherwise you'll miss it.

You can also visit Totumo on a **tour** (incl lunch COP$35,000) from Casa Viena hostel in Cartagena. It leaves at 8:30am and gets back at 2:30pm.

SAN ANDRÉS & PROVIDENCIA

The islands of San Andrés and Providencia offer a tranquil and idyllic taste of Caribbean island life, with gorgeous beaches lapped by turquoise seas rammed with pristine coral – the second-largest barrier reef in the northern hemisphere is here. For reggae, rum, sun and sand, a splurge here is well worth considering.

These Colombian territories lie 150km off Nicaragua's Miskito coast, and 800km northwest of Colombia. Both islands have a strong British influence, in food, language and architecture, and are popular snorkeling and scuba centers. The rainy season is September to December and average temperatures are 26°C to 29°C, with high humidity.

The Dutch held the islands until the British invaded in 1631 and colonized the islands, which were then home to the Raizal, an Afro-Caribbean group. The Spanish tried to take over in 1635 but failed and legendary pirate Henry Morgan operated here from 1670 onwards. Colombia won independence in 1819, and claimed the islands, in spite of Nicaraguan protestations. In 1928 a treaty granted Colombia sovereignty. The International Court of Justice reaffirmed Colombia's sovereignty in 2007.

Getting There & Away

Buy a tourist card (COP$29,000) on the mainland before checking in for your San Andrés–bound flight. The airport is in San Andrés Town, a 10-minute walk northwest of the center. Taxi is COP$9500.

Avianca (www.avianca.com) and **AeroRepública** (www.aerorepublica.com) have flights to San Andrés via Bogotá from most major Colombian cities (COP$600,000 return). **Satena Airways** (☎ 512-3139; www.satena.com; Aeropuerto Internacional Sesquicentenario) flies between Providencia and San Andrés (return COP$400,000).

SAN ANDRÉS

☎ 8 / pop 66,000

The larger of the two islands at 12.5km long and 3km wide, San Andrés has the most developed tourist infrastructure. Its isolated beaches are postcard-perfect, though the island's commercial center is far from pretty. All the amenities are in San Andrés Town: there's a **tourist office** (Secretaría de Turismo; ☎ 512-5058; www.sanandres.gov.co; Av Newball, San Andrés Town; ⏀ 8am-noon & 2-6pm Mon-Fri), an ATM at the **Banco de Bogotá** (☎ 512-4195; Av Colón 2-86, San Andrés Town), and **Bistronet** (☎ 512-6627; Centro Comercial San Andrés, San Andrés Town; per hr COP$3000; ⏀ 8:30am-9pm) provides internet.

The other two small towns, La Loma in the central hills and San Luis on the eastern coast, are far less tourist-oriented and boast some fine English-Caribbean wooden architecture.

MOMPÓS

☎ 5 / pop 62,000

Stranded on an island in the eastern backwaters of the muddy Río Magdalena, Mompós is a town lost in space and time. Founded in 1537, 230km southeast of Cartagena, Mompós became an important port – all merchandise from Cartagena passed to the interior of the colony through here, and several imposing churches and many luxurious mansions were built. It's now a Unesco World Heritage Site.

Toward the end of the 19th century shipping was diverted to the other branch of the Magdalena as the river silted up, ending the town's prosperity. Mompós has been left in isolation and little has changed since. Today, it's a startling sight, with many streets and squares looking exactly as they did in the 16th century; many buildings are still used for their original purposes.

In the evenings, the residents sit on the narrow streets and creak back and forth in rocking chairs – the town is famous for its furniture – and hundreds of bats flit about in a scene of surreal gothic tropicalia.

Mompós was the setting for *Chronicle of a Death Foretold* by Gabriel García Márquez, and features in his latest work, the controversial, neohistorical study of the final days of Simón Bolívar, *The General in His Labyrinth*.

The **Johnny Cay Natural Regional Park** is a protected coral islet 1.5km north of San Andrés Town, covered with coconut groves and surrounded by a lovely, white-sand beach.

Due to the beautiful coral reefs all around, San Andrés has become an important diving center, with more than 35 dive spots. **Karibik Diver** (☎ 512 -0101; www.karibikdiver.com; Av Newball 1-248, San Andrés Town; ☽ 8am-4pm) is a small school which provides quality equipment and personalized service.

Lodge with Raizal locals at **Cli's Place** (☎ 512-6957; luciamhj@hotmail.com; Av 20 de Julio, San Andrés Town; r per person from COP$30,000) or stay in one of nine simple, cozy rooms two blocks from the beach at **Hotel Mary May Inn** (☎ 512-5669; jfgallardo@gmail.com; Av 20 de Julio 3-74, San Andrés Town; s/d COP$40,000/60,000; ☒).

Across from the Club Nautico is **Miss Celia O'Neill Taste** (☎ 316-690-0074; Av Colombia, San Andrés Town; mains COP$15,000-20,000; ☽ lunch & dinner), with local specialties such as rundown, stewed crab and stewed fish. For nightspots in San Andrés Town head along the eastern end of Av Colombia.

PROVIDENCIA

☎ 8 / pop 5000

Lying 90km north of San Andrés, Providencia is 7km long and 4km wide, and is less commercialized than the larger island, with dozens of small villages of multicolored colonial wooden houses. Santa Isabel is the main town and is where you'll find the **tourist office** (☎ 312-315-6492; Santa Isabel), an ATM at **Banco de Bogotá** (Santa Isabel; ☽ 8-11:30am & 2-4pm Mon-Thu, 8am-11:30am & 2-4:30pm Fri) and internet at **Communication Center** (Santa Isabel; per hr COP$2500; ☽ 9am-12:30pm & 4-9pm Mon-Sat, 2:30-9pm Sun).

Diving trips and courses can be arranged with **Felipe Diving Shop** (☎ 514-8775; www.felipediving .com), run by a native Raizal. Don't miss **El Pico Natural Regional Park** for outstanding 360-degree views of the Caribbean. The most popular trail begins in Casabaja, where you can find a guide, or seek directions. Take water and sunscreen.

For accommodations, **Mr Mac** (☎ 514-8168; s/d COP$30,000/50,000) is the cheapest option in Santa Isabel, with large kitchenettes. **Aguadulce** is a quiet 20-house hamlet with more than a dozen of places to stay.

Pizza's Place (☎ 514-8224; mains COP$6000-55,000; ☽ dinner) serves sandwiches (COP$6000) and pizza (from COP$13,000) and island staples, while the specialties at **Caribbean Place** (☎ 514-8698; mains COP$18,000-53,000; ☽ lunch & dinner) include mountainous black crab, unique to the archipelago in Colombia.

Roland Roots Bar (☎ 514-8417; Bahía Manzanillo) is an atmospheric, archetypal bamboo beach bar with booming reggae and strong booze.

COLOMBIA

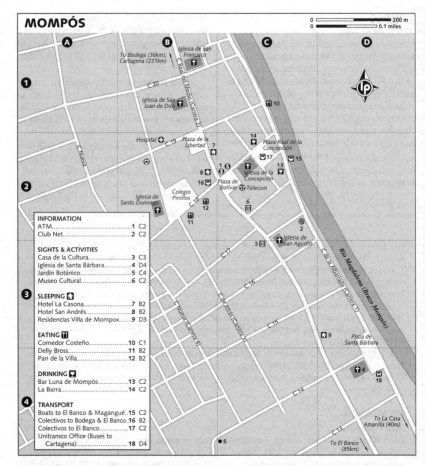

MOMPÓS

INFORMATION
ATM...1 C2
Club Net......................................2 C2

SIGHTS & ACTIVITIES
Casa de la Cultura.......................3 C3
Iglesia de Santa Bárbara..............4 D4
Jardín Botánico...........................5 C4
Museo Cultural............................6 C2

SLEEPING 🏠
Hotel La Casona..........................7 B2
Hotel San Andrés.........................8 B2
Residencias Villa de Mompox........9 D3

EATING 🍴
Comedor Costeño.......................10 C1
Delly Bross................................11 B2
Pan de la Villa...........................12 B2

DRINKING 🍸
Bar Luna de Mompós...................13 C2
La Barra....................................14 C2

TRANSPORT
Boats to El Banco & Magangué..15 C2
Colectivos to Bodega & El Banco.16 B2
Colectivos to El Banco...............17 C2
Unitransco Office (Buses to
    Cartagena).............................18 D4

Information

The tourist office has closed, so get info from Richard at La Casa Amarilla guesthouse.

ATM (BBVA; Plaza de Bolívar) Always runs out of cash. Arrive with enough.

Club Net (Carrera 1 No 16-53; per hr COP$1500; 🕔 7am-9pm) Internet cafe.

Sights

Mompós is a place to ditch this guidebook and take a wander. Most of the central streets are lined with fine whitewashed colonial houses with characteristic metal-grill windows, imposing doorways and lovely hidden patios. Six colonial churches complete the scene; all are interesting, though rarely open. Don't miss the **Iglesia de Santa Bárbara** (Calle 14) with its Moorish-

style tower, unique in Colombian religious architecture. Keep an eye out, too, for Masonic symbolism. The town is covered in it.

The **Casa de la Cultura** (Real del Medio; 🕔 8am-noon & 2-5pm Mon-Fri, 8am-5pm Sat & Sun) displays memorabilia relating to the town's history. **Museo Cultural** (Carrera 2 No 14-15; adult/child COP$3000; 🕔 8am-noon & 2-4pm Mon-Fri, 9am-noon Sat), features a collection of religious art. There's a small **Jardín Botánico** (Calle 14), with lots of hummingbirds and butterflies. Knock on the gate to be let in.

Festivals & Events

Holy Week celebrations are very elaborate in Mompós. The solemn processions circle the streets for several hours on Maundy Thursday and Good Friday nights.

Sleeping

La Casa Amarilla (☎ 301-362-7065; www
.lacasaamarillamompos.com; Carrera 1 No 13-59; dm
COP$15,000, s/d with fan COP$40,000/50,000, with air-
con COP$60,000/75,000, luxury r COP$100,000; ✵ ▢)
Excellent, renovated riverside home with
friendly, professional service. Excellent-
value dorms have just four beds in each,
private rooms are spacious with air-con
available, coffee is free, and owner Richard
will lend you his cell phone wi-fi kit. The
luxury rooms are elegant and the best
in town.

Hotel La Casona (☎ 685-5307; Real del Medio
18-58; s/d with fan COP$30,000/50,000, with air-
con COP$40,000/70,000; ✵) Well-appointed
rooms, a welcoming common area and a
friendly staff. Beware the TV in the hotel
lobby which is set to 'Colombian' on the
volume control.

Hotel San Andrés (☎ 685-5886; www.hotelsanandres
mompox.com; Real del Medio 18-23; s/d with fan
COP$30,000/50,000, with air-con COP$40,000/70,000; ✵)
Bland rooms with vile fake wall tiles and
false ceilings, but the parakeets and parrots
in the courtyard are kind of fun.

Residencias Villa de Mompox (☎ 685-5208; Real
del Medio 14-108; s/d with fan COP$30,000/60,000, with
air-con COP$40,000/80,000; ✵ ▢) Low-priced
air-con rooms.

Eating & Drinking

Plaza Santa Domingo has good, healthy street
food for a few thousand pesos a plate.

Comedor Costeño (Calle de la Albarrada 18-45; set
meal COP$3000-7000) One of several rustic, river-
front restaurants in the market area. Local
bocachica fish is a specialty.

Pan de la Villa (Calle 18 No 2-53; crepes COP$5000,
smoothies COP$2000; ✵ 7am-9pm) Specializes in
ice cream, cakes and baked goods, but also
serves crepes. Good vegetarian choices –
in relative terms. It also has wonderful *zapote* (a Colombian fruit) smoothies.

Delly Bross (Calle 18 No 2-37; mains COP$7000-16,000;
✵ breakfast, lunch & dinner) Good local food,
with local staples such as beef in a ragout
of tomatoes.

Bar Luna de Mompós (Calle de la Albarrada; ✵ 6pm-
1am Mon-Thu, to 3am Fri-Sun) Once the town's
premier riverside boozing joint, it's now
in a sound clash with neighbors. Get there
early and head on once the speaker stacks
glow red.

La Barra (Plaza Real de la Concepción; ✵ 7pm-1am
Tue-Thu, to 3:30am Fri-Sun) Head to this fancy-pants
newcomer, catering to rich local tourists, if
you actually fancy a conversation.

Getting There & Away

Mompós is well off the main routes, but can
be reached by road and river from the coast
or by road from Bucaramanga. Cartagena is
the usual departure point. Unitransco has one
direct bus daily leaving Cartagena at 7:30am
(COP$40,000, eight hours). It's faster to take
a bus to Magangué (COP$25,000, four hours);
Brasilia has half a dozen departures a day –
change for a boat to Bodega (COP$5000, 20
minutes) with frequent departures until about
3pm, and continue by *colectivo* to Mompós
(COP$7000, 40 minutes).

If you depart from Bucaramanga, set off
before 4am to make it the same day. Take
a Cootransmagdalena bus to El Banco
(COP$30,000, seven hours) and continue to
Mompós by jeep (COP$25,000, two hours).

Note that El Banco bus terminal has dozens of incredibly hectic, pestering touts who
want you on 'their' bus. They will surround
you and bellow at you. Stay cool, lower your
shades, and make your own choice.

TURBO

☎ 4 / pop 113,000
Never has a town been more aptly named.
You will want to enter and exit Turbo as
quickly as possible. It's a dirty, dangerous
and noisy port, with a grim past as a paramilitary stronghold. It is, however, the maritime gateway to Capurganá and Sapzurro
in the pristine Golfo de Urabá, a Caribbean
hideaway that could soon overshadow the
rest of Colombia's Caribbean.

Information

Banco de Bogotá (Calle 101 No 12-131) ATM.
Turbo Internet.com (☎ 827-5100; Carrera 13; per
hr COP$2000; ✵ to 8pm Mon-Fri, to 9pm Sat & Sun)
Internet cafe.

Sleeping & Eating

Residencias Florida (☎ 827-3531; Carrera 13 No 99A-
56; s/d COP$18,000/28,000) Scruffy but safe and
the owner Jhon is extremely helpful and informative. It's right on the park where the
bus will drop you, and near the dock.

Some other hotels in the area may be unsafe. If you stay near the dock you'll have

COLOMBIA

GETTING TO PANAMA

It's now possible to get to Panama from Colombia without flying or taking a sailboat trip. The basic route is Turbo–Capurganá by boat, Capurganá–Puerto Obaldia (Panama) by boat, and Puerto Obaldia–Panama City by plane. It's slow, but it's safe and it's the cheapest way to pass from South to Central America.

■ Ensure your yellow fever vaccination is up to date. Panama demands it. Make your way to Capurganá using the information in the Turbo section (below). You'll arrive in Capurganá at 10am.

■ Get your Colombian exit stamp at **Departamento Administrativo de Seguridad** (DAS, Department of Administrative Security; ☎ 311-746-6234; ☒ 8am-5pm Mon-Fri, 9am- 4pm Sat) the day before heading to Puerto Obaldia. Sleep the night in Capurganá; it's lovely.

■ Catch a motorboat from Capurganá's harbor to the first town in Panama: Puerto Obaldia (COP$20,000, 45 minutes). These leave at 7:30am on Sunday, Monday, Wednesday and Friday, and connect with onward flights from Puerto Obaldia to Panama City. Get to the docks early and skip breakfast if you suffer seasickness. It can be choppy.

■ Get a Panama entry stamp at Panamanian immigration when you arrive. From here, you can fly onward to Panama City on **Aeroperlas** (☎ in Panama +507-315-7500; www.aeroperlas.com) on Sunday, Monday, Wednesday and Friday at 10am (US$80). Panama's currency is the US dollar.

to endure the smell of raw sewage and the sound of quarrelling drug addicts and pimps. Oh, and six different sound systems competing to see who can burst their drunken clients' eardrums first.

Opposite Residencias Florida and about 50m to the left is a good restaurant without a name, or an address. It has a red awning and is owned by the partner of Jhon.

Getting There & Away

From Cartagena, take a bus to Montería (COP$35,000, 4½ hours) and change for Turbo. Leave Cartagena before 11am to make it to Turbo the same day. **Sotracor** (☎ 784-9023), **Gomez Hernandez** (☎ 784-9010) and **Coointur** (☎ 784-9008) ply the Montería–Turbo route. In Turbo, get out at the central park. Buses to Montería run from 4:30am to 4pm. **Sotrauraba** (☎ 827-2039) goes to Medellín hourly from 5am to 10pm (COP$51,000, eight hours).

Boats to Capurganá (COP$49,000, 2½ hours) leave daily from the port from 6am in high season and once at 8:30am in low season. Boats fill up quickly with locals – so arrive one hour early to buy your ticket. It can be a horrifically bumpy journey, especially if your hard plastic seat or wooden bench has no cushions, so bring one. Sit near the back of the boat, wear beachwear, take sunblock and buy a trash bag at the dock (COP$1000) to keep your luggage dry.

You'll laugh about this journey one day – if you don't bite your tongue off and smash all your teeth en-route. For continuing on to Panama, see boxed text (above).

CAPURGANÁ
☎ 4 / pop 2000

Capurganá is everything Taganga once was: a Caribbean backwater where you drop a gear the second you arrive. With its painted wooden houses, a total lack of cars, and an extremely laid-back atmosphere, it feels more like a town on Jamaica's northern coast.

Children fish from the pier in the afternoon, the taxi service is a horse and cart, and locals are in no rush to do anything. Tourism is dominated by all-inclusive hotels for wealthy Colombians, though this is changing, and there are a number of backpacker-friendly accommodations.

There are fantastic nature-watching opportunities nearby, and you can spot hundreds of varieties of bird and howler monkey troops. Fishing in the bay is said to be excellent, with huge fish landed often.

Electric power runs till 2am, so be sure to pack plenty of repellent and a mosquito net for when the fans whir down. The Gulf of Uraba, which drains away the mighty Darién jungle, is one of the wettest places on earth, with up to 10m of rain a year. The sun dries it all up in the afternoon. Note that no addresses are given – it's because none exist. The town is tiny.

Information

There are no banks, but you can sometimes get a Visa cash advance at Capurganá Tours.

Capurganá Tours (☎ 824-3173; www.capurganatours .com; ☼ 8am-noon & 2-6pm Mon-Sat) Friendly travel agency on the town's only commercial street.

DAS (☎ 311-746-6234; ☼ 8am-5pm Mon-Fri, 9am-4pm Sat) Immigration services. Near the church, three minutes' walk from the boat harbor.

Internet (per hr COP$3000; ☼ 9am-9pm Mon-Sat) In the Jasepca Building on the main park.

Panamanian Consulate (☎ 314-653-4081; ☼ 8am-4pm Mon-Fri) Near the soccer pitch.

Sights & Activities

The diving here beats Taganga on a few important points: you can dive without a wetsuit and the coral is better preserved, and closer to land. Though prices are higher, groups are smaller, and attention is more personalized. If groups of eight can be formed, you can dive the waters of the nearby Kuna Yala indigenous reserve, some of the most pristine and unfished coral in the Caribbean.

Dive & Green (☎ 316-781-6255; www.diveand green.com; ☼ 8:30am-12:30pm & 2-5:30pm), located directly left from the dock, offers two-tank dives costing COP$180,000. PADI certification costs COP$800,000.

WALKING

Sapzurro is a short and fairly easy hike through the teeming jungle just outside Capurganá. It's well signposted and you don't need a guide. **El Cielo** is another popular jungle route, with natural *piscinas* (swimming pools) to cool down in. **Aguacate** is also a pleasant one-hour walk. Wear walking shoes or trainers for all of these, as it gets muddy. **La Miel** is one of the area's loveliest beaches, and lies just inside Panama – bring ID. Ask at your accommodations for more information.

Sleeping

Hostal Los Delfines (☎ 316-866-3739; s/d COP$10,000/20,000) Near the central park area, these are best-value rooms in town with two fans, clean sheets and fair bathrooms. The restaurant does a mean red snapper for COP$10,000. The owner meets every boat at the harbor daily.

Hostal Capurganá (☎ 824-3173; Calle de Comercio; s/d COP$18,000/30,000) A great option, with new, fresh rooms and comfortable beds.

Luz de Oriente (☎ 824-3719; pier, Capurganá; r per person COP$20,000) Chilled little hotel-restaurant with sea views, and comfortable rooms and beds. And a rare novelty for anywhere with traveler presence – reggae that *isn't* Bob Marley.

Dive & Green (☎ 311-578-4021; r per person COP$20,000) Offers a COP$5000 discount on rooms in its smart cabins if you dive with them. Located on the seafront, a short walk to the right of the dock.

Hostal Marlin (☎ 315-569-3849; r per person COP$15,000) Right on the beach behind the park, with shared rooms constructed with pine and with clean beds and bathrooms.

Eating & Drinking

Most hotels offer food-included deals. Turn right from the dock to find these two excellent choices.

Hernan Patacon (Playa Blanca; mains COP$4500-12,500, ☼ 11:30am-7:30pm) Thin, crispy *patacones* (like fried plantains) topped with delicious seafood, meat or even sweet caramel, are served alfresco.

Josefina's (Playa Caleta; mains COP$20,000-30,000; ☼ lunch & dinner) Josefina serves vast portions of fresh seafood cooked with elegant simplicity. Her *pulpo al ajillo* (garlic octopus) is breathtaking. Knock at her door if she looks closed, and ask to see what delights she has in her fridge that day.

There are several bars around the park, all playing ear-splitting music to a largely blind-drunk clientele.

Getting There & Away

There are only two ways to reach Capurganá and Sapzurro. Cheapest is to catch a boat from Turbo (COP$49,000, 2½ hours), which departs daily from 6am in high season and once at 8:30am the rest of the year. In low season, the boats depart for Turbo at 7:30am.

ADA (☎ 682-8817; www.ada.aero.com) also operates flights from Medellín (around COP$307,000 one-way) on Monday, Tuesday, Thursday, Friday and Saturday at noon in low season.

SAPZURRO

☎ 4 / pop 1000

Sapzurro is an archetypal small Caribbean town, with children strolling the narrow streets carrying fresh fish, elderly ladies selling coconut ice cream with hair curlers in, men wandering about aimlessly at a snail's pace. There are no cars or sound systems. It's blissful. The beaches are pristine and the

COLOMBIA

surrounding forest is a riot of wildlife. This sleepy spot is the last stop before Panama, so it's full of bored soldiers who are actually pretty friendly. Beware: it's plagued by mosquitoes and sandflies once night falls. lazing on the beach is the only activity.

Sleeping & Eating

Camping El Chileno (☎ 313-685-9862; Sapzurro Beach; hammock COP$8000, camping with/without tent COP$6000/8000; cabaña per person COP$15,000) The ebullient owner offers a quiet spot right on the beach, with basic hammocks and a musty *cabaña* (cabin).

Reserva Natural de la Sociedad Civil Tacarcuna (☎ 314-623-149; tacarcunas@gmail.com; cabaña per person COP$25,000) Offers good beds in a private nature reserve dedicated to environmental improvements, with the owners reintroducing native plant species and trees, and using treated rainwater for all guests' needs. Ask for Martha and Fabio, in the second house on the road to La Miel.

Restaurante Las Tinajas is one of the few restaurants in Sapzurro, specializing in simple, well-prepared seafood. The prawns in garlic sauce are stellar and vegetarians are welcome. To find it ask for doña Annie and don Pacho's restaurant.

For information on how to get to Sapzurro, see the Capurganá section (p549).

BAHÍA EL AGUACATE
☎ 4 / pop 30

A tiny bay just south of Capurganá hosts two small private lodges, both of which offer superlative accommodation on small private beaches.

Ex-pilot German Piñalosa runs **Cabo Pinololo** (☎ 312-259-9967; gerdapec@hotmail.com; Bahía El Agucate; r per person COP$70,000), with a few small, well-appointed rooms set back from the beach. He also has a sailboat for excursions and is gracious and friendly. Prices include lunch and dinner.

The **Hotel Bahía Lodge** (☎ 314-812-2727; www .bahia-lodge.com, info@bahia-lodge.com; Bahía El Agucate; cabin per person for 2 nights incl breakfast COP$160,000, r per person for 2 nights COP$130,000) has a small bar, with rooms that have excellent sea views and a sandy beach. It's beyond tranquil – even the mosquitoes are on siesta, while the surrounding forest is well preserved and is home to many animals and birds.

Reservations to both hotels are via email, and the owners will meet you at the dock in Capurganá to chug you a few minutes around the corner in a small motorboat.

NORTHWEST COLOMBIA

The northwest of Colombia is mountainous with a mild climate, fertile volcanic soil that blooms with millions of flowers, verdant coffee farms, ethereal cloud forests and small, busy university towns full of hard-working *paisas,* as locals are known here.

The department of Antioquia is the biggest, richest and most populous in the region, with Medellín, a gleamingly modern and forward-looking metropolis in its center. Its inhabitants are renowned nationally for their independent and entrepreneurial spirit.

Antioquia spreads over parts of the Cordillera Occidental and the Cordillera Central. The Zona Cafetera, Colombia's major coffee-growing area, is centered on three towns, Manizales, Armenia and Pereira, which are close by to some of the country's most astounding landscapes, including the Valle de Cocora, and can be used as a launchpad to the Andes trekking areas.

MEDELLÍN
☎ 4 / pop 2,219,800

Medellín, the city of Colombia's proudest residents, the *paisas,* is back with a vengeance. Once the world's most murderous city, you'd never know it today. With a perfect, perpetual springlike climate, chic shopping malls, world-class restaurants and vibrant nightlife, the city seduces the senses and will make you feel instantly at home.

Medellín has always dwelt in the shadows of Cartagena and Bogotá, but many visitors find this city, which also has pleasant green spaces and striking public art, more relaxing than the former and more welcoming than the latter. It's got culture, class and history, and locals who'll treat you like family. It's the perfect mix between the broiling coastal fairy-tale land of Cartagena and the chilly heights of Bogotá, and tourism is flourishing.

In the 1990s, Medellín was the center of the worldwide coke trade with motorbike-riding *sicarios* (hitmen), carrying out gangland hits for the city's most notorious son, drug lord Pablo Escobar. He remains popular here with some for his generosity to the poor. Escobar was so rich he once offered to pay off Colombia's foreign debt, and paid his hitmen US$1000 for every cop they killed. The city was a no-go zone for foreigners until the kingpin was gunned down on a Medellín rooftop by security forces in 1993.

The economic engines of the city today are cut flowers, coffee and textiles, and *paisas* are known for their industriousness and shrewd business acumen. This has been coupled in recent years with intelligent local government planning and investment in infrastructure. The city boasts Colombia's only metro system, a sparkingly clean, graffiti-free, safe and affordable public transportation system that shuttles you around comfortably and quickly. The cable-car ride that swoops over poorer barrios has fostered peace, and is well worth the ride.

Medellín's character of proud self-reliance stems from its history: the town was founded in 1616 by European immigrants who worked hard, farming the land themselves to achieve their successes. The city is surrounded by lush, mountainous terrain and spills north and south down a narrow valley, with soaring buildings blooming like geometric sunflowers.

But beware: they play as hard as they work here – if you're heading for a night out with a gang of *paisas* you likely won't get home before dawn.

Information

BOOKSTORES
Centro Colombo Americano Central Medellín (Map p552; ☎ 513-4444; www.colomboworld.com; Plaza San Fernando, Carrera 45 No 53-24) Sells English-language books.
Panamericana (Map p554; ☎ 448-0999; Carrera 43A No 6S-150, El Poblado; ✆ 9:30am-9pm Mon-Sat, 11am-7:30pm Sun) This huge bookstore sells some English titles. It also sells maps of Medellín, plus electronic goods.

INTERNET ACCESS
Café Internet Doble-Click (Map p552; Calle 50 No 43-135; ✆ 7am-9pm Mon-Fri, 7am-7pm Sat, 10am-4pm Sun)
Comunicaciones La 9 (Map p554; ☎ 266-2105; Calle 9 No 41-64, El Poblado)

MONEY
Banks listed are likely to change traveler's checks at reasonable rates. The banks may also change cash, but you'll probably get similar or even better rates (and will save time) at *casas de cambio*.

Banco Santander (Map p552; Carrera 49 No 50-10)
Bancolombia (Map p554; CC Oviedo, Calle 43A No 65-15)
Citibank (off Map p554; Carrera 43A No 1A Sur-49, El Poblado)
Davivienda (off Map p554; Poblado Éxito) Inside the Éxito supermarket.
Giros & Finanzas (Map p552; Centro Comercial Villanueva, Calle 57 No 49-44, Local 241) The Western Union agent.

TOURIST INFORMATION
Fomento y Turismo (off Map p552; Subscretaria de Turismo; ☎ 444-4144; www.culturayturismomedellin.com; Av Alfonso López; ✆ 7:30am-12:30pm & 1:30-5:30pm Mon-Fri) In the Palacio de Exposiciones.

VISA INFORMATION
DAS (off Map p554; ☎ 238-9252; Calle 19 No 80A-40, Barrio Belén; ✆ 7-11am & 2-4pm Mon-Fri) For visa extensions. From El Poblado take the Circular Sur 302/303 bus heading south along Av Las Vegas, or take a taxi (COP$7000).

Sights

The **Museo de Antioquia** (Map p552; ☎ 251-3636; www.museodeantioquia.org; Carrera 52 Caraobo 52-43; admission COP$8000; ✆ 10am-6pm Mon-Sat, to 4:30pm Sun) features pre-Hispanic, colonial, independence and modern art collections, spanning Antioquia's 400-year-long history, plus Fernando Botero's donation of 92 of his own works and 22 works by international artists. His 23 large bronze sculptures have been placed in front of the museum, in Plazoleta de las Esculturas.

Across the Parque Berrío are two large murals (see Map p552) depicting Antioquia's history, the 1956 work by another of Medellín's famous and prolific sons, Pedro Nel Gómez (1899–1984). The **Casa Museo Pedro Nel Gómez** (off Map p552; ☎ 233-2633; Carrera 51B No 85-24; ✆ 9am-5pm Mon-Fri, 10am-4pm Sun), set in the house where the artist lived and worked, houses nearly 2000 of his works including watercolors, oil paintings, drawings, sculptures and murals.

Another important city museum, the **Museo de Arte Moderno de Medellín** (off Map p552; ☎ 230-2622; Carrera 64B No 51-64; ✆ 10am-5pm Tue-Fri, to 4pm Sat & Sun) stages changing exhibitions of contemporary art.

Apart from a few old churches, the city's colonial architecture has virtually disappeared. The most interesting of the historic churches is the **Basílica de la Candelaria** (Map p552; Parque Berrío), built in the 1770s and functioning as the city's cathedral until 1931. Also see the gi-

COLOMBIA

gantic neo-Romanesque **Catedral Metropolitana** (Map p552; Parque de Bolívar), completed in 1931.

Medellín has a fine botanical garden, the **Jardín Botánico Joaquín Antonio Uribe** (off Map p552; ☎ 444-5500; Carrera 52 No 73-182; ☺ 9am-5pm). A good place to chill out is the **Parque de los Pies Descalzos** (off Map p552; Barefoot Park; Carrera 57 No 42-139), where citizens are encouraged to kick

their shoes off and wade into shallow pools. Next to the park are restaurants and the **Museo Interactivo** (off Map p552; ☎ 380-6956; Carrera 57 No 42-139; admission adult/child COP$6000/4000; ☺ 10am-8pm Tue-Sat, noon-8pm Sun) featuring 200 interactive science displays – kids will love it.

For views of the city, go to the **Cerro Nutibara** (Map p552), an 80m-tall hill 2km southwest of

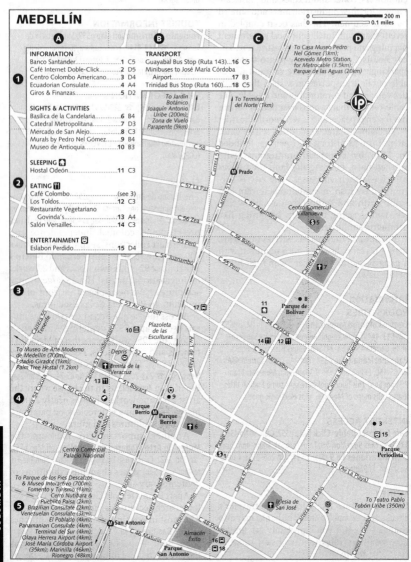

MEDELLÍN

0 — 200 m
0 — 0.1 miles

INFORMATION
Banco Santander.....................**1** C5
Café Internet Doble-Click...........**2** D5
Centro Colombo Americano........**3** D4
Ecuadorian Consulate...............**4** A4
Giros & Finanzas.....................**5** D2

SIGHTS & ACTIVITIES
Basílica de la Candelaria...........**6** B4
Catedral Metropolitana.............**7** D3
Mercado de San Alejo...............**8** C3
Murals by Pedro Nel Gómez.......**9** B4
Museo de Antioquia.................**10** B3

SLEEPING
Hostal Odeón........................**11** C3

EATING
Café Colombo.......................(see 3)
Los Toldos...........................**12** C3
Restaurante Vegetariano
  Govinda's..........................**13** A4
Salón Versailles.....................**14** C3

ENTERTAINMENT
Eslabon Perdido....................**15** D4

TRANSPORT
Guayabal Bus Stop (Ruta 143)...**16** C5
Minibuses to José María Córdoba
  Airport.............................**17** B3
Trinidad Bus Stop (Ruta 160).....**18** C5

To Casa Museo Pedro Nel Gómez (3km); Acevedo Metro Station, for Metrocable (3.5km); Parque de las Aguas (20km)

To Jardín Botánico Joaquín Antonio Uribe (200m); Zona de Vuelo Parapente (9km)

To Terminal del Norte (1km)

Centro Comercial Villanueva

Prado

Parque de Bolívar

Centro Comercial Villanueva

Plazoleta de las Esculturas

Depris

Ermita de la Veracruz

To Museo de Arte Moderno de Medellín (700m); Estadio Girardot (1km); Palm Tree Hostal (1.2km)

Parque Berrío

Parque Berrío

Centro Comercial Palacio Nacional

To Parque de los Pies Descalzos & Museo Interactivo (700m); Fomento y Turismo (1km); Cerro Nutibara & Pueblito Paisa (2km); Brazilian Consulate (2km); Venezuelan Consulate (3km); El Poblado (4km); Panamanian Consulate (4km); Terminal del Sur (4km); Olaya Herrera Airport (4km); José María Córdoba Airport (35km); Marinilla (46km); Rionegro (48km)

San Antonio

Parque San Antonio

Iglesia de San José

To Teatro Pablo Tobón Uribe (350m)

Parque Periodista

Almacén Éxito

the city center. The **Pueblito Paisa**, a replica of a typical Antioquian village, has been built on the summit and is home to several handicrafts shops. For another view of the city, take a ride on the newly installed **Metrocable** (Map p552), from Acevedo metro station.

If you're in town on the first Saturday of the month head to the Parque de Bolívar for **Mercado de San Alejo** (Map p552), a colorful craft market.

Activities

Zona de Vuelo Parapente (Map p552; ☎ 254-5943, 311-774-1175; www.zonadevueloparapentemedellin.com; Vía San Pedro de Milagros Km 5.6; flights COP$80,000) offers tandem paragliding flights over the city. It's professional, accredited and trusted.

Festivals & Events

Feria Nacional de Artesanías Craft fair held in July at the Atanasio Girardot sports complex.

Feria de las Flores Held for a week in early August, this is Medellín's biggest event. Its highlight is the Desfile de Silleteros, on August 7, when hundreds of *campesinos* (peasant farmers) come down from the mountains and parade along the streets carrying *silletas* (huge baskets) full of flowers on their backs.

Alumbrado (Christmas Light Festival) Each year at Christmas time the city ignites the riverfront with a spectacular lightshow. It lasts from December 7 until the second week in January.

Sleeping

The El Poblado *barrio*, with its shopping malls, office blocks, fancy shops and Zona Rosa filled with funky bars, clubs and restaurants has hoovered up most of the new gringos and its environs are now considered a new central district. The center is still fun, though, and is recommended if you want to experience a bustling Colombian city.

Palm Tree Hostal (off Map p552; ☎ 260-2805; www.palmtreemedellin.com; Carrera 67 No 48D-63; dm/s/d COP$17,000/25,000/34,000; 🖳) Sidelined by the Poblado boom, the Palm Tree, about 1.5km west of the center, isn't without its charms. Rooms are small, but the atmosphere is calm and social. It has a kitchen for guests and a book exchange.

Pitstop Hostel (Map p554; ☎ 352-1176; www.pitstop hostel.com; Carrera 43E No 5-110, El Poblado; dm COP$17,000-23,000, s with/without bathroom COP$60,000/30,000, d with/without bathroom COP$80,000/50,000; 🖳 💈) Huge new hostel catering to a young crowd with an Irish bar, pool, steam room, barbecue area, basket-

ball court and a huge flatscreen-TV room. Decent private rooms, airless dorms and a frat-house vibe.

Black Sheep Hostal (Map p554; ☎ 311-1589; www.blacksheepmedellin.com; Transversal 5A No 45-133, El Poblado; dm COP$40,000/50,000, without bathroom COP$40,000/50,000; 🖳) Well-managed guesthouse with every conceivable amenity including two TV rooms, barbecue, Spanish-language classes, kitchen and clean rooms. It's also adding new private rooms as foreign travelers rush into the city.

Casa Kiwi (Map p554; ☎ 268-2668; www.casakiwi.net; Carrera 36 No 7-10, El Poblado; dm COP$18,000, r with/without bathroom COP$60,000/40,000; 🖳) At the time of research, the owners were building several new rooms with private bathrooms. Great location near the Zona Rosa. Well-reviewed by residents who say it's social, but not too hectic after dark.

Tiger Paw (Map p554; ☎ 311-6079, www.tigerpawhostel.com; Carrera 36N 10-49, El Poblado; dm/s/d COP$20,000/55,000/65,000; 🖳) Fresh dorms with great beds and large under-bed lockers, a restaurant and bar on-site, and a young, party-loving crowd happy to be within stumbling distance of the bars and clubs of the Zona Rosa.

Hostal Odeón (Map p552; ☎ 513-1404; Calle 54 No 49-38; s/d/tr COP$25,000/32,000/48,000) Decent small downtown option if you want to avoid the hostel scene and be near the museums. Rooms have TV and fridge.

Eating

The center is flooded with affordable restaurants. Restaurants in the Zona Rosa at El Poblado are pricier.

Restaurante Vegetariano Govinda's (Map p552; Calle 51 No 52-17; meals COP$7000; ⏱ 9am-2:30pm Mon-Sat) Large buffet is good value for vegetarians, with soup, salad, main meal, juice and dessert.

Il Forno (Map p554; Carrera 37A No 8-9, El Poblado; mains COP$7000-18,000) Excellent pizza and lasagna, with a few passable salads.

Alex Carne de Res (Map p554; Carrera 48 No 10-70, El Poblado; mains COP$7500-14,800; ⏱ lunch & dinner) A steak so big it hangs off your plate for this price? And succulent with it? The *punta de anca* is the choicest cut – served with a chorizo; you'll waddle out the door. It's below the highway overpass near the El Poblado metro station, with thatched roofs. Vegetarians need not apply.

Salón Versailles (Map p552; Pasaje Junín 53-39; mains COP$10,900; ⏱ 7am-9pm Mon-Sat, 8am-6pm Sun) Good

COLOMBIA

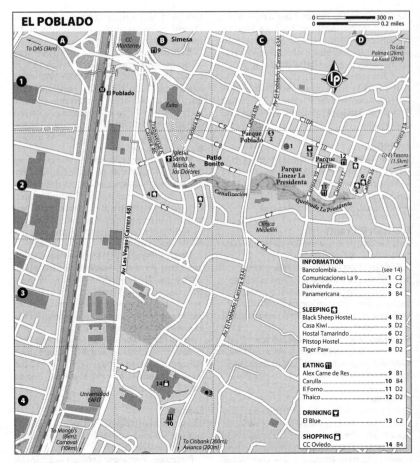

EL POBLADO

0 ━━━━ 300 m
0 ━━━━ 0.2 miles

INFORMATION	
Bancolombia	(see 14)
Comunicaciones La 9	1 C2
Davivienda	2 C2
Panamericana	3 B4

SLEEPING	
Black Sheep Hostel	4 B2
Casa Kiwi	5 D2
Hostal Tamarindo	6 D2
Pitstop Hostel	7 B2
Tiger Paw	8 D2

EATING	
Alex Carne de Res	9 B1
Carulla	10 B4
Il Forno	11 D2
Thaico	12 D2

DRINKING	
El Blue	13 C2

SHOPPING	
CC Oviedo	14 B4

lunch choice in the center, with an old-world vibe and massive cream cakes.

Los Toldos (Map p552; Calle 54 No 47-11; mains COP$15,000-18,000; ☺ lunch & dinner) The *bandeja paisa*, a meat-heavy heart attack on a plate, is trumped here with a version including a *chicharrón gigante* – a massive deep-fried pork rind.

Café Colombo (Map p552; Carrera 45 No 53-24, 10th fl; mains COP$15,000-20,000; ☺ 11am-10pm Mon-Sun) A bright minimalist eatery with a creative menu on the top floor of the Centro Colombo Americano building.

Thaico (Map p554; Calle 9A No 37-40, El Poblado; mains COP$20,000-30,000; ☺ noon-1am Mon-Sat, to 9pm Sun) Escape the tyrannical monopoly of the *comida corriente* with a Thai green curry – especially worthy are the early evening two-for-one meal deals. Cocktails go three for one.

If you're after a supermarket, head to **Carulla** (Map p552; ☎ 361-7777; Calle 43A No 6 Sur-145; ☺ 24hr).

Drinking & Entertainment

El Poblado is rammed with bars and discos, full of foreigners and Colombians looking for a good time. Las Palmas, set above the city, has late-night discos that throb till dawn. Parque Periodista in the center is grittier. Medellín's clubs operate a dress policy, so it's advisable to smarten up or you'll have to bribe the doorman.

Check the online magazine medellin.vive .in or see *Opción*, a monthly listing magazine, for cinema and theater listings.

Mango's (off Map p554; Carrera 42 No 67A-151) Surgically enhanced dancers writhing on podiums to pounding Latin music. The flashy clientele have silicone girlfriends you'd better not talk to. Gangsta-mullets are optional, but not required.

El Blue (Map p554; Calle 10 No 40-20, El Poblado; admission COP$10,000) Just off Parque Lleras, with rock and live bands. It's free to get in on Thursday, and the female clientele have cover-girl looks.

La Kasa (off Map p554; Las Palmas Km 1; admission COP$10,000, women free) Vast disco with modern techno and minimal pounding through the laser-filled air. Saturday nights are busiest.

Carnaval (off Map p554; Calle 80 Sur 50-61, Entrada La Estrella; admission COP$15,000-20,000; 10pm-6am Thu-Sat) Massive superclub playing acceptable house and techno and abominable trance, that often books international DJs. This is your classic end-up – the party only really gets going at 3am.

Eslabon Perdido (Map p552; Calle 53 No 42-55) Popular with Colombian university students, with prices to match, it has live salsa on Tuesday. It's a few blocks from Parque Periodista.

Museo de Arte Moderno de Medellín (off Map p552; 230-2622; Carrera 64B No 51-64) Medellín's best art-house cinema.

Teatro Pablo Tobón Uribe (off Map p552; 239-2674; Carrera 40 No 51-24) Medellín's major mainstream theater.

Shopping

El Tesoro (off Map p554; Carrera 25A No 1AS-45) Vast mall with free wi-fi, and imported US and foreign fashions.

CC Oviedo (Map p554; Carrera 43A No 6S-15, El Poblado) Lots of money changers and banks, plus international fashion outlets.

Getting There & Away

AIR

The main José María Córdoba airport, 35km southeast of the city, takes all international and most domestic flights except for some regional flights on light planes, which use the old Olaya Herrera airport just 4km from the city center. Frequent minibuses (COP$6000, one hour) shuttle between the city center and the main airport (leaving from behind the Nutibara Hotel) or take a cab (COP$50,000).

Avianca (Map p554; 251-7710; Calle 52 No 45-94, Local 9912) runs domestic flights throughout the country.

BUS

Medellín has two bus terminals. The Terminal del Norte, 2km north of the city center, handles buses to the north, east and southeast, including Santa Fe de Antioquia (COP$9000, two hours), Bogotá (COP$60,000, nine hours), Cartagena (COP$80,000, 13 hours) and Santa Marta (COP$80,000, 16 hours). It's seven minutes by metro from the center (alight at Estación Caribe) or take a taxi (COP$10,000).

The Terminal del Sur, 4km southwest of the center, handles all traffic to the west and south including Manizales (COP$9000, five hours), Armenia (COP$18,000, six hours), Pereira (COP$14,000 five hours) and Cali (COP$50,000, nine hours). From El Poblado, take a cab (COP$4000).

Getting Around

Medellín's metro consists of a 23km north–south line and a 6km western leg, with 25 stations. The Metrocable connects the line to low-income barrios in the hills; alight at Acevedo station to take the ride.

Apart from the metro, urban transportation is serviced by buses and *busetas*. The majority of routes originate on Av Oriental and Parque Berrío, from where you can get to almost anywhere within the metropolitan area.

AROUND MEDELLÍN

The lands surrounding Medellín are now abuzz with tourists, as Colombians and foreigners alike take to the roads, free of the threat of kidnapping or guerrilla and paramilitary action.

Santa Fe de Antioquia

4 / pop 22,600

Santa Fe de Antioquia is a popular weekend getaway for Medellín residents. The whitewashed town, founded in 1541, is the oldest in the region. It was a prosperous center during Spanish days and the capital of Antioquia until 1826. When the capital moved to Medellín it lost commercial importance; however, it retains its colonial character and makes a relaxing day trip.

SIGHTS

The town is famous for its carved wooden doorways and flower-filled patios. The 18th-century **Iglesia de Santa Bárbara** (cnr Calle 11 &

Carrera 8) is noted for its fine wide baroque stone facade.

The **Museo de Arte Religioso** (☎ 853-2345; Calle 11 No 8-12; admission COP$3000; ☒ 10am-5:30pm Sat, Sun & holidays), next door to Santa Bárbara church, has a collection of religious objects, including paintings by Gregorio Vásquez de Arce y Ceballos.

The **Puente de Occidente**, an unusual 291m bridge over the Río Cauca, is 5km east of town. When completed in 1895, it was one of the first suspension bridges in the Americas. José María Villa, its designer, was also involved in the creation of the Brooklyn Bridge in New York City. It's an exceedingly boring and hot 45-minute walk downhill, so a moto-taxi (one-way COP$3000) is money well spent. Alternatively, wait next to the Catedral in the main square for an irregular bus service (COP$1400). Be sure to climb the dirt path behind the entrance for complete aerial photos of the bridge.

FESTIVALS & EVENTS
Festival de Cine (www.festicineantioquia.com) A free four-day film festival is held outdoors in early December.

Fiesta de los Diablitos Celebrated with music, dancing, a craft fair, bullfights and a beauty contest held on December 27–31.

SLEEPING & EATING
Prices increase by 25% at weekends.

Hospedaje Franco (☎ 853-1654; Carrera 10 No 8A-14; r per person COP$15,000; ☐) This basic place has acceptable rooms around a tidy courtyard.

Hostal Alejo (☎ 853-1091; Calle 9 No 10-56; r per person COP$15,000) A small budget place with clean, fairly jaded, fan-cooled rooms, with cheap meals available. Not as nice as Hospedaje Franco.

Hotel Caserón Plaza (☎ 853-2040; halcaraz@edatel .net.co; Plaza Mayor; s/d COP$67,000/91,000; ☒) Rooms surround an attractive courtyard with a good, sunny pool area, plus a decent restaurant. The pricier rooms on the 2nd floor are much bigger and better. Also has day-time deals including access to the pool.

GETTING THERE & AWAY
There are half-a-dozen buses (COP$8000, 1½ hours) daily and another half-a-dozen minibuses (COP$9500, 1¾ hours) to and from Medellín's Terminal del Norte. Getting back is quickest in shared taxis (COP$13,000), which leave more regularly than buses.

Río Claro
Three hours east of Medellín lies the **Reserva Natural Cañón de Río Claro** (☎ 268-8855, 311-354-0119; www.rioclaroelrefugio.com; Autopista Medellín–Bogotá Km 132; campsite per person COP$5000, r per person incl 3 meals COP$55,000-90,000), a tranquil river with a marble bed that you can kayak or swim down, with great bird-watching and hiking, and a canopy zip line (COP$20,000). Local maniacs leap into the water from some of the 15m-high banks of the canyon – emulate them at your peril. The best places to stay are the open-sided cabins set back from the road, where the jungle thrum will wake you with a start and lull you to sleep. You can arrive unannounced midweek, but the owners advise early reservations, especially at weekends and holidays.

Nearby is the **Caverna de los Guácharos** (COP$8000), a spectacular cave complex filled with guacharos, a missing link in bat–bird evolution.

GETTING THERE & AWAY
From Medellín's Terminal del Norte take any one of dozens of Bogotá buses (COP$12,000, three hours), which will drop you at the entrance.

Guatape & El Peñol
☎ 4 / pop 2000
The tiny town of Guatape is a popular weekend getaway for *paisas* who want to wander its pretty streets and take trips out onto the artificial lake, El Embalse del Peñol. Looming over the lake is El Peñol, a vast granite monolith you can climb. You can do both as a day trip or spend the night in Guatape.

Much of Guatape was flooded in 1970 in order to create the lakes that now generate much of Colombia's power. Today, it is noted for its cute streets; many houses are decorated with *zocalos* (colorful concrete bas-relief scenes). They were originally designed to prevent chickens pecking at the walls, and to stop children chipping away at the buildings with ball games. Visit during the week for low prices and peace, or at weekends for a hard-drinking *paisa* jamboree.

SIGHTS
Calle de Recuerdos is a steep street decorated with many *zocalos*, and is home to the **Museo Turístico**, which, though it gets full marks for effort, is more like an antiques shop as it has no coherent theme. The **Iglesia del Calma**, on the

main square, has an unusual wooden roof and columns. It was built in 1811 as a penance by a local who killed an orange thief, according to dedicated local historian and curator of the Museo Turístico, Álvaro Idarraga (☎ 320-632-5199). Call him if you want an exhaustive history of the town. **La Casa Familiar Garcia**, just behind the church, is a large, old house which the owners leave open so tourists can snoop around inside.

El Peñol

El Peñol (The Stone) is a 220m-high granite monolith that soars above the banks of Embalse del Peñol. The dam produces 65% of the country's power. You can climb El Peñol's **649 steps** (COP$6000) to hover above the eagles and grab a magnificent view of the region. As you stand gasping at the snack bar at the top, spare a thought for the workers who dragged the cement and water to craft the staircase you just climbed.

You can get here in one of seven comical little mototaxis, rented from Umberto Arcila, in the main square of Guatape (COP$3000, 10 minutes). It's a far better option than the stiff climb up to the rock. He's a classically helpful, hospitable *paisa*.

ACTIVITIES

Boat trips out to the islands in the center of the lake are the main activity. The two-hour boat trips are a little dull, but views are good. The larger boats are slow but have a bar (per person COP$10,000); smaller boats are faster (for eight people COP$80,000). A **canopy ride** (☎ 861-1083; per ride COP$10,000; ⏱ 9am-6pm) on lakeside zip lines is fun, but pricey.

SLEEPING & EATING

El Descanso del Arriero (☎ 861-0878; Calle 30 No 28-82; s/d COP$25,000/50,000) Rooms are pokey, but clean and comfortable. The bar downstairs plays mellow music and serves cheap meals.

Hotel Guatatur (☎ 861-1212; Calle 31 No 31-04, Parque Principal, s/d COP$50,000/90,000) Chic hotel with minimal decor, smart, bright rooms, great beds and a Jacuzzi in the only suite. The restaurant downstairs is relaxed and stylish. Prices provided here are mid-week rates. At weekends prices rise and include food.

Asados Mi Casita (Calle 32 No 26-27; set lunch COP$5000, mains COP$9000-15,000; ☎ 7am-9pm) Right on the lake's shore, this has fast service and

delicious grilled trout and *marzamorra* (a corn-milk broth served with guava jelly).

There are plenty of restaurants near the main square.

GETTING THERE & AWAY

Buses to and from Medellín run on the hour all day (COP$10,000, two hours), or take a shared taxi from the northern bus terminal (COP$14,500, 1½ hours).

ZONA CAFETERA

The Zona Cafetera has exported as many sleepless nights as Colombia's coca plantations. Coffee is the world's second most traded commodity after oil, and Colombia is the world's third-biggest exporter. It's a mountainous area comprised of three cities: Manizales, a major university town (with good nightlife), an important economic engine of national trade; Pereira, a manically busy commercial center that lies near some stunning thermal springs; and Armenia, an ugly city even among its unlucky peers, and the gateway to Salento, a laid-back colonial mountain hideaway set in glorious countryside.

All three towns have been destroyed by earthquakes since their founding, around the 1850s, and have little to no historic sights. However, all three are close to some of the country's most memorable landscapes, with volcanoes, hot springs, vast mountain ranges and major national parks, and offer fun excursions.

Manizales

☎ 6 / pop 380,000

This is a wealthy town that is home to six universities and though the town is not classically pretty (your camera will hardly leave your bag), its modern houses and steep, tidy streets offer a curious contrast to all other Colombian cities. It has a fresh, chilly climate and an air of scholarly seriousness that gives way as the sun drops and the students kick back. It was founded in 1849 but was later leveled by earthquakes. From here, you can visit coffee farms and the awesome and still-active Andean volcano, Nevado del Ruiz, which stands snow-capped for much of the year at 5300m.

INFORMATION

Tourist office (☎ 884-2400, ext 153; www.caldasturistico.gov.co; Calle 19N No 21-44; ⏱ 8am-6pm Mon-Sat,

9am-1pm Sun) On the ground floor of the Palacio de Gobierno, next to the Plaza de Bolívar.

SIGHTS

The tribute to El Libertador in Plaza de Bolívar is curious: Rodrigo Arenas Betancur has cast his subject here as a condor atop a horse.

The concrete **Catedral de Manizales** (☎ 882-2600; Plaza de Bolívar; COP$5000; ☼ 9am-6pm Thu-Sun), built with the city's shaky past in mind, has a 106m-tall main tower which you can climb. It's said to be the highest in the country, and arguments grumble on over its true height. It stands opposite the **Palacio de Gobierno**.

The spaceship-like lookout point **Torre al Cielo** (☎ 880-2345; admission COP$3000; ☼ 10am-10pm Mon-Fri, 9am-10pm Sat) has wonderful views of the mountainous terrain. To get there, take any bus (COP$1100) from Cable Plaza to Chipre; they leave constantly.

TOURS

A day trip to Nevado del Ruiz, at a lung-busting 5300m, is popular, although hardened hikers will be disappointed that much of the full-day trip is spent on a bus. Tours are best arranged through **Mountain House** (trips incl lunch, insurance, jackets & gloves COP$115,000), since public transportation is patchy. They are a good deal considering that park entry is expensive (COP$53,000).

Kumanday Adventures (☎ 885-4980, 315-590-7294; kumandaycolombia@gmail.com; Av Santander 60-13) offers more adventurous options, including multiday trips to the volcano's summit. Accommodation can also be arranged in a mountain lodge with an indoor thermal pool and a waterfall on your doorstep. The management are professional and experienced.

FESTIVALS & EVENTS

Feria de Manizales Bullfights, parades and tiara-clad girls with cartoon smiles take over the town in January and prices double.

Festival Internacional de Teatro Major theatrical festival in September and October.

SLEEPING

The best places to stay are near the Zona Rosa, off Cable Plaza. Check out the old wooden cable-car tower, which used to haul goods across the ridgetops.

Mountain House (☎ 887-4736, 300-789-8840; Calle 66 No 23B-137; dm COP$18,000, s/d without bathroom incl breakfast COP$40,000/55,000; ☐) A popular hostel

with laundry, hot showers, book exchange, a pool table and occasional barbecues. It's well managed, social and gets busy; book ahead.

Kaffa Experience (☎ 890-2945, 311-745-3761; Calle 67 No 23A-33; dm/s/d COP$18,000/40,000/55,000; ☐) The sister hotel of Mountain House is larger and better-furnished with a bigger kitchen, but streetside dorms can be noisy.

Kumanday Adventures (☎ 885-4980, 315-590-7294; kumandaycolombia@gmail.com; Av Santander 60-13; dm/s/d COP$25,000/30,000/50,000) A good bet if you want to escape the hostel crowds, with clean rooms and decent common areas, though it's a little way down Av Santander.

EATING

Kibbes & Felafel (Calle 66 No 22A-56; mains COP$5000; ☼ 11am-2am daily) Just around the corner from Mountain House hostel, this unimpressive-looking drive-through-style restaurant has fantastic felafel with real tahini. You can also smoke apple tobacco through a genuine *nargile* (tobacco water pipe).

La Suiza (Carrera 23B No 64-06; mains COP$8000-12,000; ☼ 9:30am-8:30pm Mon-Sat, 10am-7:30pm Sun) A great spot for a budget breakfast, with veggie options including mushroom crepes.

Valentino's Gourmet (Carrera 23 No 63-128; pastries COP$2000-5000; ☼ 10am-10pm) Great coffee, hot chocolate and pastries.

Don Juaco (Calle 65 No 23A-44; set lunch COP$14,000; ☼ 10:30am-9:30pm) Juicy burgers, and a great-value set lunch including a main course, dessert and excellent local coffee.

DRINKING

Manizales bars change hands more times than a fake banknote, so don't be surprised if any of these spots have changed names. Av Santander is the main street leading away from Cable Plaza, head down here and see where's busy.

Barroco (Carrera 23 No 59-87; ☼ 10pm-3am Thu, to 4:30am Fri & Sat) Grungy rock bar with terrible art on the walls, but a great rear terrace and more distorted guitar than you can bang a head at.

Prenderia (Carrera 23 No 58-42; ☼ 8pm-2am Thu-Sat) Wonderfully relaxed bar with talented local musicians, laying to an older laid-back crowd. Try the lethal *carajillo* – strong espresso spiked with rum – and try not to slide off the bar stools.

Bar C (Carrera 23 No 58-42; ☼ 10pm-3am Thu to 4:30am Fri & Sat) The city's shiny end-up spot, open late with mainstream house, reggaeton and salsa rocking the well-dressed crowd.

San Telmo (Carrera 23B No 64-80; ☻ 6pm-1am Wed & Thu, to 2am Fri & Sat) Neon-lit space with no room for dancing, this busy bar gets full around 10pm with drinkers looking for crossover, *vallenato* and pop-house sounds.

GETTING THERE & AWAY
Air
Aeropuerto La Nubia (☎ 874-5451) is 8km southeast of the city center, off the Bogotá road. Take a city bus to La Enea, from where it's a five-minute walk to the terminal, or take a taxi (COP$8000). Avianca, ADA and Aires have regular flights to Bogotá, Medellín and Armenia.

Bus
The new bus terminal is now open, and the best way to get there is to take a cab to the Zona Rosa (COP$5000). Buses depart regularly to Bogotá (COP$39,000, eight hours), Medellín (COP$25,000, six hours) and Cali (COP$30,000, five hours). There are many minibuses every hour to Pereira (COP$4000, 1¼ hours) and Armenia (COP$7000, 2¼ hours).

Around Manizales
Recinto del Pensamiento (☎ 6-887-4913; www.recinto delpensamiento.com; Vía al Magdalena Km 11; admission COP$8000; ☻ 9am-4pm Tue-Sun) is a great, easy and affordable half-day excursion from Manizales. Inside the nature park, there are orchid-clad cloud forests, a butterfly farm, excellent bird-watching and a **cable-car ride** (COP$10,000). Guides are compulsory and included in admission. Take a bus headed to Sera Maltería from Cable Plaza in Manizales (COP$1100, 30 minutes, every 15 minutes), or take a taxi (COP$6000, 10 minutes).

Los Yarumos ecopark (☎ 6-875-5621; ecoparque losyarumos@epm.net.co; Calle 61B No 15A-01; basic admission COP$3200; ☻ 9am-5pm Tue-Sun) is a 40-minute walk or a short cab ride (COP$4000) from Manizales, and has great city views. As well as bird-watching, it also offers adventure sports including rock climbing, horse riding and zip-line rides. A full-day package includes all activities (COP$33,000).

Coffee-farm tourism in the Eje Cafetero tends to be expensive and is largely a preserve of wealthy Colombians, with *fincas* (farms) running to hundreds of thousands of pesos a night.

our pick Hacienda Guayabal (☎ 6-850-7831, 314-772-4856; www.haciendaguayabal.com; Vía Peaje Tarapacá Km 3, Chinchiná; s/d incl full board COP$45,000/$90,000; ☒) is one of the easiest and most affordable coffee farms to visit in the whole Zona Cafetera, and a trip here will educate, entertain and relax you. Just 40 minutes from Manizales, it's set in wonderful hills, and offers 1½-hour tours (COP$20,000) that reveal the whole coffee production process from field to cup, with roasting and selection classes at the tour's close. Harvest time is from October to December; there's a lesser crop in May and June. Most guides only speak Spanish, but English is available at a premium (COP$10,000 extra). Rooms are clean and comfortable, if a little small.

The lunch option (COP$10,000 extra) is unmissable – a delicate salad of quail eggs, marinated peppers, shaved radish and a main course of chicken in a cream and bacon sauce, with a dessert of preserved figs, *arequipe* and white cheese, with beer and coffee.

To get to Hacienda Guayabal, take any bus from Manizales to Chinchiná (COP$5000, 30 minutes), then from Chinchiná's main square, take a cab (COP$7000).

Parque Nacional Los Nevados
This snow-capped range of volcanic peaks offers some of the most stunning views in the Colombian Andes, plus some fine hiking trails through cloud forest. The Nevado del Ruiz (5325m) is the largest and the highest volcano of the chain. There is no public transportation for the park so the best way to visit is on a tour, either with Mountain House or with Kumanday Adventures, both in Manizales (see opposite).

Pereira
☎ 6 / pop 428,300
You don't come to Pereira for the architecture, nor the food, nor to hang out. Neither do Colombians – they come to make money and do business in this, the largest city of the coffee region. The streets are hectic with commercial activity, and there is really nowhere to escape the bedlam. By night, the clubs thrum with an energy that rivals Manizales.

Pereira does not offer the traveler much in the way of facilities, but if you want to experience a buzzing Colombian city in full effect, this is your spot. It's also close to some very lovely thermal baths.

COLOMBIA

The curious centerpiece of the town, **Bolívar Desnudo** (Plaza Bolívar), is a huge bronze sculpture of El Libertador riding his horse, Nevado, bareback – and fully naked. He seems to be flying furiously towards the town's grand **Catedral** across the plaza.

The **Hotel Mi Casita** (☎ 325-0947; Calle 25 No 6-20; r COP$49,000/88,000; 🖳) is the cheapest acceptable option – but it's pretty horrible. Rooms are a nausea-inducing riot of mismatched patterns, and in a uniquely hideous touch, the toilet seat is padded. There are no hostels in Pereira.

Grajales Autoservicios (Carrera 8 No 21-60; mains COP$8000-15,000; 🕒 24hr) is a self-service restaurant which has basic fodder and good breakfast choices.

The Matecaña airport is 5km west of the city center, 20 minutes by urban bus, or COP$5000 by taxi. Avianca operates around a dozens flights a day to Bogotá. The **bus terminal** (Calle 17 No 23-157) is about 1.5km south of the city center.

Thermal Baths

Termales de Santa Rosa (☎ 6-363-4959; admission COP$24,000; 🕒 9am-11pm) are 9km east of Santa Rosa de Cabal, a town on the Pereira–Manizales road. A tourist complex including thermal pools, a hotel, restaurant and bar has been built near the springs at the foot of a 170m-high waterfall. You can stay on-site, but it's overpriced. Try **Cabañas JC** (☎ 312-888-7799; s/d COP$20,000/40,000), two blocks before the thermals, and stay in lovely wooden cabins with decent beds and lot of space.

From Santa Rosa de Cabal catch a *chiva* (basic rural bus with wooden bench seats) from the market at 7am, noon and 3pm (COP$6000, 45 minutes). These *chivas* collect customers and return immediately. Jeeps (COP$20,000) also do the run, ask around in the main plaza.

A few hundred meters away are the **Balneario de Santa Rosa Termales** (☎ 6-363-4948; admission COP$20,000; 🕒 9am-midnight), which have a far nicer setting, the garden alive with the sounds of tinkling water. Again, you're better off sleeping outside the complex – and as spending the day in the pools is strangely exhausting, sleeping the night is a good idea.

Termales San Vincent (☎ 6-333-6157; www.sanvicente .com.co; admission COP$15,000) are the most relaxing and least commercial option for all water babies, with natural saunas, a 300m-long canopy line and a 30m-high waterfall, and

lots of pricey-but-worth-it lodgings (room per person COP$80,000 to COP$145,000, campsite per person COP$44,000). They are 18km east of Santa Rosa de Cabal. For reservations, especially at weekends when it gets very busy, contact the **booking office** (☎ 6-333-6157; Carrera 13 No 15-62) in Santa Rosa de Cabal. It runs a daily bus service (COP$18,000, 1¼ hours) at 9am, which returns at 5pm. The pools are closed on Monday.

Armenia
☎ 6 / pop 272,500

Like Manizales and Pereira, this departmental capital offers few sights, as most of its early architecture was destroyed by earthquakes.

If you need to kill time, check out the **Museo del Oro Quimbaya** (☎ 749-8433; cnr Av Bolívar & Calle 40N; 🕒 10am-5pm Tue-Sun), a lacklustre gold museum located in Centro Cultural, 5km northeast of the center, on the road to Pereira. For internet, try **Valencia Comunicaciones** (Calle 21 No 15-53; 🕒 8am-10pm), and there's a money-changing facility at **Bancolombia** (Calle 20 No 15-26).

Hotel Casa Real (☎ 741-4550; Carrera 18 No 18-36; s/d with bathroom COP$24,000/35,000) is a small, basic place with cable TV and new beds. The **bus terminal** (cnr Carrera 19 & Calle 35) is around 1.5km southwest of the center.

Parque Nacional del Café

This **national park** (☎ 6-741-7417; www.parque nacionaldelcafe.com; basic admission COP$18,000; 🕒 9am-4pm Wed-Sun) is basically a funfair with a shot of espresso tacked on as an afterthought: quite what a water slide and a rollercoaster have to do with the production of coffee is anyone's guess. However, the amusement park (which, tragically, does *not* include dodgems in the shape of giant coffee beans, or a whirling waltzer in the form of spinning espresso cups) gives an overview of the coffee production process. It has a few fun rides and definitely beats spending the day in Armenia. It's about 15km west of Armenia. Four buses an hour (COP$1400, 30 minutes, till 7pm) run the route.

Salento
☎ 6 / pop 7000

After the jarring concrete horrors of Manizales, Pereira and Armenia, Salento comes as a relief to the senses. The gentle rolling hills are carpeted in thick forest that embrace the undulations of the land like a mother with her newborn. Salento is fast becoming a very popular backpacker hangout, with mild weather, spectacular countryside and a small-town atmosphere. Its proximity to the fabulously beautiful Valle de Cocora makes it a required stop on any Colombian itinerary, however tight. You'll sleep like a baby here.

The streets are lined with many shops selling handicrafts and the atmosphere is supremely benign. Flirtatious old women wander the street selling rice pudding, there are many relaxing bars, cafes and billiard halls and the architecture is a chocolate-box colonial fantasy. It is also popular with Colombian holidaymakers, meaning the main square on weekends and holidays is full of families laughing, singing and dancing.

ACTIVITIES
Richie Holding of **Cycle Salento** (☎ 318-668-8763; ciclosalentocolombia@gmail.com; bike hire per day COP$35,000, per hr COP$8000) arranges mountain-bike hire on well-maintained bikes with disc brakes, and can guide you to a white-knuckle 35km all-downhill route.

SLEEPING
ourpick **Plantation House** (☎ 316-285-2603; www .theplantationhousesalento.com; Calle 7 No 1-04; dm/s/d/tr COP$15,000/40,000/45,000/60,000, s/d without bathroom COP$25,000/48,000; 🖳) Simple, comfortable rooms. The uncrowded dormitory has a fireplace and a good chilling-out area, and guests can use the kitchen – where there's endless free locally grown coffee. Cristina and Tim, a friendly and very professional Anglo-Colombian couple, will do everything they can to help you, and can arrange horse hire and guided tours of local coffee farms, including their own. Best place to stay in Salento bar none.

Hotel Las Palmas (☎ 759-3065; Calle 6 No 3-02; s/d/ tr COP$18,000/30,000/45,000) A great second choice if Plantation House is full, or if you'd prefer to be around Colombians rather than travelers. Wood-lined rooms are neat and tidy, the showers are steamingly hot and you'll want to hug the *señora* as you leave.

Balcones de Ayer (☎ 312-226-2921; Calle 6 No 5-40; s/d COP$35,000/70,000) Great value, tidy-if-small rooms in a colonial house close to the action. The restaurant downstairs is large, airy and serves excellent Colombian food.

EATING
In the main plaza many stands and kiosks sell excellent-value local dishes, including cracker-thin *patacones* loaded with tasty *aogao* (warm tomato chutney), shredded chicken and guacamole, along with delicious local trout.

Rincon de Lucy (☎ 313-471-5497; Carrera 6 No 4-02; mains COP$6000; 🍴 breakfast, lunch & dinner) Simple, generous portions of food served fast in the town's busiest and best place for *comida corriente* and cheap dinners. The beans are marvelous, and even the cheapest cuts of meat are prepared with finesse.

Donde Laurita (☎ 312-772-6313; Calle 5 No 5-34; mains COP$12,000-15,000; 🍴 lunch & dinner) More upmarket than Lucy, with kind, attentive service and more protein. Steaks and chicken are juicy and well-cooked, salads – as ever – are tiny.

DRINKING
The main plaza is lined with bars that kick out the jams at the weekends. Take your pick, they're all great.

Donde Mi A'pa (Carrera 6 No 5-22; 🍴 4pm-midnight Mon-Fri, 11am-2am Sat & Sun) Brilliantly snug bar with leglessly drunk clientele who have been carrying heavy objects up steep hills all day. A classic of its kind. Note the hundreds of envy-inspiring vinyl LPs behind the bar. Which they won't bloody sell you.

Café Jesus Martin (Carrera 6a No 6-14; 🍴 8am-midnight) Great local coffee, an OK wine list and a relaxed, smart atmosphere.

ourpick **Billar Danubio hall** (Carrera 6 No 4-30; 🍴 8am-midnight Mon-Fri, to 2am Sat & Sun) Your every Latin small-town fantasy rolled into one. Old men in nonironic ponchos and cowboy hats sip *aguardiente* as they play dominos, and the largely *ranchero* music is chosen from a vast collection of battered old vinyl. The clientele break into ragged harmony whenever an anthem of heartbreaking personal relevance is played. It's a bastion of unreconstructed male behavior, and so women may be treated as a curiosity at best. You'd be safe, though. These are total gentlemen.

GETTING THERE & AWAY
Buses to Salento from Armenia (COP$3000, 50 minutes) run every 20 to 30 minutes until 9pm.

Valle de Cocora
East of Salento, the stunning Valle de Cocora is like a lush version of Switzerland, with a

broad, green valley floor framed by rugged peaks. However, you'll remember you're a few degrees from the equator when, a short walk past Cocora, you suddenly encounter hills covered with the *palma de cera* (wax palm). The trees tower above the cloud forests in which they thrive. It is an almost hallucinatorily beautiful sight.

The most spectacular part of the valley is east of Cocora. Take the rough road heading downhill to the bridge over the Río Quindío (just a five-minute walk from the restaurants) and you will see the strange 60m-high palms. After an hour or more of walking you'll come to a signpost, with **Reserva Natural Acaime** (☎ 311-311-0701; admission COP$3000) to the right. Here you'll find a wonderful hummingbird reserve, with at least six varieties always present, with dozens of birds zipping past at once. Admission includes a hefty chunk of good cheese and a hot chocolate. You can also stay on-site (dorms per person COP$15,000).

Head back to the signpost, and either double back the way you came or take the harder road uphill towards La Montaña for some of Colombia's most mind-blowing landscapes.

Three jeeps (COP$3000, 35 minutes, 7am, 9am and 4pm) a day depart from Salento's plaza and go up the rough 11km road to Cocora.

SOUTHWEST COLOMBIA

Southwest Colombia will spin your head with its blend of ancient and modern culture. Cali, its largest city, throbs with tropical energy and a touch of danger; the ethereal archaeological sites of San Agustín and Tierradentro, nestled deep in majestic mountain landscapes, are benign and fascinating, while the Desierto de la Tatacoa is an arid anomaly.

The colonial city of Popayán, the other major tourist draw, is a living museum of Spanish rule, with many ornate churches, fascinating museums and a smart, relaxed atmosphere.

Approaching the border with Ecuador at Ipiales, the landscape gets vertiginous and the scene gets Andean; here you'll feel more like you're in Ecuador than Colombia. The beautiful Laguna de la Cocha, in Pasto, and the Santuario de las Lajas, a neo-Gothic

church in Ipiales that spans a wide gorge, are the major attractions here.

DESIERTO DE LA TATACOA

This 330-sq-km desert is a curiosity as it's surrounded by lush green fields. It is a parched spot where temperatures reach 50°C, and it features several distinct ecosystems and a variety of landscapes ranging from rippled dunes to carved cathedrals, with skipping goats, inquisitive foxes and scampering armadillos dodging between the cacti.

It's conveniently midway between Bogotá and San Agustín/Popayán, and is relatively free of tourist facilities. The locals here have a fantastic, sing-song way of speaking.

Best of all is the **observatory** (☎ 310-465-6765; admission COP$7000) for stargazing: the lack of light and development affords spectacular views. Saturn was clearly observed in March 2009, with its rings almost vertical. Local astronomer Xavier Restrepo has deep knowledge of the solar system, and can identify any one of hundreds of stars with his laser pointer. It's a surreal experience to stand and listen as he reels off the names of nebulae, galaxies, planets and constellations. Put your digital camera on the lens of the telescope for initially unimpressive shots that will astound viewers when they realize what they are really looking at.

You can arrange guided tours, which are a must for the deeper recesses of the desert. **Motorbike tours** (per day COP$50,000), or comical **mototaxi tours** (per person COP$15,000) with seats for up to five people, are available.

The small town of **Villa Vieja**, which is near the desert, has one hotel, **La Casona** (☎ 8-879-7636; hostel-lacasonavillaveija@yahoo.es; Calle 3 No 3-60; dm/s COP$15,000/20,000), with a simple large dormitory, and bare double rooms. It also serves excellent, good-value meals.

You can also stay in the desert with desert residents at simple *posadas*. Best of the bunch is **Estadero Los Hoyos** (☎ 311-536-5027; s/d/tr COP$20,000/30,000/40,000), as it's close to a fairly rustic swimming pool.

Alternatively, Xavier Restrepo, (or El Astrónomo as he's know to the entire town, which makes you feel like you've stepped into a Gabriel García Márquez novel) rents out tents, sleeping bags and camping mats (COP$15,000). The campsite is near to the observatory.

Getting There & Away

From Neiva take a bus to Villa Vieja (COP$5000, one hour); the last bus leaves at 7:30pm. There are regular buses from Bogotá (COP$20,000, five hours).

CALI

☎ 2 / pop 3.5 million

Cali is Colombia right in your face. The attitude, the heat, the traffic, the beautiful women, the music and the food all combine in a delightful, dizzying haze. Compared with Popayán's genteel politeness, Medellín's confident strut and Bogotá's refined reserve, Cali is all front – but just behind that front is a passionate, rebellious Colombian city that will love you if you love it.

If salsa is the soul music of Latin America – dancing through the pain and pleasure, the love and the loss – then it's no surprise that Cali, a tough, working town which has seen its fair share of trouble, is obsessed with it. Every city street is pasted with posters for live performances, and if you've never heard the explosive, insurrectionary power of a salsa orchestra live, this is your chance – don't miss it.

Cali doesn't cater to tourists with the same eagerness as other destinations, but this somehow contributes to its charm. Cali needs you less than you need it. It's a busy, tough, at times grimy and unsafe town (see right), but when night falls and the temperature drops on the streets, the locals seize the night with the ferociousness of people who've worked hard and who want, no, *need* to party. You're welcome along for the ride.

Orientation

Cali is built along the western edge of the Valle de Cauca. The city center is split in two by the Río Cali. To the south is the historic heart – laid out on a grid and centered around Plaza de Caycedo, where you'll find most tourist sights.

North of the river is the new center, whose main axis is Av Sexta (Av 6) with its smart shops and restaurants, and the clubs and bars that kick into life once the evening breeze sweeps in and the mercury drops.

The calmest and most relaxing neighborhood is San Antonio, an old colonial district south of the river.

Information

Banco Unión Colombiano (Carrera 3 No 11-03) Changes cash.

Bancolombia (cnr Calle 15N & Av 8N) Changes cash and traveler's checks.

Centro Cultural Comfandi (Calle 8 No 6-23, 5th fl) In the historic center.

Comunicaciones Novatec (Av 8N No 20-46) For internet.

Davivienda (cnr Av 6AN & Calle 22N)

Giros & Finanzas (Carrera 4 No 10-12) Changes cash and is a Western Union Agent.

SCI Sala de Internet (Av 6N No 13N-66) Largest central internet facility.

Secretaría de Cultura y Turismo (☎ 886-0000, ext 2410; Calle 9 No 8-60) The city tourist office is on the 2nd floor of the building of Gobernación del Valle del Cauca.

Dangers & Annoyances

Cali has an edge, especially south of the river: avoid walking alone in the old center, east of Calle 5 or in the park along the Río Cali after dark. Taxis are the safest way to travel, and the San Antonio neighborhood is safe.

Sights & Activities

The mid-16th-century **Iglesia de la Merced** (cnr Carrera 4 & Calle 7) is Cali's oldest church. The adjacent monastery houses the **Museo Arqueológico La Merced** (☎ 889-3434; Carrera 4 No 6-59; admission COP$4000; 9am-1pm & 2-6pm Mon-Sat) featuring an extensive collection of pre-Hispanic pottery.

One block away, the **Museo del Oro** (☎ 684-7757; Calle 7 No 4-69; 9am-5pm Tue-Sat) has a small but well-selected collection of gold and pottery pieces of the Calima culture.

The **Museo de Arte Moderno La Tertulia** (☎ 893-2942; Av Colombia 5 Oeste-105; admission COP$4000; 10am-6pm) presents temporary exhibitions of contemporary painting, sculpture and photography.

Zoológico de Cali (☎ 892-7474; cnr Carrera 2A Oeste & Calle 14 Oeste; admission COP$9000; 9am-4:30pm) is Colombia's best zoo. Its 10 hectares are home to about 1200 animals (belonging to about 180 species), both native and foreign.

Cali has two soccer teams. **Deportivo Cali** (www.deporcali.com) play in the Estadio Deportivo Cali near the airport in Palmira. **América de Cali** (www.america.com.co), who were funded through the 1980s and 1990s with narco-dollars, play in the city at **Estadio Pascual Guerrero** (cnr Calles 5 & 24). Any Palmira-

COLOMBIA

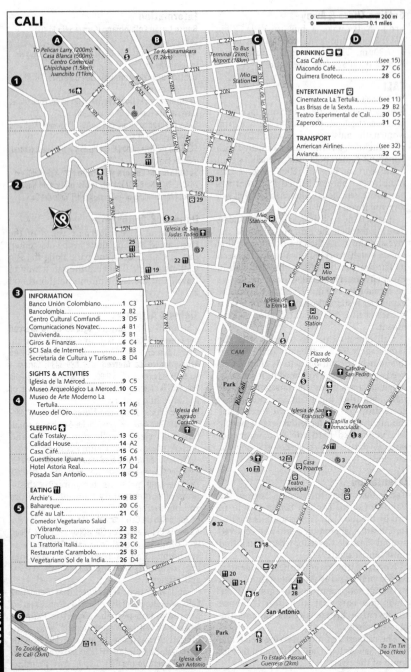

CALI

COLOMBIA

bound bus can take you to the former; to the latter, take Cali's new Mio bus.

Courses

See www.salsapower.com for dance classes if you want to stand a chance on the city's smoking dance floors.

Festivals & Events

The **Feria de Cali** is the main event, running from December 25 and extending to the end of the year with parades, salsa concerts, bullfights and a beauty pageant. The **Salsa Festival de Cali** (www.festivalsalsacali.com) features the world's greatest dancers, and runs from mid- to late September.

Sleeping

Casa Café (☎ 893-7011; Carrera 6A No 2-13; s/d COP$15,000/30,000; 🖳) Chilled gallery-cafe in creaky-but-lovely old house with occasional live performances; also rents four large rooms upstairs.

Pelican Larry (☎ 396-8659; www.pelicanlarry.com; Calle 23N No 8N-12; dm COP$16,000, s/d without bathroom COP$25,000/35,000) A new hostel with massive beds and spotless rooms in a cool, fresh house. It has rapid internet, loads of company, and a good location near bars and restaurants. There are also twice-weekly barbecues with the no-nonsense owner, Günther. Set to become Cali's top young backpacker destination.

Guesthouse Iguana (☎ 313-768-6024; www.iguana.com.co; Av 9N No 22N-46; dm COP$17,000, s/d COP$38,000/46,000, without bathroom COP$28,000/38,000; 🖳) Cali stalwart with the city's best communal kitchen, comfy lounge and balcony, and straight-up management.

Calidad House (☎ 661-2338; www.calidadhouse.com; Calle 17N No 9AN-39; dm/s/d COP$18,000/22,000/26,000; 🖳) Clean, neat and tidy hostel with the usual facilities and great location near the nightlife, but the management are, in our experience, as cold and utterly unwelcoming as a wet sleeping bag.

Café Tostaky (☎ 893-0651; Carrera 10 No 1-76; dm COP$18,000, s/d without bathroom COP$25,000/35,000; 🖳) The friendly French-Colombian owners take you to their heart. It attracts slightly older travelers who want to chill and chat over sublime espressos in the downstairs cafe. Rooms are basic, but clean and bright and not cramped. Some find the beds hard.

Casa Blanca (☎ 396-3849; Av 6bis No 26N-57; dm COP$19,000, s/d without bathroom COP$35,000/40,000;

🖳) Clean-but-small rooms on the main drag, with large kitchen and lounge for guests. Welcoming and friendly staff, who can arrange motorbike hire for accompanied excursions.

Hotel Astoria Real (☎ 883-0140; Calle 11 No 5-16; s/d COP$49,000/65,000) Latino art deco with views of the square: clean, large, bright rooms hover on the 7th floor above the traffic noise. Good value, but as in all *centro* locations in Cali, the streets aren't safe after dark.

our pick Posada San Antonio (☎ 893-7413; www.posadadesanantonio.com; Carrera 5 No 3-37; dm/s/d COP$70,000/88,000/150,000; 🖳) A beautiful colonial house, designed and converted without spoiling a single feature. Rooms are cool, fresh and clean, and there's a beautiful garden overflowing with plants. Cheaper rooms available in the back.

Eating

Café au Lait (Calle 2 No 4-73; coffee COP$2000) Excellent coffee, pastries and cakes in a soothing, calm space.

Comedor Vegetariano Salud Vibrante (Av 6 No 13N-17; set meals COP$4000) Serves up meat-free but flavorful set lunches.

Vegetariano Sol de la India (Carrera 6 No 8-48; set meals COP$4000) Vegetarian restaurant in a central location, with meat-free papas rellenas (filled potato balls deep-fried in batter) for a rare veggie street snack.

our pick Bahareque (Calle 2 No 4-23; set lunch COP$6000; 🕑 noon-2:30pm Mon-Wed, 6pm-midnight Thu-Sun) Tasty Colombian meals with a twist – soup, meat, rice and veggies as ever, but with delicious marinades on the tender meat, and fruity dressings on large salads. Airy, cool and well decorated.

D'Toluca (Calle 17N No 8N-46; dishes COP$8000-10,000; 🕑 noon-midnight) Close to the hostels, this small Mexican restaurant serves up passable enchiladas and fajitas, great juices and at night it buzzes with backpackers.

Archie's (Av 9N No 14N-22; mains COP$10,000-15,000; 🕑 noon-10pm) Gourmet pizzas and salads served under welcome air-con.

La Trattoria Italia (Calle 4 No 9-02; mains from COP$18,000; 🕑 noon-3pm Tue-Fri, 7pm-11pm Sat) Italian owned, with extensive wine list, and excellent bruschetta, pasta and Italian classics. Carefully prepared carbonara, shame about the parmesan.

Restaurante Carambolo (Calle 14N No 9N-18; mains COP$25,000) If Pedro Almodóvar owned a restaurant, it would look like this: leather

COLOMBIA

banquette sofas, neo-kitsch false flowers, elegant staff. The food's not bad either, with good meat and poultry dishes. The room and the menu are split in two, Euro versus Latino. The Latino sides wins on food, taste and style.

Drinking

Head to Calle 17N between Avs 8N and 9N for dozens of admission-free choices. San Antonio is also a great neighborhood for a few liveners before hitting the north.

Centro Comercial de Chipichape (Calle 38N No 6N-35) Plenty of outdoor cafes at this large mall.

Casa Café (Carrera 6 No 2-13; 4-11pm Tue-Sat) Relaxed cafe with board games, fresh salads, beers, juice and the occasional live band.

Macondo Café (Carrera 6 No 3-03; noon-midnight Mon-Sat, 4:30pm-midnight Sun) Relaxed San Antonio spot with delicious coffee, snacks and original tropical cocktails.

Quimera Enoteca (Carrera 9 No 3-98; 5pm-midnight Wed-Sat) Relaxed but stylish wine bar with huge selection of wines, and snacks including a cheeseboard.

Entertainment

El País newspaper has a good listing section.

Cali's dance floors are not for the fainthearted or stiff-hipped – the salsa style here is faster and more complex than elsewhere, with fancier footwork. For a casual night near the guesthouses, check out the discos of Av 6N and Calle 16N.

The city's best-known salsa nightlife is found in Juanchito, a suburb on the Río Cauca. Come on the weekend and take a taxi. Cali has seen a licensing clampdown where clubs close by 3am, but venues on the outskirts stay open later.

Las Brisas de la Sexta (Av 6N No 15N-94) One of the largest and most popular *salsotecas* (salsa clubs).

Zaperoco (Av 5N No 16N-46) Fun *salsoteca* with exuberant sounds and a torrid, tropical atmosphere.

Kukuramakara (Calle 28N No 2bis-97; admission COP$10,000; 9pm-3am Thu-Sat) Live bands. Gets full early.

Cinemateca la Tertulia (893-2939; Av Colombia 5 Oeste-105) Cali's best art-house cinema, in the Museo de Arte Moderno La Tertulia.

Teatro Experimental de Cali (884-3820; Calle 7 No 8-63) One of the city's most innovative theater companies.

Calle 5 south of the river is another good place to hang out, and less dressy than the north. **Tin Tin Deo** (Carrera 22 No 4A-27), has good salsa, a slightly faded but cool venue, and a friendly student crowd.

Getting There & Away

AIR

The Palmaseca airport is 16km northeast of the city. Minibuses between the airport and the bus terminal run every 10 minutes until about 8pm (COP$3000, 30 minutes), or take a taxi (COP$50,000).

Avianca (667-6919; Hotel Intercontinental, Av Colombia 2-72) has a regular service to all major Colombian cities.

American Airlines (666-3252; Hotel Intercontinental, Av Colombia 2-72) has flights to Miami and beyond.

BUS

The bus terminal is a 25-minute walk northeast of the city center, or 10 minutes by city bus (COP$1500). Buses run regularly to Bogotá (COP$60,000, 12 hours), Medellín (COP$45,000, nine hours) and Pasto (COP$45,000, 10 hours). Pasto buses will drop you off at Popayán (COP$17,000, three hours) and there are also hourly minibuses to Popayán (COP$20,000, three hours).

Getting Around

You can cover the new and old centers on foot. Taxis to most hostels cost around COP$5000 from the terminal. Buses (flat fare COP$1500) head south on Calle 5.

The new air-conditioned electric bus network, the **Mio** (www.metrocali.gov.co) is similar to the TransMilenio in Bogotá. It runs from north of the bus terminal along the river, through the center, and down the length of Av 5. Tickets cost COP$1500, available from lottery kiosks throughout the city. It's been plagued with teething problems, and is forcing many other buses to change routes, but is now operating with hopes to expand.

POPAYÁN

2 / pop 258,600

Popayán has the looks and history of Cartagena, the intellectual and social refinement of Bogotá, and the confidence of Medellín. But it has more style than all three. It's an immaculate example of Spanish-colonial architecture, with chalk-

---

DETOUR: PACIFIC COAST

Colombia's Pacific Coast isn't suited to budget travel. The infrastructure is poor, and traveling is improvised and expensive – mainly by riverboat and light plane, since only one road links it with the interior of the country (the Cali–Buenaventura road).

Added to that, it rains torrentially all year round (up to 15m in some parts) and until recently was dangerous, with a good deal of military, paramilitary and guerrilla activity. Now, it's swamped with well-armed Colombian soldiers who take their responsibility to visitors' safety very seriously.

Activities, too, tend to be expensive and difficult, but superlative – scuba divers need their own equipment, or a few million pesos to take once-in-a-lifetime trips diving with 200 hammerhead sharks on **Isla Malpelo**. The diving is said to be some of the best in the world. Likewise, the area is famed for its world-class sea-fishing – which runs into several hundreds of thousands of pesos per trip.

If you do choose to head to the Pacific Coast, a copy of Lonely Planet's *Colombia* is highly recommended.

---

white houses, magnificent museums set in old mansions, splendid churches and a central plaza where locals fan themselves against the midday heat in the shade of palm trees and tropical conifers.

The town also boasts one of Colombia's best universities, a well-educated population more inclined toward cafe culture than wild partying, and a deserved culinary reputation.

Founded in 1537, the town quickly became an important political, cultural and religious center, and was a key stopping point on the route between Quito and Cartagena as the Spanish plunderers looted the continent of much of its gold. The town's mild climate attracted wealthy Spanish settlers from the sugarcane farms near Cali. Several imposing churches and monasteries were built in the 17th and 18th centuries, when the city was flourishing.

In just 18 seconds, all this was unceremoniously torn down as a powerful earthquake ripped through the town on March 1, 1983, before the Maundy Thursday religious procession. The rebuilding work took more than 20 years, but all of its churches have now been restored.

Today, the town is best known for its eerie Easter Week celebrations, when huge, neo-kitsch floats depicting the Passion of Christ are carried through town by bearers in medieval costume amid a fog of incense.

Nazareth's most famous son would be disappointed to learn that hotel prices can quadruple during Holy Week.

Information

Cyber Center (Calle 5 No 9-31; per hr COP$1500; ☻ 9am-9pm) Less busy than Internet.ADSL.

Davivienda (Parque Caldas) ATM.

Euro Dollar (Carrera 7 No 6-41, Centro Comercial Luis Martínez, Local 4) Four money changers offering reasonable rates.

Internet.ADSL (☎ 822-5801; Carrera 11 No 4-36; per hr COP$1500; ☻ 8am-10pm Mon-Sat) Internet access.

Oficina de Turismo de Popayán (☎ 824-2251; Carrera 5 No 4-68; ☻ 8am-noon & 2-6pm Mon-Fri, 9am-1pm Sat & Sun) Professional and helpful.

Parques Nacionales Naturales de Colombia (☎ 823-1279; www.parquesnacionales.gov.co; Carrera 9 No 25N-6) National park office.

Policía de Turismo (☎ 822-0916; Edificio de Gobernación, Parque Caldas) Tourist police.

Sights

Popayán has some of Colombia's finest museums, most of which are set in old colonial mansions. **Casa Museo Mosquera** (☎ 824-0683; Calle 3 No 5-14; admission COP$2000; ☻ 8am-noon & 2-6pm) is a great colonial pile that was home to General Tomás Cipriano de Mosquera, Colombia's president between 1845 and 1867. The museum contains personal memorabilia and a collection of colonial art.

Museo Arquidiocesano de Arte Religioso (☎ 824-2759; Calle 4 No 4-56; admission COP$3000; ☻ 9am-12:30pm & 2-6pm Mon-Fri, 9am-2pm Sat) has an extensive collection of religious art including paintings, statues, altarpieces, silverware and liturgical vessels, most of which date from the 17th to 19th centuries.

Museo Guillermo Valencia (☎ 820-6160; Carrera 6 No 3-65; admission COP$2000; ☻ 8am-noon & 2-5pm Tue-Sun)

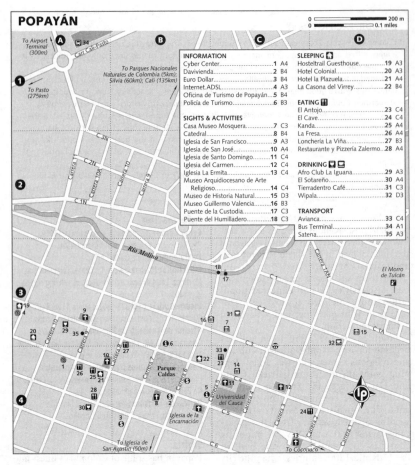

POPAYÁN

0   200 m
0   0.1 miles

To Airport
Terminal
(300m)

Carr Cali-Pasto

To Parques Nacionales
Naturales de Colombia (5km);
Silvia (60km); Cali (135km)

To Pasto
(275km)

Río Molino

To Iglesia de
San Agustín (50m)

Parque
Caldas

Universidad
del Cauca

Iglesia de la
Encarnación

To Coconuco

El Morro
de Tulcán

INFORMATION
Cyber Center...........................1 A4
Davivienda.............................2 B4
Euro Dollar.............................3 B4
Internet.ADSL.........................4 A3
Oficina de Turismo de Popayán..5 B4
Policía de Turismo...................6 B3

SIGHTS & ACTIVITIES
Casa Museo Mosquera..............7 C3
Catedral................................8 B4
Iglesia de San Francisco...........9 A3
Iglesia de San José.................10 A4
Iglesia de Santo Domingo........11 C4
Iglesia del Carmen..................12 C4
Iglesia La Ermita.....................13 C4
Museo Arquidiocesano de Arte
  Religioso.............................14 C4
Museo de Historia Natural.......15 D3
Museo Guillermo Valencia.......16 B3
Puente de la Custodia.............17 C3
Puente del Humilladero...........18 C3

SLEEPING
Hosteltrail Guesthouse.............19 A3
Hotel Colonial........................20 A3
Hotel la Plazuela....................21 A4
La Casona del Virrey...............22 B4

EATING
El Antojo..............................23 C4
El Cave................................24 C4
Kanda.................................25 A4
La Fresa..............................26 A4
Lonchería La Viña..................27 B3
Restaurante y Pizzería Zalermo..28 A4

DRINKING
Afro Club La Iguana...............29 A3
El Sotareño..........................30 A4
Tierradentro Café...................31 C3
Wipala................................32 D3

TRANSPORT
Avianca...............................33 C4
Bus Terminal.........................34 A1
Satena................................35 A3

dedicated to the Popayán-born poet who once lived here. The house is as he left it.

Museo de Historia Natural (☎ 820-1952; Carrera 2 No 1A-25; admission COP$3000; ⏰ 8am-noon & 2-5pm Tue-Sun) has collections of insects, butterflies and stuffed birds.

All the colonial churches were meticulously restored after the 1983 earthquake. The **Iglesia de San Francisco** (cnr Carrera 9 & Calle 4) is the city's largest colonial church and arguably the best, with its fine high altar and a collection of seven amazing side altarpieces. Other colonial churches famed for their rich original furnishings include **Iglesia de Santo Domingo** (cnr Carrera 5 & Calle 4), **Iglesia de San José** (cnr Calle 5 & Carrera 8) and **Iglesia de San Agustín** (cnr Calle 7 & Carrera 6).

Iglesia La Ermita (cnr Calle 5 & Carrera 2) is Popayán's oldest church (1546), worth seeing for the fragments of old frescoes, which were discovered after the earthquake. The neoclassical **Catedral** (Parque Caldas) is the youngest church in the center, built between 1859 and 1906. Hundreds died as the dome came crashing down. Today, you'd never know.

Walk north up Carrera 6 to the river to see two unusual old bridges. The small one, **Puente de la Custodia**, was constructed in 1713 to allow the priests to cross the river to bring the holy orders to the sick of the poor northern suburb. About 160 years later the 178m-long 12-arch **Puente del Humilladero** was built alongside the old bridge, and it's still in use.

COLOMBIA

Festivals & Events

Popayán is renowned for its cuisine, with a gourmet **food festival** in September. Head here during **Holy Week** and you'll see the night-time processions on Maundy Thursday and Good Friday. Popayán's Easter celebrations are the most elaborate in the country, attracting thousands of Colombians and travelers to contemplate the death and resurrection of Christ. The **festival of religious music** is held at the same time, inadvertently proving that the devil does in fact have all the best tunes.

Sleeping

Hosteltrail Guesthouse (☎ 831-7871; www .hosteltrail.com; Carrera 11 No 4-16; dm COP$20,000, s/d COP$35,000/40,000, without bathroom COP$25,000/30,000; 🖳) Welcoming backpacker hostel with all you need: dorms, kitchen, wi-fi and lockers. Friendly, informed owners.

Hotel Colonial (☎ 831-7848; Calle 4 No 10-14; s/d/tr COP$35,000/45,000/69,000; 🖳) Simple, quiet rooms, favored by Colombians. Not much natural light, but great value nonetheless.

La Casona del Virrey (☎ 824-0836; Calle 4 No 5-78; s/d COP$55,000/72,000; 🖳) Classy colonial building with many original fittings. Room 201 overlooks the square and has a killer view for the Easter parades.

Hotel la Plazuela (☎ 824-1084; hotellaplazuela@hot mail.com; Calle 5 No 8-13; s/d COP$124,000/172,000; 🖳) Carefully converted mansion with stately courtyard; best value if you're in a mood to spend.

Eating

There are plenty of budget and midrange choices available.

La Fresa (Calle 5 No 8-89; snacks COP$1500; 🕑 8am-8pm) Cheap, tasty pastries and quick snacks.

El Antojo (Carrera 5 No 13-26; dishes COP$3500; 🕑 8am-6pm, lunch till 2pm) Hearty, healthy home-cooked Colombian food. Cheap as chips and twice as healthy.

Kanda (Calle 5 No 8-53; set meals COP$4500; 🕑 8am-8pm) Three courses and a fresh juice for this price isn't to be sniffed at. Vegetarians take note: no animals were harmed in the making of your dinner.

Restaurante y Pizzería Zalermo (Carrera 8 No 5-100; mains COP$6000-10,000; 🕑 9am-10pm) It's Latin America, so the pizza's never going to be that authentic. But if you have a Jones for an approximate taste of home, it'll do.

Lonchería La Viña (Calle 4 No 7-79; set menus COP$6500, mains COP$14,000; 🕑 9am-midnight) Huge, airy room and swiftly served heaping plates of *comida típica* (the classic Latin lunch: chicken or meat, fried or stewed, with beans, salad, rice and fried plantain). Hit the grill for bargain steaks that are worth double the marked price. The *bife de chorizo* cut is the winner.

El Cave (Calle 4 No 2-07; mains COP$10,000, sandwiches COP$8000; 🕑 breakfast, lunch & dinner Mon-Fri, lunch Sat & Sun) French cuisine – meaning smallish portions of delicious food. The roast beef and gratin cheese baguette is fabulous, but service is slow.

Drinking

Tierradentro Café (Carrera 5 No 2-12) You'd be crawling the ceilings if you tried all the coffee – there are dozens of varieties.

El Sotareño (Calle 6 No 8-05; 🕑 4pm-3am Mon-Sat) Popayán institution, playing *bolero*, *ranchero* and *milonga* off original vinyl. Try not to drool in envy at the collection.

Afro Club La Iguana (Calle 4 No 9-67; 🕑 8pm-late Mon-Sat) Kicks out the salsa to a sassy crowd with mischief on their mind

Wipala (Calle 2 No 2-38; 🕑 7pm-late Mon-Sat) Art, jazz, rock and tango, sometimes live, with cheap beer and good coffee. Boho-Latino types and Euro alt-youth dominate.

Getting There & Away

AIR

The airport is just behind the bus terminal, a 15-minute walk north of the city center. Satena has daily flights to Bogotá for around COP$200,000. There's a daily flight to and from Bogotá (COP$220,000, 50 minutes) with **Avianca** (☎ 824-4505; Carrera 5 No 3-85; 🕑 8am-5pm Mon-Sat) in the early afternoon. You can only book online with a locally or US-issued credit card.

BUS

The bus terminal is a short walk north of the city center. Plenty of buses run to Cali (COP$17,000, three hours), and there are also minibuses and *colectivos* every hour or so. Buses to Bogotá run every hour or two (COP$70,000, 15 hours, night buses at 7pm and 8pm).

Buses to Pasto (COP$27,000, six hours) leave every hour. Avoid night buses as bandits have been known to attack these even when they're traveling in police-guarded caravans.

COLOMBIA

SILVIA

☎ 2 / pop 30,800

Of Colombia's 68 indigenous groups, the Guambino are the most immediately recognizable, and have survived colonialism, repression and modernization with their language, dress and customs intact. On Tuesday, they descend from their *resguardo* (reserve), which lies an hour further east, and hit Silvia for market day, to sell their produce, to buy tools and clothes, and to hang out in the main square of this small and otherwise unremarkable town.

The men and women dress in flowing, shin-length blue woolen skirts, edged with pink or turquoise, with a thin, dark woolen poncho laid over the shoulders – this is 2800m above sea level, and their reserve lies higher still. Scarves are ubiquitous, and both men and women wear a kind of felt bowler hat, some choosing to fold in the top of it so it resembles a trilby. It's a rakish look however it's worn.

Most of the older women wear many strings of small beads clustered about their necks, and carry a wooden needle which they use to spin yarn from a ball of sheep fleece which they store in their net sacks. This is the principle source of fabric for the Guambino, though the use of synthetic fibers is growing.

Keep your camera in your pocket unless you enjoy needless aggravation. True, it can be frustrating not to record such a colorful and 'foreign' scene, but you'll quickly make yourself a spectacle and cause offence, period. Also, it's a very patriarchal society, so expect odd looks if you address a woman ahead of a man.

The main square, and the market southwest of it, are where the action's at. Don't expect some kind of theme park show for your entertainment, though. This is a working town, and people are here to do business. There are few arts and crafts on sale, and you're more likely to see an indigenous elder haggling over the price of boots and saucepans or chatting on his cell phone, than offering wisdom for coins.

The best entertainment is laid on by traveling performers, snake-oil salesmen, bogus telepathists and assorted magicians and mentalists who perform in the square on market day. Stand and watch some tricksters putting on a show as the raucous church bell clangs through the cool mountain air, surrounded by the smiling, impossibly ancient faces of the Guambino and dozens of laughing Colombians, and divisions soon dissolve.

There are buses from Popayán terminal (one-way COP$5000, 6am, 7am, 8am and 10am), taking about 1½ hours. The 8am is your best bet.

Upon leaving Silvia, your bus may be stopped and you may be searched by surly police – though Westerners will likely not be searched with as much rigor or treated with such scant respect as elderly Guambino in traditional dress.

PARQUE NACIONAL PURACÉ

Out of bounds for years due to guerrilla presence, this mountainous **national park** (☎ 02-823-1223; admission COP$17,000; ☉ 8am-6pm), offers good trekking, fascinating landscapes gurgling with geysers, lurid mosses, a couple of dramatically set waterfalls and the chance to feed condors in the wild.

It's 45km east of Popayán, and overnight stays can be arranged at austere **cabins** (COP$30,000), or you can sleep with locals in nearby Puracé (pay around COP$12,000).

To feed the condors, which were released to repopulate the park, call ahead to the park's administrators to arrange a visit early on a Saturday; the birds feed at around 11am.

Take an early morning bus from Popayán to La Plata (COP$8000, 1 ½ hours), departing at 4:45am, 6:30am, 8:45am and 9:30am, to **Cruce de Pilimbalá**, the main entrance to the park.

Jump out early in Puracé to see a lovely hidden waterfall, **La Cascada de San Antonio** just behind the hospital. Ask a local to take you there. Wilson Aguilar is an expert indigenous Coconuco **guide** (☎ 313-606-0027; per day COP$25,000) based in Puracé. Local indigenous people believe that if you can see the statue of the saint that stands behind the waterfall, you'll get married within three months. Another legend states that in the 1940s, indigenous people found the statue lying mysteriously near the falls. They took it to the local priest who, for reasons known only to himself, frenziedly whipped the statue's buttocks. The following day the statue disappeared and was found behind the torrent of the 100m waterfall.

From Puracé, it's a 4km walk to the park entrance and cabins at the Cruce de Pilimbalá. Pay your entry fee here. The condor-feeding point is nearby; rangers must accompany you.

This is the starting point for a stiff five-hour hike to the crater of **Volcán Puracé**. A guide is essential. Set out early – the mist soon descends and you'll see nothing from the top.

A further 8km by bus (COP$3000) is the entry point for the **Termales de San Juan**. The path to the springs is well marked from the ranger station and is an easy 1km stroll through dripping forest creaking with the sound of frogs. The springs have an utterly otherworldly setting, swathed in mosses and lichens, with hot water bursting through the rock and gushing around in every direction. It's a duck's paradise. Sample a little of the water – it tastes just like local soda brand Bretaña. Beware the toxic clouds of sulfur, though, and don't bathe – you'll upset the ecosystem's delicate balance.

Tapirs have been seen on the paths nearby, but only by the guards who spend many weeks a year guarding the area. Just down from the Termales, there's a tiny restaurant selling trout.

If you have time, walk 2km down the road past the Termales towards Puracé and keep your ears pinned back. There's a spectacular waterfall, **Cascada Bedon**, which the Coconuco used to punish criminals by forcing them to bathe under the water.

The last bus back to Popayán leaves the Cruce de las Minas/Cruce de Pilimbalá at 5pm. Travel around here is improvised at best, be prepared to overnight at the park or in the town of Puracé.

PANCE
☎ 2 / pop 1500

A popular weekend break spot for Caleños escaping the city heat, Pance can be reached by local minibus from the bus terminal (hourly COP$2000). The main street of the town is lined with bars and restaurants running alongside the Río Pance, but these cater to Colombian weekenders. Instead, leave the bus at the bridge and take a *colectivo* (COP$1000) up the hill alongside the river to the village of Pance, and take the road to the right-hand side of the church to the **Reserva Natural Anahuac** (☎ 315-407-2724; www .reservanaturalanahuac.com/home.html; camping with/without tent COP$6000/12,000, r per person COP$15,000; 🏊). Here you'll find a private farm with tent space, but the best choice is the spacious, cool wooden lodge in the center of the site surrounded by flowing water and furnished with antiques. Simple food is available or there's an open-air kitchen.

At the time of research, the nearby **Parque Nacional los Farralones de Cali** was still closed to visitors, but it is now safe. An army battalion patrols the area and has driven guerrillas out. It's possible to enter informally, though this is illegal.

SAN AGUSTÍN
☎ 8 / pop 11,000

Long before Europeans came to the Americas, the rolling hills around San Agustín were ruled by a mysterious group of people who buried their dead and honored them with magnificent statues carved from volcanic rock. The legacy that they left behind is now one of the continent's most important archaeological sites. Hundreds of freestanding monumental statues were left next to the tombs of tribal elders of a now disappeared tribe. Pottery and gold objects were also left behind, although much of it was stolen over the centuries.

San Agustín culture flourished between the 6th and 14th centuries AD. The best statuary was made only in the last phase of the development, and the culture had presumably vanished before the Spaniards came. The statues were not discovered until the middle of the 18th century.

So far some 513 statues have been found and excavated. A great number are anthropomorphic figures – resembling masked monsters. Others are zoomorphic, depicting sacred animals including the eagle, the jaguar and the frog. The statues vary both in size, from about 20cm to 4m, and in their degree of detail.

Today, the small town captivates travelers thanks to its history and tranquility, along with the significantly reduced security risks for foreigners in the area. The countryside is beautiful, with waterfalls, rivers and canyons. The people are welcoming, prices are low and the air and light is crystalline: it's a perfect place to decompress.

Orientation & Information

The statues and tombs are scattered in groups in 19 parks on both sides of the gorge formed by the upper Río Magdalena. The main town of the region, San Agustín, is home to most of the accommodations and restaurants. From there, you can explore the region on foot, horseback or by jeep.

COLOMBIA

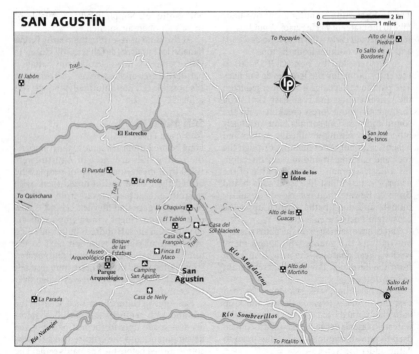

SAN AGUSTÍN

Arkos (Carrera 3 No 11-42; ☺ 8am-9pm daily) Offers the fastest internet connection in town – which really isn't saying much.

Banco Agrario de Colombia (cnr Carrera 13 & Calle 4)

Banco Ultrahuilca (Calle 3 No 12-73) One of only two ATMs in town.

Internet Galería Café (Calle 3 No 12-16; ☺ 8am-10pm daily)

Tourist office (☎ 837-3062; cnr Calle 3 & Carrera 12; ☺ 8am-noon & 2-5pm Mon-Fri) Ensure you use only this place, as it's the only official place for tourist information. Go to the town hall and look for the English sign saying 'Government Tourist Office.'

Sights & Activities

The 78-hectare **Parque Arqueológico** (admission COP$15,000; ☺ 8am-6pm, last entry 4pm), 2.5km west of San Agustín town, features some of the best statuary. The park covers several archaeological sites that include statues, tombs and burial mounds. It also has the **Museo Arqueológico** (☺ 8am-5pm), which displays smaller statues and pottery, and the **Bosque de las Estatuas** (Forest of Statues), where many statues of different origins are placed along a forest footpath.

The **Alto de los Ídolos** (☺ 8am-4pm) is another archaeological park, noted for burial mounds and large stone tombs. The largest statue, 7m tall, but with 4m visible and 3m underground, is here. The park is a few kilometers southwest of San José de Isnos, on the other side of the Río Magdalena from San Agustín town. The ticket bought at the Parque Arqueológico also covers entry to the Alto de los Ídolos and is valid for two consecutive days. For COP$20,000, hire a guide who can show you the way. The round trip is seven hours.

More than a dozen other archaeological sites are scattered over the area including **El Tablón**, **La Chaquira**, **La Pelota** and **El Purutal**, four sites close enough to each other that you can see them in one trip. The waterfalls **Salto de Bordones** and **Salto del Mortiño** are impressive, as is **El Estrecho**, where the Río Magdalena, that runs from here to the Caribbean, gushes dramatically through 2m narrows.

White-water rafting and kayaking operators **Magdalena Rafting** (☎ 311-271-5333; magdalenarafting@yahoo.fr; Vía Parque 4-12; incl snacks COP$40,000) runs half-day trips, especially in June when the river is high.

Sleeping

The best sleeping options are on foreign-owned *fincas* in the hills surrounding the town.

Camping San Agustín (☎ 837-3192; campsites COP$12,000-COP$15,000) Pitch your tent here, about 1km outside town on the way to the archaeological park.

Finca El Maco (☎ 837-3437; hammocks COP$8000, dm/s/d COP$14,000/25,000/30,000, teepee per person $16,000; ▣) Ecoranch off the road to the Parque Arqueológico. Stay in cabins, dinky chalets, and a cute teepee. Trusted tour guides offered.

our pick **Casa de François** (☎ 837-3847, 314-358-2930; dm COP$15,000, s/d without bathroom COP$15,000/32,000; ▣) French-run hostel just north of town, off the road to El Tablón. Friendly host, decent dorm, comfy rooms, and a decent wi-fi net connection.

Hospedaje El Jardín (☎ 837-3455; Carrera 11 No 4-10; r with/without bathroom COP$20,000/15,000) Basic but neat option in town near the bus offices, offering rooms with and without bathrooms.

Casa del Sol Naciente (☎ 311-587-6464; s/d COP$15,000/24,000, s/d cabaña without bathroom with river views from COP$20,000/30,000) Your own personal Shangri-La. Bamboo houses set in gorgeous grounds with million-dollar views of the Río Magdalena and the canyon. Hummingbirds and butterflies may occasionally disturb the peace. No kitchen for guests. Find trusted guides and excursions here.

Casa de Nelly (☎ 311-535-0412; hotelcasadenelly @hotmail.com; s/d without bathroom COP$15,000/40,000) One of the older hostels, with a family atmosphere and a decent bar and private kitchen. It's 1km west of the town off the very steep dirt road to La Estrella.

Eating

Head to Calle 5 for cheap eats, or take the road to the Parque Arqueológico for better options.

Mercado de San Agustín (mains COP$3000-COP$5000) Great cheap lunch option, and excellent basic provisions if you're cooking. Located a couple of blocks from the main square.

Restaurante Brahama (Calle 5 No 15-11; set meals COP$7000) Good basic diner.

Donde Richard (Vía al Parque Arqueológico; mains COP$15,000) Top choice if you have the cash and a very empty belly. Gorge on smoked leg of pork for dinner and you won't want breakfast.

Getting There & Away

All bus offices are clustered on Calle 3 near the corner of Carrera 11. Five buses a day go to Popayán (COP$16,000, six to eight hours, 7am, 9am, 11:30am, 2pm and 4pm) via a rough but spectacular road through Isnos. Coomotor has three buses daily to Bogotá (COP$$50,000, 12 hours, 6:30pm, 6:45pm and 7pm).

There are no direct buses to Tierradentro; go to La Plata (COP$20,000, four hours) and change for a bus to El Cruce de San Andrés (COP$10,000, 2½ hours), from where it's a 20-minute walk to the Tierradentro museums. La Plata has several cheap hotels.

Getting Around

The usual way of visiting San Agustín's sights (apart from the Parque Arqueológico) is by jeep tours and horse-riding excursions. The standard jeep tour includes El Estrecho, Alto de los Ídolos, Alto de las Piedras, Salto de Bordones and Salto de Mortiño. It takes seven to eight hours and costs COP$30,000 per person. Horse rental can be arranged through trusted hotel managers mentioned previously, or directly with horse owners, who often approach tourists. Never pay in advance. Horses are hired out for a specific route, for a half-day (COP$20,000). One of the most popular trips (per horse COP$21,000, around five hours) includes El Tablón, La Chaquira, La Pelota and El Purutal. If you need a guide, add COP$20,000 for the guide and another COP$21,000 for his horse.

TIERRADENTRO

☎ 2 / pop 600

Travelers who brave the rough ride along the pitted dirt roads that lead through the mountains and cliffs to Tierradentro will find tranquility, friendly locals, and one of the continent's most important and awe-inspiring archaeological sites.

Buried under the lush green fields above the tiny pueblos of San Andrés de Pisimbalá and Tierradentro are dozens of intricately designed and decorated sacred burial sites hewn out of the volcanic rock, left behind by a disappeared tribe of indigenous Colombians, who archaeologists say lived around the 7th and 9th centuries. The Páez people who live here today say they are not connected to the tomb-diggers, and so the sites' origins and age are uncertain.

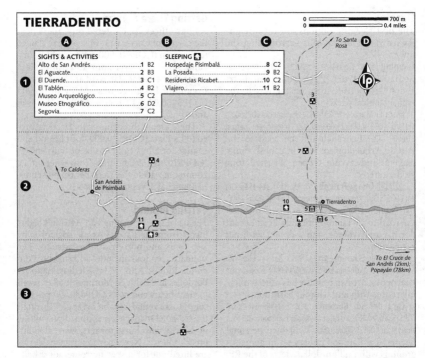

TIERRADENTRO

SIGHTS & ACTIVITIES		SLEEPING	
Alto de San Andrés.....................1	B2	Hospedaje Pisimbalá......................8	C2
El Aguacate..............................2	B3	La Posada...................................9	B2
El Duende................................3	C1	Residencias Ricabet......................10	C2
El Tablón................................4	B2	Viajero....................................11	B2
Museo Arqueológico.................5	C2		
Museo Etnográfico...................6	D2		
Segovia.................................7	C2		

The elaborate circular tombs once contained the ashes and remains of a people highly skilled in engineering, with a harmonious aesthetic sense revealed by the mysterious geometric designs etched, painted and chiseled into the walls of dozens of chambers.

You access the chambers via spiral staircases of huge stone steps. The chambers are supported by tapered columns, with faces, animals and baffling designs – many of them well-preserved – drawn in red and black and white. Urns containing the remains of tribal elders originally sat in each recess of the chambers; today they are presented tastefully in a nearby museum.

More than 100 tombs have been excavated so far; take a side trip into the woods alongside the Segovia site to see entrances to tombs as yet unexcavated due to a lack of funds. Several dozen statues similar to those found at San Agustín are also found here.

Tierradentro used to have a bad reputation (not entirely deserved) as a guerrilla stronghold but today that is no longer the case. Thanks to the negative publicity, if you visit the sites soon you'll likely be alone, staring at

the tombs with unanswered questions in your head and ripe guavas in your pocket, taken from the trees that line the paths.

Apart from the tombs, the area has cheap lodging and fresh organic food for a few dollars a plate. True, there's no internet, few restaurants and no entertainment at all, but the nearby village of San Andrés de Pisimbalá is a calming place to hang out for a few days. The landscapes here will make your soul gently soar, and the only sounds at night are cicadas and the distant rush of the Río San Andrés.

Sights

Start by checking out the two **museums** (combined ticket COP$15,000; ⏰ 8am-4pm), which stand opposite each other. One combined ticket is valid for two consecutive days to all archaeological sites and the museums. The **Museo Arqueológico** contains pottery urns that were found in the tombs; the **Museo Etnográfico** has utensils and artifacts of the Páez, including grim-looking stocks still used today to punish criminals.

You'll need at least half a day to see a good selection of tombs here, so arrive before midday. A 20-minute walk up the hill north of the museums will bring you to **Segovia**, the most important burial site. There are 28 tombs here, some with well-preserved decoration.

Other burial sites include **El Duende** (four tombs without preserved decoration) and **Alto de San Andrés** (five tombs, two of which have their original paintings). **El Aguacate** is high on a mountain ridge, a spectacular and strenuous two-hour one-way walk from the museum. There are a few dozen tombs there, but most have been destroyed by *guaqueros*

(grave robbers). Statues have been gathered together at **El Tablón**.

The tiny village of **San Andrés de Pisimbalá**, a 25-minute walk west of Tierradentro, has a beautiful 400-year-old thatched church with reeling swallows darting around the ancient rafters.

Sleeping & Eating

Whether it's walking all day or the crystal-line mountain air, every single thing you eat and drink here is delicious. You can stay

GETTING TO ECUADOR

The road to Ecuador takes in Pasto and Ipiales, neither of which will detain travelers much. **Pasto** is really only worth a stay during the crazy festival, **La Fiesta de Blancos y Negros** (Black and White Festival), held January 4 and 5, when the entire city throws paint, flour, soot and chalk at each other in commemoration of a medieval festival when slaves and owners switched face color for a day.

The only must-see is nearby **Laguna de la Cocha,** one of Colombia's largest and most beautiful lakes. It's surrounded by ramshackle wooden houses painted in bright colors, many of them budget hotels and restaurants serving fresh trout. You can rent a motorboat (per hour COP$25,000), seating up to eight people, and buzz across the lake to take a look at the island at its center. Rowboats (COP$15,000) seat five. *Colectivos* (shared taxis; COP$5000, 30 minutes, 25km) to the lake depart regularly on weekdays from the Iglesia de San Sebastián in central Pasto, and on weekends from the back of the **Hospital Departamental** (cnr Calle 22 & Carrera 7). Pay COP$5000 for each empty seat if you're in a rush.

The hulking **Volcán Galeras** has been closed for years to tourists thanks to seismic grumblings.

Pasto's best backpacker hostel is the **Koala Inn** (☎ 2-722-1101; Calle 18 No 22-37; r with/without bathroom per person COP$22,000/15,000) Open since the 1990s, it looks and smells like it. But it's cheap, central, and has a laundry and book exchange.

Pricier is the **Hotel San Sebastian** (☎ 2-721-8851; Carrera 22 No 15-78; s/d COP$31,000/49,000; 🖳). It's as characterless as a shop dummy, but has very clean rooms with hot water, wi-fi and cable TV. Budget restaurants abound in the center, and a *comida corriente* (basic set meal) will run COP$5000.

An hour and a half further down the Panamericana is **Ipiales**, a major crossing point to Ecuador. It's a functional border town saved by its famous neo-Gothic El Santuario de las Lajas. You don't need to stay overnight to visit the church. Drop your bags in the bus terminal's **left luggage** (per piece COP$1000) and take a *colectivo* (COP$5000, 20 minutes) to see the church, which spans a gorge and contains the cliff face where local man Maria Mueces says he saw an image of the Virgin appear in 1754. Pilgrims nationwide flock here and attribute thousands of miracles to the Virgin.

If you need to stay the night in Ipiales, try the **Hotel Belmont** (☎ 2-773-2771; Carrera 4; s/d COP$15,000/25,000), with simple rooms. Nearby restaurants serve up cheap meals for COP$5000.

Ipiales has a large bus terminal about 1km northeast of the center. It's linked to the center by buses (COP$1000) and taxis (COP$3500). Expreso Bolivariano has a dozen buses daily to Bogotá (COP$80,000, 25 hours) and there are regular buses to Cali (COP$30,000 to COP$40,000, 10 hours). All these will drop you in Popayán in eight hours. Daytime travel is advised. There are plenty of buses, minibuses and *colectivos* to Pasto (COP$5000, 1½ to two hours) departing from the terminal.

The border is a short taxi ride from the Ipiales bus terminal, and is open 6am to 10pm. Pay COP$1000 for a bus or around COP$5000 for a cab. There are ATMs at the border. For info on entering Colombia from Ecuador, see p622.

close to the museums in Tierradentro, which is fine for a short visit, but better choices are available in San Andrés de Pisimbalá.

Hospedaje Pisimbalá (☎ 311-605-4835; Tierradentro; s/d COP$10,000/20,000) Smallish rooms set near a gurgling river.

Residencias Ricabet (☎ 312-279-9751; Tierradentro; s/d COP$10,000/20,000) Adequate and tidy rooms though with tired sheets, arranged around a neat garden.

Viajero (☎ 312-746-5991; Calle 6 No 4-09, San Andrés de Pisimbalá; s/d COP$10,000/20,000) Basic option with cold showers, but the twinkly-eyed *señora* makes you feel like you're a visiting grandchild.

La Posada (☎ 311-601-7884; juices COP$1700, mains COP$6000; ⏰ restaurant 7am-8pm) Restaurant-hotel serving delicious organic juice, homemade ice creams, delicious meals and outstanding coffee. It's the biggest building in town. The manager Leonardo and his wife are warm and genuinely caring hosts in the best traditions of rural Colombia. He is fascinated by the tombs, and also has a dog that can guide you to the sites and back, Lassie-style. Rooms (single/double COP$15,000/30,000) are large and clean and good value.

Getting There & Away

Each day there are three to four buses to Tierradentro (COP$14,000, five to six hours) from Popayán. Those that depart at 5am, 8am, and 1pm travel only to El Cruce de San Andrés, from where it's a 20-minute walk to the museums. There's a bus at 10am that heads the extra 4km into San Andrés de Pisimbalá, passing the museums en route. Getting back to Popayán, one bus leaves San Andrés de Pisimbalá each morning at around 6:20am, also passing the museums. If you miss that, walk to El Cruce de San Andrés and flag down a bus passing at around 8am, 1pm and 4pm.

AMAZON BASIN

Colombia's Amazon makes up a third of the national territory, as large as California but with hardly a trace of infrastructure. It's mostly rainforest, woven loosely together by rivers and sparsely populated by isolated indigenous communities, many of whom shun the modern world.

There is nothing that can prepare visitors for their first glimpse of the Amazon rainforest. Not a guidebook, not a film, not a second-hand report. Its total size is staggering beyond any conception; 5.5 million sq km. Looking at its infinite forests from an airplane window is like visiting a new planet; it seems to mock human attempts to comprehend its size. Paddling through it in a canoe is exhilarating and life-affirming.

This is the most biodiverse location on earth, hosting 10% of all living species, but it is fragile, damaged and it is important to minimize the impact your presence inevitably makes here. Use small boats where possible, travel in groups, travel by public transportation, and use operators that support indigenous communities.

Much of the Amazon territory is held by guerrilla groups and coca producers and is not somewhere that fosters independent travel. However, the town of Leticia, with easy access to Peru and Brazil, is safe, and is the best place to plan activities in the region. Its small but thriving tourist industry is centered around jungle trips.

LETICIA
☎ 8 / pop 35,000

Leticia is the end of the road in Colombia, an outpost of cold beer and grilled fish, paved roads and internet cafes, tooting mopeds, ATMs, nightclubs, comfortable beds and air-con. But just a few hours away from this jungle city lie thrilling rainforest excursions, fascinating indigenous communities, and flora and fauna in abundance.

Many travelers use Leticia as a transit point for onward travel – there are boat connections to Iquitos (Peru) and Manaus (Brazil), but a trip here in its own right is definitely worth making. Leticia is a secure and easygoing place – there is no guerrilla or paramilitary activity in the town.

July and August are the only relatively dry months. The wettest period is from February to April. The Amazon River's highest level is from May to June, while the lowest is from August to October. The difference between low and high water can be as great as 15m.

Orientation

Leticia lies on the Colombia–Brazil border. Just south across the frontier is Tabatinga, a Brazilian town of similar size, with its own

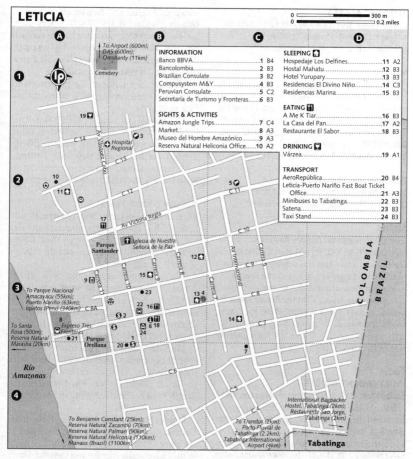

LETICIA

INFORMATION	
Banco BBVA................................**1** B4	
Bancolombia..............................**2** B3	
Brazilian Consulate...................**3** B2	
Compusystem M&Y....................**4** B3	
Peruvian Consulate....................**5** C2	
Secretaría de Turismo y Fronteras......**6** B3	
SIGHTS & ACTIVITIES	
Amazon Jungle Trips..................**7** C4	
Market.......................................**8** A3	
Museo del Hombre Amazónico....**9** A3	
Reserva Natural Heliconia Office.....**10** A2	

SLEEPING	
Hospedaje Los Delfines...............**11** A2	
Hostal Mahatu...........................**12** B3	
Hotel Yurupary..........................**13** B3	
Residencias El Divino Niño...........**14** C3	
Residencias Marina.....................**15** B3	
EATING	
A Me K Tiar...............................**16** B3	
La Casa del Pan.........................**17** A2	
Restaurante El Sabor..................**18** B3	
DRINKING	
Várzea.......................................**19** A1	
TRANSPORT	
AeroRepública............................**20** B4	
Leticia-Puerto Nariño Fast Boat Ticket	
Office....................................**21** A3	
Minibuses to Tabatinga...............**22** B3	
Satena.......................................**23** B3	
Taxi Stand.................................**24** B3	

port and airport. The towns are virtually merging together, and there are no border checkpoints between the two. Frequent *colectivos* link the towns, or you can walk. Locals and foreigners are allowed to pass between the towns without visas, but if you plan on heading further into either country you must get your passport stamped at DAS in Leticia and at Policía Federal in Tabatinga.

On the island in the Amazon opposite Leticia–Tabatinga is Santa Rosa, a Peruvian village. Boats go there from both Tabatinga and Leticia.

On the opposite side of the Amazon from Leticia, about 25km downstream, is the Brazilian town of Benjamin Constant, the main port for boats downstream to Manaus.

Tabatinga and Benjamin Constant are linked by regular boats.

Information
IMMIGRATION

DAS officials at Leticia's airport (open daily), about 3kn north of the centre, give entry or exit stamps. US, Canadian, Australian and New Zealand citizens need a visa to enter Brazil. Bring a passport photo and yellow-fever vaccination certificate to the **Brazilian consulate** (☎ 592-7530; Carrera 9 No 13-84; ☼ 8am-noon & 2-4pm Mon-Fri). If you're coming or going via Iquitos (Peru), visit the Policía Internacional Peruviano (PIP) office on Isla Santa Rosa, for entry/exit stamps or visit the **Peruvian consulate** (☎ 592-7204; Calle 11 No 5-32; ☼ 8am-1pm & 3-6pm Mon-Fri).

INTERNET ACCESS
Compusystem M&Y (Calle 8 No 7-99; per hr COP$1300, wi-fi per hr COP$1000; ☯ 8am-10pm Mon-Sat, 2-10:30pm Sun) Air-con and 10 terminals.

MONEY
Change all the money of the country you're leaving in Leticia–Tabatinga. There are *casas de cambio* on Calle 8 between Carrera 11 and the market, open weekdays from 8am or 9am until 5pm or 6pm and Saturday until around 2pm.
Banco BBVA (cnr Carrera 10 & Calle 7) ATM.
Bancolombia (Calle 8 s/n btwn Carreras 11 & 10) ATM.

TOURIST INFORMATION
Secretaría de Turismo y Fronteras (☎ 592-7569; Calle 8 No 9-75; ☯ 8am-noon & 2-5pm Mon-Fri)

Sights
The small **Museo del Hombre Amazónico** (☎ 592-7729; Carrera 11 No 9-43; ☯ 8-11:30am & 2-5pm Mon-Fri) features artifacts and household implements of indigenous groups living in the region.

Have a look around the **market** and stroll along the waterfront. Visit the **Parque Santander** before sunset for an impressive spectacle, when thousands of screeching parrots (locally called *pericos*) arrive for their nightly rest in the park's trees.

Tours
INDEPENDENT GUIDES
Enrique Arés (315-302-3493; www.omshanty.com; Km 11, Leticia), of Omshanty hostel is an ice-cool, good-humored Basque biologist, an English-speaker who has impressive first-hand knowledge of indigenous communities. Felipe Ulloa of **Selvaventura** (☎ 311-287-1307; www.amazonascolombia.com) is a seasoned Colombian professional,

---

THE ROAD TO NOWHERE
The most curious road in Colombia is to be found in Leticia. It's a superbly constructed motorway that ends after 28km, right at the edge of the jungle. It runs alongside indigenous villages which have been spruced up with soccer pitches, electric light and running water. Rumors abound that the road will one day slash through 155km of virgin rainforest in order to link Puerto Nariño, where oil speculators believe a large deposit lies, with the interior of the country. Time will tell, even if governments don't.

---

with good English and deep jungle experience. **Antonio Rengifo** (☎ 313-497-6277) offers more laid-back, slightly improvised but enormously fun trips. He's so old-school he has no email. But he does know the river well and is a great storyteller – if you speak Spanish.

All three can tailor-make excursions by land or river and are all good in different ways. Pick your style.

All charge around COP$200,000 to COP$300,000 per day for individual tours, including crocodile-spotting, piranha fishing, dolphin-watching, jungle walks and river trips, with transportation, food and accommodation included. Prices drop dramatically for groups.

JUNGLE LODGE TRIPS
There are a dozen jungle trip tour operators in Leticia. Most agencies offer standard one-day tours to Puerto Nariño – forget them unless you're incredibly timid, you can do it safely yourself for cheaper.

The real wilderness begins well off the Amazon proper, along its small tributaries, which offer better chances to observe wildlife in relatively undamaged habitat and visit indigenous settlements. It takes more time and money, but is way more rewarding.

Multiday tours are run from Leticia by several companies, four of which have built jungle lodges. All three reserves are along the lower reaches of the Río Yavarí, on the Brazil–Peru border. Traveling in groups cuts costs by up to 50%.

Reserva Natural Marasha is one hour from Leticia, just over the Amazon. Included in the price of the trip is a superb lunch, a night in the lodge and a trip around the lake. Don't miss the giant ceiba tree; in the past indigenous people used to use it as a 'jungle telephone' by beating on the trunk – the echoes could be heard up to 4km away. Book trips to this lodge at its Leticia **office** (☎ 310-280-0151; www.reservamarasha.com; Calle 12A No 5-93; per person per day COP$110,000).

Reserva Natural Zacambú is about 70km by boat from Leticia – which can take up to five hours. Its lodge is on Lake Zacambú, just off Río Yavarí on the Peruvian side of the river. The lodge is simple, rooms are basic with shared bathrooms. Call **Amazon Jungle Trips** (☎ 592-7377; amazonjungletrips@yahoo.com; Av Internacional No 6-25) to arrange a visit.

Reserva Natural Palmarí is another 20km further upstream on Río Yavarí, about 90km by

---

STRONG MEDICINE: AYAHUASCA

Most people's ideas of heavy drug use in Colombia begin and end with cocaine, but ayahuasca, a visionary jungle brew used by indigenous Amazonian shamans as a medicine for divination and healing, is gaining popularity with many travelers. Some approach it with idiotic hedonistic abandon and get their egos soundly kicked. If you have heart problems, high blood pressure or are using antidepressants, don't even dream of touching it.

Ayahuasca, a Quechua word for 'vine of the soul' contains DMT (dimethyltryptamine), the most potent psychedelic drug on earth. An average experience lasts four to five hours and may be an intensely spiritual experience. The ingredients are *Banisteriopsis caapi* vine, which contains a chemical that allows the gut to absorb the DMT contained in *Psychotria viridis* leaves.

Most users vomit and some have diarrhea, and many report extreme, sometimes terrifying hallucinations, profound personal insights and spiritual epiphanies. It's not something to undertake lightly, in fact, we advise against it. However, if you decide to do it, preparation is vital for your safety: light fasting, total abstinence from sex, alcohol, meat and animal fats for a week beforehand are advised.

---

river from Leticia. Its rambling lodge sits on the high south (Brazilian) bank of the river, overlooking a wide bend where pink and gray dolphins are often seen. The lodge features several *cabañas* with baths and a round *maloca* (central meeting house used by local indigenous communities) with hammocks. **Axel Antoine-Feill** (☎ 310-786-2770; www.palmari.org; Carrera 10 No 93-72, Bogotá) manages the lodge, and speaks English.

Reserva Natural Heliconia, about 110km from Leticia, has thatch-covered cabins, plus tours via boat or on foot of the river, creeks and jungle. There are also organized visits to indigenous villages and special tours devoted to bird-watching and dolphin-watching. The reserve is managed from an **office** (☎ 311-508-5666; www.amazonheliconia.com; Calle 13 No 11-74) in Leticia.

These operators all offer three- to six-day all-inclusive packages, except Marasha, which is best as an overnight trip. Costs for the latter three lodges run around COP$200,000 to COP$300,000 per day. Tours don't usually have a fixed timetable; the agents normally wait until they have enough people unless you don't want to wait and are prepared to pay more. Book ahead. Legally you should have a Brazilian or Peruvian visa to stay in the reserves, so check this issue with the agencies (unless nationals of your home country don't need a visa).

For a low-cost jungle fix, take trips with the locals from Puerto Nariño (p581). Bring plenty of sunscreen and mosquito repellent from Bogotá – local repellent soap brand, Nopikex, is excellent.

Sleeping

LETICIA

Omshanty (315-302-3493; www.omshanty.com; Km 11, Leticia; dm/s/d COP$10,000/30,000/40,000) Eleven kilometers on the road to nowhere – the motorway that ends at the jungle's edge – lies this hostel. Enrique Ares, a local guide, has built a wonderful reserve with comfortable, spacious cabins with small kitchens and good beds, and he offers cut-price meals and lends out boots. It's a great option if your budget won't run to a trip, as it's actually surrounded by jungle. He works closely with the local Huitoto community.

Hostal Mahatu (☎ 311-539-1265; gusrenalvaredo@hotmail.com; Carrera 7A No 9-69; dm COP$15,000, s without bathroom COP$20,000) Clean rooms with comfy beds in this small, welcoming hostel run by a very friendly, helpful Colombian owner. Guests can use the kitchen and there's a small back yard to relax in. Gustave Rene, the manager, is set to open a new, more spacious hostel on the outskirts of town, with camping.

Residencias El Divino Niño (☎ 592-5598; Av Internacional 7-23; s/d/tr/q with fan COP$30,000/40,000/50,000/70,000, with air-con COP$40,000/50,000/60,000/80,000; ✸) Good basic choice for cheap aircon rooms – saggy beds are a drawback.

Hospedaje Los Delfines (☎ 592-7488; losdelfines leticia@hotmail.com; Carrera 11 No 12-81; s/d/tr COP$45,000/60,000/90,000; ▯) Small family-run place offering eight neat rooms with fan and fridge, arranged around a leafy patio, managed by a lovely retired nun.

Hotel Yurupary (☎ 592-7983; www.hotelyurupary.col.nu; Calle 8 No 7-26; s/d/tr incl breakfast COP$79,000/85,000/125,000; ✸ ▯ ✷) Large rooms with fridge and air-con, and a lovely pool. Great value for groups, with rooms for up to four people.

TABATINGA

International Bagpacker Hostel (☎ 312-585-8855; amazondiscover@hotmail.com; Texeira 9; dm/s/d COP$15,000/25,000/35,000) It's a dump, but way better than the others nearby if you have an early boat to catch.

Eating

LETICIA

Local fish *gamitana* and *pirarúcu* – which can grow to 300kg – are delicious.

La Casa del Pan (☎ 592-7660; Calle 11 No 10-20; breakfast COP$4000; ☺ 6:30am-11pm Mon-Sat) You're in the middle of nowhere, and there's a decent bakery that does breakfast. What more could you ask for?

A Me K Tiar ☎ 592-6094; Carrera 9 No 8-15; mains COP$5000-13,000; ☺ lunch & dinner) Busy and popular *parrilla* (grillhouse) with good grilled meat.

Restaurante El Sabor (Calle 8 No 9-25; set meals COP$7000; ☺ 6am-11pm Mon-Sat) Leticia's best budget eatery, with excellent-value set meals, vegetarian burgers, banana pancakes and fruit salad, plus unlimited free juices with your meal. Great *pirarúcu*.

TABATINGA

Restaurante Sao Jorge (Av de Amistad 1941; set lunch COP$5000; ☺ 1-10pm Mon-Sat) Have a Peruvian lunch in Brazil after crossing the road from Colombia. Aside from that novelty, the food's great.

Drinking

Várzea (☎ 320-316-6083; Carrera 10 No 14-12; ☺ 6pm-2am Tue-Sun) Cool bar with European and American rock and rap, it's a strange anomaly in the jungle, but a welcome one. They're a bit keen with the mop and broom come closing time, though.

Getting There & Away

AIR

Tourists arriving at Leticia's airport are charged a compulsory COP$16,500 tax.

AeroRepública (☎ 592-7666; www.aerorepublica.com.co; Calle 7 No 10-36; ☺ 8am-noon & 2-6pm Mon-Fri, 8am-noon Sat) flies to Bogotá daily. **Satena** (☎ 592-5419; www.satena.com; Calle 9 s/n; ☺ 8am-noon & 2-6pm Mon-Fri, 8am-noon Sat) flies to Bogotá on Monday, Wednesday and Friday. Singles run about COP$300,000 for a one-way flight with both firms; Satena cuts prices on Wednesday purchases. **Trip** (www.voetrip.com.br) flies from Tabatinga International Airport to Manaus daily (COP$600,000). The airport is 4km south of Tabatinga.

BOAT

Leticia connects downstream to Manaus (Brazil) or upriver to Iquitos (Peru). See boxed text, opposite, for more information.

To get to Puerto Nariño and Parque Nacional Amacayacu, buy tickets for the Leticia–Puerto Nariño fast boat from the ticket office in the dock at Leticia. Boats leave at 8am, 10am and 2pm, take 2½ hours and cost COP$26,000. They turn around after arriving from Leticia.

THE PINK DOLPHINS OF THE AMAZON

Playful, intelligent and mysterious, the Amazonian pink dolphin, known locally as a *bufeo*, thanks to the sound they make when surfacing, are fascinating creatures, seen as good omens.

Nobody quite knows how or when they ended up living in freshwater, they may have entered the Amazon from the Pacific Ocean approximately 15 million years ago, or from the Atlantic Ocean between 1.8 million and five million years ago.

Their brains are 40% bigger than humans', and among other highly specialized evolutionary traits, their neck bone is not fused with their spine, giving their heads great mobility, allowing them to hunt for fish in the flooded rainforest. Local myths believe the dolphins shift shape and leave the water at night to impregnate girls while in human form.

Responsible tour guides should never use large boats to go and watch the dolphins. Some operators use 200HP engines, whose sound distresses the dolphins. A 10.5HP *peque peque* engine is all you need. Insist your guide does not approach the dolphins, and never interact with them physically.

GETTING TO BRAZIL & PERU

Leticia may be in the middle of nowhere, but it's a popular route to Brazil and Peru. The quickest way out is by air to Manaus in Brazil. Although slower, the more enjoyable route to is by boat to Manaus or Iquitos in Peru. Iquitos is as isolated as Leticia, if not more so.

When leaving Colombia by air or boat, you will need to get stamped out at the Departmento Administrativo de Seguridad (DAS; Department of Administrative Security) at Leticia airport.

To Manaus, two boats a week leave from Porto Fluvial de Tabatinga, at 2pm on Wednesday and Saturday and call at Benjamin Constant. The trip to Manaus takes three days and four nights and costs COP$150,000 in your own hammock, or COP$555,000 for a double cabin. Entering Brazil, you'll need to get stamped in at the Policía Federal in Tabatinga.

Upstream from Manaus to Tabatinga, the trip usually takes six days, and costs about COP$250,000 in a hammock or around COP$750,000 for a double cabin. Food is included. Bring snacks and bottled water and watch your bags.

Transtur (☎ 310-859-2897; www.transtursa.com; Marechal Mallet 248, Tabatinga) operates modern, high-speed passenger boats between Tabatinga and Iquitos. Boats leave from Tabatinga's Porto da Feira at 4am on Wednesday, Friday and Sunday, arriving in Iquitos about 10 hours later. You can carry 15kg of luggage. The boats call in at Peru's Santa Rosa immigration point. The journey costs COP$140,000 in either direction, including breakfast and lunch.

From Iquitos into Peru, you have to fly or continue by river to Pucallpa (five to seven days), from where you can go overland to Lima and elsewhere.

For more information on these border crossings, see p366 and p868.

Getting Around

The best way to travel between Leticia and Tabatinga is by taxi. It's cheap and convenient as the weather gets extremely hot here.

PARQUE NACIONAL AMACAYACU

Amacayacu takes in 2935 sq km of jungle on the northern side of the Amazon, about 55km upstream from Leticia. The luxury Decameron chain has taken over the facilities and now offers a sanitized version of the rainforest experience at sky-high prices to visitors who don't want to get their shoes dirty. The combined cost of the park entry fee (COP$31,000) and **accommodations** (dm COP$105,000) rule this out for most budget travelers.

Boats (COP$20,000, 1½ hours) from Leticia to Puerto Nariño will drop you off at the park's visitors center. Getting back to Leticia is trickier, and you can easily get stranded for hours if the fast boats from Puerto Nariño fill up before they pass.

PUERTO NARIÑO

☎ 8 / pop 2000

Puerto Nariño is a tiny town 60km up the Amazon from Leticia, and is an appealing oddity. Its streets are incredibly clean, thanks to daily cleaning patrols by proud women and girls, known as *escobitas*. There are no cars, and all rainwater is recycled – as is all garbage.

About 10km west of Puerto Nariño is **Lago Tarapoto**, a tranquil lake accessible only by river, where you can see pink dolphins playing. A half-day trip to the lake in a small boat can be informally organized with locals from Puerto Nariño (per boat for up to four people around COP$50,000).

The fantastically strange **El Alto de Águilas** (☎ 311-502-8592; dm COP$20,000) is a 20-minute walk from town, and is run by genial and brilliantly eccentric holy man, Friar Hector José Rivera. Rooms are basic, but the real fun here is the host. As the friar welcomes you into his lodge he calls his pet monkeys from the trees to swarm about you, and a pair of vividly colored macaws will swoop out from the canopy to nibble bananas and rest on a bamboo crucifix in the garden. There's a high lookout point, and Rivera can arrange canoe hire and cheap excursions into Parque Nacional Amacayacu, with all proceeds going to local indigenous families. Everyone knows him – ask around for directions.

Hotel Napu (☎ 310-488-0998; olgabeco@yahoo .com; Calle 4 No 5-72; hammocks COP$15,000, r per person without bathroom COP$25,000) offers good cheap rooms with fans. It has friendly owners and a courtyard terrace garden. The best rooms are at the back.

For cheap meals, there's only one choice: Las Margaritas, on the waterfront. Nightlife is drinking beer on the street. For breakfast, head into the market and buy an egg sandwich and a coffee from a bewildered local for COP$500.

COLOMBIA DIRECTORY

ACCOMMODATIONS

Colombia's backpacker market is growing daily, and with it comes the huge growth in facilities familiar to the continent. Every major city has at least one hostel with dormitories, internet or wi-fi, a book exchange, laundry services and travel advice. These are the cheapest and most convenient option for travelers, make for good camaraderie and are excellent sources of information. However, at times it may feel like you're on a summer camp, rather than exploring new territory.

See www.colombianhostels.com for the most popular hostels in each city.

On the local market, you can choose between *hoteles, residencias, hospedajes* and *posadas*. *Residencias* and *hospedajes* are the most common names for budget places. A *hotel* generally suggests a place of a higher standard, and almost always has private bathroom while *residencias, hospedajes* and *posadas* often have shared facilities.

Everywhere mentioned in this guide provides towels, soap and toilet paper, bed linen or blankets. You may want to bring a cotton or silk sleeping-bag liner for hygiene if you're staying in ultra-low-budget spots.

Motels rent rooms by the hour. They're found on the outskirts of the city and usually have garish signs. Many Colombians live at home until marriage, so couples check in here for a few hours of passion and privacy.

Camping is gaining popularity as the country's safety improves. Note that army-style kit is forbidden for private use. Don't leave your tent or gear unattended.

ACTIVITIES

With its amazing geographical diversity Colombia offers many opportunities for hiking. Don't go deep into the hills without checking with locals on the latest security situation.

Colombia's coral reefs provide very good conditions for snorkeling and scuba diving. The main centers are San Andrés (p544), Providencia (p544), Taganga (p532), Capurganá (p549) and Cartagena (p541), each of which has diving schools offering courses and other services. Colombia is considered one of the world's cheapest countries for diving.

Paragliding is also popular and low-priced nationwide, with Medellín (p553) and San Gil (p525) offering courses or tandem flights. White-water rafting is cheap, and is found in San Gil (p525).

Cycling is one of Colombia's favorite spectator sports, and Bogotá has a new bike-hire company (p515) as well as a car-free Sunday.

Other possible activities include mountaineering, horse riding, rock climbing, windsurfing, fishing and caving.

BOOKS

For more detailed travel information, pick up a copy of Lonely Planet's *Colombia*.

Beyond Bogotá: Diary of a Drug War Journalist in Colombia (2009) by Garry Leech is a detailed and fairly balanced examination of the impact of Plan Colombia, paramilitarism and guerrilla warfare on the rural poor of Colombia.

Out of Captivity: Surviving 1,967 Days in the Colombian Jungle (2009) by Marc Gonsalves, Tom Howes and Keith Stansell with Gary Brozek is a harrowing account of years of captivity at the hands of FARC, suffered by three US defense contractors whose helicopter crashed in the jungle in 2003. They were rescued at the same time as Ingrid Betancourt.

Inside Colombia: Drugs, Democracy & War (2003) by Grace Livingstone is a comprehensive analysis of the pre-Uribe period in Colombia.

For an account on Colombia's drug war, ready *More Terrible than Death: Violence, Drugs and America's War in Colombia* (2003) by Robin Kirk, who spent a dozen years in Colombia working for Human Rights Watch and recounts some of the most brutal incidents of the terror she witnessed during her fieldwork.

Killing Pablo: The Hunt for the World's Greatest Outlaw (2002) by Mark Bowden is a page-turning account of the life, times and death of Pablo Escobar.

BUSINESS HOURS

The office working day is usually eight hours long, from 8am to noon and 2pm to 6pm Monday to Friday. Many offices in Bogotá have adopted the *jornada continua*, a working day without a lunch break, which finishes two hours earlier. Banks (except for those in Bogotá – see p511) are open 8am to 11:30am and 2pm to 4pm Monday to Thursday, and 8am to 11:30am and 2pm to 4:30pm Friday.

Shopping hours are normally from 9am to 6pm or 7pm Monday to Saturday. Some close for lunch, others stay open. Large stores and supermarkets usually stay open until 8pm or 9pm or later. Most good restaurants in the larger cities stay open until 10pm or later; in smaller towns they usually close by 9pm or earlier. Opening hours for museums and other tourist sights vary greatly. Most museums are closed on Monday but are open on Sunday.

CLIMATE

Colombia's proximity to the equator means its temperature varies little throughout the year. Colombia, however, does have dry and wet seasons; the pattern varies nationwide. As a rule of thumb, in the Andean region and the Caribbean Coast there are two dry and two rainy seasons per year. The main dry season falls between January and March, with a shorter, less-dry period between June and August. The most pleasant time to visit Colombia is in the main dry season, when outdoor activities are more pleasant and when you'll find many festivals and fiestas. For more information and climate charts, see the South America Directory (p987).

CUSTOMS

Customs procedures are usually a formality, both on entering and on leaving the country. You will be searched, sometimes extensively, for drugs.

DANGERS & ANNOYANCES

If you use common sense, you'll find that Colombia is far safer for travelers than Venezuela, Ecuador and Brazil. Kidnapping of foreigners is almost unheard of these days, and urban attacks by FARC have been cut back to irrelevance.

Drugs

Cocaine is widely available, cheap, and you will likely be offered it at some point on your journey. If you do decide to take it, beware

that it is far stronger than in the US and UK. Paranoid delusions, tachycardia, stroke or overdose can and do occur. If somebody you are with overdoses, call an ambulance immediately, and tell the paramedics exactly what happened. Marijuana is also widely available.

Burundanga is a real concern. Dismissed by some as an urban myth, in research for this book we met three people who had been dosed with it. The usual method of administration is a spiked drink or cigarette. It is tasteless and odorless and renders victims senseless, only to wake up with no recollection of the previous few hours, minus their wallets and valuables. The drug is obtained from a nightshade species widespread in Colombia. Don't accept a drink, snack or cigarette from a stranger, especially when traveling alone, and especially on buses.

Guerrillas

The principal areas of conflict are now Chocó, Putumayo and the Amazon Basin. Since Uribe came to office in 2002, cases of kidnapping for ransom have decreased significantly. The targets are almost exclusively wealthy Colombian businessmen or their family members, as well as foreign businessmen.

Theft & Robbery

Theft is the most common traveler danger. Generally speaking, the problem is more serious in the largest cities. Rural areas are safer. The most common methods of theft are snatching your daypack, camera or watch, pickpocketing, or taking advantage of a moment's inattention to pick up your gear and run away.

DRIVER'S LICENSE

It is possible to drive a car or motorbike in Colombia, if you can handle the crazy driving. Bring along an International Driving Permit.

ELECTRICITY

Colombia uses two-pronged US-type plugs that run at 110V, 60Hz.

EMBASSIES & CONSULATES

Foreign diplomatic representatives in Colombia include the following (embassy and consulate are at the same address unless specified otherwise). For locations of these and other consulates, see individual city maps.

COLOMBIA

Australia (☎ 1-236-2828; Carrera 16 No 86A-05, Bogotá)
Brazil Bogotá (☎ 1-218-0800; Calle 93 No 14-20, 8th fl);
Leticia (Map p577; ☎ 8-592-7530; Carrera 9 No 13-84);
Medellín (Map p552; ☎ 4-265-7565; Calle 29D No 55-91)
Canada (☎ 1-657-9914; Carrera 7 No 115-33, 14th fl,
Bogotá)
Ecuador Bogotá (☎ 1-542-7121; Calle 72 No 6-30);
Ipiales (☎ 2-773-2292; Carrera 7 No 14-10); Medellín (Map
p552; ☎ 4-512-1303; Calle 50 No 52-22, Oficina 603)
France (☎ 1-638-1400; Carrera 11 No 93-12, Bogotá)
Germany (☎ 1-423-2600; Carrera 69 No 25B-44, Bogotá)
Peru Bogotá consulate (☎ 1-257-6846; Calle 90 No 14-
26); Bogotá embassy (☎ 1-257-0505; Calle 80A No 6-50);
Leticia (Map p577; ☎ 8-592-7755; Calle 11 No 5-32)
UK (☎ 1-326-8301; www.britain.gov.co; Carrera 9 No
76-49, 9th fl, Bogotá)
USA (☎ 1-315-0811; Calle 22Dbis No 47-51, Bogotá)
Venezuela Bogotá consulate (☎ 1-636-4011; Av 13 No
103-16); Bogotá embassy (☎ 1-640-1213; Carrera 11 No
87-51, 5th fl); Cartagena (off Map p539; ☎ 5-665-0382;
Carrera 3 No 8-129, Bocagrande); Cúcuta (☎ 7-579-1956;
Av Camilo Daza); Medellín (Map p552; ☎ 4-351-1614;
Calle 32B No 69-59)

FESTIVALS & EVENTS

There are more than 200 festivals and events
ranging from small, local affairs to international festivals lasting several days. Most of
the celebrations are regional, and the most
interesting ones are listed in individual
destination sections.

FOOD & DRINK

Eating reviews throughout this chapter
are given in order of budget, with the least
expensive options first.

Colombian Cuisine

Colombian cuisine is varied and regional.
Among the most typical regional dishes are
the following:

ajiaco (a·khee·a·ko) – soup with chicken and three
varieties of potato, served with corn and capers; a Bogotá
specialty
bandeja paisa (ban·de·kha pai·sa) – typical Antioquian
dish made from ground beef, sausage, red beans, rice, fried
green banana, fried egg, fried salt pork and avocado
chocolate santafereño (cho·ko·la·te san·ta·fe·re·nyo) –
cup of hot chocolate accompanied by a piece of cheese and
bread (traditionally you put the cheese into the chocolate);
another Bogotá specialty
cuy (kooy) – grilled guinea pig; typical of Nariño
hormiga culona (or·mee·ga koo·lo·na) – large fried ants;
unique to Santander
lechona (le·cho·na) – pig carcass stuffed with its own

meat, rice and dried peas and then baked in an oven; a
specialty of Tolima
tamal (ta·mal) – chopped pork with rice and vegetables
folded in a maize dough, wrapped in banana leaves and
steamed; there are many regional varieties

Variety does not, unfortunately, apply to the
basic set meal *(comida corriente)*, which is
the principal diet of most Colombians eating
out. It is a two-course meal with *sopa* (soup)
and *bandeja* or *seco* (literally 'dry,' meaning just the main course without soup). At
lunchtime (from noon to 2pm) it is called
almuerzo; at dinnertime (after 6pm) it becomes *comida*, but it is identical to lunch.
The *almuerzos* and *comidas* are the staple,
sometimes the only, offering in countless
budget restaurants. They are the cheapest way to fill yourself up, costing between
COP$4000 and COP$6000 – roughly half
the price of an à la carte dish. Breakfasts are
dull and repetitive, normally *arepa* (grilled
cornmeal patty) and eggs.

Colombia has amazing fruits, some of
which you won't find anywhere else. Try
*guanábana, lulo, curuba, zapote, mamoncillo,
uchuva, feijoa, granadilla, maracuyá, tomate
de árbol, borojó, mamey* and *tamarindo*.

Drinks

Coffee is the number one drink – *tinto* (a
small cup of black coffee) is served everywhere. Other coffee drinks are *perico* or *pintado*, a small milk coffee, and *café con leche*,
which is larger and uses more milk.

Tea is not very popular. British travelers should seek out Hindu brand tea in
supermarkets. Using two bags, you'll get a
passable imitation of the world's finest hot
beverage. *Aromáticas* – herbal teas made with
various plants such as *cidrón* (lemon balm),
yerbabuena (mint) and *manzanilla* (chamo-
mile) – are cheap and good. *Agua de panela*
(unrefined sugar melted in hot water) is tasty
with lemon.

Beer is popular, cheap and generally not
bad. Colombian wine is vile.

Aguardiente is the local alcoholic spirit,
flavored with anise and produced by several companies throughout the country. An
aguardiente hangover will make you lose
the will to live. *Ron* (rum) is good, cheap
and available everywhere. In rural areas, try
homemade *chicha* and *guarapo* (alcoholic
fermented maize or fruit drinks).

GAY & LESBIAN TRAVELERS

Bogotá has the largest gay and lesbian community and the most open gay life; head to the Chapinero district for bars and clubs. Visit www.gaycolombia.com, which lists bars, discos, events, activities, publications and other related matters.

HEALTH

Colombia has an extensive network of pharmacies, and those in the large cities are usually well stocked. The country also has a developed array of clinics and hospitals, including some world-class private facilities in Bogotá. Tap water in the large cities is supposedly safe to drink, but newcomers had best avoid it. See the Health chapter (p1011) for more information.

HOLIDAYS

The following holidays and special events are observed as public holidays in Colombia. When the dates marked with an asterisk do not fall on a Monday, the holiday is moved to the following Monday to make a three-day-long weekend, referred to as a *puente*.

Año Nuevo (New Year's Day) January 1
Los Reyes Magos (Epiphany) January 6*
San José (St Joseph) March 19
Jueves Santo (Maundy Thursday) March/April – date varies
Viernes Santo (Good Friday) March/April – date varies
Día del Trabajador (Labor Day) May 1
La Ascensión del Señor (Ascension) May – date varies
Corpus Cristi (Corpus Christi) May/June* –date varies
Sagrado Corazón de Jesús (Sacred Heart) June*
San Pedro y San Pablo (St Peter & St Paul) June 29*
Día de la Independencia (Independence Day) July 20
Batalla de Boyacá (Battle of Boyacá) August 7
La Asunción de Nuestra Señora (Assumption) August 15*
Día de la Raza (Discovery of America) October 12*
Todos los Santos (All Saints' Day) November 1*
Independencia de Cartagena (Independence of Cartagena) November 11*
Inmaculada Concepción (Immaculate Conception) December 8
Navidad (Christmas Day) December 25

There are also three local high seasons, when Colombians rush to travel: late December to mid-January, the Easter Week, and mid-June to mid-July, when buses and planes get more crowded, fares rise and hotels fill up faster.

INTERNET ACCESS

Except for La Guajira, every place mentioned in this guide has public net access, and nearly every backpacker hostel has wi-fi. Internet connections are fastest in the major urban centers, while they can be pretty slow in some remote places. Access normally costs around COP$1500 to COP$2000 per hour. Many cafes in bigger cities have wi-fi. Don't flaunt your laptop and you'll be fine to carry it around.

INTERNET RESOURCES

Useful online resources of general and tourist information about Colombia:

BBC News (news.bbc.co.uk) Best Latin American news service online.
Centro de Investigación y Educación Popular (CINEP, Center for Research and Popular Education; www.cinep.org.co) A Jesuit-run research institution with a wide-ranging analysis of the conflict in Colombia.
Colombia Journal (www.colombiajournal.org) Excellent site providing information on human rights issues.
El Tiempo (www.eltiempo.com) Colombia's leading newspaper.
Poor but Happy (www.poorbuthappy.com/colombia) Lots of tourist and practical information.
Turismo Colombia (www.turismocolombia.com) The government's official tourism website has good tourist information in Spanish and English.

LEGAL MATTERS

If arrested, you have the right to an attorney. If you don't have one, an attorney will be appointed to you (and paid for by the government). There is a presumption of innocence. You are legally allowed 20g of marijuana and 1g of cocaine, but that won't help you a jot if the police shake you down. If money is demanded, pay immediately – no more than COP$500,000 – and leave at once before their colleagues muscle in on the action. Watch out for police impostors.

MAPS

The widest selection of maps of Colombia is produced and sold by the **Instituto Geográfico Agustín Codazzi** (off Map pp512-13; IGAC; www.igac.gov.co; Carrera 30 No 48-51, Bogotá), the government mapping body. They are of poor quality and lack detail. Folded national road maps are sold at the entrance of toll roads. They're really useful for off-the-beaten-track journey planning.

MEDIA
Newspapers & Magazines
All major cities have daily newspapers. Bogotá's leading newspaper, *El Tiempo,* has reasonable coverage of national and international news, culture, sports and economics. It has the widest distribution nationwide. The leading newspapers in other large cities include *El Mundo* and *El Colombiano* in Medellín, and *El País* and *El Occidente* in Cali. *Semana* is the biggest national weekly magazine, and offers excellent impartial coverage of Colombian politics.

Radio & TV
Hundreds of AM and FM radio stations operate in Colombia and mainly broadcast music programs. In Bogotá, try the Universidad Nacional station (106.9 FM). There are three nationwide and four regional TV channels. Satellite and cable TV has boomed in Bogotá and in other major cities.

MONEY
Colombia's official currency is the peso. There are 50-, 100-, 200- and 500-peso coins, and paper notes of 1000, 2000, 5000, 10,000, 20,000 and 50,000 pesos. No one ever has change, so try to avoid the latter. Forged 50,000-peso notes are easy to spot for a local, not so for a visitor. Amex traveler's checks are the easiest to change. An emergency stash of US$100 is useful. However, ATMs are widespread, so debit and credit cards are your best bet – for safety and rates.

ATMs
There are plenty of ATMs in the cities and major towns, and they work with most foreign cards. Many ATMs are linked to Cirrus and Plus and most accept MasterCard and Visa. Advances are in Colombian pesos. This is the best way to manage your cash in Colombia, for safety, convenience and cost. Davivienda and Citibank have larger withdrawal limits (COP$400,000 and COP$700,000), meaning you save on repeated bank charges.

Bargaining
Bargaining is limited to informal trade and services such as markets, street stalls, taxis and long-distance buses. Always offer 25% less, especially at less busy times. On public holidays, save your breath.

Credit Cards
Credit cards are widely accepted in urban areas, and most banks offer peso advances. Visa is the best card for Colombia, followed by MasterCard.

Exchanging Money
Some major banks change cash (mostly US dollars) and traveler's checks (principally Amex), though these are uncommon. The most useful banks include Banco Unión Colombiano, Bancolombia and Banco Santander.

Banks are always crowded, and there's much paperwork involved in changing money, but the process itself shouldn't take more than five or 10 minutes. The queue might take an hour. Always take your passport original – not a copy.

You can also change cash at *casas de cambio* (authorized money-exchange offices), found in virtually all major cities and border towns. They deal mainly with US dollars, less often with euros, with rates similar to banks. It's quicker than using the bank. You can also change dollars on the street, but it's risky: changers are often crooks. The only street money markets worth considering are those at the borders, where there may be simply no alternative. There are money changers at every land border crossing.

The exchange rates as we went to press:

EXCHANGE RATES		
Country	**Unit**	**COP$**
Australia	A$1	1704
Canada	C$1	1863
euro zone	€1	2950
Japan	¥100	2197
New Zealand	NZ$1	1360
UK	£1	3492
USA	US$1	2000

POST
The Colombian postal service is operated by three companies: Avianca, Adpostal and Depris. All cover domestic and international post, but only Adpostal will ship overseas using surface mail (the cheapest form of postage). All three are efficient and reliable, but a postcard home to the US or Europe will cost around COP$10,000 – a ridiculous price. The poste restante system is operated by Avianca. The most reliable office is in Bogotá (p511).

RESPONSIBLE TRAVEL

Tourism in Colombia is still relatively small and has so far not had any lasting detrimental effect on indigenous cultures or the environment. You can keep it that way by adhering to common-sense practices: asking people first before photographing them (especially indigenous peoples), dressing appropriately when entering a church, and practicing safe environmental rules when hiking or scuba diving.

Talking politics in Colombia can be a dangerous thing. Because paramilitaries wear civilian clothing, you never really know who you are talking to, or who is listening to your conversation, and it can be quite easy to offend someone if you start ranting about the government or the opposition.

Encourage ecotourism projects that aim to preserve or restore local environments. Support native communities by buying their crafts but avoid those made from corals, turtles or fossils.

STUDYING

Colombia can be a good place to study Spanish. The Spanish spoken in Colombia is clear and easy to understand and there are language schools in the big cities. You can also find a teacher and arrange individual classes. Inquire in popular travelers' hostels (in Bogotá, Cartagena, Medellín and Cali), which usually have contacts with Spanish tutors. They are often students and their rates are reasonable.

TELEPHONE

The telephone system is largely automated for both domestic and international calls. Telecom is the most prominent company, with Orbitel and ETB not far behind.

Public telephones exist in cities and large towns but, except for the centers of the largest cities, they are few and far between, and many are out of order. As a rule, Telecom offices have some operable phones. Public telephones use coins, although newly installed telephones accept *tarjeta telefónica* (phone cards) that can be used for international, intercity and local calls. Local calls are charged by timed rate (not flat rate), costing around COP$200 for a three-minute call.

You can call direct to just about anywhere in Colombia, except calling a cell phone from a landline. Landline numbers are seven digits long. Area codes are single digits.

All calls go through Telecom (☎09) by default. You can choose to use Orbitel (☎05) or ETB (☎07) by dialing that before the number.

Colombia's country code is ☎57. If you are dialing a Colombian number from abroad, drop the prefix (05, 07 or 09) and dial only the area code and the local number.

Cell phone networks are operated by Movistar, Comcel and Tigo. Comcel leads the pack for network coverage. You can buy a SIM card for COP$5000 to COP$10,000. Buying a handset is a really good idea. Cellphone numbers always start with 3.

Cross-network calls are pricey, and many Colombians use their handsets to receive calls only, preferring to make calls from any of the dozens of informal cell phone vendors in the street. They're the guys and girls shouting *'llamadas'* or *'minutos'* on every corner. They buy in bulk and sell at a small profit, and are always cheaper than using your own phone, unless you have a contract.

TOURIST INFORMATION

Municipal tourist-information offices in departmental capitals and other tourist destinations administer tourist information. Some are better than others, but on the whole they lack city maps and brochures. Staff members may be friendly but often don't speak English. The practical information they provide can be lacking, and the quality of information largely depends on the person who attends you.

In some cities, tourist offices are supported by the Policía de Turismo, the police officers specially trained to attend tourists. They are mainly to be found on the street and at the major tourist attractions.

TRAVELERS WITH DISABILITIES

Colombia offers very little to people with disabilities. Wheelchair ramps and toilets are available only at a few upmarket hotels and restaurants, and public transportation will be a challenge for any person with mobility problems.

VISAS

Nationals of some countries, including most of Western Europe, the Americas, Japan, Australia and New Zealand, don't need a visa to enter Colombia. It's a good idea for you to check this before your planned trip, because visa regulations change frequently.

COLOMBIA

See lonelyplanet.com and its links for up-to-date visa information.

All visitors get an entry stamp or print in their passport from DAS (the security police who are also responsible for immigration) upon arrival at any international airport or land border crossing. Make sure your passport is stamped immediately. The stamp indicates how many days you can stay in the country; 60 days is most common. An onward ticket is legally required and you may be asked to show one. Upon departure, immigration officials put an exit stamp in your passport. Again, check it to avoid future problems.

Visa Extensions

You are entitled to a 30-day visa extension (US$30), which can be obtained from DAS in any departmental capital. The new 30-days period begins from the end of the visa that's already stamped in your passport (so there's no reason to wait until the last minute). Most travelers apply for an extension in Bogotá (see above), but you can do it in any other major city – Cartagena's office is usually pretty calm, while Medellín's can be hectic. Regardless, patience is required.

A 30-day extension can be obtained at the **DAS office** (1-408-8000; Calle 100 No 11B-27, Bogotá; ☺ 7:30am-4:30pm Mon-Fri) in Bogotá. Your passport, two photocopies of your passport (picture page and arrival stamp) and two passport-size photos are required. You also need to show an air ticket out of the country. You have to pay the US$30 fee at the bank. Extensions are issued the same day.

VOLUNTEERING

Fellowship of Reconciliation (☎ 1-510-763-1403; www.forcolombia.org; 369 15th St, Oakland, CA 94612, USA) employs volunteers for its two field teams in Bogotá and the Peace Community of San José de Apartadó in the northwestern Urabá region. The international team provides protective accompaniment for the leaders and residents of the Peace Community, a remarkable experiment in nonviolent resistance, and supports resistance to militarism by other Colombian groups and communities. Applicants must speak Spanish and English, be committed to nonviolence, work well in a team and have some relevant experience. Team members can be from the United States or other countries (except Colombia), and serve for a year. They are expected to work on raising funds to support the project, and receive a stipend, living expenses and medical insurance.

WOMEN TRAVELERS

Women traveling in Colombia's cities and rural areas are unlikely to get major hassle. Behave as you do at home in terms of security and you'll be fine: don't walk alone at night in dark streets, don't take lifts from guys you don't know, always take taxis in pairs after dark.

Culturally, you'll have to deal with a little more machismo than at home: you'll definitely receive more overtly flirtatious attention from males simply for being foreign. Double that if you're blonde. If you want to fend off unwelcome advances, wear a wedding ring.

WORKING

Although cash-in-hand teaching work can be found in some schools in the main cities, be aware that legally you need a work visa to get a job in Colombia. Some travelers try to strike a deal with hotel owners to teach staff English in return for a discount on the room. With the growth in tourism, many Colombians are keener than ever to get skilled up.

Ecuador

HIGHLIGHTS

- **Quito** (p601) Delve into the picturesque streets of the Old Town, its cobblestones criss-crossing one of Latin America's finest colonial centers.
- **The Oriente** (p643) Stay in a jungle lodge, raft on tropical rivers and spot caimans, howler monkeys and two-toed sloths in Ecuador's slice of the Amazon Basin.
- **Galápagos Islands** (p667) Snorkel with penguins, stare down meter-long iguanas, stand face to face with gigantic tortoises and scuba dive with monstrous manta rays.
- **Otavalo** (p618) Haggle over handmade treasures at one of South America's biggest open-air markets.
- **The Quilotoa Loop** (p625) Hike your way around this spectacular Andean destination, overnighting in peaceful villages along the way.
- **Off the Beaten Track** (p652) Journey up the Río Santiago to Playa de Oro, where jungle cats still roam the dense tropical forest.

FAST FACTS

- **Area:** 283,560 sq km (roughly the size of New Zealand or the US state of Nevada)
- **Budget:** US$20 to US$25 a day
- **Capital:** Quito
- **Costs:** budget hotel room in Quito US$6, bottle of beer US$1, four-hour bus ride US$4
- **Country Code:** ☎ 593
- **Languages:** Spanish, Quichua
- **Money:** US$
- **Population:** 15 million
- **Seasons:** high (June to August, December to January), low (September to November, February to May)
- **Time:** GMT minus five hours

TRAVEL HINTS

Pack lightly and you can carry your backpack inside the bus. Save money by ordering the *almuerzo* (set lunch) and shopping in the markets.

OVERLAND ROUTES

Major border crossings are at Ipiales (Colombia); at Tumbes/Aguas Verdes, Macará and La Balsa (Peru); and via Nuevo Rocafuerte/Iquitos (Peru by river).

Ecuador may be small, but this Andean nation towers above most other South American countries when it comes to natural and cultural wonders. Amazonian rainforest, Andean peaks, premontane cloud forests and the Galápagos Islands set the stage for the country's spectacular biodiversity. Wildlife-watching is just one way to enjoy Ecuador's riches, with dozens of animal and plant species found nowhere else on earth. On even a short Ecuadorian adventure, it's possible to photograph monkeys from jungle canopy towers, swim with sea lions in the Pacific and admire dozens of Ecuador's 1600 bird species in misty forests.

The blend of lush and volcanic scenery also provides the backdrop for adrenaline-charged adventures, from whitewater rafting on class-five rivers to climbing 5000m-high volcanoes. You can take dramatic treks through the *páramo* (high-altitude grassland), surf tight breaks off the west coast, and hike, mountain bike, mountaineer or simply unwind amid some of the continent's most dramatic scenery.

Ecuador harbors a rich indigenous heritage, where traditional costumes and highland markets are just a few pieces of the varied life of this country in the heart of the Andes.

CURRENT EVENTS

In recent years, Ecuador has taken a left-leaning turn on the political stage. President Rafael Correa, who describes himself as a humanist, a fervent Catholic of the left and a proponent of 21st-century socialism, has focused on social welfare since first taking the reins in 2007. In a nationwide referendum held in September 2008, voters approved a new constitution, which prohibits discrimination, increases spending on education and health care, allows civil unions for gay couples and gives more rights to indigenous groups. The 444-page document also gave rights to the environment, requiring the government to avoid actions that would destroy ecosystems or drive species to extinction – the first measure of its kind according to Ecuadorian officials.

In 2009 another ambitious plan showed the first signs of success. Two years earlier, Correa floated a controversial idea before the world community: pay us (in lost revenues) not to tap the estimated 900-million-barrel oil reserve inside the Parque Nacional Yasuní, one of South America's most biodiverse regions. The crude oil in the Yasuní region would then be incorporated into the carbon-dioxide trading system currently discussed in the EU, which would be a global benefit, keeping half a billion tons of carbon dioxide sequestered in the earth.

Petroleum, not surprisingly, is a hot topic in a country that relies on oil profits for 40% of its GDP. One of the world's biggest environmental lawsuits was still in limbo at the time of writing – namely the US$27 billion class-action lawsuit brought by 30,000 Ecuadorians against Chevron-Texaco for dumping 18 billion gallons of toxic waste in the Amazon and abandoning 900 waste pits (see also Environment, p596).

Other top stories include the rising tension with Colombia over their cross-border raid on FARC guerrillas (killing FARC's second in command) in 2008. Because of the violation of Ecuador's sovereignty, Correa withdrew his ambassador from Bogotá, and an Ecuadorian judge even ordered the arrest of a Colombian official involved with planning the raid. Colombian President Alvaro Uribe later responded by saying 'We cannot allow judicial or political terrorism to deprive Colombians of our right to recover our security.'

In the raid a laptop was captured which, according to a Wall Street Journal reporter, provides proof of a 'cozy relationship' between FARC and both Correa and Venezuelan President Hugo Chávez. Correa denied the allegations and threatened to sue the newspaper 'for their lies.' His government also pointed out the largely overlooked humanitarian crisis generated by the estimated 135,000 Colombian refugees living in Ecuador, for which Colombia should be shouldering more responsibility.

Despite the allegations, Correa remains popular, and he easily won re-election in 2009 with 51% of the vote in a field of eight candidates – the first time in 30 years a president was elected without a runoff. At the time of writing, his popularity was on the descent owing to a shrinking economy (in part due to lower oil prices), and allegations of corruption (Correa's brother, it was revealed, has received more than US$80 million worth of lucrative government contracts).

HISTORY

The land of fire and ice has certainly had a tumultuous history. Since becoming an independent nation in 1830, Ecuador has gone through nearly 100 changes in government and 20 constitutions – the most recent drafted in 2008. Fueling the Andean nation's volatility are rivalries both internal (conservative, church-backed Quito versus liberal, secular Guayaquil) and external (border disputes with Peru and Colombia).

Early Cultures

The oldest tools found in Ecuador date back to 9000 BC, meaning people were mucking about the region in the Stone Age. The most important early societies developed along the coast, which was a more habitable landscape than the frigid highlands. Ecuador's first permanent sedentary culture was the Valdivia, which emerged along the Santa Elena Peninsula nearly 6000 years ago.

By the 11th century AD, Ecuador had two dominant cultures: the expansionist Cara along the coast and the peaceful Quitu in the highlands. These cultures merged and became known as the Quitu-Caras, or the Shyris. They were the dominant force in the highlands until the 1300s, when the Puruhá of the central highlands became increasingly powerful. The third important group was the Cañari, further south. These were the cultures the Inca encountered when they began their expansion north from present-day Peru.

Land of the Four Quarters

Until the early 15th century, the Inca empire was concentrated around Cuzco, Peru. That changed dramatically during the rule of Inca Pachacutec, whose expansionist policies set into motion the creation of the vast Inca empire, Tahuantinsuyo, meaning 'Land of the Four Quarters' in Quichua (called Quechua elsewhere in South America). By the time the Inca reached Ecuador they were under the rule of Túpac Yupanqui, Pachacutec's successor, and they met with fierce resistance, both from the Cañari and the Quitu-Caras. In one battle the Inca massacred thousands of Caras and dumped them into a lake near Otavalo (p618), which supposedly turned the waters red and gave the lake its name, Laguna Yaguarcocha (Lake of Blood).

The subjugation of the north took many years, during which the Inca Túpac fathered a son with a Cañari princess. The son, Huayna Capác, grew up in present-day Ecuador and succeeded his father to the Inca throne. Huayna Capác had two sons: Atahualpa, who grew up in Quito, and Huáscar, who was raised in Cuzco.

When Huayna Capác died in 1527, he left his empire not to one son, as was traditional, but to two. Rivalry developed between the sons, which eventually boiled into civil war. After several years of fighting, Atahualpa defeated Huáscar near Ambato in central Ecuador. Atahualpa was thus ruling a weakened and still divided Inca empire when Francisco Pizarro landed in Peru in 1532.

The Spanish Play Dirty

Pizarro's advance was rapid and dramatic. He successfully exploited divisions within the Inca empire and enlisted many non-Inca ethnic groups that had been recently and reluctantly subjugated by the Inca. Most importantly, Inca warriors on foot were no match for the fully armored conquistadors on horseback who slaughtered them by the thousands. Within three years, and after betraying Inca rulers on several occasions, the Spanish controlled the former Inca empire.

Settling In

From 1535 onward, the colonial era proceeded with no major uprisings by indigenous Ecuadorians. Francisco Pizarro made his brother Gonzalo the governor of Quito in 1540. Hoping to find more gold, Gonzalo sent his lieutenant, Francisco de Orellana, to explore the Amazon. The lieutenant and his force ended up floating all the way to the Atlantic, becoming the first party to descend the Amazon and cross the continent. This feat took almost a year and is still commemorated in Ecuador.

During the first centuries of colonial rule, Lima (Peru) was the seat of Ecuador's political administration. Ecuador, originally a *gobernación* (province), became known as the Audiencia de Quito in 1563, a more important political division. In 1739 the Audiencia de Quito was transferred from the viceroyalty of Peru, of which it was a part, to the viceroyalty of Colombia (then known as Nueva Granada).

Ecuador remained a peaceful colony during these centuries, and agriculture and the arts flourished. Churches and monasteries were constructed atop every sacred indigenous site and were decorated with unique carvings and paintings, the result of a blend of Spanish and

ECUADOR

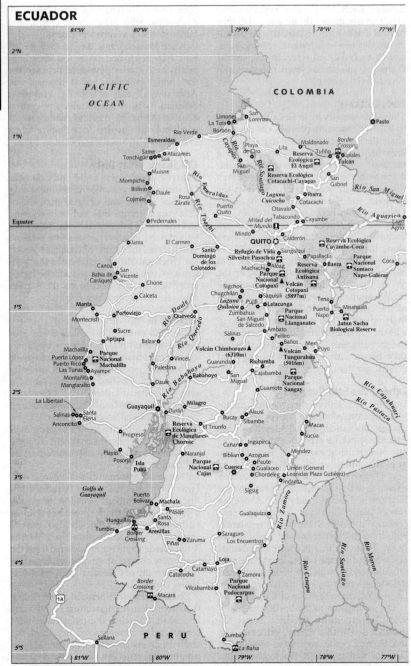

indigenous artistic influences. This so-called Escuela Quiteña (Quito school of art), still admired by visitors today, has left an indelible stamp on both the colonial buildings of the time and Ecuador's unique art history.

Life was comfortable for the ruling colonialists, but the indigenous people – and later, the *mestizos* (people of mixed Spanish and indigenous descent) – were treated abysmally under their rule. A system of forced labor was not only tolerated but encouraged, and it is no surprise that by the 18th century there were several indigenous uprisings against the Spanish ruling classes. Social unrest, as well as the introduction of cocoa and sugar plantations in the northwest, prompted landowners to import African slave laborers. Much of the rich Afro-Ecuadorian culture found in Esmeraldas province today is a legacy of this period.

Adiós, Spain

The first serious attempt at independence from Spain was made on August 10, 1809, by a partisan group led by Juan Pío Montúfar. The group took Quito and installed a government, but royalist troops regained control in only 24 days.

A decade later, Simón Bolívar, the Venezuelan liberator, freed Colombia in his march southward from Caracas. Bolívar then supported the people of Guayaquil when they claimed independence on October 9, 1820. It took another two years for Ecuador to be entirely liberated from Spanish rule. The decisive battle was fought on May 24, 1822, when Mariscal (Field Marshall) Sucre, one of Bolívar's best generals, defeated the royalists at Pichincha and took Quito.

Bolívar's idealistic dream was to form a united South America. He began by amalgamating Venezuela, Colombia and Ecuador into the independent state of Gran Colombia. This lasted only eight years, with Ecuador becoming fully independent in 1830. That same year a treaty was signed with Peru, establishing a boundary between the two nations.

Liberals Versus Conservatives

Following independence from Spain, Ecuador's history unfolded with the typically Latin American political warfare between liberals and conservatives. Quito emerged as the main center for the church-backed conservatives, while Guayaquil has traditionally been considered liberal and socialist. The rivalry between these groups has frequently escalated to extreme violence: conservative President García Moreno was shot and killed in 1875, and liberal President Eloy Alfaro was killed and burned by a mob in Quito in 1912. The rivalry between the two cities continues on a social level today (see The National Psyche, right). Over time, the military began assuming control, and the 20th century saw more periods of military than civilian rule.

War with Peru

In 1941 war broke out with Peru over border disputes. The boundary was finally redrawn by a conference of foreign-government ministers in the 1942 Protocol of Rio de Janeiro. Ecuador never recognized this border, and minor skirmishes with Peru have occurred because of it – the most serious was the short war in early 1995, when several dozen soldiers on both sides were killed. Finally, after more fighting in 1998, Peru and Ecuador negotiated a settlement in which Peru retained a majority of the land in question.

Recent Political Developments

Ecuador's most recent period of democracy began in 1979, when President Jaime Roldos Aguilera was elected. Over the next two decades, control flip-flopped democratically between liberals and conservatives.

In the 1998 elections, Jamil Mahuad, former mayor of Quito, emerged victorious and was immediately put to the test. The devastating effects of El Niño and the sagging oil market of 1997–98 sent the economy into a tailspin in 1999. The sucre, Ecuador's former currency, depreciated from about 7000 per US dollar to about 25,000 by January 2000. Things were out of control.

When Mahuad declared his plan to dump the national currency in exchange for the US dollar, the country erupted in protest. On January 21, 2000, marches shut down the capital and protesters took over the Ecuadorian congress building, forcing Mahuad to resign. The protesters were led by Antonio Vargas, Coronel Lucio Gutiérrez and former supreme court president Carlos Solórzano, who immediately turned the presidency over to former vice president, Gustavo Noboa. Noboa went ahead with 'dollarization,' and in September 2000, the US dollar became Ecuador's official currency.

Presidential Comings & Goings

President Noboa was succeeded in 2002 by former coup leader Lucio Gutiérrez, whose populist agenda led to his election. But shortly after taking office, Gutiérrez began backing down on his promises of radical reform and implemented IMF-encouraged austerity measures to finance the country's massive debt. In 2004 he also tossed out most of the supreme court, which allowed him to expel his rivals from the court and change the constitution in order to drop corruption charges against his former ally, the popularly despised ex-president, Antonio Bucaram. Not surprisingly, protests erupted in the capital, and in April 2005 the congress finally voted Gutiérrez out, replacing him with vice president Alfredo Palacios. Ousted and exiled, Gutiérrez made a surprise return to Ecuador in 2005, claiming he was the country's rightful leader. He was immediately jailed, but upon his release began campaigning for the presidency once again. However, his political days were over, and in 2006 Rafael Correa, a US-educated economist and former finance minister (under Palacios) was elected president.

THE CULTURE
The National Psyche

Most Ecuadorians have three things in common: pride in the natural beauty of their country, disdain for the seemingly endless crop of politicians who fail to deliver on their promises, and the presence of a relative in another country (some 1.5 million people – more than 10% of the population – have left Ecuador in search of work elsewhere).

From there the psyche blurs, and attitude becomes a matter of altitude. *Serranos* (people from the mountains) and *costeños* (people from the coast) can spend hours telling you what makes them different (ie better) from the other. Following the historic rivalry between conservative *quiteños* (people from Quito) and more liberal *guayaquileños* (people from Guayaquil), *serranos* call people from the coast *monos* (monkeys) and say they're lazy and would rather party than keep their cities clean. *Costeños,* on the other hand, say *serranos* are uptight and elitist and that they pepper their interactions with shallow formalities. Of course, *serranos* still pour down to the coast in droves for holidays and *costeños* speak longingly of the cool evenings of the highlands.

Lifestyle

How an Ecuadorian lives is a matter of geography, ethnicity and class. A poor *campesino* (peasant) family that cultivates the thin volcanic soil of a steep highland plot lives very differently from a coastal fishing family residing in the mangroves of Esmeraldas province, or a family staying in the slums of Guayaquil. An indigenous Saraguro family that tends communally owned cattle in the southern highlands has a dramatically different life to that of an upper-class *quiteño* family, which might have three maids, a new computer and a Mercedes in the garage.

An estimated 40% of Ecuadorians live below the poverty line, and paying for cooking fuel and putting food in the belly is a constant concern for most people. But, as most first-time visitors are astounded to experience, even the poorest Ecuadorians exude an openness, generosity and happiness all too rare in developed countries. Fiestas are celebrated with fervor by everyone, and you'll sometimes roll around in bed, kept awake until dawn by the noise of a nearby birthday bash.

Population

Ecuador has the highest population density of any South American country – about 52 people per sq km. Despite this, the country still feels incredibly wild, mainly because over 30% of the population is crammed into the cities of Quito and Guayaquil, and another 30% resides in Ecuador's other urban areas. Nearly half of the country's people live on the coast (including the Galápagos), while about 45% live in the highlands. The remainder live in the Oriente, where colonization is slowly increasing.

About 65% of the Ecuadorian people are *mestizos*, 25% are indigenous, 7% are Spanish and 3% are black. Other ethnicities account for less than 1%. The majority of the indigenous people speak Quichua and live in the highlands. A few small groups live in the lowlands.

SPORTS

The national sport – no surprise – is *fútbol* (soccer). Major-league games are played every Saturday and Sunday in Quito and Guayaquil, and impromptu games are played everywhere.

The country's best team is Barcelona (from Guayaquil), but avoid shouting that around Quito. Volleyball is also huge. Bullfighting is popular in the highlands; the biggest season is the first week of December in Quito. Finally, the *pelea de gallos* (cockfighting) also has its fan base.

RELIGION

The predominant religion (for 95% of the population) is Roman Catholicism, with a small minority of other churches. Indigenous people tend to blend Catholicism with their own traditional beliefs.

ARTS
Literature

Ecuadorian literature is mostly unknown outside Latin America, but indigenous novelist Jorge Icaza's *Huasipungo,* a naturalistic tale of the miserable conditions on Andean haciendas in the early 20th century, is available in English translation as *The Villagers.* Also worth checking out is *Fire from the Andes: Short Fiction by Women from Bolivia, Ecuador & Peru,* edited by Susan E Benner and Kathy S Leonard.

Cinema

Ecuador's most internationally applauded director is Sebastián Cordero, whose *Ratas, ratones, rateros* (1998) tells the story of a *quiteño* kid whose ex-convict cousin drags him into a nasty life of street crime. The film offers a glimpse into the capital's dark side – one you likely won't get otherwise. Cordero's more recent *Crónicas* (*Chronicles;* 2004), which takes place in a coastal lowland city, revolves around a warped deal between a serial killer and a Miami reporter. On a lighter note, check out the work of filmmaker Tania Hermida. She wrote and directed *Qué tan lejos* (How much further?; 2006), a sweet road movie of two young women on a quiet and unexpected journey of self-discovery in the highlands. It's beautifully shot in the Andean countryside.

Music

Música folklórica (traditional Andean music) has a distinctive, haunting sound that has been popularized in Western culture by songs such as Paul Simon's version of 'El cóndor pasa' ('If I Could'). Its otherworldly quality results from the use of a pentatonic (five-note) scale and pre-Columbian wind and percussion instruments that conjure the wind-swept quality of *páramo* life. It is best heard at a *peña* (folk-music club or performance).

Northwest Ecuador, particularly Esmeraldas province, is famous for its marimba music, historically the sound of Afro-Ecuadorian population. Today it's becoming increasingly difficult to hear live because many Afro-Ecuadorians have swapped it for salsa and other musical forms.

If there's one music you won't escape, it's cumbia, whose rhythm resembles that of a trotting three-legged horse. Originally from Colombia, Ecuadorian cumbia has a more raw (almost amateur), melancholic sound and is dominated by the electronic keyboard. Bus drivers love the stuff, perhaps because it so strangely complements those back-road journeys through the Andes.

When it comes to youth culture, Caribbean-born reggaeton (a blend of Puerto Rican *bomba*, dance hall and hip-hop) is the anthem among urban club-goers. There's also a new crop of rock, metal and alternative sounds emerging from Ecuador. Esto es Eso is a talented US-Ecuadorian duo blending hip-hop, pop, rock and reggae, along with *pasillo* and other traditional sounds. Sudakaya is mostly known for reggae, though they also blend other Afro-Latin rhythms like ska and calypso with bossa nova and samba. Rocola Bacalao is a top performer in the Quito scene playing a mix of ska, punk, merengue and other sounds. Ecuador also has its share of Latin pop artists, with singers like teen-idol Fausto Miño filling the airwaves.

Architecture

Many of Quito's churches were built during the colonial period, and the architects were influenced by the Escuela Quiteña (see Visual Arts, right). In addition, churches often show Moorish influences, particularly in the decorative details of interiors. Known as *mudéjar*, this reflects an architectural style that developed in Spain beginning in the 12th century. The overall architecture of colonial churches is overpoweringly ornamental and almost cloyingly rich – in short, baroque.

Many colonial houses have two stories, with the upper floors bearing ornate balconies. The walls are whitewashed and the roofs are red tile. Quito's Old Town and Cuenca are Unesco World Heritage Sites and both abound with beautifully preserved colonial architecture.

Visual Arts

The colonial religious art found in many churches and museums – especially in Quito – was produced by indigenous artists trained by the Spanish conquistadors. The artists portrayed Spanish religious concepts, yet infused their own indigenous beliefs, giving birth to a unique religious art known as the Escuela Quiteña (Quito school of art). The Quito school died out with independence.

The 19th century is referred to as the Republican period, and its art is characterized by formalism. Favorite subjects included heroes of the revolution, important members of the new republic's high society, and florid landscapes.

The 20th century saw the rise of the indigenist school, whose unifying theme is the oppression of Ecuador's indigenous inhabitants. Important *indigenista* artists include Camilo Egas (1889–1962), Oswaldo Guayasamín (1919–99), Eduardo Kingman (1913–97) and Gonzalo Endara Crow (1936–96). You can (and should!) see the works of these artists in Quito's galleries and museums. The former homes of Egas and Guayasamín, also in Quito, are now museums featuring their respective works.

ENVIRONMENT

According to ecologists, Ecuador has the highest deforestation rate and the worst environmental record in South America. In the highlands, almost all of the natural forest cover has disappeared, and only a few pockets remain, mainly in privately administered nature reserves. Along the coast, once plentiful mangrove forests have all but vanished to make way for artificial shrimp ponds.

About 95% of the forests of the western slopes and lowlands have become agricultural land, mostly banana plantations. These forests were host to more species than almost anywhere on the planet, and many of them are (or were) endemic. Scientists suggest that countless species have likely become extinct even before they have been identified, and in recent years a small preservation movement has taken root.

Although much of the rainforest in the Ecuadorian Amazon remains standing, it is being seriously threatened by fragmentation. Since the discovery of oil, roads have been laid, colonists have followed and the destruction of the forest has increased exponentially. The main drives behind the destruction are logging, cattle ranching, and oil and mineral extraction.

Clearly, these problems are linked tightly with Ecuador's economy. Oil, minerals, bananas and shrimp are some of the nation's top exports. Industry advocates claim the cost of abandoning these revenue sources is too high for a small developing country to shoulder. Environmentalists, on the other hand, claim the government has given too much free rein to big industry, which has resulted in at times catastrophic damages to the local ecology.

The rainforest's indigenous inhabitants – who depend on the rivers for drinking water and food – are also dramatically affected. Oil residues, oil treatment chemicals, erosion and fertilizers all contaminate the rivers, killing fish and rendering formerly potable water toxic. The heavy toll exacted on human life has been documented: in 2008, a team of engineers, doctors and biologists submitted a court-ordered report in conjunction with the ongoing lawsuit against Chevron (which acquired Texaco in 2001), who allegedly dumped billions of gallons of toxic waste into the Amazon. The report concluded that the toxic waste had caused 2091 cases of cancer among residents and led to 1401 deaths from 1985 to 1998. *Crude*, a documentary directed by acclaimed filmmaker Joe Berlinger, provides a fascinating portrait of this case; it premiered in late 2009.

The Land

Despite its diminutive size, Ecuador has some of the world's most varied geography. The country can be divided into three regions: the Andes form the backbone of Ecuador; the coastal lowlands lie west of the mountains; and the Oriente, to the east, comprises the jungles of the upper Amazon Basin. In only 200km as the condor flies, you can climb from the coast to snowcaps, over 6km above sea level, and then descend to the jungle on the country's eastern side. The Galápagos Islands lie on the equator, 1000km west of Ecuador's coast, and constitute one of the country's 21 provinces.

Wildlife

Ecuador is one of the most species-rich countries on the globe, deemed a 'megadiversity hot spot' by ecologists. The country has more than 20,000 plant species, with new ones discovered every year. In comparison, there are only 17,000 plant species on the entire North American continent. The tropics, in general, harbor many more species than temperate regions do, but another reason for Ecuador's biodiversity is simply that the country holds a great number of habitat types. Obviously, the Andes will support very different species than the tropical rainforests, and when intermediate biomes and the coastal areas are included, the result is a wealth of different ecosystems, a riot of life that draws nature lovers from the world over.

Bird-watchers flock to Ecuador for the great number of bird species recorded here – some 1600, or about twice the number found in any one of the continents of North America, Europe or Australia. But Ecuador isn't just for the birds: some 300 mammal species have been recorded, from monkeys in the Amazon to the rare Andean spectacled bears in the highlands.

National Parks

Ecuador has over 30 government-protected parks and reserves (of which nine carry the title of 'national park'), as well as numerous privately administered nature reserves. A total of 18% of the country lies within protected areas. Ecuador's first *parque nacional* (national park) was the Galápagos, formed in 1959. Scattered across mainland Ecuador are eight other national parks, including the most visited (from north to south):

Parque Nacional Cotopaxi (p623) The towering ice-capped cone of Volcán Cotopaxi makes for spectacular year-round hiking and mountaineering.

Parque Nacional Yasuní (p646) Amazon rainforest, big rivers and caiman-filled lagoons, plus monkeys, birds, sloths and more, mean year-round forest fun.

Parque Nacional Machalilla (p658) Coastal dry forest, beaches and islands are home to whales, seabirds, monkeys and reptiles. Hiking opportunities and beaches are superb.

Parque Nacional Sangay (p627) Volcanoes, *páramo* and cloud forest harbor spectacled bears, tapirs, pumas and ocelots, and offer hiking, climbing and wildlife-watching year-round.

Parque Nacional Cajas (p639) Shimmering lakes and moorlike *páramo* make this highland park an excellent adventure from Cuenca.

Parque Nacional Podocarpus (p642) From cloud forest to rainforest, this epic southern park is best explored from Loja, Zamora or Vilcabamba.

Many parks are inhabited by native peoples who were living in the area long before it achieved park status. In the case of the Oriente parks, indigenous hunting practices (which have a greater impact as outside interests diminish their original territories and resources) have met with concern from those seeking to protect the park. The issue of how to protect these areas from interests such as oil, timber and mining industries, while recognizing the rights of indigenous people, continues to be extremely tricky.

National park entrance fees vary. On the mainland, most highland parks charge US$10 and most lowland parks US$20 per visitor, but both fees are valid for a week. In the Galápagos Islands, the park fee is US$100 – though it may double in coming years.

TRANSPORTATION

GETTING THERE & AWAY
Air
The main international airports are in Guayaquil (p661) and Quito (p600). Direct flights go to Bogotá (Colombia), Bonaire (Netherlands Antilles), Buenos Aires (Argentina), Caracas (Venezuela), Lima (Peru), Panama City (Panama), San José (Costa Rica) and Santiago (Chile). There are also several weekly flights going to Cali (Colombia) from both Tulcán (in the northern highlands of Ecuador) and Esmeraldas (on the north coast). There are no direct flights between Quito or Guayaquil and Brazil; the best deals to Rio or São Paulo are usually via Lima.

Boat
For information on boat travel between Nuevo Rocafuerte (Ecuador) and Iquitos (Peru), see boxed text, p646.

DEPARTURE TAX

All passengers flying out of Ecuador on international flights must pay a departure tax of US$41 from Quito and US$28 from Guayaquil. This is not included in ticket prices and must be paid in cash at the airport. Short cross-border hops, such as Tulcán–Cali (Colombia), are not taxed.

Bus
International bus tickets sold in Quito often require a change of bus at the border. It's usually cheaper and just as convenient to buy a ticket to the border and another ticket in the next country. The exceptions are the international buses from Loja (p640) to Piura, Peru (via Macará), and from Guayaquil (p661) to Peru (via Huaquillas); on these, you don't have to change buses, and the immigration officials usually board the bus to take care of your paperwork. These are the primary routes between Ecuador and Peru. Zumba, south of Vilcabamba (p642), is an alternative route to/from Peru in a scenic and less used location. The main bus route between Colombia and Ecuador is via Tulcán (see boxed text, p622). Other border crossings between Colombia and Ecuador are not recommended owing to safety concerns.

GETTING AROUND
You can usually get anywhere quickly and easily. Bus is the most common mode of transportation, followed by plane. Buses can take you from the Colombian border to Peru's border in 18 hours. Boats are used in the northern coastal mangroves and in the Oriente.

Whatever form of transportation you choose, always carry your passport with you, both to board planes and to proffer during document checks on the road. People without documents may be arrested. If your passport is in order, these procedures are cursory. If you're traveling anywhere near the borders or in the Oriente, expect more frequent passport checks.

Air
With the exception of flying to the Galápagos (see p670 for details), most internal flights are relatively cheap. One-way flights average US$50 to US$75. Almost all flights originate or terminate in Quito or Guayaquil. Some domestic flights have marvelous views of the snowcapped Andes – when flying from Quito to Guayaquil, sit on the left.

Ecuador's major domestic airline is **TAME** (www.tame.com.ec). **Icaro** (www.icaro.aero) is the second-biggest, with fewer flights but newer planes. Between these two airlines, you can fly from Quito to Guayaquil, Coca, Cuenca, Esmeraldas, Lago Agrio, Loja, Macas, Machala, Manta, Tulcán and the Galápagos. From Guayaquil you can fly to Quito, Coca,

Cuenca, Loja, Machala and the Galápagos. There are no Sunday flights to the Oriente. **AeroGal** (www.aerogal.com.ec) flies mostly to the Galápagos. **LANEcuador** (www.lan.com) flies from Guayaquil to Quito and Cuenca. **VIP** (www .vipec.com) connects Quito with Lago Agrio and Coca. **Saereo** (www.saereo.com) flies from Quito to Macahala and Macas. It also has a Machala–Guayaquil run.

If you can't get a ticket for a particular flight (especially out of small towns), go to the airport early and get on the waiting list in the hope of a cancellation.

Boat

Motorized dugout canoes are the only transportation available in some roadless areas. Regularly scheduled boats are affordable, although not as cheap as a bus for a similar distance. Hiring your own boat and skipper is possible but extremely expensive. The northern coast (near San Lorenzo and Borbón) and the lower Río Napo from Coca to Peru are the places you'll most likely travel to by boat (if you get out that far).

Bus

Buses are the lifeblood of Ecuador and the easiest way to get around. Most towns have a *terminal terrestre* (central bus terminal) for long-distance buses, although in some towns buses leave from various places. To get your choice of seat, buy tickets in advance from the terminal. During holiday weekends, buses can be booked up for several days in advance.

If you're traveling lightly, keep your luggage with you inside the bus. Otherwise, heave it onto the roof or stuff it into the luggage compartment and try to keep an eye on it.

Long-distance buses rarely have toilets, but they usually stop for 20-minute meal and bladder-relief breaks at fairly appropriate times. If not, drivers will stop to let you fertilize the roadside.

Local buses are usually slow and crowded, but cheap. You can get around most towns for about US25¢. Local buses also often go out to nearby villages (a great way to explore an area).

Car & Motorcycle

Few people rent cars in Ecuador, mainly because public transportation makes getting around so easy. Ecuador's automobile association is **Aneta** (☎ 02-250-4961; www.aneta.org.ec),

which offers 24-hour roadside assistance to its members. It offers some services to members of foreign automobile clubs, including Canadian and US AAA members.

Hitchhiking

Hitchhiking is possible, but not very practical in Ecuador. Public transportation is relatively cheap and trucks are used as public transportation in remote areas, so trying to hitch a free ride isn't easy. If the driver is stopping to drop off and pick up other passengers, assume that payment will be expected. If you're the only passenger, the driver may have picked you up just to talk to a foreigner.

Taxi

Taxis are relatively cheap. Bargain the fare beforehand though, or you're likely to be overcharged. A long ride in a large city (Quito or Guayaquil) shouldn't go over US$5, and short hops in small towns usually cost about US$1. Meters are obligatory in Quito (where the minimal fare is US$1) but rarely seen elsewhere. On weekends and at night, fares are always about 25% to 50% higher. A full-day taxi hire should cost around US$50.

Train

Little remains of Ecuador's railways after the damage to lines due to the 1982–83 El Niño rains. Only the sections with tourist appeal have received enough funding to reopen. A train runs three times a week between Riobamba and Sibambe, which includes the hair-raising Nariz del Diablo (Devil's Nose), the country's railway pride and joy. The Ibarra–San Lorenzo line, which used to link the highlands with the coast, is on its deathbed; *autoferros* (buses mounted on railway chassis) only make it a fraction of the way to San Lorenzo. There's also the weekend Quito–Cotopaxi route, which stops at Area de Recreación El Boliche, adjacent to Parque Nacional Cotopaxi. At research time, this line was closed indefinitely for repairs.

Truck

In remote areas, *camiones* (trucks) and *camionetas* (pickup trucks) often double as buses. If the weather is OK, you get fabulous views; if not, you have to crouch underneath a dark tarpaulin and suck dust. Pickups can be hired to get to remote places such as climbers' refuges.

ECUADOR

QUITO

☎ 02 / pop 1.5 million

High in the Andes amid dramatic mist-covered peaks, Quito (elevation 2850m) is a beautifully set city, packed with historical monuments and architectural treasures. The jewel of Quito is its historic center, or 'Old Town,' a Unesco World Heritage Site, sprinkled with 17th-century facades, picturesque plazas and magnificent churches that blend Spanish, Moorish and indigenous elements.

Just north of there, Quito's 'New Town' is a different world entirely. For travelers, its heart is the Mariscal Sucre, a condensed area of guesthouses, travel agencies, ethnic and international eateries and a vibrant nightlife scene. This is indeed 'gringolandia' as some locals describe the area, though plenty of *quiteños* frequent the bars and restaurants of Mariscal.

Not surprisingly, the capital is a popular place to enroll in a Spanish school and stay for a while – perhaps far longer than planned, as more than a few captivated expats can attest.

ORIENTATION

Quito is Ecuador's second-largest city, after Guayaquil. It can be divided into three segments. In the center is the colonial Old Town. Modern Quito – the New Town – is in the north, with major businesses, airline offices, embassies and shopping centers. The New Town also contains the airport, middle- and upper-class homes and the Mariscal Sucre neighborhood (the travelers' ghetto known simply as El Mariscal). Av Amazonas, with its banks, hotels, crafts stores, cafes and corporate business offices, is the New Town's best-known street, although Av 10 de Agosto and Av 6 de Diciembre are the most important thoroughfares. The south comprises mostly working-class housing areas.

The **Instituto Geográfico Militar** (IGM; Map pp602-3; ☎ 254-5090, 222-9075/6; ☺ map sales room 8am-4pm Mon-Thu, 7am-12:30pm Fri), on top of steep Paz y Miño, publishes and sells Ecuador's best topographical maps. You'll need to leave your passport at the gate.

INFORMATION
Bookstores
Confederate Books (Map pp602-3; Calama 410) Ecuador's largest selection of secondhand books in English and other languages.

Libri Mundi (Map pp602-3; Mera 851) Quito's best bookstore; excellent selection of books in Spanish, English, German and French.
Libro Express (Map pp602-3; cnr Av Amazonas 816 & Veintimilla) Good for guidebooks, coffee-table books and magazines.

Emergency
Fire department (☎ 102)
General emergency (☎ 911)
Police (☎ 101)
Red Cross ambulance (☎ 131, 258-0598)

Internet Access
While the Mariscal area is bursting with cyber-cafes, they're trickier to find in the Old Town. All charge US70¢ to US$1.20 per hour.
Friends Web Café (Map pp602-3; Calama E6-19)
La Sala (Map pp602-3; cnr Calama & Reina Victoria)
Papaya Net New Town (Map pp602-3; cnr Calama 469 & Mera); Old Town (Map p605; Chile Oe4-56, Pasaje Arzobispal)

Internet Resources
Corporación Metropolitana de Turismo (www.quito.com.ec)
Gay Guide to Quito (http://gayquitoec.tripod.com)

Laundry
The following laundries will wash, dry and fold your clothes within 24 hours. All charge around US$1 per kilo.
Opera de Jabón (Map pp602-3; Pinto 325 near Reina Victoria)
Sun City Laundry (Map pp602-3; cnr Mera & Foch)
Wash & Go (Map pp602-3; Pinto 340)

Medical Services
Clínica de la Mujer (off Map pp602-3; ☎ 245-8000; cnr Av Amazonas 4826 & Gaspar de Villarroel) Private clinic specializing in women's health.
Clínica Pichincha (Map pp602-3; ☎ 256-2408, 256-2296; cnr Veintimilla 1259 & Páez) In the New Town; does lab analysis for parasites, dysentery etc.
Hospital Metropolitano (off Map pp602-3; ☎ 226-1520; cnr Mariana de Jesús & Av Occidental) Better, but pricier than Voz Andes.
Hospital Voz Andes (off Map pp602-3; ☎ 226-2142; Villalengua 267 near Avs América & 10 de Agosto) American-run hospital with outpatient and emergency rooms. Fees are low.

Money
There are several banks and *casas de cambio* (currency-exchange bureaus) in the New

Town along Av Amazonas between Av Patria and Orellana, and dozens of banks throughout town. Banks listed here have ATMs.

Banco de Guayaquil Av Amazonas (Map pp602-3; cnr Av Amazonas N22-147 & Veintimilla); Colón (Map pp602-3; cnr Av Cristóbal Colón & Reina Victoria)

Banco del Pacífico New Town (Map pp602-3; cnr Av 12 de Octubre & Cordero); Old Town (Map p605; cnr Guayaquil & Chile)

Banco del Pichincha (Map p605; cnr Guayaquil & Manabí)

Producambios (Av Amazonas 350; ⊗ 8:30am-6pm Mon-Fri, 9am-2pm Sat)

Western Union Av de la República (Map pp602-3; Av de la República 433); Colón (Map pp602-3; Av Cristóbal Colón 1333)

Post

Central post office (Map p605; Espejo 935)

Mariscal Sucre post office (Map pp602-3; cnr Av Cristóbal Colón & Reina Victoria)

Telephone

For international calls, it's much cheaper to call from an internet cafe (opposite).

Andinatel Mariscal offices Mera (Map pp602-3; cnr Mera 741 & Baquedano); Reina Victoria (Map pp602-3; Reina Victoria near Calama) In the Mariscal area.

Tourist Information

South American Explorers (SAE; Map pp602-3; ☎ 222-5228; www.saexplorers.org; cnr Washington 311 & Leonidas Plaza Gutiérrez; ⊗ 9:30am-5pm Mon-Wed & Fri, 9:30am-6pm Thu, 9:30am-noon Sat) For more information on this excellent travelers' organization, see p996.

Tourist offices (Corporación Metropolitana de Turismo; www.quito.com.ec); airport (☎ 330-0163); Mariscal (Map pp602-3; ☎ 255-1566; cnr Cordero & Reina Victoria; ⊗ 9am-5pm Mon-Fri); Old Town (Map p605; ☎ 228-1904; cnr Venezuela & Espejo, Plaza Grande; ⊗ 9am-8pm Mon-Sat, 10am-6pm Sun)

DANGERS & ANNOYANCES

Quito has its share of robberies and petty crime, and you should take precautions to avoid becoming a target. Despite the animated streets of the Mariscal area, it remains a dangerous neighborhood after dark, and muggings are all too common. It's wise to take a taxi after about 9pm – even if you have only a few blocks to walk. Sundays, when no one else is around, is a dodgy time to wander the Mariscal.

With the restoration of the Old Town and increased police presence there, the historic center is safe until 10pm or so. Don't climb up El Panecillo hill; take a taxi instead (there are plenty up top for the return trip). As usual, pickpockets work crowded buses (especially the Trole and Ecovía lines), the bus terminal and markets. If you are robbed, obtain a police report within 48 hours from the **police station** (New Town Map pp602-3; cnr Reina Victoria & Roca; Old Town Map p605; cnr Mideros & Cuenca).

If you are arriving from sea level, Quito's 2850m elevation might make you somewhat breathless and give you headaches or cotton mouth. These symptoms of *soroche* (altitude sickness) usually disappear after a day or two. To minimize symptoms, take it easy upon arrival, drink plenty of water and lay off the smokes and alcohol.

SIGHTS

If you're short on time, head straight for the beautifully restored colonial center of the Old Town.

Old Town

Built centuries ago by indigenous artisans and laborers, Quito's churches, convents, chapels and monasteries are cast in legend and steeped in history. It's a bustling area, full of yelling street vendors, ambling pedestrians, tooting taxis, belching buses, and whistle-blowing policemen trying to direct traffic in the narrow, congested one-way streets. The Old Town is closed to cars on Sunday from 8am to 4pm, which is a wonderful time to explore it.

Churches are open every day (usually until 6pm) but are crowded with worshippers on Sunday. They regularly close between 1pm and 3pm for lunch.

PLAZA GRANDE

Quito's small, exquisitely restored central plaza (also known as Plaza de la Independencia) is the perfect place to start exploring the Old Town. Its benches are great for soaking up the Andean morning sun as shoeshine boys and Polaroid photographers peddle their services around the park. The plaza is flanked by several important buildings. The low white building on the northwestern side is the **Palacio del Gobierno** (Presidential Palace; Map p605; cnr García Moreno & Chile; ⊗ guided tours 10am, 11:30am, 1pm, 2:30pm & 4pm). Visitors can enter by (free) guided tours. The president does indeed carry out business here, so sightseeing is limited to rooms not currently in use. On Monday, the changing of the guards takes place on the plaza at 11am.

ECUADOR

QUITO – NEW TOWN

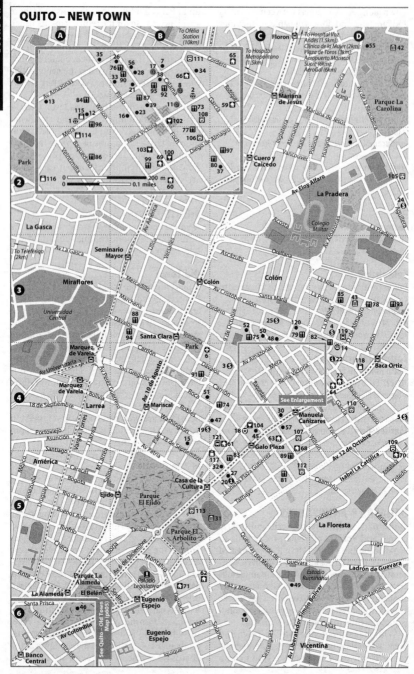

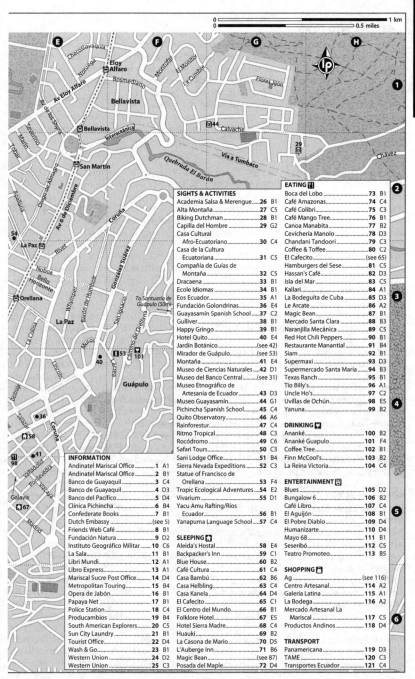

0 ____ 1 km
0 ____ 0.5 miles

SIGHTS & ACTIVITIES
Academia Salsa & Merengue	**26**	B1
Alta Montaña	**27**	C5
Biking Dutchman	**28**	B1
Capilla del Hombre	**29**	G2
Casa Cultural Afro-Ecuatoriano	**30**	C4
Casa de la Cultura Ecuatoriana	**31**	C5
Compañía de Guías de Montaña	**32**	C3
Dracaena	**33**	B1
Ecole Idiomas	**34**	B1
Eos Ecuador	**35**	A1
Fundación Golondrinas	**36**	E4
Guayasamín Spanish School	**37**	C2
Gulliver	**38**	B1
Happy Gringo	**39**	B1
Hotel Quito	**40**	B1
Jardín Botánico	(see 42)	
Mirador de Guápulo	(see 53)	
Montaña	**41**	E4
Museo de Ciencias Naturales	**42**	D1
Museo del Banco Central	(see 31)	
Museo Etnográfico de Artesanía de Ecuador	**43**	D3
Museo Guayasamín	**44**	G1
Pichincha Spanish School	**45**	C4
Quito Observatory	**46**	A6
Rainforestur	**47**	C4
Ritmo Tropical	**48**	C3
Rocódromo	**49**	C6
Safari Tours	**50**	B4
Sani Lodge Office	**51**	B4
Sierra Nevada Expeditions	**52**	C3
Statue of Francisco de Orellana	**53**	F4
Tropic Ecological Adventures	**54**	E2
Vivarium	**55**	D1
Yacu Amu Rafting/Ríos Ecuador	**56**	B1
Yanapuma Language School	**57**	C4

SLEEPING
Aleida's Hostal	**58**	B1
Backpacker's Inn	**59**	C1
Blue House	**60**	B2
Café Cultura	**61**	C4
Casa Bambú	**62**	B4
Casa Helbling	**63**	C4
Casa Kanela	**64**	D4
El Cafecito	**65**	C1
El Centro del Mundo	**66**	B1
Folklore Hotel	**67**	B5
Hotel Sierra Madre	**68**	C4
Huauki	**69**	B2
La Casona de Mario	**70**	D5
L'Auberge Inn	**71**	B6
Magic Bean	(see 87)	
Posada del Maple	**72**	D4

EATING
Boca del Lobo	**73**	B1
Café Amazonas	**74**	C4
Café Colibrí	**75**	C3
Café Mango Tree	**76**	B1
Canoa Manabita	**77**	B2
Cevichería Manolo	**78**	D3
Chandani Tandoori	**79**	C3
Coffee & Toffee	**80**	C2
El Cafecito	(see 65)	
Hamburgers del Sese	**81**	C5
Hassan's Café	**82**	D3
Isla del Mar	**83**	C5
Kallari	**84**	A1
La Bodeguita de Cuba	**85**	D3
Le Arcate	**86**	A2
Magic Bean	**87**	B1
Mercado Santa Clara	**88**	B3
Naranjilla Mecánica	**89**	C5
Red Hot Chili Peppers	**90**	B1
Restaurante Manantial	**91**	B4
Siam	**92**	B1
Supermaxi	**93**	D3
Supermercado Santa María	**94**	B3
Texas Ranch	**95**	B1
Tio Billy's	**96**	A1
Uncle Ho's	**97**	C2
Uvillas de Ochún	**98**	E5
Yanuna	**99**	B2

DRINKING
Ananké	**100**	B2
Ananké Guapulo	**101**	F4
Coffee Tree	**102**	B2
Finn McCool's	**103**	B2
La Reina Victoria	**104**	C4

ENTERTAINMENT
Blues	**105**	D2
Bungalow 6	**106**	B2
Café Libro	**107**	C4
El Aguijón	**108**	B1
El Pobre Diablo	**109**	D4
Humanizarte	**110**	D4
Mayo 68	**111**	B1
Seseribó	**112**	C5
Teatro Promoteo	**113**	B5

SHOPPING
Ag	(see 116)	
Centro Artesanal	**114**	A2
Galería Latina	**115**	A1
La Bodega	**116**	A1
Mercado Artesanal La Mariscal	**117**	C5
Productos Andinos	**118**	D4

TRANSPORT
Panamericana	**119**	D3
TAME	**120**	C3
Transportes Ecuador	**121**	C4

INFORMATION
Andinatel Mariscal Office	**1**	A1
Andinatel Mariscal Office	**2**	B1
Banco de Guayaquil	**3**	C4
Banco de Guayaquil	**4**	D3
Banco del Pacífico	**5**	D4
Clínica Pichincha	**6**	B4
Confederate Books	**7**	B1
Dutch Embassy	(see 5)	
Friends Web Café	**8**	B1
Fundación Natura	**9**	D2
Instituto Geográfico Militar	**10**	C6
La Sala	**11**	B1
Libri Mundi	**12**	A1
Libro Express	**13**	A1
Mariscal Sucre Post Office	**14**	D4
Metropolitan Touring	**15**	B4
Opera de Jabón	**16**	B1
Papaya Net	**17**	B1
Police Station	**18**	C4
Producambios	**19**	B4
South American Explorers	**20**	C5
Sun City Laundry	**21**	B1
Tourist Office	**22**	D4
Wash & Go	**23**	B1
Western Union	**24**	D2
Western Union	**25**	C3

GETTING INTO TOWN

The current airport (a new one was under construction at research time) is on Av Amazonas, about 7km north of the Mariscal Sucre neighborhood (where most of the budget hotels are). As you walk out of the airport, south is to your left. Cross Av Amazonas and flag a south-bound bus. It costs US30¢ to get from here to the Mariscal. From there, you can catch a bus or the Trole (electricity-powered bus) to the Old Town, about 2km further south. A taxi from the airport to the Mariscal should cost no more than US$5, and about US$6 to the Old Town.

The bus terminal (Terminal Terrestre Cumandá) is a few blocks south of Plaza Santo Domingo in the Old Town. Take a cab into town if you arrive at night. Avoid bus travel if you're loaded with luggage.

Quito's **cathedral** (Map p605; cnr Espejo & García Moreno; admission US$1.50; ☎ 9:30am-4pm Mon-Sat) has some fascinating religious works from artists of the Quito School (see also p596). Don't miss the painting of the Last Supper, with Christ and disciples lingering over a feast of *cuy* (whole-roasted guinea pig), *chicha* (corn drink) and *humitas* (sweet-corn tamales). Mariscal Sucre, the leading figure of Quito's independence, is buried inside. The **Palacio Arzobispal** (Archbishop's Palace; Map p605; Chile btwn García Moreno & Venezuela), now a colonnaded row of small shops and several good restaurants, stands on the plaza's northeastern side.

Just off the plaza, the **Centro Cultural Metropolitano** (Map p605; ☎ 295-0272, 258-4363; www.centrocultural-quito.com; cnr García Moreno & Espejo; ☒ 9am-5pm, patio until 7:30pm Tue-Sun) houses several temporary art exhibits, an intriguing museum, two rooftop terraces and a pleasant cafe on the interior patio. Get a glimpse of Quito's early colonial history (and a look at some rather lifelike wax figures) in the on-site **Museo Alberto Mena Caamaño** (Map p605; admission US$1.50; ☒ 9am-4:30pm Tue-Sun).

NORTH OF PLAZA GRANDE

The **Museo Camilo Egas** (Map p605; ☎ 257-2012; cnr Venezuela 1302 & Esmeraldas; admission US50¢; ☒ 9:30am-5pm Tue-Fri, 10am-4pm Sat & Sun) contains a small but iconic collection of works by the late Camilo Egas, one of the country's foremost indigenous painters.

High on a hill in the northeastern part of the Old Town stands the Gothic **Basílica del Voto Nacional** (Map p605; ☎ 258-3891; cnr Venezuela & Carchi; admission US$2; ☒ 9am-5pm), built over several decades beginning in 1926. The highlight is the basilica's towers, which you can climb to the top of if you have the nerve; the ascent requires crossing a rickety wooden plank inside the main roof and climbing steep stairs and ladders to the top.

PLAZA & MONASTERIO DE SAN FRANCISCO

With its massive stark-white towers and a mountainous backdrop of Volcán Pichincha, the **Monasterio de San Francisco** (Map p605; cnr Cuenca & Sucre; ☒ 7-11am daily, 3-6pm Mon-Thu) is one of Quito's most marvelous sights – both inside and out. It's the city's largest colonial structure and its oldest church (built from 1534 to 1604).

Although much of the church has been rebuilt because of earthquake damage, some of it is original. The **Capilla del Señor Jesús del Gran Poder**, to the right of the main altar, has original tilework, and the **main altar** itself is a spectacular example of baroque carving. To the right of the church's main entrance is the **Museo Franciscano** (Map p605; ☎ 295-2911; www.museo franciscano.com; admission US$2; ☒ 9am-1pm & 2-6pm Mon-Sat, 9am-noon Sun), which contains some of the church's finest artwork. The admission fee includes a guided tour, available in English or Spanish. Good guides will point out *mudéjar* representations of the eight planets revolving around the sun in the ceiling, and will explain how the light shines through the rear window during the solstices, lighting up the main altar. Both are examples of indigenous influence on Christian architecture.

CALLES GARCÍA MORENO & SUCRE

Beside the cathedral on García Moreno stands the 17th-century **Iglesia del Sagrario** (Map p605; García Moreno; ☒ 6am-noon & 3-6pm). Around the corner on Sucre is Ecuador's most ornate church, **La Compañía de Jesús** (Map p605; Sucre near García Moreno; admission US$2; ☒ 9:30am-5:30pm Mon-Fri, 9:30am-4:30pm Sat). The marvelously gilded Jesuit church was begun in 1605 and not completed for another 160 years. Free

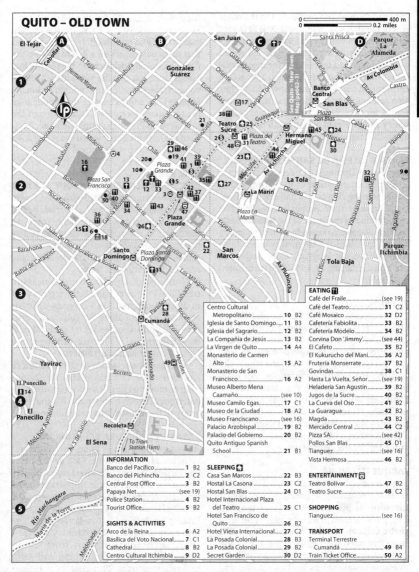

QUITO – OLD TOWN

0 ____ 400 m
0 ____ 0.2 miles

guided tours in English or Spanish highlight the church's unique features, including its Moorish elements, perfect symmetry (right down to the trompe l'oeil staircase at the rear), symbolic elements (bright red walls, a reminder of Christ's blood), and its syncretism (Ecuadorian plants and indigenous faces hidden along the pillars). *Quiteños* proudly

call it the most beautiful church in the whole country, and it's easy to see why.

Further south, the 18th-century arch, **Arco de la Reina** (Map p605; cnr García Moreno & Rocafuerte), spans García Moreno. On one side, the **Museo de la Ciudad** (Map p605; 228-3882; cnr García Moreno & Rocafuerte; admission US$2; 9:30am-5:30pm Tue-Sun) is an interesting museum depicting daily life in Quito through the centuries. On the other side of the arch stands the **Monasterio de Carmen Alto** (Map p605; cnr García Moreno & Rocafuerte), another fully functioning convent, where cloistered nuns produce and sell some of the most traditional sweets in the city. Through a revolving contraption that keeps the nuns hidden, they also sell traditional baked goods, aromatic waters for nerves and insomnia, bee pollen, honey and bottles of full-strength *mistela* (an anise-flavored liqueur).

PLAZA & IGLESIA DE SANTO DOMINGO

Plaza Santo Domingo is a regular haunt for street performers, and crowds fill the plaza to watch pouting clowns and half-cocked magicians do their stuff. A fabulous Gothic-like altar dominates the inside of the **Iglesia de Santo Domingo** (Map p605; cnr Flores & Rocafuerte; ☺ 7am-1pm & 4:30-7:30pm), and the original wooden floor was replaced not long ago. Construction of the church began in 1581 and continued until 1650.

EL PANECILLO

The small, ever-visible hill to the south of the Old Town is called **El Panecillo** (Little Bread Loaf), a major landmark in Quito. It's topped by a huge statue of **La Virgen de Quito** (Map p605) and offers marvelous views of the whole city and the surrounding volcanoes. Go early in the morning, before the clouds roll in. Definitely don't climb the stairs at the end of García Moreno on the way to the statue, though – they're unsafe. A taxi from the Old Town costs about US$4, and you can hail one at the top for the return trip.

PARQUE ITCHIMBIA

High on a hill east of the Old Town, this recently resurrected green space boasts magnificent 360-degree views of the city. The park's centerpiece, the glass-and-iron **Centro Cultural Itchimbia** (Map p605; ☎ 295-0272; Parque Itchimbia) hosts regular art exhibits and cultural events. The park has an indoor-outdoor restaurant as well as cycling and walking paths. Buses signed 'Pintado' go here from the Centro Histórico, or you can walk up (east on) Elizalde, from where signed stairways lead to the park.

TelefériQo

For spectacular views over Quito's mountainous landscape, hop aboard the **telefériQo** (off Map pp602-3; ☎ 250-0900; Av Occidental near Av La Gasca; adult/express lane US$4/7; ☺ 9:45am-9pm Mon-Thu, 9am-midnight Fri & Sat), a multimillion-dollar sky tram that takes passengers on a 2.5km ride up the flanks of Volcán Pichincha to the top of Cruz Loma. Once you're at the top (a mere 4100m), you can hike to the summit of Rucu Pichincha (4680m), an approximately three-hour hike for fit walkers (see p608). Don't attempt the hike to Rucu Pichincha until you've acclimatized in Quito for a couple of days. A taxi costs about US$3 from the Mariscal.

New Town

PARQUE LA ALAMEDA & PARQUE EL EJIDO

From the northeastern edge of the Old Town, the long, triangular Parque La Alameda begins its grassy crawl toward the New Town. In the center of the park is the **Quito Observatory** (Map pp602-3; 257-0765), the oldest European observatory on the continent. It was undergoing restoration at research time.

Northeast of La Alameda, the pleasant, tree-filled Parque El Ejido is the biggest park in downtown Quito. On weekends, open-air **art shows** are held along Av Patria, and artisans and crafts vendors set up stalls all over the northern side of the park, turning it into Quito's largest **handicrafts market**.

A solitary stone archway at the northern end of Parque El Ejido marks the beginning of modern Quito's showpiece street, Av Amazonas. North of the park, it's the main artery of the **Mariscal Sucre** neighborhood.

CASA DE LA CULTURA ECUATORIANA

Across from Parque El Ejido, the landmark, circular glass building, **Casa de la Cultura Ecuatoriana** (Map pp602-3; www.cce.org.ec), houses one of the country's most important museums, the **Museo del Banco Central** (Map pp602-3; ☎ 222-3259; cnr Avs Patria & 12 de Octubre; admission US$2; ☺ 9am-5pm Tue-Fri, 10am-4pm Sat & Sun). The museum showcases the country's largest collection of Ecuadorian art, from beautifully displayed pre-Columbian and colonial religious art to 20th-century paintings and sculpture.

PARQUE LA CAROLINA

North of the Mariscal lies the giant Parque La Carolina. On weekends it fills with families who come for paddleboats, soccer and volleyball games, and strolls along the walking paths.

The park has several museums including the **Jardín Botánico** (Map pp602-3; ☎ 246-3197; admission US$3.50; 9am-5pm), home to 300 plant and tree species from around Ecuador and a lush *orquideario* (orchid greenhouse) with nearly 1000 orchid species. Next door, the curious **Museo de Ciencias Naturales** (Map pp602-3; ☎ 244-9824; Rumipamba s/n, Parque La Carolina; admission US$2; 8:30am-1pm & 1:45-4:30pm Mon-Fri) has thousands of dead insects and arachnids on display – a good way to rile your nerves before a trip to the Oriente.

Nearby, you can provide further fodder for your jungle fears with a visit to the **Vivarium** (Map pp602-3; ☎ 227-1799; www.vivarium.org.ec; cnr Av Amazonas 3008 & Rumipamba; admission US$2.50; 9:30am-5:30pm Tue-Sun), home to 87 live reptiles and amphibians, including poisonous snakes, boa constrictors, iguanas, turtles, frogs and tortoises. It's a herpetological research and education center, and the staff periodically give up-close demonstrations with one of the snakes.

MUSEO GUAYASAMÍN & CAPILLA DEL HOMBRE

In the former home of the world-famous indigenous painter Oswaldo Guayasamín (1919–99), the **Museo Guayasamín** (Map pp602-3; (☎ 246-5265; Bosmediano 543; admission US$2; 10am-5pm Mon-Fri) houses the largest collection of his works. Guayasamín was also an avid collector, and the museum displays his outstanding collection of over 4500 pre-Columbian ceramic, bone and metal pieces from throughout Ecuador.

A few blocks away stands Guayasamín's astounding **Capilla del Hombre** (Chapel of Man; Map pp602-3; ☎ 244-6455; www.guayasamin.com; cnr Calvache & Chávez; admission US$3, with purchase of entry to Museo Guayasamín US$2; 10am-5pm Tue-Sun). The fruit of Guayasamín's greatest vision, this giant monument-cum-museum is a tribute to humankind, to the suffering of Latin America's indigenous poor, and to the undying hope for a better world. It's a moving place, and the tours (available in English, French and Spanish and included in the price) are highly recommended.

The museum and chapel are located in the neighborhood of Bellavista, northeast of downtown. You can walk uphill, or take a bus along Av 6 de Diciembre to Av Eloy Alfaro and then a Bellavista bus up the hill. A taxi costs about US$2.

MUSEO ETNOGRÁFICO DE ARTESANÍA DE ECUADOR

Just north of the Mariscal, this small but worthwhile **ethnographic museum** (☎ 223-0609; www.sinchisacha.org; cnr Reina Victoria N26-166 & La Niña; admission US$3; 9:30am-5:30pm Mon-Sat, 10:30am-4:30pm Sun) exhibits the artwork, clothing and utensils of Ecuador's indigenous people, with special emphasis on the peoples of the Oriente.

GUÁPULO

If you follow Av 12 de Octubre up the hill from the Mariscal, you'll reach **Hotel Quito** (Map pp602-3; González Suárez N27-142) at the top. Behind the hotel (which has a top-floor bar with magnificent views), steep stairs lead down toward the somewhat bohemian neighborhood of Guápulo, set in a precipitous valley. At the center of this small neighborhood stands the lovely **Santuario de Guápulo** (off Map pp602-3; 9am-noon), built between 1644 and 1693.

The best views of the church are from the **Mirador de Guápulo**, behind the Hotel Quito, at the **Statue of Francisco de Orellana** (Map pp602-3; Larrea near González Suárez). The statue shows Francisco de Orellana looking down into the valley that witnessed the beginning of his epic journey from Quito to the Atlantic, which was the first descent of the Amazon by a European.

ACTIVITIES

Quito is one of the best places to hire guides and organize both single- and multiday excursions.

Cycling

Every other Sunday, the entire length of Av Amazonas and most of the Old Town are closed to cars, and loads of peddlers take to the street for the bimonthly **ciclopaseo** (bicycle ride). Visit www.ciclopolis.ec, in Spanish, for more info.

Local mountain-biking companies rent bikes and offer excellent single- and two-day guided off-road rides in Andean settings you'd otherwise never see. Day trips cost about US$50, not including park entrance fees. Two companies with good bikes and solid reputations are **Biking Dutchman** (Map pp602-3; ☎ 256-8323; www.bikingdutchman.com; Foch 714) and **Arie's Bike Company** (☎ 238-0802; www.ariesbikecompany.com).

ECUADOR

Climbing

Climbers can get a serious fix at the **Rocódromo** (Map pp602-3; ☎ 250-8463; Queseras del Medio s/n; admission US$2; ☺ 8am-8pm Mon-Fri, to 6pm Sat & Sun), a 25m-high climbing facility located just outside the Estadio Rumiñahui (a stadium) and within walking distance from the Mariscal. There are more than a dozen routes, and all gear is available for rental (shoe rental US$1.50, ropes US$2, harnesses US$1.50). If you rent equipment, the staff will belay you.

Compañía de Guías de Montaña (Map pp602-3; ☎ 290-1551, 255-6210; www.companiadeguias.com.ec; cnr Washington 425 & Av 6 de Diciembre) is a top-notch mountain-climbing operator whose guides are all licensed instructors and speak several languages. Two-day trips up Cotopaxi or Chimborazo cost US$180 per person.

Alta Montaña (Map pp602-3; ☎ 252-4422, 09-422-9483; Washington 8-20) is another recommended climbing operator.

Montaña (Map pp602-3; ☎ 223-8954; mountain _refugeecuador@yahoo.com; cnr Cordero E12-141 & Toledo; ☺ 10am-10pm Mon-Wed, 10am-midnight Thu & Fri, 3-10pm Sat) is a meeting place for climbers from Quito. It's a good source of nonbiased information and a good place to meet local climbers.

See right for more agencies that offer climbing tours.

Hiking

Quito's new telefériQo (p606) takes passengers up to Cruz Loma (4100m). From there you can hike to the top of jagged Rucu Pichincha (4680m). Beyond the rise of Cruz Loma and past a barbed-wire fence (which no one seems to pay any attention to), trails lead to Rucu Pichincha. It's approximately three hours to the top, and some scrambling is required. Don't attempt this hike if you've just arrived in Quito; allow yourself a couple days' acclimatization. It's also essential to get the latest info on security before hiking as there have been attacks in recent years.

Whitewater Rafting

Several companies offer rafting day trips. Rates start around US$75 per person per day.

River People (☎ 290-6639; www.riverpeoplerafting ecuador.com) Family-run, affable and highly professional outfit. Trips start in Tena but go to a variety of rivers.

Yacu Amu Rafting/Ríos Ecuador (Map pp602-3; ☎ 223-6844; www.yacuamu.com; Foch 746) Whitewater rafting, kayaking trips and courses. Australian-owned, highly experienced.

COURSES
Dancing

Tired of shoe-gazing when you hit the *salsotecas* (salsa clubs)? Try salsa dance classes – they're a blast! Merengue, cumbia and other Latin dances are also taught. Private classes cost US$5 to US$6 per hour.

Academia Salsa & Merengue (Map pp602-3; ☎ 222-0427; Foch E4-256)

Casa Cultural Afro-Ecuatoriano (Map pp602-3; ☎ 222-0227; Av 6 de Diciembre Oe123-58)

Ritmo Tropical (Map pp602-3; ☎ 255-7094; ritmo tropical5@hotmail.com; cnr Av Amazonas N24-155 & Calama)

Language

Quito is one of the best places in Latin America to learn Spanish. Most schools offer one-on-one instruction and can arrange homestays with families. Rates for private lessons vary between US$6 and US$9 per hour. Some schools charge an inscription fee (usually around US$20).

Ecole Idiomas (Map pp602-3; ☎ 223-1592; info@eco travel-ecuador.com; García E6-15 near Mera) Volunteer projects available.

Guayasamín Spanish School (Map pp602-3; ☎ 254-4210; www.guayasaminschool.com; Calama E8-54 near Av 6 de Diciembre) Ecuadorian-owned; lots of reader recommendations.

Pichincha Spanish School (Map pp602-3; ☎ 222-0478; www.pichinchaspanishschool.com; Carrión 437) A small Mariscal school.

Quito Antiguo Spanish School (Map p605; ☎ 295-7023; Venezuela 1129) The Old Town's only language school with many study options.

Yanapuma Language School (Map pp602-3; ☎ 254-6709; www.yanapuma.org; Veintimilla E8-125, 2nd fl) Excellent foundation-run school with opportunities to study while traveling or volunteering, both in Quito and in remote communities.

TOURS

Organized tours are sometimes cheaper if they are booked in the town closest to where you want to go, although this demands a more flexible schedule. If you prefer to start in Quito, the following agencies and operators are well received and reliable. For cycling, rafting, climbing and other activities, see p607.

Dracaena (Map pp602-3; ☎ 254-6590; Pinto E4-453) Offers four- to eight-day tours of Cuyabeno (p644) which have received excellent reviews. Five-day tour is US$200 per person.

Eos Ecuador (Map pp602-3; ☎ 2601-3560; www
.eosecuador.travel; cnr Av Amazonas N24-66 & Pinto) Eos
offers a wide range of conventional and off-the-beaten-
path tours, including jungle tours and adventure treks.

Fundación Golondrinas (Map pp602-3; ☎ 222-6602;
www.ecuadorexplorer.com/golondrinas; Isabel La Católica
N24-679) Conservation project with volunteer opportunities;
also arranges walking tours in the *páramo* west of Tulcán.

Gulliver (Map pp602-3; ☎ 252-9297, 09-946-2265;
www.gulliver.com.ec; cnr Mera & Calama) Trekking, climbing, mountain biking and horse-riding trips in the Andes.

Happy Gringo (Map pp602-3; ☎ 222-0031; www
.happygringo.com; Foch E6-12; ☺ 9am-7pm Mon-Fri,
10am-4pm Sat & Sun) A fairly new operator that has
received numerous recommendations from travelers for its
full range of trips and tours.

Rainforestur (Map pp602-3; ☎ 223-9822; www
.rainforestur.com; cnr Av Amazonas 420 & Robles) Excellent
for Cuyabeno Reserve jungle trips. Also offers rafting trips
near Baños, and trekking and indigenous-market tours in
the Quito area.

Safari Tours (Map pp602-3; ☎ 255-2505, 250-8316;
www.safari.com.ec; Foch E5-39; ☺ 9am-7pm) Arranges
everything from jungle treks and Galápagos cruises to
volcano climbing. Loads of day trips.

Sierra Nevada Expeditions (Map pp602-3; ☎ 255-
3658; www.hotelsierranevada.com; Pinto 637 near
Cordero) Climbing, biking and river-rafting trips.

Tropic Ecological Adventures (Map pp602-3; ☎ 222-
5907; www.tropiceco.com; Av de la República E7-320,
apt 1A) Three- to six-day tours to the Oriente, Andes and
cloud forest.

FESTIVALS & EVENTS

The city's biggest party celebrates the founding of Quito in the first week of December,
when bullfights are held daily at the Plaza
de Toros (off Map pp602-3). On New Year's
Eve, life-size puppets (often of politicians) are
burned in the streets at midnight. Carnaval is
celebrated with intense water fights – no one
is spared. Colorful religious processions are
held during Easter week.

SLEEPING

Most travelers stay in the Mariscal neighborhood so they can be near the many bars, cafes
and restaurants. Unfortunately, the Mariscal
can be dangerous after dark. While lacking in
Thai restaurants and expat bars, the Old Town
offers unrivaled beauty, and its historic streets
make for some great exploring.

Adjacent to the Mariscal, the hip La
Floresta neighborhood has a few inviting
places to stay.

Old Town

The hotels between Plaza Santo Domingo and
the bus terminal are some of the cheapest, but
it's a dodgy area after sunset.

Hostal San Blas (Map p605; ☎ 228-1434; Caldas 121,
Plaza San Blas; s/d from US$6/8) This friendly, family-
run hotel on the attractive Plaza San Blas is
a good deal if you don't mind small rooms.
Rooms are dark (windows open onto a small
interior patio) but clean.

La Posada Colonial (Map p605; ☎ 228-2859; Paredes
188; r per person with/without bathroom US$8/6) Although
a bit close to the bus terminal, this wood-floor
oldie is still one of the Old Town's best values.
Beds are saggy, but it's extremely well kept
and totally secure.

Hostal La Casona (Map p605; ☎ 257-0626; Manabí
Oe1-59; s/d US$8/10) This family-run place has a
dimly lit interior patio watched over by three
floors of small rooms with low ceilings and
wide plank floors.

Secret Garden (Map p605; ☎ 295-6704; www.secret
gardenquito.com; Antepara E4-60; dm US$8, d with shared
bathroom US$20) Owned by an Ecuadorian/
Australian couple, this popular hostel has a
party vibe and attracts a mix of young backpackers. The rooms are basic and livened up
by artwork in the halls and a 5th-floor terrace
with sublime views.

Hotel Internacional Plaza del Teatro (Map p605;
☎ 295-9462; Guayaquil N8-75; s/d US$12/24) Across
from the Plaza del Teatro, this grand old
dame has seen better days but offers clean,
carpeted rooms. Some rooms have balconies;
off-street rooms lack balconies and character,
but are quieter.

Hotel San Francisco de Quito (Map p605; ☎ 228-
7758; www.sanfranciscodequito.com.ec; Sucre Oe3-17; s/d
US$14/28, s/d mini apt with kitchenettes US$28/44) This
historic converted house boasts spotless
rooms with telephone, TV and constant hot
water. Because it's a colonial building, most
rooms lack windows, but double doors open
onto a balcony over an interior courtyard. It's
popular so reserve well ahead.

Hotel Viena Internacional (Map p605; ☎ 295-4860;
www.hotelvienaint.com; cnr Flores 600 & Chile; s/d US$15/30)
Though the '70s-style wallpaper may make
your eyes water, the spotless rooms, top-notch
service and cheerful interior patio make this
fine value. Rooms have hardwood floors, TVs,
hot water and good showers.

La Posada Colonial (Map p605; ☎ 228-0282; posada
colonial@yahoo.com; cnr García Moreno 1160 & Mejía;
s/d/tr/ste US$26/36/61/71) The eight rooms at the

ECUADOR

pleasant Posada Colonial boast classic decor and all have tall ceilings, wood floors and sizeable windows (a rarity in old colonial houses). Don't confuse this with the budget hotel of the same name near the bus station.

Casa San Marcos (Map p605; ☎ 228-1811; casasanmarcos@yahoo.com; Junín 655; d US$80-150) Yet another beautifully restored colonial mansion, Casa San Marcos has just four rooms, all exquisitely set with antique furnishings, heritage artwork on the walls and tall ceilings. All rooms are bright and have windows. Also in the house is an art gallery and antiques shop; an elegant terrace cafe is in the works.

New Town

Casa Bambú (Map pp602-3; ☎ 222-6738; Solano 1758 near Av Colombia; dm/d US$5/20, s/d with shared bathroom US$7/10; 🖳) This gem boasts spacious rooms, a tiny garden, guest kitchen, a book exchange, laundry facilities and outstanding views from the rooftop hammocks. Worth the uphill hike.

El Centro del Mundo (Map pp602-3; ☎ 222-9050; www.centrodelmundo.net; García E7-26; dm/s US$6/8) A magnet among young backpackers, this French-Canadian–owned hostel has brightly painted rooms, a guest kitchen and traveler-friendly ambience.

Backpacker's Inn (Map pp602-3; ☎ 250-9669; www.backpackersinn.net; Rodríguez 245; dm/s/d from US$6/8/13; 🖳) Overlooking a peaceful street, this well-located hostel has a laid-back vibe with just a handful of simple rooms – all with decent light and wood floors.

Huaukí (Map pp602-3; ☎ 290-4286; www.hostalhuauki.com; Pinto E7-82; dm/d from US$6/20) Opened by a Japanese expat, this sleek new hostel offers small but clean colorful rooms with wood floors. The restaurant with draped fabrics is a popular traveler hangout, with Japanese and vegetarian fare.

El Cafecito (Map pp602-3; ☎ 223-4862; www.cafecito.net; Cordero E6-43; dm/d US$7/25, s/d with shared bathroom US$10/15) Cafecito is an eternally popular budget choice, and for good reason. Rooms are clean, the place has a mellow vibe and the cafe with outdoor seating serves delicious fare.

Blue House (Map pp602-3; ☎ 222-3480; www.bluehousequito.com; Pinto E8-24; dm/d US$8/20) New in 2008, this friendly guesthouse has six pleasant rooms with wood floors in a converted house on a quiet street. There's a grassy yard in front for barbecues, a comfy lounge with fireplace and a kitchen for guest use.

L'Auberge Inn (Map pp602-3; ☎ 255-2912; www.ioda.net/auberge-inn; Av Colombia N12-200; s/d US$11/19, with shared bathroom US$8/16) This clean, cheerful inn boasts a good traveler vibe with spotless rooms, a small garden area, a common room with a fireplace, a pool table and a decent in-house restaurant.

Posada del Maple (Map pp602-3; ☎ 254-4507; www.posadadelmaple.com; Rodríguez E8-49; dm US$8, s/d US$25/29, with shared bathroom US$15/19) Maple is a friendly place with clean but dated rooms, comfy lounge areas and outdoor space. It's well liked by many travelers.

La Casona de Mario (Map pp602-3; ☎ 254-4036; www.casonademario.com; Andalucía N24-115; r per person US$10) In a lovely old house, La Casona de Mario is outstanding value, with homey rooms, shared spotless bathrooms, a garden, a TV lounge and a guest kitchen.

Magic Bean (Map pp602-3; ☎ 256-6181; Foch E5-08; dm/s/d US$10/25/30) Better known for its lively restaurant below, the Magic Bean offers clean, spruce lodging. The downside: the noise from the restaurant means little rest for light sleepers.

Casa Kanela (Map pp602-3; ☎ 254-6162; www.casakanela.mamey.org; Rodríguez 147; dm/s/d/tr incl breakfast US$12/19/30/36; 🖳) An excellent new addition to Mariscal, Kanela offers minimalist but stylish rooms in a pleasant converted house on pretty Rodríguez. It's a friendly, welcoming place.

Aleida's Hostal (Map pp602-3; ☎ 223-4570; www.aleidashostal.com.ec; cnr Andalucía 559 & Salazar; s/d US$18/36, with shared bathroom US$13/26) This friendly three-story guesthouse in La Floresta is family-run and has a very spacious feel with lots of light, huge rooms, high wooden ceilings and hardwood floors.

Casa Helbling (Map pp602-3; ☎ 222-6013; www.casahelbling.de; Veintimilla 531; s/d US$22/30, with shared bathroom US$14/20; 🖳) In a homey, colonial-style house in the Mariscal, Casa Helbling is clean, relaxed and friendly. It has a guest kitchen, laundry facilities and plenty of common areas for chilling out.

Folklore Hotel (Map pp602-3; ☎ 255-4621; www.folklorehotel.com; Madrid 868 near Pontevedra; s/d incl breakfast US$19/29) This delightfully converted house in La Floresta has spacious, colorful rooms with blue-and-yellow checkered bedspreads that match the house paint job. It has a small garden and a welcoming family feel.

Hotel Sierra Madre (Map pp602-3; ☎ 250-5687; Veintimilla 464; www.hotelsierramadre.com; s/d from US$39/49) In a handsomely restored colonial building, the Sierra Madre is an inviting Ecuadorian-Belgian–run place. Rooms vary in size, but most have wood floors, excellent beds and a warm color scheme, while the best quarters have vaulted ceilings and verandas. There's a popular restaurant below.

Café Cultura (Map pp602-3; ☎ 222-4271; www.cafe cultura.com; Robles 5; s/d/tr US$79/99/109) This atmospheric boutique hotel is set in a converted mansion with a garden, crackling fireplaces and handsome mural-filled bedrooms all adding to the charm. Reservations recommended.

EATING

Quito has a rich and varied restaurant scene, with a fine mix of traditional Ecuadorian fare along with dozens of ethnic and international eateries. All budgets and tastes are catered for. You'll find everything from ubermodern sushi restaurants to classic Andean cooking served in a landmark colonial dining room, with good options for vegetarians, pizza lovers, and those simply seeking a good cafe on a drizzly afternoon.

If you're pinching pennies, stick to the standard *almuerzos* or *meriendas* (set lunches and dinners). Many restaurants close on Sunday.

Old Town

The historical center is where you'll find Quito's most traditional eateries, some of which have been honing family recipes for generations.

CAFES

El Kukurucho del Maní (Map p605; cnr Rocafuerte 0e5-02 & García Moreno; snacks US25-75¢) Great pit stop for sugary nuts, corn kernels and *haba* beans whipped up in a copper kettle.

Jugos de la Sucre (Map p605; Sucre 0e5-53; drinks US50-75¢; ☼ 7:30am-6pm) For a freshly squeezed serving of vitamins, this popular juice stand is hard to beat. Try passion fruit and orange or a dozen other flavors.

El Cafeto (Map p605; Convento de San Agustín, cnr Chile 930 & Flores; coffee US75¢-US$2) This quaint Ecuadorian-owned coffee shop serves excellent coffee made from 100% organic Ecuadorian beans.

Cafetería Fabiolita (El Buen Sanduche; Map p605; Espejo 0e4-17; sandwiches US$1, seco de chivo US$2.50; ☼ 9am-6pm) For more than 40 years this tiny eatery has served up Quito's favorite *seco de chivo* (goat stew), one of Ecuador's most traditional dishes. Arrive early, before they run out (9am

to 11am only). *Sanduiches de pernil* (ham sandwiches) are also quite satisfying.

Cafetería Modelo (Map p605; cnr Sucre & García Moreno; snacks US$1-2.50) Opened in 1950, Modelo is one of the city's oldest cafes, and a great spot to try traditional snacks like *empanadas de verde* (plantain empanadas filled with cheese), *quimbolitos* (a sweet cake steamed in a leaf), tamales and *humitas* (similar to Mexican tamales).

Café del Teatro (Map p605; Plaza del Teatro; mains US$2.50-8; ☼ 10am-7pm) Grab a table on the plaza and enjoy a drink with great views of the Teatro Sucre. Inside, you'll find a stylish multilevel cafe-restaurant, with a selection of international fare.

Tianguez (Map p605; Plaza San Francisco; mains US$3-5; ☼ 10am-6pm Mon & Tue, to 11:30pm Wed-Sun) Tucked into the stone arches beneath the Monasterio de San Francisco, this bohemian-style cafe prepares tasty appetizers (tamales, soups) as well as heartier mains.

Café Mosaico (Map p605; Samaniego N8-95 near Antepara, Itchimbia; mains US$6-11; ☼ 11am-10:30pm, from 4pm Tue) Sure, the drinks are overpriced, but you won't find a balcony view like this *anywhere* else, and tourists are a rarity.

RESTAURANTS

Govindas (Map p605; Esmeraldas 853; mains US$1.50; ☼ 8am-4pm Mon-Sat) Proudly serving 100% vegetarian cuisine, the Hare Krishnas whip up tasty fresh lunch plates from a changing menu, plus yogurt and granola, juices and sweets.

Pollos San Blas (Map p605; cnr Av Pichincha & Antepara; mains US$2-3.50; ☼ 11am-6pm) Near Plaza San Blas, this popular and casual spot is a great place for piping-hot plates of roast chicken.

Frutería Monserrate (Map p605; Espejo 0e2-12; mains US$2-5; ☼ 8am-7:30pm Mon-Fri, 9am-6:30pm Sat & Sun) A mix of travelers and locals stop in for the filling breakfasts and giant fruit salads, although empanadas and *ceviche* (raw marinated seafood) are also among the offerings.

La Guaragua (Map p605; Espejo 0e2-40 near Flores; mains US$2-6) The tables are a bit office-like, but the food is excellent. Try the *tortillas de quinoa* (quinoa patties) and empanadas.

Heladería San Agustín (Map p605; Guayaquil 1053; mains US$3-5) This family-run restaurant cooks up tasty Ecuadorian favorites in a cozy, old-world atmosphere. Save room for the handmade *helados de paila* (ice cream prepared in big copper bowls), a family recipe since 1858.

ECUADOR

Pizza SA (Map p605; Espejo Oe2-46; mains US$3-5; ⏰ 11am-11pm Mon-Sat, to 9pm Sun) Located on a restaurant-filled lane facing the Teatro Bolívar, this casual spot bakes up delicious, individually sized thin-crust pizzas. You can also enjoy sandwiches, salads and calzones. Sidewalk seating.

Café del Fraile (Map p605; Chile Oe4-22, Pasaje Arzobispal, 2nd fl; mains US$5-8; ⏰ 10am-midnight Mon-Sat, noon-10pm Sun) Country-rustic charm and balcony seating set the stage for a tasty selection of grilled dishes (including trout and corvina), sandwiches and cocktails.

Hasta La Vuelta, Señor (Map p605; ☎ 258-0887; Chile Oe4-22, Palacio Arzobispal, 3rd fl; mains US$6-10; ⏰ 11am-11pm Mon-Sat, to 8pm Sun) Ecuadorian cuisine is prepared with panache at this excellent restaurant with balcony seating. Reliable favorites include *ceviche, seco de chivo*, tilapia and sea bass.

our pick **Vista Hermosa** (Map p605; Mejía 453, 5th fl; mains US$6-10; ⏰ 1pm-2am Mon-Sat, noon-9pm Sun) A much-loved newcomer to El Centro, Vista Hermosa (literally 'beautiful view') delivers the goods with a magnificent 360-degree panorama over the Old Town from its rooftop terrace. Live music adds to the magic on Wednesday to Saturday (from 9pm onwards). Bring a jacket and arrive early to beat the crowds.

La Cueva del Oso (Map p605; Chile 1046; mains US$7-10) Lounge-like Cueva del Oso serves exquisitely prepared Ecuadorian specialties. The bar, with its low, round booths, makes for a sultry escape from the noise outside.

SELF-CATERING

Mercado Central (Map p605; Av Pichincha btwn Esmeraldas & Manabí; full meals under US$1-3; ⏰ 8am-4pm, to 3pm Sun) For stall after stall of some of Quito's most traditional (and cheapest) foods, head straight to the Mercado Central, where you'll find everything from *locro de papa* (potato soup with cheese and avocado) and seafood, and *yaguarlocro* (potato soup with chunks of fried blood sausage). Fruits and veggies too.

Corvina Don 'Jimmy' (Map p605; Mercado Central, Av Pichincha btwn Esmeraldas & Mejía; mains US$2-4; ⏰ 8am-4pm, to 3pm Sun) Open since 1953, this is the Mercado Central's most famous stall, serving huge portions of *corvina* (sea bass). Ask for it with rice if you don't want it over a big bowl of *ceviche*.

Magda (Map p605; Venezuela N3-62; ⏰ 8:30am-7pm Mon-Sat, 9am-5pm Sun) A conveniently located and well-stocked supermarket.

New Town

The city's best restaurants spread across the rolling avenues of new town, with an excellent assortment of classic and nouveau fare. This is the place to go for *ceviche*, Japanese, Thai, Tex-Mex and Italian.

CAFES

Kallari (Map pp602-3; Wilson E4-266; breakfast US$2, lunch US$2.50) Beside the fact that Kallari's chocolate bars induce orgasms on the spot, this Quichua coop serves up delicious, healthy breakfasts and lunches as well.

El Cafecito (Map pp602-3; Cordero E6-43; mains US$2-4) Serves inexpensive, mainly vegetarian meals and snacks all day long. Great breakfasts available.

Café Amazonas (Map pp602-3; cnr Av Amazonas & Roca; mains US$2-5) A Quito classic, with outdoor tables and prime people-watching.

Café Colibrí (Map pp602-3; Pinto 619; mains US$2-5) This German-owned cafe is a great spot for breakfasts, crepes (savory and sweet), sandwiches and coffee. Big glass windows, skylights and a garden-like front patio create an airy ambience.

Café Mango Tree (Map pp602-3; Foch E4-310; mains US$3-6; ⏰ 12:30pm-10pm) A pleasant cafe with an interior patio strung with hanging plants. In addition to coffee and smoothies, you'll find veggie plates, fajitas, lasagna, waffles, crepes, salads and other bistro fare.

Uvíllas de Ochún (Map pp602-3; Andalucía N24-234; mains US$3-5; ⏰ 1-9pm Mon-Fri) This friendly, colorfully decorated Cuban-owned cafe serves strong coffee and good rum, plus tasty snacks, sandwiches, pizzas and light fare. The artwork on the walls is for sale.

Magic Bean (Map pp602-3; Foch E5-08; mains US$4-8; ⏰ 7am-10pm) Longtime epicenter of the Mariscal, the Magic Bean serves well-prepared breakfasts, lunches, juices and snacks for the ever-present crowd of hungry travelers.

Coffee & Toffee (pp602-3; Calama; ⏰ 24hr) Equal parts cafe and lounge, Coffee & Toffee is a mellow and inviting place, with warmly lit brick walls, an open kitchen and a pleasant top-floor terrace. Locals and expats alike enjoy the wi-fi and the 24-hour service.

RESTAURANTS

Restaurante Manantial (Map pp602-3; 9 de Octubre N22-25; mains US$1-3; ⏰ 8am-6pm Sun-Fri) Run by a sweet vegan soul, Manantial is a simple, nonfussy spot serving healthy dishes like veggie burgers, tofu sandwiches, soups of the day and juices (try *aguacatado* – blended soy milk, avocado and plantain).

Hamburgers del Sese (Map pp602-3; cnr Tamayo & Carrión; mains US$2-3) One of many student hangouts in the area, Sese serves some of Quito's best burgers (veggie burgers too). Chow down inside or on the rooftop patio. For more cheap meals head along Carrión between Tamayo and Av 12 de Octubre.

Hassan's Café (Map pp602-3; Reina Victoria near Av Cristóbal Colón; mains US$2-6; 🕙 9:30am-8pm Mon-Sat) Lebanese food – shawarmas, hummus, kebabs, stuffed eggplant, veggie plates – is good, fresh and cheap at this 10-table restaurant.

Isla del Mar (Map pp602-3; cnr Av 6 de Diciembre & Washington; mains US$2.50-6) It doesn't look like much, but this hole-in-the-wall restaurant serves knockout *ceviche* and seafood dishes at rock-bottom prices.

La Bodeguita de Cuba (Map pp602-3; Reina Victoria 1721; mains US$3-5; 🕙 Tue-Sun) With its wooden tables and graffiti-covered walls, this is a great place for Cuban food and fun. Live bands perform from time to time, and there's outdoor seating.

Chandani Tandoori (Map pp602-3; Mera 1333; mains US$3-5; 🕙 11am-10pm Mon-Sat, to 3:30pm Sun) Bouncy Bollywood hits and sizzling platters of *tikka masala* make up the soundtrack to this good, inexpensive Indian restaurant. Other tasty menu items in the minimalist place include curry, *vindaloo* and korma.

Tio Billy's (Map pp602-3; Mera N23-78; mains US$3-5; 🕙 noon-2am Mon-Sat) This tiny expat-owned spot has earned a local following for its tasty square burgers. Outdoor tables and kitschy decor set the scene.

Uncle Ho's (Map pp602-3; Calama E8-29; mains US$3-6; 🕙 noon-10:30pm Mon-Sat) Sleek and slender, Uncle Ho's whips up tasty bowls of *pho*, sea bass with chili and lime over rice noodles, glazed spare ribs and other Vietnamese hits. Sidewalk seating.

ourpick Canoa Manabita (Map pp602-3; Calama 247; mains US$4-6; 🕙 Tue-Sun) This casual and unassuming place is extremely popular with locals for its mouth-watering servings of *ceviche* and seafood plates.

Cevichería Manolo (Map pp602-3; cnr Diego de Almagro & La Niña; mains US$4-6) Join the locals at this excellent and affordable seafood restaurant, with several types of Ecuadorian and Peruvian *ceviche* on the menu, plus great seafood dishes.

Red Hot Chili Peppers (Map pp602-3; Foch E4-314; mains US$4-6; 🕙 noon-10:30pm Mon-Sat) Think fajitas – the rest of the menu is good, but doesn't quite measure up to that sizzling plate of chicken or beef. Wash 'em down with smooth piña coladas.

Yanuna (Map pp602-3; Wilson E6-35; mains US$4-6) This colorful bohemian bistro serves a huge variety of global fare, including Indian *tahli*, Greek salads, Peruvian *ceviche*, Vietnamese *pho* and lots of vegetarian options.

Le Arcate (Map pp602-3; Baquedano 358; mains US$4-6; 🕙 12:30-3pm & 6-11pm Mon-Sat, noon-4pm Sun) This Mariscal favorite bakes more than 50 kinds of pizza in a wood-fired oven and serves reasonably priced lasagna, steak and seafood.

Texas Ranch (Map pp602-3; Mera 1140; mains US$4-7; 🕙 1pm-midnight) Texas Ranch serves up whopping burgers (that's the Texas part) and Argentine-style grilled meats.

Siam (Map pp602-3; Calama E5-10, 2nd fl; mains US$5-8; 🕙 1pm-midnight Mon-Fri, to 11pm Sat & Sun) Siam cooks up delicious Thai food, served in a cozy upstairs dining room amid Eastern art and relaxing music.

Naranjilla Mecánica (Map pp602-3; Tamayo N22-43; mains US$6-10; 🕙 Mon-Sat) This self-consciously hip restaurant serves inventive salads, tasty sandwiches and satisfying mains like grilled haddock with capers.

Boca del Lobo (Map pp602-3; Calama 284; mains US$6-12) The ambience at this hip restaurant is pure kitsch, with colored glass globes, empty birdcages and psychedelic paintings. The menu features raclette, crepes, open-faced sandwiches, baked desserts and sugary sweet cocktails.

SELF-CATERING

Mercado Santa Clara (Map pp602-3; cnr Dávalos & Versalles; 🕙 8am-5pm) Quito's main fruit and vegetable market also has cheap food stalls.

Supermercado Santa María (Map pp602-3; cnr Dávalos & Versalles; 🕙 8:30am-8pm Mon-Sat, 9am-6pm Sun) Huge supermarket facing Mercado Santa Clara.

Supermaxi (Map pp602-3; cnr La Niña & Pinzón; 🕙 daily) Biggest and best supermarket near the Mariscal.

DRINKING

Most of the nightlife in Quito is concentrated in and around the Mariscal, where things get raucous most nights (and very crowded on weekends). Remember to always take a cab home if you're out in the Mariscal at night (see p601).

Finn McCool's (Map pp602-3; Pinto 251) This Irish-owned bar is the current favorite among expats, for its welcoming vibe, pub quiz nights (currently Tuesday) and pool, darts and table football. The classic wood-lined bar also serves fish and chips, shepherd's pie, burgers and other pub grub.

Coffee Tree (Map pp602-3; cnr Reina Victoria & Foch; 24hr) A good place to start the night off is this outdoor bar anchoring lively Reina Victoria. There's great people-watching from the plaza tables, and numerous other eating and drinking spots nearby.

La Reina Victoria (Map pp602-3; Reina Victoria 530; Mon-Sat) This longtime expat watering hole is a cozy spot for a drink, with a fireplace, dartboard, bumper pool and Anglo pub ambience. There's decent pub fare including pizzas and fish and chips.

Ananké Guápulo (Map pp602-3; Camino de Orellana 781; Mon-Sat) This cozy little bar-pizzeria sits perched on the hillside in Guápulo. It has a wee terrace (complete with fireplace) and several good nooks for secreting away with a cocktail and a friend. Live music on weekends.

Ananké (Map pp602-3; cnr Diego de Almagro & Pinto) The newest branch of Ananké brings bohemian style to the Mariscal. The outdoor courtyard is a fine spot for an evening drink, and there are tasty wood-fired pizzas, plus live music some nights.

ENTERTAINMENT

For event listings, check the local newspapers *El Comercio* and *Hoy*, or pick up a copy of *Quito Cultura*, a monthly cultural magazine available free from the tourist offices.

Live Music

El Pobre Diablo our pick (Map pp602-3; ☎ 223-5194; www.elpobrediablo.com; Isabel La Católica E12-06; admission US$5-10; Mon-Sat) Locals and expats rate El Pobre Diablo as one of Quito's best places to hear live music. It's a friendly, laid-back place with live jazz, blues, world music and experimental sounds most nights. It's also a great place to dine, with satisfying fusion fare, a solid cocktail menu and a great vibe.

Café Libro (Map pp602-3; ☎ 223-4265; www.cafe libro.com; Leonidas Plaza Gutiérrez N23-56; admission US$3-5;

Mon-Sat) Live music, poetry slams, contemporary dance, tango, jazz and other performances draw an artsy and intellectual crowd to this handsomely set bohemian venue.

Nightclubs

Hitting the dance floor of one of Quito's *salsotecas* is a must. If you don't know how to salsa, try a few classes first (see p608).

Bungalow 6 (Map pp602-3; admission US$5; cnr Calama & Diego de Almagro; 7pm-3am Wed-Sat) The favorite dance spot in the Mariscal among foreigners, Bungalow 6 plays a wide mix of beats (salsa, reggae plus British and North American hits). There's a small but lively dance floor, drink specials and popular events nights (like ladies' night on Wednesdays). Arrive early to avoid being turned away.

El Aguijón (Map pp602-3; Calama E7-35; admission US$5; 9pm-3am Tue-Sat) This unpretentious nightclub attracts a good ratio of twenty-something locals and foreigners. The space is open and somewhat industrial, with video art playing on a large screen above the dance floor. DJs spin a little of everything, with live bands playing on Thursdays and salsa music on Wednesday nights.

Seseribó (Map pp602-3; Edificio Girón, cnr Veintimilla & Av 12 de Octubre; admission US$5-10; 9pm-2am Thu-Sat) Quito's best *salsoteca* is a must-stop for salsa fans. The music is tops, the atmosphere is superb, and the dancing is first-rate. Devoted *salseros* (salsa dancers) turn up on Thursdays, which makes it a great night to go.

LA RONDA

One of the Old Town's most recent areas to undergo restoration is the handsome street of Juan de Dios Morales, known as 'La Ronda.' This narrow lane is lined with picture-book 17th-century buildings, with placards along the walls describing (in Spanish) some of the street's history and the artists, writers and political figures who once resided here. A new crop of restaurants and shops has opened in recent years, though La Ronda remains a delightfully local and unpretentious affair. The street is at its liveliest on Friday and Saturday nights, when *canelazo* (rum with sugar, cinnamon and lemon juice) vendors keep everyone nice and cozy, and live music spills out of restaurant windows.

Blues (Map pp602-3; www.bluesestodo.com; Av de la República 476; admission US$7-15; ☑ 10pm-6am Thu-Sat) Quito's only late-night club, Blues is the place partyers head at 3am. DJs spin electronica and rock (with live rock bands on Thursdays) to a style-conscious *Quiteño* crowd.

Mayo 68 (Map pp602-3; García 662) This popular salsa club is small and conveniently located in the Mariscal; it has a local following.

Theater & Dance

Teatro Sucre (Map p605; ☎ 228-2136; www.teatrosucre .com; Manabí N8-131; admission US$3-20; ☑ ticket office 10am-1pm & 2-6pm) Overlooking the Plaza del Teatro, this is the city's most historical theater. Performances range from jazz and classical music to ballet, modern dance and opera.

Teatro Bolívar (Map p605; ☎ 258-2486/7; www.teatro bolivar.org, info@teatrobolivar.org; Espejo btwn Flores & Guayaquil) The Bolívar hosts not only theater, but also alternative rock shows and more.

Humanizarte (Map pp602-3; ☎ 222-6116; www.hu manizarte.com; Leonidas Plaza Gutiérrez N24-226) Presents both contemporary and Andean dance.

Teatro Prometeo (Map pp602-3; ☎ 222-6116; www .cce.org.ec; Av 6 de Diciembre 794) Affiliated with the Casa de la Cultura Ecuatoriana (p606), this inexpensive venue often has modern-dance performances and other shows that non-Spanish speakers can enjoy.

SHOPPING

Numerous stores in the Mariscal (especially along and near Av Amazonas and Mera) sell traditional indigenous crafts. Quality is often high, but so are the prices. The best deals can be found at the two crafts markets listed here, where indigenous, mostly *otavaleño* (people from Otavalo) vendors sell their goods.

Crafts Stores

La Bodega (Map pp602-3; Mera N22-24) Highest-quality crafts, old and new.

Ag (Map pp602-3; Mera N22-24) Ag's selection of rare, handmade silver jewelry from across South America is outstanding.

Centro Artesanal (Map pp602-3; Mera E5-11) This excellent shop is known for its crafts and paintings by local indigenous artists.

Tianguez (Map p605; Plaza San Francisco) Attached to the eponymous cafe (p611), Tianguez is a member of the Fair Trade Organization and sells some outstanding crafts from throughout Ecuador.

Galería Latina (Map pp602-3; ☎ 254-0380; Mera N23-69) Spread among many rooms of this well-stocked handicrafts shop is an excellent selection of high-quality items.

Productos Andinos (Map pp602-3; Urbina 111) This two-floor artisans cooperative is crammed with reasonably priced crafts.

Markets

On Saturday and Sunday, the northern end of Parque El Ejido turns into Quito's biggest crafts market and sidewalk art show. Two blocks north, the **Mercado Artesanal La Mariscal** (Map pp602-3; Mera btwn Washington & 18 de Septiembre) is an entire block filled with craft stalls.

GETTING THERE & AWAY

Air

Quito's new airport, located 25km east of the city, was scheduled to open in late 2010 at the time of writing. You can ask at the tourist office or visit www.quiport.com to find out if it's operational before you depart. At research time, all flights were operating out of the **Aeropuerto Mariscal Sucre** (off Map pp602-3; ☎ 294-4900, www.quitoairport.com; cnr Av Amazonas & Av de la Prensa), located about 7km north of the city center. Many of the northbound buses on Av Amazonas and Av 10 de Agosto go there – some have 'Aeropuerto' placards, while others say 'Quito Norte.' For more information, see Getting Into Town, p604.

In order of importance, Ecuador's principal domestic airlines are:

TAME (Map pp602-3; ☎ 396-6300; www.tame.com.ec; cnr Avs Amazonas N24-260 & Cristobal Colón)

Icaro (☎ 290-3395; www.icaro.aero; cnr Mera N26-221 & Orellana)

AeroGal (☎ 294-2800; www.aerogal.com.ec; Av Amazonas 7797) Near the airport.

There are regular flights connecting Quito with Coca, Cuenca, Esmeraldas, the Galápagos, Guayaquil, Lago Agrio, Loja, Macas, Machala, Manta and Tulcán. All mainland flights last under one hour and cost around US$60 to US$85 one way. Galápagos flights cost significantly more (US$300 to US$420 round-trip) and take 3¼ hours from Quito (including a layover in Guayaquil) and 1½ hours from Guayaquil.

ECUADOR

Bus

Quito's main bus station is the **Terminal Terrestre Cumandá** (Cumandá Bus Terminal; Map p605; cnr Morales & Piedra) in the Old Town, a few blocks south of Plaza Santo Domingo. The nearest Trole stop is the Cumandá stop. After around 6pm you should take a taxi, as this is an unsafe area at night. Don't take the Trole if you're loaded with luggage; it's notorious for pickpockets.

At some point in the future (city officials couldn't pin down a date as this book went to print), several new terminals are scheduled to open: **Terminal Quitumbe** (Av Cóndor Ñan and Av Mariscal Antonio José de Sucre), located 5km southwest of the Old Town, will handle destinations south of Quito. **Terminal Carapungo**, located in the north of the city, will service northern Ecuador. Check with the tourist office for the latest on the terminals – and where your particular bus will be departing from – before heading to the bus station.

Approximate one-way fares and journey times are shown in the following table. More expensive luxury services are available for long trips.

BUS FARES

Destination	Cost (US$)	Duration (hr)
Ambato	2	2½
Atacames	9	7
Bahía de Caráquez	9	8
Baños	3.50	3
Coca	9	9 (via Loreto)
Cuenca	10	10-12
Esmeraldas	9	5-6
Guayaquil	7	8
Huaquillas	10	12
Ibarra	2.50	2½
Lago Agrio	7	7-8
Latacunga	1.50	2
Loja	15	14-15
Machala	9	10
Manta	8	8-9
Otavalo	2	2¼
Portoviejo	9	9
Puerto López	12	12
Puyo	5	5½
Riobamba	4	4
San Lorenzo	6	6½
Santo Domingo	2.50	3
Tena	6	5-6
Tulcán	5	5

For comfortable buses to Guayaquil from the New Town, travel with **Panamericana** (Map pp602-3; ☎ 255-3690; cnr Av Cristóbal Colón & Reina Victoria) or **Transportes Ecuador** (Map pp602-3; ☎ 222-5315; Mera N21-44 near Washington). Panamericana also has long-distance buses to other towns, including Machala, Loja, Cuenca, Manta and Esmeraldas.

A few buses leave from other places for some destinations in the Pichincha province. **Cooperativa Flor de Valle/Cayambe** (☎ 252-7495) goes daily to Mindo (US$2.50, 2½ hours) from Quito's northern **Ofelia station**, reachable by taking the Metrobus line to the last stop.

Train

A weekend tourist train leaves Quito and heads south for about 3½ hours to the Area Nacional de Recreación El Boliche, adjoining Parque Nacional Cotopaxi. Unfortunately, the line was out of commission at time of research. Ask at the tourist office or train ticket office for the latest info.

The **train station** (off Map p605; ☎ 265-6142; Sincholagua & Maldonado) is located about 2km south of the Old Town. Purchase tickets in advance at the **train ticket office** (Map p605; ☎ 258-2921; cnr Bolívar 443 & García Moreno; ◷ 8am-4:30pm Mon-Fri).

GETTING AROUND

Bus

The local buses (US25¢) are fairly safe and convenient, but you should watch your bags and pockets on crowded buses. Buses have destination placards in their windows (not route numbers), and drivers will usually tell you which bus to take if you flag the wrong one.

Taxi

Cabs are yellow and have taxi-number stickers in the window. Drivers are legally required to use their *taxímetros* (meters) during the day, and most do. At night, drivers put away the meters, and you'll have to bargain. The going rate between the Mariscal and the Old Town is about US$2, though you'll have to pay more late at night and on Sundays; however, it should never be more than twice the metered rate. You can also hire a cab for about US$8 per hour, a great way to see outer city sites.

Trole, Ecovía & Metrobus

Quito has three electrically powered bus routes: the Trole, the Ecovía and the Metrobus. Each runs north–south along one of Quito's three main thoroughfares. Each line has designated stations and car-free lanes, making them speedy and efficient. However, as the fastest form of public transport, they are usually crowded and notorious for pickpockets. They run about every 10 minutes from 6am to 12:30am (more often in rush hours), and the fare is US25¢.

The Trole runs along Maldonado and Av 10 de Agosto. In the Old Town, southbound trolleys take the west route (along Guayaquil), while northbound trolleys take the east route (along Montúfar and Pichincha). The Ecovía runs along Av 6 de Diciembre, and the Metrobus runs along Av América.

AROUND QUITO

MITAD DEL MUNDO & AROUND

☎ 02

Ecuador's biggest claim to fame is its location on the equator. The **Mitad del Mundo** (Middle of the World; admission US$2; ☹ 9am-6pm Mon-Fri, 9am-7pm Sat & Sun), 22km north of Quito, is the place where Charles-Marie de la Condamine made the measurements in 1736 proving that this was the equatorial line. Although the monument constructed there isn't actually on the equator (GPS readings indicate true 0°00' latitude lies about 300m north), it remains a popular, if touristy, destination. On Sunday afternoons live salsa bands play in the central plaza area. The ethnographic museum (and its viewing platform up top), a scale model of Quito's Old Town and other attractions cost extra. Outside the Mitad del Mundo complex is the one-room **Museo de la Cultura Solar** (www.quitsato.org; donations accepted; ☹ 9:30am-5:30pm), where visitors can learn about the true equatorial line, which lies on the 1000-year-old indigenous site of Catequilla, visible across the highway. Just north of this museum is the **Museo Solar Inti Ñan** (☎ 239-5122; admission adults/children under 12 yr US$2/1; ☹ 9:30am-5:30pm), offering a fun-house atmosphere of water and energy demonstrations. You'll have to decide for yourself if the 'scientific' experiments are hoaxes.

Rumicucho (admission US$1; ☹ 9am-3pm Mon-Fri, 8am-4pm Sat & Sun) is a small pre-Inca site under excavation, 3.5km north of Mitad del Mundo. On the way to Calacalí, about 5km north of Mitad del Mundo, is the ancient volcanic crater and geobotanical reserve of **Pululahua** (admission US$5). The views (in the morning) are great from the rim, or you can hike down to the tiny village on the crater floor. You can overnight inside the crater at **Pululahua Hostal** (☎ 09-946-6636; www.pululahuahostal.com; dm per person US$12, cabañas US$24-36), an ecologically friendly guesthouse with simple, comfortable rooms. Tasty meals (mains US$2 to US$4) feature ingredients from the organic farm. Guests can hire bikes (US$3 per hour) or horses (US$8 per hour).

To get to Mitad del Mundo from Quito, take the Metrobus (US25¢) north to the last stop, Ofelia station. From there, transfer to the Mitad del Mundo bus (an additional US15¢); the entire trip takes one hour to 1½ hours. The bus drops you off right in front of the entrance.

Buses continue past the complex and will drop you off at the entrance road to Pululahua – ask for the Mirador de Ventanillas (the lookout point where the trail into the crater begins).

REFUGIO DE VIDA SILVESTRE PASOCHOA

This small but beautiful **wildlife reserve** (admission US$7), 30km southeast of Quito, has one of the last stands of undisturbed humid Andean forest left in central Ecuador. It's a recommended day trip for naturalists and bird-watchers, as more than 100 bird species and many rare plants have been recorded here. Trails range from easy to strenuous, and overnight **camping** (per person US$3) is allowed in designated areas. Facilities include latrines, picnic areas and water. A basic 20-bunk **shelter** (dm US$5) is available. The park ranger will give you a small trail map. **Fundación Natura** (☎ 02-254-7399; Moreno Bellido E6-167 btwn Avs Amazonas & Mariana de Jesús) in Quito has trail maps and information and can make overnight reservations. To reach the reserve, take the bus from La Marín station in Quito's Old Town to the village of **Amaguaña** (US$1, one hour), then hire a pickup (about US$10 per group or truck) to take you the last 7km to the park entrance.

ECUADOR

TERMAS DE PAPALLACTA

☎ 02

Home to Ecuador's most luxurious and most scenic thermal baths, the **Termas de Papallacta** (in Quito ☎ 250-4787; www.termaspapallacta.com; admission US$7, free for hotel guests; ⏲ 7am-9pm) are pure medicine for long days of travel. About 67km (two hours) from Quito, the complex, part of the posh **Hotel Termas de Papallacta**, makes for an excellent jaunt from Quito. Cheaper hotels are available outside the complex in the village of Papallacta itself, though it's easy enough to head back to Quito. It's best to go during the week since weekend crowds can swell to 2000 people.

Any of the buses from Quito heading toward Baeza, Tena or Lago Agrio can drop you off in Papallacta. To visit the Termas de Papallacta complex, ask the driver to let you off on the road to the baths, 1.5km before the village. Then catch an awaiting *camioneta* (small truck) for the US$2-ride up the bumpy road.

NORTHERN HIGHLANDS

The steep green hills, dust-blown villages, bustling provincial capitals and cultural riches of the northern highlands lie a few hours' drive from Quito. Those traveling to or from Colombia are bound to pass through the region, and there's plenty worth stopping for: the famous Otavalo market, which dates back to pre-Inca times, is the largest crafts market in South America, and several small towns are known for their handicrafts, including wood carvings and leatherwork.

OTAVALO

☎ 06 / pop 43,000

The friendly and prosperous town of Otavalo (elevation 2550m) is famous for its giant Saturday market, where traditionally dressed indigenous people sell handicrafts to hordes of foreigners who pour in every Saturday to get in on the deals. Despite the market's popularity, the *otavaleños* themselves remain self-determined and culturally uncompromised. The setting is fabulous, and the entire experience remains enchanting.

The most evident feature of the *otavaleños'* culture is their traditional dress. The men wear long single pigtails, calf-length white pants, rope sandals, reversible gray or blue ponchos and dark felt hats. The women are very striking, with beautifully embroidered blouses, long black skirts and shawls, and interesting folded head cloths.

Information

Banco del Pacífico (cnr Bolívar & García Moreno) Bank with ATM.

Banco del Pichincha (Bolívar near García Moreno) Bank with ATM.

Book Market (Roca near García Moreno) Used books.

Sights

Every day vendors hawk an astounding array of goods in the Plaza de Ponchos, the nucleus of the **crafts market**. But the real action happens on Saturday, official market day, when the market swells into adjacent roads.

There is an astounding array of traditional crafts including tapestries, blankets, ponchos, sweaters, hammocks, carvings, beads, original paintings and more.

The **animal market** (⏲ 6-10am Sat), on the western edge of town, offers an interesting break from the hustle of the crafts market. Beneath the volcanic backdrop of Cotacachi and Imbabura, indigenous men and women mill around with pigs, cows, goats and chickens and inspect, haggle and chat in the crisp morning air. The **food market** is near the southern end of Modesto Jaramillo.

The **Parque Cóndor** (☎ 292-4429; www.parque condor.org; admission US$3; ⏲ 9:30am-5pm Tue-Sun) is a Dutch-owned foundation that rehabilitates raptors, vultures and other birds of prey. It's a great opportunity to see an Andean condor up close, as well as eagles, owls, falcons and hawks. Don't miss free flight demonstrations at 11:30am and 4:30pm. The center is perched on the steep hillside of Pucara Alto, 4km from town.

Activities

There's great hiking around Otavalo, especially in the Lagunas de Mojanda area (p621). **Diceny Viajes** (☎ 269-0787; Sucre 10-11) offers warmly recommended hiking trips up Volcán Cotacachi with indigenous guides. **Runa Tupari** (☎ 292-5985; www.runatupari.com; cnr Sucre & Quiroga) partners with local indigenous communities, offering hiking, horse-riding and mountain-biking trips. Its day trips include a 2000m mountain-bike descent into tropical cloud forest and a round-trip 10-hour hike up Cotacachi (4939m). The oldest and best-known information and guide

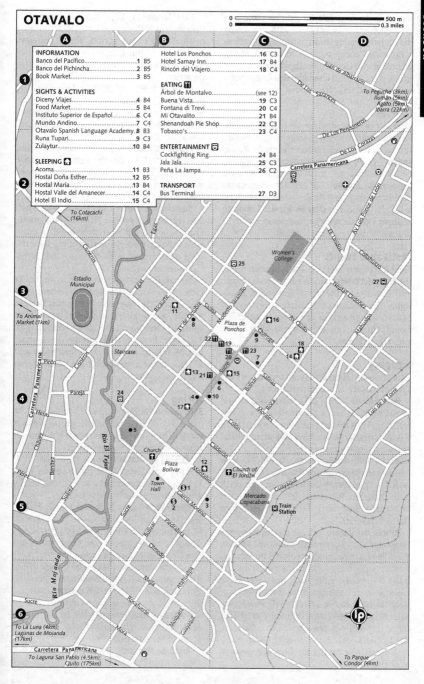

OTAVALO

0 — 500 m
0 — 0.3 miles

INFORMATION
Banco del Pacífico.........................**1** B5
Banco del Pichincha......................**2** B5
Book Market.................................**3** B5

SIGHTS & ACTIVITIES
Diceny Viajes................................**4** B4
Food Market.................................**5** B4
Instituto Superior de Español.........**6** C4
Mundo Andino..............................**7** C4
Otavalo Spanish Language Academy.**8** B3
Runa Tupari..................................**9** C3
Zulaytur......................................**10** B4

SLEEPING
Acoma...**11** B3
Hostal Doña Esther.......................**12** B5
Hostal María................................**13** B4
Hostal Valle del Amanecer............**14** C4
Hotel El Indio...............................**15** C4

Hotel Los Ponchos........................**16** C3
Hotel Samay Inn...........................**17** B4
Rincón del Viajero.........................**18** C4

EATING
Árbol de Montalvo....................(see 12)
Buena Vista.................................**19** C3
Fontana di Trevi...........................**20** C4
Mi Otavalito.................................**21** B4
Shenandoah Pie Shop...................**22** C3
Tobasco's....................................**23** C4

ENTERTAINMENT
Cockfighting Ring.........................**24** B4
Jala Jala......................................**25** C3
Peña La Jampa.............................**26** C2

TRANSPORT
Bus Terminal................................**27** D3

To Peguche (3km);
Ilumán (5km);
Agato (5km);
Ibarra (22km)

Women's
College

To Cotacachi
(16km)

Estadio
Municipal

To Animal
Market (1km)

Plaza de
Ponchos

Staircase

Church

Plaza
Bolívar

Town
Hall

Church of
El Jordán

Mercado
Copacabana

Train
Station

To La Luna (4km);
Lagunas de Mojanda
(17km)

Carretera Panamericana

To Laguna San Pablo (4.5km);
Quito (175km)

To Parque
Cóndor (4km)

service in town is **Zulaytur** (☎ 09-944-0004; www
.geocities.com/zulaytur; cnr Sucre & Colón, 2nd fl). It's run by
the knowledgeable Rodrigo Mora, who offers
a variety of cheap tours (US$26 to US$40),
including visits to indigenous weavers' homes,
where you can learn about the weaving process
and buy products off the loom.

Courses

Otavalo is a good place to learn Spanish.
Recommended language schools, with homestay and volunteer options, include **Mundo
Andino** (☎ 292-1864; www.mandinospanishschool.com;
cnr Salinas & Bolívar 4-04; lessons per hr US$5), **Instituto
Superior de Español** (☎ 299-2424; www.instituto
-superior.net; cnr Sucre & Morales; groups/individuals per
hr US$5.75/7) and the **Otavalo Spanish Language
Academy** (☎ 292-1404; www.otavalospanish.com; cnr 31
de Octubre & Salinas; lessons per hr US$6-7).

Festivals & Events

Held during the first two weeks of September,
the **Fiesta del Yamor** features processions, music
and dancing in the plaza, fireworks, cockfights, the election of the fiesta queen and, of
course, lots of *chicha de yamor* (a delicious
nonalcoholic corn drink made with seven
varieties of corn).

Sleeping

Guesthouses fill on Friday, so arrive early for
the best choice of accommodations.

Hostal María (☎ 292-0672; Modesto Jaramillo near
Colón; s/d US$6/12) Set in an unattractive green
building, Hostal María has simple rooms with
wood floors, large windows and jarring floral
curtains. Good value.

Hostal Valle del Amanecer (☎ 292-0990; www
.hostalvalledelamanecer.com; cnr Roca & Quiroga; r per person with/without bathroom US$11/9) Rooms are small
and dark, but the shady hammock-strewn
courtyard and tasty breakfasts still lure
budget travelers.

Rincón del Viajero (☎ 292-1741; www.rincondel
viajero.org; Roca 11-07; r per person with/without bathroom
US$12/10) Warm hospitality, colorful murals and
homey, snug rooms make this a great deal. It
has a TV lounge, a fireplace, hot water and a
rooftop terrace strung with hammocks.

Hotel Los Ponchos (☎ 292-2035; www.hotellos
ponchos.com; Sucre 14-15 near Av Quito; s/d US$10/20) This
dated but well-run place has a maze of clean,
tiled rooms with fuzzy animal bedspreads.
Stay street-side on the top floor for views of
Volcán Cotacachi.

Hotel Samay Inn (☎ 292-1826; samayinnhotel@hot
mail.com; Sucre 1009 near Colón; s/d US$10/20) Located
in the heart of the action, shady hallways
lead to basic but bright rooms. Balconies
offer prime people-watching, but can also
be noisy.

Hotel El Indio (☎ 292-0060; Sucre 12-14; s/d
US$15/30) A reliable hotel located near the
Plaza, El Indio offers large colorful rooms
with glossy wood trim surrounding a small,
open-air courtyard.

Acoma (☎ 292-6570; www.hotelacoma.com; Salinas
7-57; s/d US$24/37) An artfully minded midrange
guesthouse, the Acoma has lovely cedar floors,
mosaic tiles and skylights. Rooms are comfortable and airy.

Hostal Doña Esther (☎ 292-0739; www.otavalo
hotel.com; Montalvo 4-44; s/d US$25/36) This small,
Dutch-owned colonial-style hotel is cozy,
with attractive rooms surrounding a courtyard ornamented with ceramics and ferns.
Good restaurant.

For an idyllic setting outside town, try **La
Luna** (☎ 09-315-6082; www.hostallaluna.com; campsites
US$2.50, dm US$6, r per person with/without bathroom
US$12/9), a low-key, budget getaway 4.5km
south of Otavalo on the road to Lagunas de
Mojanda. Perks include pretty views, great
nearby hiking, a fireplace, dining room and
kitchen. It's an hour's walk from town, or grab
a taxi for US$4.

Eating

Shenandoah Pie Shop (Salinas 5-15; pie slices US$1.30)
Try a slice of these famous deep-dish pies à la
mode. The *mora* (blackberry) pie is thick with
fruit and perfectly tart yet sweet.

our pick **Mi Otavalito** (Sucre 11-19; mains US$4-
6) This well-loved local place serves tasty
Ecuadorian dishes amid a welcoming, family
atmosphere. Good-value *almuerzos*.

Buena Vista (Salinas, 2nd fl; mains US$4-6; Ⓥ closed
Tue) On a fine location above the Plaza de
Ponchos, this inviting low-key spot serves
grilled trout, veggie burgers, salads and bistro
fare to a mostly foreign crowd.

Tobasco's (cnr Sucre & Salinas, 2nd fl; mains US$5-6)
The rooftop patio overlooking the Plaza de
Ponchos is a fine spot for tasty enchiladas,
burritos, tacos and tropical cocktails.

Fontana di Trevi (Sucre near Salinas, 2nd fl; mains US$5-
6) Otavalo's original pizza joint still serves
some of the best pizza in town.

Árbol de Montalvo (Montalvo 4-44; mains US$5-8;
Ⓥ 6-9pm Mon-Thu, noon-10pm Fri-Sun) Make your

way to the back of Hostal Doña Esther for organic salads, seasonal vegetables and some Mediterranean-inspired pastas.

Entertainment

Otavalo is dead midweek but lively on the weekends. *Peñas* are the main hangouts.

Peña La Jampa (☎ 292-7791; cnr 31 de Octubre & Panamericana; ☼ 7pm-3am Fri & Sat) Offers a mix of live salsa, merengue, *rock en español* (Spanish rock) and *música folklórica* (folk music).

Fauno (Morales btwn Bolívar & Sucre; ☼ 2pm-3am daily) A slick three-level club attracting the younger crowd with Latin rock on weekends.

Jala Jala (☎ 292-4081; www.jalajalaotavalo.com; cnr 31 de Octubre & Av Quito; ☼ 7pm-3am Fri & Sat) One of the town's newer *peñas*, the elongated space gets busy in the wee hours.

Cockfights are held every Saturday starting at about 7pm in the ring at the southwest end of 31 de Octubre (admission US$1) .

Getting There & Around

The **bus terminal** (cnr Atahualpa & Collahuazo) is two blocks north of Av Quito. Transportes Otavalo/Los Lagos is the only company from Quito (US$2, 2½ hours) that enters the terminal. Other companies drop passengers on the Panamericana (a 10-minute walk from town) on their way north or south. Frequent buses depart the terminal to Ibarra (US50¢, 35 minutes).

AROUND OTAVALO
☎ 06

The quality of light, the sense that time has stopped, and the endless Andean vistas give the countryside around Otavalo an enchanting character. Scattered with lakes, hiking trails and traditional indigenous villages, it's an area well worth exploring. Tour agencies in Otavalo (p618) can provide information or organize hikes, or you can explore on your own.

The beautiful **Lagunas de Mojanda**, in the high *páramo* some 17km south of Otavalo, make for unforgettable hiking. Taxis from Otavalo charge about US$15 each way. You could also walk up and camp. Both Runa Tupari and Zulaytur (see p618) offer guided hikes that include transportation. For information about the lakes visit the **Mojanda Foundation/Pachamama Association** (☎ 292-2986; www.casamojanda.com/foundation.html) across from Casa Mojanda.

Strung along the eastern side of the Panamericana, a few kilometers north of Otavalo, are the mostly indigenous villages of **Peguche, Ilumán** and **Agato**. You can walk or take local buses to all three. In Peguche, **Hostal Aya Huma** (☎ 269-0333; www.ayahuma.com; s/d US$17/24, with shared bathroom US$8/12) is a beautifully set, mellow *hostal* that serves good, cheap homemade meals (veggie options too). You can also hike to a pretty **waterfall** 2km south of Peguche.

Laguna San Pablo can be reached on foot from Otavalo by heading roughly southeast on any of the paths heading over the hill behind the railway station. You can then walk the paved road that goes all the way around the lake.

The village of **Cotacachi**, some 15km north of Otavalo, is famous for its leatherwork, which is sold in stores all along the main street. There are hourly buses from Otavalo and a few hotels in Cotacachi.

About 18km west of Cotacachi, the spectacular crater lake, **Laguna Cuicocha**, lies within an extinct, eroded volcano. The lake is part of the **Reserva Ecológica Cotacachi-Cayapas** (lake admission US$1, entire park US$5), established to protect the large area of western Andean forest that extends from **Volcán Cotacachi** (4939m) to the Río Cayapas in the coastal lowlands. A walk around the lake takes about six hours (ask about safety at the ranger station at the park entrance). To get there, take a truck or taxi (each US$8, one way) from Cotacachi.

IBARRA
☎ 06 / pop 109,000

Though growth has diminished Ibarra's (elevation 2225m) former small-town allure, its colonial architecture, leafy plazas and cobbled streets make it a handsome city – at least on weekends when the streets aren't so choked with traffic. Ibarra's unique blend of students, *mestizos,* indigenous highlanders and Afro-Ecuadorians give it an interesting multicultural edge.

Ibarra's old architecture and shady plazas sit north of the center. The **tourist office** (iTur; ☎ 260-8409; www.turismoibarra.com; cnr Oveido & Sucre; ☼ 8:30am-1pm & 2-5pm Mon-Fri) is two blocks south of Parque Pedro Moncayo. **Banco del Pacífico** (cnr Olmedo & Moncayo) has an ATM.

Sleeping

Hostal Ecuador (☎ 295-6425; Mosquera 5-54; s/d US$5/10) Bare, bright rooms give a sanitarium effect, but the attention is sincere.

ECUADOR

Hostal Imbabura (☎ 264-4586; cnr Oviedo 9-33 & Sánchez; s/d with shared bathroom US$7/14) Clean, pleasant rooms with wood floors open onto a peaceful inner courtyard strung with hanging plants.

Hostal El Dorado (☎ 295-8700; cnr Oviedo 5-41 & Sucre; s/d US$8/16) The best among the budget options, El Dorado offers clean, tidy rooms. The best ones are bright and airy with wood floors.

Hostal El Ejecutivo (☎ 295-6575; Bolívar 9-69; s/d from US$8/16; 🖳) Old plaids dominate the ample rooms (some with balconies) and add a retro feel. An internet cafe is on the 1st floor.

Eating

Ibarra is known for tasty *nogadas* (nougats) and sweet *arrope de mora* (a thick blackberry syrup), available at kiosks facing Parque La Merced.

Heladería Rosalía Suárez (Oviedo 7-82; ice cream US$1.50) Ecuador's most famous ice-cream shop has been whipping up refreshing *helados de paila* (handmade sorbets) for over a century.

Antojitos de Mi Tierra (Plaza Francisco Calderón; mains US$2-4) The place to go for traditional snacks such as *chicha de arroz* (a sweetened rice drink) and tamales, *humitas* and *quimbolitos*.

Café Arte (Salinas 5-43; mains US$4-6; 🕙 5pm-midnight) A funky and relaxed artist-owned gathering spot, this is a good place to socialize and check out local bands. Food leans toward Mexican.

Órale (Sucre btwn Grijalva & Borrero; mains US$4) Tasty Mexican food is served in a casual atmosphere.

Getting There & Away

BUS

Ibarra's new bus terminal is located at the end of Av Teodoro Gómez de la Torre. You can grab a taxi to or from the center for US$1. There are regular departures to Quito (US$2.50, two to three hours), Guayaquil (US$9, 10 hours), Esmeraldas (US$8, nine hours), Atacames (US$9, nine hours), San Lorenzo (US$4, four hours), Tulcán (US$2, 2½ hours), Otavalo (US50¢, 35 minutes) and numerous other destinations.

TRAIN

The spectacular Ibarra–San Lorenzo railway, which once linked the highlands to the coast, no longer runs. However, *autoferros* go as far as Primer Paso (US$4 one way, 2½ hours), less than a quarter of the way to San Lorenzo. It's essentially a round-trip tourist attraction and should depart at 8:30am daily, though canceled departures are common. For more information, visit the **train station** (☎ 295-0390; Espejo).

WESTERN ANDEAN SLOPES
☎ 02

The western slopes of the Andes, northwest of Quito, are home to some of Ecuador's last remaining stands of tropical cloud forest. Along the old road to Santo Domingo (which continues to the coast), you'll encounter some fabulous places to explore these cloud-swept forests. The best place to start is the village of **Mindo**, which is famous for its bird-watching and its environmentally conscious inhabitants. Once in Mindo, you can hike in the

---

GETTING TO COLOMBIA

The Rumichaca border crossing, 6.5km north of **Tulcán**, is the principal gateway to Colombia and currently the only recommended crossing. Formalities are straightforward at the border, which is open 24 hours every day. Crossing is free. Minibuses (US80¢) and taxis (US$3) run regularly between the border and Tulcán's Parque Isidro Ayora, about five blocks north of the central plaza. The buses accept Colombian pesos or US dollars. Be absolutely certain that you have your papers in order and be ready for drugs and weapons searches on both sides. Once across the border, there is frequent transportation to Ipiales, the first town in Colombia, 2km away.

If you need to break your journey at Tulcán, there are many basic (but generally shabby) guesthouses. Better picks include **Hotel San Francisco** (☎ 06-298-0760; Bolívar near Atahualpa; s/d US$5/10) and **Hotel Unicornio** (☎ 06-298-0638; cnr Pichincha & Sucre; s/d US$9/18). Direct buses from Tulcán go to Ibarra (US$2.50, 2½ hours), Quito (US$5, five hours), Guayaquil (US$13, 13 hours) and Cuenca (US$17, 17 hours). The **bus terminal** (cnr Bolívar & Arellano) is 2.5km southwest of the town center, reachable by city bus (US20¢) or taxi (about US$1).

If you're crossing from Colombia, see p575.

cloud forest, hire bird-watching guides, swim in the Río Mindo and *relax*.

There are several basic but charming accommodations in town, including **Rubby Hostal** (☎ 09-340-6321; rubbyhostal@yahoo.com; r per person US$6) and **La Casa de Cecilia** (☎ 09-334-5393; casadececilia @yahoo.com; s/d US$6/12).

Direct buses run by Cooperativa Flor de Valle go daily to Mindo (US$2.50, 2½ hours) from Quito's Ofelia station.

CENTRAL HIGHLANDS

South of Quito the Panamericana winds past eight of the country's 10 highest peaks, including the picture-perfect snowcapped cone of Volcán Cotopaxi (5897m) and the glaciated behemoth, Volcán Chimborazo (6310m). For trekkers and climbers, the central highlands are a paradise, and even inexperienced climbers can have a go at summiting some of the country's highest peaks. You can also hike between remote Andean villages near the Quilotoa Loop, gorge yourself on homemade cheeses and chocolate in Guaranda and Salinas, barrel downhill to the Oriente on a rented mountain bike from Baños, hike or trek in spectacular national parks or ride the scenic train down the famous Nariz del Diablo. The central highlands are home to scores of tiny indigenous villages and many of the country's most traditional markets.

PARQUE NACIONAL COTOPAXI
☎ 03

The centerpiece of Ecuador's most popular **national park** (admission US$10) is the snowcapped and downright astonishing **Volcán Cotopaxi** (5897m), Ecuador's second-highest peak. The park is almost deserted midweek, when nature freaks can have the breathtaking (literally) scenery nearly to themselves.

The park has a small museum, an information center, a *refugio* (climbers' refuge) and some camping and picnicking areas. The gate is open from 7am to 3pm (longer on weekends), but hikers can come through any time.

The park's main entrance is via a turnoff from the Panamericana, roughly 30km north of Latacunga. From the turnoff, it's 6km to **Control Caspi**, the entrance station. Any Quito–Latacunga bus will let you off at the turnoff. Follow the main dirt roads (also signed) to

the entrance. It's another 9km or so to the museum. About 4km beyond the museum is **Laguna de Limpiopungo**, a shallow Andean lake 3830m above sea level; a trail circles the lake and takes about half an hour to walk. The *refugio* is about 12km past (and 1000m above) the lake. You can drive up a very rough road to a parking area (about 1km before the refuge) or hire a truck and driver from Latacunga for about US$40.

From the lake you can walk to the refuge, but walking at this altitude is difficult for the unacclimatized, and altitude sickness is a very real danger; acclimatize for several days in Quito or elsewhere before attempting to walk in. Continuing beyond the climbers' refuge requires snow- and ice-climbing gear and expertise. Outfitters in Quito (p608) and Latacunga (p624) offer guided summit trips and downhill mountain-biking tours of Cotopaxi.

Near the main entrance to the park, about 2km west (and across the Panamericana), the **Albergue Cuello de Luna** (☎ 09-970-0330, in Quito 02-224-2744; www.cuellodeluna.com; dm from US$11, s/d/tr/q US$23/34/45/53, s/d/tr without bathroom US$20/26/36) is friendly and popular, and serves good meals (US$7 to US$10). **Albergue de Alta Montaña Paja Blanca** (☎ 231-4234; r per person US$13), adjacent to the museum, has shared A-frames with beds, fireplaces and hot water, but no electricity at night. Next door, the restaurant by the same name serves good local trout and cold beers.

Camping in the park costs US$3 per person. A bunk in the refuge costs US$20; cooking facilities are available. Be sure to bring a warm sleeping bag.

LATACUNGA
☎ 03 / pop 87,000

Many travelers end up passing through Latacunga, either to access the Quilotoa Loop (p625), the Thursday-morning market in Saquisilí (p625), or Parque Nacional Cotopaxi (left). But for those who stick around, Latacunga also offers a quiet and congenial historic center that's famous for its Mamá Negra festival. You'd never know that such a charming city lies behind the loud and polluted section that greets visitors on the Panamericana.

Information
Banco de Guayaquil (Maldonado 7-20) Bank with ATM.
Discovery Net (Salcedo 4-16; per hr US$1) Internet access.

ECUADOR

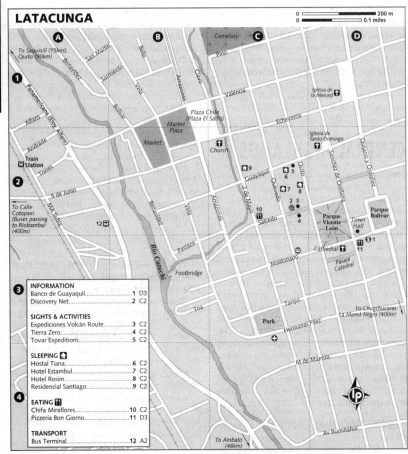

LATACUNGA

INFORMATION	
Banco de Guayaquil.....................1 D3	
Discovery Net..............................2 C2	

SIGHTS & ACTIVITIES	
Expediciones Volcán Route..........3 C2	
Tierra Zero................................4 C2	
Tovar Expeditions.......................5 C2	

SLEEPING	
Hostal Tiana...............................6 C2	
Hotel Estambul...........................7 C2	
Hotel Rosim...............................8 C2	
Residencial Santiago...................9 C2	

EATING	
Chifa Miraflores..........................10 C2	
Pizzería Bon Giorno.....................11 D3	

TRANSPORT	
Bus Terminal..............................12 A2	

Activities

Several tour operators offer day trips and two- to three-day climbing trips to Cotopaxi (p623). Day trips run about US$50 per person, depending on the size of your group and whether or not the US$10 park entrance fee is included (usually not). Two-day climbing trips to Cotopaxi cost about US$160 per person – make sure your guide is qualified and motivated if you're attempting the summit. A few recommended agencies:

Expediciones Volcán Route (☎ 281-2452; volcan route@hotmail.com; Salcedo 4-49)

Tierra Zero (☎ 280-4327; tierraazultours@hotmail.com; cnr Salcedo & Quito)

Tovar Expeditions (☎ 281-1333; tovarexpeditions @hotmail.com; Guayaquil 5-38)

Festivals & Events

Latacunga's major annual fiesta (September 23 and 24) honors La Virgen de las Mercedes. More popularly known as the **Fiesta de la Mamá Negra**, the event features processions, costumes, fireworks, street dancing and Andean music. This is one of those festivals that, although superficially Christian, has a strong indigenous influence and is well worth seeing.

Sleeping

Hotels fill up fast on Wednesday afternoon for the Thursday-morning indigenous market at Saquisilí.

Residencial Santiago (☎ 280-0899; cnr 2 de Mayo & Guayaquil; r per person with/without bathroom US$8/6) This hospitable, no-frills hotel has aging rooms with wood floors. Ask for a room with a window.

Hostal Tiana (☎ 281-0147; www.hostaltiana .com; Guayaquil 5-32; dm US$8, s/d with shared bathroom US$10/14; ▣) Latacunga's new *hostal* is situated in a century-old house with a pretty courtyard. Rooms are basic but clean and all share bathrooms. Owners are a great source of regional information, and luggage storage (US$2) is available. Dutch, English and Spanish are spoken, and tasty meals are available.

Hotel Estambul (☎ 280-0354; Quevedo 73-40; r per person with/without bathroom US$11/9) A reliable family-run budget guesthouse with comfortable rooms.

Hotel Rosim (☎ 280-2172; www.hotelrosim.com; Quito 16-49; s/d US$12/24; ▣) This good-value hotel in a 90-year-old building has high ceilings and original floors. Cable TV and wi-fi are included in the price.

Eating

Latacunga's traditional dish is the *chugchucara*, a tasty plate of *fritada* (pieces of fried pork meat), *mote* (hominy) and various sides. There are several *chugchucara* restaurants on Quijano y Ordoñez, a few blocks south of the town center. Inexpensive *pollerías* (roast-chicken restaurants) lie along Amazonas between Salcedo and Guayaquil.

Chifa Miraflores (☎ 280-9079; cnr 2 de Mayo & Salcedo; mains US$3-5; ☯ 10am-9pm) Miraflores makes mean stir-fries and other Chinese classics.

Pizzería Bon Giorno (cnr Sanchez de Orellana & Maldonado; mains US$4-7) Giant portions of hearty lasagna and good pizzas.

our pick **Chugchucaras La Mamá Negra** (☎ 280-5401; Quijano y Ordoñez 1-67; chugchucara US$6.50; ☯ closed Mon) One of the best places for *chugchucaras*.

Getting There & Away

Buses from Quito (US$1.50, two hours) will drop you off at the **bus terminal** (Panamericana) if Latacunga is their final destination. If you're taking a bus that's continuing to Ambato or Riobamba, it will drop you off at the corner of 5 de Junio and Cotopaxi, about five blocks west of the Panamericana. Buses to Ambato (US$1, 45 minutes) and Quito leave from the bus terminal. If you're heading south to Riobamba, it's easiest to catch a passing bus from the corner of 5 de Junio and Cotopaxi. Otherwise, bus to Ambato and change there.

From the terminal, Transportes Cotopaxi departs hourly for the rough but spectacular descent to Quevedo (US$4, 5½ hours) via Zumbahua (US$2, two hours). For transport information to other destinations on the Quilotoa Loop, see p626.

THE QUILOTOA LOOP
☎ 03

Bumping along the spectacular dirt roads of the Quilotoa Loop and hiking between the area's Andean villages is one of Ecuador's most exhilarating adventures. Transport is tricky but the rewards are abundant: highland markets, the breathtaking crater lake of Laguna Quilotoa, splendid hikes, and traditional highland villages. Allow yourself *at least* three days for the loop and bring warm clothes (it gets painfully cold up here), water and snacks. If you're planning a multiday hike through the area, do yourself a favor and leave your heavy backpack in a guesthouse in Latacunga (carrying only the essentials).

Latacunga to Zumbahua

Ten kilometers west of Latacunga, **Pujilí** has a Sunday market and interesting Corpus Christi and All Souls' Day celebrations. The road winds into the upper reaches of the *páramo*, passing the speck-like village of Tigua about 45km after Pujilí. Tigua is known for the bright paintings of Andean life made on sheepskin canvases. Cozy lodging is available at **Posada de Tigua** (Hacienda Agrícola-Ganadera Tigua Chimbacucho; ☎ 281-4870; www.laposadadetigua.com; Vía Latacunga–Zumbahua Km 49; r per person incl breakfast & dinner US$30), a working dairy ranch. Horse riding is also available.

Some 15km west of Tigua, the tiny village of **Zumbahua** has a small but fascinating Saturday market and is surrounded by green patchwork peaks, a setting that makes for spectacular walking.

Accommodations and food in Zumbahua are basic. The town's three lodgings fill up fast on Friday, so get there early; the best of them is **Cóndor Matzi** (☎ 281-4611; s/d US$6/12), on the square.

Zumbahua to Saquisilí

From Zumbahua buses and hired trucks trundle up the 14km of unpaved road leading north to one of Ecuador's most staggering sights – **Laguna Quilotoa**, a stunning volcanic crater lake. Near the crater rim are several

ECUADOR

extremely basic, inexpensive accommodations owned by friendly indigenous folks. Bring a warm sleeping bag.

About 14km north of the lake is the wee village of **Chugchilán**, which is an excellent base for hiking and has several traveler-friendly hotels. Rates include dinner and breakfast. **Hostal Mama Hilda** (☎ 281-4814, in Quito 02-258-2957; www .hostalmamahilda.com; r per person with/without bathroom US$21/17) is friendly and popular with backpackers. Delightful **Hostal Cloud Forest** (☎ 281-4808; jose_cloudforest@hotmail.com; r per person with/without bathroom US$15/12) is the cheapest and simplest.

Some 14km northeast of Chugchilán and just off the Quilotoa Loop, the beautiful village of **Isinliví** makes a good hike from either Chugchilán or Sigchos. A woodworking/cabinetry shop makes high-end furniture, and locals can direct you to nearby *pucarás* (pre-Inca hill fortresses). **Llullu Llama** (☎ 281-4790; www.llullullama.com; dm per person US$18; r per person US$19-25), run by the same owners as Latacunga's Hostal Tiana, is an enchanting old farmhouse with comfortable rooms and a wood-burning stove. A delicious dinner and breakfast is included in the price.

About 23km north of Chugchilán is the village of **Sigchos**, which has a couple of basic lodgings. From here, it's about 52km east to **Saquisilí**, home of one of the most important indigenous markets in the country. Each Thursday morning inhabitants of remote indigenous villages, most of whom are recognized by their felt porkpie hats and red ponchos, descend upon the market in a cacophony of sound and color. Accommodations are available in several cold-water cheapies.

Getting There & Around

No buses go all the way around the loop. From Latacunga they only travel as far as Chugchilán (US$4, four hours), and they either go clockwise (via Zumbahua and Quilotoa) or counterclockwise (via Saquisilí and Sigchos). The bus via Zumbahua departs Latacunga's bus terminal daily at noon, passing Zumbahua at around 1:30pm, Laguna Quilotoa at around 2pm, arriving in Chugchilán at about 4pm. The bus via Sigchos departs daily at 11:30am, passing Saquisilí just before noon and Sigchos at around 2pm, arriving in Chugchilán at around 3:30pm; the Saturday bus via Sigchos leaves at 10:30am.

From Chugchilán, buses returning to Latacunga via Zumbahua leave Chugchilán

Monday through Friday at 4am (good morning!), passing Quilotoa at around 6am, Zumbahua at around 6:30am, arriving in Latacunga at around 8am. On Saturday this bus leaves Chugchilán at 3am, and on Sunday at 6am and 10am. Buses via Sigchos leave Monday through Friday at 3am, passing Sigchos at around 4am, Saquisilí at around 7am, arriving in Latacunga at around 8am. On Saturday this bus departs at 7am. On Sunday you must switch buses in Sigchos.

A morning milk truck (US$1) leaves Chugchilán for Sigchos around 8:30am and will take passengers, allowing you to skip the predawn wake-up. In Zumbahua, trucks can be hired to Laguna Quilotoa or anywhere on the loop.

Be sure to confirm bus times at your guesthouse.

AMBATO
☎ 03 / pop 217,000

Compared to nearby Baños, Ambato offers little for the traveler, except the chance to experience a nontouristy Ecuadorian city. Ambato's claims to fame are its chaotic **Monday market**; its flower festival, held in the second half of February; and its *quintas* (historic country homes) outside the center. Above town, there are picturesque views of the puffing Volcán Tungurahua.

The bus terminal is 2km from downtown. City buses marked 'Centro' go to Parque Cevallos (US20¢), the central plaza.

Information

Banco del Pacífico (cnr Lalama & Cevallos) Bank and ATM.
Net Place (Montalvo 05-58 near Cevallos; per hr US$1) Internet access.
Tourist office (☎ 282-1800; cnr Guayaquil & Rocafuerte)

Sleeping & Eating

Hostal Conquistador (☎ 282-0391; Parque 12 de Noviembre; s/d US$7/8) This is a clean, comfortable, centrally located option. The upper floors are quieter.

Gran Hotel (☎ 282-4235; cnr Rocafuerte & Lalama; s/d incl breakfast US$15/21) The Gran may lack grandeur, but the carpeted rooms have hot showers and TVs, and the staff is pleasant.

Delicias del Paso (☎ 242-6048; cnr Sucre & Quito; menu items US$1-2; 10am-6pm) This cafeteria serves tasty quiches and cakes, and you can order them to go right from the street.

Mercado Central (12 de Noviembre; mains US$1.50; 7am-7pm) The 2nd floor of Ambato's indoor market has particularly good *lapingachos* (fried mashed-potato-and-cheese pancakes).

Getting There & Away

Ambato has regular bus services to Baños (US$1, one hour), Riobamba (US$1.25, one hour), Quito (US$2, 2½ hours) and Guayaquil (US$6, six hours). Less frequent, daily buses travel to Guaranda (US$2, two hours), Cuenca (US$7, seven hours) and Tena (US$5, five hours).

BAÑOS

☎ 03 / pop 14,700

Hemmed in by luxuriant green peaks, blessed with steaming thermal baths and adorned by a beautiful waterfall, Baños is one of Ecuador's most enticing and popular tourist destinations. Ecuadorians and foreigners alike flock here to hike, soak in the baths, ride mountain bikes, zip around on rented quad-runners, volcano-watch, party, and break their molars on the town's famous *melcocha* (taffy). Touristy as it is, it's a wonderful place to hang out for a few days.

Baños (elevation 1800m) is also the gateway town into the jungle via Puyo (p649). East of Baños, the road drops spectacularly toward the upper Amazon Basin and the views are best taken in over the handlebars of a mountain bike, which you can rent in town.

Baños' annual fiesta is held on December 16 and preceding days.

Information

Banco del Pichincha (cnr Ambato & Halflants) Bank with ATM.

Direct Connect (Martínez near Alfaro; per hr US$2) Internet.

La Herradura (Martínez near Alfaro; per kilo US$1) Laundry.

Tourist office (☎ 274-0483; mun_banos@andinanet .net; Halflants near Rocafuerte)

Sights & Activities

A small town in a fabulous setting, Baños offers an excellent range of outdoor adventures, plus hot baths for a refreshing soak when the day is done.

HOT BATHS

A soak in a thermal bath is an essential Baños experience. Go early in the morning (ie before 7am) to beat the crowds. Towels

are generally available for rent, though sometimes they run out. Boasting the town's best-known pools is the **Piscina de la Virgen** (daytime/night US$1.60/2; ☎ 4:30am-5pm & 6-10pm). **Piscina El Salado** (admission US$1; ☎ 4:30am-5pm), 2km west of town, is similar but has more pools of different temperatures. Catch the bus on Rocafuerte, near the market.

HIKING

Baños has some great hiking. The tourist office provides a crude but useful map showing some of the trails around town.

From the bus terminal, a short trail leads to Puente San Francisco (San Francisco Bridge), across Río Pastaza. Continue up the other side as far as you want.

At the southern end of Maldonado a footpath leads to Bellavista (the white-cross lookout high over Baños) and then to the settlement of Runtún, about 1km away. South on Mera, a footpath leads to the **Mirador de la Virgen del Agua Santa** and on to Runtún.

MOUNTAIN BIKING

Numerous companies rent bikes for about US$5 per day. You can find several outfitters along the streets south of Parque de la Basílica. Check the equipment carefully. The best paved ride is the dramatic descent to Puyo, about 60km away by road. Be sure to stop at the spectacular **Pailón del Diablo**, a waterfall about 18km from Baños. There is a passport control at the town of Shell so carry your documents. From Puyo (or anywhere along the way) take a bus back to Baños with the bike on the roof.

CLIMBING & TREKKING

The climbing conditions on Tungurahua (5016m), an active volcano, are naturally in flux. At the time of research, local authorities were carefully monitoring the situation and considering declaring the volcano open for climbing. The volcano is part of **Parque Nacional Sangay** (admission US$10).

Climbs of Cotopaxi and Chimborazo can be arranged. Reputable climbing outfitters are **Expediciones Amazónicas** (☎ 274-0506; www.amazon icas.banios.com; amazonicas2002@yahoo.com; Oriente 11-68 near Halflants) and **Rainforestur** (☎ 274-0743; www .rainforestur.com.ec; Ambato 800). The going rate for climbs with an overnight stay in the refuge is around US$120 to US$150 per person, plus park fees.

ECUADOR

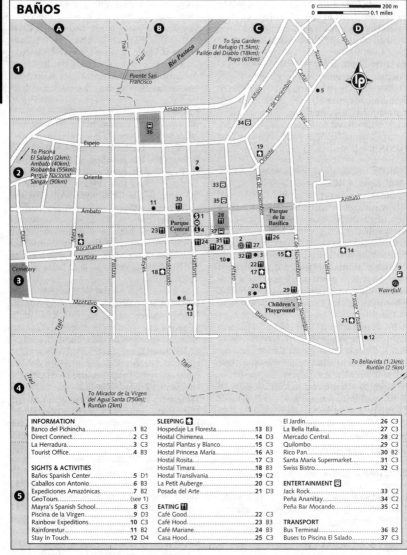

BAÑOS

HORSE RIDING
You can arrange four-hour horse-riding trips for around US$25 per person through **Caballos con Antonio** (☎ 274-1618; Montalvo near Halflants).

RIVER RAFTING
GeoTours (☎ 274-1344; www.geotoursbanios.com; cnr Ambato & Halflants) offers half-day trips on the

Río Patate for US$30 and full-day trips on the Río Pastaza (class IV-V) for US$100. The full-day trip is 10 hours, with four hours on the river. Prices include food, transportation, guides and equipment. It also offers a three-day kayaking course ($150). **Rainforestur** (☎ 274-0743; www.rainforestur.com.ec; Ambato 800) also offers rafting trips.

JUNGLE TRIPS

Loads of jungle trips are advertised from Baños, but not all guides are experienced. Those listed here have received good reports. Three- to seven-day jungle tours cost about US$30 to US$50 per person per day, depending on the destination. You won't see animals in the forests closer to Baños; if you want primary rainforest, make sure you're going as deep as the lower Río Napo area (p646).

Owned by a member of the Shuar community (an indigenous group from the southern Oriente), **Rainbow Expeditions** (☎ 08-909-2616; rainbowexpeditions2005@hotmail.com; cnr Alfaro & Martínez) is an extremely well-run operation with interesting trips. Other recommended operators are **Rainforestur** (☎ 274-0743; www.rainforestur.com.ec; Ambato 800) and **Expediciones Amazónicas** (☎ 274-0506; www.amazonicas.banios.com; amazonicas2002@yahoo.com; Oriente 11-68 near Halflants). They both lead culture and nature tours near Puyo and Lago Agrio.

MASSAGES & SPA TREATMENTS

Baños offers an endless supply of spas with medicinal mud baths, massages and other treatments (intestinal drainage, anyone?). The well-maintained **Spa Garden El Refugio** (☎ 274-0482; www.spaecuador.info; Camino Real; treatments US$5-20), just outside of town, has a good range of treatments. For excellent one-hour full-body massages ($25) and herbal facials ($20), pay a visit to **Stay In Touch** (☎ 274-0973; Ibarra).

Courses

One-on-one classes start around US$6 per hour (slightly less for small-group instruction). The following schools also offer homestays.

Baños Spanish Center (☎ 274-0632; www.spanishcenter.banios.com; Oriente 8-20 near Cañar)

Mayra's Spanish School (☎ 274-2850; www.mayraspanishschool.com; Montalvo near 16 de Deciembre)

Sleeping

There are scores of hotels in Baños, and competition is stiff, so prices are low. Rates are highest on Friday evenings and holiday weekends when every hotel in town can fill up.

Hostal Rosita (☎ 274-0396; 16 de Diciembre; r per person US$5-6) If you want space at rock-bottom prices, Hostal Rosita is hard to beat. You'll find big, basic, minimally furnished suites, most with kitchen units.

Hostal Timara (☎ 274-0599; Maldonado; r per person with/without bathroom from US$7/5) This 40-year-old family business has a range of rooms from colorful, nicely appointed rooms with private bathrooms to older basic quarters with shared facilities. Guest kitchen.

Hostal Chimenea (☎ 274-2725; lachimenea01@hotmail.com; Martínez near Vieira; r per person US$5.50-7.50; 🖳) This popular budget choice near the baths has clean, comfortable rooms with wood floors; the best rooms have good views.

Hostal Plantas y Blanco (☎ 274-0044; option3@hotmail.com; cnr Martínez & 12 de Noviembre; r per person US$5.50-8.50; 🖳) Attractively decorated and eternally popular, 'Plants and White' (you figure it out) scores big points with travelers for its rooftop terrace, outstanding breakfasts, on-site steam bathroom and overall value.

Hostal Princesa María (☎ 274-1035; holaprincesamaria1@hotmail.com; cnr Mera & Rocafuerte; r per person US$6; 🖳) This friendly, family-run *hostal* has clean, airy rooms with private bathrooms, a small front garden and a communal kitchen.

Hostal Transilvania (☎ 274-2281; www.hostal-transilvania.com; cnr 16 de Diciembre & Oriente; r per person US$7; 🖳) Popular with Israeli travelers, the Transilvania has simple, clean rooms with private bathrooms, along with free internet and a Middle Eastern restaurant on site.

La Petit Auberge (☎ 274-0936; www.lepetit.banios.com; 16 de Diciembre; r per person US$10-14) With a rustic, cozy cabin-like feel, this French-owned guesthouse has delightful rooms. The best have a fireplace and pretty views. Recommended restaurant serves French-inspired dishes (mains US$5 to US$8).

Posada del Arte (☎ 274-0083; www.posadadelarte.com; Pasaje V Ibarra; s/d from US$21/35; 🖳) This handsome little guesthouse has colorful, comfortable rooms, wood floors, a rooftop terrace, gigantic breakfasts and art all around. Great restaurant with fireplace on-site (mains US$3 to US$7).

Hospedaje La Floresta (☎ 274-1824; www.lafloresta.banios.com; cnr Montalvo & Haflants; s/d US$25/40; 🖳) This comfortable inn situated around a pretty interior garden has friendly staff and spacious rooms with big windows and comfortable beds. Free wireless internet.

Eating

Baños is famous for its *melcocha* (chewy taffy); makers pull it from wooden pegs in doorways around town.

ECUADOR

Mercado Central (cnr Alfaro & Rocafuerte; almuerzos US$1.50) For fresh fruit and vegetables and cheap, cheap *almuerzos*, visit the town's central market.

Café Good (16 de Diciembre; mains US$2-4, almuerzos US$2; ☯ 8am-10pm) Café Good serves satisfying veggies dishes with wholesome brown rice, as well as some chicken and fish.

Rico Pan (Ambato near Maldonado; breakfast US$3-4) Best bread in town and great breakfasts.

Casa Hood (Martínez btwn Halflants & Alfaro; mains US$3-5; ☯ 8am-10:15pm Wed-Mon) This excellent cafe has nourishing breakfasts, a US$2 *almuerzo* and a menu of Thai, Mexican and Middle Eastern dishes. It also has a book exchange, free movie screenings and yoga classes.

Café Hood (Maldonado, Parque Central; mains US$4-6) Some of the dishes here are simply excellent, such as the soft tacos or the chickpeas and spinach in curry sauce. Lots of veggie options.

La Bella Italia (Martínez; mains US$4-6) This elegant little Italian bistro serves pasta and pizzas in a quiet atmosphere.

El Jardín (cnr Rocafuerte & 16 de Diciembre; mains US$5-7; ☯ 1-11pm Mon-Sat) Facing the Parque de la Basílica, El Jardín has a leafy outdoor patio, where diners munch on snacks, sandwiches, steak and grilled trout.

Café Mariane (cnr Halflants & Rocafuerte; mains US$5-12) Mariane's French-Mediterranean cuisine features excellent fondues and beautifully prepared pasta and meat dishes.

Swiss Bistro (Martínez near Alfaro; mains US$6-8) This charming newcomer offers tasty European and Swiss specialties, which include fondue, steaks, fresh salads, soups (eg pumpkin) and a Swiss potato dish called Röesti.

Quilombo (cnr Montalvo & 12 de Noviembre; mains US$8-12; ☯ Wed-Sun) *Quilombo* means 'mess' or 'insanity' in Argentine slang – come see why it's a fitting name for this excellent Argentine grillhouse.

Santa María supermarket (cnr Alfaro & Rocafuerte) Stock up here.

Drinking & Entertainment

Nightlife in Baños means dancing in local *peñas* and hanging out in bars. The best place to bar-hop is the two-block strip along Alfaro, north of Ambato.

Peña Ananitay (16 de Diciembre near Espejo; ☯ 9pm-3am) This is the best place in town to catch live *música folklórica*. It can get packed, but that's part of the fun.

Peña Bar Mocambo (Alfaro near Ambato; ☯ 4pm-2am) Always a popular option thanks to its sidewalk bar, party atmosphere and upstairs billiards room.

Jack Rock (Alfaro 5-41; ☯ 7pm-2am) Jack Rock boasts a rock-and-roll theme and the best pub atmosphere in town. It plays classic rock during the week and salsa, merengue and reggaeton on weekends.

Getting There & Away

From many towns it may be quicker to change buses in Ambato, where there are frequent buses to Baños (US$1, one hour).

From Baños' **bus terminal** (cnr Espejo & Reyes) many buses leave for Quito (US$3.50, 3½ hours), Puyo (US$2, 1½ hours) and Tena (US$4, four hours). The road to Riobamba (US$2, two hours) via Penipe remained closed at the time of writing, meaning you'll have to backtrack through Ambato.

GUARANDA

☎ 03 / pop 31,000

Half the fun of Guaranda is getting there. The 99km 'highway' from Ambato reaches altitude over 4000m and passes within 5km of the glacier on Volcán Chimborazo (6310m). The road slices through windswept *páramo* grass and past little troops of *vicuña* (a wild relative of the llama) before suddenly plunging toward Guaranda.

The capital of Bolívar province, Guaranda is small and uneventful, though it is famous for its Carnaval celebrations. It's also the departure point for the delightful village of Salinas.

Information

Banco del Pichincha (Azuay near 7 de Mayo) Bank with an ATM.

Clínica Bolívar (☎ 298-1278) One of several clinics and pharmacies near Plaza Roja, south of the hospital.

Hospital (Cisneros s/n)

Sleeping & Eating

Hostal de las Flores (☎ 298-0644; Pichincha 4-02; r per person with/without bathroom US$10/8) Guaranda's most traveler-oriented hotel has cheerful rooms that open onto a small interior courtyard.

Hotel Bolívar (☎ 298-0547; Sucre 7-04; s/d US$8/16) This is another good option, with clean and welcoming rooms and a pleasant courtyard. The attached restaurant has good *almuerzos* (US$2 to US$3).

Los 7 Santos (☎ 298-0612; Convención de 1884 near 10 de Agosto; mains US$1-3; ☷ 10am-11pm Mon-Sat) Thoroughly out of place in Guaranda, Los 7 Santos is an artsy cafe with great atmosphere along with breakfast, small sandwiches and *bocaditos* (snacks) all day.

La Bohemia (☎ 298-4368; cnr Convención de 1884 & 10 de Agosto; mains US$2-4; ☷ 8am-9pm Mon-Sat) Close to Parque Bolívar, La Bohemia serves *almuerzos* (US$2) in a laid-back but attentive atmosphere. Chase your meal down with one of the giant *batidos* (fruit shakes).

Pizzería Salinerita (☎ 298-5406; Av General Enriquez; pizzas US$3-7; ☷ noon-10pm Mon-Sat) Serves good pizzas.

La Estancia (☎ 298-3157; García Moreno near Sucre; mains US$3-4.50; ☷ noon-10pm Tue-Sat, to 4pm Mon) Restaurant by day, bar by night, La Estancia is a cool little place with an old-fashioned sign, wooden tables and friendly staff. Most of the menu is steaks, chicken and pasta.

Getting There & Away

The bus terminal is 500m east of downtown, just off Av de Carvajal. Buses run to Ambato (US$2, two hours), Quito (US$5, five hours), Riobamba (US$2, two hours) and Guayaquil (US$4, five hours). The trip to Guayaquil is spectacular.

SALINAS
☎ 03 / pop 1000

Set in wild, beautiful countryside and famous for its excellent cheeses, salamis, divine chocolate and rough-spun sweaters, the tiny mountain village of Salinas, 35km north of Guaranda, makes for an interesting jaunt off the beaten track. The elevation is a whopping 3550m. Facing the main plaza, the **tourist office** (☎ 239-0022; www .salinerito.com) will organize visits to Salinas' unique cooperatives.

Directly across from El Refugio, the privately run **Hostal Samilagua** (sadehm2@latinmail.com; r per person US$6) is a simple place managed by a friendly local woman. Rooms are concrete rather than wood, but they're colorfully painted and comfortable.

Two blocks above the plaza, **El Refugio** (☎ 239-0024; r per person US$19) is a nice traveler's lodge with wood details, views of town, and a roaring fireplace in the lobby. It is owned and operated by the community of Salinas.

Buses to Salinas (US25¢, one hour) leave Plaza Roja in Guaranda at 6am and 7am daily and hourly from 10am to 4pm Monday through Friday. Cooperative-owned, white pickups that serve as collective taxis leave from the same place to Salinas (US$1, 45 minutes).

RIOBAMBA
☎ 03 / pop 182,000

Deemed 'the Sultan of the Andes,' Riobamba (elevation 2750m) is an old-fashioned, traditional city that both bores and delights travelers. It's sedate yet handsome, with wide avenues and random mismatched shops tucked into imposing 18th- and 19th-century stone buildings. The city is both the starting point for the spectacular train ride down the Nariz del Diablo, and one of the best places in the country to hire mountain guides.

Information

Banco de Guayaquil (cnr Primera Constituyente & García Moreno) Bank with ATM.
Hotel Los Shyris Internet (cnr Rocafuerte & 10 de Agosto) Internet access.
Parque Nacional Sangay office (☎ 295-3041; parquesangay@andinanet.net; Av 9 de Octubre near Duchicela; ☷ 8am-1pm & 2-5pm Mon-Fri) Get information and pay entry fees to Parque Nacional Sangay here.

Sights

On **market day** (Saturday), Riobamba's streets become a hive of activity, especially along the streets northeast of Parque de la Concepción.

The renowned **Museo de Arte Religioso** (☎ 296-5212; Argentinos; admission US$2; ☷ 9am-noon & 3-6pm Tue-Sat) houses a fascinating collection of religious art. Its signature piece is a priceless, 360kg gold monstrance inlaid with more than 1500 precious stones.

Activities

Thanks to the proximity of Volcán Chimborazo, Riobamba is one of Ecuador's most important climbing towns. Two-day summit trips start around US$160 per person for Chimborazo and include guides, climbing gear, transportation and meals, but not park entrance fees (US$10).

Mountain biking is also popular, and one-day trips start at US$35 per person. Downhill descents from the refuge on Chimborazo are an exhilarating way to take in the views.

ECUADOR

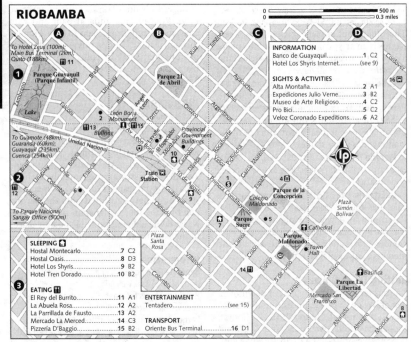

RIOBAMBA

Recommended operators:

Alta Montaña (☎ 294-2215; cnr Av León Borja & Uruguay) Excellent guided climbs.

Expediciones Julio Verne (☎ 296-3436; www .julioverne-travel.com; El Espectador 22-25; 9am-1pm & 3-6pm Mon-Fri, 9am-noon Sat) Climbing, mountain biking and more. Dutch and English spoken.

Pro Bici (☎ 295-1759; www.probici.com; cnr Primera Constituyente & Larrea) Outstanding mountain-bike trips and rentals. English spoken.

Veloz Coronado Expeditions (☎ 296-0916; www .velozexpediciones.com; cnr Chile 33-21 & Francia) Highly experienced climbing operator.

Sleeping

Hostal Oasis (☎ 296-1210; Veloz 15-32; s/d US$10/20) When it comes to friendliness, value and down-home cutesiness, it's hard to beat Oasis. Simple rooms are set around a garden, complete with squawking parrots. Free transport to and from train and bus stations.

Hotel Los Shyris (☎ 296-0323; cnr Rocafuerte & 10 de Agosto; s/d incl breakfast US$11/18; 🖥) The large and modernish Shyris is great value for its central location and clean rooms with TV. Many rooms are sunny and recently renovated.

Hotel Tren Dorado (☎ 296-4890; htrendorado@hot mail.com; Carabobo 22-35; s/d US$12/24) Conveniently close to the train station, the friendly Tren Dorado has clean, comfortable rooms done in pastel color schemes.

Hostal Montecarlo (☎ 296-1577; montecarlo @andinanet.net; 10 de Agosto 25-41; s/d US$15/19) The Montecarlo occupies an attractively restored, turn-of-the-20th-century house, though the rooms themselves are worn and some lack windows.

Hotel Zeus (☎ 296-8036; www.hotelzeus.com.ec; Av León Borja 41-29; s/d from US$24/37) Hotel Zeus is a good midrange option, with a range of room styles and amenities as well as gym access. The pricier rooms are excellent (some have views of Chimborazo).

Eating

La Abuela Rosa (cnr Brasil 37-57 & Esmeraldas; mains US$1-2) Drop by Grandma Rosa's for *comida típica* (traditional food) and tasty snacks.

Mercado La Merced (Mercado M Borja; Guayaquil btwn Espejo & Colón; mains US$1-3) A great spot to try Ecuador's classic *hornado* (whole roast pig). Best on Saturday.

El Rey del Burrito (Av León Borja 38-36; mains US$3-5; ⊙ 11am-11pm Mon-Sat, to 4pm Sun) Large burritos, tacos and enchiladas come nicely prepared in this friendly restaurant decorated with colorful murals.

Pizzería D'Baggio (Av León Borja 33-24; mains US$4-6; ⊙ noon-10pm Mon-Sat) This corner pizzeria is a popular gathering for locals and travelers alike, with dozens of satisfying medium-thick-crust pizzas, out of Baggio's wood oven.

La Parrillada de Fausto (☎ 296-7876; Uruguay 20-38; mains US$4-6; ⊙ noon-3pm & 6-10:30pm Mon-Sat) This fun, Argentine-style grill serves great barbecued steaks, trout and chicken in a ranch-style setting. Don't miss the cavelike bar in the back.

Entertainment

Nightlife, limited as it is, centers around the intersection of Av León Borja and Torres, and northwest along Av León Borja.

Tentadero (Av León Borja near Ángel León; admission US$3; ⊙ 8pm-late Fri & Sat) is the town's spiciest *discoteca,* spinning electronica and salsa well into the night.

Getting There & Away

BUS

The **main bus terminal** (☎ 296-2005; cnr Av León Borja & Av de la Prensa) is 2km northwest of the center. Buses run frequently to Quito (US$4, four hours), Guayaquil (US$5, five hours) and Alausí (US$1.50, two hours) and less frequently to Cuenca (US$6, six hours). There's at least one morning bus to Machala (US$6, seven hours). Local buses run along Av León Borja, connecting the terminal with downtown.

Buses to Baños (US$2, two hours) and the Oriente leave from the **Oriente bus terminal** (cnr Espejo & Luz Elisa Borja) just northeast of the center.

TRAIN

The spectacular train ride to Sibambe (US$11, five hours) begins in Riobamba. The train stops in Alausí (p634) just before trudging down the world-famous, hair-raising switchbacks known as the **Nariz del Diablo** (Devil's Nose). The train leaves Riobamba at 7am Wednesday, Friday and Sunday. It picks up more passengers in Alausí and goes only as far as Sibambe, immediately below the Nariz del Diablo, where there are no services. From Sibambe, the train ascends the Nariz del Diablo and returns to Alausí, where passengers can spend the night,

continue on to Cuenca by bus or return to Riobamba by bus. Owing to an accident in 2008, roof riding is now prohibited.

Heavy rains and landslides sometimes damage the tracks and cause authorities to shut down the Riobamba–Alausí run. Your best bet is to call the **train station** (☎ 296-1909; cnr Av León Borja & Unidad Nacional), which is also where you buy your tickets either the day before or the morning of the departure (starting at 6am).

VOLCÁN CHIMBORAZO

Not only is the extinct Volcán Chimborazo the highest mountain in Ecuador, but its peak (6310m), due to the earth's equatorial bulge, is also the furthest point from the center of the earth – tell that to your K2-climbing buddies. The mountain is part of the **Reserva de Producción de Fauna Chimborazo** (admission US$10), which also encompasses **Volcán Carihuairazo** (5020m).

Two small lodges on the lower slopes of Chimborazo are interesting places to see the countryside and learn a bit about local culture. **La Casa del Cóndor** (☎ 357-1379; s/d US$5/10) in the small indigenous community of **Pulinguí San Pablo** (3900m) on the Riobamba–Guaranda road offers simple accommodations; locals provide basic guiding services, mountain bikes are available, and there are fascinating interpretation trails in the area.

The two high **climbers' refuges** (beds US$10), at 4800m and 5000m, on the other hand, are pretty much a place to eat some grub and catch a few winks before heading out on an all-night climb. The refuges have mattresses, water and cooking facilities; bring warm sleeping bags.

Climbing beyond the refuge requires snow- and ice-climbing gear and mountaineering experience, as does the ascent of Carihuairazo. Contact one of the recommended guide outfits listed under Riobamba (p631) or Quito (p608). Avoid inexperienced guides; a climb at this altitude is not to be taken lightly.

There are also excellent trekking opportunities between the two mountains. Topographical maps of the region are available at the Instituto Geográfico Militar in Quito (p600). June through September is the dry season in this region, and the nights are very cold year-round.

If you're up for an 8km walk (not easy at this altitude), you can take a Guaranda-bound bus from Riobamba and ask the driver to drop you off at the park entrance road.

ALAUSÍ

☎ 03 / pop 8000

The busy little railroad town of Alausí (elevation 2350m) is the last place the train passes through before its descent down the famous Nariz del Diablo. Many jump on the train here, rather than in Riobamba, though you're more likely to score a good seat in Riobamba (see p633).

Many hotels are found along the main street (Av 5 de Junio), and most fill up on Saturday night. Spotless **Hotel Europa** (☎ 293-0200; cnr 5 de Junio 175 & Orozco; s with/without bathroom US$8/5, d with/without bathroom US$14/8) is one of the best. Other decent options include **Hotel Panamericano** (☎ 293-0156; cnr 5 de Junio & 9 de Octubre; r per person with/without bathroom US$10/6) and **Hotel Gampala** (☎ 293-0138; 5 de Junio 122; s/d US$11/20).

Buses run hourly to and from Riobamba (US$1.50, two hours) and several buses a day also go to Cuenca (US$4, four hours).

The train from Riobamba to Sibambe stops in Alausí before heading down the Nariz del Diablo (US$11 round-trip). It leaves Alausí on Wednesday, Friday and Sunday at 9:30am, and tickets go on sale at 8am.

THE SOUTHERN HIGHLANDS

As you roll down the Panamericana into the southern highlands, the giant snowcapped peaks of the central highlands fade from the rearview mirror. The climate gets a bit warmer, distances between towns become greater, and the decades clunk down by the wayside. Cuenca – arguably Ecuador's most beautiful city – and handsome little Loja are the region's only sizable towns.

Even though you won't be out scaling glaciers in the southern highlands, a variety of outdoor activities abounds. The lake-studded Parque Nacional Cajas offers excellent hiking and camping, while in Parque Nacional Podocarpus you can explore cloud forest, tropical humid forest and *páramo* within the same park. From the laid-back gringo hangout of Vilcabamba, you can spend days walking or horse riding through captivating mountain country, returning each evening to massages, hot tubs and delicious food.

CUENCA

☎ 07 / pop 470,000

Comparing the colonial beauty of Cuenca and Quito is a favorite pastime around here. In grandeur, Quito wins hands down. But Cuenca – that tidy jewel of the south – takes the cake when it comes to charm. Its narrow cobblestone streets and whitewashed red-tiled buildings, its handsome plazas and domed churches, and its setting above the grassy banks of the Río Tomebamba, all create a city that's supremely impressive. Though firmly anchored in its colonial past, Ecuador's third-largest city (elevation 2530m) also has a modern edge, with international restaurants, art galleries, cool cafes and welcoming bars tucked into its magnificent architecture.

Information

BOOKSTORES

Carolina Bookstore (Hermano Miguel 4-46)

INTERNET ACCESS

These places charge about US$1 per hour.

Azuaynet (Padre Aguirre near Lamar)

Cybercom (cnr Presidente Córdova & Borrero)

Cybernet (Benigno Malo near Larga)

LAUNDRY

La Química Borrero (Borrero near Presidente Cordova); Gran Colombia (cnr Gran Colombia & Montalvo)

Lavahora (Vásquez 6-76)

MEDICAL SERVICES

Clínica Santa Inés (☎ 281-7888; Daniel Córdova 2-113) Consultations at this clinic cost about US$20.

MONEY

Banco de Guayaquil (cnr Mariscal Sucre & Borrero) Bank with ATM.

Banco del Pichincha (cnr Solano & 12 de Abril) Bank with ATM.

POST

Post office (cnr Gran Colombia & Borrero)

TOURIST INFORMATION

Bus terminal information office (☎ 284-3888; bus terminal)

Tourist information (iTur; ☎ 282-1035; cnr Mariscal Sucre & Cordero) Extremely helpful; English spoken.

Sights

Take a walk along 3 de Noviembre, which follows the northern bank of the **Río Tomebamba**.

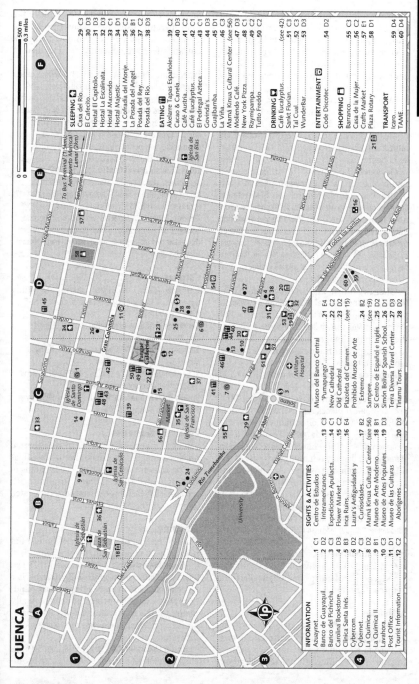

ECUADOR

The river is lined with colonial buildings, and women still dry their laundry on the river's grassy banks. A patch of **Inca ruins** lie near the river, between the east end of Larga and Av Todos los Santos. Most of the stonework was destroyed to build colonial buildings, but there are some fine niches and walls.

Parque Calderón (cnr Benigno Malo & Bolívar), the main plaza, is dominated by the handsome **'new cathedral'** (c 1885) with its huge blue domes. Opposite stands the diminutive **'old cathedral'** (construction began in 1557), known as El Sagrario.

Go smell the flowers (or at least snap a photo of them) at the **flower market** in front of the wee colonial church on **Plazoleta del Carmen** (cnr Padre Aguirre & Mariscal Sucre). Afterwards, hoof it over to the quiet **Plaza de San Sebastián** (cnr Mariscal Sucre & Talbot) and check out the **Museo de Arte Moderno** (cnr Mariscal Sucre & Talbot; admission by donation; 🕑 9am-1pm & 3-6:30pm Mon-Fri, 9am-1pm Sat & Sun), which houses a small collection of contemporary local art.

Cuenca's most important museum, the **Museo del Banco Central 'Pumapungo'** (www.museo pumapungo.com; Larga near Huayna Capac; admission US$3; 🕑 9am-6pm Mon-Fri, 9am-1pm Sat) merits a visit for the fabulous ethnographic exhibits alone, not to mention the entrancing display of *tsantsas* (shrunken heads).

Museo de las Culturas Aborígenes (Larga 5-24; admission US$2; 🕑 9am-6pm Mon-Fri, 9am-3pm Sat) houses an excellent collection of over 5000 archaeological pieces representative of about 20 Ecuadorian pre-Columbian cultures. The worthwhile **Museo de Artes Populares** (Cidap; Hermano Miguel 3-23; 🕑 9:30am-1pm & 2-6pm Mon-Fri, 10am-1pm Sat) displays changing exhibits of traditional indigenous costumes, handicrafts and artwork from around Latin America.

Clustered around the Plazoleta de la Cruz del Vado are a few interesting sites including the **Prohibido Museo de Arte Extremo** (La Condamine 12-102; admission US50¢; 🕑 noon-late), a goth-lovers' gallery, bar and cafe, and **Laura's Antiguidades y Curiosidades** (☎ 282-3312; La Condamine 12-112; 🕑 daily), which showcases a hodgepodge of curios and objets d'art in a 19th-century house.

Activities

Cuenca is a perfect base for exploring – by foot, horse or bike – nearby attractions such as Parque Nacional Cajas, the Inca ruins of Ingapirca and indigenous villages. Head out on your own or set yourself up at one of the tour operators listed here. Day trips average US$35 to US$40 per person; note that park entrance fees are generally not included in the cost.

Expediciones Apullacta (☎ 283-7815; www.apullacta .com; Gran Colombia 11-02) Day tours to Ingapirca and Cajas.

Mamá Kinua Cultural Center (☎ 284-0610; Casa de la Mujer, Torres 7-45) A community tourism project offering tours and homestays in nearby indigenous communities (per person US$48 a night; two persons minimum). No English is spoken.

Terra Diversa Travel Center (☎ 282-3782; www .terradiversa.com; Hermano Miguel 5-42) Horse riding, mountain biking and hiking, Ingapirca trips, and three-hour city tours (US$15).

Tinamu Tours (☎ 245-0143; www.tinamutours.com; Borrero 7-68) Rents camping gear, conducts tours all over the region, and offers parapenting (tandem hang-gliding) trips (US$48).

Courses

Cuenca is an excellent setting to study Spanish. One-on-one classes cost US$5 to US$7 per hour.

Centro de Estudios Interamericanos (CEDEI; ☎ 283-4353; www.cedei.org; Cordero 5-66)

Sampere (☎ 282-3960; www.sampere.es; Hermano Miguel 3-43)

Sí Centro de Español e Inglés (☎ 282-0429; www .sicentrospanishschool.com; Borrero 7-67)

Simón Bolívar Spanish School (☎ 283-9959; www .bolivar2.com; Cordero 10-25)

Festivals & Events

Cuenca's independence as a city is celebrated on November 3 with a major fiesta. Christmas Eve parades are very colorful. The founding of Cuenca (April 10 to 13) and Corpus Christi are also busy holidays. Carnaval is celebrated with boisterous water fights.

Sleeping

Cuenca has a great selection of hotels, but prices are a tad higher than elsewhere.

Hostal Majestic (☎ 283-5674; Cordero 11-29; r per person with/without bathroom US$10/5) Majestic is a whacky place in an early 20th-century building. Dalí-esque paintings adorn the walls, plants fill the lobby, and a few caged parakeets compliment the quirkiness. Most rooms lack windows.

Hostal La Escalinata (☎ 284-5758; Larga 5-83; r per person with/without bathroom US$6/5) Many rooms lack windows and the foam mattresses are soft, but the location is excellent.

Hostal El Capitolio (☎ 282-4446; Vásquez 5-66; s/d with shared bathroom US$7/14) El Capitolio is a friendly, family-run place with clean, basic rooms with shared facilities (three rooms per floor share a bathroom), plus use of the kitchen.

El Cafecito (☎ 283-2337; www.cafecito.net; Vásquez 7-36; dm/s/d/tr US$7/25/25/30, d with shared bathroom US$15) This cafe-bar and *hostal* is a longtime favorite of the *mochilero* (backpacker) and local hipster scenes. The dorm rooms right off the cafe are spacious but noisy at night, and the comfortable rooms looking onto the garden have a touch of local art.

Posada del Río (☎ 282-3111; posadadelriocuenca @yahoo.com; Hermano Miguel 4-18; r per person with/without bathroom US$10/8; 🖳) This simple and tasteful inn near the river has a rooftop terrace with views and a communal kitchen. Bright colors and woodwork adorn throughout, and the shared bathrooms are clean.

Hostal Macondo (☎ 284-0697; www.hostalmacondo .com; Tarqui 11-64; s/d US$21/30, with shared bathroom US$15/22) The colonial-style Hostal Macondo has palatial rooms in the front, older section, and small but cozy rooms situated around a big, sunny garden out back.

Casa del Río (☎ 282-9659; hostalcasadelrio@hotmail .com; Bajada del Padrón 4-07; s/d US$18/29; 🖳) Scenically set above the river, this small guesthouse with terrace has a range of rooms, from small dark quarters with carpeting to trim and tidy numbers with wood floors and pretty views.

our pick La Cofradía del Monje (☎ 283-1251; viniciocobojr@cofradiadelmonje.com; Presidente Córdova 10-33; s/d US$26/42) In a refurbished century-old home practically on top of the Iglesia de San Francisco, the 'Brotherhood of Monks' B&B has high timbered ceilings, lovely wood floors and expansive views of the plaza and market below.

Posada del Rey (☎ 284-3845; www.posadadelreyhotel .com; Benigno Malo 9-91; s/d US$30/60) In a restored colonial-style house, 10 rooms with hand-painted murals and polished wood floors surround a central courtyard. All rooms have balconies and cable TV, and the family-size attic suite also has internet.

La Posada del Angel (☎ 284-0695; www.hostalposada delangel.com; Bolívar 14-11; s/d US$37/52; 🖳) Color, character, history – the Posada del Angel has handsomely designed rooms overlooking an interior courtyard.

Eating

Most restaurants close on Sunday.

Café Austria (Benigno Malo 5-45; snacks US$1-3) Austrian-style cakes, coffee and sandwiches.

Tutto Freddo (cnr Benigno Malo & Bolívar; ice cream US$1-$3; 🕑 daily) Likely the best (and definitely the most popular) ice cream in town.

New York Pizza (Gran Colombia 10-43; mains US$1.50-4) Nonfussy spot with thin-crust pizza by the slice.

Cacao & Canela (cnr Jaramillo & Borrero; sandwiches US$2-4; 🕑 8:30am-9:30pm Mon-Sat) This charming little cafe decorated with old film posters serves decent coffee, filling breakfasts and sandwiches and other snacks.

Moliendo Café (Vásquez 6-24; light meals US$2-4) Moliendo Café serves delicious Colombian *arepas* (a corn and cheese pancake), topped with anything from beans and cheese to slow-cooked pork.

Govinda's (Jaramillo 7-27; almuerzos US$2, mains US$2-4; 🕑 8:30am-3pm Mon-Sat) Pizzas, lentil burgers and a little good karma to wash it down.

Mamá Kinua Cultural Center (Casa de la Mujer, Torres 7-45; almuerzos US$2.50; 🕑 8am-5:30pm Mon-Fri) Pop into this women-run restaurant for some of the tastiest *almuerzos* around. Food here is mostly vegetarian.

Raymipampa (Benigno Malo 8-59; mains US$3-6) This Cuenca institution serves *ceviche*, soups, crepes (sweet and savory), and many other selections amid comfortable, nonfussy ambience.

Akelarre Tapas Españoles (☎ 282-3636; Torres 8-40; tapas US$3-6, mains US$6-9) Akelarre serves petite plates of Spanish tapas, plus excellent paella on Sundays.

Guajibamba (Cordero 12-32; mains US$4-6) This atmospheric restaurant serves traditional *seco de chivo* and gourmet *fritada*. It's also one of the best places to try *cuy* (call an hour before you go for prep time).

our pick Café Eucalyptus (www.cafeeucalyptus .com; Gran Colombia 9-41; mains US$4-7; 🕑 dinner Mon-Sat) Satisfying world cuisine (chicken satay, Cuban sandwiches, black bean and veggie wraps) is served at cozy tables near roaring fireplaces, and there's live music some nights. Good selection of wines, microbrews and cocktails.

La Viña (Cordero 5-101; mains US$5-10) A delightful new place that's both casual and classy, with flickering candles, psychedelic artwork and delicious thin-crust pizzas loaded with toppings. There are also filling pastas, risotto, grilled eggplant, salads and desserts.

El Pedregal Azteca (Gran Colombia 10-29; mains US$5-9) El Pedregal serves delicious Mexican food, including lots of vegetarian options, in an atmosphere that's all ponchos and sombreros. The portions can be a bit small, however, so fill up on the free homemade corn chips.

Drinking

Café Eucalyptus (p637) is an excellent spot for a relaxed drink with a mostly gringo crowd.

WunderBar (cnr Hermano Miguel & Larga; drinks US$2-4; ✔ 11am-1am Mon-Fri, 3pm-1am Sat) This Austrian-owned place above the river has classic pub-like ambience, a sizeable menu and outdoor seating in warm weather.

Sankt Florian (Larga 7-119; drinks US$2-4) This classy cafe and bar in a historic Calle Larga house has billiards, live music, and a happy hour from 8pm to 10pm Wednesday to Saturday.

Tal Cual (Larga 7-57; drinks US$2-4) Cozy, friendly bar hosting live music Thursday through Saturday.

Entertainment

Discos are open Thursday through Saturday nights. Midweek Cuenca is pretty sedate. Along Presidente Córdova, east of Hermano Miguel, there are several popular bars with dance floors.

Code Discotec (Presidente Córdova 5-39) Of the clubs located along Presidente Córdova, this is a current favorite. It's non-stop dancing from about midnight to dawn Thursday to Saturday.

Shopping

There are several good crafts stores along Gran Colombia and on the blocks just north of Parque Calderón. The best place for a serious spree, however, is the **Casa de la Mujer** (Torres 7-33), which houses over 100 crafts stalls.

The Thursday market at **Plaza Rotary** (cnr Lamar & Hermano Miguel) exists mainly for locals, but there are also a few worthwhile crafts stalls. You're better off heading to the nearby **crafts market** (cnr Sangurima & Vargas Machuca), which has an odd but quite interesting combination of basketry, ceramics and other curios.

Cuenca produces panama and other kinds of straw hats and there are dozens of hat makers about town. **Barranco** (Larga 10-41) is a long-time seller with a small museum where you can see how panama hats were made over the years. There's also a cafe with views.

Getting There & Away

AIR

Cuenca's **Aeropuerto Mariscal Lamar** (☎ 286-2203; Av España) is 2km from downtown. **TAME** (☎ 288-9097; Astudillo 2-22) and **Icaro** (☎ 281-1450; Milenium Plaza, Astudillo s\n) fly daily to Quito (US$80) and Guayaquil (US$65).

BUS

Cuenca's **bus terminal** (Av España) is 1.5km northeast of the center. Buses to Guayaquil (US$8) go either via Parque Nacional Cajas (3½ hours) or Cañar (5½ hours). There are regular departures to Quito (US$10, 10 to 12 hours). Several buses go to Machala (US$4.50, four hours); a few continue on to Huaquillas (US$6, five hours). Buses go regularly to Alausí (US$4, four hours). Several buses a day head to Loja (US$7, 5½ hours), Macas (US$8.50, eight hours via Guarumales, 10 hours via Limón) and other Oriente towns. Buses for Gualaceo (US80¢, one hour) leave every 30 minutes.

Getting Around

Cuenca is very walkable. A taxi to or from the bus terminal or airport costs about US$2. From the front of the bus terminal buses depart regularly to downtown (US25¢).

AROUND CUENCA

☎ 07

From small indigenous villages to hot springs and hiking, there's ample opportunity for excursions from Cuenca.

Ingapirca

The most important Inca site in Ecuador, Ingapirca was built toward the end of the 15th century during the Inca expansion into present-day Ecuador. The **site** (admission US$6; ✔ 8am-6pm), 50km north of Cuenca, was built with the same mortarless, polished-stone technique used by the Inca in Peru. Although less impressive than sites in Peru, it's definitely worth a visit. A museum explains the site, and guides (both the human and the written varieties) are available. **Ingapirca village**, 1km away, has a crafts shop, simple restaurants and a basic *pensión*.

For an economical visit, catch a direct Transportes Cañar bus (US$2.50, two hours) from Cuenca's bus terminal at 9am. Buses return to Cuenca at 1pm and 4pm Monday through Friday and at 9am and 1pm on Saturday and Sunday.

THE INCA TRAIL TO INGAPIRCA

Though it sees only a fraction of the traffic that the Inca Trail to Machu Picchu gets, the three-day hike to Ingapirca is a popular trek. Parts of the approximately 40km hike follow the original royal road that linked Cuzco with Quito and Tomebamba (at present-day Cuenca).

The starting point for the hike is the village of **Achupallas**, 23km southeast of Alausí (p634). The route is faint in places and sometimes even nonexistent, so travel with a compass and three 1:50,000 topographical maps – Alausí, Juncal and Cañar – available at the IGM (p600) in Quito. There are sometimes locals around who may provide directions. Pack extra food in case you get lost. The area is remote but inhabited, so don't leave your stuff lying around outside your tent. Also be prepared for extremely persistent begging from children; most travelers refuse to hand anything over so as not to encourage the begging from future walkers.

To get to Achupallas, take one of the daily trucks from Alausí or, more reliably, hire a taxi-pickup for about US$10 to US$15 one way. Alternatively, south-bound Panamericana buses from Alausí can drop you off at La Moya (also known as Guasuntos), where you can wait for passing trucks headed to Achupallas, 12km up a slim mountain road. You can hire guides in Achupallas for about US$30 per day. If you want to go on your own, check out a hiking guide, such as *Ecuador: Climbing and Hiking Guide* by Rob Rachowiecki and Mark Thurber.

Gualaceo, Chordeleg & Sígsig

Seeing these three villages (famous for their Sunday markets) together makes a great day trip from Cuenca. If you start early, you can be back in Cuenca by the afternoon. Gualaceo has the biggest market, with fruit and vegetables, animals and various household goods. Chordeleg's market, 5km away, is smaller and more touristy. Sígsig's market is 25km from Gualaceo and is an excellent place to see the art of panama hat–making.

From Cuenca's bus terminal, buses leave every 30 minutes to Gualaceo (US80¢, one hour), Chordeleg (US$1, one hour) and Sígsig (US$1.25, 1½ hours). You can walk the 5km from Gualaceo to Chordeleg if you don't want to wait for the bus.

Parque Nacional Cajas

The stunning, chilly, moorlike *páramo* of **Parque Nacional Cajas** (admission US$10) is famous for its many lakes, great trout fishing and rugged camping and hiking. It's a good day trip from Cuenca (only 30km away). **Camping** (per person US$4) is allowed, and a small *refugio* has eight cots and a kitchen; the latter fills up fast. Hiking solo in Cajas can be dangerous – the abundance of lakes and fog is disorienting. It's best to be finished by 4pm when the fog gets thick. Shorter trails are well marked. Glossy, topographical trail maps are free with admission.

Guayaquil-bound buses pass through the park, but drivers refuse to sell reduced-fare tickets for the one-hour ride. To avoid paying the full US$8 fare to Guayaquil, you can take a Transporte Occidental bus (US$1.25, one hour) from Ricardo Darque between Av de las Américas and Victor Manuel Albornoz in Cuenca. Even after taking a taxi (US$2) to this bus stop, it will still come out cheaper. Buses depart daily at 6:15am, 7am, 10:20am, noon, 2pm, 4pm and 5pm. To return to Cuenca, you can flag any passing Cuenca-bound bus.

SARAGURO
☎ 07

South of Cuenca the road winds through eerie *páramo* until, after 165km, it reaches Saraguro, which means 'land of corn' in Quichua. Quaint little Saraguro is home to the indigenous Saraguro, the most prosperous indigenous group in the southern highlands. The group originally lived in the Lake Titicaca region of Peru but were forcibly relocated through the Inca empire's system of colonization, known as *mitimaes*.

Today, the Saraguro are readily identifiable by their traditional dress. Both men and women (but especially the women) wear striking flat white felt hats with wide brims that are often spotted on the underside. The men sport a single braid and wear a black poncho and knee-length black shorts, occasionally covered with a small white apron.

The best day to be in Saraguro is Sunday, when the local market draws Saraguros from the surrounding countryside. Sleep at friendly

ECUADOR

Residencial Saraguro (☎ 220-0286; cnr Loja & Castro; s/d US$5/10), or the pretty **Hostal Achik Wasi** (☎ 220-0331; Calle Intiñan, Barrio La Luz; s/d US$12/24) 10 minutes out of town. You'll find tasty meals at indigenous-run **Mamá Cuchara** (Parque Central; mains US$1.50-2.50; ☯ closed Sat).

Any Loja-bound bus from Cuenca (US$5, 3½ hours) will drop you off a block from the main plaza. Buses to Loja (US$2, 1½ hours) leave hourly during the day.

LOJA
☎ 07 / pop 152,000

Thanks to its proximity to the Oriente, Loja (elevation 2100m) is blessed with a delightfully temperate climate. The city is famous for its musicians (everyone seems to play something) and its award-winning parks. Although it's the provincial capital, it's still a small town at heart – so much so that you'll find a day or two plenty of time. Loja is a good base for visiting nearby Parque Nacional Podocarpus and the main stop before heading south to Vilcabamba and Peru.

Good views can be had from the **Virgen de Loja Statue** (La Salle). The annual fiesta of the **Virgen del Cisne** (September 8) is celebrated with huge parades and a produce fair.

Information
Banco de Guayaquil (Eguiguren near Bernardo Valdivieso) Bank with ATM.
Clínica San Agustín (☎ 257-0314; cnr 18 de Noviembre & Azuay) Clinic with a good reputation.

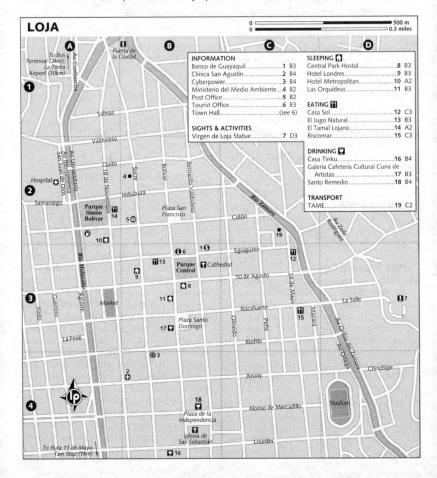

LOJA

0   500 m
0   0.3 miles

INFORMATION
Banco de Guayaquil..................1 B3
Clínica San Agustín..................2 B4
Cyberpower............................3 B4
Ministerio del Medio Ambiente....4 B2
Post Office............................5 B2
Tourist Office.........................6 B3
Town Hall.........................(see 6)

SIGHTS & ACTIVITIES
Virgen de Loja Statue...............7 D3

SLEEPING
Central Park Hostal...................8 B3
Hotel Londres.........................9 B3
Hotel Metropolitan..................10 A2
Las Orquídeas........................11 B3

EATING
Casa Sol.............................12 C3
El Jugo Natural......................13 B3
El Tamal Lojano......................14 A2
Riscomar.............................15 C3

DRINKING
Casa Tinku...........................16 B4
Galería Cafetería Cultural Cuna de
  Artistas............................17 B3
Santo Remedio.......................18 B4

TRANSPORT
TAME................................19 C2

Cyberpower (cnr Riofrío & Sucre; per hr US$1) Internet.

Ministerio del Medio Ambiente (☎ 258-5421; podocam@impsat.net.ec; Sucre 4-35) Provides information on Parque Nacional Podocarpus.

Post office (cnr Colón & Sucre)

Tourist office (iTur; ☎ 258-1251; cnr Bolívar & Eguiguren) In the Town Hall.

Sleeping

Hotel Londres (☎ 256-1936; Sucre 07-51; s/d US$5/10) With creaky wooden floors, big white walls and saggy beds, Hotel Londres is as basic as they come, but it's a tried-and-true traveler favorite.

   Las Orquídeas (☎ 258-7008; Bolívar 08-59; s/d US$10/18) This place provides small, clean, acceptable rooms. Try to score a window.

   Hotel Metropolitan (☎ 257-0007; 18 de Noviembre 6-41; s/d US$10/20) It is friendly and comfortable here, with hardwood floors, decent beds and cable TV, but most rooms lack windows.

   Central Park Hostal (☎ 256-1103; 10 de Agosto 13-64; s/d US$17/34) Pink is the color of choice on walls, curtains and satiny bedspreads, but if you can stomach it, this clean and well-run place offers good value. Some rooms overlook the park.

Eating & Drinking

our pick **El Tamal Lojano** (18 de Noviembre 05-12; mains US$1-2) People flock here for the excellent *quimbolitos, humitas* and *tamales lojanos* (all delicious variations on corn dumplings), and *empanadas de verde.* Try them all!

   Casa Sol (24 de Mayo 07-04; snacks US$1-2) Casa Sol serves drinks and traditional snacks at balcony tables overlooking a little park. It's best in the evening.

   El Jugo Natural (Eguiguren 14-20; light meals US$1-3) Fresh juices, yogurt shakes and fruit salads star at this small cafe.

   Galería Cafetería Cultural Cuna de Artistas (Bolívar 09-89; mains US$2-5) Bohemian cafe that's great for an evening drink or bite, particularly when there's live music on.

   Riscomar (Rocafuerte 09-00; mains US$6-7) Serving some of Loja's best seafood, Riscomar prepares delicious *ceviche* in an inviting but unpretentious dining room.

   Casa Tinku (Lourdes btwn Bolivar & Sucre) Casa Tinku is a spirited little bar with a great vibe. There's usually live music on weekends.

   Santo Remedio (Alonso de Mercadillo near Bernardo Valdivieso) Lively drinking spot with candlelit tables, a back patio and bands or DJs tearing things up on weekends.

GETTING TO PERU

Most people buy tickets direct to Piura, Peru from Loja aboard **Loja International** (☎ 257-9014, 257-0505). Several buses daily depart from Loja, stop at the border for passengers to take care of exits and entries and then continue on to Piura. The entire ride is nine hours (and costs US$8). Try to buy your tickets at least a day before you travel. If you want to break the journey from Loja, do so at **Catacocha**. The Loja–Piura bus stops in Catacocha and Macará, so you can get on in either town as well. To enter Ecuador from Peru, see p844.

Getting There & Away

Loja is served by La Toma airport in Catamayo, 30km west of town. **TAME** (☎ 257-0248; Av Ortega near 24 de Mayo) flies to Quito (US$82) daily and to Guayaquil (US$73) on Tuesday, Thursday and Saturday. For airport transfer (US$5, 40 minutes) call **Aerotaxi** (☎ 257-1327, 258-4423).

   Loja's bus terminal is 2km north of town. Several buses a day run to Quito (US$15, 15 hours), Macará (US$6, six hours), Guayaquil (US$9, nine hours), Machala (US$5, five hours), Zamora (US$2.50, two hours) and Cuenca (US$7, five hours), as well as other destinations.

   Buses to Vilcabamba (US$1, 1½ hours) depart hourly. Vilcabambaturis runs faster minibuses (US$1, one hour). Fastest of all are the *taxis colectivos* (shared taxis; US$1.20, 45 minutes), which leave from the **Ruta 11 de Mayo taxi stop** (Av Universitaria), 10 blocks south of Alonso de Mercadillo; ask a local taxi driver to take you.

ZAMORA

☎ 07 / pop 15,100

Perspiring peacefully on the tropical banks of the Río Zamora, this easy-going jungle town is the best launching pad for exploring the verdant lowlands of Parque Nacional Podocarpus (p642). Although it's geographically part of the Oriente, Zamora (elevation 970m) is closer to Loja by bus (two hours) than to other jungle towns, most of which are quite a long way north. Decent budget hotels in town include **Hotel Chonta Dorada** (☎ 260-6384/7055; hotelchontadorada@hotmail.com; Pío Jaramillo near Amazonas; s/d US$9/18) and **Hotel**

Gimyfa (☎ 260-6103; Diego de Vaca near Pío Jaramillo; s/d US$9/18). Outside town, bird-watchers should book a cabin in the lovely private reserve of **Copalinga** (☎ 09-347-7013; www.copalinga.com; Vía al Podocarpus Km 3; cabins per person US$23-47). Meals are also available.

Continuing north through the Oriente by bus, you will find a few basic hotels in the small towns of **Gualaquiza** (five hours), **Limón** (about nine hours), **Méndez** and **Sucúa**. **Macas** (p651) is approximately 13 to 15 hours away.

PARQUE NACIONAL PODOCARPUS

One of the most biologically rich areas in the country and a wonderful park to explore, **Parque Nacional Podocarpus** (admission US$10) protects habitats at altitudes ranging from 3600m in the *páramo* near Loja to 1000m in the steamy rainforests near Zamora. The topography is wonderfully rugged and complex, and the park is simply bursting with plant and animal life. Parque Nacional Podocarpus' namesake, Podocarpus, is Ecuador's only native conifer.

The main entrance to the highland sector of the park is **Cajanuma**, about 10km south of Loja. From here, a track leads 8.5km up to the ranger station and trailheads. The best bet for a day trip is to ride all the way up in a taxi from Loja (about US$10), hike for several hours and walk the 8.5km back to the main road where you can flag a passing bus.

To visit the tropical, lowland sector, head to Zamora and get a taxi (US$4 one way) or walk the 6km dirt road to the **Bombuscaro entrance**, where there is a ranger station, trails, swimming, waterfalls, a **camping area** (per person US$3) and a small **refugio** (per person US$5) without mattresses. Access from Vilcabamba is possible by horseback.

VILCABAMBA

☎ 07 / pop 4200

Deemed the valley of longevity, Vilcabamba (elevation 1500m) is famous for having inhabitants that just don't kick the bucket. And it's no wonder – with a setting so peaceful, weather so sublime and a pace so re-*laaaxing*, who in their right mind would want to toss in the towel? Backpackers stop here to get in on the mellowness and to hike, ride horses, enjoy the food, get massages and chill out in Vilcabamba's cheap guesthouses. It's also the perfect stopping point en route to or from Peru via Zumba.

Bring cash, because there are no banks. Telephones, cybercafes and the post office are all easy to find.

Activities

There's great hiking in the area. The most popular hike is up Cerro Mandango (but there have been reports of robberies, so enquire about safety before setting out). Most naturalists and horse guides charge about US$35 per day (not including park entrance fees). For a taste of the region's biodiversity, the small but scenic **Rumi Wilco Nature Preserve** (admission US$2) has 7km of hiking trails, where 123 bird species have been sighted. **Orlando Falco** leads walking tours to Parque Nacional Podocarpus. Find him at Primavera (Sucre 10-30), his craft shop near the plaza, or at Rumi Wilco Ecolodge (below). **Caballos Gavilan** (☎ 264-0281; gavilanhorse@yahoo.com; Sucre) offers affordable, highly recommended horse-riding trips, which can last from four hours to three days. **El Chino** (cnr Diego de la Vaca & Toledo) rents mountain bikes for US$1.50 per hour and offers biking day tours starting at US$18.

Sleeping

Rumi Wilco Ecolodge (www.rumiwilco.com; campsite per person US$3.50, s/d US$7/14) About a 12-minute walk from town, Rumi Wilco has several delightful four-person cabins (double/triple/quad US$26/30/36), serene hideaways with hammocks, kitchen and a private drinking well. The simpler adobe houses are also good value. There's camping and hiking trails on site.

Hostal Las Margaritas (☎ 264-0051; cnr Sucre & Jaramillo; s/d US$10/20; 🏊) In a big, classy house with a garden full of fruit trees, this family-run *hostal* has clean rooms with firm beds and cable TV.

Hostería y Restaurante Izhcayluma (☎ 264-0095; www.izhcayluma.com; dm US$10, s US$19-24, d US$28-36; 🏊) With sweeping views over the valley, a swimming pool, a flower-filled garden, an excellent restaurant (mains US$5 to US$6) and attractive rooms, the Hostería y Restaurante Izhcayluma is a popular destination. Located 2km south of town.

Jardín Escondido (☎ 264-0281; Sucre; dm US$11, r per person US$12-17; 🏊) Built around a tranquil interior garden with songbirds, all rooms have tall ceilings and big bathrooms, and breakfast comes with homemade bread and good coffee.

Rendez-Vous Hostal Guesthouse (☎ 09-219-1180; www.rendezvousecuador.com; Diego Vaca de Vega 06-43; s/d US$14/22) French-owned Rendez-Vous is a lovely place near the river with immaculate rooms (each has a hammock) that open onto a beautiful garden. Breakfast with homemade bread included.

Eating & Drinking

Natural Yogurt (Bolívar; mains US$2-3) Half a block from the plaza, this tiny eatery serves crepes and tasty bowls of yogurt, granola and fruit.

Al Otro Lado (Bolívar; mains US$3-5) Facing the plaza, Al Otro Lado has a small menu that changes daily and features fresh delicious fare, including quiche, soup, salad, grilled meat and often tartiflette.

Restaurante Vegetariano (cnr Salgado & Diego Vaca de la Vega; meals US$3) Enjoy a satisfying three-course vegetarian meal in a small garden at this family-run favorite.

Jardín Escondido (cnr Sucre & Agua de Hierro; mains US$3-5) This place serves Mexican food in a lovely garden setting.

Shanta's Bar (mains US$3-6; ⏰ noon-3am) On the road to Río Yambala, Shanta's serves big plates of trout, pizza and frogs' legs in an open-air, rustic setting.

Getting There & Away

Transportes Loja runs buses every 90 minutes to Loja (US$1, 1½ hours). Shared taxis leave from the bus terminal and take five passengers to Loja (US$2, 45 minutes). Buses leave daily to Zumba (US$6, six hours), near the Peruvian border.

THE ORIENTE

Ecuador's slice of the Amazon Basin – aka El Oriente – is one of the country's most thrilling travel destinations. Here you can paddle canoes up to caimans lurking in blackwater lagoons, spot two-toed sloths and howler monkeys, fish for piranhas and hike through some of the wildest plantlife you'll ever lay eyes upon. At night, after quelling your fear of the things outside, you'll be lulled to sleep by a psychedelic symphony of insects and frogs.

This section describes the Oriente from north to south (see Zamora, p641, for the region's southernmost towns). The northern Oriente sees more travelers, while the region south of Río Pastaza has a real sense of remoteness. Buses from Quito frequently go to Puyo, Tena, Coca and Lago Agrio. Buses from Cuenca (p638) go through Limón to Macas. Buses from the southern highlands town of Loja (p640) go via Zamora to Limón and on to Macas. From Macas, a road leads to Puyo and the northern Oriente. It's possible, although arduous, to travel down the Río Napo to Peru and the Amazon.

LAGO AGRIO
☎ 06 / pop 34,100

Unless you like edgy frontier towns, Lago's main tourist draw is its status as the jumping-off point for the nearby Cuyabeno wildlife reserve (p644). The Sunday morning **market** is visited by the indigenous Cofan people and might be worth a peak. Booking a tour to Cuyabeno from Lago can be difficult: most

---

GETTING TO PERU

About 125km south of Vilcabamba lies the wonderfully remote border crossing known as La Balsa, near the outpost of Zumba. From Vilcabamba (or Loja), it's an all-day journey to San Ignacio, Peru, the best place to spend the night before continuing the journey. **Transportes Nambija** (US$7.50, six hours) and Sur Oriente buses depart several times daily from Loja for Zumba, all stopping in Vilcabamba. From Zumba, several daily *rancheras* (open-sided trucks) go to the border at La Balsa (US$2, 1½ hours to 2½ hours), where you get your exit stamp. Inquire about conditions on the road between Zumba and La Balsa before setting out. Heavy rains can lead to road closure altogether.

On the other side of the 'international bridge' in Peru there are *taxis colectivos* (shared taxis) to San Ignacio (US$3, 1½ hours), where you can spend the night before heading to Jaén (three hours), on to Bagua Grande (another hour) and then to Chachapoyas (p856; three more hours), the first sizable town. From Jaén you can also travel to Chiclayo (p841), on the Peruvian coast.

For information on border crossing if you're traveling from Peru, see p844.

ECUADOR

people arrive from Quito with a tour already booked, guides show up, and everyone's gone the next morning.

If stuck in town, try **Hotel Selva Real** (☎ 283-3867; cnr Av Quito & Colombia; r per person US$15-20) or **Hotel D'Mario** (☎ 283-0172; hotelmario@andinanet.net; Av Quito 1-171; r per person US$17-40; 🔀 🖳 🕿). Both are on the main drag, where you'll find just about everything else. The latter has a popular pizzeria.

Dangers & Annoyances
With an increased pitch in the conflict in neighboring Colombia, border towns such as Lago Agrio have become safe havens for Colombian guerrillas, antirebel paramilitaries and drug smugglers. Bars can be sketchy and side streets unsafe, so stick to the main drag, especially at night. Tourists rarely have problems but be careful.

Getting There & Away
The airport is 5km east of town; taxi fare is US$3. **TAME** (☎ 283-0113; Orellana near 9 de Octubre) and **Icaro** (☎ 283-2370/1, 288-0546; at the airport) fly Monday through Saturday to Quito (US$43 to US$56); it's best to book in advance.

The bus terminal is about 2km northwest of the center. Buses head to Quito regularly (US$7, eight hours). There are one or two daily departures, mainly overnight, to Tena (US$7, eight hours), Cuenca, Guayaquil (US$14, fourteen hours) and Machala. Buses to Coca aren't usually found in the bus terminal; flag a *ranchera* (open-sided truck; US$3, 2½ hours) on Av Quito in the center – ask locally for where to wait.

RESERVA DE PRODUCCIÓN FAUNÍSTICA CUYABENO
This beautiful, 6034-sq-km **reserve** (admission US$20) protects the rainforest home of the Siona, Secoya, Cofan, Quichua and Shuar people. It also conserves the Río Cuyabeno watershed, whose rainforest lakes and swamps harbor fascinating aquatic species such as freshwater dolphins, manatees, caiman and anaconda. Monkeys abound, and tapirs, peccaries, agoutis and several cat species have been recorded. The birdlife is abundant. Though there have been numerous oil spills, huge parts of the reserve remain pristine and worth a visit. The reserve is nearly impossible to visit on your own; most visitors make arrangements in Quito (see p608) or Coca. The nearest town is Lago Agrio.

COCA
☎ 06 / pop 18,300
If you're one of those folks who dig sitting around in tropical heat guzzling beer and watching small-town street life, you'll probably find Coca oddly appealing. Otherwise, it's just a dusty, sweltering oil town and little more than a final stop before boarding an outboard canoe and heading down the mighty Río Napo. It's also a good place to hire a guide for visits to Pañacocha, Cuyabeno and Parque Nacional Yasuní (p646).

Information
Andinatel (cnr Eloy Alfaro & 6 de Diciembre)
Banco del Pinchincha (cnr Bolívar & 9 de Octubre) Bank with ATM.
Casa de Cambio 3R (cnr Napo & García Moreno) Cashes traveler's checks.
Imperial Net (García Moreno; per hr US$1.80) Internet access.
Post office (Napo near Cuenca)
Tourist office (cnr García Moreno & Quito)

Tours
Coca is closer than Misahuallí to large tracts of virgin jungle, but to hire a guide you should have a group of four or more to make it affordable. Trips down the Río Tiputini and into Parque Nacional Yasuní are possible, but require at least a week. Visiting a Huaorani village requires written permission from the community (make sure the guide you hire has this permission). Local tour companies have diminished in Coca. It's best to book from Quito, although a few independent guides operate in town.

Tropic Ecological Adventures (☎ 02-222-5907; www.tropiceco.com; Av de la República E7-320, apt 1A, Quito) provides tours to an ecologically sound lodge in Huaorani territory that is run by the Ecotourism Association of Quehueríono, which represents five communities on the upper Río Shiripuno. The group also runs day trips, one- or two-day tours into Secoya territory from Coca.

Kem Pery Tours (☎ 02-250-5600; www.kempery .com; cnr Ramíres Dávalos 117 & Amazonas, Quito; lodge 3 nights with/without bathroom US$330/310, 4 nights with/without bathroom US$370/350) leads tours to the Bataburo Lodge, on the edge of Huaorani territory, about nine hours from Coca by boat and bus. Canoes motor into the remote Ríos Tiguino and Cononaco and tours combine wildlife-viewing with cultural visits. There is a US$20 fee to enter Huaorani territory. Guides are both bilingual and native. The agency also runs longer trips in the same area that involve camping.

Native Huaorani Otobo and his family operate **Otobo's Amazon Safari** (www.rain forestcamping.com; 7-night tour incl airfare per person US$1540), a remote site on the Río Cononaco with platform tents and a thatched-roof lodge. Visitors can hike around the Parque Nacional Yasuni with a native English-speaking guide, visit lagoons and a local village. The site can be reached by small plane from Puyo and motorized canoe from Coca and the Vía Auca, or by canoe only at a reduced price.

Independent, recommended guides include **Jarol Fernando Vaca** (☎ 02-227-1094; shiripuno2004@yahoo.com), a Quito-based naturalist and butterfly specialist who can take visitors into the Shiripuno area and is authorized by Huaorani to guide in their territory; and **Sandro Ramos** (sandroidalio@hotmail.com), who leads trips into Parque Nacional Yasuni, Huaorani territory and Iquitos, Peru. **Luis Duarte** (☎ 288-2285; cocaselva@hotmail.com) organizes customized tours, including river passage to Peru or stays with Huaorani families. Find him at La Casa del Maito (right).

Sleeping & Eating

Coca's cheaper hotels are dingy, overpriced and fill up quickly with oil workers.

Hotel Oasis (☎ 288-0206; yuturilodge@yahoo.com; Camilo de Torrano s/n; s/d with fan US$9/12, with air-con US$12/25) Rooms are run-down, but there's a pleasant deck with a view of the river. The staff arranges trips to economic lodges on the Río Napo.

Hotel Lojanita (☎ 288-0032; cnr Napo & Cuenca; s/d with fan US$10/16, with air-con US$15/25; 🅿) This recently remodeled hotel is a good base for catching buses. The best rooms have white walls and linens and high ceilings.

Hostería La Misión (☎ 288-0260; Camilo de Torrano s/n; s/d US$24/36; 🅿 🅰) This longtime Coca standard has small rooms overlooking the Río Napo. Several pools and a riverside restaurant enhance the value.

Hotel El Auca (☎ 288-0127/600; helauca@ecuanex .net.ec; Napo; s/d from US$26/42) Catering to tour groups and oil workers alike (not to mention the tame jungle critters roaming the garden), the Auca is Coca's finest.

Eating & Drinking

The restaurants at **Hostería La Misión** (Camilo de Torrano s/n) and Hotel El Auca are considered to be the best in town.

Las Delicias (cnr Napo & Cuenca; mains US$1.50) Fried chicken and French fries.

La Casa del Maito (Malecón; mains US$2.50) Squeeze between the noisy locals for the heavenly house specialty, *maito* (fish cooked in leaves).

Cevichería Rincón Manaria (Quito btwn Cuenca & Bolívar; mains US$4-7) Crowded tables, big bowls of *ceviche* and loud music create a beach-party vibe at this lively joint.

Emerald Forest Blues (cnr Espejo & Quito) Friendly little bar run by a popular local guide.

El Bunker (Hostería La Misión, Camilo de Torrano s/n) Head to this steamy downstairs dance club for rapid-fire reggaeton.

Getting There & Away

AIR

The airport is 2km north of town. **TAME** (☎ 288-1078; cnr Napo & Rocafuerte) and **Icaro** (☎ 288-0997/546; www.icaro.com.ec; La Misión, Hostería La Misión) fly to Quito (US$43 to US$57) Monday through Saturday. Book ahead.

BOAT

On Monday and Thursday at 8am, **Coop de Transportes Fluviales Orellana** (☎ 288-0087; Napo near Chimborazo) offers passenger service to Nuevo Rocafuerte (US$15, 10 hours) on the Peruvian border. It returns to Coca, departing from Nuevo Rocafuerte at 5am on Sunday, Tuesday and Friday. Although there's usually a stop for lunch, you should bring some food and water for the trip. Travelers arriving and departing by river must register their passport at the *capitanía* (harbormaster's office), by the landing dock. If you're on an organized tour, your guide will usually take care of this.

BUS

There are bus offices in town and at the bus terminal, north of town. Several buses a day go to Quito (US$10, nine hours via Loreto, 13 hours via Lago Agrio), Tena (US$7, six hours) and Lago Agrio (US$3, three hours), as well as other jungle towns. Open-sided trucks called *rancheras* or *chivas* leave from the terminal for various destinations between Coca and Lago Agrio, and to Río Tiputini to the south.

GETTING TO PERU

Exit and entry formalities in Ecuador are handled in Nuevo Rocafuerte; in Peru, try your best to settle them in Pantoja, with Iquitos as backup. The official border crossing is at Pantoja, a short ride from Nuevo Rocafuerte. Boats from Nuevo Rocafuerte charge US$40 per boat to Pantoja. Timing is the key: four or five **cargo boats** (☎ 51-6-524-2082; US$35) travel from Pantoja to Iquitos (a four- to six-day trip) when they have enough cargo to justify the trip. Call the owner of one to ask about arrival dates. A hammock and 19L of water, in addition to food, are recommended; food on the boats can be dodgy. Be warned that conditions can be rough: there may only be one bathroom, crowded conditions and lots of livestock on board. Boats vary in quality, but if you've been waiting a long time for one to arrive, you may not want to be picky.

If you're traveling in the opposite direction, see p868.

RÍO NAPO
☎ 06

East of Coca, the Río Napo flows steadily toward Peru and the Amazon. This long, lonesome stretch of river contains some of Ecuador's best jungle lodges. Except aboard the boat to Nuevo Rocafuerte, independent canoe travel is expensive. If you're visiting a lodge, transport is part of the package.

Pompeya is a Catholic mission about two hours downriver from Coca on Río Napo near the **Reserva Biológica Limoncocha**. Now that there is road access and nearby oil drilling, the area is rather depressing and not ideal for spotting wildlife. The area is easily accessed by bus from the oil town of **Shushufindi**, one hour from either Coca or Lago Agrio.

About five hours downstream from Coca, **Pañacocha** is another settlement you can visit independently. You'll find a gorgeous blackwater lagoon with great piranha fishing and incredible biodiversity among cloud forest and dry forest. Tours from Coca go here but you can also take the public canoe slated for Nuevo Rocafuerte (see p645) for added adventure. Cheap accommodations are available at **Pensión Las Palmas** (riverfront; r per person US$3) but you might be more comfortable camping. Inexpensive *comedores* (eateries), including Elsita and Delicia, are within view of the boat landing.

Those who prefer comfort, wildlife guides and tasty food should consider a lodge. The least expensive in the area is **Yuturi Lodge** (Yuturi Jungle Adventures in Quito ☎ 02-250-4037/3225; www.yuturilodge.com; cnr Amazonas N24-236 & Colón; packages per person for 4 nights US$350), which has received good reports. **Sani Lodge** (in Quito, Map pp602-3; ☎ 02-255-8881; www.sanilodge.com; Roca 736, Pasaje Chantilly; packages per person for 3/4/7 nights US$510/680/1020) is a wonderful place, with outstanding guides and service while still reasonably priced.

The Río Napo flows just outside the northern border of Parque Nacional Yasuní and finally enters Peru at Nuevo Rocafuerte.

NUEVO ROCAFUERTE
☎ 06

A distant dot on the map for most, Nuevo Rocafuerte lies five hours downstream from Pañacocha (eight to 10 hours from Coca), completing a seriously arduous journey to the Peruvian border. The very basic **Parador Turístico** (☎ 238-2133; behind national police office; r per person with shared bathroom US$3-5) fills up fast, since it's the only lodging in town. A few two-shelf stores sell basic provisions; for a hot meal ask around. Electricity is only available from 6pm to 11pm. Local guides and tours up the Río Yasuní into Parque Nacional Yasuní can be arranged through Juan Carlos 'Chuso' Cuenca (☎ 238-2182).

If you are continuing to Peru, try to make arrangements well in advance. If you don't time it right, you could be stuck here for some time. Bring adequate supplies of water-purification tablets, bug repellent and food. Operators in Coca (see p644) offer jungle tours which end in Iquitos, Peru.

PARQUE NACIONAL YASUNÍ
Ecuador's largest mainland **park** (admission US$20) is a massive 9620-sq-km swath of wetlands, marshes, swamps, lakes, rivers and tropical rainforest. It contains a variety of rainforest habitats, wildlife and a few Huaorani communities. Unfortunately, poaching and (increasingly) oil exploration are damaging the park.

Visiting the park independently is difficult, but operators in Coca (p644) and Quito (p608) offer tours. Recommended independent guides include **Oscar Tapuy** (in Quito ☎ 02-288-1486; oscarta23@yahoo.com), one of the country's top bird guides and **Jarol Fernando Vaca** (in Quito ☎ 02-224-1918; shiripuno2004@yahoo.com), a Quito-based naturalist and butterfly specialist. Both speak English and Jarol is authorized by the Huaorani to guide in their territory.

TENA

☎ 06 / pop 28,000

Ecuador's de facto whitewater-rafting capital (elevation 518m) sits at the confluence of two lovely rivers, Río Tena and Río Pano, and draws paddlers from all over the world. It's an attractive, relaxed town where kayaks lie around hotel-room entrances and boaters hang out in pizza joints, rapping about their day on the rapids. Rafting is are easily arranged, and several operators offer interesting jungle trips.

Information

Banco del Austro (15 de Noviembre) Traveler's checks; ATM.

Cucupanet (main plaza at Mera; per hr US$1.20) Internet access.

Police station (☎ 288-6101; main plaza)

Sights & Activities

Stroll over a small bridge to **Parque Amazónico** (btwn Ríos Pano & Tena; admission US$2; ☾ 8:30am-5pm), a 27-hectare island with a self-guided trail passing labeled local plants and animal enclosures.

Tena's major attraction is whitewater rafting, which offers an adrenaline rush amid stunning jungle and cloud-forest scenery. Depending on difficulty, day trips run US$50

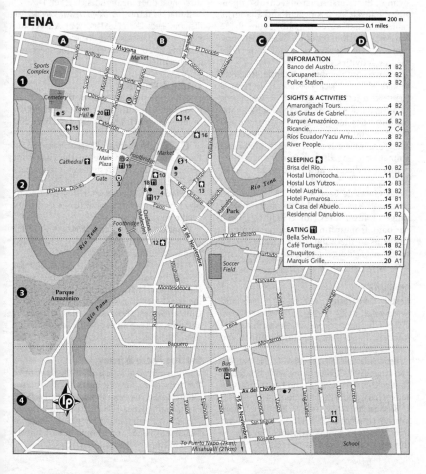

TENA

0	200 m
0	0.1 miles

INFORMATION
Banco del Austro..................................1 B2
Cucupanet...2 B2
Police Station.......................................3 B2

SIGHTS & ACTIVITIES
Amarongachi Tours...............................4 B2
Las Grutas de Gabriel...........................5 A1
Parque Amazónico................................6 B2
Ricancie..7 C4
Ríos Ecuador/Yacu Amu.......................8 B2
River People...9 B2

SLEEPING
Brisa del Río..10 B2
Hostal Limoncocha..............................11 D4
Hostal Los Yutzos................................12 B3
Hotel Austria.......................................13 B2
Hotel Pumarosa...................................14 B1
La Casa del Abuelo..............................15 A1
Residencial Danubios..........................16 B2

EATING
Bella Selva..17 B2
Café Tortuga.......................................18 B2
Chuquitos..19 B2
Marquis Grille......................................20 A1

to US$75 per person. Long in the business, **Ríos Ecuador/Yacu Amu** (☎ 288-6727; www.riosecuador. com; Orellana) offers several day trips as well as a four-day kayaking class (US$330). British-operated **River People** (☎ 288-8384; www.riverpeople raftingecuador.com; cnr 15 de Noviembre & 9 de Octubre) is a top-notch outfitter and has received positive reviews. Their outdoor cafe (Sticky Fingers) is a good spot for breakfasts.

Tours

Amarongachi Tours (☎ 288-6372; www.amarongachi .com; 15 de Noviembre 438) offers various good-time jungle excursions. On its tours (US$45 per person per day), you can stay with a family in the jungle, eat local food, go for hikes, climb up waterfalls, pan for gold and swim in the rivers. Amarongachi also operates the lovely Amarongachi and Shangrila cabins; the latter are on a bluff 100m above Río Anzu (a tributary of Río Napo) and feature great views of the river and some more mellow activities.

Also recommended is **Ricancie** (Indigenous Network of Upper Napo Communities for Cultural Coexistence & Ecotourism; ☎ 288-8479; www.ricancie .nativeweb.org; cnr Av El Chofer & Vasco). Ten Quichua communities have joined to improve life for their 200 families through ecotourism. They organize adventure tours, bird- and animal-watching, demonstrations of healing plants, handicrafts and cooking for US$45 per day.

Las Grutas de Gabriel (☎ 288-7894; www.las grutasdegabriel.com; Calderón) also offers a wide range of adventures (for US$30 to US$50 per day), from rafting adventures to multi-day trips in the jungle. The locally owned outfit uses indigenous guides and helps disadvantaged youths.

Sleeping

Hostal Limoncocha (☎ 288-7583; limoncocha @andinanet.net; Ita 533; r per person with/without bathroom US$8/5) Chipper backpacker digs with a guest kitchen, hand-painted murals and clean private bathrooms.

Residencial Danubios (☎ 288-6378; 15 de Noviembre; r per person US$6) Clean rooms with tile floors (but cold-water showers) and friendly service make this a good-value option.

Brisa del Río (☎ 288-6444/208; Orellana; r with shared bathroom per person US$7) Friendly owners and light, spacious rooms with fans have made this riverfront *hostal* a popular choice. Shared

bathrooms are spic-and-span clean. Several rooms have river views.

Hotel Austria (☎ 288-7205; Tarqui; r per person US$12) This large gated house has clipped shrubbery and Adirondack chairs. Recommended for its bright, high-ceilinged rooms with fans and hot water.

La Casa del Abuelo (☎ 288-6318; runanambi@yahoo .com; Mera 628; s/d US$15/20) An ample refurbished colonial-style home with comfortable rooms tucked away on a quiet street. Ask the owners about their rural guesthouse 5km away on the river.

Hotel Pumarosa (☎ 287-0311; Orellana; s/d US$15/25; ✗) Inviting rooms around a shaded courtyard have high wooden ceilings, large windows, reliable hot water and flourishes of artwork. The disco next door means noisy weekends.

Hostal Los Yutzos (☎ 288-6717; www.geocities.com /losyutzos; Rueda 190; s/d US$34/45; ✗) A riverside gem with spacious and attractive rooms, a relaxing balcony with wooden loungers and a lush garden.

Eating & Drinking

For the adventurous, grills by the pedestrian bridge cook up sausages, chicken and *guanta* (a jungle rodent). There's also cold beer and riverside seating.

our pick **Café Tortuga** (Orellana; mains US$2-4) Excellent Swiss-run cafe on the riverfront serving empanadas, fresh juices, crepes, coffees, breakfast and more.

Bella Selva (Orellana; mains US$2-6) Riverfront pizza parlor with tropical tunes and tasty veggie pizzas.

Chuquitos (main plaza; mains US$4-6) An old favorite for its waterside terrace and varied menu, including excellent fish.

Marquis Grille (☎ 288-6513; Amazonas 251; mains US$6-20; ✗ Mon-Sat) With white tablecloths, classical music and attentive service, this is the most formal restaurant for miles, with Chilean wines, steamed tilapia, rich pastas and lobster. Keep an eye on the thatch for the resident sloth.

Getting There & Away

The bus terminal is less than 1km south of the main plaza. Several buses a day head for Quito (US$6, six hours), Lago Agrio (US$7, eight hours), Coca (US$7, six hours), Baños (US$4, four hours) and other places. Buses for Misahuallí (US$1, one hour) depart hourly from in front of the terminal.

MISAHUALLÍ

☎ 06

One of the Oriente's sleepiest jungle towns, Misahuallí sits swathed in greenery at the junction of two major rivers at the literal end of the road. The town has popular sandy beaches and a famous cadre of monkeys adept at swiping sunglasses and cameras from visitors. While wildlife-watching isn't the draw here, there are lovely walks to be had, and a variety of jungle birds, tropical flowers, army ants, dazzling butterflies and other insects can be seen.

There's no bank, so get cash before arriving.

Activities

The dirt roads around Misahuallí make for relaxing walks to outlying villages. You can also walk to a nearby **waterfall** for swimming and picnics. To get there, take a Misahuallí–Puerto Napo bus and ask the driver to drop you off at Río Latas, about 20 minutes from Misahuallí; ask for *el camino a las cascadas* (the trail to the falls). Follow the river upstream to the falls, about an hour's walk up the river – be prepared to wade.

Be sure to visit the **Butterfly Farm** (admission US$2.50; 8:30am-12pm & 2-5pm), a block off the plaza.

Tours

If you're hoping to see any of the wildlife, make sure you're venturing well away from Misahuallí, and be sure to hire an experienced and licensed guide (not the touts in the main plaza). Tours range from one day to 10 days and prices usually include the guide, food, water, accommodations (which range from jungle camping to comfortable lodges) and rubber boots. Rates are usually around US$35 to US$45 per person per day.

The following guides and operators are all recommended:

Douglas Clarke's Expeditions (☎ 289-0002; douglasclarkeexpediciones@yahoo.com) Readers recommend this longtime operator. Most overnights involve camping and some English is spoken.

Ecoselva (☎ 289-0019; ecoselva@yahoo.es; main plaza) Pepe Tapia González takes visitors on fun one- to 10-day tours with overnights at his rustic lodge or jungle camps. He speaks English, has a biology background and is knowledgeable about plants and insects.

Luis Zapata (☎ 289-0071; zorrozz_2000@yahoo.com) An independent, recommended guide who speaks English.

Misahuallí Tours (☎ 288-7616; main plaza) Carlos Lastra runs tours on the upper Río Napo. He's experienced and well respected.

Sleeping & Eating

Water and electricity failures are frequent here, and most hotels are very basic.

Hostal Marena Internacional (☎ 289-0002; Av Principal; s/d US$6/12) Half a block from the plaza, these neat tiled rooms have hot-water bathrooms. It's owned by Douglas Clarke's Expeditions.

Hostal Shaw (☎ 289-0019; main plaza; s/d US$6/12) Run by Ecoselva, this *hostal* has simple rooms with fans and private bathrooms with hot water. There's a tasty cafe downstairs.

El Paisano (☎ 289-0027; Rivadeneyra; s/d US$8/16) Off the plaza, this backpacker haunt has cement rooms, tiny bathrooms, hot water, fans and mosquito nets. Vegetarian dishes at the open-air restaurant.

France Amazonia (☎ 289-0009; www.france-amazonia.com; Av Principal; s/d US$18/36;) Just outside town, shady thatched huts surround a sparkling pool and sandy fire pit. Beds are ultranarrow but rooms are pleasant. French-owned.

Getting There & Away

Buses to Tena (US$1, one hour) leave hourly from the plaza.

JATUN SACHA BIOLOGICAL RESERVE

On the southern bank of the Río Napo, about 7km east of Misahuallí, **Jatun Sacha Biological Reserve** (admission US$7) is a biological station and rainforest reserve protecting 850 butterfly species and 535 bird species. It is run by **Fundación Jatun Sacha** (☎ 02-331-7163; www.jatunsacha.org), an Ecuadorian nonprofit organization. You can visit the reserve on a day trip or stay at **Cabañas Aliñahui** (☎ 02-227-4510; www.ecuadoramazonlodge.com; s/d incl 3 meals US$50/100), but you'll need to book in advance.

Jatun Sacha and Cabañas Aliñahui are reached from Tena: take an Ahuano or Santa Rosa bus and ask the driver to drop you off at either entrance. Aliñahui is about 3km east of the Jatun Sacha research station, or 27km east of Tena on the road to Santa Rosa.

PUYO

☎ 03 / pop 35,000

A lazy river slinks through this concrete outpost, which is part mellow jungle town and part commercial, government hub. The streets are filled with missionaries, vendors pushing street carts and indigenous people from far-flung corners of the Amazon. Dense green jungle flourishes around the town's edges while jagged snowcapped mountains rise in the distance. It's a good starting point for reaching indigenous villages.

Marín and Atahualpa are the principal downtown streets with the most services.

Information

Banco del Austro (Atahualpa) Bank with ATM.
Cámara de Turismo (☎ 288-3681; Centro Comercial Zuñiga, Marín; ☉ 8:30am-12:30pm & 3-6pm Mon-Fri) Provides regional maps and info.

Sights & Activities

North of downtown, a bridge crossing the Río Puyo leads to the **Parque Omaere** (www .fundacionomaere.org; admission US$3; ☉ 9am-5pm), an intriguing ethnobotanical park of rainforest plants and indigenous dwellings less than 1km from the city center. A pleasant **trail** (called the *paseo turístico*) continues past Omaere for 1.7km along the river to the Puyo-Tena road, where you can flag a bus back to town every 20 minutes or return along the trail.

Visitors rave about the **Jardín Botánico Las Orquídeas** (☎ 288-4855; admission US$5; ☉ 8am-6pm), located 15 minutes south from Puyo on the road to Macas. Enthusiastic owner Omar Taeyu guides visitors through hills of lush foliage and fishponds to see gorgeous plants and countless rare orchids. Call ahead.

Tours

The recommended **Papangu-Atacapi Tours** (☎ 288-7684; papanguturismo@yahoo.es; 27 de Febrero near Sucre) is a unique Quichua-run tour operator specializing in community tourism. One- to 10-day tours (two-person minimum) start at US$40 per person per day. **Fundecopia** (☎ 09-029-4808; www.fundecopia) organizes trips to the Arutam Rainforest Reserve and Shuar homestays with some volunteer opportunities. Tourists pay US$20 per day and volunteers US$75 per week; the fees include meals and lodging.

Sleeping

Hotel Libertad (☎ 288-3282; cnr Orellana & Manzano; s/d US$6/12) This tranquil spot offers cramped but spotless rooms.

Hotel Los Cofanes (☎ 288-5560; loscofanes@yahoo .com; cnr 27 de Febrero & Marín; s/d US$10/20) The tiled rooms need a remodel, but the attention is good and rooms include phone, fan and cable TV.

Las Palmas (☎ 288-4832; cnr 20 de Julio & 4 de Enero; s/d US$13/26; ☐) This big, yellow colonial with attractive gardens and chattering parrot, has neat, bright rooms. There's on-site internet, a cafe and hammocks.

Delfín Rosado (☎ 288-8757; www.delfinrosadohotel spa.com; cnr Marín & Atahualpa; r per person incl breakfast US$15; ☐) New paint, dark wood furniture and a spiral staircase create a modern, clean option, but it's a bit loud. A Quito-based pizza chain is downstairs.

El Jardín ☎ 288-7770; www.eljardin.pastaza.net; Paseo Turístico, Barrio Obrero; s/d US$25/50; ☐) A welcoming spot set behind a large garden, this rustic wooden house has hammock balconies, wi-fi and plain but comfortable rooms.

Eating

Toke Esmeraldo (Orellana s/n; mains US$1.50) A cheery street shack where you can pull up a stool for some fresh, fast seafood including *ceviche* and fried tilapia. Sip on a range of fresh juices.

El Fariseo (☎ 288-3795; cnr Atahualpa & Villamil; mains US$2-5; ☉ Mon-Sat) Sit streetside for a frothy cappuccino and slice of cake. *Platos fuertes* include burritos and burgers.

El Toro Asado (☎ 08-494-8156; cnr Atahualpa & 27 de Febrero; mains US$4) In addition to more common meats and fish, this elegant grillhouse serves *guanta*, an Amazonian…er, rodent, five different ways.

El Jardín (☎ 288-7770; Paseo Turístico, Barrio Obrero; mains US$5-11) This highly recommended house by the river serves some of the Oriente's best cooking.

O Sole Mio (☎ 288-4768; cnr Pichincha & Guaranda; pizzas US$6; ☉ 6-10pm Wed-Sun) A modern Italian restaurant, with outdoor patio overlooking twinkling town lights, serves uncommonly authentic pizzas.

Getting There & Away

The bus terminal is 3km out of town (a taxi should cost US$1). Buses run regularly to Baños (US$2, 1½ hours), Quito (US$5, 5½ hours), Macas (US$5, four hours) and Tena (US$2.50, 2½ hours). Services to other towns are also available.

MACAS

☎ 07 / pop 17,000

Macas' slow and steady pace and approachable locals make it a welcoming stop. It's also an excellent launch pad for adventures further afield. Macas is situated above the banks of the wild Río Upano, and there are great views of the river and the Río Upano valley from behind the town's cathedral. On a clear day you can glimpse the often smoking Volcán Sangay, some 40km northwest. Though the biggest town in the southern Oriente, it's definitely a small town at heart.

Information

Banco del Austro (cnr 24 de Mayo & 10 de Agosto) Bank with ATM.

Cámara de Turismo (☎ 270-1606; Comín near Soasti) Tourist information kiosk.

Cyber Vision (Soasti; per hr US$1.50) Internet access.

Tours

Macas is the place to book trips into the southern Oriente, but services are not as comprehensive as in the north. Be aware that the Shuar don't want unguided visitors in their villages; some villages refuse visitors entirely. Multiday trips cost US$40 to US$75 per day. **Planeta Tours** (☎ 270-1328; cnr Comín & Soasti) offers cultural tours in Shuar territory, waterfall hikes, fishing, whitewater rafting on the Río Upano and canoeing. **Insondu Mundo Shuar** (☎ 270-2533; www.mundoshuar.com; cnr Soasti & Bolívar) does two- to five-day trips into Shuar territory with some English-speaking guides. Independent guides include Shuar guide **Nanki Wampankit Juank** (nanki_82@hotmail.com) and the experienced **Rafael Telcán** (☎ 09-101-1075).

Sleeping & Eating

Hotel La Orquidea (☎ 270-0970; cnr 9 de Octubre & Sucre; s/d US$8/16) A pleasant, old-fashioned *pensión* that's run by a friendly family. Wonderfully away from the noise.

Hotel Level 5 (☎ 270-1240; cnr Juan de la Cruz & Soasti; s/d US$10/20) This fairly new glass-walled hotel has small but clean and comfortable rooms with good views.

Café Bar Maravilla (☎ 270-0158; Soasti near Sucre; mains US$4-6; ⏰ 4pm-1am Mon-Sat) This wonderfully atmospheric eatery serves creative fare and delicious cocktails.

The *comedores* on Comín near Soasti sell tasty *ayampacos*, a jungle specialty of meat, chicken or fish grilled in *bijao* leaves.

Getting There & Away

TAME (☎ 270-1162/978; www.tame.com.ec) flies to Quito (US$80) on Monday, Wednesday and Friday. The bus terminal has several daily departures for Cuenca (US$8.50, eight hours), Guayaquil (US$10, 10 hours) and Riobamba (US$5, five hours). Buses to Puyo (US$4, four hours) leave 10 times daily; some continue to Tena.

PACIFIC COAST & LOWLANDS

Ecuador, land of lively Andean markets, Amazon adventures and…beaches? While not high priority for most travelers, Ecuador's northern coast offers off-the-beaten-path adventures. It's a land of giant mangroves, Afro-Ecuadorian culture and dodgy backwater villages, with a sprinkling of inviting beaches and surf spots. The more visited southern coast (from Parque Nacional Machalilla to the Peruvian border) has delectably fresh seafood and the country's best beaches, including attractive stretches along the 'Ruta del Sol' (Route of the Sun). Keep in mind the weather: June to November is the rainy season, but also the sunniest; the sun blazes both before and after the afternoon downpour. December through May is often overcast and chilly.

Getting There & Away

Most places along the northern coast can be reached from Quito in a day's travel. San Lorenzo is a seven-hour bus ride from Quito, though it can also be reached by road from Ibarra (in the northern highlands). Nearly the entire coastal highway is now paved. A spectacular road links Latacunga (see p625) in the highlands to the lowland city of Quevedo, an important junction en route to the south coast. Other handy routes are the 11-hour bus ride from Quito to lovely Puerto López (p658).

SAN LORENZO & AROUND

☎ 06

Encircled by verdant jungle, at the edge of a dank, still sea, San Lorenzo (population 15,000) is a decrepit, lively hodgepodge of blazing heat, tropical beats and crumbling storefronts. Marimba notes and salsa music flavor this mostly Afro-Ecuadorian outpost,

ECUADOR

which goes all out in August with an annual music festival. The main reason to visit is to explore the infrequently visited mangroves of the area. Boat tours can be arranged down at the port.

Orientation & Information

Imbabura is the main drag. Buses roll into town, pass the train station (on the left) and stop at the end of Imbabura at the plaza. The port is a couple of blocks further down. Money-changing opportunities are poor. Don't wander from the main drag after dark.

Sleeping & Eating

Hotels are *all* basic. Mosquito nets and fans are recommended and water shortages are frequent.

Hotel Carondelet (☎ 278-1119; Parque Central; r per person with/without bathroom US$8/6) The small rooms at Carondelet are adequate, and some offer views over the tin roofs toward the river.

Hotel Pampa de Oro (☎ 278-0214; Ortíz; s/d US$7/14) On a side street off Imbabura, this is the pick of the hotels, with clean, wood-floor rooms. Some are bright and open onto a shared balcony.

Hotel Continental (☎ 278-0125; Imbabura; r per person with fan/air-con US$8/12; ☒) This aging place has fading fishing murals and creaky floorboards. The rooms are sizable and fairly clean, with tile floors, TV and warm showers.

Ballet Azul (Imbabura; mains US$3-6; ⏱ 8:30am-10pm Mon-Sat) Shrimp is the specialty at this popular open-sided place. *Ceviche de camarón* (shrimp ceviche) and *camarones al ajillo* (garlic shrimp) mate perfectly with a *cerveza* (beer).

Getting There & Away

Buses to Ibarra (US$4, four hours) depart twice daily from the corner of Imbabura and Ortíz. Buses to Esmeraldas (US$5, five hours) and Borbón (US$1.20, one hour) depart hourly between 5am and 4pm from the central plaza.

Although boat traffic has dwindled with the completion of the road to Borbón and Esmeraldas, there are still departures at 7:30am and 10:30am for La Tola (US$5, 2½ hours) via Limones (US$3, 1½ hours). The ride through the coastal mangroves to these tiny, predominantly Afro-Ecuadorian fishing villages is quite an experience. The early departure connects in La Tola with buses to Esmeraldas.

For a tour of the mangroves, head to the port and arrange a trip through **Cooperativa San Lorenzo del Pailón** (☎ 278-0039) or **Andrés Carvache** (☎ 278-0161; andrescarvache@yahoo.es). Prices are around US$20 to US$30 per hour.

PLAYA DE ORO

Two rivers lead inland from Borbón: Río Cayapas and Río Santiago. The furthest community up Río Santiago is the remote settlement of **Playa de Oro**, near the border of Reserva Ecológica Cotacachi-Cayapas. Half an hour upstream from Playa de Oro is the **Playa de Oro Reserva de Tigrillos**, a 10,000-hectare reserve that protects native jungle cats. The best way to experience it is by staying at the community-operated riverside **jungle lodge** (www.touchthejungle.org; r per person US$50). Prices include three meals and local guides. It's an authentic and totally unique experience.

The village of Playa de Oro is about five hours upstream from Borbón, but there are no regular boats. You have to take the 7:30am bus from Borbón to Selva Alegre (US$3, two hours). From Selva Alegre, if you made a reservation, a boat from Playa de Oro will motor you up to the village or the reserve (US$50 each way). If you didn't make a reservation, your best bet is to time your visit with the once-a-week market boat that at time of research went out on Saturdays (leaving around noon and costing US$10 per person). The river trip from Selva Alegre takes two hours (2½ hours if you're going to the reserve). Reservations must be made at least two weeks in advance with **Tracy Jordan** (tracy@touchthejungle.org).

ESMERALDAS

☎ 06 / pop 98,000

Lively, noisy and notoriously dodgy, Esmeraldas is an important port and home to a major oil refinery. For travelers, it's little more than a necessary stop to make bus connections. If you need to spend the night, the old, wooden **Hostal Miraflores** (☎ 272-3077; Bolívar 6-04, 2nd fl; s/d US$5/10) on the plaza is the best bet for backpackers.

The airport is 25km up the road to San Lorenzo; taxi fare is around US$7. **TAME** (☎ 272-6863; cnr Bolívar & 9 de Octubre), near the plaza, has daily flights to Quito (US$54) and less frequent services to Guayaquil (US$98 one way) and Cali, Colombia (US$115 one way).

Buses leave from different stops within walking distance of each other and the main plaza. **Aero Taxi** (Sucre near Rocafuerte), **Transportes**

Occidentales (9 de Octubre near Sucre) and **Transportes Esmeraldas** (10 de Agosto, Plaza Central) all go to Quito (US$6 to US$7, six hours). Occidentales and Esmeraldas have many buses to Guayaquil (US$7, eight hours), Ambato, Machala and other cities. **Reina del Camino** (Piedrahita near Bolívar) serves Manta (US$8, seven hours) and Bahía de Caráquez (US$8, eight hours).

Transportes La Costeñita (Malecón Maldonado) and **Transportes del Pacífico** (Malecón Maldonado) head frequently to Atacames and Súa (each US$1, about one hour) and Muisne (US$2.20, two hours). These companies also go to Borbón (US$3.50, four hours) and San Lorenzo (US$5, five hours). These buses pass the airport.

ATACAMES
☎ 06 / pop 10,200

The raucous beach town of Atacames inspires pure excitement or dread, depending on how you like your beach vacations. For some *serranos* (highlanders), Atacames equals nonstop party, with a wide packed beach, bustling guesthouses and a jumble of thatched-roof bars blaring salsa and reggaeton at all hours of the day. Plenty of international travelers join the festive atmosphere, which reaches its peak in the high season (July to mid-September, Christmas through New Year, Carnaval and Easter).

Buses drop passengers off in the center of town, on the main road from Esmeraldas (get off at the motorized-tricycle stand). The center is on the inland side of the highway, and the beach is reached by a small footbridge over the Río Atacames or by tricycle 'eco-taxi' (US$1). Most of the hotels and bars are along the *malecón* (waterfront promenade).

Dangers & Annoyances
A powerful undertow here causes drownings every year, so keep within your limits. There have been assaults on the beach, so stick to populated areas. Don't bring anything of value to the beach.

Sleeping
Hotels fill up fast on weekends and holidays. Prices quoted here are for the high season, during which hotels generally charge a four-person minimum (the number of beds in most hotel rooms).

At the west end of the *malecón*, Las Acacias runs away from the beach toward the highway. Atacames' cheapest hotels are along this street. Most of them are simple but just fine.

Hotel Jennifer (☎ 273-1055; near Malecón; s/d from US$8/15) This simple, straightforward place has clean, Spartan rooms that get a decent amount of light. Kind staff.

Cabañas Los Bohíos (☎ 272-7478; Calle Principal; s/d US$10/20) Near the dark Río Atacames, Los Bohíos offers a mix of clean rooms and small simple bamboo cabins.

Hotel Tahiti (☎ 273-1078; Malecón; r US$20-40; 🏊) The nicely landscaped pool is the centerpiece of this whitewashed five-story hotel near the beach. Rooms are clean and fan-cooled and many have balconies with partial sea views.

Eating
Restaurants near the beach all serve the same thing – the day's catch. Locals dine on fresh *ceviche* on a tiny lane off the Malecón. Bowls start at around US$4.

Punto y Como (Malecón; mains US$3-7; 🕚 11am-10pm) Crowds pack into this small, cozy seafood restaurant.

Pizzería da Giulio (☎ 273-1603; Malecón; mains US$6-9; 🕔 5:30pm-midnight Tue-Fri, 10:30am-midnight Sat & Sun) Run by a Sicilian, this restaurant with balcony seating serves tasty thin-crust pizzas.

Getting There & Away
There are regular buses to Esmeraldas (US$1, one hour), as well as south to Súa (US30¢, 10 minutes), Same (US30¢, 15 minutes) and Muisne (US$1.50, 1½ hours). Transportes Occidentales and Aerotaxi, whose offices are near the highway, both go to Quito daily (US$7 to US$8, seven hours).

SÚA
☎ 06

This friendly fishing village, 6km west of Atacames, is far more tranquil than its party-town neighbor. The mellow bay is a fine spot for a swim, although early in the morning it's busy with trawlers.

There are fewer lodgings here than in Atacames, but they're also quieter and often better value if you aren't looking for nightlife. All have cold-water bathrooms. **Sol de Súa** (☎ 273-1021; www.folklorehotelsua.com; Malecón; cabin per person US$5) consists of nine basic wood-and-concrete cabins scattered around a sandy yard. **Hostal Las Buganvillas** (☎ 273-1008; Malecón; s/d US$8/16; 🏊) has clean-swept rooms with tile floors. **Hotel Chagra Ramos** (☎ 273-1006; Malecón; s/d US$8/16) is a friendly, wind-battered classic.

ECUADOR

SAME & TONCHIGÜE
☎ 06

Same (pronounced *sah*-may) boasts the prettiest beach in the area, a striking 3km-long stretch of palm-fringed coast only lightly touched by development. The village itself, which lies 7km southwest of Sua, is small with only a sprinkling of (pricier) guesthouses and restaurants. **La Terraza** (☎ 247-0320; Same; s/d from US$12/24) offers simple rooms in a white-washed beachfront guesthouse. There's an open-sided restaurant and other good eating options nearby.

About 3km past Same, Tonchigüe is a tiny fishing village whose beach is a continuation of the Same beach. **Playa Escondida** (☎ 273-3122, 09-973-3368; www.playaescondida.com.ec; campsite per person US$5, r per person from US$20) is 3km west of Tonchigüe and 10km down the road to Punta Galeras. It's an isolated, quiet, beautiful spot, run by a Canadian expat. It has a restaurant and lots of empty, hidden beach.

MUISNE
☎ 05

Muisne is a tumbledown, working-class island surrounded by river and sea. Its long, wide wind-swept beach is backed by a few sandy little hotels and simple restaurants. Buses stop at the dock, where boats (US20¢) cross the river to the town. On the island, the main road heads from the dock through the 'center' of town and crumbles slowly away to the beach, 1.5km away. Hire an 'eco-taxi' (tricycle, US$1) for a ride to the beach if you're feeling lazy.

Facing the beach, **Calade Spondylus** (☎ 248-0279; r/cabin per person US$6/8) has simple but clean rooms plus wooden cabins around a rustic garden. Other good options are **Hostal Las Olas** (☎ 248-0782; s/d US$10/15) and the renovated **Playa Paraíso** (☎ 248-0192; s/d US$14/28).

Buses depart from El Relleno across the river to Esmeraldas (US$2, 2½ hours) passing Same, Súa and Atacames en route. Transportes Occidentales has night buses to Quito (US$8, eight hours). Buses head daily to Santo Domingo, with connections to Quito and Guayaquil.

The easiest way to go south from Muisne is by bus to the road junction known as **El Salto** (US50¢, 30 minutes) and then grabbing a passing bus to **Pedernales** (US$3, three hours). Between El Salto and Pedernales, you sometimes have to change buses in **San José de Chamanga** (you'll recognize Chamanga by the floating piles of garbage and stilted houses). Pedernales has connections further south and into the highlands.

MOMPICHE
☎ 05

Besides a stretch of palm-fringed sand, Mompiche has little else. That's the beauty. Its claim to fame is its world-class wave – a left-hand point break that rolls to life during big swells. Get your 40 winks at **Gabeal** (☎ 09-969-6543; east beach; camping per person US$3, r per person US$15), a set of bamboo cabins with cold-water bathrooms. Horse riding and surf lessons are available. Laid-back **DMCA Surf Hostel** (campsite per person US$3, r per person US$6-8) is popular with the surf crowd.

Rancheras go to and from Esmeraldas every day (US$3.50, 3½ hours), passing Atacames on the way.

CANOA
☎ 05 / pop 6100

Surfers, fishermen and sunseekers share this gorgeous, fat strip of beach – one of the best around – and the village continues to grow. In addition to surfing and beach walks, you can arrange boat trips, go biking in the countryside and visit the lovely **Río Muchacho Organic Farm** (☎ 09-147-9849; www.riomuchacho.com; r per person US$30), which offers sustainable-farming classes and accepts volunteers.

The beachfront **Coco Loco** (☎ 09-544-7260; hotalcocoloco@yahoo.com; dm/s/d/tr US$5/16/18/28, s/d with shared bathroom US$10/14) has clean rooms and a sand- and palm-filled yard. **Hotel Bambu** (☎ 261-6370; www.ecuadorexplorer.com/bambu; r US$20, s/d with shared bathroom US$7/12) rents spotless, cottage-like rooms on the beach. The grounds are scattered with hammocks, the restaurant is excellent, and juices and cold beers make everyone happy. Two blocks from the beach, **Linda Onda** (☎ 261-6339, 08-023-5719; www.linda onda.com; dm US$6, s/d from US$10/15) is a festive guesthouse run by two Aussie expats.

Café Flor (mains US$3-6; ⏰ 9am-3pm & 6-9:30pm Mon-Sat) is a sweet, family-run cafe that serves delicious breakfasts, plus pizzas, burritos, hamburgers and veggie burgers. **Amalur** (mains US$3-7; ⏰ noon-9pm) is a Basque restaurant serving tasty fresh calamari, gazpacho, grilled pork with red peppers and other tasty options. **El Oasis** (Calle Principal; mains US$4-10; ⏰ 8am till last customer) is a simple thatched-roof restaurant serving excellent seafood.

ourpick **Mambo Bar** (Malecón; ☽ noon-late Mon-Sat) is an open-sided balcony bar facing the beach with a small dance floor that brings a good mix of travelers and locals.

SAN VICENTE
☎ 05

This busy town is a short ferry ride across the Río Chone from the more popular resort of Bahía de Caráquez. Most travelers stop only for bus connections or to catch the ferry to Bahía.

Buses leave from the market area near the pier. Costa del Norte offers hourly service to Pedernales (US$3, three hours). Coactur serves Manta, Portoviejo and Guayaquil (US$7, six hours) daily. Ferries to Bahía de Caráquez (US35¢, 10 minutes) leave often from the pier between 6am and 10pm.

BAHÍA DE CARÁQUEZ
☎ 05 / pop 20,000

Chalk-colored high-rises, red tile roofs, man-icured yards and swept sidewalks give this self-proclaimed 'eco-city' a tidy impression. Today, the town market recycles its waste, organic shrimp farms are well underway, and reforestation projects dot the hillside. There are several interesting eco and cultural tours worth checking out, but for beaches you'll have to head elsewhere.

Ferries from San Vicente cross the Río Chone and dock at the piers along Malecón Alberto Santos, on the peninsula's eastern side. **Banco de Guayaquil** (cnr Bolívar & Riofrío) has an ATM.

Tours

Tours in Bahía are unique. The operators listed here devote themselves to ecotourism and will show you local environmental projects and take you to handmade-paper cooperatives. Both companies offer day trips to Islas Fragatas in the Chone estuary. **Guacamayo Bahíatours** (☎ 269-1412; www.guacamayotours.com; cnr Bolívar & Arenas) also arranges stays at Río Muchacho Organic Farm (opposite). **Bahía Dolphin Tours** (☎ 269-0257; www.chirije.com; Av Virgílio Ratti 606) offers visits to its nearby archaeological site.

Sleeping

The cheapest places usually have water-supply problems. **Hotel Italia** (☎ 269-1137; cnr Bolívar & Checa; s/d US$10/20) An old-fashioned four-story hotel

with comfortable high-ceiling rooms, fans, hot water and cable TV.

Centro Vocational Life (☎ 269-0496; cnr Vitteri & Muñoz Dávila; s/d US$10/20; ✹) Six small cabins sit on this gated grassy lot with a playground. Each has cable TV and a kitchenette, and some have hot water.

La Herradura (☎ 269-0446; Bolívar 202; s/d from US$20/30; ✹) An old Spanish home with antiques and artwork brimming from its nooks.

Eating

Several restaurants line the waterfront near the pier.

Arena Bar (☎ 269-2024; cnr Bolívar & Riofrío; mains US$2-5; ☽ 5pm-midnight) Chow down on pizzas, inventive salads and tasty sandwiches at this easygoing spot.

Vereda (☎ 269-2755; Muñoz Dávila; mains US$3-5) This popular family-run restaurant serves regional favorites like crab, *ceviche*, grilled river fish and seafood platters.

Puerto Amistad (☎ 269-3112; www.puertoamistad ecuador.com; Malecón Alberto Santos; mains US$4-7; ☽ noon-midnight Mon-Sat) An expat favorite, Puerto Amistad serves salads, savory crepes, quesa-dillas and grilled dishes in an airy waterside setting (200m south of the ferry dock).

Getting There & Away

For boat information, see San Vicente (left). Buses stop at the southern end of Malecón Alberto Santos. Coactur buses serve Portoviejo (US$2, two hours) and Manta (US$3, three hours) every hour. Reina del Camino serves Quito (US$7 to US$9, eight hours), Esmeraldas (US$7, eight hours) and Guayaquil (US$6 to US$7, six hours).

MONTECRISTI
☎ 05

Montecristi is known throughout the world for producing the finest straw hat on the planet – the mistakenly labeled **panama hat**. In Ecuador they're called *sombreros de paja toquilla* (*toquilla* straw is a fine fibrous straw endemic to the region). Countless places in town sell hats, but for a proper *super-fino* (the finest, most tightly woven hat of all), you'll need to visit the shop and home of **José Chávez Franco** (☎ 231-0343; Rocafuerte 386), behind the church. You can pick up a beauty for less than US$100, cheaper than just about anywhere else in the world. Montecristi is 30 minutes by

ECUADOR

bus from Manta (US40¢). Cuenca (see p638) is another great place to buy panama hats.

MANTA
☎ 05 / pop 185,000

Come daylight, local fishing crews hoist in their catch and head ashore to transform **Playa Tarqui** into a scene of prattling housewives, restaurant owners and seafood buyers, all haggling for the best of the haul. Nearby, giant wooden fishing boats are still built by hand on the beach, continuing the *manteños'* (people from Manta) strong seafaring tradition. This may not be the place for empty, paradisiacal beaches, but it's an interesting place to soak up the atmosphere of a busy, relatively safe Ecuadorian port city.

Manta is named after the Manta culture (AD 500 to 1550), known for its pottery and navigational skills. The Manta sailed to Central America, Peru and possibly the Galápagos.

Orientation

A fetid inlet divides the town into Manta (west side) and Tarqui (east side); the two sides are joined by a vehicle bridge. Manta has the main offices, shopping areas and bus terminal, while Tarqui has cheaper hotels.

The airport is 3km east of Tarqui, and the bus terminal, conveniently, is in Manta, one block off the *malecón*.

Information

Banco del Pacífico ATM (cnr Av 107 & Calle 103, Tarqui)
Banco del Pichincha (cnr Av 2 & Calle 11, Manta) ATM.
Cámara de Turismo (☎ 262-0478; Malecón de Manta & Circunvalación, Tramo 1; ☾ 9am-6pm) Near Playa Murciélago.
Municipal tourist office (☎ 262-2944; Av 3 No 10-34; ☾ 8am-12:30pm & 2:30-5pm Mon-Fri) Friendly office.

Sights

The clean, wide **Playa Murciélago**, which lies 2km west of Manta's center, is popular with residents and Ecuadorian tourists. **Playa Tarqui** is less picturesque, but it's interesting in the early morning when fisherfolk haul their catches ashore in front of the boat-building area.

The **Museo del Banco Central** (Malecón de Manta & Calle 20; admission US$1, free Sun; ☾ 9am-5pm Mon-Sat, 11am-3pm Sun) houses a small but interesting collection of pre-Columbian artifacts.

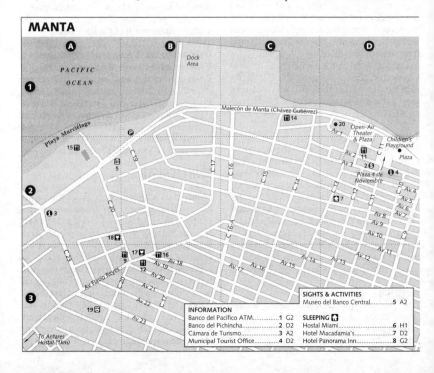

MANTA

PACIFIC OCEAN

Dock Area

Malecón de Manta (Chávez Gutiérrez)

Playa Murciélago

Open-Air Theater & Plaza
Children's Playground
Plaza

Plaza 4 de Noviembre

To Antares Hostal (1km)

SIGHTS & ACTIVITIES	
Museo del Banco Central	5 A2

INFORMATION	
Banco del Pacífico ATM	1 G2
Banco del Pichincha	2 D2
Cámara de Turismo	3 A2
Municipal Tourist Office	4 D2

SLEEPING	
Hostal Miami	6 H1
Hotel Macadamia's	7 D2
Hotel Panorama Inn	8 G2

ECUADOR

Sleeping

Prices rise during holiday weekends and the December-to-March and June-to-August high seasons, when single rooms are hard to find. While the best eating and nightlife options are in Manta proper, the cheaper hotels are in Tarqui. If you stay here, definitely take a taxi if you're out after dark.

Hotel Panorama Inn (☎ 261-1552; Calle 103 near Av 105; r per person US$7, annex s/d US$20/25) The budget version of this hotel is worn out but welcoming. Its newer incarnation across the road has air-conditioning and a courtyard pool.

Hostal Miami (☎ 261-1743; cnr Malecón de Tarqui & Calle 108; s/d from US$10/15; ✗) This friendly place offers simple but pleasant rooms, some with ocean views.

Hotel Macadamia's (☎ 261-0036; cnr Calle 13 & Av 8; s/d US$18/25; ✗) This tidy guesthouse has clean, bright accommodations (all six rooms have windows) with tile floors and sturdy furnishings.

Antares Hostal (☎ 262-6493; www.hostal-antares .com; cnr Calle 29 & Av Flavio Reyes; s/d US$25/50; ✗ ▨) In a peaceful residential neighborhood above Playa Murciélago, Antares offers trim and cheerfully painted rooms with wood details.

Eating

Cheap outdoor seafood restaurants line the eastern end of Playa Tarqui. The Playa Murciélago seafood restaurants are newer but still cheap.

Fruta del Tiempo (cnr Av 1 & Calle 12; mains US$1-3; ✆ 7:30am-11pm) Slip into a bamboo chair near the plaza for juices, breakfasts, filling lunches and ice-cream sundaes.

Trosky Burguer (cnr Avs 18 & Flavio Reyes; mains US$2-5; ✆ 6pm-3am Tue-Sun) This popular surfer-run snack spot serves juicy burgers amid rock and reef sounds. Friendly English-speaking owner.

Beachcomber (cnr Calle 20 & Av Flavio Reyes; mains US$2-7; ✆ 6pm-midnight) Popular Beachcomber is a favorite for its grilled meats. Dine in the lush backyard garden or on the open-sided front porch.

Picantería El Marino (cnr Malecón de Tarqui & Calle 110; mains US$3-7; ✆ 8am-5pm) Lunchtime favorite El Marino serves fresh seafood, including mouth-watering *ceviche*.

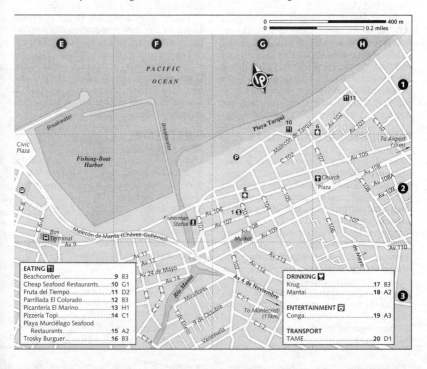

EATING 🍴
Beachcomber...............................9 B3
Cheap Seafood Restaurants.......10 G1
Fruta del Tiempo.......................11 D2
Parrillada El Colorado................12 B3
Picantería El Marino...................13 H1
Pizzería Topi..............................14 C1
Playa Murciélago Seafood
  Restaurants............................15 A2
Trosky Burguer...........................16 B3

DRINKING 🍸
Krug...17 B3
Mantai.......................................18 A2

ENTERTAINMENT 🎭
Conga...19 A3

TRANSPORT
TAME...20 D1

Parrillada El Colorado (cnr Avs 19 & Flavio Reyes; mains US$3.50; ☻ 5pm-midnight) Another popular but very casual spot, with patrons sitting at sidewalk tables next to a sizzling grill.

Pizzería Topi (Malecón de Manta; mains US$5-9; ☻ noon-11pm) A popular pizzeria.

Drinking & Entertainment

The epicenter of Manta's nightlife is the intersection of Av Flavio Reyes and Calle 20, uphill from Playa Murciélago.

Mantai (cnr Calle 17 & Av 12A; mains US$3-7; ☻ 7pm-2am Mon-Sat) Mantai has a pretty outdoor setting with good-looking wait staff, electronic music and tasty bistro fare.

Krug (cnr Av Flavio Reyes & Av 18; ☻ 5pm-3am Mon-Sat) A popular brew pub with a relaxed and welcoming atmosphere.

Conga (Av 23) Favorite club of the moment with a mix of salsa, reggaeton, meringue and electronica.

Getting There & Away

The **airport** (☎ 262-1580) is some 3km east of Tarqui; a taxi costs about US$1. **TAME** (☎ 262-2006; Malecón de Manta) flies daily to Quito (US$45).

Buses depart frequently to Portoviejo (US75¢, 40 minutes), Guayaquil (US$4.50, four hours), Quito (US$8, nine hours) and Bahía de Caráquez (US$3, 2½ hours); and to Puerto López (US$2.50, 2½ hours) and Montañita (US$5, 3½ hours). Coactur goes to Pedernales (US$5, seven hours) and Canoa regularly. Most other major destinations are also served regularly.

PARQUE NACIONAL MACHALILLA
☎ 05

Preserving isolated beaches, coral formations, two offshore islands, tropical dry forest, coastal cloud forest, archaeological sites and 20,000 hectares of ocean, Ecuador's only coastal **national park** (admission US$20) is a marvelous and unique destination. The tropical dry forest seen here used to stretch along much of the Pacific Coast of Central and South America, but it has been whacked nearly into extinction. Plants in the park include cacti, various figs and the giant kapok tree. Howler monkeys, anteaters and some 200 bird species inhabit the forest interior, while the coastal edges are home to frigate birds, pelicans and boobies, some of which nest in colonies on the offshore islands.

The beautiful beach of **Playa Los Frailes** is about 10km north of Puerto López, just before the town of Machalilla. Buses stop in front of the ranger station, from where a 3km road and a 4km trail lead to the beach. The swimming is good, seabirds are plentiful and camping is allowed.

The barren, sun-charred **Isla de la Plata**, an island 40km northwest of Puerto López, is a highlight of the park, especially from mid-June to mid-October when humpback whales mate offshore and sightings from tour boats (arranged in Puerto López; see below) are practically guaranteed. The island itself hosts nesting seabird colonies, and a short hike is usually included in the whale-watching tours. Outside the whale season you may see dolphins. It takes two to three hours to reach the island. Camping is not permitted.

From the mainland park entrance, 6km north of Puerto López, a dirt road goes 5km to **Agua Blanca** (admission US$3), a little village with an **archaeological museum** (admission free with village entry; ☎ 8am-6pm) and a Manta archaeological site nearby. The area has hiking and horse trails, and guides are available. Camping is allowed here or you can stay in people's homes.

Visitor information is available in Puerto López at the **park headquarters and museum** (☎ 260-4170; ☻ 8am-5pm Mon-Fri). The US$20 park entrance fee covers all sectors of the park (including the islands) and is valid for five days. If you plan to visit *only* Isla de la Plata, the fee is US$15; the mainland-only fee is US$12. The fee is charged in all sectors of the park, so carry your ticket.

PUERTO LÓPEZ
☎ 05 / pop 14,000

Chipped blue fishing boats bob on a beautiful fishhook bay, and cheerful hotels, a smattering of expats, slow smiles, happy cafes and a dirt-road pace of life make it tough to leave. With its unbeatable location near Parque Nacional Machalilla, Puerto López is an obligatory stop on any coastal jaunt.

There are internet cafes in town, and **Banco de Pichincha** (cnr Machalilla & Córdova) has an ATM.

Tours

Numerous outfits offer trips to Isla de la Plata and/or tours of the mainland area of the park. Most agencies charge US$35 to US$40 per person (not including the park entrance fee) for a trip to the island

and seasonal whale-watching. Licensed companies have better boats and more equipment (such as life jackets, radio and backup) than the unlicensed guides who offer the trip for nearly half the price. Companies with good reputation include **Exploramar Diving** (☎ 230-0123; www.explora diving.com; Malecón), **Machalilla Tours** (☎ 230-0234; Malecón) and **Cercapez** (☎ 230-0173; cnr Machalilla & Lascano).

Sleeping

Hostal Maxima (☎ 09-953-4282; www.hotelmaxima .org; Gonzáles Suarez near Machalilla; r per person with/ without bathroom US$6/5) This welcoming guesthouse with a spacious grassy courtyard offers a range of clean, colorful rooms. Excellent value.

Sol Inn (☎ 230-0248; hostal_solinn@hotmail.com; Montalvo near Eloy Alfaro; r per person with/without bathroom US$7/5) This mellow backpacker retreat has compact wood-and-bamboo rooms, each with front-porch hammocks; there's an outdoor kitchen and living area.

Hostería Playa Sur (☎ 293-2700; playasurpuerto lopez@hotmail.com; Malecón; s/d US$8/16) These standalone *cabañas* (cabins) at the northern end of the beach are small but cozy, each with its own private hot-water bathroom.

Hostal Flipper (☎ 230-0221; cnr Córdova & Rocafuerte; s/d US$8/16) Immaculate *hostal* with terracotta walls and airy rooms.

Hostería Itapoá (☎ 09-314-5894, in Quito 02-255-1569; Malecón; s/d US$10/20) This hospitable Brazilian-Ecuadorian place is an affordable retreat of thatched-roof *cabañas* set around a blooming garden bordered by hammocks.

Hostería Mandala (☎ 230-0181; www.hosteria mandala.info; s/d/q cabin US$27/44/83) Just north of town, this beautiful place located near the beach has a handful of ecologically minded cabins set in a labyrinthine garden. The lodge also has a bar, game room and multilingual library, and the restaurant serves delectable breakfasts, Italian fare and local seafood. Outstanding.

Eating

Patacon Pisa'o (Córdova; mains US$3) This tiny Colombian joint serves fantastic *arepas* with shredded beef, chicken or beans.

Café Bellena/Whale Café (Malecón; mains US$5-8) Serves great breakfasts, tasty grilled meats and seafood, pizzas, vegetarian meals and decadent desserts.

Bellitalia (Montalvo; mains US$6-10; ☽ from 6pm) This candlelit restaurant prepares divine Italian food, best enjoyed in the lush garden.

Along the *malecón* you'll find traditional seafood restaurants with patio dining. **Restaurant Carmita** (Malecón; mains US$5-10) is the best known.

Getting There & Away

There are several daily buses to Quito (US$12, 11 hours). Buses to Jipijapa can drop you off at the national park entrance and at other coastal points. Hourly buses head south to Santa Elena and can drop you off at points along the way.

SOUTH OF PUERTO LÓPEZ

☎ 04

This stretch of the Ruta del Sol is particularly inviting, thanks to its tiny fishing villages and wide beaches. Some 14km south of Puerto López (right after the village of Puerto Rico), **Hostería Alandaluz** (☎ 278-0686; www.andaluz hosteria.com; camping US$5, s/d from US$16/29) is one of Ecuador's first self-sustaining resorts, built from fast-growing bamboo and palm leaves. You can bask on the undisturbed beach, ride horses, play volleyball or just hang out – the atmosphere is very relaxed. Meals are also provided at reasonable prices.

The next village south (blink and you'll miss it) is **Las Tunas**. The beach here is long, wide and empty. You'll know you've reached Las Tunas when you spot the grounded bow of a giant wooden boat, which is actually the restaurant half of a hotel, appropriately called **La Barquita** (The Little Boat; ☎ 278-0051; www.labarquita-ec.com; d/tr US$35/45), with clean, comfortable doubles with hammocks out front and a few *cabañas*. Also in Las Tunas is **Hostería La Perla** (☎ 278-0701; www .hosterialaperla.net; camping per person US$5, s/d US$25/40), a romantic beach house weathered by sun and sand. Owner Mónica Fabara is a marine biologist and highly regarded local guide.

Sandwiched between verdant tropical hills and another long, wide beach, the sandy little village of **Ayampe** is about 17km south of Puerto López, right on the Guayas–Manabí provincial line. Among the handful of excellent guesthouses here is the lovely **Finca Punta Ayampe** (☎ 09-198-0982; www.fincapuntaayampe.com; r per person from US$14). On the beach, **Cabañas La Tortuga** (☎ 278-0613; www.latortuga.com.ec; tents US$8, s/d US$18/25) has well-maintained thatched-roof cabins, plus a camping annex nearby.

MONTAÑITA

☎ 04

Blessed with the country's best surf – and more budget hotels than you can shake your board at – Montañita means bare feet, baggy shorts, surf and scene. Some dig it, others despise it. Despite its rapid growth, it's as mellow and friendly as ever. Several shops in town rent boards.

There are several cybercafes in town. Banco de Guayaquil has an ATM.

Sleeping

Book a room in advance (and bring earplugs) during the December-to-April high season. Expect lower prices and fewer crowds out of season.

El Centro del Mundo (☎ 278-2831; r per person with/without bathroom US$8/7) This three-story behemoth located close to the beach offers no-frills rooms and makeshift shared toilets and showers. Communal balconies face the ocean.

Tiki Limbo Backpackers Hostel (☎ 254-0607; www .tikilimbo.com; s/d US$10/20) This longtime budget favorite on the main strip has worn, pastel-colored rooms with bamboo details, a laid-back lounge and a decent restaurant. Like other guesthouses on this street, it's noisy at night.

Hostal Pakaloro (☎ 206-0092; pakaloro2006@hotmail .com; s/d US$15/25) Beautiful craftsmanship, attention to detail, immaculate rooms, porch hammocks and polished wooden floors makes Pakaloro a popular guesthouse.

Hostal Kundalini (☎ 09-954-1745; www.hostalkun dalini.com; cabañas per person US$15) Just across the creek that marks the northern border of town, Kundalini offers a peaceful beachfront setting amid thatched-roof cabañas with bamboo walls and individual hammocks.

Paradise South (☎ 09-787-8925; s/d US$15/30) Down near the beach and great for those seeking silence, these adobe-walled cottages have ceramic floors and modern bathrooms.

Hanga-Roa Hostal (☎ 235-2955; www.montanita .com/hangaroa; s/d US$20/30) On the beach, Hanga-Roa has colorful rooms with bamboo walls and modern bathrooms. A patio over the sand is great for sunset drinks.

Charo's Hostal (☎ 206-0044; www.charoshostal .com; r US$25; ⊠ ⊇) Charo has bright, clean, straightforward hotel rooms, along with a beachfront location and a courtyard pool and Jacuzzi.

Eating

A few good restaurants on the main strip include the prime people-watching spot of the stylish cafe-restaurant **Karukera** (mains US$4-8). Nearby, **Café Hola Ola** (mains US$5-8) serves a few Israeli-inspired dishes, large breakfasts and grilled meats and seafood. Its huge back garden and bar hosts live music on weekend nights. **Funky Monkey** (mains US$4) is a mellow and mod restaurant with good grilled dishes and fusion fare. On side streets, **Café del Mar** (mains US$4) serves tasty vegetarian plates, while open-air **Latina Bistro** (mains US$4-7) has talented chefs who prepare excellent Colombian, Asian and Ecuadorian dishes. **Tiburón Restaurant** (mains US$5-7) is a top place in town for seafood and *ceviche*.

Getting There & Away

Three CLP buses a day pass Montañita on their way south to Guayaquil (US$6, 3½ hours). Buses south to Santa Elena (US$1.50, two hours) and La Libertad, or north to Puerto López (US$1.50, one hour) pass every 15 minutes.

SANTA ELENA & LA LIBERTAD

If you're heading south to Guayaquil and don't take one of the direct CLP buses (see Montañita), you'll have to change buses in one of these two cities. Santa Elena is easier – the driver will drop you off where the road forks; cross the street and flag a bus on the other fork. Avoid the busy, unpleasant port of La Libertad.

PLAYAS

☎ 04

Hovering somewhere between interesting and ugly, Playas is the nearest beach resort to Guayaquil. It's slammed from January to April, when prices rise, tents and litter adorn the beach, discos thump late into the night and the open-air seafood restaurants (which is half the fun of Playas) stay packed all day. It's almost deserted during the rest of the year.

There's some good surf around Playas; you can get information at the local surf club **Playas Club Surf** (cnr Av Paquisha & Av 7) at Restaurant Jalisco.

The cheapest hotels are concrete cells with brackish running water. The spotless, four-story **Hotel Arena Caliente** (☎ 276-1580; Av Paquisha; s/d US$25/35; ⊠ ⊇), with inviting courtyard pool, is a better option.

Transportes Villamil runs frequent buses to Guayaquil (US$2.50, 1¾ hours).

GUAYAQUIL

☎ 04 / pop 2,160,000

Although it's hot, noisy and chaotic, Guayaquil has come a long way from its dismal days as the crime-ridden port of yesteryear. The transformed *malecón* overlooking the Río Guayas has helped redefine the city. The historical neighborhood of Las Peñas, as well as Guayaquil's principal downtown thoroughfare, 9 de Octubre, have also been restored. There's much to explore in these areas, although if you're not enamored of big cities, you probably won't like this one either.

All flights to the Galápagos either stop or originate in Guayaquil. Subsequently, it's the next best place (after Quito) to set up a trip to the islands.

Orientation

Most travelers stay in the center of town, which is organized in a gridlike fashion on the west bank of Río Guayas. The main east–west street is 9 de Octubre. The Malecón 2000 (the city's rebuilt riverfront promenade) stretches along the bank of the Río Guayas, from the Mercado Sur (near the diagonal Blvd José Joaquín Olmedo) at its southern tip, to Barrio Las Peñas and the hill of Cerro Santa Ana to the north. The suburb of Urdesa, which is frequently visited for its restaurants and nightlife, is about 4km northwest and 1.5km west of the airport.

Information

BOOKSTORES

Librería Científica (Luque 225) A small selection of English-language travel guides are available here.

EMERGENCY

Police (☎ 101)
Red Cross ambulance (☎ 131)

INTERNET ACCESS

The following cybercafes charge around US$1 per hour.

CyberNet (Luque 1115) Next door to Hotel Alexander.
Internet 50¢ (Rumichaca 818 near 9 de Octubre; per hr US50¢)
Joeliki Cybernet (Moncayo near Vélez)

MEDICAL SERVICES

Clínica Kennedy (☎ 238-9666; Av del Periodista, Nueva Kennedy suburb) Guayaquil's best hospital.
Dr Serrano Saenz (☎ 256-1785; cnr Boyacá 821 & Junín) Takes drop-ins; speaks English.

MONEY

There are ATMs all over downtown, especially around Plaza de la Merced.

POST

Post office (Carbo near Aguirre)

TELEPHONE

Most internet cafes also double as phone centers.

TOURIST INFORMATION

Centro de Turismo (Malecón) Very helpful; in a train car on the Malecón.
Dirección Municipal de Turismo (☎ 252-4100, ext 3477/9; www.guayaquil.gov.ec; Pichincha 605 near 10 de Agosto) Inside the city-hall building.
Subsecretario de Turismo Litoral (☎ 256-8764; infotour@telconet.net; Paula de Icaza 203, 5th fl) Info on Guayas and Manabí provinces.

TRAVEL AGENCIES

The agencies listed here arrange Galápagos trips.

Centro Viajero (☎ 230-1283; centrovi@telconet.net; cnr Baquerizo Moreno 1119 & 9 de Octubre, Office 805, 8th fl) Great service; Spanish, English and French spoken.
Dreamkapture Travel (☎ 224-2909; www.dreamkapture.com; Alborada 12a Etapa, cnr Benjamín Carrión & Av Francisco de Orellana) French-Canadian owned, located at the Dreamkapture Hostal.
Galasam Tours (☎ 230-4488; www.galapagos-islands.com; 9 de Octubre 424, Office 9A) Great deals, but bargain hard. Some complaints.

Dangers & Annoyances

The downtown area is fine during the day, but sketchy after dark. The Malecón and the main stairway up Cerro Santa Ana are perfectly safe, even at night. There is a persistent problem with post–ATM withdrawal robberies, so be extra aware for at least a few blocks after leaving the bank. Watch your belongings in the bus terminal and in La Bahía street market.

Sights

MALECÓN 2000

If you've just arrived, head down to the reconstructed **waterfront promenade** (☯ 7am-midnight) and take in the breeze blowing (if you're lucky) off the wide Río Guayas. Known as Malecón 2000, the waterfront is Guayaquil's flagship redevelopment project, stretching 2.5km along the river, from the **Mercado Sur** at the southern end to Cerro Santa Ana and Las Peñas (see

GUAYAQUIL – CITY CENTER

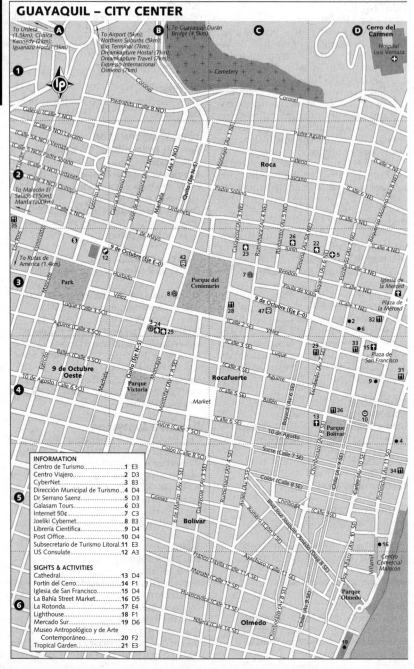

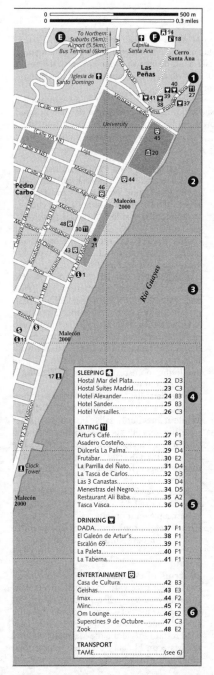

following section) to the north. The area is heavily policed and completely safe, even at night (which is when it's most pleasant).

Just north of the Mercado Sur, in the area bound by Olmedo, Chile, Colón and the waterfront, is the crowded and colorful street market **La Bahía** (Pichincha), a fascinating area to explore (but watch for pickpockets).

Bustling 9 de Octubre is Guayaquil's main commercial street; it intersects the Malecón at the impressive **La Rotonda** monument. Further north along the Malecón is a well-manicured **tropical garden** with footpaths, small ponds and shade from the sun. Nearby is the modern **Museo Antropológico y de Arte Contemporáneo** (MAAC; ☎ 230-9400; cnr Malecón & Loja; admission US$1.50, free Sun; ☼ 9:30am-5:30pm Tue-Sat, 11am-3:30pm Sun), a museum of anthropology, archaeology and contemporary Ecuadorian art. MAAC also has a theater (for plays, concerts and film), an open-air stage and a food court.

LAS PEÑAS & CERRO SANTA ANA

At the northern end of the Malecón, these two historic neighborhoods have been refurbished into an idealized version of a quaint South American hillside village – brightly painted homes, cobblestone alleyways and all. The stairway winding up Cerro Santa Ana past the brightly painted buildings is lined with informal restaurants and neighborhood bars. The views from the hilltop fort, called **Fortín del Cerro**, and the **lighthouse** are spectacular.

To the right of the stairs, the historic cobbled street of **Numa Pompillo Llona** winds past elegantly decaying wooden colonial houses propped half-heartedly on bamboo supports. Many of the houses over the river are art galleries.

DOWNTOWN AREA

Prehistoric-looking iguanas roam the handsome, tree-filled **Parque Bolívar** (Parque Seminario; cnr Chile & Ballén) and stare down children for their snacks. They're an odd sight. The modern **cathedral** is on the plaza's western side.

The main thoroughfare, **9 de Octubre**, is definitely worth a stroll to experience Guayaquil's commercial vibrancy. Guayaquil's biggest plaza, **Parque del Centenario** (cnr 9 de Octubre & Garaycoa), covers four blocks, is full of monuments and marks the center of the city. The city's most impressive church is the **Iglesia de San Francisco** (9 de Octubre near Chile), which has been reconstructed and beautifully restored since the devastating 1896 fire.

ECUADOR

GETTING INTO TOWN

The airport is about 5km north of the center on Av de las Américas. The bus terminal is 2km north of the airport. A taxi to the center should cost about US$4 from either location. If you cross the street in front of the airport, you can take a bus downtown. From the center, the best bus to take to the airport is the No 2 Especial (US25¢), which takes under an hour. It runs along the Malecón but is sometimes full, so allow plenty of time.

Buses from the center to the bus terminal leave from Parque Victoria, near 10 de Agosto and Moncayo. Several buses leave from the terminal for downtown including the No 71. You can also take faster Metrovía buses, which head downtown from the Terminal Río Daule, opposite the bus station.

MALECÓN EL SALADO
Like its more famous sister development on the Río Guayas, the Malecón El Salado is an attempt to reclaim the city's other waterfront for the everyday use of its residents. There are several eateries and cafes in a streamlined, modern mall-like building along the estuary and a walkway above.

Festivals & Events
The whole city parties during the last week of July, celebrating Simón Bolívar's birthday (July 24) and Guayaquil Foundation Day (July 25). Hotels fill up and services are disrupted. Celebrations are huge during Guayaquil's Independence Day (October 9) and Día de la Raza (October 12). New Year's Eve is celebrated with bonfires.

Sleeping
Budget hotels are generally poor value and pricey. The least expensive options are found within several blocks of the Parque del Centenario and street noise can be an annoyance.

Hotel Sander (☎ 232-0030; www.sanderguayaquil .com; Luque 1101; r per person with fan/air-con US$9/12; ✷) Despite the bare-bones rooms and large bunker-like appearance, the 24-hour security, friendly service and a working elevator make the Sander one of the better cheapies.

Dreamkapture Hostal (☎ 224-2909; www.dreamkap ture.com; Alborada 12a Etapa, Manzana 2, Villa 21; dm US$10, s/d US$18/28, with shared bathroom US$17/23; ✷ 🖳 🖭) In the northern suburb of Alborada, this small, friendly Canadian-Ecuadorian–owned *hostal* boasts spotless rooms and a small garden. There's lots of travel info (see p661), and breakfast is included. The *hostal* is on Sixto Juan Bernal near the intersection of Benjamín Carrión and Av Francisco de Orellana. There's no sign; look for the dreamy paintings.

Hostal Mar del Plata (☎ 230-7610; Junín 718 near Boyacá; s/d with fan US$12/20, s/d with air-con US$18/23; ✷) If you don't mind vintage TVs and seat-free toilets, these clean rooms are a solid choice.

Hostal Suites Madrid (☎ 230-7804; Quísquis 305; r with fan/air-con US$15/20; ✷) The large, modern rooms here are kept spotless and bright, and lack that down-and-out feeling so typical of Guayaquil's budget hotels.

our pick Iguanazú Hostal (☎ 220-1143, 09-986-7968; www.iguanazuhostel.com; Cuiadadela La Cogra, Km 3.5, Villa 2; dm/s/d US$15/40/48; ✷ 🖳 🖭) Iguanazú is an oasis of tranquility perched on a hill. The downside is that it's hard to find – it's just north of Miraflores, off Carlos Julio Arosemena. Besides charming rooms, there's a terrace with hammocks and wonderful views, a lawn, pool and living room/restaurant area. Breakfast is included and wi-fi is available.

Hotel Versailles (☎ 230-8773; infohotelversailles@ yahoo.es; cnr Junín & Ximena; r with air-con US$25; ✷ 🖳) While it inevitably falls short of its namesake, the Versailles is a remarkably good deal only a few blocks from 9 de Octubre. The large marble-floored rooms are spotless and they even sport flat-screen TVs and high-end shower fixtures.

Hotel Alexander (☎ 253-2651; hotelalexander@hot mail.com; Luque 1107; s/d US$32/36; ✷ 🖳) Central location, a pleasant on-site restaurant, internet (free wireless, too) and professional service make up for dark, unimpressive rooms.

Eating
In terms of eating, downtown Guayaquil hasn't kept pace with the northern suburbs. Informal *parrillas* (grill restaurants) are found around Parque del Centenario, and there are several concentrations of bright, clean fast-food restaurants along the Malecón 2000 and the Malecón El Salado. There's a large food court in the Mall del Sol north of downtown.

The best dining experiences are in hotels downtown or in the northwestern suburb of Urdesa.

Dulcería La Palma (Escobedo btwn Velez & Luque; snacks US$1.5-2.50) This atmospheric cafe is pleasant spot for a recharge.

Asadero Costeño (Garaycoa 929; almuerzos US$1.50) Great for cheap grilled chicken.

Menestras del Negro (cnr Malecón & Sucre; mains US$2) This Ecuadorian fast-food chain serves grilled meat, fish and chicken dishes along with heaped servings of beans.

Restaurant Ali Baba (9 de Octubre; mains US$2) You should head to Ali Baba for Middle Eastern staples like hummus, falafel and juicy shawarmas.

Frutabar (Malecón; sandwiches US$2-4) Here you can choose from over 20 types of *batidos* and sandwiches, snacks and dozens of juice creations.

Las 3 Canastas (cnr Velez & Chile; snacks US$2-4) A downtown spot for fruit shakes, fruit juices and ice cream. Outdoor tables, too.

La Parrilla del Ñato (cnr Luque & Pichincha; mains US$4-7) This two-story Guayaquil institution (there's another branch in Urdesa) is always crowded. Specializing in personalized grills – meat or seafood – fired up at your table, La Parrilla has a huge menu, including pastas, pizzas, sandwiches and *almuerzos*.

Artur's Café (Numa Pompillo Llona 127; mains US$4-7) Long-time local favorite for its hideaway atmosphere and superb location over the Río Guayas in Las Peñas, although the dishes (Ecuadorian) are fairly average.

La Tasca de Carlos (☎ 230-3661; cnr Cordova 1002 & Paula de Icaza; mains US$8-14) One of several attractive Spanish restaurants serving paellas, tortillas and other traditional dishes.

Tasca Vasca (cnr Ballén 422 & Chimborazo; mains US$8-14) This Spanish classic boasts smoky, cellar-like atmosphere, gentlemanly waiters and chalkboard menus.

Drinking

The *farra* (nightlife) in Guayaquil is spread around town, but some of the most interesting, welcoming and stylish bars are conveniently found in the neighborhood of Las Peñas. There are also some downtown gems near the Malecón 2000. The neighborhoods of Alborada, Kennedy Norte and Urdesa have their fair share of clubs and bars.

DADA (Numa Pompilio Llona 177) Hip and stylish, yet warm and welcoming, DADA has an all-wood interior and views of the river.

Escalón 69 (Cerro Santa Ana) Above the restaurant of the same name, Escalón 69 has DJs and live music on weekends.

El Galeón de Artur's (Cerro Santa Ana) Also in Las Peñas, El Galeón is a casual place for a drink if you don't mind the loud music.

La Paleta (Numa Pompilio Llona) Probably the most bohemian bar in the city, La Paleta offers cavelike nooks, comfy benches and dark wood ambience.

La Taberna (Cerro Santa Ana) Join the young neighborhood crowd at this cool-grunge drinking bar with Latin rock and pop in the background.

Entertainment

El Telégrafo and *El Universo* both publish entertainment listings.

Popular nightclubs on the Malécon include **Geishas** (cnr Malecón 602 & Imbabura; ⏰ 7pm-4am Mon-Fri), **Zook** (Panamá) and **Om Lounge** (cnr Malecón & Padre Aguirre). A few blocks away, between the MAAC and Las Peñas, is **Minc** (cnr Malecón & Vernaza y Carbo; admission US$10; ⏰ 6:30pm-late Wed-Sat).

For movies, check out the following:

Casa de Cultura (cnr 9 de Octubre & Moncayo) Foreign films and art flicks.

Imax (Malecón 2000; www.imaxmalecon2000.com; admission US$4) Connected to the MAAC.

Supercines 9 de Octubre (cnr 9 de Octubre 823 & Avilés; admission US$2) Modern multiplex.

Getting There & Away

AIR

See Getting Into Town, opposite, for details on getting to and from the airport. Departure tax for international flights is US$28. **TAME** (downtown ☎ 231-0305; Av 9 de Octubre 424, Gran Pasaje; airport ☎ 228-2062, 228-7155) has several flights daily to Quito (US$62), one or two daily to Cuenca (US$68) and three weekly to Loja (US$73). TAME and **AeroGal** (☎ 228-4218; www.aerogal.com .ec; at the airport) fly to Isla Baltra and San Cristóbal in the Galápagos (US$362 round-trip, US$318 mid-January to mid-June and September to November, 1½ hours). **Icaro** (☎ 390-5060; www .icaro.aero; at the airport) flies to Quito.

BUS

The bus terminal is 2km beyond the airport. There are services to most major towns in the country. Many buses go daily to Quito (US$9, seven to 10 hours), Manta (US$4.50, four hours), Esmeraldas (US$7, seven hours) and Cuenca (US$7, 3½ hours).

Several companies at the terminal go to Machala (US$4.50, three hours) and Huaquillas (US$5.50, four hours) on the Peruvian border. The easiest way to Peru, however, is with one of the international lines. **Rutas de América** (☎ 223-8673; cnr Los Ríos 3012 & Letamendi), whose office and terminal is southeast of downtown, has direct buses to Lima (US$50, 24 hours) on Wednesdays at 11am and Sundays at 7am and 11am. A notch above in service (and price), **Expresso Internacional Ormeno** (☎ 229-7362; Centro de Negocios El Terminal, Bahía Norte, Oficina 34, Bloque C) goes to Lima (US$65) on Sundays at 11:30am, stopping in Tumbes (US$20, eight hours). Its office and terminal is on Av de las Américas, just north of the main bus terminal. These services are convenient because you don't have to get off the bus to take care of border formalities.

Getting Around
Walking is the easiest way of getting around downtown. City buses are cheap (US25¢) but routes are complicated. A taxi within downtown costs no more than US$1.50.

MACHALA
☎ 07 / pop 228,000

The self-proclaimed 'banana capital of the world,' Machala is a chaotic, workaday city. Most travelers going to and from Peru pass through here, but few stay more than a night. Páez is a pedestrian-only zone between Rocafuerte and 9 de Octubre.

The **tourist office** (cnr 9 de Mayo & 9 de Octubre) distributes city and area maps. **Banco del Pacífico** (cnr Junín & Rocafuerte) and **Banco del Pichincha** (cnr Rocafuerte & Guayas) have ATMs and change traveler's checks.

Sleeping & Eating
There are several cheap *parrilla* restaurants serving inexpensive grilled chicken and steaks on Sucre near Colón.

Hotel Bolívar Internacional (☎ 293-0727; fal varado@hotmail.com; cnr Bolívar & Colón; s/d US$18/26; ⊠ 🖥) This squeaky clean and friendly hotel is only a short walk from the busy center.

Hostal Saloah (☎ 293-4344; Colón 1818; s/d incl breakfast US$18/29; ⊠ 🖥) On a bustling block near several bus companies, the Saloah has well-kept rooms with tiny windows. There's a rooftop patio with views.

Getting There & Away
The airport is 1km southwest of town; a taxi costs about US$1. **Saereo** (☎ 292-2630; www .saereo.com) flies once or twice daily to both Guayaquil and Quito.

There is no central bus terminal. Buses with **CIFA** (cnr Bolívar & Guayas) run regularly to Huaquillas (US$1.80, 1½ hours) at the Peruvian border, and to Guayaquil (US$4, four hours) from 9 de Octubre near Tarqui. **Rutas Orenses** (9 de Octubre near Tarqui) and **Ecuatoriana Pullman** (9 de Octubre near Colón) also serve Guayaquil; the latter has air-conditioned buses.

Panamericana (cnr Bolívar & Colón) offers several buses a day to Quito (US$10, 10 hours). **Transportes Cooperativa Loja** (cnr Tarqui & Bolívar) goes to Loja (US$4.50, five hours).

HUAQUILLAS
☎ 07 / pop 30,000

Called Aguas Verdes on the Peruvian side, Huaquillas is the main border town with Peru and lies 80km south of Machala. There's little reason to stop. Almost everything

---

GETTING TO PERU

Formalities are straightforward on both sides of the border. Many travelers report that crossing by overnight bus is easier – it allows you to avoid the crowds, touts and overzealous immigration officials (at night, officials simply want you on your way). The bus company CIFA offers direct international departures from both Machala and Guayaquil to Tumbes, Peru.

The Ecuadorian **immigration office** (⏰ 24hr) is 5km outside Huaquillas and 3km north of the border. Entrance and exit formalities are carried out here; there are no fees. The bus doesn't wait, but if you save your ticket, you can board another passing bus for free. There are also taxis.

When leaving Ecuador, you'll get an exit stamp from the Ecuadorian immigration office. After showing your passport to the international bridge guard, take a shared taxi (US50¢) to the Peruvian immigration building, about 2km beyond the border. From here, *colectivos* go to Tumbes (US$1.50; beware of overcharging).

If you're coming *from* Peru, see boxed text, p846.

happens on the long main street. Ecuadorian banks don't change money (though they have ATMs). The briefcase-toting money changers do change money, but numerous rip-offs have been reported.

If you need to spend the night, **Hotel Rodey** (☎ 299-5581; Av Tnte Cordovez & 10 de Agosto; s/d from US$5/10) is adequate.

CIFA buses run frequently to Machala (US$1.80, 1½ hours) from the main street, two blocks from the border. Panamericana goes daily to Quito (US$10, 12 hours). Ecuatoriana Pullman has buses to Guayaquil (US$5, four hours). For Loja (US$6, six hours), use Transportes Loja.

THE GALÁPAGOS ISLANDS

☎ 05 / pop 30,000

Inspiration to Charles Darwin (who came here in 1535), the Galápagos Islands may make you think differently about the world. A trip to this extraordinary region is like visiting an alternate universe, some strange utopian colony organized by sea lions – the golden retrievers of the Galápagos – and arranged on principles of mutual cooperation. What's so extraordinary for visitors is the fearlessness of the islands' famous inhabitants. Blue-footed boobies, sea lions, prehistoric land iguanas – all act as if humans are nothing more than slightly annoying paparazzi. Nowhere else can you engage in a staring contest with wild animals and lose!

Visiting the islands is expensive, however, and the only way to truly experience their marvels is by taking a cruise. It's possible to visit four of the islands independently, but you will not see the wildlife or the many smaller islands that you will aboard a cruise.

ENVIRONMENT

The Galápagos Islands were declared a national park in 1959. Organized tourism began in the 1960s and by the 1990s some 60,000 people visited annually. Today, over 180,000 people visit each year. With the boom in tourism, more people have migrated to the islands to work, and the island population has been growing about 10% annually. The dramatic increase in human activity has begun to impact the islands' fragile ecology.

The islands have faced other problems including oil spills, the poaching of sea lions for bait, overfishing, illegal fishing for shark, lobster and other marine life, and the introduction of nonnative animals. Despite conservation efforts by organizations like the **Galapagos Conservancy** (www.galapagos.org), the future of the islands remains unclear. Since 2007, Unesco has treated the World Heritage-listed islands as being 'in danger.'

ORIENTATION

The most important island is Isla Santa Cruz. On the southern side of the island is Puerto Ayora, the largest town in the Galápagos and where most of the budget tours are based. It has many hotels and restaurants. North of Santa Cruz, separated by a narrow strait, is Isla Baltra, home of the islands' main airport. A public bus and a ferry connect the Baltra airport with Puerto Ayora.

Isla San Cristóbal, the most easterly island, is home to the provincial capital, Puerto Baquerizo Moreno, which also has hotels and an airport. The other inhabited islands are Isla Isabela and Isla Santa María. Note that most of the islands have two or even three names.

INFORMATION

All foreign visitors must pay US$100 (cash only) upon arrival to the national park. The high season is from December to January, around Easter, and from June to August; during these periods, budget tours may be difficult to arrange. Galápagos time is one hour behind mainland Ecuador. For the latest news on the islands, check out the Charles Darwin Foundation's news site at www.darwinfoundation.org.

COSTS

Plan on spending more money than you want to. For an economy tour, you can count on a minimum of US$500 to US$700 for a one-week trip in the low season or US$1000 in high season, not including airfare and the US$100 park entrance fee. The cheapest (although not the best) time to go is between September and November, when the seas are rough and business is dead. You may save money if you arrange a tour independently in Puerto Ayora, though you must factor in hotel expenses.

WHAT TO BRING

Many handy (or even indispensable) items are unavailable in the Galápagos. Stock up on seasickness pills, sunscreen, insect repellent, batteries, toiletries and medication on the mainland.

VISITOR SITES

To protect the islands, the national park authorities allow access to about 50 visitor sites, in addition to the towns and public areas. Other areas are off-limits. The visitor sites are where the most interesting wildlife and geology are seen. Apart from places near Puerto Ayora and Puerto Baquerizo Moreno, most sites are reached by boat. Normally, landings are made in a *panga* (skiff). Landings are either 'wet' (you hop overboard and wade ashore in knee-deep water) or 'dry' (you get off onto a pier or rocky outcrop).

TOURS

Boat-based trips with nights spent aboard are the most common type of tour, though there are also day trips (returning to the same hotel each night) and hotel-based trips (staying on different islands). Prices do not include the US$100 park fee (which may double in coming years), airfare and bottled drinks. Neither do they include tips. On a cheap one-week tour, the crew and guide are tipped *at least* US$20 per passenger (about half to the guide).

If you're going to spend a large chunk of change getting to the islands, then seeing the Galápagos is probably important to you and you want to get as much out of it as possible. The economy-class boats are usually OK, but if something is going to go wrong, it's more likely to happen on the cheaper boats. If this is all you can afford and you really want to see the Galápagos, go! But, you might consider spending a few hundred dollars extra to go on a more comfortable, reliable boat and get a decent guide.

Boat Tours

Most visitors go on longer boat tours and sleep aboard overnight. Tours from four to eight days are the most common. You can't really do the Galápagos Islands justice on a tour shorter than a week, although five days is acceptable. To visit the outlying islands of Isabela and Fernandina, two weeks are recommended. On the first day of a prearranged tour, you arrive from the mainland by air at about noon,

so this leaves only half a day in the Galápagos; on the last day, you have to be at the airport in the morning. Thus a 'five-day' tour gives only three full days in the islands. Arranging a tour in Puerto Ayora avoids this.

Often, a one-week tour is two shorter tours combined, for example a Monday to Thursday tour combined with a Thursday to Monday tour. Try to avoid one-week trips such as this, as most of Thursday will be spent dropping off and picking up passengers.

Tour boats range from small yachts to large cruise ships. The most common type of boat is a motor sailer carrying six to 16 passengers. Tour categories range from economy and tourist to deluxe and luxury.

Seven-night/eight-day economy tours are generally aboard small boats with six to 12 bunks in double, triple and quad cabins. Bedding is provided and the accommodations are clean, but damp and cramped, with little privacy. Plenty of simple but fresh food and juice is served at all meals, and a guide accompanies the boat (few guides on economy tours speak English).

There are toilets and fresh water is available for drinking. Bathroom facilities may be saltwater deck hoses or freshwater showers on some boats. The preset itineraries allow you to visit most of the central islands and give enough time to see the wildlife.

Occasionally, things go wrong, and when they do, a refund is difficult to obtain. Problems have included last-minute changes of boat (which the contractual small print allows), poor crew, a lack of bottled drinks, not sticking to the agreed itinerary, mechanical breakdowns and overbooking. Passengers have to share cabins and are not guaranteed that their cabin mates will be of the same gender; if you are uncomfortable sharing a cabin with a stranger of the opposite sex, make sure you are guaranteed in writing that you won't have to do this. Generally speaking, the cheaper the tour, the less comfortable the boat and the less knowledgeable the guide.

Arranging Tours On-Site

Most people arrive in the islands with a prearranged tour, although it can be cheaper to arrange a tour for yourself in Puerto Ayora or Puerto Baquerizo Moreno. Generally, only the cheaper boats are available once you get to the Galápagos; the better boats are almost always booked. Therefore, don't fly to the

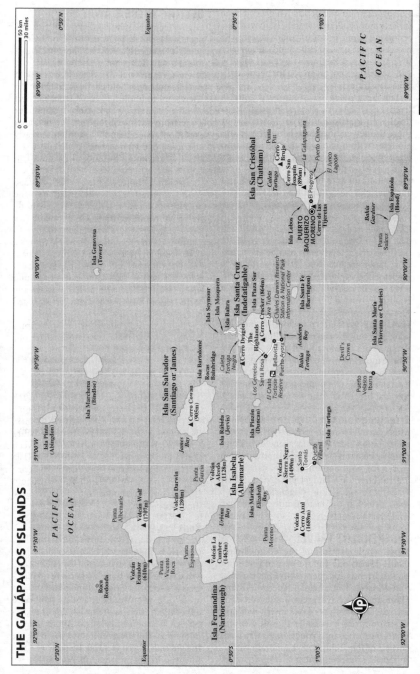

THE GALÁPAGOS ISLANDS

PACIFIC OCEAN

0   50 km
0   30 miles

Equator

Isla Fernandina (Narborough)
Roca Redonda
Volcán Ecuador (610m)
Punta Vicente Roca
Punta Espinosa
Volcán La Cumbre (1463m)

PACIFIC OCEAN

Volcán Wolf (1707m)
Punta Albemarle
Volcán Darwin (1280m)
Punta García
Volcán Alcedo (1128m)
Isla Isabela (Albemarle)
Islas Mariela
Elizabeth Bay
Urbina Bay
Punta Moreno
Volcán Cerro Azul (1689m)
Volcán Sierra Negra (1490m)
Santo Tomás
Puerto Villamil

Isla Pinta (Abingdon)
Isla Marchena (Bindloe)
Isla Genovesa (Tower)

Isla San Salvador (Santiago or James)
Cerro Cowan (905m)
James Bay
Rocas Bainbridge
Isla Bartolomé
Caleta Tortuga Negra
Isla Rábida (Jervis)
Isla Pinzón (Duncan)
Isla Tortuga

Isla Seymour
Isla Mosquera
Isla Baltra
Isla Santa Cruz (Indefatigable)
Cerro Dragón
The Highlands
Cerro Crocker (864m)
Los Gemelos
Santa Rosa
Bellavista
El Chato Tortoise Reserve
Puerto Ayora
Bahía Tortuga
Isla Plaza Sur
Lava Tubes
Charles Darwin Research Station & National Park Information Center
Academy Bay
Isla Santa Fé (Barrington)

Isla San Cristóbal (Chatham)
Caleta Tortuga
Cerro San Joaquín (896m)
El Progreso
La Galápaguera
Punta Pitt
Cerro Brujo
Puerto Chino
El Junco Lagoon
Isla Lobos
PUERTO BAQUERIZO MORENO
Cerro de las Tijeretas

Devil's Crown
Puerto Velasco Ibarra
Isla Santa María (Floreana or Charles)

Bahía Gardner
Punta Suárez
Isla Española (Hood)

Equator
0°30'N
0°30'S
1°00'S
1°00'S

92°00'W   91°30'W   91°00'W   90°30'W   90°00'W   89°30'W   89°00'W

Galápagos hoping to get on a high-end boat for less money. Flying to the Galápagos and arranging a tour is not uncommon, but it is not as straightforward as it sounds. It can take several days – sometimes a week or more – and is therefore not an option for people with time constraints.

The best place to organize a tour is from Puerto Ayora. It is also possible to do this in Puerto Baquerizo Moreno, but there are fewer boats available. If you are alone or with a friend, you'll need to find more people, as even the smallest boats take no fewer than four passengers. There are usually people looking for boats, and agencies can help in putting travelers and boats together.

Finding boats in August and around Christmas and Easter is especially difficult. The less busy months have fewer travelers on the islands, but boats are often being repaired or overhauled at this time, particularly in October. Despite the caveats, travelers who arrive in Puerto Ayora looking for a boat can almost always find one within a week (often in just a few days) if they work at it. This method isn't always cost-effective since by the time you pay for hotels and meals in Puerto Ayora, you may not save anything.

The most important thing is to find a good captain and an enthusiastic naturalist guide. You should be able to meet both and inspect the boat before booking.

Arranging Tours in Advance

Most travelers arrange tours in Quito or Guayaquil. Check various agencies to compare prices and get a departure date that works for you. Sometimes you can get on a great boat for a budget price, particularly when business is slow – agencies will drop their prices at the last minute rather than leave berths empty.

INDEPENDENT TRAVEL

Most people get around the islands by organized boat tour, but it's easy to visit some of the islands independently. Santa Cruz, San Cristóbal, Isabela and Santa María (Floreana) all have accommodations and are reachable by affordable interisland boat rides or more expensive flights. Keep in mind, however, that you'll only scratch the surface of the archipelago's natural wonders if traveling independently.

GETTING THERE & AWAY

Flights from the mainland arrive at two airports: Isla Baltra, just north of Santa Cruz, and Isla San Cristóbal. The two major airlines flying to the Galápagos Islands are **TAME** (www.tame.com.ec) and **AeroGal** (www.aerogal.com.ec); both operate morning flights daily from Quito via Guayaquil to both the San Cristóbal airport and the Isla Baltra airport (just over an hour away from Puerto Ayora by public transportation). All return flights are in the early afternoon of the same day.

Flights from Guayaquil cost round-trip US$362/318 (high/low season) and take 1½ hours. From Quito, flights cost US$412/356 round-trip and take 3½ hours, due to the layover in Guayaquil. It's also possible to fly from Quito and return to Guayaquil or vice versa; it's often more convenient to fly into Baltra and out of San Cristóbal or vice versa. A transit control fee of US$10 must be paid at the Instituto Nacional Galápagos (Ingala) office next to the ticket counter at either Quito or Guayaquil airport; the charge is already included in the price of many prearranged boat tours.

Flights to the Galápagos are sometimes booked solid, so make sure you arrange your trip well in advance.

GETTING AROUND
Air

The small airline, **Emetebe** (Guayaquil ☎ 04-229-2492; www.emetebe.com.ec; Puerto Ayora ☎ 252-6177; Puerto Villamil ☎ 252-9255; San Cristóbal ☎ 252-0615), flies a five-passenger aircraft between Baltra and Puerto Villamil (Isla Isabela), between Baltra and Puerto Baquerizo Moreno (Isla San Cristóbal), and between Puerto Baquerizo Moreno and Puerto Villamil. Fares are about US$130 one way, and there is a 9kg baggage limit per person.

Boat

Private speedboats known as *lanchas* or *fibras* (short for 'fiberglass boats') offer daily passenger ferry services between Santa Cruz and San Cristóbal and Isabela (there are no direct trips between San Cristóbal and Isabela). Fares are US$30 on any passage and are purchased either on the day before or the day of departure. Ask around in Puerto Ayora, Puerto Baquerizo Moreno and Puerto Villamil; see the Getting There & Away sections of these towns for more information.

ECUADOR

ISLA SANTA CRUZ (INDEFATIGABLE)

Most visitors only pass through the archipelago's most populous island on their way from Isla Baltra to Puerto Ayora. But Santa Cruz is a destination in and of itself, with easily accessible beaches and remote highlands that offer adventurous activities far from the tourist trail.

Puerto Ayora

Clean little Puerto Ayora is the Galápagos' main population center and the heart of the tourist industry. It's a friendly place to hang out and the best place in the islands to set up a cruise.

INFORMATION

Banco del Pacífico (Av Charles Darwin) The town's only bank has a MasterCard/Cirrus ATM and changes traveler's checks.

Cámara de Turismo (☎ 252-6206; www.galapagos tour.org; Av Charles Darwin) Tourist office; report any complaints about boats, tours, guides or crew here.

Galápagos Online (Av Charles Darwin; per hr US$3) One of many cybercafes.

Laundry Lava Flash (Av Bolívar Naveda; per kg US$1) Laundry.

ACTIVITIES

Lonesome George Travel Agency (☎ 252-6245; lone somegrg@yahoo.com; cnr Avs Opuntia & Padre Julio Herrera), among other outfits, rents snorkeling equipment (US$8 per day), kayaks (US$30 per half-day), bicycles (US$2 per hour), surfboards (US$20 per half-day) and wet suits (US$8 per day).

The best dive centers in town are **Scuba Iguana** (☎ 252-6497; www.scubaiguana.com; Av Charles Darwin), in the Hotel Galápagos, near the cemetery, and **Galápagos Sub-Aqua** (☎ 230-5514; www .galapagos-sub-aqua.com; Av Charles Darwin). Both are excellent and offer a variety of tours that include gear, boat and guide. Full PADI-certification courses are available.

TOURS

If you're setting up a cruise from Puerto Ayora, visit the following agencies to compare prices and tours. They all offer last-minute deals (when they exist).

Iguana Travel (Av Charles Darwin) Arranges day tours and books last-minute overnight yachts on the lower end of the pay scale.

Joybe Tours (☎ 252-4385; Av Bolívar Naveda) Last-minute overnight boat deals and day tours.

Moonrise Travel (☎ 252-6348; www.galapagosmoon rise.com; Av Charles Darwin) Reputable agency long in the business; can arrange camping at their private ranch in the highlands, plus boat tours.

SLEEPING

Most hotels in Puerto Ayora are along Av Charles Darwin.

Hotel Lirio del Mar (☎ 252-6212; Av Bolívar Naveda; s/d US$15/30) Three floors of colorful concrete rooms are basic but clean, and a shared terrace catches the breeze.

Hotel Salinas (☎ 252-6072; Av Bolívar Naveda; s/d from US$18/36) Two-story hotel with plain rooms, hot water, TV and fans. Try for a room on the 2nd floor.

El Peregrino B&B (☎ 252-7515; Av Charles Darwin; s/d incl breakfast US$20/40) This simple, four-room guesthouse boasts a central location and warm, family-like atmosphere.

Hotel Sir Francis Drake (☎ 252-6221; Av Padre Julio Herrera; s/d US$20/40) The bright ground-floor rooms all the way in the back have big windows and are a great value at this friendly hotel.

EATING

A handful of popular kiosks selling inexpensive and hearty meals – mainly meat and fish dishes – lie along Charles Binford, just east of Av Padre Julio Herrera.

El Chocolate (Av Charles Darwin; mains US$3-6) A popular waterfront eatery, El Chocolate has outdoor patio tables and serves seafood, sandwiches and burgers besides fresh coffee and chocolate cake.

Garrapata (Av Charles Darwin; mains US$4-9) Garrapata is a well-liked outdoor restaurant with substantial meat, seafood and chicken dishes with Italian and Ecuadorian flavors.

Familiar William's (Charles Binford; mains US$5-7; 🕑 6-10pm Tue-Sun) Famous for its *encocados* (fish, shrimp or lobster smothered in a savory coconut sauce).

Casa de Lago Café Cultural (www.galapagoscultural .com; cnr Brito & Montalvo; mains US$5) This boho cafe serves excellent homemade fruit drinks, ice cream and empanadas, and schedules periodic readings, photo exhibits and live music.

DRINKING & ENTERTAINMENT

The **Bongo Bar** (Av Charles Darwin; 🕑 6pm-2am) is a trendy spot replete with flat-screen TVs, loud music, a pool table and a mix of locals, guides and tourists. The downstairs disco, **La Panga**

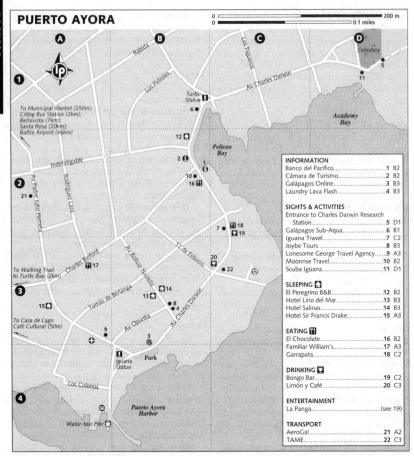

PUERTO AYORA

(Av Charles Darwin; 8:30pm-2am), is where to go to grind the night away (US$10 admission on weekends).

A more mellow, younger crowd head to the **Limón y Café** (Av Charles Darwin), a modest outdoor bar with a gravel floor and pool tables.

GETTING THERE & AWAY
For more information on flights to and from Santa Cruz see p670. Reconfirming your flight departures with **Aerogal** (252-6798; www.aerogal .com.ec; Av Padre Julio Herrera) or **TAME** (252-6527; www .tame.com.ec; Av Charles Darwin) offices is essential.

If you are traveling independently, take the public bus signed 'Muelle' from the airport to the dock (a free 10-minute ride) for the ferry to Isla Santa Cruz. A 10-minute ferry

ride (US80¢) will take you across to Santa Cruz, where you will be met by a Citteg bus to take you to Puerto Ayora, about 45 minutes away (US$1.80).

Arriving air passengers on prebooked tours will be met by a boat representative for the bus-boat-bus journey to Puerto Ayora.

Private speedboats head daily to Isabela and San Cristóbal at 2pm (three hours). Buy tickets from travel agencies or the small kiosk near the water-taxi pier.

Around Puerto Ayora
Though much of the island is off-limits without a guide, there's lots to see. Unless otherwise noted, you can visit the following sites by yourself. The **Charles Darwin Research Station** (Map

p672; www.darwinfoundation.org; 🕑 6am-6pm) is about a 20-minute walk by road northeast of Puerto Ayora. The station features an information center, a museum, a tortoise nursery and a walk-in tortoise enclosure where you can meet these Galápagos giants face to face.

Southwest of Puerto Ayora, a 3km trail takes you to the paradisiacal **Bahía Tortuga** (Turtle Bay; Map p669), which has a beautiful, white, coral-sand beach and protected swimming behind a spit. The beach is backed by mangroves, and you may spot harmless sharks (worry not), pelicans and even flamingos. Marine iguanas abound. Beware of strong currents on the exposed side of the spit. Follow the sign from Av Padre Julio Herrera.

Buses from Puerto Ayora go to the villages of **Bellavista** (Map p669) and **Santa Rosa** (Map p669), from where you can explore some of the interior. Neither of these villages has hotels. Infrequent buses depart from the Citteg bus station, 2km north of the harbor. A taxi to the bus station costs US$1. Inquire at the tourist office about the current schedule. In Puerto Ayora, you could also hire a truck or rent a mountain bike for the day (it's uphill to the villages).

From the village of Bellavista, 7km north of Puerto Ayora, you can turn either west on the main road toward Santa Rosa, or east and go about 2km to the **lava tubes** (Map p669; admission US$3). These underground tunnels stretch more than 1km in length; bring a flashlight.

A footpath north from Bellavista leads toward the highlands, including **Cerro Crocker** (Map p669) and other hills and extinct volcanoes. This is a good chance to see local vegetation and birds. It is about 6km from Bellavista to the crescent-shaped hill of Media Luna and another 3km to the base of Cerro Crocker. This is national-park land, and a guide is required.

The twin craters called **Los Gemelos** (Map p669) are 5km beyond Santa Rosa. They are sink-holes, rather than volcanic craters, and are surrounded by Scalesia forest. Vermilion fly-catchers are often seen and short-eared owls are spotted on occasion. Although less than 100m from the road, the craters are hidden by vegetation, so go with a guide.

Near Santa Rosa, **El Chato Tortoise Reserve** (Map p669; admission US$3) protects giant tortoises roaming in the wild. A trail from the village (ask for directions) leads through private property to the reserve, about 3km away. The trail is downhill and often muddy. It forks at the reserve boundary, with the right fork going up to the small hill of Cerro Chato (3km further) and the left fork going to La Caseta (2km). A guide is required. All manner of locals will offer to guide you. Bring plenty of water. Horses can be hired in Santa Rosa.

Near the reserve is **Rancho Permiso** (admission US$4) owned by the Devine family. This place always has dozens of giant tortoises. You can wander around at will and take photos for a small fee. A cafe sells coffee or herbal tea that's welcome if the highland mist has soaked you.

ISLA SAN CRISTÓBAL

Locals call San Cristóbal the capital of paradise and, since Puerto Baquerizo Moreno is the capital of Galápagos province, it technically is. The island has several easily accessible visitor sites, incredible surf and the lovely, laid-back capital itself.

Puerto Baquerizo Moreno

Often just called Cristóbal, Puerto Baquerizo Moreno is a relaxed little town, busy with tourists during the high season and sleepy the rest of the year. It's possible to arrange tours here, though it's a great spot just to unwind. Three world-class surf breaks are nearby.

The intriguing exhibits at the modern **Interpretation Center** (☎ 252-0358; 🕑 8am-6pm) on the north side of the bay explains the history and significance of the Galápagos better than anywhere else in the islands.

Air passengers arriving in Puerto Baquerizo Moreno can walk into town in a few minutes.

Cabañas Don Jorge (☎ 252-0208; Av Alsacio Northia; r per person US$8-15) On the way to Playa Mann, these rustic *cabañas* are showing their age, but are fully stocked and good for self-catering.

Hotel Mar Azul (☎ 252-0139; hotelmarazul_ex @hotmail.com; Av Alsacio Northia; s US$12-20, d US$20-25; 🖳 🖳) Despite a '70s-era facade, Mar Azul is a surprisingly decent choice – particularly for the rooms opening onto the small, sunny courtyard.

Hotel Chatham (☎ 252-0137; Av Alsacio Northia; s/d US$15/25; 🖳) Chatham's bare-bones rooms have no character, but at least there is a patio with hammocks, and it's only a short walk from the airport.

Inexpensive restaurants abound and *almuerzos* are good value (US$2.50). Be sure to have a *batido* (fruit shake) at **El Grande** (Villamil; drinks US90¢-US$1.50).

ECUADOR

Around Puerto Baquerizo Moreno

You can visit the following sites without a guide. About 1.5km southeast of Puerto Baquerizo Moreno, **Cerro de las Tijeretas** (Frigate-Bird Hill; Map p669) provides good views and can be reached on a trail without a guide. You'll pass a national park information office en route, and there's excellent snorkeling on the ocean side.

For about US$20 round-trip, taxis in Puerto Baquerizo Moreno will go to the farming center of **El Progreso** (Map p669), about 8km east at the base of the Cerro San Joaquín (896m), the highest point on San Cristóbal. From El Progreso, you can catch one of the occasional buses (or hire a jeep, hitchhike or walk the 10km) to **El Junco Lagoon** (Map p669), a freshwater lake about 700m above sea level with superb views. The road continues beyond the lagoon and branches to the isolated beach of **Puerto Chino** (Map p669), where you can camp with permission from the Galápagos **national park office** (☎ 252-0138; www.galapagospark.org) in Puerto Baquerizo Moreno. The other branch goes to **La Galapaguera** (Map p669), where giant tortoises can be seen.

About an hour north of Puerto Baquerizo Moreno by boat is tiny, rocky **Isla Lobos** (Map p669), the main sea lion and blue-footed booby colony open to visitors (a guide is required) to Isla San Cristóbal. The island has a 300m trail and you can see lava lizards here.

ISLA ISABELA

Puerto Villamil (Map p669) is the main town on seldom visited Isla Isabela. An 18km road leads from the town up to the tiny village of Santo Tomás. Puerto Villamil has a handful of places to stay.

On the road heading north to the Crianza de Tortugas (turtle nursery) is one of the cheapest options, the very basic **Pensión La Jungla** (☎ 252-9348; r US$10). In town, the **Hostería Isabela del Mar** (☎ 252-9030; www.hosteriaisabela.com.ec; s/d US$20/40) has a good restaurant and a few rooms with ocean views.

There are a few basic *comedores*, and most hotels offer meals.

ISLA SANTA MARÍA

Also known as Floreana, this island has fewer than 100 inhabitants, most spread near **Puerto Velasco Ibarra** (Map p669), the island's only settlement. There you will find **Hostal Wittmer** (☎ 05-252-9506; s/d/tr US$30/50/70), which also doubles

as the best eatery and information and guide center. Most of the beachfront rooms are in a small, white two-story building and have private balconies; meals can be provided. It's run by the family of late Margaret Wittmer, who is famous for being one of the islands' first settlers.

ECUADOR DIRECTORY

ACCOMMODATIONS

There is no shortage of places to stay in Ecuador, but during major fiestas or the night before market day, accommodations can be tight, so plan ahead. Most hotels have single-room rates, although during high season some beach towns charge for the number of beds in the room, regardless of the number of people checking in. In popular resort areas, high-season prices (running from June to August and mid-December to January) are about 30% higher than the rest of the year.

Ecuador has a growing number of youth hostels, as well as inexpensive *pensiones*. Staying with families is an option in remote villages.

ACTIVITIES

Where to begin? There are so many exciting activities in Ecuador that any list will certainly miss something. For climbers, the volcanic, snowcapped peaks of Ecuador's central highlands – including Chimborazo (a doozy at 6310m, p633) and Cotopaxi (5897m, p623) – attract mountaineers from around the world. Quito (p608), Riobamba (p631), Baños (p627) and Latacunga (p624) are the best towns to hire guides and gear.

How about hiking? The moorlike landscape of Parque Nacional Cajas (p639); the cloud forests of Parque Nacional Podocarpus (p642) or Mindo (p622); the windswept *páramo* of Lagunas de Mojanda (p621), near Otavalo; the spectacular high-Andean Quilotoa Loop area (p625); and the coastal dry forests of Parque Nacional Machalilla (p658) are just a few of Ecuador's hiking possibilities.

Ecuador is also one of the world's top bird-watching destinations, with over 1600 species on record. Mindo (p622), the lower Río Napo region of the Amazon (p646) and the Galápagos (p667) are extraordinary places for bird-watching.

Tena (p647) in the Oriente is Ecuador's kayaking and river-rafting capital, where it's easy to set up day runs down the nearby Río Napo (class III) or Río Misahuallí (class IV+).

The surfing is excellent at Montañita (p660) and on Isla San Cristóbal (p673) in the Galápagos. Playas (p660) has some decent nearby breaks, but you'll have to make friends with the locals (try the Playas Club Surf, p660) to find them. The Galápagos are also famous for scuba diving and snorkeling (think hammerhead sharks and giant manta rays).

Mountain biking is growing in popularity, with a handful of outfitters in Quito (p607) and Riobamba (p631) offering memorable trips over challenging terrain (like Volcán Chimborazo). You can also head off on your own on trips like the dramatic descent from Baños to Puyo. You can rent bikes for about US$5 per hour in places such as Baños (p627), Vilcabamba (p642) and Riobamba (p631), or go for the extreme downhill day trips offered by outfitters in those towns, as well as in Quito (p607) and Cuenca (p636).

BOOKS

Lonely Planet's *Ecuador & the Galápagos Islands* has more detailed travel information on the country.

If there's one book that nails Ecuadorian culture on the head, it's the eloquent and humorous *Living Poor,* written by Moritz Thomsen. Joe Kane's *Savages* is a more recently written account that illustrates the oil industry's impacts on the Ecuadorian Amazon.

The Panama Hat Trail, by Tom Miller, is a fascinating book about the author's search for that most quintessential and misnamed of Ecuadorian products, the panama hat. For a more literary (and surreal) impression of Ecuador, read Henri Michaux' *Ecuador: A Travel Journal,* or Kurt Vonnegut's absurd *Galápagos,* which takes place in a futuristic Guayaquil as well as on the islands.

BUSINESS HOURS

Reviews throughout this book provide opening hours only when they differ from the following standard hours: banks are generally open Monday through Friday, from 8am to between 2pm and 4pm. In bigger cities, most business and government offices are open Monday through Friday between 9am and 5:30pm, and closed for an hour at lunch, which is sometime between noon and 2pm. On the coast and in smaller towns, the lunch break can be dragged on for two or more hours. Many businesses operate midday hours on Saturday, but nearly everything – including restaurants – closes on Sunday. Restaurants generally open for lunch from around 11:30am to 3pm and for dinner from 5pm to 10pm; some stay open all day. Bars usually open sometime between 5pm and 7pm and close between midnight and 2pm. Post offices are generally open 8am to 6pm Monday through Friday and 8am to 1pm on Saturday.

CLIMATE

Ecuador's climate consists of wet and dry seasons, with significant variation among the different geographical regions (depending on whether you're in the Andes, on the coast or in the Oriente).

The Galápagos and the coast have a hot and rainy season from January to April; you can expect short torrential downpours with skin-cooking sunshine in between. You'll be a walking pool of sweat if you travel on the coast during this time. From May to December it rains infrequently, but the skies are often overcast and the beaches cool. Travel is definitely more pleasant, but you may find the beach is just a little too nippy for sunbathing. Ecuadorians hit the beaches during the wet season.

In the Oriente, it rains during most months, especially during the afternoon and evening. August and December through March are usually the driest months, and April through June are the wettest, with regional variations. Malaria is more common during the wet season, but river travel is usually easier due to higher water levels.

Travel is pleasant in the highlands year-round, although you'll definitely be dodging raindrops October through May. It doesn't rain daily though, and even April, the wettest month, averages one rainy day in two.

Daytime temperatures in Quito average a high of 21°C (70°F) and a low of 8°C (48°F) year-round.

For more information and climate charts see the South America Directory (p987).

DANGERS & ANNOYANCES

Ecuador is a fairly safe country, but you should still be careful. Pickpocketing occurs in crowded places, such as markets. Armed robbery is still unusual in most of Ecuador, although certain parts of Guayaquil and Quito's Mariscal Sucre neighborhood have a reputation for being dangerous.

Every year or so, a few long-distance night buses are robbed on the way to/from the coast. Avoid taking night buses through the provinces of Guayas or Manabí unless you have to.

There are occasional flare-ups of guerrilla activity in some areas near the Colombian border (particularly in the northern Oriente). Tours are generally safe, though it's wise to do some research before heading to this area.

Take the normal precautions as outlined in the South America Directory (see p989). If you are robbed, get a *denuncia* (police report) from the local police station within 48 hours – they won't process a report after that.

DRIVER'S LICENSE

An international driver's license, alongside a home-country license and passport, is required to drive in Ecuador.

ELECTRICITY

Ecuador uses 110V, 60 cycles, AC (the same as in North America). Plugs have two flat prongs, as in North America.

EMBASSIES & CONSULATES

As well as the information provided below, see Visas, p681. Embassies and consulates are best visited in the morning. New Zealand has no consular representation in Ecuador.

Australia Guayaquil (☎ 04-601-7529; ausconsulate @unidas.com.ec; Rocafuerte 510, 2nd fl)

Canada Guayaquil (☎ 04-229-6895; Avs Joaquin Orranita & Juan Tanca Marengo); Quito (☎ 02-245-5499; www .canadainternational.gc.ca/ecuador-equateur; Av Amazonas 4153 & Unión de Periodistas)

Colombia Guayaquil (☎ 04-263-0674/5; www.consulado decolombiagye.com; Francisco de Orellana, World Trade Center, Tower B, 11th fl); Lago Agrio (☎ 06-283-0084; Av Quito 1-52); Quito (☎ 02-222-2486; cnr Av Colón 1133 & Amazonas, 7th fl); Tulcán (☎ 06-298-0559; Av Manabi 58-087)

France Guayaquil (☎ 04-232-8442; cnr Mascote 909 & Hurtado); Quito (☎ 02-252-6361; Leonidas Plaza 107 & Av Patria)

Germany Guayaquil (☎ 04-220-6867/8; Avs Las Monjas & CJ Arosemena, Km 2.5, Edificio Berlin); Quito (☎ 02-297-0821; cnr Naciones Unidas E10-44 & República de El Salvador, Edificio Citiplaza, 12th fl)

Ireland (☎ 2-245-1577; cnr Antonio de Ulloa 2651 & Rumipamba, Quito)

Netherlands (Map pp602-3; ☎ 02-222-9229; www .embajadadeholanda.com; World Trade Center, Tower 1, 1st fl, cnr 12 de Octubre 1942 & Cordero, Quito)

Peru Guayaquil (☎ 04-228-0114; conperu@gye.satnet .net; Av Francisco de Orellana 501); Loja (☎ 07-257-9068; Sucre 10-56); Machala (☎ 07-293-0680; cnr Bolívar & Colón); Quito (☎ 02-246-8410; embpeecu@uio.satnet.net; cnr Republica de El Salvador 495 & Irlanda)

UK Guayaquil (☎ 04-256-0400; cnr Córdova 623 & Padre Solano); Quito (☎ 02-297-0800; http://ukinecuador.fco .gov.uk/en; cnr Naciones Unidas & República de El Salvador, Edificio Citiplaza, 14th fl)

USA Guayaquil (Map pp662-3; ☎ 04-232-3570; http:// guayaquil.usconsulate.gov; cnr 9 de Octubre & García Moreno); Quito (☎ 02-398-5000; http://ecuador.us embassy.gov; cnr Av Avigiras E12-170 & Eloy Alfaro)

FESTIVALS & EVENTS

Many of Ecuador's major festivals are oriented around the Roman Catholic liturgical calendar. These are often celebrated with great pageantry, especially in highland indigenous villages, where a Catholic feast day is often the excuse for a traditional indigenous fiesta with drinking, dancing, rituals and processions. The major festivals are listed here.

February
Carnaval Celebrated throughout Ecuador the last few days of Lent. Dates vary.
Fiesta de Frutas y Flores (Fruit & Flower Festival) Held in Ambato the last two weeks of February.

March
Semana Santa (Holy Week) Colorful religious processions held the week before Easter throughout Ecuador, but particularly popular in Quito.

June
Corpus Christi Religious feast day (the Thursday after the eighth Sunday after Easter) combined with the traditional harvest fiesta in many highland towns; it includes processions and street dancing.
Inti Raymi Millennia-old indigenous celebration of summer equinox celebrated throughout northern highlands, especially in Otavalo, where it's also combined with feasts of St John the Baptist (June 24) and Sts Peter and Paul (June 29). Held from June 21 to 29.

September
Fiesta del Yamor Held in Otavalo, September 1 to 15.
Fiesta de la Mamá Negra Held in Latacunga, September 23 to 24.

December
Fundación de Quito (Founding of Quito) Celebrated the first week of December with bullfights, parades and dancing.

FOOD & DRINK
Eating reviews throughout this chapter are given in order of budget, with the least expensive options first. For information about standard restaurant hours, see Business Hours, p675.

Ecuadorian Cuisine
For breakfast, eggs and bread rolls or toast are available. A good alternative is *humita*, a sweet-corn tamale often served with coffee.

Lunch is the main meal of the day for many Ecuadorians. A cheap restaurant will serve a decent *almuerzo* (lunch of the day) for as little as US$2. An *almuerzo* consists of a *sopa* (soup) and a *segundo* (second dish), which is usually a stew with plenty of rice. Sometimes the segundo is *pescado* (fish), *lentejas* (lentils) or *menestras* (generally, bean stew). Some places serve salad, juice and *postre* (dessert), as well as the two main courses.

The *merienda* (evening meal) is a set meal, usually similar to lunch. If you don't want the *almuerzo* or *merienda*, you can choose from the menu, but this is always more expensive.

A *churrasco* is a hearty dish of fried beef, fried eggs, a few veggies, fried potatoes, slices of avocado and tomato, and the inevitable rice.

Arroz con pollo is a mountain of rice with little bits of chicken mixed in. *Pollo a la brasa* is roast chicken, often served with fries. *Gallina* is usually boiled chicken, as in soups, and *pollo* is more often chicken that's been spit-roasted or fried.

Parrillas (or *parrilladas*) are grillhouses. Steaks, pork chops, chicken breasts, blood sausage, liver and tripe are all served (together or individually, depending on the establishment). Some *parrillas* do the Argentine thing and serve everything together on a tabletop grill.

Seafood can be delicious, particularly in Esmeraldas and Manabí provinces. The most common types of fish are *corvina* (technically white sea bass, but usually just a white fish) and *trucha* (trout). Popular throughout Ecuador, *ceviche* is uncooked seafood marinated in lemon and served with popcorn and sliced onions. *Ceviche* comes as *pescado* (fish), *camarones* (shrimp), *concha* (shellfish) or *mixto* (mixed). Unfortunately, improperly prepared *ceviche* is a source of cholera, so avoid it if in any doubt.

Chifas (Chinese restaurants) are generally inexpensive. Among other standards, they serve *chaulafan* (rice dishes) and *tallarines* (noodle dishes). Portions tend to be filling, with a good dose of MSG. Vegetarians will find that *chifas* are the best choice for meatless dishes. Vegetarian restaurants are rare outside touristy areas.

Restaurants usually offer a wide range of dishes, including the following classics:

caldo (kal·do) – Soup or stew. Often served in markets for breakfast. *Caldo de gallina* (chicken soup) is the most popular. *Caldo de patas* is soup made by boiling cattle hooves.

cuy (kooy) – Whole-roasted guinea pig. A traditional delicacy dating to Inca times, *cuy* tastes rather like a cross between rabbit and chicken. They're easily identified on grills with their paws and teeth sticking out.

lapingachos (la·peen·ga·chos) – Fried mashed-potato-and-cheese pancakes, often served with *fritada* (scraps of fried or roast pork).

seco (se·ko) – Literally 'dry' (as opposed to a 'wet' soup), this is stew, usually meat, served with rice. It may be *seco de gallina* (chicken stew), *de res* (beef), *de chivo* (goat) or *de cordero* (lamb).

tortilla de maíz (tor·tee·lya de ma·ees) – Tasty fried corn pancakes.

yaguarlocro (ya·gwar·lo·kro) – Another classic; potato soup with chunks of fried blood sausage floating in it. Many people prefer straight *locro*, usually with potatoes, corn and an avocado or cheese topping, without the blood sausage.

Drinks
Purify all tap water or buy bottled water. Some pharmacies, cafes and a growing number of guesthouses allow travelers to refill their water bottles from their purified source – a good option for those concerned about all the empty bottles that end up in landfills. *Agua con gas* is carbonated; *agua sin gas* is not carbonated.

Bottled drinks are cheap and all the usual soft drinks are available. The local ones have endearing names such as Bimbo or Lulu. Ask for your drink *helada* if you want it out of the refrigerator, *al clima* if you don't. Remember to say *sin hielo* (without ice) unless you really trust the water supply.

Jugos (juices) are available everywhere. Make sure you get *jugo puro* (pure) and not *con agua* (with water). The most common kinds are *mora* (blackberry), *tomate de árbol* (a strangely addictive local fruit), *naranja* (orange), *toronja* (grapefruit), *maracuyá* (passion fruit), *piña* (pineapple), *sandía* (watermelon), *naranjilla* (a local fruit that tastes like bitter orange) and papaya.

Coffee is widely available but often disappointing. Instant coffee, served *en leche* (with milk) or *en agua* (with water), is the most common. Espresso is found in better restaurants.

Té (tea) is served black with lemon and sugar. *Té de hierbas* (herb tea) and hot chocolate are also popular.

For alcoholic drinks, local *cervezas* (beers) are palatable and inexpensive. Pilsener is available in 650mL bottles, while Club comes in 330mL bottles. Imports are tough to find.

Ron (rum) is cheap and can be decent. The local firewater, *aguardiente*, is sugarcane alcohol, and is an acquired taste.

GAY & LESBIAN TRAVELERS

Ecuador is probably not the best place to be outwardly affectionate with a partner of the same sex. Homosexuality was illegal until 1997. Quito and Guayaquil have underground social scenes, but outside the occasional dance club, they're hard to find. Check out the useful **Gay Guide to Quito** (http://quito.queercity.info) or **Gayecuador** (www.gayecuador.com, in Spanish).

HOLIDAYS

On major holidays, banks, offices and other services are closed and public transportation is often very crowded; book ahead if possible. The following are Ecuador's major national holidays; they may be celebrated for several days around the actual date:

New Year's Day January 1
Epiphany January 6
Semana Santa (Easter Week) March/April
Labor Day May 1
Battle of Pichincha May 24. This honors the decisive battle of independence from Spain in 1822.
Simón Bolívar's Birthday July 24
Quito Independence Day August 10
Guayaquil Independence Day October 9. This combines with the October 12 national holiday and is an important festival in Guayaquil.
Columbus Day/Día de la Raza October 12
All Saints' Day November 1
Day of the Dead (All Souls' Day) November 2. Celebrated by flower-laying ceremonies in cemeteries, it's especially colorful in rural areas, where entire indigenous families show up at cemeteries to eat, drink and leave offerings in memory of the departed.
Cuenca Independence Day November 3. Combines with the national holidays of November 1 and 2 to give Cuenca its most important fiesta of the year.

Christmas Eve December 24
Christmas Day December 25

INTERNET ACCESS

All but the smallest of towns have internet cafes. Prices hover around US$1 per hour, though they get higher in small towns and on the Galápagos.

INTERNET RESOURCES

Most websites listed in the chapter are in English though some are in Spanish only.
The Best of Ecuador (www.thebestofecuador.com) Comprehensive tourist information.
Ecuador (www.ecuador.com) Overview site giving a condensed portrait of the country.
Ecuador Explorer (www.ecuadorexplorer.com) Extensive information and good classifieds.
Latin American Network Information Center (http://lanic.utexas.edu/la/ecuador) Links to everything Ecuadorian.
Ministerio de Turismo (www.vivecuador.com) Covers everything from health and budget issues to country highlights.

LEGAL MATTERS

Drug penalties in Ecuador for possession of even small amounts of illegal drugs (which include marijuana and cocaine) are severe. Defendants often spend months in jail before they are brought to trial, and if convicted (as is usually the case) they can expect several years in jail.

Treat plainclothes 'policemen' with suspicion. If you're asked for ID by a uniformed official in broad daylight, show your passport.

In the event of a car accident, unless extremely minor, the vehicles should stay where they are until the police arrive and make a report. If you hit a pedestrian, you are legally responsible for the pedestrian's injuries and can be jailed unless you pay, even if the accident was not your fault. Drive defensively.

MAPS

Ecuadorian bookstores carry a limited selection of Ecuadorian maps. The best selection is available from the Instituto Geográfico Militar in Quito (see p600).

Prodoguias publishes the *Quito Distrito Metropolitano* pocket guide (US$6). It's sold at the main Quito tourist office and in some pharmacies.

MEDIA

The *Quito Cultura* (www.quitocultura.com) is a free monthly magazine listing what's on in Quito. The monthly English-language *Ecuador Reporter* (www.ecuadorreporter.com), available free in Quito, has articles on the capital, nightlife reviews and travel articles covering popular destinations in Ecuador. The country's best newspapers are *El Comercio* (www.elcomercio.com) and *Hoy* (www.hoy.com.ec), published in Quito, and *El Telégrafo* (www.telegrafo.com.ec) and *El Universo* (www.eluniverso.com), published in Guayaquil.

MONEY

Ecuador's currency was the sucre until it switched to the US dollar in 2000, a process called 'dollarization' (see p594). For more on costs and money see Getting Started, p22.

ATMs

ATMs are the easiest way of getting cash. They're found in most cities and even in smaller towns, although they are sometimes out of order. Make sure you have a four-digit PIN. Banco del Pacífico and Banco del Pichincha have MasterCard/Cirrus ATMs. Banco de Guayaquil has Visa/Plus ATMs.

Bargaining

Bargaining is expected at food and crafts markets. Sometimes you can bargain on hotels during low season.

Cash

Bills are the same as those used in the US. Coins are identical in shape, size and material to their US counterparts, but instead of US presidents, they feature the faces and symbols of Ecuador. US coins are also used interchangeably.

Change is often quite difficult to come by. Trying to purchase inexpensive items with a US$20 bill (or even a US$10 bill) generally results in either you or the proprietor running from shop to shop until someone produces some change. If no one does, you're out of luck. Change bills whenever you can. To ask for change, make a deeply worried face and ask '¿Tiene suelto?' (Do you have change?).

Credit Cards

Credit cards are a fine backup, but not widely accepted. Merchants accepting credit cards will often add from 4% to 10% to the bill. Paying cash is often better value. Visa and MasterCard are the most widely accepted cards.

Exchanging Money

Foreign currencies can be exchanged into US dollars easily in Quito, Guayaquil and Cuenca, where rates are also the best. You can also change money at most of the major border crossings. In some places, however, notably the Oriente, it is quite difficult to exchange money. Exchange houses, called *casas de cambio,* are normally the best places; banks will also exchange money but are usually much slower. Generally, exchange rates are within 2% of one another in any given city.

Major towns have a black market, usually near the big *casas de cambio*. Rates are about the same, but street changing is illegal (though ignored), and counterfeits and cheating are serious risks.

Exchange rates at the time of writing included the following:

EXCHANGE RATES		
Country	**Unit**	**US$**
Australia	A$1	0.87
Canada	C$1	0.93
euro zone	€1	1.47
Japan	¥100	1.10
New Zealand	NZ$1	0.72
UK	UK£1	1.62

Traveler's Checks

Very few banks, hotels or retailers will cash traveler's checks, making them a poor option in Ecuador. Those that do typically tack on a rate of 2% to 4%. It's much more useful to have a supply of US cash and an ATM card (plus a backup ATM card just in case).

POST

It costs US$1.25 to send a letter to North America, US$2 to Europe and US$2.25 to the rest of the world. For a few cents extra, you can send them *certificado* (certified). Sending parcels of 2kg to 20kg is best done in Quito.

To receive mail in Ecuador, have the sender mail your item to the nearest post office, eg Lista de Correos, Correo Central, Quito (or town and province of your choice), Ecuador. Mail is filed alphabetically, so make sure that your last name is clear.

For members, the South American Explorers (p601) will hold mail sent to the clubhouse. If your incoming mail weighs over 2kg, you have to recover it from customs (and pay high duty).

RESPONSIBLE TRAVEL

The best way to make sure your money goes to the right people is to support local businesses, choosing small, family-run restaurants and guesthouses rather than foreign-owned places, for instance. If you plan to study Spanish in Ecuador (and it's a great place to learn), try to choose a school that invests a portion of its profits in the community, and consider living with a local family.

Ecotourism is a major buzzword used by nearly every tour operator in the country, though only a handful truly merit the label. The SAE in Quito (p601) is a good resource for finding tour operators and hotels or lodges that truly practice ecotourism.

Support local artisans by buying locally made handicrafts and artwork, and try to buy at the source. Don't buy illegal artifacts such as pre-Columbian pieces; mounted insects; items made from endangered animals; or jewelry made from sea turtle or black coral.

What you eat also affects the environment. Certain products – especially shrimp – have caused widespread destruction of mangroves and coastal ecosystems, and lobster is significantly overfished. Try to limit your intake when in Ecuador.

What you leave behind is also something to consider. Take home your plastics and batteries when you leave, as Ecuador has no means of processing these things.

When signing up for a package tour or expedition – whether it's a Galápagos tour or a rafting or climbing trip – be sure to ask lots of questions before committing. In order to minimize the impact of your visit, you'll want to choose an outfit that's sensitive to the local ecology and its resident communities. Guides shouldn't hunt, cut trees for bonfires, harass wildlife or litter, and they should support in some way the communities they visit. Try to find out if outfits use indigenous or local guides.

There are many ways for visitors to play a positive role in Ecuador, not least of which is volunteering. See opposite for a few ideas on how to get involved.

STUDYING

Ecuador is one of the best places to study Spanish on the continent. Quito (p608) and Cuenca (p636), and to a lesser extent Otavalo (p620) and Baños (p629), all have schools where you can have one-on-one classes and stay with a host family. Prices range from US$5 to US$10 per hour.

TELEPHONE

For international calls, cybercafes (prevalent in major towns and cities) provide the cheapest service, with rates ranging from US10¢ to US35¢ per minute for calls across the globe (Quito has the best rates). Calls are pricier (US25¢ to US50¢ per minute) at phone centers run by Andinatel, Pacifictel and Etapa – Ecuador's three regional companies.

Reverse-charge (collect) calls are possible to North America and most European countries. Direct dialing to a North American or European operator is also possible; the numbers are available from your long-distance service provider. From a private phone within Ecuador, dial ☎116 for an international operator.

Two-digit area codes (indicated after town headings throughout the chapter) change by province. Drop the area code if you're calling within a province. If calling from abroad, drop the 0 from the code. Ecuador's country code is ☎593.

To call locally, you can use either a Pacifictel or Andinatel office or a public phone box. Public phones operate with prepaid phone cards, which are available at kiosks.

All telephone numbers in Ecuador now have seven digits.

Cell Phones

Cell-phone numbers in Ecuador always start with the prefix ☎09. As far as bringing your own phone, only GSM cell phones operating at 850 Mhz (GSM 850) function in Ecuador. A tri-band GSM cellular will not currently work in Ecuador.

TOILETS

Ecuadorian plumbing has very low pressure. Putting toilet paper into the bowl may clog the system, so use the waste basket. This may seem unsanitary, but it's much better than clogged bowls and water overflowing onto the floor. Expensive hotels have adequate plumbing.

Public toilets are limited mainly to bus terminals, airports and restaurants. Toilets are called *servicios higiénicos* and are usually marked 'SS. HH.' People needing to use the toilet often ask to use the *baño* in a restaurant; toilet paper is rarely available – carry a personal supply.

TOURIST INFORMATION

The government-run **Ministerio de Turismo** (www.vivecuador.com) is responsible for tourist information at the national level. It is slowly opening tourist information offices – known as **iTur** offices – in important towns throughout Ecuador.

South American Explorers (SAE) has a clubhouse in Quito (see p601). For information on this organization, see p996.

TOURS

Most of the Galápagos archipelago is accessible to visitors only by guided tour (ie a cruise). Many travelers also opt to visit the Amazon on organized tours, as these are efficient, educational and often the only way to get deep into the rainforest.

TRAVELERS WITH DISABILITIES

Unfortunately, Ecuador's infrastructure for disabled travelers is virtually nonexistent.

VISAS

Most travelers entering Ecuador as tourists, including citizens of Australasian countries, Japan, the EU, Canada and the USA do not require visas. Upon entry, they will be issued a T-3 tourist card valid for 90 days. Sixty-day stamps are rarely given, but double-check if you're going to be in the country for a while. Residents of most Central American and some Asian countries require visas.

All travelers entering as diplomats, refugees, students, laborers, religious workers, businesspeople, volunteers and cultural-exchange visitors require nonimmigrant visas. Various immigrant visas are also available. Visas must be obtained from an Ecuadorian embassy and cannot be arranged within Ecuador.

Officially, to enter the country you must have a ticket out of Ecuador and sufficient funds for your stay, but border authorities rarely ask for proof of this. International vaccination certificates are not required by law, but some vaccinations, particularly against yellow fever, are advisable.

See also lonelyplanet.com and its links for up-to-date visa information.

Visa Extensions

Tourist-card extensions can be obtained from the **Jefatura Provincial de Migración** (☎ 02-224-7510; Isla Seymour 1152 near Río Coca, Quito; 🕒 8:30am-noon & 3-5pm Mon-Fri). On top of the original 90 days, you can obtain up to 30 additional days, a process that can be performed three times, for a maximum of 180 days (six months) per year. To get an extension, go to the Jefatura Provincial de Migración before your initial 90 days expire. If you overstay your visa, even by a day, you will be fined US$200.

VOLUNTEERING

Numerous organizations look for the services of volunteers, however many require at least a minimal grasp of Spanish, a minimum commitment of several weeks or months, as well as fees (anywhere from US$300 to US$600 per month) to cover the costs of room and board. Volunteers can work in conservation programs, help street kids, teach, build nature trails, construct websites, do medical or agricultural work – the possibilities are endless. Many jungle lodges also accept volunteers for long-term stays. To keep your volunteer costs down, your best bet is to look when you get to Ecuador. Plenty of places need volunteers who only have their hard work to offer.

South American Explorers (see p601) in Quito has a volunteer section where current offerings are posted. The classifieds section on **Ecuador Explorer** (www.ecuadorexplorer.com) has a list of organizations seeking volunteers.

Organizations in Ecuador that often need volunteers:

Andean Bear Conservation Project (www.andean bear.org; volunteers per month US$600) Track bears.

AmaZOOnico (☎ 09-414-3395; www.amazoonico.org) Work in animal rehabilitation sector.

Bosque Nublado Santa Lucía (www.santa-lucia.org, www.santaluciaecuador.com) Involved in reforestation, trail maintenance, construction, teaching English.

FEVI (www.fevi.org) FEVI works with children, the elderly, women's groups and indigenous communities.

Fundación Natura (www.fnatura.org) Ecuadorian nongovernment organization that needs volunteers for research and reforestation.

Jatun Sacha Foundation (www.jatunsacha.org) Plant conservation, reserve maintenance, environmental education, community service, agroforestry.

Junto con los Niños (www.juconi.org.ec) Work with street kids in the slum areas of Guayaquil.

Merazonia (☎ www.merazonia.org) A refuge for injured animals.

New Era Galápagos Foundation (www.newera galapagos.org) Sustainable tourism in the Galápagos. Volunteers live and work on Isla San Cristóbal.

Rainforest Concern (www.rainforestconcern.org) British nonprofit.

Reserva Biológica Los Cedros (www.reservaloscedros .org) In the cloud forests of the western Andean slopes.

Río Muchacho Organic Farm (www.riomuchacho.com) Volunteer opportunities in organic agriculture. See also p654.

Yanapuma Foundation (Map pp602-3; ☎ 02-254-6709; www.yanapuma.org; 2nd fl, Veintimilla E8-125, Quito) Teaching English, reforestation, building houses, coastal clean-ups.

WOMEN TRAVELERS

Generally, women travelers will find Ecuador safe and pleasant, although machismo is alive and well. Ecuadorian men often make flirtatious comments and whistle at single women. Women who firmly ignore unwanted verbal advances are often treated with respect.

On the coast, you'll find that come-ons are more predatory, and solo female travelers should take precautions such as staying away from bars and discos where they will obviously get hit on, opting for taxis over walking etc. Racy conversation with a guy, while it may be ironic or humorous, is not common here, and a man will probably assume you're after one thing.

We have received warnings from women who were molested while on organized tours. If you're traveling solo, it's essential to do some investigating before committing to a tour: find out who's leading the tour, what other tourists will be on the outing and so on. Women-only travel groups or guides are available in a few situations.

WORKING

Officially, you need a work visa to get a job in Ecuador. English-teaching positions occasionally pop up in Quito or Cuenca. The pay is low but enough to live on. Tourist services (jungle lodges, tour operators etc) are good places to look for work.

The Guianas

Mix a population of descendants of escaped and freed slaves with a strong indigenous culture; add a sprinkling of Indian, Indonesian, Laotian, Chinese and Brazilian immigrants, some French, British and Dutch colonialism and steam the whole lot on the Atlantic coast of Latin South America. The result of this unlikely recipe is one of the most diverse and least visited regions on the continent. Divided into three countries that have been defined by their colonial past, the cultural mishmash causes a little bit of chaos, some wild-hot cuisine and lots and lots of feisty and eccentric personalities. An Afro-European vibe reminds you that you that these countries consider themselves to be Caribbean before South American.

Deep, malarial jungles protected the region from getting too much European interest early on – most of the first settlers died of tropical diseases. Today, this gives these countries a trump card they have yet to fully exploit: some of the purest tropical rainforests on the planet, ideal for the most adventurous sort of ecotourism. Lack of tourist infrastructure makes traveling in any of the Guianas challenging and expensive yet incredibly rewarding. French Guiana, which is technically France, is the most tidy and organized of the three countries; the potholes increase as you travel west through kaleidoscopic Suriname, and by the time you reach Guyana you'll have lost track of the last time you had a hot shower.

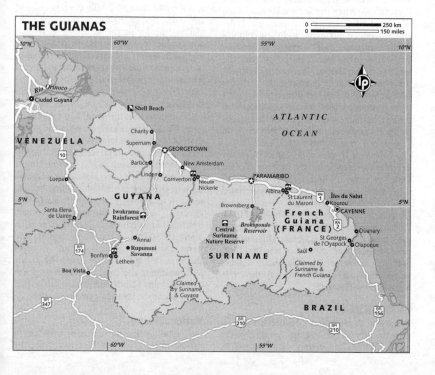

HISTORY

Spaniards saw the muddy Guiana coastline, enshrouded in mangroves and sparsely inhabited by the warlike Carib people, for the first time in 1499, but they found no prospect of gold or cheap labor and largely ignored it. Several 16th-century explorers, including Sir Walter Raleigh, placed the mythical city of El Dorado in the region, but there was still no sustained European interest in the area until the mid-17th century.

The Netherlands began to settle the land in 1615. After forming the Dutch West India Company in 1621, the colonists traded with Amerindian peoples of the interior and established plantations of sugar, cocoa and other tropical commodities. Indigenous peoples were almost wiped out by introduced diseases, so the Dutch imported West African slaves to construct canals and work the plantations. Beginning in the mid-18th century, escaped slaves (whose descendants are now called Maroons) formed settlements in the interior.

England established sugar and tobacco plantations on the west bank of the Suriname River around 1650 and founded what is now Paramaribo. After the second Anglo-Dutch War, under the Treaty of Breda (1667), the Dutch retained Suriname and their colonies on the Guyanese coast (in exchange for a tiny island now called Manhattan) but ceded the area east of the Maroni (Marowijne in Dutch) River to the French. For the next 150 years sovereignty of the region shifted between the three powers; by 1800 Britain was dominant, though Suriname remained under Dutch control, and France retained a precarious hold on Cayenne in what is now French Guiana.

At the end of the Napoleonic Wars, the Treaty of Paris reaffirmed the sovereignty of the Dutch in Suriname and of the French east of the Maroni, while Britain formally purchased the Dutch colonies in what became British Guiana. By 1834 slavery was abolished in all British colonies, and the Royal Navy suppressed the slave trade in the Caribbean. This created a need for more plantation labor, and the immigration of indentured labor from other colonies (especially India) created a unique ethnic mix in each of the Guianas.

ENVIRONMENT

Almost anywhere that rainforests exist, so does the prospect of logging, mining, drilling and hunting. The Guianas are no exception.

Especially in much poorer Suriname and Guyana, cutting ancient hardwood trees and tapping large veins of gold and bauxite spells jobs and revenue. Fortunately, the people and governments of the Guianas also recognize the enormous economic potential of ecotourism, which they can only realize through sound conservation practices. In Suriname, Conservation International assists the government in protecting and managing its land, and the Guyanese are actively promoting sustainable tourism and, in particular, birdwatching resources. A particular bright spot is the locally managed Iwokrama Rainforest Preserve in Guyana, which encompasses 371,000 hectares and successfully balances sustainable logging practices with ecotourism and conservation.

The Land

Besides a long, largely untouched coastline looking north toward the Atlantic Ocean, the Guianas' most significant feature is the Guiana Shield, a massive section of South America's continental crust that was connected to Africa 150 million years ago. At that time, the shield was already close to 2 billion years old and covered in rich vegetation. Andean uplift and glacial drift during the ice ages later created *tepui* (tabletop) mountains and the Guianese highlands region and carved out large swaths of savannah while leaving remnant patches of Amazonian rainforest.

Wildlife

This biodiversity 'hot spot' is a small land area (470,000 square kilometers) hosting more than 6000 known plants, 1600 bird species, 800 reptiles and amphibians and 200 mammals. Whew! Among these are some simply unforgettable creatures, such as the Guiana cock-of-the-rock (a bird), the golden-handed tamarin (a monkey) and the oncilla (a jungle cat). The Guianas also lay claim to many unusually large animals: the giant river otter, giant anteater, black caiman, jaguar, and harpy eagle. Even their bullet ant is one of the world's biggest. Away from the jungle and savannah, the coastal beaches welcome dolphins, shore birds and marine turtles that come ashore to lay their eggs seasonally.

National Parks

Suriname has the most extensive system of protected parks of the three countries, the largest being the 1.6-million-hectare Central Suriname Nature Reserve (p714). Guyana's largest park, Iwokrama (p729), is an inspirational example of how a population's passion for conservation can sustain a protected forest area under difficult economic circumstances. While French Guiana officially has the least protected land of the three countries, its isolated, agriculture- and extraction-free history has allowed most of it to remain relatively pristine. Thanks to conservation schemes, increased ecotourism opportunities and relatively sparse human settlement, the Guianas offer excellent chances of seeing wild animals and make an outstanding destination for a South American safari.

RESPONSIBLE TRAVEL

Ecotourism is big business in the Guianas, but some operators have their own take on what it means as far as practice goes. Poke around and get a feel for a company's 'eco-strategy' before going with it. Look for tours that are sensitive to the environment and for programs co-run by Amerindians.

Technically you need permission to visit Amerindian communities, but if you are traveling with a tour company, this should be taken care of for you. Ensure that your guide shows environmental respect – no hunting, gathering, littering etc – and, ideally, is from the culture of the village that you're visiting. On your own end, bring fishhooks and knives as trade goods and ask locals' permission before photographing them.

When visiting sea turtle nesting sites, maintain a clear distance, avoid flash photography and unnecessary flashlight use, and never touch the eggs or hatchlings.

In cities, keep an eye out for and steer clear of rare animals (like turtles) on menus, buy local products and, no matter where you are, conserve energy and water (many establishments filter their own water or collect precious rainwater).

TRANSPORTATION

Transportation is one of the biggest challenges to traveling in the Guianas. Most roads, especially in Guyana and Suriname, are in bad shape and sometimes impassable, and routes are extremely limited in the interior. A flight or boat ride is often necessary to reach more remote destinations. All of these factors add up to high transport costs and require planning and patience.

For more information about travel in the Guianas see the individual transport sections for French Guiana (p689), Suriname (p708) and Guyana (p722).

Air

International flights arrive in Georgetown (Guyana), Paramaribo (Suriname) and Cayenne (French Guiana). From North America, flights often go through one or multiple Caribbean islands, sending passengers on circuitous routes and requiring overnight stopovers. Thanks to lingering colonial ties, you can fly Amsterdam–Paramaribo,

---

STAY ALERT!

Minibus rides are a quintessential Guiana experience, and one that can leave your heart racing. They move at frightening speeds around metropolitan streets and jungle tracks, blaring music and packed to the gills with people and cargo. Breakdowns and accidents are frequent. If you feel truly endangered, request to be let out, ask for a refund (which you may or may not get), and wait, perhaps a long time, for another minibus with a free seat to stop for you – then pray that the operator doesn't drive even more recklessly.

Minibus services present ample opportunities to swindle travelers. Before you leave, verify the price of your trip and where you will be dropped off (your hotel, an intersection). River crossings usually involve vehicle changes; your driver should give you a receipt so you don't have to pay again when you meet your connection on the other side.

The minibus business is full of names – Bobby, Johnny, Brian – but the difference in the service between them is minute, and they even sometimes move passengers into their competitors' buses at transfer points without notifying them. Don't be surprised if you started your trip with Bobby and ended your trip with Johnny. The whole system is chaos, but a necessary one in a region with no public transport.

THE GUIANAS

New York–Georgetown and Paris–Cayenne unburdened by plane changes.

At the time of writing, there were limited flights linking all three countries but no non-charter flights connecting Cayenne to the other Guianas.

Bus

Almost anyone traveling in the Guianas will use a bus or minibus. 'Public buses' may be minibuses (eight- to 12-passenger minivans) and follow regulated routes with set fares, but private companies also operate minibuses, either by reservation (they'll pick you up) or from designated spots around towns (usually leaving when full). To add to the confusion, minibuses are also sometimes called 'taxis,' although taxis are your usual five-passenger sedans as well (but more expensive than minibuses); in this chapter a taxi refers to the pricier sedan option.

Large, 40-seater buses are rare and only follow a few routes in the Guianas.

Car & Motorcycle

It's possible to travel overland across all three Guianas but only near the coasts. Rainy seasons drastically affect roads, especially in Guyana and Suriname, where they are iffy even when dry. Ferries that accommodate vehicles link all three countries, and a bridge connects Brazil with French Guiana.

FRENCH GUIANA

HIGHLIGHTS

- **Îles du Salut** (p697) Cast away to an island vacation, complete with sand, sun, palm trees and penal colony ruins.
- **Centre Spatial Guyanais (Guianese Space Center)** (p697) See one of the world's busiest satellite launchers or, if you're lucky, watch one blast off.
- **Cacao** (p694) Gorge on Laotian treats and admire ornate embroidery in French Guiana's largest Hmong refugee community.
- **Best Journey** (p701) Watch the peaceful ritual of dinosaur-like leatherback turtles laying their eggs in the moonlit sand of Awala-Yalimopo.
- **Off the Beaten Track** (p695) Find Capuchin monkeys, enormous snakes, and a slew of other exotic plants and critters at the Sentier Molokoï de Cacao.

THE GUIANAS

FAST FACTS

- **Area:** 91,000 sq km (slightly smaller than Portugal or the US state of Indiana)
- **Budget:** US$50 to US$60 a day
- **Capital:** Cayenne
- **Costs:** hammock space in a traditional *carbet* (open-air hut) US$12, Indonesian fried noodles US$5, one-hour minibus ride US$12 to US$15
- **Country code:** ☎ 594
- **Languages:** French, French Guianese, Creole, Amerindian languages, Sranan Tongo
- **Money:** US$1 = €0.70
- **Population:** 221,500
- **Seasons:** high (June to September), low (September to May), rainy (November to April)
- **Time:** GMT minus three hours

TRAVEL HINTS

Bring a hammock and sleep cheap nearly anywhere besides Cayenne – and don't forget your mosquito net!

OVERLAND ROUTES

French Guiana's border crossings include Albina (Suriname) and Oiapoque (Brazil).

French Guiana is a tiny country of cleaned-up colonial architecture, eerie prison-camp history and some of the world's most diverse plant and animal life. Almost all French Guianese cities look out to sea, giving them a distinct maritime culture, and the interior is where the best wildlife action happens, with the exception of thousands of endangered sea turtles that storm the country's untouched beaches every year. Colonized by France – and thus a member of the EU – it's one of South America's wealthiest corners, with funds pouring in from Paris to promote tourism and to insure a stable base for its satellite launcher. Despite a thoroughly French veneer, this outpost of France feels more Amazonian than European; the croissants are great, but come for the pristine jungle and world-class ecotourism.

CURRENT EVENTS

Developments at the Centre Spatial Guyanais (Guianese Space Center) in Kourou are always big news. Culminating decades of effort by the European Space program to offer the EU independent access to space, the Soyuz medium-load launcher, capable of transporting satellites and humans into space, made its maiden voyage in 2009.

HISTORY

The earliest French settlement was in Cayenne in 1643, but tropical diseases and hostile local Amerindians limited plantation development. After various conflicts with the Dutch and British and an eight-year occupation by Brazil and Portugal, the French resumed control only to see slavery abolished (1848), and the few plantations almost collapsed.

About the same time, France decided that penal settlements in Guiana would reduce the cost of French prisons and contribute to colony development. Napoleon III sent the first convicts in 1852; those who survived their sentences had to remain there as exiles for an equal period of time. With 90% of them dying of malaria or yellow fever, this policy did little to increase the population or develop the colony. French Guiana became notorious for the brutality and corruption of its penal system, which lasted until 1953.

Guyane became an overseas department of France in 1946, and in 1964 work began on the Centre Spatial Guyanais, which has brought an influx of scientists, engineers, technicians and service people from Europe and elsewhere, turning the city of Kourou into a sizable, modern town responsible for 15% of all economic activity. The first Hmong refugees from Laos arrived in 1975 and settled primarily in the towns of Cacao and Javouhey. They now make up about 1.5% of the population and have become vital agricultural producers, growing about 80% of the department's produce.

Successive French governments have provided state employment and billions of euros in subsidies, resulting in a near-European standard of living in urban areas. Rural villages are much poorer, and in the hinterland many Amerindians and Maroons still lead a subsistence lifestyle.

THE CULTURE

French Guiana is a tantalizing mélange of visible history, fabulous cuisine and the sultry French language with the vastness and ethnic diversity of Amazonia. Dependent on France yet independent of European hustle and bustle, the people of this tiny department are warmhearted and tough. Though Cayenne and Kourou enjoy somewhat continental economies, the majority of the populace struggles financially and lives a modest lifestyle.

Guianese people take pride in their multicultural universe borne of multiregional influences. French Guiana has about 220,000 permanent inhabitants, with temporary and migrant workers from Haiti and Brazil making up the 60,000-and-growing balance. Two separate Hmong groups – 'green' or Mong Leng and 'white' or Hmong Der – speak different but mutually intelligible dialects. White and green Hmong were forbidden to intermarry in Laos but are allowed to in French Guiana.

RELIGION

French Guiana is predominantly Catholic, but Maroons and Amerindians follow their own religious traditions. The Hmong also tend to be Roman Catholic due to the influence of Sister Anne-Marie Javouhey, who brought them to French Guiana.

ARTS

Music and dance are the liveliest art forms in French Guiana – think Caribbean rhythms with a French accent. Maroon and Amerindian wood carvings, baskets and

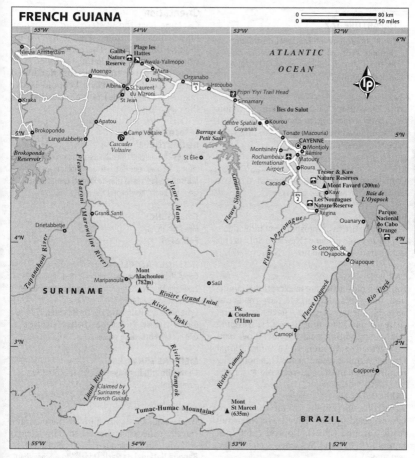

FRENCH GUIANA

tapestries are sold in markets and along the roadside. Hmong tapestries are found in Cacao and Javouhey.

ENVIRONMENT

French Guiana borders Brazil to the east and south, while the Maroni and Litani Rivers form the border with Suriname (though the southern part is disputed).

The majority of Guianese people live in the Atlantic coastal zone, which has most of French Guiana's limited road network. The coast is mostly mangrove swamp with only a few sandy beaches. The densely forested interior, whose terrain rises gradually toward the Tumac-Humac Mountains on the Brazilian frontier, is largely unpopulated.

TRANSPORTATION
Getting There & Away

All international passengers must fly through Cayenne's Rochambeau International Airport (p694).

From St Laurent du Maroni (in the west; see p701) and St Georges de l'Oyapock (in the east; see p696), ferries head to Suriname and Brazil, respectively. Both ferries carry vehicles.

Getting Around

Getting around French Guiana without your own wheels is much more difficult and costly than in mainland France, where public transport and hitchhiking are more common. Even though renting a car might blow your budget, it's probably the most cost-efficient way to

---

DEPARTURE TAX

For flights to any international destination (besides Paris, which is considered a domestic flight), the departure tax (US$20) is included in the ticket price.

---

cruise the country. Customs and Immigration frequently stop traffic to check for drugs and undocumented passengers – make sure your papers are in order.

AIR
From Cayenne, small planes operated by Air Guyane fly to Saül (see p694).

BOAT
Tours often use river transport, but individuals can try to catch a boat at Kaw and St Laurent. Catamarans sail to the Îles du Salut (p697).

CAR
Although most roads are in exceptional condition, some secondary and tertiary roads can be bad in the rainy season – have a spare tire, spare gas and spare time. If you are traveling in a group, renting a car (from €40 per day) may actually save money. An International Driving Permit is recommended but not legally required. You must be 21 years old to rent.

TAXI COLLECTIF
Taxis collectifs (minibuses) are the second-best wheeled option. They leave when full from Cayenne (p694), Kourou (p697), St Laurent (p701) and St Georges (see boxed text, p696).

CAYENNE
pop 63,000

A crossroads of the Caribbean, South America and Europe, Cayenne is a city of myriad cultures surrounded by all the colors of the Caribbean. The streets are lined with colonial wrought-iron balconies with louvered shutters painted in tropical pinks, yellows and turquoise. The vibrant markets and excellent Brazilian, Creole, French and Chinese restaurants make this town as pleasing to the belly as it is to the eye; you won't want to be skipping any meals here. Outside the city center, highways and urban sprawl reminds you that you're still in the 21st century.

Orientation
Cayenne is at the western end of a small hilly peninsula on the Cayenne River overlooking the Atlantic. The center of the action is the Place des Palmistes, lined with cafes and palm trees, in the northwest corner. To its west, Place Léopold Héder (aka Place Grenoble) is the oldest part of the city.

Information
BOOKSTORES
AJC (33 Blvd Jubelin) Offers books and maps, including Institut Géographique National topographic maps.
Maison de la Presse (Rue de Rémire) Carries French-language books, newspapers and magazines.

EMERGENCY
Fire (☎ 18)
Police (☎ 17)

INTERNET ACCESS
Copy' Print (22 Lalouette; per hr €2; ☿ 8am-noon & 2:30-6pm Mon-Fri, 8am-noon Sat) The cheapest internet cafe in the city center.
CyberCafé des Palmistes (Bar Les Palmistes, 12 Av du Général de Gaulle; ☿ 7am-midnight Mon-Sat) Have a cold beer while checking your email.

MEDICAL SERVICES
Centre Hospitalier Cayenne (☎ 39-5050; 3 Av Flamboyants)

MONEY
Banks and ATMs are all over the city, and traveler's checks can be cashed at both banks and *cambios* (currency-exchange offices).
Banque National de Paris (2 Place Victor Schoelcher)
Change Caraïbes (64 Av du Général de Gaulle; ☿ 7:30am-12:30pm & 3:30-5:30pm Mon-Fri, 8am-noon Sat) Offers competitive rates.

POST
Post Agence de Ceperou (Place Léopold Héder; ☿ 7:30am-1:30pm Mon-Fri, to 11:45am Sat)

GETTING INTO TOWN

Rochambeau International Airport is 16km southwest of Cayenne. From the airport, consider sharing a taxi (€35, 20 minutes). To the airport, it's cheaper to take a *taxi colectif* (minibus) to Matoury (€2, 15 minutes, 10km), then a taxi for the remaining 6km.

CAYENNE

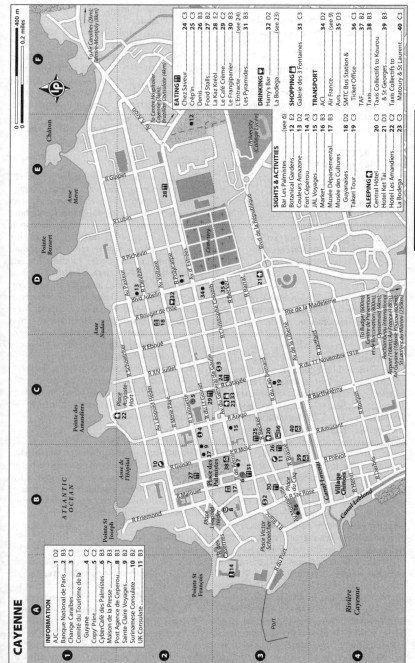

INFORMATION

AJC	**1** D2
Banque National de Paris	**2** B3
Change Caraïbes	**3** C3
Comité du Tourisme de la Guyane	**4** C2
Copy'Print	**5** C3
CyberCafé des Palmistes	**6** B3
Maison de la Presse	**7** B3
Post Agence de Ceperou	**8** B3
Sainte Claire Voyages	**9** B2
Surinamese Consulate	**10** B2
UK Consulate	**11** B3

SIGHTS & ACTIVITIES

Bar Les Palmistes	(see 6)
Botanical Gardens	**12** E2
Couleurs Amazone	**13** D2
Fort Cépérou	**14** A3
JAL Voyages	**15** C3
Market	**16** B3
Musée Départemental	**17** B3
Musée des Cultures Guyanaises	**18** D2
Takari Tour	**19** C3

SLEEPING

Central Hôtel	**20** C3
Hotel Ket Tai	**21** D3
Hotel Les Amandiers	**22** C3
La Bodega	**23** C3

EATING

Chez Saveur	**24** C3
Crépin	**25** C3
Denis	**26** B3
Food Stalls	**27** B2
La Kaz Kréol	**28** E2
Le Café Crème	**29** C2
Le Frangipanier	**30** B3
L'Entracte	(see 24)
Les Pyramides	**31** B3

DRINKING

Harry's Bar	**32** D2
La Bodega	(see 23)

SHOPPING

Galerie des 3 Fontaines	**33** C3

TRANSPORT

ACL	**34** D2
Air France	(see 9)
Avis	**35** D3
SMTC Bus Station & Ticket Office	**36** C3
TAF	**37** B2
Taxis	**38** B3
Taxis Collectifs to Kourou & St Georges	**39** B3
Taxis Collectifs to Matoury & St Laurent	**40** C3

TELEPHONE

There's no central telephone office but plenty of pay phones near Place des Palmistes.

TOURIST INFORMATION

Comité du Tourisme de la Guyane (☎ 29-6500; www.tourisme-guyane.com; 12 Lalouette; ⊙ 8am-1pm & 3-6pm Mon-Fri, 8am-noon Sat) Filled with pamphlets, maps and information, the office is always staffed with someone to answer questions. An information desk at the airport stays open late for arriving flights.

TRAVEL AGENCIES

Sainte Claire Voyages (☎ 30-0038, 17-19 Lalouette) Helpful staff can book flights and tours.

Dangers & Annoyances

Petty and violent crime is on the rise, mostly as a result of increasing drug problems. At night, walk in groups or take a taxi. The Village Chinois (aka Chicago) area, south of the market, should be reached in taxi.

Sights

Cayenne is easy to see on foot in one day. Off the gardened **Place Léopold Héder** are the remains of **Fort Cépérou**, perched on land bought in 1643 from the Galibi Indians by the first French colonists. Most of the site is now a restricted military zone, but you can still stroll around for good views of Cayenne and the river. The **Bar Les Palmistes** (12 Av du Général de Gaulle; ⊙ 7am-midnight Mon-Sat) is the best place to people-watch on the palm tree–lined **Place des Palmistes**. The sizable **Botanical Gardens** (Blvd de la République), built in 1879 and renovated in 2009, today flourish with tropical Guianese flora. After siesta, cruise Av du Général de Gaulle, the main commercial street, to experience Cayenne at its bustling peak.

Inside Cayenne's main **market** (cnr Brassé & Ste Rose; ⊙ 6:30am-1pm Wed, Fri & Sat), eager shoppers will find a vibrant jumble of Amerindian basketry, African-style paintings and carvings, piles of exotic spices at great prices, and soup stalls that serve up the best Vietnamese *pho* (€4) in the Guianas. Endless aisles of fruit and vegetable stands – overflowing with daikon, bok choy and bean sprouts – look more Southeast Asia than South America.

The centrally located **Musée Départemental** (1 Rue de Rémire; adult/child & student €1/.50; ⊙ 8am-1:15pm & 3-5:45pm Mon & Thu, 8am-1:15pm Wed & Fri) features a frighteningly large stuffed black caiman, as well as other preserved local critters, an

ethnobotanical display and an air-conditioned 'butterfly room.' The upstairs area recaptures life in the old penal colony and displays some Amerindian handicrafts.

The smaller **Musée des Cultures Guyanaises** (☎ 31-4172; 78 Payé; ⊙ 8am-12:45pm & 3-5:45pm Mon, Tue, Thu & Fri, 8am-12:45pm Wed, to 11:45am Sat) is devoted to Guiana's early history, from its geologic formation through precolonial, Amerindian times. It houses a relaxing, air-con library (upstairs) that has publications in French, English and various other languages.

Tours

French Guiana's pristine jungles are impenetrable and dangerous without a knowledgeable guide. Licensed Cayenne-based agencies run tours, often hiring out guides throughout the country (and taking a commission on their services). Using an agency will ensure that you have permission to enter Amerindian communities. The better of these include **Takari Tour** (☎ 31-1960; www.takaritour.gf; 8 Rue du Cap Bernard), the oldest and most respected operator; **JAL Voyages** (☎ 31-6820; www.jal-voyages.com; 26 Av du Général de Gaulle), which has a popular overnight jaunt on a floating *carbet* in Kaw (from €150); and **Couleurs Amazone** (☎ 28-7000; www.couleursamazone.fr; 21 Blvd Jubelin), which offers day and multiday trips on every major river in French Guiana (from €450 for five days).

A cheaper alternative is to go directly to local guides, usually found at lodgings throughout French Guiana, and make your own arrangements.

Festivals & Events

Carnaval (January to February or March; dates vary) is *the* annual festival, and it gets bigger and wilder every year, with near-perpetual live bands and parades. Schools and businesses close and hotels are often fully booked during the last week of the festivities.

Sleeping

In Cayenne, one person usually has to pay the full price of a double room. If you have wheels, you'll find better deals outside Cayenne. Skip the hotels' expensive breakfasts and hit the cafes and markets for your morning meal.

La Bodega (☎ 30-2513; www.labodega.fr; 42 Av du Général de Gaulle; d from €30, with air-con €35; ✦) The cheapest place in town, the Bodega also has a popular downstairs bar with live music on Sundays. It's great if you want to drink all night and stumble up to bed, but a little noisy if you need serious shut-eye. Rooms with a view, which are great for Carnaval, start at €40.

Hotel Ket Tai (☎ 28-9777; 72 Blvd Jubelin; d €40) With simple, if not bland, motel-style comfort, the Ket Tai is a rare bargain this close to the city center.

Hotel Les Amandiers (☎ 31-3875; amandiers@hot mail.com; Place Auguste-Hort; d/ste €58/99; ✎ ▭) Run by a lovely, English-speaking place, the beautiful Amandiers is the only hotel in Cayenne overlooking the ocean and a stretch of park. Request a room with a view and check out the delicious French-Guyanese food at the restaurant downstairs.

Central Hôtel (☎ 25-6565; www.centralhotel-cayenne .fr; cnr Molé & Rue du Lieutenant Becker; s/d €60/65; ✎ ▭) The rooms are small but have kitchenettes, balconies and bathtubs. Although the Central is generic like a business hotel, the staff are friendly and the location is tops. Internet in the lobby is free.

our pick **Oyasamaïd** (☎ 31-5684; www.oyasamaid .com; PK 4, Rte de la Madeleine; d €60; ✎ ▭ ☎) A French family pension à la Guianese, this four-room place is friendly, bright and impeccably clean. All the spacious rooms have Jacuzzi bathtubs, and a swimming pool seals the deal. An extra bed is €10, and room rates drop €5 the second night; all rooms include one free breakfast.

Eating

For the best bang for your buck, you can slurp noodles at Cayenne's daytime **market** (opposite) and browse the nighttime **food stalls** (Place des Palmistes) for crepes, fried rice and sandwiches (all from about €3). Small Chinese takeout joints and grocery shops make self-catering a breeze. The sit-down options in Cayenne can be outstanding.

Crêp'in (5 Rue du Lieutenant Becker; crepes from €2, salads €3.50, breakfasts €5; ✎ 8am-8pm Mon-Sat) One of the only places in town serving a complete breakfast. Come back again for a lunch of salads, sandwiches, sweet and savory crepes, and fresh juices.

Le Café Crème (44 Cataÿee; sandwiches from €3; ✎ 6:15am-4:30pm Mon-Fri, to 3:30pm Sat) Get Parisian-style coffee, sizable sandwiches and delicate pastries at this sidewalk cafe à la française. Your best bet for coffee before 7am.

our pick **Le Frangipanier** (7 Av Monnerville; starters €3, mains €9-12; ✎ 10am-3pm Mon, 9:30am-3pm Tue & Thu, 7am-3pm Wed, Fri & Sat) The steaming *pho* noodle

soups, fresh salads and crunchy egg rolls are worth working around this Laotian restaurant's funky hours. Overlooking the market's flower stalls, the cafe-style restaurant is great for lunch after exploring the market.

Denis (Brassé; mains around €5; ✎ 11:30am-10:30pm) One of the best of a slew of affordable Chinese restaurants. This friendly place has plenty of vegetarian options and a wide variety of meat and seafood dishes.

Chez Saveur (cnr Colomb & Cataÿee; mains €7-10; ✎ 11:30am-10:30pm Tue-Sat) There's usually a line of people at this corner takeout joint waiting for finger food like breaded prawns and cassava fries as well as hearty Guianese meat dishes. It's like upscale fast food.

L'Entracte (☎ 30-0137; 65 Cataÿee; pizzas from €9; noon-2:30pm & 6:30-10:30pm) Eat the cheapest (but tasty!) pizza in town while admiring the movie posters that cover the walls.

La Kaz Kréol (☎ 39-0697; 35 Av d'Estrées; mains €12-18; ✎ 12-2pm & 6:30-10:30pm Tue-Sun) The best sit-down Creole restaurant in Cayenne serves outstanding stuffed cassava, meat stews and seafood in a homey setting. Try the Creole breakfasts on Saturdays and Sundays.

Les Pyramides (cnr Colomb & Malouet; mains €15; ✎ noon-3pm & 7-11pm Tue-Sun) This superb Middle Eastern restaurant makes hearty, heaping platters of couscous to rave reviews.

Drinking

Live music, wine and rum punch flow freely in bars and clubs throughout Cayenne. **La Bodega** (42 Av du Général de Gaulle; ✎ 7pm-1am Sun-Fri, to 2am Sat) is a decidedly French sidewalk bar that gets lively after 11pm. Cozy **Harry's Bar** (20 Rouget de l'Isle; ✎ 7am-2:30pm & 5pm-1am Mon-Thu, to 2am Fri & Sat) boasts 50 brands of whiskey and beers.

Reggae music rocks small clubs in Village Chinois (but see the warning opposite), and a few Brazilian and Dominican bars dot Av de la Liberté.

Shopping

The **Galerie des 3 Fontaines** (Av du Général de Gaulle; ✎ 9am-12:30pm & 2-7pm Mon-Sat) sells souvenirs ranging from tacky and cheap to chic and smart, including books on French Guiana, cassava treats made by Amerindians, and every kind of wooden object you can imagine. Be warned that Hmong embroidery and weaving are only available in Cacao and other Hmong villages.

Getting There & Away

All international and domestic flights leave from **Rochambeau International Airport** (☎ 29-9700).

Airline offices in town or at Rochambeau:

Air Caraïbes (☎ 29-3636; gsa.aircaraibes@wanadoo.fr; Centre de Katoury, Rte Rocade) Services the Caribbean.

Air France (☎ 29-8700; www.airfrance.gf; 17 Lalouette) Flies to Paris and the Caribbean. Also has an airport office.

Air Guyane (☎ 29-3630; www.airguyane.com; Rochambeau International Airport) Flies to Saül.

TAF (☎ 30-7000; 2 Lalouette) Goes to Brazil.

Plan ahead and book seats well in advance to get the cheapest fares. Air Guyana flies daily to Saül (€65, 40 minutes). Some other destinations and one-way flight details:

Belém, Brazil (TAF; from €180, 2¼hr, 3 weekly)

Fort-de-France, Martinique (Air France & Air Caraïbes; from €200, 2hr, daily)

Macapá, Brazil (TAF; €150, 1¼hr, 3 weekly)

Paris, France (Air France & Air Caraïbes; from €400, 8½hr, daily)

Getting Around

BUS

Local buses leave from the **SMTC bus station** (☎ 25-4929 for schedule; cnr Rue du Cap Bernard & Molé) runs limited service Monday to Saturday around Cayenne and Montjoly's beaches (€2). You'll probably need taxis.

CAR

Renting a car can be cheaper than public transport if two or more persons are traveling together. Most companies have offices in Kourou, St. Laurent du Maroni and at the airport (some have airport-pickup surcharges of up to €20). Expect to pay from €35 per day for a compact with unlimited mileage. Cars are not allowed over the border.

ACL Airport (☎ 35-6636); Downtown (☎ 30-4756, 44 Blvd Jubelin)

ADA (☎ 25-0573; www.adaguyane.com; airport)

Avis Airport (☎ 35-3414); Downtown (☎ 30-2522, 58 Blvd Jubelin)

Budget (www.budget-gf.com) Airport (☎ 27-9780); Downtown (☎ 35-1020, 55 Zone Artisanale Galmot)

TAXI

Taxis charge a hiring fee of €1.50, plus €.50 per kilometer; the per-kilometer charge increases to €1 on Sundays and holidays, and from 7pm to 6am. There's a taxi stand on the southeast corner of Place des Palmistes.

TAXI COLLECTIF

Taxis collectifs leave when full from the *gare routière* (station) on Av de la Liberté until 6pm daily. From the corner of Rue Molé, they head to Matoury (€2, 15 minutes, 10km) and St Laurent (€35, four hours, 250km). From the corner of Rue Malouet, they depart for Kourou (€8, one hour, 60km) and St Georges (€15, two hours, 100km). Settle rates in advance and show up around 8am to get a spot.

AROUND CAYENNE

The best way to see many sights around the capital is by renting a car for a day or two.

Rémire-Montjoly

pop 19,500

Though technically two separate towns, Rémire-Montjoly, only 8km from Cayenne, functions as a single village. Its sweeping beaches are some of the country's best waterfront. Despite the persistence of mosquitoes and biting sand flies (make sure you bring repellent!), locals flock here in droves. Topless sunbathing is de rigueur at the best beach, **Plage Montjoly**, reachable by taxi or bus (see left) from Cayenne. The renovated historical ruins at **Fort Diamant** (☎ 35-4110; admission with/without guided tour €5/3), an old coastal battery dating from the early 19th century, are along the main beach road. The easy 2.5km **Salines Trail** at the end of Rue St Domenica, or the 4km **Rorota Trail** to the top of **Montagne du Mahury**, both offer excellent views of the coastal marshland and the ocean. On the RN2 heading toward the airport, the 5km hike into the **Grand Matoury Nature Reserve** is good for bird-watching.

Motel du Lac (☎ 38-0800; moteldulac@opensurf.net; Chemin Poupon, Rte de Montjoly; d €69; ⓧ ⓡ), a well-run place with a great pool near Montjoly beach and a lakeside ecological reserve. Otherwise try **Motel Beauregard 'Cric-Crac'** (☎ 35-4100; PK9, 2 Rte de Rémire; d from €70; ⓧ ⓡ), which has a bowling alley, tennis courts and a gym as well as a pool; it's endearingly kitsch and only 10km from Cayenne.

Cacao

pop 950

A tidy slice of Laos in the hills of Guiana, Cacao, about 75km southwest of Cayenne, is a village of sparkling clear rivers, vegetable plantations and no-nonsense wooden houses on stilts. The Hmong refugees who left Laos

AROUND CAYENNE

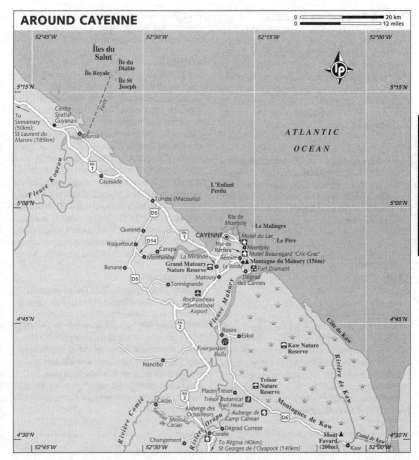

in the 1970s keep their town a safe, peaceful haven, and it's now a favorite weekend day trip among locals from Cayenne. Sunday, market day, is the best time for a visit if you want to shop for Hmong embroidery and weaving, and feast on a smorgasbord of Laotian treats (get there by 10am, before the tour buses arrive). Don't miss **Le Planeur Bleu** (☎ 27-0034; cleplaneur bleu@wanadoo.fr; admission €2.50; ⊙ 9am-1pm & 2-4pm Sun, other times by appointment) to see butterflies and arachnids, both dead and alive, or hold live tarantulas.

ourpick Chez By et Daniel (☎ 27-0998; 111 Bourg de Cacao) serves Laotian dishes – and offers a 5% discount with your Planeur Bleu ticket.

For a wildlife- and insect-spotting adventure, embark on the 18km hike along the **Sentier Molokoï de Cacao** (Cacao Molokoï Nature Trail), one of the few deep-forest jaunts that can be accomplished independently. The track links the rustic-chic **Auberge des Orpailleurs** (☎ 27-0622; www.aubergedes orpailleurs.com; PK62, RN 2; r from €24, hammock spaces per person €5.50), on the road to Régina, with the more basic **Quimbe Kio** (☎ 27-0122; Le Bourg de Cacao; hammock spaces €10, with hammock €14) in Cacao. These two *gîtes* (guesthouses) are also great places to arrange other ecotourism excursions within this region. Bring plenty of water, insect repellent and rain gear. A small refuge hut midway is the best place to overnight (€5 per person). Make reservations and get maps and advice at either *gîte*.

Trésor & Kaw Nature Reserves

The Trésor Nature Reserve is one of French Guiana's most accessible primary rainforests, and the bordering swamps of the Kaw Nature Reserve are excellent for observing caimans (best at night) and spectacular waterfowl like the scarlet ibis (best in summer). Drive 17km from Roura on the D6 (there's no bus) to Trésor's 1.75km **botanical trail** with rich diversity and protected wildlife. The paved D6 ends a few kilometers before the village of Kaw; a small beat-up road will take you the rest of the way to Kaw, where the folks at the **Restaurant Gingembre Sirop** (☎ 27-0464; hammock spaces/beds €7/15) help arrange wildlife-viewing excursions from €30. Between Trésor and Kaw, 28km from Roura, the friendly **Auberge de Camp Caïman** (☎ 30-7277; www.auberge-camp-caiman.com; hammock spaces €7, s/d €23/45) is the best place to stay in the area, offering a restaurant and all-inclusive, two-day catamaran excursions of Kaw from €135.

SAÜL
pop 150

Accessible by air from Cayenne, the defunct gold-mining village of Saül – the geographic center of French Guiana – is an untamed paradise explored mostly by professional biologists. The Big Tree path – with the largest tree ever recorded in French Guiana – is just one of hundreds of kilometers of trails built by French and American research institutes in the area.

For basic accommodations call the town hall for the **Gîtes Communal** (☎ 37-4500; s/d/tr €15/25/30). You can also organize an eight-day river-jungle-village adventure to Saül through tour agencies in Cayenne (p692).

KOUROU
pop 21,000

On a small peninsula overlooking the Atlantic Ocean and Kourou River, this small city of modern apartment blocks once existed solely to serve the mainland and offshore penal colonies. Now it seems to exist solely to serve the Centre Spatial Guyanais (Guyanese Space Center), a satellite construction facility and launch pad that employs thousands of people. A few beaches suitable for sunbathing line the easternmost part of town, but Kourou is mostly a way station for visiting the Space Center and catching a boat to the Îles du Salut. If you must hang out, head to Le Vieux Bourg (Old Town), a great strip for eating, drinking and wondering why the rest of the town isn't this hip.

Information

Guyanespace Voyages (☎ 22-3101; www.guyane space.com; 5 Cabalou) Reserve everything from transport to the Îles du Salut to international air travel.
Mediateque (Pôle Culturel de Kourou; ☼ 9am-5pm Mon-Fri) Internet is free but you need to show your passport.
Point Information Tourisme (☎ 32-9833; Av Victor Hugo; ☼ 7:30am-1:30pm Mon-Fri) Tucked away in a complex across the street from Église Notre Dame.
Taxi Phone Cyber (18 Aimaras; ☼ 9am-1pm & 3-8pm Mon-Sat, 9am-2pm Sun) Internet and international telephone service.

GETTING TO BRAZIL

It's best to avoid picking up hitchhikers or driving at night along the sketchy road connecting Régina (population 300), a near ghost town, and **St Georges de l'Oyapock** (population 2750), a sleepy outpost on the Brazilian border. St Georges serves as a departure point for visits to Amerindian villages and the ruins of Silver Mountain Penal Colony on the Oyapock River, but not much else. Accessing the villages requires permission from local authorities and an experienced guide, so it's best to contact a Cayenne-based tour company (see p692). If you get stuck in St Georges for a night, try the popular **Chez Modestine** (☎ 37-0013) or the quieter **Caz-Calé** (☎ 37-0054), both on Rue Elie-Elfort with rooms from €40. Eat at **Cappuccino** (mains €7), right down the street, which serves local-style fish and meat.

Minibuses leave when full (early mornings are best) from the town center to Cayenne (€15, two hours, 100km).

Stamp out at the **Douane** (customs office; ☼ 8am-6pm) on the riverside in St Georges, then hire a dugout (€6, 5 minutes) to take you across to Oiapoque, Brazil. A bridge linking the two towns is slated for completion sometime in 2010 (after years of delays). Once in Oiapoque, it's a 10-minute walk away from the river to the Police Federal, where you stamp into Brazil. Daily buses and planes leave Oiapoque for Macapá. For details on travel from Oiapoque to French Guiana, see p357.

Sights

In 1964 Kourou was chosen to be the site of the **Centre Spatial Guyanais** (CSG; ☎ 32-6123; www .cnes-csg.fr) because it's close to the equator, is away from tropical storm tracks and earthquake zones, and has a low population density. The launch site is the only one in the world this close to the equator (five degrees), where the earth's spin is significantly faster than further north or south; this means that the site benefits from the 'slingshot effect,' which boosts propulsion and makes launches up to 17% more energy-efficient than those at sites further away from the equator. Since 1980 two-thirds of the world's commercial satellites have been launched from French Guiana.

The center is run by CNES (Centre National d'Études Spatiales; www.cnes.fr) in collaboration with the ESA (European Space Agency; www.esa.com) and Arianespace (www.ariane space.com). Ariane 5, a heavy lift launcher, was the first rocket to take off from the center, but two more launchers, Vega (a light-lift rocket) and Soyuz (a medium-lift launcher), have recently begun service, increasing the number of liftoffs to nearly a dozen per year. This frequency makes it all that much easier to coordinate your visit with a launch, in which rockets blast off at speeds approaching 8km per second after a thrilling countdown of exploding booster fire.

Visit the ESA website to find out the launch schedule and reserve a space at one of several observation points within the space center. Email csg-accueil@cnes.fr well ahead of time, providing your full name, address, phone number and age). It's free, but children under 16 are not permitted at sites within 6km of the launch pad and those under eight are not permitted within 12km. You can watch it, reservation-free, with locals at Kourou's beaches or at the **Carapa Observation Site**, 15km west of the city center.

Space junkies will love the free three-hour **tours** (☽ 7:45am & 12:45pm Mon-Thu & 7:45am Fri) at the Space Center, which include a visit to the massive launch pad; phone ahead for reservations and bring your passport. Tour guides sometimes speak English or German; ask when you book.

Don't miss the excellent **Musée de l'Espace** (Space Museum; adult/child €5/3, with tour €7/4; ☽ 8am-6pm Mon-Fri, 2-6pm Sat), with informative displays in English and French. Note that the Space Center is closed on days after a launch.

Sleeping

Kourou has pitifully few inexpensive options. Both of the 'budget' places have reception hours from noon to 2pm and 6pm to 8pm every day. The best beds are at the welcoming **Hotel Ballahou** (☎ 22-0022; http://pagesperso-orange .fr/ballahou; 1-3 Martial; d/apt €45/55; ⚏), within short walking distance of the beaches. It can be tricky to find, but they'll pick you up in town. **Le Gros Bec** (☎ 32-9191; hotel-le grosbec@wanadoo.fr; 56 Rue du Floch; s/d/tr €55.50/63.50/69.50; ⚏), right next to Le Vieux Bourg, has spacious split-level studios with kitchenettes.

Eating & Drinking

Potholed, colorful Le Vieux Bourg, centralized along Av Général de Gaulle, is by far the most eclectic area of Kourou and the best place for cheap and delicious Indian, Creole, Chinese, Moroccan, French cuisine and more. There are also some hopping bars with live music – cruise the street and take your pick.

Outside of Le Vieux Bourg, **Le Glacier des 2 Lacs** (68 Av des Deux Lacs; ☽ 8am-11:30pm Wed-Sun) has sinful ice cream, perfect for Kourou's sunny afternoons, and **La Pizzeria** (38 King; pizzas from €6; ☽ noon-10:30pm) does Italian dishes and pizzas.

Self-catering is easy thanks to the produce **market** (Place de la Condamine; ☽ Tue & Fri) as well as ubiquitous grocery stores.

Getting There & Away

Taxis collectifs run to Cayenne (€8, one hour, 60km) and St Laurent (€30, three hours, 190km); ask at hotels about times and departure locations (they may pick you up). Two rental companies that service both Cayenne and Kourou, **Avis** (☎ 32-5299; 4 Av de France) and **Budget** (☎ 32-4861; ZI Paracaibo), enable one-way jaunts but these include a hefty fee.

AROUND KOUROU

Îles du Salut

Known in English as the Salvation Islands, these were anything but that for prisoners sent here from the French mainland by Emperor Napoleon III and subsequent French governments. The three tiny islands, 15km north of Kourou over choppy, shark-infested waters, were considered escape-proof and particularly appropriate for political prisoners, including Alfred Dreyfus (see boxed text, p698). From 1852 to 1947, some 80,000 prisoners died from disease, inhumane conditions and the guillotine on these sad isles.

THE GUIANAS

Since then, the islands have become a lackadaisical delight – a place to escape *to*. Île Royale, once the administrative headquarters of the penal settlement, has several restored prison buildings, including a restaurant-auberge, while the smaller Île St Joseph, with its eerie solitary-confinement cells and guards' cemetery, has overgrown with coconut palms.

The old **director's house** (☑ 10am-noon & 2:30-4pm Tue-Sun) has an interesting English-language history display; two-hour guided tours of Île Royale (usually in French, free) begin here at 10:30am. Surprisingly abundant wildlife includes green-winged Ara macaws, agoutis, capuchin monkeys and sea turtles. Carry a swimsuit and towel to take advantage of the white-sand beach and shallow swimming holes on St Joseph. The Centre Spatial Guyanais has a huge infrared camera on Île Royale, and the islands are evacuated when there's an eastward launch from the space center.

SLEEPING & EATING
Auberge des Îles du Salut (☎ 32-1100; www.ilesdusalut .com; Île Royale; hammock spaces €10, 'guard rooms' from €60, s/d incl full board €166/235) The welcome hasn't improved much since the days of arriving convicts, but the rooms, in the artfully renovated director's house, are something out of a breezy Bogart film. If you want a more Papillon-like experience, you can stay in simpler rooms in old guards' quarters (some with terraces) or sling a hammock in the prison dormitories

(both cleaned up and freshly painted). Don't leave without having at least one meal (set menu €34) at the restaurant, which serves the best fish soup this side of Provence. There are no cooking facilities, but bringing picnic supplies (and plenty of water – it's not potable on the islands) can keep your costs to a minimum.

It's also possible to camp for free along some of the paradisiacal littoral areas of Îles Royale and St Joseph (but bring mosquito repellent, nets and rain gear).

GETTING THERE & AWAY
Comfortable, fume-free catamarans and sailboats, which provide sunset servings of rum punch, take about 1½ to two hours to reach the islands. Most boats to the islands depart around 8am from Kourou's *ponton des pêcheurs* (fishermen's dock, at the end of Av Général de Gaulle) and return between 4pm and 6pm. Call to reserve 48 to 72 hours in advance, or book with tour operators in Cayenne (see p692) or Kourou (p696). Seafaring options:

Îles du Salut (☎ 32-3381; €39) This festive catamaran ferries up to 100 passengers to Île St Joseph and sails around Île du Diable.

Royal Ti'Punch (☎ 32-0995; €39) Owned by the auberge, this smaller catamaran includes a shuttle to Île St Joseph. Book 72 hours in advance.

Tropic Alizés (☎ 25-1010; €59) This boat leaves from the Nautical Club of Kourou; price includes round-trip transfer to Cayenne.

PAPILLON: ESCAPE ARTIST OR CON MAN?

Of all the prisoners who did hard time on Devil's Island, only Alfred Dreyfus, the Frenchman wrongly convicted of treason in 1894, achieved anything near the fame of Henry Charrière, who became known – or notorious – for his epic tail of nine remarkable escapes from French Guiana's infamous prison camps. Nicknamed Papillon (Butterfly) for a tattoo on his chest, Charrière claims in his autobiography that after being wrongly convicted of murder he escaped from Îles du Salut by floating toward the mainland on a sack full of coconuts and braved harsh malarial jungles to flee eastward. Fashioning himself into an international man of mystery living among native villagers, he eventually became a Venezuelan citizen and was portrayed by Steve McQueen in a Hollywood version of his life.

Although Papillon always claimed his innocence, research has proved otherwise. Paris police reports reveal that 'Papillon' was almost certainly guilty of the murder that incarcerated him, and firsthand accounts from prison guards describe Charrière as a well-behaved convict who worked contentedly on latrine duty.

The real Papillion is now believed to be a Parisian names Charles Brunier, who recently celebrated his 100th birthday. With a butterfly tattoo on his left arm and a documented history of three escapes from the Guiana camps, his story adds up, but time has rendered the truth as stealthy as an escaping convict.

Sinnamary & Around

Sixty kilometers northwest of Kourou, the friendly village of Sinnamary (population 2800) is perched on a picturesque bend in a river of the same name. A small Indonesian community here produces excellent woodwork, jewelry and pottery. At the town hall, you can get information and hire a guide for the 20km **Pripri Yiyi Trail**, which offers fairly easy walking through the bird-filled marshes of Yiyi. To get there yourself, follow the RN1 until Sinnamary, then take the road to Iracoubo for 10km, looking for the trailhead at **La Maison de la Nature** (☎ 34-5709; 🕑 8:30am-1:30pm & 3-6pm Tue, Wed & Fri, to 6.30pm Mon & Thu), which has a permanent exhibition and displays about the marsh ecosystem.

Restaurant-Hôtel Floria (RN1; r €35), at the southeastern entrance to Iracoubo, has authentic Creole cheerfulness and tiny rooms with bright curtains. The grandmotherly Floria serves copious Creole meals for about €15.

Another 30km eastward on the RN1 highway, in the village of Iracoubo, the **Eglise d'Iracoubo**, a 19th-century church with an elaborate altar created by a convict named Huguet, makes for a nice pit stop. If you want to see more, the **Tourism Office** (☎ 44-0316; 80 Pavant) arranges three-hour tours (€1) of the church, a local soap factory and nearby Amerindian villages. Call ahead to reserve a spot.

ST LAURENT DU MARONI
pop 33,700

St Laurent is a dozy place with some of the country's finest colonial architecture and, even 60 years after the penitentiary's closure, it's dominated by penal buildings and the ghosts of its prisoners. Along the banks of the Fleuve Maroni (Marowijne River), bordering Suriname, St Laurent is also a place to take a river trip to Maroon and Amerindian settlements.

Information

EMERGENCIES
Hôpital Franck Joly (☎ 34-1037; 16 Av du Général de Gaulle).

INTERNET ACCESS
Inkprint Cyberglacé (cnr Av Eboué & Hugo; 🕑 9am-noon & 3:30-7pm Mon-Sat, 9:30am-noon Sun) Very centrally located, offering fast and reliable internet connection.

Upgrade Computer (25 Av Eboué; 🕑 8:30am-1pm & 4-7pm Mon-Fri)

MONEY
Banks and ATMs are scattered throughout town.
Cambio COP (23 Montravel; 🕑 8am-noon) Competitive rates for euros.

POST
Post Office (3 Av du Général de Gaulle; 🕑 7:30am-1:30pm Mon-Fri, to 11:45am Sat)

TOURIST INFORMATION
Office du Tourisme (☎ 34-2398; www.97320.com; Esplanade Baudin; 🕑 7:30am-6pm Mon-Fri, 7:45am-12:45pm & 2:45-5:45pm Sat, 9am-1pm Sun; only Sat hr in Jul & Aug) The English-speaking staff give out free maps. They also organize accommodation and Camp de la Transportation and local tours.

TRAVEL AGENCIES
Ouest Voyages (☎ 34-4444; 10 Av Félix Eboué)

Sights & Activities

The eerily quiet **Camp de la Transportation**, where prisoners arrived for processing, was the largest prison in French Guiana. Convicts arrived by boatfuls of 500 to 600 men and it took 20 days to cross the Atlantic. The Tourism Office has a brochure with a map pointing out the tiny cells, leg shackles, dorm-style toilets (known to prisoners as the 'love room') and public execution areas. One cell has Papillon's name engraved near the bed, but whether this was really his cell is up to debate. The Tourism Office also offers 1½-hour **tours** (adult/child/student €5/1/2.50; 🕑 8am, 9:30am, 11am, 3pm & 4:30pm Mon-Sat, 9:30am & 11am Sun); most guides speak some English. There are no 8am tours in July or August.

For canoeing on the Maroni, rent canoes from the **Maroni Club** (☎ 23-5251; Esplanade Baudin; per 2hr €15). **Tropic-Cata** (☎ 34-2518; Esplanade Baudin) offers two-hour (€20) to two-day (€180) boat tours of the Maroni. Or take an Amerindian-led canoe tour with **Agami** (p700) from €30 for a half day.

If you ever wanted to nuzzle with a giant anaconda, here's your chance: **L'Arche de Noé** (Noah's Ark; guided visits adult/child €6.50/3; 🕑 9-11:30am & 2:30-5pm) is a zoo and refuge where more than 100 animals rescued from illegal trafficking have a home. It's 10km south of town on the road to St Jean.

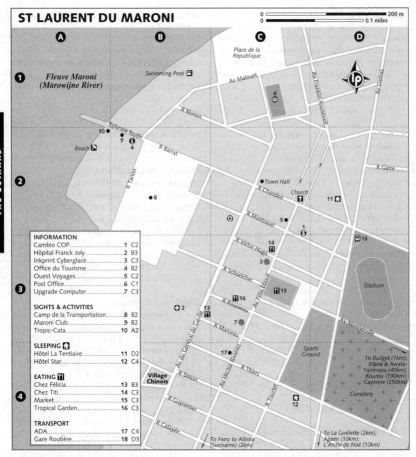

ST LAURENT DU MARONI

INFORMATION
Cambio COP.................................**1** C2
Hôpital Franck Joly.....................**2** B3
Inkprint Cyberglacé....................**3** C3
Office du Tourisme......................**4** B2
Ouest Voyages.............................**5** C3
Post Office...................................**6** C1
Upgrade Computer......................**7** C3

SIGHTS & ACTIVITIES
Camp de la Transportation........**8** B2
Maroni Club.................................**9** B2
Tropic-Cata.................................**10** A2

SLEEPING
Hôtel La Tentiaire.....................**11** D2
Hôtel Star..................................**12** C4

EATING
Chez Félicia...............................**13** B3
Chez Titi....................................**14** C3
Market.......................................**15** C3
Tropical Garden........................**16** C3

TRANSPORT
ADA...**17** C4
Gare Routière...........................**18** D3

Sleeping & Eating

St Laurent has very few hotels; two are in town, and there is cheaper hammock space available further out.

Agami (☎ 34-7403, fax 34-0153; PK 10; hammock spaces with/without hammock €12/7) Dominican Carmen and her husband have traditional Amerindian huts for hammocks in their gardens of grapefruits and bananas. The restaurant serves the best set meal (€13) of traditional Amerindian food found in the Guianas. Reasonably priced canoe tours are also available. Agami is on the road to St Jean.

ourpick Hôtel La Tentiaire (☎ 34-2600; ten tiaire@wanadoo.fr; 12 Av Franklin Roosevelt; s/d/ste €50/60/80; 🖥 🈺) The best in the center, Tentaire has classy rooms with wood accents

in a renovated administrative penitentiary building. Some rooms have balconies looking over the little adjacent park.

Hôtel Star (☎ 34-1084; 26 Thiers; d from €50/65; 🈺 🈺) With its public-high-school decor and mildewy rooms, it's a place to stay only if the Tentaire is full.

Chez Titi (11 Victor Hugo; breakfasts €7, mains & pizzas €9-17; 🕑 6am-10pm Tue-Sat) This rustic cabin-like cafe has full breakfasts and tasty lunches with fresh salads, pizzas and sandwiches.

Tropical Garden (7 Rousseau; pizzas from €9, set meals €13; 🕑 11am-1am) With its nature-meets-funk adornments, great food, a full bar and pool table, this is the most animated place in town.

Chez Félicia (23 Av du Général de Gaulle; mains €10-12) This local favorite has good Creole cuisine that you can eat in or take away.

ourpick **La Goélette** (17 Rue des Amazones, Balate Plage; mains €18-30) Feast on French dishes prepared with local seafood on this antique vessel that was originally bound for Nigeria.

Several small grocery stores and a midsize **market** (Av Felix Eboué; [clock] morning Wed & Sat) provide self-catering options. Market stalls offer filling *bami goreng* (fried noodles; €3) with a side order of satay.

Getting There & Around

St Laurent's wide, colonial streets are perfect for wandering around. Taxis running between the Albina ferry dock and downtown cost about €2.50, or you can walk the whole distance (about 2km).

Taxis collectifs leave when full for Cayenne (€35, four hours, 250km) and Kourou (€30, three hours, 190km) from the *gare routière* at the stadium.

ADA ([phone] 27-9482; 14 Av Hector Rivierez) and **Budget** ([phone] 34-0294; 328, Av Gaston Monnerville) both tack on exorbitant fees for one-way rentals to Cayenne.

AROUND ST LAURENT DU MARONI

Mana & Awala-Yalimopo

About 50km northeast of St Laurent by a potholed road lies the rustic village of Mana (population 600), which boasts a particularly scenic waterfront on the Mana River, considered one of the loveliest and least spoiled rivers in northern South America.

GETTING TO SURINAME

The ferry for Albina, Suriname, **Bac La Gabrielle** (per passenger/car €4/27; 30 min; [clock] 7am & 3pm Mon, Tue, Thu & Fri, 7am & 5:30pm Wed, 8am & 9am Sat, 3:30pm Sun), leaves from the international quay about 2km south of central St Laurent, down Av Eboué. Customs and immigration are housed in white trailers at the quay. Private *pirogues* (dugout canoes; €4, 10 minutes) also leave the quay on demand all day and drop passengers at the Albina ferry dock. Buses and taxis for Paramaribo, Suriname, meet the ferry at the other side. See p715 for more details and for information on travel from Suriname to French Guiana.

There's an ATM at the **post office** (Rue Bastille) in Mana, and the last gas station heading east is at the roundabout at the Mana entrance. There's no other way to get to this area than by car.

Amerindian settlements and ridiculously thick clouds of mosquitoes populate Awala-Yalimopo (population 1200) and **Plage Les Hattes**. The latter is one of the world's most spectacular nesting sites for giant leatherback turtles, which can grow up to 600kg; nesting occurs from April to July, and their eggs hatch between July and September. The number of turtles that come ashore is so high that one biologist has likened the scene to a tank battle.

Maison de la Reserve Natural l'Amana ([phone] 34-8404; adult/child €2/free; [clock] 8am-noon & 2-6pm Mon, Wed & Fri & Sat 2-6pm Tue & Thu) has a little museum, information about turtle biology and two nature trails leading from its premises.

In Mana, cheery French- and Spanish-speaking Isabelle brightens up the otherwise drab **Le Bougainvillier** ([phone] 34-8062; 33 Frères; d with/without bathroom €30/25; [icon]). Awala-Yalimopo lodging includes the Amerindian-style *carbets* just 50m from Les Hattes beach at **Chez Judith & Denis** ([phone] 34-2438; hammock spaces €4), and the similar but larger **L'Auberge de Jeunesse Simili** ([phone] 34-1625; hammock spaces with/without hammock €12/7). Places at both fill quickly during turtle-viewing periods. Reserve a French-Amerindian lunch or dinner at **Yalimalé** ([phone] 34-3432; mains €6-14; [clock] closed Sun dinner & Mon).

Javouhey

pop 1050

Thirteen kilometers off the St Laurent–Mana road, this Hmong village has a delightful Sunday market without the crowds found in Cacao. Buy beautiful Hmong embroidery, sample delicious Laotian food and visit the **Musée Hmong** (Museum of Hmong Culture; [phone] 34-2719; [clock] 8am-6pm Sun), which displays agricultural and musical instruments. The cozy and rustic cabins at **Auberge du Bois Diable** ([phone] 34-1935; dewevre.alain@wanadoo.fr; PK8 Rte de l'Acarouany; s/d €40/60) have large jungle-themed murals. Monkeys and jungle cats, rescued by owner/Mana river specialist Alain Dewevre (aka 'Tarzan'), animate the property. Easy to extreme jungle jaunts can be organized here.

FRENCH GUIANA DIRECTORY

Accommodations

Hotels in French Guiana are generally charmless but comfortable. Cheap hotels start at around €30 for a single, €45 for a double, but can run significantly higher during Carnaval. Most hotels have some English-speaking staff.

The most economical options include long-stay *gîtes* (inquire at tourist offices) in Cayenne, Kourou and St Laurent, and rustic *carbets* for hammocks. It's usually possible to hang a hammock in a *carbet* for €6 and up, and for free in some rural camping areas; many accommodations have hammocks and mosquito nets to rent (from €12).

Activities

Bird-watching, hiking and canoeing are popular in French Guiana. Water sports – windsurfing, kitesurfing and sailing – are a major pastime on beaches at Montjoly (p694) and Kourou (p696), but renting gear is practically impossible. Sport fishing is gaining popularity, especially around Kourou; stop by Guyanespace Voyages (p696).

Books

The best-known book on French Guiana's penal colony is Henri Charrière's autobiographical novel, *Papillon,* which was made into a legendary Hollywood film. Alexander Miles' *Devil's Island: Colony of the Damned* is a factual but very readable account. Ann Fadiman's *The Spirit Catches You and You Fall Down,* though set mostly in California, is the best work explaining the Hmong diaspora.

Business Hours

If you want to accomplish something, get up early. Many businesses close up shop in the heat of the day; generally hours are 8am to noon and 2pm to 5pm, while restaurants tend to serve from noon to 2pm and again from 7pm to 10pm or later. The country stops on Sunday and sometimes Monday, especially in St Laurent. Nightclubs and bars open at around 10pm.

Climate

Expect a soggy trip from January to June, with the heaviest rains occurring in May. The dry season, from July to December, may be the most comfortable time to visit. French Guiana maintains a toasty (average 28°C) and humid climate year round. Travel with light clothing and a poncho. For more information and climate charts, see p987.

Dangers & Annoyances

Rural French Guiana is safe, but the larger towns warrant caution at night. Crime and drug trafficking has increased throughout the country in recent years, and you'll often find customs roadblocks on coastal routes. Both locals and foreigners may be searched.

Locals hitchhike around Cayenne and west toward St Laurent, but it's riskier for travelers, who may be seen as money-laden targets. Never hitch at night or on the road between Régina and St Georges, which is more dangerous and remote.

Electricity

Currents are 220/127V, 50 Hz.

Embassies & Consulates

Brazil (off Map p691; ☎ 29-6010; 444 Chemin St Antoine, Cayenne)
Netherlands (☎ 34-0504; ZI Dégrad des Cannes, Rémire-Montjoly)
Suriname (Map p691; ☎ 30-0461; 3 Av Léopold Héder)
UK (Map p691; ☎ 31-1034; 16 Av Monnerville)

Festivals & Events

Carnaval (January to February or March; dates vary) is a gigantic, colorful occasion, with festivities rocking towns from Epiphany to several solid days of partying before Ash Wednesday. Other fabulous celebrations include the Hmong New Year (usually in December) in Cacao, and Chinese New Year (January or February) in Cayenne.

Food & Drink

Ubiquitous Asian restaurants and food stalls serve delicious and cheap Chinese, Vietnamese, Laotian and Indonesian dishes, including numerous vegetarian delights. Cafes and delis offer tasty meals for a few euros more, and upscale restaurants are rarely less than €10 for a meal.

Most restaurants charge 10% for service; if it's not on the bill, leave between 10 and 15 percent. Eating reviews throughout this chapter are given in order of budget, with the least expensive options first.

Health

Chloroquine-resistant malaria is present in the interior, and French Guiana is considered a yellow fever–infected area. If you need a vaccination while there, contact the **Centre de Prévention et de Vaccination** (off Map p691; ☎ 30-2585; Rue des Pommes Rosas, Cayenne; ⏰ 8:30am-noon Mon & Thu). Typhoid prophylaxis is recommended. Excellent medical care is available, but few doctors speak English. Water is fine in bigger towns; drink bottled or boiled water elsewhere.

See the Health chapter, p1011, for more information.

Holidays

New Year's Day January 1
Ash Wednesday February/March
Good Friday/Easter Monday March/April
Labor Day May 1
Bastille Day July 14
All Saints' Day November 1
All Souls' Day November 2
Armistice (Veterans' Day) November 11
Christmas Day December 25

Internet Access

Internet in the cities is pricey at about €4 per hour.

Internet Resources

Guiana Shield Media Project (www.gsmp.org) Good information on environmental issues (provided in five languages).
Réseau France Outre-Mer (RFO; www.guyane.rfo.fr) Up-to-date news, cultural info, links and more.

Maps

France's Institut Géographique National publishes a 1:500,000 map of French Guiana, with fine city maps of Cayenne and Kourou as well as more detailed maps of the populated coastal areas. Topographic maps (1:25,000) and a variety of tourist maps are available throughout the country.

Media

The *International Herald Tribune* arrives irregularly at local newsstands. *France-Guyane* is Cayenne's daily French-language newspaper, with good local and international coverage. French newspapers and magazines are everywhere.

Money

French Guiana is one of the most expensive regions in South America, in part because it uses the euro and imports many goods from France. It's easy to exchange traveler's checks in US dollars or euros at banks and *cambios*, but for about 5% commission instead of the usual 3% charged for cash.

Credit cards are widely accepted, and you can get Visa or MasterCard cash advances at ATMs *(guichets automatiques)*, which are on the Plus and Cirrus networks. Eurocard and Carte Bleu are also widely accepted.

Exchange rates at press time:

EXCHANGE RATES		
Country	**Unit**	**€**
Australia	A$1	0.60
Canada	C$1	0.62
Japan	¥100	0.75
New Zealand	NZ$1	0.48
UK	UK£1	1.08
USA	US$1	0.70

Post

The postal service is very reliable, although all mail is routed through France. To receive mail in French Guiana, it's best to have the letters addressed to France but using the French Guianese postal code.

Shopping

Elaborate tapestries, produced by the Hmong peoples who emigrated here from Laos in the 1970s, cannot be found elsewhere in South America. They're not cheap and are difficult to find outside Cacao and Javouhey. Maroon carvings and Amerindian crafts tend to be much more expensive here than in Suriname. Other souvenirs include pinned gigantic bugs and stunning butterflies (though it's not recommended to support this industry by buying such products).

Telephone

You can make local and international calls from any pay phone or at 'taxi phone' spots, which are often found in internet cafes; you need a phone card – available at post offices, newsstands and tobacconists – to use public telephones. Internet phone services are a cheaper option and are available at internet

THE GUIANAS

cafes throughout Cayenne. There are no area codes in French Guiana.

Tourist Information

Nearly every city and town in French Guiana has a tourist office of some sort, even if it's just a desk in the local *marché* (market).

Tours

Because public transport is so limited, especially in the interior, tours are the best way to see French Guiana. Operators and their offers are provided in individual town sections.

Visas

Passports are obligatory for all visitors, except those from France. Visitors should also have a yellow-fever vaccination certificate. Australian, New Zealand, Japanese, EU and US nationals, among others, do not need a visa for stays up to 90 days.

Those who need visas (US$80) should apply with two passport photos at a French embassy and be prepared to show an onward or return ticket. Officially, all visitors, even French citizens, should have either onward or return tickets.

See also lonelyplanet.com and its links for up-to-date visa information.

VISAS FOR ONWARD TRAVEL

Visas are required for nationals of many countries entering Brazil (see p375) and Suriname (see p718).

SURINAME

HIGHLIGHTS

- **Galibi Nature Reserve** (p715) Tread lightly on beaches where giant leatherback turtles emerge from the sea and lay their eggs in the sand.
- **Paramaribo** (p708) Stroll along this Unesco-listed capital's historic waterfront and streets lined with stately colonial architecture.
- **Brownsberg & Brokopondo Reservoir** (p714) Marvel at the strange contrast of primate-filled forests surrounding an endless, eerie artificial lake.
- **Best Journey** (p714) Drive 190km through jungle and savanna, then canoe past Amerindian villages to the Raleighvallen, gateway to the Central Suriname Nature Reserve.
- **Off the Beaten Track** (p715) Listen as Amerindian elders regale visitors with ancient tales and share unsurpassed jungle knowledge in the tranquil village of Palumeu.

THE GUIANAS

FAST FACTS

- **Area:** 163,800 sq km (roughly the size of four Netherlands, or the US state of Georgia)
- **Budget:** US$30 to US$40 a day
- **Capital:** Paramaribo
- **Costs:** guesthouse in Paramaribo US$20 to US$30, chicken-and-vegetable roti US$2.50, one-hour minibus ride US$12 to US$15
- **Country code:** ☎ 597
- **Languages:** Dutch, English, Sranan Tongo (Surinaams), Hindi, Urdu, Javanese, Maroon and Amerindian languages, Mandarin, Cantonese
- **Money:** US$1 = SR$2.78 (Suriname dollars)
- **Population:** 475,000
- **Seasons:** high (June to August), rainy (April to July and December to January)
- **Time:** GMT minus three hours

TRAVEL HINTS

At night, take inexpensive taxis to restaurants away from the city center for a more local Paramaribo experience.

OVERLAND ROUTES

Suriname's border crossings include Corriverton (Guyana) and St Laurent (French Guiana).

Suriname, the self-proclaimed 'beating heart of the Amazon,' is just that: a warm, dense convergence of rivers that thumps with the lively rhythm of ethnic diversity. From Paramaribo, the country's effervescent Dutch-colonial capital, to the fathomless jungles of the interior, the descendants of escaped African slaves, Dutch and British colonialists, Indian, Indonesian and Chinese indentured laborers and Amerindians offer a genuine welcome to their tiny country. You get the best of both worlds here: a city that's chock-full of restaurants, shopping venues and night spots and an untamed jungle utterly away from modern development. It's not easy to get around this river-heavy, forest-dense country, and the mix of languages can make it hard to communicate, sometimes even for Dutch speakers. Don't forget that a meeting of culinary traditions means the food here is as spicy and rich as the country itself.

CURRENT EVENTS

In 2007, with the help of a UN tribunal, the long-running border dispute with Guyana over a potentially oil-rich offshore region was finally resolved to all parties' satisfaction.

At the time of research, Desiré Bouterse, the former coup leader and president, was defending himself in court against charges of ordering the killing of 15 opponents in the infamous 1982 'December Murders' in Paramaribo (see below). If found guilty, his planned campaign for the presidency will be over.

HISTORY

Suriname was the last outpost of what was once a substantial Dutch presence in South America. The Netherlands controlled large parts of Brazil and the Guianas until territorial conflicts with Britain and France left them in control of only Dutch Guiana and a few Caribbean islands. During the 19th century, Hindustanis and Indonesians (locally referred to as 'Javanese') arrived as indentured plantation workers.

Despite limited autonomy, Suriname remained a colony until 1954, when the area became a self-governing state; it became independent in 1975. Since then, political developments have been uneven. A coup in 1980, led by Sergeant Major (later Lieutenant Colonel) Desiré Bouterse, brought a military regime to power and was later accused of ordering the execution of 15 prominent opponents in Fort Zeelandia – an event now called the 'December Murders' – in 1982. In 1986 the government carried out a vicious campaign to suppress Maroon rebellion, led by Ronnie Brunswijk and his Jungle Commando (the Maroon military). Many of those loyal to Brunswijk fled to French Guiana as their villages were destroyed.

In 1987 a civilian government was elected, but it was deposed by a bloodless coup in 1990.

Another civilian government led by Ronald Venetiaan was elected in 1991 and signed a peace treaty with the Jungle Commando and other armed bands in 1992.

A series of strikes and demonstrations in 1999 protested economic instability and called for the government to hold elections a year ahead of schedule. Elections were subsequently held in May 2000, and Venetiaan was re-elected; although little changed, the Netherlands stepped up its level of aid into Suriname, helping to stabilize the economy.

Suriname relies on bauxite for 70% of its foreign exchange. Agriculture, particularly irrigated rice cultivation and bananas, is a major industry for the republic, and the fishing industry is growing. The country is also making a conscious effort to develop ecotourism in the interior.

In 2004 the Suriname dollar replaced the faltering guilder, restoring confidence in the economy.

THE CULTURE

Suriname is a cultural free-for-all of incredibly friendly and generous people. Paramaribo's level of acceptance and unity is primarily undisturbed by religious and racial tension, which is remarkable given the intimacy of so many groups living in such a small corner of the world; however, Maroons and Amerindians in the interior live with high poverty levels and fewer educational opportunities, resulting in strong feelings that the government has neglected them.

Many Surinamese live or have lived in the Netherlands, either to enjoy its greater economic opportunities or to escape military repression, and are consequently knowledgeable of European trends. Dutch is the official national language, but many people speak Sranan Tongo (a creole language) and English or both.

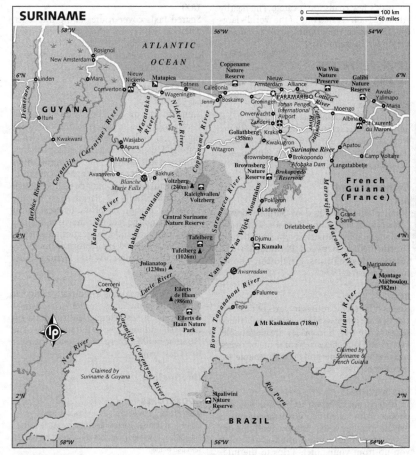

RELIGION

About 40% of the country's well-integrated population is nominally Christian, but some also adhere to traditional African beliefs. Hindus compose 26% of the population (most of the East Indian community), while 19% are Muslim (ethnic Indonesians plus a minority of East Indian origin). A small number are Buddhists, Jews and followers of Amerindian religions.

ARTS

Some cultural forms – such as Indonesian gamelan music, often heard at special events – derive from the immigrant populations. Other art forms that visitors enjoy include intricate Amerindian basketry and wood carvings by Maroons, who are widely regarded as the best carvers in tropical America.

ENVIRONMENT

Suriname is divided into a coastal region and dense tropical forest and savannas. To its west, the Corantijn (Corentyne in Guyana) River forms the border, disputed in its most southerly reaches with Guyana; the Marowijne (Maroni in French Guiana) and Litani Rivers form the border (also disputed in the south) with French Guiana. None of the parties is actively pursuing negotiations about the border disputes, opting instead for détente on the matter.

The majority of Surinamese inhabit the Atlantic coastal plain, where most of the country's few roads are located. The nearby Afobaka Dam created one of the world's largest (1550 sq km) reservoirs, Brokopondo, on the upper Suriname River.

TRANSPORTATION
Getting There & Away
International flights arrive at Suriname's outdated Zanderij airport (see p712).

From Albina (in the east of Suriname, p715) and Nieuw Nickerie, via South Drain (in the west of Suriname, p716), ferries traverse the river borders with French Guiana and Guyana, respectively.

Getting Around
AIR
Small planes, operated by **Surinam Airways** (SLM; www.slm.firm.sr) and **Gum Air** (www.gumair .com), which is mostly a charter airline, shuttle people between Paramaribo and remote destinations, including some nature reserves.

BOAT
Rivers offer scenic routes to parts of the interior that are otherwise inaccessible. Scheduled services are few, and prices are negotiable. Ferries and launches cross some major rivers, such as the Suriname and the Coppename, for very few coins.

BUS & MINIBUS
In order from cheapest to priciest, you can choose from scheduled government buses, private minibuses that leave when full from designated points, and minibuses that pick you up from your hotel. Trips to the interior cost significantly more than those on coastal routes.

CAR
Suriname's roads are limited and difficult to navigate. Passenger cars can handle the roads along the coast and to Brownsberg, but tracks into the interior are for 4WDs only. Driving is on the left. An International Driving Permit is required.

DEPARTURE TAX

Suriname's departure tax is US$20, lumped with the ticket price.

TAXI
Shared taxis cover routes along the coast. They can be several times more expensive than minibuses but are markedly faster. Local cab fares are negotiable and reasonable; set a price before getting in.

PARAMARIBO
pop 220,300

Amsterdam meets the Wild West in Paramaribo, the most vivacious and striking capital in the Guianas. Black-and-white colonial Dutch buildings line grassy squares, wafts of spices escape from Indian roti shops and mingle with car exhaust, Maroon artists sell colorful paintings outside somber Dutch forts. Inhabitants of Paramaribo, locally known as 'Parbo,' are proud of their multi-ethnicity and the fact that they live in a city where mosques and synagogues play happy neighbors. In 2002 the historical inner city was listed as a Unesco World Heritage Site.

Orientation
Parbo's historic core is a compact triangular area whose boundaries are Henk Arronstraat on the north, Zwartenhovenbrugstraat on the west, and the river to the southeast. The Paramaribo–Meerzorg bridge spans the river to its east bank.

Information
BOOKSTORES
Vaco Press (Domineestraat 26; 8am-4:30pm Mon-Fri, to 1pm Sat) Paramaribo's best bookstore sells publications in various languages and also has the best selection of maps.

EMERGENCY
Academisch Ziekenhuis (opposite) is Paramaribo's only hospital that provides emergency services.
Police, fire & rescue (115)

INTERNET ACCESS
Business Center (Kleine Waterstraat; per hr SR$6) Next to Café-Bar 't Vat.
Cyber Café (Kleine Waterstraat; per hr SR$5) Across from the Hotel Torarica.

INTERNET RESOURCES
Welcome to Parbo (www.parbo.com) A useful introduction to Paramaribo and Suriname, maintained by the Suriname Tourism Foundation.

THE GUIANAS

GETTING INTO TOWN

From Johan Pengel International Airport (aka Zanderij), 45km south of Parbo, you can grab a taxi into town (SR$80, one hour). Better yet, have your hotel arrange a cab to meet you. Better yet, have your hotel arrange a cab or minibus from **Le Ashrouf Airport Shuttle** (☎ 45-4451; SR$40); they'll take you directly between the airport and any address in town. Still cheaper minibuses go to and from Zanderij (SR$4) and the Zorg-en-Hoop airfield (SR$2) from Heiligenweg in daytime hours only. A taxi from Zorg-en-Hoop is about SR$20.

MEDICAL SERVICES

Academisch Ziekenhuis (AZ; ☎ 44-2222; Flustraat; 6-10pm Mon-Fri, 9am-10pm Sat & Sun) Has general practitioners who provide excellent care and speak English.

MONEY

You can change money or traveler's checks or get credit-card advances at most major banks, but only RBTT banks have ATMs that accept international cards. You can change US dollars or euros 24 hours a day, with no fees, at the ATM-like **exchange machine** (cnr Sommelsdijckstraat & Kleine Waterstraat), across from the Hotel Torarica.

Centrale Bank van Suriname (Waterkant 20)

RBTT Bank (Kerkplein 1)

POST

Post office (Korte Kerkstraat 1) Opposite the Dutch Reformed Church. Also has internet.

TELEPHONE

TeleSur (Heiligenweg 1) You can make international calls and buy cards for pay phones here.

TOURIST INFORMATION

Tourist Information Center (☎ 47-9200; Waterkant 1; 9am-3:30pm Mon-Fri) The friendly folks here can welcome you in several languages, provide a walking-tour map and guide you in the right direction for almost any kind of activity in Suriname.

Dangers & Annoyances

Avoid quiet streets and secluded areas after dark; the Palmentuin in particular is known for drug dealing and robberies at night. Watch for pickpockets around the market area, even in daylight hours.

Sights

This capital of colonial architecture and lively main streets could fill two days of exploring. Inside well-restored **Fort Zeelandia** (9am-5pm Tue-Sun), a star-shaped 18th-century fort built on the site where the first colonists alighted, is the **Stichting Surinaams Museum** (☎ 42-5871; admission SR$5; 9am-2pm Tue-Sat, 10am-2pm Sun, tours in Dutch 11am & 12:30pm Sun), featuring colonial-era relics, period rooms and temporary exhibitions. Southwest along Waterkant are some of the city's most impressive colonial buildings, mostly merchants' houses built after the fires of 1821 and 1832. The streets inland from here, particularly **Lim-a-Postraat**, have many old wooden buildings, some restored, others in picturesque decay.

Surrounding the centrally located **Onafhankelijkheidsplein** (Independence Square), which features a statue of legendary and portly former prime minister Pengel, are the contrasting stately 18th-century **Presidential Palace** (open to the public November 25 only) and aging colonial government buildings. Behind the palace is the **Palmentuin**, a shady haven of tall royal palms.

The 1885 Roman Catholic **St Petrus en Paulus Kathedral** (Henk Arronstraat), which the Surinamese claim is the world's largest wooden building, was intermittently closed and neglected for decades, but a full restoration of the church was completed in 2009 and it was reopened. The tourism office (left) can arrange tours. Several blocks away are some of the continent's finest examples of other religious buildings – the biggest **mosque** in the Caribbean and the expansive **Neveh Shalom synagogue**, completed in 1723 – sitting harmoniously side by side on Keizerstraat.

Not for the fainthearted, the frenzied **central market** (Waterkant) is divided into distinct areas: the fruits and vegetable section on the main floor and the sprawling Asian and Indian market, selling all the plastic objects and foodstuffs you could ever hope to find, on the second.

Tours

Most of Suriname's exemplary national parks and reserves are accessible via tours with Parbo-based operators. You should shop around, but not too much: prices are competitive, and most of the agencies work together to assemble the minimum number of participants for trips. All charge 5% extra for credit card payments.

Stinasu (Stichting Natuurbehoud Suriname; ☎ 47-6597; www.stinasu.sr; Cornelis Jongbawstraat 14), the Foundation for Nature Conservation in Suriname, donates a percentage of all trip proceeds to nature conservation. It coordi-

nates research and ecotourism expeditions, runs excellent guided trips to Brownsberg (from SR$280), the Galibi and Matapica turtle reserves (from SR$560), and Raleighvallen/ Voltzberg/Foengoe Island (SRD$1450, four days), and helps unguided visitors explore the Central Suriname Nature Reserve more or less independently.

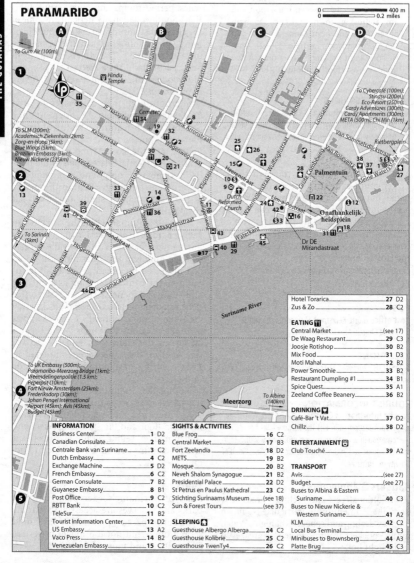

PARAMARIBO

METS (Movement for Eco-Tourism in Suriname; ☎ 47-7088; www.surinamevacations.com; JF Nassylaan 2) is an organized and professional agency that also donates proceeds to conservation and conducts a wide range of trips, including sightseeing tours of Paramaribo (SR$98, half day), nearby plantations (from SR$112) and jungle expeditions to the deep interior (SR$4330, eight days).

Spotting wild river dolphins in the waterways around Paramaribo has become popular. **Waterproof Suriname** (☎ 96-2927; www.waterproofsuriname.com) runs laid-back boat cruises (SR$265) to see them, sometimes combined with walks around the Commewijne River plantations. It also runs day trips from Parbo to see sea turtles at Matapica Beach (SR$560). The company will pick you up; it doesn't have an office.

Blue Frog (☎ 42-0808; www.bluefrog.travel; Mirandastraat 8) handles interior and coastal destinations, sets up volunteer gigs and offers an ISIC card discount. **Cardy Adventures** (☎ 42-2518; www.cardyadventures.com; Cornelis Jongbawstraat 31; ☷ 8am-6:30pm) has bike tours (from SR$140) to the nearby Commewijne plantations as well as longer tours, of up to 10 days, to the interior. **Sun & Forest Tours** (☎ 47-8383; www.sunandforesttours.com; Kleine Waterstraat 1) is another recommended full-service operator.

Sleeping

Guesthouses in Paramaribo are roughly the equivalent of hostels in neighboring countries and are the most inexpensive lodging options in town. Some guesthouses only have cold showers, which is not a big problem in Parbo's hot climate.

Guesthouse TwenTy4 (☎ 42-0751; www.twenty4suriname.com; Jessurunstraat 24; s/d SR$60/120) Owned by the Zus & Zo folks, the TwenTy4 is older and less equipped (no hot water or air-con), but the homey house is on a central, quiet backstreet, and the whole place has a relaxed, welcoming vibe. You can get breakfast (SR$17) and beer and set up your activities with the help of the staff.

Guesthouse Albergo Alberga (☎ 52-0050; www.guesthousealbergoalberga.com; Lim-a-Postraat 13; s/d SR$60/78, d with air-con SR$120; ☷ ☷) This long-running favorite is situated on a quintessentially colonial Parbo street in an endearing World Heritage–listed building. Some rooms are quite spacious, but none have hot water. The little pool out back is great for a dunk after a long day exploring Parbo.

our pick **Zus & Zo** (☎ 52-0905; www.zusenzo.suriname.com; Grote Combéweg 13A; s/d SR$60/120) A backpacker's hostel that can also please slightly more upscale travelers, the bright and inviting Zus & Zo (say it 10 times fast!) has rooms with hot water and air-con in the top floor of a classic, Paramaribo colonial-style house. Use the kitchen to make your own meals or head to the ground-floor cafe for fresh coffee, salads and sandwiches. It sometimes holds music and other artsy events and runs the city's best gift/souvenir shop. The staff can help you arrange almost any excursion in Suriname.

Cardy Apartments (☎ 42-2518; www.cardyadventures.com; Cornelis Jongbawstraat 31; s/d apt from SR$85/148) Already experienced in the tour and bike-rental business, Cardy's now has apartments, which are clean and have kitchenettes and hot water. For longer stays, their weekly and monthly rates are unbeatable.

Guesthouse Kolibrie (☎ 91-9051; www.guesthouse-kolibrie.com; Jessurunstraat 9; r with/without bathroom SR$176/156, apt from SR$126; ☷ ☷) The sprawling, palm-filled yard and breezy patio at the Hummingbird Guesthouse do indeed invite lots of little birds into this centrally located oasis. The decor is unremarkable, but the rooms (which come with breakfast) are big, bright and clean, and the apartments, suitable for longer stays, have fully equipped kitchens.

Eco-Resort (☎ 42-5522; www.ecoresortinn.com; Cornelis Jongbawstraat 16; s/d from SR$247/297; ☷) What makes this modern and professional hotel 'eco' is not clear, but the price includes a buffet breakfast, free airport transfer with a two-night stay and use of the swanky facilities at the Hotel Torarica. The more expensive 'river view' rooms don't really have river views, but they are set closer to the water than the standards.

Hotel Torarica (☎ 47-1500; www.torarica.com; Rietbergplein 1; s/d SR\$392/448; ❄ ▤) Las Vegas meets Suriname at the mirrored and chandeliered Hotel Torarica. It's known for its casino, but the big round pool and waterfront gazebo are pleasant retreats from Parbo's hot and bustling streets.

Eating

Tourists frequent 'the strip' across from Hotel Torarica, which has restaurants to fit all budgets – take your pick of Dutch pancake shops, Indonesian, Creole and others. The cheapest city-center options are at the frenetic **central market** (p709) and Indonesian stalls along Waterkant. **Eating in Suriname** (www.eteninsuriname.com) is a useful website with information on restaurants in Paramaribo.

Zeeland Coffee Beanery (cnr Domineestraat & Steenbakkerijstraat; soups & cakes from SR\$5; ❄ 7am-9pm Sun-Wed, to 11pm Thu-Sat) This local's favorite is situated on a busy street corner and is a wonderful place to watch people on parade while sipping coffee and nibbling sandwiches and pastries.

Power Smoothie (☎ 47-7047; Zwartenhovenbrugstraat 62; mains SR\$9-14; ❄ 8am-9pm Mon-Sat) Fresh and nourishing juices, smoothies (from SR\$7), sandwiches, wraps and salads make this little eat-in or take-away place a great pit stop any time of day.

Moti Mahal (Wagenwegstraat 56-58; roti from SR\$8) Huge portions of tasty roti are served in this hole-in-the-wall shop.

ourpick **Joosje Rotishop** (Zwartenhovenbrugstraat 9; roti from SR\$10; ❄ 8:30am-10pm Mon-Sat) Serving delicious roti since 1942, this is the locals' favorite for a sit-down, air-con meal. There's also a convenient take-out counter.

Restaurant Dumpling #1 (JF Nassylaan 12; mains SR\$10-30; ❄ 7am-2pm & 5-11pm Tue-Sun) The name says it all. Don't miss the succulent dumplings and other Chinese classics, like steamed spare ribs and tofu soup pot.

Chi Min (☎ 41-2155; Cornelis Jongbawstraat 83; mains SR\$12-30; ❄ 11am-11pm) A Parbo favorite just a short taxi ride north of the center, Chi Min's brightly decorated interior has tables fit for a dozen people and a menu with hundreds of Chinese dishes. A take-out counter with the same menu is at street level. Make a booking if you have a large group.

Mix Food (☎ 42-0688; Zeelandiaweg 1; mains SR\$15-22; ❄ Mon-Fri 8am-10pm; Sat 11am-10pm) This quiet, outdoor eatery overlooking the

river dishes out Parbo's best Creole food and has exceptionally friendly service. Try delicious peanut, cassava or banana soup accompanied by roast chicken and *pom*, a kind a casserole.

De Waag Restaurant (☎ 47-4514; Waterkant 5; lunch SR\$15, dinner SR\$35-45; ❄ 9am-3pm & 6-11pm Mon-Sat) This chic restaurant located in an old, renovated weight house from Parbo's shipping heyday serves stacked sandwiches and Italian specialties like lasagna and tortellini. It has live music every Tuesday and Friday evening.

Drinking & Entertainment

The night begins at **Café-Bar 't Vat** (Kleine Waterstraat 1; ❄ 8am-1am Mon-Thu, 8am-3am Fri, 9am-3am Sat, 9am-1am Sun), an outdoor bar/cafe with occasional live music. Around the corner, **Chillz** (Van Rooseveltkade 12; ❄ 5pm-late) invites you to sip cocktails on their boat-size couches on the patio or groove to mellow dance beats in the interior lounge.

Away from the Hotel Torarica area, try **Club Touché** (cnr Waldijkstraat & Dr Sophie Redmondstraat; ❄ 10pm-3am Wed-Sat), where you can dance the night away with techno downstairs and salsa upstairs.

Shopping

Good-quality clothing knockoffs and pirated DVDs (illegal) can be found for exceptionally low prices along Steenbakkerijstraat and Domineestraat. For high-quality Suriname handicrafts and jewelry, head to the gift shop at Zus & Zo (see p711).

Getting There & Away

AIR

There are two airports in Paramaribo: nearby Zorg-en-Hoop (for domestic and

Guyana flights) and the larger Johan Pengel International Airport (for all other international flights) – which is usually referred to as Zanderij – 45km south of Parbo. Noncharter service to Cayenne may also become available in the future; inquire with the airlines listed below.

Blue Wings (☎ 43-0370; www.bluewingairlines.com; Zorg-en-Hoop) Serves Georgetown, Guyana (US$185, three weekly), and domestic destinations.

Gum Air (☎ 49-8760; www.gumair.com; Kwattaweg 254) Charters dozens of domestic flights.

KLM (☎ 47-2421; Dr DE Mirandastraat 9) Services Amsterdam.

META (☎ 47-3162, Mahonylaan 50) Services Georgetown, Guyana (US$155, 50 minutes, two per week), Belém, Brazil (US$200, 2½ hours, three weekly), and Boa Vista, Brazil (US$200, 1½ hours, two weekly).

SLM (☎ 43-2700; www.slm.firm.sr; Dr Sophie Redmondstraat 219) Flies to Raleigh Falls; Belém, Brazil (US$227, two weekly); and Port of Spain, Trinidad (US$202, three weekly).

BUS & MINIBUS

Minibuses to Brownsweg (SR$40, three hours) leave from the corner of Prinsenstraat and Saramacastraat. Public buses to Nieuw Nickerie (SR$12, four hours, 235km) and other western destinations leave throughout the day from the corner of Dr Sophie Redmondstraat and Hofstraat; for a private minibus (SR$45), ask your hotel for a list of companies that will pick you up. To Albina, public buses (SR$8, three hours, 140km) leave hourly and private buses (SR$25, 3½ hours) leave when full from Waterkant at the foot of Heiligenweg. For connecting boat information, see the Albina (p715) and Nieuw Nickerie (p716) sections.

CAR

Both **Avis** (☎ 42-1567; www.avis.com) and **Budget** (☎ 42-4631; www.budgetsuriname.com) have offices at the Hotel Torarica and the airport. Compact cars rent from SR$115 per day, and 4WDs are available.

TAXI

Taxis are a fast but much more expensive option for traveling between the coastal cities. If you have a group (up to four) it can be a great deal. Expect to pay about SR$200 to Albina and SR$300 to Nieuw Nickerie. Ask at your hotel for a list of drivers and/or to call for you.

Getting Around

The Paramaribo–Meerzorg bridge has displaced ferry service, but fast and frequent **water taxis** (per person or bike SR$3) still leave from **Platte Brug** on Waterkant just south of Keizerstraat.

In good Dutch fashion, many people see Parbo and its environs, including the old plantations across the Suriname River, on bicycles. Helmets are rarely worn and are hard to rent. **Cardy Adventures** (☎ 42-2518; www .cardyadventures.com; Cornelis Jongbawstraat 31; ☽ 8am-6:30pm) has reliable road and mountain bikes from SR$14 per day and provides maps of biking routes.

Most of Parbo's buses leave from Heiligenweg. Ask at points of departure or at your guesthouse for departure times.

Taxis are usually reasonably priced but unmetered and negotiable (a short trip will cost around SR$6).

AROUND PARAMARIBO

The rivers and plantations around Parbo offer day trips full of history and wildlife that can be reached by bike or boat (or both).

Commewijne River

Opposite Paramaribo, the banks of the Suriname and Commewijne river are lined with old plantation properties divided by canals and strewn with the remains of coffee, cacao and cane-processing buildings. Many visitors rent a bike to spend a full day touring the well-defined routes past the plantations.

One route crosses the two rivers using water taxis to reach **Frederiksdorp** (☎ 30-5003; d SR$195), a plantation complex that has been lovingly restored and turned into a hotel by the preservation-focused Hagemeyer family. Boat tours also ferry visitors to plantations upriver, stopping at **Fort Nieuw Amsterdam** to see artifacts of the slave trade and an impressive Dutch-engineered system of locks holding back the river. **Peperpot**, about 10km from Parbo, stands in eerie dilapidation across the Meerzorg bridge and is a favorite birdwatchers' locale. Cardy Adventures (see p711) and the Tourist Information Center (see p709) can provide maps and information about the routes.

North of Fort Nieuw Amsterdam, **Matapica** is a tranquil and almost mosquito-free beach where sea turtles come ashore April to August. Tours generally reach it by boating through

THE GUIANAS

DIY AMAZON EXPLORATION

If you and a buddy are up for a real Surinamese adventure, grab your hammock, sunscreen and insect repellant and head up the Suriname River by boat, stopping at small Amerindian and Maroon villages along the way.

Boat schedules don't exist, so pack your patience as well. Many tiny outposts have recently started independent and bare-bones tourists projects ready to accommodate travelers with a hammock hook, and most communities also have a place to buy drinks and someone who will prepare a meal (usually fish) for you. If you don't want to backtrack, several airstrips along the way offer regular connections to Paramaribo, and some tour-agency charters might be able to offer you a seat as well.

A new organization, **Stichting Lodeholders Boven Suriname** (Association of Saramacaan Lodge Holders; www.upper-suriname.com), maintains an online map of villages and lodges that can receive travelers and is an invaluable resource if you want to cut a track into this frontier.

---

the plantation canals and a swamp rich in birdlife. Stinasu (p710) runs a small camp there.

Spotting friendly-faced river **dolphins** along the Commewijne is also popular, and most plantation boat tours will attempt to point them out to passengers when passing through the dolphins' feeding grounds. One-day boat excursions dedicated to dolphin-viewing are also available year-round (see p711).

NATURE PARKS & RESERVES

Suriname's extensive system of protected parks and reserves are its main attraction after Parbo, but independent exploration ranges from difficult to impossible and most people visit with a tour operator (see p709).

Central Suriname Nature Reserve

Any map of Suriname reveals huge swaths of protected areas. One of the biggest, covering 12% of Suriname's land area, is this 1.6-million-hectare reserve, established in 1998 with a US$1 million donation from Conservation International. Forty percent of Central Suriname Nature Reserve's plants and animals are found only in the Guianas.

Raleighvallen (Raleigh Falls) is a long staircase of cascading water on the upper Coppename River, in the heart of Maroon and Amerindian country. Resident wildlife include free-swinging spider monkeys, electric eels and Guiana Cock-of-the-Rock, a spectacular blood-orange bird with crested plumage like a Trojan warrior's helmet. Stinasu (p710) has tourist lodges – accessible by a flight or a five-hour drive and two-hour boat ride – on Foengoe Island next to

the falls. Voltzberg is a 240m granite dome accessible by a 2½-hour jungle trail and then a steep ascent.

Brownsberg Nature Reserve & Brokopondo

Brownsberg's park headquarters are located on a high plateau overlooking Brokopondo lake, about 100km from Paramaribo along a red-dirt highway. The plateau is about 500m higher than the surrounding area and has noticeably different flora and fauna. Monkeys seem to be everywhere, whether they are red howlers growling in the canopy or precious black-bearded sakis checking you out from a tree limb. Stinasu (p710) has lodges (from SR$350) for groups, and camping (SR$42) and hammock sites (SR$30) at the headquarters.

Brokopondo lake is really a man-made reservoir, created in 1964 when the government dammed the Suriname River to produce hydroelectric power for processing bauxite. Views of storm clouds moving in over the 1500-sq-km lake are breathtaking, but a closer look reveals a rainforest graveyard, in which dead trees stick up over the water's surface from what was once the forest floor. The park has interesting displays explaining how the dam project required relocating thousands of mostly Maroon and Amerindian people as well as hundreds of thousands of animals.

A 45-minute motorboat ride across Brokopondo's stump-riddled waters brings you to the small island of Tonka, which has a rustic ecotourism project run by the Saramaccan Maroons. For details contact Stinasu (p710).

It's relatively easy to visit Brownsberg on your own: minibuses run from the corner of Prinsenstraat and Saramacastraat in Paramaribo to the Maroon village of Brownswerg (SR$40, three hours). From here, arrange for Stinasu to pick you up and drive you to the park (SR$50, 30 minutes); several Parbo-based tour agencies also do Brownsberg as a (very) long day trip (see p709).

Galibi & Coppename Nature Reserves

Galibi's turtle-nesting area hosts hordes of sea turtles, including the giant leatherback, during egg-laying season (April through August). You can get there from Albina with permission from members of the local Carib community and a hired canoe, or more easily from Paramaribo with Stinasu.

The Coppename wetland reserve, at the mouth of the Coppename River, is home to the endangered manatee and is a haven for birdwatchers. Stinasu organizes trips by request.

Palumeu
pop 300

On the banks of the Boven Tapanahoni River, this tranquil Amerindian village welcomes visitors in the hope of creating a sustainable future outside the logging and hunting industries. It's possible to brave rapids over eight to 12 days to reach this area by river from Albina, or take the one-hour flight from Paramaribo over pristine jungle. Accommodations (booked through METS or Stinasu; see p709) are in basic but comfortable Amerindian-style huts lit by kerosene lanterns.

NIEUW NICKERIE
pop 13,100

This bustling border town of wide streets was once a major *balata* (natural rubber) collecting center, although now it's mostly a banana and rice production hub with a large port. It's also the last stop before Guyana and the departure point for exploring Bigi Pan, a swampy reservoir known for caimans, scarlet ibis and more than 100 other birds; all the hotels charge SR$140 for a day tour to the area.

Make phone calls and check internet at the **TeleSur Office** (Kanaalstraat 3; 7am-10pm Mon-Sat) and use the ATM at the **RBTT Bank** next door.

Both the **Concord Hotel** (23-2345; Wilhelminastraat 3; d SR$105;) and **Sea Breeze** (21-2111; Meimastraat 34; d SR$95;) are small and clean motel-style establishments. The **Residence Inn** (21-0950; Bharosstraat 84; www.resinn.com; s/d SR$165/199;) is a comfortable but rather predictable chain hotel which provides friendly service.

Melissa's Halal Food (Concord Hotel; mains SR$7-8) serves copious Indian dishes in an air-con dining room.

All buses and minibuses arrive at and leave from the market. Government buses travel to Paramaribo (SR$12, four hours) at 6am and 1pm daily, and a private bus (SR$20) leaves when full after the first government bus leaves. Taxis to Paramaribo (SR$300) take three to four hours. Minibuses to South Drain (SR$14) for the ferry to Guyana leave at 8am, and it's best to reserve with the driver the day before; your hotel can help with this.

GETTING TO FRENCH GUIANA

Destroyed during the Maroon rebellion of the 1980s and still recovering, **Albina** (population 4000) is the last stop before crossing the Marowijne River to St Laurent du Maroni, French Guiana. Some travelers pass through here on tours to the Galibi Reserve to see turtles, but there's little reason to stay. If you're stuck, try the **Creek Guesthouse** (34-2031, d SR$75), a clean place whose owners speak English and can probably find a guide to the turtle beaches.

Minibuses (SR$25, 2½ hours) and public buses (SR$10, three hours) to Paramaribo leave from central Albina. **Benito Taxi** (0864-2174; SR$200) will drop you at your guesthouse in Paramaribo.

The French **ferry** (per passenger/car SR$12/95 or €4/26; 8am & 5pm Mon-Fri, 8:30am & 9:30am Sat, 3pm & 4pm Sun) crosses the Marowijne River from Albina to St Laurent du Maroni, French Guiana, in 30 minutes; from there, *taxis collectifs* go to Cayenne (p701). **Motorboats** (per person SR$12 or €4) leave from the Albina ferry dock for the crossing (10 minutes) during daylight hours. Get your exit and entrance stamps at Immigration at the ferry docks on both sides of the river. For information on travel in the opposite direction, see p701.

GETTING TO GUYANA

From Nieuw Nickerie it's a bumpy 1½-hour ride to South Drain to catch the Canawaima ferry (SR$28, 25 minutes, 11am daily) across the Corantijn River to Moleson Creek, Guyana. After getting stamped in and passing a customs check in Guyana, you'll find several minibuses to Corriverton (G$400, 20 minutes) and Georgetown (G$2000, three hours).

If the road between Nieuw Nickerie and South Drain is impassable (because of rain), you can follow the locals and 'do the backtrack,' which is technically illegal and involves crossing the Corentyne on small motorboats to Springlands, Guyana. Your hotel or your driver from Parbo will know the road situation and can help you get to the backtrack launch if necessary. You can stamp in at the police station near the Springlands dock. Corriverton/Georgetown-bound buses meet arriving backtrackers.

Guyana is an hour behind Suriname; remember to set your watch *back* one hour.

An easy way to get directly to Georgetown from Paramaribo is through **Bobby Minibus** (☎ 49-8583, 0874-3897; SR$80) or **Johhny's Bus & Taxi** (☎ 0865-2080, 0880-5210), which leave Paramaribo at between 4am and 5am to meet the ferry in South Drain; the journey takes nine to 12 hours, depending on the roads. For information on travel in the opposite direction, see p728.

SURINAME DIRECTORY

Accommodations

Fairly affordable hotels and guesthouses are readily found in Paramaribo starting at SR$60, while sleeping in the interior can involve more rustic accommodations that are also more expensive. Nights can be hot and buggy; your mosquito net will be your friend.

Suriname's 'high season' is July to August, but prices only inflate slightly, if at all. Tour operators sometimes actually offer discounts during December, January and high season.

Activities

Suriname's best activity is experiencing nature in the interior. Bird-watching and other wildlife-spotting adventures are once-in-a-lifetime experiences, and boating and trekking opportunities are abundant. People explore by bike, but only in areas around the coastal cities.

Books

The most popular book on Suriname is Mark Plotkin's *Tales of a Shaman's Apprentice*, which also includes information on Brazil, Venezuela and the other Guianas. *The Guide to Suriname* by Els Schellekens and famous local photographer Roy Tjin is published in English and sometimes available at Vaco Press (p708). *How Dear Was the Sugar?* by Cynthia McLeod, perhaps Suriname's most important historical novelist, explores the sugarcane industry of the 18th century.

Business Hours

General business hours are 7:30am to 3pm weekdays, with perhaps a few hours on Saturday. Most restaurants serve lunch from around 11am to 2:30pm and dinner from about 6pm to 10pm. A small number of places open for breakfast at 8am.

Opening hours are not listed in reviews unless they vary widely from these.

Climate

The major rainy season is from late April to July, with a shorter one in December and January. Suriname's dry seasons – February to late April and August to early December – are the best times for a visit. For more details and climate charts, see p987.

Dangers & Annoyances

Some urban areas, such as markets, are subject to petty crime (mainly pickpockets); ask locally for places to avoid. Unlike in the other two Guianas, theft in the interior has been increasing and traveling alone is not advised.

Electricity

Currents are 110/220V, 60Hz.

Embassies & Consulates

The embassies and consulates listed below are all in Paramaribo (Map p710).
Brazil (☎ 40-0200; Maratakkastraat 2, Zorg-en-Hoop)
Canada (☎ 47-1222; Wagenwegstraat 50)
France (☎ 47-6455; Henk Arronstraat 5-7, 2nd fl)
Germany (☎ 47-1150; Domineestraat 34-36)
Guyana (☎ 477895; Henk Arronstraat 82)

Netherlands (☎ 47-7211; Van Roseveltkade 5)
UK (☎ 40-2870; VSH United Bldg, Van't Hogerhuysstraat 9-11)
USA (☎ 47-2900; Dr Sophie Redmondstraat 129) Also responsible for US citizens in French Guiana.
Venezuela (☎ 47-5401; Henk Arronstraat 23-25)

Food & Drink

Surinamese cooking reflects the nation's ethnic diversity and is often superb. Many varieties of Asian cuisine – Chinese, Indonesian, Indian and even Korean – make Suriname a relative paradise for vegetarians. The cheapest eateries are *warungs* (Javanese food stalls). Creole cooking mixes African and Amerindian elements. Menus are often in English and prices often quoted in US dollars or euros.

Parbo, the local beer, is quite good; it's customary to share a *djogo* (1L bottle) among friends. Borgoe and Black Cat are the best local rums.

Most restaurants charge 10% for service; if it's not on the bill, leave between 10 and 15 percent. Eating reviews throughout this chapter are given in order of budget, with the least expensive options first.

Health

A yellow-fever vaccination certificate is required for travelers arriving from infected areas. Typhoid and chloroquine-resistant malaria are present in the interior. Tap water is safe to drink in Paramaribo but not elsewhere. See the Health chapter, p1011 for more information.

Holidays

New Year's Day January 1; the biggest celebration of the year.
Day of the Revolution February 25
Holi Phagwah (Hindu New Year) March/April
Good Friday/Easter Monday March/April
Labor Day May 1
National Union Day/Abolition of Slavery Day July 1
Independence Day November 25
Christmas Day December 25
Boxing Day December 26
Eid-ul-Fitr (Lebaran or Bodo in Indonesian) End of Ramadan; dates vary.

Internet Access

Parbo and Nieuw Nickerie have affordable (around SR$5 to SR$6 per hour) internet cafes. Major hotels offer internet access to guests with laptops (for a fee).

Internet Resources

Surinam.Net (www.surinam.net) Info, links, live radio and forums.
Suriname Tourism Foundation (www.suriname-tourism.org) Helpful information about tourist services and what to see in Suriname.

Maps

Vaco Press (p708) and the Hotel Torarica (p712) gift shop in Paramaribo stock the excellent, current Hebri BV *toeristenkaart* (€10).

Media

Two Dutch-language dailies, *De Ware Tijd* and *De Wes*, and the *Suriname Weekly*, published in both English and Dutch, deliver the news.

TV and radio stations broadcast in Dutch, Sranan Tongo, English, Hindustani and Javanese.

Money

Although the official unit of currency is the Surinamese dollar (SR$), some businesses quote prices in euros or US dollars. Most banks will accept major foreign currencies, but you may run into difficulty trying to change Guyanese dollars and Brazilian reales.

Exchange traveler's checks and get credit card advances at RBTT banks and some hotels. Only RBTT ATMs accept foreign cards, and major hotels and travel agencies – but hardly anywhere else – accept credit cards (usually for a fee).

Locals are always changing money, and many get fair rates without a transaction fee at the ATM-like **exchange machine** (cnr Sommelsdijckstraat & Kleine Waterstraat) in Paramaribo (see p709).

Exchange rates at the time of writing:

EXCHANGE RATES		
Country	**Unit**	**SR$**
Australia	A$1	2.52
Canada	C$1	2.68
euro zone	€1	4.11
Japan	¥100	3.09
New Zealand	NZ$1	2.04
UK	UK£1	4.38
USA	US$1	2.78

THE GUIANAS

Post

Postal services in Paramaribo are reliable but may be less so in other parts of Suriname.

Shopping

Maroon handicrafts, especially tribal wood-carvings, are stunning and cheaper in Suriname than in Guyana or French Guiana. Amerindian and Javanese crafts are also attractive. The commercial center along and around Domineestraat in Paramaribo is the best place to shop.

Telephone

The national telephone company is TeleSur (Telecommunicatiebedrijf Suriname). Local and international calls, including reverse-charge (collect) calls, can be made from yellow public telephone booths with prepaid phone cards purchased from a TeleSur office. There are no area codes in Suriname.

Tourist Information

The Tourist Information Center in Paramaribo has everything to get you started.

Tours

Suriname's interior is best experienced if going with a professional tour company. See p709 for a few of the 30-something operators that specialize in nature and sociocultural (visiting Amerindian or Maroon villages) activities.

Tour prices include meals, accommodations, transport and guides. Most trips require a four-person minimum, so try to make arrangements as early as possible.

Visas

Passports are obligatory. Citizens from many countries do not require a visa, but visitors from the US, UK, Australia, Canada, New Zealand and Western Europe do. Anyone traveling to Suriname should check the visa requirements (www.surinameembassy.org) for updates. US passport holders must pay US$100 for a five-year multiple-entry visa, while all other nationalities requiring a visa have to pay from US$30 to US$175, depending on the length of stay and number of entries.

For a visa, contact Suriname's nearest overseas representation and allow approximately four weeks for a postal application. Consulates in Georgetown (Guyana) and Cayenne (French Guiana) can issue visas within a couple of hours or days. Bring a passport-size photo and your ticket out of South America.

Visitors planning to stay in Suriname for more than 30 days should register at the **Vreemdelingenpolitie** (off Map p710; Immigration Service; ☎ 40-3609; Laachmonstraat; 7am-2pm Mon-Fri) in Paramaribo within eight days of their arrival.

See also lonelyplanet.com and its links for up-to-date visa information.

Women Travelers

Female travelers, especially if traveling alone, will find local males verbally aggressive, but rarely physically threatening. Constant 'hissing' and 'sucking' noises can be annoying, if not truly disconcerting – ignoring them usually helps.

GUYANA

HIGHLIGHTS

- **Kaieteur Falls** (p728) Watch your step as you stand on the ledge of the world's highest single-drop fall, deep in the Amazon jungle.
- **Iwokrama** (p730) See the future of ecotourism in this successful reserve that ensures Amerindian cultural survival while protecting the forest's rich diversity.
- **Rupununi Savannas** (p731) Live out your safari dreams alongside some of the last thriving populations of giant river otters and black caimans.
- **Best Journey** (p728) Pass through rice-farming villages and cross rivers teeming with wildlife on the long journey from Parika to Mabaruma (Shell Beach).
- **Off the Beaten Track** Go on a cattle drive with local *vaqueros* (cowboys) in the remote Kanuku Mountains (p731).

THE GUIANAS

FAST FACTS

- **Area:** 215,000 sq km (about the size of the UK)
- **Budget:** US$40 to US$50 a day
- **Capital:** Georgetown
- **Costs:** guesthouse bed US$30, delicious pepper pot US$3, Georgetown taxi ride US$0.25 per kilometer
- **Country code:** ☎ 592
- **Languages:** English, Creole, Hindi, Urdu, Amerindian
- **Money:** US$1 = G$200 (Guyanese dollars)
- **Population:** 765,000
- **Seasons:** high (June to September), low (September to May), rainy (November to April)
- **Time:** GMT minus four hours

TRAVEL HINTS

Bring plenty of long-sleeve, lightweight clothing and mosquito repellent for the malaria-ridden interior.

OVERLAND ROUTES

Guyana's border crossings are Nieuw Nickerie (Suriname) and Bonfim (Brazil).

Described by its own tourism association as 'Conradian' and 'raw,' Guyana is a densely forested country with a troubled history of political instability and interethnic tension. Underneath the headlines of corruption and economic mismanagement, however, is a joyful and motivated mix of people who are turning Guyana into one of the continent's premier ecotourism destinations. Georgetown, the country's crumbling colonial capital, is distinctly Caribbean with a rocking nightlife, great places to eat and an edgy market; the interior of the country is more Amazonian with its Amerindian communities and unparalleled wildlife-viewing opportunities tucked quietly away from the capital's hoopla.

CURRENT EVENTS

With the help of a UN tribunal, the long-running border dispute with Suriname over a potentially oil-rich offshore region was finally resolved to all parties' satisfaction in 2007. Both nations' presidents generously proclaimed this resolution to be the beginning of a new period of friendly relations between Guyana and Suriname.

After years of talks and financing deals, the Takutu bridge, connecting Lethem in southern Guyana with Brazil, was completed in 2008; now the question remains of who will pave the road connecting Lethem to Georgetown, and when.

HISTORY

Both Carib and Arawak tribes inhabited the land that is now Guyana before the Dutch arrived in the late 16th century. Running a plantation economy dependent on African slaves, the Dutch faced a widespread rebellion, known as the Berbice Slave Revolt, in 1763. The rebel leader, Kofi, remains a national hero despite the ultimate failure of the slaves to gain their freedom.

The British took control in 1796, and in 1831 the three colonial settlements of Essequibo, Demerara and Berbice merged to become British Guiana. After the abolition of slavery in 1834, Africans refused to work on the plantations for wages, and many established their own villages in the bush and became known as Maroons. Plantations closed or consolidated because of the labor shortage, but the sugar industry was resurrected with the help of imported, indentured labor from Portugal, India, China and other countries, drastically transforming the nation's demographic and laying the groundwork for fractious racial politics that continue to be a problem today.

British Guiana was run very much as a colony until 1953, when a new constitution provided for home rule and an elected government. In 1966 the country became an independent member of the British Commonwealth with the new name, Guyana,

---

TRAGEDY AT JONESTOWN

On November 18, 1978, 913 people (including over 270 children) were killed in a mass suicide-murder in a remote corner of Guyana's northwestern rainforest. Since then, Guyana has been sadly associated with this horrific event that became known as the Jonestown Massacre.

In the 1950s Jim Jones, a charismatic American leader, started a religious congregation in Indiana called the Peoples Temple. With utopian ideas of an egalitarian agricultural community, Jones attracted hundreds of followers, but by the 1960s, after moving his church to San Francisco, he became increasingly paranoid and the Peoples Temple started to resemble a cult. Jones' next move took the congregation to the Guyanese bush, and by 1977 word leaked from escaped members that Jones was running the settlement more like a French Guiana prison camp. California congressperson Leo Ryan, along with journalists and worried family members, visited Jonestown, where they encountered several frightened Temple members who wanted to leave. Not realizing how dangerous Jones really was, Ryan tried to take several residents with him, only to meet gunfire from Jones' followers on the Jonestown airstrip. Ryan and four others were killed. That night Jones ordered his followers to drink cyanide-laced punch; while many 'drank the Kool-Aid,' others were found shot or with slit throats. Jones either shot himself or ordered someone to do it.

Director Stanley Nelson has provided a modern perspective on this mysterious tragedy in his excellent 2006 documentary *Jonestown: The Life and Death of Peoples Temple*.

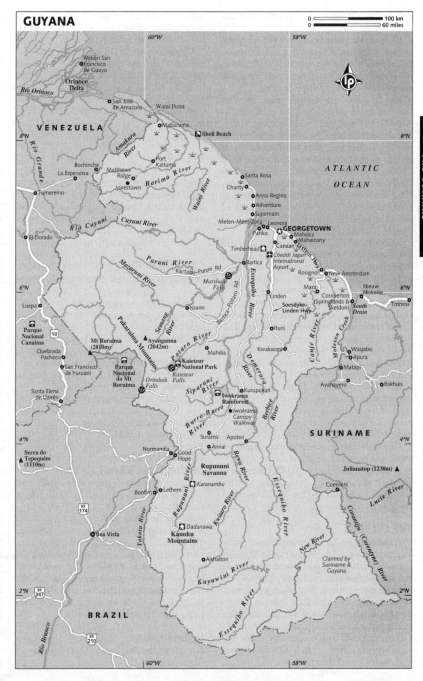

GUYANA

THE GUIANAS

and in 1970 it became a republic with an elected president.

Only a few years later, in 1978, Guyana attracted the world's attention with the mass suicide-murder of more than 900 members of American Jim Jones' expatriate religious community of Jonestown (see p720).

For decades after independence, most of the important posts had been occupied by Afro-Guyanese, but more recently Indo-Guyanese have been appointed to influential positions, fueling racial tensions between groups of African and East Indian descent. Cheddi Jagan, Guyana's first elected president, died in office in 1997 and was replaced by his US-born wife Janet, resulting in continued political tension. In 1999 Janet Jagan retired from the presidency on health grounds and named Bharrat Jagdeo her successor.

Elections scheduled for January 2001 were delayed until March 2001 because of election irregularities. This move antagonized voters in an already racially charged campaign, and entire blocks of Georgetown were set ablaze by opposition supporters as the ruling PPP/Civic (led by an Indo-Guyanese majority) was declared victor of a third consecutive term. The police and protestors clashed in the capital for weeks. Fortunately, violence on this scale has not returned to Georgetown since 2001, but racial tensions continue to be a part of Guyanese politics and daily life; however, new efforts at tolerance education have made a positive impact on Guyanese youth, and many people acknowledge that more cooperation to end racial conflict is needed.

Guyana's economy relies on commodities exports, especially bauxite but also gold, sugar, rice, timber and shrimp. Indo-Guyanese control most of the small business, while the Afro-Guyanese have, until the late '90s, dominated the government sector.

THE CULTURE

Guyana's culture is a reflection of its colonialist plantation past. African slaves lived under severe conditions that destroyed much – but not all – of their culture. East Indian laborers arrived under better circumstances and managed to keep much of their heritage intact. The main groups of Amerindians, who reside in scattered interior settlements – Arawak, Carib, Makushi and Wapishana – still live significantly off the land. Ethnic tension and distrust rack contemporary Guyanese

society, which is also increasingly distrustful of Brazilians, who are perceived to want access to Guyana's natural resources.

Guyana's population is 765,000, but some 500,000 Guyanese also live abroad, mostly in Canada, the UK, the USA and Trinidad. This imbalance leads many people to believe that more Guyanese live outside of the country than inside, but the numbers don't bear this out; still, Guyana is concerned, and probably justifiably so, about 'brain drain.'

RELIGION

Most Afro-Guyanese are Christian, usually Anglican, but a handful are Muslim. The Indo-Guyanese population is mostly Hindu, with a sizable Muslim minority, but Hindu-Muslim friction is uncommon. Since independence, efforts have been made to recognize all relevant religions in national holidays.

ENVIRONMENT

Guyana is swarming with rivers, including its three principal waterways (listed east to west): the Berbice, Demerara and Essequibo. The narrow strip of coastal lowland (with almost no sandy beaches) is 460km long and comprises 4% of the total land area but is home to 90% of the population. The Dutch, using a system of drainage canals and seawalls, reclaimed much of the marshy coastal land from the Atlantic and made it available for agriculture.

Tropical rainforest covers most of the interior, though southwestern Guyana features extensive savannas between the Rupununi River and the Brazil border.

TRANSPORTATION
Getting There & Away

Travelers flying to Guyana arrive at Cheddi Jagan International Airport (p727), south of the capital.

In the far south of Guyana, via Lethem, a new bridge connects Guyana with Boa Vista, Brazil. In the northeast, a ferry connects Corriverton (Springlands) via Moleson Creek to Suriname (p728). The only crossing between Venezuela and Guyana is the remote, difficult and dangerous road between Bochinche and Mabaruma; you're better off going through Brazil.

Getting Around

For more details about traveling around Guyana, see p727.

THE GUIANAS

DEPARTURE TAX

Outbound passengers pay a departure tax of US$20 (payable in US dollars).

AIR

Charter air services to interior destinations such as Annai, Kaieteur and Iwokrama, are available from the Ogle Aerodome in Georgetown (see p727).

BOAT

Regular ferry service crosses the Essequibo between Charity and Bartica, with a stop at Parika (reached by paved highway from Georgetown). A ferry also crosses from Rosignol to New Amsterdam, along the Eastern Hwy on the way to the Suriname border, but a new bridge also crosses the river and may completely displace ferry service in the near future. More-frequent speedboats (river taxis) carry passengers from Parika to Bartica.

BUS & MINIBUS

Cheap local buses (which are actually privately owned minibuses with regulated fares) speed between points all over Georgetown. Minibuses travel the highways connecting Georgetown with coastal and interior towns and cities. A large bus travels the highway between Georgetown and Lethem, stopping at points in between.

CAR

Rental cars are available in Georgetown, though not from the airport at the time of writing. An International Driving Permit is recommended and is required for car rental.

TAXIS

Many taxi companies travel between Georgetown and coastal destinations, although they cost significantly more than buses and minibuses. They can be a good value for a group.

GEORGETOWN

pop 240,000

Georgetown's older residents love to reminisce about the capital's glamorous bygone era, striking a nostalgic note about a time when children played in the streets past dark and the colonial-era buildings shined as if they were built yesterday. Although the glory days may be over, Georgetown's easy-to-navigate streets, dilapidated architecture and unkempt parks still offer a laid-back feel amidst real-life chaos, and seeking out the city's riches – historic monuments, a thriving intellectual scene and fabulous restaurants – behind its hard-boiled exterior is part of the adventure.

In 2007 Georgetown hosted the semifinals of the Cricket World Cup, an event that dramatically changed the tourist infrastructure of the country by introducing new hotels, sport facilities, and organizations and companies catering to tourists.

Orientation

Georgetown sits on the east bank of the Demerara River, where the river empties into the Atlantic. A long seawall prevents flooding, and a Dutch canal system drains the town, which is actually seven feet below sea level.

Georgetown is divided into several districts: Kingston (in the northwest); Cummingsburg, Alberttown, Queenstown and Newtown (in the center); Robbstown, Lacytown, Stabroek and Bourda (south of Church St); Werk-en-Rust, Wortmanville, Charlestown and Le Repentir (further south); Thomas Lands (east); and Kitty (further east).

Information

BOOKSTORES

Austin's Book Services (190 Church St; ⏰ 8am–4pm Mon-Fri, to 1pm Sat) Offers the widest selection of books and maps.

EMERGENCY

Ambulance (☎ 913)
Fire (☎ 912)
Police (☎ 911)

GETTING INTO TOWN

Bus 42 (G$400, one hour) services Cheddi Jagan International Airport to/from the Timeri Bus Park behind the Parliament Building in central Georgetown; the bus is safe enough, but at night a taxi (G$4000; may be shared) is a much wiser choice. For early-morning flights from Jagan, make taxi arrangements the day before.

THE GUIANAS

GEORGETOWN

INFORMATION
Austin's Book Services....................**1** C3
Brazilian Embassy..........................**2** E4
Canadian High Commission...........**3** B1
DHL...**4** E3
Guyana Telephone &
  Telegraph...................................**5** D1
Lapateries Cambio.........................**6** B2
Ministry of Home Affairs................**7** B4
Oasis Café......................................**8** B2
Post Internet..................................**9** B2
Post Office....................................**10** B3
Scotiabank....................................**11** B3
Scotiabank....................................**12** B2

St Joseph's Mercy Hospital...........**13** C1
Surinamese Embassy......................**14** E3
Tourism & Hospitality
  Association of Guyana................**15** C2
UK High Commission.....................**16** B2
UPS...**17** C4
US Embassy...................................**18** C1
Venezuelan Embassy......................**19** C3

SIGHTS & ACTIVITIES
Iwokrama Office............................**20** B1
Museum of Guyana.......................**21** B2
National Library.............................**22** B3
Parliament Building........................**23** B4
Rainforest Tours............................**24** B3
Shell Beach Adventures.................**25** B1
St George's Cathedral....................**26** B3
Stabroek Market............................**27** B4
State House...................................**28** B2
Town Hall......................................**29** B3

Walter Roth Museum of
  Anthropology.............................**30** B2
Wilderness Explorers.....................**31** B2
Wonderland Tours.........................**32** B3
Zoo...**33** E4

SLEEPING
Cara Lodge...................................**34** C3
Florentene's Hotel.........................**35** C3
Hotel Ariantze...............................**36** C3
Rima Guest House.........................**37** B2
Sleep' In..**38** D3
YWCA..**39** B4

EATING
Brasil Churrascaria &
  Pizzaria......................................**40** C4
Coal Pot.......................................**41** B3
House of Flavors............................**42** C4
New Thriving.................................**43** B3
Oasis Café.............................(see 8)
Shanta's.......................................**44** C2

DRINKING
Celina's Atlantic Resort.................**45** F1
Club Latino..........................(see 25)
Sidewalk Café & Jazz Club....(see 36)

SHOPPING
Hibiscus Craft Plaza......................**46** B3
Shell Beach Adventures........(see 25)

TRANSPORT
Budget..**47** D3
Delta Airlines.................................**48** B3
Intraserve Bus Office.....................**49** B3
Jerrie's..**50** C3
META..**51** C3
Minibuses to Airport.....................**52** B4
Minibuses to Parika,
  Rosignol & Corriverton...............**53** B4
Roraima Airways............................**54** E4
Timeri Bus Park.....................(see 52)

INTERNET ACCESS

Internet access in Georgetown costs about G$600 per hour; wi-fi is increasingly available and generally free.

Oasis Café (125 Carmichael St; ⏰ 8am-8pm Mon-Fri, 10am-4pm Sat) Has two terminals and wi-fi.

Post Internet (cnr Lamaha & Carmichael Sts; per hr G$200; ⏰ 8am-6pm Mon-Fri, to 1pm Sat) The cheapest but slowest internet in town.

MEDICAL SERVICES

St Joseph's Mercy Hospital (☎ 227-2072; 130-132 Parade St) This private clinic and hospital has a 24-hour emergency room and pharmacy.

MONEY

Laparties Cambio (34 Water St; ⏰ 8am-5pm Mon-Fri) At the back of Fogarty's grocery store, this safe place has the best rates in town.

Scotiabank (104 Carmichael St; ⏰ 8am-6pm Mon-Fri) Accepts international ATM cards, processes credit card advances and cashes traveler's checks. A second branch sits at the corner of Robb St and Ave of the Republic.

POST

Post Office (☎ 225-7071; Robb St) This central postal hub can be hectic.

TELEPHONE

Guyana Telephone & Telegraph (GT&T; cnr Church St & Ave of the Republic; ⏰ 7am-10pm)

TOURIST INFORMATION

Tourism & Hospitality Association of Guyana (THAG; ☎ 225-0807; 157 Waterloo St; ⏰ 8am-5pm Mon-Fri) Publishes the useful *Explore Guyana* guide and has maps and pamphlets.

Dangers & Annoyances

Although Georgetown has more crime than the other Guianese capitals, you can safely explore the city by using a good dose of precaution: be aware of your surroundings, don't wear jewelry or expensive-looking clothes or carry more cash than you need when walking. Also, you should avoid deserted streets, especially on the weekends, and use taxis, which are inexpensive, to get around at night.

Sights

The best 19th-century buildings are along Main St and especially along Ave of the Republic, just east of the Demerara River.

The most impressive building in town is the Anglican, Gothic-style **St George's Cathedral** (North Rd), said to be the world's tallest wooden building. It was completed in 1892 and was built with a native hardwood called greenheart. Further south, on Charlotte St, is the distinctive neo-Gothic **Town Hall** (1868), with its 75ft tower where colonial-period wives apparently watched for their husbands' ships to come into port. At the south end of Ave of the Republic is the well-kept **Parliament Building** (1834). The nearby landmark, **Stabroek Market** (Water St), a cast-iron building with a corrugated-iron clock tower, dates back to the late 1700s, although the current structure was built in 1880.

Andrew Carnegie built the **National Library** (cnr Ave of the Republic & Church St) in 1909; three blocks north stands the heavily louvered **State House** (cnr Main & New Market Sts), which is now the president's residence.

The **Museum of Guyana** (cnr North Rd & Hincks St; ⏰ 8am-4pm) is an old-fashioned institution documenting the nation's cultural, social and political history. Anyone interested in Amerindian cultures will find the **Walter Roth Museum of Anthropology** (61 Main St; ⏰ 8am-2pm) interesting for its artifacts and photos; be sure to check out the paintings of Guyana's nine indigenous tribes.

Worth the short ride away from the center, the **Roy Geddes Steel Pan Museum** (190 Roxanne Burnhan Gardens; ⏰ 2-5pm) displays the history and fabrication of the steel pan and has recordings of its hypnotic music. The internationally known pioneer of steel pan, Roy himself, welcomes visitors with personal tours. It's hard to find, so take a taxi.

Many bird-watching groups visit Georgetown's **botanical gardens** (Regent Rd) as an introduction to Guyana's birdlife. The garden's **zoo** (www.guyanazoo.org.gy; cnr Regent & Vlissengen Rds; adult/child G$200/100; ⏰ 7:30am-5:30pm) has a large collection of fascinating creatures kept in troublingly small and neglected cages. Check out the manatees swimming in the zoo canal, offering remarkably close glimpses of these shy creatures.

During daylight hours, the **Promenade Garden** in Cummingsburg is a quiet place to relax, read and enjoy the flowers.

Tours

Guyana is one to watch on the South American ecotourism scene, thanks to increased investment by the government to promote sustainable travel. Although it's possible to visit the interior of Guyana independently, some of the best ecotourism opportunities – such as Iwokrama and Santa Mission – require a local guide.

Annette at **Shell Beach Adventures** (☎ 225-4483; www.sbadventures.com; Le Meridien Pegasus Hotel, Seawall Rd) has an infectious enthusiasm for sea turtles, Amerindian cultures and rainforest preservation and runs some of the country's best tours. She arranges eco/socio-friendly three-day trips (G$120,000) along the coast to observe sea turtles during egg-laying season (March/April to August) or adventurous jaunts to the interior. Frank Singh's **Rainforest Tours** (☎ 227-2011; www.rftours.com; Hotel Tower, 74 Main St) arranges an adventurous five-day overland journey to Kaieteur Falls (G$110,000). **Wilderness Explorers** (☎ 227-7698; www.wilderness-explorers.com; Cara Suites, 176 Middle St) specializes in longer, customized trips to the Rupununi Savannas and Iwokrama. **Wonderland Tours** (☎ 225-3122; www.wonderlandtoursgy.com; 85 Quamina St) offers bargains on day trips to the Essequibo River, including Santa Mission (G$16,000).

Sleeping

YWCA (☎ 226-5610; 106 Brickdam St; dm G$2000) Georgetown's cheapest option has 50 dorm beds for both men and women. You don't get much more than you pay for, but it's in the heart of Georgetown and secure.

Florentene's Hotel (☎ 226-2283; 3 North Rd; d G$3000) If you don't mind the rust-stained sinks and dusty wood floors, this is a friendly, albeit crumbling, place to stay.

our pick **Rima Guest House** (☎ 225-7401; rima@networksgy.com; 92 Middle St; s/d/tr G$5500/6500/9000) This backpackers' favorite is a family-run place with giant rooms and shared bathrooms in a large colonial house. The owners are friendly and helpful.

Sleep' In (☎ 231-7667; www.sleepinguesthouse.com; 151 Church St; d with/without air-con G$9300/7000; ✱) Offering 'total convenience,' the Sleep' In is indeed centrally located, and all the rooms have hot water and wi-fi – a cut above most guesthouses in this price range.

Hotel Ariantze (☎ 226-5363; www.ariantzesidewalk.com; 176 Middle St; s/d incl breakfast G$12,800/14,000; ✱) This boutique-style hotel has colonial architecture, big, bright windows and helpful staff. All the rooms have free wi-fi, and credit cards are accepted for a 5% service fee.

Kanuku Suites (☎ 226-4001; www.kanukusuites.com; 123 Section M, Campbellville, s/d G$13,920/16,240) This tall baby-blue hotel, situated on a quiet street just east of the center, takes pride in offering all the mod-cons, from cable TV to wi-fi. It has a good seafood restaurant, and the folks here can help you set up tours to the interior.

Cara Lodge (☎ 225-5301; www.carahotels.com; 294 Quamina St; s/d G$22,500/25,600; ✱ ▯) Something about the gingerbread details and art-adorned corridors make this feel like a hideaway for glamorous film stars. There's an old-fashioned ballroom, a patio bar around a 100-year-old mango tree, and a classy, rich-and-famous-worthy restaurant downstairs. Ask for a standard room, which are actually nicer than the higher-priced rooms.

Eating

Some of the best food in the Guianas can be had for a few coins in Georgetown. *Snackettes* are small eateries that serve inexpensive small meals (you usually order at the counter and the food is brought to your table), and grocery stores and markets all over town offer self-catering options.

House of Flavors (177 Charlotte St; light meals G$200; ⌚ 6am-9pm Mon-Sat, to 4pm Sun) Serving only one dish – home-cooked rice, beans, veggies, and mango *achar* (spicy pickled condiment) – in a calabash, this Rastafarian (and vegetarian) restaurants doubles as a music store and caters to long lines of diners, many with impressive dreadlocks.

our pick **Shanta's** (225 Camp St; light meals from G$400; ⌚ 8am-6pm) For more than a half century, Shanta's has been filling Georgetown's bellies with the best roti, curries and *chokas* (roasted vegetables) this side of India. It's unbelievably inexpensive for how delicious it is. Try everything.

Coal Pot (Carmichael St; meals G$400-1000) This local Creole favorite serves stewed meats and fish over rice. Lines can be long at lunch.

Oasis Café (125 Carmichael St; www.oasiscafegy.com; snacks & sandwiches G$400-1000; ⌚ 7:30am-6:30pm Mon-Thu, 7:30am-8:30pm Fri, 9am-9:30pm Sat, 10am-6pm Sun) With real coffee, a lunchtime salad/entree bar (G$2000), rich desserts and internet, this place really is an oasis. Try the 'bake and saltfish' (fried bread with salted cod) for breakfast.

New Thriving (cnr Main & Hope Sts; mains G$800-2000; ⌚ 10:30am-9:30pm) The new luxurious branch, once described as 'Buckingham Palace meets Taj Mahal,' of Georgetown's best Chinese restaurant also serves Thai and sushi. Dim sum is the main attraction on Sundays.

Brasil Churrascaria & Pizzaria (208 Alexander St; mains G$1000-2200; ⏰ 11am-9pm Mon-Sat) With so many immigrants from its neighbor to the south, Georgetown has great Brazilian restaurants. This one has a salad bar, grilled meats and great pizzas.

Drinking & Entertainment
East of Newtown, Sheriff St is a raucous parade of bars, discos and nightclubs with an equally raucous clientele plying the streets; it might be the party you're looking for, but it's not Georgetown's safest strip. The party gets rolling about 10pm and goes until dawn. The DJ at the tamer **Club Latino** (Seawall Rd), in the faded Le Meriden Pegasus Hotel, spins Latin beats on the weekend; during the week the vibe is quieter. The oddly named **Celina's Atlantic Resort** (Seawall Rd) is just a bar, but it's in an open-air *benab* (traditional open-air structure) looking over the water. The **Sidewalk Café and Jazz Club** (176 Middle St) at the Hotel Ariantze is an ambient place for a drink any night or live jazz Thursday nights.

Shopping
You can find local handicrafts at the kiosks in **Hibiscus Craft Plaza**, in front of the post office. The **Shell Beach Adventures** (Seawall Rd) office at Le Meridien Pegasus Hotel sells organic chocolate, *casareep* (Amerindian cassava sauce), and crabtree-oil products.

Getting There & Away
AIR
International flights arrive and depart from Cheddi Jagan International Airport 41km south of Georgetown, and domestic flights run out of Ogle Aerodrome closer to town, to the east. Flights to Cayenne, French Guiana, may become available in the near future; check with the airlines. Airlines serving Georgetown and sample fares:

Delta Airlines (☎ 225-7800; www.delta.com; 126 Carmichael St) Flies nonstop to New York (US$900, 6½ hours, four weekly).
META (☎ 225-5315; cnr Middle & Thomas Sts) Serves Boa Vista, Brazil (US$195, one hour, three weekly), and Paramaribo, Suriname (US$155, 50 minutes, two weekly).
Roraima Airways (☎ 225-9648; www.roraimaairways .com; R8 Eping Ave, Bel Air Park) Flies to Paramaribo, Suriname (US$185, 50 minutes, three weekly), and Lethem & Annai (US$110, 1½ hours, three weekly).
Trans Guyana Airways (TGA; ☎ 222-2525; www .transguyana.com; Ogle Aerodome) Operates small planes into the interior, including Kaieteur (US$125, one hour, three weekly) and Lethem & Annai (US$110, 1½ hours, daily).

BUS & MINIBUS
Direct minibuses to Parika (bus 32; G$400, one hour), Corriverton (bus 63, G$1600, five to six hours) and Rosignol (bus 50; G$800, 2½ hours) leave from Stabroek Market. At Parika, you can make boat connections to Bartica (G$2000, one hour); at Rosignol, you can taxi across the new floating bridge or catch the ferry to New Amsterdam (G$70, 20 minutes). These have no fixed schedules and leave when full.

Intraserve (☎ 226-0605, 159 Charlotte St) buses and minibuses head south to destinations in the interior and to Lethem. See p730 for more information.

Getting Around
Budget (☎ 225-5595; 75 Church St) rents cars (G$10,000 per day, three-day minimum), but with bad roads full of farm animals and crazy driving, you may as well leave the driving to others.

For simplicity and safety, taxis are *the* way to get around central Georgetown; trips around the center are G$300 or so. Have your hotel call a reliable cab company or identify a taxi rank near the hotels. All registered taxi license plates start with an 'H.'

BERBICE
The Eastern Hwy follows the coastal plain from Georgetown to the Suriname border. The road travels through town after unremarkable town, passing potholes, suicidal dogs, unfenced livestock and the resultant roadkill. At **Rosignol**, about two hours' drive from Georgetown, you can cross the Berbice River to **New Amsterdam** via a new floating bridge or the massive, antique ferry (G$70, 20 minutes). Minibuses meet the ferry to take passengers to **Corriverton** (G$600, two hours).

The whole coastal region stretching from Rosignal to Corriverton is collectively known as Berbice, and Corriverton is actually the two small towns of **Springlands** and **Skeldon**, on the west bank of the Corentyne River, bordering Suriname.

Corriverton's main street, Public Rd, is a lively strip with mosques, churches, a Hindu temple, cheap hotels, eateries and bars. Brahman cattle roam round the market like the sacred cows of India. If you need to stay the night, try the friendly **Hotel Malinmar** (☎ 335-3328; 13 Public Rd; r from G$5000), with rooms looking over the river; you can eat at **Faheeda's Halal** (147 Public Rd; mains G$600-800; ☺ 9am-9pm), which overlooks the main drag.

Although most travelers speed through Berbice, the little towns do have hidden (although run-down) colonial buildings. The quintessential Berbice activity, however, is taking a ride in a Tapir, the only car ever to be manufactured in Guyana. Named after one of the most awkward and lethargic animals in the wild, these boxy cars are proudly decorated by their owners and used as taxis to ferry passengers through and between the towns.

Buses and Tapirs run from Public Rd in Corriverton to New Amsterdam and, the other way, to the Suriname ferry at Moleson Creek (G$600, 20 minutes). Be sure to depart Corriverton before 10am to reach the ferry.

NORTHWEST COAST

About 20km west of Georgetown, the coastal highway passes Meten-Meer-Zorg, where you'll find the **Guyana Heritage Museum and Toucan Inn** (☎ 275-0028; 17 Meeten-meer-Zorg; admission G$100; ☺ 7:30am-5:30pm). Owner Gary Serrao and his eclectic collection of historical artifacts and maps dating to the 17th century make for a fascinating dip into Guyanese history. Also on site is an inn (rooms with/without air-con G$5000/3000); take a dip in the pool and enjoy the rooftop views of the Essequibo rushing into the Atlantic.

Further west along the coastal highway, boats travel from **Parika** southward to the lively mining town of **Bartica** (population 11,100). Near Bartica, the Essequibo meets the Mazaruni River and **Marshall Falls**, a series of rapids and a jungle waterfall reached

by a short hike. One of the more interesting places to stay in this area is **Timberhead** (☎ 233-5108; www.timberheadguyana.com; 810 Providence, East Bank Demerara; all inclusive per person G$30,000), a small resort on Pokerero Creek with traditional thatched-roof cabins; from here you can easily access the Amerindian village of **Santa Mission**, a favorite destination for Guyanese who want to appreciate Carib and Arawak customs, such as making cassava bread. Tour operators offer day trips to all of the above places from Georgetown (see p725).

The west bank of the Essequibo River can be reached by boat from **Parika** to **Supernam**. Heading west from the Essequibo, a coastal road passes quaint rice-mill and farming villages to the town of **Charity**, about 50km away. From here you'll need a boat to go further – through bird-filled rivers, mangrove swamps and savannas – to **Shell Beach**, which extends for about 140km along the coast toward the Venezuelan border and is a nesting site for four of Guyana's eight sea turtle species. This is one of the least developed areas of the entire South American coastline; the only human alterations are in the form of temporary fishing huts and small Amerindian settlements. **Waini Point** near the beautiful town of **Mabaruma** (population 700) is the most spectacular sighting area for the scarlet ibis. Georgetown agencies can help you set up a tour through the area or arrange a flight or boat directly to Mabaruma (see p726).

THE INTERIOR
Kaieteur National Park

This area is home to one of the world's most impressive waterfalls (see boxed text opposite), a tiny population of Amerindians and the endless biodiversity of the Guiana Shield, a massive geological formation covered in rainforest

---

GETTING TO SURINAME

The Canawaima ferry to Suriname (G$2000, 25 minutes, 12:30pm daily) leaves from Moleson Creek and crosses the Corentyne River to the Surinamese border at South Drain, 1½ hours south of Nieuw Nickerie. Get to the ferry no later than 11am to stamp passports and go through customs control. Minibuses to Nieuw Nickerie and Paramaribo meet the ferry on the Suriname side. It's best to change your Guyanese currency before leaving Guyana in case no one's buying across the river. Make sure you know your rates before you make the exchange.

For direct minibus service to Paramaribo from Georgetown, call **Brian Minibus** (☎ 218-4460) or **Bobby Taxi Bus** (☎ 234-1456, 226-8668). Both pick up around 5am.

Suriname is an hour ahead of Guyana; remember to set your watch *ahead* one hour.

For information on travel in the opposite direction, see p716.

SPLURGE!

You may have been to Salto Angel or Cataratas do Iguaçu, seen Niagara or not even be particularly interested in waterfalls; it doesn't matter, go to **Kaieteur Falls** (www.kaieteurpark.gov.gy). Watching 30,000 gallons of water shooting over a 250m cliff (allegedly making this the world's highest single-drop falls) in the middle of a misty, ancient jungle without another tourist in sight is a once-in-a-lifetime experience. The brave can actually stand at the top of the falls and gaze over the precipice. Depending on the season, the falls are from 76m to 122m wide. Swifts nest under behind the falls and dart in and out of the waters around sunset each night. The trail approaching the falls is home to scarlet red Guiana Cock-of-the-Rock birds and miniscule golden frogs that produce a poison 160,000 times more potent than cocaine.

Although the low-carbon, eight-day overland journey to Kaieteur is available through Rainforest Tours (p726) in Georgetown, most folks take advantage of day trips in small planes (about G$55,000) offered by Georgetown tour operators; make early inquiries and be flexible, since the flights go only when a full load of five to eight passengers can be arranged (usually on weekends).

and savanna. It has, however, been subject to the strategies of government and mining interests to limit its boundaries since it first became a park in 1929; after several expansions and contractions, it now encompasses 62,700 hectares and is actively protected by the government – largely because the park's tourism potential depends on it being intact.

It's possible to stay in a rustic **lodge** (per person G$3600) at Kaieteur Falls. **Air Services Ltd** (☎ 222-4357; www.airservicesltd.com; Ogle Aerodrome, Georgetown) books the lodge and flights and helps with organizing food (weight limits make it difficult to bring your own). If you have the time, take the challenging but spectacular and more environmentally responsible overland route to Kaieteur with Rainforest Tours; it takes around five days (see p726).

Iwokrama Rainforest

The **Iwokrama Centre for Rainforest Conservation and Development**, established in 1996, is a unique living laboratory for tropical forest management and socioeconomic development for Amerindians. Amidst 371,000 hectares of virgin rainforest, this exceptional region is home to the world's highest recorded number of fish and bat species, South America's largest cat (jaguar), the world's largest freshwater fish (arapaima), and the world's largest otters, river turtles, anteaters, snakes, rodents, eagles and caimans.

Unlike a national park, Iwokrama is not funded by the government and must therefore take a realistic approach to economic survival without overexploiting resources. The community practices highly selective tree felling while studying sustainable logging techniques; the profits from the timber are used to help finance ecotourism work and biological research. Amerindian peoples inhabit parts of the forest and are encouraged to work with ecotourism projects, to become park rangers, harvest tropical aquarium fish and create cottage industries. Everyone involved in Iwokrama, from the director to the field-center cook to the inhabitants of the surrounding villages, beams with hope and pride for the center's projects that is truly inspirational.

Iwokrama's Georgetown **office** (☎ 225-1504; www.iwokrama.org; 77 High St) arranges transportation and accommodations; stay in riverside, eco-chic cabins or a more economical hammock camp at the **field station** (cabins s/d with full board G$39,760/50,000, hammocks with full board G$12,000). A two-day tour (about G$55,000 all inclusive, per person, depending on group size) includes visits to Amerindian villages, forest walks and nighttime caiman-spotting. Independent visits should be organized through the Georgetown office in advance.

Only 60km south of the of the field station and worthy of a day trip, Iwokrama's new **canopy walkway** (www.iwokramacanopywalkway.com; day pass G$3600), a series of suspension bridges hoisted 30m above the forest floor, offers literally bird's-eye views of native greenheart trees, high-dwelling red howler monkeys and lots of birds. To be ready for the early morning canopy action, sleep at **Atta Rainforest Camp** (hammocks with full board, guide and all fees G$18,000), which is 500m from the canopy walkway.

For information on getting to sights within Iwokrama, see the boxed text 'Do-It-Yourself Transportation' on p730.

THE GUIANAS

DO-IT-YOURSELF TRANSPORTATION

The bigger lodges and ranches offer overland 4WD and boat transportation, but the cost of fuel in the Rupununi can make these options prohibitively expensive. Sample one-way fares for a jeep for four people are: Annai to Lethem (G$46,000), Annai to Karanambu (G$72,000) and Lethem to Dadanawa (G$40,000). Traveling in groups can ease the sticker shock.

If you are not in a group, flying is your best option. Roraima and TGA (see p727) fly from Georgetown to Lethem, Annai and Karanambu (all from G$22,000 one way).

With a little patience and planning, you can also reach the Rupununi's main ports of call (Iwokrama, Annai, Lethem) on the cheaper Intraserve bus, a safe 40-seater bus that travels from Georgetown to Lethem by night (G$10,000, daily during dry season, no service Monday, Wednesday and Saturday during wet season, 12 to 18 hours), and in reverse by day. Note that you'll still need to arrange pickup from lodges, such as Karanambu and Dadanawa. Reserve your seat at the **Intraserve office** (☎ 226-0605, 159 Charlotte St) at least a day before departure; the bus fills quickly and can be canceled or delayed during the wet season. It leaves from **Jerrie's** (cnr Middle & Waterloo Sts), where you can stock up on food and water for the trip. Check in at 7pm for the 9pm departure. Going the other way, Intraserve leaves from the **Lethem ticket office** (☎ 772-2202), across from the airstrip, at 11am. The long voyage involves a ferry crossing and several police checkpoints; bring warm clothes, your passport and patience.

Intraserve books shorter distances – for example, Georgetown to Annai (G$8000) or Canopy Walkway to Annai (G$2000) – but you must reserve in advance. You can also catch minibuses that leave daily from the market (G$8320, 12 to 18 hours), but the ride will be bumpier and they're less safe than the Intraserve.

For information on hitchhiking in the Rupununi, see Dangers & Annoyances, p732.

Surama
pop 300

In case you are generally afraid of 'native-watching' experiences, the small Makushi village of **Surama** (www.wilderness-explorers.com/surama_village.htm; huts with full board & activities per person from G$25,600) will surprise you by its dignified approach to tourism and proud self-sufficiency. Local guides lead visitors through the village to learn about daily life, including cassava processing and medicinal plant usage, and the school often prepares a warm-hearted welcome of singing and dancing for village visitors. You can also climb nearby Surama Mountain (230m) for panoramic views of the savannah and Pakaraima range or float down the Burro Burro River in dugouts. Reserve through Iwokrama or Wilderness Explorers (p726), who can also arrange less expensive itineraries that allow you to camp at Carahaa Landing Camp, about 5km from the village on the river's edge.

For information on getting to Surama, check oute the boxed text 'Do-It-Yourself Transportation,' above. You can arrange Intraserve bus service – although you may have to wait a day or two – or private transportation to Surama at the Oasis Service Center or Rock View Lodge in Annai (right).

The North Rupununi

The Rupununi savannas are Africa-like plains scattered with Amerindian villages, small 'islands' of jungle (remnants of life before the last ice age) and an exceptional diversity of wildlife. Rivers full of huge caimans and the world's largest water lilies (*Victoria amazonica*) cut through plains of golden grasses and termite mounds, and a mind-boggling array of birds fly across the sky. On a human level, the Rupununi feels like a tight-knit, small town spread over 104,400 sq km, and you'd be hard-pressed to find a safer place in South America.

The heart of the north Rupununi is at **Annai** (population 300), a crossroads of Amerindian peoples with a police station and an airstrip. Colin Edwards runs the **Oasis Service Center**, where you can get breakfast (G$700) or Brazilian BBQ (G$1200), have a drink or set yourself up in a *benab* (hammock spaces with/without hammock G$2000/1000) or camp (G$1000). Edwards also owns **Rock View Lodge** (☎ 226-5412; www.rockviewlodge.com; s/d with full board G$28,000/44,000; ☒), an elegantly rustic hacienda-style retreat at the Annai airstrip; guests might share their rooms with hummingbirds that flit in and out the windows. Both establishments arrange walks and visits to several nearby Makushi villages.

About 60km south by rugged road and boat (a short trek by Rupununi standards) you'll find yourself in the middle of a real-life Jane Goodall–like experience at **Karanambu Ranch** (s/d incl meals & activities G$40,000/72,000). Diane McTurk is an extraordinary character who has devoted her life to saving the giant river otter. A few otter orphans animate the ranch, as does Diane, who is easily just as interesting. Accommodations are in ranch-meets-Amerindian-style huts with spacious and well-equipped attached bathrooms. The ranch arranges activities – from bird-watching to giant anteater tracking – in this area of unparalleled beauty.

The isolated ranch-lodges don't have phones but can be reserved through Wilderness Explorers (p726). Getting anywhere off the dirt highway passing through the Rupununi is outrageously expensive, and you still have to arrange in advance for someone from the lodges to pick you up at the highway. For information on getting around the Rupununi on your own (and for less), see the boxed text 'Do-It-Yourself Transportation,' opposite.

The South Rupununi

The biggest settlement in the Rupununi is much further south at **Lethem** (population 2500), a cowboy town right on the Brazilian border. The region attracts a collection of eccentric characters fanatical about wildlife, conservation and living life to the fullest. The surrounding area is home to Guyana's *vaqueros*, and every Easter, the Rupununi Rodeo in Lethem attracts hundreds of visitors to see the usual rodeo spectacles with a distinctly Rupununi/Amerindian touch. Local waterfalls and a cooperative cashew-processing plant are interesting year-round attractions.

Don and Shirley's shop (☎ 772-2085, ⏰ 8am-11pm daily) at Lethem's airstrip is the best place to get information about the local attractions, guides and other points of interest in the area. On a hill looking over town, **Regional Guest House** (☎ 772-2020; d from G$5000; 🔀), which also has a terrific restaurant, has nice wood-accented, well-ventilated rooms and a veranda with views of Lethem and beyond. In town, try the **Cacique Guest House** (☎ 772-2083; d from G$4400; 🔀), which has small, clean rooms with fans.

The nearby **Kanuku Mountains** – 'Kanuku' means 'rich forest' in the Makushi language – harbor an extraordinary diversity of wildlife. Seventy percent of Guyana's bird species reside here. Duane and Sandy's remote **Dadanawa Ranch** (www.dadanawaranch.com; cabins per person incl meals G$24,000), at the base of the Kanukus, is straight out of National Geographic. Extreme treks – tracking harpy eagles, jaguars and the recently rediscovered red siskin finch – complement days partaking in ranch work and or even riding on a cattle drive to Lethem.

For information on getting to south Rupununi sites, see the boxed text 'Do-It-Yourself Transportation,' opposite; for traveling to Brazil, see below.

GUYANA DIRECTORY
Accommodations

In Georgetown, the cheapest hotels often double as 'love inns,' which locals use by the hour – so be careful of questionably low rates. Modest hotels that are clean, secure and comfortable charge G$2000 to G$8000; better accommodations, with air-con, usually start at G$10,000. Rainforest lodges and savanna ranches are more expensive (G$18,000).

THE GUIANAS

GETTING TO BRAZIL

A new Brazilian-built bridge – with a cool lane-crossing system that switches from Guyana's left-hand driving to Brazil's right-hand driving – straddles the Takutu River from Lethem on Guyana's side to Bonfim, Brazil, on the other. Stamp out of customs and immigration on the Guyana side of the bridge and stamp into the corresponding office on the Brazil end. You can catch a cab in Lethem (G$600) if one is around, or just walk across the bridge (about 500m). From the Bonfim bus terminal you can catch Amatur buses to Boa Vista, where planes and buses connect to further destinations. Note that American, Canadian and Australian nationals need visas (available in Georgetown; see p375 for more information on visas for Brazil), and all need yellow-fever vaccinations, as well. Money changers abound – you can't miss 'em. For information on traveling from Brazil to Guyana, see p363.

Activities

The interior and coastal areas offer countless possibilities, from river rafting, trekking and bird-watching to wildlife-viewing and fishing. Community tourism is growing, particularly in the Rupununi. Most folks arrange adventures through Georgetown's tour agencies, but independent travel is increasing.

Books

Evelyn Waugh described a rugged trip from Georgetown across the Rupununi Savanna in *Ninety-Two Days*. Find Shiva Naipaul's moving account of the Jonestown tragedy (p363) in *Journey to Nowhere: A New World Tragedy*, published in the UK as *Black and White*. Oonya Kempadoo's *Buxton Spice* is a sexually charged account about growing up in Guyana in the 1970s. The bird-watchers' bible is *Birds of Venezuela* by Steven L Hilty.

Business Hours

Commerce awakens around 8:30am and tends to last until 4pm or so. Saturdays are half days if shops open at all, and Georgetown becomes a ghost town on Sundays. Restaurants generally serve lunch from about 11:30am to 3pm and dinner from around 6:30pm to 10pm.

Climate

Guyana has two distinct rainy seasons – May to mid-August and mid-November to mid-January – although downpours can occur even in the 'dry' seasons. August through October are the hottest months.

The best time to visit Guyana may be at the end of either rainy season, when the discharge of water over Kaieteur Falls is greatest.

For more information and climate charts, see p987.

Dangers & Annoyances

Although Guyana's interior is tranquil and safe, Georgetown is well known for crime. This reputation may be exaggerated, but a good dose of caution and common sense is warranted (see also p725). In urban areas, avoid potentially hazardous situations and flashing expensive items and jewelry, and be aware of others on the street. Steer clear of the Seawall at night – except on Sunday evening, when everyone comes out to socialize – and ask at your hotel about current dangers and places to avoid.

From Cheddi Jagan International Airport, use only registered airport taxis and drivers with official IDs (attached to their shirt pockets). Do not let yourself be separated from your luggage or backpack.

Hitchhiking is highly discouraged – the threat of robbery and physical danger is very real. An exception to this rule is the Rupununi, where thumbing is more common, but usually from a ferry or other transit point – better not to be left stranded out on the long, lonely highway.

Electricity

Currents are 127V, 60Hz.

Embassies & Consulates

The following embassies and consulates are in Georgetown (Map p724).

Brazil (☎ 225-7970; 308-309 Church St)
Canada (☎ 227-2081; cnr High & Young Sts)
Suriname (☎ 226-7844; 171 Crown St)
UK (☎ 226-5881; 44 Main St)
USA (☎ 225-4902; 100 Young St)
Venezuela (☎ 226-6749; 296 Thomas St)

Festivals & Events

Republic Day celebrations in February are the most important national cultural events of the year, though Hindu and Muslim religious festivals are also significant. **Amerindian Heritage Month** (September) features cultural events, such as handicraft exhibits and traditional dances. **Regatta**, an aquatic display of decorated boats, takes place every Easter at Bartica. An annual **Rupununi Rodeo** at Easter is held in Lethem.

Food & Drink

Guyanese food ranges from the tasty pepper pot (an Amerindian game-and-cassava stew) to the challenging *souse* (jellied cow's head). Some ubiquitous dishes are 'cook-up' (rice and beans mixed with whatever else happens to be on hand), roti and 'bake and saltfish' (fried bread and salted cod). Overall, Guyanese like spice, so if you don't, say so.

Local rum is available everywhere; El Dorado 15-year-old rum is considered one of the world's best rums, but most people settle with the less expensive but undeniably good five-year-old variety. Banks beer, brewed in Georgetown, comes in both regular and premium versions, both of which are bubbly delicious. You should also try peanut punch – made with, that's right, peanuts – and fruit punch made with rum.

Most restaurants charge 10% for service; if it's not on the bill, leave between 10 and 15 percent. Eating reviews throughout this chapter are given in order of budget, with the least expensive options first.

Health

Adequate medical care is available in Georgetown, at least at private hospitals, but facilities are few elsewhere. Chloroquine-resistant malaria is endemic, and dengue fever is also a danger, particularly in the interior and even in Georgetown – protect yourself against mosquitoes and take a malaria prophylaxis. Typhoid, hepatitis A, diphtheria/tetanus and polio inoculations are recommended. Guyana is regarded as a yellow-fever-infected area, and your next destination may require a vaccination certificate, as does Guyana when you arrive. Tap water is suspect, especially in Georgetown. Cholera outbreaks have occurred in areas with unsanitary conditions, but precautions are recommended everywhere.

See the Health chapter, p1011 for more information.

Holidays

New Year's Day January 1
Republic Day (Slave rebellion of 1763) February 23
Phagwah (Hindu New Year) March/April
Good Friday/Easter Monday March/April
Labor Day May 1
Emancipation Day August 1
Diwali (Hindu Festival of Lights) October/November
Christmas Day December 25
Boxing Day December 26
Eid-ul-Fitr (Lebaran or Bodo in Indonesian) End of Ramadan; dates vary.

Internet Access

Georgetown's internet cafes charge about G$600 per hour; in the Rupununi, satellite internet runs about G$2000 per hour. Nicer hotels also offer web access and wi-fi.

Internet Resources

Guyana News and Information (www.guyana.org) Wealth of data with heavy emphasis on current affairs.
Tourism Authority (www.guyana-tourism.com) The most thorough and up-to-date site for planning a trip to Guyana; has downloadable maps.

Maps

Country and Georgetown maps can often be found in the higher-end hotel gift shops or bookstores (p723). For detailed maps of the country, visit Georgetown's friendly **Lands & Surveys Dept, Ministry of Agriculture** (☎ 226-4051; 22 Upper Hadfield St, Durban Backlands). Have a taxi take you; it's difficult to find.

Media

Georgetown's newspapers are *Stabroek News* (www.stabroeknews.com), the most liberal paper, and *Kaieteur News*, which is the best for local gossip. The *Guyana Review* is an interesting monthly news magazine published in Georgetown.

Money

The Guyanese dollar (G$) is stable and pegged to the US dollar, which is widely accepted. You also may be able to spend your euros or even British pounds.

Credit cards are accepted at Georgetown's better hotels and restaurants, although not at gas stations or most anywhere else. Scotiabank is the easiest place to get cash advances (up to US$200), and their ATMs are the only ones that accept foreign cards.

Cash can be exchanged at banks, but *cambios* offer better rates and less red tape. Sometimes hotels change cash for a small commission.

EXCHANGE RATES		
Country	Unit	G$
Australia	A$1	180
Canada	C$1	190
euro zone	€1	300
Japan	¥100	227
New Zealand	NZ$1	148
UK	UK£1	330
USA	US$1	200

Post

Postal services are iffy. For important shipments, try these international shippers with offices in Georgetown businesses: **UPS** (Mercury Couriers; Map p724; ☎ 227-1853; 210 Camp St) and **DHL** (USA Global Export; Map p724; ☎ 225-7772; 50 E 5th St, Queenstown).

THE GUIANAS

Shopping
Nibbee fiber from forest vine is the most distinctive and appealing local product; it's used to make everything from hats to furniture. The Makushi of the southwest sculpt forest scenes from the hardened latex of the *balata* tree. Other goodies include *casareep* (an Amerindian sauce made from cassava), crabtree oil (an Amerindian cure-all), boxes, spoons and bowls carved from tropical hardwoods, and woven, Amerindian-style baby slings. The best place to buy Amerindian goods is in the villages themselves or through Iwokrama or Shell Beach Adventures (p726) in Georgetown.

Telephone
You can make direct and reverse-charge (collect) calls abroad from blue public telephones using prepaid phone cards from GT&T in Georgetown. Internet phone services are a cheaper option and available at internet cafes throughout Georgetown. Yellow public telephones are for local calls, which are free. Hotels and restaurants generally allow free local phone calls. There are no area codes in Guyana.

Tourist Information
The government has no official tourism representative abroad, but the **Tourism and Hospitality Association of Guyana** (see p725) and the **Tourism Authority** (www.guyana-tourism.com) works hard to attract visitors to Guyana and help them when they arrive.

Tours
As in the other Guianas, limited infrastructure plus tour operators equals unforgettable trips into the interior. These tours (see p725) can be costly, as can domestic airfares, which are often not included, but food and lodging are always covered. Most operators require a minimum number of people (usually four) to be booked for a tour before they'll commit to the date, so try to meet up with other travelers if you're not in a group, and start your planning as early as possible. Friday and Saturday are your best bet for a trip into the interior or to a river lodge.

Visas
All visitors must carry a passport, but travelers from the USA, Canada, EU countries, Australia, New Zealand, Japan, the UK and most Caribbean countries do not need a visa; confirm with the nearest embassy or consulate. A 90-day stay is granted on arrival in Guyana with an onward ticket. If you do need a visa, file your application at least six weeks before you leave your home country.

As well as a passport, carry an international yellow-fever vaccination certificate with you, and keep other immunizations up to date.

To stay longer than 90 days, appeal to the **Ministry of Home Affairs** (Map p724; ☎ 226-2445; 6 Brickdam Rd; ☻ 8-11:30am & 1-3pm Mon-Fri).

Visas are required for nationals of many countries entering Brazil (p375) and Suriname (p718).

Women Travelers
Guyana's not-so-safe reputation should put women travelers on particular alert. Never go out alone at night and stick to well-peopled areas if walking alone during the day in Georgetown. In the interior, traveling alone should pose few problems.

Paraguay

HIGHLIGHTS

- **National Parks in the Chaco** (p760) Watch a jaguar race through the scrub, sleep underneath billions of stars, experience the absence of humanity.
- **Itaipú Dam** (p755) Visit what is now the second-biggest dam in the world (but it's still damned big!).
- **Carnaval Encarnación** (see boxed text, p751) Get set to party at this Carnaval, which is smaller than Rio's but much more fun.
- **Trinidad** (p752) Explore the picturesque remnants of the Jesuit settlement at one of the world's least-visited Unesco World Heritage Sites.
- **Off the Beaten Track** (p758) Forget the rest of the world exists as you relax on the beach at tranquil Laguna Blanca.

FAST FACTS

- **Area:** 406,752 sq km (about the size of California)
- **Budget:** US$25 to US$40 a day
- **Capital:** Asunción
- **Costs:** *residencial* room in Asunción US$10, bus ride per hour US$2, *chipa* US$0.25
- **Country code:** ☎ 595
- **Languages:** Spanish and Guaraní (official), Plattdeutsch, Hochdeutsch
- **Money:** US$1 = 5100G (guaraní)
- **Population:** 6.5 million
- **Seasons:** hottest (December to February), coldest (June to August), rainy (October to November)
- **Time:** GMT minus four hours

TRAVEL HINTS

Don't refuse an invitation to sip *tereré* (iced herbal tea), and try fresh warm *chipa* (a type of bread made with manioc flour, eggs and cheese) – those in southern Paraguay are by far the best.

OVERLAND ROUTES

Popular entry points via bus include Foz de Iguazú, Brazil; Posadas, Argentina; or via the Ruta Trans-Chaco from Bolivia.

Little-visited, little-known Paraguay is much misunderstood. Despite its location at the heart of the continent, it is all too often passed over by backpackers who wrongly assume that there is nothing to see. True, tourism in Paraguay is underdeveloped and lacks the mega-attractions of some of its neighbors, but those who make it here are invariably glad they do.

Paraguay is a country of remarkable contrasts. It's rustic and sophisticated, extremely poor and obscenely wealthy. It boasts exotic natural reserves and massive artificial dams. Here, horses and carts pull up by Mercedes Benz cars, artisans' workshops abut glitzy shopping centers and Jesuit ruins are just a few kilometers from sophisticated colonial towns. The steamy subtropical Atlantic rainforest of the east is in stark contrast to the dry, spiny wilderness of the Chaco, home to isolated Mennonite colonies.

While Paraguayans are more used to visits from their neighbors, they are relaxed and welcoming – share a *tereré* and they will impart their country's alluring and frequently bizarre secrets.

The residual effects of dictators, corruption and contraband contribute to a sense that, for many years, much of Paraguayan life has taken place behind closed doors, while the cultural influence of the Guaraní remains as strong as ever. Paraguay is a place for those keen to have a truly authentic South American experience.

CURRENT EVENTS

The eyes of the world turned to Paraguay during the April 2008 general elections. Following a bizarre but historic turn of events, former bishop Fernando Lugo, a man with no prior political experience, was elected president of the republic. This momentous decision ended six decades of rule by the Colorado Party (the party of former dictator Alfredo Stroessner), the longest unbroken term in power by any one party in the world, ever. The strange events that led to Lugo's election involved intrigue, back-stabbing and corruption allegations of the sort that has littered Paraguayan history and ended ultimately with a new era of hope as Lugo promised to represent the masses.

The ball started rolling with outgoing President Nicanor Duarte Frutos' desperate attempts to stand for a second term in office, requiring a change in the constitution, which had been in place since the end of the dictatorship. When he found himself rebuffed by his own party he tried the next best thing, announcing his sister-in-law Blanca Ovelar as an official candidate and opting to campaign for her rather than his vice president, the young, popular and gifted orator Luis Castiglioni.

With opinion polls showing Castiglioni to be well ahead in the Colorado internals, it was to everybody's surprise when it was announced that Blanca had won by the tightest of margins. In welcoming the results Nicanor committed an important and damaging gaffe, stating that 'he' had still never lost an election, and confirming what many people had thought all along – that Blanca was merely a puppet for more 'Nicanorismo.' Castiglioni

cried 'corruption' and urged his supporters, dubbed the 'Vanguardistas,' not to vote for Blanca in the general elections. The resultant political wrangling split the Colorado Party right down the middle and for the first time opened the door for the possible election of a non-Colorado candidate.

Cue the emergence of Lino Oviedo as an independent candidate. Former head of the Paraguayan military under Stroessner, he had attempted to lead a coup d'état in 1996 (and possibly a second earlier one) and had been accused of genocide during the dictatorship. Eventually he was jailed and then acquitted for the murder of former vice president Argaña. He had an axe to grind with certain prominent Colorados whom he felt had set him up for Argaña's murder, yet he retained widespread support among the membership of the party. Of miniature stature, he was seen in some quarters as a strong, traditional leader who could whip the country back into shape. His candidature was the final nail in the Colorado coffin. As the Colorados fought amongst themselves and with Oviedo representing a return to Stroessnerism in the minds of many, support for the outsider Fernando Lugo grew exponentially.

The results were announced to much celebration in the Plaza de los Héroes. Lugo had won a historic victory with 42.3% of the vote, convincingly beating Blanca (31.8%) and Oviedo (22.8%) into second and third place. He declared that the victory showed a 'great will for change' among Paraguayans and symbolically renounced his presidential salary. Venezuelan president Hugo Chávez

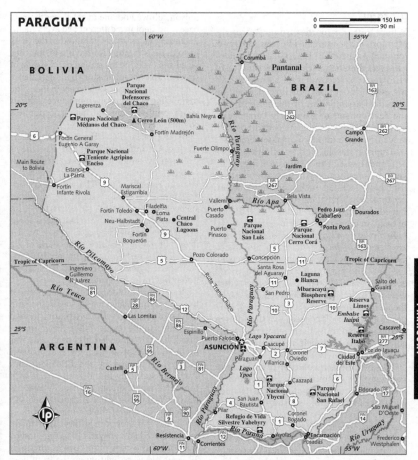

PARAGUAY

described Lugo's election as a 'victory for the Latin American revolution.'

With the honeymoon period now over, Lugo's first year in government has been plagued by controversy. Though he continues to try to implement social improvements, the remarkable renaissance of Nicanor as the head of the senate has caused friction. Lugo has been criticized by the national media for his close relationship with Chávez, while the Vatican, which had opposed his candidature, eventually accepted his resignation as a bishop after initially refusing to do so. The admission that he fathered a child while still a bishop, followed by allegations that he had another two illegitimate children by different women, has further damaged his public image.

Still, Lugo's popularity in the Paraguayan heartland remains high and for many Paraguay is at last taking steps in the right direction after decades of Colorado misrule. His biggest achievement to date is the renegotiation of the Itaipú Dam treaty. Originally agreed under the corrupt Stroessner government, benefits to the country were sacrificed in favor of benefits to the dictatorship, and ever since the renegotiation of the terms has become the Holy Grail of Paraguayan politics – often talked about but never actively sought. Lugo campaigned on a renegotiation ticket that caused many to pour scorn on his credentials as a serious candidate, but his success surprised many and represents an enormous financial gain to the nation.

HISTORY

When 350 Spaniards from Pedro de Mendoza's expedition fled Buenos Aires and founded Asunción in 1537, Guaraní hunter-gatherers dominated what is now southeastern Paraguay. Necessities on both sides saw the establishment of trade links, leading to a gradual assimilation of the cultures and the development of a uniquely Paraguayan *mestizo* (of mixed indigenous and Spanish descent) culture in the colonial settlements.

Asunción was the most significant Spanish settlement east of the Andes for nearly 50 years before Buenos Aires was fully established. It declined in importance once it became clear that the brutal Chaco region impeded the passage towards the fabled 'City of Gold' in modern-day Peru.

In the early 17th century, Jesuit missionaries created *reducciones* (settlements) where Guaraní groups were recruited as workers in the fields and put to work as wageless laborers on the grand church-building projects that were the hallmark of their settlements. Until their expulsion in 1767 (because of local jealousies and Madrid's concern that their power had become too great), the Jesuits were remarkably successful, and their influence spread to what is today Bolivia, Brazil and Argentina.

The bloodless revolution of 1811 gave Paraguay the distinction of being the first South American country to declare its independence from Spain. Its history since independence, however, has been dominated by a cast of dictators and military leaders.

Dr José Gaspar Rodríguez de Francia was the first of these leaders. Chosen as the strongest member of a governing junta, the xenophobic 'El Supremo' was initially reluctant to take charge, insisting he would accept the role only until somebody better equipped was found. That 'somebody' was never found and he ruled until his death in 1840. Francia sealed the country's borders to promote national self-sufficiency, expropriated the properties of landholders, merchants and even the church, and established the state as the only political and economic power. Under his rule Paraguay became the dominant power on the continent.

However, there was a dark side. His secret police jailed and tortured his opponents, many of whom met their end in Francia's most notorious dungeon, the 'Chamber of Truth.' After escaping an assassination attempt in 1820, El Supremo had his food and drink checked for poison, allowed no one to get closer than six paces and slept in a different bed every night. Becoming increasingly paranoid as the years passed, he is famous for having his mother killed and ordering the capital's grid system of streets with only single-story buildings, denying would-be assassins anywhere to hide. The remodeling of the city in compliance with this whim resulted in the destruction of countless colonial-era buildings.

By the early 1860s Francia's successor, Carlos Antonio López, ended Paraguay's isolation by building railroads, a telegraph system, a shipyard and a formidable army. His son, Francisco Solano López, who considered himself the Napoleon of the Americas, succeeded him. At his side was the Irish prostitute Eliza Lynch, who fantasized about being accepted into French high society. Her dream of making Asunción the 'Paris of the Americas' turned her into an unpopular Marie Antoinette figure as the country deteriorated under her husband's rule.

When Brazil invaded Uruguay, López vowed to come to the smaller nation's assistance and requested permission from Argentina to send his armies to the rescue. When Argentina refused, his arrogance led him to declare war on them too. Not surprisingly, Uruguay was quickly conquered by the Brazilians and Paraguay suddenly found itself at war with three of its neighbors simultaneously. The disastrous War of the Triple Alliance (1865–70) proved to be one of the bloodiest and most savage in Latin American history. Allied forces outnumbered Paraguayans 10 to one, and by the end of the campaign boys as young as 12 years old were fighting on the front lines armed only with farm implements. In five years Paraguay lost half of its prewar population and 26% of its national territory.

The next war wasn't too far away. In the early 1900s and with Paraguay in political turmoil, the Bolivians began to slowly advance into the Paraguayan Chaco, resulting in the eruption of full-scale hostilities in 1932. The exact reasons for the Chaco War are debated, but Bolivia's new desire for a sea port (via the Río Paraguay) and rumors of petroleum deposits in the area are often cited as factors. In the punishingly hot, arid Chaco, access to water was key to military success and the war hinged around the capture and protection of freshwater sources. Paraguay further benefited from a British-built railway line that allowed them to bring supplies to troops from Asunción. The British had earlier warned the Bolivians not to touch their railway line or risk adding another formidable enemy to their list. As a result the Paraguayan troops were able to overcome Bolivia's numerically stronger forces and even advance as far as the south Bolivian town of Villamontes. With the futility of the war becoming ever more obvious, a 1935 cease-fire left no clear victor but more than 80,000 dead.

After the Chaco War, Paraguay endured a decade of disorder before a brief civil war brought the Colorado party to power in 1949. A 1954 coup installed General Alfredo Stroessner, whose brutal 35-year, military-dominated rule (the longest South American dictatorship in history) was characterized by repression and terror. Political opponents, real or imagined, were persecuted, tortured and 'disappeared,' elections were generally considered fraudulent and corruption rampant. By the time Stroessner was overthrown, 75% of Paraguayans had known no other leader.

Stroessner was eventually driven into exile on 3 February 1989 and Paraguay's first democratic elections were held the same year. They were won by the Colorado candidate Andrés Rodríguez, who had coincidentally also masterminded the coup. The Colorados went on to win every successive election too until they were finally ousted in the historic events of 2008.

THE CULTURE
The National Psyche

Paraguayans proudly speak of their two official languages, boast about their beef and *fútbol* (soccer) teams, and accept that they live in the most bribe-hungry country outside Africa. Though things are much better than they once were, corruption remains a part of daily life. At the political level steps are being made to stamp it out, but in some areas it is so institutionalized that progress is slow. For visitors corruption is most likely to manifest itself in the form of police soliciting bribes or higher prices for gringos. Learn to live with it: it can sometimes work in your favor.

Don't let the headlines fool you either. Paraguayans are famously laid-back and rightly renowned for their warmth and hospitality. Sipping *tereré* (iced herbal tea) in the 40°C shade while shooting the breeze, interrupted only by a passing horse-drawn cart, takes the better part of a day.

Lifestyle

Statistically Paraguay is the second-poorest South American country (after Bolivia), though walking around the country's cities you might find it hard to believe. It's not uncommon to see lines of souped-up Mercedes Benz whizzing around town, classy restaurants full to bursting and houses the size of palaces. Contrast this with the lives of the rural poor in the country's heartland, where landless *campesinos* living hand to mouth are exploited by wealthy landowners and are the country's biggest social problem.

In the Chaco the disparity between the lifestyle of largely indigenous cotton-pickers and prosperous Mennonite landowners is enormous. Living side by side, the less conservative of the Mennonites enjoy German-made appliances and new trucks, while their counterparts struggle to make ends meet in semi-permanent shacks.

Paraguayan towns are frequently nicknamed 'Capital of…' after their most notable features or products. Encarnación, for example, is 'Capital de Carnaval,' Coronel Bogado is 'Capital de Chipa' and Itauguá is 'Capital de Ñandutí.'

The Paraguayan *siesta* is the most infectious slice of Paraguayan life. In some communities the siesta may extend from noon to sunset, making the early morning and dusk the busiest times of day. For an interesting and quirky guide to life in Paraguay in English see www.guidetoparaguay.com.

Population

The indigenous tribes of Paraguay belong to the Tupi/Guaraní 'family' of indigenous groups historically distributed through modern-day southern Brazil, eastern Bolivia, Paraguay, Uruguay and northern Argentina. Traditionally hunter-gatherers, the Paraguayan Guaraní comprise various tribes with distinct languages and cultures. Amongst the principal Guaraní tribal groups in Paraguay are the Chamacoco in the Chaco, the Aché of Canindeyú and the Mbyá of southern Paraguay. Though the Aché and Chamacoco still cling to their traditional cultures and beliefs, many of the other tribal groups, especially those in eastern Paraguay, have largely become assimilated into mainstream society.

Some 95% of Paraguayans are considered *mestizos*. Spanish is the language of business and is most prevalent in the cities, while in the *campaña* (countryside) Guaraní is the language of choice. Most people, however, have some knowledge of both, and Jopará (a mixture of the two) is used in some parts of the media and during social encounters. The remaining 5% of the population are descendants of European immigrants (mainly Ukrainians and Germans), Mennonite farmers and indigenous tribes. Contrary to popular belief the German population in Paraguay was present long before WWII and was not formed by escaping Nazis. There are also small but notable Asian, Arab and Brazilian communities, particularly in the south and east of the country.

More than 95% of the population lives in eastern Paraguay, only half in urban areas. Unicef reports a literacy rate of 94%, an infant mortality rate of 2.5% and an average life expectancy of 72 years. The annual population growth rate is 2.2%.

SPORTS

Paraguayans are *fútbol*-mad. It's not uncommon to see large groups of men in bars supping Pilsen (the national beer) watching the Copa Libertadores on a communal TV. The most popular teams, Olimpia and Cerro Porteño, often beat the best Argentine sides. The headquarters of **Conmebol** (☎ 021-65-0993; www.conmebol .com; Av Sudamericana Km 12), the South American football confederation, is in Luque, on the road to the airport. Tennis, basketball, volleyball, hunting and fishing are also popular.

RELIGION

Ninety percent of the population claims to be Roman Catholic, but folk variants are common. Most indigenous peoples have retained their religious beliefs, or modified them only slightly, despite nominal allegiance to Catholicism or evangelical Protestantism.

ARTS

As many local intellectuals and artists will tell you, the government gives little funding to the arts. Many artists, musicians and painters have left the country to perform or work elsewhere. Nevertheless, the country boasts some well-known figures.

Paraguay's major literary figures are poet-critic and writer Josefina Plá and poet-novelist Augusto Roa Bastos – winner of the 1990 Premio Cervantes (he died in 2005 aged 87). Despite many years in exile, Bastos focused on Paraguayan themes and history, drawing from

personal experience. His novel *Son of Man* ties together several episodes in Paraguayan history, including the Francia dictatorship and the Chaco War. Contemporary writers include Nila López, poet Jacobo A Rauskin, Luis María Martínez, Ramón Silva Ruque Vallejos, Delfina Acosta and Susy Delgado. (Interested travelers should visit Café Literario in Asunción, p747, for a summary and brief rundown – printed on the menus!)

Roland Joffe's 1986 epic film the *Mission* is a must-see even if you're not a Jesuit buff.

Paraguayan music is entirely European in origin. The most popular instruments are the guitar and the harp, while traditional dances include the lively *polkas galopadas* (literally 'galloping polkas') and the *danza de la botella*, with dancers balancing bottles on their heads.

Numerous art galleries emphasize modern, sometimes very unconventional artworks.

ENVIRONMENT

Like many developing countries, Paraguay is not known for its environmental record; the term 'lax' is being generous. The disappearance of the eastern Atlantic rainforest has been alarming, much of it logged for cropping, especially soybean and wheat crops, and mostly to the benefit of large-scale, wealthy farmers. The construction of the Itaipú hydroelectric plant (p755) was not without controversy, and a second dam at Yacyretá near Ayolas, has permanently altered the southern border of the country.

That said, many people are worried about the future of – and alleged US interest in – the country's natural resources, including the world's largest water reserve under Paraguay, Brazil and Argentina (Acuífero Guaraní).

The Land

The country is divided into two distinct regions, east and west of the Río Paraguay. Eastern Paraguay historically was a mosaic of Atlantic forest and *cerrado* (tropical savanna ecoregion), with the unique Mesopotamian flooded grasslands in the extreme south of the country. Much of the original habitat has now been converted to agriculture, especially in Itapúa and Alto Paraná departments, but substantial tracts of these pristine yet globally endangered habitats still remain. To the west is the Gran Chaco, a lush palm savanna in its lower reaches (Humid Chaco), a dense arid thorny forest (Dry Chaco) further north and west. The northeastern Chaco represents the southern extent of the great Pantanal wetland.

Wildlife

Wildlife is diverse, but the expanding rural population is putting increasing pressure on eastern Paraguay's fauna. Mammals are most abundant and easy to see in the largely unpopulated Chaco. Anteaters, armadillos, maned wolves, giant otters, lowland tapirs, jaguars, pumas, peccaries and brocket deer are all still relatively numerous here. In the mid-1970s the Chaco peccary, a species previously known only from fossilized remains, was found alive and well in the Paraguayan Chaco, where it had evaded discovery for centuries.

Birdlife is abundant, with Paraguay home to 709 bird species. The national bird is the bare-throated bellbird, named for its remarkable call, but serious bird-watchers will be in search of endangered, limited-range species, such as the white-winged nightjar, saffron-cowled blackbird, lesser nothura, helmeted woodpecker and black-fronted piping-guan. Reptiles, including caiman and anaconda, are widespread. The amphibian that will most likely catch your eye is the enormous rococo toad, attracted to lights even in urban areas.

For extensive and detailed information on the wildlife of Paraguay in English, including downloadable books, see www.faunaparaguay.com.

National Parks

Paraguay's national parks are largely remote and often inadequately protected. Most have no visitor facilities, but those covered in this book have some kind of infrastructure set up for visitors. There is also a series of excellent and well-run private reserves across the country.

Because of corruption, lack of funding and traditionally weak political will, park development is constantly disrupted. With every new politician, a totally new team and name for the national park management arrives. Thus, the parks depend heavily on outside funding and guidance from nonprofit organizations.

The body responsible for the maintenance of national parks is **SEAM** (off Map pp744–5; ☎ 021-61-5803; www.seam.gov.py; Av Madame Lynch 3500, Asunción; ✆ 7am-1pm Mon-Fri) and the tourist secretariat is **Senatur** (Map pp744–5; ☎ 021-49-4110; www.senatur.gov.py; Palma 468, Asunción; ✆ 7am-1.30pm). The impressive Mbaracayú private reserve

comes under the auspices of the **Fundación Moisés Bertoni** (☎ 021-60-8740; www.mbertoni.org.py; Argüello 208, Asunción), while the Itaipú private reserves in eastern Paraguay are managed by **Itaipú Binacional** (☎ 061-599-8989; www.itaipu.gov.py; Rodríguez 150, Ciudad del Este).

TRANSPORTATION

GETTING THERE & AWAY

Air

Paraguay's **Silvio Pettirossi International Airport** (☎ 021-64-5600) is in Luque, a satellite town of Asunción. **TAM Mercosur** (☎ 021-64-5500; www.tam.com.py) has daily flights to Asunción and Ciudad del Este from Buenos Aires (Argentina), São Paulo (Brazil) and Santiago (Chile). **Aerosur** (☎ 021-61-4743, ext 101; www.aerosur.com) heads to Santa Cruz, Bolivia on Monday, Tuesday, Friday and Sunday at 5pm. TAM has flights from a second airport in Ciudad del Este connecting to Asunción and nearby airports in Brazil, but this airport is frequently bypassed due to lack of demand.

Boat

Ferries cross into Asunción and Encarnación from Argentina. With patience and stamina, unofficial river travel from Concepción to Isla de Margarita on the Brazilian border is possible.

Bus

Negotiating Paraguayan borders can be harrowing: on the bus, off the bus… Ask the driver to stop at immigration (locals don't always need to) and be sure your papers are in order. See p752 for border crossings at Encarnación, p755 for border crossings at Ciudad del Este, and p760 for border crossings to Bolivia.

GETTING AROUND

Buses dominate transportation with cheap fares and reasonably efficient service. Journeys between Paraguayan cities typically take less

---

DEPARTURE TAX

There is a US$20 airport tax on all departing flights, payable at the desk adjacent to the entrance to the departure lounge. You will receive a sticker on your ticket in return for your payment.

than eight hours, depending on the start and end destinations. Boats are the easiest way to get between Concepción and cities higher up the Río Paraguay.

Air

Flights save time but cost more than buses, with the only scheduled flight linking Asunción with Ciudad del Este. A new airport at Encarnación is in construction. Pilot **Juan Carlos Zavala** (☎ 0971-20-1540) runs an *aerotaxi* service to the Pantanal region and the Chaco. Four passengers fit in the plane and it costs US$300 per hour. Bank on two hours to Fuerte Olimpo and three to Bahía Negra.

Boat

See p757 for details of boat travel up the Río Paraguay.

Bus

Bus quality varies from luxury services with TV, air-conditioning and comfortable reclining seats to bumpy sardine cans with windows that don't open and aisles crammed with people picked up along the way. Typically you get what you pay for; recommended companies for main routes are mentioned in the text.

Larger towns have central terminals. Elsewhere, companies are within easy walking distance of each other.

Car

It is not cheap to rent a car in Paraguay, but it can be worth it if there's a few of you. Flexibility is your main advantage, although buses go most places accessible to a car. Anywhere away from the main *rutas* (roads) and you'll need a 4WD. Companies often charge extra mileage for distances over 100km; better deals are available for longer rentals. Try **Hertz** (☎ 021-645-571; Silvio Pettirossi Airport).

Taxi

In Asunción taxi fares are metered, don't get in the taxi if it's not. In other cities they often are not, but no trip within city limits should cost more than 30,000G in Ciudad del Este and 20,000G elsewhere (usually less). Drivers in Asunción legally levy a 30% *recargo* (surcharge) between 10pm and 5am, and on Sunday and holidays.

ASUNCIÓN

☎ 021 / pop 2 million

It's hard to get your head around Asunción. At heart it's beautiful, with a sprinkling of original colonial and beaux-arts buildings, international cuisine, shady plazas and friendly people. Its more recent and modern demeanor boasts new, seemingly endless suburbs, ritzy shopping malls and smart nightclubs. Contrast this with the historic center's heavy traffic and diesel fumes, stark utilitarian architecture and shanty shacks on the banks of the Río Paraguay. Despite these blemishes, this is one of South America's more likeable capitals and it doesn't take long to learn your way about.

Asunción claims to have 2 million people, yet seems to hold many more – her sprawling suburbs swallowing up neighboring towns.

ORIENTATION

Asunción's riverside location and the haphazard growth in the 19th and 20th centuries has created irregularities in the conventional grid, centered on two plazas, the tatty Plaza Uruguaya and the handsome Plaza de los Héroes. Names of east–west streets change at Chile on the latter plaza. Much of the action, including more upmarket accommodation options and glitzy shopping areas, now takes place in the smarter suburbs to the east, notably along a series of long, broad avenues, such as España, Artigas and Mariscal López.

INFORMATION
Bookstores

There are a couple of bookstores on and around Plaza Uruguaya. Further afield are a couple of other options:

Books (Av Mariscal López 3971) Has a good selection of English-language books.

Guaraní Raity (www.guarani-raity.com; Las Perlas 3562) Sells books in and about Guaraní.

Cultural Centers

Asunción's international cultural centers offer reading material, films, art exhibitions and cultural events at little or no cost.

Alianza Francesa (☎ 21-0382; Estigarribia 1039)

Centro Cultural Paraguayo-Americano (☎ 22-4831; Av España 352)

Centro Cultural Paraguayo Japonés (☎ 60-7276; cnr Av Julio Correa & Portillo)

Instituto Cultural Paraguayo Alemán (☎ 22-6242; Juan de Salazar 310)

Emergency
Fire department (☎ 71-1132)
Medical emergency (☎ 20-4800)
Police (☎ 911)

Internet Access
Numerous *locutorios* (small telephone offices) generally also offer decent internet access for around 3000G per hour.

Laundry
Most laundries charge around 12,000G per kg; others charge per piece or per basket. Try **Lavabien** (Hernandarias 636) or **Lavandería Shalom** (15 de Agosto 230).

Medical Services
Hospital Bautista (☎ 60-0171; Av República Argentina) Recommended private hospital.
Hospital Privado Francés (☎ 29-5250; Av Brasilia 1194) Better services than the Hospital Central.

Money
All the major banks have ATMs, though most have a daily withdrawal limit of 1,000,000G and charge a usage fee of 25,000G. Along Palma and its side streets it is hardly possible to walk a block without money changers shouting '*cambio*' at you, but rates are better in the numerous *casas de cambio* (foreign currency exchange houses) in this area. There are ATMs and money changers at the bus station and airport.
Banco Sudameris (cnr Cerro Corá & Independencia Nacional)
HSBC Bank (cnr Palma & O'Leary)

Post & Telephone
Locutorios are widespread. For directory inquiries dial ☎ 112.
Main post office (cnr Alberdi & Paraguayo Independiente; ☑ 7am-7pm Mon-Fri) Send your mail *certificado* (registered) if you want it to have a hope of arriving.

GETTING INTO TOWN

Asunción's **bus terminal** (☎ 55-1740; cnr Av Fernando de la Mora & República Argentina) is several kilometers southeast of downtown. Bus 8 (US40¢) takes the most direct route to the center, but buses 10, 25, 31 and 38 also end up on Oliva. From the airport, hop on a bus headed for the center via Av Aviadores del Chaco, or grab a cab (US$15).

Tourist Information
For online city information see www.quick guide.com.py. They periodically publish an excellent magazine packed with maps and current events and available at the **tourist office** (☎ 49-4110; www.senatur.gov.py; Palma 468; ☑ 7am-7pm).

DANGERS & ANNOYANCES
Asunción is a comparatively safe city but, as with anywhere else, keep your eye on your belongings, particularly at the bus station. The Plaza Uruguaya and streets around Calle Palma are often frequented by prostitutes after dark – don't be surprised if you are solicited. On Sundays the city center is a ghost town.

SIGHTS
City Center
Center of life in Asunción is the **Plaza de los Héroes**, where a military guard protects the remains of Mariscal Francisco Solano López and other key figures of Paraguay's catastrophic wars in the **Panteón de los Héroes** (☑ 6am-6:30pm Mon-Sat, to noon Sun), the city's most instantly recognizable building. The **Casa de la Independencia** (www.casadelaindependencia.org.py; 14 de Mayo; ☑ 7am-6:30pm Mon-Fri, 8am-noon Sat) dates from 1772 and is where Paraguay became the first country on the continent to declare its independence in 1811.

North of the plaza near the waterfront is the ample **Plaza Constitución**, where you'll find the pink **Cabildo**, which was once the center of government and is now the **Museo del Congreso Nacional** (www.cabildoccr.gov.py; ☑ 10am-5pm). On the eastern side of the square is the unremarkable **Catedral Metropolitana** with an equally unremarkable **museum** (admission 4000G; ☑ 7:30am-noon Mon-Fri).

Follow Paraguayo Independiente with the waterfront on your right and you'll eventually reach the **Palacio de Gobierno** (☎ 41-4220; ☑ Thu only). In the days of Francia you would be shot for lingering too long outside but these days visits are allowed with advance reservation. Just across the street is the **Manzana de la Rivera** (Ayolas 129; ☑ 7am-9pm), a complex of eight colorful and restored houses. The oldest is Casa Viola (1750), where the **Museo Memoria de la Ciudad** houses a history of Asunción's urban development.

Asunción's other main plaza is the **Plaza Uruguaya**, four blocks east of the Plaza de los Héroes along Mariscal Estigarribia. Though frequently occupied by squatters, it is also the

PARAGUAY

DOWNTOWN ASUNCIÓN

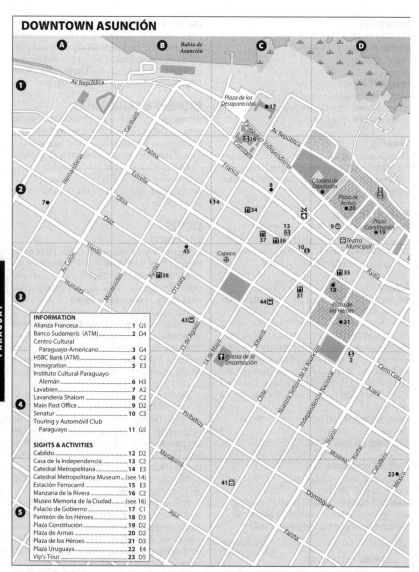

INFORMATION	
Alianza Francesa	**1** G5
Banco Sudameris (ATM)	**2** D4
Centro Cultural	
Paraguayo-Americano	**3** G4
HSBC Bank (ATM)	**4** C2
Immigration	**5** E3
Instituto Cultural Paraguayo	
Alemán	**6** H3
Lavabien	**7** A2
Lavandería Shalom	**8** C2
Main Post Office	**9** D2
Senatur	**10** C3
Touring y Automóvil Club	
Paraguayo	**11** G5

SIGHTS & ACTIVITIES	
Cabildo	**12** D2
Casa de la Independencia	**13** C2
Catedral Metropolitana	**14** E3
Catedral Metropolitana Museum	(see 14)
Estación Ferrocarril	**15** E3
Manzana de la Rivera	**16** C2
Museo Memoria de la Ciudad	(see 16)
Palacio de Gobierno	**17** C1
Panteón de los Héroes	**18** D3
Plaza Constitución	**19** D2
Plaza de Armas	**20** D2
Plaza de los Héroes	**21** D3
Plaza Uruguaya	**22** E4
Vip's Tour	**23** D5

location of the old **Estación Ferrocarril** (railway station). The Asunción–Encarnación railway line was the first in South America, and one of the first trains to run the route is on display here. These days the station is used more for concerts and recitals than anything else, but it is also the place to buy tickets for the hilarious **tourist train** (☎ 44-2448; www.ferrocarriles.com.py;

100,000G), which departs the Jardín Botánico at 10am to Areguá, returning at 5pm. A real step back in time, it is more like a mobile theater than a train, as actors in period dress mingle with passengers and perform scenes based around supposed violations of the rules of the original railway. Remember: no parrots allowed on board!

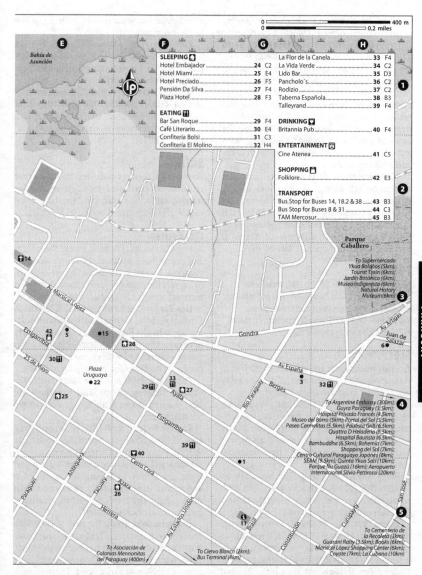

SLEEPING 🏠		
Hotel Embajador	**24**	C2
Hotel Miami	**25**	E4
Hotel Preciado	**26**	F5
Pensión Da Silva	**27**	F4
Plaza Hotel	**28**	F3

EATING 🍴		
Bar San Roque	**29**	F4
Café Literario	**30**	E4
Confitería Bolsi	**31**	C3
Confitería El Molino	**32**	H4

La Flor de la Canela	**33**	F4
La Vida Verde	**34**	C2
Lido Bar	**35**	D3
Pancho´s	**36**	C2
Rodizio	**37**	C2
Taberna Española	**38**	B3
Talleyrand	**39**	F4

DRINKING 🍷		
Britannia Pub	**40**	F4

ENTERTAINMENT 🎭		
Cine Atenea	**41**	C5

SHOPPING 🛍		
Folklore	**42**	E3

TRANSPORT		
Bus Stop for Buses 14, 18.2 & 38	**43**	B3
Bus Stop for Buses 8 & 31	**44**	C3
TAM Mercosur	**45**	B3

The Suburbs

From the center Av Artigas runs a long old way to the **Jardín Botánico** (Botanic Gardens; admission 5000G; 🕐 7am-7pm). Take bus 24 or 35 from Cerro Corá. The former estate of the ruling López dynasty, it now houses the city zoo, a small nature reserve and a couple of odd museums: a small **natural history museum** (🕐 8am-6pm Mon-Sat, to 1pm Sun) in Carlos Antonio's humble colonial house and the **Museo Indigenista** (🕐 8am-6pm Mon-Sat, to 1pm Sun) in his son Francisco's former mansion. En route to the 'Botánico' you'll pass the charred remains of the **Supermercado Ykua Bolaños**, which hit world headlines in 2006 as almost 1000 people burnt to death inside when the owner elected to 'lock-down' after a small fire broke out in the kitchen. A moving shrine to the deceased is worth a quick stop.

Everyone's favorite, **Museo del Barro** (Grabadores del Cabichui s/n; admission 8000G; 3:30-8pm Thu-Fri) displays everything from modern paintings to pre-Columbian and indigenous crafts to political caricatures of prominent Paraguayans. Take bus 30 from Oliva and get off at Shopping del Sol. It's three blocks from there off Callejón Cañada. Stay on the bus and you'll pass **Parque Ñu Guazú**, a pleasant place to pass an afternoon, with lakes and walking trails.

The **Cementerio de la Recoleta**, 3km east of the center along Av Mariscal López, is a maze of incredible mausoleums as Asunción's wealthy try to do outdo each other in the grandeur of their resting places. Eliza Lynch, hated mistress of Mariscal Francisco Solano López, is buried here.

TOURS

FAUNA Paraguay (☎ 071-20-3981; www.fauna paraguay.com) City tours, short breaks and bird-watching and ecotours with professional multilingual guides.

Vip's Tour (☎ 44-1199; www.vipstour.com.py; México 782) Organizes a smorgasbord of day trips.

SLEEPING

Accommodations are more expensive in Asunción than in the rest of the country but it won't bust anyone's budget.

Pensión Da Silva (☎ 44-6381; Ayala 843; r per person 40,000-50,000G) Great pick for value, convenience and hospitality. A family-run house with an indoor–outdoor colonial ambience. The exquisite exterior doesn't have signage – ring the bell.

Hotel Embajador (☎ 49-3393; Franco 514; s/d 50,000/70,000G;) Rough and faded but with some character and barely passable rooms; the high ceilings are indeed the highlight.

Quinta Ykua Sati (☎ 60-1230; www.quintaykuasati .com.py; Merlo; r per person 70,000G) In a residential neighborhood out near the airport, this is a tranquil rest spot with beautiful gardens. Older cabin-style rooms are a bit pokey but new rooms are spacious and modern.

Hotel Miami (☎ 44-4950; México 449; s/d 70,000/100,000G;) This hotel has a very bland hospital-type hallway, but it's clean, central and has a security door.

Plaza Hotel (☎ 44-4772; www.plazahotel.com.py; Plaza Uruguaya; s/d 130,000/180,000G;) A reliable old favorite, the Plaza's rooms could do with a makeover but it's a decent value given the buffet breakfast.

Hotel Preciado (☎ 44-7661; Azara 840; s/d 160,000/180,000G;) This modern number is a decent bet, located a couple of blocks from the center's best nightlife.

our pick Portal del Sol (☎ 60-9395; www.portaldelsol .com; Roa 1455; s/d 210,000/265,000G;) Beautiful rooms, mammoth breakfast, a pleasant splash pool, good restaurant airport pickup and parking. The lot!

EATING

Asunción's food is reflected in its diverse cultures: sophisticated local, Asian and international foods abound and vegetarians are catered for. Supermarkets are well stocked.

City Center

For typical Paraguayan food, try out the million and one options south of the center along Av Figueroa, known locally as La Quinta Avenida, or sample the *asadito* (small meat kebabs with manioc) stands (2000G) on street corners.

Lido Bar (cnr Chile & Palma; mains 7000-25,000G) A diner-style local favorite, with sidewalk seating opposite the Panteón, that serves a variety of Paraguayan specialties (excellent *sopa para-guaya* – cornbread with cheese and onion) in generous portions for breakfast and lunch.

Pancholo's (Palma near 15 de Agosto; meals 7000-40,000G) Burgers, pizzas and hot dogs are best washed down with an ice-cold *chopp* (draught beer).

Bar San Roque (☎ 44-6015; cnr Tacuary & Ayala; mains 15,000-45,000G) An Asunción landmark, with a warm turn-of-the-20th-century atmosphere. The counter displays fresh goods from the family farm and the wine list is as impressive as the menu of fish and meat dishes. As many locals will attest, a culinary must with service to match.

Confitería Bolsi (Estrella 399; mains 15,000-50,000G) More than a *confitería* (cafe/snack bar), this traditional place, which has been going since 1960, serves everything from sandwiches to curried rabbit and garlic pizza. Try the *surubí casa nostra* (a superb selection of different pasta types and flavors on one dish).

Taberna Española (☎ 44-1743; Ayolas 631; mains 15,000-195,000G) A slice of Spain in Paraguay. The energetic ambience of this 'food museum' with dangling bottles, cooking implements and bells is only the backdrop for good-value tapas and meals.

La Vida Verde (Palma; per kg 35,000G) Assess your mood by one of the 32 quirkily sculptured emotional 'faces' on the wall – 'satisfied' is how you'll feel after this eating experience. A delicious daily buffet of Chinese vegetarian delights (although they bend the rules a bit).

Rodizio (Palma near 15 de Agosto; per kg 53,000G) All-day Brazilian buffet. Hunks of meat on the grill, scores of dessert choices and a salad bar for those with a guilty conscience.

Near Plaza Uruguaya

Confitería El Molino (Av España 382; snacks 5000-25,000G) With bow-tied waiters and gourmet-style pastries and biscuits, this is one of the sweetest *confiterías* around. Great for *minutas* (short orders), snacks and excellent *licuados* (blended fruit drinks).

Café Literario (cnr Estigarribia & México; snacks 5000-25,000G; ⏰ 4-10pm) Cool air, music, books (of course) and all that jazz. This artsy, comfy cafe–bookstore is a great place to read, write or imbibe.

La Flor de la Canela (☎ 49-8928; Tacuary 167; mains 22,000-80,000G) The Peruvian food is more genuine than this smart place's faux Inca sculptures. Fish and *mariscos* (seafood) dominate the menu, and the *ceviche* (marinated raw seafood) is fantastic.

Talleyrand (☎ 44-1163; Estigarribia 932; mains 25,000-50,000G) International haute cuisine for people with their noses *haute* in the air. Lovely food and lovely prices.

East of the Center

On Sundays it's best to head to one of the large shopping centers such as **Mariscal López** (cnr Quesada 5050 & Charles de Gaulle) or **Shopping del Sol** (cnr Aviadores del Chaco & González).

Quattro D Heladería (cnr Av San Martín & Andrade; 8000G per scoop) We're not sure what the four Ds stand for in Spanish (or Italian) – but the ice cream here is divine, delightful, delicious and delectable in anyone's language!

Ciervo Blanco (Flores near Radio Operadores del Chaco; meals 35,000-50,000G) If you're looking for a traditional Paraguayan experience, this place, in Barrio Pinozá, just southeast of the center, has it. Juicy *asado* (grilled meat), traditional music and bottle-dancers will keep you entertained.

Paulista Grill (cnr San Martín & Mariscal López; buffet 60,000G) Dripping slabs of delicious meat (veggies can have the salad buffet). Popular with those in the more upmarket east, and worth going to if you're in the area.

DRINKING

Some bars and all discos charge admission for men (women usually get in free) and can be crowded at weekends. Options are limited in the center and most of the flashy clubs are a short cab ride east of downtown on Av Brasilia. For a more refined (and pricier!) scene head to Paseo Carmelitas off Av España.

Britannia Pub (☎ 44-3990; www.brittania-pub.com; Cerro Corá 851; ⏰ Tue-Sun) Casually hip with an air-conditioned international ambience and outdoor patio, the 'Brit Pub' is a favorite among foreigners and locals alike for its pub grub and even has its own beer!

Bohemia (cnr Long & España) Upscale but laid-back bar with salsa rhythms and great cocktails.

Bambuddha (☎ 66-4826; Aviadores del Chaco 1655; ⏰ Tue-Sat) One of Asunción's top bars, this is the place to be seen if you are young, trendy and aspiring to be part of the much photographed 'Asunción high' (local hip crowd).

La Cubana (Av Fernando de la Mora near Mariscal López; admission 5000G) Atmospheric, down-to-earth Paraguayan disco with dancers and live music playing salsa, merengue and *kachaka* to a local crowd.

Coyote (☎ 66-2816; Sucre 1655; admission 40,000-80,000G) Starts late, ends late – this bouncing disco is for young, wealthy, beautiful people who like to dance 'til they drop.

ENTERTAINMENT

Most of Asunción's shopping malls have multi-screen cinemas such as **Cine Atenea** (Excelsior Mall, cnr Manduvirá & Chile; tickets 20,000G) and the **Cinepremium del Sol** (Shopping del Sol, cnr Aviadores

---

POMBERO

Guaraní folklore has many colorful mythological figures, but none is so widely believed to be true as Pombero. A mischievous little imp, said to be short, muscular and hairy, he emerges at night when he should only be referred to as Karai Pyhare (Lord of the Night). His presence is used to explain anything from strange sounds and missing items to unfortunate minor accidents. Pombero's penchant for young women, accompanied or otherwise, can only be overcome by diverting his attentions with a glass of *caña* (rum) or cigarettes, left as a gift. Place it on the roadside and high-tail out of there!

del Chaco & González; tickets 20,000G). Films are often in English with Spanish subtitles.

SHOPPING

Asunción offers Paraguay's best souvenir shopping. The typical Paraguayan souvenir is a *matero, bombilla* and *termos* (cup, straw and flask) for *tereré* consumption and these are ubiquitous – though quality varies. The ground floor of the Senatur tourist office has examples of local *artesanías* (craftwork) from around the country, ranging from intricate Luque silver to fine *ñandutí* (lace). **Folklore** (cnr Estigarribia & Caballero), a little further along, also has a wide range of goods at reasonable prices. The open-air market at Plaza de los Héroes is stocked with *ao po'i* or *lienzo* (loose-weave cotton) garments and other indigenous crafts; it swells considerably on a Sunday morning. Mercado Cuatro is a lively trading lot occupying the wedge formed by the intersection of Avs Francia and Pettirossi, stretching several blocks.

GETTING THERE & AWAY

Air

Aeropuerto Internacional Silvio Pettirossi (☎ 64-5600) is in the suburb of Luque, 20km east of Asunción. It's easily reached by buses displaying 'Aeropuerto' signs heading out Av Aviadores del Chaco. See p741 for details of flights in and out of Asunción. Airport taxis are expensive, but if you flag one down on the road outside it's half the price.

Boat

The stretch of river north of Asunción is relatively uninteresting. For boat cruises on the Río Paraguay you're better off embarking in Concepción (p757).

Bus

Tickets are best purchased at the company offices on the 2nd floor of the bus terminal.

GETTING TO ARGENTINA

Crossing into Argentina via ferry from Puerto Itá Enramada, southwest of downtown, to Puerto Pilcomayo (Argentina) is possible. Ferries leave every half-hour from 7am to 5pm weekdays, and irregularly from 7am to 10am on Saturday. You must visit the office at the port for your exit stamp before you leave Asunción.

BUS FARES		
Destination	**Cost (G)**	**Duration (hr)**
Buenos Aires, Argentina	270,000	18-21
Ciudad del Este	55,000-75,000	4½-6
Concepción	60,000	4½-6
Encarnación	50,000-75,000	5-6
Filadelfia	80,000	8
Pedro Juan Caballero	75,000	6-7½
Rio de Janeiro, Brazil	300,000	24-30
Santa Cruz, Bolivia	250,000	20-24
São Paulo, Brazil	250,000	18-20

Don't be put off by the touts shouting destinations at you – take your time to choose the company you want. City buses 8 and 31 run from Oliva to the terminal, while buses 14, 18.2 and 38 run from Haedo.

GETTING AROUND

The noisy, bone-rattling kamikaze-like city buses (2300G) go almost everywhere, but few run after 10pm. Nearly all city buses start their route at the western end of Oliva and post their destinations in the front window.

Taxis are metered and reasonable but tack on a surcharge late at night and on Sunday. A taxi from the center to the bus terminal costs about 35,000G.

AROUND ASUNCIÓN

Prepare yourself for a taste of rural and historical Paraguay. Humble communities dominated by colonial buildings observe long siestas, disturbed only by occasional ox- or horse-drawn carts clacking up cobbled streets. The tourist industry plugs the area as the 'Circuito Central,' and all of the towns on the circuit are readily accessible on frequent local buses. These leave from the *subsuelo* (lower floor) of the Asunción bus terminal (platforms 30 and 35, 5000G to 7000G).

ITAUGUÁ & AREGUÁ

These two small towns are known for their artesanal cottage industries. Itauguá's women are famous for the unique weaving of multicolored spiderweb *ñandutí* ('lace' – *ñandú* is spider in Guaraní). These exquisite pieces range in size from doilies to bedspreads; smaller ones cost only a few dollars but larger ones range upward of 250,000G. In July the town celebrates its annual **Festival de Ñandutí**.

Areguá is renowned for its ceramics, displayed along the main street. The historic cobbled streets are lined with exquisite colonial homes, and the village atmosphere is completed with a church perched on the hill and an enviable position overlooking Lago Ypacaraí.

Buses to Itauguá leave hourly or so from outside the bus terminal along Av República Argentina. For Areguá, Línea 11 leaves from outside the terminal on Av Fernando de la Mora. A ferry runs from San Bernardino in the high season but the most atmospheric way to get to Areguá is on the fortnightly tourist train (p744) from Asunción.

SAN BERNARDINO
☎ 0512

Renowned as the elite escape for the privileged of Asunción, tranquil 'San Ber' offers the lot for top relaxation – pubs, discos and upmarket hotels and restaurants line the shady cobbled streets of Lago Ypacaraí's eastern shore. Despite its reputation, there's plenty for budget travelers as well. In high season a pleasure boat takes passengers for short cruises on the lake (15,000G). Unfortunately, you won't want to swim in the lake – it's filthy.

On the lakeside of the plaza is the worn and romantically Victorian **Hotel del Lago** (☎ 23-2201; cnr Av Carlos Antonio Lopez & Weiler; s/d 240,000/320,000G; ❄ ❂), full of antique furniture – each room is different. Travelers rave about **Hostal Brisas del Mediterraneo** (☎ 23-2459; camping/dm/d incl breakfast 25,000/50,000/150,000G; ❂), which is perched on the edge of the lake and offers excellent facilities. Follow the cobbled Ruta Kennedy for 2km around the lake from in front of the Copaco office.

From Asunción Cordillera de los Altos buses run hourly from platform 35 (1½ hours).

CAACUPÉ
☎ 0511

Paraguay's answer to the Vatican City, the enormous **Basilica de Caacupé** looks quite out of place in this otherwise quiet provincial town. Caacupé really comes alive on El Día de la Virgen (8 December) when crowds of worshippers undertake pilgrimages from all corners of the country to worship and ask the Virgin for favors. As many as 300,000 of the faithful may crowd onto the plaza during the festival and participate in a spectacular candlelit procession.

If you want to stay, **Hotel Katy Maria** (☎ 24-2860; Pino; s/d 120,000/150,000G) is a good choice in view of the dome. Needless to say, you should book well in advance during the festival when prices rise exponentially. Caacupé is 54km east of Asunción and Empresa Villa Serrana departs every 10 minutes from platform 35.

YAGUARÓN & PIRIBEBUY

Yaguarón, 48km southeast of Asunción, has an 18th-century **Franciscan church** that is a landmark of colonial architecture. The nearby **Museo del Doctor Francia** (☒ 7:30am-noon & 2-6pm Mon-Fri) was the first dictator's house and is interesting for its period portraiture and statues. San Buenaventura has hourly departures to Yaguarón from platform 30.

Piribebuy, 75km from Asunción, is a small rural town that was briefly the capital of the nation during the War of the Triple Alliance (1865–70). With Asunción captured, it became the site of a famous siege in 1869, when an army of children led by the local schoolteacher bravely held off the invading Brazilian forces. The remarkable events are recounted in the small **museum** (☒ 7:30am-noon & 2-6pm Mon-Fri). Empresa Piribebuy runs every 45 minutes from platform 35 in Asunción (two hours).

SOUTHERN PARAGUAY

Paraguay's southernmost region, east of the Río Paraguay, is home to some of the country's most important historical sites. The Jesuit ruins, national parks and the *locura* (madness) of Carnaval make it an eclectic and fascinating area to visit. On the way from Asunción to Encarnación you'll pass through the town of **Coronel Bogado**. Known as the 'Capital de Chipa,' this is the best place to sample this national obsession. There's no need to get off the bus – the vendors will come to you and it's cheap as *chipa* (1000G).

ENCARNACIÓN
☎ 071 / pop 105,000

Encarnación, 'La Perla del Sur,' is Paraguay's most attractive city yet retains a small-town feel. It serves as the gateway to the nearby Jesuit ruins at Trinidad and Jesús but is most famous as the 'Capital de Carnaval' (see

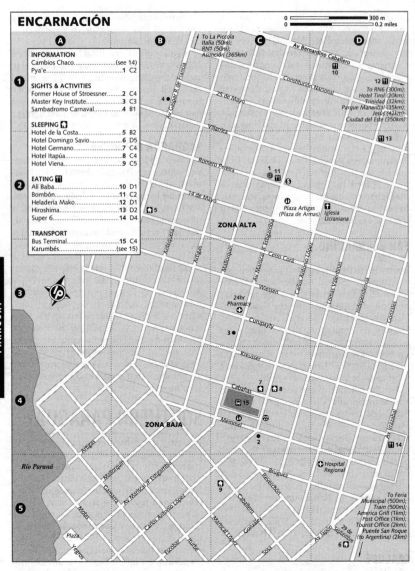

ENCARNACIÓN

INFORMATION
Cambios Chaco..........................(see 14)
Pya'e..1 C2

SIGHTS & ACTIVITIES
Former House of Stroessner........2 C4
Master Key Institute.....................3 C3
Sambadromo Carnaval.................4 B1

SLEEPING
Hotel de la Costa..........................5 B2
Hotel Domingo Savio....................6 D5
Hotel Germano.............................7 C4
Hotel Itapúa.................................8 C4
Hotel Viena...................................9 C5

EATING
Ali Baba......................................10 D1
Bombón.......................................11 C2
Heladería Mako...........................12 D1
Hiroshima....................................13 D2
Super 6..14 D4

TRANSPORT
Bus Terminal................................15 C4
Karumbés...................................(see 15)

boxed text, opposite). It is rather less proud to be the birthplace of dictator Alfredo Stroessner. His former house is now a neural hospital just behind the bus terminal.

Look out for *karumbés*, yellow horse-drawn carriages that once served as city taxis and still circulate today. Rides are free on weekends. Another blast from the past is a 19th-century steam train that carries goods, not passengers (though you could ask the driver for a ride!). Look for it near the Feria Municipal on Av Irrazábal.

Orientation

The town can be split broadly into the more modern Zona Alta (uphill), centered on the attractive Plaza de Armas, and the decaying Zona Baja (downhill), a massive market area popular with bargain-hunters and day-tripping Argentines. The latter has long been earmarked for flooding by the Yacyretá Dam (hence the lack of building maintenance!), which will drastically alter Paraguay's southern border. Latest reports suggest the waters will finally come in late 2010.

Information

INTERNET ACCESS

There are scores of internet places but the best and most central is **Pya'e** (Romero Pereira; per hr 3000G) just off the plaza.

MONEY

Most banks are on or near the plaza and all have ATMs. Money changers congregate around the bus station and at the border, but check rates before handing over any money. A more reliable option for exchanging money is **Cambios Chaco** (Av Irrazábal), next to Super 6 supermarket.

TELEPHONE

Telephone cabins are scattered around town, especially in the area around the bus terminal.

TOURIST INFORMATION

City maps are available at the tourist office, next to the immigration office at the border, but it only opens once in a blue moon. **FAUNA Paraguay** (☎ 071-20-3981; www.faunaparaguay.com), based in Encarnación, runs professional guided tours, especially ecotours, across Paraguay but is happy to answer tourist information queries by phone or email for free.

Courses

An innovative Spanish course at the **Master Key Institute** (☎ 0985-77-8198; Galería San Jorge 16, Av Mariscal JF Estigarribia; 5-day course 750,000G) holds open-air classes for all levels at the local tourist sights.

Sleeping

There are plenty of clean, reasonably priced places to choose from in Encarnación. Most of the cheaper places also have rooms with air-conditioning for about twice the price. You won't regret splashing out. Book ahead during Carnaval when prices rise considerably.

Hotel Itapúa (☎ 20-5045; López 814; s/d 35,000/70,000G, r per person with air-con 75,000G; ☒) For some cheaper digs, you can try this large and impersonal hotel.

Hotel Viena (☎ 20-5981; Caballero 568; r per person 40,000G, with air-con 75,000G; ☒) Delightful colonial veranda–styled place with the simplest of simple rooms.

Hotel Germano (☎ 20-3346; Cabañas; r per person with/without bathroom 50,000/30,000G) Across from the bus terminal, Hotel Germano couldn't be better located for late arrivals. It also happens to be the best-value budget spot in town, with spotless rooms and helpful staff. It's a favorite with the Peace Corps.

Hotel Domingo Savio (☎ 20-5800; 29 de Septiembre; s/d incl breakfast 120,000/180,000G; ☒ ☒) Decent midrange bet with nice, if unspectacular, rooms and an outdoor pool.

our pick **Hotel de la Costa** (☎ 20-0590; cnr Av Francia & Cerro Corá; s 130,000-150,000G, d 230,000-250,000G, ste 420,000G; ☒ ☒) Arguably the city's best hotel, it will have a plum location on the riverfront with views across to Argentina once the dam floods. Excellent service and a welcoming pool in the attractive garden. If you can afford it opt for the suite – with Jacuzzi and champagne breakfast, it's a steal.

CARNAVAL!

Carnaval Paraguayan-style might not be on the same scale or as famous as Rio's, but if you are young and looking for a good time, then in our opinion it is certainly much more fun. More bare flesh, louder music and obligatory crowd involvement all make for a wild night out. Don't forget your *lanzanieves* (spray snow) and a pair of sunglasses (you don't want that stuff in your eyes!), pick your place in the rickety stands and get ready to party hard with the locals – it's surprisingly infectious!

Carnaval now spans every weekend in February, from Friday to Sunday night. The *sambadromo* (parade ground) is Av Francia, also Encarnación's main strip for nightlife. Tickets (50,000G) can be bought in advance around the city or from touts on the night at a slightly higher price. Gates open around 9pm, but the action starts around 10pm. It's all over by 2am, when everybody piles into the local discos.

Eating

Encarnación has some of the best eats in Paraguay outside of Asunción, as well as an astounding number of junk-food joints. You can stock up with goodies at **Super 6** (Av Irrazábal), a supermarket that also has a great-value pay-by-weight restaurant.

Alí Baba (Av Bernardino Caballero; mains 7000-10,000G) Open all night at weekends, this is the place to head if you have the munchies after a night on the town. Give the *lomito árabe* (chopped beef wrapped in a tortilla, with vegetables, salad and sauce) a shot if you are looking for a filling snack.

Bombón (Romero Pereira; meals 10,000-30,000G) Cute little cafe with great pastries, tasty breakfasts, inventive sandwiches and good pizzas. The ice-cold *frappuccinos* go down well in the sunshine and there's a beauty parlor upstairs.

Hiroshima (☎ 20-6288; 25 de Mayo & Lomas Valentinas; mains 10,000-50,000G) Top-notch Japanese food and a deserved local favorite – unbelievable udon, sushi and tofu dishes. Food fit for a Japanese crown prince.

La Piccola Italia (☎ 20-4618; Mallorquín 609; mains 13,000-30,000G) Great-value pizza and pasta in huge portions served in distinctly Mediterranean surroundings.

America Grill (Av San Roque González; buffet 30,000G) The best of a series of Brazilian-style all-you-can-eat places. Pick your meat cuts straight from the grill, choose from the salad bar and round it off by pigging out on the dessert selection.

GETTING TO ARGENTINA

International buses (5000G) cross to Posadas in Argentina via the Puente San Roque, leaving from outside the bus terminal in Encarnación. You must get off the bus at the border immigration offices at both ends of the bridge for exit and entry stamps. Buses don't always wait – take your pack and keep your ticket to catch the next one. If you're in a group, a taxi to the Paraguayan customs costs around 20,000G, but the price rises exponentially to take it across the bridge.

Picturesque ferries (5000G) also cross the Río Paraná from the Zona Baja to/from the *costanera* (river promenade) of Posadas. For information on travel from Argentina to Encarnación, see p84.

Heladería Mako (Av Bernardino Caballero & Lomas Valentinas; ice cream per kg 35,000G) Delicious pastry delights, artesanal ice cream, great coffee and magazines make this well worth the trek.

Getting There & Away

The bus terminal is on Cabañas, more or less where the Zona Alta stops and Zona Baja starts. Frequent buses run from Encarnación to Asunción (50,000 to 70,000G, 5½ hours), with La Encarnacena and Pycasu providing the best service. The latter also runs an executive minibus service for the same cost. RYSA has the best service to Ciudad del Este (50,000G, five hours), though it is painfully slow.

TRINIDAD & JESÚS

Set atop a lush green hill northeast of Encarnación, **Trinidad** (admission 4000G; ☺ 7am-7pm) is Paraguay's best-preserved Jesuit *reducción* (settlement). Although it has been a Unesco World Heritage Site since 1993, there is little in the way of information unless you hire a Spanish-speaking guide (5000G). **Jesús** (admission 4000G; ☺ 7am-7pm), 12km north, is a nearly complete reconstruction of the Jesuit mission that was interrupted by the Jesuits' expulsion in 1767.

From Encarnación, frequent buses go to Trinidad (5000G, 28km) between 6am and 7pm, but any bus headed east along Ruta 6 to Ciudad del Este or Hohenau will drop you off there – get off when you see the power station on your right. Waiting for a return on the main road can sometimes get tedious but there is a restaurant at Trinidad at the nearby **Hotel León** (s/d 50,000/70,000G), where meals, refreshments and spacious rooms are available. Getting to Jesús without your own transport is more difficult. Walk 100m along the *ruta* to the crossroads – you'll see the sign to Jesús and wait for the Jesús–Obligado bus, which supposedly passes hourly (3000G). It will drop you at the ruins' entrance.

AROUND ENCARNACIÓN
Parque Manantial

On Ruta 6, 35km out of Encarnación near the town of Hohenau is **Parque Manantial** (☎ 0755-23-2250; entry 10,000G, camping 20,000G, pool per day 15,000G; 🏊). For much of the year you'll likely have the 200 hectares with swimming pools and forested walking tracks to yourself. Horse riding (35,000G per hour) is also available.

Hotel Tirol

A favorite with Spanish King Juan Carlos I, this timeless red-stone **hotel** (☎ 071-20-2388; www.hoteltirol.com.py; r per person incl meals 250,000G) set in 20 hectares of humid forest makes for a great day trip from Encarnación. Almost 200 bird species have been recorded here and four inviting swimming pools (10,000G for non-guests) are a great way to cool off after walking the *senderos* (trails). Should you wish to stay, book ahead in the high season (October to December), though you may have the place to yourself at other times of year.

To get there take local bus 1y2 (marked 'Capitán Miranda') from along Artigas in Encarnación. The end of the line is the entrance to the hotel. Any bus headed for Trinidad or Ciudad del Este also passes in front.

PARQUE NACIONAL SAN RAFAEL

Southern Paraguay's last great tract of Atlantic forest, gorgeous San Rafael is a lush wilderness and a bird-watchers' paradise, with over 400 species recorded. Rustic accommodation in basic wooden cabins is available on the southern tip of the reserve at **Estancia Nueva**

Gambach (☎ 0768-29-5046; r per person with/without meals 125,000/50,000G); the surroundings are beautiful, with 7km of forest trails and a gorgeous lake to cool off in. To get deeper into the park you'll need your own 4WD or a guide.

Rickety Beato Roque Gonzalez buses run from Encarnación to Ynambú, 12km outside the reserve, every morning at 8am and 11:30am (18,000G, three hours) but if you're not in a tour you'll have to arrange to be picked up from there in advance. **FAUNA Paraguay** (☎ 071-20-3981; www.faunaparaguay.com) runs recommended three- to four-day bird-watching trips to the park, including a visit to the grasslands at Estancia Kanguery. Or contact **Guyra Paraguay** (☎ 021-22-3567; www.guyra.org.py; Martino 215), which manages Kanguery and may offer basic accommodation.

EASTERN PARAGUAY

Corresponding to the region known as Alto Paraná, this area was once the domain of ancient impenetrable forests teeming with wildlife. The building of the second-largest

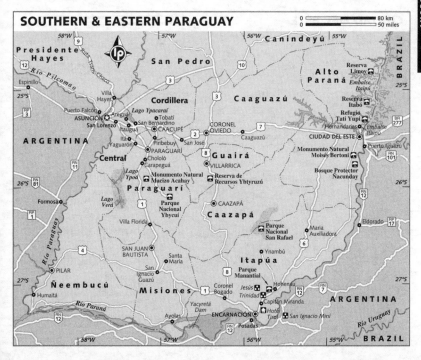

SOUTHERN & EASTERN PARAGUAY

dam in the world changed all that, flooding huge areas of pristine forest and swallowing up a set of waterfalls comparable to those at Iguazú. The dam brought development to this primeval region, leading to the founding of a city once named after a hated dictator and an invasion of Brazilian farmers bent on turning what was left of the ancient forests into soy fields. This is also Paraguay's busiest border crossing with Brazil.

CIUDAD DEL ESTE
☎ 061 / pop 356,000

Originally named Puerto Presidente Stroessner after the former dictator, the 'City of the East' is a renowned center for contraband goods, earning it the nickname 'the Supermarket of South America.' Crossing the busy border from Brazil plants you right in the middle of the market mayhem but, if you don't turn around and head straight back again, you'll find that the rest of the city is surprisingly pleasant, with some interesting attractions nearby. Of course, if you are here to shop, then you will be in your element.

Information

MONEY
Street money changers lounge around the Pioneros de Este rotunda.
ABN AMRO (Av Adrián Jara) Has an ATM.

POST
Post office (cnr García & Centro Democrático)

TOURIST INFORMATION
Tourist office (☎ 51-1626; Edificio Libano, Av Rafael Franco near Pampliega; ⏱ 7am-7pm Mon-Fri)

Sleeping
Midrange places are definitely worth the extra couple of bucks, especially once you sample the megavalue breakfast buffets, which are included in the price.

Hotel Tía Nancy (☎ 50-2974; cnr Garcete & Cruz del Chaco; s/d 50,000/70,000G, d with air-con 100,000G; ✷) Near the bus terminal, this friendly place has dark rooms but is perfectly adequate for a tranquil transit stop.

Hotel Caribe (☎ 51-2460; Fernández s/n; s/d 50,000/80,000G; ✷) A bit of grit for the gritty budget traveler, this hotel has a small

CIUDAD DEL ESTE

0 — 500 m
0 — 0.3 miles

To Ruta 6 (30km);
Ruta 2 (30km);
Airport (30km);
Encarnación (130km);
Asunción (330km)

Río Paraná

To Puente de Amistad (300m);
Foz do Iguaçu (Brazil) (1km);
Puerto Iguazú (Argentina) (5km)

To Hernandarias
(Embalse Itaipú) (20km);
Itabó (100km);
Limoy (165km)

To Faraone
(500m);
Gauchiño Grill
(500m)

To Senatur (1km);
Bus Terminal (2km);
Post Office (2km);
Hotel Tía Nancy (2km);
Salto del Monday (8km)

To Tourist
Office
(500m)

To TAM
(100m)

INFORMATION	
ABN AMRO (ATM)	1 B2
Brazilian Consulate	2 A2
Immigration & Customs Offices	3 D1

SLEEPING	
Hotel Austria	4 A1
Hotel Caribe	5 A1
Hotel Mi Abuela	6 A2
Hotel Munich	7 A1

EATING	
Hotel Austria	(see 4)
Kokorelia	8 B2
Lebanon	9 B2

TRANSPORT	
Buses to Foz do Iguaçu & Puerto Iguazú	10 D2

courtyard and shady rooms that verge on the dingy.

Hotel Mi Abuela (☎ 50-0333; Av Adrián Jara; s/d 110,000/150,000G;) Not exactly your grandmother's house, in an '80s-style building, with dark rooms around a small courtyard. Central location.

Hotel Austria (☎ 50-0883; www.hotelrestaurante austria.com; Fernández 165; s/d 120,000/150,000G;) Superclean European number with spacious rooms, big baths and even bigger breakfasts. Great restaurant, too

Hotel Munich (☎ 50-0347; Fernández 71; s/d 120,000/160,000G;) Like its neighbor Hotel Austria, this one has comfortable and spacious rooms with cable TV and a convenient location not too far from the border.

Eating

The cheapest options are the stalls along Capitán Miranda and Av Monseñor Rodríguez. Otherwise, Asian-cuisine fans, dig in.

Faraone (Av Rogelio Benítez; mains 18,000-30,000G) Top-notch à la carte meals provided at affordable rates. Finish off with a few scoops at the delicious Heladería Mita'i next door.

Kokorelia (Av Boquerón 169; mains 20,00-60,000G) Fresh and good if you're craving Asian.

Lebanon (cnr Av Adrián Jara & Abay, Edificio Salah I, 2nd fl; mains 25,000-50,000G; lunch only) For something more exotic and upscale, Lebanon serves scrumptious Middle Eastern fare for lunches only. Half portions available.

Gauchiño Grill (Av del Lago; buffet 35,000G) You'll feel the Brazilian influence here with this all-you-can-eat meat fest. Don't forget to make full use of the salad bar!

Getting There & Away

AIR

The airport is 30km west of town on Ruta 2. **TAM Mercosur** (☎ 50-6030; Curupayty) flies to Asunción three times daily, though flights are often cancelled.

BUS & TAXI

The bus terminal (☎ 51-0421) is about 2km south of the center on Chaco Boreal. City buses (2300G) shuttle frequently between here and the center, continuing on to immigration. There are frequent buses to Asunción (50,000-75,000G, five hours) and Encarnación (50,000G, five hours). Daily buses run to São Paulo, Brazil (220,000G, 14 hours).

GETTING TO BRAZIL OR ARGENTINA

The border with Brazil (Foz do Iguaçu) is at the Puente de la Amistad (Friendship Bridge). Immigration is at both ends of the bridge. Buses to Foz do Iguaçu (6000G) pass by immigration (until 8pm), as do nonstop buses to Puerto Iguazú, Argentina (you have to go via Brazil to reach Puerto Iguazú – no Brazilian visa necessary; 6000G). It's probably more convenient to walk or take a taxi to immigration and catch the bus from there. If you catch a bus to immigration, make sure you disembark to obtain all necessary exit stamps – locals don't need to stop. For information on travel from Brazil to Paraguay, see p307.

Taxis (☎ 51-0660) are fairly expensive – around 25,000G to downtown.

ITAIPÚ DAM

Paraguay's publicity machine is awash with facts and figures about the Itaipú hydroelectric project – the world's second-largest dam (China's new Three Gorges Dam is bigger). Itaipú's generators supply nearly 80% of Paraguay's electricity and 25% of Brazil's entire demand. In 1997 it churned out a staggering 12,600 megawatts, helping to make Paraguay the world's largest exporter of hydropower.

While project propaganda gushes about this disconcerting human accomplishment, it omits the US$25 billion price tag and avoids mention of environmental consequences. The 1350-sq-km, 220m deep reservoir drowned Sete Quedas, a set of waterfalls that was more impressive than Iguazú.

Free **tours** (8am, 9:30am, 1:30pm, 2:00pm & 3:00pm Mon-Sat, 8am, 9:30am & 10:30am Sun) leave from the **visitors center** (☎ 061-599-8040; www.itaipu.gov.py), north of Ciudad del Este, near the town of Hernandarias; passports are required. Any bus marked 'Hernandarias' (2300G, every 15 minutes) passes in front of the dam and Flora and Fauna Itaipú Binacional (see p756). A taxi will charge 40,000G one way or 60,000G return, including waiting time.

SALTO DEL MONDAY

This impressive 80m-high **waterfall** (admission 3000G; 8am-7pm) 10km outside of Ciudad del Este suffers from its close proximity to Iguazú on the other side of the border. If you have time on your hands, it's well worth the visit, especially as dusk falls and tens of thousands of swifts gather in the air like a cloud of mosquitoes before zipping in one after the other like miniature torpedoes to their precarious roosts on the slippery rocks behind the cascades. And in case you are wondering, it is pronounced Mon-Da-OO. A return taxi ride will cost around 60,000G, including waiting time.

ITAIPÚ ECOLOGICAL RESERVES

As a result of the catastrophic flood damage caused by Itaipú, the dam company was obliged to set up a series of eight private reserves that now protect the last remnants of the Alto Paraná Atlantic forest. Three of the most interesting are covered below.

Easiest to visit is **Refugio Tati Yupi**, 26km north of Ciudad del Este. A popular weekend spot, the reserve is best visited during the week if you hope to see animals. Serious animal-watchers will prefer **Reserva Itabó**, 100km north of the city. The forest here is undisturbed and teeming with wildlife, including friendly armadillos and endangered Vinaceous Amazon parrots. There are good accommodations, too, though occasionally occupied by school groups. The largest reserve is **Limoy**, another 65km further on, but the facilities are basic and access is difficult without a 4WD.

Unless your visit is part of a tour, you'll need your own vehicle and prior permission from **Flora and Fauna Itaipú Binacional** (☎ 061-599-8652; Hernandarias Supercarretera), 18km from the center of Ciudad del Este on the road to the dam. There is a good zoo of rescued animals and a natural history museum to make it worth the trip. Basic accommodation is available free of charge at some reserves, but you will have to bring and prepare your own food. For short guided day trips in Spanish only, contact Nelson Perez of the **Itaipú company** (☎ 0983-56-6448).

MBARACAYÚ BIOSPHERE RESERVE

Singled out by the WWF as one of the 100 most important sites for biodiversity on the planet, the 70,000 hectare Mbaracayú Biosphere Reserve is one of Paraguay's natural treasures. Consisting of pristine Atlantic forest and *cerrado* in approximately equal quantities, it is home to over 400 bird species and a swath of large mammals. Bird-watchers will be in search of the bare-throated bellbird

(Paraguay's national bird), the rare helmeted woodpecker and the endangered black-fronted piping-guan. There is also a resident Aché indigenous tribe here who are allowed to hunt using traditional methods. Look out for them in full dress at sunrise around the accommodations area at Jejui-Mi (per person 150,000G). This model reserve is run by the **Fundación Moisés Bertoni** (☎ 021-60-8740; www.mbertoni.org.py; Argüello 208, Asunción) and permission is required for access. You'll need to take all your own food and water and arrange pickup from the nearby town of Villa Ygatimi. Empresa Paraguarí runs a punishing bus service overnight from Asunción. An easier, if more expensive option is to take a guided tour (see p746).

NORTHERN PARAGUAY

Northern Paraguay is off the radar for most travelers, but the colonial city of Concepción is the best place to catch a boat heading north along the Río Paraguay. Natural wonders abound in this remote, largely unspoilt area, and the road east from **Pozo Colorado** to Concepción is famed for its abundance of wildlife.

CONCEPCIÓN

☎ 03312 / pop 70,000

'La Perla del Norte' is an easygoing city on the Río Paraguay with poetic early-20th-century buildings and a laid-back ambience. 'Action' is a trotting horse hauling a cart of watermelons along or a boatload of people and their cargo arriving at the port. Indeed, river cruises are the main reason travelers come to Concepción, whether it is for an adventurous odyssey north to Brazil or just a short weekend jaunt upriver with the locals to nearby sandy beaches.

If you don't catch the sleepy syndrome, sights include the **Museo del Cuartel de la Villa Real** (cnr Maria López & Cerro Cordillera; ☯ 7am-noon Mon-Sat), in the beautifully restored barracks that exhibit historical and war paraphernalia. Several stunning **mansions**, now municipal buildings, stand out along Estigarribia. If machines are more likely to rev you up, the open-air **Museo de Arqueología Industrial** along Agustín Pinedo features an assortment of antique industrial and agricultural machines. Perhaps the city's most eye-catching monument, however, is the enormous statue of **Maria Auxiliadora** (Virgin Mary), which towers over the northern end of the same avenue. The **market** is about as authentic as you'll get, complete with its crude *comedor* (basic cafeteria). For a leisurely meander across the river, catch a local rowboat (per person 4000G).

Information

Banco Continental and Visión on Presidente Franco have ATMs that accept foreign cards. Local resident **Celso Ruíz Díaz** (celsoruizdiaz@gmail .com) is happy to help with tourist information. His house is at the southern end of Cerro Corá, opposite the municipality building. There are several internet cafes around town, including **Cyberc@t** (Franco near Garay; per hr 5000G).

Sleeping & Eating

Hospedaje Puerta del Sol (☎ 42185; r per person 25,000G) The owners are the sweetest part of this basic place, and it's handy to the port.

Hotel Center (☎ 42360; Franco near Yegros; s 25,000-40,000G, d 40,000-60,000G; ❄) An outdated and rather dingy dive, but the air-con rooms will be welcome if you are on a budget.

our pick **Hotel Frances** (☎ 42383; cnr Franco & CA López; s/d 150,000/190,000G; ❄ 🖳 🖭) Whet your appetite in every respect at this pleasant place – lovely gardens, buffet breakfast (and restaurant) and unique handmade lamps in every room.

Hotel Piscis (☎ 41211; Estigarribia; ❄ 🖭) Due to open in 2010, this luxury pool and hotel complex has a riverfront location and promises water sports and a top-notch restaurant at accessible prices.

Ysapy (cnr Yegros & Estigarribia; mains 5000-30,000G) Packed with local youths who enjoy decent pizzas, burgers and energy drinks!

Restaurante Toninho y Jandiri (cnr Estigarribia & Iturbe; mains 40,000G) This place is worth the pressure on both stomach and purse. Come to this Brazilian *churrasquería* (restaurant featuring barbecued meat) for plentiful portions of meats and fish served on sizzle plates.

Locals flock to down-to-earth rivals **Pollería El Bigote** (Franco) and **Pollería Bulldog** (Franco; portions 10,000G) for the rotisserie chickens.

Getting There & Away
BOAT

The most traditional (but not the most comfortable) way to get to/from Concepción is by riverboat. Note that typically these are cargo boats and lack basic services (including a toilet). Boats heading upriver to Vallemí (50,000G, 30 hours) or as far as Bahía Negra (100,000G, 2½ to three days) include the *Aquidabán* (Tuesday at 11am) with returns on Sunday and the erratic *Guaraní* which passes through on Monday morning. Check schedules and boats in advance (☎ 42435) as both change frequently.

BUS

The bus terminal is eight blocks north of the center at General Garay and 14 de Mayo. Car or motorcycle taxis cost about 20,000G; *karumbés* (horse-drawn carriages) are twice as much fun (15,000G) – confirm your price before you are 'taken for a ride!'

For Asunción (60,000G, six hours) La Santaniana and La Concepcionera offer the best service. Several services head to Pedro Juan Caballero (35,000G, four hours) and Filadelfia (60,000G, six hours). There's a daily departure at 12:30pm to Ciudad del Este (70,000G, nine hours).

VALLEMÍ

Vallemí might be most famous nationally for its cement plant, but it's beginning to make a name for itself among visitors as an ecotour center for trips along the spectacular Río Apa. There's plenty to see, with *cerros* (hills) and caves in the area giving boundless opportunities for adventure tourism. There

---

UP THE LAZY RÍO PARAGUAY

North of Concepción the Paraguay river wends its way s-l-o-w-l-y through the Paraguayan Pantanal. Unlike in the Brazilian Pantanal, you are unlikely to see another tourist here, and your companions will be the wildlife: capybaras, monkeys and birds galore, including jabiru, herons, egrets, spoonbills, even macaws. Bring a hammock and a mosquito net, prepare yourself for unusual bedfellows and claim your territory early – it gets crowded. Some boats have basic cabins (around 30,000G per night) but they need to be booked well in advance. If you want to vary your diet, bring your own food. Sleepy Fuerte Olimpo is the last place to obtain an exit stamp (it's safer to get one before leaving Asunción) and services terminate in tiny Bahía Negra, near the frontiers with Bolivia and Brazil.

PARAGUAY

is even a tour of the cement plant. Tourism is highly controlled, with visits to local attractions through the municipality-sponsored **Vallemí Tour** (☎ 0351-23-0764; Río Apa near 13 de Junio), whose staff can also assist with hotel bookings and transport arrangements. See http://ciudadvallemi.tripod.com for information. Accommodation is basic, **El Prado** (☎ 0351-23-0545; r 100,000G), near the port being as good as any on account of its river views. Access is a problem and you'll need a 4WD if you are making your own way. The unrushed can catch the boat from Concepción which passes through here (50,000G, 30 hours), or you can take the bone-shaking daily buses, which leave at 5:30 and 6am (40,000G, seven hours).

PARQUE NACIONAL CERRO CORÁ

This national park protects an area of dry tropical forest and natural savanna in a landscape of steep, isolated hills. Cultural and historical features include pre-Columbian caves, petroglyphs and the site of Mariscal López' death, which, in 1870, ended the War of the Triple Alliance; it's marked with a monument at the end of a long line of busts of war heroes. There's a camping area and a small **museum**. Ask about using the cabin here, but if not the nearest accommodation is in Pedro Juan Caballero (it's pricey!). Try the retro **Eiruzú** (☎ 0336-27-2435; Mariscal López; s/d 120,000/200,000G; ❄). Buses running between Concepción and Pedro Juan Caballero (three hours from Concepción, one hour from PJC) pass the park entrance and it's a 1km walk to the visitors center.

LAGUNA BLANCA

A pristine, crystal-clear lake, Laguna Blanca is named for its white-sand beach and lakebed, so that it looks pure white when viewed from the air. If lounging around on the beach isn't your cup of tea, there are horses for rent, and the surrounding *cerrado* habitat is home to rare birds and mammals such as the maned wolf and the endangered white-winged nightjar, this being one of only three places in the world where the latter species breeds. You can camp here, or there is basic accommodation, but you'll need to bring your own food. Book in advance by calling owner **Malvina Duarte** (☎ 021-42-4760; www.lagunablanca.com.py; r per person 150,000G); she will arrange transport and food for longer stays in the ranch house. To

get there take any bus from Asunción to San Pedro or Pedro Juan Caballero and get off at Santa Rosa del Aguaray. From here infrequent local buses to Santa Barbara pass the entrance to the property. The journey may take six to eight hours by public transport and an early start is recommended. Animal lovers should contact **FAUNA Paraguay** (☎ 071-20-3981; www.faunaparaguay.com) about their three-day animal-watching trips.

THE CHACO

The Gran Chaco is *the* place to escape the crowds and experience raw wilderness. This vast plain – roughly divided into the flooded palm savannas of the Humid Chaco (first 350km west of Asunción), and the spiny forests of the Dry Chaco (the rest) – encompasses the entire western half of Paraguay and stretches into Argentina and Bolivia. Bisected by the Ruta Trans-Chaco, it's a paradise for wildlife, abounding with flocks of waterbirds and birds of prey that are easy to see along the roadside.

Although the Chaco accounts for over 60% of Paraguayan territory, less than 3% of the population lives here. Historically it was a refuge for indigenous hunter-gatherers; today the most obvious settlements are the Mennonite communities of the Central Chaco. Each September sees the Rally Transchaco, a three-day world motor-sport competition, said to be one of the toughest on the planet.

Tours

Cultural tours in the Mennonite colonies and surroundings can be arranged through the friendly and knowledgeable German- and English-speaking guide **Walter Ratzlaff** (☎ 52301). For ecotours and national park trips contact **FAUNA Paraguay** (☎ 071-20-3981; www.faunaparaguay.com).

THE MENNONITE COLONIES

Of the three Mennonite Colonies in the Central Chaco, only two are easily accessible on public transport – Filadelfia and Loma Plata. Many people are surprised by just how small these towns are. Although there's not much to do here except take in the unique atmosphere, they make for an interesting short break and are good bases for exploring the surrounding area.

MENNONITE COLONIES IN THE CHACO

Some 15,000 Mennonites inhabit the Chaco. According to their history, Canadian Mennonites were invited to Paraguay to settle what they believed to be lush, productive territory in return for their rights – religious freedom, pacifism, independent administration of their communities, permission to speak German and practice their religious beliefs. The reality of the harsh, arid Chaco came as a shock and a large percentage of the original settlers succumbed to disease, hunger and thirst as they struggled to gain a foothold.

Other Mennonite communities are elsewhere in Paraguay, but those in the Chaco are renowned for both their perseverance in the 'Green Hell,' and subsequent commercial success; their cooperatives provide much of the country's dairy products, among other things.

Today there are three main colonies in the Chaco. The oldest colony, Menno, was founded by the original settlers in 1927, and is centered around Loma Plata. Fernheim (capital Filadelfia), was founded in 1930 by refugees from the Soviet Union, followed by Neuland (capital Neu-Halbstadt), founded by Ukrainian Germans in 1947.

Filadelfia
☎ 04914 / pop 5000 (colony)

This neat Mennonite community, administrative center of Fernheim colony, resembles a suburb of Munich plonked in the middle of a sandy desert. Though dusty Av Hindenburg is the main street, the town lacks a real center; its soul is the giant dairy cooperative Trebol. For information on the Mennonites, and everything from 15th-century coins and stuffed jaguars to colorful Nivaclé headdresses, visit the **Jakob Unger Museum** (Hindenburg; ☿ 7-11:30am Mon-Fri) opposite Hotel Florida. The creaky wooden building is the original headquarters of the colony.

It's worth a trip to the gigantic, well-stocked **Cooperativa Mennonita** (cnr Unruh & Hindenburg) supermarket. It's amazing how much you can fit under one roof, but you may find yourself the only person paying; the Mennonites deal in barter more than hard currencies. There is only one ATM in town at the Portal del Chaco shopping center.

SLEEPING & EATING
Hotel Florida (☎ 32151; Hindenburg 984; dm 30,000G, s/d 100,000/150,000G; ☒ ☒) As orderly as a German train schedule and by far Filadelfia's nicest accommodation, including the cheaper rooms. Nonguests can also use the pool (per hour 7000G).

Girasol (Unruh; buffet 40,000G) Apart from Hotel Florida's restaurant, try Girasol, which serves delicious all-you-can-eat Brazilian *asados*.

GETTING THERE & AWAY
Bus companies have offices along and near Hindenburg. NASA has a daily service to Asunción (70,000G, eight hours), and a daily bus runs to Concepción (80,000G, eight hours).

Getting between the colonies by bus is tricky and buses are infrequent, usually leaving in the early morning and late evening. Ask at Hotel Florida for the latest schedules.

Loma Plata
☎ 04922 / pop 8800 (colony)

The Menno Colony's administrative center is the oldest and most traditional of the Mennonite settlements. Its excellent **museum**, in a complex of pioneer houses, has a remarkable display of original photographs and documents chronicling the colony's history, plus original artifacts and furniture.

our pick **Loma Plata Inn** (☎ 53235; s 110,000-130,000G, d 160,000-180,000G; ☒) is comfortable and the best place to stay in town. Its great restaurant, Chaco Grill, serves quality meats Brazilian-style (buffet 45,000G).

Hotel Mora (☎ 52255; Sandstrasse 803; s 65,000-100,000G, d 100,000-150,000G; ☒) has appealing, spotless rooms around a grassy setting.

AROUND THE MENNONITE COLONIES
Fortín Boquerón & Fortín Toledo
Fortín Boquerón is the site of one of the decisive battles of the Chaco War (1932–35). There is an excellent **museum** (☿ 8am-6pm Tue-Sat; admission 5000G) as well as a graveyard of the fallen and a gigantic monument constructed from the original defenses and trenches. Look for the hollowed-out *palo borracho* tree used as a sniper's nest. From the front it looks like a woodpecker hole, but despite being gutted over 70 years ago the tree is still alive!

PARAGUAY

PARAGUAY

GETTING TO BOLIVIA

The Ruta Trans-Chaco is now fully paved on the Paraguayan side, and several companies run the route from Asunción to Santa Cruz, Bolivia, daily. The journey takes about 24 hours (250,000G). All buses stop at the new *aduanas* (customs) building in Mariscal Estigarribia in the wee hours of the morning, where you must get your exit stamp before crossing an hour or two later into Bolivia at Fortín Infante Rivola (this is a border post only – no entry/exit stamps are available). Here the asphalt ends and it's another 60km to Ibibobo for Bolivian formalities. Bolivia-bound buses do not pass through the Mennonite colonies and there is no regular public transport from the colonies to Mariscal Estigarribia so, unless you fancy your chances waiting on the Trans-Chaco and hitching a lift, by far the easiest option is to head back to Asunción. The best company running this route is **Yacyretá** (☎ 021-55-1725). Buses run by other companies are much less comfortable.

Fortín Toledo also preserves Chaco War trenches but is perhaps more interesting for the **Proyecto Tagua** (Chaco peccary) breeding project (donations accepted). This pig-like creature was known only from fossil remains until its remarkable rediscovery in the 1970s. The project, initiated by San Diego Zoo, acts as a reintroduction program for this painfully shy and critically endangered species. Herds of friendly collared and frankly nasty white-lipped peccaries are also kept here, giving you a unique opportunity to compare all three species and their differing characters. Look out for the rare black-bodied woodpecker in the surroundings too.

You'll need your own transport to visit both sites as the closest accommodation is in Loma Plata. Fortín Boquerón is 65km or so from a turnoff at Cruce Los Pioneros. Fortín Toledo is accessed via a turnoff at Km 475. Follow the peccary signs.

Central Chaco Lagoons

A series of ephemeral saline lakes that form in the area to the east of Loma Plata have been declared an 'Important Bird Area' because of their importance for migrating birds. Though individual lagoons may be dry for several years before filling after a good rainstorm, the birds somehow find them. They are best from May to September when flocks of exotic ducks and flamingos obscure the water. From October to December and March to April they are used by waders on passage.

A good place to base yourself is **Laguna Capitán** (☎ 0991-65-0101; r per person 60,000G), though you'll need to book in advance and have your own transport; you'd also need a guide, or instructions on how to get there. Food can be arranged with prior warning. The lagoons are often dry here but the surroundings teem with wildlife. For waterbirds and particularly flamingos, head to **Campo Maria** (admission 10,000G), which usually has water and is a great place to see mammals like tapirs and peccaries.

NORTHWESTERN NATIONAL PARKS

Once the realm of nomadic Ayoreo foragers, **Parque Nacional Defensores del Chaco** is a wooded alluvial plain; isolated **Cerro León** (500m) is its greatest landmark. The dense thorn forest harbors large cats such as jaguars and pumas, as well as tapirs and herds of peccary. The accommodation is decent here, but you'll need to bring all your own food, drink and fuel for the generator. 'Defensores' is a long 830km from Asunción, over roads impassable to ordinary vehicles and there's no public transport. Don't attempt to visit without a guide.

A more accessible option is to visit **Parque Nacional Teniente Agripino Enciso**, which boasts a sophisticated infrastructure including an interpretation center and a visitors house with kitchen and some air-conditioned rooms (100,000G per room). Again, bring all your own food and water. NASA runs minibuses (two daily; 16 hours) from Asunción to Nueva Asunción that pass in front of the visitors center at Enciso.

A short hop further north is **Parque Nacional Médanos del Chaco**, although there are no accommodations here and it should not be attempted without a guide. The habitat is more open than at Enciso and bird-watchers should keep their eyes peeled for local species like quebracho crested-tinamou and spot-winged falconet. For expert-led animal-watching tours to any of these parks, contact **FAUNA Paraguay** (☎ 071-20-3981; www.faunaparaguay .com). To do the area justice, trips of at least five days and nights are recommended.

PARAGUAY DIRECTORY

ACCOMMODATIONS

Although worn and of a distant era, hotels and *residenciales* (guesthouses) in Paraguay are usually very clean. Camping facilities are rare. Most of the land is privately owned so you can't just pitch a tent without getting permission first. In the Chaco, formal accommodations are sparse outside the few towns, but you shouldn't really stray away from them without a guide anyway.

ACTIVITIES

Organized activities for the budget traveler are limited, but biodiversity makes Paraguay a notable destination for ecotourism, in particular bird-watching.

BOOKS

For more about Paraguay's notorious wars, pick up Harris Gaylord Warren's *Rebirth of the Paraguayan Republic,* or Augusto Roa Bastos' novel *Son of Man.* For a look into Paraguay's heinous dictators, check out Bastos' book *I the Supreme* about Francia, or Carlos Miranda's *The Stroessner Era.* An excellent fictional account of the Francisco Solano López years, focusing on Lopez' relationship with Eliza Lynch, is *The News from Paraguay* by Lily Tuck. For an anthropological slant check out Pierre Clastres' *Chronicle of the Guayaki Indians* or Matthew Pallamary's novel *Land Without Evil.* Mark Jacobs' *The Liberation of Little Heaven and Other Stories* is a collection of fictional Paraguayan shorts. History buffs should look for Andrew Nickson's *Historical Dictionary of Paraguay.* Better is *At the Tomb of the Inflatable Pig: Travels through Paraguay* by John Gimlette.

BUSINESS HOURS

Government offices are open from 7am to 1pm or 2pm. Most shops are open weekdays and Saturday from 8am to noon and from 2pm or 3pm until 7pm or 8pm. Banking hours are 8am to 1pm Monday to Friday, but *casas de cambio* (authorized currency exchange houses) keep longer hours. Restaurants normally open for lunch and dinner with a break in the afternoon. Cafes keep varying hours and, although not early starters, will be more likely to open for breakfast.

CLIMATE

Climate in Paraguay is governed by winds, a north wind bringing high temperatures from the tropics and a south wind bringing cool weather from Patagonia. Paraguay is intensely hot from November to March, averaging 35°C (95°F), with daily temperatures ranging between 25°C and 43°C (77°F to 109°F). It is coolest from April to September, though the average high in July, the coldest month, is 22°C (71°F). In this period extremely hot days as well as cold morning frosts are not unusual.

The end of June usually experiences a week or two of hot weather, known as the Veranillo de San Juan (St John's minisummer) as it frequently coincides with the Fiesta de San Juan (p762). Heavy rain and breathtaking electric storms are frequent from September to November and, less dramatically, from March to April. Typically the sun shines throughout the year, even when it is cold. For information and climate charts, see p987.

DANGERS & ANNOYANCES

Despite what you may hear from people who have never been, Paraguay is one of the continent's safest countries. With the exception of Ciudad del Este and certain parts of Asunción, cities are quite safe to walk around, even at night. The Chaco is hostile and desolate with limited infrastructure – it is highly recommended that you go with a guide. Beware of strong currents when swimming in rivers.

DRIVER'S LICENSE

Most rental agencies accept a home driver's license, but it's wise to back it up with an International Driver's License – the lack of one is a favorite scam for soliciting bribes.

ELECTRICITY

Paraguay uses 220V, 50Hz. The most common types of plugs in use are the two round pins with no grounding pin.

EMBASSIES & CONSULATES

For information about Visas see p764. For locations of these embassies see individual city maps.

Argentina (off Map pp744-5; ☎ 021-21-2320; cnr España & Perú)

Bolivia (☎ 021-61-9984; América 200)

Brazil Asunción (☎ 021-248-4000; cnr Irrazabal & Ayala); Ciudad del Este (Map p754; ☎ 061-50-0984; Pampliega 205; ☺ 7am-noon Mon-Fri)

Canada (☎ 021-22-7207; cnr Ramírez & Juan de Salazar)
Chile (☎ 021- 66-2756; Nudelman 351)
France (☎ 021-21-3840; Av España 893)
Germany (☎ 021-21-4009; Av Venezuela 241)
USA (☎ 021-21-3715; Mariscal López 1776)

FESTIVALS & EVENTS

Paraguay's celebration of **Carnaval** (February to March) is liveliest in Encarnación, though Villarrica claims to rival it. Caacupé is the most important site for the Roman Catholic **Día de la Virgen** (Immaculate Conception Day; December 8).

Other events:

Día de San Blas (Feast of San Blas) Celebration of Paraguay's patron saint held on February 3.
Fiesta de San Juan Celebrated on 23 June, with displays of dancing, singing and widespread consumption of traditional Paraguayan food.
Rally Transchaco Trans-Chaco car race held during the first week of September.

FOOD & DRINK

Eating reviews throughout this chapter are given in order of budget, with the least expensive options first.

Asado (grilled meat) is popular and a barbecue is the focal point of every social event. The beef is succulent, abundant and easily rivals that of Argentina. The best cuts are *tapa de cuadril* (similar to rump steak) and *corte americano* (akin to T-bone), though the commonest (and cheapest) are fatty *vacio* (flank) and chewy *costillas* (ribs). Grains, particularly maize, are common ingredients in traditional foods, while *mandioca* (manioc) is the standard accompaniment for every meal. *Chipa* (a type of bread made with manioc flour, eggs and cheese) is sold everywhere but is best in the southern town of Coronel Bogado (p749). Empanadas are great wherever you buy them.

Paraguayans consume massive quantities of *yerba maté* (a type of tea), most commonly as refreshing ice-cold *tereré* (iced maté) and generously spiked with *yuyos* (medicinal herbs). Roadside stands offer *mosto* (sugarcane juice), while *caña* (cane alcohol) is the fiery alcoholic alternative. Local beers, especially Baviera and Pilsen, are excellent.

The following are some other common foods you might encounter.

chipa so-ó (*chee*·pa so-ó) *Chipa* stuffed with meat.
chipa guasu (*chee*·pa *gwa*·su) Hot maize pudding with cheese and onion.
locro (*lok*·ro) Maize stew.
mazamorra (ma·sa·*mo*·ra) Sweetened corn porridge.
mbaipy he-é (*mbai*·poo he·e) A dessert of corn, milk and molasses.
mbeyú (mbe·*yoo*) A grilled manioc pancake.
sooyo (*so*·yo) Thick soup of ground meat, often with a floating poached egg.
sopa paraguaya (*so*·pa pa·ra·*gwa*·ya) Cornbread with cheese and onion.
vori-vori (vo·*ree* vo·ree) Chicken soup with cornmeal balls.

GAY & LESBIAN TRAVELERS

Paraguay is an old-fashioned country, with conservative views. Public displays of affection between same-sex couples are unknown. However, more gay bars are appearing in Asunción.

HEALTH

Paraguay presents relatively few health problems for travelers. Private hospitals are definitely better than public hospitals, and those in Asunción, Ciudad del Este and Encarnación are the best. An outbreak of dengue fever in 2008 was greatly exaggerated – there were more cases in the single Brazilian state of Rio Grande do Sul than in the whole of Paraguay. In the cities tap water is drinkable, in the countryside it should be avoided and in the Chaco it is positively salty.

Carry sunscreen, a hat and plenty of bottled water at all times to avoid becoming dehydrated. Condoms are available in most pharmacies but avoid cheap brands. For more information, see the Health chapter (p1011).

HOLIDAYS

Government offices and businesses in Paraguay are closed for the official holidays in the following list.

Año Nuevo (New Year's Day) January 1
Cerro Corá (Heroes Day) March 1
Semana Santa (Easter) March/April – dates vary
Día de los Trabajadores (Labor Day) May 1
Independencia Patria (Independence Day) May 15
Paz del Chaco (End of Chaco War) June 12
Fundación de Asunción (Founding of Asunción) August 15
Victoria de Boquerón (Battle of Boquerón) September 29
Día de la Virgen (Immaculate Conception Day) December 8
Navidad (Christmas Day) December 25

INTERNET ACCESS

Internet is *muy popular* in cities, but limited in smaller towns. An hour of use costs around 3000G to 6000G.

INTERNET RESOURCES

Desde el Chaco (www.desdelchaco.org.py) Chaco development agency with lots of information on the region.
FAUNA Paraguay (www.faunaparaguay.com) Everything you could possibly wish to know about Paraguayan wildlife.
Guaraní Ñanduti Rogue (www.staff.uni-mainz.de/lustig/guarani/welcome.html) Fascinating site covering various aspects of Guaraní culture.
Lanic (http://lanic.utexas.edu/la/sa/paraguay) Excellent collection of links from the University of Texas.
Paraguayan Current Events (www.paraguay.com) News stories about Paraguay in English.
Senatur (www.senatur.gov.py) This is the official tourist information home page.

LEGAL MATTERS

Drugs are not widely available in Paraguay and under no circumstances can you legally possess, use or traffic illegal drugs while in the country. Penalties are severe – long jail sentences and heavy fines.

MAPS

The **Touring y Automóvil Club Paraguayo** (Map pp744-5; ☎ 021-21-0550; www.tacpy.com.py; cnr 25 de Mayo & Brasil, Asunción) produce a series of road and town maps for tourists. For more detailed maps of the interior, the **Instituto Geográfico Militar** (☎ 021-20-6344; Artigas 920, Asunción) sells topographical maps that cover most of the country.

MEDIA

The following is a list of Paraguay's most important newspapers.
ABC Color (www.abc.com.py) Asunción's daily paper made its reputation opposing the Stroessner dictatorship.
Popular (www.popular.com.py) Written in Jopará, this is the country's most-read tabloid.
Última Hora (www.ultimahora.com) Editorially bold independent daily with an excellent cultural section.

MONEY

The unit of currency is the guaraní (plural *guaraníes*), indicated by 'G.' Banknote values are 1000G, 5000G, 10,000G, 20,000G, 50,000G and 100,000G; coins come in denominations of 50G, 100G, 500G and 1000G. Keep plenty of change and small notes as you go along – it comes in handy.

ATMs & Credit Cards

ATMs in major cities are connected to Visa, MasterCard and Cirrus networks. They are less frequent in other towns, but if all else fails some banks will allow you to withdraw money on a credit card on production of the proper documentation.

Plastic is rarely used outside Asunción, and even there only in midrange to top-end hotels, restaurants and shops.

Exchanging Money

Casas de cambio are abundant in Asunción and border towns and change cash and less often traveler's checks; try banks in the interior. Some *cambios* will not cash traveler's checks without the original proof of purchase receipt. Street money changers give slightly lower rates for cash only but can be helpful on evenings and weekends.

Exchange rates at press time:

EXCHANGE RATES		
Country	**Unit**	**G**
Australia	A$1	3969
Canada	C$1	4429
euro zone	€1	6952
Japan	¥100	5216
New Zealand	NZ$1	3163
UK	UK£1	8228
USA	US$	5100

PHOTOGRAPHY

Most Paraguayans will gladly smile for the camera, if you ask before shooting. Professional-quality color print and slide film is available in bigger cities.

POST

Sending a letter to the USA costs about 13,000G and it's 16,000G to Europe. Essential mail should be sent *certificado* (registered) for a small fee (4000G).

RESPONSIBLE TRAVEL

Avoid buying crafts made from wood (such as *lapacho* and *palo santo*) or wild animals. Visitors interested in natural history and conservation should contact **FAUNA Paraguay** (☎ 071-20-3981; www.faunaparaguay.com), the **Fundación Moisés Bertoni** (☎ 021-60-8740; www.mbertoni.org.py; Argüello 208, Asunción) or **Guyra Paraguay** (☎ 021-22-3567; www.guyra.org.py; Martino 215).

PARAGUAY

TELEPHONE

Copaco, the state telephone company, has offices throughout the country. Private *locutorios* (phone offices) have sprung up everywhere, often with internet service as well. Despite deregulation, international calls still run over 4000G per minute, even with lower nighttime rates.

The country code for Paraguay is ☎ 595. When calling Paraguay from another country, drop the '0' in the area code. The code for the international operator is ☎ 0010, and international direct dial code is ☎ 002. Area codes are listed under the destination headings throughout this chapter.

As a result of competition, rates for local cell-phone companies are very low and some companies offer free chips, or chips with *saldo* (credit) already charged to them for a small fee. The best companies are **Tigo** and **Claro** and *tarjetas* (cards) for charging credit to your phone are sold at every newsagent. Claro chips can be formatted to work in both Brazil and Argentina.

TOILETS

You're likely to see more jaguars than public toilets – they're rare! Most bus terminals have one – for 1000G you get a smelly loo and an (often insufficient) wad of paper. Go when you can in restaurants or hotels. Carry your own toilet paper and don't throw it down the pipes (throw the used paper into the wastebasket provided). Most buses have a toilet but the cheaper services and those in more remote areas do not.

TOURIST INFORMATION

The government-run **Senatur** (www.senatur.com.py) has tourist offices in Asunción and one or two other cities. They lack colorful brochures but staff do what they can to answer questions (in Spanish). The **Asociación de Colonias Mennonitas del Paraguay** (off Map pp744-5; ☎ 021-22-6059; www.acomepa.org; República de Colombia 1050, Asunción) has brochures about Mennonite communities.

TRAVELERS WITH DISABILITIES

Infrastructure for travelers with disabilities is negligible. Unfortunately, there are really no services for people with disabilities or special needs.

VISAS

Visitors from Australia, Canada, New Zealand and the USA need visas. Others only need a valid passport. Get your visa in advance in a neighboring country or at home. Visas may be requested and obtained in the same day at most consulates or apply online at http://paraguay.visahq.com. You will need two passport photos and two copies each of your passport, proof of onward travel and proof of sufficient funds. The cost is US$45 in cash for single entry or US$65 for multiple entry (30 to 180 days). Get your passport stamped on entering the country or face a fine upon leaving.

Visa requirements change frequently. Check lonelyplanet.com for the latest information or visit the **Immigration Office** (☎ 021-44-6673; cnr Ayala & Caballero; ⏲ 7am-1pm Mon-Fri) in Asunción.

VOLUNTEERING

FAUNA Paraguay (☎ 071-20-3981; www.faunaparaguay .com) often offers links to nonprofit volunteerships on local conservation projects. A variety of volunteer opportunities are offered by **Intercultural Experience** (☎ 021-48-2890; www.ie.com .py; cnr Av Colón & La Habana), including language immersion placements with local families. **Apatur** (☎ 021-21-0550; www.turismorural.org.py), a rural tourism association, can help make placements on *estancias* (extensive grazing establishments).

WOMEN TRAVELERS

Paraguay is a reasonably safe country for women, but solo travelers should take care. Young unaccompanied women are likely to be hit on by Paraguayan men. Generally, it's harmless – take it as a compliment and be firm but polite. Modest dress is important. Also see Women Travelers (p998) in the Directory.

Peru

HIGHLIGHTS

- **Machu Picchu** (p825) Trek a breathless rite of passage to awe-inspiring ancient Inca ruins hidden in cloud forest.
- **Cuzco** (p811) Pound colonial Andean cobblestone streets, take in historical museums and trek humbling Inca hillsides.
- **Arequipa** (p798) Embrace wild *arequipeña* nightlife under the watchful eye of imposing volcanoes and sunken canyons.
- **Lake Titicaca** (p806) Visit storybook isles on what's considered the world's largest high-altitude lake, straddling the Peru–Bolivia border.
- **Huaraz, and the Cordilleras Blanca and Huayhuash** (p846) Play high-adrenaline Andes junkie: tackle one of South America's most spectacular mountain ranges.
- **Off the Beaten Track** (p804) Go deep in the Central Andes into Cañón del Cotahuasi: dramatic volcanoes, beautiful waterfalls, unique local color and no tourists!

FAST FACTS

- **Area:** 1,285,220 sq km (five times larger than the UK)
- **Budget:** US$20 to US$30 a day
- **Capital:** Lima
- **Costs:** comfortable double room in Cuzco US$35 to US$50, 1L bottled water US$0.65, domestic flight US$65 to US$215
- **Country Code:** ☎ 51
- **Languages:** Spanish, Quechua, Aymara
- **Money:** US$1 = S2.90 (nuevos soles)
- **Population:** 29.5 million
- **Seasons:** high (June to August), rainy (November to April)
- **Time:** GMT minus five hours

TRAVEL HINT

Book Inca Trail treks at least six weeks in advance, or several months for trips during the high season (June to August).

OVERLAND ROUTES

Border crossings include Arica (Chile); Huaquillas, Guayaquil and Macará (Ecuador); Kasani and Desaguadero (Bolivia); and multiple Brazilian and Bolivian towns and river ports in the Amazon.

Imagine scenery on the epic scale of an Indiana Jones or Lara Croft flick: forgotten temples entangled in jungle vines, cobwebbed ancient tombs baking in the desert sun and bejeweled buried treasures beyond all reckoning. Wild rivers that rage, pumas prowling in the night and hallucinogenic shaman rituals – it's not just a movie here, it's real life.

Like a continent in miniature, Peru will astound you with its diversity. Not even fierce Inca warriors or Spanish conquistadors could totally dominate such jaw-dropping terrain, from glaciated Andean peaks where majestic condors soar, to almost limitless coastal deserts, to the steamy rainforests of the Amazon basin.

Take it easy on the 'Gringo Trail' encircling the country's top highlights, ending at the cloud-topping Inca citadel of Machu Picchu. Or step off the beaten path and groove to Afro-Peruvian beats, chase perfect waves off a paradisiacal Pacific beach or ride a slow boat down the Amazon.

Wherever your journey takes you in Peru, you'll be welcomed by big-hearted folks that tackle their often-unfortunate lot with gusto and a deep lust for life. Small wonder, then, that the land of the Incas is one of the continent's top picks for adventurous travelers.

CURRENT EVENTS

Try as it may, Peru remained a hotbed of political corruption as the 2000s came to a close. President Alan García Pérez gave a healthy chunk of his cabinet the pink slip in late 2008 after a widespread corruption scandal rocked his administration – audiotapes surfaced that incriminated members of his APRA party in efforts to steer lucrative petroleum contracts to favored bidders in exchange for bribes. Meanwhile, one of García's recent predecessors, the formerly exiled Alberto Fujimori, was sentenced to 25 years in prison after being found guilty on human-rights abuse charges stemming from killings and kidnappings by state-run death squads under his watch.

Speaking of violence, the Maoist Sendero Luminoso (Shining Path), Peru's most prominent though long-dormant terrorist group, ambushed a military convoy near Huancavelica in 2008, killing 19 and injuring 11. The most violent attack by the group in 10 years showed terrorism in Peru still bubbles below the surface.

But it wasn't all guns and corruption for García's administration, there were some roses too: his government has sponsored a fast and furious push to develop free-trade agreements, starting with the US, and during the APEC summit in Peru in 2008 developing agreements with Japan, South Korea and China. Peru's economy, though stalled by the global recession that began in 2007 and continues at the time of writing, has seen sustained growth during García's administration – fruits of the laborious economic stabilization efforts began by President Alejandro Toledo, who left office in 2006. Next elections are scheduled for 2011.

Meanwhile, Machu Picchu was – rightfully so – named one of the New Seven Wonders of the World in 2007. But as the site approaches its centenary in 2011, it remains embroiled in a dispute with Yale University (see boxed text, p826) over the return of long-lost artifacts.

HISTORY
Early Cultures

The Inca civilization is merely the tip of Peru's archaeological iceberg.

The country's first inhabitants were loose-knit bands of nomadic hunters, fishers and gatherers, living in caves and killing fearsome (now extinct) animals like giant sloths, saber-toothed tigers and mastodons. Domestication of the llama, alpaca and guinea pig began between 7000 and 4000 BC. Various forms of the faithful potato (Peru boasts almost 4000 varieties!) were domesticated around 3000 BC.

Roughly from 1000 to 300 BC, the Early Horizon or Chavín Period evidenced at Chavín de Huántar near Huaraz (p853) saw widespread settled communities, plus the interchange of ideas, enhanced skills and cultural complexity, although the Chavín culture inexplicably disappeared around 300 BC. The next 500 years saw the rise and fall of the Paracas culture south of Lima, who produced some of the most exquisite textiles in the Americas.

Between AD 100 and 700 pottery, metalwork and textiles reached new heights of technological development, and the Moche built their massive pyramids near Trujillo (p839) and at Sipán near Chiclayo (p842). It was also around this time that the Nazca sculpted their enigmatic lines in the desert (p795).

From about AD 600 to 1000 the first Andean expansionist empire emerged, and the influence of the Wari (Huari), from north of Ayacucho (p831), can still be seen throughout most of Peru.

TOP 10 MUST-SEE ARCHAEOLOGICAL SITES

You've come to the right country for ruins:

- misty mountaintop citadel **Machu Picchu** (p825), 'lost city' of the Incas
- enigmatic desert scratches appreciated only at 1500m: **Nazca Lines** (p795)
- dramatic hilltop funerary towers at **Sillustani** and **Cutimbo** (p809) near Lake Titicaca
- imposing Inca citadels, lush terraces and holy sites of the **Sacred Valley** (p821)
- underground tunnels at **Chavín de Huántar** (p853), a 3000-year-old ceremonial complex
- sprawling Chimú adobe metropolis **Chan Chan** (p839) near Moche pyramids, all around Trujillo
- tombs of the Lords of Sipán and Sicán at **Chiclayo** (p842)
- breathtaking cloud forest Chachapoyan fortress **Kuélap** (p857) – no crowds!
- Wiñay Wayna and the scattered ruins along the **Inca Trail** (p828), opening acts for the main event
- above Cuzco, the Inca fortress of **Saqsaywamán** (p820), site of ancient Inti Raymi festival of the sun

During the next four centuries, several states thrived, including the Chimú, who built the city of Chan Chan near Trujillo (p839) and the Chachapoyas, who erected the stone fortress of Kuélap (p857). Several smaller, warlike highland groups lived near Lake Titicaca and left impressive, circular funerary towers, including at Sillustani and Cutimbo (p809).

Inca Empire & Spanish Conquest

For all its glory, Inca pre-eminence only lasted around 100 years. The reign of the first eight Incas spanned the period from the 12th century to the early 15th century, but it was the ninth Inca, Pachacutec, who gave the empire its first bloody taste of conquest. A growing thirst for expansion had led the neighboring highland tribe, the Chankas, to Cuzco's doorstep around 1438, and Viracocha Inca fled in the belief that his small empire was lost. However, his son Pachacutec rallied the Inca army and, in a desperate battle, he famously routed the Chankas.

Buoyed by his victory, Pachacutec then embarked upon the first wave of Inca expansion, promptly bagging much of the central Andes. Over the next 25 years, the Inca empire grew until it stretched from the present-day border of Ecuador and Colombia to the deserts of northern Chile. It was during this time that scores of fabulous mountaintop citadels were built, including Machu Picchu.

When Europeans 'discovered' the New World, epidemics including smallpox swept down from Central America and the Caribbean. In 1527 the 11th Inca Huayna Capác died of such an epidemic. Before expiring he divided his empire between his two sons – Atahualpa, born of a Quitan mother, who took the north, and the pure-blooded native Cuzqueñan Huáscar, who took Cuzco and the south. Civil war eventually ensued and the slow downfall of the Inca empire began.

By 1526 Francisco Pizarro had started heading south from Panama and soon discovered the rich coastal settlements of the Inca empire. After going back to Spain to court money and men for the conquest, he returned, landing on the Ecuadorian coast and marching overland toward Peru and the heart of the Inca empire, reaching Cajamarca in 1532, by which time Atahualpa had defeated his half-brother Huáscar.

This meeting was to change the course of South American history radically. Atahualpa was ambushed by a few dozen armed conquistadors who succeeded in capturing him, killing thousands of unarmed indigenous tribespeople. In an attempt to regain his freedom, the Inca offered a ransom of gold and silver from Cuzco, including that stripped from the walls of Qorikancha.

But after holding Atahualpa prisoner for a number of months and teasing the Incas with ransom requests, Pizarro murdered him anyway, and soon marched on Cuzco (see p811). Mounted on horseback, protected by armor and swinging steel swords, the Spanish cavalry was virtually unstoppable. Despite sporadic rebellions, the Inca empire was forced to retreat into the mountains and jungle, and never recovered its glorious prestige or extent.

PERU

Colonial Peru

In 1535 Pizarro founded the capital city of Lima. Decades of turmoil ensued, with Peruvians resisting their conquerors who were fighting among themselves for control of the rich colony. Pizarro was assassinated in 1541 by the son of conquistador Diego de Almagro, whom Pizarro had put to death in 1538. Manco Inca nearly regained control of the highlands in 1536, but by 1539 had retreated to his rainforest hideout at Vilcabamba, where he was killed in 1544. Inca Túpac Amaru also attempted to overthrow the Spaniards in 1572, but was defeated and executed.

For the next two centuries Lima was the major political, social and commercial center of the Andean nations, while Cuzco became a backwater. However, this peaceful period came to an abrupt end. Indigenous people were being exploited as laborers under the *encomienda* system (whereby settlers were granted a parcel of land and native slaves). This led to the 1780 uprising under the self-proclaimed ruler Inca Túpac Amaru II. But this rebellion was also squashed, and its leaders cruelly executed.

Independence

By the early 1800s rebellion was stirring among the colonists due to high taxes imposed by Spain, plus a desire to take control of the country's rich mineral deposits, beginning with prime *guano* (seabird droppings) used for fertilizer.

Change came from two directions. After liberating Argentina and Chile from Spain, José de San Martín entered Lima and formally proclaimed Peru's independence in 1821. Meanwhile Simón Bolívar had freed Venezuela, Colombia and Ecuador. San Martín and Bolívar met in Ecuador, and as a result of this heart-to-heart – the details of which are a mystery – San Martín left Latin America altogether to live in France, while Bolívar continued into Peru. Two decisive battles were fought at Junín and Ayacucho in 1824, and the Spanish finally surrendered in 1826.

Peru also won a brief war with Spain in 1866 and lost a longer war with Chile (1879–83) over the nitrate-rich northern Atacama Desert. Chile annexed much of coastal southern Peru, but returned some areas in 1929. A little over a decade later Peru went to war with Ecuador over another border dispute.

A 1942 treaty gave Peru the area north of the Río Marañón, but Ecuador disputed this and skirmishes occurred every few years. It wasn't until 1998 that a peace treaty finally put an end to the hostilities.

Modern Times

Despite periods of civilian rule, it was coups and military dictatorships that characterized Peru's government during most of the 20th century.

In the late 1980s the country experienced severe social unrest. Demonstrations protesting the disastrous handling of the economy by President Alan García Pérez were an everyday occurrence – at one point, inflation reached 10,000%! His first term was shadowed by the disruptive activities of Maoist terrorist organization Sendero Luminoso, which waged a guerrilla war resulting in the death or 'disappearance' of at least 40,000 people, mostly in the central Andes.

In 1990 Alberto Fujimori, the son of Japanese immigrants, was elected president. Strong, semidictatorial actions led to unprecedented improvements in the economy. Popular support propelled Fujimori to a second term in 1995 (after he amended the constitution expressly so he could run again), but that support was dwindling by 1998. In September 2000 a video was released showing Vladimir Montesinos, Fujimori's hawkish head of intelligence, bribing a congressman, causing Fujimori's 10-year presidency to spiral out of control. Amid the scandal and human-rights abuse accusations, Fujimori resigned during a state trip to Asia and hid in Japan, which refused Peru's repeated extradition requests. In 2005 he was arrested while on a trip to Chile, and extradited to Peru in 2007, when he was initially tried and convicted for ordering an illegal search and sentenced to six years in prison. In 2009 Fujimori was sentenced to an additional 25 years for crimes against humanity.

Despite the blemish on the family record, Fujimori's daughter Keiko was elected to the Peruvian Congress in a landslide in 2006 and was leading the presidential prediction polls of potential candidates in the 2011 elections at the time of writing. As these things go in Latin America, she would succeed Alan García Pérez, re-elected for a second term in 2006. This time out, despite a widespread corruption scandal, García has faired wholly

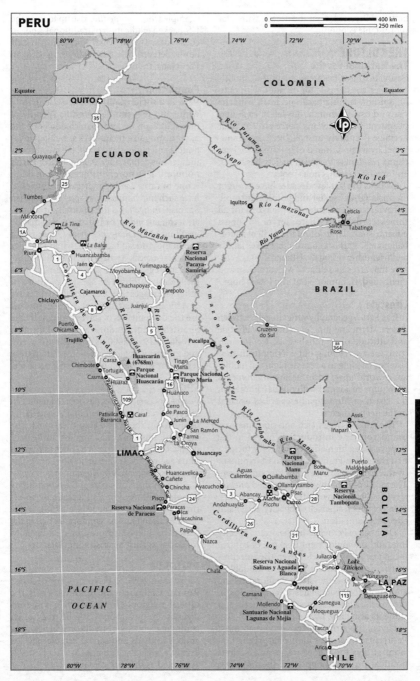

PERU

0 ————— 400 km
0 ————— 250 miles

COLOMBIA

QUITO

ECUADOR

Guayaquil

Tumbes

Máncora

La Tina

Sullana

Piura

Huancabamba

La Balsa

Jaén

Moyobamba

Yurimaguas

Cajamarca

Chachapoyas

Celendín

Chiclayo

Juanjuí

Puerto
Chicama

Trujillo

Chimbote

Caraz

Huascarán
(6768m)

Tortugas

Parque
Nacional
Huascarán

Casma

Huaraz

Patividca
Barranca

Caral

Cerro
de Pasco

Junín

La Merced

San Ramón

Tarma

La Oroya

LIMA

Chilca

Huancavelica

Cañete

Chincha

Pisco

Ayacucho

Paracas

**Reserva Nacional
de Paracas**

Ica

Huacachina

Palpa

Nazca

Chala

Camaná

Mollendo

Moquegua

Tacna

Arica

CHILE

Tingo
María

Parque Nacional
Tingo María

Huánuco

Huancayo

Aguas
Calientes

Quillabamba

Abancay

Andahuaylas

Machu
Picchu

Ollantaytambo

Pisac

Cuzco

Juliaca

Puno

*Lake
Titicaca*

Arequipa

Samegua

**Santuario Nacional
Lagunas de Mejía**

**Reserva Nacional
Salinas y Aguada
Blanca**

Yunguyo

Juli

LA PAZ

Desaguadero

Assis

Iñapari

**Parque
Nacional
Manu**

Boca
Manu

Puerto
Maldonado

**Reserva
Nacional
Tambopata**

Cruzeiro
do Sul

Río Icá

Río Yavarí

Leticia

Santa
Rosa

Tabatinga

Iquitos

Río Amazonas

Lagunas

**Reserva
Nacional
Pacaya-
Samiria**

BRAZIL

Tarapoto

Pucallpa

Río Marañón

Río Napo

Río Putumayo

A m a z o n   B a s i n

Río Ucayali

Río Huallaga

Río Urubamba

Río Manu

Cordillera   de   los   Andes

Cordillera   de   los   Andes

Cordillera   de   los   Andes

Carretera   Norte

Panamericana   Sur

BOLIVIA

*PACIFIC
OCEAN*

Equator

2°S

4°S

6°S

8°S

10°S

12°S

14°S

16°S

18°S

80°W

78°W

76°W

74°W

72°W

70°W

PERU

better as Peru rides out the decade with a far more stable economy.

THE CULTURE
The National Psyche

Peruvians have been caught up in a political roller-coaster ride for decades, with public opinion leaping back and forth with the rise and usually thunderous fall of each new president. But Peruvians' fierce pride in their heritage is entirely unshakable. Long dominated by a fair-skinned oligarchy of *limeños* (Lima residents), Peruvian society has begun embracing its indigenous roots.

Even as the last few decades have brought an onslaught of social and political turmoil, Peruvians have maintained their zeal for all things worth living. There's fervor for robust cuisine, soulful music and the thrill of a football match. This is a country that takes family and friendship seriously. Ultimately it is a culture that faces its setbacks with stoicism and plenty of dark humor – but also lots of hope.

Lifestyle

Just as Peru's geography varies hugely between desert, sierra and jungle, so does the lifestyle and attitude of its inhabitants. *Campesinos* (peasants) scratching out a living from subsistence farming in a remote highland hamlet are a world apart from urbane *arequipeños* (Arequipa residents) with holiday homes on the coast, or hunter-gatherer tribes isolated in the deep Amazon.

The gaps between rich and poor may astound you. The introduction of TV to the impoverished highlands in the 1950s fueled a first wave of migration to the coast in pursuit of the privileged lives they saw on screen. The vast influx of migrants spawned *pueblos jóvenes* (young towns) that surround Lima, many of which still lack electricity, water and adequate sanitation.

Over half of Peruvians live below the poverty line, and unemployment is so out of control it can't be measured. However, the entrepreneurial spirit is strong. Many of the jobless work as *ambulantes* (street vendors) selling anything from chocolates to clothespins in the streets, while teachers, police officers and students also drive taxis.

Given the grinding poverty that most Peruvians endure, it's hardly surprising that labor strikes for higher wages and various political protests happen all the time, for example when *campesinos* rise up to fight the US-backed eradication of traditional Andean coca crops. Travelers may find their trip suddenly delayed. It's not really a big deal to Peruvians, though.

Population

Peru is a society split between the mainly white and fair-skinned *mestizo* (people of mixed indigenous and Spanish descent – the latter distinguish themselves as being *criollo*) middle and upper classes, and the mostly poor indigenous *campesinos*. About 45% of Peru's population is purely indigenous, making it one of three Latin American countries to have such high indigenous representation. (In Spanish, *indígenas* is the culturally appropriate term, not *indios*, or Indians, which may be insulting.) Most *indígenas* speak Quechua and live in the Andean highlands, while a smaller percentage speak Aymara and inhabit the Lake Titicaca region. In the vast Amazon, various indigenous ethnicities speak a plethora of other languages. About 3% of Peruvians are of African or Asian descent. Afro-Peruvians are the descendants of slaves brought by the Spanish conquistadors. Alberto Fujimori (president 1990–2000) is of Japanese descent, and the many *chifas* (Chinese restaurants) are testimony to a widespread Chinese presence.

SPORTS

Fútbol (soccer) inspires passionate fanaticism in Peru, even though its national squad hasn't qualified for the World Cup since 1982. The big-boy teams mostly hail from Lima: the traditional *clásico* (classic match) pitches Alianza Lima against rivals Universitario (La U). The season is late March to November.

Bullfighting is also part of the bloodthirsty national culture. Lima's Plaza de Acho attracts international talent (see p788). In remote Andean hamlets, condors are tied to the back of the bull – an expression of indigenous solidarity against Spanish conquistadors.

RELIGION

More than 80% of Peruvians are declared Roman Catholics, and Catholicism is the official religion. However, while some *indígenas* are outwardly Catholic, they often combine elements of traditional beliefs into church festivals and sacred ceremonies, for example when Pachamama (Mother Earth) is venerated as the Virgin Mary.

ARTS

Literature

Peru's most famous novelist is the internationally recognized Mario Vargas Llosa (1936–), who ran unsuccessfully for president in 1990. His complex novels including *The Time of the Hero* delve into Peruvian society, politics and culture.

Considered Peru's greatest poet, César Vallejo (1892–1938) wrote *Trilce*, a book of 77 avant-garde, existentialist poems. Vallejo was known for pushing the Spanish language to its limits, inventing words when real ones no longer served him.

Two writers noted for their portrayals of indigenous communities are José María Arguedas (1911–69) and Ciro Alegría (1909–67). Women writers fill the pages of *Fire From the Andes: Short Fiction by Women from Bolivia, Ecuador and Peru*.

Rising literary stars include Peruvian-American Daniel Alarcón (1977–), whose debut novel *Lost City Radio* was a *Washington Post* 'best of' in 2007; and Sergio Bambarén (1960–), who lived in the USA and Australia before returning to Lima – his self-published *The Dolphin: The Story of a Dreamer* became a bestseller.

Music & Dance

ANDEAN

Haunting pre-Columbian music, which features wind and percussion instruments, is inescapable in the highlands. Called *música folklórica*, traditional Andean music is heard all over Peru, with bars and clubs called *peñas* specifically catering to it.

The most representative wind instruments are *quenas* and *zampoñas*. The *quena* (or *kena*) is a flute, usually made of bamboo or bone and of varying lengths depending on the pitch desired. The *zampoña* is a set of panpipes with two rows of bamboo canes, ranging from the tiny, high-pitched *chuli* to the meter-long bass *toyo*. Percussion instruments include *bombos* (drums made from hollowed-out tree trunks and stretched goatskin) and *shajshas* (rattles made of polished goat hooves).

Today's *música folklórica* groups also use stringed instruments adapted from Spain. The most typical is the *charango*, a tiny, five-stringed guitar with a box traditionally made of an armadillo shell.

COASTAL

Sassy *música criolla* has its roots in Spain and Africa. Afro-Peruvian music is unique and quite different from Caribbean or Brazilian styles. Its main instruments are guitars and the *cajón*, a wooden box on which the player sits and pounds out a rhythm. Also sharing African-Spanish roots, the bluesier *landó* has stylistic elements of call and response and lyrics often focused on slavery and social issues.

The heart of Afro-Peruvian music and dance beats strongly in Chincha (see boxed text, p791). A great introductory compilation is *Afro-Peruvian Classics: The Soul of Black Peru*, with the incomparable Susana Baca. The contemporary group Perú Negro has recently leapt onto the international scene.

The most popular coastal dance is the *marinera*, a romantic routine employing much waving of handkerchiefs. *Marinera* competitions are popular in Trujillo (p837).

MODERN

Also popular in Peru is omnipresent Caribbean salsa, as well as cumbia and *chicha*, both originally from Colombia. All three can be enjoyed in the *salsotecas* (salsa clubs), which cram in hundreds of Peruvians for all-night dance-fests. *Chicha* is a cheerful Andean fusion of traditional panpipes with electronic percussion and guitars. Deriving from cumbia is Peruvian techno-cumbia, of which prime exponents were Euforia and Rosy War, while newer bands include Agua Marina and Armonía 10. The homegrown Peruvian rock, pop, punk, hip-hop and reggaeton scenes are limited.

Architecture

While the Inca stonework of Machu Picchu is Peru's star attraction, you'll find an assortment of other architectural styles, from magnificent pre-Columbian adobe pyramids to Spanish baroque to boxy modernist. Colonial styles are well represented by the countless cathedrals, churches, monasteries and convents built after the Spanish conquistadors arrived.

Visual Arts

Indigenous artists under colonial influence created much of Peru's religious art. This unique cross-pollination gave rise to Escuela Cuzqueña (Cuzco school), a syncretic blend of Spanish and indigenous sensibilities. *Cuzqueña* canvases are proudly displayed

PERU

in many highland churches, not just in Cuzco (p814).

ENVIRONMENT

Government-backed moves to liberalize foreign land ownership of the Peruvian Amazon – 70% is now under foreign concession with plans to support energy development in the area – sparked protests from some 30,000 indigenous Peruvians from 60 tribes throughout 2009. Violent clashes in Bagua Grande resulted in over 50 deaths – Peru's worst violence since its terrorism days. In June 2009, Congress suspended President García's controversial moves.

While rainforest deforestation has caught international attention, deforestation from logging and overgrazing in the highlands are also acute problems, causing soil to deteriorate and get blown or washed away. This leads to decreased water quality, particularly in the Amazon Basin, where silt-laden water is unable to support microorganisms at the base of the food chain. Other water-related problems include pollution from mining in the highlands and from industrial waste and sewage along the coast. Some beaches have been declared unfit for swimming, and Peru's rich marine resources are threatened.

Elsewhere, responsible tourism is finally on the agenda, especially in the Amazon Basin. In addition, a US$120 million grant from the Japanese government was announced in 2009 and earmarked for preservation of 55 million hectares of Amazon rainforest over the next 10 years – a step in the right direction.

The Land

The third-largest country in South America, Peru has three distinct regions: a narrow coastal belt, the wide Andean mountains and the Amazon jungle.

The coastal strip is mainly desert, punctuated by cities and rivers down from the Andes forming agricultural oases. The country's best road, the Carretera Panamericana (Pan-American Hwy), slices through coastal Peru from border to border.

The Andes rise rapidly from the coast to spectacular heights over 6000m just 100km inland. Most mountains are between 3000m and 4000m, with jagged ranges separated by deep, vertiginous canyons. Huascarán (6768m) is Peru's highest peak.

The eastern Andes get more rainfall than the dry western slopes, and so they're covered in cloud forest that slips and slides down to merge with the rainforest of the Amazon Basin.

Wildlife

With mammoth deserts, glaciated mountain ranges, tropical rainforests and almost every imaginable habitat in between, Peru hosts a menagerie of wildlife.

Bird and marine life is abundant along the coast, with colonies of sea lions, Humboldt penguins, Chilean flamingos, Peruvian pelicans, Inca terns and the brown booby endemic to the region. Remarkable highland birds include majestic Andean condors, puna ibis and a variety of hummingbirds. The highlands are also home to camelids such as llamas, alpacas, guanacos and *vicuñas*, while cloud forests are the haunts of jaguars, tapirs and endangered spectacled bears.

Swoop down toward the Amazon and with luck you'll spot all the iconic tropical birds – parrots, macaws, toucans and many more. The Amazon is home to over a dozen species of monkeys, plus river dolphins, frogs, reptiles, fish and insects galore. Snakes? Don't panic. Many species live here, but they're mostly shy of humans.

National Parks

Peru's wealth of wildlife is protected by a system of national parks and reserves with over 55 areas covering almost 13% of the country. Yet these areas seriously lack infrastructure and are subject to illegal hunting, fishing, logging and mining. The government simply doesn't have the money to patrol the parks, though international agencies contribute money and resources to help conservation projects.

TRANSPORTATION

GETTING THERE & AWAY

For visa information, see p875.

Air

Lima's **Aeropuerto Internacional Jorge Chávez** (LIM; ☎ 01-517-3100; www.lap.com.pe) is the main hub for flights to Andean countries and Latin America, North America and Europe.

TOP WILDLIFE-WATCHING SPOTS

▓ remote jungle in **Parque Nacional Manu** (p861); your best chance to see jaguars, tapirs and monkeys

▓ the coastal reserve with penguins, flamingos and sea lions of **Islas Ballestas** and **Reserva Nacional de Paracas** (p791)

▓ **Parque Nacional Huascarán** (p852) for Andean condors, giant *Puya raimondii* plants, *vicuñas* and viscachas

▓ canopy walkways, jungle lodges and river cruises in **Iquitos** (p864)

▓ sighting capybara while cruising to a macaw's lowland salt lick at **Puerto Maldonado** (p859)

▓ the easiest place to spot Andean condors – **Cañón del Colca** (p804)

▓ oxbow lake **Yarinacocha** (p864), home to pink dolphins, huge iguanas and myriad bird species

▓ pristine rainforest reserve of **Reserva Nacional Pacaya-Samiria** (see boxed text, p867), explored by dugout canoe

▓ at **Machu Picchu** (p825), a rainbow of rare and endemic birds – over 400 species!

Boat

Boats ply the Amazon from Iquitos to Leticia, Colombia, and Tabatinga, Brazil (see boxed text, p868). It's difficult to reach Bolivia by river from Puerto Maldonado (see boxed text, p861). It's possible, but time-consuming, to travel along the Río Napo from Iquitos to Coca, Ecuador.

Bus, Car & Motorcycle

The major border crossings: Tacna to Chile (see boxed text, p798); Tumbes (see boxed text, p846), La Tina or Jaén (see boxed text, p844) to Ecuador; and Yunguyo or Desaguadero (see boxed text, p809) by Lake Titicaca to Bolivia. Brazil is reached (but not easily) via Iñapari (see boxed text, p861).

Train

There are inexpensive, twice-daily trains between Tacna and Arica, Chile (see boxed text, p798).

AIRPORT TAX

Airport taxes on all flights are charged upon departure at airports. Lima's international tax is US$31, payable in US dollars or nuevos soles (cash only). American and Delta airlines include the tax in the price of the ticket. Domestic airport taxes are between US$3 and US$6; Lima charges US$5.84 and Cuzco US$4.84.

GETTING AROUND

On the road keep your passport and Andean Immigration Card (see p875) with you, not packed in your luggage, as overland transport goes through police checkpoints.

Air

Domestic flight schedules and ticket prices change frequently. New airlines open every year, as those with poor safety records shut down (check www.airsafe.com). Another useful website is www.traficoperu.com, which details flight schedules and fare quotes between major cities. At the time of research, one-way flights on the low end averaged around S360. Early and in-country bookers get the cheapest seats (see boxed text, p774).

Most domestic airlines fly between Lima and Cuzco, as does international carrier **TACA** (www.taca.com). **LAN** (www.lan.com) serves all major and some minor routes. **Star Perú** (www.starperu .com) flies to Cuzco and the jungle cities. **LC Busre** (www.lcbusre.com.pe) provides important links to the Andean highlands. Airline offices are listed under relevant destinations in this chapter.

Flights are often late. Morning departures are more likely to be on time. Show up at least one hour early for all domestic flights (90 minutes in Lima, two hours in Cuzco). Flights are often fully booked during holidays (see p873).

PERU

SAVE!

Don't pay foreigner prices for your domestic flights in Peru! Instead, once in the country (it doesn't work from abroad), use **LAN's** (www.lan.com.pe) Peruvian website and book your flights in Spanish. Your credit card will be denied if it's not Peruvian, but you can select the option to pay at any number of supermarkets and banks throughout Peru (Wong, Metro, BCP, Interbank etc). You will receive a payment code – take this into the payment location of choice and voilà! You save up to 50% – just like locals.

Furthermore, if you're connecting through Lima on a domestic flight route, you don't need to pay the airport tax twice. Instead, go to the security guard to the right of the domestic departure entrance and they will send you through.

Boat

Small, slow motorboats depart daily from Puno for Lake Titicaca's islands (see p810).

In Peru's eastern lowlands, *peki-pekis* (dugout canoes, usually powered by an outboard engine) act as water buses on the smaller rivers. Where the rivers widen, larger cargo boats are normally available. This is the classic way to travel down the Amazon – swinging in your hammock aboard a banana boat piloted by a grizzled old captain who knows the waters better than the back of his hand. You can travel from Pucallpa or Yurimaguas to Iquitos, and on into Brazil, Colombia or Ecuador this way. These boats aren't big, but have two or more decks: the lower deck is for cargo, the upper for passengers and crew. Bring a hammock. Basic food is provided, but you may want to bring your own. To get aboard, just go down to the docks and ask for a boat to your destination. Arrange passage with the captain (nobody else). Departure time normally depends on filling up the hold. Sometimes you can sleep on the boat while awaiting departure to save costs.

Bus

Peru's notoriously dangerous buses are cheap and go just about everywhere.

Less traveled routes are served by ramshackle old chicken buses, but more popular destinations are served by fast luxury services (called *imperial* or something similar), charging up to 10 times more than *económico* (economy) buses. It's worth paying more for long-distance bus trips, if only for safety's sake. Some overnight routes offer *bus-camas* (bed-buses) with seats that fully recline. For safety, security and comfort, there is **Cruz del Sur** (www.cruzdelsur.com.pe) at the top and pretty much all goes downhill from there. Peruvians swear by **Oltursa** (www.oltursa.com.pe).

Many cities now have central bus terminals, while others have bus companies clustered around a few blocks or scattered all over town. Travel agencies are convenient for buying tickets, but will overcharge you. Instead, buy them directly from the bus company at least a day in advance. Schedules and fares change frequently. Prices skyrocket around major holidays (see p873), when tickets may be sold out several days ahead of time. Coastal buses are packed all summer long, especially on Sundays.

Buses rarely leave or arrive on time, and can be greatly delayed during the rainy season due to landslides and treacherous road conditions. Try not to take overnight buses, which are more vulnerable to fatal accidents, hijackings and luggage theft. It can get freezing cold on highland buses, so dress warmly. Long-distance buses generally stop for meals, though toilets are highly unpredictable. Some companies have their own restaurants in the middle of nowhere, practically forcing you to eat there. But you can also buy snacks from onboard vendors or bring your own food and drinks.

Car & Motorcycle

With the exception of the Carretera Panamericana and new roads leading inland from the coast, road conditions are generally poor, distances are great and renting a car is an expensive, often dangerous hassle. Keep in mind that road signage is deficient and most major roads are also toll roads: S2 to S7.50 for every 100km. *Gasolina* (petrol) averages S9 per liter, and gas stations (called *grifos*) are few and far between. Renting a private taxi for long-distance trips costs little more than renting a car, and avoids most of these pitfalls. Motorcycle rental is an option mainly in jungle towns, and there are a few outfitters in Cuzco.

Local Transportation

Taxis are unmetered, so ask locals the going rate, then haggle; drivers often double or triple the standard rate for unsuspecting foreigners. A short run in most cities costs S3 to S5 (in Lima S5 to S8). Be aware that street hawkers sell florescent taxi stickers throughout Peru, and anybody can just stick one on their windscreen. Some drivers of these unlicensed 'pirate' taxis have been known to be complicit in violent crimes against passengers, especially in Arequipa. It's safer if more expensive to take officially regulated taxis, which are typically called by telephone.

Motocarros or *mototaxis* (motorized rickshaws) are common in some of the smaller towns. *Colectivos* (shared minivans, minibuses or taxis) and trucks (in the Amazon) run between local and not so local destinations.

Train

Pricey **PeruRail** (www.perurail.com) links Cuzco and the Sacred Valley with Machu Picchu (p819). There is an unpredictable though immensely scenic thrice-weekly service that travels between Cuzco and Lake Titicaca (p809).

Other railways connect Lima and the Andean highland towns of Huancayo (p836) and Huancavelica.

LIMA

☎ 01 / pop 7,606,000

For a coastal city, Lima lacks the tropical fever of Rio de Janeiro and, though a possessor of a healthy French, Italian and German bloodline, can't boast the Euro-Latino sexiness of Buenos Aires, but the former 'City of Kings' is not without its charms.

Peru's frenetic capital, home to one-third of the country's population, can almost look like a Middle Eastern desertscape from the air, with its dust-strewn suburbs under a perpetual blanket of kicked-up earth from this arid seaside metroplex. Under the dust is a modern city with chic shopping malls, enchanting neighborhoods to explore and one of the continent's most important dining scenes – all with dramatic sea views.

Overpopulation problems have earned this fast-moving metropolis a reputation as a polluted and dangerous place. Yes and no. As you stroll from crumbling pre-Inca pyramids and the waning splendor of Spanish colonial architecture to glitzy, ultramodern shopping malls and many of the country's best museums, the most irritating inconvenience you'll probably find is the excessive use of car horns. You can escape that by tucking into fresh seafood by the ocean, going paragliding off the cliffs in Miraflores or grooving until sunrise in bohemian Barranco's bars and clubs.

HISTORY

Lima was christened the 'City of Kings' when Francisco Pizarro founded it on the Catholic feast day of Epiphany in 1535. During early Spanish colonial times it became the continent's richest, most important town, though this all changed in 1746 when a disastrous earthquake wiped out most of the city. However, rebuilding was rapid, and most of the old colonial buildings still to be seen here date from after the earthquake.

Argentinean General José de San Martín proclaimed Peruvian independence from Spain here on July 28, 1821. Three decades later the city took a crucial step over other cities on the continent by building the first railway in South America. In 1881 Lima was attacked during a war with Chile. Treasures were carried off or broken by the victorious Chileans, who occupied the town for nearly three years.

An unprecedented population explosion began in the 1920s due to rapid industrialization and an influx of rural poor from throughout Peru – especially the highlands. Such growth – and growing pains – has continued at a breakneck pace ever since. Today the city has a few wealthy and middle-class suburbs, but many people are unemployed and live with inadequate housing and no running water.

In December 1996 Túpac Amaru leftist rebels entered the Japanese ambassador's residence and took several ambassadors and ministers hostage. Four months went by before Peruvian soldiers bombed the building, entered and shot the rebels. One hostage and two Peruvian commandos died during the rescue operation.

In March 2002, a few days before a visit by US President George W Bush, a car bomb exploded near the US Embassy, killing 10 people. It was thought to have been detonated by the guerrilla group Sendero Luminoso, which had caused massive social instability in the 1980s.

PERU

METROPOLITAN LIMA

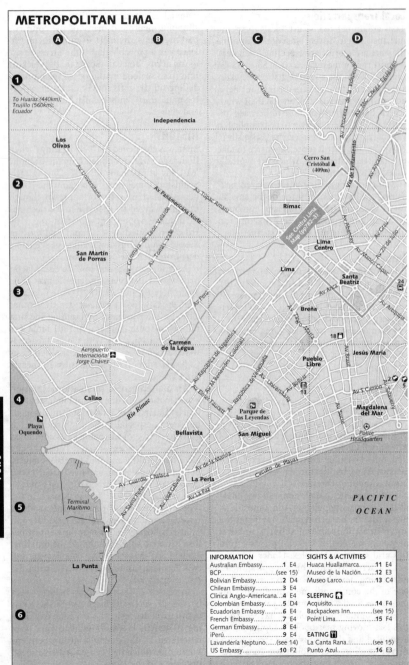

To Huaraz (440km);
Trujillo (560km);
Ecuador

Independencia

Los Olivos

Cerro San
Cristóbal ▲
(409m)

Rimac

San Martín
de Porras

Lima
Centro

Lima

Santa
Beatriz

Breña

Carmen
de la Legua

Aeropuerto
Internacional
Jorge Chávez

Pueblo
Libre

Jesús María

Callao

Parque de
las Leyendas

Magdalena
del Mar

Playa
Oquendo

Bellavista

San Miguel

Police
Headquarters

PACIFIC
OCEAN

La Perla

Terminal
Marítimo

La Punta

INFORMATION
Australian Embassy............**1** E4
BCP............................(see 15)
Bolivian Embassy.............**2** D4
Chilean Embassy..............**3** E4
Clinica Anglo-Americana....**4** E4
Colombian Embassy..........**5** D4
Ecuadorian Embassy..........**6** E4
French Embassy...............**7** E4
German Embassy..............**8** E4
iPerú...........................**9** E4
Lavandería Neptuno......(see 14)
US Embassy...................**10** F2

SIGHTS & ACTIVITIES
Huaca Huallamarca........**11** E4
Museo de la Nación........**12** E3
Museo Larco..................**13** C4

SLEEPING
Acquisito.....................**14** F4
Backpackers Inn.............(see 15)
Point Lima....................**15** F4

EATING
La Canta Rana...............(see 15)
Punto Azul....................**16** E3

PERU

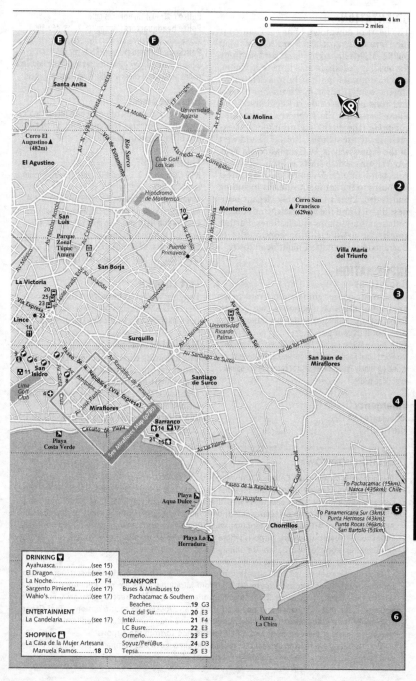

PERU

ORIENTATION

The heart of downtown Lima (El Centro) is the Plaza de Armas, aka Plaza Mayor (Map pp782–3). It's linked to Plaza San Martín by the bustling pedestrian mall Jirón de la Unión, which continues south as Jirón Belén (many streets change their names every few blocks) and runs into Paseo de la República. From Plaza Grau, the Vía Expresa – nicknamed *el zanjón* (the ditch) – is an important expressway to the suburbs. Parallel to and west of the expressway is Av Garcilaso de la Vega (Av Wilson), which starts as Jirón Tacna and runs south into Av Arequipa, the main street for buses to the southern suburbs including San Isidro, Lima's fashionably elegant business district, and the ritzy beachfront hotels, restaurants and shops of Miraflores. Further south, the artistic clifftop community of Barranco has the hottest nightlife in town.

INFORMATION
Bookstores

Foreign-language guidebooks and maps are sold at the SAE clubhouse (see Tourist Information, opposite), which has a members-only book exchange.

Zeta (Map p785; Av Espinar 219, Miraflores; 🕙 9am-9pm Mon-Sat) Good English and foreign-language selection, including Lonely Planet titles. Also at LarcoMar shopping mall (Map p785).

Emergency
Ambulance (☎ 117)
Fire (☎ 116)

Police (☎ 105) Emergencies only.
Police headquarters (Map pp776-7; ☎ 460-1060; Moore 268, Magdalena del Mar; 🕙 24hr)
Policía de Turismo (Map pp782-3; ☎ 423-3500; España, Quadra 4; 🕙 24hr) Provides reports for insurance claims or traveler's check refunds; some English spoken.

Internet Access

Some guesthouses offer free internet access. Speedy cybercafes costing about S3 per hour are ubiquitous in Miraflores.

Laundry

KTO (Map p782-3; España 481, central Lima; 🕙 9am-8pm Mon-Sat)
Lavandería 40 Minutos (Map p785; Av Espinar 154, Miraflores; 🕙 8am-8pm Mon-Sat, 9am-1pm Sun)
Lavandería Neptuno (Map pp776-7; ☎ 477-4472; Grau 912, Barranco; 🕙 hours vary)
Servirap (Map p785; Schell 601, Miraflores; 🕙 8am-10pm Mon-Sat, 10am-6pm Sun) Also has self-service.

Left Luggage

Luggage storage at the airport (domestic arrivals) costs S28 per day. Members can store their bags at the SAE clubhouse (opposite).

Medical Services

The following clinics offer emergency services and some English-speaking staff:
Clínica Anglo-Americana (Map pp776-7; ☎ 616-8900; Salazar 350, San Isidro) Stocks yellow-fever and tetanus vaccines.
Clínica Internacional (Map pp782-3; ☎ 619-6161; Washington 1471, central Lima)

GETTING INTO TOWN

The airport is in suburban Callao, 12km west of downtown (Map pp776–7).

Official taxis directly outside the terminal exit charge a whopping S45 for trips to the city center and Miraflores. Walk past these into the parking lot and you'll save S10 or so, but lose a bit of piece of mind from a security standpoint. Most hostels also offer airport pickup for S45. Alternatively, turn left outside the terminal, walk 100m to the pedestrian gate, turn right and walk 100m to the road outside the airport, where you can get an unofficial taxi for less, or a *combi* to Miraflores. Look for the 'Callao-Ate' minibus (spy the red 'S' or ask for it by its nickname, 'La S,' pronounced 'la e-se') for S1.50 (a little more for obnoxious luggage).

The cheapest way to reach the airport from downtown is on buses marked 'Faucett/Aeropuerto' running south along Alfonso Ugarte (S1.20). From Miraflores, taxis are recommended. Taking a taxi to the airport is cheapest if you just flag one down on the street and bargain. For more security, call a taxi in advance and pay the full S45 fare. A safe and secure option is **Taxi Green** (☎ 484-4001; www.taxigreen.com.pe). Maddening traffic and road construction often lead to lengthy delays, so allow at least an hour and a half for the ride to/from the airport.

Unfortunately, there is no central bus terminal in Lima. Each bus company runs its own offices and terminals, mostly in shady neighborhoods east of the city center – take a taxi.

Money

You'll find 24-hour ATMs throughout Lima. Other *casas de cambio* (foreign-exchange offices) are scattered about Camaná in central Lima and along Larco in Miraflores. Green-jacketed official money changers *(cambistas)* are all over Lima and safe to use, but get their official stamp on your bills to protect yourself against counterfeits.

Banco Continental central Lima (Map p782-3; Cuzco 286); Miraflores (Map p785; cnr Av José Larco & Tarata) Visa representative; with international ATMs.

BCP Barranco (Map pp776-7; Grau 599); central Lima (Map pp782-3; Lampa 499); Miraflores (Map p785; Av José Pardo 491); Miraflores (Map p785; cnr Av José Larco & José Gonzales); Miraflores (Map p785; cnr Av José Larco & Schell) Has 24-hour Visa/Mastercard ATMs and changes Amex traveler's checks.

HSBC (Map p785; Av José Pardo 269, Miraflores) 24hr ATM.

Interbank Miraflores (Map p785; Av José Larco 690); Miraflores (Map p785; cnr Óvalo & Av José Pardo Global ATMs but with a hefty surcharge.

LAC Dólar central Lima (Map pp782-3; ☎ 428-8127; Camaná 779; ☒ 9:30am-6:30pm Mon-Sat, 9am-2pm Sun); Miraflores (Map p785; ☎ 242-4085; Av de la Paz 211; ☒ 10am-2pm & 3-6pm Mon-Fri, 10am-2pm Sat) Reliable *casa de cambio*.

Post

Members can have mail and packages held at the SAE clubhouse (below).

DHL (Map p785; ☎ 445-4791; Av José Pardo 620, Miraflores)

FedEx (Map p785; ☎ 242-2280; Pasaje Olaya 260, Miraflores)

Main post office (Map pp782-3; Pasaje Piura, central Lima; ☒ 8am-8pm Mon-Sat, 9am-1pm Sun) Poste restante mail can be collected here, though it's not 100% reliable. Bring ID.

Serpost (Map p785; Petit Thouars 5201; ☒ 8:10am-8:45pm Mon- Sat, 9am-1pm Sun)

Tourist Information

iPerú airport (☎ 574-8000; Aeropuerto Internacional Jorge Chávez); Miraflores (Map p785; ☎ 445-9400; Larco-Mar; ☒ 11am-1pm & 2-8pm); San Isidro (Map pp776-7; ☎ 421-1627; Jorge Basadre 610; ☒ 8:30am-5pm Mon-Fri) The main office dispenses maps and offers the services of the tourist-protection agency (Indecopi). In Miraflores, you'll find helpful booths on Parque Kennedy, LarcoMar and Huaca Pucllana, among others. Inside LarcoMar is the main office, handy on weekends.

PeruRail (Map p785; ☎ 241-5068; www.perurail.com; LarcoMar; ☒ 11am-9:30pm) Get information and make bookings for Cuzco–Machu Picchu and Cuzco–Puno trains.

South American Explorers (SAE; Map p785; ☎ 445-3306; www.saexplorers.org; Piura 135, Miraflores; ☒ 9:30am-5pm Mon, Tue, Thu & Fri, to 8pm Wed, to 1pm Sat) SAE is a member-supported, nonprofit organization that functions as an invaluable information center for travelers. Also see p996.

DANGERS & ANNOYANCES

With large numbers of poor and unemployed people, Lima suffers from opportunistic crime. While you are unlikely to be physically hurt, travelers have been mugged. Take extra care on the beaches, where violent attacks have happened. Always use official regulated taxis, especially at night. Bus terminals are in disadvantaged neighborhoods and notorious for theft, so buy your tickets in advance and take a taxi. From the airport, there have been reports of thieves watching who places their valuable daypacks inside the taxis, then following them for a stoplight snatch and grab down the road. Most folks recommend placing your entire luggage in the trunk. See also p870.

SIGHTS

Central Lima is the most interesting but not the safest place to wander. It's generally OK to stroll between the Plazas de Armas, San Martín and Grau and the parklands further south. Some of Lima's best museums and other sights are in outlying suburbs.

Museums

A dominating concrete block, the state-run **Museo de la Nación** (Map pp776-7; ☎ 476-9933; Av Javier Prado Este 2466, San Borja; ☒ 9am-6pm Tue-Sun) is the best place to get your head around Peru's myriad prehistoric civilizations. Multilingual guides are available for S15. Catch a mini-bus (S1) east along Angamos Este from Av Arequipa, five blocks north of the Óvalo in Miraflores. Check with the driver that it goes to the intersection of Avs Aviación and Javier Prado Este – it's a 50m walk from there.

Museo Larco (Map pp776-7; ☎ 461-1312; www.museolarco.org; Av Bolívar 1515, Pueblo Libre; adult/student S30/15; ☒ 9am-6pm) contains an impressive collection of ceramics, highlighted by the infamous collection of pre-Columbian erotic pots, illustrating with remarkable explicitness the sexual practices of ancient Peruvian men, women, animals and skeletons in all combinations of the above. Catch a minibus marked 'Todo Bolívar' from Av Arequipa in Miraflores to the 15th block of Av Bolívar (S1.20).

PERU

In Parque de la Cultura, **Museo de Arte de Lima** (Map pp782-3; ☎ 423-4732; www.museodearte.org.pe; Paseo de Colón 125, Santa Beatriz; adult/student S12/5; ⏰ 10am-5pm) was closed during our research while undergoing a US$4.5 million renovation that includes an expansion, new cafe, museum shop and renovated galleries. It exhibits four centuries of Peruvian art, as well as pre-Columbian artifacts. The more modest **Museo Nacional de la Cultura Peruana** (Map pp782-3; ☎ 423-5892; www .museodelacultura.perucultural.org.pe; Alfonso Ugarte 650; adult/ student S3.60/1; ⏰ 10am-5pm Tue-Fri, to 2pm Sat) displays popular folk art and handicrafts. Take a taxi from Plaza San Martín (S5).

In the building used by the Spanish Inquisition from 1570 to 1820, the **Museo de la Inquisición** (Map pp782-3; ☎ 311-7777; www .congreso.gob.pe/museo.htm; Jirón Junín 548, central Lima; ⏰ 9am-1pm & 2-5pm) offers free, multilingual tours. Visitors can explore the basement where prisoners were tortured, and there's a ghoulish waxwork exhibit of life-size unfortunates on the rack or having their feet roasted.

Religious Buildings

Lima's many churches, monasteries and convents are a welcome break from the city's incessant hustle and bustle, though they are often closed for restorations or an extended lunch.

Originally built in 1555, **La Catedral de Lima** (Map pp782-3; ☎ 427-9647; Plaza de Armas; adult/child S10/2; ⏰ 9am-5pm Mon-Fri, 10am-1pm Sat) has been destroyed by earthquakes and reconstructed several times, most recently in 1746. Look for the coffin of Francisco Pizarro in the mosaic-covered chapel to the right of the main door. A debate over the authenticity of his remains raged for years after a mysterious body with multiple stab wounds and a disembodied head were unearthed in the crypt in the late 1970s. After a battery of tests, scientists concluded that the remains previously on display were of an unknown church official, and that the body from the crypt was indeed Pizarro's.

Monasterio de San Francisco (Map pp782-3; ☎ 427-1381; www.museocatacumbas.com; cnr Lampa & Ancash, central Lima; 45min guided tour adult/student S5/1; ⏰ 9:30am-5:30pm) is famous for its catacombs and remarkable library, which has thousands of antique texts, some dating back to the Spanish Conquest. The church is one of the best preserved of Lima's early colonial churches, and much of it has been restored to its original baroque style with Moorish influence. The underground catacombs are the site of an estimated 70,000 burials and the faint-hearted may find the bone-filled crypts unnerving.

Ruins

Walking up to the ceremonial platform of **Huaca Huallamarca** (Map pp776-7; ☎ 222-4124; Nicolás de Rivera 201, San Isidro; adult/child S5/1; ⏰ 9am-5pm Tue-Sun), a highly restored Maranga adobe pyramid

---

PACHACAMAC

Although it was an important Inca site and a major city when the Spanish arrived, **Pachacamac** (☎ 430-0168; http://pachacamac.perucultural.org.pe; adult/child S6/2; ⏰ 9am-5pm Mon-Fri) had been a ceremonial center for 1000 years before the expansion of the Inca empire. This sprawling archaeological complex is about 30km southeast of the city center.

The name Pachacamac, translated as 'he who animated the world' or 'he who created land and time,' comes from the powerful Wari god, whose wooden two-faced image can be seen in the on-site museum. The main temple at the site was dedicated to this deity and held a famous oracle. Pilgrims traveled to the center from great distances, and its cemetery was considered sacrosanct.

Most of the buildings are now little more than walls of piled rubble, except for the huge pyramid temples and one of the Inca complexes, the Palacio de las Mamacuñas (House of the Chosen Women), which have been excavated and reconstructed. A thorough visit of this extensive site takes two hours, following a gravel road leading from site to site.

Guided tours from Lima run around S50 per person. Going solo? Catch a minibus signed 'Pachacamac' from the corner of Ayacucho and Grau in central Lima (Map pp782-3; S4, 45 minutes). Or from Miraflores, catch any bus along Diagonal signed 'Benividas' to Ricardo Palma University (Map pp776-7; S1), head under the bridge and take any bus heading to Pachacamac (S3.50, 25 minutes). Tell the driver to let you off near the *ruinas* or you'll end up at Pachacamac village, 1km beyond the entrance. For cycling and mountain biking, see opposite.

built c AD 500, gives you a novel perspective over contemporary Lima. Take a taxi from Miraflores (S6).

More easily accessible is **Huaca Pucllana** (Map p785; ☎ 617-7138; cnr Borgoño & Tarapacá, Miraflores; admission S7; ☺ 9am-4:30pm), an adobe pyramid of the Lima culture dating from AD 400. A guided tour is included with admission. There's a tiny museum and an upscale restaurant with spectacularly romantic nighttime views over the ruins.

Plazas

The oldest part of the **Plaza de Armas** (Plaza Mayor; Map pp782–3) is its central bronze fountain, erected in 1650. To the left of the cathedral, the exquisitely balconied **Archbishop's Palace** dates from around 1924. On the cathedral's northeastern flank, the **Palacio de Gobierno** is the home of Peru's president; the changing of the guard outside takes place at noon.

The early-20th-century **Plaza San Martín** (Map pp782–3) is presided over by the aged **Gran Hotel Bolívar**. It's well worth a stop in the hotel's yesteryear bar for a sip or two of its famous *pisco sour* (cocktail made from grape brandy). Also on the plaza is a bronze statue of liberator General José de San Martín. But get closer and you'll spy the overlooked **statue of Madre Patria**. Commissioned in Spain under instruction to give the good lady a crown of flames, nobody thought to iron out the double meaning of the Spanish word for 'flame' *(llama)*, and the hapless craftsmen duly placed a delightful little llama on her head.

ACTIVITIES
Paragliding

For paragliding trips along the coast, contact **Peru Fly** (☎ 444-5004; www.perufly.com). Tandem flights (S150) take off from the beachfront cliffs in Miraflores between noon and 6pm. Meet José or Max daily at Raimondi Park on Malecón Cisneros.

Swimming & Surfing

Limeños hit the beaches in their droves during the coastal summer months of January to March, despite publicized warnings of pollution. Don't leave anything unattended for a second.

The nearby surfing hot spots **Punta Hermosa** and **San Bartolo** (off Map pp776–7) have hostels near the beach. **Punta Rocas** (off Map pp776–7) is for experienced surfers, and has one basic hostel for crashing. You'll

have to buy or rent boards in Lima, though, and hire a taxi to transport them.

To get to the southern beaches, take a 'San Bartolo' bus from the Puente Primavera (Map pp776–7; taxi from Miraflores S6). Get off where you want and hike down to the beaches, which are mostly 1km or 2km from the Carretera Panamericana.

Cycling & Mountain Biking

A popular cycling excursion is the 31km ride to Pachacamac (see boxed text, opposite).
Bike Tours of Lima (Map p785; ☎ 445-3172; www.biketoursoflima.com; Bolívar 150, Miraflores; half/full day S27/36; ☺ 9am-6pm Mon-Sat, to 1pm Sun) Rents beach cruisers.
Peru Bike (☎ 255-7607; www.perubike.com) Does all-level bike tours around Pachacamac and Totoritas as well as multiday trips all over Peru. Go Saturdays and save S30.

TOURS

Mirabús (Map p785; ☎ 476-4213; www.mirabusperu.com; Parque Kennedy) offers bilingual city tours in open-air double-decker buses. It also offers day trips to Pachacamac.

FESTIVALS & EVENTS

Check out p873 for national holidays and p871 for other festivals and events.
Festival of Lima Anniversary of the city's founding (January 18).
Feria de Santa Rosa de Lima Major processions in honor of the patron saint of Lima and the Americas. Held on August 30.
Feria del Señor de los Milagros (Lord of the Miracles) On October 18, huge (and purple) religious processions; bullfighting season starts.

SLEEPING

The *cheapest* guesthouses are generally in central Lima; the best and most popular ones are in the more upmarket and safer neighborhoods of Miraflores and Barranco.

Central Lima

Hostal España (Map pp782-3; ☎ 427-9196; www.hotelespanaperu.com; Azangaro 105; dm S14, s/d S40/50, without bathroom S28/40; 💻) If you can navigate the piles of strewn backpacks and wayward tourists, you'll find a gringo-only scene here inside a rambling old mansion full of classical busts, museum-like paintings and creaky wooden spiral staircases. Accommodations are basic with sporadic hot showers, but it's full of antiquated character.

PERU

CENTRAL LIMA

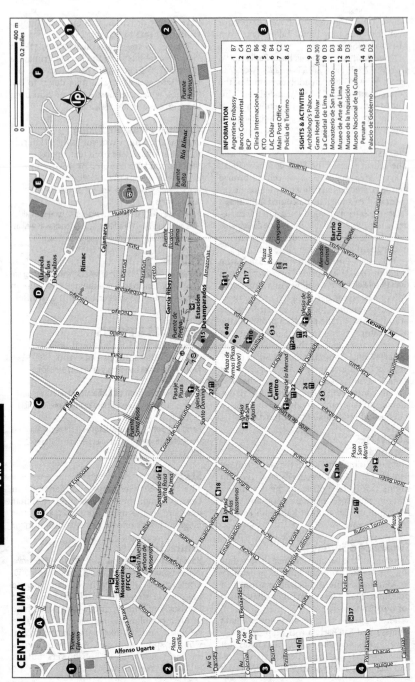

0   400 m
0   0.2 miles

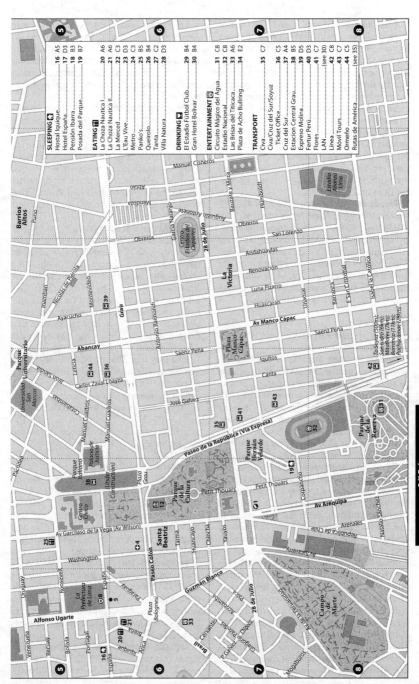

PERU

Pensión Ibarra (Map pp782-3; ☎ 427-8603; pension ibarra@gmail.com; Tacna 359, 14th & 15th fl; s/d without bathroom S20/35) This unique experience is like staying with your doting grandmother in her high-rise apartment. It's a homely *pensión* run by the helpful Ibarra sisters, who make a real effort to keep it safe, comfortable and clean. Kitchen access and views included.

Hostal Iquique (Map pp782-3; ☎ 433-4724; www .hostaliquique.com; Iquique 758; s/d S44/69, s/d/tr without bathroom S30/44/58; 🖳) A little out-of-the-way budget gem that's clean, safe, friendly and easy on the eyes with those lovely tiled archways. There's a rooftop terrace, kitchen facilities and cable TV.

Posada del Parque (Map pp782-3; ☎ 433-2412; www.incacountry.com; Parque Hernán Velarde 60; s/d/tr S113/133/182; 🖳) A lovely historic inn occupying a gorgeous colonial residential street convenient to both Centro and Miraflores. The English-speaking family is especially adorable and helpful. Breakfast and good homemade pizzas are available, but instant coffee at this level is a real bummer.

Miraflores

The area around Parque Kennedy is gringo ground zero.

Casa del Mochilero (Map p785; ☎ 444-9089; pilaryv @hotmail.com; Chacaltana 130A, 2nd fl; r without bathroom per person S15; 🖳) Beware of imposters knocking off this popular bare-bones crashpad (it's on the 2nd floor, facing the street) – they've been copied up, down and everywhere. Kitchen access and hot showers.

Loki Lima (Map p785; ☎ 651-2966; www.lokihostel .com; José Galvez 576; dm from S27, r with/without bathroom S90/80; 🖳) In a brand-new location four blocks from Parque Kennedy, this party-packer favorite boasts an airy rooftop bar and terrace, along with the same sort of nightly meals and themed evenings as its predecessors in La Paz and Cuzco. Front-desk staff isn't as informed or eager to help as they should be, however, though the owners are more than helpful.

Home Peru (Map p785; ☎ 241-9898; www.homeperu .com; Av Arequipa 4501; dm S28, s/d from S51/88, without bathroom S38/76; 🖳) Along a leafy, less frenetic block of Miraflores' main drag, steps from Huaca Pucllana, this newly popularized traveler's hub is housed inside a wonderful 1900 Patrimonio Cultural mansion full of antiques and a bird-chirpy interior garden. Breakfast is s-l-o-w, but the place is full of character. The dog-loving Peruvian owner is very helpful.

Red Psycho Llama (Map p785; ☎ 242-7486; www .redpsychollama.com; Colina 183; dm from S30, r S110; 🖳) The ecological choice, with plastic-bottle chandeliers, benches fashioned from bathtubs and a green mentality throughout. Common areas are a bit rustic, but the nice, new dorms are comfortable.

Flying Dog (Map p785; ☎ 444-5753; www.flyingdog peru.com; Lima 457; dm S31, s/d S78/80, without bathroom S56/68; 🖳) Of Flying Dog's four Lima hostels, this is the newest and the best, featuring a lovely outdoor garden bar and 3rd-floor hang room with expansive views over Parque Kennedy. Two kitchens make for a shorter line to fry up your burgers and the included breakfast is taken at the terrace restaurants across the park.

ourpick Hostal El Patio (Map p785; ☎ 444-2107; www.hostalelpatio.net; Diez Canseco 341A; s/d incl breakfast from S120/150; 🖳) This quaint inn is an urban oasis boasting a cheery English-speaking owner who takes her role as guesthouse hostess seriously. The sunny courtyard, fountain and trailing plants transcend solitude, and there are several terraces upon which to chill. Wi-fi, luggage storage and filtered water are free. Cash payments net a S15 discount.

Inka Frog (Map p785; ☎ 445-8789; www.inkafrog .com; Iglesias 271; r with/without bathroom from S140/121, tr S192; 🖳) Travelers are gushing over this stylish newcomer that's decked out in chic Andean art and retro bedspreads. Hi-tech fans, a 300-deep DVD collection, cable TV, safe boxes and humble service round out the amenities.

Barranco

Point Lima (Map pp776-7; ☎ 247-7997; www.the pointhostels.com; Malecón Junín 300; dm from S26, s/d without bathroom S50/68; 🖳) This bohemian seafront villa has ultrabasic rooms, but all the toys backpackers crave: cable TV, DVDs and ping-pong and pool tables. There's a kitchen and garden, plus free internet.

Backpackers Inn (Map pp776-7; ☎ 247-1326; www.barrancobackpackers.com; Mariscal Castilla 260; dm/d S32/97; 🖳) Newly British-owned and made over, this surf-style hostel has airy rooms with simple wooden furnishings and private bathrooms. Doubles have tranquil sea views and cable TV.

Acquisito (Map pp776-7; ☎ 247-0712; www.acquisito .com.pe; Centenario 14; s/d S48/78; 🖳) This signless, well-appointed guesthouse is remarkable for

MIRAFLORES

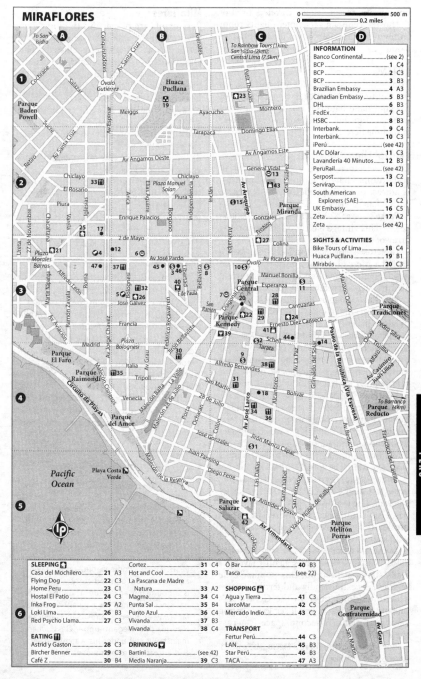

0 — 500 m
0 — 0.2 miles

PERU

To Barranco (4km);
Parque Reducto

one specific reason: single travelers tired of the hostel scene can get a hotel-quality room without being shaken down for the price of a double.

EATING

Lima's dining scene is among the best on the continent. Miraflores houses most of the gourmand haunts. *Ceviche* (raw seafood marinated in lime juice, onions and spices) is sublime here.

Central Lima

Cheap set-lunch *menús* are offered in local restaurants. Barrio Chino (Chinatown), southeast of the Plaza de Armas, is blessed with Asian eateries.

Panko's (Map pp782-3; Garcilaso de la Vega 1296; items S2-5.50) This vintage bakery offers a tempting array of sweets, pastries and drinks.

La Merced (Map pp782-3; Miró Quesada 158; menú S6-13.50) La Merced is (too) busy (for its own good) at lunch, but offers decent lunches and an intricately carved wooden ceiling.

Villa Natura (Map pp782-3; Ucayali 326; menú S7; ☯ closed Sun) One of many no-frills vegetarian pit stops in central Lima.

Queirolo (Map pp782-3; Camaná 900; mains S7.50-18.50) The Q*Bert floor design and crumbling glass cabinets reek of alcoholic enabling since God knows when at this atmospheric old restaurant popular for lunch and nightly drinks.

L'Eau Vive (Map pp782-3; ☎ 427-5612; Ucayali 370; lunch/dinner menú S15-50; ☯ closed Sun) A uniquely flavored international restaurant run by a French order of nuns, it's a welcome relief from the Lima madhouse. To enter the colonial mansion, ring the doorbell. The nuns sing 'Ave María' at 9pm.

Tanta (Map pp782-3; Pasaje Nicholas de Riviera 142; sandwiches S18-22) Chef Gastón Acurio's shady sidewalk cafe is a casual spot for fat empanadas, tasty sandwiches and one of Lima's best breakfasts, *Huevos de Gastón* (eggs scrambled with sausage and yuca).

La Choza Nautica (Map pp782-3; Breña 204; ceviche S19-33) Stainless-steel tables against lavender walls startle at first, but this popular little *cevichería* is extrafriendly and terribly tasty – a definite 'don't miss' in the Centro. It's one of the few places you'll see locals eating *ceviche* at night. A second space is across the street.

For self-catering, there's **Metro** (Map pp782-3; Cuzco 255; ☯ 9am-10pm).

Miraflores

Restaurants are pricier in Miraflores, but a few hole-in-the-wall cafes still serve cheap set menus. Fast-food joints cluster around Óvalo Gutiérrez. Open-air cafes and pizzerias surround Parque Kennedy.

Café Z (Map p785; Benavides 598; items S3.50-18.50) A godsend in Nescafé hell.

La Pascana de Madre Natura (Map p785; Chiclayo 815; mains S4.50-13) This natural-food store, bakery and cafe is herbivore Eden, serving up salads, pizza and other treats in a Zen courtyard. The divine veggie burgers are world-class. If you're vegetarian, it's Peru's best.

our pick Hot and Cool (Map p785; Berlin 511; sandwiches S8.50) It looks rudimentary, but the pristinely crafted gourmet (and cheap!) sandwiches here will knock you out. Try *Ibérico* (red wine–marinated chorizo with Manchego cheese).

Cortez (Map p785; San Martín 465; menú S10) Cozy spot; excellent set meals that include bread and a drink on top of three courses.

Punto Azul (Map p785; San Martín 595; mains S14-22; ☎ lunch) Huge portions at excellent prices make this colorful lunchtime seafooder an excellent choice for locals and foreigners alike. Awesome *ceviche* and *tiradito* (a different cut *ceviche*, minus onions) and piled-high seafood rices are the most popular dishes. The Javier Prado location (Map pp776–7) is even wilder, with mobs of standing-room-only starvivores storming the open kitchen.

Bircher Benner (Map p785; Av José Larco 413; mains S17-22) This pioneering restaurant makes excellent vegetarian treats like mushroom *ceviche*.

SPLURGE!

Astrid y Gastón (Map p785; ☎ 242-5387; www.astridygaston.com; Cantuarias 175, Miraflores; mains S39-69) Weaving a culinary ménage à trois of modern Peruvian flavors with traditional Spanish and French influences, celebrity chef–owner Gastón Acurio still hosts Lima's most special meal after 16 years. Organic guinea pig, rabbit ravioli, alpaca osso buco in red curry – each dish is a gourmand adventure. Though Gastón has since stretched his culinary empire as far away as Buenos Aires, São Paulo and Madrid, this elegant upper-class *limeño* mainstay is still under his watchful palette and a treat not to be missed.

Punta Sal (Map p785; cnr Malecón Cisneros & Tripoli; ceviche S20-38) Worth the extra soles for the excellent *ceviche* at this Lima institution, also one of the city's best spots for *leche de tigre* (literally 'tiger's milk'), an addictive aphrodisiacal concoction made from leftover *ceviche* juice.

Magma (Map p785; San Martín 512; rolls S25-30) Sushi's never cheap, but the all-you-can-eat option here for S50 (Monday to Saturday) certainly eases the pain. You need to eat three rolls to beat the house.

For self-caterers, there's **Vivanda** (Map p785; Benavides 487; 24hr). Another branch is located on Av José Pardo.

Barranco

A charming little district for a bite to eat, especially along the passageway below the Puente de los Suspiros. The specialty of the area is *anticuchos de corazón* (beef-heart shish kebabs), the waft of which permeates the entire district.

La Canta Rana (Map pp776-7; Génova 101; mains S22-40) Translated as the 'The Singing Frog,' this unpretentious lunchtime favorite is a great *cevichería*, serving all manner of seafood. The tables are as packed as the walls.

DRINKING

Lima overflows with bars, from San Isidro's pricey havens for the urbane elite to Barranco's cheap, cheerful watering holes. Plaza de Armas downtown and Miraflores have several streetfront cafes. The latter is also home to the low-rent pedestrianized San Ramón (aka Calle Pizza), where touristy pizzerias and Latin-themed clubs fight for real estate – your best bet for a cheap pub crawl (trendier options abound around the corner on Francisco de Paula Camino). In Barranco, bounce among the tight-knit nightclubs near Parque Municipal and the pedestrianized Calle Carrión all night long.

Central Lima

Drop in at the Gran Hotel Bolívar (p781) to quaff Peru's national cocktail, the *pisco sour*.

El Estadio Fútbol Club (Map pp782-3; Nicolás de Piérola 922) If there's an important match, it's on at this excellent bar devoted to soccer fanaticism. You can chug beers served in ceramic steins next to waxworks of Ronaldinho and Maradona and enjoy a select but tasty menu of Peruvian classics.

Miraflores

Tasca (Map p785; Diez Canseco 115) Flying Dog–owned tapas bar, cozily stuffed with a mix of travelers and locals. Food best avoided.

Media Naranja (Map p785; Schell 130; closed Sun) An extensive menu of Brazilian *caipirinhas* is served at this lively cafe-bar with an outdoor patio facing Parque Kennedy, but they are tiny.

Ô Bar (Map p785; F de Paula 298; from 8pm Wed-Sat) Sophisticated Italian-themed lounge with an array of creative cocktails. The long, marble bar seats 20!

Bartini (Map p785; LarcoMar; closed Mon) Glowing, sultry red, this smallish ultra lounge-style bar in LarcoMar serves up DJs and live music to an eclectic crowd. A trio of DJs makes Tuesday the best night.

Barranco

Barranco is thronged with revelers on Friday and Saturday nights.

La Noche (Map pp776-7; Bolognesi 307; admission S10-30) The party crowd is often to be found at this three-level, four-bar watering hole above a busy pedestrian parade. Expect to hear anything from Latin pop to the occasional highland folk tune.

El Dragon (Map pp776-7; Nicolás de Piérola 168; admission S20; from 10am Tue-Sat) Small but dark and sexy, this lounge boasts a hip ethos that maneuvers between resident DJs spinning a Latin cocktail of salsa and electronica to live jazz and surf guitar.

Wahio's (Map pp776-7; Plaza Espinosa; Thu-Sat) An energetic little bar with its fair share of dreadlocks, and a classic soundtrack of reggae, ska and dub.

Sargento Pimienta (Map pp776-7; Bolognesi 755; Wed-Sat) Spanish for 'Sergeant Pepper,' this huge barnlike place is so popular, parking touts start working four blocks away. DJs play a mix of international retro, plus occasional live rock, and Thursday is the best night.

our pick Ayahuasca (Map pp776-7; San Martín 130; closed Sun) This trendsetting bar is one of Lima's most atmospheric for a cocktail, from the traditional pants of the Ayucucho *tijera* dancers hanging from the ceiling in glass cases to the innovative *pisco sours* (try the *uva y camu-camu*). It's inside a restored 1860s mansion that swells with sexy *limenôs* lounging in its various art-forward rooms.

PERU

ENTERTAINMENT

Many top-end hotels downtown and in San Isidro and Miraflores have slot-machine casinos. **Circuito Mágico del Agua** (Map p782-3; Parque de la Reserva; admission S4; 4-11pm), a Bellagio-style fountain and laser show, is Lima's best entertainment bang for the buck.

Dance & Music

Peruvian music and dance is performed at *peñas*.

La Candelaria (Map pp776-7; 247-1314; www .lacandelariaperu.com; Bolognesi 292, Barranco; admission S31-37; 9:30-late Fri & Sat) and **Las Brisas del Titicaca** (Map p782-3; 332-1901; www.brisasdeltiticaca.com; Walkuski 168, central Lima; admission S48-58; 7:30pm-midnight Tue & Wed, 9:30pm-1am Thu, 10pm-3am Fri & Sat) are popular with *limeños*.

Sports

Bullfighting is popular in Lima. The main season runs from late October through November.

Plaza de Acho bullring (Map pp782-3; 481-1467; Hualgayoc 332, Rímac; tickets S30-50) Hosts bullfights during the Feria del Señor de los Milagros. The surrounding neighborhood is unsafe, so take a taxi. Buy tickets in advance.

Estadio Nacional (Map pp782-3) The major venue for soccer matches.

SHOPPING

Shopping malls include the underground LarcoMar (Map p785), with a spectacular location built right into the oceanfront cliffs, selling high-end artisan crafts, electronics, photographic supplies, outdoor gear, books and music.

Mercado Indio (Map p785; Petit Thouars 5245, Miraflores; 9am-8:30pm Mon-Sat, 10am-7pm Sun) Haggle your heart out at this enormous market, where you can browse handicrafts from all over Peru. Similar artisanal plazas abound in this area.

La Casa de la Mujer Artesana Manuela Ramos (Map pp776-7; 423-8840; Fernandini 1550, Pueblo Libre; 9am-5pm Mon-Fri) A nonprofit women's crafts cooperative off the 15th block of Brazil.

Agua y Tierra (Map p785; 444-6980; Diez Canseco 298, Miraflores; closed Sun) Specializes in Amazonian pottery, textiles and art.

GETTING THERE & AWAY
Air

Lima's **Aeropuerto Internacional Jorge Chávez** (LIM; Map pp776-7; 517-3100; www.lap.com.pe) is in Callao. Airport taxes (payable in US dollars or nuevos soles, cash only) are US$31 for international and US$5.84 for domestic flights.

Many international airlines have offices in Lima – check under 'Lineas Aéreas' in the yellow pages. Airlines offering domestic flights include the following:

LAN central Lima (Map pp782-3; 213-8200; Jirón de la Unión 908); Miraflores (Map p785; 213-8200; Av José Pardo 513)

LC Busre (Map pp776-7; 619-1313; Los Tulipones 218, Lince)

Star Perú (Map p785; 705-9000; Av José Pardo 485, Miraflores)

TACA (Map p785; 511-8222; Av José Pardo 811, Miraflores)

See regional sections later in this chapter for details of which airlines fly where. Be aware that flight schedules and ticket prices change frequently.

The official ISIC office is **InteJ** (Map pp776-7; 247-3230; www.intej.org; San Martín 240, Barranco; 9:30am-12:45pm & 2-5:45pm Mon-Fri, 9:30am-12:45pm Sat), which organizes student airfares and can change dates for flights booked through student or youth travel agencies. **Fertur Perú** (Map pp782-3; 427-2426; www.fertur-travel.com; Jirón Junín 211, central Lima; 9am-7pm Mon-Fri, 9am-2pm Sat) is also good for student airfares. They've opened a second office at Shell 485 in Miraflores (Map p785).

Bus

Lima has no central bus terminal. Each company runs its own office and station, many of which cluster around Av Javier Prado Este in La Victoria. Others are found in central Lima several blocks east of Plaza Grau, just north of Av Grau and south of 28 de Julio, on both sides of Paseo de la República. Make sure you verify which station your bus departs from when buying tickets. There are countless companies to choose from, so look carefully at the quality of the buses before deciding.

Major companies include the following:

Cruz del Sur (www.cruzdelsur.com.pe); central Lima (Map pp782-3; 424-1003; Quilca 531); La Victoria (Map pp776-7; 225-3748; Av Javier Prado Este 1109) The nicest and most reliable.

Ormeño (www.grupo-ormeno.com.pe); central Lima (Map pp782-3; 472-5000; Carlos Zavala Loayza 177); La Victoria (Map pp776-7; 472-1710; Av Javier Prado Este 1059) Quality of service varies wildly. Has extensive international service.

Rutas de América (Map pp782-3; ☎ 534-3195; www.rutasenbus.com; 28 de Julio 1145) Connects Lima with most continental capitals, including Bogotá, Buenos Aires, Caracas, La Paz, Quito, Rio de Janeiro and Santiago.

Also in central Lima, in none too pleasant areas:

Civa (Map pp782-3; ☎ 418-1111; www.civa.com.pe; 28 de Julio 1145) Also shares a ticket office with Cruz del Sur and Soyuz at Carlos Zavala Loayza and Montevideo.

Expreso Molina (Map pp782-3; ☎ 324-2137; Ayacucho 1141)

Flores (Map pp782-3; ☎ 332-1212; www.floresbus .com; Paseo de la República 683)

Línea (Map pp782-3; ☎ 424-0836; www.transportes linea.com.pe; Paseo de la República 941)

Móvil Tours (Map pp782-3; ☎ 716-8000; www.movil tours.com.pe; Paseo de la República 749)

Soyuz/PerúBus (Map pp776-3; ☎ 266-1515; www .soyuz.com.pe, www.perubus.com.pe; México 333)

Tepsa (pp776-7; ☎ 470-6666; www.tepsa.com.pe; Av Javier Prado Este 1091)

See regional sections later in this chapter for details of which bus companies go where. Approximate one-way fares and durations from Lima among the top companies follow.

BUS FARES		
Destination	**Cost (S)**	**Duration (hr)**
Arequipa	60-145	14
Ayacucho	64-90	10
Cajamarca	65-123	14
Chachapoyas	115	23
Chiclayo	84-108	10
Cuzco	144-174	20
Huancayo	25-70	6
Huaraz	63-78	7
Ica	45-66	4
Nazca	66-86	7
Piura	99-139	14
Puno (via Arequipa)	132-150	19
Tacna	113-153	18
Trujillo	34-90	7
Tumbes	120-180	19

Train

See p836 for details of highland rail services to Huancayo, which leave from Lima's **Estación Desamparados** (Map pp782-3; ☎ 263-1515; Ancash 203).

GETTING AROUND

See boxed text, p778 for details of getting to and from the airport.

Bus

By the time you read this or shortly thereafter, Lima will finally have joined the modern world and implemented a public bus system operating along the main thoroughfare of Vía Expresa as well as its main arteries around town, greatly relieving traveler confusion about the myriad privately-owned minibuses (aka *combis* or *micros*) that traverse the city in mazelike chaotic fashion. A massive underground station, **Estación Central Grau**, is the epicenter of the new system. In the meantime, most minibus fares in town run from S1 to S4 and destinations are identifiable by windscreen cards – you can flag them down or get off anywhere. The most useful routes link central Lima with Miraflores along Av Arequipa: buses are labeled 'Tdo. Arequipa' and 'Larco/Schell/Miraflores' when heading to Miraflores, or 'Tdo. Arequipa' and 'Wilson/Tacna' when leaving Miraflores for central Lima.

Taxi

Taxis don't have meters, so make sure you negotiate a price before getting in. Short rides run between S5 and S8 (depending on how local you appear) and escalate after dark. The majority of taxis in Lima are unofficial.

SOUTH COAST

The devastating earthquake of 2007 rattled and rolled Peru's south coast, a vast area characterized by sandy dunes and desertscape diving into the sea. Pisco received the brunt of the blow – 80% of the city was destroyed, while Ica, Chincha and Paracas received their fair share of destruction as well. Recovery efforts have been slow, and piles of rubble still pepper the landscape here like Legos strewn across a living-room floor. Thankfully, the area's star attractions – Islas Ballestas off the coast of Pisco, the mysterious pre-Columbian Nazca Lines, Ica's surrounding vineyards and the monstrous sand dunes of Huacachina – are welcoming tourists with open (if not outstretched and begging) arms.

PERU

TOP FIVE GRINGO TRAIL CHILL-OUT SPOTS

■ Huacachina (p793)

■ The Sacred Valley (p821)

■ Máncora (p845)

■ Cabanaconde (p805)

■ Lunahuaná (below)

LUNAHUANÁ
☎ 056 / pop 3600

Almost 15km past the surfers' beach of Cerro Azul (Carretera Panamericana Km 131), the dusty market town of San Vincente de Cañete is the gateway to the sweet wine country of Lunahuaná. It's packed for the **harvest festival** in the second week of March, but on weekends throughout the year and daily in summer, *bodegas* (wineries) and artisanal *pisco* producers set up cute booths around the plaza, which fills with revelers getting sauced at outdoor cafe tables. It's good fun!

The whitewater rafting (river-running) season on the Río Cañete is December to April, and rapids can reach Class IV. The town is packed with outfitters, but the safest and most experienced one is just by the river west of town: **Río Cañete Expediciones** (☎ 284-1271; www .riocanete.com.pe; rafting tours S35-80) also runs **Camping San Jerónimo** (☎ 284-1271; Carretera Cañete–Lunahuaná Km 33; campsites per person S6).

Near the plaza, pricy budget rooms are secure at **Hostal Casuarinas** (☎ 284-1045; Grau 295; s/d S50/60); some come with local TV and all have hot showers. At several nearby seafood restaurants, the local specialty is crawfish.

From Cañete, where coastal buses stop on the Panamericana, catch a *combi* to Imperial (S0.80, 10 minutes), then another *combi* to Lunahuaná (S4, 30 minutes), nearly 40km away. Rent mountain and quad bikes near Lunahuaná's main plaza.

PISCO
☎ 056 / pop 54,000

Though it shares its name with the white-grape brandy produced in this region, there is little buzz in Pisco these days. Eighty percent of the city was destroyed in 2007's 8.0 earthquake – where the cathedral once stood was little more than dust at the time of research (hundreds died inside when it collapsed during service). Most folks in town feel abandoned by the government and re-construction has been slow going. Many buildings are either gone or still crumbled, though most hotels were rebuilt quickly to incite tourism, the one thread holding Pisco together at the moment.

Located 235km south of Lima, Pisco is generally the base from which to see the abundant wildlife of the Islas Ballestas and Península de Paracas, but the area is also of historical and archaeological interest, having hosted one of the most highly developed pre-Inca civilizations – the Paracas culture – from 900 BC until AD 200.

Information

Internet cafes and banks with 24-hour ATMs surround the main plaza.

Dangers & Annoyances

Never walk alone after dark. Violent muggings have happened even on busy streets. The most dangerous areas are near the beaches and around the market. Women can expect lots of unwanted attention here. Since the earthquake, money flow is crippled, so petty crime has expectedly risen.

Sights & Activities

A **statue** of liberator José de San Martín peers down on the Plaza de Armas. Martín's headquarters, **Club Social Pisco** (San Martín 132), was destroyed in the quake. The **cemetery** has a few hidden secrets: buried here is suspected 19th-century English vampire, Sarah Ellen Roberts, who claimed that she would arise again after 100 years. In 1993, much to everyone's disappointment, she didn't. The cemetery is now a memorial to the more than 500 victims of the 2007 earthquake.

ISLAS BALLESTAS

Nicknamed 'the poor man's Galápagos,' these offshore islands make for a worthwhile laid-back excursion. The outward boat journey takes about 1½ hours. En route you'll see the famous three-pronged **Candelabra**, a giant figure etched into the sandy hills. An hour is spent cruising around the island's arches and caves, watching noisy sea lions sprawl on the rocks. You may also spot Humboldt penguins, Chilean flamingos and dolphins. The most common guano-producing birds are cormorants, boobies and pelicans, present in thousands-strong colonies.

RESERVA NACIONAL DE PARACAS

Beyond the village of Paracas is the entrance to this desert-filled **national reserve** (admission S5). Next to the visitors center, which has kid-friendly exhibits on conservation and ecology, the **Museo JC Tello** (admission S8; 9am-5pm) was still closed at the time of research, but was being renovated and expanded and set to reopen by fall 2009. It houses a limited collection of weavings, trophy heads and trepanned skulls (showing a medical technique used by ancient cultures whereby a slice of the skull is removed, relieving pressure on the brain resulting from injuries).

Tours

Boat tours to the Islas Ballestas leave daily at 7am (S45 plus S1 dock tax). Minibuses go from Pisco to the port at Paracas, where there is a nice seafront full of sidewalk restaurants and vendors (look out for Viviana's *chocotejas*, addictive pecans doused in caramel and covered in chocolate, a specialty of Ica). There are no cabins on the boats, so dress for wind, spray and sun. Wear a hat, as it's not unusual to receive direct guano hits. You can continue on a less interesting afternoon tour of the Península de Paracas (S25 with Islas Ballestas), which briefly stops at the visitors center and museum (entry fees not included) and whizzes by coastal geological formations.

Here are some Pisco travel agencies:

Aprotur Pisco (50-7156; aproturpisco@hotmail.com; San Francisco 112) Seven languages spoken.
Paracas Overland (53-3855; paracasoverland @hotmail.com; San Francisco 111)

Sleeping

Most travelers stay in central Pisco.

Hostal San Isidro (53-6471; San Clemente 103; www .sanisidrohostal.com; dm S20, s/d S40/60, without bathroom S25/40;) Extraordinary value here: a lovely pool, kitchen use, luggage storage, free laundry machines and a game room keep travelers and their bank accounts happy. English, French and Japanese spoken. Be weary of overcharging.

Hostal Los Inkas Inn (53-6634; www.losinkasinn .com; Barrio Nuevo 14; dm S20, s/d/tr S35/60/80;) This friendly, family-owned guesthouse has simple but colorful rooms, miniature swimming pool, rooftop terrace with billiards and foosball, and free internet.

Hostal Tambo Colorado (53-1379; www.hostaltambo colorado.com; Bolognesi 159; s/d S50/60;) Colorful art and friendly service characterize this solid midrange choice offering well-appointed rooms and an inviting plant-filled patio.

Hostal Villa Manuelita (53-5218; www.villa manuelitahostal.com; San Francisco 227; s/d incl breakfast S75/95;) Though it lost 15 rooms and its main entrance in the quake, this lovely guesthouse's then just-renovated main section escaped unharmed. There's a peaceful courtyard and rooms are spacious and as clean as a cadet's buckle on the second day of boot camp.

DETOUR

The heart of the country's Afro-Peruvian culture centers around the *peñas* (clubs with folk music) of **El Carmen** district just outside **Chincha**, at Km 202 along the Carretera Panamericana. During holidays and festivals like **Verano Negro** (late February/early March), **Fiestas Patrias** (late July) and **Fiesta de Virgen del Carmen** (December 27), these wild *peñas* are full of frenzied *limeños* (Lima inhabitants), locals and overwhelmed tourists shakin' that ass. One dance not to try at home is 'El Alcatraz,' in which a gyrating male dancer attempts to set his partner's skirt on fire with a candle. During other times, it's a dead town.

Places to bed down and sleep off your hangover (if you sleep at all) include a selection of budget *hostales* around Chincha's main plaza, like **Hostal La Posada** (056-26-2042; Santo Domingo 200; r per person S30), run by a gregarious Italian-Peruvian couple, which offers secure, antique-looking rooms. For a bit more history, check out the 300-year-old **Hacienda San José** (www .haciendasanjose.com.pe), scheduled to reopen in 2010 after suffering damage in the 2007 earthquake. African slaves worked this former sugar and honey plantation until a rebellion broke out in 1879, leading to the master being dramatically hacked to death. Guided Spanish-language tours go down into the ghoulish catacombs.

Soyuz/PerúBus has the most departures to Chincha from Lima (S26 to S28, three hours). *Combis* to El Carmen (S1.40, 30 minutes) leave from Chincha's central market, a few blocks from the main plaza. It's a short taxi ride (S3) from the Panamericana where coastal buses stop.

Eating & Drinking

Panadería San Francisco (San Juan de Dios 100; items S3.50-6.50) Your best bet for early breakfast (6:30am), cheap eats and sweet treats.

El Dorado (Progreso 171; mains S8-30) Perennially popular plaza restaurant specializing in seafood – superb *sudado* (fish stew)! – but with a little bit of everything, including vegetarian options. There's a pleasant patio out back.

Viña de Huber (Prolg Cerro Azul; ceviche S11.50-25.50; ☻ lunch) A wildly popular seafooder doing melt-in-your-mouth *ceviche* and piled-high plates of fish *chicharrones*. There's live *música criolla* amongst the tables on weekends.

Don Santiago (Callao 148; mains S13-28) Family-run spot punching above its weight class: well-presented seafood, chicken and steak dishes don't match the humble (but clean) decor.

Taberna Don Jaime (San Martín 203) Half-jars of *pisco sours* and a good selection of local wines by the bottle (S22 to S35) are the calling at Pisco's best bar. There's live music and karaoke on the weekends.

Getting There & Around

Pisco is 6km west of the Panamericana. Taxis from the highway to Centro are S8. **Soyuz/PerúBus** (☎ 53-1014; Diez Canseco s/n) has the most frequent coastal departures in either direction between Lima and Ica. From here, departures for Ica (S4 to S6, one hour) are every 10 minutes. For Nazca, switch in Ica. **Ormeño** (☎ 53-2764; San Francisco 259) has a tout-ridden bus terminal near the Plaza de Armas. It runs daily buses to Lima (S45, four hours) and many other coastal destinations. There is also direct service to Arequipa (S100, 12 hours). **Flores** (San Martín 191) also combs the coast.

Combis to Paracas leave near the market on the 5th block of Beatita de Humay when full during the day (S2, 30 minutes). Taxis to Paracas cost S15.

ICA

☎ 056 / pop 220,000

There are worse places to be stuck than Ica, the capital of the department of the same name. The bustling city boasts a thriving wine and *pisco* industry, raucous festivals and an excellent museum. The leafy plaza ain't bad either. Still, most travelers opt to bed down in nearby Huacachina. Remnants of damaged buildings from the 2007 earthquake remain, but Ica is more or less business as usual.

Information

Around the plaza, internet cafes stay open until late.

BCP (Plaza de Armas) Changes traveler's checks and cash, and has a Visa ATM.

Hospital (☎ 23-4798; Cutervo 104; ☻ 24hr) For emergencies.

Police (☎ 23-5421; JJ Elias, 5th block; ☻ 24hr) White-shirted officers patrol the plaza.

Serpost (San Martín 521)

Dangers & Annoyances

Ica has a deserved reputation for theft. Stay alert, particularly around the market, internet cafes and bus terminals – we heard about five tourist robberies around the Ormeño terminal in one week.

Sights

Three textiles were robbed from the excellent **Museo Regional de Ica** (☎ 23-4383; Jirón Ayabaca, 8th block; admission S11.50; ☻ 8am-7pm Mon-Fri, 8:30am-6pm Sat & Sun) in 2004 (one was recovered in 2007 from a private home in Lima). The museum houses an unmatched collection of artifacts from the Paracas, Nazca and Inca cultures, including superb Paracas weavings, well-preserved mummies, trepanned skulls and shrunken trophy heads. Out back is a scale model of the Nazca Lines. The museum is 1.5km southwest of the city center. Take a taxi from the Plaza de Armas (S3).

Peruvian wines and *piscos* can be sampled at **bodegas** outside town. **Vista Alegre** (☎ 23-8735; www.vistaalegre.com.pe; Camino a la Tinguiña Km 2; ☻ 8am-12:30pm & 2-4pm Mon-Fri, 8am-12:30pm Sat), 3km northeast of Ica, is the easiest commercial winery to visit (taxi S5). Tours and tastings are free from Monday to Wednesday. It's well known for Malbec, Tempranillo and Pinot Blanc. Producing Peru's most famous juice is **Tacama** (☎ 58-1030; www.tacama.com; Camino Real s/n, Tinguiña; ☻ 9am-4pm Mon-Sat, to noon Sun), 11km northeast of Ica, which offers free tours and tastings of its Tannats, Malbecs and Chardonnays, among others. Take a taxi (S15).

There are dozens of smaller, family-owned artisanal wineries, including those in suburban **Guadalupe**. *Colectivos* to Guadalupe (S1.50, 15 minutes) leave from the first block of Municipalidad near the plaza.

Festivals & Events

The harvest festival, **Fiesta de la Vendimia**, is held in early to mid-March. The religious pilgrimage of **El Señor de Luren** culminates in an all-night procession in late October. September hosts **Tourist Week**.

Sleeping

Most travelers stay in nearby Huacachina (right) where there are more popular backpacker crash pads. If you end up in Ica overnight, dozens of depressing budget hotels line the streets east of the bus terminals and north of the plaza, especially along Tacna.

Hostal El Dorado (☎ 21-5015; Lima 251; s without bathroom S20, d S50) Horrid bedspreads but otherwise clean and spacious, mere steps from the plaza.

La Florida Inn (☎ 23-7313; Los Olivos B1, Urb San Luis; s/d S60/80, without bathroom S30/60) This small, family-owned hotel not too far from the museum has quirky rooms with indigenous paintings and solar-powered hot water.

Eating

Several shops east of the main plaza sell *tejas* (caramel-wrapped candies flavored with fruits, nuts etc).

D'Lizia (Lima 155; items S4-18) This California-esque juice bar on the plaza also does breakfast, fresh salads and a wealth of upscale sandwiches at pauper prices.

El Otro Peñoncito (Bolívar 255; mains S8-28) Ica's classiest meal and one of the south coast's best. The house special, stuffed chicken with spinach in a pecan-*pisco* sauce, is well worth the soles.

Plaza 125 (Lima 125; menú S12, mains S10-30) Does efficient set lunches and a longer list of Peruvian staples in a clean, well-designed space.

Getting There & Away

Bus companies cluster on Lambayeque at the west end of Salaverry and along Manzanilla west of Lambayeque. For Lima (S20 to S55, 4½ hours), **Soyuz/PerúBus** (☎ 22-4138) and **Flores** (☎ 21-2266) have departures every 10 to 15 minutes, while less frequent luxury services go with **Cruz del Sur** (☎ 22-3333) and **Ormeño** (☎ 21-5600). To Pisco (S4, one hour), Ormeño has direct buses, while other bus companies drop passengers at the San Clemente turnoff on the Panamericana. Most companies have direct daytime buses to Nazca (S8 to S25, two hours). Services to Arequipa (S46 to S96, 12 hours) and Cuzco (S140, 18 hours) are mostly overnight. Tacna (S80, 15 hours), near the Chilean border, is serviced by Ormeño.

HUACACHINA

☎ 056 / pop 200

Surrounded by mountainous sand dunes that roll into town over the picturesque lagoon featured on the back of Peru's S50 note, there's no denying Huacachina's majestic setting. Just 5km west of Ica, this tranquil oasis boasts graceful palm trees, exotic flowers and attractive antique buildings – all testament to the bygone glamour of this resort built for the Peruvian elite. These days, it's a sandy gringo playground where backpackers tend to lose themselves for days.

Information

There's a Global ATM at El Huacanicero.
Oasis Net (Hostal Saviatierra; per hr $3; ⏱ 8:30am-9pm) Internet access.

Activities

You can rent sandboards for S3 an hour to slide, surf and somersault your way down the irresistible dunes. Thrilling rollercoaster-esque dune-buggy/sandboarding tours cost S45 (plus S3.60 'sand tax'). Go at sunset, when the scenery is at its most miraculous, rather than in the morning. All the *hostales* organize tours.

Sleeping & Eating

Camping is possible in the dunes around the lagoon – just bring a sleeping bag. For entertainment, follow the music.

Desert Nights (☎ 22-8458; www.desertadventure
.net.com; Blvd Principal s/n; dm with/without HI-card S12/15; 🖳) You don't get the pool or rowdy party scene here, but you do get a great restaurant (organic French Press coffee!), good terrace tunes, free internet, Nintendo Wii and lagoon views at this newish, American-run, HI-affiliated hostel in a historic 1920s colonial summer home on the lagoon.

Hostal Salvatierra (☎ 23-2352; www.salvatur.group
.galeon.com; Salvatierra Diaz; s/d S15/30, with hot water S20/40; 🖳 🖳) This family-run choice dates back to 1932. Creaky hardwood floors and old-school bathroom tiling give it a historic (though not overworn) edge. Economic rooms are good value if you don't mind paint-chipped walls and cold showers. There is a murky pool, too.

Carola del Sur (☎ 23-8783; Perotti s/n; dm/s/d from S15/45/60; 🖳 🖳) Affiliated with Casa de Arena and right under the lip of the dune, this large hostel has a 22-bed dormitory, private

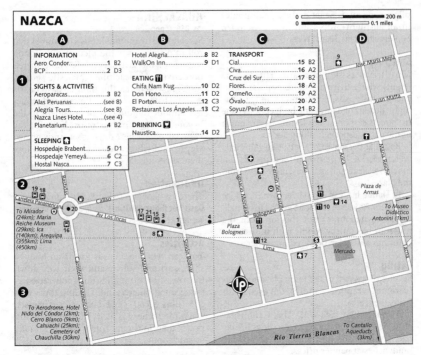

NAZCA

INFORMATION		Hotel Alegría.................8 B2		**TRANSPORT**	
Aero Condor...................1 B2		WalkOn Inn.................9 D1		Cial.............................15 B2	
BCP...............................2 D3				Civa.............................16 A2	
		EATING		Cruz del Sur................17 B2	
SIGHTS & ACTIVITIES		Chifa Nam Kug............10 D2		Flores..........................18 A2	
Aeroparacas.................3 B2		Don Hono.................11 D2		Ormeño.......................19 A2	
Alas Peruanas...........(see 8)		El Porton....................12 C3		Óvalo..........................20 A2	
Alegría Tours.............(see 8)		Restaurant Los Ángeles...13 C2		Soyuz/PerúBus.............21 A2	
Nazca Lines Hotel.......(see 4)					
Planetarium.................4 B2		**DRINKING**			
		Naustica.....................14 D2			
SLEEPING					
Hospedaje Brabent.........5 D1					
Hospedaje Yemeyá.........6 C2					
Hostal Nasca.................7 C3					

rooms and is popular with Israelis in high season. Rooms surround a large, lush plaza with plenty of hammocks and lounge spaces. English and Hebrew spoken.

Casa de Arena (☎ 23-7398; casa_de_arena@hotmail.com; Perotti s/n; dm from S20, s/d S40/609, without bathroom S30/50; ☒) Home to the best pool and bar area. Chop S5 off the room price if you sign up for a dune tour. The *discoteca* in the back buzzes until late. Fans, internet and change for your money would be nice.

Hospedaje El Huacanicero (☎ 21-7435; www.elhuacanicero.com; Perotti s/n; dm/s/d S30/100/110; ☒) A large pool and distinguished indigenous art throughout earn this guesthouse top honors in town, though private rooms are overpriced. Kitchen access, garden hammocks and a pool bar, but no internet? Inexcusable.

Casa de Bamboo (Perotti s/n; mains S7-18) Supercasual Cornwelian-run kitchen doing such culinary rarities in Peru as hummus and falafel, Thai curries and Banoffee pie.

Getting There & Away

A taxi between Ica and Huacachina costs about S5.

NAZCA

☎ 056 / pop 22,000

Bone-dry and baking hot, Nazca was a desert-scorched dead town until a flyby by American scientist Paul Kosok revealed one of Peru's most enigmatic and mysterious achievements – the world-famous Nazca Lines. In 1939 a routine ancient-irrigation research flight across the barren region unearthed the puzzling scratches in the sand, engraved on the desert floor like graffiti of giants carved with sticks the size of Redwoods. Today, travelers who come to marvel and scratch their heads over the mysterious lines, now a Unesco World Heritage Site, flood this otherwise unremarkable small town to catch a glimpse of the curious ground drawings. But despite the 2008 Indiana Jones flick, the lines do not lead to any crystal skulls. *Or do they?*

Information

Cybercafes are everywhere. A few hotels change US dollars for cash.

BCP (Lima 495) Has a Visa/Mastercard ATM; changes traveler's checks.

Sights

NAZCA LINES

Spread across 500 sq km of arid, rock-strewn plain, the Nazca Lines form a striking network of more than 800 lines, 300 geometric figures (geoglyphs), and some 70 animal and plant drawings (biomorphs). The most elaborate designs include a monkey with an extraordinarily curvaceous tail, a spider and an intriguing figure popularly called the astronaut, though some think it's a priest with an owl's head. Overflights of the lines are unforgettable, but they're not cheap (see right).

You'll get only a sketchy idea of the lines at the **mirador** (lookout; admission S1), on the Panamericana 20km north of Nazca, which has an oblique view of three figures: the lizard, tree and hands (or frog, depending on your point of view). Signs warning of land mines are a reminder that walking on the lines is strictly forbidden. To get to the observation tower, catch a northbound bus (S2) and ask the driver to let you off. To return, you'll need to flag down a southbound bus.

Another 5km north is the small **Maria Reiche Museum** (admission S10; ⏰ 9am-6pm). Though it's disappointingly scant on information, you can see where she lived, amid the clutter of her tools and obsessive sketches, and pay your respects at her tomb. To return to Nazca, flag down any passing bus.

Scripted but interesting multilingual lectures on the lines are given every evening at Nazca's small **planetarium** (☎ 52-2293; Nazca Lines Hotel, Bolognesi 147; admission S20; ⏰ 6pm in French, 7pm in English, 8:15pm in Spanish).

MUSEO DIDÁCTICO ANTONINI

On the east side of town, this **archaeological museum** (☎ 52-3444; Av de la Cultura 600; admission/cameras S15/5; ⏰ 9am-7pm) boasts an original pre-Columbian aqueduct running through

the back garden, plus reproductions of burial tombs and a scale model of the lines. You can get an overview of the Nazca culture and a glimpse of Nazca's outlying sites here.

OUTLYING SITES

It's safest to visit outlying archaeological sites with an organized tour and guide (see Tours, below), as robberies and assaults on tourists have been reported. At the **Cantallo aqueducts** (admission S10), just outside town, you can descend into the ancient stonework by means of spiraling *ventanas* (windows) – a wet, claustrophobic experience. The popular **Cemetery of Chauchilla** (admission S5), 30km south of Nazca, will satisfy any macabre urges you have to see bones, skulls and mummies. A dirt road travels 25km west to **Cahuachi**, an important Nazca center still being excavated.

Activities

An off-the-beaten-track expedition is to **Cerro Blanco**, the world's highest known sand dune (2078m). It's a real challenge for budding sandboarders fresh from Huacachina. Sandboarding tours cost S90 to S120, depending on the guide's qualifications.

Tours

Hotels and travel agencies tirelessly promote their own tours. Aggressive touts meet arriving buses to hard-sell you before you've even picked up your pack – ignore them completely, do not believe them and don't rush your decision: most agencies are clustered at the southwest end of Lima. Never hand over money on the street.

Bumpy flights over the Nazca Lines in light aircraft take off in the morning and early afternoon, if weather conditions allow. Motion sickness is common so if you're prone, keep breakfast light. Prices vary wildly

PERU

MYSTERIES IN THE SAND

The awesome, ancient Nazca Lines were made by removing sun-darkened stones from the desert surface to expose the lighter soil below. But who constructed the gigantic lines and for what reason? And why bother when they can only be properly appreciated from the air? Maria Reiche, a German mathematician and longtime researcher of the lines, theorized that they were made by the Paracas and Nazca cultures from 900 BC to AD 600, with additions by the Wari in the 7th century. She believed the lines were an astronomical calendar mapped out by sophisticated mathematics (and a long rope). Others theorize that the lines were ritual walkways connected to a water or fertility cult, giant running tracks, extraterrestrial landing sites or representations of shamans' dreams brought on by hallucinogenic drugs. Take your pick – no one really knows!

depending on season, demand and the whim of the 13 or so airlines that do the tours. Flights booked through a hotel or agency include transport to and from the aerodrome and cost around S170 in low season and up to S380 from May to August. There is a S20 tax at the aerodrome that is not included in the price of tours.

You can save the S15 or so commission being pocketed by hotels and agencies by going directly to the aerodrome yourself, but this is only worth your time if you are in a group of four or more and can split the taxi costs. If you do this, **Aeroparacas** (☎ 52-1027; www.aeroparacas.com; Lima 169), **Alas Peruanas** (☎ 52-2497; www.alasperuanas.com; Lima 168) and **Aero Condor** (☎ 52-2402; www.aerocondor.com.pe; Lima 199) are all reliable. Solo travelers can sometimes save between S15 and S30 by flying standby and occupying what would otherwise be an empty seat.

In high season, it's a good idea to book your flights several days in advance. Keep in mind, once you arrive at the aerodrome, those who have booked with powerful agencies or have offered more money will fly before you. Hurry up and wait.

Alegría Tours (☎ 52-2497; www.alasperuanas.com; Lima 168) is a reputable agency.

Sleeping

Hospedaje Brabent (☎ 52-4127; Matta 878; dm S12, s/d/tr without bathroom S20/33/50; 🖳) Though they mangled our reservation, this Dutch-Peruvian effort gets the benefit of the doubt. It's a rustic, five-room guesthouse with a hammock-filled terrace.

Hostal Nasca (☎ 52-2085; Lima 438; s/d S35/40, without bathroom S15/25) Although it caters mostly to Peruvians, this simple spot has newer rooms that are clean and offer hot water and cable TV.

WalkOn Inn (☎ 52-2566; www.walkoninn.com; Mejía 108; dm/s/d S15/25/50; 🖳 🖭) Travelers are greeted with Fanta soda and a thorough info packet at this Euro-run guesthouse with rooms surrounding a sunbaked walkway. There's a book exchange, DVD library, small solar-heated pool and all the friendliness, security and honesty you could ask for.

Hotel Nido del Cóndor (☎ 52-2402; www.nidodel condor.com; Panamericana Sur Km 447; campsite per person S20; 🖭) Opposite the aerodrome, this hotel allows camping on a grassy lawn and use of the pool and gym.

Hospedaje Yemeyá (☎ 52-3416; nazcahospedaje yemeya@hotmail.com; Callao 578; s/d without bathroom 25/30, s/d incl breakfast S35/40; 🖳) The artistic entrance hall is welcoming and clean rooms offer hot showers and cable TV, but this guesthouse utilizes touts.

Hotel Alegría (☎ 52-2702; Lima 166; s/d without bathroom S30/50, s/d/tr incl breakfast S95/126/157; 🌢 🖳 🖭) This well-heeled oasis keeps a dozen or so basic rooms with shared hot showers for budget travelers (more are on the way). There's a breezy garden and courtyard cafe.

Eating & Drinking

West of the Plaza de Armas, Bolognesi is lined with backpacker pizzerias, restaurants and bars, including Naustica.

Chifa Nam Kug (Bolognesi 448; menú S5-9.50) This cheap *chifa* has a swath of set menus under S10 that include wonton soup, main and fried rice. If you're lost, consult the picture poster on the wall.

Restaurant Los Ángeles (Bolognesi 266; mains S11-24) This Peruvian-international eatery does a lot of everything at fair prices. The veggie options are extensive (try the stuffed avocado) and it's all good.

Don Hono (Bolognesi 465; menú S12-20) Just off the main plaza, this simple spot is a local favorite for its daily changing menús of hearty comfort food. Try the lovely *cazuela* (a soupy stew with rice, corn and some meat) as a starter.

El Porton (Morsesky 120; mains S15-35) The best restaurant in Nazca is unfortunately too popular with tour groups. The food, however, like seafood rice served in a clay pot, delivers. There's an intimate bar attached.

Getting There & Around

Bus companies cluster at the west end of Lima, near the main Panamericana roundabout. Most services to Lima (S30 to S86, eight hours), Arequipa (S40 to S100, eight to 10 hours) and Tacna (S60 to S150, 12 hours) leave late in the afternoon or evening. To go directly to Cuzco (S70 to S100, 13 to 15 hours), several companies take the paved road east via Abancay. This route gets cold, so wear warm clothes. The alternative is to go via Arequipa. You can also reach Puno (S120 to S140) from here. Taxis to the aerodrome cost S3 to S5.

Ormeño (☎ 52-2058; Av Los Inkas 112) also goes to La Paz (S246).

DETOUR

South of Mollendo along an unbroken line of beaches, **Santuario Nacional Lagunas de Mejía** (☎ 054-83-5001; admission S5; ☼ sunrise-sunset) protects the largest permanent lakes in 1500km of desert coastline. More than 200 migratory and coastal bird species are best seen in early morning. The visitors center has maps of walking paths through the dunes leading to *miradores* (lookouts). Minibuses for Mejía leave Mollendo from the corner of Tacna and Arequipa (S1.20, 30 minutes).

Passing *colectivos* go deeper into the Río Tambo valley, with its irrigated rice paddies, sugarcane plantations and fields of corn and potatoes: a striking juxtaposition with the dusty backdrop of sand dunes and desert. The road rejoins the Panamericana at El Fiscal, a flyblown gas station where you can flag down standing-room-only buses back to Arequipa or south to Tacna.

TACNA
☎ 052 / pop 242,500

It's a long and dusty trail to Tacna, Peru's most heroic city, sitting staunchly at the tail end of the Carretera Panamericana, nearly 1300km southeast of Lima. In fact, this well-developed border outpost was occupied by Chile after the War of the Pacific in 1880, but townsfolk staged a border shuffle coup in 1929 and voted to return to Peru's welcoming arms. You'll also find there is added civility in this part of the country.

Information
Chilean pesos, nuevos soles and US dollars can be easily exchanged.

BCP (San Martín 574) Has a Visa/MasterCard ATM, gives Visa cash advances and changes traveler's checks.

Hospital Hipólito Unanue (☎ 42-3361; Blondell s/n; ☼ 24hr) For emergencies.

Interbank (San Martín 646) Has a global ATM.

iPerú (☎ 42-5514; San Martín 491; ☼ 8:30am-7:30pm Mon-Fri, to 2:30pm Sat) Helpful travel info on the northeast end of the plaza.

Polícia Nacional (Calderón de la Barca 353)

Serpost (Bolognesi 361) Post office.

Sights & Activities
The palm tree–studded **Plaza de Armas** features a fountain and cathedral created by French engineer Eiffel (of tower fame). Inside the train station, **Museo Ferroviario** (☎ 24-5572; cnr 2 de Mayo & Albarracin; admission S5; ☼ 8am-6pm) lets you wander amid beautiful 20th-century engines and rolling stock, plus atmospheric salons filled with historic paraphernalia.

The countryside around Tacna is known for its olive groves, orchards and *bodegas*. Catch a bus or *micro* along Bolognesi (S0.50, 10 minutes) to visit the *bodegas* and restaurants in suburban **Pocollay**.

The seaside resort of **Boca del Río** is 50km southwest of Tacna. Catch a minibus from Terminal Bolognesi (S4, one hour).

Sleeping
Hotel rooms are overpriced and fill up very fast, especially on weekends.

Hostal Inclán (☎ 24-4848; Inclán 171; s/d 27/37) The cheapest acceptable option in the center, steps from the plaza. Decent rooms for a fair price.

Lido Hospedaje (☎ 57-7001; San Martín 876A; s/d/tr S30/40/50) A dead-simple, secure guesthouse in the center that leaves us pondering what happened to the toilet seats?

Universo Hostal (☎ 71-5441; Zela 724; s/d/tr S30/40/60) A step up in comfort for the same price as Lido, this broken-in small hotel has respectable rooms with hot showers and cable TV.

Royal Inn (☎ 72-6094; Melendez 574; s/d/tr S35/45/65) North of the market, this welcoming hotel offers stuck-in-time decor and the best-value rooms with cable TV and hot water. Handy minibar by the front desk.

Eating & Drinking
Pocollay is popular with *tacneños* for its rural restaurants, which often have live bands on weekends. Many bars inhabit the first block of Arias Aragüez, where beer geeks have Münchner Brauhaus and rockers get down 'n' dirty at Jethro Pub. San Martín also comes alive on weekends, when it's pedestrianized and fills with artists and street performers.

Café Venecia (Vizquerra 130; items S4-16) Early breakfast (from 7am), good-lookin' burgers, espresso and sandwiches fuel folks at this clean cafe on Plaza Zela.

Fu Lin (Arias Araguez 396; menú S4.50; ☼ lunch Mon-Fri) A cheap vegetarian *chifa*; clean and friendly.

PERU

GETTING TO CHILE

Border-crossing formalities are straightforward. The Peruvian border post is open from 7am to midnight on weekdays, and 24 hours Friday and Saturday. Chile is an hour (two hours during daylight-saving time) ahead of Peru.

Frequent *colectivo* taxis (S15, two hours) to Arica (Chile), about 65km from Tacna, leave between 6am and 10pm from the international bus terminal opposite Terminal Terrestre. On Friday and Saturday you may find taxis willing to go outside these times, but expect to pay over the odds. Because taxi drivers help you through the border formalities, they're a safer, more convenient option than infrequent local buses. Alternatively, **Ormeño** (☎ 42-3292) offers a direct bus to Santiago (S300) on Wednesday and Sunday.

Tacna's **train station** (☎ 24-5572; cnr 2 de Mayo & Albarracín) has twice-daily services to Arica (S7, 1½ hours, at 5:45am and 4pm), which are the cheapest and most charming (but also slowest) way to cross the border. Your passport is stamped at the train station in Peru and you receive entry stamps upon arrival in Chile. Buy tickets at the station ticket office up to 1½ hours before departure.

For border crossings in the opposite direction, see p434.

Café Davinci (San Martín 596; menú S12) This civilized cafe boasts priced-for-weekending-*chilenos* dinner mains. The set lunches (S12), afternoon tea (4pm to 7pm), pizza, deserts, espresso and sandwiches are much easier on the wallet. Good bar for live music upstairs.

Getting There & Around
AIR
Tacna's **airport** (TCQ; ☎ 31-4503) is 5km west of town (taxi S10 to S12). **LAN** (☎ 42-8346; Apurímac 101) flies daily to Lima and on Wednesday and Sunday to Cuzco.

BUS
Most long-distance departures are from Terminal Terrestre (departure tax S1). Take a taxi from the center (S3). Many companies go to Lima (S60 to S148, 18 to 22 hours) and Arequipa (S25 to S36, six to seven hours) via Moquegua (S11, three hours). Most Lima-bound buses will drop you off at other coastal towns, including Nazca and Ica. Comfortable overnight buses with **Julsa** (☎ 24-7132) reach Puno (S30 to S50, 10 hours) via Desaguadero. For Cuzco, switch in Arequipa or Puno.

AREQUIPA & CANYON COUNTRY

Colonial Arequipa, with its sophisticated museums, architecture and nightlife, is surrounded by some of the wildest terrain in Peru. This is a land of active volcanoes, thermal springs, high-altitude deserts and the world's deepest canyons. Traveling overland, it's a must-stop en route to Lake Titicaca and Cuzco.

AREQUIPA
☎ 054 / pop 905,000
Rocked by volcanic eruptions and earthquakes nearly every century since the Spanish arrived in 1540, Arequipa doesn't lack for drama. The perfect cone-shaped volcano of El Misti (5822m), which rises majestically behind the cathedral on the Plaza de Armas, is flanked to the left by ragged Chachani (6075m) and to the right by Pichu Pichu (5571m). Peru's second-largest city is whitewashed in volcanic stone in a majestic mountainous setting and is one of Peru's most indebted cities to Kodak – its grand colonial buildings were built from a light-colored volcanic rock called *sillar* that dazzles in the sun and on camera. Despite its Andean setting, Arequipa boasts cosmopolitan cobblestones, gourmet restaurants and raucous nightlife.

Information
BOOKSTORES
Librería El Lector (San Francisco 221; ⊗ 9am-8pm Mon-Sat) Book exchange, local-interest titles, guidebooks and extensive selection of English titles.

EMERGENCY
Policía de Turismo (☎ 20-1258; Jerusalén 315; ⊗ 24hr)

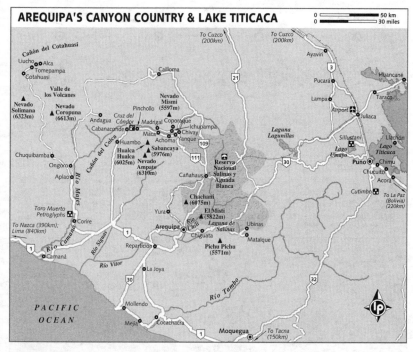

AREQUIPA'S CANYON COUNTRY & LAKE TITICACA

INTERNET ACCESS

Ciber Market (Santa Catalina 115B; per hr S1.50; ⏱ 8:00am-11pm) Quiet cabins, fast computers with printers, net-to-phone and digital-photo CD burning.

LAUNDRY

Magic Laundry (Jerusalén 404B; per kg S3-4; ⏱ 8am-8pm Mon-Sat, to 1pm Sun) Fast service.

MEDICAL SERVICES

Clínica Arequipa (☎ 25-3424; cnr Bolognesi & Puente Grau; ⏱ 24hr)

Paz Holandesa Policlinic (☎ 20-6720; www.pazholandesa.com; Av Jorge Chavez 527; ⏱ 8am-8pm Mon-Sat) Appointment-only travel clinic (English and Dutch spoken).

MONEY

Money changers are found east of the Plaza de Armas. There are also global ATMs inside Casona Santa Catalina and Terminal Terrestre.

BCP (San Juan de Dios 125) Visa ATM; changes traveler's checks.

Interbank (Mercaderes 217) Has a global ATM and changes traveler's checks.

POST

Serpost (Moral 118; ⏱ 8am-8pm Mon-Sat, 9am-1pm Sun)

TOURIST INFORMATION

iPerú airport (☎ 44-4564; Main Hall, 1st fl; ⏱ at flight arrivals); city center (☎ 22-1227; Casona Santa Calina, Santa Catalina 210; ⏱ 9am-7pm Mon-Sat, to 5pm Sun); Plaza de Armas (☎ 22-3265; Portal de la Municipalidad 110; ⏱ 8:30am-7:30pm Mon-Sat, to 4pm Sun) The main office also runs Indecopi, the tourist-protection agency that deals with complaints against travel agencies.

Dangers & Annoyances

Arequipa has an especially big problem with robberies that are carried out by taxi. All too frequently it happens that a tourist hails a *tico* (matchbox-sized yellow taxi) on the street, only to be taken to some far-flung neighborhood and held there while the bandits deplete their bank accounts with a stolen ATM card. Thieves actually rent the official-looking *ticos* solely for this purpose. It's best to only use official taxis for getting around in Arequipa.

PERU

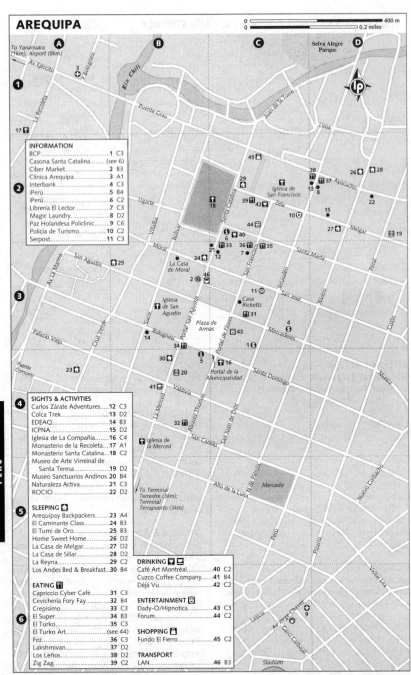

AREQUIPA

PERU

Sights

Arequipa has been baptized 'the white city' for its distinctive volcanic stonework that graces the stately Plaza de Armas and its enormous *sillar* **cathedral**, as well as many other exquisite colonial churches, convents and mansions built throughout the city. Don't miss well-preserved colonial mansions like La Casa de Moral and Casa Ricketts.

The university-run **Museo Sanctuarios Andinos** (☎ 21-5013; www.santacatalina.org.pe/santury; La Merced 110; admission S15; ☺ 9am-6pm Mon-Sat, to 3pm Sun) exhibits 'Juanita, the Ice Princess' – the frozen Inca maiden sacrificed on the summit of Ampato (6288m) over 500 years ago. For the Incas, mountains were violent deities who could kill by volcanic eruption, avalanche or climatic catastrophes, and could only be appeased by sacrifices. Multilingual tours every 20 minutes consist of a video followed by a reverent look at burial artifacts culminating with a respectful viewing of the mummy itself. Although Juanita is not on display from January through April, one of 12 other child sacrifices will be. Guides here are students working for tips.

Even if you've already overdosed on colonial edifices of yesteryear, the **Monasterio Santa Catalina** (☎ 22-9798; www.santacatalina.org.pe; Santa Catalina 301; admission S30; ☺ 9am-5pm Mon, Wed, Fri & Sat, to 8pm Tue & Thu) shouldn't be missed. Occupying a whole block and guarded by imposing high walls, it's practically a citadel within the city. A wealthy widow who chose her nuns from the richest Spanish families founded it in 1580, but her new nuns kept living it up in the style to which they were accustomed. After almost three centuries of these hedonistic goings-on, a strict Dominican nun arrived to straighten things out. The complex remained shrouded in mystery until it was forced open to the public in 1970. Today it's a meditatively mazelike place that lets you step back in time to a forgotten world of narrow twisting streets, tiny fruit-filled plazas, hidden staircases, beautiful courtyards and ascetic living quarters. Visit at night on Tuesday and Thursday for a completely different aesthetic.

One of Arequipa's oldest, the Jesuit **Iglesia de La Compañía** (☺ 9am-12:30pm & 3-6pm Mon-Fri, 11:30am-12:30pm & 3-6pm Sat, 9am-noon & 5-6pm Sun) is noted for its ornate main facade. The **San Ignacio chapel** (S4) inside has a polychrome cupola with lush murals of tropical flowers, fruits and birds, among which mingle warriors and angels.

On the west side of the Río Chili, the musty 17th-century Franciscan **Monasterio de la Recoleta** (☎ 27-0966; La Recoleta 117; admission S30; ☺ 8am-5pm) has a fascinating library with more than 20,000 historic books and maps and a museum of Amazoniana collected by missionaries. The neighborhood is dicey, so take a taxi (S3).

The gorgeous, 17th-century Carmelite convent, **Museo de Arte Virreinal de Santa Teresa** (☎ 28-1188; www.museocarmelitas.com; Melgar 303; admission S10; ☺ 9am-5pm Mon-Sat, to 1pm Sun) is celebrating its 300-year-old anniversary in 2010. It's famed for its decoratively painted walls, priceless votive objets d'art and colonial-era paintings, all explained by multilingual tour guides (tips appreciated). Don't miss the astonishing Christmas Trunk. If you show up just before noon, you can hear the nuns 'sing' their prayers in the closed chapel.

Activities

Santa Catalina and Jerusalén have dozens of fly-by-night travel agencies offering disappointingly rushed tours of the Cañón del Colca and also trekking, mountaineering and rafting trips. There are many folks muscling in on the action, so shop carefully.

Outdoor outfitters:

Carlos Zárate Adventures (☎ 20-2461; www .zarateadventures.com; Santa Catalina 204, Oficina 3) The granddaddy of *arequipeño* climbing agencies also runs mountain-biking tours, though service can be lackluster. Rents climbing gear, but inspect it carefully.

Colca Trek (☎ 20-6217; www.colcatrek.com.pe; Jerusalén 401B) Eco-conscious adventure-tour agency run by English-speaking Vlado Soto. Buys, sells and rents equipment, including camp-stove fuel, mountain bikes, climbing gear and topography maps; it also spearheads an annual Cañón cleanup. He also organizes a spectacular four-day trek into Cañón del Cotahuasi, Peru's deepest.

Naturaleza Activa (☎ 22-2257; www.peruexploration .com; Santa Catalina 211) Specializes in mountain biking and also arranges trekking and climbing tours of varying quality.

MOUNTAINEERING

Superb mountains surround Arequipa. Though many climbs in the area aren't technically difficult, they should never be undertaken lightly. Hazards include extreme weather, altitude and lack of water (carry 4L per person per day). Always check the IDs of guides carefully, and ask to see the book that identifies trained and registered guides. You should know the symptoms of altitude sickness (p1016) and carry your own medical kit.

Looming above Arequipa is the city's guardian volcano, **El Misti** (5822m), the most popular local climb. It can be tackled solo, but going with a guide helps protect against robberies, which have happened on the Apurímac route. One popular route is from Chiguata, an eight-hour hard uphill slog on rough trails to base camp (4500m). From there to the summit and back takes eight hours. The return from base camp to Chiguata takes three hours or less. **Chachani** (6075m) is one of the easiest 6000m peaks in the world, but you'll still need crampons, an ice axe and a good guide.

TREKKING

Agencies offer an array of off-the-beaten-track tours in Arequipa's canyon country, but it's better to DIY if you're just visiting the Cañón del Colca. Be sure to register at **High Mountain Rescue** (☎ 53-1165; Siglo XX, Chivay) before setting out. Optimal hiking season is from May to November. Cañón del Colca has a smattering of **campgrounds** (sites per person S5), but it's forbidden to camp by Cruz del Cóndor. For indispensable trekking maps and excellent guided trips into Cañón del Cotahuasi, contact Colca Trek.

RAFTING

The **Río Chili** is the most frequently run local river, with a half-day beginners' trip leaving daily from March to November. Further afield, the **Río Majes** passes grade II and III rapids. **Casa de Mauro** (☎ 959-33-6684; www.star.com.pe/lacasademauro; camping free, dm S20), in the village of Ongoro, 190km by road west of Arequipa, is a convenient base for rafting the Majes. The lodge can be contacted through Colca Trek. It's cheapest to take an almost hourly bus from Arequipa with Transportes del Carpio to Aplao (S2, three hours), then catch a minibus to Ongoro (S1.50).

Courses

Many schools offer Spanish classes (about S14 to S38 per hour).
EDEAQ (☎ 34-2660; www.edeaq.com; Bolognesi 132)
ICPNA (☎ 39-1020; www.cultural.edu.pe; Melgar 109)
ROCIO (☎ 28-6929; www.spanish-peru.com; Ayacucho 208, Dep 22)

Festivals & Events

Arequipeños are a proud people, and their fiery celebration of the city's founding on August 15 renews their sense of difference from coastal Lima.

Sleeping

Many more budget guesthouses lie along Puente Grau, west of Jerusalén.

La Reyna (☎ 28-6578; ulises_bc@hotmail.com; Zela 209; dm from S12, s/d S20/35, without bathroom S16/26) A rickety old standby, the cramped, meandering La Reyna is a good cheapie, with either monastery or mountaintop views. It's cheek-to-jowl with Arequipa's hottest nightlife.

Home Sweet Home (☎ 40-5982; www.homesweethome-peru.com; Rivero 509A; dm from S18, s/d/tr S40/60/90, without bathroom S30/50/75; 🖵) A popular, family-run homestay with scorching showers. Noise carries here like a delivery pigeon on meth. Rooms include internet use and a good breakfast.

Arequipay Backpackers (☎ 22-3001; www.arequipaybackpackers.com; Cruz Verde 309; dm S20, s/d without bathroom incl breakfast S36/53) Housed inside a striking, open-roofed colonial relic, this friendly option offers creaky-floored dorms, commendable bathrooms and rooftop volcano views.

Los Andes Bed & Breakfast (☎ 33-0015; losandesaqp@hotmail.com; La Merced 123; s/d S37/66, without bathroom S22/38; 🖵) Just a stone's throw south of the plaza, this airy guesthouse with hot water and sun-drenched lounges is excellent for longer stays.

La Casa de Sillar (☎ 28-4249; www.lacasadesillar.com; Rivero 504; s/d S45/75, without bathroom S35/60; 🖵) In a capacious colonial building tucked down a side alley, extraspacious rooms combine rustic style with convenience. Big common kitchen.

La Casa de Melgar (☎ 22-2459; www.lacasademelgar.com; Melgar 108A; s/d incl breakfast S117/148; 🖵) History seeps from the 18th-century walls in this colonial gem that's a perfect mid-range option for those that have outgrown the hostel scene. With its sky-high archways, antique-filled rooms and bougainvillea-draped courtyard, it's a romantic step back in time.

Also recommended:
El Caminante Class (☎ 20-3044; www.elcaminanteclass.com; Santa Catalina 207A; s/d S40/45, without bathroom S20/30; 🖵)
El Tumi de Oro (☎ 28-1319; San Agustín 311; s/d S30/50)

Eating

Trendy upscale restaurants are on San Francisco, while a few outdoor cafes line Pasaje Catedral.

Lakshmivan (Jerusalén 408; mains S4-23) One of the most extensive vegetarian menus you will see in Peru, including lacto-ovo choices.

Capriccio Cyber Café (Mercaderes 121; items S5-22) Though they serve everything from baked potatoes to three-cheese lasagna to curry sandwiches, locals and travelers alike flock to this well-conceived cafe more for a caffeine and sweet fix. There's internet upstairs.

El Turko (San Francisco 216; mains S6-14.50) The funky joint serves a hungry clubbing crowd its excellent late-night *döner kebabs*. This culinary Ottoman Empire also includes El Turko Art restaurant, Fez bar and Istanbul cafe, all nearby. Save room for the decadent baklava!

Crepisimo (Santa Catalina 208; crepes S6-16.50) Inside the Alianza Francesa, this cultural cafe offers rich coffee (comparatively speaking) and 100 kinds of scrumptious crepes.

Los Leños (Jerusalén 407; pizzas S8.50-59.50, pasta S14.50-18; ☻ dinner) Travelers say it has the best wood-burning pizza in southern Peru. It is indeed good, sold (oddly) in square tablets.

Cevichería Fory Fay (Alvarez Thomas 221; ceviche S20-25; ☻ lunch) Small and to-the-point, it offers quality *ceviche*, served here practically drowning in the marinade, and a few other seafood options.

our pick **Zig Zag** (Zela 210; mains S33-44) For those willing to shell out a few extra soles for a memorable meal, this romantic Alpine-Andean fusion haunt delivers the gourmand goods in a *sillar*-walled, candlelit setting. The specialty is stone-grilled game and fondue. One of the best restaurants in southern Peru.

El Super (Portal de la Municipalidad 130) For self-caterers.

Drinking

Arequipa's nightlife scene is not for lightweights or the easily intimidated – a slew of great bars and clubs are concentrated just north of the plaza at the corner of San Francisco and Ugarte. All of them are a good time, basically.

Cuzco Coffee Company (La Merced 135; items S2.50-11) A Starbucks rip-off, but judging by the number of foreigners here buzzed on the high-quality beans, it's not without appreciation.

Déjà Vu (San Francisco 319B) An eternally popular watering hole – on weekends, DJs spin on the rooftop terrace while live music holds court on the medievalesque ground floor. An extensive cocktail list ensures the sexy crowd is operating on liquid courage.

Café Art Montréal (Ugarte 210) A smoky, cavernous bar with live bands playing at the back on weekends. It'd be equally at home on Paris' Left Bank. Or Montréal, we suppose.

Entertainment

Forum (San Francisco 317; admission S10-15; ☻ Thu-Sat) A gutsy tropical discotheque with a thing for bamboo and waterfalls. DJs mesh cumbia, reggaeton and rock until the wee hours. Ladies free on Thursday.

Dady-O/Hipnotica (Portal de Flores 112) Sharing the same address but different spaces, Dady-O is the well-worn veteran, a raucous late-night disco and bar, while Hipnotica is the new kid on the block, a little trendier and housed inside a converted movie theater. Foreigners don't pay cover at Hipnotica and there are *folklórica* shows earlier in the evenings

---

DETOUR

The suburb of **Yanahuara** is within walking distance of downtown Arequipa. Go west on Puente Grau over the bridge, and immediately turn north on Bolognesi and walk along the park for 200m before turning west on Cuesta del Angel, which leads straight to a small plaza (look for the arches). Here the **Iglesia San Juan Batista** dates from 1750 and a **mirador** (lookout) has excellent views of Arequipa and El Misti. Afterwards, it's time to eat well. For typical *arequipeña* food, head back along Jerusalén, parallel to Lima, and just before Ejército is the well-known garden restaurant **Sol de Mayo** (☎ 25-4148; Jerusalén 207; mains S16-39). For sublime Asian fusion, continue to Ejército and turn west for two blocks to Granada and **Piquita Siu** (☎ 25-1915; Granada 102; mains S18.50-46; ☻ closed dinner Sun). For Arequipa's best *ceviche* (marinated raw seafood), it's another garden restaurant, **El Cebillano** (☎ 27-0882; Misti 110; ceviche S17-28; ☻ lunch).

Frequent minivans running along Puente Grau shuttle back and forth to Yanahuara's main plaza (S0.70).

(8:30pm). Dady-O charges a S10 cover and is only open Thursday to Saturday.

Shopping

Arequipa overflows with artisan and antique shops, especially on streets around Monasterio Santa Catalina.

Fundo El Fierro (San Francisco 200; ☽ 9am-8pm Mon-Sat, to 2pm Sun) Buy direct from the source at this *artesanía* (handicrafts) foundation's many stalls.

Getting There & Away

AIR

The **airport** (AQP; ☎ 44-3464) is 8km northwest of the center. **LAN** (☎ 20-1100; Santa Catalina 118C) serves Lima and Cuzco daily. A taxi to Centro runs S15.

BUS

Most companies leave from Terminal Terrestre or the smaller Terrapuerto bus station next door. Both are 3km south of the center (departure tax S2).

For Lima (S40 to S135, 16 to 18 hours), **Cruz del Sur** (☎ 42-7375), **Ormeño** (☎ 42-7788) and other companies operate several daily buses, mostly departing in the afternoon. Many buses stop en route at Nazca (S35 to S70, nine to 10 hours) and Ica (S35 to S70, 10 to 11 hours). Many companies also have overnight buses to Cuzco (S30 to S110, 10 to 12 hours).

Buses to Puno (S10 to S63, six hours) leave frequently, though this is one of the most notoriously dangerous routes in Peru due to a lethal combination of driver fatigue and altitude. For this reason, consider day buses only. Ormeño continues on to Desaguadero (S50, seven to eight hours) on the Bolivian border and La Paz (S144, 12 hours). Cruz del Sur has the most comfortable buses to Tacna (S35 to S40, six to seven hours) via Moquegua (S31 to S40, four hours).

For Cañón del Colca, there are a few daily buses for Chivay (S12, three hours), continuing to Cabanaconde (S15, six hours). Recommended companies include **Andalucía** (☎ 69-4060) or **Señor de los Milagros** (☎ 28-8090).

Getting Around

Minivans bound for Terminal Terrestre/ Terrapuerto (S0.70) run south along Bolívar, or you can take a taxi (S3.50 to S5). Minibuses marked 'Río Seco' or 'Zamacola' go along Puente Grau and Ejército, passing within 700m of the airport (though this walk is sketchy), or you can take a taxi direct (S10 to S13). Always use officially licensed taxi companies like **Texitel** (☎ 45-2020).

CAÑÓN DEL COLCA

One of the world's deepest canyons at 3191m, Colca ranks second only to neighboring Cañón del Cotahuasi, which is 163m deeper. Trekking is by far the best way to experience village life, although the roads are dusty. As you pass through the villages, look out for the local women's traditional embroidered clothing and hats. On an environmental note, do not dispose of trash at the bins in the canyon as they overflow and locals simply dump them in the river. Take your own trash out.

The road from Arequipa climbs north through **Reserva Nacional Salinas y Aguada Blanca**, where *vicuñas* – the endangered wild cousins of llamas and alpacas – are often sighted. The road continues through bleak *altiplano* (high Andean plateau) over the highest point of 4800m, before dropping spectacularly into Chivay.

Chivay

☎ 054 / pop 4600

The provincial capital at the head of the canyon is a small, dusty transit hub. Bring plenty of Peruvian cash, as only a few stores exchange US dollars or euros. There's slow internet access at cybercafes near the main plaza.

SIGHTS & ACTIVITIES

Soak away in Chivay's **hot springs** (admission S10; ☽ 4:00am-8pm), 3.5km northeast of town. The mineral-laden water is handy when the hot-water supply at your guesthouse packs up. Frequent *colectivos* leave from Anafi Teatro (S0.80), or it's a gorgeous walk during the day.

From where the road forks to the hot springs, stay to the left and walk beside fertile fields toward **Coporaque**, which has an arched colonial-era plaza. Then head downhill to the orange bridge across the river to **Yanque** (opposite), where passing buses or *colectivos* return to Chivay. It's an all-day walk. Alternatively, rent mountain bikes in Chivay from shops around the plaza.

A tiny **astronomical observatory** (☎ 53-1020; Casa Andina, Huayna Cápac s/n; admission S20; ☽ 7:30pm & 8:30pm for English) has nightly lectures and sky shows in Spanish and English.

SLEEPING

Though a tiny town, Chivay has plenty of *hostales* to choose from.

Casa de Anita (☎ 53-1114; Plaza de Armas 607; s/d S20/30) A little extra character for a cheapie, with its interior stone courtyard and thick, wooden doors.

Hostal Estrella de David (☎ 53-1233; Siglo XX No 209; s/d/tr S20/30/40) A simple, clean guesthouse. Some rooms boast tropical toilet seats and highly questionable pink bedspreads.

Hospedaje Rumi Wasi (☎ 53-1146; Sucre 714; s/d incl breakfast S20/40) An excellent family-run hostel with a central garden where alpacas nibble on the greenery and rooms have views of the surrounding countryside.

Colca Inn (☎ 53-1111; www.hotelcolcainn.com; Salaverry 307; s/d incl breakfast S75/101) The most comfortable, well-run midrange option in town, for those seeking added creature comforts like heaters and hotel-level service.

EATING

The best meals in Chivay are buffet restaurants catering mostly to tour groups (all-you-can-eat S18 to S25). El Balcón de Don Zacarias ranks high for cleanliness and plaza views.

Lobo's (Plaza de Armas; pizza S6-35) Has a touristy menu (with big breakfasts), brick-oven pizza and wood-stove heated confines.

Casa Blanca (Plaza de Armas 201; mains S12-26) This atmospheric spot offers pizza and a slathering of typical mains, but the real coup is the patio with mountain and plaza views.

ENTERTAINMENT

Peñas are scattered about, with shows from around 8pm nightly. **Muspay Quilla** (Leonicio Prado s/n) was the most popular at time of research.

GETTING THERE & AWAY

The bus terminal is a 15-minute walk from the plaza. There are 11 buses daily to Arequipa (S12, three hours) and six to Cabanaconde (S3, 2½ hours) via Cruz del Cóndor.

Chivay to Cabanaconde

The main road follows the south bank of the upper Cañón del Colca and leads past several picturesque villages and some of the most extensive pre-Inca terracing in Peru. One of these villages, the more culturally intact **Yanque**, has an attractive 18th-century church and an excellent, small **cultural museum** (admission S3; ☉ 7am-1:15pm & 2-6:30pm) at the plaza. A

30-minute walk to the river leads to some hot springs (admission S3). There are simple guesthouses and hotels scattered around town, but **Organización Turismo Vivencial** (☎ 995-07-8159; r per person with/without breakfast S30/20) can arrange homestays with local families. Call ahead or inquire at Killawasi Lodge on Lima.

Eventually the road reaches **Cruz del Cóndor** (entry with *boleto turístico*; see boxed text, below). Andean condors that nest here by the rocky outcrop can occasionally be seen gliding effortlessly on thermal air currents. Early morning or late afternoon are the best times to see the birds, but you'll need luck.

If you are traveling independently and plan to stop in Cruz del Cóndor before continuing on to Cabanaconde, it's best to leave Arequipa on the unfortunately timed 1am bus. You will be in Cruz del Cóndor at daybreak with enough time to enjoy it and still catch a bus on to Cabanaconde from Arequipa. Later in the afternoon, those buses are few and far between, and you could be stuck at Cruz del Cóndor for several hours.

Cabanaconde
☎ 054 / pop 1300

Cabanaconde is an excellent base for some spectacular hikes into the canyon, including the popular two-hour trek down to Sangalle (The Oasis) at the bottom, where there are natural pools for swimming (S3), simple bungalows and campsites. The return trek is thirsty work; allow three to four hours. Local guides can suggest a wealth of other treks, to waterfalls, geysers, remote villages and archaeological sites.

> ### ALERT!
> If you step foot in the Cañón del Colca, new regulations require the purchase of the *boleto turístico* (tourist ticket; S35), even if you are just passing through Chivay to Cabanaconde on a bus. There is a control point just before the entrance to Chivay, at Cruz del Cóndor, as well as rangers patrolling throughout the canyon. Do not buy the ticket from anyone who is not from **Autocolca** (☉ 53-1143; Plaza de Armas, Chivay), the regional authority governing the canyon, as used and counterfeit tickets are not uncommon. It's also a good idea to register your name at time of purchase, in case of loss or theft of your ticket.

Some hostel owners greeting tourists off the buses in the main plaza have resorted to intimidation and even become violent over persuading travelers to go to their establishments. Be wary and stick to your guns if you have come with a reservation.

ourpick Pachamama (San Pedro 209; www.pachamamahome.com; dm S10, r with/without bathroom S20/15; 🖳) is an ubercozy place offering simple dorms and rooms as complement to the canyon's best hangout spot, a candlelit pizzeria and bar (pizzas S9 to S30) run by a hip, guitar-wielding brother team from Ayacucho, who provide the sing-along soundtrack and like-a-brother hospitality to loads of nationalities cavorting over drunken travel tales. You can rent bikes, chill in the hammocks or just soak up the global vibe. This is travel.

The basic **Hostal Valle del Fuego** (☎ 20-3737; hvalledelfuego@hotmail.com; s/d S$15/30; 🖳) is an established travelers' scene. Rooms are located in an annex a block away from reception and bar (toilet seats are MIA). Some travelers, however, have been less than satisfied here.

Several daily buses bound for Chivay (S3, 2½ hours) and Arequipa (S15, six hours) via Cruz del Cóndor leave from the plaza.

LAKE TITICACA

Covering 8400 sq km and sitting at 3808m, Lake Titicaca is considered the world's largest high-altitude lake. The air looks magically clear here, as dazzling high-altitude sunlight suffuses the *altiplano* and sparkles on the deep waters. Horizons stretch until almost limitless, with ancient funerary towers and crumbling colonial churches. The port of Puno is a good base for visiting far-flung islands dotted across Lake Titicaca – from those made of artificial reeds to more remote, rural isles where villagers live much as they have for centuries.

JULIACA
☎ 051 / pop 220,000
This is a brash, unfinished eyesore on an otherwise beautiful Big Sky landscape. Principally a market town, it has the department's only commercial airport, though most tourists hightail it out of baggage claim for its more lovely lakeside neighbor, Puno.

A block northwest of the plaza, **Hostal Sakura** (☎ 32-2072; San Roman 133; s/d S45/70; 🖳)

has a positive atmosphere with hot showers and cable TV.

Ricos Pan (cnr San Roman & Chávez; items S1-5) is the best place for coffee and elaborate deserts. **Restaurant Trujillo** (San Roman 163; mains S14-386) is good for more substantial meals, though it comes across as pricey.

The **airport** (JUL; ☎ 32-4248) is 2km west of town. **LAN** (☎ 32-2228; San Roman 125) has daily flights to/from Lima, Arequipa and Cuzco. To the airport, take a taxi (S6). Direct minibuses to Puno (S15, 45 minutes) usually await incoming flights. Cheaper minibuses depart from the intersection of Piérola and 8 de Noviembre, northeast of the plaza (S2.50, 45 minutes).

PUNO
☎ 051 / pop 118,000
The gateway for Lake Titicaca's islands, the tiny port of Puno hugs the sacred Inca lake's northwestern shores. Few colonial buildings remain in town, though Puno's friendly streets bustle with local women garbed in multilayered dresses and bowler hats. You'll want to multilayer as well – nights here get bitterly cold, especially in winter when temperatures can often drop below freezing.

Information
For hospitals, it's better to go to Juliaca (left). Bolivianos can be exchanged in town or at the border. There's a global ATM inside Terminal Terrestre.
BCP (cnr Lima & Grau) Visa/MasterCard ATM; Visa cash advances.
Choza@net (Lima 339, 2nd fl; per hr S1.50; ⏰ 8am-11pm) Internet.
Dircetur (Terminal Terrestre; ⏰ 8am-6pm Mon-Sat) Traveler info in the bus terminal.
Interbank (Lima 444) Global ATM; changes traveler's checks.
iPerú (☎ 36-5088; Plaza de Armas, cnr Lima & Deustua; ⏰ 8:30am-7:30pm) Tourist information.
Lavaclin (Valcárcel 132; ⏰ 8am-noon & 2-7pm Mon-Sat) Laundry.
Policía de Turismo (Deustua 558; ⏰ 24hr) For emergencies.
Serpost (Moquegua 269; ⏰ 8am-8pm Mon-Sat)

Sights & Activities
The oldest boat on Lake Titicaca, the iron-hulled **Yavari** (☎ 36-9329; www.yavari.org; donations only; ⏰ 8am-5:15pm) was built in England and shipped in 2766 pieces around Cape Horn to Arica, then transported to Tacna by

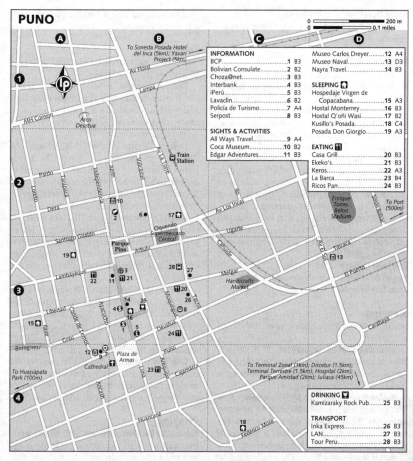

PUNO

0 — 200 m
0 — 0.1 miles

INFORMATION
BCP....................................1 B3
Bolivian Consulate.............2 B2
Choza@net........................3 B3
Interbank...........................4 B3
iPerú.................................5 B3
Lavaclin.............................6 B2
Policía de Turismo.............7 A4
Serpost..............................8 B3

SIGHTS & ACTIVITIES
All Ways Travel..................9 A4
Coca Museum..................10 B2
Edgar Adventures.............11 B3

Museo Carlos Dreyer........12 A4
Museo Naval....................13 D3
Nayra Travel....................14 B3

SLEEPING
Hospedaje Virgen de
Copacabana..................15 A3
Hostal Monterrey..............16 B3
Hostal Q'oñi Wasi.............17 B2
Kusillo's Posada...............18 C4
Posada Don Giorgio.........19 A3

EATING
Casa Grill.........................20 B3
Ekeko's............................21 B3
Keros...............................22 A3
La Barca...........................23 B4
Ricos Pan.........................24 B3

DRINKING
Kamizaraky Rock Pub........25 B3

TRANSPORT
Inka Express.....................26 B3
LAN.................................27 B3
Tour Peru.........................28 B3

PERU

train and hauled by mule over the Andes to Puno (taking a mere six years), where it was reassembled and launched in 1870. Due to a coal shortage, the engines were often powered by dried llama dung! The Peruvian navy eventually decommissioned the ship. Now moored by the Sonesta Posada Hotel del Inca (take a *mototaxi*, S3), the ship is open for tours.

The small **Museo Carlos Dreyer** (Conde de Lemos 289; admission S15; 9:30am-6:30pm) houses a beautiful collection of archaeological artifacts.

Near the port, the **Museo Naval** (cnr Titicaca & Av El Sol; 8am-1pm & 3-5pm Mon-Fri) has tiny exhibits on navigating the lake, from rudimentary reed boats to 19th-century steamers. The **Coca Museum** (☎ 951-77-0360; Deza 301;

admission S5; 9am-1pm & 3-8pm) chronicles the history of coca (in English).

Tours

Some travelers find the island-hopping tours disappointing, even exploitative; others report great fun. Ask around (eg at your guesthouse) for a local guide, preferably someone with ties to the islands, then go to the docks in the early morning and get on the next boat; or choose your tour company wisely.

All Ways Travel (☎ 35-5552; www.titicacaperu.com; Deustua 576; 8am-7pm Mon-Sat) Has multilingual staff and receives good reports from travelers.

Edgar Adventures (☎ 35-3444; Lima 328; 7am-8pm) Specializes in island tours and takes extra strides to ensure against islander exploitation.

Nayra Travel (☎ 36-4774; Lima 419;
🕑 10am-12:30pm & 2:30-8pm Mon-Sat) Personalized service for off-the-beaten-track destinations.

Festivals & Events

Puno is often named the folklore capital of Peru, celebrating wild and colorful fiestas throughout the year. Although they often occur during celebrations of Catholic feast days, many dances have their roots in preconquest celebrations tied in with the agricultural calendar. The dazzlingly ornate and imaginative costumes worn on these occasions are often worth more than an entire household's everyday clothes. Accompanying musicians play a host of traditional instruments, from Spanish-influenced brass and string to percussion and wind instruments that have changed little since Inca times. Major festivals are usually celebrated for several days before and after the actual date.

Epiphany January 6
Virgen de la Candelaria (Candlemas) February 2
Puno Day November 5

Sleeping

Some bare-bones *hostales* have only cold showers.

Hospedaje Virgen de Copacabana (☎ 36-3766; llave 228; r per person S15) This friendly, tumbledown family home offers six comfortable rooms tucked off a narrow passageway.

Hostal Q'oñi Wasi (☎ 36-5784; qoniwasi_puno @hotmail.com; Av La Torre 135; s/d/tr S20/40/60, s/d without bathroom S15/30; 🖳) A long-running backpacker haunt, quirky Q'oñi Wasi has a warren of snug, older rooms and electric showers.

Hostal Monterrey (☎ 35-1691; www.hostalmonter reypuno.com; Lima 441; s/d S30/50, with cable TV & hot water S70/105, s/d/tr without bathroom S20/35/50; 🖳) On the main pedestrian boulevard, this is a good budget option with lots of choices: 1st-floor rooms are beyond basic, those higher up give you the extra comforts, including bathtubs and hot water.

Kusillo's Posada (☎ 36-4579; kusillos@latinmail.com; Federico More 162; s/d/tr incl breakfast S40/70/105; 🖳) Run by the inconceivably welcoming Jenny Juño and her wonderful family, this heart-warming homestay steeped in homespun hospitality has cozy rooms with electric showers and lots of local love.

Posada Don Giorgio (☎ 36-3648; www.posadadongior gio.com; Tarapacá 238; s/d/tr incl breakfast S79/110/150; 🖳) This comfortable midrange choice offers spacious rooms and a bright, stained-glass atrium for breakfast.

Eating

Touristy restaurants line the rambunctious pedestrian street of Lima.

Ricos Pan (Moquegua 326; deserts S1.50-5.50, sandwiches S4.8) Puno's best bakery is a comforting find and good for decadent cakes and a handful of sandwiches, including (for this area) the rarely seen *croque monsieur*.

La Barca (Arequipa 754; mains S9-20; 🕑 lunch only) This hole-in-the-wall – it looks like a mechanic's front yard – churns out Lima-quality *ceviche* culled from both the sea and the lake. A local legend! At the time of research, a relocation was imminent, so check ahead.

Keros (Lambayeque 131; mains S15-27) Just off the main drag (and with subsequently lower prices), this often inexplicably empty spot is solid for a nice meal out. They might even often you a complimentary glass of *vino* if you're lucky.

Ekeko's (Lima 355; mains S16-23) A staple on Lima street, this traveler's hub serves up pizza, alpaca and the usual suspects under brick archways and candlelit tables. Upstairs, a late-night club with a small dance floor and ample lounge space draws travelers and locals alike.

Casa Grill (Libertad 137; mains S19-26) Forgive the cafeteria-style dining sets; this otherwise atmospheric antique house draws legions of locals for scrumptious grills and perfect fries.

Drinking

Kamizaraky Rock Pub (Pasaje Grau 158) Candles, graffiti, well-worn picnic tables, multiple Jenga sets and a cool soundtrack to tie it all together make this southern Peru's best watering hole – ideal for Puno's bone-chilling nights.

Getting There & Around

AIR

The nearest airport is in Juliaca (p806). **LAN** (☎ 36-7227; Tacna 299; 🕑 8:30am-1pm & 3:30-7pm Mon-Fri, 8:30am-4:30pm Sat) has an office in Puno.

BUS

Terminal Terrestre (☎ 36-4733; Primero de Mayo 703), located around 2km southeast of the plaza, houses Puno's long-distance bus companies (departure tax S1). Direct services go to Lima (S110 to S130, 19 to 21 hours), Arequipa (S15 to S30, 5½ to six hours) and Cuzco (S15 to S43, six to seven hours) via Juliaca (S2.50, one hour). **San Martín** (☎ 951-67-7730) has rough *económico* buses to Tacna (S30, 10 hours) via Moquegua six times daily.

Inka Express (☎ 36-5654; www.inkaexpress.com; Tacna 346) runs luxury tour buses with panoramic windows to Cuzco every morning. The worthwhile S93 fare includes beverages and an English-speaking guide who explains sites that are briefly visited en route, including Pucará, Raqchi and Andahuayillas.

Minibuses to Juliaca (S2.50, one hour), lakeshore towns and the Bolivian border leave from Terminal Zonal on Simón Bolívar, a few blocks north of Terminal Terrestre.

TAXI
A short taxi ride around town costs S3. *Mototaxis* are cheaper, but make sure the negotiated fare is per ride, not per person.

TRAIN
Trains bound for Cuzco via Juliaca purportedly leave Puno's **train station** (☎ 36-9179; Av La Torre 224; www.perurail.com; 7am-5pm Mon-Fri, 7am-noon Sat & Sun) at 8am Monday, Wednesday and Saturday (November to March), and Friday as well (April to October), arriving at 5:30pm. At the time of research, fares on the Andean Explorer train to Cuzco were S704 one-way.

AROUND PUNO
Sillustani
Sitting on rolling hills in the Lago Umayo peninsula, these ruined **towers** (admission S6) stand out for miles against the unforgiving landscape. The ancient Colla people were a warlike, Aymara-speaking tribe that buried their nobility in these impressive *chullpas* (funerary towers), made from massive coursed blocks and reaching heights of up to 12m. There are also 20 or so local *altiplano* homes in the area that welcome visitors.

Puno travel agencies run 3½-hour tours (S25 including entrance fee) that leave around 2:30pm daily. To DIY, catch any bus to Juliaca and get off where the road splits to Sillustani. From there, a taxi can deliver you directly to Sillustani (S15), or grab an occasional *combi*

GETTING TO BOLIVIA

There are two overland routes from Puno to La Paz, Bolivia. The Yunguyo route, which is safer and easier, allows you to take a break at the lakeshore resort of Copacabana. The Desaguadero route, which is slightly faster and cheaper, can be combined with a visit to the ruins at Tiwanaku (p188). Beware of immigration officials trying to charge an illegal 'entry tax' or search your belongings for 'fake dollars' to confiscate. However, as of time of research, US citizens require a visa to enter Bolivia (US$135 at border posts and US$100 at the consulate in Puno (see p871). It is also worth nothing that for those traveling to Isla del Sol, a yellow-fever certificate is not required, though some immigration officials will force the vaccine upon you if you do not have it (US$70) – you're better off making an appointment for a free one in Puno.

To enter Peru from Bolivia, see p197.

Via Yunguyo
The most convenient way to reach Bolivia is with a cross-border company like **Tour Peru** (☎ 20-6088; www.tourperu.com.pe; Tacna 282), which has daily buses departing at 7:30am that stop at the Peruvian and Bolivian border posts, then Copacabana (S19, three hours), where you board another bus to La Paz (S25, eight hours). Officials in Copacabana will make you pay just to enter town (S1).

Alternatively, frequent minibuses depart Puno's Terminal Zonal for Yunguyo (S6, 2½ hours), where you can grab a taxi for the final leg to the border (S2). In Bolivia, which is an hour ahead of Peru, the border post is open from 8:30am to 7pm daily. From the border, it's another 10km to Copacabana (*combis* B$6).

Via Desaguadero
Buses (S7) and minibuses (S7) leave Puno's Terminal Zonal and Terminal Terrestre regularly for the chaotic border town of Desaguadero (2½ hours), which has basic hotels and money changers. Border hours are 8am to 8pm, but because Bolivia is an hour ahead of Peru, plan to cross before 7pm Peruvian time. Many buses go from Desaguadero to La Paz (B$16, three hours) during daylights hours, passing the turnoff for Tiwanaku.

to the village of Atuncolla (S2, 10 minutes), a 4km walk from the ruins.

Cutimbo

Almost 20km from Puno, this dramatic windswept **site** (admission S6) has an extraordinary position atop a table-topped volcanic hill surrounded by a sprawling plain. Its modest number of exceptionally well-preserved *chullpas*, built by the Colla, Lupaca and Inca cultures, come in both square and cylindrical shapes. Look closely and you'll find several monkeys, pumas and snakes carved into the structures.

Combis leave the cemetery by Parque Amistad, 1km from Puno's town center, every half hour (S3, 30 minutes). You can't miss the site, which is a steep climb up from the right-hand (east) side of the road.

ISLAND-HOPPING

The only way to see Lake Titicaca is to spend a few days visiting its fairy-tale islands. That said, negative impacts from tourism are being felt in many communities. You could also hop over the Bolivian border to visit the more chill Isla del Sol (p197) from Copacabana.

Islas Flotantes

The unique **floating islands** (admission S5) of the Uros people – around 50 in all – have become shockingly commercialized, though there is still nothing quite like them anywhere else. The islands are built using layers of the buoyant *totora* reeds that grow abundantly in the shallows of Lake Titicaca. It's like a reed Disneyland.

Intermarriage with Aymara-speaking indigenous peoples has seen the demise of the pure-blooded Uros. Always a small tribe, they began their floating existence centuries ago in an effort to isolate themselves from the aggressive Collas and the Incas. Today several hundred people still live on the islands.

Indeed, the lives of the Uros are completely interwoven with the reeds, which are used to make their homes, boats and the crafts they churn out for tourists. The islands' reeds are constantly replenished from the top as they rot away, so the ground is always soft and springy – mind your step!

Two-hour boat tours (S20, not including island admission) leave from the dock when full from 7am until late afternoon and usually stop on Isla Taquile as well. There's a ticket

booth at the dock entrance. Trips to other islands may stop at the Islas Flotantes on the way out. You can now also sleep on some of the islands. A night in a cute hut on Uros Q'Hantati runs S120, including three meals.

Isla Taquile

Inhabited for many thousands of years, this 7 sq km **island** (admission S5) often feels like its own little world. The Quechua-speaking islanders maintain lives largely unchanged by mainland modernities and have a long tradition of weaving. Their creations can be bought in the cooperative store on the main plaza. Look for the menfolk's tightly woven woolen hats, resembling floppy nightcaps, which they knit themselves and can denote social status. The women also catch eyes in their multilayered skirts and delicately embroidered blouses.

Several hills have pre-Inca terracing and small ruins set against the backdrop of Bolivia's snowcapped Cordillera Real. Visitors are free to wander around, but you can't do that on a day trip without missing lunch or the boat back, so stay overnight if you can. Travelers will be met by islanders next to the arch atop the steep stairway up from the dock. Homestays can be arranged here (per person S10 to S20), though tourism has altered the landscape here somewhat and travelers looking for a less tainted experience should opt for sleeping on nearby Amantaní, which is still in its tourism infancy and offers a more authentic sleepover. If you do sleep on Taquile, beds are basic but clean, and facilities are minimal. You'll be given blankets, but bringing a sleeping bag and flashlight is essential.

Most island shops and restaurants close by midafternoon, when all the tour groups leave, so arrange dinner with your host family in advance. Gifts of fresh fruit from Puno's markets are appreciated. You can buy bottled drinks at the shops, though it's worth bringing purifying tablets or a water filter. Also bring small bills (change is limited) and extra money for souvenirs.

Boats for the incredibly slow 34km trip to Taquile leave Puno's dock every day around 7:30am (S20 to S25, three hours). Get to the dock early and pay the captain directly. The return boat leaves in the early afternoon, arriving in Puno around nightfall. Remember to bring sunscreen and mosquito repellent.

Puno travel agencies (p807) organize guided tours for around S35 to S45 (some with much faster boats charge upwards of S165).

Isla Amantaní

This less frequently visited **island** (admission S5) is a few kilometers northeast of Taquile. Ruins of the Tiwanaku culture top several hills. Trips here usually involve an overnight stay with islanders (around S25, including meals). Expect small periods of uncomfortable silence, dual-carb meals and limited facilities – but all in all a unique and welcoming experience. Boats to Amantaní leave Puno between 7:30am and 8:30am most mornings: pay the captain directly (S30 return, 3½ hours). Unpredictable boat connections usually make it easiest to travel from Puno to Amantaní and on to Taquile, rather than in reverse. Puno travel agencies (p807) charge S75 to S90 for a two-day tour to Amantaní, with a quick visit to Taquile and the floating islands. This is by far the most authentic choice for overnights stays.

It's important to keep in mind that Titicaca's island families will benefit more if you visit independently – there are some agencies that consistently exploit them, undercutting the agreed fee they are supposed to receive for each tourist. Go it alone, or choose your tour operator wisely.

CUZCO & THE SACRED VALLEY

As the heart of the once mighty Inca empire, the magnetic city of Cuzco heads the list of many traveler itineraries. Each year it draws hundreds of thousands of visitors to its lofty elevations, lured by the city's unique combination of colonial splendor built on hefty stone foundations of the Incas. And lying within easy hopping distance of the city is the country's biggest drawcard of all, the 'lost' city of the Incas, Machu Picchu, perched high on a remote mountaintop. The department of Cuzco also has superb trekking routes and a long list of flamboyant fiestas and carnivals in which Peru's pagan past colorfully collides with Catholic rituals and modern Latin American mayhem.

CUZCO

☎ 084 / pop 349,000

The high-flying city of Cuzco (Qosq'o in the Quechua language) sits at a 3300m crossroads of centuries-old Andean tradition and modern Peruvian life. As the continent's oldest continuously inhabited city, it was once the Inca empire's foremost stronghold, and is now both the undisputed archaeological capital of the Americas as well as one of the continent's most stanchly preserved colonial living museums. Massive Inca-built walls line steep, narrow cobblestone streets and plazas thronged with the descendants of the mighty Incas and Spanish conquistadors – who hobble about in colorful traditional wares among the hustle and bustle of contemporary *cuzqueños* making a living from the town's present-day lifeblood: tourism. And lots of it.

Though Cuzco is at the tipping point of being completely overrun with international tourism, its historical charms and breathtaking setting cannot be denied.

History

Cuzco is a city so steeped in history, tradition and myth that it can be difficult to know where fact ends and myth begins. Legends tell that in the 12th century the first Inca, Manco Capác, was charged by the ancestral sun god Inti to find the *qosq'o* (the navel of the earth). When at last Manco discovered such a point, he founded the city.

The ninth Inca Pachacutec (see p767) wasn't only a warmonger: he also proved himself a sophisticated urban developer, devising Cuzco's famous puma shape and diverting rivers to cross the city. Pachacutec also built the famous Qorikancha temple and the palace fronting what is now the Plaza de Armas.

After murdering the 12th Inca Atahualpa, the Spanish conquistador Francisco Pizarro marched on Cuzco in 1533 and appointed Manco Inca as a puppet ruler of the Incas. After a few years, Manco rebelled and laid siege to Spanish-occupied Cuzco. Only a desperate battle at Saqsaywamán saved the Spanish from annihilation. Manco was forced to retreat to Ollantaytambo and eventually into the jungle at Vilcabamba. Once the city had been safely recaptured, looted and settled, the seafaring Spaniards turned their attentions to coastal Lima, making Cuzco just another quiet colonial backwater.

PERU

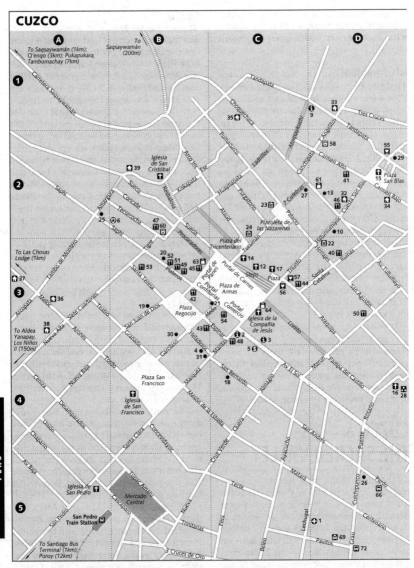

CUZCO

PERU

Few events of historical significance have rocked Cuzco since the Spanish Conquest but for earthquakes in 1650 and 1950, and a failed indigenous uprising led by Túpac Amaru II in 1780. It was the rediscovery of Machu Picchu in 1911 that has affected the city more than any event since the arrival of the Spanish.

Orientation

The city centers on the Plaza de Armas, while traffic-choked Av El Sol is the main business thoroughfare. Walking just a few blocks north or east of the plaza will lead you onto steep, twisting cobblestone streets which have changed little for centuries.

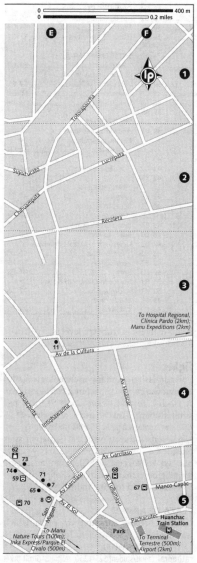

The alley off the northwest side of the plaza is Procuradores (Tax Collectors), nicknamed 'Gringo Alley' for its huddle of backpacker bars and cafes – watch out for predatory touts. Beside the cathedral, narrow Triunfo leads uphill to Plaza San Blas, the heart of Cuzco's artistic *barrio* (neighborhood).

In a resurgence of indigenous pride, the official names of many streets have been changed from Spanish back to Quechua spellings (eg Qosq'o, not Cuzco; Pisaq, not Pisac). However, maps may retain the old spellings, which are still in everyday use.

Information

BOOKSTORES
Book exchanges abound at cafes, pubs and the SAE clubhouse (p814).
Jerusalén (Heladeros 143; 🕙 10am-2pm & 4-8pm Mon-Sat)
SBS Bookshop (Av El Sol 781A; 🕙 8:30am-1:30pm & 3:30-7:30pm Mon-Sat, 8:30am-1pm Sat)

EMERGENCY
Policía de Turismo (☎ 24-9654; Saphi 510; 🕙 24hr) Offers official theft reports for insurance claims.

INTERNET ACCESS
We're not sure what's more ubiquitous – massage offers or internet call centers.

LAUNDRY
Lavanderías are clustered all around Cuzco's budget accommodations. During high season, don't bet your last pair of trekking socks on their promise of same-day service.

LEFT LUGGAGE
Many guesthouses will store your bags for free. Lock everything securely, always get a receipt and keep a copy of the contents with you.

MEDICAL SERVICES
Cuzco's medical facilities are limited. Head back to Lima for serious procedures.
Clínica Pardo (☎ 24-0997; Av de la Cultura 710; 🕙 24hr)
Clínica Paredes (☎ 22-5265; Lechugal 405; 🕙 24hr)

MONEY
Many banks on Av El Sol and shops around the Plaza de Armas have foreign card–friendly ATMs. The main bus terminal has a global ATM.
LAC Dolar (Av El Sol 150; 🕙 9:30am-1pm & 2-7pm Mon-Sat) Reliable *casa de cambio* ((exchange office).

POST
Serpost (Av El Sol 800; 🕙 8am-8pm Mon-Sat)

PERU

TOURIST INFORMATION

Dircetur (☎ 22-3702; www.dirceturcusco.gob.pe; Plaza Túpac Amaru) Cuzco's regional tourism board, with helpful info and brochures.

iPerú airport (☎ 23-7364; Main Hall, Airport; ☽ 6am-5pm); city center (☎ 25-2974; Av El Sol 103, Oficina 102; ☽ 8:30am-7:30pm) Efficient, helpful main office also runs Indecopi, the tourist-protection agency.

South American Explorers (SAE; ☎ 24-5484; www .saexplorers.org; Atoqsaykuchi 670; ☽ 9:30am-5pm Mon-Fri, to 1pm Sat) Immeasurable traveler information and maps sold. Cultural events and some volunteering info for nonmembers as well as rooms for rent by the week (s/d S224/324). Also see p779 and p875.

Dangers & Annoyances

The train stations and markets are prime areas for pickpockets and bag-slashers. Use only official taxis (look for the company's telephone number on the roof), lock your doors and never allow additional passengers. Late-night revelers returning from bars or trekkers setting off before sunrise are most vulnerable to 'choke and grab' muggings. Drug dealers and police are known to work together, especially on Procuradores, where locals warn you can make a drug deal and get busted, all within a couple of minutes. Beware of altitude sickness

if you're flying in from sea level (see p1016) – it's no joke.

Sights

For admission to many archaeological sites around Cuzco, you must buy a *boleto turístico*. A 10-day 'tourist ticket' costs S130/70 per adult/student. You can buy it at **Cosituc** (☎ 22-7037; www.cosituc.gob.pe; Av El Sol 103, Oficina 102; ☽ 8am-6pm Mon-Fri, to 1pm Sat) or at participating sites outside the city. It's also possible to buy partial one-day *boletos* costing S70. A similar scheme for religious sites, the Circuito Religioso, costs S50 and is valid for one month.

PLAZA DE ARMAS

Colonial arcades surround the plaza, which was the heart of the ancient Inca capital.

Taking almost 100 years to build, Cuzco's **cathedral** (adult/student S25/12.50, religious-circuit ticket S50/25; ☽ 10am-6pm) sits on the site of Inca Viracocha's palace and was erected using blocks from Saqsaywamán (p820). It's one of the city's greatest repositories of colonial art. Look for *The Last Supper* by Marcos Zapata, with a plump, juicy-looking roast *cuy* (guinea pig) stealing the show. Opposite the silver altar is a magnificently carved 17th-century choir. The cathedral is joined with the church of **Jesus María** (1733) and **El Triunfo** (1536), Cuzco's oldest church containing the vault of the famous Inca historian Garcilaso de la Vega, born in Cuzco in 1539.

Leaving the plaza along Loreto, **Inca walls** line both sides of the alley. On the left is the oldest Inca wall in Cuzco, part of the Acllahuasi (House of the Chosen Women). After the conquest, it became part of Santa Catalina, so it went from housing Virgins of the Sun to pious Catholic nuns. On the right is Amaruqancha (Courtyard of the Serpents), the site of the palace of Inca Huayna Capác. After the conquest, the Iglesia de la Compañía de Jesús was built here.

Exiting the plaza and heading uphill toward San Blas along Triunfo you'll reach Hatunrumiyoc, a street named after the excellently fitted **12-sided stone** on the right – children stand next to it and insist on tips just for pointing it out. This stone was part of the palace of the sixth Inca, Roca.

QORIKANCHA

This **Inca site** (Plazoleta Santo Domingo; adult/student S10/5; ☽ 8:30am-5:30pm) forms the base of the colonial church of **Iglesia de Santo Domingo**. Compare the colonial building with the Inca walls, most of which survived Cuzco's historic earthquakes with hardly a hairline crack. The site looks rather bizarre, topped with a modern protective roof of glass and metal.

In Inca times, Qorikancha (Quechua for 'golden courtyard') was literally covered with gold. It was not only used for religious rites, but was also an observatory from which priests monitored major celestial activities. Today all that remains of the Inca empire's richest temple is its masterful stonework – Spanish conquistadors looted the rest. But it's fascinating to visit nonetheless, with excellent interpretive signs for self-guided tours.

OVER THE RAINBOW

A common sight in Cuzco's Plaza de Armas is the city's much-loved flag – a brightly striped banner developed in the 1970s to represent the *arco iris* (rainbow) sacred to the Incas. Don't mistake this flag for the international gay-pride banner, to which it bears a remarkable resemblance!

MUSEUMS

Inside a Spanish colonial mansion with an Inca ceremonial courtyard, the dramatically curated **Museo de Arte Precolombino** (MAP; ☎ 23-3210; http://map.perucultural.org.pe; Plazoleta de las Nazarenas 231; adult/student S20/10; ☽ 9am-10pm) showcases a stunningly varied if small collection of priceless archaeological pieces previously buried in the vast storerooms of Lima's Museo Larco. Labels are in Spanish, English and French. It ranks right up there with the continent's best.

The modest **Museo Inka** (☎ 23-7380; cnr Tucumán & Ataúd; admission foreigners/Peruvians S10/5; ☽ 8am-7pm Mon-Fri, 9am-4pm Sat) inhabits one of the city's finest colonial buildings. It's jam-packed with metal- and goldwork, pottery, textiles, *queros* (wooden Inca drinking vessels), mummies and more. In the courtyard, highland weavers sell their traditional textiles to the public.

Originally the palace of Inca Roca, the musty **Museo de Arte del Arzobispado** (Hatunrumiyoc; adult/student S15/7.50, religious-circuit ticket S50/25; ☽ 8am-6pm Mon-Sat, 10am-6pm Sun) has an extensive religious-art collection noted for its period detail and insight into the interactions of indigenous peoples with Spanish conquistadors.

IGLESIA DE SAN BLAS

This adobe **church** (Plaza San Blas; admission S15, religious-circuit ticket S50/25; ☽ 8am-6pm Mon-Sat, 10-6pm Sun) has a pulpit which some call the finest example of colonial woodcarving in the Americas. It's the creator's skull that legend says is nestled in the topmost part.

Activities

Scores of outdoor outfitters in Cuzco offer trekking, rafting and mountain-biking adventures, as well as mountaineering, horse-riding and paragliding trips. It's dizzying, really. Be wary of outfitters lining Plateros and Santa Ana – most are just looking to cash in on the tourism bonanza.

TREKKING

The Inca Trail (p828) is on most hikers' minds, but a dizzying array of other treks surround Cuzco. Many agencies organize trips to remote Inca ruins, such as Choquequirau and Vilcabamba and around Ausangate. Prices are *not* fixed. Shop around and ask questions (eg how many people per tents, how many porters are coming, what the arrangements are for special diets). Inspect all rental gear carefully. The SAE clubhouse (p814) sells topo maps and is an excellent source of independent info.

Travelers flock to the following agencies:

Llama Path (☎ 24-0822; www.llamapath.com; San Juan de Dios 250) A popular Inca Trail outfitter, though not as personable as the others.

Peru Treks (☎ 25-2721; www.perutreks.com; Pardo 540) Locally co-owned, eco-conscious and with ethical treatment of porters.

Q'ente (☎ 222-2535; www.qente.com; Choquechaca 229) Also offers many Inca Trail alternatives.

SAS (☎ 26-1920; www.sastravelperu.com; Garcilaso 244 & 270) Everybody loves to hate the big guy, but travelers are generally pleased.

RIVER RUNNING & MOUNTAIN BIKING

White-water rafting (river running) down the **Río Urubamba** is popular, though not regulated by anyone – accidents and drownings are not uncommon. It's not very wild but offers some spectacular scenery and a chance to visit some of the best Inca ruins near Cuzco. For more remote rivers, you definitely need to book with a top-quality outfit using experienced rafting guides who know first aid, because you will be days away from help in the event of illness or accident. The same goes for mountain-biking trips.

The **Río Apurímac** has challenging rapids through deep gorges and protected rainforest, but can only be run from May to November. A wilder trip is the technically demanding **Río Tambopata**, which can be run from June to October. You'll start in the Andes, north of Lake Titicaca, and reach Reserva Nacional Tambopata in the Amazon.

If you're experienced, there are awesome mountain-biking possibilities around the Sacred Valley and downhill trips from Cuzco to the Amazon jungle. Better rental bikes cost around $45 per day, but inspect them carefully. Make sure you get a helmet, puncture repair kit, pump and tool kit.

Some reputable companies for rafting and biking trips:

Lorenzo Expeditions (☎ 26-0653; www.lorenzo expeditions.com; Plateros 348B) Travelers rave over Lorenzo Cahuana's bike-trek combo tour to Machu Picchu.

Mayuc (☎ 23-2666; www.mayuc.com; Portal Confiturías 211) Resident rafting experts.

Peru Bike (☎ 01-255-7607; www.perubike.com) Inca Trail tours by bike.

Swiss Raft (☎ 24-6414; www.swissraft-peru.com; Heladeros 129) River-rafting trips.

Courses

Cuzco is a convenient place to study Spanish.

Academia Latinoamericana (☎ 24-3364; www .latinoschools.com; Plaza Rimacpampa 565)

Fair Play (☎ 984-78-9252; www.fairplay-peru.org; Choquechaca 188 No 5)

San Blas Spanish School (☎ 24-7898; www.spanish schoolperu.com; Tandapata 688)

Tours

There are hundreds of registered travel agencies in Cuzco, but none can ever be 100% recommended. Ask around.

Blasé options include a half-day tour of the city or nearby ruins, a half-day trip to the Sunday markets at Pisac or Chinchero, or a full-day tour of the Sacred Valley (Pisac, Ollantaytambo and Chinchero). These tours are usually too rushed and not worth the money.

Even more expensive Machu Picchu tours include train tickets, the bus to/from the ruins, admission to the site, an English-speaking guide and lunch. But you only get to spend a few hours at the ruins before it's time to return to the train station, so it's better to DIY.

Cuzco is an excellent place to organize trips to the jungle, especially to Parque Nacional Manu (p861). None are cheap, though. Try the following:

Manu Expeditions (☎ 23-9974; www.manu expeditions.com; Humberto Vidal Unda G5)

Manu Nature Tours (☎ 25-2722; www.manuperu .com; Pardo 1046)

Pantiacolla (☎ 23-8322; www.pantiacolla.com; Saphi 554)

Festivals & Events

El Señor de los Temblores (The Lord of the Earthquakes) On the Monday before Easter; processions date from Cuzco's 1650 earthquake.

Qoyllur Rit'i Lesser known are these traditional Andean rites, held the Sunday before Corpus Christi near Ausangate.

Corpus Christi This feast takes place the ninth Thursday after Easter (usually early June), with fantastic religious processions and cathedral celebrations.

Inti Raymi (Festival of the Sun) Held on June 24, Cuzco's most important festival attracts thousands of visitors and culminates in a re-enactment of Inca winter-solstice ceremonies at Saqsaywamán.

Sleeping

Side streets northwest of the Plaza de Armas (especially Tigre, Tecsecocha and Suecia) are bursting with dime-a-dozen *hostales*. Budget guesthouses also surround the Plaza San Blas, though you'll have to huff and puff to get up there. Expect to pay considerably more for accommodations in Cuzco than other parts of Peru.

Las Chosas Lodge (☎ 22-3357; www.freehostal .com; 🖳) Inka Jungle Trail outfitter Lorenzo Cahuana offers no-strings-attached dorm accommodations in his home a few minutes outside town for *free*. No, that is not a typo – there is no obligation. He's very clever.

Casas de Hospedaje (☎ 24-2710; www.cusco.net/ familyhouse) Homestays cost from S40 to S50 per person, depending on the season and the facilities. Check the website for descriptions of each *cuzqueña* home, including its location and all amenities.

Loki Cuzco (☎ 24-3705; www.lokihostel.com; Santa Ana 601; dm from S21, r with/without bathroom S75/31; 🖳) This 450-year-old national monument was resurrected into a rambunctious backpacker retreat (the bar hops nightly with no remorse) with hot showers, free internet and a helpful staff at the ready with coca tea when you arrive! That hill is a bitch, though.

WalkOn Inn (☎ 23-5065; www.walkoninn.com; Suecia 504; dm S25, s/d S50/60; 🖳) Perched on a sunny green corner that feels almost rural, this tranquil place is a five-minute puff from Plaza de Armas. Gorgeous views of red-tiled roofs and green hills add to the serenity. Recently refurbished, cozy and family-friendly.

Qorichaska Hostal (☎ 22-8974; www.qorichaskaperu .com; Nueva Alta 458; s/d/tr without bathroom S25/50/75, s/ d/tr with breakfast S45/70/90) In a rickety 250-year-old colonial home, this good-value option is popular with travelers, though some have reported a noise issue.

Flying Dog Backpackers (☎ 25-3997; www.flying dogperu.com; Choquechaka 469; dm/r/tr S30/90/135, r without bathroom S75; 🖳) This Lima mainstay has set up a low-key hostel in Cuzco. It's homey and comfortable – there are even space heaters – but staff attitude is irritatingly blasé.

Aldea Yanapay (☎ 23-5870; www.aldeayanapay.org; Fierro 534; s/d/tr without bathroom S35/56/60; 🖳) Like at Los Niños, you can sleep with a clear conscience at this social-project-cum-hostel. Proceeds also benefit Cuzco street children. Volunteers can board for a month for S918 (they also run a school and cultural center). Same deal with its funky, *Dr Seuss*–like restaurant on Ruinas 415, which scores high for food as well as community service.

Casa de la Gringa I (☎ 24-1168; www.casadelagringa .com; Pasnapacana 148; d S96, d without bathroom S64-84, s without bathroom S42; 🖳) This wildly colorful hippy-dippy option is one of Cuzco's most endearing, steeped in new-agey healing and color-as-therapy. They have opened a second, less vibrant location just off Plaza San Blas.

our pick **Hostal Los Niños I** (☎ 23-1424; www .ninoshotel.com; Meloc 442; d S120, s/d without bathroom S54/108; 🖳) This sunny, Dutch-run hostel dedicates *mucho* proceeds to helping street kids. This is a delightful colonial mansion with a peaceful stone-slab courtyard and yummy firelit cafe (but the Dutch should know better than to be serving Nescafé!). A second, equally charming location resides at Fierro 476.

Amaru Hostal (☎ 22-5933; www.amaruhotel.com; Cuesta San Blas 541; s/d incl breakfast S94.50/126; 🖳) Brightly lit courtyards – one with open-air views over Cuzco – characterize this charming midrange option. Space heaters are provided, internet is extra.

Eating

Budget eateries abound on Plateros and Gringo Alley, where you can walk away for under S10. For *chicharrón* (fried pork ribs), head to 'pork street,' Pampa del Castillo.

Coca Shop (Carmen Alto 115; items S3.50-7) Supremely sedate spot to relax with organic products made from coca, including tea, brownies, chocolate (with Andean grains) and sandwiches with coca bread.

Coco Loco (Espaderos 135; snacks S7-19; ☼ 24hr) The best of the fast-food joints satiating drunken late-night munchies.

Jack's Cafe (Choquechaka 509; mains S7-20) For long-haulers on the road, this is Cuzco's best homesick remedy, serving excellent homey international fare, including veggie options, at lovely prices. A favorite.

Trotamundos (Portal Comercio 177, 2nd fl; items S7-22) Popular plaza coffeehouse with bang-up views of the cathedral.

Granja Heidi (Cuesta San Blas 525, 2nd fl; meals S8-28) This Alpine cafe does a wide range of breakfasts, crepes and comfort food, all chemical-free and wholesomely prepared.

Tearooms (Santa Teresa 364, 2nd fl; deserts S10-16, sandwiches S10-15) Part Louis IV implosion, part Casablanca dreamscape, this funky tea and desert lounge serves up global sandwiches and cocktails as well as imported teas from the UK and scrumptious deserts – a rarity!

Real McCoy (Plateros 326, 2nd fl; mains S10-27) You think fish and chips at 3300m is easy? It's not. Somehow the friendly, Brit-expat owners pull it off shockingly well, along with a wealth of other comfort pub grub.

Pizza Carlo (Maruri 381; pizza S14-31.50) We weren't familiar with the Andean pepper *rocoto* until we ordered the spicy Diavola pizza at this intimate spot boasting Cuzco's best pizza. Now we are. You have been warned.

ourpick Los Perros (Tecsecocha 436; mains S14-20) Australian-run godsend, serving exotic, Asian- and Indian-slanted bar food at stunning prices in an intimate 'couch bar.' The burger is insane.

Muse (Plateros 316, 2nd fl; mains S15-20) Bohemian cafe-lounge serving everything from a crusty veggie lasagna (a knockout!) to pesto spaghetti. On Fridays, there's often live music or DJs.

Sumaq Misky (Plateros 334, 2nd fl; mains S18-45) Hidden in an alley of souvenir stalls, this warm eatery is doing its damnedest to bring you Andean specialties in a less scary way: alpaca curries and burgers, guinea-pig tandoori – it's all good! There are veggie options too. The attached sports bar is also very popular for both American and European soccer matches.

Inka Grill (Portal de Panes 115; mains S22-45) Touristy, but a great spot to take in the gamut of Peruvian cuisine, from excellent trout *tiradito* to alpaca to coca leaf crème brûlée in a more refined Plaza de Armas environment.

Grocery shops include **Gato's Market** (Portal Belén; 8am-11pm) and the original **Market** (Mantas 119; 8am-11pm).

SPLURGE!

Don Esteban & Don Cucho (Espinar 114; mains S32-45) A cocktail is a cocktail, but occasionally one comes along and changes your views on alcoholism. The *maracuyá sour* at this upscale *comida criolla* restaurant (a damn good meal as well) is one such drink. Perfectly tart, just creamy enough, and oh so delicious. At S14, it's high-end imbibing, but you'll never want to drink anything else again. Don't discount chasing food with this dream in a glass, either – the restaurant's modern take on Peruvian classics is nearly as satisfying as the bartender's magic.

Drinking

In popular backpacker bars, especially around the Plaza de Armas, both sexes should beware of drinks being spiked – don't let go of your glass, and think twice about using free-drink coupons. Happy hour kicks off as early as 1pm.

Km 0 (Tandapata 100) Tiny space serving up Thai food and live music nightly from 9:30pm.

Norton's Rat (Santa Catalina Angosta 116; 7am-late) Down-to-earth pub which has wooden tables overlooking the plaza, and TVs, darts and billiards, plus the best sloppy burgers in town. Breakfast all day.

Paddy O'Flaherty's (Triunfo 124; 11-1am) Cramped, smoky and Irish-owned, just like Irish pubs used to be!

Entertainment

Several restaurants have evening *folklórica* music and dance shows; expect to pay S50 to S60 including buffet. Most live music venues don't charge admission.

Centro Qosqo de Arte Nativo (22-7901; Av El Sol 604; admission S15) Nightly *folklórica* shows.

Roots (Tecsecocha 282) If you like your clubs with a supreme dose of chill, this is your night out. The candlelit vibe here is part Rasta relaxed, part faux castle. The plethora of cushiony lounge chairs makes it easy to plop down and call it a night.

Ukuku's Pub (Plateros 316; 8pm-late) Usually full to bursting, Ukuku's plays a winning combination of Latin pop, reggae, alternative, salsa, ska, soul, jazz and more, and hosts live local bands nightly.

7 Angelitos (7 Angelitos 638) The way townsfolk rave about the *mojitos* here, you'd think Fidel Castro was behind the bar. They're OK, but it's more about the nightly live music and the divey atmosphere.

Shopping

Cuzco offers a cornucopia of artisan workshops and stores selling knitted woolens, woven textiles, colorful ceramics, silver jewelry and more, as well as contemporary art galleries. Near the San Pedro train station, Cuzco's Mercado Central is a handy spot to pick up fruit or that vital spare pair of clean socks, but don't go alone or take valuables, as thieves are persistent.

Andean Expressions (Choquechaca 210) A good place to pick up unique T-shirts one million other folks won't be wearing (we're talking to you, Inka Cola and Cusqueña advertisers!).

Center for Traditional Textiles of Cuzco (Av El Sol 603A) This nonprofit organization promotes the survival of traditional Andean weaving techniques, and has shop-floor demonstrations of finger-twisting complexity. Beautiful wares!

Kuna (Portal de Panes 327) You pay for the privilege, but this is the least cheesy option for alpaca wear you'd actually be caught dead in.

Trinidad Enriquez (Capila de Loreto s/n) This stylish shop houses goods that benefit five social projects ranging from child abandonment and rape to nearby rural communities. It's all top gear. It's attached to the Iglesia de la Compañía de Jesús.

Getting There & Away

AIR

Most flights from Cuzco's **airport** (CUZ; ☎ 22-2611), 2km southeast of the center, are in the morning. Airport tax is US$4.28.

AeroSur (☎ 25-4691; www.aerosur.com; Av El Sol 948, Sol Plaza) Thursday & Sunday flights to La Paz.

LAN (☎ 25-5552; www.lan.com; Av El Sol 627B) Direct flights to Lima, Arequipa, Juliaca and Puerto Maldonado.

Star Perú (☎ 23-4060; www.starperu.com; Av El Sol 627B) Thrice-daily flights to Lima.

TACA (☎ 24-5922; www.taca.com; Av El Sol 602B) Daily (except Sunday) service to/from Lima.

BUS

Long-Distance

The journey times given here are only approximate. Long delays are probable during the rainy season, especially January to April.

Cuzco's **Terminal Terrestre** (departure tax S1), 500m southeast of the city center (taxi S5), services long-distance destinations and houses all of the major bus companies including **Cruz del Sur** (☎ 24-8255), **Ormeño** (☎ 26-1704), **Cromotex** (☎ 24-9573) and **Tepsa** (☎ 24-9977). There are scores of *económico* bus operators too.

Frequent buses go to Puno (S43, six to seven hours) via Juliaca. Services to Arequipa (S90 to S106, nine hours) are mostly overnight. There are two routes to Lima. The first is via Abancay (S143 to S173, 18 to 20 hours), which is quicker but can be a rough ride and prone to crippling delays during the rainy season. The alternative is via Arequipa, a longer but more reliable route (S70, 23 hours). Buses to Abancay (S15, four hours) and Andahuaylas (S30, eight hours) go early in the morning

and evening. Change at Andahuaylas for buses bound for Ayacucho via rough highland roads that get cold at night. **Civa** (☎ 24-9961) heads to Puerto Maldonado (S60, 16 to 18 hours) every day at 3:30pm.

Inka Express (☎ 26-0272; www.inkaexpress.com; Pardo 865A) has cushy tour buses (S132) that stop at several sites en route to Puno. Buy tickets at the Pardo office, but the buses actually depart from Parque El Ovalo 500m southeast.

Buses to Quillabamba (S30, seven hours) leave a few times daily from the Santiago bus terminal in western Cuzco (taxi costs S5). One recommended company is **Ampay** (☎ 985-67-0716), which staffs another ticket counter at Cuzco's main long-distance terminal. Daytime buses are safer and have the advantage of spectacular scenery.

For other Amazon destinations you have to fly, risk a hazardous journey by truck or find an expedition. **Unancha** (☎ 25-4233; Av Huáscar 226) departs for Pillcopata from Av Huáscar on Monday, Wednesday and Friday mornings (S18 to S20, 10 hours). Trucks continue onward from Pillcopata to Itahuañia (S40, 12 hours), where you can access Parque Nacional Manu (p861).

International

Several companies offer buses to Copacabana (S70, 10 hours) and La Paz (S80, 12 hours) in Bolivia. Many swear blind service is direct, though evening buses usually stop in Puno for several hours until the border opens. Ormeño goes to La Paz (S90, 12 hours) via Desaguadero. For Tacna, near the Chilean border, Cruz del Sur has departures at 8:30pm daily (S128, 14 hours). **Internacional Litoral** (☎ 24-8989) goes to Arica, Chile (S160, 18 hours).

TRAIN

Estación Huanchac (☎ 58-1414; 7am-5pm Mon-Fri, to noon Sat & Sun) at the southeastern end of Av El Sol, serves Juliaca and Puno on Lake Titicaca. **Estación Poroy** (Carretera Cuzco–Urubamba), east of town, serves Ollantaytambo in the Sacred Valley and Machu Picchu. The two stations are unconnected, so it's impossible to travel directly from Puno to Machu Picchu. The downtown Estación San Pedro is used only for local trains, which foreigners cannot board.

A **tourist bus** to Estación Poroy departs every day at 6:15am from Av Pardo (S6). The bus also meets returning trains, dropping passengers off in Plaza Regocijo. You can also get to Poroy by taxi – S30 for a radio cab, S15 on the street.

It's possible to buy tickets at Huanchac station, but it's easier online at www.perurail .com (Visa only).

To Ollantaytambo & Machu Picchu

To get to Aguas Calientes from Cuzco by train takes about three hours, and you have two options: the Vistadome service costs S227.20 each way. It leaves Cuzco at 7am each day and returns at 3:25pm.

The luxury Hiram Bingham also departs Poroy at 9am and arrives back in Cuzco at 9pm daily except Sundays. The cheaper Backpacker Cerrojo trains now leave from Ollantaytambo (p824).

To Puno

Trains depart from Estación Huanchac at 8am, arriving to Puno around 6pm, on Mondays, Wednesdays and Saturdays from November to March, with an extra departure on Fridays from April to October ($S704). For details, see p809.

Getting Around

TO/FROM THE AIRPORT

Frequent *colectivos* run along Ayacucho to just outside the airport (S0.70). An official taxi to/from the city center costs S20/6. Be wary of rogue taxis working outside the terminal building – robberies are not uncommon. Many guesthouses offer free airport pickups by travel agents hoping to sell tours.

BUS & COLECTIVO

Daytime minibuses to Pisac (S2.40, one hour) leave from Av Tullumayo, south of Av Garcilaso. *Micros* to Urubamba (S5, 1½ hours) via Chinchero (S3, 50 minutes) depart frequently during daylight hours from the 300 block of Grau near Puente Grau. *Colectivos* for Ollantaytambo (S10, 2½ hours) and Urubamba (S6, 1½ hours) depart from Pavitos.

TAXI

Trips around town cost S5. Official taxis are much safer than 'pirate' taxis (see p814) and prices listed reflect official rates. A reliable company is **Qq'arina** (☎ 25-5000), whose drivers are licensed and carry photo ID.

AROUND CUZCO

The archaeological ruins closest to Cuzco are **Saqsaywamán**, **Q'enqo**, **Pukapukara** and **Tambomachay** (☼ 7am-6pm) – admission with a *boleto turístico* (see p814). Take a Pisac-bound bus and get off at Tambomachay, the ruin furthest away from Cuzco (and, at 3700m, the highest). It's an 8km walk back to Cuzco. Be aware that violent attacks against tourists have occurred along this route, even during daylight hours. Go in a group, and return before nightfall.

Saqsaywamán

The name means 'satisfied falcon,' though most travelers remember it by the mnemonic 'sexy woman.' The sprawling site is 2km from Cuzco. Climb steep Resbalosa street, turn right past the Iglesia de San Cristóbal and continue to a hairpin bend in the road. On the left is a stone staircase, an Inca stone road leading to the top.

Although Saqsaywamán seems huge, what today's visitor sees is only about 20% of the original structure. Soon after the conquest, the Spaniards tore down walls and used the blocks to build their own houses in Cuzco.

In 1536 the fort saw one of the fiercest battles between the Spanish and Manco Inca, who used Saqsaywamán to lay siege to the conquistadors. Thousands of dead littered the site after the Inca defeat, which attracted swarms of carrion-eating Andean condors. The tragedy was memorialized by the inclusion of eight condors in Cuzco's coat of arms.

Most striking are the magnificent three-tiered fortifications. Inca Pachachutec envisioned Cuzco in the shape of a puma, with Saqsaywamán as the head, and these 22 zigzag walls form the teeth. The parade ground is used for Inti Raymi celebrations.

If you only visit one ruin in the immediate vicinity of Cuzco, this is the one, and you're better off skipping the *boleto turístico* and paying a single admission here (S40).

Q'enqo

The name of this fascinating small ruin means 'zigzag.' It's a large limestone rock riddled with niches, steps and extraordinary symbolic carvings, including channels that may have been used for ritual sacrifices of *chicha* (corn beer), or perhaps blood. Scrambling up to the top of the boulder you'll find a flat surface used for ceremonies and laboriously etched

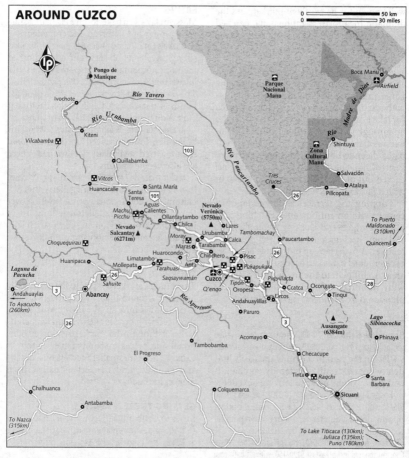

representations of animals. Back below, explore the mysterious subterranean cave with altars hewn into the rock.

The site is 2km from Saqsaywamán, on the left as you descend from Tambomachay.

Tambomachay & Pukapukara

About 300m from the main road, **Tambomachay** is a beautifully wrought ceremonial bath, still channeling clear spring water that earns it the title El Baño del Inca (Inca's Bath). On the opposite side of the road is the commanding ruin of **Pukapukara**. Its name means 'red fort,' though it was more likely a hunting lodge, guard post or stopping point for travelers. The upper esplanade has panoramic views.

THE SACRED VALLEY

The Valle Sagrado (Sacred Valley) of the Río Urubamba is about 15km north of Cuzco as the condor flies. Its star attractions are the lofty Inca citadels of Pisac and Ollantaytambo, but the valley is also packed with more peaceful Inca sites, as well as frenzied markets and high-altitude Andean villages. Investigate the idyllic countryside with Peter Frost's in-depth *Exploring Cuzco*.

Pisac

☎ 084 / pop 2000

Most visits to the Sacred Valley will begin in sleepy Pisac (elevation 2715m), just 33km northeast of Cuzco by paved road. Here you'll find a rather charming colonial village, well known for its excellent market, and the dramatic Inca fortress Intihuatana, perched precariously high atop the mountains above.

SIGHTS & ACTIVITIES

The hilltop **Inca citadel** (7am-6pm) lies high above the village on a plateau with a plunging gorge on either side. Take the steep 4km footpath starting along the left side of the church (or take a taxi for S20). It's a spectacular climb up through terraces, sweeping around mountainous flanks and along cliff-hugging footpaths defended by massive stone doorways, vertigo-inducing staircases and a short tunnel carved out of the rock. Admission is S40 or with a *boleto turístico* (see p814).

Topping the terraces is the ceremonial center, with an Intihuatana (Hitching Post of the Sun), several working water channels and some neat masonry inside well-preserved temples. A path leads up the hillside to a series of ceremonial baths and around to the military area. A cliff behind the site is honeycombed with hundreds of Inca tombs that were plundered by *guaqueros* (grave robbers).

SLEEPING

Hospedaje Beho (☎ 20-3001; artesaniasbeho@yahoo .es; Intihuatana 114; s/d/tr $30/50/60, s/d without bathroom S15/30) On the path to the ruins and easily hidden by market stalls, this family-run handicrafts shop offers no-frills lodging next door.

Hospedaje Kinsa Ccocha (☎ 20-3101; Arequipa 307; s/d S35/70, without bathroom S25/30) The comfiest budget option, down a quieter secondary street parallel to the plaza. The water is fire-heated!

Pisac Inn (☎ 20-3062; www.pisacinn.com; Plaza Constitución; s/d incl breakfast S120/150, without bathroom S90/120) One of the most colorful spots to stay in the valley, this adobe-style abode is full of Andean-chic indigenous touches and with lovely staff (though its high-season prices are up there). Massages (S90) and entry to the sauna (S35) are extra amenities. The restaurant offers some organic cuisine and focuses on local products. Not for tall folks, though.

Paz y Luz B&B (☎ 20-3204; www.pazyluzperu.com; s/d/tr incl breakfast S90/135/190; 🖳) A 1km walk east along the river, this American-run healing center has well-appointed rooms and specializes in one-day Andean-shamanic spiritual workshops (S100) and more extensive wellness stays. A new restaurant and 12 additional rooms were under construction during research.

EATING

Massive clay-oven bakeries on Mariscal Castilla vend piping-hot flatbread and empanadas.

Ulrike's Café (Plaza de Armas 828; mains S4-10) This sunny traveler's hub serves up a very limited menu of homemade pastas, sandwiches and juices (there are more choices on pizza nights). The raved-about-town cheesecake is good for South America, but Cheesecake Factory it ain't. You'll also find a global ATM here.

Ayahuasca Café (Bolognesi s/n; mains S10-15) This bohemian lounge served up the best *lomo saltado* (fried steak with rice) we had. There are also veggie options.

Mullu (Plaza de Armas 352; mains S10-30; 🕙 closed Mon) Hanging above an art gallery, this alt-cultural cafe commands a prime position over the plaza. There's a deliciously long list of juices and exotic fusion fare like ostrich stir-fry, stuffed alpaca ravioli and pumpkin stew; and Peru's best T-shirts.

SHOPPING

The Sunday market kicks into life in the early morning. Around 10am the tour buses deposit their hordes into an already chaotic scene, thronged with buyers and overrun with crafts stalls. Although the market retains a traditional side, prices are comparable to shops in Cuzco. There are smaller markets on Tuesday and Thursday and an excellent daily artisan market in the Plaza.

GETTING THERE & AWAY

Buses to Urubamba (S2, one hour) and Cuzco (S2.40, one hour) leave from near the bridge at Plazaleta Leguiz and Av Amazonas.

Urubamba

☎ 084 / pop 10,800

There is precious little to see in Urubamba (elevation 2870m), at the junction of the valley thoroughfare with the road back to Cuzco via Chinchero, but for those traipsing through the Sacred Valley, it's like a necessary transit hub. There's a global ATM at the *grifo* (gas station) on the main road, about 1km east of the bus terminal.

SIGHTS & ACTIVITIES

Many outdoor activities that are organized from Cuzco take place at Urubamba, including horse riding, mountain biking, paragliding and hot-air balloon trips. Trips often take in the amphitheater-like terraces of **Moray** (admission S10) and **Salinas** (admission S5), where thousands of salt pans have been harvested since Inca times, both nearby. **Perol Chico** (☎ 01-99-414-7267; www.perolchico.com), run by Dutch-Peruvian Eduard van Brunschot Vega, has an excellent ranch outside Urubamba with Peruvian *paso* horses. Advance bookings for horse-riding tours are required. Keep in mind – keeping horses in this part of the world is not cheap. If you go bargain bin, you are likely looking at commercially abused horses. For something a little different, **Agrotourism Chichubamba** (☎ 20-1562; www.agrotourismsacredvalley.com), in conjunction with Urubamba-based NGO Pro Peru, offers fascinating glimpses into local village life through agrotourism workshops set around themes like *chicha*, textiles and knitting, Andean chocolates or Peruvian coffee, among others. You can also spend the night in the village.

SLEEPING & EATING

Hotel Urubamba (☎ 20-1062; Bolognesi 605; s S25, d with TV S35; s/d/tr without bathroom S12/24/36) The bare-bones budget choice, if you can put up with the staff. The common bathrooms are nicer than expected, though.

Hostal Los Jardines (☎ 20-1331; www.machawasi .com; Jr Convencí 459; s/d/tr S35/60/70) Tucked away off the main road five minutes from the plaza, this is a comfortable choice. Rooms are shaken up a bit with colorful textile art and warm Andean blankets and there's a pleasant flower garden.

Café Plaza (Jr Bolívar; meals S7-25) The breakfast ham, egg and cheese on ciabatta at this homey plaza option is perfect. There's also good coffee, house-made pasta and English magazines.

Muse, Too (cnr Comercio & Grau; mains S10-20) Same food and same decor as at its popular big brother in Cuzco, but struggling to maintain the same awesome vibe (cartoons on the TV?). The *pisco sour* and Banoffee pie are memorable. Also has vegetarian dishes.

GETTING THERE & AWAY

Buses going to Cuzco (S3.30, two hours) via Pisac (S2, one hour) or Chinchero (S3.50, 50 minutes) and *colectivos* to Ollantaytambo (S1.50, 30 minutes) all leave frequently from the bus terminal. Faster *colectivos* to Cuzco (S6, 1½ hours) wait near the *grifo* further east on Av Cabo Conchatupa.

Ollantaytambo

☎ 084 / pop 2000

Tiny Ollantaytambo (elevation 2800m) is the best surviving example of Inca city planning and the most atmospheric of Sacred Valley destinations – its massive fortress stands sentinel over the cobblestoned village like a guardian to heavens itself. Nothing much has changed here in 700 years.

SIGHTS

The spectacular, steep terraces guarding the **Inca complex** (7am-5pm) – admission S40 or with a *boleto turístico* (see p814) – mark one of the few places where the conquistadors lost a major battle, when Manco Inca threw missiles and flooded the plain below. But Ollantaytambo was as much a temple as a fort to the Incas. A finely worked ceremonial area sits on top of the terracing. The stone was quarried from the mountainside high above the Río Urubamba. Transporting the huge blocks was a stupendous feat.

SLEEPING

Hospedaje Las Portadas (☎ 20-4008; Principal s/n; campsite per person S10; s/d S25/50; s/d/tr without bathroom S15/30/45) Just east of Plaza Mayor, this family guesthouse has a sunny courtyard and a small yard for camping. The makeshift terrace has some ruin views and offers panoramic vistas of neighboring construction. Rooms are very basic; some offer local TV.

Chaska Wasi (☎ 20-4045; katycusco@yahoo.es; Calle de Medio s/n; s/d S25/40, without bathroom S15/30; 🖳) North of the plaza along a narrow Inca thoroughfare, the friendly folks here offer very rustic rooms with electric showers. Breakfast costs S5 extra.

Hotel Munay Tika (☎ 20-4111; www.munaytika.com; Ferrocarril 118; s/d/tr incl breakfast S108/124/155) Meaning 'jungle flower,' this inn offers a sunny garden and hardwood floors in rustic but well-kept rooms. It's closest to the train.

EATING & DRINKING

Kusicoyllor (Plaza Araccama; mains S12-28) This stylish, underground cafe by the ruins has eclectic decor and victuals, from Amazon-grown coffee to Swiss fondue.

Hearts Café (Plaza de Armas s/n; mains S13-22) On the plaza, this British-owned cafe does it all (hummus, fajitas, breakfast, desert) and then donates all the proceeds to help local women and children.

PERU

Orishas Café (Ferrocarril s/n; mains S16-25) On the way to the train station and hanging over the river, this adorable cafe does some innovative Peruvian and international dishes and great brick-oven pizza.

GETTING THERE & AWAY

Frequent *colectivos* for Urubamba's bus terminal (S10, 30 minutes) depart just southeast of the plaza next to the market from 5am to 8pm. *Colectivos* (S20) and taxis (S120) for Cuzco mill about the train station only when trains arrive. Alternatively, head to Urubamba and transfer there.

Ollantaytambo is the halfway point for Machu Picchu trains running between Cuzco and Aguas Calientes. However, Ollantaytambo also offers additional daily Vistadome Valley trains (S169/338 one way/return) along the Sacred Valley line, as well as three cheaper Backpacker Cerrojo trains to Machu Picchu (from S108/216 one way/return).

AGUAS CALIENTES

☎ 084 / pop 2000

It won't kill you to spend a night in Aguas Calientes (also known as Machu Picchu Pueblo) – its hordes of tourist-trap restaurants and firelit bars are vaguely tolerable for an evening – but this village sustained solely by traffic to and from Machu Picchu offers little besides overpriced food and lodging (and way too many pizzerias). Though the village is nestled in the deep valley below Machu Picchu and enclosed by towering walls of stone and cloud forest, Aguas Calientes is ruined by its dependence on tourism, which has turned a scenic location into a gringo nightmare. But there is one good reason to sleep here if you're so inclined: to avoid being engulfed by day-trippers arriving by train from Cuzco, you can catch the first morning bus up the mountain to Machu Picchu and/or stay at the ruins until late afternoon when the crowds vanish.

Information

Slow internet cafes are scattered around the village. There's a post office, police station and several *lavanderías*. Everything else is a restaurant or hostel.

BCP (Av Imperio de los Incas s/n) Has a Visa ATM.
Centro de Salud (☎ 21-1037; ☯ 8am-8pm, emergencies 24hr) A small medical center.
iPerú (☎ 21-1104; Edificio del Instituto Nacional de Cultura, Pachacutec, 1st block; ☯ 9am-1pm & 2-8pm) A helpful branch.
Machu Picchu ticket office (☯ 5am-10pm) Located at the Instituto Nacional de Cultura building, next to iPerú.

Sights & Activities

By Puente Ruinas at the base of the footpath to Machu Picchu, the **Museo de Sitio Manuel Chávez Ballón** (admission S21; ☯ 9:30am-4pm) has superb multimedia displays on excavations of Machu Picchu and the ancient Incas' building methods, cosmology and culture. A small botanical garden blooms outside.

Just staggered in from the Inca Trail? Soak your aches and pains away in the somewhat suspiciously murky **hot springs** (admission S10; ☯ 5am-10:30pm), 10 minutes' walk up Pachacutec. Swimsuits and towels can be rented cheaply outside the entrance.

Sleeping

Heavy discounts are available in the off-season. Early checkout times are the norm.

Hospedaje Joe (☎ 38-3512; hostalmariaangola @hotmail.com; Mayta Cápac 102-103; s/d/tr S30/50/75; ☐) A friendly enough, somewhat damp cheapie with basic rooms and big bathrooms.

Pirwa Hostel (☎ 21-1170; www.pirwahostelscusco .com; dm/s/d/tr S36/62/93/139.50) Though staff wasn't honest with us about the availability of a room to inspect during our visit, this popular Cuzco hostel chain offers nice, clean dorms and private rooms with cable TV and well-maintained bathrooms.

Hospedaje Las Bromelias (☎ 21-1145; Colla Raymi 101; d/tr S60/90, s/d/tr without bathroom S40/65/105) Shocking *Wizard of Oz*–green bedspreads characterize this popular haunt on the plaza. There's hot water and a restaurant for breakfast, but it's really indistinguishable from any other bare-bones option around town.

Hostal Ima Sumac (☎ 23-5314; Pachacutec s/n; s/d/tr incl breakfast S45/80/110) Noise carries here like a trailer in a tornado, and staff can be oddly absent, but there's hot water and warm beds. It's at the top of Pachacutec, just before the hot springs.

Eating & Drinking

Tourist restaurants cluster alongside the railway tracks and Pachacutec toward the hot springs – almost every one of them exactly the same. You'll find backpacker bars with extralong happy hour up Pachacutec, but

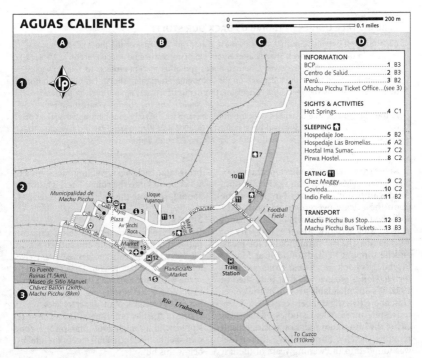

AGUAS CALIENTES

INFORMATION	
BCP	**1** B3
Centro de Salud	**2** B3
iPerú	**3** B2
Machu Picchu Ticket Office	(see 3)

SIGHTS & ACTIVITIES	
Hot Springs	**4** C1

SLEEPING	
Hospedaje Joe	**5** B2
Hospedaje Las Bromelias	**6** A2
Hostal Ima Sumac	**7** C2
Pirwa Hostel	**8** C2

EATING	
Chez Maggy	**9** C2
Govinda	**10** C2
Indio Feliz	**11** B2

TRANSPORT	
Machu Picchu Bus Stop	**12** B3
Machu Picchu Bus Tickets	**13** B3

PERU

you don't need to hear it from us – every one of them will try and lure you in.

Govinda (Pachacutec s/n; mains S10-30) This trusty vegetarian haunt has stone floors and good-value fare made by Hare Krishnas.

Chez Maggy (Pachacutec 156; pizza S18-40, mains S19-45) This place has stained-glass walls, sociable long tables, board games and an international menu that includes yummy nachos and wood-fired pizzas.

Indio Feliz (Lloque Yupanqui 4; menú S44.50, mains S24.50-34.50) Candlelit cozy but not schmaltzy, this Franco-Peruvian bistro is miles away from anything in the vicinity in quality, experience and atmosphere. The three-course set menu is superb and portions are substantial. You have one night in town: eat here.

Getting There & Around

Aguas Calientes is the final train stop for Machu Picchu. See p820 for information about trains from Cuzco, as well as opposite for details on cheaper trains starting in Ollantaytambo.

For buses to Machu Picchu, see p828.

MACHU PICCHU

For many visitors to Peru and even South America itself, a visit to the 'lost' Inca city of Machu Picchu is the defining moment of their trip. Undeniably the most spectacular archaeological site on the continent, it tantalizes with its mysterious past and is deservedly world-famous for its stunning location and craftsmanship. From June to September as many as 1000 people arrive daily. Despite such great influx, this must-see site manages to retain its air of grandeur and mystery. Many backpackers reach Machu Picchu on foot, walking along the popular Inca Trail (p828), though bus, train and car are also options.

History

For a brief history of the Inca empire, see p767.

The actual purpose and function of Machu Picchu is still a matter of speculation and educated guesswork. The citadel was never mentioned in the chronicles kept by the colonizing Spaniards, which served as a written archive of hitherto unrecorded Inca history.

PERU TO YALE UNIVERSITY: GIVE US BACK OUR STUFF!

All is not well between South America's most visited site and one of the most prestigious universities in the United States. Shortly after Hiram Bingham 'discovered' Machu Picchu in 1911, he carted off loads of ceramics, jewelry, human bones and other ancient artifacts to Yale University, where he intended to conduct research on the items and return them shortly (within 18 months) thereafter. That was 100 years ago. Peru claims thousands of artifacts remain in Yale's possession – many of which are on display at Yale's Peabody Museum – and the country wants them returned to their birthplace. Yale disagrees over the numbers, and isn't exactly coughing up what they do have, either. The he-said, she-said hit a standstill in 2008 and Peru started talking lawsuit – the country wants everything returned in time for Machu Picchu's centenary in 2011, or else.

Apart from the indigenous Quechuas, nobody knew of Machu Picchu's existence until American historian Hiram Bingham came upon the thickly overgrown ruins in 1911 while being guided by a local boy. Bingham's search was actually for the lost city of Vilcabamba, the last stronghold of the Incas, and he thought he had found it at Machu Picchu. His book *Inca Land: Explorations in the Highlands of Peru* was first published in 1922. It's downloadable for free from Project Gutenberg (www.gutenberg.org).

Despite more recent studies of the 'lost' city of the Incas, knowledge of Machu Picchu remains sketchy. Some believe the citadel was founded in the waning years of the last Incas as an attempt to preserve Inca culture or rekindle Inca predominance, while others think it may have already become a forgotten city at the time of the conquest. Another theory suggests that the site was a royal retreat abandoned upon the Spanish invasion.

Whatever the case, the exceptionally high quality of the stonework and ornamentation tell that Machu Picchu must once have been vitally important as a ceremonial center. Indeed, to some extent, it still is: Alejandro Toledo, the country's first native Quechua-speaking president, staged his colorful inauguration here in 2001.

Information

The ruins are typically open from dawn till dusk, but they are most heavily visited between 10am and 2pm. One-day tickets cost S122/61 per adult/student with ISIC card. You must buy them in advance through a tour operator, the **Instituto Nacional de Cultura** (☎ 084-23-6061; San Bernardo s/n, Cuzco; ☕ 7am-noon & 1-4:15pm Mon-Fri, 7-11am & 1-3pm Sat) or at the INC office in Aguas Calientes (p824) – they are not sold at the site itself. You aren't allowed to

bring large backpacks, walking sticks, food or water bottles into the ruins. There's a storage room just before the main entrance.

Sights

Proceed from the ticket gate along a narrow path to the mazelike main entrance to Machu Picchu, where the ruins now reveal themselves and stretch out before you. To get a visual fix of the whole site and snap the classic postcard shot, climb the zigzagging staircase to the **Hut of the Caretaker of the Funerary Rock**, which is one of the few buildings that has been restored with a thatch roof, making it a good rain shelter. The Inca Trail enters the site just below this hut.

From here, take the steps down and to the left of the plazas into the ruined sections containing the **Temple of the Sun**, a curved, tapering tower with some of Machu Picchu's finest stonework. The temple is cordoned off to visitors, but you can see into it from above. Below is an almost-hidden natural rock cave that has been carefully carved with a steplike altar and sacred niches by the Inca's stonemasons, known as the **Royal Tomb**, though no mummies were ever found here.

Climbing the stairs above the 16 nearby **ceremonial baths** that cascade down the ruins brings you to the **Sacred Plaza**, from which there is a spectacular view of the Río Urubamba valley and across to the snowcapped Cordillera Vilcabamba in the distance. The **Temple of the Three Windows** overlooks the plaza.

Behind the **Sacristy**, known for the two rocks flanking its entrance, each of which is said to contain 32 angles, a staircase climbs to the major shrine, **Intihuatana** (Hitching Post of the Sun), which lies atop a small hill. The carved rock at the summit is often called a sundial, though it was connected to the passing of the seasons rather than the time of day. The

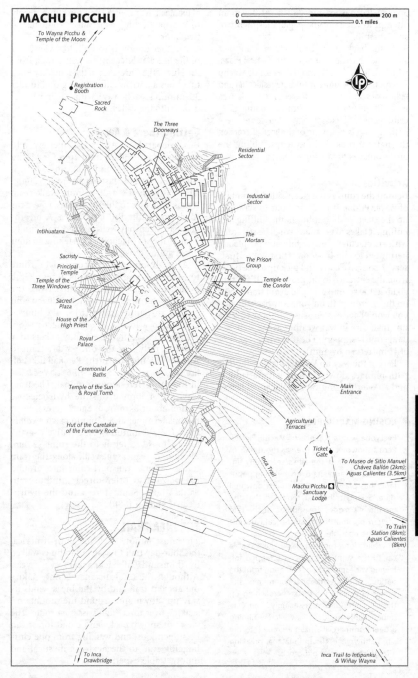

MACHU PICCHU

0 — 200 m
0 — 0.1 miles

To Wayna Picchu &
Temple of the Moon

Registration
Booth

Sacred
Rock

The Three
Doorways

Residential
Sector

Industrial
Sector

Intihuatana

The
Mortars

Sacristy

Principal
Temple

The Prison
Group

Temple of the
Three Windows

Temple of
the Condor

Sacred
Plaza

House of the
High Priest

Royal
Palace

Ceremonial
Baths

Main
Entrance

Temple of the Sun
& Royal Tomb

Hut of the Caretaker
of the Funerary Rock

Agricultural
Terraces

Ticket
Gate

Inca Trail

To Museo de Sitio Manuel
Chávez Ballón (2km);
Aguas Calientes (3.5km)

Machu Picchu
Sanctuary
Lodge

To Train
Station (8km);
Aguas Calientes
(8km)

To Inca
Drawbridge

Inca Trail to Intipunku
& Wiñay Wayna

Spaniards smashed most such shrines in an attempt to wipe out the pagan blasphemy of sun worship.

At the back of the Intihuatana is another staircase that descends to the **Central Plaza**, which divides the ceremonial sector of Machu Picchu from the more mundane **residential** and **industrial** sectors. At the lower end of this area is the **Prison Group**, a labyrinthine complex of cells, niches and passageways. The centerpiece of the group is a carving of the **head of a condor**, the natural rocks behind it resembling the bird's outstretched wings.

Activities

Behind the ruins is the steep-sided mountain of **Wayna Picchu**. It takes an hour to scramble up the steep path, but for all the huffing and puffing it takes to get there, you'll be rewarded with spectacular views. Only 400 people are permitted to climb per day (first-come, first-serve), so arrive early and pick up a free ticket from the entrance to the mountain. It's best to go up in the second group to avoid traffic jams on the narrow path on your way back down – you won't have to step aside for those coming up. Take care in wet weather as the steps get dangerously slippery. The trail entrance closes at 1pm (return by 4pm).

Part of the way up Wayna Picchu, another path plunges down to your left via ladders and an overhanging cave to the small **Temple**

---

of the Moon, from where you can climb steeply to Wayna Picchu – a circuitous route taking two hours.

Another option is to walk to a viewpoint of the **Inca drawbridge**. It's a flatter walk from the Hut of the Caretaker of the Funerary Rock that hugs a narrow cliff-clinging trail (under 30 minutes each way) with sheer vertical drops into the valley.

Getting There & Away

Buses depart from Aguas Calientes every 10 minutes from 5:30am until 1pm for Machu Picchu (S21.70, 25 minutes). Buses return when full, with the last departure at 5:30pm. Alternatively, it's a 20-minute walk from Aguas Calientes to Puente Ruinas, where the road crosses the Río Urubamba. A breathtakingly steep but well-marked trail climbs 2km further to Machu Picchu, taking an hour (less coming down!).

A newly popular, economic DIY route to Machu Picchu is via Santa Teresa. Grab a bus headed for Quillabamba from the Santiago terminal in western Cuzco and get off in Santa Maria (S15, 4½ hours), then catch a local *combi* or *colectivo* (S6, 1½ hours) to Santa Teresa. Buy tickets (day of travel only) for the once-a-day train to Aguas Calientes from the **PeruRail ticket office** (6-8am & 10am-3pm Mon-Fri, 6-8pm Wed & Sun) in the Santa Teresa bus terminal. The train leaves at 4:30pm from the hydroelectric station about 8km from Santa Teresa. Be at the bus terminal at 3:45pm to catch a *combi* there (S6, 25 minutes). Alternatively, many folks choose to leg it to the ruins (20km, 2½ hours), a pleasant walk along the train tracks. Several transport companies around the plaza also offer direct minibuses to Santa Maria, Santa Teresa and the hydroelectric station (S80).

THE INCA TRAIL

The most famous trek in South America, this four-day trail to Machu Picchu is walked by thousands of backpackers every year. Although the total distance is only 43km, the ancient trail laid by the Incas winds its way up, down and around the mountains, snaking over three high passes en route. The views of snowy peaks and cloud forest can be stupendous, and walking from one cliff-hugging ruin to the next is a mystical and unforgettable experience.

PERU

> ### LOSING MACHU PICCHU
>
> Everyone wants a piece of Machu Picchu, Peru's showpiece site. Even as thousands of visitors marvel at the site's seemingly untouchable beauty, its overwhelming popularity has placed it on a perilous downhill slide. Scientists have determined that the mountain's slopes are slipping at the rate of 1cm per month, making a catastrophic landslide possible.
>
> While a long-mooted plan to build a cable car to the summit has been scrapped following widespread condemnation from the national and international community, the threat of private interests encroaching on the site continually rears its ugly head. One unbelievable accident saw a crew filming a beer commercial smash a crane into the site's showpiece, the Intihuatana, breaking a large chip off the old block.

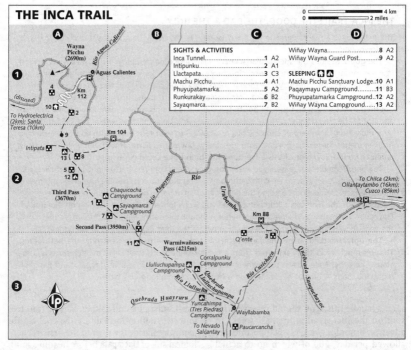

THE INCA TRAIL

SIGHTS & ACTIVITIES		
Inca Tunnel	1	A2
Intipunku	2	A1
Llactapata	3	C3
Machu Picchu	4	A1
Phuyupatamarka	5	A2
Runkurakay	6	B2
Sayaqmarca	7	B2
Wiñay Wayna	8	A2
Wiñay Wayna Guard Post	9	A2
SLEEPING		
Machu Picchu Sanctuary Lodge	10	A1
Paqaymayu Campground	11	B3
Phuyupatamarka Campground	12	A2
Wiñay Wayna Campground	13	A2

Information

You cannot hike the Inca Trail independently. All trekkers must go with a guide in an organized group (see Tours, right). You must also carry your passport (not a photocopy) and ISIC card to present at checkpoints. Don't litter or defecate in the ruins or pick plants in the national park. It is illegal to graffiti any trees or stones en route.

All trekking gear can be rented from outfitters in Cuzco. The trail gets extremely cold at night, so make sure sleeping bags are warm enough. Also remember sturdy shoes, rain gear, insect repellent, sunscreen, a flashlight (with fresh batteries), water-purification tablets, high-calorie snacks and a basic first-aid kit. Take a stash of small Peruvian currency for buying bottled water and snacks along the way, as well as for tipping the guide, cook and porters (around S100, S30 more if your hire a personal porter). You will not regret picking up a walking stick from vendors in Ollantaytambo on the first morning, either.

Tours

Guided tours depart year-round, except during February when the trail is closed for maintenance. However, in the wettest months (December to April), trails can be slippery, campsites muddy and views obscured behind a thick bank of clouds. The dry season from May to September is the most popular and crowded time to go.

The government has introduced a string of reforms in an attempt to prevent further damage to the trail. Registered tour agencies pay increasingly high taxes and have to meet minimum government standards, and their prices have consequently shot up. When choosing a tour company, realize that the cheapest agencies may care less about ecologically sensitive camping and porter welfare. For reputable companies, see p815.

For the classic four-day Inca Trail, expect to pay around S1300 for a reliable company (students with a valid ISIC card pay 50% less for their permit). That price includes a tent, food, porters, guides, a cook, admission to Machu Picchu and return to Cuzco. Tickets must be bought at least 72 hours before the trek; tour

PERU

THE INCA TRAIL: THE GOOD, THE BAD & THE UGLY

The Inca Trail is a rite of passage for many (some say too many), but what's it really like? Here's the lowdown:

The good: Besides the spectacular scenery – jaw-dropping mountain vistas, Inca ruins bathed in eerie morning mists, moss-draped cloud forests and lush lower jungle – there are some unexpected treats along the way. The food is shockingly good considering the circumstances – there is trout, lamb, beef, pork and plenty of veggie options, to name just a few of the borderline gourmet meals served en route. Kudos to the chefs. The camping equipment is in good condition and not of the cheap variety. There is even 'tent service' on some days, where the guides deliver your morning pick-me-up of choice (coca tea, coffee) to your tent along with your wake-up call. And let us not forget the porters, who are clearly not of this earth! Hiring one will incalculably enhance your enjoyment of this adventure; not hiring one could easily ruin it.

The bad: Regardless of season, you are almost guaranteed cold weather at night, bone-chillingly so on some nights, even in summer. With bathrooms almost always a considerable hike away, this makes for some excruciating nights battling the dilemma: to go or not to go? Despite the very nice tents and sleeping bags, the mats are a little skimpy, and you won't forget that you're sleeping on the ground. Egg crate–type mats would serve trekkers better. Although there are well-built bathroom facilities along the way, showers are not part of the equation before the third day. Bring lots of deodorant.

The ugly: It's difficult to find fault with this trek in all aspects except one: the bathrooms. Though much nicer than expected from a facility standpoint, their daily maintenance is atrocious. The experience hovers somewhere between European rock festival, day two, and Bangkok nightclub, 5am. A bucket of cleaner and a hose could go a long way here.

---

agents handle this. You should reserve your spot on the Inca Trail at least six weeks in advance, if not longer. Only 500 permits are allowed per day, 200 of which go to actual tourists (check availability at www.andean travelweb.com/peru/treks/inca_trail_trek _permit_availability.html). Booking several months ahead and reconfirming in advance will avoid delays caused by bottlenecks during high season. Because campsites are allotted in advance, latecomers are more likely to spend the last night several hours short of the final stretch.

The Hike

We'll say it here since nobody seems to ever want to broach the topic: this is not an easy trek. Altitude and seemingly endless climbs, especially on day two, combine to make for a very challenging walk in the mountains. Though altitude sickness does not discriminate between the fit and unfit, the long, steep climbs, generally thin air and knee-seizing steps along the way do pose a challenge for those in less than stellar physical condition. By all means go, but don't expect a breezy Sunday stroll.

Most agencies run minibuses to the start of the trail past the village of Chilca at Piscacucho (Km 82). After crossing the

Río Urubamba and taking care of trail fees and registration formalities, the trail climbs gently alongside the river to the first archaeological site of **Llactapata** before heading south down a side valley of the Río Cusichaca. The trail south leads 7km to the hamlet of **Wayllabamba** (3100m), where you can take a breather to appreciate views of snowy Nevado Verónica (5750m).

You'll cross the Río Llulucha, then climb steeply up along the river. This area is known as **Tres Piedras** (Three Stones), and from here it is a long, very steep 3km climb. The trail eventually emerges on the high, bare mountainside of **Llulluchapampa**, where the flats are dotted with campsites.

From Llulluchupampa, a good path up the left-hand side of the valley climbs for the two-hour ascent to **Warmiwañusca** (4215m), colorfully known as 'Dead Woman's Pass.' This is the highest and most difficult point of the trek, which leaves many a backpacker gasping. From Warmiwañusca, the trail continues down a long, knee-jarringly steep descent to the river, where there are large campsites at **Paqaymayu** (3500m). The trail crosses the river over a small footbridge and climbs right toward **Runkurakay**, a round ruin with superb views about an hour's walk above the river.

Above Runkurakay, the trail climbs to a false summit before continuing past two small lakes to the top of the second pass at 3950m, which has views of the snowcapped Cordillera Vilcabamba. The trail descends to the ruin of **Sayaqmarka**, a tightly constructed complex perched on a small mountain spur with incredible views, then continues downward crossing a tributary of the Río Aobamba.

The trail leads on across an Inca causeway and up again through cloud forest and an **Inca tunnel** carved into the rock to the third pass at 3670m. Soon afterward, you'll reach the beautiful, well-restored ruin of **Phuyupatamarka** (3600m above sea level). The site contains a beautiful series of ceremonial baths with water running through them.

From Phuyupatamarka, the trail takes a dizzying dive into the cloud forest below, following an incredibly well-engineered flight of many hundreds of Inca steps, affectionately known as the Gringo Killer. After passing through a tunnel, the trail eventually zigzags its way down to **Wiñay Wayna**, where a trekker's lodge sells hot showers, hot meals, cold beer and massages for those who want to pay a bit extra.

From the **Wiñay Wayna guard post**, the trail contours around through cliff-hanging cloud forest for about one hour and a half to reach **Intipunku** (Sun Gate) – where you may get lucky enough to catch your first glimpse of majestic Machu Picchu as you wait for the sun to rise over the mountaintops.

The final triumphant descent takes 30 minutes. Backpacks are not allowed into the ruins, and guards will pounce upon you to check your pack and to stamp your trail permit. Trekkers generally arrive before the morning trainloads of tourists, so you can enjoy the exhilarated exhaustion of reaching your goal without having to push through as many crushing crowds.

CENTRAL HIGHLANDS

Far off the Gringo Trail, the central Peruvian Andes are ripe for exploration. Traditions linger longer here, with delightful colonial towns among the least spoiled in the entire Andean chain. A combination of geographical isolation, harsh mountain terrain and terrorist unrest (the Sendero Luminoso was born in Ayacucho) made travel difficult for decades. Over the past decade a more stable political situation and improved transportation infrastructure are making travelers' lives easier. But visiting the region is still challenging enough, with ear-popping passes and wearisome bus journeys.

AYACUCHO

☎ 066 / pop 151,000

As the epicenter of Peru's once horrendous battle with domestic terrorism, the fascinating colonial city of Ayacucho (elevation 2750m) was off limits to travelers for the better part of the '80s and '90s – and that's part of its allure now. This modern city tucked away in the Central Andes clings fiercely to its traditional past – its Semana Santa celebrations are the country's most dazzling and famous. In town, colonial quirks abound, from hidden interior courtyards to a list of ornate 16th-, 17th- and 18th-century churches peppered about (33 in all).

Information

BCP (Portal Unión 28) Has a Visa/Mastercard ATM.
Clínica de la Esperanza (☎ 31-7436; Av Independencia 355; 🕑 8am-8pm) English spoken.
Hueco Internet (Portal Constitución 9; per hr S1.50; 🕑 7am-10pm Mon-Sat, 10am-3pm Sun)
iPerú (☎ 31-8305; Portal Municipal 45; 🕑 8:30am-7:30pm Mon-Sat, to 2:30pm Sun) For tourist information.
Policía de Turismo (☎ 31-5845; 2 de Mayo 103) Handles emergencies.
Serpost (Asamblea 293) Post office near the plaza.
Urpillay Tours (☎ 31-5074; urpillaytours@hotmail.com; Portal Constitución 9) Can provide English tours to nearby sites.
Wily Tours (☎ 31-4075; 9 de Diciembre 107) Good for travel logistics; also does local tours.

Sights

The town center has a 17th-century **cathedral**, along with a dozen other elaborate **churches** from the past 300 years, and several old **mansions** near the main plaza. Be sure to check out the striking **Templo de Santo Domingo** (9 de Diciembre, Cuadra 2), with its triple-arched belfry on the left side of the facade, where heretics were said to be punished during the Holy Inquisition.

Museo de Arte Popular (Portal Unión 28; 🕑 10am-1pm Mon-Fri) showcases Ayacucho's folkcraft specialties. To inspect Wari ceramics, **Museo Arqueológico Hipólito Unanue** (☎ 31-2056; Av Independencia 509; admission S2.50; 🕑 9am-1pm &

INCA ROADS LESS TRAVELED

Let's face it: the Inca Trail is being loved to death, and books up months in advance. Without a permit, you're SOL. But there are alternative routes to reach Machu Picchu and cover Inca ground. For some recommended trekking agencies, see p815.

Prices and availability for all of these trips depend upon demand. All below take in Machu Picchu with the exception of Ausangate:

■ The 80km, five- to six-day Ausangate jaunt takes in hot springs, turquoise lakes, Andean villages, glaciers and desert terrain over the Cordillera Vilacota mountain range culminating in the 6384m Nevado Ausangate. Quechua festivals are common in these remote areas, tourists are not.

■ Explorer Hiram Bingham documented the extensive, partially jungle-covered Inca ruins of Choquequirau two years before he 'discovered' Machu Picchu. Built on a mountain spur 1700m above the Río Apurímac, this strenuous trek varies from four to 11 days depending on the route.

■ The Valle Lares trek spends three days walking between rural Andean villages in the Sacred Valley, past hot springs, archaeological sites, lush lagoons and gorges. Trekkers finish by taking the train to Aguas Calientes from Ollantaytambo. This is more of a cultural trek, not a technical one, though the highest mountain pass (4450m) is nothing to sneeze at.

■ The snow-covered peaks of Humantay and Salcantay are the backdrop for the four- to seven-day Salcantay trek, which offers two possible routes, both around 55km. The Mollepata–Huayllabamba route tops out at 4880m and can link up with the Inca Trail (but you'll need a permit) while the Mollepata–Santa Teresa route heads through La Playa and dumps you in Aguas Calientes.

For more details on most of the above treks, see Lonely Planet's *Trekking in the Central Andes*.

3-5pm Tue-Sun) is at the university, over 1km from the center along Av Independencia. The university library has a free exhibit of mummies and skulls.

Sprawling for several kilometers along a cactus-forested roadside are the extensive ruins of **Wari** (Huari; admission S3; 9am-5pm), the capital of the Wari empire, which predated the Incas by five centuries. Beyond lies the interesting village of **Quinua**, where a huge monument and small museum mark the site of the Battle of Ayacucho (1824). This small *pueblo* (town) is famous for its unique ceramic handicrafts and makes for nice, picturesque strolling. Wari is 20km and Quinua 34km northeast of Ayacucho. *Colectivos* and *combis* go to Quinua (S3.50, one hour) via the ruins from Paradero Magdalena at the traffic circle at the east end of Cáceres in Ayacucho. Travel agencies in town offer Spanish-language tours (S25).

Festivals & Events

Ayacucho's **Semana Santa**, held the week before Easter, is Peru's finest religious festival. Celebrations begin the Friday before Palm Sunday and continue at a fevered pitch for 10 days until Easter Sunday. The Friday before Palm Sunday is marked by a procession in honor of La Virgen de los Dolores (Our Lady of Sorrows), during which it's customary to inflict 'sorrows' on bystanders by firing pebbles with slingshots. Every day sees another solemn yet colorful procession, culminating in an all-night party before Easter Sunday, with its dawn fireworks display.

Sleeping

Prices skyrocket during Semana Santa.

Hotel La Crillonesa (31-2350; www.crillones _hotel@hotmail.com; Nazareno 165; s/d S30/60, without bathroom S15/35;) Full of art and handicrafts, this budget choice dishes out hot water and offers a small cafe.

Hostal Tres Máscaras (31-2921; hotel_tres mascaras@hotmail.com; Tres Máscaras 194; s/d S30/45, without bathroom S18/30;) The undermaintained but still pleasant open-air stone courtyard with a welcoming talking parrot (*¡Hola!*) ups the character ante here. There's hot water, cable TV and a tiny pool during the hottest months.

La Colmena Hotel (☎ 31-1318; cesarde95@hotmail .com; Cuzco 140; s/d/tr S35/50/80, without bathroom S20/40/50; 🖳) If you can put up with the totally aloof owner and the staff's inability to listen, this long-standing hotel has courtyard balconies, tasteful rooms with supersized bathrooms and lush interior.

Hotel Samary (☎ 31-8575; hotelsamary@hotmail.com; Callao 329; s/d S36/52, without bathroom S22/30; 🖳) A panoramic rooftop terrace, luggage storage, 24-hour hot water, cable TV in most rooms and even DIY ironing makes this cheapie good value.

Hotel El Mesón (☎ 31-2938; www.hotelelmeson.net; Arequipa 273; s/d incl breakfast S35/45; 🖳) The arched stone exteriors of this good-value hotel offset the simple but well-kept rooms. There's hot water and cable TV, too.

Hostal Marcos (☎ 31-6867; 9 de Diciembre 143; s/d incl breakfast S45/70) A dozen spotless rooms, with 24-hour hot water and cable TV, are sequestered away at the end of an alley. It's often booked, so call ahead.

Hotel Yañez (☎ 31-4918; Cáceres 1210; s/d incl breakfast S50/70; 🖳) Subtly overpriced, but rooms are very spacious with comfy mattresses, cable TV and hot showers. Staff is friendly, too. There's a noisy downstairs casino, but we slept like a baby.

Eating

Regional specialties include *puca picante* (a curry-like potato stew in peppery peanut sauce, served with rice and a side of *chicharrones*). The colonial courtyard inside Centro Turístico Cultural San Cristóbal is full of travel-friendly bars and cafes.

La Pradera (Lima 147, Int 7; mains S2-12; 🕑 closed dinner Sun) An all-vegetarian menu is served here.

Niñachay (28 de Julio, 178; Centro Turístico Cultural San Cristóbal; menú S7, mains S5-17) It's all quality at this lovely courtyard cafe run by a travel savvy Peruvian-Ukrainian couple. It's memorable for local specialties like *puca picante* (weekends only) and *chorizo ayacuchano*; or go for trout, pasta and sandwich staples. It's all good!

Chifa Wanlin (Asamblea 257; mains S6-22) This frenzied *chifa* is always packed. Fans of sweet and sour will be happy with the *pollo tamarindo*.

Wallpa Suwa (Garcilaso de la Vega 240; mains S9.50-24; 🕑 dinner) Great chicken and actual customer service keeps this nicer-than-most *pollería* on the hot list. It's always busy and there's a piano man on weekends.

El Nino (9 de Diciembre 205; mains S10-28; 🕑 dinner) In a beautiful colonial mansion overlooking Santo Domingo temple, chronic carnivores can sink their fangs into succulent *parrillas* (grills), or pizza and pasta.

Drinking

Chill Out Café (Arequipa 298; 🕑 closed Sun) A restaurant-sized bar that's cocktails and wine only, set to an '80s soundtrack. Try the sweet Embrujo Humanguino, a creamy dose of liquid love.

Taberna Magia Negra (9 de Diciembre 293) Eclectic art on the walls and umbrellas hanging from the ceiling characterize this low-lit bar-gallery, Ayacucho's best.

Shopping

Ayacucho is famous for folk crafts. The **Galería Artesanales Shosaku Nagare** (cnr Maravillas & Quinua; 🕑 10am-8:30pm) is a good place to start.

Getting There & Away

The **airport** (PYH; 🕑 31-2088) is 4km from the town center (taxis cost S8). **LC Busre** (☎ 31-6012; 9 de Dicembre 160) has three flights daily to/from Lima.

Buses utilize a bewildering array of terminals. For Lima (S30 to S90, nine hours), there are **Empresa Molina** (☎ 31-9989; 9 de Diciembre 473) and **Cruz del Sur** (☎ 31-2813; Cáceres 1264). **Ormeño** (☎ 31-2495; Libertad 257) goes to Ica (S25, eight hours).

For Huancayo (S25 to S30, 10 to 12 hours), Empresa Molina is preferred, though if you want to continue from there to Pucallpa (S75, 30 hours), you're better off on **Turismo Central** (☎ 31-7873; Copac 499). Take note: this is a tough 250km trip, not for the faint of heart.

For Cuzco (S45 to S60, 22 hours), **Celtur** (☎ 31-3194; Pasaje Cáceres 174) has the most modern fleet and the recommended day departure time of 7am. It's a long and rough trip, but the journey can be broken at Andahuaylas (S25, 10 hours).

HUANCAYO

☎ 064 / pop 323,000

Upon first glance, there is nothing much to Huancayo, the largest city in the central highlands, its frenzied and crowded streets not seemingly dissimilar from any other workhorse Peruvian town. But despite its rambunctious and chaotic nature, Huancayo has its charms and travelers often warm up to them and hang around longer than planned. There

PERU

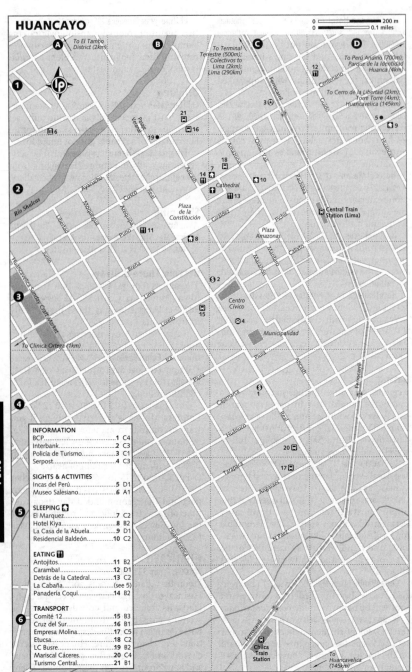

HUANCAYO

are Spanish classes to take, some 400 fiestas per year to immerse yourself in, and loads of trekking, mountain biking and cultural tours to experience in the surrounding highlands.

Information

Internet cafes are along Giráldez. BCP, Interbank and other ATMs are on Real.

Clínica Ortega (☎ 23-2921; Carrión 1124; ⏲ 24hr) For emergencies.

Policía de Turismo (☎ 21-9851; Ferrocarril 580)

Serpost (Plaza Huamamarca 350) Postal services.

Sights & Activities

Museo Salesiano (☎ 24-7763; Salesian School; admission S5; ⏲ hours vary) has Amazonian fauna, pottery and archaeology exhibits. From the center, walk 2km northeast on Giráldez to **Cerro de la Libertad**, which has good city views, then continue 2km more to the eroded sandstone towers of **Torre Torre**. About 5km from the center in the San Antonio neighborhood, **Parque de la Identidad Huanca** is a fanciful park full of stone statues and miniature buildings that supposedly represent the area's culture.

Courses

Incas del Perú (☎ 22-3303; www.incasdelperu.org; Giráldez 652) arranges Spanish lessons, which include meals and accommodations with a local family from S720 per week. Lessons can be combined with other classes, such as dancing, cooking, gourd carving or *zampoña* (panpipes).

Tours

Incas del Perú also offers guided day and cycling and horse-riding tours (S135). Mountain-bike rental costs S45 per day. They can also arrange longer mountain homestays and cloud-forest treks.

Festivals & Events

There are hundreds of fiestas in Huancayo and surrounding villages – supposedly one almost every day somewhere in the Río Mantaro valley! Huancayo's **Semana Santa** processions leading up to Easter are famous.

Sleeping

Residencial Baldeón (☎ 23-1634; Amazonas 543; r without bathroom per person S10) It's barely a step above camping, but shoestringers won't balk at the price. There's hot water, a sunny courtyard and not much else.

ourpick La Casa de la Abuela (☎ 22-3303; www .incasdelperu.com; Giráldez 691; dm/s/d S20/50/60, s/d/tr without bathroom S40/50/75, all incl breakfast; 🖳) A wonderfully charismatic hostel, full of well-worn Andean furniture, antique radios and one of the cutest families you ever did see. A garden, talking parrot, scraggly pooch, hot water, laundry, and multilingual book exchange round out the fun here. Rates include *actual* coffee for breakfast, but not internet. The hospitable owner, Lucio Hurtado, is almost singlehandedly responsible for putting Huancayo on the tourism map.

Perú Andino (☎ 22-3956; www.geocities.com/peru andino_1; Pasaje San Antonio 113; d S60, s/d without bathroom S30/60, all incl breakfast) There is a bit of a linguistic bait-and-switch happening at this traveler favorite – it's all English on the website and emails, but not a lick upon arrival. Still, it has been run by a talkative older couple since 1978 and offers all the comforts of home, though it's a bit northeast of the center.

Hotel Kiya (☎ 21-4955; kiyahotel@terra.com.pe; Giráldez 107; s/d/tr S58/68/80; 🖳) For its location on the plaza, it's hard to beat this aged option, boasting hot water, wi-fi, elevators and room service. Needs a spruce up, though.

El Marquez (☎ 21-9026; www.elmarquezhuancayo .com; Puno 294; s/d S100/140; 🖳) A midrange step up for those seeking some extra comfort after bumpy mountain travel. The rooms aren't as artsy as the lobby, but feature all the standard mod cons.

Eating & Drinking

Panadería Coqui (Puno 296; desserts S2.50-5, sandwiches S4-10) Excellent sandwiches, desserts, fine wine and espresso – what more could you want? Prompt service? Forget it.

La Cabaña (Giráldez 652; meals S5-25) The house *calientito* (a warm street brew made with herbs and vodka or *pisco*), fantastic pizza, al dente pasta and juicy grills fuel a party crowd of locals and travelers alike. *Folklórico* bands perform Thursday to Saturday nights.

Antojitos (Puno 599; pizza S20-32, mains S6-28) Desperate housewives, awkward optometrists, the town's hot-to-trot – it's all here, converging on this cozy restaurant-bar for live music nightly, pitchers of sangria and excellent bar grub. Don't miss it.

Caramba! (Jr Guido 459; mains S9.50-23.50) Perhaps a bit upscale for this book (but only just), the best *parrillada* in the central highlands offers Argentine, Brazilian or Peruvian beef, all

PERU

cooked to perfection. Besides, the ¼ rotisserie chicken goes for S9.50.

Detrás de la Catedral (Ancash 335; mains S10.90-26.90) Cozy spot equally popular with gringos and locals, all of whom come for the excellent trout *tiradito,* extra-charred burgers, and a long list of other Peruvian specialties, all identified by helpful colorful photos on the menu.

Getting There & Away

AIR

The airport (JAU) is an astonishing 50km north of town in Jauja (taxi S30 to S35). **LC Busre** (☎ 25-9415; Ayacucho 322) operates flights to/from Lima on Tuesdays, Thursdays and Saturdays.

BUS & COLECTIVO

Services vary depending on the season and demand. Some smaller long-distance buses may use the **Terminal Terrestre**, 500m north of Ayacucho.

Lima (S25 to S80, six to seven hours) is most frequently and comfortably serviced by **Etucsa** (☎ 23-6524; Puno 220) and **Cruz del Sur** (☎ 22-3367; Ayacucho 251). There's also **Mariscal Cáceres** (☎ 21-6635; Real 1241) and **Turismo Central** (☎ 22-3128; Ayacucho 274). **Comité 12** (☎ 23-3250-435681; Loreto 439) has faster *colectivo* taxis to Lima (S70, five hours).

For the rough road to Ayacucho (S28, eight to 10 hours), **Empresa Molina** (☎ 21-4902; Angaraes 334) has morning and overnight departures.

Turismo Central has (packed and uncomfortable) buses north to Huánuco (S25, seven hours) and Pucallpa (S50, 18 hours). All of the above leave from offices in the town center.

Colectivos to Lima (S50, five hours) depart from the corner of Castilla and Mariategui, 2km north of the center, when full. Ask for Pedro Laura, the only English speaker.

TRAIN

Unfortunately, train-buff favorite **Ferrocarril Central Andino** (☎ 01-226-6363; www.ferroviasperu.com.pe), which reaches a head-spinning elevation of 4829m, has been scaled back to departures at long-holiday weekends only (18 departures were scheduled for 2009), with hopes of a weekly train by 2010. Fares begin from S180 to S260 return for transportation and train meals only, and from S600 to S900 including meals and accommodations in Huancayo. The best spot to buy tickets in Lima is **Teleticket** (www.teleticket.com.pe), which operates in some Metro and Wong supermarkets.

Obviously, by the time you read this, the rail situation is likely to have changed. Check ahead.

NORTH COAST

The unruly northern coast is flush with enough ancient chronicles to fill a library of memoirs. Animated colonial towns doff their collective *campesino* hats to all who make the effort to visit. Playful seaside resorts beckon modern-day sun worshippers to their shores, while gnarly breaks have had surfers board-waxing lyrical for years. If you're heading north to Ecuador, the further you go, the better the weather gets.

TRUJILLO
☎ 044 / pop 682,800

Francisco Pizarro's Trujillo marks a notable change from other northern Peruvian cities. Here colonization *has* left an indelible mark, from the immense and beautiful Plaza de Armas to the little architectural earmarks that pepper many of the city's colorful colonial constructions. Founded by Pizarro in 1534 and named after his hometown in Spain, Trujillo quickly grew into northern Peru's biggest city, though it had been

---

DETOUR

Just 5km from Huánuco, along the long route between Pucallpa and Lima, you'll find one of Peru's oldest Andean archaeological sites: the **Temple of Kotosh** (admission S3; ⏱ 10am-5pm), aka Temple of the Crossed Hands.

If you want to break your journey here, two decent, if a little noisy, options are **Hostal Huánuco** (☎ 062-51-2050; Huánuco 777; s/d S30/35, without bathroom S15/30), an old-fashioned mansion with mismatched tiled floors, a lush garden and walls covered with art and newspaper clippings; and **Hotel Cuzco** (☎ 062-51-7653; Huánuco 614; s/d/tr S40/50/60; 🖵), a dated hotel with a cafeteria and clean, bare but good-sized rooms with cable TV and scorching showers.

ground zero for several civilizations prior to the Spanish. Nearby, 1500-year-old Moche pyramids, Las Huacas del Sol y de la Luna, and the ancient Chimú adobe metropolis of Chan Chan (see p839) loom over the desert-scape like fallen heroes, both testaments to once great empires, although built on a foundation of sand and mud.

If you want to take in the ancient culture but not the bustling city, base yourself in the nearby surfing hamlet of Huanchaco (p840), once a tranquil fishing village, now a full-on sea and sun affair.

Information

BCP (Gamarra 562)
Clínica Americano-Peruano (☎ 24-2400; Mansiche 802) The best clinic.
InterWeb (Pizarro 721; per hr S1.50; ⏲ 9am-10pm) Internet access.
iPerú (☎ 29-4561; Almagro 640; ⏲ 8am-7pm Mon-Sat, to 2pm Sun) Tourist information.
Lavanderías Unidas (Pizarro 683; per kg S8; ⏲ 9am-8:30pm) Laundry.
Policía de Turismo (☎ 29-1705; Independencia 572)

Sights

An 18th-century **cathedral** with a famous basilica fronts the Plaza de Armas.

Many other elegant colonial churches and mansions have wrought-iron grillwork and pastel coloring that typify Trujillo. **Casa de la Emancipación** (Pizarro 610), **Palacio Iturregui** (Pizarro 688) and **Casa Ganoza Chopitea** (Independencia 630), with its art gallery and two lions standing guard out front, all deserve a look.

Museo Cassinelli (Nicolás de Piérola 601; admission S7; ⏲ 9am-1pm & 2-6pm Mon-Sat) has an excellent ar-chaeological collection – in the same building as a Repsol gas station! The university-run **Museo de Arqueológia** (Junín 682; admission S5; ⏲ 8am-2:30pm Mon-Fri), in the restored Casa Risco, has artifacts from La Huaca de la Luna.

Tours

Colonial Tours (☎ 29-1034; Independencia 616), at-tached to Hostal Colonial, offers the cheap-est multilingual guided tours of nearby archaeological sites (S25).

Festivals & Events

The *marinera* dance and *caballos de paso* (horseback dressage displays) are highlights of many festivals.

La Fiesta de la Marinera The biggest of its kind, held in late January.
La Fiesta de la Primavera Held during the last week of September, with Peru's most famous parade and much dancing and entertainment.

Sleeping

Many travelers prefer the beach vibe in Huanchaco (p840).

El Conde de Arce (☎ 29-1607; Independencia 577; dm/s/d S20/30/45) Rickety hardwood floors and sink-ing mattresses characterize this weathered, courtyard-style budget inn with a dilapidated garden, right in the center.

Hostal El Ensueño (☎ 24-2583; Junín 336; s/d S40/60) Cramped quarters with mismatched door sizes are at first off-putting, but nice rooms with large bathrooms, hot water and cable TV keep this a decent budget contender.

Hotel Turismo Inn (☎ 24-3411; hotelturismo@speedy .com.pe; Gamarra 747; s/d/tr S45/69/87) Aged relic or retro chic? This decent option offers kilometer-long hallways, embroidered bed-spreads and carpeted elevators.

Hostal Colonial (☎ 25-8261; hostcolonialtruji@hot mail.com; Independencia 618; s/d S55/85; 🖳) A great location near the Plaza de Armas, this taste-fully renovated colonial mansion has pleasant courtyard, garden and restaurant with great breakfast sandwiches. Cozy rooms have hot showers (though cramped bathrooms), and some have balcony views.

Eating

Jugería San Agustín (Bolívar 526; sandwiches S2.50-6) You will salivate at the thought of your sand-wich experience at this frantically popular juice bar for years to come. A real treat.

Museo Café (Independencia 713; sandwiches S3.50-8; ⏲ closed Sun) Portions are small but made up for in antiquated atmosphere at this cafe-bar steeped in old hardwoods and aged undertones.

Mar Picante (Husares de Junín 412; ceviche S12-22; ⏲ lunch) Locals in the know pack this sea-food house for Trujillo's best *ceviche* and fish *chicharrones*. Service is swift and friendly.

Chifa Ah Chau (Gamarra 769; mains S13.50-17.50) The private curtained booths surrounding each table at this Chino-Peruvian place feel a bit like going to a culinary peep show. Huge portions can realistically serve three.

El Uruguayo (Larco 1094; mains S15-28) The greasy fries are the only downside to this carnivo-rous mainstay that serves up Uruguayan-style

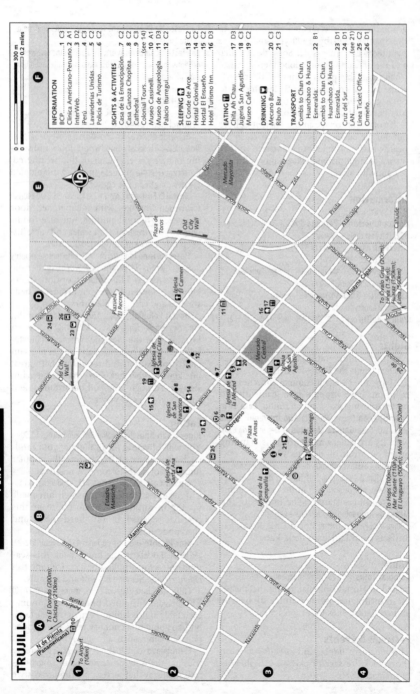

TRUJILLO

0 — 300 m
0 — 0.2 miles

DETOUR

Between Lima and Trujillo along Peru's northern coast you'll find two archaeological ruins worth seeing, though neither sits near any remarkable towns to visit. About 25km inland from Barranca lie the monumental ruins of **Caral** (admission adult/student S11.20/3.60; ☼ 9am-5pm), part of South America's oldest civilization, arising simultaneously with Egypt, India and China. **Proyecto Especial Arqueológico Caral** (☎ 01-495-1515; www.caralperu.gob.pe) has information and runs full-day tours from Lima (S160). Most coastal buses can drop you off at road marker Km 187 north of Lima, from where *colectivos* to Caral (S3.50) depart from the Mercado de Supe.

Shrouded in mystery, the well-preserved ruins at **Sechín** (admission adult/student S6/4; ☼ 8am-6pm), 5km outside Casma, date from 1600 BC. The outside walls of the main temple are covered with gruesomely realistic bas-relief carvings of warriors and captives being vividly eviscerated. Take a *mototaxi* (S3) from Casma, which is served by **Tepsa** (☎ 01-98-901-5381; Huarmey 356) from Lima and **Yungay Express** (☎ 94-360-6837; Ormeño 139) from Huaraz.

---

chops charred to your liking on tables as thick as mutant rib eyes.

Drinking

Mecano Bar (Gamarra 574; admission S10; ☼ 9pm-late) According to iPerú, this is where 'all the important people go.' You know the rest.

Hops (cnr Husares de Junín & Venezuela) Tired of Cusqueña yet? This wild, bilevel microbrewery with live music does six brews in five sizes up to a monster 3.5L that serves a small army.

Ributo Bar (Plaza de Armas, cnr Pizarro & Almagro; ☼ Wed-Sat) A popular nightspot on the plaza, with live rock Thursday to Saturday.

Getting There & Away

AIR

The **airport** (TRU; ☎ 46-4013) is 10km northwest of town. Take a taxi (S15 to S18) or a bus bound for Huanchaco and walk 1km. **LAN** (☎ 22-1469; Pizarro 340) has daily flights to/from Lima.

BUS

Buses are often full, so purchase seats in advance and double-check from where your bus leaves.

Major companies include the following:

Cruz del Sur (☎ 20-0555; Amazonas 447) To Lima (S34 to S88, nine hours).

El Dorado (☎ 29-1778; Nicolás de Piérola 1070) has rudimentary buses to Máncora (S25 to S45, eight hours) and Tumbes (S25 to S45, 10 hours).

Línea booking office (☎ 24-5181; cnr San Martín & Obregoso; ☼ 8am-9pm Mon-Sat); terminal (☎ 29-6820; América Sur 2857) Goes to Piura (S35 to S45, six hours), Cajamarca (S20 to S45, nine hours), Chiclayo (S13, 3½ hours). Buses for Lima (S40 to S110, eight hours) and Huaraz (S35 to S60, nine hours) are mostly overnight.

Móvil Tours (☎ 28-6538; América Sur 3955) Comfy overnight buses to Lima (S75, eight hours), Huaraz (S35 to S60, eight hours), Chachapoyas (S60, 13 hours) and Tarapoto (S80 to S110, 16 hours).

Ormeño (☎ 25-9782; Ejército 233) Overnight buses to Lima (S35, eight hours) and Tumbes (S60, 11 hours), as well as direct international services to Ecuador, Colombia and Venezuela.

Getting Around

White-yellow-and-orange B *combis* to La Huaca Esmeralda, Chan Chan and Huanchaco run along España past the corners of Ejército and Industrial every few minutes. Buses for La Esperanza go northwest along the Panamericana to La Huaca Arco Iris. *Combis* labeled C.M. or S.D. for Las Huacas del Sol y de la Luna depart from Óvalo Grau. These buses are worked by professional thieves – keep valuables hidden, and watch your bags carefully. Fares run S1.30 to S1.50.

AROUND TRUJILLO

The Moche and the Chimú are the two cultures that have left the greatest mark on the Trujillo area, but they are by no means the only ones – more new sites are being excavated each year.

A **combined ticket** (adult/student S11/6), valid for two days, can be purchased for Chan Chan and Huaca Esmeralda and Huaca Arco Iris, two smaller temples in the area. All are open 9am to 4pm daily.

Chan Chan

Built around AD 1300, Chan Chan must once have been a dazzling site. As you approach along the Panamericana, it's impossible not to be impressed by the vast area of crumbling mud walls stretching away into the

PERU

AROUND TRUJILLO

distance. This site once formed the largest pre-Columbian city in the Americas and the largest adobe city in the world.

At the height of the Chimú empire, Chan Chan contained about 10,000 structures, from royal palaces lined with precious metals to huge burial mounds. Although the Incas conquered the Chimú around 1460, the city was not looted until the gold-hungry Spanish arrived, and *guaqueros* finished their work.

The Chimú capital contained nine subcities, or royal compounds. The restored **Tschudi complex** is near the entrance area by the **site museum** on the main road about 500m before the Chan Chan turnoff. Tschudi's walls once stood over 10m high with impressive friezes of fish, waves and sea life. A king was once buried in the mausoleum with a treasure trove of ceremonial objects for the afterlife – and plenty of sacrificial companions.

Las Huacas del Sol y de la Luna

These **Moche temples** (www.huacadelaluna.org.pe; admission & guided tour adult/student S11/6; ☼ 9am-4pm),

---

WARNING!

It is dangerous to walk along Buenos Aires beach between Chan Chan and Huanchaco. Travelers have also been attacked while visiting archaeological sites. Go in a group, stay on the main paths and don't visit late in the day.

10km southeast of Trujillo, are 700 years older than Chan Chan.

The **Huaca del Sol** is Peru's largest pre-Columbian structure; 140 million adobe bricks were used to build it. Originally the pyramid had several levels, connected by steep stairs, huge ramps and walls sloping at 77 degrees to the horizon. Now it resembles a giant sand pile, but its sheer size makes it an awesome sight nonetheless.

The smaller **Huaca de la Luna** is riddled with rooms containing ceramics, precious metals and the beautiful polychrome friezes for which the Moche were famous. Their custom of 'burying' old temples under new ones has facilitated preservation, and archaeologists are still peeling away the layers. A new museum is under construction here.

Keep an eye out for Peruvian hairless dogs that hang out here. The body temperature of these dogs is higher than that of normal dogs, and they've traditionally been used as body-warmers for people with arthritis!

HUANCHACO

☎ 044 / pop 18,000

Once upon a time, the quaint fishing village of Huanchaco, 12km northwest of Trujillo, must have been quite a scene, what with all those high-ended, cigar-shaped *totora* boats called *caballitos* (little horses) on which fishermen paddle beyond the beakers and all. Today a few remain, but surfers and other bohemians have taken over Huanchaco and turned it into a less nocturnally oriented Máncora.

For those seeking more sun and sand between their archaeological visits in the Trujillo area, Huanchaco offers a laid-back vibe that's only disrupted by armies of bleached-blond surfers (December to April) and packs of wild Peruvian holidaymakers (weekends).

Activities

Rent surfboards and wet suits (per day S20 to S25) from several places along the main drag, including the **Wave** (☎ 46-2547; La Rivera 606).

Sleeping

You'll find budget lodgings all over town. If there's a particular restaurant or hangout whose vibe you're digging, chances are they have rooms, too.

Un Lugar (☎ 957-7170; unlugarsurfschool@hotmail .com; Atahualpa 210; dm S10) Part surf school, part surf camp. Housing is in suspect bamboo treehouse-style bungalows and there's laundry and a surf library. Lessons run S50 for two hours.

Hostal Naylamp (☎ 46-1022; www.hostalnaylamp .com; Larco 1420; campsite per person with/without tent S10/13, dms/s/d S15/30/50; 🖳) A dream budget seascape with a cafe, book exchange, luggage storage, hammocks and patios with sunset views. The issue is its location on the extreme end of the action.

Hospedaje Los Ficus de Huanchaco (☎ 46-1719; Los Ficus 215; r per person S15) This spotless house offers hot showers, breakfast on request and kitchen privileges. It's like stealing at these prices.

Chill Out (☎ 46-2320; www.chilledperu.com; Los Pinos 324; dm/d S15/35; 🖳 🍸) A Scottish takeover and makeover has turned this guesthouse, formerly in shambles, into extraordinary value. Simple but clean rooms complimented by wi-fi (with laptops for use), TV/DVD, a baby pool and a late-night cocktail bar/ restaurant featuring Indian curries.

La Casa Suiza (☎ 46-1825; www.casasuiza.com; Los Pinos 308; dm S15, s/d without bathroom S20/30; 🖳) A cozy, rock-walled home with artistically inclined rooms, plenty of plants and a rowdy rooftop and BBQ patio.

Huankarute Hospedaje (☎ 46-1705; www.hostal huankarute.com; La Rivera 233; s/d incl breakfast from S85/105; 🖳 🍸) The little beach resort that could. Top-floor doubles have sea views and bathtubs. Service is friendly and the pool is ever so inviting.

Eating

Huanchaco has oodles of seafood restaurants on the beach – the weak-stomached should be weary.

Otra Cosa (Larco 921; dishes S3.50-11) This wonderful vegetarian spot dishes up falafel, burritos and colorful daily specials, then throws in internet, massages, bike rental and a Fair Trade shop.

El Generoso (cnr Libertad & Grau; items S4-7; 🕒 dinner) An extensive burger menu.

Mochica (☎ 997-3635; cnr Larco & Independencia; meals S12-32) This Trujillo transplant is tops in town for fresh seafood.

Getting There & Away

Combis will take you from España at Industrial in Trujillo to Huanchaco's beachfront (S1.50). A taxi costs S10 to S15.

CHICLAYO

☎ 074 / pop 738,000

Lively Chiclayo saw its share of Spanish missionaries in the 16th century, though never its share of *conquistadors*, but what it lacks in colonial beauty, it more than makes up for in thrilling archaeological sites. The Moche, the Sícan and the Chimú all thrived in the area, making this well-rounded city an excellent base for exploring their ancient pyramids, tombs and artifacts.

Information

Internet cafes abound. Several banks are on the 600 block of Balta.

BCP (Balta 630) Has a 24-hour Visa ATM.

Clínica del Pacífico (☎ 23-6378; Ortiz 420) For medical attention.

iPerú (☎ 20-5703; Saenz Peña 838; 🕒 9am-7pm Mon-Sat, to 1pm Sun) Tourist info next to the police.

Lavandería Biolav (☎ 60-5297; 7 de Enero 638; per kg S5) Includes ironing and delivery.

Policía de Turismo (☎ 49-0892; Saenz Peña 830)

Sights & Activities

Don't miss the fascinating **Mercado de los Brujos** (Witches' Market), next to the sprawling Mercado Modelo, which houses a superstore of shamanistic herbs, elixirs and sagely curiosities. Need a love potion or a cure for warts? Herbalist and *brujo* (witch doctor) stalls sit side by side, vending dried herbs, bones, claws, hooves and other weird and wonderful healing charms.

PERU

During summer the coastal beaches of Pimentel and Santa Rosa are popular for **surfing**, especially at El Faro.

Tours

Moche Tours (☎ 22-4637; 7 de Enero 638; ☺ 8am-1pm & 4-8pm) offers daily tours in English and Spanish.

Sleeping

Hospedaje San Lucas (☎ 49-9269; Aguirre 412; s/d S15/30) Elementary, but trim and tidy with small artistic touches to liven things up a bit. This is the usual backpacker accommodation of choice.

Katuwira Lodge (☎ 76-1989; www.katuwira.com; campsite/r per person incl meals S30/50) A 20-minute walk south of Pimentel at Playa Las Rocas, this mystical beachside bamboo hangout sprawls. Pyramid-shaped bungalows have sea views. Seven languages spoken.

Hostal Amigos (☎ 22-6237; hostalamigos@hotmail.com; Cuglievan 616; s/d S40/60; 🖳) By far the nicest and friendliest of the budget choices, with large, bright rooms that are well kept and smartly appointed. Popular with the Peace Corps.

Hotel Paraíso (☎ 22-2070; www.hotelesparaiso.com.pe; San José 787; s/d/tr from S65/75/90; 🖳) Remarkable value, especially if you forgo breakfast. Rooms are small but tidy with great showers and all the mod cons of higher-priced options. A friendly staff and cute cafe only add to the niceties.

Eating & Drinking

Pizzería Venecia (Balta 413; pizzas S7-36; ☺ dinner Mon-Sat) Legions of locals hone in on this pizza joint for pies in five sizes and a soundtrack that teeters with the Bee Gees one minute, totters with R.E.M. the next.

Restaurant Romana (Balta 512; mains S9-23) If you can't find something on this dizzying menu, you're on a hunger strike.

Hebron (Balta 605; mains S9-23; ☺ 24hr) This flashy, fun restaurant with plush orange seating draws an eclectic crowd for three meals a day.

Ferrocol (Las Américas 168; ceviche S12-20) This hole-in-the-wall is worth a trip: chef Lucho prepares some of the best *ceviche* in Chiclayo.

Bali Lounge/Ozone (cnr Bolognesi & Ortiz; ☺ Thu-sat) The cool kids hit up this nightlife combo, starting first for drinks at Bali, then rolling upstairs to dance the night away to everything from reggaeton to cumbia at Ozone (admission S10).

Getting There & Around

AIR

The **airport** (CIX; ☎ 20-4934) is 2km southeast of town (taxi S5). **LAN** (☎ 27-4875; Izaga 770) offers daily flights to Lima. Departure tax is US$3.47.

BUS & COLECTIVO

Many bus companies are along Bolognesi, including **Cruz del Sur** (☎ 22-5508; Bolognesi 888), **Línea** (☎ 23-2951; Bolognesi 638) and **Móvil Tours** (☎ 27-1940; Bolognesi 199). Long-distance buses go to Lima (S55 to S106, 12 hours), Jáen (S45, nine hours), Tumbes (S26 to S40, eight hours), Trujillo (S15, three hours), Piura (S15, three hours), Cajamarca (S20 to S45, eight hours), Chachapoyas (S45, nine hours), Tarapoto (S50 to S60, 14 hours) and elsewhere.

The minibus terminal at the intersection of San José and Lora y Lora has regular *combis* to Lambayeque (S1.20, 20 minutes). *Combis* for Sipán (S2, one hour) leave from Terminal de Microbuses Epsel, on Piérola at Oriente, northeast of town center. *Colectivos* for Ferreñafe (S2.50, 30 minutes) depart from Prado near Sáenz Peña. For Túcume, buses leave from the 13th block of Leguia near Óvalo del Pescador (S1.80, one hour).

AROUND CHICLAYO

Guides can be hired at each of the following sites for S15 to S20 each. Guided tours from Chiclayo cost S50, not including lunch or entrance fees.

Lambayeque

The pride of northern Peru, the impressive **Museo Tumbas Reales de Sipán** (☎ 074-28-3977; www.amigosmuseosipan.com; admission S10; ☺ 9am-5pm Tue-Sun) is a world-class facility (save the Spanish-only signage) showcasing the dazzling finds of the Royal Tombs of Sipán, including that of the Lord of Sipán himself. Also in Lambayeque is the older **Bruning Museum** (☎ 074-28-3440; admission S8; ☺ 9am-5pm), which houses artifacts from the Chimú, Moche, Chavín and Vicus cultures.

Sipán

The story of this **site** (Huaca Rayada; ☎ 074-80-0048; admission S8; ☺ 9am-5pm), 30km southeast of Chiclayo, is an exciting one of buried treasure, *guaqueros*, the black market, police, archaeologists and at least one murder. Hundreds of exquisite and priceless artifacts have been recovered, and a gold-smothered royal Moche burial site – of the Lord of Sipán – was discovered in 1987. A small but well-done museum opened here in 2009 showcasing the latest finds from the 2007 opening of the chamber of the warrior priest.

Ferreñafe

About 18km northeast of Chiclayo, **Museo Nacional Sicán** (☎ 074-28-6469; http://sican.peru-cultural.org.pe; adult/student S8/3; ☼ 9am-5pm Tue-Sun) displays replicas of some of the largest tombs ever found in South America. Interestingly, the Lord of Sicán was buried upside down, in a fetal position with his head chopped off, along with a sophisticated security system to ward off *guaqueros* – a red dust that's toxic when inhaled.

Túcume

This little-known **site** (☎ 074-80-0052; adult/student S8/3; ☼ 8:30am-4:30pm Tue-Sun) can be seen from a spectacular clifftop *mirador* about 30km north of Lambayeque on the Panamericana. It's worth the climb to see the vast complex of crumbling walls, plazas and more than two dozen pyramids.

PIURA

☎ 073 / pop 377,500

Sun-scorched Piura presents itself out of the dusty tumbleweeds of the Desierto de Sechura as a mere regional transportation hub. There's little to do here, but it works just fine as a speed bump in your journey north or south – some cobblestone streets boasting character-filled houses and northern Peru's best crafts market in nearby Catacaos add to the appeal.

Information

The post office and banks with ATMs are on the Plaza de Armas.

Clínica San Miguel (☎ 30-9300; Los Cocos 111; ☼ 24hr) For medical attention.

iPerú (☎ 32-0249; Ayacucho 377; ☼ 8:30am-7pm Mon-Sat, to 2pm Sun) Has tourist information.

Sights & Activities

Museo de Vicus (☎ 32-7541; Huánuco 893; admission S3; ☼ 8am-10pm Sat, to noon Sun) is an underground gold museum, featuring a belt with a life-sized gold cat's head for a buckle.

About 12km southwest of Piura, the dusty village of Catacaos claims northern Peru's best **crafts market** (☼ 10am-6pm), which sprawls for several blocks near the plaza. Haggle for weavings, gold and silver jewelry, ceramics, wood carvings, leather goods and more – weekends are busiest.

Sleeping

Hospedaje Aruba (☎ 30-3067; Junín 851; s/d without bathroom S20/35) This spartan *hospedaje* offers tiny but clean rooms. Knock S5 off the double price without TV.

SHOPPING FOR SHAMANS

Here's a trip for daring adventurers. Deep in the eastern mountains, Huancabamba is famous for the powerful *brujos* (witch doctors) and *curanderos* (healers) that live at the nearby lakes of Huaringas. Mountains shrouded in mist surround the town itself. Because the eroding banks of the Río Huancabamba are unstable, the town is frequently subject to slippage, earning itself the nickname *la ciudad que camina* (the town that walks). Spooky.

Peruvians from all walks of life come to visit the lake district's shamans and often pay sizable amounts of money for their mystical services. They are supposed to cure an endless list of ailments, from headaches to cancer to chronic bad luck, and are particularly popular in matters of the heart – whether it's love lost, found, desired or scorned.

Ceremonies may last all night and entail hallucinogenic plants like the San Pedro cactus, as well as singing, chanting, dancing and a dip in the freezing lake waters. Some ceremonies involve more powerful substances like *ayahuasca* (Quechua for 'vine of the soul'), a potent and vile mix of jungle vines. Vomiting is a common side effect.

Combis leave Huancabamba, an eight-hour bus trip from Piura (S25), before dawn for Salala, from where horses and mules can be arranged to reach the famous lakes. Many locals (but few gringos) visit the area, so finding guides isn't difficult. Watch out for scam artists – try to get a reference beforehand. Expect to pay in the ballpark of S200 for a shaman visit. Be warned that this tradition is taken very seriously, and gawkers or skeptics will get a hostile reception.

Hospedaje San Carlos (☎ 30-6447; Ayacucho 627; s/d from 30/45; 🖳) Winning the budget stakes by a nose, this tranquil *hospedaje* has immaculate, trim rooms with TV and festive bedspreads.

Hotel Perú (☎ 33-3919; Arequipa 476; s/d S49/89, d with air-con S109; ❄ 🖳) This well-run hotel easily outpunches its budget weight class: it has the restaurant, clean rooms with cable TV, security and helpful staff of a pricier hotel for a smidgen of the price.

Eating & Drinking

Nearby Catacaos has dozens of lunchtime *picanterías* (cheap local restaurants) for trying local specialties like *seco de chabelo* (beef stew with plantains), *seco de cabrito* (goat stew), *tamales verdes* (green-corn dumplings) and *copus* (vinegar-cured goat heads stewed with vegetables).

Heladería El Chalan (Tacna 520; items S4-17) Cheap sandwiches, 30 flavors of ice cream and a tempting display case of decadent cakes and pies.

Matheo's (Tacna 532; menu S6, mains R$8-16) On Plaza de Armas, Matheo's serves I-can't-believe-it's-not-meat versions of local Peruvian dishes, salads and heaping plates of fruit and yogurt.

Capuccino (Tacna 786; sandwiches S8-20, mains S18-27; 🕑 closed Sun) Both too cool and too good for Piura, this trendy restaurant-cafe dishes up modern cuisine that cures the Peruvian food blues. No *ceviche* here.

La Santitos (Libertad 1001; mains S15-28) Festively decorated with tasteful restraint, this is the spot for local traditional food. Popular desert-dwelling dishes like succulent baby goat with rice and beans are the way to go if you have only one meal here.

El Marqués (Hotel Los Portales, Libertad 875) On Plaza de Armas, this classy tavern inside Piura's swankiest hotel is great for freeze-out air-con and interesting cocktails like Chica Morada.

Miraflores Centro Commercial (Apurímac 343) This small corner-strip mall houses Piura's best nightlife. Try Queens for dancing the night away or Atiko for drinks and other shenanigans.

Getting There & Away

AIR

The **airport** (PIU; ☎ 34-4503) is 2km southeast of the city center. **LAN** (☎ 30-5727; Grau 140) has daily flights to/from Lima.

BUS

Buses go to Lima (S75 to S139, 15 hours) with **Cruz del Sur** (☎ 33-7094; cnr Bolognesi & Lima), **Tepsa** (☎ 30-6345; Loreto 1198), Línea, Ittsa and Transportes Chiclayo.

For other destinations try the following:

El Dorado (☎ 32-5875; Cerro 1119) To Máncora (S15 to S20, three hours), Tumbes (S15 to S20, three hours) and Trujillo (S25 to S35, six hours).

GETTING TO ECUADOR

The route via La Tina/Macará to Loja, Ecuador, is more scenic but less popular than going via Tumbes (p846).

It's possible to take a bus from Piura to Sullana and switch to a *colectivo* for the border, but it's not recommended for safety reasons. **Transportes Loja** (☎ 30-5446; Cerro 1480) has a few convenient daily buses that go direct from Piura to Macará (S12, three hours) and on to Loja (S28, eight hours).

Formalities are fairly relaxed at the 24-hour border by the international Río Calvas bridge. There are no banks, but money changers at the border and in Macará, Ecuador, will change cash. Taxis and *colectivos* take travelers entering Ecuador to Macará (3km), where the Ecuadorian immigration building is found on the 2nd floor of the Municipalidad on the plaza (stop there for entry stamps). If you're riding the international Transportes Loja bus, you don't have to get off during formalities.

From Trujillo, **Ormeño** (☎ 044-25-9782; Ejército 233) offers direct buses to Quito (S256, 24 hours) and Guayaquil (S192, 18 hours).

If you're around Chachapoyas, you don't have to double back to the Peruvian coast to cross into Ecuador – it's possible to cross at the remote outpost of La Balsa. The first convenient stop in Ecuador is the lovely village of Vilcabamba (p642). You'll need to catch a bus to Bagua Grande (from Chacapoyas), then switch for Jaén and again for San Ignacio. *Colectivos* continue on to La Balsa.

To enter Peru from Ecuador, see p641.

El Sol Peruano (☎ 41-8143; Cerro 1112) Daily to Tarapoto (S60, 18 hours).

Ittsa (☎ 33-3982; Cerro 1142) To Trujillo (S25 to S45) and by *bus-cama* to Lima.

Linea (☎ 30-3894; Cerro 1215) Hourly to Chiclayo (S15, three hours).

Transportes Chiclayo (☎ 30-8455; Cerro 1121) Hourly to Chiclayo (S13, three hours), daily to Tumbes (S15, five hours) and by *bus-cama* to Lima.

For Cajamarca and the northern Andes, it's best to connect in Chiclayo (p842).

Combis for Catacaos (S1, 25 minutes) leave from Piura's Terminal Terrestre on the 1200 block of Cerro. Buses to Huancabamba depart from Terminal El Castillo 1km east of town.

MÁNCORA

☎ 073 / pop 10,000

Despite being Peru's principle beach resort and home to one of northwestern South America's best beaches, Máncora itself is little more than a glorified surfing village of shockingly rustic proportions (the fancy stuff combs its outskirts). Year-round sunshine and waves pushing 3m draw in swaths of surfers, who rub sunburnt shoulders with the Peruvian *Caras* crowd on weekends throughout the year. From December to March the scene – and price – gets deliriously rowdy.

Information

Av Piura is lined with internet cafes and *lavanderías*. There's no real bank, but there are Plus/Cirrus ATMs throughout town. Exchange US dollars at **Banco de la Nación** (☎ 25-8193; Piura 625). Tread wearily on the beach at night, as thieves pose as joggers and run away with your iPod! The website www.vivaman cora.com has useful tourist information.

Activities

You can go **surfing** year-round, but the best waves hit from November to February. Rent surfboards at the beach's southern end. **Máncora Surf Club** (☎ 70-8423; Piura 261), a British-Peruvian operation, offers surf lessons (S50 per hour). Stop by the Surfer's Bar in the same location the evening prior to make reservations. Some budget hotels teach surfing and kiteboarding, too. The best breaks in the area are on **Máncora Beach** in town and **Lobitos**, a 64km trek south. Haggle a taxi (S20 to S40).

Winds can reach 30 knots during kitesurfing season (from April to November). **Perukite** (☎ 073-96-978-6020; www.perukitemancora.com; The Birdhouse, Piura 112) can set you up with lessons (S125 per hour). Keep in mind it generally takes six hours for beginners to get riding.

Sleeping

Cheap sleeps are mostly found in the center and at the beach's southern end.

HI La Posada (☎ 25-8328; Barrio Industrial 100; dm S15, s/d S30/60; 🖳 🖳) Across the Panamericana from the beach, this HI-affiliated hostel has ultrabasic dorms and much nicer private options above the small pool.

The Point (☎ 70-6320; thepointhostels.com; Playa del Amor; dm from S20, bungalows s/d S45/64; 🖳 🖳) The Point's newest hostel sits on a more private patch of sand on the north end of town and features lovely bilevel beach bungalows and an elevated bar/TV/pool room. The downside is the 20-minute trek to other relevant action.

Loki del Mar (☎ 25-8484; www.lokihostel.com; Piura 262; dm from S25, r S76; 🖳 🖳) Elevating the hostel to entirely new levels, Loki has outdone itself (and others) with this hostel-cum-resort complete with a swimming pool, upscale cocktail menu and grub by an actual chef. Wake up to the sound of crashing waves (if you can fall asleep with the obnoxiously loud bar the night before).

Laguna Surf Camp (☎ 67-1727; www.vivaman cora.com/lagunacamp; Pasaje Veranigo s/n; s/d/tr/q incl breakfast S50/80/120/150) Laid-back Laguna has rustic Indonesian-style bamboo bungalows and kitchen facilities on the quieter side of the beach.

Eating & Drinking

Seafood rules here, but the gringo onslaught has inspired everything from breakfast burritos to Greek salads. Breakfast is well spoken for, but forget about lunch before 1pm.

Angela's Place (Piura 396; menús S6-13) Austrianrun veggie outpost with real coffee, whole-grain breads, hummus and other vegetarian delights.

Green Eggs & Ham (The Birdhouse, Piura 112; meals S12; ☉ 7:30am-1pm) A little beachfront shack good for scrumptious breakfasts.

Beef House (Piura 322; mains S16-35; ☉ dinner) Monstrous burgers and succulent steaks make this grill house the town must.

Mara Sushi (Piura 110; rolls S25) A smart little bamboo sushi joint popular with backpackers.

PERU

GETTING TO ECUADOR

The Peruvian border town of Aguas Verdes is linked by an international bridge across the Río Zarumilla with the Ecuadorian border town of Huaquillas.

For the best rates, change nuevos soles into US dollars while still in Peru. There are no entry fees into Ecuador, so be polite but insistent with any border guards trying their luck.

The last major hub north on the Peru side is **Tumbes**, not a bad little spot to shack up for a night and explore the surrounding mangroves and ecological reserves. **Preference Tours** (☎ 072-52-5518; Grau 427) can get you out and about. On the plaza, **Sí Señor** (Bolívar 115; mains S12-25) does the usual array of cheap Peruvian staples. Next door to the Cruz del Sur terminal, **Hospedaje Chicho** (☎ 072-52-2282; Tumbes 327; s/d/tr S30/45/55) is a basic crashpad for quicker overnighters. For a *little* more comfort, **Hotel Roma** (☎ 072-52-4137; hotelromatumbes@hotmail.com; Bolognesi 425; s/d/tr S45/70/95; ☐) sits on prime plaza real estate and offers wi-fi, cable TV, high-powered fans and hot showers. Beware of vicious mosquitoes in the area, and book ahead – the busy border means rooms go quickly.

From Tumbes, *colectivo* taxis (S1.50, 25 minutes) and minibuses (S3, 40 minutes) leave for the border from the 400 block of Bolívar, 26km away. It's best to take a direct bus with **Cifa** (☎ 52-7120; Tumbes 572) to Machala (S10, three hours) or Guayaquil (S25, six hours) in Ecuador, departing every two hours.

The Peruvian immigration office in Aguas Verdes is open 24 hours. On public transportation, make sure you stop there for border formalities. *Mototaxis* will then whisk you to the border (S1). About 3km to the north of the bridge, Ecuadorian immigration is also open 24 hours. Take a taxi from the bridge (US$1.50). There are basic hotels in Huaquillas, but most people catch an onward bus to Machala.

To enter Peru from Ecuador, see p666. From Tumbes, **Cruz del Sur** (☎ 52-6000; Tumbes 319) offers the most comfortable services to Lima (S110 to S180). For Máncora, **Carrucho** (☎ 52-7047; Piura 410) runs *combis*/air-con vans (S6/10) every 30 minutes from Tumbes.

Iguana's (Piura 245) Hot and sweaty locals mingle with sunburnt gringos to a soundtrack of Latin fusion in this packed bar, one of the oldest and most popular along Máncora's tiny but boisterous nightlife row.

Getting There & Away

Most southbound coastal buses headed for Lima originate in Tumbes (see boxed text, above). Frequent *combis* for Tumbes (S6 to S10, two hours) drive along Máncora's main drag. For Ecuador, see boxed text, above. **El Dorado** (☎ 25-8161; Grau 213) offers the most frequent services to more southerly towns of interest, like Piura (S15 to S20), Chiclayo (S20 to S25) and Trujillo (S25 to S35).

HUARAZ & THE CORDILLERAS

All around Huaraz, the mountainous region of the Cordilleras Blanca and Huayhuash boasts lakes of melted topaz calmly wading under the nose of snow-dusted peaks teetering on avalanche – some 22 ostentatious summits over 6000m make this the highest mountain range in the world outside the Himalayas.

Both Peru's highest point, the 6768m Huascarán, and the picture-perfect 5999m Artesonraju (rumored to be the mountain in Paramount Picture's live-action logo), loom here over Andean villages as well as the pleasant city of Huaraz, the nerve center of one of South America's premier trekking, mountain biking and climbing areas. Superlatives crash and burn in a brazen attempt to capture the awesome natural beauty of it all.

HUARAZ

☎ 043 / pop 90,000

Like Pucón in Chile, the restless Andean adventure capital of Huaraz came into its own based on a blessed location amidst some of the prettiest mountains in the world. Though nearly wiped out by the earthquake of 1970, Huaraz rebounded to become Peru's high-adrenaline showpiece, with trekking and mountaineering leading the heart-thumping charge. It buzzes with adventure seekers of all ilk in high season (May to

September) and slows to little more than a crawl rest of the year, when many folks shut up shop and head for the beaches.

Information

EMERGENCY

Casa de Guías (☎ 42-7545; Plaza Ginebra 28G; ⏲ 9am-1pm & 4-8pm Mon-Fri, 9am-1pm Sat) Arranges mountain rescues. Register here before setting out solo.

Policía de Turismo (☎ 94-310-8929; Luzuriaga 724)

LAUNDRY

Lavandería Dennys (José de la Mar 561; per kg S4; ⏲ 8am-8pm)

Lavandería Liz (José de la Mar 674; per kg S5; ⏲ 8am-1pm & 2-8pm)

MEDICAL SERVICES

Clínica San Pablo (☎ 42-8811; Huaylas 172; ⏲ 24hr) North of town. Some English spoken.

Farmacia Recuay (☎ 72-1391; Luzuriaga 497) Restocks expedition medical kits.

MONEY

BCP (Luzuriaga 691) Visa ATM and no commission on traveler's checks.

Interbank (José Sucre 687) Global ATM.

Oh-Na-Nay (Pasaje Comercio s/n) Money-exchange office.

POST

Serpost (Luzuriaga 702)

TOURIST INFORMATION

Lonely Planet's *Trekking in the Central Andes* covers the best hikes in the Cordilleras Blanca and Huayhuash.

iPerú (☎ 42-8812; Plaza de Armas, Pasaje Atusparia, Oficina 1; ⏲ 8am-6:30pm Mon-Sat, 8:30am-2pm Sun)

Dangers & Annoyances

Armed muggings of tourists on day trips around Huaraz and while trekking in the Cordilleras are unfortunately all too common. Particularly troubling spots include the hike between the ruins at Wilcahuaín and Monterrey, and in and around El Mirador de Rataquenua. Be aware of dodgy characters seemingly working for South American Explorers in and around the Cruz del Sur bus terminal – they are most certainly not affiliated.

Sights

The **Museo Regional de Ancash** (Plaza de Armas; adult/student S6/3; ⏲ 8:30am-5:15pm Tue-Sun) has small but interesting archaeology exhibits. **Monumento Nacional Wilcahuaín** (adult/student S5/2; ⏲ 8am-5pm) is a small but well-preserved Wari site with a three-story temple. The two-hour walk from town sees robberies often; take a taxi (S10) or look for *combis* by the Río Quilcay.

Activities

TREKKING & MOUNTAINEERING

The best treks are in the **Cordillera Blanca** inside Parque Nacional Huascarán (p852) and in the Cordillera Huayhuash (p853). All the equipment and help you need can be hired or bought, including trail maps, guidebooks, pack animals, *arrieros* (drivers) and local guides. Expect to pay around S120 to S150 per person per day for an all-inclusive trek or climbing expedition. Always inspect rental gear carefully.

Check certified guides and register before heading out at **Casa de Guías** (left). Reputable outfitters:

Galaxia Expeditions (☎ 42-5355; www.galaxia -expeditions.com; Parque del Periodista)

Montañero (☎ 42-6386; www.trekkingperu.com; Plaza Ginebra 30B)

Monttrek (☎ 42-1124; www.monttrekperu.com; Luzuriaga 646, 2nd fl)

MountClimb (☎ 42-4322; www.mountclimbtravel.com)

Skyline Adventures (☎ 42-7097; www.skyline -adventures.com) Based in Cashapampa.

ROCK CLIMBING

You'll find great bolted sports climbs in the Cordillera Blanca, particularly at Chancos (near Marcará), Monterrey and Recuay. For big-wall action to keep you chalked up for days, head to the famous Torre de Parón (aka the Sphinx) at Laguna Parón, 32km east of Caraz. Many trekking agencies offer rock-climbing trips and rent gear. Galaxia Expeditions has an indoor climbing wall, too.

MOUNTAIN BIKING

Mountain Bike Adventures (☎ 42-4259; www.chaki naniperu.com; Lúcar y Torre 530, 2nd fl) has been in business for over a decade. It has a good safety record and selection of bikes. The English-speaking owner is a lifelong resident of Huaraz and he knows the region's single track better than anyone. Rates start at S99 per day for guided tours. Ask about more challenging 12-day circuits of the Cordillera Blanca.

PERU

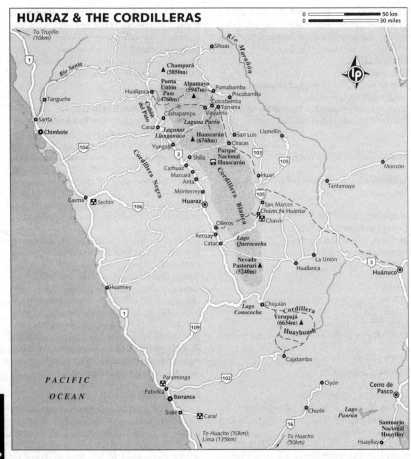

Tours

One bus tour visits the ruins at Chavín de Huántar; another goes through Yungay to the beautiful Lagunas Llanganuco, where there are spectacular views of Huascarán; a third takes you through Caraz to scenic Laguna Parón; and a fourth goes to see the extraordinary giant *Puya raimondii* plant (which can take 100 years to grow to its full height – often 10m!) and the glacier at Nevado Pastoruri (though the latter was closed indefinitely at research time). Full-day tours cost S35 to S40, excluding entry fees. Services are geared towards Peruvians – do not count on English (some of the guides speak English, but refuse to do so because the agencies stiff them on the extra pay-ment for doing so). None of the following will bowl you over with hospitality:

Huaraz Chavín Tours (☎ 42-1578; Luzuriaga 502)

Pablo Tours (☎ 42-1145; Luzuriaga 501)

Sechín Tours (☎ 42-6683; www.sechintours.com; Morales 602)

Festivals & Events

Semana Santa (Holy Week) In March/April, tongue-in-cheek funeral processions for Ño Carnavalón (King of Carnaval) are on Ash Wednesday.

El Señor de la Soledad Huaraz pays homage to its patron saint during this festival, with fireworks, music, dancing, costume parades and lots of drinking, in early May.

Semana de Andinismo International mountaineering exhibitions and competitions in June.

Sleeping

Locals meet buses to offer rooms in their houses, and *hostales* do the same. Don't pay until you've seen the room.

Jo's Place (☎ 42-5505; www.huaraz.com/josplace; Villaizán 278; campsite per person S8, dm/s/d S25/30/45) The slightly chaotic nature of English expat Jo and his modest guesthouse should suit wandering souls with its grassy camping and basic rooms, some with bathrooms. There is bacon and eggs for breakfast, as well as motorcycle parking.

Caroline Lodging (☎ 42-2588; carolinelodging.blog spot.com; Urb Avitentel Mz-D, Lt 1; dm S13, r with/without bathroom from S40/35; 🖳) Beyond the west end of 28 de Julio and down a flight of stairs, this delightful homestay offers hot-water showers, kitchen, TV lounge and mountain views. A new annex nearby offers nicer rooms and more privacy for S10 extra. A caveat: one traveler came to blows with the owners over a dispute in 2008.

Way Inn Lodge (☎ 94-346-6219; www.thewayinn .com; San Miguel de Llupa; campsite per person S15, dm S32, r with/without bathroom from S120/85) Whether you duck into the outdoor adobe sauna or tuck away into down duvets inside the cavelike dorms, this magnificent stone lodge peacefully nestled in the Cordillera Blanca above town is a true escape. UK expat Bruni is a delight, you can bolt for the trails straight from your room and dinner often comes from the frontyard trout pond. Take a taxi (S30).

Familia Meza Lodging (☎ 42-8531; familiameza _lodging@hotmail.com; Lúcar y Torre 538; r per person with-out bathroom S20) A simple family guesthouse with hot showers and a small rooftop kitchen and patios, though proximity to Café Andino might be its best quality.

Albergue Churup (☎ 42-2584; www.churup.com; Figueroa 1257; dm S25, s/d incl breakfast S70/90; 🖳) An ultrapopular Andean-chic boutique guest-house boasts quiet and cozy rooms, fireplace lounge with mountain views, book exchange, DVD library and a cheery breakfast nook and rooftop terrace. Reservations advised.

B&B My House (☎ 42-3375; www.andeanexplorers .com/micasa; 27 de Noviembre 773; s/d incl breakfast S50/ 80; 🖳) This hospitable B&B has a bright little patio and homey rooms with hot showers and writing desks. English and French spoken.

Soledad Bed & Breakfast (☎ 42-1196; www .lodgingsoledad.com; Figueroa 1267; s/d S50/90, d/tr with-out bathroom S60/90; 🖳) From the same family as Albergue Churup next door, this homey

guesthouse is a little more humble, with less Andean chic, more exposed brick. All rates include breakfast.

Olaza's Guesthouse (☎ 42-2529; www.olaza.com; Arguedas 1242; s/d incl breakfast S70/90; 🖳) An im-maculate and colorful guesthouse with scalding showers, well-appointed rooms with feather duvets, and a gorgeous rooftop fireplace lounge and terrace. Potted plants and natural sunlight are ubiquitous.

Eating

Crêperie Patrick (Luzuriaga 422; crepes from S5) Divine French-influenced, build-your-own-crepes along with the usual suspects.

Café Andino (Lúcar y Torre 530, 3rd fl; mains S8.50-25) A serious java joint (they roast their own) and Huaraz' ultimate hangout, with great mountain vistas and a well-stocked lender library in memoriam of a mountaineer. Breakfast all day and interesting mains like quinoa curries highlight the menu.

California Café (28 de Julio 562; items S9-14; ☯ closed Sun) This authentically Californian-run trave-ler hub does all-day breakfasts, light lunches and salads, rich espresso drinks and herbal teas. There's a book exchange and wi-fi.

Pizza BB (José de la Mar; pizzas from S10-18) Intimate pizzeria with an entire wall devoted to wood for the brick oven. Prices above are base – you create your own from there.

Monte Rosa (José de la Mar 661; mains S16-42) If you don't go for the fondue or raclette at this excellent Swiss-Alpine pub-restaurant, try the tasty *ají de gallina* (chicken stew in a spicy, nutty cheese sauce).

Encuentro (Morales 650; mains S18-27; ☯ 9am-11pm) This trendy eatery does well-prepared nou-veau Peruvian surrounded by contemporary art, including everyone's favorite Andean delicacy, *cuy*.

our pick **Chili Heaven** (Plaza Ginebra; mains S18-35) Tired of Peruvian? It's worth the trip to Huaraz just for the stunning Indian and Thai curries at this cozy, British-run res-taurant that also stocks 20 or so beers you haven't seen since home. It's not cheap, but portions are substantial. Chili Heaven also produces and bottles its own hot sauces.

Also recommended:

La Braza Roja (Luzuriaga 919; meals S3.50-24) Everyone's favorite *pollería*, though they grill much more than chicken.

Sabor Salud Pizzería (Luzuriaga 672, 2nd fl) The most veggie choices in town, from eggplant parmesan to a lasagna fat enough for two. There's meat, too.

PERU

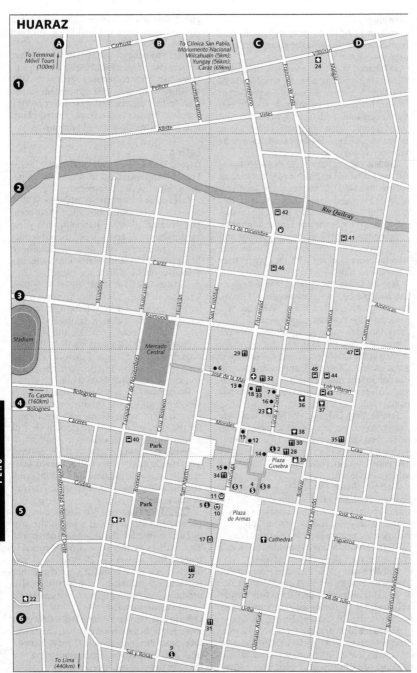

HUARAZ

PERU

To Way Inn
Lodge (14km);
Raimondi

To Mountain
Institute
(300m)

Siam de los Andes (Gamarra 560) Superb Thai food worth the price tag – when it's open, that is.

Drinking

Huaraz is the best spot in the Peruvian Andes to take a load off and get pleasantly buzzed. There are plenty of bars, discos and *peñas* around, though names and popularity change with the seasons.

El Tambo (José de la Mar 776) Don't judge a dance club by its facade: fashionable El Tambo, with its hardwood dance floor, trees as support beams throughout, and plenty of loungy areas to tuck yourself in and people-watch the night away, is far cooler than it appears. The soundtrack runs from techno-cumbia to pop to reggaeton, the crowd from young and restless to town cougars.

Los 13 Buhos (José de la Mar 812, 2nd fl) Located above Makondo's, this hip and snug bar draws the cool folks, mainly for its new, coca-infused home brew or the Long Andean Iced Tea (made with coca-infused liquors).

Also recommended is **Vagamundo Travel Bar** (Morales 753; ☽ closed Sun), an intimate spot, glowing sexy red, with good tunes.

Shopping

Tatoo (☎ 42-2966; Plaza Ginebra 686; ☽ 9am-1pm & 3-8pm Mon-Sat) Best bet for last-minute trekking and mountaineering supplies.

Getting There & Away

Many bus companies have midmorning or late-evening departures for Lima (S58 to S90, seven to eight hours). **Cruz del Sur** (☎ 42-8726; Bolívar 491) has nonstop luxury services. **Móvil Tours** (☎ 42-2555; Av Confraternidad Internacional Oeste 451) is also comfortable and has a ticket office in town (☎ 42-9541; Bolívar 542).

Línea (☎ 42-6666; Bolívar 450) and Móvil Tours go direct to Chimbote, continuing to Trujillo (S35 to S60, nine hours). Spectacular though rough rides via the amazing Cañón del Pato (that will have you scavenging for Xanax) or 4225m-high Punta Callán to Chimbote (S25, nine hours) are worth seeing with **Transportes Alas Peruanas** (☎ 42-7507; Fitzcarrald 267) and **Yungay Express** (☎ 42-4377; Raimondi 930).

Chavín Express (☎ 42-8069; Cáceres 330) goes to Chavín de Huántar (S10, two hours), continuing to Huari (S13, four hours).

Daytime minibuses for Caraz (S5.60, 1½ hours) and Yungay (S4.30, one hour) depart

PERU

frequently from near the Quilcay bridge on Fitzcarrald.

PARQUE NACIONAL HUASCARÁN

Encompassing almost the entire area of the Cordillera Blanca above 4000m, this 3400 sq km **national park** (admission day/month S5/65; ☻ 7am-3:30pm) is bursting with picturesque emerald lakes, brightly colored alpine wildflowers and red *quenua* trees.

The most popular backpacking circuit, the **Santa Cruz** trek, takes four days and rises to the Punta Unión pass (4760m), which arguably has the best Andean views in Peru. The trail, which passes by icy waterfalls and lakes, mossy meadows and verdant valleys, is well marked. *Colectivo* taxis frequently leave from Caraz for the main trailhead at Cashapampa (S10, 1½ hours).

Many other trails are available, from day hikes to ambitious two-week treks. The scenery is just as jaw-dropping, minus the crowds. Many routes aren't clearly marked, however, so go with a guide or take along top-notch topographic maps. If you are short on cash or time, the day-long trek to **Laguna 69** is stunning, dripping with marvelous mountain and waterfall views, and culminating in the Photoshop-blue lake that gives the trek its name – a perfect peek into the awesome scenery in this area. In Huaraz, the **Mountain Institute** (☎ 043-42-3446; www.mountain.org; Ricardo Palma 100) works closely with sustainable-tourism initiatives along the Inca Naani trail between Huari and Huanuco. Check with local agencies for more information.

Register with your passport at the **national park office** (☎ 043-42-2086; Sal y Rosas 555) in Huaraz and pay the park entrance fee. You can also register and pay at control stations, but their locations and operating hours vary. Don't dodge or begrudge paying the fee: the Cordillera Blanca is one of the most amazing places on the planet. Some trailhead communities, such as Cashapampa, have begun adding a surcharge of S10 per person – check current situation.

Though arbitrarily enforced, law requires a licensed guide to accompany all trekkers, unless you are a card-carrying member of a UIAA-approved mountaineering club. This is especially enforced for any mountaineering activity.

NORTH OF HUARAZ

As the Río Santa slices its way north through El Callejón de Huaylas, a paved road passes several subdued towns to Caraz, and onto the menacingly impressive **Cañón del Pato**. Many hiking trailheads are accessible from towns along this route, and two unsealed roads valiantly cross the Cordillera, one via Chacas and another via Yungay.

Lagunas Llanganuco

A dirt road climbs through the valley to two stunning **lakes**, Laguna Chinancocha and Laguna Orconcocha, 28km east of Yungay. Nestled in a glacial valley below the snow line, these pristine lagoons practically glow with bright turquoise and emerald hues. There's a 1½-hour nature trail hugging Chinacocha, passing rare *polylepis* trees. National-park entry costs S5. *Colectivos* leave from Yungay (round-trip S20) during high season (June to August). Trips during other months depend on demand. You can also take a tour from Huaraz (p848).

Caraz

☎ 043 / pop 12,000

A more traditional backdrop for your Cordillera base camp than Huaraz, the little colonial village of Caraz sees trekking and hiking trails meander in all directions from its location 67km north of Huaraz. There is far less to do in town here, but far more Andean color as well. You'll likely end up here if you tackle the Santa Cruz trek (left), as this is its traditional end point (or untraditional starting point).

Bring cash with you, as there are no ATMs. **Pony's Expeditions** (☎ 39-1642; www.ponyexpeditions .com; José Sucre 1266) rents all manner of gear, mountain bikes and arranges trekking, fishing and climbing excursions. They also sell ready-made meals (even veggie) for the mountains. Bare-bones **Hospedaje La Casona** (☎ 39-1334; Raimondi 319; s/d S15/25, without bathroom S10/15) has dark, bare and windowless rooms, but a bright courtyard. **Hostal Chavín** (☎ 39-1171; hostalchavin@latinmail.com; San Martín 1135; s/d S35/50) has a knowledgeable owner and has been renovated, with new floors, mattresses and lobby furniture.

A great place to grab an early breakfast, tiny little **Cafetería El Turista** (San Martín 1127; breakfast S3.50-6) opens at 6:15am. **Café de Rat** (above Pony's Expeditions; meals S4-10) is an atmospheric, wood-beamed restaurant doing salads (rare), pizza and other staples, as well as box lunches in high season.

Minibuses to Yungay (S1.50, 15 minutes) and Huaraz (S5.60, 1½ hours) leave from the Terminal Terrestre on the Carretera Central. *Colectivos* for Cashapampa (S7, one hour) leave from Ramón Castilla at Santa Cruz. Long-distance buses to Lima (S35, eight hours) and Trujillo (S35, nine hours) go with **Móvil Tours** (☎ 39-1922; Pasaje Olaya s/n) and other companies.

CHAVÍN DE HUÁNTAR
☎ 043 / pop 2900
Located near this small village are the ruins of **Chavín** (adult/student S11/6; ⏰ 9am-5pm Tue-Sun), built between 1200 and 800 BC by one of the continent's oldest civilizations. The site contains highly stylized cultist carvings of a jaguar or puma, Chavín's principal deity, and of condors, snakes and humans undergoing mystical (often hallucinogenic) transformations. The site's snaking underground tunnels are an exceptional feat of 3000-year-old engineering, comprising a maze of alleys, ducts and chambers – it's worth hiring a guide. Look out for the exquisitely carved, dagger-like rock known as the Lanzón de Chavín.

Don't miss the small but excellent **Museo Nacional Chavín** (⏰ 45-4011; 17 de Enero s/n; ⏰ 9am-5pm Tue-Sun), funded by the Japanese and inaugurated in 2008, which houses many of the site's important artifacts, including 19 *pututos* (shell trumpets) and 16 of the stone heads that once graced the outer walls of the complex. Here you will also find the original Tello Obelisk, one of the most important pieces of Chavín art ever discovered in the Andes.

There are a few decent hotels and restaurants in town, though most folks opt for a long day trip from Huaraz (p848).

Chavín Express buses go to Huaraz (S10, two hours).

CORDILLERA HUAYHUASH
Often playing second fiddle to the Cordillera Blanca, the Huayhuash nevertheless has an equally impressive medley of glaciers, summits and lakes all packed into an area only 30km across. Increasing numbers of travelers are discovering this rugged and remote territory, where strenuously high passes over 4500m throw down the gauntlet to the hardiest of trekkers. The feeling of utter wilderness, particularly along the unspoiled eastern edge, is a big draw. You are more likely to spot an Andean condor here than another tour group.

Several communities along the classic 10-day trekking circuit charge fees of S10 to S35 (the entire trek will run you an extra S120 to S160). These fees go toward improving security for hikers and continuing conservation work. Support local preservation efforts by paying your fees, carrying plenty of small bills and always asking for official receipts.

Travelers once used the high-altitude village of Chiquián as the gateway to the Cordillera Huayhuash, but most folks now opt to bypass it entirely via the newer road to the trailhead at Llamac, where there are basic *hospedajes* and campsites. To reach Llamac, you can catch the El Rápido bus from Huaraz (location changes yearly) at 6am to Chiquián (S15, three hours) and switch to a *combi* for Llamac (S10, one hour). There are additional charges for gear.

NORTHERN HIGHLANDS

Vast tracts of unexplored jungle and mountain ranges shrouded in mist guard the secrets of Peru's northern highlands, where Andean peaks and cloud forests stretch all the way from the coast to the deepest Amazon jungle. Interspersed with the relics of ancient warriors and Inca kings, these wild outposts are yet barely connected by disheveled, circuitous roads.

CAJAMARCA
☎ 076 / pop 162,000
The cobblestone colonial streets of Cajamarca mark the last stand for the powerful Inca empire – Atahualpa, the last Inca, was defeated here by Pizarro and later executed in the main square. Only the striking baroque, Gothic and Renaissance architecture of Cajamarca's numerous churches remains, with the lone exception of Cuarto del Rescate, where Atahualpa was held prisoner – the last Inca ruin in the city. These days, fertile farmlands carpet the entire valley around Cajamarca, which turns even lusher during the rainy season.

PERU

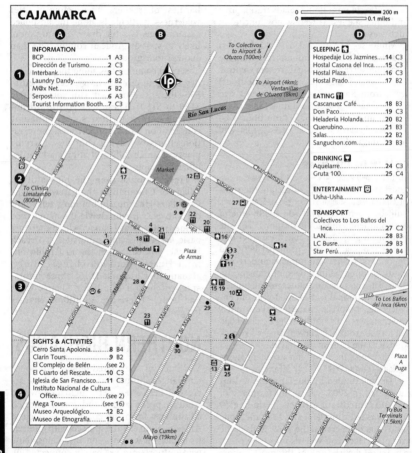

CAJAMARCA

INFORMATION
BCP...1 A3
Dirección de Turismo............2 C3
Interbank................................3 C3
Laundry Dandy.......................4 B2
M@x Net.................................5 B2
Serpost...................................6 A3
Tourist Information Booth...7 C3

SIGHTS & ACTIVITIES
Cerro Santa Apolonia..........8 B4
Clarin Tours............................9 B2
El Complejo de Belén..........(see 2)
El Cuarto del Rescate.........10 C3
Iglesia de San Francisco.....11 C3
Instituto Nacional de Cultura
   Office..............................(see 2)
Mega Tours.........................(see 16)
Museo Arqueológico.........12 B2
Museo de Etnografía.........13 C4

SLEEPING
Hospedaje Los Jazmines....14 C3
Hostal Casona del Inca.......15 C3
Hostal Plaza.........................16 C3
Hostal Prado........................17 B2

EATING
Cascanuez Café....................18 B3
Don Paco..............................19 C3
Heladería Holanda..............20 B2
Querubino.............................21 B3
Salas......................................22 B3
Sanguchon.com...................23 B3

DRINKING
Aquelarre.............................24 C3
Gruta 100..............................25 C4

ENTERTAINMENT
Usha-Usha.............................26 A2

TRANSPORT
Colectivos to Los Baños del
   Inca..................................27 C2
LAN..28 B3
LC Busre................................29 B3
Star Perú...............................30 B4

Information

BCP (cnr Lima & Apurímac) Changes traveler's checks and has a Visa/MasterCard ATM.

Clínica Limatambo (☎ 36-4241; Puno 265)

Dirección de Turismo (☎ 36-2903; El Complejo de Belén; ⏱ 7:30am-1pm & 2:30-6pm Mon-Fri)

Interbank (2 de Mayo 546) On the Plaza de Armas; changes traveler's checks and has a global ATM.

Laundry Dandy (Puga 545) Convenient.

M@x Net (Del Batán 177) Internet access.

Serpost (Apurímac 626) Postal service.

Tourist information booth Next to Iglesia de San Francisco.

Sights

The following central sights are officially open from 9am to 1pm and 3pm to 6pm

Tuesday to Saturday and from 3pm to 6pm Sunday. They don't have addresses. For admission, you must buy an all-encompassing ticket from **Instituto Nacional de Cultura** (El Complejo de Belén; admission S4.50; ⏱ 9am-1pm & 3-6pm Tue-Sun).

The only remaining Inca building here is **El Cuarto del Rescate** (Ransom Chamber). Despite the name, this is actually where Francisco Pizarro kept Inca Atahualpa prisoner before killing him off (see p767), not where the ransom was stored. Tickets include same-day admission to **El Complejo de Belén**, a sprawling 17th-century colonial complex with a small archaeology museum, and the **Museo de Etnografía**, with exhibits of traditional highland life.

Well worth visiting, the university-run **Museo Arqueológico** (Del Batán 289; ☻ 8am-2:30pm Mon-Fri) displays artifacts from pre-Inca Cajamarca culture. Facing the Plaza de Armas, **Iglesia de San Francisco** (admission S3; ☻ 9am-noon & 4-6pm Mon-Fri) has catacombs and a religious-art museum.

Hilltop **Cerro Santa Apolonia** (admission S1; ☻ 7am-6pm), with its gardens and pre-Columbian carvings, overlooks the city. Huff and puff your way up the 100m of stairs at the end of 2 de Mayo. Views are impressive.

Atahualpa was camped by **Los Baños del Inca** (admission S2, private baths per hr S4-5, sauna/massage S10-20; ☻ 5am-7:30pm), the impressive hot springs 6km east of Cajamarca, before his fateful run-in with Pizarro. Show up before 7am to avoid the rush, especially on weekends. *Colectivos* for Los Baños del Inca leave frequently from along Sabogal, near 2 de Mayo (S0.70). Bring your own towel or buy one from vendors for S5. You can also sleep here.

An astounding yet mysterious feat of pre-Inca engineering, the aqueducts at **Cumbe Mayo**, 19km outside Cajamarca, run for several kilometers across the bleak mountain-tops. The site can be reached on foot from Cerro Santa Apolonia via a signposted road. It's a four-hour walk, if you take shortcuts and ask locals for directions. Tours from Cajamarca cost S25.

Also nearby are the pre-Inca necropolises known as **Ventanillas de Otuzco**, built into a hillside 8km from Cajamarca. You can walk to Otuzco from Cajamarca or Los Baños del Inca or take a combo tour with the *baños* (S20). Buses from Cajamarca leave from north of the main plaza (S1). Better-preserved *ventanillas* (windows) at Combayo, 30km from Cajamarca, are most easily visited on a tour (S200).

Travel agents include **Mega Tours** (☎ 34-1876; www.megatours.org; Puga 691) and **Clarín Tours** (☎ 36-6829; www.clarintours.com; Del Batán 161).

Festivals & Events

The **Carnaval** involves nine days of dancing, eating, singing, partying, costumes, parades and rowdy mayhem. And water fights here are worse (or better, depending on your point of view) than elsewhere. Hotels raise their rates and fill up weeks beforehand, so hundreds of visitors end up sleeping in the plaza.

Sleeping

Hostal Plaza (☎ 36-2058; hostalplaza_cajamarca@yahoo.es; Puga 669; s/d S30/55, without bathroom S15/25) Guests can run rampant in this tattered plaza option while management tucks away behind the scenes, but the creaky rooms are the cheapest on the plaza.

Hostal Prado (☎ 36-6093; La Mar 582; s/d/tr S40/70/100, s/d without bathroom S25/35) A budget step up, with brighter lighting and well-kept rooms, though those facing the street are noisy.

Hospedaje Los Jazmines (☎ 36-1812; www.hospedajelosjazmines.com; Amazonas 775; s/d/tr S50/80/100, s/d without bathroom S40/60; ▣) This 13-room German-run *hospedaje* is well looked after and recently renovated. Rooms with cable TV and hot showers congregate around a pleasant courtyard and backyard terrace. The hotel's practice of hiring people with disabilities is commendable.

Hostal Casona del Inca (☎ 36-7527; www.casonadelincaperu.com; 2 de Mayo 460; s/d/tr S60/100/120; ▣) The quirky, fun-house atmosphere (bright, angled walls) makes this the most charismatic plaza option, but the staff is hardheaded until the death.

Eating

There are a lot of cows around Cajamarca – what to do with the brains? Eat them! The local specialty is known as *sesos*. Sweet tooths also will not suffer the bends in town – regal bakeries abound all over Centro.

Heladería Holanda (Puga 657; items S1.50-3) Northern Peru's best ice cream keeps crowds content at this bright and wonderful cafe that's not stingy with the samples. Try regional fruit flavors like *capuli*, *sauco* or *poro poro*.

Salas (Puga 637; breakfast items S3-12, mains S8-27) A venerable old-school cafeteria in place on Plaza de Armas since 1947. You can try the local specialty (*sesos* – translated here as 'crunchy' brains) if you're so inclined; otherwise there's plenty to choose from. One of the few spots open early for breakfast.

Cascanuez Café (Puga 554; mains S5-24) Good coffee and desserts.

Sanguchon.com (Junín 1137; items S5.50-12.50; ☻ dinner) Rowdy bar and burger joint, with perfectly greasy sandwiches that take the edge off a wild evening.

Don Paco (Puga 726; menu S8, meals S6-28) An eclectic menu of Peruvian and international delights draws in both locals and gringos. The *lomo saltado* sandwich slathered with *ají* is excellent. Also has vegetarian dishes.

PERU

Querubino (Puga 589; mains S15-26) This smart restaurant specializes in steak and lasagna. The green Andean curry looks like a prop from *The Exorcist*, but is damn tasty.

Drinking & Entertainment

The best bars congregate around the corner of Puga and Gálvez.

Gruta 100 (cnr Santisteban & Belén; ☽ 8pm-late Thu-Sat) Sophisticated drinking den with an attached DIY fire pit and backyard amphitheater. At the time of research, *the* place to be seen.

Aquelarre (Puga 846) This rustic watering hole takes its lead from Los Angeles (no sign, no nothing) and is reached via a clandestine doorbell. It fills up until the wee hours with locals, gringos and the Peace Corps. It's no-frills, and that's the appeal.

our pick Usha-Usha (Puga 142; admission S5; ☽ 9pm-late Mon-Sat) There is more character in this tiny, lantern-lit, graffiti-strewn hole-in-the-wall than the whole of some countries! Eccentric local musician Jaime Valera sings his heart out with his musician friends and you walk away with an unforgettable travel memory. Don't miss it.

Getting There & Away

AIR

The **airport** (CJA; ☎ 34-2689) is 4km north of town. Local buses for Otuzco, leaving from several blocks north of the plaza, pass the airport (S1); taxis are faster (S7), rickshaw-like *mototaxis* are cheaper (S3). **LAN** (☎ 36-7441; www.lan.com; Cruz de Piedra 657), **Star Perú** (☎ 36-0198; www.starperu.com; Junín 1300) and **LC Busre** (☎ 36-1098; www.lcbusre.com.pe; Lima 1024) have daily flights to/from Lima.

BUS

Most terminals are between the 2nd and 3rd blocks of Atahualpa, 1.5km southeast of town on the road to Los Baños del Inca.

Many companies have buses to Chiclayo (S25 to S45, 10 hours), Trujillo (S20 to S45, 10 hours) and Lima (S93 to S150, 16 to 18 hours). **Línea** (☎ 36-3956; Atahualpa 318) and **Tepsa** (☎ 36-3306; cnr Sucre & Reina Farje) have comfortable Lima-bound buses. Luxury *bus-camas* to Lima go with **Cruz del Sur** (☎ 36-1737; Atahualpa 600).

Línea also has buses to Piura (S39 to S49) via Chiclayo, where you can continue on to Ecuador.

A few companies go to Celendín (S10, four hours). However, beyond Celendín to Chachapoyas, transport is unreliable and the road is bad, if beautiful. It's easier to reach Chachapoyas from Chiclayo (see p842). If you must risk the treacherous journey beyond Celendín to Chacapoyas, **Móvil Tours** (☽ 34-0873; Atahualpa 405) braves the route (S50, 12 hours).

CHACHAPOYAS

☎ 041 / pop 23,000

Colonial Chachapoyas seems wildly out of place, both as the unlikely capital of the Amazonas department, and in its location surrounded by more mountainous terrain than jungle. But 'Chacas' is a bustling market town and an ideal place from which to explore Kuélap – the awesome ruins left behind by the fierce cloud forest–dwelling civilization that ruled here from AD 800 until the Incas came in the 1470s – and the surrounding waterfalls and trekking routes.

Information

Most of the following are on the Plaza de Armas, plus internet cafes and several shops changing dollars.

BCP (Plaza de Armas) Changes US dollars and traveler's checks, and has a Visa/MasterCard ATM.

Lavandería Speed Clean (Ayacucho 964; ☽ 7am-9pm Mon) Inside a travel agency.

Serpost (Ortiz Arrieta 632) Postal services; just south of the plaza.

Tourist Information (☎ 47-7292; Ortiz Arrieta 588; ☽ 9am-1pm & 3:30-8:30pm Mon-Sat, 4-8pm Sun)

Sights & Activities

Day tours from Chacas focus on Kuélap (see opposite). Travel agencies hover around the plaza. **Turismo Explorer** (☎ 47-8060; www.turismoexplorerperu.com; cnr Amazonas & Grau) has a good reputation, but competition is fierce. The dry season (May to September) is best for hiking, including the five-day **Gran Vilaya** trek to the Valle de Belén or a three-day trip to **Laguna de los Cóndores** on foot and horseback.

Sleeping

Hotel Karajía (☎ 31-2606; 2 de Mayo 546; s/d S25/35, s without bathroom & TV S15, s without bathroom S20) This budget option is in best shape and gets kudos for its priced-as-you-need scheme, allowing travelers to forgo the TVs and bathrooms for a few less soles.

Hotel Plaza (☎ 47-7787; Grau 534; s/d/tr S30/40/60) Like at Revash, there's great value here in the large, comfortable rooms with renovated bathrooms. There's an upstairs terrace restaurant overlooking the plaza, but it's on average S1 more expensive than the identically owned one below.

Hotel Revash (☎ 47-7391; revash@terra.com; Grau 517; s/d/tr S50/110/130; ⌨) The courtyard in this classic mansion is a little more overgrown than endearing, but sleeping here still offers exceptional value and scorching showers. Rooms are colorful and crotchety in a sweet way. They are pushy with tours from the in-house agency, but travelers are generally pleased with the results.

Casa Vieja (☎ 47-7353; www.casaviejaperu.com; Chincha Alta 569; s/d/tr incl breakfast S85/135/180; ⌨) Peruvian knickknacks and antique radios characterize this creaky and classy mansion on a side street off the plaza. Chirping birds inhabit the endlessly charming courtyard and rooms are bright and feature handcrafted decor, cable TV and hot showers. Breakfast (in bed!) available.

Eating & Drinking

Look for *juanes* (*bijao* leaf–steamed fish, beef or chicken with olives), made locally with yucca instead of rice.

Panificadora San José (Ayacucho 816; items S3-8.50) An excellent early-rise bakery with a small attached restaurant, where you can get good coffee, deserts, sandwiches and plenty of regional specialties like tamales, *humitas* (corn dumplings) and *juanes*.

505 Pizza-Bar (2 de Mayo 505; pizzas S4-28) Too hip for Chachapoyas, this pizza bar features 96 cocktails on the menu, the strangest of which is Sambito (malt beer, Inka Cola, *pisco*, vodka and 'rubber'), an acquired taste.

La Tushpa (Ortiz Arrieta 753; meals S6-30) The house red is terrible, which explains why locals packing this place are drinking Inka Cola with the excellently prepared steaks and chops. Slow service is quickly forgiven. The house sauces are also a highlight.

La Reina (Ayacucho 520) An artsy spot to get drunk very cheaply on exotic fruit and Amazonian liquors. Try the *maracuyá*.

Getting There & Away

Buses to Chiclayo (S30 to S40, nine to 11 hours) and on to Lima (S100 to S115, 22 hours) take a route that is paved beyond

Pedro Ruíz. Services leave with **Transervis Kuélap** (☎ 47-8128; Ortiz Arrieta 412), **Civa** (☎ 47-8048; Salamanca 956), **Transportes Zelada** (☎ 47-8066; Ortiz Arrieta 310) and comfortable **Móvil Tours** (☎ 47-8545; Libertad 464).

Transportes Roller (Grau 302) has buses to Kuélap (S15, 2½ hours) at the very non-traveler-friendly hour of 3:30am, returning at 7:30am from Kuélap. Taxis to Kuélap depart throughout the day and will wait while you take the tour (S120 return).

There are frequent *colectivos* for Tingo (S8, 1½ hours), which may continue to María (S15, three hours). *Colectivos* also go to Pedro Ruíz (S12, 1½ hours), where eastbound buses to Tarapoto (S30, six hours) stop.

KUÉLAP

Matched in grandeur only by the ruins of Machu Picchu, the fabulous ruins of this pre-Inca **citadel** (admission adult/student S12/7; ☻ 8am-noon & 1-5pm), constructed between AD 900 and 1100, are perched in the mountains southeast of Chachapoyas. The site (elevation 3000m) receives remarkably few visitors, though those who make it get to see one of the most significant and impressive pre-Columbian ruins in South America.

Though most travelers visit Kuélap on a day tour from Chachapoyas, below the ruins **Hospedaje El Bebedero** (r per person S415) has bare-bones rooms without electricity or running water – bring a sleeping bag and water-purification equipment. *Hospedajes* also abound in **María**, the nearest hamlet to the ruins. Prices run S15 per person at all of them, but **Hospedaje El Torreón** (☎ 041-81-3038) is the best.

TARAPOTO

☎ 042 / pop 117,000

A muggy and lethargic rainforest metropolis, Tarapoto balances precariously between the tropical Amazon basin and weathered Andean foothills. If it weren't for the lengthy umbilical cord that is the long, paved road back to the rest of Peru, it would sit as isolated – and nearly as manic – as Iquitos. Of late it has become a popular base for *ayahuasca* (hallucinogenic brew made from jungle vines) benders, which can be organized here, but most travelers are passing through to Yurimaguas, where boats depart for Iquitos.

PERU

Information

Internet cafes are everywhere.

BCP (Maynas 130) Cashes traveler's checks and has an ATM.

Clínica San Martín (☎ 52-3680; San Martín 274; 24hr) Offers medical care.

Tourist information office (Hurtado s/n; 8:30am-8pm Mon-Sat, 9am-1pm Sun) Tourist info on the northwest side of the plaza.

Tours

Chancas Expeditions (☎ 52-2616; www.geocities .com/amazonrainforest; Rioja 357) Offers river-rafting trips.

Kunter Journeys (☎ 52-8629; www.kunterjourneys .com; Los Flores 124) Dutch-owned upstart running sustainable-tourism trips into the jungle at Ilucanayacu, where guests stay in a hand-built rainforest lodge.

Lucho Romero Sanchez (☎ 942-61-4189; larsa_44 @hotmail.com) Trusted *ayahuasca* guide.

Quiquiriqui Tours (☎ 52-4016; www.quiquiriquitours .com; Pimentel 309; 8am-7pm) A full-service travel agency for tours of the surrounding villages and natural attractions.

Sleeping

Hospedaje Misti (☎ 52-2439; Prado 341; s/d/tr S20/40/60) The leafy courtyard and friendly front desk gives this place a leg up on what are otherwise similar options in this price range. Cold-water showers only.

Hostal San Antonio (☎ 52-5563; bonyta007@hot mail.com; Pimentel 126; s/d S25/30) The lanterns are a nice touch at this simple, value-oriented option with hot water and cable TV.

Alojamiento July (☎ 52-2087; Morey 205; s/d/ tr S30/40/60) Jungle murals, endless rows of beads and knickknacks clanking in the hallways, and sporadic rays of light give this good-value option extra charm. Rooms have electric hot showers, cable TV and minifridges.

La Patarashca (☎ 52-3899; www.lapatarashca.com; Lamas 261; s/d/tr incl breakfast S40/60/90; mains S14-26; ▣) Though it's come a bit undone of late (our room opened up to a *very* pregnant cat that had fallen through the ceiling, not to mention the urine-scented air about the place), the tropical vibe that pervades at this *hospedaje* still makes it the most charming option. There's cable TV, hammocks and cold-water showers. The bilingual macaws are a real crack-up until they steal your breakfast! The attached restaurant, serving Amazonian specialties, is the best meal in town.

Eating & Drinking

Banana's Burgers (AA de Morey 114; mains S5-12; 24hr) An all-night burger counter with a rowdy bar upstairs.

Café D'Mundo (AA de Morey 157; mains S14-2) Moody candlelight sets the tone at this sophisticated cafe-bar serving good pizza and pasta. The outdoor lounge area is an excellent spot to ride out an Amazonian evening.

La Collpa (Circunvalación 164; mains S20-28; 10am-11pm) Located in a place where you can practically taste the jungle air, this bamboo-stilt restaurant has rainforest views and specializes in jungle grills and river fish.

Stonewasi Taberna (Lamas 222; closed Sun) The happening spot in Tarapoto – a Beatles-themed bar inside, brimming patio outside. The music is as diverse as the crowd.

La Alternativa (Grau 401) A hole-in-the-wall bar with shelves of dusty bottles containing home-made Amazonian tonics. The Viborachado, a potent, snake-venom aphrodisiac, is the best seller. Try it!

Getting There & Around

The **airport** (TPP; ☎ 53-1165) is 3km southwest of the center. **LAN** (☎ 52-9318; Hurtado 103) has daily flights to/from Lima. **Star Perú** (☎ 52-8765; San Pablo de la Cruz 100) flies daily to Lima and Iquitos on Monday, Wednesday, Friday and Sunday. A *mototaxi* into town is S6.

Most bus companies are along Salaverry in the Morales district. **Móvil Tours** (☎ 52-8240) and **El Sol Peruano** (☎ 53-1861) are the best. Buses head west on the paved road to Chiclayo (S35 to 65, 14 hours), Trujillo (S80, 17 hours), Piura (S52, 17 hours) and Lima (S80 to 130, 26 hours). **Expreso Huamanga** (☎ 52-7272) goes to Pedro Ruíz (S25, seven hours), where you'll have to change to a *colectivo* taxi to reach Chachapoyas (S12, 1½ hours). Alternatively, nearly all eastbound buses stop in Pedro Ruíz as well. **Transmar** (53-2392; Amorarca 117) heads on to Pucallpa at 8am on Monday, Wednesday and Friday (S90, 19 hours).

A rough road goes east from Tarapoto to Yurimaguas. Minibuses, pickup trucks and *colectivos* traveling to Yurimaguas (S25, six hours) leave from the market in the eastern suburb of Banda de Shilcayo. Back on Salaverry, **Paredes Estrella** (☎ 52-1202) has cheaper, slower buses to Yurimaguas (S10, four hours).

A short *mototaxi* ride around town costs S2, to the bus terminal/airport S2/5.

PERU

AMAZON BASIN

Thick with primary and secondary jungle, Peru's Amazon Basin is dense and dizzying, an exotic and isolated frontier zone that spills out from all sides with exhilarating jungle-adventure opportunities. Iquitos, the area's largest city, is the gateway to once-in-a-lifetime excursions down the Amazon River, but also holds interest for its solitary, end-of-the-road atmosphere (even though the road ended in Yurimaguas). Pucallpa and Yurimaguas offer slow boats that ply the waterways to Iquitos, accessible otherwise only by air. The country's largest reserve, the bigger-than-New-Jersey Reserva Nacional Pacaya-Samiria, is also here, home to pink dolphins and 449 bird species.

Further south, the Unesco-declared Parque Nacional Manu is considered one of the world's most pristinely preserved thatches of Tarzan terrain and one of South America's best spots to see tropical wildlife. Around Puerto Maldonado, jungle lodges beckon along the Madre de Dios and Tambopata rivers (the latter is in the Reserva Nacional Tambopata) – two more of Peru's most unspoiled settings for wildlife and jungle adventure.

PUERTO MALDONADO

☎ 082 / pop 56,500

Diesel-fumed Puerto Maldonado, capital of the Madre de Dios region, is the ramshackle, almost entirely unpaved epicenter of Peru's southern Amazon. It's the least riveting tourist city in Peru – were it not the gateway to one of South America's finest jungles, it would scarcely be heard from again (save a few great bars). That may all change when the Interoceánica Hwy linking the Atlantic and Pacific Oceans via Brazil opens, but until then, do like most folks do and land here only to be swept off to a wild and exotic Amazon lodge.

Information

BCP (Plaza de Armas) ATM.

Cyberc@t (Loreto 268; per hr S2) Internet.

Dircetur airport (Baggage Claim, Airport; 🕑 10am-1pm Mon-Fri); city center (☎ 57-1164; San Martín s/n; 🕑 7am-1pm & 2-4pm) Municipal tourist info.

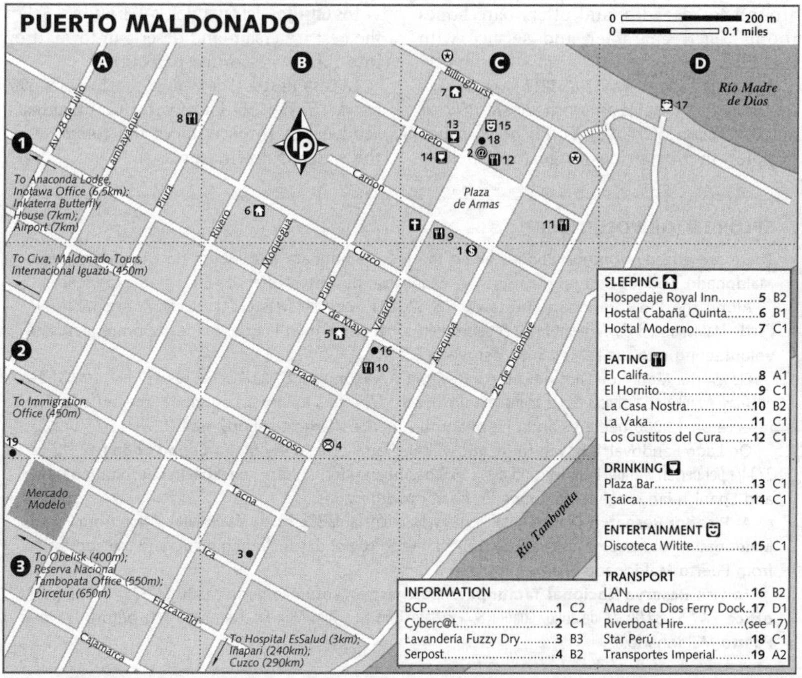
PUERTO MALDONADO
0 200 m
0 0.1 miles
A
B
C
D
1
2
3
Río Madre de Dios
Río Tambopata
Billinghurst
Loreto
Carrion
Cuzco
2 de Mayo
Prada
Troncoso
Tacna
Ica
Fitzcarrald
Cajamarca
Av 28 de Julio
Lambayaque
Piura
Rivero
Moquegua
Puno
Velarde
Arequipa
26 de Diciembre
Plaza de Armas
Mercado Modelo
To Anaconda Lodge, Inotawa Office (6.5km); Inkaterra Butterfly House (7km); Airport (7km)
To Civa, Maldonado Tours, Internacional Iguazú (450m)
To Immigration Office (450m)
To Obelisk (400m); Reserva Nacional Tambopata Office (650m); Dircetur (650m)
To Hospital EsSalud (3km); Inapari (240km); Cuzco (290km)
SLEEPING
Hospedaje Royal Inn..........5 B2
Hostal Cabaña Quinta..........6 B1
Hostal Moderno..........7 C1
EATING
El Califa..........8 A1
El Hornito..........9 C1
La Casa Nostra..........10 B2
La Vaka..........11 C1
Los Gustitos del Cura..........12 C1
DRINKING
Plaza Bar..........13 C1
Tsaica..........14 C1
ENTERTAINMENT
Discoteca Witite..........15 C1
TRANSPORT
LAN..........16 B2
Madre de Dios Ferry Dock..17 D1
Riverboat Hire..........(see 17)
Star Perú..........18 C1
Transportes Imperial..........19 A2
INFORMATION
BCP..........1 C2
Cyberc@t..........2 C1
Lavandería Fuzzy Dry..........3 B3
Serpost..........4 B2

Hospital EsSalud (☎ 57-1711) Attends tourists for emergencies only.
Lavandería Fuzzy Dry (Velarde 898; per kg S4.50) Laundry – cheaper if you don't need it same day.
Serpost (Velarde 675) Postal services.

Tours

If you haven't prearranged a river and jungle tour (see boxed text, below), there are several local guides; some quite reputable and experienced, others just interested in making quick money. Shop around, never pay for a tour beforehand and, when you agree on a price, make sure it includes the return trip! Officially licensed guides charge around S90 per person per day (excluding park fees), depending on the destination and number of people. Boat rides, which are usually needed to get out of Puerto Maldonado, are notoriously expensive.

Sleeping

Watch out for overcharging. Outside town are some jungle lodges (see boxed text, below).

Hostal Moderno (☎ 30-0043; machivj@yahoo.es; Billinghurst 359; r per person S15) Despite the name, this simple, clapboard building has been around for decades, and offers bare-bones rooms, aged character and service with a smile.

Anaconda Lodge (☎ 982-61-1039; www.anaconda junglelodge.com; campsite per person S20, s/d S100/160, without bathroom S50/80; 🐾) You'll be so much happier in this price range (and below)

staying at this newish Swiss/Thai-run lodge set amid a botanical garden next to the airport than in town, it's almost impossible to put in words. Simple but well-done bungalows with mosquito nets, a crystal-clear pool and – drumroll, please – wonderful Thai food, means there's no reason to leave before braving the jungle.

Hospedaje Royal Inn (☎ 57-3464; mitsukate@yahoo .com; 2 de Mayo 333; s/d S30/40; 🖳) Though staff is more concerned with IM'ing and the building is a half-finished monstrosity, the rooms aren't too bad. Clean and spacious. The two parrots liven up the courtyard.

Hostal Cabaña Quinta (☎ 57-1045; www.hotelcabana quinta.com.pe; Cuzco 5353; s/d with air-con S120/160, without air-con S70/120; 🖳 ❄) A fabulous midrange option with open-air, mosaic paths along jungly greens that's worth the splurge if you're stuck in town. Rates include breakfast, one of the best spreads you'll see in Peru.

Eating

Regional specialties include *chilcano* (fishchunk soup flavored with cilantro) and *parrillada de la selva* (marinated meat BBQ in an *ají*/Brazil-nut sauce).

Los Gustitos del Cura (Loreto 258; snacks S1-6) For the best ice cream and deserts in town, drop into this Swiss-owned patisserie.

La Casa Nostra (2 de Mayo 287; sandwiches S2.50-7, breakfast S7.50-11.50) Cute cafe for breakfasts, sandwiches, tropical juices and coffee (avoid the watered-down espresso).

SPLURGE! (OR VOLUNTEER?)

There are dozens of jungle lodges along the Ríos Tambopata and Madre de Dios from Puerto Maldonado. Lodges and jungle tours are expensive, but often offer life-changing experiences.

Along the Río Tambopata, **Inotawa** (☎ 57-2511; www.inotawaexpeditions.com; Av Aeropuerto 107, Puerto Maldonado; 3-day/2-night tour per person from S764) offers multilingual guides upon request and volunteering rates as low as S480 per week.

Down the Madre de Dios, **Inkaterra Reserva Amazónica** (☎ in Lima 01-610-0410, in Cuzco 084-23-4010; www.inkaterra.com; 3-day/2-night tour s/d S1924/1547) offers luxury accommodations on a private reserve on 12,000 hectares and one of South America's largest canopy walks.

On Lago Sandoval, a haven for exotic wildlife, family-run **Willy Mejía Cepa Lodge** (☎ 982-68-2734; r per person without bathroom incl meals S65) has been offering basic, backpacker accommodations and Spanish-language expeditions for nearly two decades.

At **Picaflor Research Centre** (picaflor_rc@yahoo.com; Tacna 386, Puerto Maldonado), 74km from Puerto Maldonado, volunteer prices vary by project, but S110 per day including meals and transportation from Puerto Maldonado is an example.

To visit **Reserva Nacional Tambopata**, purchase an entrance permit (S30 to S75) at the **park office** (☎ 57-3278; 28 de Julio, Cuadra 8; ☾ 8am-1pm & 3-5pm Mon-Fri, 9am-noon Sat) before leaving Puerto Maldonado.

GETTING TO BRAZIL & BOLIVIA

An unpaved road goes from Puerto Maldonado to **Iñapari** on the Brazilian border. *Colectivos* to Iñapari (S35, four hours) with **Transportes Imperial** (☎ 57-4274; lca 547) leave when they have four passengers. Iberia, 170km north of Puerto Maldonado, and Iñapari, 70km beyond Iberia, have a couple of basic hotels. At Iñapari, where Peruvian exit formalities are conducted, cross the Río Acre by ferry or bridge to Assis, Brazil, which has better hotels and a paved road via Brasiléia to Río Branco. US, Australian and Canadian citizens need to get a Brazilian visa in advance (see p375).

From Puerto Maldonado, boats can be hired for the half-day trip to the Bolivian border at Puerto Pardo for about S400. Cheaper passages are available on infrequent cargo boats. Make sure to get exit stamps before leaving Peru at Puerto Maldonado's **immigration office** (☎ 57-1069; 28 de Julio 467; ☒ 8am-1pm & 2:30-4pm Mon-Fri). From Puerto Heath, a few minutes away from Puerto Pardo by boat, it takes several days (even weeks) to arrange a boat (expensive) to Riberalta, which has road and air connections. Travel in a group to share costs and avoid months when the water is too low. Another option is to go to Brasiléia, cross the Río Acre by ferry or bridge to Cobija, on the Bolivian side, where there are hotels and erratic flights. There's also a dry-season gravel road onward to Riberalta.

To enter Peru from Brazil, see p368.

El Califa (Piura 266; mains S9-15; ☒ lunch) For an atmospheric local's lunch, look no further than this always packed staple down a dusty side street for regional specialties like palm-heart salad, *juanes* (Sunday to Monday), fried plantains and game.

La Vaka (Loreto 224; mains S11-23; ☒ dinner) Some cool kids run this trendy steakhouse-galleria specializing in *lomo* with regional sauces that are served alongside an equally saucy soundtrack.

El Hornito (Carrión 271; pizza S14-36; ☒ dinner) Big bowls of pastas and wood-fired pizzas.

Drinking & Entertainment

The best-known nightclub is **Discoteca Witite** (Velarde 151; ☒ Fri & Sat). Dueling watering holes **Plaza Bar** (Loreto 326) and **Tsaica** (Loreto 329), the former stylish and trendy, the latter indigenous-chic, fight for your drinking dollars across the street from each other on Loreto.

Getting There & Around

AIR

The **airport** (PEM) is 7km west of town; *mototaxis* cost S10. **Star Perú** (☎ 79-6551; Velarde 151) and **LAN** (☎ 57-3677; Velarde 503) have daily flights to Lima via Cuzco.

BOAT

Boat hire at the Madre de Dios ferry dock for excursions or to travel down to the Bolivian border is expensive. Upriver boats toward Manu are difficult to find.

BUS

Bus companies that comb the evolving road to Cuzco are located on the 5th block of Tambopata. It's a long and rough trip on conventional buses. **Civa** (☎ 982-72-0884), **Internacional Iguazú** (☎ 50-3859) and **Maldonado Tours** (☎ 50-3032) are the three best for the 18- to 20-hour journey (S50), with Iguazú purportedly being the safest – they randomly offer *semi-camas* (a step below *bus-camas*).

PARQUE NACIONAL MANU

Covering almost 20,000 sq km, **Parque Nacional Manu** is widely regarded as the most pristine and best-preserved thatch of jungle in the world. This Unesco Natural Heritage Site is one of the best spots in South America to see tropical wildlife. Starting in the eastern slopes of the Andes, the park plunges down into the lowlands, covering a wide range of cloud-forest and rainforest habitats containing 1000 bird species, not to mention 13 species of primates, armadillos, kinkajous, ocelots, river turtles, caiman, and countless insects, reptiles and amphibians. More elusive species include jaguars, tapirs, giant ant-eaters, tamanduas, capybaras, peccaries, the near-extinct giant river otters, and, perhaps most amazingly, uncontacted communities of hunter-gatherer tribes!

The best time to visit the park is after the rainy season (April to November). Manu is harder to access during the rainiest months (January to March), though most of the authorized companies still run (wet) tours.

PERU

It's illegal to enter the park without a licensed guide and permit, which can be arranged at Cuzco travel agencies (see p816). Transportation, accommodations and meals are also part of the tour package. Beware: not all companies enter the park itself – there are only eight agencies authorized to do so. Others offer cheaper 'Manu Tours' that cover areas outside the park, but these still boast good wildlife-watching.

Costs depend on whether you arrive/depart overland or by air, but generally hover around S3885 for five days/four nights, flying in and out, or S3585 for nine days/eight nights, all overland. Book well in advance, but be flexible with your travel plans, as tours can often return a day late. Camping is only permitted in the multiuse zone (not the reserve).

It is possible for independent travelers to reach the reserve's environs without taking a tour, but it is time-consuming and somewhat dangerous. If you're determined to go solo, buses leave Monday, Wednesday and Friday from Av Huáscar in Cuzco to Pillcopata (S18, 10 hours in good weather), where you'll need to catch a ride with a truck to Itahuania (around S40, 12 hours), to which the road now extends (the first navigable portion of the river is from Atalaya, but renting a boat from here is prohibitively expensive). At Itahuania, you can continue down the Alto Madre de Dios to the lower portion of the Madre de Dios in a cargo boat all the way to Blanquillo (around S60, six hours), where the macaws feed at the clay lick.

The boat journey down the Alto Madre de Dios to the Río Manu takes almost a day. A few minutes from the village of Boca Manu is an airstrip, often the starting or exit point for commercial trips into the park. There is a park entrance fee of S150, and continuing is only possible with a guide and permit.

Despite its preservation and world-class setting, the park sees few visitors per year, and is under a threefold threat from narcotraffickers, illegal timber exploitation and illegal gold panning.

PUCALLPA

☎ 061 / pop 205,000

A trip to tumbledown Pucallpa is like a visit with the in-laws: it ain't fun, but you gotta do it. Despite its lack of redeeming qualities, it's a welcome change of pace after the long bus ride down from the chilly and rocky Andes to the capital of the Ucayali department; and the view of the torrent Río Ucayali tearing through town from the relatively nice *malecón* (waterfront) is an impressive sight. Travelers come here in search of the riverboats combing the first navigable Amazon tributary to Iquitos or to visit indigenous communities near Yarinacocha.

Information

Several banks change money and traveler's checks and have ATMs; *casas de cambio* are along the 4th, 5th and 6th blocks of Raimondi.

BCP (cnr Raimondi & Tarapacá)

Clínica Monte Horeb (☎ 57-1689; Inmaculada 529; ☺ 24 hr) Good medical services.

Lavandería Gasparin (Portillo 526; ☺ 9am-1pm & 4-8pm Mon-Sat) Offers self-service and drop-off laundry.

Sc@rtnet (Pasaje Zegarra 189; per hr S1; ☺ 8am-11pm) Air-con internet access.

Tourist information booth (☎ 57-1303; 2 de Mayo 111) At the airport.

Sights & Activities

Most activities center around Yarinacocha (p864). Works by famed local woodcarver Agustín Rivas are displayed at his house, now also a **gallery** (☎ 57-1834; Tarapacá 861, 2nd fl; ☺ 10am-4pm Mon-Sat); ring the bell to enter or inquire in the small store below. You'll see his handy work at better establishments around town.

Sleeping

Hospedaje Barbtur (☎ 57-2532; Raimondi 670; s/d S25/35, without bathroom S13/18) Simple but perfectly decent rooms come with a bed, desk and fan, some with cable TV. The prices haven't changed since 1997!

Hostal Perú (☎ 57-5128; Raimondi 639; s/d S25/40) The best budget rooms, with freshly tiled floors and local art added during a recent makeover.

Hospedaje Komby (☎ 57-1562; hostalkomby@hotmail.com; Ucayali 360; s from S30, d/tr S45/55; ☐ ☒) Third-floor S30 rooms are spacious and high value in this otherwise forgetful option (save that pool).

Hostal Happy Day (☎ 57-1940; Huáscar 440; s/d incl breakfast with air-con S60/70, without air-con S35/45; ☒ ☐) This popular guesthouse on a quiet side street has comfortable beds, wi-fi and cable TV. Good value here; run by helpful folks.

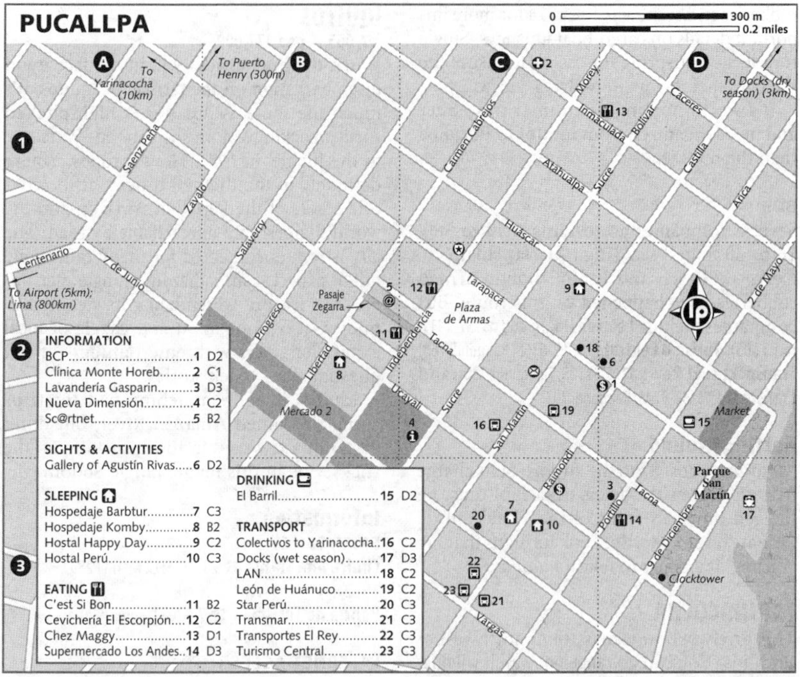
PUCALLPA
0 300 m
0 0.2 miles
To Yarinacocha (10km)
To Puerto Henry (300m)
To Docks (dry season) (3km)
To Airport (5km); Lima (800km)
Centenario
7 de Junio
Saenz Peña
Zavala
Salaverry
Progreso
Libertad
Pasaje Zegarra
Mercado 2
Independencia
Ucayali
Tacna
Sucre
San Martín
Raimondi
Portillo
9 de Diciembre
Vargas
Carmen Cabrejos
Huáscar
Tarapacá
Plaza de Armas
Atahualpa
Inmaculada
Morey
Bolívar
Cáceres
Castilla
Arica
2 de Mayo
Market
Parque San Martín
Clocktower
INFORMATION
BCP 1 D2
Clínica Monte Horeb 2 C1
Lavandería Gasparin 3 D3
Nueva Dimensión 4 C2
Sc@rtnet 5 B2
SIGHTS & ACTIVITIES
Gallery of Agustín Rivas 6 D2
SLEEPING
Hospedaje Barbtur 7 C3
Hospedaje Komby 8 B2
Hostal Happy Day 9 C2
Hostal Perú 10 C3
EATING
C'est Si Bon 11 B2
Cevichería El Escorpión 12 C2
Chez Maggy 13 D1
Supermercado Los Andes 14 D3
DRINKING
El Barril 15 D2
TRANSPORT
Colectivos to Yarinacocha 16 C2
Docks (wet season) 17 D3
LAN 18 C2
León de Huánuco 19 C2
Star Perú 20 C3
Transmar 21 C3
Transportes El Rey 22 C3
Turismo Central 23 C3

Eating & Drinking

Cevichería El Escorpión (Independencia 430; ceviche S8-25) Never mind Pucallpa's distance from the sea. This *cevichería* does the job with river fish (but avoid the just-out-of-endangerment *paiche*).

Chez Maggy (Inmaculada 643; pizza S11.50-25) This modern chain on a lively block does good thin-crust, brick-oven pizza and, depending on where you're from, try-at-your-own-risk Mexican.

Just off the southwest corner of the plaza, **C'est Si Bon** (Independencia 560; snacks S3.50-12) is a breezy spot to get ice cream, breakfasts, sandwiches – even Oreo cheesecake!

El Barril (Tarapacá 1037) does refreshing sugarcane juice, along with medicinal and alcoholic variations, right out of old wooden barrels.

Stock up at **Supermercado Los Andes** (Portillo 545) for river journeys.

Getting There & Away

AIR

Pucallpa's **airport** (PCL; ☎ 57-7329; Federico Basadre, Km 5) is 5km northwest of town. Taxis/*mototaxis* charge S15/7 for the trip. Currently scheduled flights are to Lima only with **LAN** (☎ 57-9840; Tarapacá 805) and **Star Perú** (☎ 59-0586; 7 de Junio 865). The latter flies direct to Iquitos as well.

BOAT

During high water (January to April), boats depart from next to Parque San Martín. As water levels drop, the port creeps northeast to several places along the banks, including **Puerto Henry** (Manco Capác s/n) and beyond, eventually ending up 3km northeast of center. Inquire first at Mercado 2 on Ucayali at **Nueva Dimensión** (☎ 961-62-9506; Mercado 2, Puesto 24; 🕑 6:30am-1pm Mon-Sat), where Delcio Gozarpuente keeps track of which boats are going when and from where. It's a small communications booth near the fruit juices on the southeast side of the market.

Crowded boats to Iquitos (S100 to S180) take three days. Passengers can sleep aboard on hammocks, which are sold in the market (S25 to S130) on 9 de Diciembre, or in prison-like cabins, and basic meals are provided. In the past, travelers have used Tingo María as a breaking point in this journey, but think twice: it's well regarded around Peru as a jungle no-man's-land, and readers have reported armed robberies and even rape. See p774 for more important details on cargo-boat journeys. Single travelers must spring for cabins to insure the safety of their belongings. Bring a lock.

It's worth nothing that this trip is easier and more organized from Iquitos to Pucallpa than the reverse.

BUS

Several companies go to Lima (S40 to S80, 16 to 20 hours) via Tingo María, Huánuco, Cerro de Pasco and Junín, though armed robberies have happened on this route. Bus companies include **León de Huánuco** (☎ 57-2411; Tacna 605), **Turismo Central** (☎ 57-6168; Raimondi 768) **Transportes El Rey** (☎ 57-2305; Raimondi 730) and **Transmar** (☎ 57-9778; Raimondi 793).

Getting Around

Motocarros cost S7 to the airport; taxis charge S12. *Colectivos* to Yarinacocha (S2) must be flagged down in front of the Hotel Sol de Oriente on San Martín. Look for signs that say 'Yarina.' It's easier to take a *mototaxi* (S5).

YARINACOCHA

This lovely oxbow lake is 10km northwest of Pucallpa. You can go **canoeing**, watch **wildlife**, visit matriarchal Shipibo communities and visit local **shamans**.

Popular boat trips include the **Shipibo villages** of San Francisco and Santa Clara. You can hire guides for jungle walks and overnight treks. *Peki-peki* boats with drivers cost about S20 per hour. Overnight tours are S120 per person per day (two-person minimum). Recommended guides include **Gilber Reategui Sangama** (☎ 78-8244; www.sacredheritage.com/normita) with his boat *Mi Normita*, **Gustavo Paredes** (☎ 961-85-5469) with *Poseidon*, and **Eduardo Vela** (☎ 961-92-1060) with *The Best*. It's easy to find their boats, which are all pulled up along the waterfront. Don't fall for the old 'Oh, that boat sank. Why don't you take a tour with me?' tactic.

For meditation, *ayahuasca* and other jungle healing, the new **Tierra Vida** (www.tierravidahealing.com; r per person from S50) is run by Americans. For rustic hospitality, stay across the lake at Gilber Reategui Sangama's **house** (☎ 78-8244; junglesecrets@yahoo.com; r per person incl meals S60).

There are also three pricier lakeside lodges (S100 to S125 per person including meals), including the welcoming **La Perla** (☎ 78-7551; r incl meals S100). The Shipibo village of San Francisco offers lodging from S20 per person.

IQUITOS

☎ 065 / pop 371,000

When the heat smacks you in the face upon disembarkation on the tarmac in Iquitos, it's much the same as Axl Rose's high-pitched shrill smacking you in the ears on 'Welcome to the Jungle' in 1987. How apropos. You're definitely in the thick of it here, at the chaotic cradle of the Peruvian Amazon and the world's largest city unreachable by road. The city is well documented for many things one might expect from a dizzying jungle metropolis, not least of which being its steamy humidity, sexy population and gaggle of local expat characters with entertaining – if not questionable – back stories.

Iquitos is your launching pad for trips along the famed Amazon River, but don't discount a few days in town, sucking up the sticky vibe in this manic jungle Sodom.

Information

EMERGENCY

Clínica Ana Stahl (☎ 25-2535; La Marina 285; 24hr)
Policía de Turismo (☎ 24-2081; Lores 834)

INTERNET ACCESS

Internet is big business in Iquitos. Most spots charge S2 per hour.

Cyber Coffee (Raymondi 143; 8am-midnight)
El Cyber (Arica 122; 24hr) 45 computers!

LAUNDRY

Lavandería Imperial (Putumayo 150; 8am-7pm Mon-Sat) Coin-operated.

MONEY

Many banks change traveler's checks, give credit-card advances and have ATMs. Changing Brazilian or Colombian currency is best done at the border.

BCP (Próspero, Cuadra 2) ATM.

POST

Serpost (Arica 402; 8am-6pm Mon-Fri, to 5pm Sat)

TOURIST INFORMATION

iPerú airport (☎ 26-0251; Main Hall, Airport; 6-7am & 3-9pm); city center (☎ 23-6144; Loreto 201; 8:30am-7:30pm Mon-Sat, to 2pm Sun)
Iquitos Times (www.iquitostimes.com) Very helpful English-language tourist newspaper.
Reserva Nacional Pacaya-Samiria office (☎ 60-7299; Pevas 339; 7am-3pm Mon-Fri)

IQUITOS

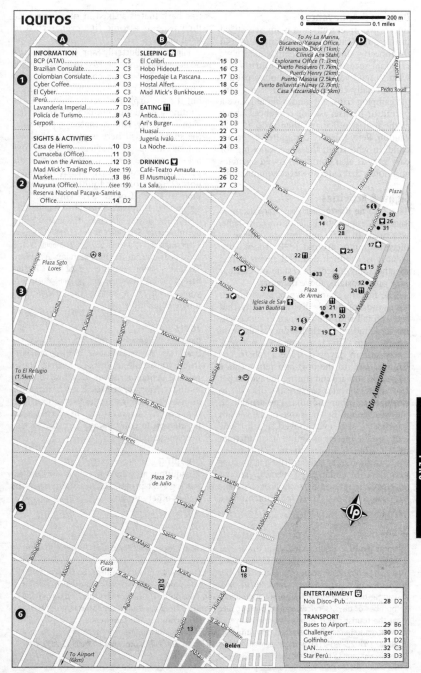

0 — 200 m
0 — 0.1 miles

INFORMATION
BCP (ATM)...........................**1** C3
Brazilian Consulate................**2** C3
Colombian Consulate.............**3** C3
Cyber Coffee.......................**4** D3
El Cyber..............................**5** C3
iPerú...................................**6** D2
Lavandería Imperial...............**7** D3
Policía de Turismo.................**8** A3
Serpost...............................**9** C4

SIGHTS & ACTIVITIES
Casa de Hierro.....................**10** D3
Cumaceba (Office)................**11** D3
Dawn on the Amazon............**12** D3
Mad Mick's Trading Post.....(see 19)
Market................................**13** B6
Muyuna (Office)................(see 19)
Reserva Nacional Pacaya-Samiria
   Office...............................**14** D2

SLEEPING
El Colibrí.............................**15** D3
Hobo Hideout......................**16** C3
Hospedaje La Pascana...........**17** D3
Hostal Alfert........................**18** C6
Mad Mick's Bunkhouse..........**19** D3

EATING
Antica.................................**20** D3
Ari's Burger.........................**21** D3
Huasai.................................**22** C3
Jugería Ivalú........................**23** C4
La Noche..............................**24** D3

DRINKING
Café-Teatro Amauta..............**25** D3
El Musmuqui........................**26** D2
La Sala................................**27** C3

To Av La Marina,
Bucanero/Yarapa Office,
El Huequito Dock (1km);
Clínica Ana Stahl,
Explorama Office (1.3km);
Puerto Pesquero (1.7km);
Puerto Henry (2km);
Puerto Masusa (2.5km);
Puerto Bellavista-Nanay (2.7km);
Casa Fitzcarraldo (3.5km)

To El Refugio
(1.5km)

To Airport
(6km)

ENTERTAINMENT
Noa Disco-Pub......................**28** D2

TRANSPORT
Buses to Airport....................**29** B6
Challenger...........................**30** D2
Golfinho..............................**31** D2
LAN....................................**32** C3
Star Perú.............................**33** D3

PERU

Dangers & Annoyances

Aggressive street touts and many self-styled jungle guides are irritatingly insistent and dishonest – don't trust them. Some have criminal records for robbing tourists and want to send you upriver without a paddle. Be especially careful when arranging jungle camping trips. All guides should have a permit or license; ask for references, check at the tourist office and then proceed with caution. Petty thievery committed by young children who roam the streets looking for easy prey is also common. Avoid agencies and hotels that cater to street commissions.

Sights & Activities

The **Casa de Hierro** (Iron House; cnr Putumayo & Raymondi), designed by Eiffel of towering fame, was made in Paris and imported piece by piece to Iquitos around 1890. It looks like what it is: a bunch of metal sheets bolted together. Stay tuned – a restaurant and bar may open upstairs above the store.

The floating shantytown of **Belén** houses thousands of people living on huts that rise and fall with the river, and canoes selling and trading jungle produce daily from around 7am. This is a poor area, but relatively safe in daylight. Take a cab to Los Chinos, walk to the port and rent a canoe to paddle you around during the November to May high-water season; it's difficult to navigate in other months. The **market**, on the west side of Belén, is one of the world's gnarliest – if it ever moved, it's for sale here, and someone is eating it: all manner of Amazonian spices, meat, fish, turtles, toucans, monkeys, caiman (there is no concern here for endangered species). There's an especially interesting section of shamanic herbs and liquors. Look for Chuchuhuasi tree bark that is soaked in rum for weeks, then used as a tonic (it's even served in local bars).

Pilpintuwasi Butterfly Farm (☎ 23-2665; www.amazonanimalorphanage.org; Padre Cocha; admission S15; ☺ 9am-4pm Tue-Sun) is a conservatorium and breeding center for Amazonian butterflies, but it's the orphaned exotic animals – including a capuchin monkey, tapir, jaguar, giant anteater and manatee – that steal the show. A visit here is pure joy and not without unexpected excitement (watch your belongings, the ornery monkeys love a little petty theft). From Puerto Bellavista-Nanay port, 2.5km north of Iquitos, take a small boat to Padre Cocha (S3). The farm is a signposted 1km walk through the village.

Built by nostalgic expats, the wacky, wonderful **Amazon Golf Club** (☎ 96-571-9444; Quistacocha; 9-hole round incl club rental S75; ☺ 7am-6pm) is the only golf course in the Peruvian Amazon. To take a swing, enquire at **Mad Mick's Trading Post** (☎ 50-7525; Putumayo 163; ☺ 9am-8pm), where you can buy, rent, sell or trade goods for a jungle expedition.

Tours

Dawn on the Amazon (☎ 22-3730; www.dawnontheamazon.com; Malecón Maldonado 185; cruises from S480) Run by a likable ex-Indiana farmer, Dawn on the Amazon offers day and custom multiday Amazon cruises. It's the best of the affordable options and the food is excellent, if not overly adventurous. They have special permission to enter Pacaya-Samiria twice as deep as anyone else.

Sleeping

Mosquitoes are rarely a serious problem, so netting isn't provided. All rooms have fans unless otherwise noted.

SPLURGE!

There are several jungle lodges in the Iquitos area, but lodges built further off into the Amazon itself offer your best chances of seeing exotic wildlife. A typical (but unforgettable) trip includes a river journey, all accommodations and meals, jungle walks and canoe trips, and a visit to an indigenous village. Price ranges for the lodges below hover around S450 to S886 per night (single occupancy) for four-night itineraries, and can go down from there depending on the number of days, services/tour and group size. Lodge offices are found in central Iquitos, or ask at the tourist office. Budget travelers have especially recommended **Cumaceba** (☎ 065-23-2229; www.cumaceba.com; Putumayo 184), **Muyuna** (☎ 065-24-2858; www.muyuna.com; Putumayo 163), **Yarapa River** (☎ 065-993-1172; www.yaropariverlodge.com; La Marina 124) and **Explorama** (☎ 065-25-2530; www.explorama.com; La Marina 340) Amazon lodges.

DETOUR

Boats from Yurimaguas to Iquitos usually stop in the remote village of **Lagunas**, which has no money-changing facilities and limited food, but it's a launching pad for visiting the wildlife-rich **Reserva Nacional Pacaya-Samiria** (admission per day S20), home to Amazon manatees, caiman, river dolphins and turtles, monkeys and abundant birdlife. Avoid visiting during the rainy season. To avoid price-cutting, there is an official guides' association, **ETASCEL** (☎ 40-1007), though travelers have reported they are less than caring or helpful. Tours cost approximately S100 per person per day, including accommodations, food and transportation, but not park entrance fees. Boats from Yurimaguas usually take 10 hours and arrive in Lagunas most days. Both towns have basic accommodation and lodging options.

In Lagunas, make sure you double-check the departure times for your boat at the port and be on alert. If you depend on others to insure you're ready to go when the boat departs, you could very well be left behind.

Mad Mick's Bunkhouse (☎ 50-7525; www.iquitos times.com; Putumayo 163; dm S10;) This popular eight-bed crash pad is in disrepair, but for the price, you can't get any closer to the action – it's 50m from the Plaza de Armas – or any more of a character running it.

Hostal Alfert (☎ 23-4105; reservacionalfert@yahoo .es; Saenz 1; s/d S15/25) In a dodgy neighborhood but with stupendous views of Belén from 2nd-floor rooms.

Hobo Hideout (☎ 23-4099; hobohideout@yahoo.com; Putumayo 437; dm S17.50, s/d without bathroom S25/35, r S50;) Justifiably popular with travelers for its *viajero* vibe on the front porch, but elsewhere the smoking front-desk staff, dead-simple, morgue-lit dorm rooms, organized hunting trips and plentiful taxidermy may be off-putting for some.

Hospedaje La Pascana (☎ 23-5581; www.pascana .com; Pevas 133; s/d/tr S35/40/50;) This is a good choice for its helpful staff and open courtyard, though charging for slow wi-fi is a tad ballsy. Pros are it's popular, friendly and that espresso machine, cons are the terrible pillows.

El Colibrí (☎ 24-1737; hostalcolibri@hotmail.com; Nauta 172; s/d S40/55) By far the best-maintained budget option, with bright rooms, cable TV and hot water on the 2nd and 3rd floors.

Casa Fitzcarraldo (☎ 60-1138; www.lacasafitzcarraldo .com; Av La Marina 2153; s/d incl breakfast S150/200;) It's a pricey midrange option, but movie buffs will want to sleep where the cast and crew of Werner Herzog's *Fitzcarraldo* were based during the filming of the 'most difficult movie ever made.' The jungly oasis has a fantastic pool and multilevel treehouse. It's run by the executive producer, Walter Saxer.

Eating

Jugería Ivalú (Lores 215; items S2-6) Fantastic find for jungle snacks like *humitas* and *juanecitos* served with colorful, spicy sauces.

La Noche (Malecón Maldonado 177; meals S6-22) This expat favorite is a quiet spot (no *mototaxis*!) with river views for hearty regional and international breakfasts and sandwiches.

Ari's Burger (Próspero 127; meals S6.50-25) Its almost legendary status is mainly due to location (on Plaza de Armas); the reality of this all-purpose America-style restaurant dubbed 'gringolandia' is very underwhelming. Vegetarian dishes are available.

Huasaí (Fitzcarrald 131; menú S9.50; lunch) Wildly popular for its homey chalkboard menu, served with air-con. A must for lunch.

Antica (Napo 159; pasta S16-32, pizza S20-30) This smart Italian, with encyclopedic pasta combinations, excellent thin-crust pizza, cheap breakfast and cozy decor supported by local Remo Caspi paddlewood, is probably the best all-things-considered dining option in Iquitos.

Bucanero (Av La Marina 124; mains S20-28; lunch) The air-con panoramic patio overlooking the river makes this a top spot for premium seafood with unstoppable views.

Al Frío y Al Fuego (Av La Marina 134B; mains S32-41; closed Mon & dinner Sun;) Iquitos' must-dining experience! It's a 10-minute motorized canoe ride to this splurge-worthy restaurant floating in the Río Itaya serving exquisite regional cuisine in a romantically lit, open-air wooden raft house. Canoes leave from El Huequito dock. Take a *mototaxi* (S2).

PERU

Drinking

El Musmuqui (Raymondi 382) Exotic cocktails laced with macerated roots and medicinal herbs are the calling here. Names ooze sexual innuendo: Take Me or Let Me Go, Old But Delicious.

Café-Teatro Amauta (Nauta 250) Antiquated tile flooring, iron staircases and, oddly, Chinese silk wallpaper, keep this a classic. Live music Thursday to Saturday.

La Sala (Putumayo 341) Never mind the cheap Latin signage, this sexy spot features a long hardwood bar bookended by two comfy, red-lit lounges with reappropriated furniture.

El Refugio (Av del Ejército 248) This kitschy, neon-lit bar is hilarious: drag queens serving suds to the real Iquitos watching the sun go down over the Río Nanay. It's in Moronacocha, 10 minutes out from the glossy, tourist bars of Centro. Take a *mototaxi* (S2.50) at 4pm on Friday or Saturday.

Entertainment

Noa Disco-Pub (Fitzcarrald 298; admission S15; ☉ Thu-Sat) The upscale, bilevel Noa pulsates from salsa to electronica.

Getting There & Away

AIR

Iquitos' **airport** (IQT; ☎ 22-8151; Abelardo Quiñones Km 6) is 6km south of town. Daily flights are currently available to Lima with **LAN** (☎ 22-4177; Próspero 232), and Lima and Pucallpa with **Star Perú** (☎ 23-6208; Napo 260). The latter also flies direct to Tarapoto four days per week.

BOAT

Most cargo boats leave from **Puerto Masusa** (☎ 77-3960; Los Rosales), 2.5km north of the town center. Dry-erase boards at the office (look for 'Aquí Radio Masusa' on the left side of Los Rosales just before the port entrance) tell you which boats are leaving when (though departures often change overnight, and boats tend to leave hours or days late). Boats to Yurimaguas

---

GETTING TO COLOMBIA, BRAZIL & ECUADOR

Colombia, Brazil and Peru share a three-way border. Even in the middle of the Amazon, border formalities must be adhered to and officials will refuse passage if your passport, tourist card and visas are not in order. Regulations change, but the riverboat captains know where to go. You can travel between the three countries without formalities, as long as you stay in the tri-border area. Otherwise, if you're leaving Peru, get an exit stamp at the Peruvian immigration post in Santa Rosa, on the south side of the river, just before the border (boats will stop long enough for this – ask the captain).

The biggest town is Leticia (Colombia), which has hotels, restaurants and a hospital. Get your passport stamped here for official entry into Colombia. Ferries from Santa Rosa (S6) reach Leticia in about 15 minutes. From Leticia you can fly to Bogotá daily with **Aero República** (www.aerorepublica.com) and three times a week on **Satena** (www.satena.com). Otherwise, infrequent boats go to Puerto Asis on the Río Putumayo, a trip of up to 12 days. From Puerto Asis, buses go further into Colombia.

Leticia is linked with Tabatinga (Brazil) by road (a short walk or COP$7000 taxi ride). Get your official entry stamp for Brazil from Tabatinga's police station. Tabatinga has an airport with flights to Manaus (Brazil) on **Trip** (www.voetrip.com.br). Boats to Manaus, about four days away, leave from downriver Wednesday and Saturday at 2pm. Hammock space runs R$150 and cabins from R$800 to R$1000. Speedboats leave from Porto Brass and run R$400 for the three-day trip. North Americans, Australians and others must obtain visas to enter Brazil; for more information, see p375.

From Iquitos, boats to Santa Rosa leave from Puerto Pesquero Monday to Saturday at 6:30pm, take three days and cost S60 for hammock space. Several companies on Raymondi at Loreto including **Golfinho** (☎ 22-5118) and **Challenger** (☎ 22-5556) offer fast launches (*más rápidos*) that take eight hours, depart at 6am most days and cost S200 including lunch.

It is also possible, though arduous, to travel by cargo boat between Iquitos and Coca, Ecuador, via the Amazon and Napo rivers. For more information on traveling this route from Ecuador to Peru, see p646.

For information on entering Peru from Brazil, see p366; from Colombia, p581.

PERU

(five days) depart Monday to Saturday at 6:30pm, give or take hours and days. Costs run S70 for a hammock (bring your own), S140 for a cabin. Tickets are sold on the boats. Be sure to pop in the port and inspect the boats before committing. *Eduardo 1-6* are considered the most comfortable to Yurimaguas.

Boats to Pucallpa (four days) depart at 6pm from **Puerto Henry** (☎ 67-8630; Av La Marina, Km 1.5). Boats leave four times a week and are pricier (S100 for a hammock, S180 for a cabin/jail cell). *Henry 6* and *7* are the most comfortable.

If you are traveling these waterways alone, a cabin is almost essential in order to secure your valuables. Without a companion to watch over them, they will be stolen. Bring a lock. Note that these boats are blatantly unfriendly to the fragile Amazon ecosystem: they dump their trash and waste straight into the river, even at port.

Getting Around

Taxis from the airport cost S15, *mototaxis* S8. Buses and trucks for nearby destinations, including the airport, leave from Arica at 9 de Dicembre. *Motocarro* rides around town cost S1.50 to S2.

PERU DIRECTORY

ACCOMMODATIONS

Lima and the tourist mecca of Cuzco are the most expensive places to stay in Peru. During high season (June through August), major holidays (p873) and festivals (p871), accommodations are likely to be full and rates can triple. At other times, the high-season rates quoted in this chapter taper off. Foreign tourists normally aren't charged the 10% sales tax on accommodations. *Incluye impuesto* (IGV) means a service charge has been included in the price. At better hotels, taxes and service charges combined may total 28%. Budget hotels usually have hot (or more likely, tepid) showers some of the time. Dormitory beds come with shared bathrooms, while single and double rooms (including those in *hostales*, which are guesthouses and not the same as backpacker hostels) have private bathrooms, unless otherwise noted.

ACTIVITIES

Most activities are available year-round, but certain times of year are better than others. Peak season for most outdoor activities is during the winter dry season (June to August). Trekking in the highlands is a muddy proposition during the wet season, especially December to March, when the heaviest rains fall. However, those hotter summer months are best for swimming and surfing along the Pacific Coast.

For your safety, avoid the cheapest, cut-rate tour agencies and outdoor outfitters. For specialized activities, bring high-quality gear from home.

If bird-watching gets you in a flap, head for the Amazon Basin (p859), Islas Ballestas (p790) and Cañón del Colca (p804) for starters. See p772 for more info on Peru's wildlife.

When it comes to mountain climbing, Huascarán (6768m), Peru's highest mountain, is experts-only, but easier peaks abound near Huaraz (p847) and Arequipa (p801). Rock and ice climbing are popular around Huaraz (p847).

Horse rentals can be easily arranged. For a real splurge, take a ride on a graceful Peruvian *paso* horse near Urubamba (p822).

Gearing up for some downhill adventures? Easy or demanding single-track trails await mountain bikers outside Huaraz (p847), Cuzco (p816) and Arequipa (p801).

Paragliding is an up-and-coming sport in Peru, especially in Lima (p781).

White-water rafting (river-running) agencies in Cuzco (p816) and Arequipa (p802) offer a multitude of day runs and longer hauls (grade III to IV+ rapids). Travelers have died on these rivers in recent years, so be especially cautious about which rafting company to trust with your life. The best place for beginners is Lunahuaná (p790).

Surfing has a big fan base in Peru. There are some radical waves up north, famously at Huanchaco (p840), Máncora and just south of Lima (p781). For something completely different, sandboard down humongous dunes in the coastal desert near Huacachina (p793) and Nazca (p795).

Trekkers, pack your boots – the variety of trails in Peru is staggering. The Cordillera Blanca (p847) can't be beaten for peaks, while the nearby Cordillera Huayhuash (p853) is similarly stunning. But if you've heard of *any* trek in Peru, you'll have heard of the world-famous Inca Trail to Machu Picchu (p828) – and everyone else has, too, so consider taking an alternative route to Machu Picchu (see boxed text, p832). The spectacular six-day Ausangate circuit (see boxed text, p832) and ancient ruins hidden in cloud forests outside Chachapoyas (p856) are a few more possibilities. Alternatively, get down into the world's deepest canyons – the Cañón del Cotahuasi (p802) and Cañón del Colca (p804).

BOOKS

Check out Lonely Planet's *Peru* guide and *Trekking in the Central Andes*.

If you read only one book about the Incas, make it the lucid and lively *Conquest of the Incas* by John Hemming. Or get a grip of *all* of Peru's bygone cultures with *The Ancient Kingdoms of Peru* by Nigel Davies.

The White Rock by Hugh Thomson describes a filmmaker's search for Inca archaeological sites throughout the Andes, with plenty of background on earlier explorers.

Eight Feet in the Andes by Dervla Murphy is a witty travelogue of the writer's 2000km journey with her daughter through remote Andean highlands from Ecuador to Cuzco, ending at Machu Picchu.

The Peru Reader: History, Culture, Politics, edited by Orin Starn, Carlos Ivan Degregori and Robin Kirk, looks at everything from the conquest of the Incas to cocaine production, guerrilla warfare and gay activism.

Touching the Void by Joe Simpson, now an award-winning British documentary film, is a harrowing account of mountaineering survival in the Cordillera Huayhuash.

The Monkey's Paw by Robin Kirk covers Peru during the violent 1980s – it's an excellent if chaotic examination of how individuals manage to survive terror.

Inca Kola by Matthew Parris is a tongue-in-cheek, often snide story about backpacking in Peru.

BUSINESS HOURS

Shops open at 9am or 10am and close from 6pm to 8pm. A two-hour lunch break is common. Shops may stay open through lunch in big cities, and there are 24-hour supermarkets in Lima. Banks are generally open 9am to 6pm Monday to Friday, to 1pm Saturday. Post offices and *casas de cambio* (money-exchange offices) keep highly variable hours. Almost everything closes on Sunday.

CLIMATE

During the coastal summer (late December to early April), many Peruvians head to the beach as the dreary *garúa* (coastal fog, mist or drizzle) clears and the sun breaks through.

In the Andes proper, the cool, dry season runs from May to September, which is peak season for tourism. The mountains can reach freezing temperatures at night, but enjoy glorious sunshine during the day. The wet season in the mountains extends from October to May, and is at its worst during January and February.

It rains all the time in the hot and humid Amazonian rainforest, but the driest months are from June to September. However, even during the wettest months (from December to May), it rarely rains for more than a few hours at a time.

For more information and climate charts, see p987.

DANGERS & ANNOYANCES

Peru has its fair share of traveler hassles, which may often be avoided by exercising common sense.

The most common problem is theft, either stealth or snatch – theft by violent mugging is rare, though not to be ruled out. Watch out for 'choke and grab' attacks, especially at archaeological sites. Robberies and fatal attacks have occurred even on popular trekking trails, notably around Huaraz.

Avoid unlicensed 'pirate' taxis, as some drivers have been known to be complicit in 'express' kidnappings. Take good-quality day buses instead of cheap, overnight services to lower the risk of having an accident or possibly being hijacked.

Do *not* get involved with drugs. Gringos who have done so are being repaid with long-term incarceration in harsh Peruvian prisons. Any suspect in a crime (which includes vehicle accidents, whether or not you're the driver at fault) is considered guilty until proven innocent.

While terrorism lingers in Peru, narco-trafficking is serious business. There was a major bust that sent shockwaves through the community in Iquitos in 2008. Areas to avoid are the Río Huallaga valley between Tingo María and Juanjui, and the Río Apurímac valley near Ayacucho, where the majority of Peru's illegal drug-growing takes place.

Not all unexploded ordinance (UXO) along the Ecuadorian border has been cleaned up. Use only official border crossings and don't stray off the beaten path in border zones.

Soroche (altitude sickness) can be fatal. For more information, see p1016.

DRIVER'S LICENSE

A driver's license from your home country is sufficient for renting a car. An International Driving Permit (IDP) is only required if you'll be driving in Peru for more than 30 days.

ELECTRICITY

Peru runs on a 220V, 60Hz AC electricity supply. Even though two-pronged outlets accept both flat (North American) and round (European) plugs, electronics built for lower voltage and cycles (eg 110V to 120V North American appliances) will function poorly or not at all, and plugging them in without using a converter can damage them.

EMBASSIES & CONSULATES

Australia (Map pp776-7; ☎ 01-222-8281; www .australia.org.pe; Suite 1301, Torre Real 3, Av Victor A Belaúnde 147, San Isidro, Lima 27)

Argentina (Map pp782-3; ☎ 01-433-3381; 28 de Julio 828, Lima 1)

Bolivia Lima (Map pp776-7; ☎ 01-442-3836; Castaños 235, San Isidro, Lima 27); Puno (Map p807; ☎/fax 051-35-1251; Arequipa 136, 3rd fl, Puno); Tacna (☎ 052-25-5121; Bolognesi 1751, Tacna)

Brazil Iquitos (Map p865; ☎ 065-23-5151; Lores 363, Iquitos); Lima (Map p785; ☎ 01-512-0830; www .embajadabrasil.org.pe; Av José Pardo 850, Miraflores, Lima 18)

Canada (Map p785; ☎ 01-319-3200; www.lima.gc.ca; Bolognesi 228, Miraflores, Lima 18)

Chile Lima (Map pp776-7; ☎ 01-221-2211; www.emba chile.peru.com.pe; Javier Prado Oeste 790, San Isidro, Lima 27); Tacna (☎ 052-42-3063; Presbitero Andía s/n, Tacna)

Colombia Iquitos (Map p865; ☎ 065-23-1461; Calvo de Araujo 431, Iquitos); Lima (Map pp776-7; ☎ 01-442-9648; www.embajadacolombia.org.pe; Jorge Basadre 1580, San Isidro, Lima 27)

Ecuador Lima (Map pp776-7; ☎ 01-421-7050; www .mecuadorperu.org.pe; Las Palmeras 356, San Isidro, Lima 27); Tumbes (☎ 072-52-5949; Bolívar 129, 3rd fl, Plaza de Armas, Tumbes)

France (Map pp776-7; ☎ 01-215-8400; www.amba france-pe.org; Av Arequipa 3415, San Isidro, Lima 27)

Germany (Map pp776-7; ☎ 01-212-5016; www .embajada-alemana.org.pe; Av Arequipa 4210, Miraflores, Lima 18)

UK (Map p785; ☎ 01-617-3000; www.ukinperu.fco .gov.uk; Edificio Parquemar, Av José Larco 1301, 22nd fl, Miraflores, Lima 18)

USA (Map pp776-7; ☎ 01-434-3000; http://lima.us embassy.gov; Av Encalada, 17th block, Monterrico, Lima)

FESTIVALS & EVENTS

See p873 for a list of national holidays.

La Virgen de la Candelaria (Candlemas) A colorful highland fiesta on February 2, particularly in the Puno area.

Carnaval In February/March – water fights galore!

Semana Santa (Holy Week) Religious processions throughout the week; March/April.

Corpus Christi Dramatic processions in Cuzco on the ninth Thursday after Easter.

Inti Raymi The great Inca festival of the sun, held on the winter solstice (June 24).

La Virgen del Carmen Street dancing in Pucara near Lake Titicaca and Paucartambo and Pisac near Cuzco on July 16.

Puno Day Spectacular costumes and dancing in Puno (November 5) to commemorate the legendary emergence of the first Inca, Manco Capác, from Lake Titicaca.

FOOD & DRINK

Food tends toward the spicy, but *ají* (chili condiments) are served separately. If you're sick of seafood, crying off *cuy* (guinea pig) or feeling ill at the very idea of Cajamarca's specialty, cow brains, don't be shy to check out a *chifa* (Chinese restaurant) or *pollería* – Peruvians can do amazing things with fried rice and rotisserie chicken. Vegetarianism is a small but fast-growing industry in Peru; hole-in-the-wall joints are popping up in major cities and tourist destinations. Many other local restaurants offer a *menú del día* (set meal, usually lunch), consisting of soup, main course and possibly dessert for around S8. Dried corn called *canchita* is a ubiquitous table snack.

Incluye impuesto (IGV) means a service charge has been included in the price. Better restaurants add 18% in taxes and 10% in tips to the bill.

Eating reviews in this chapter are given in order of budget, with the least expensive options first.

Peruvian Cuisine

Among the most typical Peruvian snacks and dishes:

ceviche (se-*vee*-che) – mixed seafood marinated in lime, chili and onions, served cold with sweet corn and a boiled yam; considered an aphrodisiac!

chirimoya (chee-ree-*mo*-ya) – reptilian-looking custard apple with sweet interior; tastes better than it looks

PERU

> **WARNING**
>
> Avoid food prepared from once or currently endangered animals. Sometimes *chanco marino* (dolphin) may be served up or, in the jungle areas, *huevos de charapa* (tortoise eggs), *paiche* (the largest scaled freshwater fish), caiman, *motelo* (turtle) or even *mono* (monkey).

cuy chactado (kooy chak·*ta*·do) – roasted guinea pig
lomo de alpaca (*lo*·mo de al·*pa*·ka) – alpaca meat tastes like beef, but has only half the fat
lomo saltado (*lo*·mo sal·*ta*·do) – chopped steak fried with onions, tomatoes and potatoes, served with rice
palta a la jardinera (*pal*·ta a la khar·dee·*nye*·ra) – avocado stuffed with cold vegetables and mayonnaise; *a la reina* is stuffed with chicken salad
rocoto relleno (ro·*ko*·to re·*ye*·no) – spicy bell pepper stuffed with ground meat; very hot!
sopa a la criolla (*so*·pa a la kree·*o*·ya) – lightly spiced, creamy noodle soup with beef and vegetables; *a la criolla* describes spicy foods.

Drinks

ALCOHOLIC DRINKS

There are about a dozen kinds of palatable and inexpensive beer, both light, lager-type beers and sweet, dark beers (called *malta* or *cerveza negra*). Cuzco and Arequipa are fiercely proud of their beers, Cuzqueña and Arequipeña.

Dating back to pre-Columbian times, traditional highland *chicha* (corn beer) is stored in earthenware pots and served in huge glasses in small Andean villages and markets, but is not usually commercially available. This homebrew is an acquired taste – the unhygienic fermentation process begins with someone chewing the corn.

Peruvian wines are decent but not up to the standard of Chilean or Argentine tipple. A white-grape brandy called *pisco* is the national drink, usually served in a *pisco sour*, a cocktail made from *pisco*, egg white, lemon juice, syrup, crushed ice and bitters. The firewater of choice in the jungle is *aguardiente* (sugarcane spirits flavored with anise). *Salud!*

NONALCOHOLIC DRINKS

Agua mineral (mineral water) is sold *con gas* (with carbonation) or *sin gas* (without carbonation). Don't leave without trying Peru's top-selling, fizzy-bubble-gum-flavored Inca Kola at least once. Ask for it *sin hielo* (without ice) unless you really trust the water supply. *Jugos* (fruit juices) are widely available. Make sure you get *jugo puro*, not *con agua* (with water). The most common juices are *naranja* (orange), *toronja* (grapefruit), *maracuyá* (passion fruit), *manzana* (apple), *naranjilla* (a local fruit tasting like bitter orange) and papaya. *Chicha morada* is a sweet, refreshing, noncarbonated drink made from purple corn. *Maté de coca* (coca-leaf tea) does wonders for warding off the effects of altitude. The coffee is fowl, usually instant in all but the biggest cities, and served with evaporated milk.

GAY & LESBIAN TRAVELERS

Peru is a strongly conservative, Catholic country. Gays and lesbians tend to keep a low profile. Homosexual rights in a political or legal context don't even exist as an issue for most Peruvians. (Note that the rainbow flag seen around Cuzco is *not* a gay-pride flag – it's the flag of the Inca empire.) When the issue does arise in public, hostility is most often the official response.

Kissing on the mouth is rarely seen in public, by either heterosexual or homosexual couples. Peruvians are physically demonstrative with their friends, though, so kissing on the cheek in greeting or an *abrazo* (backslapping hug exchanged between men) are innocuous, everyday behaviors. When in doubt, do as locals do.

Lima is the most accepting of gay people, while Cuzco, Arequipa and Trujillo are more tolerant than the norm. **Movimiento Homosexual-Lesbiana** (☎ 01-332-2945; www.mhol.org.pe) is Peru's best-known gay political organization. Lima has Peru's most open gay scene. **Deambiente** (www.deambiente.com) is a Spanish-language online magazine of politics and pop culture, plus nightlife listings. **Gayperu.com** (www.gayperu.com), another Spanish-language guide, lists bars to bathhouses. **Rainbow Tours** (☎ 01-215-

> **LIFE-CHANGING CEVICHE**
>
> - **El Cebillano** in Arequipa (see boxed text, p803)
> - **Ferrocol** in Chiclayo (p842)
> - **La Barca** in Puno (p808)
> - **La Choza Nautica** in Lima (p786)
> - **Punto Azul** in Lima (p786)

6000; www.perurainbow.com; Río de Janeiro 216, Miraflores, Lima) is a gay-owned tour agency with a multilingual website.

HOLIDAYS

On major holidays, banks, offices and other services are closed, fully booked hotels double or triple their rates, and transportation becomes overcrowded. Fiestas Patrias is the biggest national holiday, when the entire nation seems to be on the move.

Año Nuevo (New Year's Day) January 1
Good Friday March/April
Día del Trabajador (Labor Day) May 1
Inti Raymi June 24
Fiestas de San Pedro y San Pablo (Feast of St Peter & St Paul) June 29
Fiestas Patrias (National Independence Days) July 28 and 29
Fiesta de Santa Rosa de Lima August 30
Battle of Angamos Day October 8
Todos Santos (All Saints Day) November 1
Fiesta de la Purísima Concepción (Feast of the Immaculate Conception) December 8
Navidad (Christmas Day) December 25

INTERNET ACCESS

Internet cafes (locutorios) are found on every other street corner in Peru. Even small towns will have at least one cabina tucked away somewhere. Access is fast and inexpensive (around S1.50 per hour) in cities, but pricier and painfully unreliable in rural areas.

INTERNET RESOURCES

Andean Travel Web (www.andeantravelweb.com/peru) Travel directory with links to hotels, tour companies, volunteer programs etc.
Living in Peru (www.livinginperu.com) English-speaking expat's guide: an excellent source of Lima-centric news and events.
Peru Links (www.perulinks.com) Thousands of interesting links; many are in Spanish, some in English. Editor's picks and top 10 sites are always good.
PromPerú (www.peru.info) Official governmental tourism site has a good overview in Spanish, English, French, German, Italian and Portuguese.

LEGAL MATTERS

There are policía de turismo (tourist police) stations in over a dozen major cities, and they usually have someone on hand who speaks at least a little English. Although bribery is illegal, some police officers (including tourist police) may be corrupt. As most travelers won't have to deal with traffic police, the most likely place you'll be expected to pay officials a little extra is at overland border crossings. This too is illegal, and if you have the time and fortitude to stick to your guns, you will eventually be allowed in.

MAPS

The best road map of Peru, Mapa Vial (1:2,000,000) published by Lima 2000, is sold in bookstores. Topographic maps are easily available from outdoor outfitters in major cities and tourist destinations.

MONEY

The currency is the nuevo sol (S), divided into 100 céntimos.

ATMs

Most cities and some small towns have 24-hour ATMs on the Plus (Visa) and Cirrus (Maestro/MasterCard) systems. American Express and other networks are less widespread. Bigger airports and bus stations, as well as Interbank and BCP branches, have global ATMs that accept almost all foreign cards. ATMs in Peru will only accept your debit, bank or traveler's check card if you have a four-digit PIN. Both US dollars and Peruvian currency are dispensed.

Cash

The following bills are commonly in circulation: S10, S20, S50, S100. When changing money, always ask for plenty of small bills. Coins of S0.5, S0.10, S0.20, S0.50, S1, S2 and S5 are also in use. US dollars are accepted at many tourist-oriented establishments, but you'll need nuevos soles to pay for transportation, cheap meals and guesthouses etc. Counterfeiting is a major problem in Peru.

Credit Cards

Better hotels, restaurants and shops accept tarjetas de crédito (credit cards), but usually tack on a fee of 7% or more for paying with plastic.

Exchanging Money

Currencies other than US dollars can be exchanged only in major cities and at a high commission. Worn, torn or damaged bills are not accepted. Casas de cambio are open longer than banks and are much faster. Official money changers (cambistas) are

PERU

useful for exchange outside banking hours or at borders where there are no banks, but beware of 'fixed' calculators, counterfeit notes and short-changing.

Official exchange rates at press time:

EXCHANGE RATES		
Country	Unit	S
Australia	A$1	2.57
Canada	C$1	2.72
euro zone	€1	4.27
Japan	¥100	3.25
New Zealand	NZ$1	2.13
UK	UK£1	4.64
USA	US$1	2.90

POST

Serpost (www.serpost.com.pe) is the privatized postal system. It's relatively efficient, but expensive. Airmail postcards and letters cost about S5 to S6.50 each to most foreign destinations, arriving in about two weeks from Lima, longer from provincial cities.

Lista de correos (poste restante/general delivery) can be sent to any major post office. South American Explorers will hold mail and packages for members at its clubhouses in Lima (p779) and Cuzco (p814).

RESPONSIBLE TRAVEL

Archaeologists are fighting a losing battle with *guaqueros* (grave robbers), particularly along the coast. Refrain from buying original pre-Columbian artifacts, and do not contribute to wildlife destruction by eating endangered animals (see boxed text, p872) or purchasing souvenirs made from skins, feathers, horns or turtle shells. Some indigenous communities make their living from tourism. Visiting these communities may financially support their initiatives, but also weaken traditional cultures. If you go on an organized tour, make sure the company is locally owned and ask if any of the proceeds benefit the places you'll be visiting. See also Responsible Travel chapter, p4.

SHOPPING

Lima and Cuzco have the greatest selection of artisan craft shops selling antique and contemporary weavings, ceramics, paintings, woolen clothing, leather goods and silver jewelry. Lake Titicaca towns are great for knitted alpaca sweaters and knickknacks made from *totora* reeds. Huancayo is the place for carved gourds, while Ayacucho is famous for weavings and stylized ceramic churches. The Shipibo pottery sold in Yarinacocha is the best Amazon jungle craft available. Reproductions of ancient Moche pottery are sold in Trujillo; make sure objects are labeled as copies, as it's illegal to take pre-Columbian antiques out of the country. Avoid buying touristy goods made by cutting up antique textiles, which is destructive to indigenous peoples' cultural heritage.

STUDYING

Peru is lesser-known for its Spanish-language courses than other Latin American countries. However, there are several schools in Lima, Cuzco (p816) and Arequipa (p802).

TELEPHONE

Public payphones are available in even the tiniest towns. Most work with phone cards, and many with coins. Dial ☎ 109 for a Peruvian operator, ☎ 108 for an international operator and ☎ 103 for information. Internet cafes are often much cheaper for making local, long-distance and international phone calls than **Telefónica-Perú** (www.telefonica.com.pe) offices.

Cell Phones

It's possible to use a tri-band GSM world phone in Peru (GSM 1900); other systems in use are CDMA and TDMA. In major cities, you can buy cell phones from S69, then pop in a SIM card that costs around S15 – Claro offers a popular pay-as-you-go plan. Reception fades the further you head into the mountains or jungle. Cell phone rental at the airport runs around S30.70 for activation and S2.20/4.60 per minute national/international afterwards. Cell-phone numbers have nine digits and always start with 9.

Phone Cards

Called *tarjetas telefónicas,* phone cards are widely available from street vendors or kiosks. Some have an electronic chip, but most make you dial a code to obtain access. The most common are the 147 cards: dial 147, enter the code on the back of your card, listen to a message in Spanish telling you your balance, dial the number, listen to how much time you have, then your call connects. Ask around for which companies' cards offer the best deals.

Phone Codes

Peru's country code is ☎ 51. To call a foreign country, dial 00, the country code, area code and local number.

Each region of Peru (called a department) has its own area code, which begins with 0 (☎ 01 in Lima, 0 plus two digits elsewhere). To call long-distance within Peru, include the 0 in the area code. If calling from abroad, dial your international access code, the country code (☎ 51), the area code without the 0, then the local number.

TOILETS

Peruvian plumbing leaves something to be desired. Even a small amount of toilet paper in the bowl can muck up the entire system – that's why a small plastic bin is routinely provided for disposing of it. Except at museums, restaurants, hotels and bus stations, public toilets are rare in Peru. Always carry an extra roll of toilet paper with you.

TOURIST INFORMATION

PromPerú's official tourism website (www .peru.info) offers information in Spanish, Portuguese, English, French, German and Italian. PromPerú also runs **iPerú** (☎ 24hr hotline 01-574-8000) information offices in Lima, Arequipa, Ayacucho, Chiclayo, Cuzco, Huaraz, Iquitos, Piura, Puno, Tacna and Trujillo. Municipal tourist offices are found in other cities listed in this chapter. The South American Explorers clubhouses in Lima (p779) and Cuzco (p814) are good sources of information for travelers, but you'll get more help as a paying member.

TOURS

Some protected areas such as the Inca Trail and Parque Nacional Manu can only be entered with a guided tour. Other outdoor activities, such as trekking in the Andes or wildlife-watching in the Amazon, may be more rewarding with an experienced guide.

TRAVELERS WITH DISABILITIES

Peru offers few conveniences for travelers with disabilities. Peru's official tourism organization PromPerú (above) has a link to Accessible Tourism from the 'Special Interests' section of its website (www.peru.info) for reports on wheelchair-accessible hotels, restaurants and attractions in Lima, Cuzco, Aguas Calientes, Iquitos and Trujillo.

VISAS

With few exceptions (a handful of Asian, African and communist countries), visas are not required for tourism. Passports should be valid for at least six months from your departure date. For more information on entry requirements (eg onward/return tickets), see p997. Travelers are permitted a 90-day initial stay, stamped into their passports and onto an Andean Immigration Card that you must keep and return when leaving Peru. Visa extensions were discontinued in 2008, so if you want to stay beyond that, you must leave the country and re-enter for a fresh 90-day stamp (up to 180 days total per year); or, oddly, request an initial allotment of 183 days on first entry (subject to the discretion of the immigration official). Overstays are fined at US$1 per day.

While traveling around Peru, carry your passport and immigration card with you at all times, as you can be arrested if you don't have proper ID.

See also lonelyplanet.com and its links for up-to-date visa information.

VOLUNTEERING

Most volunteer programs charge you for program fees, room and board. Watch out for fake charities and illegitimate programs that are scams. Spanish-language schools usually know of casual volunteer opportunities. South American Explorers clubhouses have firsthand reports from foreign volunteers in Lima (p779) and Cuzco (p814). **ProWorld Service Corps** (ProPeru; ☎ in USA 877-429-6753, in UK 0-18-6559-6289; www.mypro world.org) organizes two- to 26-week cultural, service and academic placements in the Sacred Valley and is affiliated with NGOs throughout Peru.

WOMEN TRAVELERS

Most women encounter no serious problems in Peru, though they should come mentally prepared for being the constant center of attention. Machismo is alive and well in Peruvian towns and cities, where curious staring, whistling, hissing and *piropos* (cheeky, flirtatious or vulgar remarks) are an everyday occurrence. Ignoring provocation is generally the best response. Most men don't follow up their idle chatter with something more threatening unless they feel you've challenged or insulted their manhood.

PERU

If you appeal to locals for help, you'll find most Peruvians act protectively toward women traveling alone, expressing surprise and concern when you tell them you're traveling without your husband or family. If a stranger approaches you on the street to ask a question, *don't* stop walking, which would allow attackers to quickly surround you. Never go alone on a guided tour, and stay alert at archaeological sites, even during daylight hours. Take only authorized taxis and avoid overnight buses.

Abortions are illegal in Peru, except when they can save the life of the mother. Planned Parenthood–affiliated **Instituto Peruano de Paternidad Responsable** (Inppares; ☎ 01-583-9012; www.inppares.org.pe) runs a dozen sexual- and reproductive-health clinics for both sexes around the country.

WORKING

Officially you need a work visa in Peru, though language centers in Lima or Cuzco sometimes hire native speakers to teach English. This is illegal, and such jobs are increasingly difficult to get without a proper work visa. For internships and short-term jobs with volunteer organizations, see p875.

Uruguay

HIGHLIGHTS

- **Colonia del Sacramento** (p889) Get snap-happy on the picturesque cobbled streets of this former smugglers' port.
- **The Atlantic Coast** (p895) Hit the beach in style or in the wild along this beautiful stretch of coastline
- **Carnaval** (p886) Get those hips moving to the *candombe* rhythm at Montevideo's month-long party.
- **Termas de Daymán** (p894) Soak those weary traveling bones at the country's favorite hot springs.
- **Off the Beaten Track** (see boxed text, p897) Mingle with sea lions, penguins and whales in the secluded hippy beach town of Cabo Polonio.
- **Best Journey** (see boxed text, p903) Cross Uruguay's interior, from Chuy to Tacuarembó, through beautiful countryside few travelers ever see.

FAST FACTS

- **Area:** 187,000 sq km (roughly the size of the US state of North Dakota)
- **Budget:** US$35 to US$45 a day
- **Capital:** Montevideo
- **Costs:** budget hotel in Montevideo US$18, three-hour bus ride US$8.50, set lunch US$8
- **Country Code:** ☎ 598
- **Languages:** Spanish; Portuguese (near the Brazilian border)
- **Money:** US$1 = UR$23.4 (Uruguayan pesos)
- **Population:** 3.42 million
- **Seasons:** high (November to March), low (June to August)
- **Time:** GMT minus three hours (daylight-saving time mid-October to mid-March)

TRAVEL HINTS

Most towns have a *rotisería* (takeaway food store) and at least one lovely plaza. Instant picnic.

OVERLAND ROUTES

Uruguay's border crossings include Buenos Aires, Tigre, Colón and Concordia (all Argentina). The Gualeguaychú crossing is closed until further notice. For Brazil, most people use Chuí/Porto Alegre.

URUGUAY

Like an oasis in an often-troubled region, Uruguay moves at its own pace. Known for years as the Switzerland of South America, the country earned this reputation not just for its super-secret banking laws, but for their love of the common plebiscite and the sense of peace that pervades the nation.

There are some pretty wild contrasts here. Don't be surprised to see a horse and cart clip-clopping down Montevideo's cosmopolitan downtown streets, or a traditionally dressed *gaucho* (cowboy) toting the latest model cell phone.

Traveling in Uruguay has never been easier. The spread of hostels across the country has built on the solid foundation of an extensive bus network, good restaurants and excellent camping facilities. Even in world-class destinations such as Colonia del Sacramento or Punta del Este, finding a cheap sleep is only tricky in absolute peak periods.

People come for the wild, surf-pounded beaches, to rub shoulders with celebrities at Punta or to soak in the history in Montevideo's old town and at the smugglers' port of Colonia. They stay for the people – warm, open and sincere folk who have constructed one of South America's most progressive societies. And when they leave, they almost always say they're coming back.

CURRENT EVENTS

After a somewhat rocky beginning, Uruguay's Frente Amplio government has presided over two small social revolutions recently – the legalization of abortion in late 2007, and the sanctioning of civil unions between same-sex partners in early 2008. That said, 2009 started badly for Uruguay – a drought forced the government to announce emergency water-saving measures and beef exports fell 33%.

The lead-up to the October 2009 presidential election was dominated by debates over security, the rising crime rate and Uruguay's faltering economy which, following the global trend, entered into recession in mid-2009. At the time of writing the ruling party lead the polls, but internal bickering and expected further economic downturns gave rise to predictions that the election would be close and probably go to a second-round runoff. Under Uruguayan law, Tabaré Vázquez is not permitted to run for a second term, and his expected successor is senator and ex-Tupamaro guerilla José Mujica.

HISTORY
In the Beginning...

The Charrúa were here first, huntin' and fishin'. They had no gold and a nasty habit of killing European explorers, so the Spanish left them alone. Eventually they mellowed out, got some horses and cattle, and started trading. Once the big cattle farmers moved in, the Charrúa got pushed out and they now exist in isolated pockets around the Brazilian border.

Everybody Wants a Piece

The Jesuits were on the scene as early as 1624 and the Portuguese established present-day Colonia del Sacramento (commonly shortened to 'Colonia') in 1680 so they could smuggle goods into Buenos Aires. Spain responded by building its own citadel at Montevideo. For almost 200 years the Portuguese, Spanish and British fought to get a foothold.

From 1811 José Artigas repelled the Spanish invaders, but Brazil ended up controlling the region. Artigas was exiled to Paraguay where he died in 1850, after inspiring the 33 Orientales who, reinforced by Argentine troops, liberated the area in 1828, establishing Uruguay as a buffer between the emerging continental powers of Argentina and Brazil.

More Drama

Liberation didn't bring peace. There were internal rebellions, insurrections and coups. Argentina besieged Montevideo from 1838 to 1851 and Brazil was an ever-present threat. Uruguay's modern political parties, the Colorados and the Blancos, have their origins in this time – early party membership comprised large numbers of armed *gauchos*. By the mid-19th century the economy was largely dependent on beef and wool production. The rise of the *latifundios* (large landholdings) and commercialization of livestock led to the demise of the independent *gaucho*.

José Batlle, We Love You

In the early 20th century, visionary president José Batlle y Ordóñez introduced such innovations as pensions, farm credits, unemployment compensation and the eight-hour work day. State intervention led to the nationalization of many industries, and general prosperity. The invention of refrigerated processing and shipping facilities opened many overseas markets for Uruguayan beef. However, Batllé's reforms were largely financed through taxing the livestock sector, and when this sector faltered the welfare state crumbled.

The Wheels Fall Off

By the 1960s economic stagnation and massive inflation were reaching crisis points, and social unrest was increasing. President Oscar Gestido died in 1967 and was replaced by running mate Jorge Pacheco Areco.

Pacheco sprang into action, outlawing leftist parties and closing leftist newspapers, which he accused of supporting the guerrilla Movimiento de Liberación Nacional (commonly known as Tupamaros). The country slid into dictatorship. After Tupamaros executed suspected CIA agent Dan Mitrione (as dramatized in Costa Gavras' film *State of Siege*) and engineered a major prison escape, Pacheco put the military in charge of counterinsurgency. In 1971 Pacheco's chosen successor, Juan Bordaberry, handed control of the government over to the military.

Jobs for the Boys

The military occupied almost every position of importance in the 'national security state.' Arbitrary detention and torture became routine. The forces determined eligibility

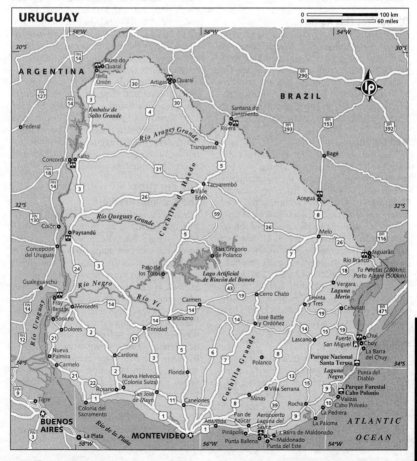

for public employment, subjected political offenses to military courts, censored libraries and even required prior approval for large family gatherings.

Voters rejected a military-drawn constitution in 1980. Four years passed before Colorado candidate Julio María Sanguinetti became president under the existing constitution. His presidency implied a return to democratic traditions, but he also supported a controversial amnesty, ratified by voters in 1989, for military human-rights abuses.

Later in 1989, the Blancos' Luis Lacalle succeeded Sanguinetti in a peaceful transition. Sanguinetti returned to office in the November 1994 elections and was succeeded by Jorge Battle Ibáñez, another Colorado candidate, in March 2000.

Oh No, Not this Again

The military were still lurking around, however – one of Ibáñez' first official duties was to dismiss the head of the army for suggesting that another coup might be in order. The Frente Amplio (Broad Front) – a coalition of leftist parties – became a serious political contender, winning popularity for its antiprivatization, prowelfare stance.

Bad Omens

When the spread of foot-and-mouth disease led to the banning of Uruguayan beef exports, it was bad news for the economy. When Argentine banks froze deposits and thousands of Argentines withdrew their cash from Uruguayan banks, it was *really* bad news. Argentine deposits made up 80% of foreign reserves in Uruguay's banks. Uruguayans watched in horror as their economy – previously one of the strongest in South America – crumbled, and inflation (3.6% in 2001) rocketed to 40% by the end of 2002. The peso plummeted in value, the economy minister resigned and the government declared a bank holiday to prevent a run on the banks.

Independence?

What followed then was a massive bailout. Ibáñez' emergency measures (cutting public spending and increasing sales tax) were rewarded by loans from the US, International Monetary Fund and World Bank, totaling US$1.5 billion. But despite that, Uruguay was still showing some pluck politically – condemning

the sanctions against Cuba, the coup in Venezuela and the war in Iraq.

Swingin' to the Left

In March 2005 Tabaré Vázquez swept into power, heading the leftist coalition Frente Amplio. Commentators saw Vázquez' election as part of a leftward swing throughout South American politics, encompassing Argentina, Bolivia, Brazil, Chile and Venezuela. Uruguayans collectively held their breath, waiting to see if the new government would live up to the rhetoric of the campaign trail, or if the country was in for more of the same.

Early signs were puzzling. Vázquez sought a free-trade deal with the US (surprising and alienating Uruguay's Mercosur trade partners), banned smoking in public (annoying pretty much everyone in this nicotine-crazed land) and granted leases to two foreign multinationals to build pulp mills on the Río Uruguay, which forms the border between Uruguay and Argentina (infuriating Argentines, environmentalists and hardcore lefties).

This last action gave rise to plenty of cross-border mud-slinging, court challenges and even an attempt at mediation by King Juan Carlos of Spain. One mill opened in late 2007, but bitterness over the issue remains, and the Gualeguaychú–Fray Bentos border bridge remains closed, blockaded by Argentine protesters.

THE CULTURE
The National Psyche

The one thing that Uruguayans will tell you that they're *not* is anything like their *porteño* (people from Buenos Aires) cousins across the water. In many ways they're right. Where Argentines are brassy and sometimes arrogant, Uruguayans are relaxed and self-assured. Where the former have always been a regional superpower, the latter have always lived in the shadow of one. Those jokes about Punta del Este being a suburb of Buenos Aires don't go down so well on this side of the border. There are lots of similarities, though – the near-universal appreciation for the arts and the Italian influence, with its love for pizza, pasta, wine and cheese. The *gaucho* thing plays a part, too, and the rugged individualism and disdain that many Uruguayans hold for *el neoliberalismo* (neoliberalism) can be traced directly back to those romantic cowboy figures.

Lifestyle

Uruguayans like to take it easy and pride themselves on being the opposite of the hot-headed Latino type. They're big drinkers, but bar-room brawls are rare. Sunday's the day for family and friends, to throw half a cow on the *asado* (barbecue), sit back and sip some maté. The population is well-educated, although public-school standards are slipping. The once-prominent middle class is disappearing as private universities become the main providers of quality education.

Population

The Uruguayan population is predominately white (88%) with 8% *mestizo* (people with mixed Spanish and indigenous blood) and 4% black. Indigenous peoples are practically non-existent. The population growth rate is 0.5%, one of the lowest in the world. Population density is 18.3 people per square kilometer.

SPORTS

In Uruguay, sport means football and football means soccer. Uruguay has won the World Cup twice, including the first tournament, played in Uruguay in 1930. The most notable teams are Montevideo-based Nacional and Peñarol. If you go to a match between these two, sit on the sidelines, not behind the goal, unless you're up for some serious passion-induced rowdiness.

The **Asociación Uruguaya de Fútbol** (off Map pp884-5; ☎ 02-400-7101; www.auf.org.uy; Guayabo 1531) in Montevideo can provide information on matches and venues.

RELIGION

Forty-seven percent of Uruguayans are Roman Catholic. There's a small Jewish minority, numbering around 10,000. Unusually for a Latin American country, a little over 17% of Uruguayans identify themselves as atheist or agnostic. Evangelical Protestantism is gaining ground and Sun Myung Moon's Unification Church (aka the Moonies) owns the afternoon daily, *Últimas Noticias.*

ARTS

Uruguay's small population produces a surprising number of talented artists and literary figures. While Juan Carlos Onetti is probably the most famous Uruguayan writer, most young Uruguayans have a big soft spot for journalist Eduardo Galeano, who has written many books and poems, including *Las venas abiertas de América Latina,* the English translation of which recently shot onto the bestseller list after Venezuelan President Hugo Chávez gave a copy to US President Barack Obama. Other major contemporary writers include author and journalist Hugo Burel, postmodernist Enrique Estrázulas, rising star Ignacio Alcuri and the late poet, essayist and novelist Mario Benedetti.

Probably the most famous film made about Uruguay is *State of Siege* (1973), which deals with the Tupamaro guerrillas' kidnapping and execution of suspected American CIA officer Dan Mitrione.

The most critically acclaimed movie to come out of Uruguay lately is *Whisky* (2004), a witty black comedy set in Montevideo and Piriápolis. It won a couple of awards at Cannes. In 2007 the documentary *Stranded* (made from the book *La socieded de la nieve*) told the story of 16 Uruguayan rugby players who survived a plane crash in the Andes. The story was made famous by the 1993 release *Alive* (yes, the one where they end up eating each other to survive), but the latest version is all the more gripping for being retold by the actual survivors.

Gigante, a beautifully shot art-house piece, is the current critics' pick for Uruguayan films – it scored three awards in 2009 at the prestigious Berlin International Film Festival.

Tango is big in Montevideo – Uruguayans claim tango legend Carlos Gardel as a native son, although the Argentines and French have other ideas. During Carnaval, Montevideo's streets reverberate to the energetic drum beats of *candombe,* an African-derived rhythm brought to Uruguay by slaves from 1750 onwards.

As far as contemporary music goes, young Uruguayans still have a lot of love for three-chord power rock. The best of the current batch of rockers is La Trampa. For something a bit lighter, try No Te Va Gustar, who blend rock with pop, electronica, ska and *murga* (athletic musical theater) rhythms.

Theater is popular and playwrights such as Mauricio Rosencof are prominent. The most renowned painters are Juan Manuel Blanes and Joaquín Torres García. Sculptors include José Belloni, whose life-size bronzes can be seen in Montevideo's parks.

URUGUAY

ENVIRONMENT

The Land

Uruguay's rolling northern hills extend from southern Brazil with two main ranges of interior hills, the Cuchilla de Haedo, west of Tacuarembó, and the Cuchilla Grande, south of Melo, neither of which exceeds 500m in height. West of Montevideo the terrain is more level. The Atlantic Coast has impressive beaches, dunes and headlands. Uruguay's grasslands and forests resemble those of Argentina's Pampas or of southern Brazil. Patches of palm savanna persist in the southeast, along the Brazilian border.

Wildlife

Nearly all large land animals have disappeared, but the occasional rhea still races across northwestern Uruguay's grasslands. Some offshore islands harbor southern fur seal and sea lion colonies.

National Parks

Uruguay isn't big on national parks. Parque Nacional Santa Teresa (p901) and Parque Nacional San Miguel are the country's only parks, but the purpose of both is to protect the colonial-era forts found within – they don't have a whole lot going on nature-wise.

TRANSPORTATION

GETTING THERE & AWAY

Air

Most international flights to and from Montevideo's Aeropuerto Carrasco pass through Buenos Aires. Direct flights go to Porto Alegre, Florianópolis, Rio de Janeiro and São Paulo (Brazil), Asunción (Paraguay) and Santiago (Chile).

Boat

Most travelers cross from Montevideo to Argentina by ferry, sometimes with bus combinations to Colonia or Carmelo. See p888.

DEPARTURE TAX

International passengers leaving from Carrasco pay US$17 departure tax if headed to Argentina, US$31 to other destinations. You can pay in pesos, US dollars or by credit card.

Bus

Direct buses theoretically run from Montevideo to Buenos Aires via Gualeguaychú, but are slower than land/river combinations across the Río de la Plata. This crossing has been closed for years now, in the wake of a dispute over Uruguayan paper plants on the bank of the Río Uruguay. There's no sign of this dispute easing up, but ask around to see if the border is now open. For the time being, buses use bridge crossings over Río Uruguay from Paysandú to Colón. There is another bridge connecting Salto and Concordia. There are multiple crossings to Brazil – the most popular is Chuy to Chuí and Pelotas. Buses generally continue through the border and passport formalities are conducted on the bus.

GETTING AROUND

Uruguayan buses and roads are well maintained. Montevideo is *the* transport hub. If you stay on the coast or river roads, you'll never be waiting long for a bus. Try something tricky like Chuy to Tacuarembó (see boxed text, p903) and you'll experience otherwise. Due to its small size, Uruguay is perfect for bus travel – the longest ride you're likely to take is a measly six hours.

Air

If you really need to get somewhere in a hurry, internal charter flights are available with **Aeromas** (☎ 02-604-6359; www.aeromas.com; Las Américas 5120, Montevideo) from Montevideo to Salto, Tacuarembó, Paysandú, Rivera and Artigas.

Bus

Most towns have a *terminal de ómnibus* (central bus terminal) for long-distance buses. To get your choice of seat, buy tickets in advance from the terminal. Local buses are slow and crowded, but cheap.

Car & Motorcycle

Due to the excellent bus network, few visitors use independent transportation to get around Uruguay. Cars and motorbikes can be hired in tourist centers such as Colonia and Punta del Este.

Hitchhiking

Hitchhikers are rare in Uruguay – you might get picked up for novelty value. It's not a particularly dangerous country, but hitching is a gamble anywhere in the world. Take the usual precautions.

Taxi

Taxis are so cheap they're hard to resist. Meters work on segments and drivers consult a photocopied chart to calculate the fare. A long ride in Montevideo shouldn't go over UR$150; short hops in small towns usually cost around UR$25. On weekends and at night, fares are 25% to 50% higher.

MONTEVIDEO

☎ 02 / pop 1.3 million

Montevideo is a favorite for many travelers. Small enough to walk around, but big enough to have some great architecture and happening nightlife.

The young *montevideanos* (people from Montevideo) who don't escape across the water to Buenos Aires have a real pride in their city, and the arts and artisan scene is particularly strong.

Many of the grand 19th-century neoclassical buildings, legacies of the beef boom, are in various stages of crumbling, although vestiges of Montevideo's colonial past still exist in the Ciudad Vieja (Old Town), the picturesque historic center.

ORIENTATION

Montevideo lies on the east bank of the Río de la Plata. Its functional center is Plaza Independencia, east of the Ciudad Vieja (old town). Av 18 de Julio is the key commercial area.

Across the harbor, the 132m Cerro de Montevideo was a landmark for early navigators of this region. East of downtown, the riverfront Rambla leads past residential suburbs and sandy beaches frequented by *montevideanos* on weekends in summer.

INFORMATION

Bookstores

Pablo Ferrando (Sarandí 675) One of the city's many bookstores, with a good selection of Uruguayan writers and music CDs.

Plaza Libros (Av 18 de Julio 892) A selection of books in English.

Cultural Centers

Alianza (☎ 901-7423; www.alianza.edu.uy; Paraguay 1217) The American-Uruguayan cultural center contains a

---

> **GETTING INTO TOWN**
>
> A taxi from the airport costs about UR$440. Airport buses cost UR$25 and take 40 minutes. Buses CA1, 21, 61, 180, 187 and 188 go from Terminal Tres Cruces to Av 18 de Julio (UR$15 to UR$20).

bookstore, a theater and a substantial library with publications in English.

Complejo Multicultural Mundo Afro (☎ 915-0247; www.mundoafro.org; Ciudadela 1229) Montevideo's Afro-Uruguayan community cultural center, upstairs in the Mercado Central.

Emergencies

Ambulance (☎ 105)
Fire (☎ 104)
Police (☎ 109)

Media

The *Guía del Ocio*, which lists cultural events, cinemas, theaters and restaurants, appears on Friday in newsstands.

Medical Services

Hospital Británico (☎ 487-1020; Italia 2420) Private, highly recommended hospital with English-speaking doctors.

Hospital Maciel (☎ 915-3000; cnr 25 de Mayo & Maciel) The public hospital, in the Ciudad Vieja.

Money

Most downtown banks have ATMs. **Exprinter** (cnr Sarandí & Juncal) and **Indumex** (Plaza Cagancha) change traveler's checks and cash.

Post & Telephone

Antel Telecentro (San José 1108; ☻ 24hr) There's another at Rincón 501.

Post office (Buenos Aires 451) This is the main post office.

Tourist Information

Hostelling International (☎ 901-3587; Paraguay 212) Information on HI-affiliated hostels around the country. Also issues ISIC student cards (UR$250).

Ministerio de Turismo (☎ 1885, ext 111; www.turismo.gub.uy; cnr Yacaré & Rambla 25 de Agosto de 1825) Better equipped than the offices.

Municipal tourist office (☎ 1950, ext 3171; Palacio Municipal) Small but well informed.

Oficina de Informes (☎ 409-7399; Tres Cruces Bus Terminal) Well equipped and handy for fresh arrivals.

Tourist police (☎ 908-3303; Colonia 1021)

MONTEVIDEO

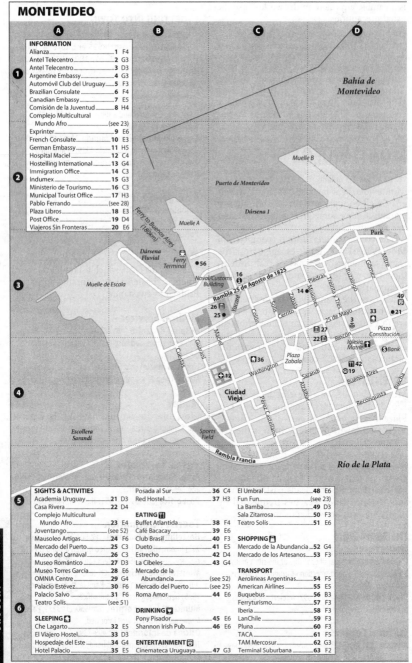

A   **B**   **C**   **D**

INFORMATION
Alianza	**1**	F4
Antel Telecentro	**2**	G3
Antel Telecentro	**3**	D3
Argentine Embassy	**4**	G3
Automóvil Club del Uruguay	**5**	F3
Brazilian Consulate	**6**	F4
Canadian Embassy	**7**	E5
Comisión de la Juventud	**8**	H4
Complejo Multicultural Mundo Afro	(see 23)	
Exprinter	**9**	E6
French Consulate	**10**	E3
German Embassy	**11**	H5
Hospital Maciel	**12**	C4
Hostelling International	**13**	G4
Immigration Office	**14**	C3
Indumex	**15**	G3
Ministerio de Tourismo	**16**	C3
Municipal Tourist Office	**17**	H3
Pablo Ferrando	(see 28)	
Plaza Libros	**18**	D4
Post Office	**19**	D4
Viajeros Sin Fronteras	**20**	E6

Bahía de Montevideo

Muelle B

Puerto de Montevideo

Dársena I

Park

Ferry to Buenos Aires (1.80km)

Muelle A

Dársena Fluvial   Ferry Terminal

●56

Muelle de Escala

Naval/Customs Building

16 ℹ️

Rambla 25 de Agosto de 1825

26 🏛️
25 ●

14 ●

49 ●
●21

33 🏨
3 🏨

Plaza Constitución

22 🏛️

Iglesia Matriz 🏛️

💲Bank

🏥36

Plaza Zabala

42 🏨
19 ⊗

🏥12

Washington

Ciudad Vieja

Escollera Sarandi

Sports Field

Reconquista

Rambla Francia

Río de la Plata

SIGHTS & ACTIVITIES
Academia Uruguay	**21**	D3
Casa Rivera	**22**	D4
Complejo Multicultural Mundo Afro	**23**	E4
Joventango	(see 52)	
Mausoleo Artigas	**24**	F6
Mercado del Puerto	**25**	C3
Museo del Carnaval	**26**	C3
Museo Romántico	**27**	D3
Museo Torres García	**28**	E6
OMNIA Centre	**29**	G4
Palacio Estévez	**30**	F3
Palacio Salvo	**31**	F6
Teatro Solís	(see 51)	

SLEEPING
Che Lagarto	**32**	E5
El Viajero Hostel	**33**	D3
Hospedaje del Este	**34**	G4
Hotel Palacio	**35**	E5

Posada al Sur	**36**	C4
Red Hostel	**37**	H3

EATING
Buffet Atlantida	**38**	F4
Café Bacacay	**39**	E6
Club Brasil	**40**	F3
Dueto	**41**	E5
Estrecho	**42**	D4
La Cibeles	**43**	G4
Mercado de la Abundancia	(see 52)	
Mercado del Puerto	(see 25)	
Roma Amor	**44**	E6

DRINKING
Pony Pisador	**45**	E6
Shannon Irish Pub	**46**	E6

ENTERTAINMENT
Cinemateca Uruguaya	**47**	G3

El Umbral	**48**	E6
Fun Fun	(see 23)	
La Bamba	**49**	D3
Sala Zitarrosa	**50**	F3
Teatro Solís	**51**	E6

SHOPPING
Mercado de la Abundancia	**52**	G4
Mercado de los Artesanos	**53**	F3

TRANSPORT
Aerolíneas Argentinas	**54**	F5
American Airlines	**55**	E5
Buquebus	**56**	B3
Ferryturismo	**57**	F3
Iberia	**58**	F3
LanChile	**59**	F3
Pluna	**60**	F3
TACA	**61**	F5
TAM Mercosur	**62**	G3
Terminal Suburbana	**63**	F2

URUGUAY

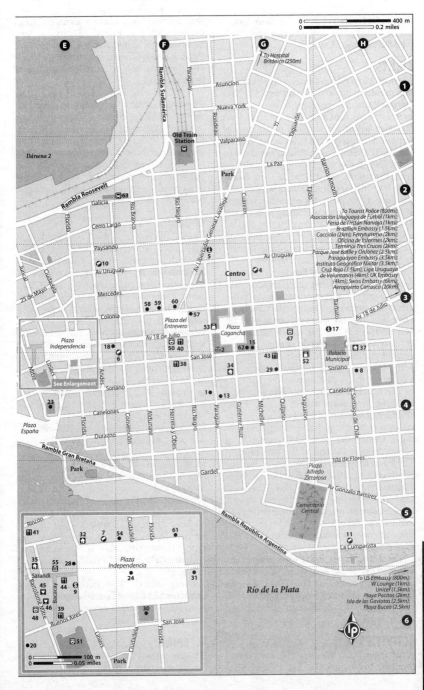

Viajeros Sin Fronteras (☎ 916-5466; Buenos Aires 618, 2nd fl) The local STA Travel affiliate can organize cheap flights, change tickets etc.

SIGHTS

Most of Montevideo's interesting buildings and museums are in the **Ciudad Vieja**. On **Plaza Independencia**, a huge statue of the country's greatest hero tops the eerie underground **Mausoleo Artigas** (☒ 9am-5pm), where fans of famous dead people can tick another one off the list. The 18th-century **Palacio Estévez** served as the Casa de Gobierno (Government House) until 1985, while the striking 26-story **Palacio Salvo** was once South America's tallest building. Just off the plaza, the recently renovated 1856 **Teatro Solís** (www.teatrosolis.org.uy; Buenos Aires 678) is Montevideo's leading theater. Guided tours (UR\$20/40 in Spanish/English; free tours in Spanish Wednesday) are available Tuesday to Sunday at 11am, midday and 4pm.

The 1868 **Mercado del Puerto** (cnr Castellano & Piedras) is a wrought-iron superstructure sheltering a gaggle of restaurants. On Saturday artists and musicians frequent the area. In the same building, the **Museo del Carnaval** (☎ 916-5493; Rambla 25 de Agosto de 1825 No 218; admission UR\$50; ☒ 11am-5pm Tue-Sun) documents past and present traditions of Montevideo's Carnaval with plenty of photos, masks, costumes and a couple of floats on display.

The neoclassical 1802 **Casa Rivera** (cnr Rincón & Misiones; ☒ noon-7pm Mon-Fri) houses a fascinating collection of indigenous artifacts, colonial treasures and oil paintings, including a spectacular panoramic depiction of Montevideo at the end of the 18th century. The **Museo Romántico** (25 de Mayo 428; ☒ 11am-6pm Mon-Fri) is filled with the opulent furnishings of Montevideo's 19th-century elite. Check out the ladies' traveling vanity case, replete with brushes, combs, scissors, perfume bottles and fold-out candleholders; you can bet there were some arguments about whose backpack *that* monster was going in.

The **Museo Torres García** (www.torresgarcia.org.uy; Sarandí 683; ☒ 9am-8pm) displays the works of Joaquín Torres García (1874–1949), the Uruguayan artist who spent much of his career in France producing abstract and Cubist work.

ACTIVITIES

Pedalers can hire a **bike** from El Viajero Hostel (available to nonguests) and go cruising along the riverfront Rambla, a walking-jogging-cycling track that leads to the city's eastern beaches. After about 2km you'll get to Playa Pocitos, which is best for **swimming** and where you should be able to jump in on a game of **beach volleyball**.

A couple of bays further along you'll get to Playa Buceo, where the yacht club offers **windsurfing** lessons for around UR\$300 per hour.

Strong **swimmers** could also strike out from here for Isla de las Gaviotas, a sandy, palm-covered island about 700m offshore.

If all that seems a bit too energetic for you, bus 64 goes from Av 18 de Julio along the coast road – just jump off when you see a beach you like.

COURSES

The following courses don't cater for the casual learner – you'd want to be staying at least a month to get your money's worth.

Academia Uruguay (☎ 915-2496; www.academia uruguay.com; Gómez 1408) Spanish tuition costs UR\$500 per hour for one-on-one or UR\$4750 for 20 hours of group classes. Can arrange homestays, private apartments and volunteer work.

Complejo Multicultural Afro Mundo (☎ 915-0247; www.afromundo.org; Mercado Central, Ciudadela 1229, 1st fl) Classes in African drumming, *capoeira* (martial art/dance performed to rhythms of an instrument called the *berimbau*; developed by Bahian slaves) and *candombe* dance.

Joventango (☎ 901-5561; www.joventango.org; Mercado de la Abundancia, cnr San José & Yaguarón) Tango classes for all levels, from gringo to expert.

OMNIA Centre (☎ 908-5564; Soriano 1245) Offers yoga, pilates, meditation and massage courses.

FESTIVALS & EVENTS

Montevideo's **Carnaval** takes place on the Monday and Tuesday before Ash Wednesday. Highlights include *candombe* dance troupes beating out African-influenced rhythms on large drums. The **Semana Criolla** (during Semana Santa) is part rodeo, part arts fair, part outdoor concert – it's *gaucho*-rama. Festivities take place at Prado, easily reached by bus 552.

Every March the two-week **Festival Cinematográfico Internacional del Uruguay** (www.cine mateca.org.uy/festivales.html) showcases Uruguayan and international films.

SLEEPING

El Viajero Hostel (☎ 915-6192; www.ciudadviejahostel .com; Ituzaingó 1436; dm UR\$365, s/tw without bathroom

UR$600/1200) Set in a grand old house with great hangout areas, compact dorms and a couple of comfortable private rooms. Rent bikes here for UR$70/150 per hour/day.

Che Lagarto (☎ 903-0175; Plaza Independencia 713; www.chelagarto.com; dm/s/d UR$375/750/1000) A sweet little hostel set in an old house right on the main plaza. Private rooms are surprisingly large – an excellent deal.

Posada al Sur (☎ 916-5782; www.posadaalsur.com.uy; Castellano 1424; dm UR$35, r with/without bathroom UR$1000/875) Exposed brick walls, arched hallways and wooden floorboards combine to give this peaceful little hostel a great atmosphere. Excellent views from the roof terrace.

Hospedaje del Este (☎ 908-5495; Soriano 1137; s/d UR$400/450) Probably the best budget hotel in town. The lobby's terribly rundown, but the rooms are great – spacious, with wood floors, new bathrooms and little balconies out onto the street.

Red Hostel (☎ 908-8514; www.redhostel.com; San José 1406; dm/s/d UR$400/900/1200) Set in a classic old house downtown, with some good common areas. An extremely high bed-to-shower ratio may be of concern.

Hotel Palacio (☎ 916-3612; www.hotelpalacio.com.uy; Mitre 1364; r UR$650) Rooms aren't huge, but they have some classy touches such as antique tile work and wooden floorboards. Ones at the front have balconies, but suffer from street noise.

EATING

La Cibeles (San José 1242; empanadas UR$23, mains UR$160) Some of the yummiest empanadas in town, in a variety of flavors (including a beguiling *dulce de leche* – caramelized milk). Full meals available, too.

Roma Amor (Bacacay 1331; mains UR$150-240) The cutest little Italian restaurant in town features a good selection of pastas, tasty pizzas and some great set lunches.

Club Brasil (Av 18 de Julio 994; mains UR$150-200) Set in the Brazilian Cultural Center, this elegant dining hall offers a few Brazilian dishes. The buffet and set meals are a bargain.

Café Bacacay (Bacacay 1306; mains UR$180-240) A sweet little lunch spot, with some good sandwiches, inventive salads and a few tasty main dishes.

ourpick Estrecho (Sarandí 460; mains UR$180-240; ☾ lunch Mon-Fri) A small but creative menu using some ingredients unusual for Uruguay. Good desserts, too.

Dueto (Mitre 1386; mains UR$180-300) Some good variations on Uruguayan classics (such as anchovy-stuffed gnocchi, UR$200) plus chicken supreme with mashed pumpkin (UR$240). Set lunches are a good deal.

Buffet Atlantida (San José 1020; all you can eat UR$210) The selection here is mind-blowing – pastas, *parrillada* and Chinese food, as well as daily specials such as roast pork. Undeniable value for those with big stomachs and small budgets.

The most fun eating is to pull up a stool at any of the *parrillas* (steakhouses) inside the **Mercado del Puerto** (cnr Castellano & Rambla 25 de Agosto de 1825; mains UR$150-250; ☾ lunch). Saturday lunchtime, when the market is crammed with locals, is the best time to visit. The more central **Mercado de la Abundancia** (cnr Yaguarón & San José; mains UR$100-250) is a popular and atmospheric spot for lunch or dinner and often has live music on weekend nights.

DRINKING

The most happening bar precinct in town is along Mitre, between Buenos Aires and Sarandí in the old city. The best idea is to go for a wander and see where the crowd is, but the classics are the **Pony Pisador** (Mitre 1326) and **Shannon Irish Pub** (Mitre 1318), which both have reasonably priced drinks, DJs and occasional live music.

ENTERTAINMENT

W Lounge (cnr Baños & Rambla Wilson; admission UR$120) For the megadisco experience, this club in the Parque Rodó, has been *the* place to shake your thang for years. Dress to impress, but don't be disappointed if you fail. A taxi from the center costs around UR$70.

Sala Zitarrosa (cnr Av 18 de Julio & Herrera y Obes) Hosts rock bands and occasional live theater.

ourpick Fun Fun (Ciudadela 1229) Located in the Mercado Central, Fun Fun attracts tango enthusiasts, with live bands on weekends and a pleasant deck area out the front.

Cinemateca Uruguaya (Av 18 de Julio 1280; www.cinemateca.org.uy; membership per month UR$185) For art-house flicks, this cinema is also a film club with a modest membership fee allowing unlimited viewing at its five cinemas.

Teatro Solís (www.teatrosolis.org.uy; Buenos Aires 678) The most prestigious playhouse in town, but there are many others. Admission starts around UR$200. Check the *Guía del Ocio* for listings for this and other theaters.

There are a few dance clubs worth checking out on Mitre. **La Bamba** (Mitre 1419; entry URS60-100) is mostly house and disco hits while **El Umbral** (Mitre 1325; entry URS$50-80) has mostly retro dance nights and occasional live music.

SHOPPING

Feria de Tristán Narvaja (Narvaja, El Cordón; ☺ 9am-3pm Sun) A bustling outdoor market that sprawls for seven blocks, selling everything from antique knickknacks and jewelry to artisan crafts and fried fish.

Mercado de los Artesanos (Plaza Cagancha) sells excellent handicrafts at reasonable prices. You'll find most of the same stuff at the **Mercado de la Abundancia** (cnr San José & Yaguarón).

Plaza Constitución hosts an enjoyable flea market on Saturday.

GETTING THERE & AWAY

Air

Montevideo's **international airport** (Aeropuerto Carrasco; ☎ 604-0329; www.aic.com.uy) is 20km east of downtown. The internet-based **Gol Airlines** (www.voegol.com.br; ☎ 606-0901) has cheap flights to Porto Alegre, Brazil. Airline offices in Montevideo include the following:

Aerolíneas Argentinas (☎ 902-3691; www.aerolineas .com.ar; Plaza Independencia 749bis)

American Airlines (☎ 916-3929; www.aa.com; Sarandí 699)

Iberia (☎ 908-1032; www.iberia.com; Colonia 975)

LANChile (☎ 902-3881; www.lan.com; Colonia 993, 4th fl)

Pluna (☎ 902-1414; www.pluna.com.uy; Colonia 1021)

TACA (☎ 000-405-1004; www.taca.com; Plaza Independencia 831, Oficina 807)

TAM Mercosur (☎ 901-8451; www.tam.com.py; Plaza Cagancha 1335, Oficina 804)

Boat

Ferryturismo (☎ 900-0045; Río Negro 1400) does bus-ferry combinations to Buenos Aires, via Colonia del Sacramento (UR$793, six hours), and with the faster Sea Cat (UR$1115, four hours). It also has a branch at **Terminal Tres Cruces** (☎ 409-8198). *Buqueaviones* (high-speed ferries) cross directly to Buenos Aires from Montevideo (from UR$1716, three hours).

Cacciola (☎ 401-9350), at Terminal Tres Cruces, runs a bus-launch service to Buenos Aires (UR$629, eight hours) via Carmelo and the Argentine Delta suburb of Tigre.

Bus

Montevideo's **Terminal Tres Cruces** (☎ 401-8998; cnr Artigas & Italia) has restaurants, clean toilets, a left-luggage facility, a *casa de cambio* (money exchange office) and ATMs.

BUS FARES		
Destination	**Cost (UR$)**	**Duration (hr)**
Chuy	330	5
Colonia	167	2½
Fray Bentos	288	4½
La Paloma	240	4
Maldonado	130	2
Mercedes	260	4
Minas	111	2
Paysandú	353	5
Punta del Diablo	296	4½
Punta del Este	135	2½
Salto	465	6
Tacuarembó	380	5
Treinta y Tres	269	4

There are daily departures to various destinations in Argentina (via Paysandú), including Buenos Aires (UR$780, 10 hours), Rosario

---

GETTING TO ARGENTINA

Ferry crossings are the most popular way to cross this border – either direct from Montevideo to Buenos Aires (from UR$1716, see above), via Colonia del Sacramento to Buenos Aires (from UR$793, see above) or via Carmelo to Tigre (from UR$403, see p892), a suburb of Buenos Aires. Immigration is carried out at the port, so try to arrive an hour ahead of your departure time. To get to Uruguay from Argentina by boat, see p68.

Local buses run across the Río Uruguay from Paysandú and Salto to their Argentine counterparts, Colón and Concordia (see p894 and p894, respectively), and are by far the cheapest way to cross. Immigration procedures are often handled on the bus, but if you have to disembark, the bus will wait. Borders are open 24 hours. The Fray Bentos–Gualeguaychú border has been closed for some time and shows no signs of reopening.

URUGUAY

(UR$1175, 10 hours), Córdoba (UR$1510, 15 hours), Paraná (UR$1050, 10 hours) and Mendoza (UR$2030, 24 hours).

EGA goes to Santiago de Chile (UR$2760, 30 hours) in Chile, and Porto Alegre (UR$1541, 11 hours), Florianópolis (UR$2437, 18 hours) and Curitiba in Brazil (UR$2857, 24 hours).

Brújula and Coit go to Asunción, Paraguay (UR$2140, 21 hours).

GETTING AROUND

Airport buses (UR$25, 40 minutes) leave from **Terminal Suburbana** (cnr Rambla Roosevelt & Río Branco). Local buses go everywhere for about UR$15.

WESTERN URUGUAY

The land west of Montevideo is in many ways the 'real' Uruguay – little river towns separated by large expanses of pampas and wheat fields. It's far off the tourist trail, mostly, except for the region's superstar, Colonia del Sacramento, whose charms attract visitors from all over the world.

COLONIA DEL SACRAMENTO

☎ 052 / pop 22,700

Take some winding, cobbled streets, add an intriguing history and put them on a gorgeous point overlooking the Río de la Plata. What do you get? A major tourist attraction.

But the snap-happy hordes can't kill the atmosphere of 'Colonia.' This place has got 'it,' whatever that is, as well as enough restaurants, bars and nightlife to keep you happy for weeks.

The Portuguese founded Colonia in 1680 to smuggle goods across the Río de la Plata into Buenos Aires. The Spanish captured it in 1762 and held it until 1777, when tax reforms finally permitted foreign goods to proceed directly to Buenos Aires.

Orientation & Information

The Barrio Histórico (historic area) is on a small peninsula – the commercial downtown, near Plaza 25 de Agosto, and the river port are a few blocks east.

Antel (Rivadavia 420)

Banco Acac (cnr Av Flores & Barbot) Has an ATM.

Banco República Operates exchange facilities at the port.

Barrio Histórico tourist office (☎ 28506; Plaza 1811) Located just outside the old town gate. Offers informative, entertaining hour-long walking tours (UR$100 per person) of the Barrio Histórico in English or Spanish.

Cambio Viaggio (cnr Av Roosevelt & Florida; ☽ closed Sun)

Central tourist office (☎ 26141; Av Flores 499)

Post office (Lavalleja 226)

Sights

Colonia's museums are open 11am to 5pm and close one day per week on a rotating basis. The UR$50 entrance ticket covers all of the following.

The Barrio Histórico begins at the restored **Puerta de Campo** (1745), on Manuel de Lobos, where a thick fortified wall runs to the river. A short distance west, off Plaza Mayor 25 de Mayo, tile-and-stucco colonial houses line narrow, cobbled **Calle de los Suspiros**; just beyond is the **Museo Portugués** (☽ closed Wed) where you'll find some great old seafaring maps and a very fanciful depiction of the Lobo family tree.

At the southwest corner of the plaza are the **Casa de Lavalleja**, formerly General Lavalleja's residence, ruins of the 17th-century **Convento de San Francisco** and the restored 19th-century **faro** (lighthouse; admission UR$15; ☽ 9am-6pm) which you can climb for great city views. At the west end, on Calle de San Francisco, the **Museo Municipal** (☽ closed Tue) has antique homewares and dinosaur remains.

At the west end of Misiones de los Tapes, the tiny **Museo de los Azulejos** (☽ closed Wed) is a 17th-century house showcasing colonial tile work. The riverfront **Paseo de San Gabriel** leads to Colegio, where a right turn onto Comercio heads to the ruined **Capilla Jesuítica** (Jesuit chapel). Turning east along Calle de la Playa will take you to Vasconcellos and the **Plaza de Armas**, where you'll find the landmark 1680 **Iglesia Matriz** (formally known as the Basílica de Sacramento), Uruguay's oldest church. Nearly destroyed by fire in 1799, it was rebuilt by Spanish architect Tomás Toribio. The interior retains its simple aesthetic appeal. **Sound and light shows** (☎ 24935; UR$40; ☽ 9:30pm Fri & Sat) here are reasonably entertaining.

Across Av Flores, the **Museo Español** (cnr España & San José; ☽ closed Thu) exhibits replicas of colonial pottery, clothing and maps. At the north end of the street is the **Puerto Viejo** (Old Port). Although it has long ceased to function as a port, it's a picturesque place to soak up some

URUGUAY

COLONIA DEL SACRAMENTO

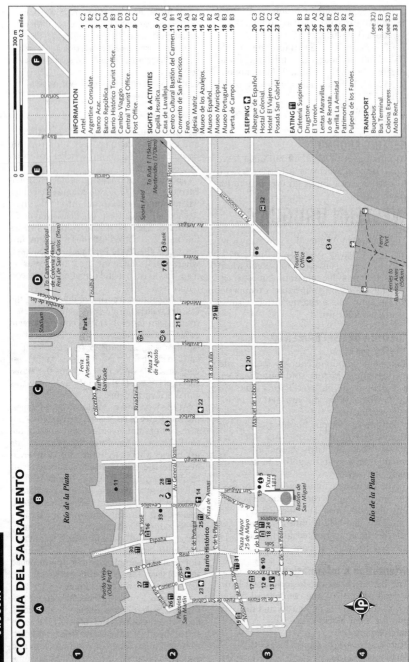

INFORMATION	
Antel..................................	1 C2
Argentine Consulate...........	2 B2
Banco Acac.........................	3 C2
Banco República.................	4 D4
Barrio Histórico Tourist Office.	5 B3
Cambio Viaggio..................	6 D3
Central Tourist Office..........	7 D2
Post Office.........................	8 C2

SIGHTS & ACTIVITIES	
Capilla Jesuítica..................	9 A2
Casa de Lavalleja................	10 A3
Centro Cultural Bastión del Carmen.	11 B1
Convento de San Francisco..	12 A3
Faro...................................	13 A3
Iglesia Matriz.....................	14 B2
Museo de los Azulejos........	15 A3
Museo Español...................	16 B2
Museo Municipal................	17 A3
Museo Portugués................	18 B3
Puerta de Campo................	19 B3

SLEEPING 🏠	
Albergue de Español...........	20 C3
Hostal Colonial...................	21 D2
Hostel El Viajero................	22 C2
Posada San Gabriel.............	23 A2

EATING 🍴	
Cafetería Suspiros...............	24 B3
Drugstore...........................	25 B2
El Torreón..........................	26 A2
Lentas Maravillas...............	27 A2
Lo de Renata......................	28 D2
Parrilla La Amistad.............	29 D2
Patrimonio.........................	30 B2
Pulpería de los Faroles.......	31 A3

TRANSPORT	
Buquebus...........................	(see 32)
Bus Terminal......................	32 E3
Colonia Express..................	(see 32)
Moto Rent..........................	33 B2

URUGUAY

of the atmosphere of the old smuggling days. One block east, the **Centro Cultural Bastión del Carmen** (cnr Cevallos & Rivadavia; ☺ 10:30am-9pm Tue-Sun) incorporates part of the ancient fortifications and now showcases traditional and contemporary art by local and international artists. Occasional live performances take place in the attached theater.

Activities
Hostel Colonial (below) organizes half-day horse treks down to the coast for UR$600. Shorter and longer rides are also available. Bicycles can be rented from the hostels.

Sleeping
Camping Municipal de Colonia (☎ 24662; campsites per person UR$100, 2-person cabañas UR$350) Near the beach at Real de San Carlos, 5km northwest of the Barrio Histórico. There are hot showers on-site and a handful of restaurants nearby.

Albergue de Español (☎ 30759; Manuel del Lobos 377; dm/d UR$200/550) Set in a charming old adobe house. Much more humble than Colonia's other hostels, and many love it for just that reason.

Hostal Colonial (☎ 30347; hostelling_colonial @hotmail.com; Av Flores 440; dm/s UR$250/300, d UR$600-900) Good courtyard rooms line this old building; out of five doubles, two come with private bathroom.

Hostel El Viajero (☎ 22683; www.elviajerocolonia .com; Barbot 164; dm UR$300-425, d UR$900; ✦) Winner of the fancy-pants hostel award, this one's all style, set in a great house with air-con dorms.

Posada San Gabriel (☎ 23283; psangabriel@adinet .com.uy; Comercio 127; r upstairs/downstairs UR$1400/1555; ✦) Set in a lovely old house in the Barrio Histórico, this little inn lays on the charm and atmosphere at a relatively low price.

Eating
Parrilla La Amistad (18 de Julio 448; mains UR$80-160) An old-style neighborhood *parrilla*. The meat dishes are superb, but the fish can be oversalted.

ourpick **Lentas Maravillas** (Santa Rita 61; dishes UR$100-250; ☺ 8am-7pm) The best breakfast/brunch/lunch spot in town is this hip little nook with a lovely grassy terrace running down to the water. The menu is small but innovative.

Cafetería Suspiros (Calle de la Peña 144; dishes UR$120-150; ☺ lunch) A shady little spot on the Plaza Mayor. The menu's standard, but the sidewalk tables are a great place to take a breather.

Drugstore (Vasconcellos 179; dishes UR$180-250) With the funkiest decor in town and a great plaza-side location, this place is rightly popular. A good, varied menu rounds out the picture. Live music on weekends.

El Torreón (Av Flores 46; dishes UR$180-350) For some of the best views in town, grab a table waterside or head up into the tower to the back deck for a more intimate vibe.

Pulpería de los Faroles (Misiones de los Tapes 101; dishes UR$200-300) Specializing in seafood and pasta – choose from the artsy interior dining room or the sea of tables out on Plaza Mayor 25 de Mayo.

Lo de Renata (Av Flores 227; dishes UR$200-320) With a better atmosphere than most of the *parrilla* joints in town, this one offers a good buffet and a truly gut-busting *chivito* (a steak sandwich with cheese, lettuce, tomato, ham and condiments) for two (UR$390).

Patrimonio (San José 111; dishes UR$300-400) Offering excellent river views from the shady deck, this is a good place to grab a drink. There's some decent food on offer here, too.

Getting There & Away
BOAT
Buquebus (☎ 130; www.buquebus.com.uy; bus terminal) has daily ferries to Buenos Aires (UR$611 to UR$933, three hours). **Colonia Express** (☎ 29677; www.coloniaexpress.com; bus terminal) does the job much quicker (UR$99 to UR$495, one hour). There are huge discounts for booking up to 20 days in advance – see the website for details. Immigration is located at the port.

BUS
Colonia's **terminal** (cnr Av Artigas & Av Roosevelt) is near the port. See the table below for domestic bus destinations, durations and costs.

BUS FARES		
Destination	**Cost (UR$)**	**Duration (hr)**
Carmelo	74	1
Mercedes	180	3
Montevideo	176	2½
Paysandú	307	6
Salto	418	8

Getting Around

Local buses leave from Av Flores to the Camping Municipal de Colonia. Bicycles can be rented from the hostels. For motorized action, try **Moto Rent** (☎ 22266; www.motorent .com.uy; Cevallos 223; golf carts & dune buggies per hr/day UR$375/1500, scooters per hr/day UR$150/500).

CARMELO

☎ 0542 / pop 17,500

A supermellow little town with a lush central square, Carmelo's streets slope down to its carefully restored waterfront. Ferries depart for the most interesting (and cheapest) of the Argentine river crossings – a two-hour ride through the delta to the Buenos Aires suburb of Tigre.

The **main tourist office** (☎ 2001; 19 de Abril 246), in the Casa de Cultura, has lots of information and a good city map. *Casas de cambio* are near Plaza Independencia.

A large park on the other side of the arroyo offers camping, swimming and a monstrous casino.

Sleeping & Eating

Camping Náutico Carmelo (☎ 2058; campsites UR$160) On the south side of Arroyo de las Vacas.

Hotel Bertolutti (☎ 2030; Uruguay 171; s/d UR$300/500) About as cheap as you want to go in this town, rooms here are basic and functional. It'll do for a night.

Posada del Navegante (☎ 3973; www.posadadelnave gante.com; Rodó 383; d with/without air-con UR$600/800; 🔀) A short walk across the bridge from the ferry, this beautiful little inn offers sweet, modern rooms 200m from a good swimming beach.

Fay Fay (18 de Julio 358; dishes UR$100-150) A fantastic little family-run restaurant on the plaza. The menu sticks closely to Uruguayan standards, but throws in a few surprises. Homemade desserts are wonderful.

Getting There & Away

Chadre/Sabelin (☎ 2987) on Plaza Independencia goes to Montevideo (UR$223, four hours), Fray Bentos (UR$130, three hours) and Paysandú (UR$223, five hours). **Berruti** (☎ 25301) is around the corner on Uruguay, with most departures for Colonia (UR$74, one hour).

Cacciola (☎ 7551; www.cacciolaviajes.com; Constituyentes s/n) has launches to the Buenos Aires suburb of Tigre (UR$403, two hours).

FRAY BENTOS

☎ 0562 / pop 24,400

Land must be cheap in Fray Bentos – the whole town is dotted with big, leafy plazas. This used to be the most popular land crossing between Argentina and Uruguay, and if the border ever opens, it will be again. If you've got a few hours to kill between buses, the town boasts a fascinating museum that's well worth checking out.

The helpful **tourist office** (☎ 2233; 33 Orientales 3260) is just off the Plaza Constitución.

Sights

The landmark 400-seat **Teatro Young** (cnr 25 de Mayo & Zorrilla), bearing the name of the Anglo-Uruguayan *estanciero* (landowner) who sponsored its construction, hosts cultural events.

Possibly the words 'tour an old meat extraction plant' don't appear on your list of must-dos for Uruguay, but **Museo de la Revolución Industrial** (☎ 2918; tours UR$40; ⏰ 10am-6pm Mon-Sat) highlights a major part of the country's history, when the British beef barons moved in and started the Uruguayan beef industry in earnest.

Sleeping & Eating

Balneario Las Cañas (☎ 2224; campsites for 2 people UR$200) A sprawling municipal campground 8km south of town.

Hotel 25 de Mayo (☎ 2586; hotel25demayo@adinet .com.uy; cnr 25 de Mayo & Lavalleja; s/d UR$380/700; 🔀) Impeccable, modern rooms a few blocks from the plaza. The Hotel Colonial (which is located on the same street) is cheaper, but way grimier.

There are plenty of *confiterías* (cafes that serve coffee, tea, desserts and simple food orders) and pizza joints scattered around the main plaza. For a wider menu, try **La Esquina de Cuqui** (cnr 18 de Julio & 19 de Abril; mains UR$150-250), which offers tasty, carefully prepared dishes and a good wine list.

Getting There & Away

The otherwise rundown **bus terminal** (☎ 2737; cnr 18 de Julio & Varela) features a grand piano and rock garden. It's 10 blocks east of Plaza Constitución. CUT goes to Mercedes (UR$28, 45 minutes) and Montevideo (UR$288, four hours). Chadre goes to Salto (UR$204, four hours), Paysandú (UR$93, two hours) and Montevideo.

MERCEDES

☎ 053 / pop 44,000

The shady, cobblestone streets of Mercedes are enchanting (unless your taxi has no suspension, in which case they're total kidney-crunchers). The riverfront is largely undeveloped, but there are plenty of grassy spots for lazing around between dips.

Plaza Independencia, located in the center of downtown, is dominated by the imposing neoclassical **cathedral** (1860).

The center is 10 blocks from the bus terminal. Either walk straight up Colón with Plaza Artigas on your right, catch any local bus or fork out UR$20 for a taxi.

The **tourist office** (☎ 22733; cnr Zorrilla de San Martín & 19 de Abril), in a new, inconvenient location down by the waterfront, has a good city map. *Casas de cambio* around the plaza change cash but not traveler's checks. The **post office** (Rodó 650) is nearby.

Activities

Club Remeros Mercedes (☎ 22534; De la Rivera 949; per hr/day UR$60/200) rents canoes, kayaks and rowboats. It also has a jetty out onto the river with high-dive platforms for bellyflopper practice.

Sleeping & Eating

Camping del Hum (campsites per person UR$50, plus per tent UR$30) On an island in the Río Negro, linked by a bridge to the mainland, with excellent facilities. Closes when the river floods.

Club Remeros Mercedes (☎ 22534; De la Rivera 949; dm/s/d UR$120/250/500) Boasts a bar, a half-decent restaurant and a jumble of pool, table tennis and *fusbol* (table soccer) tables, sporting trophies and mounted stuffed fish, all of which should be standard operating equipment in a hostel.

Hotel Mercedes (☎ 23204; Giménez 659; r with/without bathroom per person UR$300/200) An excellent deal right in the center of town, with a shady courtyard. Reservations are a good idea.

La Cabaña (cnr Costanera & Oribe; dishes UR$120-180) Mercedes is all about the riverfront and this open-air eatery down by the river has the winning combination of great food and a great atmosphere.

Getting There & Away

The **bus terminal** (☎ 30515; Plaza Artigas) has departures to Colonia (UR$180, three hours), Montevideo (UR$280, four hours) and some interior destinations.

PAYSANDÚ

☎ 072 / pop 77,100

A big (in Uruguayan terms), serious city, Paysandú wakes up every Easter for its annual **beer festival**, with plenty of live music, open-air cinema and a ready supply of a certain carbonated alcoholic beverage. The rest of the year it's kinda sleepy, but spasms into life on weekends when everybody's out and about in the restaurants, bars and discos.

Most of the fun happens down on the riverbanks, with plenty of splashing around during the day and more serious partying at night.

Av 18 de Julio, the main commercial street, runs along the south side of Plaza Constitución. The **tourist office** (☎ 26221; Av 18 de Julio 1226) is opposite Plaza Constitución. Head to **Cambio Fagalde** (Av 18 de Julio 1002) to exchange currency. **Banco Acac** (Av 18 de Julio 1020) has an ATM. If you're coming from Argentina and need Uruguayan pesos fast, Copay at the bus terminal offers bank rates.

To get to the center from the bus terminal, walk seven blocks north on Zorilla. A taxi costs around UR$50.

The **Museo Histórico** (Zorrilla 874; ☺ 9am-5pm Mon-Fri) has a great selection of hand-drawn maps, household objects and war etchings. If you thought Vista was slow, check out the slide 'n' punch 'writing machine' – a one-way ticket to Carpal Tunnel Syndrome if you ever saw one.

Sleeping & Eating

Paysandú doesn't have that many hotels, and they can fill up quickly (particularly during vacation periods). The tourist office keeps a list of *casas de familia* (family homes) offering simple accommodations for around UR$200 per person. The town's lack of hotels is matched by a surprising scarcity of restaurants.

Hotel Rafaela (☎ 24216; Av 18 de Julio 1181; r per person with/without bathroom UR$450/280) Downstairs rooms have their own bathrooms, but lack ventilation. Upstairs, the cheaper rooms with shared bathroom are a better deal and you get a shared balcony, too.

La Casona (☎ 22998; San Martín 975; r per person with/without bathroom UR$600/350) Spacious, plain rooms in a converted family house right on the plaza. Those with private patios are a good deal.

URUGUAY

Los Tres Pinos (España 1474; dishes URS100-220; ☺ lunch & dinner Mon-Sat, lunch only Sun) The *parrilla* here is excellent; try the *lechón a las brazas* (roast suckling pig).

Pan Z (cnr Pereda & Av 18 de Julio; dishes URS120-200) 'Panceta' is the most popular eating place in town – it serves pizza, pasta, *chivitos* and sangria in an informal dining room or out on the breezy outdoor deck.

Drinking & Entertainment

Club Vincenzo (cnr Brasil & Garzón) A cozy little bar with a pool table, popular for preclub drinks.

Patricia (Batllé y Ordonez s/n; admission URS60-130) The hottest dance club in town keeps the crowd moving with a beguiling mix of '80s trash and Latin beats.

Another option is to fill a bottle with something 'n' cola and hang out with everybody else in Plaza Artigas.

Getting There & Away

Paysandú's **bus terminal** (☎ 23225; cnr San Martín & Artigas) has a bus to Colón, Argentina (UR$45, 45 minutes). Domestic departures include Montevideo (UR$363, five hours), Salto (UR$116, two hours) and Tacuarembó (UR$231, six hours).

SALTO
☎ 073 / pop 105,200

People come to Salto for two reasons – to cross the border to Concordia, Argentina, and to visit the nearby **hot springs** at Daymán. Otherwise, the town's pretty enough, but unlikely to grab your attention for very long.

The **tourist office** (☎ 25194; Uruguay 1052) is vaguely useful and can supply information about visiting the local hot springs. There are *casas de cambio* downtown.

Sights & Activities

The **Museo del Hombre y la Tecnología** (cnr Brasil & Zorrilla; ☺ 2-7pm) in the former market features displays on local history.

Eight kilometers south of Salto, the **Termas de Daymán** (entry URS50; ☺ 7am-11pm) is the largest and most developed of several thermal bath complexes in northwestern Uruguay and a popular destination for Uruguayan and Argentine tourists. Look for buses running along Av Brasil with the sign 'Termas' in the windshield (URS15, 40 minutes).

Sleeping & Eating

TIA Hotel (☎ 26574; hoteltia@hotmail.com; Brasil 566; r per person URS300; ☒) The best budget deal in town offers a range of rooms in a central location.

Gran Hotel Concordia (☎ 32735; www.granhotel concordia.com.uy; Uruguay 749; r per person URS450) Reputedly Uruguay's oldest hotel, rooms overlook an attractive interior patio and are filled with antique furniture. Room 32, where famous tango singer Carlos Gardel stayed in 1933 has been turned into a minimuseum – nonguests are welcome.

El Nuevo Meson (Uruguay 564; dishes URS90-150) Straight up *parrilla* with bargain prices in a great old house.

ourpick La Caldera (Uruguay 221; dishes URS100-180) With the widest menu and best atmosphere in town, prices here are surprisingly reasonable.

Casa de Llamas (cnr Purificacón & Brasil; dishes URS180-250) The date-night favorite, with finely prepared food and a deck overlooking the river.

Getting There & Around

Bus 1 goes from the bus terminal to the center of town.

Chadre/Agencia Central goes to Concordia, Argentina (UR$50, one hour) Monday to Saturday. Immigration procedures are carried out on the bus.

Domestic buses go to Montevideo (UR$465, six hours), Bella Unión (UR$180, three hours) and Paysandú (UR$116, two hours).

From the port at the foot of Calle Brasil, **launches** (☎ 32461) cross the river to Concordia (UR$65, 10 minutes) Monday to Saturday. Immigration is at the port.

TACUAREMBÓ & AROUND
☎ 063 / pop 53,800

This is *gaucho* country. Not your 'we pose for pesos' types, but your real-deal 'we tuck our baggy pants into our boots and slap on a beret just to go to the local store' crew. It's also the alleged birthplace of tango legend Carlos Gardel (see boxed text, opposite).

The mid-March **Fiesta de la Patria Gaucho** (Cowboy Festival) merits a visit from travelers in the area.

Tacuarembó's center is Plaza 19 de Abril. The **tourist office** (☎ 27144) is in the bus terminal, but has incredibly erratic hours. The terminal's *informes* (information) office has a town map. The post office is at Ituzaingó No 262. Antel is at Sarandí No 240. The bus terminal is 2km from the center: turn left on exiting, walk through the small plaza, veer right onto Herrera and walk four blocks to 18 de Julio. A taxi costs UR$30.

The **Museo del Indio y del Gaucho** (cnr Av Flores & Artigas; ☟ 12:30-6:30pm Tue, Wed & Fri, 8:30am-6:30pm Thu, 1-5pm Sat & Sun) pays romantic tribute to Uruguay's original inhabitants and *gauchos*.

Valle Edén, a lush valley 24km southwest of Tacuarembó, is home to the **Museo Carlos Gardel** (☎ 23520; admission UR$15; ☟ 9:30am-6:30pm Tue-Sun), which documents various facets of the singer's life, including the birth certificate which Uruguayans hold as proof that Gardel was in fact born in Tacuarembó. Empresa Calibus runs infrequent buses from Tacuarembó to Valle Edén (UR$25, 20 minutes).

Sleeping & Eating
Balneario Municipal Iporá (☎ 25344; campsites free-UR$70) Seven kilometers north of town, the free campsites have clean toilets but lack showers. Buses leave from near Plaza 19 de Abril.

Residencial El Progreso (25 de Mayo 358; s/d without bathroom UR$200/400) For the 'I don't care, I just want a bed' demographic.

Hotel Plaza (☎ 27988; 25 de Agosto 247; s/d UR$470/770; ☒) Several steps up in comfort, with sweet little rooms a block and a half from the square.

La Rinconada (25 de Agosto 208; dishes UR$150-280) A dark and atmospheric local bar-restaurant serving up standard pizza and meat dishes.

La Rueda (cnr Beltrán & Av Flores; dishes UR$100-180) A friendly neighborhood *parrilla* with thatched roof and walls covered with *gaucho* paraphernalia.

Getting There & Away
The **Terminal municipal** (cnr Ruta 5 & Victorino Perera) is on the northeastern outskirts of town. Fares include Montevideo (UR$362, five hours), Salto (UR$195, five hours), Paysandú (UR$223, six hours) and Melo (UR$204, three hours). For details on going cross-country to Chuy, see boxed text, p903.

EASTERN URUGUAY

This is Uruguay's playground (and, to an extent, Brazil's, Chile's, Mexico's, Spain's etc) – a long stretch of beaches all the way from Montevideo to the Brazilian border offering something for everyone – surfers, party animals, nature freaks and family groups.

Conflicts between Spain and Portugal, and then between Argentina and Brazil, left eastern Uruguay with historical monuments such as the fortresses of Santa Teresa and San Miguel. The interior's varied landscape with palm savannas and marshes is rich in birdlife.

In the peak of summer, prices skyrocket and these towns seriously pack out. During the rest of the year you might have them to yourself.

PIRIÁPOLIS
☎ 043 / pop 8400
In the 1930s entrepreneur Francisco Piria built the landmark Hotel Argentino and an eccentric residence known as 'Piria's castle,' and ferried tourists directly from Argentina. Nowadays it's a budget alternative to beach resorts further east, mostly attracting families from Montevideo on short breaks.

The problem with this town is obvious – a four-lane highway separates it from the beach.

THE BIRTH OF A LEGEND

There's no doubt that Carlos Gardel gave birth to the tango, but – even 70 years after his death – there's still discussion over which country gave birth to Gardel.

Much like the Greek/Turkish controversy over who invented the souvlaki/doner kebab, there are three countries claiming Gardel as their own: Argentina, Uruguay and France.

The Uruguayan version goes like this: the Maestro was born here in Tacuarembó on December 11, 1887 (and to be fair, they have the documents to prove it – signed by the Argentines before Gardel became famous – in the Museo Carlos Gardel – see above).

The 'confusion' seems to have arisen because like pretty much every other Uruguayan musician, Gardel went to Buenos Aires to make it big, and then France to make it even bigger, with each country claiming him along the way.

We warmly anticipate readers' letters on the subject.

Still, if you don't mind doing the chicken run a couple of times a day, the water's clean and there are plenty of places to lay your towel.

The **tourist office** (☎ 22560; Rambla de los Argentinos 1348) has maps, brochures and current hotel prices. There's another office in the bus terminal which operates in summer. The chamber of tourism website www.piriapolistotal.com is packed with information.

There's an ATM at the corner of Piria and Buenos Aires. You can change cash at **Hotel Argentino** (Rambla de los Argentinos s/n).

Sights & Activities

For Jet Skiing, windsurfing, kayaking, banana boating and more call **Turismo Aventura** (☎ 099-120-138).

Los Criollos (☎ 709-2582; www.informes.com.uy/los criollos) offers horse rides to the top of Cerro del Indio.

SOS Rescate de Fauna Marina (☎ 33-0795; sos-fau namarina@adinet.com.uy; Punta Colorado; guided tours UR$60) runs a marine-fauna rescue operation about 10km south of town. If you want to tour the facilities, reservations are a must.

A **chairlift** (return trip UR$80; ☺ 8am-midnight summer, 10am-6pm rest of year) goes to the top of Cerro San Antonio at the eastern part of town for spectacular views over the bay and surrounds. Don't fret – there's a *parrilla* up there.

Sleeping & Eating

Camping Piriápolis FC (☎ 23275; cnr Misiones & Niza; campsites per person UR$85; ☺ mid-Dec–late Apr) Opposite the bus terminal, this place has plenty of sporting facilities.

Albergue Antón Grassi (☎ 20394; Simón del Pino 1106/36; dm/d without bathroom UR$240/520) Fairly ordinary five-bed dorms with kitchen facilities. The doubles are the best budget deal in town. Reservations are essential in January and February. Bike hire is available.

Hotel Centro (☎ 22516; Sanabria 931; r per person UR$800) Reasonably spacious rooms downtown, 50m from the beach. In the low season, when prices halve, it's a much better deal.

La Langosta (Rambla s/n; dishes UR$250-500) There are plenty of snack and pizza joints along the beachside road. This one serves up a better standard of food, including some fine seafood and pasta dishes.

Getting There & Away

The **bus terminal** (cnr Misiones & Niza) is three blocks from the beach. Destinations include Montevideo (UR$93, 1½ hours), Punta del Este (UR$56, 45 minutes) and Minas (UR$60, 45 minutes).

AROUND PIRIÁPOLIS
Pan de Azúcar

Ten kilometers north of town, there's a trail to the top of **Cerro Pan de Azúcar** (493m), Uruguay's third-highest point, crowned by a 35m-high cross and a conspicuous TV aerial. At the nearby Parque Municipal is the small but well-kept **Reserva de Fauna Autóctona**, with native species such as capybaras and gray foxes. Across the highway is the **Castillo de Piria** (☺ 10am-5pm Tue-Sun), Francisco Piria's outlandishly opulent former residence. It's worth a wander if you're in the neighborhood.

Minas & Around
☎ 044 / pop 39,000

This charming little hill town doesn't have a whole lot going for it apart from being a charming little hill town. Fans of Uruguay's bottled water Salus can check out its source, on the outskirts of town. There's a **post office** (Rodó 571) and an **Antel** (cnr Beltrán & Rodó). The **tourist office** (☎ 29796) is handily located in the bus terminal. There's another **office** (☎ 20037; Roosevelt 625) on the main plaza, inside the Paseo Artesanal, where you can also check out locally made handicrafts.

Every April 19, up to 70,000 pilgrims visit the site of **Cerro y Virgen del Verdún**, 6km west of Minas. Among the eucalyptus groves in **Parque Salus**, 10km west of town, is the source of Uruguay's best-known mineral water. Buses for the complex (which includes a reasonable restaurant) leave from Minas' bus terminal every 15 minutes (UR$20).

Located 8km out of town, the **Salto del Penitente** (☎ 3096; www.saltodelpenitente; Ruta 8 Km 125; ☺ 9:30am-5:30pm) offers canopy tours, horse riding, mineshaft rappelling (weekends only) and hiking trails. There's no public transportation – catch a taxi or call to arrange a ride with the owner in the morning.

Inexpensive camping is possible at leafy **Parque Arequita** (☎ 2503; campsites per person UR$30; ☺), 12km north on the road to Polanco (public transportation is available). The three-star hotels around the plaza have rooms for around UR$990. More humble, but totally adequate, is the **Posada Verdún** (☎ 24563; Beltrán 715; s/d UR$380/680), with good-sized rooms and leafy patios. There's plenty of *parrilla* action going on around the plaza. **Ombu** (cnr Treinta y Tres & Pérez; dishes UR$180-250) seems to be the local favorite. Make sure you stop in to **Confitería Irisarri** (Plaza Libertad; snacks UR$40-100), a local institution, and check out its subterranean dungeon-museum.

There are regular buses to Montevideo (UR$111, two hours) and Piriápolis (UR$60, 45 minutes).

MALDONADO
☎ 042 / pop 61,600

This used to be the place to stay if you wanted to avoid the outrageous prices in nearby Punta del Este, but then the Maldonado hoteliers cottoned on and jacked up all their prices. There are a couple of interesting museums and some good restaurants in town. If you're looking for a budget hotel, Maldonado's still your best bet. If you're into hostel living, Punta's the place to be.

Orientation & Information

The town center is Plaza San Fernando, but streets are irregular between Maldonado and Punta del Este. West, along the river, Rambla Claudio Williman is the main thoroughfare, while to the east, Rambla Lorenzo Batllé Pacheco follows the coast. Locations along these routes are usually identified by numbered *paradas* (bus stops).

The **tourist office** (☎ 23-0050; Parada 24, Playa Mansa; ⊙ 8am-7pm) is inconveniently located. There's a more central one in the **Intendencia** (☎ 22-0847; cnr Santa Teresa & 3 de Febrero; ⊙ 9am-3pm Mon-Fri).

Casas de cambio are clustered around Plaza San Fernando. The post office is at the corner of Ituzaingó and San Carlos.

Sights

Built between 1771 and 1797, the **Cuartel de Dragones y de Blandengues** is a block of military fortifications along 18 de Julio and Pérez del Puerto. Its **Museo Didáctico Artiguista** (⊙ 10am-11pm, guided visits 5-11pm) honors Uruguay's independence hero. Artigas was a busy guy – check out the maps of his battle campaigns, and don't miss the room with the bronze busts of the Liberators of the Americas.

The **Museo San Fernando** (cnr Sarandí & Pérez del Puerto; ⊙ 3-8pm) is a fine-arts facility. Maldonado's best museum is the **Museo Regional de Maldonado** (Ituzaingó 789; ⊙ 10am-6pm), a big jumble of old documents, knickknacks, household items, weapons, furniture, artwork and photographs, all set in a house built in 1782. There's a contemporary art gallery down the back of the garden.

Sleeping

Camping San Rafael (☎ 48-6715; campsites for 2 people UR$300; ⊙ summer only) On the eastern outskirts

---

URUGUAYAN BUDGET BEACH BREAKS

In summertime, all along the Uruguayan coast, towns fill up and hotel prices skyrocket. As well as hostels in Piriápolis, Punta del Este, La Paloma and Punta del Diablo, there are a few others dotted along the coastline which let you get your fill of sun, sand and surf without breaking the bank.

■ **Hostel Manantiales** (☎ 042-774-427; www.manantialeshostel.com; Ruta 10 Km 164; dm/s/d UR$368/460/920; 🖳 🗷) At the eastern edge of La Barra de Maldonado, outside of Punta del Este, this hostel overlooks famed Playa Bikini (although it's a good 15-minute walk to the water). Rooms are comfy and stylish, there's a good kitchen and surfboards can be hired for UR$460 per day. Buses to La Barra depart hourly from Punta del Este (UR$25, 25 minutes).

■ **El Viajero Pedrera** (☎ 0479-2252; www.lapedrerahostel.com; dm/d UR$374/690; ⊙ closed Apr-Nov) A rustic and stylish hostel 200m from the bus terminal in the little town of La Pedrera. It's a 10-minute walk to the wide sandy beach which attracts surfers from all over the world. Buses to La Pedrera leave from San Carlos, near Maldonado (UR$40, one hour) and La Paloma (UR$28, 20 minutes).

■ **Hostel Cabo Polonio** (☎ 099-000-305; www.cabopoloniohostel.com; dm/d UR$585/1400) This wonderfully rustic beach shack–hostel is set in the tiny fishing village of Cabo Polonio, which is home to a gorgeous stretch of beach and a staggering amount of wildlife – sea lions and seals March to January, penguins in July and southern right whales in October and November. To get here, catch any La Paloma–Valizas bus, get off at the turnoff and pay UR$60 for the 30-minute 4WD trip across the dunes into town. Otherwise it's a long, hot 7km hike across the sand.

of town, with fine facilities on leafy grounds. Take bus 5 from downtown.

Hotel SanCar (☎ 22-3563; Edye 597; s/d UR$500/700) A short walk north of the center, with reasonably spacious, fairly basic rooms. Some have TV.

Hotel Le Petit (☎ 22-3044; cnr Florida & Sarandí; s/d UR$600/800; 🕸) Centrally located right on the plaza, rooms here are small but comfortable. Enter through the shopping arcade off the pedestrian walkway.

Eating
Sumo (cnr Florida & Sarandí; sandwiches UR$60) This plaza-side *confitería* is a great place for breakfast, coffee or a spot of people watching.

Mundo Natural (Guerra 918; set lunch UR$65; 🕑 lunch Mon-Sat) Vegetarians: had enough of the salad bar yet? Stop in here for a range of meat-free delights, plus some yummy homemade desserts.

El Tronco (Santa Teresa 820; dishes UR$100-200) One of the coziest *parrillas* in town, with a wide menu that goes way beyond the usual suspects.

Taberna Patxi (Dodera 944; dishes from UR$200; 🕑 lunch & dinner Thu-Sat, dinner only Wed, lunch only Sun) Fine Basque specialties, including fish and shellfish and an extensive wine list.

Getting There & Away
Terminal Maldonado (☎ 25-0490; cnr Roosevelt & Sarandí) is eight blocks south of Plaza San Fernando. Plenty of buses go to Montevideo (UR$136, two hours), La Paloma (UR$99, two hours), Chuy (UR$210, three hours), Minas (UR$74, two hours) and Treinta y Tres (UR$204, four hours). Buses to La Pedrera leave from nearby San Carlos (UR$28, 15 minutes) at 8am and 8pm.

Local buses link Maldonado with Punta del Este and the beaches. They run through

---

SPLURGE!

Artist Carlos Páez Vilaró's whimsical architectural masterpiece **Casapueblo** (☎ 042-57-8611; www.clubhotel.com.ar; Punta Ballena; d from UR$2645; 🕸 🛏) is like a Mediterranean fantasyland. Rooms cascade down nine levels – numbered 0 to -9 – to a brilliant turquoise, mosaic-floored pool surrounded by a vast sun terrace. See right for details on the on-site art gallery and how to get there.

---

the center of town, saving you the trek out to the terminal – ask a local where the nearest *parada* is.

AROUND MALDONADO
Casapueblo (www.carlospaezvilaro.com; admission UR$120; 🕑 9am-sunset) is an unconventional Mediterranean villa and art gallery at scenic Punta Ballena, 10km west of Maldonado, built by famed Uruguayan artist Carlos Páez Vilaró without right angles and boasting stunning views. Nearby **Camping Internacional Punta Ballena** (☎ 042-57-8902; www.campinginternacionalpuntaballena .com; Ruta 10 Km 120; campsites UR$155, 4-person cabins UR$1350) provides the most economical accommodations in the area. Buses from Maldonado drop you at a junction 2km from the house.

PUNTA DEL ESTE
☎ 042 / pop 7000
OK, here's the plan: tan it, wax it, buff it at the gym and then plonk it on the beach at 'Punta.' Once you're done there, go out and shake it at one of the town's famous clubs.

Punta's an international beach resort, and if you like that kind of thing, you're going to love it here. If not, there are plenty of other beaches to choose from along this coast.

Orientation
Rambla Artigas circles the peninsula, passing tranquil Playa Mansa and the yacht harbor on the west side and rugged Playa Brava on the east.

Punta has two separate grids. North of a constricted neck east of the harbor is the high-rise hotel zone; the southern area is largely residential. Streets bear both names and numbers. Av Juan Gorlero is the main commercial street.

Information
The **tourist office** (☎ 44-6510; cnr Baupres & Inzaurraga) also maintains an **Oficina de Informes** (☎ 44-6519) on Plaza Artigas. Both places have reams of information and make hotel reservations.

Nearly all banks and *casas de cambio* are along Av Juan Gorlero. The post office is at Los Meros between Av Juan Gorlero and El Remanso.

Activities
Twelve kilometers off Punta's east coast, Isla de los Lobos boasts large colonies of southern fur seals and sea lions. **Fogata** (☎ 44-6822;

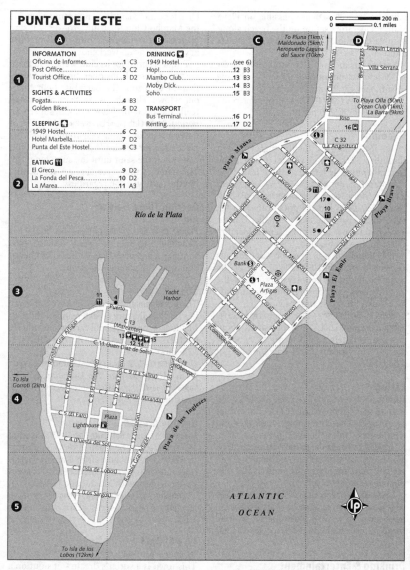

PUNTA DEL ESTE

INFORMATION	
Oficina de Informes	1 C3
Post Office	2 C2
Tourist Office	3 D2

SIGHTS & ACTIVITIES	
Fogata	4 B3
Golden Bikes	5 D2

SLEEPING	
1949 Hostel	6 C2
Hotel Marbella	7 D2
Punta del Este Hostel	8 C3

EATING	
El Greco	9 D2
La Fonda del Pesca	10 D2
La Marea	11 A3

DRINKING	
1949 Hostel	(see 6)
Hop!	12 B3
Mambo Club	13 B3
Moby Dick	14 B3
Soho	15 B3

TRANSPORT	
Bus Terminal	16 D1
Renting	17 D2

Puerto) runs tours to the island (UR$1250 per person, two hours) and to Isla Gorriti (UR$1500 per person), leaving daily in the high season, and on weekends in the low season. Make reservations in advance. Other operators have offices along the same boardwalk – it's worth going for a wander to see who has the best prices on the day.

Beach-hopping is common in Punta, depending on local conditions and the general level of action. The most popular (and fashionable) beaches, such as Bikini, are north along Playa Brava. Playa Olla gets good surf and tends to be less crowded.

During summer, **parasailing** (per 12min UR$1250), **waterskiing** (per 15min UR$1000) and **Jet**

Skiing (per 15min UR$1000) are possible on Playa Mansa. Operators set up on the beach along Rambla Claudio Williman between Paradas 2 and 20.

Surf shops in town rent **surf boards** (per day UR$500) and wetsuits during summer. In the low season, they can be much harder to find.

Golden Bikes (☎ 44-7394; El Mesana s/n) rents bikes for UR$50/200 per hour/day.

Sleeping

Prices listed here are for the high (but not absolute peak) season. If you're coming in late December to early January, add at least 30%.

Punta del Este Hostel (☎ 44-1632; www.puntadeleste hostel.com; Arrecifes 544; dm/d without bathroom UR$350/448) Nowhere near as hip as Punta's other hostel, but still a reasonable deal – smaller dorms, fewer bathrooms, but a more central location closer to the surf beach.

1949 Hostel (☎ 44-0719; www.1949hostel.com; cnr Baupres & Las Focas; dm/d UR$400/1000) One of the better hostels in the country, this one has the lot and offers good dorm rooms that include locker use, breakfast and sea views.

Hotel Marbella (☎ 44-2041; www.hotelmarbella.8m .com; Inzaurraga; r UR$2500; 🔀) Depressingly about as good as hotels get, in terms of value for money. Low season prices halve, making it a better deal.

Eating

El Greco (cnr Av Juan Gorlero & Las Focas; dishes UR$80-150) A good spot for breakfast, El Greco also does great sandwiches and homemade cakes and has plenty of sidewalk seating.

ourpick La Fonda del Pesca (Las Gaviotas; dishes UR$150-300) An atmospheric hole-in-the-wall seafood joint, decorated with murals and very popular with the locals.

La Marea (Puerto; set meals UR$335; 🕑 lunch & dinner Fri, Sat & Sun low season, lunch & dinner daily high season) Serves up some good-value set seafood meals. Grab a table out back for spectacular bay views.

Drinking & Entertainment

A good place to meet up with other travelers is the bar of the **1949 Hostel** (☎ 44-0719; www.1949hostel.com; cnr Baupres & Las Focas). Once the staff boots you out of there (around 2am or 3am), you'll have a gang together to roam the streets – either down to the port area for more drinks and electronica at the hip, minimalist Soho or sushi and cocktails at Hop! Try Moby

Dick for a more laid-back pub atmosphere or the Mambo Club for Latin grooves. All stay open as long as there's a crowd and sometimes have live music on weekends.

Punta is famed for its club scene, and there are two pieces of irony operating here. One is that the club zone (La Barra) is about 10km out of town. The other is that these places only really stay open for the one-month superpeak period. **Ocean Club** (Rambla Batllé Parada 12) is one of the best clubs operating year-round, and is the place to go for beachside dancing, where you can stomp the sand until the sun comes up. The name of this place changes frequently, but the party goes on regardless.

Getting There & Away

AIR

Pluna (☎ 49-2050, 49-0101; cnr Roosevelt & Parada 9) has daily flights to Buenos Aires (UR$6645) plus summer schedules to São Paulo (UR$14,000) and other Brazilian destinations.

BUS

The **bus terminal** (☎ 48-9467; cnr Riso & Blvd Artigas) has services that are an extension of those to Maldonado. International carriers include **TTL** (☎ 86755) to Porto Alegre, Brazil (UR$1478, 12 hours).

COT (☎ 48-3558) covers the Uruguayan coast from Montevideo to the Brazilian border. **Copsa** (☎ 48-9205) goes to Montevideo (UR$141, two hours).

Getting Around

Aeropuerto Laguna del Sauce (☎ 55-9777), west of Maldonado, can be reached by COT shuttle (UR$90). Frequent buses from Rambla Artigas (there are stops every couple of blocks) connect Punta del Este with Maldonado (UR$15).

Renting (☎ 44-8900; www.renting.com.uy; cnr Av Juan Gorlero & Las Focas) rents 125cc scooters for UR$750 for 24 hours.

LA PALOMA

☎ 0479 / pop 3400

This town is a surfer's dream – it's out on a point, and if there's no swell on the left, it'll be coming in on the right. At weekends in summer, the town often hosts free concerts down on the beach, making accommodation bookings essential.

The **tourist office** (☎ 6008; Av Nicolás Solari s/n) is in the Liga de Fomento building. There's another at the bus terminal which opens during summer. The post office and Antel are on Av Nicolás Solari.

Peteco (Av Nicolás Solari s/n) rents surfboards for UR$375 per day.

Sleeping & Eating

Camping La Aguada (☎ 6239; campsites for 2 people UR$180, 6-person cabins UR$750) At the northern approach to town, this campground has beach access, hot showers, a supermarket, a restaurant and electricity.

La Paloma Hostel (☎ 6396; www.lapalomahostel.com; dm UR$340) Nestled among the trees in Parque Andresito, this is the best hostel in town, with a huge lounge area, outdoor kitchen and great atmosphere. Prices drop in the low season.

Hotel La Tuna (☎ 6083; hlatuna@adinet.com.uy; cnr Neptune & Juno; s/d UR$500/800) The owners have kept this place in mint condition since its last overhaul back in the '70s. Front rooms have great bay views.

Restaurants here generally fall into two categories – very ornery or very snazzy. Of the former, **Rotisería Chivitería 7 Candelas** (Delfín s/n; dishes from UR$80) serves good *chivitos*, chicken and *milanesas* (breaded fish). Swankier establishments include the restaurant in **Hotel Bahia** (cnr El Sol & Av del Navio; dishes from UR$180), which serves some outrageously good seafood dishes.

Getting There & Around

Cynsa (☎ 6304) goes to Rocha (UR$30, 30 minutes) and Montevideo (UR$223, 3½ hours). **Rutas del Sol** (☎ 6019) goes to Montevideo and Punta del Diablo (UR$111, three hours), the turnoff for Cabo Polonia (UR$56, one hour) and La Pedrera (UR$28, 20 minutes).

Bikes can be rented from **Bicicletas El Topo** (Canopus; per hr/day UR$50/300). **Renting** (☎ 8900; www.renting.com.uy; Av Nicolás Solari s/n; per 24hr UR$750) hires 125cc scooters.

PUNTA DEL DIABLO

☎ 0477 / pop 700

Fabulously remote, somewhat underdeveloped and stunningly picturesque, this little fishing-surfing village of wooden cabins and winding dirt streets is like an anti–Punta del Este. It attracts a corresponding crowd – more nature-oriented and far less glamorous. Of all the towns along this coast, this one shows the greatest contrast between high and low seasons – in the winter months, it's like a ghost town, but when summer rolls around the population can swell to nearly 25,000.

Parque Nacional Santa Teresa (below) is within easy hiking distance. **Horse riding** can be arranged for about UR$250 per hour; you can ask around town or at El Diablo Tranquilo hostel.

Camping Punta del Diablo (☎ 2060; campsites for 2 people UR$260, 5-person cabins UR$820), 2km northwest of town, has excellent facilities, including a supermarket and a restaurant.

El Diablo Tranquilo (☎ 2647; www.eldiablotranquilo.com; Av Central; dm/d UR$375/1250) is one of the better hostels in the country, with roomy dorms, romantic doubles and great hangout areas. There's kitchen access and a **restaurant** (dishes from UR$150; ☼ lunch Mon-Thu, lunch & dinner Sat & Sun) a short walk away on the beachfront, serving Uruguayan classics, seafood and gringo comfort food. Surfboards rent for UR$500 per day, but are free for longer-term guests. Staff can arrange kitesurfing in summer and horseback riding year-round.

La Casa de las Boyas (☎ 2074; Calle 5; r UR$1750) is set in a cute little house perched on the hillside. Rooms are medium-sized and decorated with driftwood and other natural items. Prices drop in the low season.

There are a multitude of private *cabañas* (cabins) for rent in the village; ask in the pharmacy, supermarket and newsstand for availability. Prices start at around UR$300 per night if you supply the bedding.

Locally caught seafood is a specialty. Turning right from the bus stop, you get to the town's *patio de comidas* (food court) – basically a bunch of restaurants clustered around a parking lot. Further on is **El Viejo y el Mar** (dishes UR$140-310), a cute little six-table restaurant serving good fresh fish. Little bars open up along the seafront during summer, but the best parties happen on the beach where locals and visitors gather around beach fires to play guitars, sing songs and just generally hang out.

Rutas del Sol has buses to La Paloma (UR$111, three hours), Chuy (UR$41, one hour) and Montevideo (UR$296, four hours).

PARQUE NACIONAL SANTA TERESA

More a historical than a natural attraction, this coastal **park** (☎ 0477-2101; www.turismo.gub.uy/santateresa), 35km south of Chuy contains the hilltop **Fortaleza de Santa Teresa** (admission UR$10; ☼ 10am-7pm daily Dec-Mar, 10am-5pm Fri-Sun Apr-Nov), begun by the Portuguese but captured and finished by the Spaniards. Santa Teresa's a humble place, but visitors enjoy its uncrowded beaches and decentralized forest **camping** (campsites UR$150) with basic facilities. **Cabañas** (UR$500-1300) are also available.

The park gets crowded during Carnaval, but otherwise absorbs visitors well. Services at park headquarters include a post office, supermarket and restaurant. Rutas del Sol (UR$40, 25 minutes) travels from Punta del Diablo at 9am directly to the park headquarters, returning at 4:35pm. Buses traveling east to Chuy can also drop you off at the park entrance on Ruta 9.

CHUY & AROUND
☎ 0474 / pop 10,900

Warning: if you're not on your way to or from Brazil – or to Tacuarembó via the back road (see opposite) – you're seriously lost, buddy. Turn around and go back.

But if you are here don't miss restored **Fuerte San Miguel** (admission UR$10; ☒ 9am-5pm), a pink-granite fortress built in 1734 during hostilities between Spain and Portugal and protected by a moat. It's 7km west of Chuy.

Ten kilometers south of Chuy, a coastal lateral heads to **Camping Chuy** (☎ 9425; campsites UR$200); local buses go there.

Accommodations are available at **Hotel Internacional** (☎ 2055; Brasil 679; r standard/deluxe UR$300/650), with decent rooms in a good location. Deluxe here (TV and a recent paintjob) may not be worth the extra money.

Sadly, there are no Brazilian flavors creeping over the border onto menus here. **Hotel Plaza** (cnr Artigas & Arachanes) has a good breakfast buffet (UR$90) and **Miravos** (Brasil 505; dishes UR$130-200) has the best menu, with pasta, *parrilla,* pizza and *minutas* (short-order snacks) in a vaguely hip environment.

COT and Cynsa buses for Montevideo (UR$330, five hours) and the coast leave from near the corner of Oliviera and Brasil. Tureste leaves from the **Agencia Mesones**

office (cnr Brasil & Mauro Silva) for Treinta y Tres (UR$149, three hours).

URUGUAY DIRECTORY

ACCOMMODATIONS
Uruguay has a substantial network of youth hostels and campgrounds, especially along the coast. An International Student Identity Card (ISIC) or membership of **Minihostels** (www.minihostels.com), **HoLa** (www.holahostels.com) or **Hostelling International** (www.hihostels.com) will help with discounts in hostels. In towns, *hospedajes, residenciales* and *pensiones* offer budget accommodations from about UR$350 per person.

ACTIVITIES
Uruguay is making its mark on the world surf map. Punta del Diablo (p901) and La Paloma (p900) both get excellent waves and have stores that hire equipment. Check **Olas y Vientos** (www.olasyvientos.com.uy) for more details. Punta del Este (p898) is the place to head for upmarket beach activities, such as parasailing, waterskiing and Jet Skiing.

Bike riders can easily while away a day or two cycling around the atmospheric streets of Colonia del Sacramento (p891) and along the waterfront in Montevideo (p886).

BOOKS
Lonely Planet's *Argentina* has a dedicated Uruguay chapter which is more detailed than this book. For an account of Uruguay's Dirty War, see Lawrence Weschler's *A Miracle, a Universe: Settling Accounts with Torturers.* Onetti's novels *No Man's Land, The Shipyard, Body Snatcher* and *A Brief Life* are mostly available in Spanish and English. *The Tree of Red Stars,* Tessa Bridal's acclaimed novel set in Montevideo during the 1970s, provides one of the best descriptions of life in Uruguay available to English readers.

BUSINESS HOURS
Most shops open weekdays and Saturday from 8:30am to 12:30pm or 1pm, then close until midafternoon and reopen until 7pm or 8pm. Food shops are also open Sunday mornings.

From mid-November to mid-March, government offices are open weekdays from 7:30am to 1:30pm; the rest of the year, they are open noon to 7pm. Banks are open week-

---

GETTING TO BRAZIL

To get to Brazil, walk north along Av Artigas for about 1km to get to the immigration offices. The main street (Av Brasil/Uruguay) forms the official border here. The border is theoretically open 24 hours, but it's best to cross during normal business hours.

THE BACK ROAD: CHUY TO TACUAREMBÓ

All over the country, you'll hear the same thing: there's no way of getting from Chuy to Tacuarembó. It's true, and it's not. There's definitely no direct bus running this line, and it's certainly much quicker to backtrack via Montevideo, but where's the fun in that?

The road passes through some of Uruguay's most beautiful, least seen countryside – rolling hills where *gauchos* go about their business on horseback, swampy wetlands filled with birdlife and impressive strands of Eucalypt forest.

You need to make an early start from Chuy – Tureste has an 8:30am bus for Treinta y Tres (UR$149, three hours). In Treinta y Tres there's tourist info, budget hotels and restaurants on the plaza. The bus stations are all within a block of the plaza. **Nuñez** (☎ 0452-3703; cnr Lavalleja & Freire) has a 1:30pm departure for Melo (UR$102, two hours).

And there, unfortunately, you get stuck – there's no onward bus until the next day, but there are worse places to have to spend the night. Melo has good hotels, such as the **Principio de Asturias** (☎ 064-22064; Herrera 668; r per person UR$350) or the more basic **Cerro Largo Hotel** (☎ 064-31469; Saravia 711; r with/without bathroom UR$350/250), and fine restaurants along the main street. Tourist info is available in the bus terminal.

The next day you can take your pick – buses leave for Tacuarembó (UR$204, three hours) at the hideously early hour of 6:45am, or the much more reasonable 2:30pm.

Connections are better going back the other way – provided you take the 6:30am bus out of Tacuarembó you can easily make it to Chuy in one day, arriving around 6pm.

---

day afternoons in Montevideo; elsewhere, mornings are the rule.

Confiterías open for breakfast, usually around 8am and stay open until dinnertime. Restaurants open for lunch between noon and 3pm. Dinner is generally not eaten until after 9pm. It's not unusual (particularly in urban areas) for people to start eating at midnight.

Bars are open from 9pm, but often remain empty until at least 1am, when everybody finally gets around to going out.

Exceptions to the times mentioned here are noted in the text.

CLIMATE

Since Uruguay's major attraction is its beaches, most visitors come in summer. Between late April and November, strong winds sometimes combine with rain and cool temperatures (July's average temperature is a chilly 11°C). Along the Río Uruguay in summer, temperatures can be smotheringly hot, but the interior hill country is slightly cooler (January's average maximum is between 21°C and 26°C). For more information and climate charts, see the South America Directory (p987).

DANGERS & ANNOYANCES

Uruguay is one of the safest countries in South America, but street crime is present. Take the normal precautions; see also p989.

DRIVER'S LICENSE

Visitors to Uruguay staying less than 90 days need only a valid driver's license from their home country, although an international license may be required to hire a car.

ELECTRICITY

Uruguay runs on 220V, 50Hz. There are various types of plugs in use, the most common being the two round pins with no earthing/grounding pin.

EMBASSIES & CONSULATES

Argentina Carmelo (☎ 054-22266; Roosevelt 442); Colonia del Sacramento (Map p890; ☎ 052-22093; Av Flores 350); Montevideo (Map pp884–5; ☎ 02-902-8166; Cuariem 1470); Paysandú (☎ 072-22253; Gómez 1034); Salto (☎ 073-32931; Artigas 1162)

Brazil Chuy (0474-2049; Fernández 147); Montevideo (off Map pp884–5; ☎ 02-707-2119; Artigas 1328); Montevideo (Map pp884–5; ☎ 02-901-2024; Convención 1343, 6th fl)

Canada (Map pp884-5; ☎ 02-902-6023; Plaza Independencia 749, Oficina 102, Montevideo)

France (Map pp884-5; ☎ 02-902-0077; Uruguay 853, Montevideo)

Germany (Map pp884-5; ☎ 02-902-5222; La Cumparsita 1417, Montevideo)

Paraguay (off Map pp884-5; ☎ 02-707-2138; Artigas 1525, Montevideo)

Switzerland (off Map pp884-5; ☎ 02-711-5545; Federico Abadie 2936, 11th fl, Montevideo)

URUGUAY

UK (off Map pp884–5; ☎ 02-622-3630; Marco Bruto 1073, Montevideo)

USA (off Map pp884–5; ☎ 02-418-7777; Lauro Muller 1776, Montevideo)

FESTIVALS & EVENTS

Uruguay's Carnaval, on the Monday and Tuesday before Ash Wednesday, is livelier than Argentina's but more sedate than Brazil's. Montevideo's Afro-Uruguayan population celebrates with traditional *candombe* ceremonies. Semana Santa (Easter) has become known as Semana Turismo, with everybody from all over the country going somewhere else. Accommodations are tricky during this time, but well worth the hassle are Montevideo's Creole Week (a *gaucho* extravaganza) and Paysandú's beer festival (no explanation needed).

FOOD & DRINK

Eating reviews in this chapter are given in budget order, with the cheapest options first.

Breakfast to a Uruguayan generally means *café con leche* (coffee with milk) and a croissant or two, followed by serious amounts of maté. Most restaurants will be able to offer some *tostados* (toasted sandwiches) or an omelet to those accustomed to actually eating something in the morning. Any later than, say 10am, huge slabs of beef are the norm, usually cooked over hot coals on a *parrilla* (grill or barbecue). The most popular cut is the *asado de tira* (ribs), but *pulpo* (fillet steak) is also good. Seafood is excellent on the coast.

The standard snack is *chivito* (a steak sandwich with cheese, lettuce, tomato, ham and condiments). If you order this *al plato* (on the plate) make sure you're hungry, and be prepared for a literal pile of food. Other typical items are *puchero* (a beef stew) and *olímpicos* (club sandwiches).

Vegetarians can usually find something on the menu, often along the lines of pizza and pasta. Most vegans end up very familiar with the Uruguayan supermarket scene.

Uruguayans are probably the best dessert-makers in all of Latin America and sometimes the dessert menu is just as long as the main menu. Regional goodies include *chajá* (a meringue and ice-cream delight), *flan casero* (créme caramel) and *masini* (a custard cream pastry topped with burnt sugar). Standards such as black forest cake, chocolate mousse and tiramisu rarely disappoint.

DAY OF THE GNOCCHI

Most Uruguayan restaurants make a big deal out of serving gnocchi on the 29th of each month. A some places, this is the only day you can get it.

This tradition dates back to tough economic times when everybody was paid at the end of the month. By the time the 29th rolled around, the only thing people could afford to cook were these delicious potato dumplings.

So, in their ever-practical way, Uruguayans turned a hardship into a tradition and the 29th has been Gnocchi Day ever since.

Something to think about next time you're paying US$30 a plate at your favorite Italian restaurant back home.

Drinks

ALCOHOLIC DRINKS

Local beers, including Pilsen, Norteño and Patricia, are good. The 330mL bottles are rare outside tourist areas – generally *cerveza* (beer) means a 1L bottle and some glasses, which is a great way to meet people – pour your neighbor a beer and no doubt they'll return the favor.

Cleric is a mixture of white wine and fruit juice, while *Medio y Medio* is a mixture of sparkling wine and white wine. A shot of *grappa con miel* (grappa with honey) is worth a try – you might just like it.

NONALCOHOLIC DRINKS

Tap water's OK to drink in most places, but bottled water is cheap if you still have your doubts.

Bottled drinks are inexpensive, and all the usual soft drinks are available. Try the *pomelo* (grapefruit) flavor – it's very refreshing and not too sweet.

Jugos (juices) are available everywhere. The most common options are *naranja* (orange), *piña* (pineapple) and papaya. *Licuados* are juices mixed with either milk or water.

Coffee is available everywhere and always good, coming mostly *de la máquina* (from the machine). Uruguayans consume even more maté than Argentines and Paraguayans. If you get the chance, try to acquire the taste – there's nothing like whiling away an afternoon passing the maté with a bunch of newfound friends.

URUGUAY

Té (tea) drinking is not that common, but most cafes and bars have some lying around somewhere.

GAY & LESBIAN TRAVELERS

Uruguay has become more GLBT-friendly in recent years. In January 2008 same-sex civil unions were legally recognized. An excellent English-language web resource is **Out in Uruguay** (www.outinuruguay.com).

HOLIDAYS

Año Nuevo (New Year's Day) January 1
Epifanía (Epiphany) January 6
Viernes Santo/Pascua (Good Friday/Easter) March/April
Desembarco de los 33 (Return of the 33 Exiles) April 19
Día del Trabajador (Labor Day) May 1
Batalla de Las Piedras (Battle of Las Piedras) May 18
Natalicio de Artigas (Artigas' Birthday) June 19
Jura de la Constitución (Constitution Day) July 18
Día de la Independencia (Independence Day) August 25
Día de la Raza (Columbus Day) October 12
Día de los Muertos (All Souls' Day) November 2
Navidad (Christmas Day) December 25

INTERNET ACCESS

There are internet cafes on just about every street in cities and on the main streets in every town; access costs around UR$10 an hour.

INTERNET RESOURCES

Mercopress News Agency (www.mercopress.com) Montevideo-based internet news agency.
Ministerio de Turismo del Uruguay (www.turismo .gub.uy) Government tourist information.
Olas y Vientos (www.olasyvientos.com.uy) Everything you need to know about Uruguay's surf scene.
Red Uruguaya (www.reduruguaya.com) A guide to Uruguayan internet resources.
Uruguayan Embassy in Washington, DC (www .uruwashi.org) Historical, cultural and economic information on Uruguay.

LEGAL MATTERS

Drugs are freely available in Uruguay, but getting caught with them is as much fun as anywhere else in the world. Uruguayan police and officials are not renowned bribe-takers.

MAPS

Uruguayan road maps are only a partial guide to the highways. See the **Automóvil Club del Uruguay** (Map pp884-5; ☎ 02-1707; www.acu.com .uy; Av Libertador General Lavalleja 1532), and Shell and Ancap stations for the best ones. For more detailed maps, try the **Instituto Geográfico Militar** (off Map pp884-5; ☎ 02-481-6868; cnr 8 de Octubre & Abreu) in Montevideo.

MEDIA

Montevideo dailies include the morning *El Día*, *La República*, *La Mañana* and *El País*. *Gaceta Comercial* is the voice of the business community. Afternoon papers are *El Diario*, *Mundocolor* and *Últimas Noticias*.

MONEY

The unit of currency is the Uruguayan peso (UR$). Banknote values are five, 10, 20, 50, 100, 200, 500 and 1000. There are coins of 50 centavos, one, two, five and 10 pesos.

ATMs

For speed and convenience, nothing beats ATMs. They're found in most cities and smaller towns. Banco de la República Oriental del Uruguay seems to have the least temperamental machines. Be aware that for 'security reasons' you can only withdraw the equivalent of US$200 per transaction (with a seemingly unlimited amount of transactions possible). Check with your bank (and maybe shop around) to avoid hefty foreign transaction fees.

Credit Cards

Credit cards are useful, particularly when buying cash from a bank. Most better hotels, restaurants and shops accept credit cards.

Exchanging Money

There are plenty of *casas de cambio* in Montevideo, Colonia and the Atlantic Coast beach resorts, but banks are the rule in the interior. *Casas de cambio* offer

EXCHANGE RATES		
Country	Unit	UR$
Australia	A$1	18.70
Canada	C$1	20.61
euro zone	€1	32.51
Japan	¥100	24.21
New Zealand	NZ$1	14.95
UK	UK£1	38.18
USA	US$1	23.40

slightly lower rates and sometimes charge commissions. There's no black market for currency exchange.

POST

Postal rates are reasonable, though service can be slow. If something is truly important, send it by registered mail or private courier.

For poste restante, address mail to the main post office in Montevideo. It will hold mail for up to a month, or two months with authorization.

RESPONSIBLE TRAVEL

Responsible tourism in Uruguay is mostly a matter of common sense, and the hard and fast rules here are ones that apply all over the globe.

Bargaining isn't part of the culture here and serious red-in-the-face, veins-out-on-forehead haggling is completely out of phase with the whole Uruguayan psyche. Chances are you're paying exactly what the locals are, so ask yourself how important that 25 cents is before things get really nasty.

STUDYING

Cafes in tourist areas (particularly Colonia) often have notice boards advertising private Spanish tuition and there are options for more organized classes in Montevideo. Dance and music tuition is also available in Montevideo. See p886.

TELEPHONE

Antel is the state telephone company, but there are private *locutorios* (telephone offices) on nearly every block.

Prepaid phone cards are (finally!) starting to appear in Uruguay. Available from most newsstands, these cards invariably offer better rates for international calls than you will get at Antel offices.

Making credit-card or collect calls to the US and other overseas destinations is also often cheaper than paying locally.

Many internet cafes have headphone-microphone setups and Skype installed on their computers.

Rather than use expensive roaming plans, many travelers bring an unlocked cell phone (or buy a cheap one here) and simply insert a local SIM card. These are readily available at most kiosks, as are prepaid cards to recharge your credit. Cell-phone numbers begin with 09.

TOILETS

Toilets in Uruguay are generally clean and of a similar design to what you're probably used to. Some older establishments offer the choice of a squat toilet – a hole in the floor with a foot-stand on either side. It doesn't take much imagination to figure out what to do. If there's a wastepaper basket next to the toilet, put used toilet paper in there. Unless you want to block up the system and make a flood, that is.

NEW PHONE NUMBERS

Uruguayan phone numbers are in the midst of a major makeover. As this book goes to press, plans are underway to convert landlines nationwide to an eight-digit format. The goal is to standardize phone numbers so they can be dialed identically from any point within Uruguay, and so that they all begin with either 2 (for Montevideo) or 4 (for elsewhere in Uruguay).

It's anybody's guess whether the conversion will actually take place by the projected July 2010 effective date. Given all the uncertainty, phone numbers in this book have been left in the old format. However, by the time you read this, the change may very well have taken place. Converting to the eight-digit format is easy. Here's how it works:

- **Seven-digit Montevideo numbers** Simply add a 2 at the beginning (the old city code 02, with the zero dropped). So the old (02) 123-4567 becomes 2-123-4567.

- **Six-digit Maldonado and Punta del Este numbers** Add 42 at the beginning (again the city code with the zero dropped). So (042) 12-3456 becomes 42-12-3456.

- **Four- and five-digit numbers elsewhere in the country** Add a 4 at the beginning, plus the old city code with zero dropped, plus the number. So in Colonia (052) 12345 becomes 4-52-12345, and in Punta del Diablo (0477) 1234 becomes 4-477-1234.

- **Cell phones** These will continue to use their traditional nine-digit format (for example 099-12-3456).

TOURIST INFORMATION

Almost every municipality has a tourist office, usually on the plaza, at the bus terminal or both. Failing that, there should be an office at the *intendencia* (city hall). Hours vary widely, but they are generally open 10am to 6pm on weekdays, and 11am to 6pm on weekends. Maps are excellent, showing the town grid and surrounding attractions. The **Ministerio de Turismo** (Map pp884-5; ☎ 1885, ext 111; www.turismo.gub.uy; cnr Yacaré & Rambla 25 de Agosto de 1825) in Montevideo answers general inquiries on the country and has a fact-filled website. Uruguayan embassies and consulates overseas can sometimes help with tourist inquiries.

TOURS

Organized tours are starting to make an appearance in Uruguay, but are mostly aimed at family groups and don't go anywhere that you couldn't get to on your own, using a little common sense (and this book, of course!).

TRAVELERS WITH DISABILITIES

Uruguay is beginning to restructure for travelers with special needs, but still has a long way to go. As renovations take place (in Montevideo's Plaza Independencia and Teatro Solis for example), ramps and dedicated bathrooms are being installed. Footpaths countrywide are level(ish) but easy-access buses are nonexistent, with one exception (the CA1, which runs between downtown and the bus terminal in Montevideo). Many budget hotels have at least one set of stairs and no elevator. On the bright side, taxis are cheap and plentiful, and locals more than happy to help when they can.

VISAS

Uruguay requires passports of all foreigners, except those from neighboring countries. Nationals of Western Europe, Australia, the USA, Canada and New Zealand automatically receive a 90-day tourist card, renewable for another 90 days. Other nationals may require visas. For extensions, visit the **immigration office** (Map pp884-5; ☎ 02-916-0471; Misiones 1513) in Montevideo or local offices in border towns.

Passports are necessary for many everyday transactions, such as cashing traveler's checks, buying bus tickets and checking into hotels.

Check www.lonelyplanet.com and its links for up-to-date visa information.

VOLUNTEERING

All Uruguayan organizations which accept volunteers require a minimum commitment of one month, and many of them also expect at least basic Spanish proficiency. The following list includes some of the Montevideo-based NGOs.

Comisión de la Juventud (Map pp884-5; ☎ 02-1950-2046; cnr Santiago de Chile & Soriano) Social workers concentrating on youth issues.

Cruz Roja (off Map pp884-5; Red Cross; ☎ 02-480-0714; 8 de Octubre 2990) The Red Cross helps people avoid, prepare for and cope with emergencies.

Liga Uruguaya de Voluntarios (off Map pp884-5; ☎ 02-481-3763; Joanicó 3216) Cancer prevention and education.

Unicef (off Map pp884-5; ☎ 02-707-4972; España 2565) The local branch of the UN Children's Fund.

WOMEN TRAVELERS

Uruguayans are no slouches when it comes to *machismo*, but their easygoing nature means that in all but the most out-of-the-way places, this will probably only manifest as the odd wolf-whistle or sleazy remark (or compliment, depending on your point of view).

Venezuela

HIGHLIGHTS

- **Los Roques** (p933) Stretch out on white-sand beaches or snorkel and scuba dive the day away at these tiny, undeveloped Caribbean islands.

- **Los Llanos** (p948) Be on the lookout for capybaras, anacondas, caimans and other wildlife in the grassy flatlands of Venezuela's cowboy country.

- **Mérida** (p943) Experience nonstop outdoor activities, including paragliding, canyoning, rafting, hiking and more in the country's adventure-sports capital.

- **Salto Ángel (Angel Falls)** (p966) Marvel at the world's highest waterfall, dropping over 300 stories in Parque Nacional Canaima.

- **Best Journey** (p969) Hike to the lost world of the Roraima table mountain for moonscape scenery and unique plant life.

- **Off the Beaten Track** (p955) Spelunk through the darkness at Cueva del Guácharo, Venezuela's longest cave.

FAST FACTS

- **Area:** 912,050 sq km (twice the size of California)

- **Budget:** US$60 to US$120 a day (at official exchange rate)

- **Capital:** Caracas

- **Costs:** double room in a budget hotel US$40 to US$50, 1L bottled water US$2, 1L gasoline US$0.15 (at official exchange rate)

- **Country code:** ☎ 58

- **Language:** Spanish

- **Money:** US$1 = 2.15BsF (bolívares fuertes) – but read Money Warning, p980

- **Population:** 26.8 million

- **Seasons:** high (Christmas, Carnaval, Semana Santa, July and August), rainy (May to October)

- **Time:** GMT minus 4½ hours

TRAVEL HINTS

Bring warm clothes for bus travel as vehicles use powerful air conditioning. Keep your passport handy as there are military checkpoints along the highway.

OVERLAND ROUTES

There are four border crossings to Colombia, one to Brazil and a boat crossing to Trinidad. No official crossings exist between Venezuela and Guyana.

Venezuela receives considerably fewer visitors than other major South American countries. This is not the result of a lack of attractions. In fact, Venezuela is a land of stunning variety. The country has Andean peaks, endless Caribbean coastline, idyllic offshore islands, grasslands teeming with wildlife, the steamy Amazon and rolling savanna punctuated by flat-topped mountains called *tepuis*. The world's highest waterfall, Salto Ángel (Angel Falls), plummets 979m from the top of a *tepui* in Parque Nacional Canaima. Those seeking adventure will find hiking, snorkeling, scuba diving, kite-surfing, windsurfing, paragliding and more. Even better, most of these attractions lie within a one-day bus trip of each other.

President Hugo Chávez and his socialist 'Bolivarian Revolution' of economic reforms and social programs has drawn spectators and volunteers to the country, but he remains a deeply polarizing figure both at home and abroad.

Tourism infrastructure exists, but it's primarily geared toward domestic travelers. An odd currency situation complicates travel here, as standard bank withdrawals and credit card transactions cost twice as much as exchanging cash on an active dollar-hungry black market. Still, with these peculiarities in mind, it's easy and inexpensive to travel the country, and well worth it.

CURRENT EVENTS

President Hugo Chávez scored a major victory in 2009 when voters passed a constitutional amendment to eliminate presidential term limits. His supporters hailed it as a means for him to continue his social and economic programs to benefit ordinary Venezuelans and the poor, while his opponents viewed it as an power grab by an increasingly centralized and autocratic federal government. The major issue on people's lips is the rise in crime nationwide, referred to as *la inseguridad* (insecurity). Other themes of interest include the possibility of a less adversarial relationship with the US since the election of President Barack Obama, the large-scale revocation of media licenses for radio and television stations critical of the government, and how falling oil prices will affect the nation's oil-based economy.

HISTORY
Pre-Columbian Times

There is evidence of human habitation in northwest Venezuela going back more than 10,000 years. Steady agriculture was established around the first millennium, leading to the first year-round settlements. Formerly nomadic groups began to develop into larger cultures belonging to three main linguistic families: Carib, Arawak and Chibcha. By the time of the Spanish conquest at the end of the 15th century, some 300,000 to 400,000 indigenous people inhabited the region that is now Venezuela.

The Timote-Cuica tribes, of the Chibcha linguistic family, were the most technologically developed of Venezuela's pre-Hispanic societies. They lived in the Andes and developed complex agricultural techniques including irrigation and terracing. They were also skilled craftspeople, as we can judge by the artifacts they left behind – examples of their fine pottery are shown in museums across the country.

Spanish Conquest

Christopher Columbus was the first European to set foot on Venezuelan soil, which was also the only place where he landed on the South American mainland. On his third trip to the New World in 1498, he anchored at the eastern tip of the Península de Paria, just opposite Trinidad. He originally believed that he was on another island, but the voluminous mouth of the Río Orinoco hinted that he had stumbled into something slightly larger.

A year later Alonso de Ojeda, accompanied by the Italian Amerigo Vespucci, sailed up to the Península de la Guajira, on the western end of present-day Venezuela. On entering Lago de Maracaibo, the Spaniards saw indigenous people living in *palafitos* (thatched homes on stilts above the water). Perhaps as a bit of sarcasm, they called the waterside community 'Venezuela,' meaning 'Little Venice.' The first Spanish settlement on Venezuelan soil, Nueva Cádiz, was established around 1500 on the small island of Cubagua, just south of Isla de Margarita. The earliest Venezuelan town still in existence, Cumaná (on the mainland directly south of Isla Cubagua) dates from 1521.

Simón Bolívar & Independence

Venezuela lurked in the shadows of the Spanish empire through most of the colonial period. The country took a more primary role at the beginning of the 19th century, when Venezuela gave Latin America one of its greatest heroes, Simón Bolívar. A native of Caracas, Bolívar led the forces that put the nail in the coffin of Spanish rule over South America. He is viewed as being largely responsible for ending colonial rule all the way to the borders of Argentina.

Bolívar assumed leadership of the revolution, which had been kicked off in 1806. After unsuccessful initial attempts to defeat the Spaniards at home, he withdrew to Colombia and then to Jamaica to plot his final campaign. In 1817 Bolívar marched over the Andes with 5000 British mercenaries and an army of horsemen from Los Llanos, defeating the Spanish at the battle of Boyacá and bringing independence to Colombia. Four months later in Angostura (present-day Ciudad Bolívar), the Angostura Congress proclaimed Gran Colombia a new state, unifying Colombia (which included present-day Panama), Venezuela and Ecuador – though the last two were still under Spanish rule.

The liberation of Venezuela was completed with Bolívar's victory over Spanish forces at Carabobo in June 1821, though the royalists put up a rather pointless fight from Puerto Cabello for another two years. Gran Colombia existed for only a decade before splitting into three separate countries. Bolívar's dream of a unified republic fell apart before he died in 1830.

Caudillo Country

On his deathbed, Bolívar proclaimed 'America is ungovernable. The man who serves a revolution plows the sea. This nation will fall inevitably into the hands of the unruly mob and then will pass into the hands of almost indistinguishable petty tyrants.' Unfortunately, he was not too far off the mark. Venezuela followed independence with nearly a century of rule by a series of strongmen known as *caudillos*. It wasn't until 1947 that the first democratic government was elected.

The first of the *caudillos,* General José Antonio Páez, controlled the country for 18 years (1830–48). Despite his tough rule, he established a certain political stability and strengthened the weak economy. The period that followed was an almost uninterrupted chain of civil wars that was only stopped by another long-lived dictator, General Antonio

Guzmán Blanco (1870–88). He launched a broad program of reform, including a new constitution, and assured some temporary stability, yet his despotic rule triggered popular opposition, and when he stepped down the country fell back into civil war.

20th-Century Oil State

The first half of the 20th century was dominated by five successive military rulers from the Andean state of Táchira. The longest-lasting and most ruthless was General Juan Vicente Gómez, who seized power in 1908 and didn't relinquish it until his death in 1935. Gómez phased out the parliament and crushed the opposition on his path to monopolization of power.

The discovery of oil in the 1910s helped the Gómez regime to put the national economy on its feet. By the late 1920s, Venezuela was the world's largest exporter of oil, which not only contributed to economic recovery but also enabled the government to pay off the country's entire foreign debt.

As in most petrol states, almost none of the oil wealth made its way to the common citizen. The vast majority continued to live in poverty. Fast oil money also led to the neglect of agriculture and development of other types of production. It was easier to just import everything from abroad, which worked temporarily but proved unsustainable.

After a short flirtation with democracy and a new constitution in 1947, the inevitable coup took place and ushered in the era of Colonel Marcos Pérez Jiménez. Once in control, he smashed the opposition and plowed oil money into public works and modernizing Caracas – not making many friends in the process.

Coups & Corruption

Pérez Jiménez was overthrown in 1958 by a coalition of civilians and military officers. The country returned to democratic rule, and Rómulo Betancourt was elected president. He enjoyed popular support and was the first democratically elected president to complete his five-year term in office. There was a democratic transition of power though the country drifted to the right.

Oil money buoyed the following governments well into the 1970s. Not only did production of oil rise but, more importantly, the price quadrupled following the Arab–Israeli war in 1973. The nation went on a spending spree, building modern skyscrapers in Caracas and Maracaibo and importing all sorts of luxury goods. But what goes up must come down and by the late 1970s the bust cycle was already in full swing. And the economy continued to fall apart through the 1980s.

In 1989 the government announced IMF-mandated austerity measures, and a subsequent protest over rising transportation costs sparked the *caracazo*, a series of nationwide riots put down by military force that killed hundreds – maybe thousands – of citizens. Lingering instability brought two attempted coups d'état in 1992. The first, in February, was led by a little-known paratrooper named Colonel Hugo Chávez Frías. The second attempt, in November, was led by junior airforce officers. The air battle over Caracas, with warplanes flying between skyscrapers, gave the coup a cinematic dimension. Both attempts resulted in many deaths.

Corruption, bank failures and loan defaults plagued the government in the mid-1990s. In 1995, Venezuela was forced to devalue the currency by more than 70%. By the end of 1998, two-thirds of Venezuela's 23 million inhabitants were living below the poverty line.

A Left Turn

Nothing is better in political theater than a dramatic comeback. The 1998 election put Hugo Chávez, the leader of the 1992 failed coup, into the presidency. After being pardoned in 1994, Chávez embarked on an aggressive populist campaign: comparing himself to Bolívar, promising help (and handouts) to the poorest masses and positioning himself in opposition to the US-influenced free-market economy. He vowed to produce a great, if vague, 'peaceful and democratic social revolution.'

Since then, however, Chávez's 'social revolution' has been anything but peaceful. Shortly after taking office, Chávez set about rewriting the constitution. The new document was approved in a referendum in December 1999, granting him new and sweeping powers. The introduction of a package of new decree laws in 2001 was met with angry protests and was followed by a massive and violent strike in April 2002. It culminated in a coup d'état run by military leaders sponsored by a business lobby, in which Chávez was forced to resign. He regained power two days later, but this only intensified the conflict.

While the popular tensions rose, in December 2002 the opposition called a general strike in an attempt to oust the president. The nationwide strike paralyzed the country, including its vital oil industry and a good part of the private sector. After 63 days, the opposition finally called off the strike, which had cost the country 7.6% of its GDP and further devastated the oil-based economy. Chávez again survived and claimed victory. No one really won.

21st-Century Socialism

National politics continued to be shaky until Chávez survived a 2004 recall referendum and consolidated his power. He handily won reelection in 2006. After an unsuccessful attempt in 2007 to eliminate presidential term limits, Chávez won a referendum to amend the constitution in 2009, positioning him to run for reelection indefinitely.

Chávez has expanded his influence beyond the borders of Venezuela, reaching out to leftist leaders across the continent, oil-producing countries in the Middle East, and China, an increasingly important South American trade partner. He has allied himself with Cuba's Fidel Castro and Bolivia's Evo Morales, and stoked a combustible relationship with the US. Bad blood exists between Venezuela and neighboring Colombia over accusations that Venezuela supports FARC guerillas (Colombia's main insurgent group, Fuerzas Armadas Revolucionarias de Colombia) and shelters them within its borders.

Supporters highlight the country's programs for the poor. Under Chávez, government-sponsored projects called *misiones* (missions) now provide adult literacy classes, free medical care and subsidized food. Large land holdings are broken up in land redistribution programs and given to subsistence farmers. The government slogan is *Venezuela: Ahora es de todos* (Venezuela: Now it's for everyone). The opposition, which remains divided and feckless, criticizes the centralization of power, intolerance of political dissent, a policy of nationalization that scares off international investment and the liberal use of government funds for partisan affairs.

Dropping oil prices have pundits wondering if Chávez can sustain the extensive programs that money has funded. For the average Venezuelan, crime, persistent poverty and high inflation continue to be pressing issues.

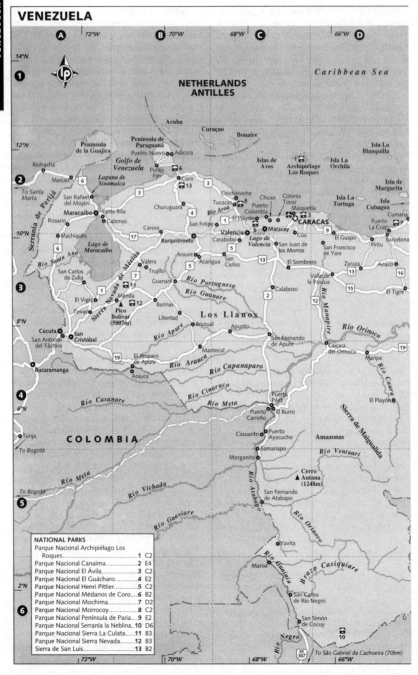

VENEZUELA

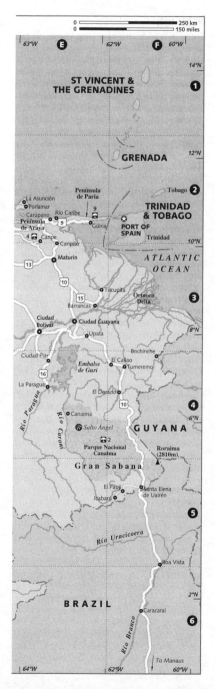

THE CULTURE
The National Psyche

Venezuela is an intensely patriotic nation that's proud of its national history. The War of Independence and the exploits of Simón Bolívar are still championed throughout the country. And it enjoys seeing itself on the world stage. Whether it's the crowning of its most recent Miss Universe or a major league baseball shutout, you can guarantee that the folks at home will be cheering.

However, unlike some neighboring South American nations, there are few defining factors of contemporary Venezuelan culture. Many attribute this to the fact that, as a petrol state, Venezuela has spent much of its existence consuming goods from abroad and not needing or bothering to produce much at home.

But just like the oil pumped out of the country, Venezuela does produce raw materials and raw talent. Two things that are produced in Venezuela, and produced prolifically, are beauty queens and baseball players. Venezuelan women have won more international beauty competitions than women of any other country, including five Miss Worlds, five Miss Universes and countless other titles.

Venezuelans have made their mark on baseball too. The North American major leagues have their fair share of Venezuelan athletes. Baseball is played throughout the country, and it is common to see pickup games in construction sites or along the side of highways. The national sport goes hand-in-hand with the national drinks of rum and ice-cold beer.

Regardless of national ills and social tensions, Venezuelans are full of life and humor. Children are given creative and sometimes downright strange names that draw on English, historical figures, indigenous languages and landmarks. People are open, willing to talk and not shy about striking up conversations with a stranger who becomes an instant *chamo* (pal or friend). Wherever you are, you're unlikely to be alone or feel isolated, especially if you can speak a little Spanish. There's always a rumba brewing somewhere.

Lifestyle

The country's climate and the restricted space of Venezuelan homes create a more open, public life where many activities take place outside. Don't be surprised to see people getting together for a beer on the street, serenaded by a car stereo at full volume. That said, noise is a constant companion, and locals are undisturbed by blaring music, ear-splitting car horns and screeching street vendors. Cell phones are also ubiquitous, with full-throated conversations the norm.

Except when driving, Venezuelans seldom seem to be in a rush. People amble at a leisurely pace best suited for the tropics. This tempo also extends to business and consumer interactions, where you may need to wait while someone finishes gabbing with coworkers or watching TV before they acknowledge your presence.

There is a significant divide between rich and poor in Venezuela, with about 30% of the population living below the poverty line, though government programs have increased access to medical care and education for many people. These days women make up about a third of Venezuela's workforce, and about half of the nation's workers earn their living within the untaxed informal economy.

Population

Venezuela has a young and mostly urban population, with half its population under 25 and 90% living in urban areas. Venezuela's population density is a low 32 people per square kilometer. However, the population is unevenly distributed: over one-fifth of the country's population lives in Caracas alone, while Los Llanos and Guayana are relatively empty.

About 70% of the population is a blend of European, indigenous and African ancestry, or any two of the three. The rest are full European (about 20%), African (8%) or indigenous (2%). Of that 2%, there are about 24 highly diverse indigenous groups comprising some 600,000 people, scattered throughout the country.

The literacy rate is 95%.

SPORTS

Soccer? What soccer? In Venezuela, *béisbol* (baseball) rules supreme. The next most popular sports are *básquetbol* (basketball, also known as *básquet* or *baloncesto*), followed by *fútbol* (soccer), which has a professional league that plays from August till May. However, soccer is still the sport of choice among the country's indigenous population.

RELIGION

Some 95% of Venezuelans are at least nominally Roman Catholic. Chávez has had words with the church in recent years and has been criticized by the Vatican. Many indigenous groups adopted Catholicism and only a few isolated tribes still practice their traditional beliefs. Evangelicals compete with Catholics for converts and are gaining ground across the country. There are small populations of Jews and Muslims, particularly in Caracas.

ARTS
Literature

The classic work in Latin American colonial literature of the treatment of the indigenous populations by the Spanish – which happens to also document Venezuela's early years – is *Brevísima relación de la destrucción de las Indias Occidentales* (A Short Account of the Destruction of the West Indies), written by Fray Bartolomé de las Casas in 1542.

As for contemporary literature, a groundbreaking experimental novel from the middle of the century is *El falso cuaderno de Narciso Espejo* by Guillermo Meneses (1911–78). Another influential work was Adriano Gonzalez Leon's (1931–2008) powerful magical-realism novel *País portátil* (Portable Country), which contrasts rural Venezuela with the urban juggernaut of Caracas.

Ednodio Quintero is another contemporary writer to look for. His work *La danza del jaguar* (The Dance of the Jaguar; 1991) is one of several translated into other languages. Other writers worth tracking down include Teresa de la Parra, Antonia Palacios, Carlos Noguera and Orlando Chirinos.

Cinema & Television
CINEMA

Venezuela's film industry is small, but has gained momentum in recent years. Most films are either contemporary social critiques or historical dramatizations.

The biggest smash in new Venezuelan cinema was 2005's *Secuestro Express* (Kidnap Express) by Jonathan Jakubowicz. The film, which was criticized by the government for its harsh portrayal of the city, takes a cold look at crime, poverty, violence, drugs and class relations in the capital. It broke all box-office records for a national production and was the first Venezuelan film to be distributed by a major Hollywood studio.

Those interested in learning more about Venezuelan film should track down a couple of films. *Oriana* (Fina Torres, 1985) recounts a pivotal childhood summer at a seaside family hacienda; *Huelepega* (Glue Sniffer; Elia Schneider, 1999) is a portrayal of Caracas street children using real street youth; *Amaneció de golpe* (A Coup at Daybreak; Carlos Azpúrua, 1999) is the story of how Chávez burst onto the political scene; and *Manuela Saenz* (Manuela Saenz; Diego Risquez, 2000) depicts the War of Independence through the eyes of Bolívar's mistress.

Also worth seeing is *The Revolution Will Not Be Televised*, a documentary shot by Irish filmmakers who were inside the presidential palace during the coup d'état of 2002.

TELEVISION

Venezuelan TV ranges from soap-opera fluff to equally kitsch government propaganda, with a few slapstick comedy shows and some baseball commentary in between. The Venezuela-based, pan–Latin American TV station TeleSur was launched in 2005. Chávez hoped it would balance out the influence of massively popular North American cable TV programs across the continent. The president's personal TV show *Aló Presidente* is a cross between an endless State of the Union address and the Oprah Winfrey show. Loquacious Chávez talks for hours (and hours…) while taking calls and addressing the questions of supporters.

Equally engaging are the *telenovelas* (soap operas). It is said that the export market for Venezuelan *telenovelas* is more than the national export of automobiles, textiles or paper products.

Music

Music is omnipresent in Venezuela. Though the country hasn't traditionally produced a lot of its own music, by law at least 50% of radio programming must now be by Venezuelan artists, and, of that music, 50% must be 'traditional.' The result has been a boon for Venezuelan musicians. The most common types of popular music are salsa, merengue and reggaeton, *vallenato* from Colombia, and North American and European pop – everything from rock to hip-hop to house. The king of Venezuelan salsa is Oscar D'León (1943–).

The country's most popular folk rhythm is the *joropo*, also called *música llanera*, which developed in Los Llanos. The *joropo* is usually sung and accompanied by the harp, *cuatro* (a small, four-stringed guitar) and maracas.

Caracas is an exciting center of Latin pop and the *rock en español* movement, which harnesses the rhythm and energy of Latin beats and combines them with international rock and alternative-rock trends. The most famous product of this scene is the Grammy-winning Los Amigos Invisibles.

Begun in 1975, a nationwide orchestra program for low-income youth has popularized classical music and trained thousands of new musicians. The top ensemble is the Simón Bolívar Youth Orchestra of Venezuela.

Architecture

There are small, and impressive, pockets of colonial architecture in Venezuela – most notably in Coro and Ciudad Bolívar – but overall the country never reached the grandeur found in other parts of the Spanish empire. Churches were mostly small and houses were usually undecorated one-story constructions. Only in the last half-century of the colonial era did a wealthier merchant class emerge that built grand residences to reflect their stature.

President Guzmán Blanco launched a dramatic overhaul of Caracas in the 1870s. He commissioned many monumental public buildings in a hodgepodge of styles, largely depending on the whim of the architect in charge. A forced march toward modernity came with oil money and culminated in the 1970s. This period was characterized by indiscriminate demolition of historic buildings and their replacement with utilitarian architecture. Still, Venezuela does have some truly remarkable modern architecture. Carlos Raúl Villanueva is considered the most outstanding Venezuelan architect. The Universidad Central de Venezuela campus in Caracas is regarded as one of his best designs and has been included on Unesco's Cultural Heritage list.

Visual Arts

Venezuela has a strong contemporary art movement. The streets and public buildings of Caracas are filled with modern art and the city houses some truly remarkable galleries.

Large-scale public art developed with the internal investment of the Guzmán Blanco regime in the late 19th century. The standout painter of that period – and one of the best in all of Venezuelan history – was Martín Tovar y Tovar (1827–1902). Some of his greatest works depicting historical events can be seen in Caracas' Asamblea Nacional (p925).

There is a rich visual arts scene among the current generation. Keep an eye out for the works of Carlos Zerpa (painting), the quirky ideas of José Antonio Hernández Díez (photo, video, installations) and the emblematic paintings, collages and sculptures of Miguel von Dangel. And you'll see plenty more in the contemporary art museum of Caracas (p925).

Jesús Soto (1923–2005) was Venezuela's number one internationally renowned contemporary artist. He was a leading representative of kinetic art (art, particularly sculpture, that contains moving parts). The largest collection of his work is in the museum dedicated to him in Ciudad Bolívar (see p963).

ENVIRONMENT

Far and away the most obvious environmental problem in Venezuela is waste management (or lack thereof). There is no recycling policy, and dumping of garbage in cities, along roads and natural areas is common practice. Untreated sewage is sometimes dumped in the sea and other water bodies. There's a general lack of clear environmental policy and little to no culture of environmental stewardship outside of the park areas. Many of the waste and pollution issues are a direct result of overpopulation in urban areas and a lack of civil planning and funds to cope with the rampant development.

Another major environmental issue is the hunting and illegal trade of fauna and flora that takes place in many parts of the country, including protected areas. A final major ecological concern is the inevitable pollution from oil refineries and mining.

The Land

About twice the size of California, Venezuela claims a multiplicity of landscapes. The traveler can encounter all four primary South American landscapes – the Amazon, the Andes, savannas and beaches – all in a single country.

The country has two mountain ranges: the Cordillera de la Costa, which separates the valley of Caracas from the Caribbean Sea, and the northern extreme of the Andes range, with its highest peaks near Mérida.

The 2150km Río Orinoco is Venezuela's main river, its entire course lying within national boundaries. The land south of the Orinoco, known as Guayana, includes the Río Caura watershed, the largely impenetrable Amazon rainforest, vast areas of sunbaked savanna and hundreds of *tepuis*.

A 2813km-long stretch of coast features a 900,000 sq km Caribbean marine zone with numerous islands and cays. The largest and most popular of these is Isla de Margarita, followed by the less developed Archipiélago Los Roques.

Wildlife

Along with the variety of Venezuelan landscape, you will encounter an amazing diversity of wildlife. Visitors often seek out anacondas, capybara, caimans and birds. There are 341 species of reptiles, 284 species of amphibians, 1791 species of fishes, 351 species of mammals and many butterflies and other invertebrates. More than 1417 species of birds – approximately 20% of the world's known species – reside in the country, and 48 of these species are endemic. The country's geographical setting on a main migratory route makes it a bird-watcher's heaven.

National Parks

Venezuela's national parks offer a diverse landscape of evergreen mountains, beaches, tropical islands, coral reefs, high plateaus and rainforests. The national parks are the number-one destination for tourism within the country. Canaima, Los Roques, Mochima, Henri Pittier, El Ávila and Morrocoy are the most popular parks. Some parks, especially those in coastal and marine zones, are easily accessible and tend to be overcrowded by locals during holiday periods and weekends; others remain unvisited. A few of the parks offer tourism facilities, but these are generally not very extensive.

Some 50% of the country is protected under national law. Many of these areas are considered national parks and natural monuments, though some are designated as wildlife refuges, forests and biosphere reserves.

TRANSPORTATION

GETTING THERE & AWAY

Air

Set at the northern edge of South America, Venezuela has the cheapest air links with Europe and is one of the fastest journeys from North America, making it a convenient northern gateway to the continent. Air-traffic disputes with the US and the government have trimmed the number of flights to and from the US, which has significantly raised transportation costs for North American visitors. The prices below are guidelines only.

BRAZIL

Flying between Brazil and Venezuela is expensive. The flight from São Paulo or Rio de Janeiro to Caracas costs 1400BsF round trip. TAM has a daily nonstop between Caracas and Manaus for 1230BsF round trip.

COLOMBIA

Avianca flies between Bogotá, Colombia and Caracas (880BsF one way, 1280BsF round trip).

GUYANA

There are no direct flights between Venezuela and Guyana. From Caracas, you need to fly via Port of Spain (Trinidad) with Caribbean Airlines (870BsF one way, 1447BsF round trip).

NETHERLANDS ANTILLES

Avior and Venezolana fly from Caracas to Aruba (760BsF to 845BsF round trip).

TRINIDAD

Caribbean Airlines flies daily between Port of Spain and Caracas (512BsF one way, 918BsF round trip). Conviasa flies between Porlamar and Port of Spain (439BsF one way, 520BsF round trip).

DEPARTURE TAX

The international airport departure tax is US$64, payable in either US dollars or bolívares, but not by credit card. There are ATMs in the airport.

Boat

Weekly passenger boats operate between Venezuela and Trinidad (see boxed text, p957). There are no longer ferries between Venezuela and the Netherlands Antilles.

Bus
BRAZIL

Only one main road connects Brazil and Venezuela; it leads from Manaus through Boa Vista to Santa Elena de Uairén and continues to Ciudad Guayana. For details see boxed text, p972.

COLOMBIA

You can enter Venezuela from Colombia at four border crossings. The two most common (and safest) are Maicao and Maracaibo, on the coastal route (see boxed text, p942), and from Cúcuta and San Antonio del Táchira (see boxed text, p949).

GUYANA

The only crossing between Venezuela and Guyana is the remote, difficult and dangerous road between Bochiche and Mabaruma; you're better off going through Brazil.

GETTING AROUND
Air

Venezuela has a number of airlines and a reasonable network of air routes. Maiquetía, where Caracas' airport is located, is the country's major aviation hub and handles flights to most airports around the country. Cities most frequently serviced from Caracas include Porlamar, Maracaibo and Puerto Ordaz (officially known as Ciudad Guayana). The most popular destinations with travelers are El Vigía, Ciudad Bolívar, Canaima, Porlamar and Los Roques. There is a tax of 27.50BsF to fly to internal destinations from Maiquetía.

Venezuela has half-a-dozen major commercial airlines servicing main domestic routes and a number of provincial carriers that cover regional and remote routes on a regular or charter basis.

Canaima and Los Roques have their own fleets of Cessnas and other smaller planes that fly for a number of smaller airlines. It is best to book these flights through an agent.

Some domestic airlines servicing Caracas:
Aeropostal (Map p924; ☎ 0800-284-6637, 0212-708-6220; www.aeropostal.com; Torre Polar Oeste, Av Paseo Colón, ground fl, Plaza Venezuela) Recently nationalized;

services Barquisimeto, Maracaibo, Porlamar, Puerto Ordaz and Valencia.

Aereotuy (LTA; Map p924; ☎ 0212-212-3110, 0295-415-5778; www.tuy.com; Edificio Sabana Grande, Blvd de Sabana Grande, 5th fl) Serves the tourism hotspots of Canaima, Los Roques and Porlamar.

Aserca (Map pp928-9; ☎ 0800-648-8356, 0212-905-5333; www.asercaairlines.com; Edificio Taeca, Calle Guaicaipuro, ground fl, El Rosal) Airline operating jet flights between several major airports, including Barcelona, Maracaibo and Porlamar.

Avior (Map pp928-9; ☎ 0501-284-67737, 0212-953-3221; www.avior.com.ve; Torre Clement, Av Venezuela, ground fl, El Rosal) Destinations include Barcelona, Barinas, Barquisimeto, Coro, Cumaná, Maturín, Porlamar, Puerto Ordaz and Valera.

Conviasa (☎ 0500-266-8427; www.conviasa.aero; Maiquetía airport) State-owned airline with destinations including Barinas, El Vigía, Maracaibo, Maturín and Puerto Ayacucho, Puerto Ordaz.

Laser (☎ 0212-202-0011; www.laser.com.ve; Maiquetía airport) Carrier with service between Caracas and Porlamar.

Rutaca (www.rutaca.com.ve) Maiquetía airport ☎ 0800-788-2221, 0212-355-1838); Caracas (Map pp928-9; ☎ 0414-624-5800; Centro Seguros La Paz, Av Francisco de Miranda) Has planes ranging from old Cessnas to newer jets and serves Canaima, Ciudad Bolívar, Porlamar, Puerto Ordaz, San Antonio del Táchira and Santa Elena de Uairén.

Santa Bárbara (Map pp928-9; ☎ 0212-204-4000; www.sbairlines.com; Miranda level, Centro Lido, Av Francisco de Miranda) Flies to El Vigía, Las Piedras and Valencia.

Venezolana (Map pp928-9; ☎ 0212-208-8400; www.ravsa.com.ve; Centro Comercial Centro Plaza, Mezzanina, Altamira) Flights to Cumaná, El Vigía, Porlamar, Maracaibo and Maturín.

Boat

Venezuela has a number of islands, but only Isla de Margarita is serviced by regular scheduled boats and ferries; see Puerto La Cruz (p951), Cumaná (p955) and Isla de Margarita (p957).

The Río Orinoco is the country's major inland waterway. The river is navigable from its mouth up to Puerto Ayacucho, with limited scheduled passenger service (p975).

Bus

As there is no passenger-train service in Venezuela (though it's in the works), almost all traveling is done by bus. Buses are generally fast and run regularly day and night between major population centers. Bus transportation is affordable and usually efficient.

Buses range from sputtering pieces of junk to the most recent models. All major companies offer *servicio ejecutivo* (executive class) in comfortable (but often icy) air-conditioned buses, which cover all of the major long-distance routes and are the dominant means of intercity transportation.

Caracas is the most important transport hub, handling buses to just about every corner of the country. In general, there's no need to buy tickets more than a couple of hours in advance for major routes, except around holidays.

Many short-distance regional routes are served by *por puestos* (literally 'by the seat'), a cross between a bus and a taxi. *Por puestos* are usually large old US-made cars (less often minibuses) that ply fixed routes and depart when all seats are filled. They cost about 40% to 80% more than buses, but they're faster and often leave more frequently.

Always travel with your passport handy, warm clothes for any bus with air-con and ear plugs for amped-up radio volume on smaller buses; as a security measure, some long-distances bus companies videotape passengers before departing.

Car & Motorcycle

Traveling by car can be a comfortable way of getting around. The country is reasonably safe, and the road network is extensive and mostly in acceptable shape. Gas stations are numerous and fuel is just about the cheapest in the world – you can fill up your tank for a dollar. This rosy picture is slightly obscured by Venezuelan traffic and local driving manners. Traffic in Venezuela, especially in Caracas, alternates between glacial and chaotic.

Bringing a car to Venezuela (or to South America in general) is time-consuming, expensive and involves plenty of paperwork, and few people do it. It's much more convenient and cheaper to rent a car locally.

Local Transport
BUS & METRO
All cities and many major towns have their own urban transportation systems, which in most places are small buses or minibuses. Depending on the region, these are called *busetas, carros, carritos, micros* or *camionetas,* and fares are usually no more than 2BsF. In many larger cities you can also find urban *por puestos,* swinging faster than buses through

the chaotic traffic. Caracas has a comprehensive subway system, and Valencia and Maracaibo have smaller offerings.

TAXI

Taxis are fairly inexpensive and worth considering, particularly for transport between the bus terminal and city center when you are carrying all your bags. Taxis don't have meters, so always fix the fare with the driver before boarding the cab. It's a good idea to find out the correct fare beforehand from an independent source, such as someone who works in the bus station or a hotel reception desk.

CARACAS

☎ 0212 / pop 6 million

A sprawling metropolis choked with traffic, Caracas incites no instant love affairs. The political and cultural capital of Venezuela is densely overpopulated and hectic, with a solid dose of crime and pollution. Few sections of the city are pedestrian-friendly and almost no quality accommodations exist for budget travelers.

That said, there's no postapocalyptic bogeyman waiting to get you, and no need to barricade yourself in a hotel room. Nestled between verdant peaks at an altitude of about 900m, the city enjoys both a spectacular setting and an unbeatable climate. Evocative fog descends from lush mountains, keeping the city comfortable year-round, and chirping *sapitos* (little frogs) form a lovely evening chorus.

Pulsing nightlife, excellent restaurants and pleasant central plazas are easily explored via an efficient, inexpensive metro system and a legion of relatively inexpensive taxis. Devotees of Simón Bolívar, the Liberator of South America, will find numerous places of worship, as will fashionistas.

Caracas isn't a primary destination for most travelers, but it has a side worth seeing.

ORIENTATION

Sprawling for 20km along a narrow coastal valley, Caracas is bordered to the north by the Parque Nacional El Ávila and to the south by a mix of modern suburbs and *barrios* (shantytowns) stacked along the steep hillsides. Downtown Caracas stretches for 8km or so west–east from the neighborhood of El

Silencio to Chacao. Museums, theaters and cinemas are clustered around Parque Central on the eastern edge of the historic center. Most accommodations and inexpensive eateries can be found here or in the bustling neighborhood of Sabana Grande. Nicer restaurants, hotels and the majority of the city's nightlife can be found to the south and east in Altamira, El Rosal and Las Mercedes.

A curiosity of Caracas is the center's street-address system. It's not the streets that bear names here, but the *esquinas* (street corners); therefore, addresses are given 'corner to corner.' So if an address is 'Piñango a Conde,' the place is between these two street corners. If a place is situated on a corner, just the corner will be named (eg Esq Conde).

INFORMATION

For a primer on the city's sights, history, services and traditions, check out **Caracas Virtual** (www.caracasvirtual.com).

Bookstores

American Book Shop (Map pp928-9; ☎ 285-8779; Nivel Jardín, Centro Comercial Centro Plaza, Los Palos Grandes) A decent selection of English titles, used books and guidebooks.

Tecni-Ciencia Libros (www.tecniciencia.com) Centro Ciudad Comercial Tamanaco (Map pp928-9; ☎ 959-5547); Centro Sambil (Map pp928-9; ☎ 264-1765); Centro Comercial San Ignacio (Map pp928-9; ☎ 264-4426) Chain bookstore with a reliable collection of texts in English and Spanish, including some Lonely Planet guidebooks.

Emergency

Emergency Center (Police, fire & ambulance ☎ 171; ☻ 24hr) Operators rarely speak English.

Immigration

Onidex (Oficina Nacional de Identificación y Extranjería; Map pp920-1; ☎ 483-2070, 483-3581; www.onidex.gov .ve; Av Baralt, Plaza Miranda, El Silencio; ☻ 8am-noon & 1-4:30pm Mon, Tue, Thu & Fri) Visas and tourist cards can be extended here for up to three months (275BsF). A passport, two photos and a letter explaining the purpose of the extension are required, plus the application form (available on the website by clicking *Extranjería*, then *Prórroga de Visa*).

Internet Access

Internet cafes are not difficult to come by, and rates are 2BsF to 3BsF per hour. The modern shopping malls tend to have cyber-cafes with the fastest connections and newest

CENTRAL CARACAS

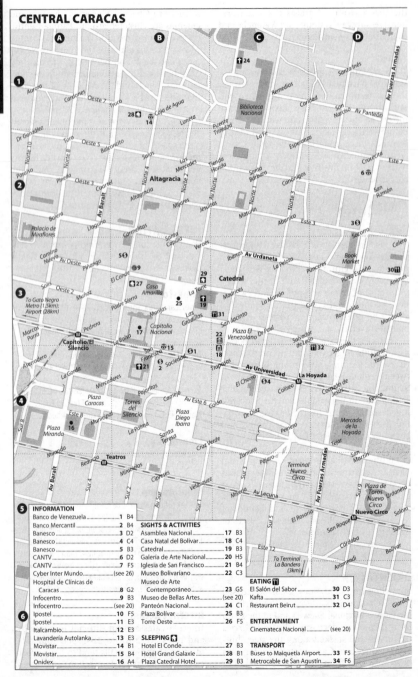

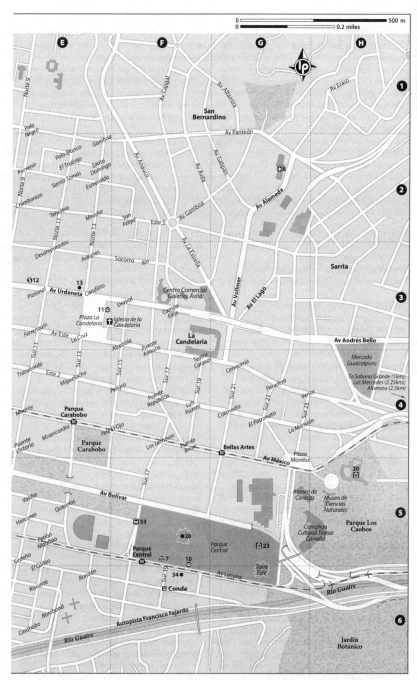

VENEZUELA

GETTING INTO TOWN

Caracas' main airport is at Maiquetía, 26km northwest of the city center. It's linked to the city by a freeway that cuts through the coastal mountain range with a variety of tunnels and bridges.

Airport–city buses (15BsF, one hour) depart from the front of the domestic and international terminals approximately every half hour from about 6am to 7pm. In the city, buses depart from Sur 17 (directly underneath Av Bolívar, next to Parque Central). During the day, the fastest option from the airport is to take the bus to Gato Negro metro station and hop on the metro, though this is not recommended after dark. Other city drop-off points include Plaza Miranda and Parque Central (the final stop).

Kiosks in both terminals sell pre-paid tickets at posted prices for the official airport taxis (150BsF to 170BsF, depending on destination and time of day; credit cards accepted). Taxis are black Ford Explorers with yellow placards on the side. Unregistered taxis are *not* recommended because of reports of robberies and kidnappings. Do not wander outside of the main airport terminals at night.

Most hotels and travel outfitters can arrange for transfers from the airport.

---

equipment. See also CANTV and Movistar, under Telephone.

There are various options:

CompuMall (Map pp928–9; Edificio Santa Ana, Av Orinoco, Las Mercedes; ⊙ 9am-9pm Mon-Sat, 11am-8pm Sun)

Cori@Red (Map pp928–9; Av Francisco de Miranda; ⊙ 8am-10pm Mon-Fri, 11am-8pm Sat & Sun) Computers upstairs with view; phones downstairs.

Cyber Inter Mundo (Map pp920–1; Nivel Lecuna, Torre Oeste, Parque Central; ⊙ 9am-6pm Mon-Fri)

Infocentro (www.infocentro.gob.ve; ⊙ 9am-4pm or 5pm Tue-Sat) Biblioteca Metropolitana Simón Rodriguez (Map pp920–1; Esq El Conde); Galería de Arte Nacional (Map pp920–1; Plaza Morelos, Los Caobos) A government project to provide internet services to all, with 30 minutes of free access available at dozens of libraries, schools and other sites. Full location list on website.

Laundry

Most hotels or hostels can do laundry. There are few self-service places. Laundromats will wash and dry clothes for 8BsF to 10BsF per 5kg load. A few recommended *lavanderías:*

Lavandería Autolanka (Map pp920–1; Centro Comercial Doral, Av Urdaneta, La Candelaria)

Lavandería Chapultepek (Map p924; Calle Bolivia, Sabana Grande) Self-service.

Medical Services

Most minor health problems can be solved in a *farmacia* (pharmacy). There's always at least one open in every neighborhood and you can easily recognize them by the neon sign that says 'Turno.' Some dependable *farmacia* chains found throughout the city include Farmatodo and FarmAhorro. These reputable medical facilities can help with more serious medical problems:

Clínica El Ávila (Map pp928–9; ☎ 276-1111; cnr Av San Juan Bosco & 6a Transversal, Altamira)

Hospital de Clínicas Caracas (Map pp920–1; ☎ 508-6111; cnr Avs Panteón & Alameda, San Bernardino)

Money

International banks and ATMs blanket the city. Cash advances on Visa and MasterCard can be easily obtained at most Caracas banks. Be cautious when using outdoor ATMs at night. Some central branches:

Banco de Venezuela Center (Map pp920–1; Av Universidad); Sabana Grande (Map p924; Av Francisco Solano)

Banco Mercantil Center (Map pp920–1; Av Universidad); Sabana Grande (Map p924; Av Las Acacias)

Banesco Altamira (Map pp928–9; Av Altamira Sur); Center (Map pp920–1; Av Fuerzas Armadas); Center (Map pp920–1; Av Universidad); Center (Map pp920–1; Esq El Conde a Esq Carmelitas); Las Mercedes (Map pp928–9; Monterrey); Sabana Grande (Map p924; Blvd de Sabana Grande)

The usual places to change foreign cash (at the official rate) are *casas de cambio* (money-exchange offices).

Amex (☎ 800-100-3555) Offers local refund assistance for traveler's checks.

Grupo Zoom (☎ 800-767-9666; www.grupozoom.com) If you need money sent to you quickly, this Western Union representative has about 75 offices around the city.

Italcambio (☎ 565-0219; www.italcambio.com; ⊙ 8am-5pm Mon-Fri, 8:30am-noon Sat) Altamira (Map pp928–9; Av Ávila); Center (Map pp920–1; Av Urdaneta); Las Mercedes (Map pp928–9; California); Maiquetía airport (International & national terminals); Sabana Grande (Map p924; Centro Comercial El Recreo, Av Casanova).

Post

FedEx (☎ 205-3333)

Ipostel (☯ 8am-noon, 1-4:30pm Mon-Fri) Altamira (Map pp928-9; Av Francisco de Miranda); La Candelaria (Map pp920-1; Plaza La Candelaria); Parque Central (Map pp920-1; Av Lecuna) Some post offices are in government services buildings called Puntos de Gestión Centralizada.

Telephone

Domestic calls can be made from public phones or stands with cell phones for rent (p981). International calls are best made from telephone centers such as the ones below.

CANTV Center (Map pp920-1; Av Fuerzas Armadas); Chacao (Map pp928-9; Centro Sambil, Av Libertador); Las Mercedes (Map pp928-9; CCCT, fl C-1, No 47-B-03); Parque Central (Map pp920-1; Av Lecuna) Internet too.

Movistar Center (Map pp920-1; Av Universidad, Esq San Francisco; ☯ 8am-8pm Mon-Sat); Center (Map pp920-1; Esq Caja de Agua; ☯ 7:30am-7:45pm Mon-Fri, 8am-7:30pm Sat & Sun) Internet too.

Tourist Information

Inatur (www.inatur.gov.ve) Maiquetía airport domestic terminal (☎ 355-1765; ☯ 7am-8pm); Maiquetía airport international terminal (☎ 355-1442; ☯ 7am-midnight) All tourist offices are at the airport.

Travel Agencies

IVI Venezuela (Map pp928-9; ☎ 993-6082; www .ivivenezuela.com; Residencia La Hacienda, Av Principal de Las Mercedes; ☯ 8am-noon & 2-6pm Mon-Fri) Offers reasonable airfares and useful information to foreign students, teachers and people under 26.

Osprey Expeditions (Map p924; ☎ 762-5975; www .ospreyvenezuela.com; Edificio La Paz, cnr Av Casanova & 2da Av de Bello Monte, Oficina 51, Sabana Grande) Helpful with travel information; arranges transportation and tours.

DANGERS & ANNOYANCES

Caracas has a justifiably bad reputation for petty crime, robbery and armed assaults. Sabana Grande and the city center are the riskiest neighborhoods, although they are generally safe during the day (but watch for pickpockets in dense crowds). Altamira and Las Mercedes are considerably safer. Travelers should always stick to well-lit main streets or use taxis after dark. Be alert about your surroundings, but don't succumb to paranoia.

Perhaps more than street crime, traffic in Caracas is the greatest danger, especially for pedestrians. Cars, but especially motorcycles, routinely ignore traffic signals and often speed up to show dominance over life forms with legs. Never assume you have the right of way in any crossing, and try to cross with others.

The Caracas airport, especially the international arrivals area, is awash in official-looking touts trying to arrange your transportation or change your cash. There is a tourism office there, but no tourism employees are roaming the halls desperately trying to 'help' you. In the past, travelers using unofficial airport transportation have been robbed or 'express kidnapped,' where they are held and forced to withdraw money from ATMs. If you haven't arranged an airport pickup, only use the official airport taxis (black Ford Explorers with yellow shields on the doors), or in the daytime, the airport bus. See the boxed text Getting into Town (opposite) for more details.

There are black-market money changers at the airport (and other locations), who may rip you off if you aren't aware of the current exchange rate or appearance of the currency. See the Money section (p980) for more information.

SIGHTS
Central Caracas
THE CENTER & AROUND

The historic sector is the heart of the original Caracas. It still retains glimpses of its colonial past but is peppered with newer buildings and a lot of questionable architecture from the last century. It's a lively area and worth visiting for its historical sites, particularly those pertaining to Simón Bolívar. In the historic quarter, addresses are given by *esquinas* (street corners), not street names.

Like any Venezuelan population center with a heartbeat, Caracas' central **Plaza Bolívar** (Map pp920–1) is dedicated to Bolívar. Its equestrian statue was cast in Europe and unveiled in 1874, after some delay when the ship carrying it foundered on Archipiélago Los Roques. The plaza is a place to hang out under jacarandas and African tulip trees, listen to soapbox politicians or browse the street stalls for religious trinkets, Chávez propaganda or souvenirs.

On the eastern side of the plaza, don't miss the **Catedral** (Map pp920-1; ☎ 862-4963; ☯ 7-11am & 4-6pm). Rebuilt from 1665 to 1713 after being flattened by an earthquake, it houses the Bolívar family chapel, where his wife and parents are buried. The chapel is in the middle of the right-hand aisle, marked by a mournful sculpture of The Liberator.

VENEZUELA

CARACAS – SABANA GRANDE

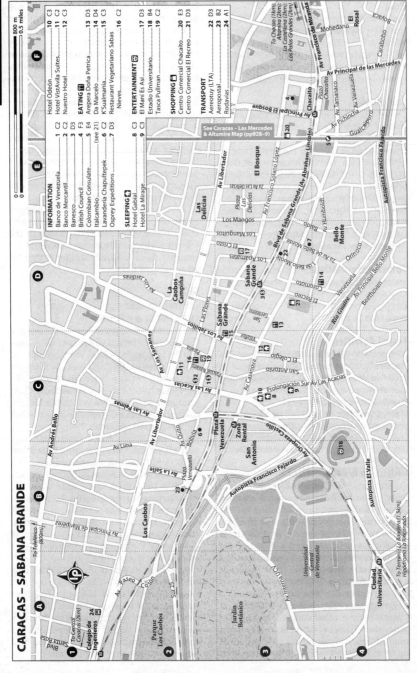

INFORMATION
Banco de Venezuela	1	C2
Banco Mercantil	2	C2
Banesco	3	D3
British Council	4	F3
Colombian Consulate	5	E4
Italcambio	(see 21)	
Lavandería Chapultepek	6	C2
Osprey Expeditions	7	D3

SLEEPING 🛏
Hotel Gabial	8	C3
Hotel La Mirage	9	C3

Hotel Odeón	10	C3
Hotel VistAvila Suites	11	C2
Nuestro Hotel	12	C3

EATING 🍴
Arepera Doña Petrica	13	D3
Da Marcelo	14	D4
K'Sualmania	15	C3
Restaurant Vegetariano Sabas Nieves	16	C2

ENTERTAINMENT 🎭
El Maní Es Así	17	D3
Estadio Universitario	18	B4
Tasca Pullman	19	C2

SHOPPING 🛍
Centro Comercial Chacaíto	20	E3
Centro Comercial El Recreo	21	D3

TRANSPORT
Aeroetuy (LTA)	22	D3
Aeropostal	23	B2
Rodovías	24	A1

The entire block just southwest of the plaza contains the **Asamblea Nacional** (Map pp920-1; ☎ 409-7185; 9:30am-12:30pm & 1:30-5pm Sat & Sun, Tue-Fri by appointment), also known as the Capitolio Nacional (National Capitol), the seat of congress built in the 1870s. In the central part of the northern building is the famous **Salón Elíptico**, an oval hall topped with an extraordinary domed ceiling with a mural depicting the battle of Carabobo. It almost seems to move as you walk beneath it.

The reconstructed interior of **Casa Natal de Bolívar** (Map pp920-1; Bolívar's Birthplace; ☎ 541-2563; San Jacinto a Traposos; 9am-4pm Tue-Fri, 10am-4pm Sat & Sun) is attractive but lacks its original detailing. In 1842, 12 years after his death, his much-celebrated funeral was held two blocks from here at the **Iglesia de San Francisco** (Map pp920-1; ☎ 482-2442; Esq San Francisco; 7am-noon & 3-6pm), after his remains had been brought back from Santa Marta, Colombia.

If you crave more Bolívar memorabilia, walk just north of Casa Natal de Bolívar to the **Museo Bolivariano** (Map pp920-1; ☎ 545-9828; San Jacinto a Traposos; 9am-4pm Tue-Fri, 10am-4pm Sat & Sun). This colonial-style museum has everything Bolívar that you can imagine, from his letters and swords to his shaving sets and medals. Also on display are the coffin in which his remains were brought back from Colombia and the *arca cineraria* (funeral ark) that bore his ashes to the Panteón Nacional.

If you have made it this far, you must continue to see the bronze sarcophagus of Bolívar in the **Panteón Nacional** (Map pp920-1; ☎ 862-1518; Av Norte; 9am-noon & 1:30-4:30pm Tue-Sun). No less than 140 white-stone tombs of other eminent Venezuelans grace the building, though there are only three women buried here.

PARQUE CENTRAL & AROUND

Not a park at all, but a series of cement high-rises, the Parque Central area is Caracas' art and culture hub, boasting half-a-dozen museums, the major performing arts center, two art cinemas and one of the best theaters in town. A jazzy new cable-car line called the **Metrocable de San Agustín** (Map pp920-1; Av Lecuna) links residents of poorer hillside *barrios* to central Caracas and was scheduled to open here in late 2009.

On the eastern end of the Parque Central complex, the **Museo de Arte Contemporáneo** (Map pp920-1; ☎ 573-8289; 9am-4pm) is by far the best art museum in the country. Here you'll find the major works of the top contemporary Venezuelan artists. There are also some remarkable paintings by international giants such as Picasso, Matisse and Monet.

The open-air viewpoint at the **Torre Oeste** (Map pp920-1; 8am-4pm) sits high on the 49th floor and has some fabulous 360-degree views of the city. To visit, check in at the tower's security department at level Sótano Uno; bring your passport for ID.

The **Galería de Arte Nacional** (Map pp920-1; ☎ 578-1818; Plaza de Los Museos, Parque Los Caobos; 9am-5pm Mon-Fri, 10am-5pm Sat & Sun) has a vast collection of artwork embracing five centuries of Venezuelan art – from pre-Hispanic to contemporary. The gallery also houses Caracas' leading art cinema.

Adjoining the gallery, the **Museo de Bellas Artes** (Map pp920-1; ☎ 578-1819; Parque Los Caobos; 9am-5pm Mon-Fri, 10am-5pm Sat & Sun) features mostly temporary exhibitions and has an excellent shop selling contemporary art and crafts. Don't miss the sculpture garden outside.

Sabana Grande & Around

Sabana Grande, 2km east of Parque Central, is an energetic district packed with hotels, love motels, restaurants and shops. Locals come en masse to stroll along its teeming market street **Boulevard de Sabana Grande** (Map p924), which stretches between Plaza Venezuela and Plaza Chacaíto.

Las Mercedes & Altamira

East of Sabana Grande lie some of Caracas' more fashionable areas, especially in **La Castellana**, **Las Mercedes** and **Altamira** (Map pp928–9). As you travel further east, you descend the social ladder, eventually reaching some of the city's most downtrodden *barrios*.

El Hatillo

El Hatillo was once its own village, but has now been absorbed into Caracas. It's a popular getaway for folks who live in the more congested urban core, with narrow central streets and plaza stacked with brightly painted colonial buildings that house restaurants, art galleries and craft shops. Located 15km southeast of the city center, this area overflows with people on the weekend. There's always a tranquil atmosphere in the afternoon and early evening, when diners and cafe-goers can sit back and relax to the sounds of crickets and *sapitos*.

VENEZUELA

Metro bus 202 (0.70BsF) leaves from near the Altamira metro station (Map pp928–9) on weekday mornings (until 10am) and afternoons (from 4pm).

ACTIVITIES

Shopping, clubbing and dining are the holy triumvirate of Caracas. The best place for **hiking** near Caracas is Parque Nacional El Ávila. Groups like the **Centro Excursionista Universitario** (www.ucv.ve/ceu.htm) and **Centro Excursionista Caracas** (www.centroexcursionistacaracas.org.ve) organize local and regional outdoor excursions for activities such as hiking and rock climbing.

TOURS

Caracas tour companies can arrange trips to almost anywhere in Venezuela, but it's usually cheaper to deal directly with the operator in the region. Caracas companies can also help by coordinating various excursions or flights for you and making reservations during busy tourism seasons.

The following companies focus on responsible tourism and have English-speaking guides (some also have guides that speak German and/or French):

Akanan Travel & Tours (Map pp928–9; ☎ 264-2769; www.akanan.com; Av Bolívar, Edificio Grano de Oro, Planta Baja, Local C, Chacao) This major operator doesn't have the most budget prices, but has reliable quality trips, including treks to Auyantepui and Roraima, and bicycle trips from La Paragua to Canaima.

Osprey Expeditions (Map p924; ☎ 762-5975; www.ospreyvenezuela.com; Edificio La Paz, cnr Av Casanova & 2da Av Bello Monte, Oficina 51, Sabana Grande) A friendly

Venezuelan-owned agency organizing tours to most parts of the country. Strong on Canaima, Orinoco Delta, Caracas and the surrounding areas.

Sociedad Conservacionista Audubón de Venezuela (SCAV; Map pp928–9; ☎ 272-8708; www.audubonvenezuela.org; Edificio Sociedad Venezolana de Ciencias Naturales, Arichuna, Urb El Marques) Organizes bird-watching tours.

FESTIVALS & EVENTS

The biggest celebrations are Christmas, Carnaval and Easter. All offices close, as do most shops, and intercity bus transportation is frantic. Flights can be fully booked.

Semana Santa (Holy Week, culminating in Easter) is also a major celebration, with festivities focused in Chacao. Traditional outlying areas celebrate holy days with more vigor than do central districts. El Hatillo boasts local feasts on several occasions during the year (including May 3, July 16 and September 4).

More characteristic of Caracas are cultural events, of which the Festival Internacional de Teatro (International Theater Festival) is the city's highlight. Initiated in 1976, it is held in March/April of every even-numbered year and attracts national and international groups to Caracas' theatres.

See boxed text, below, on the festival of Diablos Danzantes in Francisco de Yare, a day trip from Caracas.

SLEEPING

There's little to like about accommodations in Caracas for budget travelers. Most inexpensive

---

DANCING WITH DEVILS

Drums pound while hundreds of dancers clad in red devil costumes and diabolical masks writhe through the streets. This is the festival of the **Diablos Danzantes (Dancing Devils)**, a wild spectacle that takes place in Venezuela one day before Corpus Christi (the 60th day after Easter, a Thursday in May or June) and on the holy day itself.

Why devils on such a holy day in such a Catholic country? It is said that the festival demonstrates the struggle between good and evil. In the end, the costumed devils always submit to the church and demonstrate the eventual triumph of good.

The festival is a blend of Spanish and African traditions. The origins lie in Spain, where devils' images and masks were part of Corpus Christi feasts in medieval Andalusia. When the event was carried over to colonial Venezuela, it resonated with African slaves who had their own tradition of masked festivals. They also added African music and dance to the celebration. The celebrations in San Francisco de Yare and Chuao are best known throughout the country, as are their masks.

There is no direct transportation from Caracas to San Francisco de Yare. From the Nuevo Circo regional bus terminal (in central Caracas), take a frequent bus to either Ocumare del Tuy or Santa Teresa de Tuy and change for San Francisco de Yare.

rooms can only be found in love motels, which tend to be in neighborhoods that are dangerous after dark. It's worth considering staying in a midrange place in a safer neighborhood such as Altamira so you can walk around at night and breathe easier. Options like **CouchSurfing** (www.couchsurfing.org) can also be a decent way to stay here cheaply and meet the locals.

Central Caracas

Central Caracas doesn't have many good affordable accommodations. Although it's bustling during the day, the area shuts down and empties by 8pm or 9pm, so you won't want to linger outside your lodging at night. The cheapest accommodations in the center are south of Av Lecuna, but most options there are scruffy love hotels.

Hotel Grand Galaxie (Map pp920-1; ☎ 864-9011; www.hotelgrandgalaxie.com; Esq Caja de Agua; s/d 120/130BsF, ste with Jacuzzi 180BsF; ✖) Four blocks north of Plaza Bolívar, this modern eight-story tower has rather basic standard rooms, whereas suites tend to be in better condition. There's wi-fi in the lobby and an adjacent *tasca* (Spanish-style bar/restaurant).

Plaza Catedral Hotel (Map pp920-1; ☎ 564-2111; plazacatedral@cantv.net; Esq La Torre; s/d/tr incl breakfast 130/170/240BsF; ✖) Overlooking both Plaza Bolívar and the cathedral, the hotel's front corner rooms have the best sightlines, but the adjacent cathedral bells chime every quarter hour. Has a rooftop restaurant with great views.

Hotel El Conde (Map pp920-1; ☎ 862-2007; hotel conde@cantv.net; Esq El Conde; s/d/tr 330/390/425BsF; ✖ ☐) An aging 103-room lodging one block west of the Plaza Bolívar, it has an excellent location and convenient on-site restaurants and bar, though rates are a bit over the top.

Sabana Grande

Sabana Grande is the city's main budget lodging area and has plenty of places to stay, although most of them double as hourly-rate 'love motels.' The bustling neighborhood is safe during the daytime, but is dangerous at night. Stick to the main streets and walk in groups, as muggings are common.

Nuestro Hotel (Map p924; ☎ 761-5431; El Colegio, Sabana Grande; s/d/tr/q 60/90/110/130BsF) Also called the backpacker's hostel, this no-frills lodging has fan-cooled rooms with TVs and a plant-filled cement terrace. One of the few nonhourly-rates budget hotels in the city, it's a good place to meet other travelers.

Hotel Gabial (Map p924; ☎ 793-1620; fax 781-1453; Prolongación Sur Av Las Acacias; d 180-250BsF; ✖) A comfortable option are these very mirrored and somewhat modern rooms on love-hotel row, with good beds and quiet air conditioners.

Hotel VistAvila Suites (Map p924; ☎ 762-3828; www .hotelvistavila.com; Av Libertador; d 220-270BsF; ✖ ☐) A calm place to land in the city, this newly refurbished hotel has well-designed and clean, contemporary rooms with attractive accent walls.

Other inexpensive options:

Hotel Odeón (Map p924; ☎ 793-1345; Av Las Acacias, Sabana Grande; d/tr 100/115BsF; ✖) A plain Colombian-run hotel at a noisy intersection. Has eight floors of stark rooms and a decent 1st-floor cafe.

Hotel La Mirage (Map p924; ☎ 793-2733; Prolongación Sur Av Las Acacias, Sabana Grande; d 120-130BsF, tr 140BsF; ✖) An undistinguished nine-floor stack of boxy basic rooms.

Altamira

Though there are no budget options in this part of town, Altamira is a safe, leafy neighborhood where you can safely walk at night to scores of restaurants and nightlife options. It's easily accessible by metro and worth the extra price for the increased security and pleasant street life.

Hotel La Floresta (Map pp928-9; ☎ 263-1955; hotel lafloresta@cantv.net; Av Ávila, Altamira Sur; d incl breakfast 275-305BsF; ✖ ☐) Ask for a remodeled room, as an ongoing upgrade has spiffed up many of these small, comfortable rooms with new flooring, good bed lamps and attractive green and yellow bed coverings.

Hotel Altamira (Map pp928-9; ☎ 267-4284; fax 267-1846; Av José Félix Sosa, Altamira Sur; s/d 325/335BsF; ✖) On a quiet street just off the plaza, rooms have bamboo furniture and scuffed-up white-washed walls, with wicker lampshades casting trippy ceiling shadows.

Airport/Litoral Central

Many travelers use Caracas as a flight transfer point and don't bother traveling into the city itself. Additionally, staying near the airport can be a good option if you don't want to tackle getting into town after dark. The coastal towns of Catia La Mar and Macuto are near Maiquetía and have a number of good, safe places to stay. All hotels can arrange airport transfers and many will change money at

VENEZUELA

CARACAS – LAS MERCEDES & ALTAMIRA

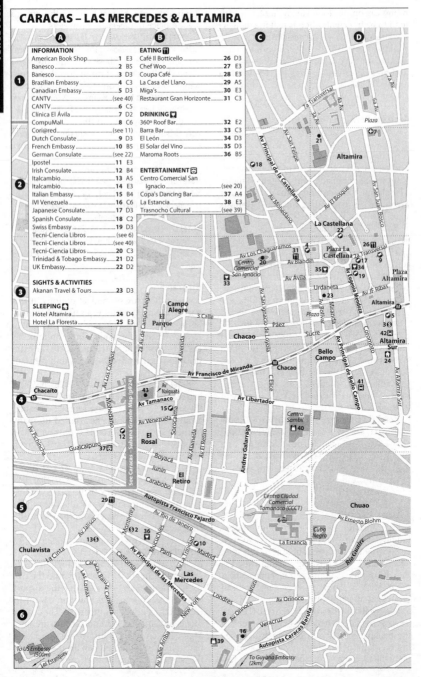

INFORMATION

American Book Shop	1	E3
Banesco	2	B5
Banesco	3	D3
Brazilian Embassy	4	C3
Canadian Embassy	5	D3
CANTV	(see 40)	
CANTV	6	C5
Clínica El Ávila	7	C6
CompuMall	8	D2
Cori@red	(see 11)	
Dutch Consulate	9	D3
French Embassy	10	B5
German Consulate	(see 22)	
Ipostel	11	E3
Irish Consulate	12	B4
Italcambio	13	A5
Italcambio	14	E3
Italian Embassy	15	B4
IVI Venezuela	16	C6
Japanese Consulate	17	D3
Spanish Consulate	18	C2
Swiss Embassy	19	D3
Tecni-Ciencia Libros	(see 6)	
Tecni-Ciencia Libros	(see 40)	
Tecni-Ciencia Libros	20	C3
Trinidad & Tobago Embassy	21	D2
UK Embassy	22	D2

SIGHTS & ACTIVITIES

Akanan Travel & Tours	23	D3

SLEEPING

Hotel Altamira	24	D4
Hotel La Floresta	25	E3

EATING

Café II Botticello	26	D3
Chef Woo	27	E3
Coupa Café	28	E3
La Casa del Llano	29	A5
Miga's	30	E3
Restaurant Gran Horizonte	31	C3

DRINKING

360° Roof Bar	32	E2
Barra Bar	33	C3
El León	34	D3
El Solar del Vino	35	D3
Maroma Roots	36	B5

ENTERTAINMENT

Centro Comercial San Ignacio	(see 20)	
Copa's Dancing Bar	37	A4
La Estancia	38	E3
Trasnocho Cultural	(see 39)	

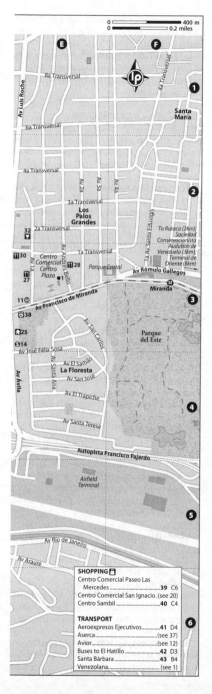

better rates than you'll find in the terminals. Daytime traffic along the coast can be fierce, but less hectic than making a morning flight from the city center. Official airport taxis to Catia La Mar are 50BsF to 55BsF.

Hotel Plazamar (☎ 339-5242; Plaza de las Palomas, Calle Macuto, Macuto; d weekday/weekend 80/100BsF, tr 120BsF; 🅿) Off a plaza dedicated to pigeon housing, Plazamar's basic rooms have cable TV, aging beds and walls with attractive marbleized paint. A laid-back place with hanging plants, a tiny enclosed upstairs terrace and breezes blowing from the beach a block away. Airport transfers 60BsF.

Hostal Tanausu (☎ 352-1704; hoteltanausu1 @yahoo.es; Av Atlántida, Catia La Mar; s/d/tr 160/190/390BsF; 🅿 💻) Rooms have interior windows and slightly lumpy beds, and corridors flaunt odd patchwork tiling. A *tasca* restaurant sprouting tree columns serves all meals.

Il Prezzano (☎ 351-2626; ilprezzano@movistar.net.ve; Av Principal de Playa Grande, Catia La Mar; d/tr 164/197BsF; 🅿 💻) A popular, safe lodging (across from a police station) with an attached restaurant and a bakery next door, this place has clean good-sized rooms, some of which face an inner patio.

Hotel La Parada (☎ 351-2148; hotel_la_parada @hotmail.com; Av Atlántida, Catia La Mar; s/tr 165/270BsF, d 200-230BsF; 🅿 💻) Kitschy nature murals enliven the hallways, and cheerful rooms have carved wooden headboards, pleasant bedspreads and interior windows, though beds are a bit thin. Round-trip airport transfer is 50BsF for one person, 70BsF for two.

EATING
Central Caracas
The center is packed with low- to mid-priced eateries.

El Salón del Sabor (Map pp920-1; Edificio Iberia, Av Urdaneta, ground fl, Esq Animas, La Candelaria; 3-course menú 28BsF; 🕒 7am-4pm Mon-Fri) A popular vegetarian lunch hall, with portions hearty enough to see you through a day of sightseeing.

Restaurant Beirut (Map pp920-1; Salvador de León a Socarrás; 2-course menú 29BsF; 🕒 11:30am-4:30pm Mon-Sat) Grab a coffee and pastry downstairs or sit upstairs for tasty Lebanese food amid turquoise walls and orange alcoves.

Kafta (Map pp920-1; Gradillas a San Jacinto; 3-course menú 35BsF; 🕒 noon-4pm Mon-Fri) Located above a busy market, Kafta has excellent Middle Eastern and Mediterranean dishes, from falafel to kebabs.

Sabana Grande

The Sabana Grande neighborhood has lots of budget lunch spots.

Arepera Doña Petrica (Map p924; Av Casanova; arepas 12-14BsF; ⊙ 24hr) This *arepa* (small, grilled corn pancake stuffed with a variety of fillings), *cachapa* (larger, flat corn pancake, served with cheese and/or ham) and sandwich restaurant serves healthy-sized, inexpensive portions to groups of beer drinking locals.

Restaurant Vegetariano Sabas Nieves (Map p924; Navarro 12; buffet 18BsF; ⊙ 7:30am-3:30pm Mon-Sat) A tranquil spot in a hectic neighborhood, its rotating fixed-price lunches can keep vegetarians entertained for the length of their stay.

K'Sualmania (Map p924; Edificio Argui, Av Los Jabillos, Sabana Grande; combo platters 22-27BsF; ⊙ 7am-4:30pm Mon-Sat) Run by a corps of kinetic young women, this spiffy little Middle Eastern joint has some of the finest falafels and *tabaquitos* (stuffed grape leaves) around.

Da Marcelo (Map p924; Coromoto; menú 23-33BsF; ⊙ 11:30am-3pm Mon-Fri) For quality Italian fare, seek out this homespun place situated down a side street. Stop to watch the flamboyant stilt walkers and jugglers practicing at the circus arts organization across the street.

Las Mercedes & Altamira

LAS MERCEDES

A fashionable dining district that becomes particularly lively in the evening, Las Mercedes mostly has restaurants that cater to an affluent clientele, but there are also some budget options.

La Casa del Llano (Map pp928-9; Av Río de Janeiro; mains 30-45BsF; ⊙ 24hr) A no-nonsense all-night diner, with *arepas*, *parrilla* (grilled meat) and other Venezuelan standards.

ALTAMIRA & LA CASTELLANA

Café Il Botticello (Map pp928-9; 2a Transversal, Altamira; pizzas 23-43BsF; pasta 14-24BsF; ⊙ noon-3pm & 6-11pm Mon-Fri, 1-11pm Sat) You need to ring the bell to enter this tiny dining room serving pastas and excellent pizzas.

Restaurant Gran Horizonte (Map pp928-9; Av Blandín; arepas & cachapas 15-25BsF; ⊙ 24hr) Tuck into your favorite *arepa* combo, a perfect sweet-corn *cachapa* or a filling plateful of BBQ meats (40BsF to 105BsF) at this cow-themed all-hours *arepera* near the Centro Comercial San Ignacio.

Chef Woo (Map pp928-9; ☎ 1a Av, Los Palos Grandes; mains 45-85BsF) Fancy some Chinese with your Polar? A raucous neighborhood restaurant popular for its tasty Szechuan fare, but visited more for cheap beer in the evening.

Miga's (Map pp928-9; cnr 1a Transversal & Av Luis Roche; sandwiches 24-37BsF; ⊙ 7am-11pm Mon-Thu, 8am-midnight Fri & Sat, 8am-11pm Sun) An indoor-outdoor bakery/cafe, with an army of servers that guarantees superfast breakfasts (20BsF to 30BsF) and hefty sandwiches.

our pick Coupa Café (Map pp928-9; Av Andrés Bello, Los Palos Grandes; breakfast 28-40BsF; ⊙ 7am-11pm Mon-Wed, to midnight Thu-Sun) A gourmet cafe emphasizing organic and fair-trade foods, Coupa serves amazing coffee from small-scale family farms, local cheeses and tasty omelets. The Moorish-accented interior and shady garden are a delightful place to sample made-to-order empanadas and nibble on excellent pastries over cappuccino. Free wi-fi.

DRINKING

Las Mercedes and La Castellana (particularly the Centro Comercial San Ignacio) hold most of the city's nightlife, but bars and discos dot other suburbs as well, including Sabana Grande, El Rosal and Altamira. Many nightclubs have basic dress codes. If a club has a cover charge, it often entitles you to your first drink or two.

Barra Bar (Map pp928-9; ☎ 264-5059; Centro Comercial Mata de Coco, Av San Marino) Tucked into a pedestrian alley next to the Seniat building, this intimate

---

PERUVIAN MARKET

Looking for a cheap bite when most restaurants are closed? On Sundays from 8am until 4pm or 5pm, follow the *caraqueños* to the bustling Peruvian market for a heaping plate of Peruvian cuisine. For about 25BsF, fill up at one of the table buffets serving dishes like *causa rellena* (potato dish stuffed with chicken, tuna or other fillings), chicken and rice, quinoa salad and ceviche, and don't skimp on the *cancha* (toasted corn kernels). Or you can shop for purple potatoes, get a bottle of homemade *chicha* (nonalcoholic corn drink) and watch the musical performances.

The weekly market is outside the Colegio de Ingenieros metro (between the Bellas Artes and Plaza Venezuela stops); exit at Av Libertador Sur/Blvr Santa Rosa and then turn right.

lounge has futuristic decor, a few couches for making out and electronica, jazz and salsa at conversation-friendly levels.

Maroma Roots (Map pp928-9; ☎ 0416-800-9301; Paris; ☿ Thu-Sat) A new reggae bar above a sushi bar (with 65BsF all-you-can-eat nights Tuesday through Thursday), with live music on Saturday and a sound system built into a mini-bus.

El Solar del Vino (Map pp928-9; ☎ 266-2873; cnr Avs Blandín & Ávila) Perfect for fresh Caracas nights, an outdoor space with a circus tent roof draws an young attractive crowd without too much attitude. Dance indoors to salsa and rock.

El León (Map pp928-9; ☎ 263-6014; Plaza La Castellana) Sit on a lofty concrete terrace and knock back cheap beers and pizza in this well-known Caracas spot.

ENTERTAINMENT

The Arts & Entertainment section of the daily newspaper *El Universal* (http://espec taculos.eluniversal.com) gives descriptions of selected upcoming events, as does the *Eventos* section of www.caracasvirtual .com. For clubs, your best bet are the listings at www.rumbacaracas.com.

Centro Comercial San Ignacio (Map pp928-9; cnr Blandín & San Ignacio) With more than a dozen nightclubs and bars, this mall comes alive at night. Dress to impress.

Cinemateca Nacional (Map pp920-1; ☎ 576-1491; www.cinemateca.gob.ve; Galería de Arte Nacional, Bellas Artes) Head here for great state-subsidized arthouse movies.

El Maní es Así (Map p924; ☎ 763-6671; cnr Av Francisco Solano López & El Cristo, Sabana Grande; ☿ 6pm-late Tue-Sun) One of the city's longest-running salsa spots, where everything revolves around the dance floor and the live salsa bands. Take a taxi after dark.

La Estancia (Map pp928-9; ☎ 208-6463; www.pdvsa .com; Av Francisco de Miranda; ☿ 9am-5pm Mon-Thu, to 7pm Fri-Sun) Sponsored by the government oil company, this arts center hosts free weekend concerts, yoga and music classes, coffee tastings and Sunday afternoon programs for kids.

Trasnocho Cultural (Map pp928-9; ☎ 993-1010; www.trasnochocultural.com; Nivel Trasnocho, Centro Comercial Paseo de Las Mercedes, Las Mercedes) A buzzing contemporary arts center buried in a mall sub-basement, it contains a theater, cinema, cafes, a yoga studio and a queer-friendly hipster bar.

> **SPLURGE!**
>
> **360° Roof Bar** (Map pp928-9; Av 1a btwn 1a & 2a Transversal, Los Palos Grandes; ☿ 5pm-midnight) Wow yourself over froufrou cocktails (35BsF) at the apex of the Hotel Altamira Suites, where this fabulous rooftop bar overlooks the entire sparkling city. Make sure you look pretty so the doormen let you in at the discreet side gate of the hotel, because this is the place that just might make you fall in love with Caracas.

Gay & Lesbian Venues

Caracas has by far the most open gay community in what is still a relatively conservative country. There are long-established gay and lesbian bars and clubs in Las Mercedes, Sabana Grande and La Castellana.

Tasca Pullman (Map p924; ☎ 761-1112; Edificio Ovidio, Av Francisco Solano López, ground fl, Sabana Grande; ☿ 8pm-late Tue-Sun) A friendly and unpretentious place, Pullman is the most popular of a group of small gay taverns in Sabana Grande. Never walk alone near here after dark.

Copa's Dancing Bar (Map pp928-9; ☎ 951-3947; Edificio Taeca, Calle Guaicaipuro, El Rosal; ☿ Wed-Sat) A mix of men and women pack the crisp white dance space, though Thursday is reserved for women. Prepare to be sized up through the front-door peephole.

Sports

Estadio Universitario (Map p924; Av Las Acacias) This baseball stadium at the Universidad Central de Venezuela hosts professional-league games from October to February and is also home to the **Leones de Caracas** (Caracas Lions; www.leones.com).

SHOPPING

Shopping is one of the city's greatest pastimes and malls are an important part of *caraqueño* life. Some of the main malls:

Centro Comercial Chacaíto (Map p924; Plaza Chacaíto, Chacaíto)

Centro Comercial El Recreo (Map p924; Av Casanova) The big one in Sabana Grande.

Centro Comercial Paseo Las Mercedes (Map pp928-9; Av Principal de Las Mercedes, Las Mercedes)

Centro Comercial San Ignacio (Map pp928-9; www .centrosanignacio.com; Av Blandín, La Castellana) Also one of the city's best centers for nightlife.

VENEZUELA

Centro Sambil (Map pp928-9; Av Libertador, Chacao; www.sambilmall.com/caracas) One of the biggest in South America.

GETTING THERE & AWAY
Air
The **Aeropuerto Internacional 'Simón Bolívar'** (www.aeropuerto-maiquetia.com.ve) is in Maiquetía, near the port of La Guaira on the Caribbean coast, 26km from central Caracas. It's generally referred to as 'Maiquetía.' There are three terminals: the **international terminal** (☎ 303-1526), the **domestic terminal** (☎ 303-1408) and an auxiliary terminal used by some smaller charter airlines. The two main terminals are separated by an easy walk of 400m, and it's about the same distance to the auxiliary terminal. There's currently no shuttle service between them.

The terminals have most conveniences, including tourist offices, car rental desks, *casas de cambio*, banks, ATMs, post and telephone offices, restaurants and a bunch of travel agencies, but no left-luggage office.

Bus
Caracas has two modern intercity bus terminals and a central terminal for shorter regional journeys. The **Terminal La Bandera** (☎ 693-6607), 3km south of the center, handles long-distance buses to anywhere in the country's west and southwest. It has good facilities, including computerized ticket booths, ATMs, telephones, a left-luggage office, an information desk and

BUS FARES

Destination	Cost (BsF)	Duration (hr)
Barinas	62-69	8½
Barquisimeto	21-45	5½
Carúpano	59-64	8½
Ciudad Bolívar	60-68	9
Ciudad Guayana	68-85	10
Coro	53-59	7
Cumaná	51-59	6½
Maracaibo	38-71	10½
Maracay	9-12	1½
Mérida	46-78	13
Puerto La Cruz	25-45	5
San Antonio del Táchira	47-84	14
San Cristóbal	45-78	13
San Fernando de Apure	23-56	8
Tucupita	40-55	11
Valencia	12-26	2½

lots of food outlets. The terminal is 300m from La Bandera metro station; you can walk the distance during the day, but take precautions at night when the area becomes unsafe. From the metro, take the Grande/Zulloaga exit, cross the avenue and turn left.

The city's other main bus terminal, the **Terminal de Oriente** (☎ 243-3253), is on the eastern outskirts of Caracas (off Map pp928-9), on the highway to Barcelona, 5km beyond Petare (about 18km from the center). It's accessible by many local buses from both the city center and Petare. It handles much of the traffic to the east and southeast of the country.

Bus companies **Aeroexpresos Ejecutivos** (Map pp928-9; ☎ 266-2321; www.aeroexpresos.com.ve; Av Principal de Bello Campo, Bello Campo) and **Rodovías** (Map p924; ☎ 577-6622; www.rodovias.com.ve; Av Libertador) have less chaotic private terminals conveniently located in the downtown area, with prices and schedules listed on their websites. They both service destinations including Ciudad Bolívar, Maracaibo, Ciudad Guayana and Puerto La Cruz.

Buses to Maiquetía airport (Map pp920-1; see boxed text, p922) depart from an underpass at Parque Central.

Car & Motorcycle
Driving into and out of Caracas is pretty straightforward. The major western access route is the Valencia–Caracas freeway, which enters the city from the south and joins Autopista Francisco Fajardo, the main east–west city artery, next to the Universidad Central de Venezuela. From anywhere in the east, access is by the Barcelona–Caracas freeway, which will take you directly to Av Francisco Fajardo.

It's best to make rental arrangements before your trip. Operators in the international terminal include **Avis** (☎ 355-1190), **Budget** (☎ 355-2799) and **Hertz** (☎ 355-1197), but they can't always provide a car on demand. You'll find desks of more local companies in the domestic terminal.

GETTING AROUND
Bus
An extensive bus network covers all suburbs within the metropolitan area, as well as major neighboring localities. Privately run *carritos* (small buses) are the main type of vehicle operating city routes, in addition to the city-run **metrobus** (www.metrodecaracas.com.ve) system. Buses run frequently but move only

VENEZUELA

as fast as traffic allows. However, they go to many destinations inaccessible by metro, are similarly priced and run later at night.

Car & Motorcycle
Driving in Caracas is only for people with lots of confidence, lots of nerves and a lot more insurance. It is easy to get lost and the traffic can be maddening. It is recommended to pay for parking in a monitored lot.

Metro
A godsend to this chaotic city, the **metro** (www .metrodecaracas.com.ve; ☾ 5:30am-11pm) is safe, fast, easy, well organized, clean and affordable – and it serves most major city attractions and tourist facilities. A single ticket for a ride of any distance is 0.50BsF, and a round trip is 0.90BsF. A 10-trip *multiabono* costs 4.50BsF and is worth it to avoid long ticket lines.

While the metro is generally safe, some opportunistic pickpockets exist.

Taxi
Identifiable by the 'Taxi' or 'Libre' sign, taxis are a fairly inexpensive means of getting around and sometimes the only option at night. None have meters, so always fix the fare before boarding – and don't be afraid to bargain. It is recommended that you use only white cars with yellow plates and preferably those from taxi ranks, of which there are plenty, especially outside shopping malls. Alternatively, many hotels or restaurants will call a reliable driver upon request.

In-a-hurry locals swear by the omnipresent Road Warrior-style *mototaxis* (motorcycle taxis). Though after you see how insanely they drive (watch your back on the sidewalk), you may choose to cool your heels.

AROUND CARACAS

Want a break from the bustle of Caracas? There are a number of exciting places to visit nearby. Because Caracas is the main jumping-off point, the Caribbean islands of Los Roques are also covered in this section.

PARQUE NACIONAL EL ÁVILA
One of the great attractions of the Caracas area, this national park encompasses some 90km of the coastal mountain range north of the city. The highest peak in the range

is Pico Naiguatá (2765m), while the most visited is Pico El Ávila (2105m). The newly nationalized and renamed **Teleférico Warairarepano** (Warairarepano cable car; ☎ 793-6050; adult/child 4-12 yr/student 25/10/15BsF; ascents ☾ noon-6pm Tue, 10am-8pm Wed & Thu, to 10pm Fri & Sat, to 6pm Sun, descents stop 2 hr later), runs 4km from Maripérez station (980m), next to Av Boyacá in Caracas, to Pico El Ávila. It's a phenomenal gondola ascent with some nail-biting heights, counting views of thick forest canopy, secret falls and the whole of Caracas. A bus (2BsF) runs to the base of the *teleférico* from the Colegio de Ingenieros metro station.

The southern slope of the range, overlooking Caracas, is uninhabited but crisscrossed with about 200km of walking trails. El Ávila provides better facilities for walkers than any other national park in Venezuela. Most of the trails are well signposted and there are a number of campgrounds.

A dozen entrances lead into the park from Caracas; all originate from Av Boyacá, commonly known as Cota Mil (at an altitude of 1000m). All routes have a short ascent before reaching a guard post, where you pay a nominal entrance fee. Because of safety concerns, solo hiking is not recommended; check with park staff about camping.

ARCHIPIÉLAGO LOS ROQUES
☎ 0237 / pop 1500
Island-hopping is the primary activity on Los Roques, a group of nearly 300 shimmering, sandy islands and islets that lie in aquamarine waters some 160km due north of Caracas. It's pricier than the mainland because everything is imported, but for those who love undeveloped beaches, snorkeling and diving, the trip is worth every bolívar. There are no high-rise hotels and you can walk barefoot on Gran Roque's sand streets. The whole archipelago, complete with the surrounding waters (2211 sq km), was made a national park in 1972.

The great majority of the islands are uninhabited except by pelicans and can be visited by boats from Gran Roque. The surrounding waters are known for their sea life, particularly lobsters (which account for 90% of national production).

For sunset views at Gran Roque, climb the hill to the remains of Faro Holandés, an 1870s lighthouse.

VENEZUELA

> **DETOUR: COLONIA TOVAR**
>
> Not your average Venezuelan town, Colonia Tovar was founded in the 19th century by German settlers. Spanish didn't become the official language until the 1940s, when a ban on marrying outside the community was abandoned.
>
> Today Colonia Tovar draws international and Venezuelan tourists (particularly on weekends). They come for the **Black Forest architecture**, mountain views, German cuisine, locally grown strawberries and the cooler climate. Accommodations here are good, but not cheap by Venezuelan standards. Bring warm clothing, as it's an all-day excursion and can get chilly.
>
> From Caracas, catch a minibus to El Junquito (3BsF, one hour) from outside the La Yaguara metro stop. At the El Junquito terminus, change for another minibus (5BsF, one hour) to town. For a spectacular and hair-raising return journey, take the southern La Victoria route back and snag a window seat on the left. Over a distance of only 30km, the road drops about 1300m through a riveting mountainous landscape. La Victoria minibuses (6.50BsF, one hour) depart regularly; from there take a bus to Terminal La Bandera (off Map pp920–1) in Caracas (7.50BsF, 1½ hours).

Orientation & Information

Gran Roque has the only village – a grid of four or so sandy car-free streets, a plaza and dozens of quaint *posadas* (small, family-run guesthouses). It's a compact place and wi-fi signals aren't difficult to find. All visitors to Los Roques pay the 55BsF national park entry fee upon arrival.

Banesco (☎ 221-1402; Plaza Bolívar; ◷ 8am-noon & 2-5pm Mon-Fri, 8am-2pm Sat) The only bank; arranges cash advances on Visa and MasterCard with a maximum of 800BsF. Also has a 24-hour ATM.

Enzosoft (per hr 20BsF; ◷ 8am-noon & 3-10pm Mon-Sat) The better internet connection and bigger rip-off. International calls cost 2BsF per minute.

Infocentro (30 min free; ◷ 8am-4:30pm & 5-8pm) Provides internet access; the state-sponsored Infocentro is near the school and across from the *panadería* (bakery).

Oscar Shop (☎ 0414-291-9160; oscarshop@hotmail .com) This small shop and informal tourist office near the airport organizes boat transportation to the islands and full-day boat tours. Also rents snorkeling equipment, surfboards, beach chairs and tents (60BsF to 80BsF per night).

Activities

SNORKELING & SCUBA DIVING

You can get snorkeling gear at many shops and most *posadas*. Scuba diving is also fabulous here; a two-dive excursion including equipment costs 475BsF.

The following are some recommended dive companies:

Aquatics Diving Center (☎ 0424-138-1240; www .adclosroques.com)

Arrecife (☎ 0414-327-8585; www.divevenezuela.com)

Ecobuzos (☎ 0414-793-1471; www.ecobuzos.com)

WINDSURFING & KITESURFING

Los Roques is also a top-notch spot for windsurfing. On the island of Francisquí de Abajo, **Vela Windsurf Center** (☎ 0414-207-2084; www .velawindsurf.com) rents equipment (US$20/35/50 per hour/half-day/day) and lessons (120BsF for two hours with equipment). Ask here for **kayak** rental and **kitesurfing** (250BsF for a four-hour class). For more on kitesurfing, inquire at **Oscar Shop** (☎ 0414-291-9160; oscarshop@hotmail.com).

Sleeping

CAMPING

Free camping is permitted on all the islands within the recreation zone, including Gran Roque. After arrival, go to **Inparques** (☎ 0414-614-2297; ◷ 8am-noon & 2-5pm Mon-Fri, 8:30am-11:30am Sat & Sun) at the far end of the village for a free camping permit and information. Oscar Shop rents tents and Roquelusa charges 15BsF per day bathroom usage for Gran Roque campers.

POSADAS

There are over 60 *posadas* providing some 500 beds on Gran Roque; almost all offer meals. Rates given here are low season per person; prices increase 30% to 70% in high season (Christmas, Carnaval, Semana Santa and August). Weekdays during low season, you can show up and bargain, especially for longer stays. Inclusive flight and lodging package deals generally don't save money.

Conserve water – it's a very precious resource here.

Doña Carmen (☎ 0414-291-9225; richardlosroques @hotmail.com; Plaza Bolívar; r per person no meals/incl breakfast & dinner 100/150BsF; ◉) The longest-running *posada* on the island (30 years), it still has the best prices. The concrete rooms are nothing special, though a couple face the beach, and there's an upstairs terrace surveying the sea.

Roquelusa (☎ 0414-369-6401; fax 221-1250; near the Inparques office; r per person incl breakfast & dinner 150BsF; ❄) This is a reliable if dingy option with small bathrooms, although all rooms have air conditioning.

El Botuto (☎ 0414-238-1589; www.posadael botuto.com; near the Inparques office; r per person incl breakfast/breakfast & dinner 210/280BsF) Known for its fantastic service and sociable dining area, beachside El Botuto has six colorful, airy rooms with small private patios and outdoor showers.

Posada La Laguna (☎ 0424-262-7913; www.la laguna.it; La Salina; r per person incl breakfast 250-400BsF; ❄) Blue cement floors and sparkling white walls give this homey Italian-run place a Mediterranean feel. Excellent multicourse dinners (50BsF) upon request.

Eating & Drinking

Most visitors eat at their posadas, but self-catering or eating out at a less expensive restaurant will cut costs. Don't expect *posadas* to permit kitchen use.

Kiosko La Sirena (empanadas 4-10BsF; burgers 25BsF; ☺ 7-10am & 7pm-late) If you're on a strict budget, settle in on a log stool at this food shack by the lagoon. Breakfast is empanadas, and hamburgers are available in the evening.

La Chuchera (Plaza Bolívar; mains 35-65BsF; ☺ 10am-10pm) La Chuchera is the main budget restaurant in town (although it's not necessarily cheap). It serves pizza, sandwiches and pasta dishes, and it's a fun place to have beers. Intermittent wi-fi available.

Aquarena Cafe (mains 38-50BsF; ☺ 8am-midnight Wed-Mon, daily in high season) Near Macanao Lodge, this beachside cafe amid billowing palms serves sushi, cooked fish, hamburgers, pizza and salads.

Bora La Mar (☺ 5pm-midnight) The cocktails are pricey (around 30BsF), but it's worth it to dig your toes in the sand and gaze at the stars by candlelight. Enter from the beach, next to the church.

For self-caterers there's a small **grocery store** (☺ 7am-1pm & 3-8pm) near the Inparques office; a **bakery** (☺ 7am-noon & 3-8pm Mon-Sat, 7am-noon Sun) by the school sells sandwich meats and fresh bread.

Getting There & Away

AIR

Maiquetía–Los Roques flights (approximately 850BsF to 1000BsF round trip) take about 40 minutes. It is easiest to book flights through an agency. Carriers include the following:

Aereotuy (LTA; ☎ 0212-212-3110, 0295-415-5778; www.tuy.com)

Chapi Air (☎ 0212-355-1965; Maiquetía domestic terminal)

Rainbow Air (☎ 0424-877-0582; makoroporlamar @gmail.com)

LTA and Rainbow Air also fly to Los Roques from Isla de Margarita (620BsF to 796BsF one way).

Normally only 15kg of free luggage is permitted on flights to Los Roques; every additional kilogram costs 5BsF.

BOAT

There are no passenger boats to Los Roques.

Getting Around

Oscar Shop (☎ 0414-291-9160; oscarshop@hotmail.com) or other boat operators in Gran Roque will take you to the island of your choice and pick you up at a prearranged time. Round-trip fares per person are Madrizquí (25BsF), the Francisquises (30BsF), and Crasquí or Noronquises (60BsF).

THE NORTHWEST

Easily reached from Caracas, the country's northwest is stocked with beaches, rain-forests, deserts, caves, waterfalls, 12 national parks and South America's largest lake. Parque Nacional Morrocoy attracts visitors with its colorful reefs, beaches and Sahara-like desert near the colonial town of Coro. Parque Nacional Henri Pittier is a favorite stop for backpackers and locals to hang out, soak up the sun and enjoy a few drinks or break out the binoculars and spot rare birds.

MARACAY

☎ 0243 / pop 610,000

A few hours from Caracas, Maracay is a busy metropolis and the 300-year-old capital of Aragua state. From 1899 to 1935 it was home base for infamous *caudillo* (provincial strongman) Juan Vicente Gómez, who built up its infrastructure and shaped it into the nation's

VENEZUELA

aviation and air force hub. The center of an important agricultural and industrial area, it's usually visited as a stopover on the way to Parque Nacional Henri Pittier and doesn't have many attractions to otherwise hold the traveler.

Orientation & Information

There are internet cafes in most malls (centros comerciales).

Banco de Venezuela (Mariño)

Banesco (Av Páez)

Ipostel (Centro Comercial 19 de Abril, cnr Avs 19 de Abril & Boyacá)

Italcambio (☎ 235-6945; No 110-K, Centro Comercial Maracay Plaza, cnr Avs Aragua & Bermúdez, 1st fl) Located 1.5km south of Plaza Bolívar.

Sleeping & Eating

Maracay's cheapest accommodations are hourly love hotels. Staying near the bus station isn't recommended; the neighborhood isn't safe after dark.

ourpick Posada El Limón (☎ 283-4925; www.posadaellimon.com; El Piñal 64, El Limón; dm/tr 50/250BsF, d 180-200BsF; ☒ 🖳 ☒) In the suburb of El Limón, this enchanting mosaic-covered posada has leafy patios and mountain views, and an inexpensive dorm with rollaway beds that often fills up on weekends. Perks include a compact pool, a restaurant serving breakfast, wi-fi and a bar. From the bus terminal, take the local bus marked 'Circunvalación,' or a cab (20BsF).

Hotel Mar del Plata (☎ 246-4313; mardelplatahotel @gmail.com; Av Santos Michelena Este 23; d 90-100BsF, tr & q 120BsF; ☒ 🖳) A quiet central budget option, Mar del Plata has 30 tidy, clean rooms with hot water and cable TV.

El Arepanito (cnr Av 19 de Abril & Junín; arepas 16-27BsF; ☒ 24hr Fri-Sun, 6am-1am Mon-Thu) Open later than most places in town, this popular restaurant serves tasty arepas, pizza and fruit juices in a pleasant plant-filled patio or in the air-conditioned dining room.

Pizza Mia (Av 19 de Abril; pizzas 18-85BsF; ☒ 10am-10:30pm) A brightly lit chain pizzeria, Pizza Mia is popular with families. It's fast food in theory only, since the pies arrive at a leisurely pace.

For a really inexpensive and filling meal, try one of the **Mercado Principal** (Av Santos Michelena; ☒ 7am-3pm) food stalls.

Getting There & Away

Two side-by-side bus terminals are located on the southeastern outskirts of the city center on Av Constitución. It's a 20-minute walk to

the Plaza Bolívar, though frequent city buses are 1BsF and a taxi across town costs 15BsF to 25BsF.

Regional buses depart from the Interurbano terminal (the eastern side), while most long-distance and air-conditioned buses depart from the new Extraurbano terminal (the western side). There are departures approximately every 15 minutes to Caracas (9BsF to 13BsF, 1½ hours) and Valencia (5BsF, one hour), and frequent departures to Barquisimeto (25BsF to 30BsF, 3½ hours), Maracaibo (50BsF to 60BsF, eight hours) and San Fernando de Apure (36BsF, seven hours). Other destinations include San Antonio del Táchira (70BsF, 12½ hours), Coro (45BsF, 6½ hours) and Mérida (60BsF, 11 hours). Direct buses to Puerto La Cruz (50BsF, seven hours) and Ciudad Bolívar (60BsF to 65BsF, nine hours) bypass Caracas, saving time and money.

PARQUE NACIONAL HENRI PITTIER

☎ 0243

Venezuela's oldest national park, Henri Pittier rolls over 1078 sq km of the rugged coastal mountain range and then plunges down to epic Caribbean beaches. There's something for everyone to love here: a glistening coastline, 600 species of birds, twisting hiking trails through verdant mountains, and quaint colonial towns with tasty food, comfortable posadas and even a bit of nightlife.

The chaotic Maracay Interurbano bus terminal is the departure point for the park, and two paved roads cross the park from north to south. The eastern road goes from Maracay north to Choroní (climbing to 1830m) and reaches the coast 2km further on at Puerto Colombia. The western road leads from Maracay to Ocumare de la Costa and El Playón, then continues to Cata; it ascends to 1128m at Paso Portachuelo. Both roads are about 55km long. There's no road connection between the coastal ends of these roads, though 10-person boats can bounce you between Puerto Colombia and El Playón (300BsF per boat one-way).

Expect crowds and traffic on holidays and weekends, and potential carsickness from the winding curves.

Puerto Colombia

Choroní may be the largest town on this side of the park, but Puerto Colombia's beachside location makes it one of the major backpacker hangouts in Venezuela. An attractive and laid-back colonial village packed with *posadas* and restaurants, most folks spend their days on the beach and evenings sipping *guarapita* (cane alcohol mixed with passion-fruit juice and lots of sugar) down on the waterfront, where drumming circles rev up on weekends.

The most popular beach is **Playa Grande**, a five- to 10-minute walk by road east of town. It's about half a kilometer long and shaded by coconut palms, but is busy and can be packed on weekends. There are several restaurants at the entrance to the beach. You can camp on the beach or sling your hammock between the palms, but don't leave your stuff unattended. Bathrooms and showers are available.

If Playa Grande is too crowded or littered, go to the undeveloped **Playa El Diario**, on the opposite (western) side of the town.

Other area beaches normally visited by boat include **Playa Aroa** (400BsF round trip per boat, 15 minutes one way), **Playa Chuao** (20BsF to 25BsF per person, 30 minutes) and **Playa Cepe** (25BsF to 30BsF per person, 45 minutes).

An internet cafe sits across from Posada Túcan, and the only bank is in Choroní.

SLEEPING

Hostal Colonial (☎ 218-5012; www.choroni.net; Morillo 37; dm/tr 20/75BsF, d 60-70BsF, without bathroom 55BsF; 🖳) Colonial is a popular backpacker spot with a wide variety of rooms, plus hot-water bathrooms, kitchen use and breakfast (16BsF to 20BsF) service on a pretty back courtyard. Reservations accepted by phone only.

Casa Luna (☎ 951-5318; www.jungletrip.de; Morillo 35; d 70-80BsF, tr 90BsF; 🖳) A friendly *posada* with a very helpful German owner, its five very clean rooms have shared cold-water bathrooms, and a five-person room is sometimes available as a dorm for 50BsF per person. There's a sociable courtyard with hammocks, as well as a kitchen and a book exchange, and Caracas airport transfers are available. Next door to Hostal Colonial.

Hostal Vista Mar (☎ 991-1107; tiegraca@gmail.com; Colón; d/tr/q with fan 150/190/230BsF, d with air-con 210-260BsF, tr with air-con 250-300BsF; 🈁) This *hostal* is right at the end of the seafront boulevard; try to snag room 20 or 21 for an ocean view. Some of its 33 rooms have fan and cold-water bathrooms, others have air-con, hot water and TV. It has lots of comfy and airy common spaces for relaxing, and rates are lower Sunday through Thursday.

EATING

Brisas del Mar (Los Cocos; mains 20-40BsF; 🕐 8:30am-10:30pm) People-watch from the front patio near the *malecón* (shoreline promenade) as you dine on pasta, seafood and meat dishes.

Bar Restaurant Araguaneyes (Los Cocos 8; mains 32-60BsF; 🕐 8am-10:30pm Mon-Thu, to 11pm Fri-Sun) Sit on the airy upstairs terrace and enjoy inter-national and *criollo* fare, including a good selection of fresh fish.

Bokú (Morillo; dinner menú 45-60BsF; 🕐 6pm-midnight) Saffron-colored tablecloths and wrought-iron chairs create a striking ambience for delectable pastas and fresh seafood. Half a block from the waterfront.

GETTING THERE & AWAY

From Anden 5 of Maracay's Interurbano ter-minal, buses depart every one or two hours (15BsF, 2¼ hours). The last bus back to Maracay theoretically departs from Puerto Colombia between 4pm and 5pm (later on weekends). Taxis leave from right behind the bus terminal (100BsF during the day, more at night, 1¼ hours); look for other travelers in the bus station to share the cost. Note that most folks refer collectively to the whole area, including Puerto Colombia, as Choroní.

From Monday through Thursday, buses run all the way to Puerto Colombia, but at weekends they terminate at a new bus sta-tion between Choroní and Puerto Colombia. *Carritos* (2BsF) marked 'Interno' run every 15 minutes or so between the two towns until about 8pm; it's about a 20-minute walk.

El Playón

Located at the end of the national park's west-ern road, El Playón is the main town in this area. It's much larger than Puerto Colombia, but has none of that town's colonial charm. There are several small beaches here, the best of which is **Playa Malibú**, close to the *malecón*. The namesake beach, **El Playón**, is right in town and has a good surfing spot on the west end. For a good place to snorkel or kayak, boats can drop you off at **La Ciénaga** (200BsF per boat one way, 15 minutes). Inquire at Posada de la Costa Eco-Lodge for trips.

Five kilometers eastward is the area's most famous beach, **Playa Cata**. The beach is a post-card crescent of sand bordering Bahía de Cata, marred only by two ugly apartment towers looming over the beach. *Carritos* (3BsF, 15 minutes) run here from El Playón.

Boats from Playa Cata take tourists to the smaller and quieter **Playa Catita** (150BsF per boat one way, 10 minutes) and the usually deserted **Playa Cuyagua** (300BsF per boat one way, 20 minutes), though both can be reached overland for a cheaper price.

The nearest ATM is in Ocumare de la Costa, on Plaza Bolívar, across from the church.

SLEEPING & EATING

There are over a dozen places to stay; many are within a couple of blocks of the waterfront. There are a few ramshackle restaurants in town and hotels generally serve food on request. Prices jump on weekends and holidays.

Posada Villa Loley (☎ 993-1252; loleyenlacosta @hotmail.com; cnr Fuerzas Armadas & Urdaneta; d/tr/q 240/260/280BsF; 🞑 🖵 🞓) A relaxing place one block from the beach, guests kick back by the tiny pool and lounge around the patio garden and bar. Rooms in this friendly *posada* sport cute fish decor, cloth window shades and attractive blue tiling, and a 30% discount is available from Sunday to Thursday.

Posada de la Costa Eco-Lodge (☎ 993-1986; www .ecovenezuela.com; California 23; d with/without sea view 435/385BsF, tr/q 472/505BsF; 🞑 🞓) Set in a tranquil garden of bougainvillea by the beach, this beautiful hotel provides neat rooms and a breezy terrace bar to survey the beach. It's worth the splurge for the rooms with sea views and balconies. Breakfast is included, and kayak and snorkeling trips are offered.

GETTING THERE & AWAY

Buses to El Playón (marked 'Ocumare de la Costa') depart from Anden 6 of Maracay's Interurbano terminal about every hour from 7am to 6pm (10BsF, two hours). Maracay's Urbanización Caña de Azúcar also has hourly minibuses to El Playón; these are handy for travelers staying in nearby El Limón.

PARQUE NACIONAL MORROCOY

☎ 0259

One of the most spectacular coastal environments in Venezuela, Parque Nacional Morrocoy comprises a strip of park on the mainland, and extends offshore to scores of islands, islets and cays. Some islands are fringed by white-sand beaches and surrounded by coral reefs. The most popular of the islands is Cayo Sombrero, which has fine (though increasingly damaged) coral reefs and some of the best beaches. Other snorkeling spots include Cayo Borracho, Playuela and Playuelita.

The park gets rather crowded on weekends, but is considerably less full during the week. Holidays are complete bumper-to-bumper madness.

Orientation & Information

The park lies between the towns of Tucacas and Chichiriviche, which are its main gateways. Chichiriviche is smaller than Tucacas, but both are somewhat unexciting and unattractive. Both towns have internet cafes and 24-hour ATMs.

Activities

Snorkeling gear can be rented from some boat operators and hotels, and many offer beach, snorkeling and bird-watching excursions.

Tucacas has three dive schools offering diving courses and guided dives. Diving certification classes run 1000BsF to 1800BsF, a two-tank dive is 350BsF to 450BsF, and snorkeling trips range from 60BsF to 200BsF.

Recommended diving companies:

Amigos del Mar (☎ 812-1754; amigos-del-mar@cantv .net; Democracia) The least expensive shop.

Frogman Dive Center (☎ 340-1824; www.frogman dive.com; Centro Comercial Bolívar, Plaza Bolívar)

Submatur (☎ 812-0082; morrocoysubmatur1@cantv .net; Ayacucho 6)

Sleeping & Eating

Camping is no longer permitted on the park's islands.

TUCACAS

Many of Tucacas' hotels and restaurants are on or near the 1km-long Av Libertador.

Posada de Carlos (☎ 812-1493; Av Principal 5; s 60BsF, r per person 40BsF; 🞑) A hand-written sign reads '*Sí, hay habitación*' (yes, there are rooms) at this good budget option with eight rooms.

Posada Amigos del Mar (☎ 812-3962; amigos-del -mar@cantv.net; Nueva; s 60BsF, r per person 40BsF) This run-down but inexpensive Belgian-owned *posada* and dive shop has good-sized fan-cooled rooms, a kitchen and a barbecue. Located behind the Ambulatorio Urbano, a quick stroll from the bus stop.

Panadería Reina del Mar (Av Libertador; mains 10-25BsF; ⏲ 7am-9pm Mon-Fri, to 10pm Sat & Sun) Close to the highway, this well-priced bakery and restaurant serves sandwiches, lasagna, chicken and the usual assortment of breakfast items.

CHICHIRIVICHE

There are lots of accommodations along the waterfront of Playa Norte. For budget eateries, try Av Zamora.

Casa Morena's Place (☎ 0424-453-3450; posada morenas@hotmail.com; Sector Playa Norte; dm 25-30BsF; s/d 50/70BsF) One block from the beach, near the Lyceo Ramon Yanez, this cheerfully cluttered budget option has laundry service and kitchen usage; English and some French are spoken.

Villa Gregoria (☎ 818-6359; aagustinm@yahoo .es; Mariño; d 100BsF; 🔊) This Spanish-run and Spanish-themed place near the bus terminus contains a small garden and comfortable rooms.

Restaurant El Rincón de Arturo (Av Zamora; breakfast 20BsF, lunch menú 22BsF; 🕑 7am-4pm Mon-Sat, 7am-6pm Sun) Two blocks from the beach, this small and popular corner eatery has tasty and straightforward meals.

Getting There & Away

Neither Tucacas nor Chichiriviche have proper bus terminals. Tucacas sits on the Valencia–Coro road, so buses run frequently to both Valencia (10BsF, 1½ hours) and Coro (25BsF, 3½ hours). Buses from Valencia pass through regularly on their way to Chichiriviche (5BsF, 40 minutes).

Chichiriviche is about 22km off the main Morón–Coro highway and is serviced by half-hourly buses from Valencia (20BsF, 2½ hours).

There's no direct bus service to Chichiriviche from Caracas or Coro. To get here from Caracas, take any of the frequent buses to Valencia (12BsF to 15BsF, 2½ hours) and change there for a Chichiriviche bus. From Coro, take any bus to Valencia, get off in Sanare (25BsF, 3¼ hours), at the turnoff for Chichiriviche, and then grab a Valencia–Chichiriviche bus.

Getting Around

Boats to the islands from both Tucacas and Chichiriviche take up to eight people and charge by the boat. Popular destinations from Tucacas include Playa Paiclás (round trip 150BsF), Playuela (200BsF) and Cayo Sombrero (250BsF). From Chichiriviche, popular trips include the close cays of Cayo Muerto, Cayo Sal and Cayo Pelón, and Cayo Sombrero.

CORO

☎ 0268 / pop 256,000

Caressed by pleasant sea breezes, Coro is one of the prettiest colonial cities in Venezuela and the entry point to the magnificent sand dunes of the Parque Nacional Médanos de Coro. The cobblestone Zamora, where most of the historic mansions are located, rivals any other colonial architecture in the country, and the city has been on Unesco's World Heritage list since 1993. An excellent base for exploring the region, especially the Península de Paraguaná and the mountainous Sierra de San Luis, it boasts a large university population and excellent budget accommodations.

Information

Araguato Expeditions (☎ 0416-866-9328; www .araguato.org; Federación 26) Tour agency based at Posada El Gallo; offers day trips (120BsF) to the Península de Paraguaná and to Sierra de San Luis.

Banco de Venezuela (Paseo Talavera)

Bancoro (cnr Av Manaure & Zamora)

Centro de Navegación Internet (cnr Av Manaure & Zamora; 🕑 8am-8:30pm)

Movistar (Falcón) Telephones.

Sights

Mesmerizing zebra stripes of sand shimmer in the breeze at the **Parque Nacional Médanos de Coro**, a spectacular desert landscape with sand dunes of 30m in height. Late afternoon is the best time to visit, when the sun is not so fierce. To get there, take the Carabobo bus from Falcón and get off 300m past the large Monumento a la Federación. From here it's a 10-minute walk north along a wide avenue to another public sculpture, the Monumento a la Madre, and then the dunes begin.

Sleeping

Coro has some of the best-value budget accommodations in the country.

Posada Turística El Gallo (☎ 252-9481; www .hosteltrail.com/posadaelgallo; Federación 26; hammock/dm 25/30BsF, s/d/tr 50/60/80BsF, without bathroom 40/50/60BsF; 🖳) In a restored colonial building with bright colors, wood beams and a lovely terrace, it's one of the best deals in town, with laundry service, regional tours, a book exchange and a kitchen. Their second posada nearby has private bathrooms.

VENEZUELA

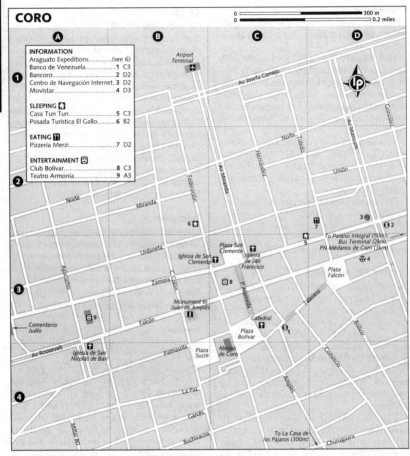

CORO

0 _____ 300 m
0 _____ 0.2 miles

INFORMATION
Araguato Expeditions............(see 6)
Banco de Venezuela................1 C3
Bancoro.................................2 D2
Centro de Navegación Internet.3 D2
Movistar................................4 D3

SLEEPING
Casa Tun Tun........................5 C3
Posada Turística El Gallo.........6 B2

EATING
Pizzería Merzi........................7 D2

ENTERTAINMENT
Club Bolívar..........................8 C3
Teatro Armonía......................9 A3

Casa Tun Tun (☎ 404-4260; www.casatuntun .com; Zamora 92; dm 30BsF, s/d/tr 60/75/95BsF, without bathroom 45/55/75BsF; 🖳) This colonial enclave sports simple, clean rooms and a basic kitchen. Reception is open from 7am to midnight.

La Casa de los Pájaros (☎ 252-8215; www.casa delospajaros.com.ve; Monzón 74; dm with fan 30BsF, d/tr/q with air-con 120/160/180BsF; ❄ 🖳) Built by architect owners, this gorgeous seven-room house dazzles with high ceilings, good lighting and artisan mosaic bathrooms.

Eating

Paraíso Integral (cnr Zamora & Gonzalez; menú 15BsF; ⏱ 7am-7pm Mon-Thu, to 5:30pm Fri, 7:30am-1pm Sun) This vegetarian eatery satiates diners with delicious soups and filling dishes like *pasticho de berengena* (eggplant lasagna), and sells hard-to-find natural foods.

Pizzería Merzi (Toledo 36; pizza from 19BsF; ⏱ 4-10pm Tue-Sun) Locals love the tasty pies served at this pizzeria, which is housed in a colonial building.

Entertainment

Club Bolívar (☎ 0414-627-2865; Zamora) This unsigned courtyard restaurant is a nighttime favorite with college students, who show up for the free live bands playing salsa and boleros.

Teatro Armonía (Zamora) Its Sala Cinemateca Coro (www.cinemateca.gob.ve) is a good bet for inexpensive arthouse movie screenings; its excellent orchestra holds free concerts on Thursdays.

Getting There & Away

AIR

The **Aeropuerto Internacional José Leonardo Chirinos** (☎ 251-5290; Av Josefa Camejo) is just a five-minute walk north of the city center. Avior has a daily flight to Caracas (269BsF). Local taxis are 10BsF.

BUS

The **Terminal de Pasajeros** (Av Los Médanos) is 2km east of the city center and accessible by frequent city transport. Ordinary buses to Punto Fijo (10BsF, 1¼ hours), Maracaibo (35BsF, four hours) and Valencia (US$7, five hours) run every half hour until about 6pm. Most of the direct buses to Caracas (53BsF to 60BsF, seven hours) depart in the evening, or take a bus to Valencia and change. Several direct buses go nightly to Mérida (64BsF, 13 hours) and San Cristóbal (70BsF, 12 hours) via Maracaibo, or you can go to Barquisimeto and change there.

ADÍCORA

☎ 0269

On the eastern coast of the Península de Paraguaná, the small blustery town of Adícora is one of the country's **windsurfing** and **kitesurfing** capitals. Pros and beginners come from all over the world to ride the local winds. It is the most popular destination on the peninsula and offers a reasonable choice of accommodations and restaurants. Windsurfing lessons run about 80BsF per

hour, and an eight- to 10-hour kitesurfing course costs 700BsF to 850BsF.

Located on Playa Sur (South Beach) at the entrance to town, a few local operators offer courses, equipment rental and accommodations with kitchen facilities. They include **Windsurf Adícora** (☎ 0416-769-6196; www.windsurfadicora.com; d 120BsF, apt 150BsF; 🖳), with good rooms and a common kitchen, and **Archie's Surf Posada** (☎ 988-8285; www.kitesurfing-venezuela.com; camping/hammock per person 30BsF, d 80BsF; 🖳), a German-run school with lots of apartment units.

Adícora is linked to Coro (9BsF, one hour) by eight buses a day, the last departing at around 5pm.

MARACAIBO

☎ 0261 / pop 2.5 million

Unless you're in the oil business, it's unlikely you'll do more than change buses in baking hot Maracaibo, Venezuela's second-largest city and the oil industry's nerve center. Some two-thirds of the national oil output comes from beneath the Lago de Maracaibo. A metropolis with vast suburbs, Maracaibo encompasses the dilapidated historic center to the south and a characterless new center of high-rises to the north. Getting between the two is easy and fast, so it doesn't really matter much where you stay. The new center offers a far better choice of hotels, restaurants and bars, and is safer at night. The old quarter boasts more colonial sights, but closes up by early evening.

LIGHTNING WITHOUT THUNDER

Centered on the mouth of the Río Catatumbo at Lago de Maracaibo, this shocking phenomenon consists of frequent flashes of lightning with no accompanying thunder. The eerie, silent electrical storm can be so strong and constant that you will be able to read this book at night.

Referred to as Relámpago de Catatumbo (Catatumbo Lightning) or Faro de Maracaibo (Maracaibo Beacon), it can be observed at night all over the region, weather permitting, from as far away as Maracaibo and San Cristóbal. You'll get a glimpse of it traveling by night on the Maracaibo–San Cristóbal or San Cristóbal–Valera roads but, the closer you get, the more impressive the spectacle becomes. Tours organized from Mérida are the easiest way to see the Catatumbo lightning close up.

Various hypotheses have been put forth to explain the lightning, but so far none have been proven. The theory that stands out is based on the topography of the region, characterized by the proximity of 5000m-high mountains (the Andes) and a vast sea-level lake (Lago de Maracaibo) – a dramatic configuration found nowhere else in the world. The clash of the cold winds descending from the freezing highlands with the hot, humid air evaporating from the lake is thought to produce the ionization of air particles responsible for the lightning.

Sightings are best from September through November, when there can be 150 to 200 flashes per minute.

VENEZUELA

Information

Banco de Venezuela Historic Center (cnr Av 5 & Calle 97); New Center (cnr Av Bella Vista & Calle 74)

Banesco New Center (cnr Av Bella Vista & Calle 71); New Center (Av Bella Vista btwn Calles 83 & 84)

Cyber @lgo Mas (Av 5 btwn Calles 96 & 97, Historic Center; ☺ 8am-4pm Mon-Fri)

Italcambio Airport (☎ 735-6206, domestic terminal); Av El Milagro (☎ 793-2983; Centro Comercial Lago Mall, Av El Milagro, New Center)

Magic Net (Centro Comercial Salto Ángel, Calle 78, New Center; internet per hr 3.50BsF; ☺ 9am-8pm Mon-Fri, 2-8pm Sun) On south side of Plaza República.

Movistar (cnr Av Bella Vista & Calle 83, New Center; ☺ 9am-6pm Mon-Thu) Phones too.

Sleeping

Although it's convenient to stay in the historic center, you will find that the options are not very appealing; also, the area is unsafe and ghost town–deserted at night. The northern suburbs are somewhat safer and provide better accommodations, but most options are unexciting.

Hotel Caribe (☎ 722-5986; hotel_caribe@cantv.net; Av 7 No 93-51, Historic Center; s 60-80BsF, d 100-190BsF, tr 225BsF; ☒ ☒) Two blocks from the Plaza Bolívar, the 90-room Caribe has an older section with good basic rooms and a newer section with better beds. A grand art-deco staircase graces the lobby.

Nuevo Hotel Unión (☎ 793-3278; Calle 84 No 4-60, New Center; d 65-70BsF, tr 100BsF; ☒) A sparse budget spot which offers 16 basic rooms with colonial tiled floors.

Hotel Nuevo Montevideo (☎ 722-2762; Calle 86A No 4-96, New Center; d 80-90BsF, tr 100BsF; ☒) Set in an old rambling house, this tranquil place has 12 large rooms with high ceilings.

Eating

Inexpensive lunch eateries abound in the Historic Center; in the New Center, the Plaza República area has upscale and evening options.

Pastelería Jeffrey's (Calle 78 btwn Avs 3H & 3G, New Center; sandwiches & salads 16-30BsF; ☺ 7am-9pm Mon-Sat, to 2pm Sun) An upscale bakery cafe near the Plaza República serving simple breakfasts, good coffee, attractive pastries, cakes and truffles and freshly made juices.

Restaurant El Enlosao (Calle 94, Historic Center; mains 22-26BsF; ☺ 11am-7:30pm) Housed in a charming historic mansion, El Enlosao serves unpretentious but tasty Venezuelan food at low prices.

Restaurant El Zaguán (cnr Calle 94 & Av 6, Historic Center; mains 30-48BsF; ☺ noon-7pm Mon-Sat) Near El Enlosao, it serves hearty local and international cuisine, with lots of coconut-based Zulia specialties. Walls of old photos document the history and architecture of colonial Maracaibo.

Restaurant Mi Vaquita (Av 3H No 76-22, New Center; mains 60-80BsF; ☺ 11:30am-4pm Mon, to 11pm Tue-Sat, noon-5pm Sun) Still sizzling after 40 years, this attractive wood-interior restaurant and bar is one of the best steakhouses in town. Live merengue, salsa and reggaeton from Thursday through Saturday.

GETTING TO COLOMBIA

A number of companies run air-conditioned buses to Cartagena via Maicao, Santa Marta and Barranquilla (all of which are in Colombia). **Bus Ven** (☎ 723-9084; bus terminal) has one 5am departure daily from Maracaibo's bus terminal (and is cheaper than its competitors): it goes to Santa Marta (220BsF, seven hours, 374km) and Cartagena (240BsF, 11 hours, 597km). The buses cross the border at **Paraguachón** (you actually change buses there) and continue through Maicao (see boxed text, p532), the first Colombian town.

It is cheaper to go by *por puesto* (shared taxi) to Maicao (60BsF, 2½ hours, 123km) and change there. *Por puestos* depart regularly from about 5am to 3pm and go as far as Maicao's bus terminal. From there, several Colombian bus companies operate buses to Santa Marta (COP$31,000, four hours) and further on; buses depart regularly until the late afternoon.

All passport formalities are done in Paraguachón on the border. Venezuelan immigration charges a 55BsF *impuesto de salida* (departure tax), paid in cash bolívares by all tourists leaving Venezuela.

Keep in mind that you need to wind your watch back one half-hour when crossing from Venezuela to Colombia. For information on traveling to Venezuela from Santa Marta, Colombia, see p532.

Getting There & Away

La Chinita international airport is 12km southwest of the city center. It's not linked by public transport; a taxi costs about 20BsF. Mostly flights go through Caracas (296BsF to 350BsF).

The busy bus terminal is 1km southwest of the center, with left luggage and an internet cafe with late hours. Regular buses run to Coro (35BsF, four hours) and Caracas (56BsF to 58BsF, 10½ hours). Several night buses run to Mérida (50BsF, nine hours) and San Cristóbal (55BsF, eight hours).

THE ANDES

Hot-blooded Venezuela is not usually associated with snow-encrusted mountains and windswept peaks. However, Venezuela is, in fact, home to the 400km-long northern end of the Andes range, crowned by the country's tallest mountain, Pico Bolívar (5007m). For those who aren't hard-core mountaineers, the region offers lush valleys of cloud forest, cascading creeks and waterfalls, and charming mountain villages accessible by narrow winding roads.

Mérida state is in the heart of the Venezuelan Andes and has the highest mountains and the best-developed facilities for travelers. The city of Mérida is one of the continent's top adventure-sports destinations, and is also the gateway to Los Llanos grasslands. The two other Andean states, Trujillo and Táchira, are less visited, but have many trekking opportunities for intrepid travelers.

MÉRIDA

☎ 0274 / pop 310,000

The adventure-sports capital of Venezuela, Mérida (elevation 1600m) is an affluent Andean city with a youthful energy and a robust arts scene. It has an unhurried, friendly and cultured atmosphere derived from the massive university and outdoor-sports presence, and active visitors will be spoiled for choice, with myriad options for hiking, canyoning, rafting, mountain biking and paragliding. The city is also the major jumping-off point for wildlife-viewing trips to Los Llanos.

Affordable and safe, Mérida has a high standard of accommodations and numerous budget eateries. While not a place to indulge in colonial architecture, it has a vibrant and unpretentious nightlife and is a major stop on backpacking circuits.

Information

INTERNET ACCESS

Fast, inexpensive internet cafes (2BsF to 3BsF per hour) are abundant in Mérida:

Cyber Blue Sky (Av 5)
Movistar (Calle 20)
Palace Cyber (Calle 24) Good screens and fast connections.

LAUNDRY

Most *posadas* offer laundry service; central *lavanderías* charge about 15BsF per load.

Lavandería Marbet (Calle 25)
Posada Patty (Calle 24)

MEDICAL SERVICES

Clínica Mérida (☎ 263-0652, 263-6395; Av Urdaneta No 45-145)

MONEY

Banco de Venezuela (Av 4)
Banesco (Calle 24)
Italcambio (☎ 263-2977; Av Urdaneta, airport)

POST

Ipostel (Calle 21)

TELEPHONE

Movistar (Calle 20) Also has internet.

TOURIST INFORMATION

Cormetur (☎ 800-637-4300, ☷ 7am-7pm; cormetur promocion@hotmail.com) Bus terminal (☎ 263-3952; Av Las Américas; ☷ 8am-6pm); Main tourist office (☎ 263-1603, 263-4701; cnr Av Urdaneta & Calle 45; ☷ 8am-noon & 2:30-6pm); Mercado Principal (☎ 262-1570; Av Las Américas; ☷ 8am-3pm Tue-Sun); Teleférico (Parque Las Heroínas; ☷ 8am-3pm Tue-Sun) One of the most helpful tourism offices in the country; English spoken at toll-free number and at main office.

Sights

The **city center** is pleasant for leisurely strolls, though it has little in the way of colonial architecture or outstanding sights. The leafy **Plaza Bolívar** is the city's heart, but it's not a colonial square. Work on the monumental **Catedral de Mérida** began in 1800, based on the plans of the 17th-century cathedral of Toledo in Spain, but it wasn't completed until 1958,

MÉRIDA

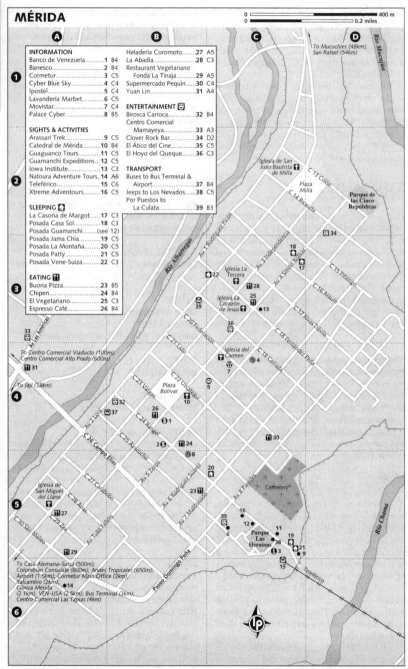

0   400 m
0   0.2 miles

INFORMATION
Banco de Venezuela..........**1** B4
Banesco.........................**2** B4
Cormetur.......................**3** C5
Cyber Blue Sky................**4** C4
Ipostel..........................**5** C4
Lavandería Marbet............**6** C5
Movistar........................**7** C4
Palace Cyber...................**8** B5

SIGHTS & ACTIVITIES
Arassari Trek...................**9** C5
Catedral de Mérida...........**10** B4
Guaguanco Tours.............**11** C5
Guamanchi Expeditions.....**12** C5
Iowa Institute.................**13** C3
Natoura Adventure Tours...**14** A6
Teleférico......................**15** C6
Xtreme Adventurs...........**16** C5

SLEEPING
La Casona de Margot.......**17** C3
Posada Casa Sol.............**18** C3
Posada Guamanchi........(see 12)
Posada Jama Chía...........**19** C5
Posada La Montaña..........**20** C5
Posada Patty..................**21** C5
Posada Vene-Suiza.........**22** C3

EATING
Buona Pizza...................**23** B5
Chipen.........................**24** B4
El Vegetariano...............**25** C3
Espresso Café................**26** B4

Heladería Coromoto........**27** A5
La Abadía......................**28** C3
Restaurant Vegetariano
   Fonda La Tinaja.........**29** A5
Supermercado Pequin......**30** C4
Yuan Lin.......................**31** A4

ENTERTAINMENT
Birosca Carioca..............**32** B4
Centro Comercial
   Mamayeya.................**33** A3
Clover Rock Bar..............**34** D2
El Ático del Cine............**35** C5
El Hoyo del Queque........**36** C3

TRANSPORT
Buses to Bus Terminal &
   Airport.....................**37** B4
Jeeps to Los Nevados......**38** C5
Por Puestos to
   La Culata..................**39** B3

and probably only then because things were sped up to meet the 400th anniversary of the city's founding. Check out the gargoyle detailing visible from Calle 22.

At the time of research, Mérida's famed **teleférico** (Parque Las Heroínas), the world's highest and longest cable-car system, was once *again* shut for repairs, which still hadn't been scheduled. When in service, it runs 12.5km from the bottom station of Barinitas (1577m) in Mérida to the top of Pico Espejo (4765m), covering the ascent in four stages. The three intermediate stations are La Montaña (2436m), La Aguada (3452m) and Loma Redonda (4045m). However, views of soaring mountains and thermal-surfing vultures still make it worthwhile to visit the Barinitas base station.

Activities

Outdoorsy adventurers will love this region for the excellent range of sports, including rock climbing, bird-watching, horse riding and rafting. See right for tour companies and p947 for more details on hiking and mountaineering.

PARAGLIDING

Paragliding is Mérida's most iconic adventure sport. There are even pictures of paragliders on the side of the city's garbage trucks. For those who want to learn to experience the joy of solo, motorless flight, **Xtreme Adventours** (☎ 252-7241; www.xatours.com; Calle 24) is the main operator, with expert instructors, though most Mérida tour agencies have their own pilots or will contract one for you.

Most visitors fly on tandem gliders with a skilled pilot, so no previous experience is necessary. The usual starting point for flights is Las González, an hour-long jeep ride from Mérida, from where you glide for 20 to 30 minutes down 850 vertical meters. The cost (260BsF to 270BsF) includes jeep transportation.

You can also take a paragliding course (about 3000BsF) that takes approximately a week, covering theory (available in English) and practice (including solo flights).

RAFTING & CANYONING

Rafting is organized on some rivers at the southern slopes of the Andes. It can be included in a tour to Los Llanos or done as a two-day rafting tour (500BsF to 650BsF per person). It's generally a wet-season activity (May through November).

Canyoning (climbing, rappelling and hiking down a river canyon and its waterfalls) is another very popular activity. Full-day, all-inclusive canyoning tours go for around 200BsF to 250BsF. **Arassari Trek** (☎ 252-5879; www.arassari .com; Calle 24) is the gold standard of rafting and canyoning tours.

MOUNTAIN BIKING

Several tour companies in Mérida organize bike trips. Shop around, as bicycle quality and rental prices may differ substantially between the companies. One of the popular bike tours is the loop around the remote mountain villages south of Mérida known as Pueblos del Sur. For a more challenging ride, try a trip up and back to El Refugio in Parque Nacional Sierra la Culata. The downhill through the high grasslands really gets the adrenaline pumping.

Courses

There are also plenty of students and tutors offering private language lessons – inquire at popular traveler hotels and tour companies. Some major institutions offering Spanish courses:

Iowa Institute (☎ 252-6404; www.iowainstitute.com; cnr Av 4 & Calle 18)

VEN-USA (☎ 263-7631; www.venusacollege.org; Edificio Tibisay, Av Urdaneta)

Tours

There are plenty of agencies in town, many of which nestle near Parque Las Heroínas and along Calle 24. Shop around, talk to other travelers and check things thoroughly before deciding. Mountain trips are popular and include treks to Pico Bolívar and Pico Humboldt. Most agencies can also book airline tickets.

An unmissable excursion out of Mérida is a wildlife safari to Los Llanos, and most companies offer this trip, usually as a four-day tour for 700BsF to 1000BsF (depending on quality of transportation, guide and accommodations). Remember that you usually get what you pay for. If you're pressed for time and cash, reserve in advance to ensure a spot in a group.

Recommended and reliable local tour companies:

Andes Tropicales (☎ 263-8633; www.andestropicales .org; cnr Av 2 & Calle 41) A non-profit development company; helps organize hiking itineraries to rural mountain homes known as *mucuposadas* (p947).

VENEZUELA

Arassari Trek (☎ 252-5879; www.arassari.com; Calle 24) The heavyweight of local operators has some of the most experienced guides, with rafting, canyoning, trekking, horse-riding and mountain biking tours. Also offers Los Llanos tours (including one- and two-day trips), and lightning trips to a camp deep in Catatumbo (p941).

Guaguanco Tours (☎ 252-3709; www.guaguanco .com.ve; Calle 24) An experienced operator with a large variety of tours, including Los Llanos, coffee plantations and hot springs.

Guamanchi Expeditions (☎ 252-2080; www .guamanchi.com; Calle 24) A long-running operator strong on mountain-related activities; also has Los Llanos trips, kayaking, bird-watching tours and bike tours. On-site *posada*.

Natoura Adventure Tours (☎ 252-4216; www .natoura.com; Calle 31) A heavyweight local operator known for mountain trekking and climbing, it runs a full range of trips. Small group tours with quality camping and mountaineering equipment.

Xtreme Adventours (☎ 252-7241; www.xatours.com; Calle 24) The main place in town for paragliding; young, adventurous Venezuelan-owned agency that has hiking, mountain biking, ATV and bridge jumping.

Sleeping

Perhaps because there's no need to pay for air-con, Mérida has some of the best-value accommodations in the country. Prices rise for traditional Venezuelan high seasons (July, August and major holidays – Christmas, Carnaval and Semana Santa). All options listed have hot-water bathrooms.

Posada Vene-Suiza (☎ 252-5775; cnr Av 2 & Calle 18; posadavene-suiza@hotmail.com; dm 35BsF, s/d/tr 80/100/150BsF, without bathroom 40/80/120BsF; 💻) A colonial-style courtyard with a quiet upstairs hammock terrace providing lovely mountain vistas. There's a kitchen, an eight-person dorm and breakfasts are available.

Posada Jama Chía (☎ 252-5767; Calle 24 No 8-223; dm 40BsF, d without bathroom 80BsF) Comfy beds and colorful fabrics enliven this unsigned and good-value three-floor posada. Kitchen use, and mountain views out back.

Posada Guamanchi (☎ 252-2080; www.guamanchi .com; Calle 24; d with/without bathroom 100/80BsF, q 140-180BsF) A popular choice for adventurous types, this rambling *posada* has two kitchens and is a good place to meet like-minded travelers. Back rooms have killer views.

Posada La Montaña (☎ 252-5977; posadala montana@intercable.net.ve; Calle 24; s 100-120BsF, d/tr/q 140/190/240BsF; 💻) A gorgeous colonial house, its comfortable rooms have decorative mosaic bedside tables, safety boxes and daily room cleaning. The restaurant serves tasty breakfasts (16BsF to 19BsF) and other meals.

Casa Alemana-Suiza (☎ 263-6503; www.casa-alemana .com; cnr Av 2 & Calle 38; s/d/tr/q 130/140/180/210BsF; 💻) A spacious building away from the more touristy center, with ample and quiet retro-style rooms, a mountain-view roof deck, a pool table and breakfast upon request.

Also recommended:

Posada Patty (☎ 251-1052; pattyclaudia@yahoo.com; Calle 24; dm 30BsF, d/tr without bathroom 60/90BsF) A friendly and familiar backpacker place with a kitchen and shared meals.

La Casona de Margot (☎ 252-3312; www.lacasonade margot.com; Av 4; s/d/tr/q 140/170/200/240, 8-person r 355BsF) Built around a cute courtyard, some of the slightly kitschy rooms have tall loft ceilings and house up to eight.

Eating

Espresso Café (Av 4; sandwiches from 15BsF; 🕙 9am-9pm Mon-Sat) Serving locally grown and organic coffee, this small upstairs arts cafe has wi-fi, a tiny balcony and uberdecadent cheesecake and brownies.

Restaurant Vegetariano Fonda La Tinaja (Calle 30; lunch menú 20BsF) This small vegetarian restaurant has excellent soups and wholemeal bread, and always gets a crowd at lunch.

Buona Pizza (Av 7; pizza 24-29BsF) Convenient, central and open late, this colorful pizza restaurant is an affordable choice popular with families.

Chipen (Av 5; mains 30-40BsF; 🕙 noon-3:30pm & 6:30-9:30pm Tue-Sun) Meat lovers' eyes will mist up at the hearty range of steaks, including a well-loved chateaubriand, served in a dark, masculine dining room with a bull's head mounted on the wall.

La Abadía (Av 3; mains 35-55BsF) This atmospheric and fun colonial mansion serves quality salads, meats and pastas and has a hookah bar in a basement catacomb, several intimate indoor and alfresco dining nooks and a

---

SPLURGE!

Posada Casa Sol (☎ 252-4164; www.posada casasol.com; Av 4; d 212-252BsF; ste 280BsF; 💻) Adorned with contemporary art, this exquisite and luxurious boutique hotel inhabits a colonial mansion with paint-textured walls, rainforest shower heads and a lovely garden with a mature avocado tree.

cybercafe offering 30 minutes' complimentary internet after your meal. Free wi-fi.

Also recommended:

Heladería Coromoto (Av 3; ice cream 5BsF; ☽ 2:15-9pm Tue-Sun) An ice-cream shop in *The Guinness World Records* for the largest number of flavors; more than 900 types, including Polar beer, trout and black bean.

El Vegetariano (cnr Av 4 & Calle 18; mains 22-33BsF; ☽ 8am-9pm Mon-Sat) Large-portioned gourmet vegetarian meals presented in a frilly dining space.

Self-caterers can stock up at the mid-sized **Supermercado Pequín** (Calle 21) and the larger **Yuan Lin** (cnr Av Las Américas & Calle 26).

Drinking & Entertainment

El Ático del Cine (Calle 25) Owned by a university film professor and her husband, college students and faculty flock to this hip loft bar and pasta and pizza restaurant (mains 20BsF to 28BsF) plastered in Venezuelan film posters.

El Hoyo del Queque (cnr Av 4 & Calle 19; admission Thu-Sat 10BsF; ☽ until 1am) This renowned and endlessly fun venue manages to fill up every night, and live bands and DJs get the party going with salsa, electronica, rock and reggae.

Clover Rock Bar (Av 4; ☽ Thu-Sat) Rockers will love this dark, boozy bar spotlighting funk, reggae and alternative music. An excellent place to see local bands.

Birosca Carioca (Calle 24) Birosca has a young, casual feel and is all about drinking and dancing and having a good time.

A number of throbbing discotheques and trendy bars can also be found in the *centros comerciales* (shopping centers) of Viaducto, Mamayeya, Las Tapias and Alto Prado.

Getting There & Away

AIR

The **airport** (Av Urdaneta) discontinued flights in 2008, but has tickets offices for a number of airlines. It's 2km southwest of Plaza Bolívar, next to the tourist office. The closest airport is an hour away in El Vigía (taxi 100BsF), and airlines including Conviasa, Venezolana and Santa Barbara have direct flights from Caracas (273BsF to 414BsF).

BUS

The bus terminal is on Av Las Américas, 3km southwest of the city center; it's linked by frequent public buses that depart from the corner of Calle 25 and Av 2.

Frequent buses service Caracas (46BsF to 78BsF, 13 hours) and Maracaibo (50BsF, nine hours). Other destinations include Coro (64BsF, 13 hours), Maracay (60BsF, 11 hours) and San Cristóbal (30BsF, five hours). Regional destinations, including Apartaderos and Jají, are serviced regularly throughout the day.

From mid-June through mid-September, Expresos Los Llanos and Expresos Mérida each run a daily bus to Ciudad Bolívar (125BsF to 144BsF, 24 hours). Otherwise, take a bus to Barinas (28BsF, four hours) and change there.

AROUND MÉRIDA

For hikers, one of the most interesting off-the-beaten-path experiences is a network of trails to indigenous mountain villages, where you can spend the night in accommodations called *mucuposadas* (*mucu* means 'place of' in the local dialect). Spaced a day's walk apart, you can traipse through cloud forest, pastureland and glacial landscapes from village to village and end the day with hot showers, cooked meals and a comfy bed. Prices are 57BsF per person per day for lodging and breakfast or 117BsF for lodging and all meals. Guides aren't necessary, but can be hired for 200BsF to 250BsF per day.

One very beautiful route that's easy to organize with public transportation includes stays at **Mucuposada Michicaba** (☎ 0274-657-7760; Gavidia), **Mucuposada El Carrizal** (☎ 0273-511-6941; Carrizal), **Mucuposada San José** (☎ 0273-416-6873; San José) and **Mucuposada Los Samanes** (☎ 0273-414-3551; Santa María de Canagua). From Mérida, take a bus 48km east to **Mucuchíes** (7.50BsF, 1½ hours), a 400-year-old town, and then a jeep to Gavidia (3BsF, one hour). At the end of the route, Los Samanes can organize your transportation or you can hike 20km to the highway and take a *por puesto* to Barinas (10BsF). Nonprofit operator **Andes Tropicales** (☎ 263-8633; www.andestropicales.org; cnr Av 2 & Calle 41, Mérida) organizes *mucuposada* walking tours.

The best known of the mountain villages is **Jají** (ha-*hee*), 38km west of Mérida and accessible by *por puesto*. It was extensively reconstructed in the late 1960s to become a manicured typical Andean town. It has a couple of budget *posadas*.

The most popular high-mountain trekking area is the **Parque Nacional Sierra Nevada**, east of Mérida, which has all of Venezuela's highest peaks. **Pico Bolívar** (5007m), Venezuela's highest point and a mere 12km from Mérida, is one of the most popular peaks to climb. Without a guide you can hike along the trail leading up to Pico Bolívar. It roughly follows the cable-car line, but be careful walking from Loma Redonda to Pico Espejo – the trail is not clear and it's easy to get lost. Venezuela's second-highest summit, **Pico Humboldt** (4942m) is also popular with high-mountain trekkers.

An easier destination is **Los Nevados**, a charming mountain village nestled at about 2700m. Jeeps to Los Nevados (50BsF, four hours) leave from Mérida's Parque Las Heroínas from 7am to noon. Simple accommodations and food are available here, or you can walk an hour to overnight in the *mucuposada* and working farm of **Hacienda El Carrizal** (☎ 0415-212-0410).

The **Parque Nacional Sierra La Culata**, to the north of Mérida, also offers some amazing hiking territory and is particularly noted for its desertlike highland landscapes. Take a *por puesto* to La Culata (departing from the corner of Calle 19 and Av 2), from where it's a three- to four-hour hike uphill to a primitive shelter known as El Refugio, at about 3700m. Continue the next day for three to four hours to the top of **Pico Pan de Azúcar** (4660m). Consider staying another night to explore local hot springs and swimming holes. The last *por puesto* back to Mérida leaves around 4pm. Other great hikes include **Pico El Águila** (4118m), **Paso del Cóndor** (4007m) and **Pico Mucuñuque** (4672m).

To overnight in the parks, Inparques charges 6BsF per person; caretakers stationed at La Mucuy and Laguna Mucubají issue on-the-spot permits.

LOS LLANOS

One of Venezuela's best destinations is the wildlife-rich Los Llanos, an immense savanna plain south of the Andes that's also the home of Venezuela's cowboys and the twangy harp music of *joropo* (traditional music of Los Llanos). Venezuela's greatest repository of wildlife, you'll be flat-out dazzled by caimans, capybaras, piranhas, anacondas and anteaters, plus an enormous variety of birds. In the rainy season, the land is half-flooded and animals are dispersed but still visible everywhere. The dry months (mid-November to April) are the high season, with a greater concentration of animals clustered near water sources. Keep in mind that wildlife-watching should be eco-friendly and not stressful for the animals (see boxed text, p231).

Several ecotourist camps, including **Hato El Frío** (www.elfrioeb.com) and **Hato El Cedral** (www .elcedral.com) offer wildlife-watching tours on their luxurious *hatos* (ranches) but they are expensive (500BsF to 600BsF per person per day). Mérida's tour companies (p945) provide similarly fascinating excursions for around 175BsF to 300BsF per day, usually as four-day all-inclusive packages.

SAN CRISTÓBAL

☎ 0276 / pop 355,000

San Cristóbal is a thriving commercial center fueled by its proximity to Colombia, just 40km away. You'll find yourself in San Cristóbal if you are traveling overland to or from anywhere in Colombia except the Caribbean Coast. Though the city is not a destination in itself, it is a modern and comfortable place with friendly inhabitants. It is worth staying a bit longer in January, when the city goes wild for two weeks celebrating its Feria de San Sebastián.

Information

Banesco (cnr Av 7 & Calle 5)
Ch@rlie's Copy (Calle 7 btwn Av 5 & Carrera 4) Internet.
Corp Banca (cnr Av 5 & Calle 8)
Movistar (cnr Av 5 & Calle 6) Telephones.

Sleeping & Eating

If you're coming by bus and just need a budget shelter for the night, check out one of several basic hotels on Calle 4, a short block south of the bus terminal. Alternatively, try one of the budget hotels in the city center (a 10-minute ride by local bus).

Hotel El Andino (☎ 343-4906; Carrera 6 btwn Calles 9 & 10; d 70BsF) Just half a block from the Plaza Bolívar, this is the most acceptable cheapie in town, secure and family run, although also a *por rato* (by the hour).

Hotel Central Park (☎ 341-9077; cnr Calle 7 & Carrera 4; s 130BsF; ❷) Though a well-positioned hotel that doubles as a residence for youthful Cuban doctors, the 70-room middle-aged building smells a bit stale.

Chung Wah (Av 5 btwn Calles 5 & 6; mains 13-28BsF) A large restaurant with the requisite *arroz frito* (fried rice), shrimp with curry and traditional *criollo* dishes, its standard Venezuelan-style Chinese dishes are nothing amazing, but it's

GETTING TO COLOMBIA

San Antonio del Táchira is the busy Venezuelan border town across from Cúcuta, Colombia. Wind your watch back 30 minutes when crossing from Venezuela to Colombia.

Onidex (☎ 0276-771-2282; Carrera 9 btwn Calles 6 & 7; ☼ 24hr) puts exit or entry stamps in passports. All tourists leaving Venezuela are charged a 55BsF *impuesto de salida* (departure tax). You must pay in cash and buy stamps for this amount in a shop (open 9am to 5pm) across the street. Buses (3BsF) and *por puestos* (6BsF) run frequently to Cúcuta in Colombia (12km). Catch a bus on Av Venezuela or save yourself the traffic time by walking to the front of the line of cars and looking for a shared taxi with extra space. Or you can walk from San Antonio across the bridge.

Nationals of most Western countries don't need a visa for Colombia, but all travelers are supposed to get an entry stamp from DAS (Colombian immigration). The DAS office is just past the bridge over the Río Táchira (the actual border), on the right. Get off at the DAS office for your Colombia entry stamp and then take another bus. Buses go as far as the Cúcuta bus terminal; most pass through the center. You can pay in Venezuelan bolívares or Colombian pesos.

From Cúcuta, there are frequent buses and flights to all major Colombian destinations; flights are at a much better price than you'd get from Maracaibo or Caracas. There are no direct flights to Colombia from San Antonio.

Roadside money changers in Colombia have decent rates, because there are no restrictions on currency transactions in that country.

For information on travel from Colombia to Venezuela, see p529.

central and open late. Don't look for vegetables beyond cabbage.

Restaurant La Bologna (Calle 5 btwn Carreras 8 & 9; menú 15-26BsF; ☼ 11am-8pm Wed-Mon) With a quiet courtyard that's a respite from city traffic noise, La Bologna brings in a steady crowd of locals to feast on its consistently good Venezuelan dishes.

Getting There & Away

AIR

About 38km southeast of the city Santo Domingo is San Cristóbal's primary airport, but the airport in San Antonio del Táchira (above) is far busier and just about the same distance away.

BUS

The busy **Terminal de Pasajeros** (☎ 346-1140; Av Manuel Felipe Rugeles, La Concordia) is 2km south of the city center and linked by frequent city bus services.

More than a dozen buses daily go to Caracas (48BsF to 70BsF, 13 hours). Most depart in the late afternoon or evening for an overnight trip via El Llano highway. Ordinary buses to Barinas (25BsF, five hours) run hourly between 5am and 6:30pm.

Buses to Mérida (27BsF to 30BsF, five hours) go every 1½ hours from 5:30am to 7pm. Five buses depart nightly for Maracaibo (54BsF to 60BsF, eight hours).

Minibuses to San Antonio del Táchira (6BsF, 1¼ hours), on the Colombian border, run every 10 or 15 minutes; it's a spectacular but busy road. If you are in a rush, consider taking a *por puesto* (18BsF).

THE NORTHEAST

Venezuela's northeast is a mosaic of natural marvels, with Caribbean beaches, coral reefs and verdant mountains. It also boasts Isla de Margarita, one of the most famous island destinations in the Caribbean, and the Cueva del Guácharo, Venezuela's biggest and most impressive cave system. Parque Nacional Mochima and the remote stretches of sand beyond Río Caribe offer the opportunity for endless beach-hopping. The city of Cumaná was also the first Spanish settlement founded on the South American mainland. Once you've spent time in the northeast, you'll understand what prompted Columbus to whimsically declare the region 'paradise on earth.'

BARCELONA

☎ 0281 / pop 590,000

Often shadowed by the creeping metropolis of nearby Puerto La Cruz, Barcelona has more charm than expected. Though modern sprawl lines its highways, at its heart is a pretty colonial center, an attractive river and a sliver of tranquility not easily found with its hectic seaside neighbor. The historic district contains a series of leafy plazas, and the pleasant stroll-worthy pedestrian mall of Av 5 de Julio (known as the *bulevar*) stretches south from Plaza Bolívar. Barcelona's airport serves as the regional terminal for Puerto la Cruz and destinations up the coast.

Information

Banco de Venezuela (Plaza Boyacá)
CANTV (Plaza Miranda; ⏰ 8am-6pm Mon-Fri, to noon Sat) Telephones and internet (per hour 3BsF).
Corp Banca (Plaza Bolívar)
Ipostel (Carrera 13 Bolívar) East of Plaza Boyacá.

Sleeping & Eating

Hotel Neverí (☎ 277-2376; cnr Avs Fuerzas Armadas & Miranda; s/d 70/100BsF; 🍴) Recognizable by the vivid mural of tropical flowers and birds adorning the outside, this place has a grand staircase, large utilitarian rooms and its own restaurant. Get a quieter room in the back.

Posada Copacabana (☎ 277-3473; Carrera Juncal; s/d/tr 100/180/270BsF; 🍴) Set your watch to the tolling cathedral bells on the adjacent Plaza Boyacá. Excellent-value Copacabana has 16 inviting rooms with handsome bathrooms.

Heladería Alaska (Av 5 de Julio btwn Carreras Freites & Bolívar; mains 13-20BsF; ⏰ 7:30am-8:30pm) You can't do much better than a cheap plateful of grilled chicken, loaded with side dishes and served on cafe tables astride a rare pedestrian strip. Well, maybe. There's also ice cream.

Mercado Municipal (⏰ 6am-2pm) Right next to the bus terminal, 1km southeast of town, the municipal market has a dozen popular and inexpensive restaurants serving typical food.

Getting There & Away

AIR
The airport is 2km south of the city center. Buses leave from the *fuente* (fountain), about 500m south of Plaza Bolívar, and go within 300m of the airport. There are daily flights to Caracas, as well as direct service to Maracaibo, Puerto Ordaz and Porlamar.

BUS
The bus terminal is 1km southeast of the city center, next to the market. Take a *buseta* (1.50BsF, 10 minutes) going south along the riverside Av Fuerzas Armadas, or walk 15 minutes.

The terminal in Puerto La Cruz has more routes, so it's better to go there instead of waiting in Barcelona. To Puerto La Cruz, catch a *buseta* from Plaza Miranda (1.50BsF, 45 minutes). They use two routes, Vía Intercomunal and Vía Alterna. Either will drop you in the center of Puerto La Cruz. Faster *por puesto* minibuses (3BsF) depart from near the *fuente*. A taxi to Puerto La Cruz is 20BsF to 25BsF.

PUERTO LA CRUZ
☎ 0281 / pop 356,000
A transit hub for Isla de Margarita and Parque Nacional Mochima, Puerto La Cruz is a bustling and rapidly expanding city. Not a particularly attractive place, its best feature is a lively waterfront boulevard, Paseo Colón, packed with hotels, bars and restaurants. This area comes to life in the late afternoon and evening as temperatures cool and street stalls open.

Beach seekers should continue further along the coastline to smaller Playa Colorada, Santa Fe or Mochima.

Information

Banco de Venezuela (Miranda)
Banco Mercantil (Arismendi)
Banesco (Freites)
CANTV (Paseo Colón; ⏰ 8am-9pm Mon-Sat, to 8:30pm Sun) Telephones and good internet access (2.50BsF per hour).
Ipostel (Freites)

Tours
Tours to the Parque Nacional Mochima are offered by a number of agencies along Paseo Colón. However, tours from Puerto La Cruz are pricier and require more transit time than those from Santa Fe or the town of Mochima.

Sleeping & Eating
Lodging in Puerto La Cruz is overpriced for what you get. Browse the Paseo Colón for the biggest selection of inexpensive international and fast-food eateries facing the water.

Hotel Neptuno (☎ 265-3261; fax 265-5790; cnr Paseo Colón & Juncal; s/d/tr 90/105/120BsF; 🍴 💻) Sea breezes buffet this waterfront hotel with aging rooms and even older bathroom fixtures. Pluses include lobby computers and an open-sided rooftop restaurant (mains 19BsF to 29BsF) with dynamite Caribbean views.

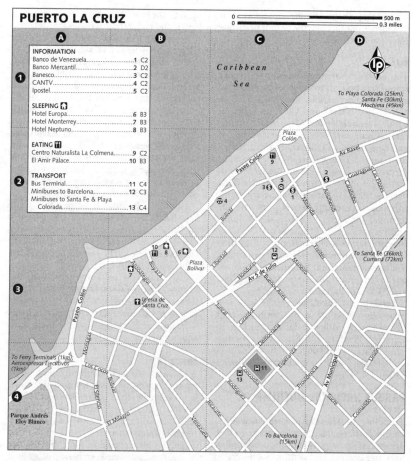

PUERTO LA CRUZ

INFORMATION	
Banco de Venezuela	1 C2
Banco Mercantil	2 D2
Banesco	3 C2
CANTV	4 C2
Ipostel	5 C2

SLEEPING	
Hotel Europa	6 B3
Hotel Monterrey	7 B3
Hotel Neptuno	8 B3

EATING	
Centro Naturalista La Colmena	9 C2
El Amir Palace	10 B3

TRANSPORT	
Bus Terminal	11 C4
Minibuses to Barcelona	12 C3
Minibuses to Santa Fe & Playa Colorada	13 C4

Hotel Monterrey (☎ 265-0523; Anzoátegui; d/tr 100/130BsF; ❄) Formerly the Family Posada, this inexpensive, small and intimate place has basic rooms and good security.

Hotel Europa (☎ 268-8157; cnr Plaza Bolívar & Sucre; s/d/tr 110/120/130BsF; ❄) Rooms are plain but spacious and there's a small common area. Angle for a sea-view terrace.

El Amir Palace (Paseo Colón 123; mains 14-45BsF; ❧ 8am-11:30pm Tue-Sun) Crisply dressed waiters shuttle Middle Eastern specialties like shawarma and falafel to your table, although its long menu also includes pasta, fish and salads.

Centro Naturalista La Colmena (Paseo Colón 27; 3-course menú 20BsF; ❧ 11:45am-2pm Mon-Fri) Hungry vegetarians will swoon for this tasty, lunch-only veggie cafe. A small covered terrace looks out across the boulevard to the sea.

Getting There & Away

AIR

The airport is in Barcelona (opposite).

BOAT

Puerto La Cruz is the major departure point for Isla de Margarita, with services offered by **Conferry** (☎ 267-7847; www.conferry.com; Sector Los Cocos) and **Naviarca/Gran Cacique** (☎ 263-0935; www.grancacique.com.ve; Sector Los Cocos). See p957 for detailed information. Smaller excursion boats leave from the small piers in town.

The ferry terminals are accessible by *por puesto* from the center, or you can take a taxi.

It's best to go in the daytime – it's a spectacular journey out through the islands of Parque Nacional Mochima.

BUS

The bustling bus terminal is three blocks from Plaza Bolívar, with lots of connections. Frequent buses service Caracas (25BsF to 45BsF, five hours) and Cumaná (7BsF to 15BsF, 1½ hours); many of the latter continue east to Carúpano (25BsF to 30BsF, four hours) and sometimes to Güiria (45BsF to 50BsF, 6½ hours). Going eastward (to Cumaná or further on), grab a seat on the left side of the bus, as there are some spectacular views over the islands of Parque Nacional Mochima. Minibuses frequently depart from near the terminal for Santa Fe (4BsF, 45 minutes) and Playa Colorada (4BsF, 30 minutes). For Barcelona, take a *buseta* from Av 5 de Julio (1.50BsF, 45 minutes). They use two routes, Vía Intercomunal and Vía Alterna. Faster *por puesto* minibuses (3BsF) depart from the same area. A taxi to Barcelona is 20BsF to 25BsF.

Aeroexpresos Ejecutivos (☎ 267-8855; www.aeroexpresos.com.ve) has a bus terminal next to the ferries, with five daily departures to Caracas (38BsF to 55BsF). *Por puestos* also run to Caracas (90BsF, four hours), Maturín (40BsF, 2½ hours) and Cumaná (30BsF to 32BsF, 1¼ hours).

PARQUE NACIONAL MOCHIMA

☎ 0293

Straddling the states of Anzoátegui and Sucre, Parque Nacional Mochima comprises a low, dry mountain range that drops down to fine bays and beaches and continues offshore to a mesmerizing constellation of three dozen arid islands. Dolphins are a common sight in the area's waters. The best beaches are on the islands and accessed by short boat trips from Santa Fe, Mochima or other coastal towns. Coral reefs surround a few of the islands and provide decent snorkeling and scuba diving. Tranquility seekers should visit midweek.

Playa Colorada

A crescent of orange sand shaded by coconut groves, Playa Colorada draws weekend hordes of young Venezuelan party-goers and sun-seekers. But it's very quiet during the week and an easy day trip from both Santa Fe and Puerto La Cruz. A few small shops sell produce, bread and other foodstuffs, and scores of food shacks open on the beach for weekends. There are no banks, and no internet access is available.

With six good-value rooms and a garden kitchen, the Swiss-run **Villa Nirvana** (☎ 808-7844; Marchán; s without bathroom 50BsF; d 80-100BsF; apt 150BsF; ❷), 500m uphill from the coastal road, can accommodate everyone from thrifty solo backpackers to small families. Breakfast is 20BsF.

An adventure-sports boot camp, Spanish language school and an excellent place to meet up with other energetic travelers, **Jakera Lodge** (☎ 808-7057; www.jakera.com; hammock/dm incl breakfast & dinner 70/90BsF;) offers dorm accommodations with communal meals and scores of scuba, canyoning and kayak outings. Look for its corrugated steel gate on the highway.

Opposite Posada Nirvana, the well-kept **Quinta Jaly** (☎ 0416-681-8113; Marchán; s/d/q 80/120/150BsF; ❷) has comfortable sitting areas and is run by an affable French-Canadian. Guests have free kitchen access, and breakfast is available for 20BsF.

The only real restaurant in town, the Portuguese-run **Café Las Carmitas** (mains 15-35BsF), serves up pizza, pasta, fish and meat dishes, as well as excellent burgers. From the highway, go one block up from the main road and turn left.

Santa Fe

A beachside town popular with international backpackers, Santa Fe comprises two separate worlds: the beach, a sedate haven of seaside *posadas* ringed with barbed-wire security fences, and the rest of the town, a rough-and-tumble fishing village.

There's little reason to leave the intimate *posada*- and cafe-lined sandy strip other than to walk to the bus terminal or visit the town's rowdy nightclub. The beach is a chill spot to sit in the sand and sip on beers and fruit juices. If you are looking for more remote and pristine beaches, small boats make day trips to the islands of Parque Nacional Mochima.

Internet junkies will need rehab if they visit the frustratingly slow *ciber* behind Posada Café del Mar and Club Náutico. Telephones are available if you contemplate falling asleep while waiting for pages to load.

Unless noted, the following are all along the beach.

A cafe, bar and *posada*, **Posada Café del Mar** (☎ 231-0009; La Marina, entering the beach; hammock 30BsF; s/d 50/70BsF) has 12 simple, fan-cooled rooms with sliding glass doors. Hang a hammock on the breezy rooftop terrace, but lock up your valuables.

Run by Santa Fe's biggest booster, the attentive **La Sierra Inn** (☎ 231-0042; cooperativasantafe demisamores@hotmail.com; d 80-90BsF, tr 120BsF; 🍽 💻), sports smart yet simple hot-water rooms and an ample shaded beach. There's a kitchen, laundry service, Spanish classes, computer usage for guests and regional tours. The fourth night is free on weekdays.

Santa Fe Resort & Dive Center (☎ 231-0051; www .santaferesort.com; d/tr 130/170BsF; 🍽) is a midrange *posada* with a range of spacious airy rooms, an on-site dive shop and boat tours.

New French owners have taken the reins at beautiful **Le Petit Jardin** (☎ 231-0036; lepetit .jardin@yahoo.com; Cochima; d/tr with breakfast 150/180BsF; 🍽 🐾), where lush hibiscus blooms around the swimming pool and continental breakfast comes with heavenly homemade jam. The five colorful rooms are contemporary and peaceful, with gorgeous bathroom tiling and lavender bedside sachets. It's a block from the beach, behind the Santa Fe Resort.

Restaurante Cochaima (breakfast 8-12BsF, mains 12-40BsF) is a breezy eatery upstairs at the Hotel Cochaima, serving all meals. Owner Margot cooks up excellent seafood dishes, pasta, *parrilla* and other typical fare.

The largest, if somewhat touristy, place to eat on the beach, open-air **Club Náutico** (La Marina, entering the beach; mains 22-35BsF; 🕑 11:30am-8:30pm Wed-Mon) has a big menu with fresh seafood, pasta and meats.

Transportation from Puerto La Cruz and Cumaná will deposit you at the bus terminal off the highway. It's a 1km walk to the beach *posadas*. Be careful at night.

Mochima

A tiny town where everyone seems to know everyone else since childhood, Mochima is a completely different experience from nearby Santa Fe. A quaint, attractive village on the edge of its namesake national park, it has no beach and is more popular with Venezuelan families than international backpackers. Frequent boats run from the waterfront to the numerous island beaches of the park. The town is nearly empty during the week.

At the central wharf, *lancheros* (boat drivers) wait on the shore for tourists. They can take you to any beach, including Playa Las Maritas (65BsF), Playa Blanca (65BsF), Playa Manare (85BsF), and Playas Cautaro and

Cautarito (75BsF). Or mix it up with a tour of five to six islands (130BsF to 150BsF). These are round-trip fares per boatload, and you can be picked up whenever you want. To camp on the islands, pick up a permit (2BsF per person nightly) at the Inparques office across from the wharf.

Both the **Aquatics Diving Center** (☎ 430-1652, 0426-581-0434; www.scubavenezuela.com) and **La Posada de los Buzos** (☎ 416-0856, 0212-961-2531) organize diving courses, dives and excursions, and handle snorkel rental. The latter also runs rafting trips on the Río Neverí.

Mochima has a good choice of accommodation and food facilities. Locals rent out rooms and houses if there is demand.

Across from a restaurant of the same name, bright blue paint enlivens the basic cold-water accommodations of **Posada El Mochimero** (☎ 417-3339; La Marina; r 70-80BsF; 🍽). Only two rooms are without air-con, but they have sets of windows to harvest the fresh sea air.

Posada Villa Vicenta (☎ 414-0868; Principal; d & tr 100BsF, q 120BsF; 🍽) has excellent vistas over the bay from four levels of terraces stepping up the hillside. Located one block back from the wharf, the pleasant no-frills rooms have cold-water bathrooms, stone walls and kitchen access, and many have space-saving fold-up beds.

For coffee and *arepas* throughout the day, cross the road to **Brasero** (arepas 6-12BsF, mains 20-40BsF; 🕑 6am-10pm). *Parrilla* is the specialty at this inexpensive and central fast-food eatery.

Moored motorboats bobble alongside **Restaurant Puerto Viejo** (mains 25-55BsF; 🕑 11am-8pm Wed-Mon), a festively painted seafood place featuring pasta, chicken as well as calamari and very fresh fish. Displays of local art and shellacked tables adorned with aquatic scenes make it a great place to linger for a meal.

Busetas departing from Cumaná will bring you to the village's center (3.50BsF, 40 minutes), next to the wharf. To Puerto La Cruz or Santa Fe, take a bus to the *crucero* (highway crossroad), then flag down the proper bus.

CUMANÁ
☎ 0293 / pop 326,000

Founded by the Spanish in 1521, Cumaná has the distinction of being the oldest remaining Spanish settlement on the South American mainland. It boasts a pretty historical district, but it's primarily used as a stepping stone to Isla de Margarita,

Península de Araya, Santa Fe, Mochima and the Cueva del Guácharo. Stock up on cash and other city conveniences here before visiting smaller nearby towns.

For the best views of the city and coastline, hoof it up to the **Castillo de San Antonio de la Eminencia** (☼ 7am-7pm), a colonial structure that has endured earthquakes and pirate attacks since it was built in 1659.

Information

Banco de Venezuela (cnr Mariño & Rojas)
Banesco (cnr Mariño & Carabobo)
Ipostel (Paraíso)
Lowett (Calle Catedral; ☼ 7:30-6pm Mon-Sat) Internet cafe inside a music shop.
Movistar (Paraíso) Telephones.

Sleeping & Eating

Hotel Astoria (☎ 433-2708; hotelastoria_7@hotmail.com; Sucre 51; s/d/tr 65/95/120BsF; ✸) A friendly cheapie featuring a small bar and pizzeria, the hotel's 18 windowless rooms have good lighting, cable TV and air-con, and often fill up.

Posada La Cazuela (☎ 432-1401; narant@hotmail.com; Sucre 63; d 100BsF; tr 110-120BsF; ✸ ▯) Artisan crafts decorate this clean and cheerful seven-room *posada* with good mattresses, cable TV and bamboo ceilings.

Bubulina's Hostal (☎ 431-4025; bubulinas@cantv.net; Callejón Santa Inés; s/tr 140/200BsF; d 160-180BsF; ✸ ▯) Down a narrow colonial street, this stylish mid-range option has lofty rooms with hot water, ceiling fans and a sunny plant-filled patio, plus a restaurant and bar for guests only.

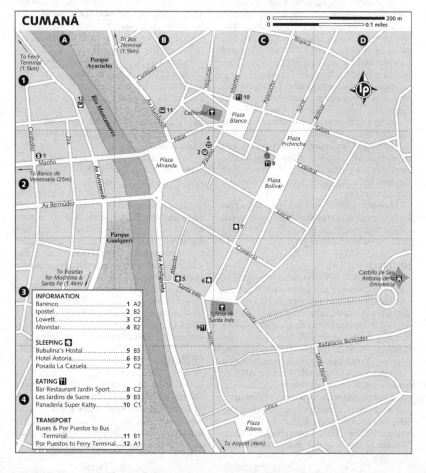

CUMANÁ

DETOUR: PENÍNSULA DE ARAYA

If supertouristy Isla de Margarita isn't your style, this is the place to visit for kilometer after kilometer of unpopulated beaches. A solitary road runs the length of this 70km-long and 10km-wide peninsula of arid red sands and scrubby dunes that pokes out between Cumaná and Isla de Margarita, and a sparse population is scattered through a handful of villages on the northern coast.

Venezuela's largest salt deposits, the **salinas** (salt pans) of Araya were discovered by the Spaniards in 1499. Natural lagoons and artificial pools evaporate in the heat, forming a multi-hued patchwork mosaic. For an overview, visit the *mirador* (lookout), 2km north of Araya on the road to Punta de Araya.

On the waterfront cliff at the southern end of the bay is **El Castillo** (the Castle), a four-pointed structure that's the biggest and oldest colonial fort in the country. Although damaged, the gargantuan coral-rock walls are an awesome sight and give a good impression of how the fort must have once looked. It's a 10-minute walk along the beach from the wharf.

The town of Araya has a half-a-dozen budget *posadas* to choose from, with many around Plaza Bolívar.

From Cumaná, Naviarca runs a ferry to the peninsula (6BsF), though small boats called *tapaditos* (3BsF, 15 minutes), located behind the Guardia Nacional post, are faster and more frequent.

Panadería Super Katty (Plaza Blanco; ✆ 6am-10pm) No seating, but this bakery has good coffee, excellent pastries and fancy cakes for on-the-road birthday celebrations.

Bar Restaurant Jardín Sport (Plaza Bolívar; mains 15-25BsF; ✆ 6am-11pm) From breakfast *arepas* (8BsF) to soups, sandwiches, burgers and *parrilla*, this courtyard restaurant and bar is a lively place to refuel. Come in the evening for cheap beer and a game of pool.

Les Jardins de Sucre (☎ 431-3689; Sucre 27; mains 25-60BsF; ✆ 6:30-9:30pm Mon, noon-2:30pm & 6:30-9:30pm Tue-Sat) One of Cumaná's best and most atmospheric dining spots, this restaurant has a dramatically lit entrance corridor leading to a tranquil water garden. Crêpes, shrimp and mushroom risotto and savory *hojaldres* (puff pastries) in white wine sauce are just a few of the scrumptious creations available at this excellent French establishment featuring a fine range of Argentine and Chilean wines.

Getting There & Away
AIR
The airport is 4km southeast of the city center. There are frequent flights to Caracas (210BsF to 290BsF) with Avior and Venezolana, and to Porlamar (150BsF to 198BsF) with Rutaca and Venezolana.

BOAT
All ferries and boats to Isla de Margarita depart from the docks next to the mouth of the Río Manzanares and go to Punta de Piedras. The principal operator is **Naviarca/**

Gran Cacique (☎ 431-5577; www.grancacique.com.ve). See p957 for more information.

The area around the ferry docks in Cumaná is not famous for its safety, so take a *por puesto* (2BsF) from just north of the bridge, or a taxi (10BsF).

BUS
The bus terminal is 1.5km northwest of the city center and linked by frequent urban buses along Av Humboldt.

Destinations include Caracas (48BsF to 54BsF, 6½ hours), Puerto La Cruz (14BsF to 20BsF, 1½ hours), Ciudad Bolívar (50BsF, six hours), Carúpano (15BsF, 2½ hours) and Güiria (40BsF, five hours).

Por puestos run to Puerto La Cruz (25BsF, 1¼ hours) and Carúpano (25BsF to 30BsF, four hours). For the Cueva del Guácharo, take a *por puesto* bound for Caripe (45BsF, 2½ hours). The cave is just before Caripe; ask to be let off at the entrance.

Busetas to Santa Fe (5BsF, 45 minutes) and Mochima (5BsF, 40 minutes) depart from near the Mercadito, one block off the Redoma El Indio.

CUEVA DEL GUÁCHARO
Venezuela's longest and most magnificent cave, **Guácharo Cave** (admission adult/child 15/5BsF; ✆ 8am-4pm Tue-Sun, last full tour at 2:30pm), 12km from Caripe toward the coast, has 10.2km of caverns. An impressive portal and cave system, it's inhabited by the shrieking *guácharo* (oilbird), which lives in total darkness and

leaves the cave only at night in search of food. *Guácharos* have a radar-location system (similar to bats) and enormous whiskers that enable them to navigate in the dark. From August to December, the population in the cave is estimated at 10,000 and occasionally up to 15,000. Within its maze of stalactites and stalagmites, the cave also shelters crabs, fish and fast-moving rodents. Arrange a late taxi pickup after closing time or camp (3BsF per tent) across from the cave entrance and witness the birds pouring out of the cave mouth at around 6:30pm and returning at about 4am.

All visits to the cave are by guided group tours; full tours take about 1½ hours. The tour visits 1200m of the cave, but high water in August and/or September occasionally limits sightseeing to 500m.

Across the road, it's a 20-minute hike to Salto La Paila, where you can swim in a chilly pool at the foot of a ribbon cascade.

RÍO CARIBE
☎ 0294 / pop 14,000
The former splendor of the old port town of Río Caribe can be spotted along the wide, tree-shaded Av Bermúdez with its once-magnificent mansions. Once a major cacao exporter, the town now serves as a laid-back holiday destination and a springboard for beaches further east. Don't miss the 18th-century church on Plaza Bolívar or the free 6pm aerobics class on the plaza at the beach end of Av Bermúdez.

A family home with 11 simple and somewhat institutional rooms, **Posada San Miguel** (☎ 416-6344; posadasanmigul@hotmail.com; Zea 83; d/tr 60/100BsF; ✖) has inexpensive lodging and kitchen privileges. Another option is **Posada Don Chilo** (☎ 646-1212; Mariño 27; d/tr 80/120BsF; ✖), with basic rooms around a small courtyard, and home-cooked meals available.

For a taste of local culture, family home **Pensión Papagayos** (☎ 646-1868; cricas@web.de; 14 de Febrero; r per person 40BsF; ✖) rents out four well-maintained rooms which share two spotless bathrooms, and you can use the kitchen.

A lush Arabic-accented courtyard cradles a lap-worthy pool at the heavenly **Posada Shalimar** (☎ 646-1135; www.posada-shalimar.com; s/d/tr 130/170/200BsF; ✖ ✖ ✖). This funky place can be addictive – even if you're not staying there – with bikes and surfboards for rent (30BsF per day), an excellent bar and restaurant (breakfast 12BsF to 24BsF, dinner mains

22BsF to 35BsF), wi-fi access and a computer for hire.

Along the *malecón* a block from Av Bermúdez, simple **Manos Benditas** (Av Gallegos; mains 14-35BsF) is a local favorite for creative *comida criolla* (creole food). Ask for the inexplicably off-the-menu *pollo a cacao* (chocolate chicken).

From Plaza Bolívar, there are frequent *por puestos* (4BsF, 30 minutes) and buses (2.50BsF) to Carúpano. Two daily buses service Caracas (60BsF, 10 hours) via Puerto La Cruz (30BsF, five hours).

AROUND RÍO CARIBE
A bonanza of two dozen beaches on the 50km coastal stretch between Río Caribe and San Juan de Unare (the last seaside village accessible by road), the coast here has some of the most gorgeous and least-visited sandy spots in the country.

The first beaches worth visiting east of Río Caribe are side-by-side **Playa Loero** and **Playa de Uva**. They lie 6km from Río Caribe by the road to Bohordal, then another 6km by a paved side road that branches off to the left.

Proceeding east, a paved road branches off 4km beyond Hacienda Bukare and goes 5km to the village of Medina then northward for 1km to a fork. The left branch goes for 2km to the crescent-shaped **Playa Medina**. The right branch leads 6km over a potholed road to the village of Pui Puy and continues for 2km to the beautiful **Playa Pui Puy**. Camping is allowed here for a small fee.

Most travelers don't venture further east, though beaches dot the coast as far as the eye can see. The seaside village of **San Juan de Las Galdonas** has especially fine beaches. Its main access road is a wholly paved 23km stretch that branches off the Río Caribe–Bohordal road 6.5km beyond the turnoff to Medina.

From San Juan de Las Galdonas, a dirt road (serviced by sporadic transportation) goes for 20km to the village of **San Juan de Unare**. Walk another hour to find the expansive Playa Cipara.

From Río Caribe, infrequent *por puesto* pickup trucks run in the morning to the villages of Medina (5BsF), Pui Puy (10BsF) and San Juan de Las Galdonas (10BsF). They don't get as far as the beaches of Medina and Pui Puy; you'll need to walk a half-hour to get the rest of the way. Locals sometimes run *mototaxis*. Trucks depart from the

---

GETTING TO TRINIDAD

Acosta Asociados (☎ 0294-982-1556; Bolívar 31; ☺ 9am-noon & 2-5:30pm Mon-Fri) operates the *Sea Prowler*, a comfortable and air-conditioned passenger boat that runs between Güiria and Chaguaramas, near Port of Spain, Trinidad. It arrives every Wednesday at around 2pm and departs back to Chaguaramas at approximately 5pm (taking 3½ hours). You should be there at 1:30pm. Fares are 632BsF one way, 1032BsF round trip, plus an 80BsF departing port tax on the outward journey (returning from Trinidad there's a port tax of US$23).

---

southeastern end of Río Caribe, opposite the gas station.

Chocoholics shouldn't miss **Chocolates Paria** (☎ 0416-282-6027; tour 15BsF; ☺ 9am-4pm), where you can tour the small-scale organic shade-grown cacao plantation and nibble on samples of varying concentration. Tours available in German, English and French. Take a *por puesto* (2.50BsF, 15 minutes) to Hacienda Bukare.

ISLA DE MARGARITA

☎ 0295 / pop 434,000

Venezuela's foremost Caribbean hotspot, Isla de Margarita is the isle of tourism. Sunseekers and bargain-hunters come from world over for its top-notch beaches and rock-bottom duty-free prices, and charter flights and package tours besiege the island from all directions. It's an urbanized and highly developed beach-vacation experience replete with fancy restaurants, high-rise international hotel chains and lots of shopping.

However, Margarita is large enough for independent travelers to find deserted beaches and a spectrum of habitats, from mangrove swamps to mountainous cloud forest and desert. While the majority of visitors stay on the east coast near Porlamar, the towns of Juangriego and El Yaque are safer and more laid-back alternatives.

Getting There & Away

AIR

Almost all the major national airlines fly into **Aeropuerto Internacional del Caribe General Santiago Mariño** (☎ 400-5057). Flight prices

are very prone to change, so use these one-way prices as guidelines only. There are frequent flights to Caracas (220BsF to 250BsF). Direct-flight destinations include Puerto Ordaz (585BsF), Cumaná (150BsF), San Antonio de Táchira (446BsF to 552BsF), Valencia (270BsF) and Maturín (190BsF). Aereotuy and Rainbow Air fly to Los Roques (616BsF to 737BsF). Avior and Conviasa fly direct to Port of Spain, Trinidad (520BsF to 950BsF round trip).

A taxi to Porlamar costs around 50BsF; there are no buses.

The following airline offices are located in the Porlamar area:

Aeropostal (☎ 262-2878; www.aeropostal.com; Centro Comercial Sambil Margarita, Av Jóvito Villaba, Pampatar)

Aereotuy (LTA; ☎ 415-5778; www.tuy.com; Av Santiago Mariño, Porlamar)

Aserca (☎ 262-0166; www.asercaairlines.com; Centro Comercial Provemed, Av Bolívar, ground fl, Pampatar)

Avior (☎ 263-9646; www.aviorairlines.com; Hotel Puerta del Sol, Los Pinos)

Laser (☎ 263-9195; www.laser.com.ve; Maneiro, Porlamar)

Rainbow Air (☎ 0424-877-0582; makoroporlamar @gmail.com; Edificio Esparta Suites, Calle Los Amendros, ground fl, Porlamar) Also called Representaciones Makoro.

Rutaca (☎ 263-9236; www.rutaca.com.ve; Centro Comercial Jumbo, Av 4 de Mayo, Porlamar)

BOAT

Isla de Margarita has links with the mainland via Puerto La Cruz and Cumaná from the ferry terminal, Punta de Piedras (29km west of Porlamar), and also has small seasickness-inducing boats that depart frequently to Chacopata (20BsF, 1½ hours) from Porlamar itself. Small buses (3BsF) regularly shuttle between Punta de Piedras and Porlamar; taxis to El Yaque are 40BsF, and 40BsF to 50BsF for Porlamar or Juangriego. On all ferries noted here, children aged two to seven and seniors over 60 pay half price.

From Puerto La Cruz

Conferry (☎ 261-6780; www.conferry.com; Calle Marcano, Porlamar; ☺ 8-11:30am & 2-4:30pm Mon-Fri, 8-11am Sat) has several departures daily; check the website for exact dates and times. Regular ferries cost from 29BsF to 37BsF for adults (depending on class) and cars are 59BsF to 71BsF (depending on size); the trip takes about 4½ hours. Express ferries take two hours and cost 62BsF to 102BsF for adults, and 109BsF to 131BsF for cars.

ISLA DE MARGARITA

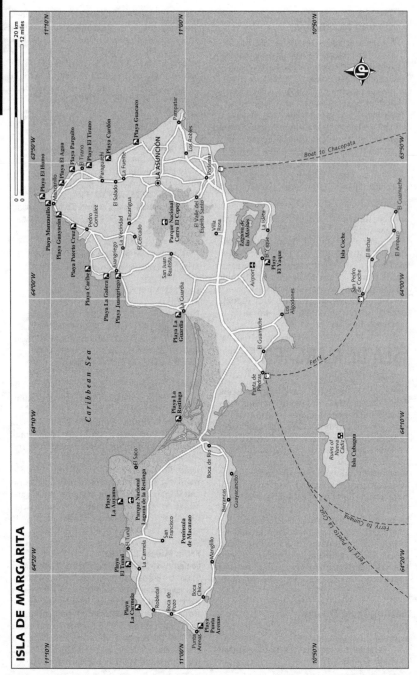

0   20 km
0   12 miles

Caribbean Sea

Playa El Humo
Playa Guayacán
Playa Manzanillo
Manzanillo
Playa Puerto Cruz
Pedro González
Playa Caribe
Playa La Galera
Playa Juangriego
Juangriego
La Vecindad
El Cercado
El Salado
Tacarigua
El Valle del Espíritu Santo
La Guardia
Playa La Guardia
San Juan Bautista
San Sebastián
Playa El Agua
Playa Parguito
El Tirano
Playa El Tirano
Playa Cardón
Paraguachí
La Fuente
Playa Guacuco
LA ASUNCIÓN
Los Robles
Pampatar
Porlamar

Boat to Chacopata

Parque Nacional Cerro El Copey
Villa Rosa
Laguna de las Marites
La Sierra
El Yaque
Playa El Yaque
Airport
Los Algodones
El Guamache

Isla Coche
El Guamache
El Bichar
El Amparo
San Pedro de Coche

Ferry

Playa La Restinga

Punta de Piedras

Ruins of Nueva Cádiz
Isla Cubagua

Ferry to Cumaná
Ferry to Puerto La Cruz

El Saco
Playa La Auyama
Parque Nacional Laguna de la Restinga
Península de Macanao
Boca de Río
Barrancas
Guayacancito
El Tunal
Playa El Tunal
San Francisco
La Carmela
Mangilllo
Playa La Carmela
Robledal
Boca de Pozo
Boca Chica
Punta Arenas
Playa Punta Arenas

64°20'W 64°10'W 64°00'W 63°50'W

11°10'N 11°00'N 10°50'N

A passenger-only hydrofoil, **Gran Cacique** (☎ 264-1160; www.grancacique.com.ve; Edificio Blue Sky, Av Santiago Mariño, Porlamar; ☼ 8am-noon & 1-5pm Mon-Fri, 8am-noon Sat) runs daily departures at 7am and 4pm (52BsF to 72BsF, two hours).

From Cumaná

From Cumaná, **Gran Cacique** (☎ 0293-432-0011), has two to three departures daily (50BsF to 65BsF, two hours), and its affiliate **Naviarca** (☎ 0293-433-5577; www.grancacique.com.ve) runs a car ferry (adults 30BsF, cars 60BsF, 3½ hours). In Margarita, Naviarca tickets are only available at Punta de Piedras (☎ 239-8232).

PORLAMAR

☎ 0295 / pop 143,000

More of a transit point and commercial center than a prime destination for independent travelers, Porlamar is Margarita's largest and busiest city. Tree-shaded Plaza Bolívar is Porlamar's historic center, but the city is rapidly expanding eastward, with new suburbs, tourist facilities, hotels and restaurants creeping along the coast toward Pampatar.

Information

Stores will accept cash dollars for payment using the official exchange rate, though some will give you the black-market rate if you negotiate. Credit cards are widely accepted in shops, upmarket hotels and restaurants.

Banco de Venezuela (Blvd Guevara)

Banesco (Av 4 de Mayo)

Cambios Cussco (☎ 261-3379; Velázquez) Money exchange.

CANTV (cnr Igualdad & Mariño) Internet and telephones. Also at Av Santiago Mariño.

Corpotur (☎ 262-2322; www.corpoturmargarita.gov.ve; Centro Artesanal Gilberto Menchini, Av Jóvito Villalba, Los Robles; ☼ 8:30am-12:30pm & 1:30-4:30pm Mon-Fri) This government-run tourist office is midway between Porlamar and Pampatar.

Digicom (Fermín) Internet.

Edikó's Lavandería (Fermín)

Ipostel (Maneiro)

Onidex (☎ 263-4766; Arismendi 7-85; ☼ 8am-noon & 1-3:45pm Mon-Fri) For visa or tourist-card extensions.

Sleeping

Porlamar has many hotels at every price. Most cheap spots are in the busy historic center, to the west and south of Plaza Bolívar.

Hotel España (☎ 261-2479; Mariño; d/tr 60/70BsF; 🕷) Sagging beds await you at this raggedy place,

although grand architectural details and intricate flooring hint to a more affluent age.

Hotel Nuevo Puerto (☎ 263-8888; La Marina; d with fan/air-con 60/80BsF; 🕷) This falling-down collection of mostly windowless rooms is little more than a place to lay your head, but the management is friendly and the labyrinthine corridors have some quirk appeal.

Hotel Jinama (☎ 261-7186; fonsoyniky@hotmail .com; Mariño; s/d/tr 80/90/100BsF; 🕷) A simple and cheerful hotel, with in-room fridges and cable TV making up for thinnish mattresses, and a pleasant common area overlooking the street.

Casa Lutecia (☎ /fax 263-8526; Campos; d/ste incl breakfast 140/180BsF; 🕷 ⛾) This Mediterranean-style posada with adobe-colored walls, a Spanish tile roof and a courtyard of brilliant bougainvillea has comfortable rooms with ceiling fans and mosquito nets for those who detest air-con. The rooftop pool is heavenly. French spoken.

Eating

Budget eateries are plentiful across the city, particularly in the old town.

Panadería 4 de Mayo (cnr Fermín & Av 4 de Mayo; snacks & sandwiches 4-12BsF; ☼ 7am-10pm) The most popular of several bustling bakeries in the vicinity, with beautiful pastries, sandwiches and cakes. Prime people-watching terrace.

Mansión China (Patiño; mains 17-50BsF) Ginger bass, roast duck and veggie dishes with tofu are just a few of the options available on the voluminous menu of this Chinese place on a ministreurant row.

Restaurant Punto Criollo (Igualdad 19; mains 20-55BsF; ☼ 10:30am-10:30pm; 🕷) A large, no-nonsense Venezuelan restaurant with a lengthy bit-of-everything menu, smartly bow-tied waiters and a long drinks list.

Casa Italia (cnr Patiño & Malavé; pizza & pasta 26-67BsF) Choose from a long list of meat and chicken offerings, or one of its almost 20 delectable pasta dishes.

Drinking & Entertainment

There's always a collection of rustic shacks, well stocked with cold beers, on the beach. Trendy nightclubs and bars are outside the city center.

Nova Café (☼ 262-7266; Los Uveros; ☼ 7pm-3am Mon-Sat) Across from the Hilton hotel, outdoor tables front this small, friendly Euro club playing electronica and lounge sounds.

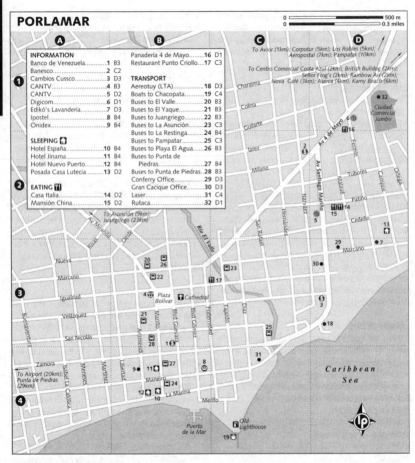

PORLAMAR

INFORMATION			
Banco de Venezuela	1	B3	
Banesco	2	C2	
Cambios Cussco	3	D3	
CANTV	4	B3	
CANTV	5	D2	
Digicom	6	D1	
Edikó's Lavandería	7	D3	
Ipostel	8	B4	
Onidex	9	B4	

SLEEPING		
Hotel España	10	B4
Hotel Jinama	11	B4
Hotel Nuevo Puerto	12	B4
Posada Casa Lutecia	13	D2

EATING		
Casa Italia	14	D2
Mansión China	15	D2

Panadería 4 de Mayo	16	D1
Restaurant Punto Criollo	17	C3

TRANSPORT		
Aereotuy (LTA)	18	D3
Boats to Chacopata	19	C4
Buses to El Valle	20	B3
Buses to El Yaque	21	B3
Buses to Juangriego	22	B3
Buses to La Asunción	23	C3
Buses to La Restinga	24	B4
Buses to Pampatar	25	C3
Buses to Playa El Agua	26	B3
Buses to Punta de Piedras	27	B4
Buses to Punta de Piedras	28	B3
Conferry Office	29	D3
Gran Cacique Office	30	D3
Laser	31	C4
Rutaca	32	D1

ourpick Kamy Beach (☎ 267-3787; Av Aldonza Marique, Playa Varadera, Pampatar; ☼ 9pm-4am Thu-Sat, nightly in high season) A slick, beachside nightclub with swaying palms, thatched-roof bars and square beds (with romantic curtains) on the sand. White lounge sofas and airy terraces overlook the beach. Live bands and DJs too.

British Bulldog (☎ 267-1527; Centro Comercial Costa Azul, Av Bolívar; ☼ 9pm-late) Plastered with Union Jacks, Margarita's first and only British-style pub has live rock Wednesday through Saturday, but no pints.

Señor Frog's (☎ 262-0451; Centro Comercial Costa Azul, Av Bolívar; ☼ 11pm-4am Tue-Sat) One of Porlamar's most popular party destinations, this gimmicky family restaurant transforms into a thumping Latin pop-orientated disco by night.

Getting Around

Small buses, locally called *micros* or *carritos*, run frequently throughout most of the island, including to Pampatar, El Yaque and Juangriego, and cost between 1.50BsF and 3.50BsF. Departure points for some of the main tourist destinations are indicated on the map.

PAMPATAR

☎ 0295 / pop 43,000

Less built-up than its neighbor Porlamar, which sits 10km to the southwest, the two towns are gradually melding into one. Pampatar was one of the earliest settlements on Margarita and once the most important port in what was to become Venezuela. It still has some colonial buildings and a nostalgic hint of faded glory. Pampatar's fort, the **Castillo de San Carlos Borromeo** (☉ 8am-6pm), is in the center of town, on the waterfront. It was built from 1662 to 1684 on the site of a previous stronghold that was destroyed by pirates.

Few travelers stay here, but there are several budget lodgings on Almirante Brión, one block back from the beach. You'll also find many open-air eateries along the beach. Minibuses between Porlamar and Pampatar run frequently; taxis are 12BsF.

JUANGRIEGO
☎ 0295 / pop 33,000

One of the nicest and most low-key beach towns on the island, Juangriego is famous for its burning sunsets. Set on the edge of a dramatic bay in the north of the island, it's a relaxing place to hang out on the beach, with rustic fishing boats, visiting yachts and pelicans. Nearby beach options are Playa La Galera, within easy walking distance and favored by locals, and the lovely Playa Caribe, 10 minutes away by taxi. When the sun sets over the peaks of Macanao far off on the horizon, the hillside **Fortín de la Galera** is the place to watch the blazing show.

El Caney (☎ 253-5059; elcaney1@hotmail.com; Guevara 17; d 100BsF, tr 120-130BsF, 6-person r 200BsF; ✷ ▢ ▣) is a colorful *posada* run by a Peruvian-Canadian couple. Nice touches include a palm-thatched terrace out front and a plunge pool with waterfall. Discounts available in low season.

Recently bought by an Irish-Venezuelan couple, and located about 200m north along the beach, **Hotel Patrick** (☎ 253-6218; www.hotel patrick.com; El Fuerte; d 100BsF, 5-person ste 180BsF; ✷ ▢) offers 10 bright rooms with wicker furniture. Bordered by a garden of lemon and banana trees, the courtyard foyer has a pool table, a TV, DVD library and a full bar and innovative restaurant that's also a wi-fi hotspot.

Grab a taxi (15BsF), head to Playa Caribe and plant yourself at **La Terraza de Playa Caribe** (☎ 0414-789-3537; mains 30-90BsF; ☉ 9am-6pm, to 10pm high season). Run by a gregarious Argentine, this beachside open-air restaurant and lounge has great seafood, *parrilla* and breakfasts, and frequently hosts reggae bands. The bar stays open later, grooving all night long for electronica full-moon parties.

Curiously, one of the best places to eat inexpensively is at the bus terminal (a 10-minute walk from the beach), which has a dozen food stalls. Numerous good seafood restaurants can be found along the beach behind Hotel Patrick

A taxi to town from Punta de Piedras or the airport costs 40BsF to 50BsF.

EL YAQUE
☎ 0295 / pop 1500

Just south of the airport, and with a guarded entrance, El Yaque has tranquil waters and steady winds that are perfect for **windsurfing** and **kitesurfing**. The beach boasts an international reputation and is a hangout for the Venezuelan and European windsurfing community (don't be surprised to see prices in euros). Several professional outfits on the beachfront offer windsurf rental (per hour/day 85/250BsF) in a variety of languages. Lessons average 110BsF per hour, or 475BsF for an advanced course of 10 hours. Kitesurfing lessons run 1140/1950/3250BsF for 1½/6/14 hours; the gear rental costs 1625BsF for 10 hours.

A taxi from the airport costs 35BsF; hourly minibuses run from Porlamar.

Right on the beach, **Warmsurfing** (☎ 0416-796-0400; www.warmsurfing.com; s/d 70/100BsF; ✷) has simple air-con rooms, a palm-roofed kitchen and a large restaurant. There's windsurfing gear for rent and a small book exchange.

Next door, at the entrance to town, **El Yaque Motion** (☎ 263-9742; www.elyaquemotion.com; d with/without bathroom 140/100BsF, tr 170BsF, apt from 200BsF; ✷ ▢) is a fine travelers' haunt with an upstairs kitchen and terrace, cheery modern rooms and a number of large apartments good for groups. In the evenings, guests often kick back over beers and communal pasta meals.

BEACHES

Isla de Margarita has some 50 beaches large enough to deserve a name, not to mention a number of other unnamed little stretches of sand. Many are built up with restaurants, bars and other facilities. Though the island is no longer a virgin paradise, you can still search out a relatively deserted spot if you look hard enough.

Playa El Agua is considered Margarita's trendiest beach. It's full of stylish Venezuelans and gawking hordes, though the true trendsetters have moved on to less-developed beaches. During holidays, the beach can get crammed with visitors but at other times it's a welcoming and wonderfully laid-back spot. It is generally an upmarket place, but there are some budget options in the back streets.

Other popular beaches include **Playa Guacuco** and **Playa Manzanillo**. Perhaps Margarita's finest beach is **Playa Puerto Cruz**, which arguably has the island's widest, whitest stretch of sand and still isn't over-developed. **Playa Parguito**, next to Playa El Agua, has strong waves good for surfing. If you want to escape from people, head for **Península de Macanao**, the wildest part of the island.

GUAYANA

The southeastern region of Guayana (not to be confused with the country Guyana) showcases Venezuela at its exotic best. The area is home to the world's highest waterfall, Salto Ángel; the impossibly lush Parque Nacional Canaima; the wildlife rich Orinoco Delta (Delta del Orinoco) and Río Caura; the Venezuelan Amazon and La Gran Sabana (The Great Savanna) where flat-topped *tepui* mountains lord over rolling grasslands. Visitors often spend an entire trip in this area of the country.

The majority of the country's indigenous groups live in Guayana, including the Warao, Pemón and Yanomami, which constitute about 10% of the region's total population.

CIUDAD BOLÍVAR
☎ 0285 / pop 462,000

Astride the Río Orinoco at its narrowest point, the namesake city of El Libertador has a *casco histórico* (historic center) preened to perfection, its restored colonial-era architecture gussied up with fresh paint. Most people visit Ciudad Bolívar as the jumping-off point to explore Parque Nacional Canaima, Salto Ángel and Guayana's various other treasures, and the city has many tour operators willing to take you there.

Simón Bolívar came here in 1817, soon after the town had been liberated from Spanish control, and set up the base for the military operations that led to the final stage of the War of Independence. The town was made the provisional capital of the yet-to-be-liberated country. The Angostura Congress convened here in 1819 and gave birth to

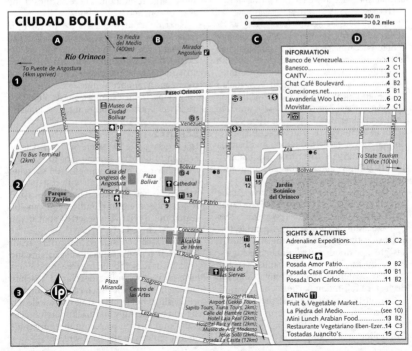

CIUDAD BOLÍVAR

INFORMATION
Banco de Venezuela..................**1** C1
Banesco.....................................**2** C1
CANTV.......................................**3** C1
Chat Café Boulevard................**4** B2
Conexiones.net.........................**5** B1
Lavandería Woo Lee................**6** D2
Movistar....................................**7** C1

SIGHTS & ACTIVITIES
Adrenaline Expeditions.............**8** C2

SLEEPING
Posada Amor Patrio...................**9** B2
Posada Casa Grande.................**10** B1
Posada Don Carlos...................**11** B2

EATING
Fruit & Vegetable Market.........**12** C2
La Piedra del Medio.............(see **10**)
Mini Lunch Arabian Food.........**13** B2
Restaurante Vegetariano Eben-Ezer..**14** C3
Tostadas Juancito's..................**15** C2

Gran Colombia, a unified republic comprising Venezuela, Colombia and Ecuador.

The historic center clears out after dark and everything is closed on Sundays. Walking alone at night is not recommended there.

Information

INTERNET ACCESS
Chat Café Boulevard (Bolívar)
Conexiones.net (Venezuela)

LAUNDRY
Lavandería Woo Lee (Zea)

MEDICAL SERVICES
Hospital Ruiz y Páez (☎ 632-4146; Av Germania)

MONEY
Banco de Venezuela (cnr Paseo Orinoco & Piar)
Banesco (cnr Dalla Costa & Venezuela)

POST
Ipostel (Av Táchira btwn Avs Cruz Verde & Guasipati)

TELEPHONES
CANTV (cnr Paseo Orinoco & Dalla Costa)
Movistar (Centro Comercial Abboud Center, Paseo Orinoco)

TOURISM INFORMATION
State tourism office (☎ 800-674-6626, 632-4525; www.turismobolivar.gob.ve; Bolívar; ⏰ 8am-noon & 2-5:30pm) Just inside the Jardín Botánico; very helpful, with English, German and Italian spoken. Toll-free information line open 8am to 8pm Monday to Saturday.

Sights

The colonial heart of the city is **Plaza Bolívar**. The lively waterfront, **Paseo Orinoco**, is lined with street vendors and old arcaded houses, some of which go back to the days of Bolívar. From the Río Orinoco shoreline or viewpoints in the city, you can see the appropriately named island **Piedra del Medio** (Rock in the Middle).

The **Museo de Arte Moderno Jesús Soto** (☎ 632-0518; cnr Avs Germania & Briceño Iragorry; ⏰ 9:30am-5:30pm Tue-Fri, 10am-5pm Sat & Sun) has an extensive collection of kinetic works by this renowned artist.

In front of the airport terminal stands the **airplane of Jimmie Angel** that landed atop what was eventually named Salto Ángel (Angel Falls).

Tours

Ciudad Bolívar is the departure point for tours to Canaima (Salto Ángel), Río Caura and onward travel to Santa Elena de Uairén (Roraima). A three-day all-inclusive tour to Salto Ángel runs about 1400BsF to 2000BsF; Adrenaline and Tiuna also sell a budget option that departs from La Paragua.

A few of the many operators:

Adrenaline Expeditions (☎ 632-4804, 0414-886-7209; adrenalinexptours@hotmail.com; Bolívar) An adventure-oriented agency catering to budget travelers, with good Río Caura, Canaima and Gran Sabana tours. Extremely helpful with regional travel information.

Gekko Tours (☎ 632-3223, 0414-854-5146; www.gekkotours-venezuela.de; airport terminal) Run by Posada La Casita; a responsible agency offering a wide range of tours and flights across the region and the country.

Sapito Tours (☎ 0414-854-8234; www.sapitotours.com; airport terminal) Representative of Bernal Tours from Canaima.

Tiuna Tours (☎ 632-8697, 0414-853-2590; tiunatours@hotmail.com; airport terminal) Ciudad Bolívar's office of the major Canaima operator.

Sleeping

Ciudad Bolívar has a number of lovely *posadas*.

ourpick Posada La Casita (☎ 617-0832, 0414-854-5146; www.posada-la-casita.com; Urbanización 24 de Julio; camping per person 20BsF, hammock 30BsF, s/d/tr 90/130/170BsF; 🅿 ⬚ ⬚) Lounge by the pool at this relaxing rural compound just outside the city. Travelers are drawn here by the wide range of sleeping options, easy access (free 24-hour pickup from the airport or bus station, and a shuttle to town) and sociable atmosphere. Snacks, drinks and inexpensive meals are available.

Posada Amor Patrio (☎ 0414-854-4925; plazabolivar@hotmail.com; Amor Patrio; hammock 25BsF, d/tr without bathrooms 75/100BsF) A historic house right behind the cathedral, with five playfully themed rooms, a rooftop hammock terrace, a kitchen and an airy salon celebrating Cuban jazz.

Posada Don Carlos (☎ 632-6017, 0414-854-6616; www.posada-doncarlos.com; Boyacá; hammock/outdoor bed 35BsF, s with fan 70-80BsF, d with fan 80-90BsF, d/tr/q with air-con 115/135/155BsF; 🅿 ⬚) An atmospheric colonial mansion with two ample patios and an antique bar, this *posada* has neat, clean accommodations, a kitchen, and meals upon request. Air-con rooms have towering ceilings and enormous wood doors. Río Caura and Salto Ángel tours can be organized.

Also recommended:

Hotel Laja Real (☎ 617-0100; www.lajareal.com; cnr Avs Andrés Bello & Jesús Soto; s 185-200BsF, d/tr 230/260BsF; ❄ ▢ ☎) An upmarket hotel directly across the street from the airport.

Posada Casa Grande (☎ 632-6706; www.cacao travel.com; cnr Venezuela & Boyacá; s/d/tr/ste 350/390/ 465/580BsF; ❄ ☎) A lovely boutique hotel in a restored colonial building; rooftop views at sunset are spectacular.

Eating & Drinking

Tostadas Juancito's (cnr Av Cumaná & Bolívar; arepas 5-12BsF, menú 20-22BsF; ☉ 6:30am-6:30pm) Hang out with the locals at this popular *arepa* and snack bar that has occupied this busy street corner forever.

Restaurante Vegetariano Eben-Ezer (Concordia; menú 20BsF; ☉ 7am-3pm Mon-Fri) A modern new vegetarian eatery, it's popular for its delicious *pasticho de berengena* (eggplant lasagna) and seitan croquettes, in addition to extensive salads and wonderful wholemeal breads and *arepas*.

Mini Lunch Arabian Food (cnr Amor Patrio & Igualdad; mains 20-30BsF; ☉ 7am-7pm) This small family-run cafe ramps up at lunchtime, with hearty vegetarian lentil soup chock-full of greens, and filling falafels; or try the tasty shawarma and kebabs.

To pick up a few nibbles in the center there's a small fruit and vegetable market behind Tostadas Juancito's that carries a bare minimum of pasta and other staples. For a late-night fast-food fix, taxi to the **Calle del Hambre** (Hungry Street; Estacionamiento del Estadio Heres), a block-long carnival of bright lights and a few dozen food stalls that buzz and sizzle until the wee hours of the morning.

SPLURGE!

La Piedra del Medio (☎ 0424-961-9836; cnr Venezuela & Boyacá; 3-course fixed-price dinner 70BsF) Chef Karla Herrera brings creativity and the best fresh local ingredients to this new restaurant inside the Posada Casa Grande. The first gourmet offering in the historic district, its soaring ceilings and warm modern accents make a cosmopolitan backdrop for an artfully presented fusion of international and traditional dishes. By reservation only; menu changes daily.

Getting There & Away

AIR

The **airport** (☎ 632-4978; Av Jesús Soto) is 2km southeast of the riverfront and linked to the city center by local transport. **Rutaca** (☎ 632-4465) flies to Caracas (290BsF) via Maturín (100BsF) Sunday through Friday, and has daily morning flights to Santa Elena de Uairén (600BsF) that often stop in Canaima. Most tour operators fly to Canaima; one-way flights without a tour cost from 350BsF to 380BsF.

BUS

The **Terminal de Pasajeros** (cnr Avs República & Sucre) is 2km south of the center. To get there, take the westbound *buseta* marked 'Terminal' from Paseo Orinoco.

Frequent buses go to Caracas (60BsF to 65BsF, nine hours); most depart in the evening. Direct buses service Maracay (60BsF to 65BsF, 9½ hours) and Valencia (48BsF to 70BsF, 10½ hours), via the shorter Los Llanos route that bypasses Caracas. Take these to go to Venezuela's northwest or the Andes without connections in Caracas.

From mid-June through mid-September, Expresos Los Llanos and Expresos Mérida each run a daily bus to Mérida (125BsF to 144BsF, 24 hours).

A few daily buses run to Puerto La Cruz (45BsF to 50BsF, four hours). Small buses depart regularly throughout the day to Puerto Ayacucho (42BsF to 50BsF, 10½ to 12 hours). To Ciudad Guayana (8BsF, 1½ hours), buses depart every 15 to 30 minutes, and a half dozen daily departures go to Santa Elena de Uairén (60BsF, 10 to 12 hours).

CIUDAD GUAYANA

☎ 0286 / pop 980,000

Officially 'founded' in 1961 to serve as an industrial center for the region, Ciudad Guayana sits on two rivers, the Río Orinoco and Río Caroní, and encompasses the unlikely twin cities of **Puerto Ordaz** and **San Félix**. The colonial town of San Félix, on the eastern side of the Caroní, is a working-class city with a historical center, but little tourist infrastructure and a reputation for being unsafe. Puerto Ordaz is a wealthy and modern prefab city, with a large middle-class population, and a smorgasbord of restaurant and entertainment options. Locals generally refer to 'San Félix' or 'Puerto Ordaz,' and tend to disregard the official title of 'Ciudad Guayana.' Don't bother to ask for Ciudad Guayana at a bus station or travel agency, because the place is little more than a name.

All listings below are in Puerto Ordaz.

Information

Banco de Venezuela (cnr Avs Las Américas & Monseñor Zabaleta)

Banco Mercantil (cnr Av Ciudad Bolívar & Vía Venezuela)

Infowarehouse (Centro Comercial Topacio, Carrera Upata) Internet.

Movistar (Carrera Upata near El Callao) Telephones.

Sights

Puerto Ordaz has three stunning parks along the Río Caroní. The 52-hectare **Parque Cachamay** (Av Guayana) has a spectacular view of the river's 200m-wide waterfalls. Pushy monkeys enliven the adjoining **Parque Loefling** (Av Guayana), which has roaming capybaras and tapirs and contains a small zoo of native wildlife. The 160-hectare **Parque La Llovizna** (Av Leopoldo Sucre Figarella) is on the other (eastern) side of the Río Caroní, with 26 wooded islands carved by thin water channels and linked by 36 footbridges. The 20m-high Salto La Llovizna kicks up the park's namesake *llovizna* (drizzle).

Sleeping

With its relative wealth and high number of business travelers, there aren't many good budget accommodations in Puerto Ordaz.

La Casa del Lobo (☎ 961-6286, 0414-871-9339; www .lobo-tours.de; Manzana 39, Zambia 2, Villa Africana; r 80BsF; 🖳) The best backpacker option in town, this German-owned house a few kilometers south of the center has five tidy rooms, a kitchen, meals prepared on request and delta tours. There's also free pickup service from Puerto Ordaz bus terminal with advance notice; taxis cost 20BsF.

Residencia Ambato 19 (☎ 923-2072; www.ambato19 .com; Ambato 19; d 150BsF; 🍴 🖳) Centrally located on a quiet street off México, this small family-run *posada* has seven tranquil and spotless rooms, all with a double bed and bathroom. It's often full, so call ahead.

Posada Turística Kaori (☎ 923-4038; kaori posada@cantv.net; Argentina, Campo B; d/tr 170/200BsF; 🍴 🖳) With small, clean and contemporary rooms with cable TV and good mattresses, this *posada* is within walking distance of the center.

Eating

RicArepa (Carrera Upata; arepas 14-19BsF; 🕐 24hr) You can choose from almost two dozen types of fillings in this buzzing *arepera*.

Bulevar de la Comida Guayanesa (Guasipati; meals 18-28BsF; 🕐 breakfast & lunch) A line of a dozen food kiosks serving typical local fare on a shaded sidewalk.

Pasta Fresca Caroní (Moitaco; pasta 18-25BsF; 🕐 11:30am-3pm Mon-Sat) Mix and match with a dozen types of fresh pasta and 15 yummy sauces.

Within view of the bus terminal, the sprawling **Orinokia Mall** (www.orinokiamall.com; Av Las Américas) contains a 20-vendor food court, a huge supermarket and a number of upscale restaurants. And if you need to kill time before your bus, there's also a multiplex cinema and a bowling alley.

Getting There & Away

Ciudad Guayana is a major transit hub for buses and flights.

AIR

A busy regional air hub, the **Aeropuerto Puerto Ordaz** (Av Guayana) is at the western end of town on the road to Ciudad Bolívar and is served by local buses. Note that the airport appears in all schedules as 'Puerto Ordaz,' not 'Ciudad Guayana.'

BUS

Ciudad Guayana has two main bus terminals, one in Puerto Ordaz, on Av Guayana 1km east of the airport, and another in San Félix. The Puerto Ordaz terminal is smaller, cleaner, quieter and safer than the busier San Félix station, and most buses stop at both terminals. If you're in a big hurry, San Félix has more *por puesto* departures. Between the terminals, taxis charge a whopping 35BsF to 40BsF, or you can get an empty seat on a bus heading that direction for 5BsF.

From Puerto Ordaz, most buses to Caracas (70BsF to 85BsF, 10½ hours) depart in the evening. Direct buses to Maracay (65BsF to 70BsF, 11 hours) and Valencia (65BsF to 70BsF, 12 hours) take the shorter Los Llanos route and bypass Caracas; they're handy for connections to the Andes and the northwest.

Buses to Ciudad Bolívar depart every half hour or so (8BsF, 1½ hours); faster *por puestos* cost 20BsF. A half dozen buses come through from Ciudad Bolívar daily on their way to

Santa Elena de Uairén (55BsF to 65BsF, nine to 11 hours); all call at San Félix, a few don't stop in Puerto Ordaz.

Across the street from the Puerto Ordaz terminal, the gleaming **Rodovías bus terminal** (☎ 951-9633; Av Guayana), has free spick-and-span bathrooms and six daily departures to its private terminal in central Caracas (68BsF to 73BsF, 10 hours).

TUCUPITA
☎ 0287 / pop 66,000

Founded in the 1920s as a Capuchin mission to convert the local indigenous population to Catholicism, Tucupita is now a steamy river port and the only sizable town in the Orinoco Delta. You can take a pleasant stroll around the central streets and along Paseo Mánamo, the riverbank esplanade, but Tucupita is mainly visited as a base for exploring the delta.

Information
Banco de Venezuela (Mánamo)
Compucenter.com (Centro Comercial Delta Center, Plaza Bolívar) Internet.
Ipostel (Pativilca)
Mi Casa (Plaza Bolívar) Convenient ATM on the main plaza.

Tours
All local operators focus on trips into the Orinoco Delta. Tours are usually all-inclusive two- to four-day excursions running 120BsF to 270BsF per person a day, depending on group size. All operators have *campamentos* (camps) serving as a base for trips in the area.
Aventura Turística Delta (☎ 721-0835, 0414-189-9063; a_t_d_1973@hotmail.com; Centurión) One of the least expensive tours and more popular agencies; has simple facilities and two basic camps with hammocks only. Near the cathedral.
Cooperativa Osibu XIV (☎ 721-3840; campamento maraisa@hotmail.com; cnr Mariño & Pativilca) The oldest local tour company, operating since 1987, and the only one that offers tours to the far eastern part of the delta. Its *campamento* in San Francisco de Guayo has *cabañas* (cabins) with beds and bathrooms.

Sleeping & Eating
Pequeño Hotel (☎ 721-0523; La Paz; s/d/tr with fan 20/30/35BsF, d/tr with air-con 50/60BsF; ✗) The family-run Pequeño Hotel has dim rooms and lumpy beds, but it's the cheapest place in town and has been welcoming travelers for more than 40 years. The *señora* locks the door by 10pm and goes to bed.

RAIN OR SHINE?

The amount of water going over Salto Ángel (Angel Falls) depends on the season, and the contrast can be dramatic. In the dry months (January to May), it can be pretty faint – just a thin ribbon of water fading into mist before it reaches the bottom. Boat access is impossible in the driest months. In the rainy season, particularly in the wettest months (August and September), the waterfall is a spectacular cascade of plummeting water – but you run the risk of rain and of the view being obscured by clouds.

Hotel Amacuro (☎ 721-0404; Bolívar; d/tr with fan 65/95BsF, with air-con 90/120BsF; ✗) Under energetic new management, this simple option just off Plaza Bolívar has reasonably clean, good-sized rooms, a restaurant and a gradual remodel are in the works.
Mi Tasca (Dalla Costa; mains 18-35BsF) Black-and-white clad waiters bring a touch of class to this *criollo* restaurant with a varied menu, good prices, generous portions and quick service.
La Mariposa Café (Centro Comercial Delta Center, Plaza Bolívar; mains 18-48BsF) Feast on *comidas internacionales* like stroganoff, steak tartar, vegetarian pastas and excellent soups.

Getting There & Away
The **Terminal de Pasajeros** (cnr Carrera 6 & Calle 10) is 1km southeast of the center. One morning and five night buses run to Caracas (40BsF to 55BsF, 11 hours) via Maturín. Daily buses to Ciudad Guayana are infrequent, so *por puestos* (40BsF, 2½ hours) are a better bet. For Caripe and Cueva del Guácharo, take a bus to Maturín (12BsF to 20BsF, four hours), or a faster and more frequently departing *por puesto* (40BsF, 2½ to three hours), and change.

SALTO ÁNGEL (ANGEL FALLS)
Salto Ángel is the world's highest waterfall and Venezuela's number-one tourist attraction. Its total height is 979m, with an uninterrupted drop of 807m – about 16 times the height of Niagara Falls. The cascade pours off the towering Auyantepui, one of the largest of the *tepuis*. Salto Ángel is not named, as one might expect, for a divine creature, but for an American bush pilot Jimmie Angel, who landed his four-seater airplane atop Auyantepui in 1937 in search of gold.

The waterfall is in a distant, lush wilderness with no road access. The village of Canaima, about 50km northwest, is the major gateway to the falls. Canaima doesn't have an overland link to the rest of the country either, but is accessed by numerous small planes from Ciudad Bolívar and Isla de Margarita.

A visit to Salto Ángel is normally undertaken in two stages, with Canaima as the stepping-stone. Most tourists fly into Canaima, where they take a light plane or boat to the falls. Most visitors who visit by boat opt to stay overnight in hammocks at one of the camps near the base of the falls. The trip upriver, the surrounding area and the experience of staying at the camp are as memorable as the waterfall itself.

Salto Ángel, Auyantepui, Canaima and the surrounding area lie within the boundaries of the 30,000-sq-km Parque Nacional Canaima. All visitors need to pay a 35BsF national-park entrance fee at Canaima airport.

CANAIMA
☎ 0286 / pop 1500

The closest population center to Salto Ángel, Canaima is a remote indigenous village that hosts and dispatches a huge number of tourists. Although it's a base to reach Venezuela's number-one natural attraction, Canaima is truly gorgeous as well. The Laguna de Canaima sits at the heart of everything, a broad blue expanse framed by a palm-tree beach, a dramatic series of seven picture-postcard

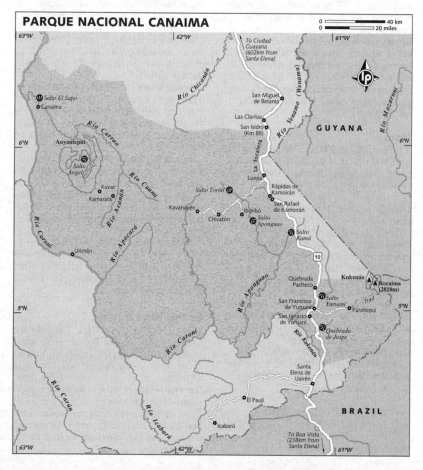

PARQUE NACIONAL CANAIMA

cascades and a backdrop of anvil-like *tepuis*. Most tours to Salto Ángel include a short boat trip and hike that allows you to walk behind some of the falls and get the backstage experience of the hammering curtains of water. Their color is a curious pink, caused by the high level of tannins from decomposed plants and trees.

The rambling Campamento Canaima is on the west of the lagoon, with the best beach for swimming and taking photos. When swimming, stay close to the main beach – a number of drownings have occurred close to the hydroelectric plant and the falls.

Information

Esedantok (per hr 10BsF) A new air-conditioned and locally owned cybercafe; the name means 'center of communications' in Pemón. Connection is slow, but same as the rest of town.

Tienda Canaima (☎ 962-0443, 0414-884-0940) Near the airport, this expensive shop stocks the biggest inventory of groceries (including ice cream), toiletries, maps and souvenirs. It also changes US dollars, euros and British pounds at an intermediary rate and gives cash on ATM cards at the official rate. Birthday cakes available upon request!

Tours

All Canaima-based tour companies run boat trips and can arrange flights. They also arrange lodging and meals. From Canaima (without flights), a three-day tour costs about 550BsF to 700BsF, but all agencies arrange full tours from Ciudad Bolívar as well.

The main operators:

Bernal Tours (☎ 0414-899-7162, 0414-854-8234; www.bernaltours.com) Family-run company based on an island in Laguna de Canaima, where participants stay and eat before and after the tour. Bernal Tours has its *campamento* on Isla Ratoncito, opposite Salto Ángel.

Excursiones Kavac (☎ 0416-685-2209) A good agency managed by the indigenous Pemón community. Marginally cheaper than Bernal Tours, it also has a *campamento* in front of Salto Ángel. Kavac tours too.

Tiuna Tours (☎ 0416-692-1536, 0286-962-4255; tiunatours@hotmail.com) The biggest and cheapest local player, with a large *campamento* in Canaima and another up the Río Carrao at the Aonda.

For the fit and adventurous, **Jakera** (www.jakera .com), based in Mérida and Playa Colorada, leads backpacking tours from La Paragua (south of Ciudad Bolívar) to Canaima.

Sleeping & Eating

There are a dozen *campamentos* and *posadas* in Canaima. Most are managed by the main tour agencies, serve all meals and will meet you at the airport. Camping on the lagoon is no longer permitted.

Campamento Churúm Venu (☎ 0416-685-2209; ssmbelk@hotmail.com; hammock space 30BsF, r per person with/without meals 215/100BsF; 🖳) Located opposite the soccer pitch, Excursiones Kavac's clean, comfortable 15-room camp often has vacancies, and it's one of the few places where you can hang a hammock (bring your own).

Campamento Tiuna (☎ 0416-692-1536, 0286-962-4255; hammock 30BsF, r per person with/without meals 300/100BsF, d 200BsF) In an open stone building at the northern part of the village, this basic *campamento* offers hammocks, six-bed dormitories and one double room. It offers free hammock lodging if you eat all meals there. Breakfast is 25BsF, lunch or dinner 60BsF. There's an office at Ciudad Bolívar airport.

Posada Kusary (☎ 962-0443, 0414-884-0940; r per person 150BsF) Run by the owners of Tienda Canaima, this well-maintained *posada* in the northern area of town has 13 rooms with fans. Breakfast is 40BsF, lunch or dinner 80BsF.

Posada Wey Tupü (☎ 0416-185-7231, 0416-997-9565; r per person with/without meals 225/100BsF; 🖳) Opposite the old school in the south part of the village, Wey Tupü has simple rooms with fans and provides some of the cheapest meals for guests. Internet costs 5BsF per hour.

Mentanai (mains 10-15BsF; 🕐 2-11pm) Next to Excursiones Kavac, this little burger and sandwich grill has a pool table and a bar serving beer and Cuba Libres plus a speck of a foodstuffs store.

Getting There & Away

Several regional carriers fly between Canaima and Ciudad Bolívar on a semi-regular or charter basis (350BsF). Various small airlines, including Aereotuy and Transmandu, go to and from Porlamar (approximately 900BsF). Rutaca's Cessna charter flights between Canaima and Santa Elena de Uairén (600BsF) have some of the best *tepui* views in the country. **Serami** (www .serami.com) has daily direct service from Puerto Ordaz (864BsF one way).

GRAN SABANA

A wide open grassland that seems suspended from endless sky, the Gran Sabana invites poetic description. Scores of waterfalls appear at every turn, and *tepuis*, the savanna's trademark table mountains, sweep across the horizon, their mesas both haunting and majestic. More than 100 of these plateaus dot the vast region from the Colombian border in the west to Guyana and Brazil in the east, but most are here in the Gran Sabana. One of the *tepuis*, Roraima, can be climbed; this trip is an extraordinary natural adventure.

The largest town is Santa Elena de Uairén, close to the Brazilian border. The rest of the sparsely populated region is inhabited mostly by the 15,000 indigenous Pemón people, who live in nearly 300 scattered villages.

Getting Around

The Ciudad Guayana–Santa Elena de Uairén Hwy provides access to this fascinating land, but public transport on this road is infrequent, making individual sightseeing inconvenient and time consuming. Tours from Ciudad Bolívar (p963) or Santa Elena de Uairén (p971) are more convenient.

RORAIMA

A stately table mountain towering into churning clouds, Roraima (2810m) lures hikers and nature-lovers looking for Venezuela at its natural and rugged best. Unexplored until 1884, and studied extensively by botanists ever since, the stark landscape contains strange rock formations and graceful arches, ribbon waterfalls, glittering quartz deposits and carnivorous plants. Frequent mist only accentuates the otherworldly feel.

Although it's one of the easier *tepuis* to climb and no technical skills are required, the trek is long and demanding. However, anyone who's reasonably fit and determined can reach the top. Be prepared for wet weather, nasty *puri puris* (invisible biting insects) and frigid nights at the summit. And give yourself at least six days round-trip so you have sufficient time to explore the vast plateau of the *tepui*.

Climbing Roraima

Roraima lies approximately 47km east of the El Dorado–Santa Elena highway, just east of San Francisco de Yuruaní. The hamlet of Paraitepui is the usual starting point for the trip. You can organize a compulsory Pemón guide in Santa Elena, San Francisco or Paraitepui. Most people opt to go on an organized tour (p971) from Santa Elena, which contracts guides and porters and arranges for meals, transportation and equipment.

The trip to the top normally takes two to three days (total net walking time is about 12 hours up and 10 hours down). There are several campsites (with water) on the way. They are Río Tek (four hours from Paraitepui), Río Kukenán (30 minutes further on) and at the foot of Roraima at the so-called *campamento base* (base camp), three hours uphill from the Río Kukenán. The steep, tough, four-hour ascent from the base camp to the top is the most spectacular (yet demanding) part of the hike.

Once atop Roraima, you'll camp in one of the dozen or so *hoteles* (hotels) – semisheltered camping spots under rock overhangs. The guides coordinate which group sleeps where.

The scenery is a moonscape sculpted by the wind and rain, with gorges, creeks, pink beaches, lookout points and gardens filled with unique flowering plants. An eerie, shifting fog often snakes across the mountaintop. While guides may have seemed superfluous on the clear trails below, they are helpful on the labyrinthine plateau. If you stay for two nights on the top you will have time to hike with your guide to some of the attractions, including **El Foso** (a crystalline pool in a massive sinkhole), the **Punto Triple** (the tri-border of Venezuela, Brazil and Guyana), **Bahia de Cristal** (a small valley brimming with quartz) and the stunning viewpoint of **La Ventana** (the Window).

The *tepui* is an ecologically delicate area. Visitors need to pack out all garbage, including human waste, and collecting quartz is strictly forbidden. Inparques searches bags at the end of the hike, and will fine you for collecting souvenirs.

Make sure to pack good rain gear, extra socks, warm clothes, insect repellant and an extra camera battery.

San Francisco de Yuruaní

San Francisco, 66km north of Santa Elena de Uairén via a gorgeous green stretch of highway, is the last large town with restaurants and lodging before the start of the Roraima trek (which departs from Paraitepui). This is the place for a hearty meal before or after your hike, and both guides and porters can be hired here for about the same price as in Paraitepui, although San Francisco has a larger population and therefore more options. Remember that, in terms of quality, you generally get what you pay for.

The town has a number of basic *posada* options along the main road (80BsF to 100BsF per room), and simple eateries serve grilled chicken and cold beer.

San Francisco de Yuruaní is on the Ciudad Guayana–Santa Elena Hwy. Eight buses a day run in either direction. Turgar has a 7:30am bus from Santa Elena (10BsF, 35 minutes) that's a good bet for Roraima hikers.

Paraitepui

The small Pemón village of Paraitepui is the gateway to the Roraima trek. It's 26km east of San Francisco; to get there, hire a jeep in San Francisco (300BsF for up to eight passengers, 500BsF from Santa Elena) or walk from San Francisco. However, the five- to seven-hour uphill walk is hot, dusty and exposed, and weary hitchhikers will be expected to pay.

The Inparques station is in Paraitepui and you must sign in before the hike (there is no park entrance fee). You are allowed to camp in the parking lot and use the covered table area, but the ranger may charge a small fee. A *comedor* (dining room) serves breakfast and dinner upon request. The town cooperative rents out stoves, tents and sleeping bags, and you can hire guides (250BsF per day per group) or porters (100BsF per day) here.

For an early start on Roraima, or to just bask in its beauty without hiking, consider overnighting at the new community-run **hotel** (☎ 0414-446-2571, 0289-540-0225; r per person incl lunch & dinner 100BsF), a very comfortable series of duplex *cabañas* on the edge of town with dreamy *tepui* views.

SANTA ELENA DE UAIRÉN
☎ 0289 / pop 18,500

A bustling low-key border town where dusty 4x4 drivers wave at their friends, Santa Elena is the primary transit point for treks to Roraima and the first stop in Venezuela for travelers entering on land from Brazil. This small yet happening town is also a good base for exploring the Gran Sabana.

SANTA ELENA DE UAIRÉN

0   200 m
0   0.1 miles

To Bus Terminal (2km);
Representaciones y Servicios
Turísticos Francisco Alvarez (2km);
Ciudad Guayana (603km);
Ciudad Bolívar (718km)

INFORMATION
Banco Guyana..............................1 A2
Banco Industrial de Venezuela.......2 A2
Centro de Comunicaciones Marcos.3 B3
Inter Top...................................4 B2
Ipostel......................................5 A2
Lavandería Pereira.......................6 B2
Money Changers..........................7 A2

SIGHTS & ACTIVITIES
Backpacker Tours.........................8 C2
Mystic Tours...............................9 B2
Ruta Salvaje..............................10 C1

SLEEPING 🏠
Hotel Lucrecia...........................11 C2
Hotel Michelle...........................12 C2
Posada Backpacker Tours............13 C2
Posada Michelle.....................(see 13)

EATING 🍴
Alfredo's Restaurant...................14 C2
Gran Sabana Deli.......................15 A2
Restaurant Michelle................(see 12)
ServeKilo Nova Opção................16 C3
Tienda Naturalista Griselda Luna..17 B3

TRANSPORT
Jeeps to El Pauji........................18 B3

Av Antonio José de Sucre

Av Mariscal Sucre

Av Perimetral

Bolívar

Roscio

Lucas Fernández Peña

Icabarú

Av Perimetral

Zea

Urdaneta

Capilla de
San Francisco

Plaza
Bolívar

To Brazilian Consulate (100m);
Hospital Rosario Vera Zurita (100m);
Airport (7km); El Pauji (73km);
Boa Vista (Brazil) (238km)

Though the city is quite safe, it's also a brazen black market and smuggling hub. Gas prices in Brazil are almost 30 times higher than those in Venezuela (where gas is cheaper than water), which means that there is serious money to be made. There's a thriving trade in gas sold from private homes, and sellers have acquired the unfortunate moniker of '*talibanes*.' Look for the huge *colas* (lines) at the gas stations and for cars and buses impounded at the border for attempting to smuggle gas into Brazil.

Information

Money changers (for US dollars and euros) work the corner of Bolívar and Urdaneta, popularly known as Cuatro Esquinas. This is the safest place in the country to delve into the black market, with the best rates, but it's technically illegal. Internet connections are v-e-r-y slow.

Banco Guyana (Plaza Bolívar)

Banco Industrial de Venezuela (Calle Bolívar)

Brazilian Consulate (☎ 995-1256; Edificio Galeno, Los Castanos, Urbanización Roraima del Casco Central; ⌚ 8am-2pm Mon-Fri) Near the hospital. A yellow-fever vaccination certificate is required to obtain a visa.

Centro de Comunicaciones Marcos (Zea) Telephones.

Hospital Rosario Vera Zurita (Icabarú) Linked to ☎ 171 emergency via radio.

Inter Top (Urdaneta; ⌚ 7am-midnight) Decent internet connection.

Ipostel (Urdaneta) Behind an unsigned door.

Lavandería Pereira (Urdaneta)

Tours

All Santa Elena tour agencies run one-, two- or three-day jeep tour around the Gran Sabana, with visits to the most interesting sights, mostly waterfalls. Budget between 170BsF to 380BsF per person per day, depending on group size and whether the tour includes just guide and transportation or food and accommodation as well.

For most visitors, the main attraction is a Roraima tour, generally offered as an all-inclusive six-day package for 1200BsF to 1700BsF (you get what you pay for). The operators who organize this tour usually also rent out camping equipment and can provide transportation to Paraitepui, the starting point for the Roraima trek, for about 500BsF per jeep each way for up to six people. Check on specifics, including group size, hiker-to-guide ratio and equipment quality before signing up for any Roraima tour.

Recommended local tour companies:

Adrenaline Expeditions (☎ 0424-970-7329; adrenaline xptours@hotmail.com) The literal sibling of the Ciudad Bolívar agency. Specializes in adventurous Gran Sabana trips.

Backpacker Tours (☎ 995-1415, 0414-886-7227; www.backpacker-tours.com; Urdaneta) The local power-house, it has the most organized, best-equipped and most expensive tours of Roraima and the region. Also rents mountain bikes.

Mystic Tours (☎ 416-0558; www.mystictours.com.ve; Urdaneta) Some of least expensive tours to Roraima, and local tours with a New Age bent.

Representaciones y Servicios Turísticos Francisco Alvarez (☎ 0414-385-2846; rstgransabana@hotmail .com; bus terminal) Personable and helpful, with regional tours and camping equipment rentals.

Ruta Salvaje (☎ 995-1134; www.rutasalvaje.com; Av Mariscal Sucre) The standard tours, plus rafting trips and paragliding.

Sleeping

Posada Michelle (☎ 995-2017; hotelmichelle@cantv.net; Urdaneta; s/d/tr/q 40/60/70/80BsF) A backpacker institution with some of the best-value budget rooms in the country. Sweat-caked Roraima hikers can take advantage of half-day rest and shower (40BsF per room) or shower only (5BsF) rates before taking the night bus out. Its brand new Hotel Michelle has minimally higher rates.

Posada Backpacker Tours (☎ 995-1415; www .backpacker-tours.com; Urdaneta; s/d/tr 60/80/120BsF; ▯) An outdoor restaurant (breakfast 18BsF) and internet cafe make this 10-room hotel the preferred evening hangout spot. Ask about its swank new *posada* with pool.

Hotel Lucrecia (☎ 995-1105; hotellucrecia@hotmail .com; Av Perimetral; s/d/tr 100/120/150BsF; ▯ ▯ ▯) Slightly removed from the central hub-bub, Lucrecia has 12 bright hot-water rooms arranged around a lush garden veranda. Breakfast and dinner are available upon request.

Eating

Restaurant Michelle (Urdaneta; mains 17-22BsF) Run by the manager of the two Michelle lodgings, the restaurant offers heaping plates of fairly authentic Chinese food.

Alfredo's Restaurant (Av Perimetral; pasta & pizza 22-40BsF, mains 45-70BsF; ⌚ 11am-3pm & 6-10pm Tue-Sun) Perhaps the best restaurant in town, Alfredo's has an unusually long menu, with fantastic pasta, reasonable steaks and fine pizzas from its wood-burning oven.

VENEZUELA

GETTING TO BRAZIL

Both Venezuelan and Brazilian passport formalities are done at the border itself, locally known as La Línea, 15km south of Santa Elena. The bus stops at the office. Be sure to have your passport stamped upon leaving or entering Venezuela and carry a yellow-fever card for entering Brazil. For information on entering Venezuela from Brazil, see p363.

ServeKilo Nova Opção (Av Perimetral; buffet per kg 30BsF; ☯ buffet 11am-4pm, mains 4-11pm) For over 16 years, this Brazilian eatery has replenished famished hikers with its scrumptious buffet. Vegetarian options available.

Also worth trying:

Gran Sabana Deli (Bolívar; pastries 8BsF; ☯ 6am-8pm Mon-Sat, to noon Sun) Mammoth two-person sandwiches (35BsF) make good on-the-go sustenance.

Tienda Naturalista Griselda Luna (Icabarú; ☯ 8am-noon & 3-6pm Mon-Sat) Stock up on dried fruit and vegetarian protein for the Roraima trek.

Getting There & Away
AIR
The tiny airport is 7km southwest of town, off the road to the Brazilian border. There's no public transport; taxis cost around 10BsF. Rutaca has flights on five-seater Cessnas to Ciudad Bolívar (600BsF), usually via Canaima (600BsF). The flight from Canaima offers spectacular *tepui* and winding river views.

BUS & JEEP
The bus terminal is on the Ciudad Guayana highway, about 2km east of the town's center. There are no buses – catch a taxi (8BsF). Eight buses depart daily to Ciudad Bolívar (45BsF to 60BsF, 10 to 12 hours), all stopping at Ciudad Guayana.

From Icabarú, two to three jeeps leave for El Pauji (35BsF, two to three hours) in the morning.

AMAZONAS

Venezuela's southernmost state, Amazonas, is predominantly Amazonian rainforest crisscrossed by rivers and sparsely populated by indigenous communities whose primary form of transportation is the dugout canoe

called a *bongo*. It covers 180,000 sq km, or one-fifth of the national territory, yet it's home to less than 1% of the country's population. The current indigenous population, estimated at 40,000, comprises three main groups (the Piaroa, Yanomami and Guajibo) and a number of smaller communities.

In contrast to the Brazilian Amazon, Venezuela's Amazonas state is topographically diverse, with *tepuis* as one of the most striking features. Though not as numerous as those in the Gran Sabana, the *tepuis* give the green carpet of rainforest a distinctive appearance. At the southernmost part of Amazonas, along the border with Brazil, is the Serranía la Neblina, a scarcely explored mountain range containing the highest South American peaks east of the Andes.

The best time to explore the region is from October to December, when the river level is high enough to navigate but rains have started to ease.

Getting Around
The region has almost no roads, so most transportation is by river or air. Other than a few short hops from Puerto Ayacucho, there's no regular passenger service on the rivers, which makes independent travel difficult, if not impossible. Tour operators in Puerto Ayacucho can take you just about everywhere, at a price.

PUERTO AYACUCHO
☏ 0248 / pop 64,000
Walk on the shady side of the street or you'll wilt in the heat of the riverside city. The only significant urban center in Venezuela's Amazon, Puerto Ayacucho is a languid and often rainy place with a slow tempo, frequent power outages and few tourists. Set on a colorful section of the Río Orinoco, just down from the spectacular rapids of Raudales Atures, it's the starting point for adventurous trips into the roadless state of Amazonas.

Information
Internet connections can be spotty.
Banco de Venezuela (Av Orinoco)
Banesco (Av Orinoco)
Biblionet (Biblioteca Pública, Av Río Negro) Offers 45 minutes free internet access.
CANTV Av Río Negro & Atabapo (8am-6pm Mon-Sat); Av Orinoco (7:30am-8pm daily) Telephones and the best internet access.

VENEZUELA

Colombian Consulate (☎ 521-0789; Calle Yacapana, Quinta Beatriz 5; ⏱ 7am-1pm & 3-5pm Mon-Fri)
Onidex (☎ 521-0198; Av Aguerrevere; ⏱ 8am-noon & 2-5pm Mon-Fri) Have your passport stamped here when leaving or entering Venezuela.

Sights

For a true sense of the city and its river history, get a bird's-eye view from one of its hills. **Cerro Perico** is a good place to survey the Río Orinoco and the city, and Cerro El Zamoro, commonly known as **El Mirador**, overlooks Orinoco's feisty Raudales Atures (rapids).

A fascinating display of regional indigenous culture, the **Museo Etnológico de Amazonas** (Av Río Negro; admission 1BsF; ⏱ 8:30-11:30am & 2:30-6pm Tue-Fri, 9am-noon & 3:30-6pm Sat, 9am-1pm Sun) displays personal items and model housing replicas from groups including the Piaroa, Guajibo, Ye'kwana and Yanomami.

Across from the museum, the **Mercado Indígena** (Av Río Negro) sells some indigenous crafts and lots of black velvet paintings.

Tours

Among the popular shorter tours are a three-day trip up the Río Cuao and a three-day trip up the Ríos Sipapo and Autana to the foot of Cerro Autana (1248m). Expect to pay from 250BsF to 350BsF per person per day.

The far southeastern part of Amazonas beyond La Esmeralda, basically all of Parque Nacional Parima-Tapirapeco, where the

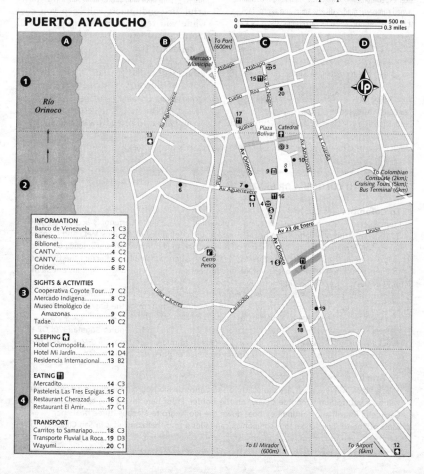

PUERTO AYACUCHO

0 — 500 m
0 — 0.3 miles

INFORMATION
Banco de Venezuela............1 C3
Banesco...............................2 C2
Biblionet.............................3 C2
CANTV................................4 C2
CANTV................................5 C1
Onidex...............................6 B2

SIGHTS & ACTIVITIES
Cooperativa Coyote Tour....7 C2
Mercado Indígena...............8 C2
Museo Etnológico de
   Amazonas.......................9 C2
Tadae...............................10 C2

SLEEPING
Hotel Cosmopolita.............11 C2
Hotel Mi Jardín..................12 D4
Residencia Internacional....13 B2

EATING
Mercadito.........................14 C3
Pastelería Las Tres Espigas..15 C1
Restaurant Cherazad.........16 C2
Restaurant El Amir............17 C1

TRANSPORT
Carritos to Samariapo........18 C3
Transporte Fluvial La Roca..19 D3
Wayumi.............................20 C1

Yanomami live, is a restricted area; you need special permits that are virtually impossible to get – some agents get around the ban by visiting Yanomami villages on the Río Siapa off Brazo Casiquiare.

Booking in advance is recommended. Puerto Ayacucho doesn't get a reliable stream of tourists, and most operators fashion individualized trips. Autana trips are more frequent.

Recommended tour operators:

Cooperativa Coyote Tour (☎ 521-4583, 0416-448-7125; coyotexpedition@cantv.net; Av Aguerrevere) In business for 20 years, its main offerings are three-day Autana and Cuao tours; also runs longer trips.

Cruising Tours (☎ 414-5036, 0416-785-5033; www.axel-expedition.com; Valle Verde Triángulo) A German-owned company; guides diverse tours and expeditions at reasonable prices and offers accommodations for tour participants.

Tadae (☎ 521-4882, 0414-486-5923; tadaevenezuela@hotmail.com; Av Río Negro) Apart from the staple Autana and Cuao tours, offers rafting on Raudales Atures.

Sleeping

Residencia Internacional (☎ 521-0242; Av Aguerrevere; d with fan/air-con 80/90BsF; ⊠) A long-time backpacker favorite, this friendly, family-operated place in a quiet residential area has a rooftop terrace and a rainbow palette of rooms around a long patio. Some kitchen use is OK.

Hotel Mi Jardín (☎ 521-4647; Av Orinoco; d 110-160BsF, tr/q 180/200BsF; ⊠ 🖵) A lovely 66-room hotel with windows that catch the breeze and look out over nearby hills. Enjoy the cooler evening air in the large open courtyard framed by bougainvillea. On-site restaurant.

Hotel Cosmopolita (☎ 521-3037; www.amazonascosmopolitahotel.com; Av Orinoco; d 180-210BsF, ste 210BsF; ⊠) A central if somewhat bland midrange option, it offers three floors of comfortable executive-style rooms with phones, TVs and fridges.

Eating

Pastelería Las Tres Espigas (Av Río Negro; pastries 3BsF; ☉ 6am-8pm Mon-Sat, to noon Sun) Four powerful air-conditioners will keep you cool while you recharge on strong coffee and morning pastries.

Restaurant El Amir (Av Orinoco; sandwiches 17BsF, mains 33-55BsF) Serving decent falafels, this local favorite has plastic tables and chairs and a reliably surly waitress.

Restaurant Cherazad (cnr Avs Aguerrevere & Río Negro; mains 25-40BsF) One of the best restaurants in town, Cherazad provides a sizable choice of pasta, steaks and fish, plus Middle Eastern dishes and pizza (from 10BsF).

GETTING TO COLOMBIA OR BRAZIL

To Colombia

From Puerto Ayacucho, the nearest large Colombian town, Puerto Carreño, is accessible via El Burro, a Venezuelan village 90km to the north, at the confluence of the Ríos Meta and Orinoco. Take a San Fernando–bound bus and get off at the wharf in El Burro, where traffic loads on ferries to cross the Río Orinoco north to Puerto Páez. Catch a *lancha* (small boat) across the Río Meta to Puerto Carreño (10BsF); boats run regularly until about 6pm. Remember to get an exit stamp in your passport at Onidex in Puerto Ayacucho before setting off.

In the small town of Puerto Carreño, go to the DAS office (Colombian immigration), for an entry stamp in your passport. The office is on Av Orinoco in front of the Casa de la Cultura. A number of shops will change bolívares to pesos.

Satena (www.satena.com) has two flights per week from Puerto Carreño to Bogotá (370COP to 470COP). Buses go only in the dry season, roughly from mid-December to mid-March, but they are not recommended because of the strong presence of guerrillas in the region.

To Brazil

Take a flight from Puerto Ayacucho south to San Carlos de Río Negro, from where irregular boats will take you to San Simón de Cocuy, on the border. From here take a bus to São Gabriel da Cachoeira (Brazil) and continue by boat down the Río Negro to Manaus (three boats per week). Most of Puerto Ayacucho's tour companies can tailor a tour that concludes in San Carlos de Río Negro, or even escort you to São Gabriel.

For an inexpensive meal or a quick empanada fix, duck into the **Mercadito** (Av Orinoco), or try one of the basic *criollo* eateries nearby on Av Amazonas.

Getting There & Away

AIR

At the airport, 6km southeast of town, Conviasa flies once daily to Caracas (275BsF) Sunday through Friday. One small local carrier, **Wayumi** (☎ 521-0635; Roa), operates scheduled and charter flights within Amazonas to a few smaller destinations.

BOAT

Transporte Fluvial La Roca (☎ 809-1595; Pasaje Orinoco, Centro Comercial Rapagna, Av Orinoco) has daily service to San Fernando de Atabapo (65BsF to 75BsF, 2½ hours).

BUS

The small bus terminal is 6km east of the center, on the outskirts of town. City buses go there from Av 23 de Enero, but are so infrequent citywide that taxis (fixed at 5BsF to anywhere in town) are the standard form of transportation. *Busetas* to Ciudad Bolívar (42BsF to 50BsF, 10½ to 12 hours) depart regularly throughout the day. Until 3pm, eight buses depart daily to San Fernando de Apure (40BsF, seven hours), from where you can get buses to Caracas, Maracay, Valencia, Barinas and San Cristóbal. *Carritos* (15BsF, 1¼ hours) and minibuses (8BsF) to Samariapo depart from Panadería Barahona on Av Orinoco.

VENEZUELA DIRECTORY

ACCOMMODATIONS

Hotels are not hard to come by in Venezuela and there are budget and midrange options in most towns (though Caracas has few quality budget accommodations). Popular tourist areas can become quite full in high season (July and August) and on major holidays (Christmas, Carnaval and Semana Santa), when beach towns will rarely have vacancies. Campgrounds are rare, though you can rough it in the countryside. Camping on the beach is popular, but be cautious and don't leave your tent unattended. Venezuela has almost no hostels. Be aware that urban budget hotels often double as hourly-rates love motels. However, even the cheapest places still provide towels and soap.

A good choice of accommodation is the *posada*, a small, family-run guesthouse. They usually have more character than hotels and offer more personalized attention. Most are budget places but there are some midrange ones and a few top-end *posadas* as well.

Another kind of countryside lodging is *campamentos* (literally 'camps'), which exist even in very remote areas. Not to be confused with campgrounds, this can be anything from a rustic shelter with a few hammocks to a posh country lodge with a swimming pool and its own airstrip. More commonly, it will be a collection of *cabañas* (cabins) plus a restaurant. *Campamentos* provide accommodation, food and usually tours, sometimes selling these services as all-inclusive packages.

As in most developing countries, prices are not set in stone and can change due to the day of the week or the mood of the person at the front desk. Never count on being able to use a credit card – even if they say that they accept plastic. Many *posadas,* especially those run by expatriates, will accept money transfers in dollars or euros.

While many accommodations list email addresses or websites, the reality is that management may not respond to queries or reservation requests in a timely manner (if at all). If possible, calling is always a better bet.

ACTIVITIES

Venezuela has many outdoor activities ranging from walking and bird-watching to adrenaline pumping paragliding and kitesurfing. Although all regions of the country have something to offer, Mérida is Venezuela's adventure sports capital.

Los Llanos is one of the best regions to see wild animals, including caimans, capybaras, anacondas, anteaters and birds. Wildlife safaris are primarily organized from Mérida (p945). For bird-watching, also consider Parque Nacional Henri Pittier.

Many of Venezuela's 40-odd national parks provide a choice of walks ranging from easy, well-signposted trails to wild jungle paths. Parque Nacional El Ávila near Caracas has some of the best easy walking trails, while the Mérida surrounds (p947) offer fabulous opportunities for high-mountain trekking. One of the most adventurous and fascinating treks is to the top of Roraima (p969).

The region around Mérida is excellent for mountain biking, and tour operators in the city organize biking trips.

Mérida is the best place for paragliding. Novices can go on a tandem flight while the more daring can take a course to learn solo flight.

Rafting trips are run on some Andean rivers (arranged in Mérida); in the Parque Nacional Mochima (from Mochima; p953), and over Orinoco rapids (from Puerto Ayacucho; p973). The Mérida region is also the home of canyoning (climbing, rappelling and hiking down a river canyon).

Venezuela has excellent snorkeling and scuba diving around the offshore archipelagos at Los Roques (p934). There's also some good snorkeling and diving around the islands closer to the mainland, including in Parque Nacional Mochima (p953) and Parque Nacional Morrocoy (p938).

Venezuela has some windsurfing and kitesurfing areas of international reputation, including Adícora and El Yaque. You can also do both at Los Roques (p934).

BOOKS

For more detailed travel information, get a copy of Lonely Planet's *Venezuela*. Of the useful local publications, *Ecotourism Guide to Venezuela* by Miro Popic is a bilingual Spanish–English guidebook focusing on ecological tourism, while *Guide to Camps, Posadas and Cabins in Venezuela* by Elizabeth Kline is a bilingual edition detailing 1200 accommodations options. Both are updated yearly.

German geographer and botanist Alexander von Humboldt describes exploring various regions of Venezuela for Volume 2 of *Personal Narratives of Travels to the Equinoctial Regions of America During the Year 1799–1804* (also abridged into the slim *Jaguars and Electric Eels*). *The Search for El Dorado* by John Hemming offers a fascinating insight into the conquest of Venezuela. Sir Arthur Conan Doyle's *The Lost World* was inspired by the Roraima *tepui*. *Venezuela: A Century of Change* by Judith Ewell provides a comprehensive 20th-century history and H Micheal Tarver and Julia Frederick's *The History of Venezuela* skims the period from Columbus' first sighting up through the Chávez presidency.

There are a dozens of books on Chávez and his 'Bolívarian Revolution,' though most sources take either a fervent pro- or anti-Chávez stance. Some of the more recent and widely sold titles are *Changing Venezuela by Taking Power* by Gregory Wilpert; *Hugo Chávez: Oil, Politics, and the Challenge to the US* by Nikolas Kozloff; and *Hugo Chávez: The Bolivarian Revolution in Venezuela* by Richard Gott and Georges Bartoli.

Serious bird-watchers may want to get *A Guide to the Birds of Venezuela* by Rodolphe Meyer de Schauensee and William H Phelps, Steven Hilty's *Birds of Venezuela* or *Birding in Venezuela* by Mary Lou Goodwin.

BUSINESS HOURS

The working day is theoretically eight hours, from 8am to noon and 2pm to 6pm Monday to Friday, but in practice many businesses work shorter hours. Shops open Monday through Friday at 9am and close at 6pm or 7pm (though laundromats open at about 7am and internet cafes may stay open later); Saturdays are usually the same, but some shops close at 1pm. Banks are open 8:30am to 3:30pm Monday through Friday. Restaurants serve from noon to 9pm or 11pm Monday through Saturday. Almost everything is closed on Sundays.

The business hours are just a guideline – don't count on them too much.

CLIMATE

Venezuela's climate features dry and wet seasons, though the tourist season runs year-round. The dry season runs roughly from December to April, while the wet season lasts the rest of the year. The dry season is more pleasant for traveling, but some sights – such as waterfalls – are more impressive in the wet season. There are many regional variations in the amount of rainfall and the length of the seasons.

For more information and climate charts, see p987.

CUSTOMS

Customs regulations don't differ much from those in other South American countries. You are allowed to bring in personal belongings and presents you intend to give to Venezuelan residents, as well as cameras, camping equipment, sports accessories, a personal computer and the like. Random searches of vehicles and buses are very common and drug penalties are stiff – don't even think about it.

DANGERS & ANNOYANCES

Venezuela is a reasonably safe place to travel. However, theft, robbery and common crime have increased over the last decade. Theft is more serious in the larger cities and urban centers than in the countryside. Caracas is, far and away, the most dangerous place in the country, and you should take care while strolling around the streets, particularly at night. Also see Dangers & Annoyances in the Caracas section, p923.

Be aware of your surroundings when withdrawing cash from an ATM at any time of the day. In our experience, police are not necessarily trustworthy (though many are), so do not blindly accept the demands of these authority figures (see also p990).

Venezuela is somewhat obsessed with identification and *cédulas* (Venezuelan ID cards) or passport numbers are often required for the most banal transactions. Always carry your passport, or you may end up explaining yourself in a police station.

Malaria and dengue fever are present in some tropical areas, and while other insect bites don't necessarily cause illness they can cause major discomfort. Overall, your biggest dangers are the standard risks of travel: sunburn, food-borne illness and traffic-related concerns.

See the Money section for an explanation of the currency situation.

DRIVER'S LICENSE

You can use any type of driver's license to operate a car in Venezuela. However, you need a superhuman level of patience and Formula 1 driving skills to make your way around Caracas in a car, as traffic lights are routinely ignored throughout the country, and police are known to pull over motorists for nonexistent infractions in an attempt to collect bribes.

ELECTRICITY

Venezuela operates on 110V at 60 Hz. The country uses US-type plugs.

EMBASSIES & CONSULATES

The following embassies are in Caracas, unless otherwise noted. If you can't find your home embassy, check a Caracas phone directory, which will include a full list.

Brazil (Map pp928-9; ☎ 0212-261-5505; www .embajadabrasil.org.ve; Centro Gerencial Mohedano, cnr Avs Los Chaguaramos & Mohedano, La Castellana, Caracas);

Santa Elena de Uairén (off Map p970; ☎ 0289-995-1256; Edificio Galeno, Los Castanos, Urbanización Roraima del Casco Central); Puerto Ordaz (☎ 0286-961-2995; Edificio Eli-Alti, Alta Vista)

Canada (Map pp928-9; ☎ 0212-600-3000; www .canadainternational.gc.ca/venezuela; cnr Avs Francisco de Miranda & Sur Altamira, Altamira, Caracas)

Colombia (Map p924; ☎ 0212-951-3631; Edificio Consulado General de Colombia, Guaicaipuro, El Rosal, Caracas); Maracaibo (☎ 0261-791-6891; Av El Milagro, Calle 72A No 72-98, Urbanización La Virginia); Puerto Ayacucho (off Map p973 ; ☎ 0248-521-0789; Yapacana off Av Rómulo Gallegos); Mérida (off Map p944; ☎ 0274-262-3105; cnr Av 2 Lora & Calle 42)

France (Map pp928-9; ☎ 0212-909-6500; www .francia.org.ve; Edificio Embajada de Francia, cnr Madrid & Av La Trinidad, Las Mercedes, Caracas)

Germany (Map pp928-9; ☎ 0212-219-2500; www .caracas.diplo.de; Torre La Castellana, Av Principal de la Castellana, La Castellana, Caracas)

Guyana (off Map pp928-9; ☎ 0212-977-1158; Quinta Roraima, Av El Paseo, Prados del Este, Caracas)

Ireland (Map pp928-9; ☎ 0212- 951-3645; irlconven @cantv.net; Torre Clement, Av Venezuela, 2nd fl, El Rosal, Caracas)

Italy (Map pp928-9; ☎ 0212-952-7311; www .ambcaracas.esteri.it; Edificio Atrium, Calle Sorocaima, El Rosal, Caracas)

Japan (Map pp928-9; ☎ 0212-261-8333; www .ve.emb-japan.go.jp; Edificio Bancaracas, Plaza La Castellana, La Castellana, Caracas)

Netherlands (Map pp928-9; ☎ 0212-276-9300; www.mfa.nl/car; Edificio San Juan, cnr 2a Transversal & Av San Juan Bosco, Altamira, Caracas)

Spain (Map pp928-9; ☎ 0212-263-2855; www.maec .es/embajadas/caracas; Quinta Marmolejo, Av Mohedano)

Switzerland (Map pp928-9; ☎ 0212-267-9585; www.eda.admin.ch/caracas; Centro Letonia, Torre Ing-Bank, Av Eugenio Mendoza y San Felipe, La Castellana)

Trinidad & Tobago (Map pp928-9; ☎ 0212-261-3748; embassytt@cantv.net; Quinta Poshika, 3a Av btwn 6a & 7a Transversal, Altamira, Caracas)

UK (Map pp928-9; ☎ 0212-263-8411; www.ukin venezuela.fco.gov.uk; Torre La Castellana, Av Principal de la Castellana, La Castellana, Caracas)

USA (off Map pp928-9; ☎ 0212-975-6411; http://caracas.usembassy.gov; cnr Calles F & Suapure, Urbanización Colinas del Valle Arriba, Caracas)

FESTIVALS & EVENTS

Given the strong Catholic character of Venezuela, many holidays follow the church calendar – Christmas, Carnaval, Easter and Corpus Christi are celebrated all over the country. Carnaval is particularly big in El

Callao. The religious calendar is dotted with saints' days, and every village and town has its own patron saint and will hold a celebration on that day.

One of Venezuela's most colorful events is the **Diablos Danzantes** (see boxed text, p926). Held on Corpus Christi, the ceremony consists of a spectacular parade and the dance of devils, performed by dancers in elaborate masks and costumes.

FOOD & DRINK

On the whole, dining options in Venezuela are good and relatively inexpensive. Various local dishes, international cuisine and an array of snacks and fast foods are all available. Budget travelers should look for restaurants that offer a *menú del día* or *menú ejecutivo*, a set meal consisting of soup and a main course. It will cost roughly 20BsF to 30BsF (a little more in Caracas), which is cheaper than any à la carte dish. A budget alternative can be roasted chicken, usually called *pollo en brasa*. Filling local choices include *pabellón criollo*, *arepas*, *cachapas* and empanadas.

For breakfast, you can visit any of the ubiquitous *panaderías* (bakeries), which sell sandwiches, pastries and yogurt, plus delicious espresso.

Venezuela is very much a meat-eating country. Vegetarian restaurants exist in most larger cities and they usually sell dried *carne de soya* (textured vegetable protein) and other items for self-catering. Meatless *arepas* are a reliable option, and Chinese, Middle Eastern and Italian eateries often have a veggie dish. For bus journeys with limited food stops, non-meat-eaters should pack sandwiches.

In almost every dining or drinking establishment, a 10% service charge will automatically be added to the bill. It's customary to leave a small tip at fancier places.

Venezuelan Cuisine

This list includes some typical Venezuelan dishes and a few international foods that have different names in Venezuelan Spanish.

arepa (a·*re*·pa) – small, grilled corn pancake stuffed with a variety of fillings
cachapa (ka·*cha*·pa) – larger, flat corn pancake, served with cheese and/or ham
cachito (ka·*chee*·to) – croissant filled with chopped ham and served hot
cambur (kam·*boor*) – banana
carabina (ka·ra·*bee*·na) – Mérida version of *hallaca*
caraota (ka·ra·*o*·ta) – black bean
casabe (ka·*sa*·be) – huge, flat bread made from yucca; a staple in indigenous communities
empanada (em·pa·*na*·da) – deep-fried cornmeal turnover stuffed with various fillings
guasacaca (gwa·sa·*ka*·ka) – a green sauce made of peppers, onions and seasoning
hallaca (a·*ya*·ka) – maize dough with chopped meat and vegetables, wrapped in banana leaves and steamed; like a Mexican tamale
lau lau (low low) – catfish
lechosa (le·*cho*·sa) – papaya
muchacho (moo·*cha*·cho) – hearty roast-beef dish
pabellón criollo (pa·be·*yon* cree·*o*·yo) – shredded beef, rice, black beans, cheese and fried plantain; Venezuela's national dish
papelón (pa·pe·*lon*) – crude brown sugar; also drink flavoring
parchita (par·*chee*·ta) – passion fruit
parrilla (pa·*ree*·ya) – mixed grill
pasapalos (pa·sa·*pa*·los) – hors d'oeuvres, small snacks, finger food
patilla (pa·*tee*·ya) – watermelon
quesillo (ke·*see*·yo) – caramel custard
tequeño (te·*ke*·nyo) – cheese strips wrapped in pastry and deep fried
teta (*te*·ta) – iced fruit juice in plastic wrap, consumed by sucking

Drinks

Venezuela has good, strong espresso coffee at every turn. Ask for *café negro* if you want it black; *café marrón* if you prefer half coffee, half milk; or *café con leche* if you like milkier coffee.

A staggering variety of fruit juices is available in restaurants, cafes and even in some fruit stores. Juices come as *batidos* (pure or cut with water) or as *merengadas* (made with milk).

The number-one alcoholic drink is *cerveza* (beer), particularly Polar and Solera (also owned by Polar). Beer is sold everywhere in cans or tiny bottles at close to freezing temperature. Among spirits, *ron* (rum) and whiskey lead the pack in popularity.

GAY & LESBIAN TRAVELERS

Homosexuality isn't illegal in Venezuela, but it is suppressed and frowned upon by the overwhelmingly Catholic society. Homosexual men, in particular, should be very discreet in smaller towns and rural areas. At the same time, pockets of tolerance do exist. Caracas has the largest gay and lesbian community and the most open gay life, including an annual gay pride festival in June that draws tens of thousands.

When looking for gay-oriented venues, the code phrase to watch out for is *en ambiente*. Some club listings can be found at www.rumbacaracas.com.

HEALTH

Venezuela has a wide array of pharmacies, clinics and hospitals. Good medical care is available in Caracas, but may be difficult to find in rural areas. Public hospitals and clinics are free, but the quality of medical care is better in private facilities. If you need hospital treatment in Venezuela, by far the best facilities are in Caracas. Smaller issues can be dealt with directly in pharmacies, as they are allowed to give injections and administer a wide range of medicines.

Tap water is generally fine for brushing your teeth, but is not recommended for consumption. Be cautious of street snacks, sun overexposure and insect bites, and be doubly careful when crossing city streets.

HOLIDAYS

Keep in mind that Venezuelans usually take holidays over Christmas, Carnaval (several days prior to Ash Wednesday), Semana Santa (the week before Easter Sunday) and during July and August. In these periods, you'll have to plan ahead as it can be tricky to find a place to stay in more popular destinations. The upside is that they really come alive with holiday merrymakers.

Some official public holidays:
New Year's Day January 1
Carnaval Monday and Tuesday prior to Ash Wednesday, February/March
Easter Maundy Thursday and Good Friday, March/April
Declaration of Independence April 19
Labor Day May 1
Battle of Carabobo June 24
Independence Day July 5
Bolívar's Birthday July 24
Discovery of America October 12
Christmas Day December 25

INTERNET ACCESS

All cities and most towns have cybercafes, and wi-fi has become common in *posadas* and larger hotels. An hour of internet access costs between 2BsF and 3BsF. Mérida and Caracas have the most widespread number of cybercafes and some of the best prices. CANTV and Movistar outlets have fast, inexpensive computers. The government **Infocentro** (www.infocentro.gob.ve) program offers free 30-minute blocks at locations nationwide.

Most websites listed in this chapter are in Spanish only; they are included for the benefit of Spanish speakers.

INTERNET RESOURCES

Some useful websites for information on Venezuela:
Online Newspapers (www.onlinenewspapers.com/venezuel.htm) Links to at least 50 Venezuelan online newspapers.
Rumba Venezuela (www.rumbavenezuela.com) Club listings for the major cities.
University of Texas (http://lanic.utexas.edu/la/venezuela) Impressive directory of Venezuelan websites from the Latin American Network Information Center.
Venezuela Analysis (www.venezuelanalysis.com) Website containing articles analyzing the current political and economic issues.
Venezuela Tuya (www.venezuelatuya.com) A comprehensive tourism portal for Venezuelan tourism.

LEGAL MATTERS

Venezuela police are to be treated with respect, but with a healthy dose of caution. Cases of police corruption, abuse of power and use of undue force are unfortunately common.

Penalties for trafficking, possessing and using illegal drugs are some of the heaviest in all of Latin America.

MAPS

The best general map of Venezuela is published by **International Travel Maps** (www.itmb.com), but it's not generally available in the country. Within Venezuela, folded road maps of the country are produced by several local publishers and are available in bookstores, limited tourism offices and some hotels and stores that cater to foreign visitors.

MEDIA

All major cities have daily newspapers. The two leading Caracas papers, *El Universal* (www.eluniversal.com) and *El Nacional* (www.el-nacional.com), have countrywide distribution. Both have reasonable coverage of national and international affairs, sports, economics and culture. The *Daily Journal* (www.thedailyjournalonline.com) is the main English-language newspaper published in Venezuela. It's available at major newsstands and select bookshops in Caracas.

A number of private and government-run TV stations operate out of Caracas and reach most of the country.

MONEY

ATMs

Cajeros automáticos (ATMs) are the easiest way of getting cash. ATMs can be found at most major banks, including Banco de Venezuela, Banco Mercantil, Banco Provincial and Banesco. ATMs are normally open 24 hours. Always have a backup, as some machines will eat cards.

Bargaining

As in most Latin American countries, bargaining in Venezuela is part of everyday life. Since part of the economy is informal, quasilegal or uncontrolled, prices for some goods and services (including products purchased at the market), taxi fares and rates in hotels are to some extent negotiable.

Black Market

There is a thriving black market for American dollars – and euros, to a lesser extent – and many people will ask to change currency in airports, bus stations or the center of towns.

If you do exchange money, talk to in-the-know locals or check websites like www.dollar.nu and www.venezuelafx.blogspot.com for current exchange rates.

Credit Cards

Visa and MasterCard are the most useful credit cards in Venezuela, though it's important to note that credit card transactions will always be more costly because they are calculated using the official exchange rate. Cards are accepted as a means of payment for goods and services (though many tour operators may refuse payment by credit card or charge 10% more for the service). They are also useful for taking cash advances from banks or ATMs. Make sure you know the number to call if you lose your credit card, and be quick to cancel it if it's lost or stolen, as credit card fraud is not uncommon. Also remember that just because an establishment claims that it takes credit cards it doesn't mean that its machine functions.

Cash

In 2008 Venezuela lopped three zeros off its currency and issued new money called 'bolívares fuertes,' abbreviated to BsF. There are now coins of 1, 5, 10, 12½ and 50 *céntimos* and 1BsF, and paper notes of 2, 5, 10, 20, 50 and 100.

However, many people cling to the old ways and will still quote prices in *miles* (thousands). You may occasionally encounter the old currency (50-, 100- and 500-bolívar coins, and 1000, 2000, 5000 and 10,000 bolívar notes) which is still good. A 100-bolívar coin and 10 *céntimo* coin (and the 500-bolívar and 50 *céntimo*) are worth the same amount; the new coins have the denominations in large type. There's a helpful conversion chart with pictures at www.reconversionbcv.org.ve.

Unless you're near the border, it's impossible to get Venezuelan currency before you enter the country.

Exchanging Money

US dollars, euros and American Express traveler's checks are the most popular and

---

MONEY WARNING!

Currency controls peg the bolívar fuerte to the US dollar at an artificially high rate, resulting in a two-tier market for changing money within Venezuela. The official exchange rate is fixed at 2.15BsF per dollar. When changing traveler's checks, using credit cards or exchanging money at a bank or *casa de cambio*, you will always receive this rate.

An active black market (also called the *dólar paralelo*, or parallel dollar) buys and sells the more stable dollars and euros, with rates boomeranging between 3BsF to 7BsF per dollar.

Though they don't advertise it, many established *posadas* and tour operators will accept payment (or sometimes give you cash at the black-market rate) through online money transfers to international bank accounts when taking bookings from abroad.

Venezuela has one of the highest rates of inflation in South America and prices are especially vulnerable to change. Prices in this chapter should be used as guidelines only.

accepted in Venezuela. They can be exchanged in some banks, but very few banks handle foreign-exchange transactions.

The *casas de cambio* (authorized money-exchange offices) are more likely to exchange your money, but may pay less and charge higher commission. The best-known *casa de cambio* is Italcambio, which has offices in most major cities and exchanges both cash and traveler's checks. Note that *casas de cambio* don't buy back Venezuelan money. The ubiquitous black market has the best rates for exchanging currencies, but is still illegal.

Official exchange rates at press time included the following:

EXCHANGE RATES

Country	Unit	BsF
Australia	A$1	1.57
Canada	C$1	1.81
euro zone	€1	2.85
Japan	¥1	.02
UK	UK£1	3.20
USA	US$1	2.15

Tipping
Most restaurants include a 10% service charge. A small tip of 5% to 10% beyond the service charge is standard in a nicer restaurant, but not required. Taxi drivers are not usually tipped unless they help carry bags. Tipping of hotel employees, dive masters, guides and so on is left to your discretion. It is rarely required but always appreciated. The simple act of buying a drink for a boat driver or cook can go a long way.

Traveler's Checks
Casas de cambio (such as Italcambio) are often the only place that will accept traveler's checks and will charge a commission of about 3% or more. Some tour operators will accept traveler's checks as payment.

POST
Ipostel (www.ipostel.gov.ve), the postal service, has post offices throughout the country. Some are in combined government services offices called Puntos de Gestión Centralizada (Central Administration Offices). The usual opening hours are 8:30am to 11:30am and 1:30pm to 5pm Monday to Friday, with regional variations. Offices in the main cities may open longer hours and on Saturday. Airmailing a letter up to 20g costs 3BsF to anywhere in the Americas or Europe, but the service is extremely unreliable and slow. Mail can take up to a month to arrive, if it arrives at all. If you are mailing something important or time-sensitive, use a reliable international express mail carrier.

RESPONSIBLE TRAVEL
Visiting a different culture can pose a great deal of challenges and you'll need to remind yourself how important it is to minimize the negative impact of your visit. Be sensitive to the needs and beliefs of the local people, and resist trying to impose your standards and way of life.

Resist the temptation to stuff your pockets with crystals, jasper or jade from the waterfalls and creeks of the Gran Sabana. Never touch coral or take home seashells found while snorkeling or diving. Refrain from purchasing articles made from tropical shells, tortoises or corals, no matter how beautiful. Don't even dream of the belt you could make from the caiman leather you saw in the market and stay away from the arts and crafts with the bits of jaguar or anaconda skin (the story about how it was killed to defend a child is an old con). The purchasing of drugs and partaking in sexual tourism cause rippling societal damage that continues long after you have returned home.

Encourage and use truly ecological tourist companies and projects. Many tour operators use the 'eco' label as a sales strategy. Find out what they do for the protection of the environment, how they minimize impact and how they contribute to local communities.

STUDYING
Venezuela has a number of language schools in most big cities. You can also find an independent teacher and arrange individual classes. Mérida is a popular place to study Spanish as it is an attractive, affordable city with a major university population (see p945).

TELEPHONE
Call centers (owned by Movistar, CANTV or independents known as *centros de comunicaciones*) are the best option for international calls. In large cities, these centers are everywhere and are normally open from about 7am to 9pm daily.

During the day entrepreneurs set up small tables at street corners and bus terminals with a few cell phones, and they charge by the minute for calls. For domestic calls, this can be more convenient (but usually noisier) than seeking out a call center, and you can also send text messages.

Bright blue CANTV public phones are everywhere, though most of them don't work. Phone cards for these phones come in a few different values and can be purchased at many stores and kiosks.

Those who plan to stay longer in Venezuela may opt to purchase a cell phone or buy a local SIM card for their own handset. The malls all have numerous competing cell-phone offices. The less expensive services generally have poorer reception, especially in areas outside of Caracas. Movistar is the major operator, followed by Movilnet and Digitel. Venezuela has one of the highest cell-phone-per-capita ratios in Latin America.

All phone numbers in the country are seven digits and area codes are three digits. Area codes are listed under the destination headings throughout this guide. The country code for Venezuela is ☎ 58. To call Venezuela from abroad, dial the international access code of the country you're calling from, Venezuela's code (☎ 58), the area code (drop the initial 0) and the local phone number. To call internationally from Venezuela, dial the international access code (00), then the country code, area code and local number.

TOILETS

Since there are no self-contained public toilets in Venezuela, use the toilets of establishments such as restaurants, hotels, museums, shopping malls and bus terminals. Don't rely on a public bathroom to have toilet paper and remember to always throw the used paper into the wastebasket provided.

The most common word for toilet is *baño*. Men's toilets will usually bear a label reading *señores* or *caballeros*, whereas women's toilets will be marked *señoras* or *damas*.

TOURIST INFORMATION

Inatur (Instituto Autónomo de Turismo de Aragua; www .inatur.gov.ve) is the Caracas-based government agency that promotes tourism and provides tourist information; it has offices at Maiquetía airport (p923). Outside the capital, tourist information is handled by regional tourist bodies. Some are better than others, but on the whole they lack city maps and brochures, and the staff members rarely speak English.

TOURS

Independent travelers who have never taken an organized tour in their lives will find themselves signing up with a group in Venezuela. As vast areas of the country are virtually inaccessible by public transport (eg the Orinoco Delta or Amazon Basin) or because a solitary visit to scattered sights in a large territory (eg the Gran Sabana) may be inconvenient, time-consuming and expensive, tours are a standard option in Venezuelan travel.

Although under some circumstances it makes sense to prebook tours from Caracas (eg when stringing together various tours in a short period of time), it is most cost-effective to arrange a tour from the regional center closest to the area you are going to visit.

TRAVELERS WITH DISABILITIES

Venezuela offers very little to people with disabilities. Wheelchair ramps are available only at a few upmarket hotels and restaurants, curb cuts are a rare afterthought, and public transportation will be a challenge for any person with mobility limitations. Hardly any office, museum or bank provides special facilities for persons with disabilities, and wheelchair-accessible toilets are virtually nonexistent.

VISAS

Nationals of the US, Canada, Australia, New Zealand, Japan, the UK and most of Western and Scandinavian Europe do not need a visa to enter Venezuela; a free tourist card *(tarjeta de ingreso)* is all that is required. The card is normally valid for 90 days (unless immigration officers note a shorter period) and can be extended. Airlines flying into Venezuela provide these cards to passengers while on the plane. Overland visitors bearing passports of the countries listed above can obtain the card from the immigration official at the border crossing.

On entering Venezuela, your passport and tourist card will be stamped (make sure this happens) by Oficina Nacional de Identificación y Extranjería (Onidex) border officials. Keep the copy of the tourist card while traveling in Venezuela (you may be asked for it during passport controls) and return it to immigration officials when leaving the country – although not all are interested in collecting the cards.

Visa and tourist-card extensions are handled by the office of Onidex in Caracas (p919). Check lonelyplanet.com and its links for up-to-date visa information.

VOLUNTEERING

It is difficult to find volunteer opportunities from outside the country, partially because many organizations don't respond to queries. The government literacy program, **Mission Robinson** (www.misionrobinson.me.gob.ve), is one option for Spanish-speakers.

WOMEN TRAVELERS

Like most of Latin America, Venezuela is very much a man's country. Women travelers will attract more curiosity, attention and advances from local men, who will quickly pick you out in a crowd and are not shy to show their admiration through whistles, endearments and flirtatious comments. These advances are usually lighthearted (no one got the memo that 'hey, baby' isn't really a desirable English greeting), though they can be very rude.

The best way to deal with unwanted attention is simply to ignore it. Dressing modestly will make you less conspicuous to the local piranhas. Although Venezuelan women wear revealing clothes, they're a lot more aware of the culture and the safety of their surroundings.

Women will constantly be asked about their marital status and whether they have children.

WORKING

Travelers looking for a paid job in Venezuela will almost always be disappointed. The economy is just not strong enough to take on foreigners for casual jobs. Qualified English teachers have the best chance of getting a job, yet it's still hard to arrange work. Try English-teaching institutions such as the **British Council** (Map p924; ☎ 0212-952-9965; www.britishcouncil.org; Torre Credicard, Av Principal de El Bosque, 3rd fl, Chacaíto, Caracas), private-language schools or linguistic departments at universities. To work legally in Venezuela, a work visa is mandatory.

South America Directory

CONTENTS

This directory provides general information on South America, from activities and books to toilets and telephones. Specific information for each country is listed in the Directory sections at the end of each country chapter.

ACCOMMODATIONS

Throughout the book's Sleeping sections, we list accommodations in order of price, with the cheapest listed first. For those nights when you need a break from shared showers and thin mattresses, we've also included a few midrange options as well as a few splurges for a real break from the long-haul grind.

Accommodation costs vary from country to country, with Andean countries (especially Bolivia) being the cheapest (from around US$5 per night) and Chile, Brazil and the Guianas the costliest (upwards of US$30).

Some excellent online resources can help you find a cheap sleep, including **CouchSurfing** (www.couchsurfing.com) and **Hostel World** (www.hostelworld.com).

Camping

Camping is an obvious choice in parks and reserves and a useful budget option in pricier countries such as Chile. In the Andean countries (Bolivia, Ecuador and Peru), there are few organized campgrounds. In Argentina, Chile, Uruguay and parts of Brazil, however, camping holidays have long been popular.

Bring all your own gear. While camping gear is available in large cities and in trekking and activities hubs, it's expensive and choices are usually minimal. Camping gear can be rented in areas with substantial camping and trekking action (eg the Lake District, Mendoza and Huaraz), but quality is sometimes dubious.

An alternative to tent camping is staying in *refugios* (simple structures within parks and reserves), where a basic bunk and kitchen access are usually provided. For climbers, most summit attempts involve staying in a *refugio*.

Hostels

Albergues (hostels) have become increasingly popular throughout South America and, as throughout the world, are great places to socialize with other travelers. You'll rarely find an official *albergue juvenil* (youth hostel); most hostels accept all ages and are not affiliated with Hostelling International (HI).

Hotels

When it comes to hotels, both terminology and criteria vary. The costliest in the genre are *hoteles* (hotels) proper. A step down in price are *hostales* (small hotels or, in Peru, guesthouses). The cheapest places are *hospedajes, casas de huéspedes, residenciales, alojamientos* and *pensiones*. A room in these places includes a bed with (hopefully) clean sheets and a blanket, maybe a table and chair and sometimes a fan. Showers and toilets are generally shared, and there may not be hot water. Cleanliness varies widely, but many places are remarkably tidy. In some areas, especially southern Chile, the cheapest places may be *casas familiares*, family houses whose hospitality makes them excellent value.

In Brazil, Argentina and some other places, prices often include breakfast, the quality of which is usually directly related to the room price.

Hot-water supplies are often erratic, or may be available only at certain hours of the day. It's something to ask about (and consider paying extra for), especially in the highlands and far south, where it gets cold.

When showering, beware the electric shower head, an innocent looking unit that heats cold water with an electric element. Don't touch the shower head or anything metal when the water is on, or you may get shocked – never strong enough to throw you across the room, but hardly pleasant.

In Sleeping sections throughout this book, dormitory prices are for rooms with shared bathrooms, while room prices include private bathrooms, unless otherwise noted.

ACTIVITIES

Whether you take to the jungle, the mountain or the ocean blue, opportunities for serious adventure are virtually boundless in South America.

Cycling

Pedaling in South America can prove an arduous undertaking, but the rewards are beyond anything the bus-bound can imagine. You can cycle the 'World's Most Dangerous Road' (p182), scream down the flanks of an Ecuadorian volcano and dodge sheep herds in Patagonia. No matter where you end up

riding, bring everything from home as equipment is hard to find outside major cities, and even then it can be painfully expensive.

If you're not bringing your bike, you'll find opportunities to rent for a day or join a mountain-biking tour. Online, check out **South American Bicycle Touring Links** (www.trans amazon.de/links) for a long list of touring links. The **Warm Showers List** (www.warmshowers.org) is a list of cyclists around the world who offer long-haulers a free place to crash.

Diving

Major destinations for divers are the Caribbean coast of Colombia (particularly Taganga) and Venezuela, islands such as Providencia (a Colombian island that is actually nearer to Nicaragua), the Galápagos and Brazil's Fernando de Noronha (p338).

Hiking & Trekking

South America is a brilliant hiking and trekking destination. Walking in the Andean countries is not limited to the national parks: because the network of dirt roads is so extensive, you can pretty much walk anywhere and, with the region's indigenous population often doing the same, you won't be alone.

The Andean countries are famous for their old Inca roads, which are ready-made for scenic excursions. The overtrodden, four-day tramp along the Inca Trail (p828) to Machu Picchu is, of course, the classic, but alternative routes are more highly recommended because they are cheaper, less touristed, more scenic and less destructive. See p832 for some alternatives. There are other treks along Inca trails as well, including Ecuador's lesser-known Inca trail to Ingapirca and numerous trails along ancient Inca routes through Bolivia's Cordilleras (p191) to the Yungas.

The national parks of southern South America, including Chile's Torres del Paine (p484), those within the Argentine Lake District, and even Argentina's storm-pounded but spectacular Fitz Roy range (p144), are superb and blessed with excellent trail infrastructure and accessibility. And for getting well off the beaten path, Northern Patagonia (p469) in Chile has some excellent treks.

Lesser-known mountain ranges, such as Colombia's Sierra Nevada de Santa Marta (principally to Ciudad Perdida) and Venezuela's Sierra Nevada de Mérida, also have great potential. The two- to three-day hike to the top of Venezuela's Roraima is one of the continent's most unforgettable experiences.

When trekking in the Andes, especially the high parks and regions of Bolivia, Ecuador and Peru, altitude sickness is a very real danger; for more information, see p1016. Elevations in the southern Andes are much lower. Most capital cities have an Instituto Geográfico Militar, which is usually the best place for official topographical maps.

Mountaineering

On a continent with one of the world's greatest mountain ranges, climbing opportunities are almost unlimited. Ecuador's volcanoes, the high peaks of Peru's Cordillera Blanca (p846) and Cordillera Huayhuash, Bolivia's Cordillera Real and Argentina's Aconcagua (the western hemisphere's highest peak; p122) all offer outstanding mountaineering opportunities. Despite its relatively low elevation, Argentina's Fitz Roy range (p144) – home to Cerro Torre, one of the world's most challenging peaks – chalks in as one of the world's top five climbing destinations.

River Rafting

Chile churns with good white water: the Maipó (p400), Trancura (p448) and Futaleufú (p470) rivers are all world-class. River running is also possible on the scenic Río Urubamba (p816) and other rivers near Cuzco, the Río Cañete (p790) south of Lima, and in the canyon country around Arequipa (p802), in Peru. In Argentina, several rivers around Bariloche and Mendoza are worth getting wet in. Baños and especially Tena in Ecuador are both rafting hubs.

Skiing & Snowboarding

South America's most important downhill ski areas are in Chile and Argentina – see those chapters for more details. The season is roughly June to September.

Surfing

Brazil is South America's best-known surfing destination, with great breaks near Rio and in the Southeast, and sprinkled all along the coast from Santa Catarina to São Luís. June to August is the best season. You'll find good waves on the northern coast of Peru (but you'll need a wet-suit), on Chile's central and northern coasts, Ecuador, Uruguay and Venezuela. For more far-flung possibilities there's the Galápagos Islands and Rapa Nui (Easter Island).

For detailed information, get a copy of the *Surf Report* from **Surfer Publications** (www.surfermag.com). It has individual reports on most parts of the South American coast. On the web, check out **Wannasurf** (www.wannasurf.com). For forecasts, subscribe to **Surfline** (www.surfline.com).

Wind Sports

Windsurfing and kitesurfing are becoming more popular. Adícora and Isla de Margarita in Venezuela, San Andrés in Colombia and numerous places along Brazil's northeast coast – especially Jericoacoara and Canoa Quebrada – are outstanding kitesurfing and windsurfing destinations. In Argentina, San Juan province's Cuesta del Viento reservoir (ask about it at the San Juan tourist office, p123) is one of the best wind-sport destinations in the world.

Paragliding and hang-gliding also have their followers. Top destinations include Iquique (Chile), Mérida (Venezuela) and Medellín (Colombia) and you can even fly from urban locations like Miraflores in Lima (p781) and Pedra Bonita in Rio de Janeiro (p268).

BOOKS

To understand the roots of Bolivarism (indeed, the book was presented by Hugo Chávez to US President Barack Obama in 2009), read *Open Veins of Latin America*. Written by the renowned Uruguayan writer Eduardo Galeano, it is a classic and eloquent polemic on the continent's cultural, social and political struggles.

Tropical Nature, by Adrian Forsyth and Ken Miyata, is a wonderfully readable (and occasionally hilarious) introduction to neotropical rainforest ecology. You can dive deeper into tropical ecosystems with John Kricher's friendly *A Neotropical Companion*.

An engaging combination of travelogue and botanical guide, *Tales of a Shaman's Apprentice* is the wonderful story of Mark Plotkin's travels in Amazonia and the Guianas in search of medicinal plants.

John A Crow's *The Epic of Latin America* is a daunting but accessible volume that covers Mexico to Tierra del Fuego, from prehistory to the present. George Pendle's *A History of Latin America* is a readable but very general account of the region since the European invasions.

Conquest of the Incas, by John Hemming, is one of the finest interpretations of the clash between the Spaniards and the Inca.

Travel Literature

Driving from Tierra del Fuego to the North Slope of Alaska in 23½ days takes a little extra something and Tim Cahill's got it in spades – hilarious run-ins with customs officials and other bureaucrats make his *Road Fever* a great read. *Chasing Che: A Motorcycle Journey in Search of the Guevara Legend,* by Patrick Symmes, follows Che's journey through South America. Of course, you can go to the source by picking up a copy of *The Motorcycle Diaries,* by Ernesto Guevara himself.

Peter Matthiessen describes a journey from the rivers of Peru to the mountains of Tierra del Fuego in *The Cloud Forest.* Alex Shoumatoff's *In Southern Light* explores firsthand some of the fantastic legends of the Amazon.

Chilean writer Luis Sepúlveda's gripping personal odyssey takes him to different parts of the continent and beyond in *Full Circle: A South American Journey,* translated into English for Lonely Planet's travel literature series.

You'll find loads more travel lit recommendations in the Directory sections of individual country chapters.

Lonely Planet

Lonely Planet produces regularly updated travel guides for individual South American countries, with heaps of information, numerous maps and color photos. Titles include *Argentina*; *Bolivia*; *Brazil*; *Chile & Easter Island*; *Colombia*; *Ecuador & the Galápagos Islands*; *Peru*; and *Venezuela.*

For even more detailed information, see the Lonely Planet city guides to *Buenos Aires* and *Rio de Janeiro.*

Also useful are the *Brazilian Portuguese, Latin American Spanish* and *Quechua* phrasebooks.

For detailed information on some outdoor activities, look at Lonely Planet's *Trekking in the Patagonian Andes* and *Watching Wildlife Galápagos Islands.*

If you're planning to visit Central America as well as South America, get a copy of Lonely Planet's *Central America on a Shoestring,* which covers the region from Panama to Belize.

BUSINESS HOURS

Generally, businesses are open from 8am or 9am to 8pm or 9pm Monday through Friday, with a two-hour lunch break around noon. Businesses are often open on Saturday, usually with shorter hours. Banks usually only change money Monday through Friday. On Sunday, nearly everything is closed. In the Andean countries, businesses tend to close earlier. More precise hours are given in the Business Hours section of each country's Directory section.

CLIMATE

Climate in South America is a matter of latitude and altitude, although warm and cold ocean currents, trade winds and topography play their part. More than two-thirds of South America is tropical, including the Amazon Basin, most of Brazil, the Guianas and the west coasts of Colombia and Ecuador. These areas of tropical rainforest have average daily maximum temperatures of about 30°C (86°F) year-round and more than 2500mm of rain annually. Less humid tropical areas, such as the Brazilian highlands and the Orinoco Basin, are still hot but enjoy cool nights and a distinct dry season.

South of the Tropic of Capricorn, Paraguay and southern Brazil are humid subtropical zones, while much of Argentina, Chile and Uruguay have temperate mid-latitude climates with mild winters and warm summers ranging from 12°C (54°F) in July to 25°C (77°F) in January, depending on landforms and latitude. Rainfall, occurring mostly in winter, varies from 200mm to 2000mm annually, depending on winds and the rain-shadow effect of the Andes. (Most of the rain dumps on the Chilean side, while Argentina remains relatively dry but receives strong winds.)

The main arid regions are northern Chile (the Atacama Desert is one of the world's driest) and Peru, between the Andes and the Pacific Coast, where the cold Humboldt Current creates a cloudy but dry climate. There are two smaller arid zones, along the north coast of Colombia and Venezuela and the Brazilian *sertão* (the drought-prone backlands of the country's northeast).

The high Andes, which have altitudes of more than 3500m, and far southern Chile and Argentina are cool-climate zones, where average daily temperatures fall below 10°C (50°F) and temperatures can dip below freezing.

SOUTH AMERICA DIRECTORY

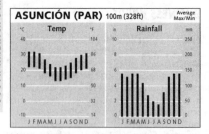

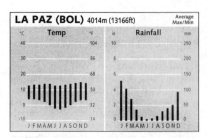

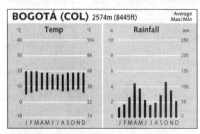

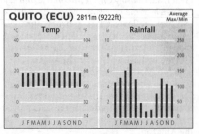

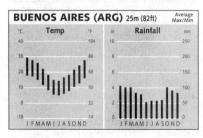

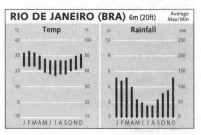

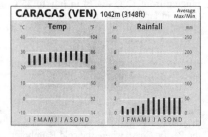

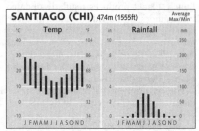

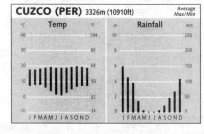

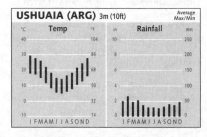

Below the equator, summer is from December to February, while winter is from June to August.

El Niño & La Niña

About every seven years, large-scale changes in ocean circulation patterns and rising sea-surface temperatures create 'El Niño,' bringing heavy rain and floods to desert areas, plunging tropical areas into drought and disrupting weather patterns worldwide. The 1997–98 winter was particularly destructive and traumatic for Peru and Ecuador. The name 'El Niño' (The Child) refers to the fact that this phenomenon usually appears around Christmas.

El Niño is often followed by La Niña the next year, where the opposite effects are observed and can include bridge and road destruction, flooding of entire villages and subsequent refugee crises, raging forest fires in drought areas, malaria epidemics due to stagnant floodwater and lower fish catches due to increased water temperatures.

CUSTOMS REGULATIONS

Customs vary slightly from country to country, but you can generally bring in personal belongings, camera gear, laptops, handheld devices and other travel-related gear. All countries prohibit the export (just as home countries prohibit the import) of archaeological items and goods made from rare or endangered animals (snake skins, cat pelts, jewelry made with teeth etc). Avoid carrying plants, seeds, fruits and fresh meat products across borders. If you're traveling overland to/from Colombia, expect thorough customs inspections on both sides of the border.

DANGERS & ANNOYANCES

There are potential dangers to traveling in South America, but with sensible precautions, you are unlikely to encounter serious problems. Your greatest annoyances will likely be reckless drivers, pollution, fiesta fireworks and low-hanging objects (watch your head!). For thoughts on bus safety, see p1008. Also see the Dangers & Annoyances sections in individual chapter Directories; the Brazil section (p370) contains some tips that are useful throughout all of South America.

Confidence Tricks & Scams

Tricks involving a quantity of cash being 'found' on the street, whereby the do-gooder tries to return it to you, elaborate hard-luck stories from supposed travelers, and 'on-the-spot fines' by bogus police are just some of the scams designed to separate you from your money. Be especially wary if one or more 'plainclothes' cops demand to search your luggage or examine your documents, traveler's checks or cash. Insist that you will allow this only at an official police station or in the presence of a uniformed officer, and don't allow anyone to take you anywhere in a taxi or unmarked car. Thieves often work in pairs to distract you while lifting your wallet. Simply stay alert. See also p994.

Drugs

And now a word from your mother: marijuana and cocaine are big business in parts of South America, and are available in many places but illegal everywhere. Indulging can either land you in jail or worse. Unless you're willing to take these risks, avoid illegal drugs.

Beware that drugs are sometimes used to set up travelers for blackmail and bribery. Avoid any conversation with someone proffering drugs. If you're in an area where drug trafficking is prevalent, ignore it entirely, with conviction.

Lonely Planet has received letters from travelers who were unwittingly drugged and robbed after accepting food from a stranger. You can see the mistake made here.

In Bolivia and Peru, coca leaves are sold legally in *tiendas* (stores) or markets for about US$0.75 to US$1.50 for a pocket-size bag (including chewing paraphernalia). *Maté de coca* is a tea made by infusing coca leaves in boiling water. It's served in many cafes and restaurants in the Andean region, and coca-leaf 'tea bags' are also available. Although *maté de coca* is widely believed to combat the effects of altitude, there is no evidence that conclusively supports this, and a cup of *maté de coca* has no immediate stimulant effect.

The practice of chewing coca leaves goes back centuries and is still common among *campesinos* (peasant farmers) of the *altiplano* (Andean high plain). The leaves are chewed with a little ash or bicarbonate of soda, as the alkalinity releases the mild stimulant contained in the leaf cells. Prolonged chewing dulls the pangs of hunger, thirst, cold and fatigue, but the initial effect just makes your mouth go numb. Without the alkaline catalyst, chewing coca leaves doesn't do much at all. See p168 for leaf-chewing methodology 101.

Be aware that someone who has chewed coca leaves or taken *maté de coca* may test positive for cocaine in the following weeks.

More refined forms of coca are illegal everywhere and transporting coca leaves over international borders is also illegal.

Natural Hazards

The Pacific Rim 'ring of fire' loops through eastern Asia, Alaska and all the way down through the Americas to Tierra del Fuego in a vast circle of earthquake and volcanic activity that includes the whole Pacific side of South America. In 1991, for example, Volcán Hudson in Chile's Aisén region erupted, burying parts of southern Patagonia knee-deep in ash. Chile has seen more recent activity of Volcán Llaima and Volcán Chaitén (both still active); the town of Chaitén has been evacuated and regional transportation may be affected. In Ecuador, Volcán Tungurahua, near Baños, sparked to life in 1999, and remains one of Ecuador's most active volcanoes. Major eruptions occurred in 2006 and 2008. Volcanoes usually give some notice before blowing and are therefore unlikely to pose any immediate threat to travelers. Earthquakes are not uncommon, occur without warning and can be very serious. The last big one in the region was a 7.9-magnitude quake that hit the south coast of Peru (in Ica province, 265km south of Lima), killing more than 300 people. Recovery has come slowly, and parts of the region remain visibly devastated. Andean construction rarely meets seismic safety standards; adobe buildings are particularly vulnerable. If you're in an earthquake, shelter in a doorway or dive under a table; don't go outside.

Other Hazards

There have been reports of brutal attacks on travelers. Be extremely cautious when scoping out your taxi driver before hopping into a cab. Trust your instincts: if something makes you uneasy, find another driver. And never ride in a vehicle that already has a passenger in it.

Police & Military

If you haven't heard, the police enjoy a poor reputation in Latin America. Folks in this line of work are generally poorly paid, and corruption can occasionally rear its ugly head. In some places, in our experience, they are not beyond enforcing minor regulations in hopes of extracting a bribe.

If you are stopped by 'plainclothes policemen,' never get into a vehicle with them. Don't give them any documents or show them any money, and don't take them to your hotel. If the police appear to be the real thing, insist on going to a police station on foot.

The military often maintains considerable influence, even under civilian governments. Avoid approaching military installations, which may display warnings such as 'No stopping or photographs – the sentry will shoot.' In the event of a coup or other emergency, state-of-siege regulations suspend civil rights. Always carry identification and be sure someone knows your whereabouts. Contact your embassy or consulate for advice.

Theft

Theft can be a problem, but remember that fellow travelers can also be accomplished crooks, so where there's a backpacker scene, there may also be thievery. Here are some common-sense suggestions to limit your liability:

- A small padlock is useful for securing your pack zippers and hostel door, if necessary. When used to secure your pack, zippers, twist ties, paper clips or safety pins can be another effective deterrent.
- Even if you're just running down the hall, never leave your hotel door unlocked.
- Always conceal your money belt and its contents, preferably beneath your clothing.
- Keep your spending money separate from the big stuff (credit cards, traveler's checks, tickets etc).
- Pack lightly and you can stash your pack under your seat on the bus. Otherwise you'll enjoy the anxiety of wondering if your pack is staying on the roof every time you stop. It usually does, but… Some swear by grain sacks – buy one at a market, stick your pack in it and it looks just like the local haul, as well as keeping your pack from getting dirty.
- To deter pack slashers, keep moving when you're wearing a backpack and wear your daypack on your chest in crowded markets or terminals.

Trouble Spots

Some countries and areas are more dangerous than others. The more dangerous places (see individual country chapters for details) warrant extra care, but don't feel you should avoid them altogether. Colombia is much safer than it has been in years, but certain regions are still off-limits. The northern border region of Ecuador, specifically in the Oriente, can be dodgy due to guerrilla activity. Travelers have been assaulted at remote and even well-touristed archaeological sites, primarily in Peru; stay informed. La Paz (Bolivia), Caracas (Venezuela), the Copacabana neighborhood in Rio (Brazil) and the Mariscal Sucre neighborhood of Quito (Ecuador) are all notorious for assaults on tourists.

For more detailed information about trouble spots in specific countries see the Dangers & Annoyances sections in the individual country Directories.

DISCOUNT CARDS

A Hostelling International–American Youth Hostel (HI-USA) membership card can be useful in Brazil and Chile (and to a lesser extent in Argentina and Uruguay) where there are many hostels, and accommodations tend to be, or traditionally have been, costlier. Elsewhere on the continent, cheap hotels and *pensiones* typically cost less than affiliated hostels.

An International Student Identity Card (ISIC) can provide discounted admission to archaeological sites and museums. It may also entitle you to reductions on bus, train and air tickets. In less developed countries, student discounts are rare, although high-ticket items such as the entrance to Machu Picchu (discounted 50% for ISIC holders under 26) may be reduced. In some countries, such as Argentina, almost any form of university identification will suffice where discounts are offered.

DISCRIMINATION

Discrimination in South America – and it's a different beast in every country – is complex and full of contradictions. The most serious reports of racism experienced by travelers have been from black travelers who were denied access to nightclubs, in some cases until the doorperson realized they were foreigners. Some black travelers describe experiencing genuine curiosity from people who simply aren't used to seeing folks of black African descent. Brazil, with its huge Afro-Brazilian population, is among the most welcoming places for travelers of color.

See also Women Travelers (p998) and Gay & Lesbian Travelers (below).

EMBASSIES & CONSULATES

For embassy and consulate addresses and phone numbers, see the Directory section in individual country chapters.

As a visitor in a South American country, it's important to realize what your own embassy – the embassy of the country of which you are a citizen – can and cannot do. Generally speaking, it won't be much help in emergencies where you're even remotely at fault. Remember that you are bound by the laws of the country you are in. Your embassy will not be sympathetic if you end up in jail after committing a crime locally, even if such actions are legal in your own country.

In genuine emergencies you may get some assistance, but only if other channels have been exhausted. For example, if you have all your money and documents stolen, it might assist in getting a new passport, but a loan for onward travel will be out of the question.

FESTIVALS & EVENTS

South America has some fabulous fiestas, from indigenous harvest festivals to wild New Year parties. Some festivals, such as **Carnaval**, which is celebrated everywhere in Brazil (but best known in Salvador and Rio) in the days leading up to Ash Wednesday in February/March, are worth planning your trip around. However, keep in mind that, for big festivals, places will be crowded and hotel rates will be at a premium, and it will be more difficult to find accommodations.

For more information, see Festivals & Events in the individual country Directory sections.

GAY & LESBIAN TRAVELERS

Buenos Aires, Rio de Janeiro and São Paulo are the most gay-friendly cities, though gay couples are openly out only in certain neighborhoods. Salvador (Brazil), Bogotá, and to a lesser extent Santiago, also have lively gay scenes. Elsewhere on the continent, where public displays of affection by same-sex couples may get negative reactions, do as the locals do – be discreet to avoid problems.

Despite a growing number of publications and websites devoted to gay travel, few have specific advice on South America. One exception is **Purple Roofs** (www.purpleroofs.com), an excellent guide to gay-friendly accommodations throughout South America.

There's far more gay and lesbian information on country-specific websites (see respective chapter Directory sections), and there are a few sites with general information on South America. There are heaps of helpful travel links listed under the Businesses and Regional pages at **Pridelinks.com** (www.pridelinks.com).

INSURANCE

A travel insurance policy covering theft, loss, accidents and illness is highly recommended. Many policies include a card with toll-free numbers for 24-hour assistance, and it's good practice to carry it with you. Note that some policies compensate travelers for misrouted or lost luggage. Baggage insurance is worth its price in peace of mind. Also check that the coverage includes worst-case scenarios: ambulances, evacuations or an emergency flight home. Some policies specifically exclude 'dangerous activities,' such as scuba diving, motorcycling, even trekking. If such activities are on your agenda, avoid this sort of policy.

There are a wide variety of policies available and your travel agent will be able to make recommendations. The policies handled by **STA Travel** (www.statravel.com) and other student-travel organizations usually offer good value. If a policy offers lower and higher medical-expense options, the low-expenses policy should be OK for South America – medical costs are not nearly as high here as elsewhere in the world.

If you have baggage insurance and need to make a claim, the insurance company may demand a receipt as proof that you bought the stuff in the first place. You must usually inform the insurance company by airmail and report the loss or theft to local police within 24 hours. Make a list of stolen items and their value. At the police station, you complete a *denuncia* (statement), a copy of which is given to you for your insurance claim. The *denuncia* usually has to be made on *papel sellado* (stamped paper), which you can buy at any stationer's.

For information on health insurance, see p1011; for car insurance, p1008.

Worldwide travel insurance is available at www.lonelyplanet.com/travel_services. You can buy, claim and extend online anytime – even if you're already on the road.

INTERNET ACCESS

Internet access is widely available. Rates range from US50¢ to US$6 per hour, but generally hover near the lower end of this spectrum. This book lists internet access points in most towns and cities. Either 'Alt + 64' or 'Alt-Gr + 2' is the command to get the '@' symbol on almost any Spanish-language keyboard.

INTERNET RESOURCES

In planning a trip, www.lonelyplanet.com is a good place to begin. You'll find succinct summaries on traveling to most places on earth, postcards from other travelers and the Thorn Tree forum, where you can ask questions before you go, make plans to meet up with other travelers on the road or dispense advice upon your return. You'll also find travel news and useful links.

Most of the other interesting internet sites about South America are devoted to specific countries within the continent – see the individual country chapters for suggestions. For websites dealing with responsible travel, see the Responsible Travel section on p4. The following are all useful sites related to the continent or travel as a whole:

Latin American Network Information Center
(Lanic; www.lanic.utexas.edu) University of Texas' outstanding list of links to all things Latin American.
South American Explorers (www.saexplorers.org) Excellent starting point for internet research.
UK Foreign & Commonwealth Office (FCO; www .fco.gov.uk) British government site with travel advisories and the like.
US State Department (www.state.gov) Travel advisories and tips; rather alarmist.

LANGUAGE

Spanish is the first language of most South American countries, followed by Portuguese, which is spoken in Brazil. Without a basic knowledge of Spanish, travel in South America can be difficult and your interaction with local people will be limited. Consider taking a crash course in *español* during your trip (see p996 for a few good places in which to learn). French is spoken in French Guiana, Dutch and English are spoken in Suriname, and English is spoken in Guyana.

Lonely Planet publishes the handy, pocket-size *Latin American Spanish* and *Brazilian Portuguese* phrasebooks. For a very brief introduction to Spanish and

Portuguese, including some useful phrases, see the Language chapter (p1020).

There are hundreds of distinct indigenous languages in South America, although some of them are spoken by only a few people. In the Andean countries and parts of Chile and Argentina, millions of people speak Quechua or Aymara as a first language, and many do not use Spanish at all. Quechua was the official language of the Inca empire and is most widely spoken in the Inca heartland of Peru and Ecuador (where it's called Quichua). Aymara was the language of the pre-Inca Tiwanaku culture, and it survives around Lake Titicaca and in much of Bolivia. For a few useful words and phrases, see p1031. If you're serious about learning more, or will be spending a lot of time in remote areas, look around La Paz or Cuzco for a good language course. Lonely Planet's *Quechua* phrasebook is primarily for travelers to Peru and contains grammar and vocabulary in the Cuzco dialect, but will also be useful for visitors to the Bolivian and Ecuadorian highlands.

LEGAL MATTERS

In city police stations, an English-speaking interpreter is a rarity: in most cases you'll either have to speak the local language or provide an interpreter. Some cities have a tourist police service, which can be more helpful.

Replacing a lost or stolen passport will likely be expensive and time-consuming. If you are robbed, photocopies (even better, certified copies) of original passports, visas and air tickets and careful records of credit card numbers and traveler's checks will prove invaluable during replacement procedures. Replacement passport applications are usually referred to the home country, so it helps to leave a copy of your passport details with someone back home.

For more information, see p989.

MAPS

International Travel Maps & Books (www.itmb.com) produces a range of excellent maps of Central and South America. For the whole continent, they have a reliable three-sheet map at a 1:4,000,000 scale and a memorial edition of their classic 1:500,000 map. The maps are huge for road use, but they're helpful for pre-trip planning. More detailed ITMB maps are available for the Amazon Basin, Ecuador, Bolivia and Venezuela. All are available on the ITMB website.

Maps of the South American continent as a whole are widely available; check any well-stocked map or travel bookstore. **South American Explorers** (www.saexplorers.org) has scores of reliable maps, including topographical, regional and city maps. For more information, see p996.

MONEY

Prices quoted in this book are given in the locally used currency (listed in Fast Facts at the start of each destination chapter). Note that US dollars are used in Ecuador, and euros in French Guiana. For exchange rates, see www.xe.com.

ATMs

An ATM card is essential. ATMs are available in most cities and large towns, and are almost always the most convenient, reliable and economical way of getting cash. The rate of exchange is usually as good as any bank or legal money changer. Many ATMs are connected to the Cirrus or Plus network, but many countries prefer one over the other. If your ATM card gets swallowed by a machine, generally the only thing you can do is call your bank and cancel the card. Although such events are rare, it's well worth having an extra ATM card (to a different account), should something go wrong.

If possible, sign up with a bank that doesn't charge a fee for out-of-network ATM withdrawals. Also, find a bank that offers a low exchange rate fee (1 to 2%). Before hitting the road, call your bank, informing them of your travel plans – that way the bank won't put a hold on foreign withdrawals while you're on the road.

Many ATMs will accept a personal identification number (PIN) of only four digits; find out whether this applies to the specific countries you're traveling to before heading off.

Bargaining

Bargaining is accepted and expected when contracting long-term accommodations and when shopping for craft goods in markets. Haggling is a near sport in the Andean countries, with patience, humor and respect serving as the ground rules of the game. Bargaining is much less common in the Cono Sur (Southern Cone; a collective term for Argentina, Chile, Uruguay and parts of Brazil and Paraguay). When you head into the bargaining trenches, remember that the point is to have fun while reaching a mutually satisfying end: the merchant should not try to fleece you, but you shouldn't try to get something for nothing either.

Black Market

Nowadays, official exchange rates are generally realistic in most South American countries, so the role of the black market is declining. Most people end up using the *mercado negro* (black market) when crossing isolated borders, where an official exchange facility might be hours away. Some travelers might still want to use street money changers if they need to exchange cash outside business hours, but with the convenience of ATM cards, this necessity is declining. The one notable exception to this is Venezuela, where ATM withdrawals and credit-card transactions cost about twice as much as exchanging cash on the black market (for more details see boxed text, p980).

Street money changers may be legal or not legal (but are often tolerated), and the practice of changing money on the street is prone to scams – one such trick consist of money changers handing their client the agreed amount less a few pesos; when the client complains, they will take it back adding the few pesos while making a few larger notes disappear. Money changers may also distract their customers during the transaction alerting them to supposed alarms such as 'police' or any other 'danger,' use fixed calculators which give an exchange rate favorable only to the money changer, or pass counterfeit, torn, smudged or tattered bills.

Cash

It's convenient to have a small wad of US cash tucked away (in 20-dollar denominations and less; 100-dollar bills are difficult to exchange). US currency is by far the easiest to exchange – everywhere in South America. Of course, unlike traveler's checks, nobody will give you a refund for lost or stolen cash. When you're about to cross from one country to another, it's handy to change some cash. Trying to exchange worn notes can be a hassle, so procure crisp bills before setting out.

In some countries, especially in rural areas, *cambio* (change) can be particularly hard to come by. Businesses even occasionally refuse to sell you something if they can't or don't want to change your note. So break down those larger bills whenever you have

the opportunity, such as at busy restaurants, banks and larger businesses.

Credit Cards

The big-name credit cards are accepted at most large stores, travel agencies and better hotels and restaurants. Credit card purchases sometimes attract an extra *recargo* (surcharge) on the price (from 2% to 10%), but they are usually billed to your account at quite favorable exchange rates. Some banks issue cash advances on major credit cards. The most widely accepted card is Visa, followed by MasterCard (those with UK Access should insist on its affiliation with MasterCard). American Express and Diners Club are also accepted in some places. Beware of credit card fraud (especially in Brazil) – never let the card out of your sight.

Exchanging Money

Traveler's checks and foreign cash can be changed at *casas de cambio* (currency-exchange offices) or banks. Rates are usually similar, but *casas de cambio* are quicker, less bureaucratic and open longer hours. Street money changers, who may or may not be legal, will only handle cash. Sometimes money can also be changed unofficially at hotels or in shops that sell imported goods (electronics dealers are an obvious choice).

It is preferable to bring money in US dollars, although banks and *casas de cambio* in capital cities will change euros, pounds sterling, Japanese yen and other major currencies. Changing these currencies in smaller towns and on the street is next to impossible.

Traveler's Checks

Traveler's checks are not nearly as convenient as ATM cards, and you may have difficulty cashing them – even at banks. High commissions (from 3% to upwards of 10%) also make them an unattractive option. If you do take traveler's checks, American Express is the most widely accepted brand, while Visa, Thomas Cook and Citibank are the next best options. To facilitate replacement in case of theft, keep a record of check numbers and the original bill of sale in a safe place. Even with proper records, replacement can be a tedious, time-intensive process.

PASSPORT

A passport is essential – make sure it's valid for at least six months beyond the projected end of your trip and has plenty of blank pages for stamp-happy officials. Carrying a photocopy of your passport (so you can leave the original in your hotel) is sometimes enough if you're walking around a town, but *always* have the original if you travel anywhere (never get on a bus leaving town without it). To reduce the risk of hassles in the event you are asked for your papers, keep the original with you at all times.

PHOTOGRAPHY & VIDEO

Consumer electronics are readily available throughout South America, but taxes can kick prices through the roof. You'll probably find better deals at home. Old-fashioned souls can still find film, including B&W and slide, in bigger cities.

Digital

Most travelers find a digital camera an essential item in the packing list. The best solution for storing photos on the road is a portable hard drive, which can double as an MP3 player, or a compact memory card/stick. It's also possible to burn your photos to CD at nearly any of South America's plethora of cybercafes.

Photographing People

Ask for permission before photographing individuals, particularly indigenous people. If someone is giving a public performance (such as a street musician or a dancer at Carnaval), or is incidental to a photograph (in a broad cityscape, for example), permission is not usually necessary – but if in doubt, ask or refrain. If you're after local-market pictures, purchasing items from a vendor may result in permission to photograph them or their wares. Paying folks for their portrait is a personal decision; in most cases, the subject will tell you right off the going rate for a photo.

Restrictions

Some tourist sites charge an additional fee for tourists with cameras. Don't take photos of military installations, military personnel or security-sensitive places like police stations. Such activities may be illegal and could even endanger your life (see p990). In most churches, flash photography (and sometimes photography period) is not allowed.

Video & DVD

Go digital. If you can't, 8mm cassettes for video cameras are available if you really search. Tourist sites that charge for still cameras often charge more for a video camera. If you want to buy a prerecorded videocassette, remember that different countries use different TV and video systems. For example, Colombia and Venezuela use the NTSC system (as in the USA), while Brazil uses PAL, and French Guiana uses the French SECAM system. DVDs in South America are generally coded for Zone 4 (the same as in Mexico, Australia and New Zealand). If you don't have a multiregion DVD player, and you are from outside the zone, you may not be able to view a disc purchased in South America.

POST

International postal rates can be quite expensive. Generally, important mail and parcels should be sent by registered or certified service; otherwise, they may go missing. Sending parcels can be awkward: often an *aduana* (customs) officer must inspect the contents before a postal clerk can accept them, so wait to seal your package until after it has been checked. Most post offices have a parcels window, usually signed *encomiendas* (parcels). The place for posting overseas parcels is sometimes different from the main post office.

UPS, FedEx, DHL and other private postal services are available in some countries, but are prohibitively expensive.

Local Addresses

Some South American addresses in this book contain a post-office box number as well as a street address. A post-office box is known as an *apartado* (abbreviated as 'Ap' or 'Apto') or a *casilla de correos* (abbreviated 'Casilla' or 'CC'). When addresses do not have an official number, which happens regularly in rural areas, the abbreviation 's/n' for *sin número* (without number) is often used.

Receiving Mail

The simplest way to receive mail is to have letters sent to you c/o Lista de Correos ('Posta Restante' in Brazil), followed by the name of the city and country where you expect to be. Mail addressed like this will always be sent to that city's main post office. In most places, the service is free or almost so. Most post offices hold mail for a month or two. American Express operates a mail service for clients.

Bring your passport when collecting mail. If awaited correspondence seems to have gone missing, ask the clerk to check under every possible combination of your initials. To simplify matters, have your letters addressed with only your first name and surname, with the latter underlined and in capital letters.

STUDYING

Spanish-language courses are available in most South American cities, with Cuzco (Peru), Arequipa (Peru), Cuenca (Ecuador) and Buenos Aires (Argentina) being some of the best. For Portuguese, Rio de Janeiro is a great place to spend some time studying. For Quechua and Aymara, try Cochabamba (Bolivia) or Cuzco.

For country-specific details, see individual country chapters, and for school listings, see individual cities. Several good websites to begin researching online are **Travel Tree** (www.traveltree.co.uk) and **Language Schools Guide** (www.languageschoolsguide.com).

TELEPHONE

Internet cafes with net-to-phone service provide the cheapest way to make international calls, with rates varying between US10¢ and US50¢ per minute to the USA and Europe.

From traditional landlines, the most economical way of calling abroad is by phone cards (see right). You can also try direct-dial lines, accessed via special numbers and billed to an account at home. There are different access numbers for each telephone company in each country – get a list from your phone company before you leave.

It is sometimes cheaper to make a collect (reverse-charge) or credit-card call overseas than to pay for the call at the source. Many towns and cities have a telephone office with a row of phone booths for local and international calls. Rates can be high.

Cell Phones

Cell-phone numbers in South America often have different area codes than fixed-line numbers, even if the cell-phone owner resides in the same city. Calling a cell phone number is always more expensive (sometimes exorbitantly so) than calling a fixed line.

If you plan to carry your own cell phone, a GSM tri- or quad-band phone is your best bet. Another option is purchasing a prepaid SIM card (or cards) for the countries where you plan on traveling. You will need a compatible international GSM cell phone that is SIM-unlocked.

For information on phone coverage, visit www.gsmworld.com.

Phone Cards

Usually, the cheapest way to make an international call is by using a phone card, the type you purchase at a kiosk or corner store. These allow you to call North America or Europe for as little as US5¢ per minute with a good card. The caveat is that you need a private phone line or a permissive telephone kiosk operator to use them.

TOILETS

There are two toilet rules for South America: always carry your own toilet paper and don't ever throw anything into the toilet bowl. Except in the most developed places, South American sewer systems can't handle toilet paper, so all paper products must be discarded in the wastebasket. Another general rule is to use public bathrooms whenever you can, as you never know when your next opportunity will be. Folks posted outside bathrooms proffering swaths of paper require payment. For a list of clean bathrooms worldwide – and proof that you can find anything online – check out the **Bathroom Diaries** (www.thebathroomdiaries.com).

TOURIST INFORMATION

Every country in South America has government-run tourist offices, but their quality and breadth of coverage vary. Local tourist offices are mentioned in this book wherever they exist.

South American Explorers (SAE; www.saexplorers .org) is one of the most helpful organizations for travelers to South America. Founded in 1977, SAE functions as an information center for travelers, adventurers and researchers. It supports scientific fieldwork, mountaineering and other expeditions, wilderness conservation and social development in Latin America. It has traveler clubhouses in Buenos Aires (p51), Lima (p779), Cuzco (p814) and Quito (p601), as well as the **US office** (☎ 607-277-0488; 126 Indian Creek Rd, Ithaca, NY 14850), which publishes the quarterly magazine *South American Explorer*. The clubhouses have extensive libraries of books, maps and traveler's reports, plus a great atmosphere. The club itself sells maps, books and other items at its offices and by mail order.

Annual SAE membership is US$60/90 per individual/couple or US$35 per person with a group of four or more and includes four issues of *South American Explorer* magazine. Members receive access to the club's information service, libraries, storage facilities, mail service and book exchange, and discounts at numerous hotels and travel services.

TRAVELERS WITH DISABILITIES

In general, South America is not well set up for disabled travelers, but the more modernized Southern Cone countries are slightly more accommodating – notably Chile, Argentina and perhaps the main cities of Brazil. Unfortunately, cheap local lodgings probably won't be well equipped to deal with physically challenged travelers; air travel will be more feasible than local buses (although this isn't impossible); and well-developed tourist attractions will be more accessible than off-the-beaten-track destinations. Start your research here:

Access-able Travel Source (www.access-able.com) Offers little information specifically on South America, but provides some good general travel advice.

Emerging Horizons (www.emerginghorizons.com) Features well-written articles and regular columns full of handy advice.

Mobility International (www.miusa.org) This US-based outfit advises travelers with disabilities and runs educational-exchange programs – a good way to visit South America.

Royal Association for Disability and Rehabilitation (www.radar.org.uk) Good resource for travelers from the UK.

Society for Accessible Travel & Hospitality (SATH; www.sath.org) Good, general travel information; based in the USA.

VISAS

A visa is an endorsement in your passport permitting you to enter a country and remain for a specified period of time. It's obtained from a foreign embassy or consulate of that country, not *in* that country. You can often get them in your home country, but it's also possible to get them en route, which may be better if you have a flexible itinerary: most visas are only good for a limited period after they're issued.

Nationals of most European countries and Japan require few visas, but travelers from the USA need some, and those from Australia,

New Zealand or South Africa might need several. Carry a handful of passport-size photographs for visa applications (although most border towns have a photographer who can do the honors).

Visa requirements are given in the Directory section at the end of each country chapter, but a summary follows. Some countries issue tourist cards to visitors on arrival; while traveling within those countries, carry your tourist card with you at all times. Residents of most countries will not need visas for Argentina, Chile, Colombia, Ecuador, French Guiana or Peru; consult the following list for other destinations.

Bolivia Residents of the USA now require visas (p244). Most other nationalities do not require them.

Brazil Residents of Canada, the USA, Australia and Japan require visas (p375).

Falkland Islands (Islas Malvinas) For non-Britons, visa requirements are generally the same as those for foreigners visiting the UK, although Argentines must obtain an advance visa. Any queries regarding entry requirements for the Falkland Islands should be directed to the British embassy in your home country.

Paraguay Residents of Canada, the USA, Australia and New Zealand require visas (p764).

Suriname Residents of Canada, the USA, Australia, New Zealand, France, Germany, the UK and the Netherlands require visas (p718).

If you need a visa for a country and arrive at a land border without one, be prepared to backtrack to the nearest town with a consulate to get one. Airlines won't normally let you board a plane for a country to which you don't have the necessary visa. Also, a visa in itself does not guarantee entry: you may still be turned back at the border if you don't have 'sufficient funds' or an onward or return ticket.

Onward or Return Tickets

Some countries require you to have a ticket out of their country before they will admit you at the border, grant you a visa or let you board their national airline. (See individual country Directory sections for specifics.) The onward or return ticket requirement can be a major nuisance for travelers who want to fly into one country and travel overland through others. Officially, Peru, Colombia, Ecuador, Venezuela, Bolivia, Brazil, Suriname and French Guiana demand onward tickets, but only sporadically enforce it. Still, if you arrive in one of the countries technically requiring an onward ticket or sufficient funds and a border guard is having a power trip, he or she *can* enforce these rules (yet another reason to be courteous and neatly dressed at border crossings).

While proof of onward or return tickets is rarely asked for by South American border officials, airline officials, especially in the US, have begun to refuse boarding passengers with one-way tickets who cannot show proof of onward or return travel or proof of citizenship (or residency) in the destination country. One way around this is to purchase a cheap, fully refundable ticket (from, say, Caracas to Miami) and cash it in after your arrival. The downside is that the refund can take up to three months. Before purchasing the ticket, you should also ask specifically where you can get a refund, as some airlines will only refund tickets at the office of purchase or at their head office.

Any ticket out of South America plus sufficient funds are usually an adequate substitute for an onward ticket. Having a major credit card or two may help.

Sufficient Funds

Sufficient funds are often *technically* required but rarely asked for. Immigration officials may ask (verbally or on the application form) about your financial resources. If you lack 'sufficient funds' for your proposed visit, officials may limit the length of your stay, but once you are in the country, you can usually extend your visa by producing a credit card or two.

VOLUNTEERING

Poking around on the internet or browsing volunteer publications definitely makes one thing clear: your work alone is not enough. Most international volunteer organizations require a weekly or monthly fee (sometimes up to US$1500 for two weeks, not including airfare), which can feel a bit harsh. This is usually to cover the costs of housing you, paying the organization's staff, rent, website fees and all that stuff. Whether it seems fair or not, your money is usually going to a good cause (or at least to the cause's bureaucracy).

If you just want to donate your hard work, there are plenty of local organizations that will take you on, though you'll have better luck looking once in the country.

If you want to peek at what's available before you go, check the following websites:

Amerispan (www.amerispan.com/volunteer_intern) Volunteer and internship programs in Argentina, Bolivia, Brazil, Chile, Ecuador and Peru.

Australian Volunteers International (www.ozvol .org.au) Sends qualified Australian volunteers to several spots in South America for one- to two-year volunteer stints.

Cross Cultural Solutions (www.crossculturalsolutions .org) Volunteer programs with an emphasis on cultural and human interaction in Brazil and Peru.

Go Abroad (www.goabroad.com) Extensive listings of volunteer and study-abroad opportunities.

Idealist.org (www.idealist.org) Action Without Borders' searchable database of thousands of volunteer positions throughout the world. Excellent resource.

Rainforest Concern (www.rainforestconcern.org) British nonprofit offering affordable volunteer positions in forest environments in several South American countries. Volunteers pay a weekly fee.

Travel Tree (www.traveltree.co.uk) Excellent website listing volunteer opportunities by duration, region and type of work. Also a great resource for language study, gap years abroad and teaching positions.

Transitions Abroad (www.transitionsabroad.com) Useful portal for both paid and volunteer work.

UN Volunteers (www.unv.org) The lofty international organization offers volunteer opportunities for peace and development projects across the globe.

Volunteer Abroad (www.volunteerabroad.com) Vast website housing links to hundreds of volunteer positions throughout South America. Great place to start.

Volunteer Latin America (www.volunteerlatinamerica .com) Worth a peek for its interesting programs throughout Latin America.

Working Abroad (www.workingabroad.com) Online network of grassroots volunteer opportunities with trip reports from the field.

WOMEN TRAVELERS

At one time or another, solo women travelers will find themselves the object of curiosity – sometimes well intentioned, sometimes not. Avoidance is an easy, effective self-defense strategy. In the Andean region, particularly in smaller towns and rural areas, modest dress and conduct are the norm, while in Brazil and the more liberal Southern Cone, standards are more relaxed, especially in beach areas; note, however, that virtually nowhere in South America is topless or nude bathing customary. When in doubt, follow the lead of local women.

Machista (macho) attitudes, stressing masculine pride and virility, are fairly widespread among South American men (although less so in indigenous communities). They are often expressed by boasting and in exaggerated attention toward women. Snappy put-down lines or other caustic comebacks to unwanted advances may make the man feel threatened, and he may respond aggressively. Most women find it easier to invent a husband and leave the guy with his pride intact, especially in front of others.

There have been isolated cases of South American men raping women travelers. Women trekking or taking tours in remote or isolated areas should be especially aware. Some cases have involved guides assaulting tour group members, so it's worth double-checking the identity and reputation of any guide or tour operator. Also be aware that women (and men) have been drugged, in bars and elsewhere, using drinks, cigarettes or pills. Police may not be very helpful in rape cases – if a local woman is raped, her family usually seeks revenge rather than calling the police. Tourist police may be more sympathetic, but it's possibly better to see a doctor and contact your embassy before reporting a rape to police.

Tampons are generally difficult to find in smaller towns, so stock up in cities or bring a supply from home. Birth control pills are sometimes tricky to find outside metropolitan areas, so you're best off bringing your own supply from home. If you can't bring enough, carry the original package with you so a pharmacist can match a local pill to yours. Pills in most South American countries are very inexpensive. 'Morning after' pills are readily available in some countries, notably Brazil.

The **International Planned Parenthood Federation website** (www.ippf.org) offers a wealth of information on member clinics (Family Planning Associations) throughout South America that provide contraception (and abortions, where legal).

WORKING

Aside from teaching or tutoring English, opportunities for employment are few, low-paying and usually illegal. Even tutoring, despite good hourly rates, is rarely remunerative because it takes time to build up a clientele. The best opportunities for teaching English are in the larger cities, and, although you won't save much, it will allow you to stick around longer. Santiago, Rio and the larger cities of Brazil are the best bets for decent pay. Other work opportunities may exist for skilled guides or in restaurants and bars catering to travelers. Many people find work at foreign-owned lodges and inns.

There are several excellent online resources, including the following:

Association of American Schools in South America (AASSA; www.aassa.com) Places accredited teachers in many academic subjects in schools throughout South America.

Dave's ESL Café (www.eslcafe.com) Loads of message boards, job boards, teaching ideas, information, links and more.

EnglishClub.com (www.englishclub.com) Great resource for ESL teachers and students.

TEFL Net (www.tefl.net) This is another rich online resource for teachers from the creators of EnglishClub.com.

Transformation

GETTING THERE & AWAY

AIR

Every South American country has an international airport in its capital and often in major cities as well. Main gateways include Buenos Aires (Argentina); Caracas (Venezuela); La Paz (Bolivia); Lima (Peru); Quito (Ecuador); Rio de Janeiro (Brazil) and São Paulo (Brazil); and Santiago (Chile). Less frequently used international gateways include Asunción (Paraguay); Bogotá (Colombia); Guayaquil (Ecuador); Manaus, Recife and Salvador (Brazil); Montevideo (Uruguay); Río Gallegos (Argentina); and Santa Cruz (Bolivia).

Owing to massive changes in the airline industry, some countries no longer have a 'flag carrier.' New airlines appear, just as old ones go into bankruptcy. At press time, these were the biggest South American airlines:

Aerolíneas Argentinas/Austral (www.aerolineas.com.ar; Argentina)

Aerosur (www.aerosur.com; Bolivia)

Avianca (www.avianca.com; Colombia)

Conviasa (www.conviasa.aero; Venezuela)

Gol Airlines (www.voegol.com.br; Brazil)

LAN (www.lan.com; Chile, Ecuador & Peru) Umbrella for LANChile, LANEcuador and LANPeru.

TAM (www.tam.com.br; Brazil)

North American, European and Australian airlines offering regular South American connections include the following:

Air France (www.airfrance.com)

American Airlines (www.aa.com)

British Airways (www.britishairways.com)

Continental Airlines (www.continental.com)

Delta (www.delta.com)

Iberia (www.iberia.com)

KLM (www.klm.com)

Swiss (www.swiss.com)

Qantas (www.qantas.com.au)

Tickets

Airfares to South America depend on the usual criteria: point and date of departure, destination, your access to discount travel agencies and whether you can take advantage of advance-purchase fares and special offers. Airlines are the best source for finding information on routes, timetables and standard fares, but they rarely sell the cheapest tickets.

Flights from North America, Europe, Australia and New Zealand may permit a stopover in South America en route to your destination city. This gives you a free air connection within the region, so it's worth considering when comparing flights. International flights may also include an onward connection at a much lower cost than a separate fare.

Flights, tours and rail tickets can also be booked online at www.lonelyplanet.com/travelservices.

COURIER FLIGHTS

Courier flights offer outstanding value if you can tolerate the restrictions. Only the major cities are served, with London, Los Angeles and

---

CLIMATE CHANGE & TRAVEL

Climate change is a serious threat to the ecosystems that humans rely upon, and air travel is the fastest-growing contributor to the problem. Lonely Planet regards travel, overall, as a global benefit, but believes we all have a responsibility to limit our personal impact on global warming.

Flying & Climate Change

Pretty much every form of motor travel generates CO_2 (the main cause of human-induced climate change) but planes are far and away the worst offenders, not just because of the sheer distances they allow us to travel, but also because they release greenhouse gases high into the atmosphere. The statistics are frightening: two people taking a return flight between Europe and the US will contribute as much to climate change as an average household's gas and electricity consumption over a whole year.

Carbon Offset Schemes

Climatecare.org and other websites use 'carbon calculators' that allow jetsetters to offset the greenhouse gases they are responsible for with contributions to energy-saving projects and other climate-friendly initiatives in the developing world – including projects in India, Honduras, Kazakhstan and Uganda.

Lonely Planet, together with Rough Guides and other concerned partners in the travel industry, supports the carbon offset scheme run by climatecare.org. Lonely Planet offsets all of its staff and author travel.

For more information check out our website: lonelyplanet.com.

New York being the most common departure points. If you can get to one of these gateway cities and connect with a courier flight, you might save a big amount to occasional served destinations such as Rio de Janeiro or Buenos Aires. Courier operators include **International Association of Air Travel Couriers** (www.courier.org).

RTW TICKETS

Some of the best deals for travelers visiting many countries on different continents are Round-the-World (RTW) tickets. Itineraries from the US, Europe or Australia can include five or more stopovers. Similar 'Circle Pacific' fares allow excursions between Australasia and South America. The downside is that you must choose your destinations at the time of purchase (although all but the first destination can usually be left open) and you may not be able stay more than 60 days in a country. Another option is putting together your own ticket with two or three stops and a return from another country. If you work with a travel agent, it might work out cheaper than an RTW ticket.

Fares for RTW and Circle Pacific tickets can vary widely, but to get an idea, shop around at the following websites:

Airbrokers (www.airbrokers.com) US based. Offers customized RTW tickets that don't require you to stick within airline affiliates.

Airtreks (www.airtreks.com) US-based.
Oneworld (www.oneworld.com) Alliance between nine airlines that offer circle and multi-continent tickets.
Roundtheworldflights.com (www.roundtheworldflights.com) UK based.
Star Alliance (www.staralliance.com) Airline alliance that allows you to build your own RTW ticket.

You can sometimes buy a RTW ticket online, but it's usually best (and often required) that you buy it through a travel or airline agent due to the complexity of the ticket. And for your own sanity, nothing is better than a good agent when planning this type of ticket.

FREE STOPOVERS

If your flight to South America connects through Miami, Los Angeles, Houston or other cities in the US, or through cities in Mexico or Central America, you may be able to arrange a free stopover. This would allow you to spend some time in these countries before continuing south. Ask your travel agent about this possibility.

From Australia

Excursion fares from Australia to South America aren't cheap. The most direct routes on Qantas and its partners are from Sydney to Santiago or Buenos Aires. Fares are usually the same from Melbourne, Sydney or Brisbane, but from other Australian cities you may have to add the cost of getting to Sydney.

In terms of airfare only, it may be marginally cheaper to go to South America via the US, but even a day in Los Angeles would cost more than the savings in airfares, so it's not good value unless you want to visit the US anyway. It may be worth it for travel to Colombia or Venezuela, but not for cities further south.

The best RTW options are probably those with Aerolíneas Argentinas combined with other airlines, including Air New Zealand, British Airways, Iberia, Singapore Airlines, Thai Airways or KLM. The Qantas version of an RTW ticket is its 'Oneworld Explorer' fare, which allows you to visit four to six continents.

Some of the cheapest tickets are available through **STA Travel** (www.statravel.com.au) and **Flight Centre** (www.flightcentre.com.au), both of which have dozens of offices in the country. For online bookings, try www.travel.com.au.

From Central America

Flights from Central America are usually subject to high tax, and discounted flights are almost unobtainable. Nevertheless, it's cheaper, easier and safer to fly between Central and South America than to go overland.

You must have an onward ticket to enter Colombia, and airlines in Panama and Costa Rica are unlikely to sell you a one-way ticket to Colombia unless you already have an onward ticket or are willing to buy a round-trip flight. Venezuela and Brazil also demand an onward ticket. If you have to purchase a round-trip ticket, check whether the airline will give you a refund for unused portions of the ticket. See also p997.

VIA ISLA DE SAN ANDRÉS

Copa Airlines (www.copaair.com) flies from Panama City to the Colombian island of Isla de San Andrés (see boxed text, p544), off the coast of Nicaragua. From San Andrés, you can continue on a domestic Colombian flight to Bogotá, Cali, Cartagena or Medellín.

FROM COSTA RICA

Flights to Quito from Costa Rica are generally about US$100 more than from Panama. The Costa Rican student organization **OTEC** (www.turismojoven.com) offers some cheap tickets.

FROM PANAMA

There are direct flights from Panama City to Bogotá, Cartagena and Medellín. The Colombian airline **Avianca** (www.avianca.com) and the Panamanian carrier **Copa** (www.copaair.com) generally offer the cheapest deals to these places. Colombia officially requires proof of onward travel, but Copa offices in Cartagena, Barranquilla and Medellín should refund unused returns; check in advance. Refunds, in Colombian currency only, take up to four days. You can also fly from Panama City to Quito, Ecuador.

From Continental Europe

The best places in Europe for cheap airfares are 'student' travel agencies (you don't have to be a student to use them) in Amsterdam, Berlin, Brussels, Frankfurt and Paris, and sometimes in Athens. If airfares are expensive where you live, try contacting a London agent, who may be able to issue an electronic ticket or a paper ticket by mail. The cheapest destinations in South America are generally Caracas, Buenos Aires and possibly Rio de Janeiro or Recife, Brazil. High-season months are from early June to early September, and mid-December to mid-January. The cheapest flights from Europe are typically charters, usually with fixed dates for both outward and return flights.

The following travel agencies are good possibilities for bargain fares from Continental Europe.

FRANCE

Expedia (www.expedia.fr)
Lastminute (www.fr.lastminute.com)
Nouvelles Frontières (www.nouvelles-frontieres.fr)
Voyages Wasteels (www.wasteels.fr)
Voyageurs du Monde (www.vdm.com)

GERMANY

Expedia (www.expedia.de)
Lastminute (www.lastminute.de)
STA Travel (www.statravel.de) For travelers under the age of 26.

ITALY

One recommended agency is **CTS Viaggi** (www.cts.it), which specializes in student and youth travel.

NETHERLANDS

Airfair (www.airfair.nl)
NBBS Reizen (www.nbbs.nl) Student agency.

TRANSPORTATION

From New Zealand

The two chief options are to fly **Aerolíneas Argentinas** (www.aerolineas.com.ar) from Auckland to Buenos Aires (with connections to neighboring countries) or to fly with **Air New Zealand** (www.airnz.co.nz) from Auckland to Papeete, Tahiti, connecting with a **LANChile** (www.lanchile.com) flight via Easter Island to Santiago. Onward tickets, eg to Lima, Rio de Janeiro, Guayaquil, Bogotá or Caracas, are much cheaper if purchased in conjunction with a long-haul flight from the same carrier. A 'Visit South America' fare, valid for three months, allows you two stops in South America plus one in the US, then returns to Auckland. Various open-jaw options are possible, and you can make the trip in either direction.

Both **Flight Centre** (www.flightcentre.co.nz) and **STA Travel** (www.statravel.co.nz) have branches throughout the country. For online bookings try www.travel.co.nz.

From the UK

Fares from London are some of the best in Europe, with the cheapest destinations in South America generally including Buenos Aires, Caracas, Bogotá and São Paulo.

Some London agencies specialize in South American travel. One very good agency is **Journey Latin America** (www.journeylatinamerica.co.uk). Other places to try are **South American Experience** (www.southamericanexperience.co.uk) and **Austral Tours** (www.latinamerica.co.uk).

Other recommended travel agencies in the UK include the following:
Ebookers (www.ebookers.com)
Flight Centre (http://flightcentre.co.uk)
North South Travel (www.northsouthtravel.co.uk) North South Travel donates part of its profits to projects in the developing world.
Quest Travel (www.questtravel.com)
STA Travel (www.statravel.co.uk) For travelers under the age of 26.
Trailfinders (www.trailfinders.co.uk)
Travel Bag (www.travelbag.co.uk)

From the USA & Canada

Major gateways are Los Angeles, Miami and New York; Miami is usually cheapest. Newark (New Jersey), Washington DC, and Dallas and Houston (Texas), also have direct connections to South America. As a general rule, Caracas and Lima are probably the cheapest South American destinations, while Buenos Aires, Santiago and La Paz are the most expensive.

Inexpensive tickets from North America usually have restrictions; often there's a two-week advance-purchase requirement, and usually you must stay no more than three months. High season for most fares is from early June to early September, and mid-December to mid-January. Look in major newspapers and alternative weeklies for sample fares and deals.

Travel agencies known as 'consolidators' typically have the best deals. They buy tickets in bulk, then discount them to their customers, or sell 'fill-up fares,' which can be even cheaper (with additional restrictions). Look for agencies that specialize in South American travel, such as **eXito** (www.exitotravel.com). The largest student travel company in the USA is **STA Travel** (www.statravel.com). The **Adventure Travel Company** (www.theadventuretravelcompany.com), is also recommended; it has offices in the US and Canada.

Most flights from Canada involve connecting via one of the US gateways. **Travel Cuts** (www.travelcuts.com) is Canada's national student travel agency. For online bookings try www.expedia.ca and www.travelocity.ca.

For US bookings online, you can try the following:
Cheap Tickets (www.cheaptickets.com)
Expedia (www.expedia.com)
Lowestfare.com (www.lowestfare.com)
Orbitz (www.orbitz.com)
Travelocity (www.travelocity.com)
STA Travel (www.sta.com) Best for travelers under the age of 26.

For occasional steals, try an air-ticket auction site such as **Priceline.com** (www.priceline.com) or **SkyAuction.com** (www.skyauction.com), where you bid on your own fare.

LAND

From North America, you can journey overland only as far south as Panama. There is no road connection onward to Colombia: the Carretera Panamericana (Pan-American Hwy) ends in the vast wilderness of the Darién Province, in southeast Panama. This roadless area between Central and South America is called the Darién Gap. In the past it has been difficult, but possible, to trek across the gap with the help of local guides, but since around 1998 it has been prohibitively dangerous, especially on the Colombian side. The region is effectively controlled by guerrillas and is positively unsafe.

BORDER CROSSINGS

There are ample border crossings in South America, so you generally never have to travel too far out of your way to get where you eventually want to go. This is particularly true in Argentina and Chile, where a shared 3500km-long frontier provides many opportunities (especially in Patagonia) to slide between countries. Most crossings are by road (or bridge), but there are a few that involve boat travel (such as across the Río de la Plata between Buenos Aires and Uruguay; several lake crossings between Argentina and Chile, and across Lake Titicaca between Bolivia and Peru).

With the influx of footloose foreigners in the region, border police are used to backpackers turning up at their often isolated corner of the globe. That said, crossing is always easier if you appear at least somewhat kempt, treat the guards with respect, and make an attempt at Spanish or Portuguese. If, on the off chance, you encounter an officer who tries to extract a little *dinero* from you before allowing you through (it does happen occasionally), maintain your composure. If the amount is small (and it generally is), it's probably not worth your trouble trying to fight it. Just consider it one small part of the great South American tale you'll be recounting in years to come. Generally, border police are courteous and easy going.

Detailed information on border crossings is provided in local sections throughout this book; major crossings are listed at the start of each chapter. Before heading to a border, be sure to get the latest information on visas – whether or not you need one – with a little on-the-ground research. Also, have a look at the Visas section in the South America Directory (p997) and in individual chapter Directory sections for specific requirements.

SEA

A few cruise ships from Europe and the US call on South American ports, but they are much more expensive than any air ticket. Some cargo ships from Houston, New Orleans, Hamburg and Amsterdam will take a limited number of passengers to South American ports, but they are also expensive.

Some small cargo ships sail between Colón, Panama and the Colombian port of Barranquilla, but many of them are involved in carrying contraband and may be too shady for comfort. Nevertheless, some of these ships take paying passengers.

There are occasional reports of pirate attacks off the coast of South America, most of which occur in the Caribbean region.

One of the most popular modes of travel between Central and South America is by booking passage on one of the foreign sailboats that travel between Cartagena and the San Blás islands, with some boats continuing to Colón. The typical passage takes four to six days and costs around US$350. The best place for up-to-date information regarding schedules and available berths is at Casa Viena (p541) in Cartagena.

Officially, both Panama and Colombia require an onward or return ticket as a condition of entry. This may not be enforced in Colombia, but it's wise to get one anyway, or have lots of money and a plausible itinerary.

Panama requires a visa or tourist card, an onward ticket and sufficient funds, and has been known to turn back arrivals who don't meet these requirements. The Panamanian consulate in Cartagena is reportedly helpful.

GETTING AROUND

Whether aboard a rickety *chiva* (open-sided bus) on the Ecuadorian coast, a motorized canoe in the Amazon, or a small aircraft humming over the Andes, transport on this continent is a big part of the South American adventure.

AIR

There is an extensive network of domestic flights, with refreshingly low price tags, especially in the Andean countries (Bolivia, Ecuador and Peru). After 18-hour bus rides across 350km of mountainous terrain on atrocious roads, you may decide, as many travelers do, to take the occasional flight.

There are drawbacks to flying, however. Airports are often far from city centers, and public buses don't run all the time, so you may end up spending a bit on taxis (it's usually easier to find a cheap taxi *to* an airport than *from* one). Airport taxes also add to the cost of air travel; they are usually higher for international departures. If safety concerns you, check out the 'Fatal Events by Airline' feature at **AirSafe.com** (www.airsafe.com).

In some areas, planes don't depart on time. Avoid scheduling a domestic flight with a close connection for an international flight or vice versa. Many a traveler has been stranded after setting too tight an itinerary that hinges on their international flight arriving on time and connecting with a domestic leg to a far-flung outpost. Reconfirm all flights 48 hours before departure and turn up at the airport at least an hour before flight time (two to three hours for international flights).

Flights from North America and Europe may permit stopovers on the way to the destination city. It's worth considering this when shopping for an international flight, as it can effectively give you a free air connection within South America. Onward connections in conjunction with an international flight can also be a cheap way to get to another South American city (for more, see p1001).

Air Passes

Air passes offer a number of flights within a country or region, for a specified period, at a fixed total price. Passes are an economical way to cover long distances in limited time, but they have shortcomings. Some are irritatingly inflexible: once you start using the pass, you're locked into a schedule and can't change it without paying a penalty. The validity period can be restrictive and some passes require that you enter the country on an international flight – you can't travel overland to the country and then start flying around with an air pass. Citizens of some countries are not eligible for certain air passes, etc. For an overview of the various passes and their minutiae, see Air Passes in the Flight pages (under Planning) of **Last Frontiers** (www.lastfrontiers.com) or Exito Airpass (under Book a Flight) of **eXito** (www.exitotravel.com).

MULTICOUNTRY AIR PASSES

A few South America air passes exist and can save you a bit of money, provided you can deal with a fixed itinerary. These mileage-based passes allow travelers to fly between cities in a limited set of countries. The restrictions vary, but flights must be completed within a period ranging from 30 days to 12 months. The cost is typically based on the number of standard air miles (not kilometers) you want to cover; prices range from US$400 to US$1500 for 1200 to 8200 miles. You'll pay higher rates (or be ineligible) if you arrive in South America on a carrier other than the one sponsoring the

air pass. You can read more about the following air passes on www.latinamerica.co.uk:

Aerolíneas Argentinas Airpass (www.aerolineas.com.ar) Includes Argentina, Bolivia, southern Brazil, Chile, Colombia, Paraguay, Peru, Uruguay and Venezuela.

One World Alliance Visit South America Airpass (www.oneworld.com) Includes LAN flights serving Argentina, Bolivia, southern Brazil, Chile, Colombia, Ecuador, Peru, Uruguay and Venezuela.

TAM South America Airpass (www.tam.com.br) Includes Argentina, Bolivia, Brazil, Chile, Paraguay, Peru, Uruguay and Venezuela.

SINGLE-COUNTRY AIR PASSES

Most air passes are only good within one country and are usually purchased in combination with a return ticket to that country. In addition, most air passes must be purchased outside the destination country; check with a travel agent. Argentina, Brazil, Chile and Peru all offer domestic air passes.

Sample Airfares

Unless noted otherwise, the following chart shows sample mid-season, one-way airfares, quoted directly by airlines for purchase in South America. With some savvy you may find better fares. Sometimes, purchasing an

AIRFARES

Origin	Destination	Cost (US$)
Asunción	Buenos Aires	210
Bogotá	Quito	250-320
Buenos Aires	La Paz	540
Buenos Aires	Santiago	200-480
Buenos Aires	Ushuaia	150
Guayaquil	Galápagos Islands	320-70 (round trip)
Guayaquil	Lima	280-400
Lima	La Paz	160-320
Punta Arenas	Falkland Islands	610 (round trip)
Punta Arenas	Santiago	415
Quito	Galápagos Islands	360-420 (round trip)
Rio de Janeiro	Manaus	200-500
Rio de Janeiro	Montevideo	250-350
Rio de Janeiro	Santa Cruz, Bolivia	250-350
Salvador	Rio de Janeiro	60-150
Santa Cruz, Bolivia	Florianópolis	330-450
Santiago	Rapa Nui (Easter Island)	500-900 (round trip)
Santiago	La Paz	525
Santiago	Lima	650

ida y vuelta (return-trip) ticket is cheaper than buying a one-way ticket; be sure to ask.

BICYCLE

Cycling South America is a challenging yet highly rewarding alternative to public transport. While better roads in Argentina and Chile make the Cono Sur (Southern Cone; a collective term for Argentina, Chile, Uruguay and parts of Brazil and Paraguay) countries especially attractive, the entire continent is manageable by bike, or – more precisely – by mountain bike. Touring bikes are suitable for paved roads, but only a *todo terreno* (mountain bike) allows you to tackle the spectacular back roads (and often main roads!) of the Andes.

There are no multicountry bike lanes or designated routes. Mountain bikers have cycled the length of the Andes, and a select few have made the transcontinental journey from North to South America. As for road rules, forget it – except for the logical rule of riding with traffic on the right-hand side of the road, there are none. Hunt down good maps that show side roads, as you'll have the enviable ability to get off the beaten track at will.

Bring your own bicycle since locally manufactured ones are less dependable and imported bikes are outrageously expensive. Bicycle mechanics are common even in small towns, but will almost invariably lack the parts you'll need. Before setting out, learn bicycle mechanics and purchase spares for the pieces most likely to fail. A basic road kit will include extra spokes and a spoke wrench, a tire patch kit, a chain punch, inner tubes, spare cables and a cycling-specific multitool. Some folks box up spare tires, leave them with a family member back home and have them shipped to South America when they need them.

Drawbacks to cycling include the weather (fierce rains, blasting winds), high altitude in the Andes, poor roads and reckless drivers – the biggest hazard for riders. Safety equipment such as reflectors, mirrors and a helmet are highly recommended. Security is another issue: always take your panniers with you, lock your bike (or pay someone to watch it) while you sightsee and bring your bike into your hotel room overnight.

Before you fly, remember to check your airline's baggage requirements; some allow bikes to fly free, while others don't. It's also essential that you box your bike up correctly to avoid damage during handling.

Although it's well over a decade old, Walter Sienko's *Latin America by Bike: A Complete Touring Guide (By Bike)* makes for an informative pre-trip read. For tips on packing, shipping and flying with a bike, check out www.bikeaccess.net. For loads of tips and such from others who have done it, check out **South America Bicycle Touring Links** (www.transamazon.de /links). Also see p985 for more information.

BOAT

From cruises through the mystical fjords of Chilean Patagonia and riverboat chugs up the mighty Amazon to outboard canoe travel in the coastal mangroves of Ecuador, South America offers ample opportunity to travel by boat. Safety is generally not an issue, especially for the established ferry and cruise operators in Chile and Argentina. There have been a couple of recent problems with tourist boats in the Galápagos (including one that sank in 2005), so don't scrimp if you don't have to.

Lake Crossings

There are outstanding (but expensive) lake excursions throughout southern Chile and Argentina, as well as on Lake Titicaca, in and between Bolivia and Peru. For details, see the individual country chapters. Some of the most popular routes:

- Copacabana (Bolivia) to the Lake Titicaca islands of Isla del Sol and Isla de la Luna
- Lago General Carrera (Chile) to Chile Chico and Puerto Ingeniero Ibáñez (Chile)
- Puerto Montt and Puerto Varas (Chile) to Bariloche (Argentina)
- Puno (Peru) to the Lake Titicaca islands

Riverboat

Long-distance travel on major rivers such as the Orinoco or Amazon is possible, but you'll have a more idyllic time on one of the smaller rivers such as the Mamoré or Beni, where boats hug the shore and you can see and hear the wildlife. On the Amazon, you rarely even see the shore. The river is also densely settled in its lower reaches, and its upper reaches have fewer passenger boats than in the past. Other river journeys include the Río Paraguay from Asunción (Paraguay) to Brazil, or the Río Napo from Coca (Ecuador) to Peru.

Riverboats vary greatly in size and standards, so check the vessel before buying a ticket and shop around. When you pay the fare, get a ticket with all the details on it. Downriver travel is faster than upriver, but boats going upriver travel closer to the shore and offer more interesting scenery. The time taken between ports is unpredictable, so river travel is best for those with an open schedule.

Food is usually included in ticket prices and means lots of rice and beans and perhaps some meat, but bring bottled water, fruit and snacks as a supplement. The evening meal on the first night of a trip is not usually included. Drinks and extra food are generally sold on board, but at high prices. Bring some spare cash and insect repellent.

Unless you have cabin space, you'll need a hammock and rope to sling it. It can get windy and cool at night, so a sleeping bag is recommended. There are usually two classes of hammock space, with space on the upper deck costing slightly more; it's cooler there and worth the extra money. Be on the boat at least eight hours prior to departure to get a good hammock space away from engine noise and toilet odors.

Overcrowding and theft on boats are common complaints. Don't allow your baggage to be stored in an insecure locker; bring your own padlock. Don't entrust your bag to any boat officials unless you are quite certain about their status – bogus officials have been reported.

For more tips on riverboat travel see p351.

Sea Trips

The best-known sea trip, and a glorious one at that, is the **Navimag** (www.navimag.com) ferry ride down the Chilean coast, from Puerto Montt to Puerto Natales. Short boat rides in some countries take you to islands not far from the mainland, including Ilha Grande and Ilha de Santa Catarina in Brazil, Isla Grande de Chiloé in Chile and Isla Grande de Tierra del Fuego in Argentina. More distant islands are usually reached by air. In parts of coastal Ecuador, outboard canoes act as public transport through the mangroves.

BUS

If there's one form of transport in South America that's guaranteed to give you fodder for your travel tales, it's the bus. Whether you're barreling down a treacherous Andean road in a bus full of chickens in Ecuador, or relaxing in a reclining leather chair sipping sparkling wine with dinner on an Argentine long-hauler, you will rarely be short on entertainment. In general, bus transport is well developed throughout the continent. Note that road conditions, bus quality and driver professionalism, however, vary widely.

Highland Peru, Bolivia and Ecuador have some of the worst roads, and bad stretches are found in parts of Colombia and the Brazilian Amazon. Much depends on the season: vast deserts of red dust in the dry season become oceans of mud in the rainy season. In Argentina, Uruguay, coastal and southern Brazil, and most of Venezuela, roads are generally better. Chile and much of Argentina have some of the best-maintained roads and most comfortable and reliable bus services in South America.

Most major cities and towns have a *terminal de autobuses* or *terminal de ómnibus* (bus terminal); in Brazil, it's called a *rodoviária*, and in Ecuador it's a *terminal terrestre*. Often, terminals are on the outskirts of town, and you'll need a local bus or taxi to reach it. The biggest and best terminals have restaurants, shops, showers and other services, and the surrounding area is often a good (but frequently ugly) place to look for cheap sleeps and eats. Village 'terminals' in rural areas often amount to dirt lots flanked by dilapidated metal hulks called 'buses' and men hawking various destinations to passersby; listen for your town of choice.

Some cities have several terminals, each serving a different route. Sometimes each bus company has its own terminal, which is particularly inconvenient. This is most common in Colombia, Ecuador and Peru, particularly in smaller towns.

Classes

Especially in the Andean countries, buses may be stripped nearly bare, tires are often treadless, and rock-hard suspension ensures a less-than-smooth ride, particularly for those at the back of the bus. After all seats are taken, the aisle is packed beyond capacity, and the roof is loaded with cargo to at least half the height of the bus, topped by the occasional goat or pig. You may have serious doubts about ever arriving at your destination, but the buses usually make it. Except for long-distance routes, different classes often don't exist: you ride what's available.

At the other extreme, you'll find luxurious coaches in Argentina, Brazil, Chile, Colombia, Uruguay, Venezuela and even Bolivia along main routes. The most expensive buses usually feature reclining seats, and meal, beverage and movie services. Different classes are called by a variety of names, depending on the country; for more information see each country's individual Transportation sections. In Argentina, Chile and Peru, the deluxe sleeper buses, called *coche-cama* or *bus-cama* (literally 'bed-bus') – or *leito* (sleeping berth) in Brazil – are available for most long-distance routes.

Costs

In the Andean countries, bus rides generally add up to about US$1 per hour of travel. When better services (such as 1st class or *coche-cama*) are offered, they can cost double the fare of a regular bus. Still, overnighters obviate the need for a hotel room, thereby saving you money.

Reservations

It's always wise to purchase your ticket in advance if you're traveling during peak holiday seasons (January through March in the Southern Cone; and around Easter week and during holiday weekends everywhere). At best, bus companies will have ticket offices at central terminals and information boards showing routes, departure times and fares. Seats will be numbered and booked in advance. In places where tickets are not sold in advance, showing up an hour or so before your departure will usually guarantee you a seat.

Safety

Anyone who has done their share of traveling in South America can tell you stories of horrifying bus rides at the mercy of crazed drivers. In the Andean countries, where roads are bad and machismo gets played out on the road, these stories surface more often. And there are *occasionally* accidents. But remember this: in countries where the vast majority of people travel by bus, there are bound to be more bus wrecks. Choosing more expensive buses is no guarantee against accidents; high-profile crashes sometimes involve well-established companies. Some roads, particularly those through the Andes, can be frightening to travel. A few well-placed flights can reduce bus anxiety.

CAR & MOTORCYCLE

Driving around South America can be mentally taxing and at times risky, but a car allows you to explore out-of-the-way places – especially parks – that are totally inaccessible by public transport. In places like Patagonia and other parts of Chile and Argentina, a short-term rental car can be well worth the expense. If you're driving your own car, so much the better.

There are some hurdles to driving. First off, you need an International Driving Permit to supplement your license from home. Vehicle security can be a problem anywhere in South America. Avoid leaving valuables in your car, and always lock it up. Parking is not always secure or even available; be mindful of where you leave your car, lest it be missing when you return.

Bring Your Own Vehicle

Shipping your own car or motorcycle to South America involves a lot of money and planning. Shipping arrangements should be made at least a month in advance. Stealing from vehicles being shipped is big business, so remove everything removable (hubcaps, wipers, mirrors), and take everything visible from the interior. Shipping your vehicle in a container is more secure, but more expensive. Shipping a motorcycle can be less costly.

If you're driving from North America, remember there is no road connecting Panama and Colombia, so you'll have to ship your vehicle around the Darién Gap.

Inspirational **VWVagabonds.com** (www.vwvagabonds.com) is bursting with information on shipping and driving a vehicle to South America.

Driver's License

If you're planning to drive anywhere, obtain an International Driving Permit or Inter-American Driving Permit (Uruguay theoretically recognizes only the latter). For about US$10 to US$15, any motoring organization will issue one, provided you have a current driver's license.

Insurance

Home auto insurance policies generally do not cover you while driving abroad. Throughout South America, if you are in an accident that injures or kills another person, you can be jailed until the case is settled, regardless of culpability. Fender benders are generally dealt with on the spot, without involving the police or insurance agents. When you rent, be certain your contract includes *seguro* (insurance).

Purchase

If you're spending several months in South America, purchasing a car is worth considering. It will be cheaper than hiring if you can resell it at the end of your stay. On the other hand, any used car can be a financial risk, especially on rugged roads, and the bureaucracy involved in purchasing a car can be horrendous.

The best countries in which to purchase cars are Argentina, Brazil and Chile, but, again, expect exasperating bureaucracies. By reputation, Santiago, Chile is the best place to buy a car, and Asunción, Paraguay is the best place to sell one. Be certain of the title; as a foreigner, getting a notarized document authorizing your use of the car is a good idea, since the bureaucracy may take its time transferring the title. Taking a vehicle purchased in South America across international borders may present obstacles.

Officially, you need a *carnet de passage* or a *libreta de pasos por aduana* (customs permit) to cross most land borders in your own vehicle, but you'll probably never have to show these documents. The best source of advice is the national automobile club in the country where you buy the car. In North America, the Canadian Automobile Association may be more helpful in getting a *carnet* than the American Automobile Association.

Rental

Major international rental agencies such as Hertz, Avis and Budget have offices in South American capitals, major cities and at major airports. Local agencies, however, often have better rates. To rent a car, you must be at least 25 and have a valid driver's license from home and a credit card. If your itinerary calls for crossing borders, know that some rental agencies restrict or forbid this; ask before renting.

Rates can fluctuate wildly (ranging from US$40 to US$80 per day). It's always worth getting a group together to defray costs. If the vehicle enables you to camp out, the saving in accommodations may offset much of the rental cost, especially in Southern Cone countries.

Road Rules

Except in Guyana and Suriname, South Americans drive on the right-hand side of the road. Road rules are frequently ignored and seldom enforced; conditions can be hazardous; and many drivers, especially in Argentina and Brazil, are reckless and even willfully dangerous. Driving at night is riskier than the day due to lower visibility and the preponderance of tired and/or intoxicated nighttime drivers sharing the road.

Road signs can be confusing, misleading or nonexistent – a good sense of humor and patience are key attributes. Honking your horn on blind curves is a simple, effective safety measure; the vehicle coming uphill on a one-way road usually has the right of way. If you're cruising along and see a tree branch or rock in the middle of the road, slow down: this means there's a breakdown, rock slide or some other trouble up ahead. Speed bumps can pop up anywhere, most often smack in the center of town, but sometimes inexplicably in the middle of a highway.

HITCHHIKING

Hitchhiking is never entirely safe in any country. Travelers who decide to hitch should understand they are taking a potentially serious risk. Hitching is less dangerous if you travel in pairs and let someone know where you are planning to go.

Though it is possible to hitch all over South America, free lifts are the rule only in Argentina, Chile, Uruguay and parts of Brazil. Elsewhere, hitching is virtually a form of public transport (especially where buses are infrequent) and drivers expect payment. There are generally fixed fares over certain routes; ask the other passengers what they're paying. It's usually about equal to the bus fare, marginally less in some places. You get better views from the top of a truck, but if you're hitching on the *altiplano* (Andean high plain of Peru, Bolivia, Chile and Argentina) or *páramo* (humid, high-altitude grassland) take warm clothing. Once the sun goes down or is obscured by clouds, it gets very cold.

There's no need to wait at the roadside for a lift, unless it happens to be convenient. Almost every town has a central truck park, often around the market. Ask around for a truck going your way and how much it will cost; be there about 30 minutes before the departure time given by the driver. It is often worth soliciting a ride at *servicentros* (gas stations) on the outskirts of large cities, where drivers refuel their vehicles.

TRANSPORTATION

Online, check out the South America section of **digihitch** (www.digihitch.com).

LOCAL TRANSPORTATION

Local and city bus systems tend to be thorough and reliable throughout South America. Although in many countries you can flag a bus anywhere on its route, you're best off finding the official bus stop. Still, if you can't find the stop, don't hesitate to throw your arm up to stop a bus you know is going your direction. Never hesitate to ask a bus driver which is the right bus to take; most of them are very generous in directing you to the right bus.

As in major cities throughout the world, pickpockets are a problem on crowded buses and subways. If you're on a crowded bus or subway, always watch your back. Avoid crowded public transport when you're loaded down with luggage. See also Dangers & Annoyances, p989.

Taxis in most big cities (but definitely not all) have meters. When a taxi has a meter, make sure the driver uses it. When it doesn't, always agree on a fare *before* you get in the cab. In most cities, fares are higher on Sundays and after around 9pm.

TRAIN

Trains are slowly fading from the South American landscape, but several spectacular routes still operate, offering some of the most unforgettable train rides on earth. Other non-touristy trains are often cheaper than buses (even in 1st class) but they're slower. If you're a railway enthusiast, or just a sucker for fun, try the following routes:

Curitiba–Paranaguá (Brazil) Descending steeply to the coastal lowlands, Brazil's best rail journey offers unforgettable views (p297).

Oruro–Uyuni–Tupiza–Villazón (Bolivia) The main line from Oruro continues south from Uyuni to Tupiza (another scenic rail trip through gorge country) and on to Villazón at the Argentine border (p203).

Puno–Juliaca–Cuzco (Peru) From the shores of Lake Titicaca and across a 4600m pass, this train runs for group bookings in high season. Departures are unpredictable, but when it does run, it's open to nongroup passengers (p809).

Riobamba–Sibambe (Ecuador) Jostle for a spot on the roof to enjoy the death-defying Nariz del Diablo (Devil's Nose), an exhilarating, steep descent via impossible switchbacks (p633).

Salta–La Polvorilla (Argentina) The Tren a las Nubes (Train to the Clouds) negotiates switchbacks, tunnels, spirals and death-defying bridges during its ascent into the Andean *puna* (highlands). Unfortunately, schedules are extremely unreliable (p103).

There are several types of passenger trains in the Andean countries. The *ferrobus* is a relatively fast, diesel-powered single or double car that caters to passengers going from A to B but not to intermediate stations. Meals are often available on board. These are the most expensive trains and can be great value.

The *tren rápido* is more like an ordinary train, pulled by a diesel or steam engine. It is relatively fast, makes few stops and is generally cheaper than a *ferrobus*. Ordinary passenger trains, sometimes called *expresos,* are slower, cheaper and stop at most intermediate stations. There are generally two classes, with 2nd class being very crowded. Lastly, there are *mixtos,* mixed passenger and freight trains; these take everything and everyone, stop at every station and a lot of other places in between, take forever and are dirt cheap.

The few remaining passenger trains in Chile and Argentina are generally more modern, and the salon and Pullman classes are very comfortable and quite inexpensive. The *economía* or *turista* classes are slightly cheaper, while the *cama* (sleeper class) is even more comfortable.

Health

CONTENTS

Medically speaking, there are two South Americas: tropical South America, which includes most of the continent except for the southernmost part, and temperate South America, including Chile, Uruguay, southern Argentina and the Falkland Islands. The diseases found in tropical South America are comparable to those found in tropical areas in Africa and Asia. Particularly important are mosquito-borne infections, including malaria, yellow fever and dengue fever, which are not a significant concern in temperate regions.

Prevention is the key to staying healthy while in South America. Travelers who receive the recommended vaccines and follow common-sense precautions usually go away with nothing more than a little diarrhea.

BEFORE YOU GO

Bring medications in their original, clearly labeled containers. A signed and dated letter from your physician describing your medical conditions and medications, including generic names, is also a good idea. If carrying syringes or needles, be sure to have a physician's letter documenting their medical necessity.

INSURANCE

If your health insurance doesn't cover you for medical expenses abroad, consider get-

ting extra insurance. Find out in advance if your insurance plan will make payments directly to providers or reimburse you later for overseas health expenditures. (In many countries doctors expect payment in cash.)

RECOMMENDED VACCINATIONS

Since most vaccines don't produce immunity until at least two weeks after they're given, visit a physician four to eight weeks before departure. Ask your doctor for an International Certificate of Vaccination (otherwise known as the yellow booklet), which will list all the vaccinations you've received. This is mandatory for countries that require proof of yellow-fever vaccination upon entry, but it's a good idea to carry it wherever you travel.

The only required vaccine is yellow fever, and that's only if you're arriving from a yellow fever–infected country in Africa or the Americas. (The exception is French Guiana, which requires yellow-fever vaccine for all travelers.) However, a number of vaccines are recommended (see above).

H1N1

The H1N1 virus (commonly referred to as 'swine flu') was given a 'Phase 6' rating by the World Health Organization in June 2009. A 'Phase 6' alert means the virus is now considered a global pandemic. All South American countries have been affected, some more than others.

At press time, airport staff in some countries were screening arriving passengers for symptoms of the H1N1 flu. Check with the embassy of the country you're visiting to see if they have imposed any travel restrictions. It's best not to travel if you have flu-like symptoms of any sort.

For the latest information, check with the World Health Organization (ww.who.intl).

MEDICAL CHECKLIST
- acetaminophen (Tylenol) or aspirin
- acetazolamide (Diamox; for altitude sickness)
- adhesive or paper tape
- antibacterial ointment (eg Bactroban; for cuts and abrasions)

RECOMMENDED VACCINATIONS

Vaccine	Recommended for	Dosage	Side effects
chickenpox	travelers who've never had chickenpox	two doses one month apart	fever; mild case of chickenpox
hepatitis A	all travelers	one dose before trip; booster 6-12 months later	soreness at injection site; headaches; body aches
hepatitis B	long-term travelers in close contact with the local population	3 doses over 6-month period	soreness at injection site; low-grade fever
measles	travelers born after 1956 who've had only one measles vaccination	one dose	fever; rash; joint pains; allergic reactions
rabies	travelers who may have contact with animals and may not have access to medical care	three doses over 3-4 week period	soreness at injection site; headaches; body aches
tetanus-diphtheria	travelers who haven't had booster within 10 years	one dose lasts 10 years	soreness at injection site
typhoid	all travelers	four capsules by mouth, one taken every other day	abdominal pain; nausea; rash
yellow fever	travelers to jungle areas at altitudes above 2300m	one dose lasts 10 years	headaches; body aches; severe reactions are rare

- antibiotics for diarrhea (eg Norfloxacin, Ciprofloxacin or Azithromycin)
- antihistamines (for hay fever and allergic reactions)
- anti-inflammatory drugs (eg ibuprofen)
- bandages, gauze, gauze rolls
- diarrhea 'stopper' (eg loperamide)
- insect repellent containing DEET for the skin
- iodine tablets (for water purification)
- oral rehydration salts
- permethrin-containing insect spray for clothing, tents and bed nets
- pocket knife
- scissors, safety pins, tweezers
- steroid cream or cortisone (for poison ivy and other allergic rashes)
- sun block
- syringes and sterile needles
- thermometer

INTERNET RESOURCES

There is a wealth of travel health advice on the internet. For further information, the **Lonely Planet website** (www.lonelyplanet.com) is a good place to start. The **World Health Organization** (www.who.int/ith) also publishes a superb book called *International Travel and Health*, which is revised annually and available online at no cost. Another resource of general interest is **MD Travel Health website** (www.mdtravelhealth.com), which provides complete travel health recommendations

for every country in the world; information is updated daily.

It's usually a good idea to consult your government's travel health website before departure, if one is available:

Australia (www.dfat.gov.au/travel)
Canada (www.travelhealth.gc.ca)
UK (www.doh.gov.uk/traveladvice)
US (www.cdc.gov/travel)

FURTHER READING

For further information, see Lonely Planet's *Healthy Travel Central & South America*. If you're traveling with children, Lonely Planet's *Travel with Children* may be useful. The *ABC of Healthy Travel*, by E Walker et al, is another valuable resource.

IN TRANSIT

DEEP VEIN THROMBOSIS (DVT)

Blood clots may form in the legs (deep vein thrombosis or DVT) during plane flights, chiefly because of prolonged immobility. The longer the flight, the greater the risk. Though most blood clots are reabsorbed uneventfully, some may break off and travel through the blood vessels to the lungs, where they could cause life-threatening complications.

The chief symptom of deep vein thrombosis is swelling or pain of the foot, ankle or calf, usually – but not always – on just one side. When a blood clot travels to the lungs, it may cause chest pain and difficulty breathing. Travelers who have any of these symptoms should immediately seek medical attention.

To prevent the development of DVT on long flights, you should walk about the cabin, perform isometric compressions of the leg muscles (ie flex the leg muscles while sitting), drink plenty of fluids and avoid alcohol and tobacco.

JET LAG & MOTION SICKNESS

Jet lag is common when crossing more than five time zones, resulting in insomnia, fatigue, malaise or nausea. To avoid jet lag, try drinking plenty of (nonalcoholic) fluids and eating light meals. Upon arrival, get exposure to natural sunlight and readjust your schedule (for meals, sleep etc) as soon as possible.

Antihistamines such as dimenhydrinate (Dramamine) and meclizine (Antivert, Bonine) are usually the first choice for treating motion sickness. Their main side effect is drowsiness. A herbal alternative is ginger, which works like a charm for some people.

IN SOUTH AMERICA

AVAILABILITY & COST OF HEALTH CARE

Good medical care may be more difficult to find in smaller cities and impossible to locate in rural areas. Many doctors and hospitals expect payment in cash, regardless of whether you have travel health insurance. If you develop a life-threatening medical problem, you'll probably want to be evacuated to a country with state-of-the-art medical care. Since this may cost tens of thousands of dollars, be sure you have insurance to cover this before you depart. You can find a list of medical evacuation and travel insurance companies on the **US State Department website** (travel.state.gov/medical.html).

INFECTIOUS DISEASES
Cholera

Cholera is an intestinal infection acquired through ingestion of contaminated food or water. The main symptom is profuse, watery diarrhea, which may be so severe that it causes life-threatening dehydration. The key treatment is drinking oral rehydration solution. Antibiotics are also given (usually

tetracycline or doxycycline) though quinolone antibiotics such as ciprofloxacin and levofloxacin are also effective.

Cholera is rare among travelers. Cholera vaccine is no longer required, and is in fact no longer available in some countries, including the US, because the old vaccine was relatively ineffective and caused side effects. There are new vaccines that are safer and more effective, but they're not available in many countries and are only recommended for those at particularly high risk.

Dengue

Dengue fever is a viral infection found throughout South America. Dengue is transmitted by Aedes mosquitoes, which bite preferentially during the daytime and are usually found close to human habitations, often indoors. They breed primarily in artificial water containers, such as jars, barrels, cans, cisterns, metal drums, plastic containers and discarded tires. As a result, dengue is especially common in densely populated, urban environments.

Dengue usually causes flu-like symptoms, including fever, muscle aches, joint pains, headaches, nausea and vomiting, often followed by a rash. The body aches may be quite uncomfortable, but most cases resolve uneventfully in a few days. Severe cases usually occur in children under age 15 who are experiencing their second dengue infection.

There is no treatment for dengue fever except to take analgesics such as acetaminophen/paracetamol (Tylenol) and drink plenty of fluids. Severe cases may require hospitalization for intravenous fluids and supportive care. There is no vaccine. The cornerstone of prevention is protection against insects (see p1017).

Keep an eye out for outbreaks in areas where you plan to visit. In 2009 Bolivia was experiencing its worst dengue outbreak in history, with more than 60,000 people infected. Brazil (particularly in Bahia) with 225,000 suspected cases and Argentina with 25,000 cases have also had serious outbreaks.

A good website on the latest information is the **CDC** (www.cdc.gov/travel).

Hepatitis A

Hepatitis A is the second most common travel-related infection (after travelers' diarrhea). It's a viral infection of the liver that's usually acquired by ingestion of contaminated water, food or ice, though it may also be acquired by direct contact with infected persons. The illness occurs throughout the world, but the incidence is higher in developing nations. Symptoms may include fever, malaise, jaundice, nausea, vomiting and abdominal pain. Most cases resolve themselves without complications, though hepatitis A occasionally causes severe liver damage. There is no treatment.

The vaccine for hepatitis A is extremely safe and highly effective. If you get a booster six to 12 months later, it lasts for at least 10 years. You really should get it before you go to any developing nation. The safety of hepatitis A vaccine has not been established for pregnant women or children under two years – instead, they should be given a gamma-globulin injection.

Hepatitis B

Like hepatitis A, hepatitis B is a liver infection that occurs worldwide but is more common in developing nations. Unlike hepatitis A, the disease is usually acquired by sexual contact or by exposure to infected blood, generally through blood transfusions or contaminated needles. The vaccine is recommended only for long-term travelers (on the road more than six months) who expect to live in rural areas or have close physical contact with the local population. Additionally, the vaccine is recommended for anyone who anticipates sexual contact with the local inhabitants or a possible need for medical, dental or other treatments while abroad, especially if a need for transfusions or injections is expected.

Hepatitis B vaccine is safe and highly effective. However, a total of three injections is necessary to establish full immunity. Several countries added hepatitis B vaccine to the list of routine childhood immunizations in the 1980s, so many young adults are already protected.

Malaria

Malaria occurs in every South American country except Chile, Uruguay and the Falkland Islands. It's transmitted by mosquito bites, usually between dusk and dawn. The main symptom is high spiking fevers, which may be accompanied by chills, sweats, headache, body aches, weakness, vomiting or diarrhea. Severe cases may involve the central nervous system and lead to seizures, confusion, coma and death.

There is a choice of three malaria pills, all of which work about equally well. Mefloquine (Lariam) is taken once weekly in a dosage of 250mg, starting one to two weeks before arrival and continuing through the trip and for four weeks after your return. The problem is that a certain percentage of people (the number is disputed) develop neuropsychiatric side effects, which may range from mild to severe. Atovaquone/proguanil (Malarone) is a newly approved combination pill taken once daily with food starting two days before arrival and continuing through the trip and for seven days after departure. Side effects are typically mild. Doxycycline is a third alternative, but may cause an exaggerated sunburn reaction.

In general, Malarone seems to cause fewer side effects than mefloquine and is becoming more popular. The chief disadvantage is that it has to be taken daily. For longer trips, it's probably worth trying mefloquine; for shorter trips, Malarone will be the drug of choice for most people.

Protecting yourself against mosquito bites is just as important as taking malaria pills (for recommendations, see p1017), since none of the pills are 100% effective.

If you do not have access to medical care while traveling, bring along additional pills for emergency self-treatment, which you should take if you can't reach a doctor and you develop symptoms that suggest malaria, such as high spiking fevers. One option is to take four tablets of Malarone once daily for three days. However, Malarone should not be used for treatment if you're already taking it for prevention. An alternative is to take 650mg quinine three times daily and 100mg doxycycline twice daily for one week. If you start self-medication, see a doctor at the earliest possible opportunity.

If you develop a fever after returning home, see a physician, as malaria symptoms may not occur for months.

Plague

The plague is usually transmitted to humans by the bite of rodent fleas, typically when rodents die off. Symptoms include fever, chills, muscle aches and malaise, associated with the development of an acutely swollen, extremely painful lymph node, known as a bubo, most often in the groin. Cases of the plague are reported from Peru, Bolivia and Brazil nearly every year. Most travelers are at extremely low risk for this disease. However, if you might have contact with rodents or their fleas, you should bring along a bottle of doxycycline, to be taken prophylactically during periods of exposure. Those less than eight years old or allergic to doxycycline should take trimethoprim-sulfamethoxazole instead. In addition, avoid areas containing rodent burrows or nests, never handle sick or dead animals, and follow the guidelines in this chapter for protecting yourself against insect bites (see p1017).

Rabies

Rabies is a viral infection of the brain and spinal cord that is almost always fatal. The rabies virus is carried in the saliva of infected animals and is typically transmitted through an animal bite, though contamination of any break in the skin with infected saliva may result in rabies. Rabies occurs in all South American countries.

Rabies vaccine is safe, but a full series requires three injections and is quite expensive. Those at high risk for rabies, such as animal handlers and spelunkers (cave explorers), should certainly get the vaccine. In addition, those at lower risk for animal bites should consider asking for the vaccine if they might be traveling to remote areas and might not have access to appropriate medical care if needed. The treatment for a possibly rabid bite consists of rabies vaccine with rabies-immune globulin. It's effective, but must be given promptly. Most travelers don't need rabies vaccine.

All animal bites and scratches must be promptly and thoroughly cleansed with large amounts of soap and water, and local health authorities should be contacted to determine whether further treatment is necessary. Also see p1017.

Typhoid

Typhoid fever is caused by ingestion of food or water contaminated by a species of salmonella known as *Salmonella typhi*. Fever occurs in virtually all cases. Other symptoms may include headache, malaise, muscle aches, dizziness, loss of appetite, nausea and abdominal pain. Either diarrhea or constipation may occur. Possible complications include intestinal perforation, intestinal bleeding, confusion, delirium or (rarely) coma.

Unless you expect to take all your meals in major hotels and restaurants, typhoid vaccine is a good idea. It's usually given orally, but is also available as an injection. Neither vaccine is approved for use in children under two years.

The drug of choice for typhoid fever is usually a quinolone antibiotic such as ciprofloxacin (Cipro) or levofloxacin (Levaquin), which many travelers carry for treatment of travelers' diarrhea. However, if you self-treat for typhoid fever, you may also need to self-treat for malaria, since the symptoms of the two diseases may be indistinguishable.

Yellow Fever

Yellow fever is a life-threatening viral infection transmitted by mosquitoes in forested areas. The illness begins with flu-like symptoms, which may include fever, chills, headache, muscle aches, backache, loss of appetite, nausea and vomiting. These symptoms usually subside in a few days, but one person in six enters a second, toxic phase characterized by recurrent fever, vomiting, listlessness, jaundice, kidney failure and hemorrhage, leading to death in up to half of the cases. There is no treatment except for supportive care.

Yellow-fever vaccine can be given only in approved yellow-fever vaccination centers, which provide validated International Certificates of Vaccination (yellow booklets). The vaccine should be given at least 10 days before any potential exposure to yellow fever and remains effective for approximately 10 years. Reactions to the vaccine are generally mild and may include headaches, muscle aches, low-grade fevers, or discomfort at the injection site. Severe, life-threatening reactions have been described but are extremely rare. In general, the risk of becoming ill from the vaccine is far less than the risk of becoming ill from yellow fever, and you're strongly encouraged to get the vaccine.

Taking measures to protect yourself from mosquito bites (p1017) is an essential part of preventing yellow fever.

Other Infections
BARTONELLOSIS (OROYA FEVER)

Bartonellosis (Oroya fever) is carried by sand flies in the arid river valleys on the western slopes of the Andes in Peru, Colombia and Ecuador between altitudes of 800m and 3000m. (Curiously, it's not found anywhere else in the world.) The chief symptoms are fever and severe body pains. Complications may include marked anemia, enlargement of the liver and spleen, and sometimes death. The drug of choice is chloramphenicol, though doxycycline is also effective.

CHAGAS' DISEASE

Chagas' disease is a parasitic infection that is transmitted by triatomine insects (reduviid bugs), which inhabit crevices in the walls and roofs of substandard housing in South and Central America. In Peru, most cases occur in the southern part of the country. The triatomine insect lays its feces on human skin as it bites, usually at night. A person becomes infected when he or she unknowingly rubs the feces into the bite wound or any other open sore. Chagas' disease is extremely rare in travelers. However, if you sleep in a poorly constructed house, especially one made of mud, adobe or thatch, be sure to protect yourself with a bed net and a good insecticide.

GNATHOSTOMIASIS

Gnathostomiasis is an intestinal parasite acquired by eating raw or undercooked freshwater fish, including *ceviche* (marinated, uncooked seafood).

HISTOPLASMOSIS

Histoplasmosis is caused by a soil-based fungus that is acquired by inhalation, often when the soil has been disrupted. Initial symptoms may include fever, chills, dry cough, chest pain and headache, sometimes leading to pneumonia. Histoplasmosis has been reported in spelunkers who have visited caves inhabited by bats.

HIV/AIDS

HIV/AIDS has been reported in all South American countries. Be sure to use condoms for all sexual encounters.

LEISHMANIASIS

Leishmaniasis occurs in the mountains and jungles of all South American countries except for Chile, Uruguay and the Falkland Islands. The infection is transmitted by sand flies, which are about one-third the size of mosquitoes. Leishmaniasis may be limited to the skin, causing slow-growing ulcers over exposed parts of the body or (less commonly) disseminate to the bone marrow, liver and spleen. The disease may be particularly severe

in those with HIV. There is no vaccine. To protect yourself from sand flies, follow the same precautions as for mosquitoes (opposite), except that netting must be finer-mesh (at least 18 holes to the linear inch).

LEPTOSPIROSIS

Leptospirosis is acquired by exposure to water contaminated by the urine of infected animals. Outbreaks often occur at times of flooding, when sewage overflow may contaminate water sources. The initial symptoms, which resemble a mild flu, usually subside uneventfully in a few days, with or without treatment, but a minority of cases are complicated by jaundice or meningitis. There is no vaccine. You can minimize your risk by staying out of bodies of fresh water that may be contaminated by animal urine. If you're visiting an area where an outbreak is in progress, you can take 200mg of doxycycline once weekly as a preventive measure. If you develop leptospirosis, the treatment is 100mg of doxycycline twice daily.

ENVIRONMENTAL HAZARDS
Altitude Sickness

Altitude sickness may develop in those who ascend rapidly to altitudes greater than 2500m. Being physically fit offers no protection. Those who have experienced altitude sickness in the past are prone to future episodes. The risk increases with faster ascents, higher altitudes and greater exertion. Symptoms may include headaches, nausea, vomiting, dizziness, malaise, insomnia and loss of appetite. Severe cases may be complicated by fluid in the lungs (high-altitude pulmonary edema) or swelling of the brain (high-altitude cerebral edema).

To protect yourself against altitude sickness, take 125mg or 250mg acetazolamide (Diamox) twice or three times daily starting 24 hours before ascent and continuing for 48 hours after arrival at altitude. Possible side effects include increased urinary volume, numbness, tingling, nausea, drowsiness, myopia and temporary impotence. Acetazolamide should not be given to pregnant women or anyone with a history of sulfa allergy. For those who cannot tolerate acetazolamide, the next best option is 4mg dexamethasone taken four times daily. Unlike acetazolamide, dexamethasone must be tapered gradually upon arrival at altitude, since there is a risk that altitude sickness will occur as the dosage is reduced. Dexamethasone is a steroid, so it should not be given to diabetics or anyone for whom steroids are contraindicated. A natural alternative is gingko, which some people find quite helpful.

When traveling to high altitudes, it's also important to avoid overexertion, eat light meals and abstain from alcohol.

If your symptoms are more than mild or don't resolve promptly, see a doctor. Altitude sickness should be taken seriously; it can be life-threatening when severe.

Animal Bites

Do not attempt to pet, handle or feed any animal, with the exception of domestic animals known to be free of any infectious disease. Most animal injuries are directly related to a person's attempt to touch or feed the animal.

Any bite or scratch by a mammal, including bats, should be promptly and thoroughly cleansed with large amounts of soap and water, followed by application of an antiseptic such as iodine or alcohol. The local health authorities should be contacted immediately for possible post-exposure rabies treatment, whether or not you've been immunized against rabies. It may also be advisable to start an antibiotic, since wounds caused by animal bites and scratches frequently become infected. One of the newer quinolones, such as levofloxacin (Levaquin), which many travelers carry in case of diarrhea, would be an appropriate choice.

Snakes and leeches are a hazard in some areas of South America. In the event of a bite from a venomous snake, place the victim at rest, keep the bitten area immobilized, and move the victim immediately to the nearest medical facility. Avoid tourniquets, which are no longer recommended.

Cold Exposure & Hypothermia

Cold exposure may be a significant problem in the Andes, particularly at night. Be sure to dress warmly, stay dry, keep active, consume plenty of food and water, get enough rest, and avoid alcohol, caffeine and tobacco. Watch out for the 'umbles' – stumbles, mumbles, fumbles and grumbles – which are important signs of impending hypothermia.

Hypothermia occurs when the body loses heat faster than it can produce it and the core temperature of the body falls. If you're trekking at high altitudes or simply taking a long

bus trip over mountains, particularly at night, be prepared. In the Andes, you should always be prepared for cold, wet or windy conditions even if it's just for a few hours. It is best to dress in layers, and a hat is important, as a lot of heat is lost through the head.

The symptoms of hypothermia include exhaustion, numbness, shivering, slurred speech, irrational or violent behavior, lethargy, stumbling, dizzy spells, muscle cramps and violent bursts of energy. To treat mild hypothermia, first get people out of the wind or rain, remove their clothing if it's wet and give them something warm and dry to wear. Make them drink hot liquids – not alcohol – and some high-calorie, easily digestible food. Do not rub victims – instead allow them to slowly warm themselves. This should be enough to treat hypothermia's early stages. Early detection and treatment of mild hypothermia is the only way to prevent severe hypothermia, which is a critical condition.

Heatstroke

To protect yourself from excessive sun exposure, you should stay out of the midday sun, wear sunglasses and a wide-brimmed sun hat, and apply sunscreen with SPF 15 or higher, with both UVA and UVB protection. Sunscreen should be generously applied to all exposed parts of the body approximately 30 minutes before sun exposure and should be reapplied after swimming or vigorous activity. Travelers should also drink plenty of fluids and avoid strenuous exercise when the temperature is high.

Insect Bites & Stings

To prevent mosquito bites, wear long sleeves, long pants, a hat and shoes (rather than sandals). Bring along a good insect repellent, preferably one containing DEET, which should be applied to exposed skin and clothing, but not to eyes, mouth, cuts, wounds or irritated skin. Products containing lower concentrations of DEET are as effective, but for shorter periods of time. In general, adults and children over 12 years should use preparations containing 25% to 35% DEET, which usually lasts about six hours. Children between two and 12 years of age should use preparations containing no more than 10% DEET, applied sparingly, which will usually last about three hours. Neurologic toxicity has been reported from DEET, especially in children, but appears to be

HEALTH

extremely uncommon and generally related to overuse. DEET-containing compounds should not be used on children under age two.

Insect repellents containing certain botanical products, including oil of eucalyptus and soybean oil, are effective but last only 1½ to two hours. DEET-containing repellents are preferable for areas where there is a high risk of malaria or yellow fever. Products based on citronella are not effective.

For additional protection, you can apply permethrin to clothing, shoes, tents and bed nets. Permethrin treatments are safe and remain effective for at least two weeks, even when items are laundered. Permethrin should not be applied directly to skin.

Don't sleep with the window open unless there is a screen. If sleeping outdoors or in accommodations that allow entry of mosquitoes, use a bed net, preferably treated with permethrin, with edges tucked in under the mattress. The mesh size should be less than 1.5mm. If the sleeping area is not otherwise protected, use a mosquito coil, which will fill the room with insecticide through the night. Wristbands impregnated with repellent are not effective.

Parasites

Intestinal parasites occur throughout South America. Common pathogens include Cyclospora, amoebae and Isospora. A tapeworm called Taenia solium may lead to a chronic brain infection called cysticercosis. If you exercise discretion in your choice of food and beverages, you'll sharply reduce your chances of becoming infected. Choose restaurants or market stalls that are well attended. If there's a high turnover, it means food hasn't been sitting around that long. At markets and street vendors, check out how the plates and cutlery are washed. If there's anything that strikes you as particularly unhygienic, move on.

A parasitic infection called schistosomiasis, which primarily affects the blood vessels in the liver, occurs in Brazil, Suriname and parts of north-central Venezuela. The disease is acquired by swimming, wading, bathing or washing in fresh water that contains infected snails. It's therefore best to stay out of bodies of fresh water, such as lakes, ponds, streams and rivers, in places where schistosomiasis might occur. Toweling yourself dry after exposure to contaminated water may reduce

your risk of becoming infected, but doesn't eliminate it. Chlorinated pools are safe.

A liver parasite called Echinococcus (hydatid disease) is found in many countries, especially Peru and Uruguay. It typically affects those in close contact with sheep. A lung parasite called Paragonimus, which is ingested by eating raw infected crustaceans, has been reported from Ecuador, Peru and Venezuela.

Travelers' Diarrhea

To prevent diarrhea, avoid tap water unless it has been boiled, filtered, irradiated with UV light (as performed by a SteriPEN) or chemically disinfected (with iodine tablets); only eat fresh fruits or vegetables if cooked or peeled; be wary of dairy products that might contain unpasteurized milk; and be highly selective when eating food from markets and street vendors.

If you develop diarrhea, be sure to drink plenty of fluids, preferably an oral rehydration solution containing salt and sugar. Gastrolyte works well for this. A few loose stools don't require treatment but you may want to take antibiotics if you start having more than three watery bowel movements within 24 hours, and it's accompanied by at least one other symptom – fever, cramps, nausea, vomiting or generally feeling unwell. Effective antibiotics include Norfloxacin, Ciprofloxacin or Azithromycin – all will kill the bacteria quickly. Note that an antidiarrheal agent (such as loperamide) is just a 'stopper' and doesn't get to the cause of the problem. Don't take loperamide if you have a fever or blood in your stools. Seek medical attention quickly if you don't respond to an appropriate antibiotic.

Water

Tap water is generally not safe to drink. Vigorous boiling for one minute is the most effective means of water purification. At altitudes greater than 2000m, boil for three minutes.

The latest method of purification is with a handheld water purifier that uses ultraviolet light to purify water. A SteriPEN – available online and in some camping stores – is a safe, effective and lightweight device for accomplishing this. Another option is to disinfect water with iodine. You can add 2% tincture of iodine to 1L of water (five drops to clear water, 10 drops to cloudy water) and let stand for 30 minutes. If the water is cold, longer times may be required. Or you can buy iodine pills such as Globaline, Potable-Aqua and Coghlan's, available at most pharmacies. Instructions are enclosed and should be carefully followed. The taste of iodinated water may be improved by adding vitamin C (ascorbic acid). Iodinated water should not be consumed for more than a few weeks. Pregnant women, those with a history of thyroid disease, and those allergic to iodine should not drink iodinated water.

A number of water filters are on the market. Those with smaller pores (reverse osmosis filters) provide the broadest protection, but they are relatively large and readily plugged by debris. Those with somewhat larger pores (microstrainer filters) are ineffective against viruses, although they remove other organisms. Manufacturers' instructions must be carefully followed.

TRADITIONAL MEDICINE

Some common traditional remedies include:

TRADITIONAL MEDICINE	
Problem	**Treatment**
altitude sickness	gingko
jet lag	melatonin
mosquito-bite prevention	eucalyptus oil, soybean oil
motion sickness	ginger

WOMEN'S HEALTH

It may be difficult to find quality obstetric care, if needed, outside major cities. In addition, it isn't advisable for pregnant women to spend time at altitudes where the air is thin. Lastly, yellow-fever vaccine is strongly recommended for travel to all jungle areas at altitudes less than 2300m, but should not be given during pregnancy because the vaccine contains a live virus that may infect the fetus.

HEALTH

Language

CONTENTS

LATIN AMERICAN SPANISH

Latin American Spanish is the language of choice for travelers in all parts of South America except for Brazil (where Portuguese is the national tongue) and the Guianas (where French, Dutch or English are largely spoken). For a more in-depth guide to the language, get a copy of Lonely Planet's *Latin American Spanish* phrasebook.

PRONUNCIATION

Latin American Spanish is easy, as most of the sounds are also found in English. If you follow our pronunciation guides (included alongside the Spanish phrases), you'll have no problems being understood.

Vowels

There are four sounds that roughly correspond to diphthongs (vowel sound combinations) in English.

a	as the 'a' in 'father'
ai	as in 'aisle'
ay	as in 'say'
e	as the 'e' in 'met'
ee	as the 'ee' in 'meet'
o	as the 'o' in 'more' (without the 'r')
oo	as the 'oo' in 'zoo'
ow	as in 'how'
oy	as in 'boy'

Consonants

Pronunciation of Spanish consonants is similar to their English counterparts. The exceptions are given in the following list.

kh	as the throaty 'ch' in the Scottish *loch*
ny	as the 'ny' in 'canyon'
r	as in 'run' but stronger and rolled, especially at the beginning of a word and in all words with *rr*
s	not lisped (unlike in Spain)

The letter 'h' is invariably silent (ie never pronounced) in Spanish.

Note also that the Spanish **b** and **v** sounds are very similar – they are both pronounced as a very soft 'v' in English (somewhere between 'b' and 'v').

You may also hear some variations in spoken Spanish as part of the regional accents across Latin America. The most notable of these variations is the pronunciation of the letter *ll*. In some parts of the continent it's pronounced as the 'lli' in 'million,' while in Argentina, Uruguay and highland Ecuador it sounds like the 's' in 'measure.' You don't need to worry about these distinctions, however – in much of Latin America the letter 'll' is pronounced as 'y' (eg as in 'yes'), and this is how it's represented in our pronunciation guides, so you'll be understood across the continent.

Word Stress

In general, Spanish words ending in vowels or the consonants -*n* or -*s* are stressed on the second-last syllable, while those with other endings have stress on the last syllable. Written accents denote stress, and override the rules above, eg *sótano* (basement), *América, porción* (portion).

In our pronunciation guides the stressed syllable is indicated with italics, so you needn't worry about these rules.

GENDER & PLURALS

In Spanish, nouns are either masculine or feminine, and there are rules to help determine gender. Feminine nouns generally end with -*a*, -*ad*, -*z* or -*ión*. Other endings, particularly -*o*, typically signify a masculine noun. Endings for adjectives also change to agree with the gender of the noun they modify (masculine/feminine -*o*/-*a*). Where both masculine and feminine forms are included in this chapter, they are separated by a slash, with the masculine form given first, eg *perdido/a*.

If a noun or adjective ends in a vowel, the plural is formed by adding *-s*. If it ends in a consonant, the plural is formed by adding *-es* to the end of the word.

ACCOMMODATIONS

I'm looking	Estoy	e·stoy
for a ...	buscando ...	boos·kan·do ...
Where's a ...?	¿Dónde hay ...?	don·de ai ...
camping	un terreno de	oon te·re·no de
ground	cámping	kam·peen
climbers'	un refugio	oon re·foo·khyo
refuge		
guesthouse	una pensión/	oo·na pen·syon/
	un hostal/	oon os·tal/
	un hospedaje	oon os·pe·da·khe
hotel	un hotel	oon o·tel
youth hostel	un albergue	oon al·ber·ge
	juvenil	khoo·ve·neel

I'd like a ...	Quisiera una	kee·sye·ra oo·na
room.	habitación ...	a·bee·ta·syon ...
double	doble	do·ble
single	individual	een·dee·vee·dwal
twin	con dos camas	kon dos ka·mas

How much is it	¿Cuánto cuesta	kwan·to kwes·ta
per ...?	por ...?	por ...
night	noche	no·che
person	persona	per·so·na
week	semana	se·ma·na

Does it include breakfast?
¿Incluye el desayuno? een·*kloo*·ye el de·sa·*yoo*·no
Can I see the room?
¿Puedo ver la pwe·do ver la
habitación? a·bee·ta·*syon*
I don't like it.
No me gusta. no me *goos*·ta
It's fine, I'll take it.
OK, la alquilo. o·*kay* la al·*kee*·lo
I'm leaving now.
Me voy ahora. me voy a·o·ra

cheaper	más económico	mas e·ko·no·mee·ko
discount	descuento	des·kwen·to
private/shared	baño privado/	ba·nyo pree·va·do/
bathroom	compartido	kom·par·tee·do
too expensive	demasiado caro	de·ma·sya·do ka·ro

MAKING A RESERVATION
(for phone or written requests)

From ...	De ...
To ...	A ...
Date	Fecha
I'd like to book ...	Quisiera reservar ...
in the name of ...	en nombre de ...
for the nights of ...	para las noches del ...
credit card	tarjeta de crédito
expiry date	fecha de vencimiento
number	número
Please confirm ...	¿Puede confirmar ...?
availability	la disponibilidad
price	el precio

CONVERSATION & ESSENTIALS

In their public behavior, South Americans are very conscious of civilities, sometimes to the point of ceremoniousness. Never approach a stranger for information without extending a greeting and use only the polite form of address, especially with the police and public officials. Young people may be less likely to expect this, but it's best to stick to the polite form unless you're sure you won't offend by using the informal mode. The polite form is used in this chapter; where options are given, the form is indicated by the abbreviations 'pol' and 'inf.'

Hello. (inf)	Hola.	o·la
Good morning.	Buenos días.	bwe·nos dee·as
Good afternoon.	Buenas tardes.	bwe·nas tar·des
Good evening/	Buenas noches.	bwe·nas no·ches
night.		
Goodbye.	Adiós.	a·dyos
See you later.	Hasta luego.	as·ta lwe·go
Yes./No.	Sí./No.	see/no
Please.	Por favor.	por fa·vor
Thank you.	Gracias.	gra·syas
Many thanks.	Muchas gracias.	moo·chas gra·syas
You're welcome.	De nada.	de na·da
Pardon.	Perdón.	per·don
Excuse me.	Permiso.	per·mee·so
(asking permission)		
Forgive me.	Disculpe.	dees·kool·pe
(apologizing)		
How are things?	¿Qué tal?	ke tal

What's your name?
¿Cómo se llama? ko·mo se ya·ma (pol)
¿Cómo te llamas? ko·mo te ya·mas (inf)

My name is ...
Me llamo ...   me *ya*·mo ...
It's a pleasure to meet you.
Mucho gusto.   moo·cho *goos*·to
The pleasure is mine.
El gusto es mío.   el *goos*·to es *mee*·o
Where are you from?
¿De dónde es/eres?   de *don*·de es/e·res (pol/inf)
I'm from ...
Soy de ...   soy de ...
Where are you staying?
¿Dónde está alojado/a?   don·de es·*ta* a·lo·*kha*·do/a (pol)
¿Dónde estás alojado/a? don·de es·*tas* a·lo·*kha*·do/a (inf)
May I take a photo?
¿Puedo sacar una foto?   pwe·do sa·*kar* oo·na *fo*·to

DIRECTIONS
How do I get to ...?
¿Cómo puedo   ko·mo *pwe*·do
llegar a ...?   ye·*gar* a ...
Is it far?
¿Está lejos?   es·ta *le*·khos
Go straight ahead.
Vaya todo derecho.   va·ya *to*·do de·*re*·cho
Turn left/right.
Voltée a la izquierda/   vol·*te*·e a la ees·*kyer*·da/
derecha.   de·*re*·cha
Can you show me (on the map)?
¿Me lo podría indicar   me lo po·*dree*·a een·dee·*kar*
(en el mapa)?   (en el *ma*·pa)

north	norte	nor·te
south	sur	soor
east	este/oriente	es·te/o·ryen·te
west	oeste/occidente	o·es·te/ok·see·den·te

here	aquí	a·kee
there	allí	a·yee
avenue	avenida	a·ve·nee·da
block	cuadra	kwa·dra
highway	carretera	ka·re·te·ra
street	calle/paseo	ka·ye/pa·se·o

SIGNS

Abierto	Open
Cerrado	Closed
Comisaría	Police Station
Entrada	Entrance
Información	Information
Prohibido	Prohibited
Salida	Exit
Servicios/Baños	Toilets
Hombres/Varones	Men
Mujeres/Damas	Women

EMERGENCIES

Help!	¡Socorro!	so·ko·ro
Fire!	¡Incendio!	een·sen·dyo
I was robbed.	Me robaron.	me ro·ba·ron
Go away!	¡Déjeme!	de·khe·me
Get lost!	¡Váyase!	va·ya·se

Call ...!	¡Llame a ...!	ya·me a ...
an ambulance	una ambulancia	oo·na am·boo·lan·sya
a doctor	un médico	oon me·dee·ko
the police	la policía	la po·lee·see·a

It's an emergency.
Es una emergencia.   es oo·na e·mer·*khen*·sya
Can you help me, please?
¿Me puede ayudar,   me *pwe*·de a·yoo·*dar*
por favor?   por fa·*vor*
I'm lost.
Estoy perdido/a.   es·*toy* per·*dee*·do/a
Where are the toilets?
¿Dónde están los baños? don·de es·*tan* los *ba*·nyos

HEALTH
I'm sick.
Estoy enfermo/a.   es·toy en·*fer*·mo/a
I need a doctor.
Necesito un médico.   ne·se·*see*·to oon *me*·dee·ko
Where's the hospital?
¿Dónde está el hospital? don·de es·*ta* el os·pee·*tal*
I'm pregnant.
Estoy embarazada.   es·*toy* em·ba·ra·*sa*·da
I've been vaccinated.
Estoy vacunado/a.   es·*toy* va·koo·*na*·do/a

I'm allergic to ...	Soy alérgico/a a ...	soy a·ler·khee·ko/a a ...
antibiotics	los antibióticos	los an·tee·byo·tee·kos
nuts	las nueces	las nwe·ses
penicillin	la penicilina	la pe·nee·see·lee·na

I'm ...	Soy ...	soy ...
asthmatic	asmático/a	as·ma·tee·ko/a
diabetic	diabético/a	dya·be·tee·ko/a
epileptic	epiléptico/a	e·pee·lep·tee·ko/a

I have (a) ...	Tengo ...	ten·go ...
altitude sickness	soroche	so·ro·che
cough	tos	tos
diarrhea	diarrea	dya·re·a
headache	un dolor de cabeza	oon do·lor de ka·be·sa
nausea	náusea	now·se·a

LANGUAGE DIFFICULTIES

Do you speak English?

¿Habla/Hablas inglés?   a·bla/a·blas een·gles (pol/inf)

Does anyone here speak English?

¿Hay alguien que hable   ai al·gyen ke a·ble
inglés?   een·gles

I (don't) understand.

Yo (no) entiendo.   yo (no) en·tyen·do

How do you say ...?

¿Cómo se dice ...?   ko·mo se dee·se ...

What does ... mean?

¿Qué quiere decir ...?   ke kye·re de·seer ...

Could you	¿Puede ..., por	pwe·de ... por
please ...?	favor?	fa·vor
repeat that	repetirlo	re·pe·teer·lo
speak more	hablar más	a·blar mas
slowly	despacio	des·pa·syo
write it down	escribirlo	es·kree·beer·lo

NUMBERS

1	uno	oo·no
2	dos	dos
3	tres	tres
4	cuatro	kwa·tro
5	cinco	seen·ko
6	seis	says
7	siete	sye·te
8	ocho	o·cho
9	nueve	nwe·ve
10	diez	dyes
11	once	on·se
12	doce	do·se
13	trece	tre·se
14	catorce	ka·tor·se
15	quince	keen·se
16	dieciséis	dye·see·says
17	diecisiete	dye·see·sye·te
18	dieciocho	dye·see·o·cho
19	diecinueve	dye·see·nwe·ve
20	veinte	vayn·te
21	veintiuno	vayn·tee·oo·no
30	treinta	trayn·ta
31	treinta y uno	trayn·ta ee oo·no
40	cuarenta	kwa·ren·ta
50	cincuenta	seen·kwen·ta
60	sesenta	se·sen·ta
70	setenta	se·ten·ta
80	ochenta	o·chen·ta
90	noventa	no·ven·ta
100	cien	syen
101	ciento uno	syen·to oo·no
200	doscientos	do·syen·tos
1000	mil	meel
5000	cinco mil	seen·ko meel
10,000	diez mil	dyes meel
50,000	cincuenta mil	seen·kwen·ta meel
100,000	cien mil	syen meel
1,000,000	un millón	oon mee·yon

SHOPPING & SERVICES

I'd like to buy ...

Quisiera comprar ...   kee·sye·ra kom·prar ...

I'm just looking.

Sólo estoy mirando.   so·lo es·toy mee·ran·do

May I look at it?

¿Puedo mirar(lo/la)?   pwe·do mee·rar(·lo/·la)

How much is it?

¿Cuánto cuesta?   kwan·to kwes·ta

That's too expensive for me.

Es demasiado caro   es de·ma·sya·do ka·ro
para mí.   pa·ra mee

Could you lower the price?

¿Podría bajar un poco   po·dree·a ba·khar oon po·ko
el precio?   el pre·syo

I don't like it.

No me gusta.   no me goos·ta

I'll take it.

Lo llevo.   lo ye·vo

Do you	¿Aceptan ...?	a·sep·tan ...
accept ...?		
American	dólares	do·la·res
dollars	americanos	a·me·ree·ka·nos
credit cards	tarjetas de	tar·khe·tas de
	crédito	kre·dee·to
traveler's	cheques de	che·kes de
checks	viajero	vya·khe·ro
more	más	mas
less	menos	me·nos
large	grande	gran·de
small	pequeño/a	pe·ke·nyo/a
I'm looking	Estoy	es·toy
for (the) ...	buscando ...	boos·kan·do ...
ATM	el cajero	el ka·khe·ro
	automático	ow·to·ma·tee·ko
bank	el banco	el ban·ko
bookstore	la librería	la lee·bre·ree·a
chemist/	la farmacia/	la far·ma·sya/
pharmacy	botica	bo·tee·ka
embassy	la embajada	la em·ba·kha·da
exchange house	la casa de	la ka·sa de
	cambio	kam·byo
general store	la tienda	la tyen·da
laundry	la lavandería	la la·van·de·ree·a
post office	el correo	el ko·re·o
(super)market	el (super-)	el (soo·per·)
	mercado	mer·ka·do
tourist office	la oficina de	la o·fee·see·na de
	turismo	too·rees·mo

What time does it open/close?

¿A qué hora abre/cierra?   a ke o·ra a·bre/sye·ra

I want to change some money/traveler's checks.

Quiero cambiar dinero/   kye·ro kam·byar dee·ne·ro/
cheques de viajero.   che·kes de vya·khe·ro

What is the exchange rate?

¿Cuál es el tipo de   kwal es el tee·po de
cambio?   kam·byo

I want to call ...

Quiero llamar a ...   kye·ro ya·mar a ...

airmail	*correo aéreo*	ko·re·o a·e·re·o
black market	*mercado negro*	mer·ka·do ne·gro
letter	*carta*	kar·ta
registered mail	*certificado*	ser·tee·fee·ka·do
stamps	*estampillas*	es·tam·pee·yas

TIME & DATES

What time is it?	*¿Qué hora es?*	ke o·ra es
It's one o'clock.	*Es la una.*	es la oo·na
It's (seven) o'clock.	*Son las (siete).*	son las (sye·te)
It's half past (two).	*Son las (dos) y media.*	son las (dos) ee me·dya
It's quarter to (three).	*Son las (tres) menos quarto.*	son las (tres) me·nos kwar·to
midnight	*medianoche*	me·dya·no·che
noon	*mediodía*	me·dyo·dee·a

yesterday	*ayer*	a·yer
today	*hoy*	oy
now	*ahora*	a·o·ra
tonight	*esta noche*	es·ta no·che
tomorrow	*mañana*	ma·nya·na

Monday	*lunes*	loo·nes
Tuesday	*martes*	mar·tes
Wednesday	*miércoles*	myer·ko·les
Thursday	*jueves*	khwe·ves
Friday	*viernes*	vyer·nes
Saturday	*sábado*	sa·ba·do
Sunday	*domingo*	do·meen·go

January	*enero*	e·ne·ro
February	*febrero*	fe·bre·ro
March	*marzo*	mar·so
April	*abril*	a·breel
May	*mayo*	ma·yo
June	*junio*	khoo·nyo
July	*julio*	khoo·lyo
August	*agosto*	a·gos·to
September	*septiembre*	sep·tyem·bre
October	*octubre*	ok·too·bre
November	*noviembre*	no·vyem·bre
December	*diciembre*	dee·syem·bre

TRANSPORTATION
Public Transportation

What time does the ... leave/arrive?	*¿A qué hora sale/llega el ...?*	a ke o·ra sa·le/ye·ga el ...
bus	*autobus*	ow·to·boos
minibus	*colectivo*	ko·lek·tee·vo
plane	*avión*	a·vyon
ship	*barco/buque*	bar·ko/boo·ke
train	*tren*	tren

airport	*el aeropuerto*	el a·e·ro·pwer·to
bus station	*el terminal de autobuses*	el ter·mee·nal de ow·to·boo·ses
bus stop	*la parada de autobuses*	la pa·ra·da de ow·to·boo·ses
luggage check room	*guardería de equipaje*	gwar·de·ree·a de e·kee·pa·khe
ticket office	*la boletería*	la bo·le·te·ree·a
train station	*la estación de ferrocarril*	la es·ta·syon de fe·ro·ka·reel

I'd like a ticket to ...

Quisiera un boleto a ...   kee·sye·ra oon bo·le·to a ...

What's the fare to ...?

¿Cuánto cuesta hasta ...?   kwan·to kwes·ta a·sta ...

1st class	*primera clase*	pree·me·ra kla·se
2nd class	*segunda clase*	se·goon·da kla·se
one-way	*ida*	ee·da
round-trip	*ida y vuelta*	ee·da ee vwel·ta
taxi/shared taxi	*taxi/colectivo*	tak·see/ko·lek·tee·vo

Private Transportation

I'd like to hire a ...	*Quisiera alquilar ...*	kee·sye·ra al·kee·lar ...
4WD	*un todo terreno*	oon to·do te·re·no
bicycle	*una bicicleta*	oo·na bee·see·kle·ta
car	*un auto*	oon ow·to
motorbike	*una moto*	oo·na mo·to

hitchhike	*hacer dedo*	a·ser de·do
pickup (truck)	*camioneta*	ka·myo·ne·ta
truck	*camión*	ka·myon

Is this the road to ...?

¿Se va a ... por esta carretera?   se va a ... por es·ta ka·re·te·ra

Where's a gas/petrol station?

¿Dónde hay una gasolinera?   don·de ai oo·na ga·so·lee·ne·ra

Please fill it up.

Lleno, por favor.   ye·no por fa·vor

I'd like (20) liters.

Quiero (veinte) litros.   kye·ro (vayn·te) lee·tros

ROAD SIGNS

Acceso	Entrance
Aparcamiento	Parking
Ceda el Paso	Give Way
Despacio	Slow
Dirección Única	One Way
Mantenga Su Derecha	Keep to the Right
No Adelantar/ No Rebase	No Passing
Pare/Stop	Stop
Peaje	Toll
Peligro	Danger
Prohibido Aparcar/ No Estacionar	No Parking
Prohibido el Paso	No Entry
Salida de Autopista	Freeway Exit

diesel	*diesel*	*dee*·sel
gas/petrol	*gasolina*	ga·so·*lee*·na
leaded (regular)	*gasolina con plomo*	ga·so·*lee*·na kon *plo*·mo
unleaded	*gasolina sin plomo*	ga·so·*lee*·na seen *plo*·mo

(How long) Can I park here?
¿(Por cuánto tiempo) (por *kwan*·to *tyem*·po)
Puedo aparcar aquí? pwe·do a·par·*kar* a·*kee*
Where do I pay?
¿Dónde se paga? *don*·de se *pa*·ga
I need a mechanic.
Necesito un ne·se·*see*·to oon
mecánico. me·*ka*·nee·ko
The car has broken down (in …).
El carro se ha averiado el *ka*·ro se a a·ve·*rya*·do
(en …). (en …)
The motorbike won't start.
No arranca la moto. no a·*ran*·ka la *mo*·to
I have a flat tyre.
Tengo un pinchazo. *ten*·go oon peen·*cha*·so
I've run out of gas/petrol.
Me quedé sin gasolina. me ke·*de* seen ga·so·*lee*·na
I've had an accident.
Tuve un accidente. *too*·ve oon ak·see·*den*·te

TRAVEL WITH CHILDREN

I need …
Necesito … ne·se·*see*·to …
Do you have …?
¿Hay …? ai …
  a babysitter (who speaks English)
  una niñera *oo*·na nee·*nye*·ra
  (de habla inglesa) (de *a*·bla een·*gle*·sa)

  a car seat for babies
  un asiento de seguridad oon a·*syen*·to de se·goo·ree·*da*
  para bebés *pa*·ra be·*bes*
  a child-minding service
  un servicio de cuidado oon ser·*vee*·syo de kwee·*da*·do
  de niños de *nee*·nyos
  a children's menu
  una carta infantil *oo*·na *kar*·ta een·fan·*teel*
  a creche
  una guardería *oo*·na gwar·de·*ree*·a
  (disposable) diapers/nappies
  pañoles pa·*nyo*·les
  (de usar y tirar) (de oo·*sar* ee tee·*rar*)
  a highchair
  una trona *oo*·na *tro*·na
  milk formula
  leche en polvo *le*·che en *pol*·vo
  a potty
  una pelela *oo*·na pe·*le*·la
  a pusher/stroller
  un cochecito oon ko·che·*see*·to

Do you mind if I breast-feed here?
¿Le molesta que dé le mo·*les*·ta ke de
de pecho aquí? de *pe*·cho a·*kee*
Are children allowed?
¿Se admiten niños? se ad·*mee*·ten *nee*·nyos

BRAZILIAN PORTUGUESE

Given that around 90% of the world's Portuguese speakers live in Brazil, South America's largest country, it's clear that a few words in the language will be very handy.

For a more thorough guide to the language, check out Lonely Planet's *Brazilian Portuguese* phrasebook.

PRONUNCIATION

The pronunciation guides explained below are included next to the Portuguese phrases throughout this section.

Vowels

a	as the 'u' in run
aa	as the 'a' in father
ai	as in 'aisle'
aw	as in 'saw'
ay	as in 'day'
e	as in 'bet'
ee	as in 'bee'
o	as in 'go'
oo	as in 'moon'
ow	as in 'how'
oy	as in 'boy'

Nasal Vowels

A characteristic feature of Brazilian Portuguese is the use of nasal vowels. They are pronounced as if you're trying to force the sound out of your nose rather than your mouth. English also has nasal vowels to some extent – when you say 'sing' in English, the 'i' is nasalized by the 'ng.' In Brazilian Portuguese, vowels followed by a nasal consonant (**m** or **n**) or those written with a tilde over them (eg **ã**) will be nasal. In our pronunciation guides, we've used 'ng' after nasal vowels to indicate a nasal sound.

Consonants

ly	as the 'lli' in 'million'
ny	as in 'canyon'
r	as in 'run'
rr	as the 'r' in 'run' but stronger and rolled
zh	as the 's' in 'pleasure'

Word Stress

In Portuguese word stress generally occurs on the second-last syllable of a word. When a word ends in *-r* or is pronounced with a nasalized vowel, the stress falls on the last syllable. Also, if a vowel has an accent marked over it, the stress falls on the syllable containing that vowel.

In our pronunciation guides the stressed syllables are indicated with italics.

GENDER & PLURALS

All nouns in Portuguese are either masculine or feminine. Feminine nouns generally end with *-a* or *-dade*, while masculine nouns often end in *-o*, *-ema*, *-oma* or *-ama*. Endings for adjectives also change to agree with the gender of the noun they modify (masculine/feminine *-o/-a*).

You can make a noun plural by adding *-s*. If the noun ends in *-s*, *-z* or *-r* and the final syllable is stressed, the plural is formed by adding *-es*.

ACCOMMODATIONS

I'd like a ... room.

Eu gostaria um quarto de ...	e·oo gos·ta·*ree*·a oom *kwarr*·to de ...
double	
casal	ka·*zow*
single	
solteiro	sol·*tay*·ro
twin	
duplo	*doo*·plo

I'm looking for ...

Estou procurando por ...	es·*to* pro·koo·*rang*·do porr ...

Where is a ...?

Onde tem ...?	*on*·de teng ...
room	
um quarto	oom *kwarr*·to
bed and breakfast	
uma pensão	*oo*·ma pen·*sowng*
camping ground	
um local para acampamento	oom lo·*kow* pa·ra a·kam·pa·*meng*·to
guesthouse	
uma hospedaria	*oo*·ma os·pe·da·*ree*·a
hotel	
um hotel	oom o·*tel*
youth hostel	
um albergue da juventude	oom ow·*berr*·ge da zhoo·veng·*too*·de

How much is it per ...?

Quanto custa por ...?	*kwan*·to *koos*·ta porr ...
night	
noite	*noy*·te
person	
pessoa	pe·*so*·a
week	
semana	se·*ma*·na

What's the address?

Qual é o endereço?	kwow e o en·de·*re*·so

Do you have a ... room?

Tem um quarto de ...?	teng oom *kwarr*·to de ...

For (three) nights.

Para (três) noites.	pa·ra (tres) *noy*·tes

Does it include breakfast?
   Inclui café   eeng·kloo·ee ka·fe
   da manhã?   da ma·nyang
May I see it?
   Posso ver?   po·so verr
I'll take it.
   Eu fico com ele.   e·oo fee·ko kom e·lee
I don't like it.
   Não gosto.   nowng gos·to
I'm leaving now.
   Estou indo embora   es·to een·do em·bo·ra
   agora.   a·go·ra

Can I pay by ...?
Posso pagar com ...?   po·so pa·garr kom ...
   credit card
   cartão de crédito   karr·towng de kre·dee·to
   traveler's check
   traveler cheque   tra·ve·ler she·kee

CONVERSATION & ESSENTIALS

Hello.
   Olá.   o·la
Hi.
   Oi.   oy
Good day.
   Bom dia.   bong dee·a
Good evening.
   Boa noite.   bo·a noy·te
See you later.
   Até mais tarde.   a·te mais tarr·de
Goodbye.
   Tchau.   chow
How are you?
   Como vai?   ko·mo vai
Fine, and you?
   Bem, e você?   beng e vo·se
I'm pleased to meet you.
   Prazer em conhecê-lo/   pra zerr eng ko·nye·se·lo/
   conhecê-la.   ko·nye·se·a
Yes.
   Sim.   seem
No.
   Não.   nowng
Please.
   Por favor.   por fa·vorr
Thank you (very much).
   (Muito) Obrigado/a.   (mween·to) o·bree·ga·do/a
You're welcome.
   De nada.   de na·da
Excuse me.
   Com licença.   kom lee·seng·sa
Sorry.
   Desculpa.   des·kool·pa

What's your name?
   Qual é o seu nome?   kwow e o se·oo no·me
My name is ...
   Meu nome é ...   me·oo no·me e ...
Where are you from?
   De onde você é?   de ong·de vo·se e
I'm from ...
   Eu sou da/do/de ...   e·oo so da/do/de ...
May I take a photo (of you)?
   Posso tirar uma foto   po·so tee·rarr oo·ma fo·to
   (de você)?   (de vo·se)

DIRECTIONS

Where is ...?
   Onde fica ...?   on·de fee·ka ...
Can you show me (on the map)?
   Você poderia me   vo·se po·de·ree·a me
   mostrar (no mapa)?   mos·trarr (no ma·pa)
What's the address?
   Qual é o endereço?   kwow e o en·de·re·so
How far is it?
   Qual a distância   kwow a dees·tan·see·a
   daqui?   da·kee
How do I get there?
   Como é que eu chego lá?   ko·mo e ke e·oo she·go la

Turn ...	*Vire ...*	vee·re ...
at the corner	*à esquina*	a es·kee·na
at the traffic	*no sinal de*	no see·now de
lights	*trânsito*	tran·zee·to
left	*à esquerda*	a es·kerr·da
right	*à direita*	a dee·ray·ta
far	*longe*	long·zhe
here	*aqui*	a·kee
near ...	*perto ...*	perr·to ...
straight ahead	*em frente*	eng freng·te
there	*lá*	la
north	*nort*	norr·te
south	*sul*	sool
east	*leste*	les·te
west	*oeste*	o·es·te

SIGNS	
Banheiro	Bathroom/Toilet
Delegacia de Polícia	Police Station
Hospital	Hospital
Não Tem Vaga	No Vacancy
Polícia	Police
Pronto Socorro	Emergency Department
Tem Vaga	Vacancy

LANGUAGE

EMERGENCIES

Help!
Socorro!   so-ko-ho
It's an emergency.
É uma emergência.   e oo-ma e-merr-zheng-see-a
I'm lost.
Estou perdido/a.   es-to perr-dee-do/a
Where are the toilets?
Onde tem um banheiro?   on-de teng oom ba-nyay-ro
Go away!
Vai embora!   vai eng-bo-ra

Call …!
Chame a …!   sha-me a …
  an ambulance
  uma ambulância   oo-ma am-boo-lan-see-a
  a doctor
  um médico   oom me-dee-ko
  the police
  a polícia   a po-lee-sya

HEALTH
I'm ill.
Estou doente.   es-to do-eng-te
I need a doctor (who speaks English).
Eu preciso de um médico   e-oo pre-see-zo de oom me-dee-ko
(que fale inglês).   (ke fa-le een-gles)
It hurts here.
Aqui dói.   a-kee doy
I've been vomiting.
Fui vomitando.   foo-ee vo-mee-tan-do
I'm pregnant.
Estou grávida.   es-to gra-vee-da

Where's the nearest …?
Onde fica … mais perto?   on-de fee-ka … mais perr-to
  (night) chemist/pharmacist
  a farmácia (noturna)   a farr-ma-see-a (no-toor-na)
  dentist
  o dentista   o deng-tees-ta
  doctor
  o médico   o me-dee-ko
  hospital
  o hospital   o os-pee-tow
  medical centre
  a clínica médica   a klee-nee-ka me-dee-ka

I feel …
Estou me sentindo …   es-to me seng-teeng-do …
  dizzy
  tonto/a   tong-to/a
  nauseous
  enjoado/a   eng-zho-a-do/a

asthma	asma	as-ma
diarrhea	diarréia	dee-a-he-ee-a
fever	febre	fe-bre
nausea	náusea	now-ze-a
pain	dor	dorr

I'm allergic to …
Tenho alergia à …   te-nyo a-lerr-zhee-a a …
  antibiotics
  antibióticos   an-tee-bee-o-tee-kos
  aspirin
  aspirina   as-pee-ree-na
  bees
  abelhas   a-be-lyas
  peanuts
  amendoims   a-meng-do-eengs
  penicillin
  penicilina   pe-nee-see-lee-na

  antiseptic
  antiséptico   an-tee-sep-tee-ko
  contraceptives
  anticoncepcionais   an-tee-kon-sep-syo-now
  painkillers
  analgésicos   a-now-zhe-zee-ko

LANGUAGE DIFFICULTIES
Do you speak English?
Você fala inglês?   vo-se fa-la een-gles
Does anyone here speak English?
Alguém aqui fala inglês?   ow-geng a-kee fa-la een-gles
Do you understand?
Você entende?   vo-se en-teng-de
I (don't) understand.
Eu (não) entendo.   e-oo (nowng) en-teng-do
What does … mean?
O que quer dizer …?   o ke kerr dee-zerr …

Could you please …?
Você poderia por favor …?   vo-se po-de-ree-a porr fa-vorr …
  repeat that
  repetir isto   he-pe-teerr ees-to
  speak more slowly
  falar mais devagar   fa-larr mais de-va-garr
  write it down
  escrever num papel   es-kre-verr noom pa-pel

NUMBERS
0	zero	ze-ro
1	um	oom
2	dois	doys
3	três	tres
4	quatro	kwa-tro
5	cinco	seen-ko
6	seis	says

7	sete	se·te
8	oito	oy·to
9	nove	naw·ve
10	dez	dez
11	onze	ong·ze
12	doze	do·ze
13	treze	tre·ze
14	quatorze	ka·torr·ze
15	quinze	keen·ze
16	dezesseis	de·ze·says
17	dezesete	de·ze·se·te
18	dezoito	de·zoy·to
19	dezenove	de·ze·naw·ve
20	vinte	veen·te
21	vinte e um	veen·te e oom
22	vinte e dois	veen·te e doys
30	trinta	treen·ta
40	quarenta	kwa·ren·ta
50	cinquenta	seen·kwen·ta
60	sessenta	se·seng·ta
70	setenta	se·teng·ta
80	oitenta	oy·teng·ta
90	noventa	no·veng·ta
100	cem	seng
200	duzentos	doo·zeng·tos
1000	mil	mee·oo
1,000,000	um milhão	oom mee·lyowng

SHOPPING & SERVICES

I'd like to buy ...
Gostaria de comprar ... gos·ta·ree·a de kom·prarr ...
I'm just looking.
Estou só olhando. es·to so o·lyan·do
May I look at it?
Posso ver? po·so verr
How much?
Quanto? kwan·to
That's too expensive.
Está muito caro. es·ta mweeng·to ka·ro
Can you lower the price?
Pode baixar o preço? po·de ba·sharr o pre·so
Do you have something cheaper?
Tem uma coisa mais teng oo·ma koy·za mais
barata? ba·ra·ta
I'll give you (five reals).
Dou (cinco reais). do (seen·ko he·ais)
I don't like it.
Não gosto. nowng gos·to
I'll take it.
Vou levar isso. vo le·var ee·so

more	mais	mais
less	menos	me·nos
large	grande	grang·de
small	pequeno/a	pe·ke·no/a

Where is ...?
Onde fica ...? on·de fee·ka ...
  an ATM
  um caixa automático oom kai·sha ow·to·ma·tee·ko
  a bank
  o banco o ban·ko
  a bookstore
  uma livraria oo·ma lee·vra·ree·a
  a chemist/pharmacy
  uma farmácia oo·ma far·ma·sya
  the ... embassy
  a embaixada de ... a eng·bai·sha·da de ...
  a foreign-exchange office
  uma loja de câmbio oo·ma lo·zha de kam·bee·o
  a laundrette
  uma lavanderia oo·ma la·vang·de·ree·a
  a (super)market
  o (super)mercado o (soo·perr·)merr·ka·do
  the police station
  a delegacia de polícia a de·le·ga·see·a de po·lee·sya
  the post office
  o correio o ko·hay·o
  the tourist office
  a secretaria de a se·kre·ta·ree·a de
  turismo too·rees·mo

What time does ... open?
A que horas abre ...? a ke aw·ras a·bre ...
Do you have any others?
Você tem outros? vo·se teng o·tros
How many?
Quantos?/Quantas? (m/f) kwan·tos/kwan·tas

I want to buy ...
Quero comprar ... ke·ro kom·prarr ...
  an aerogram
  um aerograma oom a·e·ro·gra·ma
  an envelope
  um envelope oom eng·ve·lo·pe
  a phone card
  um cartão telefônico oom kar·towng te·le·fo·nee·ko
  a postcard
  um cartão-postal oom karr·towng pos·tow
  stamps
  selos se·los

Do you accept ...?
Vocês aceitam ...? vo·ses a·say·tam ...
  credit cards
  cartão de crédito karr·towng de kre·dee·to
  traveler's checks
  traveler cheques tra·ve·ler she·kes

| **letter** | uma carta | oo·ma karr·ta |
| **parcel** | uma encomenda | oo·ma eng·ko·meng·da |

LANGUAGE

Where can I ...?
Onde posso ...?   on·de po·so ...
   change a traveler's check
   trocar traveler cheques   tro·karr tra·ve·ler she·kes
   change money
   trocar dinheiro   tro·kar dee·nyay·ro
   check my email
   checar meu e-mail   she·karr me·oo e·mail
   get internet access
   ter acesso à internet   terr a·se·so a een·terr·net

TIME & DATES
What time is it?
   Que horas são?   ke aw·ras sowng
It's (10) o'clock.
   São (dez) horas.   sowng (des) aw·ras

yesterday	*ontem*	on·teng
today	*hoje*	o·zhe
this morning	*esta manhã*	es·ta ma·nyang
in the morning	*da manhã*	da ma·nyang
now	*agora*	a·go·ra
this afternoon	*esta tarde*	es·ta tarr·de
in the afternoon	*da tarde*	da tarr·de
tonight	*hoje à noite*	o·zhe a noy·te
tomorrow	*amanhã*	a·ma·nyang

Monday	*segunda-feira*	se·goon·da·fay·ra
Tuesday	*terça-feira*	terr·sa·fay·ra
Wednesday	*quarta-feira*	kwarr·ta·fay·ra
Thursday	*quinta-feira*	keen·ta·fay·ra
Friday	*sexta-feira*	ses·ta·fay·ra
Saturday	*sábado*	sa·ba·doo
Sunday	*domingo*	do·meen·go

January	*janeiro*	zha·nay·ro
February	*fevereiro*	fe·ve·ray·ro
March	*março*	marr·so
April	*abril*	a·bree·oo
May	*maio*	ma·yo
June	*junho*	zhoo·nyo
July	*julho*	zhoo·lyo
August	*agosto*	a·gos·to
September	*setembro*	se·teng·bro
October	*outubro*	o·too·bro
November	*novembro*	no·veng·bro
December	*dezembro*	de·zeng·bro

TRANSPORTATION
Public Transportation
When's the ...	*Quando sai o ...*	kwang·do sai o ...
(bus)?	*(ônibus)?*	(o·nee·boos)
first	*primeiro*	pree·may·ro
last	*último*	ool·tee·mo
next	*próximo*	pro·see·mo

Which ... goes	*Qual o ... que*	kwow o ... ke
to (...)?	*vai para (...)?*	vai pa·ra (...)
boat	*barco*	barr·ko
bus	*ônibus*	o·nee·boos
city/intercity	*ônibus local/*	o·nee·boos lo·kow/
bus	*interurbano*	een·terr·ur·ba·no
ferry	*barca*	barr·ka
plane	*avião*	a·vee·owng
train	*trem*	treng

What time does it leave?
   Que horas sai?   ke aw·ras sai
What time does it get to (Parati)?
   Que horas chega   ke aw·ras she·ga
   em (Parati)?   eng (pa·ra·tee)

A ... ticket	*Uma passagem*	oo·ma pa·sa·zhem
to (...).	*de ... para (...).*	de ... pa·ra (...)
1st-class	*primeira classe*	pree·may·ra kla·se
2nd-class	*segunda classe*	se·goon·da kla·se
one-way	*ida*	ee·da
round-trip	*ida e volta*	ee·da e vol·ta

How much is it?
   Quanto é?   kwan·to e
Is this the bus to ...?
   Este ônibus vai para ...? es·te o·nee·boos vai pa·ra ...
Do I need to change?
   Preciso trocar de trem? pre·see·so tro·karr de treng
the luggage check room
   o balcão de guarda   o bal·kowng de gwarr·da
   volumes   vo·loo·me
a luggage locker
   um guarda volume   oom gwarr·da vo·loo·me
Is this taxi free?
   Este táxi está livre?   es·te tak·see es·ta lee·vre
Please put the meter on.
   Por favor ligue o   porr fa·vorr lee·ge o
   taxímetro.   tak·see·me·tro
How much is it to ...?
   Quanto custa até ...?   kwan·to koos·ta a·te ...
Please take me to (this address).
   Me leve para (este   me le·ve pa·ra (es·te
   endereço), por favor.   en·de·re·so) porr fa·vorr

Private Transportation
I'd like to hire	*Gostaria de*	gos·ta·ree·a de
a ...	*alugar ...*	a·loo·garr ...
4WD	*um quatro*	oom kwa·tro
	por quatro	por kwa·tro
bicycle	*uma bicicleta*	oo·ma
		bee·see·kle·ta
car	*um carro*	oom ka·ho
motorbike	*uma motocicleta*	oo·ma
		mo·to·se·kle·ta

ROAD SIGNS

Entrada	Entrance
Estrada dê Preferência	Give Way
Mão Única	One Way
Pare	Stop
Pedágio	Toll
Proibido Entrar	No Entry
Rua Sem Saída	Dead End
Saída	Freeway Exit

diesel	*diesel*	dee·sel
ethanol	*álcool*	ow·kol
LPG	*gás*	gas
unleaded	*gasolina*	ga·zo·lee·na
	comum	ko·moon

Is this the road to …?
Esta é a estrada para …?   es·ta e a es·tra·da pa·ra …

(How long) Can I park here?
(Quanto tempo) Posso   (kwan·to teng·po) po·so
estacionar aqui?   es·ta·see·o·narr a·kee

Where's a gas/petrol station?
Onde tem um posto   on·de teng oom pos·to
de gasolina?   de ga·zo·lee·na

Please fill it up.
Enche o tanque,   en·she o tan·ke
por favor.   porr fa·vorr

I'd like … liters.
Coloque … litros.   ko·lo·ke … lee·tros

The car/motorbike has broken down …
O carro/A motocicleta   o ka·ho/a mo·to·se·kle·ta
quebrou em …   ke·bro eng …

The car won't start.
O carro não está   o ka·ho nowng es·ta
pegando.   pe·gang·do

I need a mechanic.
Preciso de um   pre·see·zo de oom
mecânico.   me·ka·nee·ko

I've run out of gas/petrol.
Estou sem gasolina.   es·to seng ga·zo·lee·na

I've had an accident.
Sofri um acidente.   so·free oom a·see·den·te

TRAVEL WITH CHILDREN

I need …
Preciso de …   pre·see·zo de …

Do you have …?
Aqui tem …?   a·kee teng …

  a babysitter (who speaks English)
  uma babá   oo·ma ba·ba
  (que fale ingles)   (ke fa·le een·gles)

  a booster seat
  um assento de elevação   oom a·seng·to de e·le·va·sowng

  a car seat for babies
  um assento de criança   oom a·seng·to de kree·an·sa

  a change room for babies
  uma sala para trocar   oo·ma sa·la pa·ra tro·karr
  bebê   be·be

  a child-minding service
  um serviço de babá   oom serr·vee·so de ba·ba

  a children's menu
  um cardápio para   oom kar·da·pee·o pa·ra
  criança   kree·an·sa

  (disposable) diapers/nappies
  fraldas (descartáveis)   frow·das (des·karr·ta·vays)

  a highchair
  uma cadeira de criança   oo·ma ka·day·ra de kree·an·sa

  milk formula
  leite em pó   lay·te eng po

  a potty
  um troninho   oom tro·nee·nyo

  a pusher/stroller
  um carrinho de bebê   oom ka·hee·nyo de be·be

Do you mind if I breast-feed here?
Você se importa se eu   vo·se se eeng·porr·ta se e·oo
amamentar aqui?   a·ma·meng·tarr a·kee

Are children allowed?
É permitida a entrada   e perr·mee·tee·da a eng·tra·da
de crianças?   de kree·an·sas

INDIGENOUS LANGUAGES

AYMARA & QUECHUA

The few Aymara and Quechua words and phrases included here will be useful for those travelling in the Andes. Aymara is spoken by the Aymara people, who inhabit the highland regions of Bolivia and Peru and smaller adjoining areas of Chile and Argentina.

While the Quechua included here is from the Cuzco dialect, it should prove helpful wherever you travel in the Andes. The exception is Ecuador, where it is known as Quichua – the dialect that's most removed from the Cuzco variety. For a comprehensive guide to Quechua, pick up a copy of Lonely Planet's *Quechua* phrasebook.

In the following list, Aymara is the first entry after the English, Quechua the second. The principles of pronunciation for both languages are similar to those found in Spanish (see the Spanish pronunciation guide, p1020). An apostrophe (') represents a glottal stop – the 'nonsound' that occurs in the middle of 'uh-oh.'

Hello.	Kamisaraki.	Napaykullayki.
Please.	Mirá.	Allichu.
Thank you.	Yuspagara.	Yusulipayki.
Yes./No.	Jisa./Janiwa.	Ari./Mana.

How do you say ...?
Cun sañasauca'ha ...?   Imainata nincha chaita ...?
It's called ...
Ucan sutipa'h ...   Chaipa'g sutin'ha ...
Please repeat.
Uastata sita.   Ua'manta niway.
How much?
K'gauka?   Maik'ata'g?

father	auqui	tayta
food	manka	mikiuy
mother	taica	mama
river	jawira	mayu
snowy peak	kollu	riti-orko
water	uma	yacu

1	maya	u'
2	paya	iskai
3	quimsa	quinsa
4	pusi	tahua
5	pesca	phiska
6	zo'hta	so'gta
7	pakalko	khanchis
8	quimsakalko	pusa'g
9	yatunca	iskon
10	tunca	chunca

SRANAN TONGO (SURINAAMS)

While Dutch is the official language of Suriname and English is understood by most people, in everyday situations the lingua franca is Sranan Tongo, a creole that combines elements of Dutch, English, Portuguese and African languages. Locals often speak Sranan Tongo among themselves as a form of casual, friendly conversation. The following words and phrases might come in handy and will make the art of communication that little bit more rewarding.

Hello.	Fi-go.
What's your name?	Sah yu neng?
My name is ...	Me neng ...
Thank you.	Dan-key.
Yes./No.	Ay./No.
Do you speak English?	Yu tah-key eng-els?
How much is it?	Ow meh-nee?
When does it leave?	Ow lah-tee ah gwa?
Where is ...?	Pa-ah da ...?

boat	bo-to
far	fah-rah
near	cros-by
today	tee-day
tomorrow	tah-mah-rah
yesterday	ess-day

I	mi
you (sg)	yu
he/she/it	a
we	wi
you (pl)	unu
they	de

1	wan
2	tu
3	dri
4	fo
5	feyfi
6	siksi
7	seybi
8	ayti
9	neygi
10	tin

Also available from Lonely Planet:
Latin American Spanish,
Brazilian Portuguese and
Quechua phrasebooks

Glossary

Unless otherwise indicated, the terms listed in this glossary refer to Spanish-speaking South America in general, but regional variations in meaning are common. Portuguese phrases, which are only used in Brazil, are indicated with 'Bra.'

aduana – customs
aerosilla – (Arg) chairlift
aguardiente – sugarcane alcohol or similar drink
ahu – stone platforms which support the *moai* (Easter Island)
ají – chili condiments
alameda – street lined with trees
albergue – hostel
albergue juvenil – youth hostel; in Brazil, *albergue da juventud*
alcaldía – town hall; virtually synonymous with *municipalidad*
alerce – large coniferous tree, once common in parts of the southern Argentine and Chilean Andes; it has declined greatly due to overexploitation for timber
almuerzo – lunch; often an inexpensive fixed-price meal
alojamiento – usually a rock-bottom (or close to it) accommodations choice with shared toilet and bathroom facilities
altiplano – Andean high plain of Peru, Bolivia, Chile and Argentina
ambulante – street vendor
apartado – post-office box (abbreviated 'ap' or 'apto')
apartamento – apartment or flat; (Bra) hotel room with private bathroom
api – in Andean countries, a syrupy *chicha* made of maize, lemon, cinnamon and sugar
arepera – (Ven) snack bar
arequipeño/a – native or resident of Arequipa
arrayán – reddish-barked tree of the myrtle family, common in forests of southern Argentina and Chile
arriero – mule driver
artesanía – handicrafts; crafts shop
asado/a – roasted; (Arg) barbecue, often a family outing in summer
ascensor – elevator
asunceño/a – native or resident of Asunción
audiencia – colonial administrative subdivision under a president who held civil power in an area where no viceroy was resident
autoferro – (Ecu) bus mounted on railway chassis
autopista – freeway or motorway
ayahuasca – hallucinogenic brew made from jungle vines

Aymara – indigenous people of highland Bolivia, Peru and Chile (also called *Kolla*); also their language
azulejo – ceramic tile, usually blue, of Portuguese origin

balneario – bathing resort or beach
bandeirante – (Bra) colonial slaver and gold prospector from São Paulo who explored the interior
baños – baths
barraca – (Bra) any stall or hut, including food and drink stands at the beach or the park
barrio – neighborhood, district or borough; (Ven) shantytown; in Brazil, *bairro*
batido – fruit shake
bicho de pé – (Bra) literally 'foot bug'; burrowing parasite found near beaches and in some rainforest areas
bloco – (Bra) group of musicians and dancers who perform in street parades during Brazil's Carnavals
bocadito – snack
bodega – winery or storage area for wine
boleadoras – heavily weighted thongs, once used for hunting *guanaco* and rhea; also called *bolas*
brujo – witch doctor
burundanga – (Col) drug obtained from a plant commonly known as *borrachero* or *cacao sabanero;* used to intoxicate unsuspecting tourists in order to rob them
bus-cama – literally 'bus-bed'; very comfortable bus with fully reclining seats; also called *coche-cama*

cabaña – cabin
cabildo – colonial town council
cachaça – (Bra) sugarcane rum, also called *pinga,* produced by hundreds of small distilleries throughout the country; Brazil's national drink
cachoeira – (Bra) waterfall
cacique – Indian chief
caipirinha – (Bra) Brazil's national cocktail
cajero automático – ATM
calle – street
camanchaca – (Chi) dense convective fog on the coastal hills of the Atacama Desert; equivalent to Peru's *garúa*
cambista – street money changer
camino – road, path, way
camión – open-bed truck; popular form of local transport in the Andean countries
camioneta – pickup or other small truck; form of local transport in the Andean countries
campamento – campsite
campesino/a – rural dweller who practices subsistence agriculture; peasant
campo – the countryside; field or paddock

caña – rum

Candomblé – (Bra) Afro-Brazilian religion of Bahia

capoeira – (Bra) martial art/dance developed by Bahian slaves

carabinero – police officer

caraqueño/a – native or resident of Caracas

carioca – (Bra) native or resident of Rio de Janeiro

Carnaval – all over Latin America, pre-Lenten celebration

casa de cambio – authorized foreign-currency exchange house

casa de familia – modest family accommodations

casa de huésped – literally 'guesthouse'; form of economical lodging where guests may have access to the kitchen, garden and laundry facilities

casilla de correos – post-office box (abbreviated 'CC')

casona – large house, usually a mansion; term often applied to colonial architecture in particular

catarata – waterfall

caudillo – in 19th-century South American politics, a pro-vincial strongman whose power rested more on personal loyalty than political ideals or party organization

cazuela – hearty stew

ceiba – common tropical tree; can reach a huge size

cena – dinner; often an inexpensive set menu

cerro – hill; also refers to very high Andean peaks

certificado – registered (for mail)

cerveza – beer

ceviche – marinated raw seafood (it can be a source of both cholera and gnathostomiasis)

chachacoma – native Andean plant which yields a tea that helps combat mild symptoms of altitude sickness

chacra – garden; small, independent farm

charango – Andean stringed instrument, traditionally made with an armadillo shell as a soundbox

chicha – in Andean countries, a popular beverage (often alcoholic) made from ingredients like yucca, sweet potato or maize

chifa – Chinese restaurant (term most commonly used in Peru, Bolivia and Ecuador)

Chilote – (Chi) person from the island of Chiloé

chiva – (Col) basic rural bus with wooden bench seats

churrasquería – restaurant featuring barbecued meat; in Brazil, *churrascaria*

cinemateca – art-house cinema

cocalero – coca grower

coche-cama – see *bus-cama*

colectivo – depending on the country, either a bus, a minibus or a shared taxi

combi – small bus or minibus; also called *micro*

comedor – basic eatery or dining room in a hotel

comida corriente – (Col) basic set meal

comida criolla – creole food

comum – (Bra) taxi

confitería – cafe that serves coffee, tea, desserts and simple food orders

Cono Sur – Southern Cone; collective term for Argentina, Chile, Uruguay and parts of Brazil and Paraguay

cordillera – mountain range

corregidor – in colonial Latin America, governor of a provincial city and its surrounding area; usually associated with the *cabildo*

correo – post office; in Brazil, *correio*

cospel – token used for subway, public telephones etc, in lieu of coins

costanera – in the Southern Cone, a seaside, riverside or lakeside road

costeño – inhabitant of the coast

criollo/a – Spaniard born in colonial South America; in modern times, a South American of European descent

cumbia – big on horns and percussion, a cousin to salsa, merengue and lambada

curandero – healer

curanto – Chilean seafood stew

custodia – secure place to leave bags, eg at a bus station

cuy – roasted guinea pig, a traditional Andean food

cuzqueño/a – native or resident of Cuzco

dendê – (Bra) palm-tree oil, a main ingredient in Bahian cuisine

denuncia – affidavit or statement, usually in connection with theft or robbery

desayuno – breakfast

dique – seawall, jetty or dock; also a reservoir used for recreational purposes

edificio – building

encomienda – colonial labor system under which indigenous communities had to provide labor and tribute to a Spanish *encomendero* (landholder) in exchange for religious and language instruction

Escuela Cuzqueña and **Escuela Quiteña** – Cuzco and Quito schools of art; both results of a blend of Spanish and indigenous artistic influences

esquina – corner (abbreviated to 'esq')

estancia – extensive grazing establishment, either for cattle or sheep, with a dominant owner or manager *(estanciero)* and dependent resident labor force

FARC – Fuerzas Armadas Revolucionarias de Colombia (Revolutionary Armed Forces of Colombia); guerrilla movement

farinha – (Bra) manioc flour; staple food of indigenous peoples before colonization, and of many Brazilians today

farmacia – pharmacy

favela – (Bra) slum or shantytown

fazenda – (Bra) large ranch or farm, roughly equivalent to *hacienda*

ferrobus – type of passenger train

ferrocarril – railway, railroad

ferroviária – (Bra) railway station

flota – fleet; often a long-distance bus line
fundo – *hacienda* or farm
fútbol – soccer; in Brazil, *fútebol*

gare routière – (Gui) station
garúa – (Per) convective coastal fog
gaucho – (Arg, Uru) cowboy, herdsman; in Brazil, *gaúcho*
gîte – (Gui) guesthouse
golpe de estado – coup d'état
grifo – (Per) gas station
gringo/a – throughout Latin America, a foreigner or person with light hair and complexion; not necessarily a derogatory term
guanaco – undomesticated relative of the llama
guaquero – robber of pre-Columbian tombs
guaraná – Amazonian shrub, the berry of which is believed to have magical and medicinal powers; (Bra) a popular soft drink
Guaraní – indigenous people of Argentina, Brazil, Bolivia and Paraguay; also their language
guayaquileño/a – native or resident of Guayaquil

hacienda – large rural landholding with a dependent resident labor force under a dominant owner *(hacendado)*; (Chi) also called *fundo*
hidroviária – boat terminal
hospedaje – budget accommodations with shared bathroom; usually a family home with an extra room for guests
hostal – small hotel or guesthouse
huaquero – see *guaquero*
huaso – cowboy
humita – a sweet-corn tamale or dumpling

ida y vuelta – return trip
iglesia – church; in Brazil, *igreja*
Inca – dominant indigenous civilization of the central Andes at the time of the Spanish Conquest; refers both to the people and, individually, to their leader
indígena – native American; indigenous person
indigenismo – movement in Latin American art and literature which extols indigenous traditions
isla – island; in Brazil, *ilha*
IVA – *impuesto de valor agregado,* a value-added tax (VAT)

Jopará – mixture of Spanish and *Guaraní,* spoken in Paraguay

Kolla – another name for the *Aymara*
Kollasuyo – 'Land of the Kolla'; early indigenous name for the area now known as Bolivia

lago – lake
laguna – lagoon; shallow lake
lanchero – boat driver

lanchonete – (Bra) stand-up snack bar
latifundio – large landholding, such as a *hacienda* or cattle *estancia*
lavandería – laundry
leito – (Bra) luxury overnight express bus
licuado – fruit shake blended with milk or water
limeño/a – native or resident of Lima
lista de correos – poste restante
llanos – plains
locutorio – small telephone office
loma – mound or hill; a coastal hill in the Atacama Desert
lunfardo – street slang of Buenos Aires
lustrabotes – shoeshine boys

machismo – exaggerated masculine pride of the Latin American male
malecón – shoreline promenade
manta – shawl or bedspread
Mapuche – indigenous people of northern Patagonia
marcha español – (Arg) aggressive drum beats, bleepy noises and chanted lyrics
marinera – (Per) traditional Peruvian dance employing much waving of handkerchiefs
marisquería – seafood restaurant
maté – see *yerba maté*
maté de coca – coca-leaf tea
Medellín Cartel – Colombia's principal drug cartel in the 1980s, led by Pablo Escobar
menú del día – inexpensive set meal
mercado – market
mercado negro – black market
mercado paralelo – euphemism for black market
mestizo/a – a person of mixed indigenous and Spanish descent
micro – small bus or minibus; also called *combi*
migración – immigration office
mineiro – (Bra) miner; person from Minas Gerais state
minuta – (Arg, Par, Uru) short-order snack
mirador – viewpoint or lookout, usually on a hill but often in a building
moai – enormous stone statues on Easter Island
montevideano/a – native or resident of Montevideo
mototaxi – (Per) three-wheeled motorcycle rickshaw; also called *motocarro*
mudéjar – a Moorish-influenced architectural style that developed in Spain beginning in the 12th century
mulato/a – person of mixed African and European ancestry
municipalidad – city or town hall
museo – in Brazil, *museu;* museum
música criolla – creole music
música folklórica – traditional Andean music

ñandú – large, flightless bird, resembling the ostrich
nevado – snow-covered peak

NS – (Bra) Nosso Senhor (Our Father) or Nossa Senhora (Our Lady); often used in the name of a church
nueva canción – 1950s and '60s folk music with political undertones in Argentina, Chile and Uruguay

oferta – promotional fare, often seasonal, for plane or bus travel
oficina – office (abbreviated to 'of')
onces – morning or afternoon tea; snack
orixá – (Bra) god of Afro-Brazilian religion

paceño/a – native or resident of La Paz
Pachamama – Mother Earth, deity of the indigenous Andean people
panadería – bakery
parada or **paradero** – bus stop
páramo – humid, high-altitude grassland of the northern Andean countries
parque nacional – national park
parrilla or **parrillada** – barbecued or grilled meat; also used to refer to a steakhouse restaurant or the grill used to cook meat
pasarela – catwalk
paseo – avenue, promenade
patio de comidas – food court
paulistano – (Bra) native or resident of São Paulo
peatonal – pedestrian mall
pehuén – the monkey-puzzle tree of southern South America
peki-peki – (Per) dugout canoe
peña – club/bar that hosts informal folk music gatherings; performance at such a club
peninsular – in colonial South America, Spaniard born in Europe (as opposed to *criollo*)
pensión – short-term budget accommodations in a family home, which may also have permanent lodgers
petiscos – (Bra) appetisers; plates of bar food to share
pingüinera – penguin colony
pirogue – (Gui) dugout canoe
piropo – sexist remark, ranging from relatively innocuous to very offensive
pisco – white-grape brandy, Peruvian national drink; most frequently served as a *pisco sour* cocktail
Planalto – huge plateau covering much of southern Brazil
pollería – restaurant serving grilled chicken
por puesto – (Ven) shared taxi or minibus
porteño/a – (Arg) native or resident of Buenos Aires; (Chi) native or resident of Valparaíso
posada – small family-owned guesthouse; term sometimes also used for a hotel; in Brazil, *pousada*
prato feito or **prato do día** – (Bra) literally 'made plate' or 'plate of the day'; typically an enormous and very cheap, fixed-price meal
precordillera – foothills of the Andes
propina – tip (eg in a restaurant or cinema)

pucará – an indigenous Andean fortification
pueblo jóven – (Per) literally 'young town'; shantytown surrounding Lima
puna – Andean highlands, usually above 3000m

quarto – (Bra) hotel room with shared bathroom
quebracho – 'axe-breaker' tree of the Chaco, a natural source of tannin
quebrada – ravine, normally dry
Quechua – indigenous language of the Andean highlands, spread by Inca rule and widely spoken today; 'Quichua' in Ecuador
quena – simple reed flute
quilombo – (Bra) community of runaway slaves
quinoa – native Andean grain, the dietary equivalent of rice in the pre-Columbian era
quiteño/a – native or resident of Quito

ranchera – (Ecu) open-sided truck
rancho – rural house
realismo mágico – magic realism; literary genre typically associated with the novelists of the 1960s boom in Latin American literature, such as Gabriel García Márquez
recargo – surcharge; added by many businesses to credit-card transactions
reducción – in colonial Latin America, the concentration of native populations in central settlements, usually to aid political control or religious instruction; also known as *congregación*
refugio – rustic shelter in a national park or remote area
reggaeton – Caribbean-born popular music which combines Latin rhytms with rap
remise – (Arg) taxi booked over the phone
residencial – budget accommodations, sometimes only seasonal; in general, *residenciales* are in buildings designed expressly for short-stay lodging
río – river; in Brazil, *rio*
rock en español – fusion of Latin rhythms and rock sound
rodoferroviária – (Bra) combined bus and train station
rodoviária – (Bra) bus station
rollo/a – native or resident of Bogotá
rompepiernas – literally 'leg-breakers'; FARC's low-tech land mines designed to injure rather than kill
rotisería – takeaway food store
ruta – route or highway

s/n – *sin número;* indicating a street address without a number
salar – salt lake or salt pan, usually in the high Andes or Argentine Patagonia
salsoteca – salsa club
salteña – meat and vegetable pasty, generally a spicier version of empanada

sambadromo – samba parade ground
santiaguino/a – native or resident of Santiago
saudade – (Bra) nostalgic, often deeply melancholic longing for something
selva – natural tropical rainforest
Semana Santa – celebrated all over South America, Holy Week, the week before Easter
Sendero Luminoso – Shining Path; Peru's Maoist terrorist group which led a guerrilla war in the late 1980s
serrano – inhabitant of the mountains
sertão – (Bra) dry interior region of northeast Brazil
servicentro – gas station
sobremesa – conversation over a meal
soroche – altitude sickness
Southern Cone – see *Cono Sur*
Sranan Tongo – creole widely spoken in Suriname; also called Surinaams
suco – (Bra) fruit juice; fruit-juice bar
sudado – (Per) fish stew

Tahuantinsuyo – Spanish name of the Inca empire; in Quechua, Tawantinsuyu
tambo – in Andean countries, a wayside market and meeting place; an inn
tarjeta telefónica – phone card
tasca – Spanish-style bar-restaurant
taxi collectif – (Gui) shared taxi or minibus
teleférico – cable car
telenovela – TV soap opera
tenedor libre – (Arg) 'all-you-can-eat' buffet

tepui – flat-topped mountain; home to unique flora
termas – hot springs
terminal de ómnibus – bus station; also called *terminal terrestre*
tienda – store
tinto – red wine; (Col) small cup of black coffee
todo terreno – mountain bike
torrentismo – rappelling down a waterfall
totora – type of reed, used as a building material
tranca – (Bol) police checkpoint
Tropicalismo – Brazilian music style, a mix of local sound and North American rock and pop
Tupamaros – Uruguay's urban guerrilla movement from the 1960s

vaquero – cowboy; in Brazil, *vaqueiro*
vicuña – wild relative of the domestic llama and alpaca, found only at high altitudes in the south-central Andes
viscacha – also written as *vizcacha;* wild relative of the domestic chinchilla

yerba maté – 'Paraguayan tea' *(Ilex paraguariensis);* consumed regularly in Argentina, Paraguay, Uruguay and Brazil

zampoña – pan flute featured in traditional Andean music
zona franca – duty-free zone
zonda – (Arg) in the central Andes, a powerful, dry north wind

Behind the Scenes

THIS BOOK

This 11th edition of *South America on a Shoestring* was written by an outstanding team of authors led by Regis St. Louis. Regis wrote the front and back chapters as well as the Ecuador chapter. He was assisted by the following contributing authors: Sandra Bao (Argentina), Gregor Clark (Brazil), Aimée Dowl (the Guianas), Beth Kohn (Venezuela), Carolyn McCarthy (Chile), Anja Mutić (Bolivia), Mike Power (Colombia), Kevin Raub (Brazil and Peru), Paul Smith (Paraguay), Andy Symington (Brazil) and Lucas Vidgen (Argentina and Uruguay). David Goldberg, MD wrote the Health chapter. The Bolivia chapter was adapted in part from research and writing by Kate Armstrong and Paul Smith. *Gracias* also to the authors of the previous 10 editions, especially Danny Palmerlee, who coordinated the 9th and 10th editions. This guidebook was commissioned in Lonely Planet's Oakland office and produced by the following:

Commissioning Editor Kathleen Munnelly
Coordinating Editor Branislava Vladisavljevic
Coordinating Cartographer Andy Rojas
Coordinating Layout Designer Adrian Blackburn
Managing Editor Annelies Mertens
Managing Cartographer Alison Lyall
Managing Layout Designer Indra Kilfoyle
Assisting Editors Adrienne Costanzo, Kate Daly, Kate Evans, Melissa Faulkner, Amy Karafin, Helen Yeates
Assisting Cartographers Alissa Baker, Valeska Cañas, Dennis Capparelli, Tony Fankhauser, Karen Grant, Eve Kelly, Khahn Luu, Ross Macaw, Marc Milinkovic, Andrew Smith
Assisting Layout Designer Frank Deim
Cover Research Chris Ong, lonelyplanetimages.com
Internal Image Research Sabrina Dalbesio, lonelyplanetimages.com
Project Managers Anna Metcalfe, Sarah Sloane

Thanks to Lucy Birchley, Helen Christinis, Melanie Dankel, Sally Darmody, Eoin Dunlevy, Mark Germanchis, Chris Girdler, Rachel Imeson, Margie Jung, Glenn van der Knijff, Katie Lynch, Raphael Richards, John Taufa, Juan Winata

THANKS

REGIS ST. LOUIS

Many thanks to all my coauthors for their hard work on this ever-demanding title. At Lonely Planet, I'd like to thank in-house staff who plodded away behind the scenes, especially Kathleen Munnelly for her tireless dedication to all things South American. I also want to thank Danny Palmerlee and my coauthors on *Ecuador 8* for laying a strong foundation for my own Ecuador research. On the road, sending warmest thanks to the countless travelers and the many great Ecuadorians who provided useful advice and friendship along the way. Heartfelt gratitude to my family, especially Cassandra and Magdalena, for continued love and support throughout the Lonely Planet journey.

SANDRA BAO

My editor Kathleen Munnelly is tops, and Chile coauthor Carolyn McCarthy was loads of fun to hike with down south – and a great help with co-ordinating write-up. Along my travels I appreciate help from Alejandro and Frances in Ushuaia, Gerardo and Javier in El Chaltén, Christie and Ron in Bariloche. In BA, thanks always to my godmother Elsa (plus Jorge and Christina), Sylvia, Lucas, Mindy, Bob and, last but not least, Graciela. My husband Ben is a big support, especially in keeping the home fires burning – though the house could've been tidier. Love always to my parents, David and Fung, and to my brother Daniel.

GREGOR CLARK

I would like to thank the countless Brazilians who have brightened my days with their smiles, positive attitudes and thumbs-up signs. Extra-special *abraços* go to Ailton Lara, Christoph Hrdina, Laurenz Pinder, Junia Larissa Fuchs, Tise Sipinski, Bianca Reinert, Alisson Buzinhani, Mario Dobleck, Maria Helena, Ricardo and Luis Hernán. Thanks also to my commissioning editor Kathleen Munnelly and coordinating authors Regis St. Louis and Kevin Raub for their ongoing support and assistance. Last but not least, big hugs and kisses to Gaen, Meigan and Chloe, who always make coming home the best part of the trip.

AIMÉE DOWL

Thank you, *merci, bedankt* and *tangi* to all the generous and warm-hearted Guianese who helped me along the way, including the knowledgeable staff at Wilderness Explorers, Stinasu, and Couleurs Amazone; the friendly hosts at Zus & Zo and Rima Guesthouse; and all the pilots who put us down intact on remote jungle airstrips. Hearty thanks also goes to Rupununi ambassadors Colin Edwards and Diane McTurk, who helped me decipher their 'hometown,' and Angus and Jason who kept me company while I was there. As always, the biggest appreciation – and love – goes to Derek, who makes sunrise tramps through mosquito-infested forests the best time a girl could have.

BETH KOHN

A huge thanks to the fabulous Kathleen Munnelly for getting me out on the road, Alison Lyall and her carto crew for geographic attentiveness and Regis St. Louis for making sense of it all. Steven Bodzin wins top in-country billing for his help and support in Caracas. Thanks also go to Eric and Nella Migliore, Fabricio Mosegue, Raquel and Tom Evenou, Sonia Riera, Karla Herrera and Patrick, Francisco Álvarez, Osmel Cadenas Plaza of the Mérida tourism office and Rodrigo Alberto Torres Delepianí of the Ciudad Bolívar tourism office. A shout out to Menno Van Loon and all the wonderful fellow travelers I met along the way. Besos a Claudio.

CAROLYN MCCARTHY

This project took me from the tip to tail of Chile and put me in contact with dedicated, generous individuals who shared their time and knowledge. Were there enough ripe limes in Chile to mix up sufficient pisco sours in thanks! Especially to Peter in Pucón, Ben and Pilar in Santiago, Randy down south and Ercio in Copiapó. Bjorn was a cheerful traveling companion throughout the desert and its trials. On Rapa Nui, maururu to my fellow campers and Sharon, Hilaria, Tute and Coni. A big 'thank you' goes to Regis St. Louis and to the in-house team. Lastly, my appreciation goes out to Kathleen Munnelly, who is always a wise captain.

ANJA MUTIĆ

Thank you to my inspiring father who waited for my return from Bolivia to Croatia before passing to the other side. Tata, I dedicate this book to you. Hvala mama, Hoji and my whole family in Croatia, Barcelona and New York for their support. I profusely thank my editor Kathleen and everyone at Lonely Planet for their understanding and sympathy during a difficult time. Many thanks to my coauthors Paul and Kate. Gracias a Dirko and Virna in Sucre for their incredible kindness and generosity and Johnny Montes in Potosí for being such great help. I also thank Liz Rojas, Fabiola Mitru, Javier and Janette, Chris Sarage and Christian Schoettle.

MIKE POWER

Behind the scenes support was provided by…German Escobar – thanks for the laughs, the beers, the wisdom, and your generous good humor that saw me through a few rainy days in Bogotá. Johann and Yoli from Aquantis, whose sardonic insights into Taganga life cannot be equaled, and whose endless hospitality can never be repaid. Fredy Builes, simply by being Fredy Builes. ¿Sí o no, parcero? El Nueve in Medellín. Get well soon, parcero. Don Leonardo and his wife at La Portada in Tierradentro, who put me to bed when I was puking with a migraine on my knees by the roadside and bought me juice. Lady Emma Hamilton, whose giggle, phone calls and filthy limericks sustained a tired mind through many hours of need. Chris Power, for the constant backup – in every sense of the word.

KEVIN RAUB

Special thanks to my wife, Adriana Schmidt, and her knowledgeable and helpful father, Marcelo Schmidt, for helping dissect Brazilian news and politics. At Lonely Planet, Kathleen Munnelly, Regis St. Louis, Katy Shorthouse, Gregor Clark and Andy Symington. Along the way: Mike Watson, Karina Oliva, Mike Weston, Jess Ferguson, Boris Gomez, Marianne von Vlaardingen, SAE, Lucho Hurtado, Sinead Lowe and my fellow Inca Trail trekkers, Edgar Frisancho, Joao Rodrigues, Joao Veloso Jr, Brett Forrest, Denise Wedren, Paulo Coelho de Andrade, Talita Furtado, Beth Paiva, Claude Walker, Karla Ássimos, Camille Ulmer, Dave Cassidy, Chris Benway, Bill Grimes, Marmalita, Analía Sarfati, Vlado Soto, SP Turis.

PAUL SMITH

Thanks to everybody who has helped me out over the years in Paraguay and to Paraguayans in general for accepting me as one of their own. Particular thanks to Nelson Perez, Hugo del Castillo and Doris Clay for filling in the gaps on this edition, Arne and Karen for a great breakfast, Rob Clay for getting me a Lessonia and Robert Owen for giving me a place to stay in Asunción. Extra special thanks to mum, dad, Carol, Shawn and Yolanda for their love and support.

ANDY SYMINGTON

I owe much to many Brazilians, too many to name, who helped out with friendly information and advice on this update. Particular thanks go to Reinhard Sahre, an old Brazil hand who was excellent company (as always) in Recife, to David Rosenberg, Nieves Pérez Álvarez and Ángela González for helping out with information, to Pedro Félix Barroso for the Sol, to Mike Burren and Richard Prowse for keeping the flat warm, and especially to my family for their constant support, and to Ruth Nieto Huerta for the love and messages from across the Atlantic.

LUCAS VIDGEN

Once again, thanks firstly to the Argentines and Uruguayans who have made their countries such joyful places in which to work, live and travel. To name just a few, Ana Navarta, Lucas Mendoza and Marcela Fernández. June Fujimoto was a great on-again/off-again travel companion, and everybody who sent readers letters was, by turns, helpful, fascinating and just plain weird. Thanks also to Sandra Bao for tips and tricks and Kathleen Munnelly for letting me do my thing again. Back home, big ups to Alma de López and James Gray for taking care of business in my absence and to Sofía and América for being there when I got back.

OUR READERS

Many thanks to the travelers who used the last edition and wrote to us with helpful hints, useful advice and interesting anecdotes:

A Kate Adlam, Jorge Jaime Aguirre Ramirez, Debbie Amos, Clare Anderson, Sally Anderson, Ana Andrade, Luigi Andretto, Patrik Aqvist, Warren Aston, Andrea Avgousti **B** Amber Bacca, Goele Baert, Sarito Balkaran, Barbara Bansemer, Titus Baptist, Jennifer Bardell, Mark Barr, Hadas Bashan, Jose Benavides, Pedro Benitez, Stephen Benjamin, Hilary Benson, Maria Celina Bentancor, Hannu Berghall, Tim Bewer, Tara Bickis, Sarah Bienemann, Urs Bieri, Donna Billington, Andrew Birdsey, Susan Bishop, Marina Bitelman, Fred Black, Paul Boehlen, Rick and Liselotte Boerkamp, Conor Bolger, Iona Borthwick, Sabrina Bos, Madeleine Brady, Andrew Brennan, Jessica Brewer, Martin Brewerton, Cassandra Brooks, Tom Brosnan, Eric Brown, Jerome Brun, Katharina Buchanan, Christine Buchholz, Mirjam Buitelaar, Neil Bulman-Fleming, Anne Burrows, Susanne Burstein, Lachlan Buwalda, Allegra Buyer, David Byrne **C** Craig Campbell, Fiona Campbell, Mark Campbell, Elizabeth Carosella, Bo Christensen, Chiara Ciccarelli, Acacia Clark, Vanessa Clarke, Jonathan Clements, David Connell, Donal Convery, Valerie Cooper, Jean Copland, Camilla Corr, Barry Cracknell, Marisa Cruickshank, Stephanie Curry **D** Jonathan Deayan, Francisco De Belaustegui, Jonas De Jong, Jan De Reus, Hubert De Vries, Paul De Vries, Beata Debarge, John Delmont, Hanneke Den Ouden, Dominic Desjardins, Sylvain Deslandes, Gabriela Diriwächter, Wendy Doedel, Derek Doeffinger, Berard Dominique, Rosemarie Doyle, Timothy Doyle, Kate Duffy, Julie Dupuis **E** David Eddington, Tim Edwards, Julianne Ellis, Gary Ellison, Sophie Eustis, Mike Evans, Laura Ewles **F** Nizar Farsakh, Anthony Faughey, Manoel Ferreira, Robert Finch, Frauke Finster, Sue Fisher, Dave Foot, Hotel Frances, Andrew French, Petra Frodyma, June Fujimoto, Peter Fumberger

G Taylor Gaar, Peter Gammons, Valeria Gancitano, Mirja Gångare, Patrick Garrett, Tatjana Gazibara, Frank Geboers, Thomas Geerts, Pierre-Rudolf Gerlach, Juliette Giannesini, Manoel Giffoni, Cristina Giraldo, Chris Goldsmith, Amy Goodinge, Katharine Gordon, Cathy Grace, Sassoon Grigorian **H** Danny Hall, Kevin Hall, Richard Hall, Amy Halls, Catherine Ham, Bashar Hamarneh, Rainer Hamet, Paola Hanna, Bill Hatfield, Estelle Hayler, Kurt Healey, Laura Heckman, Kelly Heekin, Megan Heller, Katherine Helliwell, Britta Hillen, Jodie Hitchcock, Teja Hlacer, Anke Hoekstra, Daniel Hoenig, Suzanne Holmes-Walker, Charlotte Houston, Eleanor Howard, Henry Hubbard, Alice Hughes **I** David Ilian **J** Hans Jakobs, Heidi Jakobs, Nicola Jenns, Matt Joaquin, Andrea Johnston, Gwen Jones, Nikki Jones, Jessica Jormtun, Joaquin Julia Salmeron **K** David Katz, Alexis Keech, Ulrich Kellermann, Patrick Kilday, Drew Kimberley, Marie Kinsella, Diana Kirkland, Sally Kitajima, Joce Kitt, Ellen Kjoele, Lisa Knappich, Juleen Konkel, George Kostanza, Kirsty Kothakota, Stefanie Kraus, Kirstine Kristensen, Christiane Kunze, Silvie Kuratli, Matthias Kuster **L** Amy Laitinen, Robert Landsburgh, Rune Larsen, Mariko Lawson, Yasmin Lee, Elisabeth Lhoest, Tal Lichtenstein, Tom Lynar **M** Kenneth Macdonald, Kim Macquarrie, Nima Mahak, Ali Maher, Orla Maher, Jorge Malacara, Joel Marchal, Kerouedan Marie, William Marshall, Ben May, Stephan Mayer, Michelangelo Mazzeo, Michael Mc Govern, Kim Mcharg, Duncan Mclean, Peter Mcnamara, Francisco Mejia, Erna Mertens, Ville Mikkolainen, John Millan, Paul Millward, Milton Miltiadous, Anouk Minnebach, Janet Mitchelson, Dennis Mogerman, Amanda Molenaar, Leeron Morad, Thor Morales, Louise Moscrop, Dino Moutsopoulos,

SEND US YOUR FEEDBACK

We love to hear from travelers – your comments keep us on our toes and help make our books better. Our well-traveled team reads every word on what you loved or loathed about this book. Although we cannot reply individually to postal submissions, we always guarantee that your feedback goes straight to the appropriate authors, in time for the next edition. Each person who sends us information is thanked in the next edition and the most useful submissions are rewarded with a free book.

To send us your updates – and find out about Lonely Planet events, newsletters and travel news – visit our award-winning website: **lonelyplanet.com/contact**.

Note: we may edit, reproduce and incorporate your comments in Lonely Planet products such as guidebooks, websites and digital products, so let us know if you don't want your comments reproduced or your name acknowledged. For a copy of our privacy policy visit lonelyplanet.com/privacy.

Elanor Murphy, Hilary Murphy, Caroline Murray-Lyon, Karoline Myklebust **N** Beto N A, Emma Naylor, Ilka Neugebauer, Yindi Newman, Miruna Nichita, Dennis Nicoll, Alexandra Nisbeck, Christopher and Anja Nitsche, Kamilla Norrman, Marco Nueesch, Guilherme Nunes **O** Michaela Oberhofer, Ben Ogden, Thomas Olsen, Annelies Oosterkamp, Alisha Ousman **P** Zoë Paton, Allison Pelensky, Matt Pepe, Vanessa Percival, Heidi Perez, Ann Persson, Scott Petersen, Henning Petzold, Emile Phaneuf, Rochelle Pincini, Kyle Pinniger, Cecilia Pinto Oppe, Steve Ponich, Cynthia Port, Christian Prendergast **Q** Evan Quin **R** Luis Ramos, Nathalia Rampini De Queiroz, Terrence Reid, Ken Rider, Garry Ridgway, Anton Rijsdijk, Adrianne Ripoll, John Robinson, Sarah Robinson, Julia Rodriguez, Patrick Roman, Cristina Rondolino, Lucia Rosan, Carene Ross, Josiane Ruggeri, Achim Rumi, Justin Ruppel, Priska Rutishauser **S** Lauren Saikaly, Shawn Sanders, Chris Sapwell, Anne Sargent, Chris Saunders, Nina Saunders, Christian Schade, Jürgen Schenk, Andrea Schmitt, Klaus Schwab, Martin Severino, Eldivia Sidenta, Timothy Silvers, Peter Sims, Andrew Smart, Julie Smith, Paola Smith, Victoria Smith, Diego Sogorb, Ivo Sotorp, Adrienne Speidel, Dominik Spoden, Tim Squires, Beth Stark, Charles Stauffer, Dennis Steinfort, Florian Stoettner, Meaghan Stolk, Nick Stott, Michael Stout, Mojca Stritar, Samantha Sutherland, Anne Sved-Williams, Ruth Swailes, Alan Swanton, Rebecca Swart, Claudia Szabo **T** Trevor Takayama, Yvonne Tan, Christian Tavera, Alysanne Taylor, Olivia Taylor, Harry Ter Horst, Erik Thomann, Fran Thomas, Nicole Thrope, Ciska Tillema, Joey Tonis, Lynn Touzel, Fabiola Travi, Karsten Triebe, Kariina Tsursin, Nathalie Tzaud **U** Horatiu Urs **V** Marlous Van Merkenstein, Jonny Vancutsem, Marta Vidal, Liz Vincent, Oscar Vos **W** Robert Walker, Laura Wallace, Mat Ward, Luke Weatherill, Tom Weiss, Anne Welcenbach, Dorien Westrienen Van, Jonathan Wickens, Thomas Wiese, Vivian Williamson, Jessica Winkler, Carina Wolfram, Rolf Wrelf, Berbel Würth, Victoria Wymark **Y** Yolanda Yebra, Tina Yuen **Z** Andrew Ziebro, Mihael Znidersic, Michael Zysman

ACKNOWLEDGMENTS

Many thanks to the following for the use of their content:

Globe on title page ©Mountain High Maps 1993 Digital Wisdom, Inc.

Index

INDEX

INDEX

INDEX

000 Map pages
000 Photograph pages

GreenDex

GOING GREEN

In South America, sustainable travel is still a new concept, but one that's gaining much attention following the media spotlight on eco-consciousness that's spreading around the globe.

We define sustainability in three ways: environmental (minimizes negative environmental impacts and, where possible, makes positive contributions – through reforestation and the like); cultural (respects native cultures and traditions and fosters an authentic interaction between travelers and hosts) and economic (brings financial benefits to local communities and operates on principles of fair trade).

Criteria for this list include involvement in the local community and culture; participation in local conservation efforts; production or utilization of local, organic foods; use of renewable-energy sources, effective recycling and waste-management programs. This list also includes organizations owned and operated by local and indigenous operators, which thereby maintain and preserve local identity and culture.

You can help us improve this list by sending your recommendations to www.lonelyplanet.com/feed back. Learn more about sustainable travel by visiting www.lonelyplanet.com/responsibletravel.

THE LONELY PLANET STORY

Fresh from an epic journey across Europe, Asia and Australia in 1972, Tony and Maureen Wheeler sat at their kitchen table stapling together notes. The first Lonely Planet guidebook, *Across Asia on the Cheap*, was born.

Travellers snapped up the guides. Inspired by their success, the Wheelers began publishing books to Southeast Asia, India and beyond. Demand was prodigious, and the Wheelers expanded the business rapidly to keep up. Over the years, Lonely Planet extended its coverage to every country and into the virtual world via lonelyplanet.com and the Thorn Tree message board.

As Lonely Planet became a globally loved brand, Tony and Maureen received several offers for the company. But it wasn't until 2007 that they found a partner whom they trusted to remain true to the company's principles of travelling widely, treading lightly and giving sustainably. In October of that year, BBC Worldwide acquired a 75% share in the company, pledging to uphold Lonely Planet's commitment to independent travel, trustworthy advice and editorial independence.

Today, Lonely Planet has offices in Melbourne, London and Oakland, with over 500 staff members and 300 authors. Tony and Maureen are still actively involved with Lonely Planet. They're travelling more often than ever, and they're devoting their spare time to charitable projects. And the company is still driven by the philosophy of *Across Asia on the Cheap*: 'All you've got to do is decide to go and the hardest part is over. So go!'

Published by Lonely Planet

ABN 36 005 607 983

© Lonely Planet 2010

© photographers as indicated 2010

Cover montage by James Hardy. Photographs by Lonely Planet Images: Holger Leue, Brent Winebrenner, Paul Kennedy, Ralph Hopkins, John Pennock, Terry Carter, Daniel Boag, John Maier Jr. Responsible Travel photograph: Travellers preparing for hike up to top of Roraima, Venezuela, Krzysztof Dydynski, Lonely Planet Images. Many of the images in this guide are available for licensing from Lonely Planet Images: lonelyplanetimages.com.

Printed by Fabulous Printers Pte Ltd
Printed in Singapore.

LONELY PLANET OFFICES

Australia (Head Office)
Locked Bag 1, Footscray, Victoria 3011
☎ 03 8379 8000, fax 03 8379 8111
talk2us@lonelyplanet.com.au

USA
150 Linden St, Oakland, CA 94607
☎ 510 250 6400, toll free 800 275 8555
fax 510 893 8572
info@lonelyplanet.com

UK
2nd fl, 186 City Rd
London EC1V 2NT
☎ 020 7106 2100, fax 020 7106 2101
go@lonelyplanet.co.uk

Mixed Sources
Product group from well-managed forests and other controlled sources
www.fsc.org Cert no. SGS-COC-005002
© 1996 Forest Stewardship Council

Although the authors and Lonely Planet have taken all reasonable care in preparing this book, we make no warranty about the accuracy or completeness of its content and, to the maximum extent permitted, disclaim all liability arising from its use.